THE OXFORD POPULAR ENGLISH DICTIONARY

Based on The Oxford Current English Dictionary © Oxford University Press 1990.
This edition first published 1998 by Parragon Book Service Ltd and Magpie Books Ltd, an imprint of Robinson Publishing Ltd, London by arrangement with Oxford University Press

ISBN 0 75252 663 4

Typeset by the Oxford Text System
Printed in the EC

Contents

Notes

1. Pronunciation

Guidance on pronunciation follows the system of the International Phonetic Alphabet (see p. ix); it indicates the pronunciation that is standard in southern England.

2. Inflexion

See p. xi.

3. Etymology

This is given in square brackets at the end of an entry. It is usually omitted where the headword is a compound of two or more words (for which etymologies are given in their separate entries) or of an easily identifiable prefix (e.g. *anti-*, *pre-*, *un-*) and a whole word, or where the derivation is clear from the definition (e.g. *Chippendale*, *Spode*).

4. Proprietary status

This dictionary includes some words which are, or are asserted to be, proprietary names or trade marks. Their inclusion does not imply that they have acquired for legal purposes a non-proprietary or general significance, nor is any other judgement implied concerning their legal status. In cases where the editor has some evidence that a word is used as a proprietary name or trade mark this is indicated by the letter [P] but no judgement concerning the legal status of such words is made or implied thereby.

Pronunciation

1. Consonants

b, *d*, *f*, *h*, *k*, *l*, *m*, *n*, *p*, *r*, *s*, *t*, *v*, *w*, and *z* have their usual English values. Other symbols are used as follows:

g (game)	ŋ (lo*ng*)	ʃ (*sh*ip)
tʃ (*ch*air)	θ (*th*in)	ʒ (measure)
dʒ (*j*et)	ð (*th*ere)	j (*y*es)
x (Scots etc.: lo*ch*)		

Other consonants as in ar*c*, *c*ob, *c*ry (but soft *c* before *e*, *i*, *y* as in ice and city); *ch*ur*ch*; bla*ck*, lo*dge*; *g*ame, ba*g* (but soft *g* before, *e*, *i*, *y* as in age and *g*in); *j*et; si*ng*; bla*nk*; *ph*oto; *qu*een; *sh*ot; bi*tch*; *th*in; bo*x*; *y*et.

2. Vowels

short vowels		*long vowels*		*diphthongs*	
æ	(b*a*t)	ɑː	(d*ar*k)	eɪ	(s*ay*)
e	(b*e*t)	iː	(s*ee*m)	aɪ	(b*uy*)
ə	(*a*go)	ɔː	(b*or*n)	ɔɪ	(t*oy*)
ɪ	(s*i*t)	ɜː	(t*er*m)	əʊ	(s*o*)
ɒ	(t*o*p)	uː	(m*oo*n)	aʊ	(n*ow*)
ʌ	(b*u*t)			ɪə(r)	(p*eer*)
ʊ	(p*u*t)			eə(r)	(f*air*)
				ʊə(r)	(p*oor*)

(ə) signifies the indeterminate sound as in gard*e*n, carn*a*l, and rhyth*m*; (r) signifies a final r which is pronounced when the following word begins with a vowel sound.

Other vowels as in g*ai*n, f*air*, f*ar*, d*are*, s*aw*, s*ay*, b*ea*n, f*ear*, s*eer*, h*er*d, h*ere*, f*ew*, thi*ef*, b*ier*, b*ir*d, t*ire*, b*oa*t, b*oar*d, h*oe*, j*oi*n, m*oo*n, p*oor*, b*or*n, l*ou*d, s*our*, n*ow*, t*oy*, d*ue*, b*ur*n, p*ure*.

The following signify sounds not natural in English:

æ̃ (b*ai*n-marie, t*i*mbre)	ø (p*eu*)
ɑ̃ (contret*e*mps)	œ (b*œ*uf)
ɔ̃ (b*on* voyage)	œ̃ (br*un*)

3. Stress

Main stress is indicated by preceding the relevant syllable; no attempt is made to indicate secondary stress.

Pronunciation of words of one syllable is not given when it conforms with the following basic pattern:

Single-letter vowels a = /æ/, e = /e/, i = /ɪ/, o = /ɒ/, u = /ʌ/; when lengthened by a succeeding single consonant followed by *e*, a = /eɪ/, e = /i:/, i = /aɪ/, o = /əʊ/, u = /ju:/ (as in m*a*t and m*a*te; m*e*t and m*e*te, s*i*t and s*i*te, t*o*t and t*o*te, t*u*n and t*u*ne).

Pronunciation of two-syllable words is usually omitted when the first syllable is stressed and follows the basic pattern.

Pronunciation of compound words of easily recognized elements (e.g. *bathroom*, *headache*) is not given when the stress is on the first element.

Pronunciation of regularly formed derivates is not given when it can be easily deduced from the headword or from a preceding main word (e.g. *casually* from *casual* and *catty* from *cat*), unless there is a change of stress or some other notable feature (as with *certification*).

The following combinations, beginning a word, have the values shown: kn = /n/, rh = /r/, wh = /w/ or (by some speakers) /hw/ (not shown in individual entries), wr = /r/.

Pronunciation of the following suffixes and terminations should be noted:

-able /-əb(ə)l/
-age /-ɪdʒ/
-al (preceded by consonant) /-(ə)l/
-dom /-dəm/
-d (after *d* or *t*) /-ɪd/; (after other voiceless consonant) /-t/; (elsewhere) /-d/
-ess /-ɪs/
-est -ɪst/
-ful /-fʊl/
-fy /-faɪ/
-ible /-ɪb(ə)l/
-ism /-ɪz(ə)m/
-ive /-ɪv/
-less /-lɪs/
-ment /-mənt/
-ness /-nɪs/
-ous /-əs/
-sion /-ʃ(ə)n or -ʒ(ə)n/
-some /-səm/
-tion /-ʃ(ə)n/
-y (preceded by consonant, but cf. **-fy**) /-ɪ/

Inflexion

1. Plurals of Nouns

Nouns that form their plural regularly by adding *-s* (or *-es* when they end in *-s, -x, -z, -sh*, or soft *-ch*) receive no comment in the dictionary. Plural forms of those ending in *-o* (preceded by any letter other than another *o*) are always given. Other irregular forms are also given, except when the word is a compound of obvious formation (e.g. *footman, schoolchild*).

2. Forms of Verbs

(a) The following regular forms receive no comment in the dictionary:

- (i) third person singular present forms adding *-s* to the stem (or *-es* to stems ending in *-s, -x, -z, -sh*, or soft *-ch* and stems in *-o* preceded by any letter other than another *o*), or changing *-y* (preceded by a consonant or *qu*) to *-ies* (e.g. *cries, defies*).
- (ii) past tenses and past participles adding *-ed* to the stem, changing final *-y* (preceded by a consonant or *qu*) to *-ied* (e.g. *cried, defied*).
- (iii) present participles adding *-ing* to the stem, dropping a final silent *e* (e.g. *changing, dancing*).

(b) A doubled consonant in verbal inflexions (e.g. *rubbed, rubbing, sinned, sinning*) is shown in the form (**-bb-**, **-nn-**, etc.).

3. Comparative and Superlative of Adjectives and Adverbs

The following regular forms receive no comment:

- (i) Words of one syllable adding *-er* and *-est*, those ending in silent *e* dropping the *e* (e.g. *braver, bravest*) and those ending in a final consonant (except *h, w*, or *x*) preceded by a single-letter vowel doubling the consonant (e.g. *hotter, hottest*).
- (ii) Words of one or two syllables ending in *-y* (preceded by a consonant or *qu*) changing *-y* to *-ier* and *-iest* (e.g. *drier, driest; happier, happiest*).

4. Adjectives in *-able* formed from Transitive Verbs

Verbs generally drop silent final *-e* except after *c* and *g* (e.g. *movable* but *changeable*).

Words of more than one syllable ending in *-y* (preceded by a consonant or *qu*) change *y* to *i* (e.g. *enviable, undeniable*).

A final consonant is doubled as in normal inflexion (*conferrable, regrettable*): cf. 2(b) above.

Abbreviations

abbr./eviation etc.
abs./olute(ly)
acc./ording
adj./ective etc.
adjs. adjectives
adv./erb etc.
advs. adverbs
AF Anglo-French
Afr./ican
Afrik./aans
alt./eration etc.
app./arently
approx./imately
Arab./ic
Archit./ecture
assim./ilated etc.
assoc./iated etc.
Astrol./ogy
Astron./omy
attrib./utive(ly)
Austral./ian
aux./iliary

Biol./ogy
Bot./any

c. century
c. circa
Chem./istry
Chin./ese
cogn./ate
collect./ive(ly)
colloq./uial(ly)
compar./ative
conj./unction
contr./action etc.
corrupt./ion

D = disputed usage (applied to a use that, although widely found, is still the subject of much adverse comment by informed users)
d./ied
dat./ive
derog./atory
dial./ect etc.
dim./inutive etc.
dist./inguished
Du./tch

Electr./icity
emphat./ic
Engl./ish
erron./eous(ly)
esp./ecially
euphem./ism etc.
exc./ept
excl./amation etc.

F French
f. from
fem./inine
fig./urative(ly)
fl./oruit
Flem./ish
foll./owing entry
freq./ently
frequent./ative
fut./ure

G German
Gael./ic
gen./itive
Geol./ogy
Gk Greek
Gmc Germanic
Gram./mar

Heb./rew
hist./orical(ly)
Hung./arian

i. intransitive
Icel./andic
ill./ustration etc.
imit./ative etc.
imper./ative(ly)
infl./uenced
int./erjection
interrog./ative(ly)
Ir./ish
iron./ically
irreg./ular(ly)
It./alian

Jap./anese
joc./ular(ly)

L Latin
LDu. Low Dutch
LG Low German
lit./eral(ly)

masc.uline
Math./ematics
MDu. Middle Dutch
Mex./ican
MHG Middle High German
Min./eralogy
MLG Middle Low German
Mus./ic etc.
myth./ology

n. noun
Naut./ical
neg./ative(ly)
N. Engl. north of England
neut./er
Norw./egian
ns. nouns

obj./ective
obs./olete
occas./ional(ly)
OE Old English
OF Old French
OHG Old High German
ON Old Norse
ONorw. Old Norwegian
opp. (as) opposed (to)
orig./in(ally)

P proprietary name
partic./iple
pass./ive(ly)
perh./aps
Pers./ian
phr./ase
Phys./ics
pl./ural
poet./ical(ly)
pop./ular(ly)
Port./uguese
poss./essive
p.p. past participle
pr./onounced
prec./eding entry
predic./ative(ly)
Print./ing
prob./able etc.
pron./oun
pronunc./iation
prop./er(ly)
Prov./ençal

redupl./icated etc.
ref./erence etc.
refl./exive(ly)
rel./ated; relative
repr./esenting
rhet./orical(ly)
Rom./an, Romanic
Russ./ian

S.Afr. South Africa(n)
S.Amer. South America(n)
Sc./ottish
Scand./inavian
sing./ular
Skr. Sanskrit
Slav./onic
Sp./anish
superl./ative
Sw./edish

Theol./ogy
transl./ation etc.
Turk./ish

ult./imately
unkn./own
usu./al(ly)

v. verb
var./iant
v.aux. auxiliary verb
v.i. intransitive verb
v.refl. reflexive verb
v.t. transitive verb
v.t./i. transitive and intransitive verb
vulg./ar

w./ith
wd word

Aa

A, a *n.* **1** the first letter of the alphabet. **2** (*Mus.*) the sixth note in the scale of C major. —**A1,** (*colloq.*) first-rate, in perfect condition.

A *abbr.* ampere(s).

Å *abbr.* ångström(s).

a /ə, *emphatic* eɪ/ *adj.* (called the *indefinite article*) **1** one person or thing but not any specific one; one like. **2** per. [OE]

a- *prefix* **1** on (*afoot*), to (*ashore*), towards (*aside*). **2** in (*nowadays*). **3** in the process of (*a-begging, a-flutter*). [OE]

aardvark /ˈɑːdvɑːk/ *n.* a nocturnal African animal (*Orycteropus afer*), with a bulky pig-like body, long ears, and a thick tail, that feeds on termites. [Afrik., = earth-pig]

ab- *prefix* (**abs-** before *c, t*; **a-** before *m, p, v*) off, away, from. [F or f. L]

aback /əˈbæk/ *adv.* **taken aback,** disconcerted. [OE]

abacus /ˈæbəkəs/ *n.* (*pl.* **abacuses**) **1** a frame containing grooves or parallel rods or wires with beads that slide to and fro, used for counting. **2** (*Archit.*) the flat upper section of a capital, supporting the architrave. [L f. Gk *abax* slab, drawing-board f. Heb., = dust (from use of board sprinkled with sand or dust for drawing geometrical diagrams)]

abaft *adv.* in the stern half of a ship. —*prep.* nearer to the stern than. [f. A- + *baft* f. OE (*be* by, *æftan* behind)]

abalone /æbəˈləʊnɪ/ *n.* (*US*) an edible mollusc of the genus *Haliotis*, with an ear-shaped shell lined with mother-of-pearl. [Amer. Sp.]

abandon /əˈbændən/ *v.t.* **1** to go away from without intending to return; to give up, to cease work on. **2** to yield completely to an emotion or impulse. —*n.* reckless freedom of manner. —**abandonment** *n.* [f. OF (*à bandon* under another's control)]

abandoned /əˈbændənd/ *adj.* (of a person or behaviour) showing abandon, depraved. [f. prec.]

abase /əˈbeɪs/ *v.t.* to humiliate, to degrade. —**abasement** *n.* [f. OF f. L (*bassus* short)]

abashed /əˈbæʃt/ *adj.* embarrassed, disconcerted, ashamed. [f. OF (*baïr* astound)]

abate /əˈbeɪt/ *v.t./i.* to make or become less, to weaken. —**abatement** *n.* [f. OF f. L (AD-, *battuere* beat)]

abattoir /ˈæbətwɑː(r)/ *n.* a slaughterhouse. [F, as prec.]

abbacy /ˈæbəsɪ/ *n.* the office or jurisdiction of an abbot or abbess. [f. L (as ABBOT)]

abbé /ˈæbeɪ/ *n.* a Frenchman entitled to wear ecclesiastical dress, with or without official duties. [F f. L (as ABBOT)]

abbess /ˈæbes/ *n.* a woman who is head of an abbey of nuns. [f. OF (as ABBOT)]

abbey /ˈæbɪ/ *n.* **1** a building occupied by a community of monks or nuns. **2** this community. **3** a church or house that was formerly an abbey. —**the Abbey,** Westminster Abbey. [f. OF f. L *abbatia* abbacy]

abbot /ˈæbət/ *n.* a man who is head of an abbey of monks (now chiefly in Benedictine and Augustinian orders), usually elected by the monks for life or for a period of years and frequently holding certain episcopal rights. [OE, ult. f. Aram. *abba* father]

abbreviate /əˈbriːvɪeɪt/ *v.t.* to shorten (esp. a word or title). —**abbreviation** /-ˈeɪʃ(ə)n/ *n.* [f. L *abbreviare* (*brevis* short)]

ABC *n.* **1** the alphabet. **2** the elementary facts of a subject. **3** an alphabetically arranged guide. —*abbr.* Australian Broadcasting Corporation (formerly Commission).

abdicate /ˈæbdɪkeɪt/ *v.t./i.* to renounce, to resign from a throne, right, or high office. —**abdication** /-ˈkeɪʃ(ə)n/ *n.* [f. L *abdicare* (AB-, *dicare* dedicate)]

abdomen /ˈæbdəmən/ *n.* **1** the part of the body containing the stomach, bowels, intestines, and other digestive organs; the front surface of the body from waist to groin. **2** the hinder part of an insect, crustacean, spider, etc. —**abdominal** /-ˈdɒmɪn(ə)l/ *adj.* [L]

abduct /æbˈdʌkt/ *v.t.* to carry off (a person) illegally by force or deception. —**abduction** *n.*, **abductor** *n.* [f. L *abducere* (AB-, *ducere* lead)]

abed /əˈbed/ *adv.* (*archaic*) in bed. [OE (as A-, BED)]

aberrant /æˈberənt/ *adj.* departing from the normal type or accepted standard. [f. L *aberrare* (AB-, *errare* stray)]

aberration /æbəˈreɪʃ(ə)n/ *n.* **1** departure from what is normal or accepted or regarded as right; a moral or mental lapse. **2** (*Optics*) distortion of an image, the non-convergence of rays of light from a point to a single focus; *chromatic aberration*, a form of aberration due to the fact that light of different colours is refracted by different amounts as it passes through a lens, so that the resulting image is fringed with colours. **3** (*Astron.*) the apparent change in the position of a celestial body caused by the observer's motion and the finite speed of light. [as prec.]

abet /əˈbet/ *v.t.* (**-tt-**) to encourage or assist (an offender or offence). —**abetter** (in legal use **abettor**) *n.*, **abetment** *n.* [f. OF (*à* to, *beter* bait)]

abeyance /əˈbeɪəns/ *n.* **in abeyance,** (of a right or rule or problem etc.) suspended for a time. [f. OF (*à* to, *beer* gape)]

abhor /əbˈhɔː(r)/ *v.t.* (**-rr-**) to detest, to regard with disgust. —**abhorrence** /-ˈhɒrəns/ *n.* [f. L *abhorrere* shrink in dread]

abhorrent /əbˈhɒrənt/ *adj.* disgusting or hateful (*to* a person or one's beliefs); not according *to* (a principle). [as prec.]

abide /əˈbaɪd/ *v.t./i.* **1** to tolerate, to endure. **2** (*archaic, past* **abode** *or* **abided**) to remain, to dwell. —**abide by,** to act in accordance with (a promise etc.). [OE]

abiding *adj.* enduring, permanent. [f. prec.]

abigail /ˈæbɪgeɪl/ *n.* a lady's maid. [character in Beaumont and Fletcher's *Scornful Lady*; cf. 1 Sam. 25]

ability /əˈbɪlɪtɪ/ *n.* the quality that makes an action or process possible; cleverness, talent. [f. OF f. L (*habilis* deft)]

ab initio /æb ɪˈnɪʃɪəʊ/ from the beginning. [L]

abject /ˈæbdʒekt/ *adj.* lacking all pride, made humble; wretched, without resources. —**abjectly** *adv.*, **abjection** /-ˈdʒekʃ(ə)n/ *n.* [f. L *abjectus* (AB-, *jacere* throw)]

abjure /əbˈdʒʊə(r)/ *v.t.* to renounce or repudiate. —**abjuration** /-ˈreɪʃ(ə)n/ *n.* [f. L *abjurare* deny on oath]

ablative /ˈæblətɪv/ *n.* (*Gram.*) the case (especially in Latin) that indicates the agent, instrument, or location of an action. —*adj.* (*Gram.*) of or in the ablative. [f. OF or L (*ablatus* carried away)]

ablaut /ˈæblaʊt/ *n.* a change of vowel in related words (e.g. *sing, sang, sung*), characteristic of Indo-European languages. [G]

ablaze /əˈbleɪz/ *predic. adj.* blazing; glittering; greatly excited. [f. A- + BLAZE]

able /ˈeɪb(ə)l/ *adj.* having the ability or capacity (*to* do something); clever, talented, competent. —**able-bodied** *adj.* fit and strong. —**ably** *adv.* [f. OF f. L *habilis* deft]

-able *suffix* forming adjectives in sense 'that may' (*comfortable, suitable*), now always in passive sense 'that can, may, or must be -d' (*eatable, payable*), 'that can be made the subject of' (*objectionable*), 'that is relevant to or in accordance with' (*fashionable*). [F, f. L *-abilis*]

ablution /əˈbluːʃ(ə)n/ *n.* (usu. in *pl.*) ceremonial washing of hands, vessels, etc.; (*colloq.*) ordinary washing of the body, a place for doing this. [f. OF or L *ablutio* (AB-, *luere* wash)]

abnegate /ˈæbnɪgeɪt/ *v.t.* to give up or renounce (a pleasure or right etc.). —**abnegation** /-ˈgeɪʃ(ə)n/ *n.* [f. L *abnegare* refuse]

abnormal /æbˈnɔːm(ə)l/ *adj.* different from what is normal. —**abnormally** *adv.*, **abnormality** /-ˈmælɪtɪ/ *n.* [f. F f. Gk (as ANOMALOUS)]

aboard /əˈbɔːd/ *adv.* & *prep.* on or into a ship, aircraft, train, etc. [f. A- + BOARD]

abode[1] /əˈbəʊd/ *n.* (*archaic* or *literary*) a dwelling-place. [f. ABIDE]

abode[2] /əˈbəʊd/ *past* of ABIDE.

abolish /əˈbɒlɪʃ/ *v.t.* to put an end to (a custom, institution, etc.). [f. F f. L *abolēre* destroy]

abolition /æbəˈlɪʃ(ə)n/ *n.* abolishing, being abolished, especially with reference to capital punishment or (*hist.*) Black slavery and the 19th.-c. movement against this. [F or f. L (as prec.)]

abolitionist *n.* one who favours abolition, especially of capital punishment. [f. prec.]

abominable /əˈbɒmɪnəb(ə)l/ *adj.* detestable, loathsome; (*colloq.*) unpleasant. —**Abominable Snowman,** a large unidentified manlike or bearlike animal said to exist in the Himalayas, a yeti. —**abominably** *adv.* [f. OF f. L (as foll.)]

abominate /əˈbɒmɪneɪt/ *v.t.* to detest, to loathe. [f. L *abominari* deprecate]

abomination /əbɒmɪˈneɪʃ(ə)n/ *n.* **1** detesting, loathing. **2** an object of disgust. [f. OF (as prec.)]

aboriginal /æbəˈrɪdʒɪn(ə)l/ *adj.* indigenous, inhabiting a land from an early period, especially before the arrival of colonists; directly descended from early inhabitants. —*n.* an aboriginal inhabitant, especially (**Aboriginal**) of Australia. [f. L (as foll.)]

aborigines /æbəˈrɪdʒɪniːz/ *n.pl.* (*sing.* **aborigine** is used informally, but *aboriginal* is preferable) aboriginal inhabitants, especially (**Aborigines**) of Australia. [L, prob. f. *ab origine* from the beginning]

abort /əˈbɔːt/ *v.t./i.* **1** to cause an abortion of or to; to undergo abortion. **2** to remain undeveloped, to stop (a growth or disease) in its early stages. **3** to end prematurely and unsuccessfully. [f. L *aboriri* miscarry]

abortion /əˈbɔːʃ(ə)n/ *n.* **1** the expulsion (either spontaneous or induced) of a foetus from the womb before it is able to survive, especially in the first 28 weeks of pregnancy. **2** a stunted or misshapen creature or thing. [as prec.]

abortionist *n.* a person who practices abortion, esp. illegally. [f. prec.]

abortive /əˈbɔːtɪv/ *adj.* **1** producing abortion. **2** unsuccessful. [f. OF f. L (as ABORT)]

abound /əˈbaʊnd/ *v.i.* to be plentiful; to be rich *in*, to teem *with*. [f. OF f. L *abundare* overflow]

about /əˈbaʊt/ *prep.* **1** in connection with, on the subject of. **2** at a time near to. **3** all round. **4** near to hand. **5** here and there in, at points throughout. —*adv.* **1** approximately. **2** at points near by, here and there. **3** on the move, in action. **4** all round, in every direction. **5** in rotation or succession. (Tending to be replaced in many uses by *around* and *round*.) —**about turn,** a turn made so as to face the opposite direction; a reversal of opinion or policy etc. **be about to,** to intend to (do something) immediately; to be on the point or verge of. [OE (A-, *būtan* but)]

above /əˈbʌv/ *prep.* **1** over, on the top of, higher than; over the level of. **2** more than. **3** higher in rank or importance etc. than. **4** beyond the reach of; too good etc. for. —*adv.* **1** at or to a higher point, overhead. **2** in addition. **3** further back on a page or in a book. **4** (*rhet.*) in heaven. —*adj.* said, mentioned, or written above. —*n.* that which is above. —**above-board** *adv.* & *adj.* without concealment, open(ly). **above himself** etc., carried away by high spirits or conceit. [f. A- + OE *bufan* (*be* by, *ufan* above)]

abracadabra /æbrəkəˈdæbrə/ *n.* **1** a supposedly magic formula or spell. **2** gibberish. [L f. Gk; a cabbalistic word of a Gnostic sect, supposed when written triangularly, and worn, to cure fevers etc.; it is first found in a poem by Q. Serenus Sammonicus (early 3rd c. AD)]

abrade /əˈbreɪd/ *v.t.* to scrape or wear away by rubbing. [f. L *abradere* (AB-, *radere* scrape)]

abrasion /əˈbreɪʒ(ə)n/ *n.* scraping or wearing away; an area of damage caused thus. [as ABRADE]

abrasive /əˈbreɪsɪv/ *adj.* **1** causing abrasion; capable of polishing by rubbing or grinding. **2** harsh and offensive in manner. —*n.* an abrasive substance. [as prec.]

abreaction /æbrɪˈækʃ(ə)n/ *n.* free expression and release of a previously repressed emotion. [f. AB- + REACTION]

abreast /əˈbrest/ *adv.* **1** side by side and facing the same way. **2** keeping up, not behind (*of* or *with* developments). [f. A- + BREAST]

abridge /əˈbrɪdʒ/ *v.t.* to shorten into fewer words. —**abridgement** *n.* [f. OF f. L (as ABBREVIATE)]

abroad /əˈbrɔːd/ *adv.* **1** in or to a foreign country. **2** over a wide area, in different directions. **3** in circulation. [f. A- + BROAD]

abrogate /ˈæbrəgeɪt/ *v.t.* to repeal, to cancel. —**abrogation** /-ˈgeɪʃ(ə)n/ *n.* [f. L *abrogare* (AB-, *rogare* propose law)]

abrupt /əˈbrʌpt/ *adj.* **1** sudden; disjointed, not smooth; curt. **2** steep, precipitous. —**abruptly** *adv.*, **abruptness** *n.* [f. L *abruptus* (AB-, *rumpere* break)]

abscess /ˈæbsɪs/ *n.* a swollen area of body tissue in which pus gathers. [f. L *abscessus* a going away (AB-, *cedere* go)]

abscissa /æbˈsɪsə/ *n.* (*pl.* **-ae** /-iː/) (*Math.*) a coordinate measured parallel to a horizontal axis. [f. L (AB-, *scindere* cut)]

abscond /əbˈskɒnd/ *v.i.* to go away furtively, especially after wrongdoing. —**absconder** *n.* [f. L *abscondere* (AB-, *condere* stow)]

abseil /ˈæbseɪl/ *v.i.* to descend a steep rock-face using a doubled rope fixed at a higher point. —*n.* this process. [f. G (*ab* down, *seil* rope)]

absence /ˈæbs(ə)ns/ *n.* being away, the period of this; non-existence or lack *of*; inattentiveness (*of mind*). [as foll.]

absent /ˈæbs(ə)nt/ *adj.* not present; not existing. —/əbˈsent/ *v.refl.* to keep *oneself* away. —**absent-minded** *adj.* forgetful; with one's mind on other things. —**absently** *adv.* [f. OF or L *absens* (*abesse* be away)]

absentee /æbs(ə)nˈtiː/ *n.* one who absents himself. —**absentee landlord,** one not residing at the property he leases out. —**absenteeism** *n.* [f. prec.]

absinthe /ˈæbsɪnθ/ *n.* a liqueur originally flavoured with wormwood, now usually with other herbs. [f. F f. L f. Gk *apsinthion*]

absolute /ˈæbsəluːt, -juːt/ *adj.* complete, perfect; unrestricted, independent; not relative. —**absolute magnitude,** see MAGNITUDE. **absolute majority,** a majority over all rivals combined. **absolute pitch,** the ability to recognize or reproduce exactly the pitch of a note in music. **absolute temperature,** one measured from absolute zero. **absolute zero,** the temperature (−273.15 C) at which the motion of particles that constitutes heat is at a minimum. [f. L (as ABSOLVE)]

absolutely /ˈæbsəluːtlɪ/ *adv.* **1** completely, utterly, unreservedly. **2** actually. **3** in an absolute sense. **4** /-ˈluːtlɪ/ quite so, yes. [f. prec.]

absolution /æbsəˈluːʃ(ə)n/ *n.* formal forgiveness of a penitent's sins, declared by a priest. [f. OF f. L (as foll.)]

absolve /əbˈzɒlv/ *v.t.* **1** to clear *from* or *of* blame or guilt; to give absolution to. **2** to free *from* an obligation. [f. L *absolvere* (AB-, *solvere* loosen)]

absorb /əb'sɔ:b/ *v.t.* to take in, to incorporate as part of itself or oneself; to reduce the effect of, to deal easily with (shock etc.); to engross the attention of. —**absorbency** *n.*, **absorbent** *adj.* & *n.*, **absorption** *n.* [f. F or L *absorbēre* (AB-, *sorbēre* suck in)]

absorptive /əb'sɔ:ptɪv/ *adj.* able to absorb things; engrossing. [f. L (as prec.)]

abstain /əb'steɪn/ *v.i.* to restrain oneself, especially from drinking alcohol; to decline to use one's vote. —**abstainer** *n.*, **abstention** *n.* [f. AF f. L *abstinere* withhold]

abstemious /æb'sti:mɪəs/ *adj.* sparing or not self-indulgent, especially in eating and drinking. —**abstemiously** *adv.*, **abstemiousness** *n.* [f. L *abstemius* (AB-, *temetum* strong drink)]

abstinence /'æbstɪnəns/ *n.* abstaining, especially from food or alcohol. —**abstinent** *adj.* [f. OF f. L (as ABSTAIN)]

abstract[1] /'æbstrækt/ *adj.* **1** having no material existence. **2** theoretical rather than practical. —*n.* **1** a summary. **2** an abstract quality or idea. **3** an example of abstract art. —**abstract art** painting or sculpture that does not represent things pictorially. **abstract noun,** a noun denoting quality or state. —**abstractly** *adv.*, **abstractness** *n.* [f. OF or L *abstractus* (AB-, *trahere* draw)]

abstract[2] /æb'strækt/ *v.t.* **1** to take out, to remove. **2** to make a written summary of. —**abstracted** *adj.* inattentive, with one's mind on other things. —**abstractor** *n.* [f. prec.]

abstraction /æb'strækʃ(ə)n/ *n.* **1** abstracting, removing. **2** an abstract idea. **3** inattentiveness. [F or f. L (as ABSTRACT[1])]

abstruse /æb'stru:s/ *adj.* hard to understand, profound. —**abstrusely** *adv.*, **abstruseness** *n.* [F or f. L *abstrudere* conceal]

absurd /əb'sɜ:d/ *adj.* wildly inappropriate; ridiculous. —**absurdity** *n.*, **absurdly** *adv.* [f. F or L (AB-, *surdus* deaf, dull)]

abundant /ə'bʌndənt/ *adj.* more than enough, plenty; rich *in*. —**abundantly** *adv.*, **abundance** *n.* [f. L (as ABOUND)]

abuse /ə'bju:z/ *v.t.* **1** to make a bad or wrong use of; to maltreat. **2** to attack verbally. —/ə'bju:s/ *n.* **1** misuse; an unjust or corrupt practice. **2** abusive words, insults. [f. OF f. L (AB-, *uti* use)]

abusive /ə'bju:sɪv/ *adj.* using insulting language, criticizing harshly. —**abusively** *adv.* [as prec.]

abut /ə'bʌt/ *v.t./i.* (**-tt-**) to adjoin, to border *on*; to touch at one side. [f. OF (*but* end) & L]

abutment /ə'bʌtmənt/ *n.* a lateral supporting structure of a bridge, arch, etc. [f. prec.]

abysmal /ə'bɪzm(ə)l/ *adj.* extremely bad; extreme and deplorable. —**abysmally** *adv.* [f. OF f. L (as ABYSS)]

abyss /ə'bɪs/ *n.* a bottomless or deep chasm; an immeasurable depth. [f. L f. Gk *abussos* bottomless (*a-* not, *bussos* depth)]

abyssal /ə'bɪs(ə)l/ *adj.* at or of the ocean depths or floor, especially those below 1,000 metres containing relatively little marine life. [f. prec.]

AC, a.c. *abbr.* alternating current.

Ac *symbol* actinium.

acacia /ə'keɪʃə/ *n.* a tree or shrub of the genus *Acacia*, some members of which yield gum arabic; a related tree, the false acacia or locust-tree (*Robinia pseudoacacia*) grown for ornament. [L f. Gk]

Academe /'ækədi:m/ *n.* (*literary*) **Groves of Academe,** a university environment. [f. Gk (as ACADEMY)]

academic /ækə'demɪk/ *adj.* **1** of a college or university; scholarly as opposed to technical or practical. **2** not of practical relevance. —*n.* a member of an academic institution. —**academically** *adv.* [f. F or L (as ACADEMY)]

academician /əkædə'mɪʃ(ə)n/ *n.* a member of an Academy. [f. ACADEMY.]

academy /ə'kædəmɪ/ *n.* **1** a school, especially for specialized training; (*Sc.*) a secondary school. **2** a society of scholars or artists etc.; **the Academy,** the Royal Academy of Painting, Sculpture, and Architecture. —**Academy award,** any of the awards of the Academy of Motion Picture Arts and Sciences (Hollywood, USA) given annually for success in the film industry. [f. Gk *Akadēmia* name of garden where Plato taught, called after *Akadēmos* Gk hero]

acanthus /ə'kænθəs/ *n.* a Mediterranean herbaceous plant of the genus *Acanthus*, with prickly leaves; (*Gk Archit.*) a representation of its leaf. [L f. Gk (*akantha* thorn)]

ACAS /'eɪkæs/ *abbr.* Advisory, Conciliation, and Arbitration Service. The service was set up in 1975 to provide such facilities as a means of avoiding or resolving industrial disputes, and to promote the improvement of collective bargaining.

accede /æk'si:d/ *v.i.* **1** to take office, to come *to* the throne. **2** to agree *to* (a proposal etc.). [f. L *accedere* (AD-, *cedere* go)]

accelerate /ək'selereɪt/ *v.t./i.* to move faster or happen earlier; to cause to do this; to increase the speed of a motor vehicle. —**acceleration** /-'reɪʃ(ə)n/ *n.* [f. L *accelerare* (AD-, *celer* swift)]

accelerator /ək'seləreɪtə(r)/ *n.* a device for increasing speed, a pedal that controls the throttle in a motor vehicle; an apparatus for imparting high speeds to charged particles. [f. prec.]

accelerometer /əkselə'rɒmɪtə(r)/ *n.* an instrument for measuring acceleration or vibrations. [f. ACCELERATE + -METER]

accent /'æksent/ *n.* 1 prominence given to a syllable by stress or pitch. 2 a mark used with a letter or word to indicate pitch, stress, quality of vowel, etc. 3 a particular (esp. local or national) mode of pronunciation. 4 a distinctive feature or emphasis. —/æk'sent/ *v.t.* 1 to pronounce with an accent. 2 to write accents on. 3 to accentuate. —**accentual** /æk'sentju:əl/ *adj.* [f. L *accentus* (AD-, *cantus* song)]

accentor /ək'sentə(r)/ *n.* a bird of the genus *Prunella*, e.g. the hedge-sparrow. [L, f. *ad* to + *cantor* singer]

accentuate /ək'sentju:eɪt/ *v.t.* to emphasize, to make prominent. —**accentuation** /-'eɪʃ(ə)n/ *n.* [f. L (as ACCENT)]

accept /ək'sept/ *v.t.* 1 to consent to receive, to take willingly; to answer (an invitation or suitor) affirmatively. 2 to regard favourably; to tolerate or submit to. 3 to take as valid. 4 to undertake (a responsibility etc.). —**acceptance** *n.*, **acceptor** *n.* [f. OF or L *acceptare* (AD-, *capere* take)]

acceptable *adj.* worth accepting, welcome; tolerable. —**acceptably** *adv.*, **acceptability** /-'bɪlɪtɪ/ *n.* [as prec.]

access /'ækses/ *n.* 1 a way in, a means of approaching, reaching, or using. 2 an outburst *of* emotion. —*v.t.* 1 to obtain (data) from a computer. 2 to accession. [f. OF or L (as ACCEDE)]

accessible /ək'sesɪb(ə)l/ *adj.* that may be reached or obtained. —**accessibility** /-'bɪlɪtɪ/ *n.*, **accessibly** *adv.*, [F or f. L (as ACCEDE)]

accession /ək'seʃ(ə)n/ *n.* 1 acceding or attaining (*to* a throne, office, etc.). 2 a thing added. —*v.t.* to record the addition of (a new item) to a library or museum. [as prec.]

accessory /ək'sesərɪ/ *n.* 1 an additional or extra thing; (usu. in *pl.*) a small attachment or fitting. 2 a person who helps in or is privy *to* an act, especially a crime. —*adj.* additional, contributing in a minor way. [f. L (as ACCEDE)]

accidence /'æksɪd(ə)ns/ *n.* the part of grammar that deals with the way words are inflected. [f. L. (as foll.)]

accident /'æksɪd(ə)nt/ *n.* an event that is unexpected or without apparent cause; an unintentional act, chance; an unfortunate (esp. a harmful) event. [f. OF f. L *accidens* (AD-, *cadere* fall)]

accidental /æksɪ'dent(ə)l/ *adj.* happening or done by accident. —*n.* (*Mus.*) a sign indicating temporary departure from a key signature. —**accidentally** *adv.* [f. L (as prec.)]

acclaim /ə'kleɪm/ *v.t.* to welcome with shouts of approval, to applaud enthusiastically; to hail as. —*n.* a shout of applause or welcome. —**acclamation** /æklə'meɪʃ(ə)n/ *n.* [f. L *acclamare* (AD-, *clamare* shout)]

acclimatize /ə'klaɪmətaɪz/ *v.t./i.* to make or become used to a new climate or conditions. —**acclimatization** /-'zeɪʃ(ə)n/ *n.* [f. F (*à* to, *climat* climate)]

acclivity /ə'klɪvɪtɪ/ *n.* an upward slope. [f. L *acclivitas* (AD-, *clivus* slope)]

accolade /ækə'leɪd/ *n.* 1 bestowal of praise. 2 a sign at the bestowal of a knighthood, now usually a tap on the shoulder with the flat of a sword. [F (as AD, L *collum* neck)]

accommodate /ə'kɒmədeɪt/ *v.t.* 1 to provide lodging or room for. 2 to do a favour to, to oblige or supply (a person *with*). 3 to adapt, to harmonize. [f. L *accommodare* (AD-, *commodus* fitting)]

accommodating *adj.* obliging, compliant. [f. prec.]

accommodation /əkɒmə'deɪʃ(ə)n/ *n.* 1 lodging, living-premises. 2 adaptation, adjustment; a convenient arrangement. —**accommodation address**, one used on letters to a person unable to give a permanent address. [F or f. L (as ACCOMMODATE)]

accompaniment /ə'kʌmpənɪmənt/ *n.* 1 an instrumental or orchestral part supporting or partnering a solo instrument, voice, or group. 2 an accompanying thing. [f. F (as ACCOMPANY)]

accompanist /ə'kʌmpənɪst/ *n.* one who plays a musical accompaniment. [f. foll.]

accompany /ə'kəmpənɪ/ *v.t.* 1 to go with, to travel with as a companion or helper; to be done or found with. 2 to provide in addition. 3 (*Mus.*) to support or partner with an accompaniment. [f. F (as COMPANION)]

accomplice /ə'kʌmplɪs/ *n.* a partner in crime or wrongdoing. [f. F *complice* f. L (*complex* confederate)]

accomplish /ə'kʌmplɪʃ/ *v.t.* to succeed in doing, to complete. [f. OF f. L (AD-, *complere* complete)]

accomplished /ə'kʌmplɪʃt/ *adj.* skilled, having many accomplishments. [f. prec.]

accomplishment /ə'kʌmplɪʃmənt/ *n.* 1 an acquired skill, especially a social one. 2 accomplishing, completion. 3 a thing achieved. [f. ACCOMPLISH]

accord /ə'kɔ:d/ *v.t./i.* 1 to be consistent *with*. 2 to grant, to give. —*n.* conformity, agreement. —**of one's own accord**, without being asked or compelled. [f. F f. L *cor* heart]

accordance /ə'kɔ:d(ə)ns/ *n.* conformity, agreement. —**accordant** *adj.* [as prec.]

according *adv.* **according as**, in a manner or to a degree that varies as. **according to**, in a manner corresponding to; as stated by. [f. ACCORD]

accordingly *adv.* as the (stated) circumstances suggest. [f. prec.]

accordion /əˈkɔːdɪən/ *n.* a portable musical instrument with bellows, metal reeds, and keys and/or buttons. —**accordionist** *n.* [f. G. f. It. *accordare* tune]

accost /əˈkɒst/ *v.t.* to approach and speak to; (of a prostitute) to solicit. [f. F f. It. f. L *costa* rib)]

account /əˈkaʊnt/ *n.* **1** a statement of money, goods, or services received or expended; a credit or similar business arrangement with a bank or firm; a record of this. **2** a description, a report. **3** importance, advantage. **4** a reckoning. —*v.t./i.* to regard as. —**account for,** to give a reckoning of; to provide or serve as an explanation for; to kill or overcome. **on account of,** because of. [f. OF *aconter* (AD-, *conter* count)]

accountable *adj.* having to account (*for* one's actions); explicable. —**accountability** /-ˈbɪlɪtɪ/ *n.* [f. prec.]

accountant *n.* one who keeps or examines business accounts. —**accountancy** *n.* [as ACCOUNT]

accounting *n.* keeping or examining accounts; accountancy. [f. ACCOUNT]

accoutrements /əˈkuːtrəmənts/ *n.pl.* equipment, trappings. [F]

accredit /əˈkredɪt/ *v.t.* **1** to attribute, to credit (*with* a saying etc.). **2** to send (an ambassador etc.) with credentials. **3** to gain belief or influence for. —**accreditation** /-ˈteɪʃ(ə)n/ *n.*, **accredited** *adj.* [f. F (as AD-, CREDIT)]

accretion /əˈkriːʃ(ə)n/ *n.* a growth or increase by gradual addition; matter added, adhesion of this. [f. L *accretio* (AD-, *crescere* grow)]

accrue /əˈkruː/ *v.t./i.* to come as a natural increase or advantage; to accumulate. [f. AF f. L (as prec.)]

accumulate /əˈkjuːmjuːleɪt/ *v.t./i.* to get more and more of; to increase in quantity or mass. —**accumulation** /-ˈleɪʃ(ə)n/ *n.* [f. L *accumulare* (AD-, *cumulus* heap)]

accumulator /əˈkjuːmjuːleɪtə(r)/ *n.* **1** a rechargeable electric cell, a storage battery. **2** a bet placed on a series of events with winnings from each staked on the next. **3** a storage register in a computer. [f. prec.]

accurate /ˈækjʊərət/ *adj.* precise, conforming exactly to a standard or to truth. —**accuracy** *n.*, **accurately** *adv.* [f. L *accuratus* done carefully (AD-, *curare* care)]

accursed /əˈkɜːsɪd/ *adj.* lying under a curse; (*colloq.*) detestable, annoying. [OE (A-, CURSE)]

accusation /ækjuːˈzeɪʃ(ə)n/ *n.* **1** a statement accusing a person. **2** accusing, being accused. [f. OF (as ACCUSE)]

accusative /əˈkjuːzətɪv/ *n.* (*Gram.*) the case expressing the object of a verb or preposition. —*adj.* (*Gram.*) of or in the accusative. [f. OF or L]

accusatorial /əkjuːzəˈtɔːrɪəl/ *adj.* (of procedure) in which the prosecutor is distinct from the judge (opp. *inquisitorial*). [f. L (as ACCUSE)]

accusatory /əˈkjuːzətərɪ/ *adj.* of or conveying an accusation. [f. L (as foll.)]

accuse /əˈkjuːz/ *v.t.* to state that one lays the blame for a fault or crime etc. upon. —**accuser** *n.* (f. OF f. L *accusare* (AD-, *causa* cause)]

accustom /əˈkʌstʌm/ *v.t.* to make or become used *to.* [f. OF f. L (as CUSTOM)]

accustomed /əˈkʌstəmd/ *adj.* customary; used *to.* [f. prec.]

ace /eɪs/ *n.* **1** a playing-card etc. with one spot. **2** one who excels in some activity. **3** a stroke in tennis (especially a service) that is too good for an opponent to return. **4** a point scored in rackets, badminton, etc. —**within an ace of,** on the verge of. [f. OF f. L *as* one]

acerbity /əˈsɜːbɪtɪ/ *n.* **1** sharpness in speech or manner. **2** sourness. [f. L *acerbus* sour-tasting]

acetate /ˈæsɪteɪt/ *n.* **1** a salt or ester of acetic acid, especially its cellulose ester used to make textiles and gramophone records. **2** fabric made from cellulose acetate. [f. foll.]

acetic /əˈsiːtɪk/ *adj.* of or like vinegar. —**acetic acid,** the acid that gives vinegar its characteristic taste and smell. [f. F f. L *acetum* vinegar]

acetone /ˈæsɪtəʊn/ *n.* a colourless volatile liquid that dissolves organic compounds. [f. prec.]

acetylene /əˈsetɪliːn/ *n.* a hydrocarbon gas that burns with a bright flame used for cutting and welding metal. [as prec.]

ache /eɪk/ *n.* a continuous or prolonged dull pain or mental distress. —*v.i.* to suffer or be the source of this. —**achy** *adj.* [f. OE]

achene /əˈkiːn/ *n.* a small dry one-seeded fruit that does not open, e.g. a strawberry pip. [f. Gk *a* not, *khainō* gape]

achieve /əˈtʃiːv/ *v.t.* to reach or attain by effort; to earn (a reputation etc.); to accomplish. [f. OF (*a chief* to a head)]

achievement /əˈtʃiːvmənt/ *n.* **1** something achieved; an act of achieving. **2** (in heraldry) an escutcheon with adjuncts, or a bearing, especially in memory of a distinguished feat. [f. prec.]

Achilles /əˈkɪliːz/ *n.* **Achilles' heel,** a weak or vulnerable point. **Achilles' tendon,** a tendon attaching the calf muscles to the heel. [f. *Achilles*, hero in Gk legend, invulnerable except in his heel]

achromatic /ækrəˈmætɪk/ *adj.* (in optics) free from colour; transmitting light without decomposing it into constituent colours. [f. F f. Gk (*a* not, CHROMATIC)]

acid /ˈæsɪd/ *n.* any of a class of substances that contain hydrogen and neutralize alkalis, turn blue litmus red, and of which the principal types are sour and able to corrode or dissolve metals; any sour substance. —*adj.* sharp-tasting, sour; looking or sounding bitter. —**acid house** a kind of synthesized music with a simple repetitive beat. **acid rain**, rain made acid by contamination, especially by waste gases from power stations, factories, etc. **acid test**, a crucial and conclusive test. (Acid is applied to a metal to test whether it is gold or not.) —**acidic** /ə'sɪdɪk/ *adj.*, **acidity** /ə'sɪdɪtɪ/ *n.* [f. F or L (*acēre* be sour)]

acidify /ə'sɪdɪfaɪ/ *v.t.* to make or become sour. [f. ACID]

acidosis /æsɪ'dəʊsɪs/ *n.* an over-acid condition of blood or body tissue. [as prec.]

acidulate /ə'sɪdjʊleɪt/ *v.t.* to make somewhat acid. [f. L *acidulus* somewhat sour]

acidulous /ə'sɪdʊləs/ *adj.* somewhat acid. [as prec.]

acknowledge /ək'nɒlɪdʒ/ *v.t.* **1** to agree to the truth or validity of, to admit. **2** to report the receipt of. **3** to show appreciation of. —**acknowledgement** *n.* [f. obs. v. *knowledge*]

acme /'ækmɪ/ *n.* the highest point, the point of perfection. [Gk, = highest point]

acne /'æknɪ/ *n.* inflammation of the oil-glands of the skin, producing red pimples. [f. erron. Gk *aknas* for *akmas* (*akmē* facial eruption; cf. prec.)]

acolyte /'ækəlaɪt/ *n.* a person assisting a priest in certain church services; an assistant. [f. F or L f. Gk *akolouthos* follower]

aconite /'ækənaɪt/ *n.* a perennial plant of the buttercup family (genus *Aconitum*) with a poisonous root; a drug obtained from this. —**winter aconite**, a yellow-flowered plant of the genus *Eranthis*, blooming in winter. [f. F or L f. Gk]

acorn /'eɪkɔːn/ *n.* the fruit of the oak-tree, with a cup-like base. [OE]

acoustic /ə'kuːstɪk/ *adj.* of sound or the sense of hearing; of acoustics. —*n.* acoustics. —**acoustics** *n.pl.* the properties or qualities (of a room etc.) affecting the transmission of sound; (as *sing.*) the science of sound. —**acoustical** *adj.*, **acoustically** *adv.* [f. Gk (*akouō* hear)]

acquaint /ə'kweɪnt/ *v.t.* to make aware or familiar. —**be acquainted with**, to know slightly. [f. OF f. L *accognitare* (AD-, *cognoscere* know)]

acquaintance *n.* **1** being acquainted. **2** a person one knows slightly. [as prec.]

acquiesce /ækwɪ'es/ *v.i.* to agree (tacitly), to raise no objection. —**acquiesce in**, to accept (an arrangement etc.). —**acquiescence** *n.*, **acquiescent** *adj.* [f. L *acquiescere* (AD-, *quiescere* rest)]

acquire /ə'kwaɪə(r)/ *v.t.* to gain by and for oneself. —**acquired taste**, a liking gained by experience, not instantly. —**acquirement** *n.*, **acquisition** /ækwɪ'zɪʃ(ə)n/ *n.* [f. OF f. L *acquirere* (AD-, *quaerere* seek)]

acquisitive /ə'kwɪzɪtɪv/ *adj.* keen to acquire things. —**acquisitively** *adv.*, **acquisitiveness** *n.* [f. L (as prec.)]

acquit /ə'kwɪt/ *v.t.* (**-tt-**) to declare (a person) to be not guilty (*of* an offence etc.). —**acquit oneself**, to perform, to conduct oneself. [f. OF f. L *acquitare* pay debt]

acquittal /ə'kwɪt(ə)l/ *n.* **1** a verdict acquitting a person. **2** performance (*of* a duty). [f. prec.]

acre /'eɪkə(r)/ *n.* a measure of land, originally as much as a yoke of oxen could plough in a day, afterwards limited by statute to 4840 sq. yds. (0.405 ha); a stretch of land. [OE]

acreage /'eɪkərɪdʒ/ *n.* the total number of acres; an extent of land. [f. prec.]

acrid /'ækrɪd/ *adj.* bitterly pungent; bitter in manner or temper. —**acridity** /ə'krɪdɪtɪ/ *n.* [f. L *acer* keen]

acrimonious /ækrɪ'məʊnɪəs/ *adj.* bitter in manner or temper. —**acrimoniously** *adv.*, **acrimony** /'ækrɪmənɪ/ *n.* [f. F or L (as ACRID)]

acrobat /'ækrəbæt/ *n.* a performer of spectacular gymnastic feats. —**acrobatic** /-'bætɪk/ *adj.*, **acrobatically** *adv.* [f. F f. Gk (*akron* summit, *bainō* walk)]

acrobatics /ækrə'bætɪks/ *n.pl.* acrobatic feats. [f. prec.]

acronym /'ækrənɪm/ *n.* a word formed from the initial letters of other words, e.g. *Nato, laser*. [f. Gk *akron* extremity, *onoma* name]

acropolis /ə'krɒpəlɪs/ *n.* the citadel or upper fortified part of an ancient Greek city. —**the Acropolis**, that at Athens, containing the Parthenon, Erechtheum, and other noted buildings, mostly dating from the 5th c. BC. [f. Gk *akron* summit, *polis* city]

across /ə'krɒs/ *prep.* & *adv.* **1** from side to side (of). **2** to or on the other side (of). **3** forming a cross with. **4** so as to be understood or accepted. —**across the board**, applying to all. **come** *or* **run across**, to meet or find by chance. [f. OF (*croix* cross)]

acrostic /ə'krɒstɪk/ *n.* a word-puzzle or poem in which certain letters (usually the first or first and last in each line) form word(s). [f. F or Gk (*akron* end, *stikhos* row)]

acrylic /ə'krɪlɪk/ *adj.* of material made from a synthetic polymer derived from acrylic acid. —*n.* an acrylic fibre, plastic, or resin. —**acrylic acid**, an unsaturated organic acid. [f. L *acer* pungent, *olēre* smell]

ACT *abbr.* Australian Capital Territory.

act *n.* **1** a thing done; the process of doing something. **2** a piece of entertainment. **3** a pretence. **4** a main division of a play or opera. **5** a decree or law made by a parliament.

—*v.t./i.* **1** to perform actions, to behave; to perform functions; to have an effect. **2** to be an actor or actress. **3** to perform (a part) in a play etc.; to portray by actions. —**act of God,** the operation of uncontrollable natural forces. **Acts (of the Apostles),** a book of the New Testament immediately following the Gospels, relating the early history of the Church and dealing largely with the lives and work of St Peter and St Paul. It is traditionally ascribed to St Luke. [f. OF & L *actus* (*agere* do)]

actinic /æk'tɪnɪk/ *adj.* having photochemical properties, as of short-wavelength radiation. [f. Gk *aktis* ray]

actinide /'æktɪnaɪd/ *n.* any of a series of fifteen radioactive metallic elements ranging from actinium (atomic number 89) to lawrencium (103). [f. foll.]

actinium /æk'tɪnɪəm/ *n.* a radioactive metallic element, symbol Ac, atomic number 89, which occurs in pitchblende. [f. Gk *aktis* ray]

action /'ækʃ(ə)n/ *n.* **1** the process of doing or performing, exertion of energy or influence. **2** a thing done; a series of events in a drama etc. **3** a battle, fighting. **4** a way of moving or functioning, the mechanism of an instrument. **5** a lawsuit. —**action replay,** a play-back (at normal speed or in slow motion) of a televised incident in a sports match. **out of action,** not working. [f. OF f. L (as ACT)]

actionable *adj.* providing ground for an action at law. [f. prec.]

activate /'æktɪveɪt/ *v.t.* **1** to make active. **2** to make radioactive. —**activation** /-'veɪʃ(ə)n/ *n.*, **activator** *n.* [f. foll.]

active /'æktɪv/ *adj.* **1** consisting in or characterized by action, energetic; working, operative; having an effect. **2** radioactive. **3** (*Gram.*) attributing the action of the verb to the person or thing whence it proceeds (e.g. in *we saw him*). —*n.* (*Gram.*) the active voice or form of a verb. —**active voice,** (*Gram.*) that comprising the active forms of verbs. —**actively** *adv.*, **activeness** *n.* [f. OF or L (as ACT)]

activist /'æktɪvɪst/ *n.* one who follows a policy of vigorous action in a cause, especially in politics. —**activism** *n.* [f. prec.]

activity /æk'tɪvətɪ/ *n.* **1** being active, the exertion of energy. **2** a sphere or kind of action. **3** (esp. in *pl.*) actions, occupations. **4** radioactivity. [as ACTIVE]

actor *n.* a performer in a drama, film, etc. —**actress** *n.fem.* [L, = doer (as ACT)]

actual /'æktʃʊəl/ *adj.* existing in fact, real; current. [f. OF f. L (as ACT)]

actuality /æktʃʊ'ælɪtɪ/ *n.* reality; (in *pl.*) existing conditions. [f. prec.]

actually /'æktʃʊəlɪ/ *adv.* **1** really. **2** at present. **3** strange as it may seem. [f. ACTUAL]

actuary /'æktʃʊərɪ/ *n.* an expert in statistics, especially one who calculates insurance risks and premiums. —**actuarial** /-'eərɪəl/ *adj.* [f. L *actuarius* bookkeeper]

actuate /'æktʃʊeɪt/ *v.t.* to activate (a movement or process), to cause to function; to cause (a person) to act. —**actuation** /-'eɪʃ(ə)n/ *n.*, **actuator** *n.* [f. L (as ACTUAL)]

acuity /ə'kju:ətɪ/ *n.* sharpness, acuteness. [f. F or L (as ACUTE)]

acumen /'ækju:mən/ *n.* shrewdness. [L, = sharp thing]

acupuncture /'ækju:pʌnktʃə(r)/ *n.* a method (originating in China) of pricking the tissues of the body with fine needles as medical treatment or to relieve pain. —**acupuncturist** *n.* [f. L *acu* with a needle + PUNCTURE]

acute /ə'kju:t/ *adj.* **1** sharp or severe in its effect. **2** shrewd, perceptive. **3** (of a disease) not chronic, coming to a crisis. **4** (of sound) high, shrill. —**acute accent,** a mark (´) over a vowel to show its quality or length. **acute angle,** one of less than 90°. —**acutely** *adv.*, **acuteness** *n.* [f. L *acutus* (*acuere* sharpen)]

AD *abbr.* of the Christian era. [abbr. of ANNO DOMINI]

ad *n.* (*colloq.*) an advertisement. [abbr.]

ad- *prefix* (usu. assimilated to **ac-** before *c, k, q,* to **af-** etc. before *f, g, l, n, p, r, s, t*; reduced to **a-** before *sc, sp, st*) implying motion or direction to; change into; addition, adherence, increase; simple intensification. [f. OF or L *ad* to]

adage /'ædɪdʒ/ *n.* a traditional maxim, a proverb. [F f. L *adagium* (*ad* to, *aiere* say)]

adagio /ə'dɑ:ʒɪəʊ/ *adv.* (*Mus.*) in slow time. —*n.* (*pl.* **-os**) (*Mus.*) a movement to be played in this way. [It.]

Adam /'ædəm/ (in Hebrew tradition) the first man. —**Adam's apple,** the projection of cartilage at the front of the neck, especially in men. [f. Heb., = man]

adamant /'ædəmənt/ *adj.* stubbornly resolute. —**adamantine** /-'mæntaɪn/ *adj.* [f. OF f. L f. Gk *adamas* very hard metal or stone]

adapt /ə'dæpt/ *v.t./i.* to make or become suitable for a new use or situation etc. —**adaptation** /-'teɪʃ(ə)n/ *n.* [f. F f. L *adaptare* (AD-, *aptus* fit)]

adaptable *adj.* able to be adapted or to adapt. —**adaptability** /-'bɪlɪtɪ/ *n.* [f. prec.]

adaptor *n.* **1** a device for making equipment compatible. **2** a device for connecting several electric plugs to one socket. [f. ADAPT]

ADC *abbr.* aide-de-camp.

add *v.t./i.* **1** to join (a thing *to* another) as an increase or supplement. **2** to put (numbers or amounts) together to get their total. **3** to make as a further remark. —**add up,** to find the total of; to amount *to*; (*colloq.*) to make sense, to seem reasonable. —**adder** *n.* [f. L *addere* put together]

addendum /əˈdendəm/ *n.* (*pl.* **-a**) something added; (in *pl.*) additional matter at the end of a book. [L, f. *addere* add]

adder *n.* **1** a small venomous snake, especially the common viper. **2** any of various harmless snakes of North America. **3** (also **death adder**) a venomous snake of the cobra family, *Acanthophis antarcticus*, found in Australia and nearby islands. [OE, orig. *nadder*]

addict /ˈædɪkt/ *n.* a person who is addicted, especially to drugs. [as foll.]

addicted /əˈdɪktɪd/ *adj.* having an addiction *to*. [f. L *addicere* assign]

addiction /əˈdɪkʃ(ə)n/ *n.* the condition of doing or using something as a habit or compulsively (esp. of drug-taking, with adverse effects on ceasing); devotion *to* an interest. [as prec.]

addictive /əˈdɪktɪv/ *adj.* causing addiction. [as ADDICT]

addition /əˈdɪʃ(ə)n/ *n.* adding; a thing added. —**in addition,** as something added (*to*). [f. OF or L (as ADD)]

additional *adj.* added, extra. —**additionally** *adv.* [f. prec.]

additive /ˈædɪtɪv/ *n.* a thing added, especially a substance with special properties. —*adj.* involving addition. [f. L (as ADD)]

addle *v.t./i.* **1** (of an egg) to become rotten and produce no chick. **2** to muddle, to confuse. [OE, = filth]

address /əˈdres/ *n.* **1** the place where a person lives or a firm is situated; particulars of this, especially for postal purposes. **2** a speech to an audience. **3** the part of a computer instruction that specifies the location of an item of stored information. —*v.t.* **1** to write postal directions on. **2** to speak or write to; to direct a remark or written statement to. **3** to apply *oneself* or direct one's attention to. **4** to take aim at (the ball, in golf). [f. OF f. L (as DIRECT)]

addressee /ædreˈsiː/ *n.* a person to whom a letter etc. is addressed. [f. prec.]

adduce /əˈdjuːs/ *v.t.* to cite as an instance or proof. [f. L *adducere* (AD-, *ducere* bring)]

adducible *adj.* that may be adduced. [f. prec.]

adenoids /ˈædənɔɪdz/ *n.pl.* enlarged lymphatic tissue between the back of the nose and throat, often hindering breathing. —**adenoidal** *adj.* [f. Gk *adēn* gland]

adenoma /ædɪˈnəʊmə/ *n.* a gland-like benign tumour. [as prec.]

adept /ˈædept/ *adj.* thoroughly proficient (*in* or *at*). —*n.* an adept person. [f. L (*adipisci* attain)]

adequate /ˈædɪkwət/ *adj.* sufficient, satisfactory; passable but not outstandingly good. —**adequacy** *n.*, **adequately** *adv.* [f. L *adaequare* make equal]

adhere /ədˈhɪə(r)/ *v.i.* **1** to stick. **2** to give one's support or allegiance *to*. **3** to behave according *to* a rule etc. [f. F or L *adhaerēre* (AD-, *haerēre* stick)]

adherent *n.* a supporter (*of* a party or doctrine). —*adj.* adhering or sticking *to*. —**adherence** *n.* [as prec.]

adhesion /ədˈhiːʒ(ə)n/ *n.* **1** adhering (*lit.* or *fig.*). **2** the growing together of normally separate tissues as a result of inflammation or injury; such a formation. [f. F or L (as ADHERE)]

adhesive /ədˈhiːsɪv/ *adj.* having the property of adhering, sticky. —*n.* an adhesive substance. —**adhesive tape,** a strip of paper or transparent material coated with adhesive, used for fastening packages etc. —**adhesiveness** *n.* [f. F (as ADHERE)]

ad hoc /æd ˈhɒk/ for this purpose, special(ly). [L]

adieu /əˈdjuː/ *int.* & *n.* goodbye. [f. F (*à* to, *Dieu* God)]

Adi Granth /ɑːdɪ grʌnt/ the single sacred scripture of Sikhism, compiled by religious teachers, containing religious poetry in several languages. [Hindi (= first book), f. Skr.]

ad infinitum /æd ɪnfɪˈnaɪtəm/ without limit, for ever. [L]

adipose /ˈædɪpəʊs/ *adj.* of animal fat, fatty. —**adiposity** /-ˈpɒsɪtɪ/ *n.* [f. L *adeps* fat]

adjacent /əˈdʒeɪs(ə)nt/ *adj.* lying near, contiguous (*to*). [f. L *adjacēre* (AD-, *jacēre* lie)]

adjective /ˈædʒɪktɪv/ *n.* a word indicating an attribute, used to describe or modify a noun. —**adjectival** /-ˈtaɪv(ə)l/ *adj.*, **adjectivally** *adv.* [f. OF f. L *adjicere* (AD- *jacere* throw)]

adjoin /əˈdʒɔɪn/ *v.t.* to be next to and joined with. [f. OF f. L *adjungere* (AD-, *jungere* join)]

adjourn /əˈdʒɜːn/ *v.t./i.* to postpone, to break off temporarily for later resumption. —**adjournment** *n.* [f. OF f. L (AD-, *diurnum* day)]

adjudge /əˈdʒʌdʒ/ *v.t.* to pronounce judgement on; to pronounce or award judicially. —**adjudg(e)ment** *n.* [f. OF f. L *adjudicare* (AD-, *judex* judge)]

adjudicate /əˈdʒuːdɪkeɪt/ *v.t./i.* to act as judge; to adjudge. —**adjudication** /-ˈkeɪʃ(ə)n/ *n.*, **adjudicator** *n.* [as prec.]

adjunct /ˈædʒʌnkt/ *n.* a thing added or attached but subordinate (*to* or *of*). [f. L, as ADJOIN]

adjure /əˈdʒʊə(r)/ *v.t.* to command or urge solemnly. —**adjuration** /-ˈeɪʃ(ə)n/ *n.* [f. L *adjurare* put to an oath]

adjust /əˈdʒʌst/ *v.t./i.* **1** to arrange, to put into the correct order or position etc.; to regulate. **2** to make suitable (*to* a need or purpose); to harmonize (discrepancies); to adapt oneself to new conditions. **3** to assess (loss or damage). —**adjuster** *n.*, **adjustment** *n.* [f. F f. L *juxta* near]

adjustable *adj.* that may be adjusted. [f. prec.]

adjutant /ˈædjʊt(ə)nt/ *n.* an army officer assisting

a superior officer in administrative duties; an assistant. —**adjutant bird,** a large stork of the genus *Leptoptilus*, of which the largest (*L. dubius*), found in India, is 1.8-2.1 m (6-7 ft.) tall. [f. L, frequent. of *adjuvare* help]

ad lib *v.t./i.* (**-bb-**) (*colloq.*) to speak impromptu, to improvise. —*adj.* (*colloq.*) improvised. —*adv.* as one pleases, to any desired extent. [abbr. L *ad libitum* according to pleasure]

admin /ˈædmɪn/ *n.* (*colloq.*) administration. [abbr.]

administer /ədˈmɪnɪstə(r)/ *v.t./i.* **1** to manage (business affairs). **2** to give out (justice, a sacrament) formally; to present (an oath) to; to provide. **3** to act as administrator. [f. F f. L *administrare* (AD-, *ministrare* minister)]

administrate /ədˈmɪnɪstreɪt/ *v.t./i.* to act as administrator (of). [f. L (as prec.)]

administration /ədmɪnɪˈstreɪʃ(ə)n/ *n.* **1** administering, especially of public affairs. **2** the government. [f. OF or L (as ADMINISTER)]

administrative /ədˈmɪnɪstrətɪv/ *adj.* of or involving administration. [f. F or L (as prec.)]

administrator /ədˈmɪnɪstreɪtə(r)/ *n.* a manager of business affairs; one who is capable of organizing things; one authorized to manage an estate. [as ADMINISTER]

admirable /ˈædmərəb(ə)l/ *adj.* worthy of admiration; excellent. —**admirably** *adv.* [F f. L (as ADMIRE)]

admiral /ˈædmər(ə)l/ *n.* the commander-in-chief of a navy; a naval officer of high rank, the commander of a fleet or squadron. There are four grades: *Admiral of the Fleet*, *Admiral*, *Vice Admiral*, *Rear Admiral*. —**red admiral, white admiral,** European species of butterfly (*Vanessa atalanta* and *Ladoga camilla*), perhaps originally called *the admirable*. [f. OF f. L f. Arab., = commander (cf. AMIR)]

Admiralty /ˈædmərəltɪ/ *n.* the former name of the department of State administering the Royal Navy. [as prec.]

admire /ədˈmaɪə(r)/ *v.t.* to regard with approval, respect, or satisfaction; to express admiration of. —**admiration** /ædmɪˈreɪʃ(ə)n/ *n.*, **admirer** *n.* [f. F or L *admirari* (AD-, *mirari* wonder at)]

admissible /ədˈmɪsəb(ə)l/ *adj.* (of an idea etc.) worthy of being accepted or considered; (of evidence) allowable in law. —**admissibility** /-ɪˈbɪlɪtɪ/ *n.* [f. F or L (as ADMIT)]

admission /ədˈmɪʃ(ə)n/ *n.* **1** an acknowledgement (*of*). **2** admitting, being admitted; the fee for this. [f. foll.]

admit /ədˈmɪt/ *v.t./i.* (**-tt-**) **1** to recognize as true or valid; to confess *to*. **2** to allow to enter; to have room for. **3** to accept (a plea or statement). —**admit of,** to allow (a doubt, improvement, etc.) as possible. —**admittance** *n.* [f. L *admittere* (AD-, *mittere* send)]

admittedly /ədˈmɪtɪdlɪ/ *adv.* as an acknowledged fact. [f. prec.]

admixture /ædˈmɪkstʃə(r)/ *n.* a thing added as an ingredient; the adding of this. [f. AD- + MIXTURE]

admonish /ədˈmɒnɪʃ/ *v.t.* to reprove mildly but firmly; to urge or advise seriously; to warn. —**admonishment** *n.*, **admonition** /-ˈnɪʃ(ə)n/ *n.* [f. OF f. L *admonere* (AD-, *monēre* warn)]

admonitory /ədˈmɒnɪtərɪ/ *adj.* admonishing. [as prec.]

ad nauseam /æd ˈnɔːzɪæm/ to an excessive or sickening degree. [L]

ado /əˈduː/ *n.* fuss, busy activity, trouble. [orig. in *much ado* = much to do]

adobe /əˈdəʊbɪ/ *n.* brick made of clay and dried in the sun; clay for this, used extensively in South America, the south-western USA, and Africa. [Sp. f. Arab., = the brick]

adolescent /ædəˈles(ə)nt/ *adj.* growing up, between childhood and maturity. —*n.* an adolescent person. —**adolescence** *n.* [f. OF f. L *adolescere* grow up]

adopt /əˈdɒpt/ *v.t.* **1** to take into one's family *as* a relation, especially as one's child with legal guardianship; to choose (a course etc.); to take over (a name, idea, etc.); to choose as a candidate for office. **2** to accept responsibility for maintenance of (a road etc.). **3** to approve or accept (a report, accounts). —**adoption** /-ʃ(ə)n/ *n.* [f. F or L *adoptare* (AD-, *optare* choose)]

adoptive *adj.* related by adoption. [f. OF f. L (as prec.)]

adorable /əˈdɔːrəb(ə)l/ *adj.* worthy of adoration, very lovable; (*colloq.*) delightful. —**adorably** *adv.* [f. foll.]

adore /əˈdɔː(r)/ *v.t.* **1** to love deeply. **2** to worship as divine. **3** (*colloq.*) to like very much. —**adoration** /-ˈreɪʃ(ə)n/ *n.*, **adorer** *n.* [f. OF f. L *adorare* worship (AD-, *orare* pray)]

adorn /əˈdɔːn/ *v.t.* to be an ornament to, to decorate with ornaments. —**adornment** *n.* [f. OF f. L *adornare* decorate]

adrenal /əˈdriːn(ə)l/ *n.* an adrenal gland. —**adrenal gland,** either of two ductless glands above the kidneys, secreting adrenalin. [f. AD- + RENAL]

adrenalin /əˈdrenəlɪn/ *n.* a hormone that stimulates the nervous system, secreted by the adrenal glands or prepared synthetically. [f. prec.]

adrift /əˈdrɪft/ *adv.* & *predic. adj.* **1** drifting. **2** (*colloq.*) amiss, out of touch, unfastened. [f. A- + DRIFT]

adroit /əˈdrɔɪt/ *adj.* skilful, ingenious. —**adroitly** *adv.*, **adroitness** *n.* [F (*à droit* according to right)]

adsorb /ædˈsɔːb/ *v.t.* (of a solid) to hold (particles

of a gas or liquid) to its surface. —**adsorbent** *adj*., **adsorption** *n*., **adsorptive** *adj*. [f. AD-, after *absorb*]

adulation /ædjʊˈleɪʃ(ə)n/ *n*. obsequious flattery. —**adulatory** *adj*. [f. L *adulari* fawn on]

adult /ˈædʌlt/ *adj*. mature, grown-up. —*n*. an adult person. —**adulthood** *n*. [f. L (as ADOLESCENT)]

adulterant /əˈdʌltərənt/ *n*. a substance added in adulterating. [as foll.]

adulterate /əˈdʌltəreɪt/ *v.t.* to make impure or poorer in quality by an admixture of other substance(s). —**adulteration** /-ˈreɪʃ(ə)n/ *n*. [f. L *adulterare* corrupt]

adulterer /əˈdʌltərə(r)/ *n*. a person (esp. a man) who commits adultery. —**adulteress** *n.fem*. [f. F f. L (as prec.)]

adultery /əˈdʌltərɪ/ *n*. voluntary sexual intercourse of a married person with someone other than his or her spouse. —**adulterous** *adj*. [f. OF f. L]

adumbrate /ˈædʌmbreɪt/ *v.t.* **1** to indicate faintly; to foreshadow. **2** to overshadow. —**adumbration** /-ˈbreɪʃ(ə)n/ *n*. [f. L *adumbrare* (AD-, *umbra* shade)]

advance /ədˈvɑːns/ *v.t./i.* **1** to move or put forward; to progress; to rise in rank; **2** to lend, to pay before a due date. **3** to present (a suggestion or claim etc.). **4** to bring (an event) to an earlier date. **5** to raise (a price). —*n*. **1** a forward movement, progress. **2** a rise in price. **3** a loan, payment beforehand. **4** (in *pl*.) attempts to establish a friendly or business relationship. —*attrib. adj*. **1** going before others. **2** done or provided in advance. —**in advance,** ahead in time or place. [f. OF f. L (*ab* away, *ante* before)]

advanced *adj*. **1** far on in progress or life; not elementary. **2** (of ideas etc.) new and not yet generally accepted. [f. prec.]

advancement *n*. promotion of a person or plan. [f. ADVANCE]

advantage /ədˈvɑːntɪdʒ/ *n*. **1** a favourable circumstance; benefit; superiority. **2** the next point after deuce in tennis. —*v.t.* to be or give an advantage to. —**take advantage of,** to make use of, to exploit. —**advantageous** /ædvænˈteɪdʒəs/ *adj*., **advantageously** *adv*. [f. OF (as ADVANCE)]

Advent /ˈædvənt/ *n*. **1** the season (with four Sundays) before Christmas Day; the coming of Christ. **2 advent,** the arrival of an important person, event, or development. [OE f. OF f. L *adventus* arrival (AD-, *venire* come)]

Adventist /ˈædvəntɪst/ *n*. a member of any of various sects believing that the second coming of Christ is imminent. [f. prec.]

adventitious /ædvenˈtɪʃəs/ *adj*. **1** accidental, casual. **2** added from outside. **3** (*Biol*., of roots etc.) occurring in an unusual place —**adventitiously** *adv*. [f. L (as ADVENT)]

adventure /ədˈventʃə(r)/ *n*. **1** an unusual and exciting or dangerous experience. **2** willingness to take risks. —**adventure playground,** a playground where children are provided with discarded materials etc. to use imaginatively in play. —**adventurous** *adj*., **adventurously** *adv*. [f. OF (as ADVENT)]

adventurer *n*. **1** one who seeks adventures. **2** one who is ready to take risks or be unscrupulous for personal gain. —**adventuress** *n.fem*. [f. prec.]

adverb /ˈædvɜːb/ *n*. a word indicating manner, degree, circumstance, etc., used to modify an adjective, verb, or another adverb. —**adverbial** /ədˈvɜːbɪəl/ *adj*., **adverbially** *adv*. [f. F or L (*ad* to, *verbum* word)]

adversarial /ædvəˈseərɪəl/ *adj*. **1** involving adversaries, contested. **2** opposed, hostile. —**adversarially** *adv*. [f. foll.]

adversary /ˈædvəsərɪ/ *n*. an opponent, an enemy. [as foll.]

adverse /ˈædvɜːs/ *adj*. unfavourable; harmful. [f. OF f. L *adversus* (AD-, *vertere* turn)]

adversity /ədˈvɜːsɪtɪ/ *n*. misfortune, trouble. [as prec.]

advert /ˈædvɜːt/ *n*. (*colloq*.) an advertisement. [abbr.]

advertise /ˈædvətaɪz/ *v.t./i.* to praise publicly in order to promote sales; to make generally known; to offer or ask *for* by a notice in a newspaper etc. —**advertiser** *n*. [f. OF f. L (as ADVERSE)]

advertisement /ədˈvɜːtɪsmənt/ *n*. a public announcement advertising (for) something; advertising. [f. F (as prec.)]

advice /ədˈvaɪs/ *n*. **1** an opinion given as to future action. **2** information, news; formal notice of a transaction. —**take advice,** to seek it, to act according to it. [f. OF f. L (*ad* to, *vidēre* see)]

advisable /ədˈvaɪzəb(ə)l/ *adj*. worth recommending, expedient. —**advisability** /-ˈbɪlɪtɪ/ *n*. [f. foll.]

advise /ədˈvaɪz/ *v.t./i.* **1** to give advice (to), to recommend. **2** to inform. —**adviser** *n*. [as ADVICE]

advisory /ədˈvaɪzərɪ/ *adj*. giving advice. [f. prec.]

advocacy /ˈædvəkəsɪ/ *n*. **1** the advocating *of* a policy etc. **2** the function of an advocate. [f. foll.]

advocate /ˈædvəkət/ *n*. one who advocates or speaks in favour *of*; one who pleads on behalf of another, especially in a lawcourt. —/-keɪt/ *v.t.* to recommend, to be in favour of. [f. OF f. L *advocatus* (AD-, *vocare* call)]

adze /ædz/ *n*. an axe-like tool with an arched blade, for trimming large pieces of wood. [OE]

aegis /ˈiːdʒɪs/ *n.* protection, sponsorship. [L f. Gk, = mythical shield of Zeus or Athene]

aeolian /iːˈəʊlɪən/ *adj.* wind-borne. —**aeolian harp,** a stringed instrument giving musical sounds on exposure to wind. **Aeolian Islands,** the ancient name of the Lipari Islands. [f. *Aeolus*, Gk god of the winds]

aeon /ˈiːən/ *n.* a long or indefinite period. [f. L f. Gk, = age]

aepyornis /iːpɪˈɔːnɪs/ *n.* a gigantic flightless extinct bird of the genus *Aepyornis*, resembling a moa, known from remains found in Madagascar. [L f. Gk *aipus* high, *ornis* bird]

aerate /ˈeəreɪt/ *v.t.* **1** to expose to the action of air. **2** to charge with carbon dioxide. —**aeration** /-ˈreɪʃ(ə)n/ *n.*, **aerator** *n.* [f. L *aer* air]

aerial /ˈeərɪəl/ *n.* a wire or rod for transmitting or receiving aerial waves. —*adj.* **1** from the air or aircraft. **2** existing in the air. **3** like air. [f. L (as AIR)]

aero- /eərəʊ-/ *in comb.* air, aircraft. [f. Gk (*aēr* air)]

aerobatics /eərəˈbætɪks/ *n.pl.* feats of expert flying of aircraft, especially for display. [f. AERO-, after *acrobatics*]

aerobic /eəˈrəʊbɪk/ *adj.* **1** using oxygen from the air. **2** (of exercises) designed to increase the intake of oxygen and strengthen the heart and lungs. —**aerobics** *n.pl.* exercises of this kind. [f. F (as AERO- + Gk *bios* life)]

aerodrome /ˈeərədrəʊm/ *n.* an airfield or airport. [f. AERO- + Gk *dromos* course]

aerodynamics /eərəʊdaɪˈnæmɪks/ *n.* (also as *pl.*) the dynamics of solid bodies moving through air. —**aerodynamic** *adj.*

aerofoil /ˈeərəfɔɪl/ *n.* a body (e.g. an aircraft wing, fin, or tailplane) shaped to produce a desired aerodynamic reaction (e.g. lift) when it passes through air [f. AERO- + FOIL¹]

aeronaut /ˈeərənɔːt/ *n.* a balloonist or other aviator. [f. AERO- + Gk *nautēs* sailor]

aeronautics /eərəˈnɔːtɪks/ *n.* the science, art, or practice of the flight of aircraft. —**aeronautic** *adj.*, **aeronautical** *adj.* [f. AERO- + NAUTICAL]

aeroplane /ˈeərəpleɪn/ *n.* a power-driven heavier-than-air aircraft with wings. [f. F (as AERO-, PLANE¹)]

aerosol /ˈeərəsɒl/ *n.* a container holding a liquid or other substance and a propellent gas packed under pressure, dispensing its contents as a fine spray when the pressure is released; this substance. [f. AERO- + SOL]

aerospace /ˈeərəʊspeɪs/ *n.* **1** earth's atmosphere and outer space. **2** the technology of aviation in this.

aesthete /ˈiːsθiːt/ *n.* a person who claims to have great understanding and appreciation of what is beautiful, especially in the arts. [f. Gk (as foll.)]

aesthetic /iːsˈθetɪk/ *adj.* concerned with or sensitive to what is beautiful; artistic, tasteful. —**aesthetics** *n.pl.* a branch of philosophy dealing with the principles of beauty and tastefulness. —**aesthetically** *adv.*, **aestheticism** /-sɪz(ə)m/ *n.* [f. Gk (*aisthanomai* perceive)]

aetiology /iːtɪˈɒlədʒɪ/ *n.* **1** the study of causation. **2** the study of the causes of disease. **3** the cause of a disease. —**aetiological** /-əˈlɒdʒɪk(ə)l/ *adj.*, **aetiologically** *adv.* [f. L f. Gk (*aitia* cause)]

afar /əˈfɑː(r)/ *adv.* far off, far away. [f. A- + FAR]

affable /ˈæfəb(ə)l/ *adj.* polite and friendly. —**affability** /-ˈbɪlɪtɪ/ *n.*, **affably** *adv.* [F f. L *affabilis* (AD-, *fari* speak)]

affair /əˈfeə(r)/ *n.* **1** a matter, a concern; a thing done or to be done. **2** a temporary sexual relationship between two persons who are not married to each other. **3** (*colloq.*) a thing or event. **4** (in *pl.*) public or private business. [f. AF (*à faire* to do)]

affect /əˈfekt/ *v.t.* **1** to produce an effect on; (of disease) to attack; to touch the feelings of. **2** to pretend, to pose as. **3** to make a show of liking or using. [f. F or L *afficere* influence (AD-, *facere* do)

affectation /æfekˈteɪʃ(ə)n/ *n.* a studied display (*of* modesty etc.); an artificial manner, pretence. [f. prec.]

affected /əˈfektɪd/ *adj.* **1** pretended, artificial. **2** full of affectation. [f. AFFECT]

affection /əˈfekʃ(ə)n/ *n.* **1** love, a liking. **2** a disease or diseased condition. [as prec.]

affectionate /əˈfekʃ(ə)nət/ *adj.* showing affection, loving. —**affectionately** *adv.* [f. prec.]

affiance /əˈfaɪəns/ *v.t.* to promise in marriage. [f. OF f. L *affidare* entrust]

affidavit /æfɪˈdeɪvɪt/ *n.* a written statement confirmed by an oath. [L, = has stated on oath]

affiliate /əˈfɪlɪeɪt/ *v.t.* to connect as a member or branch. —*n.* an affiliated person or organization. [f. L *affiliare* adopt (AD-, *filius* son)]

affiliation /əfɪlɪˈeɪʃ(ə)n/ *n.* affiliating, being affiliated. —**affiliation order,** a court order compelling the putative father of an illegitimate child to help support it. [f. prec.]

affinity /əˈfɪnɪtɪ/ *n.* **1** a liking or attraction. **2** a relationship, especially by marriage. **3** a resemblance or connection suggesting that there is a relationship. **4** (*Chem.*) the tendency of substances to combine with others. [f. F f. L *affinis* bordering on]

affirm /əˈfɜːm/ *v.t./i.* to assert, to state as a fact; to declare solemnly in place of taking an oath. —**affirmation** /-ˈmeɪʃ(ə)n/ *n.*, **affirmatory** /əˈfɜːm-/ *adj.* [f. OF f. L *affirmare* (AD-, *firmus* strong)]

affirmative /əˈfɜːmətɪv/ *adj.* affirming, answering that a thing is so. —*n.* an affirmative word or statement. —**affirmatively** *adv.* [as prec.]

affix /əˈfɪks/ *v.t.* **1** to stick on, to fasten. **2** to add (a signature etc.) in writing. —/ˈæfɪks/ *n.* a thing affixed; (*Gram.*) a prefix or suffix. [f. F or L *affigere* (AD-, *figere* fix)]

afflict /əˈflɪkt/ *v.t.* to distress physically or mentally. [f. L (AD-, *fligere* strike)]

affliction /əˈflɪkʃ(ə)n/ *n.* distress, suffering; a cause of this. [as prec.]

affluent /ˈæflʊənt/ *adj.* wealthy; abundant. —*n.* a tributary stream. —**affluence** *n.*, **affluently** *adv.* [f. OF f. L *affluere* (AD-, *fluere* flow)]

afford /əˈfɔːd/ *v.t.* **1** to have enough money, means, or time etc. for; to be able to spare; to be in a position *to* do. **2** to provide. [f. OE, = promote]

afforest /əˈfɒrɪst/ *v.t.* to convert into forest, to plant with trees. —**afforestation** /-ˈteɪʃ(ə)n/ *n.* [f. L *afforestare* (AD-, *foresta* forest)]

affray /əˈfreɪ/ *n.* a breach of the peace by fighting or rioting in public. [f. AF f. L, = remove from peace]

affront /əˈfrʌnt/ *n.* an open insult. —*v.t.* **1** to insult openly. **2** to face, to confront. [f. OF f. L (AD-, *frons* face)]

Afghan /ˈæfgæn/ *n.* **1** a native of Afghanistan. **2** the language spoken there, Pashto. **3** (also **Afghan hound**) a dog of a breed with long silky hair. [f. Pashto]

aficionado /əfɪsjəˈneɪdəʊ/ *n.* (*pl.* **-os**) a devotee of a sport or pastime. [Sp.]

afield /əˈfiːld/ *adv.* away from home, to or at a distance. [f. A- + FIELD]

afire /əˈfaɪə(r)/ *adv.* & *predic. adj.* on fire. [f. A- + FIRE]

aflame /əˈfleɪm/ *adv.* & *predic. adj.* **1** in flames, burning. **2** very excited [f. A- + FLAME]

afloat /əˈfləʊt/ *adv.* & *predic. adj.* **1** floating; at sea, on board ship. **2** flooded. **3** out of debt or difficulty. **4** in circulation, current. [f. A- + FLOAT]

afoot /əˈfʊt/ *adv.* & *predic. adj.* progressing, in operation. [f. A- + FOOT]

afore /əˈfɔː(r)/ *adv.* & *prep.* (*archaic* or *dial.* exc. in *Naut.* use) before. [f. A- + FORE]

aforesaid /əˈfɔːsed/ *adj.* mentioned previously.

aforethought /əˈfɔːθɔːt/ *adj.* premeditated.

a fortiori /eɪ fɔːtɪˈɔːraɪ/ with yet stronger reason (than a conclusion already accepted). [L]

afraid /əˈfreɪd/ *predic. adj.* **1** alarmed, frightened, anxious about consequences etc. **2** (*colloq.*) politely regretful. [orig. f. AFFRAY]

afresh /əˈfreʃ/ *adv.* anew, beginning again. [f. A- + FRESH]

African /ˈæfrɪkən/ *n.* **1** of Africa or its people. **2** (*S.Afr.*) Bantu. —*n.* **1** an African Black. **2** (*S.Afr.*) a Bantu of South Africa. —**African marigold**, an annual garden plant (*Tagetes erecta*) with yellow flowers, originally from Mexico. —**African violet**, an East African plant of the genus *Saintpaulia*, with purple, pink, or white flowers, grown as a house-plant in Britain. [f. *Africa* name of continent]

Africanize /ˈæfrɪkənaɪz/ *v.t.* to make African, to place under the control of African Blacks. —**Africanization** /-ˈzeɪʃ(ə)n/ *n.* [f. AFRICAN]

Afrikaans /æfrɪˈkɑːns/ *n.* a language derived from Dutch, used in the Republic of South Africa. [Du., = African]

Afrikaner /æfrɪˈkɑːnə(r)/ *n.* a white person in South Africa, especially a descendant of Dutch settlers, whose native language is Afrikaans. [Afrik.]

Afro /ˈæfrəʊ/ *adj.* (of a hair-style) full and bushy, as that naturally grown by some Blacks. [f. foll., or abbr. AFRICAN]

Afro- /æfrəʊ-/ *in comb.* African. [f. L *Afer* African]

Afro-American *adj.* of American Blacks or their culture. —*n.* an American Black.

Afro-Asiatic *adj.* (of languages) Hamito-Semitic.

afrormosia /æfrɔːˈməʊzɪə/ *n.* an African tree of the genus *Afrormosia*; its teak-like wood, used for furniture. [f. AFRO- + *Ormosia* genus of trees]

aft *adv.* in, near, or to the stern of a ship or the rear of an aircraft. [prob. f. earlier *baft* (see ABAFT)]

after *prep.* **1** behind in place or order; later than. **2** in spite of. **3** as a result of. **4** in pursuit or search of. **5** about, concerning. **6** in imitation or honour of. —*adv.* behind; later. —*conj.* at or in a time later than. —*adj.* later, following; nearer the stern in a boat. —**after-care** *n.* attention after leaving hospital etc. **after-effect** *n.* an effect that arises or persists after the primary action of something. [OE]

afterbirth *n.* the placenta and foetal membrane discharged from the womb after childbirth.

afterlife *n.* life in a later part of a person's lifetime, or after death.

aftermath /ˈɑːftəmæθ/ *n.* **1** consequences, after-effects. **2** new grass growing after mowing or harvest. [f. AFTER + *math* mowing]

aftermost *adj.* last, furthest aft. [f. AFTER + -MOST]

afternoon /ɑːftəˈnuːn/ *n.* the time from noon to evening.

afters /ˈɑːftəz/ *n.pl.* (*colloq.*) a course following the main course at a meal.

aftershave *n.* a lotion for use after shaving.

afterthought *n.* something thought of or added later.

afterwards /ˈɑːftəwədz/, *US* **afterward** *adv.* later, subsequently. [OE f. AFT + *-wards* in the direction of]

Ag *symbol* silver. [f. L *argentum*]

again /əˈgeɪn, əˈgen/ *adv.* **1** another time, once more; as before; in addition. **2** furthermore, besides, likewise; on the other hand. [OE]

against /əˈgeɪnst, əˈgenst/ *prep.* **1** in opposition to; to the disadvantage of; in contrast to. **2** into collision or contact with. **3** in anticipation of, in preparation for; so as to cancel or lessen the effect of; in return for. [f. prec.]

agapanthus /ægəˈpænθəs/ *n.* an ornamental lily of the genus *Agapanthus*, native to South Africa, with blue or white flowers. [L f. Gk *agapē* love, *anthos* flower]

agape /əˈgeɪp/ *predic. adj.* gaping, open-mouthed. [f. A- + GAPE]

agar /ˈeɪgɑ:(r)/ *n.* (also **agar-agar**) any of certain seaweeds of SE Asian seas, especially *Gracilaria lichenoides*, from which a gelatinous substance is extracted, used as a solidifying agent in bacterial culture media and in the East as food. [Malay]

agaric /ˈægərɪk/ *n.* a fungus of the family Agaricaceae, with a cap and stalk, including the common mushroom. [f. L f. Gk]

agate /ˈægət/ *n.* a kind of hard semiprecious stone, a variety of chalcedony, with streaked colouring. [F f. L f. Gk]

agave /əˈgɑ:vɪ/ *n.* a plant of the genus *Agave*, especially a tropical American plant with spiny leaves and a tall stem up to 12m (40ft.) high. [f. Gk *Agauē* woman in myth (*agauos* illustrious)]

age *n.* **1** the length of past life or existence. **2** (*colloq.*, esp. in *pl.*) a long time. **3** a historical or other distinct period. **4** the later part of life, old age. —*v.t./i.* (*partic.* **ageing**) to become or cause to become old or show signs of age; to mature. —**age-long, age-old** *adjs.* having existed for a very long time. **of age,** having reached the age (18, formerly 21) at which one has an adult's legal rights and obligations. **under age,** below this age. [f. OF f. L *aetas* age]

aged *adj.* **1** /eɪdʒd/ of the age of (*aged* 3). **2** /ˈeɪdʒɪd/ very old. [f. AGE]

ageless *adj.* never growing or appearing old or outmoded; eternal. [f. AGE + -LESS]

agency /ˈeɪdʒənsɪ/ *n.* **1** the business or establishment of an agent. **2** active or intervening action. [f. L (*agere* do)]

agenda /əˈdʒendə/ *n.* (*pl.* **-as**) a programme of items of business to be dealt with at a meeting etc. [L, f. *agere* do]

agent /ˈeɪdʒənt/ *n.* **1** a person who acts for another in business etc. **2** one who or that which exerts power or produces an effect. **3** (also **secret agent**) a spy. [as prec.]

agent provocateur /æʒɑ̃ prəvɒkəˈtɜ:(r)/ (*pl.* **-ts -rs,** *pr.* same) a person employed to detect suspected offenders by tempting them to overt action. [F, = provocative agent]

agglomerate /əˈglɒmərert/ *v.t./i.* to collect into a mass. —/-ət/ *n.* a mass, especially of fused volcanic fragments. —/-ət/ *adj.* collected into a mass. —**agglomeration** /-ˈreɪʃ(ə)n/ *n.* [f. L *agglomerare* (AD-, *glomus* ball)]

agglutinate /əˈglu:tɪneɪt/ *v.t./i.* **1** to stick or fuse together, to coalesce. **2** (of language) to combine simple words without change of form to express compound ideas. —**agglutination** /-ˈeɪʃ(ə)n/ *n.*, **agglutinative** /-ətɪv/ *adj.* [f. L *agglutinare* (AD-, *gluten* glue)]

aggrandize /əˈgrændaɪz/ *v.t.* to increase the power, rank, or wealth of; to make seem greater. —**aggrandizement** /-ɪzmənt/ *n.* [f. F f. It. *aggrandire* f. L (AD-, *grandis* large)]

aggravate /ˈægrəveɪt/ *v.t.* **1** to increase the gravity of. **2** (*colloq.*, **D**) to annoy. —**aggravation** /-ˈveɪʃ(ə)n/ *n.* [f L *aggravare* make heavy (AD-, *gravis* heavy)]

aggregate /ˈægrɪgət/ *n.* **1** a total, an amount assembled. **2** broken stone, gravel, etc., used in making concrete. **3** a mass of particles or minerals. —*adj.* combined, total. —/-geɪt/ *v.t./i.* to collect or form into an aggregate; to unite; (*colloq.*) to amount to. —**in the aggregate,** as a whole. —**aggregation** /-ˈgeɪʃ(ə)n/ *n.* [f. L *aggregare* herd together (AD-, *grex* flock)]

aggression /əˈgreʃ(ə)n/ *n.* unprovoked attacking or attack; a hostile act or behaviour. [f. F or L *aggressio* attack (AD-, *gradi* step)]

aggressive /əˈgresɪv/ *adj.* apt to make attacks, showing aggression; forceful, self-assertive. —**aggressively** *adv.*, **aggressiveness** *n.* [as prec.]

aggressor /əˈgresə(r)/ *n.* one who makes an unprovoked attack or begins hostilities. [as AGGRESSION]

aggrieved /əˈgri:vd/ *adj.* having a grievance. [f. OF *agrever* make heavier (as GRIEF)]

aghast /əˈgɑ:st/ *adj.* filled with consternation or dismay. [f. obs. *v. agast* frighten]

agile /ˈædʒaɪl/ *adj.* nimble, quick-moving; lively. —**agilely** *adv.*, **agility** /əˈdʒɪlɪtɪ/ *n.* [F f. L (*agere* do)]

agitate /ˈædʒɪteɪt/ *v.t./i.* **1** to disturb, to excite. **2** to stir up (public) interest or concern. **3** to shake briskly. —**agitation** /-ˈteɪʃ(ə)n/ *n.*, **agitator** *n.* [f. L *agitare* frequent. of *agere* drive]

agley /əˈgleɪ/ *adv.* (*Sc.*) askew, awry. [f. A- + Sc. *gley* squint]

aglow /əˈgləʊ/ *pred. adj.* glowing. —*adv.* glowingly. [f. A- + GLOW]

AGM *abbr.* annual general meeting.

agnail /ˈægneɪl/ *n.* = HANGNAIL. [OE, = tight (metal) nail, hard excrescence in flesh]

agnostic /ægˈnɒstɪk/ *n.* one who believes that nothing can be known of the existence of God or of anything but material phenomena. —*adj.* of this view. —**agnosticism** /-sɪz(ə)m/ *n.* [f. Gk *a-* not + GNOSTIC]

ago /ə'gəʊ/ *adv*. in the past. [f. obs. *agone* gone by]

agog /ə'gɒg/ *adv*. & *predic. adj*. eager, expectant. [f. F *en gogues* in fun]

agonize /'ægənaɪz/ *v.t./i*. **1** to suffer mental anguish; to suffer agony. **2** to pain greatly. [f. foll.]

agony /'ægənɪ/ *n*. extreme mental or physical suffering; a severe struggle. —**agony aunt**, (*colloq*.) the (female) editor of an agony column. **agony column**, the personal column of a newspaper; a regular newspaper or magazine feature containing readers' questions about personal difficulties, with replies from the columnist. [f. OF or L f. Gk (*agōn* struggle)]

agoraphobia /ægərə'fəʊbɪə/ *n*. abnormal fear of crossing open spaces. —**agoraphobic** *adj*. & *n*. [f. Gk *agora* marketplace + PHOBIA]

AGR *abbr*. advanced gas-cooled reactor.

agrarian /ə'greərɪən/ *adj*. relating to agricultural land or its cultivation, or to landed property. [f. L (*ager* land)]

agree /ə'gri:/ *v.t./i*. **1** to hold a similar opinion; to consent (*to*). **2** to become or be in harmony, to suit or be compatible *with*. **3** to approve as correct; to reach agreement about. —**be agreed**, to have reached a similar opinion. [f. OF f. L (AD-, *gratus* pleasing)]

agreeable /ə'gri:əb(ə)l/ *adj*. **1** pleasing. **2** willing to agree. —**agreeably** *adv*. [as prec.]

agreement /ə'gri:mənt/ *n*. **1** agreeing, harmony in opinion or feeling. **2** a contract or promise. [as AGREE]

agribusiness /'ægrɪbɪznɪs/ *n*. the group of industries concerned with the processing and distribution of agricultural produce or with farm machinery. [f. AGRICULTURE + BUSINESS]

agriculture /'ægrɪkʌltʃə(r)/ *n*. the process of cultivating land and rearing livestock. —**agricultural** /-'kʌltʃər(ə)l/ *adj*., **agriculturist** /-'kʌl-/ *n*. [F, or f. L (*ager* field, *cultura* culture)]

agrimony /'ægrɪmənɪ/ *n*. a perennial plant of the genus *Agrimonia*, especially one with small yellow flowers. —**hemp agrimony**, a wild perennial plant with mauve flowers and hairy leaves. [f. OF f. L f. Gk *argemōnē* poppy]

agronomy /ə'grɒnəmɪ/ *n*. the science of soil management and crop production. [f. F f. Gk (*agros* land, *nemō* arrange)]

aground /ə'graʊnd/ *adv*. on or to the bottom of shallow water. [f. A- + GROUND]

ague /'eɪgju:/ *n*. malarial fever; a fit of shivering. [f. OF f. L *acuta* (*febris*) acute fever]

AH *abbr*. of the Muslim era (see HEGIRA). [f. L *anno Hegirae*]

ah *int*. expressing surprise, delight, pity, etc. [f. F]

aha *int*. expressing surprise or triumph. [f. AH + HA]

ahead /ə'hed/ *adv*. further forward in space, time, or progress etc.; in advance. [orig. Naut., f. A- + HEAD]

ahimsa /ə'hɪmsɑ:/ *n*. (in Hinduism, Buddhism, Jainism) the doctrine of non-violence or non-killing. [Skr. (*a* without, *himsa* injury)]

ahoy /ə'hɔɪ/ *int*. (*Naut*.) a call used in hailing. [f. AH + HOY]

aid *n*. **1** help. **2** one who or that which helps. —*v.t*. to help. [f. OF f. L (AD-, *juvare* help)]

aide /eɪd/ *n*. an aide-de-camp; an assistant. [F]

aide-de-camp /eɪd də 'kɑ̃:/ *n*. (*pl*. **aides-de-camp** *pr*. same) an officer assisting a senior officer. [F]

AIDS /eɪdz/ *abbr*. (also **Aids**) acquired immune deficiency syndrome, a condition that breaks down a person's natural defences against illness.

ail *v.t./i*. (*archaic*) to make ill or uneasy; to be in poor health. [OE (*egle* troublesome)]

aileron /'eɪlərɒn/ *n*. a hinged flap on an aeroplane wing, controlling lift and lateral balance. [F, dim. of *aile* wing f. L *ala*]

ailing *adj*. ill, in poor health or condition. [f. AIL]

ailment *n*. a minor illness. [f. AIL]

aim *v.t./i*. **1** to point, direct, or send towards a target; to take aim. **2** to make an attempt, to intend. —*n*. **1** the act of aiming. **2** purpose, intention; goal. [f. OF f. L *aestimare* reckon]

aimless *adj*. without a purpose. —**aimlessly** *adv*., **aimlessness** *n*. [f. AIM + -LESS]

ain't (*colloq*.) am not, is not, are not; has not, have not. [contr.]

Ainu /'aɪnu:/ *n*. (*pl*. same or **-s**) a member of the non-Mongoloid aboriginal inhabitants of the Japanese archipelago whose physical characteristics (light skin colour, round eyes, and exceptionally thick wavy hair) set them apart dramatically from the majority population of the islands. [Ainu, = man]

air *n*. **1** the mixture of gases (mainly oxygen and nitrogen) surrounding the earth and breathed by all land animals and plants. **2** the atmosphere, open space in this; this as the place where aircraft operate. **3** a light wind. **4** an impression given; an affected manner. **5** a melody, a tune. —*v.t./i*. **1** to expose or be exposed to fresh or warm air so as to remove staleness or damp. **2** to express publicly. —**air bed**, an inflatable mattress. **air brick**, a brick with holes to allow ventilation. **air-conditioned** *adj*. supplied with **air conditioning**, a system for regulating the humidity and temperature of a building. **air-cushion** *n*. an inflatable cushion; a layer of air providing support, especially for a vehicle of the hovercraft type. **air force**, a branch of the armed forces equipped for attacking and defending by means of aircraft (in Britain, the Royal Air Force, constituted in 1918 by amalgamating the Royal Flying Corps, formed in 1912, with the Royal Naval Air Service). **air freight,** freight carried by air. **air-freight** *v.t.* to send as air freight. **air letter,** a folding sheet of light paper that may be sent cheaply by airmail. **air pocket,** a partial vacuum in the air causing aircraft in flight to drop suddenly. **air raid,** an attack by aircraft with bombs etc. **by air,** in or by aircraft. **in the air,** current, prevalent; uncertain, not yet decided. **on the air,** broadcast or broadcasting by radio or television. —**airer** *n.* [f. OF f. L f. Gk; sense 4 F, prob. f. OF *aire* disposition f. L *area*; sense 5 f. It *aria*]

airborne *adj.* **1** transported by air or by aircraft. **2** in flight after taking off.

aircraft *n.* (*pl.* same) a machine or structure designed for flight in the air. —**aircraft-carrier** *n.* a ship carrying and used as a base for aircraft.

aircraftman *n.* the lowest rank in the RAF.

aircraftwoman *n.* the lowest rank in the WRAF.

aircrew *n.* the crew manning an aircraft.

Airedale /ˈeədeɪl/ *n.* a terrier of a large rough-coated breed. [place in W.Yorkshire]

airfield *n.* an area of land equipped with runways etc. for aircraft.

airflow *n.* a flow of air.

airgun *n.* a gun using compressed air to propel a missile.

airless *adj.* stuffy; without wind, calm and still. [f. AIR + -LESS]

airlift *n.* large-scale transport of troops, supplies, etc. by air, especially in an emergency. —*v.t.* to transport thus.

airline *n.* a service of air transport for public use; a company providing this.

airliner *n.* a large passenger-carrying aircraft.

airlock *n.* **1** stoppage of a flow by trapped air in a pump or pipe. **2** a compartment with an airtight door at each end, providing access to a pressurized chamber.

airmail *n.* mail carried by air. —*v.t.* to send by airmail.

airman *n.* (*pl.* **-men**) a male member of an air force; a male aviator.

airport *n.* an airfield with facilities for passengers and goods.

airscrew *n.* an aircraft propeller.

airship *n.* a power-driven aircraft that is lighter than air.

airsick *adj.* affected with nausea from the motion of an aircraft. —**airsickness** *n.*

airspace *n.* the air above a country and subject to its jurisdiction.

airstrip *n.* a strip of ground prepared for take-off and landing of aircraft.

airtight *adj.* impermeable to air or gas.

airway *n.* **1** a regular route of aircraft. **2** a ventilating passage in a mine. **3** a passage for air into the lungs; a device to secure this.

airwoman *n.* (*pl.* **-women**) a female member of an air force; a female aviator.

airworthy *adj.* (of aircraft) fit to fly. —**airworthiness** *n.*

airy *adj.* **1** well-ventilated; breezy. **2** light as air; unsubstantial. **3** casual and light-hearted. —**airy-fairy** *adj.* fanciful, impractical. —**airily** *adv.*, **airiness** *n.* [f. AIR]

aisle /aɪl/ *n.* **1** a side part of a church, divided by pillars from the main nave. **2** a passage between rows of pews or seats. [f. OF f. L *ala* wing]

aitch /eɪtʃ/ *n.* the letter H, h. [f. F]

aitchbone /ˈeɪtʃbəʊn/ *n.* the rump-bone of an animal; a cut of beef lying over this. [orig. *nache-bone* f. OF f. L *natis* buttock]

ajar /əˈdʒɑː(r)/ *adv.* & *predic. adj.* slightly open. [f. A- + obs. *char* turn]

akimbo /əˈkɪmbəʊ/ *adv.* (of arms) with hands on hips and elbows turned outwards. [orig. *in kenebow*, prob. f. ON, = bent in a curve]

akin /əˈkɪn/ *adj.* similar; related. [f. A- + KIN]

Al *symbol* aluminium.

à la /ɑː lɑː/ after the manner of. [F]

alabaster /ˈæləbɑːstə(r)/ *n.* a translucent usually white form of gypsum, often carved into ornaments. —*adj.* of alabaster; white or smooth as alabaster. [f. OF f. L f. Gk]

à la carte /ɑː lɑː ˈkɑːt/ ordered as separate items from a menu. [F]

alacrity /əˈlækrɪtɪ/ *n.* prompt and eager readiness. [f. L (*alacer* brisk)]

à la mode /ɑː lɑː ˈməʊd/ in fashion, fashionable. [F]

alarm /əˈlɑːm/ *n.* **1** a warning sound or signal; a device giving this. **2** an alarm clock. **3** fear caused by expectation of danger or difficulty. —*v.t./i.* to frighten; to arouse to a sense of danger. —**alarm clock,** a clock with a device that rings at a set time. [f. OF f. It. (*all'arme!* to arms!)]

alarmist *n.* one who raises unnecessary or excessive alarm. [f. prec.]

alas /əˈlæs/ *int.* expressing sorrow or distress. [f. OF f. L *lassus* weary]

alb *n.* a white vestment reaching to the feet, worn by some priests at church services. [OE f. L *albus* white]

albacore /ˈælbəkɔː(r)/ *n.* a tunny of a large West Indian or related species. [f. Port. f. Arab., = the young camel]

albatross /ˈælbətrɒs/ *n.* **1** a long-winged bird related to the petrel, inhabiting the Pacific and Southern Oceans. **2** (in golf) a score of 3 under par at a hole. [f. Sp. & Port. f. Arab., = the jug]

albedo /æl'bi:dəʊ/ *n.* (*pl.* **-os**) the fraction of incident radiation reflected by a surface. [L, = whiteness (*albus* white)]

albeit /ɔ:l'bi:ɪt/ *conj.* (*literary*) although. [f. *all be it*, = let it be completely true that]

albino /æl'bi:nəʊ/ *n.* (*pl.* **-os**) a person or animal with a congenital lack of colouring pigment in the skin and hair (which are white) and the eyes (usually pink); a plant lacking normal colouring. —**albinism** /'ælbɪnɪz(ə)m/ *n.* [Sp. & Port. f. L *albus* white]

album /'ælbəm/ *n.* **1** a blank book in which a collection of postage stamps, photographs, autographs, etc. can be kept. **2** a long-playing gramophone record with several items; a set of records. [L, = blank tablet (*albus* white)]

albumen /'ælbjʊmɪn/ *n.* white of eggs [L (*albus* white)]

albumin /'ælbjʊmɪn/ *n.* any of a class of water-soluble proteins found in egg-white, milk, blood, and some plants. [f. F (as prec.)]

alchemy /'ælkəmɪ/ *n.* a medieval form of chemistry. —**alchemist** *n.* [f. OF f. L f. Arab., = the art of transmuting metals]

alcohol /'ælkəhɒl/ *n.* a colourless volatile liquid, the intoxicant present in wine, beer, and spirits, also used as a solvent and fuel; liquor containing this; (*Chem.*) a compound of the same type as alcohol. [F or L f. Arab., = the kohl]

alcoholic /ælkə'hɒlɪk/ *adj.* of or containing alcohol; caused by alcohol. —*n.* a person who suffers from alcoholism. [f. prec.]

alcoholism /'ælkəhɒlɪz(ə)m/ *n.* habitual heavy drinking of alcohol; a diseased condition caused by this. [f. ALCOHOL]

alcove /'ælkəʊv/ *n.* a recess in a wall, room, etc. [F f. Sp. f. Arab., = the vault]

aldehyde /'ældɪhaɪd/ *n.* a volatile fluid with a suffocating smell, got by oxidation of alcohol; (*Chem.*) a compound of the same structure as this. [f. L, = alcohol deprived of hydrogen]

al dente /æl 'dentɪ/ cooked so as to be still firm when bitten. [It., = to the tooth]

alder /'ɔ:ldə(r)/ *n.* a tree of the genus *Alnus*, related to the birch; any of various similar trees (*black, red, white alder*) not related. [OE]

alderman /'ɔ:ldəmən/ *n.* (*pl.* **-men**) **1** (chiefly *hist.*) a co-opted member of an English county or borough council, next below mayor. **2** (*US & Austral.*) an elected governor of a city. [f. OE *aldor* patriarch (*ald* old)]

ale /eɪl/ *n.* beer, especially (**real ale**) that regarded as brewed and stored in the traditional way, with secondary fermentation in the container from which it is dispensed. [OE]

aleatory /'eɪlɪətərɪ/ *adj.* depending on the throw of a die etc. or on chance; (in music and art) involving random choice, e.g. in the ordering of fragments of composed music or depending on chance procedures, such as the tossing of a coin, for its composition. [f. L (*alea* die)]

alembic /ə'lembɪk/ *n.* an apparatus formerly used in distilling. [f. OF f. L f. Arab. (= the still), f. Gr *ambix* cup]

alert /ə'lɜ:t/ *adj.* watchful, vigilant; nimble. —*n.* a warning signal, notice to stand ready; a state or period of special vigilance. —*v.t.* to make alert, to warn of danger. [f. F f. It. *all' erta* to the watch-tower]

alexandrine /ælɪg'zændraɪn/ *n.* a verse of six iambic feet. —*adj.* in this metre. [f. F f. *Alexandre* = Alexander (the Great), subject of a poem in this metre]

alfalfa /æl'fælfə/ *n.* lucerne. [Sp. f. Arab., = a green fodder]

alfresco /æl'freskəʊ/ *adj.* & *adv.* in the open air. [f. It.]

alga /'ælgə/ *n.* (usu. in *pl.* **algae** /-dʒi:, -gi:/) any of a large group of primitive mainly aquatic non-flowering photosynthetic plants, including seaweeds and many plankton. [L]

algebra /'ældʒɪbrə/ *n.* the branch of mathematics that deals with formulae and equations in which symbols (usually letters) stand for unknown numbers or other entities. —**algebraic** /-'breɪɪk/ *adj.*, **algebraically** *adv.* [It., Sp., & L f. Arab., = reunion of broken parts]

ALGOL *n.* a high-level computer language using algebra. [f. ALGO(RITHMIC) + L(ANGUAGE)]

algorithm /'ælgərɪð(ə)m/ *n.* a process or rules for calculation, especially by computer. [f. OF f. L f. Pers. *Al-Khuwārizmī* (name of 9th-c. mathematician)]

alias /'eɪlɪəs/ *adv.* called (by a certain name) at other times. —*n.* an assumed name. [L, = at another time]

alibi /'ælɪbaɪ/ *n.* (*pl.* **-bis**) **1** a plea that an accused person was elsewhere when a specified act took place. **2** (**D**) an excuse. [L, = at another place]

alidade /'ælɪdeɪd/ *n.* a sighting device for angular measurement, formerly used with a quadrant, astrolabe, etc., now with a plane table. [f. L f. Arab., = the revolving radius]

alien /'eɪlɪən/ *n.* **1** a foreign-born resident who is not naturalized in the country where he or she lives. **2** a being from another world. —*adj.* **1** foreign, not one's own, unfamiliar. **2** differing in nature, inconsistent. **3** repugnant. [f. OF f. L (*alius* other)]

alienate /'eɪlɪəneɪt/ *v.t.* **1** to estrange, to make unfriendly or hostile. **2** to transfer the ownership of; to divert. —**alienation** /-'neɪʃ(ə)n/ *n.* [f. L (as prec.)]

alight[1] /ə'laɪt/ *predic. adj.* on fire, lit up. [prob. f. *on a light* (= lighted) *fire*]

alight[2] /ə'laɪt/ *v.i.* to get down or off; to descend and settle. [OE]

align /əˈlaɪn/ *v.t.* **1** to place in or bring into line, to co-ordinate. **2** to ally with a party or cause. —**alignment** *n.* [f. F (*à ligne* into line)]

alike /əˈlaɪk/ *predic. adj.* like one another. —*adv.* in a like manner. [f. OE]

alimentary /ælɪˈmentərɪ/ *adj.* of food or nutrition; nourishing. —**alimentary canal,** the tubular passage through which food passes from mouth to anus in being digested and absorbed by the body. [f. L *alimentarius* (*alere* nourish)]

alimony /ˈælɪmənɪ/ *n.* (*hist.*) an allowance (now called *maintenance*) payable to a woman from her (ex-)husband pending or after a divorce or legal separation; (*US*) an allowance paid to a spouse or child. [as prec.]

aliphatic /ælɪˈfætɪk/ *adj.* (*Chem.*, of compounds) related to fats; in which carbon atoms form open chains. [f. Gk *aleiphar* fat]

aliquot /ˈælɪkwɒt/ *adj.* that produces a quotient without a fraction when a given larger number is divided by it. —*n.* **1** an aliquot part. **2** a representative portion of a substance. [f. F f. L, = several]

alive /əˈlaɪv/ *pred. adj.* **1** living. **2** lively, active; alert or responsive *to.* **3** teeming (*with*). [OE]

alkali /ˈælkəlaɪ/ *n.* (*pl.* **-is**) any of a class of substances that neutralize acids and form caustic or corrosive solutions in water; a substance with similar but weaker properties, e.g. sodium carbonate. [f. L f. Arab., = the calcined ashes]

alkaline /ˈælkəlaɪn/ *adj.* having the properties of an alkali. —**alkalinity** /-ˈlɪnɪtɪ/ *n.* [f. prec.]

alkaloid /ˈælkəlɔːɪd/ *n.* any of a large group of nitrogenous bases of plant origin, many of which are used as drugs (e.g. quinine). [f. G (as prec.)]

alkyl /ˈælkɪl/ *n.* (usu. *attrib.*) derived from or related to a hydrocarbon of the paraffin series. [f. G (as ALCOHOL)]

all /ɔːl/ *adj.* **1** the whole amount, quantity, or extent of. **2** the greatest possible. **3** any whatever. —*n.* **1** all persons concerned, everything. **2** (in games) on both sides. —*adv.* entirely, quite; (*colloq.*) very. —**after all,** in spite of what has been said, done, or expected. **All Blacks,** the New Zealand international Rugby football team, so called from the colour of their uniforms. **all-clear** *n.* a signal that a danger or difficulty is over. **All-Hallows** *n.* All Saints' Day. **all in,** exhausted. **all-in** *attrib.* inclusive of all. **all in all,** when everything is considered; of supreme importance. **all out,** using all possible strength, effort, etc. **all over,** completely finished; in or on all parts (of); typically; (*colloq.*) excessively or effusively attentive to. **all-purpose** *adj.* having many uses. **all right,** (*predic.*) satisfactory, safe and sound, in good condition; satisfactorily, as desired; (as *int.*) I consent or agree, (*iron.*) you deserve this. **all round,** in all respects; for each person. **all-round** *adj.* (of a person) versatile. **all-rounder** *n.* a versatile person. **All Saints' Day,** 1 Nov. **all set,** (*colloq.*) ready to start. **All Souls' Day,** 2 Nov. **all there,** (*colloq.*) mentally alert or normal. **all the same,** in spite of this. **all-time** *adj.* hitherto unsurpassed. **at all,** in any way, to any extent. **in all,** in total, altogether. [OE]

Allah /ˈælə/ *n.* the Muslim name of God. [f. Arab., = the god]

allay /əˈleɪ/ *v.t.* to diminish (fear, suspicion, etc.); to relieve or alleviate pain. [OE (A-, LAY[1])]

allegation /ælɪˈgeɪʃ(ə)n/ *n.* an assertion, especially one made without proof; alleging. [f. AF or L (*allegare* adduce)]

allege /əˈledʒ/ *v.t.* to declare, especially without proof; to advance as an argument or excuse. [f. AF f. L (*litigare* dispute at law, confused in sense w. *allegare* allege)]

allegedly /əˈledʒɪdlɪ/ *adv.* as is said to be the case. [f. prec.]

allegiance /əˈliːdʒ(ə)ns/ *n.* support of a sovereign, government, or cause etc.; loyalty. [f. AF (as LIEGE)]

allegorize /ˈælɪgəraɪz/ *v.t.* to treat as or by means of an allegory. [f. foll.]

allegory /ˈælɪgərɪ/ *n.* a narrative or description in which things have a figurative or symbolical meaning. —**allegorical** /-ˈgɒrɪk(ə)l/ *adj.*, **allegorically** *adv.* [f. OF f. L f. Gk (*allos* other, *-agoria* speaking)]

allegretto /ælɪˈgretəʊ/ *adv.* & *adj.* (*Mus.*) in fairly brisk time. —*n.* (*pl.* **-os**) (*Mus.*) an allegretto passage. [It., dim. of ALLEGRO]

allegro /əˈlegrəʊ/ *adv.* (*Mus.*) in quick or lively tempo. —*n.* (*pl.* **-os**) (*Mus.*) an allegro passage. [It., = lively]

alleluia /ælɪˈluːjə/ *int.* & *n.* praise to God. [f. L f. Gk f. Heb., = praise the Lord]

allemande /ˈælmɑːnd/ *n.* **1** any of several German dances; music for one of these, especially as a suite movement. **2** a country-dance figure. [F, = German (dance)]

allergen /ˈælədʒ(ə)n/ *n.* a substance that causes an allergic reaction. —**allergenic** /-ˈdʒenɪk/ *adj.* [f. ALLERGY]

allergic /əˈlɜːdʒɪk/ *adj.* having an allergy or (*colloq.*) antipathy *to*; caused by allergy. [f. foll.]

allergy /ˈælədʒɪ/ *n.* a condition of reacting adversely to certain substances; (*colloq.*) an antipathy. [f. G f. Gk *allos* other + ENERGY]

alleviate /əˈliːvɪeɪt/ *v.t.* to lessen, to make less severe. —**alleviation** /-ˈeɪʃ(ə)n/ *n.*, **alleviator** /-ˈliː-/ *n.* [f. L *alleviare* lighten (AD-, *levare* raise)]

alley *n.* **1** a narrow passage, especially between or behind buildings. **2** a channel for balls in bowling etc. **3** a path bordered by hedges or shrubbery. [f. OF (*aller* go) f. L *ambulare* walk]

alliance /əˈlaɪəns/ *n.* a union or agreement to co-operate, especially of a State by treaty or families by marriage. [f. OF (as ALLY)]

allied /ˈælaɪd/ *adj.* **1** having a similar origin or character. **2** in alliance with foreign States; **Allied,** of the Allies (see ALLY). [f. ALLY]

alligator /ˈælɪgeɪtə(r)/ *n.* crocodilian of the genus *Alligator*, found especially in the rivers of tropical America (*A. mississippiensis*); a smaller species (*A. sinensis*) found in the Yangtze region of China. [f. Sp. *el lagarto* (L *lacerta* lizard)]

alliteration /əlɪtəˈreɪʃ(ə)n/ *n.* occurrence of the same letter or sound at the beginning of several words in succession (as in *sing a song of sixpence*). —**alliterative** /əˈlɪtərətɪv/ *adj.* [f. L *littera* letter]

allocate /ˈæləkeɪt/ *v.t.* to assign or allot. —**allocable** /ˈæləkəb(ə)l/ *adj.*, **allocation** /-ˈkeɪʃ(ə)n/ *n.* [f. L *allocare* (AD-, *locus* place)]

allot /əˈlɒt/ *v.t.* (**-tt-**) to distribute officially; to apportion as a share or task. [f. OF (*a* to, LOT)]

allotment /əˈlɒtmənt/ *n.* **1** a small piece of (public) land let out for cultivation. **2** apportioning. **3** a share. [f. prec.]

allotrope /ˈælətrəʊp/ *n.* an allotropic form (for example, diamond and graphite are allotropes of carbon). [f. foll.]

allotropy /əˈlɒtrəpɪ/ *n.* the existence of several forms of a chemical element in the same state (gas, liquid, solid) but with different physical or chemical properties. —**allotropic** /æləˈtrɒpɪk/ *adj.* [f. Gk (*allos* different, *tropos* manner)]

allow /əˈlaʊ/ *v.t./i.* **1** to permit, to let happen. **2** to assign (a fixed sum) to. **3** to add or deduct in estimating. **4** to acknowledge as true or acceptable. —**allow for,** to take into consideration; to provide for. [orig. = praise, f. OF f. L (AD-, *laudare* praise, *locare* place)]

allowable /əˈlaʊəb(ə)l/ *adj.* that may be allowed. —**allowably** *adv.* [f. prec.]

allowance /əˈlaʊəns/ *n.* an amount or sum allowed; a deduction or discount. —*v.t.* to make an allowance to. —**make allowances for,** to regard as a mitigating circumstance. [as ALLOW]

alloy /ˈælɔɪ/ *n.* **1** a substance that is a mixture wholly or mainly of metals. **2** an inferior metal mixed especially with gold or silver. —*v.t.* **1** to mix (metals). **2** to debase by an admixture; to weaken or spoil (pleasure etc. *with*). [f. OF (as ALLY)]

allspice /ˈɔːlspaɪs/ *n.* spice obtained from the berry of the pimento; this berry.

allude /əˈljuːd/ *v.i.* to refer in passing or indirectly *to* (a thing presumed known). [f. L *alludere* (AD-, *ludere* play)]

allure /əˈljʊə(r)/ *v.t.* to entice; to attract or charm. —**allurement** *n.* [f. OF (*a* to, LURE)]

allusion /əˈluːʒ(ə)n/ *n.* a passing or indirect reference (*to*). [F or f. L (as ALLUDE)]

allusive /əˈluːsɪv/ *adj.* containing allusions. —**allusively** *adv.* [as prec.]

alluvium /əˈluːvɪəm/ *n.* (*pl.* **-ia**) a deposit of earth, sand, etc., left by a flood or flow, especially in a river valley. —**alluvial** *adj.* [L f. AD-, *luere* wash]

ally /ˈælaɪ/ *n.* a State or person co-operating with another for a special purpose, especially by treaty. —*v.t.* to combine in an alliance. —**the Allies,** the nations allied in opposition to the Central Powers in the First World War or to the Axis Powers in the Second World War. [f. OF f. L *alligare* (AD-, *ligare* bind)]

Almagest /ˈælmədʒest/ **1** the title of an Arabic version of Ptolemy's astronomical treatise. **2** (in the Middle Ages; also **almagest**) any of various other celebrated textbooks on astrology and alchemy. [f. Arab. *al* the, Gk *megistē* (*suntaxis*) the great (system)]

Alma Mater /ælmə ˈmeɪtə(r)/ the title used of a university or school by its past or present members. [L, = bounteous mother]

almanac /ˈɔːlmənæk/ *n.* **1** (also **almanack**) an annual publication containing a calendar with astronomical data and sometimes other information. **2** a yearbook of sport, theatre, etc. [f. L f. Gk]

almighty /ɔːlˈmaɪtɪ/ *adj.* all-powerful; (*colloq.*) very great. —**the Almighty,** God. [OE (ALL, MIGHTY)]

almond /ˈɑːmənd/ *n.* the nut-like kernel of the fruit of two trees (*sweet* and *bitter almond*), varieties of *Prunus dulcis*, allied to the plum and peach; either of these trees. [f. OF f. L f. Gk]

almoner /ˈɑːmənə(r)/ *n.* an official distributor of alms. [f. AF f. L (as ALMS)]

almonry /ˈɑːmənrɪ/ *n.* a place for the distribution of alms. [as prec.]

almost /ˈɔːlməʊst/ *adv.* all but; as the nearest thing to. [OE (as ALL, MOST)]

alms /ɑːmz/ *n.* (*pl.* same) (*hist.*) a donation of food or money given to the poor. [OE f. L f. Gk (*eleos* pity)]

almshouse *n.* a house founded by charity for the accommodation of poor (usually elderly) people.

almucantar /ælmjuːˈkæntə(r)/ *n.* a line of constant altitude above the horizon. [f. L or F f. Arab., = sundial (*kantara* arch)]

aloe /ˈæləʊ/ *n.* a plant of the genus *Aloe*, native to Africa, with erect spikes of flowers and with leaves that yield a bitter juice; (in *pl.*) a purgative drug made from this juice. —**American aloe,** a kind of agave. [OE f. L f. Gk]

aloft /əˈlɒft/ *adv.* high up, overhead; upward. [f. ON, = in air]

alone /əˈləʊn/ *predic. adj.* without anyone or anything else, without company, assistance, or addition. —*adv.* only, exclusively. [earlier *al one* (ALL, ONE)]

along /əˈlɒŋ/ *adv.* **1** onward, into a more advanced state. **2** in company with oneself or others. **3** beside or through a part or the whole of a thing's length. —*prep.* beside or through (part of) the length of. —**all along,** from the beginning. **along with,** in addition to. [OE, orig. adj. = facing against]

alongshore *adv.* along or beside the shore.

alongside *adv.* at or to the side; close to the side of a ship, pier, or wharf. —*prep.* close to the side of.

aloof /əˈlu:f/ *adj.* unconcerned, lacking in sympathy. —*adv.* away, apart. —**aloofness** *n.* [orig. Naut., f. A- + LUFF]

aloud /əˈlaʊd/ *adv.* in a normal voice so as to be audible; (*archaic*) loudly. [f. A- + LOUD]

alpaca /ælˈpækə/ *n.* **1** a kind of llama of South America with long wool. **2** its wool; fabric made from this. **3** any of various similar fabrics. [Sp. f. Quechua (*pako* reddish-brown)]

alpenhorn /ˈælpənhɔ:n/ *n.* a long wooden horn formerly used by herdsmen in the Alps. [G, = Alpine horn]

alpenstock /ˈælpənstɒk/ *n.* a long iron-tipped staff used in mountain-climbing. [G, = Alpine stick]

alpha /ˈælfə/ *n.* **1** the first letter of the Greek alphabet, = a. **2** a first-class mark in an examination. **3** a designation of the brightest star in a constellation, or sometimes a star's position in a group. —**Alpha and Omega,** the beginning and the end. **alpha particles** *or* **rays,** helium nuclei emitted by radioactive substances (originally regarded as rays). [L f. Gk]

alphabet /ˈælfəbet/ *n.* a set of letters used in a language; these in a fixed order; symbols or signs for these. —**phonetic alphabet,** symbols used to represent the sounds of speech. [f. L f. Gk *alpha, bēta,* first two letters of Gk alphabet]

alphabetical /ælfəˈbetɪk(ə)l/ *adj.* in the order of the letters of the alphabet; using an alphabet. —**alphabetically** *adv.* [f. prec.]

alphabetize /ˈælfəbətaɪz/ *v.t.* to put into alphabetical order. —**alphabetization** /-ˈzeɪʃ(ə)n/ *n.* [f. ALPHABET]

alphanumeric /ælfənju:ˈmerɪk/ *adj.* containing both alphabetical and numerical symbols. [f. ALPHABET + NUMERICAL]

Alpine /ˈælpaɪn/ *adj.* of the Alps or other high mountains. —*n.* a plant suited to mountain regions or grown in rock gardens. [f. L f. Gk]

already /ɔ:lˈredɪ/ *adv.* before the time in question; as early or soon as this. [f. ALL + READY]

Alsatian /ælˈseɪʃ(ə)n/ *n.* a dog of a large strong smooth-haired breed of wolfhound. [f. L *Alsatia* Alsace]

also /ˈɔ:lsəʊ/ *adv.* in addition, besides. —**also-ran** *n.* a horse or dog not among the first three to finish in a race; a person who has failed to win distinction in his activities. [OE (ALL, SO)]

altar /ˈɒltə(r)/ *n.* the table on which bread and wine are consecrated in the Eucharist; any structure on which offerings are made to a god. [OE f. L (*altus* high)]

alter /ˈɒltə(r)/ *v.t./i.* to make or become different, to change in character, size, place, etc. —**alteration** /-ˈreɪʃ(ə)n/ *n.* [f. OF f. L (*alter* other)]

altercate /ˈɒltəkeɪt/ *v.i.* to dispute angrily, to wrangle. —**altercation** /-ˈkeɪʃ(ə)n/ *n.* [f. L *altercari*]

alter ego /æltər ˈi:gəʊ/ (*pl.* **-os**) an intimate friend; another aspect of oneself. [L, = other self]

alternate[1] /ɒlˈtɜ:nət/ *adj.* (of things of two kinds) coming each after one of the other kind; (with *pl. n.*) every second one. —**alternate angles,** two angles on opposite sides and at opposite ends of a line that crosses two others. —**alternately** *adv.* [f. L, = do things by turns (*alter* other)]

alternate[2] /ˈɒltəneɪt/ *v.t./i.* to arrange, perform, or occur alternately; to consist of alternate things. —**alternating current,** electric current that reverses direction at regular intervals. —**alternation** *n.* [as prec.]

alternative /ɒlˈtɜ:nətɪv/ *adj.* available in place of something else; (of life-style, medical treatment, etc.) using practices other than the conventional ones. —*n.* a choice available in place of another; each of two or more possibilities. —**Alternative Service Book,** a book containing the public liturgy of the Church of England published in 1980 for use as the alternative to the Book of Common Prayer. —**alternatively** *adv.* [as prec.]

alternator /ˈɒltɜ:neɪtə(r)/ *n.* a dynamo producing alternating current. [f. ALTERNATE[2]]

although /ɔ:lˈðəʊ/ *conj.* though. [f. ALL + THOUGH]

altimeter /ˈæltɪmi:tə(r)/ *n.* an instrument measuring altitude. [f. L *altus* + METER]

altitude /ˈæltɪtju:d/ *n.* height, especially as measured above sea-level or (of a star) above the horizon. [f. L (*altus* high)]

alto /ˈæltəʊ/ *n.* (*pl.* **-os**) **1** the highest adult male singing-voice; a female voice of similar range, a contralto; a singer with such a voice; a part written for it. **2** an instrument of the second or third highest pitch in its family. [It., = high (singing)]

altocumulus /æltəʊˈkju:mju:ləs/ *n.* (*pl.* **-li** /-laɪ/) cloud like cumulus but at a higher level. [f. L *altus* high + CUMULUS]

altogether /ɔ:ltəˈgeðə(r)/ *adv.* entirely, totally; on the whole. —**in the altogether,** (*colloq.*) nude. [f. ALL + TOGETHER]

altostratus /æltəʊˈstreɪtəs/ *n.* (*pl.* **-ti** /-taɪ/) clouds forming a continuous layer at medium altitude. [f. L. *altus* high + STRATUS]

altruism /ˈæltruɪz(ə)m/ *n.* regard for others as a principle of action, unselfishness. —**altruist** *n.*, **altruistic** /-ˈɪstɪk/ *adj.*, **altruistically** *adv.* [f. F f. It. *altrui* somebody else]

alum /ˈæləm/ *n.* a double sulphate of aluminium and another element, especially potassium, used in medicine and in dyeing. [f. OF f. L *alumen*]

alumina /əˈlu:mɪnə/ *n.* an oxide of aluminium, e.g. corundum. [f. L *alumen* alum]

aluminium /æljʊˈmɪnɪəm/ *n.* a light silvery-white metallic element, symbol Al, atomic number 13. [alt. (after *sodium* etc.) f. *aluminum*, earlier *alumium* f. ALUM]

aluminize /əˈlu:mɪnaɪz/ *v.t.* to coat with aluminium. [f. prec.]

aluminum /əˈlu:mɪnəm/ *n.* (*US*) aluminium. [see ALUMINIUM]

alumnus /əˈlʌmnəs/ *n.* (*pl.* **-ni** /-naɪ/) a former pupil or student. [L, = nursling, pupil (*alere* nourish)]

alveolus /ælˈvi:ələs/ *n.* (*pl.* **-li** /-laɪ/) **1** a small cavity such as a tooth-socket or a cell in a honeycomb. **2** any of the tiny air-filled sacs in the lungs from which oxygen passes into the blood and through which carbon dioxide is removed from it. [L, dim. of *alveus* cavity]

always /ˈɔ:lweɪz/ *adv.* at all times, on all occasions; whatever the circumstances; repeatedly. [f. ALL + WAY]

alyssum /ˈælɪsəm/ *n.* any of various cruciferous plants of the genus *Alyssum* etc. with small usually yellow or white flowers. [L f. Gk, = curing (canine) madness]

Am *symbol* americium.

am 1st person sing. pres. of BE.

a.m. *abbr.* before noon. [abbr. of L *ante meridiem*]

amalgam /əˈmælgəm/ *n.* a mixture or blend; an alloy of mercury with another metal. [f. F or L, prob. f. Gk *malagma* emollient]

amalgamate /əˈmælgəmeɪt/ *v.t./i.* to mix, to combine; (of metals) to alloy with mercury. —**amalgamation** /-meɪʃ(ə)n/ *n.* [f. L (as prec.)]

amanuensis /əmænjʊˈensɪs/ *n.* (*pl.* **-enses**) a literary assistant, especially one who writes from dictation. [L, f. *a manu* at hand]

amaryllis /æməˈrɪlɪs/ *n.* a South African plant of the genus *Amaryllis*, with lily-like flowers, growing from a bulb; any of various related plants. [L f. Gk (girl's name)]

amass /əˈmæs/ *v.t.* to heap together, to accumulate. [f. F or L (AD-, *massa* mass)]

amateur /ˈæmətə(r)/ *n.* one who does something as a pastime not as a profession; one who lacks professional skill. —**amateurish** *adj.* [F f. It. f. L *amator* lover (*amare* love)]

amatory /ˈæmətərɪ/ *adj.* of or showing sexual love. [f. L (*amare* love)]

amaze /əˈmeɪz/ *v.t.* to surprise greatly, to overwhelm with wonder. —**amazement** *n.* [f. OE]

amazon /ˈæməz(ə)n/ *n.* a tall and strong or athletic woman; a female warrier. —**amazonian** /-ˈzəʊnɪən/ *adj.* [f. *Amazon*, female warrior in Gk legend]

ambassador /æmˈbæsədə(r)/ *n.* a diplomat sent by a sovereign or State as a permanent representative or on a mission to another; an official messenger.—**ambassadorial** /-ˈdɔ:rɪəl/ *adj.* [f. F, ult. f. L *ambactus* servant]

amber *n.* **1** a yellowish-brown translucent fossil resin used in jewellery etc.; its colour. **2** a yellow traffic-light used as a cautionary signal between red (= stop) and green (= go). —*adj.* made of or coloured like amber. [f. OF f. Arab.]

ambergris /ˈæmbəgrɪs/ *n.* a grey waxlike substance found floating in tropical seas and present in the intestines of the sperm whale, used as a fixative in perfumes. [f. OF, = grey amber]

ambidextrous /æmbɪˈdekstrəs/ *adj.* able to use either hand equally well. [f. L (*ambi-* on both sides, *dexter* right-handed)]

ambience /ˈæmbɪəns/ *n.* surroundings. [as foll.]

ambient /ˈæmbɪənt/ *adj.* surrounding. [f. F or L (*ambi-* on both sides, *ire* go)]

ambiguous /æmˈbɪgjʊəs/ *adj.* having more than one possible meaning; doubtful, uncertain. —**ambiguously** *adv.*, **ambiguity** /-ˈgju:ɪtɪ/ *n.* [f. L, = doubtful (*ambi-* both ways, *agere* drive)]

ambit *n.* scope or extent; bounds. [f. L *ambitus* circuit (as AMBIENT)]

ambition /æmˈbɪʃ(ə)n/ *n.* desire for distinction or for a specific attainment; its object. [f. OF f. L, = canvassing]

ambitious /æmˈbɪʃəs/ *adj.* full of ambition; needing great effort etc., on a large scale. —**ambitiously** *adv.* [as prec.]

ambivalence /æmˈbɪvələns/ *n.* co-existence in one person of opposite feelings towards a person or thing. —**ambivalent** *adj.* [f. G f. L (*ambo* both)]

amble *v.i.* to walk in a leisurely or casual manner. —*n.* a leisurely pace. [f. OF f. L *ambulare* walk]

ambrosia /æmˈbrəʊzɪə/ *n.* the food of the gods in classical mythology; something delicious. —**ambrosial** *adj.* [L f. Gk, = elixir of life (*ambrotos* immortal)]

ambulance /ˈæmbjʊləns/ *n.* a specially equipped vehicle for conveying the sick or injured to hospital. (The word was used originally of a mobile field hospital.) [F (as foll.)]

ambulant /ˈæmbjʊlənt/ *adj.* able to walk about, not confined to bed. [f. L *ambulare* walk]

ambulatory /ˈæmbjʊlətərɪ/ *adj.* of or for walking; ambulant. —*n.* a place for walking, as in a cloister. [f. L (as prec.)]

ambuscade /æmbəsˈkeɪd/ *n.* an ambush. —*v.t.* to ambush. [f. F (as foll.)]

ambush /ˈæmbʊʃ/ *n.* the placing of troops etc. in concealment to make a surprise attack; such an attack. —*v.t.* to attack from an ambush, to lie in wait for. [f. OF (as BUSH)]

ameliorate /əˈmi:lɪəreɪt/ *v.t./i.* to make or become better. —**amelioration** /-ˈreɪʃ(ə)n/ *n.* [f. OF f. L (*melior* better)]

amen /ɑ:ˈmen, eɪ-/ *int.* (in prayers) so be it. [f. L f. Gk f. Heb., = certainly]

amenable /əˈmi:nəbəl/ *adj.* **1** tractable, responsive. **2** answerable (*to* the law etc.). —**amenability** /-ˈbɪlɪtɪ/ *n.*, **amenably** *adv.* [AF f. F *amener* bring (as AD- + L *minare* drive animals f. *minari* threaten)]

amend /əˈmend/ *v.t.* to correct an error in; to make minor alterations in. —**amendment** *n.* [f. OF f. L, = emend]

amende honorable /æmɑ̃d ɒnɔ:ˈrɑbl/ a public or open apology and reparation. [F, = honourable reparation]

amends /əˈmendz/ *n.pl.* **make amends,** to give compensation. [f. OF, = penalties (as AMEND)]

amenity /əˈmi:nɪtɪ/ *n.* a pleasant or useful feature or facility of a place etc.; a pleasant quality. [f. OF or L (*amoenus* pleasant)]

American /əˈmerɪkən/ *adj.* of the continent of America, especially the USA. —*n.* **1** a citizen of the USA; a native of America. **2** the English language as spoken and written in the USA. **American Indian** any of the original inhabitants of the continent of America (other than Eskimos) or their descendants. [f. *America*]

Americanism *n.* a word, sense, or phrase peculiar to or originating in the USA. [f. AMERICAN]

Americanize /əˈmerɪkənaɪz/ *v.t.* to make American in form or character. —**Americanization** /-ˈzeɪʃ(ə)n/ *n.* [as prec.]

americium /æməˈrɪsɪəm,-ʃɪəm/ *n.* an artificially made transuranic radioactive metallic element, symbol Am, atomic number 95. [f. *America* (where first made)]

amethyst /ˈæməθɪst/ *n.* a precious stone, purple or violet quartz. [f. OF f. L f. Gk, = not drunken (the stone being supposed to prevent drunkenness)]

Amharic /æmˈhærɪk/ *n.* the official language of Ethiopia. —*adj.* of or in this language. [f. *Amhara*, region of Ethiopia]

amiable /ˈeɪmɪəb(ə)l/ *adj.* friendly and pleasant; likeable. —**amiability** /-ˈbɪlɪtɪ/ *n.*, **amiably** *adv.* [f. OF f. L, = amicable (confused with F *aimable* lovable]

amicable /ˈæmɪkəb(ə)l/ *adj.* friendly, showing friendly feeling. —**amicably** *adv.* [f. L (*amicus* friend)]

amice[1] /ˈæmɪs/ *n.* a square of white linen worn by celebrant priests, formerly on the head, now on the neck and shoulders. [ult. f. L *amictus* garment]

amice[2] /ˈæmɪs/ *n.* a cap, hood, or cape of religious orders. [f. OF f. L *amucia*; orig. unkn.]

amid /əˈmɪd/ *prep.* in the middle of, among. [f A- + MID]

amidships /əˈmɪdʃɪps/ *adv.* in or to the middle of a ship. [f. midship(s), after AMID]

amidst /əˈmɪdst/ var. of AMID.

amine /ˈeɪmi:n/ *n.* a compound in which an alkyl or other non-acidic radical replaces a hydrogen atom of ammonia. [f. AMMONIA]

amino acid /əˈmi:nəʊ/ an organic acid derived from ammonia, especially as a constituent of proteins. [f. AMMONIA]

amir /əˈmɪə(r)/ *n.* a title of various Muslim rulers. [f. Arab., = commander]

amiss /əˈmɪs/ *predic. adj.* wrong, astray, faulty. —*adv.* wrongly; inappropriately. [prob. f. ON *á mis* so as to miss]

amity /ˈæmɪtɪ/ *n.* friendship, a friendly relationship. [f. OF f. L *amicus* friend]

ammeter /ˈæmɪtə(r)/ *n.* an instrument for measuring electric current, usually in amperes. [f. AMPERE + METER]

ammonia /əˈməʊnɪə/ *n.* a pungent gas with a strong alkaline reaction; a solution of this in water. [f. SAL AMMONIAC]

ammonite /ˈæmənaɪt/ *n.* a fossil cephalopod of the order Ammonoidea, usually with a coil-shaped shell. [f. L, = horn of (Jupiter) Ammon]

ammunition /æmjʊˈnɪʃ(ə)n/ *n.* **1** a supply of projectiles (especially bullets, shells, grenades) fired by guns etc. or hurled. **2** points that can be used to advantage in an argument etc. [f. F *la munition* taken as *l'amunition*]

amnesia /æmˈni:zjə/ *n.* loss of memory. —**amnesiac** *adj.* & *n.* [L f. Gk, = forgetfulness (*a-* not, *mnaomai* remember)]

amnesty /ˈæmnɪstɪ/ *n.* a general pardon, especially for political offences. [f. F or L f. Gk *amnēstia* forgetting (see prec.)]

amniocentesis /æmnɪəʊsenˈti:sɪs/ *n.* (*pl.* **-teses**) a prenatal diagnostic technique in which a sample of amniotic fluid is withdrawn from the uterus through a hollow needle and analysed for information about the foetus. [f. foll. + Gk *kentēsis* pricking]

amnion /ˈæmnɪɒn/ *n.* (*pl.* **-ia**) the innermost membrane enclosing the foetus and the fluid that surrounds it before birth. —**amniotic** /-ˈɒtɪk/ *adj.* [Gk, = caul (*amnos* lamb)]

amoeba /əˈmi:bə/ *n.* (*pl.* **-as**) a microscopic

aquatic protozoan that constantly changes shape. —**amoebic** *adj*. [L f. Gk, = change]

amok /ə'mɒk/ *adv*. **run amok,** to run about wildly in violent rage. [Malay, = rushing in frenzy]

among /ə'mʌŋ/ *prep*. in an assembly of, surrounded by; in the number of; between. [OE, = in a crowd]

amongst /ə'mʌŋst/ var. of AMONG.

amoral /eɪ'mɒrəl/ *adj*. not based on or not having moral principles, neither moral nor immoral. —**amoralism** *n*. [f. Gk *a*- not + MORAL]

amorous /'æmərəs/ *adj*. of, showing, or feeling sexual love. —**amorously** *adv*., **amorousness** *n*. [f. OF f. L (*amor* love)]

amorphous /ə'mɔ:fəs/ *adj*. having no definite shape or form; vague, not organized; (*Min*., *Chem*.) uncrystallized. [f. L f. Gk (*a*- not, *morphē* form)]

amortize /ə'mɔ:taɪz/ *v.t*. to pay off a debt gradually by means of a sinking fund; to write off the initial costs of (assets) gradually. —**amortization** /-'zeɪʃ(ə)n/ *n*. [f. OF f. L (*ad mortem* to death)]

amount /ə'maʊnt/ *v.i*. to be equivalent in total value, quantity, significance, etc., *to*. —*n*. the total to which a thing amounts; a quantity. [f. F f. L (*ad montem* upward)]

amour propre /æmʊə 'prɒpr/ self-esteem, vanity. [F]

amp *n*. **1** an ampere. **2** (*colloq*.) an amplifier. [abbr.]

amperage /'æmpərɪdʒ/ *n*. the strength of electric current, measured in amperes. [f. AMPERE]

ampere /'æmpeə(r)/ *n*. the base unit of electric current (symbol A; established in 1948 for international use), that constant current which, if maintained in two straight parallel conductors of infinite length, of negligible circular cross-section, and placed 1 metre apart in a vacuum, would produce between these conductors a force equal to 2×10^{-7} newton per metre of length. [f. A.-M. *Ampère*, French physicist (d. 1836)]

ampersand /'æmpəsænd/ *n*. the sign & (= and). [corrupt. of '& *per se and*', = 'the sign & by itself is *and*']

amphetamine /æm'fetəmi:n/ *n*. a synthetic drug used as a stimulant and decongestant. [abbr. of chemical name]

amphibian /æm'fɪbɪən/ *n*. **1** an animal living both on land and in water; a vertebrate animal of the class Amphibia, typically having an aquatic larval stage with gills (e.g. a tadpole) and an air-breathing four-legged adult stage. **2** an amphibious vehicle etc. [f. Gk (*amphi* both, *bios* life)]

amphibious /æm'fɪbɪəs/ *adj*. **1** living or operating both on land and in water. **2** involving military forces landed from the sea. [as prec.]

amphitheatre /'æmfɪθɪətə(r)/ *n*. an oval or circular unroofed building with tiers of seats surrounding a central space. [f. L f. Gk (*amphi* all round, *theatron* theatre]

amphora /'æmfərə/ *n*. (*pl*. **-ae** /-i:/) a Greek or Roman vessel with a narrow neck and two handles, tapering at the base, used for transporting and storing wine or oil. [L f. Gk (*amphi*- two, *pherō* carry)]

ample *adj*. plentiful, extensive; quite enough; large, of generous proportions. —**ampleness** *n*., **amply** *adv*. [f. F f. L *amplus*]

amplifier /'æmplɪfaɪə(r)/ *n*. an apparatus for increasing the strength of sounds or electrical signals. [f. foll.]

amplify /'æmplɪfaɪ/ *v.t./i*. **1** to increase the strength of (sound or electrical signals). **2** to add detail to (a story etc.); to expatiate. —**amplification** /-'keɪʃ(ə)n/ *n*. [f. OF f. L (as AMPLE)]

amplitude /'æmplɪtju:d/ *n*. **1** spaciousness, abundance. **2** the maximum departure from average of oscillation, alternating current, etc. [F or f. L (as AMPLE)]

ampoule /'æmpu:l/ *n*. a small sealed glass vessel holding a liquid, especially for injection. [F f. L *ampulla*]

amputate /'æmpjʊteɪt/ *v.t*. to cut off by surgical operation. —**amputation** /-'teɪʃ(ə)n/ *n*. [f. L *amputare* (*amb*- about, *putare* prune)]

amputee /æmpju:'ti:/ *n*. a person who has had a limb etc. amputated. [f. prec.]

amuck var. of AMOK.

amulet /'æmjʊlɪt/ *n*. a thing worn as a charm against evil. [f. L]

amuse /ə'mjʊz/ *v.t*. **1** to cause to laugh or smile. **2** to occupy pleasantly. —**amusement** *n*. [f. OF (*a* to, *muser* stare)]

an /ən, *emphatic* æn/ *adj*. the form of *a* (the indefinite article) used before vowel sounds other than u /ju:, jʊ/.

ana- /ænə-/ *prefix* (usu. **an-** before a vowel) **1** up (in place or time). **2** again. [f. Gk *ana* up]

Anabaptist /ænə'bæptɪst/ *n*. a member of any of various 16th-c. religious groups practising adult baptism. [f. L f. Gk (ANA-, *baptismos* baptism]

anabolism /ə'næbəlɪz(ə)m/ *n*. constructive metabolism, the synthesis of complex substances for body tissue etc. (opp. CATABOLISM). —**anabolic** /ænə'bɒlɪk/ *adj*. [f. Gk *anabolē* ascent (ANA-, *ballō* throw)]

anachronism /ə'nækrənɪz(ə)m/ *n*. attribution of a custom or event etc. to a period to which it does not belong; a thing thus attributed; a person or thing out of harmony with the period. —**anachronistic** /-'nɪstɪk/ *adj*. [f. F or Gk (ANA-, *khronos* time)]

anacoluthon /ænəkəˈlju:θən/ *n.* (*pl.* **-tha**) a sentence or construction that lacks a proper grammatical sequence. [L f. Gk (*an-* not, *akolouthos* following)]

anaconda /ænəˈkɒndə/ *n.* a large aquatic and arboreal boa of tropical South America. [f. Sinhalese, = whip-snake; orig. of a snake in Sri Lanka]

anaemia /əˈni:mɪə/ *n.* deficiency of red cells or of their haemoglobin in blood. [f. Gk, = lack of blood]

anaemic /əˈni:mɪk/ *adj.* suffering from anaemia; pale; lacking vitality. [f. prec.]

anaesthesia /ænɪsˈθi:zɪə/ *n.* loss of sensation, especially that induced by anaesthetics. [f. Gk (*an-* without, *aisthēsia* sensation)]

anaesthetic /ænɪsˈθetɪk/ *n.* a substance (e.g. a drug or gas) that produces loss of sensation and of ability to feel pain. —*adj.* having this effect. [as prec.]

anaesthetize /əˈni:sθətaɪz/ *v.t.* to administer an anaesthetic to. —**anaesthetist** *n.*, **anaesthetization** /-ˈzeɪʃ(ə)n/ *n.* [f. ANAESTHESIA]

anagram /ˈænəgræm/ *n.* a word or phrase formed by transposing the letters of another. [f. F f. ANA- + Gk *gramma* letter]

anal /ˈeɪn(ə)l/ *adj.* of or near the anus. [f. ANUS]

analgesia /ænælˈdʒi:zɪə/ *n.* relief of pain, loss of ability to feel pain while still conscious. [f. Gk (*an-* without, *algēsia* pain)]

analgesic /ænælˈdʒi:zɪk/ *adj.* producing analgesia. —*n.* an analgesic drug. [as prec.]

analogize /əˈnælədʒaɪz/ *v.t./i.* to represent or explain by analogy; to use analogy. [f. ANALOGY]

analogous /əˈnæləgəs/ *adj.* partially similar or parallel (*to*). —**analogously** *adv.* [f. L f. Gk (as ANALOGY)]

analogue /ˈænəlɒg/ *n.* an analogous thing. [F f. Gk (*ana-* according to, *logos* proportion)]

analogy /əˈnælədʒɪ/ *n.* correspondence or partial similarity of things; reasoning from parallel cases. —**analogical** /ænəˈlɒdʒɪk(ə)l/ *adj.* [f. F or L f. Gk (as prec.)]

analyse /ˈænəlaɪz/ *v.t.* **1** to examine in detail. **2** to ascertain the elements or structure of. **3** to psychoanalyse. —**analysable** *adj.* [f. foll.]

analysis /əˈnæləsɪs/ *n.* (*pl.* **analyses**) **1** the process of analysing; a statement of the result of this. **2** psychoanalysis. **3** the mathematical theory of functions and limiting operations on them, continuity, differentiation, and integration, treated by the strictest standards of logical reasoning. —**analytic** /ænəˈlɪtɪk/ *adj.*, **analytical** *adj.*, **analytically** *adv.* [L f. Gk (ANA-, *luō* loosen)]

analyst /ˈænəlɪst/ *n.* **1** one skilled in analysis, especially of chemical substances. **2** a psychoanalyst. [f. F (as prec.)]

anapaest /ˈænəpi:st/ *n.* a metrical foot with two short or unstressed syllables followed by one long or stressed syllable. [f. L f. Gk *anapaistos* (*ana* reversed (dactyl), *-paistos* f. *paiō* strike)]

anarchist /ˈænəkɪst/ *n.* one who believes that government and law should be abolished. —**anarchism** *n.*, **anarchistic** /-ˈkɪstɪk/ *adj.* [as foll.]

anarchy /ˈænəkɪ/ *n.* disorder (esp. political), lack of government or control. —**anarchic** /æˈnɑ:kɪk/ *adj.* [f. L f. Gk (*an-* without, *arkhē* rule)]

anastigmatic /ænəstɪgˈmætɪk/ *adj.* free from astigmatism. [f. Gk *an-* not + ASTIGMATISM]

anathema /əˈnæθəmə/ *n.* **1** a detested thing. **2** a formal curse of the Church, excommunicating a person or denouncing a doctrine etc. [L f. Gk, = thing assigned (to evil)]

anathematize /əˈnæθəmətaɪz/ *v.t.* to curse. [f. prec.]

anatomize /əˈnætəmaɪz/ *v.t.* **1** to dissect. **2** to analyse. [as foll.]

anatomy /əˈnætəmɪ/ *n.* **1** the science of bodily structure; the bodily structure of an animal or plant. **2** analysis. —**anatomical** /ænəˈtɒmɪk(ə)l/ *adj.*, **anatomically** *adv.* [f. F or L f. Gk (ANA-, *temnō* cut)]

ANC *abbr.* African National Congress.

ancestor /ˈænsestə(r)/ *n.* **1** a person from whom one is descended, especially one more remote than grandparents. **2** an early type of animal, plant, or thing from which later ones have evolved. —**ancestral** /-ˈsestr(ə)l/ *adj.*, **ancestress** /ˈæn-/ *n.fem.*, **ancestry** *n.* [f. OF f. L (*ante* before, *cedere* go)]

anchor /ˈæŋkə(r)/ *n.* **1** a heavy metal weight used to moor a ship to the sea-bottom or a balloon etc. to the ground. **2** a thing that gives stability. —*v.t./i.* to secure or be moored with an anchor, to cast an anchor; to fix firmly. —**anchor man,** one who co-ordinates activities, especially the compère in a broadcast; a strong member of a sports team who plays a vital part, e.g. the last runner in a relay race. [f. OE f. L f. Gk *agkura*]

anchorage /ˈæŋkərɪdʒ/ *n.* **1** a place for anchoring. **2** lying at anchor. [f. prec.]

anchorite /ˈæŋkəraɪt/ *n.* a hermit, a religious recluse. [f. L f. Gk (*anakhōreō* retire)]

anchovy /ˈæntʃəvɪ/ *n.* a small rich-flavoured fish of the herring family. [f. Sp. & Port. *anchova*]

ancient /ˈeɪnʃ(ə)nt/ *adj.* of times long past; having lived or existed for a long time. [f. AF f. L *ante* before]

ancillary /ænˈsɪlərɪ/ *adj.* subordinate, auxiliary (*to*). [f. L (*ancilla* handmaid)]

and /ənd, emphatic ænd/ *conj.* **1** connecting words, clauses, and sentences in a simple relation or implying progression, causation, consequence, duration, number, addition, or variety. **2** (*colloq.*) to (as in *go and, try and*). —**and/or,** together with or as an alternative. [OE]

andante /æn'dæntɪ/ *adv.* (*Mus.*) in moderately slow tempo. —*n.* (*Mus.*) a movement to be played in this way. [It., = going]

andiron /'ændaɪən/ *n.* a metal stand (usually one of a pair) supporting logs in a fireplace. [f. OF *andier*, assim. to IRON]

androgen /'ændrəgən/ *n.* a male sex hormone or other substance that can cause certain male characteristics to develop or be maintained. [f. Gk *andro-* male]

androgynous /æn'drɒdʒɪnəs/ *adj.* hermaphrodite; (of a plant) with stamens and pistils in the same flowers. [f. Gk as prec. + *gunē* woman]

android /'ændrɔːɪd/ *n.* a robot with an apparently human form. [as ANDROGEN]

anecdote /'ænɪkdəʊt/ *n.* a short account of an entertaining or interesting incident. —**anecdotal** /-'dəʊt(ə)l/ *adj.* [F or f. Gk *anekdota* unpublished things]

anechoic /ænɪ'kəʊɪk/ *adj.* free from echo. —**anechoic chamber,** a room designed to absorb nearly all the reverberation produced in it, used in acoustic experiments. [f. Gk *an-* without + ECHO]

anemometer /ænɪ'mɒmɪtə(r)/ *n.* an instrument for measuring the force of wind. [f. Gk *anemos* wind + METER]

anemone /ə'nemənɪ/ *n.* a plant of the genus *Anemone*, related to the buttercup, with white, red, or purple flowers. [f. L f. Gk, = wind-flower (*anemos* wind)]

anent /ə'nent/ *prep.* (*Sc.*) concerning. [OE *an efen* on a level with]

aneroid /'ænərɔːɪd/ *n.* an **aneroid barometer,** a barometer measuring air-pressure by the action of air on the lid of a box containing a vacuum, which causes a pointer to move, not by the height of a fluid column. [f. F f. Gk *a-* not, *nēros* water]

aneurysm /'ænjʊrɪz(ə)m/ *n.* permanent abnormal dilatation of an artery. [f. Gk (*aneurinō* widen)]

anew /ə'njuː/ *adv.* again; in a different way. [earlier *of newe*]

angel /'eɪndʒ(ə)l/ *n.* **1** an attendant or messenger of God; a representation of this, conventionally in human form with wings. **2** a very virtuous, kind, or obliging person. —**angel cake,** very light sponge-cake. **angel-fish** *n.* a fish with wing-like fins. [f. OF f. L f. Gk *aggelos* messenger]

angelic /æn'dʒelɪk/ *adj.* of or like an angel. —**Angelic Doctor,** the nickname of St Thomas Aquinas. —**angelically** *adv.* [as prec.]

angelica /æn'dʒelɪkə/ *n.* an aromatic umbelliferous plant; its candied stalks, used in cookery. [f. L, = angelic (herb)]

angelus /'ændʒɪləs/ *n.* a prayer of the Roman Catholic Church said at morning, noon, and sunset in commemoration of the Incarnation; a bell rung to announce this. [L *Angelus Domini* (= angel of the Lord), opening words of prayer]

anger /'æŋgə(r)/ *n.* extreme or passionate displeasure. —*v.t.* to make angry. [f. ON *angr* grief]

Angevin /'ændʒɪvɪn/ *n.* **1** a native or inhabitant of Anjou in France. **2** a Plantagenet. —*adj.* of the Angevins. [F]

angina /æn'dʒaɪnə/ *n.* (also **angina pectoris**) pain in the chest brought on by exertion, owing to an inadequate blood supply to the heart. [L f. Gk (*agkhonē* strangling)]

angiosperm /'ændʒɪəspɜːm/ *n.* a member of the group of flowering plants that have seeds enclosed in an ovary (opp. GYMNOSPERM). [f. Gk *aggeion* vessel + *sperma* seed]

Angle /'æŋg(ə)l/ *n.* a member of a North German tribe who came to England in the 5th c., founding kingdoms in Mercia, Northumbria, and East Anglia, and finally gave their name to England and the English. [f. L f. *Angul* name of district in Germany]

angle[1] *n.* **1** the space between two lines or surfaces that meet; the inclination of two lines etc. to each other; a corner. **2** a point of view. —*v.t./i.* **1** to move or place obliquely. **2** to present (information etc.) from a particular point of view. [f. F or L *angulus*]

angle[2] *v.i.* **1** to fish with hook and line. **2** to seek an objective deviously. —**angler** *n.* [OE]

Anglican /'æŋglɪkən/ *adj.* of the reformed Church of England or any Church in communion with it. —*n.* a member of the Anglican Church. —**Anglicanism** *n.* [f. L *Anglicanus* ANGLE]

Anglicism /'æŋglɪsɪz(ə)m/ *n.* a peculiarly English word or custom. [f. L *Anglicus* of Angles]

Anglicize /'æŋglɪsaɪz/ *v.t.* to make English in form or character. [as prec.]

Anglo- *in comb.* English; of English origin; English or British and. [as ANGLE]

Anglo-Catholic *adj.* of the section of the Church of England that emphasizes its unbroken connection with the early Church and seeks maximum accordance with the doctrine of the Catholic Church. —*n.* an adherent of Anglo-Catholic belief.

Anglophile /'æŋgləʊfaɪl/ *n.* one who greatly admires England or the English. [f. ANGLO- + *-phile* (Gk *philos* dear)]

Anglo-Saxon *adj.* of English Saxons before the Norman Conquest. —*n.* **1** an Anglo-Saxon person. **2** the English language of this period, also called Old English. **3** a person of English descent.

angora /æŋ'gɔːrə/ *n.* **1** a long-haired variety of cat, goat, or rabbit. **2** soft fluffy fabric or yarn made from the hair of an angora rabbit or goat. [f. *Angora*, the former name of Ankara]

angostura /æŋgəˈstjʊərə/ *n.* the aromatic bitter bark of a South American tree, used as a flavouring. [f. *Angostura* (now Ciudad Bolívar), town in Venezuela]

angry /ˈæŋgrɪ/ *adj.* **1** feeling or showing anger. **2** inflamed. —**angrily** *adv.* [f. ANGER]

angst /æŋst/ *n.* anxiety; a feeling of guilt or remorse. [G]

ångström /ˈæŋgstrəm/ *n.* a unit of length used in measuring wavelengths of light. [f. *A. J. Ångström*, Swedish physicist (d. 1874)]

anguish /ˈæŋgwɪʃ/ *n.* severe (especially mental) suffering. —**anguished** *adj.* [f. OF f. L *angustia* tightness]

angular /ˈæŋgjʊlə(r)/ *adj.* **1** having sharp corners or features, not plump or smooth. **2** forming an angle. **3** measured by angle. —**angularity** /-ˈlærɪtɪ/ *n.* [f. L *angulus* angle]

aniline /ˈænɪli:n/ *n.* an oily liquid got from coal tar, used in dye-making. [f. G (*anil* indigo, whence orig. obtained) f. Arab. *al nil* the indigo]

animadvert /ænɪmədˈvɜ:t/ *v.i.* to pass hostile criticism or censure (*on*). —**animadversion** /-ˈvɜ:ʃ(ə)n/ *n.* [f. L (*animus* mind, *vertere* turn)]

animal /ˈænɪm(ə)l/ *n.* **1** a living thing having sensation and usually the ability to move; such a being other than man; a quadruped. **2** a brutish or uncivilized person. —*adj.* **1** of or like an animal. **2** bestial; carnal. [f. L *animalis* having breath (*anima* breath)]

animalcule /ænɪˈmælkju:l/ *n.* a microscopic animal. [f. prec. + dim. *-cule*]

animate /ˈænɪmət/ *adj.* having life; lively. —/-eɪt/ *v.t.* **1** to enliven. **2** to give life to. **3** to produce as an animated cartoon. **4** to motivate. —**animated cartoon,** a film made by photographing a series of drawings or positions of puppets to create an illusion of movement. —**animation** /-ˈmeɪʃ(ə)n/ *n.*, **animator** *n.* [f. L *animare* give life to (*anima* life)]

animism /ˈænɪmɪz(ə)m/ *n.* attribution of a living soul to inanimate objects and natural phenomena. —**animistic** /-ˈmɪstɪk/ *adj.* [f. L *anima* life, soul]

animosity /ænɪˈmɒsɪtɪ/ *n.* a spirit or feeling of hostility. [f. OF or L (as foll.)]

animus /ˈænɪməs/ *n.* a display of animosity; ill-feeling. [L, = spirit, mind]

anion /ˈænaɪən/ *n.* a negatively charged ion. —**anionic** /-ˈɒnɪk/ *adj.* [f. Gk *ana* up + ION]

aniseed /ˈænɪsi:d/ *n.* the aromatic seed of an umbelliferous plant *Pimpinella anisum*, used for flavouring. [f. OF f. L f. Gk *anison* dill]

ankh /æŋk/ *n.* a cross with a loop as its upper arm, used in ancient Egypt as a symbol of life. [Egyptian, = life]

ankle *n.* the joint connecting the foot with the leg; the part of the leg between this and the calf. [f. ON]

anklet /ˈæŋklɪt/ *n.* an ornament or fetter worn round the ankle. [f. prec. + *-let* (as in *bracelet*)]

ankylosis /æŋkaɪˈləʊsɪs/ *n.* stiffening of a joint by fusion of bones. [f. Gk (*agkulos* crooked)]

annals /ˈænəlz/ *n.pl.* a narrative of events year by year; written records. —**annalistic** /-ˈlɪstɪk/ *adj.* [f. F or L (*annus* year)]

anneal /əˈni:l/ *v.t.* to heat (metal or glass) and allow it to cool slowly, especially to toughen it. [OE, = bake]

annelid /ˈænəlɪd/ *n.* a segmented worm of the phylum Annelida, e.g. earthworm. [f. F f. L (*an(n)ulus* ring)]

annex /æˈneks/ *v.t.* **1** to add or append as a subordinate part. **2** to incorporate (territory) into one's own. **3** (*colloq.*) to take without right. —**annexation** /-ˈseɪʃ(ə)n/ *n.* [f. F f. L *annectere* (AD-, *nectere* bind)]

annexe /ˈæneks/ *n.* a building attached to a larger or more important one or forming a subordinate part of a main building. [as prec.]

annihilate /əˈnaɪɪleɪt/ *v.t.* to destroy completely. —**annihilation** /-ˈleɪʃ(ə)n/ *n.* [f. L *annihilare* (AD-, *nihil* nothing)]

anniversary /ænɪˈvɜ:sərɪ/ *n.* the date on which an event took place in a previous year; a celebration of this. [f. L (*annus* year, *versus* turned)]

Anno Domini /ænəʊ ˈdɒmɪnaɪ/ *adv.* in the year of the Christian era. —*n.* (*colloq.*) advancing age. [L, = in the year of the Lord]

annotate /ˈænəʊteɪt/ *v.t.* to add explanatory notes to. —**annotation** /-ˈteɪʃ(ə)n/ *n.* [f. L *annotare* (AD-, *nota* mark)]

announce /əˈnaʊns/ *v.t.* to make publicly known; to make known the arrival or imminence of; to be a sign of. —**announcement** *n.* [f. OF f. L *annuntiare* (AD-, *nuntius* messenger)]

announcer *n.* one who announces items in broadcasting. [f. prec.]

annoy /əˈnɔɪ/ *v.t.* to anger slightly; to be troublesome to, to molest. —**annoyance** *n.* [f. OF f. L *in odio* hateful)]

annoyed /əˈnɔɪd/ *adj.* somewhat angry. [f. prec.]

annual /ˈænjʊəl/ *adj.* **1** reckoned by the year; recurring once every year. **2** (of plants) living or lasting only one year or season. —*n.* **1** a book etc. published in yearly issues. **2** an annual plant. —**annual ring,** a ring in the cross-section of a tree, fish, etc., from one year's growth. —**annually** *adv.* [f. OF f. L (*annus* year)]

annuity /əˈnju:ɪtɪ/ *n.* an investment yielding a fixed annual sum; a yearly grant or allowance. [as prec.]

annul /əˈnʌl/ *v.t.* (**-ll-**) to declare to be invalid; to cancel, to abolish. —**annulment** *n*. [f. OF f. L *annullare* (AD-, *nullus* none)]

annular /'ænjʊlə(r)/ *adj*. ring-shaped, forming a ring. —**annular eclipse**, see ECLIPSE. [f. F or L (*an(n)ulus* ring)]

annulet /'ænju:lɪt/ *n*. a small ring; an encircling band. [f. L *an(n)ulus*]

Annunciation /ənʌnsɪ'eɪʃ(ə)n/ *n*. the announcement by the angel Gabriel to the Virgin Mary that she was to be the mother of Christ; the festival commemorating this (25 Mar.), also called Lady Day. [f. OF f. L (as ANNOUNCE)]

anode /'ænəʊd/ *n*. the electrode by which current enters a device. [f. Gk *anodos* way up (*ana* up, *hodos* way)]

anodize /'ænədaɪz/ *v.t*. to coat (metal) with a protective layer by electrolysis. [f. prec.]

anodyne /'ænədaɪn/ *adj*. relieving pain, soothing. —*n*. an anodyne drug or circumstance. [f. L f. Gk (*an-* without, *odunē* pain)]

anoint /ə'nɔɪnt/ *v.t*. to apply oil or ointment to, especially as a religious ceremony; to smear (*with* grease etc.). [f. AF f. L *inungere*]

anomalous /ə'nɒmələs/ *adj*. deviant, irregular, abnormal. —**anomalously** *adv*. [f. L f. Gk (*an-* not, *homalos* even)]

anomaly /ə'nɒməlɪ/ *n*. an anomalous thing. [as prec.]

anon /ə'nɒn/ *adv*. soon, shortly. [OE *on an* into one]

anon. *abbr*. anonymous.

anonymous /ə'nɒnɪməs/ *adj*. with a name that is not known or not made public; written or given by such a person. —**anonymously** *adv*., **anonymity** /ænɒ'nɪmɪtɪ/ *n*. [f. L f. Gk (*an-* without, *onoma* name)]

anorak /'ænəræk/ *n*. a waterproof jacket, usually with a hood attached. [Eskimo]

anorexia /ænə'reksɪə/ *n*. lack of appetite for food. —**anorexia nervosa** /nə'vəʊsə/, chronic anorexia caused by a psychological condition. —**anorexic** *n*. [L f. Gk (*an-* not, *orexis* appetite)]

another /ə'nʌðə(r)/ *adj*. additional, one more; a different (*thing* etc.); some other. —*n*. another person or thing. [earlier *an other*]

anserine /'ænsəraɪn/ *adj*. of or like a goose. [f. L (*anser* goose)]

answer /'ɑ:nsə(r)/ *n*. something said, written, or done in reaction to a question, statement, or circumstance; the solution to a problem. —*v.t./i*. **1** to make an answer (to). **2** to respond to the summons or signal of. **3** to suit (a need or purpose). **4** to be responsible *for* or *to*. **5** to correspond *to* a description. —**answer back**, to answer a rebuke impudently. [OE, = swear against (a charge)]

answerable *adj*. **1** responsible *to* or *for*. **2** that can be answered. [f. prec.]

ant *n*. a small wingless or hymenopterous insect, all species of which live in highly organized groups. —**ant-eater** *n*. any of various mammals that feed on ants and termites. [OE]

antacid /æn'tæsɪd/ *adj*. preventing or correcting acidity. —*n*. an antacid substance. [f. ANTI- + ACID]

antagonism /æn'tægənɪz(ə)m/ *n*. active opposition, hostility. [as foll.]

antagonist *n*. an opponent. [f. F or L f. Gk (as ANTAGONIZE)]

antagonistic /æntægə'nɪstɪk/ *adj*. showing antagonism, hostile. [as foll.]

antagonize /æn'tægənaɪz/ *v.t*. to arouse antagonism in. [f. Gk, = struggle against (*agōn* contest)]

Antarctic /æn'tɑ:ktɪk/ *adj*. of the south polar regions. —*n*. the regions (both land and sea) round the South Pole. —**Antarctic Circle**, the parallel of latitude 66° 33′ S, south of which the sun does not rise at midwinter or set at midsummer. [f. OF or L f. Gk *anti* opposite + ARCTIC]

ante /'æntɪ/ *n*. a stake put up by a poker player before drawing new cards; an amount to be paid in advance. —*v.t*. to put up (an ante). [f. ANTE-]

ante- *prefix* before, preceding. [L, = before]

antecedent /æntɪ'si:d(ə)nt/ *n*. **1** a preceding thing or circumstance. **2** (*Gram*.) a word or phrase to which another word (especially a relative pronoun) refers. **3** (in *pl*.) a person's or thing's past history. —*adj*. previous. [f. F or L (ANTE-, *cedere* go)]

antechamber *n*. an ante-room. [f. ANTE- + CHAMBER]

antedate /æntɪ'deɪt/ *v.t*. to be of earlier date than; to give a date earlier than the true one to. [f. ANTE- + DATE¹]

antediluvian /æntɪdɪ'lu:vɪən/ *adj*. of the time before the Flood; (*colloq*.) very old. [f. ANTE- + L *diluvium* deluge]

antelope /'æntɪləʊp/ *n*. (*pl*. same or **-s**) a swift-running deerlike animal (e.g. chamois, gazelle) found especially in Africa. [f. OF or L f. Gk *antholops*]

antenatal /æntɪ'neɪt(ə)l/ *adj*. before birth; relating to pregnancy. [f. ANTE- + NATAL]

antenna /æn'tenə/ *n*. **1** (*pl*. **-ae**) either of a pair of flexible sensory organs found on the heads of insects, crustaceans, etc., a feeler. **2** (*pl*. **-as**) a radio aerial. [L, = sail-yard]

antepenultimate /æntɪpɪ'nʌltɪmət/ *adj*. last but two.

ante-post /æntɪ'pəʊst/ *adj*. (of racing bets) made before the runners' numbers are displayed.

anterior /æn'tɪərɪə(r)/ *adj*. nearer the front; prior (*to*). [f. F or L, compar. of *ante* before]

ante-room /'æntɪru:m/ *n*. a small room leading to a main one.

anthem /ˈænθəm/ *n.* **1** a short choral composition, usually based on a passage of Scripture, for church use; a song of praise or gladness. **2** a national anthem (see NATIONAL). [OE f. L (as ANTIPHON)]

anther /ˈænθə(r)/ *n.* the part of a stamen containing pollen. [f. F or L f. Gk (*anthos* flower)]

anthill /ˈænthɪl/ *n.* a mound of soil formed by ants over their nest.

anthology /ænˈθɒlədʒɪ/ *n.* a collection of passages from literature, especially poetry and song. —**anthologist** *n.* [f. F or L f. Gk (*anthos* flower, *-logia* collection)]

anthozoan /ænθəˈzəʊən/ *n.* a marine animal of the class Anthozoa which includes corals and sea anemones. [f. L f. Gk *anthos* flower, *zōa* animals]

anthracite /ˈænθrəsaɪt/ *n.* a hard form of coal that burns with little flame and smoke. [f. Gk *anthrax* coal, carbuncle]

anthrax /ˈænθræks/ *n.* a disease of sheep and cattle that can be transmitted to people. [L f. Gk (as prec.)]

anthropocentric /ænθrəpəˈsentrɪk/ *adj.* regarding mankind as the centre of existence. [f. Gk *anthrōpos* human being]

anthropoid /ˈænθrəpɔɪd/ *adj.* like a human in form. —*n.* an anthropoid ape. [as prec.]

anthropology /ænθrəˈpɒlədʒɪ/ *n.* the study of mankind, now usually divided into two main sub-disciplines: study of the social organization and cultural systems of human groups (**social anthropology**), and study of the structure and evolution of man (**physical** or **biological anthropology**). —**anthropological** /-əˈlɒdʒɪk(ə)l/ *adj.*, **anthropologist** *n.* [f. Gk *anthrōpos* human being + -LOGY]

anthropomorphism /ænθrəpəˈmɔːfɪz(ə)m/ *n.* the attribution of human form or personality to a god, animal, or thing. —**anthropomorphic** *adj.* [as foll.]

anthropomorphous /ænθrəpəˈmɔːfəs/ *adj.* of human form. [f. Gk (*anthrōpos* human being, *morphē* form)]

anti /ˈæntɪ/ *prep.* opposed to. —*n.* one who is opposed to a policy etc. [f. foll.]

anti- *prefix* opposed to; preventing. [f. Gk *anti* against]

anti-aircraft *adj.* used in attacking enemy aircraft.

antibiotic /æntɪbaɪˈɒtɪk/ *n.* a substance capable of destroying or preventing the growth of bacteria or similar organisms. —*adj.* functioning in this way. [f. F f. Gk (ANTI-, *bios* life)]

antibody /ˈæntɪbɒdɪ/ *n.* a protein produced in the body in response to and then counteracting antigens. [transl. G *antikörper* (ANTI-, *körper* body)]

antic *n.* (usu. in *pl.*) absurd movements intended to cause amusement; odd or foolish behaviour. [f. It. *antico* antique, used as = grotesque]

Antichrist /ˈæntɪkraɪst/ *n.* an enemy of Christ, the great personal opponent of Christ expected by the early Christians to appear before the end of the world.

anticipate /ænˈtɪsɪpeɪt/ *v.t.* **1** to deal with or use before the proper time. **2** to forestall. **3** to be ahead of (a person) in taking some action etc.; to foresee and provide for. **4** (D) to expect. [f. L *anticipare* (*anti* = ante, *capere* take)]

anticipation /æntɪsɪˈpeɪʃ(ə)n/ *n.* anticipating; eager expectation. —**anticipatory** /-ˈpeɪtərɪ/ *adj.* [f. prec.]

anticlimax /ˈæntɪklaɪmæks/ *n.* a trivial conclusion to something significant or impressive, especially where a climax was expected.

anticline /ˈæntɪklaɪn/ *n.* a land formation in which strata are folded so that they slope down on opposite sides of a ridge. —**anticlinal** *adj.* [f. ANTI- + Gk *klinō* lean]

anticlockwise /æntɪˈklɒkwaɪz/ *adj.* & *adv.* moving in a curve in the opposite direction to the hands of a clock (see CLOCKWISE).

anticyclone /æntɪˈsaɪkləʊn/ *n.* a system of winds rotating outwards from an area of high barometric pressure, producing fine weather.

antidote /ˈæntɪdəʊt/ *n.* a substance that counteracts the effect of a poison; anything that counteracts unpleasant effects. —**antidotal** *adj.* [F or L f. Gk *antidotos* given against]

antifreeze *n.* a substance added to water (especially in the radiator of a motor vehicle) to lower its freezing-point and therefore make it less likely to freeze.

antigen /ˈæntɪdʒən/ *n.* a substance (e.g. a toxin) that causes the body to produce antibodies. [G (ANTI-, Gk *-genēs* of a kind)]

anti-hero *n.* a central character in a story or drama who noticeably lacks conventional heroic attitudes.

antihistamine /æntɪˈhɪstəmiːn/ *n.* a substance that counteracts the effects of histamine, used in treating allergies.

antiknock *n.* a substance added to motor fuel to prevent or reduce knock.

antilog /ˈæntɪlɒg/ *n.* (*colloq.*) an antilogarithm. [abbr.]

antilogarithm /æntɪˈlɒgərɪð(ə)m/ *n.* the number to which a given logarithm belongs.

antimacassar /æntɪməˈkæsə(r)/ *n.* a former name for a short cover put over the backs or arms of chairs etc. to keep them from getting dirty, or as an ornament. [f. ANTI- + *Macassar*, because originally used as a protection against the Macassar oil that was used on hair]

antimatter /ˈæntɪmætə(r)/ *n*. (hypothetical) matter composed solely of antiparticles (see ANTIPARTICLE).

antimony /ˈæntɪmənɪ/ *n*. a semi-metallic element, symbol Sb, atomic number 51, existing as a brittle silvery-white metal and in several non-metallic forms. [f. L *antimonium* (orig. unkn.)]

anting *n*. the rubbing or placing of ants etc. in their feathers by birds, perhaps in order to kill parasites. [f. ANT]

antinomy /ænˈtɪnəmɪ/ *n*. contradiction between two laws or authorities that are both reasonable. [as prec.]

antinovel *n*. a novel in which the conventions of the form are studiously avoided.

antiparticle *n*. an elementary particle having the same mass as a given particle but an opposite electric charge or magnetic moment.

antipathy /ænˈtɪpəθɪ/ *n*. a strong or deep-seated aversion; its object. —**antipathetic** /-ˈθetɪk/ *adj*. [f. F or L f. Gk (*antipathēs* opposed in feeling)]

antiperspirant /æntɪˈpɜːspɪrənt/ *n*. a substance that prevents or reduces perspiration.

antiphon /ˈæntɪfən/ *n*. a hymn or psalm etc. in which versicles or phrases are sung alternately by two sections of a choir; a versicle or phrase from this. [f. L f. Gk (ANTI-, *phonē* sound)]

antiphonal /ænˈtɪfən(ə)l/ *adj*. sung alternately by two sections of a choir. [f. prec.]

antipodes /ænˈtɪpədiːz/ *n.pl.* places diametrically opposite each other on the earth; **the Antipodes**, Australasia in relation to Europe. —**antipodal** *adj*., **antipodean** /-ˈdiːən/ *adj*. [F or L f. Gk, = having the feet opposite]

antipope *n*. a person set up as pope in opposition to one held by some supporters to be canonically chosen.

antiquarian /æntɪˈkweərɪən/ *adj*. of or dealing in antiques or rare books. —*n*. an antiquary. [as foll.]

antiquary /ænˈtɪkwərɪ/ *n*. one who studies or collects antiques or antiquities. [f. L (*antiquus* ancient)]

antiquated /ˈæntɪkweɪtɪd/ *adj*. old, out of date, old-fashioned. [f. L (as foll.)]

antique /ænˈtiːk/ *n*. an object of considerable age, especially an item of furniture or a decorative object sought by collectors. —*adj*. of or existing from an early date; old; old-fashioned. [F, or f. L = former, ancient (*ante* before)]

antiquity /ænˈtɪkwɪtɪ/ *n*. **1** ancient times, especially before the Middle Ages. **2** great age. **3** (in *pl.*) remains from ancient times. [f. OF f. L (as prec.)]

antirrhinum /æntɪˈraɪnəm/ *n*. a plant of the genus *Antirrhinum* with a flower that has an aperture between closed 'lips'. [L, f. Gk (*anti* counterfeiting, *rhis* snout)]

antiscorbutic /æntɪskɔːˈbjuːtɪk/ *adj*. that prevents or cures scurvy. —*n*. an antiscorbutic medicine. [f. ANTI- + L *scorbutus* scurvy]

anti-Semitic /æntɪsɪˈmɪtɪk/ *adj*. hostile to Jews. —**anti-Semite** /-ˈsiːmaɪt/ *n*., **anti-Semitism** /-ˈsemɪtɪz(ə)m/ *n*.

antisepsis /æntɪˈsepsɪs/ *n*. the process or principles of using antiseptics.

antiseptic /æntɪˈseptɪk/ *adj*. that counteracts sepsis, especially by destroying bacteria. —*n*. an antiseptic substance.

antisocial /æntɪˈsəʊʃ(ə)l/ *adj*. **1** opposed or harmful to social institutions and laws; interfering with amenities enjoyed by others. **2** not sociable.

antistatic /æntɪˈstætɪk/ *adj*. that counteracts the effects of static electricity.

antithesis /ænˈtɪθəsɪs/ *n*. (*pl*. **-eses** /-əsiːz/) a direct opposite; contrast; contrast of ideas emphasized by the parallelism of contrasted words. —**antithetic** /-ˈθetɪk/ *adj*., **antithetical** *adj*. [L f. Gk (*antitithēmi* set against)]

antitoxin /æntɪˈtɒksɪn/ *n*. an antibody that counteracts a toxin. —**antitoxic** *adj*.

antitrades /ˈæntɪtreɪdz/ *n.pl.* winds blowing above and in the opposite direction to trade winds. [f. ANTI- + TRADE (winds)]

antitrust *adj*. (*US*) opposed to trusts or other monopolies.

antitype *n*. **1** one of the opposite type. **2** that which a type or symbol represents. [f. Gk *antitupos* corresponding as an impression to the die (ANTI-, *tupos* stamp)]

antivivisection /æntɪvɪvɪˈsekʃ(ə)n/ *n*. opposed to experiments on live animals. —**antivivisectionist** *n*.

antler *n*. a branched horn of a stag or other (usually male) deer. —**antlered** *adj*. [f. AF; orig. unkn.]

antonym /ˈæntənɪm/ *n*. a word that is opposite in meaning to another. [f. F (ANTI-, Gk *onoma* name)]

antrum *n*. (*pl*. **-tra**) a cavity of the body, especially one of a pair in the upper jaw-bone. [L f. Gk, = cave]

anus /ˈeɪnəs/ *n*. the excretory opening at the end of the alimentary canal. [L]

anvil *n*. an iron block on which a smith hammers metal into shape. [OE (*an* on, *filt*- beat)]

anxiety /æŋˈzaɪətɪ/ *n*. the state of being anxious; something causing this. [f. F or L (as foll.)]

anxious /ˈæŋʃəs/ *adj*. **1** troubled, uneasy in mind. **2** causing or marked by worry. **3** eagerly wanting (*to*). —**anxiously** *adv*. [f. L *anxius* (*angere* choke)]

any /ˈenɪ/ *adj*. **1** one or some (but no matter which) from three or more or from a quantity.

2 an appreciable or significant (amount etc.). 3 whichever is chosen. —*pron.* any one, any number or amount. —*adv.* at all, in some degree. [OE]

anybody /ˈenɪbɒdɪ/ *n.* & *pron.* 1 any person. 2 a person of importance. [f. ANY + BODY (= person)]

anyhow /ˈenɪhaʊ/ *adv.* 1 anyway. 2 in a disorderly manner.

anyone /ˈenɪwʌn/ *n.* & *pron.* anybody.

anything /ˈenɪθɪŋ/ *n.* & *pron.* any thing, a thing of any sort. —**anything but,** not at all. **like anything,** with great intensity.

anyway /ˈenɪweɪ/ *adv.* in any way or manner; in any case.

anywhere /ˈenɪ(h)weə(r)/ *adv.* in or to any place. —*pron.* any place.

Anzac /ˈænzæk/ *n.* 1 a member of the Australian and New Zealand Army Corps (1914–18). 2 an Australian or a New Zealand person, especially a serviceman. —*adj.* of Anzacs. —**Anzac Day,** 25 April, commemorating the landing of the corps in Gallipoli. [acronym]

Anzus /ˈænzəs/ the combination of Australia, New Zealand, and the USA for the security of the Pacific. [acronym]

aorist /ˈeɪərɪst/ *n.* the unqualified past tense of a verb (especially in Greek), without reference to duration or completion. [f. Gk, = indefinite]

aorta /eɪˈɔːtə/ *n.* the main artery carrying blood from the left ventricle of the heart. —**aortic** *adj.* [f. Gk (*aeirō* raise)]

apace /əˈpeɪs/ *adv.* swiftly. [f. OF *à pas* at (a considerable) pace]

Apache /əˈpætʃɪ/ *n.* (*pl.* same or **-s**) a member of an Athapaskan-speaking American Indian tribe. [Mexican Sp.]

apache /əˈpæʃ/ *n.* a violent street ruffian, originally in Paris *c.*1900. [f. prec.]

apart /əˈpɑːt/ *adv.* 1 separately, not together. 2 into pieces. 3 aside, to or at a distance. —**apart from,** excepting, not considering. **tell apart,** to distinguish between. [f. OF (*à* to, *part* side)]

apartheid /əˈpɑːtheɪt/ *n.* the South African policy of racial separation and discrimination, separating Europeans and non-Europeans. [Afrik. (as APART, -HOOD)]

apartment /əˈpɑːtmənt/ *n.* 1 (in *pl.*) a suite of rooms, usually rented furnished. 2 (*US*) a flat. [f. F f. It. (*a parte* apart)]

apathy /ˈæpəθɪ/ *n.* lack of interest or concern, indifference. —**apathetic** /-ˈθetɪk/ *adj.*, **apathetically** *adv.* [f. F f. L f. Gk (*a-* without, *pathos* suffering)]

apatite /ˈæpətaɪt/ *n.* a crystalline mineral of calcium phosphate and fluoride. [f. G f. Gk *apatē* deceit (from its deceptive forms)]

ape *n.* a monkey, especially of the tailless kind (gorilla, chimpanzee, orang-utan, gibbon). —*v.t.* to imitate. —**ape-man** *n.* an extinct primate postulated by Haeckel as intermediate between ape and man; a primitive man. [OE]

aperient /əˈpɪərɪənt/ *adj.* laxative. —*n.* a laxative medicine. [f. L *aperire* to open]

aperitif /əˈperɪtiːf/ *n.* an alcoholic drink taken before a meal. [f. F f. L (as prec.)]

aperture /ˈæpətjʊə(r)/ *n.* an opening or gap; a space for admitting light in a camera or optical instrument. [f. L (as prec.)]

apex /ˈeɪpeks/ *n.* (*pl.* **apexes**) the highest point; the pointed end, the tip. [L]

aphelion /əˈfiːlɪən/ *n.* (*pl.* **-ia**) the point in a planet's or comet's orbit when it is furthest from the sun. [f. Gk *aph' hēliou* from the sun]

aphid /ˈeɪfɪd/ *n.* a plant louse such as greenfly or blackfly. [f. foll.]

aphis /ˈeɪfɪs/ *n.* (*pl.* **-ides** /-ɪdiːz/) an aphid. [the word was invented by Linnaeus, perh. a misreading of Gk *koris* bug]

aphorism /ˈæfərɪz(ə)m/ *n.* a short pithy saying. [f. F or L f. Gk *aphorismos* definition (*horos* boundary)]

aphrodisiac /æfrəˈdɪsɪæk/ *adj.* arousing sexual desire. —*n.* an aphrodisiac substance. [f. Gk f. *Aphrodite*, Gk goddess of love]

apiary /ˈeɪpɪərɪ/ *n.* a place with a number of hives where bees are kept. —**apiarist** *n.* [f. L (*apis* bee)]

apical /ˈeɪpɪk(ə)l/ *adj* of, at, or forming an apex. [f. APEX]

apiculture /ˈeɪpɪkʌltʃə(r)/ *n.* bee-keeping. —**apiculturist** *n.* [f. L *apis* bee + CULTURE]

apiece /əˈpiːs/ *adv.* for each one. [orig. *a piece*]

aplomb /əˈplɒm/ *n.* assurance, self-confidence. [F, = straight as a plummet]

Apocalypse /əˈpɒkəlɪps/ *n.* 1 the *Revelation of St John the Divine*, containing a prophetic description of the end of the world. 2 **apocalypse,** great and dramatic events like those described in the Apocalypse. —**apocalyptic** /əpɒkəˈlɪptɪk/ *adj.*, **apocalyptically** *adv.* [f. OF f. L f. Gk, = uncovering]

Apocrypha /əˈpɒkrɪfə/ the Biblical books received by the early Church as part of the Greek version of the Old Testament, but not included in the Hebrew Bible.

apocryphal /əˈpɒkrɪf(ə)l/ *adj.* untrue, invented; of doubtful authenticity. [f. prec.]

apogee /ˈæpədʒiː/ *n.* the highest point, a climax; the point in the orbit of the moon or any planet or satellite when it is at its furthest point from the earth. [f. F or Gk *apogeion* away from the earth (*gē* earth)]

apolitical /eɪpəˈlɪtɪk(ə)l/ *adj.* not interested in or concerned with politics. [f. Gk *a-* not + POLITICAL]

apologetic /əpɒləˈdʒetɪk/ *adj.* making an apology; diffident. —**apologetics** *n.pl.* a reasoned defence, especially of Christianity. —**apologetically** *adv.* [f. F f. L f. Gk (*apologeomai* speak in defence)]

apologia /æpəˈləʊdʒɪə/ *n.* a formal defence of belief or conduct. [L f. Gk (see APOLOGY)]

apologist /əˈpɒlədʒɪst/ *n.* one who makes a formal defence of a belief etc. by argument. [f. F f. Gk *apologizomai* render an account]

apologize /əˈpɒlədʒaɪz/ *v.i.* to make an apology. [f. Gk (see prec.)]

apology /əˈpɒlədʒɪ/ *n.* **1** regretful acknowledgement of an offence or failure. **2** an explanation or defence of a belief etc. —**apology for,** a poor or scanty specimen of. [f. F or L f. Gk *apologia* (as APOLOGETIC)]

apophthegm /ˈæpəθem/ *n.* a terse or pithy saying. [f. F or Gk (*apophtheggomai* speak out)]

apoplectic /æpəˈplektɪk/ *adj.* of, suffering from, or liable to apoplexy; (*colloq.*) liable to fits of rage in which the face becomes very red. —**apoplectically** *adv.* [as foll.]

apoplexy /ˈæpəpleksɪ/ *n.* a sudden inability to feel and move, caused by blockage or rupture of a brain artery. [f. OF f. L f. Gk (*apoplēssō* disable by a stroke)]

apostasy /əˈpɒstəsɪ/ *n.* renunciation of one's religious faith or one's principles or party etc. [f. L f. Gk, = defection]

apostate /əˈpɒsteɪt/ *n.* one who renounces his former belief, principles, or party, etc. [f. OF or L f. Gk *apostatēs* deserter]

apostatize /əˈpɒstətaɪz/ *v.i.* to become an apostate. [f. prec.]

a posteriori /eɪ pɒsterɪˈɔ:raɪ/ reasoning from effects back to their causes. [L, = from what comes after]

Apostle /əˈpɒs(ə)l/ *n.* **1** the name given in the Gospels and later to the twelve chief disciples of Christ. **2 apostle,** the first successful Christian missionary in a country; the leader of a new faith or reform. —**Apostle spoon,** a spoon with a figure of an Apostle on the handle. [OE f. L f. Gk (*apostellō* send forth)]

apostolic /æpəˈstɒlɪk/ *adj.* of the Apostles or their teaching; of the pope. —**apostolic succession,** the uninterrupted transmission of spiritual authority through successive popes and other bishops from the Apostles. [as prec.]

apostrophe /əˈpɒstrəfɪ/ *n.* **1** the sign (') showing the possessive case, omission of letters or numbers, or the plurals of letters. **2** an exclamatory passage addressed to a person or persons or an abstract idea. [L f. Gk (*apostrephō* turn away)]

apostrophize /əˈpɒstrəfaɪz/ *v.t.* to address in an apostrophe. [f. prec.]

apothecary /əˈpɒθɪkərɪ/ *n.* (*archaic*) a pharmaceutical chemist. [f. OF f. L f. Gk *apothēkē* storehouse]

apotheosis /æpəθɪˈəʊsɪs/ *n.* (*pl.* **-oses**) **1** deification. **2** a deified ideal; the highest development of a thing. [L f. Gk (*theos* god)]

appal /əˈpɔ:l/ *v.t.* (**-ll-**) to fill with horror or dismay, to shock deeply. —**appalling** *adj.* [f. OF *apalir* grow pale]

apparatus /æpəˈreɪtəs/ *n.* **1** equipment for performing something, e.g. gymnastics or scientific experiments; bodily organs effecting a natural process. **2** a complicted organization. [L (AD-, *parare* make ready)]

apparel /əˈpær(ə)l/ *n.* (*archaic*) clothing. —*v.t.* (**-ll-**) (*archaic*) to clothe. [f. OF f. Rom., = make ready (AD-, dim. of L *par* equal)]

apparent /əˈpærənt/ *adj.* **1** readily visible or perceivable. **2** seeming but not real. —**apparently** *adv.* [f. OF f. L (as APPEAR)]

apparition /æpəˈrɪʃ(ə)n/ *n.* something remarkable or expected that appears; a ghost. [f. F or L (as APPEAR)]

appeal /əˈpi:l/ *v.t./i.* **1** to make an earnest or formal request; to call attention or resort *to* (evidence etc.) as support; to make a request (*to* a higher court) for alteration of the decision of a lower court; (in cricket) to ask the umpire to declare a batsman out. **2** to be attractive or of interest *to*. —*n.* **1** an act of appealing. **2** an appealing quality, attraction. **3** a request for donations to a cause. [f. F f. L *appellare* address (AD-, *pellere* drive)]

appear /əˈpɪə(r)/ *v.i.* **1** to become or be visible; to give an impression, to seem. **2** to present oneself formally or publicly. **3** to be published. [f. OF f. L *apparēre* come in sight]

appearance *n.* appearing; an outward form as perceived, a semblance. —**keep up appearances,** to maintain a display or pretence of prosperity, good behaviour, etc. [as prec.]

appease /əˈpi:z/ *v.t.* to make calm or quiet by making concessions etc. or by satisfying demands. —**appeasement** *n.* [f. AF (*à* to, *pais* peace)]

appellant /əˈpelənt/ *n.* (*Law*) a person making an appeal to a higher court. [f. F (as APPEAL)]

appellation /æpəˈleɪʃ(ə)n/ *n.* a name or title; nomenclature. [as prec.]

append /əˈpend/ *v.t.* to attach; to add, especially to a written document. [f. L *appendere* (AD-, *pendere* hang)]

appendage /əˈpendɪdʒ/ *n.* a thing attached to or forming a natural part of something larger or more important. [f. prec.]

appendicitis /əpendɪˈsaɪtɪs/ *n.* inflammation of the appendix. [f. foll. + -ITIS]

appendix /əˈpendɪks/ *n.* (*pl.* **-ices** /-ɪsi:z/) **1** supplementary matter at the end of a book etc. **2** a small blind tube of tissue forming an outgrowth of the caecum. [L (as APPEND)]

appertain /æpəˈteɪn/ *v.i.* to belong or relate *to*. [f. OF f. L *appertinere* (AD-, *pertinēre* pertain)]

appetite /ˈæpɪtaɪt/ *n.* a natural craving or relish, especially for food or something pleasurable. [f. OF f. L *appetere* seek after]

appetizer /ˈæpɪtaɪzə(r)/ *n.* a small savoury or drink taken before a meal to stimulate the appetite. [f. foll.]

appetizing /ˈæpɪtaɪzɪŋ/ *adj.* (of food) stimulating the appetite, attractive to eat. —**appetizingly** *adv.* [f. F (as APPETITE)]

applaud /əˈplɔːd/ *v.t./i.* to express strong approval (of), especially by clapping; to commend, to praise. —**applause** *n.* [f. L *applaudere* (AD-, *plaudere* clap hands)]

apple *n.* a round firm fruit with juicy flesh; the tree bearing this. —**apple of one's eye,** a cherished person or thing. **apple-pie order,** extreme neatness. [OE]

appliance /əˈplaɪəns/ *n.* a device, a utensil; a fire-engine. [f. APPLY]

applicable /ˈæplɪkəb(ə)l/ *adj.* that may be applied (*to*), appropriate. —**applicability** /-ˈbɪlɪtɪ/ *n.* [OF or f. L (as APPLY)]

applicant /ˈæplɪkənt/ *n.* one who applies for something, especially employment. [f. foll.]

application /æplɪkeɪʃ(ə)n/ *n.* **1** the act of applying something. **2** a thing applied. **3** a formal request. **4** sustained effort, diligence. **5** relevance. [f. F f. L (as APPLY)]

applicator /ˈæplɪkeɪtə(r)/ *n.* a device for applying a substance. [f. prec.]

applied /əˈplaɪd/ *adj.* (of knowledge etc.) put to practical use. [f. APPLY]

appliqué /əˈpliːkeɪ/ *n.* ornamental work in which fabric is cut out and attached to the surface of another fabric. —*v.t.* (**-quéd, -quéing**) to decorate with appliqué. [F (as foll.)]

apply /əˈplaɪ/ *v.t./i.* **1** to make a formal request. **2** to put into contact, to spread on a surface. **3** to bring into use or action. **4** to be relevant. —**apply oneself,** to give one's attention and energy (*to* a task). [f. OF f. L *applicare* fasten to]

appoint /əˈpɔɪnt/ *v.t.* **1** to assign (a person) to a job or office; to set up by choosing members. **2** to fix or decide (a date or place etc.). —**well-appointed** *adj.* well-equipped or furnished. [f. OF (*à point* to a point)]

appointee /æpɔɪnˈtiː/ *n.* a person appointed. [f. prec.]

appointment /əˈpɔɪntmənt/ *n.* **1** an arrangement to meet or visit at a particular time. **2** appointing a person to a job; the person appointed. **3** (in *pl.*) fittings, furnishings. [f. APPOINT]

apportion /əˈpɔːʃ(ə)n/ *v.t.* to share out; to assign as a share (*to*). —**apportionment** *n.* [f. F or L (as PORTION)]

apposite /ˈæpəsɪt/ *adj.* (of a remark) appropriate. —**appositely** *adv.*, **appositeness** *n.* [f. L (*apponere* apply)]

apposition /æpəˈsɪʃ(ə)n/ *n.* juxtaposition, especially (*Gram.*) of elements sharing a syntactic function. [as prec.]

appraise /əˈpreɪz/ *v.t.* to estimate the value or amount of; to fix a price for (a thing) officially. —**appraisal** *n.* [earlier *apprise*, assim. to PRAISE]

appreciable /əˈpriːʃəb(ə)l/ *adj.* enough to be seen or felt, considerable. —**appreciably** *adv.* [F (as foll.)]

appreciate /əˈpriːʃɪeɪt/ *v.t./i.* **1** to value greatly; to be grateful for. **2** to recognize, to be sympathetically aware of; to assess realistically. **3** to raise or rise in value. —**appreciation** /-ˈeɪʃ(ə)n/ *n.* [f. L *appretiare* appraise (AD-, *pretium* price)]

appreciative /əˈpriːʃəɪv/ *adj.* expressing appreciation. [f. prec.]

appreciatory /əˈpriːʃətərɪ/ *adj.* (of remarks etc.) expressing appreciation. [f. APPRECIATE]

apprehend /æprɪˈhend/ *v.t.* **1** to arrest, to seize. **2** to understand. **3** to expect with fear or anxiety. [f. F or L *apprehendere* (AD-, *prehendere* grasp)]

apprehensible /æprɪˈhensɪb(ə)l/ *adj.* able to be grasped by the mind or perceived by the senses. [as prec.]

apprehension /æprɪˈhenʃ(ə)n/ *n.* **1** dread, fearful, expectation. **2** arrest, capture. **3** understanding. [F or f. L (as APPREHEND)]

apprehensive /æprɪˈhensɪv/ *adj.* feeling apprehension, anxious. —**apprehensively** *adv.*, **apprehensiveness** *n.* [f. F or L (as APPREHEND)]

apprentice /əˈprentɪs/ *n.* one who is learning a craft and is bound to an employer for a specified term by legal agreement in return for instruction; a novice (jockey). —*v.t.* to bind as an apprentice. —**apprenticeship** *n.* [f. OF (*apprendre* learn)]

apprise /əˈpraɪz/ *v.t.* to inform, to notify. [f. F (*apprendre* learn; as APPREHEND)]

appro /ˈæprəʊ/ *n.* (*colloq.*) approval. [abbr.]

approach /əˈprəʊtʃ/ *v.t./i.* **1** to come near or nearer (to) in space or time. **2** to be similar or approximate to. **3** to make a tentative proposal to. **4** to set about (a task). —*n.* **1** an act or means of approaching. **2** a way of dealing with a person or thing. **3** an approximation. **4** the final part of an aircraft's flight before landing. [f. OF f. L *appropiare* draw near (AD-, *prope* near)]

approachable /əˈprəʊtʃəb(ə)l/ *adj.* able to be approached; friendly, easy to talk to. —**approachability** /-ˈbɪlɪtɪ/ *n.* [f. prec.]

approbation /æprəˈbeɪʃ(ə)n/ *n.* approval, consent. [f. OF f. L *approbatio* (AD-, *probare* test)]

appropriate[1] /əˈprəʊprɪət/ *adj.* suitable, proper. —**appropriately** *adv.*, **appropriateness** *n.* [f. L *appropriare* (AD-, *proprius* one's own)]

appropriate[2] /əˈprəʊprɪeɪt/ *v.t.* to take and use as one's own; to devote (money etc.) to a special purpose. —**appropriation** /-ˈeɪʃ(ə)n/ *n.*, **appropriator** *n.* [f. prec.]

approval /əˈpru:v(ə)l/ *n.* **1** approving; favourable opinion. **2** consent. —**on approval,** returnable to the supplier (without obligation to purchase) if not suitable. [f. foll.]

approve /əˈpru:v/ *v.t./i.* **1** to give or have a favourable opinion (*of*). **2** to give assent to. [f. OF f. L *approbare* test (AD-, *probus* good)]

approximate[1] /əˈprɒksɪmət/ *adj.* almost (but not completely) exact or correct, near to the actual. —**approximately** *adv.* [f. L *approximare* (AD-, *proximus* very near)]

approximate[2] /əˈprɒksɪmeɪt/ *v.t./i.* to be or make approximate or near (*to*). —**approximation** /-ˈmeɪʃ(ə)n/ *n.* [f. prec.]

appurtenances /əˈpɜ:tɪnənsɪz/ *n.pl.* belongings, accessories. [f. AF (as APPERTAIN)]

après-ski /æpreɪˈski:/ *adj.* done or worn after skiing. [F]

apricot /ˈeɪprɪkɒt/ *n.* an orange-yellow stone-fruit allied to the plum and peach; its colour; the tree bearing it. [f. Port. or Sp. f. Arab. *al* the + *barkuk*, f. Gk f. L *praecox* early-ripe]

April /ˈeɪpr(ə)l/ *n.* the fourth month of the year. —**April fool,** the victim of a hoax on **April Fool's Day** (1 April). [f. L *Aprilis*]

a priori /eɪ praɪˈɔ:raɪ/ **1** reasoning from causes to effects. **2** assumed without investigation. **3** (of knowledge) existing in the mind independently of sensory experience. [L, = from what is before]

apron /ˈeɪprən/ *n.* **1** a garment worn over the front part of the body to protect the wearer's clothes. **2** a hard-surfaced area on an airfield where aircraft are manœuvred or loaded and unloaded. **3** an extension of a stage in front of a curtain. [orig. *naperon*, f. OF *nape* table-cloth f. L *mappa*]

apropos /ˈæprəpəʊ, -ˈpəʊ/ *adj.* & *adv.* **1** relevant(ly). **2** by the way. —**apropos of,** concerning, with reference to. [f. F *à propos* to the purpose]

apse *n.* a recess with an arched or domed roof, especially at the end of a church. [as APSIS]

apsidal /ˈæpsɪd(ə)l/ *adj.* **1** of the form of an apse. **2** of apsides. [f. prec.]

apsis /ˈæpsɪs/ *n.* (*pl.* **apsides** /ˈæpsɪdi:z/) each of the points, on the orbit of a planet or satellite etc., nearest to or furthest from the body round which it moves. [L f. Gk (*h*)*apsis* arch, vault]

apt *adj.* **1** suitable, appropriate. **2** having a tendency. **3** quick at learning. —**aptly** *adv.*, **aptness** *n.* [f. L *aptus* fitted]

apteryx /ˈæptərɪks/ *n.* a kiwi. [f. Gk *a-* without, *pterux* wing]

aptitude /ˈæptɪtju:d/ *n.* a natural ability or skill. [F f. L (as APT)]

aqualung /ˈækwəlʌŋ/ *n.* a portable underwater breathing apparatus consisting of cylinders of compressed air connected to a face-mask. [f. L *aqua* water + LUNG]

aquamarine /ækwəməˈri:n/ *n.* a bluish-green beryl; its colour. [f. L *aqua marina* sea water]

aquaplane /ˈækwəpleɪn/ *n.* a board on which a person stands for riding on water, pulled by a speedboat. —*v.i.* **1** to ride on an aquaplane. **2** (of a vehicle) to glide uncontrollably on a wet surface. [f. L *aqua* water + PLANE[1]]

aquarium /əˈkweərɪəm/ *n.* (*pl.* **-ums**) a tank or artificial pond for keeping and showing living fish and other aquatic life; a building containing such tanks etc. [f. L *aquarius* of water]

aquatic /əˈkwætɪk/ *adj.* growing or living in or near water; taking place in or on water. [f. F or L (*aqua* water)]

aquatint /ˈækwətɪnt/ *n.* a print resembling a watercolour, produced from a copper plate engraved with nitric acid. [f. F f. It. *acqua tinta* coloured water]

aqueduct /ˈækwɪdʌkt/ *n.* an artificial channel carrying water across country, especially in the form of a bridge across a valley or low ground. [f. L *aquae ductus* conduit (*aqua* water, *ducere* lead)]

aqueous /ˈeɪkwɪəs/ *adj.* of or like water; produced by water. —**aqueous humour,** see HUMOUR. [f. L (*aqua* water)]

aquilegia /ækwɪˈli:dʒjə/ *n.* a plant of the genus *Aquilegia*, a columbine, especially with blue flowers. [L, of unknown meaning]

aquiline /ˈækɪlaɪn/ *adj.* of or like an eagle; hooked like an eagle's beak. [f. L (*aquila* eagle)]

Ar *symbol* argon.

Arab *n.* **1** a member of a Semitic people originally inhabiting the Arabian peninsula and neighbouring countries, now also other parts of the Middle East and North Africa. **2** a horse of a breed native to Arabia. —*adj.* of Arabs. [f. F, ult. f. Arab. *ʻarab*]

arabesque /ærəˈbesk/ *n.* **1** an elaborate design using intertwined leaves, branches, and scrolls. **2** a ballet dancer's position in which one leg is extended horizontally backwards and the arms are outstretched. **3** a short usually florid piece of music. [F f. It. (*Arabo* Arab)]

Arabian /əˈreɪbɪən/ *adj.* of Arabia or the Arabs (esp. with geographical reference). [f. *Arabia*]

Arabic /ˈærəbɪk/ *n.* the language of the Arabs.

—*adj.* of or in the Arabic language. —**arabic numerals,** the numerals 1, 2, 3, 4, etc. [f. OF f. L f. Gk *Arabikos*]

arable /ˈærəb(ə)l/ *adj.* (of land) suitable for growing crops. —*n.* land of this kind. [F or f. L (*arare* plough)]

arachnid /əˈræknɪd/ *n.* a member of the class Arachnida, comprising spiders, scorpions, ticks, and mites. [f. F or L f. Gk *arachnē* spider]

Aramaic /ærəˈmeɪɪk/ *n.* a Semitic language of ancient Syria. —*adj.* of or in Aramaic. [f. *Aram*, biblical name of Syria]

Aran /ˈærən/ *adj.* of a type of patterned knitwear characteristic of the **Aran Islands,** a group of three islands off the west coast of Ireland.

arbiter /ˈɑːbɪtə(r)/ *n.* **1** a person with great control or influence over something. **2** a judge, an arbitrator. [L]

arbitrary /ˈɑːbɪtrərɪ/ *adj.* **1** based on random choice or whim; capricious. **2** despotic. —**arbitrarily** *adv.*, **arbitrariness** *n.* [f. F or L, = of an ARBITER]

arbitrate /ˈɑːbɪtreɪt/ *v.t./i.* to act as an arbitrator, to settle (a dispute) thus. —**arbitration** /-ˈtreɪʃ(ə)n/ *n.* [f. L *arbitrari* judge]

arbitrator /ɑːbɪtreɪtə(r)/ *n.* an impartial person chosen to settle a dispute between parties. [L]

arbor /ˈɑːbə(r)/ *n.* an axle or spindle on which a wheel etc. revolves in mechanism. [L, = tree]

arboreal /ɑːˈbɔːrɪəl/ *adj.* of trees; living in trees. [f. L *arboreus* (*arbor* tree)]

arboretum /ɑːbəriːtəm/ *n.* (*pl.* **-ta**) a place where trees are grown for study and display. [L (*arbor* tree)]

arbour /ˈɑːbə(r)/ *n.* a shady retreat enclosed by trees or climbing plants. [f. AF f. L *herba* herb, assim. to L *arbor* tree]

arbutus /ɑːˈbjuːtəs/ *n.* **1** an evergreen of the genus *Arbutus*, one with strawberry-like fruits. **2** (*US*) a trailing plant that bears fragrant pink flowers in spring. [L]

arc *n.* **1** part of the circumference of a circle or other curve; anything shaped like this. **2** a large luminous flow of electric current through gas. —*v.i.* (**arced, arcing** /-k-/) to form an arc, to move in a curve. —**arc lamp,** a lamp in which an arc is used to produce light. [f. OF f. L *arcus* bow, curve]

arcade /ɑːˈkeɪd/ *n.* **1** a covered walk, especially one lined with shops. **2** a series of arches supporting or along a wall. [F (as ARCH)]

arcane /ɑːˈkeɪn/ *adj.* mysterious, secret, understood by few. [F, or f. L (*arcēre* shut up, *arca* chest)]

arch[1] *n.* a structure (usually curved) supporting the weight of what is above it or used ornamentally; something curved like this. —*v.t./i.* to form (into) an arch; to span with or like an arch. [f. OF f. L *arcus* arc]

arch[2] *adj.* consciously or affectedly playful. —**archly** *adv.*, **archness** *n.* [f. foll. (2)]

arch- *prefix* **1** chief, superior. **2** pre-eminent, extremely bad. [f. OE or OF, f. L f. Gk (*arkhos* chief)]

archaeology /ɑːkɪˈɒlədʒɪ/ *n.* the study of civilizations through their material remains. —**archaeological** /-əˈlɒdʒɪk(ə)l/ *adj.*, **archaeologist** *n.* [f. Gk, = ancient history (*arkhaios* old, -LOGY)]

archaic /ɑːˈkeɪɪk/ *adj.* ancient, of an early period in a culture; antiquated; (of a word) no longer in ordinary use. —**archaically** *adv.* [f. F f. Gk (*arkhē* beginning)]

archaism /ˈɑːkeɪɪz(ə)m/ *n.* an archaic word or expression; use of what is archaic. —**archaistic** /-ˈɪstɪk/ *adj.* [f. Gk (as prec.)]

archaize /ˈɑːkeɪaɪz/ *v.t./i.* **1** to imitate the archaic. **2** to render archaistic. [f. Gk, = be old-fashioned (as prec.)]

archangel /ˈɑːkeɪndʒ(ə)l/ *n.* an angel of the highest rank. [OE, ult. f. Gk (as ARCH-, ANGEL)]

archbishop /ɑːtʃˈbɪʃəp/ *n.* the chief bishop of a Church province. —**archbishopric** *n.* his office or diocese. [OE (as ARCH-, BISHOP)]

archdeacon /ɑːtʃˈdiːkən/ *n.* a church dignitary ranking next below bishop. —**archideaconal** /ɑːkɪdɪˈækən(ə)l/ *adj.* [OE, ult. f. Gk (as ARCH-, DEACON)]

archdeaconry *n.* an archdeacon's office or residence.

archdiocese /ɑːtʃˈdaɪəsɪs/ *n.* the diocese of an archbishop.

archduchy /ˈɑːtʃdʌtʃɪ/ *n.* the territory of an archduke. [as foll.]

archduke /ˈɑːtʃdjuːk/ *n.* the chief duke; (*hist.*) the title of the son of the Emperor of Austria. —**archduchess** *n.fem.* [f. OF f. L (as ARCH-, DUKE)]

archer *n.* **1** one who shoots with bow and arrows. **2** the Archer, the constellation or sign of the zodiac Sagittarius. [f. OF f. L *arcus* bow]

archery *n.* the use of bow and arrows, especially as a sport. [f. prec.]

archetype /ˈɑːkɪtaɪp/ *n.* **1** the original model from which others are copied. **2** a typical example. —**archetypal** *adj.* [f. L f. Gk (ARCH-, *tupos* stamp)]

archiepiscopal /ɑːkɪɪˈpɪskəp(ə)l/ *adj.* of an archbishop or archbishopric. [f. L f. Gk (as ARCH-, *episkopos* bishop)]

archimandrite /ɑːkɪˈmændraɪt/ *n.* the superior of a large monastery in the Orthodox Church. [F or f. L f. Gk (as ARCH-, *mandra* monastery)]

archipelago /ɑːkɪˈpeləgəʊ/ *n.* (*pl.* **-os**) a sea with many islands; a group of islands. [f. It. f. Gk (as ARCH-, *pelagos* sea, orig. = the Aegean Sea)]

architect /ˈɑːkɪtekt/ *n.* a designer of buildings and large structures who prepares plans and supervises construction; a designer or creator *of*. [f. F, ult. f. Gk (as ARCH-, *tektōn* builder)]

architectonic /ɑ:kɪtekˈtɒnɪk/ *adj*. **1** of architecture or architects. **2** constructive. [f. L f. Gk (as prec.)]

architecture /ˈɑ:kɪtektʃə(r)/ *n*. the art or science of designing and constructing buildings; a style of building. —**architectural** /-ˈtektʃər(ə)l/ *adj*., **architecturally** *adv*. [F or f. L (as ARCHITECT)]

architrave /ˈɑ:kɪtreɪv/ *n*. a horizontal beam resting on the tops of columns; a moulded frame round a doorway or window. [F f. It. (as ARCH-, *trave* f. L *trabs* beam)]

archive /ˈɑ:kaɪv/ *n*. (freq. in *pl*.) a collection of the historical documents or records of an institution or community. [f. F f. L f. Gk *arkheia* public records]

archivist /ˈɑ:kɪvɪst/ *n*. one in charge of archives. [f. prec.]

archway /ˈɑtʃweɪ/ *n*. an arched entrance or passage.

Arctic /ˈɑ:ktɪk/ *adj*. **1** of the region round the North Pole. **2 arctic,** very cold. *n*. the Arctic regions. —**Arctic Circle,** an imaginary line round the Arctic region at the parallel of 66° 33′ N. [f. OF f. L f. Gk (*arktos* bear, Ursa Major)]

ardent /ˈɑ:d(ə)nt/ *adj*. eager, fervent, passionate. —**ardency** *n*., **ardently** *adv*. [f. OF f. L *ardens* burning]

ardour /ˈɑ:də(r)/ *n*. zeal, enthusiasm, passion. [f. OF f. L (*ardēre* burn)]

arduous /ˈɑ:djʊəs/ *adj*. hard to accomplish; needing much effort, laborious. —**arduously** *adv*. [f. L *arduus* steep, difficult]

are[1] 2nd person sing. and 1st, 2nd, & 3rd person pl. of BE.

are[2] /ɑ:(r)/ *n*. a metric unit of measure, 100 square metres. [F f. L *area* (see foll.)]

area /ˈeərɪə/ *n*. **1** the extent or measure of a surface. **2** a region; a space set aside for a purpose. **3** the field of an activity or subject. **4** a space in front of the basement of a building. [L, = vacant piece of level ground]

areca /əˈri:kə/ *n*. a tropical Asiatic palm-tree of the genus *Areca*. [Port., f. Malayalam]

arena /əˈri:nə/ *n*. **1** the level area in the centre of an amphitheatre or sports stadium etc. **2** a scene of conflict, a sphere of action. [L, = sand]

aren't /ɑ:nt/ (*colloq*.) are not. [contr.]

arête /æˈreɪt/ *n*. a sharp ridge on a mountain. [F f. L *arista* spiny process]

argent /ˈɑ:dʒənt/ *n*. & *adj*. (*Her*.) silver or white (colour). [F f. L *argentum* silver]

argon /ˈɑ:gɒn/ *n*. an element of the noble gas group, symbol Ar, atomic number 18. [f. Gk *argos* idle (*a*- not, *ergon* work)]

argosy /ˈɑ:gəsɪ/ *n*. (*poet*.) a merchant-ship; a fleet of these. [prob. f. It. *Ragusa nave* ship of Ragusa (in Dalmatia)]

argot /ˈɑ:gəʊ/ *n*. the special jargon of a group. [F]

arguable /ˈɑ:gjʊəb(ə)l/ *adj*. **1** that may be asserted. **2** open to doubt. —**arguably** *adv*. [f. foll.]

argue /ˈɑ:gju:/ *v.t./i*. **1** to exchange views or angry words with expression of disagreement. **2** to reason (*for*, *against*, or *that*); to treat by reasoning; to prove or indicate; to persuade *into* or *out of*. [f. OF f. L *argutari* prattle (*arguere* prove)]

argument /ˈɑ:gjʊmənt/ *n*. **1** a discussion involving disagreement; a quarrel. **2** a reason advanced; a chain of reasoning. [as prec.]

argumentation /ɑ:gjʊmenˈteɪʃ(ə)n/ *n*. arguing. [F f. L (as ARGUE)]

argumentative /ɑ:gjʊˈmentətɪv/ *adj*. fond of arguing. —**argumentatively** *adv*. [f. F or L (as prec.)]

argy-bargy /ˈɑ:dʒɪbɑ:dʒɪ/ *n*. (*colloq*.) a heated argument. [orig. Sc.]

aria /ˈɑ:rɪə/ *n*. an extended piece for solo voice and accompaniment, especially in an opera or oratorio. [It.]

arid /ˈærɪd/ *adj*. **1** dry, parched. **2** uninteresting. —**aridly** *adv*., **aridity** /-ˈrɪdɪtɪ/ *n*., **aridness** *n*. [f. F or L (*arēre* be dry)]

Aries /ˈeəri:z/ a constellation and the first sign of the zodiac, the Ram, which the sun enters at the vernal equinox. Arian *adj*. & *n*. [L, = ram]

aright /əˈraɪt/ *adv*. rightly. [OE (A-, RIGHT)]

arise /əˈraɪz/ *v.i*. (*past* **arose,** *p.p*. **arisen** /əˈrɪz(ə)n/) **1** to come into existence or to people's notice; to originate or result. **2** (*archaic*) to get up; to rise from the dead. [OE (A-, RISE)]

aristocracy /ærɪsˈtɒkrəsɪ/ *n*. **1** the hereditary upper classes, the nobility or élite. **2** a State governed by these. **3** the best representatives (*of* a category). —**aristocratic** /-təˈkrætɪk/ *adj*. [f. F f. Gk (*aristos* best, -*kratia* power)]

aristocrat /ˈærɪstəkræt/ *n*. a member of the aristocracy. [f. F (as prec.)]

arithmetic[1] /əˈrɪθmətɪk/ *n*. **1** the part of mathematics that deals with numbers and the operations of addition, subtraction, multiplication, and division. **2** calculation by means of numbers. —**arithmetic unit,** the part of a computer where data are processed, as distinct from storage or control units. [f. OF f. L f. Gk *arithmētikē* (*tekhnē*) (art) of counting (*arithmos* number)]

arithmetic[2] /ærɪθˈmetɪk/ *adj*. (also **arithmetical**) of arithmetic. —**arithmetical progression,** a sequence of numbers showing increase or decrease by a constant quantity, e.g. 1, 3, 5, 7. —**arithmetically** *adv*. [as prec.]

ark *n*. **1** Noah's boat or a model of this. **2 Ark of the Covenant,** a wooden chest in which the writings of Jewish Law were kept. [OE, f. L *arca* chest]

arm[1] *n.* **1** either of the two upper limbs of the human body from shoulder to hand; something covering this, a sleeve. **2** a raised side part of a chair, supporting a sitter's arm. **3** a thing resembling an arm in shape or function. **4** a control, a means of reaching. —**arm-band** *n.* a band worn round the arm or sleeve. [OE]

arm[2] *n.* **1** (usu. in *pl.*) a weapon. **2** a branch of military forces. **3** (in *pl.*) heraldic devices. —*v.t./i.* **1** to equip with weapons etc.; to equip oneself in preparation for war. **2** to make (a bomb etc.) ready to explode. —**up in arms,** protesting vigorously. [f. OF f. L *arma* weapons]

armada /ɑːˈmɑːdə/ *n.* a fleet of warships, especially (**Armada**) a Spanish naval invasion force sent against England in 1588 by Philip II of Spain. [Sp. f. Rom., = army]

armadillo /ɑːməˈdɪləʊ/ *n.* (*pl.* **-os**) a burrowing mammal of South America with a body encased in bony plates, often rolling itself into a ball when captured. [Sp., dim. of *armado* armed man (ARM²)]

Armageddon /ɑːməˈged(ə)n/ *n.* an ultimate or large-scale conflict, especially that between the forces of good and evil at the end of the world (Rev. 16: 16); the scene of this.

armament /ˈɑːməmənt/ *n.* **1** (usu. in *pl.*) military weapons and equipment. **2** the process of equipping for war. [f. L (as ARM²)]

armature /ˈɑːmətʃə(r)/ *n.* **1** the wire-wound core of a dynamo or electric motor. **2** a bar placed in contact with the poles of a magnet. **3** a framework round which a clay or plaster sculpture is modelled. [F f. L *armatura* armour]

armchair *n.* **1** a chair with side supports for a sitter's arms. **2** (*attrib.*) theorizing, not practical or participating; amateur.

armful *n.* a quantity that is as much as the arm can hold. [f. ARM¹ + -FUL]

armhole *n.* an opening in a garment through which the arm is inserted.

armistice /ˈɑːmɪstɪs/ *n.* a stopping of hostilities; a short truce. —**Armistice Day,** 11 Nov., the anniversary of the armistice that ended the First World War, now replaced by Remembrance Sunday and (in the USA) Veterans Day. [F or f. L (*arma* arms, *sistere* make stand)]

armlet /ˈɑːmlɪt/ *n.* a band worn round the arm or sleeve. [f. ARM¹ + -LET]

armorial /ɑːˈmɔːrɪəl/ *adj.* of coats of arms, heraldic. [f. foll.]

armour /ˈɑːmə(r)/ *n.* **1** a protective covering for the body, formerly worn in fighting; a protective metal covering for an armed vehicle, ship, etc. **2** armoured fighting vehicles collectively. [f. OF f. L (as ARM²)]

armoured /ˈɑːməd/ *adj.* **1** furnished with armour. **2** equipped with armoured vehicles. [f. prec.]

armourer /ˈɑːmərə(r)/ *n.* **1** an official in charge of small arms. **2** a maker of arms or armour. [f. ARMOUR]

armoury /ˈɑːmərɪ/ *n.* a place where arms are kept. [as prec.]

armpit *n.* the hollow under the arm below the shoulder. [f. ARM + PIT]

army *n.* **1** an organized force armed for fighting on land. **2** a vast group. **3** a body of people organized for a cause. [f OF (as ARM²)]

arnica /ˈɑːnɪkə/ *n.* a composite plant of the genus *Arnica*, with yellow flowers; a substance prepared from this, formerly used to treat bruises. [orig. unkn.]

aroma /əˈrəʊmə/ *n.* a smell, especially a pleasant one. [L f. Gk, = spice]

aromatic /ærəˈmætɪk/ *adj.* **1** fragrant, having a pleasantly strong smell. **2** (*Chem.*, of compounds) containing one or more rings of six carbon atoms, as in benzene. —*n.* an aromatic substance. —**aromatically** *adv.* [f. OF f. L f. Gk (as AROMA)]

arose /əˈrəʊz/ *past* of ARISE.

around /əˈraʊnd/ *adv.* **1** on every side, all round; here and there. **2** (*colloq.*) near at hand. —*prep.* **1** on or along the circuit of; on every side of. **2** about, (*US*) approximately at. [f. A- + ROUND]

arouse /əˈraʊz/ *v.t.* to rouse; to induce. [f. A- + ROUSE]

arpeggio /ɑːˈpedʒɪəʊ/ *n.* (*pl.* **-os**) the sounding of the notes of a chord in succession; a chord so played. [It. (*arpa* harp)]

arrack /ˈærək/ *n.* a kind of alcoholic spirit, especially that made from coco sap or rice. [f. Arab. *'arak*]

arraign /əˈreɪn/ *v.t.* to indict, to accuse; to find fault with (an action or statement), to challenge. —**arraignment** *n.* [f. AF f. L (AD-, *ratio* reason)]

arrange /əˈreɪndʒ/ *v.t./i.* **1** to put into the required order, to adjust or place. **2** to plan or prepare; to take measures or give instructions. **3** to adapt, especially (music) for performance with different instruments or voices. —**arrangement** *n.* [f. OF (*à* to, *rangier* range)]

arrant /ˈærənt/ *adj.* downright, utter. [var. of ERRANT, orig. in *arrant* (= outlawed roving) *thief*]

arras /ˈærəs/ *n.* a richly decorated tapestry or wall-hanging. [f. *Arras*, town in France famous in the 13th–16th c. for tapestry weaving]

array /əˈreɪ/ *n.* an imposing series, a display; an ordered arrangement. —*v.t.* to arrange in order, to marshal (forces). [f. AF f. L (AD-, READY)]

arrears /əˈrɪəz/ *n.* the amount that is still outstanding or uncompleted, especially of a debt or of work to be done. —**in arrears,** not paid or done when it was due. [f. OF f. L (AD-, *retro* backwards)]

arrest /əˈrest/ *v.t.* **1** to seize (a person) by the authority of the law. **2** to stop or check (a movement or process). **3** to catch and hold (attention). —*n.* **1** an act of arresting, legal seizure of a person. **2** a stoppage. —**arrester** *n.*, **arrestor** *n.* [f. OF f. L (*restare* remain)]

arrestable /əˈrestəb(ə)l/ *adj.* (of an offence) such that the offender may be arrested without a warrant. [f. prec.]

arrière-pensée /ærɪeərˈpɑ̃seɪ/ *n.* an ulterior motive; a mental reservation. [F, = behind thought]

arris /ˈærɪs/ *n.* the sharp edge formed where two surfaces meet to form an angle, especially in architecture. [f. F *areste* = ARÊTE]

arrival /əˈraɪv(ə)l/ *n.* **1** arriving, appearance on the scene. **2** a person or thing that has arrived. [f. foll.]

arrive /əˈraɪv/ *v.i.* **1** to reach a destination or a certain point on a journey. **2** (of a time) to come. **3** to be recognized as having achieved success in the world. **4** (*colloq.*, of a baby) to be born. —**arrive at,** to reach (a decision or conclusion). [f. OF f. L (AD-, *ripa* shore)]

arriviste /æri:ˈvi:st/ *n.* a person ruthlessly and obsessively aspiring to advancement. [F (*arriver* arrive)]

arrogant /ˈærəgənt/ *adj.* proud and overbearing through an exaggerated feeling of one's superiority. —**arrogance** *n.*, **arrogantly** *adv.* [f. OF (as foll.)]

arrogate /ˈærəgeɪt/ *v.t.* **1** to claim or seize without right. **2** to attribute unjustly. —**arrogation** /-ˈgeɪʃ(ə)n/ *n.* [f. L *arrogare* (AD-, *rogare* ask)]

arrow /ˈærəʊ/ *n.* a straight thin pointed shaft to be shot from a bow; a representation of this, especially to show direction. [OE]

arrowhead /ˈærəʊhed/ *n.* the pointed tip of an arrow.

arrowroot /ˈærəʊru:t/ *n.* a nutritious starch prepared from the root of an American plant; this plant.

arse *n.* (*vulg.*) the buttocks. [OE]

arsenal /ˈɑ:s(ə)n(ə)l/ *n.* a place where weapons and ammunition are stored or manufactured. [F or f. It. f. Arab., = workshop]

arsenic /ˈɑ:s(ə)nɪk/ *n.* a semi-metallic element, symbol As, atomic number 33, existing as a brittle steel-grey solid and in several other allotropic forms; (*pop.*) arsenic trioxide, its main commercial compound. —**arsenical** /ɑ:ˈsenɪk(ə)l/ *adj.* [f. OF, ult. f. Pers. (*zar* gold)]

arson /ˈɑ:s(ə)n/ *n.* the deliberate and criminal act of setting fire to a house or other building. —**arsonist** *n.* [AF f. L (*ardēre* burn)]

art[1] *n.* **1** human creative skill or its application; the branch of creative activity concerned with the production of imitative and imaginative designs and expression of ideas, especially in painting; products of this. **2** any skill; a craft or activity requiring imaginative skill. **3** (in *pl.*) branches of learning (e.g. languages, literature, and history) requiring sympathetic understanding and creative skill as distinct from the technical skills of science. **4** a specific ability, a knack. **5** cunning, artfulness; a trick or stratagem. [f. OF f. L *ars*]

art[2] (*archaic*) 2nd person sing. pres. of BE.

artefact /ˈɑ:tɪfækt/ *n.* a man-made object, especially a tool, weapon, or vessel as an archaeological item. [f. L *arte* by art, *facere* make]

arteriosclerosis /ɑ:tɪərɪəʊsklɪəˈrəʊsɪs/ *n.* hardening of the walls of arteries, so that blood circulation is hindered. [f. ARTERY + SCLEROSIS]

artery /ˈɑ:tərɪ/ *n.* **1** any of the tubes conveying blood away from the heart to all parts of the body. **2** a main road or railway line. —**arterial** /ɑ:ˈtɪərɪəl/ *adj.* [f. L f. Gk (prob. f. *airō* raise)]

artesian well /ɑ:ˈti:ʒ(ə)n/ a well in which water rises to the surface by natural pressure through a vertically drilled hole. [f. F (*Artois* an old province of France)]

artful *adj.* crafty, cunningly clever at getting what one wants. —**artfully** *adv.*, **artfulness** *n.* [f. ART[1]]

arthritis /ɑ:ˈθraɪtɪs/ *n.* a condition in which there is pain and stiffness in a joint or joints. —**arthritic** /ɑ:ˈθrɪtɪk/ *adj.* & *n.* [L f. Gk (*arthron* joint)]

arthropod /ˈɑ:θrəpɒd/ *n.* an animal of the phylum Arthropoda, with a segmented body and jointed limbs, and typically encased in a hard outer skeleton. [f. Gk *arthron* joint + *pous podos* foot]

artichoke /ˈɑ:tɪtʃəʊk/ *n.* a plant allied to the thistle; its flower, with thick leaf-like scales used as a vegetable: —**Jerusalem artichoke,** a kind of sunflower with tubers that are used as a vegetable. [f. It. f. Arab.; *Jerusalem* is a corrupt. of It. *girasole* sunflower]

article /ˈɑ:tɪk(ə)l/ *n.* **1** a particular item or commodity. **2** a short self-contained piece of writing, in a newspaper, journal, etc., or in an encyclopaedia. **3** a clause or item of an agreement. **4** the definite or indefinite article (see below). —*v.t.* to bind by articles of apprenticeship. —**definite article,** 'the', **indefinite article,** 'a' or 'an' (or their equivalents in another language). [f. OF f. L *articulus* dim. of *artus* joint]

articular /ɑ:ˈtɪkjʊlə(r)/ *adj.* of a joint or joints of the body. [f. L (as prec.)]

articulate[1] /ɑːˈtɪkjʊlət/ *adj*. **1** to express oneself clearly and fluently. **2** (of speech) spoken clearly, in words. **3** having joints. —**articulacy** *n*., **articulately** *adv*., **articulateness** *n*. [f. L (as ARTICLE)]

articulate[2] /ɑːtɪkjʊleɪt/ *v.t./i*. **1** to speak or express clearly, to pronounce distinctly. **2** to form a joint *with*. —**articulation** /-ˈleɪʃ(ə)n/ *n*. [as prec.]

articulated /ɑːˈtɪkjʊleɪtɪd/ *adj*. with parts connected or divided by a (flexible) joint or joints. [f. prec.]

artifice /ˈɑːtɪfɪs/ *n*. trickery, a piece of cunning; skill, ingenuity. [F f. L (*ars* art, *facere* make)]

artificer /ɑːˈtɪfɪsə(r)/ *n*. a skilled workman or mechanic. [f. F (as prec.)]

artificial /ɑːtɪˈfɪʃ(ə)l/ *adj*. produced by human art or effort, not originating naturally; affected, insincere. —**artificial insemination**, injection of semen into the uterus other than by copulation. **artificial respiration**, manual or mechanical stimulation of breathing. —**artificiality** /-ʃɪˈælɪtɪ/ *n*., **artificially** *adv*. [f. OF or L (as ARTIFICE)]

artillery /ɑːˈtɪlərɪ/ *n*. heavy guns used for fighting on land; a branch of an army equipped with these. —**artilleryman** *n*. [f. OF (*artiller* equip)]

artisan /ɑːtɪˈzæn, ˈɑː-/ *n*. a skilled workman, a mechanic. [F f. It. f. L (*artire* instruct in arts)]

artist /ˈɑːtɪst/ *n*. **1** one who practises any of the fine arts, especially painting. **2** one who does something with skill or taste. **3** an artiste. —**artistry** *n*. [f. F f. It. (*arte* art)]

artiste /ɑːˈtiːst/ *n*. a professional performer, especially a singer or dancer. [F (as prec.)]

artistic /ɑːˈtɪstɪk/ *adj*. of art or artists; skilfully or tastefully done; showing aptitude for the fine arts. —**artistically** *adv*. [f. prec.]

artless /ˈɑːtlɪs/ *adj*. **1** free from artfulness, ingenuous. **2** not resulting from art, natural. **3** crude, clumsy. —**artlessly** *adv*., **artlessness** *n*. [f. ART[1]]

arty /ˈɑːtɪ/ *adj*. (*colloq*.) pretentiously or quaintly artistic. —**artiness** *n*. [f. ART[1]]

arum /ˈeərəm/ *n*. a plant of the genus *Arum* with small flowers enclosed in bracts. —**arum lily**, a cultivated white arum. [L f. Gk *aron*]

Aryan /ˈeərɪən/ *adj*. **1** of the Indo-European family of languages. **2** of the ancient inhabitants of the Iranian plateau speaking a language of this family. —*n*. **1** a member of the Aryan peoples. **2** (in Nazi Germany) a non-Jewish European, a person of Nordic racial type. [f. Skr. *āryas* noble, earlier used as a national name]

As *symbol* arsenic.

as /əz, emphat. æz/ *adv*. & *conj*. **1** to the same extent; in the manner in which; in the capacity or form of; for instance. **2** during or at the time of. **3** for the reason that, seeing that. —*rel. pron*. that, who, which. —**as from**, on or after (a specified date). **as if**, as would be the case if. **as it were**, as if it was actually so, in a way. **as of**, as from, as at (a specified time). **as though**, as if. **as to**, with regard to. **as well**, advisable, desirable, reasonably. **as well (as)**, in addition (to). **as yet**, until now. [f. OE *alswā* also]

asafoetida /æsəˈfiːtɪdə/ *n*. a resinous strong-smelling plant gum formerly used in medicine. [L f. Pers. *azā* mastic; *fetida* fetid]

asbestos /æsˈbestɒs/ *n*. a fibrous silicate mineral; a fire-resistant substance made from this. [f. OF f. L f. Gk, = unquenchable]

asbestosis /æsbesˈtəʊsɪs/ *n*. a lung disease caused by inhaling asbestos particles. [f. prec.]

ascend /əˈsend/ *v.t./i*. to move upwards, to rise; to climb. —**ascend the throne**, to become king or queen. [f. L *ascendere* (AD-, *scandere* climb)]

ascendancy /əˈsendənsɪ/ *n*. dominant power or control (*over*). [f. foll.]

ascendant /əˈsend(ə)nt/ *adj*. ascending, rising; gaining ascendancy; (*Astron*.) rising towards the zenith; (*Astrol*., of a sign) just above the eastern horizon. —*n*. (*Astrol*.) the point of the ecliptic that is ascendant at a given time, e.g. at the birth of a child. —**in the ascendant**, at or near the peak of one's fortunes; (*pop*.) rising. [f. OF f. L (as ASCEND)]

ascension /əˈsenʃ(ə)n/ *n*. ascent, especially (**Ascension**) that of Christ into Heaven, witnessed by the Apostles. —**Ascension Day**, the Thursday on which this is commemorated, the 40th day after Easter. [as prec.]

ascent /əˈsent/ *n*. **1** ascending; rise. **2** a way up, an upward path or slope. [f. ASCEND]

ascertain /æsəˈteɪn/ *v.t*. to find out for certain, especially by making enquiries. **ascertainable** *adj*., **ascertainment** *n*. [f. OF (as CERTAIN)]

ascetic /əˈsetɪk/ *adj*. severely abstinent, austere; having the appearance of an ascetic. —*n*. a person leading an ascetic life, especially one doing this in a religious cause. —**ascetically** *adv*., **asceticism** /-ɪsɪz(ə)m/ *n*. [f. L or f. Gk (*askētēs* monk, *askeō* exercise)]

ascidian /əˈsɪdɪən/ *n*. a tunicate of the order Ascidiacea, especially a sea-squirt. [f. Gk, dim. of *askos* wine-skin]

ascorbic acid /əˈskɔːbɪk/ vitamin C, which prevents scurvy, found especially in citrus fruits and in vegetables. [f. Gk *a*- not + SCORBUTIC]

ascribable /əˈskraɪbəb(ə)l/ *adj*. that may be ascribed. [f. foll.]

ascribe /əˈskraɪb/ *v.t*. to attribute. **ascription** /-ˈskrɪpʃ(ə)n/ *n*. [f. L *ascribere* (AD-, *scribere* write)]

asdic /ˈæzdɪk/ *n*. an early form of sonar. [f. initials of *A*nti-*S*ubmarine *D*etection *I*nvestigation *C*ommittee]

asepsis /eɪˈsepsɪs/ *n.* aseptic methods or conditions (see ANTISEPTIC). [f. Gk *a-* not + SEPSIS]

aseptic /eɪˈseptɪk/ *adj.* free from sepsis, especially that caused by micro-organisms, surgically sterile; aiming at the absence rather than the counteraction (cf. ANTISEPTIC) of septic matter. —**aseptically** *adv.* [f. Gk *a-* not + SEPTIC]

asexual /eɪˈseksjʊəl/ *adj.* without sex or sexuality; (of reproduction) not involving the fusion of gametes, —**asexually** *adv.* [f. Gk *a-* not + SEXUAL]

ash[1] *n.* (freq. in *pl.*) the whitish grey powdery residue left after combustion of any substance; (in *pl.*) the remains of a human body after cremation. —**the Ashes,** a trophy for the winner of a series of test matches in cricket between England and Australia. **Ash Wednesday,** the first day of Lent, so called from the former custom of sprinkling ashes on penitents' heads. [OE]

ash[2] *n.* a tree of the genus *Fraxinus* with silver-grey bark and pinnate foliage; its hard close-grained wood. [OE]

ashamed /əˈʃeɪmd/ *adj.* (usu. *predic.*) feeling or affected by shame; reluctant or hesitant through shame. [OE (as A-, SHAME)]

ashbin *n.* a dustbin. [f. ASH[1]]

ashen *adj.* of or like ashes, pale as ashes. [f. ASH[1]]

ashlar /ˈæʃlə(r)/ *n.* square-hewn stones, masonry made of these; thin slabs of this used for facing walls. [f. OF f. L, dim. of *axis* board]

ashore /əˈʃɔ:(r)/ *adv.* to or on shore; on land. [f. A- + SHORE]

ashram /ˈæʃræm/ *n.* (in India etc.) a place of religious learning or retreat. [f. Skr., = hermitage]

ashtray *n.* a receptacle for tobacco ash.

ashy *adj.* like ash, ashen; covered with ashes. [f. ASH[1]]

Asian /ˈeɪʃ(ə)n, ˈeɪʒ-/ *adj.* of the continent of Asia. —*n.* an Asian person. [f. L f. Gk]

Asiatic /eɪzɪˈætɪk/ *adj.* of Asia. [as prec.]

aside /əˈsaɪd/ *adv.* to or on one side, away from the main part or group. —*n.* words spoken aside. [f. A- + SIDE]

asinine /ˈæsɪnaɪn/ *adj.* like an ass, silly, stupid. —**asininity** /-ˈnɪnɪtɪ/ *n.* [f. L (*asinus* ass)]

ask /ɑ:sk/ *v.t./i.* **1** to call for an answer to or about, to address a question to. **2** to seek to obtain from someone. **3** to invite. [OE]

askance /əˈskæns/ *adv.* with a sideways look. —**look askance at,** to regard with distrust or disapproval. [orig. unkn.]

askew /əˈskju:/ *adv.* & *pred. adj.* not straight or level, oblique(ly). [f. A- + SKEW]

aslant /əˈslɑ:nt/ *adv.* on a slant, obliquely. —*prep.* obliquely across. [f. A- + SLANT]

asleep /əˈsli:p/ *predic. adj.* sleeping; (of a limb etc.) numb. —*adv.* into a state of sleep. [f. A- + SLEEP]

asocial /ˈeɪsəʊʃ(ə)l/ *adj.* not social; not sociable; (*colloq.*) inconsiderate. [f. Gk *a-* not + SOCIAL]

asp *n.* a small poisonous viper of Africa and southern Europe. [f. OF or L f. Gk]

asparagus /əˈspærəgəs/ *n.* a plant of the genus *Asparagus*, especially a species (*A. officinalis*) whose young shoots are cooked and eaten as a vegetable; this food. [L f. Gk]

aspect /ˈæspekt/ *n.* **1** a person's or thing's appearance, especially to the mind, a feature by which a matter is considered. **2** the direction a thing faces, the side of a building etc. facing a particular direction. **3** (*Astrol.*) the relative position of planets etc., regarded as influencing events. [f. L (*adspicere* look at)]

aspen *n.* a kind of poplar with especially tremulous leaves. [OE (earlier *asp*)]

asperity /əˈsperɪtɪ/ *n.* harshness of temper or tone. [f. OF or L (*asper* rough)]

aspersion /əˈspɜ:ʃ(ə)n/ *n.* a damaging or derogatory remark. —**cast aspersions on,** to attack the reputation of. [f. L *aspergere* sprinkle]

asphalt /ˈæsfælt/ *n.* a tarlike bitumen made from petroleum; a mixture of this with sand and gravel for use in paving etc. —*v.t.* to coat or pave with asphalt. [f. L f. Gk]

asphodel /ˈæsfədel/ *n.* a plant of the genus *Asphodeline* or *Asphodelus*, of the lily family; (*poet.*) an immortal flower growing in Elysium. [f. L f. Gk]

asphyxia /æsˈfɪksɪə/ *n.* lack of oxygen in the blood through impaired respiration, causing unconsciousness or death; suffocation. [f. Gk (*a-* not, *sphuxis* pulse)]

asphyxiate /æsˈfɪksɪeɪt/ *v.t./i.* to cause asphyxia in; to suffocate. —**asphyxiation** /-ˈeɪʃ(ə)n/ *n.* [f. prec.]

aspic /ˈæspɪk/ *n.* a savoury jelly for holding meat, fish, egg, etc. [F, = asp (the colours of the jelly being compared to those of the asp)]

aspidistra /æspɪˈdɪstrə/ *n.* a plant of the genus *Aspidistra*, with broad tapering leaves, often grown as a house-plant. [f. Gk *aspis* shield]

aspirant /ˈæspɪrənt, əˈspaɪər-/ *n.* one who aspires, especially to an honour or position. —*adj.* aspiring. [F or f. L (as ASPIRE)]

aspirate[1] /ˈæspəreɪt/ *v.t.* **1** to pronounce with an initial *h* or with release of breath. **2** to draw (fluid) by suction from a cavity etc. [f. L (as ASPIRE)]

aspirate[2] /ˈæspərət/ *n.* the sound of *h*; a consonant pronounced with this. —*adj.* pronounced with an aspirate. [as prec.]

aspiration /æspəˈreɪʃ(ə)n/ *n.* **1** ambition, strong desire. **2** aspirating. **3** the drawing of breath. [as ASPIRE]

aspirator /ˈæspəreɪtə(r)/ *n.* a device for drawing fluid from a cavity etc. [as foll.]

aspire /əˈspaɪə(r)/ *v.i.* to have an ambition or strong desire. [f. F or L *adspirare* breathe upon]

aspirin /ˈæsp(ə)rɪn/ *n.* a white powder, acetylsalicylic acid, used to relieve pain and reduce fever; a tablet of this. [G]

ass[1] *n.* **1** a quadruped of the horse genus with long ears, a donkey, regarded in ancient times as the embodiment of lust quite as much as stupidity. **2** a stupid person. [OE f. L *asinus*]

ass[2] *n.* (*US, vulg.*) = ARSE.

assail /əˈseɪl/ *v.t.* **1** to attack physically or verbally. **2** to begin (a task) resolutely. —**assailant** *n.* [f. OF f. L *assilire* (AD-, *salire* leap)]

assassin /əˈsæsɪn/ *n.* **1** one who assassinates another. **2 Assassin,** any of a number of Muslim fanatics in the time of the Crusades, notorious for a series of killings of political and religious opponents. [ult. f. Arab. (pl.), = hashish-takers, so called because they acted as if crazed by hashish]

assassinate /əˈsæsɪneɪt/ *v.t.* to kill (an important person) by violent means, usually for political or religious motives. —**assassination** /-ˈneɪʃ(ə)n/ *n.*, **assassinator** *n.* [as prec.]

assault /əˈsɔːlt/ *n.* a violent physical or verbal attack; (*euphem.*) rape; (*Law*) a threat or display of violence against a person. —*v.t.* to make an assault on, to attack. [f. OF f. L (as ASSAIL)]

assay /əˈseɪ/ *n.* a test of metal or ore to determine its ingredients and quality. —*v.t./i.* **1** to make an assay of (metal). **2** (*archaic*) to attempt. [f. OF, var. of *essai* essay]

assegai /ˈæsɪgaɪ/ *n.* a light iron-tipped spear of South African peoples. [f. F or Port. f. Arab., = the spear]

assemblage /əˈsemblɪdʒ/ *n.* **1** coming together. **2** an assembly; things assembled. [f. foll.]

assemble /əˈsemb(ə)l/ *v.t./i.* to bring or come together; to fit or put (components, or a completed whole) together. —**assembler** *n.* [f. OF f. L (*ad* to, *simul* together)]

assembly /əˈsemblɪ/ *n.* **1** assembling. **2** an assembled group; a deliberative body. —**assembly line,** machinery arranged in a sequence by which a product is progressively assembled. [as prec.]

assent /əˈsent/ *n.* (official) consent or approval. —*v.i.* to express agreement, to consent. —**assenter** *n.* [f. OF f. L *assentari* (AD-, *sentire* think)]

assert /əˈsɜːt/ *v.t.* **1** to declare as true, to state. **2** to enforce a claim to (rights). —**assert oneself,** to insist on one's rights or recognition; to take effective action. —**assertion** *n.*, **assertive** *n.* [f. L *asserere* (AD-, *serere* join)]

assess /əˈses/ *v.t.* to estimate the value of (property) for taxation; to decide or fix the amount of (a tax, penalty, etc.). —**assessment** *n.* [f. F f. L *assidēre* sit by]

assessor /əˈsesə(r)/ *n.* **1** one who assesses, especially for tax or insurance. **2** one who advises a judge in court on technical matters. [f. OF f. L, = assistant-judge]

asset /ˈæset/ *n.* a possession having value, especially that which can be used or sold to meet debts etc.; a useful quality, skill, or person. [f. AF f. L (*ad* to, *satis* enough)]

asseverate /əˈsevəreɪt/ *v.t.* to state solemnly. —**asseveration** /-ˈreɪʃ(ə)n/ *n.* [f. L *asseverare* (AD-, *severus* serious)]

assiduous /əˈsɪdjuəs/ *adj.* persevering, working with diligence and close attention. —**assiduity** /æsɪˈdjuːɪtɪ/ *n.* **assiduously** *adv.*, **assiduousness** *n.* [f. L (as ASSESS)]

assign /əˈsaɪn/ *v.t.* to allot; to put aside or specify for a particular purpose; to designate; to ascribe or attribute; (*Law*) to transfer formally. —**assignable** *adj.* [f. OF f. L *assignare* mark out to (*signum* sign)]

assignation /æsɪgˈneɪʃ(ə)n/ *n.* **1** an appointment to meet, especially by lovers in secret. **2** assigning. [as prec.]

assignment /əˈsaɪnmənt/ *n.* **1** a thing assigned, especially a task or duty; a share. **2** assigning. [f. ASSIGN]

assimilate /əˈsɪmɪleɪt/ *v.t./i.* **1** to absorb or become absorbed. **2** to make alike or similar (*to*). —**assimilable** *adj.*, **assimilation** /-ˈleɪʃ(ə)n/ *n.* [f. L *assimilare* (AD-, *similis* like)]

assist /əˈsɪst/ *v.t./i.* to help. —**assistance** *n.* [f. F f. L *assistere* take one's stand by]

assistant /əˈsɪst(ə)nt/ *n.* one who assists, a helper; one who serves customers in a shop. —*adj.* assisting, helping a senior and ranking next below him or her. [as prec.]

assizes /əˈsaɪzɪz/ *n.pl.* a periodical county session, held until 1972, for the administration of civil and criminal justice. [f. F f. L (as ASSESS)]

associate[1] /əˈsəʊsɪeɪt, -ʃɪeɪt/ *v.t./i.* **1** to connect in one's mind. **2** to join as a companion or colleague etc.; to act together for a common purpose; to have frequent dealings (*with*). **3** to declare (oneself) as being in agreement *with*. —**associative** *adj.* [f. L *associare* (AD-, *socius* sharing, allied)]

associate[2] /əˈsəʊsɪət, -ʃɪət/ *n.* **1** a subordinate member of a society etc. **2** a partner or colleague. —*adj.* **1** associated **2** having subordinate membership. [as prec.]

association /əsəʊsɪˈeɪʃ(ə)n, -ʃɪ-/ *n.* **1** a body of persons organized for a common purpose. **2** a mental connection of ideas. **3** associating, companionship. —**Association football,** the kind of football played between two teams of 11 players with a round ball which may not be handled in play except by the goalkeeper.

assonance /ˈæs(ə)nəns/ *n.* resemblance of sound between two syllables; a rhyme depending on identity in vowel-sounds only (as *sonnet/porridge*) or in consonants only (as *killed/cold*). **assonant** *adj.*, **assonantal** /-ˈnænt(ə)l/ *adj.* [F f. L *assonare* (AD-, *sonus* sound)]

assort /əˈsɔːt/ *v.t./i.* **1** to arrange in sorts, to classify. **2** to suit or harmonize (*with*). [f. OF (*à* to, *sorte* sort)]

assorted /əˈsɔːtɪd/ *adj.* **1** of various sorts, mixed. **2** matched. [f. prec.]

assortment /əˈsɔːtmənt/ *n.* **1** an assorted group or mixture. **2** classification. [f. ASSORT]

assuage /əˈsweɪdʒ/ *v.t.* to soothe, to make less severe; to appease (an appetite). —**assuagement** *n.* [f. OF f. L *suavis* sweet]

assume /əˈsjuːm/ *v.t.* **1** to take as true or sure to happen. **2** to put on oneself (a role or attitude etc.); to undertake (an office). [f. L *assumere* (AD-, *sumere* take)]

assuming /əˈsjuːmɪŋ/ *adj.* presumptuous, arrogant. [f. prec.]

assumption /əˈsʌmpʃ(ə)n/ *n.* assuming, a thing assumed. —**the Assumption,** the taking of the Virgin Mary in bodily form into heaven; the festival commemorating this (15 Aug.).

assurance /əˈʃʊərəns/ *n.* **1** a formal declaration or promise, a guarantee. **2** self-confidence. **3** certainty. **4** insurance, especially of life. Insurance companies tend to use the term *assurance* of policies where a sum is payable after a fixed number of years or on the death of the insured person, and *insurance* of policies relating to events such as fire, accident, or death within a limited period. In popular usage the word *insurance* is used in both cases. [f. foll.]

assure /əˈʃʊə(r)/ *v.t.* **1** to make (a person) sure (*of* a fact), to convince; to tell confidently. **2** to ensure the happening etc. of, to guarantee. **3** to insure (especially life). [f. OF f. L AD-, *securus* safe]

assured /əˈʃʊəd/ *adj.* made sure; confident. —**assuredly** /-rɪdlɪ/ *adv.* certainly. [f. prec.]

astatine /ˈæstətiːn/ *n.* a radioactive element, symbol At, atomic number 85. [f. Gk *astatos* unstable]

aster *n.* a composite plant of the genus *Aster* with bright daisy-like flowers. [L f. Gk, = star]

asterisk /ˈæstərɪsk/ *n.* a star-shaped symbol (*) used to mark words etc. for reference or distinction. —*v.t.* to mark with an asterisk. [f. L f. Gk, = little star]

astern /əˈstɜːn/ *adv.* **1** in or to the rear of a ship or aircraft, behind. **2** backwards. [f. A- + STERN]

asteroid /ˈæstərɔɪd/ *n.* **1** any of the minor planets. **2** a starfish. [f. Gk (*astēr* star)]

asthma /ˈæsmə/ *n.* a respiratory disease (frequently connected with an allergy), often with paroxysms of difficult breathing. —**asthmatic** /æsˈmætɪk/ *adj.* & *n.* [f. L f. Gk (*azō* breathe hard)]

astigmatism /əˈstɪgmətɪz(ə)m/ *n.* a defect in an eye or lens, preventing rays of light from a point from being brought to a common focus. —**astigmatic** /æstɪgˈmætɪk/ *adj.*, **astigmatically** *adv.* [f. Gk *a-* not + *stigma* point]

astir /əˈstɜː(r)/ *adv.* & *predic. adj.* in motion; out of bed. [f. A- + STIR]

astonish /əˈstɒnɪʃ/ *v.t.* to surprise very greatly. —**astonishment** *n.* [f. OF f. L (*tonare* thunder)]

astound /əˈstaʊnd/ *v.t.* to shock with surprise. [as prec.]

astragal /ˈæstrəg(ə)l/ *n.* a small moulding, of semicircular section, placed round the top or bottom of a column. [f. L f. Gk]

astrakhan /æstrəˈkæn/ *n.* the dark tightly curled fleece of lambs from Astrakhan in Russia; an imitation of this.

astral /ˈæstrəl/ *adj.* of or connected with stars. —**astral body,** a supposed ethereal counterpart of the body. [f. L (*astrum* star)]

astray /əˈstreɪ/ *adv.* out of the right way. —**go astray,** to be missing; to fall into error or wrongdoing. [f. OF f. L *extra* away, *vagari* wander]

astride /əˈstraɪd/ *adv.* with one leg on either side (*of*); with feet wide apart. —*prep.* astride of; extending across. [f. A- + STRIDE]

astringent /əˈstrɪndʒənt/ *adj.* **1** that causes contraction of body tissue and checks bleeding. **2** severe, austere. —*n.* an astringent substance. —**astringency** *n.* [F f. L (AD-, *stringere* bind)]

astrolabe /ˈæstrəleɪb/ *n.* an instrument formerly used for measuring the altitudes of stars etc. until replaced by the sextant. [f. OF f. L f. Gk, = star-taking]

astrology /əˈstrɒlədʒɪ/ *n.* study of the positions and movements of stars regarded as having an influence on human affairs —**astrologer** *n.*, **astrological** /æstrəˈlɒdʒɪk(ə)l/ *adj.*, **astrologically** *adv.* [f. OF f. L f. Gk (*astron* star, -LOGY)]

astronaut /ˈæstrənɔːt/ *n.* a traveller in space. [f. Gk *astron* star, *nautēs* sailor]

astronautics /æstrəˈnɔːtɪks/ *n.* the science of space travel and its technology. —**astronautical** *adj.* [as prec.]

astronomical /æstrəˈnɒmɪk(ə)l/ *adj.* **1** of astronomy. **2** vast in amount. —**astronomically** *adv.* [as foll.]

astronomy /əˈstrɒnəmɪ/ *n.* the science of the heavenly bodies and their movements. —**astronomer** *n.* [f. OF f. L f. Gk (*astron* star, *nemō* arrange)]

astrophysics /æstrəʊˈfɪzɪks/ *n.* the branch of astronomy concerned with the physics and chemistry of the heavenly bodies. —**astrophysical** *adj.*, **astrophysicist** *n.* [f. Gk *astron* star + PHYSICS]

astute /əˈstju:t/ *adj.* shrewd, seeing how to gain an advantage. —**astutely** *adv.*, **astuteness** *n.* [f. F or L (*astus* craft)]

asunder /əˈsʌndə(r)/ *adv.* (*formal*) apart, in pieces. [OE *on sundran* into pieces]

asylum /əˈsaɪləm/ *n.* **1** a place of refuge (formerly for criminals). **2** (in full **political asylum**) protection given by a State to a political refugee from another country. **3** (*hist.*) an institution for the care and shelter of insane or destitute persons. [f. L f. Gk, = refuge (*a-* not, *sulon* right of seizure)]

asymmetry /æˈsɪmətrɪ, eɪ-/ *n.* lack of symmetry. —**asymmetric** /-ˈmetrɪk/ *adj.*, **asymmetrical** *adj.* [f. Gk *a-* not + SYMMETRY]

At *symbol* astatine.

at /ət, *emphatic* æt/ *prep.* **1** having as position, time of day, state, or price. **2** with motion or aim towards. —**at it,** working, in activity. [OE]

atavism /ˈætəvɪz(ə)m/ *n.* resemblance to remote ancestors rather than to parents, reversion to an earlier type. —**atavistic** /-ˈvɪstɪk/ *adj.* [f. F f. L *atavus* ancestor]

ate /et, eɪt/ *past* of EAT.

atheism /ˈeɪθɪɪz(ə)m/ *n.* belief that no God or gods exist(s). —**atheist** *n.*, **atheistic** /-ˈɪstɪk/ *adj.* [f. F f. Gk (*a-* not, *theos* god)]

atherosclerosis /æθərəʊsklɪəˈrəʊsɪs/ *n.* formation of fatty deposits in arteries, often with hardening. [f. G f. Gk *athērē* gruel]

athlete /ˈæθli:t/ *n.* one who competes or excels in physical games and exercises. —**athlete's foot,** a fungous disease of the feet. [f. L f. Gk (*athlon* prize)]

athletic /æθˈletɪk/ *adj.* of athletes; physically strong and active, muscular. —**athleticism** *n.* [f. F or L (as prec.)]

athletics *n.pl.* (occas. treated as *sing.*) the practice of or competition in physical exercises (running, jumping, throwing, etc.); (*US*) physical sports and games of any kind. [f. prec.]

athwart /əˈθwɔ:t/ *adv.* & *prep.* across from side to side. [f. A- + THWART]

Atlantic /ətˈlæntɪk/ *adj.* of the Atlantic Ocean. —*n.* the Atlantic Ocean, lying between Europe and Africa on the east and North and South America on the west. [as foll.]

atlas /ˈætləs/ *n.* a book of maps. [f. *Atlas*, a Titan who held up the universe]

atman /ˈætmən/ *n.* (*Hinduism*) the self; the supreme principle of life in the universe. [Skr., = self; essence, highest personal principle of life]

atmosphere /ˈætməsfɪə(r)/ *n.* **1** the mixture of gases surrounding the earth or a heavenly body. **2** the air in a room etc. **3** a psychological environment; the tone or mood pervading a book or work of art etc. **4** pressure of about 1 kg per sq. cm, being that exerted by the atmosphere on the earth's surface. —**atmospheric** /-ˈferɪk/ *adj.* [f. Gk *atmos* vapour + SPHERE]

atmospherics /ætməsˈferɪks/ *n.* or *n.pl.* electrical disturbance in the atmosphere; interference in telecommunications caused by this.

atoll /ˈæt(ə)l/ *n.* a ring-shaped coral reef enclosing a lagoon. [f. Maldive *atolu*]

atom /ˈætəm/ *n.* **1** the smallest particle of a chemical element; this as a source of atomic energy. **2** a minute portion or thing. —**atom bomb,** an atomic bomb. [f. OF f. L f. Gk *atomos* indivisible]

atomic /əˈtɒmɪk/ *adj.* **1** of an atom or atoms. **2** using energy from atoms. —**atomic bomb** a bomb whose destructive power comes from the rapid release of nuclear energy by fission of heavy atomic nuclei. **atomic energy,** nuclear energy. **atomic mass,** = atomic weight. **atomic number,** the number of unit positive charges carried by the nucleus of an atom. **atomic theory,** the theory that all matter consists of atoms. **atomic weight,** the ratio between the mass of one atom of an element or isotope and one-twelfth the weight of an atom of the isotope carbon 12. [as prec.]

atomism /ˈætəmɪz(ə)m/ *n.* the philosophical theory that all matter consists of minute individual particles. —**atomistic** /-ˈmɪstɪk/ *adj.* [f. ATOM]

atomize /ˈætəmaɪz/ *v.t.* to reduce to atoms or fine particles. —**atomization** /-ˈzeɪʃ(ə)n/ *n.* [f. ATOM]

atomizer *n.* a device for reducing liquids to a fine spray. [f. prec.]

atonal /eɪˈtəʊn(ə)l/ *adj.* (*Mus.*) not written in any one key. —**atonality** /-ˈnælɪtɪ/ *n.* [f. Gk *a-* not + TONAL]

atone /əˈtəʊn/ *v.i.* to make amends (*for*). —**atonement** *n.* —**the Atonement,** the expiation of man's sin by Christ. **Day of Atonement,** the most solemn religious fast of the Jewish year, eight days after the Jewish New Year. [f. *at one*]

atrium /ˈeɪtrɪəm/ *n.* (*pl.* **-ia** or **-iums**) **1** the central court of an ancient Roman house. **2** either of the two upper cavities in the heart. [L]

atrocious /əˈtrəʊʃəs/ *adj.* very bad; wicked. —**atrociously** *adv.* [f. L *atrox* cruel]

atrocity /əˈtrɒsɪtɪ/ *n.* a wicked or cruel act,

wickedness; a repellent thing. [f. F or L (as prec.)]

atrophy /ˈætrəfɪ/ *n.* wasting away through under-nourishment or lack of use; emaciation. —*v.t./i.* to cause atrophy in; to suffer atrophy. [f. F or L f. Gk (*a-* without, *trophē* food)]

atropine /ˈætrəpɪn, -piːn/ *n.* a poisonous alkaloid found in deadly nightshade, used in medicine. [f. foll.]

attach /əˈtætʃ/ *v.t./i.* **1** to fix to something else. **2** to join (oneself) as a companion etc.; to assign (a person) to a particular group. **3** to accompany or form part of. **4** to attribute; to be attributable. **5** to seize by legal authority. —**be attached to,** to be very fond of. [f. OF, = fasten]

attachable *adj.* that may be attached. [f. prec.]

attaché /əˈtæʃeɪ/ *n.* a person attached to an ambassador's staff and having responsibility in a specific capacity. —**attaché case,** a small rectangular case for carrying documents etc. [F (as ATTACH)]

attachment /əˈtætʃmənt/ *n.* **1** attaching, being attached. **2** a thing (esp. a device) attached. **3** affection, devotion. **4** legal seizure. [f. ATTACH]

attack /əˈtæk/ *v.t./i.* **1** to act violently against; to make an attack. **2** to criticize strongly. **3** to act harmfully on. **4** to undertake (a task) with vigour. —*n.* **1** an act of attacking. **2** strong criticism. **3** a sudden onset of illness etc. —**attacker** *n.* [f. F f. It., = join battle]

attain *v.t./i.* to succeed in accomplishing, obtaining, or reaching. [f. AF f. L (AD-, *tangere* touch)]

attainable /əˈteɪnəb(ə)l/ *adj.* that may be attained. [f. prec.]

attainment /əˈteɪnmənt/ *n.* **1** attaining. **2** (usu. in *pl.*) what is attained, an achievement. [f. ATTAIN]

attar /ˈætə(r)/ *n.* a fragrant oil, especially from rose-petals. [Pers. f. Arab. (*'itr* perfume)]

attempt /əˈtempt/ *v.t.* to make an effort to accomplish. —*n.* an effort to accomplish, overcome, or surpass something; an attack. [f. OF f. L *attemptare* (AD-, *temptare* try)]

attend /əˈtend/ *v.t./i.* **1** to be present (at); to go regularly to. **2** to apply one's mind; to accompany. —**attendance** *n.* [f. OF f. L *attendere* (AD-, *tendere* stretch)]

attendant /əˈtend(ə)nt/ *n.* a person attending, especially to provide service. —*adj.* accompanying; waiting *on*. [f. prec.]

attention /əˈtenʃ(ə)n/ *n.* **1** applying one's mind, mental concentration; awareness. **2** consideration, care. **3** putting into good condition. **4** an attitude of concentration or readiness (also as a command). **5** (in *pl.*) small acts of kindness or courtesy. —*int.* an order to take notice or to assume an attitude of attention. [f. L (as ATTEND)]

attentive /əˈtentɪv/ *adj.* paying attention; devotedly courteous or considerate. —**attentively** *adv.*, **attentiveness** *n.* [f. F (as ATTEND)]

attenuate /əˈtenjʊeɪt/ *v.t.* **1** to make slender or thin. **2** to reduce in force or value. —**attenuation** /-ˈeɪʃ(ə)n/ *n.* [f. L *attenuare* (AD-, *tenuis* thin)]

attest /əˈtest/ *v.t./i.* **1** to be evidence or proof of. **2** to declare to be true or genuine. —**attestation** /ætesˈteɪʃ(ə)n/ *n.* [f. F f. L *attestari* (AD-, *testis* witness)]

Attic /ˈætɪk/ *adj.* **1** of Athens or Attica. **2** of the ancient Greek dialect used there. —*n.* this dialect. [f. L f. Gk]

attic /ˈætɪk/ *n.* a room in the top storey of a house, immediately below the roof. [f. F, as prec.; orig. used of a small architectural feature above a larger one]

attire /əˈtaɪə(r)/ *n.* (*formal*) clothes. [f. OF (*à tire* in order)]

attired /əˈtaɪəd/ *adj.* (*formal*) clothed. [f. prec.]

attitude /ˈætɪtjuːd/ *n.* **1** a way of regarding, a disposition or reaction (*to*). **2** a position of the body or its parts. **3** the position of an aircraft etc. in relation to given points. [F f. It. f. L (*aptus* fitted)]

atto- /ætəʊ-/ *prefix* denoting a factor of 10^{-18} (*attometre*). [f. Da. or Norw. *atten* eighteen]

attorney /əˈtɜːnɪ/ *n.* one appointed to act for another in business or legal affairs; (*US*) a lawyer. —**Attorney-General** *n.* the chief legal officer, appointed by the government holding office. [f. OF (*atorner* assign)]

attract /əˈtrækt/ *v.t.* **1** to draw towards itself by unseen force. **2** to arouse interest, pleasure, or admiration in. —**attraction** *n.* [f. L *attrahere* (AD-, *trahere* pull)]

attractive /əˈtræktɪv/ *adj.* **1** that attracts or can attract. **2** good-looking. —**attractively** *adv.*, **attractiveness** *n.* [f. F f. L (as prec.)]

attributable /əˈtrɪbjuːtəb(ə)l/ *adj.* that may be attributed. [f. foll.]

attribute[1] /əˈtrɪbjuːt/ *v.t.* (with *to*) to regard as belonging to, caused by, or originated by. —**attribution** /-ˈbjuːʃ(ə)n/ *n.* [f. L *attribuere* (AD-, *tribuere* allot)]

attribute[2] /ˈætrɪbjuːt/ *n.* **1** a quality ascribed to or characteristic of a person or thing. **2** an object associated with or symbolizing a person. [as prec.]

attributive /əˈtrɪbjʊtɪv/ *adj.* expressing an attribute; (*Gram.*, of an adjective) placed before the noun it qualifies (cf. PREDICATIVE). —**attributively** *adv.* [f. F (as ATTRIBUTE[1])]

attrition /əˈtrɪʃ(ə)n/ *n.* **1** wearing away by friction. **2** gradual wearing down of strength and morale by harassment. [f. L *attritio* (AD-*terere* rub)]

attune /əˈtju:n/ *v.t.* **1** to harmonize or adapt (one's mind etc.) *to* a matter or idea. **2** to bring into musical accord. [f. AD- + TUNE]

atypical /eɪˈtɪpɪk(ə)l/ *adj.* not belonging to any type. [f. Gk *a-* not + TYPICAL]

Au *symbol* gold. [f. L *aurum*]

aubergine /ˈəʊbəʒi:n/ *n.* **1** the fruit of the egg-plant, used as a vegetable. **2** its dark-purple colour. [F, ult. f. Skr.]

aubrietia /ɔ:ˈbri:ʃə/ *n.* a low-growing perennial rock-plant with mauve, purple, or pink flowers. [f. Claude *Aubriet*, Fr. botanist (d. 1743)]

auburn /ˈɔ:bən/ *adj.* (of hair) reddish-brown. [orig. = yellowish-white, f. OF f. L (*albus* white)]

auction /ˈɔ:kʃ(ə)n/ *n.* a sale in which each article is sold to the highest bidder. —*v.t.* to sell by auction. [f. L (*augēre* increase)]

auctioneer /ɔ:kʃəˈnɪə(r)/ *n.* one whose business is to conduct auctions. —*v.t.* to sell by auction. [f. prec.]

audacious /ɔ:ˈdeɪʃəs/ *adj.* daring, bold. —**audaciously** *adv.*, **audacity** /ɔˈdæsəɪtɪ/ *n.* [f. L (*audēre* dare)]

audible /ˈɔ:dɪb(ə)l/ *adj.* that can be heard (distinctly). —**audibility** /-ˈbɪlɪtɪ/ *n.*, **audibly** *adv.* [f. L (*audire* hear)]

audience /ˈɔ:dɪəns/ *n.* **1** a group of listeners or spectators. **2** a formal interview. [f. OF f. L (as prec.)]

audio /ˈɔ:dɪəʊ/ *n.* (*pl.* **-os**) and *in comb.* audible sound reproduced mechanically; its reproduction. —**audio frequency,** a frequency comparable to that of ordinary sound. **audio typist,** one who types from a recording. **audio-visual** *adj.* using both sight and sound. [f. L *audire* hear]

audit /ˈɔ:dɪt/ *n.* an official scrutiny of accounts to see that they are in order. —*v.t.* to conduct an audit of. [f. L *auditus* hearing (as prec.)]

audition /ɔ:ˈdɪʃ(ə)n/ *n.* a trial performance to test the suitability of an actor etc. for a part. —*v.t./i.* give an audition to; have an audition. [as AUDIO]

auditor /ˈɔ:dɪtə(r)/ *n.* **1** one authorized to audit accounts. **2** a listener. [f. AF f. L (as AUDIO)]

auditorium /ɔ:dɪˈtɔrɪəm/ *n.* (*pl.* **-ums**) the part of a theatre etc. occupied by an audience. [L (as foll.)]

auditory /ˈɔ:dɪtərɪ/ *adj.* of or concerned with hearing. [f. L (as AUDITOR)]

au fait /əʊ ˈfeɪ/ well acquainted *with* a subject. [F]

auger /ˈɔ:gə(r)/ *n.* a tool for boring holes in wood, having a long shank with a helical groove, and a transverse handle. [OE (*nafu* nave of wheel, *gār* piercer)]

aught /ɔ:t/ *n.* (*archaic* or *poet.*) anything. [OE]

augment[1] /ɔ:gˈment/ *v.t.* to increase, to make greater. —**augmentation** /-ˈteɪʃ(ə)n/ *n.* [f. F or L (*augēre* increase)]

augment[2] /ˈɔ:gmənt/ *n.* a vowel prefixed to past tenses in Greek and Sanskrit. [as prec.]

au gratin /əʊ ˈgrætæ̃/ cooked with a crust of breadcrumbs and grated cheese. [F (*gratter* grate)]

augur /ˈɔ:gə(r)/ *n.* an ancient Roman religious official who observed and interpreted omens in natural phenomena; a soothsayer. —*v.t./i.* to portend; to serve as an omen. —**augural** *adj.* [L]

August /ˈɔ:gʌst/ *n.* the eighth month of the year. [OE, f. *Augustus*, first Roman emperor (d. AD 14)]

august /ɔ:ˈgʌst/ *adj.* majestic, imposing. [f. F or L, = consecrated, venerable]

auk /ɔ:k/ *n.* a sea-bird of the family Alcidae, e.g. the great auk (flightless and extinct), little auk, guillemot, puffin, razorbill. [f. ON *álka*]

auld lang syne /ɔ:ld læŋ ˈsaɪn/ (*Sc.*) days of long ago. [Sc., = old long since]

aunt /ɑ:nt/ *n.* a sister or sister-in-law of one's father or mother; (*colloq.*) an unrelated friend of a parent. —**Aunt Sally,** a figure used as a target in a throwing-game; a target of general abuse. [f. AF f. L *amita*]

auntie, aunty /ˈɑ:ntɪ/ *n.* (*colloq.*) an aunt.

au pair /əʊ ˈpeər/ (in full **au pair girl**) a young woman, usually from abroad, helping with housework etc. in return for board and lodging. [F]

aura /ˈɔ:rə/ *n.* (*pl.* **-as**) the distinctive atmosphere attending a person or thing; a subtle emanation. [L f. Gk, = breeze]

aural /ˈɔ:r(ə)l/ *adj.* of or concerning the ear or hearing. —**aurally** *adv.* [f. L *auris* ear]

aureola /ɔ:ˈri:ələ/, **aureole** /ˈɔrɪəʊl/ *n.* **1** a celestial crown or halo, especially round the head or body of a portrayed divine figure. **2** a corona round the sun or moon. [L, = golden crown]

au revoir /əʊ rəˈvwɑ:r/ goodbye for the moment. [F]

auricle /ˈɔ:rɪk(ə)l/ *n.* **1** the external part of the ear. **2** an atrium of the heart; a small appendage to this. —**auricular** /ɔˈrɪkjʊlə(r)/ *adj.* [f. L, dim. of *auris* ear]

auriferous /ɔ:ˈrɪfərəs/ *adj.* yielding gold. [f. L (*aurum* gold, *ferre* bear)]

aurochs /ˈɔ:rəks/ *n.* **1** an extinct European wild ox. **2** a European bison. [G]

aurora /ɔ:ˈrɔrə/ *n.* (*pl.* **-as, -ae** /-i:/) a luminescent display of colours in the atmosphere at high northern (**aurora borealis**) or southern (**aurora australis**) latitudes, arising from electrical interactions between the Earth's magnetic field and streams of energetic charged particles from the sun. [f. L, = dawn]

auscultation /ɔ:skʊl'teɪʃ(ə)n/ *n.* listening to the sounds of the heart, lungs, etc., for diagnosis. [f. L (*auscultare* listen to)]

auspice /ɔ:spɪs/ *n.* **1** an omen. **2** (in *pl.*) patronage. [orig. = observation of bird-flight (in divination); F or f. L (*avis* bird)]

auspicious /ɔ:'spɪʃəs/ *adj.* showing signs that promise well, favourable. —**auspiciously** *adv.*, **auspiciousness** *n.* [f. prec.]

Aussie /'ɒzɪ/ *n.* & *adj.* (*colloq.*) Australian. [abbr.]

austere /ɔ:'stɪə(r)/ *adj.* stern, grim; severely simple; severe in self-discipline or abstinence. —**austerely** *adv.*, **austerity** /ɔ'sterətɪ/ *n.* [f. OF f. L f. Gk *austēros* severe]

austral /'ɔ:str(ə)l/ *adj.* **1** southern. **2** Austral, Australian; Australasian. [f. L *australis* (*Auster* south wind)]

Australasian /ɒstrə'leɪʒ(ə)n, ɔ:-/ *adj.* of Australia, New Zealand, and neighbouring islands in the South Pacific. —**Australasian** *n.* an Australasian person. [f. *Australia*, *Asia*]

Australian /ɒ'streɪlɪən, ɔ:-/ *adj.* of Australia or its people. —*n.* a native or inhabitant of Australia. [f. *Australia*]

autarchy /'ɔ:tɑ:kɪ/ *n.* despotism, absolute rule. [f. Gk *autos* self, *arkhē* rule]

autarky /'ɔ:tɑ:kɪ/ *n.* self-sufficiency, especially in economic affairs. [f. Gk (*autos* self, *arkeō* suffice)]

authentic /ɔ:'θentɪk/ *adj.* genuine, of legitimate or undisputed origin; trustworthy. —**authentically** *adv.*, **authenticity** /-'tɪsɪtɪ/ *n.* [f. OF f. L f. Gk, = principal, genuine]

authenticate /ɔ:'θentɪkeɪt/ *v.t.* to establish as valid or authentic. —**authentication** /-'keɪʃ(ə)n/ *n.*, **authenticator** *n.* [f. L (as prec.)]

author /'ɔ:θə(r)/ *n.* **1** the writer of a book or books, article(s), etc. **2** the originator *of* a plan or policy etc. —**authorship** *n.* [f. AF f. L *auctor* (*augēre* increase)]

authoritarian /ɔ:θɒrɪ'teərɪən/ *adj.* favouring or characterized by unqualified obedience to authority. —*n.* an authoritarian person. [f. AUTHORITY]

authoritative /ɔ:'θɒrɪtətɪv/ *adj.* reliable, as having authority; official. —**authoritatively** *adv.* [f. foll.]

authority /ɔ:'θɒrɪtɪ/ *n.* **1** the power or right to enforce obedience. **2** (esp. in *pl.*) a body having authority. **3** personal influence arising from knowledge or position etc., a testimony based on this. **4** a person to whom knowledge or influence is attributed; an expert. [f. OF f. L (as AUTHOR)]

authorize /'ɔ:θəraɪz/ *v.t.* to give authority to (a person) or for (an action etc.); to recognize officially. **Authorized Version** the English translation of the Bible (1611), ordered by King James I. —**authorization** /-'zeɪʃ(ə)n/ *n.* [as prec.]

autism /'ɔ:tɪz(ə)m/ *n.* a mental condition, especially in children, preventing proper response to the environment. —**autistic** /ɔ'tɪstɪk/ *adj.* [as AUTO-]

auto /'ɔ:təʊ/ *n.* (*pl.* **-os**) (*US colloq.*) a motor car. [abbr. of AUTOMOBILE]

auto- /'ɔ:tə(ʊ)/ *in comb.* self; own; of or by oneself or itself, automatic. [f. Gk *autos* self]

autobahn /'ɔ:təbɑ:n/ *n.* a German, Austrian, or Swiss motorway. [G (*auto* motor car, *bahn* road)]

autobiography /ɔ:təbaɪ'ɒgrəfɪ/ *n.* the story of a person's life written by himself or herself; the writing of this. —**autobiographical** /-'græfɪk(ə)l/ *adj.*

autochthonous /ɔ:'tɒkθənəs/ *adj.* indigenous, aboriginal. [f. Gk, = sprung from that land itself (as AUTO-, *khthōn* land)]

autoclave /'ɔ:təʊkleɪv/ *n.* **1** a strong vessel used for chemical reactions at high pressures and temperatures. **2** a sterilizer using high-pressure steam. [f. AUTO- + L *clavus* nail or *clavis* key]

autocracy /ɔ:'tɒkrəsɪ/ *n.* absolute government by one person; dictatorship. [f. Gk (as foll.)]

autocrat /'ɔ:təkræt/ *n.* a sole ruler with absolute power; an authoritarian person. —**autocratic** /-'krætɪk/ *adj.*, **autocratically** *adv.* [f. F f. Gk (as AUTO-, *kratos* power)]

autocross /'ɔ:təʊkrɒs/ *n.* motor-racing across country or on unmade roads. [f. AUTO(MOBILE) + CROSS]

Autocue /'ɔ:təʊkju:/ *n.* [P] a device showing a television speaker the script as an aid to memory.

auto-da-fé /ɔ:təʊdɑ:'feɪ/ *n.* (*pl.* **-os-**) the ceremonial judgement of heretics by the Spanish Inquisition; the execution of heretics by public burning. [Port., = act of the faith]

autogiro /ɔ:tə'dʒaɪrəʊ/ *n.* (*pl.* **-os**) an aircraft in which the lift comes from its rotating wings. [Sp. (as AUTO-, *giro* gyration)]

autograph /'ɔ:təgrɑ:f/ *n.* **1** a person's signature, his or her handwriting. **2** a manuscript in the author's handwriting. **3** a document signed by its author. —*v.t.* to sign or write on in one's own hand. [F, or f. L f. Gk (*graphō* write)]

auto-immunity *n.* the state produced by the presence either of antibodies produced by an organism and reacting against a constituent of it, or of lymphoid cells sensitized against a constituent of the body's own tissues. —**auto-immune** *adj.*

automate /'ɔ:təmeɪt/ *v.t.* to apply automation to, to operate by automation. [back-formation f. AUTOMATION]

automatic /ɔ:tə'mætɪk/ *adj.* **1** working of itself without direct human intervention in the process. **2** done from habit without conscious thought. **3** following necessarily. **4** (of a firearm) having a mechanism for continuous loading and firing. —*n.* **1** an automatic gun etc. **2** a motor vehicle with automatic transmission. —**automatic pilot,** a device in an aircraft or ship to keep it on a set course. **automatic transmission,** a system in a motor vehicle for automatic gear-change. —**automatically** *adv.* [as AUTOMATON]

automation /ɔ:təˈmeɪʃ(ə)n/ *n.* the production of goods etc. by automatic processes; use of automatic equipment in place of human effort. [f. prec.]

automatism /ɔ:ˈtɒmətɪz(ə)m/ *n.* **1** involuntary action. **2** unthinking routine. [f. F (as foll.)]

automaton /ɔ:ˈtɒmət(ə)n/ *n.* (*pl.* **-tons,** *collect.* **-ta**) **1** a machine responding to automatic (esp. electronic) control. **2** a person acting mechanically. [L f. Gk, = acting of itself]

automobile /ˈɔ:təməbi:l/ *n.* (*US*) a motor car. [F (as AUTO-, MOBILE)]

automotive /ɔ:təˈməʊtɪv/ *adj.* concerned with motor vehicles.

autonomic /ɔ:təˈnɒmɪk/ *adj.* functioning involuntarily. [as foll.]

autonomous /ɔ:ˈtɒnəməs/ *adj.* self-governing, acting independently. [f. Gk (AUTO- *nomos* law)]

autonomy /ɔ:ˈtɒnəmɪ/ *n.* the right of self-government, independence. [as prec.]

autopilot /ˈɔ:təʊpaɪlət/ *n.* an automatic pilot.

autopsy /ˈɔ:tɒpsɪ/ *n.* a post-mortem. [f. F f. Gk (*autoptēs* eyewitness)]

autostrada /ˈɔ:təstrɑ:də/ *n.* (*pl.* **-de** /-deɪ/) an Italian motorway. [It. (as AUTOMOBILE, *strada* road)]

auto-suggestion *n.* suggestion arising unconsciously from within a person to influence his own actions etc.

autumn /ˈɔ:təm/ *n.* the season between summer and winter; a time of incipient decline. —**autumnal** /ɔ:ˈtʌmn(ə)l/ *adj.* [f. OF f. L *autumnus*]

auxiliary /ɔ:gˈzɪljərɪ/ *adj.* giving help; additional, subsidiary. —*n.* **1** an auxiliary person or thing. **2** an auxiliary verb. **3** (in *pl.*) foreign or allied troops in the service of a nation at war. —**auxiliary verb,** a verb used to form tenses, moods, etc. of other verbs (e.g. *have* in *they have gone*). [f. L (*auxilium* help)]

auxin /ˈɔ:ksɪn/ *n.* a substance that stimulates the growth of plants, a growth hormone. [G, f. Gk *auxō* increase]

AV *abbr.* Authorized Version.

avail /əˈveɪl/ *v.t./i.* to be of use or advantage (to). —*n.* effectiveness, advantage. —**avail oneself of,** to make use of. [f. OF f. L *valēre* be strong]

available /əˈveɪləb(ə)l/ *adj.* capable of being used; at one's disposal. —**availability** /-ˈbɪlɪtɪ/ *n.* [f. prec.]

avalanche /ˈævəlɑ:nʃ/ *n.* **1** a mass of dislodged snow, rock, etc., sliding rapidly down a mountain. **2** a great onrush. [F (*avaler* descend)]

avant-garde /ævɑ̃ˈgɑ:d/ *n.* a leading group of innovators, especially in art and literature. —*adj.* (of ideas) new, progressive. [F, = vanguard]

avarice /ˈævərɪs/ *n.* greed for wealth or gain. —**avaricious** *adj.*, **avariciously** *adv.* [f. OF f. L (*avarus* greedy)]

avatar /ˈævətɑ:(r)/ *n.* (*Hinduism*) **1** the descent to earth of a deity in a manifest form. **2** any of the ten incarnations of Vishnu. [f. Skr., = descent]

Ave /ˈɑvɪ, ˈɑveɪ/ *n.* (in full **Ave Maria,** = Hail, Mary) a devotional recitation and prayer to the Virgin Mary (cf. Luke 1: 28 & 42). [L, imper. of *avēre* fare well]

avenge /əˈvendʒ/ *v.t.* to take vengeance for (an injury) or on behalf of (a person). —**avenger** *n.* [f OF f. L (*vindicare* vindicate)]

avenue /ˈævənju:/ *n.* **1** a broad main street; a tree-lined approach or path. **2** a way of approach. [F f. *avenir* come to f. L (AD-, *venire* come)]

aver /əˈvɜ:(r)/ *v.t.* (**-rr-**) to assert, to affirm. —**averment** *n.* [f. OF (*a-* to + L *verus* true)]

average /ˈævərɪdʒ/ *n.* **1** the generally prevailing rate, degree, or amount. **2** a number obtained by adding several quantities together and dividing the total by the number of quantities. **3** (*Law*) damage to or loss of a ship or cargo. —*adj.* of the usual or ordinary standard; calculated by making an average. —*v.t.* to amount to or produce as an average; to calculate the average of. [f. F f. It. f. Arab., = damaged goods]

averse /əˈvɜ:s/ *predic. adj.* unwilling, opposed, disinclined (*to* or *from*). [f. L (as AVERT)]

aversion /əˈvɜ:ʃ(ə)n/ *n.* **1** a strong dislike (*to* or *from*), unwillingness. **2** an object of dislike. [F or f. L (as foll.)]

avert /əˈvɜ:t/ *v.t.* **1** to turn away (eyes, thoughts, etc.). **2** to prevent (a disaster etc.) from happening. [f. L (AB-, *vertere* turn)]

Avesta /əˈvestə/ *n.* the sacred scripture of Zoroastrianism, compiled by Zoroaster as a means of reforming an older tradition. (See ZEND-AVESTA.) —**Avestan** *adj.* & *n.* [f. Pers. *avastāk* text]

aviary /ˈeɪvɪərɪ/ *n.* a large cage or building for keeping birds. [f. L (*avis* bird)]

aviation /eɪvɪˈeɪʃ(ə)n/ *n.* the practice or science of flying aircraft. [F f. L (*avis* bird)]

aviator /ˈeɪvɪeɪtə(r)/ *n.* a pilot or member of an aircraft crew in the early days of aviation. [as prec.]

avid /ˈævɪd/ *adj.* eager, greedy. —**avidity** /əˈvɪdɪtɪ/ *n.*, **avidly** *adv.* [f. F or L (*avēre* crave)]

avionics /eɪvɪˈɒnɪks/ *n.* or *n.pl.* the science of electronics applied to aeronautics. [f. AVI(ATION) + ELECTRONICS]

avocado /ævəˈkɑːdəʊ/ *n.* (*pl.* **-os**) **1** a pear-shaped tropical fruit with rough skin and creamy flesh. **2** its dark green colour. [Sp. (= advocate) f. Aztec]

avocation /ævəˈkeɪʃ(ə)n/ *n.* a secondary activity done in addition to one's main work; (*colloq.*) one's occupation. [f. L (*avocare* call away)]

avocet /ˈævəset/ *n.* a wading bird with long legs and an upturned bill. [f. F f. It.]

avoid /əˈvɔɪd/ *v.t.* to keep away or refrain from; to escape or evade. —**avoidable** *adj.*, **avoidance** *n.* [f. AF, = clear out]

avoirdupois /ævədəˈpɔɪz/ *n.* a system of weights based on a pound of 16 ounces or 7,000 grains. [F, = goods of weight]

avow /əˈvaʊ/ *v.t.* to declare, to admit. —**avowal** *n.*, **avowedly** /əˈvaʊɪdlɪ/ *adv.* [f. OF f. L (*vocare* call)]

avuncular /əˈvʌŋkjʊlə(r)/ *adj.* of or like a kindly uncle. [f. L *avunculus* maternal uncle (dim. of *avus* grandfather)]

await /əˈweɪt/ *v.t.* to wait for; to be in store for. [f. AF (as WAIT)]

awake /əˈweɪk/ *v.t./i.* (*past* **awoke** /əˈwəʊk/, *p.p.* **awoken** /əˈwəʊkən/) **1** to wake, to cease from sleep; to become active. **2** to rouse from sleep. —*predic. adj.* no longer or not yet asleep; alert. [OE]

awaken /əˈweɪkən/ *v.t.* to awake; to draw the attention of (a person *to* a fact etc.). [OE]

award /əˈwɔːd/ *v.t.* to give by official decision as a payment, prize, or penalty. —*n.* **1** a decision of this kind. **2** an amount or prize etc. awarded. [AF *awarder* (as WARD)]

aware /əˈweə(r)/ *predic. adj.* having knowledge or realization (*of* or *that*). [OE]

awash /əˈwɒʃ/ *predic. adj.* washed over by water or waves. [f. A- + WASH]

away /əˈweɪ/ *adv.* **1** to or at a distance; into nonexistence. **2** constantly, persistently. **3** without delay. —*adj.* played or playing on an opponent's ground. —*n.* an away match or (in football pools) victory in this. [OE (A-, WAY)]

awe /ɔː/ *n.* respect or admiration charged reverence or fear. —*v.t.* to fill or inspire with awe. [ON]

aweigh /əˈweɪ/ *adv.* (of an anchor) just lifted from the bottom in weighing anchor. [f. A- + WEIGH]

awesome /ˈɔːsəm/ *adj.* inspiring awe. [f. AWE + -SOME]

awestricken, awestruck *adjs.* filled with awe.

awful /ˈɔːf(ə)l/ *adj.* **1** (*colloq.*) very bad or poor; notable of its kind. **2** awe-inspiring, terrifying. [f. AWE + -FUL]

awfully /ˈɔːfʊlɪ, *colloq.* ˈɔːflɪ/ *adv.* **1** in a way that inspires awe. **2** (*colloq.*) very; badly.

awhile /əˈwaɪl/ *adv.* for a short time. [OE, = *a while*]

awkward /ˈɔːkwəd/ *adj.* **1** clumsy, having little skill. **2** difficult to handle, use, or deal with. **3** embarrassing, inconvenient; embarrassed. —**awkwardly** *adv.*, **awkwardness** *n.* [f. obs. *awk* perverse, f. ON, = turned the wrong way]

awl *n.* a small pointed tool for pricking holes, especially in leather or wood. [OE]

awn *n.* the bristly head of the sheath of barley, oats, etc. [f. ON]

awning *n.* a canvas or plastic sheet stretched by supports from a wall as a shelter against sun and rain. [orig. unkn.]

awoke *past* of AWAKE.

awoken *p.p.* of AWAKE.

awry /əˈraɪ/ *adv.* **1** crookedly, out of the true position. **2** amiss. —*predic. adj.* crooked. [f. A- + WRY]

axe *n.* a chopping-tool with a long handle and a heavy blade. —*v.t.* to eliminate or reduce drastically. —**have an axe to grind,** to have a personal interest involved and to be anxious to take care of it. [OE]

axial /ˈæksɪəl/ *adj.* **1** of or forming an axis. **2** round an axis. —**axially** *adv.* [f. AXIS]

axil *n.* the upper angle where a leaf joins a stem, or between a branch and the trunk of a tree. [f. L *axilla* armpit (dim. of *ala* wing)]

axiology /æksɪˈɒlədʒɪ/ *n.* (*Philos.*) the theory of value. —**axiological** /-ˈlɒdʒɪk(ə)l/ *adj.* [f. F f. Gk *axia* value]

axiom /ˈæksɪəm/ *n.* an established or accepted principle; a self-evident truth. —**axiomatic** /-ˈmætɪk/ *adj.* [f. F or L f. Gk (*axios* worthy)]

axis /ˈæksɪs/ *n.* (*pl.* **axes** /-siːz/) **1** an imaginary line about which an object rotates; a line about which a regular figure is symmetrically arranged. **2** any of a set of reference lines for measurement of coordinates etc. **3** the relation between countries, regarded as a common pivot on which they revolve, especially (**the Axis**) the political association of 1936 (becoming in 1939 a military alliance) between Italy and Germany, and later Japan. [L, = axle, pivot]

axle *n.* the bar or rod on which a wheel or wheels revolve(s); the rod connecting a pair of wheels of a vehicle. [f. ON]

Axminster /ˈæksmɪnstə(r)/ *n.* a machine-woven tufted carpet with cut pile. [name of town in Devon]

axolotl /æksəˈlɒt(ə)l/ *n.* a newtlike amphibian found in Mexican lakes. [Nahuatl (*atl* water, *xolotl* servant)]

axon /ˈæksɒn/ *n.* a long appendage of a nerve cell, usually carrying signals from it. [f. Gk, = axis]

ayatollah /aɪəˈtɒlə/ *n.* a Shiite religious leader in Iran. [Pers. f. Arab., = token of God]

aye[1] /aɪ/ *adv.* (*archaic, dial., nautical*, or *formal*) yes, —*n.* an affirmative answer or vote. [prob. f. pron. *I* expressing assent]

aye[2] /aɪ/ *adv.* (*archaic*) always. [f. ON]

azalea /əˈzeɪlɪə/ *n.* a flowering shrubby plant of the genus or subgenus *Azalea*. [f. Gk, = dry (from the dry soil in which Linnaeus believed that it flourished)]

azimuth /ˈæzɪməθ/ *n.* **1** an arc of the sky from the zenith to the horizon. **2** the distance (measured as an angle) along the horizon clockwise from the north point to the point where the azimuth through a particular object (e.g. a star) meets the horizon. **3** a directional bearing. —**azimuthal** /-ˈmu:θ(ə)l/ *adj.* [f. OF f. Arab. (*al* the, *sumūt* directions)]

Aztec /ˈæztek/ *n.* **1** a member of the native people dominant in central Mexico at the time of the Spanish conquest (1521). **2** their language, also called Nahuatl. —*adj.* of the Aztecs or their language. [f. F or Sp. f. Nahuatl, = men of the north]

azure /ˈæʒə(r), ˈæʒjʊə(r)/ *adj.* & *n.* sky-blue; (in heraldry) blue. [f. OF f. L f. Arab. *al* the, *lāzaward* (f. Pers.) lapis lazuli]

Bb

B, b *n.* **1** the second letter of the alphabet. **2** (*Mus.*) the seventh note in the scale of C major.

B *symbol* boron.

b. *abbr.* born.

BA *abbr.* Bachelor of Arts.

Ba *symbol* barium.

baa /bɑː/ *n.* the bleat of a sheep or lamb. —*v.i.* (**baaed, baa'd**) to bleat. [imit.]

baba /ˈbɑːbɑː/ *n.* (also **rum baba**) a sponge-cake soaked in rum syrup. [F]

babble *v.t./i.* **1** to make incoherent sounds; to talk inarticulately or excessively; to say incoherently. **2** to repeat or divulge foolishly. **3** (of a stream etc.) to murmur as it trickles. —*n.* **1** incoherent or foolish talk. **2** a confused murmur. [imit.]

babe *n.* **1** (*poet.*) a baby. **2** an inexperienced or guileless person. **3** (*US slang*) a young woman. [imit. of child's *ba ba*]

babel /ˈbeɪb(ə)l/ *n.* **1** a confused noise, especially of voices. **2** a scene of confusion. [f. Heb. *babel* Babylon f. Semitic *bab ili* gate of God; cf. *balal* confuse]

baboon /bəˈbuːn/ *n.* a large African and Arabian monkey with a doglike snout. [f. OF or L]

baby /ˈbeɪbɪ/ *n.* **1** a very young child or animal. **2** the youngest member of a family etc.; a thing small of its kind; a childish person. **3** (*slang*) a sweetheart. **4** (*slang*) one's own concern or activity. —*v.t.* to treat like a baby. —**baby grand,** a small grand piano. **baby-sit** *v.i.* to look after a young child while its parents are out. **baby-sitter** *n.* one who baby-sits. —**babyhood** *n.*, **babyish** *adj.* [as BABE]

baccalaureate /bækəˈlɔːrɪət/ *n.* the degree of a Bachelor of Arts or Science etc. [f. L *baccalaureus* (see BACHELOR), with pun on *bacca lauri* laurel berry]

baccarat /ˈbækərɑː/ *n.* a gambling card-game, played against the banker by punters each in turn staking that their hand will total nine. [F]

bachelor /ˈbætʃ(ə)lə(r)/ *n.* **1** an unmarried man. **2** one who holds the degree of Bachelor of Arts or Science etc. —**bachelor flat,** one suitable for a person living alone. **Bachelor of Arts** *or* **Science** etc., a person who has obtained a first degree in arts or sciences, or other faculty. [f. OF *bacheler* aspirant to knighthood]

bacillus /bəˈsɪləs/ *n.* (*pl.* **bacilli** /-laɪ/) a rod-shaped bacterium, especially one causing disease by entering and multiplying in animal and other tissues. —**bacillary** *adj.* [L, dim. of *baculus* stick]

back[1] *n.* **1** the hinder surface of the human body from shoulder to hip; the corresponding part of an animal's body. **2** a similar ridge-shaped part, the keel of a ship. **3** an outer or rear surface; the less active, less important, or less visible part; the side or part normally away from the spectator or direction of motion. **4** the part of a garment covering the back. **5** a defensive player near the goal in football etc. —*adj.* **1** situated behind or in the rear. **2** of or for past time. **3** (of vowels) formed at the back of the mouth (as in *hard, hot*). —*adv.* **1** to the rear, away from the front. **2** in or into an earlier or normal position or condition; in or into the past. **3** at a distance; in check. **4** in return. —**at the back of one's mind,** borne in mind but not consciously thought of. **back-bencher** *n.* an MP not entitled to sit on the front benches in Parliament, i.e. one without senior office either in government or in opposition. **back boiler,** a boiler behind a domestic fire. **back formation,** an apparent root-word formed from a word that looks like (but is not) its derivative, as *laze* from *lazy*; formation of words in this way. **back of beyond,** (*colloq.*) a remote and benighted region. **back seat,** a seat at the back; a less prominent position. **back-seat driver,** a person who has no responsibility but is eager to advise someone who has. **back slang,** a form of slang using words spelt backwards, as *yob* for *boy*. **back-to-back** *adj.* (of houses) built with juxtaposed backs. **back to front,** with the back placed where the front should be. **get** *or* **put a person's back up,** to annoy or irritate him. **get off a person's back,** to stop annoying him. **have one's back to the wall,** to be fighting for survival. **put one's back into,** to put all one's strength into (efforts). **see the**

back of, to be rid of. **turn one's back on,** to repudiate (former associates etc.). [OE]

back[2] *v.t./i.* **1** to help with money, to give encouragement or support to; to lay a bet on the success of. **2** to go or cause to go backwards. **3** to provide with a lining or support at the back; to provide a musical accompaniment to. **4** to be so situated that its rear abuts *on*. **5** (of wind) to change gradually in an anticlockwise direction. —**back down,** to abandon a claim, viewpoint, etc. **back out,** to withdraw from an agreement. **back up,** to give encouragement or support to; to confirm (a statement). **back water,** to reverse a boat's forward motion by using the oars. —**backer** *n.* [f. BACK[1]]

backache *n.* pain in the back.

backbiting *n.* spiteful talk about a person, especially in his or her absence.

backblocks *n.pl.* (*Austral.* & *NZ*) land in the remote interior.

backbone *n.* **1** the spine. **2** the main support of a structure. **3** firmness of character.

backchat *n.* (*colloq.*) impudent repartee.

backdate *v.t.* to assign an earlier date than the actual one to (a document etc.); to make (agreements etc.) retrospectively valid.

backdrop *n.* a flat painted curtain at the back of a stage set.

backfire /bækˈfaɪə(r)/ *v.i.* **1** (of an engine or vehicle) to undergo premature explosion in the cylinder or exhaust-pipe. **2** (of a plan etc.) to go wrong, especially so as to recoil on its originator. —*n.* an instance of backfiring.

backgammon /ˈbækgæmən/ *n.* a game for two, played on a special double board with pieces like draughtsmen moved according to the throw of a dice. [f. BACK[1] (because pieces go back and re-enter) + obs. *gamen* game]

background *n.* **1** the back part of a scene etc., especially as the setting for the chief part; an unimportant or unobtrusive position. **2** a person's education, knowledge, or social circumstances; explanatory or contributory information or circumstances.

backhand *n.* a stroke, especially in tennis, made with the back of one's hand towards one's opponent; the side of the court or player on which such strokes are made.

backhanded *adj.* **1** delivered with the back of the hand. **2** (of a compliment) oblique, ambiguous.

backhander *n.* **1** a back-handed stroke. **2** (*slang*) a reward for services rendered, a bribe.

backing *n.* **1** support, encouragement; a body of supporters. **2** material used to support or line the back of something. **3** a musical accompaniment to a singer. [f. BACK[2]]

backlash *n.* a violent usually hostile reaction.

backless *adj.* without a back; (of a dress) cut low at the back. [f. BACK[1] + -LESS]

backlog *n.* arrears of uncompleted work etc. (orig. = a large log placed at the back of a fire to sustain it).

backpack *n.* a rucksack; a package of equipment carried similarly.

back-pedal *v.i.* (-**ll**-) **1** to work the pedals of a bicycle backwards. **2** to reverse one's previous action or opinion.

backside *n.* (*colloq.*) the buttocks.

backslide *v.i.* to relapse into error or bad ways.

backspace *v.i.* to cause a typewriter carriage or 'golf ball' to move backwards one space.

backstage *adj.* & *adv.* behind the curtain of a theatre, especially in the wings or dressing-rooms.

backstitch *v.t./i.* to sew by inserting the needle each time behind the place where it has just been brought out. —*n.* a stitch made in this way.

backstroke *n.* a swimming stroke performed on the back.

backtrack *v.i.* to retrace one's steps; to reverse one's action.

backward /ˈbækwəd/ *adj.* **1** directed towards the back or to the starting-point. **2** slow to make (mental etc.) progress. **3** lacking confidence to come forward, shy. —*adv.* backwards. —**backwardness** *n.* [earlier *abackward*]

backwards /ˈbækwədz/ *adv.* **1** towards the direction away from one's front; back foremost. **2** (of the motion of a thing) towards its starting-point. **3** in the reverse of the usual order; into a worse state; into the past. —**bend** *or* **lean over backwards,** to go to great lengths (*to*). **know something backwards,** to know it exhaustively. [as prec.]

backwash *n.* receding waves created by a moving ship.

backwater *n.* **1** a stretch of stagnant water beside a stream. **2** a place indifferent to progress or new ideas.

backwoods *n.* **1** remote uncleared forest, as in North America. **2** a remote or backward area. —**backwoodsman** *n.* (*pl.* **-men**)

backyard *n.* a yard at the back of a house.

bacon /ˈbeɪkən/ *n.* dried and salted meat from the back or side of a pig. —**bring home the bacon,** (*slang*) to succeed in an undertaking. **save one's bacon,** (*slang*) to escape injury or punishment. [f. OF]

bactericide /bækˈtɪərɪsaɪd/ *n.* a substance that kills bacteria. —**bactericidal** *adj.* [f. BACTERIUM + -CIDE]

bacteriology /bæktɪərɪˈɒlədʒɪ/ *n.* the scientific

study of bacteria. —**bacteriological** /-ˈlɒdʒɪk(ə)l/ *adj.*, **bacteriologist** *n.* [f. foll. + -LOGY]

bacterium /bækˈtɪərɪəm/ *n.* (*pl.* **-ia**) any of several types of microscopic or ultra-microscopic single-celled organisms. —**bacterial** *adj.* [f. Gk *baktērion* dim. of *baktron* stick]

bad *adj.* (*compar.* WORSE, *superl.* WORST) **1** of poor quality, defective. **2** putrid, decaying. **3** in poor health, injured. **4** morally defective, wicked; (of a child) naughty. **5** unwelcome, disagreeable; harmful, detrimental; (of something unwelcome) serious, severe. —*adv.* (*US*) badly. —**bad blood,** unfriendly feelings. **bad debt,** one not recoverable. **bad language,** swear-words. **feel bad about,** to feel guilt or remorse about. **go to the bad,** to become criminal, dissolute, or immoral. **not bad,** (*colloq.*) good, fairly good. —**badness** *n.* [perh. f. OE *bæddel* hermaphrodite, womanish man]

bade /bæd, beɪd/ *past* of BID.

badge *n.* something worn to show one's rank, membership, etc. [orig. unkn.]

badger /ˈbædʒə(r)/ *n.* a grey nocturnal burrowing animal of the weasel family. —*v.t.* to pester. [perh. f. BADGE, from the distinctive markings on its head]

badinage /ˈbædɪnɑːʒ/ *n.* good-humoured mockery. [F]

badly *adv.* (**worse, worst**) **1** defectively, improperly. **2** so as to inflict much injury, severely. **3** (*colloq.*) very much. [f. BAD]

badminton /ˈbædmɪnt(ə)n/ *n.* a volleying game played by one or two players opposing an equivalent number across a net, using rackets and a shuttlecock. [f. *Badminton* in Avon]

baffle *v.t.* **1** to perplex, to bewilder. **2** to frustrate. —*n.* a screen preventing the passage of sound etc. —**bafflement** *n.* [orig. unkn.]

bag *n.* **1** a receptacle for carrying things, made of flexible material with an opening at the top; this with its contents. **2** anything resembling this, as loose folds of skin under the eyes. **3** the total number of game shot by a sportsman. **4** (in *pl.*, *slang*) a great quantity *of*. —*v.t.* (**-gg-**) **1** to put in a bag. **2** (*slang*) to secure possession of. —**bag and baggage,** with all one's belongings. **in the bag,** as good as secured. —**bagful** *n.* (*pl.* **-fuls**) [perh. f. ON]

bagatelle /bægəˈtel/ *n.* **1** a board game in which small balls are struck into holes. **2** a thing of no importance. **3** a short piece of music, especially for the piano. [F f. It.]

baggage /ˈbægɪdʒ/ *n.* **1** luggage, especially that carried by sea or air. **2** the portable equipment of an army. [f. OF (*bagues* bundles)]

baggy *adj.* hanging in loose folds. [f. BAG]

bagpipe *n.* (also in *pl.*) an instrument with reeds that are sounded by the pressure of wind emitted from a bag squeezed by the player's arm and fed with air either by breath or by means of small bellows strapped to the waist.

bah /bɑː/ *int.* expressing contempt or disgust. [prob. f. F]

Baha'i /bɑːˈhɑːɪ/ *n.* a monotheistic religion, or a follower of this, founded in Persia in the 19th c. by Baha-ullah (1817-92) and his son Abdul Baha (1844-1921). —**Baha'ism** *n.* [f. Pers. *bahā* splendour]

bail[1] *n.* **1** money or property pledged as security that an arrested person will appear in court to stand trial if released temporarily. **2** permission for a person's release on such security. —*v.t.* to procure the release of (an arrested person) by becoming security for him or her. —**bail out,** to rescue from financial difficulties. —**on bail,** released after bail is pledged. [f. OF (*bailler* take charge of) f. L *baiulare* carry a load]

bail[2] *n.* **1** (in cricket) either of the two cross-pieces resting on the three stumps of the wicket. **2** a bar separating horses in an open stable. **3** a bar holding paper against the platen of a typewriter. [f. OF *bailler* enclose]

bail[3] *v.t.* to scoop out (water) that has entered a boat; to clear (a boat) of water. [f. F *baille* bucket]

bailey /ˈbeɪlɪ/ *n.* the outer wall of a castle; a court enclosed by this. [rel. to BAIL[2]]

Bailey bridge /ˈbeɪlɪ/ a bridge made in prefabricated sections designed for rapid assembly. [f. D. C. *Bailey* (d. 1985), the designer]

bailie /ˈbeɪlɪ/ *n.* a municipal officer and magistrate in Scotland. [as foll.]

bailiff /ˈbeɪlɪf/ *n.* **1** a sheriff's officer who serves writs and performs arrests. **2** a landlord's agent or steward. **3** the leading civil officer in each of the Channel Islands. [f. OF f. L (*baiulus* manager)]

bailiwick /ˈbeɪlɪwɪk/ *n.* the jurisdiction of a bailie or (in the Channel Islands) a bailiff. [f. BAILIE + *wick* district]

bain-marie /bæ̃mæˈriː/ *n.* a vessel of hot water in which a dish of food is placed for slow cooking. [F f. L *balneum mariae* bath of Mary (supposed Jewish alchemist)]

Bairam /baɪˈrɑːm/ *n.* either of two annual Muslim festivals, **Greater Bairam,** celebrated concurrently with the annual pilgrimage (*hadj*) in the twelfth month of the Muslim lunar calendar and continuing for 3-4 days, and **Lesser Bairam,** which follows the month of ritual fasting (Ramadan), the ninth month of the year, and lasts 2-3 days. [Turk. & Pers.]

bairn /beən/ *n.* (*Sc.*) a child. [OE, rel. to BEAR[1]]

bait *n.* food (real or sham) used to entice fish etc.; an enticement. *—v.t.* **1** to put bait on or in (a fish-hook, trap, etc.). **2** to attack (a chained bear etc.) with dogs for sport; to torment or provoke. [f. ON, rel. to BITE]

baize *n.* a coarse usually green woollen material used to cover tables, doors, etc. [f. F *bai* chestnut-coloured]

bake *v.t./i.* **1** to cook or be cooked by dry heat, especially in an oven. **2** to harden or be hardened by exposure to heat. **—baked beans,** cooked haricot beans (usually tinned and prepared with tomato sauce). [OE]

bakehouse *n* a house or room for baking bread.

bakelite /ˈbeɪk(ə)laɪt/ *n.* a plastic made from phenol etc. and formaldehyde, used in electrical appliances etc. as an insulator. [G, f. L. H. *Baekeland* Belgian-American inventor (d. 1944)]

baker *n.* one who bakes and sells bread. **—baker's dozen,** thirteen (from the old custom of giving the retailer a free loaf for every twelve he bought). [f. BAKE]

bakery *n.* a place where bread is made or sold. [as prec.]

Bakewell tart /ˈbeɪkwel/ a tart containing an almond-flavoured pudding mixture over a layer of jam. [town in Derbyshire]

baking *adj.* (*colloq.*, of weather etc.) intolerably hot. [f. BAKE]

baking-powder *n.* a mixture of sodium bicarbonate, cream of tartar, etc., used as a raising agent

baksheesh /bækˈʃi:ʃ/ *n.* (in the Middle East) a gratuity, alms. [Pers.]

Balaclava /bæləˈklɑ:və/ *n.* (in full **Balaclava helmet**) a knitted cap covering the head and neck, with an opening for the face. [f. *Balaclava* in the Crimea, site of a battle in 1854]

balalaika /bæləˈlaɪkə/ *n.* a guitar-like instrument (made in various sizes) with a triangular body, popular in Slavonic countries. [Russ.]

balance /ˈbæləns/ *n.* **1** a weighing-apparatus with two scales or pans hanging from a cross-bar. **2** (also **balance-wheel**) a mechanism regulating the speed of a clock or watch. **3** the stable condition arising from even distribution of weight or amount. **4** a preponderating weight or amount. **5** the agreement or difference between credits and debits; a statement of this. **6** the difference between a sum paid and a sum due; the amount left over. *—v.t./i.* **1** to offset, to weigh (considerations etc.) against each other. **2** to distribute (weights) evenly; to be, put, or keep in a state of balance. **3** to compare the credit and debit sides of (an account) and make any necessary entry to equalize them; (of an account) to have its two sides equal. **—balance of payments,** the difference in value between the amount paid by a country for its imports and that paid to it for its exports (including invisible earnings). **balance of power,** a situation in which the chief States have roughly equal power; the power to decide events, held by a small group when the larger groups are of equal strength to each other. **balance of trade,** the difference in value between imports and exports. **balance sheet,** a written statement of assets and liabilities. **in the balance,** with the outcome still undecided. **on balance,** taking all things into consideration. [f. OF f. L *bilanx* two-scaled (balance) (BI-, *lanx* scale)]

balcony /ˈbælkənɪ/ *n.* **1** a platform with a rail or balustrade, on the outside of a building, with access from an upper-storey door or window. **2** an upper tier of seats in a cinema or above the dress circle in a theatre. [f. It., as BALK]

bald /bɔ:ld/ *adj.* **1** with a hairless scalp; (of animals etc.) lacking the usual hairs, feathers, etc. of the species. **2** (of a tyre) having its tread worn away. **3** (of style) plain and unelaborated. **—bald eagle,** a kind of eagle (*Haliaetus leucocephalus*) with white feathers on its head and neck, the emblematic bird of the USA. [orig. unkn.]

baldachin /ˈbældəkɪn/ *n.* (also **baldaquin**) a canopy over a throne etc. [f. It. *Baldaco* (=Baghdad), where the original brocade of the canopy was made]

balderdash /ˈbɔ:ldədæʃ/ *n.* nonsense. [earlier sense (16th c.) 'frothy liquid'; orig. unkn.]

balding /ˈbɔ:ldɪŋ/ *adj.* becoming bald. [f. BALD]

baldric /ˈbɔ:ldrɪk/ *n.* a strap, worn across the body, on which a shield or sword is hung. [f. OF *baudrei*]

bale[1] *n.* a large bundle of merchandise (e.g. cloth) or hay. *—v.t.* to make into a bale. **—baler** *n.* [f. MDu., rel. to BALL[1]]

bale[2] *v.i.* **bale out,** to escape from an aircraft by parachute. [=BAIL[1]]

baleen /bæˈli:n/ *n.* whalebone. [f. OF f. L *balaena* whale]

baleful /ˈbeɪlfəl/ *adj.* having a deadly or malign influence. **—balefully** *adv.* [f. *bale* (OE *b(e)alu*) destruction, evil]

balk /bɔ:k/ *v.t./i.* **1** to shy or jib *at.* **2** to thwart. [= BAULK]

Balkan /ˈbɔ:lkən, ˈbɒl-/ *adj.* of the peninsula of SE Europe, south of the Danube and Sava rivers, or its peoples or countries. [Turk.]

ball[1] /bɔ:l/ *n.* **1** a rounded object, solid or hollow, especially for use in a game. **2** a single delivery of a ball by a bowler in cricket or a pitcher in baseball. **3** a rounded mass or part; (in *pl.*, *vulg.*) the testicles. —*v.t./i.* to form into a ball. —**ball (and socket) joint,** a form of joint with a rounded end in a concave cup or socket, having great freedom of movement. **ball-bearing** *n.* a bearing using small steel balls. **ball-point (pen),** a pen with a tiny ball as its writing-point. **on the ball,** (*colloq.*) alert. **set the ball rolling,** to open a discussion. [f. ON]

ball[2] /bɔ:l/ *n.* a formal social gathering for dancing. [f. F f. L f. Gk]

ballad /ˈbæləd/ *n.* a simple song, especially one with a repeated melody; a poem or song in short stanzas telling a story. [f. OF f. Prov. *balada* dancing-song (as BALL[2])]

ballade /bæˈlɑ:d/ *n.* a poem with one or more sets of three verses with 7, 8, or 10 lines each ending with the same refrain line, and a short final verse. [F, = prec.]

balladeer /bæləˈdɪə(r)/ *n.* a composer or performer of ballads. [f. BALLAD]

ballast /ˈbæləst/ *n.* **1** heavy material placed in the hold of a ship or the car of a balloon to give it stability. **2** coarse stones etc. forming the bed of a railway or road. —*v.t.* to weight with ballast. [f. LG or Scand.]

ballcock *n.* a device with a floating ball controlling the water-level in a cistern.

ballerina /bæləˈri:nə/ *n.* a woman ballet-dancer, especially one taking leading roles in classical ballet. [It. (*ballare* dance)]

ballet /ˈbæleɪ/ *n.* a form of dancing and mime to music; a performance of this. [F f. It. (as BALL[2])]

balletomane /ˈbælɪtəmeɪn/ *n.* a ballet enthusiast. [f. prec. + *-mane* (as MANIA)]

ballista /bəˈlɪstə/ *n.* (*pl.* **-ae**) a machine of ancient warfare for hurling large stones etc. [L, f. Gk *ballō* throw]

ballistic /bəˈlɪstɪk/ *adj.* of projectiles. —**ballistic missile,** one powered only during the initial stages of its flight and falling by gravity on its target. [f. prec.]

ballistics *n.* the science of projectiles and firearms. [f. prec.]

balloon /bəˈlu:n/ *n.* **1** a small inflatable rubber bag with a neck, used as a child's toy or decoration. **2** a large rounded envelope inflated with hot air or gas to make it rise in the air, often one with a basket etc. for passengers. **3** a balloon-shaped line containing the words or thoughts of a character in a comic strip or cartoon. —*v.t./i.* **1** to swell out like a balloon. **2** to travel by balloon. **3** to hit or kick (a ball) high in the air. [f. F or It. (*balla* ball)]

balloonist *n.* one who travels by balloon. [f. prec.]

ballot /ˈbælət/ *n.* the process of voting to select a representative or course of action etc. usually in secret and on ballot-papers; the total of votes cast by this method. —*v.t./i.* to vote or cause to vote by ballot. —**ballot-box** *n.* a container for ballot-papers. **ballot-paper** *n.* a paper used in voting by ballot, usually having the names of candidates etc. printed on it. [f. It., = small ball; such voting was orig. by small balls]

ballroom *n.* a large room for formal dancing.

bally /ˈbælɪ/ *adj.* & *adv.* (*colloq.*) a milder form of intensive 'bloody'. [voicing of *bl—y*, squeamish printing of BLOODY]

ballyhoo /bælɪˈhu:/ *n.* loud noise, fuss; extravagant publicity. [orig. unkn.]

balm /bɑ:m/ *n.* **1** a fragrant medicinal gum exuded by certain trees, balsam. **2** an aromatic ointment. **3** a healing or soothing influence. **4** a herb (*Melissa officinalis*) with lemon-scented leaves. [f. OF f. L, = BALSAM]

balmy /ˈbɑ:mɪ/ *adj.* **1** resembling balm, fragrant or soothing; (of air) soft and warm. **2** (*slang*) = BARMY. [f. BALM]

baloney /bəˈləʊnɪ/ *n.* var. of BOLONEY.

balsa /ˈbɔ:lsə/ *n.* (also **balsa-wood**) a very light strong wood from a tropical American tree (*Ochroma pyramidale*), used for models etc. [Sp., = raft]

balsam /ˈbɔ:lsəm/ *n.* **1** a resinous exudation from certain trees, balm; an ointment, especially of a substance dissolved in oil or turpentine; a tree producing balsam. **2** any of various flowering plants of the genus *Impatiens*, especially one cultivated for its showy flowers. [OE f. L *balsamum*]

Baltic /ˈbɔ:ltɪk, ˈbɒl-/ *adj.* of the Baltic Sea, an almost landlocked sea of NE Europe. —*n.* the Baltic Sea. [f. L (*Balthae* dwellers near the Baltic Sea)]

baluster /ˈbæləstə(r)/ *n.* a short pillar with a curving outline, especially in a balustrade; a post helping to support a rail. [f. F, ult. f. Gk *balaustion* flower of wild pomegranate, from resemblance in shape]

balustrade /bæləˈstreɪd/ *n.* a row of balusters with a rail or coping as an ornamental parapet to a balcony, terrace, etc. [F, as prec.]

bamboo /bæmˈbu:/ *n.* any of a large group of tree-like grasses of the genus *Bambusa*, especially characteristic of eastern Asia; its hollow stem used to make canes, furniture, etc., or as food. [f. Du. f. Port. *Mambu*, f. Malay]

bamboozle /bæmˈbu:z(ə)l/ *v.t.* (*colloq.*) to hoax, to cheat; to mystify, to perplex. —**bamboozlement** *n.* [orig. unkn.]

ban *v.t.* (**-nn-**) to prohibit officially (*from*); to forbid. —*n.* an official prohibition. [OE, = summon]

banal /bəˈnɑ:l/ *adj.* commonplace, trite.

—**banality** /bəˈnælɪtɪ/ *n.* [F (as BAN); orig. = 'compulsory', hence = 'common to all']

banana /bəˈnɑːnə/ *n.* a long finger-shaped yellow fruit; the tropical tree (*Musa sapientum*) bearing it. —**banana republic,** (*derog.*) a small tropical country dependent on its fruit exports and regarded as economically unstable. [Port. or Sp., f. Afr. name]

band[1] *n.* **1** a narrow strip, hoop, or loop. **2** a range of values, wavelengths, etc. between two given limits. —*v.t.* to put a band on or round. —**band-saw** *n.* a power saw consisting of a toothed steel belt running over wheels. [f. ON, rel. to BIND]

band[2] *n.* **1** an organized group of people with a common purpose. **2** a group of musicians (especially players of wind and percussion instruments) organized for playing together. —*v.t./i.* to unite in an organized group. [f. OF, perh. f. Goth. *bandwa* signal]

bandage /ˈbændɪdʒ/ *n.* a strip of material used to bind a wound. —*v.t.* to bind with a bandage. [F, as BAND[1]]

bandanna /bænˈdænə/ *n.* a large handkerchief with spots or other pattern. [f. Hindi, = tie-dyeing (rel. to BAND[1], BIND)]

bandbox *n.* a box for hats etc.

bandeau /ˈbændəʊ/ *n.* (*pl.* **-eaux** /-əʊz/) a strip of material worn round the hair or inside a hat. [F, as BAND[1]]

bandicoot /ˈbændɪkuːt/ *n.* **1** a kind of very large rat (*Bandicota indica*) in India. **2** a ratlike Australasian marsupial of the family Peramelidae. [Telugu, = pig-rat]

bandit *n.* a robber or outlaw, especially one of a gang attacking travellers. —**banditry** *n.* [f. It., = outlawed (as BANISH)]

bandmaster *n.* the conductor of a musical band.

bandoleer, bandolier /bændəˈlɪə(r)/ *n.* a shoulder-belt with loops for ammunition. [f. Du. or F, prob. rel. to BANNER]

bandstand *n.* a platform for musicians, especially outdoors.

bandwagon /ˈbændwægən/ *n.* a wagon for a band of musicians to ride in, as in a parade. —**climb** *or* **jump on the bandwagon,** to attach oneself to a successful party or cause.

bandwidth *n.* (in telecommunications etc.) a range of frequencies.

bandy[1] *v.t.* to exchange (words etc. *with*); to pass on (a rumour etc.) thoughtlessly. —*n.* a game resembling ice hockey but played with a ball not a puck. [perh. f. F *bander* take sides, oppose]

bandy[2] *adj.* (of legs) curving apart at the knees. [perh. f. obs. *bandy* hockey-stick]

bane *n.* **1** a cause of ruin or trouble. **2** (*archaic*) a poison (now only in plant-names, as *henbane*). —**baneful** *adj.* [OE]

bang *v.t./i.* **1** to make a sudden loud noise like an explosion; to strike or shut noisily. **2** to collide. —*n.* **1** a banging noise. **2** a sharp blow. —*adv.* **1** with a banging sound. **2** (*colloq.*) abruptly, exactly. [imit.]

banger *n.* anything that makes a loud bang, as a firework; (*colloq.*) a noisy old car; (*slang*) a sausage. [f. BANG]

bangle *n.* a large decorative ring worn round the arm or ankle. [f. Hindi *bangrī*]

banian /ˈbænjən/ *n.* an Indian fig-tree (*Ficus benghalensis*) with spreading branches from which roots grow downwards to the ground and form new trunks. [Port. f. Skr., = trader (from such a tree under which traders built a pagoda)]

banish *v.t.* **1** to condemn to exile. **2** to dismiss from one's mind or presence. —**banishment** *n.* [f. OF, rel. to BAN]

banister /ˈbænɪstə(r)/ *n.* any of the posts supporting a stair handrail; (in *pl.*) these posts together with the rail. [corrupt. of BALUSTER]

banjo /ˈbændʒəʊ/ *n.* (*pl.* **-os**) a stringed instrument like a guitar, with a circular body. —**banjoist** *n.* [corrupt. of earlier *bandore*, ult. f. Gk *pandoura* three-stringed lute]

bank[1] *n.* **1** a stretch of sloping ground, especially that on either side of a river. **2** a raised mass of sand etc. in the bed of the sea or of a river. **3** a flat-topped mass of snow or cloud. —*v.t./i.* **1** to provide with or form a bank. **2** to heap; to pile coal-dust etc. on (a fire) so that it burns slowly. **3** to tilt laterally in rounding a curve. [f. ON, rel. to BENCH]

bank[2] *n.* **1** an establishment where money is deposited in accounts, withdrawn, and borrowed. **2** a place for storing a reserve supply (e.g. of blood). **3** the pool of money in a gambling-game. —*v.t./i.* to deposit (money) at a bank; to have an account *at* or *with* a bank. —**bank holiday,** a weekday kept as a public holiday, when banks are officially closed. [f. F or It. (as foll.), referring to the fact that early bankers transacted their business at a bench (*banco*) in the market-place]

bank[3] *n.* a series of similar objects grouped in a row; a tier of oars in a galley. [f. OF *banc* bench (as BANK[1])]

banker *n.* **1** one who runs a bank. **2** the keeper of the bank in a gambling-game. [f. BANK[2]]

banking *n.* the business of running a bank. [f. BANK[2]]

banknote *n.* a strip of paper serving as currency, originally a promissory note from a bank.

bankrupt /ˈbæŋkrʌpt/ *adj.* **1** declared by a court of law to be unable to meet debts in full, the estate therefore being administered on behalf of creditors; financially ruined, insolvent. **2** destitute *of*. —*n*. a person officially declared bankrupt. —*v.t.* to make bankrupt. —**bankruptcy** *n*. [f. It., = broken bench (cf. BANK²)]

banner *n*. **1** a large cloth carrying an emblem or slogan, carried on a crossbar or between two poles at public demonstrations. **2** the flag of a king, knight, etc., serving as a rallying-point. —**banner headline,** one extending across a newspaper page. [f. AF f. L *bandum* standard]

bannock /ˈbænək/ *n*. (*Sc. & N. Engl.*) a round flat loaf, usually unleavened. [OE]

banns *n.pl.* an announcement in church, usually read out on three successive Sundays, of an intended marriage, to give opportunity of objection. [pl. of BAN]

banquet /ˈbæŋkwɪt/ *n*. a sumptuous meal; an elaborate and formal dinner. —*v.i.* to take part in a banquet. —**banqueter** *n*. [f. F, dim. of *banc* bench]

banshee /ˈbænʃi:/ *n*. (*Ir. & Sc.*) a female spirit whose wail outside a house is superstitiously believed to portend death within. [Ir., = woman of the fairies]

bantam /ˈbæntəm/ *n*. a kind of small domestic fowl, of which the cock is very pugnacious. [f. *Bantam* seaport in Java]

bantamweight *n*. a boxing-weight between flyweight and featherweight (see BOXING-WEIGHT).

banter *n*. playful good-humoured teasing. —*v.t./i.* to exchange banter, to joke in a good-humoured way; to chaff. [orig. unkn.]

Bantu /bænˈtu:/ *n*. (*pl.* same or **-us**) **1** a large group of Black peoples in central and southern Africa; a member of this group. **2** the group of languages spoken by them. —*adj*. of the Bantu or their languages. [Bantu, = people]

Bantustan /bæntu:ˈstɑ:n/ *n*. any of the territories, officially called Bantu homelands, reserved for Black Africans in the Republic of South Africa. [f. prec. + *-stan* (as in HINDUSTANI)]

banyan /ˈbænɪən/ *n*. var. of BANIAN.

baobab /ˈbeɪəʊbæb/ *n*. an African tree (*Adansonia digitata*) with a massive trunk and large edible pulpy fruit. [prob. native name]

bap *n*. a soft flat bread roll. [Sc.; orig. unkn.]

baptism /ˈbæptɪz(ə)m/ *n*. admission to the Church by the rite of sprinkling with or immersing in water, chiefly administered to infants, with name-giving. —**baptism of fire,** initiation in a painful experience, such as exposure to gunfire. —**baptismal** /-ˈtɪzm(ə)l/ *adj*. [as BAPTIZE]

Baptist /ˈbæptɪst/ *n*. **1** a member of a Christian sect practising baptism of adults by immersion (see below). **2 the Baptist,** the title of St John who baptized Christ. [as BAPTIZE]

baptistery /ˈbæptɪstərɪ/ *n*. a part of a church, or (formerly) a separate building, used for baptism; an immersion receptacle in a Baptist chapel. [f. Gk *baptistērion* bathing-place (as foll.)]

baptize /bæpˈtaɪz/ *v.t.* **1** to administer baptism to, to christen. **2** to name or nickname. [f. OF f. L f. Gk *baptizō* immerse, baptize]

bar¹ *n*. **1** a long piece of rigid material; an oblong piece (of chocolate, soap, etc.); the heating element of an electric fire. **2** a strip of silver below the clasp of a medal, serving as an extra distinction. **3** a band of colour etc., a stripe. **4** a rod or pole that fastens, confines, or obstructs something; a barrier; a sandbank or shoal at the mouth of a harbour or estuary; a restriction. **5** (*Mus.*) any of the vertical lines dividing a piece of music into equal units; a section between two of these. **6** a partition (real or imaginary) across a lawcourt, separating the judge, jury, and certain lawyers from the public; **the Bar,** barristers. **7** a counter across which alcoholic drinks are served; the room containing this; a counter for special service (e.g. *heel bar* for shoe repairs). —*v.t.* (**-rr-**) **1** to fasten with a bar, bolt, etc.; to shut *in* or *out*. **2** to obstruct, prevent, or prohibit; to exclude. —*prep*. excluding. [f. OF *barre*]

bar² *n*. a unit of pressure, 10^5 newton per sq. metre, approximately one atmosphere, used especially in meteorology. [f. Gk. *baros* weight]

barathea /bærəˈθi:ə/ *n*. a kind of fine cloth, especially of wool woven with silk. [orig. unkn.]

barb *n*. **1** a small spine curving back from the point of an arrow or fish-hook, making it difficult to withdraw from what it has pierced. **2** a wounding remark. **3** a fleshy appendage from the mouth of some fishes. **4** a lateral filament branching from the shaft of a feather. [f. OF f. L. *barba* beard]

barbarian /bɑ:ˈbeərɪən/ *n*. an uncivilized person. —*adj*. uncivilized. [as BARBAROUS]

barbaric /bɑ:ˈbærɪk/ *adj*. typical of a barbarian, rough and unrefined. [as BARBAROUS]

barbarism /ˈbɑ:bərɪz(ə)m/ *n*. **1** an uncivilized condition or practice. **2** an unacceptable linguistic usage. [as BARBAROUS]

barbarity /bɑ:ˈbærɪtɪ/ *n*. savage cruelty; a savagely cruel act. [as BARBAROUS.]

barbarous /ˈbɑ:bərəs/ *adj*. uncivilized; savagely cruel. —**barbarously** *adv*. [f. L. f. Gk, orig. = non-Greek, then = outside the Romano-Greek world]

barbecue /ˈbɑːbɪkjuː/ *n.* a metal frame or portable grill for cooking meat, especially over an open fire; meat so cooked; an open-air party using this. *—v.t.* to cook on a barbecue. [f. Sp. f. Haitian]

barbed *adj.* **1** furnished with a barb or barbs. **2** (of remarks) having cruel undertones. **—barbed wire,** wire set with small spikes, used as fencing. [f. BARB]

barbel /ˈbɑːb(ə)l/ *n.* **1** a beardlike filament at the mouth of some fishes. **2** a large European freshwater fish of the genus *Barbus* with such filaments. [f. OF (as BARB)]

barbell *n.* a metal rod used in weight-lifting, with adjustable weighted discs at either end.

barber *n.* a men's hairdresser. **—barber-shop** *adj.* of a style of highly chromatic part-singing by male quartets. [AF f. L *barba* beard].

barbican /ˈbɑːbɪkən/ *n.* an outer defence of a castle or city, especially a double tower over a gate or bridge. [f. OF; orig. unkn.]

barbiturate /bɑːˈbɪtjʊrət/ *n.* a soporific and sedative drug derived from barbituric acid. [f. foll.]

barbituric acid /bɑːbɪˈtjʊərɪk/ an acid, malonyl urea, from which barbiturates are derived. [f. F f. G, f. *Barbara* woman's name]

barbule /ˈbɑːbjuːl/ *n.* a filament branching from the barb of a feather. [f. L (dim. of *barba* beard)]

barcarole /bɑːkəˈrɒl, -ˈrəʊl/ *n.* **1** a gondolier's song. **2** a piece of music with steady lilting rhythm, especially for piano. [f. F f. It. (*barca* boat)]

bard[1] *n.* **1** a Celtic minstrel; a Welsh poet honoured at an Eisteddfod. **2** (*archaic*) a poet. **—the Bard of Avon,** Shakespeare. [Celtic]

bard[2] *v.t.* to place slices of bacon over (meat etc.) before roasting. [f. F *barde* (orig. = horse's breastplate), ult. f. Arab.]

bare *adj.* **1** not clothed, not covered; scantily furnished. **2** empty. **3** plain, not elaborated. **4** scanty, only just sufficient. *—v.t.* to uncover, to reveal. **—barely** *adv.*, **bareness** *n.* [OE]

bareback *adj.* & *adv.* on a horse without a saddle.

barefaced *adj.* shameless, impudent.

barefoot *adj.* & *adv.* without shoes, stockings, etc., on the feet.

bareheaded *adj.* without a hat.

barely *adv.* scarcely, only just. [f. BARE]

bargain /ˈbɑːgɪn/ *n.* an agreement made with obligations on both sides, or on the terms of a sale; something obtained as a result of this, a thing got cheaply. *—v.i.* **1** to discuss the terms of a sale or agreement. **2** to expect or be prepared *for*. [f. OF *bargaignier*]

barge *n.* a long flat-bottomed boat carrying freight on rivers or canals; a large ornamental boat for State occasions etc. *—v.i.* to lurch or move clumsily *into, around*, etc. **—barge in,** to intrude without ceremony. [f. OF, perh. f. L & rel. to BARQUE]

barge-board *n.* a board or ornamental screen under the edge of a gable. [orig. unkn.]

bargee /bɑːˈdʒiː/ *n.* a person in charge of a barge (for freight); a member of its crew. [f. BARGE]

baritone /ˈbærɪtəʊn/ *n.* a male voice between tenor and bass; a singer having such a voice; a part written for it. [f. It. f. Gk *barus* heavy]

barium /ˈbeərɪəm/ *n.* a silver-white metallic element of the alkaline-earth metal group, symbol Ba, atomic number 56. **—barium meal,** a mixture including barium sulphate, which is opaque to X-rays, used in radiography of the alimentary canal. [f. BARYTA]

bark[1] *n.* the tough outer skin of the trunks and branches of trees. *—v.t.* **1** to strip bark from (trees). **2** to scrape the skin off (part of the body) accidentally. [f. Scand., perh. rel. to BIRCH]

bark[2] *v.t./i.* **1** (of a dog or fox) to utter a sharp explosive cry. **2** to speak or utter in a sharp commanding tone. *—n.* a sound of or like barking. **—bark up the wrong tree,** to direct one's efforts to the wrong quarter. [OE, perh. var. of BREAK]

barley /ˈbɑːlɪ/ *n.* a cereal plant of the genus *Hordeum*, or its grain, used as food and in making malt liquors and spirits. **—barley sugar,** a sweet made of boiled sugar. **barley-water** *n.* a drink made from pearl barley (see PEARL). [OE]

barmaid *n.* a woman who serves behind the bar of a public house etc.

barman *n.* (*pl.* **-men**) a man who serves behind the bar of a public house etc.

bar mitzvah /ˈmɪtzvə/ **1** a Jewish boy aged 13 when he takes on the responsibilities of an adult under the Jewish law. **2** the solemnization of this event by calling upon the boy to read from the Scriptures in a synagogue service. [Heb., = son of commandment]

barmy *adj.* (*slang*) crazy. [f. OE *barm* froth on top of fermenting liquor]

barn *n.* a simple roofed building for storing grain etc. on a farm. **—barn dance,** a kind of country dance; a social gathering for dancing, originally held in a barn. **barn owl,** a kind of owl, brownish above with white under-parts. [OE, = barley-house]

barnacle /ˈbɑːnək(ə)l/ *n.* a shellfish that clings to coastal rocks, ships' bottoms, etc. **—barnacle goose,** an Arctic goose (*Branta Leucopsis*) visiting Britain in winter. [orig. unkn.]

barney /ˈbɑːnɪ/ *n.* (*slang*) a noisy dispute. [orig. unkn.; perh. dial.]

barnstorm *v.i.* to travel through rural areas as an actor or political campaigner. —**barnstormer** *n.*

barograph /ˈbærəgrɑːf/ *n.* a self-recording barometer. [as foll. + Gk *grapho* write]

barometer /bəˈrɒmɪtə(r)/ *n.* an instrument measuring atmospheric pressure, used to forecast weather. —**barometric** /bærəˈmetrɪk/ *adj.* [f. Gk *baros* weight, *metron* measure]

baron /ˈbærən/ *n.* **1** a member of the lowest order of the British peerage, styled *Lord* —; a foreign nobleman of equivalent rank (styled *Baron* —). **2** one who controls the trade in a specified commodity, a magnate. **3** (*hist.*) one who held land from the king in the Middle Ages. —**baroness** *n.fem.* [f. AF f. L *baro* man (prob. = free man or king's man; orig. not a title of dignity)]

baronet /ˈbærənɪt/ *n.* a member of the lowest hereditary titled British order, ranking next below a baron. —**baronetcy** *n.* [f. BARON]

baronial /bəˈrəunɪəl/ *adj.* of or suitable for a baron. [as prec.]

barony /ˈbærənɪ/ *n.* the rank or domain of a baron. [f. BARON]

baroque /bəˈrɒk/ *adj.* of the ornate style of architecture and art of the 17th and 18th c.; of comparable musical developments *c.*1600-1750. —*n.* baroque style or ornamentation; baroque art collectively. [F f. Port., orig. = misshapen pearl]

barouche /bəˈruːʃ/ *n.* a four-wheeled horse-drawn carriage with seats for two couples facing each other. [f. G f. It. f. L *birotus* (BI-, *rota* wheel)]

barque /bɑːk/ *n.* a sailing-ship square-rigged on the foremast and mainmast and fore-and-aft rigged on the mizen. [f. F, prob. f. L *barca* ship's boat]

barquentine /ˈbɑːkəntiːn/ *n.* a three-masted vessel with the foremast square-rigged, the main and mizen fore-and-aft rigged. [f. prec., after *brigantine*]

barrack /ˈbærək/ *v.t./i.* (of spectators etc.) to shout derisively (at). [prob. = Austral. sl. *borak* banter, of Aboriginal orig.]

barracks /ˈbærəks/ *n.* a large building or group of buildings in which soldiers are housed; a large plain and ugly building. —**barrack-room lawyer,** a pompously argumentative person. [f. F f. It. or Sp., = soldier's tent]

barracuda /bærəˈkuːdə/ *n.* **1** a large voracious West Indian sea-fish of the family Sphyraenidae. **2** (also **barracouta** /-ˈkuːtə/) a long slender sea-fish (*Thyrsites atun*) of the Pacific etc. (In South Africa the same fish is called *snoek*.) [Amer. Sp.]

barrage /ˈbærɑːʒ/ *n.* **1** a heavy continuous artillery bombardment; a rapid succession of criticisms, questions, etc. **2** an artificial barrier in a river, acting as a dam. —**barrage balloon,** a large balloon anchored to the ground, as part of a barrier against aircraft. [F, as BAR[1]]

barratry /ˈbærətrɪ/ *n.* fraud or culpable negligence by a ship's master or crew at the expense of the owner or insurer. [f. OF (*barat* deceit)]

barre /bɑː(r)/ *n.* a horizontal bar at waist-level, used by dancers to steady themselves when exercising. [F, = BAR[1]]

barrel /ˈbær(ə)l/ *n.* **1** a large rounded usually wooden container for liquids etc., with slightly bulging sides and flat circular ends. **2** the amount it contains, often used as a measure of capacity (in brewing = 36 imperial gallons; in the oil industry = 35 imperial or 42 US gallons). **3** a cylindrical tube-like part, especially the part of a gun through which the shot is fired. —*v.t.* (**-ll-**) to store in a barrel. —**barrel vault,** a vault with a uniform concave roof. [f. OF, perh. as BAR[1]]

barrel-organ *n.* **1** an automatic pipe-organ much used in churches in the 19th c. **2** a 19th-c. street-instrument (not of the organ type) producing notes by means of metal tongues struck by pins fixed in the barrel.

barren /ˈbærən/ *adj.* **1** (of land) unable to produce crops or vegetation, infertile. **2** unable to bear young; not producing fruit. **3** not productive of results. [f. AF, ult. orig. unkn.]

barricade /bærɪˈkeɪd/ *n.* a barrier, especially one hastily erected across a street. —*v.t.* to block or defend with a barricade. [F, f. Sp. *barrica* cask (as BARREL)]

barrier /ˈbærɪə(r)/ *n.* **1** a fence, rail, etc., barring advance or preventing access. **2** a gate at a railway-station where tickets have to be shown. **3** a circumstance that prevents progress or communication etc. —**barrier reef,** a coral reef cut off from the nearest land by a channel. [f. AF (as BAR[1])]

barrister /ˈbærɪstə(r)/ *n.* a lawyer entitled to represent clients in the higher lawcourts. [f. BAR[1]]

barrow[1] /ˈbærəu/ *n.* **1** a two-wheeled hand-cart, especially for selling things in the street. **2** a wheelbarrow. [OE, rel. to BEAR[1]]

barrow[2] /ˈbærəu/ *n.* a mound of earth constructed in ancient times to cover one or more burials. [OE, = hill, hillock]

bartender /ˈbɑːtendə(r)/ *n.* a barman or barmaid.

barter /ˈbɑːtə(r)/ *v.t./i.* to part with (goods) in exchange for others of equivalent value; to trade in this way. —*n.* such trade or exchange. [prob. f. OF *barater*, as BARRATRY]

baryon /ˈbærɪɒn/ *n.* a nucleon or hyperon. [f. Gk *barus* heavy; so called because their mass is greater than, or equal to, that of the proton]

baryta /bəˈraɪtə/ *n.* barium oxide or hydroxide. [f. Gk *barus* heavy]

barytes /bəˈraɪti:z/ *n.* barium sulphate, used in some white paints. [as prec.]

basal /ˈbeɪs(ə)l/ *a.* of or forming the base of something. [f. BASE¹]

basalt /ˈbæsɔ:lt/ *n.* a dark igneous rock, often forming columnar strata. —**basaltic** /bəˈsɔ:ltɪk/ *adj.* [f. L f. Gk (*basanos* touchstone)]

bascule /ˈbæskju:l/ *n.* a lever apparatus used in a **bascule bridge,** a kind of drawbridge worked by counterweights. [F, = see-saw]

base¹ *n.* **1** the lowest part of anything, the part on which it rests. **2** a basis; a main principle or starting-point. **3** the headquarters of an expedition or military force etc., from where its operations are directed. **4** the main or underlying ingredient of a mixture. **5** a substance, (not necessarily soluble in water) that can combine with an acid to form a salt. **6** the number on which a system of calculation is based, e.g. 10 in decimal counting, 2 in the binary system. **7** (in baseball) any of the four stations that a batsman must reach in turn in scoring a run. —*v.t.* to use as a base or foundation, or as evidence for a conclusion etc. [F, or f. L f. Gk *basis* stepping]

base² *adj.* **1** lacking moral worth, cowardly, contemptible. **2** (of metals) not precious; (of coins) adulterated with inferior metal. —**basely** *adv.*, **baseness** *n.* [f. F *bas* of low height, f. L *bassus* short]

baseball *n.* a game evolved from rounders, with teams of 9 players who in turn seek to strike the ball thrown by an opponent (the *pitcher*) and traverse a circuit of four points (*bases*).

baseless *adj.* with no foundation in fact. [f. BASE¹ + -LESS]

baseline *n.* a line used as a base or starting-point; the line at each end of a tennis-court.

basement /ˈbeɪsmənt/ *n.* a storey below ground level. [prob. Du., as BASE¹]

basenji /bəˈsendʒɪ/ *n.* a breed of small rarely-barking African hunting-dog. [Bantu]

bash *v.t.* **1** to strike violently. **2** to attack violently with blows, words, or hostile actions. —*n.* a heavy blow. —**have a bash,** (*colloq.*) to have a try. [imit., perh. B(ANG + SM)ASH]

bashful *adj.* self-consciously shy. —**bashfully** *adv.*, **bashfulness** *n.* [f. obs. *bash* (*v.*) = ABASH + -FUL]

BASIC /ˈbeɪsɪk/ *n.* a computer language using familiar English words. [acronym, *B*eginner's *A*ll-purpose *S*ymbolic *I*nstruction *C*ode]

basic /ˈbeɪsɪk/ *adj.* **1** forming a base or starting-point; forming a standard minimum before additions. **2** of fundamental importance. **3** (of rock or soil) having a low silica content in proportion to the lime or other bases present. —**Basic English,** a simplified form of English with a select vocabulary of 850 words for international use. **basic slag,** a fertilizer containing phosphates, formed as a by-product in steel manufacture. —**basically** *adv.* [f. BASE¹]

basil /ˈbæz(ə)l/ *n.* an aromatic herb of the genus *Ocimum*. [f. OF f. L f. Gk *basilikos* royal]

basilica /bəˈzɪlɪkə/ *n.* an oblong hall or church with a double colonnade and an apse. [L f. Gk, = royal (house)]

basilisk /ˈbæzɪlɪsk/ *n.* **1** a mythical reptile (also called a *cockatrice*), hatched by a serpent from a cock's egg. Its breath, and even its glance, was fatal. **2** a tropical crested lizard of the genus *Basiliscus*. [f. L f. Gk, dim. of *basileus* king (so called, acc. to Pliny, from a spot resembling a crown on its head)]

basin /ˈbeɪs(ə)n/ *n.* **1** a rounded open vessel for liquids etc.; a wash-basin. **2** a depression where water collects; the tract of country drained by a river. **3** an almost land-locked harbour. —**basinful** *n.* [f. OF f. L *ba(s)cinus*, perh. f. Gaulish]

basis /ˈbeɪsɪs/ *n.* (*pl.* **bases** /ˈbeɪsi:z/) **1** a foundation or support. **2** a main principle, a starting-point. [L f. Gk, = BASE¹]

bask /bɑ:sk/ *v.i.* (usu. with *in*) to lie or rest comfortably in a pleasant warmth; to enjoy (one's popularity, glory, etc.). —**basking shark,** a very large shark (*Cetorhinus maximus*) accustomed to lie near the surface of water. [f. ON, rel. to BATHE]

basket /ˈbɑ:skɪt/ *n.* a container made of interwoven cane, wire, etc.; the amount contained in it. —**basket weave,** one with a pattern resembling basketwork. —**basketful** *n.* [AF & OF; orig. unkn.]

basketball *n.* a game played between teams of 5 or 6 players in which a goal is scored when the ball is thrown into a net fixed on a ring about 3 m (10 ft.) above the ground.

basketry /ˈbɑ:skɪtrɪ/ *n.* **1** baskets and other objects woven from flexible canes etc. **2** the art of weaving these. [f. BASKET]

basketwork *n.* basketry.

Basque /bɑ:sk/ *n.* **1** a member of a people living in the western Pyrenees on both sides of the French-Spanish border. **2** their language. —*adj.* of the Basques or their language. [F f. L *Vasco*]

bas-relief /ˈbæsrɪli:f/ *n.* low relief; a sculpture or carving in low relief. [f. It. *basso rilievo*]

bass[1] /beɪs/ *adj.* deep-sounding; of the lowest musical pitch. —*n.* **1** a male voice of the lowest range; a singer with such a voice; a part written for it. **2** bass pitch. **3** (*colloq.*) a double-bass; a bass guitar. —**bass-viol** *n.* a viola da gamba. [as BASE², alt. after It. *basso*]

bass[2] /bæs/ *n.* (*pl.* **basses,** *collect.* **bass**) any of several marine fish of the perch family. [OE]

basset /ˈbæsɪt/ *n.* (in full **basset-hound**) a short-legged hound of a kind originally used for hunting hares. [F, dim. of *bas* low]

bassinet /bæsɪˈnet/ *n.* a child's wicker cradle with a hood. [F, dim. of *bassin* basin]

bassoon /bəˈsuːn/ *n.* a bass instrument of the oboe family. —**bassoonist** *n.* [f. F f. It. *bassone* (*basso* BASE²)]

bast /bæst/ *n.* fibrous material obtained from the inner bark of the lime-tree or other sources and used for matting etc.; phloem. [OE]

bastard /ˈbɑːstəd/ *adj.* **1** born of parents not married to each other. **2** hybrid. **3** (*Bot.* & *Zool.*) resembling (the species whose name is appropriated). —*n.* **1** a bastard person. **2** (*colloq.*) a disliked or difficult person or thing. [f. OF f. L, perh. f. *bast* pack-saddle (used by muleteers as a bed)]

bastardize *v.t.* to declare (a person) illegitimate. [f. prec.]

bastardy *n.* the condition of being a bastard, illegitimacy. [f. BASTARD]

baste[1] /beɪst/ *v.t.* to moisten (roasting meat) with melted fat to prevent it from drying. [orig. unkn.]

baste[2] /beɪst/ *v.t.* to stitch loosely together (preparatory to regular sewing). [f. OF, = sew lightly]

bastinado /bæstiˈnɑːdəʊ/ *n.* (*pl.* **-os**) a torture consisting of repeated blows with a light cane on the soles of the feet. —*v.t.* to torture in this way. [f. Sp. (*baston* stick)]

bastion /ˈbæstɪən/ *n.* **1** a projecting part of a fortification. **2** a fortified place near hostile territory. **3** an institution etc. serving as a stronghold. [F f. It. (*bastire* build)]

bat[1] **1** *n.* an implement (usually of wood) with handle and a flat or curved surface for striking the ball in games; a turn at using this. **2** a batsman. —*v.t./i.* (**-tt-**) to use a bat; to hit with a bat. —**off one's own bat,** without prompting or assistance. [f. OE *batt* club f. OF (*battre* hit)]

bat[2] *n.* a furry mouselike mammal of the order Chiroptera, active at night, flying by means of a winglike membrane on its forelimbs. —**blind as a bat,** completely blind. [f. Scand., orig. *bakke*]

bat[3] *v.t.* (**-tt-**) to flutter. —**not bat an eyelid,** (*colloq.*) to show no surprise or alarm. [var. of obs. *bate* flutter]

batch /bætʃ/ *n.* **1** a quantity of loaves or cakes produced at a single baking. **2** a quantity or number of persons or things coming or dealt with together; an instalment. [f. OE, rel. to BAKE]

bated /ˈbeɪtɪd/ *adj.* **with bated breath,** holding one's breath in anxiety or suspense. [f. ABATE]

bath /bɑːθ/ *n.* (*pl.* **baths** /bɑːðz/) **1** a long open vessel in which one sits to wash the body; water for this; the process of washing in it; (in *pl.*) a building where baths may be taken by the public. **2** (in *pl.*) a public swimming-pool. **3** a liquid in which something is immersed; its container. —*v.t./i.* to immerse in a bath; to take a bath. —**Order of the Bath,** an order of knighthood, so called from the ceremonial bath which originally preceded installation. [OE]

Bath bun /bɑːθ/ a round spiced bun with currants and icing. [*Bath,* spa town in Avon]

bath chair a kind of wheelchair for invalids. [as prec.]

bathe /beɪð/ *v.t./i.* **1** to immerse in or treat with liquid; to lie immersed in water etc. **2** to go swimming. **3** (of light or warmth) to envelop. —*n.* an instance of bathing. —**bathing-suit** *n.* a garment worn for swimming. —**bather** *n.* [rel. to BATH¹]

bathos /ˈbeɪθɒs/ *n.* unintentional descent from the sublime to the commonplace or absurd. [Gk, = depth]

bathroom *n.* a room with a bath, wash-basin, etc.; (*euphem.*) a lavatory.

bathyscaphe /ˈbæθɪskæf/ *n.* a manned vessel for deep-sea diving, with special buoyancy gear. [F, f. Gk *bathus* deep + *skaphos* ship]

bathysphere /ˈbæθɪsfɪə(r)/ *n.* a spherical diving-vessel for deep-sea observation. [f. Gk *bathus* deep + SPHERE]

batik /ˈbætɪk/ *n.* a method, originally Javanese, of printing coloured designs on textiles by waxing the parts not to be dyed, so as to repel the pigment; fabric treated thus. [Javanese, = painted]

batiste /bæˈtiːst/ *n.* a fine light cotton or linen fabric. [F, f. *Baptiste* of Cambrai, first maker]

batman /ˈbætmən/ *n.* (*pl.* **-men**) a soldier acting as personal servant to an officer. [f. OF f. L *bastum* pack-saddle]

baton /bæt(ə)n/ *n.* **1** a long thin stick used by a conductor to direct performers; a short stick carried and passed on in a relay race; a drum major's stick; a staff of office; a policeman's truncheon. **2** (in heraldry) a narrow bend truncated at each end. **3** a stroke replacing a figure on the face of a clock or watch. —**baton sinister,** (in heraldry) a baton from sinister to dexter, used as a mark of bastardy. [f. F f. L *bastum* stick]

batrachian /bəˈtreɪkɪən/ *n.* any of a class of amphibians (Batrachia or Salientia) that discard gills and tails, e.g. frog and toad. *—adj.* of these animals. [f. Gk *batrachos* frog]

batsman /ˈbætsmən/ *n.* (*pl.* **-men**) a player who is batting in cricket or baseball; one who is good at this. [f. BAT¹]

battalion /bəˈtælɪən/ *n.* a large body of men ready for battle, especially an infantry unit forming part of a brigade; a large group of persons with a common purpose. [f. F f. It. (*battaglia* battle)]

batten¹ /ˈbæt(ə)n/ *n.* **1** a long narrow piece of squared timber. **2** a strip of wood or metal fastening or holding something in place. *—v.t.* to strengthen or fasten with battens. [f. OF (*battre* beat)]

batten² /ˈbæt(ə)n/ *v.i.* to grow fat or prosperous *on*. [ON, rel. to BETTER]

Battenberg /ˈbæt(ə)nbɜːg/ *n.* (in full **Battenberg cake**) a kind of cake made in a rectangular shape with alternating pink and yellow squares, covered with marzipan. [perh. f. name of village in W. Germany]

batter¹ *v.t./i.* to hit with repeated hard blows; to knock heavily and insistently *at*. *—n.* a beaten mixture of flour, eggs, and milk for cooking. **—battered baby, wife,** etc., one subjected to repeated violence. [f. AF (as BATTERY]

batter² *n.* a batsman in baseball. [f. BAT¹]

battering-ram *n.* a swinging beam, formerly with an iron ram's-head end, used to breach walls etc. [f. BATTER¹]

battery /ˈbætərɪ/ *n.* **1** a portable container of a cell or cells for converting chemical into electrical energy. **2** a series of cages for the intensive keeping of poultry or cattle etc. **3** a set of connected similar units of equipment. **4** (*Law*) unlawful physical violence inflicted on a person. [f. F f. L *battuere* beat]

battle *n.* **1** a fight between large organized forces. **2** a contest; a hard struggle. *—v.i.* to struggle hard. **—battle-cry** *n.* a war-cry; a slogan. [f. OF f. L, = gladiatorial exercises (as prec.)]

battleaxe *n.* **1** a heavy axe used in ancient warfare. **2** (*colloq.*) a formidable or domineering woman.

battledore /ˈbæt(ə)ldɔː(r)/ *n.* a small racket used with a shuttlecock in the volleying game of **battledore and shuttlecock**. [perh. f. Prov. *batedor* beater, orig. a paddle-like instrument used in washing etc.]

battledress *n.* the everyday uniform of a soldier etc.

battlefield *n.* the site of a battle.

battleground *n.* a battlefield.

battlement /ˈbæt(ə)lmənt/ *n.* (usu. in *pl.*) a parapet with lower sections at intervals, originally for firing from. [f. OF *batailler* fortify (as BATTLE)]

battleship *n.* a warship with the heaviest armour and largest guns.

batty /ˈbætɪ/ *adj.* (*slang*) crazy; eccentric. [f. BAT²]

bauble /ˈbɔːb(ə)l/ *n.* a showy but valueless ornament. [f. OF *ba(u)bel* toy]

baud /bəʊd/ *n.* (in telecommunications and computers) a unit of signal transmission speed equal to one information unit per second; (*loosely*) a unit of data transmission speed of one bit per second. [f. J. M. E. *Baudot*, French engineer (d. 1903)]

baulk /bɔːk/ *n.* **1** a strip of ground left unploughed; a strip of earth left between excavation trenches. **2** the area of a billiard-table within which the cue balls are placed at the start of a game. **3** a roughly squared length of timber. [OE f. ON]

bauxite /ˈbɔːksaɪt/ *n.* an earthy mineral, the chief source of aluminium. [F, f. *Les Baux* in S. France]

bawdy /ˈbɔːdɪ/ *adj.* humorously indecent. *—n.* bawdy talk or writing. **—bawdily** *adv.*, **bawdiness** *n.* [f. obs. *bawd* woman brothel-keeper]

bawl /bɔːl/ *v.t./i.* to call out loudly; to weep noisily. **—bawl out,** (*colloq.*) to reprimand severely. [imit.]

bay¹ *n.* a broad inlet of the sea where the land curves inwards. [f. OF f. Sp. *bahia*]

bay² *n.* **1** a section of wall between buttresses or columns. **2** a recess in a room or building, especially one formed by a projecting window. **3** any of a series of compartments in a building or structure; a partitioned or marked area forming a unit. **4** the cul-de-sac where a side-line terminates at a railway station. **—bay window,** a window projecting from the line of a building. [f. OF (*ba(y)er* gape)]

bay³ *n.* the Mediterranean laurel *Laurus nobilis*, with fragrant deep-green leaves that are used for seasoning. **—bay rum,** perfume (especially for the hair) originally distilled from rum and bayberry leaves. [f. OF f. L *baca* berry]

bay⁴ *n.* the deep drawn-out cry of a large dog or of hounds in pursuit of a hunted animal. *—v.i.* to utter this cry. **—at bay,** facing one's attackers, as a cornered animal. **hold** *or* **keep at bay,** to fight off (pursuers). [f. OF (as BAY²)]

bay⁵ *adj.* (esp. of a horse) reddish-brown. *—n.* a reddish-brown horse. [f. OF f. L *badius*]

bayberry *n.* a fragrant West Indian tree, *Pimenta acris*. [as prec.]

bayonet /ˈbeɪənɪt/ *n.* a stabbing blade that can be attached to the muzzle of a rifle for use in hand-to-hand fighting. *—v.t.* to wound with a bayonet. **—bayonet fitting,** a type of attachment in which a cylindrical part is pushed into a socket and twisted slightly so that it is secured by engagement of parts. [f. F, perh. f. *Bayonne* in SW France, where the weapon is said to have been first made or first used]

bazaar /bəˈzɑː(r)/ *n.* **1** a market in oriental countries. **2** a sale of goods to raise funds for charity. [f. Pers.]

bazooka /bəˈzuːkə/ *n.* a tubular anti-tank rocket-launcher. [orig. = trombone-like instrument; perh. rel. to Du. *bazuin* trumpet]

BBC *abbr.* British Broadcasting Corporation.

BC *abbr.* before Christ (in dating).

BCE *abbr.* before the Common Era (in dating).

bdellium /ˈdelɪəm/ *n.* a resin used especially as a perfume; the tree (esp. of the genus *Commiphora*) yielding this. [L f. Gk f. Heb.]

Be *symbol* beryllium.

be /bɪ, *emphatic* biː/ *v.i.* (*pres.* **am, are, is**; *past* **was, were**; *p.p.* **been**; *partic.* **being**) **1** to exist; to occur; to occupy a given position in space or time. **2** to have a certain quality, identity, meaning, cost, etc. —*v.aux.* used with parts of other verbs to form passive, continuous tenses, or (with infin.) to express destiny, duty, etc. —**be-all (and end-all)** *n.* one's consuming purpose. **be that as it may,** whatever the facts of the matter may be. **for the time being,** for the moment. **have been,** (*colloq.*) to have come or gone as a visitor. **let be,** to leave undisturbed. **the — to be,** the future (person of a named function). [OE]

be- *prefix* **1** forming verbs implying transitive action (*bemoan*), completeness (*becalm*), thoroughness (*belabour*), attitude or treatment (*befriend*). **2** forming adjectives with the suffix *-ed* in sense 'having' (*bespectacled*). [OE, = BY]

beach *n.* a pebbly or sandy shore, especially of the sea between high and low water-mark. —*v.t.* to haul up (a boat) on the beach. —**beach-head** *n.* a fortified position set up on a beach by landing forces. [orig. unkn.]

beachcomber /ˈbiːtʃkəʊmə(r)/ *n.* one who lives by salvaging objects washed up on the beach; a loafer who lives on what he can earn casually on a waterfront. —**beachcombing** *n.*

beacon /ˈbiːkən/ *n.* **1** a signal-fire set up in a high or prominent position; a high hill suitable for such a fire. **2** a warning or guiding light; a Belisha beacon. **3** a signal station such as a lighthouse. [OE]

bead *n.* **1** a small perforated piece of hard material for making necklaces etc.; (in *pl.*) a necklace or string of beads, a rosary. **2** a drop of moisture; a small bubble. **3** a small knob forming the sight of a gun. **4** a strip on the inner edge of a pneumatic tyre for gripping the wheel. **5** a small globular moulding, often applied in rows like a series of beads. —*v.t.* **1** to adorn with beads. **2** to coat (a surface) with beads of moisture. —**draw a bead on,** to take aim at. [OE, = prayer (from its use in rosaries)]

beading *n.* **1** a decoration of beads. **2** a moulding or carving like a series of beads. **3** a strip of material with one side rounded, used to trim the edge of wood. **4** the bead of a tyre.

beadle /ˈbiːd(ə)l/ *n.* **1** a ceremonial officer of a church, college, etc. **2** (*Sc.*) a church officer attending on a minister. **3** (*hist.*) a minor officer of a parish, dealing with petty offenders etc. [f. OF f. Gmc]

beady *adj.* (of eyes) small and glittering. [f. BEAD]

beagle /ˈbiːg(ə)l/ *n.* a small hound of a kind originally used in hunting hares etc. on foot. [f. OF *beegueule* noisy person, prob. f. *beer* open wide + *gueule* throat]

beagling *n.* hunting with beagles. [f. prec.]

beak *n.* **1** a bird's horny projecting jaws. **2** a similar mouth-like part or other projection. —**beaked** *adj.* [f. OF, of Celtic origin]

beaker /ˈbiːkə(r)/ *n.* **1** a tall narrow drinking-cup, often without a handle. **2** an open glass vessel with straight sides and a lip for pouring liquids, used in laboratories. **3** a wide-mouthed pottery vessel found in graves of the late neolithic period (3rd millennium BC) in western Europe. [ON, perh. f. Gk *bikos* drinking-vessel]

beam *n.* **1** a long sturdy piece of timber or other solid material used in building houses etc. **2** the cross-bar of a balance. **3** (in *pl.*) the horizontal cross-timbers of a ship; a ship's greatest breadth. **4** a ray or stream of light or other radiation. **5** radio waves transmitted undispersed, especially as used to guide aircraft or missiles. **6** a radiant look, a smile. —*v.t./i.* **1** to radiate (light, affection, etc.). **2** to direct (radio signals); to shine. **3** to smile radiantly. —**on one's beam-ends,** (*colloq.*) near the end of one's resources. [OE, = tree]

bean *n.* **1** any of the oval edible seeds of various leguminous plants; a plant producing beans. **2** a similar-shaped seed of other plants (e.g. cocoa, coffee). —**full of beans,** (*colloq.*) lively, in high spirits. **spill the beans,** (*slang*) to divulge secrets. [OE]

beanfeast *n.* a festive entertainment, originally one given annually by an employer to his employees. [f. prec., beans and bacon being regarded as an indispensable dish]

beano /ˈbiːnəʊ/ *n.* (*pl.* **-os**) (*slang*) a party, a merry time. [abbr. BEANFEAST]

bear[1] /beə(r)/ *v.t./i.* (*past* **bore;** *p.p.* **borne**) **1** to carry; to support. **2** to bring or take. **3** to have as a visible feature or as a name, meaning, etc. **4** to hold or cherish in the mind. **5** to give birth to; to produce (fruit or flowers). **6** to hold up (a load) without collapsing; to sustain (a cost); to endure, to tolerate; to be fit for. **7** to make one's way in a given direction. **8** to exert pressure, to thrust. —**bear on,** to be relevant to. **bear out,** to confirm. **bear up,** to remain cheerful, not despair. **bear with,** to tolerate patiently. **bear witness to,** to provide evidence of the truth of. **bring to bear,** to focus (pressure etc.). **be borne in upon,** to become convincing to. [OE]

bear[2] /beə(r)/ *n.* **1** a large heavy powerful mammal of the family Ursidae, with thick fur. **2** a rough uncouth or surly person. **3** one who sells shares on the Stock Exchange for future delivery, hoping to buy them at a lower price in the mean time. The term (which dates from the 18th c.) is probably derived from the proverb 'to sell the bear's skin before one has caught the bear'. The associated term *bull* appears later, and was perhaps suggested by *bear*. —**bear-hug** *n.* a powerful hug. **Great Bear, Little Bear,** constellations near the North Pole. [OE]

bearable *adj.* endurable. [f. BEAR[1]]

beard /bɪəd/ *n.* hair on the chin etc. of an adult man; similar hair in certain animals, e.g. goats. —*v.t.* to confront boldly. —**bearded** *adj.* [OE]

bearer *n.* **1** one who carries or helps to carry a load, especially equipment on an expedition. **2** one who brings a letter or message; the actual presenter of a cheque. [f. BEAR[1]]

beargarden *n.* (*colloq.*) a scene of rowdy behaviour.

bearing *n.* **1** bodily attitude as expressing character. **2** relationship, relevance. **3** (usu. in *pl.*) the part of a machine bearing the friction. **4** the compass direction of one point in relation to another; (in *pl.*) relative position. **5** a heraldic charge or device. [f. BEAR[1]]

bearskin *n.* a guardsman's tall furry cap.

beast *n.* **1** an animal, especially a wild four-footed kind. **2** an offensively brutal or sensuous man; (*colloq.*) any objectionable person. [f. OF f. L *bestia*]

beastly *adj.* **1** of or like a beast, especially in obedience to animal instincts. **2** (*colloq.*) objectionable, highly unpleasant. [f. prec.]

beat *v.t./i.* (*past* **beat**; *p.p.* **beaten**) **1** to hit repeatedly, especially with a stick; to strike persistently; to shape or flatten by blows. **2** to mix vigorously to a frothy or smooth consistency. **3** (of the heart) to pulsate rhythmically. **4** to overcome, to do better than; to be too difficult for. **5** to sail to windward by a series of alternate tacks across the wind. —*n.* **1** a regular repeated stroke, a sound of this; the rhythmic pulsation of the heart. **2** the principal recurring accent in music or verse; a form of pop music with strongly-marked rhythm. **3** a route regularly patrolled by a policeman or sentinel. —*predic. adj.* (*slang*) exhausted, tired out. —**beat about the bush,** to approach a subject in a roundabout way. **beat a retreat,** to withdraw to a safer position. **beat down,** to force (a seller) to lower his price; (of the sun, rain, etc.) to come down with great force. **beaten track,** a well-worn or frequented route. **beat it,** (*slang*) to go away. **beat off,** to repel (an attacker). **beat the bounds,** to perform the ancient ceremony of going round a parish boundary striking certain points with willow rods. **beat time,** to wave a stick or tap in time with music. **beat up,** to assault systematically with punches, kicks, etc. [OE]

beater *n.* **1** an implement for beating things; a device for tapping a triangle (percussion instrument). **2** a person employed to rouse game at a shoot. [f. BEAT]

beatific /bi:əˈtɪfɪk/ *adj.* **1** (of smiles etc.) showing great happiness. **2** making blessed. [f. F or L (*beatus* blessed, *facere* make)]

beatify /bi:ˈætɪfaɪ/ *v.t.* to make blessed; (of the pope) to declare (a person) to be in heaven (the first step to canonization). —**beatification** /-fɪˈkeɪʃ(ə)n/ *n.* [as prec.]

beatitude /bi:ˈætɪtju:d/ *n.* **1** blessedness. **2** (in *pl.*) the pronouncements by Christ in the Sermon on the Mount beginning 'Blessed are . . .' (Matt.5:3-11). [f. L (*beatus* blessed)]

Beaufort scale /ˈbəʊfət/ a scale of wind velocity ranging from 0 (calm) to 12 (hurricane). [f. Sir F. *Beaufort*, English admiral (d. 1857), the inventor]

Beaujolais /ˈbəʊʒəleɪ/ *n.* a red or white burgundy from Beaujolais, France.

beautician /bju:ˈtɪʃ(ə)n/ *n.* one who gives beautifying treatments to the face or body. [f. BEAUTY]

beautiful /ˈbju:tɪf(ə)l/ *adj.* **1** having beauty, pleasing to the eye, ear, or mind. **2** admirable or excellent of its kind. —**beautifully** *adv.* [f. BEAUTY + -FUL]

beautify /ˈbju:tɪfaɪ/ *v.t.* to make beautiful. —**beautification** /-fɪˈkeɪʃ(ə)n/ *n.* [f. foll.]

beauty /ˈbju:tɪ/ *n.* **1** qualities of form, face, etc., that together please one or more of the senses or the mind; a person or thing having these. **2** a fine specimen; a pleasing or advantageous feature. —**beauty parlour,** an establishment giving beautifying treatments. **beauty queen,** a woman judged the most beautiful in a contest. **beauty sleep,** sleep that is said to make or keep a person beautiful. **beauty spot** a place famous for its beautiful scenery; a birthmark or artificial patch on the face, said to heighten beauty. [f. AF f. L (*bellus* pretty)]

beaver[1] *n.* **1** an amphibious rodent of the genus *Castor* with soft brown fur and a broad tail, able to cut down trees by gnawing and to build dams in which to make lodges and raise young. **2** its fur; a hat made of this. **3 Beaver,** a member of a junior branch of the Scout Association, consisting of boys aged six and seven. *—v.i.* **beaver away,** to work hard. [OE]

beaver[2] *n.* (*hist.*) the lower portion of the face-guard of a helmet, when worn with a visor. [f. OF *baviere* bib]

bebop /ˈbi:bɒp/ *n.* a kind of jazz with highly syncopated rhythms. [imit.]

becalm /bɪˈkɑ:m/ *v.t.* (usu. in *pass.*) to keep (a ship) motionless through absence of wind. [f. BE- + CALM]

became *past* of BECOME.

because /bɪˈkɒz/ *conj.* for the reason that, since. *—adv.* by reason *of.* [f. BE- + CAUSE]

béchamel sauce /ˈbeʃəm(ə)l/ a kind of fine white sauce. [invented by Marquis de *Béchamel* (d. 1703), courtier of Louis XIV]

beck[1] *n.* (*archaic*) a gesture. **—at the beck and call of,** subject to constant orders from. [f. *beck* (*v.*) inferred from BECKON]

beck[2] *n.* (*N.Engl.*) a brook, a stream. [ON]

beckon /ˈbekən/ *v.t./i.* to signal or summon by a gesture. [OE, rel. to BEACON]

become /bɪˈkʌm/ *v.t./i.* (*past* **became;** *p.p.* **become**) **1** to come or grow to be, to begin to be. **2** to suit, to be becoming to. **—become of,** to happen to. [f. BE- + COME]

becoming *adj.* giving a pleasing appearance or effect, suitable. **—becomingly** *adv.* [f. prec.]

becquerel /ˈbekər(ə)l/ *n.* a unit of radioactivity, corresponding to one disintegration per second. [f. A.-H. *Becquerel,* French physicist (d. 1908)]

bed *n.* **1** a base or support to sleep or rest on, a piece of furniture with a mattress and covering. **2** a garden plot in which plants are grown. **3** the bottom of the sea or a river etc.; the foundation of a road or railway. **4** a stratum or layer. *—v.t./i.* **(-dd-) 1** to put or go to bed. **2** to plant in a garden bed. **3** to place or fix in a foundation. [OE]

bedaub /bɪˈdɔ:b/ *v.t.* to smear all over, especially with paint. [f. BE- + DAUB]

bedbug *n.* a small flat evil-smelling blood-sucking insect (*Cimex lectularius*) infesting dirty beds.

bedclothes *n.pl.* sheets, blankets, etc., used on a bed.

bedding *n.* **1** things used to make a bed (e.g. mattress, bedclothes; straw and hay for horses etc.). **2** geological strata. **—bedding plant,** a plant suitable for a garden bed. [f. BED]

bedevil /bɪˈdev(ə)l/ *v.t.* **(-ll-)** to trouble or vex; to confuse or perplex; to torment or abuse. **—bedevilment** *n.* [f. BE- + DEVIL]

bedfellow *n.* one occupying the same bed; an associate.

bedizen /bɪˈdaɪz(ə)n/ *v.t.* to deck out gaudily. [f. BE- + obs. *dizen* deck out]

bedlam /ˈbedləm/ *n.* a scene of wild confusion or uproar. [f. St Mary of *Bethlehem,* mental hospital formerly in London]

bedouin /ˈbedʊɪn/ *n.* (*pl.* same) a nomadic Arab of the desert. [f. OF ult. f. Arab. (*bedw* desert)]

bedpan *n.* a pan for use as a lavatory by a person confined to bed.

bedpost *n.* any of the upright supports of a bedstead.

bedraggled /bɪˈdraeg(ə)ld/ *adj.* wet and dishevelled. [f. BE- + DRAGGLE]

bedridden /ˈbedrɪd(ə)n/ *adj.* permanently confined to bed by infirmity. [f. BED + *ridden* (see RIDE)]

bedrock *n.* **1** solid rock beneath loose soil. **2** basic facts or principles.

bedroom *n.* a room with a bed and other furniture for sleeping in.

Beds. *abbr.* Bedfordshire.

bedside *n.* a position by a bed.

bedsit, bedsitter *ns.* (*colloq.*) a bed-sitting-room. [f. foll.]

bed-sitting-room *n.* a room serving as bedroom and sitting-room.

bedsore *n.* a sore caused by prolonged lying in bed.

bedspread *n.* a cloth or cover put over a bed when this is not in use.

bedstead /ˈbedsted/ *n.* the framework of a bed.

bedstraw *n.* a herbaceous plant of the genus *Galium,* formerly used as straw for beds.

bee *n.* a four-winged stinging insect, living in colonies and collecting nectar and pollen to produce wax and honey. **—a bee in one's bonnet,** (*colloq.*) an obsession. [OE]

beech *n.* **1** a forest tree of the genus *Fagus,* with smooth bark and glossy leaves. **2** any of various similar chiefly evergreen trees of the genus *Notofagus,* growing in cooler regions of the countries of the southern hemisphere. **3** the wood of any of these. [OE]

beechmast /ˈbi:tʃmɑ:st/ *n.* beech nuts collectively. [f. BEECH + MAST[2]]

beef *n.* **1** the meat of an ox, bull, or cow; (*pl.* **beeves**) an ox etc. bred for meat. **2** (*colloq.*) muscular strength, brawn. **3** (*slang*) a complaint. *—v.i.* (*slang*) to grumble. **—beef tea,** stewed extract of beef, given to invalids etc. **beef up,** (*slang*) to strengthen, to reinforce. [f. AF f. L *bos bovis* ox]

beefeater /ˈbi:fi:tə(r)/ *n.* a guard at the Tower of London, or a member of the Yeomen of the Guard, wearing Tudor dress as uniform. [f. obs. sense 'dependant, well-fed menial']

beefy *adj.* like beef; brawny, muscular. —**beefiness** *n.* [f. BEEF]

beehive *n.* a hive.

beeline *n.* a straight line of travel between two points. —**make a beeline for,** to head directly for.

been *p.p.* of BE.

beep *n.* a short high-pitched sound, especially that of a car-horn. —*v.i.* to make this sound. [imit.]

beer *n.* an alcoholic drink made from fermented malt and flavoured especially with hops. —**small beer,** something insignificant. —**beery** *adj.* [OE]

beeswax /ˈbi:zwæks/ *n.* wax secreted by bees for honeycombs and used for polishing wood.

beeswing /ˈbi:zwɪŋ/ *n.* a filmy crust on old port wine.

beet *n.* (*pl.* same or **-s**) a plant of the genus *Beta* grown for its succulent root and for sugar. [OE f. L]

beetle[1] *n.* an insect of the order Coleoptera, with front wings converted to hard wing-cases closing over its back wings; (*pop.*) a similar (often black) insect. [OE, rel. to BITE]

beetle[2] *n.* a heavy-headed tool for crushing or ramming things. [OE, rel. to BEAT[1]]

beetle-browed *adj.* with brows projecting in a threatening way. [f. *beetle* (orig. unkn.) + BROW]

beetling *adj.* projecting threateningly, overhanging. [as prec.]

beetroot *n.* the red root of the garden beet, used in salads etc.

befall /bɪˈfɔ:l/ *v.i./t.* (*past* **befell;** *p.p.* **befallen**) to happen (to). [f. BE- + FALL]

befit /bɪˈfɪt/ *v.t.* (**-tt-**) to be suited to or proper for. [f. BE- + FIT]

befog /bɪˈfɒg/ *v.t.* (**-gg-**) to envelop as with fog, to confuse. [f. BE- + FOG]

before /bɪˈfɔ:(r)/ *adv.* & *prep.* **1** ahead (of), in front (of); in the presence of. **2** at a time previous (to). **3** in preference to. —*conj.* earlier than the time when. —**before Christ,** (of a date) reckoned backwards from the birth of Christ. [f. BE- + FORE]

beforehand *adv.* in advance, in readiness or anticipation.

befriend /bɪˈfrend/ *v.t.* to act as a friend to, to help. [f. BE- + FRIEND]

befuddle /bɪˈfʌd(ə)l/ *v.t.* to stupefy, to confuse with or as with alcoholic drink. [f. BE- + FUDDLE]

beg *v.t./i.* (**-gg-**) **1** to ask for as a gift or favour, to request earnestly or humbly; to live by seeking charity. **2** to ask for formally; to take or ask leave to do something. —**beg the question,** to assume the truth, in reasoning, of a thing that is still to be proved. **go begging,** to be available but unwanted. [rel. to BID]

began *past* of BEGIN.

beget /bɪˈget/ *v.t.* (**-tt-**; *past* **begot** (*archaic* **begat**); *p.p.* **begotten**) to be the father of; to give rise to (an effect). [f. BE- + GET]

beggar /ˈbegə(r)/ **1** one who lives by begging; a very poor person. **2** (*colloq.*) a person, a fellow. —*v.t.* **1** to reduce to extreme poverty. **2** to render (description etc.) inadequate —**beggarly** *adj.*, **beggary** *n.* [f. BEG]

begin /bɪˈgɪn/ *v.t./i.* (**-nn-**; *past* **began;** *p.p.* **begun**) **1** to perform the earliest or first part of (an activity or process etc.). **2** to be the first to do something; to take the first step, to start speaking; (*colloq.*) to show any likelihood. **3** to come into existence. **4** to have its first element or starting-point (at some point in space or time). [OE]

beginner *n.* one who is just beginning, especially to learn a skill. —**beginner's luck,** good luck supposed to attend a beginner. [f. prec.]

beginning *n.* the first part of something; the time or place at which something begins; source, origin. —**beginning of the end,** the first clear signs of an (often unfavourable) outcome. [f. BEGIN]

begone /bɪˈgɒn/ *int.* go away at once! [f. BE + GONE]

begonia /bɪˈgəʊnɪə/ *n.* a garden plant of the genus *Begonia* with showy flowers and brightly coloured leaves. [f. M. *Bégon*, French patron of science (d. 1710)]

begot, begotten *past* & *p.p.* of BEGET.

begrudge /bɪˈgrʌdʒ/ *v.t.* to grudge. [f. BE- + GRUDGE]

beguile /bɪˈgaɪl/ *v.t.* **1** to charm or divert; to make (time) pass pleasantly. **2** to deceive, to trick. —**beguilement** *n.* [f. BE- + obs. *guile* deceive]

beguine /bɪˈgi:n/ *n.* a West Indian dance; its music or rhythm. f. F (*béguin* infatuation)]

begum /ˈbeɪgəm/ *n.* (in Pakistan and India) the title of a Muslim married woman, = Mrs; a Muslim woman of high rank. [f. Urdu f. Turk., = princess]

begun *p.p.* of BEGIN.

behalf /bɪˈhɑ:f/ *n.* **on behalf of,** in the interests of, as the representative of. [earlier *bihalve* on the part of (BE-, *half* side)]

behave /bɪˈheɪv/ *v.i.* **1** to act or react (in a specified way). **2** to show good manners; to conduct (oneself) well. [f. BE- + HAVE]

behaviour /bɪˈheɪvjə(r)/ *n.* a way of behaving, manners. [f. prec.]

behavioural *adj.* of or concerned with behaviour. —**behavioural science,** any discipline that studies behaviour, e.g. sociology. [f. prec.]

behaviourism *n.* the study of actions by analysis into stimulus and response; advocacy of this as the only valid method in psychology. —**behaviourist** *n.*, **behaviouristic** /-ˈrɪstɪk/ *adj.* [f. BEHAVIOUR]

behead /bɪˈhed/ *v.t.* to cut off the head of, especially in execution. [f. BE- + HEAD]

beheld *past* of BEHOLD.

behest /bɪˈhest/ *n.* (*literary*) a command, a request. [OE]

behind /bɪˈhaɪnd/ *adv.* & *prep.* **1** to the rear (of); further back in space or time (than). **2** in an inferior position (to). **3** in support (of). **4** remaining after others have left. **5** in arrears (with). —*n.* (*colloq.*) the buttocks. —**behind the times,** antiquated in ideas or practices. **behind time,** late, unpunctual. [OE]

behindhand /bɪˈhaɪndhænd/ *adv.* & *predic. adj.* in arrears; behind time; out of date.

behold /bɪˈhəʊld/ *v.t.* (*past* & *p.p.* **beheld**) (*archaic* or *literary*) to observe, to see. [f. BE- + HOLD]

beholden /bɪˈhəʊld(ə)n/ *predic. adj.* under an obligation (to). [obs. p.p. of BEHOLD]

behoove /bɪˈhu:v/ *v.t. impers.* (*US*) = BEHOVE.

behove /bɪˈhəʊv/ *v.t. impers.* to be incumbent on ; to be fitting for. [f. BE- + OE *hof* rel. to HEAVE]

beige /beɪʒ/ *adj.* & *n.* sandy fawn. [F]

being /ˈbi:ɪŋ/ *n.* **1** existence. **2** essence or nature, constitution. **3** something (esp. a person) that exists and has life. [f. BE]

bejewelled /bɪˈdʒu:əld/ *adj.* adorned with jewels. [f. BE- + JEWEL]

bel *n.* a unit (= ten decibels) used in comparing power levels in electrical communication. [f. A. G. *Bell*, Scottish inventor (d. 1922)]

belabour /bɪˈleɪbə(r)/ *v.t.* **1** to attack physically or verbally. **2** to labour (a subject). [f. BE- + LABOUR]

belated /bɪˈleɪtɪd/ *adj.* coming late or too late. —**belatedly** *adv.* [f. BE- + LATE]

belay /bɪˈleɪ/ *v.t.* to secure (a rope) by winding it round a peg or spike etc. —*n.* the securing of a rope in this way. [f. Du. *beleggen*]

bel canto /bel ˈkæntəʊ/ a style of operatic singing concentrating on beauty of sound and vocal technique. [It., = fine song]

belch *v.t./i.* **1** to emit wind from the stomach through the mouth. **2** (of a chimney, gun, etc.) to discharge (smoke etc.). —*n.* an act of belching. [OE]

beleaguer /bɪˈli:gə(r)/ *v.t.* (*literary*) **1** to besiege. **2** to harass or oppress. [f. Du. *belegeren* camp round (*leger* camp)]

belemnite /ˈbeləmnaɪt/ *n.* a common fossil of sharp-pointed tapering shape. [f. Gk *belemnon* dart]

belfry /ˈbelfrɪ/ *n.* a bell tower (chiefly attached to a church); the bell-chamber in this. [orig. = siege-tower; f. OF f. Gmc]

belie /bɪˈlaɪ/ *v.t.* (*past* & *p.p.* **belied;** *pres. p.* **belying**) **1** to fail to confirm, to show to be untrue; to fail to live up to (one's reputation, promise, etc.). **2** to give a false idea of. [f. BE- + LIE[1]]

belief /bɪˈli:f/ *n.* **1** the act of believing. **2** something firmly believed. **3** trust, confidence *in*. **4** acceptance of a doctrine etc., one's religion. [f. BELIEVE]

believable /bɪˈli:vəb(ə)l/ *adj.* that may be believed. [f. foll.]

believe /bɪˈli:v/ *v.t./i.* **1** to accept as true or conveying truth. **2** to think, to suppose. **3** to have (religious) faith; to have faith *in*; to have confidence *in*. —**believer** *n.* [OE]

Belisha beacon /bɪˈli:ʃə/ a flashing orange globe on a striped post, marking a pedestrian crossing. [f. L. Hore-*Belisha*, Minister of Transport 1934]

belittle /bɪˈlɪt(ə)l/ *v.t.* to imply to be of little consequence. —**belittlement** *n.* [f. BE- + LITTLE]

bell[1] *n.* **1** a cup-shaped metal instrument that makes a ringing sound when struck. **2** the sound of a bell, used as a signal (*one* to *eight bells* indicating the half-hours of a nautical watch). **3** a bell-shaped object or flower. **4** a device making a ringing or buzzing sound for attracting attention in a house etc. —**bell-bottomed** *adj.* (of trousers) widening from the knee down. **bell-ringing** *n.* the ringing of church bells or handbells with changes etc. [OE]

bell[2] *n.* the bay of a stag. —*v.i.* to make this sound. [OE]

belladonna /beləˈdɒnə/ *n.* deadly nightshade, a plant (*Atropa belladonna*) with purple flowers and poisonous black berries; a drug prepared from this. [f. It., = beautiful lady]

belle /bel/ *n.* a beautiful or the most beautiful woman. [F f. L (*bellus* beautiful)]

belle époque /bel ɪˈpɒk/ the period of settled and comfortable life preceding the First World War. [F, = fine period]

belles-lettres /belˈletr/ *n.pl.* writings or studies of a literary nature. [F, = fine letters]

bellicose /ˈbelikəʊz/ *adj.* eager to fight, warlike. —**bellicosity** /-ˈkɒsɪtɪ/ *n.* [f. L (*bellum* war)]

belligerent /bɪˈlɪdʒərənt/ *adj.* engaged in a war or conflict; bellicose. —*n.* a person or nation participating in a war. —**belligerence** *n.*, **belligerency** *n.* [f. L (*bellum* war, *gerere* wage)]

bellow /ˈbeləʊ/ *v.i./t.* to emit a deep loud roar; to utter loudly. —*n.* a loud roar, originally that of a bull. [orig. unkn.]

bellows /ˈbeləʊz/ *n.pl.* **1** a device which, when squeezed, drives a blast of air into a fire, through organ pipes, etc. **2** the expandable part of a camera etc. [rel. to foll.]

belly /ˈbelɪ/ *n.* **1** the abdomen; the stomach. **2** the underside of a four-legged animal. **3** the cavity or bulging part of anything. —*v.i./t.* to swell out. —**belly-ache** *n.* stomach pain; (*v.i.*) (*slang*) to complain querulously. **belly-dance** *n.* an oriental dance by a woman, with voluptuous movements of the belly. **belly-dancer** *n.* [OE, = bag]

belong /bɪˈlɒŋ/ *v.i.* **1** (with *to*) to be the property of; to be rightly assigned to as a duty, right, part, etc.; to be a member of (a club, family, etc.). **2** to fit an environment etc.; to be rightly placed. [f. BE- + obs. *long* belong]

belongings *n.pl.* personal possessions. [f. prec.]

beloved /bɪˈlʌvɪd/ *adj.* much loved (*predic.* /-ˈlʌvd/). —*n.* a beloved person. [f. BE- + LOVE]

below /bɪˈləʊ/ *adv.* **1** at or to a lower point or level. **2** further down a page, further on in a book etc. —*prep.* lower in position, amount, rank, etc., than; downstream from. [f. BE- + LOW[1]]

belt *n.* **1** a strip of leather etc. worn round the waist or diagonally across the chest to secure clothes or hold weapons etc. **2** a strip of colour, a special surface, trees, etc., round or on something; a zone or region. **3** a flexible strip carrying machine-gun cartridges; an endless strap connecting pulleys etc. **4** (*slang*) a heavy blow. —*v.t.* **1** to put a belt round. **2** to thrash with a belt; (*slang*) to hit with force. **3** to move rapidly. —**below the belt,** unfair, unfairly. **belt up,** to fasten one's safety belt; (*slang*) to stop talking. **tighten one's belt,** to live more frugally. [OE f. L *balteus*]

beluga /bɪˈlu:gə/ *n.* **1** a large white sturgeon (*Huso huso*); caviare from this. **2** a white whale (*Delphinapterus leucas*). [Russ. (*belyi* white)]

belvedere /ˈbelvɪdɪə(r)/ *n.* a raised turret or summer-house from which to view scenery. [It., = beautiful view]

bemoan /bɪˈməʊn/ *v.t.* to lament, complain of. [f. BE- + MOAN]

bemuse /bɪˈmju:z/ *v.t.* to stupefy or bewilder. [f. BE- + MUSE]

bench *n.* **1** a long seat of wood or stone. **2** a work-table for a carpenter, scientist, etc. **3** a judge's seat in court; a lawcourt; (*collect.*) judges and magistrates. —**bench-mark** *n.* a surveyor's mark indicating a point in a line of levels; a standard or point of reference. **King's** *or* **Queen's Bench,** a division of the High Court of Justice. **on the bench,** serving as a judge or magistrate. [OE, rel. to BANK[1]]

bencher *n.* a senior member of any of the Inns of Court. [f. BENCH]

bend[1] *v.t./i.* (*past* & *p.p.* **bent** exc. in *bended knee*) **1** to force (what was straight) into a curve or angle; to become curved or angular; to modify (rules) to suit oneself. **2** to direct (one's energies) *to.* **3** to incline from the vertical; to submit or bow (*to, before*); to force to submit. **4** to turn (one's steps etc.) in a new direction. —*n.* **1** a curve, departure from a straight course; the bent part of a thing. **2** (in *pl.*) sickness due to too rapid decompression e.g. after diving. [OE, rel. to BIND]

bend[2] *n.* **1** any of various knots used to tie one rope to another. **2** (in heraldry) a stripe from the dexter chief to the sinister base. —**bend sinister,** (in heraldry) a stripe from the sinister chief to the dexter base, sometimes used as a sign of bastardy. [OE, = band, bond]

beneath /bɪˈni:θ/ *adv.* & *prep.* **1** below, under. **2** not worthy of. —**beneath contempt,** not even worth despising. [OE (rel. to NETHER)]

benediction /benɪˈdɪkʃ(ə)n/ *n.* a spoken blessing, especially at the end of a religious service or as a special Roman Catholic service. —**benedictory** *adj.* [f. OF f. L (*benedicere* bless)]

benefaction /benɪˈfækʃ(ə)n/ *n.* a charitable gift or endowment, especially to an institution. [as foll.]

benefactor /ˈbenɪfæktə(r)/ *n.* one who has given financial or other help, especially to an institution. —**benefactress** *n.fem.* [f. L (as BENEFIT)]

benefice /ˈbenɪfɪs/ *n.* a living held by a vicar, rector, etc. [f. OF f. L *beneficium* kind deed]

beneficent /bɪˈnefɪs(ə)nt/ *adj.* conferring blessings or favours. —**beneficence** *n.* [f. L (as BENEFIT)]

beneficial /benɪˈfɪʃ(ə)l/ *adj.* advantageous, having benefits. —**beneficially** *adj.* [f. L (as BENEFICE)]

beneficiary /benɪˈfɪʃərɪ/ *n.* a recipient of benefits, especially as designated in a will. [f. L (as BENEFICE)]

benefit /ˈbenɪfɪt/ *n.* **1** a favourable, helpful, or profitable factor or circumstance. **2** a payment to which one is entitled from an insurance policy or government funds. **3** a public performance or game of which the proceeds go to a charitable cause etc. —*v.t./i.* **1** to do good to. **2** to receive benefit (*from* or *by*). —**benefit of clergy,** the privilege, to which clergymen were formerly entitled, of being tried before an ecclesiastical court not a secular one, or (in certain cases) of being exempt from the sentence imposed. **benefit of the doubt,** concession that a person is innocent, correct, etc., although doubt exists. **benefit society,** a society for mutual insurance against illness or the effects of old age. [f. AF f. L benefactum (*bene facere* do well)]

benevolent /bɪˈnev(ə)lənt/ *adj.* wishing to do good to others, friendly and helpful; (of a fund) charitable. —**benevolence** *n.*, **benevolently** *adv.* [f. OF f. L *bene volens* well wishing]

benighted /bɪˈnaɪtɪd/ *adj.* **1** overtaken by night. **2** intellectually or morally ignorant. [f. BE- + NIGHT]

benign /bɪˈnaɪn/ *adj.* kindly; propitious; (of climate) mild; (of disease) mild, not malignant. —**benignly** *adv.* [f. OF f. L *benignus*]

benignant /bɪˈnɪgnənt/ *adj.* kindly, especially to inferiors; beneficial. —**benignancy** *n.*, **benignantly** *adv.* [f. prec.]

benignity /bɪˈnɪgnɪtɪ/ *n.* kindliness. [f. BENIGN]

benison /ˈbenɪ:z(ə)n/ *n.* (*archaic*) a blessing. [f. OF f. L *benedictio* benediction]

bent[1] *p.p.* of BEND[1]. —*adj.* curved or having an angle; (*slang*) dishonest, illicit. —*n.* a natural tendency or bias; a talent (*for*). —**bent on,** determined on, seeking to do.

bent[2] *n.* **1** any of various coarse stiff grasses etc. **2** the flower-stalk of grasses, especially when old and dry. [= OE *beonet*]

benthos /ˈbenθɒs/ *n.* the flora and fauna found at the bottom of a sea or lake. [Gk, = depth of sea]

bentwood *n.* wood artificially curved for making furniture.

benumb /bɪˈnʌm/ *v.t.* to make numb; to paralyse or deaden. [f. BE- + NUMB]

benzene /ˈbenzi:n/ *n.* a substance obtained from coal-tar and used as a solvent, fuel, and in the manufacture of plastics. [f. BENZOIN]

benzine /ˈbenzi:n/ *n.* a spirit obtained from petroleum and used as a cleansing agent. [f. foll.]

benzoin /ˈbenzəʊɪn/ *n.* the aromatic resin of an East Indian tree, *Styrax benzoin*; a white crystalline constituent of this. —**benzoic** /-ˈzəʊɪk/ *adj.* [f. F f. Arab. *lubān jāwī* incense of Java]

benzol /ˈbenzɒl/ *n.* benzene, especially in its unrefined state. [f. prec.]

bequeath /bɪˈkwi:ð/ *v.t.* to leave (personal estate) to a person by will; to transmit to posterity. [OE (BE- + root of QUOTH)]

bequest /bɪˈkwest/ *n.* bequeathing; a thing bequeathed. [rel. to prec.]

berate /bɪˈreɪt/ *v.t.* to scold or rebuke severely. [f. BE- + RATE]

berberis /ˈbɜ:bərɪs/ *n.* a cultivated prickly yellow-flowered shrub of the genus *Berberis*. [f. L & OF (orig. unkn.)]

berceuse /beəˈsɜ:z/ *n.* an instrumental piece of music in the style of a lullaby. [F (*bercer* rock to sleep)]

bereave /bɪˈri:v/ *v.t.* (chiefly in *pass.*; *p.p.* **bereaved**) to deprive of a near relative, spouse, etc., by death. [OE (*reave* take away forcibly)]

bereft /bɪˈreft/ *adj.* deprived (*of*). [f. prec.]

beret /ˈbereɪ/ *n.* a round flat cap of felt or cloth. [F, rel. to BIRETTA]

berg *n.* an iceberg. [abbr.]

bergamot /ˈbɜ:gəmɒt/ *n.* **1** a perfume from the rind of a citrus fruit; the tree (*Citrus bergamia*) bearing this fruit. **2** an aromatic herb, especially *Monardia didyma*. [f. *Bergamo* in Italy]

beriberi /berɪˈberɪ/ *n.* a tropical disease of the nervous system, caused by deficiency of vitamin B. [Sinhalese, f. *beri* weakness]

berkelium /bɜ:kˈi:lɪəm, ˈbɜ:klɪəm/ *n.* an artificially made transuranic radioactive metallic element, symbol Bk, atomic number 97, first obtained in 1949 by bombarding americium with helium ions. [f. *Berkeley* in California (where first made)]

Berks. *abbr.* Berkshire.

berry *n.* any small roundish juicy fruit without a stone; (*Bot.*) a fruit with seeds enclosed in pulp (e.g. banana, tomato). [OE]

berserk /bəˈsɜ:k/ *adj.* uncontrollably violent. —**go berserk,** to fly into a violent rage, to lose control. [orig. = Norse warrior, f. Icel. = bear-coat]

berth *n.* **1** a fixed bunk on a ship, train, etc., for sleeping in. **2** a ship's place at a wharf; room for a ship to swing at anchor. —*v.t./i.* **1** to moor (a ship) in a berth; to come to a mooring. **2** to provide with a sleeping-berth. —**give a wide berth to,** to keep at a safe distance from. [f. BEAR[2]]

beryl /ˈberɪl/ *n.* a transparent often pale-green precious stone; a mineral species including this and the emerald. [f. OF f. L f. Gk *bērullos*]

beryllium /bəˈrɪlɪəm/ *n.* a very light hard greyish-white metallic element of the alkaline-earth metal series, symbol Be, atomic number 4. [f. prec.]

beseech /bɪˈsi:tʃ/ *v.t.* (*past* & *p.p.* **besought** /-ˈsɔ:t/) to implore, to ask earnestly for. [f. BE- + SEEK]

beset /bɪˈset/ *v.t.* (**-tt-**; *past* & *p.p.* **beset**) to surround, to hem in; (of troubles etc.) to assail persistently. [f. BE- + SET]

beside /bɪˈsaɪd/ *prep.* **1** by the side of; near. **2** compared with. —**beside oneself,** frantic with worry, anger, etc. **beside the point,** irrelevant. [f. BE- + SIDE]

besides /bɪˈsaɪdz/ *adv.* & *prep.* in addition (to). [f. prec.]

besiege /bɪˈsi:dʒ/ *v.t.* **1** to lay seige to. **2** to crowd round oppressively, to harass with requests etc. [f. BE- + SIEGE]

besom /ˈbi:z(ə)m/ *n.* a broom made of twigs tied round a stick. [OE]

besot /bɪˈsɒt/ *v.t.* (**-tt-**; esp. in *pass.*) to infatuate. [f. BE- + SOT]

bespeak /bɪˈspi:k/ *v.t.* (*past* **bespoke**; *p.p.* **bespoken,** as *adj.* **bespoke**) **1** to engage beforehand; to commission (a product). **2** to be an indication of. [f. BE- + SPEAK]

bespectacled /bɪˈspektək(ə)ld/ *adj*. wearing spectacles. [f. BE- + SPECTACLE]

bespoke /bɪˈspəʊk/ *adj*. (of clothes etc.) made to order; (of a tailor etc.) dealing in such goods. [f. BESPEAK]

best *adj*. (*superl*. of GOOD) of the most excellent or desirable kind. —*adv*. (*superl*. of WELL) in the best manner; to the greatest degree; most usefully. —*n*. that which is best; the chief merit; (*colloq*.) one's best clothes. —*v.t*. (*colloq*.) to defeat or outwit. —**at best,** on the most hopeful or favourable view. **best end,** the rib end of neck of lamb, meatier than the scrag end. **best man,** a bridegroom's chief attendant. **best part,** most *of*. **best-seller** *n*. a book that sells in very large numbers. **do one's best,** do all one can. **get** *or* **have the best of,** to win (a fight etc.). **make the best of,** to be as contented as possible with; to do what one can with (something of limited potential). [OE, for *betest* (cf. BETTER)]

bestial /ˈbestɪəl/ *adj*. of a beast; beast-like in cruelty, blind lust, etc. —**bestiality** /-ˈælɪtɪ/ *n*. [f. OF f. L (*bestia* beast)]

bestiary /ˈbestɪərɪ/ *n*. a medieval treatise on beasts. [f. L (as prec.)]

bestir /bɪˈstɜː(r)/ *v.t*. (**-rr-**) to rouse or exert (*oneself*). [f. BE- + STIR]

bestow /bɪˈstəʊ/ *v.t*. to confer. —**bestowal** *n*. [f. BE- + STOW]

bestrew /bɪˈstruː/ *v.t*. (*p.p*. **bestrewed, bestrewn**) to strew; to lie scattered over. [f. BE- + STREW]

bestride /bɪˈstraɪd/ *v.t*. (*past* **bestrode**; *p.p*. **bestridden**) **1** to sit astride on. **2** to stand astride over. [f. BE- + STRIDE]

bet *v.i./t*. (**-tt-**; *past* & *p.p*. **bet, betted**) **1** to risk one's money against another's on the outcome of an event; to risk (an amount) thus. **1** (*colloq*.) to think most likely. —*n*. **1** an act of betting. **2** a sum staked. —**you bet,** (*slang*) you may be sure. [perh. = ABET]

beta /ˈbiːtə/ *n*. **1** the second letter of the Greek alphabet, = b. **2** a second-class mark in an examination. **3** a designation of the second brightest star in a constellation, or sometimes a star's position in a group. —**beta-blocker** *n*. a drug that prevents the stimulation of receptors (**beta receptors**) in the central nervous system that cause increased cardiac activity. **beta particles** *or* **rays,** fast-moving electrons emitted by radioactive substances, formerly regarded as rays. [f. Gk]

betake /bɪˈteɪk/ *v.refl*. (*past* **betook**; *p.p*. **betaken**) to go *to*. [f. BE- + TAKE]

betatron /ˈbiːtətrɒn/ *n*. an apparatus for accelerating electrons in a circular path. [f. BETA + (ELEC)TRON]

betel /ˈbiːt(ə)l/ *n*. the leaf of the plant *Piper betle*, chewed in the east with betel-nut. —**betel-nut** *n*. the areca nut. [f. Port. f. Malayalam]

bête noire /beɪt ˈnwɑː(r)/ (*pl*. **bêtes noires** *pr*. same) a person's chief dislike. [F, lit. = black beast]

bethink /bɪˈθɪŋk/ *v.refl*. (*past* & *p.p*. **bethought**) to stop to think, to recollect. [f. BE- + THINK]

betide /bɪˈtaɪd/ *v.t./i*. to happen (to), now chiefly in **woe betide** (a person), orig. a curse, now a warning. [f. BE- + obs. *tide* befall]

betimes /bɪˈtaɪmz/ *adv*. (*literary*) in good time, early. [f. BE- + TIME]

betoken /bɪˈtəʊkən/ *v.t*. to be a sign of, to indicate. [f. BE- + TOKEN]

betony /ˈbetənɪ/ *n*. a purple-flowered plant *Betonica officinalis*, formerly used in medicine. [f. OF f. L, perh. f. name of Iberian tribe]

betray /bɪˈtreɪ/ *v.t*. **1** to be disloyal to; to give up or reveal disloyally (to an enemy). **2** to reveal involuntarily; to be evidence of. **3** to lead astray. —**betrayal** *n*., **betrayer** *n*. [f. BE- + obs. *tray* f. F f. L *tradere* hand over]

betroth /bɪˈtrəʊð/ *v.t*. to engage to marry a specified person. —**betrothal** *n*., **betrothed** *adj*. & *n*. [f. BE- + TRUTH]

better *adj*. (*compar*. of GOOD) **1** of a more excellent or desirable kind. **2** partly or fully recovered from illness. **3** greater (*part* etc.). —*adv*. (*compar*. of WELL[1]) in a better manner; to a greater degree; more usefully. —*n*. that which is better; (in *pl*.) one's superiors. —*v.t*. to improve; to surpass (a feat). —*v.refl*. to improve one's position in life. —**better half,** (*colloq*.) one's spouse. **get the better of,** to defeat or outwit. **had better,** would find it more advantageous to. [OE]

betterment *n*. improvement. [f. prec.]

betting-shop *n*. a bookmaker's shop or office.

between /bɪˈtwiːn/ *adv*. & *prep*. **1** in the space, time, condition, etc., bounded by (two limits). **2** to and from; reciprocally felt or done by. **3** by the sharing or joint action of. **4** taking one and rejecting the other of. —**between ourselves, between you and me,** speaking in confidence. **in between**, in an intermediate position. [OE (ult. rel. to TWO)]

betwixt /bɪˈtwɪkst/ *prep*. & *adv*. between, now only in **betwixt and between,** (*colloq*.) neither one thing nor the other. [f. OE (as prec.)]

bevel /ˈbev(ə)l/ *n*. **1** a joiner's or mason's tool for adjusting angles. **2** a slope from the horizontal or vertical; a sloping edge or surface. —*v.t./i*. (**-ll-**) to reduce (a square edge) to a sloping one; to slope at an angle. [f. OF (*baer* gape)]

beverage /ˈbevərɪdʒ/ *n*. any drink. [f. OF f. L *bibere* drink]

bevy /ˈbevɪ/ *n*. a large group (*of*). [orig. unkn.]

bewail /bɪˈweɪl/ *v.t*. to wail over, to mourn for. [f. BE- + WAIL]

beware /bɪˈweə(r)/ *v.i.* (only *imper.* & *infin.*) to be on one's guard. —**beware of,** to be cautious of, to guard against. [f. BE + obs. *ware* cautious]

bewilder /bɪˈwɪldə(r)/ *v.t.* to perplex or confuse. —**bewilderment** *n.* [f. BE- + obs. *wilder* to lose one's way]

bewitch /bɪˈwɪtʃ/ *v.t.* **1** to captivate, to delight greatly. **2** to cast a spell on. [f. BE- + WITCH]

beyond /bɪˈjɒnd/ *adv.* & *prep.* **1** at or to the far side (of). **2** outside the scope or understanding of. **3** in addition (to). —*n.* the unknown after death. [OE (*be* by, rel. to YON)]

bezel /ˈbez(ə)l/ *n.* **1** the sloping edge of a chisel; an oblique face of a cut gem. **2** a rim holding a glass cover etc. or a gem in position. [f. OF; orig. unkn.]

bezique /bɪˈzi:k/ *n.* a card-game for two players, using a double pack of 64 cards (ace to seven only); a combination of the queen of spades and jack of diamonds in this game. [F, perh. f. Pers. = juggler]

bhakti /ˈbɑ:ktɪ/ *n.* (*Hinduism*) devotional worship directed to one supreme deity, usually Vishnu (especially in his incarnations as Rama and Krishna) or Siva, by whose grace salvation may be attained by all regardless of sex, caste, or class. [Skr.]

bhang /bæŋ/ *n.* Indian hemp; its dried leaves smoked or chewed as a narcotic and intoxicant. [f. Port. f. Skr.]

Bi *symbol* bismuth.

bi- /baɪ-/ *prefix* two, twice (*bilateral, bi-weekly*). [L]

biannual /baɪˈænjʊəl/ *adj.* twice-yearly.

bias /ˈbaɪəs/ *n.* **1** a predisposition or prejudice. **2** distortion of a statistical result by a neglected factor. **3** (in bowls) the oblique course of a bowl or the lopsided form causing it. **4** an oblique direction in cutting cloth. —*v.t.* (*p.t.* & *p.p.* **biased**) to give a bias to, to influence unfairly. —**bias binding**, a strip of material cut diagonally, used to bind edges. [f. OF, perh. ult. f. Gk *epikarsios* oblique]

bib *n.* **1** a cloth etc. tied over a child's chest at meals to protect its clothes. **2** the part of an apron or overall covering the chest. [perh. f. archaic *bib* drink (f. L *bibere*)]

Bible /ˈbaɪb(ə)l/ *n.* **1** the Christian scriptures (Old and New Testament). **2 bible,** a copy of these; the scriptures of another religion; an authoritative book. [f. OF f. L f. Gk *biblia* books, orig. dim of *bublos* papyrus]

biblical /ˈbɪblɪk(ə)l/ *adj.* of or in the Bible. [f. prec.]

bibliography /bɪblɪˈɒgrəfɪ/ *n.* **1** a list of books by a given author or on a given topic. **2** the study of the history of books and their production. —**bibliographer** *n.*, **bibliographical** /-ˈgraefɪk(ə)l/ *adj.* [f. Gk (as prec., *graphia* writing)]

bibliophile /ˈbɪblɪəfaɪl/ *n.* a lover of books. [f. F (as prec. + Gk *philos* friend)]

bibulous /ˈbɪbjʊləs/ *adj.* addicted to alcoholic drink. [f. L *bibere* drink)]

bicameral /ˈbaɪkæmər(ə)l/ *adj.* having two legislative chambers. [f. BI- + L *camera* chamber]

bicarbonate /baɪˈkɑ:bəneɪt/ *n.* a carbonate containing a double proportion of carbon dioxide, especially sodium bicarbonate.

bicentenary /baɪsenˈti:nərɪ/ *n.* a two-hundredth anniversary.

bicentennial /baɪsenˈtenɪəl/ *adj.* occurring every two hundred years. —*n.* a bicentenary.

biceps /ˈbaɪseps/ *n.* a muscle with two heads or attachments, especially that which bends the elbow. [L, = two-headed]

bicker *v.i.* to quarrel pettily. [orig. unkn.]

biconcave /baɪˈkɒnkeɪv/ *adj.* (of a lens) concave on both sides.

biconvex /baɪˈkɒnveks/ *adj.* (of a lens) convex on both sides.

bicuspid /baɪˈkʌspɪd/ *adj.* having two cusps. —*n.* any of the eight bicuspid teeth (between the molars and canines). [f. BI- + L *cuspis* sharp point]

bicycle /ˈbaɪsɪk(ə)l/ *n.* a road vehicle with two wheels one behind the other, driven by pedals worked by the rider. —*v.i.* to ride on a bicycle. —**bicycle clip**, each of a pair of clips for securing a cyclist's trouser-leg at the ankle. —**bicyclist** *n.* [f. F (BI-, Gk *kuklos* wheel)]

bid *v.t./i.* (**-dd-**; *past* & *p.p.* **bid**) **1** to offer (a certain sum) as the price one is willing to pay, especially at an auction; to make a bid or bids; (in card-games) to state (the number of tricks) one undertakes to win in a given suit. **2** (*past* **bade**, *p.p.* **bidden** or **bid**) to instruct or invite to; to utter (a greeting, farewell). —*n.* **1** an act of bidding; a sum etc. bid. **2** an attempt. —**bid fair to,** to seem likely to. **make a bid for,** to attempt to secure. [OE]

biddable /ˈbɪdəb(ə)l/ *adj.* docile, obedient. [f. BID]

bidding *n.* **1** a person's command or invitation. **2** the bids made at an auction or in a card-game. [f. BID]

biddy *n.* **old biddy,** (*slang*) an elderly woman. [pet-form of woman's Christian name *Bridget*]

bide *v.t./i.* (*archaic* or *dial.*) to remain. —**bide one's time,** to await one's best opportunity. [OE]

bidet /ˈbi:deɪ/ *n.* a low basin for sitting astride to wash the genital and anal regions. [F, = pony]

biennial /baɪˈenɪəl/ *adj.* **1** lasting or living for two years. **2** happening every second year. —*n.* a plant that springs one year and flowers, fruits, and dies the next. [f. L (BI-, *annus* year)]

bier /bɪə(r)/ *n.* a movable stand on which a coffin or corpse rests. [OE (rel. to BEAR[2])]

biff *n.* (*slang*) a smart blow. —*v.t.* to strike (a person). [imit.]

bifid /ˈbaɪfɪd/ *adj.* divided by a deep cleft into two parts. [f. L (BI-, *findere* split)]

bifocal /baɪˈfəʊk(ə)l/ *adj.* having two foci (of spectacle lenses having part for near and part for distant vision). —**bifocals** *n.pl.* spectacles with such lenses (see SPECTACLE).

bifurcate /ˈbaɪfɜːkeɪt/ *v.t./i.* to divide into two branches. —**bifurcation** /-ˈkeɪʃ(ə)n/ *n.* [f. L *bifurcare* (BI-, *furca* fork)]

big *adj.* (**-gg-**) **1** large in size, amount, or intensity; outstandingly large of its kind; grown up, elder. **2** important, outstanding. **3** boastful; (*colloq.*) ambitious, generous. **4** advanced in pregnancy (especially of animals). —*adv.*(*colloq.*) on a grand scale, ambitiously. —**Big Brother,** a seemingly benevolent but in fact ruthless dictator. [character in George Orwell's novel *1984*] **big end,** the end of a connecting-rod in an engine, encircling the crankshaft. **big-head** *n.* (*colloq.*) a conceited person. **big-hearted** *adj.* generous. **big time,** (*slang*) the highest rank among entertainers etc. **big top,** the main tent at a circus. [orig. unkn.]

bigamy /ˈbɪgəmɪ/ *n.* the crime of making a second marriage while a first is still valid. —**bigamist** *n.*, **bigamous** *adj.* [f. OF f. L (BI-, Gk *gamos* marriage)]

bighorn *n.* either of two North American sheep (*Ovis canadensis* and *O. dalli*) with transversely ribbed horns that in the male may curve in a huge spiral.

bight /baɪt/ *n.* **1** a loop of rope. **2** a wide shallow bay on a coast. [OE]

bigot /ˈbɪgət/ *n.* an obstinate and intolerant adherent of a creed or view. —**bigoted** *adj.*, **bigotry** *n.* [F]

bigwig *n.* (*colloq.*) an important person.

bijou /ˈbiːʒuː/ *adj.* small and elegant. [F, = jewel]

bike *n.* (*colloq.*) a bicycle or motor cycle. —*v.i.* (*colloq.*) to ride on this. [abbr.]

bikini /bɪˈkiːnɪ/ *n.* a woman's scanty two-piece beach garment. [f. *Bikini*, an atoll in the West Pacific where an atomic bomb was tested in 1946]

bilateral /baɪˈlætər(ə)l/ *adj.* of, on, or having two sides; involving two parties. —**bilateralism** *n.*, **bilaterally** *adv.* [f. L (BI-, *latus* side)]

bilberry /ˈbɪlbərɪ/ *n.* a small shrub (*Vaccinium myrtillus*) growing on heaths, moors, etc.; its purple-black berry. [Scand.]

bile *n.* **1** a bitter yellowish fluid produced by the liver and stored in the gall-bladder, aiding digestion of fats. **2** (*archaic*) one of the four humours (see HUMOUR). —**bile duct,** a duct conveying bile to the duodenum. [f. F f. L *bilis*]

bilge /bɪldʒ/ *n.* **1** the nearly flat part of a ship's bottom. **2** (also **bilge-water**) the foul water that collects there. **3** (*slang*) worthless ideas or talk. [prob. var. of BULGE]

bilharzia /bɪlˈhɑːtsɪə/ *n.* a tropical disease caused by a flatworm parasitic in the pelvis. [f. T. *Bilharz*, German physician (d. 1862)]

bilingual /baɪˈlɪŋgw(ə)l/ *adj.* speaking or written in two languages. [f. L (BI-, *lingua* language)]

bilious /ˈbɪljəs/ *adj.* **1** affected by sickness assumed to be caused by a disorder of the bile. **2** of a sickly yellowish hue. —**biliousness** *n.* [f. BILE]

bilk *v.t.* to cheat (*of* what is due); to avoid paying (a creditor etc.). [orig. unkn.]

bill[1] *n.* **1** a statement of charges for goods or services supplied. **2** the draft of a proposed law. **3** a poster or placard; a programme of entertainment. **4** (*US*) a banknote. —*v.t.* **1** to announce on a poster or in a programme. **2** to advertise *as*. **3** to send a note of charges to. —**bill of exchange,** a written order to pay a sum on a given date to the drawer or a named person. **bill of fare,** a menu. **bill of lading,** an inventory of goods to be shipped, signed by the carrier. [f. AF f. L *bulla* seal]

bill[2] *n.* **1** a bird's beak, especially when slender or flattened. **2** a narrow promontory. —*v.i.* (of doves) to stroke each other's bills. —**bill and coo,** to exchange caresses. [OE]

bill[3] *n.* (*hist.*) a weapon with a hooked blade. [OE]

billabong /ˈbɪləbɒŋ/ *n.* (*Austral.*) a river branch forming a backwater or stagnant pool. [f. Aboriginal *Bilibang* Bell River (*billa* water)]

billboard *n.* a hoarding for advertisements. [f. BILL[1] + BOARD]

billet[1] /ˈbɪlɪt/ *n.* **1** an order to a householder to lodge and board soldiers etc.; a place so provided. **2** (*colloq.*) a job. —*v.t.* to place (soldiers etc.) in a billet. [f. AF (dim. of *bille* BILL[1])]

billet[2] /ˈbɪlɪt/ *n.* **1** a thick piece of firewood. **2** a small bar of metal. [f. F (dim. of *bille* tree-trunk)]

billet-doux /bɪlɪˈduː/ *n.* (*pl.* **billets-doux** -ˈduːz/) (*joc.*) a love-letter. [F, = sweet note]

billhook *n.* a tool with a hooked blade, used for pruning etc. [f. BILL[3] + HOOK]

billiards /ˈbɪljədz/ *n.* a game played on an oblong cloth-covered table with three balls struck with cues. —**bar billiards,** a game in which balls are to be struck into holes on a table. [f. F *billard* cue, dim. of *bille* tree-trunk]

billingsgate /ˈbɪlɪŋzgeɪt/ *n.* coarse abuse. [f. *Billingsgate*, a London fish-market dating from the 16th c., known for the invective traditionally ascribed to the fish-porters]

billion /ˈbɪljən/ *adj.* & *n.* (*pl.* **billion** except as below) **1** a million million. **2** (*US* and increasingly *British*) a thousand million. **3** billions (*pl.*, *colloq.*) great numbers *of*. —**billionth** *adj.* [f. F (BI-, MILLION)]

billow /ˈbɪləʊ/ *n.* a large wave. —*v.i.* to rise or roll like waves. —**billowy** *adj.* [f. ON]

billy *n.* a billycan. [abbr.]

billycan /ˈbɪlɪkæn/ *n.* a tin or enamelled container with a lid and handle, used as a cooking-vessel, especially in Australia. [perh. f. Aboriginal *billa* water]

billy-goat /ˈbɪlɪgəʊt/ *n.* a male goat. [f. *Billy* pet-form of *William* + GOAT]

bimetallic /baɪmɪˈtælɪk/ *adj.* using or made of two metals.

bin *n.* a large rigid container, usually with a lid, for storing coal, grain, flour, etc.; a receptacle for rubbish. [OE]

binary /ˈbaɪnərɪ/ *adj.* involving a pair or pairs. —*n.* a binary star. —**binary compound,** one containing two chemical elements or radicals. **binary digit,** either of the two digits used in the binary scale. **binary scale,** a numerical system using only the two digits 0 and 1. **binary star,** a gravitationally-bound pair of stars revolving round a common centre. [f. L *bini* two together]

binaural /baɪnˈɔːr(ə)l, bɪ-/ *adj.* of or used with both ears; (of sound) recorded by two microphones and usually transmitted separately to the two ears. [f. BI- + AURAL]

bind /baɪnd/ *v.t./i.* (*past* & *p.p.* **bound**) **1** to tie or fasten together; to encircle *with*; to bandage (*up*). **2** to secure or restrain by fastening; to fasten sheets of (a book) into a cover; to cover the edge of (a thing) with strengthening or decorative material. **3** to be obligatory; to compel, to impose a duty on. **4** to stick together. **5** to constipate. **6** (*slang*) to grumble. —*n.* (*slang*) a nuisance, a bore. —**bind over,** (*Law*) to put under an obligation (*to* keep the peace etc.). [OE]

binder /ˈbaɪndə(r)/ *n.* **1** a loose cover for papers. **2** a bookbinder. **3** a substance that binds things together. **4** a machine that binds harvested corn into sheaves. [f. prec.]

bindery *n.* a bookbinder's workshop. [f. prec.]

binding /ˈbaɪndɪŋ/ *n.* something that binds, especially the gluing etc. and covers of a book. —*adj.* obligatory (*on*). [f. BIND]

bindweed /ˈbaɪndwiːd/ *n.* convolvulus.

bine *n.* the twisting stem of a climbing plant, especially the hop. [dial. form of BIND]

binge /bɪndʒ/ *n.* (*slang*) a drinking-bout or spree. [prob. dial., = soak]

bingo[1] /ˈbɪŋgəʊ/ *int.* an exclamation at a sudden action or event. [imit. of sudden sound; cf. dial. *bing*]

bingo[2] /ˈbɪŋgəʊ/ *n.* a popular gambling game that is a variety of lotto, played with cards on which numbered squares have to be covered as the numbers are called at random. The player first covering all or a set of these wins a prize. [perh. f. winner's exclam. of *bingo* (see prec.)]

binnacle /ˈbɪnək(ə)l/ *n.* a case or stand for a ship's compass. [earlier *bittacle*, f. Sp. or Port. f. L *habitaculum* lodging]

binocular /bɪˈnɒkjʊlə(r), baɪ-/ *n.* (usu. in *pl.* and /bɪ-/) field- or opera-glasses etc. for use with both eyes. —/usu. baɪ-/ *adj.* for or using both eyes. [f. L *bini* two together, *oculus* eye]

binomial /baɪˈnəʊmɪəl/ *n.* an algebraic expression consisting of two terms linked by a plus or minus sign. —*adj.* consisting of two terms so linked. —**binomial theorem,** formula for finding any power of a binomial without multiplying at length. [f. F (BI-, Gk *nomos* part)]

binturong /ˈbɪntjʊərɒŋ/ *n.* a prehensile-tailed civet (*Arctitis binturong*) of South Asia. [Malay]

bio- /baɪəʊ-/ *prefix* of life or living things. [f. Gk *bios* life]

biochemistry /baɪəʊˈkemɪstrɪ/ *n.* the study of the chemistry of living organisms. —**biochemical** *adj.*, **biochemist** *n.*

biodegradable /baɪəʊdɪˈgreɪdəb(ə)l/ *adj.* capable of being decomposed by bacteria.

bioengineering /baɪəʊendʒɪˈnɪərɪŋ/ *n.* the application of engineering techniques to biological processes.

biography /baɪˈɒgrəfɪ/ *n.* a written account of a person's life; the writing of biographies. —**biographer** *n.*, **biographical** /baɪəˈgræfɪk(ə)l/ *adj.* [f. BIO- + -GRAPHY]

biological /baɪəˈlɒdʒɪk(ə)l/ *adj.* of or relating to biology. —**biological warfare,** the use of organisms to spread disease among the enemy. —**biologically** *adv.* [f. foll.]

biology /baɪˈɒlədʒɪ/ *n.* the science of living organisms, dealing with their morphology, physiology, anatomy, behaviour, origin, and distribution. —**biologist** *n.* [f. BIO- + -LOGY]

biometry /baɪˈɒmɪtrɪ/ *n.* the analysis of biological phenomena by statistical methods. —**biometric** /baɪəˈmetrɪk/ *adj.* [f. BIO- + Gk *metron* measure]

bionic /baɪˈɒnɪk/ *adj.* forming or possessing an electronically operated body part or parts. [f. BIO-, after *electronic*]

biophysics /baɪəʊˈfɪzɪks/ *n.* the science of the physical properties of living organisms and their constituents, and the investigation of biological phenomena in general by means of the techniques of modern physics. —**biophysical** *adj.*, **biophysicist** *n.*

biopsy /ˈbaɪɒpsɪ/ *n.* an examination of tissue cut from the living body, as a means of diagnosis; surgical removal of such tissue. [f. BIO-, after *autopsy*]

biorhythm /ˈbaɪəʊrɪð(ə)m/ *n.* any of the internal

cycles said to govern a person's physiological, emotional, and intellectual activity.

biosphere /ˈbaɪəsfɪə(r)/ *n.* the regions of the earth's crust and atmosphere occupied by living organisms.

biotic /baɪˈɒtɪk/ *adj.* of life or living things. [f. F or L f. Gk (*bios* life)]

biotin /ˈbaɪətɪn/ *n.* a vitamin in yeast and egg-yolks, controlling growth. [G, as prec.]

bipartisan /baɪpɑːtɪˈzæn/ *adj.* involving or agreed to by two parties.

bipartite /baɪˈpɑːtaɪt/ *adj.* consisting of two parts; shared by two parties. [f. L (BI-, *partiri* divide)]

biped /ˈbaɪped/ *n.* a two-footed animal. —*adj.* two-footed. [f. L (BI-, *pes* foot)]

biplane /ˈbaɪpleɪn/ *n.* an aeroplane with two sets of wings, one above the other.

bipolar /baɪˈpəʊlə(r)/ *adj.* having two poles or extremities.

birch /bɜːtʃ/ *n.* **1** a tree of the genus *Betula* with smooth bark and slender branches. **2** a rod of birch twigs, used for flogging delinquents. —*v.t.* to flog with a birch. [OE]

bird /bɜːd/ *n.* **1** an egg-laying vertebrate animal of the class Aves, with feathers, two wings, and two feet. **2** (*slang*) a young woman; a person (especially a strange one). **3** (*rhyming slang*, f. *birdlime* = time) a prison sentence. —**bird of paradise,** a New Guinea bird with brilliant plumage. **bird of passage,** a migrant, a transient visitor. **bird-watcher** *n.* one who studies birds in their natural surroundings. [orig. unkn.]

birdie /ˈbɜːdɪ/ *n.* **1** (*children's colloq.*) a bird. **2** (in golf) a hole played in one stroke under par. [f. BIRD]

biretta /bɪˈretə/ *n.* a square cap worn by (esp. Roman Catholic) priests. [f. It. or Sp. dim. f. L *birrus* cape]

Biro /ˈbaɪrəʊ/ *n.* [P] a kind of ball-point pen. [f. L. *Biró*, Hungarian inventor (d. 1985)]

birth *n.* **1** the emergence of young from the mother's body. **2** origin, parentage. —**birth certificate,** an official document giving the date and place etc. of a person's birth. **birth-control** *n.* prevention of undesired pregnancy. **birth-rate** *n.* the number of births in one year for every 1,000 people. **give birth to,** to produce (young); to cause. [f. ON (rel. to BEAR[2])]

birthday *n.* the anniversary of the day of one's birth.

birthmark *n.* an unusual coloured mark on a person's skin at or from the time of birth.

birthplace *n.* the place of a person's birth.

birthright *n.* rights belonging to a person by birth, especially as the eldest son.

birthstone *n.* (in astrology) a gemstone associated with a particular month or sign of the zodiac and thought to bring good luck if worn by a person born then.

biscuit /ˈbɪskɪt/ *n.* **1** a flat thin unleavened cake, usually dry and crisp. **2** porcelain after firing but before glazing. **3** a light-brown colour. [f. OF f. L *biscoctus* twice baked]

bisect /baɪˈsekt/ *v.t.* to divide into two (strictly, equal) parts. —**bisection** *n.*, **bisector** *n.* [f. BI- + L *secare* cut]

bisexual /baɪˈseksjʊəl/ *adj.* **1** sexually attracted both to men and women. **2** having male and female sexual organs in one individual. —**bisexuality** /-ˈælɪtɪ/ *n.*

bishop /ˈbɪʃəp/ *n.* **1** a senior clergyman in charge of a diocese. **2** a mitre-shaped chess piece. [OE, ult. f. Gk. *episkopos* overseer]

bishopric /ˈbɪʃəprɪk/ *n.* the office or diocese of a bishop. [f. prec.]

bismuth /ˈbɪzməθ/ *n.* a brittle reddish-white metallic element, symbol Bi, atomic number 83; a compound of it used as a medicine. [f. G *wismut*, orig. unkn.]

bison /ˈbaɪs(ə)n/ *n.* (*pl.* same) **1** the European wild ox *Bison bonasus* (no longer surviving in the wild state). **2** the North American buffalo *Bison bison*. [f. L f. Gmc]

bisque[1] /bɪsk/ *n.* an extra turn, stroke, etc., allowed to an inferior player in some games. [F]

bisque[2] /biːsk/ *n.* unglazed white porcelain. [f. BISCUIT]

bisque[3] /bɪsk/ *n.* rich soup made from shellfish. [F; orig. unkn.]

bistre /ˈbɪstə(r)/ *n.* a brown pigment prepared from soot; the colour of this. [F; orig. unkn.]

bistro /ˈbiːstrəʊ/ *n.* (*pl.* **-os**) a continental wine-bar or small restaurant. [F]

bit[1] *n.* a small piece or quantity; a short distance or time; a small coin. —**a bit,** (*colloq.*) somewhat. **bit by bit,** gradually. **bit part,** a small part in a play or film. [OE (rel. to BITE)]

bit[2] *n.* **1** the mouthpiece of a bridle. **2** the part of a tool that cuts, grips, etc.; the boring-piece of a drill. [OE (rel. to BITE)]

bit[3] *n.* (in computers) a unit of information expressed as a choice between two possibilities. [f. *b(inary dig)it*)]

bit[4] *past* of BITE.

bitch *n.* **1** a female dog; a female fox, otter, etc. **2** (*derog.*) a spiteful or unpleasant woman. —*v.i.* to speak spitefully; (*colloq.*) to grumble. [OE]

bitchy /ˈbɪtʃɪ/ *adj.* spiteful, catty. —**bitchiness** *n.* [f. prec.]

bite *v.t./i.* (*past* **bit**; *p.p.* **bitten**) **1** to cut into or wound with the teeth; to take (a piece) *off* with the teeth. **2** (of an insect) to sting; (of a snake) to pierce with its fangs. **3** to snap *at*; (of a fish) to accept bait. **4** to cause smarting pain. **5** (of a wheel, screw, etc.) to grip the surface. —*n.* **1** an act of biting; a wound made by biting etc. **2** a mouthful of food; a snack. **3** the taking of bait by a fish. **4** incisiveness, pungency. [OE]

bitter *adj.* **1** having a sharp astringent taste, not sweet; (of beer) strongly flavoured with hops. **2** piercingly cold. **3** painful to the mind. **4** showing grief or resentment; virulent, resentful. —*n.* bitter beer; (in *pl.*) liquors impregnated with bitter herbs. —**bitter-sweet** *adj.* sweet but with a bitter element. **to the bitter end,** to the last extremity however painful. —**bitterly** *adv.*, **bitterness** *n.* [OE (prob. rel. to BITE)]

bittern /ˈbɪtɜːn/ *n.* a marsh bird of the genus *Botaurus*, allied to herons, especially one known for the male's booming note in the breeding-season. [f. OF f. L *butio* bittern, *taurus* bull]

bitty *adj.* made up of bits, scrappy. [f. BIT[1]]

bitumen /ˈbɪtjʊmɪn/ *n.* a mixture of tarlike hydrocarbons derived from petroleum. —**bituminous** /-ˈtjuːmɪnəs/ *adj.* [L]

bivalve /ˈbaɪvælv/ *adj.* (of shellfish) having two shells united by a hinge. —*n.* a bivalve shellfish, e.g. the oyster.

bivouac /ˈbɪvʊæk/ *n.* an encampment without tents, as of troops in the field. —*v.i.* (**-ck-**) to camp thus. [f. F, prob. f. G *beiwacht* additional guard; orig. of the citizens' patrol at Aargau and Zurich, assisting the night-watch at times of special need]

bizarre /bɪˈzɑː(r)/ *adj.* strikingly odd in appearance or effect. [F, orig. = brave, soldierly]

Bk *symbol* berkelium.

blab *v.t./i.* (**-bb-**) to talk indiscreetly, to let out (secrets) by indiscreet talk. [prob. imit.]

black *adj.* **1** colourless from the absence or absorption of light, of the colour of coal or soot. **2** dark-skinned; **Black,** of or for Negroes; of their culture etc. **3** (of the sky) dusky, overcast. **4** sinister, wicked; dismal, sullen, frowning; portending trouble or difficulty; (of humour) morbid, cynical. **5** (of goods etc.) banned by workers on strike from being handled by other trade-unionists. —*n.* **1** black colour or pigment; black (especially mourning) clothes or material. **2** a black ball or piece in a game. **3** the credit side of an account; *in the black*, solvent. **4** **Black,** a Negro. —*v.t.* **1** to make black. **2** to polish with blacking. **3** to declare (goods) to be 'black'. —**black and blue,** discoloured by bruises. **black and white,** photographed etc. in shades of grey and not in colour; comprising only opposite extremes; *in black and white*, recorded in writing or print. **black box,** the flight-recorder in an aircraft. **black bread,** coarse rye bread. **black coffee,** coffee without milk. **Black Country,** the industrial district of the Midlands west of Birmingham, so called from the smoke and dust of the coal and iron trades in the 19th c. **black eye,** one with the surrounding skin darkened by bruises. **Black Friars,** Dominicans, so called from their black cloaks. **black hole,** a region in outer space with a strong gravitational field from which matter and radiation cannot escape. **black ice,** thin transparent ice on a road etc. **black letter,** a heavy style of type used by early printers. **black magic,** magic involving the invocation of devils. **Black Maria,** a police vehicle for conveying prisoners. **black mark,** a mark of discredit. **black market,** illicit traffic in rationed or officially restricted goods. **black mass,** a sacrificial rite in honour of Satan, parodying the Eucharist. **Black Monk,** a Benedictine, so called from the colour of the habit. **black-out** *n.* a covering of all windows etc. to prevent light being seen by enemy aircraft; a temporary ban on the release of news; (*colloq.*) a momentary loss of consciousness. **black out,** to impose a black-out on; to suffer a 'black-out'. **black pepper,** pepper from the unripe berries complete with husks. **Black Power,** a movement seeking civil rights, political power, etc., for Blacks. **black sheep,** a discreditable character in an otherwise well-behaved group. **black tie,** a man's black bow-tie worn with a dinner-jacket. **black widow,** a venomous spider of the genus *Latrodectus*, found in tropical and subtropical regions. The female of the North American species *L. mactans* devours its mate. —**blackly** *adv.*, **blackness** *n.* [OE]

blackball *v.t.* to reject (a proposed member of a club etc.) in a ballot, originally by voting with a black ball.

blackberry *n.* the dark edible fruit of the bramble; this shrub.

blackbird *n.* **1** a songbird of the thrush family (*Turdus merula*), the male of which is black. **2** (*US*) the grackle or a similar bird.

blackboard *n.* a board with a smooth dark surface, used in classrooms etc. for writing on in chalk.

blackcock *n.* a male black grouse.

blackcurrant *n.* the small dark edible berry of the shrub *Ribes nigrum*; this shrub.

blacken /ˈblækən/ *v.t./i.* **1** to make or become black. **2** to speak ill of, to defame. [f. BLACK]

blackfly *n.* a black aphid infesting plants.

blackguard /ˈblægɑːd/ *n.* an unprincipled villain, a scoundrel. —**blackguardly** *adj.* [f. BLACK + GUARD; orig. collect. n., = royal scullions, vagrants, etc.]

blackhead *n.* a black-topped pimple on the face etc.

blacking *n.* black polish for shoes. [f. BLACK]

blacklead *n.* graphite.

blackleg *n.* (*derog.*) a person who refuses to join an appropriate trade union, or who participates in strike-breaking by working for an employer whose regular workmen are on strike. —*v.i.* (**-gg-**) to act as a blackleg. [f. BLACK + LEG, for unknown reason]

blacklist /ˈblæklɪst/ *n.* a list of persons etc. in disfavour. —*v.t.* to put on a blacklist.

blackmail *n.* exaction of payment in return for not carrying out a threat, especially to reveal discreditable secrets; payment exacted thus; use of threats or moral pressure. —*v.t.* to exact payment by blackmail; to threaten, to coerce. —**blackmailer** *n.* [f. obs. *mail* rent]

blacksmith *n.* a smith who works in iron.

blackthorn *n.* a thorny shrub *Prunus spinosa* bearing white flowers and sloes.

bladder *n.* a sac in the bodies of humans and animals for holding liquids, especially the urinary bladder; an animal's bladder, or a bag resembling this, inflated or otherwise prepared for various uses. —**bladder-wrack** *n.* a seaweed with air-filled swellings among its fronds. [OE]

blade *n.* **1** the cutting part of a knife etc.; the flat wide part of a spade, oar, etc. **2** the flat narrow leaf of grasses; the broad part of a leaf, as distinct from its stalk. **3** a broad flattish bone. [OE]

blame *v.t.* to hold responsible and criticize (*for*); to fix the responsibility for (misfortunes etc.) *on* a person. —*n.* responsibility for a bad result or attribution of it to a person. —**blameless** *adj.*, **blameworthy** *adj.* [f. OF, ult. = BLASPHEME]

blanch /blɑːntʃ/ *v.t./i.* **1** to make white by extracting the colour from or by depriving (plants) of light. **2** to peel (almonds) by scalding; to dip (vegetables) in boiling water. **3** to become pale with fear etc. [f. OF (as BLANK)]

blancmange /bləˈmɒnʒ/ *n.* a flavoured jelly-like pudding made with cornflour and milk. [f. OF, = white food]

bland *adj.* mild in flavour or properties; insipid, dull; soothing in manner, suave. —**blandly** *adj.*, **blandness** *n.* [f. L *blandus* soft, caressing]

blandish /ˈblændɪʃ/ *v.t.* to flatter, to cajole. —**blandishment** *n.* (usu. in *pl.*) [f. OF *blandir* flatter f. L (as prec.)]

blank *adj.* **1** not written, printed, or recorded on; with spaces left for details or signature. **2** showing no interest or emotion. **3** sheer, unadorned. —*n.* **1** a blank space in a document etc.; an empty surface. **2** a dash put in place of an omitted word. **3** a blank cartridge. —*v.t.* to screen *off* or *out*. —**blank cartridge,** one containing no bullet. **blank cheque,** one with the amount left for the payee to fill in. **blank verse,** unrhymed verse, usually in iambic pentameters. **draw a blank,** to be unsuccessful, to get no response. [f. OF *blanc* white f. Gmc]

blanket /ˈblæŋkɪt/ *n.* **1** a thick covering made of woollen or other fabric, used for warmth, chiefly as bedding. **2** a thick covering mass or layer. —*adj.* general, covering all cases or classes. —*v.t.* **1** to cover with a blanket. **2** to suppress (a scandal etc.). [f. OF (dim. of *blanc* BLANK)]

blare /bleə(r)/ *v.i./t.* to make a loud sound like a trumpet; to utter loudly. —*n.* a blaring sound. [f. Du., imit.]

blarney / ˈblɑːnɪ/ *n.* deceptive flattery. —*v.t./i.* to use or subject to such flattery. [f. *Blarney* Castle near Cork, a stone of which is said to confer a cajoling tongue on anyone kissing it]

blasé /ˈblɑːzeɪ/ *adj.* bored or unimpressed, especially through familiarity. [F]

blaspheme /blæsˈfiːm/ *v.t./i* to utter blasphemy against, to talk impiously. —**blasphemer** *n.* [f. OF f. L f. Gk *blasphēmeō* speak ill of]

blasphemy /ˈblæsfəmɪ/ *n.* grossly irreverent talk about God or sacred things. —**blasphemous** *adj.* [as prec.]

blast /blɑːst/ *n.* **1** an explosion, a destructive wave of air from this; a strong gust of wind etc. **2** the loud sound made by a trumpet, car horn, etc. —*v.t.* **1** to blow up (rocks etc.) with explosives. **2** to blow destructively on, to wither or blight (*lit.*, and in curses or as *int.* of annoyance). —**(at) full blast,** at full capacity or speed. **blast off,** (of a rocket or spacecraft) to launch into space. **blast-off** *n.* this launching. [OE (rel. to BLOW)]

blasted /ˈblɑːstɪd/ *adj.* cursed, damnable. —*adv.* damnably. [f. BLAST]

blast-furnace *n.* a smelting-furnace into which compressed hot air is driven.

blatant /ˈbleɪt(ə)nt/ *adj.* flagrant, unashamed; loudly obtrusive. —**blatantly** *adv.* [orig. = clamorous; coined by Spenser]

blather /ˈblæθə(r)/ *v.i.* (*colloq.*) to chatter foolishly. —*n.* (*colloq.*) foolish chatter. [f. ON]

blaze[1] *n.* **1** a bright flame or fire. **2** a brilliant display (*of* lights, colours, publicity). **3** a dramatic outburst of emotion. —*v.i.* **1** to burn or shine fiercely. **2** to display sudden emotion, usually anger. —**blaze away,** to fire a gun continuously. [OE, = torch]

blaze[2] *n.* **1** a white mark on the face of an animal, especially a horse. **2** a mark made in the bark of a tree to indicate a route. —*v.t.* to mark (a tree or path) with blazes. —**blaze a trail,** to show the way for others to follow. [orig. unkn.]

blaze[3] *v.t.* to proclaim. [f. MLG & MDu., rel. to BLOW[1]]

blazer /ˈbleɪzə(r)/ *n.* a light jacket often in the

colours, or with the badge, of a team or school. [f. BLAZE[1]]

blazon /ˈbleɪz(ə)n/ *n.* a heraldic shield, a coat of arms. —*v.t.* to proclaim; to describe or paint (a coat of arms); to inscribe with arms, names, etc., in colours. —**blazonry** *n.* [f. OF *blason* shield]

bleach *v.t./i.* to whiten by chemicals or exposure to sunlight. —*n.* a bleaching substance or process. —**bleaching powder,** chloride of lime. [OE]

bleak *adj.* **1** cold and wind-swept. **2** unpromising, dreary, grim. —**bleakly** *adv.*, **bleakness** *n.* [orig. = pale; rel. to BLEACH]

bleary *adj.* dim-sighted from watering of the eyes. —**blearily** *adv.* [f. LG]

bleat *n.* the tremulous cry of a sheep, goat, or calf. —*v.i.* to utter this cry; to say or speak feebly or plaintively. [OE, imit.]

bleed *v.t./i* (*past & p.p.* **bled**) **1** to leak blood or other fluid; (of a dye) to run. **2** to draw off blood or surplus fluid from; (*colloq.*) to extort money from. —*n.* an act of bleeding. [OE (rel. to BLOOD)]

bleep *v.i.* to emit an intermittent high-pitched signal. —*n.* such a signal. [imit.]

blemish /ˈblemɪʃ/ *v.t.* to spoil the beauty or perfection of. —*n.* a defect, a flaw. [f. OF *blesmir* make pale]

blench *v.i.* to flinch. [OE, = deceive; rel. to BLINK]

blend *v.t./i.* **1** to mix (different varieties) to get a required flavour, texture, etc. **2** to mingle or merge (*with*). **3** (of colours etc.) to pass imperceptibly into each other. **4** to harmonize. —*n.* a mixture of different varieties. [f. ON]

blende /blend/ *n.* native zinc sulphide. [G (*blenden* deceive, because while often resembling lead ore it yielded no lead)]

blender *n.* a device for blending soft or liquid foods. [f. BLEND]

blenny *n.* a small sea-fish (especially of the genus *Blennius*) with spiny fins and slimy scales. [f. L f. Gk *blennos* mucus, from the mucous coating of its scales]

bless *v.t.* **1** to invoke God's favour on; to sanctify by the sign of the cross; to consecrate (food etc.). **2** to glorify (God); to attribute one's good luck to (one's stars etc.). —**be blessed with,** to be fortunate enough to possess. [OE, rel. to BLOOD]

blessed /ˈblesɪd/ *predic. adj.* holy; beatified; (*iron. slang*) cursed.

blessing *n.* **1** an invocation of God's favour; a grace before or after a meal. **2** something one is thankful for, a benefit. [f. BLESS]

blether var. of BLATHER.

blew *past* of BLOW.

blewits /ˈbluːɪts/ *n.* an edible mushroom with a lilac stem. [prob. f. BLUE]

blight /blaɪt/ *n.* **1** a disease causing plants to shrivel up etc.; a fungus or aphid causing it. **2** an obscure malignant influence. —*v.t.* **1** to affect (plants) with blight. **2** to frustrate or spoil. [orig. unkn.]

blighter /ˈblaɪtə(r)/ *n.* (*colloq.*) a person or thing, especially an annoying one. [f. prec.]

Blighty /ˈblaɪtɪ/ *n.* (*military slang*) home (especially Britain) after service abroad; a wound ensuring one's return home. [f. Hind., = foreign, European]

blimey /ˈblaɪmɪ/ *int.* of astonishment, contempt, etc. [corrupt. of (*God*) *blind me*]

blimp *n.* **1** a small non-rigid airship. **2** a soundproof cover for a cine-camera. **3 (Colonel) Blimp,** a diehard reactionary (named after a cartoon character representing a pompous obese elderly man). [orig. unkn.]

blind /blaɪnd/ *adj.* **1** lacking the power of sight; (of a corner etc.) not allowing a clear view of the road ahead; (of flying) relying solely on instruments. **2** without foresight or discernment; reckless; not governed by purpose. —*v.t.* to deprive of sight; to dazzle with bright light; to beguile so as to rob of judgement; to overawe. —*n.* **1** a screen for a window; a shop's awning. **2** a pretext, a ruse. —**blind alley,** a street closed at one end. **blind date,** a social engagement between a man and woman who have not previously met. **blind spot,** a spot in the retina insensitive to light (ill. BODY2); an area in which discernment is lacking. **blind stitch** etc., sewing visible on one side only. **turn a blind eye to,** to pretend not to notice. —**blindly** *adv.*, **blindness** *n.* [OE]

blindfold *adj.* & *adv.* with the eyes bandaged. —*n.* a cloth placed over a person's eyes. —*v.t.* to block the sight of with a blindfold. [orig. *blindfelled* = struck blind]

blindworm *n.* a slow-worm [from its small eyes].

blink *v.t./i.* **1** to move the eyelids quickly down and up; to look with eyes opening and shutting. **2** to shine with an unsteady or intermittent light. **3** to shirk consideration of (facts etc.). —*n.* **1** an act of blinking. **2** a momentary gleam. [rel. to BLENCH]

blinkers *n.pl.* screens on a horse's bridle to prevent it seeing sideways. [f. BLINK]

blinking *adj.* & *adv.* (*slang*, *euphem.*) bloody (= damned). [f. BLINK]

blip *n.* a spot of light on a radar screen; a quick popping sound. —*v.i.* (**-pp-**) to make a blip. [imit.]

bliss *n.* perfect happiness; the perfect joy of heaven. —**blissful** *adj.*, **blissfully** *adv.* [OE f. Gmc (= blithe)]

blister *n.* a bubble on the skin filled with watery

fluid, caused by friction etc.; a similar swelling on painted wood etc. —*v.t./i* **1** to develop blisters; to raise blisters on. **2** to criticize sharply. [orig. unkn.]

blithe /blaɪð/ *adj*. joyous, carefree; casual, careless. [OE]

blitz /blɪts/ *n*. a sudden intensive (usually aerial) attack; **the Blitz,** the German air-raids on London in 1940. —*v.t.* to attack or destroy by a blitz. [abbr. of foll.]

blitzkrieg /ˈblɪtskri:g/ *n*. an intensive campaign intended to bring about a speedy victory, especially as used by Germany against various countries of Europe in the Second World War. [G, = lightning war]

blizzard /ˈblɪzəd/ *n*. a severe snowstorm. [orig. unkn.]

bloat *v.t.* to cause to swell out, to make turgid. [f. obs. *bloat* swollen (orig. unkn.)]

bloated *adj*. puffed up with pride of wealth, self-indulgence, etc. [f. BLOAT]

bloater *n*. a herring half-dried in smoke. [perh. rel. to ON *blautr* soaked]

blob *n*. a thick drop; a small round mass. [imit.]

bloc /blɒk/ *n*. a combination of countries, parties, etc., to foster a common interest. [F, = BLOCK]

block *n*. **1** a solid piece of wood, stone, or other hard substance; this as used for chopping or hammering on, or from which horses are mounted; **the block,** that on which condemned people were beheaded. **2** a large building divided into flats or offices. **3** a group of buildings bounded by streets. **4** an obstruction; an inability or mental resistance caused by psychological factors. **5** a large section of seats, shares, etc. as a unit; (*attrib.*) made or treated as a large unit. **6** a piece of wood or metal engraved for printing. **7** a pulley mounted in a case. —*v.t.* **1** to obstruct or impede; to restrict the use or conversion of (currency). **2** to sketch *in* or *out* roughly. —**block and tackle,** a system of pulleys and ropes, especially for lifting things. **block-buster** *n*. a bomb powerful enough to destroy a whole block of buildings. **block diagram,** one showing the general arrangement of parts in an apparatus. **block letters,** letters written separately as in print, usually in capitals. **block mountain,** one formed by faults. **block vote,** a vote by a delegate to a conference etc. proportional in value to the number of persons represented. [f. OF f. LDu.]

blockade /blɒˈkeɪd/ *n*. the cutting off of a place by enemy forces to prevent goods etc. reaching or leaving it. —*v.t.* to subject to a blockade. [f. BLOCK]

blockage /ˈblɒkɪdʒ/ *n*. **1** something that blocks. **2** the state of being blocked. [f. BLOCK]

blockhead *n*. a slow-witted person.

blockhouse *n*. a reinforced concrete military shelter; a timber building used as a fort, with loopholes for guns.

bloke *n*. (*colloq.*) a man, a fellow. [Shelta]

blond (of a woman or her hair usu. **blonde**) *adj*. fair-haired; (of hair) fair. —*n*. a fair-haired person. [f. F f. L, = yellow]

blood /blʌd/ *n*. **1** the fluid, usually red, circulating in the arteries and veins of animals. **2** the taking of life. **3** passion, temperament. **4** race, descent, parentage; blood-relations. **5** a dandy. —*v.t.* to give (hounds) their first taste of blood; to initiate (a person). —**blood-bath** *n*. a massacre. **blood count,** the number of corpuscles in a given volume of blood. **blood-curdling** *adj*. extremely horrific. **blood group,** any of the types into which human blood is divided according to its compatibility in transfusion. **blood-money** *n*. a fine paid by a killer to his victim's next-of-kin. **blood orange,** a variety of orange with red-streaked pulp. **blood-poisoning** *n*. infection of the bloodstream by bacteria. **blood pressure,** varying pressure of blood in the vessels, measured for diagnosis. **blood-relation** *n*. one related by birth, not marriage. **blood sports,** sports involving the killing of animals. **blood-stained** *adj*. stained with blood; guilty of bloodshed. **blood test,** an examination of a person's blood for diagnosis etc. **blood-vessel** *n*. a vein, artery, or capillary conveying blood. **in cold blood,** with premeditated violence. [OE]

bloodhound *n*. a large keen-scented dog used in tracking.

bloodless *adj*. **1** without blood, pale from loss of blood. **2** involving no bloodshed. **3** without vitality; unemotional. [f. BLOOD + -LESS]

bloodshed *n*. the spilling of blood, slaughter.

bloodshot *adj*. (of eyeballs) tinged with blood.

bloodstock *n*. pedigree horses.

bloodstream *n*. the blood circulating in the body.

bloodsucker *n*. **1** a creature that sucks blood, a leech. **2** an extortionate person.

bloodthirsty *adj*. eager for bloodshed.

bloody /ˈblʌdɪ/ *adj*. **1** of, like, or smeared with blood. **2** involving bloodshed; cruel, bloodthirsty. **3** (*slang*) cursed, damnable. —*adv*. (*slang*) damnably. —*v.t.* to stain with blood. **bloody-minded** *adj*. deliberately uncooperative. —**bloodily** *adv*., **bloodiness** *n*. [f. BLOOD]

bloom *n*. **1** the flower of a plant (especially one grown chiefly for this). **2** greatest beauty or perfection; freshness; flush, glow. **3** the powdery deposit on grapes, plums, etc. —*v.i.* **1** to bear blooms, to be in bloom. **2** to be in full beauty or vigour. —**in bloom,** flowering. [f. ON]

bloomer *n.* (*slang*) a blunder. [f. BLOOM]

bloomers *n.pl.* **1** loose knee-length trousers formerly worn by women. **2** (*colloq.*) knickers with legs. [f. Mrs A. *Bloomer*, Amer. social reformer (d. 1894) who advocated costume called 'rational dress' for women, invented by Mrs E. S. Miller and consisting of a short jacket, full skirt reaching to just below the knee, and trousers down to the ankle]

blooming *adj. & adv.* **1** in bloom; flourishing. **2** (*slang*, expressing mild annoyance or dislike) confounded. [f. BLOOM]

blossom /ˈblɒsəm/ *n.* a flower or mass of flowers, especially of a fruit tree. —*v.i.* **1** to open into blossom. **2** to evolve or mature *into*. **3** to thrive. [OE]

blot *n.* **1** a small stain of ink etc. **2** a disfiguring feature. **3** something bringing disgrace. —*v.t.* (**-tt-**) **1** to stain with ink or other liquid. **2** to dry with blotting-paper. —**blot out,** to obliterate; to obscure from view. **blotting-paper** *n.* absorbent paper for drying wet ink. [prob. f. Scand.]

blotch /blɒtʃ/ *n.* a discoloured patch on the skin; any large irregular patch of colour. —**blotchy** *adj.* [f. obs. *plotch* and BLOT]

blotter *n.* a pad of blotting-paper. [f. BLOT]

blotto /ˈblɒtəʊ/ *adj.* (*slang*) very drunk. [orig. unkn.]

blouse /blaʊz/ *n.* **1** a shirt-like garment worn by women. **2** a waist-length jacket forming part of a soldier's or airman's battledress. [F; orig. unkn.]

blow[1] /bləʊ/ *v.t./i* (*past* **blew** /blu:/; *p.p.* **blown** /bləʊn/) **1** to direct a current of air from the mouth; to move rapidly as a current of air; to breathe hard; (of a whale) to eject air and water when surfacing. **2** to sound (a wind instrument), (of such an instrument) to sound; to send out (bubbles etc.) or clear (the nose) by breathing. **3** to break open with explosives, to send flying (*off* etc.) by explosion; to melt (a fuse) or be melted under an overload. **4** to propel by a current of air; to shape (molten glass) by blowing. **5** (*slang*) to reveal (a secret etc.). **6** (*slang*, esp. as *int.*) to curse. **7** (*slang*) to squander; to bungle. —*n.* an act of blowing; exposure to fresh air. —**blow-dry** *v.t.* to use a hand-held drier to style washed hair while drying it. **blow-hole** *n.* a hole for blowing or breathing through; an outlet for the escape of air or gas etc. **blow one's own trumpet,** to boast. **blow-out** *n.* an uncontrolled eruption of oil or gas from a well; a burst in a tyre; (*colloq.*) a large meal. **blow up,** to shatter or be shattered in an explosion; to inflate with air; (*colloq.*) to enlarge (a photograph). [OE]

blow[2] /bləʊ/ *n.* a hard stroke with the hand or a weapon; a sudden shock or misfortune. [orig. unkn.]

blowfly *n.* a fly that lays its eggs on meat.

blowlamp *n.* a portable burner producing a very hot flame that can be directed on to a small area.

blowpipe *n.* **1** a tube for blowing air through, to increase the heat of a flame or in glass-blowing. **2** a tube through which poisonous darts are blown.

blowzy /ˈblaʊzɪ/ *adj.* red-faced, coarse-looking; slatternly. [f. obs. *blowze* beggar's wench]

blubber *n.* whale fat. —*v.i.* to sob noisily. —*adj.* (of lips) thick, swollen. [prob. imit.]

bludgeon /ˈblʌdʒ(ə)n/ *n.* a short stick with a heavy end. —*v.t.* **1** to beat with a bludgeon. **2** to coerce. [orig. unkn.]

blue /blu:/ *adj.* **1** having the colour of the clear sky. **2** sad, despondent. **3** indecent. —*n.* **1** blue colour or pigment; blue clothes or material. **2** the distinction of representing Oxford or Cambridge in a sport; one holding this. **3** (in *pl.*) a despondent state, slow melancholy music of Black American origin. —*v.t.* (*partic.* **blueing**) **1** to make blue. **2** (*colloq.*) to squander. —**blue baby,** one with congenital blueness of the skin from a heart defect. **blue blood,** aristocratic birth. **blue book,** a Parliamentary or Privy-Council report. **blue cheese,** cheese with veins of blue mould. **blue-collar worker,** a manual or industrial worker. **blue-eyed boy,** (*colloq.*) a favourite. **blue-pencil** *v.t.* to delete with a blue pencil, to censor. **Blue Peter,** a blue flag with a white square raised when a ship leaves port. **Blue Riband** (*or* **Ribbon**) **of the Atlantic,** a trophy for the ship making the fastest sea-crossing of the Atlantic. **blue ribbon,** the ribbon of the Garter; the highest honour in any sphere; a small strip of blue ribbon formerly worn by certain abstainers from alcoholic beverages. **blue tit,** a tit with bright blue tail, wings, and top of head. **blue whale,** a rorqual, the largest known living mammal. **once in a blue moon,** very rarely. **out of the blue,** unexpectedly. —**blueness** *n.* [f. OF *bleu* f. Gmc]

bluebell *n.* a plant with blue bell-shaped flowers, the wild hyacinth (*Endymion non-scriptus*) or (*Sc.*) harebell (*Campanula rotundifolia*).

bluebottle *n.* a large buzzing fly with a blue body.

blueprint *n.* a blue-and-white photographic print of plans, technical drawings, etc.; a detailed plan.

bluestocking *n.* a pretentiously intellectual woman. [f. the '*Blue Stocking* Club', 18th-c. literary coterie]

bluff[1] *v.t./i.* to make pretence of strength etc. to gain an advantage; to deceive by this. —*n.* an act of bluffing. [orig. a term in the game of poker, f. Du. *bluffen* brag]

bluff[2] *adj.* **1** (of cliffs etc.) having a vertical or steep broad front. **2** frank or abrupt and hearty in manner. —*n.* a bluff cliff or headland. [orig. unkn.]

bluish /ˈbluːɪʃ/ *adj.* fairly blue. [f. BLUE]

blunder *v.i.* to make a serious or foolish mistake; to move clumsily and uncertainly. —*n.* a serious or foolish mistake. [prob. f. Scand.]

blunderbuss /ˈblʌndəbəs/ *n.* a type of muzzle-loading usually flintlock gun for close-range use, common in the 18th c., with a flared muzzle, firing many balls at one shot. [f. Du., = thunder-gun]

blunt *adj.* **1** without a sharp edge or point, not sharp. **2** abrupt and outspoken. —*v.t.* to make blunt or less sharp. —**bluntly** *adv.*, **bluntness** *n.* [perh. f. Scand. (ON *blunda* shut the eyes)]

blur *v.t.* (**-rr-**) to make or become less distinct; to smear (writing etc.). —*n.* **1** a thing seen or heard indistinctly. **2** a smear. [perh. rel. to BLEARY]

blurb *n.* descriptive or commendatory matter, especially a description of a book printed on its jacket. [said to have been originated in 1907 by G. Burgess, Amer. humorist, in a comic book jacket embellished with a drawing of a pulchritudinous young lady whom he facetiously dubbed Miss Blinda Blurb]

blurt *v.t.* (usu. with *out*) to utter abruptly or tactlessly. [imit].

blush *v.i.* **1** to develop a pink tinge in the face from shame or embarrassment; to be ashamed or embarrassed *to*. **2** to be red or pink. —*n.* an act of blushing; a rosy glow. [OE]

bluster *v.i.* to behave noisily or boisterously; (of winds etc.) to blow fiercely. —*n.* noisy self-assertive talk, threats. —**blustery** *adj.* [imit.]

BMX *n.* **1** organized bicycle racing on a dirt track. **2** a kind of bicycle for use in this. [abbr. *bicycle moto-cross*]

boa /ˈbəʊə/ *n.* **1** a large South American non-poisonous snake of the genus *Boa* that kills its prey by constriction so that it suffocates; (*loosely*) a snake of similar habits elsewhere, a python. **2** a woman's long furry or feathered wrap for the throat. —**boa constrictor**, a Brazilian species of boa. [L]

boar *n.* **1** a wild pig (*Sus scrofa*) formerly common in forested areas of Europe. **2** an uncastrated male domestic pig. [OE]

board *n.* **1** a flat thin piece of sawn timber, usually long and narrow; a flat piece of wood or other firm substance used in games, for posting notices, etc. **2** material resembling boards, made of compressed fibres; thick stiff card used for book-covers. **3** provision of meals, usually for payment. **4** the directors of a company or other official group meeting together. **5** (in *pl.*) a theatre stage, the acting profession. —*v.t./i.* **1** to go aboard (a ship, aircraft, etc.). **2** to cover or close *up* with boards. **3** to provide with or receive meals, usually for payment. —**board game**, a game played on a specially marked board. **on board**, on or on to a ship, aircraft, oil rig, etc. [OE]

boarder *n.* one who boards with a person, especially a pupil who boards at a boarding-school. [f. prec.]

boarding-house *n.* a house at which board and lodging may be obtained for payment. [f. BOARD]

boarding-school *n.* a school that provides pupils with board and lodging. [f. BOARD]

boardroom *n.* a room in which a board of directors etc. regularly meet.

boast *v.t./i.* to speak with great pride and try to impress people, to extol one's own excellence etc.; to be the proud possessor of. —*n.* an act of boasting; something one boasts of. [f. AF; orig. unkn.]

boastful *adj.* boasting frequently, full of boasting. —**boastfully** *adv.*, **boastfulness** *n.* [f. BOAST + -FUL]

boat *n.* **1** a small vessel propelled on water by paddle, oars, sail, or engine; (*loosely*) a ship; (*US*) a sea-going vessel. **2** a boat-shaped vessel for gravy etc. —*v.i.* to go in a boat, especially for pleasure. —**boat-hook** *n.* a long pole with a hook and spike at the end for moving boats. **boat-house** *n.* a shed at the water's edge in which boats are kept. **boat-train** *n.* one timed to catch a boat. **in the same boat**, suffering the same troubles. [OE]

boater *n.* a flat-topped straw hat with a brim. [f. BOAT]

boatman *n.* (*pl.* **-men**) one who conveys by boat or hires out boats.

Boat Race an annual rowing competition on the Thames in London between eights of Oxford and Cambridge Universities.

boatswain /ˈbəʊs(ə)n/ *n.* a ship's officer in charge of the crew, rigging, etc.

bob[1] *v.i.* (**-bb-**) to make a jerky movement, to move quickly up and down; to curtsy quickly. —*n.* a bobbing movement. —**bob up**, (*colloq.*) to appear or re-emerge suddenly. [imit.]

bob[2] *n.* **1** a hair-style in which the hair is cut short to hang evenly. **2** a weight on a pendulum. —*v.t.* to cut (the hair) in a bob. [orig. unkn.]

bob[3] *n.* (*pl.* same) (*slang*) a shilling, five pence. [orig. unkn.]

bobbin /ˈbɒbɪn/ *n.* a cylinder holding a spool of thread in machine sewing, lace-making, etc. [f. F]

bobble *n.* a small ornamental woolly ball. [dim. of BOB[2]]

bobby /ˈbɒbɪ/ *n.* (*colloq.*) a policeman. [f. Sir

Robert Peel, Home Secretary at the passing of the Metropolitan Police Act, 1828]

bob-sleigh /ˈbɒbsleɪ/, **bob-sled** *ns.* a sleigh with two axles, each of which has two runners, steered either by ropes or by a wheel; the winter sport in which such sleighs, normally manned by crews of four or two, are guided down a specially prepared descending track of solid ice with banked bends. —**bob-sleighing, bob-sledding** *ns.* [perh. f. BOB²]

bobstay *n.* a rope holding the bowsprit down. [perh. f. BOB¹]

bobtail *n.* a docked tail, a horse or dog having such a tail. [f. BOB²]

bode *v.t./i.* to be a sign of, to portend. —**bode ill** *or* **well,** to be a bad or good sign. [OE]

bodega /bəˈdi:gə/ *n.* a cellar or shop selling wine. [Sp.]

bodice /ˈbɒdɪs/ *n.* **1** the upper part of a woman's dress, down to the waist. **2** a woman's vest-like undergarment. [orig. *pair of bodies* = whalebone corset]

bodily /ˈbɒdɪlɪ/ *adj.* of the human body or physical nature. —*adv.* **1** as a whole. **2** in the body, in person. [f. BODY]

bodkin /ˈbɒdkɪn/ *n.* a blunt thick needle for drawing tape etc. through a hem. [orig. unkn.]

body /ˈbɒdɪ/ *n.* **1** the physical structure, including bones, flesh, and organs, of a human being or animal (alive or dead). **2** a corpse. **3** the trunk apart from the head and limbs; the main or central part of something; the majority *of.* **4** a group of persons or things regarded as a unit. **5** (*colloq.*) a person. **6** a distinct piece of matter. **7** solidity, substantial character etc. —**body-blow** *n.* a very severe setback. **body-building** *n.* strengthening of the body by exercises. **body language,** involuntary movements or attitudes by which a person communicates his feelings or moods etc. (usually unwittingly) to others. **bodyline bowling,** (*Cricket*) persistent fast bowling on the leg side, threatening the batsman's body. **body politic,** the nation in its corporate character. **in a body,** collectively. [OE]

bodyguard *n.* a person or group of persons escorting and guarding a dignitary etc.

body-snatcher *n.* (*hist.*) one who illicitly disinterred corpses for dissection. —**body-snatching** *n.*

bodywork *n.* the structure of a vehicle body.

Boer /ˈbəʊə(r), bʊə(r)/ *n.* an Afrikaner; (*hist.*) an early Dutch inhabitant of the Cape. —*adj.* of Boers. [Du., = farmer]

boffin /ˈbɒfɪn/ *n.* (*colloq.*) a person engaged in (esp. secret) scientific research. [orig. unkn.]

bog *n.* a piece of wet spongy ground, especially on peat. —*v.t.* (**-gg-**; usu.in *pass.* with *down*) to stick fast in wet ground; to impede the progress of. —**bog myrtle,** a fragrant-leaved shrub found in bogs. **bog oak,** wood of oak etc. preserved in peat. —**boggy** *adj.* [f. Ir. or Gael. *bogach*]

bogey /ˈbəʊgɪ/ *n.* (in golf) a score of one stroke above par at a hole. [perh. f. BOGY as imaginary player]

boggle *v.i.* to take alarm or hesitate (*at*). [f. dial. *bogle* = BOGY]

bogie /ˈbəʊgɪ/ *n.* a wheeled undercarriage pivoted below a locomotive etc. [orig. unkn.]

bogus /ˈbəʊgəs/ *adj.* sham, spurious. [orig. unkn.]

bogy /ˈbəʊgɪ/ *n.* an evil spirit; an object of dread. [orig. (*Old*) *Bogey* the Devil]

bogyman /ˈbəʊgɪmæn/ *n.* (*pl.* **-men**) a person (often imaginary) causing fear or difficulty. [f. prec.]

Bohemian /bəʊˈhi:mɪən/ *adj.* **1** of Bohemia, an area of Czechoslovakia. **2** of irregular and socially unconventional habits. —*n.* a person of Bohemian habits. [f. *Bohemia.*]

boil¹ *v.t./i.* **1** to bubble up (of liquid reaching the temperature at which it gives off vapour, or of the containing vessel); to bring to boiling-point; to cook or be cooked in boiling liquid, to subject to the heat of boiling liquid. **2** (of the sea etc.) to seethe like boiling liquid. **3** to be greatly disturbed by anger or other strong emotion. —*n.* the act or point of boiling. —**boil over,** to spill over in boiling. [f. AF f. L *bullire* (*bulla* bubble)]

boil² *n.* an inflamed pus-filled swelling under the skin. [OE]

boiler *n.* **1** a tank in which a house's hot water is stored; a closed vessel in which water is heated to supply steam for an engine etc. **2** a large tub for boiling laundry. [f. BOIL¹]

boiling-point *n.* **1** the temperature at which a liquid begins to boil. **2** a state of great anger or excitement. [f. BOIL¹]

boisterous /ˈbɔɪstərəs/ *adj.* noisily exuberant; (of the wind or sea) stormy, turbulent. [orig. unkn.]

bold /bəʊld/ *adj.* **1** confident and courageous, adventurous; shameless, impudent. **2** standing out distinctly, conspicuous. —**bold face,** type with thick heavy lines. —**boldly** *adv.*, **boldness** *n.* [OE]

bole *n.* the trunk of a tree. [f. ON]

bolero *n.* (*pl.* **-os**) **1** /bəˈleərəʊ/ a Spanish dance; the music for this. **2** /ˈbɒlərəʊ/ a woman's short jacket with no front fastening. [Sp.]

boll/ bəʊl/ *n.* a round seed-vessel (of cotton, flax, etc.) —**boll-weevil** *n.* a destructive insect infesting the cotton-plant. [f. MDu. *bolle,* rel. to BOWL¹]

bollard /ˈbɒləd/ *n.* **1** each of a line of short posts for keeping traffic off a path etc. **2** a post on a ship or quay to which a mooring rope may be tied. [perh. f. BOLE]

boloney /bəˈləʊnɪ/ *n.* (*slang*) nonsense. [orig. unkn.]

Bolshevik /ˈbɒlʃɪvɪk/ *n.* **1** a member of the wing of the Social-Democratic party in Russia which, from 1903, favoured revolutionary tactics. **2** (*loosely*) any socialist extremist. —**Bolshevism** *n.*, **Bolshevist** *n.* [Russ., = member of the majority; cf. *Menshevik*]

Bolshie /ˈbɒlʃɪ/ *adj.* (*slang*) **1** Bolshevik, left-wing. **2** rebellious, uncooperative. —*n.* (*slang*) a Bolshevik. [abbr.]

bolster /ˈbəʊlstə(r)/ *n.* **1** a long under-pillow across a bed. **2** a pad or support in a machine or instrument. —*v.t.* to support or prop (*up*), to strengthen. [OE]

bolt[1] /bəʊlt/ *n.* **1** a bar sliding into a socket, for fastening a door. **2** a heavy pin for holding metal plates etc. together, usually secured with a nut. **3** an act of bolting. **4** a discharge of lightning. **5** an arrow shot from a crossbow. —*v.t./i* **1** to secure (a door) with bolts, to keep *in* or *out* by bolting a door; to fasten together with metal bolts. **2** to eat (food) very rapidly. **3** to dash off suddenly, (of a horse) to run off out of control. **4** to run to seed prematurely. —**bolt-hole** *n.* a means or place of escape. **bolt upright,** rigidly upright. [OE]

bolt[2] bəʊlt/ *v.t.* to sift (flour etc). [f. OF *bul(e)ter* (orig. unkn.)]

bomb /bɒm/ *n.* a destructive device containing explosive or incendiary material, gas, etc., which is thrown, dropped from an aircraft, or placed in position; **the bomb,** a nuclear bomb as the ultimate weapon. —*v.t.* to attack with bombs, especially from the air. [f. F, ult. f. Gk *bombos* loud humming]

bombard /bɒmˈbɑːd/ *v.t.* **1** to attack persistently with heavy guns. **2** to assail *with* questions, abuse, etc. **3** (*Physics*) to direct a stream of high-speed particles at. —**bombardment** *n.* [f. F (as prec.)]

bombardier /bɒmbəˈdɪə(r)/ *n.* **1** a non-commissioned officer in the artillery. **2** (*US*) a person in an aircraft who releases bombs. [f. F (as prec.)]

bombast /ˈbɒmbæst/ *n.* pompous or grandiloquent language. —**bombastic** /-ˈbæstɪk/ *adj.*, **bombastically** *adv.* [f. obs. *bombace* cotton wadding]

Bombay duck a small fish eaten as a relish when dried, especially with curry. [corrupt. of *bombil*, Indian name of the fish]

bombazine /ˈbɒmbəziːn/ *n.* a twilled worsted dress-material, especially the black kind formerly much used for mourning. [f. F ult. f. Gk (*bombux* silk)]

bomber /ˈbɒmə(r)/ *n.* **1** an aircraft used to drop bombs. **2** a person using bombs illegally. [f. BOMB]

bombshell *n.* an overwhelming surprise or disappointment.

bona-fide /bəʊnə ˈfaɪdɪ/ *adj.* genuine, sincere. —**bona fides** /-iːz/, honest intention, sincerity. [L, = (in) good faith]

bonanza /bəˈnænzə/ *n.* a source of wealth or prosperity, an unexpected success (orig. a mining term). [Sp., = fair weather, prosperity]

bon-bon *n.* a sweet. [F (*bon* good)]

bond *n.* **1** something that binds together or (usu. in *pl.*) restrains. **2** a binding agreement; a deed by which a person binds himself to pay another; a certificate issued by a government or company, undertaking to repay borrowed money together with any due interest. **3** the linkage of atoms in a molecule. **4** any of various methods (*English bond*, *Flemish bond*, etc.) of holding a wall together by making bricks overlap. —*v.t.* **1** to unite or reinforce with a bond. **2** to place goods in bond. —**bond (paper),** a high-quality writing paper. **in bond,** stored by the Customs in special warehouses until the importer has paid the duty. [var. of BAND[1]]

bondage *n.* slavery, captivity; subjection to any constraining force. [f. OE *bonda* husbandman, later assoc. with BOND]

bonded *adj.* (of goods) placed in bond; (of warehouses) containing such goods. [f. BOND]

bone *n.* **1** any of the hard pieces (other than teeth, nails, and cartilage) making up the skeleton in vertebrates; (in *pl.*) a skeleton, especially as remains. **2** the material of which bones consist or a similar substance. **3** (in *pl.*) the basic essentials of a thing. —*v.t.* to remove the bones from. —**bone china,** china made of clay mixed with bone ash. **bone-dry** *adj.* completely dry. **bone-meal** *n.* ground bones used as fertilizer. **bone of contention,** the subject of a dispute. **bone-shaker** *n.* an old jolting vehicle; (hist.) an early type of bicycle. **have a bone to pick,** to have something to complain about or dispute *with*. **make no bones about,** to admit or allow without fuss. **to the bone,** to the bare minimum. [OE].

bonfire *n.* a large open-air fire. —**Bonfire Night,** that of 5 November, when bonfires are lit in memory of the Gunpowder Plot. [earlier *bonefire* = fire in which bones are burnt]

bongo /ˈbɒŋgəʊ/ *n.* (*pl.* **-os, -oes**) each of a pair of small drums usually held between the knees and beaten with the fingers. [Amer. Sp.]

bonhomie /ˈbɒnəmiː/ *n.* friendly geniality. [F (f. *bonhomme* good-natured man)]

bonnet /ˈbɒnɪt/ *n.* **1** an outdoor head-dress tied with strings below the chin, now chiefly worn by babies. **2** a Scotch cap. **3** a hinged cover over the engine of a motor vehicle. [f. OF *bonet* (orig. = the material of which caps were made]

bonny /ˈbɒnɪ/ *adj.* (chiefly *Sc.*) **1** handsome,

healthy-looking. **2** pleasant. [perh. f. F *bon* good]

bonsai /ˈbɒnsaɪ/ *n.* an artificially dwarf potted tree or shrub; the method of growing these. [Jap.]

bonus /ˈbəʊnəs/ *n.* something paid or given in addition to the normal amount; an extra benefit. [L, = good]

bon voyage /bɔ̃ vwɑːˈjɑːʒ/ an expression of good wishes to someone beginning a journey. [F]

bony /ˈbəʊnɪ/ *adj.* of or like bone; thin with prominent bones; (of fish) having a skeleton of bone rather than cartilage (see FISH[1]). —**boniness** *n.* [f. BONE]

bonze *n.* a Buddhist priest in Japan or adjacent countries. [f. F or Port. f. Jap.]

boo *int.* expressing disapproval or contempt. —*n.* the sound *boo.* —*v.t./i.* to utter boos, to jeer at. [imit.]

boob[1] *n.* (*slang*) **1** a silly mistake. **2** a foolish person. —*v.i.* (*slang*) to make a silly mistake. [f. BOOBY]

boob[2] *n.* (usu. in *pl.*; *slang*) a woman's breast. [f. earlier *bub*, *bubby*; cf. G dial. *bübbi* teat]

booby *n.* a stupid or childish person. —**booby prize,** a prize awarded to the person coming last in a contest. **booby trap,** a hidden trap rigged up for a practical joke; a disguised explosive device. **booby-trap** *v.t.* to place a booby trap in or on. [f. Sp. *bobo* f. L *balbus* stammering]

boogie-woogie /buːgɪˈwuːgɪ/ *n.* a style of playing blues on the piano, marked by persistent bass rhythm. [orig. unkn.]

book /bʊk/ *n.* **1** a set of printed sheets bound together in a cover for reading; a written work intended for printing as a book. **2** a bound set of blank sheets for writing notes, accounts, exercises, etc. in; (in *pl.*) a set of accounts. **3** a series of cheques, stamps, tickets, etc., bound together like a book. **4** a main division of a literary work, or of the Bible. **5** a record of bets made. **6** a libretto, the script of a play. —*v.t./i.* **1** to enter the name of in a book or list; to record a charge against. **2** to reserve in advance; to make a reservation. —**book club,** a society supplying its members with selected books on special terms. **book-ends** *n.* a pair of props designed to keep a row of unshelved books upright. **book in,** to register one's arrival at a hotel etc. **book-plate** *n.* a label with the owner's name etc. pasted at the front of a book. **book token,** a voucher exchangeable for books of a given value. **bring to book,** to call to account. **by the book,** strictly in accordance with regulations. [OE]

bookbinder *n.* one who binds books professionally. —**bookbinding** *n.*

bookcase *n.* a piece of furniture with shelves for books.

bookie /ˈbʊkɪ/ *n.* (*colloq.*) a bookmaker. [abbr.]

bookish /ˈbʊkɪʃ/ *adj.* addicted to reading; deriving one's knowledge from books, not from experience. [f. BOOK]

bookkeeper *n.* one who keeps accounts, especially as a profession. —**bookkeeping** *n.*

booklet /ˈbʊklɪt/ *n.* a small thin usually paper-covered book. [f. BOOK + -LET]

bookmaker *n.* a professional taker of bets. —**bookmaking** *n.*

bookmark *n.* a strip of card, leather, etc. inserted in a book to mark the reader's place.

bookseller *n.* a dealer in books.

bookshop *n.* a shop selling books.

bookworm *n.* **1** a person addicted to reading. **2** a larva that feeds on paper etc. in books.

boom[1] *n.* a deep resonant sound. —*v.i.* to make or speak with a boom. [imit.]

boom[2] *n.* a period of sudden prosperity or commercial activity. —*v.i.* to enjoy a boom. [perh. = BOOM[1]]

boom[3] *n.* **1** a long pole fixed at one end to support the bottom of a sail, microphone, etc. **2** a barrier across a harbour. [f. Du., = BEAM]

boomerang /ˈbuːməræŋ/ *n.* **1** a flat curved strip of wood, used by Australian Aborigines, usually of a kind that when thrown returns to the thrower. **2** a scheme etc. that recoils unfavourably on its originator. —*v.i.* (of a scheme) to recoil thus. [Aboriginal]

boon[1] *n.* something to be thankful for, a blessing. [f. ON, = prayer]

boon[2] *adj.* **boon companion,** a pleasant sociable companion. [f. OF f. L *bonus* good]

boor /bʊə(r)/ *n.* an ill-mannered person. —**boorish** *adj.*, **boorishness** *n.* [f. LDu.]

boost *v.t.* to increase the strength or reputation of; (*colloq.*) to push from below. —*n.* an act of boosting. [orig. unkn.]

booster *n.* a device for increasing voltage or signal strength; an auxiliary engine or rocket for initial acceleration; an injection etc. renewing the effect of an earlier one. [f. BOOST]

boot[1] *n.* **1** an outer foot-covering, often of leather, coming above the ankle. **2** a luggage compartment at the back of a car. —*v.t.* to kick. [f. ON]

boot[2] *n.* **to boot,** as well, into the bargain. [OE, = advantage]

bootee /buːˈtiː/ *n.* a baby's knitted or crocheted boot. [f. BOOT[1]]

booth /buːð/ *n.* a small temporary shelter for a stall etc. at a market or fair; an enclosure or compartment for telephoning, voting, etc. [f. ON]

bootleg *adj.* smuggled, illicit (orig. of liquor so called because concealed in the boots). —**bootlegger** *n.*

bootless *adj.* unavailing. [f. BOOT[2] + -LESS]

booty /ˈbuːtɪ/ *n.* plunder gained in war etc., loot. [f. G, = exchange]

booze *n.* (*colloq.*) alcoholic drink. —*v.i.* (*colloq.*) to drink heavily. —**boozer** *n.*, **boozy** *adj.* [f. Du., = drink to excess]

bop *n.* bebop. [abbr.]

boracic /bəˈræsɪk/ *adj.* of borax. —**boracic acid,** boric acid. [f. BORAX]

borage /ˈbɒrɪdʒ/ *n.* a herb (*Borago officinalis*) with blue flowers and hairy leaves. [f. OF, ult. f. Arab., = father of sweat (from its use as a diaphoretic)]

borax /ˈbɔːræks/ *n.* a white powder, a compound of boron, used in making glass, enamels, and detergents. [f. OF, ult. f. Pers.]

border /ˈbɔːdə(r)/ *n.* **1** an edge or boundary; the part near this. **2** the dividing-line between two countries; the district on either side of this. **3** a strip of ground round the edge of a garden. **4** an edging to a garment etc. —*v.t./i.* **1** to provide with a border; to serve as a border to. **2** (with *on*) to adjoin; to come close to (a condition). —**the Border,** that between England and Scotland. [f. OF *bordure*, rel. to BOARD]

borderland *n.* **1** the district near a border. **2** a condition between two extremes. **3** an area for debate.

borderline *n.* a boundary; the limit of a category etc. —*adj.* on or near the borderline.

bore[1] *v.t./i.* **1** to make (a hole or well etc.), especially with a revolving tool; to make a hole (in) thus; to drill (the shaft of a well). **2** to hollow out (a tube) evenly. **3** (of a racehorse) to push another horse out of the way. —*n.* **1** the hollow of a gun barrel or of the cylinder in an internal-combustion engine; its diameter. **2** a borehole made to find water etc. [OE; cf. ON *bora* borehole]

bore[2] *v.t.* to weary by tedious talk or dullness. —*n.* a dull or wearisome person or thing. —**boredom** *n.*, **boring** *adj.* [orig. unkn.]

bore[3] *n.* a high tidal wave with a steep front that occurs when two tides meet or when the spring flood tide rushes up a narrowing estuary. [f. Scand.]

bore[4] *past* of BEAR[1].

borehole *n.* a deep hole bored in the ground especially to find water.

boric acid /ˈbɔːrɪk/ an acid derived from borax, used as an antiseptic. [f. BORON]

born *p.p.* of BEAR[1]. —*adj.* **1** existing as a result of birth. **2** qualified by natural disposition or ability. **3** destined or of a certain status or origin by birth. —**born of,** owing its origin to.

-borne *adj.* with prefixed noun in sense 'carried or transported by'. [*p.p.* of BEAR[1]]

boron /ˈbɔːrɒn/ *n.* a non-metallic element, symbol B, atomic number 5, which can exist in crystalline form or as a brown powder. [f. BORAX w. ending of *carbon*, which it resembles in some respects]

borough /ˈbʌrə/ *n.* **1** an administrative division of London or of New York City; a territorial division in Alaska, corresponding to a county. **2** a town with a corporation and with privileges conferred by royal charter or defined by statute; (*hist.*) a town sending representatives to Parliament. [OE; orig. = fortress, fortified town]

borrow /ˈbɒrəʊ/ *v.t./i.* to get the temporary use of (a thing) on condition that it is returned; to obtain money thus; to adopt or use (ideas etc. originated by another). [OE]

Borstal /ˈbɔːst(ə)l/ *n.* the former name for an institution for reforming and training young offenders. [f. *Borstal* in Kent]

bortsch /bɔːtʃ/ *n.* a highly seasoned Russian or Polish soup of various ingredients including beetroot and cabbage. [f. Russ. *borshch*]

borzoi /ˈbɔːzɔɪ/ *n.* a large Russian wolfhound with a narrow head and silky coat. [Russ., = swift]

bosh *n.* & *int.* (*slang*) nonsense. [f. Turk., = empty]

bos'n /ˈbəʊs(ə)n/ contr. of BOATSWAIN.

bosom /ˈbʊz(ə)m/ *n.* the breast, especially of a woman, or the part of a dress covering it; the enclosing space formed by the breast and arms. —**bosom friend,** an intimate friend. [OE]

boson /ˈbəʊzɒn/ *n.* a particle obeying the relations stated by Bose and Einstein, with integral spin. [f. S. N. *Bose*, Indian physicist (d. 1974)]

boss[1] *n.* (*colloq.*) an employer or manager. —*v.t.* (*colloq.*) to be the boss of; to order *about*. [f. Du. *baas* master]

boss[2] *n.* a round projecting knob or stud, as in the centre of a shield; a carved projection where ribs of vaulting cross. [f. OF; orig. unkn.]

boss-eyed *adj.* cross-eyed, having only one good eye. [f. *boss* miss a shot; orig. unkn.]

bossy *adj.* (*colloq*) fond of ordering people about. —**bossiness** *n.* [f. BOSS[1]]

bosun, bo'sun /ˈbəʊs(ə)n/ contr. of BOATSWAIN.

botanize /ˈbɒtənaɪz/ *v.i.* to collect or study plants. [f. foll.]

botany /ˈbɒtənɪ/ *n.* the science of the structure, physiology, classification, and distribution of plants. —**botanical** /bəˈtænɪk(ə)l/ *adj.* [f. F or L f. Gk (*botanē* plant)]

botch *v.t.* to bungle, to do badly; to patch or put together clumsily. —*n.* bungled or spoilt work. [orig. unkn.]

both /bəʊθ/ *adj.* & *pron.* the two, not only one. —*adv.* with equal truth in two cases. [f. ON]

bother /ˈbɒðə(r)/ *v.t./i.* **1** to give trouble, worry, or annoyance to. **2** to take trouble. **3** to concern oneself *with*. —*n*. a person or thing causing bother. [orig. unkn.]

bothersome /ˈbɒðəsəm/ *adj*. troublesome. [f. prec. + -SOME]

bo-tree /ˈbəʊtri:/ *n*. the Buddhist name for a large Indian fig-tree (*Ficus religiosa*) related to the banyan, sometimes worshipped as a symbol of the Buddha since he attained nirvana beneath such a tree. [Sinhalese *bo* (Skr. *boahi* perfect knowledge)]

bottle *n*. **1** a narrow-necked glass or plastic container for storing liquid; the amount that will fill it. **2** a hot-water bottle. **3** a baby's feeding-bottle. **4** (*slang*) courage. —*v.t.* **1** to seal or store in bottles or jars. **2** (with *up*) to confine; to restrain (feelings etc.). —**bottle-brush** *n*. a cylindrical brush for cleaning inside bottles; any of various plants with flowers of this shape. **bottle-green** *adj*. dark green. **bottle-neck** *n*. a narrow stretch of road where traffic cannot flow freely. **bottle-party** *n*. one to which each guest brings a bottle of drink. [f. OF, rel. to BUTT[4]]

bottom /ˈbɒtəm/ *n*. **1** the lowest part of anything, that on which it rests; the buttocks. **2** the lowest or most distant point; the less honourable end of a table, class, etc. **3** the ground under a stretch of water. **4** a ship's keel or hull; a ship. —*adj*. lowest in position, rank, or degree. —*v.t./i.* **1** to provide with a bottom. **2** (of prices, usu. with *out*) to reach the lowest level. —**at bottom,** basically. **bottom line,** the amount of total assets after profit and loss etc. are calculated; (*fig*.) the essential thing. **get to the bottom of,** to find the real cause of. [OE]

botulism /ˈbɒtjʊlɪz(ə)m/ *n*. poisoning by a bacillus found in inadequately preserved food etc. [f. L *botulus* sausage]

bouclé /ˈbu:kleɪ/ *n*. yarn with looped or curled ply; a fabric made from this. [F, = curled]

boudoir /ˈbu:dwɑ:(r)/ *n*. a woman's private room. [F (*bouder* sulk)]

bougainvillaea /bu:gənˈvɪlɪə/ *n*. a tropical shrub of the genus *Bougainvillaea*, with large coloured bracts. [f. L. A. de Bougainville, French explorer (d. 1811)]

bough /baʊ/ *n*. any of the main branches of a tree. [OE]

bought *past* & *p.p.* of BUY.

bouillon /ˈbu:jɔ̃/ *n*. thin clear soup. [F (*bouillir* boil)]

boulder /ˈbəʊldə(r)/ *n*. a large stone worn smooth by weather or water. [f. Scand.]

boulevard /ˈbu:ləvɑ:d/ *n*. a broad often tree-lined street (in France etc.); (*US*) a broad main road. [F. f. G, = bulwark (orig. of promenade on demolished fortification)]

boult var. of BOLT[2].

bounce *v.t./i.* **1** to rebound or cause to rebound; (*slang*, of a cheque) to be returned by the bank as worthless. **2** to rush noisily or boisterously. —*n*. **1** an act or the power of bouncing. **2** a self-confident manner, swagger. —**bouncy** *adj*. [orig. unkn.]

bouncer *n*. **1** a bumper in cricket. **2** a person employed to eject troublesome people from a night-club etc. [f. prec.]

bouncing *adj*. (usu. of a baby) big and healthy. [f. BOUNCE]

bound[1] *v.i.* to spring or leap, to move by leaps; (of a ball etc.) to recoil from a wall or the ground. —*n*. a springy upward or forward movement; the recoil of a ball etc. [f. AF, orig. = resound]

bound[2] *n*. (usu. in *pl.*) the limit of a territory; a limitation, a restriction. —*v.t.* to set bounds to; to be the boundary of. —**beat the bounds,** see BEAT[1]. **out of bounds,** beyond one's permitted area. [f. AF. f. L; orig. unkn.]

bound[3] *adj*. heading *for* a place or in a given direction. [f. ON, = ready]

bound[4] *p.p.* of BIND. —*adj*. **1** obliged by law or duty *to;* certain *to*. **2** tied or fastened. —**bound up with,** closely associated with.

boundary /ˈbaʊndərɪ/ *n*. **1** a line marking the limit of land etc. **2** (in cricket) the limit of the field; a hit to this, scoring 4 or 6 runs. —**boundary layer,** the layer of fluid adjacent to the surface of a moving body, or of air to an aircraft in motion. [F. BOUND[2]]

bounden /ˈbaʊnd(ə)n/ *adj*. (of duty etc.) obligatory. [archaic p.p. of BIND[1]]

boundless *adj*. unlimited. [f. BOUND[2] + -LESS]

bountiful /ˈbaʊntɪfʊl/ *adj*. **1** generous in giving. **2** ample. [f. BOUNTY]

bounty /ˈbaʊntɪ/ *n*. **1** liberality in giving; a generous gift. **2** a sum paid as an official reward, especially by the State. [f. OF f. L (*bonus* good)]

bouquet /bu:ˈkeɪ/ *n*. **1** a bunch of flowers for carrying in the hand. **2** a compliment. **3** the perfume of a wine. —**bouquet garni** /ˈgɑ:nɪ/, a bunch or bag of mixed herbs for flavouring a stew etc. [F, f. OF *bois* wood)]

bourbon /ˈbɜ:bən/ *n*. (*US*) whisky distilled from maize and rye. [f. *Bourbon* County, Kentucky, where first made]

bourgeois /ˈbʊəʒwɑ:/ *adj*. of or associated with the middle classes; conventional, materialistic. —*n*. a bourgeois person. [F, = BURGESS]

bourgeoisie /bʊəʒwɑ:ˈzi:/ *n*. (usu. *derog*.) the bourgeois class. [F. (f. prec.)]

bourn /bʊən/ *n*. a small stream. [S. Engl. var. of BURN[2]]

bourne /bɔ:n/ *n*. (*archaic*) a limit. [f. F *borne* f. OF *bodne*, = BOUND[2]]

bourse /bʊəs/ *n*. a money-market; **Bourse,** the

Paris equivalent of the Stock Exchange. [F, = purse, f. L *bursa*]

bout *n.* **1** a turn or spell of an activity; an attack *of* an illness. **2** a boxing or wrestling match. [f. obs. *bought* bending]

boutique /bu:ˈti:k/ *n.* a small shop or department selling clothes and other items of fashion. [F]

bouzouki /bu:ˈzu:kɪ/ *n.* a Greek stringed instrument of the lute family, plucked with a plectrum, played in popular music. [mod. Gk]

bovine /ˈbəʊvaɪn/ *adj.* of or like an ox; dull, stupid. [f. L (*bos* ox)]

bow[1] /bəʊ/ *n.* **1** a shallow curve or bend; a thing of this form. **2** a weapon for shooting arrows, with string stretched across the ends of a curved piece of wood etc. **3** a flexible stick with stretched horsehair for playing a violin etc. **4** a knot made with a loop or loops, a ribbon etc. so tied. —*v.t.* to use the bow on (a violin etc., or *abs.*). —**bow-legged** *adj.* having bandy legs. **bow-tie** *n.* a necktie tied in a bow. **bow-window** *n.* a curved bay window. [OE]

bow[2] /baʊ/ *v.t./i.* **1** to incline the head or body, especially in formal salutation; to incline (the head) thus. **2** to cause to bend under a weight. —*n.* an act of bowing. —**bow and scrape,** to be obsequiously polite. **take a bow,** to acknowledge applause. [OE]

bow[3] /baʊ/ *n.* (often in *pl.*) the fore-end of a boat or ship; the rower nearest the bow. [f. LG or Du., rel. to BOUGH]

bowdlerize /ˈbaʊdləraɪz/ *v.t.* to expurgate (a book or author). —**bowdlerization** /-ˈzeɪʃ(ə)n/ *n.* [f. T. *Bowdler*, who in 1818 published an expurgated edition of Shakespeare]

bowel /ˈbaʊəl/ *n.* a division of the alimentary canal below the stomach, the intestine; (in *pl.*) innermost parts. [f. OF f. L (dim. of *botulus* sausage)]

bower /ˈbaʊə(r)/ *n.* a leafy shelter, an arbour. —**bower-bird** *n.* any of various passerine birds native to Australia and New Guinea, the males of which build decorated 'bowers' during courtship. [OE, = dwelling]

bowie /ˈbəʊɪ/ *n.* (in full **bowie knife**) a long hunting-knife with a double-edged point. [f. J. *Bowie* Amer. soldier (d. 1836)]

bowl[1] /bəʊl/ *n.* **1** a round open vessel for food or liquid. **2** the rounded part of a tobacco-pipe, spoon, etc. **3** the contents of a bowl. **4** (*US*) an outdoor stadium (orig. bowl-shaped) for football. [OE]

bowl[2] /bəʊl/ *n.* a hard ball weighted or shaped so as to run in a curve; (in *pl.*) a game played with these on grass, or with round balls in tenpin bowling or skittles. —*v.t.* **1** to play bowls; to roll (a ball etc.) along the ground. **2** (in cricket) to deliver (a ball); to dismiss (a batsman) by delivering a ball that hits the wicket. **3** to move (*along*) rapidly in a vehicle etc. —**bowling-alley** *n.* one of a series of enclosed channels for playing skittles; a building containing these. **bowling-green** *n.* a lawn for playing bowls. **bowl over,** to knock down; to amaze or disconcert. [f. F f. L *bulla* bubble]

bowler[1] /bəʊlə(r)/ *n.* **1** one who plays bowls. **2** (in cricket) the player who delivers the ball. [f. BOWL[2]]

bowler[2] /bəʊlə(r)/ *n.* a stiff felt hat with a rounded crown. [f. J. *Bowler*, London hatter who designed it, 1850]

bowline /ˈbəʊlɪn/ *n.* **1** a rope from a ship's bow keeping the sail taut against the wind. **2** a knot forming a non-slipping loop at the end of a rope. [f. BOW[3] + LINE]

bowling /ˈbəʊlɪŋ/ (also **tenpin bowling**) an indoor game for individual players or for teams, in which a player tries to knock down with a ball ten 'pins' placed in a triangle

bowsprit /ˈbəʊsprɪt/ *n.* a long spar running forward from a ship's bow. [f. MLG or MDu. (as BOW[3], SPRIT]

box[1] *n.* **1** a container for solids, usually with flat sides and a lid; the quantity contained in this. **2** a separate compartment, as for several people in a theatre, for horses in a stable etc., or witnesses in a lawcourt. **3** a box-like shelter, as for a sentry, person telephoning, etc.; a small country-house for shooting, fishing, etc. **4** a confined space. **5** a receptacle at a newspaper office for replies to an advertisement. **6** a coachman's seat. —*v.t.* to put in or provide with a box. —**box girder,** a girder made of plates fastened in a box shape. **box in** *or* **up,** to shut into a small space restricting movement. **box junction,** a road intersection with a yellow-striped area which a vehicle may not enter (except when turning right) until its exit is clear. **box number,** the number of a box in a newspaper office. **box-office** *n.* an office for booking seats at a theatre etc. **box-pleat** *n.* a combination of two parallel pleats forming a raised strip. **box-room** *n.* a room for storing boxes etc. **box-spring** *n.* each of a set of vertical springs in a mattress. [OE, f. L *pyxis*, *buxis* (as BOX[3])]

box[2] *v.t./i.* **1** to fight with the fists, especially in boxing-gloves as a sport. **2** to slap (a person's ears). —*n.* a hard slap on the ears etc. [orig. unkn.]

box[3] *n.* an evergreen shrub (*Buxus sempervirens*) much used in hedging and topiary; its wood. [OE f. L *buxus*, var. of L *pyxis* box of boxwood]

boxer *n.* **1** one who boxes for sport. **2** a dog of a breed of medium size with a smooth brown coat. [f. BOX[2]]

boxing *n.* the sport of fist-fighting by two men (usually wearing padded gloves) in a roped square. —**boxing-glove** *n.* a padded glove worn in the sport of boxing. **boxing-weight** *n.* the weight at which boxers are matched. British professional scale, upper weight limits: flyweight 8 stone, bantamweight 8 stone 6 lbs, featherweight 9 stone, lightweight 9 stone 9 lbs, light welterweight 10 stone, welterweight 10 stone 7 lbs, light middleweight 11 stone, middleweight 11 stone 6 lbs, light heavyweight 12 stone 7 lbs, heavyweight (no limit; any weight above 12 stone 7 lbs). The weights and divisions are modified in the amateur scale. [f. BOX[1]]

Boxing Day the first weekday after Christmas, when Christmas-boxes used to be presented. [f. (money-)BOX[1]]

boy *n.* **1** a male child. **2** a young man. **3** a (young) male employee or servant. —**the boys,** a group of men, especially in a social context. **boy-friend** *n.* a girl's or woman's regular male companion. —**boyhood** *n.*, **boyish** *adj.* [orig. unkn.]

boycott /ˈbɔɪkɒt/ *v.t.* to combine in refusing to have dealings with (a person, group, etc.) or handle (goods etc.). —*n.* an act of boycotting. [f. Capt. *Boycott*, land-agent in Ireland, so treated in 1880. The Irish Land League ordered him to reduce rents after a bad harvest, and when he refused the tenants avoided any communication with him]

BP *abbr.* before the present (esp. in geological dating).

Br *symbol* bromine.

bra /brɑː/ *n.* a brassière. [abbr.]

brace *n.* **1** a device that clamps things together or holds and supports them in position. **2** (in *pl.*) straps to hold up the trousers, fastened to the waistband and passing over the shoulders. **3** (esp. of game; *pl.* same) a pair. **4** a rope attached to the yard of a ship for trimming a sail. **5** a connecting mark { or } in printing. —*v.t.* **1** to clamp or hold up by a brace, to fasten tightly, to steady against pressure or shock. **2** to invigorate. —**brace and bit,** a revolving tool with a D-shaped handle, for boring holes. [f. OF f. L *bracchia* arms]

bracelet /ˈbreɪslɪt/ *n.* an ornamental band or chain worn on the wrist or arm. [f. OF, dim. of *bracel* f. L *bracchiale* (as prec.)]

brachiopod /ˈbrækɪəpɒd/ *n.* an invertebrate of the phylum Brachiopoda like a bivalve mollusc, found especially as a fossil. [f. Gk *brakhiōn* arm + *pous podos* foot]

brachiosaurus /brækɪəˈsɔːrəs/ *n.* a huge dinosaur of the genus *Brachiosaurus*, with the forelegs longer than the hind legs. [f. Gk *brakhiōn* arm + *sauros* lizard]

brachycephalic /brækɪsɪˈfælɪk/ *adj.* having a short rounded skull. —**brachycephalous** /-ˈsefələs/ *adj.*, **brachycephaly** *n.* [f. Gk *brakhus* short, *kephalē* head]

bracken /ˈbrækən/ *n.* a large fern of heaths and hillsides; a mass of such ferns. [f. ON]

bracket /ˈbrækɪt/ *n.* **1** a flat-topped projection from a wall supporting a statue, arch, etc.; a shelf fixed with an angled prop to a wall. **2** a mark used in pairs ( ) [ ] { } to enclose words or figures. **3** a group of people classified together as similar or falling between given limits. —*v.t.* **1** to enclose (words etc.) in brackets. **2** to group in the same category. —**bracket clock,** a clock designed to stand on a shelf or wall-bracket. [f. Sp. f. L *bracae* breeches]

brackish *adj.* (of water) slightly saline. [f. LG or Du.]

bract *n.* a small modified often scale-like leaf below the calyx of a flower. [f. L *bractea* thin metal sheet]

brad *n.* a thin flat nail with the head in the form of a slight enlargement at the top. [f. ON, = spike]

bradawl /ˈbrædɔːl/ *n.* a small non-spiral hand-tool for boring holes for brads and screws. [f. BRAD + AWL]

brae /breɪ/ *n.* (*Sc.*) a steep slope, a hillside. [f. ON, = eyelash]

brag *v.t./i.* (**-gg-**) to talk boastfully; to boast. —*n.* boastful talk. [orig. unkn.]

braggart /ˈbrægət/ *n.* boastful person. —*adj.* boastful. [f. BRAG]

brahman /ˈbrɑːmən/ var. of BRAHMIN.

brahmin /ˈbrɑːmɪn/ *n.* a member of the Hindu priestly class, versed in sacred knowledge (i.e. the Veda). —**brahminical** /-ˈmɪnɪk(ə)l/ *adj.*, **brahminism** *n.* [as BRAHMAN]

braid *n.* **1** a woven band of silk or thread used for trimming. **2** a plaited tress of hair. —*v.t.* **1** to trim with braid. **2** to plait. **3** (esp. in *p.p.*; of a stream) to divide (esp. at low water) into several channels. [OE]

Braille /breɪl/ *n.* a system of representing letters etc. by raised dots, which blind people can read by touch. —*v.t.* to represent in Braille. [f. L. *Braille*, its inventor (d. 1852), a blind French teacher who perfected his system in 1834]

brain *n.* **1** that part of the nervous system in the vertebrate that is contained in the skull; a structure of analogous function found in many invertebrates. **2** an intelligent person; (also in *pl.*) one who organizes a complex plan or idea. **3** (often in *pl.*) intellectual power. **4** an electronic device with functions comparable to the brain's. —*v.t.* to kill by a heavy blow on the head. —**brain-child** *n.* a person's inspired idea. **brain-drain** *n.* the loss of talented or professional people by emigration. **brain-stem** *n.* the stemlike portion of the brain connecting the cerebral hemispheres with the spinal cord. **brains trust,** a group of experts giving impromptu answers to questions (as a form of entertainment). **on the brain,** obsessively in one's thoughts. [OE]

brainless *adj.* lacking intelligence. [f. BRAIN + -LESS]

brainpower *n.* mental ability or intelligence.

brainstorm *n.* **1** a sudden extreme mental disturbance. **2** (*US*) a sudden bright idea.

brainstorming *n.* (*US*) a spontaneous discussion in a search for new ideas.

brainwash *v.t.* to implant new ideas in the mind of (a person) and eliminate established ones by subjecting him systematically to great mental pressure.

brainwave *n.* **1** an electrical impulse in the brain. **2** (*colloq.*) a sudden bright idea.

brainy *adj.* intellectually active or clever. —**braininess** *n.* [f. BRAIN]

braise /breɪz/ *v.t.* to cook (meat) slowly in fat or with very little liquid in a closed vessel. [f. F (*braise* live coals)]

brake[1] *n.* a device for checking the motion of a wheel, vehicle, etc. —*v.t./i.* to apply a brake; to retard by a brake. —**brake-drum** *n.* a cylinder attached to a wheel, on which the brake-shoe presses. **brake-horsepower** *n.* the power of an engine measured by the force needed to brake it. **brake-shoe** *n.* a long curved block acting on a wheel to brake it. [orig. unkn.]

brake[2] *n.* a clump of bushes, a thicket. [f. OE, = branch, stump]

brake[3] *n.* an estate car. [var. of *break* carriage-frame, wagonette (orig. unkn.)]

bramble *n.* a rough prickly shrub of the genus *Rubus* with long trailing shoots, especially the blackberry; its fruit. —**brambly** *adj.* [OE, rel.to BROOM]

brambling *n.* a small brightly coloured finch (*Fringilla montifringilla*). [f. G, rel. to prec.]

bran *n.* ground husks of grain, sifted out from the flour. —**bran-tub** *n.* a lucky dip with prizes hidden in bran. [f. OF; orig. unkn.]

branch /brɑːntʃ/ *n.* **1** a limb from the trunk or bough of a tree. **2** a lateral extension of a river, road, railway, etc. **3** a subdivision of a family, study, etc. **4** a local establishment of a bank or other central organization. —*v.t.* to diverge from the main part; (often with *off*) to divide into branches; to put out branches. —**branch out,** to extend one's field of interest. [f. OF f. L *branca* paw]

brand *n.* **1** a trade mark, identifying label, etc., on goods; a particular make of goods. **2** a mark of ownership burnt on livestock with a hot iron, the iron used for this. **3** a stigma, mark of disgrace. **4** a piece of burning or charred wood. —*v.t.* **1** to assign a trade mark or proprietary label to (goods). **2** to mark with a hot iron as a mark of ownership or disgrace; to stigmatize. **3** to impress on the memory. —**brand-new** *adj.* completely new. [OE]

brandish /ˈbrændɪʃ/ *v.t.* to wave (weapons etc.) threateningly or in display. [f. OF f. Gmc]

brandy /ˈbrændɪ/ *n.* a strong spirit distilled from wine. —**brandy-snap** *n.* a crisp rolled gingerbread wafer. [f. Du. *brandewijn* burnt (distilled) wine]

brash *adj.* vulgarly or obnoxiously self-assertive, impudent. [dial.]

brass /brɑːs/ *n.* **1** a widely-used alloy of copper and zinc, sometimes including minor constituents such as tin. **2** brass objects or wind-instruments collectively; a brass memorial tablet in a church; a brass ornament worn by a horse. **3** (*hist.*) bronze. **4** (*colloq.*) money. **5** (*slang*) impudence. —*adj.* made of brass. —**brass band,** a band playing brass instruments. **brass-rubbing** *n.* the taking of impressions on paper of memorial brasses. **brass tacks,** (*colloq.*) essential details. [OE]

brasserie /ˈbræsərɪ/ *n.* a bar where food can be obtained as well as drinks; an informal licensed restaurant. [F, = brewery (*brasser* brew)]

brassica /ˈbræsɪkə/ *n.* a plant of the genus *Brassica* (cabbage, turnip, etc.). [L]

brassière /ˈbræsɪeə(r)/ *n.* a woman's undergarment supporting the breasts. [F]

brassy /ˈbrɑːsɪ/ *adj.* **1** bold and vulgar; pretentious, showy. **2** loud and strident. —**brassiness** *n.* [f. BRASS]

brat *n.* (*derog.*) a child. [orig. unkn.]

bravado /brəˈvɑːdəʊ/ *n.* an outward display of fearlessness. [Sp.]

brave *adj.* able or ready to face danger, pain, etc. **2** splendid, spectacular. —*v.t.* to face bravely or defiantly. —*n.* a North American Indian warrior. —**bravely** *adj.*, **bravery** /ˈbreɪvərɪ/ *n.* [f. F. f. Sp.]

bravo[1] /ˈbrɑːvəʊ/ *n.* (*pl.* **-os**) & *int.* a cry of approval; well done! [F f. It. (as foll.)]

bravo[2] /ˈbrɑːvəʊ/ *n.* (*pl.* **-oes**) a hired ruffian or killer. [F f. It. (as BRAVE)]

bravura /brəˈvʊərə/ *n.* a brilliant or ambitious performance; a piece of vocal etc. music calling for technical virtuosity. [It.]

brawl *n.* a noisy quarrel or fight. —*v.i.* **1** to take part in a brawl. **2** (of a stream) to flow noisily. —**brawler** *n.* [f. Prov., rel. to BRAY]

brawn *n.* **1** muscle, muscular strength. **2** pressed jellied meat made from a pig's head etc. —**brawny** *adj.* [f. AF f. Gmc]

bray *n.* a donkey's loud strident cry; any loud harsh sound. —*v.i.* to emit a bray. [f. OF, perh. f. Celtic]

braze *v.t.* to solder with an alloy of brass and zinc. [f. F *braser* (*braise* live coals)]

brazen /ˈbreɪz(ə)n/ *adj.* **1** shameless and defiant. **2** of or like brass; harsh in tone or colour. —*v.t.*

to face (a situation) *out* boldly and defiantly after doing wrong. [OE, as BRASS]

brazier[1] /ˈbreɪzɪə(r)/ *n.* a metal stand with burning coal as a portable heater. [f. F *brasier* (*braise* hot coals)]

brazier[2] /ˈbreɪzɪə(r)/ *n.* a worker in brass. [prob. f. BRASS, after *glass, glazier*]

breach *n.* **1** a breaking of or failure to observe a law, contract, etc. **2** a breaking of relations, estrangement. **3** a gap or opening (in fortifications etc). —*v.t.* to make a breach in. —**breach of the peace,** a disturbance, an affray. **breach of promise,** the breaking of a promise to marry. [f. OF f. Gmc, rel. to BREAK]

bread /bred/ *n.* flour moistened, kneaded, and baked in loaves, usually with leaven. —*v.t.* to coat with breadcrumbs for frying. —**bread-fruit** *n.* the fruit of a Pacific tree (*Artocarpus communis*) with white pulp like new bread. [OE]

breadboard *n.* **1** a board for cutting bread on. **2** a board on which an experimental electric circuit is set out.

breadcrumbs *n.pl.* bread crumbled for use in cooking.

breadth /bredθ/ *n.* **1** the distance or measurement from side to side of a thing. **2** great extent. **3** freedom from limitations set by prejudice, intolerance, etc. [f. OE, rel. to BROAD]

breadwinner *n.* the member of a family who earns the money to support the other(s).

break /breɪk/ *v.t./i.* (*past* **broke**; *p.p.* **broken**) **1** to separate or cause to separate into pieces under a blow or strain; to damage, to make or become inoperative; to break the bone in (a part of the body). **2** to stop for a time, to make or become discontinuous; (of weather) to change suddenly after a fine spell. **3** to fail to keep (a law or promise etc.). **4** to make a way suddenly or violently. **5** to emerge or appear suddenly (from); to reveal (news etc.); to become known. **6** to surpass (a record). **7** to solve (a cipher). **8** to make or become weak; to overwhelm with grief etc.; to destroy the spirit etc. of (a person). **9** to change course etc. suddenly; (of a voice) to change its even tone, either with emotion or (of a boy's voice) by becoming suddenly deeper at puberty; (of waves) to fall in foam. **10.** (of boxers) to come out of a clinch. —*n.* **1** the act or process of breaking. **2** a point where a thing is broken, a gap. **3** an interval, an interruption, a pause in activity. **4** a sudden dash. **5** (*slang*) a piece of luck. **6** (in cricket) a change of direction of a ball on bouncing. **7** points scored continuously in billiards etc. —**break away,** to free oneself from constraint; to secede. **break the bank,** to exhaust its funds (in gambling etc.). **break dancing,** a kind of street dancing to a loud beat, with wriggling and bending of the arms and legs, in which the dancers may spin to the floor and revolve on their backs. **break down,** to experience mechanical failure; to make or become ineffective; to suffer an emotional collapse; to reduce to its constituent parts by chemical action or analysis. **break even,** to emerge from a transaction with neither profit nor loss. **break in,** to enter forcibly; to interpose a remark; to accustom to a habit or duties etc.; to wear until comfortable. **break-in** *n.* a forcible entry by a thief etc. **breaking-point,** *n.* the point at which a person or thing gives way under stress. **break into,** to enter forcibly; to begin suddenly to utter, perform, etc. **break off,** to detach by breaking; to bring abruptly to an end; to cease talking etc. **break open,** to use force to open. **break out,** to escape by force from prison etc.; to begin or develop suddenly; to become suddenly covered *in* a rash. **break-out** *n.* a forcible escape. **break up,** to break into small pieces; to separate, (of schoolchilden) to disperse for the holidays. **break wind,** to emit wind from the anus. **break with,** to end one's friendship with. [OE]

breakable *adj.* easily broken. [f. prec.]

breakage *n.* damage by breaking; an instance of this. [f. BREAK]

breakaway *n.* a breaking of one's ties, secession. —*adj.* that has broken away or seceded.

breakdown *n.* **1** a failure of mechanical action health, mental stability, etc. **2** an analysis of statistics.

breaker *n.* a heavy wave breaking on a coast or over a reef. [f. BREAK]

breakfast /ˈbrekfəst/ *n.* the first meal of the day. —*v.i.* to have breakfast. [f. BREAK + FAST[2]]

breakneck *adj.* (of speed) dangerously fast.

breakthrough *n.* **1** a major advance or discovery. **2** the act of breaking through an obstacle etc.

breakup *n.* disintegration, collapse; dispersal.

breakwater *n.* a barrier protecting a harbour etc. against heavy waves.

bream *n.* (*pl.* same) a yellowish freshwater fish of the genus *Abramis*; (also **sea-bream**) a similarly shaped fish of the family Sparidae. [f. OF]

breast /brest/ *n.* **1** either of the two protuberant milk-secreting organs on the upper front of a woman's body; the corresponding (usually rudimentary) part of a man's body. **2** the upper front of the human body or of a garment covering it; the corresponding part in animals. **3** the breast as a source of emotion. —*v.t.* to advance to meet with one's breast; to reach the top of (a hill). —**breast-feed** *v.t.* to feed (a baby) with milk from the breast. **breast-stroke** *n.* a swimming stroke performed face downwards, with sweeping movements of the arms. [OE]

breastbone *n.* the flat vertical bone in the chest joined to the ribs.

breastplate *n.* a piece of armour covering the chest.

breastwork *n.* a low temporary defensive wall or parapet.

breath /breθ/ *n.* **1** air drawn into and expelled from the lungs; exhaled air as perceived by the senses. **2** a breathing in; breathing, ability to breathe. **3** a slight movement of air; a whiff (of perfume). **4** a hint or slight rumour (of suspicion etc.). —**breath-test,** a test of breath to discover the amount of alcohol in the body. **hold one's breath,** to cease breathing temporarily from excitement etc. **out of breath,** panting after strenuous exercise. **under one's breath,** in a whisper. [OE]

breathalyse /ˈbreθəlaɪz/ *v.t.* to test with a breathalyser. [f. foll.]

breathalyser *n.* an instrument measuring the amount of alcohol in a person's blood from a sample of his exhaled breath. [f. BREATH + ANALYSE]

breathe /bri:ð/ *v.t./i.* **1** to draw air into and expel it from the lungs; to be alive; to draw into or expel from the lungs on the breath. **2** to utter or mention; to speak softly. **3** to pause for breath. **4** to exude or instil (a quality or feeling). —**breathe again** *or* **freely,** to feel relieved of fear etc. **breathing-space** *n.* time to breathe, a chance to recover from effort. [f. BREATH]

breather /ˈbri:ðə(r)/ *n.* a pause for rest; a spell of fresh air. [f. prec.]

breathless *adj.* panting after exertion; holding one's breath with excitement. [f. BREATH + -LESS]

breathtaking *adj.* spectacular, very exciting.

bred *past & p.p.* of BREED.

breech *n.* **1** the back part of a rifle or gun barrel. **2** (*archaic*) the buttocks. —**breech birth,** a birth in which the baby's buttocks or feet emerge first. [OE]

breeches /ˈbrɪtʃɪz/ *n.pl.* knee-length trousers, now worn for riding or in ceremonial dress. —**breeches buoy,** a lifebuoy with canvas breeches, slung on a rope for hauling people off a wreck etc. [pl. of prec.]

breed *v.t./i.* (*past & p.p.* **bred**) **1** to bear young. **2** to keep (animals) in order to produce young. **3** to train or bring up. **4** to give rise to. **5** to produce (fissile material) in a breeder reactor. —*n.* **1** a strain of an animal or plant species evolved by selective breeding. **2** family, lineage. **3** a sort or kind. [OE, rel. to BROOD]

breeder *n.* one who breeds animals. —**breeder reactor,** a nuclear reactor which can create more fissile material than it consumes. [f. prec.]

breeding *n.* **1** the production of young from animals, propagation. **2** good manners resulting from training or background. [f. BREED]

breeze[1] *n.* a cool or gentle wind. —*v.i.* (*colloq.*) to come *in*, to move *along* etc., in a casual jaunty manner. [f. Sp. *briza* north-east wind]

breeze[2] *n.* small cinders. —**breeze block,** a lightweight building block made from breeze with sand and cement. [f. F *braise* live coals]

breezy *adj.* **1** pleasantly windy or wind-swept. **2** casual and jaunty in manner. [f. BREEZE[1]]

brent-goose *n.* (also **brent**) the smallest kind of wild goose, *Branta bernicla*. [orig. unkn.]

brethren /ˈbreðrɪn/ *n.pl.* brothers (*archaic* except with ref. to monastic orders, certain sects, etc.). [f. BROTHER]

Breton /ˈbretɒn/ *adj.* of the Bretons or their language. —*n.* **1** a native or inhabitant of Brittany. **2** the language of the Bretons. [OF, = Briton]

breve /bri:ˈv/ *n.* **1** a mark (˘) placed over a short or unstressed vowel. **2** (*Mus.*) a note equal to two semibreves. [var. of BRIEF]

breviary /ˈbri:vɪərɪ/ *n.* a book containing the daily office of the Roman Catholic Church. [f. L *breviarium* summary (*brevis* brief)]

brevity /ˈbrevɪtɪ/ *n.* conciseness of written or spoken expression; shortness, especially of duration. [f. L (as prec.)]

brew /bru:/ *v.t./i.* **1** to make (beer etc.) by infusion, boiling, and fermentation; to make (tea etc.) by infusion; to undergo such processes. **2** (of evil results) to develop, to gather force. —*n.* a liquid or amount of liquid made by brewing; the process of brewing; the quality of what is brewed. —**brewer** *n.* [OE]

brewery /ˈbru:ərɪ/ *n.* a place where beer is brewed commercially. [f. prec.]

briar[1,2] var. of BRIER[1,2].

bribe *n.* money etc. offered to procure a corrupt action or decision in favour of the giver. —*v.t.* to give a bribe to. —**bribery** /ˈbraɪbərɪ/ *n.* [f. OF *briber* beg]

bric-à-brac /ˈbrɪkəbræk/ *n.* miscellaneous old ornaments, furniture, trinkets, etc. [f. obs. F, = at random]

brick *n.* **1** a small usually rectangular block of baked or dried clay, used in building; the material of this; building work consisting of such blocks. **2** a brick-shaped loaf, block of ice-cream, etc. —*adj.* made of brick. —*v.t.* to block *up* or fill *in* with bricks. —**brick-red** *adj.* having the red colour of bricks. [f. LG or Du.]

brickbat *n.* **1** a piece of brick, especially as a missile. **2** an uncomplimentary remark.

bricklayer *n.* a workman who builds with bricks.

brickwork *n.* a structure of or building in bricks.

bridal /ˈbraɪd(ə)l/ *adj.* of a bride or wedding. [OE, orig. as n. = wedding feast]

bride *n.* a woman on or just before her wedding-day; a newly-married woman. [OE]

bridegroom *n.* a man on or just before his wedding-day; a newly-married man.

bridesmaid *n.* an unmarried woman or girl attending the bride at a wedding.

bridge[1] *n.* **1** a structure carrying a road, railway, etc. over a river, ravine, etc.; a thing joining or connecting parts. **2** the upper bony part of the nose. **3** a piece of wood etc. over which the strings of a violin are stretched. **4** the raised platform on a ship from which the captain directs its course. **5** a false tooth or teeth supported by the natural teeth on each side. —*v.t.* to connect by or as by a bridge. —**bridging loan** a loan to cover the short interval between buying one thing and selling another (especially houses). [OE]

bridge[2] /brɪdʒ/ *n.* a card-game derived from whist, in which one player's cards are exposed and played by his partner. [orig. unkn., but prob. of Levantine origin since some form of the game seems to have been long known in the Near East]

bridgehead *n.* a fortified position established in hostile territory, especially on the far side of a river as a base for further advance.

bridle /ˈbraɪd(ə)l/ *n.* the harness round a horse's head by which the rider controls it; a restraining thing or influence. —*v.t./i.* **1** to put a bridle on; to curb or restrain. **2** to draw up the head in pride or resentment. —**bridle-path** *n.* one suitable for horse-riding. [OE]

Brie /briː/ *n.* a kind of soft ripe cheese. [f. *Brie* in N. France.]

brief *adj.* **1** of short duration. **2** concise. —*n.* **1** a summary of the facts of a case drawn up for a barrister; a case taken on by a barrister. **2** (in *pl.*) very short pants. —*v.t.* to give a brief to (a barrister); to provide with the essential facts beforehand. —**briefly** *adv.*, **briefness** *n.* [f. AF f. L *breve* dispatch (*brevis* short)]

briefcase *n.* a flat case for carrying documents.

brier[1] /ˈbraɪə(r)/ *n.* a wild rose or other prickly bush. [OE]

brier[2] /ˈbraɪə(r)/ *n.* a shrubby heath (*Erica arborea*) of southern Europe; a tobacco-pipe made from its woody root. [f. F *bruyère* heath]

brig *n.* a square-rigged sailing-ship with two masts. [abbr. BRIGANTINE]

brigade /brɪˈgeɪd/ *n.* **1** a military unit forming part of a division. **2** a body of people organized for a special purpose. [f. F. f. It. *brigata* company (*brigare* be busy with, f. *briga* strife)]

brigadier /brɪgəˈdɪə(r)/ *n.* an officer commanding a brigade; a staff officer with similar status, next in rank above a colonel. [F (as prec.)]

brigand /ˈbrɪgənd/ *n.* a member of a robber gang, a bandit. —**brigandage** *n.* [f. OF f. It. (as BRIGADE)]

brigantine /ˈbrɪgəntiːn/ *n.* a sailing-ship with two masts, the foremast square-rigged, used in the 18th and 19th c. for short coastal and trading voyages. [f. OF or It. (as BRIGAND)]

bright /braɪt/ *adj.* **1** emitting or reflecting much light, shining. **2** (of colour) intense, conspicuous. **3** intelligent, talented. **4** cheerful, vivacious. —*adv.* brightly. —**brightly** *adv.*, **brightness** *n.* [OE]

brighten /ˈbraɪt(ə)n/ *v.t./i.* to make or become brighter. [f. prec.]

brill *n.* a European flat-fish (*Scophthalmus rhombus*). [orig. unkn.]

brilliant /ˈbrɪlɪənt/ *adj.* **1** bright, sparkling. **2** strikingly talented or intelligent. **3** showy. —*n.* a diamond of the finest cut and brilliance, with many facets. —**brilliance** *n.*, **brilliancy** *n.* [f. F *brillant* shining, f. It. *brillare*; orig. unkn.]

brilliantine /ˈbrɪljəntiːn/ *n.* a substance to make the hair glossy. [f. F (as prec.)]

brim *n.* the edge or lip of a cup or other vessel; the projecting edge of a hat. —*v.t./i.* (**-mm-**) to fill or be full to the brim. —**brim over,** to overflow. [orig. unkn.]

brimstone *n.* (*archaic*) sulphur. [f. BURN[1] + STONE]

brindled /ˈbrɪnd(ə)ld/ *adj.* (esp. of dogs or cattle) brownish or tawny with streaks of other colour. [f. Scand.]

brine *n.* water saturated with salt. —*v.t.* to soak in brine. —**briny** *adj.* [OE]

bring *v.t./i.* (*past* & *p.p.* **brought** /brɔːt/) **1** to come carrying, leading, etc. **2** to cause to be present, to result in. **3** to put forward (charges etc.) in court. **4** to cause to reach a given state. **5** to induce *to*. —**bring about,** to cause to happen. **bring-and-buy-sale,** a sale at which people bring items for sale and buy those brought by others. **bring down,** to cause to fall; to lower (prices). **bring forth,** to give birth to. **bring forward,** to move to an earlier time; to transfer from a previous page or account. **bring in,** to introduce; to yield as income or profit. **bring off,** to attempt successfully. **bring on,** to cause to develop rapidly. **bring out,** to bring into prominence; to publish. **bring up,** to supervise the education etc. of (a growing child); to call attention to (a subject); to vomit; to come to a sudden halt. [OE]

brink *n.* **1** the edge of a steep place or stretch of water. **2** the point immediately before some dangerous action, experience, etc. [f. ON]

brinkmanship *n.* the art of pursuing a dangerous policy to the brink of war etc. before desisting. [f. prec., after *sportsmanship*]

brio /ˈbriːəʊ/ *n.* vivacity. [It.]

briquette /brɪˈket/ *n.* a block of compressed coal-dust. [F, dim. of *brique* BRICK]

brisk *adj.* moving quickly, active, lively. —**briskly** *adv.*, **briskness** *n.* [prob. f. F BRUSQUE]

brisket /ˈbrɪskɪt/ *n.* a joint of meat cut from an animal's breast. [f. AF, perh. f. ON]

brisling /ˈbrɪzlɪŋ/ *n.* a small herring or sprat. [Norw. & Da.]

bristle /ˈbrɪs(ə)l/ *n.* **1** a short stiff hair. **2** one of the stiff pieces of hair or wire etc. in a brush. —*v.t./i* **1** to show anger or temper. **2** (of hair or feathers) to stand upright; (of an animal etc.) to make the hair bristle. —**bristle with,** to have in abundance. [OE]

bristly /ˈbrɪslɪ/ *adj.* full of bristles; rough and prickly. [f. BRISTLE]

Britannic /brɪˈtænɪk/ *adj.* of Britain (chiefly in *His* or *Her Britannic Majesty*). [as prec.]

Briticism /ˈbrɪtɪsɪzm/ *n.* an idiom used in Britain but not in the USA etc. [f. foll., after *Gallicism*]

British /ˈbrɪtɪʃ/ *adj.* of Great Britain or the United Kingdom. —**the British,** the people of Great Britain or the United Kingdom. [OE]

Briton /ˈbrɪt(ə)n/ *n.* **1** a member of the people living in South Britain before the Roman conquest. **2** a native of Great Britain. [f. L f. Celt.]

brittle *adj.* hard but fragile; easily destroyed. —**brittleness** *n.* [OE]

broach¹ *v.t.* **1** raise (a subject) for discussion. **2** to pierce (a cask) to draw liquor. —*n.* **1** a tool for enlarging holes. **2** a roasting-spit. —**broach spire,** a church spire rising from a square tower without a parapet. [f. OF f. L *broccus* projecting]

broach² *v.t./i.* (usu. with *to*) to veer or cause (a ship) to veer and present its side to the wind and waves. [orig. unkn.]

broad /brɔːd/ *adj.* **1** large in extent from one side to the other, wide; (after measurements) in breadth; extensive. **2** full and complete; (of hints) explicit; (of accent) strongly regional. **3** tolerant, liberal. **4** in general terms, not detailed. **5** (of humour) somewhat coarse. —*n.* the broad part. —**broad bean,** an edible bean, *Vicia faba*, or one of its large flat seeds. **Broad Church,** the section of the Anglican Church favouring toleration, not strict adherence to dogma. **broad-minded** *adj.* having tolerant views. **the Broads,** large areas of open fresh water in East Anglia, formed by the widening of rivers. [OE]

broadcast *v.t./i* (*past* & *p.p.* **broadcast**) **1** to transmit (programmes or information) by radio or television; to speak or perform thus. **2** to disseminate (information) widely. **3** to scatter (seed) at random rather than in rows. —*n.* a radio or television programme or transmission. —*adv.* by random sowing. —**broadcaster** *n.*

broadcloth *n.* a fine woollen or worsted cloth used in tailoring (orig. woven on a wide loom).

broaden /ˈbrɔːd(ə)n/ *v.t./i.* to make or become broad. [f. BROAD]

broadloom *adj.* (of carpets) woven in broad widths.

broadsheet *n.* a large sheet of paper printed on one side only, especially with information.

broadside *n.* **1** the firing of all the guns that are on one side of a ship. **2** a fierce verbal attack. **3** the side of a ship above the water between bow and quarter. —**broadside on,** sideways on.

broadsword *n.* a sword with a broad blade for cutting rather than thrusting.

brocade /brəˈkeɪd/ *n.* a fabric woven with raised pattern. —*v.t.* to weave thus. [f. Sp. and Port. f. It. (*brocco* twisted thread)]

broccoli /ˈbrɒkəlɪ/ *n.* a hardy variety of cauliflower with greenish flower-heads. [It.]

broch /brɒk, brɒx/ *n.* a circular dry-stone tower of a type found in northern Scotland and the adjacent islands, dating from *c.*100 BC–100 AD. [f. ON *borg* castle]

brochure /ˈbrəʊʃʊə(r)/ *n.* a booklet or pamphlet giving descriptive information. [F, = stitching (*brocher* stitch)]

broderie anglaise /brəʊdrɪɑ̃gˈleɪz/ open embroidery on white linen or cambric. [F, = English embroidery]

brogue¹ /brəʊg/ *n.* a strong outdoor shoe with ornamental perforated bands; a rough shoe of untanned leather. [f. Ir. & Gael. f. ON]

brogue² /brəʊg/ *n.* a strong regional, especially Irish, accent. [perh. allusive use of prec.]

broil *v.t./i.* to cook (meat) on a fire or gridiron; to make or become very hot, as from sunshine. [f. OF *bruler* burn]

broiler *n.* a young chicken reared for broiling or roasting. [f. prec.]

broke *past* of BREAK. —*adj.* (*colloq.*) having no money, bankrupt.

broken *p.p.* of BREAK. —*adj.* that has been broken; (of a person) crushed in spirit, beaten; (of a language) spoken imperfectly (by a foreigner); (of sleep or time) disturbed, interrupted. —**broken chord,** (*Mus.*) a chord in which the notes are played successively, not simultaneously. **broken-down** *adj.* worn or sick, inoperative through mechanical failure. **broken-hearted** *adj.* overwhelmed by grief. **broken home,** a family lacking one parent, as by divorce or separation. **broken reed,** a person who proves unreliable in an emergency.

broker *n.* **1** an agent buying and selling for others; a dealer on the Stock Exchange. **2** an official licensed to sell or appraise distrained goods. [f. AF; orig. unkn.]

brokerage /ˈbrəʊkərɪdʒ/ *n.* a broker's fee or commission. [f. prec.]

brolly *n.* (*colloq.*) an umbrella. [abbr.]

bromide /ˈbrəʊmaɪd/ *n.* **1** a compound of bromine, used in sedatives. **2** a soothing statement. [f. foll.]

bromine /ˈbrəʊmi:n/ *n.* a non-metallic dark-red liquid element of the halogen group with a poisonous rank-smelling vapour, symbol Br, atomic number 35. [f. F f. Gk *brōmos* stench]

bronchial /ˈbrɒŋkɪəl/ *adj.* of the bronchi (see BRONCHUS) or the smaller tubes into which they divide. [f. BRONCHUS]

bronchitis /brɒŋˈkaɪtɪs/ *n.* inflammation of the mucous membrane in the bronchial tubes. [f. foll.]

bronchus /ˈbrɒŋkəs/ *n.* (*pl.* **-chi** /-kaɪ/) either of the two main divisions of the windpipe, leading to the lungs. [L f. Gk.]

bronco /ˈbrɒŋkəʊ/ *n.* (*pl.* **-os**) a wild or half-tamed horse of the western USA. [Sp., = rough]

brontosaurus /brɒntəˈsɔ:rəs/ *n.* a large herbivorous dinosaur of the genus *Brontosaurus* of the Jurassic and Cretaceous periods. [f. Gk *brontē* thunder + *sauros* lizard]

bronze *n.* **1** an alloy of copper and tin. **2** its brownish colour. **3** an object (especially a work of art) made of bronze. —*adj.* made of or coloured like bronze. —*v.t.* to give a bronze surface or colour to; (of the sun etc.) to tan. —**Bronze Age** the period when certain weapons and tools were made of bronze rather than stone. **bronze medal,** one awarded as the third prize. [f. F f. It., prob. f. Pers. *birinj* copper]

brooch /brəʊtʃ/ *n.* an ornamental clasp fastening by a pin at the back. [f. as BROACH[1]]

brood *n.* **1** the young of a bird or other creature produced at one hatching or birth. **2** the children in a family. —*v.i.* **1** to ponder anxiously or resentfully. **2** to sit as a hen on eggs to hatch them. [OE]

broody *adj.* **1** (of a hen) wanting to brood. **2** engrossed and thoughtful. [f. prec.]

brook[1] /brʊk/ *n.* a small stream. [OE]

brook[2] /brʊk/ *v.t.* (usu. with negative) to tolerate, to allow. [OE]

broom *n.* **1** a yellow-flowered shrub of acid soils, *Cytisus* (or *Sarothamnus*) *scoparius*; any shrub of the genus *Cytisus* or the allied genus *Genista*, with yellow, white, etc. flowers. **2** a long-handled implement for sweeping floors, originally made with twigs from this. —**new broom,** a newly appointed person eager to make changes. [OE]

broomstick *n.* a broom-handle.

broth /brɒθ/ *n.* the water in which meat or fish has been boiled; a soup made from this. [OE]

brothel /ˈbrɒθ(ə)l/ *n.* a house where prostitutes may be visited. [orig. = worthless man, prostitute, f. OE]

brother /ˈbrʌðə(r)/ *n.* **1** a man or boy in relation to the other sons and daughters of his parents. **2** a man who is a close friend or associate; a male fellow member of the same church, trade union, or other association, or of the human race. **3** a monk who is not a priest. —**brother-in-law** *n.* (*pl.* **brothers-in-law**) the brother of one's husband or wife; the husband of one's sister. —**brotherly** *adj.* [OE]

brotherhood /ˈbrʌðəhʊd/ *n.* **1** friendly feeling as between brothers. **2** an association of men with common (often religious) beliefs or interests. [f. BROTHER + -HOOD]

brougham /ˈbru:əm/ *n.* (*hist.*) a one-horse closed carriage with the driver's seat outside; a motor-car with the driver's seat open. [f. Lord *Brougham* (d. 1868)]

brought /brɔ:t/ *past* & *p.p.* of BRING.

brow /braʊ/ *n.* **1** (usu. in *pl.*) an eyebrow. **2** the forehead. **3** the projecting upper part or edge of a hill or cliff. [OE]

browbeat *v.t.* to intimidate.

brown /braʊn/ *adj.* of a colour between orange and black; dark-skinned, sun-tanned; (of bread) brown from the colour of the wholemeal, or other coarse flour used. —*n.* brown colour or pigment; brown clothes or material. —*v.t./i.* to make or become brown. —**brown bear,** a large bear (*Ursus arctos*) of the northern hemisphere with shaggy usually brownish fur. **brown paper,** unbleached paper used for packing. **brown sugar,** sugar only partially refined. [OE]

brownie /ˈbraʊnɪ/ *n.* **1** a benevolent elf. **2 Brownie,** a junior Guide. [f. BROWN]

browning *n.* browned flour or other additive to colour gravy. [f. BROWN]

browse /braʊz/ *v.i.* **1** to read or inspect items on display etc. casually. **2** (of animals) to crop or feed *on* leaves and young shoots. —*n.* an act or spell of browsing. [f. OF *broust* young shoot, prob. f. Gmc]

brucellosis /bru:səˈləʊsɪs/ *n.* a bacterial disease causing abortion in domestic animals and recurrent fever in humans consuming their products. [f. Sir D. *Bruce*, Scottish physician (d. 1931)]

bruise /bru:z/ *n.* an injury caused by a blow etc. that discolours the skin without breaking it. —*v.t./i.* to injure in this way; to be susceptible to bruises; to hurt mentally. [orig. = crush, f. OE]

bruit /bru:t/ *v.t.* (*archaic*) to spread (a report) *abroad* or *about*. [F, = noise]

brunch *n.* (*colloq.*) a meal combining breakfast and lunch. [portmanteau word]

brunette /bru:ˈnet/ *n.* a woman with dark brown hair. [F, dim. of *brun* brown]

brunt *n.* the chief stress or strain (*of* an attack or responsibility etc.). [orig. unkn.]

brush *n.* **1** an implement with bristles, hairs, etc., set in a solid base for cleaning, painting, dressing the hair, etc.; an application of this. **2** a fox's bushy tail. **3** a brushlike piece of carbon or metal for making an electrical connection, especially with a moving part. **4** a short, usually unpleasant, encounter *with*. —*v.t.* **1** to sweep clean, arrange, etc., with a brush. **2** to touch lightly in passing. **3** to apply or remove with a brush. —**brush aside,** to dismiss as irrelevant. **brush off,** to dismiss abruptly. **brush-off** *n.* an abrupt dismissal, a rebuff. **brush up,** to clean or smarten up; to revive one's former knowledge of. [f. AF *brousse*, OF *brosse*]

brushed *adj.* (of fabrics) finished with a nap. [f. prec.]

brushwood *n.* cut or broken twigs etc.; undergrowth.

brushwork *n.* manipulation of the brush in painting; a painter's style in this.

brusque /brʊsk/ *adj.* abrupt or offhand in manner. —**brusquely** *adv.*, **brusqueness** *n.* [F, f. It. *brusco* sour]

Brussels sprouts /ˈbrʌs(ə)lz/ the edible leaf-buds, resembling tiny cabbages, growing thickly on the stem of a variety of cabbage (*Brassica oleracea gemmifera*). [f. *Brussels*, capital of Belgium.]

brutal /ˈbru:t(ə)l/ *adj.* very cruel, merciless. —**brutality** /-ˈtælɪtɪ/ *n.*, **brutally** *adv.* [f. BRUTE]

brutalize *v.t./i.* to make or become brutal; to treat brutally. [f. prec.]

brute *n.* a brutal or (*colloq.*) disagreeable person. —*adj.* unable to reason; animal-like in stupidity, sensuality, etc.; unthinking, exerted etc. without mental effort. —**brutish** *adj.* [f. F. f. L *brutus* stupid]

bryony /ˈbraɪənɪ/ *n.* either of two climbing hedge-plants, *Bryonia dioica* and *Tamus communis*. [f. L f. Gk]

bryophyte /ˈbraɪəfaɪt/ *n.* a member of the Bryophyta, a group of plants comprising the mosses and liverworts. [ult. f. Gk (*bruon* moss, *phuton* plant)]

Brythonic /braɪˈθɒnɪk/ *adj.* of the Celts of southern Britain or their languages. —*n.* the southern group of the Celtic languages, including Welsh, Cornish, and Breton. [f. Welsh *Brython* Britons]

B.Sc. *abbr.* Bachelor of Science.

BSE *abbr.* bovine spongiform encephalopathy, popularly known as 'mad cow disease', a virus disease of cattle that attacks the brain tissue and makes it spongy, and affects the central nervous system.

bubble *n.* **1** a globular film of liquid enclosing air or gas; an air-filled cavity in glass etc. **2** a transparent domed canopy. —*v.t.* to send up or rise in bubbles; to make the sound of bubbles. —**bubble and squeak,** cooked potato and cabbage fried together in a cake. **bubble gum,** chewing-gum that can be blown into bubbles. —**bubbly** *adj.* [imit.]

bubonic /bju:ˈbɒnɪk/ *adj.* **bubonic plague,** a contagious bacterial disease characterized by inflamed swellings (*buboes*) in the groin or armpit. [f. Gk *boubōn* groin]

buccaneer /bʌkəˈnɪə(r)/ *n.* a pirate, originally on the Spanish-American coast; an unscrupulous adventurer. —**buccaneering** *adj.* & *n.* [f. F (*boucan* barbecue, of Brazilian origin)]

buck[1] *n.* **1** a male deer, rabbit, or hare. **2** (*archaic*) a fashionable young man. —*v.t./i.* (of a horse) to jump vertically with back arched; to throw (the rider) thus. —**buck up,** (*slang*) to hurry up; to cheer up. [OE]

buck[2] *n.* (in poker) an object placed as a reminder before the player whose turn it is to deal. —**pass the buck,** (*colloq.*) to shift responsibility (and possible blame) to another. [orig. unkn.]

buck[3] *n.* (*US slang*) a dollar [orig. unkn.]

bucket /ˈbʌkɪt/ *n.* **1** a round flat-bottomed container with a handle, for carrying liquids etc.; the amount contained in this. **2** a scoop in a dredger etc.; a compartment in a water-wheel. —*v.t./i.* **1** to travel or drive fast and bumpily. **2** to rain or pour down heavily. [perh. f. OE, = pitcher]

buckle *n.* a metal clasp with a hinged pin for securing a strap, belt, etc. —*v.t./i.* **1** to fasten with a buckle. **2** to crumple or cause to crumple under pressure. [f. OF f. L *buccula* cheek-strap of helmet]

buckler *n.* a small round shield with a handle. [as prec.]

buckram /ˈbʌkrəm/ *n.* coarse linen or cloth stiffened with paste, used for binding books etc. [f. AF, perh. f. *Bokhara* in central Asia]

Bucks. *abbr.* Buckinghamshire.

buckshee /bʌkˈʃi:/ *adj.* & *adv.* (*slang*) free of charge. [corrupt of BAKSHEESH]

buckshot *n.* coarse lead shot. [f. BUCK[1] + SHOT]

buckskin *n.* leather from a buck's skin; a thick smooth cotton or woollen fabric.

buckthorn *n.* a thorny shrub (*Rhamnus cathartica*) with berries that were formerly used as a purgative. [f. BUCK[1] + THORN]

buckwheat *n.* a plant of the genus *Fagopyrum*, with dark seeds used for horse and poultry food etc. [Du., = beech-wheat.]

bucolic /bju:ˈkɒlɪk/ *adj.* of herdsmen or shepherds, pastoral. —*n.* a pastoral poem. [f. L f. Gk (*boukolos* herdsman)]

bud *n.* the rudiment of a shoot, foliage, or flower; a leaf or flower not fully open; an asexual growth separating from an organism to form a new animal. —*v.t./i.* (**-dd-**) **1** to put forth buds. **2** to graft the bud of (a plant) on another plant. **3** (esp. in *partic.*) to begin to grow or develop. [orig. unkn.]

Buddha /ˈbʊdə/ *n.* the title of the Indian philosopher Gautama (5th c. BC) and his successors; a representation of Gautama. [Skr., = enlightened (*budh* wake up, know)]

Buddhism /ˈbʊdɪz(ə)m/ *n.* the religion founded by Gautama the Buddha. —**Buddhist** *n.* & *adj.* [f. prec.]

buddleia /ˈbʌdlɪə/ *n.* a garden shrub or tree of the genus *Buddleia*, with small fragrant lilac, white, red, pink, or yellow flowers in clusters, especially *B. davidii* which bears lilac flowers that attract many butterflies. [f. A. *Buddle* English botanist (d. 1715)]

buddy *n.* a friend, a mate. [perh. f. BROTHER]

budge /bʌdʒ/ *v.t./i.* (chiefly in negative contexts) **1** to move in the least degree. **2** to abandon or cause to abandon an opinion. [f. F *bouger*]

budgerigar /ˈbʌdʒərɪgɑ:(r)/ *n.* an Australian grass parakeet, often kept as a cage-bird. [Aboriginal, = good cockatoo]

budget /ˈbʌdʒɪt/ *n.* an estimate or plan of income and expenditure, especially those of a country; the amount of money needed or available. —*v.t./i.* to allot or allow *for* in a budget. —**budgetary** *adj.* [f. OF f. L *bulga* bag]

budgie /ˈbʌdʒɪ/ *n.* (*colloq.*) a budgerigar. [abbr.]

buff *n.* **1** a velvety dull-yellow leather; the colour of this. **2** (*colloq.*) an enthusiast [orig. for going to fires, from the buff uniforms once worn by New York volunteer firemen]. —*v.t.* to polish (metal etc.) by rubbing; to make velvety like buff. —**in the buff,** naked. [orig. = buffalo, f. F *buffle*]

buffalo /ˈbʌfələʊ/ *n.* (*pl* **-oes**, *collect.* **-o**) an ox, especially *Bubalis bubalis* of Asia, or *Syncerus caffer* of Africa, or (especially) *Bison bison* of North America. [prob. f. Port. f. L f. Gk *boubalos*]

buffer[1] *n.* **1** thing that deadens impact, especially a shock-absorber fitted (in pairs) on a railway vehicle or at the end of a track. **2** a substance that maintains the degree of acidity in a solution. —**buffer state,** a small country between two powerful ones, thought to reduce the chance of war between these. [f. *buff* sound as of a soft body when struck]

buffer[2] *n.* (*slang*) a man, a fellow. [perh. f. prec.]

buffet[1] /ˈbʊfeɪ/ *n.* **1** a place where light meals may be bought (usually at a counter) and eaten. **2** /also ˈbʌfɪt/ a sideboard or recessed cupboard for dishes etc. **3** provision of food where guests serve themselves. —**buffet car,** a railway coach in which refreshments are served. [F, = stool]

buffet[2] /ˈbʌfɪt/ *n.* a blow, especially with the hand. —*v.t.* to deal such blows to; to contend with (waves etc.) [f. OF, dim. of *bufe* blow]

buffoon /bəˈfu:n/ *n.* a jester, a clown. —**buffoonery** *n.* [f. F f. It. f. L *buffo* clown]

bug *n.* **1** a hemipterous insect, especially a bedbug; any small insect. **2** (*colloq.*) a virus, an infection; an obsessive enthusiasm or enthusiast. **3** (*slang*) a concealed microphone. **4** (*slang.*) a defect in a machine etc. —*v.t.* (**-gg-**) (*slang*) **1** to conceal a microphone in. **2** to annoy. [orig. unkn.]

bugbear *n.* a cause of annoyance; an object of baseless fear, a bogy. [f. obs. *bug* bogy]

bugger *n.* (*vulgar*) a hateful or contemptible person or thing; a sodomite. —*int.* (*vulgar*) expressing annoyance. [f. Du., ult. f. L *Bulgarus* Bulgarian heretic]

buggery *n.* sodomy. [as prec.]

buggy *n.* a light horse-drawn vehicle for one or two persons; a small sturdy motor vehicle. [orig. unkn.]

bugle[1] /ˈbju:g(ə)l/ *n.* an instrument like a small trumpet, for sounding signals. —*v.i.* to sound a bugle. —**bugler** *n.* [orig. = buffalo; f. OF f. L *buculus* young bull]

bugle[2] /ˈbju:g(ə)l/ *n.* a creeping woodland plant (*Ajuga reptans*) with blue flowers. [f. L *bugula*]

bugloss /ˈbju:glɒs/ *n.* **1** a plant related to borage, of various genera. **2** a plant of the genus *Echium*, especially *E. vulgare* (also called **viper's bugloss**) with white bristly hairs and blue flowers. [f. F or L f. Gk *bouglossos* ox-tongued, with ref. to the shape and roughness of its leaves]

buhl /bu:l/ *n.* inlaid work of brass, tortoiseshell, etc. [f. A. C. *Boule*, French wood-carver (d. 1732)]

build /bɪld/ *v.t.* (*past* & *p.p.* **built** /bɪlt/) to construct by putting parts or material together; to develop or establish (a reputation etc.). —*n.* style of construction; proportions of the body. —**build up,** to establish or be established gradually. [OE]

builder *n.* one who builds, especially a contractor who builds houses. [f. prec.]

building *n.* **1** the construction of houses etc. **2** a permanent built structure that can be entered. —**building society,** a society of investors that lends money to people buying houses etc.

build-up *n.* **1** a favourable description in advance. **2** a gradual approach to a climax.

built /bɪlt *past* & *p.p.* of BUILD. —*adj.* having a specified bodily build. —**built-up** *adj.* increased in height etc. by the addition of parts; (of an area) fully occupied by houses etc.

bulb *n.* **1** the globular base of the stem in plants

such as the onion and daffodil, from which roots grow down and leaves grow up. **2** an object or part shaped like this; an electric lamp, its glass container. —**bulbous** /ˈbʌlbəs/ *adj.* [f. L f. Gk *bolbos* onion]

bulge *n.* **1** an irregularly rounded swelling. **2** (*colloq.*) a temporary increase in numbers. —*v.i.* to form a bulge. [f. L *bulga* bag]

bulk *n.* **1** size or magnitude, especially when great. **2** the greater part *of*. **3** a large shape, body, or person. **4** a large quantity. —*v.t./i.* **1** to increase the size or thickness of. **2** to seem (*large* etc.) in size or importance. —**bulk buying,** buying in large amounts, especially by one buyer of much of a producer's output. [ON]

bulkhead *n.* an upright partition between compartments in a ship, aircraft, etc. [f. *bulk* stall + HEAD]

bulky *adj.* taking up much space, inconveniently large. —**bulkiness** *n.* [f. BULK]

bull[1] /bʊl/ *n.* **1** an uncastrated male of the ox family; the male of the whale, elephant, and other large animals. **2 the Bull,** the constellation or sign of the zodiac Taurus. **3** the bull's-eye of a target. **4** one who buys shares on the Stock Exchange in the hope of selling them at a higher price later (cf. BEAR[2]). —**bull-nosed** *adj.* with a rounded end. **bull-terrier** *n.* a dog of a breed originally produced by crossing a bulldog and a terrier. [f. ON]

bull[2] /bʊl/ *n.* a papal edict. [f. L *bulla* seal]

bulldog *n.* a dog of strong courageous breed with a broad head and short thick neck.

bulldoze /ˈbʊldəʊz/ *v.t.* **1** to move or clear with a bulldozer. **2** (*colloq.*) to intimidate; to force one's *way*. [orig. = coerce by threats of violence; perh. f.BULL[1], DOSE]

bulldozer *n.* a powerful tractor with a broad vertical blade in front for moving earth etc. [f. prec.]

bullet /ˈbʊlɪt/ *n.* a small cylindrical projectile fired from a gun etc. [f. F (dim. of *boule* ball)]

bulletin /ˈbʊlɪlɪn/ *n.* a short official statement of news, the condition of a patient, etc. [F f. It. dim. of *bulletta* passport (L *bulla* seal)]

bullfighting *n.* the sport of baiting and usually killing a bull. —**bullfighter** *n.*

bullfinch *n.* a songbird with a short beak and pinkish breast.

bullfrog *n.* a large American frog with a bellowing cry.

bullion /ˈbʌljən/ *n.* gold or silver in bulk before coining, or valued by weight. [AF, = mint (as BOIL[1])]

bullock /ˈbʊlək/ *n.* a castrated bull. [OE, dim. of BULL[1]]

bull's-eye *n.* **1** the centre of a target. **2** a large hard minty sweet. **3** a hemisphere or thick disc of glass as a window in a ship, a small circular window; a hemispherical lens, a lantern with this; a boss at the centre of a sheet of blown glass. [f. BULL[1]]

bully[1] /ˈbʊlɪ/ *n.* a person using strength or power to hurt or coerce others by intimidation. —*v.t.* to behave as a bully towards, to intimidate. [prob. f. Du., orig. as a term of endearment]

bully[2] /ˈbʊlɪ/ *n.* the start of play in hockey, at which two opposing players tap the ground and each other's sticks three times before hitting the ball. —*v.i.* to start play thus. [orig. unkn.]

bulrush /ˈbʊlrʌʃ/ *n.* any of several tall reed-like plants, *Scirpus lacustris* or (now more usually) *Typha latifolia*. [f. BULL[1], in sense 'coarse']

bulwark /ˈbʊlwək/ *n.* **1** a defensive wall, especially of earth; a protecting person or thing. **2** (usu. in *pl.*) a ship's side above deck. [f. MDu.]

bum[1] *n.* (*slang*) the buttocks. [orig. unkn.]

bum[2] *n.* (*US slang*) a loafer, a dissolute person. [f. G *bummler* loafer]

bumble *v.i.* **1** to blunder, to act ineptly. **2** to ramble *on* in speaking. **3** to buzz loudly. [f. BOOM[1]]

bumble-bee *n.* a large bee with a loud hum.

bummalo /ˈbʌmələʊ/ *n.* (*pl.* same) a small fish (*Harpodon nehereus*) of South Asian coasts. [perh. f. *bombil* (as *Bombay duck*)]

bump *n.* **1** a dull-sounding blow or impact. **2** a swelling produced by this. **3** any lump or unevenness on a surface; a prominence on the skull, associated by phrenologists with mental faculties. —*v.t./i* to hit or come (*against* or *into*) with a bump; to hurt thus; to travel with jolts. —**bump into,** (*colloq.*) to meet by chance. **bump off,** (*slang*) to murder. **bump up,** to increase (prices etc.). —**bumpily** *adv.*, **bumpiness** *n.*, **bumpy** *adj.* [imit.]

bumper *n.* **1** a horizontal bar attached at either end of a motor vehicle to reduce damage in a collision. **2** (in cricket) a ball that rises high after pitching. **3** a wine-glass filled to the brim. —*adj.* (of crops etc.) exceptionally abundant. [f. BUMP]

bumpkin *n.* an awkward or simple country person. [f. Du.]

bumptious /ˈbʌmpʃəs/ *adj.* offensively self-confident. [f. BUMP, after *fractious*]

bun *n.* **1** a small round cake often with currants. **2** hair fastened in a rounded mass at the back of the head. [orig. unkn.]

bunch *n.* **1** a set of things growing or fastened together. **2** (*slang*) a gang or group. —*v.t./i.* **1** to make into a bunch. **2** to gather into close folds. **3** to form a group or crowd. —**bunchy** *adj.* [orig. unkn.]

bundle *n.* a collection of things fastened or wrapped together. —*v.t.* **1** to make into a bundle. **2** to throw hastily *into* a receptacle; to send (a person) unceremoniously *out* etc. [perh. f. OE, = binding; also f. Du. *bundel*]

bung *n.* a large stopper, especially for the mouth of a cask. —*v.t.* **1** to stop with a bung. **2** (*slang*) to throw, to put. —**bunged up,** blocked. [f. Du.]

bungalow /ˈbʌŋgələʊ/ *n.* a one-storeyed house. [orig. in India, f. Gujarati f. Hindi, = of Bengal]

bungle *v.t.* to mismanage, to blunder through lack of skill. —*n.* a bungled attempt. —**bungler** *n.* [imit., cf. *bumble*]

bunion /ˈbʌnjən/ *n.* a swelling on the foot, especially on the big toe. [f. OF (*buigne* bump on head)]

bunk[1] *n.* a shelf-like bed, usually one in a tiered series, as in a ship etc. [orig. unkn.]

bunk[2] *n.* **do a bunk,** (*slang*) to go away hurriedly. [orig. unkn.]

bunk[3] *n.* (*slang*) bunkum. [abbr.]

bunker *n.* **1** a compartment for coal; a reinforced underground shelter. **2** a sandy hollow constructed as an obstacle on a golf-course. —*v.t.* to fill the bunkers of (a ship) with fuel. [orig. unkn.]

bunkum *n.* nonsense, claptrap. [f. a verbose congressman from *Buncombe* County in North Carolina *c.*1820]

bunny *n.* (*children's colloq.*) a rabbit. [f. dial. *bun* rabbit]

bunting[1] *n.* flags and similar festive decorations; a loosely-woven fabric used for these. [orig. unkn.]

bunting[2] *n.* a small bird allied to the finches. [orig. unkn.]

buoy /bɔɪ/ *n.* **1** an anchored float marking a navigable course or reefs etc. **2** a lifebuoy. —*v.t.* **1** to mark with a buoy. **2** (also with *up*) to keep afloat, to sustain and encourage (a person, courage, etc.). [prob. f. MDu., perh. f. OF *boie* chain ult. f. Gk *boeiai* (*dorai*) ox-hides, straps]

buoyant /ˈbɔɪənt/ *adj.* **1** able to stay afloat. **2** constantly cheerful or light-hearted. —**buoyancy** *n.* [f. F or Sp. (as prec.)]

bur *n.* a seed or seed-head with hooked bristles, clinging to the hair or clothes. [f. Scand.]

burble *v.i.* to make a murmuring noise; to speak ramblingly. [imit.]

burbot /ˈbɜːbət/ *n* an eel-like freshwater fish (*Lota lota*). [rel. to OF *barbote*]

burden *n.* **1** a thing carried, especially something heavy; an oppressive responsibility, expense, etc. **2** a ship's carrying capacity. **3** the refrain of a song; the main theme of a speech etc. —*v.t.* to place a heavy load on, to encumber; to oppress. —**burden of proof,** the obligation to prove one's case. [OE, f. BEAR[1]]

burdensome *adj.* troublesome, oppressive. [f. prec. + -SOME]

burdock /ˈbɜːdɒk/ *n.* a plant of the genus *Arctium*, with dock-like leaves and bur-like flower-heads. [f. BUR + DOCK[4]]

bureau /ˈbjʊərəʊ/ *n.* (*pl.* **-eaux**) **1** a writing-desk with drawers. **2** an office or department for transacting specific business; a government department. [F, = desk, orig. its baize covering, ult. f. Gk *purros* red]

bureaucracy /bjʊəˈrɒkrəsɪ/ *n.* government by the officials of a central administration rather than by elected representatives; such officials, often regarded as inflexible or unimaginative; excessive official routine. [f. prec., after *aristocracy* etc.]

bureaucrat /ˈbjʊərəkræt/ *n.* an official in a bureaucracy. —**bureaucratic** /-ˈkrætɪk/ *adj.* [as prec.]

burette /bjʊəˈret/ *n.* a graduated glass tube with a tap, for measuring small amounts of liquid in chemical analysis. [F]

burgee /bɜːˈdʒiː/ *n.* a small triangular or swallow-tailed flag on a yacht. [perh. for *burgee's* (owner's) *flag* f. F *bourgeois* owner etc.]

burgeon /ˈbɜːdʒ(ə)n/ *v.i.* (*literary*) to begin to grow rapidly, to flourish. [f. OF f. L *burra* wool]

burgess /ˈbɜːdʒɪs/ *n.* a citizen of a town or borough; (*hist.*) an MP for a borough, corporate town, or university. [f. OF f. L *burgus* borough]

burgh /ˈbʌrə/ *n.* a Scottish borough. [Sc. form of BOROUGH]

burgher /ˈbɜːgə(r)/ *n.* a citizen of a (chiefly foreign) town. [f. G or Du. (*burg* BOROUGH)]

burglar /ˈbɜːglə(r)/ *n.* one who commits burglary. —**burglarious** /-ˈgleərɪəs/ *adj.* [f. AF *burgler* plunderer]

burglary /ˈbɜːglərɪ/ *n.* illegal entry into a building to commit theft etc. [as prec.]

burgle *v.t.* to enter and rob (a house), to rob the house of (a person). [f. BURGLAR]

burgomaster /ˈbɜːgəmɑːstə(r)/ *n.* the mayor of a Dutch or Flemish town. [Du. (*burg* borough)]

burgundy /ˈbɜːgəndɪ/ *n.* a red or white wine from Burgundy in eastern France; a similar wine from elsewhere. [place-name]

burial /ˈberɪəl/ *n.* **1** the burying of a dead body; a funeral. **2** (*Archaeol.*) a grave or its remains. [f. BURY]

burin /ˈbjʊərɪn/ *n.* a tool for engraving on copper or wood; a prehistoric flint tool with a narrow chisel edge. [F]

burlesque /bɜːˈlesk/ *n.* a composition in which a serious subject is treated comically or a trivial one with mock solemnity; this as a branch of literature etc. —*adj.* of the nature of burlesque. —*v.t.* to make or give a burlesque of. [F. f. It. (*burla* mockery)]

burly *adj.* of strong sturdy build. [orig. = stately; prob. f. BOWER]

Burmese /bɜːˈmiːz/ *adj.* of Burma (from 1989

officially called Myanmar), a country in SE Asia, or its people or language. —*n.* (*pl.* same) **1** a native of Burma. **2** the official language of Burma. [f. Burma.]

burn[1] *v.t./i.* (*past & p.p.* **burned, burnt**) **1** to consume or be consumed by fire; to blaze or glow with fire. **2** to use or be used as fuel; to give out or cause to give out light or heat. **3** to injure by fire or great heat, to suffer such injury; to scorch or char in cooking. **4** to produce (a mark etc.) by fire; to harden (bricks) by fire. **5** to feel a hot sensation. **7** to be filled *with* a violent emotion. —*n.* a mark or injury caused by burning. —**burn down,** to destroy or be destroyed by burning. **burning-glass** *n.* a lens to concentrate the sun's rays on an object and burn it. [OE]

burn[2] *n.* (*Sc.*) a brook. [OE]

burner *n.* the part of a lamp, gas cooker, etc., that emits and shapes the flame. [f. BURN[1]]

burning *adj.* **1** that burns; ardent, intense. **2** (of a question) hotly discussed. [f. BURN[1]]

burnish /ˈbɜːnɪʃ/ *v.t.* to polish by rubbing. [f. OF *brunir* (*brun* brown)]

burnous /bɜːˈnuːs/ *n.* an Arab or Moorish hooded cloak. [F f. Arab. f. Gk *birros* cloak]

burnt *past & p.p.* of BURN[1]. —*adj.* **burnt ochre, sienna,** etc., pigment darkened by burning. **burnt offering,** a sacrifice offered by burning.

burp *v.t./i.* (*colloq.*) to belch; to cause (a baby) to belch. —*n.* (*colloq.*) a belch. [imit.]

burr[1] *n.* **1** a whirring sound; a rough pronunciation of the letter r; a regional accent characterized by this. **2** a rough edge on metal or paper. **3** a small drill. —*v.i.* to make a burr. [imit.]

burr[2] var. of BUR.

burrow /ˈbʌrəʊ/ *n.* a hole or tunnel dug by a fox, rabbit, etc. as a dwelling. —*v.t./i.* **1** to dig a burrow; to form by burrowing. **2** to investigate or search (*into*). [var. of BOROUGH]

bursar /ˈbɜːsə(r)/ *n.* **1** a person who manages the finances of a college etc. **2** a student holding a bursary. [f. F or L (*bursa* bag)]

bursary *n.* **1** a grant or scholarship awarded to a student. **2** the bursar's office in a college. [f. prec.]

burst *v.t./i.* (*past & p.p.* **burst**) **1** to force open by internal pressure; to be full to overflowing. **2** to make one's way with sudden violence; to appear or come suddenly. —*n.* **1** a bursting, a split. **2** a sudden outbreak or explosion. **3** a sudden effort, a spurt. —**burst into,** to break into (blossom, flame, tears, etc.). **burst out,** to exclaim suddenly; to begin suddenly. [OE]

bury /ˈberɪ/ *v.t.* **1** to deposit (a corpse) in the earth, a tomb, or the sea; to put underground; to put out of sight. **2** to involve *oneself* deeply *in* (a study etc.). —**bury the hatchet,** to cease quarrelling. [OE]

bus *n.* (*pl.* **buses**) a long-bodied passenger vehicle, especially one serving the public on a fixed route. —*v.t./i.* (**bused, busing**) to go by bus; to transport by bus, especially to counteract racial segregation. [abbr. of OMNIBUS]

busby /ˈbʌzbɪ/ *n.* a tall fur cap worn by hussars as part of military ceremonial uniform. [orig. unkn.]

bush[1] /bʊʃ/ *n.* **1** a shrub or clump of shrubs; a thick growth (of hair etc.). **2** wild uncultivated country, forest (in Australia, Africa, etc.). —**bush-baby** *n.* a small African tree-climbing lemur. [f. OE & ON]

bush[2] /bʊʃ/ *n.* **1** a metal lining for a round hole in which something fits or revolves. **2** an electrically insulating sleeve. —*v.t.* to fit with a bush. [f. MDu. *busse* box]

bushel /ˈbʊʃ(ə)l/ *n.* a measure of capacity (8 gallons, about 36.4 litres) for corn, fruit, etc. [f. OF *buissel*, perh. of Gaulish orig.]

bushman *n.* (*pl.* **-men**) **1** a dweller or traveller in the Australian bush. **2 Bushman,** a member or the language of an aboriginal people in South Africa.

bushranger *n.* (*hist.*) an Australian brigand living in the bush.

bushy /ˈbʊʃɪ/ *adj.* **1** growing thickly like a bush. **2** covered with bushes. [f. BUSH[1]]

business /ˈbɪznɪs/ *n.* **1** a person's regular occupation or profession. **2** a thing that is one's concern, a task or duty. **3** a thing or things needing to be dealt with. **4** (*derog.*) an affair, subject, or device. **5** buying and selling, trade; a commercial house or firm. —**business man** *or* **woman,** one engaged in commerce. **mean business,** to be in earnest. **mind one's own business,** to refrain from meddling. [OE (as BUSY)]

businesslike *adj.* practical, methodical. [f. prec. + -LIKE]

busker *n.* a singer or other entertainer who performs in the street. —**busking** *n.* [f. obs. *busk* peddle]

buskin *n.* a thick-soled boot worn by tragic actors in ancient Greece. [prob. f. OF]

bust[1] *v.t./i.* (*past & p.p.* **bust, busted**) (*colloq.*) to break or burst. —*adj.* (*colloq.*) broken, burst; bankrupt. —*n.* (*colloq.*) a sudden (esp. financial) failure. —**bust-up** *n.* a quarrel. [f. BURST]

bust[2] *n.* **1** a sculptured representation of the head, shoulders, and chest. **2** the upper front of a woman's etc. body; the measurement round this. [f. F f. It.]

bustard /ˈbʌstəd/ *n.* a large tall ostrich-like swift-running bird of the family Otididae. [prob. f. AF f. L *avis tarda* slow bird ('slow' unexplained)]

bustle[1] /ˈbʌs(ə)l/ *v.i.* to make a show of activity,

to hurry (*about*). —*n.* excited activity. [perh. f. obs. *busk* prepare, rel. to BOUND[4]]

bustle[2] /ˈbʌs(ə)l/ *n.* (*hist.*) a pad used to puff out a woman's skirt at the back. [orig. unkn.]

busy /ˈbɪzɪ/ *adj.* **1** actively engaged in doing something; ceaselessly active, always employed; meddlesome. **2** full of business or activity. —*v.t.* to occupy or keep busy. —**busily** *adv.* [OE]

busybody *n.* a meddlesome person.

but /bət, *emphatic* bʌt/ *conj.* nevertheless, however; on the other hand; otherwise than; without the result that. —*prep.* except, apart from, other than. —*adv.* only, no more than. —*n.* an objection. [OE (f. BY, OUT); orig. = outside]

butane /ˈbju:teɪn/ *n.* a hydrocarbon of the paraffin series, used in liquid form as fuel. [f. BUTYL]

butch /bʊtʃ/ *adj.* (*slang*) masculine, tough-looking. [orig. unkn.]

butcher /ˈbʊtʃə(r)/ *n.* **1** a dealer in meat; one who slaughters animals for food. **2** one who kills or has people killed needlessly or brutally. —*v.t.* **1** to slaughter or cut up (an animal) for meat. **2** to kill needlessly or cruelly. **3** to perform or deal with very ineptly. [f. OF *bo(u)chier* (*boc* buck)]

butler /ˈbʌtlə(r)/ *n.* the chief manservant of a household, in charge of the wine-cellar. [f. AF *buteler* (*bouteille* bottle)]

butt[1] *v.t./i.* **1** to push with the head like a ram or goat. **2** to meet or cause to meet edge to edge. —*n.* **1** an act of butting. **2** a butted join. —**butt in,** to interfere. [f. AF *buter* strike, thrust]

butt[2] *n.* **1** an object *of* ridicule etc.; a person habitually mocked or teased. **2** a mound behind a target; (in *pl.*) a shooting-range. [f. OF *but* goal]

butt[3] *n.* the thicker end of a tool or weapon; the stub of a cigarette or cigar. [f. Du. *bot* stumpy]

butt[4] *n.* a large cask. [f. AF f. L *buttis*]

butter *n.* a fatty food substance made from cream by churning. —*v.t.* to spread, cook, or serve with butter. —**butter-bean** *n.* a large dried white Lima bean. **butter-fingers** *n.* a clumsy person always dropping things. **butter muslin,** thin loosely woven cloth originally used for wrapping butter. **butter up,** (*colloq.*) to flatter. [OE, ult. f. Gk *bouturon*]

buttercup *n.* a meadow plant of the genus *Ranunculus* with yellow cup-shaped flowers.

butterfly *n.* any of a large group of insects of the order Lepidoptera, distinguished from moths in most instances by diurnal behaviour, clubbed or dilated antennae, thin bodies, and the usually erect position of the wings when at rest. —**butterfly nut,** a kind of wing-nut. **butterfly stroke,** (in swimming) a stroke in which both arms are lifted forwards simultaneously. [orig. unkn.]

buttermilk *n.* the somewhat acid liquid left after churning butter.

butterscotch *n.* a hard kind of toffee. [perh. orig. of *Scotch* manufacture]

buttery[1] *adj.* like or containing butter.

buttery[2] /ˈbʌtərɪ/ *n.* a place in a college etc. where provisions are kept and supplied. [f. BUTT[4]]

buttock /ˈbʌtək/ *n.* (usu. in *pl.*) either of the two fleshy rounded parts on the lower rear of a human or animal body. [dim. of *butt* ridge]

button /ˈbʌt(ə)n/ *n.* **1** a small disc or knob attached to a garment etc. to fasten it by passing through a hole, or to serve as an ornament or badge. **2** a small rounded object of similar form, especially a knob to operate an electrical device. —*v.t./i.* to fasten (*up*) with buttons. —**button mushroom,** a small unopened mushroom. [f. OF *bouton*]

buttonhole *n.* **1** a slit through which a button is passed to fasten clothing etc. **2** a flower worn in the buttonhole of a coat-lapel. —*v.t.* to accost and detain (a reluctant listener).

buttress /ˈbʌtrɪs/ *n.* **1** a projecting support built against a wall. **2** a support or reinforcement. —*v.t.* **1** to support with a buttress or buttresses. **2** to give support and help to. [f. OF (*ars*) *bouterez* thrusting (arch), f. *bouter* BUTT[1]]

butyl /ˈbju:tɪl/ *n.* the radical C_4H_9 derived from butane. [f. L *butyrum* butter]

buxom /ˈbʌksəm/ *adj.* (esp. of women) plump and healthy-looking. [earlier = *pliant*, rel. to BOW[2]]

buy /baɪ/ *v.t.* (*past* & *p.p.* **bought** /bɔ:t/) **1** to obtain in exchange for money etc.; to win over by bribery. **2** (*slang*) to believe, to accept the truth of. —*n.* a purchase. —**buy off,** to pay to be rid of. **buy out,** to pay (a person) to give up an ownership etc. **buy up,** to buy all available stock of; to absorb (a firm) by purchase. [OE]

buyer *n.* one who buys; an agent who selects and purchases stock for a large shop. —**buyer's market,** trading conditions favourable to the buyer. [f. BUY]

buzz *v.t./i.* **1** to make a sibilant hum like a bee; to be filled with a confused murmur. **2** to be filled with activity or excitement; to move excitedly *about* etc. **3** to threaten (an aircraft) by flying close to it. —*n.* a buzzing sound; (*slang*) a telephone call. —**buzz off,** (*slang*) to go away. **buzz word,** a word (esp. technical or jargon) used more to impress than to inform. [imit.]

buzzard /ˈbʌzəd/ *n.* a large kind of predatory hawk of the genus *Buteo*. [f. OF f. L *buteo* falcon]

buzzer *n.* an electrical device producing a buzzing sound as a signal. [f. BUZZ]

bwana /ˈbwɑːnə/ *n.* sir, master (a form of address in Africa). [Swahili]

by /baɪ/ *prep.* **1** near, beside. **2** along, via, passing through or beside; avoiding. **3** in circumstances of, during. **4** through the agency or means of; (of an animal) having as its sire. **5** as soon as, not later than. **6** according to, using a standard or unit. **7** succeeding, with a succession of. **8** to the extent of. **9** concerning, in respect of. **10.** as surely as one believes in (God etc.). —*adv.* **1** close at hand. **2** aside, in reserve. **3** past. —*adj.* subordinate, incidental; secondary, side. —*n.* = BYE[1]. —**by and by,** before long. **by the by** (*or* **bye**), incidentally. **by and large,** on the whole. **by oneself,** without companions; by one's own unaided efforts. [OE]

bye[1] /baɪ/ *n.* **1** (in cricket) a run scored from a ball that passes the batsman without being hit. **2** the status of an unpaired competitor in a game, who proceeds to the next round as if having won. [= BY]

bye[2] /baɪ/ *int.* (also **bye-bye**) (*colloq.*) goodbye. [abbr.]

by-election *n.* the election of an MP in place of one who has died or resigned.

bygone *adj.* past, antiquated. —*n.* (in *pl.*) a past offence or injury (in phr. *let bygones be bygones*).

by-law *n.* a regulation made by a local authority or corporation. [perh. f. Scand. *by* town, assoc. with BY]

byline *n.* a line in a newspaper etc. naming the writer of an article.

bypass *n.* **1** a main road taking through traffic round a town or congested area. **2** a secondary channel, pipe, etc. for use when the main one is closed. —*v.t.* **1** to avoid by means of a bypass; to provide with a bypass. **2** to avoid consulting (a person) or omit (procedures etc.) in order to act quickly.

by-play *n.* subsidiary action in a play, usually without speech.

by-product *n.* a product arising incidentally in the manufacture of something else; a secondary result.

byre /ˈbaɪə(r)/ *n.* a cow-shed. [OE, rel. to BOWER]

by-road *n.* a minor road.

byssinosis /bɪsɪˈnəʊsɪs/ *n.* a lung disease caused by prolonged inhalation of textile fibre dust. [f. Gk *bussinos* made of linen]

bystander *n.* one who stands by but does not take part in something, a mere spectator.

byte /baɪt/ *n.* a fixed number of binary digits in a computer, often representing a single character. [orig. unkn.]

byway *n.* a minor road or path.

byword *n.* a person or thing cited as a notable example; a familar saying.

Byzantine /bɪˈzæntaɪn, baɪ-/ *adj.* of Byzantium or the Eastern Roman Empire; resembling its complicated and devious politics. —*n.* a native or inhabitant of Byzantium. [f. *Byzantium* ancient city (now Istanbul)]

Cc

C, c *n.* **1** the third letter of the alphabet. **2** (*Mus.*) the first note of the natural major scale. **3** (as a Roman numeral) 100.

C *abbr.* **1** Celsius, centigrade, **2** coulomb.

C *symbol* **1** carbon. **2** (also ©) copyright.

c. *abbr.* **1** century. **2** chapter. **3** cent.

c. *abbr. circa*, about.

Ca *symbol* calcium.

cab *n.* **1** a taxi; (*hist.*) a cabriolet or its improved successor the hansom; any of various types of horse-drawn public carriage with two or four wheels. **2** the driver's compartment in a train, lorry, or crane. [abbr. of CABRIOLET]

cabal /kəˈbæl/ *n.* **1** a secret intrigue. **2** a political clique. [f. F f. L, = CABBALA]

cabaret /ˈkæbəreɪ/ *n.* an entertainment provided in a restaurant or night-club while guests eat or drink at tables; such a night-club etc. [F, = tavern]

cabbage /ˈkæbɪdʒ/ *n.* **1** a vegetable with thick green or purple leaves, usually forming a round head. **2** (*colloq.*) a person who lives inactively or without interest. [f. OF *caboche* head]

cabbala /kəˈbɑːlə/ *n.* a pretended tradition of mystical interpretation of the Old Testament, using esoteric methods (including ciphers), that reached the height of its influence in the later Middle Ages. [L f. Heb., = tradition]

cabbalistic /kæbəˈlɪstɪk/ *adj.* of or like the cabbala; having a mystical sense, occult. [f. prec.]

cabby, cabbie /ˈkæbɪ/ *n.* (*colloq.*) a taxi-driver. [f. CAB]

caber /ˈkeɪbə(r)/ *n.* a roughly-trimmed tree-trunk used in the Scottish Highland sport of **tossing the caber.** [f. Gael. *cabar* pole]

cabin /ˈkæbɪn/ *n.* **1** a small shelter or house, especially of wood. **2** a room or compartment in a ship, aircraft, etc., for passengers or crew. **3** a driver's cab. —**cabin-boy** *n.* a man or boy waiting on officers or passengers on a ship. **cabin cruiser,** a large motor boat with a cabin. [f. OF f. L *capanna*]

cabinet /ˈkæbɪnɪt/ *n.* **1** a cupboard or container with drawers, shelves, etc., for storing or displaying articles; a piece of furniture housing a radio or television set etc. **2 Cabinet,** the group of ministers reponsible for implementing government policy. —**cabinet-maker** *n.* a skilled joiner. [f. prec.]

cable /ˈkeɪb(ə)l/ *n.* **1** a thick rope of wire or hemp; an encased group of insulated wires for transmitting electricity or for telecommunications; the anchor chain of a ship. **2** a cablegram. **3** (in full **cable stitch**) a knitted pattern looking like twisted rope. —*v.t./i.* to communicate with or transmit by cablegram. —**cable-car** *n.* any of the cars in a **cable railway,** mounted on an endless cable and drawn up and down a mountain side etc. by an engine at one end. **cable television,** transmission of television programmes by cable to subscribers. [f. AF f. L *caplum* halter, f. Arab.]

cablegram *n.* a telegraph message sent by undersea cable. [f. CABLE + -GRAM]

caboose /kəˈbuːs/ *n.* (*US*) a guard's van, especially on a goods train. [f. Du.; orig. unkn.]

cabriole /ˈkæbrɪəʊl/ *n.* a kind of curved leg characteristic of 17th–18th-c. furniture, especially that of Chippendale type. [F, f. It. *capriolare* leap in the air; from resemblance to a leaping animal's foreleg]

cabriolet /ˈkæbrɪəleɪ/ *n.* a light two-wheeled carriage with a hood, drawn by one horse, introduced into London from Paris in the early 19th c. [F, f. *cabriole* goat's leap]

cacao /kəˈkeɪəʊ/ *n.* (*pl.* **-os**) the seed from which cocoa and chocolate are made; the tree (*Theobroma cacao*) producing it. [Sp. f. Nahuatl]

cachalot /ˈkæʃəlɒt/ *n.* a sperm whale. [F f. Sp. & Port.]

cache /kæʃ/ *n.* a place for hiding treasures or stores; things so hidden. —*v.t.* to put in a cache. [F (*cacher* hide)]

cachet /ˈkæʃeɪ/ *n.* **1** a distinguishing mark or seal. **2** prestige. **3** internal evidence of authenticity. **4** a wafer enclosing an unpleasant medicine. [F (*cacher* press, f. L *coactare* constrain)]

cackle *n.* **1** the clucking of a hen. **2** noisy inconsequential talk. **3** a loud silly laugh. —*v.i.* to emit a cackle; to utter or express with a cackle. —**cut the cackle,** (*colloq.*) to come to the point. [imit.]

cacophony /kə'kɒfənɪ/ *n.* harsh discordant sound. —**cacophonous** *adj.* [f. F f. Gk (*kakos* bad, *phōnē* sound)]

cactus /'kæktəs/ *n.* (*pl.* **-i** /-aɪ/, **-uses**) a succulent plant of the family Cactaceae, with a thick fleshy stem, usually spines but no leaves, and brilliantly coloured flowers. [L f. Gk]

cad *n.* a person (especially a man) who behaves dishonourably. —**caddish** *adj.* [abbr. of CADDIE in the sense 'odd-job man']

cadaver /kə'deɪvə(r)/ *n.* a corpse. [f. L (*cadere* fall)]

cadaverous /kə'dævərəs/ *adj.* corpselike, gaunt and pale. [as prec.]

caddie /'kædɪ/ *n.* **1** a person who assists a golfer during a match, carrying his clubs etc. **2** a small container holding articles ready for use. —*v.i.* to act as caddie. [orig. Sc., f. F CADET]

caddis-fly /'kædɪsflaɪ/ *n.* a feebly flying frequently nocturnal insect of the order Trichoptera, living near water. —**caddis-worm** *n.* its larva. [orig. unkn.]

caddy[1] /'kædɪ/ *n.* a small box for holding tea. [earlier *catty* weight of 1⅓ lb., f. Malay *kātī*]

caddy[2] /'kædɪ/ var. of CADDIE.

cadence /'keɪd(ə)ns/ *n.* **1** the fall of the voice, especially at the end of a phrase or sentence; tonal inflection. **2** rhythm in sound. **3** a melodic or harmonic progression or device conventionally associated with the end of a musical composition, section, or phrase. [f. It. *cadenza* f. L *cadere* fall]

cadency /'keɪd(ə)nsɪ/ *n.* the status of a younger branch of a family. [as prec.]

cadenza /kə'denzə/ *n.* a flourish inserted into the final cadence of any section of a vocal aria or a movement in a concerto, sonata, or other solo instrumental work. [see CADENCE]

cadet /kə'det/ *n.* **1** a member of a corps receiving elementary military or police training. **2** a younger son. [F, f. dim. of L *caput* head]

cadge /kædʒ/ *v.t./i.* to ask for as a gift; to beg. —**cadger** *n.* [orig. unkn.]

cadmium /'kædmɪəm/ *n.* a bluish-white metallic element, symbol Cd, atomic number 48. [f. obs. *cadmia* calamine, ult. f. Gk *kadm(e)ia (gē)* Cadmean (earth), f. *Cadmus* in Gk legend]

cadre /'kɑ:də(r)/ *n.* a group forming a nucleus of trained persons round which a military or political unit can be formed. [F f. It. f. L *quadrus* square]

caecilian /sɪ'sɪlɪən/ *n.* a member of the order Apoda of amphibians, mainly tropical and wormlike. [f. L *caecilia* a kind of lizard]

caecum /'si:kəm/ *n.* (*pl.* **-ca**) a tubular pouch forming the first part of the large intestine. [L (*caecus* blind)]

Caesarean /sɪ'zeərɪən/ *adj.* **Caesarean birth** *or* **section**, delivery of a child by cutting into the mother's womb through the wall of the abdomen, so called from the story that Julius Caesar was born in this way.

caesium /'si:zɪəm/ *n.* a soft silver-white metallic element of the alkali metal group, symbol Cs, atomic number 55. [f. L *caesius* bluish- or greyish-green, f. its spectrum lines]

caesura /sɪ'zjʊərə/ *n.* a short pause in the rhythm of a line of verse. [L (*caedere* cut)]

café /'kæfeɪ/ *n.* a tea-shop or small restaurant. [F, = coffee (-house)]

cafeteria /kæfɪ'tɪərɪə/ *n.* a restaurant in which customers serve themselves from a counter or display. [f. Amer. Sp., = coffee-shop]

caffeine /'kæfi:n/ *n.* an alkaloid stimulant found in tea leaves and coffee beans. [f. F (*café* coffee)]

caftan /'kæft(ə)n/ *n.* **1** a long coat-like garment, often with a sash or belt, worn by men in countries of the Near East. **2** a woman's long loose dress. [f. Turk.]

cage *n.* **1** a structure with bars or wires, especially for containing animals or birds. **2** any similar framework, an enclosed platform in which people travel in a lift or the shaft of a mine. —*v.t.* to confine in a cage. [f. OF f. L *cavea*]

cagey /'keɪdʒɪ/ *adj.* (*colloq.*) cautious about giving information, secretive. —**cagily** *adv.*, **caginess** *n.* [orig. unkn.]

cagoule /kə'gu:l/ *n.* a thin hooded waterproof jacket reaching to the knees. [F]

cahoots /kə'hu:ts/ *n.pl.* (*US slang*) **in cahoots with**, in collusion with. [orig. unkn.]

Cainozoic /kaɪnə'zəʊɪk/ *adj.* of the most recent era of geological time, following the Mesozoic era and lasting from about 65 million years ago to the present day. —*n.* this era. [f. Gk *kainos* new + *zōion* animal]

caique /kaɪ'i:k/ *n.* a light rowing-boat used on the Bosporus; a Levantine sailing-ship. [F f. It. f. Turk. *kayik*]

cairn *n.* a mound of rough stones set up as a monument or landmark. —**cairn terrier**, a small shaggy terrier with short legs. [f. Gael. *carn*]

cairngorm *n.* a yellow or wine-coloured semi-precious stone from the Cairngorm mountains in Scotland. [f. Gael. *carn gorm* blue cairn]

caisson /'keɪs(ə)n/ *n.* a watertight chamber inside which work can be carried out on underwater structures. [F f. It. *cassone*]

cajole /kə'dʒəʊl/ *v.t.* to coax. —**cajolery** *n.* [f. F *cajoler*]

cake *n.* **1** a baked sweet breadlike food made from a mixture of flour, fats, sugar, eggs, etc. **2** other food cooked in a flat round shape. **3** a flattish compact mass. **4** cattle-cake. —*v.t./i.* to form into a compact mass; to encrust *with* a hardened or sticky mass. [ON]

calabash /ˈkæləbæʃ/ *n.* **1** a tropical American tree of the genus *Crescentia*, with fruit in the form of large gourds. **2** this or a similar gourd whose shell serves for holding liquid etc. **3** a bowl or pipe made from a gourd. [f. F f. Sp., perh. f. Pers. *karbuz* melon]

calabrese /kæləˈbreɪseɪ/ *n.* a variety of sprouting broccoli. [It., = Calabrian]

calamine /ˈkæləmaɪn/ *n.* a pink powder, chiefly zinc carbonate or oxide, used especially in skin lotions. [f. F f. L *cadmia* (see CADMIUM)]

calamity /kəˈlæmɪtɪ/ *n.* a grievous disaster or adversity. —**calamitous** /-mɪtəs/ *adj.* [f. F f. L]

calcareous /kælˈkeərɪəs/ *adj.* of or containing calcium carbonate. [f. L *calx* lime]

calceolaria /kælsɪəˈleərɪə/ *n.* a South American plant of the genus *Calceolaria*, with a slipper-shaped flower. [f. L, dim. of *calceus* shoe]

calcify /ˈkælsɪfaɪ/ *v.t./i.* to harden by a deposit of calcium salts; to convert or be converted into calcium carbonate. —**calcification** /-ˈkeɪʃ(ə)n/ *n.* [f. L *calx* lime]

calcine /ˈkælsaɪn/ *v.t./i.* to reduce (a substance) or be reduced to quicklime or powder by heating to a high temperature without melting it. —**calcination** /-sɪˈneɪʃ(ə)n/ *n.* [f. OF or L (as prec.)]

calcite /ˈkælsaɪt/ *n.* crystalline calcium carbonate. [as foll.]

calcium /ˈkælsɪəm/ *n.* a greyish-white metallic element of the alkaline-earth metal group, symbol Ca, atomic number 20. [f. L *calx* lime]

calculable /ˈkælkjʊləb(ə)l/ *adj.* that may be calculated. [f. foll.]

calculate /ˈkælkjʊleɪt/ *v.t./i.* **1** to ascertain, especially by using mathematics or by reckoning. **2** to plan deliberately; to rely *on*. **3** (*US colloq.*) to suppose, to believe. —**calculation** /-ˈleɪʃ(ə)n/ *n.* [f. L (as CALCULUS)]

calculated *adj.* **1** done with awarenesss of the likely consequences. **2** designed or suitable *to* do. [f. prec.]

calculating *adj.* (of a person) shrewd, scheming. [f. CALCULATE]

calculator *n.* a device, especially a small electronic one, used in making calculations. [as prec.]

calculus /ˈkælkjʊləs/ *n.* **1** a particular system of calculation or reasoning, especially the branch of mathematics that deals with differentiation and integration. **2** (*pl.* **-li**) a stone or concretion found in some part of the body. [L, = small stone (used on an abacus)]

Caledonian /kælɪˈdəʊnɪən/ *adj.* of Scotland or (in Roman times) Caledonia (= northern Britain). —*n.* (usu. *joc.*) a Scotsman. [f. L *Caledonia*]

calendar /ˈkælɪndə(r)/ *n.* **1** a system fixing a year's beginning, length, and subdivision. **2** a chart showing the days, weeks, and months of a particular year; an adjustable device showing the day's date etc. **3** a register or list of special dates or events, documents chronologically arranged, etc. —*v.t.* **1** to enter in a calendar. **2** to analyse and index (documents). [f. AF f. L *calendarium* account-book (as CALENDS)]

calender /ˈkælɪndə(r)/ *n.* a machine for rolling cloth, paper, etc. to glaze or smooth it. —*v.t.* to press in a calender. [f. F]

calends /ˈkælɪndz/ *n.pl.* the first day of the month in the ancient Roman calendar. [f. OF f. L *calendae* (from the proclaiming of the order of days)]

calf[1] /kɑ:f/ *n.* (*pl.* **calves** /kɑ:vz/) young of cattle, also of the deer, elephant, whale, and certain other animals; calfskin. —**calf-love** *n.* immature romantic love. [OE]

calf[2] /kɑ:f/ *n.* (*pl.* **calves** /kɑ:vz/) the fleshy hind part of the human leg below the knee. [ON]

calfskin *n.* leather made from the skin of calves. [f. CALF[1]]

calibrate /ˈkælɪbreɪt/ *v.t.* **1** to mark (a gauge) with a scale of readings; to correlate the readings of (an instrument etc.) with a standard. **2** to find the calibre of. —**calibration** /-ˈbreɪʃ(ə)n/ *n.*, **calibrator** *n.* [f. foll.]

calibre /ˈkælɪbə(r)/ *n.* **1** the internal diameter of a gun-barrel or tube; the diameter of a bullet or shell. **2** strength or quality of character; ability, importance. [f. F, ult. f. Arab., = mould]

calico /ˈkælɪkəʊ/ *n.* (*pl.* **-oes**) cotton cloth, especially plain white or unbleached; (*US*) printed cotton fabric. —*adj.* **1** of calico. **2** (*US*) multicoloured. [f. *Calicut* town in India]

californium /kælɪˈfɔ:nɪəm/ *n.* an artificially made transuranic radioactive metallic element, symbol Cf, atomic number 98. [f. *California*, State of USA (where first made)]

caliph /ˈkælɪf, ˈkeɪ-/ *n.* (*hist.*) a leader of the Muslim community in matters both temporal and spiritual. —**caliphate** *n.* [f. OF f. Arab., = successor (i.e. one succeeding Muhammad)]

calix /ˈkeɪlɪks/ *n.* (*pl.* **-ices** /-ɪsi:z/) a cuplike cavity or organ. [L, = cup]

call /kɔ:l/ *v.t./i.* **1** to shout or speak *out* loudly to attract attention; (of a bird etc.) to utter its call. **2** to summon; to order to take place; to invite (attention etc.). **3** to rouse deliberately from sleep, to summon to get up. **4** to name, describe, or regard as. **5** to communicate or converse with by telephone or radio. **6** to name (a suit) in bidding at cards; to attempt to predict the result of tossing a coin etc. **7** to make a brief visit (*at* a place, *on* a person). —*n.* **1** a shout or cry; the characteristic cry of a bird etc.; a signal on a bugle etc. **2** a summons, an invitation; a demand or claim; a need, an occasion. **3** a player's right or turn to bid or call trumps at cards; a bid etc. thus made. **4** an act of telephoning, a conversation over the telephone. **5** the option of buying stock at a given date. —**call-box** *n.* a telephone kiosk. **call-girl** *n.* a prostitute accepting appointments by telephone. **call up,** to summon to do military service. **call-up** *n.* a summons to do military service. **on call,** ready or available when needed. —**caller** *n.* [OE f. ON]

calligraphy /kəˈlɪgrəfɪ/ *n.* beautiful handwriting; handwriting. —**calligrapher** *n.*, **calligraphist** *n.*, **calligraphic** /kælɪˈgræfɪk/ *adj.* [f. Gk (*kallos* beauty, *graphē* writing)]

calling *n.* a profession or trade; a vocation. [f. CALL]

calliper /ˈkælɪpə(r)/ *n.* (usu. in *pl.*) **1** a pair of hinged arms for measuring diameters. **2** a metal support for a weak or injured leg. [var. of CALIBRE]

callisthenics /kælɪsˈθenɪks/ *n.pl.* exercises to develop elegance and grace of movement. [f. Gk *kallos* beauty + *sthenos* strength]

callosity /kəˈlɒsɪtɪ/ *n.* abnormal hardness of the skin; a callus. [f. F or L (as foll.)]

callous /ˈkæləs/ *adj.* **1** unfeeling, unsympathetic. **2** (of skin) hardened. [f. L *callosus* (as CALLUS)]

callow /ˈkæləʊ/ *adj.* immature and inexperienced. —**callowly** *adv.*, **callowness** *n.* [OE, prob. f. L *calvus* bald]

callus /ˈkæləs/ *n.* an area of hard thickened skin or tissue; bony material formed when a bone-fracture heals. [L]

calm /kɑːm/ *adj.* **1** quiet and still, not windy. **2** not excited or agitated. **3** confident. —*n.* a calm condition or period. —*v.t./i.* to make or become calm. —**calmly** *adv.*, **calmness** *n.* [f. L f. Gk *kauma* heat]

calomel /ˈkæləmel/ *n.* a compound of mercury, used as a purgative. [perh. f. Gk *kalos* beautiful, *melas* black]

Calor gas /ˈkælə/ [P] liquefied butane etc. stored under pressure in containers for use where mains gas is not available. [L *calor* heat]

caloric /ˈkælərɪk/ *adj.* of heat; of calories. [f. F (as foll.)]

calorie /ˈkælərɪ/ *n.* a unit of quantity for measuring heat, the amount needed to raise one gram (*small calorie*) or one kilogram (*large calorie*) of water 1 C; a large calorie as a unit for measuring the energy value of foods. [F f. L *calor* heat]

calorific /kæləˈrɪfɪk/ *adj.* producing heat. [f. L (*calor* heat)]

calorimeter /kæləˈrɪmɪtə(r)/ *n.* an instrument for measuring the quantity of heat in a body. [as prec. + -METER]

calumniate /kəˈlʌmnɪeɪt/ *v.t.* to slander, to defame. —**calumniation** /-ˈeɪʃ(ə)n/ *n.* [f. L *calumniari*]

calumny /ˈkæləmnɪ/ *n.* slander; malicious representation. —**calumnious** /kəˈlʌmnɪəs/ *adj.* [f. L]

calve /kɑːv/ *v.i.* to give birth to a calf. [OE (as CALF¹)]

Calvinism /ˈkælvɪnɪz(ə)m/ *n.* the theological system of the Swiss Protestant John Calvin (1509-64) and his successors, stressing predestination and divine grace. —**Calvinist** *n.*, **Calvinistic** *adj.* [f. *Calvin*]

calx *n.* (*pl.* **calces** /ˈkælsiːz/) the powdery or friable substance left after the burning of a metal or mineral. [L, = lime]

calypso /kəˈlɪpsəʊ/ *n.* (*pl.* **-os**) a West Indian song with a variable rhythm and topical, usually improvised, lyrics. [orig. unkn.]

calyx /ˈkeɪlɪks/ *n.* (*pl.* **calyces** /-ɪsiːz/) a whorl of leaves forming the outer case of a bud or the envelope of a flower. [L f. Gk (*kaluptō* hide)]

cam *n.* a projecting part on a wheel or shaft in machinery, shaped so that its circular motion, as it turns, transmits an up-and-down or back-and-forth motion to another part. [f. Du. *kam* comb (*kamrad* cog-wheel)]

camaraderie /kæməˈrɑːdərɪ/ *n.* comradeship, mutual trust and friendship. [F]

camber /ˈkæmbə(r)/ *n.* a convex or arched shape given to the surface of a road, deck, etc.; the banked outer curve of a bend in a road etc. —*v.t.* to construct with a camber. [f. F (= arched) f. L *camurus* curved inwards]

cambium /ˈkæmbɪəm/ *n.* cellular tissue from which xylem and phloem grow. [L, = exchange]

Cambrian /ˈkæmbrɪən/ *adj.* **1** Welsh. **2** of the first period of the Palaeozoic era. —*n.* this period. [f. L *Cambria* var. of *Cumbria* f. Welsh (as CYMRIC)]

cambric /ˈkæmbrɪk/ *n.* thin linen or cotton cloth. [f. *Cambrai*, town in N. France where orig. made]

Cambs. *abbr.* Cambridgeshire.

came *past* of COME.

camel /ˈkæm(ə)l/ *n.* **1** a large ruminant quadruped with a long neck and one hump (*Arabian camel*) or two humps (*Bactrian camel*), adapted to living in sandy deserts. **2** fawn colour. —**camel('s) hair,** fabric made of this or similar hair; fine soft hair used in artists' brushes. [OE f. L f. Gk f. Semitic]

camellia /kəˈmelɪə/ *n.* a shrub of the genus *Camellia*, especially a flowering evergreen from China and Japan. [f. J. *Camellus*, 17th-c. Jesuit and botanist]

Camembert /ˈkæməmbeə(r)/ *n.* a kind of small soft rich cheese. [name of town in Normandy, France, where orig. made]

cameo /ˈkæmɪəʊ/ *n.* (*pl.* **-os**) **1** a small piece of hard stone carved in relief, especially with two coloured layers cut so that one serves as a background to the design. **2** something small but well executed, especially a short descriptive literary sketch or an acted scene. [f. OF & L]

camera /ˈkæmərə/ *n.* an apparatus for taking photographs, motion pictures, or television pictures. —***in camera,*** (*Law*) in a judge's private room; privately, not in public. [L, = vault, f. Gk *kamara* thing with arched cover]

cameraman *n.* (*pl.* **-men**) a person whose job is to operate a camera, especially in film-making or television.

camera obscura /əbˈskjʊərə/ an apparatus that uses a darkened box or room with an aperture for projecting an image of a distant object on a screen within. [L, = dark chamber]

camisole /ˈkæmɪsəʊl/ *n.* a woman's bodice-like garment or undergarment. [F f. It. or Sp., = shirt]

camomile /ˈkæməmaɪl/ *n.* an aromatic composite plant of the genus *Anthemis* or *Matricaria* with flowers that are used as a tonic. [f. OF f. L f. Gk, = earth-apple (from the apple-like smell of the flowers)]

camouflage /ˈkæməflɑːdʒ/ *n.* the disguising of guns, ships, etc. by colouring or covering them to make them blend with their surroundings; this disguise; a means of disguise or concealment. —*v.t.* to hide by camouflage. [F (*camoufler* disguise) f. It.]

camp[1] *n.* **1** a place where troops are lodged or trained. **2** an ancient fortified site. **3** temporary accommodation of tents, huts, etc. for holiday-makers, detainees, etc. **4** the adherents of a doctrine or party. —*v.i.* to live in a camp; to make a camp. —**camp-bed** *n.* a folding portable bed. **camp-follower** *n.* a hanger-on providing services to a military camp etc. or sympathetic to a group or theory. —**camper** *n.* [F f. It. f. L *campus* level ground]

camp[2] *adj.* affectedly exaggerated for theatrical effect; effeminate, homosexual. —*n.* a camp manner or style. —*v.t./i.* to act in a camp way. [orig. unkn.]

campaign /kæmˈpeɪn/ *n.* **1** a series of military operations in a definite area or for a particular objective. **2** an organized course of action for a particular purpose, especially to arouse public interest. —*v.i.* to take part in a campaign. —**campaigner** *n.* [f. F, = open country (as CAMP[1])]

campanology /kæmpəˈnɒlədʒɪ/ *n.* the study of bells and their founding, ringing, etc. —**campanologist** *n.* [f. L *campana* bell]

campanula /kəmˈpænjʊlə/ *n.* a plant of the genus *Campanula* with bell-shaped usually blue, pink, or white flowers. [dim. of L *campana* bell]

camphor /ˈkæmfə(r)/ *n.* a white translucent strong-smelling crystalline substance used in insect-repellents and medicines and in making plastics. [f. OF or L f. Arab. f. Skr.]

camphorated /ˈkæmfəreɪtɪd/ *adj.* containing camphor. [f. prec.]

campion /ˈkæmpɪən/ *n.* a plant of the genus *Silene, Melandrium,* or *Lychnis,* with usually pink or white notched flowers. [orig. unkn.; transl. of Gk name of a plant used for garlands]

campsite *n.* a camping-site, especially one equipped for holiday-makers.

campus /ˈkæmpəs/ *n.* the grounds of a university or college; a university, especially as a teaching institution. [L, = field]

camshaft *n.* a shaft carrying cams.

can[1] /kən, emphatic kæn/ *v.aux.* (3 *sing. pres.* **can;** *past* **could**) **1** to be able to, to know how to. **2** to have the right to, to be permitted to. [OE, = know]

can[2] *n.* a metal or plastic container for liquids; a tin container in which food or drink is hermetically sealed for preservation. —*v.t.* (**-nn-**) to put or preserve in a can. —**canned music,** music recorded for reproduction. [OE]

Canadian /kəˈneɪdɪən/ *adj.* of Canada or its people. —*n.* a native or inhabitant of Canada. [f. *Canada*, country in N. America]

canal /kəˈnæl/ *n.* **1** an artificial channel carrying water for irrigation, drainage, or power, or for inland navigation. **2** a tubular passage in a plant or animal body. [f. OF or It. f. L *canalis*]

canalize /ˈkænəlaɪz/ *v.t.* **1** to make a canal through; to provide with canals. **2** to channel. —**canalization** /-ˈzeɪʃ(ə)n/ *n.* [f. F (as CANAL)]

canapé /ˈkænəpeɪ/ *n.* a small piece of bread, pastry, or biscuit with a savoury topping. [F]

canary /kəˈneərɪ/ *n.* a small songbird with yellow feathers, the finch *Serinus canarius.* [f. *Canary* Islands, f. L *canis* dog, one of the islands being noted in Roman times for large dogs]

canasta /kəˈnæstə/ *n.* a card-game of Uruguayan origin, resembling rummy. [Sp., = basket]

cancan /ˈkænkæn/ *n.* a lively stage-dance with high kicking, performed by women in long skirts and petticoats.

cancel /ˈkæns(ə)l/ *v.t./i.* (**-ll-**) **1** to state that (a previous arrangement or decision) will not take place or be executed; to discontinue; to annul, to make void. **2** to neutralize, to counterbalance. **3** to obliterate or delete (writing etc.); to mark so as to prevent further use. **4** (*Math.*) to strike out (an equal factor) on each side of an equation etc. —**cancellation** /-ˈleɪʃ(ə)n/ *n.* [f. F f. L (*cancelli* cross-bars)]

Cancer /ˈkænsə(r)/ a constellation and the fourth sign of the zodiac, the Crab, which the sun enters at the summer solstice. —**tropic of Cancer,** see TROPIC. [L, = crab]

cancer /ˈkænsə(r)/ *n.* **1** a tumour, especially a malignant one; a disease featuring this. **2** an evil influence or corruption. —**cancerous** *adj.*, **cancroid** /ˈkæŋkrɔɪd/ *adj.* [as prec.]

candela /kænˈdi:lə/ *n.* the base unit of luminous intensity (symbol cd), the luminous intensity, in the perpendicular direction, of a surface of 1/600,000 square metre of a black body at the temperature of freezing platinum under a pressure of 101,325 newtons per square metre. [L, = candle (*candēre* shine)]

candelabrum /kændɪˈlɑ:brəm/ *n.* (*pl.* **-bra**) a large branched candlestick or light-holder. [L (as prec.)]

candid *adj.* **1** frank, not hiding one's thoughts. **2** (in photography) informal, of a picture taken usually without the subject's knowledge. —**candidly** *adv.*, **candidness** *n.* [f. F or L *candidus* white]

candidate /ˈkændɪdət/ *n.* **1** a person who seeks or is nominated for an office, award, etc. **2** a person or thing likely to gain a specified distinction or position. **3** one taking an examination. —**candidacy** *n.*, **candidature** *n.* [f. F or L, = white-robed (see prec.), from the white robes worn by Roman candidates for office]

candle *n.* a usually cylindrical stick of wax or tallow enclosing a wick for giving light when burning. —**candle-light** *n.* the light of candles. **cannot hold a candle to,** is very inferior to. [OE f. L (*candēre* shine)]

Candlemas /ˈkænd(ə)lməs/ *n.* the feast of the Purification of the Virgin Mary (2 Feb.), when candles are blessed. [OE (as CANDLE, MASS²)]

candlepower *n.* a unit of luminous intensity.

candlestick *n.* a holder for one or more candles.

candlewick *n.* a fabric with a raised tufted pattern worked in thick soft cotton yarn; this yarn.

candour /ˈkændə(r)/ *n.* candid speech or quality, frankness. [f. F or L *candor* whiteness (*candēre* shine)]

candy *n.* **1** sugar crystallized by repeated boiling and slow evaporation. **2** (*US*) sweets, a sweet. —*v.t.* to preserve (fruit etc.) by coating or impregnating with candy. —**candy-floss** *n.* a fluffy mass of spun sugar round a stick. **candy-stripes** *n.pl.* alternate stripes of white and colour. **candy-striped** *adj.* [earlier *sugar candy*, f. F f. Arab. (*kand* sugar, ult. f. Skr.)]

candytuft *n.* a garden plant of the genus *Iberis* with white, pink, or purple flowers in flat tufts. [f. *Candia* in Crete]

cane *n.* **1** the hollow jointed stem of tall reeds and grasses (e.g. bamboo, sugar-cane); the solid stem of slender palms (e.g. Malacca); a plant with such a stem; the stems of these used as material for wickerwork etc. **2** a stem or a length of it, or a slender rod, used as a walking-stick or to support a plant etc. or as a stick for use in corporal punishment. —*v.t.* **1** to beat with a cane. **2** to weave cane into (a chair etc.). —**cane-sugar,** sugar obtained from the juice of sugar-cane. [f. OF f. L f. Gk *kanna* reed, f. Semitic]

canine /ˈkeɪnaɪn/ *adj.* of a dog or dogs. —*n.* **1** a dog. **2** a canine tooth. —**canine tooth,** a strong pointed tooth between the incisors and molars. [f. L *caninus* (*canis* dog)]

canister /ˈkænɪstə(r)/ *n.* a metal box or other container; a cylinder, filled with shot or tear-gas, that bursts and releases its contents on impact. [f. L f. Gk *kanastron* wicker basket (*kanna* reed)]

canker /ˈkæŋkə(r)/ *n.* **1** a disease that destroys the wood of trees and plants; a disease causing ulcerous sores in animals. **2** a corrupting influence. —**cankerous** *adj.* [OE f. L (as CANCER)]

canna /ˈkænə/ *n.* a tropical plant of the genus *Canna*, with ornamental leaves and bright yellow, red, or orange flowers. [L (as CANE)]

cannabis /ˈkænəbɪs/ *n.* a hemp plant of the genus *Cannabis;* a preparation of this for smoking or chewing as an intoxicant or hallucinogenic drug. [L f. Gk]

cannery /ˈkænərɪ/ *n.* a canning-factory. [f. CAN²]

cannibal /ˈkænɪb(ə)l/ *n.* a person who eats human flesh; an animal that eats its own species. —**cannibalism** *n.*, **cannibalistic** /-ˈlɪstɪk/ *adj.* [f. Sp., var. of *Caribes* name of West Indian tribe (Caribs) formerly noted for their practice of cannibalism]

cannibalize /ˈkænɪb(ə)laɪz/ *v.t.* to use (a machine etc.) as a source of spare parts for others. —**cannibalization** /-ˈzeɪʃ(ə)n/ *n.* [f. prec.]

cannon /ˈkænən/ *n.* **1** (*pl.* same) an old type of large heavy gun of a size which required it to be mounted for firing, discharging solid metal balls. **2** an automatic shell-firing gun used in aircraft. **3** the hitting of two balls successively by a player's ball in billiards. —*v.i.* to collide heavily *against* or *into*. —**cannon-bone** *n.* a tube-shaped bone between a horse's hock and fetlock. **cannon-fodder** *n.* men regarded merely as material to be expended in war. [f. F f. It., = great tube (as CANE); sense 2 formerly *carom*]

cannonade /kænəˈneɪd/ *n.* continuous heavy gunfire. —*v.t.* to bombard with a cannonade. [as prec.]

cannot /ˈkænɒt/ = can not. [CAN¹]

canny /ˈkænɪ/ *adj.* shrewd and cautious; worldly-wise. —**cannily** *adv.*, **canniness** *n.* [f. CAN¹]

canoe /kəˈnu:/ *n.* a keelless boat, pointed at both ends and propelled by a paddle or paddles, in which the paddler faces forward, often in a kneeling position. —*v.i.* (*partic.* **canoeing**) to go in or paddle a canoe. —**canoeist** *n.* [f. Sp. & Haitian *canoa*]

canon /ˈkænən/ *n.* **1** a general rule, law, principle, or criterion; a church decree or law. **2** a member of a cathedral chapter. **3** a body of sacred or other writings accepted as genuine. **4** the central unchanging part of the RC Mass. **5** (*Mus.*) a passage or piece of music in which a theme is taken up by several parts successively. —**canon law**, ecclesiastical law, based on the New Testament, tradition, pronouncements by popes and councils of the Church, and decisions in particular cases. [OE f. L f. Gk *kanōn* rule]

canonical /kəˈnɒnɪk(ə)l/ *adj.* **1** according to or ordered by canon law. **2** included in the canon of Scripture; authoritative, accepted. **3** of a cathedral canon or chapter. **4** (in *pl.*) the canonical dress of clergy. [f. L (as prec.)]

canonize /ˈkænənaɪz/ *v.t.* **1** to declare officially to be a saint, usually with a ceremony. **2** to admit to the canon of Scriptures. **3** to sanction by church authority. —**canonization** /-ˈzeɪʃ(ə)n/ *n.* [f. L (as CANON)]

canopy /ˈkænəpɪ/ *n.* **1** a hanging cover forming a shelter above a throne, bed, or person etc.; any similar covering. **2** the expanding part of a parachute. —*v.t.* to supply or be a canopy to. [f. L f. Gk, = mosquito-net (*kōnōps* gnat)]

cant[1] *n.* **1** insincere pious or moral talk. **2** jargon. —*v.i.* to use cant. [prob. f. L *cantare* (see CHANT)]

cant[2] *n.* a tilted or sloping position; a sloping surface, a bevel. —*v.t./i.* to tilt, to slope. [LG or Du., = edge, f. L *cant(h)us* iron tire]

can't /kɑ:nt/ (*colloq.*) cannot. [CAN[1]]

Cantab. *abbr.* Cantabrigian, of Cambridge University.

cantabile /kænˈtɑ:bɪlɪ/ *adv.* (*Mus.*) in a smooth flowing style. —*n.* (*Mus.*) a piece to be performed in this way. [It., = suitable for singing]

Cantabrigian /kæntəˈbrɪdʒɪən/ *adj.* of Cambridge or Cambridge University. —*n.* a citizen of Cambridge; a member of Cambridge University. [f. *Cantabrigia*, Latinized name of CAMBRIDGE]

cantaloup /ˈkæntəlu:p/ *n.* a small round ribbed melon with orange flesh. [F, f. *Cantaluppi* near Rome, where first grown in Europe]

cantankerous /kænˈtæŋkərəs/ *adj.* bad-tempered, quarrelsome. —**cantankerously** *adv.*, **cantankerousness** *n.* [perh. f. Ir. *cant* outbidding + *rancorous*]

cantata /kænˈtɑ:tə/ *n.* (*Mus.*) a short narrative or descriptive composition with vocal solos and usually a chorus and orchestral accompaniment. [It., = sung (air) f. *cantare* sing]

canteen /kænˈti:n/ *n.* **1** a restaurant for the employees of a factory, office, etc.; a shop for provisions or liquor in a barracks or camp. **2** a case or box containing a set of cutlery. **3** a soldier's or camper's water-flask. [f. F or Ir., = cellar]

canter *n.* a gentle gallop. —*v.t./i.* to go or cause to go at a canter. [short for *Canterbury gallop* etc., from the supposed easy pace of medieval pilgrims to Canterbury in Kent]

cantharides /kænˈθærɪdi:z/ *n.pl.* the dried remains of a kind of beetle (*Lytta vesicatoria*). It has been used in medicine for its irritant action on the skin, and as an aphrodisiac. [L f. Gk]

canticle /ˈkæntɪk(ə)l/ *n.* **1** a song or chant with words taken from the Bible. **2 Canticles**, the Song of Solomon. [f. OF or L, dim. of *canticum* (*cantus* song)]

cantilever /ˈkæntɪli:və(r)/ *n.* a projecting beam, bracket, or girder supporting a balcony, bridge, or similar structure; a beam or girder fixed at one end only. [orig. unkn.]

cantle *n.* the upward-curving hind part of a saddle. [f. AF f. L *cantellus*, dim. of *cantus* (see CANT[2])]

canto /ˈkæntəʊ/ *n.* (*pl.* **-os**) any of the sections into which a long poem is divided. [It., = song, f. L *cantus* (as CHANT)]

canton /ˈkæntɒn/ *n.* a subdivision of a country; a State of the Swiss confederation. [OF, = corner (rel. to CANT[2])]

Cantonese /kæntəˈni:z/ *n.* (*pl.* same) **1** a native or inhabitant of the city of Canton in China. **2** a Chinese language spoken in southern China and in Hong Kong. —*adj.* of Canton or its people or language. [name of city]

cantor /ˈkæntɔ:(r)/ *n.* the leader of the liturgical singing of a church choir; a precentor in a synagogue. —**cantorial** /-ˈtɔ:rɪəl/ *adj.* [L, = singer (*canere* sing)]

canvas /ˈkænvəs/ *n.* **1** strong coarse cloth used for making tents and sails and as a surface for oil-painting; a painting on canvas. **2** a racing-boat's covered end. [f. OF f. L CANNABIS]

canvass /ˈkænvəs/ *v.t./i.* **1** to solicit votes (from); to ascertain the opinions of; to ask for custom from. **2** to propose (an idea or plan etc.). —*n.* canvassing, especially of electors. —**canvasser** *n.* [f. prec., orig. = toss in a sheet, hence = shake up, agitate]

canyon /ˈkænjən/ *n.* a deep gorge. [f. Sp., = tube, f. L (as CANE)]

caoutchouc /ˈkaʊtʃʊk/ *n.* unvulcanized rubber. [F f. Carib *cahuchu*]

CAP *abbr.* Common Agricultural Policy (of the EEC), a system for establishing common prices for most agricultural products, a single fund for price supports, and levies on imports.

cap *n.* **1** a soft brimless head-covering, usually with a peak. **2** a head-covering worn in a particular profession; an academic mortar-board; a cap awarded as a sign of membership of a sports team. **3** a caplike cover or top. —*v.t.* (**-pp-**) **1** to put a cap on; to cover the top or end of **2** to award a sports cap to. **3** to form the top of. **4** to surpass, to excel. [f. OE f. L *cappa*, perh. f. *caput* head]

capable /ˈkeɪpəb(ə)l/ *adj*. having a certain ability or capacity *of;* competent. —**capability** /-ˈbɪlɪtɪ/ *n*., **capably** *adv*. [F f. L (*capere* hold)]

capacious /kəˈpeɪʃəs/ *adj*. roomy, able to hold much. —**capaciously** *adv*., **capaciousness** *n*. [f. L *capax* (*capere* hold)]

capacitance /kəˈpæsɪt(ə)ns/ *n*. ability to store an electric charge; the measure of this, the ratio of the change in the electric charge of a body to a corresponding change in its potential. [f. CAPACITY]

capacitor /kəˈpæsɪtə(r)/ *n*. a device having capacitance, usually consisting of conductors separated by an insulator. [f. foll.]

capacity /kəˈpæsɪtɪ/ *n*. **1** the ability to contain or accommodate. **2** ability, capability. **3** the maximum amount that can be contained or produced etc. **4** function, position, legal competency. —**to capacity,** fully, to the full. [f. F f. L (as CAPACIOUS)]

caparison /kəˈpærɪs(ə)n/ *n*. a horse's trappings; equipment, finery. —*v.t.* to adorn. [f. F f. Sp., = saddle-cloth (as CAPE[1])]

cape[1] *n*. a cloak; a similarly shaped part or garment covering the shoulders. [F f. L *cappa* CAP]

cape[2] *n*. a coastal promontory. —**the Cape,** the Cape of Good Hope; the province containing it, Cape Province. [f. OF f. L *caput* head]

caper[1] /ˈkeɪpə(r)/ *v.i.* to jump or run about playfully. —*n*. **1** a playful jump or leap. **2** a prank. **3** (*slang*) an activity. [abbr. of CABRIOLE]

caper[2] /ˈkeɪpə(r)/ *n*. a bramble-like shrub; (in *pl.*) its buds pickled for use in sauces etc. [f. L f. Gk *kapparis*]

capercaillie /kæpəˈkeɪlɪ/ *n*. the largest kind of European grouse, *Tetrao urogallus*. [f. Gaelic, = horse of the forest]

capillary /kəˈpɪlərɪ/ *adj*. like a hair, hairlike in diameter. —*n*. **1** a capillary tube. **2** any of the very fine ramified blood-vessels connecting arteries and veins. —**capillary attraction, repulsion,** the tendency of liquid to be drawn up or down in a capillary tube. —**capillarity** /-ˈlærɪtɪ/ *n*. [f. L (*capillus* hair)]

capital /ˈkæpɪt(ə)l/ *n*. **1** the most important town or city of a country or region, usually its seat of government and administrative centre. **2** the money or other assets with which a company starts business; accumulated wealth; capitalists collectively. **3** a capital letter. **4** the head of a column or pillar. —*adj*. **1** principal, most important; (*colloq.*) excellent. **2** involving punishment by death; very serious. **3** (of letters of the alphabet) of the form and size used to begin a name or sentence. —**capital gain,** profit from the sale of investment or property. **capital punishment,** infliction of death by an authorized public authority as punishment for a crime. **capital sum,** a lump sum of money, especially that payable to an insured person. **capital transfer tax,** a tax on capital that is transferred from one person or another, as by gift or bequest. **make capital out of,** to use (a situation etc.) to one's own advantage. [f. OF f. L (*caput* head)]

capitalism /ˈkæpɪt(ə)lɪz(ə)m/ *n*. an economic system in which trade and industry are controlled by private owners and for profit. [f. prec.]

capitalist /ˈkæpɪt(ə)lɪst/ *n*. **1** a person using or possessing capital, a rich person. **2** a believer in capitalism. —*adj*. of or favouring capitalism. —**capitalistic** /-ˈɪstɪk/ *adj*. [as prec.]

capitalize /ˈkæpɪt(ə)laɪz/ *v.t./i.* **1** to convert into capital; to provide with capital. **2** to write or print with a capital letter; to begin (a word) with a capital letter. —**capitalize on,** to use to one's advantage. —**capitalization** /-ˈzeɪʃ(ə)n/ *n*. [f. F (as CAPITAL)]

capitation /kæpɪˈteɪʃ(ə)n/ *n*. a tax or fee levied per person. [F or f. L, = poll-tax (*caput* head)]

capitulate /kəˈpɪtjuleɪt/ *v.i.* to surrender. —**capitulation** /-ˈleɪʃ(ə)n/ *n*. [f. L *capitulare* put under headings, f. *capitulum* dim. of *caput* head]

capon /ˈkeɪpən/ *n*. a domestic cock castrated and fattened for eating. [OE f. AF f. L *capo*]

caprice /kəˈpri:s/ *n*. **1** a whim; a tendency to capricious behaviour. **2** a work of lively fancy in art or music. [F f. It. *capriccio* sudden start (orig. = horror)]

capricious /kəˈprɪʃəs/ *adj*. guided by caprice, impulsive; unpredictable. —**capriciously** *adv*., **capriciousness** *n*. [as prec.]

Capricorn /ˈkæprɪkɔ:n/ a constellation and the tenth sign of the zodiac, the Goat, which the sun enters at the winter solstice. —**tropic of Capricorn,** see TROPIC. [f. OF f. L (*caper* goat, *cornu* horn)]

capsicum /ˈkæpsɪkəm/ *n*. the sweet pepper, a tropical plant of the genus *Capsicum* with hot-tasting seeds; its fruit. [perh. f. L *capsa* case]

capsize /kæpˈsaɪz/ *v.t./i.* to overturn (a boat); to be overturned. [perh. f. Sp. *capuzar* sink by the head (*cabo* head, *chapuzar* dive)]

capstan /ˈkæpst(ə)n/ *n*. **1** a thick revolving post round which a cable or rope is wound as it turns, e.g. to raise a ship's anchor. **2** a revolving spindle carrying the spool on a tape-recorder. —**capstan lathe,** a lathe with a revolving tool-holder. [f. Prov. f. L (*capere* seize)]

capsule /ˈkæpsju:l/ *n*. **1** a small soluble case in which a dose of medicine is enclosed for swallowing. **2** a plant's seed-case that splits open when ripe. **3** a detachable compartment of an aircraft or nose-cone of a rocket. —*adj.* concise, highly condensed. [F f. L (*capsa* case)]

capsulize /ˈkæpsjʊlaɪz/ *v.t.* to put (information etc.) into a compact form. [f. prec.]

captain /ˈkæptɪn/ *n.* **1** a person given authority over a group or team. **2** the person commanding a ship; a naval officer ranking next below commodore. **3** an army officer ranking next below major. **4** the pilot of a civil aircraft. —*v.t.* to be captain of. —**captaincy** *n.* [f. OF f. L, = chief (*caput* head)]

caption /ˈkæpʃ(ə)n/ *n.* a short title or heading; a description or explanation printed with an illustration etc.; words shown on a cinema or television screen. —*v.t.* to provide with a caption. [f. L (*capere* take)]

captious /ˈkæpʃəs/ *adj.* fond of finding fault, raising petty objections. —**captiously** *adv.*, **captiousness** *n.* [f. OF or L (as prec.)]

captivate /ˈkæptɪveɪt/ *v.t.* to capture the affection or fancy of, to charm. —**captivation** /-ˈveɪʃ(ə)n/ *n.* [f. L *captivare* take captive (as foll.)]

captive /ˈkæptɪv/ *adj.* taken prisoner; restrained, confined; (of an audience or market) having no choice but to listen or comply. —*n.* a captive person or animal. [f. L *captivus* (*capere* take)]

captivity /kæpˈtɪvɪtɪ/ *n.* the state of being held captive. —**the Captivity,** that of the Jews in Babylon, to which they were deported by Nebuchadnezzar in 586 BC and from which they were released by Cyrus in 538 BC. [as prec.]

captor /ˈkæptə(r)/ *n.* one who captures. [L (as CAPTURE)]

capture /ˈkæptʃə(r)/ *v.t.* **1** to take prisoner, to seize; to obtain by force, trickery, attraction, or skill. **2** to portray (a likeness etc.) in permanent form. **3** to absorb (an atomic particle). **4** (of a stream) to divert the upper course of (another) into its own waters by encroaching on the other's basin. **5** (of a star or planet) to bring (an object) within its gravitational field. **6** to put (data) into a form accessible by computer. —*n.* **1** the act of capturing. **2** a thing or person captured. [F f. L (as prec.)]

Capuchin /ˈkæpjʊtʃɪn/ *n.* **1** a Franciscan friar of the new rule of 1528. **2** capuchin, a monkey or pigeon with a hood-like crown. [F f. It. (*cappuccio* cowl)]

capybara /kæpɪˈbɑːrə/ *n.* a large South American rodent (*Hydrochoerus capybara*) allied to the guinea-pig. [Tupi]

car *n.* **1** a motor car. **2** a railway carriage of a specified type; (*US*) any railway carriage or van. **3** the passenger compartment of an airship, balloon, cable railway, or lift. —**car-park** *n.* an area for parking cars. [f. AF f. L *carrum*]

caracul var. of KARAKUL.

carafe /kəˈræf/ *n.* a glass container in which water or wine is served at table. [F, ult. f. Arab., = drinking-vessel]

caramel /ˈkærəm(ə)l/ *n.* **1** burnt sugar or syrup used for colouring or flavouring food. **2** a kind of toffee tasting like this. **3** light-brown colour. [F f. Sp.]

caramelize /ˈkærəməlaɪz/ *v.t./i.* to turn into caramel. —**caramelization** /-ˈzeɪʃ(ə)n/ *n.* [f. prec.]

carapace /ˈkærəpeɪs/ *n.* the upper shell of a tortoise or crustacean. [F f. Sp.]

carat /ˈkærət/ *n.* a unit of weight for precious stones, 200 mg; a unit of measurement for the purity of gold, pure gold being 24 carat. [F, ult. f. Gk *keration* fruit of carob (dim. of *keras* horn)]

caravan /ˈkærəvæn/ *n.* **1** an enclosed carriage equipped for living in, able to be towed by a vehicle; a covered cart used similarly, towed by a horse. **2** a company (especially of merchants) travelling together, especially across desert country. —*v.i.* (**-nn-**) to travel or live in a caravan. [f. F f. Pers.]

caravanserai /kærəˈvænsərɪ/ *n.* (in eastern countries) an inn with a large central courtyard for accommodation of travelling caravans. [f. Pers., = caravan-place]

caraway /ˈkærəweɪ/ *n.* an aromatic umbelliferous plant (*Carum carvi*) with spicy seeds that are used for flavouring cake etc. [f. Sp. f. Arab., perh. f. Gk *caron* cumin]

carbide /ˈkɑːbaɪd/ *n.* a binary compound of carbon, especially calcium carbide which is used in making acetylene gas. [f. CARBON]

carbine /ˈkɑːbaɪn/ *n.* a short rifle, originally for cavalry use. [earlier & F *carabine*, weapon of the *carabin* mounted musketeer]

carbohydrate /kɑːbəˈhaɪdreɪt/ *n.* **1** an energy-producing compound of carbon with oxygen and hydrogen, e.g. starch, sugar, glucose. **2** starchy food, considered to be fattening. [f. CARBON + HYDRATE]

carbolic /kɑːˈbɒlɪk/ *adj.* **carbolic acid,** phenol. **carbolic soap,** soap containing this. [f. foll.]

carbon /ˈkɑːbən/ *n.* **1** a non-metallic element, symbol C, atomic number 6. **2** a carbon copy; carbon paper. **3** a rod of carbon used in an arc lamp. —**carbon copy,** a copy made with carbon paper; an exact copy. **carbon dioxide,** a colourless odourless gas formed by burning carbon or breathed out by animals in respiration. **carbon 14,** a radioisotope with mass 14 used in dating prehistoric objects. **carbon monoxide,** a poisonous colourless almost odourless gas formed by burning carbon incompletely, occurring e.g. in the exhaust of motor engines. **carbon paper,** thin pigmented paper placed between sheets of paper for reproducing what is written or typed on the top sheet. **carbon tetrachloride,** a colourless liquid used as a solvent in dry cleaning etc. [f. F f. L *carbo* charcoal]

carbonaceous /kɑ:bəˈneɪʃəs/ *adj.* consisting of or containing carbon; of or like coal or charcoal. [f. prec.]

carbonade /kɑ:bəˈneɪd/ *n.* a rich beef stew containing beer. [F]

carbonate /ˈkɑ:bəneɪt/ *n.* a salt of carbonic acid. —*v.t.* to impregnate with carbon dioxide; to make (drinks) effervescent with this. [f. F. (as CARBON)]

carbonic /kɑ:ˈbɒnɪk/ *adj.* of carbon. —**carbonic acid,** a weak acid formed from carbon dioxide and water. [f. CARBON]

carboniferous /kɑ:bəˈnɪfərəs/ *adj.* **1** producing coal. **2 Carboniferous,** of the fifth period of the Palaeozoic era, lasting from about 360 to 286 million years ago. —**Carboniferous** *n.* this period. [f. CARBON + *-ferous* bearing (L *ferre* bear)]

carbonize /ˈkɑ:bənaɪz/ *v.t.* **1** to convert into carbon; to reduce to charcoal or coke. **2** to coat with carbon. —**carbonization** /-ˈzeɪʃ(ə)n/ *n.* [f. CARBON]

carborundum /kɑ:bəˈrʌndəm/ *n.* a compound of carbon and silicon, used especially as an abrasive. [f. CARBON + CORUNDUM]

carboy /ˈkɑ:bɔɪ/ *n.* a large globular bottle enclosed in a frame, used for transporting liquids safely. [f. Pers., = large glass flagon]

carbuncle /ˈkɑ:bʌŋk(ə)l/ *n.* **1** a severe abscess in the skin. **2** a bright-red gem cut in a knob-like shape. [f. OF f. L, = small coal (*carbo* coal)]

carburation /kɑ:bjʊˈreɪʃ(ə)n/ *n.* the process of charging air with a spray of liquid hydrocarbon fuel. [f. CARBON]

carburettor /kɑ:bjʊˈretə(r)/ *n.* an apparatus for the carburation of air in an internal-combustion engine. [as prec.]

carcass /ˈkɑ:kəs/ *n.* **1** the dead body of an animal, especially one prepared for cutting up as meat; the bony part of the body of a bird before or after cooking. **2** a framework; the foundation structure of a tyre. [f. AF; orig. unkn.]

carcinogen /kɑ:ˈsɪnədʒən/ *n.* a substance that induces cancer. —**carcinogenic** /-ˈdʒenɪk/ *adj.* [f. foll.]

carcinoma /kɑ:sɪˈnəʊmə/ *n.* (*pl.* **-mata**) a cancerous tumour. [L f. Gk (*karkinos* crab)]

card[1] *n.* **1** thick stiff paper or thin cardboard; a piece of this for writing or printing on, especially to send messages or greetings or to record information; a flat usually rectangular piece of thin pasteboard, plastic, etc., recording membership or identifying the bearer; (in *pl.*, *colloq.*) an employee's documents held by his employer. **2** a playing-card; (in *pl.*) card-playing. **3** a programme of events at a race-meeting etc. **4** (*colloq.*) an odd or amusing person. —**card-carrying** *adj.* being a registered member of a political party, trade union, etc. **card-sharp** *n.* a swindler at card-games. **card vote,** a block vote (see BLOCK). **on the cards,** likely, possible. [f. OE f. L f. Gk *khartēs* papyrus-leaf]

card[2] *n.* a toothed instrument or wire brush for raising nap on cloth or for disentangling fibres before spinning. —*v.t.* to brush or comb with a card. [f. OF f. L *carere* card]

cardamom /ˈkɑ:dəməm/ *n.* spice from the seed-capsules of various East Indian plants, especially *Elettaria cardamomum*, a plant of the ginger family. [f. L or F f. Gk (*kardamon* cress, *amōmon* a spice-plant)]

cardboard *n.* stiff paper or pasteboard, especially for making cards or boxes.

cardiac /ˈkɑ:dɪæk/ *adj.* of the heart. [f. F or L f. Gk (*kardia* heart)]

cardigan /ˈkɑ:dɪgən/ *n.* a knitted jacket. [named after 7th Earl of Cardigan (d. 1868), who led the disastrous Charge of the Light Brigade in the Crimean War]

cardinal /ˈkɑ:dɪn(ə)l/ *adj.* **1** chief, fundamental. **2** deep scarlet as worn by cardinals. —*n.* **1** a member of the Sacred College of the Roman Catholic Church. Cardinals hold the highest rank next to the pope, who is chosen from their number. **2** a small scarlet American songbird of the genus *Richmondena*. —**cardinal numbers,** the whole numbers (1, 2, 3, etc.) representing a quantity, as opposed to ordinal numbers. **cardinal points,** the four main points of the compass, North, South, East, and West. **cardinal virtues,** justice, prudence, temperance, fortitude, faith, hope, charity. [f. OF f. L (*cardo* hinge)]

cardiology /kɑ:dɪˈɒlədʒɪ/ *n.* the branch of medicine concerned with diseases and abnormalities of the heart. —**cardiological** /-ˈlɒdʒɪk(ə)l/ *adj.*, **cardiologist** *n.* [f. Gk *kardia* heart + -LOGY]

care /keə(r)/ *n.* **1** serious attention and thought; caution to avoid damage or loss. **2** protection, charge, supervision. **3** a thing to be done or seen to. —*v.t./i.* **1** to feel concern or interest. **2** to feel affection or a liking *for* or willingness *to* do. **3** to provide *for*. —**care of,** at the address of (one who will deliver or forward things). **in care,** taken into the care of a local authority. [OE, = sorrow]

careen /kəˈri:n/ *v.t.* **1** to tilt, to lean over. **2** (*US*) to swerve. [f. F f. It. f. L *carina* keel]

career /kəˈrɪə(r)/ *n.* **1** one's advancement through life, especially in a profession; a profession or occupation, especially one offering advancement. **2** swift forward movement. —*v.i.* to move swiftly or wildly. [f. F, ult. f. L *carrus* car]

careerist *n.* a person who is predominantly concerned with advancement in a career. [f. prec.]

carefree *adj.* light-hearted through being free from anxiety or responsibility.

careful *adj.* giving serious attention and thought, painstaking; done with care and attention; cautious. —**carefully** *adv.*, **carefulness** *n.* [f. CARE + -FUL]

careless *adj.* not giving or given serious attention and thought; unthinking, insensitive; casual and lighthearted. —**carelessly** *adv.*, **carelessness** *n.* [f. CARE + -LESS]

carer *n.* one who looks after a sick or disabled person at home.

caress /kəˈres/ *v.t.* to touch or stroke lovingly, to caress. —*n.* a loving touch, a kiss. [f. F f. L *carus* dear]

caret /ˈkærət/ *n.* a mark showing an omission (and intended insertion) in something printed or written. [L, = is lacking]

caretaker *n.* **1** a person employed to look after a house or building etc. **2** (*attrib.*) exercising temporary power.

careworn *adj.* showing the effects of prolonged worry.

cargo *n.* (*pl.* **-oes**) goods carried on a ship or aircraft. [Sp., as CHARGE]

caribou /ˈkærɪbu:/ *n.* (*pl.* same) a North American reindeer. [F, prob. f. Amer. Ind.]

caricature /ˈkærɪkətjʊə(r)/ *n.* a grotesque representation, especially of a person by exaggeration of characteristics; a ridiculously poor imitation or version. —*v.t.* to make or give a caricature of. —**caricaturist** *n.* [F f. It. (*caricare* exaggerate)]

caries /ˈkeəri:z/ *n.* (*pl.* same) decay in bones or teeth. [L]

carillon /kəˈrɪljən, ˈkæ-/ *n.* a set of bells sounded either from a keyboard or mechanically. [F]

carioca /kærɪˈəʊkə/ *n.* a Brazilian dance resembling the samba; music for this. [Port.]

Carmelite /ˈkɑ:məlaɪt/ *n.* a member of the Carmelite order of friars or nuns. —*adj.* of the Carmelite order. [f. L, f. Mt. *Carmel* in Palestine, place of foundation]

carminative /ˈkɑ:mɪnətɪv/ *adj.* curing flatulence. —*n.* a carminative drug. [f. F or L *carminare* heal (by incantation)]

carmine /ˈkɑ:maɪn/ *adj.* of vivid crimson colour. —*n.* **1** this colour. **2** a red pigment made from cochineal. [f. F or L (perh. as CRIMSON)]

carnage /ˈkɑ:nɪdʒ/ *n.* great slaughter. [F f. It. f. L *caro* flesh]

carnal /ˈkɑ:n(ə)l/ *adj.* of the body or flesh, not spiritual; sensual, sexual. —**carnality** /-ˈnælɪtɪ/ *n.*, **carnally** *adv.* [f. L (as prec.)]

carnassial /kɑ:ˈnæsɪəl/ *n.* a carnassial tooth. —*adj.* **carnassial tooth**, a carnivore's premolar tooth, adapted for cutting. [f. F *carnassier* carnivorous]

carnation /kɑ:ˈneɪʃ(ə)n/ *n.* a cultivated clove-scented pink. [earlier *coronation*]

carnelian /kɑ:ˈni:lɪən/ var. of CORNELIAN².

carnet /ˈkɑ:neɪ/ *n.* the documents of identification etc. that are needed to permit a vehicle to be driven across a frontier or to use a camping-site. [F, = notebook]

carnival /ˈkɑ:nɪvəl/ *n.* **1** festivities and public merrymaking, usually with a procession. **2** (*US*) a fun-fair or circus. [f. It. f. L *carnelevarium* Shrove-tide, f. *caro* meat, *levare* put away, with ref. to the austerities of Lent]

carnivore /ˈkɑ:nɪvɔ:(r)/ *n.* a carnivorous animal or plant. [f. foll.]

carnivorous /kɑ:ˈnɪvərəs/ *adj.* feeding on flesh or other animal matter; belonging to the Carnivora, a large order of mainly carnivorous mammals (bears, cats, dogs, foxes, seals, etc.). [f. L (*caro* flesh)]

carob /ˈkærəb/ *n.* the horn-shaped edible pod of a Mediterranean evergreen tree, *Ceratonia siliqua*. [f. F, ult. f. Arab.]

carol /ˈkærəl/ *n.* a joyful song, especially a Christmas hymn. —*v.t./i.* (**-ll-**) to sing carols; to sing joyfully. —**caroller** *n.* [f. OF; orig. unkn.]

carotid /kəˈrɒtɪd/ *adj.* of the two main arteries, one on each side of the neck, carrying blood to the head. —*n.* a carotid artery. [f. F f. Gk (*karoō* stupefy, compression of these arteries being thought to cause stupor)]

carouse /kəˈraʊz/ *v.i.* to have a noisy or lively drinking-party. —*n.* such a party. —**carousal** *n.* [f. G *gar aus* (drunk) right out]

carousel /kærʊˈsel/ *n.* **1** (*US*) a merry-go-round. **2** a rotating conveyor or delivery system. [F f. It.]

carp¹ *n.* (*pl.* same) a freshwater fish of the genus *Cyprinus*, especially a species often bred in ponds. [f. OF f. Prov. or L]

carp² *v.i.* to find fault, to complain pettily. [f. ON, = brag]

carpal /ˈkɑ:p(ə)l/ *adj.* of the wrist-bone. [f. CARPUS]

carpel /ˈkɑ:p(ə)l/ *n.* any of the segments of a compound pistil of a flower; a simple pistil, in which the seeds develop. [f. F f. Gk *karpos* fruit]

carpenter /ˈkɑ:pɪntə(r)/ *n.* a craftsman in woodwork, one who makes or repairs wooden structures. —*v.t./i.* to do or make by carpenter's work. —**carpentry** *n.* [f. OF f. L (*carpentum* wagon)]

carpet /ˈkɑ:pɪt/ *n.* **1** a thick textile covering for floors or stairs. **2** a carpet-like expanse, a thick layer underfoot. —*v.t.* **1** to cover with or as with a carpet. **2** (*colloq.*) to reprimand. —**carpet-bag** *n.* a travelling-bag of the kind formerly made of carpet-like material. **carpet-bagger** *n.* a political candidate without local connections; (*hist.*) any of the adventurers from the northern States who went into the southern States after the American Civil War, in order to profit from the post-war reorganization (so called from the carpet-bag which held all their possessions). **carpet-sweeper** *n.* a household device with revolving brushes for sweeping carpets. **on the carpet,** (*colloq.*) being reprimanded. [f. OF or L (*carpere* pull to pieces)]

carport *n.* an open-sided shelter for a car, projecting from the side of a house.

carpus /ˈkɑːpəs/ *n.* (*pl.* **-pi** /-paɪ/) the set of small bones connecting the hand and forearm, especially the wrist in man. [f. Gk *karpos* wrist]

carriage /ˈkærɪdʒ/ *n.* **1** a wheeled passenger vehicle, usually horse-drawn. **2** a railway passenger vehicle. **3** the conveying of goods etc.; the cost of this. **4** a moving part carrying or holding something in a machine. **5** a gun-carriage. **6** the posture of the body when walking. —**carriage clock,** a small portable clock with a rectangular case and a handle on top. [as CARRY]

carriageway *n.* the part of the road on which vehicles travel.

carrier /ˈkærɪə(r)/ *n.* **1** a person or thing that carries something; a person or company conveying goods or passengers for payment. **2** a support or receptacle for carrying something; a carrier bag. **3** a person or animal that transmits a disease without being affected by it. **4** an aircraftcarrier. —**carrier bag,** a paper or plastic bag, with handles, for holding shopping etc. **carrier pigeon,** a homing pigeon used to carry messages tied to its leg or neck. **carrier wave,** a high-frequency electromagnetic wave modulated in amplitude or frequency to convey a telecommunications signal. [f. CARRY]

carrion /ˈkærɪən/ *n.* dead putrefying flesh. —**carrion crow,** a black crow (*Corvus corone*) that feeds on carrion and small animals. [f. AF f. L *caro* flesh]

carrot /ˈkærət/ *n.* **1** an umbelliferous plant (*Daucus carota*) with a tapering orange-coloured edible root; this root, used as a vegetable. **2** a means of enticement. —**carroty** *adj.* [f. F f. L f. Gk *karōton*]

carry /ˈkærɪ/ *v.t./i.* **1** to hold up or support while moving; to take with one from one place to another. **2** to support the weight or responsibility of. **3** to be pregnant with. **4** to conduct or transmit. **5** to take (a process etc.) to a specified point. **6** to involve, to entail or imply. **7** to transfer (a figure) to a column of higher value. **8** to hold (the body or oneself) in a specified way. **9** (of a newspaper or broadcast etc.) to include in its contents; (of a shop) to keep a regular stock of. **10** (of sound) to be audible at a distance; (of a gun etc.) to propel to a specified distance. **11** to win or capture; to win over (an audience); to win victory or acceptance for (a proposal etc.). —*n.* an act of carrying; (in golf) the flight of a ball before pitching. —**be carried away,** to be uncontrollably excited. **carry-cot** *n.* a portable cot for a baby. **carry forward,** to transfer to a new page or account. **carry off,** to take away (especially by force); (of a disease) to cause the death of; to win (a prize); to deal with (a situation) successfully. **carry on,** to continue; to engage in; (*colloq.*) to behave excitedly, to complain lengthily; to flirt or have an affair (*with*). **carry out,** to put (an idea etc.) into practice. **carry over,** to carry forward; to postpone. **carry weight,** to be influential or important. [f. AF (as CAR)]

cart *n.* a small strong vehicle with two or four wheels for carrying loads, usually drawn by a horse; a light vehicle for pulling by hand. —*v.t.* **1** to convey in a cart. **2** (*slang*) to carry or take laboriously. —**cart-horse** *n.* a horse of heavy build, fit for drawing carts. **cart-wheel** *n.* a handspring in which the body turns with limbs spread like the spokes of a wheel, balancing on each hand in turn. **cart-wright** *n.* a maker of carts. [ON & OE]

carte blanche /kɑːt blɑ̃ʃ/ full discretionary power given to a person. [F, = blank paper]

cartel /kɑːˈtel/ *n.* a union of business firms to control prices etc. [f. G. f. F f. It., dim. of *carta* card]

Cartesian /kɑːˈtiːzjən/ *adj.* of Descartes (1596–1650). —*n.* a follower of Descartes. —**Cartesian coordinates,** those measured from intersecting straight axes. **Cartesian diver,** a toy device that rises and falls in liquid when the cover of a vessel is subjected to varying pressure. [f. L (*Cartesius* Descartes)]

Carthusian /kɑːˈθjuːzɪən/ *n.* a member of the Carthusian order of monks or nuns. —*adj.* of the Carthusian order. [f. L *Cart(h)usia* Chartreuse]

cartilage /ˈkɑːtɪlɪdʒ/ *n.* tough flexible tissue attached to the bones of vertebrates; a structure of this. [F f. L *cartilago*]

cartilaginous /kɑːtɪˈlædʒɪnəs/ *adj.* of or like cartilage; (of fish) having a cartilaginous skeleton. [f. prec.]

cartography /kɑːˈtɒgrəfɪ/ *n.* map-drawing. —**cartographer** *n.*, **cartographic** /-ˈgræfɪk/ *adj.* [f. F (*carte* map)]

carton /ˈkɑːt(ə)n/ *n.* a light box or container made of cardboard or plastic. [F, f. as foll.]

cartoon /kɑːˈtuːn/ *n.* **1** a humorous drawing in a newspaper etc., especially as a topical comment; a sequence of such drawings telling a comic or serial story; an animated cartoon on film. **2** an artist's full-size drawing as a sketch for a work of art. —*v.t.* to draw a cartoon of. —**cartoonist** *n.* [f. It. (*carta* card)]

cartouche /kɑː'tuːʃ/ *n.* **1** a scroll-like ornamentation in architecture etc. **2** an oval emblem containing hieroglyphics that give the birth-name and coronation name of an ancient Egyptian king. [F, = cartridge (as prec.)]

cartridge /'kɑːtrɪdʒ/ *n.* **1** a case containing a charge of propellant explosive for firearms or blasting, with bullet or shot if for small arms. **2** a sealed container holding film, magnetic tape, etc., ready for insertion as a unit. **3** a component on the pick-up head of a record-player, carrying the stylus. —**cartridge paper,** thick strong paper for drawing etc. [f. prec.]

carve *v.t./i.* **1** to produce or shape by cutting; to cut designs etc. in (hard material). **2** to cut (meat) into slices for serving. **3** to make (a career etc.) by effort. —**carve up,** to divide into parts or shares. [OE]

carvel-built /'kɑːv(ə)l'bɪlt/ *adj.* (of a boat) made with planks joined smoothly and not overlapping. [f. F, ult. f. Gk *karabos* light ship]

carver *n.* **1** one who carves. **2** a knife or (in *pl.*) knife and fork for carving meat. **3** a chair with arms that forms one of a set of dining-room chairs. [f. CARVE]

carving *n.* a carved object or design. [f. CARVE]

caryatid /kærɪ'ætɪd/ *n.* a sculptured female figure used as a supporting pillar in a building. [f. F, ult. f. Gk, = priestess of Caryae in Greece]

Casanova /kæzə'nəʊvə, kæs-/ *n.* a man notorious for many love-affairs. [f. G. J. Casanova de Seingalt, Italian adventurer (d. 1798), famous for his memoirs, in French, describing his adventurous life, and particularly his pursuit of women, in a large number of European countries]

cascade /kæs'keɪd/ *n.* a small waterfall, especially one in a series; something arranged like this. —*v.i.* to fall in or like a cascade. [F, ult. f. L *casus* case]

cascara /kæs'kɑːrə/ *n.* the bark of a North American buckthorn, used as a laxative. [Sp., = sacred bark]

case[1] *n.* **1** an instance of a thing's occurring; an actual or hypothetical situation. **2** a condition of disease or injury, a person suffering from this. **3** an instance or condition of one receiving professional guidance, especially by a doctor. **4** a matter under investigation e.g. by police. **5** a lawsuit; the sum of arguments on one side in this; a set of facts or arguments supporting something. **6** (*Gram.*) the relation of a word to others in a sentence; the form of a noun, adjective, or pronoun expressing this. —**case-law** *n.* law as established by cases decided. **in any case,** whatever the facts are. **in case,** lest something should happen; in the event *of*. [f. OF f. L *casus* (*cadere* fall)]

case[2] *n.* **1** a container or protective covering; this with its contents. **2** a suitcase or other item of luggage. **3** (*Printing*) a partitioned receptacle for type. —*v.t.* to enclose in a case. —**case-harden** *v.t.* to harden the surface of (metal, especially iron by carbonizing); to make unfeeling or unsympathetic. **lower case,** non-capital letters in printing-type. **upper case,** capital letters in printing-type. [f. OF f. L *capsa* box (*capere* hold)]

casemate /'keɪsmeɪt/ *n.* **1** a room built inside the thick wall of a fortification. **2** an armoured enclosure for guns on a warship. [F & It., perh. f. Gk *khasma* gap]

casement /'keɪsmənt/ *n.* a window hinged to open at the side; (*poet.*) a window. [f. L *cassimentum* (*cassa* CASE[2])]

cash *n.* money in coin or notes; immediate payment at the time of purchase; (*colloq.*) wealth. —*v.t.* to give or obtain cash for. —**cash and carry,** a system of (esp. wholesale) trading in which the buyer pays for goods in cash and takes them away himself. **cash crop,** a crop grown for selling. **cash flow,** movement of money out of and into a business, affecting its ability to make payments. **cash in (on),** to profit (from); to use to one's advantage. **cash on delivery,** a system of paying for goods when they are delivered. **cash register,** a machine in a shop etc. with mechanism for recording the amount of each sale. [f. F (as CASE[2])]

cashew /'kæʃuː/ *n.* an edible kidney-shaped nut; the tropical tree (*Anacardium occidentale*) producing this. [f. Port. f. Tupi]

cashier[1] /kæ'ʃɪə(r)/ *n.* a person in charge of cash transactions in a bank or shop etc. [f. Du. or F (as CASH)]

cashier[2] /kæ'ʃɪə(r)/ *v.t.* to dismiss from service, especially with disgrace. [f. Flemish f. F f. L *cassare* quash]

cashmere /'kæʃmɪə(r)/ *n.* a very fine soft wool, especially that of the Kashmir goat; fabric made from this. [f. *Kashmir* in Asia]

casing /'keɪsɪŋ/ *n.* a protective covering. [f. CASE[2]]

casino /kə'siːnəʊ/ *n.* (*pl.* **-os**) a public room or building for gambling and other amusements. [It., dim. of *casa* house f. L *casa* cottage]

cask /kɑːsk/ *n.* a barrel, especially one for alcoholic liquor; its contents. [f. F or Sp. (*casco* helmet)]

casket /'kɑːskɪt/ *n.* **1** a small usually ornamental box for holding valuables etc. **2** (*US*) a coffin. [perh. f. AF, ult. f. L *capsa* CASE[2]]

cassata /kə'sɑːtə/ *n.* an ice-cream cake containing fruit and nuts. [It.]

cassava /kəˈsɑːvə/ *n.* a tropical plant of the genus *Manihot*, with tuberous roots; starch or flour from this, used to make bread and tapioca. [f. Amer. Ind. *casavi*]

casserole /ˈkæsərəʊl/ *n.* a covered dish in which meat etc. is cooked and served; food cooked in this. —*v.t.* to cook in a casserole. [F, ult. f. Gk *kuathion* little cup]

cassette /kəˈset/ *n.* a small sealed case containing a reel of film or magnetic tape. [F, dim. of *casse* CASE[2]]

cassia /ˈkæsɪə/ *n.* **1** a kind of cinnamon. **2** a plant of the genus *Cassia*, yielding senna-leaves. [f. L f. Gk f. Heb.]

cassock /ˈkæsək/ *n.* a long usually black or red garment worn by certain clergy and members of a church choir. [f. F f. It. *cassaca* horseman's coat]

cassowary /ˈkæsəweərɪ/ *n.* a large flightless bird of the genus *Casuarius*, related to the emu. [f. Malay]

cast /kɑːst/ *v.t./i.* (*past & p.p.* **cast**) **1** to throw, to emit; to shed. **2** to send, direct, or cause to fall (*on*, *over*, etc.). **3** to record or register (a vote). **4** to shape (molten metal or plastic material) in a mould; to make (a product) thus. **5** to assign (an actor) *as* a character; to allocate roles in (a play or film etc.). **6** to utter (aspersions *on*). **7** to reckon or add *up* (figures); to calculate (a horoscope). —*n.* **1** the throwing of a missile, dice, fishing-line or net, etc. **2** an object of metal, clay, etc., made in a mould; a moulded mass of solidified material, especially plaster protecting a broken limb. **3** a set of actors taking parts in a play or film etc. **4** the form, type, or quality (*of* features, the mind, etc.). **5** a tinge of colour. **6** a slight squint. —**cast about for,** to try to find or think of. **cast down,** to depress, to deject. **casting vote,** the deciding vote when votes on two sides are equal. **cast iron,** a hard alloy of iron, carbon, and silicon, cast in a mould. **cast-iron** *adj.* made of cast iron; very strong, unchallengeable. **cast off,** to discard; to release a ship from its moorings; (in knitting) to loop stitches off a needle to form an edge. **cast-off** *n.* an abandoned thing; a garment that the owner will not wear again. **cast on,** (in knitting) to make the first row of loops on a needle. [f. ON]

castanet /kæstəˈnet/ *n.* (usu. in *pl.*) a small concave piece of hardwood, ivory, etc., struck against another by the fingers as a rhythmic accompaniment, especially to a Spanish dance. [f. Sp. f. L *castanea* chestnut]

castaway /ˈkɑːstəweɪ/ *n.* a shipwrecked person. —*adj.* **1** discarded. **2** shipwrecked.

caste /kɑːst/ *n.* **1** a Hindu hereditary class; this class system; the position it confers. **2** a more or less exclusive social class or system of classes. —**casteism** /-tɪz(ə)m/ *n.* [f. Sp. & Port. *casta* lineage, fem. of *casto* pure (as CHASTE)]

castellated /ˈkæstəleɪtɪd/ *adj.* built with battlements; castle-like. —**castellation** /-ˈleɪʃ(ə)n/ *n.* [f. L (as CASTLE)]

caster var. of CASTOR.

castigate /ˈkæstɪgeɪt/ *v.t.* to rebuke or punish severely. —**castigation** /-ˈgeɪʃ(ə)n/ *n.*, **castigator** *n.* [f. L *castigare* reprove (*castus* pure)]

castle /ˈkɑːs(ə)l/ *n.* **1** a large fortified building or group of buildings. **2** (in chess) a rook (ROOK[2]). —*v.t./i.* (in chess) to move (the king) two squares towards a rook and the rook to the square which the king has crossed; (of the king or player) to make such a move. —**castles in the air,** a visionary unattainable scheme, a day-dream. [f. AF f. L, dim. of *castrum* fort]

castor /ˈkɑːstə(r)/ *n.* **1** a small swivelled wheel (often one of a set) fixed to the leg or underside of a piece of furniture so that this can be moved easily. **2** a small container for sugar or salt, with a perforated top for sprinkling the contents. —**castor sugar,** finely granulated white sugar. [f. CAST]

castor oil /ˈkɑːstə(r)/ oil from seeds of the plant *Ricinus communis*, used as a purgative and lubricant. [orig. unkn.]

castrate /kæˈstreɪt/ *v.t.* **1** to remove the testicles of, to geld. **2** to deprive of vigour. —**castration** *n.* [f. L *castrare*]

castrato /kæˈstrɑːtəʊ/ *n.* (*pl.* **-ti** /-tiː/) (*hist.*) a male singer castrated in boyhood to preserve a soprano or alto voice. [It. (as prec.)]

casual /ˈkæzjʊəl/ *adj.* **1** happening by chance. **2** unconcerned, made or done without great care or thought. **3** not regular or permanent. **4** (of clothes) informal. —*n.* **1** a casual worker. **2** (usu. in *pl.*) casual clothes or shoes. —**casually** *adv.*, **casualness** *n.* [f. OF & L (*casus* CASE[1])]

casualty /ˈkæzjʊəltɪ/ *n.* **1** a person killed or injured in war or in an accident; a thing lost or destroyed in some occurrence. **2** an accident or mishap. [f. L (as prec.)]

casuarina /kæzjʊəˈriːnə/ *n.* a tree of the genus *Casuarina*, native to Australia and tropical SE Asia, with jointed branches resembling gigantic horse-tails. [f. CASSOWARY, f. fancied resemblance to its feathers]

casuistry /ˈkæzjʊɪstrɪ/ *n.* clever but often false reasoning, especially about moral issues. —**casuist** *n.*, **casuistic** /-ˈɪstɪk/ *adj.* [f. F f. Sp. f. L *casus* CASE[1]]

cat *n.* **1** a small furry domesticated carnivorous quadruped, *Felis catus*; a member of the genus *Felis* (e.g. lion, tiger, leopard (*the great Cats*)); a catlike animal of other species. **2** (*colloq.*) a malicious or spiteful woman. **3** the cat-o'-nine-tails. —**cat-and-dog life,** one full of quarrels. **cat-and-mouse game,** the practice of taking slight action repeatedly against a weaker party. **cat burglar,** one who enters by climbing a wall or drainpipe etc. to an upper storey. **cat-o'-nine-tails** *n.* a whip with nine knotted lashes. **cat's cradle,** a child's game with string forming looped patterns between the fingers. **Cats-eye** *n.* [P] any of a line of reflector studs marking the centre or edge of a road (patented in 1934). **cat's-paw** *n.* a person used as a tool by another (from the fable of the monkey who used the paw of his friend the cat to rake roasted chestnuts out of the fire). [OE f. L *cattus*]

cata- /kætə-/ *prefix* (usu. **cat-** before a vowel or h) **1** down (*cataract*). **2** wrongly (*catachresis*). [f. Gk *kata* down]

catabolism /kəˈtæbəlɪz(ə)m/ *n.* destructive metabolism, the breakdown of complex substances in the body (opp. ANABOLISM). —**catabolic** /kætəˈbɒlɪk/ *adj.* [f. Gk (CATA-, *bolē* throwing)]

catachresis /kætəˈkri:sɪs/ *n.* incorrect use of words. —**catachrestic** *adj.* [L f. Gk (CATA-, *khrēsis* f. *khraomai* use)]

cataclysm /ˈkætəklɪz(ə)m/ *n.* a violent upheaval or disaster; a sudden great change caused by this. [f. F f. L f. Gk (CATA-, *klusmos* flood)]

cataclysmic /kætəˈklɪzmɪk/ *adj.* of or involving a cataclysm. —**cataclysmic variable,** a class of variable star which includes dwarf novae, classical novae, and others exhibiting single or repeated outbursts. [f. prec.]

catacomb /ˈkætəku:m/ *n.* a subterranean place for burial of the dead, consisting of galleries of passages with recesses excavated in their sides for tombs. [f. F f. L *catacumbas*; orig. unkn.]

catafalque /ˈkætəfælk/ *n.* a decorated platform for supporting the coffin of a distinguished person during a funeral or lying-in-state. [F f. It.; orig. unkn.]

catalepsy /ˈkætəlepsɪ/ *n.* a trance or seizure with un- consciousness and rigidity of the body. —**cataleptic** /-ˈleptɪk/ *adj.* & *n.* [f. F or L f. Gk (CATA-, *lēpsis* seizure)]

catalogue /ˈkætəlɒg/ *n.* a list of items, usually in systematic order and often with a description of each. —*v.t.* to make a catalogue of; to enter in a catalogue. —**cataloguer** *n.* [F f. L f. Gk (CATA-, *legō* choose)]

catalyse /ˈkætəlaɪz/ *v.t.* to accelerate or produce by catalysis. [f. foll.]

catalysis /kəˈtælɪsɪs/ *n.* (*pl.* **-lyses** /-si:z/) the action of a catalyst. [f. Gk, = dissolution (CATA-, *luō* set free)]

catalyst /ˈkætəlɪst/ *n.* a substance that aids or accelerates a chemical reaction without itself undergoing change; a person or thing that precipitates a change. [f. prec.]

catalytic /kætəˈlɪtɪk/ *adj.* of or using a catalyst; of catalysis. —**catalytic converter,** a device with a catalyst for converting pollutant gases into harmless products. **catalytic cracker,** a device in which catalytic cracking is carried out. **catalytic cracking,** the cracking of petroleum oils by a process using a catalyst. [f. CATALYSIS]

catamaran /kætəməˈræn/ *n.* **1** a boat with twin hulls side by side. **2** a raft of yoked logs or boats. [f. Tamil, = tied wood]

catamite /ˈkætəmaɪt/ *n.* the passive partner (especially a boy) in homosexual practices. [f. L f. Gk]

catapult /ˈkætəpʌlt/ *n.* **1** a forked stick etc. with elastic for shooting small stones. **2** an ancient type of military machine for hurling large stones etc. **3** a mechanical device for launching a glider, an aircraft from a ship's deck, etc. —*v.t./i.* **1** to launch with or hurl from a catapult. **2** to fling forcibly. **3** to leap or be hurled forcibly. [f. F or L f. Gk (CATA- *pellō* hurl]

cataract /ˈkætərækt/ *n.* **1** a large waterfall; a rush of water. **2** a condition in which the lens of the eye becomes progressively opaque. [f. L f. Gk, = down-rushing; sense 2 prob. f. obs. sense = portcullis]

catarrh /kəˈtɑ:(r)/ *n.* inflammation of mucous membrane; a watery discharge in the nose or throat due to this. —**catarrhal** *adj.* [f. F f. L f. Gk (CATA-, *rheō* flow)]

catastrophe /kəˈtæstrəfɪ/ *n.* a great and usually sudden disaster; a disastrous end. **catastrophic** /kætəˈstrɒfɪk/ *adj.*, **catastrophically** *adv.* [f. L f. Gk (CATA-, *strephō* turn)]

catatonia /kætəˈtəʊnɪə/ *n.* schizophrenia with intervals of catalepsy and occasionally violence; catalepsy. —**catatonic** /-ˈtɒnɪk/ *adj.* & *n.* [f. Gk (CATA-, *tonos* tension)]

catcall *n.* a shrill whistle of disapproval. —*v.i.* to make a catcall.

catch *v.t./i.* (*past* & *p.p.* **caught** /kɔ:t/) **1** to capture in a trap, in the hand(s) etc., or after a chase; to lay hold of; to catch out (a batsman). **2** to be in time for and board (a train etc.). **3** to detect or surprise; to trap into a mistake or contradiction etc. **4** to get or contract by infection, contagion, or example. **5** to grasp with the senses or mind; to perceive and reproduce (a likeness etc.). **6** to become or cause to become fixed or entangled; to check suddenly. **7** to draw the attention of, to captivate. **8** to begin to burn. —*n.* **1** the act of catching. **2** something caught or worth catching. **3** a concealed difficulty or disadvantage; a question etc. involving this for a victim. **4** a device for fastening something. **5** (*Mus.*) a round, especially with words arranged to produce a humorous effect. —**catch-all** *n.* a thing for including many items. **catch-as-catch-can** *n.* wrestling in which few or no holds are barred. **catch crop,** a crop that grows quickly and is harvested while the main crop is growing. **catch hold of,** to grasp, to seize in the hand(s). **catch it,** (*colloq.*) to be scolded or punished. **catch on,** (*colloq.*) to become popular; to understand what is meant. **catch out,** to detect in a mistake; to get (a batsman) out by catching the ball direct from his bat. **catch-phrase** *n.* a phrase in frequent current use; a slogan. **catch up,** to come abreast with (a person etc. ahead); to make up arrears. [f. AF f. L *captare* try to catch (*capere* take)]

catcher *n.* one who catches; a baseball fielder who stands behind the batter. [f. prec.]

catching *adj.* infectious; catchy. [f. CATCH]

catchment *n.* collection of rainfall. —**catchment area,** an area from which rainfall drains into a river or reservoir; an area served by a school, hospital, etc. [as prec.]

catchpenny *adj.* intended to sell quickly.

catch-22 *n.* (*colloq.*) a dilemma where the victim is bound to suffer, no matter which course of action etc. he takes. [title of a comic novel by J. Heller (1961), set in the Second World War, in which the hero wishes not to fly any more missions and decides to go crazy, only to be told that anyone who wants to get out of combat duty is not really crazy]

catchweight *adj.* & *n.* (*Sport*) accepting a contestant at the weight he happens to be, not a fixed weight.

catchword *n.* **1** a memorable word or phrase in frequent current use, a slogan. **2** a word so placed as to draw attention.

catchy *adj.* **1** (of a tune etc.) easy to remember. **2** tricky, involving a catch. [f. CATCH]

catechism /ˈkætɪkɪz(ə)m/ *n.* a summary of the principles of a religion in the form of questions and answers; a series of questions. [f. L (as foll.)]

catechize /ˈkætɪkaɪz/ *v.t.* to put a series of questions to; to instruct by use of the Church catechism. [f. L f. Gk (*katēkhēō* make clear)]

catechumen /kætɪˈkjuːmən/ *n.* a convert to Christianity who is being instructed before baptism. [as prec.]

categorical /kætɪˈɡɒrɪk(ə)l/ *adj.* unconditional, explicit. —**categorically** *adv.* [f. CATEGORY]

categorize /ˈkætɪɡəraɪz/ *v.t.* to place in a category. —**categorization** /-ˈzeɪʃ(ə)n/ *n.* [f. foll.]

category /ˈkætɪɡərɪ/ *n.* a class or division (of things etc.). [f. F or L f. Gk, = statement (*katēgoros* accuser)]

catenary /kəˈtiːnərɪ/ *n.* a curve formed by a uniform chain hanging freely from two points that are not in the same vertical line. —*adj.* forming or like such a curve. [f. L *catena* chain]

cater /ˈkeɪtə(r)/ *v.i.* **1** to supply food; to provide meals, amusements, etc. *for*. **2** to pander *to* (bad inclinations). [f. obs. *cater* (now *caterer*), f. OF *acater* buy]

caterer /ˈkeɪtərə(r)/ *n.* one whose trade is to supply food for social events. [f. prec.]

caterpillar /ˈkætəpɪlə(r)/ *n.* the larva of a butterfly or moth; a similar larva of various insects. [f. F, lit. = hairy cat]

Caterpillar track [P] a band of linked steel plates passing round wheels on each side of a tractor etc. for travel on rough ground.

caterwaul /ˈkætəwɔːl/ *v.i.* to make a cat's shrill howling cry. [f. CAT + *-waul* (imit.)]

catfish *n.* a large fish of the sub-order Siluroidea, with whisker like barbels round its mouth.

catgut *n.* fine strong thread made from the dried intestines of sheep etc., used for the strings of musical instruments and for surgical suture. [some have conjectured a humorous reference to the resemblance of the sound to caterwauling]

catharsis /kəˈθɑːsɪs/ *n.* **1** purgation. **2** relief of strong feelings or tension, e.g. by giving vent to these in drama or art (the emotional effect of tragedy described in Aristotle's *Poetics*). [f. Gk (*kathairō* cleanse)]

cathartic /kəˈθɑːtɪk/ *adj.* effecting catharsis; purgative. —*n.* a cathartic substance. [f. prec.]

cathedral /kəˈθiːdr(ə)l/ *n.* the principal church of a bishop's see. —*adj.* of or having a cathedral. [f. OF or L f. Gk *kathedra* seat]

Catherine wheel /ˈkæθərɪn/ a firework that rotates when lit. [f. St *Catherine*, said to have been tortured on a spiked wheel (and then beheaded) at Alexandria in the 4th c.]

catheter /ˈkæθɪtə(r)/ *n.* a tube inserted into a body-cavity (especially the bladder) to drain fluid. [f. Gk (*kathiēmi* send down)]

cathode /ˈkæθəʊd/ *n.* the electrode by which current leaves a device. —**cathode-ray tube,** a vacuum tube in which a beam of electrons from the cathode produces a luminous image on a fluorescent screen (as in a television set and an oscilloscope). [f. Gk *kathodos* way down (*kata* down, *hodos* way)]

catholic /ˈkæθəlɪk/ *adj.* universal, including many or most things. —**catholicity** /-ˈlɪsɪtɪ/ *n.* [f. OF or L f. Gk (*kata* in respect of, *holos* whole)]

Catholic *adj.* **1** including all Christians, or all of the Western Church. **2** Roman Catholic. —*n.* a Roman Catholic. —**Catholicism** /-ˈθɒlɪsɪz(ə)m/ *n.* [= prec.]

cation /ˈkætaɪən/ *n.* a positively charged ion (opp. *anion*). —**cationic** /-ˈɒnɪk/ *adj.* [f. Gk. *kata* down + ION]

catkin *n.* a spike of small soft flowers (usually hanging) on trees such as willow and hazel. [f. Du., = kitten]

catmint *n.* a blue-flowered plant (*Nepeta cataria*) with a strong smell that is attractive to cats.

catnap *n.* a short sleep. —*v.i.* (**-pp-**) to have a catnap.

catnip *n.* catmint.

catsuit *n.* a close-fitting garment covering the body from neck to feet, with sleeves and trouser legs.

cattle *n.pl.* cows, bulls, oxen. —**cattle-grid** *n.* a grid covering a ditch, allowing vehicles to pass over but not cattle, sheep, etc. [f. OF *chatel* (cf. CHATTEL), as CAPITAL]

catty *adj.* catlike; malicious, speaking spitefully. —**cattily** *adv.*, **cattiness** *n.* [f. CAT]

catwalk /ˈkætwɔːk/ *n.* a raised narrow pathway.

caucus /ˈkɔːkəs/ *n.* **1** (often *derog.*) the committee of a local branch of a political party, making plans, decisions, etc. **2** (*US*) a meeting of party leaders to decide policy etc. **3** (*Austral.*) the parliamentary members of a political party who decide policy etc.; a meeting of these. [US wd, perh. f. Algonquin, = adviser]

caudal /ˈkɔːd(ə)l/ *adj.* of, like, or at the tail. [f. L *cauda* tail]

caudate /ˈkɔːˈdeɪt/ *adj.* having a tail. [as prec.]

caught *past* & *p.p.* of CATCH.

caul /kɔːl/ *n.* a membrane enclosing a foetus in the womb; part of this sometimes found on a child's head at birth. [perh. f. OF, = small cap]

cauldron /ˈkɔːldrən/ *n.* a large deep cooking-pot for boiling things in. [f. AF f. L *caldarium* hot bath]

cauliflower /ˈkɒlɪflaʊə(r)/ *n.* a cabbage with a large white flower-head. —**cauliflower ear,** an ear thickened by repeated blows. [f. F *chou fleur* flowered cabbage]

caulk /kɔːk/ *v.t.* to make watertight by filling seams or joints with waterproof material, or by driving edges of plating together. [f. OF f. L *calcare* tread]

causal /ˈkɔːz(ə)l/ *adj.* of or forming a cause; relating to cause and effect. —**causally** *adv.* [f. L (as CAUSE)]

causality /kɔːˈzælɪtɪ/ *n.* the relationship between cause and effect; the principle that everything has a cause. [f. prec.]

causation /kɔːˈzeɪʃ(ə)n/ *n.* the act of causing; causality. [F or f. L (as CAUSE)]

causative /ˈkɔːzətɪv/ *adj.* acting as or expressing a cause. [f. OF or L (as CAUSE)]

cause /kɔːz/ *n.* **1** a thing that produces an effect; a person or thing that makes something happen. **2** a reason or motive; justification. **3** a principle, belief, or purpose for which efforts are made, a movement or charity. **4** a matter to be settled at law; a case offered at law. —*v.t.* to be the cause of, to produce, to make happen. [f. OF f. L *causa*]

cause célèbre /kɔːz seˈlebrə/ (*pl.* **-s -s,** pr. same) a lawsuit or other issue that rouses great interest. [F]

causeway /ˈkɔːzweɪ/ *n.* a raised road across low or wet ground. [earlier *cauce(way)*, f. OF f. L *calx* limestone]

caustic /ˈkɔːstɪk/ *adj.* **1** that burns or corrodes things by chemical action. **2** sarcastic. —**caustic curve,** a curve formed by the intersection of rays reflected or refracted from a curved surface. **caustic soda,** sodium hydroxide. —**causticity** /-ˈtɪsɪtɪ/ *n.*, **caustically** *adv.* [f. L f. Gk (*kaustos* burnt)]

cauterize /ˈkɔːtəraɪz/ *v.t.* to burn (tissue) with a caustic substance or hot iron to destroy infection or stop bleeding. —**cauterization** /-ˈzeɪʃ(ə)n/ *n.* [f. F f. L f. Gk (*kautērion* branding-iron)]

caution /ˈkɔːʃ(ə)n/ *n.* **1** avoidance of rashness, attention to safety. **2** a warning against danger etc.; a warning and reprimand. **3** (*colloq.*) an amusing person or thing. —*v.t.* to warn; to warn and reprimand. [f. OF f. L (*cavere* take heed)]

cautionary /ˈkɔːʃ(ə)nərɪ/ *adj.* that gives or serves as a warning. [f. prec.]

cautious /ˈkɔːʃəs/ *adj.* having or showing caution. —**cautiously** *adv.*, **cautiousness** *n.* [f. CAUTION]

cavalcade /ˈkævəlkeɪd/ *n.* a procession or company of people on horseback or in cars etc. [F f. It. (*cavalcare* ride, f. L *caballus* horse)]

Cavalier /kævəˈlɪə(r)/ *n.* a supporter of Charles I in the English Civil War. [F f. It. (as CHEVALIER)]

cavalier /kævəˈlɪə(r)/ *n.* a courtly gentleman. —*adj.* arrogant, offhand. [as prec.]

cavalry /ˈkæv(ə)lrɪ/ *n.* (usu. as *pl.*) troops who fight on horseback or in armoured vehicles. [f. F f. It. f. L *caballus* horse]

cave *n.* a hollow in the side of a hill or cliff, or underground. —*v.i.* to explore caves. —**cave-painting** *n.* picture(s) of animals etc. on the interior of a cave, especially by prehistoric peoples. **cave in,** to fall or cause to fall inwards, to collapse; to withdraw one's opposition. [f. OF f. L *cavus* hollow]

caveat /ˈkævɪæt/ *n.* a warning; a proviso. [L, = let him beware]

caveman *n.* (*pl.* **-men**) a prehistoric man living in caves; a man with a rough primitive manner towards women.

cavern /ˈkævən/ *n.* a large cave. —**cavernous** *adj.* [f. OF or L (*cavus* hollow)]

caviare /ˈkævɪɑː(r)/ *n.* the pickled roe of sturgeon or other large fish. [f. It. f. Turk.]

cavil /ˈkævɪl/ *v.i.* (**-ll-**) to raise petty objections (*at*). —*n.* a petty objection. [f. F f. L (*cavilla* mockery)]

cavity /ˈkævɪtɪ/ *n.* a hollow within a solid body. —**cavity wall,** a double wall with an internal space. [f. F or L (as CAVE)]

cavort /kəˈvɔːt/ *v.i.* to prance or caper excitedly. [perh. f. CURVET]

caw *n*. the harsh cry of a rook, raven, or crow etc. —*v.i.* to make a caw. [imit.]

cayenne /keɪˈen/ *n*. (in full **cayenne pepper**) pungent red powdered pepper made from capsicum. [f. Tupi, assim. to *Cayenne* capital of French Guiana]

cayman /ˈkeɪmən/ *n*. (*pl*. **-s**) a South American alligator, especially of the genus *Caiman*. [f. Sp. & Port. f. Carib]

CB *abbr*. citizens' band.

CBI *abbr*. Confederation of British Industry, the employers' federation in the UK, founded in 1965.

Cd *symbol* cadmium.

cd *abbr*. candela.

CE *abbr*. Common Era.

Ce *symbol* cerium.

cease /si:s/ *v.t./i.* to bring or come to an end; to stop. —**cease-fire** *n*. a signal (in war) to stop firing; a halt in hostilities. [f. OF f. L *cessare*]

ceaseless *adj*. without cease, not ceasing. [f. prec. + -LESS]

cedar /ˈsi:də(r)/ *n*. an evergreen coniferous tree of the genus *Cedrus*; its hard fragrant wood. [f. OF f. L f. Gk *kedros*]

cede /si:d/ *v.t.* to give up one's rights to or possession of. [f. L *cedere* yield]

cedilla /sɪˈdɪlə/ *n*. a mark written under *c* especially in French, to show that it is sibilant (as in *façade*). [f. Sp., dim. of *zeda* z]

ceilidh /ˈkeɪlɪ/ *n*. (orig. *Sc*. & *Ir*.) an informal gathering for traditional music, dancing, etc. [Gael.]

ceiling /ˈsi:lɪŋ/ *n*. **1** the under-surface of the top of a room etc. **2** the maximum altitude a given aircraft can normally reach. **3** an upper limit (of prices, performance, etc.). [orig. unkn.]

celandine /ˈseləndaɪn/ *n*. either of two yellow-flowered plants, **greater celandine** (*Chelidonium majus*) and **lesser celandine** (*Ranunculus ficaria*). [f. OF f. L f. Gk (*chelidon* the swallow)]

celebrant /ˈselɪbrənt/ *n*. an officiating priest, especially at the Eucharist. [as foll.]

celebrate /ˈselɪbreɪt/ *v.t./i.* **1** to mark (an occasion) with festivities; to engage in such festivities. **2** to perform (religious rites); to officiate at the Eucharist etc. **3** to praise widely, to extol. —**celebration** /-ˈbreɪʃ(ə)n/ *n*. [f. L *celebrare* (*celeber* renowned)]

celebrated *adj*. widely known. [f. prec.]

celebrity /sɪˈlebrɪtɪ/ *n*. a well-known person; fame. [as CELEBRATE]

celeriac /sɪˈlerɪæk/ *n*. a variety of celery with large edible root. [f. CELERY]

celerity /sɪˈlerɪtɪ/ *n*. (*archaic* & *literary*) swiftness. [f. L (*celer* swift)]

celery /ˈselərɪ/ *n*. a vegetable (*Apium graveolens*) with blanched stems eaten raw in salads or cooked. [f. F, ult. f. Gk *selinon* parsley]

celesta /sɪˈlestə/ *n*. a small keyboard instrument with hammers striking metal plates to give a bell-like sound. [f. F *céleste* (as foll.)]

celestial /sɪˈlestɪəl/ *adj*. **1** of the sky or heavenly bodies. **2** of heaven, divine. —**celestially** *adv*. [f. L (*caelum* sky)]

celibate /ˈselɪbət/ *adj*. remaining unmarried or abstaining from sexual relations, especially for religious reasons. —*n*. a celibate person. —**celibacy** *n*. [f. L *caelebs* bachelor]

cell *n*. **1** a very small room, e.g. for a monk in a monastery or for confining a prisoner. **2** a compartment in a honeycomb. **3** a microscopic structure which is effectively the unit of life. **4** a container with materials for producing electricity by chemical action; a device for converting chemical or radiant energy into electrical energy. **5** a small group of people forming a centre or nucleus of political (often subversive) activities. [f. L *cella* store-room]

cellar /ˈselə(r)/ *n*. **1** a room below ground-level, used for storage (especially of wine). **2** a person's or institution's stock of wine. [f. AF f. L *cellarium* (as prec.)]

cello /ˈtʃeləʊ/ *n*. (*pl*. **-os**) a violoncello, an instrument like a large violin with four strings and a range of over three octaves, played supported on the floor in an upright or slanting position between the seated player's knees. —**cellist** *n*. [abbr. of VIOLONCELLO]

Cellophane /ˈseləfeɪn/ *n*. [P] a thin transparent wrapping material made from viscose (first produced in Switzerland in 1908). [f. CELLULOSE, cf. DIAPHANOUS]

cellular /ˈseljʊlə(r)/ *adj*. consisting of cells; (of blankets etc.) woven with an open mesh. —**cellularity** /-ˈlærɪtɪ/ *n*. [f. foll.]

cellule /ˈselju:l/ *n*. a small cell or cavity. [F, or f. L *cellula* (*cella* CELL)]

celluloid /ˈseljʊlɔɪd/ *n*. a plastic made from camphor and cellulose nitrate. [f. foll.]

cellulose /ˈseljʊləʊz, -əʊs/ *n*. **1** the main constituent of plant-cell walls and derived textile fibres. **2** (*pop*.) paint or lacquer made from solutions of cellulose acetate or nitrate. [f. F or L (as CELLULE)]

Celsius /ˈselsɪəs/ *adj*. of or using the Celsius (centigrade) scale of temperature. [f. A. *Celsius* (1701–44), Swedish astronomer who advocated this scale]

Celt /kelt/ *n*. a member of one of a group of western European peoples (including the ancient Gauls and Britons, and modern Bretons, Cornish, Gaels, Irish, Manx, and Welsh). [f. L f. Gk *Keltoi*]

Celtic /ˈkeltɪk/ *adj*. of the Celts and kindred peoples, or their languages. —*n*. a sub-group of the Indo-European language group, today spoken in the British Isles and in Brittany, divided into two groups, Goidelic (consisting of Irish, Scots Gaelic, and Manx) and Brythonic (consisting of Welsh, Cornish, and Breton). [f. L (as CELT) or F]

cement /sɪˈment/ *n.* a grey powder made by burning lime and clay, which sets to a stonelike mass when mixed with water and is used as a building material, mortar, etc.; any soft substance that sets firm. —*v.t.* to join with or like cement; to apply cement to, to line with cement. —**cementation** /-ˈteɪʃ(ə)n/ *n.* [f. OF f. L *caementum* quarry stone]

cemetery /ˈsemɪtərɪ/ *n.* a burial ground other than a churchyard. [f. L f Gk *koimeterion* dormitory]

cenotaph /ˈsenətɑ:f/ *n.* a sepulchral monument to persons buried elsewhere. [f. Gk, = empty tomb]

censer /ˈsensə(r)/ *n.* a small container in which incense is burnt, swung on chains in a religious ceremony to disperse its fragrance. [f. AF (as INCENSE[1])]

censor /ˈsensə(r)/ *n.* an official with the power to suppress parts of books, films, letters, news, etc., on grounds of obscenity, risk to security, etc. —*v.t.* to treat (books, films, etc.) in this way. —**censorship** *n.* [L, = magistrate who registered citizens and could exclude from public functions on moral grounds]

censorious /senˈsɔ:rɪəs/ *adj.* severely critical, fault-finding. [f. prec.]

censure /ˈsenʃə(r)/ *n.* strong criticism or condemnation, a rebuke. —*v.t.* to blame and rebuke. [f. OF f L (*censēre* assess; cf. CENSOR)]

census /ˈsensəs/ *n.* an official count of a population or of a class of things. [L, as CENSOR]

cent *n.* one hundredth of a US dollar or certain other metric units of currency; a coin of this value. [f. F, It. or L (*centum* hundred)]

Centaur /ˈsentɔ:(r)/ *n.* (*Gk myth.*) a member of a tribe of wild creatures with the upper part of a man and the hindquarters of a horse.

centaury /ˈsentɔ:rɪ/ *n.* a plant of the genus *Centaurium* with small pink flowers usually in clusters, especially the common centaury of the herbalists (*C. erythraea*). [f. L f. Gk, = centaur, because said to have been discovered and used medicinally by Chiron the Centaur, tutor of Achilles]

centenarian /sentɪˈneərɪən/ *n.* a person a hundred or more years old. [as foll.]

centenary /senˈti:nərɪ/ *n.* a hundredth anniversary. —*adj.* of such an anniversary. [f. L (*centeni* 100 each)]

centennial /senˈtenɪəl/ *adj.* & *n.* centenary. [as prec.]

centesimal /senˈtesɪm(ə)l/ *adj.* reckoning or reckoned by hundredths. [f. L (*centum* hundred)]

centi- *in comb.* **1** one hundredth. **2** a hundred. [f. L *centum* hundred]

centigrade /ˈsentɪgreɪd/ *adj.* of or having a temperature scale of a hundred degrees, 0° being the freezing-point and 100° the boiling-point of water. [f. CENTI- + L *gradus* step]

centigram /ˈsentɪgræm/ *n.* one hundredth of a gram.

centilitre /ˈsentɪli:tə(r)/ *n.* one hundredth of a litre.

centimetre /ˈsentɪmi:tə(r)/ *n.* one hundredth of a metre, about 0.4 inch.

centipede /ˈsentɪpi:d/ *n.* a many-legged arthropod of the class Chilopoda, having one pair of legs to each segment (cf. MILLEPEDE). [f. F or L (*centum* hundred, *pes pedis* foot)]

central /ˈsentr(ə)l/ *adj.* **1** of, at, from, or forming the centre. **2** chief, most important. —**central bank,** a national (not commercial) bank, issuing currency. **central heating,** a method of warming a building from one source by circulating hot water, hot air, or steam in pipes, or by linked radiators. **Central Intelligence Agency,** a federal agency in the USA, established in 1947, responsible for co-ordinating government intelligence activities. **central nervous system,** the brain and spinal cord. **Central Powers,** Germany and Austria-Hungary before 1914. —**centrality** /-ˈtrælɪtɪ/ *n.*, **centrally** *adv.* [F or f. L (*centrum* centre)]

centralism /ˈsentrəlɪz(ə)m/ *n.* a centralizing policy, especially in administration. —**centralist** *n.* [f. prec.]

centralize /ˈsentrəlaɪz/ *v.t.* to concentrate (administration etc.) at a single centre; to subject to such a system. —**centralization** /-ˈzeɪʃ(ə)n/ *n.* [f. CENTRAL]

centre /ˈsentə(r)/ *n.* **1** the middle point or part; a pivot or axis of rotation. **2** a point towards which interest is directed or from which administration etc. is organized; a main source of dispersal. **3** a place where certain activities or facilities are concentrated. **4** those members of a political party or group holding moderate opinions, between two extremes. **5** a centre-forward. —*adj.* of or at the centre. —*v.t./i.* **1** to place in or at the centre. **2** to concentrate or be concentrated *in* or *on*. **3** to kick or hit from the wing towards the middle of the pitch in football or hockey. —**centre-forward, centre-half** *ns.* the middle player in the forward (or half-back) line in football etc. **centre of gravity,** the point round which the mass of a body is evenly distributed. **centre-piece** *n.* an ornament for the middle of a table etc., a principal item. [f. OF or L f. Gk *kentron* sharp point]

centrifugal /senˈtrɪfjʊg(ə)l, -ˈfju:-/ *adj.* moving

away from the centre or axis. —**centrifugal force,** the apparent tendency of a rotating body to move outwards from the centre of rotation (see CENTRIFUGE). **centrifugal machine,** one in which the rotation causes this. —**centrifugally** *adv.* [f. L *centrum* centre + *fugere* flee]

centrifuge /ˈsentrɪfju:dʒ/ *n.* a machine using centrifugal force to separate substances of different densities (e.g. milk and cream. —*v.t.* to subject to centrifugal motion; to separate by using a centrifuge. [F (as prec.)]

centripetal /senˈtrɪpɪt(ə)l, -ˈpi:-/ *adj.* moving towards the centre or axis. [f. L (*centrum* centre, *petere* seek)]

centrist /ˈsentrɪst/ *n.* one who adopts a middle position in politics etc. —**centrism** *n.* [f. CENTRE]

centurion /cenˈtjʊərɪən/ *n.* an officer in the Roman army, originally one commanding a hundred infantrymen. [f. L (as foll.)]

century /ˈsentjʊrɪ, -tʃərɪ/ *n.* **1** a period of a hundred years, especially one reckoned from the birth of Christ. **2** a score of 100; (in cricket) a batsman's score of at least one hundred runs in an innings. [f. L *centuria* (*centum* hundred)]

cephalic /sɪˈfælɪk/ *adj.* of or in the head. —**cephalic index,** the ratio of the maximum skull width to maximum skull length, multiplied by 100. [f. F f. L f. Gk (*kephalē* head)]

cephalopod /ˈsefələpɒd/ *n.* a mollusc of the class Cephalopoda, having a distinct head with a ring of tentacles round the mouth. [f. Gk *kephalē* head + *pous podos* foot]

ceramic /sɪˈræmɪk/ *adj.* of pottery or similar substances. —*n.* **1** a ceramic article or substance. **2** (in *pl.*) the art of making pottery etc. [f. Gk (*keramos* pottery)]

cereal /ˈsɪərɪəl/ *adj.* of edible grain. —*n.* **1** edible grain or the grass producing it. **2** a breakfast food made from this. [f. L *cerealis* f. *Ceres*, ancient Italian corn-goddess]

cerebellum /serɪˈbeləm/ *n.* a small part of the brain, located in the back of the skull. [L, dim. of CEREBRUM]

cerebral /ˈserɪbr(ə)l/ *adj.* of the brain; intellectual. —**cerebral palsy,** spastic paralysis resulting from brain damage before or at birth, with jerky or uncontrolled movements. [f. L *cerebrum* brain]

cerebration /serɪˈbreɪʃ(ə)n/ *n.* activity of the brain. [as prec.]

cerebro-spinal /serɪbrəʊˈspaɪn(ə)l/ *adj.* of the brain and spinal cord. [f. foll. + SPINAL]

cerebrum /ˈserɪbrəm/ *n.* the principal part of the brain, located in the front of the skull. [L]

ceremonial /serɪˈməʊnɪəl/ *adj.* of a ceremony, used in ceremonies; formal. —*n.* ceremony; a system of rules for ceremonies. —**ceremonially** *adv.* [f. L (as CEREMONY)]

ceremonious /serɪˈməʊnɪəs/ *adj.* full of ceremony; elaborately performed. —**ceremoniously** *adv.* [as foll.]

ceremony /ˈserɪmənɪ/ *n.* **1** a set of formal acts, especially those used on a religous or public occasion. **2** formal or elaborate politeness. [f. OF or L *caerimonia* religous worship]

cerise /səˈri:z/ *adj.* & *n.* light clear red. [F, = cherry]

cerium /ˈsɪərɪəm/ *n.* a soft iron-grey metallic element of the lanthanide series, symbol Ce, atomic number 58. [f. *Ceres*, asteroid discovered (1801) just before the element]

certain /ˈsɜ:t(ə)n/ *adj.* **1** feeling sure, convinced. **2** known without doubt; that can be relied on to happen, be effective, etc. **3** that will not be further specified or defined. **4** small in amount but definitely there. [f. OF f. L *certus* settled]

certainly *adv.* without doubt; yes. [f. prec.]

certainty *n.* **1** an undoubted fact; an indubitable prospect. **2** absolute conviction. [f. AF (as CERTAIN)]

certifiable /ˈsɜ:tɪfaɪəb(ə)l/ *adj.* that can be certified. [f. CERTIFY]

certificate /səˈtɪfɪkət/ *n.* an official written or printed statement attesting certain facts. —**certificated** *adj.*, **certification** /-ˈkeɪʃ(ə)n/ *n.* [f. F or L (as foll.)]

certify /ˈsɜ:tɪfaɪ/ *v.t.* to state formally on a certificate; to declare (a person) officially to be insane. [f. OF f. L (as CERTAIN)]

certitude /ˈsɜ:tɪtju:d/ *n.* a feeling of certainty. [as prec.]

cerulean /səˈru:lɪən/ *adj.* sky-blue. [f. L *caeruleus* (*caelum* sky)]

cervix /ˈsɜ:vɪks/ *n.* (*pl.* **-vices** /-vɪsi:z/) the neck; a necklike structure, especially the opening of the womb. —**cervical** /səˈvaɪk(ə)l, ˈsɜ:vɪk(ə)l/ *adj.* [L]

cessation /seˈseɪʃ(ə)n/ *n.* ceasing; a pause. [f. L (*cessare* cease)]

cession /ˈseʃ(ə)n/ *n.* the act of ceding. [f. OF or L (as CEDE)]

cesspit /ˈsespɪt/ *n.* a covered pit for temporary storage of liquid waste or sewage. [f. foll.]

cesspool /ˈsespu:l/ *n.* = prec. [perh. alt. f. earlier *cesperalle* f. *suspiral* water-pipe]

cetacean /sɪˈteɪʃ(ə)n/ *n.* a member of the mammalian order Cetacea, containing whales, dolphins, and porpoises. —*adj.* of cetaceans. [f. L f. Gk *kētos* whale]

cetane /ˈsi:teɪn/ *n.* a hydrocarbon of the paraffin series, found in petroleum. [f. SPERMACETI]

Cf *symbol* californium.

cf. *abbr.* compare. [f. L *confer*]

CFC *abbr.* chloro-flurocarbon, any of various usually gaseous substances thought to be harmful to the ozone layer in the earth's atmosphere.

Chablis /ˈʃæbli:/ *n.* a white burgundy. [f. *Chablis* in E. France]

chadar, chador *ns.* variants of CHUDDAR.

chafe /tʃeɪf/ *v.t./i.* **1** to rub (the skin etc.) to restore warmth. **2** to make or become sore by rubbing. **3** to become irritated or impatient. [f. OF *chauffer* f. L *calefacere* make warm]

chafer /ˈtʃeɪfə(r)/ *n.* a large slow-moving beetle, especially a cockchafer. [OE]

chaff /tʃɑ:f/ *n.* **1** corn-husks separated from the seed by threshing etc.; chopped hay or straw as cattle-food; worthless stuff. **2** good-humoured teasing or joking. —*v.t.* to tease or joke in a good-humoured way. [OE]

chaffer /ˈtʃæfə(r)/ *v.i.* to bargain or haggle. [OE]

chaffinch /ˈtʃæfɪntʃ/ *n.* a common European finch (*Fringilla coelebs*). [OE (as CHAFF, FINCH)]

chafing-dish /ˈtʃeɪfɪŋ/ *n.* a pan with a heater under it for cooking food or keeping it warm at the table. [f. CHAFE]

chagrin /ˈʃægrɪn/ *n.* a feeling of annoyance and embarrassment or disappointment. —*v.t.* to affect with chagrin. [F]

chain *n.* **1** a series of connected metal links or rings, used for hauling, supporting, or restraining things or worn as an ornament; a connected series or sequence. **2** a number of shops, hotels, etc., owned by a single company. **3** a unit of length for measuring land, 66 ft. —*v.t.* to fasten or restrain with a chain. —**chain-gang** *n.* a group of prisoners chained together for manual work. **chain-letter** *n.* a letter of which the recipient is asked to make copies and send these to others, who will do the same. **chain-mail** *n.* armour made from interlaced rings. **chain reaction,** a chemical or nuclear reaction the products of which themselves cause further reactions; a series of events in which each causes or influences the next. **chain-saw** *n.* a saw consisting of an endless loop of chain with teeth set in it. **chain-smoke** *v.i* to smoke many cigarettes in a continuous succession. **chain-stitch** *n.* an ornamental sewing or crochet stitch like a chain; a stitch made by a sewing machine using a single thread that is hooked through its own loop on the under-side of the fabric sewn. **chain store,** one of a series of shops owned by the same firm and selling similar goods. [f. OF f. L *catena*]

chair *n.* **1** a movable seat with a back, for one person. **2** a position of authority at a meeting, the chairmanship. **3** a professorship. **4** (*US*) the electric chair. —*v.t.* **1** to seat in a chair of honour. **2** to carry in triumph on the shoulders of a group. **3** to act as chairman of. —**chair-lift** *n.* a series of chairs suspended from an endless cable for carrying passengers up a mountain etc. [f. AF f. L f. Gk *cathedra*]

chairman *n.* (*pl.* **-men**) the person presiding over a meeting; the regular president of a committee, board of directors, etc. —**chairwoman** *n.* (*pl.* **-women**), **chairperson** *n.*, **chairmanship** *n.*

chaise longue /ʃeɪz ˈlɒŋ/ a low chair with the seat long enough to support the sitter's legs. [F, = long chair]

chalcedony /kælˈsed(ə)nɪ/ *n.* a type of quartz including many varieties of precious stone, e.g. onyx and jasper. [f. L f. Gk]

chalcolithic /kælkəˈlɪθɪk/ *adj.* of a period in which both stone and bronze implements were used. [f. Gk *khalkos* copper + *lithos* stone]

chalet /ˈʃæleɪ/ *n.* **1** a Swiss mountain hut or cottage; a house in similar style. **2** a small hut in a holiday camp etc. [Swiss F]

chalice /ˈtʃælɪs/ *n.* a vessel like a large goblet for holding wine, one from which wine is drunk at the Eucharist. [f. OF f. L *calix* cup]

chalk /tʃɔ:k/ *n.* a white soft limestone used for burning into lime; a stick of this or similar substance, white or coloured, used for writing or drawing. —*v.t.* to mark, draw, rub, etc., with chalk. —**by a long chalk,** by far. **chalk-stripe** *n.* a textile pattern of thin white stripes on a dark background. **chalk up,** to register (a success etc.). —**chalky** *adj.* [OE f. L CALX]

challenge /ˈtʃælɪndʒ/ *n.* **1** a call to demonstrate one's ability or strength, especially in a contest. **2** a call or demand to respond, a sentry's call for a person to identify himself. **3** a formal objection, e.g. to a juryman. **4** a challenging task. —*v.t.* **1** to issue a challenge to. **2** to raise a formal objection to. **3** to question the truth or rightness of. **4** (*abs.*, usu. in *partic.*) to offer problems that test one's abilities, to be stimulating. —**challenger** *n.* [f. OF f. L *calumnia* calumny]

chalybeate /kəˈlɪbɪət/ *adj.* (of water or springs) impregnated with iron salts. [f. L f. Gk *khalups* steel]

chamber /ˈtʃeɪmbə(r)/ *n.* **1** an assembly hall; the council or other body that meets in it. **2** (in *pl.*) a set of rooms in a larger building, a judge's room for hearing cases that do not need to be taken in court. **3** a cavity or compartment in the body of an animal or plant, or in machinery. **4** (*archaic*) a room, especially a bedroom. —**chamber music,** music written for a small number of players, suitable for performing in a room or small hall. **Chamber of Commerce,** an association of business men etc. to promote local commercial interests. **chamber-pot** *n.* a receptacle for urine etc., used in the bedroom. [f. OF f. L *camera* vaulted chamber]

chamberlain /ˈtʃeɪmbəlɪn/ *n.* an official managing a royal or noble household. [f. OF f. Gmc (as CHAMBER)]

chambermaid *n.* a woman employed to clean and tidy bedrooms in a hotel etc.

chameleon /kəˈmiːlɪən/ *n.* **1** a small lizard able to change colour according to its surroundings. **2** a changeable or inconstant person. [f. L. f. Gk, = ground-lion]

chamfer /ˈtʃæmfə(r)/ *v.t.* to bevel symmetrically. —*n.* a chamfered edge or corner. [f. F (*chant* edge, *fraint* broken)]

chamois /ˈʃæmwɑː/ *n.* **1** (*pl.* same /-wɑːz/) a small wild antelope of goat size, found in the mountains of Europe and Asia. **2** /ˈʃæmɪ/ (also **chamois-leather**) soft yellowish leather from sheep, goats, deer, etc., or a piece of this, used for washing or polishing things. [F]

chamomile var. of CAMOMILE.

champ *v.t./i.* **1** to munch noisily; to make a chewing action or noise. **2** to show impatience. [imit.]

champagne /ʃæmˈpeɪn/ *n.* **1** a naturally sparkling white wine from Champagne in France; a similar wine from elsewhere. **2** a pale straw colour. [f. *Champagne*, former province in E. France]

champion /ˈtʃæmpɪən/ *n.* **1** (freq. *attrib.*) a person or thing that has defeated or surpassed all rivals in a competition. **2** a person who fights or argues in support of another or of a cause. —*v.t.* to support as a champion. [f. OF f. L *campio* fighter (*campus* field)]

championship *n.* **1** the status of a champion in a sport etc.; a contest held to decide the champion. **2** advocacy, defence (of a cause etc.). [f. prec. + -SHIP]

champlevé /ˈʃɑ̃ləveɪ/ *adj.* of or using a style of enamel-work decoration in which hollows are made in a metal surface and filled with enamel. —*n.* this style. [F, = raised field]

chance /tʃɑːns/ **1** the way things happen without known cause or agency; the supposed force governing such happenings, luck, fate. **2** a possibility, likelihood. **3** an opportunity. —*adj.* happening by chance. —*v.t./i.* **1** to happen by chance. **2** to take one's chance of, to risk. —**by chance,** as it turns or turned out; without being planned. **chance on,** to come upon or find by chance. **chance one's arm,** (*colloq.*) to take a chance although failure is possible. **take a chance,** to take a risk, to act in the hope that a particular thing will (or will not) happen. **take chances,** to behave riskily. **take one's chance,** to trust to luck. [f. AF f. L *cadere* fall]

chancel /ˈtʃɑːns(ə)l/ *n.* the part of a church, often screened off, containing the altar. [f. OF f. L *cancelli* grating]

chancellery /ˈtʃɑːns(ə)lərɪ/ *n.* **1** a chancellor's department, residence, or staff. **2** = CHANCERY 2. [f. CHANCERY]

chancellor /ˈtʃɑːns(ə)lə(r)/ *n.* **1** a State or law official of various kinds; the chief minister of State in West Germany and Austria. **2** the non-resident head of a university. —**Chancellor of the Exchequer,** the finance minister of the UK, who prepares the budget. [f. AF f. L *cancellarius* secretary]

Chancery /ˈtʃɑːnsərɪ/ *n.* the Lord Chancellor's division of the High Court of Justice. [contr. of CHANCELLERY]

chancery /ˈtʃɑːnsərɪ/ *n.* **1** a public records office. **2** an office attached to an embassy or consulate. [= prec.]

chancy /ˈtʃɑːnsɪ/ *adj.* risky, uncertain. [f. CHANCE]

chandelier /ʃændəˈlɪə(r)/ *n.* an ornamental branched support for a number of lights, hung from a ceiling. [f. F (as CANDLE)]

chandler /ˈtʃɑːndlə(r)/ *n.* a dealer in ropes, canvas, and other supplies for ships. [f. F (CANDLE)]

change /tʃeɪndʒ/ *v.t./i.* **1** to make or become different; to pass from one form or phase into another. **2** to take or use another instead of; to put fresh clothes or coverings etc. on; to go from one (vehicle, route, etc.) to another; to exchange. **3** to give small money in change for; to give different currency for. —*n.* **1** changing, alteration; substitution of one thing for another, variety; a reserve (of clothing etc.); a fresh occupation or surroundings. **2** money in small units; money returned as the balance when the price is less than the amount tendered. **3** the menopause. **4** (in bell-ringing, usu. in *pl.*) the different orders in which the bells of a peal may be rung. —**change hands,** to pass to a new owner. **change of heart,** a great alteration in one's attitude or feelings. **change of life,** the menopause. **change one's mind,** to adopt a new purpose or way of thinking. **change over,** to change from one system or situation to another. **change-over** *n.* such a change. **change-ringing** *n.* ringing a peal of bells in a series of different orders. [f. AF f. L *cambire* barter]

changeable /ˈtʃeɪndʒəb(ə)l/ *adj.* liable to change, inconstant. [f. prec.]

changeling /ˈtʃeɪndʒlɪŋ/ *n.* a child or thing believed to have been substituted secretly for another, especially by elves etc. [f. CHANGE + -LING]

channel *n.* **1** the sunken bed of a watercourse; the navigable part of a waterway. **2** a piece of water (wider than a strait) connecting two seas. **3** a passage along which a liquid may flow; a sunken course or line along which something may move. **4** any course by which news or information etc. may travel. **5** a band of broadcasting frequencies reserved for a particular programme. **6** a path for transmitting electrical signals or (in computers) data. —*v.t.* (**-ll-**) **1** to form channels or grooves in. **2** to direct along a channel or desired route. —**the Channel,** the English Channel (see ENGLISH). [f. OF f. L *canalis* canal]

Channel Tunnel a tunnel under the English Channel, linking the coasts of England and France.

chant /tʃɑ:nt/ *n.* **1** a melody for psalms and other unmetrical texts, in which an indefinite number of syllables are sung to one opening note. **2** a measured monotonous song. —*v.t.* to sing, especially a chant; to shout or call rhythmically. [f. OF f. L *cantare* sing]

chanter *n.* **1** one who chants. **2** the melody-pipe of bagpipes. [f. prec.]

chanterelle /ʃɑ:ntəˈrel/ *n.* a yellow edible funnel-shaped fungus (*Cantharellus cibarius*). [F, f. L f. Gk *kantharos* drinking-vessel]

chantry /ˈtʃɑ:ntrɪ/ *n.* a chapel endowed for the saying of masses for the founder's soul. [f. AF (*chanter* chant)]

chaos /ˈkeɪɒs/ *n.* **1** utter confusion or disorder. **2** formless primordial matter. —**chaotic** /-ˈɒtɪk/ *adj.*, **chaotically** *adv.* [F or L f. Gk]

chap[1] *n.* (*colloq.*) a man, a fellow. [abbr. of archaic *chapman* pedlar]

chap[2] *v.t./i.* (**-pp-**) (of skin) to split or crack, (of wind etc.) to cause to develop chaps. —*n.* (usu. in *pl.*) a crack in the skin. [perh. rel. to Du. *kappen* chop off]

chap[3] *n.* the lower jaw or half of the cheek, especially of a pig, as food. [var. of CHOP[3]; orig. unkn.]

chaparral /tʃæpəˈræl, ʃæ-/ *n.* (*US*) dense tangled brushwood, especially in the south-western USA and Mexico. [Sp. (*chaparra* evergreen oak)]

chapati, chapatti variants of CHUPATTY.

chap-book *n.* (*hist.*) a small pamphlet of tales, ballads, tracts, etc., hawked by chapmen. [as CHAPMAN]

chapel /ˈtʃæp(ə)l/ *n.* **1** a place used for Christian worship, other than a cathedral or parish church; a service in this. **2** a separate part of a cathedral or church, with its own altar. **3** a section of a trade union in a printing works. [f. OF f. L, dim. of *cappa* cloak; the first chapel was a sanctuary in which St Martin's sacred cloak was kept by *capellani* (chaplains)]

chaperon /ˈʃæpərəʊn/ *n.* an older or married woman in charge of a young unmarried woman on social occasions. —*v.t.* to act as a chaperon to —**chaperonage** *n.* [F, = hood]

chaplain /ˈtʃæplɪn/ *n.* a clergyman attached to a private chapel, institution, regiment, ship, etc. —**chaplaincy** *n.* [f. AF f. L (see CHAPEL)]

chaplet /ˈtʃæplɪt/ *n.* **1** a wreath for the head. **2** a short rosary. [f. OF f. L *cappa* cap]

chapman *n.* (*pl.* **-men**) (*hist.*) a pedlar. [OE (*cēap* barter, MAN)]

chapter /ˈtʃæptə(r)/ *n.* **1** a division of a book; (*fig.*) a period of time. **2** the canons of a cathedral or the monks of a particular order etc.; a meeting of these. —**chapter house,** a building used for such meetings. [f. OF f. L *capitulum*, dim. of *caput* head]

char[1] *v.t./i.* (**-rr-**) to make or become black by burning; to burn to charcoal. [back-formation f. CHARCOAL]

char[2] *n.* a charwoman. —*v.i.* (**-rr-**) to work as a charwoman. [earlier *chare* f. OE *cerr* a turn]

char[3] *n.* (*pl.* same) a small trout of the genus *Salvelinus*. [orig. unkn.]

charabanc /ˈʃærəbæŋ/ *n.* a long vehicle, originally horse-drawn and open, later an early form of motor coach, with seating on transverse benches facing forward. [f. F *char-à-bancs* benched carriage]

character /ˈkærɪktə(r)/ *n.* **1** the distinguishing qualities of a person, group, or thing; a person's moral qualities; moral strength. **2** reputation; good reputation. **3** a person having specified qualities; an eccentric. **4** a person in a play, novel, etc. **5** a description of a person's qualities, a testimonial. **6** (often in *pl.*) an inscribed letter or graphic symbol, as in an alphabet. **7** a physical characteristic of a biological species. [f. OF f. L f. Gk, = stamp, impression]

characteristic /kærɪktəˈrɪstɪk/ *adj.* distinctive of a particular individual, class, etc. —*n.* a characteristic feature or quality. —**characteristically** *adv.* [f. F or L (as prec.)]

characterize /ˈkærɪktəraɪz/ *v.t.* **1** to sum up the qualities of. **2** to be characteristic of. —**characterization** /-ˈzeɪʃ(ə)n/ *n.* [f. F or L f. Gk (as CHARACTER)]

charade /ʃəˈrɑ:d/ *n.* **1** (in *pl.*) a game in which a word has to be guessed from clues to each syllable given in acted scenes. **2** an absurd pretence. [F f. Prov. (*charra* chatter)]

charcoal /ˈtʃɑ:kəʊl/ *n.* the black carbonized residue of partially burnt wood etc., ued as a filtering material, as fuel, or for drawing. —**charcoal grey,** very dark grey. [rel. to COAL]

charge *n.* **1** the price asked for goods or services. **2** a formal accusation. **3** an admonition given about one's duty or responsibility; a task or duty. **4** custody. **5** an impetuous attack in battle etc. **6** the quantity of material used in an apparatus in a single operation, especially of explosive in a gun. **7** the amount of electricity contained in a substance; energy stored chemically for conversion into electricity. **8** a heraldic device or bearing. —*v.t./i.* **1** to ask as a price; to ask (a person) for a price; to debit (a cost) *to* an account. **2** to accuse formally of a crime. **3** to entrust *with* a task; to admonish *to*. **4** to advance impetuously; to attack thus. **5** to give an electric charge to; to store energy in; to load with the requisite amount of explosive etc. **6** to saturate with liquid, vapour, or chemical. —**in charge,** in command. **take charge,** to take control. [f. OF f. L *carricare* load (*carrus* car)]

chargé d'affaires /ʃɑːʒeɪ dæˈfeə(r)/ (*pl.* **-es** /-eɪ/) an ambassador's deputy; an envoy to a minor country. [F, = entrusted with affairs]

charger *n.* **1** a cavalry horse. **2** an apparatus for charging a battery. [f. CHARGE]

chariot /ˈtʃærɪət/ *n.* a two-wheeled horse-drawn vehicle used in ancient warfare and racing. —**charioteer** /-ɪəˈtɪə(r)/ *n.* [f. OF (*char* car)]

charisma /kəˈrɪzmə/ *n.* the capacity to inspire devotion and enthusiasm; divinely conferred power or talent. —**charismatic** /kærɪzˈmætɪk/ *adj.* [L f. Gk (*kharis* favour, grace)]

charitable /ˈtʃærɪtəb(ə)l/ *adj.* **1** generous in giving to those in need; lenient in judging others. **2** connected with organized charities. —**charitably** *adv.* [f. foll.]

charity /ˈtʃærɪtɪ/ *n.* **1** kindness or voluntary giving to those in need; an organization for helping those in need; help so given. **2** leniency in judging others; love towards others. [f. OF f. L *caritas* (*carus* dear)]

charlady *n.* a charwoman. [f. CHAR²]

charlatan /ˈʃɑːlətən/ *n.* one falsely claiming to have a special knowledge or skill. —**charlatanism** *n.* [F f. It., = babbler]

Charleston /ˈtʃɑːlstən/ *n.* a lively American dance of the 1920s, with side-kicks from the knee. [f. *Charleston* in S. Carolina]

charlock /ˈtʃɑːlɒk/ *n.* a mustardlike weed (*Sinapis arvensis*) with yellow flowers. [OE]

charlotte /ˈʃɑːlɒt/ *n.* **1** a pudding made of stewed apple or other fruit with a covering or layer of crumbs, biscuits, etc. **2** a moulded dessert consisting of a creamy filling enclosed in sponge fingers. [F]

charm *n.* **1** attractiveness, the power of arousing love or admiration; an attractive feature. **2** an act, object, or words believed to have occult power; a trinket on a bracelet etc. —*v.t.* **1** to delight; to influence by personal charm. **2** to influence by or as if by magic. —**charmer** *n.* [f. OF f. L *carmen* song, spell]

charming *adj.* delightfully attractive. —**charmingly** *adv.* [f. prec.]

charnel-house /ˈtʃɑːn(ə)l/ a place where the bodies or bones of the dead are kept. [F f. L (as CARNAL)]

Charollais /ˈʃærəleɪ/ *n.* a French breed of large white beef-cattle; an animal of this breed. [f. Monts du *Charollais* in E. France]

chart *n.* **1** a map for those navigating on water or in the air; an outline map for showing special information. **2** a diagram, graph, or table giving information in tabular form; (in *pl.*) those listing the recordings currently most popular. —*v.t.* to make a chart of, to map. [f. F f. L *charta* card]

charter *n.* **1** a document from a ruler or government, conferring rights or laying down a constitution. **2** the chartering of an aircraft, ship, etc. —*v.t.* **1** to grant a charter to; to found by charter. **2** to let or hire (an aircraft, ship, etc.) for private use. —**chartered accountant, surveyor,** etc., one belonging to a professional body that has a royal charter. **charter flight,** a flight by chartered aircraft. [f. OF f. L, dim. of *charta* card]

Chartism *n.* a popular movement in Britain for electoral and social reform, 1837–48, whose principles were set out in a manifesto called *The People's Charter*. —**Chartist** *n.* [f. prec.]

chartreuse /ʃɑːˈtrɜːz/ *n.* **1** a pale green or yellow aromatic brandy liqueur. **2** its green colour. **3** fruit enclosed in jelly. [f. *Chartreuse*, monastery near Grenoble]

charwoman *n.* (*pl.* **-women**) a woman hired by the hour to clean a house or other building. [f. CHAR²]

chary /ˈtʃeərɪ/ *adj.* cautious, wary; sparing *of*. [OE, rel. to CARE]

chase¹ /tʃeɪs/ *v.t./i.* **1** to go quickly after in order to capture, overtake, or drive away. **2** to hurry. **3** (*colloq.*) to try to attain. —*n.* **1** chasing, pursuit; hunting, especially as a sport. **2** unenclosed park-land, originally for hunting. [f. OF f. L *captare* (*capere* catch)]

chase² /tʃeɪs/ *v.t.* to engrave or emboss (metal). [f. F (as CASE²)]

chaser *n.* **1** a horse for steeplechasing. **2** a drink taken after another of a different kind. [f. CHASE¹]

chasm /ˈkæz(ə)m/ *n.* **1** a very deep cleft in the ground etc. **2** a wide difference of feeling, interests, etc. [f. L f. Gk, = gaping hollow]

chassis /ˈʃæsɪ, -iː/ *n.* (*pl.* **chassis** /-iːz/) the base-frame of a motor vehicle, carriage, etc.; a metal frame to carry radio etc. equipment. [f. F f. L (CASE²)]

chaste /tʃeɪst/ *adj.* **1** virgin, celibate; not having sexual intercourse except with one's spouse. **2** simple in style, not ornate. —**chastely** *adv.* [f. OF f. L *castus*]

chasten /ˈtʃeɪs(ə)n/ *v.t.* to subdue the pride *of*. [f. OF f. L *castigare* castigate]

chastise /tʃæˈstaɪz/ *v.t.* to punish, especially by beating. —**chastisement** *n.* [app. rel. to prec.]

chastity /ˈtʃæstɪtɪ/ *n.* **1** virginity, celibacy. **2** simplicity of style. [f. OF f. L (*castus* chaste)]

chasuble /ˈtʃæzjʊb(ə)l/ *n.* a loose sleeveless outer vestment worn by a priest celebrating the Eucharist. [f. OF, ult. f. L *casula* hooded cloak, dim. of *casa* cottage]

chat *n.* a friendly informal conversation. —*v.i.*

(**-tt-**) to hold a chat. —**chat up,** (*colloq.*) to chat to a person flirtatiously or with a particular motive. **chat show,** a television programme in which people are interviewed. [f. CHATTER]

château /ˈʃætəʊ/ *n.* (*pl.* **-eaux** /-əʊz/) a large French country house or castle. [F, = castle]

chatelaine /ˈʃæt(ə)leɪn/ *n.* **1** the mistress of a large house. **2** (*hist.*) a set of short chains attached to a woman's belt, for carrying keys etc. [F (as prec.)]

chattel /ˈʃæt(ə)l/ *n.* (usu. in *pl.*) a movable possession (as opposed to a house or land). [f. OF (as CATTLE)]

chatter /ˈtʃætə(r)/ *v.i.* **1** to talk quickly, incessantly, trivially, or indiscreetly. **2** (of a bird) to emit short quick notes. **3** (of the teeth) to click repeatedly together. —*n.* chattering talk or sound. [imit.]

chatterbox *n.* a talkative person.

chatty *adj.* **1** fond of chatting. **2** resembling chat. —**chattily** *adv.*, **chattiness** *n.* [f. CHAT]

chauffeur /ˈʃəʊfə(r), ʃəʊˈfɜ:(r)/ *n.* a person employed to drive a car. —*v.t.* to drive as chauffeur. —**chauffeuse** /-z/ *n.fem.* [F, = stoker]

chauvinism /ˈʃəʊvɪnɪz(ə)m/ *n.* **1** exaggerated or aggressive patriotism. **2** excessive or prejudiced support or loyalty for one's cause or group. —**chauvinist** *n.*, **chauvinistic** /-ˈnɪstɪk/ *adj.* [f. *Chauvin*, Napoleonic veteran, character in French play (1831)]

cheap *adj.* **1** low in price, worth more than it cost; charging low prices, offering good value; **2** poor in quality, of low value; showy but worthless, silly. —*adv.* cheaply. —**cheaply** *adv.*, **cheapness** *n.* [f. obs. phr. *good cheap* (*cheap* bargain, f. OE ult. f. L *caupo* innkeeper)]

cheapen *v.t./i.* to make or become cheap; to depreciate, to degrade. [f. prec.]

cheapjack *n.* a seller of shoddy goods at low prices. —*adj.* of poor quality, shoddy.

cheat *v.t./i.* to trick or deceive, to deprive *of* by trickery; to act fraudulently or dishonestly. —*n.* **1** one who cheats. **2** a deception, a trick. [as ESCHEAT]

check[1] *n.* **1** a stopping or slowing of motion, a pause; a loss of the scent in hunting. **2** a restraint. **3** a control to secure accuracy; a test or examination to see that something is correct or in good working order. **4** a receipt; a bill in a restaurant. **5** (*US*) a cheque. **6** (in chess) exposure of a king to possible capture. —*v.t./i.* **1** to stop or slow the motion of suddenly, to restrain; to make a sudden stop. **2** to test or examine for correctness or good working order. **3** (*US*) to correspond when compared. **4** (in chess) to threaten (an opponent's king). —**check in,** to register one's arrival at a hotel, airport, etc. **check on** *or* **up** *or* **up on**, to examine or investigate the correctness, honesty, etc., of. **check out,** to leave a hotel, airport, etc., with proper formalities; to test (a possibility). **check-out** *n.* checking out; a place where goods are paid for by customers in a supermarket. **check-up** *n.* a thorough examination, especially a medical one. [f. OF, ult. f. Pers., = king]

check[2] *n.* a cross-lined pattern of small squares. [prob. f. CHEQUER]

checked *adj.* having a check pattern. [f. CHECK[2]]

checkers *n.pl.* (usu. treated as *sing.*) (*US*) the game of draughts. [var. of CHEQUER]

checkmate *n.* **1** (in chess) a check from which the king cannot escape. **2** a final defeat. —*v.t.* **1** to put in checkmate. **2** to defeat finally, to foil. [f. OF, ult. f. Pers. *shāh māt* the king is dead]

Cheddar /ˈtʃedə(r)/ *n.* a hard cheese of a kind originally made at Cheddar in Somerset.

cheek *n.* **1** either side of the face below the eye. **2** impudent speech; quiet arrogance. —*v.t.* to speak impudently to. —**cheek-bone** *n.* the bone below the eye. **cheek by jowl,** in juxtaposition. [OE]

cheeky *adj.* impertinent, saucy. —**cheekily** *adv.*, **cheekiness** *n.* [f. CHEEK]

cheep *n.* the weak shrill cry of a young bird. —*v.i.* to make this cry. [imit.]

cheer *n.* **1** a shout of encouragement or applause. **2** cheerfulness. —*v.t./i.* **1** to raise a cheer; to applaud or urge *on* with cheers. **2** to comfort or gladden. —**cheer up,** to make or become more cheerful. [f. AF, = face, ult. f. Gk *kara* head]

cheerful *adj.* in good spirits, visibly happy; pleasantly bright. —**cheerfully** *adv.*, **cheerfulness** *n.* [f. CHEER + -FUL]

cheerio /tʃɪərɪˈəʊ/ *int.* (*colloq.*) expressing good wishes on parting; goodbye. [f. CHEER]

cheerless *adj.* gloomy, comfortless. [f. CHEER + -LESS]

cheery *adj.* ebulliently cheerful. —**cheerily** *adv.* [f. CHEER]

cheese /tʃi:z/ *n.* **1** a food made from milk curds or occasionally from whey; a shaped mass of this. **2** a thick stiff jam. —**cheese-paring** *adj.* & *n.* stingy, stinginess. —**cheesy** *adj.* [OE, f. L *caseus*]

cheesecake *n.* a tart filled with sweetened curds.

cheesecloth *n.* a thin loosely woven cotton fabric.

cheetah /ˈtʃi:tə/ *n.* a very swift feline resembling a leopard, sometimes used in hunting. [Hindi, perh. f. Skr. *chitraka* speckled]

chef /ʃef/ *n.* a male cook (esp. the head cook) in a restaurant etc. [F, = head]

chef-d'œuvre /ʃeɪˈdəvr/ *n.* (*pl.* ***chefs-d'œuvre***, *pr.* same) a masterpiece. [F]

Chelsea /ˈtʃelsɪ/ *n.* **Chelsea bun,** a kind of rolled currant bun. **Chelsea pensioner,** an inmate of Chelsea Royal Hospital for old or disabled soldiers. **Chelsea ware,** a kind of porcelain made at Chelsea in the 18th c. [name of London borough]

chemical /ˈkemɪk(ə)l/ *adj.* of, using, or produced by chemistry or chemicals —*n.* a substance obtained by or used in a chemical process. —**chemical engineering,** the industrial applications of chemistry. **chemical warfare,** warfare using poison gas and other chemicals. —**chemically** *adv.* [f. F f. L (as ALCHEMY)]

chemise /ʃəˈmi:z/ *n.* a loose-fitting undergarment formerly worn by women, hanging straight from the shoulders; a dress of similar shape. [f. OF f. L *camisia* shirt]

chemist /ˈkemɪst/ *n.* **1** a dealer in medicinal drugs etc. **2** a scientist specializing in chemistry. [f. F (as ALCHEMIST)]

chemistry /ˈkemɪstrɪ/ *n.* **1** the scientific study of substances and their elements and of how they react when combined, etc. **2** the chemical properties, reactions, etc., of a substance. [f. prec.]

chemotherapy /keməʊˈθerəpɪ/ *n.* treatment of disease by drugs and other chemical substances. [f. CHEMICAL + THERAPY]

chenille /ʃəˈni:l/ *n.* a tufty velvety cord or yarn, used for trimming furniture; a fabric made from this. [F, = hairy caterpillar, f. L *canicula* little dog]

cheongsam /tʃɪɒŋˈsæm/ *n.* a Chinese woman's garment with a high neck and slit skirt. [Chinese]

cheque /tʃek/ *n.* a written order for a bank to pay a stated sum from the drawer's account; a printed form for writing this. —**cheque-book** *n.* a book of printed forms for writing cheques. **cheque card,** a card issued by a bank, guaranteeing payment of cheques up to a stated amount. [var. of CHECK[1]]

chequer /ˈtʃekə(r)/ *n.* (chiefly in *pl.*) a pattern of squares of alternating colours, as on a chessboard. —*v.t.* **1** to mark with such a pattern; to variegate. **2** to vary with different elements; (in *p.p.*) marked by vicissitudes of fortune. [f. EXCHEQUER]

cherish /ˈtʃerɪʃ/ *v.t.* to tend lovingly; to be fond of; to cling to (a hope or feeling). [f. OF (*cher* f. L *carus* dear)]

cheroot /ʃəˈru:t/ *n.* a cigar with both ends open. [f. F f. Tamil]

Cherokee /ˈtʃerəki:/ *n.* (*pl.* same) a member of an American Indian tribe formerly inhabiting much of the southern USA. [native name]

cherry /ˈtʃerɪ/ *n.* **1** a small soft round stone-fruit. **2** a tree of the genus *Prunus* bearing this or grown for its ornamental flowers; the wood of this tree. **3** the bright red colour of ripe cherries. —*adj.* bright red. —**cherry brandy,** a liqueur of brandy in which cherries have been steeped. [f. OF f. L perh. f. Gk *kerasos*]

chert /tʃɜ:t/ *n.* a flintlike form of quartz. [orig. unkn.]

cherub /ˈtʃerəb/ *n.* **1** (*pl.* **cherubim**) an angelic being of an order usually grouped with the seraphim. **2** a representation, in art, of a winged chubby child; a pretty or well-behaved child. —**cherubic** /-ˈru:bɪk/ *adj.* [OE, f. Heb.]

chervil /ˈtʃɜ:vɪl/ *n.* a herb (*Anthriscus cerefolium*) used to flavour salads etc. [OE f. L f. Gk *khairephullon*]

Ches. *abbr.* Cheshire.

Cheshire /ˈtʃeʃə(r)/ a north midlands county of England. —**Cheshire cheese,** a crumbly cheese originally made in Cheshire. **like a Cheshire cat,** with a broad fixed grin.

chess *n.* a game of skill played between two persons on a chequered board divided into 64 squares. Each player has 16 'men', which are moved according to strict rules. [f. OF *esches*, pl. of *eschec* (CHECK[1])]

chessboard *n.* the board used in chess (see prec.).

chest *n.* **1** a large strong box for storing or transporting things. **2** the part of the body enclosed by the ribs and breast-bone; the upper front surface of the body. —**chest of drawers,** a piece of furniture consisting of a set of drawers in a frame, for storing clothes etc. [OE f. L f. Gk *kistē*]

chesterfield /ˈtʃestəfiəld/ *n.* a sofa with padded back, seat, and ends. [f. 19th-c. Earl of *Chesterfield*]

chestnut /ˈtʃesnʌt/ *n.* **1** a tree with hard brown nuts, those of the Spanish or sweet chestnut (*Castanea sativa*) being edible; its nut; the wood of this tree. **2** deep reddish-brown. **3** a horse of reddish-brown or yellowish-brown colour. **4** a small hard patch on a horse's leg. **5** an old joke or anecdote. —*adj.* deep reddish-brown or (of horses) yellowish-brown. [f. obs. *chesten* (f. OF f. L f. Gk *kastanea*) + NUT]

cheval-glass /ʃəˈvæl/ *n.* a tall mirror swung on an upright frame. [f. F *cheval* horse, frame]

chevalier /ʃevəˈlɪə(r)/ *n.* a member of certain orders of knighthood, or of the French Legion of Honour etc. [f. AF f. L (*caballus* horse)]

chevron /ˈtʃevrən/ *n.* a V-shaped line, stripe, or bar, especially one worn on the sleeve of a uniform to denote rank. [f. OF f. L *caper* goat; cf. L *capreoli* pair of rafters]

chew *v.t.* to work or grind between the teeth; to make this movement. —*n.* the act of chewing; something for chewing. —**chewing-gum** *n.* flavoured gum for prolonged chewing. **chew over,** (*colloq.*) to think over. [OE]

chez /ʃeɪ/ *prep.* at the home of. [F, f. OF f. L *casa* cottage]

chi /kaɪ/ *n.* the twenty-second letter of the Greek alphabet, = kh, ch.

Chianti /kɪˈæntɪ/ *n.* a dry, usually red, Italian wine. [name of town in Tuscany]

chiaroscuro /kɪɑːrəˈskʊərəʊ/ *n.* treatment of light and shade in painting; light and shade effects in nature. [It. (*chiaro* bright, *oscuro* dark)]

chic /ʃiːk/ *n.* fashionable elegance or stylishness in dress etc. —*adj.* fashionably elegant, stylish. [F]

chicane /ʃɪˈkeɪn/ *v.t./i.* to practise or subject to chicanery; to trick. —*n.* **1** chicanery. **2** an artificial barrier on a motor-racing course etc. [F, = quibble]

chicanery /ʃɪˈkeɪnərɪ/ *n.* quibbles or subterfuges used to gain an advantage. [f. F (as prec.)]

chick *n.* **1** a young bird before or after hatching. **2** (*slang*) a young woman. [f. CHICKEN]

chicken /ˈtʃɪkɪn/ *n.* **1** a young bird, especially of the domestic fowl. **2** the flesh of the domestic fowl as food. —*adj.* (*slang*) afraid to do something, cowardly. —*v.i.* (*slang*) to opt *out* through cowardice. —**chicken-feed** *n.* (*colloq.*) an unimportant or small amount of money etc. **chicken-hearted** *adj.* cowardly. **chicken-pox** *n.* a disease, especially of children, with an eruption of small blisters. **chicken-wire** *n.* light wire netting with hexagonal mesh. [OE]

chick-pea *n.* the legume *Cicer arietinum*; its edible seed. [*chick* for earlier *chich* f. F f. L *cicer*]

chickweed *n.* a small weed, *Stellaria media*, with tiny white flowers.

chicle /ˈtʃɪk(ə)l/ *n.* a gum-like substance obtained from the sapodilla tree, used chiefly in chewing-gum. [Sp., f. Nahuatl]

chicory /ˈtʃɪkərɪ/ *n.* **1** a blue-flowered plant (*Cichorium intybus*) grown for salads etc.; its root ground for use with or instead of coffee. Its crown is known in the USA as *endive*. **2** (*US*) = ENDIVE 1. [f. F f. L f. Gk]

chide *v.t.* (*past* **chided, chid;** *p.p.* **chided, chidden**) (*archaic & literary*) to scold. [OE]

chief *n.* **1** a leader or ruler; the head of a tribe, clan, etc.; a person with the highest authority. **2** (in heraldry) the upper third of a shield. —*adj.* highest in rank or authority; most important. [f. OF f. L *caput* head]

chiefly *adv.* pre-eminently, above all; mainly but not exclusively. [f. prec.]

chieftain /ˈtʃiːftən/ *n.* the chief of a clan or tribe. [f. OF f. L *capitaneus* captain]

chiff-chaff *n.* a small songbird (*Phylloscopus collybita*) of the warbler family. [imit.]

chiffon /ˈʃɪfɒn/ *n.* **1** a light diaphanous fabric of silk, nylon, etc. **2** a very light-textured pudding made with beaten egg-white. [F (*chiffe* rag)]

chiffonier /ʃɪfəˈnɪə(r)/ *n.* **1** a movable low cupboard with a top used as a sideboard. **2** (*US*) a tall chest of drawers. [f. F, = rag-picker, chest of drawers for odds and ends]

chigger *n.* a chigoe; a harvest-bug. [var. of CHIGOE]

chignon /ˈʃiːnjɔ̃/ *n.* a coil or mass of hair worn by women at the back of the head. [F, orig. = nape]

chigoe /ˈtʃɪgəʊ/ *n.* a tropical flea that burrows into the skin. [Carib]

chihuahua /tʃɪˈwɑːwə/ *n.* a dog of a very small smooth-haired breed originating in Mexico. [f. *Chihuahua* State and city in Mexico]

chilblain /ˈtʃɪlbleɪn/ *n.* an inflamed swelling on a finger, toe, etc., caused by exposure to cold and by poor blood- circulation. [f. CHILL + OE *blain* swelling, sore]

child /tʃaɪld/ *n.* (*pl.* **children** /ˈtʃɪldrən/) **1** a young person of either sex before puberty; an unborn or newborn human being; a childish person. **2** a son or daughter; a descendant; a product *of*. —**child's play,** something very easy to do. [OE]

childbirth *n.* the process of giving birth to a child.

childhood *n.* the period or condition of being a child. [f. CHILD + -HOOD]

childish *adj.* immature like a child; unsuited to an adult. —**childishly** *adv.*, **childishness** *n.* [f. CHILD]

childless *adj.* having no children. [f. CHILD + -LESS]

childlike *adj.* having the good qualities of a child, simple and innocent.

chill *n.* **1** unpleasant coldness. **2** an illness with feverish shivering. **3** coldness of manner.—*adj.* chilly. —*v.t./i.* **1** to make or become cold; to harden (molten metal) by contact with cold material; to preserve (meat etc.) at a low temperature without freezing. **2** to depress or dispirit. [OE]

chilli /ˈtʃɪlɪ/ *n.* (*pl.* **chillies**) the small red hot-tasting dried pod of a type of capsicum, used as a relish or made into seasoning. [f. Sp. f. Aztec]

chilly *adj.* rather cold, unpleasantly cold; cold and unfriendly in manner. [f. CHILL]

chime *n.* a tuned set of bells; a series of notes sounded by these. —*v.t./i.* (of bells) to sound; (of a clock) to indicate (the hour) by chiming. —**chime in,** to interject a remark; to agree or correspond *with*. [OE f. L f. Gk *kumbalon* cymbal]

chimera /kɪˈmɪərə/ *n.* a thing of hybrid character. —**chimerical** /-ˈmerɪk(ə)l/ *adj.* [f. Gk *Chimera*, mythological monster with lion's head, serpent's body, and goat's tail]

chimney /ˈtʃɪmnɪ/ *n.* **1** a structure carrying off the smoke or steam of a fire, furnace, engine, etc.; the part of this projecting above a roof. **2** a glass tube protecting the flame of a lamp. **3** a narrow vertical cleft in a rock-face. —**chimney-breast** *n.* the projecting part of a wall round a chimney-flue. **chimney-pot** *n.* an earthenware or metal tube at the top of a chimney. **chimney-stack** *n.* a number of chimneys standing together. **chimney-sweep** *n.* one who removes soot from inside chimneys. [f. OF f. L f. Gk *kaminos* oven]

chimpanzee /tʃɪmpən'zi:/ *n.* a Central and West African ape of the genus *Pan*, of which there are two species: *P. troglodytes*, which resembles man more closely than does any other ape, and the pygmy chimpanzee *P. paniscus*. [f. F f. African native name]

chin *n.* the front of the lower jaw. [OE]

china /'tʃaɪnə/ *n.* fine earthenware, porcelain. —**china clay,** kaolin. [f. Pers. f. *China*, country in E. Asia]

chinagraph /'tʃaɪnəgrɑ:f/ *n.* a kind of pencil that can write on china and glass. [f. CHINA + -GRAPH]

chinchilla /tʃɪn'tʃɪlə/ *n.* **1** a small South American rodent of the genus *Chinchilla*; its soft grey fur. **2** a variety of silver-coloured domestic cat. **3** a variety of rabbit bred for its fur; this fur. [Sp., dim. of *chinche* bug]

Chindit /'tʃɪndɪt/ *n.* a member of the allied forces fighting behind Japanese lines in Burma 1943-5. [f. Burmese *chinthé* a mythical creature]

chine[1] *n.* **1** an animal's backbone; a joint of meat containing part of this. **2** a mountain ridge. —*v.t.* to cut through the backbone of (a carcass). [f. OF f. Gmc (rel. to SHIN and L *spina* spine)]

chine[2] *n.* a deep narrow ravine on the Isle of Wight or Dorset coast. [OE *cinu* chink]

Chinese /tʃaɪ'ni:z/ *n.* (*pl.* same) **1** a native of China; a person of Chinese descent. **2** the language spoken in China. —*adj.* of China or its people or language. —**Chinese lantern,** a collapsible paper lantern; a plant (*Physalis alkekengi*) grown for its inflated papery orange calyx. [f. *China*, country in E. Asia]

chink[1] *n.* a narrow opening or slit. [rel. to CHINE[2]]

chink[2] *n.* a sound like glasses or coins being struck together. —*v.t./i.* to make or cause to make this sound. [imit.]

chinoiserie /ʃɪn'wɑ:zərɪ/ *n.* imitation of Chinese motifs in furniture or decoration; examples of this. [F]

chinook /tʃɪ'nʊk/ *n.* a warm dry wind which blows down the eastern slopes of the Rocky Mountains; (*erron.*) a warm wet oceanic wind west of them. [f. *Chinook*, tribe of N. Amer. Indians]

chintz *n.* a cotton fabric with a printed pattern, usually glazed, used for furnishings. [f. Hindi f. Skr. *citra* variegated]

chip *v.t./i.* (**-pp-**) **1** to knock or break (a piece) *off*, *away*; to break the edge or surface of; to shape or carve thus. **2** to make (potatoes) into chips. —*n.* **1** a piece chipped off; the mark left by this. **2** a long fried strip of potato. **3** a counter used in a game. **4** a microchip. —**chip off the old block,** a child who is very like his father. **chip on one's shoulder,** a feeling of resentment or bitterness about something. **chip in,** (*colloq.*) to interrupt; to contribute money. [f. OE *cipp*, *cyp* beam]

chipboard *n.* material made of compressed wood chips and resin.

chipmunk /'tʃɪpmʌŋk/ *n.* a small striped North American animal of the genus *Tamias*, resembling a squirrel. [Algonquian]

chipolata /tʃɪpə'lɑ:tə/ *n.* a small spicy sausage. [F f. It. (*cipolla* onion)]

Chippendale /'tʃɪpəndeɪl/ *n.* an elegant 18th-c. style of furniture, named after its designer, Thomas Chippendale, English cabinet-maker (d. 1779).

chiromancy /'kaɪrəmænsɪ/ *n.* palmistry. —**chiromancer** *n.* [f. Gk *kheir* hand]

chiropody /kɪ'rɒpədɪ/ *n.* treatment of ailments of the foot. —**chiropodist** *n.* [f. Gk *kheir* hand + *pous* foot]

chiropractic /kaɪrə'præktɪk/ *n.* treatment of disease by manipulation of the spine and joints. —**chiropractor** *n.* [f. Gk *kheir* hand + *praktikos* (cf. PRACTICAL)]

chirp *n.* the short sharp note of a small bird or a grasshopper. —*v.i.* to make this sound. [imit.]

chirrup /'tʃɪrəp/ *n.* a series of chirps. —*v.i.* to make this sound. [trilled form of CHIRP]

chisel /'tʃɪz(ə)l/ *n.* a tool with a bevelled cutting-edge for shaping wood, stone, or metal. —*v.t.* (**-ll-**) to cut or shape with a chisel. [f. OF f. L *caedere* cut]

chit[1] *n.* a shoot, a sprout. —*v.i.* (of seed) to sprout, to germinate. [orig. unkn.]

chit[2] *n.* a young child; a small young woman. [orig. = whelp, cub, kitten, perh. f. CHIT[1]]

chit[3] *n.* a short written note, especially of an order made, a sum owed, etc. [earlier *chitty*, f. Hindi f. Skr. *citra* mark]

chit-chat *n.* chat, gossip. [redupl. of CHAT]

chitin /'kaɪtɪn/ *n.* a substance forming the horny constituent in the exoskeleton of arthropods. —**chitinous** *adj.* [f. F f. Gk *khitōn* garment]

chitterlings *n.pl.* the smaller intestines of a pig, cooked as food. [orig. unkn.]

chivalry /'ʃɪv(ə)lrɪ/ *n.* courtesy and consideration, especially to weaker people; the medieval knightly system with its ethical and social code. —**chivalrous** *adj.* [f. OF f. L, = horseman (as CAVALIER)]

chive *n.* (chiefly in *pl.*) a small herb (*Allium*

schoenoprasum) related to the onion, used for flavouring. [f. OF f. L *cepa* onion]

chivvy /ˈtʃɪvɪ/ *v.t.* to keep urging (a person) to hurry, to harass. [f. *chevy*, prob. f. ballad of *Chevy Chase*, place on Scottish Border]

chloral /ˈklɔːr(ə)l/ *n.* (in full **chloral hydrate**) a white crystalline compound used as a sedative or anaesthetic. [F (*chlore* chlorine, *alcool* alcohol)]

chloride /ˈklɔːraɪd/ *n.* a binary compound of chlorine; a bleaching agent containing this. [f. CHLORINE]

chlorinate /ˈklɔːrɪneɪt/ *v.t.* to treat or disinfect with chlorine. —**chlorination** /-ˈneɪʃ(ə)n/ *n.* [f. foll.]

chlorine /ˈklɔːriːn/ *n.* a non-metallic gaseous element of the halogen group, symbol Cl, atomic number 17. [f. Gk *khlōros* green]

chloroform /ˈklɒrəfɔːm/ *n.* a thin colourless liquid whose inhaled vapour produces unconsciousness. —*v.t.* to make unconscious with this. [f. F (as prec.)]

chlorophyll /ˈklɒrəfɪl/ *n.* the green colouring-matter in plants. [f. F f. Gk *khlōros* green, *phullon* leaf]

choc *n.* (*colloq.*) chocolate; a chocolate. —**choc-ice** *n.* a small bar of ice-cream coated with chocolate. [abbr.]

chock *n.* a block or wedge used to prevent something from moving. —*v.t.* to wedge with a chock or chocks. —**chock-a-block** *adj.* & *adv.* crammed or crowded together. **chock-full** *adj.* crammed full. [prob f. OF *ço(u)che*; orig. unkn.]

chocolate /ˈtʃɒk(ə)lət/ *n.* **1** an edible powder, paste, or solid block made from cacao seeds; a sweet made of or coated with this; a drink made with it. **2** dark-brown colour. —*adj.* **1** made of chocolate; flavoured or coated with chocolate. **2** chocolate-coloured. [f. F or Sp. f. Aztec *chocolatl*]

choice *n.* the act or power of choosing; a person or thing chosen; a variety from which to choose. —*adj.* of special quality. [f. OF f. Gmc, rel. to CHOOSE]

choir /kwaɪə(r)/ *n.* **1** an organized body of singers especially in a church. **2** the part of a church etc. where they sit. [f. OF f. L *chorus*]

choke /tʃəʊk/ *v.t./i.* **1** to stop the breathing of by compressing or blocking the windpipe or (of smoke etc.) by being unfit to breathe; to be unable to breathe from such a cause; to make or become speechless from emotion. **2** to clog, to smother. —*n.* **1** choking, a choking sound. **2** a valve controlling the flow of air into a petrol engine. **3** an inductance coil to smooth variations of alternating current. —**choke off,** (*colloq.*) to silence or discourage, usually by snubbing. [f. OE *ācēocian* (A-, *cēoce* cheek)]

choker *n.* a high collar; a close-fitting necklace. [f. prec.]

choler /ˈkɒlə(r)/ *n.* **1** (*hist.*) one of the four humours. **2** (*poet.* or *archaic*) anger, irascibility. [f. OF f. L f. Gk (*kholē* bile)]

cholera /ˈkɒlərə/ *n.* an infectious often fatal disease with acute diarrhoea. [f. L (as prec.)]

choleric /ˈkɒlərɪk/ *adj.* irascible; angry. [f. OF (as CHOLER)]

cholesterol /kəˈlestərɒl/ *n.* a fatty steroid alcohol found in animal tissues and thought to promote arteriosclerosis. [f. Gk *kholē* bile + *stereos* stiff]

chondrite /ˈkɒndraɪt/ *n.* a meteorite containing granules (*chondrules*), the most abundant type of meteorite in the solar system. [f. G f.Gk *khondros* granule]

chook /tʃʊk/ *n.* (*Austral.* & *NZ*) a domestic fowl, a chicken. [prob. f. dial. *chuck* chick]

choose /tʃuːz/ *v.t./i.* (*past* **chose** /tʃəʊz/; *p.p.* **chosen** /ˈtʃəʊz(ə)n/) to select from a greater number; to decide or desire as a matter of preference. [OE]

choosey /ˈtʃuːzɪ/ *adj.* (*colloq.*) careful and cautious in choosing, hard to please. [f. prec.]

chop[1] *v.t./i.* (**-pp-**) **1** to cut with a heavy blow, usually with an axe or knife; to cut up small in cookery; to make a chopping blow *at*. **2** to strike (a ball) with a heavy edgewise blow. —*n.* **1** a chopping stroke or blow. **2** a thick slice of meat, usually including a rib. [var. of CHAP[2]]

chop[2] *v.t./i.* (**-pp-**) **chop and change,** to keep changing. [perh. var. of obs. *chap* barter]

chop[3] *n.* (usu. in *pl.*) the jaws of a person or animal. [var. of CHAP[3]]

chopper *n.* **1** a short axe with large blade; a butcher's cleaver. **2** (*slang*) a helicopter. [f. CHOP[1]]

choppy *adj.* **1** (of the sea) full of short broken waves. **2** jerky, abrupt. —**choppiness** *n.* [f. CHOP[1]]

chopsticks *n.pl.* a pair of sticks held in one hand and used in China etc. to lift food to the mouth. [f. pidgin English *chop* quick]

chop-suey /tʃɒpˈsuːɪ/ *n.* a Chinese dish of small pieces of meat fried with rice and vegetables. [Chinese, = mixed bits]

choral /ˈkɔːr(ə)l/ *adj.* written for a choir or chorus; sung or spoken by these. —**choral society,** a society formed to sing choral music. [f. L (as CHORUS)]

chorale /kɒˈrɑːl/ *n.* a metrical hymn sung in unison, originally in the Lutheran Church; a harmonized form of this. [f. G (as prec.)]

chord[1] /kɔːd/ *n.* a group of notes sounded together in harmony. [orig. *cord* f. ACCORD]

chord[2] /kɔːd/ *n.* **1** a straight line joining the ends of an arc. **2** (*poet.*) a string of a harp etc. [var. of CORD]

chordate /ˈkɔːdeɪt/ *adj.* of the phylum Chordata, having a notochord. —*n.* a member of this phylum, which includes all the vertebrates as well as a few invertebrate groups, characterized by having a notochord at some stage of the life cycle. [f. L *chorda* CHORD[1], after *Vertebrata* etc.]

chore /tʃɔ:(r)/ *n.* a recurrent or tedious task. [rel. to CHAR[2]]

choreograph /ˈkɒrɪəgrɑ:f/ *v.t.* to provide choreography for. [f. foll.]

choreography /kɒrɪˈɒgrəfɪ/ *n.* the composition of ballet or stage-dances. —**choreographer** *n.*, **choreographic** /-ˈgræfɪk/ *adj.* [f. Gk *khoreia* choral dancing to music (as CHORUS)]

chorister /ˈkɒrɪstə(r)/ *n.* a member of a church choir. [f. OF (*quer* choir)]

chortle *n.* a loud gleeful chuckle. —*v.i.* to utter a chortle. [blend of CHUCKLE and SNORT]

chorus /ˈkɔ:rəs/ *n.* **1** an organized group of singers; a group of singing dancers in an opera, musical comedy, etc. or in an ancient Greek play. **2** a thing sung or said by many at once; the refrain of a song, which the audience join the performer in singing. **3** a character speaking the prologue etc. in a play. —*v.t./i.* to say or sing in chorus. [L f. Gk]

chose, chosen *past* & *p.p.* of CHOOSE.

chough /tʃʌf/ *n.* a red-legged crow of the genus *Pyrrhocorax*. [imit.]

choux pastry /ʃu:/ a very light pastry enriched with eggs. [F, orig. = cabbages]

chow /tʃaʊ/ *n.* a long-haired dog of a Chinese breed. [short for *chow-chow*, perh. f. pidgin English]

chowder /ˈtʃaʊdə(r)/ *n.* (*US*) a thick soup of clams (or fish) and vegetables. [perh. f. F (*chaudière* pot)]

chow mein /tʃaʊ ˈmeɪn/ a Chinese dish of fried noodles usually with shredded meat and vegetables. [f. Chinese, = fried flour]

chrism /ˈkrɪz(ə)m/ *n.* consecrated oil. [OE f. L f. Gk *khrisma* anointing]

Christ /kraɪst/ *n.* the Messiah of Jewish prophecy; the title (now treated as a name) of Jesus, regarded as fulfilling this prophecy. [OE f. L f. Gk *khristos* anointed one (transl. of Heb., = Messiah)]

christen /ˈkrɪs(ə)n/ *v.t.* to admit to the Christian Church by baptism; to give a name or nickname to. [OE, = make Christian]

Christian /ˈkrɪstjən/ *adj.* **1** of the doctrines of Christianity, believing in or based on these. **2** showing the qualities of a Christian, kindly, humane. —*n.* **1** an adherent of Christianity. **2** a kindly or humane person. —**Christian era**, the era reckoned from the birth of Christ. **Christian name**, a personal name given at baptism. **Christian Science**, a system of health and healing, without medical treatment, by the mental effect of a person's Christian faith. **Christian Sicentist**, an adherent of this. [f. L (*Christus* Christ)]

Christiania /krɪstɪˈɑ:nɪə/ *n.* (in skiing) a turn in which the skis are kept parallel, used for stopping short. [former name of Oslo]

Christianity /krɪstɪˈænɪtɪ/ *n.* **1** the Christian religion, based on the belief that Christ was the incarnate Son of God and on his teaching. **2** Christian character or quality. [f. OF (as prec.)]

christie /ˈkrɪstɪ/ *n.* = Christiania. [abbr.]

Christingle /krɪˈstɪŋg(ə)l/ *n.* a lighted candle set in an orange received at a Christingle service. —**Christingle service**, a children's Advent service, originally in the Moravian Church and recently popularized outside it, at which each participant is given an orange (symbolizing the world) set with a candle (symbolizing Christ as the Light of the World) and other symbolical decorations. [f. CHRIST; origin of second element unknown]

Christmas /ˈkrɪsməs/ *n.* the Christian festival commemorating the birth of Christ; the festive period about this time. —**Christmas-box** *n.* a present or gratuity given at Christmas, especially to employees. **Christmas card**, a card sent with greetings at Christmas. **Christmas Day**, 25 Dec. **Christmas Eve**, 24 Dec. **Christmas pudding**, rich plum pudding eaten at Christmas. **Christmas rose**, a white-flowered winter-blooming hellebore, *Helleborus niger*. **Christmas tree**, a young conifer (or imitation of one) decorated with lights etc. at Christmas. [OE, = CHRIST, MASS[2]]

chromatic /krəˈmætɪk/ *adj.* **1** of colour, in colours. **2** (*Mus.*) with notes not belonging to the diatonic scale. —**chromatic scale**, one that proceeds by semitones. [f. F or L f. Gk (*khrōma* colour)]

chromatin /ˈkrəʊmətɪn/ *n.* a readily stained constituent of the nucleus of a cell. [G, f. Gk *khrōma* colour]

chromatography /krəʊməˈtɒgrəfɪ/ *n.* separation of a mixture into its component substances by passing it over material which absorbs these at different rates so that they appear as layers, often of different colours. [f. G (as prec. + -GRAPHY)]

chrome /krəʊm/ *n.* chromium, especially as a plating; a yellow pigment obtained from a compound of chromium. [F, f. Gk *khrōma* colour, from the brilliant colours of its compounds]

chromium /ˈkrəʊmɪəm/ *n.* a hard metallic element, symbol Cr, atomic number 24. [f. CHROME]

chromosome /ˈkrəʊməsəʊm/ *n.* any of a number of rod-like or threadlike structures found in the nuclei of the cells of living organisms and containing the genes. [G, f. Gk *khrōma* colour *sōma* body)]

chronic /ˈkrɒnɪk/ *adj.* (of diseases etc.) long-lasting, persistent; suffering from a chronic disease. —**chronically** *adv.* [f. F f. L f. Gk (*khronos* time)]

chronicle /ˈkrɒnɪk(ə)l/ *n.* a record of events in the order of their occurrence. —*v.t.* to record in a chronicle. —**Chronicles,** either of two books of the Old Testament recording the history of Israel and Judah from the Creation until the return from Exile (536 BC). —**chronicler** *n.* [f. AF f. L f. Gk *khronika* (as prec.)]

chronogram /ˈkrɒnəgræm/ *n.* a phrase etc. of which the Roman-numeral letters, when added, give a date, e.g. LorD haVe MerCIe Vpon Vs = 50 + 500 + 5 + 1000 + 100 + 1 + 5 + 5 = 1666. [f. Gk *khronos* time + -GRAM]

chronology /krəˈnɒlədʒɪ/ *n.* arrangement of events according to date or in order of occurrence. —**chronological** /krɒnəˈlɒdʒɪk(ə)l/ *adj.*, **chronologically** *adv.* [f. Gk *khronos* time + -LOGY]

chronometer /krəˈnɒmɪtə(r)/ *n.* a time-measuring instrument, especially one keeping accurate time in spite of movement or of variations in temperature, humidity, and air pressure. [f. Gk *khronos* time + -METER]

chrysalis /ˈkrɪsəlɪs/ *n.* (*pl.* **chrysalides** /-ˈsælɪdiːz/) a butterfly or moth at the quiescent stage between the larval and adult phases; the case enclosing it. [f. L f. Gk (*khrusos* gold)]

chrysanthemum /krɪˈsænθəməm/ *n.* an autumn-flowering plant of the genus *Chrysanthemum*, grown in many colours. [L f. Gk (*khrusos* gold, *anthemon* flower)]

chryselephantine /krɪselɪˈfæntaɪn/ *adj.* (of sculpture) overlaid with gold and ivory. [f. Gk (*khrusos* gold, *elephas* ivory)]

chrysoberyl /krɪsəʊˈberɪl/ *n.* a yellowish-green gem. [f. L f. Gk (*khrūsos* gold, BERYL)]

chrysolite /ˈkrɪsəlaɪt/ *n.* a precious stone, a variety of olivine. [f. OF f. L f. Gk (*khrūsos* gold, *lithos* stone)]

chub *n.* (*pl.* same) a thick-bodied river-fish (*Leuciscus cephalus*) of the carp family. [orig. unkn.]

chubby *adj.* plump, plump-faced. [f. CHUB]

chuck[1] *v.t.* **1** (*colloq.*) to throw carelessly or casually. **2** to touch playfully (*under the chin*). —*n.* an act of chucking. —**chuck out,** (*slang*) to expel; to throw away. [perh. f. F *chuquer* knock]

chuck[2] *n.* **1** the part of a lathe holding the workpiece; the part of a drill holding the bit. **2** a cut of beef from the neck to the ribs. [var. of CHOCK]

chuckle *n.* a quiet or suppressed laugh. —*v.i.* to give a chuckle. [f. *chuck* cluck]

chuddar /ˈtʃʌdə(r)/ *n.* a large piece of cloth worn as a kind of cloak, leaving only the face exposed, by Muslim women in certain countries. [f. Pers.]

chug *n.* the dull short repeated sound of an engine running slowly. —*v.i.* (**-gg-**) to move with or make this sound. [imit.]

chukker /ˈtʃʌkə(r)/ *n.* (also **chukka**) a period of play in polo. [f. Hindi f. Skr. *cakra* wheel]

chum *n.* (*colloq.*) a close friend. —*v.i.* (**-mm-**) —**chum up,** (*colloq.*) to form a close friendship. [prob. abbr. of *chamber-fellow*]

chummy *adj.* (*colloq.*) friendly. —**chumminess** *n.* [f. CHUM]

chump *n.* **1** the thick blunt end of loin of lamb etc. **2** (*colloq.*) a stupid person. [blend of CHUNK and LUMP]

chunk *n.* a thick lump cut off; a substantial amount. [prob. var. of CHUCK[2]]

chunky *adj.* **1** in chunks, containing chunks. **2** short and thickset. [f. prec.]

chupatty /tʃʌˈpætɪ/ *n.* a small flat thin cake of coarse unleavened bread. [f. Hindi]

church *n.* a building for public Christian worship; a service in this. —*v.t.* to perform the church service of thanksgiving for (a woman after childbirth). —**the Church,** the whole body of Christian believers; a particular group of these; the clergy, the clerical profession. **Church of England,** the Church in England recognized by the State and rejecting papal authority. [OE f. Gk *kuriakon* Lord's (house)]

churchman *n.* (*pl.* **-men**) **1** a clergyman. **2** a member of a Church.

churchwarden *n.* **1** a lay representative of a parish who helps with the business of a church. **2** a long-stemmed clay pipe.

churchyard *n.* the enclosed ground round a church, especially as used for burials.

churlish *adj.* rude and unfriendly, ungracious; mean, grudging. —**churlishly** *adv.*, **churlishness** *n.* [OE]

churn *n.* **1** a vessel in which milk or cream is shaken to produce butter. **2** a large milk-can in which milk is carried from a farm. —*v.t./i.* **1** to shake (milk or cream) in a churn; to produce (butter) thus. **2** to stir or swirl violently, to break *up* the surface of. —**churn out,** to produce in quantity. [OE]

Churrigueresque /tʃʌrɪgəˈresk/ *adj.* of the lavishly ornamented late Spanish baroque style. [f. J. de *Churriguera*, Spanish architect (d. 1725)]

chute /ʃuːt/ *n.* a sloping or vertical channel or slide for conveying things to a lower level. [F, = fall, with some senses of SHOOT]

chutney /ˈtʃʌtnɪ/ *n.* a pungent relish of fruits, vinegar, spices, etc. [f. Hindi]

CIA *abbr.* Central Intelligence Agency.

ciborium /sɪˈbɔːrɪəm/ *n.* (*pl.* **-ia**) **1** (*Archit.*) a canopy; a canopied shrine. **2** a covered receptacle for the reservation of the Eucharist. [L f. Gk, = seed-vessel of water-lily, cup made from it]

cicada /sɪˈkɑːdə/ *n.* a grasshopper-like insect of the genus *Cicada*, that makes a loud rhythmic chirping. [L]

cicatrice /ˈsɪkətrɪs/ *n.* the scar left by a healed wound. [f. OF or L]

cicely /ˈsɪs(ə)lɪ/ *n.* **sweet cicely**, an aromatic umbelliferous herb, *Myrrhis odorata*. [f. L f. Gk *seselis*, assim. to the woman's name *Cicely*]

cicerone /tʃɪtʃəˈrəʊnɪ, sɪs-/ *n.* (*pl.* **-ni** /-niː/) a guide who shows antiquities to visitors. [It. f. L *Cicero* 1st c. BC), Roman statesman]

CID *abbr.* Criminal Investigation Department.

-cide *suffix* person or substance that kills (*regicide*, *insecticide*); killing (*homicide*). [f. L *caedere* kill]

cider /ˈsaɪdə(r)/ *n.* a fermented drink made from apples. [f. OF, ult. f. Heb., = strong drink]

cigar /sɪˈgɑː(r)/ *n.* a roll of tobacco leaves for smoking. [f. F or Sp.]

cigarette /sɪgəˈret/ *n.* a small cylinder of shredded tobacco etc. rolled in thin paper for smoking. [F, dim. of *cigare*]

ciliate /ˈsɪlɪət/ *adj.* having cilia. —*n.* a member of the class Ciliata consisting of protozoa which have a relatively complex body structure and are characterized by possessing cilia. [f. CILIUM]

cilium /ˈsɪlɪəm/ *n.* (*pl.* **cilia**) a minute hair fringing a leaf, an insect's wing, etc; a hairlike vibrating organ on animal or vegetable tissue. [L, = eyelid]

cinchona /sɪŋˈkəʊnə/ *n.* a South American evergreen tree or shrub of the genus *Cinchona*; its bark, the source of quinine. [f. Countess of *Chinchón* who introduced the drug to Spain, 1640]

cincture /ˈsɪŋktʃə(r), -tʃʊə(r)/ *n.* (*literary*) a girdle, belt, or border. —*v.t.* to surround with a cincture. [f. L *cinctura* (*cingere* gird)]

cinder /ˈsɪndə(r)/ *n.* the residue of coal, wood, etc., after it has ceased to flame; (in *pl.*) ashes. [OE]

cine- /sɪnɪ-/ *prefix* cinematographic (as in *cine-camera*, *cine-projector*). [abbr.]

cinema /ˈsɪnəmə/ *n.* **1** a theatre where motion-picture films are shown. **2** films as an art or industry. —**cinematic** /-ˈmætɪk/ *adj.* [f. F *cinéma* abbr. *cinématographe* (see CINEMATOGRAPH)]

CinemaScope /ˈsɪnəməskəʊp/ *n.* [P] a wide-screen process in which special lenses are used to compress a wide image into a standard frame and then expand it again during projection.

cinematheque /sɪnəməˈtek/ *n.* a film library or repository; a small cinema. [f. F (CINEMA, *bibliothèque* library)]

cinematograph /sɪnəˈmætəgrɑːf/ *n.* a machine for projecting motion-picture films on to a screen. [f. F *ciné- matographe* (machine patented by the Lumière brothers in 1895), f. Gk *kinēma* motion + -GRAPH]

cinematography /sɪnɪməˈtɒgrəfɪ/ *n.* the art of making motion-picture films. —**cinematographer** *n.*, **cinematographic** /-ˈgræfɪk/ *adj.* [as prec.]

cinéma-vérité /sɪnemə ˈverɪteɪ/ *n.* a style of documentary film-making developed in the late 1950s and early 1960s. [F, = film truth]

cineraria /sɪnəˈreərɪə/ *n.* a composite plant, a variety of *Senecio cruentus*, with bright daisy-like flowers. [L, = of ashes, f. the hoary leaves of allied species]

cinerary urn /ˈsɪnərərɪ/ an urn for holding a dead person's ashes after cremation. [f. L (as prec.)]

cinnabar /ˈsɪnəbɑː(r)/ *n.* **1** red mercuric sulphide; the pigment obtained from this, vermilion. **2** a moth with reddish-marked wings. [f. L f. Gk]

cinnamon /ˈsɪnəmən/ *n.* a spice from the aromatic inner bark of a SE Asian tree; its colour, a yellowish-brown. [f. OF f. L, ult. f. Semitic]

cinquefoil /ˈsɪŋkfɔɪl/ *n.* **1** a plant of the genus *Potentilla*, with a compound leaf of five leaflets. **2** a five-cusped ornament etc. [f. L (*quinque* five, *folium* leaf)]

cipher /ˈsaɪfə(r)/ *n.* **1** a set of letters or symbols representing others, used to conceal the meaning of a message etc. **2** the symbol O, representing nought or zero. **3** any Arabic numeral. —*v.t.* to write in cipher. [f. OF f. L f. Arab., = zero]

circa /ˈsɜːkə/ *prep.* about (a specified date or number). [L]

circadian /sɜːˈkeɪdɪən/ *adj.* (of physiological activities etc.) occurring about once every twenty-four hours. [f. L *circa* about, *dies* day]

circle /ˈsɜːk(ə)l/ *n.* **1** a round plane figure with its circum- ference equidistant from the centre at all points. **2** a circular or roundish structure, enclosure, etc.; a curved upper tier of seats at a theatre etc.; a road or railway without ends, on which traffic circulates continuously. **3** persons grouped round a centre of interest; a restricted group or set. —*v.t./i.* **1** to move in a circle; to revolve round. **2** to form a circle round, to surround. [f. OF f. L *circulus* dim. of *circus* ring]

circlet /ˈsɜːklɪt/ *n.* an ornamental band worn round the head. [f. prec. + -LET]

circuit /ˈsɜːkɪt/ *n.* **1** a line enclosing an area, the route or distance round; a motor-racing track. **2** a closed path for an electric current; the apparatus through which a current passes. **3** a judge's itinerary through a district to hold courts, such a district; a group of Methodist churches served by a set of itinerant preachers. **4** a chain of theatres, cinemas, etc., under a single management. **5** a sequence of sporting events. —**circuit-breaker** *n.* an automatic device for interrupting an electric current. [f. OF f. L *circuitus* (*circum* round, *ire* go)]

circuitous /sɜːˈkjuːɪtəs/ *adj.* going a long way round, indirect. [f. L (as prec.)]

circuitry /ˈsɜːkɪtrɪ/ *n.* a system of electric circuits; the equipment forming this. [f. CIRCUIT]

circular /ˈsɜːkjʊlə(r)/ *adj.* **1** in the form of a circle. **2** travelling in a circle; (of reasoning) following a vicious circle. **3** (of letters etc.) addressed to a number of people, not individual. —*n.* a circular letter, leaflet, etc. —**circular saw**, a rotating toothed disc for sawing wood etc. —**circularity** /-ˈlærɪtɪ/ *n.* [f. AF f. L *circularis* (*circulus* circle)]

circularize /ˈsɜːkjʊləraɪz/ *v.t.* to send circulars to. [f. prec.]

circulate /ˈsɜːkjʊleɪt/ *v.t./i.* **1** to go round continuously; to hand or be passed from person to person. **2** to send circulars to. [f. L (as CIRCLE)]

circulation /sɜːkjʊˈleɪʃ(ə)n/ *n.* **1** movement from and back to a starting-point, especially that of the blood from and to the heart. **2** transmission or distribution (of information, books, etc.). **3** the number of copies of a newspaper etc. sold or distributed. [f. prec.]

circulatory /sɜːkjʊˈleɪtərɪ/ *adj.* of the circulation of the blood. [f. CIRCULATE]

circumcise /ˈsɜːkəmsaɪz/ *v.t.* to cut off the foreskin of (a male person) as a religious rite or surgically; to cut off the clitoris of (a female person), to perform the operation of infibulation on. —**circumcision** /-ˈsɪʒ(ə)n/ *n.* [f. OF f. L (*circum* round, *caedere* cut)]

circumference /sɜːˈkʌmfərəns/ *n.* the line enclosing a circle or circular object; the distance round this. [f. OF f. L (*circum* round, *ferre* carry)]

circumflex /ˈsɜːkəmfleks/ *n.* (in full **circumflex accent**) a mark (ˆ) over a vowel to show contraction, length, or special quality. [f. L (*circum* round, *flexus* bent)]

circumlocution /sɜːkəmləˈkjuːʃ(ə)n/ *n.* speaking in a roundabout or indirect way; a roundabout expression. —**circumlocutory** /-ˈlɒkjʊtərɪ/ *adj.* [f. L (*circum* round, *locutio* speaking)]

circumnavigate /sɜːkəmˈnævɪgeɪt/ *v.t.* to sail round (the world etc.). —**circumnavigation** /-ˈgeɪʃ(ə)n/ *n.* [f. L (*circum* round, *navigare* navigate)]

circumscribe /ˈsɜːkəmskraɪb/ *v.t.* **1** to draw a line round; (in geometry) to draw (a figure) round another so as to touch it at points without cutting it. **2** to mark the limits of, to restrict. —**circumscription** /-ˈskrɪpʃ(ə)n/ *n.* [f. L (*circum* round, *scribere* write)]

circumspect /ˈsɜːkəmspekt/ *adj.* cautious, taking everything into account. —**circumspection** /-ˈspekʃ(ə)n/ *n.* [f. L (*circum* round, *specere* look)]

circumstance /ˈsɜːkəmstəns/ *n.* **1** a fact or occurrence. **2** (in *pl.*) the conditions connected with or affecting an event or person or action, financial position. **3** ceremony, fuss. [f. OF f. L (*circum* round, *stare* stand)]

circumstantial /sɜːkəmˈstænʃ(ə)l/ *adj.* **1** giving full details. **2** (of evidence) consisting of facts that strongly suggest something without providing direct proof. —**circumstantiality** /-ʃɪˈælɪtɪ/ *n.*, **circumstantially** *adv.* [f. L (as prec.)]

circumvent /sɜːkəmˈvent/ *v.t.* to evade or find a way round (a difficulty); to outwit. —**circumvention** *n.* [f. L (*circum* round, *venire* come)]

circus /ˈsɜːkəs/ *n.* **1** a travelling show of performing animals, acrobats, clowns, etc. **2** (*colloq.*) a scene of lively action. **3** (*colloq.*) a group of people in a common activity, especially sport. **4** an open space in a town, on which streets converge. **5** (*hist.*) an arena for sports and games. [L, = ring]

cire perdue /sɪər ˈpɜːdjuː/ a method of casting bronze by using an inner and an outer mould, with molten metal poured in after the wax layer between these has been melted away. [F, = lost wax]

cirque /sɜːk/ *n.* a deep bowl-shaped hollow at the head of a valley or on a mountain-side. [F f. L *circus* ring]

cirrhosis /sɪˈrəʊsɪs/ *n.* a chronic disease of the liver, especially suffered by alcoholics, in which the liver hardens into many small projections. [f. Gk *kirrhos* tawny]

cirriped /ˈsɪrɪped/ *n.* a marine crustacean in a valved shell, e.g. a barnacle. [f. L *cirrus* curl (from form of legs) + *pes* foot]

cirrocumulus /sɪrəʊˈkjuːmjuːləs/ *n.* (*pl.* **-li** /-laɪ/) a form of usually high cloud consisting of small roundish fleecy clouds in contact with one another, known as 'mackerel sky'. [f. CIRRUS + CUMULUS]

cirrostratus /sɪrəʊˈstreɪtəs/ *n.* (*pl.* **-ti** /-taɪ/) thin usually high white cloud composed mainly of fine ice-crystals and producing halo phenomena. [f. foll. + STRATUS]

cirrus /ˈsɪrəs/ *n.* (*pl.* **cirri** /-raɪ/) **1** a form of cloud, usually high, with diverging filaments or wisps. **2** a tendril or appendage of a plant or animal. [L, = curl]

cissy var. of SISSY.

cist /kɪst/ *n.* a prehistoric burial chest or chamber excavated in rock or formed of stones or hollowed tree-trunks, especially a stone coffin formed of slabs placed on edge and covered on the top by one or more horizontal slabs. [Welsh, = chest]

Cistercian /sɪs'tɜːʃ(ə)n/ *n.* a member of the Cistercian order. —*adj.* of the Cistercian order. [f. F f. L *Cistercium* Cîteaux near Dijon in France, where founded]

cistern /'sɪstɜːn/ *n.* a tank for storing water (especially in a roof-space) supplying taps, or as part of a flushing lavatory; an underground reservoir. [f. OF f. L (*cista* box, f. Gk *kistē*)]

cistus *n.* a shrub of the genus *Cistus* with large white, pink, or purple flowers. [f. Gk]

citadel /'sɪtəd(ə)l/ *n.* **1** a fortress, usually on high ground, protecting or dominating a city. **2** a meeting-hall of the Salvation Army. [f. F or It., f. L *civitas* city]

cite /saɪt/ *v.t.* **1** to quote or mention as an example or to support an argument. **2** to mention in an official dispatch. **3** to summon to appear in a lawcourt. —**citation** /-'teɪʃ(ə)n/ *n.* [f. F f. L (*ciēre* set moving)]

citizen /'sɪtɪz(ə)n/ *n.* a native or naturalized member *of* a State; an inhabitant of a city. —**citizens' band,** a system of local radio intercommunication by individuals on special frequencies. —**citizenry** *n.*, **citizenship** *n.* [f. AF f. L *civitas* city]

citrate /'sɪtreɪt/ *n.* a salt of citric acid. [f. foll.]

citric /'sɪtrɪk/ *adj.* derived from citrus fruit. —**citric acid,** the sharp-tasting acid in lemon-juice etc. [f. F f. L *citrus* citron]

citron /'sɪtrən/ *n.* a large yellow-skinned fruit like a lemon; the tree (*Citrus medica*) bearing it. [F f. L *citrus*]

citronella /sɪtrə'nelə/ *n.* a fragrant oil obtained from a grass (*Cymbopogon nardus*) of S. Asia; this grass. [as prec.]

citrus /'sɪtrəs/ *n.* a tree of the genus *Citrus*, including citron, lemon, and orange; the fruit of such a tree. [L]

city /'sɪtɪ/ *n.* a large town, especially one created by royal charter and containing a cathedral. —**the City,** the part of London governed by the Lord Mayor and Corporation; the business quarter of this; commercial circles. **city fathers,** the officials administering a city. **city-state** *n.* (*hist.*) a city that is also an independent State, characteristic of ancient Greece. [f. OF f. L *civitas* (*civis* citizen)]

cityscape *n.* a view of a city, city scenery. [f. CITY, after *landscape*]

civet /'sɪvɪt/ *n.* **1** (in full **civet-cat**) any of various small catlike animals of the family Viverridae, especially *Civettictis civetta* of central Africa. **2** the strong musky perfume obtained from its anal glands. [f. F, ult. f. Arab., = the perfume]

civic /'sɪvɪk/ *adj.* of a city; of citizens or citizenship. —**civic centre,** the area where municipal offices are situated. [f. OF or L (*civis* citizen)]

civics /'sɪvɪks/ *n.pl.* the study of the rights and duties of citizenship. [f. prec.]

civil /'sɪv(ə)l, -ɪl/ *adj.* **1** of or belonging to citizens. **2** of ordinary citizens, non-military. **3** polite, obliging, not rude. **4** (*Law*) concerning private rights and not criminal offences. **5** (of the length of the day, year, etc.) fixed by custom or law, not natural or astronomical. —**civil defence,** an organization for protecting civilians in an air raid or other enemy action. **civil disobedience,** refusal to comply with a law or laws as a peaceful protest. **civil engineer,** one who designs or maintains works of public utility, e.g. roads and bridges. **civil liberty,** freedom of action subject to the law. **civil list,** the annual allowance by Parliament for the sovereign's household expenses etc. It is made in lieu of the revenues from royal patrimonies, which are assigned to the Treasury for public use. **civil marriage,** one solemnized with a civil (not religious) ceremony. **civil rights,** the rights of citizens, especially (*US*) of Blacks, to liberty, equality, etc. **Civil Service,** the body of persons employed by a State in the administration of civil (non-military) affairs. **Civil Servant,** a member of the Civil Service. **civil war,** war between people of the same country. —**civilly** *adv.* [f. OF f. L *civilis* (as CIVIC)]

civilian /sɪ'vɪljən/ *n.* a person not in the armed forces or police force. —*adj.* of or for civilians. [f. prec.]

civility /sɪ'vɪlɪtɪ/ *n.* politeness; an act of politeness. [f. OF f. L (as CIVIL)]

civilization /sɪvɪlaɪ'zeɪʃ(ə)n/ *n.* **1** an advanced stage or system of social development; those peoples of the world regarded as having this. **2** a people or nation (especially of the past) regarded as an element of social evolution. [f. foll.]

civilize /'sɪvɪlaɪz/ *v.t.* to bring out of a barbarous or primitive stage of society to a more developed one; to refine and educate. [f. F *civiliser* (as CIVIL)]

civvies /'sɪvɪz/ *n.pl.* (*slang*) civilian clothes. [abbr.]

Civvy Street (*slang*) civilian life. [abbr.]

Cl *symbol* chlorine.

cl *abbr.* centilitre(s).

clack *v.i.* to make a sharp sound as of boards struck together; to chatter. —*n.* a clacking noise or talk. [imit.]

clad[1] *past & p.p.* of CLOTHE.

clad[2] *v.t.* (**-dd-**) to provide with cladding. [f. prec.]

cladding *n.* a protective coating or covering on a structure, material, etc. [f. prec.]

clade /kleɪd/ *n.* a group of organisms that have

evolved from a common ancestor. [f. Gk *klados* branch]

cladistics /klə'dıstıks/ *n.* the systematic classification of groups of organisms on the basis of the order of their assumed divergence from ancestral species. [f. prec.]

claim *v.t.* **1** to demand as one's due or property. **2** to represent oneself as having; to profess *to*; to assert *that*. **3** to have as an achievement or victim etc.; to deserve (attention etc.). —*n.* **1** a demand for a thing considered one's due. **2** the right or title (*to*). **3** an assertion. **4** a thing (especially land) claimed. [f. OF f. L *clamare* call out]

claimant *n.* a person making a claim, especially in a lawsuit. [f. prec.]

clairvoyance /kleə'vɔıəns/ *n.* the supposed faculty of seeing mentally things in the future or out of sight; exceptional insight. —**clairvoyant** *n.* & *adj.* [F (*clair* clear, *voyant* seeing)]

clam *n.* an edible bivalve mollusc, especially *Mercenaria mercenaria* and *Mya arenaria.* —*v.i.* **(-mm-) clam up,** (*slang*) to become silent. [app. f. *clam* clamp]

clamber *v.i.* to climb laboriously with hands and feet. —*n.* a difficult climb. [prob. f. *clamb* (obs. past tense of CLIMB)]

clammy *adj.* unpleasantly damp and sticky. —**clammily** *adv.*, **clamminess** *n.* [f. *clam* daub]

clamour /'klæmə(r)/ *n.* a loud or vehement shouting or noise; a loud protest or demand. —*v.t. /i.* to make a clamour; to utter with a clamour. —**clamorous** *adj.* [f. OF f. L (*clamare* call out)]

clamp[1] *n.* a device, especially a brace or band of iron etc., for strengthening, pressing, or holding things together. —*v.t.* to strengthen or fasten with a clamp; to fix firmly. —**clamp down on,** to become strict about, to suppress. **clamp-down** *n.* [f. LG or Du.]

clamp[2] *n.* a pile of bricks for burning; potatoes etc. stored in the open under straw and earth, peat, etc. [prob. f. Du., rel. to CLUMP]

clan *n.* a group of families with a common ancestor, especially in Scotland; a large family or social group; a group with a strong common interest. —**clannish** *adj.*, **clansman** *n.* [f. Gael. f. L *planta* sprout]

clandestine /klæn'destın/ *adj.* surreptitious, secret. —**clandestinely** *adv.* [f. F or L (*clam* secretly)]

clang *n.* a loud resonant metallic sound. —*v.t./i.* to make or cause to make a clang. [imit.; cf. L *clangere* resound]

clangour /'klæŋgə(r)/ *n.* prolonged clanging. —**clangorous** *adj.* [f. L (as prec.)]

clank *n.* a metallic sound as of metal striking metal. —*v.t./i.* to make or cause to make a clank. [imit.]

clap *v.t./i.* **(-pp-) 1** to strike the palms (or *hands*) repeatedly together, especially in applause; to applaud thus. **2** to put or place with vigour or determination. —*n.* **1** an act of clapping, especially as applause; an explosive sound, especially of thunder. **2** a friendly slap. —**clap eyes on,** (*colloq.*) to catch sight of. **clapped out,** (*slang*) worn out, exhausted. [OE, = throb, beat]

clapper *n.* the tongue or striker of a bell. —**clapper-board** *n.* a device in film-making that makes a sharp clap for synchronizing picture and sound. [f. CLAP]

clapper bridge a rough bridge consisting of a series of slabs or planks resting on piles of stones. [perh. f. L. *claperius* heap of stones (orig. unkn.)]

claptrap *n.* insincere or pretentious talk, nonsense.

claque /klæk/ *n.* a hired group of applauders in a theatre etc. [F (*claquer* clap)]

claret /'klærət/ *n.* **1** red wine, especially from Bordeaux. **2** reddish-violet colour. [F, orig. = clarified wine (L *clarus* clear)]

clarify /'klærıfaı/ *v.t./i.* **1** to make or become clear to see or easier to understand. **2** to free (a liquid etc.) from impurity or opaqueness. —**clarification** /-fı'keıʃ(ə)n/ *n.* [f. OF f. L (*clarus* clear)]

clarinet /klærı'net/ *n.* a single-reed wood-wind instrument. —**clarinettist** *n.* [f. F, dim. of *clarine* a kind of bell]

clarion /'klærıən/ *n.* **1** a clear rousing sound. **2** (*hist.*) a shrill war-trumpet. [f. L (*clarus* clear)]

clarity /'klærıtı/ *n.* clearness. [as prec.]

clash *v.t./i.* **1** to strike making a loud harsh sound as of light metal objects struck together. **2** to conflict, to disagree; to coincide inconveniently (*with*). **3** (of colours) to produce an unpleasant visual effect by not being harmonious. —*n.* **1** a sound of clashing. **2** conflict, a disagreement. **3** a clashing of colours. [imit.]

clasp /klɑ:sp/ *n.* **1** a device with interlocking parts for fastening. **2** a grasp, a handshake, an embrace. **3** a bar on a medal-ribbon. —*v.t.* **1** to fasten with a clasp. **2** to grasp, to hold closely or embrace. —**clasp-knife** *n.* a folding knife with a catch to hold the blade open. [orig. unkn.]

class /klɑ:s/ *n.* **1** a set of persons or things grouped together, or graded or differentiated (especially by quality) from others; a division or order of society; a division of candidates by merit in an examination; a grouping of animals or plants next below a phylum. **2** distinction, high quality. **3** a set of students taught together; the occasion when they meet. —*v.t.*

to place in a class, to classify. [f. L *classis* division of Roman people]

classic /ˈklæsɪk/ *adj*. **1** of acknowledged excellence; outstandingly important, remarkably typical. **2** of ancient Greek and Roman art, literature, and culture; resembling this, especially in harmony and restraint. **3** having historic associations. —*n*. **1** a classic work, example, writer, etc. **2** (in *pl*.) the study of ancient Greek and Roman literature, culture, etc. [f. L *classicus* of the highest class (as CLASS)]

classical /ˈklæsɪk(ə)l *adj*. **1** of ancient Greek and Roman art, literature, culture, etc. **2** simple and harmonious in style. **3** (of music) serious, following established forms; of the period *c*.1750-1800. —**classical scholar,** an expert in ancient Greek and Roman languages and culture. —**classically** *adv*. [as prec.]

classicism /ˈklæsɪsɪz(ə)m/ *n*. following of the classic style. [f. CLASSIC]

classicist /ˈklæsɪsɪst/ *n*. a classical scholar. [as prec. + IST]

classifiable /ˈklæsɪfaɪəb(ə)l/ *adj*. that can be classified. [f. CLASSIFY]

classificatory /klæsɪfɪˈkeɪtərɪ/ *adj*. of or involving classification. [as prec.]

classify /ˈklæsɪfaɪ/ *v.t*. **1** to arrange in classes or categories; to assign a class to. **2** to designate as officially secret or not for general disclosure. —**classification** /-ˈkeɪʃ(ə)n/ *n*. [back-formation f. *classification* f. F (as CLASS)]

classless *adj*. without distinctions of social class. [f. CLASS + -LESS]

classroom *n*. a room where a class of students is taught.

classy /ˈklɑːsɪ/ *adj*. (*colloq*.) superior, stylish. —**classily** *adv*., **classiness** *n*. [f. CLASS]

clatter *n*. a sound as of hard objects struck together or falling; noisy talk. —*v.i*. to make a clatter; to fall, move, etc., with a clatter. [OE (imit.)]

clause /klɔːz/ *n*. **1** a distinct part of a sentence, containing a finite verb. **2** a single part in a treaty, law, contract, etc. [f. OF f. L *clausula* conclusion (as CLOSE)]

claustrophobia /klɔːstrəˈfəʊbɪə/ *n*. abnormal fear of being in a confined space. —**claustrophobic** *adj*. [f. L *claustrum* enclosed space + PHOBIA]

clavichord /ˈklævɪkɔːd/ *n*. a stringed keyboard instrument with a very soft tone, developed in the 14th c. and in use from the early 15th.[f. L (*clavis* key, *chorda* string)]

clavicle /ˈklævɪk(ə)l/ *n*. the collar-bone. [f. L, dim. of *clavis* key]

clavier /ˈkleɪvɪə(r)/ *n*. a keyboard; an instrument with this; an organ manual. [F, or f. G f. L, orig. = key-bearer (*clavis* key)]

claw *n*. **1** the pointed nail of an animal's or bird's foot; a foot armed with claws. **2** the pincers of a shellfish. **3** a device for grappling and holding things. —*v.t*. to scratch or maul or pull with the claws; to scratch with the finger-nails. —**claw back,** to recoup (money etc.) that has just been given away, e.g. in taxation. **claw-hammer** *n*. a hammer with one side of the head forked for extracting nails. [OE]

clay *n*. a stiff sticky earth, especially used for making bricks, pottery, etc. —**clay pigeon,** a breakable disc thrown up from a trap as a target for shooting. [OE]

claymore *n*. **1** a Scottish two-edged broadsword. **2** a broadsword (often single-edged) with a basket-like structure protecting the hilt. [Gael., = great sword]

clean *adj*. **1** free from dirt or impurities, not soiled; not yet used, preserving what is regarded as the original state; free from obscenity or indecency; attentive to personal hygiene and cleanness; (of a nuclear weapon) producing relatively little fall-out; containing nothing dishonourable, (of a licence) without endorsements. **2** complete, clear-cut; evenly shaped, without projections or roughness. —*adv*. **1** completely, entirely. **2** in a clean manner. —*v.t./i*. to make or become clean. —*n*. a process of cleaning. —**clean-cut** *adj*. sharply outlined. **clean out,** to clean the inside of; (*slang*) to use up all the supplies or money of. **clean-shaven** *adj*. with beard or moustache shaved off. **clean sheet,** a record not showing any offences. **clean up,** to make clean or tidy; to restore order or morality to; (*colloq*.) to make a gain or profit. **make a clean breast of,** to confess fully about. —**cleanness** *n*. [OE]

cleaner *n*. **1** a person employed to clean rooms. **2** (usu. in *pl*.) an establishment for cleaning clothes. **3** a device or substance for cleaning things. [f. prec.]

cleanly[1] /ˈkliːnlɪ/ *adv*. in a clean manner. [f. CLEAN]

cleanly[2] /ˈklenlɪ/ *adj*. habitually clean, with clean habits. —**cleanliness** *n*. [as prec.]

cleanse /klenz/ *v.t*. to make clean or pure. —**cleanser** *n*. [f. CLEAN]

clear *adj*. **1** not clouded or murky or spotted; transparent; (of the conscience) free from guilt. **2** readily perceived by the senses or mind. **3** able to discern readily and accurately; confident or convinced (*about*, *that*). **4** (of a road etc.) unobstructed, open. **5** net, without deduction, complete; unhampered, free (*of* debt, commitments, etc.). —*adv*. clearly; completely; apart, out of contact. —*v.t./i*. **1** to make or become clear. **2** to free from or *of* obstruction, suspicion, etc.; to show or declare to be innocent (*of*); to approve (a person) for special duty, access to information, etc.; to pass (a cheque) through a clearing-house. **3** to pass over or by without touching; to pass through (a customs office etc.). **4** to make (an amount of money) as a net gain or to balance expenses. —**clear away,** to remove completely; to remove used crockery etc. after a meal; (of mists etc.) to disappear. **clear-cut** *adj.* sharply defined. **clearing bank,** a large bank belonging to a clearing-house. **clearing-house** *n.* a bankers' establishment where cheques etc. are exchanged, only the balances being paid in cash; an agency for collecting or distributing information etc. **clear off,** to get rid of, to complete payment of (a debt etc.); (*colloq.*) to go away. **clear out,** to empty; to remove; (*colloq.*) to go away. **clear up,** to tidy up; to solve (a mystery etc.); (of weather) to become fine. **clear a thing with,** to get approval or authorization of it from (a person). —**clearly** *adv.*, **clearness** *n.* [f. OF f. L *clarus* bright, clear]

clearance *n.* **1** the act or process of clearing or being cleared; permission, authorization. **2** a space allowed for one object to move within or past another. [f. prec.]

clearing *n.* an open space in woodland from which trees have been cleared. [f. CLEAR]

clearway *n.* a main road (other than a motorway) on which vehicles may not ordinarily stop.

cleat *n.* **1** a projecting piece of metal, wood, etc., bolted on for securing ropes to, or to strengthen woodwork. **2** a projecting piece fastened to a spar, gangway, boot, etc., to prevent slipping. **3** a wedge serving as a support. [OE]

cleavage *n.* **1** the process of splitting, the way in which a thing tends to split. **2** the hollow between full breasts. [f. foll.]

cleave[1] *v.t./i.* (*past* **clove, cleft, cleaved;** *p.p.* **cloven** /ˈkləuv(ə)n/, **cleft, cleaved**) to chop, to split or become split, especially along the grain or line of cleavage; to make a way through (the air etc.). [OE]

cleave[2] *v.i.* (*literary*) to stick fast or adhere *to* [OE]

cleaver *n.* a heavy chopping tool used by butchers. [f. CLEAVE[1]]

cleavers *n.* (as *sing.* or *pl.*) a plant (*Galium aparine*) with hooked bristles on its stem that catch in clothes etc. [f. CLEAVE[2]]

clef *n.* a symbol on a staff in a musical score, locating a particular note on it and showing the pitch of the notes following that symbol, e.g. **alto** (*or* **C**) **clef, bass** (*or* **F**) **clef, treble** (*or* **G**) **clef.** [F, = key]

cleft *p.p.* of CLEAVE[1]. —*adj.* split, partly divided. —*n.* a space made by cleaving, a fissure. —**cleft palate,** a congenital split in the roof of the mouth. **in a cleft stick,** in a dilemma.

clematis /ˈklemətɪs/ *n.* a climbing plant of the genus *Clematis*, chiefly with white, pink, or purple flowers. [L f. Gk (*klēma* vine branch)]

clement /ˈklemənt/ *adj.* **1** (of weather) mild. **2** merciful. —**clemency** *n.* [f. L]

clementine /ˈklemənti:n/ *n.* a kind of small orange. [F]

clench *v.t.* **1** to close (the teeth or fingers) tightly; to grasp firmly. **2** to clinch (a nail or rivet). —*n.* a clenching action, a clenched state. [OE]

clerestory /ˈklɪəstərɪ/ *n.* the part of the wall of a cathedral or large church, with a series of windows, above the aisle roof. [f. CLEAR + STOREY]

clergy *n.* (usu. as *pl.*) the body of those ordained for religious service; clergymen. [f. OF (as CLERK)]

clergyman *n.* (*pl.* **-men**) a member of the clergy, especially of the Church of England.

cleric /ˈklerɪk/ *n.* a clergyman. [f. L f. Gk (*klēros* heritage, priestly order)]

clerical /ˈklerɪk(ə)l/ *adj.* **1** of the clergy or a clergyman. **2** of or done by clerks. —**clerical collar,** an upright white collar fastening at the back, worn by clergy. [as prec.]

clerihew /ˈklerɪhju:/ *n.* a short witty, comic, or nonsensical verse, usually in two rhyming couplets with free metre in lines of unequal length. [f. E. *Clerihew* Bentley, English writer (d. 1956), its inventor]

clerk /klɑ:k/ *n.* **1** a person employed in an office, bank, etc., to keep records, accounts, etc. **2** a secretary or agent of a local council (*town clerk*), court, etc. **3** a lay officer of a church (*parish clerk*). —**clerk of (the) works,** an overseer of building works etc. [f. OE & OF (as CLERIC)]

clever /ˈklevə(r)/ *adj.* quick at learning or understanding things, skilful; ingenious. —**cleverly** *adj.*, **cleverness** *n.* [perh. rel. to CLEAVE[2], w. sense 'quick to seize']

clevis /ˈklevɪs/ *n.* a U-shaped piece of metal at the end of a beam for attaching tackle etc. [f. OE, rel. to CLEAVE[1]]

clew /klu:/ *n.* the lower or after corner of a sail; the small cords suspending a hammock. —*v.t.* to draw the lower ends of (a sail) *up* to the upper yard or mast for furling. [OE, orig. = ball of thread]

cliché /ˈkli:ʃeɪ/ *n.* a hackneyed phrase or opinion. [F, orig. = metal casting of stereotype]

click *n.* a slight sharp sound as of a dropping latch. —*v.t./i.* **1** to make or cause to make a click; to fasten with a click. **2** (*slang*) to become clear or understandable; to be successful; to become friendly *with*. [imit.]

client /ˈklaɪənt/ *n.* a person using the services of a lawyer, architect, or professional person other than a doctor, or of a business; a customer. [f. L *cliens* (*cluere* hear, obey)]

clientele /kli:ɒn'tel/ *n.* clients or customers collectively. [f. L & F (as prec.)]

cliff *n.* a steep rock-face, especially on the coast. —**cliff-hanger** *n.* a serial film etc. in which the viewer etc. is left in suspense at the end of each episode. [OE]

climacteric /klaɪ'mæktərɪk/ *n.* the period of life when physical powers begin to decline. [f. F or L f. Gk (as CLIMAX)]

climactic /klaɪ'mæktɪk/ *adj.* of a climax. [f. CLIMAX]

climate /'klaɪmət/ *n.* **1** the prevailing weather conditions of an area; a region with certain weather conditions. **2** the prevailing trend of opinion or feeling. —**climatic** /-'mætɪk/ *adj.* [f. OF or L f. Gk *klima* slope]

climax /'klaɪmæks/ *n.* **1** the event or point of the greatest intensity or interest, culmination. **2** sexual orgasm. —*v.t./i.* to reach or bring to a climax. [L f. Gk, = ladder]

climb /klaɪm/ *v.t./i.* **1** to go up or over by effort. **2** to move upwards, to go higher; (of a plant) to grow up a support. **3** to rise in social rank etc. by one's own efforts. —*n.* **1** the action of climbing. **2** a hill etc. climbed or to be climbed. —**climb down,** to go downwards by effort; to retreat from a position taken up in argument. **climb-down** *n.* such a retreat. **climbing-frame** *n.* a structure of jointed bars etc. for children to climb on. [OE]

climber *n.* **1** a mountaineer. **2** a climbing plant. **3** one who strives to rise socially. [f. prec.]

clime *n.* (*literary*) a region; a climate. [f. L *clima* (as CLIMATE)]

clinch *v.t./i.* **1** to confirm or settle (an argument or bargain) conclusively. **2** (of boxers) to come too close together for a full-arm blow; (*colloq.*) to embrace. **3** to secure (a nail or rivet) by driving the point sideways when it is through. —*n.* a clinching action, a clinched state. [var. of CLENCH]

clincher *n.* a decisive point that settles an argument, proposition, etc. [f. prec.]

cling *v.i.* (*past & p.p.* **clung**) **1** to maintain one's grasp, to hold on tightly. **2** to become attached, to stick fast. **3** to be stubbornly faithful. [OE]

clingstone *n.* a kind of peach or nectarine in which the stone is difficult to separate from the flesh.

clinic /'klɪnɪk/ *n.* **1** a private or specialized hospital. **2** a place or session at which specialized medical treatment or advice is given. [f. F f. Gk (as foll.)]

clinical /'klɪnɪk(ə)l/ *adj.* **1** of or for the treatment of patients; taught or learnt at the hospital bedside. **2** dispassionate, coldly detached. —**clinical death,** death judged by observation of a person's condition. —**clinically** *adv.* [f. L f. Gk (*klinē* bed)]

clinician /klɪ'nɪʃ(ə)n/ *n.* one who is skilled in the practice of clinical medicine, psychiatry, etc. [f. CLINIC]

clink[1] *n.* a sharp ringing sound. —*v.t./i.* to make or cause to make this sound. [f. Du.; imit.]

clink[2] *n.* (*slang*) prison. [orig. unkn.]

clinker *n.* a mass of slag or lava; the stony residue from burnt coal. [f. Du. (as CLINK[1])]

clinker-built *adj.* (of a boat) having its external planks overlapping and secured with clinched nails. [f. *clink*, dial. var. of CLINCH]

clip[1] *n.* **1** a device for holding things together or affixing something. **2** a piece of jewellery fastened by a clip. **3** a set of attached cartridges for a firearm. —*v.t.* (**-pp-**) to grip tightly; to fix with a clip. —**clip-on** *adj.* attached by a clip. [OE]

clip[2] *v.t.* (**-pp-**) **1** to cut or trim with shears or scissors. **2** to punch a small piece from (a ticket etc.) to show that it has been used; to cut from a newspaper etc. **3** to omit (letters etc.) from (a word pronounced). **4** (*colloq.*) to hit sharply. —*n.* **1** the act of clipping. **2** something clipped; a yield of wool clipped from sheep; an extract from a film. **3** (*colloq.*) a sharp blow. **4** (*colloq.*) a rapid pace. [f. ON, prob. imit.]

clipboard *n.* a small portable board with a spring clip for holding papers.

clipper *n.* **1** a fast sailing-ship. **2** (usu. in *pl.*) an instrument for clipping hair. [f. CLIP[2]]

clipping *n.* a piece clipped off; a newspaper cutting. [f. CLIP[2]]

clique /kli:k/ *n.* a small exclusive group of people. —**cliquish** *adj.*, **cliquy** *adj.* [F, orig. = clicking noise]

clitoris /'klɪtərɪs/ *n.* a small erectile part of the female genitals, at the upper end of the vulva. —**clitoral** *adj.* [L f. Gk]

cloaca /kləʊ'eɪkə/ *n.* (*pl.* **-ae** /-i:/) the excretory opening at the end of the intestinal canal in birds, reptiles, etc. [L, = sewer]

cloak *n.* a sleeveless outdoor garment hanging loosely from the shoulders. —*v.t.* **1** to cover with a cloak. **2** to conceal, to disguise. —**cloak-and-dagger** *adj.* involving intrigue and espionage. [f. OF *cloke*, var. of *cloche* bell (from its shape)]

cloakroom *n.* a room where outdoor clothes and luggage may be left by visitors; (*euphem.*) a lavatory.

clobber[1] *n.* (*slang*) clothing, personal belongings. [orig. unkn.]

clobber[2] *v.t.* (*slang*) **1** to hit repeatedly, to beat up. **2** to defeat. **3** to criticize severely. [orig. unkn.]

cloche /klɒʃ/ *n.* **1** a portable translucent cover for protecting outdoor plants. **2** a woman's close-fitting bell-shaped hat (ill. DRESS). [F, = bell, f. L (as foll.)]

clock[1] *n.* **1** an instrument measuring and

recording the passage of time, with a regulating device (so that it operates at a uniform speed) and constant motive power, usually indicating hours, minutes, etc., by hands on a dial or by displayed figures. **2** a clocklike measuring device; (*colloq.*) a speedometer, taximeter, or stop-watch. **3** the seed-head of a dandelion. —*v.t.* to time (a race) with a stop-watch; (also with *up*) to attain or register (a stated time, distance, or speed). —**clock golf,** a game in which a golf-ball is putted into a hole from successive points round a circle. **clock in** *or* **on,** to register one's arrival at work, especially by means of an automatic clock. **clock off** *or* **out,** to register one's departure similarly. [f. LG or Du. f. L *clocca* bell]

clock[2] *n.* an ornamental pattern on the side of a stocking or sock. [orig. unkn.]

clockwise *adj.* & *adv.* moving in a curve from left to right, corresponding in direction to the hands of a clock.

clockwork *n.* a mechanism with spring and gears, like that used (from the 15th c., instead of weights) to drive clocks; (*attrib.*) driven by clockwork.

clod *n.* a lump of earth, clay, etc. [var. of CLOT]

clodhoppers *n.pl.* (*colloq.*) large heavy shoes.

clog *n.* a shoe with a thick wooden sole. —*v.t./i.* (**-gg-**) to cause an obstruction in; to become blocked. [orig. unkn.]

cloisonne /klwɑːˈzɒneɪ/ *n.* a technique of enamel decoration in which the colours are kept apart by thin metal strips. —*adj.* of or using this technique. [F, f. *cloison* partition, ult. f. L *claudere* close]

cloister *n.* **1** a covered walk, often round a quadrangle with a wall on the outer and a colonnade on the inner side, especially in a monastery, convent, college, or cathedral. **2** monastic life or seclusion. —*v.t.* to seclude in a convent etc. —**cloistral** *adj.* [f. OF f. L *claustrum* enclosed place (*claudere* shut)]

cloistered *adj.* secluded, sheltered; monastic. [f. prec.]

clone *n.* a group of plants or organisms produced asexually from one stock or ancestor; one such organism; (*colloq.*) a person regarded as identical with another. —*v.t.* to propagate as a clone. —**clonal** /ˈkləʊn(ə)l/ *adj.* [f. Gk *klōn* twig]

clonk *n.* a sharp heavy sound of an impact. —*v.t./i.* **1** to make this sound. **2** (*colloq.*) to hit. [imit.]

close[1] /kləʊs/ *adj.* **1** near in space or time; near in relationship or association; nearly alike; (of a race or contest) in which the competitors are almost equal. **2** dense, compact, with only slight intervals; detailed, leaving no gaps or weaknesses. **3** oppressively warm or humid. **4** closed, shut; limited to certain persons. **5** hidden, secret; secretive. **6** niggardly. —*adv.* at a short distance or interval. —*n.* **1** a street closed at one end. **2** a precinct of a cathedral. —**at close quarters,** very close together. **close harmony,** harmony in which the notes of a chord are close together. **close-hauled** *adj.* with sails hauled aft to sail close to the wind. **close-knit** *adj.* closely united. **close season,** the season when the killing of game etc. is illegal. **close shave,** a narrow escape. **close-up** *n.* a photograph etc. taken at close range. —**closely** *adv.*, **closeness** *n.* [f. OF f. L *clausus* (*claudere* shut)]

close[2] /kləʊz/ *v.t./i.* **1** to shut, to block up. **2** to bring or come to an end; to be or declare to be not open to the public. **3** to bring or come closer or into contact; to make (an electric circuit etc.) continuous. —*n.* a conclusion, an end. —**closed-circuit** *adj.* (of television) transmitted by wires to a restricted circuit of receivers. **close down,** to cease working, trading, or transmitting. **closed shop,** a business etc. where employees must belong to an agreed trade union. **close in,** to approach from all sides so as to shut in or entrap; (of days) to get successively shorter. **close with,** to accept the offer made by (a person); to join battle or start fighting with. **closing-time** *n.* the time when a public house etc. ends business. [f. OF *clos* f. L *claudere* shut]

closet /ˈklɒzɪt/ *n.* a cupboard or small room; a water-closet. —*v.t.* to shut away, especially in private conference or study. [f. OF, dim. of *clos* enclosed space (as prec.)]

closure /ˈkləʊʒə(r)/ *n.* a closing or closed state; a decision in Parliament to take a vote without further debate. —*v.t.* to apply closure to (a motion, speaker, etc.). [f. OF f. L *clausura* (*claudere* close)]

clot *n.* a thick mass of coagulated liquid, especially of blood exposed to air. —*v.i.* (**-tt-**) to form into clots. —**clotted cream,** thick cream obtained by slow scalding. [OE]

cloth *n.* **1** woven or felted material; a piece of this for a special purpose; a dishcloth, tablecloth, etc. **2** clerical clothes, the clergy. [OE]

clothe /kləʊð/ *v.t.* (*past* & *p.p.* **clothed** *or* **clad**) to put clothes on, to provide with clothes; to cover as with clothes. [OE (as CLOTH)]

clothes /kləʊðz, -əʊz/ *n.pl.* things worn to cover the body and limbs; bedclothes. —**clothes-horse** *n.* a frame for airing washed clothes. **clothes-line** *n.* a rope or wire on which washed clothes are hung out to dry. **clothes-peg** *n.* a clip or forked device for securing clothes to a clothes-line. [OE (orig. pl. of CLOTH)]

clothier /ˈkləʊðɪə(r)/ *n.* a seller of men's clothes. [f. CLOTH]

clothing /ˈkləʊðɪŋ/ *n.* clothes collectively. [f. CLOTH]

cloud *n.* **1** a visible mass of condensed watery vapour floating high above the ground. **2** a mass of smoke or dust; a large moving mass of insects etc. in the sky. **3** a state of gloom, trouble, or suspicion. —*v.t./i.* to cover or darken with clouds or gloom or trouble; to become overcast or gloomy. —**cloud chamber,** a device containing vapour for tracking the paths of charged particles, X-rays, and gamma rays. **cloud-cuckoo-land** *n.* a realm of fantasy or unrealistic ideas (transl. of Gk name of realm in Aristophanes' *Birds* built by the birds to separate the gods from mankind). [OE]

cloudburst *n.* a sudden violent rainstorm.

cloudless *adj.* without clouds. [f. CLOUD + -LESS]

cloudy *adj.* **1** covered with clouds, overcast. **2** not clear, not transparent. —**cloudiness** *n.* [f. CLOUD]

clout *n.* **1** a heavy blow. **2** (*archaic*) a piece of cloth or clothing. —*v.t.* to hit hard. [OE]

clove[1] *n.* the dried flower-bud of a tropical myrtle (*Eugenia caryophyllata*) used as a spice. [f. OF f. L *clavus* nail (from the shape)]

clove[2] *n.* a small segment of a compound bulb, especially of garlic. [OE, rel. to CLEAVE[1]]

clove[3] *past* of CLEAVE[1].

clove hitch a knot used for securing a rope to a spar or to another rope. [old p.p. of CLEAVE[1]]

cloven *p.p.* of CLEAVE[1]. —*adj.* split, partly divided. —**cloven hoof,** a hoof that is divided, as of oxen, sheep, or goats.

clover *n.* a fodder plant of the genus *Trifolium,* with leaves of three leaflets. —**in clover,** in ease and luxury. [OE]

clown *n.* a performer, especially in a circus, who does comical tricks and actions; a person acting like a clown. —*v.i.* to behave like a clown. —**clownish** *adj.* [orig. unkn.]

cloy *v.t.* to satiate or sicken, especially with richness, sweetness, or excess. [f. AF (cf. ENCLAVE)]

club *n.* **1** a heavy stick thick at one end, used as a weapon etc.; a stick with a shaped head, used in golf. **2** a playing-card of the suit (**clubs**) marked with black clover-leaves. **3** an association of persons meeting periodically for a shared activity; an organization or premises offering its members social amenities, meals, temporary accommodation, etc.; an organization offering subscribers certain benefits. —*v.t./i.* (**-bb-**) **1** to strike with a club etc. **2** to combine, especially in making up a sum of money for a purpose. —**club-foot** *n.* a congenitally deformed foot. **club-moss** *n.* a pteridophyte with upright spikes of spore-cases. **club-root** *n.* a disease of cabbages etc. with a swelling at the base of the stem. [ON]

clubbable *adj.* sociable, fit for membership of a club. [f. CLUB]

clubhouse *n.* the premises used by a club.

cluck *n.* a guttural cry like that of a hen. —*v.i.* to emit a cluck. [imit.]

clue *n.* a fact or idea that gives a guide to the solution of a problem; a word or words indicating what is to be inserted in a crossword puzzle. —*v.t.* to provide with a clue. —**not to have a clue,** (*colloq.*) to be ignorant or incompetent. [var. of CLEW]

clump *n.* a cluster or mass (of trees, tall plants, etc.). —*v.t.* **1** to form a clump, to arrange in a clump. **2** to walk with a heavy tread. **3** (*colloq.*) to hit. [f. LG or Du.]

clumsy /ˈklʌmzɪ/ *adj.* heavy and lacking in dexterity or grace; large and difficult to handle or use; done without tact or skill. —**clumsily** *adv.*, **clumsiness** *n.* [f. obs. *clumse* be numb with cold, prob. f. Scand.]

clung *past* & *p.p.* of CLING.

cluster *n.* a small close group; a group of stars bound together by gravity. —*v.t./i.* to gather in a cluster. [OE]

clutch[1] *v.t./i.* to seize eagerly, to grasp tightly; try to grasp *at.* —*n.* **1** a tight grasp; (in *pl.*) grasping hands, cruel or relentless grasp or control. **2** (in motor vehicles) a device for connecting the engine to the transmission; the pedal operating this. [OE]

clutch[2] *n.* a set of eggs for hatching; the chickens hatched from these. [var. of N. Engl. *cletch,* f. ON]

clutter *n.* a crowded untidy collection of things; untidy state. —*v.t.* to crowd untidily, to fill with clutter. [rel. to CLOT]

Clydesdale /ˈklaɪdzdeɪl/ *n.* a breed of heavy draught-horses originally bred near the River Clyde; an animal of this breed.

Cm *symbol* curium.

cm *abbr.* centimetre(s).

CND *abbr.* Campaign for Nuclear Disarmament.

Co *symbol* cobalt.

Co. *abbr.* company.

c/o *abbr.* care of.

co- *prefix* together with, jointly. [L]

coach *n.* **1** a single-decker bus, usually comfortably equipped for longer journeys; a railway carriage; a closed horse-drawn carriage. **2** an instructor or trainer in sport; a private tutor. —*v.t.* to train or teach as a coach. —**coach screw,** a large screw with a square head, turned by a spanner. [f. F f. Magyar]

coachwork *n.* the bodywork of a road or railway vehicle.

coagulant /kəʊˈægjʊlənt/ *n.* a substance that causes coagulation. [f. foll.]

coagulate /kəʊˈægjʊleɪt/ *v.t./i.* to change from a

liquid to a semisolid; to clot, to curdle. —**coagulation** *n.* [f. L *coagulare* (*coagulum* rennet)]

coal *n.* a hard black mineral, found below ground and used as fuel and in making gas, tar, etc.; a piece of this, one that is burning. —*v.t./i.* to put coal into (a ship etc.); to take in a supply of coal. —**coal-face** *n.* the exposed surface of coal in a mine. **coal gas,** mixed gases extracted from coal and used for lighting and heating. **coal measures,** a series of rocks formed by seams of coal and intervening strata. **coals to Newcastle,** a thing brought to a place where it is already plentiful, an unnecessary action. **coal-scuttle** *n.* a container for coal to supply a domestic fire. **coal tar,** tar extracted from bituminous coal. **coal-tit** *n.* a small greyish bird with a dark head. [OE]

coalesce /kəʊəˈles/ *v.i.* to come together and form one whole. —**coalescence** *n.*, **coalescent** *adj.* [f. L *coalescere* (co-, *alescere* grow up)]

coalfield *n.* an area yielding coal.

coalition /kəʊˈlɪʃ(ə)n/ *n.* fusion into one whole; a temporary alliance of political parties. [f. L (as COALESCE)]

coaming *n.* a raised border round a ship's hatches etc. to keep out water. [orig. unkn.]

coarse *adj.* **1** rough or loose in texture, made of large particles. **2** lacking refinement of manner or perception, crude, vulgar; (of language) obscene. **3** inferior, common. —**coarse fish,** freshwater fish other than salmon and trout. —**coarsely** *adv.*, **coarseness** *n.* [orig. unkn.]

coarsen *v.t./i.* to make or become coarse. [f. prec.]

coast *n.* the border of the land nearest the sea, the sea-shore. —*v.i.* **1** to ride or move, usually downhill, without the use of power. **2** to sail along the coast. —**coastal** *adj.* [f. OF f. L *costa* rib, flank]

coaster *n.* **1** a ship that travels along the coast. **2** a small tray or mat for a bottle or glass. [f. COAST]

coastguard *n.* a body of persons employed to keep watch on coasts, prevent smuggling, etc.; a member of this.

coastline *n.* the line of the sea-shore, especially with regard to its configuration.

coat *n.* **1** an outer garment with sleeves and often extending below the hips, an overcoat, jacket, etc. **2** a natural covering, especially an animal's fur or hair. **3** a covering of paint etc. laid on a surface at any one time. —*v.t.* to cover *with* a coat or layer; (of paint etc.) to form a covering to. —**coat of arms,** the heraldic bearings or shield of a person or corporation. **coat of mail,** *see* MAIL². [f. OF f. Gmc]

coating *n.* **1** a covering layer. **2** material for coats. [f. COAT]

co-author *n.* a joint author. —*v.t.* to be joint author of.

coax *v.t.* **1** to persuade gradually or by flattery; to obtain by such means. **2** to manipulate carefully or slowly. [f. 'make a *cokes* of' (obs. *cokes* fool)]

coaxial /kəʊˈæksɪəl/ *adj.* having a common axis; (of an electric cable or line) transmitting by means of two concentric conductors separated by an insulator. [f. CO- + AXIAL]

cob *n.* **1** a roundish lump. **2** a corn-cob (see CORN¹). **3** a sturdy riding-horse with short legs. **4** a male swan. **5** a large hazel-nut. **6** a loaf rounded on the top. [orig. unkn.]

cobalt /ˈkəʊbɔːlt, -ɒlt/ *n.* **1** a hard silvery-white metallic element similar in many respects to nickel, symbol Co, atomic number 27. **2** a pigment made from cobalt. —*adj.* the deep-blue colour characteristic of this pigment. [f. G *kobalt*, prob. = *kobold* goblin or demon of the mines, the ore having been so called by the miners on account of its worthlessness (as then supposed) and from its bad effects upon their health and upon the silver ores with which it occurred, effects due mainly to the arsenic and sulphur with which it was combined]

cobber *n.* (*Austral.* & *N.Z. colloq.*) a friend, a mate. [perh. f. dial. *cob* take a liking to]

cobble¹ *n.* (in full **cobble-stone**) a small rounded stone used for paving. —*v.t.* to pave with cobbles. [f. COB]

cobble² *v.t.* to mend or patch up (especially shoes); to repair or put together roughly. [back-formation f. foll.]

cobbler *n.* **1** a shoe-repairer. **2** an iced drink of wine, sugar, and lemon. **3** a fruit pie topped with scones. [orig. unkn.]

COBOL /ˈkəʊbɒl/ *n.* a computer language for use in commerce. [*Co*mmon *B*usiness *O*riented *L*anguage]

cobra /ˈkəʊbrə, ˈkɒ-/ *n.* a venomous hooded Indian or African snake of the genus *Naja*. [Port., f. L *colubra* snake]

cobweb *n.* the fine network spun by a spider; a thread of this. —**cobwebby** *adj.* [f. obs. *coppe* spider]

coca /ˈkəʊkə/ *n.* a South American shrub, *Erythroxylon coca*; its leaves, chewed as a stimulant. [Sp. f. Quechua]

cocaine /kɒˈkeɪn, kəʊ-/ *n.* a drug from coca, used as a local anaesthetic and as a stimulating drug. [f. COCA]

coccyx /ˈkɒksɪks/ *n.* (*pl.* **coccyges** /-dʒiːz/) a small triangular bone at the base of the spinal column. [L f. Gk *kokkux* cuckoo (from being shaped like its bill)]

cochineal /ˈkɒtʃɪniːl/ *n.* a bright-red colouring matter made from the dried bodies of a Mexican insect *Dactylopius coccus*. [f. F or Sp. f. L *coccinus* scarlet f. Gk]

cochlea /ˈkɒklɪə/ *n.* (*pl.* **cochleae** /-lɪi:/) the spiral cavity of the inner ear. [L, = snail-shell, f. Gk]

cock[1] *n.* **1** a male bird, especially of the domestic fowl. **2** the firing-lever in a gun, raised to be released by the trigger; a cocked position. **3** a tap or valve controlling the flow of a liquid. —*v.t.* **1** to make upright or erect; to move (the eye or ear) attentively or knowingly; to set aslant or turn up the brim of (a hat). **2** to raise the cock of (a gun). —**cock-a-doodle-doo** *int.* the sound of a cock crowing. **cock-a-hoop** *adj.* exultant. **cock-a-leekie** *n.* a Scottish soup of cock boiled with leeks. **cock-and-bull story,** one that is absurd or incredible. **cock a snook,** see SNOOK. **cock-crow** *n.* dawn. **cocked hat,** a brimless triangular hat pointed at front, back, and top. **cock-eyed** *adj.* (*colloq.*) crooked, askew; absurd, not practical. **cock-fight** *n.* a fight between cocks as a sport. **cock-shy** *n.* a target for throwing at, a throw at this; an object of ridicule or criticism. [f. OE & F]

cock[2] *n.* a small conical pile of hay or straw. [perh. f. Scand.]

cockade /kɒˈkeɪd/ *n.* a rosette etc. worn in the hat as a badge. [f. F (as COCK[1])]

cockatoo /kɒkəˈtu:/ *n.* a crested parrot. [f. Du. f. Malay]

cockchafer /ˈkɒktʃeɪfə(r)/ *n.* a large pale-brown beetle.

cocker *n.* (in full **cocker spaniel**) a small spaniel with a golden-brown coat. [f. COCK[1], as starting woodcock]

cockerel /ˈkɒkər(ə)l/ *n.* a young cock. [dim. of COCK[1]]

cockle *n.* **1** an edible bivalve shellfish; its shell. **2** a pucker or wrinkle in paper, glass, etc. **3** (in full **cockle-shell**) a small shallow boat. —*v.t./i.* to make or become puckered. [f. OF *coquille* shell f. L f. Gk (as CONCH)]

cockney /ˈkɒknɪ/ *n.* **1** a native of London, especially of the East End (according to Minsheu (early 17th c.) 'one born within the sound of Bow Bells'). **2** the dialect or accent historically associated with this area. —*adj.* of cockneys or their dialect. [f. obs. *cokeney* cock's egg, orig. sense prob. small or ill-shaped egg, hence 'milksop', 'townsman']

cockpit *n.* **1** the compartment for the pilot (and crew) of an aircraft or spacecraft; the driver's seat in a racing-car; a space for the helmsman in some small yachts. **2** an arena of war or other conflict. **3** a place made for cock-fights.

cockroach *n.* a dark-brown beetle-like insect infesting kitchens and bathrooms. [f. Sp. *cucaracha*]

cockscomb *n.* the crest of a cock.

cocksure *adj.* presumptuously or arrogantly confident; absolutely sure. [f. *cock* = God + SURE]

cocktail *n.* **1** a mixed alcoholic drink, especially of spirit with bitters etc. **2** an appetizer containing shellfish or fruit. [orig. unkn.]

cocky *adj.* pertly self-confident. —**cockily** *adv.*, **cockiness** *n.* [f. COCK[1]]

coco /ˈkəʊkəʊ/ *n.* a tropical palm-tree (*Cocos nucifera*) from which coconuts come. [Sp. & Port., = grimace]

cocoa /ˈkəʊkəʊ/ *n.* a powder made with crushed cacao seeds, often with other ingredients; a drink made from this. —**cocoa bean,** a cacao seed. **cocoa butter,** a fatty substance obtained from this. [alt. of CACAO]

coconut /ˈkəʊkənʌt/ *n.* the large brown seed of the coco, with a hard shell and edible white lining enclosing a milky juice. —**coconut matting,** matting made of fibre from coconut husks. **coconut shy,** a fairground amusement where balls are thrown to dislodge coconuts from a stand. [f. coco + NUT]

cocoon /kəˈku:n/ *n.* the silky case spun by an insect larva to protect itself as a chrysalis, especially that of a silkworm; a protective covering. —*v.t.* to wrap or coat in a cocoon. [f. F f. Prov. (*coca* shell)]

cocotte /kəˈkɒt/ *n.* a small fireproof dish for serving food. [F]

COD *abbr.* cash (*US* collect) on delivery.

cod *n.* (*pl.* same) a large sea fish (also **codfish**). —**cod-liver oil,** oil from cod livers, rich in vitamins A and D. [orig. unkn.]

coda *n.* the final passage of a movement or piece of music, often elaborate and distinct; the concluding section of a ballet. [It. f. L *cauda* tail]

coddle *v.t.* **1** to treat as an invalid; to protect attentively, to pamper. **2** to cook (an egg) in water just below boiling-point. [prob. var. of CAUDLE]

code *n.* **1** a system of words, letters, or symbols used to represent others for secrecy or brevity. **2** a system of prearranged signals for transmitting messages. **3** a set of instructions used in programming a computer. **4** a systematic set of laws or rules. **5** a prevailing standard of moral behaviour. —*v.t.* to put into code. [f. OF f. L *codex*]

codeine /ˈkəʊdi:n/ *n.* an alkaloid obtained from opium, used to relieve pain or induce sleep. [f. Gk *kōdeia* poppy-head]

codex /ˈkəʊdeks/ *n.* (*pl.* **codices** /-dɪsi:z/) **1** an ancient manuscript text in the book-form which between 1st–4th c. AD gradually replaced the continuous roll previously used for written documents. **2** a collection of pharmaceutical descriptions of drugs etc. [L, = wood block, tablet, book (as these tablets were often coated with wax and inscribed)]

codger /ˈkɒdʒə(r)/ *n.* (*colloq.*) a person, especially a strange one. [perh. var. of CADGER]

codicil /ˈkɒdɪsɪl/ *n.* an addition to a will

explaining, modifying, or revoking it or part of it. [f. L, dim. of CODEX]

codify /ˈkəʊdɪfaɪ/ *v.t.* to arrange (laws etc.) systematically into a code. —**codification** /-ˈkeɪʃ(ə)n/ *n.*, **codifier** *n.* [f. CODE]

codling[1] *n.* (also **codlin**) **1** a kind of cooking apple, usually oblong and yellowish. **2** a moth whose larva feeds on apples. [f. F *quer de lion* lion-heart]

codling[2] *n.* a small codfish. [f. COD]

codpiece *n.* an appendage like small bag or a flap at the front of a man's breeches in 15th-16th-c. dress. [f. obs. *cod* scrotum]

coeducation /kəʊedjuːˈkeɪʃ(ə)n/ *n.* education of pupils of both sexes together. —**coeducational** *adj.*

coefficient /kəʊɪˈfɪʃ(ə)nt/ *n.* (*Math.*) a quantity placed before and multiplying another quantity; (*Physics*) a multiplier or factor by which a property is measured.

coelacanth /ˈsiːləkænθ/ *n.* a fish of the family Coelacanthidae, originally thought to have a hollow spine, extinct but for one species (*Latimeria chalumnae*). [f. Gk *koilos* hollow + *acantha* spine]

coelenterate /siːˈlentəreɪt/ *n.* a member of the phylum Coelenterata, aquatic animals (including sea-anemones, hydras, jellyfish, and corals) with a simple tube-shaped or cup-shaped body and a digestive system with a single opening surrounded by a ring of tentacles. —*adj.* of coelenterates. [f. Gk *koilos* hollow + *enteron* intestine]

coeliac /ˈsiːlɪæk/ *adj.* of the belly. —**coeliac disease,** an intestinal disease causing defective digestion of fats. [f. L f. Gk (*koilia* belly)]

coenobite /ˈsiːnəbaɪt/ *n.* a member of a monastic community. —**coenobitic** /-ˈbɪtɪk/ *adj.*, **coenobitical** *adj.* [f. OF or L f. Gk *koinobion* convent (*koinos* common, *bios* life)]

coequal /kəʊˈiːkwəl/ *adj.* & *n.* (*archaic* or *literary*) equal.

coerce /kəʊˈɜːs/ *v.t.* to impel or force (*into* obedience etc.). —**coercion** *n.* [f. L *coercēre* (co-, *arcēre* restrain)]

coercive /kəʊˈɜːsɪv/ *adj.* using coercion. [as prec.]

coeval /kəʊˈiːvəl/ *adj.* having the same age, existing at the same epoch. —*n.* a coeval person, a contemporary. [f. L *coaevus* (co-, *aevum* age)]

coexist /kəʊɪgˈzɪst/ *v.i.* to exist together (*with*). [f. L *coexistere* (co-, *existere* exist)]

coexistence *n.* coexisting. —**peaceful coexistence,** mutual tolerance of nations with different ideologies or political and social systems. —**coexistent** *adj.* [f. prec.]

coextensive /kəʊɪkˈstensɪv/ *adj.* extending over the same space or time.

C. of E. *abbr.* Church of England.

coffee /ˈkɒfiː/ *n.* **1** a drink made from the roasted and ground beanlike seeds of a tropical shrub of the genus *Coffea*; a cup of this; these seeds; the shrub. **2** the pale brown colour of coffee mixed with milk. —**coffee bar,** a place serving coffee and light refreshments from a counter. **coffee morning,** a morning social gathering at which coffee is served, usually in aid of a good cause. **coffee shop,** an informal restaurant, especially at a hotel. **coffee-table** *n.* a small low table. **coffee-table book,** a large expensive illustrated book, too large for a bookshelf. [f. Turk. f. Arab.]

coffer *n.* **1** a large strong box for valuables; (in *pl.*) a treasury, funds. **2** a sunken panel in a ceiling etc. —**coffer-dam** *n.* a watertight enclosure pumped dry for work in building bridges etc., or for repairing a ship. [f. OF f. L f. Gk *kophinos* basket]

coffin *n.* a box in which a corpse is buried or cremated. —*v.t.* to put in a coffin. [f. OF, = little basket (as prec.)]

cog *n.* any of a series of projections on the edge of a wheel or bar transferring motion by engaging with another series; an unimportant member of an organization etc. —**cog-wheel** *n.* a wheel with cogs. [prob. f. Scand.]

cogent /ˈkəʊdʒ(ə)nt/ *adj.* convincing, compelling. —**cogency** *n.*, **cogently** *adv.* [f. L *cogere* compel]

cogging *n.* the process of passing heated metal ingots between a pair of rollers as the first stage in rolling them into the shape required. [f. COG]

cogitate /ˈkɒdʒɪteɪt/ *v.t./i.* to ponder, to meditate. —**cogitation** /-ˈteɪʃ(ə)n/ *n.*, **cogitative** *adj.* [f. L *cogitare* think]

cognac /ˈkɒnjæk/ *n.* brandy, especially that distilled in the town of Cognac in western France. [f. *Cognac*]

cognate /ˈkɒgneɪt/ *adj.* related or descended from a common ancestor; (of a word) having the same linguistic family or derivation. —*n.* a relative; a cognate word. [f. L *cognatus* (co-, *gnatus* born)]

cognition /kɒgˈnɪʃ(ə)n/ *n.* knowing, perceiving, or conceiving as an act or faculty distinct from emotion and volition; the result of this. —**cognitional** *adj.*, **cognitive** /ˈkɒgnɪtɪv/ *adj.* [f. L *cognoscere* (co-, *gnoscere* know)]

cognizance /ˈkɒgnɪz(ə)ns/ *n.* **1** knowledge or awareness, perception. **2** sphere of observation or concern. **3** a distinctive device or mark. [f. OF f. L (as prec.)]

cognizant /ˈkɒgnɪz(ə)nt/ *adj.* having knowledge or taking note of. [f. prec.]

cognomen /kɒgˈnəʊmen/ *n.* a nickname; an ancient Roman's personal name or epithet. [L]

cognoscente /kɒnjɒˈʃentɪ/ *n.* (*pl.* **-ti**) a connoisseur. [It.]

cohabit /kəʊˈhæbɪt/ *v.i.* to live together as husband and wife (usually of a couple who are not married to each other). —**cohabitation** /-ˈteɪʃ(ə)n/ *n.* [f. L *cohabitare* (co-, *habitare* dwell)]

cohere /kəʊˈhɪə(r)/ *v.i.* **1** (of parts or a whole) to stick together, to remain united. **2** (of reasoning etc.) to be logical or consistent. [f. L *cohaerēre* (co-, *haerēre* stick)]

coherent /kəʊˈhɪərənt/ *adj.* cohering; (of reasoning) connected logically; not rambling in speech or in reasoning. —**coherence** *n.*, **coherently** *adv.* [as prec.]

cohesion /kəʊˈhiːʒ(ə)n/ *n.* sticking together; the force with which molecules cohere, a tendency to cohere. —**cohesive** *adj.* [as COHERE]

cohort /ˈkəʊhɔːt/ *n.* **1** a Roman military unit, one tenth of a legion; a band of warriors. **2** persons banded or grouped together; a group having a common statistical characteristic. [f. F or L *cohors*]

coif *n.* (*hist.*) a close-fitting cap. [f. OF f. L *cofia* helmet]

coiffeur /kwɑːˈfɜː(r)/ *n.* a hairdresser. —***coiffeuse*** *n.fem.* [F]

coiffure /kwɑːˈfjʊə(r)/ *n.* a hairstyle. [F]

coign /kɔɪn/ *n.* a projecting corner, chiefly in **coign of vantage,** a place from which a good view can be obtained. [old form of COIN (Shak. *Macbeth* I. vi. 7)]

coil *v.t./i.* to arrange or be arranged in spirals or concentric rings; to move sinuously. —*n.* a coiled length of rope etc.; a coiled arrangement; a single turn of a coiled thing; a flexible loop as a contraceptive device in the womb; a coiled wire for the passage of an electric current. [f. OF f. L *colligere* collect]

coin *n.* a small stamped disc of metal as official money; coins collectively. —*v.t.* **1** to make (money) by stamping metal; to make (metal) into coins. **2** to invent (a new word or phrase). [f. OF, = stamping-die, f. L *cuneus* wedge]

coinage /ˈkɔɪnɪdʒ/ *n.* **1** coining; coins; a system of coins in use. **2** a coined word or phrase. [as prec.]

coincide /kəʊɪnˈsaɪd/ *v.i.* **1** to occur at the same time; to occupy the same portion of space. **2** to agree or be identical (*with*). [f. L *coincidere* (co-, *incidere* fall on)]

coincidence /kəʊˈɪnsɪd(ə)ns/ *n.* coinciding; a remarkable concurrence of events or circumstances without apparent causal connection. —**coincident** *adj.* [as prec.]

coincidental /kəʊɪnsɪˈdent(ə)l/ *adj.* occurring by coincidence; in the nature of a coincidence. —**coincidentally** *adv.* [f. prec.]

Cointreau /ˈkwæntrəʊ/ *n.* [P] a colourless orange-flavoured liqueur.

coir /kɔɪə(r)/ *n.* coconut fibre used for ropes, matting, etc. [f. Malayalam, = cord]

coition /kəʊˈɪʃ(ə)n/ *n.* coitus. [f. L *coire* (co-, *ire* go)]

coitus /ˈkəʊɪtəs/ *n.* sexual intercourse. —**coital** *adj.* [L, as prec.]

coke *n.* the solid substance left after gases have been extracted from coal. —*v.t.* to convert (coal) into coke. [prob. f. dial. *colk* core (orig. unkn.)]

col /kɒl/ *n.* **1** a depression in a chain of mountains. **2** a region of low pressure between anticyclones. [F f. L, = neck]

col- *prefix* see COM-.

cola /ˈkəʊlə/ *n.* a West African tree with seed producing an extract used as a tonic etc.; a carbonated drink flavoured with this. [West African]

colander /ˈkʌləndə(r)/ *n.* a perforated bowl-shaped vessel used to strain off liquid in cooking. [f. L *colare* strain]

cold *adj.* **1** of or at a low temperature, especially when compared with the human body; not heated, cooled after heat; feeling cold. **2** dead; (*slang*) unconscious. **3** lacking geniality, affection, or enthusiasm. **4** depressing, dispiriting. **5** (of colour) suggestive of cold. **6** remote from the thing sought; (of the scent in hunting) grown faint. **7** unrehearsed. —*adv.* in a cold state. —*n.* **1** prevalence of low temperature; cold condition. **2** an infectious illness of the nose or throat or both, with catarrh and sneezing. —**cold-blooded** *adj.* having a body temperature that varies with that of the environment; callous, cruel. **cold chisel,** a toughened steel chisel. **cold comfort,** poor consolation. **cold cream,** an ointment for cleansing and softening the skin. **cold frame,** an unheated frame for growing small plants. **cold shoulder,** deliberate unfriendliness. **cold-shoulder** *v.t.* to be unfriendly to. **cold storage,** storage in a refrigerator; *in cold storage*, put aside but still available. **cold war,** hostilities short of armed conflict, consisting in threats, violent propaganda, subversive political activities or the like, specifically those between the USSR and the Western powers after the Second World War. **get** *or* **have cold feet,** to feel afraid or reluctant. **throw** *or* **pour cold water on,** to be discouraging about, to belittle. —**coldly** *adv.*, **coldness** *n.* [OE, cogn. w. L *gelu* frost]

cole *n.* any of various plants of the cabbage family, especially (**cole-seed**) rape. [f. ON f. L *caulis*]

coleopterous /kɒlɪˈɒptərəs/ *adj.* of the order Coleoptera (comprising beetles and weevils) of insects with front wings serving as sheaths for the hinder wings. [f. Gk (*koleon* sheath, *pteron* wing)]

coleslaw /ˈkəʊlslɔː/ *n.* a salad of sliced raw cabbage coated in dressing. [f. COLE]

coleus /ˈkəʊlɪəs/ *n.* a plant of the genus *Coleus* with variegated coloured leaves. [f. Gk *koleos* sheath]

colic /ˈkɒlɪk/ *n.* a severe spasmodic abdominal pain. —**colicky** *adj.* [f. F f. L (as COLON[2])]

colitis /kəˈlaɪtɪs/ *n.* inflammation of the lining of the colon. [f. COLON[2]]

collaborate /kəˈlæbəreɪt/ *v.i.* to work jointly (*with*), especially at a literary or artistic production; to co-operate with the enemy. —**collaboration** /-ˈreɪʃ(ə)n/ *n.*, **collaborator** *n.* [f. L *collaborare* (COL-, *laborare* work)]

collage /kɒˈlɑːʒ/ *n.* a form or work of art in which various materials are arranged and glued to a backing. [F, = gluing]

collagen /ˈkɒlədʒ(ə)n/ *n.* a protein found in animal tissue and bone, yielding gelatin on boiling. [f. F f. Gk *kolla* glue]

collapse /kəˈlæps/ *v.t./i.* **1** to fall down or in suddenly. **2** to lose strength, force, or value suddenly; to cause to collapse. —*n.* the act or process of collapsing; a breakdown. [f. L *collapsus* (COL-, *labi* slip)]

collapsible /kəˈlæpsɪb(ə)l/ *adj.* made so as to fold compactly. [f. prec.]

collar /ˈkɒlə(r)/ *n.* **1** a neckband, upright or turned over, of a coat, dress, shirt, etc. **2** a strap of leather etc. put round an animal's neck. **3** a restraining or connecting band, ring, or pipe in a machine etc. —*v.t.* (*slang*) to seize, to appropriate. —**collar-beam** *n.* a horizontal beam connecting two rafters. **collar-bone** *n.* the bone joining the breast-bone and shoulder-blade, the clavicle. [f. AF f. L (*collum* neck)]

collate /kəˈleɪt/ *v.t.* to compare (texts etc.) in detail (*with*); to collect and arrange systematically. —**collator** *n.* [f. L *collat-* p.p. stem of *conferre* bring together]

collateral /kəˈlætərəl/ *adj.* **1** side by side, parallel; additional but subordinate, contributory; connected but aside from the main subject, course, etc. **2** descended from the same stock but by a different line. —*n.* a collateral person or security. —**collateral security,** an additional security pledged; a security lodged by a third party, or consisting of stocks, shares, property, etc., as opposed to a personal guarantee. —**collaterally** *adv.* [f. L (COL-, *lateralis* lateral)]

collation /kəˈleɪʃ(ə)n/ *n.* **1** collating, being collated. **2** a light meal. [f. L (as COLLATE); sense 2 f. *Collationes Patrum* (= *Lives of the Fathers*) read in Benedictine monasteries and followed by a light repast]

colleague /ˈkɒliːg/ *n.* a fellow official or worker, especially in a profession or business. [f. F f. L *collega* partner in office (COL, *legare* depute)]

collect[1] /kəˈlekt/ *v.t./i.* **1** to bring or come together, to assemble, to accumulate; to seek and obtain (books, stamps, etc.) systematically for addition to others; to get (contributions, tax, etc.) from a number of people. **2** to call for, to fetch. **3** to regain control of, to concentrate, to recover (*oneself*, one's thoughts, courage, etc.); (in p.p.) not perturbed or distracted. —*adj.* & *adv.* (*US*) to be paid for by the recipient (of a telephone call, parcel, etc.). —**collection** *n.*, **collector** *n.* [f. OF f. L *colligere* (COL-, *legere* pick)]

collect[2] /ˈkɒlekt/ *n.* a short prayer of the Anglican or Roman Catholic Church, usually to be read on an appointed day. [as prec.]

collectable /kəˈlektəb(ə)l/ *adj.* suitable for being collected. —*n.* (usu. in *pl.*) a collectable item. [f. COLLECT[1]]

collective /kəˈlektɪv/ *adj.* formed by, constituting, or denoting a collection; taken as a whole, aggregate, common. —*n.* **1** a collective farm. **2** a collective noun. —**collective bargaining,** negotiation of wages etc. by an organized body of employees. **collective farm,** a jointly operated amalgamation of several smallholdings. **collective noun,** a singular noun denoting a collection or number of individuals (e.g. *cattle*, *flock*, *troop*). **collective ownership,** ownership of land etc. by all for the benefit of all. —**collectivity** /-ˈtɪvɪtɪ/ *n.*, **collectively** *adv.* [f. F or L (as COLLECT[1])]

collectivism *n.* the theory or practice of collective ownership of land and means of production. —**collectivist** *n.* [f. prec.]

colleen /kəˈliːn/ *n.* (*Ir.*) a girl. [Ir., dim. of *caile* countrywoman]

college /ˈkɒlɪdʒ/ *n.* **1** an establishment for higher or professional education; a body of teachers and students within a university, their premises; a small university; a school. **2** an organized body of persons with shared functions and privileges. —**College of Arms,** a royal corporation, founded in 1483, exercising jurisdiction in matters armorial, recording proved pedigrees, and granting armorial bearings. [f. OF or L (as COLLEAGUE)]

collegiate /kəˈliːdʒɪət/ *adj.* of a college or college student. —**collegiate church,** a church (other than a cathedral) with a chapter of canons but without bishops, or (*Sc.* & *US*) associated jointly with others under a group of pastors. [f. L (as COLLEGE)]

collide /kəˈlaɪd/ *v.i.* to come into collision or conflict (*with*). [f. L *collidere* (COL, *laedere* strike and hurt)]

collie /ˈkɒlɪ/ *n.* a sheep-dog with a long pointed muzzle and usually long hair. [perh. f. *coll* coal (as being orig. black)]

collier /ˈkɒlɪə(r)/ *n.* **1** a coal-miner. **2** a ship that carries coal as its cargo. [f. COAL]

colliery *n.* a coal-mine and its buildings. [as prec.]

collision /kəˈlɪʒ(ə)n/ *n.* colliding, the striking of one body against another. —**collision course,** a course or action that is bound to end in a collision. [f. L (as COLLIDE)]

collocate /ˈkɒləkeɪt/ *v.t.* to place (esp. words) together or side by side. —**collocation** /-ˈkeɪʃ(ə)n/ *n.* [f. L *collocare* (COL-, *locare* place)]

colloid /ˈkɒlɔɪd/ *n.* **1** a gluey substance. **2** a non-crystalline substance with very large molecules, forming a viscous solution with special properties; a finely divided substance dispersed in a gas, liquid, or solid. —**colloidal** *adj.* [f. Gk *kolla* glue]

collop /ˈkɒləp/ *n.* a slice of meat, an escalope. [f. Scand., = fried bacon and eggs]

colloquial /kəˈləʊkwɪəl/ *adj.* belonging or proper to ordinary or familiar conversation, not formal or literary. —**colloquially** *adv.* [as COLLOQUY]

colloquialism *n.* a colloquial word or phrase; use of these. [f. prec.]

colloquy /ˈkɒləkwɪ/ *n.* talk, a conversation. [f. L *colloquium* (COL-, *loqui* speak)]

collusion /kəˈlu:ʒ(ə)n/ *n.* a secret agreement or co-operation, especially for fraud or deceit. —**collusive** *adj.* [f. OF or L *collusio* (COL-, *ludere* play)]

collywobbles /ˈkɒlɪwɒb(ə)lz/ *n.pl.* (*colloq.*) rumblings or pain in the stomach; an apprehensive feeling. [f. COLIC + WOBBLE]

cologne /kəˈləʊn/ *n.* eau-de-Cologne or other lightly scented liquid, used to cool or scent the skin. [abbr.]

colon[1] /ˈkəʊlən/ *n.* a punctuation mark (:), used (i) to show that what follows is an example, list, or summary of what precedes it, or a contrasting idea; (ii) between numbers that are in proportion. [f. L f. Gk *kōlon* limb, clause]

colon[2] /ˈkəʊlɒn/ *n.* the lower and greater part of the large intestine. —**colonic** /-ˈlɒnɪk/ *adj.* [f. OF or L f. Gk]

colonel /ˈkɜ:n(ə)l/ *n.* an officer commanding a regiment, of rank next below brigadier. —**colonelcy** *n.* [f. F f. It. (*colonna* column)]

colonial /kəˈləʊnɪəl/ *adj.* of a colony or colonies. —*n.* an inhabitant of a colony. [F, or f. COLONY]

colonialism *n.* the policy of acquiring or maintaining colonies; (*derog.*) an alleged policy of exploitation of colonies. —**colonialist** *n.* [f. prec.]

colonist /ˈkɒlənɪst/ *n.* a settler in or inhabitant of a colony. [f. COLONY]

colonize /ˈkɒlənaɪz/ *v.t./i.* to establish a colony (in); to join a colony. —**colonization** /-ˈzeɪʃ(ə)n/ *n.* [as prec.]

colonnade /kɒləˈneɪd/ *n.* a row of columns, especially supporting entablature or roof. [F (*colonne* column)]

colony /ˈkɒlənɪ/ *n.* **1** a settlement or settlers in a new country fully or partly subject to the mother country; their territory. **2** a group of one nationality, occupation, etc., forming a community in a city. **3** a group of animals that live close together. [f. L (*colonus* farmer, f. *colere* cultivate)]

colophon /ˈkɒləfən/ *n.* a tailpiece in a manuscript or book, giving the writer's or printer's name, date, etc.; a publisher's or printer's imprint, especially on a title-page. [L f. Gk, = summit, finishing touch]

coloration /kʌləˈreɪʃ(ə)n/ *n.* colouring; an arrangement of colours. [F or f. L (*colorare* colour)]

coloratura /kɒlərəˈtʊərə/ *n.* an elaborate ornamentation of a vocal melody; a soprano skilled in coloratura singing. [It. f. L (as prec.)]

colossal /kəˈlɒs(ə)l/ *adj.* immense; (*colloq.*) remarkable, splendid. —**colossally** *adv.* [F (*colosse* colossus)]

colossus /kəˈlɒsəs/ *n.* (*pl.* **-i**) **1** a statue of more than life size. **2** a gigantic person or personified empire etc. [L f. Gk]

colostomy /kəˈlɒstəmɪ/ *n.* an artificial opening through which the bowel can empty, made surgically by bringing part of the colon to the surface of the abdomen. [f. as COLON[2] + Gk *stoma* mouth]

colour /ˈkʌlə(r)/ *n.* **1** the sensation produced on the eye by rays of light resolved (as by a prism) into different wavelengths or by selective reflection (*black* being the effect produced by no light or by a surface reflecting no rays, and *white* the effect produced by rays of unresolved light). **2** a particular variety of this. **3** the use of all colours (not only black and white), e.g. in photography. **4** a colouring substance. **5** pigmentation of the skin, especially when dark. **6** ruddiness of complexion. **7** (in *pl.*) a coloured ribbon etc. given to regular or leading members of a sports team; the flag of a ship or regiment. **8** a show of reason; a pretext. **9** quality, mood, or variety in music, literature, etc. —*v.t./i.* **1** to put colour on, to paint, stain, or dye; to take on colour, to blush. **2** to give a special character or bias to. —**colour bar,** discrimination between white and non-white persons. **colour-blind** *adj.* unable to distinguish between certain colours. **colour scheme,** a systematic combination of colours. **primary colours,** (of light) red, green, and violet, (of paints etc.) red, blue, and yellow, giving all others by mixture. **secondary colour,** a mixture of two primary colours. [f. OF f. L]

colourant /ˈkʌlərənt/ *n.* colouring-matter. [f. prec.]

coloured *adj.* having colour; wholly or partly of non-white descent, or (**Coloured,** in South Africa) of mixed white and non-white descent. —*n.* a coloured person; **Coloured,** (in South Africa) a person of mixed white and non-white descent. [f. COLOUR]

colourful *adj.* full of colour or interest; with vivid details. —**colourfully** *adv.* [f. COLOUR + -FUL]

colouring *n.* **1** the disposition of colours. **2** a substance giving colour. **3** an artist's use of colour. **4** facial complexion. [f. COLOUR]

colourless *adj.* without colour; lacking character or vividness. [f. COLOUR + -LESS]

colt /kəult/ *n.* **1** a young male horse. **2** an inexperienced player in a team. [OE, = young donkey or camel]

coltsfoot /ˈkəultsfut/ *n.* a weed (*Tussilago farfara*) with large leaves and yellow flowers. Its Latin name refers to the fact that a cough medicine (L *tussis* cough) was formerly made from it.

columbine /ˈkɒləmbaın/ *n.* a garden plant (aquilegia) with slender pointed projections on its petals. [f. OF f. L *columba* pigeon, from the resemblance of the flower to clustered pigeons]

column /ˈkɒləm/ *n.* **1** a pillar, usually of circular section and with a base and capital. **2** something shaped like this. **3** a vertical division of a page in printed matter; a part of a newspaper devoted to a particular subject or by a regular writer. **4** a vertical row of figures in accounts etc. **5** a long narrow formation of troops or vehicles etc. —**columnar** /kəˈlʌmnə(r)/ *adj.* [f. OF & L, = pillar]

columnist /ˈkɒləmıst/ *n.* a person regularly writing a newspaper column. [f. prec.]

com- *prefix* (becoming **col-** before l, **cor-** before r, and **con-** before other consonants) with, jointly; altogether. [f. L *cum* with]

coma /ˈkəumə/ *n.* (*pl.* **-ae**) a state of prolonged deep unconsciousness. [f. L f. Gk, = deep sleep]

Comanche /kəˈmæntʃı/ *n.* **1** a North American Indian people of Texas and Oklahoma. **2** their language. —*adj.* of this people or their language. [Sp.]

comatose /ˈkəumətəus/ *adj.* in a coma, drowsy. [f. COMA]

comb /kəum/ *n.* **1** a toothed strip of rigid material for tidying and arranging the hair or for keeping it in place; part of a machine having a similar design or purpose. **2** the red fleshy crest of a fowl, especially the cock. **3** a honeycomb. —*v.t./i.* to draw a comb through (hair); to dress (wool etc.) with a comb; (*colloq.*) to search (a place etc.) thoroughly. —**comb out,** to remove with a comb; (*colloq.*) to search out and get rid of (anything unwanted). [OE]

combat /ˈkɒmbæt/ *n.* a fight, struggle, or contest. —*v.t./i.* to engage in a contest (with); to oppose, to strive against. [f. F f. L (COM-, *batuere* fight)]

combatant /ˈkɒmbət(ə)nt/ *adj.* fighting, for fighting. —*n.* a person engaged in fighting. [as prec.]

combative /ˈkɒmbətıv/ *adj.* pugnacious. [f. COMBAT]

combe /ku:m/ var. of COOMB.

combination /kɒmbıˈneıʃ(ə)n/ *n.* **1** combining, being combined; a combined state. **2** a combined set of persons or things; a sequence of numbers or letters used to open a combination lock. **3** (in *pl.*) a one-piece undergarment for body and legs. —**combination lock,** a lock which can be opened only by a specific sequence of movements. —**combinative** /ˈkɒmbınətıv/ *adj.* [as foll.]

combine[1] /kəmˈbaın/ *v.t./i.* to join or be joined into a group, set, or mixture; to co-operate. [f. OF or L *combinare* (COM-, *bini* two together)]

combine[2] /ˈkɒmbaın/ *n.* a combination of persons or firms acting together in business. —**combine harvester,** a combined reaping and threshing machine. [f. prec.]

combings /ˈkəumıŋs/ *n.pl.* loose hair removed by a brush or comb. [f. COMB]

combust /kəmˈbʌst/ *v.t.* to subject to combustion. [as COMBUSTION]

combustible /kəmˈbʌstıb(ə)l/ *adj.* capable of or used for burning. —*n.* a combustible thing. —**combustibility** /-ˈbılıtı/ *n.* [as foll.]

combustion /kəmˈbʌstʃ(ə)n/ *n.* the process of burning, a chemical process (accompanied by heat and light) in which substances combine with oxygen. [f. F or L (*combustere* burn up)]

come /kʌm/ *v.i.* **1** to move, be brought towards, or reach a place thought of as near or familiar to the speaker or hearer. **2** to reach a specified point, condition, or result. **3** to occur, to happen, to become present instead of future. **4** to take or occupy a specified position in space or time. **5** to become perceptible or known. **6** to be available. **7** to be descended, to be the result (*of*). **8** (*colloq.*) to behave like. **9** (in *imper.*) an exclamation of mild protest or encouragement. —**come about,** to happen. **come across,** to meet or find unexpectedly. **come along,** to make progress; (as *imper.*) hurry up. **come-back** *n.* a return to one's former successful position; (*colloq.*) a retort or retaliation. **come by,** to obtain. **come-down** *n.* a downfall; an anticlimax. **come-hither** *adj.* flirtatious, inviting. **come out,** to emerge, to become known; to go on strike; to be published; to declare oneself (*for* or *against*); to be satisfactorily visible in a photograph etc.; to erupt, to become covered *in* (a rash etc.); to emerge from an examination etc. with a specified result; to be solved. **come out with,** to say, to disclose. **come over,** (of a feeling etc.) to affect (a person); (*colloq.*) to be affected with (a feeling). **come round,** to pay an informal visit; to recover consciousness; to be converted to another person's opinion; (of a date) to recur. **come to,** to amount to, to be equivalent to; to recover consciousness. **come to pass,** to happen. **come up,** to arise for discussion etc., to occur. **come-uppance** *n.* (*colloq.*) a deserved punishment or rebuke. **come up with,** to present or produce (an idea etc.); to draw level with. —**comer** *n.* [OE]

Comecon /ˈkɒmɪkɒn/ the English name for an economic organization of Soviet-bloc countries, founded in 1949 and analogous to the European Economic Community. [short for *Co*uncil for *M*utual *Econ*omic Aid (or Assistance), transl. Russ. title]

comedian /kəˈmeiːdɪən/ *n.* a humorous performer on the stage, television, etc.; an actor who plays comic parts. —**comedienne** /-ˈen/ *n.fem.* [as COMEDY.]

comedy /ˈkɒmɪdɪ/ *n.* **1** a light amusing play or film, usually with a happy ending; the branch of drama that consists of such plays. **2** humour, humorous incidents in life. [f. OF f. L f. Gk (*kōmos* revel)]

comely /ˈkʌmlɪ/ *adj.* handsome, good-looking. **comeliness** *n.* [prob. as BECOME]

comestibles /kəˈmestɪb(ə)lz/ *n.pl.* (*formal* or *joc.*) things to eat. [f. F f. L (*comedere* eat)]

comet /ˈkɒmɪt/ *n.* a luminous object seen in the night sky, consisting of an icy nucleus and a tail of evaporated gas and dust particles. —**cometary** *adj.* [f. F f. L f. Gk, = long-haired]

comfit /ˈkʌmfɪt/ *n.* (*archaic*) a sweet consisting of a nut etc. in sugar. [f. OF f. L *confectum* (CON-, *facere* make)]

comfort /ˈkʌmfət/ *n.* **1** a state of physical or mental well-being or contentment. **2** relief of suffering or grief, consolation; a person or thing that gives this. **3** (in *pl.*) things that allow ease or well-being in life. —*v.t.* to give comfort to, to soothe in grief, to console. —**comforter** *n.* [f. OF f. L *confortare* strengthen (CON-, *fortis* strong)]

comfortable /ˈkʌmfətəb(ə)l/ *adj.* **1** giving or feeling ease and contentment; not close or restricted. —**comfortably** *adv.* [as prec.]

comfrey /ˈkʌmfrɪ/ *n.* a tall bell-flowered plant of the genus *Symphytum*, growing in damp shady places. [f. AF f. L *conferva* (CON-, *fervēre* boil)]

comfy /ˈkʌmfɪ/ *adj.* (*colloq.*) comfortable. [abbr.]

comic /ˈkɒmɪk/ *adj.* of or like comedy; causing amusement or laughter. —*n.* **1** a comedian. **2** a paper (usually for children) with series of strip cartoons. —**comical** *adj.*, **comically** *adv.* [f. L (as COMEDY)]

coming /kʌmɪŋ/ *adj.* approaching next; likely to be important in the near future. —*n.* arrival. [f. COME]

comity /ˈkɒmɪtɪ/ *n.* courtesy, friendship; an association of nations etc. for their mutual benefit. —**comity of nations,** nations' friendly recognition of each other's laws and customs. [f. L (*comis* courteous)]

comma *n.* the punctuation-mark (,), indicating a slight pause or break between parts of a sentence, or separating words or figures in a list. [f. L f. Gk, = clause]

command /kəˈmɑːnd/ *n.* **1** a statement, given with authority, that some action must be performed. **2** the right to control others, authority. **3** ability to use something, mastery. **4** forces or a district under a commander. —*v.t./i.* **1** to give a command or order to; to have authority over. **2** to deserve and get. **3** to dominate (a strategic position) from a superior height, to look down over. —**Command paper,** a paper laid before Parliament by royal command. **command performance,** a performance of a film, show, etc., by royal request. [f. AF f. L, = COMMEND]

commandant /ˈkɒmənd(ə)nt/ *n.* a commanding officer, especially of a military academy or prisoner-of-war camp. [F (as COMMAND)]

commandeer /kɒmənˈdɪə(r)/ *v.t.* to seize for military use; to seize for one's own purposes. [f. S.Afr. Du. f. F, = command]

commander /kəˈmɑːndə(r)/ *n.* **1** one who commands, especially a naval officer of rank next below captain. **2** (in full **Knight Commander**) a member of the higher class in some orders of knighthood. —**commander-in-chief** *n.* the supreme commander. [f. OF (as COMMAND)]

commandment /kəˈmɑːndmənt/ *n.* a divine command, especially (**Commandment**) one of the ten given to Moses (Exod. 20: 1-17). [as prec.]

commando /kəˈmɑːndəʊ/ *n.* (*pl.* **-os**) **1** a party called out for military purposes. **2** (in the Boer War) a unit of the Boer army composed of the militia of an electoral district. **3** (in the Second World War) a member of a military unit specially trained for making raids and assaults; such a unit. [Port. (as COMMAND)]

comme il faut /kɒm iːl ˈfəʊ/ proper, properly, as it should be. [F, = as is necessary]

commemorate /kəˈmeməreɪt/ *v.t.* to keep in memory by a celebration or ceremony; to be a memorial to. —**commemoration** /-ˈreɪʃ(ə)n/ *n.*, **commemorative** *adj.* [f. L *commemorare* (COM-, *memor* mindful)]

commence /kəˈmens/ *v.t.* to begin. —**commencement** *n.* [f. OF f. L (COM-, *initiare* initiate)]

commend /kəˈmend/ *v.t.* **1** to praise; to recommend. **2** to entrust, to commit.

—**commendation** /-ˈdeɪʃ(ə)n/ *n*. **commendatory** /-ˈmen-/ *adj*. [f. L *commendare* (COM-, *mandare* entrust)]

commendable /kəˈmendəb(ə)l/ *adj*. praiseworthy. —**commendably** *adv* [f. OF (as prec.)]

commensal /kəˈmens(ə)l/ *adj* living in a form of symbiosis that is beneficial to one species and neither harmful nor beneficial to the other. —*n*. a plant or animal living thus. —**commensalism** *n* [f. F or L (COM-, *mensa* table)]

commensurable /kəˈmenʃərəb(ə)l/ *adj*. measurable by the same standard (*with* or *to*); proportionate *to*. [f. L (as MEASURE)]

commensurate /kəˈmenʃərət/ *adj*. coextensive (*with*); proportionate (*to* or *with*). [as prec.]

comment /ˈkɒment/ *n*. a brief critical or explanatory remark or note, an opinion. —*v.i.* to utter or write comments. [f. L. = contrivance, interpretation (*comminisci* devise)]

commentary /ˈkɒmentərɪ/ *n* a series of descriptive comments on an event or performance; a set of explanatory notes on a text etc. [as prec.]

commentate /ˈkɒmənteɪt/ *v.i.* to act as a commentator. [f. foll.]

commentator *n*. the speaker or writer of a commentary; one who comments on current events. [L (as COMMENT)]

commerce /ˈkɒməs/ *n*. buying and selling, all forms of trading, including banking, insurance, etc. [F or f. L *commercium* (COM-, *merx* merchandise)]

commercial /kəˈmɜːʃ(ə)l/ *adj*. of or engaged in commerce; concerned chiefly with financial profit; (of broadcasting) in which advertisements are included to provide finance. —*n*. a broadcast advertisement. —**commercial traveller,** a firm's representative visiting shops etc. to obtain orders. —**commercially** *adv*. [f. prec.]

commercialism *n*. commercial practices and attitudes. [f. prec.]

commercialize *v.t.* to make commercial; to seek to make profitable. —**commercialization** /-ˈzeɪʃ(ə)n/ *n*. [f. COMMERCIAL]

Commie /ˈkɒmɪ/ *n*. (*slang*, *derog*.) a Communist. [abbr.]

commination /kɒmɪˈneɪʃ(ə)n/ *n*. threatening of divine vengeance. —**comminatory** /ˈkɒmɪneɪtərɪ/ *adj*. [f. L (COM-, *minare* threaten)]

commingle /kəˈmɪŋg(ə)l/ *v.t./i.* (*literary*) to mix together. [f. COM- + MINGLE]

comminute /ˈkɒmɪnjuːt/ *v.t.* **1** to reduce to small fragments. **2** to divide (property) into small portions. —**comminuted fracture,** one producing multiple fragments of bone. —**comminution** /-ˈnjuːʃ(ə)n/ *n*. [f. L *comminuere* (COM-, *minuere* lessen)]

commiserate /kəˈmɪzəreɪt/ *v.i.* to express pity, to sympathize. —**commiseration** /-ˈreɪʃ(ə)n/ *n*., **commiserative** *adj*. [f. L *commiserari* (COM-, *miserari* pity)]

commissar /ˈkɒmɪsɑː(r)/ *n*. (*hist.*) a head of a government department of the USSR. [f. Russ. f. F (as COMMISSARY)]

commissariat /kɒmɪˈseərɪət/ *n*. **1** the department responsible for the supply of food etc. for an army; the food supplied. **2** (*hist.*) a government department of the USSR. [F (as foll.)]

commissary /ˈkɒmɪsərɪ/ *n*. **1** a deputy, a delegate. **2** (*US*) a store where food and other supplies are sold at a military base. **3** (*US*) a restaurant in a film studio or factory etc. [f. L, = person in charge (as COMMIT)]

commission /kəˈmɪʃ(ə)n/ *n*. **1** the giving of authority to a person to perform a task; the task so given; such a person's authority or instructions. **2** a body or board of persons constituted to perform certain duties. **3** a warrant conferring authority, especially that of an officer in the armed forces above a certain rank. **4** the payment or percentage received by an agent. **5** committing, performance (e.g. of a crime). —*v.t.* **1** to give a commission to; to employ (a person) *to* do a piece of work. **2** to prepare (a ship) for active service. **3** to bring (a machine etc.) into operation. —**commission agent,** a bookmaker. **in** *or* **out of commission,** ready or not ready for use. [f. OF f. L (as COMMIT)]

commissionaire /kəmɪʃ(ə)ˈneə(r)/ *n*. an attendant at the door of a theatre, office, etc. [F, as foll.]

commissioner /kəˈmɪʃ(ə)nə(r)/ *n*. **1** one who is appointed by commission (e.g. the head of Scotland Yard). **2** a member of a commission. **3** an official representing the government in a district, department, etc. —**Commissioner for Oaths,** a solicitor authorized to administer oaths in affidavits etc. [f. L (as COMMISSION)]

commissure /ˈkɒmɪsjʊə(r)/ *n*. the joint between two bones; a junction or seam. [f. L, = junction]

commit /kəˈmɪt/ *v.t.* (**-tt-**) **1** to be the doer of (a crime etc.). **2** to entrust for safe keeping or treatment. **3** to pledge, to bind with an obligation. —**commit to memory,** to memorize. [f. L *committere* entrust (COM-, *mittere* send)]

commitment /kəˈmɪtmənt/ *n*. **1** committing, being committed. **2** an engagement or involvement that restricts freedom of action or choice. **3** an obligation or pledge. [f. prec.]

committal /kəˈmɪt(ə)l/ *n*. the action of committing, especially to prison or for burial or cremation. [as prec.]

committee mɪtɪ/ *n.* a group of persons appointed by and usually out of) a larger body, to attend to s ecial business or manage the business of club etc. [f. COMMIT]

commode /kə məʊd/ *n.* **1** a chamber-pot mounted in a chair or box with a cover. **2** a chest of draw ers. [F f. L *commodus* convenient]

commodious /kəˈməʊdɪəs/ *adj.* roomy. [f. F f. L, as prec.]

commodity /k əˈmɒdɪtɪ/ *n.* an article of trade, especially a product as opposed to a service. [f. OF or L (as COMMODE)]

commodore ˈkɒmədɔ:(r)/ *n.* a naval officer next below rear-admiral; the commander of a squadron or other division of a fleet; the president of a yacht club. [f. Du. f. F, = commander]

common /ˈkɒmən/ *adj.* **1** shared by, coming from, or affecting all concerned; of or belonging to the whole community, public. **2** occurring often; ordinary, of the most familiar or numerous kind. **3** without special rank or position; (in *pl.*) the common people. **4** of inferior quality; ill-bred, unrefined. **5** (*Gram.*, of a noun) referring to any one of a class; (of gender) referring to individuals of either sex. — *n.* an area of unfenced grassland for all to use. —**Common Era,** the Christian era. **common law,** unwritten law based on custom and precedent. **common-law husband** *or* **wife,** one recognized by common law without an official ceremony, usually after a period of cohabitation. **Common Market,** the European Economic Community. **common or garden,** (*colloq.*) ordinary. **common-room** *n.* a room for social use by students or teachers at a college etc. **common sense,** good practical sense in everyday matters. **common time,** (*Mus.*) four crotchets in a bar. **in common,** shared by several (especially as an interest or characteristic); in joint use. **the Commons,** the House of Commons. **commonly** *adv.*, **commonness** *n.* [f. OF f. L]

commonality /kɒməˈnælɪtɪ/ *n.* **1** the sharing of an attribute. **2** a common occurrence. [var. of foll.]

commonalty /ˈkɒmən(ə)ltɪ/ *n.* the common people; the general body (of mankind etc.). [as COMMON]

commoner /ˈkɒmənə(r)/ *n.* **1** a member of the common people (below the rank of peer). **2** a student without financial support from a college. [as COMMON]

commonplace *adj.* ordinary, usual; lacking in originality or individuality. —*n.* a commonplace event, topic, etc., or remark. [transl. of L & Gk (lit. common place), = general theme]

commonsensical /kɒmənˈsensɪk(ə)l/ *adj.* having or marked by common sense. [f. *common sense*]

commonwealth /ˈkɒmənwelθ/ *n.* **1** an independent State or community. **2** a republic or democratic State. **3** a federation of States. —**the Commonwealth,** (i) the republican government of Britain between the execution of Charles I in 1649 and the Restoration in 1660; (ii) an association of the UK and various independent States (previously subject to Britain) and dependencies. **New Commonwealth,** those countries which have achieved self-government within the Commonwealth since 1945. [f. COMMON + WEALTH]

commotion /kəˈməʊʃ(ə)n/ *n.* uproar, fuss and disturbance. [f. OF or L (as COM-, MOTION)]

communal /ˈkɒmjʊn(ə)l/ *adj.* shared between the members of a group or community. —**communally** *adv.*, **communalistic** /-ˈlɪstɪk/ *adj.* [F f. L (as foll.)]

commune[1] /ˈkɒmju:n/ *n.* **1** a group of people, not all of one family, sharing living arrangements and goods. **2** a small district of local government in France and certain other European countries. [f. L *communia* (*communis* common)]

commune[2] /kɒˈmju:n/ *v.i.* to communicate mentally or spiritually, to feel in close touch (*with*). [f. F, = share]

communicable /kəˈmju:nɪkəb(ə)l/ *adj.* that can be communicated. [f. OF or L (as COMMUNICATE)]

communicant /kəˈmju:nɪkənt/ *n.* **1** a person who receives Holy Communion; one who does this regularly. **2** one who communicates information [as foll.]

communicate /kəˈmju:nɪkeɪt/ *v.t./i.* **1** to impart, to transmit; to make known; to succeed in conveying information. **2** to have social dealings (*with*). **3** to be connected. **4** to receive Holy Communion. [f. L *communicare* (as COMMON)]

communication /kəmju:nɪˈkeɪʃ(ə)n/ *n.* **1** communicating. **2** something that communicates information, sent or transmitted from one person to another; a letter or message. **3** a means of communicating, e.g. a road, railway, telegraph line, radio, etc. **4** (in *pl.*) the science and practice of transmitting information. —**communications satellite,** one used for intercontinental television and telephone etc. communications. [as prec.]

communicative /kəˈmju:nɪkətɪv/ *adj.* ready and willing to talk and impart information. [as COMMUNICATE]

communion /kəˈmju:nɪən/ *n.* **1** fellowship, having ideas and beliefs in common. **2** a body of Christians of the same denomination. **3** social dealings. —**(Holy) Communion,** the

Eucharist. **communion of saints,** fellowship of Christians past and present. [f. OF or L (*communis* common)].

communiqué /kəˈmju:nɪkeɪ/ *n.* an official communication or report. [F, = communicated]

communism /ˈkɒmju:nɪz(ə)m/ *n.* 1. a system of society with vesting of property in the community, each member working for the common benefit according to his capacity and receiving according to his needs. **2 Communism,** a movement or political party advocating communism, especially as derived from Marxism; a communistic form of society established in the 20th c. in the USSR and elsewhere. [f. F (*commun* common)]

communist /ˈkɒmjʊnɪst/ *n.* **1** a supporter of communism. **2 Communist,** a member or supporter of a Communist Party. —**communistic** /-ˈnɪstɪk/ *adj.* [as prec.]

community /kəˈmju:nɪtɪ/ *n.* **1** a body of people living in one place, district, or country; a group having a religion, race, profession, etc., in common; a commune. **2** fellowship (*of* interest etc.); the state of being shared or held in common; joint ownership or liability. —**community centre,** a place providing social, recreational, and educational facilities for a neighbourhood. **community charge,** a form of local tax introduced in Scotland in 1989 and in England and Wales in 1990, replacing domestic rates. **community home,** a centre for housing young offenders. **community service,** performance of specified unpaid services to the community as an alternative to a prison sentence. **community singing,** organized singing in chorus by a large gathering of people. [f. OF f. L (as COMMON)]

commutative /kəˈmju:tətɪv/ *adj.* (of a mathematical operation) producing the same result regardless of the order in which the quantities are taken (e.g. 3 + 4 = 7, 4 + 3 = 7). [f. F or L (as foll.)]

commute /kəˈmju:t/ *v.t./i.* **1** to travel regularly by train, bus, or car to and from one's daily work in a city etc. **2** to exchange *for*; to change (one form of payment or obligation) *for* or *into* another; to change (a punishment) *to* another less severe. —**commutation** /-ˈteɪʃ(ə)n/ *n.* [f. L *commutare* (COM-, *mutare* change)]

commuter *n.* one who commutes to and from work. [f. prec.]

compact[1] /kəmˈpækt/ *adj.* closely or neatly packed together; concise. —*v.t.* to make compact. —/ˈkɒm-/ *n.* a small flat case for face-powder. —**compact disc,** a disc without grooves, on which sound is recorded digitally for reproduction by means of a laser beam directed on to it. —**compactly** *adv.*, **compactness** *n.* [f. L *compingere* (COM-, *pingere* fasten)]

compact[2] /ˈkɒmpækt/ *n.* an agreement, a contract. [f. L *compactum* (COM-, as PACT)]

companion /kəmˈpænjən/ *n.* **1** one who associates with or accompanies another; a woman paid to live with and accompany another. **2** a member of the lowest grade of some orders of knighthood. **3** a handbook or reference book dealing with a specified subject. **4** a thing that matches or accompanies another. —**companion-way** *n.* a staircase from a ship's deck to the saloon or cabins. —**companionship** *n.* [f. OF f. L (COM-, *panis* bread)]

companionable *adj.* sociable, friendly. —**companionably** *adv.* [f. prec.]

company /ˈkʌmpənɪ/ *n.* **1** being with another or others. **2** a number of people assembled, guests; a person's associates; a body of persons assembled for a common (esp. commercial) object; a group of actors etc.; a subdivision of an infantry battalion. —**part company,** to go different ways after being together; to cease associating (*with*). [f. AF (as COMPANION)]

comparable /ˈkɒmpərəb(ə)l, (D) -ˈpær-/ *adj.* that can be compared (*with* or *to*). —**comparability** /-ˈbɪlɪtɪ/ *n.*, **comparably** *adv.* [f. OF f. L (as COMPARE)]

comparative /kəmˈpærətɪv/ *adj.* perceptible or estimated by comparison; of or involving comparison; considered in relation to each other. —*n.* (*Gram.*) the comparative degree. —**comparative adjective, adverb,** one in the comparative degree. **comparative degree,** the form expressing a higher degree of a quality (e.g. *braver, more quickly*). [f. L (as foll.)]

compare /kəmˈpeə(r)/ *v.t./i.* **1** to estimate the similarity of (one thing *with* or *to* another; two things); to liken or regard as similar (*to*); to bear comparison *with*. **2** to form the comparative and superlative degrees of (an adjective or adverb). —*n.* (*literary*) comparison. [f. OF f. L *comparare* (COM-, *par* equal)]

comparison /kəmˈpærɪs(ə)n/ *n.* comparing. —**bear comparison,** to be able to be compared favourably *with*. **degrees of comparison,** (*Gram.*) the positive, comparative, and superlative (of adjectives and adverbs). [as prec.]

compartment /kəmˈpɑ:tmənt/ *n.* a division separated by partitions, e.g. in a railway carriage; a watertight division of a ship. [f. F f. It. f. L *compartiri* (COM-, *partiri* share)]

compartmental /kɒmpɑ:tˈment(ə)l/ *adj.* of or divided into compartments or categories. [f. prec.]

compartmentalize /kɒmpɑ:tˈment(ə)laɪz/ *v.t.* to divide into compartments or categories. [f. prec.]

compass /ˈkʌmpəs/ *n.* **1** an instrument showing the magnetic north and bearings from it.

2 (often in *pl.*) an instrument for taking measurements and describing circles, with two legs connected at one end by a movable joint. **3** circumference, boundary; area, extent, scope; the range of a voice or musical instrument. —**compass rose,** a circle showing the 32 principal points of the compass. [f. OF f. L (COM-, *passus* step)]

compassion /kəmˈpæʃ(ə)n/ *n.* a feeling of pity inclining one to be helpful or show mercy. [f. OF f. L (COM-, *pati* suffer)]

compassionate/kəmˈpæʃənət/*adj.* sympathetic, showing compassion. —**compassionate leave,** leave granted on grounds of bereavement etc. —**compassionately** *adv.* [f. prec.]

compatible /kəmˈpætɪb(ə)l/ *adj.* **1** able to coexist (*with*); mutually tolerant. **2** (of equipment etc.) able to be used in combination. —**compatibility** /-ˈbɪlɪtɪ/ *n.* [F f. L (as COMPASSION)]

compatriot /kəmˈpætrɪət/ *n.* a fellow-countryman. [f. F f. L (COM-, *patria* mother country)]

compeer /kəmˈpɪə(r)/ *n.* a person of equal standing; a comrade. [f. OF (as COM-, PEER²)]

compel /kəmˈpel/ *v.t.* (**-ll-**) **1** to use irresistible force or influence so as to cause (a person etc.) to do something; to allow no choice of action. **2** to arouse (a feeling) irresistibly. [f. L *compellere* (COM-, *pellere* drive)]

compelling *adj.* arousing strong interest or admiration. [f. prec.]

compendious /kəmˈpendɪəs/ *adj.* comprehensive but brief. [f. OF f. L (as foll.)]

compendium /kəmˈpendɪəm/ *n.* (*pl.* **-ia**) **1** a concise summary or abridgement. **2** a collection of table-games etc. [L, = saving, short cut (COM-, *pendere* weigh)]

compensate /ˈkɒmpənseɪt/ *v.t./i.* **1** to make suitable payment in return for (loss, damage, etc.); to recompense. **2** to counterbalance. —**compensatory** *adj.* [f. L *compensare* (COM-, frequent. of *pendere* weigh)]

compensation /kɒmpənˈseɪʃ(ə)n/ *n.* compensating, being compensated; a thing (esp. money) that compensates. [f. OF f. L (as prec.)]

compère /ˈkɒmpeə(r)/ *n.* a person who introduces artistes at a variety show etc. —*v.t.* to act as compère to. [F, = godfather]

compete /kəmˈpi:t/ *v.i.* to take part in a contest, race, etc.; to strive (*with* or *against*). [f. L *competere* strive after (COM-, *petere* seek)]

competence /ˈkɒmpɪtəns/ *n.* (also **competency**) **1** being competent, ability; legal capacity. **2** a comfortably adequate income. [f. foll.]

competent /ˈkɒmpɪt(ə)nt/ *adj.* having the required knowledge, ability, or authority; effective, adequate. —**competently** *adv.* [f. OF or L (as COMPETE)]

competition /kɒmpɪˈtɪʃ(ə)n/ *n.* **1** an event in which persons compete. **2** competing (*for*) by examination, in trade, etc. **3** those competing with one. [as COMPETE]

competitive /kəmˈpetɪtɪv/ *adj.* of or involving competition; (of prices etc.) comparing favourably with those of rivals. —**competitively** *adv.* [as COMPETE]

competitor /kəmˈpetɪtə(r)/ *n.* one who competes; a rival, especially in trade. [as prec.]

compile /kəmˈpaɪl/ *v.t.* to collect and arrange (information) into a list, volume, etc.; to produce (books etc.) thus. —**compilation** /-ˈleɪʃ(ə)n/ *n.*, **compiler** *n.* [f. OF or L *compilare* plunder]

complacent /kəmˈpleɪsənt/ *adj.* self-satisfied, calmly content. —**complacency** *n.*, **complacently** *adv.* [f. L *complacēre* (COM-, *placēre* please)]

complain /kəmˈpleɪn/ *v.i.* to express dissatisfaction. —**complain of,** to say that one is suffering from (a pain etc.); to state a grievance concerning. [f. OF f. L (COM-, *plangere* lament)]

complainant /kəmˈpleɪnənt/ *n.* the plaintiff (in certain lawsuits). [as prec.]

complaint /kəmˈpleɪnt/ *n.* **1** a statement of dissatisfaction, utterance of a grievance, a formal accusation. **2** a cause of dissatisfaction; an illness. [as COMPLAIN]

complaisant /kəmˈpleɪz(ə)nt/ *adj.* inclined to please or defer to others; acquiescent. —**complaisance** *n.* [F (as COMPLACENT)]

complement /ˈkɒmpləmənt/ *n.* that which makes a thing complete; the full number required to man a ship, fill a conveyance, etc.; the word or words added to a verb to complete the predicate; the deficiency of an angle from 90°. —*v.t.* to complete; to form a complement to. [f. L (as COMPLETE)]

complementary /kɒmpləˈmentərɪ/ *adj.* completing, forming a complement; (of two or more things) complementing each other. —**complementary colour,** a colour of light that when combined with a given colour makes white light (e.g. blue with yellow). [f. prec.]

complete /kəmˈpli:t/ *adj.* having all its parts, entire; finished; thorough, in every way. —*v.t.* to make complete; to finish; to fill in (a form etc.). —**complete with,** having as an important feature or addition. —**completely** *adv.*, **completeness** *n.* [f. OF or L *complere* fill]

completion /kəmˈpli:ʃ(ə)n/ *n.* completing, being completed. [as prec.]

complex /ˈkɒmpleks/ *adj.* consisting of several parts, composite; complicated. —*n.* **1** a complex whole. **2** a group of usually repressed ideas etc. causing abnormal behaviour or mental state. **3** a set of buildings. —**complexity** *n.* [f. F or L *complecti* embrace, assoc. with *complexus* plaited]

complexion /kəm'plekʃ(ə)n/ *n.* **1** the natural colour, texture, and appearance of the skin, especially of the face. **2** character, aspect. [f. OF f. L (as prec.)]

compliant /kəm'plaɪənt/ *adj.* complying, obedient. —**compliance** *n.* [f. COMPLY]

complicate /'kɒmplɪkeɪt/ *v.t.* to make involved, intricate, or difficult. [f. L *complicare* (COM-, *plicare* fold)]

complication /kɒmplɪ'keɪʃ(ə)n/ *n.* **1** an involved condition, an entangled state of affairs. **2** a complicating circumstance; a secondary disease or condition aggravating an already existing one. [as prec.]

complicity /kəm'plɪsɪtɪ/ *n.* partnership in evil action. [f. obs. *complice* accomplice]

compliment /'kɒmplɪmənt/ *n.* a polite expression of praise; an act implying praise; (in *pl.*) formal greetings accompanying a note, present, etc. —/-ment/ *v.t.* to pay a compliment to. [F f. L (as COMPLEMENT)]

complimentary /kɒmplɪ'mentərɪ/ *adj.* expressing a compliment; given free of charge by way of compliment. [f. prec.]

compline /'kɒmplɪn/ *n.* the last of the canonical hours of prayer; the service said at this. [f. OF f. L (as foll.)]

comply /kəm'plaɪ/ *v.i.* to act in accordance (*with*). [f. It. f. L *complēre* fill up]

component /kəm'pəʊnənt/ *adj.* forming one of the parts of a whole. —*n.* a component part. [f. L (as COMPOUND¹)]

comport /kəm'pɔːt/ *v.t./i.* (*literary*) to conduct or behave *oneself*. —**comport with,** to suit, to befit. —**comportment** *n.* [f. L *comportare* (COM-, *portare* carry)]

compose /kəm'pəʊz/ *v.t.* **1** to create in music or writing. **2** to form, to make up. **3** (in printing) to set up (type), to arrange (an article etc.) in type. **4** to arrange artistically, neatly, or for a specified purpose. **5** to make (oneself, one's feelings, etc.) calm. —**composed of,** made up of, consisting of. [f. F f. L *componere* (COM-, *ponere* put)]

composed *adj.* calm, self-possessed. —**composedly** /-ɪdlɪ/ *adv.* [f. prec.]

composer *n.* one who composes (esp. music). [f. COMPOSE]

composite /'kɒmpəzɪt, -zaɪt/ *adj.* **1** made up of various parts. **2** (of a plant, e.g. daisy, dandelion) of the family Compositae, in which the flower-head is made up of many individual flowers which together look like one bloom. **3** (*Archit.*) of mixed Ionic and Corinthian style. —*n.* a composite thing or plant. [F f. L (as COMPOUND¹)]

composition /kɒmpə'zɪʃ(ə)n/ *n.* **1** an act or method of putting together into a whole, composing. **2** a thing composed, a piece of writing or (esp.) music. **3** the constitution of a substance etc.; the arrangement of parts in a picture etc. **4** a compound artificial substance, especially one serving the purpose of a natural one. **5** a financial compromise. —**compositional** *adj.* [f. OF f. L (as prec.)]

compositor /kəm'pɒzɪtə(r)/ *n.* one who sets up type for printing. [f. AF f. L (as COMPOSE)]

compost /'kɒmpɒst/ *n.* a mixture of decayed organic mixture used as a fertilizer; a mixture usually of soil and other ingredients for growing seedlings, cuttings, etc. —*v.t.* to make into compost; to treat with compost. [f. OF f. L (as COMPOSITE)]

composure /kɒm'pəʊʒə(r)/ *n.* tranquil demeanour, calmness. [f. COMPOSE]

compote /'kɒmpəʊt, -pɒt/ *n.* fruit preserved or cooked in syrup. [F (as COMPOSITE)]

compound¹ /'kɒmpaʊnd/ *n.* a thing made up of two or more ingredients; a substance consisting of two or more elements chemically united in fixed proportions; a word formed by a combination of words. —/kəm'paʊnd/ *v.t./i.* **1** to mix or combine (ingredients or elements); to make up (a composite whole); to increase or complicate (difficulties etc.). **2** to settle (a matter) by mutual agreement; to condone or conceal (an offence or liability) for personal gain; to come to terms (*with* a person). —/'kɒmpaʊnd/ *adj.* made up of two or more ingredients; combined, collective. —**compound fracture,** one complicated by a wound. **compound interest,** see INTEREST. **compound time,** (*Mus.*) that with a ternary subdivision of the unit (e.g. into three, six, nine). [f. OF f. L *componere* put together]

compound² /'kɒmpaʊnd/ *n.* an enclosure or fenced-in space; (in India, China, etc.) the enclosure in which a house or factory stands. [f. Port. or Du. f. Malay *kampong*]

comprehend /kɒmprɪ'hend/ *v.t.* **1** to grasp mentally, to understand. **2** to include. —**comprehensible** *adj.*, **comprehension** *n.* [f. OF or L *comprehendere* (COM-, *prehendere* grasp, seize)]

comprehensive *adj.* including much or all, inclusive. —*n.* a comprehensive school. —**comprehensive school,** a large secondary school providing courses for children of all abilities. —**comprehensively** *adv.* [as prec.]

compress /kəm'pres/ *v.t.* to squeeze together; to bring into a smaller space. —/'kɒmpres/ *n.* a pad of lint etc. pressed on to some part of the body to stop bleeding, relieve inflammation, etc. [f. OF or L *compressare* frequent. of *comprimere* (COM-, *premere* press)]

compression /kəm'preʃ(ə)n/ *n.* compressing;

reduction in the volume of fuel mixture in an internal-combustion engine before ignition. [f. prec.]

compressor /kəmˈpresə(r)/ *n*. a machine for compressing air or other gases. [f. COMPRESS]

comprise /kəmˈpraɪz/ *v.t.* to include, to consist of. [f. F (as COMPREHEND)]

compromise /ˈkɒmprəmaɪz/ *n*. **1** a settlement made by each side giving up part of its demands; the process of making this. **2** an intermediate way *between* conflicting courses, opinions, etc. —*v.t./i.* **1** to settle (a dispute) or modify (principles) by compromise; to make a compromise. **2** to bring under suspicion or into danger by indiscreet action. [f. OF f. L *compromittere* (COM-, *promittere* put forth)]

comptroller *n*. var. of CONTROLLER (in titles of some financial officers).

compulsion /kəmˈpʌlʃ(ə)n/ *n*. compelling, being compelled; an irresistible urge. [f. F f. L (as COMPEL)]

compulsive /kəmˈpʌlsɪv/ *adj*. tending to compel; resulting or acting from or as if from compulsion, especially contrary to one's conscious wishes; irresistible. [as prec.]

compulsory /kəmˈpʌlsərɪ/ *adj*. that must be done, required by the rules etc. —**compulsorily** *adv*. [as COMPULSION]

compunction /kəmˈpʌŋkʃ(ə)n/ *n*. pricking of the conscience; a slight regret or scruple. [f. OF f. L (COM-, *pungere* prick)]

computable /kəmˈpju:təb(ə)l/ *adj*. that can be computed. —**computability** /-ˈbɪlɪtɪ/ *n*. [f. foll.]

compute /kəmˈpju:t/ *v.t./i.* to reckon or calculate; to use a computer. —**computation** /kɒmpju:ˈteɪʃ(ə)n/ *n*. [f. F or L *computare* reckon]

computer /kəmˈpju:tə(r)/ *n*. **1** an automatic electronic apparatus for analysing and storing data, making calculations, or controlling operations that are expressible in numerical or logical terms. **2** one who or that which computes. [f. prec.]

computerize /kəmˈpju:təraɪz/ *v.t.* to equip with, perform, or produce by computer. —**computerization** /-ˈzeɪʃ(ə)n/ *n*. [f. prec.]

comrade /ˈkɒmrəd/ *n*. an associate or companion in some activity; a fellow socialist or communist. —**comradely** *adj*., **comradeship** *n*. [f. F f. Sp., orig. = room-mate (as CHAMBER)]

con[1] *v.t.* (**-nn-**) (*slang*) to persuade or swindle (a person) after winning his confidence. —*n*. (*slang*) a confidence trick. [abbr. of CONFIDENCE]

con[2] *v.t.* (**-nn-**) to peruse, study, or learn by heart. [form of CAN[1]]

con[3] *v.t.* (**-nn-**) to direct the steering of (a ship). [orig. *cond* f. F *conduire* (as CONDUCT)]

con[4] *adv. & prep.* (of an argument or reason) against. —*n*. a reason against (see PRO[2]). [f. L *contra* against]

con- *prefix* see COM-.

concatenate /kənˈkætɪneɪt/ *v.t.* to link together, to form a sequence of. —**concatenation** /-ˈneɪʃ(ə)n/ *n*. [f. L *concatenare* (CON-, *catena* chain)]

concave /kɒnˈkeɪv/ *adj*. curved like the interior of a circle or sphere. —**concavity** /-ˈkævɪtɪ/ *n*. [f. L (CON-, *cavus* hollow)]

conceal /kənˈsi:l/ *v.t.* to keep secret or hidden. —**concealment** *n*. [f. OF f. L *concelare* hide]

concede /kənˈsi:d/ *v.t.* **1** to admit to be true. **2** to grant (a privilege, right, etc.) **3** to admit defeat in (a contest, election, etc.). [f. F or L *concedere* (CON-, *cedere* cede)]

conceit /kənˈsi:t/ *n*. **1** excessive pride in oneself. **2** a fanciful notion. [f. CONCEIVE]

conceited *adj*. having too high an opinion of one's qualities or attributes. [f. prec.]

conceivable /kənˈsi:vəb(ə)l/ *adj*. that can be (mentally) conceived. —**conceivably** *adv*. [f. foll.]

conceive /kənˈsi:v/ *v.t./i.* **1** to become pregnant (with). **2** to form (ideas etc.) in the mind; to imagine, to think *of*. [f. OF f. L *concipere* (CON-, *capere* take)]

concentrate /ˈkɒnsəntreɪt/ *v.t./i.* **1** to employ all one's thought, attention, efforts, etc. (*on*); to bring or come together to one place. **2** to increase the strength of (a liquid etc.) by removing water etc. —*n*. a concentrated substance. [f. after F *concentrer* (as CON-, CENTRE)]

concentrated *adj*. **1** (of a liquid) having more than the natural or original strength, not diluted. **2** intense. [f. prec.]

concentration /kɒnsənˈtreɪʃ(ə)n/ *n*. **1** concentrating, being concentrated. **2** the amount or strength of a substance in a mixture; a mental state of exclusive attention. —**concentration camp**, a place for the detention of political prisoners etc., especially in Nazi Germany.

concentric /kənˈsentrɪk/ *adj*. having a common centre. —**concentrically** *adv*. [f. OF f. L (as CENTRE)]

concept /ˈkɒnsept/ *n*. a generalized idea or notion. [f. L (as CONCEIVE)]

conception /kənˈsepʃ(ə)n/ *n*. **1** conceiving, being conceived. **2** the result of this, an idea. —**conceptional** *adj*. [f. OF f. L (as prec.)]

conceptual /kənˈseptjʊ(ə)l/ *adj*. of mental concepts. [as CONCEPT]

conceptualism /kənˈseptjʊəlɪz(ə)m/ *n*. the theory that universals exist, but only as mental concepts. —**conceptualist** *n*. [f. prec.]

conceptualize /kənˈseptjʊ(ə)laɪz/ *v.t.* to form a mental concept of. [f. CONCEPTUAL]

concern /kən'sɜ:n/ *v.t.* to be relevant or important to; to affect or worry; to relate to, to be about. —*n.* **1** a thing of interest or importance to one. **2** anxiety, worry. **3** (in *pl.*) one's affairs. **4** a business or firm; (*colloq.*) a thing. —**be concerned in,** to take part in. **concern oneself,** to feel an interest or anxiety (*in, about,* etc.); to have a desire to deal *with.* —**concernment** *n.* [f. F or L *concernere* (CON-, *cernere* sift, discern)]

concerned *adj.* **1** anxious, troubled. **2** involved, interested. —**concernedly** /-ɪdlɪ/ *adv.*, **concernedness** /-ɪdnɪs/ *n.* [f. prec.]

concerning *prep.* about, with regard to. [f. CONCERN]

concert /'kɒnsət/ *n.* **1** a musical entertainment by several performers. **2** a combination of voices or sounds. **3** agreement, working together. —**concert pitch,** a pitch, slightly higher than the ordinary, internationally agreed for concert performances. [F f. It. (as CONCERTO)]

concerted /kən'sɜ:tɪd/ *adj.* **1** effected by mutual agreement, done in co-operation. **2** (*Mus.*) arranged in parts for voices or instruments. [as prec.]

concertina /kɒnsə'ti:nə/ *n.* a portable musical instrument like an accordion but smaller. —*v.t./i.* to compress or collapse in folds like those of a concertina. [f. CONCERT]

concerto /kən'tʃɜ:təʊ/ *n.* (*pl.* **-os** or **-i** /-i:/) a composition (usually in three movements) for one or more solo instruments accompanied by an orchestra. —**concerto grosso** /'grəʊsəʊ/, a composition with a small group of solo instruments accompanied by an orchestra. [It., f. *concertare* bring into harmony, *grosso* big]

concession /kən'seʃ(ə)n/ *n.* **1** conceding. **2** a thing conceded, especially a grant of land for extraction of minerals, trading rights, etc.; a reduction in price for certain categories of person. —**concessionary** *adj.* [f. F or L (as CONCEDE)]

concessionaire /kənseʃə'neə(r)/ *n.* the holder of a concession. [F (as prec.)]

concessive /kən'sesɪv/ *adj.* (*Gram.*) expressing a concession, of words such as *although* or *even if.* [f. L (as CONCEDE)]

conch /kɒntʃ/ *n.* the spiral shell of certain shellfish; such a shellfish, especially a large gastropod. [f. L *concha* f. Gk]

conchology /kɒŋ'kɒlədʒɪ/ *n.* the study of shells and shellfish. —**conchologist** *n.* [f. CONCH + -LOGY]

concierge /'kɒnsɪeəʒ/ *n.* (in France and French-speaking areas) a doorkeeper or porter (esp. of a block of flats). [F, f. L *conservius* fellow-slave]

conciliate /kən'sɪlɪeɪt/ *v.t.* to win over from anger or hostility, to win the goodwill of; to reconcile (disagreeing parties). —**conciliation** /-'eɪʃ(ə)n/ *n.* **conciliator** *n.*, **conciliatory** *adj.* [f. L *conciliare* combine, gain (*concilium* council)]

concise /kən'saɪs/ *adj.* brief but comprehensive in expression. —**concisely** *adv.*, **conciseness** *n.*, **concision** /-'sɪʒ(ə)n/ *n.* [f. F or L (CON-, *caedere* cut)]

conclave /'kɒnkleɪv/ *n.* a private meeting; a meeting-place or assembly of cardinals for the election of a pope. [f. OF f. L, = lockable room (*clavis* key)]

conclude /kən'klu:d/ *v.t./i.* **1** to bring or come to an end; to arrange or settle (a treaty etc.) finally. **2** to draw a conclusion (*that*). [f. L *concludere* (CON-, *claudere* shut)]

conclusion /kən'klu:ʒ(ə)n/ *n.* **1** ending, an end. **2** a settling or concluding (of peace etc.). **3** a judgement or opinion based on reasoning; a proposition in logic reached from previous ones. [as prec.]

conclusive /kən'klu:sɪv/ *adj.* decisive, completely convincing. —**conclusively** *adv.* [as CONCLUDE]

concoct /kən'kɒkt/ *v.t.* to prepare, especially by mixing a variety of ingredients; to invent (a story or plot). —**concoction** /-'kɒkʃ(ə)n/ *n.* [f. L *concoquere* (CON-, *coquere* cook)]

concomitant /kən'kɒmɪtənt/ *adj.* accompanying. —*n.* an accompanying thing. —**concomitance** *n.* [f. L *concomitari* (CON-, *comes* companion)]

concord /'kɒŋkɔ:d/ *n.* **1** agreement, harmony. **2** (*Mus.*) a chord or interval satisfactory in itself. **3** (*Gram.*) agreement between words in gender, number, etc. —**concordant** /kən'kɔ:dənt/ *adj.* [f. OF f. L (CON-, *cor* heart)]

concordance /kən'kɔ:dəns/ *n.* **1** agreement. **2** an alphabetical index of the words used by an author or in a book. [as prec.]

concordat /kən'kɔ:dæt/ *n.* an official agreement, especially between Church and State. [f. F or L p.p. of *concordare* (as CONCORD)]

concourse /'kɒŋkɔ:s/ *n.* **1** a crowd, a gathering. **2** a large open area in a railway station etc. [f. OF f. L (as CONCUR)]

concrete /'kɒnkri:t/ *n.* a mixture of cement with sand or gravel, used in building. —*adj.* **1** existing in material form, real. **2** definite, positive. **3** (*Gram.*, of a noun) denoting a thing, not a quality or state etc. —*v.t./i.* **1** to cover with or embed in concrete. **2** /kən'kri:t/ to form into a mass, to solidify. —**concrete music,** music prepared from recorded (natural or man-made) sounds. **concrete poetry,** poetry using typographical devices to enhance its effect. [f. F f. L *concrescere* grow together]

concretion /kən'kri:ʃ(ə)n/ *n.* a hard solid mass; the forming of this by coalescence. [as prec.]

concubine /'kɒnkjʊbaɪn/ *n.* a woman cohabiting with a man to whom she is not married; a secondary wife in polygamous societies.

—**concubinage** /kən'kju:bɪnɪdʒ/ *n.* [f. OF f. L (CON-, *cubare* lie)]

concupiscence /kən'kju:pɪsəns, kɒnkjʊ'pɪ-/ *n.* intense sexual desire. —**concupiscent** *adj.* [f. L *concupiscere* begin to desire]

concur /kən'kɜ:(r)/ *v.i.* (**-rr-**) **1** to agree in opinion. **2** to happen together, to coincide. [f. L *concurrere* (CON-, *currere* run)]

concurrence /kən'kʌrəns/ *n.* **1** agreement. **2** simultaneous occurrence of events. [f. prec.]

concurrent /kən'kʌrənt/ *adj.* **1** existing or acting together or at the same time. **2** running in the same direction; (of three or more lines) meeting at or tending to one point. —**concurrently** *adv.* [as CONCUR]

concuss /kən'kʌs/ *v.t.* to subject to concussion. [f. L *concutere* (CON-, *quatere* shake)]

concussion /kən'kʌʃ(ə)n/ *n.* **1** injury to the brain caused by a heavy blow, fall, etc. **2** violent shaking. [as prec.]

condemn /kən'dem/ *v.t.* **1** to express utter disapproval of. **2** to pronounce guilty, to convict; to sentence *to* a punishment; to assign an unpleasant future or fate to. **3** to pronounce unfit for use or habitation. —**condemnation** /kɒndem'neɪʃ(ə)n/ *n.*, **condemnatory** /kən'demnətərɪ/ *adj.* [f. OF f. L *condemnare* (CON-, *damnare* damn)]

condensation /kɒnden'seɪʃ(ə)n/ *n.* **1** condensing. **2** condensed material (esp. water on cold windows etc.). **3** abridgement. [f. L (as foll.)]

condense /kən'dens/ *v.t./i.* **1** to make denser or more concentrated. **2** to change or be changed from gas or vapour into liquid. **3** to express in few words. —**condensed milk,** milk thickened by evaporation and sweetened. [f. F or L *condensare* (CON-, *densus* thick)]

condenser *n.* **1** an apparatus or vessel for condensing vapour. **2** a capacitor. **3** a lens system for concentrating light. [f. prec.]

condescend /kɒndɪ'send/ *v.i.* to be gracious enough (*to* do), especially while showing one's feeling of dignity or superiority; to disregard one's superiority (*to* a person). —**condescension** *n.* [f. OF f. L *condescendere* (CON-, *descendere* descend)]

condign /kən'daɪn/ *adj.* (of punishment etc.) severe and well-deserved. [f. OF f. L (CON-, *dignus* worthy)]

condiment /'kɒndɪmənt/ *n.* a seasoning or relish for food. [f. L (*condire* pickle)]

condition /kən'dɪʃ(ə)n/ *n.* **1** a stipulation, a thing upon the fulfilment of which depends something else. **2** the state of being of a person or thing. **3** a state of physical fitness or (of things) fitness for use. **4** an ailment or abnormality. **5** (in *pl.*) circumstances, especially those affecting the functioning or existence of something. —*v.t.* **1** to bring into the desired state or condition; to make fit; to train or accustom. **2** to modify, to have a strong effect on. —**conditioned reflex,** a reflex response to a non-natural stimulus, established by training. **on condition that,** with the condition that. [f. OF f. L, = thing agreed on (CON-, *dicere* say)]

conditional *adj.* **1** dependent (*on*); not absolute, containing a condition or stipulation. **2** (*Gram.*, of a clause, mood, etc.) expressing a condition. —**conditionally** *adv.* [f. prec.]

condole /kən'dəʊl/ *v.i.* to express sympathy (*with* a person *on* a loss etc.). —**condolence** n. [f. L *condolēre* (CON-, *dolēre* grieve)]

condom /'kɒndəm/ *n.* a contraceptive sheath. [orig. unkn.]

condominium /kɒndə'mɪnɪəm/ *n.* joint control of a State's affairs by two or more other States. [L (CON-, *dominium* sovereignty)]

condone /kən'dəʊn/ *v.t.* to forgive or overlook (an offence or wrongdoing). —**condonation** /kɒndə'neɪʃ(ə)n/ *n.* [f. L *condonare* (CON-, *donare* give)]

condor /'kɒndə(r)/ *n.* a very large vulture (*Vultur gryphus*) of South America; a smaller (and rare) vulture, the California condor (*Gymnogyps californianus*) of North America. [Sp. f. Quechua *cuntur*]

conduce /kən'dju:s/ *v.i.* to tend to lead or contribute *to* (a result). —**conducive** *adj.* [f. L (as foll.)]

conduct /'kɒndʌkt/ *n.* **1** behaviour (esp. in its moral aspect). **2** the manner of directing and managing (a business or war). —/kən'dʌkt/ *v.t.* **1** to lead or guide. **2** to direct or manage (a business etc.). **3** to be conductor of (an orchestra etc.). **4** to transmit (heat, electricity, etc.) by conduction. —**conduct oneself,** to behave (*well*, *badly*, etc.). [f. OF f. L *conducere* (CON-, *ducere* lead)]

conductance /kən'dʌkt(ə)ns/ *n.* the power of a specified body to conduct electricity. [f. prec.]

conduction /kən'dʌkʃ(ə)n/ *n.* the transmission or conducting of heat, electricity, etc. [as CONDUCT]

conductive /kən'dʌktɪv/ *adj.* having the property of conducting heat or electricity. —**conductivity** /kɒndʌk'tɪvɪtɪ/ *n.* [f. CONDUCT]

conductor /kən'dʌktə(r)/ *n.* **1** a person who directs the performance of an orchestra, choir, etc. **2** one who collects fares in a bus etc. **3** a substance that conducts heat or electricity. [f. F f. L (as CONDUCT)]

conductress /kən'dʌktrɪs/ *n.fem.* a woman bus conductor. [f. prec.]

conduit /'kɒndɪt, -djuɪt/ *n.* a channel or pipe for conveying liquids; a tube or trough for protecting insulated electric wires. [f. OF f. L (as CONDUCT)]

condyle /'kɒndaɪl/ *n.* a rounded process at the

end of a bone, forming an articulation with another bone. [F f. L f. Gk *kondulos* knuckle]

cone *n.* **1** a solid figure with a circular plane base, narrowing to a point; a thing of similar shape, solid or hollow. **2** the dry fruit of a pine or fir. **3** an ice-cream cornet. [f. F f. L f. Gk]

coney *n.* var. of CONY.

confabulate /kən'fæbjʊleɪt/ *v.i.* to converse, to chat. —**confabulation** /-'leɪʃ(ə)n/ *n.* [f. L *confabulari* (CON-, *fabula* tale)]

confection /kən'fekʃ(ə)n/ *n.* a dish or delicacy made with sweet ingredients; a cake or sweet. [f. OF f. L (*conficere* prepare)]

confectioner *n.* a maker or retailer of confectionery. [f. prec.]

confectionery *n.* confections, especially sweets. [f. prec.]

confederacy /kən'fedərəsɪ/ *n.* a league or alliance, especially (**the Confederacy**) that of the Confederate States. [f. AF (as foll.)]

confederate /kən'fedərət/ *adj.* allied. —*n.* **1** an ally, especially (in bad sense) an accomplice. **2 Confederate,** a supporter of the Confederate States. —/-reɪt/ *v.t./i.* to bring or come into alliance (*with*). —**Confederate States,** the 11 southern States which seceded from the United States in 1860-1 and formed a confederacy of their own (thus precipitating the American Civil War) which was finally overthrown in 1865, after which they were reunited to the USA. [f. L (CON-, FEDERATE)]

confederation /kənfede'reɪʃ(ə)n/ *n.* **1** forming or being formed in alliance etc. **2** a union or alliance of States. [f. prec.]

confer /kən'fɜː(r)/ *v.t./i.* (**-rr-**) **1** to grant, to bestow. **2** to hold a conference or discussion. —**conferrable** *adj.* [f. L *conferre* (CON-, *ferre* bring)]

conference /'kɒnfərəns/ *n.* consultation; a meeting (esp. a regular one) for discussion. [as prec.]

conferment /kən'fɜːmənt/ *n.* the conferring (of a degree, honour, etc.). [f. CONFER]

confess /kən'fes/ *v.t./i.* **1** to acknowledge, own, or admit (a fault, wrongdoing, etc.); to admit reluctantly. **2** to declare one's sins formally, especially to a priest. **3** (of a priest) to hear the confession of. [f. OF f. L *confitēri* (CON-, *fatēri* declare, avow)]

confessedly /kən'fesɪdlɪ/ *adv.* by personal or general admission. [f. prec.]

confession /kən'feʃ(ə)n/ *n.* **1** the confessing (of an offence etc., or of sins to a priest). **2** a thing confessed; a declaration of one's religious beliefs, a statement of one's principles. [as prec.]

confessional *n.* an enclosed stall in a church, in which a priest sits to hear confessions. —*adj.* of a confession. [f. prec.]

confessor *n.* **1** a priest who hears confessions and gives spiritual counsel. **2** one who avows his religion in the face of danger. [f. AF f. L (as CONFESS)]

confetti /kən'fetɪ/ *n.* small bits of coloured paper thrown by wedding guests at the bride and bridegroom. [It. (as CONFECTION)]

confidant /kɒnfɪ'dænt/ *n.* (*fem.* **confidante** *pr.* same) a person trusted with knowledge of one's private affairs. [as foll.]

confide /kən'faɪd/ *v.t./i.* **1,** to tell (secrets *to*). **2** to entrust (an object of care or a task *to*). —**confide in,** to talk confidentially to. [f. L *confidere* (CON-, *fidere* trust)]

confidence /'kɒnfɪd(ə)ns/ *n.* **1** firm trust; a feeling of certainty, sense of self-reliance, boldness. **2** something told confidentially. —**confidence man,** one who robs by means of a confidence trick. **confidence trick,** a swindle in which the victim is persuaded to trust someone who gives a false impression of honesty. **in a person's confidence,** trusted with his secrets. [f. L (as prec.)]

confident *n.* feeling or showing confidence, bold. [F f. It. (as CONFIDE)]

confidential /kɒnfɪ'denʃ(ə)l/ *adj.* **1** spoken or written in confidence. **2** entrusted with secrets. **3** confiding. —**confidentiality** /-ʃɪ'ælɪtɪ/ *n.*, **confidentially** *adv.* [f. prec.]

configuration /kənfɪgjʊə'reɪʃ(ə)n/ *n.* manner of arrangement, shape, outline. [f. L *configuratio* (CON-, *figurare* fashion)]

confine /kən'faɪn/ *v.t.* to keep or restrict within certain limits; to imprison. —/'kɒnfaɪn/ *n.* (usu. in *pl.*) a limit or boundary of an area. —**be confined,** to be undergoing childbirth. [f. F f. L (CON-, *finis* limit)]

confinement *n.* **1** confining, being confined. **2** the period of childbirth. [f. prec.]

confirm /kən'fɜːm/ *v.t.* **1** to provide support for the truth or correctness of. **2** to establish more firmly; to encourage (*in* an opinion etc.). **3** to make formally definite or valid. **4** to administer the rite of confirmation to. —**confirmative** *adj.*, **confirmatory** /-'fɜː-/ *adj.* [f. OF f. L *confirmare* (CON-, *firmus* firm)]

confirmation /kɒnfə'meɪʃ(ə)n/ *n.* **1** confirming; corroboration. **2** a religious rite confirming a baptized person as a member of the Christian Church. [as prec.]

confirmed *adj.* firmly settled in some habit or condition. [f. CONFIRM]

confiscate /'kɒnfɪskeɪt/ *v.t.* to take or seize by authority. —**confiscation** /-'keɪʃ(ə)n/ *n.* [f. L *confiscare* (CON-, *fiscus* treasure)]

conflagration /kɒnflə'greɪʃ(ə)n/ *n.* a great and destructive fire. [f. L *conflagratio* (CON-, *flagrare* blaze)]

conflate /kən'fleɪt/ *v.t.* to blend or fuse together

(especially two variant texts into one) —**conflation** *n.* [f. L *conflare* (CON-, *flare* blow)]

conflict /ˈkɒnflɪkt/ *n.* **1** a fight, a struggle. **2** the clashing (*of* opposed principles etc.). —/kənˈflɪkt/ *v.i.* **1** to struggle (*with*). **2** to clash or be incompatible. [f. L *confligere* (CON-, *fligere* strike)]

confluence /ˈkɒnflʊəns/ *n.* flowing together; the place where the two rivers unite. [as foll.]

confluent /ˈkɒnflʊənt/ *adj.* flowing together, uniting. —*n.* a stream joining another. [f. L *confluere* (CON-, *fluere* flow)]

conform /kənˈfɔ:m/ *v.t./i.* **1** to comply *with* rules or general custom. **2** to make or be conformable. —**conform to** *or* **with,** to comply or be in accordance with. [f. OF f. L *conformare* (CON-, *forma* shape)]

conformable *adj.* **1** similar (*to*). **2** consistent (*with*), adaptable (*to*). —**conformably** *adv.* [as prec.]

conformation /kɒnfəˈmeɪʃ(ə)n/ *n.* the way in which a thing is formed, its structure. [as CONFORM]

conformist /kənˈfɔ:mɪst/ *n.* one who conforms to an established practice. —**conformism** *n.* [as prec.]

conformity *n.* conforming with established practice; agreement, suitability. [f. OF f. L (as CONFORM)]

confound /kənˈfaʊnd/ *v.t.* **1** to perplex, to baffle; to confuse. **2** (*archaic*) to defeat or overthrow. —*int.* of annoyance (*confound it!*). [f. AF f. L *confundere* mix up]

confounded *adj.* (*colloq.*) damned. [f. prec.]

confrère /ˈkɒnfreə(r)/ *n.* a fellow-member of a profession etc. [F, = fellow-brother]

confront /kənˈfrʌnt/ *v.t.* **1** to meet or stand facing; to face in hostility or defiance. **2** (of a difficulty etc.) to present itself to. **3** to bring (a person) face to face *with* (accusers etc.). —**confrontation** /kɒnfrʌnˈteɪʃ(ə)n/ *n.* [f. F f. L *confrontare* (CON-, *frons* face)]

Confucianism /kənˈfju:ʃ(ə)nɪz(ə)m/ *n.* a system of philosophical and ethical teachings founded by the Chinese philospher Confucius in the 6th c. BC. [f. *Confucius*]

confuse /kənˈfju:z/ *v.t.* **1** to bring into disorder, to mix up. **2** to throw the mind or feelings of (a person) into disorder; to destroy the composure of. **3** to mix up in the mind, to fail to distinguish between. **4** to make unclear. —**confusedly** /-ˈfju:zɪdlɪ/ *adv.* [back-formation f. *confused* (as CONFOUND)]

confusion *n.* the act or result of confusing; a confused state. [as prec.]

confute /kənˈfju:t/ *v.t.* to prove (a person or thing) to be in error. —**confutation** /kɒnfju:ˈteɪʃ(ə)n/ *n.* [f. L *confutare* restrain]

conga /ˈkɒŋgə/ *n.* a Latin-American dance of African origin, usually with a number of persons in a single line. —**conga drum,** a tall narrow low-toned drum beaten with the hands. [Amer. Sp., f. Sp *conga* of the Congo]

congé /ˈkɔ̃ʒeɪ/ *n.* unceremonious dismissal; leave-taking. [f. OF f. L *commeatus* leave of absence (*commeare* go and come)]

congeal /kənˈdʒi:l/ *v.t./i.* to become or cause to become semi-solid by cooling; (of blood etc.) to coagulate. —**congelation** /ˈkɒndʒəˈleɪʃ(ə)n/ *n.* [f. OF f. L *congelare* freeze (CON-, *gelu* ice)]

congener /ˈkɒndʒenə(r)/ *n.* a thing or person of the same kind or class. [f. L (CON-, GENUS)]

congenial /kənˈdʒi.nɪəl/ *adj.* pleasant because like oneself in temperament or interests; suited or agreeable (*to*). —**congeniality** /-ˈælɪtɪ/ *n.*, **congenially** *adv.* [f. CON- + GENIAL]

congenital /kənˈdʒenɪt(ə)l/ *adj.* existing or as such from birth. —**congenitally** *adv.* [f. L (CON-, *genitus* begotten)]

conger /ˈkɒŋgə(r)/ *n.* a large sea eel of the family Congridae. [f. OF f. L f. Gk]

congeries /kənˈdʒɪəri:z/ *n.* (*pl.* same) a disorderly collection, a mass or heap. [L (as foll.)]

congest /kənˈdʒest/ *n.* (usu. in *p.p.*) to affect with congestion. [f. L *congere* (CON-, *gerere* bring)]

congestion /kənˈdʒestʃ(ə)n/ *n.* abnormal accumulation or obstruction, especially of traffic etc. or of blood in a part of the body. [as prec.]

conglomerate /kənˈglɒmərət/ *adj.* gathered into a rounded mass. —*n.* **1** a conglomerate mass. **2** a group or corporation formed by the merging of separate firms. —/-reɪt/ *v.t.* to collect into a coherent mass. —**conglomeration** /-ˈreɪʃ(ə)n/ *n.* [f. L *conglomerare* (CON-, *glomus* ball)]

congratulate /kənˈgrætjʊleɪt/ *v.t.* to express pleasure at the happiness, excellence, or good fortune of (a person *on* an event etc.). —**congratulate oneself,** to think oneself fortunate. —**congratulatory** *adj.* [f. L *congratulari* (CON-, *gratulari* show joy)]

congratulation /kəngrætjʊˈleɪʃ(ə)n/ *n.* congratulating; an expression of this. [as prec.]

congregate /ˈkɒŋgrɪgeɪt/ *v.t./i.* to collect or gather into a crowd. [f. L *congregare* (CON-, *grex* flock)]

congregation /kɒŋgrɪˈgeɪʃ(ə)n/ *n.* a gathering of persons, especially for religious purposes; a body of persons regularly attending a particular church etc. [f. OF or L (as prec.)]

congregational *adj.* **1** of a congregation. **2 Congregational,** of or adhering to Congregationalism. [f. prec.]

Congregationalism *n.* a form of church organization in which each local church is independent and autonomous. —**Congregationalist** *n.* [f. prec.]

congress /ˈkɒŋgres/ *n.* **1** a formal meeting of delegates for discussion. **2 Congress,** a national legislative assembly; that of the USA. [f. L (CON-, *gradi* walk)]

congressional /kənˈgreʃən(ə)l/ *adj.* of a congress. [f. prec.]

congruent /ˈkɒŋgruənt/ *adj.* **1** suitable, consistent (*with*). **2** (of geometric figures) coinciding exactly when superimposed. —**congruence** *n.*, **congruency** *n.* [f. F or L (*congruere* agree)]

congruous /ˈkɒŋgruəs/ *adj.* suitable, agreeing; fitting. —**congruity** /-ˈgruːɪtɪ/ *n.* [f. L *congruus* (as prec.)]

conic /ˈkɒnɪk/ *adj.* of a cone. —**conic section,** a figure formed by the intersection of a cone and a plane. [f. L f. Gk (as CONE)]

conical /ˈkɒnɪk(ə)l/ *adj.* cone-shaped. [as prec.]

conifer /ˈkɒnɪfə(r), ˈkəʊn-/ *n.* a tree that bears cones. —**coniferous** /-ˈnɪfərəs/ *adj.* [f. L (as CONE, *ferre* bear)]

conjectural /kənˈdʒektʃər(ə)l/ *adj.* based on or involving conjecture. [as foll.]

conjecture /kənˈdʒektʃə(r)/ *n.* **1** formation of an opinion on incomplete grounds; guessing. **2** a guess. —*v.t./i.* to guess. [f. OF or L *conjicere* (CON-, *jacere* throw)]

conjoin /kənˈdʒɔɪn/ *v.t./i.* to join or combine. [f. OF f. L *conjungere* (CON-, *jungere* join)]

conjoint /ˈkɒndʒɔɪnt/ *adj.* associated, conjoined. [as prec.]

conjugal /ˈkɒndʒʊg(ə)l/ *adj.* of marriage or the relationship of husband and wife. —**conjugally** *adv.* [f. L (*conjunx* spouse)]

conjugate /ˈkɒndʒʊgeɪt/ *v.t./i.* **1** to give the different forms of (a verb). **2** to unite; to become fused. —*adj.* joined together, coupled, fused. —*n.* a conjugate word or thing. [f. L *conjugare* yoke together (CON-, *jugum* yoke)]

conjugation /kɒndʒʊˈgeɪʃ(ə)n/ *n.* (*Gram.*) a system of verbal inflection. [as prec.]

conjunct /kənˈdʒʌŋkt/ *adj.* joined together; combined; associated. [f. L (as CONJOIN)]

conjunction /kənˈdʒʌŋkʃ(ə)n/ *n.* **1** joining, connection. **2** (*Gram.*) a word used to connect clauses or sentences, or words in the same clause (e.g. *and*, *but*, *if*). **3** a combination of events or circumstances. **4** the apparent proximity of two heavenly bodies. [as prec.]

conjunctiva /kɒndʒʌŋkˈtaɪvə/ *n.* the mucous membrane connecting the eyeball and inner eyelids. [L (as foll.)]

conjunctive /kənˈdʒʌŋktɪv/ *adj.* serving to join; (*Gram.*) of the nature of a conjunction. [as CONJOIN]

conjunctivitis /kəndʒʌŋktɪˈvaɪtɪs/ *n.* inflammation of the conjunctiva. [f. CONJUNCTIVA]

conjuncture /kənˈdʒʌŋktʃə(r)/ *n.* a combination of events; a state of affairs. [F f. It. (as CONJOIN)]

conjure /ˈkʌndʒə(r)/ *v.t./i.* **1** to perform tricks which appear to be magical, especially by movements of the hands. **2** to summon (a spirit) to appear. —**conjure up,** to produce as if from nothing; to evoke. [f. OF *conjurer* plot, exorcize, f. L *conjurare* bind together by oath]

conjuror *n.* a skilled performer of conjuring tricks. [f. prec.]

conker *n.* a horse-chestnut fruit; (in *pl.*) a children's game played with these on strings. [f. dial. *conker* snail-shell]

connate /ˈkɒneɪt/ *adj.* **1** born with a person, innate. **2** formed at the same time. **3** (of leaves etc.) united from the start of life. [f. L *connatus* (CON-, *nasci* be born]

connect /kəˈnekt/ *v.t./i.* **1** to join, to be joined; to construct a line etc. from (one point to another). **2** to associate mentally or practically; (usu. in *pass.*) to unite or associate in a relationship etc. **3** (of a train etc.) to be synchronized at its destination *with* another, allowing passengers to transfer. **4** to be meaningful or relevant; to form a logical sequence. —**connecting-rod** *n.* the rod between the piston and the crankpin etc. [f. L *connectere* (CON-, *nectere* bind)]

connection /kəˈnekʃ(ə)n/ *n.* **1** connecting; being connected or related. **2** a relationship or association of ideas. **3** a connecting part. **4** a relative or close associate. **5** a group of associates or clients. **6** a connecting train etc. [as prec.]

connective *adj.* serving to connect, especially of body tissues connecting and supporting organs etc. [f. CONNECT]

connector *n.* a thing that connects others. [as prec.]

conning-tower *n.* a raised structure on a submarine, containing the periscope; an armoured pilot-house on a warship. [f. CON[3]]

connive /kəˈnaɪv/ *v.i.* **connive at,** to disregard or tacitly consent to (wrongdoing). —**connivance** *n.* [f. F or L *connivēre* shut the eyes to]

connoisseur /kɒnəˈsɜː(r)/ *n.* an expert judge (*of* or *in* matters of taste, especially in the fine arts). [F (*connaître* know)]

connote /kəˈnəʊt/ *v.t.* (of words) to imply in addition to the literal meaning; to mean, to signify. —**connotation** /kɒnəˈteɪʃ(ə)n/ *n.*, **connotative** /ˈkɒnəteɪtɪv/ *adj.* [f. L *connotare* (CON-, *notare* note)]

connubial /kəˈnjuːbɪəl/ *adj.* of marriage or the relation of husband and wife. [f. L (CON-, *nubere* marry)]

conquer /ˈkɒŋkə(r)/ *v.t./i.* to overcome and control militarily; to be victorious; to overcome by effort. —**conqueror** *n.* [f. AF f. L *conquirere* win]

conquest /ˈkɒnkwest/ *n.* **1** conquering. **2** conquered territory; something won; a person whose affections have been won. —**the Conquest** *or* **Norman Conquest,** the conquest of England by William of Normandy in 1066. [as prec.]

conquistador /kɒnˈkwɪstədɔː(r)/ *n.* (*pl.* **-ores** /-ɔːriːz/) a conqueror, especially one of the Spanish soldiers and adventurers who conquered South and Central America in the 16th c. [Sp.]

consanguineous /kɒnsæŋˈgwɪnɪəs/ *adj.* descended from the same ancestor, akin. —**consanguinity** *n.* [f. L (CON-, *sanguis* blood)]

conscience /ˈkɒnʃ(ə)ns/ *n.* the moral sense of right and wrong, especially as felt by a person and affecting his behaviour. —**conscience clause,** a clause in a law, ensuring respect for the consciences of those affected. **conscience money,** a sum paid to relieve one's conscience. **conscience-stricken** *adj.* made uneasy by a bad conscience. [f. OF f. L (as CONSCIOUS)]

conscientious /kɒnʃɪˈenʃəs/ *adj.* obedient to conscience; showing or done with careful attention. —**conscientious objector,** a person who for reasons of conscience objects to military service etc. —**conscientiously** *adv.*, **conscientiousness** *n.* [as prec.]

conscious /ˈkɒnʃəs/ *adj.* **1** awake and aware of one's surroundings and identity. **2** knowing, aware (*of* or *that*). **3** (of actions, emotions, etc.) realized or recognized by the doer etc., intentional. —*n.* the conscious mind. —**consciously** *adv.* [f. L *conscire* be privy to (CON-, *scire* know)]

consciousness *n.* awareness; a person's conscious thoughts and feelings as a whole. [f. prec.]

conscript /kənˈskrɪpt/ *v.t.* to summon for compulsory State (esp. military) service. —/ˈkɒnskrɪpt/ *n.* a conscripted person. [back-formation f. *conscription* f. L *conscribere* enrol]

consecrate /ˈkɒnsɪkreɪt/ *v.t.* **1** to make or declare sacred, to dedicate formally to a religious or divine purpose. **2** to devote *to* a purpose. —**consecration** /-ˈkreɪʃ(ə)n/ *n.* [f. L *consecrare* (CON-, *sacrare* dedicate)]

consecutive /kənˈsekjʊtɪv/ *adj.* **1** following continuously, in unbroken or logical order. **2** (*Gram.*) expressing consequence. —**consecutively** *adv.* [f. F f. L (CON-, *sequi* follow)]

consensus /kənˈsensəs/ *n.* agreement in opinion; a majority view. [L (as foll.)]

consent /kənˈsent/ *v.i.* to express willingness or agree (*to*), to give permission (*that*). —*n.* voluntary agreement, permission. —**age of consent,** the age at which a girl's consent to sexual intercourse is valid in law. [f. OF f. L *consentire* agree (CON-, *sentire* feel)]

consequence /ˈkɒnsɪkwəns/ *n.* **1** what follows logically or effectively from some causal action or condition. **2** importance. [as foll.]

consequent /ˈkɒnsɪkwənt/ *adj.* following as a consequence (*on* or *upon*); logically consistent. —*n.* a thing that follows another. —**consequently** *adv.* [f. OF f. L *consequi* (as CONSECUTIVE)]

consequential /kɒnsɪˈkwenʃ(ə)l/ *adj.* **1** consequent; resulting indirectly. **2** self-important. —**consequentially** *adv.* [f. L *consequentia* consequence]

conservancy /kənˈsɜːvənsɪ/ *n.* a body controlling a port, river, etc., or concerned with the preservation of natural resources. [f. AF f. L (as foll.)]

conservation /kɒnsəˈveɪʃ(ə)n/ *n.* preservation, especially of the natural environment. —**conservation of energy,** the principle that the quantity of energy of any system of bodies not subject to external action remains constant. [as CONSERVE]

conservationist *n.* a supporter or advocate of environmental conservation. [f. prec.]

conservative /kənˈsɜːvətɪv/ *adj.* **1** tending to conserve, averse to rapid changes; (of views, taste, etc.) avoiding extremes. **2** (of an estimate etc.) purposely low. —*n.* **1** a conservative person. **2 Conservative,** a member or supporter of the Conservative Party. —**Conservative Party,** a political party disposed to maintain existing institutions and promote private enterprise. —**conservatism** *n.*, **conservatively** *adv.* [f. L (as CONSERVE)]

conservatoire /kənˈsɜːvətwɑː(r)/ *n.* a (usually European) school of music or other arts. [F (as foll.)]

conservatory /kənˈsɜːvətərɪ/ *n.* a greenhouse for tender plants, especially one with a communicating entrance from a house. [as CONSERVE]

conserve /kənˈsɜːv/ *v.t.* to keep from harm, decay, or loss, especially for future use. —*n.* jam, especially that made from fresh fruit. [f. OF f. L *conservare* (CON-, *servare* keep safe)]

consider /kənˈsɪdə(r)/ *v.t.* **1** to think about, especially in order to reach a conclusion; to examine the merits of; (in *p.p.*, of an opinion etc.) formed after careful thought. **2** to make allowances or be thoughtful for. **3** to think to be; to have the opinion *that.* **4** to look attentively at. [f. OF f. L *considerare* (orig. an augural term, f. *sidus* star)]

considerable /kənˈsɪdərəb(ə)l/ *adj.* not negligible, fairly great in amount or extent etc.; of some importance. —**considerably** *adv.* [as prec.]

considerate /kənˈsɪdərət/ *adj.* thoughtful for

others, careful not to cause inconvenience or hurt. —**considerately** *adv.* [f. L (as CONSIDER)]

consideration /kənsɪdəˈreɪʃ(ə)n/ *n.* **1** careful thought. **2** being considerate, kindness. **3** a factor influencing a decision or course of action. **4** a compensation, reward. —**in consideration of,** in return for, on account of. **take into consideration,** to make allowance for. [f. OF f. L (as prec.)]

considering *prep.* in view of, taking into consideration; (*ellipt., colloq.*) in view of the circumstances. [f. CONSIDER]

consign /kənˈsaɪn/ *v.t.* to hand over or deliver; to assign or commit *to*; to send (goods) *to*. [f. F or L *consignare* mark with a seal]

consignee /kɒnsaɪˈniː/ *n.* a person to whom something is consigned. [f. prec.]

consignment *n.* **1** consigning. **2** a batch of goods etc. consigned. [f. CONSIGN]

consist /kənˈsɪst/ *v.i.* **1** to be composed *of*. **2** to be consistent *with*. —**consist in,** to have as its basis or essential feature. [f. L *consistere* exist (CON-, *sistere* stop)]

consistency /kənˈsɪstənsɪ/ *n.* **1** degree of density, firmness, or solidity, especially of thick liquids. **2** being consistent. [f. F or L (as prec.)]

consistent /kənˈsɪst(ə)nt/ *adj.* **1** compatible or in harmony (*with*). **2** (of a person) constant to the same principles of thought or action. —**consistently** *adv.* [as CONSIST]

consistory /kənˈsɪstərɪ/ *n.* **1** a council of cardinals, or of the pope and cardinals. **2 Consistory (Court),** an Anglican bishop's court to deal with ecclesiastical problems and offences. [f. AF f. L (as CONSIST)]

consolation /kɒnsəˈleɪʃ(ə)n/ *n.* consoling; a consoling circumstance. —**consolation prize,** a prize given to a competitor who just fails to win one of the main prizes. —**consolatory** *adj.* [as foll.]

console[1] /kənˈsəʊl/ *v.t.* to comfort, especially in grief or disappointment. [f. F f. L *consolari*]

console[2] /ˈkɒnsəʊl/ *n.* **1** a bracket supporting a shelf etc. **2** a frame containing the keys and stops of an organ; a panel for switches, controls, etc. **3** a cabinet for radio etc. equipment. [F]

consolidate /kənˈsɒlɪdeɪt/ *v.t./i.* **1** to make or become strong or solid. **2** to combine into one whole. —**consolidation** /-ˈdeɪʃ(ə)n/ *n.* [f. L *consolidare* (CON-, *solidus* solid)]

consols /ˈkɒnsɒlz/ *n.pl.* British government securities. [abbr. of *consolidated annuities*]

consommé /kənˈsɒmeɪ/ *n.* clear meat soup. [F]

consonance /ˈkɒnsənəns/ *n.* agreement or harmony. [as foll.]

consonant /ˈkɒnsənənt/ *n.* a speech sound in which the breath is at least partially obstructed, combining with a vowel to form a syllable; a letter representing this. —*adj.* in agreement or harmony *with*; agreeable *to*. —**consonantal** /-ˈnænt(ə)l/ *adj.* [f. F f. L *consonare* (CON-, *sonare* sound)]

consort[1] /ˈkɒnsɔːt/ *n.* **1** a wife or husband, especially of a reigning monarch. **2** a ship sailing with another. —/kənˈsɔːt/ *v.i.* **1** to associate or keep company (*with, together*). **2** to be in harmony (*with*). [f. F f. L *consors* sharer (CON-, *sors* lot)]

consort[2] /ˈkɒnsɔːt/ *n.* an ensemble of voices and/or instruments in English music from about 1570 to 1720. [earlier form of CONCERT]

consortium /kənˈsɔːtɪəm/ *n.* (*pl.* **-ia**) an association, especially of several business companies. [L (as CONSORT[1])]

conspectus /kənˈspektəs/ *n.* a general view or survey; a synopsis. [L (*conspicere* look at attentively)]

conspicuous /kənˈspɪkjʊəs/ *adj.* clearly visible, attracting attention; noteworthy, striking. —**conspicuously** *adv.*, **conspicuousness** *n.* [f. L (as prec.)]

conspiracy /kənˈspɪrəsɪ/ *n.* an act of conspiring; an unlawful combination or plot. —**conspiracy of silence,** an agreement not to talk about something. [as CONSPIRE]

conspirator /kənˈspɪrətə(r)/ *n.* a person who conspires. —**conspiratorial** /-ˈtɔrɪəl/ *adj.*, **conspiratorially** *adv.* [as foll.]

conspire /kənˈspaɪə(r)/ *v.i.* **1** to plan secretly with others, especially for some unlawful purpose. **2** (of events) to seem to be working together. [f. OF f. L *conspirare* agree, plot (CON-, *spirare* breathe)]

constable /ˈkɒnstəb(ə)l, ˈkʌn-/ *n.* **1** a policeman; a policeman or policewoman of the lowest rank. **2** the governor of a royal castle. **3** (*hist.*) the principal officer of the royal household. —**Chief Constable,** the head of the police force of an area. [f. OF f. L *comes stabuli* count of the stable]

constabulary /kənˈstæbjʊlərɪ/ *n.* a police force. [as prec.]

constancy /ˈkɒnst(ə)nsɪ/ *n.* the quality of being unchanging and dependable; faithfulness. [as foll.]

constant /ˈkɒnst(ə)nt/ *adj.* **1** continuous; frequently occurring. **2** unchanging, faithful, dependable. —*n.* anything that does not vary; (*Math. & Physics*) a quantity or number of constant value. —**constantly** *adv.* [f. OF f. L *constare* (CON-, *stare* stand)]

constellation /kɒnstəˈleɪʃ(ə)n/ *n.* a group of stars forming a recognizable pattern in the sky and identified by some imaginative name describing their form or identifying them with a mythological figure. [f. F f. L *constellatio* (CON-, *stella* star)]

consternation /kɒnstəˈneɪʃ(ə)n/ *n.* amazement

or dismay causing mental confusion. [f. F or L (CON-, *sternere* throw down)]

constipate /ˈkɒnstɪpeɪt/ *v.t.* to affect with constipation. [f. L *constipare* (CON-, *stipare* stuff full)]

constipation /kɒnstɪˈpeɪʃ(ə)n/ *n.* a condition with hardened faeces and difficulty in emptying the bowels. [as prec.]

constituency /kənˈstɪtjʊənsɪ/ *n.* a body of voters who elect a representative; an area so represented. [as foll.]

constituent /kənˈstɪtjʊənt/ *adj.* **1** composing or helping to make a whole. **2** able to make or change a constitution; electing a representative. —*n.* **1** a constituent part. **2** a member of a constituency. [as foll.]

constitute /ˈkɒnstɪtju:t/ *v.t.* **1** to compose, to be the essence or components of. **2** to appoint or set up (an assembly etc.) in legal form. **3** to form or establish. [f. L *constituere* (CON-, *statuere* set up)]

constitution /kɒnstɪˈtju:ʃ(ə)n/ *n.* **1** an act or method of constituting, composition. **2** the condition of a person's body as regards health, strength, etc. **3** the form in which a State is organized; the body of fundamental principles by which a State or organization is governed. [as prec.]

constitutional *adj.* of, in harmony with, or limited by the constitution. —*n.* a walk taken regularly as healthy exercise. —**constitutionality** /-ˈnælɪtɪ/ *n.*, **constitutionally** *adv.* [f. prec.]

constitutive /ˈkɒnstɪtju:tɪv/ *adj.* **1** able to form or appoint, constituent. **2** essential. [as CONSTITUTE]

constrain /kənˈstreɪn/ *v.t.* **1** to urge irresistibly or by necessity. **2** to confine forcibly, to imprison. **3** (in *p.p.*) forced, embarrassed. [f. OF f. L *constringere* (CON-, *stringere* bind)]

constraint /kənˈstreɪnt/ *n.* constraining, being constrained; a restriction; restraint of natural feelings, a constrained manner. [as prec.]

constrict /kənˈstrɪkt/ *v.t.* to compress, to make narrow or tight. —**constriction** *n.*, **constrictive** *adj.* [f. L (as CONSTRAIN)]

constrictor *n.* **1** a muscle that draws together or narrows a part. **2** a snake that kills by compressing its prey. [f. prec.]

construct /kənˈstrʌkt/ *v.t.* **1** to make by fitting parts together, to build or form. **2** (*Geom.*) to delineate (a figure). —/ˈkɒn-/ *n.* a thing constructed, especially by the mind. —**constructor** /-ˈstrʌktə(r)/ *n.* [f. L *construere* (CON-, *struere* pile, build)]

construction /kənˈstrʌkʃ(ə)n/ *n.* **1** constructing; a thing constructed. **2** the syntactical connection of words in a sentence. **3** an interpretation or explanation of a statement or action. —**constructional** *adj.* [as prec.]

constructive /kənˈstrʌktɪv/ *adj.* tending to form a basis for ideas, positive, helpful. —**constructively** *adv.* [as CONSTRUCT]

constructivism /kɒnˈstrʌktɪvɪz(ə)m/ *n.* a kind of art using various materials combined into usu. non-pictorial forms. —**constructivist** *n.* [f. Russ. *konstruktivizm* (as prec.)]

construe /kənˈstru:/ *v.t.* **1** to interpret (words or actions). **2** to combine (words *with* others) grammatically. **3** to analyse the syntax of (a sentence). **4** to translate word for word. [as CONSTRUCT]

consubstantial /kɒnsəbˈstænʃ(ə)l/ *adj.* of one substance. [f. L (as CON-, SUBSTANTIAL)]

consubstantiation /kɒnsəbstænʃɪˈeɪʃ(ə)n/ *n.* the doctrine, associated especially with Luther, that in the Eucharist, after consecration of the elements, the real substances of the body and blood of Christ coexist with those of the bread and wine. [as prec.]

consul /ˈkɒns(ə)l/ *n.* **1** an official appointed by the State to live in a foreign city and protect the State's citizens and other interests there. **2** (*hist.*) either of the two annually elected chief magistrates in ancient Rome. —**consular** /ˈkɒnsjʊlə(r)/ *adj.* [L, rel. to CONSULT]

consulate /ˈkɒnsjʊlət/ *n.* the position, office, or residence of a consul. [as prec.]

consult /kənˈsʌlt/ *v.t./i.* **1** to seek information or advice from (a person, book, etc.); to take counsel (*with*). **2** to take (feelings etc.) into consideration. [f. F f. L *consultare* frequent. of *consulere* take counsel]

consultant /kənˈsʌltənt/ *n.* a person qualified to give expert professional advice, especially in a branch of medicine. —**consultancy** *n.* [as prec.]

consultation /kɒnsəlˈteɪʃ(ə)n/ *n.* consulting; a meeting for this purpose. [f. OF or L (as CONSULT)]

consultative /kənˈsʌltətɪv/ *adj.* of or for consultation. [f. CONSULT]

consume /kənˈsju:m/ *v.t.* **1** to eat or drink; to use up; to destroy. **2** (in *p.p.*) possessed *by* or entirely preoccupied *with* (envy etc.). —**consumable** *adj.* [f. L *consumere* (CON-, *sumere* take up)]

consumer *n.* one who consumes, especially one who uses a product; a person who buys or uses goods or services. [f. prec.]

consumerism *n.* **1** protection or promotion of consumers' interests. **2** high consumption of goods, the belief in this. [f. prec.]

consummate /kənˈsʌmɪt/ *adj.* complete; perfect; supremely skilled. —/ˈkɒnsəmeɪt/ *v.t.* to make perfect or complete; to complete (a marriage) by sexual intercourse. —**consummation** /kɒnsəˈmeɪʃ(ə)n/ *n.* [f. L *consummare* complete (CON,- *summus* utmost)]

consumption /kənˈsʌmpʃ(ə)n/ *n.* **1** consuming;

the amount consumed. **2** the purchase and use of goods etc. **3** pulmonary tuberculosis. [as CONSUME]

consumptive /kən'sʌmptɪv/ *adj.* tending to or affected with pulmonary tuberculosis. —*n.* a consumptive person. [as prec.]

contact /'kɒntækt/ *n.* **1** the condition or state of touching, meeting, or communicating. **2** a person who is or may be contacted for information, assistance, etc. **3** a person likely to carry a contagious disease through being near an infected person. **4** a connection for the passage of an electric current. —/also kən'tækt/ *v.t.* to get in touch with (a person); to begin communication or personal dealings with. —**contact lens,** a small usually plastic lens placed against the eyeball to correct faulty vision. [f. L *contingere* (CON-, *tangere* touch)]

contagion /kən'teɪdʒən/ *n.* the spreading of disease by bodily contact; a disease so transmitted; a corrupting moral influence. [f. L *contagio* (as prec.)]

contagious /kən'teɪdʒəs/ *adj.* (of a person) likely to transmit disease by bodily contact; (of a disease) transmitted in this way. [f. L *contagiosus* (as CONTAGION)]

contain /kən'teɪn/ *v.t.* **1** to have, hold, or be able to hold within itself; to include or comprise; to consist of, to be equal to; (of a number) to be divisible by (a factor) without remainder. **2** to enclose, to prevent from moving or extending; to control or restrain (feelings etc.). [f. OF f. L *continēre* (CON-, *tenēre* hold)]

container *n.* **1** a box, jar, etc., for containing particular things. **2** a large boxlike receptacle of standard design for the transport of goods. [f. prec.]

containerize *v.t.* to transport by container; to convert to this method of transporting goods. —**containerization** /-'zeɪʃ(ə)n/ *n.* [f. prec.]

containment *n.* the action or policy of preventing the expansion of a hostile country or influence. [f. CONTAIN]

contaminate /kən'tæmɪneɪt/ *v.t.* to pollute, especially with radioactivity; to infect. —**contaminant** *n.*, **contamination** /-'neɪʃ(ə)n/ *n.*, **contaminator** *n.* [f. L *contaminare* (CON-, *tamin-* rel. to *tangere* touch)]

contemn /kən'tem/ *v.t.* (*literary*) to despise; to disregard. [f. OF or L *contemnere* despise]

contemplate /'kɒntəmpleɪt/ *v.t./i.* **1** to survey with the eyes or mind. **2** to regard (an event) as possible; to intend. **3** to meditate. —**contemplation** /-'pleɪʃ(ə)n/ *n.* [f. L *contemplari* (CON-, *templum* area within which an augur took the auspices)]

contemplative /kən'templətɪv/ *adj.* of or given to (esp. religious) contemplation, meditative. —*n.* a person devoted to religious contemplation. [f. OF f. L (as prec.)]

contemporaneous /kəntempə'reɪnɪəs/ *adj.* existing or occurring at the same time (*with*). —**contemporaneity** /-'ni:ɪtɪ/ *n.* [f. L *contemporaneus* (CON-, *tempus* time)]

contemporary /kən'tempərərɪ/ *adj.* **1** belonging to the same time or period; of the same age. **2** modern in style or design. —*n.* a contemporary person or thing. [f. L (as prec.)]

contempt /kən'tempt/ *n.* **1** the feeling that a person or thing is worthless or beneath consideration, or deserving extreme reproach or scorn; the condition of being held in contempt. **2** (in full **contempt of court**) disrespect for or disobedience to a court of law. [as CONTEMN]

contemptible /kən'temptɪb(ə)l/ *adj.* deserving contempt. —**contemptibility** /-'bɪlɪtɪ/ *n.*, **contemptibly** *adv.* [as CONTEMN]

contemptuous *adj.* feeling or showing contempt. —**contemptuously** *adv.*, **contemptuousness** *n.* [as CONTEMPT]

contend /kən'tend/ *v.i.* **1** to struggle or compete; to argue (*with*). **2** to assert or maintain (*that*). —**contender** *n.* [f. OF or L *contendere* (CON-, *tendere* stretch, strive)]

content[1] /'kɒntent/ *n.* **1** (usu. in *pl.*) what is contained in a thing, especially in a vessel, book, or house. **2** capacity, volume. **3** the amount (of a constituent) contained. **4** the substance (of a speech etc.) as distinct from the form. [f. L (as CONTAIN)]

content[2] /kən'tent/ *predic. adj.* satisfied, adequately happy; willing (*to* do). —*v.t.* to make content, to satisfy. —*n.* a contented state, satisfaction. [f. OF f. L (as CONTAIN)]

contented /kən'tentɪd/ *adj.* satisfied; willing to be content *with*. —**contentedly** *adv.* [f. prec.]

contention /kən'tenʃ(ə)n/ *n.* **1** contending, argument or dispute. **2** the point contended for in an argument. [f. prec.]

contentious /kən'tenʃəs/ *adj.* **1** quarrelsome. **2** likely to cause argument. [as prec.]

contentment *n.* a contented state, tranquil happiness. [f. CONTENT[2]]

conterminous /kɒn'tɜ:mɪnəs/ *adj.* having a common boundary (*with*). [f. L *conterminus* (CON-, *terminus* boundary)]

contest /'kɒntest/ *n.* contending, strife; a competition. —/kən'test/ *v.t.* **1** to dispute (a claim or statement). **2** to contend or compete for (a prize, a seat in parliament, etc.) or in (an election). [f. L *contestari* (CON-, *testis* witness)]

contestant /kən'testənt/ *n.* one who takes part in a contest. [f. prec.]

context /'kɒntekst/ *n.* **1** the parts that precede and follow a word or passage and fix its precise meaning. **2** attendant circumstances. —**contextual** /kən'tekstjʊəl/ *adj.* [f. L (CON-, *texere* weave)]

contiguous /kən'tɪgjʊəs/ *adj* next (*to*) touching, in contact. —**contiguity** /kɒntɪ'gju:ɪtɪ/ *n* **contiguously** *adv*. [as CONTINGENT]

continent[1] /'kɒntɪnənt/ *n* any of the main continuous bodies of land (Europe, Asia, Africa, North America, South America Australia, Antarctica) —**the Continent**, the mainland of Europe as distinct from the British Isles. [f. L *terra continens* continuous land (as foll.)]

continent[2] /'kɒntɪnənt/ *adj* able to control the movements of the bowels and bladder —**continence** *n*. [f. L (as CONTAIN)]

continental /kɒntɪ'nent(ə)l/ *adj*. 1 of or characteristic of a continent. 2 **Continental**, characteristic of the Continent. —**Continental breakfast**, a light breakfast of coffee and rolls etc. **continental quilt**, a duvet. **continental shelf**, the shallow sea-bed bordering a continent. [f. prec.]

contingency /kən'tɪndʒ(ə)nsɪ/ *n*. an event that may or may not occur: an unknown or unforeseen circumstance. [as foll.]

contingent /kən'tɪndʒ(ə)nt/ *adj*. conditional or dependent (*on* or *upon* especially an uncertain event or circumstance); that may or may not occur; fortuitous. —*n*. a body of troops, ships, etc., forming part of a larger group. —**contingently** *adv* [f L (as CONTACT)]

continual /kən'tɪnjʊəl/ *adj* constantly or frequently recurring, always happening —**continually** *adv*. [as CONTINUE]

continuance /kən'tɪnjʊəns/ *n*. continuing in existence or operation; duration. [as CONTINUE]

continuation /kəntɪnjʊ'eɪʃ(ə)n/ *n*. continuing; a thing that continues something else. [as CONTINUE]

continue /kən'tɪnju:/ *v.t./i*. 1 to maintain or keep up, not to stop (an action etc.). 2 to resume or prolong (a narrative, journey, etc., or *abs*.); to prolong, to be a sequel to. 3 to remain, to stay; not to become other than. [f. OF f. L *continuare* (as CONTINUOUS)]

continuity /kɒntɪ'nju:ɪtɪ/ *n*. 1 being continuous; unbroken succession; logical sequence. 2 maintenance of consistency in successive shots or scenes of a film etc. 3 linkage between broadcast items. [as CONTINUOUS]

continuo /kən'tɪnjʊəʊ/ *n*. (*pl*. **-os**) (*Mus*.) a continuous bass accompaniment played usually on a keyboard instrument. [It. (as foll.)]

continuous /kən'tɪnjʊəs/ *adj*. without an interval or break, uninterrupted; connected throughout in space or time. —**continuously** *adv*. [f. L (as CONTAIN)]

continuum /kən'tɪnjʊəm/ *n*. (*pl*. **-nua**) a thing of continuous structure. [L (as prec.)]

contort /kən'tɔ:t/ *v.t*. to twist or force out of normal shape. —**contortion** *n*. [f. L *contorquēre* (CON-, *torquēre* twist)]

contortionist /kən'tɔ:ʃənɪst/ *n* a performer who can twist his body into unusual positions [f. prec.]

contour /'kɒntʊə(r)/ *n* 1 an outline. 2 a line on a map joining points at the same altitude. 3 a line separating differently coloured parts of a design. —*v.t*. to mark with contour lines. [f. F f. It. (*contornare* draw in outline)]

contra- *prefix* against. opposed to. [f. L *contra* against]

contraband /'kɒntrəbænd/ *n* smuggled goods, smuggling, prohibited trade. —*adj* forbidden to be imported or exported. [f. Sp. f It. (as CONTRA-, *bando* proclamation)]

contraception /kɒntrə'sepʃ(ə)n/ *n*. prevention of pregnancy, the use of contraceptives. [f. CONTRA- + (CON)CEP·TION]

contraceptive /kɒntrə'septɪv/ *adj*. preventing pregnancy. —*n*. a contraceptive device or drug. [as prec.]

contract /'kɒntrækt/ *n*. a written or spoken agreement, especially one enforceable by law; the document recording it. —/kən'trækt/ *v.t./i*. 1 to make or become smaller; to draw (muscles, the brow, etc.) together 2 to shorten (a word) by combination or elision. 3 to make a contract (*with*): to form or enter into (a marriage, debt, etc.); to arrange for (work) to be done by contract —**contract bridge**, a form of bridge in which only tricks bid and won count towards the game. **contract in** *or* **out**, to elect to enter or not to enter a scheme or commitment. [f. OF f. L *contractus* (CON-, *trahere* draw)]

contractable *adj*. (of disease) that may be contracted. [f. prec.]

contractible *adj*. able to be made smaller or drawn together. [f. CONTRACT]

contractile /kən'træktaɪl/ *adj*. capable of or producing contraction. —**contractility** /kɒntræk'tɪlɪtɪ/ *n*. [as prec.]

contraction /kən'trækʃ(ə)n/ *n*. 1 contracting. 2 shortening a word or words by combination or elision; a contracted form. [f. CONTRACT]

contractor /kən'træktə(r)/ *n*. one who makes a contract, especially to build houses. [as prec.]

contractual /kən'træktjʊəl/ *adj*. of or in the nature of a contract. —**contractually** *adv*. [f. CONTRACT]

contradict /kɒntrə'dɪkt/ *v.t*. to deny; to deny the statement made by; (of facts, statements, etc.) to be at variance or conflict with. —**contradiction** *n*., **contradictory** *adj*. [f. L *contradicere* (CONTRA-, *dicere* say)]

contradistinction /kɒntrədɪs'tɪŋkʃ(ə)n/ *n*. distinction by contrast; contrast.

contraflow *n*. a flow (esp. of road traffic) in a direction opposite to, and alongside, that of the usual or established flow.

contralto /kən'træltəʊ/ *n*. (*pl*. **-os**) the lowest

female singing-voice; a singer with such a voice; a part written for it. [It. (CONTRA-, ALTO)]

contraption /kən'træpʃ(ə)n/ *n.* a machine or device, especially a strange or cumbersome one. [orig. unkn.]

contrapuntal /kɒntrə'pʌnt(ə)l/ *adj.* of or in counterpoint. —**contrapuntally** *adv.* [f. It. *contrappunto* counterpoint]

contrariwise /kən'treərɪwaɪz/ *adv.* on the other hand, in the opposite way; perversely. [f. foll.]

contrary[1] /'kɒntrərɪ/ *adj.* opposed in nature, tendency, or direction; in opposition *to*; (of a wind) impeding, unfavourable. —*n.* the opposite of a person or thing. —*adv.* in opposition or contrast *to.* —**on the contrary,** in contrast to what has just been implied or stated. [f. AF f. L *contrarius* (*contra* against)]

contrary[2] /kən'treərɪ/ *adj.* doing the opposite of what is expected or advised, wilful. —**contrariness** *n.* [var. pronunc. of prec.]

contrast /'kɒntrɑ:st/ *n.* **1** juxtaposition or comparison showing striking differences; a difference so revealed. **2** a person or thing having noticeably different qualities (*to*). **3** the degree of difference between tones in a photograph or television picture. —/kən'trɑ:st/ *v.t./i.* to set in opposition to reveal a contrast; to have or show a contrast (*with*). [f. F f. It. f. L *contrastare* (CONTRA-, *stare* stand)]

contravene /kɒntrə'vi:n/ *v.t.* to violate or infringe (a law); to contradict, to conflict with. —**contravention** /-'venʃ(ə)n/ *n.* [f. L *contravenire* (CONTRA-, *venire* come)]

contretemps /'kɔ̃trətɑ̃/ *n.* an unfortunate occurrence; an unexpected mishap. [F]

contribute /kən'trɪbju:t, (D) 'kɒn-/ *v.t./i.* to give jointly with others (*to* a common fund); to supply (an article) for publication with others. —**contribute to,** to help to bring about. —**contributor** *n.* [f. L *contribuere* (CON-, *tribuere* bestow)]

contribution /kɒntrɪ'bju:ʃ(ə)n/ *n.* contributing; a thing contributed. [f. OF or L (as prec.)]

contributory /kən'trɪbjʊtərɪ/ *adj.* that contributes; using contributions. [as CONTRIBUTE]

contrite /'kɒntraɪt/ *adj.* penitent, feeling great guilt. —**contritely** *adv.*, **contrition** /kən'trɪʃ(ə)n/ *n.* [f. OF f. L *contritus* bruised (CON-, *terere* rub)]

contrivance /kən'traɪv(ə)ns/ *n.* contriving; something contrived, especially a device or plan. [f. foll.]

contrive /kən'traɪv/ *v.t./i.* to devise, plan, or make resourcefully or with skill; to manage (*to* do). —**contriver** *n.* [f. OF *controver* find, imagine, f. It.]

control /kən'trəʊl/ *n.* **1** the power of directing or restraining; self-restraint; a means of restraining or regulating; (usu. in *pl.*) switches and other devices by which a machine is controlled. **2** a place where something is controlled or verified. **3** a standard of comparison for checking the results of an experiment. **4** a personality said to direct the actions and words of a spiritualist medium. —*v.t.* **1** to have control of, to regulate; to serve as a control to. **2** to check or verify. —**control tower,** a tall building at an airport from which air traffic is controlled. **in control,** in charge (*of*). **out of control,** unrestrained, without control. —**controllable** *adj.* [f. AF *contreroller* keep copy of accounts, f. L (CONTRA-, *rotulus* roll)]

controller *n.* a person or thing that controls; a person in charge of expenditure. [as prec.]

controversial /kɒntrə'vɜ:ʃ(ə)l/ *adj.* causing or subject to controversy. [as foll.]

controversy /'kɒntrəvɜ:sɪ, (D) kən'trɒvəsɪ/ *n.* a prolonged argument or dispute. [as foll.]

controvert /'kɒntrəvɜ:t/ *v.t.* to dispute or deny. [f F f. L (CONTRA-, *vertere* turn)]

contumacy /'kɒntjʊməsɪ/ *n.* stubborn refusal to obey or comply. —**contumacious** /kɒntjʊ'meɪʃəs/ *adj.* [f. L *contumax* (CON-, perh. rel. to *tumēre* swell)]

contumely /'kɒntju:mlɪ/ *n.* insulting language or treatment; disgrace. —**contumelious** /kɒntju:'mi:lɪəs/ *adj.* [f. L (perh. as prec.)]

contuse /kən'tju:z/ *v.t.* to bruise. —**contusion** *n.* [f. L *contundere* (CON-, *tundere* thump)]

conundrum /kə'nʌndrəm/ *n.* a riddle or hard question, especially one with a pun in its answer. [orig. unkn.]

conurbation /kɒnɜ:'beɪʃ(ə)n/ *n.* an extended urban area, especially consisting of several towns and merging suburbs. [f. CON- + L *urbs* city]

convalesce /kɒnvə'les/ *v.i.* to recover health after an illness. [f. L *convalescere* (CON-, *valescere* grow strong)]

convalescent /kɒnvə'les(ə)nt/ *adj.* recovering from an illness. —*n.* a convalescent person. —**convalescence** *n.* [f. prec.]

convection /kən'vekʃ(ə)n/ *n.* **1** the transmission of heat by movement of the heated substance. **2** (*Meteorol.*) a vertical movement of air. —**convective** *adj.* [f. L *convectio* (CON-, *vehere* carry)]

convector /kən'vektə(r)/ *n.* a heating appliance that circulates warm air. [as prec.]

convene /kɒn'vi:n/ *v.t./i.* to summon or arrange (a meeting etc.); to assemble. —**convener** *n.* [f. L *convenire* (CON-, *venire* come)]

convenience /kən'vi:nɪəns/ *n.* **1** the quality of being convenient, suitability; freedom from difficulty or trouble; advantage. **2** a useful thing; a lavatory, especially a public one. —**convenience food,** food requiring very little preparation. [as prec.]

convenient /kən'vi:nɪənt/ *adj.* serving one's comfort or interests, suitable, free of trouble or difficulty; available or occurring at a suitable time or place. —**conveniently** *adv.* [f. L *convenire* suit, agree with (as CONVENE)]

convent /'kɒnvənt/ *n.* a religious community, especially of nuns, under vows; a building occupied by this. [f. AF f. L (as CONVENE)]

conventicle /kən'ventɪk(ə)l/ *n.* (chiefly *hist.*) a secret meeting, especially of religious dissenters. [f. L (as prec.)]

convention /kən'venʃ(ə)n/ *n.* **1** a formal assembly or conference. **2** a formal agreement or treaty. **3** general agreement on social behaviour etc. by the implicit consent of the majority. **4** a custom or customary practice. [f. OF f. L (as CONVENE)]

conventional *adj.* depending on or according with a convention; (of a person) attentive to social conventions; usual, of agreed significance; not spontaneous or sincere or original; (of weapons or a power) non-nuclear. —**conventionalism** *n.*, **conventionality** /-'nælɪtɪ/ *n.*, **conventionally** *adv.* [f. F or L (as prec.)]

converge /kən'vɜ:dʒ/ *v.i.* to come together or towards the same point. —**converge on,** to approach from different directions. —**convergence** *n.*, **convergent** *adj.* [f. L *convergere* (CON-, *vergere* incline)]

conversant /kən'vɜ:sənt/ *adj.* well acquainted (*with* a subject etc.). [f. OF (as CONVERSE[1])]

conversation /kɒnvə'seɪʃ(ə)n/ *n.* the informal exchange of ideas by spoken words; an instance of this. [f. OF f. L (as CONVERSE[1])]

conversational *adj.* of or in a conversation; colloquial. —**conversationally** *adv.* [f. prec.]

conversationalist *n.* a person fond of or good at conversation. [f. prec.]

converse[1] /kən'vɜ:s/ *v.i.* to hold a conversation, to talk (*with*) —/'kɒnvɜ:s/ *n.* (*archaic*) conversation. [f. OF f. L *conversari* keep company (as CONVERT)]

converse[2] /'kɒnvɜ:s/ *adj.* opposite, contrary, reversed. —*n.* a converse statement, idea or proposition. —**conversely** /kən'vɜ:slɪ/ *adv.* [f. L (as CONVERT)]

convert /kən'vɜ:t/ *v.t./i.* **1** to change or be able to be changed in form or function (*into*). **2** to cause (a person) to change his beliefs, opinion, party, etc. **3** to change (money etc.) into a different form or currency. **4** to make structural alterations in (a building) for a new purpose. **5** to complete (a try in Rugby football) by kicking a goal. —/'kɒnvɜ:t/ *n.* a person converted, especially to a new religion. —**conversion** *n.*, **converter** *n.* [f. OF f. L *convertere* (CON-, *vertere* turn)]

convertible /kən'vɜ:tɪb(ə)l/ *adj.* able to be converted. —*n.* a motor car with a folding or detachable roof. —**convertibility** /-'bɪlɪtɪ/ *n.* [OF f. L (as prec.)]

convex /'kɒnveks/ *adj.* with the outline or surface curved like the exterior of a sphere or circle. —**convexity** /kən'veksɪtɪ/ *n.* [f. L *convexus* vaulted]

convey /kən'veɪ/ *v.t.* **1** to transport or carry (goods, passengers, etc.). **2** to communicate (an idea, meaning, etc.). **3** to transfer the legal title to (property). **4** to transmit (sound etc.). —**conveyable** *adj.* [f. OF f. L *conviare* (CON-, *via* way)]

conveyance *n.* **1** conveying. **2** a means of transport, a vehicle. **3** the transfer of property; a deed effecting this. —(in legal sense) **conveyancer** *n.*, **conveyancing** *n.* [f. prec.]

conveyor *n.* (also **conveyer**) a person or thing that conveys. —**conveyor belt,** an endless moving belt for conveying articles in a factory etc. [f. CONVEY]

convict /kən'vɪkt/ *v.t.* to prove or find guilty (*of*). —/'kɒnvɪkt/ *n.* a convicted prisoner. [f. L *convincere* (CON-, *vincere* conquer)]

conviction /kən'vɪkʃ(ə)n/ *n.* **1** convicting, being convicted. **2** being convinced, a convinced state; a firm belief. [as prec.]

convince /kən'vɪns/ *v.t.* to persuade firmly (*of*, *that*). —**convincible** *adj.* [f. L (as CONVICT)]

convivial /kən'vɪvɪəl/ *adj.* fond of good company, sociable and lively. —**conviviality** /-'ælɪtɪ/ *n.* **convivially** *adv.* [f. L *convivium* feast (CON-, *vivere* live)]

convocation /kɒnvə'keɪʃ(ə)n/ *n.* convoking; an assembly convoked, especially the provincial synod of Anglican clergy or the legislative assembly of a university. —**convocational** *adj.* [as foll.]

convoke /kən'vəʊk/ *v.t.* to call together; to summon to assemble. [f. L *convocare* (CON-, *vocare* call)]

convoluted /'kɒnvəlu:tɪd/ *adj.* coiled, twisted; complex. [f. L *convolutus* (CON-, *volvere* roll)]

convolution /kɒnvə'lu:ʃ(ə)n/ *n.* coiling; a coil or twist; complexity; a sinuous fold in the surface of the brain. [as prec.]

convolvulus /kən'vɒlvjʊləs/ *n.* a twining plant of the genus *Convolvulus* or *Calystegia*, bindweed. [L (as CONVOLUTED)]

convoy /'kɒnvɔɪ/ *v.t.* to escort as a protection. —*n.* **1** convoying. **2** a group of ships, vehicles, etc., travelling together or escorted. [f. OF (as CONVEY)]

convulse /kən'vʌls/ *v.t.* (usu. in *pass.*) to affect with convulsions; to cause to laugh uncontrollably. —**convulsive** *adj.* [f. L *convellere* (CON-, *vellere* pull)]

convulsion /kən'vʌlʃ(ə)n/ *n.* **1** (often in *pl.*) a violent irregular motion of the limbs or body caused by involuntary contraction of the muscles. **2** a violent disturbance. **3** (in *pl.*) uncontrollable laughter. [as prec.]

cony /ˈkəʊnɪ/ *n.* a rabbit; its fur. [f. AF f. L *cuniculus*]

coo *n.* a soft murmuring sound like that of the dove. —*v.t.*/*i.* to emit a coo; to talk or say in a soft or amorous voice. [imit.]

cooee /ˈku:ɪ/ *n.* a cry used to attract attention. —*v.i.* to emit a cooee. —*int.* (*colloq.*) used to attract attention. [imit., orig. Aboriginal]

cook /kʊk/ *v.t.*/*i.* **1** to prepare (food) by heating; to undergo cooking. **2** (*colloq.*) to alter or falsify (accounts etc.). —*n.* one who cooks, esp. professionally or in a specified way. —**cook up,** (*colloq.*) to invent or concoct (a story, an excuse, etc.). [OE f. L *coquus*]

cooker *n.* **1** an appliance or vessel for cooking food. **2** a fruit (esp. an apple) suitable for cooking. [f. prec.]

cookery *n.* the art or practice of cooking. [f. COOK]

cookie /ˈkʊkɪ/ *n.* **1** (*US*) a sweet biscuit. **2** (*Sc.*) a plain bun. [f. Du. *koekje* dim. of *koek* cake]

cool *adj.* **1** of or at a fairly low temperature, fairly cold, not hot; suggesting or achieving coolness. **2** calm, unexcited; lacking enthusiasm, restrained; calmly audacious. —*n.* coolness; cool air, a cool place. —*v.t.*/*i.* (often with *down* or *off*) to make or become cool. —**cooling tower,** a tall structure for cooling hot water before reuse, especially in industry. **cooling-off period,** an interval to allow for a change of mind before action. **cool off,** to calm down. —**coolly** /ˈku:llɪ/ *adv.*, **coolness** *n.* [OE, rel. to COLD]

coolant /ˈku:lənt/ *n.* a cooling agent, especially a fluid to remove heat from an engine. [f. prec.]

cooler *n.* **1** a vessel in which a thing is cooled. **2** (*slang*) a prison cell. [f. COOL]

coolie /ˈku:lɪ/ *n.* an unskilled native labourer in Eastern countries. [perh. f. *Kuli*, tribe in India]

coomb /ku:m/ *n.* a valley on the side of a hill; a short valley running up from the coast. [OE]

coop *n.* a cage for keeping poultry. —*v.t.* to keep in a coop; (often with *in* or *up*) to confine (a person). [f. LG or Du., ult. f. L *cupa* cask]

cooper *n.* a maker or repairer of casks and barrels. [as prec.]

co-operate /kəʊˈɒpəreɪt/ *v.i.* to work or act together (*with*). —**co-operation** /-ˈreɪʃ(ə)n/ *n.*, **co-operator** *n.* [f. L *cooperari* (co-, *opus* work)]

co-operative /kəʊˈɒpərətɪv/ *adj.* **1** of or providing co-operation; willing to co-operate. **2** (of a business) owned and run jointly by its members with profits shared among them. —*n.* a co-operative farm or society. —**co-operatively** *adv.* [as prec.]

co-opt /kəʊˈɒpt/ *v.t.* to appoint to membership of a body by the invitation or votes of the existing members. —**co-option** *n.*, **co-optive** *adj.* [f. L *cooptare* (co-, *optare* choose)]

co-ordinate /kəʊˈɔ:dɪnət/ *adj.* equal in rank or importance (esp. of the parts of a compound sentence); consisting of co-ordinate things. —*n.* **1** a co-ordinate thing. **2** (*Math.*, usu. **coordinate**) each of a system of magnitudes used to fix the position of a point, a line, or a plane. **3** (in *pl.*) matching items of clothing. —/-neɪt/ *v.t.* to make co-ordinate; to bring (parts, movements, etc.) into a proper relationship; to cause (the limbs, parts, etc.) to function together or in proper order. —**co-ordinately** *adv.*, **co-ordination** /-ˈneɪʃ(ə)n/ *n.*, **co-ordinative** *adj.*, **co-ordinator** *n.* [f. co- + L *ordinare* arrange, order]

coot *n.* a water-bird of the genus *Fulica* with a horny white patch on its forehead. [prob. f. LG]

cop *n.* (*slang*) a policeman. —*v.t.* (**-pp-**) (*slang*) **1** to catch or arrest (an offender). **2** to receive, to obtain or suffer. —**cop out,** (*slang*) to withdraw, to give up. **cop-out** *n.* (*slang*) a cowardly evasion or escape. [perh. f. obs. F *cap* arrest f. *caper* seize]

copal /ˈkəʊp(ə)l/ *n.* the resin of various tropical trees, used for varnish. [Sp. f. Aztec]

copartner /kəʊˈpɑ:tnə(r)/ *n.* a partner or associate. —**copartnership** *n.* [f. co- + PARTNER]

cope[1] *v.i.* to deal effectively or contend *with*; (*colloq.*) to manage successfully. [f. OF f. L f. Gk *kolaphos* blow with fist]

cope[2] *n.* a long cloaklike vestment worn by priests in ceremonies and processions. —*v.t.* to cover with a cope or coping. [OE, f. L *cappa* cap, cape]

copeck /ˈkəʊpek/ *n.* a Russian coin, one hundredth of a rouble. [f. Russ. *kopeika*]

copier /ˈkɒpɪə(r)/ *n.* a person or machine that copies (documents etc.). [f. COPY]

co-pilot /ˈkəʊpaɪlət/ *n.* the second pilot in an aircraft.

coping /ˈkəʊpɪŋ/ *n.* the top (usually sloping) row of masonry in a wall. —**coping-stone** *n.* a stone used in a coping. [f. COPE[2]]

coping saw /ˈkəʊpɪŋ/ a D-shaped saw for cutting curved outlines in wood. [f. OF *coper* cut (as COPE[2])]

copious /ˈkəʊpɪəs/ *adj.* abundant, plentiful; producing much. —**copiously** *adv.* [f. OF or L (*copia* plenty)]

copper[1] /ˈkɒpə(r)/ *n.* **1** a reddish-brown ductile metallic element, symbol Cu, atomic number 29. **2** a bronze coin; a penny. **3** a large metal vessel for boiling things, especially laundry. —*adj.* made of or coloured like copper. —*v.t.* to cover with copper. —**Copper Age,** the prehistoric period when some weapons and tools were made of copper, either before or in place of bronze. **copper beech,** a variety of beech with copper-coloured leaves. **copper-bottomed** *adj.* having the bottom sheathed with copper (esp. of a ship or pan); reliable; genuine. [OE f. L *cuprum* = *cyprium aes* Cyprus metal (Cyprus was the principal source of copper in Roman times)]

copper² *n.* (*slang*) a policeman. [f. COP]

copperhead *n.* a venomous American or Australian snake with a reddish-brown head.

copperplate *n.* **1** a polished copper plate for engraving or etching; a print made from this. **2** a fine style of handwriting.

coppice /ˈkɒpɪs/ *n.* an area of small trees and undergrowth. [f. OF f. L (as COPE²)]

copra /ˈkɒprə/ *n.* dried coconut-kernels. [Port. f. Malayalam]

copse *n.* a coppice. [shortened form]

Copt *n.* **1** a native Egyptian in and after the Hellenistic period. **2** a member of the Coptic Church. [f. F f. Arab., ult. f. Gk *Aiguptios* Egyptian]

Coptic /ˈkɒptɪk/ *adj.* of the Copts or Coptic. —*n.* the language of the Copts, now used only in the Coptic Church. —**Coptic Church,** the native Christian Church in Egypt, traditionally founded by St Mark. [f. prec.]

copula /ˈkɒpjʊlə/ *n.* a connecting word, especially a part of the verb *to be* connecting the predicate with the subject. [L, = fastening]

copulate /ˈkɒpjʊleɪt/ *v.i.* to come together sexually (*with*), as in the act of mating. —**copulation** /-ˈleɪʃ(ə)n/ *n.* [f. L *copulare* fasten together]

copy /ˈkɒpɪ/ *n.* **1** a thing made to look like another; a specimen of a book, magazine, etc. **2** matter to be printed; material for a newspaper article. **3** the text of an advertisement. —*v.t./i.* to make a copy (of); to imitate, to do the same as. —**copy-typist** *n.* one who makes typewritten copies of documents etc. **copy-writer** *n.* a writer of copy for publication, especially publicity material. [f. OF f. L *copia* abundance, in medieval sense = transcript, f. phr. *facere copiam describendi* give permission to transcribe]

copy-book *n.* a book containing models of handwriting for learners to imitate. —*adj.* tritely conventional; exemplary.

copyhold *n.* (*hist.*) tenure of land in accordance with the transcript of manorial records; land so held.

copyist *n.* a person who makes copies; an imitator. [f. COPY]

copyright *n.* the exclusive legal right to print, publish, perform, film, or record literary, artistic, or musical material, normally vested in the creator of such material. —*adj.* protected by copyright. —*v.t.* to secure a copyright of (material).

coquette /kɒˈket/ *n.* a flirtatious woman or girl. —*v.i.* to flirt. —**coquettish** *adj.*, **coquetry** /ˈkɒkɪtrɪ/ *n.* [F, = wanton, dim. of *coq* cock]

cor- *prefix* see COM-.

coracle /ˈkɒrək(ə)l/ *n.* a small boat, constructed of wickerwork and made watertight originally with animal hides but more recently with pitch or some other watertight material, used for river and coastal transport by the ancient Britons and still used by fishermen on the rivers and lakes of Wales and Ireland. [f. Welsh *corwgl* (*corwg* = Ir. *currach* boat)]

coral /ˈkɒr(ə)l/ *n.* **1** a hard usually red, pink, or white calcareous substance secreted by many species of coelenterates for support or habitation, and sometimes building up to form reefs and islands; that forming the skeleton of the precious coral (*corallium*) of the Mediterranean and Red Sea; (*loosely*) a similar substance produced by marine algae etc. **2** a structure formed of such substances. **3** any of numerous species of usually colonial marine coelenterates producing a horny, calcareous, or soft skeleton; an individual polyp or colony of these, especially of the order Madreporaria (the stony or true corals) which have a calcareous skeleton and are the main reef-forming types. **3** the yellowish- or reddish-pink colour of some corals. —*adj.* **1** made of coral. **2** yellowish- or reddish-pink. [f. OF f. L f. Gk *korallion*, prob. of Semitic origin]

coralline /ˈkɒrəlaɪn/ *adj.* of or like coral. —*n.* a seaweed with a hard jointed stem. [f. It. *corallino* dim. of *corallo* (as prec.)]

cor anglais /kɔːr ˈɑ̃gleɪ/ an alto woodwind instrument of the oboe family. [F, = English horn]

corbel /ˈkɔːb(ə)l/ *n.* a stone or timber projection from a wall, acting as a supporting bracket. —**corbelled** *adj.* [f. OF, dim. of *corp* crow (as foll.)]

corbie /ˈkɔːbɪ/ *n.* (*Sc.*) a raven, a black crow. [f. OF *corb*, *corp* f. L *corvus*]

cord *n.* **1** thick string or a piece of this; a similar structure in the body; electric flex. **2** a ribbed fabric, especially corduroy; (in *pl.*) corduroy trousers. **3** a measure of cut wood (usually 128 cu. ft, 3.6 cu. m). —*v.t.* **1** to secure with cord. **2** (in *p.p.*, of cloth) ribbed. [f. OF f. L f. Gk *khordē* string of musical instrument]

cordial /ˈkɔːdɪəl/ *adj.* heartfelt, sincere; warm, friendly. —*n.* a fruit-flavoured drink. —**cordiality** /-ˈælɪtɪ/ *n.*, **cordially** *adv.* [f. L *cordialis* (*cor* heart)]

cordite /ˈkɔːdaɪt/ *n.* a cordlike smokeless explosive. [f. CORD]

cordon /ˈkɔːd(ə)n/ *n.* **1** a line or circle of police, soldiers, guards, etc., esp. one preventing access to or from an area. **2** an ornamental cord or braid. **3** a fruit-tree trained to grow as a single stem. —*v.t.* (often with *off*) to enclose or separate with a cordon of police. [f. It. & F (as CORD)]

cordon bleu /kɔ:dɔ̃ 'blɜ:/ **1** of the highest class in cookery. **2** a cook of this class. [F, = blue ribbon, orig. that worn by Knights-grand-cross of the French order of the Holy Ghost, the highest order of chivalry under the Bourbon kings; hence extended to other first-class distinctions]

corduroy /'kɔ:dərɔɪ/ *n.* a thick cotton fabric with velvety ribs; (in *pl.*) corduroy trousers. [f. CORD ribbed fabric + obs. *duroy* coarse woollen fabric]

core *n.* **1** the horny central part of certain fruits, containing the seeds. **2** the central or most important part of anything; the central region of the earth. **3** the region of fissile material in a nuclear reactor. **4** a unit of structure in a computer, storing one bit (see BIT²) of data. **5** the inner strand of an electric cable. **6** the piece of soft iron forming the centre of a magnet or induction coil. —*v.t.* to remove the core from. [orig. unkn.]

coreopsis /kɒrɪ'ɒpsɪs/ *n.* a plant of the genus *Coreopsis*, with daisy-like usually yellow flowers. [L, f. Gk *koris* bug + *opsis* appearance (from the shape of the seed)]

co-respondent /kəʊrɪ'spɒnd(ə)nt/ *n.* the person (esp. the man) said to have committed adultery with the respondent in a divorce case.

corgi /'kɔ:gɪ/ *n.* a dog of short-legged Welsh breed with a foxlike head. [Welsh]

coriander /kɒrɪ'ændə(r)/ *n.* an aromatic herb, *Coriandrum sativum*; its seeds used as flavouring. [f. OF f. L f. Gk]

Corinthian /kə'rɪnθɪən/ *adj.* **1** of ancient Corinth in southern Greece. **2** (*Archit.*) of the order characterized by acanthus-leaf capitals and ornate decoration, used especially by the Romans. [f. L f. Gk *Korinthios*]

cork *n.* **1** the outer bark of a South European oak (*Quercus suber*), a buoyant light-brown substance. **2** a bottle-stopper of cork or other material. **3** a float made of cork. —*v.t.* (often with *up*) to stop or confine; to restrain (the feelings etc.). [f. LG or Du. f. Sp. *alcorque*]

corkage /'kɔ:kɪdʒ/ *n.* a charge made by a restaurant etc. for serving wine (esp. when brought from elsewhere). [f. prec.]

corked *adj.* stopped with cork; (of wine) spoilt by a decayed cork. [f. CORK]

corkscrew *n.* **1** a spiral steel device for extracting corks from bottles. **2** (often *attrib.*) a thing with a spiral shape. —*v.i.* to move spirally, to twist.

corm *n.* the bulblike underground stem of certain plants. [f. L f. Gk *kormos* trunk with boughs lopped off]

cormorant /'kɔ:mərənt/ *n.* a large black voracious sea-bird, *Phalocrorax carbo*. [f. OF f. L *corvus marinus* sea-raven]

corn¹ *n.* a cereal before or after harvesting, especially wheat, oats, barley, or (*US*) maize; a grain or seed of a cereal plant. —**corn-cob** *n.* the cylindrical centre of an ear of maize, to which the grains are attached. **corn on the cob**, maize cooked and eaten in this form. **corn dolly**, a symbolic or decorative figure made of plaited straw. [OE]

corn² *n.* a small tender horny place on the skin, especially on the toe. [f. AF f. L *cornu* horn]

Corn. *abbr.* Cornwall.

corncrake *n.* a bird (*Crex crex*) with a harsh grating cry. [f. CORN¹]

cornea /'kɔ:nɪə/ *n.* the transparent membrane covering the iris and pupil of the eyeball. —**corneal** *adj.* [f. L *cornea* (*tela*) horny tissue (*cornu* horn)]

corned *adj.* (of beef) preserved in salt or brine. [f. CORN¹]

cornel /'kɔ:n(ə)l/ *n.* a tree of the genus *Cornus*, e.g. cornelian cherry, dogwood. [f. G, ult. f. L *cornus*]

cornelian /kɔ:'ni:lɪən/ *n.* a dull red variety of chalcedony. [f. OF, after L *caro* flesh]

cornelian cherry /kɔ:'ni:lɪən/ a European berry-bearing tree, *Cornus mas*. [f. CORNEL]

corner *n.* **1** a place where converging sides or edges meet; a projecting angle, especially where two streets meet. **2** an internal space or recess formed by the meeting of two walls etc.; an angle of a ring in boxing etc., especially one where a contestant rests between rounds; a difficult position, especially one with no escape. **3** a secluded or remote place; a region or quarter, especially a remote one. **4** the action or result of buying the whole available stock of a commodity. **5** a free kick or hit from the corner of the field in football and hockey. —*v.t./i.* **1** to force (a person) into a difficult or inescapable position. **2** to establish a corner in (a commodity). **3** (esp. of or in a vehicle) to go round a corner. —**corner-stone** *n.* a stone in the projecting angle of a wall, a foundation-stone; an indispensable part or basis. [f. AF f. L *cornarium* (*cornu* horn)]

cornet /'kɔ:nɪt/ *n.* **1** a brass instrument resembling a trumpet but shorter and wider. **2** a conical wafer for holding ice-cream. —**cornettist, cornetist** /-'netɪst/ *n.* [f. OF dim. f. L *cornu* horn, trumpet]

cornflakes *n.pl.* a breakfast cereal of toasted maize flakes.

cornflour *n.* fine-ground flour made from maize, rice, etc.

cornflower *n.* a plant (especially a blue-flowered kind, *Centaurea cyanus*) that grows wild in cornfields.

cornice /ˈkɔːnɪs/ *n.* a horizontal moulding in relief, especially along the top of an internal wall or as the topmost part of an entablature. [f. F f. It.]

Cornish /ˈkɔːnɪʃ/ *adj.* of Cornwall or its people or language. —*n.* the ancient Celtic language of Cornwall. —**Cornish pasty,** seasoned meat and vegetables baked in a pastry envelope. [f. *Cornwall*, county of SW England]

cornucopia /kɔːnjʊˈkəʊpɪə/ *n.* a symbol of plenty consisting of a goat's horn overflowing with flowers, fruit, and corn; abundance. [L (*cornu copiae* horn of plenty)]

corny *adj.* (*colloq.*) trite; feebly humorous; sentimental, old-fashioned. —**cornily** *adv.*, **corniness** *n.* [f. CORN¹]

corolla /kəˈrɒlə/ *n.* the whorl of petals forming the inner envelope of a flower. [L, dim. of CORONA]

corollary /kəˈrɒlərɪ/ *n.* a proposition that follows from one already proved; the natural consequence (*of*). [f. L *corollarium* money paid for garlands, gratuity]

corona /kəˈrəʊnə/ *n.* (*pl.* **-ae** /-iː/) **1** the outermost region of the sun, normally visible only during a total solar eclipse, when it is seen as a pearly glow round the disc of the obscuring moon. **2** a glow round an electric conductor. **3** any of various crownlike parts of the body. **4** (in a flower) an appendage on top of a seed or on the inner side of a corolla. —**coronal** *adj.* [L, = garland, crown]

coronary /ˈkɒrənərɪ/ *adj* of the arteries supplying blood to the heart. —*n.* a coronary artery or thrombosis. —**coronary thrombosis,** blockage of a coronary artery by a clot of blood. [as prec.]

coronation /kɒrəˈneɪʃ(ə)n/ *n.* the ceremony of crowning a sovereign or consort. [f. OF f. L *coronatio* (*coronare* crown)]

coroner /ˈkɒrənə(r)/ *n.* an officer holding inquests into deaths thought to be violent or accidental, and inquiries into cases of treasure trove. [f. AF (as CROWN)]

coronet /ˈkɒrənɪt, -net/ *n.* **1** a small crown; a band of jewels worn as a head-dress. **2** the lowest part of a horse's pastern. [f. OF, dim. of *corone* crown]

corpora *pl.* of CORPUS.

corporal¹ /ˈkɔːpər(ə)l/ *n.* a non-commissioned army or RAF officer next below a sergeant. [f. F f. It.]

corporal² /ˈkɔːpərəl/ *adj.* of the human body. —**corporal punishment,** that inflicted on the body, especially by beating. —**corporality** /-ˈælɪtɪ/ *n.* [f. OF f. L (*corpus* body)]

corporate /ˈkɔːpərət/ *adj.* forming a corporation or group; of or belonging to a group. [f. L *corporare* form into a body (as prec.)]

corporation /kɔːpəˈreɪʃ(ə)n/ *n.* **1** a group of people authorized to act as an individual, especially in business. **2** the civic authorities of a borough, town, or city. **3** (*colloq.*) a protruding abdomen. [as prec.]

corporative /ˈkɔːpərətɪv/ *adj.* of a corporation; governed by or organized in corporations, especially of employers and employed. [f. CORPORATE]

corporeal /kɔːˈpɔːrɪəl/ *adj.* bodily, physical; material. —**corporeality** /-ˈælɪtɪ/ *n.*, **corporeally** *adv.* [f. L (*corpus* body)]

corposant /ˈkɔːpəz(ə)nt/ *n.* a luminous electrical discharge (also known as *St Elmo's fire*) sometimes seen on a ship or aircraft during a storm. [f. Sp. *corpo santo* holy body]

corps /kɔː(r)/ *n.* (*pl.* same /kɔːz/) **1** a military force or division. **2** a group of persons engaged in some activity. [F (as CORPSE)]

corps de ballet /kɔː də ˈbæleɪ/ a company of ballet-dancers. [F]

corps diplomatique /kɔː dɪpləmæˈtiːk/ the diplomatic corps (see DIPLOMATIC). [F]

corpse *n.* a dead (usu. human) body. [f. OF f. L *corpus* body]

corpulent /ˈkɔːpjʊlənt/ *adj.* bulky in body, fat. —**corpulence** *n.* [f. L *corpulentus* (as foll.)]

corpus /ˈkɔːpəs/ *n.* (*pl.* **corpora** /ˈkɔːpərə/) a body or collection of writings, texts, etc. —**Corpus Christi,** (= body of Christ) the feast commemorating the institution and gift of the Eucharist, celebrated on the Thursday after Trinity Sunday. [L, = body]

corpuscle /ˈkɔːpʌs(ə)l/ *n.* a minute body or cell in an organism, especially (in *pl.*) the red or white cells in the blood of vertebrates. —**corpuscular** /-ˈpʌskjʊlə(r)/ *adj.* [f. L *corpusculum* dim. of prec.]

corral /kɒˈrɑːl/ *n* an enclosure for wild animals or (*US*) cattle or horses. —*v.t.* (**-ll-**) to put or keep in a corral. [Sp. & Port., f. as KRAAL]

correct /kəˈrekt/ *adj.* **1** true, accurate. **2** (of conduct) proper, in accordance with taste or a standard. —*v.t.* **1** to set right (an error, omission, etc.); to mark the errors in; to substitute the right thing for (a wrong one). **2** to admonish; to punish (a person or fault). **3** to counteract (a harmful or divergent tendency etc.); to eliminate an aberration from (a lens etc.); to bring into accordance with a standard. —**correctly** *adv.*, **correctness** *n.*, **corrector** *n.* [f. L *corrigere* (COR-, *regere* guide)]

correction /kəˈrekʃ(ə)n/ *n.* **1** correcting. **2** a thing substituted for what is wrong. **3** (*archaic*) punishment. [f. OF f. L (as CORRECT)]

correctitude /kəˈrektɪtjuːd/ *n.* consciously correct behaviour. [blend of CORRECT, RECTITUDE]

corrective /kəˈrektɪv/ *adj.* serving to correct or counteract something harmful. —*n.* a corrective measure or thing. [F or f. L (as CORRECT)]

correlate /ˈkɒrəleɪt/ *v.t./i.* to have or bring into a mutual relation or dependence (*with* or *to*). —*n.* each of two related or complementary things. —**correlation** /-ˈleɪʃ(ə)n/ *n.* [f. L *correlatio* (COR-, *relatio* relation)]

correlative /kɒˈrelətɪv/ *adj.* having a mutual relationship; (*Gram.*, of words) corresponding to each other and used regularly together (as *neither* and *nor*). —**correlativity** /-ˈtɪvɪtɪ/ *n.* [f. L (COR-, *relativus* relative)]

correspond /kɒrɪˈspɒnd/ *v.i.* **1** to be analogous (*to*) or in agreement (*with*). **2** to communicate by interchange of letters (*with*). [f. F f. L *correspondere* (COR-, *respondere* answer)]

correspondence *n.* **1** agreement or similarity. **2** communication by letters; the letters sent or received. —**correspondence course,** a course of study conducted by post. [f. OF f. L (as prec.)]

correspondent *n.* **1** a person writing letters to another, esp. regularly. **2** a person employed by a newspaper to write regularly on a particular subject. [as prec.]

corridor /ˈkɒrɪdɔ:(r)/ *n.* **1** a passage from which doors lead into rooms; a passage in a train giving access to compartments along its length. **2** a strip of territory of one State passing through that of another. **3** a route which aircraft must follow, especially over foreign territory. [F f. It. (*correre* run)]

corrie *n.* (*Sc.*) a round hollow on a mountainside. [Gaelic]

corrigendum /kɒrɪˈgendəm/ *n.* (*pl.* **-da**) a thing to be corrected, especially an error in a book. [L (*corrigere* correct)]

corrigible /ˈkɒrɪdʒɪb(ə)l/ *adj.* able to be corrected; submissive. —**corrigibly** *adv.* [f. F f. L (as prec.)]

corroborate /kəˈrɒbəreɪt/ *v.t.* to confirm or give support to (a person, a statement or belief). —**corroboration** /-ˈreɪʃ(ə)n/ *n.*, **corroborative** /kəˈrɒbərətɪv/ *adj.* **corroborator** *n.*, **corroboratory** /kəˈrɒbərətərɪ/ *adj.* [f. L *corroborare* (COR-, *robur* strength)]

corroboree /kəˈrɒbərɪ/ *n.* a festive or warlike dance of Australian aboriginals; a noisy party. [Aboriginal]

corrode /kəˈrəʊd/ *v.t./i.* to wear away, especially by chemical action; to destroy gradually; to decay. —**corrosion** *n.* [f. L *corrodere* (COR-, *rodere* gnaw)]

corrosive /kəˈrəʊsɪv/ *adj.* tending to corrode. —*n.* a corrosive substance. [f. OF (as prec.)]

corrugated /ˈkɒrʊgeɪtɪd/ *adj.* formed into regular alternate folds and grooves, especially so as to strengthen (iron etc., or for use as roofing) or make (cardboard or paper) more resilient. —**corrugation** /-ˈgeɪʃ(ə)n/ *n.* [f. L *corrugare* (COR-, *ruga* wrinkle)]

corrupt /kəˈrʌpt/ *adj.* **1** morally depraved, wicked; influenced by or using bribery. **2** (of a text etc.) made suspect or unreliable by errors or alterations. —*v.t./i.* to make or become corrupt. —**corruption** *n.*, **corruptive** *adj.* [f. OF or L *corruptus* (COR-, *rumpere* break)]

corruptible /kəˈrʌptɪb(ə)l/ *adj.* able to be (esp. morally) corrupted. —**corruptibility** /-ˈbɪlɪtɪ/ *n.* [f. prec.]

corsage /kɔ:ˈsɑ:ʒ/ *n.* (*US*) a small bouquet worn by a woman. [f. OF (as CORPSE)]

corsair *n.* a pirate ship; a pirate. [f. F f. L *cursarius* (as COURSE)]

corselette /ˈkɔ:slɪt/ *n.* a woman's foundation garment combining corset and brassière. [f. CORSLET]

corset /ˈkɔ:sɪt/ *n.* a close-fitting undergarment worn to compress and shape the figure or as a surgical support. —*v.t.* **1** to provide with a corset. **2** to control closely. —**corsetry** *n.* [f. OF dim. of *cors* body (as CORPSE)]

corslet /ˈkɔ:slɪt/ *n.* **1** a garment (usually tight-fitting) covering the body. **2** (*hist.*) armour covering the trunk of the body. [f. OF, as prec.]

cortège /kɔ:ˈteɪʒ/ *n.* a procession, especially for a funeral. [F]

cortex /ˈkɔ:teks/ *n.* (*pl.* **cortices** /-ɪsi:z/) the outer covering of the kidney or other organ; the outer grey matter of the brain. —**cortical** *adj.*, **corticated** *adj.* [L, = bark]

cortisone /ˈkɔ:tɪzəʊn/ *n.* a hormone used medically against inflammation and allergy. [abbr. of chemical name]

corundum /kəˈrʌndəm/ *n.* extremely hard crystallized alumina, used especially as an abrasive. [f. Tamil f. Skr., = ruby]

coruscate /ˈkɒrəskeɪt/ *v.i.* to sparkle, to shine. —**coruscation** /-ˈskeɪʃ(ə)n/ *n.* [f. L *coruscare* glitter]

corvette /kɔ:ˈvet/ *n.* a small naval escort vessel; (*hist.*) a flush-decked warship with one tier of guns. [F, f. MDu. *corf* kind of ship]

corymb /ˈkɒrɪmb/ *n.* a flat-topped cluster of flowers on a long stem with the stems lengthening away from the centre. [f. F or L f. Gk, = cluster]

cos¹ /kɒs/ *n.* a crisp lettuce with narrow leaves. [f. *Cos*, island in the Aegean, where it originated]

cos² /kɒs, -z/ *abbr.* cosine.

cos³ /kɒz/ *conj.* (*colloq.*) because. [abbr.]

cosec. /ˈkəʊsek/ *abbr.* cosecant.

cosecant /kəʊˈsi:kənt/ *n.* the secant of the complement of a given angle. [f. co- + SECANT]

cosh *n.* (*colloq.*) a heavy blunt weapon. —*v.t.* (*colloq.*) to hit with a cosh. [orig. unkn.]

cosine /ˈkəʊsaɪn/ *n.* the ratio of the side adjacent

to the acute angle (in a right-angled triangle) to the hypotenuse. [f. co- + SINE]

cosmetic /kɒzˈmetɪk/ *adj*. **1** designed to beautify the skin, hair, etc.; (of a body treatment or surgery) improving or restoring the normal appearance. **2** superficially improving or beneficial. —*n*. a cosmetic preparation, especially for the face. —**cosmetically** *adv*. [f. F f. Gk (*kosmeō* adorn)]

cosmic /ˈkɒzmɪk/ *adj*. of the cosmos, especially as distinct from the earth; of or for space travel. —**cosmic rays** *or* **radiation,** high energy radiation from outer space. [f. COSMOS¹]

cosmogony /kɒzˈmɒgənɪ/ *n*. the origin of the universe; a theory about this. [f. Gk (as COSMOS¹, *-gonia* begetting)]

cosmology /kɒzˈmɒlədʒɪ/ *n*. the science of the creation and development of the universe. —**cosmological** /-ˈlɒdʒɪk(ə)l/ *adj*., **cosmologist** *n*. [f. COSMOS + -LOGY]

cosmonaut /ˈkɒzmənɔːt/ *n*. a Russian astronaut. [f. COSMOS¹, after *astronaut*]

cosmopolitan /kɒzməˈpɒlɪt(ə)n/ *adj*. of or from many parts of the world; free from national limitations or prejudices. —*n*. a cosmopolitan person. —**cosmopolitanism** *n*. [f. Gk *kosmopolitēs* citizen of the world]

cosmos¹ /ˈkɒzmɒs/ *n*. the universe as a well-ordered whole. [Gk, = order, ornament, world, or universe]

cosmos² /ˈkɒzmɒs/ *n*. a garden plant of the genus *Cosmos*, with pink, white, or purple flowers. [as prec.]

Cossack /ˈkɒsæk/ *n*. a member of those Russians who sought a free life in the steppes or on the frontiers of imperial Russia and were allowed privileges in return for service in protecting the frontiers; a descendant of these, noted for warlike qualities and for horsemanship. [ult. f. Turki, = nomad, adventurer (first used of an unrelated nomadic people, the Kazakhs, of S. Siberia)]

cosset /ˈkɒsɪt/ *v.t*. to pamper. [f. earlier n. = pet lamb, f. AF f. OE *cotsǣta* cottager]

cost *v.t*. **1** (*past* & *p.p*. **cost**) to be obtainable for (a certain sum), to have as a price; to require as an effort; to involve as a loss or sacrifice. **2** (*past* & *p.p*. **costed**) to fix or estimate the cost of. —*n*. what a thing costs, a price; an expenditure of time or effort; a loss or sacrifice; (in *pl*.) legal expenses. —**at all costs,** no matter what the cost or risk may be. **cost-effective** effective in relation to its cost. **cost of living,** the level of prices especially of basic necessities. **cost price,** the price paid for a thing by one who later sells it. [f. OF f. L *constare* stand at a price]

costal /ˈkɒst(ə)l/ *adj*. of the ribs. [f. F f. L (*costa* rib)]

co-star *n*. a cinema or stage star appearing with another or others of equal importance. —*v.t*. (-rr-) to include as a co-star.

coster *n*. a costermonger. [abbr.]

costermonger /ˈkɒstəmʌŋgə(r)/ *n*. a person who sells fruit, vegetables, etc., from a barrow in the street. [f. *costard* large apple f. OF *coste* rib (as COSTAL)]

costive /ˈkɒstɪv/ *adj*. constipated. [f. OF f. L (as CONSTIPATE)]

costly *adj*. costing much, expensive. —**costliness** *n*. [f. COST]

costume /ˈkɒstjuːm/ *n*. a style of dress, especially as associated with a particular place or time; a set of clothes; clothes or a garment for a particular activity; an actor's clothes for a part. —**costume jewellery,** jewellery made of inexpensive materials. [F f. It., f. L *consuetudo* custom]

costumier /kɒˈstjuːmɪə(r)/ *n*. one who makes or deals in costumes. [F (as prec.)]

cosy /ˈkəʊzɪ/ *adj*. comfortable and warm, snug. —*n*. a cover to keep hot a teapot or boiled egg. —*v.t*. (often with *along*) (*colloq*.) to reassure, to delude. —**cosily** *adv*., **cosiness** *n*. [orig. Sc.; etym. unkn.]

cot¹ *n*. a bed with high sides for a baby or very young child; a small light bed. —**cot-death** *n*. an unexplained death of a sleeping baby. [f. Hindi, = bedstead, hammock]

cot² *n*. a small shelter; a cote; (*poetic*) a cottage. [OE, rel. to COTE]

cot³ *abbr*. cotangent.

cotangent /ˈkəʊtændʒ(ə)nt/ *n*. the tangent of the complement of a given angle. [f. co- + TANGENT]

cote *n*. a shed, stall, or shelter, especially for birds or animals. [OE]

coterie /ˈkəʊtərɪ/ *n*. an exclusive group of people sharing an interest. [F, orig. = association of tenants]

cotoneaster /kətəʊnɪˈæstə(r)/ *n*. a shrub or small tree bearing red or orange berries. [f. L *cotoneum* quince]

cottage /ˈkɒtɪdʒ/ *n*. a small simple house, especially in the country. —**cottage cheese,** a soft white cheese made from curds of skim milk without pressing. **cottage industry,** one carried on at home. **cottage pie,** a dish of minced meat topped with mashed potato. [f. AF (as COT²)]

cottager *n*. one who lives in a cottage. [f. prec.]

cottar /ˈkɒtə(r)/ *n*. (also **cotter**¹) (*hist*. & *Sc*.) a farm-labourer having free use of a cottage. [f. COT²]

cotter *n*. a bolt or wedge for securing parts of machinery etc. —**cotter pin,** a cotter, a split pin put through a cotter to keep it in place. [orig. unkn.]

cotton /ˈkɒt(ə)n/ *n*. a soft white fibrous substance

covering the seeds of tropical plants of the genus *Gossypium*; such a plant; thread or cloth made from this. —*v.i.* **cotton on (to),** (*slang*) to understand; to form a liking or attachment for. —**cotton wool,** fluffy wadding of a kind originally made from raw cotton. —**cottony** *adj.* [f. OF f. Arab.]

cotyledon /kɒtɪ'li:d(ə)n/ *n.* the first leaf produced by a plant embryo. [L f. Gk (*kotulē* cup)]

couch[1] /kaʊtʃ/ *n.* **1** a piece of furniture like a sofa but with the back extending along half its length and only one raised end; a sofa or settee. **2** a bed-like structure on which a doctor's patient can lie for examination. —*v.t./i.* **1** to express *in* words of a certain kind. **2** to lay as on a couch. **3** to lie in a lair etc. or in ambush. **4** to lower (a spear) to the position for attack. [f. OF f. L *collocare* lay in place]

couch[2] /ku:tʃ, kaʊtʃ/ *n.* (in full **couch-grass**) a grassy weed (*Elymus repens*) with long creeping roots. [var. of QUITCH]

couchant /'kaʊtʃ(ə)nt/ *adj.* (in heraldry, of an animal) lying with the body resting on the legs and the head raised. [F, as COUCH[1]]

couchette /ku:'ʃet/ *n.* a railway carriage with seats that are convertible into sleeping-berths; a berth in this. [F, = little bed]

cougar /'ku:gə(r)/ *n.* (*US*) a puma. [F, f. Guarani]

cough /kɒf/ *v.t./i.* **1** to expel air or other matter from the lungs with a sudden sharp sound; (of an engine etc.) to make a similar sound. **2** (*slang*) to confess. —*n.* the act or sound of coughing; a condition of the respiratory organs causing coughing. —**cough mixture,** a medicine to relieve a cough. **cough up,** to eject or say with coughs; (*slang*) to bring out or give (money or information) reluctantly. [imit., rel. to Du. *kuchen*]

could /kʊd/ *v.aux.* **1** *past* of CAN[1]. **2** to feel inclined to. —**could be,** (*colloq.*) might be; that may be true.

couldn't /'kʊd(ə)nt/ (*colloq.*) = could not.

coulomb /'ku:lɒm/ *n.* a unit of electric charge, the quantity of electricity conveyed in one second by a current of one ampere. [f. C.-A. de *Coulomb* (1736-1806), French military engineer]

coulter /'kəʊltə(r)/ *n.* a vertical blade in front of a ploughshare. [OE f. L *culter* knife]

council /'kaʊns(ə)l/ *n.* an advisory, deliberative, or administrative body; a meeting of the local administrative body of a county, city, town, etc. —**council house,** a house owned and let by a local council. [f. AF f. L *concilium* assembly; cf. COUNSEL]

councillor /'kaʊns(ə)lə(r)/ *n.* a member of a council, especially of a local administrative council. [alt. of COUNSELLOR]

counsel /'kaʊns(ə)l/ *n.* **1** advice formally given; consultation, especially to seek or give advice; professional guidance. **2** a legal adviser (esp. a barrister); a group of these. —*v.t.* (**-ll-**) **1** to advise, to recommend. **2** to give professional guidance to (a person in need of psychological help). —**counsel of despair,** an action to be taken when all else fails. **counsel of perfection,** ideal but impracticable advice. **keep one's own counsel,** not to confide in others. **King's** *or* **Queen's Counsel,** counsel to the Crown, taking precedence over other barristers. **take counsel,** to consult *with*. [f. OF f. L *consilium* (*consulere* consult)]

counsellor /'kaʊns(ə)lə(r)/ *n.* an adviser; one who gives counsel. [as prec.]

count[1] /kaʊnt/ *v.t./i.* **1** to find the number of (things etc.), especially by assigning successive numerals; to repeat numerals in order. **2** to include or be included in a reckoning or consideration. **3** to have a certain value or significance. **4** to regard or consider. —*n.* **1** counting, a calculation. **2** a total. **3** any of the points being considered. **4** each of the charges in a legal indictment. —**count on,** to rely on, to expect. **count out,** to exclude, to disregard; to complete a count of 10 seconds over (a fallen boxer etc.); to procure an adjournment of (the House of Commons) for lack of a quorum. **count up,** to find the total of. **keep** *or* **lose count,** to know or not know how many there have been. **out for the count,** defeated, unconscious. [f. OF f. L *computare* compute]

count[2] /kaʊnt/ *n.* a foreign nobleman equivalent in rank to an earl. [f. OF f. L *comes* companion]

countdown *n.* counting numerals backwards to zero, especially before launching a spacecraft etc.

countenance /'kaʊntɪnəns/ *n.* **1** a facial expression, the face; composure of the face. **2** moral support or approval. —*v.t.* to give approval to (an act); to encourage or connive at (a person or practice). —**keep one's countenance,** to maintain composure, to refrain from laughing. [f. OF (*contenir* contain)]

counter[1] /'kaʊntə(r)/ *n.* **1** a flat-topped fitment in a shop etc. over which goods are sold or served or business is conducted with customers. **2** a small disc used in table-games for scoring etc. **3** a token representing a coin. **4** a device for counting. —**under the counter,** surreptitiously, illegally. [f. OF f. L *computatorium* (as COMPUTE)]

counter[2] /'kaʊntə(r)/ *v.t./i.* **1** to oppose, to contradict. **2** to make or meet by a countermove; to baffle or frustrate thus. **3** to give a return blow in boxing. —*adv.* in the opposite direction or manner. —*adj.* opposite. —*n.* **1** a return action or blow; a countermove. **2** the stiff part of a shoe or boot round the heel. **3** the curved part of a ship's stern. [f. foll.]

counter- *prefix* forming verbs, nouns, adjectives, and adverbs, implying retaliation or reversal (*counterstroke, counter-clockwise*), rivalry or opposition (*counter-attraction, counter-current*), reciprocity or correspondence (*countersign, counterpart*). [f. OF *contre* f. L *contra* against]

counteract /kaʊntəˈrækt/ *v.t.* to neutralize, hinder, or defeat by contrary action. —**counteraction** *n.*, **counteractive** *adj.*

counter-attack *n.* an attack made to meet an enemy's or opponent's attack. —*v.t./i.* to make a counter-attack (on).

counterbalance *n.* a weight or influence that balances another. —*v.t.* to be a counterbalance to, to neutralize thus.

countercheck *n.* **1** an obstruction checking movement or operating against another check. **2** a second test for verifying another. —*v.t.* to verify by a second test.

counter-clockwise *adj.* & *adv.* anticlockwise.

counter-espionage *n.* action taken to uncover and frustrate enemy espionage.

counterfeit /ˈkaʊntəfɪt, -fi:t/ *adj.* made in imitation and of inferior material, usually to defraud; not genuine, forged. —*n.* a counterfeit thing. —*v.t.* to make a counterfeit of in order to defraud, to forge. [f. p.p. of OF *contrefaire* f. L, = make in opposition]

counterfoil /ˈkaʊntəfɔɪl/ *n.* the part of a cheque, receipt, etc., retained as a record by the person issuing it.

counter-intelligence *n.* counter-espionage.

countermand /kaʊntəˈmɑ:nd/ *v.t.* to revoke or cancel (a command). —*n.* a command cancelling a previous one. [f. OF f. L *contramandare* (CONTRA-, *mandare* order)]

countermarch *n.* a march in the opposite direction. —*v.t./i.* to march or cause to march back.

countermeasure *n.* an action taken to counteract a danger or threat.

countermove *n.* a move or action taken in opposition to another.

counterpane /ˈkaʊntəpeɪn/ *n.* a bedspread. [f. OF f. L *culcita puncta* quilted mattress]

counterpart /ˈkaʊntəpɑ:t/ *n.* a person or thing like or naturally complementary to another; a duplicate.

counterpoint *n.* a melody added as an accompaniment to a given melody; the art or mode of adding melodies as an accompaniment according to fixed rules. —*v.t.* to add counterpoint to; to set in contrast. [f. OF f. L *contrapunctum* pricked or marked opposite, i.e. to the original melody]

counterpoise /ˈkaʊntəpɔɪz/ *n.* the balancing of each other by two weights or forces; a counterbalancing weight or force. —*v.t.* to counterbalance; to compensate for. [f. OF f. L (CONTRA-, *pensum* weight)]

counter-productive *adj.* having the opposite of the desired effect.

Counter-Reformation *n.* the revival of the Roman Catholic Church in Europe from the mid-16th–mid-17th c.

counter-revolution *n.* a revolution opposing a former one or reversing its results.

countersign /ˈkaʊntəsaɪn/ *v.t.* to add a confirming signature to (a document already signed by another). —*n.* a word required in answer to a sentry's challenge; an identificatory mark. —**countersignature** /-sɪg-/ *n.* [f. F f. It. (as COUNTER-, SIGN)]

countersink /ˈkaʊntəsɪŋk/ *v.t.* (*past* & *p.p.* **-sunk**) to shape the top of (a screw-hole) with a tapered enlargement so that a screw-head lies level with or below the surface; to sink (a screw etc.) in such a hole.

counterstroke /ˈkaʊntəstrəʊk/ *n.* a stroke given in return.

counter-tenor *n.* a male singing-voice higher than tenor but with its quality; a singer with such a voice; a part written for it.

countervail /ˈkaʊntəveɪl/ *v.t.* to counterbalance; to avail against. [f. AF f. L *contra valēre* be of worth against]

counterweight /ˈkaʊntəweɪt/ *n.* a counterbalancing weight.

countess /ˈkaʊntɪs/ *n.* the wife or widow of an earl or count; a woman holding the rank of an earl or count. [f. OF f. L *comitissa* (as COUNT[2])]

countless /ˈkaʊntlɪs/ *adj.* too many to be counted.

countrified /ˈkʌntrɪfaɪd/ *adj.* rustic in appearance or manners. [f. foll.]

country /ˈkʌntrɪ/ *n.* **1** the territory of a nation; the State of which one is a member. **2** the national population (esp. as electors). **3** a land or region with regard to its aspect or associations. **4** open regions of fields and woods etc. as distinct from towns or the capital (often *attrib.*). **5** country-and-western. —**country-and-western** *n.* rural or cowboy songs to the guitar. **country club,** a sporting social club in a rural area. **country dance,** a traditional English dance, often with couples face to face in lines. **go to the country,** to appeal to the body of electors after an adverse or doubtful vote in the House of Commons, or at the end of a government's term of office, by effecting the dissolution of Parliament and holding a general election. [f. OF f. L *contrata* (*terra*) land lying opposite (as CONTRA-)]

countryman *n.* (*pl.* **-men**) **1** a person living in rural parts. **2** a fellow-member of a State or district. —**countrywoman** *n.fem.* (*pl.* **-women**)

countryside *n.* country districts.

country-wide *adj.* extending throughout a nation.

county /ˈkaʊntɪ/ *n.* **1** a territorial division of a country, forming the chief unit of local administration and justice; (*US*) a political and administrative division next below a State. **2** the people of a county; long-established families of a high social level. —**county council,** the elected governing body of an administrative county. **county court,** a local court for civil cases. **county town,** a town that is the administrative centre of a county. [f. AF f. L *comitatus* (as COUNT²)]

coup /ku:/ *n.* a successful stroke or move, a *coup d'état*. [F f. L *colpus* blow]

coup de grâce /ku: də ˈgrɑ:s/ a finishing stroke. [F]

coup d'état /ku: deɪˈtɑ:/ the sudden overthrow of a government, especially by force. [F]

coupé /ˈku:peɪ/ *n.* a closed two-door car with a sloping back. [F (*couper* cut)]

couple /ˈkʌp(ə)l/ *n.* **1** a man and woman who are engaged or married to each other. **2** a pair of partners in a dance etc. **3** two things, or (*loosely*) several things. —*v.t./i.* **1** to link or associate together. **2** to copulate. [f. OF f. L *copula* fastening]

couplet /ˈkʌplɪt/ *n.* two successive lines of verse, especially when rhyming and of the same length. [F (as prec.)]

coupling /ˈkʌplɪŋ/ *n.* **1** a link connecting two railway vehicles or two parts of machinery. **2** the arrangement of items on a gramophone record.

coupon /ˈku:pɒn/ *n.* **1** a small often detachable piece of printed paper entitling the holder to specified goods or a service or some concession. **2** a small printed form of application or entry for a competition etc. [F (*couper* cut)]

courage /ˈkʌrɪdʒ/ *n.* readiness to face and endure danger or difficulty; the ability to control or suppress fear or its disturbing effects; a courageous mood or inclination. —**have the courage of one's convictions,** to have the courage to do what one believes to be right. [f. OF f. L (*cor* heart)]

courageous /kəˈreɪdʒəs/ *adj.* having or showing courage. —**courageously** *adv.* [as prec.]

courgette /kʊəˈʒet/ *n.* a small green or yellow vegetable marrow. [F (*courge* gourd)]

courier /ˈkʊrɪə(r)/ *n.* **1** a special messenger. **2** a person employed to guide and assist a group of tourists. [f. F f. It. *corriere* f. L (*currere* run)]

course /kɔ:s/ *n.* **1** an onward movement in space or time; a direction taken or intended; the direction or channel followed by a river etc. **2** the successive development *of* events, the ordinary sequence or order; a line of conduct or action. **3** a series *of* lectures, lessons, etc., in a particular subject; a sequence *of* medical treatment. **4** each successive part of a meal. **5** a golf-course; a racecourse. **6** a continuous row of masonry at one level in a building. —*v.t./i.* **1** to use hounds to hunt (esp. hares). **2** to move or flow freely. —**in the course of,** in the process of. **in due course,** at about the expected time. **of course,** as is or was to be expected, without doubt, admittedly. [f. OF f. L *cursus* (*currere* run)]

courser /ˈkɔ:sə(r)/ *n.* **1** a fast-running African or Asian bird. **2** (*poetic*) a swift horse. [f. L (as prec.)]

court /kɔ:t/ *n.* **1** a courtyard; a yard surrounded by houses, with entry from the street. **2** an enclosed or marked area for some games, e.g. squash and tennis. **3** (also **Court**) a sovereign's establishment with courtiers and attendants; this as representing a country; a reception at court. **4** (in full **court of law**) a judicial body hearing legal cases; the place where this meets; *the* judges of a court. —*v.t.* to treat flatteringly or with special attention; to seek to attract the favour or love of; to seek to win; to make oneself vulnerable to. —**court-card** *n.* a playing-card that is a king, queen, or jack. **court-house** *n.* the building in which a court of law is held; (*US*) the building containing the administrative offices of a county. **court martial,** (*pl. courts martial*) a judicial court of naval, military, or air force officers for trying charges involving offences against military law; trial by such a court. **court-martial** *v.t.* (**-ll-**) to try by court martial. **court shoe,** a woman's light shoe with a low-cut upper. **go to court,** to take legal action. **hold court,** to preside over one's admirers. **out of court,** (of a settlement) without reaching trial; not worth discussing. **pay court to,** to court (a person) to win favour. **put out of court,** to refuse or make it inappropriate to consider. [f. AF f. L *cohors* yard, retinue]

courteous /ˈkɜ:tɪəs/ *adj.* polite, considerate. —**courteously** *adv.* [f. OF (as prec.)]

courtesan /kɔ:tɪˈzæn/ *n.* a prostitute with clients among the wealthy or nobility. [f. F f. It. (*cortigiano* courtier)]

courtesy /ˈkɜ:təsɪ/ *n.* courteous behaviour, a courteous act. —**by courtesy of,** by permission of. **courtesy light,** a light in a car that is switched on automatically by opening the door. [f. OF (as COURTEOUS)]

courtier /ˈkɔ:tɪə(r)/ *n.* a companion of the sovereign at court. [f. AF (as COURT)]

courtly /ˈkɔ:tlɪ/ *adj.* polished or refined in manners. —**courtly love,** the conventional medieval tradition of knightly love and etiquette. —**courtliness** *n.* [f. COURT]

courtship *n.* courting, especially of an intended wife; a period of courting.

courtyard *n.* a space enclosed by walls or buildings.

couscous /ˈku:sku:s/ *n.* a North African dish of crushed wheat or coarse flour steamed over broth, often with meat or fruit added. [F f. Arab. (*kaskasa* to pound)]

cousin /ˈkʌz(ə)n/ *n.* 1 (also **first cousin, cousin german**) a son or daughter of one's uncle or aunt; (also **first cousin once** (*or* **twice** etc.) **removed**) a son or daughter (or grandson etc.) of one's first cousin, one's parent's (or grandparent's etc.) cousin; (also **second cousin**) a son or daughter of one's parent's first cousin. **2** (*hist.*) the title used by one sovereign addressing another. —**cousinly** *adj.* [f. OF f. L *consobrinus*]

couture /ku:ˈtjʊə(r)/ *n.* the design and making of high-quality fashionable clothes. [F, = sewing, dressmaking]

couturier /ku:ˈtjʊrɪeɪ/ *n.* a fashion designer. —**couturière** /-ɪeə(r)/ *n.fem.* [F]

couvade /ku:ˈvɑ:d/ *n.* a custom of some primitive peoples by which the husband feigns illness and is put to bed when his wife is giving birth to a child. [F (*couver* hatch f. L *cubare* lie down)]

cove[1] *n.* **1** a small bay or inlet of the coast; a sheltered recess. **2** a curved moulding at the junction of a ceiling and a wall. —*v.t.* **1** to provide (a room etc.) with a cove. **2** to slope (the sides of a fireplace) inwards. [OE, = chamber]

cove[2] *n.* (*slang*) a fellow, a man. [orig. unkn.]

coven /ˈkʌv(ə)n/ *n.* an assembly of witches. [f. OF *covent* (as CONVENT)]

covenant /ˈkʌvənənt/ *n.* a formal agreement, (*Law*) a sealed contract; the biblical compact between God and the Israelites. —*v.t./i.* to agree, especially by legal covenant (*with* a person). [f. OF *co(n)venir* (as CONVENE)]

covenanter *n.* **1** one who covenants. **2 Covenanter,** a supporter of the Scottish National Covenant of 1638 and the Solemn League and Covenant (1643), proclamations defending Presbyterianism and resisting the religious policies of Charles I. [f. prec.]

Coventry /ˈkɒvəntrɪ/ **send to Coventry,** to refuse to speak to or associate with. [name of town in W. Midlands]

cover /ˈkʌvə(r)/ *v.t.* **1** to lie or extend over, to form or occupy the whole surface of. **2** to conceal or protect (a thing) by placing something on or in front of it; to provide (a person) with something that covers; to protect, to clothe; to strew thoroughly *with* **3** to enclose or include; to deal with (a subject) **4** to travel (a specified distance etc.). **5** to be enough money to pay for. **6** to investigate or describe as a reporter. **7** (of a fortification or gun etc.) to have within its range; to protect from a commanding position; to keep a gun aimed at; to have within one's range of fire; to protect by firing against the enemy. **8** to protect or oppose (another player) in field-games. **9** (of a stallion etc.) to mate with. **10.** to deputize temporarily *for*. **11.** (in *p.p.*) wearing a hat, having a roof. —*n.* **1** a thing that covers, a lid, a top. **2** the binding of a book; one board of this. **3** an envelope or other postal wrapping. **4** shelter, protection. **5** a screen, a pretence; a pretended identity. **6** funds from an insurance to meet a liability or contingent loss, protection by insurance. **7** a supporting force protecting another from attack. **8** an individual place-setting at a meal. **9** cover- point. —**cover charge,** an extra charge per person in a restaurant etc. **cover girl,** a girl whose picture appears on magazine covers. **covering letter** *or* **note,** one sent with and explaining goods or documents. **cover note,** a temporary certificate of current insurance. **cover-point** *n.* a cricket fieldsman covering point. **cover-up** *n.* a concealment, especially of facts. **take cover,** to seek shelter. **under cover,** in secret, sheltered from the weather. **under cover of,** hidden or protected by (e.g. darkness); with an outward show of (e.g. friendship). [f. OF f. L *cooperire* (co-, *operire* cover)]

coverage /ˈkʌvərɪdʒ/ *n.* the area or amount covered or reached; the reporting of events in a newspaper etc. [f. prec.]

coverall /ˈkʌvərɔ:l/ *n.* a thing that covers entirely; (usu. in *pl.*) a full-length protective garment.

coverlet /ˈkʌvəlɪt/ *n.* a covering, especially a bedspread. [f. AF (as COVER, *lit* bed)]

covert /ˈkʌvət/ *adj.* disguised, not open or explicit. —*n.* **1** a wood or thicket affording cover for game. **2** a feather covering the base of a bird's wing-feather or tail-feather. —**covertly** *adv.* [as COVER]

covet /ˈkʌvɪt/ *v.t.* to envy another the possession of, to long to possess. [f. OF f. L (as CUPIDITY)]

covetous /ˈkʌvɪtəs/ *adj.* coveting, avaricious, grasping. —**covetously** *adv.*, **covetousness** *n.* [as prec.]

covey /ˈkʌvɪ/ *n.* **1** a brood of partridges (esp. flying together). **2** a small group of people. [f. OF f. L (*cubare* lie)]

cow[1] *n.* (*pl.* **cows,** *archaic* **kine**) **1** the fully-grown female of any bovine animal, especially of the domestic species used as a source of milk and beef. **2** the female of other large animals, especially the elephant, whale, or seal. —**cow-lick** *n.* a projecting lock of hair. **cow-pat** *n* a flat round piece of cow-dung. [OE]

cow[2] *v t* to intimidate, to dispirit. [f. ON *kúga* oppress]

coward /ˈkaʊəd/ *n.* a person easily giving way to fear and lacking courage. [f. OF f. L *cauda* tail]

cowardice /ˈkaʊədɪs/ *n.* cowardly feelings or conduct. [as prec.]

cowardly *adj.* of or like a coward, lacking courage; (of an action) done against one who cannot retaliate. —**cowardliness** *n.* [f. COWARD]

cowbell *n.* a bell hung round a cow's neck.

cowboy *n.* **1** (in the western US) a man in charge of cattle. **2** (*colloq.*) an unscrupulous or reckless business man.

cowcatcher *n.* a fender fitted on the front of a locomotive to push aside cattle or other obstacles on the line.

cower *v.i.* to crouch or shrink back, especially in fear; to huddle up. [f. LG *kūren* lie in wait]

cowherd *n.* a person who looks after cows at pasture.

cowhide *n.* a cow's hide; leather or a whip made from this.

cowl *n.* **1** a monk's hood or hooded garment. **2** a hood-shaped covering, especially of a chimney or shaft. [OE f. L *cucullus* hood of cloak]

cowling *n.* a removable cover over the engine of a vehicle or aircraft. [f. prec.]

co-worker *n.* one who works in collaboration with another.

cowpox *n.* a disease of cows, caused by a virus which is used in vaccination against smallpox.

cowrie /ˈkaʊrɪ/ *n.* a gastropod of the family Cypraeidae, with a glossy shell and an opening that consists of a slit running the length of one side. [f. Urdu & Hindi]

cowslip *n.* a wild plant (*Primula veris*) with small yellow flowers. [OE (as cow¹, *slyppe* slimy substance, i.e. dung)]

cox *n.* a coxswain, especially of a racing boat. —*v.t./i.* to act as cox (of). [abbr.]

coxcomb /ˈkɒkskəʊm/ *n.* **1** a conceited showy person. **2** (*hist.*) a medieval jester's cap. —**coxcombry** *n.* [=*cock's comb*]

coxswain /ˈkɒksweɪn, ˈkɒks(ə)n/ *n.* **1** the steersman of a rowing-boat or other small boat. **2** the senior petty officer in a small ship. —*v.t./i.* to act as coxswain (of). [f. obs. *cock* small boat + SWAIN]

coy *adj.* affectedly modest or bashful; archly reticent. —**coyly** *adv.*, **coyness** *n.* [f. OF f. L *quietus* quiet]

coyote /kɔɪˈəʊtɪ, ˈkɔɪəʊt/ *n.* the North American prairie-wolf (*Canis latrans*). [Mex. Sp. f. Aztec]

coypu /ˈkɔɪpu:/ *n.* a beaver-like water-rodent, originally from South America. [native name in Chile]

cozen /ˈkʌz(ə)n/ *v.t./i.* (*literary*) to cheat, to defraud; to act deceitfully. —**cozenage** *n.* [perh. rel. to COUSIN]

c.p. *abbr.* candlepower.

Cpl. *abbr.* Corporal.

c.p.s. *abbr.* cycles per second.

Cr *symbol* chromium.

crab *n.* **1** a shellfish, especially of the group Brachyura, with ten legs, of which the front pair are modified into pincers; the flesh of this as food. **2 the Crab,** the constellation or sign of the zodiac Cancer. —*v.t./i.* (*colloq.*) (**-bb-**) to criticize adversely or captiously; to act so as to spoil. —**catch a crab,** to get an oar jammed underwater by a faulty stroke in rowing. **crab-apple** *n.* the fruit of an apple tree, *Malus sylvestris*, that bears small fruit with a harsh sour flavour. **crab-louse** *n.* a parasite infesting the hairy parts of the body. [OE, rel. to LG *krabben*, ON *krafla* scratch]

crabbed /ˈkræbɪd/ *adj.* **1** bad-tempered, crabby. **2** (of writing) difficult to read or decipher. [f. CRAB]

crabby *adj.* irritable, morose. —**crabbily** *adv.*, **crabbiness** *n.* [as prec.]

crabwise *adv.* & *adj.* sideways or backwards like the movement of a crab.

crack *n.* **1** a sudden sharp explosive sound. **2** a sharp blow. **3** a narrow opening; a line of division where something is broken but has not come completely apart. **4** (*colloq.*) a wisecrack, a joke. —*adj.* (*colloq.*) first-rate. —*v.t./i.* **1** to break without coming completely apart; to become broken thus; to gape with cracks. **2** to make or cause to make the sound of a crack; to hit sharply. **3** to break the case of (a nut); to break into (a safe etc.); to find the solution to (a code or problem). **4** (of the voice) to become suddenly harsh, as with emotion. **5** to yield suddenly or cease to resist under strain. **6** to tell (a joke). **7** to break down (heavy oils) in order to produce lighter ones. **8** (in *p.p.*, *colloq.*) crazy, infatuated. —**crack a bottle,** to open it and drink the contents. **crack-brained** *adj.* crazy. **crack down on,** (*colloq.*) to take severe measures against. **crack of dawn,** daybreak. **crack up,** (*colloq.*) to have a physical or mental breakdown; to praise highly (usu. in *pass.*, esp. in *not all it* etc *is cracked up to be*). **get cracking,** (*colloq.*) to make a start. **have a crack at,** (*colloq.*) to attempt. [OE, = resound]

cracker *n.* **1** an explosive firework. **2** a small paper toy in the form of a roll that makes a cracking sound when pulled apart. **3** a thin crisp savoury biscuit; (*US*) a biscuit. [f. prec.]

crackers *predic. adj.* (*slang*) crazy. [f. prec.]

crackle /ˈkræk(ə)l/ *n.* the sound of repeated slight cracks as of burning wood. —*v.i.* to emit a crackle. [f. CRACK]

crackling *n.* the crisp skin of roast pork. [f. prec.]

cracknel /ˈkrækn(ə)l/ *n.* a light crisp kind of biscuit. [f. F f. MDu. (as CRACK)]

crackpot *adj.* (*colloq.*) eccentric, unpractical. —*n.* (*colloq.*) an eccentric or unpractical person.

-cracy /krəsɪ/ *suffix* with sense 'rule or ruling body of'. [f. F f. Gk (*kratos* strength)]

cradle /ˈkreɪd(ə)l/ *n.* **1** a small bed or cot for a baby, usually on rockers. **2** a place regarded as the origin of something. **3** a supporting framework or structure. —*v.t.* to place in a cradle; to contain or shelter as in a cradle. [OE]

craft /krɑːft/ *n.* **1** a special skill or technique; an occupation needing this. **2** cunning, craftiness. **3** (*pl.* same) a ship or boat, an aircraft or spacecraft. —*v.t.* to make in a skilful manner. [OE, = OHG *kraft* strength]

craftsman *n.* (*pl.* **-men**) one who practises a craft; a skilled person. —**craftsmanship** *n.*

crafty *adj.* cunning, using underhand methods; ingenious. —**craftily** *adv.*, **craftiness** *n.* [as CRAFT]

crag *n.* a steep rugged rock. —**craggy** *adj.*, **cragginess** *n.* [Celtic]

crake *n.* a bird of the rail family, especially the corncrake. [f. ON, imit. of cry]

cram *v.t./i.* (**-mm-**) **1** to fill to excess; to force (*in* or *into*). **2** to feed to excess. **3** to study intensively for an examination. [OE]

cramp *n.* **1** a sudden painful involuntary contraction of muscle(s). **2** (in full **cramp-iron**) a kind of clamp, especially for holding masonry or timbers. —*v.t.* **1** to affect with cramp. **2** to restrict or confine narrowly. **3** to fasten with a cramp. —**cramp a person's style,** to prevent him from acting freely or to his best ability. [f. OF f. MDu., f. adj. meaning 'bent']

cramped *adj.* (of a space) too narrow; (of handwriting) small and with the letters close together. [f. prec.]

crampon /ˈkræmpən/ *n.* an iron plate with spikes fixed to a boot for climbing on ice. [f. F (as prec.)]

cranberry /ˈkrænbərɪ/ *n.* a small acid red berry; the shrub bearing it (*Vaccinium oxycoccus* or *V. macrocarpon*). [after G *kranbeere* crane-berry]

crane *n.* **1** a machine for moving heavy objects, usually by suspending them from a projecting arm or beam. **2** a large wading bird of the family Gruidae, with long legs, neck, and bill. —*v.t./i.* to stretch (one's neck) in order to see something. —**crane-fly** *n.* a two-winged insect of the family Tipulidae, with very long legs. **crane's-bill** *n.* a plant of the genus *Geranium*. [OE]

cranium /ˈkreɪnɪəm/ *n.* (*pl.* **-ia**) the bones enclosing the brain; the skull. —**cranial** *adj.* [L f. Gk]

crank[1] *n.* the part of an axle or shaft bent at right angles for converting reciprocal into circular motion, or vice versa. —*v.t.* to move by means of a crank; to start (*up*) (a car engine) by turning a crank. [OE]

crank[2] *n.* an eccentric person. [back-formation f. CRANKY]

crankcase *n.* the case enclosing a crankshaft.

crankpin *n.* the pin by which the connecting-rod is attached to the crank.

crankshaft *n.* a shaft driven by a crank.

cranky *adj.* **1** shaky. **2** crotchety, eccentric; ill-tempered. —**crankily** *adv.*, **crankiness** *n.* [perh. f. obs. *crank* rogue feigning sickness]

crannog /ˈkrænəg/ *n.* a lake-dwelling in Scotland or Ireland, examples of which are found from the neolithic period until medieval times. [Irish (*crann* tree, beam)]

cranny *n.* a crevice. —**crannied** *adj.* [f. OF f. L *crena* notch]

crap *n.* (*vulgar*) faeces; nonsense, rubbish. —*v.i.* (**-pp-**) (*vulgar*) to defecate. —**crappy** *adj.* [f. Du.; orig. = chaff, refuse from fat-boiling]

crape *n.* crêpe, usually of black silk etc., especially for mourning dress. [as CRÊPE]

craps *n.pl.* a game of chance played with dice, popular in the USA. —**shoot craps,** to play this. [perh. f. *crab* lowest throw at dice]

crapulent /ˈkræpjʊlənt/ *adj.* suffering or resulting from intemperance. —**crapulence** *n.*, **crapulous** *adj.* [f. L f. Gk *kraipalē* drunken headache]

crash[1] *n.* **1** a sudden violent percussive noise as of something breaking by impact; a fall or impact accompanied by this; a burst of loud sound. **2** a sudden downfall or collapse (especially of a government or a business). **3** (*attrib.*) done rapidly or urgently. —*v.t./i.* **1** to fall, collide, or proceed with a crash, to cause to do this; to make the noise of a crash. **2** (of an aircraft or pilot) to fall violently to land or sea. **3** to collapse financially. **4** to pass (an instruction etc. to stop, especially a red light). **5** (*colloq.*) to enter or take part in (a party etc.) uninvited. —*adv.* with a crash. —**crash-dive** *v.i.* (of a submarine) to submerge hurriedly in an emergency; (of an aircraft) to dive and crash; (*n.*) the action of this. **crash-helmet** *n.* a helmet worn to protect the head in case of a crash. **crash-land** *v.t./i.* (of an aircraft or pilot) to land hurriedly with a crash. [imit.]

crash[2] *n.* a coarse plain linen or cotton fabric. [f. Russ. *krashenina*]

crashing *adj.* (*colloq.*) overwhelming. [f. CRASH[1]]

crass /kræs/ *adj.* gross; grossly stupid. —**crassly** *adv.*, **crassness** *n.* [f. L *crassus* thick]

-crat *suffix* forming nouns meaning 'a supporter or member of a -cracy'. [f. F f. Gk (as -CRACY)]

crate *n.* **1** a packing-case made of wooden slats, for conveying fragile goods. **2** a divided container for holding milk-bottles. **3** (*slang*) an old aircraft or car. —*v.t.* to pack in a crate. [perh. f. Du. *krat* basket]

crater /ˈkreɪtə(r)/ *n.* the mouth of a volcano; a bowl-shaped cavity, especially that made by the explosion of a shell or bomb. [L f. Gk, = mixing-bowl]

cravat /krəˈvæt/ *n.* **1** a short scarf. **2** a broad neck-tie. [f. F f. G f. Serbo-Croatian, = Croat]

-cratic, -cratical *suffixes* forming adjectives from nouns in *-crat.* [f. -CRAT]

crave *v.t./i.* to desire greatly, to long *for;* to ask earnestly for. [OE]

craven /ˈkreɪv(ə)n/ *adj.* cowardly, abject. —*n.* a craven person. [perh. f. OF *cravanté* f. L *crepare* burst]

craving *n.* a strong desire, an intense longing. [f. CRAVE]

craw *n.* the crop of a bird or insect. —**stick in one's craw,** to be unacceptable. [f. MLG or Du.]

crawfish *n.* a large spiny sea-lobster. [var. of CRAYFISH]

crawl *v.i.* **1** to progress with the body on or close to the ground or other surface, or on hands and knees. **2** to walk or move or (of time) pass slowly. **3** (*colloq.*) to seek favour by behaving in a servile way. **4** to be covered or filled *with.* **5** (of the skin etc.) to creep. —*n.* **1** crawling. **2** a slow rate of motion. **3** a high-speed overarm swimming stroke. [orig. unkn.]

crayfish *n.* a small lobster-like freshwater crustacean; a crawfish. [f. OF *crevice* crab f. G]

crayon /ˈkreɪən/ *n.* a stick or pencil of coloured wax etc. for drawing. —*v.t.* to draw or colour with crayons. [F (*craie* chalk)]

craze *n.* a great but usually temporary enthusiasm; the object of this. —*v.t.* to make crazy. [orig. = break, shatter; perh. f. ON]

crazy /ˈkreɪzɪ/ *adj.* **1** insane; foolish, lacking sense. **2** (*colloq.*) extremely enthusiastic (*about*). **3** (of a building etc.) unsound. —**crazy paving,** paving made up of irregular pieces. —**like crazy,** (*colloq.*) like mad, very much. —**crazily** *adv.*, **craziness** *n.* [f. prec.]

creak *n.* a harsh strident noise, as of an unoiled hinge. —*v.i.* to make or move with a creak; to be in poor condition. —**creaky** *adj.*, **creakily** *adv.* [imit.]

cream *n.* **1** the part of milk with a high fat content; its yellowish-white colour. **2** a creamlike preparation or ointment; a food or drink with the consistency of or compared to cream. **3** the best part *of.* —*v.t./i.* **1** to remove the cream from (milk). **2** to make creamy; to beat to a creamy consistency. **3** to apply cosmetic cream to. **4** to form cream, froth, or scum. —**cream cheese,** a soft rich cheese made of cream or unskimmed milk without pressing. **cream off,** to remove the best or a required part of. **cream of tartar,** purified tartar used in medicine and cooking. [f. OF f. L (as CHRISM)]

creamery /ˈkri:mərɪ/ *n.* a place where dairy products are processed or sold. [f. prec.]

creamy *adj.* like cream; rich in cream. —**creamily** *adv.*, **creaminess** *n.* [f. CREAM]

crease *n.* **1** a line caused by folding or crushing. **2** a line defining the position of the bowler or batsman in cricket. —*v.t./i.* **1** to make creases in; to develop creases. **2** (*slang*) to stun, to tire out. [earlier *creast* = CREST]

create /kri:ˈeɪt/ *v.t./i.* **1** to bring into existence, to give rise to; to originate. **2** to invest (a person) with a rank. **3** (*slang*) to make a fuss. [f. L *creare*]

creation /krɪˈeɪʃ(ə)n/ *n.* **1** creating. **2** all created things. **3** a thing created, especially by human intelligence. —**the Creation,** the creation of the world. [f. OF f. L (as prec.)]

creationism *n.* the theory attributing the origin of matter and biological species to special creation, not to evolution. [f. prec.]

creative /krɪˈeɪtɪv/ *adj.* able to create; inventive, imaginative. —**creativity** /-ˈtɪvɪtɪ/ *n.*, **creatively** *adv.* [f. CREATE]

creator /krɪˈeɪtə(r)/ *n.* one who creates something; **the Creator,** God. [f. OF f. L (as CREATE)]

creature /ˈkri:tʃə(r)/ *n.* **1** a created being, especially an animal; a person. **2** one in a subservient position. —**creature comforts,** good food, clothes, surroundings, etc. [f. OF f. L (as CREATE)]

crèche /kreɪʃ/ *n.* a day nursery for babies. [F]

credence /ˈkri:d(ə)ns/ *n.* **1** belief. **2** a small table, shelf, or niche for the Eucharistic elements before consecration. [f. OF f. L (as CREDIT)]

credentials /krɪˈdenʃ(ə)lz/ *n.pl.* a letter or letters of introduction; evidence of achievement or trustworthiness. [f. L (as CREDIT)]

credibility /kredɪˈbɪlɪtɪ/ *n.* being credible. —**credibility gap,** the seeming difference between what is said and what is true. [f. foll.]

credible /ˈkredɪb(ə)l/ *adj.* believable, worthy of belief. —**credibly** *adv.* [f. L (as CREDIT)]

credit /ˈkredɪt/ *n.* **1** belief or confidence in a person, his words, or actions. **2** a source of honour or good reputation; the power or influence it gives. **3** acknowledgement of merit or achievement; (usu. in *pl.*) the acknowledgement of a contributor's services to a book, film, etc. **4** trust that a person will pay later for goods supplied; power to buy in this way; a person's financial standing. **5** the sum at a person's disposal in a bank; an entry in an account of a sum paid into it; this sum. **6** the side of an account recording such entries. **7** (*US*) a certificate of the completion of a course by a student. —*v.t.* **1** to believe, to take to be true or reliable. **2** to enter on the credit side of an account (an amount *to* a person, a person *with* an amount). **3** to attribute. —**credit card,** a card authorizing the purchase of goods on credit. **credit with,** to ascribe (a quality or feeling) to. **give credit for,** to recognize that (a person) has a quality etc. **on credit,** by arrangement to pay later. **to one's credit,** in one's favour. [f. F f. L (*credere* believe, trust)]

creditable *adj.* praiseworthy, bringing honour or respect. —**creditably** *adv.* [f. prec.]

creditor /ˈkredɪtə(r)/ *n.* a person to whom money is owed. [f. AF f. L (as prec.)]

credo /ˈkriːdəʊ, ˈkreɪ-/ *n.* (*pl.* **-os**) a creed. [L, = I believe]

credulity /krɪˈdjuːlɪtɪ/ *n.* an inclination to believe too readily. [f. foll.]

credulous /ˈkredjʊləs/ *adj.* too ready to believe; (of behaviour) showing credulity. —**credulously** *adv.* [f. L (as CREDIT)]

creed *n.* a system of religious belief; a formal summary of Christian doctrine; a set of beliefs or principles. —**creedal** *adj.* [OE f. L *credo*]

creek *n.* an inlet on the sea-coast; a short arm of a river; (*Austral.* & *NZ*) a stream, a brook; (*US*) a tributary of a river. —**up the creek,** (*slang*) in difficulties; crazy. [f. ON or MDu.; ult. orig. unkn.]

creel *n.* a fisherman's large wicker basket. [orig. Sc; ult. orig. unkn.]

creep *v.i.* (*past* & *p.p.* **crept**) **1** to move slowly with the body prone and close to the ground; to move stealthily or cautiously, to advance very gradually; (of a plant) to grow along the ground or up a vertical surface. **2** to experience a shivering sensation due to repugnance or fear. **3** to develop gradually. —*n.* **1** creeping. **2** (*slang*) an unpleasant person. **3** a gradual change in the shape of a metal under stress. —**the creeps,** (*colloq.*) a nervous feeling of revulsion or fear. [OE]

creeper *n.* a person or thing that creeps; a creeping or climbing plant. [f. prec.]

creepy *adj.* causing nervous revulsion or fear; having this feeling. —**creepy-crawly** *n.* (*colloq.*) a small creeping insect. —**creepily** *adv.*, creepiness *n.* [f. CREEP]

creese *n.* var. of KRIS.

cremate /krɪˈmeɪt/ *v.t.* to dispose of a corpse by burning it to ashes. —**cremation** *n.* [f. L *cremare* burn]

crematorium /kreməˈtɔːrɪəm/ *n.* (*pl.* **-ia**) a place where corpses are cremated. [L (as prec.)]

crematory /ˈkremətərɪ/ *adj.* of or pertaining to cremation. —*n.* (*US*) a crematorium. [f. CREMATE]

crème de menthe /krem də ˈmɑ̃t/ *n.* a green peppermint liqueur. [F, = cream of mint]

crenate /ˈkriːneɪt/ *adj.* with a notched edge or rounded teeth. —**crenated** *adj.* [f. L *crena* notch]

crenel /ˈkren(ə)l/ *n.* an open space or indentation in an embattled parapet, originally for shooting through etc. [f. OF f. dim. of L *crena* notch]

crenellate /ˈkrenəleɪt/ *v.t.* to furnish with battlements or loopholes. —**crenellation** /-ˈleɪʃ(ə)n/ *n.* [f. F (as prec.)]

Creole /ˈkriːəʊl/ *n.* **1** a descendant of European settlers in the West Indies or Central or South America; a white descendant of French settlers in the southern USA. **2** a person of mixed European and Black descent. **3** a creolized language. —*adj.* **1** that is a Creole; of Creole or Creoles. **2 creole,** of local origin or descent. [f. F f. Sp., prob. f. Port. *crioulo* home-born slave]

creolize /ˈkriːəlaɪz/ *v.t.* to make (the language of a dominant group, in modified form) into the sole language of the group dominated. [f. prec.]

creosote /ˈkriːəsəʊt/ *n.* a dark-brown oil distilled from coal tar, used as a wood preservative; a colourless oily fluid distilled from wood tar, used as an antiseptic. —*v.t.* to treat with creosote. [f. G f. Gk, = flesh-preserver]

crêpe /kreɪp/ *n.* **1** a gauzelike fabric with a wrinkled surface. **2** a durable wrinkled sheet rubber used for shoe-soles etc. —**crêpe paper,** a thin crinkled paper. **crêpe Suzette,** a small sweet pancake served flambé. [F f. L (as CRISP)]

crepitate /ˈkrepɪteɪt/ *v.i.* to make a crackling sound. —**crepitation** /ˈteɪʃ(ə)n/ *n.* [f. L *crepitare* (frequent. of *crepare* creak)]

crept *past* & *p.p.* of CREEP.

crepuscular /krɪˈpʌskjʊlə(r)/ *adj.* **1** of twilight; (of animals) appearing or active in twilight. **2** dim, not yet fully enlightened. [f. L *crepusculum* twilight]

crescendo /krɪˈʃendəʊ/ *adv.* (*Mus.*) with a gradual increase of loudness. —*n.* (*pl.* **-os**) **1** a passage to be played this way. **2** progress towards a climax. [It. (as foll.)]

crescent /ˈkres(ə)nt/ *n.* **1** the waxing moon; the moon as seen in the first or last quarter; this as an emblem of Turkey or Islam. **2** anything of crescent shape, especially a street of houses. —*adj.* **1** increasing. **2** crescent-shaped. [f. AF f. L (*crescere* grow)]

cress *n.* any of various cruciferous plants with pungent edible leaves. [OE]

crest *n.* **1** a comb or tuft on a bird's or animal's head. **2** a plume, as on a helmet etc. **3** the top of a mountain, roof, or ridge; the surface line of the neck in animals; a curl of foam on a wave. **4** a device above the shield and helmet on a coat of arms, or on notepaper etc. —*v.t./i.* **1** to reach the crest of. **2** (of a wave) to form a crest. **3** to serve as a crest to, to crown. [f. OF f. L *crista*]

crestfallen *adj.* dejected, abashed.

cretaceous /krɪˈteɪʃ(ə)s/ *adj.* **1** of the nature of chalk. **2 Cretaceous,** of the final period of the Mesozoic era, lasting from about 144 to 65 million years ago. —**Cretaceous** *n.* this period. [f. L *cretaceus* (*creta* chalk)]

cretin /ˈkretɪn/ *n.* a person with deformity and mental retardation caused by thyroid deficiency; (*colloq.*) a stupid person. —**cretinism** *n.*, **cretinous** *adj.* [f. Swiss F (as CHRISTIAN)]

cretonne /ˈkretɒn/ *n.* a colour-printed cotton cloth used for chair-covers etc. [F, f. *Creton* in Normandy]

crevasse /krɪˈvæs/ *n.* a deep open crack, especially in the ice of a glacier. [F (as foll.)]

crevice /ˈkrevɪs/ *n.* a narrow opening or fissure especially in a rock or wall. [f. OF *crevace* (*crever* burst)]

crew[1] /kru:/ *n.* **1** the body of persons manning a ship, aircraft, etc.; these other than the officers. **2** a group of people, especially working together. —*v.t./i.* to act as a crew (for); to supply a crew for. —**crew cut,** a closely cropped man's haircut. **crew neck,** a close-fitting round neckline, especially of a pullover. [orig. = reinforcement; f. OF *creue* increase f. L (*crescere* grow)]

crew[2] *past* of CROW.

crewel /ˈkru:əl/ *n.* a thin worsted yarn for tapestry and embroidery. —**crewel-work** *n.* a design in this on linen. [orig. unkn.]

crib *n.* **1** a wooden framework for holding animals' fodder. **2** a child's bed or cot. **3** a model of the manger scene at Bethlehem. **4** the cards given by other players to the dealer at cribbage; (*colloq.*) cribbage. **5** a literal translation for the use of students; (*colloq.*) an instance of plagiarism. —*v.t./i.* (**-bb-**) **1** to confine in a small space. **2** to pilfer; to copy unfairly or without acknowledgement. [OE]

cribbage *n.* a card-game for two or more persons, with a 'crib' (see CRIB 4). [orig. unkn.]

crick *n.* a sudden painful stiffness in the neck or back. —*v.t.* to cause a crick in. [orig. unkn.]

cricket[1] /ˈkrɪkɪt/ *n.* an open-air summer game played with ball, bats, and two wickets between teams of 11 players each. —**not cricket,** (*colloq.*) not fair play (from the game's tradition of fair play and generous applause for the achievements of players of both sides). —**cricketer** *n.* [orig. unkn.]

cricket[2] /ˈkrɪkɪt/ *n.* a jumping chirping insect. [f. OF (*criquer* creak); imit.]

cri de coeur /kri: də kɜ:/ a passionate appeal, a complaint or protest. [F, = cry from the heart]

cried *past & p.p.* of CRY.

crier /ˈkraɪə(r)/ *n.* one who cries, especially an official making public announcements in lawcourts or in the street. [f. AF (as CRY)]

crikey /ˈkraɪkɪ/ *int.* (*slang*) expressing astonishment. [euphem. for *Christ*]

crime *n.* an act (usually a serious offence) punishable by law; an evil act; such acts collectively; (*colloq.*) a shame, a senseless act. [f. OF f. L *crimen* accusation, offence]

criminal /ˈkrɪmɪn(ə)l/ *n.* a person guilty of crime. —*adj.* of, involving, or concerning crime; guilty of crime. —**criminality** /-ˈnælɪtɪ/ *n.* **criminally** *adv.* [f. L (as CRIME)]

criminology /krɪmɪˈnɒlədʒɪ/ *n.* the scientific study of crime. —**criminologist** *n.* [as CRIME + -LOGY]

crimp *v.t.* to press into small folds or ridges; to corrugate; to make waves in (hair). —*n.* a crimped thing or form. [prob. f. MDu. or MLG]

crimson /ˈkrɪmz(ə)n/ *adj.* of a rich deep red inclining to purple. —*n.* crimson colour. [ult. f. Arab. (as KERMES)]

cringe /krɪndʒ/ *vi.* to shrink back in fear, to cower; to behave obsequiously (*to*). [rel. to CRANK[1]]

crinkle *n.* a wrinkle, a crease. —*v.t./i.* to form crinkles (in). —**crinkly** *adj.* [frequent. of OE *crincan* yield (rel. to prec.)]

crinoid /ˈkrɪnɔɪd/ *adj.* lily-shaped —*n.* a crinoid echinoderm. [f. Gk *krinoeidēs* (*krinon* lily)]

crinoline /ˈkrɪnəlɪn, -li:n/ *n.* **1** a stiffened or hooped petticoat formerly worn to make a long skirt stand out. **2** a stiff fabric of horsehair etc. used for linings, hats, etc. [F f. L (*crinis* hair, *linum* thread)]

cripes /kraɪps/ *int.* (*vulgar*) expressing astonishment. [perversion of CHRIST]

cripple *n.* a person who is permanently lame. —*v.t.* to make a cripple of, to lame; to disable, to weaken or damage seriously. [OE, cogn. w. CREEP]

crisis /ˈkraɪsɪs/ *n.* (*pl.* **crises** /-si:z/) a decisive moment; a time of danger or great difficulty. [L f. Gk, = decision]

crisp *adj.* **1** hard but brittle, breaking with a snap; slightly stiff. **2** (of air) cold and bracing. **3** (of style or manner) brisk and decisive. —*n.* a thin fried slice of potato (sold in packets etc.). —*v.t./i.* to make or become crisp. —**crisply** *adv.*, **crispness** *n.*, **crispy** *adj.* [f. L *crispus* curled]

crispbread *n.* a thin crisp biscuit of crushed rye etc.

criss-cross *n.* a pattern of crossing lines. —*adj.* crossing, in cross lines. —*adv.* crosswise, at cross purposes. —*v.t./i.* to mark or form or move in a criss-cross pattern. [orig. f. *Christ's cross*]

criterion /kraɪˈtɪərɪən/ *n.* (*pl.* **-ia**) a principle or standard by which a thing is judged. [Gk, = means of judging (as foll.)]

critic /ˈkrɪtɪk/ *n.* **1** one who censures. **2** one who reviews or judges the merit of literary, artistic, etc., works. [f. L f. Gk (*kritēs* judge)]

critical /ˈkrɪtɪk(ə)l/ *adj.* **1** fault-finding,

censorious; expressing criticism. **2** of or at a crisis, decisive, crucial. **3** marking the transition from one state etc. to another; (of a nuclear reactor) maintaining a self-sustaining chain-reaction. —**critical path,** the sequence of stages determining the minimum time needed for a complex operation. —**critically** *adv.* [f. L (as prec.)]

criticism /ˈkrɪtɪsɪz(ə)m/ *n.* **1** finding fault, censure. **2** the work of a critic; a critical article, essay, or remark. [f. CRITIC]

criticize /ˈkrɪtɪsaɪz/ *v.t./i.* **1** to find fault (with), to censure. **2** to discuss critically. [as prec.]

critique /krɪˈti:k/ *n.* **1** a critical essay or analysis. **2** a criticism. [F (as CRITIC)]

croak *n.* a deep hoarse cry or sound as of a raven or frog. —*v.t./i.* **1** to utter or speak with a croak. **2** (*slang*) to die; to kill. [imit.]

Croat /ˈkrəʊæt/ *n.* **1** a native or inhabitant of Croatia in Yugoslavia. **2** the language of the Croats. —**Croatian** /-ˈeɪʃ(ə)n/ *adj.* & *n.* [f. L f. Serbo-Croatian *Hrvat*]

crochet /ˈkrəʊʃeɪ/ *n.* needlework in which the yarn is looped into a pattern of stitches by means of a hooked needle. —*v.t./i.* to make in or do crochet. [F (*croc* hook)]

crock[1] *n.* (*colloq.*) a person who suffers from ill health or lameness etc.; a worn-out vehicle, ship, etc. [orig. Sc., perh. f. Flem.]

crock[2] *n.* an earthenware pot or jar; a broken piece of this. [OE]

crockery *n.* earthenware vessels, plates, etc. [f. CROCK[2]]

crocket /ˈkrɒkɪt/ *n.* a small ornamental carving on the inclined side of a pinnacle etc. [f. OF (as CROCHET)]

crocodile /ˈkrɒkədaɪl/ *n.* **1** a reptile of the order Crocodilia, found in tropical regions, with a long snout. **2** its skin, used to make bags, shoes, etc. **3** (*colloq.*) a line of schoolchildren etc. walking in pairs. —**crocodile tears,** insincere grief (from the belief that the crocodile wept while devouring, or to allure, its victim). [f. OF f. L f. Gk *krokodilos*]

crocus /ˈkrəʊkəs/ *n.* a dwarf spring-flowering plant of the genus *Crocus*, growing from a corm, with yellow, purple, or white flowers. —**autumn crocus,** a similar plant blooming in autumn after its leaves have died down. [L f. Gk, of Semitic orig.]

croft *n.* an enclosed piece of (usually arable) land; a small rented farm, especially in the Scottish Highlands. —*v.i.* to farm a croft; to live as a crofter. [OE]

crofter *n.* one who rents a croft. [f. prec.]

croissant /ˈkrwɑ:sɑ̃/ *n.* a crescent-shaped bread roll. [F, = crescent]

cromlech /ˈkrɒmlek/ *n.* **1** a megalithic chamber tomb, a dolmen. **2** (in Brittany) a circle of upright prehistoric stones. [Welsh (*crwm* curved, *llech* flat stone)]

crone *n.* a withered old woman. [f. Du. *croonje* carcass]

crony *n.* a close friend. [f. Gk *khronios* of long standing (*khronos* time)]

crook /krʊk/ *n.* **1** the hooked staff of a shepherd or bishop. **2** a bent or curved thing; a hook; a bend, a curve. **3** (*colloq.*) a rogue, a swindler; a professional criminal. —*adj.* (*Austral.* & *NZ*) unsatisfactory, unpleasant; ailing, injured. —*v.t./i.* to bend, to curve. [f. ON]

crooked /ˈkrʊkɪd/ *adj.* **1** not straight or level; bent, curved, twisted. **2** not straightforward, dishonest. —**crookedly** *adv.*, **crookedness** *n.* [f. prec.]

croon *v.t./i.* to hum or sing in a low subdued voice and sentimental manner. —*n.* such singing. —**crooner** *n.* [orig. Sc. & N. Engl., f. MDu., MLG *kronen* groan, lament]

crop *n.* **1** the produce of cultivated plants, especially cereals; a season's total yield; a group or amount produced at one time. **2** the handle of a looped whip. **3** hair cut very short. **4** the pouch in a bird's gullet where food is prepared for digestion. —*v.t./i.* (**-pp-**) **1** to cut or bite off; to cut (hair) very short. **2** to sow (land) *with* a crop; to bear crops. —**crop-eared** *adj.* with the ears or hair cut short. **crop up,** to occur unexpectedly or by chance. [OE]

cropper *n.* a crop-producing plant of a specified quality. —**come a cropper,** (*slang*) to fall heavily, to fail badly. [f. prec.]

croquet /ˈkrəʊkeɪ/ *n.* **1** a game, played on a lawn, in which wooden balls are driven with mallets through square-topped hoops. **2** an act of croqueting. —*v.t./i.* to drive away (an opponent's ball) by placing one's own against it and striking one's own. [perh. dial. var. of F *crochet* hook]

croquette /krəʊˈket/ *n.* a roll of potato, meat, etc. coated in breadcrumbs and fried. [F (*croquer* crunch)]

crore /krɔ:(r)/ *n.* (in India) 10 million, one hundred lakhs. [f. Hindi f. Skr. *koti* apex]

crosier /ˈkrəʊzɪə(r),-ʒə(r)/ *n.* the hooked staff carried by a bishop as a symbol of office. [f. OF *crossier* crook-bearer, *croisier* cross-bearer]

cross[1] *n.* **1** an upright post with a transverse bar, as used in antiquity for crucifixion, especially (**the Cross**) that on which Christ was crucified; a representation of this as the emblem of Christianity, a staff surmounted by a cross; a monument in the form of a cross. **2** a thing or mark of similar shape, especially the figure made by two short intersecting lines (+ or ×). **3** a decoration indicating rank in some orders of knighthood or awarded for personal valour. **4** an intermixture of breeds, a hybrid; a mixture or compromise *between* two or more things. **5** a crosswise movement of an actor, football, boxer's fist, etc. **6** a trouble or annoyance. —*adj*. **1** transverse, reaching from side to side; intersecting. **2** contrary, opposed, reciprocal. **3** annoyed or angry (*with*) —**be at cross purposes,** to misunderstand or conflict with one another. **on the cross,** diagonally. —**crossly** *adv*., **crossness** *n*. [OE, ult. f. L *crux*]

cross[2] *v.t./i.* **1** to go across (a road, river, sea, any area), to cross a road etc. **2** to intersect or be across one another; to cause to be in this position. **3** to draw a line or lines across. **4** to make the sign of the cross over (esp. *oneself*). **5** to pass in opposite or different directions. **6** to thwart, to frustrate; to anger by refusing to acquiesce. **7** to interbreed; to cross-fertilize. —**cross one's heart,** to make the sign of the cross over it as a sign of sincerity. **cross one's mind,** (of an idea etc.) to occur to one. **cross off,** to remove from a list etc. **cross out,** to cancel, to obliterate. [f. prec.]

crossbar *n*. a horizontal bar, especially between uprights.

cross-bench *n*. a bench in Parliament for members not belonging to the government or main opposition.

crossbill *n*. a bird of the genus *Loxia* with a bill whose jaws cross when closed.

crossbow *n*. a bow fixed across a wooden stock, with a groove for the arrow and a mechanism for drawing and releasing the string.

cross-breed *v.t.* to produce a hybrid of. —*n*. a hybrid animal or plant. —**cross-bred** *adj*. hybrid.

cross-check *v.t./i.* to check by an alternative method of verification. —*n*. a check of this kind.

cross-country *adj*. & *adv*. across fields, not keeping to main or direct roads.

cross-cut *n*. a diagonal cut, path, etc. —**cross-cut saw,** a saw for cutting across the grain of wood.

crosse *n*. the netted crook used in lacrosse. [F (as CROCHET)]

cross-examine *v.t.* to examine (especially an opposing witness in a lawcourt) so as to check or extend previous testimony. —**cross-examination** *n*.

cross-eyed *adj*. having one or both eyes turned towards the nose.

cross-fertilize *v.t.* to fertilize (an animal or plant) from one of a different species. —**cross-fertilization** *n*.

crossfire *n*. a firing of guns in two crossing directions; opposition, interrogation, etc., from several sides at once.

cross-grained *adj*. **1** (of wood) with the grain in crossing directions. **2** (of a person) perverse, intractable.

crossing *n*. **1** place where things cross. **2** a place at which one may cross. **3** a journey across water. [f. CROSS[2]]

cross-legged *adj*. with the legs crossed, or with the ankles crossed and knees apart.

cross-patch *n*. a bad-tempered person.

cross-ply *adj*. (of a tyre) having the fabric layers with the cords lying crosswise.

cross-question *v.t.* to cross-examine.

cross-reference *n*. a reference from one part of a book etc. to another.

crossroads *n.pl.* the intersection of two roads. —**at the crossroads,** at the point where a decision must be made or a course of action chosen.

cross-section *n*. **1** a transverse section; a representation or diagram of a thing as if cut through. **2** a representative sample. —**cross-sectional** *adj*.

cross-stitch *n*. a stitch formed by two crossing stiches.

cross-talk *n*. **1** unwanted transfer of signals between communication channels. **2** repartee.

crossways *adv*. = CROSSWISE.

cross-wind *n*. a wind blowing across the direction of travel.

crosswise *adv*. (also **crossways**) in the manner of a cross, across, with one crossing the other.

crossword *n*. a puzzle in which vertically and horizontally crossing words indicated by clues have to be fitted into a grid of squares.

crotch *n*. the place where things (especially the legs of a body or a garment) fork. [perh. f. OF *croc(he)* hook]

crotchet /ˈkrɒtʃɪt/ *n*. (*Mus*) a note equal to two quavers or half a minim. [f. OF (as prec.)]

crotchety *adj*. peevish. [f. prec.]

crouch *v.i.* to lower the body with the knees bent close against the chest; to be in this position. —*n*. crouching. [f. OF *crochir* be bent (as CROTCH)]

croup[1] /kru:p/ *n*. an inflammation of the larynx and trachea of children, with a hard cough and difficult breathing. [f. *croup* to croak (imit.)]

croup[2] /kru:p/ *n*. the rump (especially of a horse. [f. OF (rel. to CROP)]

croupier /ˈkru:pɪə(r)/ *n*. a person in charge of a gambling-table raking in and paying out money. [F, orig. = rider on the croup]

croûton /ˈkru:tɒn/ *n*. a small piece of fried or toasted bread served with soup etc. [F (as CRUST)]

crow /krəʊ/ *n*. **1** a large black bird of the genus *Corvus* or family Corvidae, including the jackdaw, raven, and rook. **2** the cry of a crow, the crowing of a cock. —*v.i.* (*past* in 1st sense also **crew** /kru:/ **1** (of a cock) to utter a loud shrill cry. **2** (of a baby) to utter happy sounds. **3** to express gleeful satisfaction (*over*). —**as**

the crow flies, in a straight line. **crow's foot,** a wrinkle at the outer corner of the eye. **crow's nest** *n.* a barrel fixed at the mast-head of a sailing ship as a shelter for the look-out. [OE]

crowbar *n.* an iron bar with a flattened end, used as a lever.

crowd *n.* a large number of people gathered together without orderly arrangement; a mass of spectators, an audience; (*colloq.*) a company, a set, a lot. —*v.t./i.* to come or cause to come together in a crowd; to fill, to occupy, to cram (*into* or *with*); to inconvenience by crowding or coming aggressively close to. —**crowd out,** to keep out by crowding. —**crowded** *adj.* [OE *crūdan* press, drive]

crown *n.* **1** a monarch's ornamental and usually jewelled headdress. **2** (often **Crown**) *the* monarch (especially as head of State); *the* power or authority of the monarch. **3** a wreath for the head, as an emblem of victory; a reward for or consummation of effort. **4** the top part of a thing, especially of the head or a hat; the highest or central point of an arched or curved thing; the part of a tooth projecting from the gum, an artificial replacement for this or a part of this. **5** a figure of a crown as a mark or emblem. **6** a British coin worth 25p (formerly 5 shillings). **7** a former size of paper, 504 × 384 mm. —*v.t.* **1** to put a crown on; to invest with a regal crown or office; to be a crown to, to encircle or rest on the top of; to be the consummation, reward, or finishing-touch to. **2** (*slang*) to hit on the head. **3** to promote (a piece in draughts) to king. —**Crown Colony,** a colony subject to direct control by the British government. **Crown Court,** a court of criminal jurisdiction in England and Wales. **Crown Derby,** a kind of china made at Derby and often marked with a crown. **crown jewels,** the sovereign's regalia, including a crown, sceptre, and orb, used on ceremonial occasions. **Crown Prince,** the male heir to a throne. **Crown Princess,** the wife of a Crown Prince; the female heir to a throne. **crown wheel,** a wheel with teeth or cogs at right angles to its plane. [f. AF f. L *corona*]

crozier var. of CROSIER.

CRT *abbr.* cathode-ray tube.

cruces *pl.* of CRUX.

crucial /ˈkru:ʃ(ə)l/ *adj.* decisive, critical; (*colloq.*) (**D**) very important. —**crucially** *adv.* [F, f. L *crux* cross]

crucible /ˈkru:sɪb(ə)l/ *n.* a melting-pot for metals etc.; a severe test. [f. L *crucibulum* (as prec.)]

cruciferous /kru:ˈsɪfərəs/ *adj.* of the family Cruciferae, having flowers with four equal petals arranged crosswise. [f. L, = cross-bearing (as CRUCIAL)]

crucifix /ˈkru:sɪfɪks/ *n.* a model of the cross, especially with a figure of Christ on it. [f. OF f. L, = fixed to a cross]

crucifixion /kru:sɪˈfɪkʃ(ə)n/ *n.* crucifying, being crucified; **the Crucifixion,** that of Christ. [f. L (as prec.)]

cruciform /ˈkru:sɪfɔ:m/ *adj.* cross-shaped. [f. L *crux* cross + -FORM]

crucify /ˈkru:sɪfaɪ/ *v.t.* **1** to put to death by fastening to a cross. **2** to persecute, to torment; to destroy in argument etc. [f. OF f. L (as CRUCIFIX)]

cruck /krʌk/ *n.* one of the paired curved timbers extending to the ground in the framework of a house-roof. [var. of CROOK]

crude /kru:d/ *adj.* in the natural state, not refined; lacking finish, unpolished; rude, blunt. —**crudely** *adv.*, **crudity** *n.* [f. L *crudus* raw, rough]

cruel /ˈkru:əl/ *adj.* indifferent to or gratified by another's suffering; causing pain or suffering. —**cruelly** *adv.*, **cruelty** *n.* [f. OF f. L *crudelis* (as prec.)]

cruet /ˈkru:ɪt/ *n.* a small glass bottle for holding oil or vinegar for use at table; a stand holding this and salt, pepper, and mustard pots. [f. OF, dim. of *crue* pot (rel. to CROCK²)]

cruise /kru:z/ *v.i.* **1** to sail about without precise destination, or calling at a series of places. **2** (of a motor vehicle or aircraft) to travel at a moderate economical speed. **3** (of a vehicle or driver) to travel at random, esp. slowly. —*n.* a cruising voyage. —**cruise missile,** one able to fly at low altitude and guide itself by reference to the features of the region traversed. [prob. f. Du. (*kruis* cross)]

cruiser /ˈkru:zə(r)/ *n.* a warship of high speed and medium armament; a cabin cruiser (see CABIN). [f. Du. (as prec.)]

cruiserweight *n.* light heavyweight (see HEAVYWEIGHT).

crumb /krʌm/ *n.* **1** a small fragment, especially of bread; a small particle or amount *of.* **2** the soft inner part of bread. —*v.t.* **1** to cover with bread crumbs. **2** to crumble (bread). —**crumby** *adj.* [OE]

crumble *v.t./i.* to break or fall into small fragments; (of power, reputation, etc.) to collapse gradually. —*n.* a dish of cooked fruit with a crumbly topping. —**crumbly** *adj.* [f. prec.]

crumbs /krʌmz/ *int.* expressing dismay or surprise. [euphem. for *Christ*]

crummy *adj.* (*slang*) dirty, squalid; inferior, worthless. —**crumminess** *n.* [var. of CRUMBY]

crumpet /ˈkrʌmpɪt/ *n.* **1** a flat soft cake of yeast mixture, toasted and eaten with butter. **2** (*slang*) the head. **3** (*slang*) a sexually attractive woman or women. [orig. unkn.]

crumple *v.t./i.* to crush or become crushed into

creases; to collapse, to give way. [f. obs. *crump* curl up]

crunch *v.t./i.* to crush noisily with the teeth; to grind under foot (gravel, dry snow, etc.); to make a crunching sound. —*n.* **1** crunching; a crunching sound. **2** (*colloq.*) a decisive event. —**when it comes to the crunch,** (*colloq.*) when there is a show-down. [imit.]

crupper *n.* a strap holding a harness back by passing under a horse's tail. [f. AF (as CROUP[2])]

crusade /kruːˈseɪd/ *n.* **1 Crusade,** any of a series of military expeditions undertaken by Christian western Europe in the 11th-13th c. to rescue the Holy Land from the Saracens . **2** a vigorous campaign in favour of a cause. —*v.t./i.* to engage in a crusade. [earlier *croisade* (F, f. *croix* cross)]

crusader *n.* **1** one who engages in a crusade. **2 Crusader,** one who took part in the Crusades. [f. prec.]

cruse /kruːz/ *n.* (*archaic*) an earthenware pot or jar. [OE]

crush *v.t./i.* **1** to press heavily or with violence so as to break, injure or wrinkle; to squeeze tightly; to press or pound into small fragments. **2** to become crushed. **3** to defeat or subdue completely. —*n.* **1** a crowded mass of people pressed together. **2** a drink made from the juice of crushed fruit. **3** (*slang*) an infatuation. [f. OF *croissir* gnash (the teeth)]

crushable /ˈkrʌʃəb(ə)l/ *adj.* that can be crushed; easily crushed. [f. prec.]

crust *n.* **1** the hard outer part of bread; the similar casing of anything. **2** the rocky outer skin of the earth. **3** a deposit, especially from wine on a bottle. **4** (*slang*) impudence. —*v.t./i.* to cover with or form into a crust; to become covered with a crust. —**crustal** *adj.* [f. OF f. L *crusta* rind, shell]

crustacean /krʌˈsteɪʃ(ə)n/ *n.* a member of the Crustacea, a large class of hard-shelled mainly aquatic animals including crabs, lobsters, shrimps, wood-lice, etc. —*adj.* of crustaceans. [f. L (as prec.)]

crusty *adj.* **1** having a crisp crust. **2** irritable, curt. —**crustily** *adv.*, **crustiness** *n.* [f. CRUST]

crutch *n.* **1** a support for a lame person, usually with a cross-piece fitting under the armpit or shaped so that the weight is supported on the forearm; any support. **2** the crotch. [OE]

crux /krʌks/ *n.* (*pl.* **cruces** /ˈkruːsiːz/) the decisive point, the crucial element of a problem. [L, = cross]

cry /kraɪ/ *v.t./i.* (*past* & *p.p.* **cried**) **1** to make a loud shrill sound; to call out loudly in words; (of an animal) to utter its cry. **2** to shed tears. **3** (often with *out*) to appeal, demand, or show need *for*. **4** (of a hawker etc.) to proclaim (wares) for sale. —*n.* **1** a loud inarticulate utterance of pain, grief, joy, etc.; a loud excited utterance of words; the loud natural utterance of an animal, that of hounds on a scent. **2** an urgent appeal or entreaty; a public demand. **3** a watchword, a rallying call. **4** a spell of weeping. —**cry-baby** *n.* a person who weeps easily or without good reason. **cry down,** to disparage. **cry off,** to withdraw from a promise or undertaking. **cry up,** to praise, to extol. **cry wolf,** see WOLF. **in full cry,** in close pursuit. [f. OF f. L *quiritare* wail]

crying *adj.* (esp. of injustice) flagrant, demanding redress. [f. prec.]

cryogenics /kraɪəˈdʒenɪks/ *n.* the branch of physics dealing with very low temperatures and their effects. [f. Gk *kruos* frost + -GENIC]

cryosurgery /kraɪəʊˈsɜːdʒərɪ/ *n.* surgery in which local application of intense cold is used for anaesthesia or therapy. [f. Gk *kruos* frost + SURGERY]

crypt /krɪpt/ *n.* a vault, especially one beneath a church, used as a burial-place. [f. L f. Gk *kruptē* (*kruptos* hidden)]

cryptic /ˈkrɪptɪk/ *adj.* secret, mysterious; obscure in meaning. —**cryptically** *adv.* [as prec.]

cryptogam /ˈkrɪptəgæm/ *n.* a plant with no true flowers or seeds, e.g. a fern, moss, or fungus. —**cryptogamous** /-ˈtɒgəməs/ *adj.* [f. F (as CRYPT, Gk *gamos* marriage)]

cryptogram /ˈkrɪptəgræm/ *n.* a thing written in cipher. [as CRYPT + -GRAM]

cryptography /krɪpˈtɒgrəfɪ/ *n.* the art of writing in or deciphering codes or ciphers. —**cryptographer** *n.*, **cryptographic** /-təˈgræfɪk/ *adj.* [as CRYPT + -GRAPHY]

crystal /ˈkrɪst(ə)l/ *n.* **1** a kind of clear transparent colourless mineral; a piece of this. **2** highly transparent glass, flint glass; articles made of this. **3** an aggregation of molecules with a definite internal structure and the external form of a solid enclosed by symmetrically arranged plane faces. —*adj.* made of crystal; like or clear as crystal. —**crystal ball,** a glass globe used in crystal-gazing. **crystal-gazing** *n.* concentrating one's gaze oh a crystal to obtain a picture by hallucination etc. [OE f. OF, ult. f. Gk *krustallos* ice, crystal]

crystalline /ˈkrɪst(ə)laɪn/ *adj.* **1** of, like, or clear as crystal. **2** having the structure and form of a crystal. —**crystallinity** /-ˈlɪnɪtɪ/ *n.* [f. OF (as prec.)]

crystallize /ˈkrɪstəlaɪz/ *v.t./i.* **1** to form into crystals. **2** (of ideas or plans) to become definite. —**crystallized fruit,** fruit preserved in sugar. —**crystallization** /-ˈzeɪʃ(ə)n/ *n.* [f. CRYSTAL]

crystallography /krɪstəˈlɒgrəfɪ/ *n.* the science of crystal structure. —**crystallographer** *n.* [f. CRYSTAL + -GRAPHY]

crystalloid /ˈkrɪst(ə)lɔɪd/ *n.* a substance having a crystalline structure. [f. CRYSTAL]

Cs *symbol* caesium.

c/s *abbr.* cycles per second.

CSE *abbr.* Certificate of Secondary Education.

Cu *symbol* copper.

cu. *abbr.* cubic.

cub *n.* **1** the young of a fox, bear, lion, etc. **2** an ill-mannered young man. **3** (*colloq.*) an inexperienced reporter. **4 Cub,** a Cub Scout. —*v.t./i.* (**-bb-**) **1** to bring forth (cubs). **2** to hunt fox-cubs. —**Cub Scout,** a member of the junior branch of the Scout Association, consisting of boys aged eight to ten-and-a-half. [orig. unkn.]

cubby-hole /ˈkʌbɪhəʊl/ *n.* a very small room; a small snug place. [f. dial. *cub* stall f. LG]

cube /kju:b/ *n.* **1** a solid contained by six equal squares; a cube-shaped block. **2** the product of a number multiplied by its square. —*v.t.* **1** to find the cube of (a number). **2** to cut (food) into small cubes. —**cube root,** the number which produces a given number when cubed. [F or L f. Gk]

cubic /ˈkju:bɪk/ *adj.* **1** of three dimensions. **2** involving the cube (and no higher power) of a number. —**cubic metre** etc., the volume of a cube whose edge is one metre etc. [f. F or L (as prec.)]

cubical /ˈkju:bɪk(ə)l/ *adj.* cube-shaped. [f. prec.]

cubicle /ˈkju:bɪk(ə)l/ *n.* a small separate sleeping-compartment; an enclosed space screened for privacy. [f. L (*cubare* lie)]

cubism /ˈkju:bɪz(ə)m/ *n.* a style of art (esp. painting) in which objects are so presented as to give the effect of an assemblage of geometrical figures. —**cubist** *n.* [f. F (as CUBE)]

cubit /ˈkju:bɪt/ *n.* an ancient measure of length, approximately equal to the length of the forearm. [f. L *cubitum* elbow]

cuboid /ˈkju:bɔɪd/ *adj.* cube-shaped, like a cube. —*n.* a rectangular parallelepiped. [f. Gk (as CUBE)]

cuckold /ˈkʌkəʊld/ *n.* a husband whose wife is unfaithful to him. —*v.t.* to make a cuckold of. —**cuckoldry** *n.* [f. OF (*cucu* cuckoo)]

cuckoo /ˈkʊku:/ *n.* **1** a migratory bird (*Cuculus canorus*) with a characteristic cry, which deposits its eggs in the nests of small birds. **2** a bird of the family Cuculidae, with or without this habit. —*adj.* (*slang*) crazy, foolish. —**cuckoo-pint** *n.* wild arum (*Arum maculatum*). **cuckoo-spit** *n.* a froth exuded by the larvae of certain insects on leaves, stems, etc. [f. OF (imit.)]

cucumber /ˈkju:kʌmbə(r)/ *n.* a long green fleshy vegetable used in salads; the plant producing this. [f. OF f. L *cucumer*]

cud *n.* the half-digested food that a ruminant chews at leisure. —**chew the cud,** to reflect, to ponder. [OE, rel. to OHG *kuti, quiti* glue]

cuddle *v.t./i.* to hug, to embrace fondly; to lie close and snug; to nestle together. —*n.* a prolonged and fond hug. —**cuddlesome** *adj.*, **cuddly** *adj.* [perh. f. dial. *couth* snug]

cudgel /ˈkʌdʒ(ə)l/ *n.* a short thick stick used as a weapon. —*v.t.* (**-ll-**) to beat with a cudgel. —**cudgel one's brains,** to think hard about a problem. **take up the cudgels for,** to defend vigorously. [OE]

cue[1] *n.* something said or done (especially by an actor in a play) which serves as a signal for another to say or do something; a stimulus to perception etc.; a signal, a hint. —*v.t.* to give a cue to. —**cue in,** to insert a cue for; to give information to. [orig. unkn.]

cue[2] *n.* a billiard-player's rod for striking the ball. —*v.t./i.* to use a cue; to strike with a cue. [var. of QUEUE]

cuff[1] *n.* **1** the thicker end-part of a sleeve; a separate band worn round the wrist. **2** (in *pl.*, *colloq.*) handcuffs. —**cuff-link** *n.* one of a pair of fasteners for shirt cuffs. **off the cuff,** extempore, without preparation. [orig. unkn.]

cuff[2] *v.t.* to strike with the open hand. —*n.* a cuffing blow. [perh. imit.]

cuirass /kwɪˈræs/ *n.* a piece of armour consisting of a breastplate and back-plate fastened together. [f. OF f. L *coriaceus* (*corium* leather)]

cuisine /kwɪˈzi:n/ *n.* a style or method of cooking. [F, = kitchen]

cul-de-sac /ˈkʌldəsæk, ˈkʊl-/ *n.* (*pl.* **culs-de-sac** *pr.* same) a street or passage closed at one end. [F, = sack-bottom]

culinary /ˈkʌlɪnərɪ/ *adj.* of or for cooking. [f. L (*culina* kitchen)]

cull *v.t.* **1** to pick (a flower etc.), to select. **2** to select from a herd etc. and kill (surplus animals). —*n.* culling; an animal or animals culled. [f. OF f. L *colligere* collect]

culminate /ˈkʌlmɪneɪt/ *v.i.* to reach its highest point (*in*). —**culmination** /-ˈneɪʃ(ə)n/ *n.* [f. L *culminare* (*culmen* summit)]

culottes /kju:ˈlɒts/ *n.pl.* women's trousers styled to resemble a skirt. [F, = knee-breeches]

culpable /ˈkʌlpəb(ə)l/ *adj.* deserving blame. —**culpability** /-ˈbɪlɪtɪ/ *n.*, **culpably** *adv.* [f. OF f. L (*culpare* to blame)]

culprit /ˈkʌlprɪt/ *n.* a person accused of or guilty of an offence. [perh. abbr. of AF formula said by Clerk of Crown to prisoner pleading Not Guilty, *Culpable: prest d'averrer* etc. (You are) guilty: (I am) ready to prove it]

cult *n.* a system of religious worship especially as expressed in ritual; devotion or homage to a person or thing. [f. F or f. L (*colere* cultivate, worship)]

cultivate /ˈkʌltɪveɪt/ *v.t.* **1** to prepare and use

(soil) for crops. **2** to produce (crops) by tending them. **3** to apply oneself to improving or developing (the mind, an acquaintance, etc.). **4** to spend time and care in developing; to develop the friendship of. —**cultivation** /-ˈveɪʃ(ə)n/ *n.* [f. L *cultivare* (*cultiva* (*terra*) arable land, as prec.)]

cultivator /ˈkʌltɪveɪtə(r)/ *n.* **1** a device for breaking up ground. **2** one who cultivates. [f. prec.]

culture /ˈkʌltʃə(r)/ *n.* **1** refined understanding of the arts and other human intellectual achievement. **2** the customs and civilization of a particular time or people. **3** improvement by care and training. **4** the cultivation of plants, rearing of bees, silkworms, etc. **4** a quantity of bacteria grown for study. —*v.t.* to grow (bacteria) for study. —**cultural** *adj.* [f. F or L (as CULT)]

cultured *adj.* having or showing culture. —**cultured pearl,** a pearl formed by an oyster after the insertion of a foreign body into its shell. [f. prec.]

culvert /ˈkʌlvət/ *n.* a drain that crosses under a road, canal, etc. [orig. unkn.]

cum /kʊm/ *prep.* with, together with; also used as. [L]

cumber *v.t.* (*literary*) to hamper, to hinder, to inconvenience. [f. ENCUMBER]

cumbersome /ˈkʌmbəsəm/ *adj.* hampering; inconvenient in size, weight, or shape. [f. CUMBER]

cumin /ˈkʌmɪn/ *n.* a herb (*Cuminum cyminum*) with aromatic seeds. [f. OF f. L f. Gk (prob. of Semitic origin)]

cummerbund /ˈkʌməbʌnd/ *n.* a sash worn round the waist. [f. Hindi & Pers., = loin-band]

cumquat var. of KUMQUAT.

cumulate /ˈkju:mjʊleɪt/ *v.t./i.* to accumulate; to combine (catalogue entries etc.). [f. L *cumulare* (*cumulus* heap)]

cumulative /ˈkju:mjʊlətɪv/ *adj.* increasing or increased in amount, force, etc., by successive additions. —**cumulatively** *adv.* [as prec.]

cumulonimbus /kju:mjʊləʊˈnɪmbəs/ *n.* a form of cloud consisting of a tall dense mass, present during thunderstorms. [f. foll. + NIMBUS]

cumulus /ˈkju:mjʊləs/ *n.* (*pl.* **-li**) a form of cloud consisting of rounded masses heaped on a horizontal base. [L, = heap]

cuneiform /ˈkju:nɪfɔ:m/ *adj.* of or using an ancient system of writing with wedge-shaped marks impressed on soft clay with a straight length of reed, bone, wood, or metal, or incised into stone etc. —*n.* this writing. [f. F f. L *cuneus* wedge + *forma* shape]

cunning *adj.* **1** skilled in ingenuity or deceit, selfishly clever or crafty; ingenious. **2** (*US*) attractive, quaint. —*n.* craftiness, skill in deceit. [f. ON, = knowing (as CAN¹)]

cunt *n.* (*vulgar*) the female genitals. [f. ON *kunta*, MLG, MDu. *kunte*]

cup *n.* **1** a small bowl with a handle, used for drinking from; its contents, the amount that it holds. **2** a cup-shaped thing. **3** flavoured wine, cider, etc. **4** an ornamental vessel as the prize for a race or contest. **4** one's fate or fortune. —*v.t.* (**-pp-**) to form (esp. one's hands) into the shape of a cup; to take or hold as in a cup. —**Cup Final,** the final football etc. match in a competition for a cup. —**cupful** *n.* (*pl.* **-fuls**) [OE]

cupboard /ˈkʌbəd/ *n.* a recess or piece of furniture with a door and (usually) shelves, in which things may be stored. —**cupboard love,** a display of affection meant to secure some gain.

cupidity /kjʊˈpɪdɪtɪ/ *n.* greed for gain. [f. OF or L (*cupiditas* desire)]

cupola /ˈkju:pələ/ *n.* **1** a small dome on a roof. **2** a furnace for melting metals. **3** a ship's or fort's revolving gun-turret. [It. f. L (*cupa* cask)]

cuppa /ˈkʌpə/ *n.* (*colloq.*) a cup of (tea). [corrupt.]

cupreous /ˈkju:prɪəs/ *adj.* of or like copper. [f. L (*cuprum* copper)]

cupric /ˈkju:prɪk/ *adj.* of copper. [as prec.]

cupro-nickel /kju:prəʊˈnɪk(ə)l/ *n.* an alloy of copper and nickel. [as CUPREOUS]

cur *n.* **1** a worthless or bad-tempered dog. **2** a contemptible person. [perh. f. ON *kurr* grumbling]

curable /ˈkjʊərəb(ə)l/ *adj.* that can be cured. [f. CURE]

curaçao /ˈkjʊərəsəʊ/ *n.* a liqueur flavoured with the peel of bitter oranges. [name of Caribbean island producing these oranges]

curacy /ˈkjʊərəsɪ/ *n.* a curate's office; the tenure of it. [f. CURATE]

curare /kjʊəˈrɑ:rɪ/ *n.* the bitter extract of various plants, used by South American Indians as a poison on arrows. [f. Carib]

curate /ˈkjʊərət/ *n.* the assistant to a parish priest. [f. L (as CURE)]

curator /kjʊəˈreɪtə(r)/ *n.* a person in charge of a museum or other collection. [as prec.]

curative /ˈkʊərətɪv/ *adj.* tending or able to cure. —*n.* a curative thing. [F f. L (as CURE)]

curb *n.* **1** a check, a restraint. **2** a strap or chain fastened to a bit and passing under a horse's lower jaw, used as a check. **3** a border or edging, the frame round the top of a well; a kerb. —*v.t.* **1** to restrain. **2** to put a curb on (a horse). [f. OF f. L *curvare* (as CURVE)]

curd *n.* (often in *pl.*) a coagulated substance formed by the action of acids on milk, made into cheese or eaten as food. [orig. unkn.]

curdle *v.t./i.* to congeal, to form into curds. —**make one's blood curdle,** to fill one with horror. [f. prec.]

cure *v.t.* **1** to restore to health; to relieve *of* a disease; to eliminate (a disease, evil, etc.). **2** to preserve (meat, fruit, tobacco, or skins) by salting, drying, etc. **3** to vulcanize (rubber). —*n.* a thing that cures; a restoration to health; a course of medicinal or healing treatment. [f. OF f. L *curare* take care of (*cura* care)]

curé /ˈkjʊəreɪ/ *n.* a parish priest in France etc. [F (as CURATE)]

curette /kjʊəˈret/ *n.* a surgeon's small scraping-instrument. —*v.t.* to scrape with this. —**curettage** *n.* [F, f. *curer* cleanse (as CURE)]

curfew /ˈkɜːfjuː/ *n.* a signal or time after which people must remain indoors; (*hist.*) a signal for the extinction of fires at a fixed evening hour. [f. AF *coeverfu* (as COVER, FUEL)]

Curia /ˈkjʊərɪə/ *n.* the papal court, especially those functionaries through whom the government of the Roman Catholic Church is administered. [L, = senate-house at Rome]

curie /ˈkjʊərɪ/ *n.* **1** a unit of radioactivity, corresponding to 3.7×10^{10} disintegrations per second. **2** a quantity of radioactive substance having this activity. [f. P. *Curie* (1859–1906), French physicist]

curio /ˈkjʊərɪəʊ/ *n.* (*pl.* **-os**) a rare or unusual object. [abbr. of foll.]

curiosity /kjʊərɪˈɒsɪtɪ/ *n.* **1** an eager desire to know; inquisitiveness. **2** a strange or rare thing. [as foll.]

curious /ˈkjʊərɪəs/ *adj.* **1** eager to know or learn; inquisitive. **2** strange, surprising, odd. —**curiously** *adv.* [f. OF f. L *curiosus* careful (as CURE)]

curium /ˈkjʊərɪəm/ *n.* an artificially made transuranic radioactive metallic element, symbol Cm, atomic number 96. [f. M. *Curie* (1867–1934) and P. *Curie* (see CURIE)]

curl *v.t./i.* **1** to bend or coil into a spiral; to move in a spiral form. **2** to play curling. —*n.* **1** a coiled lock of hair; anything spiral or curved inwards. **2** a curling movement. —**curl up,** to lie or sit with the knees drawn up; to writhe with horror, shame, etc. [f. obs. *crulle* curly f. Du.]

curler *n.* a device for curling the hair. [f. prec.]

curlew /ˈkɜːljʊ/ *n.* a wading bird of the genus *Numenius*, with a long slender curved bill. [f. OF]

curlicue /ˈkɜːlɪkjuː/ *n.* a decorative curl or twist. [f. CURLY + CUE² (= pigtail) or Q]

curling *n.* a game played on ice, in which large flat rounded stones are hurled along a defined space (the *rink*) towards a mark (the *tee*). [f. CURL]

curly *adj.* having or arranged in curls; moving in curves. [f. CURL]

curmudgeon /kəˈmʌdʒ(ə)n/ *n.* a bad-tempered person. [orig. unkn.]

currant /ˈkʌrənt/ *n.* **1** the dried fruit of a small seedless grape, used in cookery. **2** any of various shrubs of the genus *Ribes* producing black, red, or white berries; such a berry. [f. AF, = (grapes of) Corinth, the orig. source)]

currawong /ˈkʌrəwɒŋ/ *n.* a small crowlike Australian bird of the genus *Strepera*, with a resonant call. [Aboriginal]

currency /ˈkʌrənsɪ/ *n.* **1** the money in use in a country. **2** being current, prevalence. [f. foll.]

current /ˈkʌrənt/ *adj.* **1** belonging to the present time, happening now. **2** (of money, an opinion, rumour, word) in general circulation or use. —*n.* **1** a body of water, air, etc., moving in a definite direction, especially through a stiller surrounding body. **2** the general tendency or course *of* events or opinions. **3** the movement of electrically charged particles; a quantity representing the intensity of this. —**current account,** a bank account from which money may be drawn without notice. [f. OF f. L *currere* run]

currently *adv.* at the present time. [f. prec.]

curricle /ˈkʌrɪk(ə)l/ *n.* a light open horse-drawn carriage, usually with two horses abreast. [f. L *curriculum* (see foll.)]

curriculum /kəˈrɪkjʊləm/ *n.* (*pl* **-la**) a course of study. —**curriculum vitae** /ˈviːtaɪ/, an account of one's previous career. [L, = racecourse (*currere* run)]

currier /ˈkʌrɪə(r)/ *n.* a leather-dresser. [f. OF f. L (*corium* leather)]

curry¹ *n.* a dish of meat, fish, eggs, etc., cooked with hot-tasting spices, usually served with rice. —*v.t.* to make (meat etc.) into a curry. —**curry powder,** a preparation of turmeric and other spices for making curry. [f. Tamil *kari* sauce]

curry² *v.t.* **1** to groom (a horse) with a curry-comb. **2** to treat (tanned leather) to improve its properties. —**curry-comb** *n.* a pad with rubber or plastic projections for grooming a horse. —**curry favour,** to ingratiate oneself. [f. OF f. L *conredare* f. Gmc (as READY)]

curse *n.* **1** a solemn utterance wishing a person to suffer destruction or punishment; an evil resulting from this. **2** a violent exclamation of anger, a profane oath. **3** a thing that causes evil or harm. —*v.t./i.* to utter a curse against; to utter expletive curses. —**the curse,** (*colloq.*) menstruation. **be cursed with,** to have as a burden or source of harm. [OE]

cursed /ˈkɜːsɪd/ *adj.* damnable, abominable. [f. prec.]

cursive /ˈkɜːsɪv/ *adj.* (of writing) done with joined characters. —*n.* cursive writing. [f. L (*scriptura*) *cursiva* f. *currere* run]

cursor /ˈkɜːsə(r)/ *n.* **1** a transparent slide with a hair-line, forming part of a slide-rule. **2** the indicator on a VDU screen, showing a particular position in displayed matter. [L, = runner (as prec.)]

cursory /ˈkɜːsərɪ/ *adj.* hasty, hurried. —**cursorily** *adv.* [f. L, = of a runner (as prec.)]

curt *adj.* noticeably or rudely brief. —**curtly** *adv.*, **curtness** *n.* [f. L *curtus* cut short]

curtail /kɜːˈteɪl/ *v.t.* to cut short, to reduce. —**curtailment** *n.* [f. obs. *curtal* horse with docked tail f. OF (as prec.)]

curtain /ˈkɜːt(ə)n/ *n.* a piece of cloth etc. hung up as a screen, usually movable sideways or upwards, especially at a window or between the stage and auditorium of a theatre; the rise or fall of the stage curtain at the beginning or end of an act or scene; (in *pl.*, *slang*) the end. —*v.t.* to furnish or cover with curtains; to shut *off* with a curtain or curtains. —**curtain-call** *n.* an audience's summons to an actor or actors to take a bow after the fall of the curtain. **curtain-raiser** *n.* a short opening theatre-piece; a preliminary event. **curtain-wall** *n.* the plain wall of a fortified place, connecting two towers etc. [f. OF f. L *cortina* transl. Gk *aulaia* (*aulē* court)]

curtsy /ˈkɜːtsɪ/ *n.* a woman's or girl's salutation made by bending the knees and lowering the body. —*v.i.* to make a curtsy. [var. of COURTESY]

curvaceous /kɜːˈveɪʃəs/ *adj.* (*colloq.*) (of a woman) having a shapely curved figure. [f. CURVE]

curvature /ˈkɜːvətʃə(r)/ *n.* curving; curved form. [f. OF f. L (as foll.)]

curve *n.* a line of which no part is straight; a surface of which no part is flat; a curved form or thing; a curved line on a graph. —*v.t./i.* to bend or shape so as to form a curve. —**curvy** *adj.* [f. L *curvus* curved]

curvet /kɜːˈvet/ *n.* a horse's short frisky leap. —*v.i.* to perform a curvet. [f. It. dim. of *corva* (as prec.)]

curvilinear /kɜːvɪˈlɪnɪə(r)/ contained by or consisting of curved lines. [f. CURVE, after *rectilinear*]

cushion /ˈkʊʃ(ə)n/ *n.* **1** a fabric case filled with a mass of soft or springy material, used to make a seat etc. more comfortable. **2** a soft pad or other means of support or of protection against jarring; a means of protection against shock; the elastic lining of the rim of a billiard table, from which the balls rebound. **3** the body of air supporting a hovercraft etc. —*v.t.* **1** to provide or protect with a cushion or cushions. **2** to mitigate the adverse effects of. [f. OF f. L *culcita* mattress]

cushy /ˈkʊʃɪ/ *adj.* (*colloq.*, of a job etc.) pleasant and easy. [f. Hindi, = pleasant]

cusp *n.* a point at which two curves meet; a projecting point between small arcs in Gothic tracery; the horn of the crescent moon etc. [f. L *cuspis* point, apex]

cuss *n.* (*colloq.*) **1** a curse. **2** an awkward or difficult person. —*v.t./i.* (*colloq.*) to curse. [vulgar pronunc. of CURSE]

cussed /ˈkʌsɪd/ *adj.* (*colloq.*) awkward and stubborn. —**cussedness** *n.* [f. prec.]

custard /ˈkʌstəd/ *n.* a dish or sauce made with milk and beaten eggs, usually sweetened; a sweet sauce made with milk and flavoured cornflour. [f. AF f. OF *crouste* crust]

custodian /kʌsˈtəʊdɪən/ *n.* a guardian or keeper, especially of a public building. [f. foll.]

custody /ˈkʌstədɪ/ *n.* **1** guardianship, protective care. **2** imprisonment. —**take into custody,** to arrest. —**custodial** /-ˈstəʊdɪəl/ *adj.* [f. L *custodia* (*custos* guardian)]

custom /ˈkʌstəm/ *n.* **1** the usual way of behaving or acting; established usage as a power or as having the force of law. **2** a business patronage, regular dealings or customers. **3** (in *pl.*) the duty levied on imports; (often treated as *sing.*) the government department or officials administering this. —**custom-built** *adj.* built to a customer's order. **custom-house** *n.* an office at a port or frontier etc. at which customs duties are levied. [f. OF f. L *consuetudo*]

customary *adj.* in accordance with custom, usual. —**customarily** *adv.* [f. L (as prec.)]

customer *n.* a person who buys goods or services from a shop or business; (*colloq.*) a person one has to deal with. [f. AF (as CUSTOM)]

cut *v.t./i.* (**-tt-**) (*past* and *p.p.* **cut**) **1** to penetrate or wound with a sharp-edged instrument (also *fig.*) **2** to divide or detach with a knife etc.; to shape, make, or shorten thus; to be able to cut or be cut; to have (a tooth) appear through the gum. **3** to execute (*a caper* etc.) or make (*a sorry figure* etc.). **4** to reduce by removing part of; to cease to provide; to switch off (electricity, an engine, etc.). **5** to divide a pack of cards; to select (a card) thus. **6** to absent oneself from; to renounce (a connection), to ignore or refuse to recognize (a person). **7** to edit (a film); to go quickly *to* another shot. **8** to hit (a ball) with a chopping motion in cricket etc. **9** to pass *through* etc. as a shorter way. **10.** (*US*) to dilute (spirits for drinking). —*n.* **1** the act of cutting; a division, wound, or hurt made by this; a stroke with a sword, whip, or cane. **2** a piece of meat cut from a carcass. **3** the way a thing is cut, the style in which clothes are made. **4** a reduction or cessation. **5** an excision of part of a play, film, book, etc. **6** (*slang*) a commission, a share of the profits etc. **7** a stroke made by cutting a ball in cricket etc. **8** a cutting remark. **9** the ignoring of or refusal to recognize a person etc. —**a cut above,** noticeably superior to. **cut and dried,** prepared in advance, ready; inflexible. **cut and run,** (*slang*) to run away. **cut**

back, to reduce, to prune. **cut-back** *n.* a reduction. **cut both ways,** to serve both sides of an argument. **cut corners,** to do a task etc. perfunctorily or incompletely. **cut down,** to reduce (expenses etc.). **cut in,** to interrupt; to move in front of another vehicle (especially in overtaking) leaving too little space. **cut it out,** (*slang*, in *imper.*) stop doing that. **cut line,** a line above which service must be made in squash. **cut one's losses,** to abandon an unprofitable scheme before the losses become too great. **cut no ice,** (*slang*) to be of no importance or effect. **cut off,** to end abruptly; to intercept, to interrupt; to prevent from continuing; to disinherit. **cut-off** *n.* the point at which a thing is cut off; a device for stopping a flow. **cut out,** to remove, to omit; to outdo or supplant; to cease or cause to cease functioning; (in *pass.*) to be suited (*for, to* be or do). **cut-out** *n.* a thing cut out; a device for automatic disconnection; the release of exhaust gases, etc. **cut-price** *adj.* for sale at a reduced price. **cut-rate** *adj.* available at a reduced rate. **cut a tooth,** to have a tooth beginning to emerge from the gum. **cut one's teeth on,** to acquire experience from. **cut up,** to cut into small pieces; (in *pass.*) to be greatly distressed. **cut up rough,** to show anger or resentment. [perh. OE]

cutaneous /kju:ˈteɪnɪəs/ *adj.* of the skin. [f. L (as CUTIS)]

cutaway *adj.* **1** (of a diagram etc.) having some parts absent to reveal the interior. **2** (of a coat) with the front below the waist cut away.

cute /kju:t/ *adj.* (*colloq.*) clever, ingenious; (*US*) attractive, quaint. —**cutely** *adv.*, **cuteness** *n.* [f. ACUTE]

cuticle /ˈkju:tɪk(ə)l/ *n.* the skin at the base of the finger-nail or toe-nail. [f. L *cuticula* (as foll.)]

cutis /ˈkju:tɪs/ *n.* the true skin beneath the epidermis. [L, = skin]

cutlass /ˈkʌtləs/ *n.* (*hist.*) a short sword with a slightly curved blade. [f. F f. L (as foll.)]

cutlery /ˈkʌtlərɪ/ *n.* knives, forks, and spoons for use at table. [f. OF f. L *cultellus* dim. of *culter* knife]

cutlet /ˈkʌtlɪt/ *n.* a neck-chop of mutton or lamb; a small piece of veal etc. for frying; a flat cake of minced meat etc. [f. OF f. L (*costa* rib)]

cutter *n.* **1** a tailor etc. who takes measurements and cuts cloth. **2** a small fast sailing-ship. **3** a small boat carried by a large ship. [f. CUT]

cutting *n.* **1** a piece cut from a newspaper etc. **2** a piece cut from a plant for propagation. **3** an excavated channel through high ground, for a railway or road. [f. CUT]

cutthroat *n.* **1** a murderer. **2** a razor with a long blade set in a handle. —*adj.* **1** intense and ruthless. **2** (of a card-game) three-handed.

cuttlefish /ˈkʌt(ə)lfɪʃ/ *n.* a ten-armed mollusc of the genus *Sepia* that ejects a black fluid when threatened. [OE, rel. to *cod* bag (ref. to the ink-bag)]

cutwater *n.* **1** the forward edge of a ship's prow. **2** a wedge-shaped projection from a pier or bridge.

c.v. *abbr.* curriculum vitae.

cwm /ku:m/ *n.* (in Wales) = COOMB; a cirque. [Welsh]

cwt. *abbr.* hundredweight.

cyan /ˈsaɪən/ *adj.* & *n.* (in photography) greenish-blue. [f. Gk *kuan(e)os* dark blue]

cyanic /saɪˈænɪk/ *adj.* of or containing cyanogen. [f. CYANOGEN]

cyanide /ˈsaɪənaɪd/ *n.* a highly poisonous substance used in the extraction of gold and silver. [f. foll.]

cyanogen /saɪˈænədʒɪn/ *n.* an inflammable poisonous gas. [f. F f. Gk *kuanos* dark-blue mineral + -GEN]

cyanosis /saɪəˈnəʊsɪs/ *n.* blue discoloration of the skin due to lack of oxygen in the blood. [as prec.]

cybernetics /saɪbəˈnetɪks/ *n.* the science of the systems of control and communications in animals and machines. —**cybernetic** *adj.* [f. Gk *kubernētēs* steersman]

cyclamate /ˈsaɪkləmeɪt, ˈsɪk-/ *n.* an artificial sweetening agent. [f. chemical name]

cyclamen /ˈsɪkləmən/ a plant of the genus *Cyclamen*, with pink, red, or white flowers with reflexed petals. [L f. Gk (perh. f. *kuklos* circle)]

cycle /ˈsaɪk(ə)l/ *n.* **1** a recurrent round or period (of events, phenomena, etc.); the time needed for one such round or period; cycles per second, hertz. **2** a recurrent series of operations or states; a series of songs, poems, etc., usually on a single theme. **3** a bicycle, a tricycle, or motor cycle. —*v.i.* **1** to ride a bicycle or tricycle. **2** to move in cycles. [f. OF, or f. L f. Gk *kuklos* circle]

cyclic /ˈsaɪklɪk/ *adj.* **1** recurring in cycles; belonging to a chronological cycle. **2** (*Chem.*) with the constituent atoms forming a ring. [f. F or L (as prec.)]

cyclist /ˈsaɪklɪst/ *n.* a rider of a bicycle. [f. CYCLE]

cyclo- *comb. form* of CYCLE.

cyclo-cross /ˈsaɪkləʊkrɒs/ *n.* cross-country racing on bicycles.

cyclone /ˈsaɪkləʊn/ *n.* a system of winds rotating inwards to an area of low barometric pressure; a violent hurricane of a limited diameter. —**cyclonic** /-ˈklɒnɪk/ *adj.* [f. Gk *kuklōma* wheel, coil of snake (as CYCLE)]

Cyclopean /saɪkləˈpi:ən/ *adj.* (of ancient masonry) made of massive irregular blocks. [f. L f. Gk (*Kuklops* Cyclops, mythical giant)]

cyclostyle /ˈsaɪkləstaɪl/ *n.* an apparatus printing

copies of writing from a stencil. —*v.t.* to print or reproduce with this. [f. CYCLO- + STYLE]

cyclotron /ˈsaɪklətrɒn/ *n.* an apparatus for accelerating charged atomic particles by subjecting them repeatedly to an electric field as they revolve in orbits of increasing diameter in a constant magnetic field. [f. CYCLO- + -TRON]

cygnet /ˈsɪgnɪt/ *n.* a young swan. [f. AF f. L (as foll.)]

cylinder /ˈsɪlɪndə(r)/ *n.* a uniform solid or hollow body with straight sides and a circular section; a thing of this shape, e.g. a container for liquid gas etc., or a part of a machine, especially the piston-chamber in an engine. —**cylindrical** /-ˈlɪndrɪk(ə)l/ *adj.* [f. L f. Gk (*kulindō* to roll)]

cymbal /ˈsɪmb(ə)l/ *n.* each of a pair of concave brass plates forming a musical instrument, clashed together or struck to make a ringing sound. —**cymbalist** *n.* [f. L f. Gk (*kumbē* cup)]

cyme /saɪm/ *n.* a flower group with a single terminal flower on each stem. [F, var. of *cime* summit [f. L f. Gk]

Cymric /ˈkɪmrɪk/ *adj.* Welsh. [f. Welsh *Cymru* Wales]

Cynic /ˈsɪnɪk/ *n.* a member of an ancient Greek sect of philosophers characterized by an ostentatious contempt for ease, wealth, and the enjoyments of life. —*adj.* of the Cynics. [f. L f. Gk *Cynosarges*, place where the sect was founded]

cynic /ˈsɪnɪk/ *n.* one who has little faith in human sincerity or goodness. —**cynical** *adj.*, **cynically** *adv.*, **cynicism** *n.* [= prec.]

cynosure /ˈsaɪnəzjʊə(r), ˈsɪn-/ *n.* a centre of attraction or admiration. [F, or f. L f. Gk, = dog's tail (name for Ursa Minor)]

cypher var. of CIPHER.

cypress /ˈsaɪprəs/ a coniferous tree of the genus *Cupressus*, with dark foliage, taken as a symbol of mourning. [f. OF f. L f. Gk]

Cypriot /ˈsɪprɪət/ *n.* **1** a native or inhabitant of Cyprus. **2** the dialect of Greek used there. —*adj.* of Cyprus or its people or language. [f. *Cyprus*]

Cyrillic /sɪˈrɪlɪk/ *adj.* of one of the two principal Slavonic alphabets (the other is the Roman) in use today. [f. St *Cyril* (9th c.), Gk missionary]

cyst /sɪst/ *n.* a sac containing fluid or soft matter formed on or in the body. [f. Gk *kustis* bladder]

cystic *adj.* **1** of the bladder. **2** like a cyst. [f. F (as prec.)]

cystitis /sɪsˈtaɪtɪs/ *n.* inflammation of the bladder. [f. Gk *kustis* bladder]

-cyte /-saɪt/ *suffix* denoting a mature biological cell. [as foll.]

cytology /saɪˈtɒlədʒɪ/ *n.* the study of biological cells. —**cytological** /-ˈlɒdʒɪk(ə)l/ *adj.* [f. Gk *kutos* vessel + -LOGY]

cytoplasm /ˈsaɪtəplæz(ə)m/ *n.* the protoplasmic content of a cell other than the nucleus. —**cytoplasmic** *adj.* [f. CYTO- + PLASMA]

czar var. of TSAR.

Czech /tʃek/ *n.* **1** a native of the western and central parts of Czechoslovakia. **2** the Slavonic language of people in these parts. **3** a Czechoslovakian. —*adj.* of the Czechs or their language. [Polish spelling of Bohemian *Cech*]

Czechoslovak /tʃekəˈsləʊvæk/ (also **Czechoslovakian** /-vækɪən/) *n.* a native of Czechoslovakia. —*adj.* of Czechoslovakia or its people. [f. prec. + SLOVAK]

Dd

D, d *n.* **1** the fourth letter of the alphabet. **2** (*Mus.*) the second note in the scale of C major. **3** (as a Roman numeral) 500. **4** = DEE.

d. *abbr.* **1** daughter. **2** died. **3** (until 1971) penny, pence (short for L *denarius*).

dab[1] *v.t./i.* **(-bb-) 1** to press briefly and lightly. **2** to aim a feeble blow (*at*), to strike lightly. —*n.* **1** an act of dabbing, a light blow. **2** a small amount of a soft substance applied to a surface. **3** (in *pl.*, *slang*) fingerprints. [imit.]

dab[2] *n.* & *adj.* (*colloq.*, also **dab hand**) an adept [orig. unkn.]

dab[3] *n.* a flat-fish of the genus *Limanda*. [orig. unkn.]

dabble *v.t./i.* **1** to wet partly or intermittently; to move the feet, hands, or bill lightly in water or mud. **2** to study or work casually (*in* a subject). [f. DAB[1]]

dabchick *n.* a small water-bird of the grebe family. [prob. f. *dap* dip + CHICK]

dace /deɪs/ *n.* (*pl.* same) a small freshwater fish, especially of the genus *Leuciscus*, related to the carp. [f. OF *dars* dart]

dachshund /ˈdækshʊnd/ *n.* a small dog of a short-legged long-bodied breed. [G, = badger-dog]

dactyl /ˈdæktɪl/ *n.* a metrical foot with one long or stressed syllable followed by two short or unstressed syllables. —**dactylic** /-ˈtɪlɪk/ *adj.* [f. Gk *dactulos* finger]

dad *n.* (*colloq.*) father. [imit. of child's *da da*]

Dada /ˈdɑːdɑː/ *n.* an international movement in art and literature about 1915–20, repudiating conventions and intended to shock. —**Dadaism** /-dəɪz(ə)m/ *n.*, **Dadaist** *n.* [f. F *dada* hobby-horse]

daddy *n.* (*colloq.*) father; the oldest or most important person or thing. [f. DAD]

daddy-long-legs *n.* a crane-fly.

dado /ˈdeɪdəʊ/ *n.* (*pl.* **-os**) **1** the lower part of the wall of a room etc. when it is coloured or faced differently from the upper part. **2** the plinth of a column. **3** the cube of a pedestal. [It., = DIE[1]]

daemon *n.* see DEMON.

daffodil /ˈdæfədɪl/ *n.* a yellow narcissus with a trumpet-shaped crown. [earlier *affodil*, f. as ASPHODEL]

daft /dɑːft/ *adj.* (*colloq.*) silly, foolish, crazy. [OE, = mild]

dagger *n.* **1** a short pointed two-edged weapon used for stabbing. **2** an obelus. —**at daggers drawn,** hostile and on the point of quarrelling. **look daggers,** to glare angrily. [perh. f. *dag* pierce]

daguerreotype /dəˈgerəʊtaɪp/ *n.* an early kind of photograph taken on a silver-coated copper plate and developed by exposure to mercury vapour, giving a positive image of white on silver. [f. name of inventor, Louis *Daguerre* (d. 1851)]

dahlia /ˈdeɪlɪə/ *n.* a composite plant of the genus *Dahlia*, of Mexican origin, cultivated for its many-coloured single or double flowers. [f. name of A. *Dahl* (d. 1789), Swedish botanist]

Dáil /dɔɪl/ *n.* (also **Dáil Éireann** /ˈeɪrən/) the lower house of parliament in the Republic of Ireland. [Irish, = assembly (of Ireland)]

daily /ˈdeɪlɪ/ *adj.* done, produced, or occurring every day or weekday. —*adv.* every day. —*n.* **1** a daily newspaper. **2** (*colloq.*) a charwoman employed on a daily basis. —**daily bread,** one's livelihood. [f. DAY]

dainty *adj.* **1** small and pretty, delicate. **2** fastidious, especially about food. —*n.* a delicacy. —**daintily** *adv.*, **daintiness** *n.* [f. OF f. L *dignitas* worth]

daiquiri /ˈdaɪkɪrɪ/ *n.* a cocktail of rum, lime-juice, etc. [f. *Daiquiri*, a rum-producing district in Cuba]

dairy *n.* a room or building where milk and milk products are processed; a shop where these are sold. —**dairy farm,** a farm producing chiefly milk and its derivatives. [OE, = kneader of dough]

dairymaid *n.* a woman employed in a dairy.

dairyman *n.* (*pl.* **-men**) a dealer in milk etc.

dais /ˈdeɪɪs/ *n.* a low platform, especially at one end of a room or hall. [f. L *discus* disc, in med. L = table]

daisy /ˈdeɪzɪ/ *n.* a small European composite flower (*Bellis perennis*) with a yellow disc and white rays; any of various similar flowers. —**daisy wheel,** a disc with characters on its circumference used as a printer in word processing. [OE, = day's eye]

Dalai Lama /dælaɪ ˈlɑːmə/ the head lama of Tibet. [Mongolian *dalai* ocean + LAMA]

dale *n.* a valley, especially in north England. [OE]

dally *v.i.* **1** to dawdle, to waste time. **2** to amuse oneself; to flirt. —**dalliance** *n.* [f. OF *dalier* chat]

Dalmatian /dælˈmeɪʃ(ə)n/ *adj.* of Dalmatia, the central region of the coast of Yugoslavia. —*n.* a dog of a large white breed with dark spots.

dalmatic /dælˈmætɪk/ *n.* a long loose vestment with slit sides and wide sleeves, worn by deacons and bishops on ceremonial occasions. [f. L *dalmatica (vestis)* robe of Dalmatian wool]

dam[1] *n.* a barrier built across a river etc. to hold back water and control its flow. —*v.t.* (**-mm-**) **1** to hold back with a dam. **2** to obstruct, to block (*up*). [f. G *tam*]

dam[2] *n.* the mother especially of a quadruped. [var. of DAME]

damage /ˈdæmɪdʒ/ *n.* **1** something done or suffered that reduces the value or usefulness of the thing affected or spoils its appearance. **2** (*slang*) the cost. **3** (in *pl.*) money claimed or awarded as compensation for loss or injury. —*v.t.* to cause damage to. [OF f. L *damnum* loss]

damascene /ˈdæməsiːn/ *v.t.* to decorate (metal) with inlaid or wavy patterns. [f. *Damascus* capital of Syria]

damask /ˈdæməsk/ *n.* figured woven silk or linen, especially white table-linen with designs shown up by reflection of light. —*adj.* **1** made of damask. **2** coloured like a damask rose, velvety pink. —**damask rose,** a fragrant rose grown especially to make attar. [as *damascene*]

dame *n.* **1 Dame**, the title of a woman Knight Commander or holder of the Grand Cross in orders of chivalry; a woman with this title. **2** a comic middle-aged female character in modern pantomime, usually played by a man. **3** (*archaic, joc.*, or *US slang*) a woman. —**dame school,** (*hist.*) a small primary school of the 18th c., usually kept by one female teacher, for the children of poor families. [f. OF f. L *domina* lady]

damn /dæm/ *int.* an exclamation of anger or annoyance. —*v.t.* **1** to curse. **2** to condemn as a failure, to censure. **3** to doom to hell. **4** to be the ruin of; to show to be guilty. —*n.* an uttered curse. —*adj.* & *adv.* (*colloq.*) damned. —**damn all,** (*slang*) nothing at all. [f. OF f. L (*damnum* loss)]

damnable /ˈdæmnəb(ə)l/ *adj.* hateful, annoying. —**damnably** *adv.* [f. DAMN]

damnation /dæmˈneɪʃ(ə)n/ *n.* eternal punishment in hell. —*int.* damn. [f. DAMN]

damned /dæmd/ *adj.* hateful, annoying. —*adv.* extremely. —**do one's damnedest,** to do one's utmost. [f. DAMN]

damp *adj.* slightly or moderately wet. —*n.* **1** diffused moisture, especially as an inconvenience or danger. **2** foul or explosive gas in a mine. —*v.t.* **1** to make damp. **2** to make sad or dull, to discourage; to reduce the vigour of. **3** to reduce the vibration of. —**damp course,** a layer of damp-proof material built into a wall near the ground to prevent damp from rising. —**damply** *adv.*, **dampness** *n.* [f. G, = vapour]

dampen *v.t.* to damp. [f. DAMP]

damper *n.* **1** a device that reduces shock, noise, vibration, or oscillation; a pad that silences a piano-string except when removed by a note's being struck or by use of a pedal. **2** a movable metal plate that regulates the flow of air into the fire in a stove or furnace. [f. DAMP]

damsel /ˈdæmz(ə)l/ *n.* (*archaic* or *literary*) a young woman. [f. OF, dim. of L *domina* (see DAME)]

damselfly /ˈdæmz(ə)lflaɪ/ *n.* an insect of the order Odonata, like a dragonfly but with wings that fold while it rests. [f. prec.]

damson /ˈdæmz(ə)n/ *n.* a small dark-purple plum; its colour; the tree that bears it. [f. L *damascenum (prunum)* Damascus plum]

dan *n.* a degree of proficiency in judo etc.; one who reaches this. [Jap.]

dance /dɑːns/ *v.t./i.* **1** to move with rhythmical steps or movements, usually to music; to perform (a specified dance). **2** to move in a lively way, to bob up and down. —*n.* **1** a piece of dancing, a special form of this. **2** a social gathering for dancing. **3** a piece of music for dancing to. —**dance attendance on,** to follow about and help dutifully. **lead a person a dance,** to cause him much trouble. —**dancer** *n.* [f. OF *danser*, ult. orig. unkn.]

dandelion /ˈdændɪlaɪən/ *n.* a common composite plant (*Taraxacum officinale*) with jagged leaves and a large bright-yellow flower on a hollow stalk, succeeded by a globular head of seeds with downy tufts. [f. F *dent-de-lion*, f. L (= lion's tooth)]

dander *n.* (*colloq.*) anger, fighting spirit. [orig. unkn.]

dandified /ˈdændɪfaɪd/ *adj.* like a dandy. [f. DANDY]

dandle *v.t.* to dance (a child) on one's knees or in one's arms. [orig. unkn.]

dandruff /ˈdændrʌf/ *n.* flakes of scurf on the scalp and amongst the hair. [orig. unkn.]

dandy *n.* **1** a man who pays excessive attention to the smartness of his appearance and clothes. **2** (*colloq.*) an excellent thing. —*adj.* (*colloq.*) splendid, first-rate. [perh. orig. = *Andrew* in *Jack-a-dandy*]

Dane *n.* **1** a native of Denmark. **2** (*hist.*) a Northman invader of England in the 9th-11th c.

—**Great Dane,** a dog of a large short-haired breed. [f. ON *Danir* (L *Dani*)]

Danegeld /ˈdeɪngeld/ *n.* a land-tax levied in Anglo-Saxon England (especially 991-1016), originally to bribe the invading Danes to go away, turned into a permanent levy for national defence by the Norman kings. [OE, = Dane payment]

Danelaw /ˈdeɪnlɔː/ *n.* the NE part of England settled or held by the Danes from the late 9th c. and administered according to their laws until after the Norman Conquest. [OE, = Danes' law]

danger /ˈdeɪndʒə(r)/ *n.* liability or exposure to harm or death; a thing that causes this. [f. OF f. L *dominus* lord]

dangerous /ˈdeɪndʒərəs/ *adj.* involving or causing danger. —**dangerously** *adv.* [f. prec.]

dangle *v.t./i.* **1** to hang loosely; to hold or carry (a thing) so that it sways loosely. **2** to hold out (a bait or temptation) enticingly. [corresp. to Sw. *dangla*]

Danish /ˈdeɪnɪʃ/ *adj.* of Denmark or its people or language. —*n.* the official language of Denmark. —**Danish blue,** a soft white cheese with veins of blue mould. **Danish pastry,** a yeast cake topped with icing, nuts, etc. [f. L *Danensis*]

dank *adj.* unpleasantly cold and damp. [prob. f. Scand. (Sw. *dank* marshy spot)]

daphne /ˈdæfnɪ/ *n.* a flowering shrub of the genus *Daphne* (e.g. spurge laurel), mezereon. [f. Gk, = laurel]

dapper /ˈdæpə(r)/ *adj.* neat and smart, especially in dress. [f. MLG, MDu., = strong, stout]

dapple *v.t.* to mark with spots or patches of colour or shade. [orig. unkn.]

dapple-grey *adj.* grey with darker markings. —*n.* a dapple-grey horse. [f. prec.]

Darby and Joan a devoted old married couple. The source of the names is usually considered to be a poem in the *Gentleman's Magazine* (1735) containing the lines 'Old Darby, with Joan by his side, You've often regarded with wonder: He's dropsical, she is sore-eyed, Yet they're never happy asunder'.

dare /deə(r)/ *v.t.* (3 sing. pres. usu. **dare** before an expressed or implied infinitive without *to*) **1** to have the courage or impudence (*to*); to face as a danger. **2** to challenge to do something risky. —*n.* a challenge to do something risky. —**I dare say,** I am prepared to believe, I do not deny, it is very likely. [OE (cf. Gk *tharseō* be bold)]

daredevil *n.* a recklessly daring person.

daring /ˈdeərɪŋ/ *n.* adventurous courage. —*adj.* bold, adventurous; boldly dramatic or unconventional. [f. DARE]

dariole /ˈdærɪəʊl/ *n.* a savoury or sweet dish cooked and served in a small mould; this mould. [f. OF]

dark *adj.* **1** with little or no light. **2** (of colour) of a deep shade closer to black than to white; having a brown or black skin, complexion, or hair. **3** gloomy, dismal. **4** secret; mysterious; remote and unexplored. —*n.* **1** absence of light; a time of darkness, night or nightfall. **2** a dark colour or area. —**Dark Ages** the period (*c.*500-1100) between the fall of the Roman Empire and the high Middle Ages. **Dark Continent,** Africa. **dark horse,** a competitor of whose abilities little is known before the contest. **dark-room** *n.* a room where light is excluded so that photographs can be processed. **in the dark,** with no light; lacking information. —**darkly** *adv.*, **darkness** *n.* [OE]

darken *v.t./i.* to make or become dark. —**never darken a person's door,** to stay away from him because one is unwelcome. [f. DARK]

darling *n.* a beloved or lovable person or thing, a favourite. —*adj.* beloved; (*colloq.*) charming. [OE, = little dear]

darn[1] *v.t.* to mend by weaving yarn across a hole. —*n.* a place mended by darning. —**darning** *n.* a piece of such mending; things to be darned. **darning-needle** *n.* a long sewing-needle used in darning. [orig. unkn.]

darn[2], **darned** /dɑːnd/ = DAMN, DAMNED. [corruption]

darnel /ˈdɑːnəl/ *n.* a grass (*Lolium temulentum*) that grows in some countries as a weed among corn. [f. F dial. *darnelle*]

dart *n.* **1** a small pointed missile used as a weapon or in the game of *darts*. **2** a darting movement. **3** a tapering stitched tuck in a garment. —*v.t./i.* **1** to spring or move suddenly (*out, past*, etc.). **2** to direct (a glance etc.) rapidly. —**dartboard** *n.* the target in the game of darts, a board marked with concentric circles. [f. OF *dars*]

dash *v.t./i.* **1** to run rapidly, to rush. **2** to knock, drive, or throw forcefully, to shatter thus; to destroy (hopes etc.); to daunt. **3** to write hastily. **4** (*slang*) damn. **5** (*slang*) to give as a bribe. —*n.* **1** a short rapid run, a rush; (*US*) a sprinting-race. **2** impetuous vigour; lively spirit or appearance. **3** a slight admixture (*of* liquid or flavouring). **4** a horizontal stroke (—) in writing or printing to mark a break in the sense, omitted words, etc. **5** the longer of the two signals used in the Morse code. **6** a dashboard. —**cut a dash,** to make a brilliant show in appearance or behaviour. [imit.]

dashboard *n.* a board below the windscreen of a motor vehicle, carrying various instruments and controls.

dashing *adj.* spirited, lively; showy. [f. DASH]

dastardly /ˈdæstədlɪ/ *adj.* contemptible and

cowardly. [prob. f. *dazed*, or obs. *dasart* dullard]

data /ˈdeɪtə, ˈdɑː-/ *n.pl.*, also ((D) as *sing.*, although the sing. form is **datum**) facts or information used as a basis for inference or reckoning, or prepared for being processed by a computer; quantities or characters for such processing. —**data bank,** a large store or source of data. **data processing,** automatic performance of operations on data. [L, = things given (*dare* give)]

database /ˈdeɪtəbeɪs/ *n.* an organized store of data for computer processing.

datable /ˈdeɪtəb(ə)l/ *adj.* capable of being dated. [f. DATE¹]

date¹ *n.* **1** the numbered day of the month. **2** a statement (usually day, month, and year) on a document, coin, etc., of when it was composed or issued; the period to which something belongs; the time at which a thing happens or is to happen. **3** (*colloq.*) an appointment to meet; (*US*) a person of the opposite sex with whom one has a social engagement. —*v.t./i.* **1** to mark with a date; to assign a date *to*. **2** to have existed *from*. **3** to be or become out of date; to show up the age of. **4** (*colloq.*) to make a social engagement with. —**out of date,** no longer fashionable, current, or valid. **to date,** until now. **up to date,** in current fashion; in accordance with what is now known or required. [f. OF f. L *data* = (letter) given (at specified time and place)]

date² *n.* the oblong brown sweet edible fruit of a palm tree (*Phoenix dactylifera*) of western Asia and North Africa; (also **date-palm**) this tree. [f. OF f. L f. Gk *daktulos* finger, from the shape of its leaf]

date-line *n.* **1** the imaginary north-south line through the Pacific Ocean, partly along the meridian farthest (i.e. 180°) from Greenwich, east and west of which the date differs (east being one day earlier).

date-stamp *n.* an adjustable rubber stamp for marking the date of receipt etc. on a document; its mark. —*v.t.* to mark with a date-stamp.

dative /ˈdeɪtɪv/ *n.* (*Gram.*) the case expressing the indirect object or a recipient. —*adj.* (*Gram.*) of or in the dative. [f. L (*casus*) *dativus* (case) of giving]

datum /ˈdeɪtəm, ˈdɑː-/ *n.* **1** (*pl.* **data**) see DATA. **2** (*pl.* **-ums**) the starting-point from which something is measured or calculated. [sing. of DATA]

daub /dɔːb/ *v.t.* **1** to coat or smear roughly with a soft substance; to lay on (such a substance). **2** to paint crudely or unskilfully. —*n.* **1** plaster or other substance daubed on a surface, a smear. **2** a crude painting. [f. OF f. L *dealbare* to whitewash (DE-, *albus* white)]

daughter /ˈdɔːtə(r)/ *n.* **1** a female child in relation to her parents(s); a female descendant or product *of*. **2** (*Phys. & Biol., attrib.*) an element or cell etc. produced by disintegration or division of another. —**daughter-in-law** *n.* a son's wife. [OE]

daunt /dɔːnt/ *v.t.* to discourage, to intimidate. [f. OF f. L *domitare* (*domare* tame)]

dauntless *adj.* not to be daunted, intrepid. [f. DAUNT + -LESS]

dauphin /ˈdɔːfɪn/ *n.* the title borne by the eldest son of the king of France from 1349 to 1830. [f. L *delphinus* dolphin]

davenport /ˈdævənpɔːt/ *n.* **1** a writing-desk with drawers and a hinged flap. **2** (*US*) a large sofa. [19th-c. maker's name]

davit /ˈdævɪt/ *n.* a kind of small crane on board ship. [f. AF, dim. of *Davi* David]

Davy lamp /ˈdeɪvɪ/ an early type of safety lamp for miners, with wire gauze enclosing the flame. [f. Sir Humphry *Davy* who invented it in 1816]

daw *n.* a jackdaw. [OE]

dawdle *v.i.* to proceed slowly and idly. [orig. unkn.]

dawn *n.* **1** the first light of day. **2** the beginning *of*. —*v.i.* **1** to begin to grow light. **2** to begin to appear or become evident. —**dawn chorus,** early-morning bird-song. **dawn on,** to begin to be understood by. [f. OE, as DAY]

day *n.* **1** the time between sunrise and sunset; daylight; the time for one rotation of the earth, 24 hours, especially from one midnight to the next; the hours given to work. **2** a specified or appointed date; a period, era, or lifetime. **3** a period of prosperity or success. **4** a day's endeavour, especially as bringing success. —**day-bed** *n.* a bed for daytime rest. **day-boy, day-girl** *ns.* a school pupil attending a boarding school but living at home. **day centre,** a place where social and other facilities are provided for elderly or handicapped people during the day. **day in, day out,** continuously. **day nursery,** a place where young children are looked after while their parents are at work. **day release,** a system of allowing employees days off work for education. **day-return** *n.* a ticket sold at a reduced rate for a journey both ways in one day. **day-room** *n.* a room for use during the day only. **day-star** *n.* the sun or other morning star. [OE]

daybreak *n.* the first light of day, dawn.

day-dream *n.* a pleasant fantasy or reverie. —*v.i.* to indulge in day-dreams.

daylight *n.* **1** the light of day; dawn. **2** understanding or knowledge that has dawned. —**daylight robbery,** (*colloq.*) an excessive charge. **daylight saving,** the achieving of longer evening daylight, especially in summer, by making clocks show a later time. **scare the (living) daylights out of,** (*slang*) to terrify.

daytime *n.* the time of daylight.

daze *v.t.* to stupefy, to bewilder. —*n.* a state of being dazed. [f. ON, = weary]

dazzle *v.t.* **1** to make temporarily unable to see by excess of light. **2** to impress or overpower by a display of knowledge, ability, etc. —*n.* bright dazzling light. [f. prec.]

dB *abbr.* decibel(s).

DC *abbr.* **1** (also **d.c.**) direct current. **2** District of Columbia.

D-Day *n.* **1** the day (6 June 1944) on which British and American forces invaded northern France in the Second World War. **2** the day on which an important operation is to begin. [*D* for *day*]

DDT *n.* a white chlorinated hydrocarbon used as an insecticide. [f. chemical name]

de- *prefix* **1** down, away. **2** completely. **3** removing, reversing. [f. L *de* off, from]

deacon /ˈdi:k(ə)n/ *n.* (in Episcopal churches) a clergyman ranking below bishop and priest; (in Nonconformist churches) a layman attending to church business; (in the early Church) a minister of charity. —**deaconess** *n.fem.* [OE f. L f. Gk *diakonos* servant]

dead /ded/ *adj.* **1** no longer alive. **2** numb, having lost sensation. **3** unappreciative, insensitive *to*. **4** no longer effective or in use, extinct; inactive; lacking vigour, interest, or activity; (of a ball in games) out of play. **5** abrupt, complete; exact, unqualified. —*adv.* completely, exactly. —*n.* an inactive or silent time. —**dead-alive** *adj.* very dreary. **dead beat,** (*colloq.*) exhausted. **dead-beat escapement,** one that stops 'dead' without recoil. **dead end,** the closed end of a passage etc.; a course etc. with no prospects. **dead heat,** the result of a race in which two or more competitors finish exactly level. **dead letter,** a law or practice that is no longer observed. **dead man's handle,** a controlling-handle on an electric train etc. that disconnects the power supply if released. **dead march,** a funeral march. **dead nettle,** a plant of the genus *Lamium* with nettle-like leaves but not stinging. **dead-pan** *adj.* & *adv.* with an expressionless face. **dead reckoning,** calculation of a ship's position by log and compass etc. when observations are impossible. **dead set,** a determined attack. **dead shot,** one who never misses the target. **dead water,** the water in a ship's wake close to the stern. **dead weight,** a heavy inert weight. **dead wood,** useless persons or things. [OE]

deaden /ˈded(ə)n/ *v.t./i.* to deprive of or lose vitality, loudness, feeling, etc.; to make insensitive *to*. [f. DEAD]

deadline *n.* a time-limit. [orig. = the line round a military prison (at Andersonville, Georgia, USA; *c.*1864) beyond which a prisoner was liable to be shot down]

deadlock *n.* a situation in which no progress can be made. —*v.t./i.* to bring or come to a deadlock.

deadly /ˈdedlɪ/ *adj.* **1** causing or able to cause fatal injury, death, or serious damage. **2** intense; deathlike. **3** accurate. —*adv.* as if dead; extremely. —**deadly nightshade,** see BELLADONNA. **seven deadly sins,** those held to result in damnation for a person's soul (traditionally pride, covetousness, lust, envy, gluttony, anger, sloth. —**deadliness** *n.* [as DEAD]

deaf /def/ *n.* **1** wholly or partly without hearing. **2** refusing to listen. —**deaf aid,** a hearing-aid. **deaf mute,** a person who is both deaf and dumb. —**deafness** *n.* [OE]

deafen /ˈdef(ə)n/ *v.t.* to overwhelm with sound; to make deaf or temporarily unable to hear by a very loud noise. —**deafening** *adj.* [f. DEAF]

deal[1] *v.t./i.* (*past* & *p.p.* **dealt** /delt/) **1** to distribute or hand *out* among several people etc.; to distribute cards to players. **2** to assign as a share or deserts; to inflict. **3** to do business; to trade *in*. —*n.* **1** dealing or a player's turn to deal at cards; the round of play following this. **2** (*colloq.*) a business transaction or agreement. **3** (*colloq.*) treatment. **4** (*colloq.*) a large amount. —**deal with,** to do business with; to take action about; to be what is needed by (a situation etc.); to discuss (a subject) in a book or speech etc. [OE]

deal[2] *n.* sawn fir or pine timber; a deal board of standard size. [f. MLG, MDu. *dele* plank]

dealer *n.* **1** a person dealing at cards. **2** a trader. **3** a jobber on the Stock Exchange. [f. DEAL[1]]

dealings *n.pl.* a person's conduct or transactions *with* another. [f. DEAL[1]]

dean *n.* **1** a clergyman who is head of the chapter of a cathedral or collegiate church. **2** a college fellow responsible for student discipline; the head of a university faculty or department or of a medical college. —**area** *or* **rural dean,** the head of clergy in a division of an archdeaconry. [f. AF f. L *decanus* (*decem* ten); orig. = chief of group of ten]

deanery *n.* **1** a dean's house or office. **2** a rural dean's group of parishes. [f. DEAN]

dear *adj.* **1** much loved; cherished; precious *to*. **2** (as a polite form of address) esteemed. **3** costing more than it is worth; having high prices. —*n.* a dear person. —*adv.* dearly, at a high price. —*int.* expressing surprise, distress, or pity. —**dearly** *adv.*, **dearness** *n.* [OE]

dearth /dɜ:θ/ *n.* scarcity, lack. [as DEAR]

death /deθ/ *n.* **1** the process of dying, the end of life; final cessation of vital functions; the state of being dead. **2** an event etc. that ends life, a cause of death. **3** the ending or destruction of something. —**at death's door,** close to death. **death cap,** a poisonous toadstool (*Amanita phalloides*). **death certificate,** an official statement of the date, place, and cause of a person's death. **death duty,** (*hist.*) a tax levied on property after the owner's death. **death knell,** the tolling of a bell to mark a person's death; an event that heralds a thing's extinction. **death-mask** *n.* a cast taken of a dead person's face. **death penalty,** punishment by being put to death. **death rate,** the number of deaths per thousand of population per year. **death-roll** *n.* a list or number of those killed in an accident, battle, etc. **death's head,** a picture of a skull as a symbol of death. **death-trap** *n.* a dangerous place, vehicle, etc. **death-warrant** *n.* an order for the execution of a condemned person; something that causes the end of an established practice etc. **death-watch beetle,** a small beetle whose larva bores in wood and makes a ticking sound, formerly supposed to portend a death. **death-wish** *n.* a desire (usually unconscious) for the death of oneself or another. **put to death,** to kill, to execute. **to death,** extremely, to the utmost limit. **to the death,** until one or other is killed. [OE]

deathbed *n.* a bed on which a person is dying or dies.

deathly *adj.* suggestive of death. —*adv.* in a deathly way. [f. DEATH]

deb *n.* (*colloq.*) débutante. [abbr.]

débâcle /deɪˈbɑːkl/ *n.* a sudden disastrous collapse, rout, etc. [F (*débâcler* unbar)]

debar /dɪˈbɑː(r)/ *v.t.* (**-rr-**) to exclude, to prohibit.

debase /dɪˈbeɪs/ *v.t.* to lower in quality or value; to depreciate (coins) by use of an alloy etc. —**debasement** *n.* [f. DE- + obs. *base* abase]

debatable /dɪˈbeɪtəb(ə)l/ *adj.* open to dispute. [f. foll.]

debate /dɪˈbeɪt/ *n.* a formal discussion, an open argument. —*v.t./i.* to hold a debate about; to discuss, to consider. [f. F (as DE-, BATTLE)]

debauch /dɪˈbɔːtʃ/ *v.t.* to make dissolute; to lead into debauchery. —*n.* a bout of debauchery. [f. F; ult. orig. unkn.]

debauchery /dɪˈbɔːtʃərɪ/ *n.* excessive sensual indulgence. [f. prec.]

debenture /dɪˈbentʃə(r)/ *n.* a certificate or bond acknowledging a debt and providing for payment of interest at fixed intervals. [f. L *debentur* are owing (*debēre* owe)]

debilitate /dɪˈbɪlɪteɪt/ *v.t.* to cause debility in. [f. L (as foll.)]

debility /dɪˈbɪlɪtɪ/ *n.* feebleness, weakness, especially of health. [f. OF f. L (*debilis* weak)]

debit /ˈdebɪt/ *n.* an entry in an account-book of a sum owed; the sum itself, the total of such sums. —*v.t.* to enter as a debit (in). [f. F f. L *debitum* debt]

debonair /debəˈneə(r)/ *adj.* having a carefree self-assured manner. [f. OF (*de bon aire* of good disposition)]

debouch /dɪˈbaʊtʃ/ *v.i.* to come out from a ravine or wood etc. into open ground; (of a river or road) to merge into a larger or wider one. [f. F (DE-, *bouche* mouth)]

debrief /diːˈbriːf/ *v.t.* to interrogate (a person) about a completed undertaking in order to obtain information about it.

debris /ˈdebriː, ˈdeɪ-/ *n.* scattered broken pieces, rubbish, wreckage. [f. F (DE- *briser* break)]

debt /det/ *n.* money etc. that is owed; an obligation; a state of owing. [f. OF f. L *debitum* (*debēre* owe)]

debtor /ˈdetə(r)/ *n.* a person owing money etc. [as prec.]

debug /diːˈbʌg/ *v.t.* (**-gg-**) **1** to remove bugs from. **2** (*slang*) to remove concealed listening devices from (a room etc.) or defects from (a machine etc.).

debunk /diːˈbʌŋk/ *v.t.* (*colloq.*) to show the good reputation of (a person etc.) to be false; to expose the falseness of (a claim etc.).

début /ˈdeɪbuː, -bjuː/ *n.* a first appearance (as a performer, in society, etc.). [F (*débuter* lead off)]

débutante /ˈdebjuːtɑːnt/ *n.* a young woman making her social début. [F (as prec.)]

Dec. *abbr.* December.

deca- *in comb.* **1** tenfold, having ten. **2** ten (esp. of a unit in the metric system, as *decagram*). [f. Gk *deka* ten]

decade /ˈdekeɪd/ *n.* a ten-year period; a series or group of ten. [f. F f. L f. Gk (*deka* ten)]

decadence /ˈdekəd(ə)ns/ *n.* **1** deterioration, decline (esp. of a nation, art or literature after reaching a peak). **2** decadent attitude or behaviour. [f. F f. L (as foll.)]

decadent /ˈdekəd(ə)nt/ *adj.* **1** declining, of a period of decadence. **2** self-indulgent. [f. F f. L (as DECAY)]

decaffeinated /diːˈkæfɪneɪtɪd/ *adj.* having had the caffeine removed or reduced. [f. DE- + CAFFEINE]

decagon /ˈdekəgən/ *n.* a plane figure with ten sides and ten angles. —**decagonal** /-ˈkægən(ə)l/ *adj.* [f. L f. Gk (DECA-, *-gōnos* angled)]

decagram /ˈdekəgræm/ *n.* a metric unit of mass, equal to 10 grams.

decalitre /ˈdekəliːtə(r)/ *n.* a metric unit of capacity, equal to 10 litres.

Decalogue /ˈdekəlɒg/ *n.* the Ten Commandments. [f. OF or L f. Gk (*hoi deka logoi* the ten commandments)]

decametre /ˈdekəmiːtə(r)/ *n.* a metric unit of length, equal to 10 metres.

decamp /dɪˈkæmp/ *v.i.* **1** to break up or leave

camp. **2** to take oneself off, to abscond. [f. F (as DE-, CAMP[1])]

decanal /dɪˈkeɪn(ə)l, ˈdekə-/ *adj.* of a dean; of the dean's or south side of a choir. [f. L (*decanus* dean)]

decant /dɪˈkænt/ *v.t.* to pour off (wine, liquid, a solution) leaving a sediment behind; to transfer as if by pouring. [f. L *decanthare* f. Gk *kanthos* lip of beaker]

decanter /dɪˈkæntə(r)/ *n.* a stoppered glass bottle into which wine or spirit is decanted. [f. prec.]

decapitate /dɪˈkæpɪteɪt/ *v.t.* to behead. —**decapitation** /-ˈteɪʃ(ə)n/ *n.* [f. L (DE-, *caput* head)]

decapod /ˈdekəpɒd/ *n.* a ten-footed crustacean, e.g. a crab. [f. F f. L f. Gk (as DECA-, *pous pod-* foot)]

decarbonize /diːˈkɑːbənaɪz/ *v.t.* to remove the carbon from (an internal-combustion engine etc.). —**decarbonization** /-ˈzeɪʃ(ə)n/ *n.* [f. DE- + CARBON]

decathlon /dɪˈkæθlən/ *n.* an athletic contest in which each competitor takes part in the ten different events which it comprises. [f. Gk *deka* ten, *athlon* contest]

decay /dɪˈkeɪ/ *v.t./i.* **1** to rot or decompose, to cause to do this. **2** to decline or cause to decline in quality, power, wealth, energy, beauty, etc. **3** (of a substance) to undergo change by radioactivity. —*n.* **1** a rotten or ruinous state. **2** decline in health, loss of quality. **3** radioactive change. [f. OF f. L (DE-, *cadere* fall)]

decease /dɪˈsiːs/ *n.* (chiefly *Law*) death. —*v.i.* to die. [f. OF f. L *decessus* (*cedere* go)]

deceased *adj.* dead. —*n.* a person who has died (esp. recently). [f. prec.]

deceit /dɪˈsiːt/ *n.* the concealing of truth in order to mislead, a dishonest trick; the tendency to use deceit. —**deceitful** *adj.*, **deceitfully** *adv.*, **deceitfulness** *n.* [as foll.]

deceive /dɪˈsiːv/ *v.t./i.* **1** to make (a person) believe what is false, to mislead purposely; to use deceit. **2** to be unfaithful to, esp. sexually. —**deceive oneself,** to persist in a mistaken belief. —**deceiver** *n.* [f. OF f. L *decipere* (DE-, *capere* take)]

decelerate /diːˈseləreɪt/ *v.t./i.* to reduce the speed (of). —**deceleration** /-ˈreɪʃ(ə)n/ *n.* [f. DE-, after ACCELERATE]

December /dɪˈsembə(r)/ *n.* the twelfth month of the year. [f. OF f. L (*decem* ten, because orig. the tenth month in the Roman calendar)]

decency /ˈdiːs(ə)nsɪ/ *n.* correct and tasteful behaviour; compliance with recognized propriety; avoidance of obscenity; (in *pl.*) the requirements of correct behaviour. [f. L (as DECENT)]

decennial /dɪˈsenɪ(ə)l/ *adj.* lasting for ten years; recurring every ten years. [f. L (*decem* ten, *annus* year)]

decent /ˈdiːs(ə)nt/ *adj.* **1** seemly, not immodest or obscene or indelicate; respectable. **2** acceptable, quite good. **3** (*colloq.*) kind, obliging. —**decently** *adv.* [f. F or L (*decēre* be seemly)]

decentralize /diːˈsentrəlaɪz/ *v.t.* to transfer from a central to a local authority; to distribute among local centres. —**decentralization** /-ˈzeɪʃ(ə)n/ *n.*

deception /dɪˈsepʃ(ə)n/ *n.* deceiving, being deceived; a thing that deceives. [f. OF or L (as DECEIVE)]

deceptive /dɪˈseptɪv/ *adj.* apt to mislead, easily mistaken for something else. —**deceptively** *adv.* [as prec.]

deci- *in comb.* one-tenth. [f. L *decimus* tenth]

decibel /ˈdesɪb(e)l/ *n.* a unit used in the comparison of power levels in electrical communication or the intensities of sounds, freq. used to express a single power level or sound intensity relative to some reference level (stated or understood).

decide /dɪˈsaɪd/ *v.t./i.* to bring or come to a resolution; to settle (an issue etc.) in favour of one side or another; to give a judgement. [f. F or L (DE-, *caedere* cut)

decided *adj.* **1** (usu. *attrib.*) definite, unquestionable. **2** having clear opinions, determined. —**decidedly** *adv.* [f. prec.]

decider *n.* a game, race, etc., to decide between competitors finishing equal in a previous contest. [f. DECIDE]

deciduous /dɪˈsɪdjʊəs/ *adj.* (of a tree) shedding its leaves annually; (of leaves, horns, teeth, etc.) shed periodically or normally. [f. L [DE-, *cadere* fall)]

decigram /ˈdesɪgræm/ *n.* a metric unit of mass, equal to one-tenth of a gram.

decilitre /ˈdesɪliːtə(r)/ *n.* a metric unit of capacity, equal to one-tenth of a litre.

decimal /ˈdesɪm(ə)l/ *adj.* of tenths or ten, proceeding or reckoning by tens; of decimal coinage. —*n.* a decimal fraction. —**decimal coinage** *or* **currency,** that in which the units are decimal multiples or fractions of each other. **decimal fraction,** one with a power of 10 as the denominator, especially when written as figures after the decimal point. **decimal point,** the dot placed after the unit figure in the decimal notation. **decimal system,** that in which each denomination, weight, or measure is 10 times the value of the one immediately below it. [f. L *decimus* tenth (*decem* ten)]

decimalize /ˈdesɪməlaɪz/ *v.t.* to express as a decimal, to convert to a decimal system. —**decimalization** /-ˈzeɪʃ(ə)n/ *n.* [f. prec.]

decimate /ˈdesɪmeɪt/ *v.t.* to destroy one-tenth of; (D) to destroy a large proportion of.

—**decimation** /-ˈmeɪʃ(ə)n/ *n.* [f. L *decimare* take the tenth man (*decimus* tenth), referring to the ancient Roman custom of putting to death one in every ten soldiers taking part in a mutiny or similar crime]

decimetre /ˈdesɪmiːtə(r)/ *n.* a metric unit of length, equal to one-tenth of a metre.

decipher /dɪˈsaɪfə(r)/ *v.t.* to convert (a text written in cipher or unfamiliar script) into an understandable script or language; to establish the meaning of (poor writing, anything puzzling). —**decipherment** *n.*

decipherable *adj.* able to be deciphered. [f. prec.]

decision /dɪˈsɪʒ(ə)n/ *n.* **1** an act of deciding. **2** settlement (of an issue etc.). **3** a conclusion reached, a resolve made. **4** the tendency to decide firmly. [f. OF or L (as DECIDE)]

decisive /dɪˈsaɪsɪv/ *adj.* **1** that decides an issue or contributes to a decision. **2** showing decision and firmness, positive. —**decisively** *adv.* [f. F f. L (as prec.)]

deck *n.* **1** a platform in a ship covering the hull's area (or part of this) at any level and serving as a floor; a ship's accommodation on a particular deck. **2** a floor or compartment of a bus etc. **3** the component that carries the magnetic tape, disc, etc., in sound-reproduction equipment or a computer. **4** (*US*) a pack of cards. **5** (*slang*) the ground. —*v.t.* **1** to furnish with or cover as a deck. **2** (often with *out*) to array, to adorn. —**below deck(s)**, in(to) the space under the main deck. **deck-chair** *n.* a portable folding chair (orig. used on deck in passenger ships). **deck-hand** *n.* a man employed on a ship's deck in cleaning and odd jobs. [f. MDu., = roof, cloak]

-decker *in comb.* having a specified number of decks. [f. DECK]

declaim /dɪˈkleɪm/ *v.t./i.* to speak or utter rhetorically or affectedly; to practise oratory; to inveigh *against*. —**declamation** /dekləˈmeɪʃ(ə)n/ *n.*, **declamatory** /dɪˈklæmətərɪ/ *adj.* [f. F or L (as CLAIM)]

declaration /dekləˈreɪʃ(ə)n/ *n.* declaring; an emphatic or deliberate statement; a formal announcement. [f. L (as DECLARE)]

declare /dɪˈkleə(r)/ *v.t./i.* **1** to announce openly or formally; to pronounce; to assert emphatically; (in *p.p.*) that is such by his own admission. **2** to acknowledge the possession of (dutiable goods, income, etc.). **3** (in cricket) to choose to close one's side's innings before all the wickets have fallen. **4** to name the trump suit in a card-game. —**declare oneself**, to reveal one's intentions or identity. —**declarative** /-ˈklærətɪv/ *adj.*, **declaratory** /-ˈklærətərɪ/ *adj.* [f. L *declarare* (DE-, *clarus* clear)]

declension /dɪˈklenʃ(ə)n/ *n.* **1** variation of the form of a noun etc. to give its grammatical case; the class by which a noun etc. is declined. **2** falling-off, deterioration. [f. OF (as DECLINE)]

declination /deklɪˈneɪʃ(ə)n/ *n.* **1** a downward bend. **2** the angular distance of a star etc. north or south of the celestial equator. **3** the deviation of a compass needle east or west from the true north. —**declinational** *adj.* [f. L (as foll.)]

decline /dɪˈklaɪn/ *v.t./i.* **1** to deteriorate, to lose strength or vigour, to decrease. **2** to refuse (an invitation or challenge) formally and courteously; to give or send a refusal. **3** to slope downwards; to bend down, to droop. **4** (*Gram.*) to give the forms of (a noun or adjective) corresponding to the cases. —*n.* **1** declining, a gradual loss of vigour etc. **2** deterioration, decay. [f. OF f. L *declinare* (DE-, *clinare* bend)]

declivity /dɪˈklɪvɪtɪ/ *n.* a downward slope. [f. L *declivitas* (DE-, *clivus* slope)]

declutch /diːˈklʌtʃ/ *v.i.* to disengage the clutch of a motor vehicle.

decoct /dɪˈkɒkt/ *v.t.* to make a decoction of. [f. L *decoquere* boil down]

decoction /dɪˈkɒkʃ(ə)n/ *n.* boiling down to extract an essence; the essence produced. [f. OF or L (as prec.)]

decode /diːˈkəʊd/ *v.t.* to convert (a coded message) into an understandable language.

decoke /diːˈkəʊk/ *v.t.* (*colloq.*) to decarbonize. —*n.* (*colloq.*) the process of decarbonizing.

décolletage /deɪkɒlˈtɑːʒ/ *n.* a low neckline of a woman's dress etc. [F (DE-, *collet* collar of dress)]

décolleté /deɪˈkɒlteɪ/ *adj.* having a low neckline. [F (as prec.)]

decompose /diːkəmˈpəʊz/ *v.t./i.* **1** to decay, to rot. **2** to separate (a substance) into its elements. —**decomposition** /-kɒmpəˈzɪʃ(ə)n/ *n.*

decompress /diːkəmˈpres/ *v.t.* to subject to decompression.

decompression /diˈkəmˈpreʃ(ə)n/ *n.* release from compression; the gradual reduction of air pressure on a person who has been subjected to it (especially underwater). —**decompression chamber**, an enclosed space for this. **decompression sickness**, the condition caused by a sudden lowering of the air pressure and the formation of bubbles in the blood.

decongestant /diːkənˈdʒest(ə)nt/ *n.* a medicinal substance that relieves congestion.

decontaminate /diːkənˈtæmɪneɪt/ *v.t.* to remove (esp. radioactive) contamination from. —**decontamination** /-ˈneɪʃ(ə)n/ *n.*

décor /ˈdeɪkɔː(r), de-/ *n.* the furnishing and decoration of a room or stage. [F (as foll.)]

decorate /ˈdekəreɪt/ *v.t.* **1** to furnish with adornments; to serve as an adornment to. **2** to paint or paper etc. (a room or house). **3** to invest with an order, medal, or other award. —**Decorated style,** a style of English Gothic architecture (*c.*1250–1350) with increasing use of decoration. —**decorative** /ˈdekərətɪv/ *adj.* [f. L *decorare* (*decus* beauty)]

decoration /dekəˈreɪʃ(ə)n/ *n.* **1** decorating; a thing that decorates; (in *pl.*) flags etc. put up on a festive occasion. **2** a medal etc. conferred and worn as an honour. [f. F or L (as prec.)]

decorator /ˈdekəreɪt(ə)r/ *n.* a person who decorates, especially one who paints or papers houses professionally. [f. DECORATE]

decorous /ˈdekərəs/ *adj.* having or showing decorum. —**decorously** *adv.* [f. L *decorus* seemly]

decorum /diˈkɔːrəm/ *n.* behaviour or usage conforming with decency or politeness, seemliness. [L (as prec.)]

decoy /ˈdiːkɔɪ/ *n.* a thing or person used to lure an animal or other person into a trap or danger; a bait, an enticement. —/dɪˈkɔɪ/ *v.t.* to lure by means of a decoy. [perh. f. Du. (*de* the, *kooi* f. L *cavea* cave)]

decrease /dɪˈkriːs/ *v.t./i.* to make or become smaller or fewer. —/ˈdiː-/ *n.* decreasing; the amount by which a thing decreases. [f. OF f. L *decrescere* (DE-, *crescere* grow)]

decree /dɪˈkriː/ *n.* an official or authoritative order having legal force; a judgement or decision of certain law-courts. —*v.t.* to ordain by decree. —**decree nisi** /ˈnaɪsaɪ/, a provisional order for divorce, made absolute unless cause to the contrary is shown within a fixed period (L *nisi* unless). [f. OF f. L *decretum* thing decided]

decrepit /dɪˈkrepɪt/ *adj.* weakened by age or hard use, dilapidated. —**decrepitude** *n.* [f. L (DE-, *crepare* creak)]

decretal /dɪˈkriːt(ə)l/ *n.* a papal decree. [f. L (as DECREE)]

decry /dɪˈkraɪ/ *v.t.* to disparage, to depreciate.

dedicate /ˈdedɪkeɪt/ *v.t.* to devote to a sacred person or purpose; to devote (esp. *oneself*) to a special task or purpose; (of an author or composer) to address (a book, piece of music, etc.) *to* a person as an honour or recognition; (in *p.p.*) devoted to a vocation etc., having single-minded loyalty. —**dedicator** *n.* [f. L *dedicare* (DE-, *dicare* declare)]

dedication /dedɪˈkeɪʃ(ə)n/ *n.* dedicating; the words with which a book etc. is dedicated. [f. OF or L (as prec.)]

dedicatory /ˈdedɪkeɪtərɪ/ *adj.* of or forming a dedication. [f. DEDICATE]

deduce /dɪˈdjuːs/ *v.t.* to infer, to draw as a logical conclusion. —**deducible** *adj.* [f. L *deducere* (DE-, *ducere* lead)]

deduct /dɪˈdʌkt/ *v.t.* to subtract, to take away; to withhold (a portion or amount). [f. L (as prec.)]

deductible *adj.* that may be deducted, especially from one's tax or taxable income. [f. prec.]

deduction /dɪˈdʌkʃ(ə)n/ *n.* **1** deducting; an amount deducted. **2** deducing, the inferring of particular instances from a general law. **3** a conclusion reached. [f. OF or L (as DEDUCE)]

deductive *adj.* of or reasoning by deduction. [f. L (as DEDUCE)]

dee *n.* the letter D; a thing shaped like this. [name of the letter]

deed *n.* **1** a thing consciously done; a brave, skilful, or conspicuous act. **2** actual fact, performance. **3** a document effecting the legal transfer of ownership and bearing the disposer's signature. —**deed-box** *n.* a strong box for keeping deeds and other documents. **deed of covenant,** an agreement to pay a regular amount annually to a charity etc., enabling the charity to recover the tax paid by the donor on this amount of his outcome. **deed poll,** a deed made by one party only, especially to change a name. [OE, rel. to DO¹]

deem *v.t.* to regard, to consider, to judge. [OE]

deemster /ˈdiːmstə(r)/ *n.* either of the two judges in the Isle of Man. [f. prec.]

deep *adj.* **1** extending far down or in from the top, surface, or edge; extending to or lying at a specified depth. **2** situated far down, back, or in. **3** coming or brought from far down or in; low-pitched, full-toned, not shrill. **4** intense, vivid, extreme. **5** heartfelt, absorbing; fully absorbed or overwhelmed. **6** profound, penetrating, difficult to understand. —*n.* **1** a deep place (esp. *the* sea) or state. **2** the position of a fieldsman distant from the batsman in cricket. —*adv.* deeply; far down or in. —**deep-fry** *v.t.* to fry (food) in fat or oil that covers it. **deep-laid** *adj.* (of a scheme) secret and elaborate. **deep-rooted, -seated** *adjs.* (of feelings or convictions) firmly established, profound. **go off the deep end,** to give way to anger or emotion. **in deep water,** in trouble or difficulty. —**deeply** *adv.*, **deepness** *n.* [OE]

deepen *v.t./i.* to make or become deep or deeper. [f. DEEP]

deep-freeze /diːpˈfriːz/ *n.* a freezer; storage in a freezer. —*v.t.* (*past* **deep-froze**; *p.p.* **deep-frozen**) to store in a deep-freeze.

deer *n.* (*pl.* same) a four-footed ruminant animal of the family Cervidae, of which the male usually has antlers. [OE]

deerskin *n.* leather from a deer's skin.

deerstalker /ˈdɪəstɔːkə(r)/ *n.* a soft cloth cap with peaks in front and behind.

deface /dɪˈfeɪs/ *v.t.* to spoil the appearance of; to make illegible. —**defacement** *n.*

de facto /diː ˈfæktəʊ, deɪ/ in fact, existing in fact (whether by right or not). [L]

defalcate /ˈdiːfælkeɪt/ *v.i.* to misappropriate

money. —**defalcator** *n.* [f. L *defalcare* lop with a sickle (DE-, *falx* sickle)]

defalcation /di:fælˈkeɪʃ(ə)n/ *n.* **1** misappropriation of money; the amount misappropriated. **2** a shortcoming. [f. prec.]

defame /dɪˈfeɪm/ *v.t.* to attack the good reputation of, to speak ill of. —**defamation** /defəˈmeɪʃ(ə)n/ *n.*, **defamatory** /dɪˈfæmətərɪ/ *adj.* [f. OF f. L *diffamare* (DIS-, *fama* report)]

default /dɪˈfɔ:lt, -ˈfɒlt/ *n.* failure to fulfil an obligation, especially to appear, pay, or act in some way. —*v.i.* to fail to meet an (esp. pecuniary) obligation. —**go by default,** to be absent, to be ignored because of absence. **in default of,** because of or in case of the lack or absence of. [f. OF f. L (as FAIL)]

defaulter *n.* one who defaults, especially a soldier guilty of a military offence. [f. prec.]

defeat /dɪˈfi:t/ *v.t.* to overcome in a battle or other contest; to frustrate, to baffle. —*n.* defeating, being defeated. [f. AF f. L *disfacere* (DIS-, *facere* do)]

defeatist *n.* one who expects or accepts defeat too readily. —**defeatism** *n.* [f. prec.]

defecate /ˈdi:fɪkeɪt/ *v.i.* to expel faeces from the bowels. —**defecation** /-ˈkeɪʃ(ə)n/ *n.* [f. L *defaecere* purify (DE-, *faex* dregs)]

defect /dɪˈfekt/ *n.* /also ˈdi:-/ a lack of something essential to adequacy or completeness, an imperfection; a shortcoming, a failing. —*v.i.* to abandon one's country or cause in favour of another. —**defector** *n.* [f. L *deficere* fail]

defection /dɪˈfekʃ(ə)n/ *n.* the abandonment of one's country or cause. [f. L (as prec.)]

defective /dɪˈfektɪv/ *adj.* **1** having defects, imperfect, incomplete. **2** mentally subnormal. —**defectively** *adv.*, **defectiveness** *n.* [f. OF or L (as DEFECT)]

defence /dɪˈfens/ *n.* **1** defending from or resistance against attack; a means of achieving this; (in *pl.*) fortifications etc. **2** a justification put forward in response to an accusation. **3** the defendant's case in a lawsuit; counsel for the defendant. **4** the players in the defending position in a game. —**defence mechanism,** the body's reaction against disease organisms; a mental process avoiding conscious conflict. [f. OF f. L (as DEFEND)]

defenceless *adj.* having no defence, unable to defend oneself. [f. prec. + -LESS]

defend /dɪˈfend/ *v.t./i.* **1** to resist an attack made on, to protect. **2** to uphold by argument, to speak or write in favour of; to conduct the defence in a lawsuit. —**defender** *n.* [f. OF f. L *defendere* (DE-, *fendere* strike)]

defendant *n.* the person accused or sued in a lawsuit. [f. prec.]

defensible /dɪˈfensɪb(ə)l/ *adj.* able to be defended or justified. —**defensibility** /-ˈbɪlɪtɪ/ *n.*, **defensibly** *adv.* [f. L (as DEFEND)]

defensive *adj.* done or intended for defence, protective. —**on the defensive,** in an attitude or position of defence; expecting criticism. —**defensively** *adv.* [f. F f. L (as DEFEND)]

defer[1] /dɪˈfɜ:(r)/ *v.t.* (**-rr-**) to put off to a later time, to postpone. —**deferred payment,** payment by instalments for goods supplied. **deferred shares** (*or* **stock**), shares or stock with the least entitlement to a dividend. —**deferment** *n.*, **deferral** *n.* [orig. same as DIFFER]

defer[2] /dɪˈfɜ:(r)/ *v.i.* (**-rr-**) to yield or make concessions in opinion or action (*to* a person). [f. F f. L *deferre* confer, give]

deference /ˈdefərəns/ *n.* courteous regard, compliance with another's wishes or advice. —**in deference to,** out of respect for. [f. F (as prec.)]

deferential /defəˈrenʃ(ə)l/ *adj.* showing deference. —**deferentially** *adv.* [f. prec.]

defiance /dɪˈfaɪəns/ *n.* defying, open disobedience, bold resistance. [f. OF (as DEFY)]

defiant /dɪˈfaɪənt/ *adj.* showing defiance. —**defiantly** *adv.* [f. prec.]

deficiency /dɪˈfɪʃ(ə)nsɪ/ *n.* being deficient; a lack or shortage (*of*); a thing lacking, a deficit. —**deficiency disease,** a disease caused by lack of some essential element in the diet. [f. foll.]

deficient /dɪˈfɪʃ(ə)nt/ *adj.* incomplete or insufficient in some essential respect. [f. L *deficere* be lacking]

deficit /ˈdefɪsɪt/ *n.* the amount by which a total falls short of what is required; the excess of liabilities over assets. [f. F f. L (as prec.)]

defile[1] /dɪˈfaɪl/ *v.t.* to make dirty, to pollute; to corrupt. —**defilement** *n.* [for earlier *defoul* f. OF, = trample down]

defile[2] /dɪˈfaɪl/ *n.* /also ˈdi:-/ a gorge or pass through which troops etc. can pass only in file. —*v.i.* to march in file. [f. F (as DE-, FILE[1])]

definable /dɪˈfaɪnəb(ə)l/ *adj.* able to be defined. [f. foll.]

define /dɪˈfaɪn/ *v.t.* **1** to give the exact meaning of (a word etc.). **2** to describe or explain the scope of. **3** to outline clearly, to mark out the boundary of. [f. OF f. L *definire* finish (*finis* boundary)

definite /ˈdefɪnɪt/ *adj.* having exact and discernible limits; clear and distinct, not vague. —**definite article,** see ARTICLE. —**definitely** *adv.* [f. L (as prec.)]

definition /defɪˈnɪʃ(ə)n/ *n.* **1** defining; a statement of the precise meaning of a word etc. **2** the degree of distinctness in the outline of an object or image. [f. OF f. L (as prec.)]

definitive /dɪˈfɪnɪtɪv/ *adj.* (of an answer, treaty, verdict, etc.) final, decisive, unconditional; (of an edition of a book etc.) most authoritative. [as prec.]

deflate /dɪˈfleɪt/ *v.t./i.* **1** to let out the air or gas from (a balloon, tyre, etc.). **2** to lose or cause to lose confidence or conceit. **3** to apply deflation to (the economy), to pursue a policy of deflation. [f. DE- + INFLATE]

deflation /dɪˈfleɪʃ(ə)n/ *n.* deflating; reduction of the amount of money in circulation to increase its value as a measure against inflation. —**deflationary** *adj.* [f. prec.]

deflect /dɪˈflekt/ *v.t./i.* to turn aside from a straight course or intended purpose; to deviate or cause to deviate (*from*). —**deflexion, deflection** *ns.*, **deflector** *n.* [f. L *deflectere* (DE-, *flectere* bend)]

deflower /diːˈflaʊə(r)/ *v.t.* **1** to deprive (a woman) of virginity; to ravage. **2** to remove the flowers from (a plant). [f. OF f. L (as DE-, FLOWER)]

defoliate /diːˈfəʊlɪeɪt/ *v.t.* to remove the leaves from, especially as a military tactic. —**defoliant** *n.*, **defoliation** /-ˈeɪʃ(ə)n/ *n.* [f. L *defoliare* (DE-, *folium* leaf)]

deform /dɪˈfɔːm/ *v.t.* to spoil the appearance or form of, to put out of shape. —**deformation** /diːfɔːˈmeɪʃ(ə)n/ *n.* [f. L *deformare* (DE- *forma* shape)]

deformed *adj.* misshapen. [f. prec.]

deformity /dɪˈfɔːmɪtɪ/ *n.* deformed state; a malformation, especially of a body or limb. [as DEFORM]

defraud /dɪˈfrɔːd/ *v.t.* to cheat by fraud. [f. OF or L (DE-, *fraus* fraud)]

defray /dɪˈfreɪ/ *v.t.* to provide the money to pay (a cost or expense). —**defrayal** *n.* [f. F f. L *fredum* fine]

defrost /diːˈfrɒst/ *v.t.* to remove the frost or ice from; to unfreeze (frozen food).

deft *adj.* neatly skilful or dextrous, adroit. —**deftly** *adv.*, **deftness** *n.* [var. of DAFT in obs. sense 'meek']

defunct /dɪˈfʌŋkt/ *adj.* no longer existing or in use; extinct, dead. [f. L (DE-, p.p. of *fungi* perform)]

defuse /diːˈfjuːz/ *v.t.* to remove the fuse from (an explosive, a bomb); to reduce the tension or potential danger in (a crisis, difficulty, etc.).

defy /dɪˈfaɪ/ *v.t.* **1** to resist openly, to refuse to obey. **2** (of a thing) to present insuperable obstacles to. **3** to challenge (a person) to do or prove something. [f. OF f. L *fides* faith]

degauss /diːˈgaʊs/ *v.t.* to demagnetize; to neutralize the magnetism of (a ship) by means of an encircling current-carrying conductor, as a precaution against magnetic mines.

degenerate[1] /dɪˈdʒenərət/ *adj.* having lost the qualities that are normal and desirable or proper to its kind. —*n.* a degenerate person or animal. —**degeneracy** *n.* [as foll.]

degenerate[2] /dɪˈdʒenəreɪt/ *v.i.* to become worse or lower in standard; to become degenerate. —**degeneration** /-ˈreɪʃ(ə)n/ *n.* [f. L (*degener* ignoble, f. DE-, *genus* race)]

degrade /dɪˈgreɪd/ *v.t.* **1** to reduce to a lower rank. **2** to bring into dishonour or contempt. **3** to reduce to a lower organic type or a simpler structure. —**degradation** /degrəˈdeɪʃ(ə)n/ *n.* [f. OF f. L *degradare* (DE-, *gradus* step)]

degrading /dɪˈgreɪdɪŋ/ *adj.* humiliating, lowering one's self-respect. [f. prec.]

degree /dɪˈgriː/ *n.* **1** a stage in an ascending or descending series; a stage in intensity or amount etc.; a category of crime or criminality; a step in direct genealogical descent. **2** a unit of measurement in an angle or arc; a unit in a scale of temperature, hardness, etc. **3** an academic diploma awarded for proficiency in a specified subject, or as an honour. —**by degrees**, a little at a time, gradually. [f. OF f. L (DE-, *gradus* step)

dehisce /dɪˈhɪs/ *v.i.* to gape, to burst open (especially of a seed-vessel). —**dehiscence** *n.*, **dehiscent** *adj.* [f. L *dehiscere* (DE-, *hiscere* begin to gape)]

dehumanize /diːˈhjuːmənaɪz/ *v.t.* to remove human characteristics from; to make impersonal. —**dehumanization** /-ˈzeɪʃ(ə)n/ *n.* [f. DE- + HUMAN]

dehydrate /diːˈhaɪdreɪt/ *v.t./i.* to remove the water or moisture from; to make or become dry. —**dehydration** /-ˈdreɪʃ(ə)n/ *n.* [f. DE- + Gk *hudōr* water]

de-ice /diːˈaɪs/ *v.t.* to remove the ice from; to prevent the formation of ice on. —**de-icer** *n.*

deify /diːˈɪfaɪ/ *v.t.* to make a god of; to regard or worship as a god. —**deification** /-fɪˈkeɪʃ(ə)n/ *n.* [f. OF f. L *deificare* (*deus* god)]

deign /deɪn/ *v.i.* to think fit or condescend *to* do. [f. OF f. L *dignari* (*dignus* worthy)]

deism /ˈdiːɪz(ə)m/ *n.* belief in the existence of a god (creator of the world) without accepting revelation (cf. THEISM). —**deist** *n.*, **deistic** /-ˈɪstɪk/ *adj.* [f. L *deus* god]

deity /ˈdiːɪtɪ, (D) ˈdeɪ-/ *n.* divine status or nature; a god; **the Deity**, God. [f. OF f. L (as prec.)]

déjà vu /deɪʒɑː ˈvuː/ the illusory feeling of having already experienced a present situation; something tediously familiar. [F, = already seen]

deject /dɪˈdʒekt/ *v.t.* (often in *p.p.*) to put in low spirits, to depress. —**dejectedly** *adv.*, **dejection** *n.* [f. L *dejicere* cast down (DE-, *jacere* throw)]

de jure /diː ˈdʒʊərɪ, deɪ ˈjʊəreɪ/ rightful; by right. [L]

dekko /ˈdekəʊ/ *n.* (*slang*) a look. [f. Hindi]

delay /dɪˈleɪ/ *v.t./i.* to make or be late, to hinder; to postpone, to defer; to wait, to loiter. —*n.* an act or process of delaying; a hindrance; the time lost by inaction or inability to proceed. —**delayed-action** *adj.* operating after an interval of time. [f. OF (prob. as DIS-, *laier* leave)]

delectable /dɪˈlektəb(ə)l/ *adj.* delightful, enjoyable. —**delectably** *adv.* [f. OF f. L (*delectare* delight)]

delectation /di:lekˈteɪʃ(ə)n/ *n.* enjoyment, delight. [f. OF (as prec.)]

delegacy /ˈdelɪgəsɪ/ *n.* a body of delegates. [f. foll.]

delegate /ˈdelɪgət/ *n.* a person appointed as a representative; a member of a deputation or committee. —/-geɪt/ *v.t.* to appoint or send as a representative; to entrust (a task) *to* an agent. [f. L *delegare* (DE-, *legare* depute)]

delegation /delɪˈgeɪʃ(ə)n/ *n.* **1** delegating. **2** a body of delegates. [as prec.]

delete /dɪˈli:t/ *v.t.* to cross out or remove (a letter, word, etc.). —**deletion** *n.* [f. L *delēre* efface]

deleterious /delɪtˈɪərɪəs/ *adj.* harmful to the body or mind. [f. L f. Gk]

delft *n.* (also **delftware**) a kind of glazed earthenware, usually decorated in blue, made at Delft in Holland. [name of town]

deliberate /dɪˈlɪbərət/ *adj.* **1** intentional, fully considered. **2** unhurried, slow and careful. —/-reɪt/ *v.i.* to think carefully (about); to take counsel. —**deliberately** *adv.* [f. L *deliberare* (DE-, *librare* weigh f. *libra* balance)]

deliberation /dɪlɪbəˈreɪʃ(ə)n/ *n.* careful consideration; careful slowness. [f. OF f. L (as prec.)]

deliberative /dɪˈlɪbərətɪv/ *adj.* of or for deliberation. [f. F or L (as DELIBERATE)]

delicacy /ˈdelɪkəsɪ/ *n.* **1** delicateness. **2** avoidance of immodesty or giving offence. **3** a choice food. [f. foll.]

delicate /ˈdelɪkət/ *adj.* **1** fine or pleasing in texture or construction etc.; (of colour or taste etc.) pleasantly subtle, not strong. **2** deft, sensitive; (esp. of actions) considerate. **3** tender, easily harmed; liable to illness; requiring deftness or tact. **4** avoiding coarseness or impropriety. —**delicately** *adv.*, **delicateness** *n.* [f. OF or L; orig. unkn.]

delicatessen /delɪkəˈtes(ə)n/ *n.* a shop selling prepared foods and delicacies; such food. [Du. or G f. F *délicatesse* (as prec.)]

delicious /dɪˈlɪʃəs/ *adj.* highly pleasing, especially to the taste or smell. —**deliciously** *adv.* [f. OF f. L (*deliçiae* delight)]

delight /dɪˈlaɪt/ *v.t./i.* **1** to please greatly. **2** to take great pleasure *in*; to be highly pleased *to* do. —*n.* great pleasure; a thing that gives it. [f. OF f. L *delectare*]

delightful *adj.* giving delight. —**delightfully** *adv.* [f. prec.]

delimit /dɪˈlɪmɪt/ *v.t.* to fix the limits or boundaries of. —**delimitation** /-ˈteɪʃ(ə)n/ *n.* [f. F f. L *delimitare* (DE-, *limes* boundary)]

delineate /dɪˈlɪnɪeɪt/ *v.t.* to show by a drawing or description. **delineation** /-ˈeɪʃ(ə)n/ *n.* [f. L *delineare* (DE-, *linea* line)]

delinquent /dɪˈlɪŋkwənt/ *adj.* committing an offence; failing in a duty. —*n.* an offender (esp. **juvenile delinquent**). —**delinquency** *n.* [f. L *delinquere* offend]

deliquesce /delɪˈkwes/ *v.i.* to become liquid, to melt; to dissolve in moisture absorbed from the air. —**deliquescence** *n.*, **deliquescent** *adj.* [f. L *deliquescere* begin to be liquid)]

delirious /dɪˈlɪrɪəs/ *adj.* affected with delirium; raving, wildly excited; ecstatic. —**deliriously** *adv.* [f. foll.]

delirium /dɪˈlɪrɪəm/ *n.* a disordered state of mind with incoherent speech and hallucinations; a mood of frenzied excitement. —**delirium tremens** /ˈtri:menz/, a form of delirium with tremors and terrifying delusions due to prolonged consumption of alcohol. [L, f. *delirare* be deranged, orig. = deviate from a ridge in ploughing]

deliver /dɪˈlɪvə(r)/ *v.t.* **1** to convey or distribute (letters or goods etc.) to a destination or destinations; to transfer possession of, to give *up* or hand *over* to another. **2** to utter (a speech or sermon); to aim or launch (a blow, attack, ball). **3** to set free, to rescue (*from*). **4** to assist at the birth of or in giving birth; (also **be delivered of**) to give birth to. —**deliver the goods**, (*colloq.*) to carry out one's part of a bargain. —**deliverer** *n.* [f. OF (as DE-, LIBERATE)]

deliverance *n.* rescue, setting free. [as prec.]

delivery *n.* delivering, being delivered; the periodical distribution of letters or goods etc.; the manner of delivering a ball, speech, etc. [f. AF (as DELIVER)]

dell *n.* a small wooded hollow. [OE, rel. to DALE]

delouse /di:ˈlaʊs/ *v.t.* to rid of lice.

Delphic /ˈdelfɪk/ *adj.* of or like the ancient Greek oracle at Delphi; obscure, enigmatic. [f. *Delphi*]

delphinium /delˈfɪnɪəm/ *n.* a garden plant of the genus *Delphinium*, with tall spikes of usually blue flowers. [L f. Gk, = larkspur (*delphin* dolphin)]

delta *n.* **1** the fourth letter of the Greek alphabet, = d. **2** a triangular alluvial tract at a river's mouth enclosed or watered by diverging outlets. **3** a designation of the fourth-brightest star in a constellation, or sometimes the star's position in a group. —**delta wing**, a triangular sweptback wing of an aircraft. —**deltaic** /delˈteɪɪk/ *adj.* [Gk, f. Phoenician *daleth* door]

delude /dɪˈlu:d/ *v.t.* to fool, to deceive. [f. L *deludere* (DE-, *ludere* play)]

deluge /ˈdelju:dʒ/ *n.* **1** a great flood; **the Deluge,** Noah's flood. **2** a heavy fall of rain. **3** an overwhelming rush. —*v.t.* to flood; to overwhelm. [f. OF f. L *diluvium*]

delusion /dɪˈlu:ʒ(ə)n/ *n.* a false belief or impression; a vain hope; a hallucination. —**delusive** *adj.* [f. L (as DELUDE)]

de luxe /də ˈlʌks, ˈlʊks/ of a superior kind or quality; sumptuous. [F, = of luxury]

delve *v.t./i.* **1** to search (*into* books etc.) for information. **2** (*archaic*) to dig. [OE]

demagnetize /di:ˈmægnɪtaɪz/ *v.t.* to remove the magnetization of. —**demagnetization** /-ˈzeɪʃ(ə)n/*n.*

demagogue /ˈdeməgɒg/ *n.* a political agitator appealing to popular wishes or prejudices. —**demagogic** /-ˈgɒgɪk/ *adj.*, **demagogy** /ˈdem-/ *n.* [f. Gk [*dēmos* people, *agōgos* leading)]

demand /dɪˈmɑ:nd/ *n.* **1** a request made as of right or peremptorily; an urgent claim. **2** popular desire for goods or services. —*v.t.* **1** to make a demand for. **2** to insist on being told. **3** to require, to call for. —**in demand,** much sought after. **on demand,** as soon as asked for. [f. OF f. L *demandare* (DE-, *mandare* to commission)]

demanding *adj.* requiring much skill or effort; making many demands. [f. prec.]

demarcation /di:mɑ:ˈkeɪʃ(ə)n/ *n.* the marking of a boundary or limits, especially between work considered by trade unions to belong to different trades. [f. Sp. (*demarcar* mark bounds of)]

démarche /ˈdeɪmɑ:ʃ/ *n.* a step or proceeding in diplomacy, especially one initiating a fresh policy. [F (*démarcher* take steps)]

dematerialize /di:məˈtɪərɪəlaɪz/ *v.t./i.* to make or become non-material or spiritual.

demean /dɪˈmi:n/ *v.t.* to lower the dignity of. [f. DE- + MEAN²]

demeanour /dɪˈmi:nə(r)/ *n.* bearing, outward behaviour. [f. OF (as DE-, L *minare* drive animals f. *minari* threaten)]

demented /dɪˈmentɪd/ *adj.* driven mad, crazy. [f. OF or L (*demens* out of one's mind)]

dementia /dɪˈmenʃə/ *n.* insanity with loss of intellectual power due to brain disease or injury. —**dementia praecox** /ˈpri:kɒks/, schizophrenia. [L (as prec.)]

demerara /deməˈreərə/ *n.* a kind of raw cane-sugar, originally and chiefly from Demerara, a region of Guyana, the crystals of which have a yellowish-brown colour.

demerit /di:ˈmerɪt/ *n.* a fault, an undesirable quality. [f. OF or L (*demerēri* deserve)]

demesne /dɪˈmi:n, -meɪn/ *n.* **1** the land attached to a mansion etc.; territory, a domain; landed property, an estate. **2** possession (of land) as one's own. **3** a region or sphere (*of*). [f. AF, = belonging to a lord, f. L (*dominus* lord)]

demi- /ˈdemɪ/ *prefix* half-. [f. F f. L *dimidius*]

demigod /ˈdemɪgɒd/ *n.* a partly divine being; the offspring of a mortal and a god or goddess; a godlike person.

demijohn /ˈdemɪdʒɒn/ *n.* a large bottle in a wicker case. [corruption of F *dame-jeanne* Lady Jane]

demilitarize /di:ˈmɪlɪtəraɪz/ *v.t.* to remove military organization or forces from (a zone etc.). —**demilitarization** /-ˈzeɪʃ(ə)n/ *n.*

demi-mondaine /demɪmɔ̃ˈdeɪn/ *n.* a woman of the *demi-monde.* [f. foll.]

demi-monde /ˈdemɪmɒnd/ *n.* **1** women of doubtful repute in society. **2** a group behaving with doubtful legality etc. [F, = half-world]

demise /dɪˈmaɪz/ *n.* **1** death. **2** transfer of an estate by lease or a will. —*v.t.* to transfer (an estate or title) to another. [f. AF, = abdicate (as DISMISS)]

demisemiquaver /demɪˈsemɪkweɪvə(r)/ *n.* a note in music equal to half a semiquaver.

demist /di:ˈmɪst/ *v.t.* to clear mist from (a windscreen etc.). —**demister** *n.*

demo /ˈdeməʊ/ *n.* (*pl.* **-os**) (*colloq.*) a demonstration, especially to express opinion. [abbr.]

demob /di:ˈmɒb/ *v.t.* (**-bb-**) (*colloq.*) to demobilize. [abbr.]

demobilize /di:ˈməʊbɪlaɪz/ *v.t.* to release from military service. —**demobilization** /-ˈzeɪʃ(ə)n/ *n.*

democracy /dɪˈmɒkrəsɪ/ *n.* **1** government by all the people, direct or representative; a State having this. **2** a form of society ignoring hereditary class distinctions and tolerating minority views. [f. F f. L f. Gk (*dēmos* the people, -CRACY)]

democrat /ˈdeməkræt/ *n.* **1** an advocate of democracy. **2** —**Democrat,** (*US*) a member of the Democratic Party. [f. F (as prec. + -CRAT)]

democratic /deməˈkrætɪk/ *adj.* of or according to democracy; supporting or constituting democracy. —**Democratic Party,** one of the two chief political parties in the USA (the other being the Republican Party). —**democratically** *adv.* [f. F f. L f. Gk (as DEMOCRACY)]

democratize /dɪˈmɒkrətaɪz/ *v.t.* to make democratic. —**democratization** /-ˈzeɪʃ(ə)n/ *n.* [f. DEMOCRATIC]

demodulation /di:mɒdjʊˈleɪʃ(ə)n/ *n.* the process of extracting a modulating radio signal from a modulated wave etc.

demography /dɪˈmɒgrəfɪ/ *n.* the study of statistics of births, deaths, diseases, etc., as illustrating the conditions of life in communities. —**demographic** /demə'græfɪk/ *adj.*, **demographically** *adv.* [f. Gk *dēmos* the people + -GRAPHY]

demolish /dɪ'mɒlɪʃ/ *v.t.* **1** to pull or knock down (a building); to destroy. **2** to refute (a theory); to overthrow (an institution). **3** (*joc.*) to eat up. —**demolition** /demə'lɪʃ(ə)n/ *n.* [f. F f. L *demoliri* (DE-, *moliri* construct)]

demon /'di:mən/ *n.* **1** a devil, an evil spirit; a cruel or forceful person; a personified evil passion. **2** (also **daemon**) a supernatural being in Greek mythology. —**demonic** /dɪ'mɒnɪk/ *adj.* [f. L f. Gk *daimōn* inferior deity, spirit]

demonetize /di:'mɒnɪtaɪz/ *v.t.* to withdraw (a coin etc.) from use as money. —**demonetization** /-'zeɪʃ(ə)n/ *n.* [f. F (as DE-, L *moneta* money)]

demoniac /dɪ'məʊnɪæk/ *adj.* **1** possessed by an evil spirit. **2** of or like a demon. **3** fiercely energetic, frenzied. —*n.* a demoniac person. —**demoniacal** /di:mə'naɪək(ə)l/ *adj.* [f. OF f. L f. Gk (*daimonion* dim. of *daimōn*; see prec.)]

demonology /di:mə'nɒlədʒɪ/ *n.* the study of beliefs about demons. [f. DEMON + -LOGY]

demonstrable /'demənstrəb(ə)l/ *adj.* able to be shown or proved. —**demonstrably** *adv.* [f. L (as foll.)]

demonstrate /'demənstreɪt/ *v.t./i.* **1** to show evidence of; to describe and explain by help of specimens or experiments; to prove the truth of logically. **2** to take part in a public demonstration. [f. L *demonstrare* (DE-, *monstrare* show)]

demonstration /demən'streɪʃ(ə)n/ *n.* **1** demonstrating; an instance of this. **2** a show of feeling. **3** an organized gathering or procession to express the opinion of a group publicly. **4** a display of military force. [f. OF or L (as prec.)]

demonstrative /dɪ'mɒnstrətɪv/ *adj.* **1** showing or proving. **2** given to or marked by the open expression of feelings. **3** (*Gram.*, of an adjective or pronoun) indicating the person or thing referred to (e.g. *this, those*). —**demonstratively** *adv.* [f. OF f. L (as DEMONSTRATE)]

demonstrator /'demənstreɪtə(r)/ *n.* one who demonstrates; one who teaches by demonstration, especially in a laboratory. [f. L (as DEMONSTRATE)]

demoralize /dɪ'mɒrəlaɪz/ *v.t.* to weaken the morale of, to dishearten. —**demoralization** /-'zeɪʃ(ə)n/ *n.* [f. F (as DE-, MORAL)]

demote /di:'məʊt/ *v.t.* to reduce to a lower rank or class. —**demotion** *n.* [f. DE- + PROMOTE]

demotic /dɪ'mɒtɪk/ *adj.* (of language or writing) of the popular form. —*n.* **1** demotic script, the popular simplified form of ancient Egyptian writing. **2** the popular form of modern Greek. [f. Gk (*dēmos* people)]

demur /dɪ'mɜ:(r)/ *v.t.* (**-rr-**) to raise objections, to be unwilling. —*n.* objecting (usu. in *without demur*). [f. OF f. L DE-, *morari* delay]

demure /dɪ'mjʊə(r)/ *adj.* quiet and serious or affectedly so. —**demurely** *adv.*, **demureness** *n.* [perh. f. p.p. of OF *demorer* remain (as prec.)]

demurrer /dɪ'mʌrə(r)/ *n.* a legal objection to the relevance of an opponent's point. [f. AF (as DEMUR)]

den *n.* **1** a wild beast's lair. **2** a place of crime or vice. **3** a small private room for study etc. [OE]

denarius /dɪ'neərɪəs/ *n.* (*pl.* **-rii** /-rɪaɪ/) an ancient Roman silver coin. [L (*deni* ten each)]

denary /'di:nərɪ/ *adj.* of ten, decimal. [f. L (as prec.)]

denationalize /di:'næʃ(ə)nəlaɪz/ *v.t.* to transfer (an industry, institution, etc.) from national to private ownership. —**denationalization** /-'zeɪʃ(ə)n/*n.*

denature /di:'neɪtʃə(r)/ *v.t.* **1** to change the nature or properties of. **2** to make (alcohol) unfit for drinking. [f. F (as DE-, NATURE)]

dendrochronology /dendrəʊkrə'nɒlədʒɪ/ *n.* a method of dating timber by study of its annual growth-rings. [f. Gk *dendron* tree + CHRONOLOGY]

dendrology /den'drɒlədʒɪ/ *n.* the study of trees. [f. Gk *dendron* tree + -LOGY]

dene /di:n/ *n.* a narrow wooded valley. [OE, rel. to DEN]

dengue /'deŋgɪ/ *n.* an infectious tropical fever causing acute pain in the joints. [West Indian Sp. f. Swahili]

deniable /dɪ'naɪəb(ə)l/ *adj.* able to be denied. [f. DENY]

denial /dɪ'naɪ(ə)l/ *n.* **1** denying. **2** refusal of a request or wish. **3** a statement that a thing is not true or existent. **4** a disavowal. [f. DENY]

denier /'denjə(r)/ *n.* a unit of weight for measuring the fineness of silk, rayon, or nylon yarn. [orig. name of small coin; f. OF f. L *denarius*]

denigrate /'denɪgreɪt/ *v.t.* to blacken the reputation of; to defame. —**denigration** /-'greɪʃ(ə)n/ *n.*, **denigrator** *n.* [f. L *denigrare* (DE-*niger* black)]

denim /'denɪm/ *n.* a twilled cotton fabric used for overalls, jeans, etc.; (in *pl.*) a garment made of this. [for *serge de Nim* (*Nîmes* in S. France)]

denizen /'denɪz(ə)n/ *n.* **1** an inhabitant or occupant (of a place). **2** a foreigner admitted to residence and certain rights. **3** a naturalized foreign word, animal, or plant. [f. AF (*deinz* within f. L *de intus*)]

denominate /dɪ'nɒmɪneɪt/ *v.t.* to give a name to; to call or describe (a person or thing) as. [f. L *denominare* (as DE-, NOMINATE)]

denomination /dɪnɒmɪˈneɪʃ(ə)n/ *n.* **1** a name or designation, especially a characteristic or class name. **2** a Church or religious sect. **3** a class of units of measurement or money. [f. OF or L (as prec.)]

denominational /dɪnɒmɪˈneɪʃ(ə)n(ə)l/ *adj.* of a particular religious denomination. [f. prec.]

denominator /dɪˈnɒmɪneɪtə(r)/ *n.* the number below the line in a vulgar fraction, showing how many parts the whole is divided into, the divisor. —**least** *or* **lowest common denominator,** the lowest common multiple of the denominators of several fractions; the common feature of the members of a group. [f. F or L (as DENOMINATE)]

denote /dɪˈnəʊt/ *v.t.* **1** to be the name for, to be the sign or symbol of. **2** to indicate, to give to understand; to signify. —**denotation** /diːnəʊˈteɪʃ(ə)n/ *n.* [f. F or L *denotare* (DE-, *notare* mark)]

dénouement /deɪˈnuːmɑ̃/ *n.* the unravelling of a plot, especially the final resolution in a play, novel, etc. [F, = unknotting]

denounce /dɪˈnaʊns/ *v.t.* **1** to inform against, to accuse publicly. **2** to announce withdrawal from (a treaty etc.). [f. OF f. L *denuntiare* make known (DE-, *nuntius* messenger)]

de novo /diː ˈnəʊvəʊ/ afresh, starting again. [L]

dense *adj.* **1** closely compacted in substance; crowded together. **2** crass, stupid. —**densely** *adv.*, **denseness** *n.* [f. F or L *densus*]

density /ˈdensɪtɪ/ *n.* **1** closeness of substance. **2** the degree of consistency measured by the quantity of mass in a unit volume. **3** the opacity of a photographic image. [f. F or L (as prec.)]

dent *n.* a depression in a surface left by a blow or pressure. —*v.t./i.* to make a dent in; to become dented. [prob. f. INDENT]

dental /ˈdent(ə)l/ *adj.* **1** of or for the teeth; of dentistry. **2** (of a consonant) pronounced with the tongue-tip against the upper front teeth or the ridge of the teeth. —**dental floss,** fine strong thread used to clean between the teeth. **dental surgeon,** a dentist. [f. L *dentalis* (*dens* tooth)]

dentate /ˈdenteɪt/ *adj.* toothed, having toothlike notches. [f. L *dentatus* (as prec.)]

dentifrice /ˈdentɪfrɪs/ *n.* a powder, paste, etc., for cleaning the teeth. [F f. L (*dens* tooth, *fricare* rub)]

dentine /ˈdentiːn/ *n.* the hard dense tissue forming the main part of teeth. [f. L *dens* tooth]

dentist /ˈdentɪst/ *n.* a person who is qualified to treat the teeth, extract them, fit artificial ones, etc. —**dentistry** *n.* [f. F f. L (*dens* tooth)]

dentition /denˈtɪʃ(ə)n/ *n.* **1** the type and arrangement of teeth in a species etc. **2** teething. [f. L (*dentire* teethe)]

denture /ˈdentʃə(r)/ *n.* a set of artificial teeth. [F f. L (as DENTAL)]

denude /dɪˈnjuːd/ *v.t.* to make naked or bare; to strip of a covering, property, etc. —**denudation** /diːnjuːˈdeɪʃ(ə)n/ *n.* [f. L *denudare* strip (DE-, *nudus* naked)]

denunciation /dɪnʌnsɪˈeɪʃ(ə)n/ *n.* denouncing. —**denunciatory** /dɪˈnʌnsɪətərɪ/ *adj.* [f. F or L (as DENOUNCE)]

deny /dɪˈnaɪ/ *v.t.* **1** to declare untrue or non-existent. **2** to disavow or repudiate. **3** to refuse (a request, applicant, thing *to* a person). —**deny oneself,** to restrict (one's food, drink, or pleasure). [f. OF f. L *denegare* (DE-, *negare* say no)]

deodar /ˈdiːədɑː(r)/ *n.* the Himalayan cedar (*Cedrus deodara*), the tallest of the cedars (sometimes 60 m in height), with pendulous tips to its slightly drooping branches and bearing large barrel-shaped cones. [f. Hindi f. Skr., = divine tree]

deodorant /dɪˈəʊdərənt/ *adj.* that removes or conceals unwanted odours. —*n.* a deodorant substance. [f. foll.]

deodorize /dɪˈəʊdəraɪz/ *v.t.* to destroy the odour of. —**deodorization** /-ˈzeɪʃ(ə)n/ *n.* [f. DE- + L *odor* smell]

deoxyribonucleic acid /dɪɒksɪraɪbəʊnjuːˈkliːɪk/ see DNA. [f. DE- + OXYGEN + RIBONUCLEIC]

dep. *abbr.* **1** departs. **2** deputy.

depart /dɪˈpɑːt/ *v.i.* to go away, to leave; (of a train, bus, etc.) to set out, to leave; to diverge or deviate. —**depart this life,** to die. [f. OF f. L *dispertire* divide]

departed *adj.* & *n.* bygone; (*the*) deceased. [f. prec.]

department *n.* **1** a separate part of a complex whole, a branch, especially of a municipal or State administration, university, or shop. **2** an administrative district in France etc. **3** an area of activity. —**department store,** a large shop supplying many kinds of goods from various departments. —**departmental** /diːpɑːtˈment(ə)l/ *adj.* [f. F (as DEPART)]

departure /dɪˈpɑːtʃə(r)/ *n.* **1** going away; a deviation *from* (the truth, a standard); the starting of a train, aircraft, etc. **2** setting out on a course of action or thought. [f. OF (as DEPART)]

depend /dɪˈpend/ *v.i.* **1** (with *on* or *upon*, or *absol.*) to be controlled or determined by. **2** (with *on* or *upon*) to be unable to do without, to need for success etc. **3** to trust confidently, to feel certain about. **4** (*archaic*) to hang down. [f. OF f. L *dependēre* (DE-, *pendēre* hang)]

dependable *adj.* that may be depended on. —**dependability** /-ˈbɪlɪtɪ/ *n.*, **dependably** *adv.* [f. prec.]

dependant *n.* one who depends on another for support. [f. F (as DEPEND)]

dependence *n.* depending, being dependent; reliance. [as prec.]

dependency *n.* a country or province controlled by another. [as DEPENDANT]

dependent *adj.* **1** depending (*on*). **2** unable to do without something (especially a drug). **3** maintained at another's cost. **4** (of a clause, phrase, or word) in a subordinate relation to a sentence or word. —*n.* (*US*) = DEPENDANT. [var. of DEPENDANT]

depict /dɪˈpɪkt/ *v.t.* to represent in drawing or colours; to portray in words, to describe. —**depiction** *n.* [f. L *depingere* (DE-, *pingere* paint)]

depilate /ˈdepɪleɪt/ *v.t.* to remove hair from. —**depilation** /-ˈleɪʃ(ə)n/ *n.* [f. L *depilare* (DE-, *pilus* hair)]

depilatory /dɪˈpɪlətərɪ/ *adj.* that removes unwanted hair. —*n.* a depilatory substance. [f. prec.]

deplete /dɪˈpliːt/ *v.t.* to empty, to exhaust; to reduce the numbers or quantity of. —**depletion** *n.* [f. L *deplere* (DE-, *plēre* fill)]

deplorable /dɪˈplɔːrəb(ə)l/ *adj.* lamentable, regrettable; exceedingly bad, shocking. —**deplorably** *adv.* [f. foll.]

deplore /dɪˈplɔː(r)/ *v.t.* to regret deeply; to find deplorable. [f. F or It. f. L *deplorare* (DE-, *plorare* bewail)]

deploy /dɪˈplɔɪ/ *v.t.* **1** to spread (troops) out from a column into a line. **2** to bring (forces, arguments, etc.) into effective action. —**deployment** *n.* [f. F f. L *displicare* scatter and *deplicare* explain (*plicare* fold)]

deponent /dɪˈpəʊnənt/ *adj.* (of a verb, esp. in Greek and Latin) passive in form but active in meaning. —*n.* **1** a deponent verb. **2** a person making a deposition under oath. [f. L *deponere* put down, lay aside]

depopulate /diːˈpɒpjʊleɪt/ *v.t.* to reduce the population of. —**depopulation** /-ˈleɪʃ(ə)n/ *n.* [f. L *depopulari* lay waste (DE-, *populus* people)]

deport /dɪˈpɔːt/ *v.t.* **1** to remove (an unwanted person) from a country. **2** to behave or conduct *oneself* (in a specified manner). [f. OF f. L *deportare* (DE-, *portare* carry)]

deportation /diːpɔːˈteɪʃ(ə)n/ *n.* the removal of an unwanted person from a country. [f. prec.]

deportee /diːpɔːˈtiː/ *n.* a person who has been or is to be deported. [f. DEPORT]

deportment /dɪˈpɔːtmənt/ *n.* bearing, behaviour. [f. F (as DEPORT)]

depose /dɪˈpəʊz/ *v.t./i.* **1** to remove from power; to dethrone. **2** to bear witness *that*, to testify *to*, especially on oath in court. [f. OF f. L (as foll.)]

deposit /dɪˈpɒzɪt/ *n.* **1** a thing stored or entrusted for safe-keeping; a sum placed in a bank. **2** a sum required and paid as a pledge or first instalment. **3** a layer of precipitated matter, a natural accumulation. —*v.t.* **1** to store or entrust for keeping (esp. a sum in a bank). **2** to pay as a pledge. **3** to lay down; (of water etc.) to leave (matter) lying. —**deposit account**, a savings account at a bank requiring notice for withdrawal. [f. p.p. of L *deponere* (as DEPONENT)]

depositary /dɪˈpɒzɪtərɪ/ *n.* a person to whom a thing is entrusted. [f. L (as prec.)]

deposition /depəˈzɪʃ(ə)n, diː-/ *n.* **1** deposing; a dethronement. **2** sworn evidence, the giving of this. **3** the taking down of Christ from the Cross. [f. OF f. L (as DEPOSE)]

depositor *n.* a person who deposits money or property. [f. DEPOSIT]

depository /dɪˈpɒzɪtərɪ/ *n.* a storehouse; = DEPOSITARY. [f. L (as DEPOSIT)]

depot /ˈdepəʊ/ *n.* **1** a storehouse, especially one for military supplies. **2** the headquarters of a regiment. **3** a place where goods are deposited or from which goods, vehicles, etc., are dispatched; a bus station; (*US*) a railway station. [f. F (as DEPOSIT)]

deprave /dɪˈpreɪv/ *v.t.* to make morally bad, to corrupt. —**depravation** /deprəˈveɪʃ(ə)n/ *n.* [f. OF or L *depravare* (DE-, *pravus* crooked)]

depravity /dɪˈprævɪtɪ/ *n.* moral corruption, wickedness. [f. DE- + obs. *pravity* f. L (as prec.)]

deprecate /ˈdeprɪkeɪt/ *v.t.* **1** to express a wish against or disapproval of. **2** to try to avert (a person's anger etc.). —**deprecation** /-ˈkeɪʃ(ə)n/ *n.*, **deprecatory** /ˈdeprɪkətərɪ/ *adj.* [f. L *deprecari* pray (a thing) away (DE-, *precari* pray)]

depreciate /dɪˈpriːʃɪeɪt/ *v.t./i.* **1** to diminish in value, price, or purchasing power. **2** to disparage, to belittle. [f. L *depretiare* (DE-, *pretiare* value f. *pretium* price)]

depreciation /dɪpriːʃɪˈeɪʃ(ə)n/ *n.* a decline in value, especially that due to wear and tear; the allowance made for this. [f. prec.]

depreciatory /dɪˈpriːʃətərɪ/ *adj.* disparaging. [f. DEPRECIATE]

depredation /deprɪˈdeɪʃ(ə)n/ *n.* (usu. in *pl.*) plundering, destruction. [f. F f. L (DE-, *praedari* plunder)]

depress /dɪˈpres/ *v.t.* **1** to lower the spirits of, to sadden. **2** to reduce the activity of (esp. trade). **3** to press down (a lever etc.). —**depressed area**, an area of economic depression. [f. OF f. L *depressare* (DE-, *premere* press)]

depressant *adj.* causing depression. —*n.* a depressant agent or influence. [f. prec.]

depression /dɪˈpreʃ(ə)n/ *n.* **1** a state of extreme dejection, often with physical symptoms. **2** a long period of financial and industrial slump.

3 a lowering of atmospheric pressure; the winds caused by this. **4** a sunken place or hollow on a surface. **5** pressing down. [as DEPRESS]

depressive *adj*. tending to depress; involving mental depression. —*n*. a person suffering from depression. [f. F or L (as DEPRESS)]

deprivation /deprɪˈveɪʃ(ə)n/ *n*. depriving; loss of a desired thing. [f. foll.]

deprive /dɪˈpraɪv/ *v.t.* to prevent from the use or enjoyment *of*; to dispossess or strip *of*. —**deprived child,** one lacking a normal home life. —**deprival** *n*. [f. OF f. L *deprivare* (DE-, *privare* deprive)]

Dept. *abbr*. Department.

depth *n*. **1** deepness; the measurement from the top down, from the surface inwards, or from the front to the back. **2** profundity, abstruseness; sagacity. **3** intensity of a colour, darkness, etc. **4** (often in *pl.*) the deepest or most central part. —**depth charge,** a bomb exploding under water, for dropping on a submerged submarine etc. **in depth,** thoroughly. **in-depth** *adj*. thorough. **out of one's depth,** in water too deep to stand in; engaged on a task beyond one's powers. [as DEEP]

deputation /depjʊˈteɪʃ(ə)n/ *n*. a body of persons appointed to represent others. [f. L (as foll.)]

depute /dɪˈpjuːt/ *v.t.* to delegate (a task) to a person; to appoint as one's deputy. [f. OF f. L *deputare* regard as, allot]

deputize /ˈdepjʊtaɪz/ *v.i.* to act as deputy (*for*). [f. foll.]

deputy /ˈdepjʊtɪ/ *n*. **1** a person appointed to act as a substitute for another. **2** a parliamentary representative in some countries. [f. p.p. of OF *deputer* (as DEPUTE)]

derail /dɪˈreɪl/ *v.t.* to cause (a train) to leave the rails. —**derailment** *n*. [f. F (as DE-, RAIL[1])]

derange /dɪˈreɪndʒ/ *v.t.* to throw into confusion, to disrupt; to make insane. —**derangement** *n*. [f. F (as DE-, *rang* rank, order)]

Derby /ˈdɑːbɪ/ *n*. **1** an annual horse-race for three-year-olds, run on Epsom Downs in England on the last Wednesday in May or the first Wednesday in June. **2** a similar race elsewhere. **3** an important sporting contest.

Derby. *abbr*. Derbyshire.

derelict /ˈderɪlɪkt/ *adj*. abandoned, left to fall into ruin (esp. of a ship at sea or decrepit property). —*n*. an abandoned property, especially a ship; a person forsaken by society, a social misfit. [f. L *derelictus* (DE-, *relinquere* leave behind)]

dereliction /derɪˈlɪkʃ(ə)n/ *n*. **1** abandoning, being abandoned. **2** neglect *of duty*. **3** a shortcoming. [f. L (as prec.)]

derestrict /diːrɪˈstrɪkt/ *v.t.* to remove a restriction (esp. a speed-limit) from. —**derestriction** *n*.

deride /dɪˈraɪd/ *v.t.* to laugh scornfully at; to treat with scorn. [f. L *deridēre* (DE-, *ridēre* laugh)]

de rigueur /də rɪˈgɜː(r)/ required by custom or etiquette. [F, = of strictness]

derision /dɪˈrɪʒ(ə)n/ *n*. scorn, ridicule. [f. OF f. L (as DERIDE)]

derisive /dɪˈraɪsɪv/ *adj*. scornful, showing derision. —**derisively** *adv*. [f. prec.]

derisory /dɪˈraɪsərɪ/ *adj*. **1** showing derision. **2** deserving derision; too insignificant for serious consideration. [f. L (as DERIDE)]

derivation /derɪˈveɪʃ(ə)n/ *n*. **1** deriving. **2** the formation of a word from a word or root; the tracing or a statement of this. [f. F or L (as DERIVE)]

derivative /dɪˈrɪvətɪv/ *adj*. derived from a source, not original. —*n*. **1** a derivative word or thing. **2** (*Math.*) a quantity measuring the rate of change of another. [f. F f. L (as foll.)]

derive /dɪˈraɪv/ *v.t./i.* **1** to trace or obtain *from* a source. **2** to originate, to be descended, *from*. **3** to show or assert the descent or formation of (a word etc.) *from*. [f. OF or L *derivare* (as DE-, *rivus* stream)]

dermatitis /dɜːməˈtaɪtɪs/ *n*. inflammation of the skin. [f. Gk *derma* skin]

dermatology /dɜːməˈtɒlədʒɪ/ *n*. the study of the skin and its diseases. —**dermatologist** *n*. [as prec. + -LOGY]

dermis /ˈdɜːmɪs/ *n*. the layer of skin below the epidermis. [after EPIDERMIS]

derogate /ˈderəgeɪt/ *v.i.* to detract *from* (a merit, right, etc.). —**derogation** /-ˈgeɪʃ(ə)n/ *n*. [f. L *derogare* (DE-, *rogare* ask)]

derogatory /dɪˈrɒgətərɪ/ *adj*. involving disparagement or discredit; depreciatory. [as prec.]

derrick /ˈderɪk/ *n*. **1** a kind of crane with an arm pivoted at the base of a central post or to a floor. **2** the framework over an oil-well etc., holding the drilling machinery. [orig. = gallows, f. name of London hangman *c.*1600]

derring-do /derɪŋˈduː/ *n*. (*literary*) heroic courage or action. [orig. = *daring to do*]

derris /ˈderɪs/ *n* **1** a tropical climbing plant of the genus *Derris*. **2** an insecticide made from its powdered root. [L f. Gk, = leather covering (in allusion to its pods)]

derv *n*. a fuel oil used in heavy road-vehicles. [f. *d*iesel- *e*ngined *r*oad *v*ehicle]

dervish /ˈdɜːvɪʃ/ *n*. a member of any of several Sufi religious groups, vowed to poverty and austerity and holding esoteric beliefs. [f. Turk. f. Pers., = poor, a mendicant]

desalinate /dɪˈsælɪneɪt/ *v.t.* to remove the salt

from (esp. sea-water). —**desalination** /-ˈneɪʃ(ə)n/ *n.* [f. DE- + SALINE]

descant /ˈdeskænt/ *n.* a free soprano part added to a tune; (*poetic*) a song, a melody. —/dɪsˈkænt/ *v.i.* to talk lengthily *upon.* [f. OF f. L (DIS-, *cantus* song)]

descend /dɪˈsend/ *v.t./i.* **1** to go or come down; to slope downwards. **2** to make a sudden attack or unexpected visit (*on*). **3** to sink or stoop *to* (an unworthy act), to pass by inheritance *to.* —**be descended from,** to come by descent from (a specified person etc.). [f. OF f. L *descendere* (DE-, *scandere* climb)]

descendant *n.* a person descended from another. [f. F (as prec.)]

descent /dɪˈsent/ *n.* **1** the act of descending. **2** a way by which one may descend; a downward slope. **3** lineage, family origin. **4** a sudden attack. **5** decline, fall. [as DESCEND]

describe /dɪˈskraɪb/ *v.t.* **1** to set forth in words; to recite the characteristics of. **2** to mark out, to draw, to move in (a specified line or curve). [f. L *describere* (DE-, *scribere* write)]

description /dɪˈskrɪpʃ(ə)n/ *n.* **1** describing; an account or verbal picture. **2** a sort or class. [as prec.]

descriptive /dɪˈskrɪptɪv/ *adj.* serving or seeking to describe; (of linguistics or grammar etc.) studying the structure of a language at a given time, avoiding comparisons with other languages or other historical phases and without social evaluations. [as DESCRIBE]

descry /dɪˈskraɪ/ *v.t.* to catch sight of, to succeed in discerning. [f. OF *descrier* (as CRY); orig. = announce, proclaim]

desecrate /ˈdesɪkreɪt/ *v.t.* to treat (a sacred thing) with irreverence or disrespect. —**desecration** /-ˈkreɪʃ(ə)n/ *n.*, **desecrator** *n.* [f. DE- + CONSECRATE]

desegregate /di:ˈsegrɪgeɪt/ *v.t.* to abolish racial segregation in. —**desegregation** /-ˈgeɪʃ(ə)n/ *n.*

desert[1] /dɪˈzɜ:t/ *v.t./i.* to abandon, to leave without intention of returning; to leave military service unlawfully. —**deserter** *n.*, **desertion** *n.* [f. F f. L (*deserere* forsake)]

desert[2] /ˈdezət/ *n.* a dry barren often sand-covered area of land. —*adj.* uninhabited, barren. [f. OF f. L *desertus* (as prec.)]

desert[3] /dɪˈzɜ:t/ *n.* **1** deserving, being worthy of reward or punishment. **2** (in *pl.*) a deserved recompense. [f. OF (as DESERVE)]

deserve /dɪˈzɜ:v/ *v.t.* to be entitled to, especially by one's conduct or qualities. [f. OF f. L *deservire* (DE-, *servire* serve)]

deservedly /dɪˈzɜ:vɪdlɪ/ *adv.* as deserved, justly. [f. prec.]

deserving *adj.* worthy (*of*), worth rewarding or supporting. [f. DESERVE]

déshabillé /deɪzæˈbi:eɪ/ *n.* the state of being only partly dressed. [F, = undressed]

desiccate /ˈdesɪkeɪt/ *v.t.* to remove the moisture from; to dry (a foodstuff) to preserve it. —**desiccation** /-ˈkeɪʃ(ə)n/ *n.*, **desiccator** *n.* [f. L *desiccare* (DE-, *siccus* dry)]

desideratum /dɪsɪdəˈreɪtəm, -ˈrɑ:-/ *n.* (*pl.* **-ta**) a thing that is lacking but needed or desired. [L (as DESIRE)]

design /dɪˈzaɪn/ *n.* **1** a preliminary outline or drawing for something that is to be made; the art of producing these. **2** a scheme of lines or shapes forming a decoration. **3** a general arrangement or layout; an established form of a product. **4** an intention or purpose; a mental plan, a scheme of attack or approach. —*v.t./i.* **1** to prepare a design for; to be a designer. **2** to intend or set aside for some purpose. —**by design,** on purpose. **have designs on,** to plan to harm or appropriate. [f. F f. L (as foll.)]

designate /ˈdezɪgneɪt/ *v.t.* **1** to specify, to indicate as having some function. **2** to describe as, to give or serve as a name or distinctive mark to. **3** to appoint to a position. —/-nət/ *adj.* appointed to but not yet installed in office. [f. L *designare* (DE-, *signum* mark)]

designation /dezɪgˈneɪʃ(ə)n/ *n.* designating; a name or title. [f. OF or L (as prec.)]

designedly /dɪˈzaɪnɪdlɪ/ *adv.* intentionally. [f. DESIGN]

designer *n.* one who makes designs, especially for clothes or manufactured products. [f. DESIGN]

designing *adj.* crafty, scheming. [as prec.]

desirable *adj.* worth having or wishing for; causing desire; (of a course of action) advisable. [f. foll.]

desire /dɪˈzaɪə(r)/ *n.* **1** an unsatisfied longing, a feeling of potential pleasure or satisfaction in obtaining or possessing something. **2** an expression of this, a request. **3** an object of desire. **4** strong sexual urge. —*v.t./i.* to have a desire for; to ask for; (*archaic*) to wish. —**leaves much to be desired,** is very imperfect. [f. OF f. L *desiderare* long for]

desirous *predic. adj.* having a desire, desiring. [f. AF (as prec.)]

desist /dɪˈzɪst, -ˈsɪst/ *v.i.* to cease (*from*). [f. OF f. L *desistere* (DE-, *sistere* stop)]

desk *n.* **1** a piece of furniture with a flat or sloped surface serving as a rest for writing or reading at. **2** a counter behind which a receptionist or cashier sits. **3** the section of a newspaper office dealing with specified topics. **4** the position of the music-stand at which a player (especially of a stringed instrument) sits in an orchestra. [f. L (as DISCUS)]

desolate /ˈdesələt/ *adj.* **1** left alone, solitary. **2** deserted, uninhabited, barren, dismal. **3** forlorn and wretched. —/-leɪt/ *v.t.* **1** to depopulate, to devastate. **2** to make (a person) wretched. [f. L *desolatus* (DE-, *solus* alone)]

desolation /desəˈleɪʃ(ə)n/ *n.* **1** a desolate or barren state. **2** being forsaken, loneliness. **3** grief, wretchedness. [as prec.]

despair /dɪsˈpeə(r)/ *n.* complete loss or absence of hope; a thing that causes this. —*v.i.* to lose all hope (*of*). [f. OF f. L *desperare* (DE-, *sperare* hope)]

despatch var. of DISPATCH.

desperado /despəˈrɑːdəʊ/ *n.* (*pl.* **-oes**) a desperate or reckless person, especially a criminal. [as foll. w. Sp. suffix]

desperate /ˈdespərət/ *adj.* **1** leaving no or little room for hope; extremely dangerous or serious. **2** reckless from despair; violent, lawless. **3** staking all on a small chance. —**desperately** *adv.* [as prec.]

desperation /despəˈreɪʃ(ə)n/ *n.* despair; a reckless state of mind, readiness to take any way out of a desperate situation. [f. L (as DESPAIR)]

despicable /ˈdespɪkəb(ə)l, dɪˈspɪk-/ *adj.* deserving to be despised, contemptible. —**despicably** *adv.* [f. L (*despicari* despise, as foll.)]

despise /dɪsˈpaɪz/ *v.t.* to regard as inferior or worthless; to feel contempt for. [f. OF f. L *despicere* look down on (DE-, *specere* look at)]

despite /dɪˈspaɪt/ *prep.* in spite of. —*n.* (*literary*) **1** disdain. **2** malice, hatred. [f. OF f. L *despectus* (as prec.)]

despoil /dɪˈspɔɪl/ *v.t.* (*literary*) to plunder, to rob. —**despoliation** /dɪspəʊlɪˈeɪʃ(ə)n/ *n.* [f. OF or L (as SPOIL)]

despond /dɪˈspɒnd/ *v.i.* to lose heart, to be dejected. [f. L *despondēre* abandon (DE-, *spondēre* promise)]

despondent /dɪˈspɒndənt/ *adj.* having lost heart, dejected. —**despondency** *n.*, **despondently** *adv.* [as prec.]

despot /ˈdespɒt/ *n.* an absolute ruler; a tyrant. [f. F f. L f. Gk *despotēs* master]

despotic /deˈspɒtɪk/ *adj.* having unrestricted power, tyrannous. —**despotically** *adv.* [f. prec.]

despotism /ˈdespətɪz(ə)m/ *n.* rule by a despot; a country ruled by a despot. [f. DESPOT]

dessert /dɪˈzɜːt/ *n.* the sweet course of a meal; a course of fruit, nuts, etc., at the end of dinner. [f. F *desservir* clear the table]

dessertspoon *n.* a spoon between a tablespoon and a teaspoon in size. —**dessertspoonful** *n.* (*pl.* **-fuls**) [f. prec.]

destination /destɪˈneɪʃ(ə)n/ *n.* a place to which a person or thing is going. [f. OF or L (as foll.)]

destine /ˈdestɪn/ *v.t.* to settle or determine the future of; to appoint, to set apart for a purpose. [f. F f. L *destinare*]

destiny /ˈdestɪnɪ/ *n.* fate considered as a power; what is destined to happen to a person etc.; the predetermined course of events. [f. OF (as prec.)]

destitute /ˈdestɪtjuːt/ *adj.* without resources, in great need of food, shelter, etc.; devoid *of*. —**destitution** /-ˈtjuːʃ(ə)n/ *n.* [f. L *destituere* forsake (DE-, *statuere* place)]

destroy /dɪˈstrɔɪ/ *v.t.* **1** to pull or break down; to make useless. **2** to kill (esp. a sick or unwanted animal) deliberately. **3** to nullify, to neutralize the effect of; to put out of existence. [f. OF f. L *destruere* (DE-, *struere* build)]

destroyer *n.* **1** a person or thing that destroys. **2** a fast warship designed to protect other ships. [f. prec.]

destruct /dɪˈstrʌkt/ *v.t./i.* (*US*) to destroy (one's own equipment) deliberately; to be destroyed thus. —*n.* (*US*) the action of destructing. [f. L (as DESTROY), or back-formation f. DESTRUCTION]

destructible *adj.* able to be destroyed. [F or f. L (as DESTROY)]

destruction /dɪˈstrʌkʃ(ə)n/ *n.* destroying, being destroyed; a cause of this. [f. OF f. L (as DESTROY)]

destructive /dɪˈstrʌktɪv/ *adj.* **1** destroying, causing destruction. **2** (of criticism etc.) merely negative, refuting etc. without offering amendments or alternatives. [as prec.]

desuetude /dɪˈsjuːɪtjuːd/ *n.* a state of disuse. [f. F or L *desuetudo* (DE-, *suescere* be accustomed)]

desultory /ˈdesəltərɪ/ *adj.* going constantly from one subject to another; disconnected, unmethodical. —**desultorily** *adv.*, **desultoriness** *n.* [f. L (*desultor* one who vaults, f. *salire* leap)]

detach /dɪˈtætʃ/ *v.t.* **1** to unfasten or separate and remove (*from*). **2** to send (part of a force) on a separate mission. [f. F (as DE-, ATTACH)]

detached *adj.* **1** separate, standing apart. **2** unemotional, impartial. [f. prec.]

detachment *n.* **1** detaching, being detached. **2** a lack of emotion or concern, impartiality. **3** a portion of an army etc. separately employed. [f. F (as DETACH)]

detail /ˈdiːteɪl/ *n.* **1** an item, a small or subordinate particular; these collectively, the treatment of them. **2** minor decoration in a building, picture, etc. **3** a small military detachment. —*v.t.* **1** to give particulars of, to describe fully. **2** to assign for special duty. —**in detail,** describing the individual parts or events fully. [f. F (DE-, *tailler* cut)]

detailed *adj.* having or involving many details; thorough. [f. prec.]

detain /dɪˈteɪn/ *v.t.* **1** to keep in confinement or under restraint. **2** to keep waiting, to delay. [f. OF f. L *detinēre* (DE-, *tenēre* hold)]

detainee /dɪteɪˈniː/ *n.* a person detained in custody, usually on political grounds. [f. prec.]

detect /dɪˈtekt/ *v.t.* to discover the existence or

presence of; to discover (a person) *in* the performance of some wrong or secret act. —**detector** *n.* [f. L *detegere* (DE-, *tegere* cover)]

detectable *adj.* that may be detected. [f. prec.]

detection /dɪˈtekʃ(ə)n/ *n.* detecting, being detected; the work of a detective. [f. DETECT]

detective /dɪˈtektɪv/ *n.* a person, especially a member of a police force, employed to investigate crimes. —*adj.* serving to detect. —**detective story** etc., one describing a crime and the detection of criminals. [f. DETECT]

détente /deɪˈtɑ̃t/ *n.* the easing of strained relations, especially between States. [F, = relaxation]

detention /dɪˈtenʃ(ə)n/ *n.* detaining, being detained; being kept in school after hours as a punishment. —**detention centre**, an institution for the brief detention of young offenders. [f. F or L (as DETAIN)]

deter /dɪˈtɜ:(r)/ *v.t.* (**-rr-**) to discourage or prevent (*from*) through fear or dislike of the consequences. —**determent** *n.* [f. L *deterrere* (DE-, *terrēre* frighten)]

detergent /dɪˈtɜ:dʒ(ə)nt/ *n.* a cleansing agent, especially a synthetic substance used with water for removing dirt etc. —*adj.* cleansing. [f. L *detergēre* (DE-, *tergēre* wipe)]

deteriorate /dɪˈtɪərɪəreɪt/ *v.t./i.* to make or become worse. —**deterioration** /-ˈreɪʃ(ə)n/ *n.* [f. L (*deterior* worse)]

determinant /dɪˈtɜ:mɪnənt/ *adj.* determining, decisive. —*n.* **1** a determining factor. **2** the quantity obtained by adding the products of the elements of a square matrix according to a certain rule. [f. L (as DETERMINE)]

determinate /dɪˈtɜ:mɪnət/ *adj.* limited, of definite scope or nature. [as prec.]

determination /dɪtɜ:mɪˈneɪʃ(ə)n/ *n.* **1** firmness of purpose, resoluteness. **2** the process of deciding, determining, or calculating. [f. OF f. L (as DETERMINE)]

determinative /dɪˈtɜ:mɪnətɪv/ *adj.* serving to define, qualify, or direct. —*n.* a determinative thing. [f. F (as foll.)]

determine /dɪˈtɜ:mɪn/ *v.t./i.* **1** to find out or calculate precisely; to settle, to decide; to be the decisive factor in regard to. **2** to decide firmly, to resolve. —**be determined,** to have decided firmly. [f. OF f. L *determinare* (DE-, *terminus* end, limit)]

determined *adj.* showing determination, resolute, unflinching. —**determinedly** *adv.* [f. prec.]

determinism /dɪˈtɜ:mɪnɪz(ə)m/ *n.* the theory that human action is not free but is determined by motives regarded as external forces acting on the will. —**determinist** *n.*, **deterministic** /-ˈnɪstɪk/ *adj.* [f. DETERMINE]

deterrent /dɪˈterənt/ *adj.* deterring. —*n.* a deterrent thing or factor. [f. L (as DETER)]

detest /dɪˈtest/ *v.t.* to hate, to loathe. —**detestation** /-ˈsteɪʃ(ə)n/ *n.* [f. L *detestari* call to witness]

detestable *adj.* intensely disliked, hateful. [f. prec.]

dethrone /di:ˈθrəun/ *v.t.* to remove from a throne, to depose. —**dethronement** *n.*

detonate /ˈdetəneɪt/ *v.t./i.* to explode or cause to explode with a loud report. —**detonation** /-ˈneɪʃ(ə)n/ *n.* [f. L *detonare* (DE-, *tonare* thunder)]

detonator *n.* a device for detonating an explosive. [f. prec.]

detour /ˈdi:tuə(r)/ *n.* a divergence from one's direct or intended route, a roundabout course. [f. F *détourner* turn away (as DE-, TURN)]

detract /dɪˈtrækt/ *v.t./i.* to take away (some amount) *from* a whole. —**detract from,** to reduce the credit due to, to depreciate. —**detraction** *n.*, **detractor** *n.* [f. L *detrahere* (DE-, *trahere* draw)]

detriment /ˈdetrɪmənt/ *n.* harm, damage; a thing causing this. —**detrimental** /-ˈment(ə)l/ *adj.*, **detrimentally** *adv.* [f. OF or L *detrimentum* (*deterere* wear away)]

detritus /dɪˈtraɪtəs/ *n.* matter produced by erosion, as gravel or rock-debris. [f. F f. L (as prec.)]

de trop /də ˈtrəu/ not wanted, in the way. [F, = excessive]

deuce[1] /dju:s/ *n.* **1** (in tennis) the score of 40 all, at which two consecutive points are needed to win. **2** the two on dice. [f. OF f. L *duos* (*duo* two)]

deuce[2] /dju:s/ *n.* misfortune, the Devil (*colloq.* used esp. as an exclamation of surprise or annoyance). [f. LG *duus* (as prec.), the two at dice being the worst throw]

deuced /ˈdju:sɪd, djust/ *adj.* & *adv.* damned. [f. prec.]

deus ex machina /ˈdeɪəs eks ˈmækɪnə/ an unexpected power or event saving a seemingly impossible situation, especially in a play or novel. [L transl. Gk, = god from the machinery (w. ref. to the machinery by which, in ancient Greek theatre, gods were shown in the air)]

deuterium /dju:ˈtɪərɪəm/ *n.* a heavy isotope of hydrogen, symbol D or ^{2}H, atomic number 1. [f. Gk *deuteros* second]

deuteron /ˈdju:tərɒn/ *n.* the nucleus of a deuterium atom, consisting of a proton and a neutron. [as prec.]

Deutschmark /ˈdɔɪtʃmɑ:k/ *n.* the currency unit in Germany. [G, = German mark (MARK[2])]

devalue /di:ˈvælju:/ *v.t.* to reduce the value of, to reduce the value of (a currency) in relation to other currencies or to gold. —**devaluation** /-ˈeɪʃ(ə)n/*n.*

Devanagari /deɪvəˈnɑ:gərɪ/ *n.* the alphabet in

which Sanskrit, Hindi, and several North Indian languages are usually written. [Skr., = of the divine town]

devastate /ˈdevəsteɪt/ *v.t.* to lay waste, to cause great destruction to. —**devastation** /-ˈsteɪʃ(ə)n/ *n.* [f. L *devastare* (DE-, *vastare* lay waste)]

devastating *adj.* crushingly effective, overwhelming. [f. prec.]

develop /dɪˈveləp/ *v.t./i.* **1** to make or become bigger, fuller, or more elaborate or systematic; to bring or come to an active or visible state or to maturity, to reveal or be revealed. **2** to begin to exhibit or suffer from. **3** to construct new buildings on (land); to convert (land) to a new use so as to use its resources. **4** to treat (a photographic film etc.) to make the picture visible. —**developing country,** a poor or primitive country that is developing better economic and social conditions. —**developer** *n.* [f. F *développer*]

development *n.* **1** developing, being developed. **2** a thing that has developed, especially an event or circumstance. **3** developed land. **4** (*Mus.*) elaboration of a theme, especially in the second part of a sonata movement. —**development area,** one where new industries are encouraged in order to counteract unemployment there. —**developmental** /-ˈment(ə)l/ *adj.* [f. prec.]

deviant /ˈdi:vɪənt/ *adj.* that deviates from the normal. —*n.* a deviant person or thing. [as foll.]

deviate /ˈdi:vɪeɪt/ *v.i.* to turn aside or diverge (*from* a course of action, rule, etc.). —**deviator** *n.* [f L. *deviare* (DE-, *via* way)]

deviation /di:vɪˈeɪʃ(ə)n/ *n.* deviating; departing from an accepted political (esp. Communist) doctrine. —**deviationist** *n.* [f. F f. L (as prec.)]

device /dɪˈvaɪs/ *n.* **1** a thing made or adapted for a particular purpose. **2** a plan, a scheme; a trick. **3** an emblematic or heraldic design. —**leave a person to his own devices,** to leave him to do as he wishes without help or advice. [f. OF f. L (as DEVISE)]

devil /ˈdev(ə)l/ *n.* **1** the supreme spirit of evil (usu. **the Devil**); an evil spirit, a demon, a superhuman malignant being; a personified evil spirit, force, or quality. **2** a wicked or cruel person; a mischievously energetic, clever, or self-willed person. **3** (*colloq.*) a person, a fellow. **4** fighting spirit, mischievousness. **5** (*colloq.*) something difficult or awkward. **6** a literary hack used by an employer; a junior legal counsel. —*v.t./i.* (**-ll-**) **1** to cook (food) with hot seasoning. **2** to act as a devil (for an author or barrister). **3** (*US*) to harass, to worry. —**between the devil and the deep blue sea,** in a dilemma. **a devil of,** (*colloq.*) a considerable or remarkable. **devil-may-care** *adj.* cheerful and reckless. **devil's advocate,** one who tests a proposition by arguing against it. **devil's coach-horse,** a large rove-beetle. **the devil's own,** very difficult or unusual. **the devil to pay,** trouble to be expected. **give the Devil his due,** to acknowledge the merits or achievement of a person otherwise disfavoured. **play the devil with,** to cause severe damage to. [OE f. L f. Gk *diabolos* slanderer]

devilish *adj.* of or like a devil; mischievous. —*adv.* (*colloq.*) very, extremely. [f. prec.]

devilment *n.* mischief, wild spirits. [f. DEVIL]

devilry *n.* wickedness, reckless mischief; black magic. [f. DEVIL]

devious /ˈdi:vɪəs/ *adj.* winding, circuitous; not straightforward, underhand. —**deviously** *adv.*, **deviousness** *n.* [f. L *devius* (DE-, *via* way)]

devise /dɪˈvaɪz/ *v.t.* **1** to plan or invent by careful thought. **2** (*Law*) to leave (real estate) by will. [f. OF f. L *dividere* divide]

devoid /dɪˈvɔɪd/ *predic. adj.* (with *of*) quite lacking or free from. [f. OF (as DE-, VOID)]

devolution /di:vəˈlu:ʃ(ə)n/ *n.* delegation of power, especially by a central government to a local or regional administration. [f. L (as foll.)]

devolve /dɪˈvɒlv/ *v.i.* (of work or duties) to pass or be passed on to another; (of property etc.) to descend or pass (*to* or *upon*). [f. L *devolvere* (DE-, *volvere* roll)]

devote /dɪvəʊt/ *v.t.* to apply or give over *to* a particular activity or purpose. [f. L *devovēre* (DE-, *vovēre* vow)]

devoted *adj.* showing devotion, very loyal or loving. —**devotedly** *adv.* [f. prec.]

devotee /devəˈti:/ *n.* a person who is devoted to something, an enthusiast. [f. DEVOTE]

devotion /dɪˈvəʊʃ(ə)n/ *n.* **1** great love or loyalty, enthusiastic zeal. **2** religious worship; (in *pl.*) prayers. —**devotional** *adj.* [f. OF or L (as DEVOTE)]

devour /dɪˈvaʊə(r)/ *v.t.* **1** to eat hungrily or greedily. **2** (of fire etc.) to engulf, to destroy. **3** to take in greedily with the eyes or ears. **4** to absorb the attention of. [f. OF f. L *devorare* (DE-, *vorare* swallow)]

devout /dɪˈvaʊt/ *adj.* earnestly religious; earnest, sincere. —**devoutly** *adv.* [f. OF f. L *devotus* (as DEVOTE)]

dew *n.* atmospheric vapour condensing in small drops on cool surfaces between evening and morning; beaded or glistening moisture resembling this. —**dew-claw** *n.* the rudimentary inner toe of some dogs. **dew-point** *n.* the temperature at which the air can hold no more water vapour, and dew forms. **dew-pond** *n.* a shallow, usually artificial, pond once supposed to be fed by atmospheric condensation. —**dewy** *adj.* [OE]

dewar /ˈdju:ə(r)/ *n.* a double-walled flask with

the space between its walls evacuated to reduce transfer of heat. [f. Sir J. *Dewar*, British physicist (d. 1923)]

dewberry *n.* a bluish fruit like a blackberry; the shrub (*Rubus caesius*) bearing it.

dewdrop *n.* a drop of dew.

dewlap *n.* a fold of loose skin hanging from the throat of cattle and other animals. [f. DEW + LAP[1]]

dexter *adj.* (in heraldry) of or on the right-hand side (the observer's left) of a shield etc. [L, = on the right]

dexterity /dekˈsterɪtɪ/ *n.* skill in handling things; manual or mental adroitness. [f. F f. L (as DEXTER)]

dexterous var. of DEXTROUS.

dextrous /ˈdekstrəs/ *adj.* having or showing dexterity. —**dextrously** *adv.* [f. L (as prec.)]

DFC *abbr.* Distinguished Flying Cross.

DFM *abbr.* Distinguished Flying Medal.

dharma /ˈdɑːmə/ *n.* **1** the Hindu moral law; right behaviour; social rules. **2** (in Buddhism) truth. [Skr., = law, custom]

dhoti /ˈdəʊtɪ/ *n.* the loincloth worn by male Hindus. [Hindi]

dhow /daʊ/ *n.* a lateen-rigged ship of the Arabian Sea. [orig. unkn.]

di- *prefix* two, double-. [Gk (*dis* twice)]

dia- *prefix* (**di-** before a vowel) **1** through. **2** apart. **3** across. [Gk *dia* through]

diabetes /daɪəˈbiːtiːz/ *n.* a disease (also called **diabetes mellitus**) in which sugar and starch are not properly metabolized by the body. [orig. = siphon; L f. Gk (*diabainō* go through)]

diabetic /daɪəˈbetɪk/ *adj.* of or having diabetes, for diabetics. —*n.* a person suffering from diabetes. [f. prec.]

diabolic, diabolical /daɪəˈbɒlɪk, -k(ə)l/ *adjs.* of the Devil; devilish, inhumanly cruel or wicked; fiendishly clever or cunning or annoying. —**diabolically** *adv.* [f. OF or L (as DEVIL)]

diabolism /daɪˈæbəlɪz(ə)m/ *n.* worship of the Devil; sorcery. [f. Gk (as DEVIL)]

diachronic /daɪəˈkrɒnɪk/ *adj.* concerned with the historical development of a subject. —**diachronic linguistics**, historical linguistics (see HISTORICAL). [f. F (DIA-, Gk *khronos* time)]

diaconal /daɪˈækən(ə)l/ *adj.* of a deacon. [f. L (as DEACON)]

diaconate /daɪˈækənət/ *n.* **1** the office of a deacon. **2** a body of deacons. [as prec.]

diacritical /daɪəˈkrɪtɪk(ə)l/ *adj.* distinguishing, distinctive. —**diacritical mark** (*or* **sign**), a sign used to indicate different sounds or values of a letter (an accent, diaeresis, cedilla, etc.). [f. Gk (as DIA-, CRITICAL)]

diadem /ˈdaɪədem/ *n.* **1** a crown or headband worn as a sign of sovereignty. **2** sovereignty. **3** a crowning distinction or glory. [f. OF f. L f. Gk (*deō* bind)]

diaeresis /daɪˈɪərəsɪs/ *n.* (*pl.* **-reses** /-siːz/) a mark (as in *naïve*) over a vowel indicating that it is sounded separately. [L f. Gk, = separation]

diagnose /ˈdaɪəgnəʊz/ *v.t.* to make a diagnosis of (a disease, a mechanical fault, etc.); to infer the presence of (a specified disease etc.) from symptoms. [f. foll.]

diagnosis /daɪəgˈnəʊsɪs/ *n.* (*pl.* **-oses** /-siːz/) the identification of a disease by means of the patient's symptoms, a formal statement of this; the ascertainment of the cause of a mechanical fault etc. [L f. Gk (DIA-, *gignōskō* recognize)]

diagnostic /daɪəgˈnɒstɪk/ *adj.* of or assisting diagnosis. —*n.* a symptom. —**diagnostician** /-ˈstɪʃ(ə)n/ *n.* [f. Gk (as prec.)]

diagonal /daɪˈægən(ə)l/ *adj.* crossing a straight-sided figure from corner to corner, slanting, oblique. —*n.* a straight line joining two opposite corners. —**diagonally** *adv.* [f. L f. Gk (DIA-, *gōnia* angle)]

diagram /ˈdaɪəgræm/ *n.* a drawing showing the general scheme or outline of an object and its parts; a graphic representation of a course or the results of an action or process. —**diagrammatic** /-ˈmætɪk/ *adj.*, **diagrammatically** *adv.* [f. L f. Gk (as DIA-, -GRAM)]

dial /ˈdaɪəl/ *n.* **1** the plate on the front of a clock or watch, marking the hours etc.; a similar flat plate marked with a scale for the measurement of something, and having a movable pointer indicating the amount registered. **2** a movable disc with finger-holes over a circle of numbers, manipulated in order to make a connection with another instrument; a plate or disc etc. on a radio or television set for selecting a wavelength or channel. **3** (*slang*) a person's face. —*v.t./i.* (**-ll-**) to select or regulate by means of a dial; to make a telephone connection by using a dial or numbered buttons; to ring up (a number etc.) thus. [f. L (*dies* day)]

dialect /ˈdaɪəlekt/ *n.* a form of speech peculiar to a district or class; a subordinate variety of a language showing sufficient differences from the standard language in vocabulary, pronunciation, or idiom for it to be considered as distinct. —**dialectal** /-ˈlekt(ə)l/ *adj.*, **dialectology** *n.* [f. F or L f. Gk, = discourse (*dialegomai* converse)]

dialectic /daɪəˈlektɪk/ *n.* **1** (also in *pl.*, occas. treated as *sing.*) the art of investigating the truth of opinions; the testing of truth by discussion, logical disputation. **2** criticism dealing with metaphysical contradictions and their solutions; the existence or action of opposing social forces etc. —*adj.* of disputation or dialectics. [f. OF or L f. Gk *dialektikē* (*tekhnē* art) of debate]

dialectical /daɪəˈlektɪk(ə)l/ *adj.* of dialectic. —**dialectical materialism,** the theory propagated by Marx and Engels according to which political events or social phenomena are to be interpreted as a conflict of social forces (the 'class struggle') produced by the operation of economic causes. [f. prec.]

dialogue /ˈdaɪəlɒg/ *n.* a conversation; the written form of this; a passage of conversation in a novel etc.; a discussion between the representatives of two groups etc. [f. OF f. L f. Gk (*dialegomai* converse)]

dialysis /daɪˈælɪsɪs/ *n.* (*pl.* **-lyses** /-si:z/) the separation of particles by differences in their ability to pass through a suitable membrane; the process of allowing blood to flow past such a membrane on the other side of which is another liquid, so that certain dissolved substances in the blood may pass through the membrane and the blood itself be purified or cleansed in cases of renal failure, poisoning, etc.; an occasion of undergoing this process. [f. L f. Gk, = dissolution (as DIA-, *luō* set free)]

diamanté /dɪəˈmɑ̃teɪ/ *adj.* decorated with powdered crystal or other sparkling substance. [F, = set with diamonds]

diameter /daɪˈæmɪtə(r)/ *n.* a straight line passing from side to side through the centre of a circle or sphere; a transverse measurement, width, or thickness; the unit of linear magnifying power. [f. OF f. L f. Gk, = measuring across (as DIA-, -METER)]

diametrical /daɪəˈmetrɪk(ə)l/ *adj.* **1** of or along a diameter. **2** (of opposites etc.) complete, direct. —**diametrically** *adv.* (f. Gk (as prec.)]

diamond /ˈdaɪəmənd/ *n.* **1** a very hard transparent precious stone of pure crystallized carbon. **2** a rhombus; a rhombus-shaped thing. **3** a playing-card of the suit (**diamonds**) marked with red rhombuses. —**diamond wedding,** the 60th (or 75th) anniversary of a wedding. [f. OF f. L f. Gk *adamas* adamant]

dianthus /daɪˈænθəs/ *n.* a flowering plant of the genus *Dianthus*, including the carnation. [f. Gk *Dios* of Zeus + *anthos* flower]

diapason /daɪəˈpeɪs(ə)n, -z-/ *n.* the entire compass of a musical instrument or voice; a fixed standard of musical pitch; either of the two main organ-stops extending through the whole compass. [f. L f. Gk, = through all (notes)]

diaper /ˈdaɪəpə(r)/ *n.* (*US*) a baby's nappy. [f. OF f. L f. Gk (as DIA-, *aspros* white)]

diaphanous /daɪˈæfənəs/ *adj.* (of a fabric etc.) light and delicate and almost transparent. [f. L f. Gk (DIA-, *-phanēs* showing)]

diaphragm /ˈdaɪəfræm/ *n.* **1** the muscular partition between the thorax and the abdomen in mammals **2** a thin sheet used as a partition etc.; a vibrating disc in a microphone, telephone, loudspeaker, etc., and acoustic systems etc. **3** a device for varying the lens aperture in a camera etc. **4** a thin contraceptive cap fitting over the cervix of the uterus. [f. L f. Gk (DIA-, *phragma* fence)]

diarist /ˈdaɪərɪst/ *n.* one who keeps a diary. [f. DIARY]

diarrhoea /daɪəˈri:ə/ *n.* the condition of excessively frequent and loose bowel movements. [f. L f. Gk (DIA-, *rheō* flow)]

diary /ˈdaɪərɪ/ *n.* a daily record of events or thoughts; a book for this or for noting future engagements. [f. L *diarium* (*dies* day)]

Diaspora /daɪˈæspərə/ *n.* the Dispersion of the Jews (see DISPERSION); the Jews thus dispersed. [Gk, f. *dia* through, *speirō* scatter]

diastase /ˈdaɪəsteɪs/ the enzyme converting starch to sugar, important in digestion. [F f. Gk, = separation]

diastole /daɪˈæst(ə)lɪ/ *n.* the dilatation of the heart rhythmically alternating with systole to form the pulse. —**diastolic** /daɪəˈstɒlɪk/ *adj.* [L f. Gk (DIA-, *stellō* send)]

diathermy /ˈdaɪəθəmɪ/ *n.* the application of high-frequency electric currents to produce heat within the body. —**diathermic** *adj.* [f. G f. Gk *dia* through, *thermon* heat]

diatom /daɪˈætəm/ *n.* a microscopic one-cell alga of the division Bacillariophyta, found as plankton and forming fossil deposits. [f. L f. Gk, = cut in half]

diatomic /daɪəˈtɒmɪk/ *adj.* consisting of two atoms; having two replaceable atoms or radicals. [f. DI- + ATOM]

diatonic /daɪəˈtɒnɪk/ *adj.* (*Mus.*, of a scale, interval, etc.) involving only notes proper to the prevailing key without chromatic alteration. [f. F or L f. Gk (DIA-, *tonikos* tonic)]

diatribe /ˈdaɪətraɪb/ *n.* a forceful verbal attack, abusive criticism. [F f. L f. Gk *diatribē* spending of time, discourse]

dibber /ˈdɪbə(r)/ *n.* a hand-tool for making holes in the ground for seeds or young plants. [f. foll.]

dibble /ˈdɪb(ə)l/ *n.* a dibber. —*v.t./i.* to prepare (soil) with a dibble, to sow or plant with a dibble. [perh. rel. to DAB[1]]

dice *n.* (properly *pl.* of DIE[2] but often as *sing.*) a small cube with the faces bearing usually 1-6 spots used in games of chance; a game played with one or more of these. —*v.t./i.* **1** to gamble with dice. **2** to cut into small cubes. —**no dice,** (*slang*) no success or prospect of it. [f. DIE[2]]

dicey /ˈdaɪsɪ/ *adj.* (*slang*) risky, unreliable. [f. prec.]

dichotomy /daɪˈkɒtəmɪ/ *n.* a division into two parts or kinds. [f. L f. Gk (*dikho-* apart, *-tomia* cutting)]

dichromatic /daɪkrəˈmætɪk/ *adj.* **1** two-coloured. **2** having vision sensitive to only two of the three primary colours. [f. DI- + Gk *khrōma* colour]

dickens /ˈdɪkɪnz/ *n.* (*colloq.*) deuce, the Devil (esp. in exclamations). [prob. f. surname *Dickens*]

Dickensian /dɪˈkenzɪən/ *adj.* of the novelist Charles Dickens (1812-70) or his works; resembling situations described in them. [f. *Dickens*]

dicker *v.i.* to bargain, to haggle. [perh. f. *dicker* set of ten (hides), as unit of trade]

dicky *adj.* (*slang*) unsound, likely to collapse or fail. —*n.* (*colloq.*) a false shirt-front. [f. *Dicky* dim. of Richard]

dicotyledon /daɪkɒtɪˈli:d(ə)n/ *n.* a flowering plant having two cotyledons. —**dicotyledonous** *adj.*

Dictaphone /ˈdɪktəfəʊn/ *n.* [P] a machine for recording and playing back dictated words. [f. DICTATE + Gk *phōnē* voice]

dictate /dɪkˈteɪt/ *v.t./i.* **1** to say or read aloud (words to be written down or recorded). **2** to state or order with the force of authority; to give peremptory orders. —/ˈdɪkteɪt/ *n.* (usu. in *pl.*) an authoritative instruction. —**dictation** /-ˈteɪʃ(ə)n/ *n.* [f. L *dictare* (*dicere* say)]

dictator /dɪkˈteɪtə(r)/ *n.* a ruler (often a usurper) with unrestricted authority; a person with supreme authority in any sphere; a domineering person. —**dictatorship** *n.* [f. L (as prec.)]

dictatorial /dɪktəˈtɔ:rɪəl/ *adj.* of or like a dictator; imperious, overbearing. —**dictatorially** *adv.* [as prec.]

diction /ˈdɪkʃ(ə)n/ *n.* **1** a person's manner of enunciation in speaking or singing. **2** the choice of words and phrases in speech or writing. [f. F or L *dictio* (*dicere* say)]

dictionary /ˈdɪkʃ(ə)nərɪ/ *n.* a book that lists (usually in alphabetical order) and explains the words of a language (often with information on pronunciation, inflected forms, and etymology) or gives the equivalent words in another language; a similar book explaining the terms of a particular subject. [f. L (as prec.)]

dictum /ˈdɪktəm/ *n.* (*pl.* **-ta**) a formal expression of opinion; a saying. [L (p.p. of *dicere* say)]

did *past* of DO[1].

didactic /dɪˈdæktɪk, daɪ-/ *adj.* meant to instruct; (of a person) tediously pedantic. —**didactically** *adv.*, **didacticism** /-tɪsɪz(ə)m/ *n.* [f. Gk (*didaskō* teach)]

diddle *v.t.* (*slang*) to cheat, to swindle. [back-formation f. Jeremy *Diddler*, character in play (1803)]

didn't (*colloq.*) = did not.

die[1] /daɪ/ *v.i.* (*partic.* **dying** /daɪɪŋ/) **1** to cease to live, to expire, to lose vital force. **2** to cease to exist or function, to disappear, to fade away; (of flame) to go out. **3** to wish longingly or intently. **4** to be exhausted or tormented. —**die away,** to become weaker or fainter to the point of extinction. **die back,** (of a plant) to decay from the tip towards the root. **die down,** to become less loud or strong. **die-hard** *n.* a conservative or stubborn person. **die out,** to become extinct, to cease to exist. **never say die,** keep up courage, not give in. [prob. f. ON]

die[2] /daɪ/ *n.* **1** see DICE. **2** an engraved device for stamping a design on coins, medals, etc.; a device for stamping, cutting, or moulding material into a particular shape. —**diecasting** *n.* a process or product of casting from metal moulds. **die-sinker** *n.* an engraver of dies. **die-stamping** *n.* embossing paper etc. with a die. **straight as a die,** quite straight, very honest. [f. OF f. L *datum* p.p. of *dare* give]

dielectric /daɪəˈlektrɪk/ *adj.* that does not conduct electricity. —*n.* a dielectric substance usable for insulating. [f. Gk *dia* through + ELECTRIC]

diesel /di:z(ə)l/ *n.* **1** (also **diesel engine**) a type of internal-combustion engine in which ignition of fuel is produced by the heat of air that has been highly compressed. **2** a vehicle driven by such an engine. **3** the fuel for this. —**diesel-electric** *adj.* driven by electric current from a generator driven by a diesel engine. **diesel oil,** the heavy petroleum fraction used in diesel engines. [f. R. *Diesel* (d. 1913), German engineer]

diet[1] /ˈdaɪət/ *n.* the sort of foods one habitually eats; a precribed course of food to which a person is restricted. —*v.t./i.* to restrict oneself to a special diet, especially in order to control one's weight; to restrict (a person) to a special diet. —**dietary** *adj.* [f. OF f. L f. Gk *diaita* way of life]

diet[2] /ˈdaɪət/ *n.* a conference or congress (especially as the English name for some foreign parliamentary assemblies). [f. L *dieta* (*dies* day)]

dietetic /daɪətetɪk/ *adj.* of diet and nutrition. [f. L f. Gk (as DIET[1])]

dietetics *n.pl.* the scientific study of diet and nutrition. [f. prec.]

dietitian /daɪəˈtɪʃ(ə)n/ *n.* an expert in dietetics. [f. DIET[1]]

differ *v.i.* **1** to be unlike; to be distinguishable *from.* **2** to disagree in opinion (*from*). [f. OF f. L *differre* orig. = bear apart]

difference *n.* **1** being different or unlike. **2** a point in which things differ; the amount or degree of unlikeness. **3** the quantity by which amounts differ, the remainder left after subtraction. **4** a disagreement in opinion, a dispute, a quarrel. —**make all the difference,** to be very important or significant. **split the**

difference, to take the average of two proposed amounts. [f. OF f. L (as foll.)]

different *adj.* unlike, of other nature, form, or quality (*from* or (**D**) *to*); separate, distinct; unusual. —**differently** *adv.* [f. OF f. L (as DIFFER)]

differential /dɪfəˈrenʃ(ə)l/ *adj.* **1** of or showing or depending on a difference; constituting or relating to specific differences. **2** (*Math.*) relating to infinitesimal differences. —*n.* **1** an agreed difference in wage between industries or between different classes of workers in the same industry. **2** a difference between rates of interest etc. **3** a differential gear. —**differential calculus,** a method of calculating rates of change, maximum and minimum values, etc. **differential gear,** a gear enabling a motor vehicle's driven wheels to revolve at different speeds in rounding corners. [f. L (as DIFFERENCE)]

differentiate /dɪfəˈrenʃɪeɪt/ *v.t.* **1** to constitute the difference between or in. **2** to recognize as different, to distinguish, to discriminate. **3** to develop differences, to become different. **4** (*Math.*) to calculate the derivative of. —**differentiation** /-ˈeɪʃ(ə)n/ *n.* [as prec.]

difficult /ˈdɪfɪk(ə)lt/ *adj.* needing much effort or skill; troublesome, perplexing; not easy to please or satisfy. [back form. f. foll.]

difficulty /ˈdɪfɪk(ə)ltɪ/ *n.* being difficult; a difficult problem or thing, a hindrance to progress; (often in *pl.*) trouble or distress, especially shortage of money. [f. L *difficultas* (as FACULTY)]

diffident /ˈdɪfɪd(ə)nt/ *adj.* lacking self-confidence, hesitating to put oneself or one's ideas forward. —**diffidence** *n.*, **diffidently** *adv.* [f. L *diffidere* mistrust (DIS-, *fidere* trust)]

diffract /dɪˈfrækt/ *v.t.* to break up (a beam of light) into a series of dark and light bands or coloured spectra, or (a beam of radiation or particles) into a series of high and low intensities. —**diffractive** *adj.* [f. L, = break apart (DE-, *frangere* break)]

diffraction /dɪˈfrækʃ(ə)n/ *n.* diffracting. —**diffraction grating,** a plate of glass or polished metal ruled with very close equidistant parallel lines, producing a spectrum by means of the transmitted or reflected light. [f. prec.]

diffuse /dɪˈfjuːs/ *adj.* spread out, not concentrated; wordy, not concise. —/-ˈfjuːz/ *v.t.* to spread widely or thinly; (esp. of fluids) to intermingle by diffusion. —**diffusible** /-z-/ *adj.*, **diffusive** /-s-/ *adj.* [f. F or L *diffusus* extensive (*fundere* pour)]

diffusion /dɪˈfjuːʒ(ə)n/ *n.* diffusing, being diffused; the interpenetration of substances by the natural movement of their particles. [f. L (as prec.)]

dig *v.t./i.* (**-gg-**; *past* & *p.p.* **dug**) **1** to break up and remove or turn over (ground etc.) with a tool, the hands, claws, etc.; to make (a way, hole, etc.) or obtain by digging; to excavate archaeologically. **2** to thrust (a sharp object) *into* or *in*; to prod or nudge. **3** to make a search (*for* or *into*). —*n.* **1** a piece of digging; an archaeological excavation. **2** a prod or nudge. **3** a cutting or sarcastic remark. **4** (in *pl.*, *colloq.*) lodgings. —**dig one's heels** *or* **toes in,** to be obstinate, to refuse to give way. **dig in,** to mix into the soil by digging; (*colloq.*) to begin eating. **dig oneself in,** to dig a defensive trench or pit; to establish one's position. [perh. f. OE]

digest /dɪˈdʒest/ *v.t.* **1** to assimilate food in the stomach and bowels. **2** to understand and assimilate mentally. **3** to summarize. —/ˈdaɪdʒest/ *n.* a methodical summary, especially of laws; a periodical synopsis of current literature or news. [f. L *digerere* distribute, dispose]

digestible /dɪˈdʒestɪb(ə)l/ *adj.* able to be digested. [f. prec.]

digestion /dɪˈdʒestʃ(ə)n/ *n.* the process of digesting; the power of digesting food. [f. DIGEST]

digestive /dɪˈdʒestɪv/ *adj.* of or aiding digestion. —*n.* a digestive substance. —**digestive biscuit,** a sweet kind of wholemeal biscuit. [f. OF or L (as DIGEST)]

digger *n.* **1** one who digs; a mechanical excavator. **2** (*colloq.*) an Australian or New Zealander.

diggings *n.pl.* **1** a mine or goldfield. **2** (*colloq.*) lodgings. [f. DIG]

digit /ˈdɪdʒɪt/ *n.* **1** any of the numerals from 0 to 9. **2** a finger or toe. [f. L *digitus* finger, toe]

digital /ˈdɪdʒɪt(ə)l/ *adj.* of digits. —**digital clock, watch,** one showing the time by displayed digits, not by hands. **digital recording,** a recording with sound-information represented in digits for more accurate transmission. —**digitally** *adv.* [f. L *digitalis* (as prec.)]

digitalis /dɪdʒɪˈteɪlɪs/ *n.* a drug prepared from dried foxglove leaves, used as a heart-stimulant. [as prec., generic name of foxglove, f. its thimble-shaped flower]

dignified *adj.* having or showing dignity. [f. foll.]

dignify /ˈdɪgnɪfaɪ/ *v.t.* to confer dignity on, to ennoble; to give a high-sounding name to. [f. OF f. L (*dignus* worthy)]

dignitary /ˈdɪgnɪtərɪ/ *n.* a person holding a high rank or position, especially ecclesiastical. [f. foll.]

dignity /ˈdɪgnɪtɪ/ *n.* **1** a composed and serious manner or style, showing suitable formality. **2** worthiness of honour or respect. **3** a high rank or position. —**beneath one's dignity,** not worthy enough for one to do. **stand on one's**

dignity, to insist on being treated with respect. [f. L *dignitas* (*dignus* worthy)]

digraph /ˈdaɪgrɑːf/ *n.* a union of two letters representing one sound (as *ph*, *ea*). [f. DI- + Gk -*graphos* written]

digress /daɪˈgres/ *v.i.* to depart from the main subject temporarily in speech or writing. —**digression** *n.* [f. L *digredi* depart (*gradus* step)]

dike /daɪk/ *n.* a long wall or embankment against flooding; a ditch; a low wall of turf or stone. —*v.t.* to provide or protect with dikes. [f. ON or Du.]

diktat /ˈdɪktɑːt/ *n.* a categorical statement or decree. [G, = DICTATE]

dilapidated /dɪˈlæpɪdeɪtɪd/ *adj.* in a state of disrepair or ruin. —**dilapidation** /-ˈdeɪʃ(ə)n/ *n.* [f. L *dilapidare* squander (*lapis* stone)]

dilatation /dɪləˈteɪʃ(ə)n/ *n.* dilation; widening of the cervix, e.g. for surgical curettage. [as foll.]

dilate /daɪˈleɪt/ *v.t./i.* **1** to make or become wider or larger. **2** to speak or write at length. —**dilation** *n.* [f. OF f. L *dilatare* spread out (*latus* wide)]

dilatory /ˈdɪlətərɪ/ *adj.* **1** slow to act, not prompt. **2** designed to cause delay. [f. L *dilatorius* (*dilator* delayer)]

dilemma /dɪˈlemə, daɪ-/ *n.* a situation in which a choice has to be made between alternatives that are both undesirable; (**D**) a difficult situation. [L f. Gk, = double proposition]

dilettante /dɪlɪˈtæntɪ/ *n.* (*pl.* **-ti** /-tiː/, **-tes**) who dabbles in a subject without serious study of it. —**dilettantism** *n.* [It., f. *dilettare* (f. L *delectare*) delight]

diligent /ˈdɪlɪdʒ(ə)nt/ *adj.* careful and hard-working; showing care and effort. —**diligence** *n.*, **diligently** *adv.* [f. OF f. L *diligens* assiduous f. *diligere* love]

dill *n.* a yellow-flowered herb (*Anethum graveolens*) with scented leaves and seeds used for flavouring pickles. [OE]

dilly-dally *v.i.* to waste time by indecision etc. [redupl. of DALLY]

dilute /daɪˈljuːt/ *v.t.* **1** to reduce the strength of (a fluid) by adding water or other solvent. **2** to weaken or reduce the forcefulness of. —*adj.* diluted. —**dilution** *n.* [f. L *diluere* wash away, dilute]

dim *adj.* **1** faintly luminous or visible, not bright. **2** indistinct, not clearly perceived or remembered. **3** not seeing clearly; (*colloq.*) stupid. —*v.t./i.* (**-mm-**) to become or make dim. —**dimly** *adv.*, **dimness** *n.* [OE]

dime /daɪm/ *n.* (*US*) a ten-cent coin. [orig. = tithe, f. OF f. L *decima* (*pars*) tenth part]

dimension /daɪˈmenʃ(ə)n/ *n.* a measurable extent of any kind, as length, breadth, thickness, area, or volume; (in *pl.*) size; extent or scope in a particular aspect. —**dimensional** *adj.* [f. OF f. L (DI-, *mensio* measure)]

dimidiate /dɪˈmɪdɪət/ *adj.* halved, split in two. —**dimidiation** /-ˈeɪʃ(ə)n/ *n.* [f. L *dimidiare* (DI-, *midium* half)]

diminish /dɪˈmɪnɪʃ/ *v.t./i.* to make or become smaller or less (in fact or appearance); to lessen the reputation of (a person). —**law of diminishing returns,** the fact that expenditure, taxation, etc., beyond a certain point does not produce a proportionate yield. [f. earlier *minish* (f. OF, as MINCE) and *diminue* f. OF f. L *diminuere* break up small]

diminuendo /dɪmɪnjʊˈendəʊ/ *adv.* (*Mus.*) with a gradual decrease of loudness. —*n.* (*pl.* **-os**) (*Mus.*) a passage to be played in this way. [It. (as prec.)]

diminution /dɪmɪˈnjuːʃ(ə)n/ *n.* diminishing, being diminished; decrease. [f. OF f. L (as DIMINISH)]

diminutive /dɪˈmɪnjʊtɪv/ *adj.* **1** remarkably small, tiny. **2** (of a derivative or suffix) used to imply something small (actually or in token of affection etc.) of the kind denoted by the simple word. —*n.* a diminutive word. [as prec.]

dimity /ˈdɪmɪtɪ/ *n.* a cotton fabric woven with checks or stripes of heavier thread. [f. It. or L f. Gk *dimitos* of double thread]

dimple *n.* a small hollow or dent, especially in the cheek or chin. —*v.t./i.* to produce dimples in; to show dimples. [prob. f. OE, cf. OHG *tumphilo* deep place in water]

din *n.* a prolonged loud and distracting noise. —*v.t./i.* (**-nn-**) **1** to force (information) *into* a person by continually repeating it. **2** to make a din. [OE]

dinar /ˈdiːnɑː(r)/ *n.* a currency unit in Yugoslavia and in several countries of the Middle East and North Africa. [f. Arab. & Pers. f. Gk f. L *denarius* silver coin]

dine *v.t./i.* **1** to eat dinner. **2** to give dinner to (esp. socially). —**dining-car** *n.* a railway coach in which meals are served. **dining-room** *n.* a room in which meals are eaten. [f. OF *di(s)ner* f. L *disjejunare* break one's fast (DIS-, *jejunare* fast)]

diner *n.* **1** a person who dines. **2** a small dining-room. **3** a dining-car on a train. [f. prec.]

ding-dong *n.* the sound of alternating strokes as of two bells. —*adj.* (of a contest) in which each contestant alternately has the advantage. —*adv.* with vigour and energy. [imit.]

dinghy /ˈdɪŋgɪ, -ŋɪ/ *n.* a ship's small boat; a small pleasure boat; a small inflatable rubber boat. [f. Hindi, = Indian river-boat]

dingle *n.* a deep wooded valley or dell. [orig. unkn.]

dingo /ˈdɪŋgəʊ/ *n.* (*pl.* **-oes**) a wild or half-domesticated Australian dog, *Canis dingo*. [Aboriginal]

dingy /ˈdɪndʒɪ/ *adj.* dull-coloured, drab; dirty-looking. —**dingily** *adv.*, **dinginess** *n.* [orig. unkn.]

dinkum /ˈdɪŋkəm/ *adj.* (*Austral. & NZ colloq.*) genuine, real. [orig. unkn.]

dinky *adj.* (*colloq.*) neat and attractive; small, dainty. [dim. of Sc. *dink* neat, trim]

dinner *n.* the chief meal of the day, whether at midday or evening; a formal evening meal in honour of a person or event. —**dinner-jacket,** a man's short usually black jacket for evening wear. [f. OF (as DINE)]

dinosaur /ˈdaɪnəsɔː(r)/ *n.* an extinct reptile of the Mesozoic era, often of enormous size. [f. L f. Gk (*deinos* terrible, *sauros* lizard)]

dint *n.* a dent. —*v.t.* to mark with dints. —**by dint of,** by force or means of. [f. OE & ON; ult. orig. unkn.]

diocese /ˈdaɪəsɪs/ *n.* the district under the pastoral care of a bishop. —**diocesan** /daɪˈɒsɪs(ə)n/ *adj.* [f. OF f. L f. Gk *dioikēsis* administration]

diode /ˈdaɪəʊd/ *n.* a thermionic valve having two electrodes; a semiconductor rectifier having two terminals. [f. DI- + ELECTRODE]

dioecious /daɪˈiːʃəs/ *adj.* **1** (*Bot.*) with male and female organs on separate plants. **2** (*Zool.*) having the two sexes in separate individuals. [f. DI- + Gk *-oikos* -housed]

dioptre /daɪˈɒptə(r)/ *n.* a unit of refractive power of a lens. [f. F f. L f. Gk *dioptra* optical instrument]

diorama /daɪəˈrɑːmə/ *n.* **1** a scenic painting in which changes in colour and direction of illumination simulate sunrise etc. **2** a small representation of a scene with three-dimensional figures, viewed through a window etc. **3** a small-scale model or film-set. [f. Gk *dia* through + *horama* thing seen]

dioxide /daɪˈɒksaɪd/ *n.* an oxide containing two atoms of oxygen.

dip *v.t./i.* (**-pp-**) **1** to put or let down into a liquid, to immerse; to dye (a fabric) thus; to wash (sheep) in vermin-killing liquid; to go under water and emerge quickly; to go down, to go below any surface or level. **2** to lower for a moment and then raise again; to lower the beam of (a vehicle's headlights) to reduce dazzle. **3** to slope or extend downwards. **4** to put a hand or ladle etc. *into* to take something out; to look cursorily *into* (a book etc.). —*n.* **1** dipping, being dipped. **2** (*colloq.*) a bathe in the sea etc. **3** a liquid in which a thing is dipped; a sauce or dressing in which food is dipped before eating. **4** the downward slope of a road etc.; a depression in the skyline etc. —**dipstick** *n.* a rod for measuring the depth of a liquid, especially oil in a vehicle's engine. **dip-switch** *n.* a switch for dipping a vehicle's headlights. [OE]

diphtheria /dɪfˈθɪərɪə/ *n.* an acute infectious bacterial disease with inflammation of a mucous membrane especially of the throat. [f. F f. Gk *diphthera* piece of leather, f. the toughness of the false membrane developed]

diphthong /ˈdɪfθɒŋ/ *n.* a union of two vowels (letters or sounds) pronounced in one syllable (as in *coin, loud, toy*). —**diphthongal** /-ˈθɒŋg(ə)l/ *adj* [f. F f. L f. Gk (DI-, *phthongos* sound)]

diplodocus /dɪˈplɒdəkəs/ *n.* a giant herbivorous dinosaur of the order Sauropoda. [f. Gk *diploos* double + *dokos* beam]

diploid /ˈdɪplɔɪd/ *adj.* having chromosomes in homologous pairs. —*n.* a diploid cell or organism. [G, f. Gk *diplous* double + *eidos* form]

diploma /dɪˈpləʊmə/ *n.* **1** a certificate awarded by a college etc. to a person who has successfully completed a course of study; a document conferring honour or privilege. **2** an official document, a charter. [L f. Gk, = folded paper (*diplous* double)]

diplomacy /dɪˈpləʊməsɪ/ *n.* the management of international relations or skill in this; tact. [f. F (as DIPLOMATIC)]

diplomat /ˈdɪpləmæt/ *n.* **1** a member of the diplomatic service. **2** a tactful person. [f. F (as foll.)]

diplomatic /dɪpləˈmætɪk/ *adj.* of or involved in diplomacy; tactful. —*n.* (in *sing.* or *pl.*) the palaeographic and critical study of diplomas (sense 2). —**diplomatic immunity,** exemption of diplomatic staff etc. abroad from arrest, taxation, etc. **diplomatic service,** the branch of public service concerned with the representation of a country abroad. —**diplomatically** *adv.* [f. F (as DIPLOMA)]

diplomatist /dɪˈpləʊmətɪst/ *n.* a diplomat.

dipper *n.* **1** a thing that dips. **2** a diving bird, especially the water ouzel. [f. prec.]

dipsomania /dɪpsəˈmeɪnɪə/ *n.* an uncontrollable craving for alcohol. —**dipsomaniac** *n.* [f. Gk *dipsa* thirst + MANIA]

dipterous /ˈdɪptərəs/ *adj.* two-winged, belonging to the order Diptera (insects with one pair of membranous wings, e.g. fly, mosquito). [f. Gk (DI-, *pteron* wing)]

diptych /ˈdɪptɪk/ *n.* a painting, especially an altar-piece, on two leaves closing like a book. [f. L f. Gk, = pair of writing tablets (DI-, *ptukhē* fold)]

dire *adj.* dreadful, calamitous, ominous; extreme and requiring urgent remedy. [f. L *dirus*]

direct /dɪˈrekt, daɪ-/ *adj.* **1** extending or moving in a straight line or by the shortest route, not crooked or oblique. **2** straightforward, going straight to the point; frank, not ambiguous. **3** without intermediaries; personal. **4** (of descent) linear, not collateral. **5** complete, greatest possible. —*adv.* in a direct way or manner; by a direct route. —*v.t.* **1** to control, to manage, to govern the actions of; to command; to supervise the acting etc. of (a play or film etc.). **2** to tell (a person) the way (*to*); to address (a letter etc. *to*). **3** to cause (a blow, remark, effort, attention, etc.) to have a specified direction or target. —**direct action,** exertion of pressure on the community by action (e.g. a strike or sabotage) seeking an immediate effect, rather than by parliamentary means. **direct current,** an electric current flowing in one direction only. **direct debit,** the regular debiting of a person's bank account at the request of a creditor. **direct-grant school,** one receiving money from the government and not from a local authority, and in return observes certain conditions as to the admission of pupils. **direct object,** the primary object of action of a transitive verb. **direct speech,** words quoted as actually spoken, not modified by being reported. **direct tax,** one levied on income as distinct from one on goods or services. —**directness** *n.* [f. L *dirigere* (*regere* keep straight, rule)]

direction *n.* **1** directing, supervision. **2** (usu. in *pl.*) an order or instruction. **3** a line along which or a point to or from which a person or thing moves or looks; the tendency or scope of a subject, aspect. [f. F or L (as prec.)]

directional *adj.* **1** of or indicating direction. **2** sending or receiving radio signals in one direction only. [f. prec.]

directive *n.* a general instruction for a procedure or action. —*adj.* serving to direct. [as DIRECT]

directly *adv.* in a direct line or manner; at once, without delay. —*conj.* as soon as. [f. DIRECT]

director *n.* one who directs, especially a member of the board managing the affairs of a company etc.; a person who directs a play, film, etc.; a spiritual advisor. —**directorial** /-ˈtɔːrɪəl/ *adj.*, **directorship** *n.*, **directness** *n.fem.* [f. AF f. L, = governor (as DIRECT)]

directorate *n.* **1** the office of director. **2** a board of directors. [f. prec.]

directory *n.* a book with a list of telephone subscribers, inhabitants of a district, members of a profession etc., with various details. [as DIRECT]

dirge *n.* a slow mournful song; a lament for the dead. [f. L *dirige* imper. of *dirigere* direct, first wd in Latin antiphon (from Psalm 5: 8) in Office of the Dead]

dirigible /ˈdɪrɪdʒɪb(ə)l/ *adj.* capable of being guided. —*n.* a dirigible balloon airship. or [as DIRECT]

dirk *n.* a kind of dagger, especially of a Scottish Highlander. [orig. unkn.]

dirndl /ˈdɜːnd(ə)l/ *n.* a woman's dress imitating Alpine peasant costume, with a fitted bodice and full skirt; (also **dirndl skirt**) a full gathered skirt with a tight waistband. [G, dim. of *dirne* girl]

dirt *n.* **1** unclean matter that soils something. **2** earth, soil. **3** foul or malicious words or talk. **4** excrement. —**dirt cheap,** (*colloq.*) very cheap. **dirt road,** a road without a made surface. **dirt-track** *n.* a racing track made of earth or rolled cinders etc. **treat like dirt,** to treat (a person) with contempt. [ON, = excrement]

dirty *adj.* **1** soiled by dirt, unclean; (of a nuclear weapon) causing considerable fall-out. **2** obscene, lewd. **3** dishonourable, unfair. **4** (of weather) rough, squally. **5** (of a colour) not pure or clear. —*v.t./i.* to make or become dirty. —**dirty look,** (*colloq.*) a look of disapproval or disgust. **dirty word,** an obscene word; a word for something disapproved of. —**dirtily** *adv.*, **dirtiness** *n.*

dis- *prefix* (**di-** before certain consonants) implying reversal of an action or state, the direct opposite of the simple word, the removal of a thing or quality, completeness or intensification of the action, expulsion from. [L]

disability /dɪsəˈbɪlɪtɪ/ *n.* something that disables or disqualifies a person; a physical incapacity caused by injury, disease, etc.

disable /dɪsˈeɪb(ə)l/ *v.t.* to deprive of an ability; (esp. in *p.p.*) to cripple, to deprive of or reduce the power of acting, walking, etc. —**disablement** *n.*

disabuse /dɪsəˈbjuːz/ *v.t.* to free *of* a false idea etc., to disillusion.

disadvantage /dɪsədˈvɑːntɪdʒ/ *n.* an unfavourable circumstance or condition; damage to one's interest or reputation. —*v.t.* to put at a disadvantage. —**disadvantageous** /-ˈteɪdʒəs/ *adj.*

disadvantaged *adj.* in unfavourable conditions; lacking normal social etc. opportunities. [f. prec.]

disaffected /dɪsəˈfektɪd/ *adj.* discontented; disloyal. —**disaffection** *n.*

disagree /dɪsəˈgriː/ *v.i.* **1** to hold a different opinion; to quarrel. **2** (of factors or circumstances) to fail to correspond. —**disagree with,** to differ in opinion from; to have an adverse effect on. —**disagreement** *n.*

disagreeable *adj.* unpleasant, not to one's liking; (of a person) not amiable. —**disagreeably** *adv.*

disallow /dɪsəˈlaʊ/ *v.t.* to refuse to allow or accept as valid.

disappear /dɪsəˈpɪə(r)/ *v.i.* to cease to be visible, to pass from sight or existence. —**disappearance** *n.*

disappoint /dɪsəˈpɔɪnt/ *v.t.* to fail to fulfil the

desire or expectation of; to frustrate (a hope, purpose, etc.). [f. OF (as DIS-, APPOINT)]

disappointment *n*. a person, thing, or event that proves disappointing; the resulting distress. [f. prec.]

disapprobation /dɪsæprəˈbeɪʃ(ə)n/ *n*. disapproval.

disapprove /dɪsəˈpru:v/ *v.i.* to have or express an unfavourable opinion (*of*) —**disapproval** *n*.

disarm /dɪˈsɑ:m/ *v.t.*/*i.* **1** to deprive of weapons or the means of defence; to reduce or give up one's own armaments. **2** to defuse (a bomb). **3** to pacify the hostility or suspicions of. [f. OF (as DIS-, ARM[2])]

disarmament /dɪsˈɑ:məmənt/ *n*. the reduction of military forces and armaments. [f. prec.]

disarrange /dɪsəˈreɪndʒ/ *v.t.* to undo the arrangement of, to disorganize. —**disarrangement** *n*.

disarray /dɪsəˈreɪ/ *n*. disorder. —*v.t.* to throw into disorder.

disassociate /dɪsəˈsəʊsɪeɪt/ *v.t.* = DISSOCIATE.

disaster /dɪˈzɑ:stə(r)/ *n*. a sudden or great misfortune; a complete failure. —**disastrous** *adj*., **disastrously** *adv*. [f. F f. It. (as DIS-, L *astrum* star, planet)]

disavow /dɪsəˈvaʊ/ *v.t.* to disclaim knowledge of or responsibility for. —**disavowal** *n*.

disband /dɪsˈbænd/ *v.t.*/*i.* to break up (a group etc.); (of a group) to disperse. —**disbandment** *n*.

disbar /dɪsˈbɑ:(r)/ *v.t.* (**-rr-**) to deprive (a barrister) of the right to practise law. —**disbarment** *n*.

disbelieve /dɪsbɪˈli:v/ *v.t.*/*i.* to refuse or be unable to believe; to be sceptical. —**disbelief** *n*., **disbeliever** *n*.

disburden /dɪsˈbɜ:d(ə)n/ *v.t.* to relieve of a burden; to remove (a load, anxieties, etc.).

disburse /dɪsˈbɜ:s/ *v.t.* to pay out (money). —**disbursal** *n*., **disbursement** *n*. [f. OF (as DIS-, *bourse* purse)]

disc *n*. **1** a thin circular plate of any material; something shaped or looking like this, as the sun's face. **2** a layer of cartilage between the vertebrae. **3** a gramophone record. **4** (in computers) a disc with a surface on which data can be recorded (usu. magnetically) and stored. —**disc brake,** a brake consisting of a disc operated by the action of friction pads on it. **disc drive,** (in computers) a device for controlling and using a disc pack, having a rotation mechanism. **disc jockey,** a presenter of a broadcast programme featuring recordings of popular music. **disc pack,** a data storage medium consisting of an assembly of rigid magnetic discs mounted on a spindle, with a removable protective cover. [f. F or f. L *discus*]

discard /dɪsˈkɑ:d/ *v.t.* to put aside as useless or unwanted; to reject (a playing card) from a hand. —/ˈdɪs-/ *n*. a discarded thing.

discern /dɪˈsɜ:n/ *v.t.* to perceive clearly with the mind or senses; to make out by thought or by gazing, listening, etc. [f. OF f. L *discernere* (DIS-, *cernere* separate)]

discernible *adj*. able to be discerned. [f. prec.]

discerning *adj*. having good judgement or insight. [f. DISCERN]

discernment *n*. good judgement or insight. [as prec.]

discharge /dɪsˈtʃɑ:dʒ/ *v.t.*/*i.* **1** to send out or emit (missiles, liquids, etc.), (of a wound etc.) to emit a liquid; to unload from a ship. **2** to release (a prisoner); to allow (a patient, jury, etc.) to leave; to relieve (a bankrupt) of residual liability; to dismiss from employment or office. **3** to acquit oneself of, to pay or perform (a duty or obligation). **4** to fire (a gun); to release the electric charge of; to remove the cargo from (a ship etc.). —/also ˈdɪs-/ *n*. **1** discharging, being discharged. **2** that which is discharged, especially matter from a wound or sore. **3** the release of an electric charge, especially with a spark. **4** a written certificate of release, dismissal, etc. [f. OF (as DIS-, CHARGE)]

disciple /dɪˈsaɪp(ə)l/ *n*. a follower or adherent of a leader, teacher, etc.; one of Christ's original followers. [f. L *discipulus* (*discere* learn)]

disciplinarian /dɪsɪplɪˈneərɪən/ *n*. one who enforces or believes in strict discipline. [f. foll.]

disciplinary /ˈdɪsɪplɪnərɪ, -ˈplɪn-/ *adj*. of or for discipline. [as foll.]

discipline /ˈdɪsɪplɪn/ *n*. **1** training or a way of life aimed at self-control and obedience; order maintained or observed among pupils, soldiers, and others under control; control exercised over the members of an organization. **2** punishment given to correct a person or enforce obedience. **3** a branch of instruction or learning. —*v.t.* to train to obedience and order; to punish. [f. L (*discere* learn)]

disclaim /dɪsˈkleɪm/ *v.t.* to renounce a claim to, to disown, to deny (responsibility etc.).

disclaimer *n*. a statement disclaiming something; a renunciation. [f. prec.]

disclose /dɪsˈkləʊz/ *v.t.* **1** to make known. **2** to expose to view. —**disclosure** *n*. [f. OF (as DIS-, CLOSE[2])]

disco *n*. (*pl*. **-os**) (*colloq*.) a discothèque; a dancing-party with records; equipment for this. [abbr.]

discolour /dɪsˈkʌlə(r)/ *v.t.*/*i.* to spoil the colour of, to stain; to become changed in colour or stained. —**discoloration** /-ˈreɪʃ(ə)n/ *n*. [f. OF or L (as DIS-, *colorare* colour)]

discomfit /dɪsˈkʌmfɪt/ *v.t.* to humiliate or disconcert completely. —**discomfiture** /-fɪtʃə(r)/ *n*. [f. OF *desconfire* (as DIS-, L *conficere* put together)]

discomfort /dɪsˈkʌmfət/ *n.* lack of comfort; a thing causing this. —*v.t.* to make uncomfortable.

discompose /dɪskəmˈpəʊz/ *v.t.* to disturb the composure of. —**discomposure** *n.*

disconcert /dɪskənˈsɜːt/ *v.t.* to disturb the self-possession of, to fluster. [f. F (as DIS-, CONCERT)]

disconnect /dɪskəˈnekt/ *v.t.* to break the connection of; to put out of action by disconnecting parts. —**disconnection** *n.*

disconnected *adj.* (esp. of speech or writing) lacking orderly connection, having abrupt transitions. [f. prec.]

disconsolate /dɪsˈkɒns(ə)lət/ *adj.* forlorn, downcast, disappointed. [f. L *disconsolatus* (DIS-, *consolare* console)]

discontent /dɪskənˈtent/ *n.* dissatisfaction, lack of contentment; a grievance. —*v.t.* to make dissatisfied. —**discontentment** *n.*

discontented *adj.* dissatisfied, feeling discontent. [f. prec.]

discontinue /dɪskənˈtɪnjuː/ *v.t./i.* to cease, to cause to cease; to cease from, to give up. —**discontinuance** *n.* [f. OF f. L *discontinuare* (DIS- *continuare* continue)]

discontinuous /dɪskənˈtɪnjʊəs/ *adj.* lacking continuity in space or time, intermittent. —**discontinuity** /-ˈjuːɪtɪ/ *n.*

discord /ˈdɪskɔːd/ *n.* **1** opposition of views, strife; a harsh noise, clashing sounds. **2** (*Mus.*) a lack of harmony between notes sounded together. [f. OF f. L (as DIS-, *cor* heart)]

discordant /dɪsˈkɔːd(ə)nt/ *adj.* disagreeing; not in harmony, clashing. —**discordance** *n.* [as prec.]

discothèque /ˈdɪskəʊtek/ *n.* a club etc. where amplified recorded popular music is played for dancing; the equipment for playing such records. [F, = record-library]

discount /ˈdɪskaʊnt/ *n.* an amount deducted from the full or normal price; an amount deducted for the immediate payment of a sum not yet due (e.g. on a bill of exchange. —*v.t.* **1** /-ˈkaʊnt/ to disregard partly or wholly. **2** /ˈdɪs-/ to buy or sell at a discount; to deduct an amount from (a price etc.). —**at a discount,** below full or normal price; (*fig.*) not at the true value. [f. F or It. (as DIS-, COUNT[1])]

discountenance /dɪsˈkaʊnt(ə)nəns/ *v.t.* **1** to refuse to approve of. **2** to disconcert.

discourage /dɪsˈkʌrɪdʒ/ *v.t.* to deprive of courage or confidence; to dissuade, to deter; to show disapproval of. —**discouragement** *n.* [f. OF (as DIS-, COURAGE)]

discourse /ˈdɪskɔːs/ *n.* **1** conversation; a speech or lecture. **2** a written treatise on a subject. —/-ˈkɔːs/ *v.i.* **1** to converse; to speak or write at length on a subject. **2** to utter a discourse. [f. L *discursus* (as DISCURSIVE)]

discourteous /dɪsˈkɜːtɪəs/ *adj.* lacking courtesy. —**discourteously** *adv.*, **discourtesy** *n.*

discover /dɪsˈkʌvə(r)/ *v.t.* to acquire knowledge or sight of by effort or chance; to be the first to do this in a particular case. [f. OF f. L *discooperire* (DIS-, *cooperire* cover)]

discovery *n.* discovering; a thing discovered. [f. prec.]

discredit /dɪsˈkredɪt/ *v.t.* **1** to harm the good reputation of. **2** to refuse to believe; to cause to be disbelieved. —*n.* **1** harm to a reputation, a person or thing causing this. **2** lack of credibility.

discreditable *adj.* bringing discredit, shameful. —**discreditably** *adv.* [f. prec.]

discreet /dɪsˈkriːt/ *adj.* **1** showing caution and good judgement in what one does; not giving away secrets. **2** unobtrusive. —**discreetly** *adv.* [f. OF f. L *discretus* separate, *discretio* discernment]

discrepancy /dɪsˈkrepənsɪ/ *n.* a difference, failure to correspond, inconsistency. —**discrepant** *adj.* [f. L, = discordance of sound]

discrete /dɪsˈkriːt/ *adj.* separate, individually distinct; discontinuous. [f. L (*discernere* distinguish, separate)]

discretion /dɪsˈkreʃ(ə)n/ *n.* **1** good judgement, prudence; ability to keep secrets. **2** freedom or authority to act according to one's judgement. —**years** *or* **age of discretion,** the age at which a person is considered capable of managing his own affairs. [f. OF f. L (as DISCERN)]

discretionary *adj.* done or used at a person's discretion. [f. prec.]

discriminate /dɪsˈkrɪmɪneɪt/ *v.t./i.* **1** to make or see a distinction (between); to distinguish unfairly *against* or *in favour of* a person on grounds of sex, race, colour, etc. **2** to have good taste or judgement. —**discrimination** /-ˈneɪʃ(ə)n/ *n.*, **discriminatory** /-ˈkrɪm-/ *adj.* [f. L (*discrimen* distinction)]

discriminating *adj.* showing good judgement, discerning. [f. prec.]

discursive /dɪsˈkɜːsɪv/ *adj.* wandering from topic to topic. [f. L (*discurrere* run to and fro)]

discus /ˈdɪskəs/ *n.* a heavy thick-centred disc thrown in ancient and modern sports. [L f. Gk *diskos*]

discuss /dɪsˈkʌs/ *v.t.* to consider (a subject) by talking or writing about it; to hold a conversation about. —**discussion** *n.* [f. L *discutere* shake to pieces]

disdain /dɪsˈdeɪn/ *n.* scorn, contempt. —*v.t.* to regard with disdain; to refrain or refuse from disdain. —**disdainful** *adj.*, **disdainfully** *adv.* [f. OF f. L *dedignare* think unworthy]

disease /dɪˈziːz/ *n.* an unhealthy condition of the body, a plant, or some part thereof, caused by infection, diet, or faulty functioning of a physiological process; a particular kind of this; an abnormal mental condition. [f. OF (as DIS-, EASE)]

diseased *adj*. affected with disease; abnormal, disordered. [f. prec.]

disembark /dɪsɪm'bɑ:k/ *v.t./i.* to go or put ashore. —**disembarkation** /-'keɪʃ(ə)n/ *n.*

disembarrass /dɪsɪm'bærəs/ *v.t.* **1** to free from embarrassment. **2** to rid or relieve (*of*). —**disembarrassment** *n.*

disembody /dɪsɪm'bɒdɪ/ *v.t.* to free (a soul, spirit, etc.) from the body or concrete form. —**disembodiment** *n.*

disembowel /dɪsɪm'baʊəl/ *v.t.* (**-ll-**) to remove the bowels or entrails of. —**disembowelment** *n.* [f. DIS- = utterly + obs. *embowl* disembowel]

disenchant /dɪsɪn'tʃɑ:nt/ *v.t.* to free from enchantment or illusion. —**disenchantment** *n.*

disencumber /dɪsɪn'kʌmbə(r)/ *v.t.* to free from encumbrance.

disengage /dɪsɪn'geɪdʒ/ *v.t./i.* to detach, to loosen, to release from engagement; to become detached. —**disengagement** *n.*

disengaged *adj*. at leisure, uncommitted; detached. [f. prec.]

disentangle /dɪsɪn'tæŋg(ə)l/ *v.t./i.* to free or become free of tangles or complications. —**disentanglement** *n.*

disestablish /dɪsɪ'stæblɪʃ/ *v.t.* to end the established state of, to deprive (the Church) of its State connection. —**disestablishment** *n.*

disfavour /dɪs'feɪvə(r)/ *n.* dislike, disapproval; being disliked. —*v.t.* to regard or treat with disfavour.

disfigure /dɪs'fɪgə(r)/ *v.t.* to spoil the appearance of. —**disfigurement** *n.*

disfranchise /dɪs'fræntʃaɪz/ *v.t.* to deprive of rights as a citizen or of a franchise held. —**disfranchisement** *n.*

disgorge /dɪs'gɔ:dʒ/ *v.t.* to eject from the throat; to pour forth.

disgrace /dɪs'greɪs/ *n.* loss of favour or respect, downfall from a position of honour; a thing that causes this. —*v.t.* to bring disgrace to, to degrade; to dismiss from favour or honour. [f. F f. It. (as DIS-, GRACE)]

disgraceful *adj*. causing disgrace, shameful. —**disgracefully** *adv*. [f. prec.]

disgruntled /dɪs'grʌnt(ə)ld/ *adj*. sulkily discontented. [f. DIS- = utterly + *gruntle* obs. frequent. of GRUNT]

disguise /dɪs'gaɪz/ *v.t.* to conceal the identity of, to make unrecognizable; to conceal or obscure. —*n.* something worn to disguise one's identity; a disguised state. [f. OF (as DIS- GUISE]

disgust /dɪs'gʌst/ *n.* strong dislike, repugnance. —*v.t.* to cause disgust in. [f. OF f. It. (as DIS-, GUSTO)]

dish *n.* **1** a shallow flat-bottomed container for holding food; its contents; (in *pl.*) all the utensils after use at a meal. **2** a particular kind of food. **3** a dish-shaped object or cavity. **4** (*colloq.*) an attractive young woman. —*v.t.* **1** to make dish-shaped. **2** (*colloq.*) to frustrate, to ruin. —**dish out,** (*slang*) to distribute (carelessly). **dish up,** to put (food) in dishes ready for serving, to prepare to serve a meal; (*slang*) to present as fact or argument. **dish-water** *n.* water in which dishes have been washed. [OE f. L *discus* disc]

dishabille /dɪsə'bi:l/ var. of DÉSHABILLÉ.

disharmony /dɪs'hɑ:mənɪ/ *n.* lack of harmony, discord. —**disharmonious** /-'məʊnɪəs/ *adj.*

dishcloth *n.* a cloth for washing dishes.

dishearten /dɪs'hɑ:t(ə)n/ *v.t.* to make despondent, to cause to lose courage or confidence. —**disheartenment** *n.*

dishevelled /dɪ'ʃev(ə)ld/ *adj*. ruffled and untidy. —**dishevelment** *n.* [f. OF (as DIS-, *chevel* hair)]

dishonest /dɪs'ɒnɪst/ *adj*. not honest. —**dishonestly** *adv*., **dishonesty** *n.*

dishonour /dɪs'ɒnə(r)/ *n.* loss of honour or respect, shame or disgrace; a thing that causes this. —*v.t.* **1** to bring dishonour upon, to disgrace. **2** to refuse to accept or pay (a cheque etc.). [f. OF f. L *dishonorare* (DIS-, HONOUR)]

dishonourable /dɪs'ɒnərəb(ə)l/ *adj*. bringing dishonour, shameful, ignominious. —**dishonourably** *adv*. [f. prec.]

dishwasher *n.* **1** a machine for washing dishes. **2** a water wagtail.

disillusion /dɪsɪ'lu:ʒ(ə)n/ *v.t.* to free from illusion or mistaken belief. —*n.* being disillusioned. —**disillusionment** *n.*

disincentive /dɪsɪn'sentɪv/ *n.* a thing or factor discouraging a particular action.

disincline /dɪsɪn'klaɪn/ *v.t.* to make unwilling. —**disinclination** /-klɪ'neɪʃ(ə)n/ *n.*

disinfect /dɪsɪn'fekt/ *v.t.* to cleanse of infection, to remove bacteria from. —**disinfection** *n.*

disinfectant *adj*. having disinfecting properties. —*n.* a disinfecting substance. [f. prec.]

disinflation /dɪsɪn'fleɪʃ(ə)n/ *n.* a policy designed to counteract inflation without producing the disadvantages of deflation. —**disinflationary** *n.*

disingenuous /dɪsɪn'dʒenjʊəs/ *adj*. insincere, giving a false appearance of candour. —**disingenuously** *adv*., **disingenuousness** *n.*

disinherit /dɪsɪn'herɪt/ *v.t.* to reject as one's heir, to deprive of the right of inheritance (esp. by making a new will). —**disinheritance** *n.* [f. DIS- + INHERIT in obs. sense 'make heir']

disintegrate /dɪ'sɪntɪgreɪt/ *v.t./i.* to separate or cause to separate into component parts, to break up; to deprive of or lose cohesion; (of a nucleus) to emit one or more particles or divide into smaller nuclei. —**disintegration** /-ˈgreɪʃ(ə)n/ *n*., **disintegrator** *n*.

disinter /dɪsɪnˈtɜ:(r)/ *v.t*. (**-rr-**) to dig up (esp. a corpse) from the ground. —**disinterment** *n*.

disinterest /dɪsˈɪntərest/ *n*. **1** impartiality. **2** (**D**) lack of concern.

disinterested *adj*. **1** impartial, not influenced by involvement or advantage. **2** (**D**) uninterested. —**disinterestedly** *adv*., **disinterestedness** *n*. [f. prec.]

disjoin /dɪsˈdʒɔɪn/ *v.t*. to separate, to disunite, to part. [f. OF f. L *disjungere* (DIS-, *jungere* join)]

disjoint /dɪsˈdʒɔɪnt/ *v.t*. to take to pieces at the joints; to dislocate; to disturb the working or connection of. [as prec.]

disjointed *adj*. (of talk) disconnected. [f. prec.]

disjunction /dɪsˈdʒʌŋkʃ(ə)n/ *n*. disjoining, separation. [f. OF or L (as DISJOIN)]

disjunctive /dɪsˈdʒʌŋktɪv/ *adj*. involving separation; (of conjunctions such as *or* and *but*) introducing an alternative or contrast. [f. L (as prec.)]

disk var. of DISC.

diskette /dɪsˈket/ *n*. a floppy disc, not necessarily of small size. [f. prec. + -ETTE]

dislike /dɪsˈlaɪk/ *n*. a feeling that a person or thing is unpleasant, unattractive, etc.; the object of this. —*v.t*. to have a dislike for, not to like.

dislocate /ˈdɪsləkeɪt/ *v.t*. to disturb the normal connection of, to displace a bone in (a joint); to disrupt, to put out of order. —**dislocation** /-ˈkeɪʃ(ə)n/ *n*. [f. OF or L *dislocare* (DIS-, *locare* place)]

dislodge /dɪsˈlɒdʒ/ *v.t*. to disturb or move from an established position. —**dislodgement** *n*.

disloyal /dɪsˈlɔɪəl/ *adj*. unfaithful, lacking loyalty. —**disloyally** *adv*., **disloyalty** *n*.

dismal /ˈdɪzm(ə)l/ *adj*. causing or showing gloom, miserable, dreary; (*colloq*.) feeble, inept. —**dismally** *adv*. [f. OF f. L *dies mali* unlucky days (of which there were held to be two in each month)]

dismantle /dɪsˈmænt(ə)l/ *v.t*. to pull down, to take to pieces; to deprive of defences, equipment, etc.

dismay /dɪsˈmeɪ/ *n*. a feeling of helplessness and alarm in the face of some danger or difficulty. —*v.t*. to fill with dismay. [f. OF (as DIS-, MAY[1])]

dismember /dɪsˈmembə(r)/ *v.t*. **1** to remove the limbs from. **2** to partition (a country etc.), to divide up. —**dismemberment** *n*. [f. OF (as DIS-, L *membrum* limb)]

dismiss /dɪsˈmɪs/ *v.t*. **1** to send away, to cause to leave one's presence; to disperse. **2** to order to terminate employment or service (esp. with dishonour). **3** to put out of one's thoughts, to cease to feel or discuss; to treat (a subject) summarily; to reject (a lawsuit etc.) without further hearing. **4** to put out (a batsman or side) in cricket (*for* a stated score). —**dismissal** *n*., **dismissive** *adj*. [f. OF f. L *dimissus* (as DIS-, *mittere* send)]

dismount /dɪsˈmaʊnt/ *v.t./i*. **1** to get off or down from an animal one is riding; to cause to fall off, to unseat. **2** to remove (a thing, esp. a gun) from its mounting.

disobedient /dɪsəˈbi:dɪənt/ *adj*. disobeying, rebellious. —**disobedience** *n*., **disobediently** *adv*.

disobey /dɪsəˈbeɪ/ *v.t./i*. fail or refuse to obey; to disregard (a rule, order, etc.).

disorder /dɪsˈɔ:də(r)/ *n*. **1** lack of order, confusion; a commotion, a riot. **2** disturbance of a normal state or function; an ailment, a disease. —*v.t*. to put into disorder, to upset. [f. OF (as DIS-, ORDAIN)]

disorderly *adj*. untidy, confused; riotous, contrary to public order or morality. —**disorderly house**, a brothel. [f. prec.]

disorganize /dɪsˈɔ:gənaɪz/ *v.t*. to upset the order or system of, to throw into confusion. —**disorganization** /-ˈzeɪʃ(ə)n/ *n*.

disorient /dɪsˈɔ:rɪənt/ *v.t*. to disorientate.

disorientate /dɪsˈɔ:rɪənteɪt/ *v.t*. to confuse (a person) as to his bearings. —**disorientation** /-ˈteɪʃɪ(ə)n/*n*.

disown /dɪsˈəʊn/ *v.t*. to refuse to recognize or acknowledge, to repudiate; to reject connection with.

disparage /dɪsˈpærɪdʒ/ *v.t*. to speak slightingly of, to belittle. —**disparagement** *n*., **disparagingly** *adv*. [f. OF *desparagier* marry unequally (as DIS-, *parage* equality of rank f. L *par* equal)]

disparate /ˈdɪspərət/ *adj*. essentially different, unrelated, not comparable. [f. L *disparare* separate, infl. in sense by *dispar* unequal]

disparity /dɪsˈpærɪtɪ/ *n*. inequality, difference, incongruity. [f. F f. L (*dispar* unequal)]

dispassionate /dɪsˈpæʃ(ə)nət/ *adj*. free from emotion, impartial. —**dispassionately** *adv*.

dispatch /dɪˈspætʃ/ *v.t*. **1** to send off to a destination or for a purpose. **2** to give the death-blow to, to kill; to finish or dispose of promptly or quickly. —*n*. **1** dispatching, being dispatched. **2** promptness, efficiency. **3** a written (official) message; a news report sent to a newspaper or news agency. —**dispatch-box** *n*. a case for carrying official documents. **dispatch-rider** *n*. an official messenger on a motor cycle. [f. It. *dispacciare* or Sp. *despachar*]

dispel /dɪˈspel/ *v.t*. (**-ll-**) to drive away, to scatter (darkness, fog, fears, etc.). [f. L *dispellere* (DIS-, *pellere* drive)]

dispensable /dɪˈspensəb(ə)l/ *adj*. that can be dispensed with. [f. L (as DISPENSE)]

dispensary /dɪˈspensərɪ/ *n*. a place (especially a

room) where medicines are dispensed. [f. L (as DISPENSE)]

dispensation /dispen'seɪʃ(ə)n/ *n.* **1** dispensing, distributing. **2** ordering or management, especially of the world by Providence. **3** an exemption from a penalty, rule, or obligation. [f. OF or L (as foll.)]

dispense /dɪ'spens/ *v.t./i.* to distribute, to deal out, to administer; to make up and give out (medicines etc.) according to prescriptions. —**dispense with,** to do without; to make unnecessary. [f. OF f. L *dispensare*, frequent. of *dispendere* weigh or pay out]

dispenser *n.* **1** a person who dispenses (especially medicine). **2** a device for dispensing commodities in fixed quantities. [f. prec.]

disperse /dɪ'spɜ:s/ *v.t./i.* **1** to scatter; to drive, go, or send in different directions. **2** to send to or station at different points. **3** to put in circulation, to disseminate. **4** to separate (white light) into coloured constituents. —**dispersal** *n.*, **dispersive** *adj.* [f. L *dispergere* (DIS-, *spargere* scatter)]

dispersion /dɪ'spɜ:ʃ(ə)n/ *n.* **1** dispersing, being dispersed. **2 the Dispersion,** the scattering of Jews among Gentiles from the time of the Captivity onwards; the Jews thus scattered. [f. prec.]

dispirit /dɪ'spɪrɪt/ *v.t.* (often in *p.p.*) to make despondent. [f. DIS- + SPIRIT]

displace /dɪs'pleɪs/ *v.t.* to move from its place; to oust, to take the place of; to remove from office. —**displaced person,** one removed from his home country by military or political pressure; originally, a civilian deported from a German-occupied country to work in Germany during the Second World War and thereafter homeless.

displacement *n.* **1** displacing, being displaced. **2** the amount of fluid displaced by a thing floating or immersed in it; the amount by which a thing is shifted from its place. [f. prec.]

display /dɪ'spleɪ/ *v.t.* to exhibit, to show; to reveal, to betray, to allow to appear. —*n.* **1** displaying. **2** a thing or things displayed, a show; ostentation. **3** a bird's special pattern of behaviour as a means of visual communication. [f. OF f. L *displicare* (DIS-, *plicare* fold)]

displease /dɪs'pli:z/ *v.t.* to arouse the disapproval or indignation of, to offend; to be unpleasing to. [f. OF (as DIS-, L *placēre* please)]

displeasure /dɪs'pleʒə(r)/ *n.* a displeased feeling, indignation, dissatisfaction. [as prec.]

disport /dɪ'spɔ:t/ *v.t./i.* to play, to frolic; to enjoy *oneself*. [f. OF (as DIS-, L *portare* carry)]

disposable *adj.* able to be disposed of; at one's disposal; designed to be thrown away after use. —*n.* a disposable article. [f. DISPOSE]

disposal *n.* disposing, disposing of. —**at one's disposal,** available for one's use. [f. foll.]

dispose /dɪ'spəʊz/ *v.t./i.* **1** to place suitably or in order, to arrange. **2** to incline, to make willing or desirous; to bring (a person, the mind) into a certain state; (in *pass.*) to have a specified tendency of mind. **3** to determine the course of events. —**dispose of,** to get rid of; to deal with, to finish; to prove (an argument etc.) incorrect. [f. OF (as POSE), assoc. with foll.]

disposition /dɪspə'zɪʃ(ə)n/ *n.* **1** setting in order, arrangement. **2** the relative position of parts. **3** a temperament; a natural tendency, an inclination. **4** (usu. in *pl.*) a plan, preparations. [f. OF f. L (*disponere* arrange)]

dispossess /dɪspə'zes/ *v.t.* to deprive (a person) of the possession *of*; to oust, to dislodge. —**dispossession** *n.*

disproof /dɪs'pru:f/ *n.* disproving, a refutation.

disproportion /dɪsprə'pɔ:ʃ(ə)n/ *n.* lack of proportion; being out of proportion.

disproportionate /dɪsprə'pɔ:ʃ(ə)nət/ *adj.* out of proportion, relatively too large or too small. —**disproportionately** *adv.* [f. prec.]

disprove /dɪs'pru:v/ *v.t.* to prove to be false.

disputable /dɪs'pju:təb(ə)l/ *adj.* open to dispute, not certainly true. [F, or f. L (as DISPUTE)]

disputant /dɪs'pju:tənt/ *adj.* a person involved in disputation. [f. DISPUTE]

disputation /dɪspju:'teɪʃ(ə)n/ *n.* **1** an argument, a debate. **2** a formal discussion of a set question or thesis. [f. F or L (as DISPUTE)]

disputatious /dɪspju:'teɪʃəs/ *adj.* fond of argument. [as prec.]

dispute /dɪs'pju:t/ *v.t./i.* **1** to argue, to debate. **2** to quarrel. **3** to question the truth or validity of. —*n.* **1** an argument, a debate. **2** a quarrel. —**in dispute,** being argued about. [f. OF f. L *disputare* estimate (DIS-, *putare* reckon)]

disqualify /dɪs'kwɒlɪfaɪ/ *v.t.* to make or declare ineligible or unsuitable; to debar from a competition. —**disqualification** /-'keɪʃ(ə)n/ *n.*

disquiet /dɪs'kwaɪət/ *n.* uneasiness, anxiety. —*v.t.* to cause disquiet to.

disquietude /dɪs'kwaɪətju:d/ *n.* a state of disquiet.

disquisition /dɪskwɪ'zɪʃ(ə)n/ *n.* a long elaborate treatise or discourse upon a subject. [F f. L (DIS-, *quaerere* seek)]

disregard /dɪsrɪ'gɑ:d/ *v.t.* to pay no attention to, to treat as of no importance. —*n.* lack of attention, indifference, neglect.

disrepair /dɪsrɪ'peə(r)/ *n.* bad condition due to lack of repairs.

disreputable /dɪs'repjʊtəb(ə)l/ *adj.* of bad repute, not respectable in character or appearance; discreditable. —**disreputably** *adv.*

disrepute /dɪsrɪ'pju:t/ *n.* lack of good repute, discredit.

disrespect /dɪsrɪ'spekt/ *n.* lack of respect, discourtesy. —**disrespectful** *adj.*, **disrespectfully** *adv.*

disrobe /dɪs'rəʊb/ *v.t./i.* to remove clothes (from).

disrupt /dɪs'rʌpt/ *v.t.* to interrupt the flow or continuity of, to bring disorder to; to break apart. —**disruption** *n.*, **disruptive** *adj.* [f. L *disrumpere* (DIS-, *rumpere* break)]

dissatisfaction /dɪsætɪs'fækʃ(ə)n/ *n.* lack of satisfaction or contentment; a cause of this.

dissatisfy /dɪ'sætɪsfaɪ/ *v.t.* to fail to satisfy, to make discontented.

dissect /dɪ'sekt/ *v.t.* **1** to cut into pieces, especially so as to examine parts or structure. **2** to analyse, to examine or criticize in detail. —**dissection** *n.*, **dissector** *n.* [f. L *dissecare* (DIS-, *secare* cut)]

dissemble /dɪ'semb(ə)l/ *v.t./i.* to conceal or disguise (intention, character, feeling, etc.); to talk or act hypocritically or insincerely. [f. OF f. L *dissimulare* (DIS-, *simulare* simulate)]

disseminate /dɪ'semɪneɪt/ *v.t.* to scatter about, to spread (ideas etc.) widely. —**dissemination** /-'neɪʃ(ə)n/ *n.*, **disseminator** *n.* [f. L *disseminare* (DIS-, *semen* seed)]

dissension /dɪ'senʃ(ə)n/ *n.* discord arising from dissent. [f. OF f. L (as foll.)]

dissent /dɪ'sent/ *v.i.* to disagree openly, to hold a different view or belief (*from*). —*n.* such a difference of view or belief; an expression of this. [f. L *dissentire* (DIS-, *sentire* feel)]

dissenter *n.* one who dissents; **Dissenter**, a member of a sect that has separated from the Church of England, a Nonconformist. [f. prec.]

dissentient /dɪ'senʃɪənt, -ʃ(ə)nt/ *adj.* dissenting from an established view. —*n.* a dissentient person. [as DISSENT]

dissertation /dɪsə'teɪʃ(ə)n/ *n.* a detailed discourse, especially as submitted for a higher degree in a university. [f. L *dissertare*, frequent. of *disserere* examine]

disservice /dɪs'sɜ:vɪs/ *n.* a harmful action, especially one done in a misguided attempt to help.

dissident /'dɪsɪd(ə)nt/ *adj.* disagreeing, at variance. —*n.* a person who is at variance, especially with established authority. —**dissidence** *n.* [F, or f. L *dissidēre* (DIS-, *sedēre* sit)]

dissimilar /dɪ'sɪmɪlə(r)/ *adj.* unlike, not similar. —**dissimilarity** /-'lærɪtɪ/ *n.*

dissimulate /dɪ'sɪmjʊleɪt/ *v.t./i.* to dissemble. —**dissimulation** /-'leɪʃ(ə)n/ *n.* [f. L *dissimulare* (DIS-, *simulare* simulate)]

dissipate /'dɪsɪpeɪt/ *v.t./i.* to dispel, to disperse; to squander, to fritter away. [f. L *dissipare* scatter around]

dissipated *adj.* given to dissipation, dissolute. [f. prec.]

dissipation /dɪsɪ'peɪʃ(ə)n/ *n.* dissipating; a frivolous or dissolute way of life. [as DISSIPATE]

dissociate /dɪ'səʊsɪeɪt, -ʃɪ-/ *v.t./i.* to separate or disconnect in thought or fact; to become dissociated. —**dissociate oneself from**, to declare oneself unconnected with. **dissociation** /-'eɪʃ(ə)n/ *n.*, **dissociative** *adj.* [f. L *dissociare* (DIS-, *socius* companion)]

dissoluble /dɪ'sɒljʊb(ə)l/ *adj.* that can be disintegrated, loosened, or disconnected. [F, or f. L (DIS-, SOLUBLE)]

dissolute /'dɪsəlu:t, -lju:t/ *adj.* morally lax, licentious. [f. L (as DISSOLVE)]

dissolution /dɪsə'lu:ʃ(ə)n, -'lju:-/ *n.* **1** dissolving, being dissolved, especially of a partnership or of a parliament for a new election; the breaking up or abolition (of an institution). **2** death. [f. OF or L (as foll.)]

dissolve /dɪ'zɒlv/ *v.t./i.* **1** to make or become liquid, especially by immersion or dispersion in a liquid. **2** to disappear gradually; to cause to do this. **3** to dismiss or disperse (an assembly, especially a parliament). **4** to annul or put an end to (a marriage or partnership). —**dissolve into**, to give way to (tears, laughter). [f. L *dissolvere* (DIS-, *solvere* loosen)]

dissonant /'dɪsənənt/ *adj.* not in harmony, harsh-toned; incongruous. —**dissonance** *n.* [f. OF or L *dissonare* (DIS-, *sonare* sound)]

dissuade /dɪ'sweɪd/ *v.t.* to give advice or exercise influence to discourage or divert (a person *from*). —**dissuasion** *n.*, **dissuasive** *adj.* [f. L *dissuadēre* (DIS-, *suadēre* persuade)]

distaff /'dɪstɑ:f/ *n.* a cleft stick holding wool or flax for spinning. —**distaff side**, the branch of a family descended from a female parent or ancestor. [OE (as MLG *dise(ne)* bunch of flax, STAFF)]

distance /'dɪstəns/ *n.* **1** the length of space between one point and another; a space of time. **2** a distant point, a remoter field of vision. **3** being far off; remoteness, reserve. —*v.t.* **1** to place or cause to seem far off. **2** to leave far behind in a race etc. —**keep one's distance**, to remain apart or aloof. [f. OF f. L (*distare* stand apart)]

distant *adj.* **1** far away, at a specified distance; remote in position, time, relationship, or concept. **2** avoiding familiarity, aloof. —**distantly** *adv.* [as prec.]

distaste /dɪs'teɪst/ *n.* a dislike, an aversion (*for*).

distasteful *adj.* causing distaste, disagreeable *to*. —**distastefully** *adv.* [f. prec.]

distemper[1] /dɪ'stempə(r)/ *n.* a disease of dogs and some other animals, with catarrh and weakness. —*v.t.* (*archaic*, usu. in *p.p.*) to upset, to derange. [f. L *distemperare* (DIS-, *temperare* mix in correct proportion)]

distemper[2] /dɪ'stempə(r)/ *n.* a kind of paint using glue or size instead of an oil-base, for use on walls. —*v.t.* to paint with this. [f. OF or L *distemperare* soak (as prec.)]

distend /dɪˈstend/ *v.t./i.* to swell or stretch out by pressure from within. —**distensible** *adj.*, **distension** *n.* [f. L *distendere* (DIS-, *tendere* stretch)]

distich /ˈdɪstɪk/ *n.* a verse couplet. [f. L f. Gk (DI-, *stikhos* line)]

distil /dɪˈstɪl/ *v.t.*(**-ll-**) **1** to purify, to extract the essence from (a substance) by vaporizing it with heat then condensing it with cold and re-collecting the resulting liquid; to make (whisky, an essence, etc.) by distilling raw materials. **2** to fall or cause to fall in drops. —**distillation** /-ˈleɪʃ(ə)n/ *n.* [f. L *distillare* (DE-, *stilla* drop)]

distillate /dɪˈstɪleɪt/ *n.* a product of distillation. [f. prec.]

distiller *n.* one who distils, especially a maker of alcoholic liquor. [f. DISTIL]

distillery *n.* a place where alcoholic liquor is distilled. [as prec.]

distinct /dɪˈstɪŋkt/ *adj.* **1** not identical, separate, different in quality or kind. **2** clearly perceptible, definite, and unmistakable. —**distinctly** *adv.*, **distinctness** *n.* [f. p.p. of L *distinguere* (as DISTINGUISH)]

distinction /dɪˈstɪŋkʃ(ə)n/ *n.* **1** seeing or making a difference, discrimination. **2** a difference seen or made; a thing that differentiates. **3** distinguished character, excellence. **4** the showing of special consideration. **5** a title or mark of honour. [f. OF f. L (as DISTINGUISH)]

distinctive *adj.* distinguishing, characteristic. —**distinctively** *adv.* [as prec.]

distingué /dɪˈstæŋgeɪ/ *adj.* having a distinguished air or manners. [F (as foll.)]

distinguish /dɪˈstɪŋgwɪʃ/ *v.t./i.* **1** to observe or identify a difference in; to differentiate, to draw distinctions (*between*); to characterize, to be a mark or property of. **2** to make out by listening, looking, etc. **3** to make *oneself* prominent or noteworthy (*by* some achievement). [f. F or L *distinguere* (DIS-, *stinguere* extinguish)]

distinguishable *adj.* able to be distinguished. [f. prec.]

distinguished *adj* eminent, having distinction. [f. DISTINGUISH]

distort /dɪˈstɔːt/ *v.t.* to pull or twist out of shape; to transmit (a sound etc.) inaccurately; to misrepresent (facts etc.). —**distortion** *n.* [f. L *distorquēre* (DIS-, *torquēre* twist)]

distract /dɪˈstrækt/ *v.t.* to draw away the attention of (a person, the mind, etc.); to confuse, to bewilder. [f. L (DIS-, *trahere* draw)]

distraction /dɪˈstrækʃ(ə)n/ *n.* **1** distracting, being distracted. **2** a thing that distracts the attention or impairs concentration. **3** an amusement, a relaxation. **4** mental confusion or distress. [f. OF or L (as prec.)]

distrain /dɪˈstreɪn/ *v.i.* to levy distraint (*upon* a person or goods). [f. OF f. L *distringere* (DIS-, *stringere* draw tight)]

distraint /dɪˈstreɪnt/ *n.* the seizure of goods as a method of enforcing payment. [f. prec.]

distrait /dɪˈstreɪ/ *adj.* (*fem.* ***distraite*** /-eɪt/) inattentive; distraught. [F (as DISTRACT)]

distraught /dɪˈstrɔːt/ *adj.* much troubled in mind; demented with worry etc. [alt. of obs. *distract* adj. (as DISTRACT)]

distress /dɪˈstres/ *n.* **1** anguish or suffering caused by pain, sorrow, worry, or exhaustion; a state of difficulty or helplessness; lack of money or necessaries. **2** (*Law*) distraint. —*v.t.* to cause distress to, to make unhappy. [f. OF (rel. to DISTRAIN)]

distressed *adj.* affected by distress, impoverished. —**distressed area,** a region of much poverty and unemployment. [f. prec.]

distributary /dɪˈstrɪbjʊtərɪ/ *n.* a river or glacier branch that does not return to the main stream after leaving it (as in a delta). [f. foll.]

distribute /dɪˈstrɪbjuːt, (**D**) ˈdɪs-/ *v.t.* to divide and give a share of to each of a number; to spread about, to scatter, to put at different points; to arrange, to classify. —**distribution** /-ˈbjuːʃ(ə)n/ *n.* [f. L *distribuere* (DIS-, *tribuere* assign)]

distributive /dɪˈstrɪbjʊtɪv/ *adj.* of, concerned with, or produced by distribution; (*Gram. & Logic*) referring to each individual of a class, not to the class collectively. —*n.* a distributive word (e.g. *each*, *neither*, *every*). [f. F or L (as prec.)]

distributor /dɪˈstrɪbjʊtə(r)/ *n.* **1** one who distributes things, especially an agent who markets goods. **2** a device in an internal-combustion engine for passing the current to each sparking-plug in turn. [f. DISTRIBUTE]

district /ˈdɪstrɪkt/ *n.* a region or territory regarded as a geographical or administrative unit; a division of a county. —**district attorney,** (*US*) the prosecuting officer of a district. **district nurse,** a local nurse visiting patients at their homes. [F f. L, = territory of jurisdiction (as DISTRAIN)]

distrust /dɪsˈtrʌst/ *n.* lack of trust, suspicion. —*v.t.* to feel distrust in. —**distrustful** *adj.*

disturb /dɪˈstɜːb/ *v.t.* **1** to break the rest or quiet or calm of; to agitate, to worry. **2** to move from a settled position. **3** (in *p.p.*) emotionally or mentally unstable or abnormal. [f. OF f. L *disturbare* (DIS-, *turbare* to disorder)]

disturbance *n.* an interruption of tranquillity; agitation; a tumult, an uproar. [as prec.]

disunion /dɪsˈjuːnɪən/ *n.* separation, lack of union; discord.

disunite /dɪsju:ˈnaɪt/ *v.t./i.* to remove unity from; to cause to separate, to experience separation. —**disunity** /-ˈju:nɪtɪ/ *n.*

disuse /dɪsˈju:z/ *v.t.* to cease to use. —/-ˈju:s/ *n.* a disused state.

disyllable /dɪˈsɪləb(ə)l, daɪ-/ *n.* a word or metrical foot of two syllables. —**disyllabic** /-ˈlæbɪk/ *adj.* [f. DI- + SYLLABLE]

ditch *n.* a long narrow excavated channel, especially for drainage or to mark a boundary. —*v.t./i.* **1** to make or repair ditches. **2** to drive (a vehicle) into a ditch; (*slang*) to make a forced landing on the sea, to bring (an aircraft) down thus. **3** (*slang*) to abandon, to discard, to leave in the lurch; to frustrate. —**dull as ditch-water,** very dull. [OE]

dither /ˈdɪðə(r)/ *v.i.* to be nervously hesitant or unsure; to tremble, to quiver. —*n.* a state of dithering, nervous excitement or apprehension. [var. of *didder* = DODDER[1]]

dithyramb /ˈdɪθɪræm/ *n.* a Greek choric hymn, wild in character; a passionate or inflated poem, speech, or writing. —**dithyrambic** /-ˈræmbɪk/ *adj.* [f. L f. Gk]

dittany /ˈdɪtənɪ/ *n.* a herb of the genus *Dictamnus*, formerly supposed to be of medicinal value. [f. OF f. L *dictamnus* f. Gk (perh. f. *Diktē* mountain in Crete where (among other places) the herb grew)]

ditto /ˈdɪtəʊ/ *n.* (*pl.* **-os**) the aforesaid, the same (in accounts, inventories, etc.), symbolized by two small marks (*ditto marks* ,,) placed under the word or item repeated; (*colloq.*) an expression of agreement. [It. f. L (as DICTUM)]

ditty *n.* a short simple song. [f. OF *dité* composition f. L (as DICTATE)]

diuretic /daɪʊəˈretɪk/ *adj.* causing an increased secretion of urine. —*n.* a diuretic drug. [f. OF or L f. Gk (DIA-, *oureō* urinate)]

diurnal /daɪˈɜ:n(ə)l/ *adj.* **1** of the day, not nocturnal. **2** daily; occupying one day. [f. L (*dies* day)]

diva /ˈdi:və/ *n.* a great woman singer, a prima donna. [It. f. L, = goddess]

divalent /daɪˈveɪlənt/ *adj.* (*Chem.*) having a valence of two. [f. DI- + *-valent* (as VALENCE)]

divan /dɪˈvæn/ *n.* a low couch or bed without a back or ends. [f. F or It. ult. f. Pers., = bench]

dive *v.t./i.* **1** to plunge, especially head first, into water; (of an aircraft) to plunge steeply downwards; (of a submarine or diver) to submerge; to go down or out of sight suddenly. **2** to rush or move suddenly. **3** to put (one's hand) *into* one's pocket, handbag, etc. —*n.* **1** an act of diving; a sharp downward movement or fall. **2** (*colloq.*) a disreputable place, a drinking-den. —**dive-bomb** *v.t.* to drop bombs on from a diving aircraft. **diving-bell** *n.* an open-bottomed structure supplied with air, in which a diver can be lowered into deep water. **diving-board** *n.* a springboard for diving from. **diving-suit** *n.* a watertight suit, usually with a helmet and an air-supply for work underwater. [OE; rel. to DEEP, DIP]

diver *n.* **1** one who dives, especially a person who works underwater in a diving-suit. **2** a diving bird, especially of the genus *Gavia*. [f. prec.]

diverge /daɪˈvɜ:dʒ/ *v.i.* to go in different directions from a common point, to become further apart; to go aside *from* a track or path. —**divergent** *adj.*, **divergence** *n.* [f. L (DIS-, *vergere* incline)]

divers /ˈdaɪvəz/ *adj.* (*archaic*) various, several. [f. OF (as foll.)]

diverse /daɪˈvɜ:s/ *adj.* of different kinds, varied. [f. L *diversus* (DIS-, *vertere* turn)]

diversify /daɪˈvɜ:sɪfaɪ/ *v.t.* to make diverse, to vary; to spread (an investment) over several enterprises or products. —**diversification** /-fɪˈkeɪʃ(ə)n/ *n.* [f. OF f. L (as prec.)]

diversion /daɪˈvɜ:ʃ(ə)n/ *n.* **1** diverting something from its course. **2** the diverting of attention, a manœuvre to achieve this; a pastime, a recreation. **3** an alternative route when a road is temporarily closed to traffic. —**diversionary** *adj.* [f. L (as foll.)]

diversity /daɪˈvɜ:sɪtɪ/ *n.* being diverse; a variety. [f. OF (as DIVERS)]

divert /daɪˈvɜ:t/ *v.t.* **1** to turn aside from its course; to cause to go by a different route. **2** to distract (the attention); to entertain or amuse. [f. F f. L (DIS-, *vertere* turn)]

divertissement /di:vɜ:ˈti:smɑ̃/ *n.* a short ballet etc. between acts or longer pieces; a diversion or entertainment. [F (as prec.)]

divest /daɪˈvest/ *v.t.* to strip (a person) *of* clothes; to deprive or rid *of*. [f. OF (as DIS-, L *vestire* clothe)]

divide /dɪˈvaɪd/ *v.t./i.* **1** to separate *into* parts, to split or break up; to separate (one thing) from another; to become or be able to be divided. **2** to mark out into parts or groups, to classify. **3** to cause to disagree, to set at variance. **4** to distribute, to share out. **5** to find how many times a number contains another. **6** to separate (an assembly etc.) into two sets in voting, to be thus separated. —*n.* **1** a watershed. **2** (*fig.*) a dividing line. —**divided skirt,** culottes. [f. L *dividere* force apart]

dividend /ˈdɪvɪdend/ *n.* **1** a number to be divided. **2** a share of profits paid to shareholders or to winners in a football pool. **3** the benefit from an action. [f. AF f. L (as prec.)]

divider *n.* **1** a screen etc. dividing a room. **2** (in *pl.*) measuring compasses. [f. prec.]

divination /dɪvɪˈneɪʃ(ə)n/ *n.* insight into the unknown or the future by allegedly supernatural means. [f. OF or f. L (as DIVINE[2])]

divine[1] /dɪˈvaɪn/ *adj.* **1** of, from, or like God or a god; sacred. **2** (*colloq.*) excellent, delightful. —*n.* a theologian or clergyman. —**divinely** *adv.* [f. OF f. L (*divus* god)]

divine[2] /dɪˈvaɪn/ *v.t./i.* to discover by intuition, inspiration, or guessing; to foresee; to practise divination. —**divining-rod** *n.* a dowsing-rod (see DOWSE). —**diviner** *n.* [f. F f. L *divinare* (as prec.)]

divinity /dɪˈvɪnɪtɪ/ *n.* **1** being divine; a god; godhead. **2** theology. [f. OF f. L (as DIVINE[1])]

divisible /dɪˈvɪzɪb(ə)l/ *adj.* able to be divided. —**divisibility** /-ˈbɪlɪtɪ/ *n.* [F or f. L (as DIVIDE)]

division /dɪˈvɪʒ(ə)n/ *n.* **1** dividing, being divided; a process of dividing a number by another; a disagreement or discord; (in Parliament) the separation of members into two sections for counting votes. **2** one of the parts into which a thing is divided; a major unit of administration or organization. —**division sign,** the sign ÷ indicating that one quantity is to be divided by another. —**divisional** *adj.* [f. OF f. L (as DIVIDE)]

divisive /dɪˈvaɪsɪv/ *adj.* tending to cause disagreement. [f. L (as DIVIDE)]

divisor /dɪˈvaɪzə(r)/ *n.* the number by which another is to be divided. [f. F or L (as DIVIDE)]

divorce /dɪˈvɔːs/ *n.* **1** legal dissolution of a marriage. **2** severance, separation. —*v.t.* **1** to separate by divorce; to end a marriage with (one's husband or wife) by divorce. **2** to detach, to separate. [f. OF f. L (DIS-, *vortere* = *vertere* turn)]

divorcee /dɪvɔːˈsiː/ *n.* a divorced person. [f. prec.]

divot /ˈdɪvət/ *n.* a piece of turf cut out by a blow, especially by the head of a golf-club. [orig. Sc.; etym. unkn.]

divulge /daɪˈvʌldʒ/ *v.t.* to disclose or reveal (a secret etc.). —**divulgence** *n.* [f. L (DIS-, *vulgare* publish)]

divvy *n.* (*colloq.*) a dividend. —*v.t.* (*colloq.*, with *up*) to share out. [abbr. of DIVIDEND]

Diwali /dɪˈwɑːlɪ/ *n.* the Hindu festival of lights celebrated in October or November in honour of the goddess of wealth (Lakshmi). [f. Hindi f. Skr., = row of lamps (*dīpa* lamp)]

Dixie /ˈdɪksɪ/ *n.* the Southern States of the USA. [orig. unkn.]

dixie *n.* a large iron cooking-pot used by campers etc. [f. Hindi *degchī* f. Pers., dim. of *deg* pot]

Dixieland *n.* **1** Dixie. **2** a kind of jazz with a strong two-beat rhythm. [f. DIXIE]

DIY *abbr.* do-it-yourself.

dizzy *adj.* giddy, feeling confused; making giddy. —*v.t.* to make dizzy, to bewilder. —**dizzily** *adv.*, **dizziness** *n.* [OE]

DJ *abbr.* **1** a disc jockey. **2** a dinner-jacket.

dl *abbr.* decilitre(s).

D.Litt. *abbr.* Doctor of Letters. [f. L *Doctor Litterarum*]

dm *abbr.* decimetre(s).

DNA *abbr.* deoxyribonucleic acid, a substance that is a major constituent of chromosomes.

D-notice *n.* an official request to news editors not to publish items on specified subjects, for reasons of security. [f. *de*fence + NOTICE]

do[1] /dʊ, *emphat.* duː/ *v.t./i.* (3 *sing. pres.* **does** /dʌz/; *past* **did**; *p.p.* **done** /dʌn/; *partic.* **doing**) **1** to perform, to carry out, to fulfil or complete. **2** to produce, to make; to bring about, to provide. **3** to deal with, to set in order; to work out, to solve; to work at, to be occupied with; to cook; to translate or transform; (*slang*) to cheat, to rob or burgle; to prosecute or convict. **4** to cover in travelling; (*colloq.*) to visit, to see the sights of. **5** to undergo. **6** to provide food etc. for; (*colloq.*) to satisfy, to be suitable or convenient to. **7** to produce (a play etc.); to play the part of, to act like. **8** to fare, to get on, to achieve something. **9** to be suitable or acceptable, to serve a purpose. **10** to be in progress. —*v. aux.*, with infinitive or elliptically, for emphasis, in inversion, in questions and negations, or in place of the verb. —**do away with,** to get rid of, to abolish, to kill. **do down,** (*colloq.*) to overcome, to cheat, to swindle. **do for,** to be satisfactory or sufficient for; (*colloq.*) to destroy, to ruin, to kill; (*colloq.*) to act as a housekeeper for. **do-gooder** *n.* person meaning to do social good but unrealistic or intrusive in the process. **do in,** (*slang*) to ruin, to kill; (*colloq.*) to exhaust, to tire out. **do-it-yourself** *adj.* & *n.* (work) done or to be done by an amateur handyman at home. **do or die,** to persist regardless of danger. **do out,** to clean or redecorate (a room). **do over,** (*slang*) to attack, to beat up. **do something for,** (*colloq.*) to enhance the appearance or quality of. **do up,** to fasten, to wrap up; to refurbish, to renovate. **do with,** to use, to treat. **do without,** to forgo, to manage without. **to do with,** in connection with, related to. [OE]

do[2] /duː/ *n.* (*pl.* **dos, do's**) **1** an elaborate event, party, or operation. **2** (*colloq.*) a swindle, a hoax. —**dos and don'ts,** the rules of behaviour. **fair dos,** fair shares. [f. prec.]

do[3] var. of DOH.

Dobermann pinscher /ˈdəʊbəmən ˈpɪnʃə(r)/ a large dog of a German breed with a smooth coat and docked tail. [f. L *Dobermann* (19th-c. German dog-breeder), G *pinscher* terrier]

doc *n.* (*colloq.*) doctor. [abbr.]

docile /ˈdəʊsaɪl/ *adj.* submissive, easily managed. —**docilely** *adv.*, **docility** /-ˈsɪlɪtɪ/ *n.* [f. L (*docēre* teach)]

dock[1] *n.* an artificially enclosed body of water for the loading, unloading, and repair of ships; (in *pl.*) a range of docks with wharves and offices. —*v.t./i.* **1** to bring or come into dock. **2** to join (two or more spacecraft) together in space, to become joined thus. —**in dock,** (*colloq.*) in hospital or (of a vehicle) laid up for repairs. [f. MDu. *docke*]

dock[2] *n.* an enclosure in a criminal court for the accused. [prob. f. Flem. *dok* cage]

dock[3] *n.* a weed of the genus *Rumex*, with broad leaves that are rubbed on the skin to alleviate the pain of nettle-stings. [OE]

dock[4] *v.t.* **1** to cut short (an animal's tail). **2** to reduce or take away a part of (wages, supplies, etc.). [f. *dock* fleshy part of tail, perh. rel. to MLG *dokke* bundle of straw]

dock[5] *n.* **1** the solid fleshy part of an animal's tail; the crupper of a saddle or harness. [perh. f. MLG *dokke* bundle of straw]

docker *n.* a person employed to load and unload ships. [f. DOCK[1]]

docket /ˈdɒkɪt/ *n.* a document or label listing goods delivered or the contents of a package, or recording the payment of customs dues etc. —*v.t.* to enter on a docket, to label with a docket. [orig. unkn.]

dockland *n.* the district near docks. [f. DOCK[1]]

dockyard *n.* an area with docks and equipment for building and repairing ships. [f. DOCK[1]]

doctor /ˈdɒktə(r)/ *n.* **1** a qualified practitioner of medicine, a physician. **2** a person who holds a doctorate. —*v.t.* **1** to treat medically. **2** to castrate or spay (an animal). **3** to patch up (machinery etc.); to tamper with or falsify. [f. OF f. L (*docēre* teach)]

doctoral /ˈdɒktər(ə)l/ *adj.* of or for the degree of doctor. [f. prec.]

doctorate /ˈdɒktərət/ *n.* the highest university degree in any faculty. [f. DOCTOR]

doctrinaire /dɒktrɪˈneə(r)/ *n.* a person who applies principles pedantically without allowance for circumstances. —*adj.* theoretical and unpractical. [F (as foll.)]

doctrine /ˈdɒktrɪn/ *n.* what is taught, a body of instruction; a principle of religion, a political etc. belief, a set of such principles. —**doctrinal** /-ˈtraɪn(ə)l/ *adj.* [f. OF f. L (as DOCTOR)]

document /ˈdɒkjʊmənt/ *n.* a thing, especially a title-deed, writing, or inscription, that provides a record or evidence. —*v.t.* to prove by or provide with documents. —**documentation** /-ˈteɪʃ(ə)n/ *n.* [f. OF f. L, = proof (as DOCTOR)]

documentary /dɒkjʊˈmentərɪ/ *adj.* consisting of documents; providing a factual record or report. —*n.* a documentary film. [f. prec.]

dodder[1] *v.i.* to tremble or totter, especially from age. —**dodderer** *n.*, **doddery** *adj.* [var. of obs. dial. *dadder*]

dodder[2] *n.* a threadlike climbing parasitic plant of the genus *Cascuta*. [= MLG *dod(d)er*, MHG *toter*]

dodecagon /dəʊˈdekəgən/ *n.* a plane figure with twelve sides and angles. [f. Gk (*dōdeka* twelve, *-gonos* angled)]

dodecahedron /dəʊdekəˈhi:drən/ *n.* a solid figure with twelve faces. [f. Gk (*dōdeka* twelve, *hedra* base)]

dodecaphonic /dəʊdekəˈfɒnɪk/ *adj.* of a compositional method, in which the twelve notes of the octave are treated equally, without the focusing on a 'home-note' (the tonic) of traditional harmony. [f. Gk *dōdeka* twelve + PHONIC]

dodge /dɒdʒ/ *v.t./i.* to move quickly to one side, or *round*, *about*, or *behind* an obstacle, to elude a pursuer, blow, etc.; to evade by cunning or trickery. —*n.* a quick movement to avoid something; a clever trick or expedient. [orig. unkn.]

dodgem /ˈdɒdʒəm/ *n.* a small electrically driven car in an enclosure at a fun-fair, in which the driver tries to bump other cars and dodge those trying to bump his or her car. [f. prec. + 'EM]

dodgy *adj.* (*colloq.*) awkward, unreliable, tricky. [f. DODGE]

dodo /ˈdəʊdəʊ/ *n.* (*pl.* **-os**) a large extinct bird (*Raphus cucullatus*) of Mauritius etc. —**as dead as the dodo,** entirely obsolete. [f. Port., = simpleton]

DOE *abbr.* Department of the Environment.

doe /dəʊ/ *n.* the female of the fallow deer, reindeer, hare, or rabbit. [OE]

doer /ˈdu:ə(r)/ *n.* one who does something; one who acts rather than merely talking or thinking. [f. DO[1]]

does /dʌz/ see DO[1].

doeskin *n.* the skin of a fallow deer; leather made from this.

doesn't /ˈdʌzn(ə)t/ (*colloq.*) = does not.

doff *v.t.* to take off (a hat or clothing). [= *do off*]

dog *n.* **1** a four-legged carnivorous animal of the genus *Canis*, of many breeds (wild and domesticated); the male of this or of a fox or wolf. **2** a person, a despicable person. **3** a mechanical device for gripping something. —*v.t.* to follow closely and persistently, to pursue, to track. —**dog-collar** *n.* a collar for a dog; (*colloq.*) a clerical collar. **dog days,** the hottest period of the year. **dog-eared** *adj.* (of a book) with the corners worn or battered with use. **dog-eat-dog** *n.* ruthless competition. **dog-end** *n.* (*slang*) a cigarette-end. **dog in the manger,** one who clings to a thing he cannot use, preventing others from enjoying it. **dog's breakfast,** (*colloq.*) a mess. **dog's life,** a life of misery or harassment. **dog-star** *n.* the chief star of the constellation Canis Major or Minor, especially Sirius. **dog-tired** *adj.* tired out. **dog-watch** *n.* one of the two-hour watches on a ship (4-6 or 6-8 p.m.). **go to the dogs,** (*slang*) to deteriorate, to be ruined. [OE]

dogcart *n.* a two-wheeled driving-cart with cross seats back to back.

doge /dəʊdʒ/ *n.* (*hist.*) the chief magistrate in the former republics of Venice and Genoa. [F f. It. f. L *dux* leader]

dogfight *n.* **1** a close combat between fighter aircraft. **2** an uproar, a fight like that between dogs.

dogfish *n.* (*pl.* usu. same) any of several small sharks, especially *Scyliorhinus canicula*.

dogged /ˈdɒgɪd/ *adj.* tenacious, grimly persistent. — **doggedly** *adv.* [f. DOG]

doggerel /ˈdɒgər(ə)l/ *n.* poor or trivial verse. [app. f. DOG (with disparaging force as in *dogrose*)]

doggie /ˈdɒgɪ/ *n.* (*children's colloq.*) a dog. [f. DOG]

doggo *adv.* **lie doggo,** (*slang*) to lie motionless or hidden. [prob. f. DOG]

doggy *adj.* of or like a dog; devoted to dogs. —*n.* = DOGGIE. [f. DOG]

doghouse *n.* (*US*) a dog's kennel. —**in the doghouse,** (*slang*) in disgrace.

dogma /ˈdɒgmə/ *n.* **1** a principle or tenet; a system of these, especially as laid down by the authority of a Church. **2** an arrogant declaration of opinion. [L f. Gk (*dokeō* seem)]

dogmatic /dɒgˈmætɪk/ *adj.* **1** of or in the nature of a dogma. **2** asserting or given to asserting dogmas or opinions; intolerantly authoritative. —**dogmatically** *adv.* [f. prec.]

dogmatism /ˈdɒgmətɪz(ə)m/ *n.* the tendency to be dogmatic. [as foll.]

dogmatize /ˈdɒgmətaɪz/ *v.t./i.* to speak dogmatically; to express (a principle etc.) as a dogma. [f. F f. L f. Gk (as DOGMA)]

dogrose *n.* a wild hedge-rose, *Rosa canina*.

dogsbody /ˈdɒgzbɒdɪ/ *n.* (*colloq.*) a drudge.

dogwood *n.* a shrub (*Cornus sanguinea*) with dark red branches, greenish-white flowers, and purple berries, found in woods and hedgerows.

doh /dəʊ/ *n.* (*Mus.*) the first note of a major scale in tonic sol-fa (see entry). [f. It. *do*]

doily /ˈdɔɪlɪ/ *n.* a small ornamental lace or paper mat used on a plate for cakes etc. [orig. name of a fabric, f. surname]

doing /ˈdu:ɪŋ/ *partic.* of DO¹. —*n.* **1** activity, effort. **2** (in *pl.*, *slang*) adjuncts, things needed. [f. DO¹]

Dolby /ˈdɒlbɪ/ *n.* [P] a system used in tape-recording to reduce unwanted sounds at high frequency. [f. R. *Dolby* (1933-) the inventor]

doldrums /ˈdɒldrəmz/ *n.pl.* **1** low spirits; a period of inactivity. **2** an equatorial ocean region often marked by calms. [perh. after *dull* and *tantrum*]

dole *n.* **1** a charitable distribution, a thing given sparingly or reluctantly. **2 the dole,** (*colloq.*) a State benefit payable to insured persons who are unable to obtain employment. —*v.t.* to deal *out* sparingly. —**on the dole,** (*colloq.*) receiving State benefit for the unemployed. [OE, rel. to DEAL¹]

doleful /ˈdəʊlf(ə)l/ *adj.* mournful, sad; dreary, dismal. —**dolefully** *adv.* [f. *dole* grief f. OF f. L (*dolēre* grieve)]

dolerite /ˈdɒlərait/ *n.* a coarse basaltic rock. [f. F f. Gk *doleros* deceptive (because its contents are difficult to distinguish)]

dolichocephalic /dɒlɪkəʊsɪˈfælɪk/ *adj.* having a skull that is longer than it is wide. —**dolichocephalous** /-ˈsefələs/ *adj.*, **dolichocephalism** /-ˈsef-/ *n.*, **dolichocephaly** /-ˈsef-/ *n.* [f. Gk *dolikhos* long + CEPHALIC]

doll *n.* **1** a small model of a human figure, especially a baby or child, as a child's toy; a ventriloquist's dummy. **2** (*slang*) a young woman. —*v.t.* (*colloq.*) to dress *up* smartly. [pet- form of name *Dorothy*]

dollar /ˈdɒlə(r)/ *n.* the currency unit in the USA and certain other countries. [f. LG f. G *thaler* (*Joachimsthaler*, coin from *Joachimstal* in Germany)]

dollop /ˈdɒləp/ *n.* (*colloq.*) a shapeless lump of food etc. [perh. f. Scand.]

dolly *n.* **1** (*children's colloq.*) a doll. **2** a movable platform for a cine-camera. —**dolly-bird** *n.* (*colloq.*) an attractive and stylish young woman. [f. DOLL]

dolman sleeve /ˈdɒlmən/ a loose sleeve cut in one piece with the body of a garment. [f. Turk.]

dolmen /ˈdɒlmən/ *n.* a megalithic chamber tomb with a large flat stone laid on upright ones. [F, perh. f. Cornish *tolmēn* hole of stone]

dolomite /ˈdɒləmaɪt/ *n.* a mineral or rock of calcium magnesium carbonate. —**dolomitic** /-ˈmɪtɪk/ *adj.* [F, f. D. de *Dolomieu* French geologist (d. 1802)]

dolour /ˈdɒlə(r)/ *n.* (*literary*) sorrow, distress. —**dolorous** *adj.* [f. OF f. L (as DOLEFUL)]

dolphin *n.* a sea mammal (*Delphinus delphis*) like a porpoise but larger and with a slender pointed snout.[f. L. *delphinus* f. Gk]

dolt /dəʊlt/ *n.* a stupid person. [prob. rel. to *dol* obs. var. of DULL]

Dom /dɒm/ *n.* a title prefixed to the names of some Roman Catholic dignitaries, and Benedictine and Carthusian monks. [f. L *dominus* master]

-dom *suffix* forming nouns, (1) from nouns or adjectives, denoting rank, condition, or domain (*earldom, freedom, kingdom*), (2) from nouns, denoting collective plural or in sense 'the ways of —s' (*officialdom*). [OE]

domain /dəˈmeɪn/ *n.* an area under one rule, a realm; an estate or lands under one control; a sphere of control or influence. [f. F, var. of DEMESNE]

dome /dəʊm/ *n.* a rounded vault forming a roof; a dome-shaped thing. [f. F f. It. *duomo* cathedral f. L *domus* house]

domed *adj.* having a dome or domes; shaped like a dome. [f. prec.]

domestic /də'mestɪk/ *adj.* of the home or household or family affairs; of one's own country, not foreign or international; fond of home life; (of an animal) kept by or living with man. —*n.* a household servant. —**domestic science,** home economics (see HOME). —**domestically** *adv.* [f. F f. L (*domus* house)]

domesticate /də'mestɪkeɪt/ *v.t.* to tame (an animal) to live with humans; to accustom to home life and management. [f. L (as prec.)]

domesticity /dɒməs'tɪsɪtɪ/ *n.* being domestic; domestic or home life. [f. DOMESTIC]

domicile /'dɒmɪsaɪl/ *n.* a dwelling-place; (*Law*) a place of permanent residence, the fact of residing. [f. OF f. L (*domus* house)]

domiciled *adj.* having a domicile at or in. [f. prec.]

domiciliary /dɒmɪ'sɪlɪərɪ/ *adj.* of a dwelling-place (especially of the visit of a doctor, officials, etc., to a person's home). [f. F f. L (as DOMICILE)]

dominant /'dɒmɪnənt/ *adj.* dominating, prevailing; (of an inherited characteristic) appearing in offspring even when a corresponding opposite characteristic is also inherited. —*n.* (*Mus.*) the fifth note of the diatonic scale of any key. —**dominance** *n.* [F, f. L *dominari* (as foll.)]

dominate /'dɒmɪneɪt/ *v.t./i.* to have a commanding influence over; to be the most influential or conspicuous; (of a high place) to have a commanding position over. —**domination** /-'neɪʃ(ə)n/ *n.* [f. L *dominari* (*dominus* lord)]

domineer /dɒmɪ'nɪə(r)/ *v.i.* to behave in an arrogant and overbearing way. [f. Du. f. F *dominer* (as prec.)]

dominion /də'mɪnjən/ *n.* **1** sovereignty, control. **2** the territory of a sovereign or government, a domain. **3** (*hist.*) the title of the self-governing territories of the British Commonwealth. [f. OF f. L (*dominus* lord)]

domino[1] /'dɒmɪnəʊ/ *n.* a loose cloak with a mask for the upper part of the face, formerly worn at masquerades. [F, prob. as prec. but unexplained]

domino[2] /'dɒmɪnəʊ/ *n.* each of 28 small oblong pieces marked with (usually) 0–6 pips in each half; (in *pl.*) the game played with these. —**domino theory,** the theory that one (especially a political) event precipitates others in a causal sequence, like a row of dominoes falling over. [perhaps named from the semblance of the black back of the domino to the masquerade garment of the same name: see prec.]

don[1] *n.* **1** a head, fellow, or tutor of a college, especially at Oxford or Cambridge. **2 Don,** a Spanish title prefixed to a man's Christian name. [Sp., f. L *dominus* lord]

don[2] *v.t.* (**-nn-**) to put on (clothing etc.). [= do on]

donate /dəʊ'neɪt/ *v.t.* to give or contribute (money etc.), especially voluntarily to a fund or institution. [back-formation f. foll.]

donation /dəʊ'neɪʃ(ə)n/ *n.* an act of donating; an amount donated. [f. OF f. L (*donum* gift)]

done /dʌn/ *p.p.* of DO[1]. —*adj.* **1** completed; cooked. **2** (of an action or behaviour etc.) socially acceptable. **3** (as *int.* in reply to an offer etc.) accepted. **4** (*colloq.*) tired out (often with *in* or *up*). —**be done with,** to have finished with. **done for,** in serious trouble. **have done with,** to finish dealing with.

donjon /'dɒndʒ(ə)n/ *n.* the great tower or keep of a castle. [archaic spelling of DUNGEON]

donkey /'dɒŋkɪ/ *n.* **1** a domestic ass (see ASS[1]). **2** (*colloq.*) a stupid person. —**donkey engine,** a small auxiliary engine. **donkey jacket,** a workman's thick weatherproof jacket. **donkey's years,** (*colloq.*) a very long time. **donkey-work** *n.* the laborious part of a job. [perh. f. proper name *Duncan* (cf. NEDDY)]

Donna /'dɒnə/ *n.* the title of an Italian, Spanish, or Portuguese lady. [It., f. L *domina* mistress; cf. DON[1]]

donnish *adj.* like a college don; pedantic. [f. DON[1]]

donor /'dəʊnə(r)/ *n.* one who gives or donates something; one who provides blood for transfusion, semen for insemination, or an organ or tissue for transplantation. [f. AF f. L *donator* (as DONATION)]

don't /dəʊnt/ (*colloq.*) = do not. —*n.* a prohibition. [f. DO[1]]

doodle *v.t./i.* to scribble or draw, esp. absent-mindedly. —*n.* a scribble or drawing made by doodling. [orig. = foolish person; cf. LG *dudelkopf*]

doom *n.* a grim fate or destiny, death or ruin; a condemnation. —*v.t.* to condemn or destine *to*. [OE, = statute]

doomsday /'du:mzdeɪ/ *n.* the day of the Last Judgement. —**till doomsday,** for ever. [f. prec.]

door /dɔ:(r)/ *n.* **1** a hinged, sliding, or revolving barrier for closing the entrance to a building, room, cupboard, etc.; this as representing a house etc.; a doorway. **2** an entrance or exit, the means of access or approach. —**door-keeper** *n.* a doorman. **door-to-door** *adj.* (of selling etc.) done at each house in turn. [OE]

doorbell *n.* a bell in a house rung at the front door by visitors to signal arrival.

doorknob *n.* a knob for turning to release the latch of a door.

doorman *n.* (*pl.* **-men**) a person on duty at the entrance to a large building.

doormat *n.* **1** a mat at an entrance, for wiping the shoes. **2** a feebly submissive person.

doorstep *n.* **1** a step leading to the outer door of a house etc.; a point in front of this. **2** (*slang*) a thick slice of bread. —**on one's doorstep,** very close.

doorstop *n.* a device for keeping a door open or to prevent it from striking a wall etc. when opened.

doorway *n.* an opening filled by a door.

dope *n.* **1** a thick liquid used as a lubricant etc.; varnish. **2** (*slang*) a drug, especially a narcotic; a drug or stimulant given to an athlete etc. to affect performance. **3** (*slang*) information. **4** (*slang*) a stupid person. —*v.t./i.* **1** to treat with dope. **2** to give a drug or stimulant to; to take addictive drugs. [f. Du. *doop* sauce]

dopey /ˈdəʊpɪ/ *adj.* (*slang*) half asleep; stupefied by or as by a drug; stupid. —**dopiness** *n.* [f. prec.]

doppelgänger /ˈdɒp(ə)lgeŋə(r)/ *n.* the wraith of a living person. [G, = double-goer]

Doppler effect /ˈdɒplə(r)/ the apparent increase (or decrease) in the frequency of sound, light, and other waves when the source and the observer become closer (or more distant). [f. C. J. *Doppler* Austrian physicist (d. 1853)]

dorado /dəˈrɑːdəʊ/ *n.* (*pl.* **-os**) a blue and silver sea-fish of the genus *Coryphaena*, showing brilliant colours when it dies out of water. [Sp., = gilt]

Doric /ˈdɒrɪk/ *adj.* **1** (of a dialect) broad, rustic. **2** (*Archit.*) of the oldest and simplest of the Greek orders. —*n.* rustic English or (esp.) Scots. [f. L f. Gk (*Doris* in Greece)]

dormant /ˈdɔːmənt/ *adj.* sleeping, lying inactive as in a sleep; temporarily inactive; (of plants) alive but not actively growing. —**dormancy** *n.* [f. partic. of OF *dormir* sleep f. L *dormire*]

dormer *n.* a projecting upright window in a sloping roof. [f. OF (as prec.)]

dormitory /ˈdɔːmɪtərɪ/ *n.* **1** a sleeping-room with several beds, especially in a school or institution. **2** (in full **dormitory town**) a small town or suburb from which people travel to work in a city etc. [f. L (*dormire* sleep)]

dormouse /ˈdɔːmaʊs/ *n.* (*pl.* **-mice** /-maɪs/) a mouselike hibernating rodent of the family Gliridae. [orig. unkn.]

dormy /ˈdɔːmɪ/ *adj.* as many holes ahead in the score of golf as there are holes left to play. [orig. unkn.]

dorsal /ˈdɔːs(ə)l/ *adj.* of or on the back. —**dorsally** *adv.* [F, or f. L (*dorsum* back)]

dory /ˈdɔːrɪ/ *n.* (also **John Dory**) an edible sea-fish, *Zeus faber*. [f. F *dorée* gilded]

dosage /ˈdəʊsɪdʒ/ *n.* the giving of a dose; the size of a dose. [f. foll.]

dose *n.* **1** the amount of medicine to be taken at one time; an amount of flattery, punishment, etc.; an amount of radiation received by a person or thing. **2** (*slang*) a venereal infection. —*v.t.* to give a dose or doses of medicine to; to treat (a person or animal) *with*. [F f. L f. Gk *dosis* gift]

dosimeter /dəʊˈsɪmɪtə(r)/ *n.* a device for measuring the amount of a dose; a recording device to measure ionizing radiation, especially one worn by a person exposed to potentially harmful radiation. [f. DOSE + -METER]

doss *v.i.* (*slang*) to sleep, especially in a doss-house. —**doss down,** (*slang*) to sleep on a makeshift bed. **doss-house** *n.* (*slang*) a cheap lodging-house. [prob. = *doss* ornamental cover for seat-back, f. OF *dos* back (as DORSAL)]

dossier /ˈdɒsɪə(r), -ɪeɪ/ *n.* a set of documents containing information about a person or event. [F, f. label on back (*dos*, as prec.)]

dot *n.* **1** a small round mark or spot; this as part of *i* or *j* or as a decimal point. **2** the shorter of the two signals used in the Morse code. —*v.t.* (**-tt-**) **1** to mark with a dot or dots; to cover partly as with dots. **2** (*slang*) to hit. —**dotted line,** a line of dots on a document to show the place for a signature. **dot the i's and cross the t's,** to be minutely accurate; to emphasize details. **on the dot,** exactly on time. **the year dot,** (*colloq.*) far in the past. [perh. = OE *dott* head of boil]

dotage /ˈdəʊtɪdʒ/ *n.* feeble-minded senility. [f. DOTE]

dotard /ˈdəʊtəd/ *n.* a person who is in his dotage. [f. foll.]

dote *v.i.* to be silly or infatuated. —**dote on,** to be excessively fond of. [cf. MDu. *doten* be silly]

dotterel /ˈdɒtər(ə)l/ *n.* a small migrant plover, *Eudromias morinellus*. [f. prec.; named from the ease with which it is caught, a supposed sign of stupidity]

dottle *n.* the remnant of unburnt tobacco in a pipe. [f. DOT]

dotty *adj.* (*colloq.*) feeble-minded, eccentric, silly. —**dottiness** *n.* [f. DOT]

double[1] /ˈdʌb(ə)l/ *adj.* **1** consisting of two parts or things. **2** twofold, multiplied by two; twice as much or many. **3** having twice the usual quantity, size, strength, etc.; having some part double; (of a flower) having more than one circle of petals. **4** folded, stooping. **5** ambiguous, deceitful, hypocritical. **6** (of a musical instrument) lower in pitch by an octave. —*adv.* at or to twice the amount etc.; two together. —*n.* **1** a double quantity or thing; a double measure of spirits etc.; twice as much or many. **2** the counterpart of a person or thing, a person who looks exactly like another. **3** (in *pl.*) a game between two pairs of players. **4** a pair of victories over the same team or of championships at the same game etc.; a system of betting in which the winnings and stake from the first bet are transferred to a second; a doubling of an opponent's bid in bridge; a hit on the narrow ring between the outer circles in darts. —**at the double,** running, hurrying. **double agent,** one who spies simultaneously for two rival countries. **double-barrelled** *adj.* (of a gun) having two barrels; (of a name) having two parts with a hyphen. **double-bass** /beɪs/ *n.* the largest and lowest-pitched instrument of the violin family, now possessing four strings (formerly three) and sounding an octave below the cello, with a range of nearly three octaves. **double-breasted** *adj.* (of a coat etc.) having fronts that overlap to fasten across the breast. **double-check** *v.t.* to verify twice or in two ways. **double chin,** a chin with a fold of loose flesh below it. **double cream,** thick cream with a high fat-content. **double-cross** *v.t.* to deceive or betray (a person one is supposedly helping); (as *n.*) an act of doing this. **double-dealing** *n.* deceit, especially in business; (as *adj.*) practising deceit. **double-decker** *n.* a bus with two decks. **double Dutch,** gibberish. **double eagle,** a figure of a two-headed eagle. **double-edged** *adj.* having two cutting-edges; (*fig.*) damaging to the user as well as his opponent. **double entry,** a system of book-keeping in which each transaction is entered as a debit in one account and a credit in another. **double figures,** the numbers from 10 to 99. **double glazing,** two layers of glass in a window to reduce loss of heat and exclude noise. **double helix,** a pair of parallel helices with a common axis, especially in the structure of the DNA molecule. **double-jointed** *adj.* having joints that allow unusual bending of the fingers etc. **double or quits,** a gamble to decide whether a player's loss or debt be doubled or cancelled. **double-park** *v.i.* to park a vehicle alongside one that is already parked at the roadside. **double pneumonia,** that affecting both lungs. **double-quick** *adj.* & *adv.* very quick(ly). **double standard,** a rule or principle applied more strictly to some than to others (or to oneself). **double star,** two stars that are actually or apparently very close together. **doublestopping** *n.* the sounding of two strings at once on a violin etc. **double take,** a delayed reaction to a situation etc. immediately after one's first reaction. **double-talk** *n.* verbal expression that is (usually deliberately) ambiguous or misleading. **double-think** *n.* a mental capacity to accept contrary opinions at the same time. **double time,** payment of an employee at twice the normal rate. —**doubly** *adv.* [f. OF f. L *duplus*]

double[2] /ˈdʌb(ə)l/ *v.t./i.* **1** to make or become double, to increase twofold, to multiply by two; to amount to twice as much. **2** to fold or bend over on itself, to become folded. **3** to act (two parts) in the same play etc.; to be an understudy etc. (*for*); to play a twofold role (**as**). **4** to turn sharply in flight or pursuit; (of a ship) to sail round (a headland). **5** to make a call in bridge increasing the value of points to be won or lost on (an opponent's bid). —**double back,** to take a new direction opposite to the previous one. **double up,** to bend or curl up with pain or laughter, to cause to do this; to share or cause to share a room, quarters, etc., with another or others. [as prec.]

double entendre /du:bl ɑ̃ˈtɑ̃dr/ a phrase affording two meanings, one usually indecent. [obs. F, = double understanding]

doublet /ˈdʌblɪt/ *n.* **1** a man's close-fitting jacket, with or without sleeves, worn in the 15th-17th c. **2** either of a pair of similar things. [as DOUBLE[1]]

doubloon /dʌbˈlu:n/ *n.* a former Spanish gold coin. [f. F or Sp. (as DOUBLE[1])]

doubt /daʊt/ *n.* a feeling of uncertainty about something, an undecided state of mind; an inclination to disbelieve; an uncertain state of things; a lack of full proof or clear indication. —*v.t./i.* to feel uncertain or undecided (about); to hesitate to believe; to call in question. —**no doubt,** certainly, probably, admittedly. **without (a) doubt,** certainly. —**doubter** *n.* [f. OF f. L *dubitare*]

doubtful *adj.* feeling doubt; causing doubt, unreliable, undecided. —**doubtfully** *adv.*, **doubtfulness** *n.* [f. DOUBT + -FUL]

doubtless *adv.* certainly, probably. [f. DOUBT + -LESS]

douche /du:ʃ/ *n.* a jet of liquid applied to a part of the body for cleansing or for a medicinal purpose; a device for producing such a jet. —*v.t./i.* to treat with a douche; to use a douche. [F f. It. *doccia* pipe f. L (as DUCT)]

dough /dəʊ/ *n.* **1** a thick mixture of flour etc. and liquid, for baking. **2** (*slang*) money. —**doughy** *adj.* [OE]

doughnut /ˈdəʊnʌt/ *n.* a small sweetened fried cake of dough. [f. prec.]

doughty /ˈdaʊtɪ/ *adj.* (*archaic* or *joc.*) valiant, stouthearted. —**doughtily** *adv.*, **doughtiness** *n.* [OE]

Douglas /ˈdʌgləs/ *n.* **Douglas fir, pine,** *or* **spruce,** a large conifer of the genus *Pseudotsuga*, originally of western North America. [f. D. *Douglas*, Sc. botanist (d. 1834)]

dour /dʊə(r)/ *adj.* stern, severe, obstinate. —**dourly** *adv.*, **dourness** *n.* [prob. f. Gaelic *dúr* dull, obstinate]

douse /daʊs/ *v.t.* **1** to plunge into water, to throw water over. **2** to extinguish (a light). [perh. rel. to MDu., LG *dossen* strike]

dove /dʌv/ *n.* **1** a bird of the family Columbidae,

with short legs, small head, and large breast. **2** an advocate of peace or peaceful policy. **3** a gentle or innocent person. [f. ON (perh. imit.)]

dovecote /ˈdʌvkɒt/ *n.* a shelter with nesting-holes for domesticated pigeons.

dovetail *n.* a joint formed by a mortise with a tenon shaped like a dove's spread tail. —*v.t./i.* **1** to fit together with dovetails. **2** to fit together or combine neatly.

dowager /ˈdaʊədʒə(r)/ *n.* a woman with a title or property derived from her late husband; (*colloq.*) a dignified elderly woman. [f. OF (*douage*, as DOWER)]

dowdy /ˈdaʊdɪ/ *adj.* (of clothes) unattractively dull; (of a person) dressed in dowdy clothes. —**dowdily** *adv.*, **dowdiness** *n.* [orig. unkn.]

dowel /ˈdaʊəl/ *n.* a headless wooden or metal pin for holding two pieces of wood or stone together. —*v.t.* (**-ll-**) to fasten with a dowel. [f. MLG *dovel*]

dowelling *n.* round rods for cutting into dowels. [f. prec.]

dower /ˈdaʊə(r)/ *n.* **1** a widow's share for life of her husband's estate. **2** (*archaic*) a dowry. —*v.t.* **1** (*archaic*) to give a dowry to. **2** to endow *with* talent etc. —**dower house,** a smaller house near a big one, forming part of a widow's dower. [f. OF f. L *dotarium* (*dos* dowry)]

Dow–Jones index or **average** /daʊˈdʒəʊnz/ a figure indicating the relative price of American securities based on the current average rates of an agreed select list of industrial and other stocks. [f. C. H. *Dow* (d. 1902) and E. D. *Jones* (d. 1920), Amer. economists]

down[1] /daʊn/ *adv.* **1** at, in, or towards a lower place, level, value, or condition, or a place etc. regarded as lower; to a finer consistency or smaller amount or size; southwards, further south; away from a central place or capital city or university; in or into a less strong or less active or losing position or condition; into quiescence; incapacitated *with* (an illness etc.). **2** from an erect or vertical position to a horizontal one. **3** so as to be deflated. **4** from an earlier to a later time. **5** in writing; in or into a recorded form. **6** to its source or place. **7** as a payment at the time of purchase. —*prep.* **1** downwards along, through, or into; from the top to the bottom of; along. **2** at or in a lower part of. —*adj.* directed downwards; (of travel) away from a capital or centre. —*v.t.* (*colloq.*) to knock or bring down; to swallow. —*n.* **1** an act of putting down. **2** a reverse of fortune (often in *ups and downs*). —**down and out,** penniless, destitute. **down-and-out** *n.* a destitute person. **down-hearted** *adj.* dejected. **down in the mouth,** looking unhappy. **down on,** holding in disfavour. **down payment,** a partial payment made at the time of purchase. **down stage,** at or to the front of a theatre stage. **down-to-earth** *adj.* practical, realistic. **down tools,** to cease work; to go on strike. **down to the ground,** (*colloq.*) completely. **down under,** in the antipodes, especially Australia. **down with** *int.* of disgust with or rejection of a stated person or thing. **have a down on,** to hold in disfavour. [f. earlier *adown* (f. DOWN[3])]

down[2] *n.* the first covering of young birds, a bird's underplumage; fine soft feathers or short hairs; a fluffy substance. [f. ON]

down[3] *n.* **1** (also **downland**) an area of high open land. **2** (in *pl.*) chalk uplands especially of southern England. [OE, rel. to DUNE]

downbeat *n.* an accented beat in music, when the conductor's baton moves downwards. —*adj.* **1** pessimistic, gloomy. **2** relaxed.

downcast *adj.* **1** (of the eyes) looking downwards. **2** (of a person) dejected.

downfall *n.* a fall from prosperity or power; a cause of this.

downgrade *v.t.* to lower in grade or rank.

downhill *adv.* down a slope; in a descending direction. —*adj.* sloping downwards, declining. —**go downhill,** to deteriorate.

downpipe *n.* a pipe for carrying rain-water from a roof to a drain.

downpour *n.* a heavy fall of rain.

downright *adj.* plain, straightforward; utter, complete. —*adv.* thoroughly, completely.

Down's syndrome /daʊnz/ an abnormal congenital condition in which a person has a broad flattened skull, slanting eyes, and mental deficiency (also called *mongolism* from some physical resemblance to Mongoloid peoples). [f. J. L. H. *Down* physician (d. 1896)]

downstairs *adv.* down the stairs; to or on a lower floor. —*adj.* situated downstairs. —*n.* a downstairs floor.

downstream *adj.* & *adv.* in the direction in which a stream flows; moving downstream.

downtown *adj.* (*US*) of a lower or more central part of a town or city. —*adv.* (*US*) in or into this part. —*n.* (*US*) a downtown area.

downtrodden *adj.* oppressed, badly treated.

downturn *n.* a decline, especially in an economic or business activity.

downward /ˈdaʊnwəd/ *adv.* (also **downwards** /-z/) towards what is lower, inferior, less important, or later. —*adj.* moving or extending downwards. [f. DOWN[1] + -WARD]

downwind *adj.* & *adv.* in the direction in which the wind is blowing.

downy *adj.* **1** of or like down, soft and fluffy. **2** (*slang*) aware, knowing. [f. DOWN[2]]

dowry /ˈdaʊərɪ/ *n.* property or money brought by a bride to her husband. [f. AF & OF, = dower]

dowse[1] /daʊz/ *v.i.* to search for underground water or minerals by holding a Y-shaped stick or rod (*dowsing-rod*) which dips abruptly when over the right spot. —**dowser** *n.* [orig. unkn.]

dowse² /daʊs/ var. of DOUSE.

doxology /dɒkˈsɒlədʒɪ/ *n.* a liturgical formula of praise to God. [f. L f. Gk (*doxa* glory, -LOGY)]

doyen /ˈdɔɪən/ *n.* a senior member of a body of colleagues. —**doyenne** /-ˈen/ *n.fem.* [F. (as DEAN)]

doz. *abbr.* dozen.

doze *v.i.* to be half asleep, to sleep lightly. —*n.* a short light sleep. —**doze off,** to fall lightly asleep. [orig. unkn.]

dozen /ˈdʌz(ə)n/ *n.* **1** (for plural usage see HUNDRED) twelve, a set of twelve. **2** (in *pl.*) very many. —**talk nineteen to the dozen,** to talk incessantly. [f. OF ult. f. L *duodecim* twelve]

dozy /ˈdəʊzɪ/ *adj.* drowsy; (*colloq.*) stupid, lazy. [f. DOZE]

D.Phil. *abbr.* Doctor of Philosophy.

DPP *abbr.* Director of Public Prosecutions.

Dr *abbr.* Doctor.

drab *adj.* **1** dull, uninteresting. **2** of a dull brownish colour. —*n.* drab colour. —**drably** *adv.*, **drabness** *n.* [f. obs. *drap* cloth f. OF f. L]

drachm /dræm/ *n.* a weight formerly used by apothecaries, one eighth of an ounce. [f. OF or L (as foll.)]

drachma /ˈdrækmə/ *n.* (*pl.* **-as**) **1** the unit of currency of Greece. **2** silver coin of ancient Greece. [L f. Gk *drakhmē*]

Draconian /drəˈkəʊnɪən/ *adj.* (of laws) very harsh, cruel. [f. *Drakōn* (*c.*620 BC), said to have established severe laws in ancient Athens]

draft /drɑːft/ *n.* **1** a rough preliminary outline of a scheme or written version of a speech, document, etc. **2** a written order for the payment of money by a bank; drawing of money by this. **3** a detachment from a larger group for a special duty or purpose; selection of this; (*US*) conscription. —*v.t.* **1** to prepare a draft of (writing or a scheme). **2** to select for a special duty or purpose; (*US*) to conscript. [phonetic spelling of DRAUGHT]

draftsman *n.* (*pl.* **-men**) one who drafts documents.

drag *v.t./i.* (**-gg-**) **1** to pull or pass along with effort, difficulty, or friction; to trail or allow to trail along the ground; (*colloq.*) to take (a person *to*, especially against his will). **2** to use a grapnel, to search (the bottom of a lake or river etc.) with grapnels, nets, etc. **3** (*colloq.*) to draw *on* or *at* (a cigarette etc.). —*n.* **1** a hindrance to progress; a longitudinal retarding force exerted by air on aircraft etc. in flight. **2** a retarded motion. **3** (*colloq.*) a boring or tiresome person, duty, etc. **4** a lure drawn before hounds as a substitute for a fox; a hunt using this; an apparatus for dredging etc.; a drag-net. **5** (*slang*) a draw on a cigarette etc. **6** (*slang*) women's clothes worn by men. —**drag one's feet,** to be deliberately slow or reluctant to act. **drag in,** to introduce (a subject) irrelevantly. **drag-net** *n.* a net drawn through a river or across ground to trap fish or game; a systematic hunt for criminals etc. **drag on,** to continue tediously. **drag out,** to prolong at length. **drag race,** an acceleration race between cars over a short distance. **drag up,** (*colloq.*) to introduce or revive (an unwelcome subject). [OE or ON (as DRAW)]

draggle *v.t./i.* to make dirty, wet, or limp by trailing; to hang trailing. [f. prec.]

dragon /ˈdrægən/ *n.* **1** a mythical monster like a reptile, usually with wings and able to breathe out fire. **2** a fierce person. [f. OF f. L f. Gk *drakōn* serpent]

dragon-fly *n.* an insect of the order Odonata, with a long body and two pairs of transparent wings.

dragoon /drəˈguːn/ *n.* **1** a cavalryman (orig. a mounted infantryman). **2** a fierce fellow. —*v.t.* to force *into* doing something. [orig. = carbine, f. F *dragon* (as prec.)]

drain *v.t./i.* **1** to draw off liquid from; to draw off (a liquid). **2** to flow or trickle away. **3** to dry or become dry as liquid flows away; to exhaust of strength or resources. **4** to drink (a liquid), to empty (a glass etc.) by drinking the contents. —*n.* **1** a channel, conduit, or pipe carrying off a liquid, sewage, etc. **2** a constant outlet or expenditure. —**down the drain,** (*colloq.*) lost, wasted. **drain-pipe** *n.* a pipe for carrying off surplus water or liquid sewage from a building. **draining-board** *n.* a sloping grooved surface beside a sink on which washed dishes etc. are left to drain

drainage *n.* **1** draining; a system of drains. **2** what is drained off. [f. prec.]

drake *n.* a male duck. [app. f. second element in OHG *antrehho*]

dram *n.* **1** a small drink of spirits. **2** = DRACHM. [f. OF *drame* or L *drama* (as DRACHM)]

drama /ˈdrɑːmə/ *n.* **1** a play for acting on stage or for broadcasting. **2** the art of writing and presenting plays. **3** a dramatic series of events; dramatic quality. [L f. Gk (*draō* do)]

dramatic /drəˈmætɪk/ *adj.* of drama, sudden and exciting or unexpected; vividly striking; (of a gesture etc.) overdone or absurd. —**dramatically** *adv.* [f. L f. Gk (as prec.)]

dramatics *n.pl.* (often treated as *sing.*) **1** the performance of plays. **2** exaggerated behaviour. [f. prec.]

dramatis personae /ˈdræmətɪs pɜːˈsəʊnaɪ/ the characters in a play; a list of these. [L, = persons of the drama]

dramatist /ˈdræmətɪst/ *n.* a writer of dramas. [f. DRAMA]

dramatize /ˈdræmətaɪz/ *v.t./i.* **1** to make (a novel

etc.) into a play. **2** to make a dramatic scene of; to behave dramatically. —**dramatization** /-ˈzeɪʃ(ə)n/ *n.* [as prec.]

drank *past* of DRINK.

drape *v.t.* to cover loosely, hang, or adorn, with cloth etc.; to arrange (clothes, hangings) in graceful folds. —*n.* (in *pl.*, *US*) curtains. [f. OF f. L *drappus* cloth]

draper *n.* a retailer of textile fabrics. [as prec.]

drapery *n.* **1** a draper's trade or fabrics. **2** fabric arranged in loose folds. [f. prec.]

drastic /ˈdræstɪk/ *adj.* having a strong or far-reaching effect, severe. —**drastically** *adv.* [f. Gk *drastikos* (*draō* do)]

drat *int.* of anger or annoyance, (*colloq.*) curse. —**dratted** *adj.* [for '*Od* (= God) *rot*]

draught /drɑːft/ *n.* **1** a current of air in a room etc., or in a chimney. **2** pulling, traction. **3** the depth of water needed to float a ship. **4** the drawing of liquor from a cask etc. **5** a single act of drinking; the amount so drunk. **6** the drawing in of a fishing-net; the fish caught in this. —**draught beer,** beer drawn from a cask, not bottled. **draught-horse** *n.* a horse used for pulling heavy loads, a cart, plough, etc. **feel the draught,** (*slang*) to feel the effect of financial or other difficulties. [perh. f. ON]

draughts /drɑːfts/ *n.* a game for two players, with initially 12 pieces (of equal value) each, on a **draughtboard** (the same as a chessboard). [pl. of prec.]

draughtsman *n.* (*pl.* **-men**) **1** one who makes drawings, plans, or sketches. **2** a piece in the game of draughts. —**draughtsmanship** *n.* [f. DRAUGHT]

draughty *adj.* (of a room etc.) letting in sharp currents of air. [as prec.]

Dravidian /drəˈvɪdɪən/ *n.* **1** a member of a dark-skinned people of southern India and Sri Lanka. **2** the group of languages spoken by them. —*adj.* of the Dravidians or their languages. [f. Skr. *Dravida*, a province of S. India]

draw *v.t./i.* (*past* **drew**/druː/; *p.p.* **drawn**) **1** to pull or cause to move towards or after one; to pull up, over, or across; to pull (curtains etc.) open or shut. **2** to attract; to take in; to elicit or evoke; to induce. **3** to take out, to remove; to obtain by lot, to draw lots. **4** to take or get from a source; to obtain (water) from a well or tap; to bring out (liquid from a vessel, blood from the body); to disembowel. **5** to infer (a conclusion). **6** to trace (a line or mark); to produce (a picture) by lines and marks; to represent (a thing) thus. **7** to formulate or perceive (a comparison, distinctions). **8** to compose or write out (a document, cheque, etc.). **9** to finish (a contest or game) with neither side winning. **10** to make one's way, to move. **11** to make a call *on* a person, his skill, etc. **12** (of a ship) to require (a specified depth of water) to float in. **13** to search (a cover) for game. —*n.* **1** an act of drawing, a pull. **2** a person or thing that draws custom, attention, etc. **3** a drawing of lots, a raffle. **4** a drawn game. **5** a suck on a cigarette etc. —**draw back,** to withdraw from an undertaking. **draw in,** (of days) to become shorter; to persuade to join. **draw in one's horns,** to become less assertive or ambitious. **draw the line at,** to set a limit (of tolerance etc.) at. **draw on,** to approach, to come near. **draw out,** to prolong; to elicit, to induce to talk; (of days) to become longer. **draw-string** *n.* one that can be pulled to tighten an opening. **draw up,** to compose or draft (a document etc.); to bring into order; to come to a halt; to make *oneself* stiffly erect. **quick on the draw,** quick to react. [OE (as DRAG)]

drawback *n.* a thing that impairs satisfaction, a disadvantage.

drawbridge *n.* a bridge, especially over a moat, hinged at one end for drawing up.

drawer /ˈdrɔːə(r)/ *n.* **1** one who or that which draws, especially a person who draws a cheque etc. **2** (also /drɔː/) a boxlike storage compartment without a lid, for sliding in and out of a table etc. **3** (in *pl.*) an undergarment worn next to the body below the waist. [f. DRAW]

drawing *n.* **1** the art of representing by line with a pencil etc. **2** a picture etc. drawn thus. —**drawing-board** *n.* a board on which paper is stretched while a drawing is made. **drawing-pin** *n.* a flat-headed pin for fastening paper etc. to a surface.

drawing-room *n.* a room for comfortable sitting or entertaining in a private house. [f. earlier *withdrawing-room*]

drawl *v.t./i.* to speak with drawn-out vowel-sounds. —*n.* a drawling utterance or way of speaking. [prob. f. LG, Du. *dralen* linger]

drawn *p.p.* of DRAW. —*adj.* looking strained from fear or anxiety.

dray *n.* a low cart without sides for heavy loads, especially beer-barrels. —**drayman** *n.* (*pl.* **-men**) [OE, = drag-net (as DRAW)]

dread /dred/ *v.t.* to fear greatly; to look forward to with great apprehension. —*n.* great fear or apprehension. —*adj.* dreaded; (*archaic*) dreadful, awe-inspiring. [OE]

dreadful *adj.* terrible; (*colloq.*) troublesome, very bad. —**dreadfully** *adv.* [f. DREAD + -FUL]

dream *n.* **1** a series of pictures or events in the mind of a sleeping person. **2** a day-dream, a fantasy; an ideal or aspiration. **3** a beautiful or ideal person or thing. —*v.t./i.* (*past* & *p.p.* **dreamt** /dremt/ or **dreamed**) **1** to experience a dream; to imagine as in a dream. **2** (with *neg.*) to think of as a possibility. —**dream-land** *n.* an ideal or imaginary land. **dream up,** to imagine, to invent. **like a dream,** (*colloq.*) easily, effortlessly. —**dreamer** *n.* [f. OE]

dreamless *adj.* without dreaming. [f. DREAM]

dreamy *adj.* **1** dreamlike. **2** given to dreaming or fantasy, vague. —**dreamily** *adv.*, **dreaminess** *n.* [as prec.]

dreary *adj.* dismal, dull, gloomy. —**drearily** *adv.*, **dreariness** *n.* [OE (*drêor* gore)]

dredge[1] /dredʒ/ *n.* an apparatus for bringing up oysters etc. or clearing out mud etc. from a river or the sea bottom. —*v.t./i.* to bring *up* or clean out with a dredge; to use a dredge. [f. Sc. *dreg* perh. rel. to MDu. *dregghe*]

dredge[2] *v.t.* to sprinkle with flour, sugar, etc. [f. obs. *dredge* sweetmeat f. OF perh. ult. f. Gk *tragēmata* spices]

dredger[1] *n.* a dredge, a boat with a dredge. [f. DREDGE[1]]

dredger[2] *n.* a container with a perforated lid, used for sprinkling flour etc. [f. DREDGE[2]]

dregs *n.pl.* sediment, grounds, lees; the worst or most useless part. [prob. f. ON]

drench *v.t.* **1** to make thoroughly wet. **2** to force (an animal) to take a dose of medicine. —*n.* a dose of medicine for an animal. [OE (as DRINK)]

Dresden /ˈdrezd(ə)n/ *n.* **1** (also **Dresden china** etc.) china of a kind made at Meissen near Dresden in East Germany, with elaborate decoration and delicate colourings. **2** (*attrib.*) characterized by delicate or frail prettiness.

dress *v.t./i.* **1** to put clothes upon; to provide oneself with and wear clothes; to put on one's clothes; to put on evening dress. **2** to arrange or adorn (the hair, a shop window, etc.). **3** to clean or treat (a wound etc.). **4** to prepare (a bird, crab, or salad) for cooking or eating. **5** to finish the surface of (a fabric, leather, stone). **6** to apply manure to. **7** to correct the alignment of (troops). —*n.* **1** clothing, especially the visible part of it; formal or ceremonial costume. **2** a woman's or girl's garment of bodice and skirt. **3** an external covering, an outward form. —**dress-circle** *n.* the first gallery in a theatre, where evening dress was formerly required. **dress down,** to scold, to reprimand. **dress rehearsal,** the final rehearsal in full costume. **dress up,** to put on special clothes; to make (a thing) more attractive or interesting. [f. OF f. L *directus* direct]

dressage /ˈdresɑːʒ/ *n.* the training of a horse in obedience and deportment; a display of this. [F (*dresser* train, as prec.)]

dresser[1] *n.* a kitchen sideboard with shelves for dishes etc. [f. OF (*dresser* prepare, as DRESS]

dresser[2] *n.* **1** one who helps to dress actors or actresses. **2** a surgeon's assistant in operations. [f. DRESS]

dressing *n.* **1** putting clothes on. **2** a sauce or stuffing etc. for food. **3** a bandage, ointment, etc., for a wound. **4** manure etc. spread over the land. **5** a substance used to stiffen textile fabrics during manufacture. —**dressing down,** a scolding. **dressing-gown** *n.* a loose gown worn when one is not fully dressed. **dressing-room** *n.* a room for dressing or changing clothes, especially in a theatre etc., or attached to a bedroom. **dressing-table** *n.* a piece of bedroom furniture with a mirror and usually drawers, for use while dressing, arranging the hair, applying make-up, etc.

dressmaker *n.* a person who makes women's clothes. —**dressmaking** *n.*

dressy *adj.* smart, elegant, wearing stylish clothes. —**dressily** *adv.*

drew *past* of DRAW.

drey /dreɪ/ *n.* a squirrel's nest. [orig. unkn.]

dribble *v.t./i.* **1** to allow saliva to flow from the mouth; to flow or cause to flow in drops. **2** to move the ball forward in football or hockey with slight touches of the feet or stick. —*n.* **1** an act of dribbling. **2** a dribbling flow. [frequent. of *drib* obs. var. of DRIP]

driblet /ˈdrɪblɪt/ *n.* a small amount. [as prec. + -LET]

dribs and drabs small scattered amounts. [*drib* as DRIBBLE; *drab* redupl.]

drier /ˈdraɪə(r)/ *n.* a device for drying hair, laundry, etc. [f. DRY]

drift *n.* **1** being driven along, especially by a current; a slow movement or variation; a slow deviation of a ship, projectile, etc. from a course. **2** a mass of snow or sand driven along or heaped up by the wind; fragments of rock heaped up by wind, water, etc. **3** the policy of merely waiting on events, inaction. **4** (in mining) a horizontal passage following a mineral vein. **5** (*S. Afr.*) a ford. —*v.t./i.* **1** to be carried by or as if by a current of air or water, (of a current) to cause to drift; to heap or be heaped in drifts. **2** to move casually or aimlessly. —**drift mine,** a mine using a horizontal passage (see sense 4). **drift-net** *n.* a net used in sea-fishing and allowed to drift with the tide. [f. ON & MHG *trift* movement of cattle (cogn. w. DRIVE)]

drifter *n.* **1** an aimless person. **2** a boat used for fishing with a drift-net. [f. prec.]

driftwood *n.* wood floating on moving water or washed ashore by it.

drill[1] *n.* **1** a tool or machine for boring holes or sinking wells. **2** instruction in military exercises; thorough training, especially by a repeated routine; (*colloq.*) a recognized procedure. —*v.t./i.* **1** to make (a hole) with a drill; to use a drill on. **2** to train or be trained by means of drill. [f. MDu. *drillen* bore]

drill[2] *n.* **1** a small furrow for sowing seed in. **2** a machine for making a furrow, sowing, and covering the seed. **3** a row of seeds so sown.

—*v.t.* to plant in drills. [perh. = obs. *drill* rivulet]

drill[3] *n.* a strong twilled cotton or linen fabric. [f. G *drilich* f. L *trilix* having three threads]

drill[4] *n.* a West African baboon (*Mandrillus leucophaeus*) related to the mandrill. [prob. African name; cf. MANDRILL]

drily /ˈdraɪlɪ/ *adv.* in a dry manner. [f. DRY]

drink *v.t./i.* (*past* **drank**; *p.p.* **drunk**) **1** to swallow (a liquid); to swallow the contents of (a vessel); to take alcoholic liquor, especially to excess; to bring (*oneself*) to a specified state by drinking. **2** (of a plant, sponge, etc.) to absorb (moisture). —*n.* liquid for drinking; a glass etc. or portion of this, especially alcoholic; intoxicating liquor, the excessive use of it. —**the drink,** (*slang*) the sea. **drink a person's health,** to pledge good wishes to him by drinking. **drink in,** to listen to or understand eagerly. **drink to,** to drink a toast to, to wish success to. **drink up,** to drink all or the remainder (of). —**drinker** *n.* [OE]

drinkable *adj.* suitable for drinking. [f. prec.]

drip *v.t./i.* (**-pp-**) to fall or let fall in drops; to be so wet (*with* a liquid) as to shed drops. —*n.* **1** a small falling drop of liquid; a liquid falling in drops, the sound of this; a drip-feed. **2** (*slang*) a feeble or dull person. [f. MDa. *drippe* (cf. DROP)]

drip-dry *v.t./i.* to dry easily when hung up; to leave to dry in this way. —*adj.* made of a fabric that will dry easily without creasing.

drip-feed *n.* feeding by liquid a drop at a time, especially intravenously; apparatus for this. —*v.t.* to apply a drip-feed to.

dripping *n.* fat melted from roasting meat. [f. DRIP]

dripstone *n.* a projection above a wall or window etc., to divert water from the parts below.

drive *v.t./i.* (*past* **drove**; *p.p.* **driven** /ˈdrɪv(ə)n/) **1** to urge in some direction by blows, threats, violence, etc. **2** to cause to go in some direction; to direct and control (a vehicle or locomotive); to convey in a vehicle; to operate a motor vehicle, to be competent to do so; to travel in a private vehicle. **3** to impel or carry along; to hit (a ball) forcibly; to force or hit (a nail or stake) *into*; to bore (a tunnel etc.); (of a power-source) to set or keep (machinery) going. **4** to compel; to force into a state of being (*mad* etc.); to overwork. **5** to be moved by wind, esp. rapidly. **6** to carry on, to conclude. **7** to dash, to rush; to work hard *at*. —*n.* **1** an excursion or journey in a vehicle. **2** a street or road, especially a scenic one. **3** a driveway. **4** a forcible stroke of a ball. **5** capacity or desire to achieve things; organized effort to some end. **6** the transmission of power to machinery, the wheels of a motor vehicle etc.; the position of the steering-wheel of a motor vehicle. **7** a social event of numerous simultaneous card-games etc. —**drive at,** to seek, to intend, to mean. **drive-in** *adj.* (of a cinema, bank, etc.) for the use of passengers seated in cars; (*n.*) a cinema, bank, etc., of this type. **driving-licence** *n.* a licence permitting one to drive a motor vehicle. **driving-test** *n.* an official test of competence to drive a motor vehicle. **driving-wheel** *n.* a wheel communicating motive power in machinery. [OE]

drivel /ˈdrɪv(ə)l/ *n.* silly talk, nonsense. —*v.i.* (**-ll-**) **1** to talk drivel. **2** to run at the nose or mouth. [OE]

driven *p.p.* of DRIVE.

driver *n.* **1** a person who drives (especially a motor vehicle). **2** a golf-club for driving from a tee. [f. DRIVE]

driveway *n.* a road serving as an approach for vehicles, especially a private one to a house etc.

drizzle *n.* very fine rain. —*v.i.* (of rain) to fall in very fine drops. —**drizzly** *adj.* [perh. rel. to OE *drēosan* fall]

drogue /drəʊg/ *n.* a truncated cone of fabric used as a brake for a landing aircraft or as a target, wind-sock, etc. [orig. unkn.]

droll /drəʊl/ *adj.* oddly or strangely amusing. —**drolly** /ˈdrəʊl-lɪ/ *adv.* [f. F *drôle*]

drollery /ˈdrəʊlərɪ/ *n.* quaint humour. [f. prec.]

dromedary /ˈdrɒmɪdərɪ, ˈdrʌm-/ *n.* a light one-humped (esp. Arabian) camel bred for riding. [f. F or L f. Gk *dromas* runner]

drone *n.* **1** a non-working male of the honey-bee; an idler. **2** a deep humming sound; the bass-pipe of a bagpipe, its continuous note. —*v.t./i.* to make a deep humming sound; to speak or utter monotonously. [OE]

drool /dru:l/ *v.i.* to dribble, to slobber; to show unrestrained admiration (*over*). [contr. of DRIVEL]

droop /dru:p/ *v.t./i.* to bend or hang downwards, especially through tiredness or weakness; to languish, to flag; to let (the eyes or head) drop. —*n.* a drooping attitude, a loss of spirit. —**droopy** *adj.* [f. ON (as foll.)]

drop *n.* **1** a small round portion of liquid such as hangs or falls separately or adheres to a surface; a thing in the shape of a drop, especially a sweet or a pendant; (in *pl.*) a liquid medicine to be measured by drops; a minute quantity; a glass etc. of intoxicating liquor. **2** an act of dropping, a fall of prices, temperature, etc. **3** a thing that drops or is dropped; a drop-curtain. **4** a steep or vertical descent; the distance of this. **5** (*slang*) a hiding-place for stolen or illicit goods etc. **6** (*slang*) a bribe. —*v.t./i.* **1** to fall by the force of gravity from not being held; to allow to fall, to cease to hold. **2** to fall or cause to fall in drops; to shed (tears, blood). **3** to set down (a passenger, parcel, etc.). **4** to fell with a blow, bullet, etc.; to sink to the ground, esp. from exhaustion or injury. 5 to fall naturally *asleep*, (*back*) *into* a habit, etc. 6 to fall in a direction, condition, amount, degree, or pitch. 7 to lower, to direct downwards; to become lower; to perform (a curtsy). 8 to move to or be left in a position further back. 9 to cease to associate with, deal with, or discuss; to cease, to lapse. 10 to utter or be uttered casually; to send casually; to come or go casually *by* or *in* as a visitor, or *into* a place. 11 to lose (money, esp. in gambling); to omit in speech. 12 to send (the ball) or score (a goal) in football by a drop-kick. 13 to give birth to (esp. a lamb). —**at the drop of a hat,** promptly, instantly. **drop-curtain** *n.* a painted curtain that can be lowered on to a theatre stage. **drop-kick** *n.* a kick at football made by dropping the ball and kicking it as it touches the ground. **drop off,** to fall asleep; to drop (a passenger). **drop on a person,** to be severe with him. **drop out,** to cease to take an active part. **drop-out** *n.* one who withdraws from conventional society. **drop scone,** a scone made by dropping a spoonful of mixture on a cooking surface. [OE]

droplet *n.* a small drop. [f. DROP]

dropper *n.* a device for releasing a liquid in drops. [f. DROP]

droppings *n.pl.* what falls or has fallen in drops, especially the dung of some animals and birds. [f. DROP]

dropsy *n.* a disease in which watery fluid collects in the cavities or tissues of the body. —**dropsical** *adj.* [for earlier *hydropsy* f. OF f. L f. Gk (*hudōr* water)]

drosophila /drəˈsɒfɪlə/ *n.* a fruit-fly of the genus *Drosophila*, used extensively in genetic research. [f. Gk *drosos* dew, moisture + *philos* loving]

dross /drɒs/ *n.* scum separated from metals in melting; impurities, rubbish. [OE]

drought /draʊt/ *n.* an abnormally prolonged spell without rain. [OE (as DRY)]

drove[1] *n.* a herd or flock being driven or moving together; a moving crowd. [OE (as DRIVE)]

drove[2] *past* of DRIVE.

drover *n.* a driver of cattle. [f. DROVE[1]]

drown *v.t./i.* 1 to suffocate by submersion in water or other liquid; to flood, to drench. 2 to alleviate (a sorrow etc.) with drink. 3 to overpower (a sound) with a louder noise. —**drowned valley,** a valley that has become submerged at its lower end by the sea or a lake. [rel. to ON *drukna* be drowned; cogn. w. DRINK]

drowse /draʊz/ *v.i.* to be lightly asleep. [back-formation f. foll.]

drowsy /ˈdraʊzɪ/ *adj.* very sleepy, almost asleep. —**drowsily** *adv.*, **drowsiness** *n.* [rel. to OE *drūsian* be languid]

drub *v.t.* (**-bb-**) to beat, to thrash; to defeat thoroughly. —**drubbing** *n.* [ult. f. Arab.]

drudge *n.* one who does dull, laborious, or menial work. —*v.i.* to work hard or laboriously, to toil. —**drudgery** *n.* [perh. rel. to DRAG]

drug *n.* a medicinal substance; a narcotic, hallucinogen, or stimulant, especially one causing addiction. —*v.t./i.* (**-gg-**) to add a drug to (food or drink); to give drugs to, to stupefy; to take drugs as an addict. —**drug on the market,** a commodity that is plentiful but no longer in demand. [f. OF *drogue*]

drugget /ˈdrʌgɪt/ *n.* a coarse woven fabric used for floor coverings etc. [f. F *droguet*]

druggist *n.* a pharmaceutical chemist. [f. F (as DRUG)]

drugstore *n.* (*US*) a chemist's shop also selling light refreshments and other articles.

Druid /ˈdru:ɪd/ *n.* 1 a priest of the ancient Celts in Gaul, Britain, and Ireland. 2 a member of any of various movements attempting to revive Druid practices. 3 an officer of the Gorsedd. —**Druidism** *n.*, **Druidic** /-ˈɪdɪk/ *adj.*, **Druidical** *adj.* [f. F or L f. Celtic]

drum *n.* 1 a musical instrument or toy sounded by striking, made of a hollow cylinder or hemisphere with skin or parchment stretched over the opening(s); its player; the sound produced by striking it; (in *pl.*) the percussion section of an orchestra or band. 2 a cylindrical object, structure, or container. 3 the ear-drum. —*v.t./i.* (**-mm-**) 1 to play a drum; to make the sound of a drum, to tap or beat continuously or rhythmically with the fingers etc. 2 to drive facts or a lesson *into* a person by persistence. 3 (of a bird or insect) to make a loud noise with the wings. —**drum brake,** a brake consisting of shoes acting on a revolving drum. **drum major,** the leader of a marching band. **drum majorette,** a female drum major. **drum out,** to dismiss with ignominy. **drum up,** to produce or obtain by vigorous effort. [f. LG *trommel*]

drumhead *n.* the part of a drum that is struck.

drumlin /ˈdrʌmlɪn/ *n.* a long oval mound of matter deposited by a glacier, flood, etc., with its longer axis parallel to the direction of the flow. [f. Gael. & Ir. *druim* ridge]

drummer *n.* a player of a drum. [f. DRUM]

drumstick *n.* 1 a stick for beating a drum. 2 the lower joint of the leg of a cooked fowl.

drunk *adj.* lacking proper control of oneself from the effects of alcoholic drink; overcome *with* joy, success, etc. —*n.* 1 a drunken person. 2 (*slang*) a bout of drinking. [p.p. of DRINK]

drunkard /ˈdrʌŋkəd/ *n.* a person who is habitually drunk. [f. prec.]

drunken *adj.* drunk, often drunk; involving or caused by excessive alcoholic drinking. —**drunkenly** *adv.*, **drunkenness** /-kən-nɪs/ *n.* [as DRUNK]

drupe /dru:p/ *n.* a fleshy or pulpy fruit enclosing

a stone with a kernel, e.g. a plum. [f. L f. Gk *druppa* olive]

Druse /druːz/ *n.* a member of a political and religious sect of Muslim origin, concentrated in Lebanon, with smaller groups in Syria and Israel. [F f. Arab., prob. f. their founder *al-Darazī* (11th c.)]

dry /draɪ/ *adj.* **(drier, driest) 1** without moisture, not wet; not rainy, deficient in rainfall; not yielding water, milk, etc.; parched, dried up; (*colloq.*) thirsty. **2** prohibiting or opposed to the sale of alcoholic liquor at some or all times. **3** unconnected with or not using liquid. **4** solid, not liquid. **5** without butter etc. **6** (of a liquid) having disappeared by evaporation, draining, wiping, etc. **7** (of a wine) free from sweetness. **8** plain, unelaborated, uninteresting; cold, impassive; (of wit) expressed with pretended seriousness. —*v.t./i.* to make or become dry; to preserve (food) by the removal of moisture. —**dry battery** *or* **cell,** a battery or cell in which the electrolyte is absorbed in a solid. **dry-clean** *v.t.* to clean (clothes etc.) with organic solvents that evaporate quickly, without using water. **dry dock,** a dry enclosure for building or repairing ships. **dry-fly** *adj.* (of fishing) using an artificial fly that floats. **dry-ice** *n.* solid carbon dioxide used as a refrigerant. **dry land,** land as distinct from sea etc. **dry measure,** a measure for dry goods. **dry out,** to make or become fully dry; (of a drug addict etc.) to undergo treatment to cure an addiction. **dry-point** *n.* a needle for engraving without acid on a bare copper plate; an engraving produced by this. **dry rot,** a decayed state of wood when not well ventilated; the fungi causing this; any moral or social decay. **dry run,** (*colloq.*) a rehearsal. **dry-shod** *adj.* & *adv.* without wetting one's shoes. **dry up,** to dry washed dishes; to make completely dry; to cease to yield liquid; to become unproductive; (of an actor) to forget one's lines; (in *imper.*) to cease to talk. —**dryness** *n.* [OE]

dryad /ˈdraɪæd/ *n.* a wood-nymph. [f. OF f. L f. Gk (*drus* oak)]

dryer var. of DRIER.

dryly var. of DRILY.

drystone *adj.* (of a wall etc.) made of stones without mortar.

DSC *abbr.* Distinguished Service Cross.

D.Sc. *abbr.* Doctor of Science.

DSM *abbr.* Distinguished Service Medal.

DSO *abbr.* Distinguished Service Order.

d.t., d.t.'s *abbr.* delirium tremens.

dual /ˈdjʊəl/ *adj.* composed of two parts, twofold, double. —*n.* (*Gram.*) a dual number or form. —**dual carriageway,** a road with a dividing strip between traffic flowing in opposite directions. **dual-control** *n.* two linked sets of controls, enabling either of two persons to operate a car or aircraft. —**duality** /djʊˈælɪtɪ/ *n.* [f. L *dualis* (*duo* two)]

dub[1] *v.t.* **(-bb-) 1** to make (a person) a knight by touching his shoulders with a sword. **2** to give a specified name to. **3** to smear (leather) with grease. [f. OF *adober* equip with armour, repair]

dub[2] *v.t.* **(-bb-)** to make an alternative sound-track of (a film) especially in a different language; to add (sound effects, music) to a film or broadcast. [abbr. of DOUBLE]

dubbin *n.* (also **dubbing**) a thick grease for softening and waterproofing leather. [f. DUB[1]]

dubiety /djuːˈbaɪətɪ/ *n.* a feeling of doubt. [f. L (as foll.)]

dubious /ˈdjuːbɪəs/ *adj.* **1** hesitating, doubtful. **2** unreliable; of questionable or suspected character. —**dubiously** *adv.* [f. L *dubiosus* (*dubium* doubt)]

ducal /ˈdjuːk(ə)l/ *adj.* of or like a duke. [f. F (as DUKE)]

ducat /ˈdʌkət/ *n.* a gold coin formerly current in most European countries. [f. It. or L, = duchy]

duchess /ˈdʌtʃɪs/ *n.* the wife or widow of a duke; a woman holding the rank of duke in her own right. [f. OF f. L *ducissa* (as DUKE)]

duchy /ˈdʌtʃɪ/ *n.* the territory of a duke or duchess; the royal dukedom of Cornwall or Lancaster. [f. OF f. L *ducatus* (as DUKE)]

duck[1] *n.* **1** a swimming bird of the genus *Anas* and kindred genera, especially the domesticated form of the mallard or wild duck; the female of this; its flesh as food. **2** the score of 0 in cricket. **3** (*colloq.*, esp. as a form of address) dear. —*v.t./i.* **1** to bob down, especially to avoid being seen or hit; to dip the head under water and emerge; to plunge (a person) briefly in water. **2** (*colloq.*) to dodge or avoid (a task etc.). —**duck-boards** *n.pl.* wooden slats forming a narrow path in a trench or over mud. **ducks and drakes,** the game of making a flat stone skim along the surface of water (*play ducks and drakes with*, to squander). **like water off a duck's back,** producing no effect. [OE (*dūcan* dive)]

duck[2] *n.* a strong linen or cotton cloth; (in *pl.*) trousers made of this. [f. MDu.]

duckbill *n.* a platypus.

duckling *n.* a young duck. [f. DUCK[1] + -LING]

duckweed *n.* a plant of the genus *Lemna* that forms a covering on the surface of still water.

ducky *n.* (*colloq.*, esp. as a form of address) dear. [f. DUCK[1]]

duct *n.* a channel or tube for conveying a fluid, cable, etc.; a tube in the body conveying secretions etc. —*v.t.* to convey through a duct. [f. L *ductus* aqueduct (*ducere* lead)]

ductile /ˈdʌktaɪl/ *adj.* **1** (of a metal) capable of being drawn into wire. **2** pliable, docile. —**ductility** /-ˈtɪlɪtɪ/ *n.* [f. F or L (as prec.)]

ductless *adj.* without a duct. —**ductless gland,** a gland that passes its secretions directly into the bloodstream, not through a duct. [f. DUCT + -LESS]

dud *n.* (*slang*) **1** a thing that fails to work, a useless thing. **2** (in *pl.*) clothes, rags. —*adj.* (*slang*) defective, useless. [orig. unkn.]

dude /dju:d/ *n.* (*US*) a dandy; a city man. [prob. f. G dial. *dude* fool]

dudgeon /ˈdʌdʒ(ə)n/ *n.* resentment, indignation, usu. in *in high dudgeon*, very angry. [orig. unkn.]

due /dju:/ *adj.* **1** owed as a debt or obligation; payable immediately. **2** merited, appropriate; that ought to be given *to* a person. **3** ascribable *to* a cause, agent, etc. **4** under engagement *to* do something or arrive at a certain time; to be looked for or foreseen. —*adv.* (of a point of the compass) exactly, directly. —*n.* **1** what one owes; (usu. in *pl.*) a fee or amount payable. **2** a person's right, what is owed him. —**become** *or* **fall due,** to become payable. **due to, (D)** because of. [f. OF f. L *debitus* (*debēre* owe)]

duel /ˈdju:əl/ *n.* a formal fight with deadly weapons between two persons; a two-sided contest. —*v.i.* **(-ll-)** to fight a duel. —**duellist** *n.* [f. It. *duello* or L *duellum* (= *bellum*) war]

duenna /djuˈenə/ *n.* an older woman acting as a chaperon to girls, especially in a Spanish family. [Sp. f. L *domina* (as DON[1])]

duet /dju:ˈet/ *n.* a musical composition for two performers; the performers. —**duettist** *n.* [f. G or It. f. L (*duo* two)]

duff[1] *adj.* (*slang*) worthless, useless, counterfeit. —*n.* a boiled pudding. [northern pronunc. of DOUGH]

duff[2] *v.t.* (*slang*) to bungle. [perh. back-formation f. DUFFER]

duffel var. of DUFFLE.

duffer *n.* an inefficient or stupid person. [perh. f. Sc. *doufart* stupid person]

duffle *n.* a heavy woollen cloth. —**duffle bag,** a cylindrical canvas bag closed by a draw-string. **duffle coat,** a hooded overcoat of duffle, fastened with toggles. [f. *Duffel* town in Belgium]

dug[1] *past* & *p.p.* of DIG.

dug[2] *n.* an udder, a teat. [orig. unkn.]

dugong /ˈdu:gɒŋ/ *n.* an Asian sea-mammal, *Dugong dugon*. [f. Malay]

dug-out *n.* **1** a canoe made by hollowing a tree-trunk. **2** a roofed shelter, especially for troops in the trenches.

duke /dju:k/ *n.* a person holding the highest hereditary title of nobility; a sovereign prince ruling a duchy or small State. —**dukedom** *n.* [f. OF f. L (*dux* leader)]

dulcet /ˈdʌlsɪt/ *adj.* sweet-sounding. [f. OF f. L (*dulcis* sweet)]

dulcimer /ˈdʌlsɪmə(r)/ *n.* **1** a musical instrument consisting of a shallow closed box over which metal strings are stretched to be struck by wood, cane, or wire hammers, the prototype of the piano. **2** a musical instrument of the zither type, fretted and with steel strings which are stopped with one hand and plucked with a plectrum by the other, played in Kentucky and Alabama as an accompaniment to songs and dances. [f. OF perh. f. L *dulce melos* sweet melody]

dull *adj.* **1** not bright, vivid, or clear; (of weather) overcast. **2** tedious, not interesting or exciting. **3** not sharp; (of pain) indistinctly felt; (of sound) not resonant. **4** slow in understanding, stupid; without keen perception. **5** listless, depressed; (of trade etc.) slow, sluggish. —*v.t./i.* to make or become dull. —**dully** /ˈdʌl-lɪ/ *adv.*, **dullness** *n.* [f. MLG, MDu. *dul* = OE *dol* stupid]

dullard /ˈdʌləd/ *n.* a mentally dull person. [f. prec.]

duly /ˈdju:lɪ/ *adv.* in due time or manner; rightly, properly, sufficiently. [f. DUE]

dumb /dʌm/ *adj.* **1** unable to speak; silenced by surprise, shyness, etc.; inarticulate; taciturn, reticent. **2** stupid, ignorant. **3** (of action) performed without speech. **4** giving no sound. —**dumb show,** gestures instead of speech. **dumb waiter,** a small movable set of shelves for serving food; a lift for food etc. —**dumbly** *adv.*, **dumbness** *n.* [OE]

dumb-bell *n.* a short bar with a weight at each end used in pairs for exercising the muscles.

dumbfound /dʌmˈfaʊnd/ *v.t.* to nonplus, to make speechless with surprise. [f. DUMB + CONFOUND]

dumdum bullet /ˈdʌmdʌm/ a soft-nosed bullet that expands on impact. [f. *Dum-Dum* in India, where first produced]

dummy *n.* **1** a model of the human form, especially as used to display clothes or by a ventriloquist; an imitation object, an object serving to replace a real or normal one. **2** a baby's rubber teat. **3** a stupid person; a person taking no real part, a figure-head. **4** a player or an imaginary player in some card-games, whose cards are exposed and played by a partner. —*adj.* sham, imitation. —*v.i.* to use a feigned pass or swerve in football etc. —**dummy run,** a trial attempt, a rehearsal. [f. DUMB]

dump *v.t.* **1** to deposit as rubbish; to put down firmly or clumsily; (*colloq.*) to abandon or get rid of. **2** to sell (excess goods) in a new market (especially abroad) at a lower price than in an original market. —*n.* **1** a place or heap for depositing rubbish; an accumulated pile of ore, earth, etc.; a temporary store of ammunition etc. **2** (*colloq.*) an unpleasant or dreary place. [perh. rel. to Norw. *dumpa* fall suddenly]

dumpling /ˈdʌmplɪŋ/ *n.* **1** a baked or boiled ball of dough, as part of a stew or containing apple etc. **2** a small fat person. [perh. f. *dump* small round object + -LING]

dumps *n.pl.* (*colloq.*) low spirits, depression, usu. in *down in the dumps*. [prob. f. MDu. *domp* exhalation, mist (as DAMP)]

dumpy *adj.* short and stout. —**dumpiness** *n.* [f. *dump* (cf. DUMPLING)]

dun[1] *adj.* greyish-brown; (of a horse) having a golden sand-coloured body. —*n.* **1** dun colour. **2** a dun horse. [OE]

dun[2] *v.t.* (**-nn-**) to ask persistently for payment of a debt. —*n.* a demand for payment. [abbr. of obs. *dunkirk* privateer, f. *Dunkirk* in France]

dunce *n.* one who is slow at learning, a dullard. [f. *Duns Scotus* (d. 1308), philosopher]

Dundee cake /dʌnˈdi:/ a rich fruit-cake usually decorated with split almonds. [f. *Dundee* city in Scotland]

dunderhead /ˈdʌndəhed/ *n.* a stupid person. [perh. rel. to dial. *dunner* resounding noise]

dune /dju:n/ *n.* a mound or ridge of sand etc. formed by wind. [F, f. MDu. (as DOWN[3])]

dung *n.* the excrement of animals; manure. —*v.t.* to apply dung to, to manure (land). —**dung-beetle** *n.* a beetle whose larvae develop in dung. [OE]

dungaree /dʌŋgəˈri:/ *n.* a strong coarse cotton cloth; (in *pl.*) overalls or trousers made of this. [f. Hindi]

dungeon /ˈdʌndʒ(ə)n/ *n.* an underground cell for prisoners. [f. OF f. L *domnio* (*dominus* lord)]

dunghill *n.* a heap of dung or refuse in a farmyard.

dunk *v.t.* to dip (bread etc.) into a soup or beverage before eating it; to immerse. [f. G *tunken* dip]

dunlin /ˈdʌnlɪn/ *n.* the red-backed sandpiper, *Calidris alpina*. [prob. f. DUN[1]]

dunnock /ˈdʌnək/ *n.* the hedge-sparrow, *Prunella modularis*. [f. DUN[1]]

duo /ˈdju:əʊ/ *n.* (*pl.* **-os**) a pair of performers; a duet. [L, = two]

duodecimal /dju:əʊdesɪm(ə)l/ *adj.* of twelfths or twelve; proceeding or reckoning by twelves. [f. L (*duodecim* twelve)]

duodenum /dju:əʊˈdi:nəm/ *n.* the first part of the small intestine immediately below the stomach. —**duodenal** *adj.* [L (as prec.), from its length of 12 fingers' breadth]

duologue /ˈdju:əlɒg/ *n.* a dialogue between two persons. [f. L or Gk *duo* two, after MONOLOGUE]

dupe /dju:p/ *n.* a victim of deception. —*v.t.* to deceive, to trick. [F, lit. = hoopoe]

duple /ˈdju:p(ə)l/ *adj.* of two parts. —**duple time**, (*Mus.*) that with two beats to the bar. [f. L (*duo* two)]

duplex /ˈdju:pleks/ *adj.* having two parts; (of a set of rooms) on two floors. [L, = double]

duplicate /ˈdju:plɪkət/ *adj.* exactly like another example; existing in two examples, having two corresponding parts; doubled, twice as large or as many; (of card-games) with the same hand played by different players. —*n.* one of two things exactly alike, especially that made after the other; an exact copy of a letter or document. —/-keɪt/ *v.t.* to make or be an exact copy of; to double; to multiply by two; to repeat (an action etc.) especially unnecessarily. —**duplication** /-ˈkeɪʃ(ə)n/ *n.* [f. L (as prec.)]

duplicator *n.* a machine for producing documents in multiple copies. [f. prec.]

duplicity /dju:ˈplɪsɪtɪ/ *n.* double-dealing, deceitfulness. —**duplicitous** *adj.* [f. OF or L (as DUPLEX)]

Dur. *abbr.* Durham (county).

durable /ˈdjʊərəb(ə)l/ *adj.* likely to last; (of goods) remaining useful for a long period; resisting wear, decay, etc. —**durability** /-ˈbɪlɪtɪ/ *n.* [f. OF f. L (*durare* endure)]

duration /djʊəˈreɪʃ(ə)n/ *n.* the time during which a thing continues. [as prec.]

duress /djʊəˈres/ *n.* the use of force or threats, esp. illegally; imprisonment. [f. OF f. L *duritia* (*durus* hard)]

during /ˈdjʊərɪŋ/ *prep.* throughout or at a point in the duration of. [f. obs. *dure* continue f. OF (as DURATION)]

dusk *n.* the darker stage of twilight. [f. OE *dox* dark, swarthy]

dusky *adj.* shadowy, dim; dark-coloured. —**duskily** *adv.*, **duskiness** *n.* [f. prec.]

dust *n.* **1** finely powdered earth or other matter. **2** pollen; a fine powder of any material. **3** a dead person's remains. **4** confusion, turmoil. —*v.t.* **1** to clear of dust by wiping; to clear furniture etc. of dust. **2** to sprinkle (powder or dust) over, to sprinkle (an object) thus. —**bite the dust**, to be killed. **dust-cart** *n.* a vehicle for collecting household refuse. **dust-cover** *n.* a sheet or cloth to keep the dust off furniture etc.; a dust-jacket. **dust-jacket** *n.* a paper wrapper on a book. **dust-sheet** *n.* a dust-cover for furniture. **dust-up** *n.* (*colloq.*) a fight, a disturbance. **throw dust in (a person's) eyes**, to mislead him. [OE]

dustbin *n.* a container for household refuse.

dust-bowl *n.* an arid or unproductive dry region.

duster *n.* a cloth for dusting furniture etc. [f. DUST]

dustman *n.* (*pl.* **-men**) a man employed to empty dustbins.

dustpan *n.* a pan into which dust is brushed from a floor.

dusty *adj.* **1** covered with or full of dust. **2** like dust. **3** (of a colour) dull or vague. —**dusty answer,** a curt rejection of a request. **not so dusty,** (*colloq.*) fairly good. —**dustily** *adv.*, **dustiness** *n.* [OE (as DUST)]

Dutch *adj.* of the Netherlands or its people or language. —*n.* the Dutch language. —**the Dutch,** the people of the Netherlands. **Dutch auction,** one in which the price is reduced until a buyer is found. **Dutch barn,** a farm shelter for hay etc., consisting of a roof on poles. **Dutch cap,** a contraceptive diaphragm. **Dutch courage,** courage induced by alcoholic drink. **Dutch elm disease,** a fungous disease of elms, first found in the Netherlands. **Dutch oven,** a metal box for cooking, of which the open side is turned towards an ordinary fire; a covered cooking-pot. **Dutch treat,** a party, outing, etc., at which each participant pays for his own share. **go Dutch,** to share the expenses on an outing etc. **in Dutch,** (*slang*) in disgrace. **talk like a Dutch uncle,** to speak severely but kindly. [f. MDu. *dutsch*, OHG *diutisc* national]

dutch *n.* (*slang*) a costermonger's wife. [abbr. of DUCHESS]

Dutchman *n.* (*pl.* **-men**) a man of Dutch birth or nationality. —**I'm a Dutchman,** a phrase implying refusal or disbelief.

duteous /ˈdjuːtɪəs/ *adj.* (*literary*) dutiful. [f. DUTY]

dutiable /ˈdjuːtɪəb(ə)l/ *adj.* requiring payment of duty. [f. DUTY]

dutiful /ˈdjuːtɪf(ə)l/ *adj.* doing or observant of one's duty, obedient. —**dutifully** *adv.* [f. DUTY + -FUL]

duty /ˈdjuːtɪ/ *n.* **1** a moral or legal obligation, what one is bound or ought to do; the binding force of what is right; a business, office, or function arising from these, an engagement in these. **2** deference, an expression of respect to a superior. **3** a tax levied on certain goods, imports, events, or services. —**do duty for,** to serve as or pass for (something else). **duty-bound** *adj.* obliged by duty. **duty-free shop,** a shop at an airport etc. at which goods can be bought free of duty. **on, off, duty,** actually engaged, not engaged, in one's regular work or some obligation. [f. AF (as DUE)]

duvet /ˈduːveɪ/ *n.* a thick soft quilt used instead of bedclothes. [F]

dwarf /dwɔːf/ *n.* (*pl.* **-fs**) **1** a person, animal, or plant much below normal size. **2** a small mythological being with magical powers. —*adj.* of a kind very small in size. —*v.t.* **1** to stunt in growth. **2** to make seem small by contrast or distance. [OE]

dwell *v.i.* (*past* & *p.p.* **dwelt**) to live as an occupant or inhabitant. —**dwell on** *or* **upon,** to think or speak or write at length on. —**dweller** *n.* (OE, = lead astray]

dwelling *n.* a house, a residence. [f. prec.]

dwindle *v.i.* to become gradually less or smaller; to lose importance. [f. *dwine* fade away f. OE]

Dy *symbol* dysprosium.

Dyak /ˈdaɪæk/ *n.* **1** a member of the indigenous non-Muslim inhabitants of Borneo. **2** their language, = Iban. [f. Malay *dayak* up-country]

dybbuk /ˈdɪbək/ *n.* (*pl.* **-im, -s**) (in Jewish folklore) the malevolent spirit of a dead person that enters and controls the body of a living person until exorcized. [f. Heb. (*dābak* cling)]

dye /daɪ/ *n.* a substance used to change the colour of hair, fabric, wood, etc.; a colour produced by this. —*v.t.* (*partic.* **dyeing**) to impregnate with dye; to make (a thing) a specified colour thus. —**dyed in the wool,** out-and-out, unchangeable. —**dyer** *n.* [OE]

dying see DIE[1].

dyke var. of DIKE.

dynamic /daɪˈnæmɪk/ *adj.* **1** of motive force (opp. *static*). **2** of force in actual operation (opp. *potential*). **3** of dynamics. **4** (of a person) active, energetic. —**dynamically** *adv.* [f. F f. Gk (*dunamis* force, power)]

dynamics *n.* (usu. treated as *sing.*) **1** the mathematical study of motion and the forces causing it; the branch of any science in which forces or changes are considered. **2** motive forces, physical or moral, in any sphere. **3** (*Mus.*) gradations or amount of volume of sound. [f. prec.]

dynamism /ˈdaɪnəmɪz(ə)m/ *n.* energizing or dynamic action or power. [f. Gk *dunamis* power]

dynamite /ˈdaɪnəmaɪt/ *n.* **1** a high explosive. **2** a potentially dangerous person or thing. —*v.t.* to charge or blow up with dynamite. [as prec.]

dynamo /ˈdaɪnəməʊ/ *n.* (*pl.* **-os**) a machine converting mechanical into electrical energy, especially by rotating coils of copper wire in a magnetic field. [abbr. of *dynamo-electric machine* (as DYNAMIC)]

dynamometer /daɪnəˈmɒmɪtə(r)/ *n.* an instrument measuring the energy expended. [f. F f. Gk *dunamis* force + -METER]

dynast /ˈdɪnæst/ *n.* a ruler; a member of a dynasty. [f. L f. Gk (*dunamai* be able)]

dynasty /ˈdɪnəstɪ/ *n.* a line of hereditary rulers; a succession of leaders in any field. —**dynastic** /-ˈnæstɪk/ *adj.* [f. F or L f. Gk (as prec.)]

dyne /daɪn/ *n.* a unit of force, the force that, acting for 1 second on a mass of 1 g, gives it a velocity of 1 cm per second. [F, f. Gk *dunamis* force]

dys- *prefix* bad, difficult. [f. Gk *dus-*]

dysentery /ˈdɪs(ə)ntrɪ/ *n.* a disease with inflammation of the intestines, causing severe diarrhoea. [f. OF or L f. Gk (DYS-, *entera* bowels)]

dyslexia /dɪsˈleksɪə/ *n.* abnormal difficulty in

reading and spelling, caused by a condition of the brain. —**dyslexic** *adj*. & *n*. [f. G f. Gk (DYS-, *lexis* speech)]

dyspepsia /dɪsˈpepsɪə/ *n*. indigestion. —**dyspeptic** *adj*. & *n*. [L f. Gk (DYS-, *peptos* cooked, digested]

dysprosium /dɪsˈprəʊzɪəm/ *n*. a soft metallic element of the lanthanide series, symbol Dy, atomic number 66. [f. Gk *dusprositos* hard to get at]

dystrophy /ˈdɪstrəfɪ/ *n*. defective nutrition. —**muscular dystrophy**, hereditary progressive weakening and wasting of the muscles. [L f. Gk (DYS-, *-trophia* nourishment)]

Ee

E, e *n.* **1** the fifth letter of the alphabet. **2** (*Mus.*) the third note in the scale of C major.

E *symbol* (preceding a number) indicating conformity with an EEC standard of quantities and capacities permitted for certain prepackaged products.

E. *abbr.* east, eastern.

e *symbol* indicating conformity with EEC standards for the indicated weights or volume of certain prepackaged products.

each *adj.* every one of (two or more persons or things) regarded separately. —*pron.* each person or thing. —**each other,** one another. **each way,** (of a bet) backing a horse etc. to win and to be placed. [OE, = ever alike]

eager /ˈiːgə(r)/ *adj.* full of keen desire, enthusiastic. —**eager beaver,** (*colloq.*) a very or excessively diligent person. —**eagerly** *adv.*, **eagerness** *n.* [f. AF f. L *acer*]

eagle *n.* **1** a large bird of prey of the family Accipitridae, with keen vision and powerful flight; the figure of an eagle, especially as the symbol of the USA or (*hist.*) as a Roman or French ensign. **2** (in golf) a hole played in two under par or bogey. —**eagle eye,** keen sight or watchfulness. —**eagle-eyed** *adj.* [f. AF f. L *aquila*]

eaglet /ˈiːglɪt/ *n.* a young eagle. [f. prec. + -LET]

E. & O.E. *abbr.* errors and omissions excepted.

ear[1] *n.* **1** the organ of hearing in man and animals, especially the external part of this. **2** the faculty of discriminating sound. **3** an ear-shaped thing. —**all ears,** listening attentively. **ear-drum** *n.* the internal membrane of the ear. **ear-piercing** *adj.* shrill. **ear-plug** *n.* a piece of wax etc. placed in the ear to protect against water, noise, etc. **ear-ring** *n.* an ornament worn on the lobe of the ear. **ear-splitting** *adj.* extremely loud. **ear-trumpet** *n.* a trumpet-shaped tube formerly used as an aid to hearing by the partially deaf. **give one's ears,** to make any sacrifice *for* a thing, *to* do, *if.* **have** *or* **keep an ear to the ground,** to be alert to rumours or the trend of opinion. **have a person's ear,** to have a person's favourable attention. **up to the ears,** (*colloq.*) deeply involved or occupied (*in*). [OE]

ear[2] *n.* the seed-bearing head of a cereal plant. [OE]

earache *n.* pain in the inner ear.

earful *n.* (*colloq.*) **1** copious talk. **2** a reprimand. [f. EAR[1] + -FUL]

earl /ɜːl/ *n.* a British nobleman ranking between marquis and viscount. —**Earl Marshal,** the officer presiding over the Heralds' College, with ceremonial duties on royal occasions. [OE]

earldom /ˈɜːldəm/ *n.* the position or domain of an earl. [f. EARL + -DOM]

early /ˈɜːlɪ/ *adj.* & *adv.* before the due, usual, or expected time; not far on in day, night, or time; not far on in a period, development, or process of evolution; forward in flowering, ripening, etc. —**early bird,** (*colloq.*) one who arrives or gets up early. **early days,** early in time for something (to happen etc.). **Early English (style),** the first stage of English Gothic architecture (13th c.), with narrow pointed windows and pointed arches. **early on,** at an early stage. [OE (as ERE)]

earmark *n.* an identifying mark; an owner's mark on the ear of an animal. —*v.t.* **1** to set aside for a special purpose. **2** to mark (an animal) with an earmark.

earn /ɜːn/ *v.t.* **1** to bring in as income or interest. **2** (of a person, conduct, etc.) to obtain or be entitled to as a reward of work or merit. [OE]

earnest[1] /ˈɜːnɪst/ *adj.* ardently serious, showing intense feeling. —**in earnest,** serious, seriously, with determination. —**earnestly** *adv.*, **earnestness** *n.* [OE (cf. ON *ern* vigorous)]

earnest[2] /ˈɜːnɪst/ *n.* money paid as an instalment, especially to confirm a contract; a token, a foretaste. [prob. var. of *erles* f. L *arrhula* dim. of *arr(h)a* pledge]

earnings *n.pl.* money earned. [f. EARN]

earphone *n.* a device worn over or put to the ear to receive radio or telephone etc. communication.

earshot *n.* hearing-distance.

earth /ɜːθ/ *n.* **1** (also **Earth**) the planet on which we live. **2** the present abode of man, as distinct from heaven and hell. **3** land and sea, as distinct from sky; dry land, the ground. **4** soil. **5** connection to earth as the completion of an electrical circuit, either accidental (with resulting leakage of current or dangerous differences of potential) or intentional (as for the purpose of providing a return path for a current). **6** the hole of a badger, fox, etc. **7** (*colloq.*) a huge sum, a vast amount. —*v.t.* **1** to connect (an electrical circuit) to earth. **2** to cover (the roots of a plant) with earth. —**come back to earth,** to return to realities. **earth-nut** *n.* any of various plants or their tubers, especially the peanut. **earth sciences,** those concerned with the earth or part of it. **earth-shaking** *adj.* having a violent effect. **gone to earth,** in hiding. **on earth,** existing anywhere. **run to earth,** to find after a long search. [OE]

earthbound *adj.* **1** attached (*lit.* or *fig.*) to the earth or earthly things. **2** moving towards the earth.

earthen *adj.* made of earth or baked clay. [f. EARTH]

earthenware *n.* pottery made of coarse baked clay.

earthly *adj.* of the earth or man's life on it, terrestrial. —**no earthly,** (*colloq.*) absolutely no. **not an earthly,** (*slang*) no chance whatever. —**earthliness** *n.* [f. EARTH]

earthquake *n* a convulsion of the earth's surface.

earthwork *n.* an artificial bank of earth in a fortification or in road-building.

earthworm *n* an annelid worm (of various genera) living in the ground.

earthy *adj.* **1** of or like earth or soil. **2** gross, coarse. **3** worldly. —**earthiness** *n.* [f. EARTH]

earwig *n.* a small insect of the order Dermaptera, with pincers at its tail end. [OE (EAR[1], *wig* prob. rel. to *wiggle*); once thought to enter the head through the ear]

ease /i:z/ *n.* **1** freedom from pain or trouble; freedom from constraint. **2** facility. —*v.t./i.* **1** to relieve from pain or anxiety. **2** to relax, to slacken, to make or become less burdensome. **3** to cause to move by gentle force. —**at ease,** free from anxiety or constraint; (of soldiers etc.) in a relaxed attitude, with the feet apart. **ease off** *or* **up,** to become less burdensome or severe. [f. OF *aise* f. L *adjacens* lying near]

easel /ˈi:z(ə)l/ *n.* a standing wooden support for an artist's canvas, a blackboard, etc. [f. Du. *ezel* ass]

easement /ˈi:zmənt/ *n.* a legal right of way or similar right over another's ground or property. [f. OF (as EASE)]

easily /ˈi:zɪlɪ/ *adv.* **1** in an easy manner, without difficulty. **2** by far. **3** very probably. [f. EASE]

east *n.* **1** the point of the horizon where the sun rises at the equinoxes; the compass point corresponding to this; the direction in which this lies. **2** (usu. **East**) the part of a country or town lying to the east; the regions or countries lying to the east of Europe; the Communist States of eastern Europe. —*adj.* **1** towards, at, or facing the east. **2** (of wind) blowing from the east. —*adv.* towards, at, or near the east. —**East End,** the eastern part of London, including the docks. **east-north-east, east-south-east** *adjs.* & *advs.* midway between east and north-east, or south-east; (*ns.*) the compass point in this position. **East Side,** the eastern part of Manhattan. [OE]

Easter /ˈi:stə(r)/ *n.* the Christian feast of the Resurrection of Christ, the greatest and oldest feast of the Christian Church, celebrated on the first Sunday after the first full moon after the vernal equinox (21 March). —**Easter egg,** an edible artificial (usually chocolate) egg given as a gift at Easter. [OE]

easterly /ˈi:stəlɪ/ *adj.* & *adv.* in an eastern position or direction; (of wind) blowing from the east (approximately). [f. EAST]

eastern /ˈi:stən/ *adj.* of or in the east. —**Eastern Church,** the Orthodox Church. —**easternmost** *adj.* [f. EAST]

easterner *n.* a native or inhabitant of the east. [f. prec.]

easting *n.* (*Naut.* etc.) **1** a distance travelled or measured eastward. **2** an easterly direction. [f. EAST]

eastward /ˈi:stwəd/ *adj.* & (also **eastwards** /-z/) *adv.* towards the east. —*n.* an eastward direction or region. [f. EAST + -WARD]

easy /ˈi:zɪ/ *adj.* **1** not difficult, achieved without great effort. **2** free from pain, trouble, or anxiety. **3** free from awkwardness, strictness, etc., relaxed and pleasant. **4** compliant, obliging. —*adv.* with ease, in an effortless or relaxed manner; (as *int.*) go carefully. —**easy chair,** a large comfortable chair. **easy on the eye,** pleasant to look at. **Easy Street,** (*colloq.*) a state of affluence. **go easy,** to be sparing or cautious (*with* or *on*). **I'm easy,** (*colloq.*) I have no preference. **take it easy,** to proceed gently, to relax. —**easiness** *n.* [f. AF (as EASE)]

easygoing *adj.* placid and tolerant, relaxed in manner.

eat *v.t./i.* (*past* **ate** /et, eɪt/, *p.p.* **eaten**) **1** to take into the mouth, to chew and swallow (food); to consume food, to take a meal. **2** (often with *away*) to destroy, to consume; (also with *at*) to trouble, to vex. —**eat one's heart out,** to suffer greatly from anxiety or longing. **eating apple** etc., one suitable for eating raw. **eats** *n.pl.* (*colloq.*) food, a meal. **eat up,** to eat or consume completely; to traverse (distance) rapidly. **eat one's words,** to retract them abjectly. [OE]

eatable *adj*. that may be eaten. —*n*. (usu. in *pl*.) food. [f. EAT]

eater *n*. **1** one who eats. **2** an eating apple etc. [f. EAT]

eau-de-Cologne /əʊdəkəˈləʊn/ *n*. a perfume originally made at Cologne. [F, = water of Cologne]

eaves *n.pl*. the projecting lower edge of a roof. [OE, rel. to OVER]

eavesdrop /ˈi:vzdrɒp/ *v.i*. (**-pp-**) to listen secretly to a private conversation. —**eavesdropper** *n*. [f. prec.]

ebb *n*. **1** the outward movement of the tide, away from the land. **2** decline, poor condition. —*v.i*. to flow back; to recede, to decline. [OE]

ebonite /ˈebənaɪt/ *n*. vulcanite. [f. foll.]

ebony /ˈebənɪ/ *n*. the hard heavy black wood of a tropical tree especially of the genus *Diospyros*. —*adj*. made of ebony; black like ebony. [f. L f. Gk *ebenos* ebony-tree]

ebullient /ɪˈbʌlɪənt/ *adj*. exuberant, high-spirited. —**ebullience** *n*., **ebulliency** *n*. [f. L *ebullire* (EX-, *bullire* boil)]

ebullition /ebəˈlɪʃ(ə)n/ *n*. boiling; a sudden outburst of passion or emotion. [as prec.]

EC *abbr*. **1** East Central. **2** European Commission. **3** European Community.

eccentric /ɪkˈsentrɪk/ *adj*. **1** odd or capricious in behaviour or appearance. **2** not placed centrally; not having its axis placed centrally; (of a circle) not concentric (*to* another circle); (of an orbit) not circular. —*n*. **1** an eccentric person. **2** a disc fixed eccentrically on a revolving shaft, for changing rotatory to to-and-fro motion. —**eccentrically** *adv*., **eccentricity** /-ˈtrɪsɪtɪ/ *n*. [f. L f. Gk (*ek* out of, *kentron* centre)]

Eccles cake /ˈek(ə)lz/ a round cake of pastry filled with currants. [f. *Eccles* in Greater Manchester]

ecclesiastic /ɪkli:zɪˈæstɪk/ *n*. a clergyman. [f. F or L f. Gk (*ekklēsia* church)]

ecclesiastical *adj*. of the Church or clergy. [f. prec.]

ecclesiology /ɪkli:zɪˈɒlədʒɪ/ *n*. the study of church building and decoration. [f. Gk *ekklēsia* church + -LOGY]

ECG *abbr*. electrocardiogram.

echelon /ˈeʃəlɒn/ *n*. **1** a formation of troops or ships, aircraft, etc., in parallel rows with the end of each row projecting further laterally than the one in front. **2** a grade or rank in an organization. [F, = rung of ladder]

echidna /ɪˈkɪdnə/ *n*. an Australian egg-laying animal (*Tachyglossus aculeatus*) resembling a hedgehog. [L f. Gk, = viper]

echinoderm /ɪˈkaɪnədɜ:m, ˈekɪn-/ *n*. an animal of the phylum Echinodermata, a group of marine invertebrates including starfish and sea-urchins, many of which have spiny skins. [f. Gk *ekhinos* hedgehog, sea-urchin + *derma* skin]

echo /ˈekəʊ/ *n*. (*pl*. **-oes**) **1** repetition of sound by the reflection of sound-waves; a secondary sound so produced. **2** a reflected radio or radar beam. **3** a close imitation or imitator. —*v.t./i*. **1** (of a place) to resound with an echo; to repeat (a sound) thus; (of a sound) to be repeated, to resound. **2** to repeat (a person's words); to imitate the opinions of. —**echo-sounder** *n*. a sounding apparatus for determining the depth of sea beneath a ship by measuring the time taken for an echo to be received (see ASDIC, SONAR). **echo-sounding** *n*. [f. OF or L f. Gk]

echoic /eˈkəʊɪk/ *adj*. (of a word) imitating the sound it represents, onomatopoeic. —**echoically** *adv*. [f. ECHO]

echolocation /ekəʊləˈkeɪʃ(ə)n/ *n*. the location of objects by means of the echo reflected from them by a sound-signal, as of ultrasonic sounds emitted by bats or by man-made devices.

éclair /eɪˈkleə(r), ɪ-/ *n*. a finger-shaped cake of choux pastry filled with cream and iced. [F, = lightning]

éclat /ˈeɪklɑ:/ *n*. brilliant success or display; renown, esteem. [F, lit. = burst of light]

eclectic /ɪˈklektɪk/ *adj*. selecting ideas or beliefs from various sources. —*n*. an eclectic person. —**eclectically** *adv*., **eclecticism** /-sɪz(ə)m/ *n*. [f. Gk (*eklegō* pick out)]

eclipse /ɪˈklɪps/ *n*. **1** the obscuring of light from one heavenly body by another. **2** loss of light, brilliance, or importance. —*v.t*. **1** to cause an eclipse of; to intercept (light). **2** to outshine, to surpass. —**annular eclipse,** one leaving a complete ring of the solar surface open to view, occurring when the moon passes before the sun at a greater distance than average. **partial eclipse,** one that is not total. **total eclipse,** one where the entire surface of the luminous body is obscured. [f. OF, ult. f. Gk *ekleipō* fail to appear]

ecliptic /ɪˈklɪptɪk/ *n*. the apparent path across the heavens of the sun during the year, so called because lunar and solar eclipses will occur only when the moon crosses this path. —*adj*. of an eclipse or the ecliptic. [f. L f. Gk (as prec.)]

eclogue /ˈeklɒg/ *n*. a short poem, especially a pastoral dialogue such as those of Theocritus and Virgil. [f. L f. Gk, = selection (as ECLECTIC)]

eco- *prefix* ecology, ecological. [f. ECOLOGY]

ecoclimate /ˈi:kəʊklaɪmət/ *n*. climate as an ecological factor. [f. ECO- + CLIMATE]

ecology /i:ˈkɒlədʒɪ/ *n*. the study of organisms in relation to one another and to their surroundings. —**ecological** /-ˈlɒdʒɪk(ə)l/ *adj.*, **ecologist** *n.* [f. Gk *oikos* home + -LOGY]

economic /iːkəˈnɒmɪk, ek-/ *adj.* **1** of economics. **2** maintained for profit, on business lines; adequate to pay or recoup expenditure with some profit; practical, considered with regard to human needs. —**economically** *adv.* [f. F or L f. Gk (as ECONOMY)]

economical *adj.* careful in the use of resources, avoiding waste; thrifty. —**economically** *adv.* [as prec.]

economics *n.* **1** the science of the production and distribution of wealth; the application of this to a particular subject. **2** (as *pl.*) the financial aspects of something. [f. ECONOMIC]

economist /ɪˈkɒnəmɪst/ *n.* an expert on or student of economics. [f. Gk (as ECONOMY)]

economize /ɪˈkɒnəmaɪz/ *v.t./i.* to be economical, to make economies, to reduce expenditure; (usu. with *on*) to use sparingly. [as prec.]

economy /ɪˈkɒnəmɪ/ *n.* **1** the wealth and resources of a community; the administration or condition of these. **2** careful management of (esp. financial) resources, frugality; an instance of this. [f. F or L f. Gk *oikonomia* stewardship (*oikos* house, *nemō* manage)]

ecosystem /ˈiːkəʊsɪstəm/ *n.* a system of interacting organisms in a particular habitat. [f. ECO- + SYSTEM]

ecru /ˈeɪkruː/ *n.* a light fawn colour. [F, = unbleached]

ecstasy /ˈekstəsɪ/ *n.* an overwhelming feeling of joy, rapture. —**ecstatic** /ekˈstætɪk/ *adj.*, **ecstatically** *adv.* [f. OF f. L f. Gk *ekstasis* standing outside oneself]

ECT *abbr.* electroconvulsive therapy.

ecto- *prefix* outside. [f. Gk *ektos*]

ectomorph /ˈektəmɔːf/ *n.* a person with a lean build of body, thought likely to be an introvert. [f. ECTO- + Gk *morphē* form]

-ectomy /-ektəmɪ/ *suffix* forming nouns, denoting a surgical operation in which some part is removed (*tonsillectomy*). [f. Gk *ektomē* excision]

ectopic /ekˈtɒpɪk/ *adj.* (*Path.*) in an abnormal place or position. [f. Gk *ektopos* out of place]

ectoplasm /ˈektəplæz(ə)m/ *n.* a viscous substance supposed to emanate from the body of a spiritualist medium during a trance. [f. ECTO- + PLASMA]

Ecu /ˈeɪkjuː, ˈiː-/ *n.* (also **ecu**) the European currency unit. [abbr.]

ecumenical /iːkjuːˈmenɪk(ə)l/ *adj.* of or representing the whole Christian world; seeking world-wide Christian unity. —**ecumenicalism** *n.*, **ecumenism** /iːˈkjuːmənɪz(ə)m/ *n.* [f. L f. Gk (*oikoumenē* the inhabited earth)]

eczema /ˈeksɪmə/ *n.* a skin disorder with inflammation and itching. —**eczematous** /ekˈziːmətəs/ *adj.* [L f. Gk (*ek* out, *zeō* boil)]

Edam /ˈiːdæm/ *n.* a spherical Dutch cheese, usually pale yellow with a red rind. [f. *Edam* in Holland]

eddy /ˈedɪ/ *n.* an area of water swirling in a circular motion; smoke, fog, etc., moving like this. —*v.t./i.* to move in eddies. [f. OE *ed-* again, back]

edelweiss /ˈeɪd(ə)lvaɪs/ *n.* an alpine plant (*Leontopodium alpinum*) with woolly white bracts round the flower-heads. [G (*edel* noble, *weiss* white)]

edentate /ɪˈdenteɪt/ *adj.* having few or no teeth. —*n.* an edentate animal, especially a mammal. [f. L *edentatus* (EX-, *dens* tooth)]

edge /edʒ/ *n.* **1** the cutting side of a blade; the sharpness of this; (*fig.*) effectiveness. **2** an edge-shaped thing, especially the crest of a ridge. **3** the meeting-line of surfaces; the boundary-line of a region or surface; the brink of a precipice. —*v.t./i.* **1** to give or form a border to. **2** to insinuate (a thing or *oneself*, *in* etc.). **3** to advance (esp. gradually and obliquely). **4** to give a sharp edge to. —**have the edge on,** (*colloq.*) to have an advantage over. **on edge,** tense and irritable. **set one's teeth on edge,** (of a taste or sound) to cause an unpleasant nervous sensation. **take the edge off,** to dull, to weaken, to make less intense. [OE]

edgeways *adv.* (also **edgewise**) with the edge foremost or uppermost. —**get a word in edgeways,** to contribute to a conversation dominated by another or others.

edging *n.* a thing forming an edge, a border. [f. EDGE]

edgy *adj.* irritable, anxious, on edge. —**edgily** *adv.*, **edginess** *n.* [f. EDGE]

edible /ˈedɪb(ə)l/ *adj.* fit to be eaten. —*n.* an edible thing. —**edibility** /-ˈbɪlɪtɪ/ *n.* [f. L (*edere* eat)]

edict /ˈiːdɪkt/ *n.* an order proclaimed by authority. [f. L (*edicere* proclaim)]

edifice /ˈedɪfɪs/ *n.* a building, especially a large imposing one. [f. OF f. L *aedificium*]

edify /ˈedɪfaɪ/ *v.t.* to benefit spiritually; to improve morally. —**edification** /-fɪˈkeɪʃ(ə)n/ *n.* [f. OF f. L *aedificare* build]

edit /ˈedɪt/ *v.t.* **1** to assemble or prepare (written material) for publication; to arrange or modify (another's work) for publication. **2** to act as editor of (a newspaper etc.). **3** to prepare (data) for processing by computer. **4** to take extracts from and collate (a film etc.) so as to form a unified sequence. **5** to reword for a purpose. [f. F (as foll.)]

edition /ɪˈdɪʃ(ə)n/ *n.* **1** the edited or published form of a book etc. **2** the copies of a book, newspaper, etc., issued at one time; the whole number of products of the same kind issued at one time. **3** a person etc. considered as resembling another. [f. F f. L (*edere* publish)]

editor /ˈedɪtə(r)/ *n.* **1** one who edits. **2** one who directs the content and writing of a newspaper or a particular section of one. **3** the head of a department of a publishing house. —**editorship** *n.* [L (as EDIT)]

editorial /edɪˈtɔːrɪəl/ *adj.* of an editor or editing. —*n.* a newspaper article commenting on a current topic, written or sanctioned by the editor. —**editorially** *adv.* [f. prec.]

EDP *abbr.* electronic data processing.

educable /ˈedjʊkəb(ə)l/ *adj.* able to be educated. [f. foll.]

educate /ˈedjuːkeɪt/ *v.t.* to train or instruct intellectually, morally, and socially; to provide schooling for. —**educated guess**, one based on experience. —**educative** *adj.*, **educator** *n.* [f. L (rel. to EDUCE)]

education /edjuːˈkeɪʃ(ə)n/ *n.* systematic instruction; a course of this; development of character or mental powers. —**educational** *adj.*, **educationally** *adv.* [f. F or L (as prec.)]

educationist *n.* (also **educationalist**) an expert in educational methods. [f. prec.]

educe /ɪˈdjuːs/ *v.t.* to bring out, to develop from latent or potential existence. —**eduction** /ɪˈdʌkʃ(ə)n/ *n.* [f. L *educere* draw out]

Edwardian /edˈwɔːdɪən/ *adj.* belonging to or characteristic of the reign of Edward VII (1901-10). —*n.* a person of this period. [f. EDWARD]

EEC *abbr.* European Economic Community.

EEG *abbr.* electroencephalogram.

eel *n.* **1** a snakelike fish. **2** an evasive person. [OE]

eerie /ˈɪərɪ/ *adj.* gloomy and strange, weird. —**eerily** *adv.*, **eeriness** *n.* [OE; orig. = timid]

efface /ɪˈfeis/ *v.t.* **1** to rub or wipe out (a mark, recollection, or impression). **2** to surpass, to eclipse. —**efface oneself**, to treat or regard oneself as unimportant. —**effacement** *n.* [f. F (as EX-¹, FACE)]

effect /ɪˈfekt/ *n.* **1** a result or consequence of an action etc. **2** the state of being operative; efficacy. **3** an impression produced on a spectator or hearer etc. **4** (in *pl.*) property. **5** (in *pl.*) sounds and visual features giving realism to a play, film, etc. —*v.t.* to bring about, to accomplish, to cause to occur. —**bring** *or* **carry into effect**, to accomplish. **give effect to**, to make operative. **in effect**, for practical purposes, in reality. **take effect**, to become operative. **to that effect**, having that result or implication. **with effect from**, coming into operation at (a stated time). [f. OF or L (as EFFICIENT)]

effective /ɪˈfektɪv/ *adj.* **1** having an effect, powerful in effect; striking, remarkable. **2** actual, existing. **3** operative. —**effectively** *adv.*, **effectiveness** *n.* [f. L (as prec.)]

effectual /ɪˈfektʃʊəl, -tjʊəl/ *adj.* answering its purpose, sufficient to produce an effect; valid. —**effectually** *adv.* [f. L (as EFFECT)]

effectuate /ɪˈfektʃʊeɪt, -tjʊeɪt/ *v.t.* to cause to happen. [as prec.]

effeminate /ɪˈfemɪnət/ *adj.* (of a man) womanish in appearance or manner. —**effeminacy** *n.* [f. L *effeminatus* (EX-¹, *femina* woman)]

effervesce /efəˈves/ *v.i.* **1** to give off bubbles of gas. **2** to show great liveliness. —**effervescence** *n.*, **effervescent** *adj.* [f. L *effervescere* (EX-¹, *fervescere* begin to be hot)]

effete /ɪˈfiːt/ *adj.* worn out, lacking vitality; feeble. —**effeteness** *n.* [f. L *effetus* worn out by bearing young (as FOETUS)]

efficacious /efɪˈkeɪʃəs/ *adj.* producing or able to produce the desired effect. —**efficacy** /ˈefɪkəsɪ/ *n.* [f. L *efficax* (as foll.)]

efficient /ɪˈfɪʃ(ə)nt/ *adj.* **1** productive with the minimum waste of effort. **2** (of a person) capable, acting effectively. **3** producing an effect. —**efficiency** *n.* **efficiently** *adv.* [f. L *efficere* accomplish (EX-¹, *facere* make, do)]

effigy /ˈefɪdʒɪ/ *n.* a portrait or image of a person. [f. L *effigies* (EX-¹, *fingere* fashion)]

effloresce /eflɔːˈres/ *v.i.* **1** to burst into flower. **2** (of a substance) to turn to fine powder on exposure to air; (of salts) to come to the surface and crystallize; (of a surface) to become covered with such salt particles. —**efflorescence** *n.*, **efflorescent** *adj.* [f. L *efflorescere* (EX-¹, *florescere* begin to bloom)]

effluence /ˈeflʊəns/ *n.* a flowing out of light or electricity etc.; that which flows out. [as foll.]

effluent /ˈeflʊənt/ *adj.* flowing out. —*n.* a thing that flows out, especially a stream from a larger stream, or sewage. [f. L *effluere* flow out]

effluvium /eˈfluːvɪəm/ *n.* (*pl.* **-ia**) an outflow of a substance, especially an unpleasant or harmful one. [L (as prec.)]

efflux /ˈeflʌks/ *n.* an outflow. [f. L *effluxus* (as EFFLUENT)]

effort /ˈefət/ *n.* **1** strenuous physical or mental exertion; the application of this, an attempt; the force exerted. **2** (*colloq.*) something accomplished. [F, f. OF *esforcier* f. L *fortis* strong]

effortless *adj.* done without effort, requiring no effort. —**effortlessly** *adv.* [f. prec. + -LESS]

effrontery /ɪˈfrʌntərɪ/ *n.* shameless insolence, impudence. [f. F f. L *effrons* shameless (EX-¹, *frons* forehead)]

effulgent /ɪˈfʌldʒ(ə)nt/ *adj.* radiant, bright. —**effulgence** *n.* [f. L *effulgēre* (EX-¹, *fulgēre* shine)]

effuse /ɪ'fju:z/ *v.t.* to pour forth, to send out (a liquid or light, or *fig.*). [f. L *effundere* (EX-[1], *fundere* pour)]

effusion /ɪ'fju:ʒ(ə)n/ *n.* an outpouring, especially (*derog.*) of unrestrained literary work. [f. OF or L (as prec.)]

effusive /ɪ'fju:sɪv/ *adj.* demonstrative, gushing. —**effusively** *adv.*, **effusiveness** *n.* [f. L (as EFFUSE)]

eft *n.* a newt. [OE]

EFTA /'eftə/ *abbr.* European Free Trade Association.

e.g. *abbr.* for example. [abbr. of L *exempli gratia*]

egalitarian /ɪgælɪ'teərɪən/ *adj.* of or advocating equal rights for all. —*n.* an egalitarian person. —**egalitarianism** *n.* [f. F (*égal* equal)]

egg[1] *n.* **1** a spheroidal body produced by the female of birds etc. containing the germ of a new individual, especially that of the domestic fowl for eating; a female ovum. **2** (*colloq.*) a person (qualified in some way). —**egg-cup** *n.* a small cup for holding a boiled egg. **egg-flip, egg-nog** *ns.* a drink of alcoholic spirit with beaten egg, milk, etc. **egg-plant** *n.* a plant (*Solanum melongena*) with deep purple fruit used as a vegetable; its fruit, aubergine. **with egg on one's face,** (*colloq.*) made to look foolish. —**eggy** *adj.* [f. ON]

egg[2] *v.t.* to urge *on.* [f. ON (as EDGE)]

egghead *n.* (*colloq.*) an intellectual person.

eggshell *n.* the shell of an egg. —*adj.* **1** (of china) thin and fragile. **2** (of paint) with a slight gloss.

eglantine /'egləntaɪn/ *n.* sweet-brier. [f. F f. L *acus* needle]

ego /'i:gəʊ, 'e-/ *n.* (*pl.* **-os**) **1** the self, the part of the mind that reacts to reality and has a sense of individuality. **2** self-esteem. —**ego-trip** *n.* (*colloq.*) an activity undertaken to boost one's own self-esteem or feelings. [L, = I]

egocentric /egəʊ'sentrɪk/ *adj.* self-centred. —**egocentricity** /-'trɪsɪtɪ/ *n.* [f. EGO + -CENTRIC]

egoism /'egəʊɪz(ə)m/ *n.* **1** self-interest as the moral basis of behaviour; systematic selfishness. **2** egotism. —**egoist** *n.*, **egoistic** /-'ɪstɪk/ *adj.*, **egoistically** *adv.* [f. EGO]

egotism /'egəʊtɪz(ə)m/ *n.* the practice of talking too much about oneself; self-conceit; selfishness. —**egotist** *n.*, **egotistic** /-'tɪstɪk/ *adj.*, **egotistically** *adv.* [f. EGO, with intrusive -t-]

egregious /ɪ'gri:dʒəs/ *adj.* outstandingly bad; (*archaic*) remarkable. [f. L, = illustrious, lit. 'standing out from the flock']

egress /'i:gres/ *n.* an exit; the right of going out. [f. L (*egredi* walk out)]

egret /'i:grɪt/ *n.* a kind of heron (*Egretta alba*) with long white feathers. [f. F *aigrette*]

Egyptian /ɪ'dʒɪpʃ(ə)n/ *adj.* of Egypt or its people or language. —*n.* **1** a native or inhabitant of Egypt. **2** the language of the ancient Egyptians. [f. *Egypt* country in NE Africa]

Egyptology /i:dʒɪp'tɒlədʒɪ/ *n.* the study of Egyptian antiquities. —**Egyptologist** *n.* [as prec. + -LOGY]

eh /eɪ/ *int.* (*colloq.*) expressing inquiry or surprise, or inviting assent, or asking for repetition or explanation. [instinctive excl.]

eider /'aɪdə(r)/ *n.* a large northern duck, especially of the genus *Somateria*. [f. Icel.]

eiderdown *n.* a quilt stuffed with feathers, down, or other soft material. [f. prec.]

eight /eɪt/ *adj.* & *n.* **1** one more than seven; the symbol for this (8, viii, VIII). **2** a size etc. denoted by eight. **3** an eight-oared rowing-boat or its crew. —**have one over the eight,** (*slang*) to get slightly drunk. [OE]

eighteen /eɪ'ti:n/ *adj.* & *n.* **1** one more than seventeen; the symbol for this (18, xviii, XVIII). **2** a size etc. denoted by eighteen. —**eighteenth** *adj.* & *n.* [f. EIGHT + -TEEN]

eightfold *adj.* & *adv.* **1** eight times as much or as many. **2** consisting of eight parts. [f. EIGHT + -FOLD]

eighth /eɪtθ/ *adj.* next after the seventh. —*n.* one of eight equal parts of a thing. —**eighthly** *adv.* [OE (cf. EIGHT)]

eightsome *adj.* for eight people. —**eightsome reel,** a lively Scottish dance for eight people. [f. EIGHT + -SOME]

eighty /'eɪtɪ/ *adj.* & *n.* **1** eight times ten; the symbol for this (80, lxxx, LXXX). **2** (in *pl.*) the numbers, years, or degrees of temperature from 80 to 89. —**eightieth** *adj.* & *n.* [OE (cf. EIGHT)]

einsteinium /aɪn'staɪnɪəm/ *n.* an artificially made transuranic radioactive metallic element, symbol Es, atomic number 99. [f. A. *Einstein* scientist (d. 1955)]

eisteddfod /aɪs'teðvɒd/ *n.* an annual meeting of Welsh poets and musicians for competitions. [Welsh, = session]

either /'aɪðə(r), 'i:ðə(r)/ *adj.* & *pron.* one or the other of two; each of two. —*adv.* or *conj.* **1** as one possibility; as one choice or alternative, which way you will. **2** (with neg. or interrog.) any more than the other, moreover. [OE]

ejaculate /ɪ'dʒækjʊleɪt/ *v.t./i.* **1** to utter suddenly, to exclaim. **2** to emit (esp. semen) from the body. —**ejaculation** /-'leɪʃ(ə)n/ *n.*, **ejaculatory** *adj.* [f. L *ejaculari* shoot out (*jaculum* javelin)]

eject /ɪ'dʒekt/ *v.t.* **1** to expel, to compel to leave; to dispossess (a tenant). **2** to send out, to emit. —**ejection** *n.*, **ejectment** *n.* [f. L (EX-[1], *jacere* throw)]

ejector *n.* a device for ejecting something.

—**ejector seat,** a device for the ejection of the pilot of an aircraft etc. in an emergency. [f. prec.]

eke /iːk/ *v.t.* (with *out*) to make (a living) or support (an existence) with difficulty; to supplement (an income etc.). [OE; cogn. w. L *augēre* increase]

elaborate[1] /ɪˈlæbərət/ *adj.* minutely worked out; highly developed or complicated. —**elaborately** *adv.* [f. L *elaborare* (EX-[1], *laborare* work)]

elaborate[2] /ɪˈlæbəreɪt/ *v.t./i.* to work out or explain in detail. —**elaboration** /-ˈreɪʃ(ə)n/ *n.* [as prec.]

élan /eɪˈlɑ̃/ *n.* vivacity, dash. [F (*élancer* launch)]

eland /ˈiːlənd/ an African antelope of the genus *Taurotragus*, the largest of living antelopes, with spirally twisted horns. [Du., = elk]

elapse /ɪˈlæps/ *v.i.* (of time) to pass away. [f. L *elabi* (EX-[1], *labi* glide)]

elasmobranch /ɪˈlæzməbræŋk/ *n.* a fish of the class Chondrichthyes (shark, skate, etc.). [f. Gk *elasmos* beaten metal + *bragkhia* gills]

elastic /ɪˈlæstɪk/ *adj.* **1** able to resume its normal length, bulk, or shape after being stretched or crushed; springy. **2** (of the feelings or a person) buoyant; flexible, adaptable. —*n.* elastic cord or fabric, usually woven with strips of rubber. —**elastically** *adv.*, **elasticity** /-ˈstɪsɪtɪ/ *n.* [f. Gk, = propulsive (*elaunō* drive)]

elasticated /ɪˈlæstɪkeɪtɪd/ *adj.* (of fabric) made elastic by weaving with rubber thread. [f. prec.]

elastomer /ɪˈlæstəmə(r)/ *n.* a natural or synthetic rubber or rubber-like plastic. —**elastomeric** /-ˈmerɪk/ *adj.* [f. ELASTIC, after *isomer*]

elate /ɪˈleɪt/ *v.t.* to inspirit, to stimulate; (esp. in *p.p.*) to make pleased or proud. —**elation** *n.* [f. L *efferre elat-* raise]

elbow /ˈelbəʊ/ *n.* **1** the joint between the forearm and upper arm; the corresponding part in an animal. **2** the part of the sleeve of a garment covering this. **3** an elbow-shaped bend etc. —*v.t.* to thrust or jostle (*oneself* or *one's way in*, *out*, etc.). —**elbow-grease** *n.* (*colloq.*) vigorous polishing; hard work. **elbow-room** *n.* plenty of room to move or work in. **out at (the) elbows,** worn, ragged, poor. [OE (as ELL, BOW[1])]

elder[1] *adj.* (of persons, especially related ones) senior, of greater age. —*n.* **1** (in *pl.*) persons of greater age or venerable because of age. **2** an official in the early Christian Church and some modern Churches. —**elder statesman,** an influential experienced person (especially a politician) of advanced age. [OE (compar. of OLD)]

elder[2] *n.* a tree (*Sambucus nigra*) with white flowers and dark berries. [OE]

elderberry *n.* the berry of the elder tree.

elderly *adj.* somewhat old, past middle age. [f. ELDER[1]]

eldest *adj.* first-born, oldest surviving. [OE (superl. of OLD)]

eldorado /eldəˈrɑːdəʊ/ *n.* (*pl.* **-os**) a place of great abundance. [f. Spanish *el dorado* the gilded]

eldritch /ˈeldrɪtʃ/ *adj.* (*Sc.*) weird; hideous. [perh. rel. to ELF]

elecampane /elɪkæmˈpeɪn/ *n.* a plant (*Inula helenium*) with bitter aromatic leaves and root. [corruption of medieval name *Enula campana*]

elect /ɪˈlekt/ *v.t.* to choose by voting; to choose (a thing, *to* do); (*Theol.* of God) to choose (a person) for salvation. —*adj.* chosen; select, choice; (after a noun) chosen but not yet in office. [f. L *eligere* pick out]

election /ɪˈlekʃ(ə)n/ *n.* **1** electing, being elected; the process of electing, especially Members of Parliament. **2** (*Theol.*) God's choice of some persons in preference to others. [as prec.]

electioneer /ɪlekʃəˈnɪə(r)/ *v.i.* to take part in an election campaign. [f. prec.]

elective /ɪˈlektɪv/ *adj.* **1** chosen or appointed by election. **2** (of a body) having power to elect. **3** optional, not urgently necessary. [f. F f. L (as ELECT)]

elector /ɪˈlektə(r)/ *n.* **1** one who has the right to elect or take part in an election. **2** Elector, (*hist.*) any of the German princes entitled to elect the Emperor.

electoral /ɪˈlektər(ə)l/ *adj.* of or ranking as electors. —**electoral college,** a body of persons who cast votes for the election of a leader; (in the USA) the body of electors, chosen by popular vote in each State, who elect the US President and vice-president. [f. prec.]

electorate /ɪˈlektərət/ *n.* **1** the body of electors. **2** the office or dominions of a German Elector. [f. ELECTOR]

electric /ɪˈlektrɪk/ *adj.* **1** of, worked by, or charged with electricity; producing or capable of generating electricity. **2** causing sudden and dramatic excitement. —*n.* an electric light, vehicle, etc.; (in *pl.*) electrical equipment. —**electric blanket,** a blanket heated by an internal electric element. **electric chair,** a chair used to electrocute as a form of execution. **electric eel,** an eel-like fish (*Electrophorus electricus*) capable of giving an electric shock. **electric eye,** a photoelectric cell operating a relay when a beam of light is broken. **electric field,** see FIELD. **electric fire,** an appliance giving heat from an electrically charged wire coil or bar. **electric light,** a light produced by electricity in any of various devices (e.g. an incandescent lamp, fluorescent lamp, arc lamp). **electric shock,** the effect of a sudden discharge of electricity through the body of a person etc. [f. L f. Gk *ēlektron* amber, from the static electricity found in it]

electrical /ɪ'lektrɪk(ə)l/ *adj.* **1** of or concerned with electricity. **2** suddenly exciting. —**electrically** *adv.* [f. prec.]

electrician /ɪlek'trɪʃ(ə)n/ *n.* a person whose profession is installing and maintaining electrical equipment. [f. ELECTRIC]

electricity /ɪlek'trɪsɪtɪ/ *n.* **1** a form of energy occurring in elementary particles (electrons, protons) and hence in larger bodies containing them; the branch of science concerned with this. **2** a supply of electricity. [as prec.]

electrify /ɪ'lektrɪfaɪ/ *v.t.* **1** to charge with electricity. **2** to convert (a railway, factory, etc.) to the use of electric power. **3** to excite or startle suddenly. —**electrification** /-fɪ'keɪʃ(ə)n/ *n.* [f. ELECTRIC]

electro- /ɪlektrəʊ-/ *in comb.* of, by, or caused by electricity. [as ELECTRIC]

electrocardiogram /ɪlektrəʊ'kɑ:dɪəgræm/ *n.* the record obtained by an electrocardiograph. [f. ELECTRO- + CARDIO- + -GRAM]

electrocardiograph /ɪlektrəʊ'kɑ:dɪəgrɑ:f/ *n.* an instrument that receives electrical impulses as they vary during the cardiac cycle and transforms them into a graphic record. [as prec. + -GRAPH]

electroconvulsive therapy /ɪlektrəʊkən'vʌlsiv/ therapy using the convulsive response to electric shocks.

electrocute /ɪ'lektrəkju:t/ *v.t.* to kill or execute by electric shock. —**electrocution** /-'kju:ʃ(ə)n/ *n.* [f. ELECTRO-, after *execute*]

electrode /ɪ'lektrəʊd/ *n.* a conductor through which electricity enters or leaves an electrolyte, gas, vacuum, etc. [f. ELECTRIC + Gk *hodos* way]

electrodynamics /ɪlektrəʊdaɪ'næmɪks/ *n.* the study of electricity in motion.

electroencephalogram /ɪlektrəʊen'sefələgræm/ *n.* a record traced by an electroencephalograph. [f. ELECTRO- + ENCEPHALO- + -GRAM]

electroencephalograph /ɪlektrəʊen'sefələgrɑ:f/ *n.* an instrument recording the electrical activity of the brain. [as prec. + -GRAPH]

electrolyse /ɪ'lektrəlaɪz/ *v.t.* to subject to or treat by electrolysis. [f. foll.]

electrolysis /ɪlek'trɒlɪsɪs/ *n.* chemical decomposition by electric action; the breaking up of tumours, hair-roots, etc., by electric action. —**electrolytic** /-ə'lɪtɪk/ *adj.* [f. ELECTRO- + -LYSIS]

electrolyte /ɪ'lektrəlaɪt/ *n.* a solution able to conduct an electric current, especially in an electric cell or battery; a substance that can dissolve to produce this. [f. ELECTRO- + -LYTE]

electromagnet /ɪlektrəʊ'mægnɪt/ *n.* a soft metal core made into a magnet by an electric current passing through a coil surrounding it.

electromagnetic /ɪlektrəʊmæg'netɪk/ *adj.* having both electrical and magnetic properties. —**electromagnetic radiation,** the kind of radiation that includes visible light, radio waves, gamma rays, etc., in which electric and magnetic fields vary simultaneously. —**electromagnetically** *adv.*

electromagnetism /ɪlektrəʊ'mægnətɪz(ə)m/ *n.* magnetic forces produced by electricity; the study of these.

electromotive /ɪlektrəʊ'məʊtɪv/ *adj.* producing or tending to produce an electric current. —**electromotive force,** a force set up by difference of potential in an electric circuit.

electron /ɪ'lektrɒn/ *n.* a stable elementary particle with an indivisible charge of negative electricity, found in all atoms and acting as a carrier of electricity in solids, with mass of approximately 9×10^{-31} kg. —**electron lens,** a device for focusing a stream of electrons by electric and magnetic fields. **electron microscope,** a type of microscope giving high magnification and resolution by employing a beam of electrons instead of light and focusing it by means of magnetic or electrostatic fields. **electron-volt** *n.* a unit of energy, the amount gained by an electron when accelerated through a potential difference of one volt. [f. ELECTRIC]

electronic /ɪlek'trɒnɪk/ *adj.* **1** produced by or involving a flow of electrons. **2** of electrons or electronics. —**electronic music,** music produced by electronic means and recorded on tape. —**electronically** *adv.* [f. prec.]

electronics *n.* **1** the branch of physics and technology dealing with the behaviour of electrons in a vacuum, gas, semiconductor, etc. **2** (as *pl.*) electronic circuits. [f. prec.]

electroplate /ɪ'lektrəʊpleɪt/ *v.t.* to coat with a thin layer of silver, chromium, etc., by electrolysis. The commercial use of this process dates from the mid-19th c. —*n.* objects so plated.

electroscope /ɪ'lektrəskəʊp/ *n.* an instrument for detecting and measuring electricity, especially to indicate the ionization of air by radioactivity. [f. ELECTRO- + -SCOPE]

electro-shock /ɪlektrəʊ'ʃɒk/ *n.* electric shock. —**electro-shock therapy,** electroconvulsive therapy.

electrostatics /ɪlektrəʊˈstætɪks/ *n.* the study of electricity at rest.

electrotechnology /ɪlektrəʊtekˈnɒlədʒɪ/ *n.* the science of the technological application of electricity.

electrotherapy /ɪlektrəʊˈθerəpɪ/ *n.* the treatment of diseases by the use of electricity. [f. ELECTRO- + THERAPY]

elegant /ˈelɪgənt/ *adj.* graceful in appearance or manner; tasteful, refined. —**elegance** *n.*, **elegantly** *adv.* [f. F or L, rel. to *eligere* (as ELECT)]

elegiac /elɪˈdʒaɪək/ *adj.* used for elegies; mournful. —*n.* (in *pl.*) elegiac verses. —**elegiac couplet** *or* **metre,** a dactylic hexameter and pentameter. [f. F or L (as foll.)]

elegy /ˈelɪdʒɪ/ *n.* a sorrowful or serious poem or song; a lament for the dead; a poem in elegiac metre. [f. F or L f. Gk (*elegos* mournful poem)]

element /ˈelɪmənt/ *n.* **1** a component part, a contributing factor. **2** a substance composed of atoms of the same atomic number. **3** any of the four substances (earth, water, air, and fire) in ancient and medieval philosophy. **4** a being's natural abode or environment. **5** a wire that gives out heat in an electric cooker, heater, etc. **6** (in *pl.*) atmospheric agencies, especially wind and storm. **7** (in *pl.*) the bread and wine of the Eucharist. —**in one's element,** in one's accustomed or preferred surroundings, doing what one is skilled at and enjoys. [f. OF f. L]

elemental /elɪˈment(ə)l/ *adj.* **1** of or like the elements or the forces of nature, powerful, tremendous. **2** basic, essential. [f. prec.]

elementary /elɪˈmentərɪ/ *adj.* **1** dealing with the simplest facts of a subject, rudimentary. **2** (*Chem.*) not analysable. —**elementarily** *adv.*, **elementariness** *n.* [f. L (as ELEMENT)]

elementary particle any of several subatomic particles which are not known to be composed of simpler particles and which are characterized by having a definite mass, a lifetime that is long compared with the interaction time, and well-defined electromagnetic properties, and are capable of an independent existence.

elephant /ˈelɪfənt/ *n.* the largest living land animal, with a trunk and ivory tusks, the Indian elephant (*Elephas maximus*) and the African (*Loxodonta africana*). [f. OF f. L f. Gk *elephas*, orig. = ivory]

elephantiasis /elɪfənˈtaɪəsɪs/ *n.* a skin disease causing gross enlargement of a limb etc. [L f. Gk (as prec.)]

elephantine /elɪˈfæntaɪn/ *adj.* **1** of elephants. **2** huge, clumsy, unwieldy. [f. L f. Gk (as ELEPHANT)]

elevate /ˈelɪveɪt/ *v.t.* to raise or lift up; to enhance morally or intellectually; (in *p.p.*) exalted in rank or status. [f. L *elevare* lift (EX-[1], *levis* light)]

elevation /elɪˈveɪʃ(ə)n/ *n.* **1** elevating, being elevated. **2** the height above a given (especially sea) level; a high position; the angle (especially of a gun or the direction of a heavenly body) with the horizontal. **3** a flat drawing showing one side of a building. [f. OF or L (as prec.)]

elevator *n.* **1** a person or thing that elevates; a hoisting-machine. **2** the movable part of a tailplane, used for changing an aircraft's attitude to its flight-path. **3** (*US*) a lift (see LIFT *n.* 3). [f. ELEVATE]

eleven /ɪˈlev(ə)n/ *adj.* & *n.* **1** one more than ten; the symbol for this (11, xi, XI). **2** a size etc. denoted by eleven. **3** a team of eleven players at cricket, football, etc. —**eleven-plus** *n.* an examination taken in some districts of England and Wales at the age 11-12 before entering secondary school. [OE, perh. = one left over (ten)]

elevenfold *adj.* & *adv.* eleven times as much or as many; consisting of eleven parts. [f. prec. + -FOLD]

elevenses /ɪˈlevənzɪz/ *n.* light refreshment taken at about 11 a.m. [f. ELEVEN]

eleventh *adj.* next after the tenth. —*n.* one of eleven equal parts. —**eleventh hour,** the last possible moment. [OE (as ELEVEN)]

elf *n.* (*pl.* **elves** /elvz/) a supernatural being in Germanic mythology; a dwarf, a little creature. —**elfish** *adj.* [OE]

elfin /ˈelfɪn/ *adj.* of elves, elflike. [f. ELF]

elicit /ɪˈlɪsɪt/ *v.t.* to draw out (a latent thing, especially a response etc.). [f. L *elicere* (EX-[1], *lacere* entice)]

elide /ɪˈlaɪd/ *v.t.* to omit (a vowel or syllable) in pronunciation. [f. L *elidere* crush out]

eligible /ˈelɪdʒɪb(ə)l/ *adj.* fit or entitled to be chosen (*for* an office, award, etc.); desirable or suitable, especially for marriage. —**eligibility** /-ˈbɪlɪtɪ/ *n.* [f. F f. L (as ELECT)]

eliminate /ɪˈlɪmɪneɪt/ *v.t.* to remove, to get rid of; to exclude from consideration; to exclude from a further stage of competition through defeat etc. —**elimination** /-ˈneɪʃ(ə)n/ *n.*, **eliminator** *n.* [f. L *eliminare* (EX-[1], *limen* threshold)]

elision /ɪˈlɪʒ(ə)n/ *n.* omission of a vowel or syllable in pronouncing (as in *I'm*, *let's*; *e'en*) or of a passage in a book etc. [f. L (as ELIDE)]

élite /eɪˈliːt/ *n.* **1** a select group or class; *the* best (of a group). **2** a size of letters in typewriting (12 per inch). [f. F (as ELECT)]

élitism /eɪˈliːtɪz(ə)m/ *n.* recourse to or advocacy of leadership or dominance by a select group. —**élitist** *n.* [f. prec.]

elixir /ɪˈlɪksə(r)/ *n.* **1** an alchemist's preparation designed to change metal into gold or (*elixir of life*) to prolong life indefinitely; a remedy for all ills. **2** an aromatic medicinal drug. [f. L f. Arab., prob. f. Gk *xērion* powder for wounds]

Elizabethan /ɪlɪzəˈbi:θ(ə)n/ *adj.* belonging to or characteristic of the reign of Queen Elizabeth I (1533-1603). —*n.* a person of this period. [f. *Elizabeth*]

elk *n.* **1** a large deer (*Alces alces*) of northern Europe and Asia, the moose. **2** (*US*) the wapiti. [prob. OE]

ell *n.* (*hist.*) a measure of length, = 45 inches. [OE, = forearm (cogn. with L *ulna*)]

ellipse /ɪˈlɪps/ *n.* a regular oval, the figure produced when a cone is cut by a plane making a smaller angle with the base than the side of the cone makes. [f. F f. L f. Gk *elleipsis* deficit]

ellipsis /ɪˈlɪpsɪs/ *n.* (*pl.* **ellipses** /-si:z/) the omission of words needed to complete a construction or sense; a set of three dots etc. indicating such an omission. [as prec.]

ellipsoid /ɪˈlɪpsɔɪd/ *n.* a solid of which all plane sections through one axis are ellipses and all other plane sections are ellipses or circles. [f. ELLIPSE]

elliptical /ɪˈlɪptɪk(ə)l/ *adj.* **1** of or in the form of an ellipse. **2** of or containing an ellipsis. —**elliptically** *adv.* [f. Gk (as ELLIPSE)]

elm *n.* a tree of the genus *Ulmus*, especially *U. procera* with rough serrated leaves; its wood. [OE]

elocution /eləˈkju:ʃ(ə)n/ *n.* the art or style of expressive speaking. —**elocutionary** *adj.*, **elocutionist** *n.* [f. L (as ELOQUENT)]

elongate /ˈi:lɒŋgeɪt/ *v.t.* to lengthen, to extend, to draw out. —**elongation** /-ˈgeɪʃ(ə)n/ *n.* [f. L *elongare* (EX-[1], *longus* long)]

elope /ɪˈləʊp/ *v.i.* to run away secretly with a lover, especially in order to get married. —**elopement** *n.* [f. AF, perh. rel. to LEAP]

eloquence /ˈeləkwəns/ *n.* fluent and effective use of language. [f. OF f. L (as foll.)]

eloquent *adj.* having eloquence; expressive (*of*). —**eloquently** *adv.* [f. OF f. L *eloqui* (EX-[1], *loqui* speak)]

else *adv.* (with indefinite or interrog. pronoun) besides; instead; otherwise, if not. —**or else**, (*colloq.*) expressing threat or warning. [OE, rel. to L *alius* other]

elsewhere *adv.* in or to some other place.

elucidate /ɪˈlu:sɪdeɪt/ *v.t.* to throw light on, to explain. —**elucidation** /-ˈdeɪʃ(ə)n/ *n.*, **elucidatory** *adj.* [f. L *elucidare* (EX-[1], *lucidus* bright)]

elude /ɪˈlju:d/ *v.t.* to escape adroitly from (danger etc.); to avoid compliance with or fulfilment of (a law, obligation, etc.); to baffle (a person or the memory etc.). —**elusion** *n.*, **elusive** *adj.* [f. L *eludere* (EX-[1], *ludere* play)]

elver *n.* a young eel. [var. of *eelfare* (EEL, FARE)]

elves *pl.* of ELF.

elvish *adj.* = ELFISH.

Elysium /ɪˈlɪzɪəm/ **1** (*Gk myth.*) the abode of the blessed after death. **2** a place of ideal happiness. —**Elysian** *adj.* [f. L f. Gk *Elusion* (*pedion* plain)]

em *n.* (*Printing*) a unit of measurement equal to the space occupied by m. [name of letter *M*]

'em /əm/ *pron.* (*colloq.*) them.

em- see EN-.

emaciate /ɪˈmeɪsɪeɪt, -ʃ-/ *v.t.* to make thin or feeble. —**emaciation** /-ˈeɪʃ(ə)n/ *n.* [f. L *emaciare* (EX-[1], *macies* leanness)]

emanate /ˈeməneɪt/ *v.t./i.* to originate or proceed (*from* a source, person, etc.); to cause to do this. —**emanation** /-ˈneɪʃ(ə)n/ *n.* [f. L *emanare* (EX-[1], *manare* flow)]

emancipate /ɪˈmænsɪpeɪt/ *v.t.* to free from slavery or from (esp. political or social) restraint. —**emancipation** /-ˈpeɪʃ(ə)n/ *n.*, **emancipator** *n.*, **emancipatory** *adj.* [f. L *emancipare* (EX-[1], *mancipare* transfer ownership of)]

emasculate /ɪˈmæskjʊleɪt/ *v.t.* **1** to castrate. **2** to deprive of strength or force. —/-ət/ *adj.* **1** castrated; effeminate. **2** deprived of strength or force. —**emasculation** /-ˈleɪʃ(ə)n/ *n.*, **emasculatory** *adj.* [f. L *emasculare* (EX-[1], *masculus* dim. of *mas* male)]

embalm /ɪmˈbɑ:m/ *v.t.* **1** to preserve (a corpse) from decay. **2** to preserve from decay or oblivion. **3** to make fragrant. —**embalmment** *n.* [f. OF (as EM-, BALM)]

embankment /ɪmˈbæŋkmənt/ *n.* an earth or stone bank keeping back water or carrying a road, railway, etc. [f. EM- + BANK]

embargo /emˈbɑ:gəʊ/ *n.* (*pl.* **-oes**) an order forbidding foreign ships to enter, or any ships to leave, the country's ports; a prohibition or restraint, especially of commerce. —*v.t.* to place under an embargo. [Sp., f. *embargar* arrest (as IN-[1], BAR[1])]

embark /ɪmˈbɑ:k/ *v.t./i.* **1** to put or go on board ship (*for* a destination). **2** to engage *in* or *on* an enterprise. [f. F (as EM-, BARQUE)]

embarkation /embɑ:ˈkeɪʃ(ə)n/ *n.* embarking on a ship. [f. prec.]

embarrass /ɪmˈbærəs/ *v.t.* **1** to make (a person) feel awkward or ashamed. **2** to encumber; to perplex; to complicate (a question etc.). —**embarrassment** *n.* [f. F f. Sp. f. It. (*imbarrare* bar in)]

embassy /ˈembəsɪ/ *n.* the offices or residence of an ambassador; an ambassador and his staff; a deputation to a foreign government. [f. OF (as AMBASSADOR)]

embattled /ɪmˈbæt(ə)ld/ *adj.* **1** prepared or

arrayed for battle. **2** fortified with battlements. [f. EM- + BATTLE]

embed /ɪmˈbed/ *v.t.* **(-dd-)** to fix firmly in a surrounding mass.

embellish /ɪmˈbelɪʃ) *v.t.* to beautify, to adorn; to enhance (a narrative) with fictitious additions. —**embellishment** *n.* [f. OF *embellir* (*bel* handsome f. L)]

ember *n.* (usu. in *pl.*) a small piece of live coal etc. in a dying fire. [OE]

ember days a group of three days in each season, observed as days of fasting and prayer in some Churches. [OE, perh. f. *ymbryne* period]

embezzle /ɪmˈbez(ə)l/ *v.t.* to divert (money etc.) fraudulently to one's own use. —**embezzlement** *n.*, **embezzler** *n.* [f. AF (*besiler* = OF *besillier* maltreat, ravage)]

embitter /ɪmˈbɪtə(r)/ *v.t.* to arouse bitter feelings in; to make bitter. —**embitterment** *n.*

emblazon /ɪmˈbleɪz(ə)n/ *v.t.* to blazon. —**emblazonment** *n.*

emblem /ˈembləm/ *n.* a symbol; a heraldic or representative device. —**emblematic** /-ˈmætɪk/ *adj.* [f. L *emblēma* inlaid work f. Gk (*emballō* insert)]

embody /ɪmˈbɒdɪ/ *v.t.* **1** to make (an idea etc.) actual or discernible; (of a thing) to be an expression of. **2** to include, to comprise. —**embodiment** *n.*

embolden /ɪmˈbəʊld(ə)n/ *v.t.* to make bold, to encourage. [f. EM- + BOLD]

embolism /ˈembəlɪz(ə)m/ *n.* an obstruction of an artery etc. by a clot of blood, an air-bubble, etc. [f. L f. Gk (*emballō* insert)]

embolus /ˈembələs/ *n.* (*pl.* **-li** /-laɪ/) a thing causing an embolism. [as prec.]

emboss /ɪmˈbɒs/ *v.t.* to carve or decorate with a design in relief. —**embossment** *n.* [f. OF (as EM-, BOSS[2])]

embrace /ɪmˈbreɪs/ *v.t.* **1** to hold closely in the arms, especially as a sign of affection; (*absol.* of two people) to embrace each other; to clasp, to enclose. **2** to accept, to adopt (an idea, belief, etc.). **3** to take in with the eye or mind. —*n.* holding in the arms, a clasp. [f. OF f. L *bracchium* arm]

embrasure /ɪmˈbreɪʒə(r)/ *n.* **1** the bevelling of a wall at the sides of a window etc. **2** an opening between the merlons of an embattled parapet. [f. F (*embraser* splay)]

embrocation /embrəˈkeɪʃ(ə)n/ *n.* a liquid for rubbing on the body to relieve muscular pain. [f. F or L f. Gk *embrokhē* lotion]

embroider /ɪmˈbrɔɪdə(r)/ *v.t.* **1** to decorate (cloth etc.) with needlework. **2** to embellish (a narrative). [f. AF *enbrouder* f. Gmc]

embroidery *n.* **1** embroidering; embroidered work. **2** elaboration, as of a narrative by inessential detail. [f. prec.]

embroil /ɪmˈbrɔɪl/ *v.t.* **1** to bring (affairs etc.) into confusion. **2** to involve (a person) in hostility (*with* another). —**embroilment** *n.* [f. F *embrouiller* entangle, mix]

embryo /ˈembrɪəʊ/ *n.* (*pl.* **-os**) an unborn or unhatched offspring; a human offspring in the first eight weeks from conception; a rudimentary plant in a seed; a thing in a rudimentary stage. —*adj.* undeveloped, immature. —**in embryo** undeveloped. —**embryonic** /-ˈɒnɪk/ *adj.* [L f. Gk *embruon* (EM-, *bruō* swell, grow)]

embryology /embrɪˈɒlədʒɪ/ *n.* the science of the embryo. [f. prec. + -LOGY]

emend /ɪˈmend/ *v.t.* to correct or remove errors from (a text etc.), to seek to do this. —**emendation** /i:menˈdeɪʃ(ə)n/ *n.* [f. L *emendare* (EX-[1], *menda* fault)]

emerald /ˈemər(ə)ld/ *n.* a bright-green precious stone; the colour of this. —**Emerald Isle,** Ireland. [f. OF f. L *smaragdus* f. Gk]

emerge /ɪˈmɜ:dʒ/ *v.i.* to come up or out into view; to become known or recognized, (of facts) to be revealed; (of a difficulty) to occur. —**emergence** *n.*, **emergent** *adj.* [f. L *emergere* (EX-[1], *mergere* plunge)]

emergency /ɪˈmɜ:dʒ(ə)nsɪ/ *n.* a sudden state of danger, conflict, etc., requiring immediate action; a condition needing immediate treatment, a patient with this. —*adj.* for use in an emergency. [f. L (as prec.)]

emeritus /ɪˈmerɪtəs/ *adj.* retired and retaining a title as an honour. [L, = that has earned his discharge by service]

emery /ˈemərɪ/ *n.* a coarse corundum for polishing metal etc. —**emery-board** *n.* emery-coated nail-file. [f. F f. It. f. Gk *smēris* polishing powder]

emetic /ɪˈmetɪk/ *adj.* that causes vomiting. —*n.* an emetic medicine. [f. Gk (*emeō* vomit)]

EMF *abbr.* electromotive force.

emigrant /ˈemɪgrənt/ *n.* one who emigrates. —*adj.* emigrating. [as foll.]

emigrate /ˈemɪgreɪt/ *v.i.* to leave one's own country to settle in another. —**emigration** /-ˈgreɪʃ(ə)n/ *n.* [f. L *emigrare* (EX-[1], MIGRATE)]

émigré /ˈemɪgreɪ/ *n.* an emigrant, especially a political exile. [F (as prec.)]

eminence /ˈemɪnəns/ *n.* **1** distinction, recognized superiority. **2** a piece of rising ground. —**His, Your,** etc., **Eminence,** a title used in addressing or referring to a cardinal. [f. L (as EMINENT)]

éminence grise /eɪmɪnɑ̃s ˈgri:z/ one who exercises power or influence without holding office. [F, = grey cardinal (orig. applied to Cardinal Richelieu's secretary)]

eminent /ˈemɪnənt/ *adj.* distinguished, notable, outstanding. —**eminently** *adv.* [f. L, orig. = jutting out]

emir /eˈmɪə(r)/ *n.* the title of various Muslim rulers. [f. F (as AMIR)]

emirate /ˈemɪərət/ *n.* the rank, domain, or reign of an emir. [f. prec.]

emissary /ˈemɪsərɪ/ *n.* a person sent on a special diplomatic mission. [f. L, = scout, spy (as foll.)]

emit /ɪˈmɪt/ *v.t.* (**-tt-**) to send out (light, heat, etc.); to utter (a cry etc.). —**emission** *n.*, **emissive** *adj.* [f. L *emittere* (EX-[1], *mittere* send)]

emollient /ɪˈmɒlɪənt/ *adj.* softening or soothing the skin. —*n.* an emollient substance. [f. L *emollire* (EX-[1], *mollis* soft)]

emolument /ɪˈmɒljʊmənt/ *n.* a profit from employment, a salary. [f. OF or L, prob. orig. = payment for corn-grinding (*molere* grind)]

emote /ɪˈməʊt/ *v.i.* to act with a show of emotion. [back-formation f. foll.]

emotion /ɪˈməʊʃ(ə)n/ *n.* a strong mental or instinctive feeling such as love or fear. [f. F (*émouvoir* excite, as MOVE)]

emotional *adj.* of or expressing emotion(s); liable to excessive emotion. —**emotionalism** *n.*, **emotionally** *adv.* [f. prec.]

emotive /ɪˈməʊtɪv/ *adj.* of or tending to excite emotion; arousing feeling. [f. L *emovere* disturb (EX-[1], *movere* move)]

empanel /ɪmˈpæn(ə)l/ *v.t.* (**-ll-**) to enter (a jury) on a panel. [f. AF (as EM-, PANEL)]

empathize /ˈempəθaɪz/ *v.t./i.* to treat with empathy; to use empathy. [f. foll.]

empathy /ˈempəθɪ/ *n.* the power of identifying oneself mentally with (and so fully comprehending) a person or object of contemplation. —**empathic** /-ˈpæθɪk/ *adj.* [transl. G *einfühlung* (*ein* in, *fühlung* feeling), after Gk *empatheia* (EM-, *pathēs* f. *pathos* feeling)]

emperor /ˈempərə(r)/ *n.* the sovereign of an empire. —**emperor penguin,** the largest known species of penguin, *Aptenodytes forsteri*. [f. OF f. L *imperator* (*imperare* command)]

emphasis /ˈemfəsɪs/ *n.* (*pl.* **emphases** /-si:z/) **1** special importance or prominence attached to a thing. **2** the stress on a syllable or word(s) or on note(s) in music. **3** vigour or intensity of expression, feeling, etc. [L f. Gk *emphainō* exhibit]

emphasize /ˈemfəsaɪz/ *v.t.* to put emphasis on, to stress. [f. prec.]

emphatic /ɪmˈfætɪk/ *adj.* full of emphasis, forcibly expressive; (of words) bearing stress, used to give emphasis. —**emphatically** *adv.* [f. L f. Gk (as EMPHASIS)]

emphysema /emfɪˈsi:mə/ *n.* a swelling due to air in body tissues. [L f. Gk (*emphusaō* puff up)]

empire /ˈempaɪə(r)/ *n.* **1** an extensive group of countries or States under the supreme rule of one State or person. **2** a large commercial organization etc. owned or directed by one person or group. **3** supreme dominion (*over*). —**empire-building** *n.* deliberate accumulation of territory, authority, etc. [f. OF f. L *imperium* (as EMPIRE)]

empirical /emˈpɪrɪk(ə)l/ *adj.* relying on observation and experiment, not on theory. —**empirically** *adv.* [f. Gk (*empeiria* experience)]

empiricism /ɪmˈpɪrɪsɪz(ə)m/ *n.* **1** the use of empirical methods. **2** the theory that regards sense-experience(s) as the only source of knowledge. —**empiricist** *n.* [f. L f. Gk *empeirikos* (as prec.)]

emplacement /ɪmˈpleɪsmənt/ *n.* **1** putting in position. **2** a platform for guns. [f. F (as EM-, PLACE)]

employ /ɪmˈplɔɪ/ *v.t.* to use the services of (a person) in return for payment; to use (a thing, time, energy, etc.) to some effect; to keep occupied. —*n.* **in the employ of,** employed by. —**employer** *n.* [f. OF f. L *implicari* be involved]

employable *adj.* able to be employed. [f. prec.]

employee /emplɔɪˈi:, -ˈplɔɪi/ *n.* a person employed for wages. [f. EMPLOY]

employment *n.* employing, being employed; one's regular trade or profession. —**employment exchange,** a State office concerned with finding employment for those seeking it. [as prec.]

emporium /emˈpɔ:rɪəm/ *n.* (*pl.* **-ia, -iums**) a centre of commerce, a market; a large shop, a store. [L f. Gk (*emporos* merchant)]

empower /ɪmˈpaʊə(r)/ *v.t.* to give power or authority to.

empress /ˈemprɪs/ *n.* the wife or widow of an emperor; a woman emperor. [f. OF (as EMPEROR)]

empty *adj.* **1** containing nothing; (of a house etc.) unoccupied or unfurnished. **2** (*colloq.*) hungry. **3** foolish, meaningless, vacuous. —*v.t./i.* to remove the contents of; to transfer (the contents of one thing *into* another); to become empty; (of a river) to discharge itself. —*n.* an empty bottle, box, etc. —**empty-handed** *adj.* having or bringing nothing. **empty-headed** *adj.* foolish, lacking sense. —**emptily** *adv.*, **emptiness** *n.* [OE (*æmetta* leisure)]

empyrean /empaɪˈri:ən/ *n.* the highest heaven, as the sphere of fire in ancient cosmology or the abode of God. —*adj.* of this. —**empyreal** *adj.* [f. L f. Gk (*pur* fire)]

EMS *abbr.* European Monetary System.

emu /ˈi:mju:/ *n.* a large flightless Australian bird, *Dromaius novaehollandiae*, capable of running at speeds of up to 50 k.p.h. (30 m.p.h.). [f. Port. *ema* crane]

emulate /ˈemjʊleɪt/ *v.t.* to try to equal or excel; to imitate. —**emulation** /-ˈleɪʃ(ə)n/ *n.*, **emulative** *adj.*, **emulator** *n.* [f. L *aemulari* (as foll.)]

emulous /ˈemjʊləs/ *adj.* eagerly or jealously imitative (*of*); actuated by rivalry. [f. L *aemulus* rival]

emulsify /ɪˈmʌlsɪfaɪ/ *v.t.* to convert into an emulsion. [as foll.]

emulsion /ɪˈmʌlʃ(ə)n/ *n.* **1** a fine dispersion of one liquid in another, especially as paint, medicine, etc. **2** a mixture of a silver compound in gelatin etc. as a coating for a photographic plate or film. —**emulsive** *adj.* [f. F f. L *emulgēre* (EX-[1], *mulgēre* milk)]

en *n.* (*Printing*) a unit of measurement equal to half an em. [name of letter *N*]

en- *prefix* (**em-** before *b, m, p*) **1** = IN-[1], forming verbs (1) from nouns, in the sense 'put into or on' (*embed*), (2) from nouns or adjectives, in the sense 'bring into the condition of' (*enslave*), often with suffix -EN (*enlighten*), (3) from verbs, in the sense 'in, into, on' (*enfold*) or intensively (*entangle*). [f. F f. L *in*-]. **2** in, inside (*energy, enthusiasm*). [f. Gk *en*-]

enable /ɪˈneɪb(ə)l/ *v.t.* to give the means or authority (*to do*); to make possible.

enact /ɪˈnækt/ *v.t.* **1** to ordain, to decree. **2** to play (a part on the stage or in life). —**enactive** *adj.*

enactment *n.* a law enacted. [f. prec.]

enamel /ɪˈnæm(ə)l/ *n.* **1** a glasslike (usually opaque) ornamental or preservative coating on metal. **2** a hard smooth coating; a cosmetic simulating this; the hard coating of teeth. **3** a painting done in enamel. —*v.t.* (**-ll-**) to coat, inlay, or portray with enamel. [f. AF f. Gmc]

enamour /ɪˈnæmə(r)/ *v.t.* (usu. in *p.p.*) to inspire with love or liking (*of*). [f. OF *enamourer* (*amour* love)]

en bloc /ɒn ˈblɒk/ in a block, all at the same time. [F]

encamp /ɪnˈkæmp/ *v.t./i.* to settle in a military or other camp. —**encampment** *n.*

encapsulate /ɪnˈkæpsjʊleɪt/ *v.t.* **1** to enclose (as) in a capsule. **2** to summarize; to isolate. —**encapsulation** /-ˈleɪʃ(ə)n/ *n.* [f. EN- + L *capsula* capsule]

encase /ɪnˈkeɪs/ *v.t.* to confine (as) in a case. —**encasement** *n.*

encash /enˈkæʃ/ *v.t.* to convert into cash. —**encashment** *n.*

encaustic /enˈkɔ:stɪk/ *adj.* (of painting) using pigments mixed with hot wax, which are burned in as an inlay. —*n.* the art or product of this. [f. L f. Gk (as EN-, CAUSTIC)]

enceinte /ɑ̃ˈsæ̃t/ *adj.* pregnant. [F, = ungirdled]

encephalitis /ensefəˈlaɪtɪs/ *n.* inflammation of the brain. [f. Gk *egkephalos* brain]

encephalogram /enˈsefələgræm/ *n.* an electroencephalogram. [as prec. + -GRAM]

encephalograph /enˈsefələgrɑ:f/ *n.* an electroencephalograph. [as ENCEPHALITIS + -GRAPH]

enchain /ɪnˈtʃeɪn/ *v.t.* **1** to chain up. **2** to hold (the attention or emotions) fast. [f. F (as EN-, CHAIN)]

enchant /ɪnˈtʃɑ:nt/ *v.t.* to charm, to delight; to bewitch. —**enchanter, enchantment** *ns.*, **enchantress** *n.fem.* [f. F f. L *incantare*, frequent. of *canere* sing]

encircle /ɪnˈsɜ:k(ə)l/ *v.t.* to surround; to form a circle round. —**encirclement** *n.* [f. EN- + CIRCLE]

enclave /ˈenkleɪv/ *n.* the territory of one State surrounded by that of another. [F (*enclaver* shut in, f. L *clavis* key)]

enclitic /enˈklɪtɪk/ *adj.* (of a word) pronounced with so little emphasis that it forms part of the preceding word. —*n.* such a word. [f. L f. Gk (EN-, *klinō* lean)]

enclose /ɪnˈkləʊz/ *v.t.* **1** to shut in on all sides, to surround with a wall or fence etc.; to shut up in a receptacle (esp. in an envelope besides a letter). **2** (in *p.p.*, of a religious community) secluded from the outside world. [f. OF f. L (as INCLUDE)]

enclosure /ɪnˈkləʊʒə(r)/ *n.* **1** the act of enclosing; the enclosing of common land to make it private property. **2** an enclosed space or area. **3** a thing enclosed with a letter. [as prec.]

encode /ɪnˈkəʊd/ *v.t.* to put into code. —**encoder** *n.*

encomium /enˈkəʊmɪəm/ *n.* (*pl.* **-ums**) formal or bombastic praise. [L f. Gk]

encompass /ɪnˈkʌmpəs/ *v.t.* to surround; to contain.

encore /ˈɒŋkɔ:(r)/ *n.* an audience's demand for further performance or repetition of an item; such an item. —*v.t.* to call for an encore of (an item), to call back (a performer) for this. —/also -ˈkɔ:(r)/ *int.* again, once more. [F, = once more]

encounter /ɪnˈkaʊntə(r)/ *v.t.* **1** to meet by chance or unexpectedly. **2** to find oneself faced with (a problem etc.). **3** to meet as an adversary. —*n.* a meeting by chance or in conflict. [f. OF f. L *contra* against]

encourage /ɪnˈkʌrɪdʒ/ *v.t.* **1** to give courage or confidence to. **2** to urge; to stimulate, to promote. —**encouragement** *n.* [f. F (as EN-, COURAGE)]

encroach /ɪn'krəʊtʃ/ *v.i.* to intrude (*on* or *upon*); to advance gradually beyond due limits. —**encroachment** *n.* [f. OF *encrochier* (*croc* hook)]

encrust /ɪn'krʌst/ *v.t./i.* to cover with or form a crust; to overlay with a crust of silver etc. [f. F (as EN-, CRUST)]

encumber /ɪn'kʌmbə(r)/ *v.t.* to be a burden to; to hamper, to impede. [f. OF f. Rom.]

encumbrance *n.* a burden, an impediment. [f. prec.]

encyclical /ɪn'sɪklɪk(ə)l/ *adj.* for wide circulation. —*n.* a papal encyclical letter. [f. L f. Gk (EN-, *kuklos* circle)]

encyclopaedia /ensaɪklə'pi:dɪə/ *n.* a book or set of books giving information on many subjects, or on many aspects of one subject. [L f. Gk *egkuklios* all-round, *paideia* education]

encyclopaedic *adj.* (of knowledge or information) comprehensive. [f. prec.]

encyclopaedist *n.* a writer of an encyclopaedia. [f. ENCYCLOPAEDIA]

end *n.* **1** the extreme limit, the furthest point; the extreme part or surface of a thing. **2** a finish or conclusion; the latter part; destruction, death. **3** a purpose, an object. **4** a result, an outcome. **5** a remnant, a piece left over. **6** the half of a sports pitch etc. occupied by one side. **7** the part or share with which a person is concerned. —*v.t./i.* to bring or come to an end, to finish; to result *in*. —**the end,** (*colloq.*) the limit of endurability. **end it all,** (*colloq.*) to commit suicide. **end on,** with the end facing one or adjoining the end of the next object. **end-product** *n.* the final product of manufacture, a transformation, etc. **ends of the earth,** the remotest regions. **end to end,** with the end of one adjoining the end of the next in a series. **end up,** to reach a certain state or action eventually. **in the end,** finally. **keep one's end up,** to do one's part despite difficulties. **make ends meet,** to live within one's income. **no end,** (*colloq.*) to a great extent. **no end of,** (*colloq.*) much or many of. **on end,** upright; continuously. **put an end to,** to stop, to abolish, to destroy. [OE]

endanger /ɪn'deɪndʒə(r)/ *v.t.* to bring into danger.

endear /ɪn'dɪə(r)/ *v.t.* to make dear (*to*).

endearment *n.* **1** an act or words expressing affection. **2** liking, affection. [f. prec.]

endeavour /ɪn'devə(r)/ *v.t.* to try earnestly (*to do*). —*n.* an earnest attempt. [f. EN- + F *devoir* duty]

endemic /en'demɪk/ *adj.* regularly or only found among a (specified) people or in a (specified) country. —*n.* an endemic disease or plant. —**endemically** *adv.* [f. F or L f. Gk (EN-, *dēmos* people)]

ending *n.* the end or final part, especially of a story; the inflected final part of a word. [f. END]

endive /'endɪv/ *n.* **1** a curly leaved plant (*Cichorium endivia*) used in salads. **2** (*US*) a chicory crown. [f. OF, ult. f. L *intibum*]

endless /'endlɪs/ *adj.* without end, infinite; incessant; continual; (*colloq.*) innumerable. —**endless belt** *or* **chain** etc., one with the ends joined for continuous action over wheels etc. [f. END + -LESS]

endmost *adj.* nearest the end. [f. END + -MOST]

endo- *prefix* internal(ly). [f. Gk *endon* within]

endocrine /'endəʊkraɪn, -krɪn/ *adj.* (of a gland) secreting directly into the blood. [f. ENDO- + Gk *krinō* sift]

endogenous /en'dɒdʒɪnəs/ *adj.* growing or originating from within. [f. ENDO- + -GENOUS]

endomorph /'endəʊmɔ:f/ *n.* a person with a soft round build of the body, thought likely to be an extrovert. [f. ENDO- + Gk *morphē* form]

endorphin /en'dɔ:fɪn/ *n.* any of a group of peptides that occur naturally in the brain and have an effect similar to that of morphine, serving to inhibit pain. [f. F (as ENDO-, MORPHINE)]

endorse /ɪn'dɔ:s/ *v.t.* **1** to confirm, to approve. **2** to write a comment etc. on (a document); to sign the back of (a cheque). **3** to enter the details of a conviction for an offence on (a licence). —**endorsement** *n.* [f. L *indorsare* (IN-[1], *dorsum* back)]

endoscope /'endəskəʊp/ *n.* an instrument used for viewing the internal parts of the body. —**endoscopy** /'dɒskəpɪ/ *n.* [f. ENDO- + -SCOPE]

endow /ɪn'daʊ/ *v.t.* **1** to bequeath or give a permanent income to (a person, institution, etc.). **2** (esp. in *p.p.*) to provide with talent or ability. [f. AF (as EN-, DOWER)]

endowment *n.* endowing; an endowed income. —**endowment assurance** *or* **insurance policy** etc., a form of life insurance with payment of a fixed sum to the insured person on a specified date, or to his estate if he dies earlier. [f. prec.]

endpaper *n.* a stout blank leaf of paper fixed across the beginning or end of a book and the inside cover.

endue /ɪn'dju:/ *v.t.* to provide (a person *with* qualities etc.). [f. OF f. L *inducere* draw on, assoc. with *induere* put on (clothes)]

endurable *adj.* able to be endured. [f. ENDURE]

endurance *n.* **1** the power of enduring. **2** the ability to withstand prolonged strain. [OF (as ENDURE]

endure /ɪn'djʊə(r)/ *v.t./i.* **1** to undergo (pain etc.); to tolerate, to bear. **2** to last. [f. OF f. L *indurare* harden (IN-[1], *durus* hard)]

endways *adv.* (also **endwise**) **1** with the end uppermost or foremost. **2** end to end.

enema /ˈenɪmə/ *n.* the insertion of liquid through the anus into the rectum, especially to expel its contents; a liquid or syringe used for this. [L f. Gk (*eniēmi* inject)]

enemy /ˈenəmɪ/ *n.* a person actively hostile to another and seeking to defeat or harm him; a hostile nation or army, a member of this; an adversary, an opponent. —*adj.* of or belonging to the enemy. [f. OF f. L *inimicus* (IN-², *amicus* friend)]

energetic /enəˈdʒetɪk/ *adj.* full of energy; powerfully active. —**energetically** *adv.* [f. Gk (as ENERGY)]

energize /ˈenədʒaɪz/ *v.t.* to give energy to; to provide (a device) with energy for operation. [f. foll.]

energy /ˈenədʒɪ/ *n.* **1** capacity for activity, force, vigour. **2** the ability of matter or radiation to do work (see below). [f. F or L f. Gk *energeia* (*ergon* work)]

enervate /ˈenəveɪt/ *v.t.* to deprive of vigour or vitality. —**enervation** /-ˈveɪʃ(ə)n/ *n.* [f. L *enervare* (EX-¹, *nervus* sinew)]

enfant terrible /ɑ̃fɑ̃ teˈriːbl/ a person who causes embarrassment by indiscreet behaviour; an unruly child. [F, = terrible child]

enfeeble /ɪnˈfiːb(ə)l/ *v.t.* to make feeble. —**enfeeblement** *n.* [f. OF (as EN-, FEEBLE)]

enfilade /enfɪˈleɪd/ *n.* gunfire directed along a line from end to end. —*v.t.* to direct an enfilade at. [F, f. *enfiler* (EN-, *fil* thread)]

enfold /ɪnˈfəʊld/ *v.t.* to wrap (a person *in* or *with*); to clasp, to embrace.

enforce /ɪnˈfɔːs/ *v.t.* to compel observance of (a law etc.); to impose (an action or one's will etc. *on* a person); to persist in (a demand etc.). —**enforceable** *adj.*, **enforcement** *n.* [f. OF *enforci(e)r* f. L *fortis* strong]

enfranchise /ɪnˈfræntʃaɪz/ *v.t.* **1** to give (a person) the right to vote. **2** to give (a town) municipal rights, especially representation in parliament. **3** to free (a slave etc.). —**enfranchisement** /-ɪzmənt/ *n.* [f. OF *enfranchir* (*franc* free)]

engage /ɪnˈgeɪdʒ/ *v.t./i.* **1** to take into one's employment, to hire. **2** to arrange beforehand to occupy (a room, seat, etc.). **3** to promise, to pledge. **4** to occupy the attention of; to occupy oneself. **5** to come or bring into battle (with). **6** to interlock (parts of a gear etc.) so as to transmit power; to become interlocked thus. [f. F (as IN-, GAGE¹)]

engaged *adj.* **1** having promised to marry. **2** occupied or reserved by a person etc.; occupied with business etc. **3** (of a telephone line) already in use. [f. prec.]

engagement *n.* **1** engaging, being engaged. **2** an appointment made with another person. **3** a promise to marry a specified person. **4** a battle. —**engagement ring,** a finger-ring given by a man to a woman when they promise to marry. [F (as ENGAGE)]

engaging *adj.* attractive, charming. [f. ENGAGE]

engender /ɪnˈdʒendə(r)/ *v.t.* to give rise to (a feeling etc.). [f. OF f. L (as IN-¹, GENERATE)]

engine /ˈendʒɪn/ *n.* **1** a mechanical contrivance of parts working together, especially as a source of power. **2** a railway locomotive; a fire-engine; a steam-engine. **3** (*archaic*) a machine of war; an instrument; a means. [f. OF f. L *ingenium* talent, device]

engineer /endʒɪˈnɪə(r)/ *n.* **1** a person skilled in some branch of engineering; a civil engineer (see CIVIL). **2** a person who makes or is in charge of engines or other equipment. **3** one who designs and constructs military works, especially a soldier so trained. —*v.t./i.* **1** to act as an engineer; to plan and construct or control as engineer. **2** (*colloq.*) to contrive, to bring about. [f. OF f. L *ingeniator* (as prec.)]

engineering *n.* the application of science for the control and use of power, especially in roads and other works of public utility, machines, and electrical apparatus. [f. prec.]

English /ˈɪŋglɪʃ/ *adj.* of England or its people or language. —*n.* the language of England; its literary or standard form. —**english** *v.t.* (*archaic*) to render into English. —**the English,** the people of England. **the King's** *or* **Queen's English,** the English language correctly spoken or written. [OE (as ANGLES)]

Englishman *n.* (*pl.* **-men**) one who is English by birth, descent, or naturalization. —**Englishwoman** *n.fem.* (*pl.* **-women**)

engorged /ɪnˈgɔːdʒd/ *adj.* crammed full; congested with blood. [f. F (as EN-, GORGE)]

engraft /ɪnˈgrɑːft/ *v.t.* to graft (a shoot of one plant *on* or *into* another); to implant; to incorporate (a thing *into* another).

engrave /ɪnˈgreɪv/ *v.t.* **1** to inscribe or cut (a design) on a hard surface; to inscribe (a surface) thus. **2** to impress deeply *on* the memory.

engraving *n.* a print made from an engraved plate. [f. prec.]

engross /ɪnˈgrəʊs/ *v.t.* **1** to absorb the attention of, to occupy fully. **2** to write out in large letters or in legal form. —**engrossment** *n.* [f. AF *engrosser* (*en gros* wholesale); f. *en* in, *grosse* large writing]

engulf /ɪnˈgʌlf/ *v.t.* to flow over and swamp, to overwhelm.

enhance /ɪnˈhɑːns/ *v.t.* to heighten or intensify (a quality or power etc.). —**enhancement** *n.* [f. AF prob. alt. f. OF *enhaucier* f. L *altus* high]

enigma /ɪˈnɪgmə/ *n.* a puzzling thing or person; a riddle or paradox. —**enigmatic** /-ˈmætɪk/ *adj.*, **enigmatically** *adv.* [f. L f. Gk *ainigma*]

enjoin /ɪnˈdʒɔɪn/ *v.t.* to command, to order; to

impose (an action *on* a person); (*Law*) to prohibit by injunction (*from* doing). [f. OF f. L *injungere* attach]

enjoy /ɪnˈdʒɔɪ/ *v.t.* to take pleasure in; to have the use or benefit of; to experience. —**enjoy oneself**, to experience pleasure. —**enjoyment** *n.* [f. OF (as EN-, JOY)]

enjoyable *adj.* pleasant, giving enjoyment. —**enjoyably** *adv.* [f. prec.]

enkephalin /enˈkef(ə)lɪn/ *n.* either of two morphine-like peptides in the brain thought to be concerned with the perception of pain. [f. Gk *egkephalos* brain]

enkindle /ɪnˈkɪnd(ə)l/ *v.t.* to cause to blaze up; to arouse.

enlarge /ɪnˈlɑ:dʒ/ *v.t./i.* **1** to make or become larger or wider; to reproduce (a photograph) on a larger scale. **2** to describe in greater detail. —**enlargement** *n.* [f. OF (as EN-, LARGE)]

enlighten /ɪnˈlaɪt(ə)n/ *v.t.* to instruct or inform (a person *on* a subject); to free from superstition etc.

enlightenment *n.* enlightening. —**the Enlightenment**, the 18th-c. philosophy allegedly placing too much emphasis on reason and individualism as against tradition. [f. prec.]

enlist /ɪnˈlɪst/ *v.t./i.* **1** to enrol in the armed services. **2** to secure as a means of help or support. —**enlistment** *n.*

enliven /ɪnˈlaɪv(ə)n/ *v.t.* to make lively or cheerful. —**enlivenment** *n.*

en masse /ã ˈmæs/ all together. [F]

enmesh /ɪnˈmeʃ/ *v.t.* to entangle (as) in a net.

enmity /ˈenmɪtɪ/ *n.* the state or feeling of being an enemy, hostility. [f. OF (as ENEMY)]

ennoble /ɪˈnəʊb(ə)l/ *v.t.* to make (a person) a noble; to make noble. —**ennoblement** *n.* [f. F (as EN-, NOBLE)]

ennui /ˈɒnwi:, ɒˈnwi:/ *n.* mental weariness caused by idleness or lack of interest, a feeling of boredom. [F, f. L *in odio* hateful]

enormity /ɪˈnɔ:mɪtɪ/ *n.* **1** monstrous wickedness; a dreadful crime; a serious error. **2** (**D**) great size. [f. F f. L (as foll.)]

enormous /ɪˈnɔ:məs/ *adj.* extraordinarily large, vast, huge. —**enormously** *adv.* [f. L *enormis* (EX-[1], *norma* pattern, standard)]

enough /ɪˈnʌf/ *adj.* as much or as many as required. —*n.* the amount or quantity that is enough. —*adv.* to the required degree, adequately; fairly; very, quite. —**have had enough of**, to want no more of; to be satiated with or tired of. **sure enough**, undeniably, as expected. [OE]

enounce /ɪˈnaʊns/ *v.t.* to enunciate, to pronounce. [f. F *énoncer* (as ENUNCIATE)]

en passant /ã ˈpæsã/ by the way. [F, = in passing]

enquire /ɪnˈkwaɪə(r)/ *v.t./i.* to ask to be told (a person's name, business, etc.); to seek information (*about* etc.). —**enquiry** *n.* [= INQUIRE]

enrage /ɪnˈreɪdʒ/ *v.t.* to make furious. [f. F (as EN-, RAGE)]

enrapture /ɪnˈræptʃə(r)/ *v.t.* to delight intensely.

enrich /ɪnˈrɪtʃ/ *v.t.* to make rich or richer; to increase the strength or wealth or value of. —**enrichment** *n.* [f. OF (as EN-, RICH)]

enrol /ɪnˈrəʊl/ *v.t./i.* (**-ll-**) to write the name of (a person) on a list; to enlist; to incorporate as a member; to enrol oneself. —**enrolment** *n.* [f. OF (as EN-, ROLL)]

en route /ã ˈru:t/ on the way. [F]

ensconce /ɪnˈskɒns/ *v.t.* to settle comfortably.

ensemble /ãˈsãbl/ *n.* **1** a thing viewed as a sum of its parts. **2** a set of matching items of dress. **3** a group of actors, dancers, musicians, etc., performing together; (*Mus.*) a concerted passage for an ensemble. [F, f. L *insimul* (IN-[1], *simul* at the same time)]

enshrine /ɪnˈʃraɪn/ *v.t.* to enclose (as) in a shrine; to serve as a shrine for.

enshroud /ɪnˈʃraʊd/ *v.t.* to cover completely (as) with a shroud; to hide from view.

ensign /ˈensaɪn, -s(ə)n/ *n.* **1** a banner or flag, especially a nation's military or naval flag. **2** a standard-bearer. **3** (*hist.*) the lowest commissioned infantry officer. **4** (*US*) the lowest commissioned officer in the navy. [f. OF f. L *insignia*]

ensilage /ˈensɪlɪdʒ/ *n.* silage. [F (as EN-, SILAGE)]

enslave /ɪnˈsleɪv/ *v.t.* to make into a slave. —**enslavement** *n.*

ensnare /ɪnˈsneə(r)/ *v.t.* to catch (as) in a snare.

ensue /ɪnˈsju:/ *v.i.* to happen later or as a result. [f. OF f. L (IN-[1], *sequi* follow)]

en suite /ã ˈswi:t/ forming a single unit. [F, = in sequence]

ensure /ɪnˈʃʊə(r)/ *v.t.* to make certain or secure; to make safe (*against* risks). [f. AF (as EN-, SURE)]

ENT *abbr.* ear, nose, and throat.

entablature /ɪnˈtæblətʃə(r)/ *n.* (*Archit.*) an upper part supported by columns, including the architrave, frieze, and cornice. [f. It., f. *intavolare* board up (*tavola* table)]

entail /ɪnˈteɪl/ *v.t.* **1** to necessitate or involve unavoidably. **2** (*Law*) to bequeath (an estate) inalienably to a named succession of beneficiaries. —*n.* an entailed estate or succession.

entangle /ɪnˈtæŋg(ə)l/ *v.t.* to cause to get caught in a snare or tangle; to involve in difficulties; to complicate. —**entanglement** *n.*

entente /ãˈtãnt/ *n.* a friendly understanding

or association, especially between States. —**entente cordiale** /kɔ:dɪ'ɑ:l/, that between Britain and France resulting from diplomatic exchanges in 1904. [F, = understanding (as INTENT)]

enter *v.t./i.* **1** to go or come in or into; to come on stage (esp. as a direction); to penetrate. **2** to write (a name, details, etc.) in a list, book, etc.; to register as a competitor; to record (a plea etc.) formally. **3** to admit or obtain admission for (a pupil, a person as a member, etc.). —**enter into,** to take part in (a conversation etc.); to subscribe to or become bound by (an agreement, contract, etc.); to form part of (a calculation, plan, etc.); to sympathize with (feelings). **enter on** *or* **upon,** to assume possession of (property) or the functions of (an office); to begin; to begin to deal with. [f. OF f. L *intrare* (*intra* within)]

enteric /en'terɪk/ *adj.* of the intestines. [f. Gk (*enteron* intestine)]

enteritis /entə'raɪtɪs/ *n.* inflammation of the intestines. [as prec. + -ITIS]

enterprise /'entəpraɪz/ *n.* an undertaking, especially a bold or difficult one; readiness to be involved in such undertakings. [f. OF *entreprendre* var. of *emprendre* f. L (as IN-[1], *prehendere* take)]

enterprising *adj.* showing enterprise; energetic and resourceful. [f. prec.]

entertain /entə'teɪn/ *v.t.* **1** to amuse, to occupy agreeably. **2** to receive as a guest; to receive guests. **3** to harbour, to cherish, to consider favourably (an idea etc.). [f. F f. L (INTER-, *tenēre* hold)]

entertainer *n.* one who provides entertainment, especially as a professional. [f. prec.]

entertaining *adj.* amusing, diverting. [f. ENTERTAIN]

entertainment *n.* entertaining; a thing that entertains, especially before a public audience. [f. prec.]

enthral /ɪn'θrɔ:l/ *v.t.* (**-ll-**) to captivate, to please greatly. —**enthralment** *n.* [f. EN- + THRALL]

enthrone /ɪn'θrəʊn/ *v.t.* to place on a throne, especially ceremonially. —**enthronement** *n.*

enthuse /ɪn'θju:z, -'θu:z/ *v.t./i.* (*colloq.*) to be or make enthusiastic. [back-formation f. foll.]

enthusiasm /ɪn'θju:zɪæz(ə)m, -'θu:-/ *n.* intensity of feeling or interest, great eagerness. [f. F or L f. Gk (*entheos* possessed by a god)]

enthusiast *n.* a person full of enthusiasm for something. [as prec.]

enthusiastic /ɪnθju:zɪ'æstɪk, -θu:-/ *adj.* having or showing enthusiasm. —**enthusiastically** *adv.* [f. prec.]

entice /ɪn'taɪs/ *v.t.* to persuade by an offer of pleasure or reward. —**enticement** *n.* [f. OF prob. f. L *titio* firebrand]

entire /ɪn'taɪə(r)/ *adj.* **1** whole, complete. **2** in one piece; continuous. **3** unqualified, absolute. [f. AF f. L *integer* (IN-[2], *tangere* touch)]

entirely *adv.* wholly, solely. [f. prec.]

entirety /ɪn'taɪərətɪ/ *n.* completeness; the sum total (*of*). —**in its entirety,** in its complete form. [f. ENTIRE]

entitle /ɪn'taɪt(ə)l/ *v.t.* **1** to give a right or just claim *to*. **2** to give a title to (a book etc.). —**entitlement** *n.* [f. AF f. L *intitulare* (IN-[1], *titulus* title)]

entity /'entɪtɪ/ *n.* a thing with distinct existence; a thing's existence in itself. [f. F or L (*ens* partic. of *esse* be)]

entomb /ɪn'tu:m/ *v.t.* to place in a tomb; to serve as a tomb for. —**entombment** *n.*

entomology /entə'mɒlədʒɪ/ *n.* the study of insects. —**entomological** /-'lɒdʒɪk(ə)l/ *adj.*, **entomologist** *n.* [f. F or L f. Gk (*entomon* insect)]

entourage /ɒntʊə'rɑ:ʒ/ *n.* the people attending an important person. [F (*entourer* surround)]

entr'acte /'ɒntrækt/ *n.* an interval between the acts of a play; a dance or music etc. performed then. [F (*entre* between, *acte* act)]

entrails /'entreɪlz/ *n.pl.* **1** the bowels, the intestines. **2** the inner parts of a thing. [f. OF f. L *intralia* (*inter* among)]

entrance[1] /'entrəns/ *n.* **1** going or coming in; the coming of an actor on to a stage. **2** a door or passage etc. by which one enters. **3** the right of admission; the fee charged for this. [f. OF (as ENTER)]

entrance[2] /ɪn'trɑ:ns/ *v.t.* **1** to enchant, to delight. **2** to put into a trance. —**entrancement** *n.*

entrant /'entrənt/ *n.* one who enters an examination, profession, etc. [F (as ENTER)]

entrap /ɪn'træp/ *v.t.* (**-pp-**) to catch (as) in a trap; to beguile. [f. OF (as EN-, TRAP)]

entreat /ɪn'tri:t/ *v.t.* to ask earnestly, to beg. [f. OF (as EN-, TREAT)]

entreaty *n.* an earnest request. [f. prec.]

entrecôte /'ɒntrəkəʊt/ *n.* a boned steak cut off a sirloin. [F, = between-rib]

entrée /'ɒntreɪ/ *n.* **1** the right of admission. **2** a dish served between fish and meat courses; (*US*) the main dish of a meal. [F, = entry]

entrench /ɪn'trentʃ/ *v.t.* **1** to establish firmly (in a position, office, etc.). **2** to surround with a trench as a fortification. —**entrenchment** *n.*

entrepôt /'ɒntrəpəʊ/ *n.* a warehouse for temporary storage of goods in transit. [F (*entreposer* store, as INTERPOSE)]

entrepreneur /ɒntrəprə'nɜ:(r)/ *n.* one who undertakes a commercial enterprise with a chance of profit or loss; a contractor acting as an intermediary. —**entrepreneurial** *adj.* [F (as ENTERPRISE)]

entropy /ˈentrəpɪ/ *n.* a measure of the disorder of the molecules in substances etc. that are mixed or in contact with each other, indicating the amount of energy that (although it still exists) is not available for use because it has become more evenly distributed instead of being concentrated. [f. G (as EN-, Gk *tropē* transformation)]

entrust /ɪnˈtrʌst/ *v.t.* to give (an object of care) with trust; to assign responsibility *to* (a person).

entry /ˈentrɪ/ *n.* **1** entering; the liberty to do this. **2** a place of entrance, a door, gate, etc. **3** a passage between buildings. **4** an item entered in a diary, list, etc.; the recording of this. **5** a person or thing entered in a race, competition, etc.; a list of such competitors. [f. OF (as ENTER)]

entwine /ɪnˈtwaɪn/ *v.t.* to twine round; to interweave.

enumerate /ɪˈnju:məreɪt/ *v.t.* to count; to specify (items). —**enumeration** /-ˈreɪʃ(ə)n/ *n.*, **enumerative** *adj.* [f. L *enumerare* (EX-[1], *numerare* number)]

enumerator *n.* a person employed in census-taking. [f. prec.]

enunciate /ɪˈnʌnsɪeɪt/ *v.t.* **1** to pronounce (words) clearly. **2** to state in definite terms. —**enunciation** /-ˈeɪʃ(ə)n/ *n.* [f. L *enuntiare* (EX-[1], *nuntiare* announce)]

enuresis /enjʊəˈri:sɪs/ *n.* involuntary urination. [f. Gk *enoureō* urinate in (*ouron* urine)]

envelop /ɪnˈveləp/ *v.t.* to wrap up; to surround, to cover on all sides. —**envelopment** *n.* [f. OF (as EN-; cf. DEVELOP)]

envelope /ˈenvələʊp, ˈɒn-/ *n.* **1** a folded paper container for a letter etc. **2** a wrapper, a covering. **3** the gas container of a balloon or airship. [f. F (as prec.)]

enviable /ˈenvɪəb(ə)l/ *adj.* such as to cause envy, desirable. —**enviably** *adv.* [f. ENVY]

envious /ˈenvɪəs/ *adj.* feeling or showing envy. —**enviously** *adv.* [f. AF (as ENVY)]

environment /ɪnˈvaɪərənmənt/ *n.* surroundings, especially as affecting people's lives; conditions or circumstances of living. —**environmental** /-ˈment(ə)l/ *adj.* [f. OF (as ENVIRONS)]

environmentalist /ɪnvaɪərenˈment(ə)lɪst/ *n.* one who is concerned with the protection of the environment from pollution etc. [f. prec.]

environs /ɪnˈvaɪərənz/ *n.pl.* the district round a town etc. [f. OF (*viron* circuit, neighbourhood, f. *virer* turn)]

envisage /ɪnˈvɪzɪdʒ/ *v.t.* to have a mental picture of (a thing or conditions not yet existing); to conceive as possible or desirable. [f. OF (as EN- VISAGE)]

envoy /ˈenvɔɪ/ *n.* **1** a messenger or representative. **2** (in full **envoy extraordinary**) a diplomatic agent ranking below ambassador. [f. F (*envoyer* send)]

envy /ˈenvɪ/ *n.* a feeling of discontented longing aroused by another's better fortune etc.; the object of this feeling. —*v.t.* to feel envy of. [f. OF f. L *invidia*]

enwrap /ɪnˈræp/ *v.t.* (**-pp-**) to wrap or enfold.

enzyme /ˈenzaɪm/ *n.* any of a class of large molecules, consisting entirely or chiefly of protein, found in all cells and essential to life, that act as catalysts of biochemical reactions in all living organisms. [f. Gk *en* in + *zumē* leaven]

eolithic /i:əˈlɪθɪk/ *adj.* of the earliest age of man that is represented by the use of worked flint implements. [f. F f. Gk *ēōs* dawn + *lithos* stone]

EP *abbr.* extended-play (record).

epaulette /ˈepəlet/ *n.* an ornamental shoulder-piece worn on a uniform. [f. F (*épaule* shoulder)]

épée /eɪˈpeɪ/ *n.* a sharp-pointed sword used (with the end blunted) in fencing. [F]

epergne /ɪˈpɜ:n/ *n.* an ornament for a dinner-table, with small bowls or vases on branched supports. [orig. unkn.]

ephedrine /ˈefədrɪn/ *n.* an alkaloid drug used to relieve asthma etc. [f. *Ephedra*, genus of plants yielding it]

ephemera /ɪˈfemərə/ *n.pl.* things of only short-lived usefulness. [f. L f. Gk (as foll.)]

ephemeral /ɪˈfemər(ə)l/ *adj.* lasting or living only a day or a few days; transitory. [f. Gk *ephēmeros* lasting only a day (*epi* on, *hēmera* day)]

ephod /ˈefəd/ *n.* a Jewish priestly vestment. [f. Heb.]

epi- /epɪ-/ *prefix* upon, above, in addition. [f. Gk]

epic /ˈepɪk/ *n.* a long poem narrating the adventures or achievements of a heroic figure or a nation; a book or film based on this. —*adj.* of or like an epic; grand, heroic. [f. L f. Gk (*epos* word, narrative song)]

epicanthus /epɪˈkænθəs/ *n.* a downward fold of skin which sometimes covers the inner angle (*canthus*) of the eye, especially in Mongolian peoples. —**epicanthic** *adj.* [f. EPI- + L *canthus* corner of the eye]

epicene /ˈepɪsi:n/ *adj.* of, for, or denoting both sexes; having the characteristics of both sexes or of neither sex. —*n.* an epicene person. [f. L f. Gk (EPI-, *koinos* common)]

epicentre /ˈepɪsentə(r)/ *n.* the point at which an earthquake reaches the earth's surface; the central point of a difficulty. [f. Gk (as EPI-, CENTRE)]

epicure /ˈepɪkjʊə(r)/ *n.* a person of refined

tastes in food and drink etc. —**epicurism** *n.* [f. L f. EPICURUS]

epicurean /epɪkjʊəˈriːən/ *adj.* fond of refined sensuous pleasure and luxury. —*n.* a person with epicurean tastes. [f. *Epicurus*, Gk philosopher (3rd c. BC)]

epidemic /epɪˈdemɪk/ *adj.* (esp. of a disease) prevalent among a community at a particular time. —*n.* an epidemic disease. [f. F f. L f. Gk *epidēmia* prevalence of disease (EPI-, *dēmos* the people)]

epidemiology /epɪdiːmɪˈɒlədʒɪ/ *n.* the branch of medicine concerned with the control of epidemics. [as prec. + -LOGY]

epidermis /epɪˈdɜːmɪs/ *n.* the outer layer of the skin, the cuticle. —**epidermal** *adj.* [L f. Gk (EPI-, *derma* skin)]

epidiascope /epɪˈdaɪəskəʊp/ *n.* an optical projector giving images of both opaque and transparent objects. [f. EPI- + DIA- + -SCOPE]

epidural /epɪˈdjʊər(ə)l/ *adj.* (of an anaesthetic) injected into the dura mater round the spinal cord. —*n.* an epidural injection. [f. EPI- + DURA (MATER)]

epiglottis /epɪˈglɒtɪs/ *n.* the cartilage at the root of the tongue, depressed to cover the wind-pipe in swallowing. —**epiglottal** *adj.* [Gk (EPI-, *glōtta* tongue)]

epigram /ˈepɪgræm/ *n.* a short poem with a witty ending; a pointed saying. —**epigrammatic** /-grəˈmætɪk/ *adj.* [f. F or L f. Gk (as EPI-, -GRAM)]

epigraph /ˈepɪgrɑːf/ *n.* an inscription. —**epigraphic** /-ˈgræfɪk/ *adj.* [f. Gk (as EPI-, -GRAPH)]

epigraphy /eˈpɪgrəfɪ/ *n.* the study of inscriptions. —**epigraphist** *n.* [as prec.]

epilepsy /ˈepɪlepsɪ/ *n.* a nervous disorder with seizures accompanied by changes in the rhythm of the electrical currents of the brain. —**epileptic** /-ˈleptɪk/ *adj.* & *n.* [f. F or L f. Gk (*epilambanō* take hold of)]

epilogue /ˈepɪlɒg/ *n.* the concluding part of a book etc.; a speech or short poem addressed to an audience by an actor at the end of a play. [f. F f. L f. Gk (EPI-, *logos* speech)]

Epiphany /ɪˈpɪfənɪ/ *n.* a feast of the Church kept on 6 Jan., celebrating the manifestation of Christ to the Gentiles in the persons of the Magi. [f. OF f. L f. Gk (EPI-, *phainō* show)]

episcopacy /eˈpɪskəpəsɪ/ *n.* government by bishops. —**the episcopacy,** the bishops. [f. L (as foll.)]

episcopal /eˈpɪskəp(ə)l/ *adj.* of a bishop or bishops; (of a Church) governed by bishops. —**episcopally.** *adv.* [f. F or L (*episcopus* bishop)]

episcopalian /epɪskəˈpeɪlɪən/ *adj.* of episcopacy. —*n.* an adherent of episcopacy; a member of an episcopal Church. —**episcopalianism** *n.* [f. prec.]

episcopate /eˈpɪskəpət/ *n.* the office or tenure of a bishop. —**the episcopate,** the bishops. [f. L (as EPISCOPAL)]

episiotomy /epɪsɪˈɒtəmɪ/ *n.* a surgical cut made at the opening of the vagina during childbirth, to aid delivery. [f. Gk *epision* pubic region + -TOMY]

episode /ˈepɪsəʊd/ *n.* an incident in a narrative, one part of several in a serial story; an incident or event as part of a sequence; an incidental narrative or series of events. [f. Gk (EPI-, *eisodos* entrance)]

episodic /epɪˈsɒdɪk/ *adj.* sporadic, occurring irregularly; incidental. —**episodically** *adv.* [f. prec.]

epistemology /epɪstɪˈmɒlədʒɪ/ *n.* the theory of the method or grounds of knowledge. —**epistemological** /-əˈlɒdʒɪk(ə)l/ *adj.* [f. Gk *epistēmē* knowledge + -LOGY]

epistle /ɪˈpɪs(ə)l/ *n.* **1** any of the letters in the New Testament, written by or attributed to one of the Apostles. **2** (usu. *joc.*) any letter. **3** a poem etc. in the form of a letter. [f. OF f. L f. Gk *epistolē* (EPI-, *stellō* send)]

epistolary /ɪˈpɪstələrɪ/ *adj.* of or suitable for letters. [f. F or L (as prec.)]

epitaph /ˈepɪtɑːf/ *n.* the words inscribed on a tomb or appropriate to a dead person. [f. OF f. L f. Gk *epitaphion* funeral oration (EPI-, *taphos* tomb)]

epithalamium /epɪθəˈleɪmɪəm/ *n.* (*pl.* **-ia**) a nuptial song or poem. [f. L f. Gk (EPI-, *thalamos* bridal chamber)]

epithelium /epɪˈθiːlɪəm/ *n.* (*pl.* **-ia**) the tissue forming the outer layer of the body or lining an open cavity; the epidermis of young cells. —**epithelial** *adj.* [L (EPI-, Gk *thēlē* teat)]

epithet /ˈepɪθet/ *n.* an adjective expressing a quality or attribute, a descriptive word. —**epithetic** /-ˈθetɪk/ *adj.*, **epithetically** *adv.* [f. F or L f. Gk (EPI-, *tithēmi* place)]

epitome /eˈpɪtəmɪ/ *n.* a person who embodies a quality etc.; a thing that represents another in miniature. [L f. Gk, = abridgement]

epitomize *v.t.* to be an epitome of. [f. prec.]

EPNS *abbr.* electroplated nickel silver.

epoch /ˈiːpɒk/ *n.* a period of history etc. marked by notable events; the beginning of an era in history, life, etc.; the division of a geological period, corresponding to a series in rocks. —**epoch-making** *adj.* very important or remarkable. —**epochal** *adj.* [f. L f. Gk, = pause]

eponym /ˈepənɪm/ *n.* a person after whom a place etc. is named. —**eponymous** /ɪˈpɒnɪməs/ *adj.* [f. Gk (EPI-, *onoma* name)]

epoxy /ɪˈpɒksɪ/ *adj.* of or derived from a

compound in which an oxygen atom and two carbon atoms form a ring. —**epoxy resin,** a synthetic thermosetting resin. [f. EPI- + OXY-]

epsilon /ep'saɪlən/ *n.* the fifth letter of the Greek alphabet, = e. [Gk, = bare E (*psilos* bare)]

Epsom salts /'epsəm/ magnesium sulphate used as a purgative etc. [f. *Epsom* in Surrey]

equable /'ekwəb(ə)l/ *adj.* even, not varying; (of climate) moderate; (of a person) not easily disturbed. —**equably** *adv.* [f. L *aequabilis* (as foll.)]

equal /'i:kw(ə)l/ *adj.* the same in number, size, degree, merit, etc.; evenly balanced; having the same rights or status; uniform in operation. —*n.* a person or thing equal to another, especially a person equal in rank or status. —*v.t.* (**-ll-**) to be equal to; to achieve something that is equal to. —**be equal to,** to have the strength or capacity for. —**equally** *adv.* [f. L *aequalis* (*aequus* even, equal)]

equalitarian /i:kwɒlɪ'teərɪən/ *adj.* var. of EGALITARIAN.

equality /i:'kwɒlɪtɪ/ *n.* the condition of being equal. [f. OF f. L (as EQUAL)]

equalize /'i:kwəlaɪz/ *v.t./i.* to make or become equal; (in games) to reach an opponent's score. —**equalization** /-'zeɪʃ(ə)n/ *n.* [f. EQUAL]

equalizer *n.* a goal etc. that equalizes a score. [f. prec.]

equanimity /ekwə'nɪmɪtɪ, i:k-/ *n.* mental composure; acceptance of fate. [f. L (*aequus* even, *animus* mind)]

equate /ɪ'kweɪt/ *v.t.* to regard as equal or equivalent (*to* or *with*). [f. L *aequare* (*aequus* equal)]

equation /ɪ'kweɪʒ(ə)n/ *n.* **1** equating, making equal, balancing. **2** a statement of equality between two mathematical expressions (conveyed by the sign =). **3** a formula indicating a chemical reaction by the use of symbols. [f. OF or L (as prec.)]

equator /ɪ'kweɪtə(r)/ *n.* an imaginary line round the earth or other body, equidistant from the poles. —**celestial equator,** see CELESTIAL. [f. OF or L (as EQUATE)]

equatorial /ekwə'tɔ:rɪəl/ *adj.* of or near the equator. [f. prec.]

equerry /'ekwərɪ/ *n.* an officer of the British royal household attending members of the royal family. [earlier *esquiry* f. obs. F *escurie* stable]

equestrian /ɪ'kwestrɪən/ *adj.* of horse-riding; on horseback. —*n.* a rider or performer on a horse. [f. L *equestris* (*equus* horse)]

equi- *prefix* equal. [f. L *aequi-* (*aequus* equal)]

equiangular /i:kwɪ'æŋgjʊlə(r)/ *adj.* having equal angles.

equidistant /i:kwɪ'dɪst(ə)nt/ *adj.* at equal distances.

equilateral /i:kwɪ'lætər(ə)l/ *adj.* having all sides equal. [f. EQUI- + L *latus* side]

equilibrate /i:kwɪ'laɪbreɪt/ *v.t./i.* to cause (two things) to balance; to balance. —**equilibration** /-'breɪʃ(ə)n/ *n.* [f. L *aequilibrare* (EQUI-, *libra* balance)]

equilibrium /i:kwɪ'lɪbrɪəm/ *n.* (*pl.* **-ia**) a state of balance; composure. [L (as prec.)]

equine /'ekwaɪn/ *adj.* of or like a horse. [f. L (*equus* horse)]

equinoctial /i:kwɪ'nɒkʃ(ə)l, ek-/ *adj.* of, happening at or near, an equinox. —*n.* the celestial equator. —**equinoctial line,** the celestial equator. **equinoctial point,** see EQUINOX. [as foll.]

equinox /'ekwɪnɒks/ *n.* **1** the time or date at which the sun crosses the equator, and day and night are everywhere of equal length. **2** the position of the sun on the celestial sphere at either of these times (also called the *equinoctial point*). —**autumn** *or* **autumnal equinox,** about 22 Sept. **spring** *or* **vernal equinox,** about 20 March. [f. OF or L (as EQUI-, *nox* night)]

equip /ɪ'kwɪp/ *v.t.* (**-pp-**) to supply with what is needed. [f. F, prob. f. ON *skipa* man (ship)]

equipage /'ekwɪpɪdʒ/ *n.* requisites, an outfit; a carriage and horses with attendants. [as prec.]

equipment /ɪ'kwɪpmənt/ *n.* equipping; the necessary outfit, tools, apparatus, etc. [as EQUIP]

equipoise /'ekwɪpɔɪz, 'i:k-/ *n.* **1** equilibrium. **2** a counter-balancing thing. [f. EQUI- + POISE]

equitable /'ekwɪtəb(ə)l/ *adj.* fair, just; valid in equity rather than law. —**equitably** *adv.* [f. F (as EQUITY)]

equitation /ekwɪ'teɪʃ(ə)n/ *n.* riding on a horse; horsemanship. [f. F or L (*equitare* ride horse)]

equity /'ekwɪtɪ/ *n.* **1** fairness; the principles of justice as supplementing law. **2** the value of shares issued by a company. **3** (in *pl.*) stocks and shares not bearing fixed interest. [f. OF f. L *aequitas* (*aequus* equal, fair)]

equivalent /ɪ'kwɪv(ə)lənt/ *adj.* equal in value, amount, importance, etc.; corresponding; meaning the same; having the same result. —*n.* an equivalent thing, amount, etc. —**equivalence** *n.* [f. OF f. L (as EQUI-, *valere* be worth)]

equivocal /ɪ'kwɪvək(ə)l/ *adj.* of double or doubtful meaning; of uncertain nature; questionable, dubious. —**equivocally** *adv.* [f. L *aequivocus* (as EQUI-, *vocare* call)]

equivocate /ɪ'kwɪvəkeɪt/ *v.i.* to use equivocal terms to conceal the truth. —**equivocation** /-'keɪʃ(ə)n/ *n.*, **equivocator** *n.* [f. L (as prec.)]

ER *abbr.* **1** Queen Elizabeth (L *Elizabetha Regina*). **2** King Edward (L *Edwardus Rex*).

Er *symbol* erbium.

er /ɜ:(r), ə(r)/ *int.* expressing hesitation. [imit.]

era /ˈɪərə/ *n.* a system of chronology starting from a noteworthy event; a historical or other period, the date beginning this; a major division of geological time. [L, = number expressed in figures (orig. pl. of *aes* money)]

eradicable /ɪˈrædɪkəb(ə)l/ *adj.* able to be eradicated. [f. foll.]

eradicate /ɪˈrædɪkeɪt/ *v.t.* to root out, to destroy completely. —**eradication** /-ˈkeɪʃ(ə)n/ *n.*, **eradicator** *n.* [f. L *eradicare* (EX-¹, *radix* root)]

erase /ɪˈreɪz/ *v.t.* to rub out; to obliterate, to remove all traces of; to remove a recording from (magnetic tape). [f. L *eradere* (EX-¹, *radere* scrape)]

eraser *n.* a thing that erases, especially a piece of rubber etc. for removing pencil marks. [f. prec.]

erasure /ɪˈreɪʒə(r)/ *n.* **1** erasing. **2** an erased word etc. [f. ERASE]

erbium /ˈɜ:bɪəm/ *n.* a soft metallic element of the lanthanide series, symbol Er, atomic number 68. [f. *Ytterby* in Sweden]

ere /eə(r)/ *prep.* & *conj.* (*archaic* or *poetic*) before. [OE, orig. a compar. (cf. ERSTWHILE)]

erect /ɪˈrekt/ *adj.* upright, vertical; (of hair) bristling; (of the penis etc.) enlarged and rigid from sexual excitement. —*v.t.* **1** to raise, to set upright, to build. **2** to establish. —**erection** *n.* [f. L *erigere* set up]

erectile /ɪˈrektaɪl/ *adj.* that can become erect (esp. of body tissue by sexual excitement). [f. F (as prec.)]

erector *n.* a person or thing that erects something; a muscle causing erection. [f. ERECT]

eremite /ˈerɪmaɪt/ *n.* a hermit, especially a Christian recluse. —**eremitic** /-ˈmɪtɪk/ *adj.*, **eremitical** *adj.* [f. OF (as HERMIT)]

erg *n.* a unit of work or energy. [f. Gk *ergon* work]

ergo /ˈɜ:gəʊ/ *adv.* therefore. [L]

ergonomics /ɜ:gəˈnɒmɪks/ *n.* the study of the efficiency of persons in their working environment. —**ergonomic** *adj.*, **ergonomically** *adv.* [f. Gk *ergon* work + *-nomics* (as ECONOMICS)]

ergot /ˈɜ:gət/ *n.* **1** a disease of rye etc. caused by a fungus. **2** a drug prepared from the fungus. **3** a horny protuberance on the inner side of a horse's fetlock. [F, f. OF *argot* cock's spur (from the appearance of the diseased grain etc.)]

ermine /ˈɜ:mɪn/ *n.* **1** an animal of the weasel family (*Mustela erminea*) with brown fur turning white (except for the dark tip of its tail) in winter (cf. STOAT). **2** its white fur, used in the robes of judges, peers, etc. [f. OF, prob. f. L (*mus*) *Armenius* Armenian (mouse)]

erne /ɜ:n/ *n.* the sea eagle, *Haliaetus albicilla*. [OE]

Ernie /ˈɜ:nɪ/ a device used (from 1956) for drawing the prize-winning numbers of Premium Bonds. [f. initial letters of *electronic random number indicator equipment*]

erode /ɪˈrəʊd/ *v.t.* to wear away or destroy gradually. —**erosion** *n.*, **erosional** *adj.*, **erosive** *adj.* [f. F or L *erodere* (EX-¹, *rodere* gnaw)]

erogenous /ɪˈrɒdʒɪnəs/ *adj.* causing sexual desire, particularly sensitive to sexual stimulation. [f. Gk *erōs* sexual love + -GENOUS]

erotic /ɪˈrɒtɪk/ *adj.* of or causing sexual excitement or desire. —**erotically** *adv.* [f. F f. Gk (*erōs* sexual love)]

erotica /ɪˈrɒtɪkə/ *n.pl.* erotic literature or art. [f. prec.]

eroticism /ɪˈrɒtɪsɪz(ə)m/ *n.* erotic character, sexual excitement. [f. EROTIC]

err /ɜ:(r)/ *v.i.* to be mistaken or incorrect; to do wrong, to sin. [f. OF f. L *errare* wander, stray]

errand /ˈerənd/ *n.* a short journey for taking a message, collecting goods, etc.; the object of a journey. —**errand of mercy,** a journey to relieve distress etc. [OE]

errant[1] /ˈerənt/ *adj.* erring. [as ERR]

errant[2] /ˈerənt/ *adj.* travelling in search of adventure. —**errantry** *n.* [f. OF f. L *itinerare* (*iter* journey)]

erratic /ɪˈrætɪk/ *adj.* uncertain in movement; irregular in conduct or opinion etc. —**erratic block,** a large rock brought from a distance by a glacier. —**erratically** *adv.* [f. OF f. L *erraticus* (as ERR)]

erratum /eˈrɑ:təm/ *n.* (*pl.* **-ta**) an error in printing or writing. [L (as ERR)]

erroneous /ɪˈrəʊnɪəs/ *adj.* incorrect. —**erroneously** *adv.* [f. OF or L (*erro* vagabond, as ERR)]

error /ˈerə(r)/ *n.* a mistake; the condition of being wrong in opinion or conduct; a wrong opinion; the amount of inaccuracy in a calculation or measurement. [f. OF f. L (as ERR)]

ersatz /ˈeəzæts/ *n.* a substitute or imitation. —*adj.* synthetic, imitation. [G, = replacement]

Erse /ɜ:s/ *adj.* & *n.* Irish Gaelic (see GAELIC). [early Sc. form of IRISH]

erstwhile /ˈɜ:stwaɪl/ *adj.* former, previous. —*adv.* (*archaic*) formerly. [OE superl. (as ERE) + WHILE]

eructation /i:rʌkˈteɪʃ(ə)n/ *n.* belching. [f. L (EX-¹, *ructare* belch)]

erudite /ˈeru:daɪt/ *adj.* learned, showing great learning. —**erudition** /-ˈdɪʃ(ə)n/ *n.* [f. L *erudire* instruct (EX¹, *rudis* untrained)]

erupt /ɪˈrʌpt/ *v.i.* **1** to break out suddenly or

dramatically. **2** (of a volcano) to shoot out lava etc. **3** (of a rash) to appear on the skin. —**eruption** *n.*, **eruptive** *adj.* [f. L *erumpere* (EX-[1], *rumpere* break)]

erysipelas /erɪˈsɪpɪləs/ *n.* acute inflammation of the skin, with deep red coloration. [L f. Gk]

erythrocyte /ɪˈrɪθrəʊsaɪt/ *n.* a red blood-corpuscle. [f. Gk *eruthros* red + -CYTE]

Es *symbol* einsteinium.

escalate /ˈeskəleɪt/ *v.t./i.* to increase or develop (usually rapidly) by stages; to become more intense, to cause to do so. —**escalation** /-ˈleɪʃ(ə)n/ *n.* [back-formation f. foll.]

escalator /ˈeskəleɪtə(r)/ *n.* a staircase with an endless chain of steps moving up or down. [f. *escalade* climb wall by ladder + ELEVATOR]

escalope /ˈeskələʊp/ *n.* a slice of boneless meat, especially from a leg of veal. [F, orig. = shell]

escapade /eskəˈpeɪd/ *n.* a piece of daring or reckless adventure. [F, f. Prov. or Sp. (as foll.)]

escape /ɪˈskeɪp/ *v.t./i.* to get free of restriction or control, to get free *from*; (of gas etc.) to leak from a container etc.; to elude, to avoid (punishment, commitment, etc.); to elude the notice or memory of; (of words etc.) to issue unawares from (a person, the lips). —*n.* escaping; a means or act or the fact of escaping; a leakage of gas etc.; temporary relief from reality or worry. —**escape clause,** one specifying the conditions under which a party to a contract is free from obligations. **escape velocity,** the minimum velocity needed to escape from the gravitational field of a body. —**escaper** *n.* [f. AF f. EX-[1] + L *cappa* cloak]

escapee /eskeɪˈpiː/ *n.* one who has escaped. [f. prec.]

escapement /ɪˈskeɪpmənt/ *n.* the part of a watch or clock mechanism connecting and regulating its motive power. [f. F (as ESCAPE)]

escapism /ɪˈskeɪpɪz(ə)m/ *n.* a tendency to seek distraction or relief from reality. —**escapist** *n.* [f. ESCAPE]

escapology /eskəˈpɒlədʒɪ/ *n.* the methods and technique of escaping from captivity or confinement. —**escapologist** *n.* [f. ESCAPE + -LOGY]

escarpment /ɪˈskɑːpmənt/ *n.* a long steep slope at the edge of a plateau. [f. F (as SCARP)]

eschatology /eskəˈtɒlədʒɪ/ *n.* a doctrine of death and the afterlife. —**eschatological** /-ˈlɒdʒɪk(ə)l/ *adj.* [f. Gk *eskhatos* last + -LOGY]

escheat /ɪsˈtʃiːt/ *n.* (*hist.*) the lapse of property to the government etc. on the owner's dying intestate without heirs; the property so lapsing. —*v.t./i.* to hand over or revert as an escheat; to confiscate. [f. OF f. L *excidere* (EX-[1], *cadere* fall)]

eschew /ɪsˈtʃuː/ *v.t.* to avoid, to abstain from. [f. OF f. Gmc (as SHY[1])]

escort /ˈeskɔːt/ *n.* a person or group of persons, vehicles, ships, etc., accompanying a person or thing for protection or as a courtesy; a person accompanying another of the opposite sex socially. —/ɪˈskɔːt/ *v.t.* to act as an escort to. [f. F f. It. (*scorgere* conduct)]

escritoire /eskrɪˈtwɑː(r)/ *n.* a writing-desk with drawers etc. [F, f. L *scriptorium*]

escudo /eˈskjuːdəʊ/ *n.* (*pl.* **-os**) the monetary unit of Portugal. [Sp. & Port., f. L *scutum* shield]

esculent /ˈeskjʊlənt/ *adj.* fit for food. —*n.* an esculent substance. [f. L (*esca* food)]

escutcheon /ɪˈskʌtʃ(ə)n/ *n.* a shield or emblem bearing a coat of arms. —**blot on one's escutcheon,** a stain on one's reputation. [f. AF f. L *scutum* shield]

esker /ˈeskə(r)/ *n.* a long ridge of gravel in a river valley, originally deposited by a stream formed from the melting of ice under a glacier. [f. Ir. *eiscir*]

Eskimo /ˈeskɪməʊ/ *n.* (*pl.* **-os** or same) a member or the language of a people inhabiting the Arctic coast of North America and of eastern Siberia. —*adj.* of the Eskimos or their language. [Da. f. F f. Algonquian, lit. = 'eaters of raw flesh']

ESN *abbr.* educationally subnormal.

esoteric /iːsəʊˈterɪk/ *adj.* intelligible only to those with special knowledge. [f. Gk (compar. of *esō* within)]

ESP *abbr.* extra-sensory perception.

espadrille /espəˈdrɪl/ *n.* a light canvas shoe with a plaited fibre sole. [F f. Prov. (as ESPARTO)]

espalier /ɪˈspælɪə(r)/ *n.* a lattice-work along which the branches of a tree or shrub are trained; a tree or shrub so trained. [F f. It. (*spalla* shoulder)]

esparto /eˈspɑːtəʊ/ *n.* a coarse grass (*Stipa tenacissima*) of Spain and North Africa, used in paper-making. [Sp. f. L f. Gk *sparton* rope]

especial /ɪˈspeʃ(ə)l/ *adj.* special, exceptional. [f. OF f. L (as SPECIAL)]

especially *adv.* particularly, more than in other cases. [f. prec.]

Esperanto /espəˈræntəʊ/ *n.* an artificial language designed as a medium of communication for persons of all languages. [pen-name (f. L *sperare* hope) of its inventor]

espionage /ˈespɪənɑːʒ/ *n.* spying, the use of spies. [F (*espion* spy)]

esplanade /espləˈneɪd/ *n.* a level open area, especially for walking on or separating a fortress from a town. [F f. Sp. f. L *explanare* make level]

espousal /ɪˈspaʊz(ə)l/ *n.* **1** the espousing of a

cause. **2** (often in *pl.*) betrothal, marriage. [f. OF f. L *sponsalia* (as foll.)]

espouse /ɪˈspaʊz/ *v.t.* **1** to adopt or support (a cause). **2** to marry; to give (a woman) in marriage. [f. OF f. L *sponsare* (*spondēre* betroth)]

espresso /eˈspresəʊ/ *n.* (*pl.* **-os**) strong concentrated coffee made under steam pressure; a machine for making this. [It., = pressed out]

esprit /ˈespriː/ *n.* sprightliness; wit. —***esprit de corps*** /də ˈkɔː(r)/ devotion and loyalty to a body by its members. [F, = SPIRIT]

espy /ɪˈspaɪ/ *v.t.* to catch sight of. [f. OF (as SPY)]

Esq. *abbr.* esquire.

-esque /-esk/ *suffix* forming adjectives in the sense 'after the style of' (*romanesque*). [F f. It. f. L *-iscus*]

esquire /ɪˈskwaɪə(r)/ *n.* **1** a title added to a man's surname when no other title is used, especially as a form of address in letters. **2** (*archaic*) a squire. [f. OF f. L *scutarius* shield-bearer (*scutum* shield)]

-ess /-ɪs/ *suffix* forming nouns denoting females (*actress, goddess*). [f. F, ult. f. Gk *-issa*]

essay /ˈeseɪ/ *n.* a short prose composition on a subject; an attempt. —/eˈseɪ/ *v.t.* to attempt. [f. F f. L *exagium* weighing; = ASSAY]

essayist /ˈeseɪɪst/ *n.* a writer of essays. [f. prec.]

essence /ˈes(ə)ns/ *n.* **1** all that makes a thing what it is; an indispensable quality or element. **2** an extract got by distillation etc.; a perfume, a scent. —**in essence,** fundamentally. **of the essence,** indispensable. [f. OF f. L *essentia* (*esse* be)]

essential /ɪˈsenʃ(ə)l/ *adj.* necessary, indispensable; of or constituting a thing's essence. —*n.* an indispensable or fundamental element or thing. —**essential oil,** a volatile oil with an odour characteristic of the plant from which it is extracted. —**essentiality** /-ʃɪˈælɪtɪ/ *n.*, **essentially** *adv.* [f. L (as ESSENCE)]

establish /ɪˈstæblɪʃ/ *v.t.* **1** to set up (a system, business, etc.) on a permanent basis; to settle (a person etc. *in* an office etc.). **2** to cause to be generally accepted, to prove, to place beyond dispute. —**Established Church,** the Church recognized by the State. [f. OF f. L *stabilire* make stable]

establishment *n.* **1** establishing, being established. **2** an organized body permanently maintained (e.g. the army, navy, Civil Service). **3** a business firm or public institution. **4** a household, a staff of servants etc. **5** a church system established by law. —**the Establishment,** people established in positions of power and authority, exercising influence in public life or other activity and thought of as a group generally resisting changes. [f. prec.]

estate /ɪˈsteɪt/ *n.* **1** landed property. **2** a residential or industrial area with an integrated design or purpose. **3** a person's assets and liabilities, especially at death. **4** a property where rubber, tea, grapes, etc., are cultivated. **5** a class forming part of the body politic and sharing in government. **6** (*archaic*) state, condition. —**estate agent,** one whose business is the sale or lease of houses and land, the steward of an estate. **estate car,** a motor car with the interior extended at the rear to accommodate passengers and goods. **the Three Estates (of the Realm),** (in England) the Lords Spiritual, Lords Temporal, and the commons. [f. OF f. L *status*]

esteem /ɪˈstiːm/ *v.t.* to have a high regard for, to think favourably of; to consider to be. —*n.* high regard or favour. [f. OF f. L (as ESTIMATE)]

ester /ˈestə(r)/ *n.* a chemical compound formed by the interaction of an acid and an alcohol. [G, prob. f. *essig* vinegar + = *äther* ether]

estimable /ˈestɪməb(ə)l/ *adj.* worthy of esteem. [F, f. L (as foll.)]

estimate /ˈestɪmət/ *n.* an approximate judgement of number, amount, quality, character, etc.; a price quoted for work etc. to be undertaken. —/-eɪt/ *v.t.* **1** to form an estimate or opinion of; to form an estimate *that.* **2** to fix by estimate (*at*). —**estimator** *n.* [f. L *aestimare* fix price of]

estimation /estɪˈmeɪʃ(ə)n/ *n.* estimating; a judgement of worth. [f. OF or L (as prec.)]

estoile /eˈstɔɪl/ *n.* (in heraldry) a charge in the form of a star with wavy points or rays. [OF, = star]

estrange /ɪˈstreɪndʒ/ *v.t.* to cause (a person) to turn away in feeling or affection (*from* another). —**estrangement** *n.* [f. AF f. L *extraneare* treat as a stranger (as STRANGE)]

estuary /ˈestjʊərɪ/ *n.* the wide tidal mouth of a river. [f. L *aestuarium* tidal channel (*aestus* tide)]

ETA *abbr.* **1** estimated time of arrival. **2** /ˈetə/ a Basque separatist movement [Basque abbr.].

eta /ˈiːtə/ *n.* the seventh letter of the Greek alphabet, = ē. [Gk]

et al. *abbr.* and others. [f. L *et alii*, etc.]

etc. *abbr.* et cetera.

et cetera /et ˈsetərə/ and the rest, and so on. —**etceteras** *n.pl.* extras, sundries. [L]

etch *v.t./i.* **1** to reproduce (a picture etc.) by engraving a metal plate with acid, especially to print copies; to engrave (a plate) with acid; to practise this craft (see foll.). **2** (*fig.*) to impress deeply (*on*). [f. Du. f. G f. OHG *azzen* cause to eat]

etching *n.* a print made from an etched plate; the art of producing etched prints. [f. prec.]

ETD *abbr.* estimated time of departure.

eternal /ɪˈtɜ:n(ə)l/ *adj.* existing always, without end or (usually) beginning; unchanging; constant, too frequent. —**the Eternal,** God. —**eternally** *adv.* [f. L *aeternus* (*aevum* age)]

eternity /ɪˈtɜ:nɪtɪ/ *n.* infinite (esp. future) time; endless life after death; being eternal; (*colloq.*) a very long time. —**eternity ring,** a finger-ring with gems set all round it. [f. OF f. L (as prec.)]

ethane /ˈeθeɪn, ˈi:θ-/ *n.* a hydrocarbon gas of the paraffin series. [as ETHER]

ether /ˈi:θə(r)/ *n.* **1** a volatile liquid produced by the action of acids on alcohol, used as a solvent or anaesthetic. **2** clear sky, the upper air. **3** the medium formerly assumed to permeate space and transmit electromagnetic radiation. [f. OF or L f. Gk *aithēr* (*aithō* burn, shine)]

ethereal /ɪˈθɪərɪəl/ *adj.* light, airy; delicate, especially in appearance; heavenly. —**ethereally** *adv.* [f. L f. Gk (as prec.)]

ethic /ˈeθɪk/ *n.* a set of moral principles. —*adj.* ethical. [f. OF or L f. Gk (as ETHOS)]

ethical *adj.* **1** relating to morals, especially as concerning human conduct. **2** morally correct. **3** (of a medicine or drug) not advertised to the general public and usually available only on a doctor's prescription. —**ethically** *adv.* [f. prec.]

ethics *n.* **1** the science of morals in human conduct. **2** (as *pl.*) moral principles or code. [f. ETHIC]

ethnic /ˈeθnɪk/ *adj.* **1** of a group of mankind distinguished from others by race or by having a common national or cultural tradition. **2** (of clothes etc.) resembling the peasant clothes of an ethnic group or primitive people. —**ethnical** *adj.*, **ethnically** *adv.* [f. L f. Gk (*ethnos* nation)]

ethnology /eθˈnɒlədʒɪ/ *n.* the comparative scientific study of human peoples. —**ethnological** /-əˈlɒdʒɪk(ə)l/ *adj.*, **ethnologist** *n.* [as prec. + -LOGY]

ethology /i:ˈθɒlədʒɪ/ *n.* **1** the science of character-formation. **2** the science of animal behaviour. —**ethologist** *n.* [f. Gk *ēthos* character, disposition + -LOGY]

ethos /ˈi:θɒs/ *n.* the characteristic spirit or attitudes of a community etc. [Gk, = character, disposition]

ethyl /ˈeθɪl/ *n.* a radical derived from ethane, present in alcohol and ether. [G (as ETHER)]

ethylene /ˈeθɪli:n/ *n.* a hydrocarbon of the olefin series. [f. prec.]

etiolate /ˈi:tɪəleɪt/ *v.t.* to make (a plant) pale by excluding light; to give a sickly hue to (a person). —**etiolation** /-ˈleɪʃ(ə)n/ *n.* [f. F f. Norman *étieuler* make into haulm f. L *stipula* straw]

etiquette /ˈetɪket/ *n.* conventional rules of social behaviour or professional conduct. [F, = ticket]

Etruscan /ɪˈtrʌskən/ *adj.* of ancient Etruria (see below) or its people or language. —*n.* **1** a native of ancient Etruria. **2** its language in Italy. [f. L *Etruscus*]

et seq. *abbr.* (also ***et seqq.***) and the following (page(s), matter, etc.). [f. L *et sequentia*]

-ette /-et/ *suffix* forming nouns denoting smallness (*kitchenette*), imitation or substitution (*flannelette*), or female status (*suffragette*). [f. F]

étude /eɪˈtju:d/ *n.* a short musical composition (usually for one instrument). [F, = study]

etymology /etɪˈmɒlədʒɪ/ *n.* **1** the origin and development of a word's form and its meaning; an account of this. **2** the study of the origin of words. —**etymological** /-ˈlɒdʒɪk(ə)l/ *adj.*, **etymologist** *n.* [f. OF f. L f. Gk (*etumon* original form of word)]

Eu *symbol* europium.

eu- *prefix* well, easily. [Gk]

eucalyptus /ju:kəˈlɪptəs/ *n.* **1** (also **eucalypt**) a tall evergreen tree of the genus *Eucalyptus*. **2** an oil obtained from it used as an antiseptic etc. [f. EU- + Gk *kaluptos* covered (the unopened flower being protected by a cap)]

Eucharist /ˈju:kərɪst/ *n.* **1** a Christian sacrament in which bread and wine are consecrated and consumed. **2** the consecrated elements, especially the bread. —**Eucharistic** /-ˈrɪstɪk/ *adj.* [f. OF f. L f. Gk, = thanksgiving]

euchre /ˈju:kə(r)/ *n.* an American card-game for 2, 3, or 4 persons, played with a pack of 32 cards. [orig. unkn.]

eugenics /ju:ˈdʒenɪks/ *n.* the science of the production of fine (esp. human) offspring by control of inherited qualities. —**eugenic** *adj.*, **eugenically** *adv.* [f. EU- + Gk *gen-* give birth to]

eulogize /ˈju:lədʒaɪz/ *v.t.* to extol, to praise. [f. foll.]

eulogy /ˈju:lədʒɪ/ *n.* a speech or writing in praise of a person; an expression of praise. —**eulogistic** /-ˈdʒɪstɪk/ *adj.* [f. L f. Gk *eulogia* praise (as EU-, -LOGY)]

eunuch /ˈju:nək/ *n.* a castrated man, especially one formerly employed in a harem or as a court official especially in the Orient or under the Roman Empire. [f. L f. Gk, = bedchamber attendant]

euphemism /ˈju:fɪmɪz(ə)m/ *n.* the use of a mild or indirect expression instead of a blunt or direct one; such an expression. —**euphemistic** /-ˈmɪstɪk/ *adj.*, **euphemistically** *adv.* [f. Gk (EU-, *phēmē* speaking)]

euphonium /ju:ˈfəʊnɪəm/ *n.* a tenor tuba. [as foll.]

euphony /ˈju:fənɪ/ *n.* pleasantness of sounds, especially of words; a pleasing sound. —**euphonious** /-ˈfəʊnɪəs/ *adj.* [f. F f. L f. Gk (EU-, *phōnē* sound)]

euphoria /ju:ˈfɔ:rɪə/ *n.* a feeling of well-being or elation. —**euphoric** /-ˈfɒrɪk/ *adj.* [f. Gk *euphoros* (EU-, *pherō* bear)]

euphuism /ˈju:fju:ɪz(ə)m/ *n.* an affected or high-flown style of writing. —**euphuistic** /-ˈɪstɪk/ *adj.*, **euphuistically** *adv.* [orig. of writing in imitation of Lyly's *Euphues* (16th c.)]

Eurasian /jʊəˈreɪʒ(ə)n/ *adj.* **1** of mixed European and Asian parentage. **2** of Europe and Asia. —*n.* a Eurasian person. [f. EUROPEAN + ASIAN]

Euratom /jʊərˈætəm/ *n.* the European Atomic Energy Community. [abbr.]

eureka /jʊəˈri:kə/ *int.* (announcing a discovery etc.) I have found it. [Gk *heurēka* (*heuriskō* find); attributed to Archimedes]

eurhythmics /ju:ˈrɪðmɪks/ *n. pl.* harmony of bodily movement, especially as developed with music and dance into a system of education. [f. EU- + Gk *rhuthmos* proportion, rhythm]

Euro- /jʊərəʊ/ *in comb.* Europe, European.

Eurocommunism *n.* Communism in the countries of Western Europe, independent of Soviet influence.

Eurocrat /ˈjʊərəʊkræt/ *n.* a bureaucrat of the European Communities. [f. EURO- + -CRAT]

Eurodollar *n.* a dollar held in a bank in Europe etc.

European /jʊərəˈpi:ən/ *adj.* **1** of the continent of Europe. **2** of the European (Economic) Community. —*n.* **1** a native or inhabitant of Europe; a descendant of such persons. **3** one who is concerned with European matters. [f. F f. L f. Gk]

europium /jʊəˈrəʊpɪəm/ *n.* a soft metallic element of the lanthanide series, symbol Eu, atomic number 63. [as prec.]

Eustachian tube /ju:ˈsteɪʃɪən/ the narrow passage from the pharynx to the cavity of the middle ear. [f. B. *Eustachi* It. anatomist (d. 1574)]

euthanasia /ju:θəˈneɪzɪə/ *n.* the bringing about of a gentle and easy death in the case of incurable and painful disease; such a death. [Gk (as EU-, *thanatos* death)]

eV *abbr.* electron-volt(s).

evacuate /ɪˈvækjʊeɪt/ *v.t.* **1** to send (people) away from a place of danger; to empty (a place) thus; to withdraw from. **2** to make empty; to empty the contents of. —**evacuation** /-ˈeɪʃ(ə)n/ *n.* [f. L *evacuare* (EX-[1], *vacuus* empty)]

evacuee /ɪvækju:ˈi:/ *n.* a person sent away from a place of danger. [f. prec.]

evade /ɪˈveɪd/ *v.t.* to avoid or escape from, especially by guile or trickery; to avoid doing or answering directly. [f. F f. L (EX-[1], *vadere* go)]

evaluate /ɪˈvæljʊeɪt/ *v.t.* to find or state the number or amount of; to appraise, to assess. —**evaluation** /-ˈeɪʃ(ə)n/ *n.* [f. F (as EX-[1], VALUE)]

evanesce /i:vəˈnes, e-/ *v.i.* to fade from sight, to disappear. [f. L *evanescere* (EX-[1], *vanus* empty)]

evanescent *adj.* (of an impression etc.) quickly fading. —**evanescence** *n.* [f. prec.]

evangelical /i:vænˈdʒelɪk(ə)l/ *adj.* **1** of the Protestant Churches, as basing their claim pre-eminently on the gospel. **2** (formerly, in Germany and Switzerland) the Lutheran Churches as contrasted with the Calvinist (Reformed) Churches. **3** (in the Church of England) of the school (originating in the 18th c.) that lays special stress on personal conversion and salvation by faith in the Atonement. —**evangelicalism** *n.* [f. L f. Gk (as EVANGELIZE)]

evangelism /ɪˈvændʒəlɪz(ə)m/ *n.* preaching or promulgation of the gospel. [as prec.]

evangelist /ɪˈvændʒ(ə)lɪst/ *n.* **1** the writer of any one of the four Gospels. **2** a preacher of the gospel. —**evangelistic** /-ˈlɪstɪk/ *adj.* [f. OF f. L (as foll.)]

evangelize /ɪˈvændʒ(ə)laɪz/ *v.t.* to preach the gospel to; to convert to Christianity. —**evangelization** /-ˈzeɪʃ(ə)n/ *n.* [f. L f. Gk (*euaggelion* good news)]

evaporable /ɪˈvæpərəb(ə)l/ *adj.* able to be evaporated. [f. foll.]

evaporate /ɪˈvæpəreɪt/ *v.t./i.* **1** to turn into vapour; to lose or cause to lose moisture as vapour. **2** to become lost or disappear; to cause to do this. —**evaporated milk,** unsweetened milk concentrated by partial evaporation and tinned. —**evaporation** /-ˈreɪʃ(ə)n/ *n.* [f. L *evaporare* (EX-[1], as VAPOUR)]

evasion /ɪˈveɪʒ(ə)n/ *n.* **1** evading. **2** an evasive answer etc. [f. OF f. L (as EVADE)]

evasive /ɪˈveɪsɪv/ *adj.* seeking to evade; not direct in answer etc. —**evasively** *adv.*, **evasiveness** *n.* [as prec.]

eve /i:v/ *n.* the evening or day before a festival etc.; the time just before an event; (*archaic*) evening. [= EVEN[2]]

even[1] /ˈi:v(ə)n/ *adj.* **1** level, free from irregularities, smooth. **2** uniform in quality, constant. **3** equal in amount, value, etc.; equally balanced. **4** in the same plane or line (with). **5** equable, calm. **6** (of a number such as 4 or 6) integrally divisible by 2; bearing such a number; not involving fractions. —*v.t./i.* (often with *up*) to make or become even or equal. —*adv.* (*a*) inviting comparison of the negation, assertion, etc., with an implied one that is less strong or remarkable; (*b*) introducing an extreme case. —**be** *or* **get even with,** to have one's revenge on. **even chance,** an equal chance of success or failure. **even-handed** *adj*. impartial, fair. **even money, evens** *n.pl.* betting-odds offering a gambler the chance of winning the amount he staked. **even now,** now as well as previously, at this very moment. **even so,** despite some other consideration. —**evenly** *adv*., **evenness** *n*. [OE]

even[2] /ˈiːv(ə)n/ *n*. (*poetic*) evening. [OE]

evening /ˈiːvnɪŋ/ *n*. **1** the end of the day, especially from about 6 p.m. (or earlier sunset) to bedtime. **2** the decline or last period (of life etc.). —**evening dress,** formal dress for evening wear. **evening primrose,** a plant of the genus *Oenothera*, with yellow flowers that open in the evening. **evening star,** a planet, especially Venus, when seen in the west after sunset. [OE]

evensong *n*. the service of evening prayer in the Church of England. [f. EVEN² + SONG]

event /ɪˈvent/ *n*. a thing that happens or takes place, especially one of importance; the fact of a thing occurring; an item in an (especially sports) programme. —**at all events, in any** *or* **either event,** whatever happens. **in the event,** as it turned out. **in the event of,** if (the specified event) occurs. **in the event that,** if. [f. L (*evenire* happen)]

eventful *adj*. marked by noteworthy events. —**eventfully** *adv*. [f. prec.]

eventide /ˈiːvəntaɪd/ *n*. (*archaic*) evening. [f. EVEN² + TIDE]

eventual /ɪˈventʃʊ(ə)l/ *adj*. occurring in due course or at last. —**eventually** *adv*. [as EVENT]

eventuality /ɪventʃʊˈælɪtɪ/ *n*. a possible event or result. [f. prec.]

eventuate /ɪˈventʃʊeɪt/ *v.i.* to result, to be the outcome. [as EVENT]

ever /ˈevə(r)/ *adv*. **1** at all times, always; at any time. **2** (as an emphatic word) in any way, at all. —**did you ever?,** (*colloq*.) did you ever hear or see the like? **ever since,** throughout the period since (then). **ever so,** (*colloq*.) very; very much. **ever such a,** (*colloq*.) a very. [OE]

evergreen *adj*. retaining its green leaves throughout the year. —*n*. an evergreen tree or shrub.

everlasting /evəˈlɑːstɪŋ/ *adj*. **1** lasting for ever; lasting a long time. **2** (of flowers) keeping their shape and colour when dried. —*n*. **1** eternity. **2** an everlasting flower, especially one of the genus *Helichrysum*. —**everlastingly** *adv*.

evermore /evəˈmɔː(r)/ *adv*. for ever, always.

every /ˈevrɪ/ *adj*. **1** each single. **2** each at a specified interval in a series. **3** all possible; the utmost degree of. —**every bit as,** (*colloq*.) quite as. **every now and then,** from time to time. **every one,** each one. **every other,** each second in a series. **every so often,** at intervals, occasionally. [OE, = ever each]

everybody *pron*. every person.

everyday *adj*. occurring or used every day; ordinary, commonplace.

Everyman /ˈevrɪmæn/ an ordinary or typical person. [name of leading character in 15th-c. morality play]

everyone *pron*. everybody.

everything *pron*. **1** all things. **2** the thing of chief importance.

everywhere *adv*. in every place; (*colloq*.) in many places.

evict /ɪˈvɪkt/ *v.t.* to expel (a tenant) by legal process. —**eviction** *n*. [f. L (EX-¹, *vincere* conquer)]

evidence /ˈevɪd(ə)ns/ *n*. **1** an indication, a sign, the facts available as proving or supporting a notion etc. **2** (*Law*) information given personally or drawn from a document etc. and tending to prove a fact; testimony admissible in court. —*v.t.* to indicate, to be evidence of. —**in evidence,** conspicuous. **turn King's** *or* **Queen's evidence,** said of an accused person who testifies for the prosecution against the person(s) associated with him in an alleged crime. [f. OF f. L (as foll.)]

evident *adj*. obvious, plain, manifest. —**evidently** *adv*. [f. OF or L (EX-¹, *vidēre* see)]

evidential /evɪˈdenʃ(ə)l/ *adj*. of or providing evidence. [f. EVIDENCE]

evil /ˈiːv(ə)l, -ɪl/ *adj*. morally bad, wicked; harmful, tending to harm; disagreeable. —*n*. an evil thing; wickedness. —**evil eye,** a malicious look superstitiously believed to do material harm. —**evilly** *adv*. [OE]

evildoer *n*. a sinner. —**evildoing** *n*.

evince /ɪˈvɪns/ *v.t.* to indicate or exhibit (a quality). [f. L (as EVICT)]

eviscerate /ɪˈvɪsəreɪt/ *v.t.* to disembowel. —**evisceration** /-ˈreɪʃ(ə)n/ *n*. [f. L *eviscerare* (EX-¹, *viscera* bowels)]

evocative /ɪˈvɒkətɪv/ *adj*. tending to evoke (esp. feelings or memories). [f. foll.]

evoke /ɪˈvəʊk/ *v.t.* to inspire or draw forth (memories, a response, etc.). —**evocation** /evəˈkeɪʃ(ə)n/ *n*. [f. L *evocare* (EX-¹, *vocare* call)]

evolute /ˈiːvəljuːt, -luːt/ *n*. the locus of the centres of curvature of another curve that is its involute. [f. L (as EVOLVE)]

evolution /iːvəˈluːʃ(ə)n/ *n*. **1** evolving. **2** the origination of species by development from earlier forms, not by special creation; the gradual development of a phenomenon, organism, etc. **3** a change in the disposition of troops or ships. —**evolutionary** *adj.* [f. L, = unrolling (as EVOLVE)]

evolutionist *n.* one who upholds the theory that species developed by evolution rather than by special creation. [f. prec.]

evolve /ɪ'vɒlv/ *v.t./i.* **1** to develop gradually by a natural process; **2** to work out or devise (a theory, plan, etc.). **3** to unfold, to open out. **4** to give off (gas, heat, etc.). [f. L (EX-[1], *volvere* roll)]

ewe /ju:/ *n.* a female sheep. [OE]

ewer /'ju:ə(r)/ *n.* a water-jug with a wide mouth. [f. OF f. L *aqua* water]

ex[1] *prep.* **1** (of goods) sold from. **2** outside, without, exclusive of. —**ex dividend,** (of stocks and shares) not including the next dividend. [L, = out of]

ex[2] *n.* (*colloq.*) a former husband or wife. [f. EX-[1]]

ex-[1] *prefix* (**ef-** before f; **e-** before some consonants) forming (1) verbs in the sense 'out', 'forth' (*exclude, exit*), 'upward' (*extol*), 'thoroughly' (*excruciate*), 'bring into a state' (*exasperate*), (2) nouns from the titles of office, status, etc., in the sense 'formerly' (*ex-convict*). [f. L *ex* out of]

ex-[2] *prefix* = 'out' (*exodus*). [f. Gk]

exa- *in comb.* denoting a factor of 10^{18}. [perh. f. HEXA-]

exacerbate /ek'sæsəbeɪt/ *v.t.* to make (pain, anger, etc.) worse; to irritate. —**exacerbation** /-'beɪʃ(ə)n/ *n.* [f. L *exacerbare* (EX-[1], *acerbus* bitter)]

exact /ɪg'zækt/ *adj.* accurate, correct in all details; precise, (of a person) tending to precision. —*v.t.* to demand and enforce payment etc. of; to demand, to require urgently, to insist on. —**exact science,** one in which absolute precision is possible. —**exactness** *n.*, **exactor** *n.* [f. L *exigere* (EX-[1], *agere* drive)]

exacting *adj.* making great demands, calling for much effort. [f. prec.]

exaction /ɪg'zækʃ(ə)n/ *n.* **1** exacting (*of* money etc.). **2** the thing exacted. **3** an illegal or exorbitant demand, extortion. [f. EXACT]

exactitude /ɪg'zæktɪtju:d/ *n.* exactness, precision. [as prec.]

exactly *adv.* **1** accurately, precisely. **2** (said in reply) I quite agree. [f. EXACT]

exaggerate /ɪg'zædʒəreɪt/ *v.t.* to make (a thing, or *absol.*) seem larger or greater than it really is, in speech or writing; to enlarge or alter beyond normal or due proportions. —**exaggeration** /-'reɪʃ(ə)n/ *n.* [f. L *exaggerare* heap up (EX-[1], *agger* heap)]

exalt /ɪg'zɔ:lt/ *v.t.* **1** to raise in rank or power etc. **2** to praise highly. **3** to dignify, to ennoble. —**exaltation** /-'teɪʃ(ə)n/ *n.* [f. L *exaltare* (EX-[1], *altus* high)]

exam /ɪg'zæm/ *n.* (*colloq.*) an examination. [abbr.]

examination /ɪgzæmɪ'neɪʃ(ə)n/ *n.* examining, being examined; the testing of proficiency or knowledge by oral or written questions; the formal questioning of a witness etc. in a lawcourt. [f. OF f. L (as foll.)]

examine /ɪg'zæmɪn/ *v.t.* **1** to inquire into the nature or condition etc. of. **2** to look closely at. **3** to test the proficiency of by a series of questions or exercises. **4** to question formally. —**examiner** *n.* [f. OF f. L *examinare* (*examen* tongue of balance)]

examinee /ɪgzæmɪ'ni:/ *n.* one who is being examined, especially in a test of proficiency. [f. prec.]

example /ɪg'zɑ:mp(ə)l/ *n.* **1** a thing characteristic of its kind or illustrating a general rule; a problem or exercise designed to do this. **2** a person or thing or conduct worthy of imitation. **3** a fact or thing seen as a warning to others. —**for example,** by way of illustration. [f. OF f. L *exemplum*]

exasperate /ɪg'zæspəreɪt, -'zɑ:s-/ *v.t.* to irritate intensely. —**exasperation** /-'reɪʃ(ə)n/ *n.* [f. L *exasperare* (EX-[1], *asper* rough)]

ex cathedra /eks kə'θi:drə/ with full authority (esp. of a papal pronouncement). [L, = from the chair]

excavate /'ekskəveɪt/ *v.t.* to make (a hole or channel) by digging, to dig out (soil); to reveal or extract by digging. —**excavation** /-'veɪʃ(ə)n/ *n.*, **excavator** *n.* [f. L *excavare* (EX-[1], *cavus* hollow)]

exceed /ɪk'si:d/ *v.t.* **1** to be more or greater than, to surpass. **2** to go beyond (a limit etc.); to do more than is warranted by (instructions etc.). [f. OF f. L *excedere* go beyond]

exceedingly *adv.* very, extremely. [f. prec.]

excel /ɪk'sel/ *v.t./i.* (**-ll-**) to be superior to; to be pre-eminent. [f. L *excellere*; cf. *celsus* lofty]

excellence /'eksələns/ *n.* great worth or quality. [f. OF or L (as prec.)]

Excellency *n.* **His, Her, Your,** etc., **Excellency,** a title used in addressing or referring to certain high officials. [f. L (as EXCEL)]

excellent *adj.* extremely good. —**excellently** *adv.* [f. OF (as EXCEL)]

excentric var. (in technical senses) of ECCENTRIC.

except /ɪk'sept/ *v.t.* to exclude from a general statement or condition etc. —*prep.* not including, other than. —*conj.* (*archaic*) unless. [f. L *excipere* take out]

excepting *prep.* except. [f. prec.]

exception /ɪk'sepʃ(ə)n/ *n.* **1** excepting. **2** a thing or case excepted or apart, especially a thing not following a general rule. —**take exception,** to object (*to*). **with the exception of,** except. [f. OF f. L (as EXCEPT)]

exceptionable *adj*. open to objection. [f. prec.]

exceptional *adj*. forming an exception, unusual; outstanding. —**exceptionally** *adv*. [f. EXCEPT]

excerpt /ˈeksɜːpt/ *n*. a short extract from a book, film, etc. —/ɪkˈsɜːpt/ *v.t*. to take excerpts from. —**excerption** /-ˈsɜːpʃ(ə)n/ *n*. [f. L *excerpere* (EX-¹, *carpere* pluck)]

excess /ɪkˈses/ *n*. **1** the exceeding of due limits; (usu. in *pl*.) immoderate or outrageous behaviour. **2** the amount by which one number or quantity exceeds another. **3** an agreed amount subtracted by an insurer from the total payment to be made to an insured person who makes a claim. —/ˈekses/ *adj*. that exceeds a limit or given amount; required as an excess. —**excess baggage**, that exceeding the weight-allowance and liable to an extra charge. **in excess of**, more than. [f. OF f. L (as EXCEED)]

excessive /ɪkˈsesɪv/ *adj*. too much, too great, more than what is normal or necessary. —**excessively** *adv*. [f. prec.]

exchange /ɪksˈtʃeɪndʒ/ *n*. **1** the act or process of giving one thing and receiving another in its place; the giving of money for its equivalent in money of the same or another country. **2** the central telephone office of a district, where connections are effected. **3** the place where merchants, brokers, etc., gather to transact business. **4** an office where certain information is given. **5** a system of settling debts between persons (especially in different countries) without the use of money, by bills of exchange (see BILL¹). —*v.t./i*. to give or receive (a thing) in place of (or *for*) another; to give one and receive another of (things or persons); to make an exchange *with* someone else. —**exchange rate**, the value of one currency in terms of another. **in exchange**, as a thing exchanged (*for*). [f. OF (as EX-¹, CHANGE)]

exchangeable *adj*. able to be exchanged. [f. prec.]

exchequer /ɪksˈtʃekə(r)/ *n*. **1 Exchequer**, the former government department dealing with national revenue; a royal or national treasury. **2** one's private funds. [f. OF f. L *scaccarium* chess-board, w. ref. to former keeping of accounts on chequered table-cloth]

excise¹ /ˈeksaɪz/ *n*. duty or tax levied on goods produced or sold within a country, and on various licences etc. —*v.t*. to charge excise on; to make (a person) pay excise. [f. MDu. (as CENSUS)]

excise² /ɪkˈsaɪz/ *v.t*. to remove by cutting out or away (a passage from a book, tissue from the body, etc.). —**excision** /-ˈsɪʒ(ə)n/ *n*. [f. L *excidere* (EX-¹, *caedere* cut)]

excitable /ɪkˈsaɪtəb(ə)l/ *adj*. (esp. of a person) easily excited. —**excitability** /-ˈbɪlɪtɪ/ *n*. [f. foll.]

excite /ɪkˈsaɪt/ *v.t*. to rouse the feelings or emotion of (a person); to bring into play, to rouse up (feelings etc.); to provoke or bring about (an action etc.); to stimulate (a bodily organ etc.) to activity. [f. OF or L *excitare*, frequent. of *exciēre* set in motion]

excitement *n*. **1** a thing that excites. **2** an excited state of mind. [f. prec.]

exciting *adj*. arousing great interest or enthusiasm. —**excitingly** *adv*. [f. EXCITE]

exclaim /ɪkˈskleɪm/ *v.t./i*. to cry out, especially in anger, surprise, pain, etc.; to utter or say in this manner. [f. F or L *exclamare* (EX-¹, *clamare* shout)]

exclamation /ekskləˈmeɪʃ(ə)n/ *n*. **1** exclaiming. **2** a word or words etc. exclaimed. —**exclamation mark**, the punctuation mark (!) placed after and indicating an exclamation. [f. OF or L (as prec.)]

exclamatory /ɪkˈsklæmətərɪ/ *adj*. of or serving as an exclamation. [as prec.]

exclude /ɪkˈskluːd/ *v.t*. **1** to shut or keep out from a place, group, or privilege etc. **2** to remove from consideration. **3** to make impossible, to preclude. —**exclusion** *n*. [f. L *excludere* (EX-¹, *claudere* shut)]

exclusive /ɪksˈkluːsɪv/ *adj*. excluding, not inclusive; excluding all others; tending to exclude others, esp. socially; (of shops or goods) high-class, catering for the wealthy; (of goods for sale, a newspaper article, etc.) not available or appearing elsewhere. —**exclusive of**, not counting. —**exclusively** *adv*., **exclusiveness** *n*., **exclusivity** /-ˈsɪvɪtɪ/ *n*. [as prec.]

excommunicate /ekskəˈmjuːnɪkeɪt/ *v.t*. to deprive (a person) of membership and especially the sacraments of the Church. —/-ət/ *adj*. excommunicated. —/-ət/ *n*. an excommunicated person. —**excommunication** /-ˈkeɪʃ(ə)n/ *n*. [f. L *excommunicare* put out of the community (EX-¹, *communis* common)]

excoriate /eksˈkɔːrɪeɪt/ *v.t*. **1** to remove part of the skin of (a person etc.), as by abrasion; to strip off (skin). **2** to censure severely. —**excoriation** /-ˈeɪʃ(ə)n/ *n*. [f. L *excoriare* (EX-¹, *corium* hide)]

excrement /ˈekskrɪmənt/ *n*. faeces. —**excremental** /-ˈment(ə)l/ *adj*. [f. F or L (as EXCRETE)]

excrescence /ɪkˈskresəns/ *n*. an abnormal or morbid outgrowth on a body or plant; an ugly addition. —**excrescent** *adj*. [f. L (EX-¹, *crescere* grow)]

excreta /ekˈskriːtə/ *n.pl*. faeces and urine. [L (as foll.)]

excrete /ɪkˈskriːt/ *v.t*. to expel from the body as waste. —**excretion** *n*., **excretory** *adj*. [f. L (EX-¹, *cernere* sift)]

excruciating /ɪk'skru:ʃɪeɪtɪŋ/ *adj.* acutely painful; (*colloq.*) (of humour etc.) shocking, poor. [f. L *excruciare* torment (EX-[1], *crux* cross)]

exculpate /'ekskʌlpeɪt/ *v.t.* to free from blame; to clear (a person *from* a charge). —**exculpation** /-'peɪʃ(ə)n/ *n.*, **exculpatory** /-'kʌlpətərɪ/ *adj.* [f. L *exculpare* (EX-[1], *culpa* blame)]

excursion /ɪk'skɜ:ʃ(ə)n/ *n.* a short journey or ramble for pleasure and returning to the starting-point. [f. L (EX-[1], *currere* run)]

excursive *adj.* digressive. [as prec.]

excusable *adj.* that may be excused. [f. foll.]

excuse /ɪk'skju:z/ *v.t.* **1** to try to lessen the blame attaching to (an act or fault or the person committing it); (of a fact or circumstance) to mitigate or justify thus; to overlook or forgive (a person or offence). **2** to release from an obligation or duty; to gain exemption for. **3** to allow to leave. —/ɪk'skju:s/ *n.* a reason put forward to mitigate or justify an offence; an apology. —**excuse me,** a polite apology for interrupting or disagreeing etc. **excuse oneself,** to ask permission or apologize for leaving. [f. OF f. L *excusare* (EX-[1], *causa* accusation)]

ex-directory *adj.* (of a telephone number) omitted from the directory at the subscriber's request.

exeat /'eksɪæt/ *n.* leave of absence from college etc. [L, = let him go out]

execrable /'eksɪkrəb(ə)l/ *adj.* abominable. —**execrably** *adv.* [f. OF f. L (as foll.)]

execrate /'eksɪkreɪt/ *v.t./i.* to express loathing for, to detest; to utter curses. —**execration** /-'kreɪʃ(ə)n/ *n.* [f. L *ex(s)ecrari* (EX-[1], *sacrare* devote f. *sacer* sacred, accursed)]

executant /ɪg'zekjʊt(ə)nt/ *n.* a performer, especially of music. [f. F (as foll.)]

execute /'eksɪkju:t/ *v.t.* **1** to carry into effect, to perform (a plan, duty, etc.). **2** to produce (a work of art). **3** to inflict capital punishment on. **4** to make (a legal document) valid by signing, sealing, etc. [f. OF f. L *executare* (EX-[1], *sequi* follow)]

execution /eksɪ'kju:ʃ(ə)n/ *n.* **1** carrying out, performance. **2** an infliction of capital punishment. **3** skill in or manner of a performance. [f. OF f. L (as prec.)]

executioner *n.* one who carries out a death sentence. [f. prec.]

executive /ɪg'zekjʊtɪv/ *adj.* concerned with executing laws, agreements, etc., or with other administration or management. —*n.* a person or body having executive authority or in an executive position in a business organization etc.; the executive branch of government etc. [f. L (as EXECUTE)]

executor /ɪg'zekjʊtə(r)/ *n.* a person appointed by a testator to carry out the terms of a will. —**executorial** /-'tɔ:rɪəl/ *adj.*, **executrix** *n.fem.* [f. AF f. L (as EXECUTE)]

exegesis /eksɪ'dʒi:sɪs/ *n.* (*pl.* **exegeses** /-si:z/) an explanation, especially of a passage of Scripture. —**exegetic** /-'dʒetɪk/ *adj.* [f. Gk, f. *exēgeomai* interpret]

exemplar /ɪg'zemplə(r)/ *n.* a model, a type; an instance. [f. OF f. L (as EXAMPLE)]

exemplary /ɪg'zemplərɪ/ *adj.* **1** fit to be imitated, very good. **2** serving as an example or as a warning. [f. L (as EXAMPLE)]

exemplify /ɪg'zemplɪfaɪ/ *v.t.* to give or serve as an example of. —**exemplification** /-'keɪʃ(ə)n/ *n.* [f. L (as EXAMPLE)]

exempt /ɪg'zempt/ *adj.* freed (*from* an obligation or liability etc. imposed on others). —*v.t.* to make exempt (*from*). —**exemption** *n.* [f. L (*eximere* take out)]

exequies /'eksɪkwɪz/ *n. pl.* funeral rites. [f. OF f. L *exsequiae* (as EXECUTE)]

exercise /'eksəsaɪz/ *n.* **1** activity requiring physical effort, done to improve the health; (often in *pl.*) a particular bodily task devised for this. **2** the use or application (of a mental faculty, right, etc.); the practice (of a virtue or function etc.). **3** (often in *pl.*) military drill or manœuvres. —*v.t.* **1** to use or apply (a mental faculty, right, etc.); to practise (a virtue or function etc.). **2** to take or cause to take exercise; to give exercise to. **3** to perplex, to worry. [f. OF f. L (*exercēre* keep at work)]

exert /ɪg'zɜ:t/ *v.t.* to bring into use, to bring (influence, pressure, etc.) to bear. —**exert oneself,** to use efforts or endeavours. —**exertion** *n.* [f. L *exserere* put forth]

exeunt /'eksɪʊnt/ *v.i.* (as a stage direction) they leave the stage. ***exeunt omnes*** /'ɒmni:z/, all go off. [L (as EXIT[2])]

exfoliate /eks'fəʊlɪeɪt/ *v.i.* to come off in scales or layers; (of a tree) to throw off bark thus. —**exfoliation** /-'eɪʃ(ə)n/ *n.* [f. L *exfoliare* (EX-[1], *folium* leaf)]

ex gratia /eks 'greɪʃə/ done or given as a concession, not from an (especially legal) obligation. [L, = from kindness]

exhale /eks'heɪl/ *v.t./i.* to breathe out; to give off or be given off in a vapour. —**exhalation** /-hə'leɪʃ(ə)n/ *n.* [f. OF f. L *exhalare* (EX-[1], *halare* breathe)]

exhaust /ɪg'zɔ:st/ *v.t.* **1** to consume or use up the whole of; to use up the strength or resources of, to tire out. **2** to empty (a vessel etc. *of* its contents); to draw off (air). **3** to study or expound on (a subject) completely. —*n.* **1** the expulsion or exit of steam or waste gases from an engine etc.; such gases etc. **2** the pipe or system through which they are expelled. [f. L *exhaurire* drain]

exhaustible *adj.* liable to be exhausted. [f. prec.]

exhaustion /ɪɡˈzɔːstʃ(ə)n/ *n.* exhausting, being exhausted; complete loss of strength. [as EXHAUST]

exhaustive *adj.* that exhausts a subject; thorough, comprehensive. —**exhaustively** *adv.* [f. EXHAUST]

exhibit /ɪɡˈzɪbɪt/ *v.t.* to show or display, especially publicly; to manifest (a quality etc.). —*n.* a thing exhibited, especially in an exhibition or as evidence in a lawcourt. —**exhibitor** *n.* [f. L *exhibēre* (EX-¹, *habēre* hold)]

exhibition /eksɪˈbɪʃ(ə)n/ *n.* **1** exhibiting, being exhibited. **2** a public display of works of art etc. **3** a minor scholarship, especially from the funds of a school or college etc. [f. OF f. L (as prec.)]

exhibitioner *n.* a student receiving an exhibition. [f. prec.]

exhibitionism *n.* a tendency towards display or extravagant behaviour; a perverted mental condition characterized by indecent exposure of the genitals. —**exhibitionist** *n.* [f. EXHIBITION]

exhilarate /ɪɡˈzɪləreɪt/ *v.t.* to enliven or gladden. —**exhilaration** /-ˈreɪʃ(ə)n/ *n.* [f. L *exhilarare* (EX-¹, *hilaris* cheerful)]

exhort /ɪɡˈzɔːt/ *v.t.* to urge or admonish earnestly. —**exhortation** /egzɔːˈteɪʃ(ə)n/ *n.*, **exhortative** *adj.*, **exhortatory** *adj.* [f. L (EX-¹, *hortari* exhort)]

exhume /eksˈhjuːm/ *v.t.* to dig up or unearth (especially a buried corpse). —**exhumation** /-ˈmeɪʃ(ə)n/ *n.* [f. F f. L (EX-¹, *humare* bury)]

ex hypothesi /eks haɪˈpɒθəsɪ/ according to the hypothesis proposed. [L]

exigency /ˈeksɪdʒənsɪ/ *n.* (also **exigence**) an urgent need or demand; an emergency. —**exigent** *adj.* [f. F & L *exigere* (as EXACT)]

exiguous /egˈzɪɡjʊəs/ *adj.* scanty, small. —**exiguity** /-ˈɡjuːɪtɪ/ *n.*, **exiguousness** *n.* [f. L *exiguus* scanty (*exigere* weigh exactly)]

exile /ˈekzaɪl, eg-/ *n.* **1** being expelled from one's native country; a long absence abroad. **2** a person in exile. —*v.t.* to send into exile. —**the Exile,** the Captivity of the Jews in Babylon. [f. OF f. L *exilium* banishment]

exist /ɪɡˈzɪst/ *v.i.* **1** to have a place in reality. **2** (of circumstances etc.) to occur, to be found. **3** to live, to sustain life; to continue in being. [prob. back-formation f. foll. (cf. L *existere*)]

existence /ɪɡˈzɪst(ə)ns/ *n.* **1** the fact or a manner of existing or living; continuance in life or being. **2** all that exists. —**existent** *adj.* [f. OF or L *existentia* (EX-¹, *sistere* redupl. of *stare* stand)]

existential /egzɪˈstenʃ(ə)l/ *adj.* of or relating to existence; concerned with human experience as viewed by existentialism. —**existentially** *adv.* [f. L (as prec.)]

existentialism /egzɪˈstenʃ(ə)lɪz(ə)m/ *n.* a philosophical theory that emphasizes the existence of the individual, who, being free and responsible, is held to be what he makes himself by the self-development of his essence through acts of the will (which, in the Christian form of the theory, leads to God). —**existentialist** *n.* [f. G (as prec.)]

exit¹ /ˈeksɪt, ˈegz-/ *n.* **1** the act or right of going out. **2** a passage or door as the way out. **3** an actor's departure from the stage. —*v.i.* to make one's exit. [f. L *exitus* going out (as foll.)]

exit ² /ˈeksɪt, ˈegz-/ *v.i.* (as a stage direction) he or she leaves the stage. [L (*exire* go out)]

exo- *prefix* external(ly). [f. Gk *exō* outside]

exocrine /ˈeksəkraɪn, -krɪn/ *adj.* (of a gland) secreting through a duct. [f. EXO- + Gk *krinō* sift]

exodus /ˈeksədəs/ *n.* a mass departure, esp. (**Exodus**) that of the Israelites from Egypt. [L f. Gk, = way out]

ex officio /eks əˈfɪʃɪəʊ/ by virtue of one's office. —**ex-officio** *adj.* of a position held thus. [L]

exonerate /ɪɡˈzɒnəreɪt/ *v.t.* to free or declare free from blame. —**exoneration** /-ˈreɪʃ(ə)n/ *n.*, **exonerative** /ɪɡˈzɒnərətɪv/ *adj.* [f. L *exonerare* (EX-¹, *onus* burden)]

exorbitant /ɪɡˈzɔːbɪtənt/ *adj.* (of a price or demand etc.) grossly excessive. [f. L (as EX-¹, ORBIT)]

exorcise /ˈeksɔːsaɪz/ *v.t.* to drive out (an evil spirit) by invocation etc.; to free (a person or place) thus. —**exorcism** *n.*, **exorcist** *n.* [f. F or L f. Gk *exorkizō* (*horkos* oath)]

exordium /ekˈsɔːdɪəm/ *n.* (*pl.* **-iums**) the introductory part of a discourse or treatise. [L (EX-¹, *ordiri* begin)]

exotic /ɪɡˈzɒtɪk/ *adj.* introduced from abroad, not native; remarkably strange or unusual. —*n.* an exotic plant etc. —**exotically** *adv.* [f. L f. Gk (as EXO-)]

exotica /ɪɡˈzɒtɪkə/ *n.pl.* remarkably strange or rare objects. [L (as prec.)]

expand /ɪkˈspænd/ *v.t./i.* **1** to increase in size, bulk, or importance. **2** to unfold or spread out. **3** to express at length (condensed notes, an algebraic expression, etc.). **4** to be genial or effusive. —**expander** *n.* [f. L *expandere* spread]

expanse /ɪkˈspæns/ *n.* a wide area or extent of land, space, etc. [as prec.]

expansible /ɪkˈspænsɪb(ə)l/ *adj.* that can be expanded. —**expansibility** /-ˈbɪlɪtɪ/ *n.* [f. EXPAND]

expansion /ɪkˈspænʃ(ə)n/ *n.* expanding; an enlargement, an increase. [as prec.]

expansionism *n.* advocacy of expansion, especially in territory. —**expansionist** *n.* [f. prec.]

expansive /ɪkˈspænsɪv/ *adj.* **1** able or tending to expand. **2** extensive. **3** effusive, genial. —**expansively** *adv.*, **expansiveness** *n.* [as EXPAND]

expatiate /ɪkˈspeɪʃɪeɪt/ *v.i.* to speak or write at length (*on*). —**expatiation** /-ˈeɪʃ(ə)n/ *n.*, **expatiatory** *adj.* [f. L *exspatiari* walk about (EX-¹, *spatium* space)]

expatriate /eksˈpætrɪeɪt/ *v.t.* to expel, or to remove *oneself*, from one's native country. —/-ət/ *adj.* expatriated. —/-ət/ *n.* an expatriated person. —**expatriation** /-ˈeɪʃ(ə)n/ *n.* [f. L *expatriare* (EX-¹, *patria* native land)]

expect /ɪkˈspekt/ *v.t.* **1** to regard as likely, to assume as a future event or occurrence. **2** to look for as due. **3** (*colloq.*) to think, to suppose. —**be expecting,** (*colloq.*) to be pregnant. [f. L *ex(s)pectare* (*spectare* look)]

expectancy *n.* a state of expectation; a prospect or prospective chance. [f. prec.]

expectant *adj.* expecting, having expectation. —**expectant mother,** a pregnant woman. —**expectantly** *adv.* [as EXPECT]

expectation /ekspekˈteɪʃ(ə)n/ *n.* **1** expecting, looking forward with hope or fear etc. **2** what one expects; the probability (*of* an event); the probable duration (*of* life); (in *pl.*) prospects of inheritance. [as prec.]

expectorant /ekˈspektərənt/ *adj.* that causes one to expectorate. —*n.* an expectorant medicine. [as foll.]

expectorate /ekˈspektəreɪt/ *v.t./i.* to cough or spit out (phlegm etc.) from the chest or lungs; to spit. —**expectoration** /-ˈreɪʃ(ə)n/ *n.* [f. L *expectorare* (EX-¹, *pectus* breast)]

expedient /ɪkˈspiːdɪənt/ *adj.* advantageous, advisable on practical rather than moral grounds; suitable, appropriate. —*n.* a means of achieving an end, a resource. —**expedience** *n.*, **expediency** *n.*, **expediently** *adv.* [f. L *expedire* (as foll.)]

expedite /ˈekspɪdaɪt/ *v.t.* to assist the progress of, to hasten (an action, measure, etc.); to accomplish (business) quickly. [f. L *expedire* free from difficulties, put in order]

expedition /ekspəˈdɪʃ(ə)n/ *n.* **1** a journey or voyage for a particular purpose especially exploration; the people or ships etc. undertaking this. **2** promptness, speed. [f. OF f. L (as prec.)]

expeditionary *adj.* of or used in an expedition [f. prec.]

expeditious /ekspəˈdɪʃəs/ *adj.* acting or done with speed and efficiency. —**expeditiously** *adv.* [as prec.]

expel /ɪkˈspel/ *v.t.* (**-ll-**) to send or drive out by force; to compel (a person) by process of law to leave a school or country etc. [f. L *expellere* (EX-¹, *pellere* drive)]

expend /ɪkˈspend/ *v.t.* to spend or use up (money, time, etc.). [f. L *expendere* (EX-¹, *pendere* weigh)]

expendable *adj.* that may be sacrificed or dispensed with; not worth preserving. [f. prec.]

expenditure /ekˈspendɪtʃə(r)/ *n.* expending (especially of money); the amount expended. [f. EXPEND]

expense /ɪkˈspens/ *n.* a cost incurred; (in *pl.*) the costs incurred in doing a job etc., reimbursement for these; the spending of money, a thing on which money is spent. —**at the expense of,** so as to cause loss or damage or discredit to. **expense account,** the record of an employee's expenses payable by an employer. [f. OF f. L *expensa* (as EXPEND)]

expensive *adj.* costing much, of a high price. —**expensively** *adv.*, **expensiveness** *n.* [as EXPEND]

experience /ɪkˈspɪərɪəns/ *n.* personal observation of or involvement with a fact, event, etc.; knowledge or skill based on this; an event that affects one. —*v.t.* to have experience of, to undergo; to feel. [f. OF f. L (*experiri* make trial of)]

experienced *adj.* having had much experience; skilled from this. [f. prec.]

experiential /ɪkspɪərɪˈenʃ(ə)l/ *adj.* involving or based on experience. [f. EXPERIENCE]

experiment /ɪkˈsperɪmənt/ *n.* a procedure tried on the chance of success, or to test an hypothesis etc. or demonstrate a known fact. —/also -ent/ *v.i.* to make an experiment (*on* or *with*). —**experimentation** /-ˈteɪʃ(ə)n/ *n.* [f. OF or L (as EXPERIENCE)]

experimental /ɪksperɪˈment(ə)l/ *adj.* of, based on, or using an experiment; in the nature of an experiment. —**experimentalism** *n.*, **experimentally** *adv.* [f. prec.]

expert /ˈekspɜːt/ *adj.* highly practised and skilful, or well informed, in a subject. —*n.* a person who is expert in a subject; (*attrib.*) of or being an expert. —**expertly** *adv.* [f. OF f. L (as EXPERIENCE)]

expertise /ekspɜːˈtiːz/ *n.* expert skill or knowledge or judgement. [F]

expiate /ˈekspɪeɪt/ *v.t.* to make amends for (a wrong); to pay the penalty of. —**expiable** *adj.*, **expiation** /-ˈeɪʃ(ə)n/ *n.*, **expiatory** *adj.* [f. L *expiare* seek to appease (EX-¹, *pius* devout)]

expiratory /ɪkˈspaɪrətərɪ/ *adj.* of breathing out. [f. foll.]

expire /ɪkˈspaɪə(r)/ *v.t./i.* **1** (of a period, the validity of a thing, etc.) to come to an end. **2** to breathe out (air, or *absol.*); to die. —**expiration** /ekspɪˈreɪʃ(ə)n/ *n.* [f. OF f. L *exspirare* (EX-¹, *spirare* breathe)]

expiry /ɪk'spaɪrɪ/ *n.* the termination of a period of validity. [f. prec.]

explain /ɪk'spleɪn/ *v.t.* to make clear or intelligible, to give the meaning of; to make known in detail; to account for (conduct etc.). —**explain away**, to minimize the significance of. **explain oneself**, to justify one's conduct or attitude etc. [f. L *explanare* (EX-¹, *planus* flat, plain)]

explanation /eksplə'neɪʃ(ə)n/ *n.* explaining; a statement or circumstance that explains something. [as prec.]

explanatory /ɪk'splænətərɪ/ *adj.* serving or intended to explain. [as EXPLAIN]

expletive /ɪk'spli:tɪv/ *n.* an oath or meaningless exclamation; a word used to fill out a sentence etc. —*adj.* serving as an expletive. [f. L (*explēre* fill out)]

explicable /'eksplɪkəb(ə)l, ɪk'splɪk-/ *adj.* that can be explained. [as foll.]

explicate /'eksplɪkeɪt/ *v.t.* to explain or develop (an idea etc.). —**explication** /-'keɪʃ(ə)n/ *n.* [f. L *explicare* unfold (EX-¹, *plicare* fold)]

explicit /ɪk'splɪsɪt/ *adj.* **1** expressly stated, not merely implied; stated in detail; definite. **2** outspoken. —**explicitly** *adv.*, **explicitness** *n.* [f. F or L (as prec.)]

explode /ɪk'spləʊd/ *v.t./i.* **1** to expand suddenly with a loud noise owing to the release of internal energy; to cause to do this. **2** to give vent suddenly to emotion or violence. **3** to increase suddenly or rapidly. **4** to expose or discredit (a theory etc.). **5** (usu. in *p.p.*) to show parts of (a diagram etc.) in relative positions but somewhat separated. [f. L *explodere* drive off the stage by clapping (EX-¹, *plaudere* clap)]

exploit /'eksplɔɪt/ *n.* a bold or daring feat. —/ɪk'splɔɪt/ *v.t.* to use or develop for one's own ends, to take advantage of. —**exploitation** /-'teɪʃ(ə)n/ *n.* [f. OF (as EXPLICATE)]

explore /ɪk'splɔ:(r)/ *v.t.* **1** to travel extensively through (a country etc.) in order to learn or discover about it. **2** to inquire into. **3** to examine by touch. —**exploration** /eksplə'reɪʃ(ə)n/ *n.*, **exploratory** /ɪk'splɒrətərɪ/ *adj.*, **explorer** *n.* [f. F f. L *explorare*]

explosion /ɪk'spləʊʒ(ə)n/ *n.* **1** exploding; a loud noise due to this. **2** a sudden outbreak of feeling etc. **3** a sudden or rapid increase. [f. L (as EXPLODE)]

explosive /ɪk'spləʊsɪv/ *adj.* **1** able or tending or likely to explode. **2** likely to cause a violent outburst etc., dangerously tense. —*n.* an explosive substance. —**explosively** *adv.* [f. prec.]

exponent /ɪk'spəʊnənt/ *n.* **1** a person who explains or interprets something. **2** a person who favours or promotes an idea etc. **3** a type or representative. **4** a raised symbol beside a numeral (e.g. 3 in 2^3) indicating how many times it is to be multiplied by itself. [f. L *exponere* (EX-¹, *ponere* put)]

exponential /ekspə'nenʃ(ə)l/ *adj.* **1** of or indicated by a mathematical exponent. **2** (of an increase etc.) more and more rapid. —**exponential curve**, one based on an exponential equation, increasing sharply in steepness. [f. prec.]

export /'ekspɔ:t/ *v.t.* /also -'spɔ:t/ to send out (goods) for sale in another country. —*n.* **1** exporting. **2** an exported article; (usu. in *pl.*) the amount exported. —**exportation** /-'teɪʃ(ə)n/ *n.*, **exporter** /-'pɔ:t-/ *n.* [f. L *exportare* (EX-¹, *portare* carry)]

exportable /ɪk'spɔ:təb(ə)l/ *adj.* that can be exported. [f. prec.]

expose /ɪk'spəʊz/ *v.t.* **1** to leave uncovered or unprotected, especially from the weather; to allow light to reach (a photographic film or plate); to leave (a baby) in the open to die. **2** to subject *to* (a risk etc.). **3** to reveal, to make known or visible; to show up in a true (usually unfavourable) light. —**expose oneself**, to expose one's body indecently. [f. OF f. L (as EXPONENT)]

exposé /ek'spəʊzeɪ/ *n.* an orderly statement of facts; a revealing of a discreditable thing. [F (as prec.)]

exposition /ekspə'zɪʃ(ə)n/ *n.* **1** expounding, an explanatory account. **2** a large public exhibition. **3** (*Mus.*) the part of a movement in which themes are presented. [f. OF or L (as EXPOSE)]

ex post facto /eks pəʊst 'fæktəʊ/ retrospective, retrospectively. [L, = from what is done afterwards]

expostulate /ɪk'spɒstjʊleɪt/ *v.i.* to make a reasoned protest, to remonstrate. —**expostulation** /-'leɪʃ(ə)n/ *n.*, **expostulatory** *adj.* [f. L (as EX-¹, POSTULATE)]

exposure /ɪk'spəʊʒə(r)/ *n.* **1** exposing, being exposed. **2** the exposing of a photographic film or plate; the duration of this; the part of a film exposed for one picture. [f. EXPOSE]

expound /ɪk'spaʊnd/ *v.t.* to set forth in detail; to explain, to interpret. [f. OF (as EXPONENT)]

express /ɪk'spres/ *v.t.* **1** to represent or make known in words or by gestures, conduct, etc. **2** to squeeze out (juice etc.). **3** to send by express service. —*adj.* **1** definitely stated, explicit. **2** sent or delivered by a specially fast service. **3** (of a train) travelling at high speed and with few stops. —*n.* **1** an express train etc. **2** (*US*) a service for the rapid transport of parcels etc. —*adv.* at high speed, by express. —**express oneself**, to say what one means or thinks. —**expressly** *adv.* [f. OF f. L *exprimere*, orig. = press out]

expressible /ɪk'spresɪb(ə)l/ *adj.* that can be expressed. [f. prec.]

expression /ɪk'spreʃ(ə)n/ *n.* **1** expressing; a word or phrase; a collection of symbols in mathematics expressing a quantity. **2** a look or facial aspect; the showing of feeling in the manner of speaking or of performing music; the representation of feeling in art. [as EXPRESS]

expressionism /ɪk'spreʃ(ə)nɪz(ə)m/ *n.* a style of painting in which the artist or writer seeks to express emotional experience rather than impressions of the physical world, especially through the use of violent colour and linear distortions; a similar style or movement in literature, drama, music, etc. —**expressionist** *n.* & *adj.* [f. prec.]

expressionless *adj.* without positive expression, not revealing one's thoughts or feelings. [f. prec. + -LESS]

expressive *adj.* serving to express; full of expression. —**expressively** *adv.*, **expressiveness** *n.* [f. F f. L (as EXPRESS)]

expressway *n.* (*US*) an urban motorway.

expropriate /eks'prəʊprɪeɪt/ *v.t.* to take away (property) from its owner; to dispossess (a person). —**expropriation** /-'eɪʃ(ə)n/ *n.* [f. L *expropriare* (EX-[1], *proprium* property)]

expulsion /ɪk'spʌlʃ(ə)n/ *n.* expelling, being expelled. [f. L (as EXPEL)]

expulsive /ɪk'spʌlsɪv/ *adj.* expelling. [f. prec.]

expunge /ɪk'spʌndʒ/ *v.t.* to erase or remove (a passage *from* a book etc.). [f. L *expungere* prick out (for deletion)]

expurgate /'ekspɜ:geɪt/ *v.t.* to remove matter thought to be objectionable from (a book etc.); to remove (such matter). —**expurgation** /-'geɪʃ(ə)n/ *n.*, **expurgator** *n.* [f. L *expurgare* (EX-[1], *purgare* cleanse)]

exquisite /'ekskwɪzɪt, (D) ek'skwɪzɪt/ *adj.* **1** extremely beautiful or delicate. **2** highly sensitive; acute, keen. —*n.* a person of refined (especially affected) tastes. —**exquisitely** *adv.* [f. L *exquirere* search out (EX-[1], *quaerere* seek)]

ex-serviceman /eks'sɜ:vɪsmən/ *n.* (*pl.* **-men**) a former member of the armed forces.

extant /ek'stænt, 'ek-/ *adj.* still existing. [f. L *ex(s)tare* (EX-[1], *stare* stand)]

extemporaneous /ekstempə'reɪnɪəs/ *adj.* spoken or done without preparation. —**extemporaneously** *adv.* [as EXTEMPORE]

extemporary /ɪk'stempərərɪ/ *adj.* extemporaneous. [as foll.]

extempore /ek'stempərɪ/ *adj.* & *adv.* without preparation, offhand. [L, lit. = out of the time (*ex* out of, *tempus* time)]

extemporize /ɪk'stempəraɪz/ *v.t./i.* to speak, utter, or perform extempore. —**extemporization** /-'zeɪʃ(ə)n/ *n.* [f. prec.]

extend /ɪk'stend/ *v.t./i.* **1** to lengthen in space or time; to increase in scope. **2** to stretch or lay out at full length; to reach or be continuous over a certain area; to have a certain scope. **3** to offer or accord a feeling, invitation, etc., *to*. —**extended family,** one including relatives living near. **extended-play** *adj.* (of a gramophone record) playing for longer than most singles. **extend oneself** *or* **be extended,** to have one's abilities taxed to the utmost. —**extender** *n.* [f. L *extendere* (EX-[1], *tendere* stretch)]

extensible /ɪk'stensɪb(ə)l/ *adj.* (also **extendible**) that can be extended. [f. prec.]

extension /ɪk'stenʃ(ə)n/ *n.* **1** extending, being extended. **2** a part enlarging or added on to a main structure etc.; an additional period of time; a subsidiary telephone on the same line as the main one, its number. **3** extramural instruction by a university or college etc. [as EXTENT]

extensive *adj.* large; far-reaching. —**extensively** *adv.*, **extensiveness** *n.* [f. F or L (as EXTEND)]

extent /ɪk'stent/ *n.* the space over which a thing extends; a large area; range, scope, or degree. [f. AF f. L (as EXTEND)]

extenuate /ɪk'stenjʊeɪt/ *v.t.* to lessen the seeming seriousness of (an offence or guilt) by partial excuse. —**extenuation** /-'eɪʃ(ə)n/ *n.* [f. L *extenuare* (EX-[1], *tenuis* thin)]

exterior /ɪk'stɪərɪə(r)/ *adj.* outer, outward; coming from outside. —*n.* the exterior part or aspect; an outdoor scene in filming. [f. L, compar. of *exterus* outside]

exterminate /ɪk'stɜ:mɪneɪt/ *v.t.* to destroy (a disease, people, etc.) utterly. —**extermination** /-'neɪʃ(ə)n/ *n.*, **exterminator** *n.* [f. L *exterminare* (EX-[1], *terminare* put an end to, f. *terminus* boundary]

external /ek'stɜ:n(ə)l/ *adj.* of or situated on the outside or visible part; coming from the outside or an outside source; of a country's foreign affairs; outside the conscious subject; (of medicine etc.) for use on the outside of the body; of students taking the examinations of, but not attending, a university. —*n.* (in *pl.*) external features or circumstances; non-essentials. —**externality** /-'nælɪtɪ/ *n.*, **externally** *adv.* [f. L *externus* (as EXTERIOR)]

externalize /ek'stɜ:n(ə)laɪz/ *v.t.* to give or attribute external existence to. —**externalization** /-'zeɪʃ(ə)n/ *n.* [f. prec.]

extinct /ɪk'stɪŋkt/ *adj.* no longer existing, obsolete; no longer burning, (of a volcano) no longer active. [f. L *exstinguere* (EX-[1], *stinguere* quench)]

extinction /ɪk'stɪŋkʃ(ə)n/ *n.* making or becoming extinct, dying out. [as prec.]

extinguish /ɪk'stɪŋgwɪʃ/ *v.t.* **1** to cause (a fire or light etc.) to cease to burn or function. **2** to terminate, to make extinct, to destroy; to wipe out (a debt). [f. L (as EXTINCT)]

extinguisher *n.* a fire extinguisher (see FIRE). [f. prec.]

extirpate /ˈekstɜːpeɪt/ *v.t.* to destroy, to root out. —**extirpation** /-peɪʃ(ə)n/ *n.* [f. L *exstirpare* (EX-¹, *stirps* stem)]

extol /ɪkˈstəʊl/ *v.t.* (-ll-) to praise enthusiastically. [f. L *extollere* (EX-¹, *tollere* raise)]

extort /ɪkˈstɔːt/ *v.t.* to obtain (money, a secret, etc.) by force, threats, or intimidation etc. [f. L *extorquere* (EX-¹, *torquere* twist)]

extortion /ɪkˈstɔːʃ(ə)n/ *n.* extorting, especially of money; illegal exaction. [as prec.]

extortionate /ɪkˈstɔːʃ(ə)nət/ *adj.* (of prices) excessively high; (of demands) excessive. —**extortionately** *adv.* [f. prec.]

extortioner *n* one who practises extortion. [f. EXTORTION]

extra /ˈekstrə/ *adj.* additional; more than is usual or necessary or expected. —*adv.* more than usually; additionally. —*n.* an extra thing; a thing charged extra; a person engaged temporarily for a minor part in a film etc.; a special issue of a newspaper etc.; a run in cricket not scored from a hit with the bat. [prob. for EXTRAORDINARY]

extra- *prefix* forming adjectives in the sense 'outside', 'beyond the scope of'. [f. L *extra* outside]

extract /ɪkˈstrækt/ *v.t.* **1** to take out by effort or force (anything firmly rooted or fixed). **2** to obtain (money, an admission etc.) against a person's will **3** to obtain (juice etc.) by pressure, distillation, etc. **4** to derive (pleasure etc *from*). **5** to quote or copy out (a passage from a book etc.). **6** to find (the root of a number) —/ˈekstrækt/ *n.* **1** a short passage from a book etc. **2** a substance got by distillation etc.; a concentrated preparation. [f. L *extrahere* (EX-¹, *trahere* draw)]

extraction /ɪkˈstrækʃ(ə)n/ *n.* **1** extracting, especially of a tooth. **2** lineage. [f. F f. L (as prec.)]

extractive /ɪkˈstræktɪv/ *adj.* of or involving extraction. —**extractive industry,** one obtaining minerals etc. from the ground. [f. EXTRACT]

extractor /ɪkˈstræktə(r)/ *n.* a person or thing that extracts —**extractor fan,** a ventilating fan in a window etc. to remove stale air. [as prec.]

extra-curricular /ekstrəkəˈrɪkjʊlə(r)/ *adj.* not part of the normal curriculum.

extraditable /ˈekstrədaɪtəb(ə)l/ *adj.* liable to or (of a crime) warranting extradition. [f. foll.]

extradite /ˈekstrədaɪt/ *v.t.* to hand over (a person accused of a crime) to the State wishing to try him. —**extradition** /-ˈdɪʃ(ə)n/ *n.* [f. F (as EX-¹, TRADITION)]

extramarital /ekstrəˈmærɪt(ə)l/ *adj.* (of sexual relationships) outside marriage.

extramural /ekstrəˈmjʊər(ə)l/ *adj.* (of university teaching) additional to normal degree courses. [f. L *extra muros* outside the walls]

extraneous /ɪkˈstreɪnɪəs/ *adj.* of external origin; not belonging (*to* the matter in hand). —**extraneously** *adv.* [f. L *extraneus* (*extra* outside)]

extraordinary /ɪkˈstrɔːdɪnərɪ, ekstrəˈɔːd-/ *adj.* unusual or remarkable; out of the usual course, additional; specially employed; unusually great. —**extraordinarily** *adv.* [f. L (*extra ordinem* outside the usual order)]

extrapolate /ekˈstræpəleɪt/ *v.t./i.* to estimate from known values, data, etc. (others which lie outside the range of those known). —**extrapolation** /-ˈleɪʃ(ə)n/ *n.* [f. EXTRA- + INTERPOLATE]

extra-sensory /ekstrəˈsensərɪ/ *adj.* (of perception) derived by means other than the known senses.

extra-terrestrial /ekstrətɪˈrestrɪ(ə)l/ *adj.* outside the earth or its atmosphere.

extravagant /ɪkˈstrævəgənt/ *adj.* **1** spending (especially money) excessively. **2** costing much. **3** passing the bounds of reason, absurd. —**extravagance** *n.*, **extravagantly** *adv.* [f. L (EXTRA-, *vagari* wander)]

extravaganza /ekstrævəˈgænzə/ *n.* a fanciful literary, musical, or dramatic composition; a spectacular theatrical production. [f. It. *estravaganza* (as prec.)]

extravasate /ekˈstrævəseɪt/ *v.t./i.* to force out (blood etc.) from its vessel; (of blood, lava, etc.) to flow out. —**extravasation** /-ˈseɪʃ(ə)n/ *n.* [f. L *extra* outside + *vas* vessel]

extreme /ɪkˈstriːm/ *adj.* reaching a high or the highest degree; severe, going to great lengths; politically far to the left or right; outermost, furthest from the centre; utmost; last. —*n.* one or other of two things as remote or as different as possible, the thing at either end; an extreme degree; the first or last of a series. —**go to extremes,** to take an extreme course of action. **in the extreme,** to an extreme degree. [f. OF f. L (superl. of *exterus* outer)]

extremely *adv.* in an extreme degree, very. [f. prec.]

extremist *n.* one who holds extreme (esp. political) views. —**extremism** *n.* [f. EXTREME]

extremity /ɪkˈstremɪtɪ/ *n.* an extreme point, an end; extreme distress or difficulty; (in *pl.*) the hands and feet. [f. OF or L (as EXTREME)]

extricable /ˈekstrɪkəb(ə)l/ *adj.* that can be extricated. [f. foll.]

extricate /ˈekstrɪkeɪt/ *v.t.* to free or disentangle

(*from* a difficulty etc.). —**extrication** /-ˈkeɪʃ(ə)n/ *n.* [f. L *extricare* (EX-¹, *tricae* entanglements)]

extrinsic /ekˈstrɪnsɪk/ *adj.* not inherent or intrinsic; extraneous, not belonging (*to*). —**extrinsically** *adv.* [f. L *extrinsecus* outwardly (as EXTRA-)]

extrovert /ˈekstrəvɜːt/ *adj.* (also **extroverted**) directing one's thoughts and interests to things outside oneself; socially unreserved. —*n.* an extrovert person. —**extroversion** /-ˈvɜːʃ(ə)n/ *n.* [as EXTRA- + *vertere* turn]

extrude /ekˈstruːd/ *v.t.* to thrust or force out; to shape (metal, plastics, etc.) by forcing through a die. —**extrusion** *n.*, **extrusive** *adj.* [f. L (EX-¹, *trudere* thrust)]

exuberant /ɪgˈzjuːbərənt/ *adj.* lively, effusive, high-spirited; (of a plant etc.) prolific, luxuriant; (of health, emotion, etc.) overflowing, abundant. —**exuberance** *n.*, **exuberantly** *adv.* [f. F f. L *exuberare* (EX-¹, *uber* fruitful)]

exude /ɪgˈzjuːd/ *v.t./i.* to ooze out; to give out (moisture); to emit (a smell); to show (pleasure etc.) freely. —**exudation** /eksjuːˈdeɪʃ(ə)n/ *n.* [f. L (EX-¹, *sudare* sweat)]

exult /ɪgˈzʌlt/ *v.i.* to rejoice greatly. —**exultation** /eksʌlˈteɪʃ(ə)n/ *n.* [f. L (EX-¹, *saltare* dance)]

exultant *adj.* exulting, rejoicing. [f. prec.]

eye /aɪ/ *n.* **1** the organ of sight in man and animals; the iris of an eye; the region round an eye. **2** a particular visual faculty. **3** a thing like an eye, e.g. a spot on a peacock's tail or butterfly's wing, the leaf-bud of a potato; the hole of a needle; a calm region in the centre of a hurricane etc. —*v.t.* (*partic.* **eyeing**) to look at, to observe (esp. with curiosity or suspicion). —**all eyes,** watching intently. **all my eye,** (*slang*) nonsense. **cast** *or* **run an eye over,** to examine quickly. **catch a person's eye,** to succeed in attracting a person's attention. **close** *or* **shut one's eyes to,** to ignore, to disregard. **do in the eye,** to defraud or thwart. **an eye for an eye,** retaliation in kind. **eye-liner** *n.* a cosmetic applied as a line round the eye. **eye-opener** *n.* a surprising or revealing fact or circumstance. **eye-rhyme** *n.* correspondence of words in spelling but not in pronunciation (e.g. *dear* and *pear*). **eye-shade** *n.* a device to protect the eyes from strong light. **eye-shadow** *n.* a cosmetic applied to the skin round the eyes. **eye-strain** *n.* weariness of the eyes. **eye-tooth** *n.* a canine tooth in the upper jaw, below the eye. **get one's eye in,** to become accustomed to prevailing conditions especially in sport. **half an eye,** the slightest degree of perceptiveness. **have eyes for,** to be interested in, to wish to acquire. **in** *or* **through the eyes of,** from the point of view of, in the judgement of. **in the public eye,** receiving much publicity. **keep an eye on,** to watch carefully, to take care of. **keep an eye open** *or* **out for,** to watch for. **keep one's eyes open** *or* (*slang*) **peeled** *or* **skinned,** to be watchful. **make eyes at,** to look at amorously or flirtatiously. **one in the eye,** a setback or discomfiture (*for*). **see eye to eye,** to agree. **set eyes on,** to catch sight of. **up to the eyes,** deeply engaged or involved *in*. **with an eye to,** with a view to. [OE]

eyeball *n.* the ball of the eye, within the lids and sockets. —**eyeball to eyeball,** (*colloq.*) confronting closely.

eyebath *n.* a small cup shaped to fit round the eye, for applying lotion to the eye.

eyebright *n.* a plant of the genus *Euphrasia*, formerly used as a remedy for weak eyes.

eyebrow *n.* the fringe of hair growing on the ridge above the eye-socket. —**raise an eyebrow** *or* **one's eyebrows,** to show surprise or disbelief.

eyeful *n.* a thing thrown or blown into the eye; (*colloq.*) a thorough look; (*colloq.*) a visually striking person or thing. [f. EYE + -FUL]

eyeglass *n.* a lens for a defective eye.

eyehole *n.* **1** the socket containing the eye. **2** a hole to look through.

eyelash *n.* any of the fringe of hairs on the edge of the eyelid.

eyelet /ˈaɪlɪt/ *n.* a small hole for passing cord or rope through; a metal ring for strengthening this. [f. OF *oillet* dim. of *oil* eye]

eyelid *n.* either of the two folds of skin that can be moved together to cover the eye.

eyepiece *n.* the lens or lenses to which the eye is applied at the end of a microscope, telescope, etc.

eyesight *n.* the faculty or power of seeing.

eyesore *n.* a thing that offends the sight; an ugly object etc.

eyewash *n.* **1** a lotion for the eye. **2** (*slang*) nonsense, insincere talk.

eyewitness *n.* a person who can give evidence of an incident from personal observation of it.

eyrie /ˈaɪərɪ, ˈɪərɪ/ *n.* the nest of an eagle or other bird of prey built high up; a house etc. perched high up. [f. OF *aire* lair f. L *ager* piece of ground]

Ff

F, f *n.* (*pl.* **Fs, F's**) **1** the sixth letter of the alphabet. **2** (*Mus.*) the fourth note in the scale of C major.

F *abbr.* **1** Fahrenheit. **2** farad(s). **3** Fellow of. **4** fine (pencil-lead).

F *symbol* fluorine.

f. *abbr.* **1** female; feminine. **2** focal length. **3** folio. **4** following page etc.

f *abbr.* (*Mus.*) forte.

FA *abbr.* Football Association.

fa var. of FAH.

fab *adj.* (*colloq.*) marvellous. [abbr. of FABULOUS]

Fabian /ˈfeɪbɪən/ *n.* a member of the Fabian Society, an English socialist society advocating social change through gradual reform rather than by violent revolutionary action. —**Fabianism** *n.* [f. *Fabius*, Roman general (d. 203BC)]

fable /ˈfeɪb(ə)l/ *n.* **1** a story, especially a supernatural one, not based on fact; a short moral tale especially about animals; legendary tales. **2** a lie, lies. **3** a thing only supposed to exist. [f. OF f. L *fabula* discourse]

fabled *adj.* celebrated in fable, legendary. [f. prec.]

fabric /ˈfæbrɪk/ *n.* **1** woven, knitted, or felted material; a plastic resembling this. **2** the walls, floors, and roof of a building. **3** a structure (*lit.* or *fig.*). [f. F f. L (*faber* metal-worker)]

fabricate /ˈfæbrɪkeɪt/ *v.t.* **1** to construct, to manufacture. **2** to invent (a story); to forge (a document). —**fabrication** /-ˈkeɪʃ(ə)n/ *n.*, **fabricator** *n.* [f. L (as prec.)]

fabulous /ˈfæbjʊləs/ *adj.* **1** famed in fable, legendary. **2** incredible, absurd. **3** (*colloq.*) marvellous. —**fabulously** *adv.* [f. F or L (as FABLE)]

façade /fəˈsɑːd/ *n.* **1** the face or front of a building. **2** an outward (esp. deceptive) appearance. [F (as foll.)]

face *n.* **1** the front of the head from the forehead to the chin; the expression of the facial features; a grimace. **2** the surface of a thing, especially the functional surface of a tool etc.; the upper or forward-facing side, the front; the dial-plate of a clock. **3** an outward appearance, an aspect. **4** composure; effrontery, nerve. **5** esteem. **6** a typeface. —*v.t./i.* **1** to have or turn the face towards; to be opposite to. **2** to meet resolutely, not to shrink from; to meet (an opponent) in a contest; to present itself to. **3** to cover the surface of (a wall etc.) with a facing; to put a facing on (a garment etc.). —**face card,** a court card. **face-cloth** *n.* a face-flannel; a smooth-surfaced woollen cloth. **face-flannel** *n.* a cloth for washing one's face. **face-lift** *n.* the operation of having one's face lifted; a procedure to improve a thing's appearance. **face to face,** facing, confronting each other. **face up to,** to face resolutely. **face value,** the value printed or stamped on money; what a thing seems to mean or imply. **have the face,** to be shameless enough. **in (the) face of,** despite. **lose face,** to be humiliated. **make** *or* **pull a face,** to grimace. **on the face of it,** to outward appearances. **put a bold** *or* **good face on,** to accept (a difficulty etc.) cheerfully. **save face,** to preserve esteem, to avoid humiliation. **set one's face against,** to resist determinedly. **show one's face,** to let oneself be seen. **to a person's face,** openly in his presence. [f. OF f. L *facies*]

faceless /ˈfeɪslɪs/ *adj.* **1** without identity, purposely not identifiable. **2** lacking character. [f. FACE + -LESS]

facer *n.* a sudden unexpected difficulty. [f. FACE]

facet /ˈfæsɪt/ *n.* **1** one aspect of a problem etc. **2** one side of a many-sided cut gem etc. —**faceted** *adj.* [f. F (as FACE)]

facetious /fəˈsiːʃəs/ *adj.* intending or intended to be amusing. —**facetiously** *adv.*, **facetiousness** *n.* [f. F f. L *facetiae* wit]

facia /ˈfeɪʃə/ *n.* **1** the instrument panel of a motor vehicle. **2** the plate over a shop-front with the name etc. [var. of FASCIA]

facial /ˈfeɪʃ(ə)l/ *adj.* of or for the face. —*n.* a beauty treatment for the face. —**facially** *adv.* [f. L (as FACE)]

facile /ˈfæsaɪl/ *adj.* **1** easily achieved but of little value. **2** easy, easily done; working easily, fluent. [f. F or L *facilis* (*facere* make, do)]

facilitate /fəˈsɪlɪteɪt/ *v.t.* to make easy or less difficult; to make (an action or result) more easily achieved. —**facilitation** /-ˈteɪʃ(ə)n/ *n.* [f. F f. It. (as prec.)]

facility /fəˈsɪlɪtɪ/ *n.* **1** ease, absence of difficulty; fluency, dexterity. **2** (esp. in *pl.*) the opportunity or equipment for doing something. [f. F or L (as FACILE)]

facing *n.* a layer of material over a part of a garment etc., for contrast or strength; an outer layer covering the surface of a wall etc. [f. FACE]

facsimile /fækˈsɪmɪlɪ/ *n.* an exact copy of writing, a picture, etc. [L, = make a likeness]

fact *n.* a thing that is known to be true or to exist; truth, reality; a thing assumed as a basis for argument. —**facts and figures,** the precise details. **facts of life,** (*colloq.*) the realities of a situation; knowledge of human sexual functions. **in fact,** in reality, in short. [f. L *factum* (as FACILE)]

faction /ˈfækʃ(ə)n/ *n.* a small group with special aims within a larger one. —**factional** *adj.* [f. F f. L]

factious /ˈfækʃəs/ *adj.* of a faction, characterized by factions. [f. F or L (as FACTION)]

factitious /fækˈtɪʃəs/ *adj.* made for a special purpose; artificial. —**factitiously** *adv.* [f. L (as FACILE)]

factor /ˈfæktə(r)/ *n.* **1** a circumstance etc. contributing to a result. **2** a whole number etc. that when multiplied with another produces a given number. **3** a business agent; an agent or deputy; (*Sc.*) a land-steward. **4** a gene or other agent determining a hereditary character. [f. F or L (*facere* make, do)]

factorial /fækˈtɔːrɪ(ə)l/ *n.* the product of a number and all the whole numbers below it. —*adj.* of a factor or factorial. [f. prec.]

factorize /ˈfæktəraɪz/ *v.t.* to resolve into factors. —**factorization** /-ˈzeɪʃ(ə)n/ *n.* [f. FACTOR]

factory /ˈfæktərɪ/ *n.* a building or buildings in which goods are manufactured. —**factory farm,** one employing industrial or intensive methods of rearing livestock. **factory ship,** one that processes and freezes its catch while still at sea. [f. Port. or L (as FACTOR)]

factotum /fækˈtəʊtəm/ *n.* an employee doing all kinds of work. [L, = do the whole lot]

factual /ˈfæktjʊ(ə)l/ *adj.* based on or concerning facts. —**factually** *adv.* [f. FACT]

faculty /ˈfæk(ə)ltɪ/ *n.* **1** an aptitude or ability for a particular activity; an inherent mental or physical power. **2** a department of a university teaching a particular subject; (*US*) the staff of a university or college. **3** authorization, especially by Church authority. [f. OF f. L *facultas* (*facilis* easy)]

fad *n.* a craze; a peculiar notion. —**faddish** *adj.* [prob. f. FIDDLE-FADDLE]

faddy *adj.* having arbitrary likes and dislikes, especially about food. —**faddiness** *n.* [f. prec.]

fade *v.t./i.* to lose or cause to lose colour, freshness, or strength; to disappear gradually; to bring (a sound or picture) gradually *in* or *out* of perception. —*n.* an act of fading. —**fade away** *or* **out,** to become weaker or less distinct; to die away; to disappear. [f. OF (*fade* dull, insipid)]

faeces /ˈfiːsiːz/ *n.pl.* waste matter discharged from the bowels. —**faecal** /ˈfiːk(ə)l/ *adj.* [L]

fag[1] *v.t./i.* (**-gg-**) **1** to tire (*out*), to exhaust. **2** to toil; (as a junior schoolboy) to run errands for a senior boy. —*n.* **1** (*colloq.*) drudgery. **2** (*slang*) a cigarette. **3** a schoolboy who fags. —**fag-end** *n.* a cigarette end. [orig. unkn.]

fag[2] *n.* (*US slang*) a homosexual. [abbr. of foll.]

faggot /ˈfægət/ *n.* **1** a ball or roll of seasoned chopped liver etc. baked or fried. **2** a bundle of sticks, herbs, metal rods, etc. **3** (*slang*) an unpleasant woman. **4** (*US slang*) a homosexual. [f. OF f. It.]

faggoting *n.* embroidery in which threads are fastened together like faggots. [f. prec.]

fah /fɑː/ *n.* (*Mus.*) the fourth note of the major scale in tonic sol-fa (see entry). [f. *famuli* (see GAMUT)]

Fahrenheit /ˈfærənhaɪt/ *adj.* of the scale of temperature on which water freezes at 32° and boils at 212°. [f. G. *Fahrenheit* German physicist (d. 1736)]

faience /ˈfaɪɑ̃s/ *n.* decorated and glazed earthenware and porcelain. [f. F f. *Faenza* in Italy]

fail *v.t./i.* **1** not to succeed; to be unsuccessful in (an examination etc.); to grade (a candidate) as not having passed an examination. **2** to disappoint, to let down. **3** to neglect or forget, to be unable. **4** to be absent or deficient; (of crops) to produce a very poor harvest. **5** to become weak or ineffective, to cease functioning; to become bankrupt. —*n.* a failure in an examination. —**fail-safe** *adj.* reverting to a safe condition in the event of a breakdown etc. **without fail,** for certain, whatever happens. [f. OF f. L *fallere* deceive]

failed *adj.* unsuccessful. [f. prec.]

failing *n.* a fault, a weakness. —*prep.* in default of, if not. [f. FAIL]

failure /ˈfeɪljə(r)/ *n.* **1** failing, non-performance, lack of success. **2** cessation of normal function through weakness etc. **3** deficiency, as through a poor harvest. **4** an unsuccessful person or thing. [f. FAIL]

fain *predic. adj.* willing or obliged (*to*). —*adv.* gladly. [OE]

faint *adj.* **1** indistinct, pale, dim. **2** weak from hunger etc. **3** timid; feeble. —*v.i.* to lose consciousness, to become faint. —*n.* an act of fainting; a state of having fainted. —**faint-hearted** *adj.* cowardly, timid.

—faintly *adv.*, **faintness** *n.* [f. OF, p.p. of *feindre* feign]

fair[1] *adj.* **1** just, unbiased, in accordance with the rules. **2** blond, not dark, pale. **3** of only moderate quality or amount. **4** favourable, satisfactory, promising; unobstructed. **5** (of a copied document) neat, without corrections. **6** beautiful. **7** (*slang*) complete, unquestionable. *—adv.* **1** in a fair manner. **2** exactly, completely. **—fair and square,** exactly; above-board, straightforward(ly). **fair game,** a thing one may reasonably or legitimately pursue etc. **fair play,** equitable conduct or conditions. **the fair sex,** women. **fair-weather friend,** a friend or ally who is unreliable in difficulties. **in a fair way to,** likely to. [OE]

fair[2] *n.* **1** a periodical gathering for the sale of goods, often with entertainments. **2** a fun-fair. **3** an exhibition, especially to promote particular products. [f. OF f. L *feriae* holiday]

fairground *n.* an outdoor area where a fair is held.

fairing[1] *n.* a streamlining structure added to a ship or aircraft. [f. FAIR[1]]

fairing[2] *n.* an object bought at a fair. [f. FAIR[2]]

Fair Isle an island about half-way between the Orkneys and Shetlands, noted for the characteristic coloured designs in knitting which are named after it.

fairly *adv.* **1** in a fair manner. **2** moderately. **3** to a noticeable degree. [f. FAIR[1]]

fairway *n.* **1** a navigable channel. **2** a part of a golf-course between a tee and the green, kept free of rough grass.

fairy *n.* **1** a small imaginary being with magical powers. **2** (*slang*) a male homosexual. **—fairy godmother,** a benefactress. **fairy lights,** small coloured lights especially for outdoor decorations. **fairy ring,** a ring of darker grass caused by fungi. **fairy story** *or* **-tale** *n.* a tale about fairies; an incredible story, a falsehood. [f. OF (as FAY, -ERY)]

fairyland /ˈfeərɪlænd/ *n.* the home of the fairies; an enchanted place.

fait accompli /feɪt əˈkɒmpli:/ a thing that has been done and is past arguing against. [F]

faith *n.* **1** complete trust, unquestioning confidence. **2** strong belief, especially in a religious doctrine; a system of beliefs, a religion. **3** loyalty, trustworthiness. **—bad faith,** dishonest intention. **faith-cure, -healing,** etc., a cure etc. depending on faith rather than on medical treatment. **good faith,** sincere intention. [f. AF f. L *fides*]

faithful *adj.* **1** showing faith; loyal, trustworthy, constant. **2** accurate. **3** the Faithful, believers in a religion, followers. **—faithfulness** *n.* [f. FAITH + -FUL]

faithfully *adv.* in a faithful manner. **—yours faithfully,** a formula for ending a business or formal letter. [f. prec.]

faithless *adj.* **1** false, unreliable, disloyal. **2** without religious faith. [f. FAITH + -LESS]

fake *n.* a thing or person that is not genuine. *—adj.* counterfeit, not genuine. *—v.t.* to make (a thing) so that it falsely appears genuine; to feign. [f. obs. *feak*, *feague* thrash f. G]

fakir /ˈfeɪkɪə(r)/ *n.* a Muslim or Hindu religious mendicant or ascetic. [Arab., = poor man]

falchion /ˈfɔ:ltʃ(ə)n/ *n.* a broad curved sword. [f. OF f. L *falx* scythe]

falcon /ˈfɔ:lkən/ *n.* a small hawk trained to hunt game-birds for sport. [f. OF f. L *falco*]

falconry *n.* the breeding and training of hawks. [f. F (as prec.)]

fall /fɔ:l/ *v.i.* (*past* **fell**; *p.p.* **fallen**) **1** to go or come down freely, to descend. **2** to cease to stand, to come suddenly to the ground from a loss of balance etc. **3** to become detached and descend, to slope or hang down; to become lower, to subside; to lose status or position; to yield to temptation; to succumb (*to*); to be overthrown or vanquished, to perish; (of the face) to show dismay or disappointment. **4** to take or have a particular direction or place; to come by chance or duty. **5** to occur. **6** to pass *in* or *into* a specified condition; to become. *—n.* **1** the act or manner of falling; succumbing to temptation. **2** the amount by which something falls; the amount that falls. **3** (esp. in *pl.*) a waterfall. **4** a wrestling-bout; a throw in this in which both shoulders touch the mat for one second. **5** (*US*) autumn. **—the Fall (of man),** the first act of disobedience of Adam and Eve (Gen. 2 ff.) whereby man lost his primal innocence and happiness and entered upon his actual condition of sin and toil. **fall away,** to become few or thin; to desert; to vanish. **fall back,** to retreat. **fall back on,** to have recourse to in an extremity. **fall down (on),** to fail (in). **fall flat,** to be a failure, to fail to win applause. **fall for,** (*colloq.*) to be captivated or deceived by. **fall foul of,** to collide or quarrel with. **fall-guy** *n.* (*slang*) an easy victim, a scapegoat. **fall in,** to take or cause to take one's place in a military formation; (of a building etc.) to collapse. **fall in with,** to meet (by chance); to agree or coincide with. **fall off,** to decrease; to deteriorate. **fall on** *or* **upon,** to assault; to meet. **fall on one's feet,** to get out of a difficulty successfully. **fall out,** to quarrel; to result, to occur; to leave or cause to leave one's place in a military formation. **fall-out** *n.* radioactive debris in the air, from a nuclear explosion. **fall over,** to stumble and come to the ground. **fall over oneself,** (*colloq.*) to be eager or hasty; to be very confused. **fall short,** to be deficient or inadequate. **fall short of,** to fail to reach or obtain. **fall through,** to fail, (of a plan etc.) to come to nothing. **fall to,** to begin. [OE]

fallacy /ˈfæləsɪ/ *n.* a mistaken belief; faulty reasoning or misleading argument; a tendency to mislead or delude. —**fallacious** /fəˈleɪʃəs/ *adj.* [f. L (*fallere* deceive)]

fallible /ˈfælɪb(ə)l/ *adj.* capable of making mistakes. —**fallibility** /-ˈbɪlɪtɪ/ *n.*, **fallibly** *adv.* [as prec.]

Fallopian tube /fəˈləʊpɪən/ either of two tubes along which egg-cells travel from the ovaries to the womb. [f. *Fallopius*, Italian anatomist (d. 1562)]

fallow[1] /ˈfæləʊ/ *adj.* (of land) ploughed but left unsown; uncultivated. —*n.* fallow land. [OE]

fallow[2] /ˈfæləʊ/ *adj.* of a pale brownish or reddish yellow. —**fallow deer,** a species (*Dama dama*) smaller than the red deer. [OE]

false /fɔːls, fɒls/ *adj.* **1** wrong, incorrect. **2** deceitful, treacherous, unfaithful *to*; deceptive. **3** spurious, sham, artificial. **4** improperly so called. —**false alarm,** an alarm needlessly given. **false pretences,** misrepresentation with intent to deceive. **false teeth,** artificial teeth. —**falsely** *adv.*, **falseness** *n.* [f. OE & OF f. L *falsus* (*fallere* deceive)]

falsehood *n.* an untrue thing; a lie, lying. [f. prec. + -HOOD]

falsetto /fɔːlˈsetəʊ, fɒl-/ (*pl.* **-os**) an artificial voice above the normal range, especially by a male tenor. [It., dim. of *falso* false]

falsies /ˈfɔːlsɪz, ˈfɒl-/ *n.pl.* (*colloq.*) pads etc. to make the breasts seem larger. [f. FALSE]

falsify /ˈfɔːlsɪfaɪ, ˈfɒl-/ *v.t.* to alter fraudulently; to misrepresent (facts etc.). —**falsification** /-fɪˈkeɪʃ(ə)n/ *n.* [f. F or L (*falsificus* making false)]

falsity *n.* being false. [f. FALSE]

falter /ˈfɔːltə(r)/ *v.t./i.* to stumble; to move or function unsteadily; to say or speak hesitatingly; to lose strength. [orig. unkn.]

fame *n.* renown; the state of being famous; (*archaic*) reputation. [f. OF f. L *fama*]

famed *adj.* famous, much spoken of (*for*). [f. FAME]

familial /fəˈmɪlɪ(ə)l/ *adj.* of or relating to a family or its members. [F, f. L *familia* family]

familiar /fəˈmɪlɪə(r)/ *adj.* **1** well acquainted *with*. **2** well known (*to*); often encountered or experienced. **3** informal, esp. excessively so. —*n.* **1** an intimate friend. **2** a familiar spirit. —**familiar spirit,** a demon serving a witch etc. —**familiarity** /-ˈærɪtɪ/ *n.*, **familiarly** *adv.* [f. OF f. L (as FAMILY)]

familiarize /fəˈmɪlɪəraɪz/ *v.t.* **1** to make well acquainted. **2** to make well known. —**familiarization** /-ˈzeɪʃ(ə)n/ *n.* [f. F (as FAMILIAR)]

family /ˈfæmɪlɪ/ *n.* **1** a set of parents and children or of relatives; a person's children; the members of a household. **2** all the descendants of a common ancestor; lineage; a race or group of peoples from a common stock; a group of languages derived from one early language. **3** a group of objects distinguished by common features. **4** a group of allied genera of animals or plants, usually a subdivision of an order. —**family man,** one with a family; one who is fond of home life. **family name,** a surname. **family planning,** birth-control. **family tree,** a genealogical chart. **in the family way,** (*colloq.*) pregnant. [f. L *familia* household (*famulus* servant)]

famine /ˈfæmɪn/ *n.* extreme scarcity, especially of food. [f. OF f. L *fames* hunger]

famish /ˈfæmɪʃ/ *v.t./i.* to reduce or be reduced to extreme hunger. —**be famished** *or* **famishing,** (*colloq.*) to be very hungry. [f. OF (as prec.)]

famous /ˈfeɪməs/ *adj.* **1** well known, celebrated. **2** (*colloq.*) excellent. —**famously** *adv.* [f. AF & OF f. L (as FAME)]

fan[1] *n.* **1** a mechanical apparatus with rotating blades for ventilation. **2** a device (usually folding and sector-shaped when spread out) waved in the hand to cool the face etc.; anything spread out in this shape. —*v.t./i.* (**-nn-**) **1** to cool or kindle by agitating the air around; to blow gently upon. **2** to spread (*out*) in a fan shape. —**fan belt,** the belt transmitting the torque from a motor-vehicle engine to the fan which cools the radiator. **fan-jet** *n.* a turbofan. **fan tracery** *or* **vault(ing),** ornamental vaulting with fanlike ribs. [OE, f. L *vannus* winnowing-basket]

fan[2] *n.* a devotee of a specified amusement, performer, etc. —**fan club,** one organized for a celebrity's admirers. **fan mail,** letters to a celebrity from fans. [abbr. of foll.]

fanatic /fəˈnætɪk/ *n.* a person filled with excessive and often misguided enthusiasm for something. —*adj.* excessively enthusiastic. —**fanatical** *adj.*, **fanatically** *adv.*, **fanaticism** /-ɪsɪz(ə)m/ *n.* [f. F or L (*fanum* temple)]

fancier /ˈfænsɪə(r)/ *n.* a connoisseur, an enthusiast; an amateur breeder of some plant or animal. [f. FANCY]

fanciful /ˈfænsɪf(ə)l/ *adj.* **1** existing only in imagination or fancy. **2** indulging in fancy. —**fancifully** *adv.* [f. foll. + -FUL]

fancy /ˈfænsɪ/ *n.* **1** the faculty of imagination; a mental image. **2** a supposition. **3** a caprice; a liking or whim. **4** those who have a certain hobby, fanciers. —*adj.* **1** elaborate, ornamental. **2** capricious, extravagant. —*v.t.* **1** to imagine. **2** (*colloq.*) to feel a desire for; to find sexually attractive; to have an unduly high opinion of (*oneself*, one's ability, etc.).

3 to be inclined to think (*that*). **4** to breed or grow (animals or plants) with attention to certain points. —**fancy dress,** costume for masquerading as a different person etc. at a party etc. **fancy-free** *adj*. not in love. **fancy man,** (*slang*) a woman's lover, a pimp. **fancy that!** *or* **just fancy!,** how strange! **fancy woman,** (*slang*) a mistress. [contr. of FANTASY]

fandango /fæn'dæŋgəʊ/ *n*. (*pl*. **-oes**) a lively Spanish dance; music for this. [Sp., perh. of Black orig.]

fanfare /'fænfeə(r)/ *n*. a short showy or ceremonious sounding of trumpets etc. [F, imit.]

fang *n*. **1** a canine tooth, especially of a dog or wolf. **2** a serpent's venom-tooth. **3** the root of a tooth or its prong. [OE f. ON]

fanlight *n*. a small (orig. semi-circular) window over a door or other window. [f. FAN[1] + LIGHT[1]]

fanny /'fænɪ/ *n*. (*slang*) the female genitals; the buttocks. [orig. unkn.]

fantail *n*. a pigeon with a fan-shaped tail.

fantasia /fæntə'zɪə, -'teɪzɪə/ *n*. a musical or other composition in which form is subordinate to imagination, or which is based on familiar tunes. [It., = fantasy]

fantasize /'fæntəsaɪz/ *v.t./i*. to imagine, to create a fantasy (about); to day-dream. [f. FANTASY]

fantastic /fæn'tæstɪk/ *adj*. **1** extravagantly fanciful, fabulous; grotesque, quaint. **2** (*colloq*.) excellent, extraordinary. —**fantastically** *adv*. [f. OF f. L f. Gk (as foll.)]

fantasy /'fæntəsɪ/ *n*. **1** imagination, especially when extravagant; a mental image, a day-dream. **2** a fanciful invention or composition, a book or film etc. relating fanciful events. [f. OF f. L f. Gk *phantasia* appearance]

far *adv*. (*compar*. **farther, further;** *superl*. **farthest, furthest**) **1** at, to, or by a great distance; a long way or a long way off in space or time. **2** to a great extent or degree, by much. —*adj*. distant, remote; more distant. —**as far as,** right to (a place); to the extent that. **by far,** by a great amount. **far and away,** by far. **far and wide,** over a large area. **far-away** *adj*. remote; (of a look) dreamy; (of a voice) sounding as if from a distance. **a far cry,** a long way. **Far East,** China, Japan, and other countries of East and SE Asia. **far-fetched** *adj*. (of an explanation etc.) strained, unconvincing. **far-flung** *adj*. extending far. **far-reaching** *adj*. of wide application or influence. **far-seeing** *adj*. showing foresight, prudent. **Far West,** the regions of North America in the Rocky Mountains and along the Pacific coast; (*formerly*) the area west of the earliest European settlements (now called the *Middle West*). **in so far as,** to the extent that. **so far,** to such an extent, to this point; until now. **so far as,** as far as; in so far as. [OE]

farad /'færəd/ *n*. a unit of capacitance such that one coulomb of charge causes a potential difference of one volt. [f. M. *Faraday*, English physicist (d. 1867)]

farandole /færən'dəʊl/ *n*. a lively Provençal dance; the music for this. [F f. Prov.]

farce *n*. **1** a comedy based on ludicrously improbable events; this genre of theatre. **2** absurdly futile proceedings or pretence. —**farcical** *adj*., **farcically** *adv*. [F (orig. = stuffing) f. OF f. L *farcire* to stuff (with ref. to interludes)]

fare /feə(r)/ *n*. **1** the price charged to a passenger on public transport; a fare-paying passenger. **2** food provided. —*v.i*. to progress, to get on. [OE]

farewell /feə'wel/ *int*. goodbye! —*n*. a leave-taking.

farina /fə'raɪnə, fə'ri:nə/ *n*. flour or meal of corn, nuts, or starchy roots. [L]

farinaceous /færɪ'neɪʃəs/ *adj*. of or like farina, starchy. [f. prec.]

farm *n*. an area of land and its buildings used under one management for growing crops, rearing animals, etc.; any place for breeding animals; a farmhouse. —*v.t./i*. **1** to use (land) for growing crops, rearing animals, etc.; to breed (fish etc.) commercially; to work as a farmer. **2** to take the proceeds of (a tax) on payment of a fixed sum. —**farm-hand** *n*. a worker on a farm. **farm out,** to delegate (work) to others. [f. OF f. L *firma* fixed payment; orig. applied to leased land]

farmer *n*. an owner or manager of a farm. [f. FARM]

farmhouse *n*. a dwelling-place attached to a farm.

farmost *adj*. furthest. [f. FAR]

farmstead /'fɑ:msted/ *n*. a farm and its buildings.

farmyard *n*. the yard of a farmhouse.

faro /'feərəʊ/ *n*. a gambling card-game. [f. F *pharaon* pharaoh (said to have been name of king of hearts)]

farrago /fə'rɑ:gəʊ/ *n*. (*pl*. **-os**) a hotchpotch, a medley. [L, = mixed fodder (*far* corn)]

farrier /'færɪə(r)/ *n*. a smith who shoes horses. —**farriery** *n*. [f. OF f. L *ferrarius* (*ferrum* iron, horseshoe)]

farrow /'færəʊ/ *v.t./i*. (of a sow) to give birth, to give birth to (pigs). —*n*. farrowing; a litter of pigs. [OE]

Farsi /'fɑ:sɪ/ *n*. the Persian language. [Pers.; cf. PARSEE]

fart *v.i*. (*vulgar*) to emit wind from the anus.

—*n.* (*vulgar*) an emission of wind from the anus. [OE]

farther /ˈfɑːðə(r)/ *adv.* & *adj.* at or to a greater distance, more remote. [var. of FURTHER]

farthest /ˈfɑːðɪst/ *adv.* & *adj.* at or to the greatest distance, most remote. [var. of FURTHEST]

farthing /ˈfɑːðɪŋ/ *n.* (*hist.*) a quarter of a penny, a coin of this value (legal tender until 1961). [OE, f. *fēortha* fourth]

farthingale /ˈfɑːðɪŋgeɪl/ *n.* (*hist.*) a hooped petticoat. [f. F *verdugale* f. Sp. (*verdugo* rod)]

fasces /ˈfæsiːz/ *n.* a bundle of rods with a projecting axe-blade carried before an ancient Roman magistrate as a symbol of authority. [L, pl. of *fascis* bundle]

fascia /ˈfeɪʃə/ *n.* **1** (*Archit.*) a long flat surface of wood or stone. **2** a stripe, a band. **3** = facia. [L, = band, door-frame]

fascicle /ˈfæsɪk(ə)l/ *n.* an instalment of a book. [f. L *fasciculus* dim. of *fascis* bundle]

fascinate /ˈfæsɪneɪt/ *v.t.* **1** to capture the interest of; to charm irresistibly. **2** (of a snake etc.) to paralyse (a victim) with fear. —**fascination** /-ˈneɪʃ(ə)n/ *n.*, **fascinator** *n.* [f. L *fascinare* (*fascinum* spell)]

Fascism /ˈfæʃɪz(ə)m/ *n.* an extreme right-wing totalitarian political system or such views. —**Fascist** *n.* & *adj.* [f. It. (*fascio* bundle, organized group, f. L *fascis* bundle; see FASCES)]

fashion /ˈfæʃ(ə)n/ *n.* **1** the current popular custom or style, especially in dress. **2** a manner of doing something. —*v.t.* to form or make (*into*). —**after a fashion,** to some extent, barely adequately. **in fashion,** fashionable at the present time. **out of fashion,** no longer fashionable. [f. AF f. L *factio* (*facere* make)]

fashionable *adj.* following or in keeping with the current fashion; characteristic of or patronized by fashionable people. —**fashionably** *adv.* [f. prec.]

fast[1] /fɑːst/ *adj.* **1** moving or done quickly; enabling or causing quick motion; (of a clock etc.) showing a time later than the correct time; (of photographic film) very sensitive to light and needing only a short exposure. **2** (of a person) immoral, dissipated. **3** firm, fixed, firmly attached; (of a colour) not fading when washed etc.; (of a friend) close. —*adv.* **1** quickly, in quick succession. **2** firmly, tightly. —**fast breeder (reactor),** a reactor using mainly fast neutrons. **fast neutron,** a neutron with high kinetic energy. **fast one,** (*slang*) an unfair or deceitful action. [OE]

fast[2] /fɑːst/ *v.i.* to abstain from food or certain food, especially as a religious observance. —*n.* fasting; a period of fasting. [OE]

fasten /ˈfɑːs(ə)n/ *v.t./i.* **1** to fix firmly, to tie or join together; to join or close *up.* **2** to fix (one's glance or attention) intently. **3** to become fastened. —**fasten off,** to tie or secure the end of a thread etc. **fasten on** *or* **upon,** to seize on (as a victim etc.). [OE (as FAST[1])]

fastener /ˈfɑːsnə(r)/ *n.* (also **fastening**) a device that fastens something. [f. prec.]

fastidious /fæˈstɪdɪəs/ *adj.* very careful in matters of choice or taste; easily disgusted, squeamish. —**fastidiously** *adv.*, **fastidiousness** *n.* [f. L (*fastidium* aversion)]

fastness /ˈfɑːstnɪs/ *n.* a stronghold. [OE (as FAST[1])]

fat *adj.* **1** very plump; well-fed; (of an animal) made plump for slaughter. **2** containing much fat; covered with fat. **3** thick, substantial. **4** fertile. —*n.* **1** an oily or greasy substance found in animal bodies etc. **2** the fat part of an animal's flesh (opp. *lean*). —*v.t.* (**-tt-**) to fatten. —**a fat chance,** (*slang*) very little chance. **fat-head** (*colloq.*) a stupid person. **the fat is in the fire,** there will be trouble. **a fat lot,** (*slang*) very little. **kill the fatted calf,** to celebrate, especially at a prodigal's return. **live off the fat of the land,** to live luxuriously. —**fatness** *n.* [OE]

fatal /ˈfeɪt(ə)l/ *adj.* causing or ending in death; ruinous, disastrous, fateful. —**fatally** *adv.* [f. OF or L (as FATE)]

fatalism /ˈfeɪtəlɪz(ə)m/ *n.* the belief that all that happens is predetermined and therefore inevitable. —**fatalist** *n.*, **fatalistic** /-ˈlɪstɪk/ *adj.* [f. prec.]

fatality /fəˈtælɪtɪ/ *n.* **1** a death by accident or in war etc. **2** a fatal influence; a predestined liability to disaster. [f. F or L (as FATAL)]

fate *n.* **1** an irresistible power or force controlling all events. **2** what is destined; a person's destiny or fortune; death, destruction. —*v.t.* (esp. in *pass.*) to preordain. —**the Fates,** (*Gk myth.*) the goddesses who presided over the birth and life of men. [f. It. & L *fatum*]

fateful *adj.* controlled by fate; decisive, important. —**fatefully** *adv.* [f. FATE + -FUL]

father /ˈfɑːðə(r)/ *n.* **1** a male parent; a male guardian through adoption. **2** (usually in *pl.*) a forefather; a founder or originator, an early leader; (in *pl.*) elders, leading members. **3 Father,** God, especially the first person of the Trinity. **4** a priest, especially of a religious order, or as a title or form of address. **5** venerable person, especially as a title in personifications. —*v.t.* **1** to beget; to originate (a scheme etc.). **2** to fix the paternity of (a child) or the responsibility for (a book, idea, etc.) *on* or *upon.* —**father-figure** *n.* an older man who is respected like a father, a trusted leader. **father-in-law** *n.* (*pl.* **fathers-in-law**) one's wife's or husband's father. **Father of the**

House, the member of the House of Commons with the longest continuous service. **Father's Day,** a day (usually the third Sunday in June) for a special tribute to fathers. **Fathers (of the Church),** those early ecclesiastical writers, especially of the first five centuries, whose writings on Christian doctrines were regarded as especially authoritative. —**fatherhood** *n.* [OE]

fatherland *n.* one's native country.

fatherly *adj.* of or like a father. [f. FATHER]

fathom /ˈfæð(ə)m/ *n.* a measure of 6 feet, especially in soundings. —*v.t.* **1** to understand. **2** to measure the depth of (water). [OE, = the outstretched arms]

fatigue /fəˈtiːg/ *n.* **1** extreme tiredness. **2** weakness in metals etc. from variations of stress. **3** a soldier's non-combatant duty; (in *pl.*) clothing worn for this. —*v.t.* to cause fatigue in; to tire. [f. F f. L *fatigare* exhaust]

fatstock *n.* livestock fattened for slaughter.

fatten *v.t./i.* to make or become fat. [f. FAT]

fatty *adj.* like or containing fat. —**fatty acid,** a member of a series of acids occurring in or derived from natural fats etc. [f. FAT]

fatuous /ˈfætjʊəs/ *adj.* silly, purposeless. —**fatuity** /fəˈtjuːɪtɪ/ *n.*, **fatuously** *adv.* [f. L *fatuus*]

faucet /ˈfɔːsɪt/ *n.* a tap for a barrel etc.; (*US*) any tap. [f. F *fausset* vent-peg f. Prov. (*falsar* bore)]

fault /fɔːlt, fɒlt/ *n.* **1** a defect or blemish. **2** an offence or misdeed; the responsibility or blame for this; (in tennis etc.) an incorrect serve; (in show-jumping) a penalty for an error. **3** a break in the continuity of rock strata. —*v.t./i.* **1** to find fault with, to blame. **2** to cause a fault in (rock strata); (of rock) to have a fault. —**at fault,** blameworthy. **find fault with,** to criticize unfavourably. **to a fault,** excessively. [f. OF f. L *fallere* deceive]

faultless *adj.* without faults. —**faultlessly** *adv.* [f. FAULT + -LESS]

faulty *adj.* having a fault or faults, imperfect. —**faultily** *adv.*, **faultiness** *n.* [f. FAULT]

faun /fɔːn/ *n.* a Latin rural deity with a goat's horns, legs, and tail. [f. OF or L *Faunus*, Latin god identified with Gk Pan]

fauna /ˈfɔːnə/ *n.* (*pl.* **-as**) the animals of a particular region or period. [f. name of rural goddess, sister of Faunus (see prec.)]

faute de mieux /fəʊt də ˈmjɜː/ for want of any better alternative. [F]

faux pas /fəʊ ˈpɑː/ *n.* (*pl.* same /ˈpɑːz/) a tactless mistake, a blunder. [F, = false step]

favour /ˈfeɪvə(r)/ *n.* **1** liking, goodwill, approval. **2** a kind or helpful act. **3** partiality. **4** a badge or ornament worn as a mark of favour. —*v.t.* **1** to regard or treat with favour or partiality. **2** to support, to promote, to prefer; to oblige *with*; to be to the advantage of, to facilitate. **3** (*colloq.*) to resemble in features. **4** (in *p.p.*) having special advantages; having specified looks. —**in** *or* **out of favour,** approved or disapproved of. **in favour of,** in support of; to the advantage of. [f. OF f. L *favor* (*favere* show goodwill to)]

favourable *adj.* **1** well disposed, approving. **2** pleasing. **3** satisfactory; helpful, suitable. —**favourably** *adv.* [as prec.]

favourite /ˈfeɪvərɪt/ *adj.* preferred to all others. —*n.* a favourite person or thing, especially a person favoured by a monarch or superior; (in sport) a competitor thought most likely to win. [f. obs. F f. It. (as FAVOUR)]

favouritism *n.* unfair favouring of one person or group at the expense of another. [f. prec.]

fawn[1] *n.* **1** a deer in its first year. **2** a light yellowish-brown colour. —*adj.* fawn-coloured. [f. OF f. L *fetus* offspring]

fawn[2] *v.i.* (esp. of a dog etc.) to try to win affection by grovelling etc.; to lavish caresses (*on* or *upon*); to behave servilely. [OE (as FAIN)]

fax *n.* **1** facsimile reproduction of a document etc. by electronic transmission. **2** this reproduction. —*v.t.* transmit by fax. [abbr. FACSIMILE]

fay *n.* (*literary*) a fairy. [f. OF f. L *fata* the Fates]

FBA *abbr.* Fellow of the British Academy.

FBI *abbr.* (*US*) Federal Bureau of Investigation.

Fe *symbol* iron.

fealty /ˈfiːəltɪ/ *n.* the duty of a feudal tenant or vassal to his lord; allegiance. [f. OF f. L (as FIDELITY)]

fear *n.* **1** an unpleasant emotion caused by exposure to danger, the expectation of pain, etc.; alarm. **2** awe and reverence. **3** a danger, a likelihood. —*v.t./i.* **1** to have fear, to expect with fear or anxiety; to be afraid of; to shrink from (*doing*). **2** to revere (God). —**no fear!,** (*colloq.*) certainly not! [OE, = sudden calamity, danger]

fearful *adj.* **1** afraid, reluctant through fear. **2** causing fear. **3** (*colloq.*) extreme, annoying. —**fearfully** *adv.* [f. prec. + -FUL]

fearless *adj.* without fear, brave. —**fearlessly** *adv.*, **fearlessness** *n.* [f. FEAR + -LESS]

fearsome *adj.* frightening, formidable. [f. FEAR + -SOME]

feasible /ˈfiːzɪb(ə)l/ *adj.* practicable, possible. —**feasibility** /-ˈbɪlɪtɪ/ *n.*, **feasibly** *adv.* [f. OF f. L *facere* do]

feast *n.* **1** a large meal, a banquet. **2** a joyful religious festival. **3** something giving great pleasure. —*v.t./i.* **1** to partake of a feast, to eat and drink heartily (*on*). **2** to give a feast to. **3** to give pleasure to, to regale. [f. OF f. L (*festus* festal)]

feat *n.* a remarkable act or achievement. [f. OF f. L (as FACT)]

feather /ˈfeðə(r)/ *n.* **1** any of the appendages growing from a bird's skin, with a horny stem and fine strands on both sides; a piece of this as a decoration etc. **2** (*collect.*) plumage; game-birds. —*v.t.*/*i.* **1** to cover or line with feathers. **2** to turn (an oar) so that it passes through the air edgeways; to make this movement. —**feather bed,** a mattress stuffed with feathers. **feather-bed** *v.t.* to make things easy for, to pamper. **feather-brained, -headed** *adjs.* silly. **feather in one's cap,** an achievement to one's credit. **feather one's nest,** to enrich oneself. —**feathery** *adj.* [OE]

feathering *n.* **1** plumage. **2** the feathers of an arrow. **3** a feather-like structure or marking. [f. prec.]

featherweight *n.* **1** a boxing-weight between bantamweight and lightweight (see BOXING-WEIGHT). **2** a person or thing of very light weight.

feature /ˈfiːtʃə(r)/ *n.* **1** (usu. in *pl.*) a part of the face, especially with regard to the appearance. **2** a characteristic or notable part of a thing. **3** a prominent article in a newspaper etc. **4** a feature film. —*v.t.*/*i.* **1** to give prominence to. **2** to be a feature of. **3** to be a participant (*in*). —**feature film,** the main film in a cinema programme. [f. OF f. L *factura* formation (*facere* make)]

featureless *adj.* lacking distinct features. [f. prec. + -LESS]

Feb. *abbr.* February.

febrile /ˈfiːbraɪl/ *adj.* of a fever, feverish. [f. F or L (*febris* fever)]

February /ˈfebrʊərɪ/ *n.* the second month of the year. [f. OF f. L (*februa* purification feast held in this month)]

feckless *adj.* feeble, incompetent, helpless. —**fecklessness** *n.* [f. Sc. *feck* (*effeck* var. of EFFECT) + -LESS]

fecund /ˈfiːkənd/ *adj.* prolific, fertile; fertilizing. —**fecundity** /fɪˈkʌndɪtɪ/ *n.* [f. F or L *fecundus* fruitful]

fecundate /ˈfiːkəndeɪt/ *v.t.* to make fecund, to fertilize. —**fecundation** /-ˈdeɪʃ(ə)n/ *n.* [f. L *fecundare* (as prec.)]

fed *past* & *p.p.* of FEED.

federal /ˈfedər(ə)l/ *adj.* **1** of a system of government in which several States unite but remain independent in internal affairs; of such States or their central government. **2** relating to or favouring central as opposed to provincial government. **3** Federal, (*US*) of the northern States in the American Civil War. —**federalism** *n.*, **federalist** *n.*, **federally** *adv.* [f. L (*foedus* covenant)]

federalize *v.t.* to make federal, to organize in a federal system. —**federalization** /-ˈzeɪʃ(ə)n/ *n.* [f. prec.]

federate /ˈfedəreɪt/ *v.t.*/*i.* to unite on a federal basis or for a common object. —/ˈfedərət/ *adj.* so united. [f. L *foederare* (as FEDERAL)]

federation /fedəˈreɪʃ(ə)n/ *n.* **1** an act of federating. **2** a federal group. —**federative** /ˈfedərətɪv/ *adj.* [f. F f. L (as FEDERAL)]

fee *n.* **1** the sum payable to an official or professional person for services; the charge for joining a society, taking an examination, etc.; the money paid for the transfer to another employer of a footballer etc.; (in *pl.*) regular payment for instruction at a school etc. **2** an inherited estate of land, unlimited (**fee simple**) or limited (**fee-tail**) as to the class of heir. —**in fee,** in absolute ownership. [f. AF f. L *feudum*, perh. f. Frankish *fehu-od* cattle-property]

feeble *adj.* weak; lacking strength, energy, or effectiveness. —**feeble-minded** *adj.* mentally deficient. —**feebleness** *n.*, **feebly** *adv.* [f. OF f. L *flebilis* lamentable]

feed *v.t.*/*i.* (*past* & *p.p.* **fed**) **1** to supply with food, to put food into the mouth of; to give as food to animals. **2** (esp. of animals or babies, or *colloq.*) to take food, to eat. **3** to maintain a supply of (material required *into* a machine etc.), to keep (a machine, fire, etc.) supplied thus. **4** to gratify; to encourage *with*. **5** to send passes to (a player) in football etc. —*n.* **1** food for animals; a measured allowance of this. **2** feeding. **3** a meal (esp. for babies, or *colloq.*). **4** material supplied to machines etc. —**fed up,** (*colloq.*) discontented or bored (*with*). **feed on,** to consume; to be nourished or strengthened by. [OE]

feedback *n.* **1** return to the input of a part of the output of a system or process; a signal so returned. **2** information about the result of an experiment etc.; response.

feeder *n.* **1** one that feeds in a specified way. **2** the feeding apparatus in a machine. **3** a child's bib. **4** a tributary, branch road, branch railway line, etc., that links with the main system. [f. prec.]

feel *v.t.*/*i.* (*past* & *p.p.* **felt**) **1** to examine or search by touch; to perceive by touch, to have a sensation of. **2** to be conscious of (an emotion etc.). **3** to experience, to be affected by (an emotion or physical condition). **4** to seem, to give an impression of being. **5** to have a vague or emotional impression; to consider, to think; to be consciously, to consider oneself. **6** to sympathize *with*, to have pity *for*. —n. **1** an act of feeling; the sense of touch. **2** the sensation characterizing a material, situation, etc. —**feel like,** (*colloq.*) to have a wish for, to be inclined towards. **feel one's way,** to proceed cautiously (*lit.* or *fig.*). [OE]

feeler *n.* **1** an organ in certain animals for testing things by touch. **2** a tentative proposal or suggestion. —**feeler gauge,** a gauge with blades that can be inserted to measure gaps. [f. prec.]

feeling *n.* **1** the capacity to feel, the sense of touch. **2** an emotion; (in *pl.*) emotional susceptibilities. **3** an opinion or notion. **4** sympathy with others. **5** earnestness. —*adj.* sensitive, sympathetic; heartfelt. [f. FEEL]

feet *pl.* of FOOT.

feign /feɪn/ *v.t.* to pretend; to simulate. [f. OF f. L *fingere* mould, fashion]

feint /feɪnt/ *n.* a sham attack, blow, etc. to divert an opponent's attention from the main attack; a pretence. —*v.i.* to make a feint. —*adj.* (of paper etc.) having faintly ruled lines. [f. F (as prec.)]

feldspar /ˈfeldspɑ:(r)/ *n.* any of a group of usually white or flesh-red rock-forming minerals which are aluminium silicates combined with various other metallic ions. [f. G *feldspat(h)* (*feld* field, *spat(h)* spar)]

felicitate /fɪˈlɪsɪteɪt/ *v.t.* to congratulate. [f. L *felicitare* make very happy (*felix* happy)]

felicitation /fɪlɪsɪˈteɪʃ(ə)n/ *n.* (usu. in *pl.*) a congratulation. [f. prec.]

felicitous /fɪˈlɪsɪtəs/ *adj.* well-chosen, apt. —**felicitously** *adv.* [f. foll.]

felicity /fɪˈlɪsɪtɪ/ *n.* **1** great happiness. **2** a pleasing manner or style. [f. OF f. L (*felix* happy)]

feline /ˈfi:laɪn/ *adj.* of cats; catlike. —*n.* an animal of the cat family. —**felinity** /fɪˈlɪnɪtɪ/ *n.* [f. L (*feles* cat)]

fell[1] *v.t.* **1** to cut down (a tree); to strike down by a blow or cut. **2** to stitch down (the edge of a seam). [OE (causative of FALL)]

fell[2] *n.* a hill; a stretch of hills or moorland, especially in northern England. [ON]

fell[3] *adj.* ruthless, destructive. —**at one fell swoop,** in a single (deadly) action. [f. OF (as FELON)]

fell[4] *n.* an animal's skin or hide with the hair. [OE]

fell[5] *past* of FALL.

fellatio /feˈlɑ:tɪəʊ/ *n.* stimulation of the penis by sucking. [f. L *fellare* suck]

fellow /ˈfeləʊ/ *n.* **1** a comrade or associate. **2** a counterpart, an equal. **3** (*colloq.*) a man or boy. **4** an incorporated senior member of a college; a research student receiving a fellowship. **5** a member of a learned society. —*attrib.* or *adj.* of the same class, associated in a joint action. —**fellow-feeling** *n.* sympathy with a person whose experience etc. one shares. **fellow-traveller** *n.* a sympathizer with but not a member of a political (esp. the Communist) party. [OE f. ON]

fellowship *n.* **1** friendly association with others, companionship. **2** a body of associates. **3** the position or income of a fellow of a college or learned society; the stipend granted to a graduate for a period of research. [f. prec.]

felon /ˈfelən/ *n.* one who has committed a felony. [f. OF f. L *fel(l)o* (orig. unkn.)]

felony /ˈfelənɪ/ *n.* (*hist.*) any of a class of crimes which may loosely be said to have been regarded by the law as of graver character than those called misdemeanours. —**felonious** /fɪˈləʊnɪəs/ *adj.*, **feloniously** *adv.* [f. OF (as prec.)]

felspar var. of FELDSPAR.

felt[1] *n.* a cloth of matted and pressed fibres of wool etc. —*v.t./i.* to make into felt; to cover with felt; to become matted. —**felt(-tip** *or* **-tipped) pen,** a pen with a felt point. [OE]

felt[2] *past & p.p.* of FEEL.

felucca /fɪˈlʌkə/ *n.* a small ship with lateen sails and/or oars, used on Mediterranean coasts. [f. It. f. Sp. f. Arab., perh. f. Gk *epholkion* small boat towed after a ship]

female /ˈfi:meɪl/ *adj.* **1** of the sex that can bear offspring or produce eggs; (of plants) fruit-bearing; of women or female animals or plants. **2** (of a screw, socket, etc.) made hollow to receive the corresponding inserted part. —*n.* a female person, animal, or plant. [f. OF f. L *femella* (*femina* woman), assim. to MALE]

feminine /ˈfemɪnɪn/ *adj.* **1** of a woman; having qualities associated with women. **2** (*Gram.*) of or denoting the gender proper to women's names. **3** (of a rhyme or line-ending) having a stressed syllable followed by an unstressed one. —*n.* the feminine gender; a feminine word. —**femininity** /-ˈnɪnɪtɪ/ *n.* [f. OF or L (*femina* woman)]

feminism /ˈfemɪnɪz(ə)m/ *n.* advocacy of women's rights on the basis of the equality of the sexes. —**feminist** *n.* [as prec.]

femme fatale /fæm fæˈtɑ:l/ *n.* a dangerously attractive woman. [F]

femto- /femtəʊ-/ *in comb.* denoting a factor of 10^{-15} (*femtometre*). [f. Da. or Norw. *femten* fifteen]

femur /ˈfi:mə(r)/ *n.* the thigh-bone. —**femoral** /ˈfemər(ə)l/ *adj.* [L, = thigh]

fen *n.* a low marshy area of land. —**the Fens,** low-lying districts of Lincolnshire, Cambridgeshire, and neighbouring counties in eastern England. [OE]

fence *n.* **1** a barrier or railing enclosing a field, garden, etc.; a structure for a horse to jump over in a competition etc. **2** a guard or guide or gauge in a machine. **3** a dealer in stolen goods. —*v.t./i.* **1** to surround (as) with a fence; to enclose or separate with a fence. **2** to practise the sport of fencing; to be evasive, to parry. **3** to deal in (stolen goods). [f. DEFENCE]

fencing /ˈfensɪŋ/ *n.* **1** fences; material for fences. **2** the sport of fighting with foils or other kinds of sword. [f. prec.]

fend *v.t./i.* **1** to ward *off*, to repel. **2** to provide *for*. [f. DEFEND]

fender *n.* **1** a low frame bordering a fireplace to keep in falling coals etc. **2** a pad or bundle of rope etc. hung over a vessel's side to protect it against impact. **3** (*US*) the bumper of a motor vehicle. [f. prec.]

fennel /ˈfen(ə)l/ *n.* a yellow-flowered herb (*Foeniculum vulgare*) used for flavouring. [OE & f. OF f. L *faeniculum*]

fenny *adj.* characterized by fens. [f. FEN]

fenugreek /ˈfenju:gri:k/ *n.* a leguminous plant (*Trigonella foenum-graecum*) with aromatic seeds. [f. OF f. L, = Greek hay]

feoff /fef/ *n.* a fief. [AF var. of FIEF]

feral /ˈfɪər(ə)l/ *adj.* wild; uncultivated; in a wild state after escape from captivity; brutal. [f. L *ferus* wild]

ferial /ˈfɪərɪəl/ *adj.* (of a day) not a festival or fast. [f. OF or L *ferialis* (*feriae* holiday)]

Ferm. *abbr.* Fermanagh.

ferment /ˈfɜ:ment/ *n.* **1** fermentation; a fermenting agent. **2** excitement. —/fəˈment/ *v.t./i.* **1** to undergo or subject to fermentation. **2** to excite. [f. OF or L *fermentum* (*fervēre* boil)]

fermentation /fɜ:menˈteɪʃ(ə)n/ *n.* **1** a chemical change involving effervescence and the production of heat, induced by an organic substance such as yeast. **2** excitement. —**fermentative** /fəˈmentətɪv/ *adj.* [f. L (as prec.)]

fermion /ˈfɜ:mɪɒn/ *n.* a particle obeying the relations stated by Fermi and Dirac, with half-integral spin. [f. E. *Fermi*, physicist (d. 1954)]

fermium /ˈfɜ:mɪəm/ *n.* an artificially made transuranic radioactive metallic element, symbol Fm, atomic number 100. [as prec.]

fern *n.* a kind of flowerless plant, usually with feathery fronds. —**ferny** *adj.* [OE]

ferocious /fəˈrəʊʃəs/ *adj.* fierce, savage. —**ferociously** *adv.*, **ferocity** /fəˈrɒsɪtɪ/ *n.* [f. L *ferox*]

ferret /ˈferɪt/ *n.* a variety of the common polecat, used in catching rabbits, rats, etc. —*v.t./i.* **1** to hunt with ferrets. **2** to rummage, to search. —**ferret out**, to discover or produce by searching. [f. OF f. L (*fur* thief)]

ferric /ˈferɪk/ *adj.* of iron; containing iron in trivalent form. [f. L *ferrum* iron]

Ferris wheel /ˈferɪs/ a giant revolving vertical wheel with passenger cars on its periphery, used for rides at fun-fairs etc. [f. name of inventor G. W. G. *Ferris*, Amer. engineer (d. 1896)]

ferro- *in comb.* containing iron; of iron. [as FERRIC]

ferroconcrete /ferəʊˈkɒnkri:t/ *n.* reinforced concrete.

ferromagnetism /ferəʊˈmægnɪtɪz(ə)m/ *n.* a form of magnetism found in substances (such as iron, cobalt, nickel, and their alloys) with high magnetic permeability and with some ability to retain their magnetization after the magnetizing field is removed. —**ferromagnetic** /-mægˈnetɪk/ *adj.*

ferrous /ˈferəs/ *adj.* containing iron; containing iron in divalent form. [f. L *ferrum* iron]

ferrule /ˈferəl, -u:l/ *n.* a metal ring or cap strengthening the end of a stick etc. [f. OF *virelle* f. L (*viriae* bracelet)]

ferry /ˈferɪ/ *v.t./i.* **1** to go or convey in a boat across water; (of a boat) to pass to and fro across water. **2** to transport from one place to another, especially as a regular service. —*n.* a boat etc. used for ferrying; the place or service of ferrying. —**ferryman** *n.* [f. ON]

fertile /ˈfɜ:taɪl/ *adj.* **1** (of soil) rich in the materials needed to support vegetation; fruitful (*lit.* or *fig.*). **2** (of animals and plants) able to produce young or fruit. **3** (of seeds or eggs) capable of developing into a new plant or animal. **4** (of the mind) easily producing ideas, inventive. **5** (of nuclear material) able to become fissile by the capture of neutrons. —**fertility** /fəˈtɪlɪtɪ/ *n.* [f. F f. L *fertilis*]

fertilize /ˈfɜ:tɪlaɪz/ *v.t.* **1** to make (soil etc.) fertile. **2** to introduce pollen or sperm into (a plant, egg, or female animal) so that seed or young develops. —**fertilization** /-ˈzeɪʃ(ə)n/ *n.* [f. prec.]

fertilizer *n.* a chemical or natural substance added to soil to make it more fertile. [f. prec.]

fervent /ˈfɜ:v(ə)nt/ *adj.* ardent, impassioned. —**fervency** *n.*, **fervently** *adv.* [f. OF f. L (*fervēre* boil)]

fervid /ˈfɜ:vɪd/ *adj.* fervent. —**fervidly** *adv.* [f. L (as prec.)]

fervour /ˈfɜ:və(r)/ *n.* passion, zeal. [as FERVENT]

fescue /ˈfeskju:/ *n.* a grass of the genus *Festuca*, valuable for pasture and fodder. [f. OF f. L *festuca* stalk, straw]

fess *n.* (in heraldry) a horizontal stripe across the middle of a shield, broader than a bar. [f. OF f. L *fascia* band]

festal /ˈfest(ə)l/ *adj.* of a feast or festival; joyous. —**festally** *adv.* [f. OF f. L (as FEAST)]

fester *v.t./i.* **1** to make or become septic. **2** to cause continuing annoyance. **3** to rot, to stagnate. [f. OF f. L *fistula* pipe, flute]

festival /ˈfestɪv(ə)l/ *n.* **1** a day or time of celebration. **2** a cultural event comprising a series of concerts, plays, films, etc., held regularly. [f. OF f. L (as foll.)]

festive /ˈfestɪv/ *adj*. of or characteristic of a festival; joyous. —**festively** *adv*. [f. L (*festum*, as FEAST)]

festivity /feˈstɪvɪtɪ/ *n*. gaiety, festive celebration; (in *pl*.) festive proceedings. [f. OF or L (as prec.)]

festoon /feˈstu:n/ *n*. a chain of flowers, ribbons, etc., hung in a curve as a decoration; something arranged similarly. —*v.t*. to adorn with or form into festoons. [f. F f. It. (as FEAST)]

Festschrift /ˈfestʃrɪft/ *n*. a published collection of writings in honour of a scholar. [G, = festival-writing]

fetch /fetʃ/ *v.t./i*. **1** to go for and bring back. **2** to cause to come, to draw forth; to be sold for (a price). **3** (*colloq*.) to deal (a blow etc.). **4** (*Naut*.) to arrive at; to sail close-hauled without tacking. —*n*. **1** an act of fetching. **2** a dodge, a trick. —**fetch up**, (*colloq*.) to arrive, to stop; to vomit. [OE]

fetching *adj*. attractive. [f. prec.]

fête /feɪt/ *n*. an outdoor function with a sale of goods, amusements, etc., especially to raise funds for some purpose. —*v.t*. to honour or entertain lavishly. [F (as FEAST)]

fetid /ˈfetɪd, ˈfi:t-/ *adj*. stinking. [f. L (*fetēre* stink)]

fetish /ˈfetɪʃ/ *n*. **1** an object worshipped as magical by primitive peoples. **2** a thing evoking irrational devotion or respect. **3** a thing abnormally stimulating or attracting sexual desire. —**fetishism** *n*., **fetishist** *n*. [f. F f. Port. *feitiço* charm, orig. adj. = made by art, f. L *facticius*]

fetlock *n*. the part of the back of a horse's leg above the hoof where a tuft of hair grows. [rel. to G *fessel* pastern]

fetter /ˈfetə(r)/ *n*. a shackle for holding a prisoner by the ankle; a bond, (in *pl*.) captivity; a restraint. —*v.t*. to put into fetters; to restrict. [OE, rel. to FOOT]

fettle *n*. condition, trim. [OE, = girdle]

fetus /ˈfi:təs/ var. of FOETUS.

feu /fju:/ *n*. (*Sc*.) a perpetual lease at a fixed rent; land so held. —*v.t*. (*Sc*.) to grant (land) on feu. [f. OF (as FEE)]

feud[1] /fju:d/ *n*. a prolonged mutual hostility, especially between families or groups. —*v.i*. to conduct a feud. [f. OF f. MDu. (rel. to FOE)]

feud[2] /fju:d/ *n*. a fief. [f. L *feudum* (as FEE)]

feudal /ˈfju:d(ə)l/ *adj*. of, resembling, or according to the feudal system. —**feudal system**, a medieval European politico-economic system based on the relation of vassal and superior arising from the holding of lands on condition of homage and military service or labour. —**feudalism** *n*., **feudalist** *n*., **feudalistic** /-ˈlɪstɪk/ *adj*. [f. L *feudalis* (as prec.)]

fever /ˈfi:və(r)/ *n*. **1** an abnormally high body temperature, often with delirium; a disease characterized by this. **2** nervous agitation or excitement. —*v.t*. to affect with fever or excitement. —**fever pitch**, a state of extreme excitement. [f. OE & AF f. L *febris*]

feverfew /ˈfi:vəfju:/ *n*. an aromatic herb (*Chrysanthemum parthenium*) with feathery leaves, formerly used to reduce fever. [OE f. L *febrifuga* (as prec., *fugare* put to flight)]

feverish *adj*. having the symptoms of fever; excited, restless. —**feverishly** *adv*., **feverishness** *n*. [f. FEVER]

few *adj*. not many. —*n*. a small number. —**a few**, some, several. **few and far between**, scarce. **a good** *or* **quite a few**, a fair number (of). **no fewer than**, as many as. —**fewness** *n*. [OE]

fey /feɪ/ *adj*. strange, other-worldly; (*Sc*.) fated to die soon. —**feyness** *n*. [OE]

fez *n*. (*pl*. **fezzes**) a flat-topped conical red cap with a tassel worn by men in some Muslim countries. [Turk., perh. f. *Fez* in Morocco]

ff. *abbr*. following pages etc.

ff *abbr*. (*Mus*.) fortissimo.

fiancé /fɪˈɑ̃seɪ/ *n*. a man or (**fiancée**) woman to whom a person is engaged to be married. [F (*fiancer* betroth)]

fiasco /fɪˈæskəʊ/ *n*. (*pl*. **-os**) a ludicrous or humiliating failure. [It., = bottle (with unexplained allusion)]

fiat /ˈfaɪæt/ *n*. an authorization; a decree. [L, = let it be done]

fib *n*. a trivial lie. —*v.i*. (**-bb-**) to tell a fib. —**fibber** *n*. [perh. f. obs. *fible-fable* nonsense (f. FABLE)]

fibre /ˈfaɪbə(r)/ *n*. **1** any of the threads or filaments forming animal and vegetable tissue and textile substance. **2** a piece of glass in the form of a thread. **3** a substance formed of fibres. **4** character. —**fibre optics**, the use of thin flexible fibres of glass or other transparent solids to transmit light-signals. [f. F f. L *fibra*]

fibreboard *n*. flexible board made of compressed fibres of wood etc.

fibreglass *n*. glass in fibrous form; material made from this (e.g. fabric for curtains, matter for use in thermal insulation); plastic containing such glass.

fibril /ˈfaɪbrɪl/ *n*. a small fibre. [dim. of FIBRE]

fibroid /ˈfaɪbrɔɪd/ *adj*. of or like fibrous tissue. —*n*. a fibroid tumour in the uterus. [f. FIBRE]

fibrosis /faɪˈbrəʊsɪs/ *n*. development of excessive fibrous tissue. [f. FIBRE]

fibrositis /faɪbrəˈsaɪtɪs/ *n*. rheumatic

inflammation of fibrous tissue. [as foll. + -ITIS]

fibrous /ˈfaɪbrəs/ *adj.* of or like fibre. [as FIBRE]

fibula /ˈfɪbjʊlə/ *n.* (*pl.* **-ae** /-iː/) **1** the bone on the outer side of the lower leg. **2** an ancient brooch or clasp. [L, = brooch]

fiche /fiːʃ/ *n.* (*pl.* same) a microfiche. [abbr.]

fickle *adj.* inconstant, changeable, especially in loyalty. —**fickleness** *n.*, **fickly** *adv.* [OE]

fiction /ˈfɪkʃ(ə)n/ *n.* **1** an invented idea, statement, or narrative; literature describing imaginary events and people. **2** a conventionally accepted falsehood. —**fictional** *adj.* [f. OF f. L (as FEIGN)]

fictionalize *v.t.* to make into a fictional narrative. [f. prec.]

fictitious /fɪkˈtɪʃəs/ *adj.* imagined or made up, not real or genuine. [f. L (as prec.)]

fictive /ˈfɪktɪv/ *adj.* created or creating by imagination. [f. F or L (as FICTION)]

fiddle *n.* **1** (*colloq.* or *derog.*) a stringed instrument played with a bow, especially a violin. **2** (*slang*) an instance of cheating or fraud. —*v.t./i.* **1** to play restlessly (*with*), to move aimlessly. **2** (*slang*) to cheat, to swindle, to falsify, to get by cheating. **3** to play (on) the fiddle. —**as fit as a fiddle,** in very good health. **play second fiddle,** to take a subordinate role. [OE, ult. as VIOL]

fiddle-faddle /ˈfɪd(ə)lfæd(ə)l/ *n.* trivial matters. —*v.i.* to fuss, to trifle. —*int.* nonsense. [redupl. of prec.]

fiddler *n.* **1** a player on the fiddle. **2** (*slang*) a swindler. **3** a small crab of the genus *Uca*, the male having one large claw held in a position like a violinist's arm. [f. FIDDLE]

fiddlesticks *int.* nonsense.

fiddling *adj.* petty, trivial. [f. FIDDLE]

fiddly *adj.* (*colloq.*) awkward to do or use. [as prec.]

fidelity /fɪˈdelɪtɪ/ *n.* **1** faithfulness, loyalty. **2** accuracy; precision in the reproduction of sound. [f. F or L (*fidelis* faithful)]

fidget /ˈfɪdʒɪt/ *v.t./i.* to move or act restlessly or nervously; to be or make uneasy. —*n.* **1** one who fidgets. **2** (in *pl.*) fidgeting movements. —**fidgety** *adj.* [f. obs. or dial. *fidge* twitch]

fiduciary /fɪˈdjuːʃɪərɪ/ *adj.* of, held, or given in trust; (of a paper currency) depending for its value on public confidence or securities. —*n.* a trustee. [f. L (*fiducia* trust)]

fie /faɪ/ *int.* expressing disgust or shame. [f. OF f. L]

fief /fiːf/ *n.* **1** land held under a feudal system or in fee. **2** one's sphere of operation or control. [F, as FEE]

field /fiːld/ *n.* **1** an area of open land, especially for pasture or crops; an area rich in some natural product, e.g. a coalfield, oilfield. **2** a piece of land for a specified purpose, especially an area marked out for a game. **3** the participants in a contest or sport; all the competitors or all but the one(s) specified; the fielding side in cricket. **4** an expanse of ice, sea, snow, etc. **5** a place of battle or campaign. **6** an area or sphere of operation, observation, intellectual activities, etc. **7** the area in which a force is effective, the force exerted by such a field. **8** the background of a picture, coin, flag, etc.; (in heraldry) the surface of an escutcheon. **9** (in computers) a part of a record, representing a unit of information. —*attrib.* **1** (of an animal or plant) found in open country, wild. **2** (of artillery etc.) light and mobile for use on campaign. **3** carried out or working in the natural environment, not in the laboratory etc. —*v.t./i.* **1** to act as a fieldsman in cricket etc.; to stop and return (a ball). **2** to select (a team or individual) to play in a game. **3** to deal with (a succession of questions etc.). —**field-day** *n.* a military exercise or review, an important or successful occasion. **field-events** *n.pl.* athletic sports other than races. **field-glasses** *n.pl.* binoculars for outdoor use. **Field-Marshal** *n.* an army officer of the highest rank. **field officer,** an army officer of a rank above a captain and below a general. **field sports,** outdoor sports, especially hunting, shooting, and fishing. **hold the field,** not to be superseded. **take the field,** to begin a campaign. [OE]

fielder *n.* a fieldsman. [f. prec.]

fieldfare *n.* a kind of thrush (*Turdus pilaris*). [perh. f. FIELD + FARE]

fieldsman *n.* (*pl.* **-men**) a player (other than the bowler or pitcher) of the side deployed in the field while the opposing players are batting in cricket, baseball, etc.

fieldwork *n.* **1** practical work done outside libraries and laboratories by surveyors, scientists, etc. **2** a temporary fortification. —**fieldworker** *n.*

fiend /fiːnd/ *n.* **1** an evil spirit, a devil; a very wicked or cruel person. **2** (*slang*) a devotee or addict. —**fiendish** *adj.*, **fiendishly** *adv.* [OE]

fierce *adj.* vehemently aggressive or frightening in temper or action, violent; eager, intense; strong or uncontrolled. —**fiercely** *adv.*, **fierceness** *n.* [f. OF f. L *ferus* savage]

fiery /ˈfaɪərɪ/ *adj.* **1** consisting of fire, flaming; like fire in appearance, bright red; intensely hot. **2** spirited, passionate, intense. —**fierily** *adv.*, **fieriness** *n.* [f. FIRE]

fiesta /fɪˈestə/ *n.* a festival, a holiday. [Sp. (as FEAST)]

fife /faɪf/ *n.* a small shrill flute used in military music. [f. G *pfeife* pipe]

fifteen /fɪfˈtiːn/ *adj.* & *n.* **1** one more than fourteen; the symbol for this (15, xv, XV).

2 the size etc. denoted by fifteen. **3** a team of fifteen players, especially in rugby football. —**fifteenth** *adj.* & *n.* [OE (as FIVE, -TEEN)]

fifth *adj.* next after the fourth. —*n.* **1** one of five equal parts of a thing. **2** (*Mus.*) an interval or chord spanning five alphabetical notes (e.g. C to G). —**fifth column,** a group working for the enemy within a country at war. The term dates from the Spanish Civil War when General Mola, leading four columns of troops towards Madrid, declared that he had a fifth column inside the city. **fifth columnist,** a member of this, a traitor. —**fifthly** *adv.* [OE (cf. FIVE)]

fifty /ˈfɪftɪ/ *adj.* & *n.* **1** five times ten; the symbol for this (50, l, L). **2** (in *pl.*) the numbers, years, or degrees of temperature from 50 to 59. —**fifty-fifty** *adj.* & *adv.* equal, equally. —**fiftieth** *adj.* & *n.* [OE (as FIVE)]

fig[1] *n.* **1** a soft pear-shaped fruit; the tree bearing it (*Ficus carica*). **2** a thing of little value. —**fig-leaf** *n.* a device for concealing something, especially the genitals. [f. OF f. L *ficus*]

fig[2] *n.* dress, equipment; condition. [f. obs. *feague* (as FAKE)]

fig. *abbr.* figure.

fight /faɪt/ *v.t./i.* (*past* & *p.p.* **fought** /fɔːt/) **1** to contend or struggle (against) in physical combat or in war; to carry on (a battle). **2** to contend or struggle in any way (about), to strive *for*; to strive to overcome. **3** to make *one's way* by fighting or effort. —*n.* **1** fighting, a battle or combat; a conflict or struggle, a vigorous effort. **2** the power or inclination to fight. **3** a boxing-match. —**fighting chance,** an opportunity of succeeding by a great effort. **fighting fit,** fit and ready. **fight shy of,** to avoid. [OE]

fighter *n.* **1** one who fights; one who does not yield without a struggle. **2** a fast military aircraft designed for attacking other aircraft. [f. prec.]

figment /ˈfɪgmənt/ *n.* a thing invented or existing only in the imagination. [f. L *figmentum* (as FEIGN)]

figuration /fɪgjʊˈreɪʃ(ə)n/ *n.* an act or mode of formation; ornamentation. [f. F or L (as FIGURE)]

figurative /ˈfɪgjʊrətɪv, -gə-/ *adj.* **1** metaphorical, not literal; characterized by figures of speech. **2** of pictorial or sculptural representation. —**figuratively** *adv.* [f. L (as foll.)]

figure /ˈfɪgə(r)/ *n.* **1** external form, bodily shape; a geometrical space enclosed by lines or surfaces. **2** a person as seen but not identified, or as contemplated mentally; an appearance as giving a certain impression. **3** a representation of the human form etc.; an image or likeness. **4** a diagram, an illustration; a decorative pattern; a series of movements forming a single unit in dancing etc.; a succession of notes forming a single idea in music. **5** the symbol of a number, a numeral (especially 0-9); a value, an amount of money; (in *pl.*) arithmetical calculations. —*v.t./i.* **1** to appear or be mentioned, esp. prominently. **2** to represent in a diagram or picture. **3** to imagine, to picture mentally. **4** to embellish with a pattern. **5** to mark with numbers or prices. **6** to calculate, to do arithmetic. **7** to be a symbol of. **8** (*US*) to understand, to consider; (*colloq.*) to be likely or understandable. —**figure-head** *n.* a carved image at a ship's prow; a person nominally at the head but with no real power. **figure (of speech),** an expression using words differently from their literal meaning, especially a metaphor. **figure out,** to work out by arithmetic or logic. [f. OF f. L *figura* (*fingere* fashion)]

figurine /ˈfɪgjʊriːn/ *n.* a statuette. [F f. It. (as prec.)]

filament /ˈfɪləmənt/ *n.* a threadlike strand or fibre; the conducting wire or thread in an electric bulb (now usually of tungsten). —**filamentary** /-ˈmentərɪ/ *adj.* [f. F or L (*filum* thread)]

filbert /ˈfɪlbət/ *n.* a nut of the cultivated hazel; the tree bearing it (*Corylus maxima*). [f. AF *philbert*, the nut being ripe about St Philibert's day (20 Aug.)]

filch *v.t.* to pilfer, to steal. [orig. unkn.]

file[1] *n.* **1** a folder or box etc. for holding loose papers; its contents. **2** a collection of (usually related) data stored under one reference in a computer. **3** a line of people or things one behind the other. —*v.t./i.* **1** to place in a file or among records; to submit (an application for divorce, a petition, etc.); (of a reporter) to send (a story etc.) to a newspaper. **2** to walk in a line. [f. F f. L *filum* thread]

file[2] *n.* a tool with a roughened steel surface for smoothing or shaping wood etc. —*v.t.* to smooth or shape with a file. [OE]

filial /ˈfɪlɪ(ə)l/ *adj.* of or due from a son or daughter. —**filially** *adv.* [f. OF or L (*filius* son, *filia* daughter)]

filibuster /ˈfɪlɪbʌstə(r)/ *n.* **1** a person engaging in unauthorized warfare against a foreign State. **2** one who obstructs progress in a legislative assembly; such obstruction. —*v.i.* to act as a filibuster. [ult. f. Du. *vrijbuiter* (as FREEBOOTER)]

filigree /ˈfɪlɪgriː/ *n.* fine ornamental work in gold etc. wire; similar delicate work. —**filigreed** *adj.* [f. F *filigrane* f. It. (L *filum* thread, *granum* seed)]

filing *n.* (usu. in *pl.*) a particle rubbed off by a file. [f. FILE[2]]

Filipino /fɪlɪ'pi:nəʊ/ *n.* (*pl.* **-os**) a native of the Philippine Islands. —*adj.* of Filipinos or the Philippine Islands. [Sp., = Philippine]

fill *v.t./i.* **1** to make or become full (*with*); to occupy completely, to spread over or through; to block up (a cavity or hole); to drill and put a filling into (a decayed tooth); (of a sail) to be distended by the wind. **2** to appoint a person to hold (a vacant post); to hold or discharge the duties of (an office etc.); to carry out or supply (an order, commission, etc.); to occupy (vacant time). —*n.* as much as one wants or can bear of food etc.; enough to fill a thing. —**fill the bill,** to be suitable or adequate. **fill in,** to add information to complete (a form or document etc.); to complete (a drawing etc.) within the outline; to fill (a hole etc.) completely; to act as a substitute (*for*); to spend (time) in a temporary activity; (*colloq.*) to give the required information to. **fill out,** to enlarge to the required size; to become enlarged or plump. **fill up,** to make or become completely full; to fill in (a document); to fill the petrol tank of (a car etc.). [OE (cf. FULL)]

filler *n.* material used to fill a cavity or increase the bulk; an item filling space in a newspaper etc. [f. FILL]

fillet /'fɪlɪt/ *n.* **1** a boneless piece of meat or fish. **2** a headband, a hair ribbon; a narrow strip or ridge. **3** (*Archit.*) a narrow flat band between mouldings. —*v.t.* **1** to remove the bones from; to divide (a fish etc.) into fillets. **2** to bind or provide with a fillet or fillets. [f. OF f. L *filum* thread]

filling *n.* **1** the material used to fill a cavity in a tooth. **2** the material between the bread in a sandwich. —**filling-station** *n.* an establishment selling petrol etc. to motorists. [f. FILL]

fillip /'fɪlɪp/ *n.* **1** a stimulus, an incentive; **2** a flick with the finger or thumb. —*v.t.* to give a fillip to. [imit.]

filly /'fɪlɪ/ *n.* **1** a young female horse. **2** (*slang*) a lively young woman. [f. ON (as FOAL)]

film *n.* **1** a thin coating or covering layer. **2** a strip or sheet of plastic or some other flexible base coated with a light-sensitive emulsion for exposure in a camera. **3** a motion picture; a story represented by this; (in *pl.*) the cinema industry. **4** a slight veil or haze etc.; a dimness or morbid growth affecting the eyes. —*v.t.* **1** to make a film or motion picture of (a scene, story, etc.). **2** to cover or become covered with a film. —**film star,** a celebrated actor or actress in films. **film-strip** *n.* a series of transparencies in a strip for projection. [OE *filmen* membrane]

filmy *adj.* thin and transparent. —**filmily** *adv.*, **filminess** *n.* [f. prec.]

filter *n.* **1** a device for removing impurities from a liquid or gas passed through it; a screen for absorbing or modifying light, X-rays, etc.; a device for suppressing electrical or sound waves of frequencies not required. **2** an arrangement for filtering traffic. —*v.t./i.* **1** to pass or cause to pass through a filter; to make a way gradually (*through, into,* etc.), to leak *out.* **2** (of traffic) to be allowed to pass in a certain direction while other traffic is held up (especially at traffic lights). —**filter-paper** *n.* a porous paper for filtering. **filter-tip** *n.* a cigarette with a filter for purifying smoke; the filter itself. [f. F f. L f. Gmc (as FELT[1], the earliest filters being of felt)]

filth *n.* repugnant or extreme dirt; obscenity. [OE (cf. FOUL)]

filthy *adj.* **1** extremely or disgustingly dirty; obscene. **2** (*colloq.*, of the weather) very unpleasant. —*adv.* in a filthy way; (*colloq.*) extremely. —**filthily** *adv.*, **filthiness** *n.* [f. prec.]

filtrate /'fɪltreɪt/ *v.t.* to filter. —*n.* a filtered liquid. —**filtration** /-'treɪʃ(ə)n/ *n.* [f. FILTER]

fin *n.* **1** a thin flat organ for propelling and steering, growing on fish and cetaceans at various parts of the body; an underwater swimmer's flipper. **2** a small projection on an aircraft or rocket for ensuring stability; any similar projection or attachment. [OE]

finagle /fɪ'neɪg(ə)l/ *v.t./i.* (*colloq.*) to act or obtain dishonestly. [f. dial. *fainaigue* cheat]

final /'faɪn(ə)l/ *adj.* situated at the end, coming last; conclusive, decisive. —*n.* **1** the last or deciding heat or game in sports etc. **2** the last edition of a day's newspaper. **3** (usu. in *pl.*) a final examination. —**final cause,** an ultimate purpose. **final clause,** (*Gram.*) a clause expressing purpose. —**finally** *adv.* [f. OF or L (*finis* end, goal)]

finale /fɪ'nɑ:lɪ/ *n.* the last movement or section of a piece of music or drama etc. [It. (as prec.)]

finalist /'faɪnəlɪst/ *n.* a competitor in the final of a competition etc. [f. FINAL]

finality /faɪ'nælɪtɪ/ *n.* the quality or fact of being final. [f. F or L (as FINAL)]

finalize /'faɪnəlaɪz/ *v.t.* to put into a final form, to complete. —**finalization** /-'zeɪʃ(ə)n/ *n.* [f. FINAL]

finance /faɪ'næns, fɪ-, 'faɪ/ *n.* **1** the management of money; support in money for an enterprise. **2** (in *pl.*) money resources. —*v.t.* to provide the capital for (a person or enterprise). —**finance company** *or* **house,** a company concerned mainly with providing money for hire-purchase transactions. [f. OF (*finer* settle debt, as FINE[2])]

financial /faɪ'nænʃ(ə)l, fɪ-/ *adj.* of finance. —**financial year,** a year reckoned from 1 or 6 April for taxing and accounting. —**financially** *adv.* [f. prec.]

financier /faɪˈnænsɪə(r), fɪ-/ *n.* a person engaged in large-scale finance. [F (as FINANCE)]

finch *n.* any of several small songbirds, especially of the genus *Fringilla.* [OE]

find /faɪnd/ *v.t* (*past & p.p.* **found** /faʊnd/) **1** to discover or get possession of by chance or effort; to become aware of. **2** to obtain, to succeed in obtaining. **3** to seek out and provide. **4** to ascertain by inquiry, calculation, etc. **5** to perceive or experience; to regard or discover from experience. **6** (of a jury, judge, etc.) to decide and declare. **7** to reach by a natural process. —*n.* a discovery; a thing or person discovered, especially when of value. —**find oneself,** to discover what one is, to discover one's vocation. **find one's feet,** to be able to walk; to develop one's independent ability. **find out,** to discover or detect (a wrongdoer etc.); to get information (about). [OE]

finder *n.* **1** one who finds. **2** a small telescope attached to a large one to locate an object. **3** a viewfinder. [f. FIND]

finding *n.* (often in *pl.*) a conclusion reached by an inquiry etc. [f. FIND]

fine[1] *adj.* **1** of high quality; excellent, of notable merit (also *iron.*); pure, refined; (of gold or silver) containing a specified proportion of pure metal. **2** of handsome appearance or size, beautiful, imposing; in good health. **3** (of the weather) bright; free from rain, fog, etc. **4** small, thin, or sharp of its kind; in small particles. **5** (of speech) tritely complimentary, euphemistic. **6** smart, showy, ornate. **7** fastidious, affectedly refined. **8** (in cricket) behind and at a narrow angle to the wicket. —*n.* **1** fine weather. **2** (in *pl.*) small particles in mining, milling, etc. —*adv.* finely; (*colloq.*) very well. —*v.t./i.* (often with *away, down, off*) to make or become pure, clear, thinner, etc. —**cut** *or* **run it fine,** to allow very little margin of time etc. **fine arts,** those appealing to the mind or the sense of beauty, especially painting, sculpture, and architecture. **fine-spun** *adj.* delicate; (of a theory) too subtle, unpractical. **fine-tooth comb,** a comb with narrow close-set teeth (*go over with a fine-tooth comb,* to search thoroughly). **not to put too fine a point on it,** to speak bluntly. —**finely** *adv.*, **fineness** *n.* [f. OF f. L *finire* finish]

fine[2] *n.* a sum of money (to be) paid as a penalty. —*v.t.* to punish by a fine. —**in fine,** in sum. [f. OF f. L *finis* end (in medieval times = sum paid on settling lawsuit)]

finery /ˈfaɪnərɪ/ *n.* showy dress or decoration. [f. FINE[1]]

fines herbes /fi:nz ˈeəb/ *n.pl.* mixed herbs used in cooking. [F, = fine herbs]

finesse /fɪˈnes/ *n.* **1** refinement; subtle or delicate manipulation; artful tact in handling a difficulty. **2** (in card-games) an attempt to win a trick by playing a card that is not the highest held. —*v.t./i.* **1** to achieve by finesse. **2** (in card-games) to make a finesse (with). [F (as FINE[1])]

finger /ˈfɪŋgə(r)/ *n.* **1** any of the five terminal members of the hand, any of these excluding the thumb. **2** the part of a glove for a finger. **3** a finger-like object or structure. **4** a measure of liquor in a glass, based on the breadth of a finger. —*v.t.* to feel or turn about with the fingers; to play (music or an instrument) with the fingers. —**finger-board** *n.* a flat strip at the top end of a stringed instrument, against which the strings are pressed to determine notes. **finger-bowl** *n.* a small bowl for rinsing the fingers during a meal. **finger-mark** *n.* a mark left on a surface by a finger. **finger-nail** *n.* the nail at the tip of a finger. **finger-plate** *n.* a plate fixed to a door above the handle to prevent finger-marks. **finger-stall** *n.* a sheath to cover an injured finger. **get** *or* **pull one's finger out,** (*slang*) to cease prevaricating and start to act. **put one's finger on,** to locate or identify exactly. [OE]

fingering *n.* the manner or technique of using the fingers, especially to play an instrument; an indication of this in a musical score. [f. prec.]

fingerprint *n.* an impression made on a surface by the fleshy pad at the end of a finger, especially as a means of identification.

fingertip *n.* the tip of a finger. —**have at one's fingertips,** to be thoroughly familiar with (a subject etc.).

finial /ˈfɪnɪ(ə)l/ *n.* an ornamental top to a gable, canopy, etc. [f. AF f. L *finis* end]

finicky /ˈfɪnɪkɪ/ *adj.* (also **finical, finicking**) **1** excessively detailed, fiddly. **2** over-particular, fastidious. [prob. slang extension of FINE[1]]

finis /ˈfɪnɪs, ˈfi:n-/ *n.* the end, especially of a book. [L]

finish /ˈfɪnɪʃ/ *v.t./i.* (often with *off* or *up*) to bring or come to an end, to come to the end of; to complete the manufacture of (cloth etc.) by surface treatment. —*n.* **1** the end, the last stage; the point at which a race etc. ends. **2** a method, material, or texture used for surface treatment of wood, cloth, etc. —**finishing-school** *n.* a private school where girls are prepared for entry into fashionable society. **finish off,** to end, (*colloq.*) to kill. **finish with,** to have no more to do with. [f. OF f. L (*finis* end)]

finite /ˈfaɪnaɪt/ *adj.* limited, not infinite; (of a part of the verb) having a specific number and person. [f. L (*finire* end, set limit to)]

Finn *n.* a native of Finland. [OE]

finnan /ˈfɪnən/ *n.* (also **finnan haddock**) haddock cured with the smoke of green wood, turf, or peat. [f. *Findhorn* in Scotland]

Finnic /ˈfɪnɪk/ *adj.* **1** of the group of peoples allied to the Finns. **2** of the group of languages allied to Finnish. [f. FINN]

Finnish /ˈfɪnɪʃ/ *adj.* of the Finns or their language. —*n.* the language of Finland. [f. FINN]

fiord /fjɔːd/ *n.* (also **fjord**) a long narrow inlet of the sea between high cliffs. [Norw. f. ON; cf. FIRTH]

fipple /ˈfɪp(ə)l/ *n.* the plug at the mouth-end of a wind instrument. —**fipple flute,** a flute played by blowing endwise, e.g. a recorder. [cf. Icel. *flipi* lip of horse]

fir *n.* an evergreen coniferous tree of the genus *Abies* or various other genera, with needles placed singly on the shoots; its wood. —**fir-cone** *n.* its fruit. **noble fir,** a common fir (*Abies procera*) of fine and lofty appearance. [prob. f. ON]

fire *n.* **1** the state or process of combustion causing heat and light, the active principle operative in this, flame or incandescence. **2** destructive burning. **3** burning fuel in a grate or furnace; an electric or gas fire (see ELECTRIC, GAS). **4** the firing of guns. **5** angry or excited feeling, enthusiasm, vivacity. **6** burning heat, fever. —*v.t./i.* **1** to send (a missile) from a gun etc.; to detonate. **2** to deliver or utter in rapid succession. **3** to dismiss (an employee) from a job. **4** to set fire to with the intention of destroying. **5** to catch fire; (of an internal-combustion engine) to undergo ignition. **6** to supply (a furnace etc.) with fuel. **7** to stimulate (the imagination); to fill with enthusiasm. **8** to bake or dry (pottery, bricks, etc.). **9** to become heated or excited. **10** to cause to glow, to redden. —**catch fire,** to ignite, to start to burn. **fire-alarm** *n.* a device giving warning of a fire. **fire-ball** *n.* a large meteor; a ball of flame from a nuclear explosion; an energetic person. **fire-bomb** *n.* an incendiary bomb. **fire-break** *n.* an obstacle to the spread of fire in a forest etc. **fire-brick** *n.* a fireproof brick used in a grate. **fire-brigade** *n.* an organized body of men trained and employed to extinguish fires. **fire-clay** *n.* a clay used to make fire-bricks. **fire-drill** *n.* a rehearsal of the procedure to be used in case of fire. **fire-eater** *n.* a conjuror who appears to swallow fire; a quarrelsome person. **fire-engine** *n.* a vehicle carrying the equipment for fighting large fires. **fire-escape** *n.* an emergency staircase or apparatus for escape from a building on fire. **fire extinguisher,** an apparatus with a jet for discharging liquid chemicals or foam to extinguish a fire. **fire-guard** *n.* a protective screen or grid placed in front of a fire. **fire-irons** *n.pl.* the tongs, poker, and shovel for tending a domestic fire. **fire-lighter** *n.* a piece of inflammable material used to help start a fire in a grate. **fire-power** *n.* the destructive capacity of guns etc. **fire-practice** *n.* fire-drill. **fire-raising** *n.* arson. **fire station,** the headquarters of a fire-brigade. **fire-storm** *n.* a high wind or storm following a fire caused by bombs. **fire-trap** *n.* a building without proper provision for escape in case of fire. **fire-watcher** *n.* a person keeping watch for fires, especially those caused by bombs. **fire-water** *n.* (*colloq.*) strong alcoholic liquor. **on fire,** burning; excited. **open fire,** to start firing guns etc. **set fire to, set on fire,** to cause to burn or ignite. **set the world on fire,** to do something remarkable or sensational. **under fire,** being fired on (by the enemy etc.); being rigorously criticized or questioned. —**firer** *n.* [OE]

firearm *n.* (usu. in *pl.*) a gun, pistol, or rifle.

firebox *n.* the fuel-chamber of a steam-engine or boiler.

firebrand *n.* **1** a piece of burning wood. **2** a person who causes trouble.

firecracker *n.* (*US*) an explosive firework.

firedamp *n.* a miners' name for methane, which is explosive when mixed in a certain proportion with air.

firedog *n.* an andiron.

firefly *n.* a kind of beetle emitting phosphorescent light (there are about 2,000 species).

firelight *n.* light from the fire in a fireplace.

fireman *n.* (*pl.* **-men**) **1** a member of a fire-brigade. **2** one who tends the furnace of a steam-engine fire.

fireplace *n.* an open recess for a domestic fire, at the base of a chimney; its surrounding structure.

fireproof *adj.* able to resist fire or great heat. —*v.t.* to make fireproof.

fireside *n.* the area round a fireplace; one's home or home-life.

firewood *n.* wood for use as fuel.

firework *n.* **1** a device containing combustible chemicals that cause explosions or spectacular effects. **2** (in *pl.*) an outburst of passion, especially anger.

firing *n.* **1** the discharge of guns. **2** fuel. —**firing-line** *n.* the front line in a battle, the leading part in an activity etc. **firing-squad** *n.* a group that fires the salute at a military funeral or shoots a condemned person.

firm[1] *adj.* solid, stable, steady, not fluctuating; resolute, determined; not easily shaken; (of an offer etc.) not liable to cancellation after acceptance. —*adv.* firmly. —*v.t./i.* to become or cause to become firm or secure. —**firmly** *adv.* [f. OF f. L *firmus*]

firm[2] *n.* a business concern or its members. [earlier = signature, f. Sp. & It. f. L *firmare* ratify (as prec.)]

firmament /ˈfɜːməmənt/ *n.* the sky regarded as a vault or arch. [f. OF f. L (as FIRM¹)]

first *adj.* **1** foremost in time, order, or importance. **2** most willing or likely. **3** basic, evident. —*n.* **1** the person or thing that is first; the first day of a month; a first occurrence of something notable. **2** first-class honours in a university degree. —*adv.* **1** before anyone or anything else; before someone or something else. **2** for the first time. **3** in preference. —**at first,** at the beginning. **at first hand,** directly, from the original source. **first aid,** help given to the injured until medical treatment is available. **first blood,** the first success in a contest. **first-born** *adj.* eldest; (*n.*) the eldest child. **first class,** the best group or category; the best accommodation in a train, ship, etc.; the class of mail to be most quickly delivered; the highest category of achievement in an examination. **first-class** *adj.* & *adv.* of or by the first class; excellent. **first-day cover,** an envelope with stamps postmarked on the first day of issue. **first finger,** that next to the thumb. **first-foot** *n.* (*Sc.*) the first person to cross the threshold in the New Year; (*v.i.*) to be the first to do this. **first-fruit** *n.* (usu. in *pl.*) the first agricultural produce of the season; the first results of work etc. **First Lady,** (*US*) the wife of the President. **first light,** dawn. **first night,** the first public performance of a play etc. **first offender,** one against whom no previous conviction is recorded. **first officer,** the mate on a merchant ship. **first past the post,** winning an election by having most votes though not necessarily an absolute majority. **first-rate** *adj.* & *adv.* excellent; (*colloq.*) very well. **in the first place,** as the first consideration. [OE (superl. from stem of FORE)]

firsthand *adj.* & *adv.* from the original source, direct.

firstly *adv.* first, to begin with. [f. FIRST]

firth *n.* a narrow inlet of sea; an estuary. [f. ON (as FIORD)]

fiscal /ˈfisk(ə)l/ *adj.* of the public revenue. —*n.* a legal official in some countries; (*Sc.*) a procurator fiscal. [f. F or L (*fiscus* treasury)]

fish[1] *n.* (*pl.* usu. same) **1** a vertebrate cold-blooded animal with gills and fins living wholly in water; any animal living in water, e.g. a cuttlefish, a jellyfish. **2** the flesh of fish as food. **3** (*colloq.*) a person. **4** (in *pl.*) **the Fish** or **Fishes,** the constellation or sign of the zodiac Pisces. —*v.t./i.* **1** to try to catch fish (in). **2** to search (for) in water or by reaching into something; (*colloq.*) to bring *out* thus. **3** to seek *for* (compliments, information, etc.) by hinting or indirect questioning. —**fish cake,** a small fried cake of shredded fish and mashed potato. **fish-eye lens,** a wide-angled lens with a distorting effect. **fish finger,** a small oblong piece of fish in batter or bread-crumbs. **fish-hook** *n.* a barbed hook for catching fish. **fish-kettle** *n.* an oval pan for boiling fish. **fish-meal** *n.* ground dried fish as a fertilizer etc. **fish-net** *adj.* (of a fabric) made with an open mesh. **fish out of water,** a person not in his element. **fish-tail** *n.* a thing shaped like a fish's tail. **other fish to fry,** more important things to do. [OE]

fish[2] *n.* a piece of wood or iron etc. to strengthen a mast, beam, etc. —**fish-plate** *n.* a flat plate of iron etc. connecting railway rails. [f. F *ficher* fix f. L *figere*]

fisher *n.* **1** a fishing animal. **2** (*archaic*) a fisherman. [f. FISH¹]

fishery *n.* **1** a place where fish are caught. **2** the business of fishing. [f. FISH¹]

fishing *n.* the sport of trying to catch fish. —**fishing-line, -rod** *ns.* a line and rod with a fish-hook, used in this. [f. FISH¹]

fishmonger *n.* a dealer in fish.

fishwife *n.* a woman who sells fish.

fishy *adj.* **1** of or like a fish. **2** (*slang*) dubious, suspect. —**fishily** *adv.*, **fishiness** *n.* [f. FISH¹]

fissile /ˈfisaɪl/ *adj.* capable of undergoing nuclear fission; tending to split. [f. L (as FISSURE)]

fission /ˈfiʃ(ə)n/ *n.* **1** a method of biological reproduction by the division of a cell etc. **2** nuclear fission. —*v.t./i.* to undergo or cause to undergo fission. —**fission bomb,** an atomic bomb. [f. L (as foll.)]

fissionable *adj.* capable of undergoing nuclear fission. [f. prec.]

fissure /ˈfiʃə(r)/ *n.* a cleft made by splitting or separation of parts. —*v.t./i.* to split, to crack. [f. OF or L (*findere fiss-* cleave)]

fist *n.* the tightly closed hand. [OE]

fisticuffs /ˈfistɪkʌfs/ *n.pl.* fighting with the fists. [f. *fisty* (obs. adj. f. prec.) + CUFF]

fistula /ˈfistjʊlə/ *n.* **1** a long pipelike ulcer. **2** an abnormal or surgically made passage in the body. —**fistular** *adj.*, **fistulous** *adj.* [L, = pipe]

fit[1] *adj.* **1** well suited or qualified. **2** competent, worthy; in a suitable condition, ready. **3** in good health or condition. **4** proper, befitting. —*v.t./i.* (**-tt-**) **1** to make or be of the right shape and size (for). **2** to put or go into position. **3** to adapt, to make or be suitable or competent. **4** to supply or equip *with.* —*n.* the way a thing fits. —**fit in,** to be or cause to be harmonious or in a suitable relationship; to find space or time for. **fit out** *or* **up,** to supply or equip *with.* **see** *or* **think fit,** to decide or choose (*to do*). —**fitly** *adv.*, **fitness** *n.* [orig. unkn.]

fit[2] *n.* **1** a sudden seizure of epilepsy, hysteria, etc., usually with unconsciousness; a brief attack of an illness or its symptoms. **2** a sudden short bout or burst. —**by** *or* **in fits and starts,** spasmodically. **have a fit,** (*colloq.*) to be greatly surprised or outraged. **in fits,** laughing uncontrollably. [orig. = position of danger; etym. unkn.]

fitful *adj.* active or occurring spasmodically or intermittently. —**fitfully** *adv.* [f. FIT[2] + -FUL]

fitment *n.* a piece of fixed furniture. [f. FIT[1]]

fitter *n.* **1** a person concerned with the fitting of clothes etc. **2** a mechanic who fits together and adjusts machinery. [f. FIT[1]]

fitting *n.* **1** the process of having a garment etc. fitted. **2** (in *pl.*) the fixtures and fitments of a building. —*adj.* proper, befitting. [f. FIT[1]]

five *adj.* & *n.* **1** one more than four; the symbol for this (5, v, V). **2** the size etc. denoted by five. —**five-year plan,** a plan for the economic development of the USSR in five years, inaugurated in 1928 (and later repeated); a similar plan adapted in other countries. [OE]

fivefold *adj.* & *adv.* **1** five times as much or as many. **2** consisting of five parts. [f. FIVE + -FOLD]

fiver *n.* (*colloq.*) a £5 note. [f. FIVE]

fives /faɪvz/ *n.* a ball-game played with padded gloves in a walled court, with three walls (**Eton fives**) or four (**Rugby fives**). [*pl.* of FIVE]

fix *v.t./i.* **1** to make firm or stable, to fasten, to secure; to implant (an idea or memory) in the mind. **2** to place definitely or permanently. **3** to decide, to settle, to specify (a price, date, etc.). **4** to direct (the eyes or attention) steadily. **5** to determine the exact nature, position, etc., of; to identify, to locate. **6** to make (the eyes or features) rigid; to become rigid; to congeal, to stiffen. **7** to repair. **8** (*colloq.*) to punish or kill. **9** (*colloq.*) to secure the support of (a person) or result of (a race etc.) fraudulently. **10** (*slang*) to inject (*oneself*) with a narcotic. **11** to make (a colour, photographic image, etc.) fast or permanent. **12** (of a plant) to assimilate (nitrogen, carbon dioxide) by forming a non-gaseous compound. —*n.* **1** a dilemma, a difficult position. **2** the act of finding a position, or a position found, by bearings etc. **3** (*slang*) a dose of a narcotic drug. —**be fixed (for),** (*colloq.*) to be situated (as regards). **fixed star,** a star so far from Earth as to appear motionless except for the diurnal revolution of the heavens (opp. *planet*, *comet*, etc.). **fix on** *or* **upon,** to choose, to decide on. **fix up,** to arrange, to organize; to accommodate. [ult. f. L *figere fix-* fix]

fixate /fɪk'seɪt/ *v.t.* **1** to direct one's gaze on. **2** (chiefly in *pass.*) to cause to acquire an abnormal attachment to persons or things. [f. L (as FIX)]

fixation /fɪk'seɪʃ(ə)n/ *n.* **1** the act or process of being fixated. **2** an obsession, a concentration on one idea. **3** the process of fixing (see FIX 12). [f. L (*fixare* fix)]

fixative /'fɪksətɪv/ *adj.* tending to fix or secure. —*n.* a fixative substance. [f. FIX]

fixedly /'fɪksɪdlɪ/ *adv.* in a fixed way, intently. [f. FIX]

fixer *n.* a person or thing that fixes; (*colloq.*) one who makes (esp. illicit) arrangements; a substance for fixing a photographic image etc. [f. FIX]

fixings *n.pl.* (*US*) **1** apparatus, equipment. **2** the trimmings of a dress or dish. [f. FIX]

fixity *n.* fixed state, stability, permanence. [f. obs. *fix* fixed]

fixture /'fɪkstʃə(r)/ *n.* **1** a thing fixed in position; (in *pl.*) articles belonging to a house etc. **2** a sporting event or date fixed for it. [alt. of obs. *fixure* (as FIX)]

fizz *v.i.* **1** to effervesce. **2** to hiss, to splutter. —*n.* **1** a hissing sound. **2** effervescence; (*colloq.*) an effervescent drink. [imit.]

fizzle *v.i.* to make a feeble hiss. —*n.* a fizzling sound. —**fizzle out,** to end feebly. [as prec.]

fizzy *adj.* effervescent. —**fizziness** *n.* [f. FIZZ]

fjord var. of FIORD.

fl. *abbr.* **1** floruit. **2** fluid.

flab *n.* (*colloq.*) fat, flabbiness. [imit. or f. FLABBY]

flabbergast /'flæbəgɑːst/ *v.t.* (*colloq.*) to astound. [perh. f. foll. + AGHAST]

flabby *adj.* limp and hanging loose; feeble. —**flabbily** *adv.*, **flabbiness** *n.* [alt. of *flappy* (f. FLAP)]

flaccid /'flæksɪd/ *adj.* flabby; drooping. —**flaccidity** /-'sɪdɪtɪ/ *n.*, **flaccidly** *adv.* [f. F or L (*flaccus* flabby)]

flag[1] *n.* **1** a piece of material, usually oblong or square and attached by one edge to a pole, rope, etc., used as a country's emblem or as a standard, signal, etc. **2** a small metal plate showing that a taxi is for hire. **3** a small paper etc. device resembling a flag. —*v.t.* (**-gg-**) **1** to inform or signal (as) with a flag, especially (often with *down*) to signal (a vehicle or driver) to stop. **2** to mark with a flag or tag. —**flag-day** *n.* a day on which money is raised from passers-by etc. for a cause and small paper flags are given as tokens. **flag of convenience,** a foreign flag under which a ship is registered to avoid taxes etc. **flag-officer** *n.* an admiral, vice-admiral, or rear-admiral; the commodore of a yacht-club. **flag of truce,** a white flag, indicating a desire to parley. **flag-pole** *n.* a flagstaff. [perh. f. obs. *flag* drooping]

flag[2] *v.i.* (**-gg-**) to lose momentum or vigour; to become limp or feeble. [as prec.; orig. unkn.]

flag[3] *n.* a flagstone; (in *pl.*) a pavement of these. —*v.t.* (**-gg-**) to pave with flags. [cf. ON *flaga* slab of stone]

flag[4] *n.* a plant with a bladed leaf (especially *Iris pseudacorus*), usually growing on moist ground. [orig. unkn.]

flagellant /ˈflædʒələnt/ *n.* one who flagellates himself or others. —*adj.* of flagellation. [f. L *flagellare* whip (as FLAGELLUM)]

flagellate[1] /ˈflædʒəleɪt/ *v.t.* to whip, to flog, especially as a religious discipline or sexual stimulus. —**flagellation** /-ˈleɪʃ(ə)n/ *n.* [as prec.]

flagellate[2] /ˈflædʒələt/ *adj.* having flagella (see foll.). —*n.* a protozoon having flagella. [f. foll.]

flagellum /fləˈdʒeləm/ *n.* (*pl.* **-a**) **1** (*Bot.*) a runner, a creeping shoot. **2** (*Biol.*) a lashlike appendage. [L, = whip, dim. of *flagrum* scourge]

flageolet /flædʒəˈlet/ *n.* a fipple flute with two thumb-holes. [F f. Prov.]

flagon /ˈflægən/ *n.* a large rounded vessel for holding liquids, usually with a handle and lid. [f. AF f. L (as FLASK)]

flagrant /ˈfleɪgrənt/ *adj.* glaringly bad; notorious or scandalous. —**flagrancy** *n.*, **flagrantly** *adv.* [f. F or L (*flagrare* blaze)]

flagship *n.* a ship that carries an admiral and flies his flag; the principal vessel of a shipping-line.

flagstaff *n.* a pole on which a flag is hoisted.

flagstone *n.* a flat slab of stone for paving.

flail *n.* a short heavy stick swinging at the end of a wooden staff, used as an implement for threshing. —*v.t./i.* to wave or swing wildly; to beat (as) with a flail. [OE, prob. f. L *flagellum* whip]

flair *n.* a natural ability or talent for selecting or doing what is best, useful, etc.; style, finesse. [F, = power of scent]

flak *n.* **1** anti-aircraft fire. **2** a barrage of criticism. —**flak jacket,** a heavy protective jacket reinforced with metal. [G, abbr. of *fliegerabwehrkanone* pilot-defence-gun]

flake *n.* **1** a small light piece, e.g. of snow; a thin broad piece shaved or split off. **2** dog-fish as food. —*v.t./i.* to take or come *away* or *off* in flakes; to fall in or sprinkle with flakes. —**flake out,** (*colloq.*) to fall asleep or faint (as) with exhaustion. —**flaky** *adj.* [cf. ON *flakna* flake off]

flambé /ˈflɑ̃beɪ/ *adj.* (of food) covered with spirit and served alight. [F, = singed]

flamboyant /flæmˈbɔɪənt/ *adj.* showy or florid in appearance or manner. —**flamboyance** *n.*, **flamboyantly** *adv.* [F (as prec.)]

flame *n.* **1** ignited gas burning visibly; a tongue-shaped portion of this. **2** a bright light or bright red colour. **3** passion, especially of love. —*v.i.* **1** to burn with flames, to blaze. **2** (of a person or temper) to explode in anger. **3** to shine or glow like a flame. —**flame-thrower** *n.* a weapon throwing a jet of flame. **flame-tree** *n.* any of several trees with brilliant red or yellow flowers. [f. OF f. L *flamma*]

flamenco /fləˈmeŋkəʊ/ *n.* (*pl.* **-os**) a Spanish gypsy style of song or dance. [Sp., = Flemish]

flaming *adj.* **1** burning with flames. **2** very hot or bright. **3** (*colloq.*) passionate. **4** (*colloq.*) damned. [f. FLAME]

flamingo fləˈmɪŋgəʊ/ *n.* (*pl.* **-os**) a tall long-necked wading-bird of the family Phoenicopteridae, with pink, scarlet, and black plumage. [f. Port. f. Prov. (as FLAME)]

flammable /ˈflæməb(ə)l/ *adj.* that may be set on fire. —**flammability** /-ˈbɪlɪtɪ/ *n.* [f. L (as FLAME)]

flan *n.* an open sponge or pastry case filled or spread with a fruit or savoury filling. [F, orig. = round cake]

flange /flændʒ/ *n.* a rim or projection, especially for strengthening or attachment to another object. [perh. f. *flange, flanch* widen outwards]

flank *n.* **1** the fleshy part of the side of the body between the ribs and the hip. **2** the side of a mountain etc. **3** the left or right side of a body of troops. —*v.t.* to be or be posted at or move along the flank or side of. [f. OF f. Gmc]

flannel *n.* **1** a kind of woven woollen usually napless cloth; (in *pl.*) flannel garments, especially trousers. **2** a cloth used for washing oneself. **3** (*slang*) nonsense, flattery. —*v.t.* (**-ll-**) **1** to wash with a flannel. **2** (*slang*) to flatter. —**flannelled** *adj.* [perh. f. Welsh *gwlanen* (*gwlan* wool)]

flannelette /flæn(ə)lˈet/ *n.* a napped cotton fabric resembling flannel. [f. prec.]

flap *v.t./i.* (**-pp-**) **1** to swing or sway about; to cause to do this, to move up and down. **2** to hit at (a fly etc.) with a flat object. **3** (*colloq.*, of ears) to listen intently. **4** (*colloq.*) to be agitated or panicky. —*n.* **1** a flat broad piece attached at one edge, acting as a cover, extension, etc.; an aileron on an aircraft, a hinged or sliding section used to control lift. **2** the action or sound of flapping. **3** a light blow, usually with something flat. **4** (*colloq.*) a state of agitation or fuss. —**flappy** *adj.* [prob. imit.]

flapdoodle /ˈflæpdu:d(ə)l/ *n.* nonsense. [orig. unkn.]

flapjack *n.* **1** a sweet oatcake. **2** a small pancake. [f. FLAP (in dial. sense 'toss') + JACK]

flapper *n.* **1** a broad flat device, a flap. **2** (*colloq.*) a young (esp. unconventional) woman in the 1920s. [f. FLAP]

flare /fleə(r)/ *v.t./i.* **1** to blaze with a bright unsteady flame. **2** to burst into sudden activity or anger. **3** to widen gradually. —*n.* **1** a flame or bright light used as a signal or for illumination. **2** an outburst of flame. **3** a dazzling unsteady light; unwanted light resulting from reflection within a lens. **4** a flared shape, a gradual widening. —**flare path,** a line of lights to guide aircraft landing or taking off. **flare up,** to burst into flame; to become suddenly angry. [orig. unkn.]

flash *n.* **1** a sudden short blaze of flame or light. **2** a brief outburst of feeling, a transient display of wit etc.; an instant; a brief news item on the radio etc. **3** a photographic flashlight. **4** a coloured cloth patch as an emblem on military uniform. —*v.t./i.* **1** to give out a flash, to gleam. **2** to burst suddenly into view or perception. **3** to send or reflect like a flash or in flashes; to cause to shine briefly. **4** to rush past suddenly. **5** to send (news etc.) by radio or telegraph. **6** (*colloq.*) to show suddenly or ostentatiously; (*slang*) to display oneself indecently. —*adj.* (*colloq.*) gaudy, showy, smart. —**flash cube,** a set of four flashbulbs arranged as a cube and operated in turn. **flash in the pan,** a seemingly brilliant but fleeting success; a promising start followed by failure. [orig. imit., of the sea]

flashback *n.* a return to a past event, especially as a scene in a film.

flashbulb *n.* a bulb giving a bright light for flashlight photography.

flasher *n.* **1** an automatic device for flashing lights intermittently. **2** (*slang*) a person who exposes himself indecently. [f. FLASH]

flashing *n.* a strip of metal acting as waterproofing at a joint of roofing etc. [f. dial. *flash* seal with lead sheets, or obs. *flash* lightning]

flashlight *n.* **1** a device producing a brief bright light for indoor etc. photography. **2** an electric torch.

flashpoint *n.* the temperature at which vapour from oil etc. will ignite; the point at which anger breaks out.

flashy *adj.* gaudy, showy, cheaply attractive. —**flashily** *adv.*, **flashiness** *n.* [f. FLASH]

flask /flɑːsk/ *n.* **1** a vacuum flask. **2** a narrow-necked bulbous bottle as used in chemistry. **3** a small flat bottle for spirits, carried in the pocket etc. [f. F & It. f. L (cf. FLAGON)]

flat *adj.* **1** horizontal, level; spread out, lying at full length. **2** smooth, without bumps or indentations. **3** absolute, downright; dull, uninteresting, monotonous; (of a drink) that has lost its effervescence; (of a battery etc.) no longer able to generate electric current. **4** (of a tyre) deflated, especially from a puncture. **5** (*Mus.*, of a note) below the normal or correct pitch; a semitone lower than the corresponding note or key of natural pitch. —*adv.* **1** in a flat manner. **2** (*Mus.*) below the correct pitch. **3** (*colloq.*) absolutely, completely, exactly. —*n.* **1** a group of rooms, usually on one floor, forming a residence. **2** a flat thing or part, level ground; low land; (*colloq.*) a flat tyre; a section of stage scenery mounted on a frame. **3** (*Mus.*) a note that is a semitone lower than the corresponding one of natural pitch; the sign indicating this. —**the flat,** the season of flat races for horses. **flat-fish** *n.* a type of fish with a flattened body (e.g. sole, plaice). **flat feet,** feet with less than the normal arch beneath. **flat-footed** *adj.* having flat feet; (*colloq.*) resolute, uninspired, unprepared. **flat-iron** *n.* a heavy iron for pressing linen etc., heated by external means. **flat out,** at top speed, using all one's strength or resources. **flat race,** a race over level ground, without jumps. **flat rate,** an unvarying rate or charge. **flat spin,** a nearly horizontal spin in an aircraft; (*colloq.*) agitation or panic. **that's flat,** (*colloq.*) that is definite. —**flatly** *adv.*, **flatness** *n.* [f. ON]

flatlet /ˈflætlɪt/ *n.* a small flat, usually of one or two rooms. [f. FLAT + -LET]

flatten *v.t./i.* **1** to make or become flat. **2** to defeat or refute decisively, to humiliate. [f. FLAT]

flatter *v.t.* to pay exaggerated or insincere compliments to, especially to win favour; to cause to feel honoured; (of a portrait etc.) to represent (a person) too favourably. —**flatter oneself,** to delude oneself smugly. —**flatterer** *n.* [perh. rel. to OF *flater* smooth down]

flattery *n.* exaggerated or insincere praise. [f. prec.]

flatulent /ˈflætjʊlənt/ *adj.* **1** causing, caused by, or troubled with the formation of gas in the alimentary canal. **2** inflated, pretentious. —**flatulence, flatulency** *ns.* [F f. L (*flatus* wind in stomach)]

flatworm *n.* a type of worm with a flattened body, e.g. the tapeworm.

flaunt *v.t./i.* to display proudly; to show off, to parade. [orig. unkn.]

flautist /ˈflɔːtɪst/ *n.* a flute-player. [f. It. (*flauto* flute)]

Flavian /ˈfleɪvɪən/ *adj.* of the dynasty of Roman emperors including Vespasian and his sons Titus and Domitian. —*n.* a member of this dynasty. [f. L *Flavius* name of family]

flavour /ˈfleɪvə(r)/ *n.* a distinctive taste; a mingled sensation of smell and taste; an indefinable characteristic quality. —*v.t.* to give a flavour to, to season. —**flavoursome**

adj. [f. OF *flaor*, perh. f. L *flatus* blowing & *foetor* stench, assim. to *savour*]

flavouring *n.* a thing used to flavour food or drink. [f. prec.]

flaw[1] *n.* an imperfection, a blemish; a crack, a breach; an invalidating defect in a document etc. —*v.t.* to make a flaw in, to spoil. [perh. f. ON *flaga* slab (as FLAG[1])]

flaw[2] *n.* a squall of wind. [f. MDu. *vlaghe*]

flax *n.* a blue-flowered plant (*Linum usitatissimum*) cultivated for its seed and for the textile fibre obtained from its stem; its fibre. —**flax-seed** *n.* linseed. [OE]

flaxen *adj.* of flax; pale yellow. [f. FLAX]

flay *v.t.* **1** to strip off the skin or hide of; to peel off. **2** to criticize severely. [OE]

F-layer *n.* the highest and most strongly ionized layer in the ionosphere.

flea *n.* a small wingless jumping insect feeding on human and other blood. —**flea-bite** *n.* a slight injury or inconvenience. **flea-bitten** *adj.* bitten by or infested with fleas; shabby. **a flea in one's ear,** a sharp reproof. **flea market,** (*colloq.*) a street market selling second-hand goods etc. [OE]

fleck *n.* a small spot of colour; a small particle, a speck. —*v.t.* to mark with flecks. [f. ON, or MLG or Du.]

fled *past* & *p.p.* of FLEE.

fledge *v.t.* **1** to provide (a bird, arrow, etc.) with feathers or down. **2** to rear (a young bird) until it can fly. **3** (in *p.p.*) able to fly; mature, independent, trained. [f. obs. adj. *fledge* fit to fly]

fledgeling /ˈfledʒlɪŋ/ *n.* **1** a young bird. **2** an inexperienced person. [f. prec.]

flee *v.t./i.* (*past* & *p.p.* **fled**) to run away (from), to leave hurriedly; to seek safety in flight; to vanish. [OE]

fleece *n.* **1** the woolly coat of a sheep etc.; the wool shorn from a sheep in one shearing. **2** a soft fabric for lining etc. —*v.t.* **1** to strip or rob of money, property, etc. **2** to remove the fleece from (a sheep). —**fleecy** *adj.* [OE]

fleet *n.* **1** a naval force, a navy; a group of ships under one commander. **2** a number of vehicles under one proprietor. —*v.i.* to pass rapidly. —*adj.* swift, nimble. —**fleetly** *adv.*, **fleetness** *n.* [OE]

fleeting *adj.* brief, passing rapidly. [OE, = float, swim]

Flemish /ˈflemɪʃ/ *adj.* of Flanders or its people or their language. —*n.* this language, which is essentially the same language as Dutch. —**Flemish bond,** see BOND[1]. [f. Du. (as prec.)]

flesh *n.* **1** the soft substance between the skin and bones. **2** the tissue of animal bodies (excluding fish and sometimes fowl) as food. **3** the body as opposed to the mind or soul. **4** the visible surface of the human body; the pulpy part of a fruit or plant; plumpness, fat. —*v.t./i.* (with *out*) to make or become substantial. —**the flesh,** the physical or sensual appetites. **flesh and blood,** the human body, human nature, mankind (*one's flesh and blood*, near relations). **flesh-coloured** *adj.* yellowish pink. **flesh-wound** *n.* a wound not reaching a bone or vital organ. **in the flesh,** in bodily form, in person. [OE]

fleshly *adj.* **1** mortal, worldly. **2** sensual. [OE]

fleshpots *n.pl.* luxurious living.

fleshy *adj.* of or like flesh, plump, pulpy. —**fleshiness** *n.* [f. FLESH]

fleur-de-lis /flɜːdəˈliː/ *n.* (also **-lys**; *pl.* **fleurs-** *pr.* same) the heraldic lily of three petals; the former royal arms of France. [f. OF, = flower of lily]

flew *past* of FLY[1].

flex[1] *v.t.* to bend (a joint or limb); to move (a muscle) to bend a joint. [f. L *flectere flex-* bend]

flex[2] *n.* flexible insulated wire. [abbr. of foll.]

flexible /ˈfleksɪb(ə)l/ *adj.* **1** that bends easily without breaking, pliable. **2** adaptable to circumstances. **3** easily persuaded, manageable. —**flexibility** /-ˈbɪlɪtɪ/ *n.*, **flexibly** *adv.* [f. OF or L (as FLEX[1])]

flexion /ˈflekʃ(ə)n/ *n.* bending; a bent state or part. [f. L *flexio* (as FLEX[1])]

flexitime /ˈfleksɪtaɪm/ *n.* a system of flexible working hours. [f. FLEXIBLE + TIME]

flibbertigibbet /flɪbətɪˈdʒɪbɪt/ *n.* a gossiping or frivolous person. [imit. of chatter]

flick *n.* **1** the sudden release of a bent finger or thumb. **2** a quick light blow or stroke. **3** (*colloq.*) a cinema film; **the flicks,** a cinema performance. —*v.t.* to strike or knock or move with a flick. —**flick-knife** *n.* a knife with a blade that springs out when a button etc. is pressed. **flick through,** to look cursorily through (a book etc.). [imit.]

flicker *v.i.* **1** to burn or shine unsteadily or fitfully. **2** to quiver, to flutter. **3** (of hope etc.) to occur briefly. —*n.* **1** a flickering light or movement. **2** a brief spell (of hope, recognition, etc.). [OE]

flier var. of FLYER.

flight[1] /flaɪt/ *n.* **1** an act or manner of flying; the movement or passage of a thing through the air; the distance flown. **2** a journey made by an aircraft or airline. **3** a group of birds etc. flying together; a volley (*of* arrows etc.). **4** a series (*of* stairs in a straight line, of hurdles etc. for racing). **5** an exceptional effort *of* fancy etc. **6** the tail of a dart. —**flight-deck** *n.* the cockpit of a large aircraft; the deck of an aircraft-carrier. **flight-lieutenant** *n.* an RAF officer next below squadron leader. **flight-recorder** *n.* an electronic device in an aircraft, recording information about its flight. **flight sergeant,** the RAF rank next above sergeant. **in the first** *or* **top flight,** taking a leading place, excellent of its kind. [OE (cf. FLY¹)]

flight² /flaɪt/ *n.* fleeing, an escape from danger etc. —**put to flight,** to cause to flee. **take (to) flight,** to flee. [OE (as FLEE)]

flightless /ˈflaɪtlɪs/ *adj.* (of a bird) lacking the power of flight. [f. FLIGHT + -LESS]

flighty *adj.* (usu. of a woman) frivolous, changeable. —**flightily** *adv.*, **flightiness** *n.* [f. FLIGHT]

flimsy /ˈflɪmzɪ/ *adj.* **1** lightly or carelessly assembled; easily damaged or knocked apart. **2** (of an excuse etc.) unconvincing. —**flimsily** *adv.*, **flimsiness** *n.* [orig. unkn.]

flinch *v.i.* to draw back, to shrink (*from* an action); to wince. [f. OF *flenchir* f. Gmc]

fling *v.t./i.* (*past* & *p.p.* **flung**) **1** to throw, esp. forcefully or hurriedly. **2** to put or send hurriedly or summarily. **3** to put *on* or take *off* (clothes) hurriedly or casually. **4** to rush, to go angrily or violently. —*n.* **1** the action of flinging. **2** a vigorous dance. **3** a short bout of self-indulgence. [perh. f. ON]

flint *n.* **1** a hard stone of nearly pure silica found in pebbly lumps steel-grey within and encrusted with white; a piece of this, especially as a prehistoric tool or weapon. **2** a piece of hard alloy used to produce a spark. **3** anything hard and unyielding. —**flinty** *adj.* [OE]

flintlock *n.* an old type of gun fired by a spark from a flint.

flip¹ *v.t.* (**-pp-**) to turn over quickly, to flick; to toss (a thing) with a jerk so that it turns over in the air. —*n.* **1** the action of flipping. **2** (*colloq.*) a short trip. —**flip side,** the reverse side of a gramophone record. **flip through,** to look cursorily through (a book etc.). [prob. f. FILLIP]

flip² *n.* a drink of heated beer and spirit. [perh. = prec.]

flip³ *adj.* (*colloq.*) glib, flippant. [f. FLIP¹]

flippant /ˈflɪpənt/ *adj.* treating a serious matter lightly, disrespectful. —**flippancy** *n.*, **flippantly** *adv.* [f. FLIP¹]

flipper *n.* **1** a limb used by turtles, seals, etc., in swimming. **2** a flat rubber etc. attachment worn on the foot in underwater swimming. **3** (*slang*) the hand. [f. FLIP¹]

flipping *adj.* & *adv.* (*slang*, expressing mild annoyance) damned. [f. FLIP¹]

flirt *v.t./i.* **1** to behave lightheartedly in an amorous manner, to pretend courtship. **2** to toy *with* an idea etc., to interest oneself superficially. **3** to trifle *with* a danger etc. **4** to wave or move briskly in short jerks. —*n.* one who flirts amorously. —**flirtation** /-ˈteɪʃ(ə)n/ *n.*, **flirtatious** /-ˈteɪʃəs/ *adj.*, **flirtatiously** *adv.* [imit., orig. = move or throw with a jerk]

flit *v.i.* (**-tt-**) **1** to move lightly and rapidly. **2** to make short flights. **3** to abscond, to disappear secretly (especially from one's abode to escape a creditor). —*n.* an act of flitting. [f. ON (rel. to FLEET)]

flitch *n.* a side of bacon. [OE]

flitter *v.i.* to flit about. —**flitter-mouse** *n.* a bat (BAT²). [f. FLIT]

float *v.t./i.* **1** to rest or move on the surface of a liquid; to cause to do this; to move or be suspended *in* a liquid or gas. **2** (*slang*) to move about in a leisurely way. **3** to hover *before* the eyes or mind. **4** (of a currency) to have a fluctuating exchange rate; to cause or allow (a currency) to have this. **5** to start (a company, scheme, etc.). —*n.* **1** a raft. **2** a floating device to control the flow of water, petrol, etc. **3** a structure enabling an aircraft to float on water. **4** a cork or quill used on a fishing-line as an indicator; a cork supporting the edge of a fishing-net. **5** a low-bodied lorry or cart, especially one used for display in a procession. **6** a sum of money retained for minor expenditure or change-giving. **7** a tool for smoothing plaster. **8** (in *sing.* or *pl.*) the footlights in a theatre. —**floating dock,** a floating structure usable as a dry dock. **floating kidney,** one unusually movable. **floating population,** a population not settled in a definite place. **floating rib,** any of the ribs not joined to the breastbone. **floating voter,** a voter not permanently supporting any one political party. [OE]

floatation var. of FLOTATION.

flocculent /ˈflɒkjʊlənt/ *adj.* like tufts of wool; in or showing tufts. —**flocculence** *n.* [f. L (as FLOCK²)]

flock¹ *n.* **1** a number of sheep, goats, or birds regarded as a group or unit. **2** a large crowd of people; a number of people in the care of a priest or teacher etc. —*v.i.* to move or assemble in large numbers. [OE]

flock² *n.* a lock or tuft of wool etc.; wool or cotton waste used as a stuffing. [f. OF f. L *floccus*]

floe /fləʊ/ *n.* a sheet of floating ice. [f. Norw.]

flog *v.t.* (**-gg-**) **1** to beat with a whip, stick, etc. **2** (*slang*) to sell. —**flog a dead horse,** to waste one's efforts. **flog to death,** (*colloq.*) to talk about or promote at tedious length. —**flogging** *n.* [orig. unkn.]

flood /flʌd/ *n.* **1** an influx or the overflowing of water beyond its normal confines, especially over land; the water that overflows; an outpouring, an outburst of great quantity. **2** the inflow of the tide. **3** (*colloq.*) a floodlight. —*v.t./i.* **1** to overflow; to cover or be covered with a flood. **2** to come (*in*) in great quantities.

3 to drive *out* (of a home etc.) by flood. 4 to have a uterine haemorrhage. —**the Flood,** that brought by God upon the earth in the time of Noah (Gen. 6 ff.). **flood plain,** the level area over which a river spreads in flood. **flood-tide** *n.* a rising tide. [OE, rel. to FLOW]

floodgate *n.* a gate that can be opened or closed to control the flow of water, especially the lower gate of a lock.

floodlight *n.* a large powerful light (usually one of several) to illuminate a building, sportsground, etc. —*v.t.* to illuminate with this.

floor /flɔː(r)/ *n.* 1 the lower surface of a room, on which one stands. 2 the bottom of the sea, a cave, etc. 3 the rooms etc. on the same level in a building. 4 the part of a legislative assembly etc. where members sit and speak; the right to speak next in a debate etc. 5 a level area. 6 a minimum level for prices, wages, etc. —*v.t.* 1 to provide with a floor. 2 to knock (a person) down. 3 to baffle or nonplus; to overcome. —**floor manager,** the stage manager of a television production. **floor show,** an entertainment presented on the floor of a night-club etc. [OE]

floorboard *n.* a long wooden board used for flooring.

floorcloth *n.* a cloth for washing floors.

flooring *n.* boards etc. used as a floor. [f. FLOOR]

floozie *n.* (also **floosie**) (*colloq.*) a woman, especially a disreputable one. [cf. FLOSS and dial. *floosy* fluffy]

flop *v.i.* (-pp-) 1 to fall or sit etc. (*down*) suddenly, awkwardly, or with a slight thud. 2 to hang or sway limply or heavily. 3 to make a dull flapping sound. 4 (*slang*) to fail. —*n.* 1 a flopping motion or sound. 2 (*slang*) a failure. —*adv.* with a flop. [var. of FLAP]

floppy *adj.* tending to flop, not firm or rigid. —**floppy disc,** a flexible disc for the storage of machine-readable data. —**floppiness** *n.* [f. FLOP]

flora /ˈflɔːrə/ *n.* (*pl.* **-as**) the plants of a particular region or period. [L, f. prec.]

floral /ˈflɔːr(ə)l, ˈflɒ-/ *adj.* of or decorated with flowers. —**florally** *adv.* [f. L (as FLOWER)]

Florentine /ˈflɒrəntaɪn/ *adj.* of Florence in Italy. —*n.* a native of Florence. [f. F or L]

florescence /flɔːˈres(ə)ns, flɒ-/ *n.* flowering time or state (*lit.* or *fig.*). [f. L *florescere* (*florēre* bloom)]

floret /ˈflɔːrɪt/ *n.* a small flower; each of the small flowers of a composite flower. [f. L *flos floris* flower]

floribunda /flɒrɪˈbʌndə/ *n.* a rose or other plant bearing dense clusters of flowers. [L, = freely flowering (as prec. + *-bund-* (cf. *moribund*) infl. by L *abundus* copious)]

florid /ˈflɒrɪd/ *adj.* 1 ornate, elaborate, showy. 2 ruddy, flushed. [f. F or L *floridus* (*flos floris* flower)]

florin /ˈflɒrɪn/ *n.* a gold or silver coin, especially the former English two-shilling coin (10p). [f. OF f. It. (*fiore* flower), the original coin having the figure of a lily]

florist /ˈflɒrɪst/ *n.* one who deals in or grows flowers. [f. L *flos floris* flower]

floruit /ˈflɒruɪt/ *n.* the period or date at which a person lived or worked. [L, = he or she flourished]

floss *n.* 1 the rough silk enveloping a silkworm's cocoon. 2 untwisted silk thread for embroidery. 3 dental floss (see DENTAL). —**flossy** *adj.* [f. F *floche*]

flotation /fləʊˈteɪʃ(ə)n/ *n.* the launching of a commercial enterprise etc. [alt. of *floatation*, f. FLOAT after *rotation* etc.]

flotilla /flɒˈtɪlə/ *n.* a small fleet; a fleet of small ships. [Sp. (*flota* fleet)]

flotsam /ˈflɒtsəm/ *n.* wreckage found floating. —**flotsam and jetsam,** odds and ends; vagrants etc. [f. AF (*floter* float)]

flounce[1] *v.i.* to go or move abruptly or angrily, with jerking movements. —*n.* a flouncing movement. [perh. imit.]

flounce[2] *n.* an ornamental frill round a woman's skirt etc. —*v.t.* to trim with flounces. [alt. of *frounce* fold, pleat, f. OF]

flounder[1] *v.i.* to move or struggle helplessly or clumsily; to progress with great difficulty, to struggle. —*n.* an act of floundering. [imit.]

flounder[2] *n.* a flat-fish, especially a small edible species (*Pleuronectes flesus*). [f. AF, prob. f. Scand.]

flour /ˈflaʊə(r)/ *n.* a fine meal or powder made by milling and usually sifting cereals, especially wheat; a fine soft powder. —*v.t.* to sprinkle with flour. —**floury** *adj.* [different spelling of FLOWER in sense 'finest part']

flourish /ˈflʌrɪʃ/ *v.t./i.* 1 to grow vigorously and healthily; to prosper, to thrive, to be in one's prime. 2 to wave, to brandish. —*n.* 1 an ornamental curve in writing. 2 a dramatic gesture with the hand etc. 3 (*Mus.*) a florid passage, a fanfare. [f. OF f. L *florēre* (as FLORET)]

flout /flaʊt/ *v.t.* to disobey openly and scornfully. [perh. f. Du. *fluiten* whistle, hiss (cf. FLUTE)]

flow /fləʊ/ *v.i.* 1 to glide along as a stream, to move freely like a liquid or gas. 2 (of blood, money, or electric current) to circulate. 3 to proceed steadily and continuously. 4 to hang easily, to undulate. 5 to be plentiful; to be plentifully supplied *with*. 6 to gush out (*from*); to result from. 7 (of the tide) to rise. —*n.* 1 a flowing movement or mass; a flowing liquid, the amount of this. 2 an outpouring. 3 a rise of the tide. —**flow chart** *or* **diagram** *or* **sheet,** a diagram showing the movement or development of things through a series of processes. [OE]

flower /ˈflaʊə(r)/ *n.* the part of a plant from which the fruit or seed is developed; a blossom (and its stem) used especially in groups for decoration; a plant cultivated or noted for its flowers. —*v.t./i.* **1** to bloom or blossom, to cause to do this. **2** to reach a peak. —**the flower of,** the best part of. **flowers of sulphur,** the fine powder produced when sulphur evaporates and condenses. **in flower,** with the flowers out. [f. OF f. L *flos floris*]

flowerpot *n.* a pot in which a plant may be grown.

flowery *adj.* **1** abounding in flowers. **2** (of language) ornate, elaborate. —**floweriness** *n.* [f. FLOWER]

flown *p.p.* of FLY[1].

flu /flu:/ *n.* (*colloq.*) influenza. [abbr.]

fluctuate /ˈflʌktjʊeɪt/ *v.i.* to vary erratically, to rise and fall. —**fluctuation** /-ˈeɪʃ(ə)n/ *n.* [f. L *fluctuare* (*fluctus* wave)]

flue /flu:/ *n.* the smoke-duct in a chimney; a channel for conveying heat. [orig. unkn.]

fluent /ˈflu:ənt/ *adj.* (of a person) able to speak quickly and easily; (of speech) flowing easily, coming readily. —**fluency** *n.*, **fluently** *adv.* [f. L (*fluere* flow)]

fluff *n.* **1** a light downy substance, e.g. that shed from fabric. **2** (*slang*) a bungle or mistake (in a performance etc.). —*v.t./i.* **1** to shake or puff into a soft mass. **2** (*slang*) to make a mistake in, to bungle. [prob. dial. alt. of *flue* fluff]

fluffy /ˈflʌfɪ/ *adj.* having or covered with a mass of fluff. —**fluffily** *adv.*, **fluffiness** *n.* [f. prec.]

fluid /ˈflu:ɪd/ *n.* a substance, as a gas or liquid, that is capable of flowing freely; a fluid part or secretion. —*adj.* able to flow freely; not solid or rigid, fluctuating. —**fluid mechanics,** the study of the mechanical properties of fluids. **fluid ounce,** one twentieth of a pint; (*US*) one sixteenth of a pint. —**fluidity** /-ˈɪdɪtɪ/ *n.* [f. F or L (*fluere* flow)]

fluidics /flu:ˈɪdɪks/ *n.* the technique of using small interacting flows and fluid jets for amplification, switching, etc. [f. prec.]

fluidize /ˈflu:ɪdaɪz/ *v.t.* to cause (a mass of granular material, e.g. sand) to behave like a fluid by passing a current of gas, vapour, or liquid upwards through it. —**fluidization** /-ˈzeɪʃ(ə)n/ *n.* [f. FLUID]

fluke[1] /flu:k/ *n.* a thing that happens or succeeds by chance, a piece of luck. —*v.t.* to achieve, hit, etc., by a fluke. —**fluky** *adj.* [perh. f. dial. *fluke* guess]

fluke[2] /flu:k/ *n.* **1** a flat-fish, a flounder. **2** a parasitic worm of the class Trematoda, found in sheep's liver. [OE]

fluke[3] /flu:k/ *n.* **1** the triangular flat end of an anchor arm. **2** the lobe of a whale's tail. [perh. f. prec.]

flummery /ˈflʌmərɪ/ *n.* **1** a sweet milk dish. **2** nonsense, empty talk. [f. Welsh *llymru*]

flummox /ˈflʌməks/ *v.t.* (*colloq.*) to bewilder, to disconcert. [prob. dial., imit.]

flung *past* & *p.p.* of FLING.

flunk *v.t./i.* (*US colloq.*) to fail, especially in an examination. [cf. FUNK and obs. *flink* be a coward]

flunkey /ˈflʌŋkɪ/ *n.* (usu. *derog.*) **1** a footman. **2** a toady, a snob. **3** (*US*) a cook, waiter, etc. [perh. f. FLANK, with sense 'one who flanks']

fluoresce /flʊəˈres/ *v.i.* to be or become fluorescent. [f. foll.]

fluorescent *adj.* (of a substance) absorbing radiation and emitting it in the form of light. —**fluorescent lamp,** one with such a substance. —**fluorescence** *n.* [f. FLUORSPAR, after *opalescent*]

fluoridate /ˈflʊərɪdeɪt/ *v.t.* to add traces of fluoride to (drinking-water etc.), especially to prevent tooth-decay. —**fluoridation** /-ˈdeɪʃ(ə)n/ *n.* [f. foll.]

fluoride /ˈflʊraɪd/ *n.* a binary compound of fluorine. [f. FLUORINE]

fluorinate /ˈflʊərɪneɪt/ *v.t.* to fluoridate; to introduce fluorine into. [f. foll.]

fluorine /ˈflʊəri:n/ *n.* a pale yellow non-metallic gaseous element of the halogen group, symbol F, atomic number 9. [F (as FLUORSPAR)]

fluorocarbon /flʊərəʊˈkɑ:bən/ *n.* a synthetic compound of carbon and fluorine. [f. prec. + CARBON]

fluorspar /ˈflʊəspɑ:(r)/ *n.* calcium fluoride as a mineral. [f. *fluor* mineral used as flux (L, f. *fluere* flow) + SPAR[3]]

flurry /ˈflʌrɪ/ *n.* a gust, a squall; a sudden burst of activity; nervous hurry, agitation. —*v.t.* to confuse or agitate. [imit.]

flush[1] *v.t./i.* **1** to become or cause to become red in the face, to blush. **2** to cleanse (a drain, lavatory, etc.) by the flow of water; to dispose of (a thing) thus. **3** (of water) to rush or spurt out. **4** to inflame with pride or passion. **5** to make level. —*n.* **1** a reddening of the face, a blush; a feeling of feverish heat. **2** a rush of excitement or elation. **3** a rush of water; cleansing by flushing. **4** freshness, vigour. —*adj.* **1** level, in the same plane. **2** (*colloq.*) having plenty of money etc. [perh. = foll., influenced by *flash* and *blush*]

flush[2] *v.t./i.* **1** to take wing and fly up or away, to cause to do this. **2** to reveal, to drive *out*. [imit.; cf. *fly*, *rush*]

flush[3] *n.* a hand of cards all of one suit.

—**straight flush,** a flush that is also a sequence. **royal flush,** a straight flush headed by an ace. [f. OF f. L (as FLUX)]

fluster *v.t./i.* to confuse or agitate; to make nervous; to bustle. —*n.* a confused or agitated state. [orig. unkn.]

flute /flu:t/ *n.* **1** an instrument of the wood-wind family made in silver, stainless steel, or occasionally wood, having holes along it stopped by fingers or (since the 19th c.) keys, and a blow-hole in the side near the end. **2** its player. **3** a semicylindrical vertical groove in a pillar; a similar groove elsewhere. —*v.t./i.* **1** to play (on) the flute. **2** to speak or utter in flute-like tones. **3** to make ornamental grooves in. [f. OF, prob. f. Prov. *flaut*]

fluting /'flu:tɪŋ/ *n.* a series of ornamental grooves. [f. FLUTE]

flutter *v.t./i.* **1** to flap (the wings) in flying or trying to fly. **2** to wave or flap quickly and irregularly; to move about restlessly; (of the pulse) to beat feebly and irregularly. —*n.* **1** fluttering. **2** a state of nervous excitement. **3** a rapid fluctuation in pitch or loudness. **4** (*colloq.*) a small bet or speculation. [OE (as FLEET)]

fluvial /'flu:vɪ(ə)l/ *adj.* of or found in rivers. [f. L (*fluvius* river)]

flux *n.* **1** a continuous succession of changes. **2** flowing; the inflow of the tide. **3** a substance mixed with a metal etc. to aid fusion. [f. OF or L *fluxus* (*fluere* flow)]

fly[1] /flaɪ/ *v.t./i.* (*past* **flew** /flu:/, *p.p.* **flown** /fləʊn/) **1** to move through the air by means of wings. **2** (of an aircraft etc. or its occupants) to travel through the air or space; to transport in an aircraft. **3** (of a cloud etc.) to pass quickly through the air. **4** to go or move quickly, to pass swiftly; to flee (from); (*colloq.*) to depart hastily. **5** (of a flag, the hair, etc.) to wave; to raise (a flag) so that it waves. **6** to make (a kite) rise and stay aloft. **7** to be driven or scattered; to come or be forced suddenly *off*, *open*, etc. —*n.* **1** flying. **2** a flap on a garment to contain or cover a fastening, (usu. in *pl.*) this fastening on trousers; a flap at the entrance of a tent. **4** (in *pl.*) the space over the proscenium in a theatre. **5** the part of a flag furthest from the staff. —**fly a kite,** (*colloq.*) to sound out public opinion. **fly-by-night** *adj.* unreliable, irresponsible; (*n.*) a person of this kind. **fly-half** *n.* the stand-off half in Rugby football. **fly in the face of,** to disregard or disobey openly. **fly off the handle,** (*colloq.*) to become uncontrollably angry. **fly-past** *n.* a ceremonial flight of aircraft past a person or place. [OE]

fly[2] /flaɪ/ *n.* **1** a two-winged insect, especially of the order Diptera. **2** some other winged insect, e.g. a firefly, mayfly. **3** a disease of plants or animals caused by flies. **4** a natural or artificial fly as a bait in fishing. —**fly-blown** *adj.* (of meat etc.) tainted by flies' eggs. **fly-fish** *v.i.* to fish with a fly. **fly in the ointment,** a minor irritation that spoils enjoyment. **fly on the wall,** an unnoticed observer. **fly-paper** *n.* a sticky treated paper for catching flies. **fly-spray** *n.* a liquid sprayed from a canister to kill flies. **fly-trap** *n.* a plant (*Dionaea muscipula*) able to catch flies. **there are no flies on him,** (*slang*) he is very astute. [OE (as foll.)]

fly[3] *adj.* (*slang*) knowing, clever. [orig. unkn.]

flycatcher *n.* a bird (especially of the genus *Muscicapa*) that catches insects in the air.

flyer *n.* **1** an airman or airwoman. **2** a fast-moving animal or vehicle. **3** an ambitious or outstanding person. [f. FLY[1]]

flying *n.* flight. —*adj.* **1** that flies. **2** (of a flag etc.) fluttering, waving. **3** hasty. **4** (of an animal) able to make long leaps by the use of membranes etc. **5** (of a vehicle etc.) designed for rapid movement. —**flying boat,** an aircraft that can land on and take off from water and whose main body is a hull which supports it in the water. **flying buttress,** a buttress formed from a separate column, usually forming an arch with the wall it supports. **flying fish,** a tropical fish of either of two genera (*Dactylopterus* and *Exocetus*) with winglike fins, able to rise into the air. **flying fox,** a fruit-eating bat of the genus *Pteropus*. **flying officer,** an RAF officer next below flight lieutenant. **flying picket,** a picket organized for moving from place to place. **flying saucer,** an unidentified saucer-shaped object reported as seen in the sky. **flying squad,** a police detachment or other body organized for rapid movement. **flying start,** a start in which the starting-point is passed at full speed; (*fig.*) a vigorous start giving an initial advantage. **with flying colours,** with great credit gained in a test etc. [f. FLY[1]]

flyleaf *n.* a blank leaf at the beginning or end of a book.

flyover *n.* a bridge that carries one road or railway over another.

flysheet *n.* a tract or circular of 2 or 4 pages.

flyweight *n.* the lightest professional boxing-weight (see BOXING-WEIGHT).

flywheel *n.* a heavy wheel on a revolving shaft to regulate machinery or accumulate power.

FM *abbr.* **1** Field Marshal. **2** frequency modulation.

Fm *symbol* fermium.

f-number /ef-/ *n.* the ratio of the focal length and effective diameter of a lens, used in photography to calculate the amount of light passing through the lens. [f. *f*ocal + NUMBER]

FO *abbr.* **1** Flying Officer. **2** (*hist.*) Foreign Office.

foal *n.* the young of the horse or a related animal. —*v.t.* (of a mare etc.) to give birth to (a foal, or *abs.*). —**in** *or* **with foal,** (of a mare etc.) pregnant. [OE]

foam *n.* **1** a collection of small bubbles formed on or in a liquid by agitation, fermentation, etc.; the froth of saliva or perspiration. **2** a substance resembling foam, e.g. rubber or plastic in a cellular mass. —*v.i.* to emit foam, to froth; to run in a foam. —**foam at the mouth,** to be very angry. —**foamy** *adj.* [OE]

fob[1] *n.* **1** an ornamental attachment to a watch-chain, key-ring, etc. **2** a small pocket for a watch etc. in the waistband of trousers. [prob. f. G]

fob[2] *v.t.* (**-bb-**) **fob off,** to deceive into accepting or being satisfied (*with* an inferior thing, excuse, etc.); to palm or pass off (a thing) *on* (*to*) a person. [f. obs. *fop* to dupe]

f.o.b. *abbr.* free on board.

focal /ˈfəʊk(ə)l/ *adj.* of or at a focus. —**focal distance** *or* **length,** the distance between the centre of a mirror or lens and its focus. —**focally** *adv.* [f. L (as FOCUS)]

focus /ˈfəʊkəs/ *n.* (*pl.* **focuses, foci** /ˈfəʊsaɪ/) **1** the point at which rays or waves meet after reflection or refraction; the point from which rays etc. appear to proceed; the point at which an object must be situated for a lens or mirror to give a well-defined image; an adjustment of the eye or a lens to give a clear image; a state of clear definition. **2** a centre of interest or activity etc. —*v.t./i.* (*p.t.* **focused**) **1** to bring into focus; to adjust the focus of (a lens or the eye); to converge or cause to converge to a focus. **2** to concentrate or be concentrated *on*. [L, = hearth]

fodder *n.* dried hay or straw etc. for horses, cattle, etc. —*v.t.* to give fodder to. [OE, rel. to FOOD]

foe *n.* (chiefly *poetic*) an enemy. —**foeman** *n.* [OE]

foetid /ˈfiːtɪd/ var. of FETID.

foetus /ˈfiːtəs/ *n.* an unborn or unhatched offspring, especially a human embryo more than eight weeks after conception. —**foetal** *adj.* [f. L *fetus* young offspring]

fog *n.* **1** a thick cloud of water droplets or smoke suspended at or near the earth's surface. **2** cloudiness obscuring the image on a photographic negative etc. —*v.t./i.* (**-gg-**) **1** to cover or become covered (as) with fog. **2** to perplex. —**fog-bank** *n.* a mass of fog at sea. **fog-bound** *adj.* unable to leave because of fog. **fog-horn** *n.* a horn sounding a warning to ships in fog. **fog-lamp** *n.* a powerful lamp for use in fog. [perh. = *fog* rank grass, perh. of Scand. orig.]

foggy *adj.* full of fog; of or like fog, indistinct. —**not have the foggiest,** (*colloq.*) to have no idea at all. —**fogginess** *n.* [f. FOG]

fogy /ˈfəʊgɪ/ *n.* (also **fogey**) an old-fashioned person (usu. *old fogy*). [orig. unkn.]

foible /ˈfɔɪb(ə)l/ *n.* a small weakness in a person's character. [F, obs. form of *faible* (as FEEBLE)]

foil[1] *v.t.* to baffle, to frustrate, to defeat. [perh. f. OF *fouler* to full cloth, to trample, f. L (as FULLER)]

foil[2] *n.* **1** metal hammered or rolled into thin sheets. **2** a person or thing that enhances the qualities of another by contrast. [f. OF f. L *folium* leaf]

foil[3] *n.* a light blunt-edged sword used in fencing. [orig. unkn.]

foist *v.t.* to force (an inferior, unwelcome, or undeserved thing) *on* (a person). [orig. of palming false dice, f. Du. *vuisten* take in the hand]

fold[1] /fəʊld/ *v.t./i.* **1** to bend or close (a flexible thing) over upon itself; to bend part of (a thing) *back* or *down*; to become or be able to be folded. **2** to embrace (*in* the arms or *to* the breast); to clasp (the arms etc.) *about* or *round*; to wrap, to envelop. **3** (in cookery) to mix (an ingredient) *in* lightly without stirring or beating. —*n.* **1** folding. **2** a folded part; a line made by folding. **3** a hollow among hills. **4** a curvature of geological strata. —**fold one's arms,** to place them across the chest, together or entwined. **fold one's hands,** to clasp them. **fold up,** to collapse (*lit.* or *fig.*); to cease to function. [OE]

fold[2] *n.* **1** a sheep-fold. **2** the body of believers, the members of a Church. —*v.t.* to enclose (sheep) in a fold. [OE]

-fold /fəʊld/ *suffix* forming adjectives and adverbs from cardinal numbers, in sense 'in an amount multiplied by', 'with so many parts'. [OE, orig. = folded in so many layers]

folder *n.* **1** a folding cover or holder for loose papers. **2** a folded leaflet. [f. FOLD[1]]

foliaceous /fəʊlɪˈeɪʃəs/ *adj.* of or like leaves; laminated. [f. L (*folium* leaf)]

foliage /ˈfəʊlɪɪdʒ/ *n.* leaves, leafage. [f. F *feuillage* (*feuille* leaf, as prec.)]

foliar /ˈfəʊlɪə(r)/ *adj.* of leaves. —**foliar feed,** a feed supplied to the leaves of plants. [f. L *folium* leaf]

foliate /ˈfəʊlɪət/ *adj.* leaflike, having leaves. —/-eɪt/ *v.t./i.* to split or beat into thin layers. —**foliation** /-ˈeɪʃ(ə)n/ *n.* [as prec.]

folic /ˈfəʊlɪk, ˈfɒ-/ *adj.* **folic acid,** a B-group vitamin, deficiency of which causes human anaemia. [f. L *folium* leaf (because found especially in green leaves)]

folio /ˈfəʊlɪəʊ/ *n.* (*pl.* **-os**) **1** a leaf of paper etc., especially one numbered only on the front.

2 a sheet of paper folded once, making two leaves of a book; a book made of such sheets. —*adj.* (of a book etc.) made of folios, of the largest size. —**in folio,** made of folios. [L, ablative of *folium* leaf]

folliot /'fəʊlɪət, 'fɒ-/ *n.* a type of clock escapement consisting of a bar with adjustable weights on the ends [f. OF, perh. f. *folier* play the fool, dance about]

folk /fəʊk/ *n.* **1** a nation or people. **2** the people of a specified class; (often in *pl.*) people in general; one's parents or relatives. **3** folk-music. —*attrib.* of popular origin. —**folk-music, folk-song,** *ns.* music or song traditional in a country, or in the style of this.

folklore *n.* the traditional beliefs etc. of a community; the study of these. —**folklorist** *n.*

folksy /'fəʊksɪ/ *adj.* adopting the characteristics of ordinary people or of folk-art; simple, unpretentious, friendly. [f. FOLK]

folkweave *n.* a rough loosely woven fabric.

follicle /'fɒlɪk(ə)l/ *n.* a small sac or vesicle in the body, especially one containing a hair-root. —**follicular** /fɒ'lɪkjʊlə(r)/ *adj.* [f. L (dim. of *follis* bellows)]

follow /'fɒləʊ/ *v.t./i.* **1** to go or come after (a person or thing proceeding ahead). **2** to go along (a road etc.). **3** to come next in order or time. **4** to take as a guide or leader, to conform to; to practise (a trade or profession), to undertake (a course of study etc.). **5** to understand the meaning or tendency of (an argument, speaker). **6** to be aware of the present state or progress of (events etc.). **7** to provide *with* a sequel or successor. **8** to result *from*; to be necessarily true as a result of something else. —**follow on,** to continue; (of a cricket team) to have to bat again immediately after a first innings. **follow-on** *n.* an instance of this. **follow out,** to carry out, to adhere strictly to (instructions etc.). **follow suit,** to play a card of the suit led; to conform to another's actions. **follow through,** to continue (an action etc.) to its conclusion. **follow up,** to pursue; to develop; to supplement (one thing *with* another). **follow-up** *n.* a further or continued action, a measure, etc. [OE]

follower *n.* one who follows; a supporter or devotee. [f. prec.]

following *n.* a body of supporters or devotees. —*adj.* that follows or comes after. —*prep.* after in time, as a sequel to. —**the following,** what follows; now to be given or named. [f. FOLLOW]

folly *n.* **1** foolishness; a foolish act, behaviour, idea, etc. **2** a costly ornamental building that serves no practical purpose. [f. OF *folie* (*fol* mad, as FOOL)]

foment /fə'ment/ *v.t.* to instigate or stir up (trouble, discontent, etc.). [f. F f. L *fomentum* poultice (*fovēre* warm, cherish)]

fomentation /fəʊmen'teɪʃ(ə)n/ *n.* **1** fomenting. **2** a hot lotion applied to part of the body to relieve pain or inflammation. [f. OF or L (as prec.)]

fond *adj.* **1** affectionate, loving; doting. **2** (of hopes, beliefs, etc.) foolishly credulous or optimistic. —**fond of,** having a liking for. —**fondly** *adv.*, **fondness** *n.* [f. obs. *fon* fool, be foolish]

fondant /'fɒnd(ə)nt/ *n.* a soft sweet of flavoured sugar. [F, = melting f. L *fundere* pour]

fondle *v.t.* to caress. [back-formation f. *fondling* fondled person, f. FOND]

fondue /'fɒndju:, -du:/ *n.* a dish of flavoured melted cheese. [F, p.p. of *fondre* melt (as FONDANT)]

font[1] *n.* a receptacle in a church for baptismal water. —**fontal** *adj.* [OE f. OIr. f. L *fons* fountain]

font[2] *US* var. of FOUNT[1].

fontanelle /fɒntə'nel/ *n.* the membranous space in an infant's skull at the angles of the parietal bones. [f. F (*fontaine* fountain)]

food *n.* **1** any substance(s) that can be taken into the body to maintain life and growth. **2** a solid substance of this kind. —**food-chain** *n.* (similarly **food-pyramid**) a series of plants and animals each of which serves as a source of nourishment for the one(s) above it in the series. **food for thought,** something that needs thinking about. **food-gatherer** *n.* a member of a people at a primitive stage of civilization obtaining food from natural sources not through agriculture. **food-gathering** *n.* this practice. **food-poisoning** *n.* an illness caused by bacteria or toxins in food. **food processor,** an electrically driven device with blades for mixing or slicing food. **food value,** the nourishing power of a food. **food-web** *n.* an interdependent group of food-chains. [OE, rel. to FEED]

foodstuff *n.* a substance used as a food.

fool[1] *n.* **1** a person who acts or thinks unwisely or imprudently, a stupid person. **2** (*hist.*) a jester, a clown. **3** a dupe. —*v.t./i.* to act in a joking or teasing way; to play or trifle (*about, around*); to cheat or deceive (a person) *out of* something or *into doing*. —**act** *or* **play the fool,** to behave in a silly way. **be no** *or* **nobody's fool,** to be shrewd or prudent. **fool's errand,** a fruitless errand. **fool's gold,** iron pyrites. **fool's paradise,** illusory happiness. **make a fool of,** to make (a person) look foolish; to trick or deceive. [f. OF *fol* f. L *follis* bellows, empty-headed person]

fool[2] *n.* a dessert of fruit crushed and mixed with cream or custard. [perh. f. prec.]

foolery *n.* foolish acts or behaviour. [f. FOOL[1]]

foolhardy *adj.* rashly or foolishly bold, reckless. —**foolhardiness** *n.* [f. OF (as FOOL[1], HARDY)]

foolish *adj.* (of a person or action) lacking good sense or judgement, unwise. —**foolishly** *adv.*, **foolishness** *n.* [f. FOOL[1]]

foolproof *adj.* (of a procedure, machine, etc.) so straightforward or simple as to be incapable of misuse or mistake.

foolscap /'fu:lskæp, -lz-/ *n.* a size of paper, about 330 × 200 (or 400) mm. [f. use of fool's cap (jester's cap with bells) as watermark]

foot /fʊt/ *n.* (*pl.* **feet**) **1** the end part of the leg beyond the ankle. **2** the lowest part of a page, table, hill, etc.; the end of a bed where the feet are normally put. **3** the part of a sock etc. covering the foot. **4** (*pl.* also **foot**) a linear measure of 12 inches (30.48 cm) originally based on the measurement of a man's foot. **5** a division of verse including one stressed syllable. **6** step, pace, tread. **7** (*hist.*) infantry. —*v.t.* to pay (a bill). —**feet of clay,** a fundamental weakness in a person of supposed merit. **foot-and-mouth (disease),** a contagious virus disease of cattle etc. **foot-brake** *n.* a foot-operated brake on a vehicle. **foot-bridge** *n.* a bridge for pedestrians only. **foot-slog** *v.i.* (*colloq.*) to walk or march. **have one foot in the grave,** to be near death or very old. **my foot!** (*colloq.*) an exclamation of contemptuous contradiction. **on foot,** walking not riding. **put one's feet up,** to have a rest. **put one's foot down,** to be firm or insistent; to accelerate a motor vehicle. **put one's foot in it,** to blunder. **under one's feet,** in the way (*lit.* & *fig.*). **under foot,** on the ground. [OE]

footage *n.* a length in feet, especially of exposed cinema film. [f. FOOT]

football *n.* **1** a large inflated ball, usually of leather. **2** an outdoor game between two teams, played with this. —**football pool(s),** a form of gambling on the results of football matches, the entry money being awarded in prizes. —**footballer** *n.*

footfall *n.* the sound of a footstep.

foothill *n.* one of the low hills near the bottom of a mountain or range.

foothold *n.* a place where the foot can be supported securely; (*fig.*) a secure initial position.

footing *n.* **1** a foothold, a secure position. **2** the position or status of a person in relation to others. [f. FOOT]

footlights *n.pl.* a row of lights at the front of a stage at the level of the actors' feet.

footling /'fu:tlɪŋ/ *adj.* (*slang*) trivial, silly. [f. *footle* play the fool (orig. unkn.)]

footloose *adj.* free to act as one pleases.

footman *n.* (*pl.* **-men**) a liveried servant for attending at the door or at table.

footnote *n.* a note printed at the foot of a page.

footpad *n.* (*hist.*) an unmounted highwayman. [f. FOOT + *pad* (archaic slang) = road, f. Du. & LG *pad* path]

footpath *n.* a path for pedestrians, a pavement.

footplate *n.* a platform for the crew of a locomotive.

footprint *n.* an impression left by a foot or shoe.

footsore *adj.* with sore feet, especially from walking.

footstep *n.* a step taken in walking; the sound of this. —**follow in a person's footsteps,** to do as he did.

footstool *n.* a stool for resting the feet on when sitting.

footway *n.* a path for pedestrians only.

footwear *n.* shoes, socks, etc.

footwork *n.* the use or manner of using the feet in sports, dancing, etc.

fop *n.* a dandy. —**foppery** *n.*, **foppish** *adj.* [perh. f. obs. *fop* fool]

for /fə(r), *emphat.* fɔ:(r)/ *prep.* **1** in defence, support, or favour of; in the interest or to the benefit of. **2** suitable or appropriate to. **3** in respect or reference to, regarding, so far as concerns. **4** at the price of; in exchange with, corresponding to; as a penalty or reward resulting from. **5** with a view to, in hope or quest of, in order to get. **6** in the direction of, towards, to reach. **7** so as to have begun by (a specified time). **8** through or over (a distance or period), during. **9** in the character of, as being. **10** because of, on account of. **11** in spite of, notwithstanding. **12** considering or making due allowance in respect of. —*conj.* seeing that, since, because. —**be for it,** (*colloq.*) to be about to get punishment or other trouble. **for ever,** for all time (see also FOREVER). **O** *or* **oh for,** I wish I had. [OE (prob. as FORE)]

for- *prefix* forming verbs etc. meaning (1) away or off (*forget, forgive*); (2) prohibition (*forbid*); (3) abstention or neglect (*forgo, forsake*). [OE]

f.o.r. *abbr.* free on rail.

forage /'fɒrɪdʒ/ *n.* **1** food for horses and cattle. **2** foraging. —*v.t./i.* to go searching, to rummage; to collect forage (from). —**forager** *n.* [f. OF f. Gmc (as FODDER)]

forasmuch /fɒrəz'mʌtʃ/ *adv.* **forasmuch as,** (*archaic*) since, because. [= *for as much*]

foray /'fɒreɪ/ *n.* a sudden attack, a raid. —*v.i.* to make a foray. [f. OF *forrier* forager (as FODDER)]

forbade, forbad *past* of FORBID.

forbear[1] /fɔ:'beə(r)/ *v.t./i.* (*past* **forbore**; *p.p.* **forborne**) to abstain (from) or refrain. [OE (FOR-, BEAR[1])]

forbear[2] var. of FOREBEAR.

forbearance *n.* patient self-control, tolerance. [f. FORBEAR[1]]

forbid /fəˈbɪd/ *v.t.* (**-dd-**; *past* **forbade** /-ˈbæd/, **forbad**; *p.p.* **forbidden**) to order not *to do*; to refuse to allow (a thing, or a person to have a thing); to refuse a person entry to. [f. FOR-, BID]

forbidding *adj.* uninviting, repellent, stern. [f. prec.]

forbore *past* of FORBEAR[1].

forborne *p.p.* of FORBEAR[1].

force[1] *n.* **1** strength, power, impetus, intense effort; coercion, compulsion; military strength. **2** an organized body of soldiers, police, workers, etc. **3** binding power, validity, effect, precise significance. **4** influence, efficacy. **5** a measurable and determinable influence tending to cause the motion of a body; the intensity of this; a person or thing likened to this.—*v.t./i.* **1** to constrain (a person) by force or against his will. **2** to make (a way) into or through by force, to break open by force. **3** to drive or propel violently or against resistance. **4** to impose or press (a thing) *on* or *upon* a person. **5** to cause or produce by effort. **6** to strain or increase to the utmost, to overstrain. **7** to hasten the growth or maturity of (a plant, pupil, etc.) artificially. —**forced labour,** compulsory labour, usually under harsh conditions. **forced landing,** an unavoidable landing of an aircraft in an emergency. **forced march,** a lengthy and vigorous march especially by troops. **force-feed** *v.t.* to feed (esp. a prisoner) against his will. **force a person's hand,** to make him act prematurely or unwillingly. **force the issue,** to make an immediate decision necessary. **in force,** valid, in great strength or numbers. [f. OF f. L *fortis* strong]

force[2] *n.* (*N. Engl.*) a waterfall. [f. ON *fors*]

forceful *adj.* powerful and vigorous; (of speech) impressive, compelling. —**forcefully** *adv.*, **forcefulness** *n.* [f. FORCE[1] + -FUL]

force majeure /fɔːs mæˈʒɜː(r)/ irresistible force; unforeseen circumstances excusing a person from the fulfilment of a contract. [F, = superior strength]

forcemeat /ˈfɔːsmiːt/ *n.* meat etc. chopped and seasoned for a stuffing or garnish. [f. OF *farsir* stuff (as FARCE)]

forceps /ˈfɔːseps/ *n.* (*pl.* same) surgical pincers. [L]

forcible /ˈfɔːsɪb(ə)l/ *adj.* done by or involving force; forceful. —**forcibly** *adv.* [f. OF (as FORCE[1])]

ford *n.* a shallow place where a river or stream may be crossed by wading, in a motor vehicle, etc. —*v.t.* to cross (water) thus. —**fordable** *adj.* [OE (rel. to FARE)]

fore *adj.* situated in front. —*n.* the front part, the bow of a ship. —*int.* (in golf) as a warning to a person likely to be hit by a ball. —**fore and aft,** at the bow and stern; all over the ship. **fore-and-aft** *adj.* (of a sail or rigging) lengthwise, not on yards. **to the fore,** in front, conspicuous. [OE]

fore- *prefix* forming (1) verbs in senses 'in front' (*foreshorten*), 'beforehand' (*forewarn*); (2) nouns in senses 'situated in front' (*forecourt*), 'front part of' (*forehead*), 'of or near the bow of a ship' (*forecastle*), 'preceding' (*forerunner*). [f. prec.]

forearm[1] /ˈfɔːrɑːm/ *n.* the arm between the elbow and the wrist or fingertips; the corresponding part in an animal.

forearm[2] /fɔːrˈɑːm/ *v.t.* to arm beforehand, to prepare.

forebear /ˈfɔːbeə(r)/ *n.* (usu. in *pl.*) an ancestor. [f. FORE- + obs. *beer* (BE)]

forebode /fɔːˈbəʊd/ *v.t.* to be an advance sign of, to portend; to have a presentiment of (usu. evil) or *that*.

foreboding *n.* an expectation of trouble. [f. prec.]

forecast /ˈfɔːkɑːst/ *v.t.* (*past* & *p.p.* **-cast** or **-casted**) to predict or estimate beforehand. —*n.* forecasting; a prediction.

forecastle /ˈfəʊks(ə)l/ *n.* the forward part of a ship where formerly the crew were accommodated.

foreclose /fɔːˈkləʊz/ *v.t.* **1** to take possession of the mortgaged property of (a person) when the loan is not duly repaid; to stop (a mortgage) from being redeemable. **2** to exclude, to prevent. —**foreclosure** *n.* [f. OF *forclore* (*for-* out of, as CLOSE[1])]

forecourt *n.* an enclosed space in front of a building; the part of a filling-station where petrol is dispensed.

foredoom /fɔːˈduːm/ *v.t.* to doom or condemn beforehand.

forefather *n.* (usu. in *pl.*) an ancestor, a member of a past generation of a family or people.

forefinger *n.* the finger next to the thumb.

forefoot *n.* (*pl.* **-feet**) a front foot of an animal.

forefront *n.* the foremost part; the leading position.

foregoing /fɔːˈgəʊɪŋ/ *adj.* preceding, previously mentioned. [as foll.]

foregone /ˈfɔːgɒn/ *adj.* previous, preceding. —**foregone conclusion,** an easily foreseen or predictable result. [OE (as FORE-, GO)]

foreground *n.* **1** the part of a view or picture nearest the observer. **2** the most conspicuous position.

forehand *n.* (in tennis etc.) a stroke made with the palm of the hand facing the opponent.

—*adj*. (also **forehanded**) of or made with this stroke.

forehead /ˈfɒrɪd, ˈfɔːhed/ *n*. the part of the head above the eyebrows.

foreign / ˈfɒrən/ *adj*. 1 of, from, situated in, or characteristic of a country or language other than one's own; dealing with other countries; of another district, society, etc. 2 unfamiliar, strange, uncharacteristic. 3 coming from outside. —**foreign aid,** money etc. given or lent by one country to another. **Foreign and Commonwealth Office,** the UK government department dealing with foreign affairs. **Foreign Secretary,** the head of this. **foreign legion,** a military formation of foreign volunteers, especially in the French army. [f. OF f. L *foris* outside]

foreigner *n*. a person born in or coming from another country. [f. prec.]

foreknow /fɔːˈnəʊ/ *v.t.* to know beforehand. —**foreknowledge** /fɔːˈnɒlɪdʒ/ *n*.

foreland *n*. a promontory, a cape.

foreleg *n*. a front leg of an animal.

forelimb *n*. a front limb of an animal.

forelock *n*. a lock of hair just above the forehead. —**take time by the forelock,** to seize an opportunity.

foreman *n*. (*pl*. **-men**) 1 a workman supervising others. 2 the president and spokesman of a jury.

foremast *n*. the mast nearest the bow of a ship.

foremost *adj*. most advanced in position; most notable, best. —*adv*. in the first place, most importantly. [f. superl. of OE *forma* first, assim. to FORE and -MOST]

forename *n*. a first or Christian name.

forenoon *n*. the day till noon, the morning.

forensic /fəˈrensɪk/ *adj*. of or used in courts of law. —**forensic medicine,** the application of medical knowledge to legal problems. —**forensically** *adv*. [f. L (as FORUM)]

foreordain /fɔːrɔːˈdeɪn/ *v.t.* to destine beforehand. —**foreordination** /-dɪˈneɪʃ(ə)n/ *n*.

forepaw *n*. a front paw of an animal.

foreplay *n*. stimulation preceding sexual intercourse.

forerunner *n*. a predecessor; an advance messenger.

foresail /ˈfɔːseɪl/, -s(ə)l/ *n*. the principal sail on the foremast.

foresee /fɔːˈsiː/ *v.t.* (*past* **-saw**; *p.p.* **-seen**) to see or be aware of beforehand.

foreseeable /fɔːˈsiːəb(ə)l/ *adj*. able to be foreseen. —**in the foreseeable future,** in the period ahead during which the general course of events can reasonably be predicted. [f. prec.]

foreshadow /fɔːˈʃædəʊ/ *v.t.* to be a warning or indication of (a future event).

foreshore *n*. the shore between high- and low-water marks.

foreshorten /fɔːˈʃɔːt(ə)n/ *v.t.* to show or portray (an object) with apparent shortening due to visual perspective.

foresight *n*. 1 regard or provision for the future. 2 foreseeing. 3 the front sight of a gun.

foreskin *n*. the loose skin covering the end of the penis.

forest /ˈfɒrɪst/ *n*. a large area of land covered chiefly with trees and undergrowth; the trees in this; a dense concentration (of things). —*v.t.* to plant with trees, to make into a forest. [f. OF f. L *forestis* (*silva* wood) outside (walls of park)]

forestall /fɔːˈstɔːl/ *v.t.* to act in advance of in order to prevent; to deal with beforehand. [f. OE, = an ambush, plot (as FORE-, STALL)]

forestay *n*. a stay from the head of the foremast to a ship's deck to support the foremast.

forester *n*. 1 an officer in charge of a forest. 2 a dweller in a forest. [f. FOREST]

forestry *n*. the science or management of forests. [as prec.]

foretaste *n*. a taste or experience of something in advance.

foretell /fɔːˈtel/ *v.t.* (*past* & *p.p.* **-told**) to predict, to prophesy; to be a precursor of.

forethought *n*. care or provision for the future, deliberate intention.

forever /fəˈrevə(r)/ *adv*. continually, persistently.

forewarn /fɔːˈwɔːn/ *v.t.* to warn beforehand.

forewoman *n*. (*pl*. **-women**) 1 a woman worker supervising others. 2 the woman foreman of a jury.

foreword *n*. the introductory remarks at the beginning of a book, often by a person other than the author.

forfeit /ˈfɔːfɪt/ *n*. a penalty, a thing surrendered as a penalty. —*v.t.* to lose or surrender as a penalty. —*adj*. lost or surrendered as a forfeit. —**forfeiture** *n*. [f. OF *forfaire* transgress f. L *foris* outside, *facere* do]

forgather /fɔːˈgæðə(r)/ *v.i.* to assemble, to associate. [f. Du. *vergaderen*]

forgave *past* of FORGIVE.

forge[1] *v.t.* 1 to make or write in fraudulent imitation. 2 to shape (metal) by heating and hammering. —*n*. a furnace etc. for melting and refining metal; a workshop with this; a blacksmith's workshop. —**forger** *n*. [f. OF f. L *fabrica* (as FABRIC)]

forge[2] *v.i.* to advance or move forward gradually or steadily. [perh. alt. f. FORCE[1]]

forgery /ˈfɔːdʒərɪ/ *n*. 1 the act of forging. 2 a forged document etc. [f. FORGE[1]]

forget /fəˈget/ *v.t./i.* (**-tt-**; *past* **forgot**; *p.p.*

forgotten, *US* **forgot**) to lose remembrance of or *about*, not to remember; to neglect or overlook; to cease to think of. —**forget oneself,** to put others' interests first; to behave without due dignity. [OE (as FOR-, GET)]

forgetful *adj*. apt to forget, neglectful. —**forgetfully** *adv*., **forgetfulness** *n*. [f. prec. + -FUL]

forget-me-not *n*. a plant of the genus *Myosotis* with small blue flowers.

forgive /fə'gɪv/ *v.t.* (*past* **forgave**; *p.p.* **forgiven** /-'gɪv(ə)n/) **1** to cease to feel angry or resentful towards (a person) or about (an offence). **2** to pardon. **3** to remit (a debt). [OE (as FOR-, GIVE)]

forgiveness *n*. the act of forgiving; the state of being forgiven. [f. prec.]

forgiving *adj*. inclined readily to forgive. [f. FORGIVE]

forgo /fɔː'gəʊ/ *v.t.* (*past* **forwent**; *p.p.* **forgone**) to go without, to relinquish; to omit or decline to take or use (a pleasure, advantage, etc.). [OE (as FOR-, GO)]

forgot *past* (& *US p.p.*) of FORGET.

forgotten *p.p.* of FORGET.

fork *n*. **1** a pronged implement used in eating and cooking; a similar much larger implement used for digging, lifting, etc. **2** a divergence of a stick, road, etc, into two parts; the place of this; one of the two parts. **3** the forked support for a bicycle wheel. **4** a pronged device pushed under a load to be lifted. —*v.t./i.* **1** to form a fork or branch by separating into two parts; to take one road at a fork. **2** to dig, lift, or throw with a fork. —**fork-lift truck,** a vehicle with a fork for lifting and carrying loads. **fork out,** (*slang*) to pay (usu. reluctantly). [OE f. L *furca*]

forlorn /fɔː'lɔːn/ *adj*. sad and abandoned; in a pitiful state. —**forlorn hope,** a faint remaining hope or chance. —**forlornly** *adv*. [p.p. of obs. *forlese* (as FOR-, LOSE); *forlorn hope* f. Du. *verloren hoop* lost troop (orig. of storming-party)]

form *n*. **1** shape, arrangement of parts, visible aspect. **2** a person or animal as visible or tangible. **3** the mode in which a thing exists or manifests itself. **4** a printed document with blank spaces for information to be inserted. **5** a class in school. **6** a customary method; a set order of words. **7** a species, a kind. **8** behaviour according to rule or custom; correct procedure. **9** (of an athlete, horse, etc.) condition of health and training; (in racing etc.) details of previous performances; (*slang*) a criminal record. **10** one of the ways in which a word may be spelt, pronounced, or inflected. **11** the arrangement and style in a literary or musical composition. **12** a bench. **13** a hare's lair. —*v.t./i.* **1** to fashion or shape. **2** to mould by discipline, to train or instruct. **3** to develop or establish as a concept, institution, or practice; to organize (*into* a company etc.) **4** to be the material of, to make up, to be. **5** to take shape, to come into existence. **6** to construct (a word) by inflexion etc. **7** (often with *up*) to bring or move into formation. —**on** *or* **off form,** performing or playing well or badly. [f. OF f. L *forma*]

-form *suffix* forming adjectives (usu. as **-iform**) in senses 'having the form of' (*cuneiform*), 'having such a number of forms' (*uniform*). [as prec.]

formal /'fɔːm(ə)l/ *adj*. **1** used or done or held in accordance with rules, convention, or ceremony; excessively stiff or methodical. **2** valid or correctly so called because of its form; explicit. **3** of or concerned with (outward) form, especially as distinct from content or matter. **4** perfunctory, following form only. **5** precise, symmetrical. —**formally** *adv*. [f. L (as FORM)]

formaldehyde /fɔː'mældɪhaɪd/ *n*. the aldehyde of formic acid, used as a disinfectant and preservative. [f. FORMIC + ALDEHYDE]

formalin /'fɔːməlɪn/ *n*. an aqueous solution of formaldehyde. [f. prec.]

formalism /'fɔːməlɪz(ə)m/ *n*. **1** strict or excessive adherence to or concern with form or forms. **2** treatment of mathematics as the manipulation of meaningless symbols. **3** a symbolic and stylized manner of theatrical production. —**formalist***n*. [f. FORMAL]

formality /fɔː'mælɪtɪ/ *n*. a formal act, regulation, or custom (often lacking real significance); a thing done simply to comply with a rule; rigid observance of rules or convention. [f. F or L (as FORMAL)]

formalize /'fɔːməlaɪz/ *v.t.* to make formal; to give a definite (esp. legal) form to. —**formalization** /-'zeɪʃ(ə)n/ *n*. [f. FORMAL]

format /'fɔːmæt/ *n*. **1** the shape and size (of a book etc.). **2** style or manner of arrangement or procedure. **3** the arrangement of data etc. for a computer. —*v.t.* (**-tt-**) to arrange in a format, especially for a computer. [F f. G, f. L *formatus* (*liber*) shaped (book), as foll.]

formation /fɔː'meɪʃ(ə)n/ *n*. **1** forming. **2** a thing formed; a particular arrangement (e.g. of troops); a set of rocks or strata with a common characteristic. [f. OF or L (*formare* to shape, as FORM)]

formative /'fɔːmətɪv/ *adj*. serving to form or fashion; of formation. [f. OF or L (as prec.)]

forme /fɔːm/ *n*. a body of type secured in a chase for printing at one impression. [var. of FORM]

former *adj*. of the past, earlier. —**the former,** (often *absol*.), the first or first-mentioned of two. [compar. of OE *forma* first (cf. FOREMOST)]

formerly *adv.* in former times. [f. prec.]

Formica /fɔːˈmaɪkə/ *n.* [P] a hard durable plastic laminate used on surfaces. [orig. unkn.]

formic acid /ˈfɔːmɪk/ a colourless irritant volatile acid contained in the fluid emitted by ants. [f. L *formica* ant]

formidable /ˈfɔːmɪdəb(ə)l, (D) -ˈmɪd-/ *adj.* **1** inspiring fear or dread. **2** likely to be difficult to overcome or deal with. —**formidably** *adv.* [F, or f. L (*formidare* dread)]

formless *adj.* without a definite or regular form. [f. FORM + -LESS]

formula /ˈfɔːmjʊlə/ *n.* (*pl.* **-as, -ae** /-iː/) **1** a set of chemical symbols showing the constituents of a substance. **2** a mathematical rule expressed in figures. **3** a fixed form of words, especially one used on social or ceremonious occasions; a form of words embodying or enabling an agreement. **4** a list of ingredients. **5** the classification of a racing car, especially by engine capacity. **6** (*US*) an infant's food made according to a prescribed recipe. —**formulaic** /-ˈleɪɪk/ *adj.* [L, dim. of *forma* form]

formulary /ˈfɔːmjʊlərɪ/ *n.* a collection of formulas or set forms. [f. F or L (as prec.)]

formulate /ˈfɔːmjʊleɪt/ *v.t.* to express in a formula; to express clearly and precisely. —**formulation** /-ˈleɪʃ(ə)n/ *n.* [f. FORMULA]

fornicate /ˈfɔːnɪkeɪt/ *v.i.* (of people not married to each other) to have sexual intercourse voluntarily. —**fornication** /-ˈkeɪʃ(ə)n/ *n.*, **fornicator** *n.* [f. L *fornicare* (*formix* brothel)]

forsake /fɔːˈseɪk/ *v.t.* (*past* **forsook** /-ˈsʊk/; *p.p.* **forsaken**) **1** to give up, to renounce. **2** to withdraw one's help or companionship from. [OE (as FOR-, *sacan* quarrel)]

forsooth /fɔːˈsuːθ/ *adv.* (*archaic*, now usu. *iron.*) indeed, truly, no doubt. [OE (as FOR, SOOTH)]

forswear /fɔːˈsweə(r)/ *v.t.* (*past* **forswore**; *p.p.* **forsworn**) **1** to abjure, to renounce. **2** (in *p.p.*) perjured. —**forswear oneself,** to perjure oneself. [OE (as FOR-, SWEAR)]

forsythia /fɔːˈsaɪθɪə/ *n.* an ornamental shrub of the genus *Forsythia*, with bright yellow flowers. [f. W. *Forsyth* English botanist (d. 1804)]

fort *n.* a fortified military building or position. —**hold the fort,** to act as a temporary substitute, to cope with an emergency. [f. F or It. f. L *fortis* strong]

forte[1] /ˈfɔːteɪ/ *n.* one's strong point, a thing in which one excels. [f. F *fort* strong (as prec.)]

forte[2] /ˈfɔːteɪ/ *adj.* & *adv.* (*Mus.*) loud, loudly. —*n.* (*Mus.*) loud playing; a passage played loudly. [It., = strong, loud]

fortepiano /ˈfɔːtɪpɪænəʊ/ *n.* (*pl.* **-os**) a pianoforte, especially with reference to an instrument of the 18th to early 19th c. [It. (*forte* loud, *piano* soft)]

forth *adv.* (*archaic* exc. in set phrases) forward, into view; onwards in time; forwards; out from a starting-point. [OE]

forthcoming *adj.* **1** approaching, coming or available soon; **2** produced when wanted. **3** (of a person). **3** willing to give information, responsive.

forthright *adj.* straightforward; outspoken; decisive.

forthwith /fɔːθˈwɪð/ *adv.* at once, without delay. [f. earlier *forthwithal* (FORTH, WITH, ALL)]

fortification /fɔːtɪfɪˈkeɪʃ(ə)n/ *n.* **1** the act of fortifying. **2** (usu. in *pl.*) defensive works, walls, etc. [f. F f. L (as foll.)]

fortify /ˈfɔːtɪfaɪ/ *v.t./i.* **1** to strengthen physically, mentally, morally, etc. **2** to provide with or erect fortifications. **3** to strengthen (wine) with alcohol; to add extra nutrients, especially vitamins, to (food). [f. OF f. L *fortificare* (*fortis* strong)]

fortissimo /fɔːˈtɪsɪməʊ/ *adj.* & *adv.* (*Mus.*) very loud, very loudly. —*n.* (*pl.* **-os**) (*Mus.*) very loud playing; a passage played very loudly. [It., superl. of FORTE[2]]

fortitude /ˈfɔːtɪtjuːd/ *n.* courage in pain or adversity. [f. F f. L (*fortis* strong, brave)]

fortnight *n.* two weeks. [OE, = fourteen nights]

fortnightly *adj.* done, produced, or occurring once a fortnight. —*adv.* every fortnight. —*n.* a fortnightly magazine etc. [f. prec.]

fortran /ˈfɔːtræn/ *n.* a computer language used especially for scientific calculations. [f. *Formula Translation*]

fortress /ˈfɔːtrɪs/ *n.* a fortified building or town. [f. OF f. L *fortis* strong]

fortuitous /fɔːˈtjuːɪtəs/ *adj.* happening by chance, accidental. —**fortuitously** *adv.*, **fortuitousness** *n.*, **fortuity** *n.* [f. L (*forte* by chance)]

fortunate /ˈfɔːtjʊnət, -tʃənət/ *adj.* lucky, auspicious. —**fortunately** *adv.* [f. L (as foll.)]

fortune /ˈfɔːtjuːn, -tʃuːn/ *n.* **1** chance or luck as a force in human affairs. **2** the luck (good or bad) that befalls a person or enterprise. **3** a person's destiny. **4** good luck; prosperity, great wealth, a huge sum of money. —**fortune-teller** *n.* a person who claims to foretell one's destiny. **make a fortune,** to become very rich. [f. L *fortuna* luck, chance]

forty *adj.* & *n.* **1** four times ten; the symbol for this (40, xl, XL). **2** (in *pl.*) the numbers, years, degrees of temperature, etc., from 40 to 49. —**forty winks,** a short sleep. —**fortieth** *adj.* & *n.* [OE (as FOUR)]

forum /ˈfɔːrəm/ *n.* **1** the public square or market-place in an ancient Roman city, used for judicial and other business. **2** a place of or meeting for public discussion; a court, a tribunal. [L]

forward /ˈfɔːwəd/ *adj.* **1** lying in one's line of motion, onward or towards the front. **2** relating to the future. **3** precocious, bold in manner, presumptuous. **4** approaching maturity or completion; (of a plant etc.) well-advanced, early. *—n.* an attacking player near the front in football, hockey, etc. *—adv.* **1** to the front, into prominence; in advance, ahead. **2** onward so as to make progress. **3** towards the future. **4** (also **forwards**) towards the front in the direction one is facing; in the normal direction of motion or of traversal; with a continuous forward motion. *—v.t.* **1** to send (a letter etc.) on to a further destination; to dispatch (goods etc.). **2** to help to advance; to promote. **—forwardness** *n.* [OE (as FORTH, -WARD)]

fosse /fɒs/ *n.* a long ditch or trench, especially in fortification. [f. OF f. L *fossa* ditch]

fossick /ˈfɒsɪk/ *v.i.* (*Austral. & NZ slang*) to rummage, to search *about*; to search for gold etc. in abandoned workings. [per. f. dial. *fossick* bustle about]

fossil /ˈfɒs(ə)l/ *n.* **1** the remains or impression of a (usu. prehistoric) plant or animal hardened in a rock. **2** an antiquated or unchanging person or thing. *—adj.* **1** of or like a fossil. **2** found buried, dug from the ground. **—fossil fuel,** coal, oil, etc. formed in the geological past (esp. opp. *nuclear fuel*). [f. F f. L *fossilis* (*fodere* dig)]

fossilize /ˈfɒsɪlaɪz/ *v.t./i.* to become or cause to become a fossil. **—fossilization** /-ˈzeɪʃ(ə)n/ *n.* [f. prec.]

foster *v.t.* **1** to promote the growth or development of; to encourage or harbour (a feeling); (of circumstances) to be favourable to. **2** to bring up a child that is not one's own. *—adj.* (in *comb.*, as *foster-brother*, *-mother*) having a family connection by fostering not by birth. **—foster home,** a home in which a foster-child is brought up. [OE, = nourishment (as FOOD)]

fought *past* & *p.p.* of FIGHT.

foul *adj.* **1** offensive, loathsome, stinking; filthy, soiled; (*colloq.*) disgusting. **2** (of language etc.) obscene, disgustingly abusive. **3** (of weather) rough, stormy. **4** containing noxious matter; clogged, choked; overgrown with barnacles etc. **5** unfair, against the rules. **6** in collision; (of a rope etc.) entangled. *—n.* **1** a foul stroke or piece of play. **2** a collision, an entanglement. *—adv.* unfairly, contrary to the rules. *—v.t./i.* **1** to make or become foul. **2** to commit a foul against (a player). **3** to become or cause to become entangled; to collide with. **—foul-mouthed** *adj.* using abusive or offensive language. **foul play,** unfair play in sport; a treacherous or violent act, especially murder. **foul up,** to become or cause to become blocked or entangled; to spoil or bungle. **—foully** *adv.* [OE]

foulard /fuːˈlɑːd/ *n.* a thin soft material of silk or silk and cotton. [F]

found[1] *v.t.* **1** to establish, especially with an endowment; to originate or initiate (an institution etc.), to be the original builder of (a town etc.). **2** to lay the base of (a building); to construct or base (a story, theory, rule, etc.) *on* or *upon*. **—ill-founded** *adj.* unjustified. **well-founded** *adj.* justified, reasonable. **—founder**[1] *n.* [f. OF f. L *fundare* (*fundus* bottom)]

found[2] *v.t.* to melt and mould (metal); to fuse (the materials for glass); to make (a thing) thus. **—founder**[2] *n.* [f. OF f. L *fundere* pour]

found[3] *past* & *p.p.* of FIND.

foundation /faʊnˈdeɪʃ(ə)n/ *n.* **1** establishing, especially of an endowed institution; such an institution (e.g. a college, hospital, school) or its revenues. **2** the solid ground or base on which a building rests; (in *sing.* or *pl.*) the lowest part of a building usually below ground-level. **3** a basis, an underlying principle. **4** the material or part on which other parts are overlaid; (in full **foundation garment**) a woman's supporting undergarment, e.g. a corset. **—foundation-stone** *n.* a stone laid ceremonially to celebrate the founding of a building; (*fig.*) a basis. [f. OF f. L (as FOUND[1])]

founder[1,2] see FOUND[1,2].

founder[3] *v.i.* (of a horse or rider) to fall to the ground, to fall from lameness, to stick in mud etc.; (of a plan etc.) to fail; (of a ship) to fill with water and sink. [f. OF f. L *fundus* bottom]

foundling *n.* an abandoned infant of unknown parents. [f. p.p. of FIND]

foundry *n.* a workshop for or the business of casting metal. [f. FOUND[2]]

fount[1] /faʊnt, fɒnt/ *n.* a set of printing-type of the same face and size. [f. F (as FOUND[2])]

fount[2] *n.* a source; (*poetic*) a spring, a fountain. [back-formation f. foll.]

fountain /ˈfaʊntɪn/ *n.* **1** a jet or jets of water made to spout for ornamental purposes or for drinking; a structure provided for this. **2** a spring; the source (*of* wisdom etc.). **—fountain-head** *n.* the source. **fountain-pen** *n.* a pen with a reservoir holding ink. [f. OF f. L *fontana* (*fons fontis* spring)]

four /ˈfɔː(r)/ *adj.* & *n.* **1** one more than three; the symbol for this (4, iv, IV). **2** the size etc. denoted by four. **3** a team of four; a four-oared boat or its crew. **—four-in-hand** *n.* a vehicle with four horses driven by one person. **the four last things,** death, judgement, heaven, and hell. **four-letter word,** a short word referring to the sexual or excretory functions and regarded as vulgar or obscene. **four-poster** *n.* a bed with four posts supporting a canopy. **four-square** *adj.* solidly based, steady; (*adv.*) squarely, resolutely. **four-stroke** *adj.* (of an internal-combustion engine) having a cycle of four strokes of a piston, in which a cylinder fires once. **four-wheel drive,** drive acting on all four wheels of a vehicle. **on all fours,** on hands and knees. [OE]

fourfold *adj.* & *adv.* four times as much or as many; consisting of four parts. [f. FOUR + -FOLD]

foursome *n.* a group of four persons; a golf match between two pairs with partners playing the same ball. [f. FOUR + -SOME]

fourteen /fɔːˈtiːn/ *adj.* & *n.* **1** one more than thirteen; the symbol for this (14, xiv, XIV). **2** the size etc. denoted by fourteen. —**fourteenth** *adj.* & *n.* [OE (as FOUR, -TEEN)]

fourth *adj.* next after the third. —*n.* one of the four equal parts of a thing. —**fourth estate,** the press. —**fourthly** *adv.* [OE (cf. FOUR)]

fowl *n.* (*pl.* **fowls** or *collect.* **fowl**) **1** a domestic cock or hen kept for eggs and flesh; the flesh of birds as food. **2** a bird (*archaic* exc. in *comb.*) —*v.i.* to hunt or shoot or snare wildfowl. —**fowler** *n.* [OE]

fox *n.* **1** a wild four-legged animal (*Vulpes vulpes*) of the dog family with red fur and a bushy tail; its fur. **2** a cunning person. —*v.t.* **1** to deceive, to baffle; **2** (esp. in *p.p.*) to discolour (the pages of a book etc.) with brownish marks. —**fox-terrier** *n.* a kind of short-haired terrier. [OE]

foxglove *n.* a tall plant (*Digitalis purpurea*) with purple or white flowers like glove-fingers.

foxhole *n.* a hole in the ground used as a shelter against missiles or as a firing-point.

foxhound *n.* a kind of hound bred and trained to hunt foxes.

foxtrot *n.* a ballroom dance with slow and quick steps; the music for this. —*v.i.* to dance the foxtrot.

foxy *adj.* **1** foxlike. **2** sly, cunning. **3** reddish-brown. —**foxily** *adv.*, **foxiness** *n.* [f. FOX]

foyer /ˈfɔɪeɪ, ˈfwæjeɪ/ *n.* the entrance hall or an open space in a theatre etc. for the audience's use during an interval; the entrance hall of a hotel etc. [F, = hearth, home]

Fr *symbol* francium.

Fr. *abbr.* **1** Father. **2** French.

fr. *abbr.* franc(s).

fracas /ˈfrækɑː/ *n.* (*pl.* same /-kɑːz/, (*US*) **fracases**) a noisy disturbance or quarrel. [F f. It.]

fraction /ˈfrækʃ(ə)n/ *n.* **1** a numerical quantity that is not a whole number (e.g. ½, 0.5). **2** a small part, piece, or amount. **3** a portion of a mixture obtained by distillation etc. [f. OF f. L (*frangere* break)]

fractional *adj.* **1** of fractions; being a fraction. **2** very slight. —**fractional distillation,** separation of parts of a mixture by making use of their different physical properties. —**fractionally** *adv.* [f. prec.]

fractionate /ˈfrækʃəneɪt/ *v.t.* to break up into parts; to separate (a mixture) by fractional distillation. —**fractionation** *n.*, **fractionator** *n.* [f. FRACTION]

fractious /ˈfrækʃəs/ *adj.* irritable, peevish. —**fractiously** *adv.*, **fractiousness** *n.* [f. prec. in obs. sense 'brawling']

fracture /ˈfræktʃə(r)/ *n.* a breakage, especially of a bone or cartilage. —*v.t./i.* to cause a fracture in; to suffer a fracture. [f. F or L (as FRACTION)]

fragile /ˈfrædʒaɪl/ *adj.* easily broken, weak; of delicate constitution, not strong. —**fragilely** *adv.*, **fragility** /frəˈdʒɪlɪtɪ/ *n.* [f. F or L *fragilis* (as FRACTION)]

fragment /ˈfrægmənt/ *n.* a part broken off; the remainder of an otherwise lost or destroyed whole; the extant remains or an unfinished portion of a book etc. —/also -ˈment/ *v.t./i.* to break or separate into fragments. —**fragmentary** *adj.*, **fragmentation** /-ˈteɪʃ(ə)n/ *n.* [f. F or L *fragmentum* (as prec.)]

fragrance /ˈfreɪgrəns/ *n.* sweetness of smell; a sweet scent. [f. F or L (as foll.)]

fragrant /ˈfreɪgrənt/ *adj.* sweet-smelling. —**fragrantly** *adv.* [f. F or L (*fragrare* smell sweet)]

frail *adj.* fragile, delicate; transient; morally weak. —**frailly** *adv.* [f. OF (as FRAGILE)]

frailty *n.* frail quality; a weakness, a foible. [as prec.]

frame *v.t.* **1** to construct, to put together or devise (a complex thing, idea, theory, etc.); to adapt or fit *to* or *into*. **2** to articulate (words). **3** to set in a frame; to serve as a frame for; (*slang*) to concoct a false charge or evidence against, to devise a plot against. —*n.* **1** the case or border enclosing a picture, window, door, etc. **2** the human or animal body, especially with reference to its size. **3** the basic rigid supporting structure of a building, motor vehicle, aircraft, bicycle, etc.; (in *pl.*) the structure of spectacles holding the lenses. **4** construction, build, structure; the established order or system; a temporary state (*of mind*). **5** a single complete image or picture on a cinema film or transmitted in a series of lines by television. **6** a boxlike structure of glass etc. for protecting plants. **7** the triangular structure for positioning the balls in snooker etc.; a round of play in snooker etc. **8** (*US slang*) a frame-up. —**frame of reference,** a system of geometrical axes for defining position, a set of standards or principles governing behaviour, thought, etc. **frame-up** *n.* (*colloq.*) a conspiracy to make an innocent person appear guilty. [OE, = be helpful]

framework *n.* an essential supporting structure; a basic system.

franc *n.* the unit of currency in France, Belgium, Switzerland, etc. [f. OF f. *Francorum Rex* king of the Franks, legend on the earliest gold coins so called (14th c.)]

franchise /ˈfræntʃaɪz/ *n.* **1** the right to vote in a State election. **2** full membership of a corporation or State, citizenship. **3** a right or privilege granted to a person or corporation. **4** authorization to sell a company's goods etc. in a particular area. —*v.t.* to grant a franchise to. [f. OF (*franc* free, as FRANK)]

Franciscan /frænˈsɪskən/ *adj.* of the order founded by St Francis of Assisi (d. 1226). —*n.* a monk or nun of the Franciscan order. [f. F f. L (*Franciscus* Francis)]

francium /ˈfrænsɪəm/ *n.* a radioactive metallic element, symbol Fr, atomic number 87. [f. FRANCE, country of its discoverer (M. Perey)]

Franco- *in comb.* French and (*Franco-German*). [f. L (as FRANK)]

franglais /ˈfrɑ̃gleɪ/ *n.* a corrupt version of French using many words and phrases borrowed from English. [F (*français* French, *anglais* English)]

Frank *n.* a member of a Germanic people that conquered Gaul in the 6th c. —**Frankish** *adj.* [OE]

frank *adj.* candid, open, outspoken, undisguised, unmistakable. —*v.t.* to mark (a letter etc.) to record the payment of postage. —*n.* a franking signature or mark. —**frankly** *adv.*, **frankness** *n.* [f. OF f. L *francus* free (as foll., since only Franks had full freedom in Frankish Gaul)]

frankfurter /ˈfræŋkfɜːtə(r)/ *n.* a seasoned smoked sausage. [f. G *Frankfurter wurst* Frankfurt sausage (*Frankfurt* in Germany)]

frankincense /ˈfræŋkɪnsens/ *n.* an aromatic gum resin burnt as incense. [f. OF (as FRANK in obs. sense 'of high quality', INCENSE²)]

frantic /ˈfræntɪk/ *adj.* wildly excited, frenzied; characterized by great hurry or anxiety, desperate, violent; (*colloq.*) extreme. —**frantically** *adv.* [f. OF f. L (as PHRENETIC)]

frappé /ˈfræpeɪ/ *adj.* (esp. of wine) iced, chilled. [F, p.p. of *frapper* strike, ice (drinks)]

fraternal /frəˈtɜːn(ə)l/ *adj.* of brothers, brotherly. —**fraternal twins,** twins developed from separate ova and not necessarily similar. —**fraternally** *adv.* [f. L (*frater* brother)]

fraternity /frəˈtɜːnɪtɪ/ *n.* **1** a religious brotherhood. **2** a guild or group of people sharing interests or beliefs etc. **3** brotherliness. **4** (*US*) a male students' society in a college or university. [f. OF f. L (as prec.)]

fraternize /ˈfrætənaɪz/ *v.i.* to associate or make friends (*with*); (of troops) to enter into friendly relations *with* enemy troops or inhabitants of an occupied country. —**fraternization** /-ˈzeɪʃ(ə)n/ *n.* [f. F & L (as FRATERNAL)]

fratricide /ˈfrætrɪsaɪd/ *n.* **1** the crime of killing one's own brother or sister. **2** one who is guilty of this. —**fratricidal** *adj.* [F, or f. L (*frater* brother, -CIDE)]

Frau /fraʊ/ *n.* (*pl.* **Frauen**) a German woman; the title of a German wife or widow, = Mrs. [G]

fraud /frɔːd/ *n.* **1** criminal deception. **2** a dishonest artifice or trick; an impostor. **3** a person or thing not fulfilling a claim or expectation. [f. OF f. L]

fraudulent /ˈfrɔːdjʊlənt/ *adj.* of, involving, or guilty of fraud. —**fraudulence** *n.*, **fraudulently** *adv.* [f. OF or L (as prec.)]

fraught /frɔːt/ *adj.* **1** filled or attended *with* (danger etc.). **2** (*colloq.*) causing or suffering anxiety or distress. [p.p. of obs. *fraught* load with cargo, f. MDu. (as FREIGHT)]

Fräulein /ˈfrɔɪlaɪn/ *n.* an unmarried German woman; the title of a German spinster, = Miss. [G, dim. of FRAU]

fray[1] *v.t./i.* to become or cause to become worn through by rubbing; to become ragged at the edge (*lit.*, or *fig.* of nerves, temper, etc.). [f. F f. L *fricare* rub]

fray[2] *n.* a fight, a conflict; a brawl. [as AFFRAY]

frazzle *n.* a worn or exhausted state. [perh. f. FRAY¹ + dial. *fazzle* tangle]

freak *n.* **1** a capricious or unusual idea, act, etc. **2** a monstrosity, an abnormal person or thing. **3** an unconventional person; one who freaks out; a drug addict. —*v.t./i.* (with *out*) (*slang*) **1** to undergo or cause to undergo hallucinations through drug-taking etc. or a strong emotional experience. **2** to adopt an unconventional life-style. —**freak-out** *n.* (*slang*) the experience of freaking out. —**freakish** *adj.* [prob. f. dial.]

freckle *n.* a light brown spot on the skin. —*v.t./i.* to spot or be spotted with freckles. [f. ON]

free *adj.* (*compar.* **freer** /ˈfriːə(r)/, *superl.* **freest** (ˈfriːɪst/) **1** not a slave or under the control of another, having personal rights and social and political liberty; (of a State, citizens, or institutions) subject neither to foreign domination nor to despotic government. **2** not fixed or held down, able to move without hindrance; permitted *to* do; unrestricted, not controlled by rules; (of a translation) not literal. 3 (with *of* or *from*) without, not subject to or affected by. 4 without payment, costing nothing to the recipient. 5 not occupied or in use; without engagements; clear of obstructions. 6 coming, given, or giving readily; impudent. 7 (*Chem.*) not combined; (*Phys.*) not bound in an atom or molecule; (of power or energy) disengaged, available. —*adv.* freely; without cost or payment. —*v.t.* to make free, to set at liberty; to relieve *from*; to rid or ease *of*; to clear, to disentangle. —**free and easy,** informal. **free association,** association of ideas, by a person undergoing a psychological test, without suggestion or control by the tester. **free-born** *adj.* born as a free citizen. **Free Church,** a nonconformist Church. **Free Church of Scotland,** that which seceded from the Presbyterian establishment 1843-1929. **free enterprise,** freedom of private business from State control. **free fall,** movement under the force of gravity only. **free fight,** a general fight in which all present may join, without rules. **free-for-all** *n.* a free fight, an unrestricted discussion etc. **free hand,** freedom to act at one's own discretion. **free-hand** *adj.* (of a drawing) done without instruments such as a ruler or compasses. **free-handed** *adj.* generous. **free house,** an inn or public house not controlled by a brewery and therefore able to sell any brand of beer etc. **free kick,** a kick in football taken without interference from opponents, as a minor penalty. **free lance,** a person whose services are available to any would-be employer, not one only. **free-lance** *adj.* of a free lance; (*v.i.*) to act as a free lance. **free-loader** *n.* (*slang*) a sponger. **free love,** sexual relations irrespective of marriage. **free market,** a market in which prices are determined by unrestricted competition. **free on board** *or* **rail,** without charge for delivery to a ship, railway wagon, etc. **free port,** one open to all traders, or free from duty on goods in transit. **free-range** *adj.* (of hens etc.) given freedom of movement in seeking food etc. **free speech,** the freedom to express opinions of any kind. **free-spoken** *adj.* not concealing one's opinions. **free-standing** *adj.* not supported by another structure. **free-style** *adj.* (of a swimming-race) in which any stroke may be used; (of wrestling) with few restrictions on the holds permitted. **free-thinker** *n.* one who rejects dogma or authority in religious belief. **free trade,** trade left to its natural course without import restrictions etc. **free vote,** a parliamentary vote in which members are not bound by party policy. **free wheel,** the driving-wheel of a bicycle able to revolve with the pedals at rest. **free-wheel** *v.i.* to ride a bicycle with the pedals at rest; to move or act without constraint. **free will,** the power of acting without the constraint of necessity or fate, the ability to act at one's own discretion. **free world,** the non-Communist countries' collective name for themselves. —**freely** *adv.* [OE]

-free *in comb.* free of or from (*duty-free*, *fancy-free*). [f. prec.]

freeboard *n.* the part of a ship's side between the water-line and the deck.

freebooter *n.* a pirate. [f. Du. *vrijbuiter* (as FREE, BOOTY)]

freedman *n.* (*pl.* **-men**) an emancipated slave. [f. p.p. of *free* v. (FREE) + MAN]

freedom /ˈfriːdəm/ *n.* 1 the condition of being free or unrestricted; personal or civic liberty; liberty of action (*to*). 2 frankness, undue familiarity. 3 exemption (*from*); the unrestricted use (*of* a house etc.); honorary membership or citizenship. —**freedom of speech,** the right to express one's views freely. [OE (cf. FREE)]

freehold *n.* the holding of land or property in absolute possession. —*adj.* owned thus. —**freeholder** *n.*

freeman *n.* (*pl.* **-men**) 1 one who is not a slave or serf. 2 one who has the freedom of a city etc.

Freemason /ˈfriːmeɪs(ə)n/ *n.* a member of an international fraternity for mutual help and fellowship, called *Free and Accepted Masons*, having an elaborate ritual and system of secret signs.

Freemasonry *n.* 1 the system and institutions of Freemasons (see prec.). 2 freemasonry, a secret or tacit fellowship, instinctive sympathy. [f. prec.]

freesia /ˈfriːzjə, -ʒə/ *n.* a bulbous African plant of the genus *Freesia*, with fragrant flowers. [f. F. T. H. *Freese* German physician (d. 1876)]

freeway *n.* an express highway, especially with limited access.

freeze *v.t./i.* (*past* **froze**; *p.p.* **frozen**) 1 to turn into ice or some other solid by cold; to cover or become covered with ice. 2 to be or feel very cold; to make or become rigid from cold; to adhere by frost. 3 to preserve (food) by refrigeration below freezing-point. 4 to become or cause to become motionless through fear, surprise, etc. 5 to fix (prices, wages, etc.) at a certain level; to make (assets) unavailable. —*n.* 1 a state or period of frost; the coming of a period of frost. 2 the fixing or stabilization of prices, wages, etc. —**freeze-dry** *v.t.* to freeze and dry by evaporation of ice in a high vacuum. **freeze on to,** (*slang*) to take or keep a tight hold of. **freeze up,** to freeze completely; to obstruct by the formation of ice etc. **freeze-up** *n.* a period or conditions of extreme cold. **freezing-point**

n. the temperature at which a liquid, especially water, freezes. [OE]

freezer *n.* a refrigerated container or compartment in which food is preserved at a very low temperature. [f. prec.]

freight /freɪt/ *n.* **1** the transport of goods in containers or by water or air (or (*US*) by land). **2** the goods transported, a cargo, a load. **3** a charge for the transport of goods. —*v.t.* to transport (goods) by freight; to load with freight. [f. MLG or MDu. *vrecht* var. of *vracht* (as FRAUGHT)]

freighter *n.* a ship or aircraft designed to carry freight; (*US*) a freight-wagon. [f. prec.]

freightliner *n.* a train carrying goods in containers.

French *adj.* of France or its people or language; having French characteristics. —*n.* **1** the French language. **2** (*euphem.*) bad language. **3** dry vermouth. —**the French** (*pl.*), the people of France. **French bean,** the kidney or haricot bean used as unripe sliced pods or as ripe seeds. **French bread,** bread in a long crisp loaf. **French chalk,** finely powdered talc used as a marker, dry lubricant, etc. **French dressing,** a salad dressing of seasoned oil and vinegar. **French fried potatoes** *or* **fries,** (*US*) potato chips. **French horn,** an instrument of the brass family, a coiled tube with a wide-flaring bell facing backwards. **French leave,** absence without permission. **French letter,** (*colloq.*) a condom. **French polish,** shellac polish for wood. **French window,** a glazed door in an outside wall. [OE (as FRANK)]

frenchify /ˈfrentʃɪfaɪ/ *v.t.* (usu. in *p.p.*) to make French in form, manners, etc. [f. prec.]

Frenchman *n.* (*pl.* **-men**) a man of French birth or nationality. —**Frenchwoman** *n.fem.* (*pl.* **-women**)

frenetic /frəˈnetɪk/ *adj.* frantic, frenzied; fanatic. —**frenetically** *adv.* [f. OF f. L f. Gk (*phren* mind)]

frenzy /ˈfrenzɪ/ *n.* wild excitement or agitation; a delirious fury. —*v.t.* (usu. in *p.p.*) to drive to frenzy. —**frenziedly** *adv.* [f. OF f. L *phrenesia* f. Gk (as prec.)]

frequency /ˈfri:kwənsɪ/ *n.* **1** commonness of occurrence; frequent occurrence. **2** the rate of recurrence (of vibration etc.); the number of cycles of a carrier wave per second; a band or group of such values. —**frequency modulation,** the varying of a carrier-wave frequency. [f. L (as foll.)]

frequent /ˈfri:kwənt/ *adj.* occurring often or in close succession; habitual, constant. —/frɪˈkwent/ *v.t.* to attend or go to habitually. —**frequently** *adv.*, **frequentation** /-ˈteɪʃ(ə)n/ *n.* [f. F or L *frequens*, orig. = crowded]

frequentative /frɪˈkwentətɪv/ *adj.* (*Gram.*, of a verb etc.) expressing frequent repetition or intensity of action. —*n.* a frequentative verb etc. [as prec.]

fresco /ˈfreskəʊ/ *n.* (*pl.* **-os**) a method of wall-painting, or a picture done, in which pure powdered pigments, mixed only in water, are applied to a wet freshly laid lime-plaster ground. [It., = cool, fresh]

fresh *adj.* **1** newly made or obtained; other, different, not previously known or used. **2** lately arrived *from*. **3** not stale or musty; not faded. **4** (of food) not preserved by salting, tinning, freezing, etc. **5** not salty. **6** pure, untainted; refreshing. **7** not weary, vigorous; (of a wind) brisk. **8** cheeky, amorously impudent; inexperienced. —*adv.* newly, recently (esp. in comb.: *fresh-baked, fresh-cut*). —**freshly** *adv.*, **freshness** *n.* [f. OF *freis fresche* f. Gmc]

freshen *v.t./i.* to make or become fresh. [f. prec.]

fresher *n.* (*slang*) a freshman. [f. FRESH]

freshet /ˈfreʃɪt/ *n.* a stream of fresh water flowing into the sea; a flood of a river. [f. OF (as FRESH)]

freshman *n.* (*pl.* **-men**) a first-year student at university or (*US*) high school.

freshwater *adj.* (of fish etc.) of fresh (not salt) water, not of the sea.

fret[1] *v.t./i.* (**-tt-**) **1** to worry, to vex; to be worried or distressed. **2** to wear or consume by gnawing or rubbing. —*n.* worry, vexation. [OE *fretan* (as FOR-, EAT)]

fret[2] *n.* an ornamental pattern of continuous combinations of straight lines joined usually at right angles. —*v.t.* (**-tt-**) to adorn with a fret or with carved or embossed work. [f. OF *frete* trellis-work]

fret[3] *n.* a bar or ridge on the finger-board of a guitar etc. to guide fingering. [orig. unkn.]

fretful *adj.* constantly fretting, querulous. —**fretfully** *adv.* [f. FRET[1] + -FUL]

fretsaw *n.* a narrow saw stretched on a frame for cutting thin wood in patterns. [f. FRET[2] + SAW[1]]

fretwork *n.* ornamental work in wood with a fretsaw.

Freudian /ˈfrɔɪdɪən/ *adj.* of Freud or his theories or methods of psychoanalysis. —**Freudian slip,** an unintentional error that seems to reveal unconscious feelings. [f. S. *Freud*, Austrian neurologist (d. 1939)]

Fri. *abbr.* Friday.

friable /ˈfraɪəb(ə)l/ *adj.* easily crumbled. —**friability** /-ˈbɪlɪtɪ/ *n.* [f. F or L (*friare* crumble)]

friar /ˈfraɪə(r)/ *n.* a member of certain non-enclosed religious orders of men (especially Augustinians, Carmelites,

Dominicans, and Franciscans), founded in the Middle Ages. —**friar's balsam,** a tincture of benzoin etc. used especially for inhaling. [f. OF f. L *frater* brother]

friary *n.* a monastery of friars. [f. prec.]

fricassee /ˈfrɪkəsiː, -ˈsiː/ *n.* a dish of stewed or fried pieces of meat served in a thick sauce. —*v.t.* to make a fricassee of. [F (*fricasser* cut up and stew in sauce)]

fricative /ˈfrɪkətɪv/ *adj.* (of a consonant, e.g. *f*, *th*) sounded by the friction of the breath in a narrow opening. —*n.* a fricative consonant. [f. L (as foll.)]

friction /ˈfrɪkʃ(ə)n/ *n.* **1** the rubbing of one object against another. **2** the resistance an object encounters in moving over another. **3** clash of wills, temperaments, opinions, etc. —**frictional** *adj.* [f. F f. L (*fricare* rub)]

Friday /ˈfraɪdeɪ, -dɪ/ *n.* the day of the week following Thursday. —*adv.* (*colloq.*) on Friday. —**girl** *or* **man Friday,** an assistant doing general duties in an office etc. [f. Man Friday, character in Defoe's *Robinson Crusoe*]. [OE, = day of FRIGGA]

fridge *n.* (*colloq.*) a refrigerator. [abbr.]

friend /frend/ *n.* **1** a person with whom one enjoys mutual affection and regard (usu. exclusive of sexual or family bonds). **2** a sympathizer, a helper; a helpful thing or quality; one who is not an enemy. **3** some person already mentioned or under discussion. **4** (usu. in *pl.*) a regular contributor of money or other assistance to an institution. **5 Friend,** a member of the Society of Friends (see SOCIETY), a Quaker. [OE]

friendless *adj.* without friends. [f. prec. + -LESS]

friendly *adj.* acting as or like a friend, well-disposed, kindly; on amicable terms (*with*); characteristic of friends, showing or prompted by kindness. —*n.* a friendly match. —*adv.* in a friendly manner. —**friendly match,** a match played for enjoyment and not in competition. **Friendly Society,** a society for insurance against sickness etc. —**friendliness** *n.* [f. FRIEND]

friendship *n.* a friendly relationship or feeling. [OE (as FRIEND, -SHIP)]

frier var. of FRYER.

Friesian /ˈfriːʒjən/ *n.* one of a breed of large black-and-white dairy cattle, originally from Friesland, a northern province of the Netherlands. [var. of FRISIAN]

frieze /friːz/ *n.* **1** the part of an entablature between the architrave and the cornice; a horizontal band of sculpture filling this. **2** a band of decoration, especially along a wall near the ceiling. [f. F f. L *Phrygium* (*opus*) Phrygian work]

frigate /ˈfrɪgɪt/ *n.* a naval escort-vessel like a large corvette; (*hist.*) the warship next in size to ships of the line. [f. F f. It.]

fright /fraɪt/ *n.* **1** sudden or extreme fear; an instance of this. **2** a person or thing looking grotesque or ridiculous. [OE]

frighten *v.t.* to fill with fright; to force or drive (*away* or *off*) by fright. [f. prec.]

frightful *adj.* dreadful, shocking, ugly; (*colloq.*) extreme, extremely bad. —**frightfully** *adv.* [f. FRIGHT + -FUL]

frigid /ˈfrɪdʒɪd/ *adj.* **1** lacking friendliness or enthusiasm, dull. **2** (of a woman) sexually unresponsive. **3** (esp. of climate or air) cold. —**frigidity** /-ˈdʒɪdɪtɪ/ *n.*, **frigidly** *adv.* [f. L *frigidus* (*frigēre* be cold)]

frill *n.* **1** a strip of material gathered or pleated and fixed along one edge as a trimming. **2** (in *pl.*) unnecessary embellishments or accomplishments. —*v.t.* to decorate with a frill. —**frilled** *adj.*, **frilly** *adj.* [orig. unkn.]

fringe *n.* **1** a border or edging of tassels or loose threads. **2** the front hair hanging over the forehead; **3** the margin or outer limit of an area, population, etc. **4** an area or part of minor importance. —*v.t.* to adorn with a fringe; to serve as a fringe to. —**fringe benefit,** an employee's benefit additional to the normal wage or salary. —**fringe medicine,** systems of treatment of diseases, injuries, etc., that are not regarded by the medical profession as part of orthodox treatment. [f. OF f. L *fimbria* fibres, fringe]

frippery /ˈfrɪpərɪ/ *n.* showy finery or ornament, especially in dress; empty display in speech, literary style, etc. [f. F *friperie* (OF *frepe* rag)]

Frisbee /ˈfrɪzbɪ/ *n.* [P] a concave plastic disc for skimming through the air as an outdoor game. [perh. f. *Frisbie* American baker whose pie-tins could be used similarly]

Frisian /ˈfrɪzɪən/ *adj.* of Friesland, a northern province of the Netherlands, or its people or language. —*n.* **1** a native of Friesland. **2** the Germanic language spoken there. [f. L *Frisii* (pl.) f. OFris.]

frisk *v.t./i.* **1** to leap or skip playfully. **2** (*slang*) to feel over and search (a person) for a weapon etc. —*n.* **1** a playful leap or skip. **2** (*slang*) a search of a person. [f. OF *frisque* lively]

frisky *adj.* lively, playful. —**friskily** *adv.*, **friskiness** *n.* [f. prec.]

frisson /ˈfriːsɔ̃/ *n.* an emotional thrill. [F, = shiver]

frith var. of FIRTH.

fritter[1] *v.t.* (usu. with *away*) to waste (money, time, energy, etc.) triflingly or indiscriminately. [f. obs. *fritters* fragments]

fritter[2] *n.* a small flat piece of fried batter containing meat or fruit etc. [f. OF *friture* f. L *frigere* fry]

frivolous /ˈfrɪvələs/ *adj.* paltry, trifling; lacking seriousness, silly. —**frivolity** /-ˈvɒlɪtɪ/ *n.*, **frivolously** *adv.* [f. L *frivolus* silly, trifling]

frizz *v.t.* to form (hair) into a mass of small curls. —*n.* frizzed hair or a frizzed state. —**frizzy** *adj.* [f. F *friser*]

frizzle[1] *v.t./i.* **1** to fry or cook with a sizzling noise. **2** to burn or shrivel (up). [f. obs. *frizz* fry, with imit. ending]

frizzle[2] /ˈfrɪz(ə)l/ *v.t./i.* to form into tight curls. —*n.* frizzled hair. —**frizzly** *adj.* [orig. unkn.; earlier than FRIZZ]

fro /frəʊ/ *adv.* **to and fro,** see TO. [f. ON, = from]

frock *n.* **1** a woman's or girl's dress. **2** a monk's or priest's gown. **3** a smock. —*v.t.* to invest with priestly office. —**frockcoat** *n.* a man's long-skirted coat not cut away in front; a military coat of this shape. [f. OF *froc*]

frog[1] *n.* **1** a small tailless smooth-skinned leaping amphibian of the order Anura, especially the common frog (genus *Rana*). **2** Frog, (*derog.*) a Frenchman (with ref. to use of edible frogs' legs in French cooking). **3** the horny substance in the sole of a horse's foot. —**frog in one's throat,** (*colloq.*) hoarseness. [OE]

frog[2] *n.* an ornamental coat-fastening of a spindle-shaped button and loop. [orig. unkn.]

frogman *n.* (*pl.* **-men**) a person equipped with a rubber suit and flippers etc. for underwater swimming.

frogmarch *v.t.* to hustle forward holding and pinning the arms from behind; to carry (a person) face downwards by means of four persons each holding a limb. —*n.* the process of frogmarching a person.

frolic /ˈfrɒlɪk/ *v.i.* (**-ck-**) to play about cheerfully. —*n.* cheerful play; a prank; a merry party. [f. Du. *vrolijk* (*vro* glad)]

frolicsome *adj.* merry, playful. [f. prec. + -SOME]

from /frəm, *emphat.* frɒm/ *prep.* expressing separation or origin, followed by: a person, place, time, etc., that is the starting-point of a motion or action; a place, object, etc., whose distance or remoteness is stated; a source, giver, sender; a thing or person avoided, deprived, etc.; a reason, cause, motive; a thing distinguished or unlike; a lower limit; a state changed for another; adverbs or prepositions of time or place. [OE]

frond *n.* a leaflike part of a fern or palm. [f. L *frons frondis* leaf]

front /frʌnt/ *n.* **1** the side or part normally nearer or towards the spectator or direction of motion. **2** any face of a building, especially that of the main entrance. **3** the foremost part of an army, a line of battle, the ground towards the enemy, the scene of actual fighting; a sector of activity compared to a military front; an organized political group. **4** a forward or conspicuous position. **5** an outward appearance; a bluff, a pretext; a person etc. serving to cover subversive or illegal activities. **6** the promenade of a seaside resort. **7** the forward edge of an advancing mass of cold or warm air. **8** the auditorium of a theatre. —*adj.* of the front; situated in front; (of vowels) formed at the front of the mouth (as in *see*). —*v.t./i.* **1** to have the front facing or directed (*on, to, towards, upon*). **2** (*slang*) to act as a front or cover *for*. **3** to furnish with a front. —**front-bencher** *n.* a leading member of the government or opposition in Parliament. **front runner,** the contestant most likely to succeed. **in front,** in an advanced or facing position. **in front of,** before, in advance of; in the presence of, confronting. [f. OF f. L *frons frontis* forehead]

frontage *n.* **1** the front of a building. **2** the land abutting on a street or water, or between the front of a building and a road. **3** the extent of a front. **4** the way a thing faces; an outlook. [f. prec.]

frontal *adj.* **1** of or on the front; of the front as seen by an onlooker. **2** of the forehead. —*n.* **1** a covering for the front of an altar. **2** a façade. [as FRONT]

frontier /ˈfrʌntɪə(r)/ *n.* **1** a border between two countries, the district on each side of it. **2** the limits of attainment or knowledge in a subject. [f. AF f. L (as FRONT)]

frontispiece /ˈfrʌntɪspi:s/ *n.* an illustration facing the title-page of a book. [f. F or L, = façade (as prec., *specere* look)]

frost *n.* **1** freezing; the prevalence of a temperature below the freezing-point of water. **2** frozen dew or vapour. **3** a chilling influence, unfriendliness. —*v.t./i.* **1** to cover (as) with frost; to injure (a plant etc.) with frost. **2** to make (glass) non-transparent by giving it a rough frostlike surface. —**frost-bite** *n.* injury to the tissue of the body due to freezing. **frost-bitten** *adj.* affected with frost-bite. [OE (as FREEZE)]

frosting *n.* a sugar icing for cakes. [f. prec.]

frosty *adj.* **1** cold with frost; covered (as) with frost. **2** unfriendly in manner. —**frostily** *adv.*, **frostiness** *n.* [f. FROST]

froth /frɒθ/ *n.* **1** foam. **2** idle talk or ideas. —*v.t./i.* to emit or gather froth; to make (beer etc.) froth. —**frothy** *adj.* [f. ON]

froward /ˈfrəʊəd/ *adj.* (*archaic*) perverse, difficult to deal with. [f. FRO + -WARD]

frown *v.i.* to wrinkle the brows, especially in displeasure or deep thought. —*n.* the action of frowning; a look of displeasure or deep thought. —**frown at** *or* **on,** to disapprove of. [f. OF (*froigne* surly look, f. Celt.)]

frowsty *adj.* stuffy, fusty. [var. of foll.]

frowzy *adj.* **1** fusty. **2** slatternly, dingy. [orig. unkn.]

froze, frozen *past & p.p.* of FREEZE.

FRS *abbr.* Fellow of the Royal Society.

fructify /ˈfrʌktɪfaɪ/ *v.t./i.* to bear or cause to bear fruit. [f. OF f. L (as FRUIT)]

fructose /ˈfrʌktəʊz/ *n.* a sugar found in fruit juice, honey, etc. [f. L (as FRUIT)]

frugal /ˈfruːg(ə)l/ *adj.* **1** sparing or economical, especially as regards food. **2** meagre, costing little. —**frugality** /-ˈgælɪtɪ/ *n.*, **frugally** *adv.* [f. L (*frugi* thrifty)]

fruit /fruːt/ *n.* **1** the product of a plant or tree that contains seed; this used as food; these products collectively. **2** (usu. in *pl.*) vegetable products fit for food. **3** the product of action, the result; (in *pl.*) profits. —*v.t./i.* to bear or cause to bear fruit. —**fruit-cake** *n.* one containing dried fruit. **fruit machine,** a coin-operated gambling machine, often using symbols resembling fruit. **fruit sugar,** fructose. [f. OF f. L *fructus* (*frui* enjoy)]

fruiterer /ˈfruːtərə(r)/ *n.* a dealer in fruit. [f. prec.]

fruitful /ˈfruːtfəl/ *adj.* **1** producing much fruit. **2** producing good results, successful. —**fruitfully** *adv.*, **fruitfulness** *n.* [f. FRUIT + -FUL]

fruition /fruːˈɪʃ(ə)n/ *n.* the bearing of fruit (*lit.* or *fig.*); the realization of aims or hopes. [f. OF f. L (*frui* enjoy), erron. assoc. with FRUIT]

fruitless /ˈfruːtlɪs/ *adj.* **1** not bearing fruit. **2** useless, unsuccessful. —**fruitlessly** *adv.*, **fruitlessness** *n.* [f. FRUIT + -LESS]

fruity /ˈfruːtɪ/ *adj.* **1** of fruit, tasting or smelling like fruit; full of fruit. **2** (of a voice etc.) of a full rich quality. **3** (*colloq.*) full of rough humour or (usu. scandalous) interest. —**fruitily** *adv.*, **fruitiness** *n.* [f. FRUIT]

frump *n.* an unattractive dowdy woman. —**frumpish** *adj.* [perh. f. dial. *frumple* wrinkle f. MDu. (as FOR-, RUMPLE)]

frustrate /frʌˈstreɪt/ *v.t.* to make (efforts) ineffective; to prevent (a person) from achieving a purpose; (in *p.p.*) discontented because unable to achieve desires. —**frustration** *n.* [f. L (*frustra* in vain)]

frustum /ˈfrʌstəm/ *n.* (*pl.* **-ta**) the lower part of a cone or pyramid whose top is cut off by a plane parallel to the base. [L, = piece cut off]

fry[1] *v.t./i.* to cook or be cooked in hot fat. —*n.* **1** the internal parts of animals usually eaten fried. **2** fried food. —**frying-pan** *n.* a shallow pan used in frying (*out of the frying-pan into the fire*, from a bad situation to a worse). **fry-up** *n.* miscellaneous fried food. [f. OF f. L *frigere*]

fry[2] *n.* young or newly hatched fishes. —**small fry,** people of little importance; children. [f. ON, = seed]

fryer *n.* **1** one who fries. **2** a vessel for frying food, especially fish. [f. FRY[1]]

ft. *abbr.* foot, feet.

fuchsia /ˈfjuːʃə/ *n.* a shrub of the genus *Fuchsia*, with drooping red or purple or white flowers. [f. L *Fuchs*, German botanist (d. 1566)]

fuck *v.t./i.* (*vulgar*) **1** to have sexual intercourse (*with*). **2** to make *off*; to idle *about* or *around*. **3** to mess *up*. —int. (*vulgar*) expressing anger or annoyance. —*n.* (*vulgar*) **1** the act of or a partner in sexual intercourse. **2** the slightest amount. —**fucking** *adj.* & *adv.* (*vulgar*, often as a mere intensive). [orig. unkn.]

fuddle *v.t.* to confuse or stupefy, especially with alcoholic liquor. —*n.* confusion; intoxication. [orig. unkn.]

fuddy-duddy /ˈfʌdɪdʌdɪ/ *adj.* (*slang*) old-fashioned or quaintly fussy. —*n.* (*slang*) such a person. [orig. unkn.]

fudge *n.* **1** a soft toffee-like sweet made of milk, sugar, and butter. **2** nonsense. —*v.t.* to put together in a makeshift or dishonest way, to fake. [perh. f. obs. *fadge* fit]

fuel /ˈfjuː(ə)l/ *n.* **1** material for burning as a fire or as a source of heat or power; material used as a source of nuclear energy. **2** food as a source of energy. **3** a thing that sustains or inflames passion etc. —*v.t./i.* (**-ll-**) **1** to supply with fuel; to inflame (a feeling etc.). **2** to take in or get fuel. —**fuel cell,** a cell producing electricity direct from a chemical reaction. **fuel injection,** the direct introduction of fuel under pressure into the combustion unit of an internal-combustion engine. [f. AF f. L *focus* hearth]

fug *n.* (*colloq.*) stuffiness of the air in a room. —**fuggy** *adj.*, **fugginess** *n.* [orig. unkn.]

fugitive /ˈfjuːdʒɪtɪv/ *adj.* **1** fleeing, that runs or has run away. **2** fleeting, transient; (of literature) of passing interest, ephemeral. —*n.* one who flees, e.g. from justice or an enemy. [f. OF f. L (*fugere* flee)]

fugue /fjuːg/ *n.* a piece of music in which three or more parts or 'voices' (described thus whether vocal or instrumental) enter successively in imitation of each other. [F or f. It., f. L *fuga* flight]

führer /ˈfjʊərə(r)/ *n.* a tyrannical leader. [G, = leader (part of title assumed by Adolf Hitler)]

-ful /-fʊl/ *suffix* forming (1) adjectives from nouns, in sense 'full of' (*beautiful*), 'having the qualities of' (*masterful*), or from adjectives (*direful*); or from verbs in sense 'apt to' (*forgetful*); (2) nouns (*pl.* **-fuls**) in sense 'amount that fills' (*glassful, handful, spoonful*). [f. FULL]

fulcrum /ˈfʊlkrəm/ *n.* (*pl.* **fulcra**) the point on

which a lever is supported. [L, = post of couch (*fulcire* prop)]

fulfil /fʊl'fɪl/ *v.t.* (**-ll-**) to carry out (a task, prophecy, promise, command, or law); to satisfy (conditions, a desire, a prayer); to answer (a purpose). —**fulfil oneself,** to develop fully one's gifts and character. —**fulfilment** *n.* [OE (as FULL[1], FILL)]

full[1] /fʊl/ *adj.* **1** holding all that its limits will allow; having eaten to one's limit or satisfaction. **2** abundant, copious, satisfying. **3** having an abundance *of*. **4** engrossed in thinking *of*. **5** complete, perfect, reaching the specified or usual or utmost limit. **6** (of a tone) clear and deep. **7** plump, rounded; (of clothes) made of much material hanging in folds. —*adv.* **1** very; quite, fully. **2** exactly. —**full back,** a defensive player near the goal in football, hockey, etc. **full-blooded** *adj.* vigorous, sensual; not hybrid. **full-blown** *adj.* fully developed. **full board,** the provision of bed and all meals at a hotel etc. **full-bodied** *adj.* rich in quality, tone, etc. **full brother, sister,** a brother or sister with both parents the same. **full face,** with all the face visible to the spectator. **full house,** a large or full attendance at a theatre etc.; a hand in poker with three of a kind and a pair. **full-length** *adj.* not shortened or abbreviated; (of a mirror or portrait) showing the whole of the human figure. **full moon,** the moon with the whole disc illuminated; the time when this occurs. **full pitch,** a full toss. **full-scale** *adj.* not reduced in size, complete. **full stop,** the punctuation mark (.) used at the end of a sentence or abbreviation; a complete cessation. **full time,** the total normal duration of work etc. **full-time** *adj.* occupying or using the whole of the available working time. **full toss,** a ball pitched right up to the batsman in cricket. **in full,** without abridgement, to or for the full amount. **in full view,** entirely visible. **to the full,** to the utmost extent. [OE]

full[2] /fʊl/ *v.t.* to clean and thicken (cloth). [back-formation f. FULLER]

fuller *n.* one who fulls cloth. —**fuller's earth,** a type of clay used in fulling. [OE f. L *fullo*]

fullness *n.* being full. —**the fullness of time,** the appropriate or destined time. [f. FULL[1]]

fully *adv.* completely, entirely; no less than. —**fully-fashioned** *adj.* (of women's clothing) shaped to fit the body. [f. FULL[1]]

fulmar /'fʊlmə(r)/ *n.* an Arctic sea-bird (*Fulmarus glacialis*) related to the petrel. [f. ON (as FOUL, *mar* gull)]

fulminant /'fʊlmɪnənt/ *adj.* **1** fulminating. **2** (of a disease) developing suddenly. [f. F or L (as foll.)]

fulminate /'fʌlmɪneɪt, 'fʊ-/ *v.i.* **1** to express censure loudly and forcefully. **2** to explode violently, to flash like lightning. —**fulmination** /-'neɪʃ(ə)n/ *n.*, **fulminator** *n.* [f. L (*fulmen* lightning)]

fulsome /'fʊlsəm/ *adj.* (of flattery etc.) cloying, disgustingly excessive. [f. FULL[1]]

fumble *v.t./i.* to use the hands awkwardly, to grope about; to handle clumsily or nervously. —*n.* an act of fumbling. [f. LG or Du.]

fume /fju:m/ *n.* (usu. in *pl.*) exuded gas, smoke, or vapour, especially when harmful or unpleasant. —*v.t./i.* **1** to emit fumes; to issue in fumes. **2** to be very angry. **3** to subject to fumes, especially of ammonia to darken oak etc. [f. OF f. L *fumus* smoke]

fumigate /'fju:mɪgeɪt/ *v.t.* to disinfect or purify with the action of fumes. —**fumigation** /-'geɪʃ(ə)n/ *n.*, **fumigator** *n.* [f. L (as prec.)]

fun *n.* lively or playful amusement; a source of this. —**for** *or* **in fun,** not seriously. **make fun of** *or* **poke fun at,** to tease, to ridicule. [f. obs. v. *fun* befool (as FOND)]

function /'fʌŋkʃ(ə)n/ *n.* **1** the activity proper to a person or institution or by which a thing fulfils its purpose; an official or professional duty. **2** a public ceremony or occasion. **3** a social gathering, especially a large one. **4** (*Math.*) a quantity whose value depends on varying values (of others). —*v.i.* to fulfil a function, to operate. [f. F f. L (*fungi funct-* perform)]

functional *adj.* **1** of or serving a function; designed or intended to be practical rather than necessarily attractive or pleasing. **2** affecting a function of a bodily organ but not its structure. —**functionally** *adv.* [f. prec.]

functionalism *n.* belief in or stress on the practical application of a thing. —**functionalist** *n.* [f. prec.]

functionary *n.* a person or official performing certain duties. [as prec.]

fund *n.* **1** a permanently available stock. **2** a stock of money, especially one set apart for a purpose; (in *pl.*) money resources. —*v.t.* to provide with money; to make (a debt) permanent at a fixed interest. —**in funds,** having money to spend. [f. L *fundus* bottom]

fundamental /fʌndə'ment(ə)l/ *adj.* of, affecting, or serving as a base or foundation, essential, primary. —*n.* **1** (usu. in *pl.*) a fundamental rule or principle. **2** (in full **fundamental note**) the lowest note of a chord. —**fundamental particle,** an elementary particle. —**fundamentally** *adv.* [f. F or L (*fundamentum* foundation, as prec.)]

fundamentalism *n.* strict maintenance of traditional orthodox religious beliefs. —**fundamentalist** *n.* [f. prec.]

funeral /'fju:nər(ə)l/ *n.* **1** a burial or cremation of the dead with ceremonies. **2** (*slang*) one's (usu. unpleasant) concern. —*attrib. adj.* of or used at funerals. [f. OF f. L (*funus funer-* burial)]

funerary /ˈfjuːnərərɪ/ *adj.* of or used at a funeral or funerals. [f. L (as prec.)]

funereal /fjuːˈnɪərɪəl/ *adj.* of or appropriate to a funeral, dismal, dark. —**funereally** *adv.* [as prec.]

fun-fair *n.* a fair consisting of amusements and side-shows.

fungicide /ˈfʌndʒɪsaɪd/ *n.* a substance that kills fungus. —**fungicidal** /-saɪd(ə)l/ *adj.* [f. FUNGUS + -CIDE]

fungoid /ˈfʌŋgɔɪd/ *adj.* fungus-like. —*n.* a fungoid plant. [f. foll.]

fungus /ˈfʌŋgəs/ *n.* (*pl.* **-gi** /-gaɪ/) any of a large group of non-flowering plants including mushrooms, toadstools, moulds, and yeasts. **2** a spongy morbid growth. —**fungal** *adj.*, **fungous** *adj.* [L]

funicular /fjuːˈnɪkjʊlə(r)/ *adj.* (of a railway especially on a mountain) operating by a cable with ascending and descending cars counterbalanced. —*n.* such a railway. [f. L *funiculus* dim. of *funis* rope]

funk *n.* (*slang*) **1** fear, panic. **2** a coward. —*v.t./i.* (*slang*) to be afraid (of); to try to evade. —**blue funk,** (*slang*) extreme panic. [orig. unkn.]

funky /ˈfʌŋkɪ/ *adj.* (*slang*) **1** (esp. of music) down-to-earth, emotional. **2** fashionable. **3** having a strong smell. [orig. unkn.]

funnel /ˈfʌn(ə)l/ *n.* **1** a narrow tube or pipe widening at the top, for pouring liquid etc. into a small opening. **2** a metal chimney on a steam-engine or ship. —*v.t./i.* (**-ll-**) to move or cause to move (as) through a funnel. [f. Prov. *fonilh* f. L (*in*)*fundibulum* f. IN-¹, *fundere* pour]

funny *adj.* **1** amusing, comical. **2** strange, hard to account for; (*colloq.*) slightly unwell, eccentric, etc. —**funny-bone** *n.* the part of the elbow over which a very sensitive nerve passes. —**funnily** *adv.*, **funniness** *n.* [f. FUN]

fur *n.* **1** the short fine soft hair of certain animals. **2** an animal skin with the fur on it, used especially for making or trimming clothes etc.; a garment made or lined with this. **3** (in heraldry) a representation of tufts on a plain ground. **4** (*collect.*) furred animals. **5** the crust or coating formed on the tongue in sickness, in a kettle by hard water, etc. —*v.t./i.* (**-rr-**) **1** (esp. in *p.p.*) to line or trim with fur. **2** (often with *up*) to make or become coated with a fur deposit. —**make the fur fly,** to cause trouble or dissension. [f. OF *forrer* (*forre, fuerre* sheath)]

furbelow /ˈfɜːbɪləʊ/ *n.* **1** a gathered strip or pleated border of a skirt or petticoat. **2** (in *pl.*) showy ornaments. [f. F *falbala*]

furbish /ˈfɜːbɪʃ/ *v.t.* (often with *up*) to polish, to clean up or renovate. [f. OF *forbir*]

furcate /ˈfɜːkeɪt/ *adj.* forked, branched. —*v.i.* to fork, to divide. —**furcation** /-ˈkeɪʃ(ə)n/ *n.* [f. L (*furca* fork)]

furious /ˈfjʊərɪəs/ *adj.* very angry, full of fury, raging, frantic. —**furiously** *adv.* [f. OF f. L (as FURY)]

furl *v.t./i.* to roll up and bind (a sail etc.); to become furled. [f. F *ferler* f. OF (*ferm* firm, *lier* bind)]

furlong /ˈfɜːlɒŋ/ *n.* one-eighth of a mile. [OE (as FURROW, LONG¹)]

furlough /ˈfɜːləʊ/ *n.* leave of absence, especially that granted to a serviceman. —*v.t./i.* (*US*) to grant a furlough to; to spend a furlough. [f. Du. (as FOR-, LEAVE)]

furnace /ˈfɜːnɪs/ *n.* an enclosed structure for intense heating by fire, especially of metals or water; a very hot place. [f. OF f. L *fornax* (*fornus* oven)]

furnish /ˈfɜːnɪʃ/ *v.t.* **1** to provide (a house or room etc.) with furniture. **2** to supply *with* a thing. [f. OF *furnir* (cf. FRAME, FROM)]

furnishings *n.pl.* the furniture and fitments in a house or room etc. [f. prec.]

furniture /ˈfɜːnɪtʃə(r)/ *n.* **1** the movable equipment of a house or room etc., e.g. tables, chairs, and beds. **2** a ship's equipment. **3** accessories, e.g. the handles and lock on a door. [f. F (as FURNISH)]

furore /fjʊəˈrɔːrɪ/ *n.* an uproar of enthusiastic admiration or fury. [It., f. L *furor* madness]

furrier /ˈfʌrɪə(r)/ *n.* a dealer in or dresser of furs. [f. OF]

furrow /ˈfʌrəʊ/ *n.* **1** a narrow cut in the ground made by a plough. **2** a rut, a groove, a wrinkle. **3** a ship's track. —*v.t.* **1** to plough. **2** to make furrows or grooves etc. in. [OE]

furry /ˈfɜːrɪ/ *adj.* like or covered with fur. [f. FUR]

further /ˈfɜːðə(r)/ *adv.* **1** more far in space or time. **2** more, to a greater extent. **3** in addition. —*adj.* **1** more distant or advanced. **2** more, additional. —*v.t.* to promote or favour (a scheme etc.). —**further education,** that for persons above school age. [OE (compar. of FORTH)]

furtherance *n.* the furthering of a scheme etc. [f. prec.]

furthermore *adv.* in addition, besides.

furthermost *adj.* most distant.

furthest /ˈfɜːðɪst/ *adj.* most distant. —*adv.* to or at the greatest distance. [superl. f. FURTHER]

furtive /ˈfɜːtɪv/ *adj.* done by stealth; sly, stealthy. —**furtively** *adv.*, **furtiveness** *n.* [f. F or L (*furtum* theft)]

fury /ˈfjʊərɪ/ *n.* **1** wild and passionate anger, rage. **2** the violence of a storm, disease, etc. **3** **Fury,** each of the Furies, avenging goddesses of Greek mythology. **4** an angry or malignant woman. —**like fury,** (*colloq.*) with great force or effort. [f. OF f. L *furia* (as FURORE)]

furze *n.* a spiny evergreen shrub of the genus *Ulex* with yellow flowers, gorse. —**furzy** *adj.* [OE]

fuse[1] /fju:z/ *v.t./i.* **1** to melt with intense heat; to blend into a whole by melting. **2** to mix or blend together. **3** to provide (an electric circuit) with a fuse or fuses. **4** (of an appliance) to fail owing to the melting of a fuse; to cause (an appliance) to do this. —*n.* a device with a strip or wire of easily melted metal placed in an electric circuit so as to interrupt an excessive current by melting. [f. L *fundere fus-* pour, melt]

fuse[2] /fju:z/ *n.* a device or component of combustible matter for detonating a bomb etc. or an explosive charge. —*v.t.* to fit a fuse to. [f. It. f. L *fusus* spindle]

fuselage /ˈfju:zəlɑ:ʒ/ *n.* the body of an aeroplane. [F (*fuseler* cut in spindle form, as prec.)]

fusible /ˈfju:zɪb(ə)l/ *adj.* that may be melted. —**fusibility** /-ˈbɪlɪtɪ/ *n.* [f. L (as FUSE[1])]

fusil /ˈfju:zɪl/ *n.* (*hist.*) a light musket. [F f. L (*focus* hearth)]

fusilier /fju:zɪˈlɪə(r)/ *n.* a member of any of several British regiments formerly armed with fusils. [F (as prec.)]

fusillade /fju:zɪˈleɪd/ *n.* **1** a continuous discharge of firearms. **2** a sustained outburst of criticism etc. [F (*fusiller* shoot, as prec.)]

fusion /ˈfju:ʒ(ə)n/ *n.* **1** fusing or melting together; blending, coalition. **2** nuclear fusion (see NUCLEAR). [f. F or L (as FUSE[1])]

fuss *n.* **1** excited commotion, bustle. **2** excessive concern about a trivial thing. **3** a sustained protest or dispute. —*v.t./i.* to behave with nervous concern; to agitate, to worry. —**make a fuss,** to complain vigorously. **make a fuss of,** to treat with excessive attention etc. [orig. unkn.]

fusspot *n.* (*colloq.*) a person given to fussing.

fussy *adj.* inclined to fuss; over-elaborate, fastidious. —**fussily** *adv.*, **fussiness** *n.* [f. FUSS]

fustian /ˈfʌstɪən/ *n.* **1** a thick twilled cotton cloth usually dyed dark. **2** bombast. —*adj.* **1** made of fustian. **2** bombastic, worthless. [f. OF f. L, orig. ref. to cloth from *Fostat* suburb of Cairo]

fusty *adj.* musty, stuffy, stale-smelling; antiquated. —**fustiness** *adj.* [f. OF, = smelling of the cask (*fust* cask)]

futile /ˈfju:taɪl/ *adj.* useless, ineffectual, frivolous. —**futility** /-ˈtɪlɪtɪ/ *n.* [f. L *futilis*, lit. = leaky]

future /ˈfju:tʃə(r)/ *adj.* **1** belonging to the time coming after the present; about to happen or be or become. **2** (*Gram.*, of a tense) describing an event yet to happen. —*n.* **1** future time, events, or condition. **2** a prospect of success etc. **3** (*Gram.*) a future tense. **4** (in *pl.*) goods and stocks for future delivery. —**in future,** from this time onwards. [f. OF f. L *futurus* fut. partic. of *esse* be]

futurism *n.* a 20th-c. movement in art, literature, music, etc., departing from traditional forms so as to express movement and growth. —**futurist** *n.* [f. prec.]

futuristic /fju:tʃəˈrɪstɪk/ *adj.* **1** suitable for the future, ultra-modern. **2** of futurism. [f. FUTURE]

futurity /fju:ˈtjʊərɪtɪ/ *n.* future time; (in *sing.* or *pl.*) future events. [as prec.]

futurology /fju:tʃəˈrɒlədʒɪ/ *n.* the forecasting of the future, especially from present trends in society. [f. FUTURE + -LOGY]

fuzz[1] *n.* **1** fluff; fluffy or frizzed hair. [prob. f. LG or Du.]

fuzz[2] *n.* (*slang*) the police; a policeman. [orig. unkn.]

fuzzy *adj.* **1** like fuzz. **2** blurred, indistinct. —**fuzzily** *adv.*, **fuzziness** *n.* [f. FUZZ]

Gg

G, g /dʒiː/ *n.* (*pl.* **Gs, G's**) **1** the seventh letter of the alphabet. **2** (*Mus.*) the fifth note in the scale of C major.

G *abbr.* **1** gauss. **2** giga-.

g. *abbr.* **1** gram(s). **2** gravity; acceleration due to gravity.

Ga *symbol* gallium.

gab *n.* (*colloq.*) talk, chatter. —**gift of the gab,** eloquence, loquacity. [var. of GOB[2]]

gabardine /ˈgæbədiːn/ *n.* a twill-woven cloth, especially of worsted. [var. of GABERDINE]

gabble *v.t./i.* to talk or utter inarticulately or too fast. —*n.* fast unintelligible talk. —**gabbler** *n.* [f. MDu., imit.]

gabby *adj.* (*colloq.*) talkative. [f. GAB]

gaberdine /ˈgæbədiːn/ *n.* **1** (*hist.*) a loose long upper garment worn especially by Jews. **2** gabardine. [f. OF *gauvardine*]

gable /ˈgeɪb(ə)l/ *n.* **1** the triangular upper part of a wall at the end of a ridged roof; an end wall with a gable. **2** a gable-shaped canopy. —**gabled** *adj.* [f. ON & OF]

gad[1] *v.i.* **(-dd-)** to go *about* idly or in search of pleasure. [f. obs. *gadling* companion f. OE]

gad[2] *int.* (also **by gad**) expressing surprise or emphatic assertion. [= *God*]

gadabout /ˈgædəbaʊt/ *n.* one who gads about.

gadfly *n.* **1** a fly that bites cattle. **2** an irritating person. [f. obs. *gad* spike f. ON]

gadget /ˈgædʒɪt/ *n.* a small mechanical device or tool. —**gadgetry** *n.* [orig. unkn.]

gadoid /ˈgeɪdɔɪd/ *adj.* of the cod family Gadidae. —*n.* a gadoid fish. [f. Gk *gados* cod]

gadolinium /gædəˈlɪnɪəm/ *n.* a metallic element of the lanthanide series, symbol Gd, atomic number 64. [f. J. *Gadolin*, Finnish mineralogist (d. 1852)]

Gael /geɪl/ *n.* a Scottish Celt; a Gaelic-speaking Celt. [f. Gaelic *Gaidheal*]

Gaelic /ˈgeɪlɪk, ˈgæ-/ *n.* a Celtic language spoken in Ireland and Scotland in two distinct varieties, referred to also as Irish (or Erse) and Scots Gaelic respectively. —*adj.* of Gaelic or the Gaels. [f. GAEL]

gaff[1] *n.* **1** a stick with an iron hook for landing large fish; a barbed fishing-spear. **2** a spar to which the head of a fore-and-aft sail is bent. —*v.t.* to seize (a fish) with a gaff. [f. Prov. *gaf* hook]

gaff[2] *n.* **blow the gaff,** (*slang*) to divulge a plot or secret. [orig. unkn.]

gaffe /gæf/ *n.* a social blunder. [F]

gaffer *n.* **1** an old fellow (also as a title or form of address). **2** a foreman, a boss. [prob. contraction of GODFATHER]

gag *n.* **1** a thing thrust into or tied across the mouth to prevent speech or hold the mouth open for an operation. **2** a joke or comic scene in a play, film, etc. **3** a thing restricting free speech; a Parliamentary closure. —*v.t./i.* **(-gg-)** **1** to apply a gag to. **2** to silence, to deprive of free speech. **3** to make gags in a play, film, etc. **4** to choke, to retch. [perh. imit. of choking]

gaga /ˈgɑːgɑː/ *adj.* (*slang*) senile; fatuous, slightly crazy. [F]

gage[1] *n.* **1** a pledge, a thing deposited as security. **2** the symbol of a challenge to fight, especially a glove thrown down. [f. OF (cf. WED)]

gage[2] *n.* a greengage. [abbr.]

gage[3] *US* & *Naut.* var. of GAUGE.

gaggle *n.* **1** a flock of geese. **2** a disorderly group. [imit.]

gaiety /ˈgeɪətɪ/ *n.* being gay, mirth; merry-making, amusement; bright appearance. [f. F (as GAY)]

gaily *adv.* in a gay manner. [f. GAY]

gain *v.t./i.* **1** to obtain or secure. **2** to acquire as profit etc., to earn; to make a profit; to be benefited, improve, or advance *in* some respect. **3** to obtain as an increment or addition. **4** (of a clock etc.) to become fast, or fast by (a specified time). **5** to come closer to something pursued, to catch up *on* or *upon*. **6** to reach (a desired place). **7** to win (land from the sea, a battle). —*n.* **1** an increase of wealth or possessions. **2** an improvement, an increase in amount or power. **3** the acquisition of wealth. —**gain ground,** to make progress. **gain time,** to improve one's chances by causing or accepting a delay. —**gainer** *n.* [f. OF *gaigner* till, acquire]

gainful *adj.* (of employment) paid; lucrative. —**gainfully** *adv.* [f. GAIN + -FUL]

gainsay /geɪnˈseɪ/ *v.t.* to deny, to contradict. [f. obs. *gain-* against + SAY]

gait *n.* manner of walking; the manner of forward motion of a horse etc. [var. of dial. *gate* road, going]

gaiter *n.* a covering of cloth, leather, etc., for the leg below the knee, for the ankle, or for part of a machine etc. [f. F *guètre*]

gal *n.* (*colloq.*) a girl. [repr. var. pronunc.]

gal. *abbr.* gallon(s).

gala /ˈgɑːlə, ˈgeɪlə/ *n.* a festive occasion; a festive gathering for sports. [f. F or It. f. Sp. f. Arab., = presentation garment]

galactic /gəˈlæktɪk/ *adj.* of a galaxy or galaxies. [f. Gk *galaktias*, var. of *galaxias* (as GALAXY)]

galantine /ˈgæləntiːn/ *n.* white meat boned, spiced, etc., and served cold. [f. OF, alt. f. *galatine* jellied meat]

galaxy /ˈgæləksɪ/ *n.* **1** an aggregate of gas, dust, and millions or billions of stars, bound together by gravity, in form either elliptical, irregular, or disc-shaped; **Galaxy,** that which contains the Earth. **2 Galaxy,** the Milky Way. **3** a brilliant company. [f. OF f. L f. Gk *galaxias* (*gala* milk)]

gale[1] *n.* **1** a very strong wind, especially (on the Beaufort scale) of 32-54 m.p.h.; a storm. **2** an outburst, especially of laughter. **3** (*poetic*) a breeze. [orig. unkn.]

gale[2] *n.* (usu. in **sweet-gale**) bog myrtle (*Myrica gale*). [OE]

gall[1] /gɔːl/ *n.* **1** the bile of animals. **2** bitterness; asperity, rancour. **3** (*slang*) impudence. —**gall-bladder** *n.* a vessel containing bile after its secretion by the liver. [ON]

gall[2] /gɔːl/ *n.* a sore made by chafing; mental soreness or its cause; a place rubbed bare. —*v.t.* **1** to rub sore. **2** to vex, to humiliate. [f. MLG or MDu.]

gall[3] /gɔːl/ *n.* a growth produced by insects etc. on plants and trees, especially the oak. [f. OF f. L *galla*]

gallant /ˈgælənt/ *adj.* **1** brave. **2** fine, stately. **3** /also gəˈlænt/ very attentive to women. —*n.* /also gəˈlænt/ a ladies' man. [f. OF (*galer* make merry)]

gallantry /ˈgæləntrɪ/ *n.* **1** bravery. **2** devotion to women. **3** a polite act or speech. [f. F (as prec.)]

galleon /ˈgæljən/ *n.* a type of ship (esp. Spanish used in the late 16th-17th c. [f. MDu. f. F *galion*, or f. Sp. *galeón*]

gallery /ˈgælərɪ/ *n.* **1** a room or building for showing works of art. **2** a balcony, especially in a hall or church; the highest tier of seats in a theatre; its occupants. **3** a covered walk partly open at the side, a colonnade; a narrow passage in the thickness of a wall or on corbels, open towards the interior of a building. **4** a long narrow room or passage. **5** a group of spectators at a golf match etc. **6** a horizontal underground passage in a mine etc. —**play to the gallery,** to seek to win approval by appealing to unrefined taste. [f. F f. It. f. L *galeria*]

galley /ˈgælɪ/ *n.* **1** (*hist.*) a long flat one-decked vessel usually rowed by slaves or criminals. **2** an ancient oared warship. **3** a kitchen in a ship or aircraft. **4** a long tray for set-up type in printing. **5** (in full **galley proof**), a proof in a long narrow form. [f. OF f. L or Gk]

Gallic /ˈgælɪk/ *adj.* **1** of Gaul or the Gauls. **2** typically French. [f. L (*Gallus* a Gaul)]

Gallicism /ˈgælɪsɪz(ə)m/ *n.* a French idiom. [f. prec.]

gallinaceous /gælɪˈneɪʃəs/ *adj.* of the order including domestic poultry, pheasants, etc. [f. L (*gallina* hen)]

gallium /ˈgælɪəm/ *n.* a soft bluish-white metallic element, symbol Ga, atomic number 31, which liquefies at 30 °C. [f. L *Gallia* Gaul, in honour of France, country of its discoverer (Lecoq de Boisbaudran)]

gallivant /gælɪˈvænt/ *v.i.* (*colloq.*) to gad about. [perh. corrupt. of *gallant* to flirt (as GALLANT)]

Gallo- /gæləʊ-/ *in comb.* French. [f. L *Gallus* a Gaul]

gallon /ˈgælən/ *n.* a measure of capacity (4546 cc; for wine, or *US*, 3785 cc); (usu. in *pl.*, *colloq.*) a large amount. [f. OF *jalon* f. Rom.]

gallop /ˈgæləp/ *n.* the fastest pace of a horse etc., with all the feet off the ground together in each stride; a ride at this pace. —*v.t./i.* **1** (of a horse etc. or its rider) to go at a gallop; to make (a horse) gallop. **2** to read, talk, etc., fast; to progress rapidly. [f. OF (as WALLOP)]

galloway /ˈgæləweɪ/ *n.* **1** a horse of a small strong breed from Galloway, an area in SW Scotland; a small horse. **2** an animal of a breed of cattle from Galloway.

gallows /ˈgæləʊz/ *n. pl.* (usu. treated as *sing.*) a structure, usually of two uprights and a cross-piece, for the hanging of criminals. [f. ON]

gallstone /ˈgɔːlstəʊn/ *n.* a small hard stony mass formed in the gall-bladder. [f. GALL[1] + STONE]

Gallup poll /ˈgæləp/ an assessment of public opinion by the questioning of a representative sample, especially as the basis of forecasts of voting etc. [f. G. H. *Gallup*, American statistician (1901-84) who devised such assessment]

galop /ˈgæləp/ *n.* a lively dance in duple time; the music for this. [F, = GALLOP]

galore /gəˈlɔː(r)/ *adv.* in plenty. [f. Ir.]

galosh /gəˈlɒʃ/ *n.* a waterproof overshoe. [f. OF f. L *gallicula* small Gallic shoe]

galumph /gəˈlʌmf/ *v.i.* (*colloq.*) to go prancing

in triumph; to move noisily or clumsily. [coined by Lewis Carroll in *Through the Looking-glass*, perh. f. GALLOP, TRIUMPH]

galvanic /gæl'vænɪk/ *adj.* **1** producing an electric current by chemical action; (of electricity) produced by chemical action. **2** stimulating, full of energy; sudden and remarkable. —**galvanically** *adv.* [f. L. *Galvani*, Italian anatomist (d. 1798)]

galvanize /'gælvənaɪz/ *v.t.* **1** to stimulate by or as by electricity *into* activity. **2** to coat (iron) with zinc to protect from rust. —**galvanization** /-'zeɪʃ(ə)n/ *n.* [as prec.]

galvanometer /gælvə'nɒmɪtə(r)/ *n.* an instrument for measuring small electric currents. [as prec. + -METER]

gambit /'gæmbɪt/ *n.* **1** a chess opening in which a player sacrifices a pawn or piece for the sake of later advantage. **2** an opening move in a discussion etc.; a trick, a device. [f. It. *gambetto* tripping up]

gamble *v.t./i.* to play games of chance for money; to risk much in hope of great gain. —*n.* gambling; a risky undertaking. —**gamble away,** to lose by gambling. **gamble on,** to act in the hope of (an event). [f. obs. *gamel* to sport (as GAME[1])]

gambler *n.* one who gambles, esp. habitually. [f. prec.]

gamboge /gæm'bu:ʒ, -bəʊʒ/ *n.* a gum resin used as a yellow pigment and as a purgative. [f. *Cambodia*, where the substance is obtained]

gambol /'gæmb(ə)l/ *v.i.* (**-ll-**) to jump about playfully. —*n.* a gambolling movement. [f. *gambade* leap f. It. (*gamba* leg)]

game[1] *n.* **1** a form of play or sport, especially a competitive one organized with rules, penalties, etc. **2** a portion of play forming a scoring unit e.g. in bridge or tennis; the winning score in a game; the state of the score. **3** (in *pl.*) a series of athletic etc. contests. **4** a scheme, undertaking, etc. **5** wild animals or birds hunted for sport or food; their flesh as food. —*adj.* spirited, eager and willing. —*v.i.* to gamble for money stakes. —**the game is up,** the scheme is revealed or foiled. **game theory,** the branch of mathematics that deals with the selection of best strategies for participants. **give the game away,** to reveal intentions or a secret. **make game of,** to ridicule. **on the game,** (*slang*) involved in prostitution or thieving. —**gamely** *adv.*, **gameness** *n.* [OE]

game[2] *adj.* (of a leg, arm, etc.) crippled. [orig. unkn.]

gamecock *n.* a cock bred and trained for cock-fighting.

gamekeeper *n.* a person employed to breed and protect game.

gamelan /'gæməlæn/ *n.* the standard instrumental ensemble of Indonesia, comprising sets of tuned gongs, gong-chimes, and other percussion instruments as well as string and wood-wind instruments. [Javanese]

gamesmanship *n.* the art of winning games by gaining a psychological advantage over an opponent, first described by Stephen Potter (1947). [f. GAME[1], after *sportsmanship*]

gamesome /'geɪmsəm/ *adj.* playful, sportive. [f. GAME + -SOME]

gamester /'geɪmstə(r)/ *n.* a gambler.

gamete /'gæmi:t/ *n.* a mature germ-cell which unites with another in sexual reproduction. —**gametic** /gə'metɪk/ *adj.* [f. Gk, = wife (*gamos* marriage)]

gamin /'gæmɪn/ *n.* a street urchin; an impudent child. [F]

gamine /gə'mi:n/ *n.* a girl with mischievous charm. [F (fem. of prec.)]

gamma /'gæmə/ *n.* **1** the third letter of the Greek alphabet, = g. **2** a third-class mark in an examination. **3** a designation of the third-brightest star in a constellation, or sometimes the star's position in a group. —**gamma radiation** *or* **rays,** X-rays of very short wavelength emitted by radioactive substances. [Gk]

gammon /'gæmən/ *n.* the bottom piece of a flitch of bacon including a hind leg; pig's ham cured like bacon. [f. OF *gambon* (*gambe* leg)]

gammy *adj.* (*slang*) game (GAME[2]). [f. dial. form of GAME[2]]

gamut /'gæmət/*n.* **1** the lowest note in the medieval sequence of hexachords, = modern G on the lowest line of the bass staff. **2** the whole series of notes used in medieval or modern music; the major diatonic scale; the compass of a voice or instrument. **3** the entire series or range. [f. L *gamma ut* (GAMMA taken as name for note one tone lower than A of classical scale, *ut* first of six arbitrary names of notes forming hexachord, being italicized syllables of a 7th-c. Latin hymn: *Ut* queant laxis *re*sonare fibris *Mi*ra gestorum *fa*muli tuorum, *Sol*ve polluti *la*bii reatum, Sancte Ioannes)]

gamy /'geɪmɪ/ *adj.* smelling or tasting like high game. [f. GAME[1]]

gander *n.* **1** a male goose. **2** (*slang*) a look, a glance. [OE]

gang[1] *n.* **1** a band of persons associating for some (usu. criminal) purpose. **2** a set of workers, slaves, or prisoners. **3** a set of tools working in co-ordination. —*v.t.* to arrange (tools etc.) to work in co-ordination. —**gang up,** to act in concert (*with*). **gang up on,** (*colloq.*) to combine against. [f. ON, = GOING]

gang[2] *v.i.* (*Sc.*) to go. —**gang agley,** (of a plan etc.) to go wrong. [OE (as prec.; cf. GO)]

ganger *n.* the foreman of a gang of workers. [f. GANG[1]]

gangling /ˈgæŋglɪŋ/ *adj.* (of a person) loosely built, lanky. [frequent. of GANG[2]]

ganglion /ˈgæŋglɪən/ *n* (*pl.* **-ia**) **1** an enlargement or knot on a nerve forming a centre for the reception and transmission of impulses. **2** a centre of activity etc. —**ganglionic** /-ˈɒnɪk/ *adj.* [Gk]

gangplank *n.* a movable plank for walking into and out of a boat etc. [f. GANG[1] + PLANK]

gangrene /ˈgæŋgriːn/ *n.* **1** death of body tissue, usually caused by obstructed blood-circulation. **2** moral corruption. —*v.t./i.* to affect or become affected with gangrene. —**gangrenous** /-grɪnəs/ *adj.* [f. F f. L f. Gk]

gangster *n.* a member of a gang of violent criminals. [f. GANG[1]]

gangue /gæŋ/ *n.* valueless earth etc. in which ore is found. [F, f. G *gang* lode (= GANG[1])]

gangway *n.* **1** a passage, especially between rows of seats. **2** the opening in a ship's bulwarks; a bridge from this to the shore. [f. GANG[1] + WAY]

gannet /ˈgænɪt/ *n.* a large sea-bird of the genus *Sula*. [OE, cogn. with GANDER]

gantlet /ˈgæntlɪt/ *n. US* var. of GAUNTLET.

gantry /ˈgæntrɪ/ *n.* a structure supporting a travelling crane, railway signals, equipment for a rocket-launch, etc. [prob. f. dial. form of GALLON + TREE]

gaol /dʒeɪl/ *n.* a public prison; confinement in this. —*v.t.* to put in gaol. [= JAIL; f. OF *jaiole* f. Rom. dim. of L *cavea* cage]

gaolbird *n.* a habitual criminal; a prisoner.

gaolbreak *n.* an escape from gaol.

gaoler *n.* a person in charge of a gaol or the prisoners in it. [f. GAOL]

gap *n.* **1** a breach in a hedge, fence, or wall. **2** an empty space; an interval. **3** a deficiency. **4** a wide divergence in views etc. **5** a gorge or pass. —**gappy** *adj.* [f. ON, = chasm (rel. to foll.)]

gape *v.i.* to open the mouth wide; (of the mouth etc.) to open or be open wide; to stare *at*; to yawn. —*n.* an open-mouthed stare; a yawn; an open mouth. [f. ON]

garage /ˈgærɑːdʒ, -ɑːʒ, -ɪdʒ/ *n.* **1** a building for housing a motor vehicle or vehicles. **2** an establishment repairing and selling motor vehicles. —*v.t.* to put or keep (a vehicle) in a garage. [F (*garer* shelter)]

garb *n.* clothing, especially of a distinctive kind. —*v.t.* (usu. in *pass* or *refl.*) to dress, especially in distinctive clothes. [f. F f. It. f. Gmc (as GEAR)]

garbage /ˈgɑːbɪdʒ/ *n.* rubbish or refuse of any kind; domestic waste. [f. AF]

garble *v.t.* to distort or confuse (facts, messages, etc.). [f. It. f. Arab. *garbala* sift (cf. L *cribrum* sieve)]

garden /ˈgɑːd(ə)n/ *n.* **1** a piece of ground for growing flowers, fruit, or vegetables. **2** (*attrib.*) cultivated. **3** (esp. in *pl.*) grounds laid out for public enjoyment. —*v.i.* to cultivate a garden. —**garden centre,** an establishment selling garden plants and equipment. **garden city,** a town laid out with many open spaces and trees. **garden party,** a party held in a garden. [f. OF *gardin* (F *jardin*) (as YARD[2])]

gardener /ˈgɑːdnə(r)/ *n.* a person who gardens; a person employed to tend a garden. [f. prec.]

gardenia /gɑːˈdiːnɪə/ *n.* a tree or shrub of the genus *Gardenia*, with large fragrant white or yellow flowers; its flower. [f. Dr A. *Garden*, Scottish naturalist (d. 1791)]

garderobe /ˈgɑːdrəʊb/ *n.* (*hist.*) **1** a store-room or wardrobe. **2** a lavatory. [F (*garder* keep, ROBE)]

garfish /ˈgɑːfɪʃ/ *n.* (*pl.* same) a fish with a long spearlike snout. [f. OE *gar* spear + FISH]

gargantuan /gɑːˈgæntjʊən/ *adj.* gigantic. [f. *Gargantua* giant in book by Rabelais]

gargle *v.t.* to wash (the throat) with a liquid held there and kept in motion by the breath (or *abs.*). —*n.* a liquid so used. [f. F (as foll.)]

gargoyle /ˈgɑːgɔɪl/ *n.* a grotesque carved face or figure as a spout from the gutter of a building. [f. OF *gargouille* throat]

garibaldi /gærɪˈbɔːldɪ/ *n.* a biscuit containing a layer of currants. [f. *Garibaldi*, Italian patriot (d. 1882)]

garish /ˈgeərɪʃ/ *adj.* obtrusively bright, showy, gaudy. [app. f. obs. *gaure* stare]

garland /ˈgɑːlənd/ *n.* a wreath, usually of flowers, worn on the head or hung on an object as a decoration. —*v.t.* to deck with garlands; to crown with a garland. [f. OF]

garlic /ˈgɑːlɪk/ *n.* a plant of the genus *Allium* (usually *A. sativum*) with a pungent strong-smelling bulb used in cookery. —**garlicky** /ˈgɑːlɪkɪ/ *adj.* [OE (*gar* spear, LEEK)]

garment /ˈgɑːmənt/ *n.* an article of dress; an outward covering. [f. OF (as GARNISH)]

garner /ˈgɑːnə(r)/ *v.t.* to store; to collect. —*n.* (*literary*) a storehouse, a granary (*lit.* or *fig.*). [f. OF f. L, = GRANARY]

garnet /ˈgɑːnɪt/ *n.* a vitreous silicate mineral, especially a red kind used as a gem. [f. OF f. L *granatum* pomegranate]

garnish /ˈgɑːnɪʃ/ *v.t.* to decorate (esp. a dish for the table). —*n.* a decorative addition. —**garnishment** *n.* [f. OF *garnir*]

garotte var. of GARROTTE.

garret /ˈgærɪt/ *n.* an attic or room in the roof, especially a dismal one. [f. OF *garite* watch-tower (as GARRISON)]

garrison /ˈgærɪs(ə)n/ *n.* troops stationed in a town etc. to defend it. —*v.t.* to provide with or occupy as a garrison. [f. OF (*garir* defend)]

garrotte /gəˈrɒt/ *n.* **1** a Spanish method of capital punishment by strangulation with a metal collar; the apparatus for this. **2** a cord or wire used to strangle a victim. —*v.t.* to execute or strangle with a garrotte. [f. F or Sp. (*garrote* cudgel)]

garrulous /ˈgærʊləs/ *adj.* talkative. —**garrulity** /gəˈru:lɪtɪ/ *n.*, **garrulously** *adv.*, **garrulousness** *n.* [f. L (*garrire* chatter)]

garter *n.* **1** a band worn near the knee to keep up a sock etc. **2** the Garter, the highest order of English knighthood; the badge or membership of this. —**garter stitch,** rows of plain stitch in knitting. [f. OF *gartier* (*garet* bend of knee)]

garth *n.* **1** (*archaic*) a close or yard, a garden or paddock. **2** an open space within cloisters. [f. ON (cf. YARD)]

gas *n.* (*pl.* **gases** /ˈgæsɪz/) **1** any substance which is compressible, expands to fill any space in which it is enclosed, and consists of molecules which are not bound together but move about relatively independently; a substance which is a gas at normal temperatures and pressures; a gas which at a given temperature cannot be liquefied by pressure alone (other gases generally being known as 'vapours' in this context). **2** such a substance (especially coal gas or natural gas) used for heating, lighting, or cooking. **3** nitrous oxide or other gas used as an anaesthetic. **4** a poisonous gas used to disable an enemy in war. **5** (*US colloq.*) petrol, gasoline. **6** (*colloq.*) idle talk, boasting. —*v.t./i.* (**-ss-**) **1** to expose to gas; to poison or injure by gas. **2** (*colloq.*) to talk idly or boastfully. —**gas chamber,** an enclosed space that can be filled with poisonous gas to kill animals or people. **gas fire,** a domestic heater burning gas. **gas-fired** *adj.* using gas as a fuel. **gas mask,** a device worn over the face as protection against poison gas. **gas ring,** a hollow perforated ring fed with gas for cooking etc. **gas turbine,** one driven by a flow of gas or by gas from combustion. **step on the gas,** (*colloq.*) to accelerate a motor vehicle. [word invented by J. B. van Helmont, Dutch chemist (d. 1644), after Gk *khaos* chaos]

gasbag *n.* **1** a container of gas. **2** (*slang*) an idle talker.

gaseous /ˈgæsɪəs, ˈgeɪ-/ *adj.* of or like gas. [f. GAS]

gash *n.* a long deep cut, wound, or cleft. —*v.t.* to make a gash in, to cut. [var. of earlier *garce* f. OF (*garcer* wound)]

gasholder /ˈgæshəʊldə(r)/ *n.* a large receptacle for storing gas, a gasometer.

gasify /ˈgæsɪfaɪ/ *v.t.* to convert into a gas. —**gasification** /-fɪˈkeɪʃ(ə)n/ *n.* [f. GAS]

gasket /ˈgæskɪt/ *n.* **1** a sheet or ring of rubber etc. to seal a junction of metal surfaces. **2** a small cord securing a furled sail to a yard. [perh. f. F *garcette* little girl, thin rope]

gaskin /ˈgæskɪn/ *n.* the hinder part of a horse's thigh. [perh. erron. f. *galligaskins* wide hose of 16th- 17th c.]

gaslight *n.* the light given by burning gas.

gasoline /ˈgæsəli:n/ *n.* (*US*) petrol. [f. GAS]

gasometer /gæˈsɒmɪtə(r)/ *n.* a large tank from which gas is distributed by pipes. [f. F *gazomètre* (as GAS, -METER)]

gasp /gɑ:sp/ *v.t./i.* to catch the breath with an open mouth as in exhaustion or surprise; to utter with gasps. —*n.* a convulsive catching of the breath. —**at one's last gasp,** at the point of death, exhausted. [f. ON]

gassy *adj.* **1** of, like, or full of gas. **2** verbose. [f. GAS]

gastric /ˈgæstrɪk/ *adj.* of the stomach. —**gastric flu,** (*colloq.*) sickness and diarrhoea of unknown cause. **gastric juice,** the digestive fluid secreted by the stomach glands. [f. Gk (*gastēr* stomach)]

gastro- /gæstrəʊ-/ *in comb.* stomach. [f. Gk (as prec.)]

gastro-enteritis /gæstrəʊentəˈraɪtɪs/ *n.* inflammation of the stomach and intestine.

gastronome /ˈgæstrənəʊm/ *n.* a connoisseur of eating and drinking. [F (as foll.)]

gastronomy /gæˈstrɒnəmɪ/ *n.* the science of good eating and drinking. —**gastronomic** /-ˈnɒmɪk/ *adj.* [f. F f. Gk (GASTRO-, *-nomia* f. *nomos* law]

gastropod /ˈgæstrəpɒd/ *n.* a mollusc, such as a snail or limpet, of the class Gastropoda, moving by means of a muscular ventral organ and possessing both tentacles and eyes. [f. F (GASTRO-, Gk *pous podos* foot)]

gastroscope /ˈgæstrəskəʊp/ *n.* an instrument that can be passed down the throat for looking inside the stomach. [f. GASTRO- + -SCOPE]

gasworks *n.pl.* a place where gas for lighting and heating is manufactured.

gate *n.* **1** a barrier, usually hinged, used to close an opening made for entrance and exit through a wall, fence, etc. **2** such an opening; a means of entrance or exit; a numbered place of access to an aircraft at an airport. **3** a device regulating the passage of water in a lock etc. **4** the number entering by payment at gates to see a football match etc.; the amount of money thus taken. —*v.t.* to confine to a college or school, especially after a fixed hour. —**gate-leg** *adj.*, **gate-legged** *adj.* (of a table) with the legs in a gatelike frame which swings back to allow the top to fold down. [OE]

gateau /ˈgætəʊ/ *n.* a large rich cake often filled with cream, or cream and fruit, and highly decorated. [f. F *gâteau* cake]

gatecrash *v.t./i.* to go to (a private party etc.) without having been invited. —**gatecrasher** *n.*

gatehouse *n.* the lodge of a park etc.; the entrance building of a castle.

gateway *n.* an opening which can be closed with a gate; a means of access (*lit.* or *fig.*).

gather /ˈgæðə(r)/ *v.t./i.* **1** to bring or come together. **2** to collect, to obtain gradually; to summon up (energy etc.). **3** to infer or deduce. **4** to pluck, to collect as harvest. **5** to increase (speed etc.) gradually. **6** to draw together in folds or wrinkles. **7** to develop a purulent swelling. —*n.* (usu. in *pl.*) a fold or pleat. —**gather up,** to bring together; to pick up from the ground; to draw into a small compass. [OE]

gathering *n.* **1** an assembly. **2** a purulent swelling. **3** a group of leaves taken together in bookbinding. [f. prec.]

GATT /gæt/ *abbr.* General Agreement on Tariffs and Trade (a treaty to which more than 80 countries are parties, in operation since 1948, to promote trade and economic development).

gauche /gəʊʃ/ *adj.* lacking in ease and grace of manner, awkward and tactless. [F, lit. = left(-handed)]

gaucherie /ˈgəʊʃəri:/ *n.* gauche manners, a gauche act. [F (as prec.)]

gaucho /ˈgaʊtʃəʊ/ *n.* (*pl.* **-os**) a mounted herdsman in the South American pampas. [Sp., f. Quechua]

gaudy[1] /ˈgɔ:dɪ/ *adj.* tastelessly showy or bright. —**gaudily** *adv.*, **gaudiness** *n.* [prob. f. OF f. L *gaudēre* rejoice]

gaudy[2] /ˈgɔ:dɪ/ *n.* an annual entertainment, especially a college dinner for old members etc. [f. L *gaudium* joy (cf. prec.)]

gauge /geɪdʒ/ *n.* **1** a standard measure especially of the capacity or contents of a barrel, fineness of textile, diameter of a bullet, or thickness of sheet metal; the distance between rails or opposite wheels. **2** a graduated instrument used as a measuring device; a device for measuring the dimensions of tools, wire, etc.; a carpenter's adjustable tool for marking parallel lines. **3** capacity, extent. **4** a means of estimating, a criterion, a test. **5** (*Naut.*) relative position with respect to the wind. —*v.t.* **1** to measure exactly; to measure the content or capacity of (a cask etc.). **2** to estimate (a person or character). [f. OF; orig. unkn.]

gaunt /gɔ:nt/ *adj.* **1** lean, haggard. **2** grim, desolate. —**gauntness** *n.* [orig. unkn.]

gauntlet[1] /ˈgɔ:ntlɪt/ *n.* **1** a glove with a long loose wrist. **2** (*hist.*) an armoured glove. —**pick up the gauntlet,** to accept a challenge. **throw down the gauntlet,** to issue a challenge. [f. OF (*gant* glove)]

gauntlet[2] /ˈgɔ:ntlɪt/ *n.* **run the gauntlet,** to pass between rows of persons who strike one with sticks etc., orig. as a naval or military punishment; to undergo criticism etc. [f. Sw. *gattlopp* (*gata* lane, *lopp* course)]

gauss /gaʊs/ *n.* (*pl.* same) an electromagnetic unit of magnetic induction. [f. K. F. *Gauss*, German physicist (d. 1855)]

gauze /gɔ:z/ *n.* a thin transparent fabric of silk, cotton, wire, etc. —**gauzy** *adj.* [f. F f. *Gaza* in Palestine]

gave *past* of GIVE.

gavel /ˈgæv(ə)l/ *n.* a hammer used for calling attention by an auctioneer or chairman or judge. [orig. unkn.]

gavotte /gəˈvɒt/ *n.* a medium-paced dance in common time; the music for this. [F f. Prov. (*Gavot* native of region in Alps)]

gawk *v.i.* (*colloq.*) to stare stupidly. —*n.* an awkward or bashful person. [rel. to obs. *gaw* gaze]

gawky *adj.* awkward, ungainly. —**gawkily** *adv.*, **gawkiness** *n.* [as prec.]

gawp *v.i.* (*colloq.*) to gawk. [f. obs. *galpen* yawn (as YELP)]

gay *adj.* **1** light-hearted and cheerful, happy and full of fun. **2** brightly-coloured, dressed or decorated in bright colours. **3** (*colloq.*) homosexual; of or for homosexuals. —*n.* (*colloq.*) a homosexual person. —**gayness** *n.* [f. OF *gai*; etym. unkn.]

gaze *v.i.* to look long and steadily. —*n.* a long steady look. [orig. unkn.]

gazebo /gəˈzi:bəʊ/ *n.* (*pl.* **-os**) a summer-house, turret, etc., with a wide view. [perh. joc. f. prec.]

gazelle /gəˈzel/ *n.* a small graceful antelope, especially of the genus *Gazella*. [F, prob. f. Sp. f. Arab.]

gazette /gəˈzet/ *n.* **1** (used in titles) a newspaper. **2** an official publication with announcements etc. —*v.t.* to publish, or announce the appointment of (a person), in an official gazette. [F f. It.]

gazetteer /gæzɪˈtɪə(r)/ *n.* a geographical index. [f. F f. It. (as prec.)]

gazump /gəˈzʌmp/ *v.t.* (*slang*) to raise a price after accepting an offer from (a buyer); (*slang*) to swindle. [orig. unkn.]

GB *abbr.* Great Britain.

GC *abbr.* George Cross.

GCE *abbr.* General Certificate of Education.

GCSE *abbr.* General Certificate of Secondary Education.

Gd *symbol* gadolinium.

GDP *abbr*. gross domestic product.

GDR *abbr*. German Democratic Republic.

Ge *symbol* germanium.

gear /gɪə(r)/ *n*. **1** (often in *pl*.) a set of toothed wheels working on one another to transmit rotational motion from one shaft to another, especially those connecting a vehicle's engine to its road wheels; a particular setting of these (*high* with faster revolutions of the driven part relative to the driving part, *low* with slower). **2** equipment, apparatus, etc. **3** (*colloq*.) clothing; rigging. —*v.t.* **1** to put in gear, to provide with gear(s). **2** to adjust or adapt *to*. **3** to harness (*up*). —**gear-lever** *n*. a lever used to engage or change a gear. **gear-shift** *n*. (*US*) a gear-lever. **in gear,** with a gear engaged. **out of gear,** with the gears disengaged; not proceeding or produced uniformly (*with*). [f. ON f. Gmc, = prepare]

gearbox *n*. a case enclosing the gears of a vehicle or other machine.

gearing *n*. a set or arrangement of gears. [f. GEAR]

gearwheel *n*. a toothed wheel in a set of gears.

gecko /ˈgekəʊ/ *n*. (*pl*. **-os**) a tropical house-lizard of the family Geckonidae. [Malay, imit. its cry]

gee[1] *int*. (also **gee whiz**) expressing surprise etc. [perh. abbr. of *Jesus*]

gee[2] *int*. (usu. with *up*) a command to a horse etc. to start or go faster. [orig. unkn.]

gee-gee /ˈdʒi:dʒi:/ *n*. (*colloq*.) a horse. [orig. a child's word, f. prec.]

geese *pl*. of GOOSE.

geezer /ˈgi:zə(r)/ *n*. (*slang*) a person, especially an old man. [dial. pronunc. of *guiser* mummer, f. GUISE]

Geiger counter /ˈgaɪgə(r)/ a device for detecting and measuring radioactivity etc. [f. H. *Geiger*, German physicist (d. 1945)]

geisha /ˈgeɪʃə/ *n*. a Japanese woman trained to entertain men. [Jap.]

gel /dʒel/ *n*. a semi-solid colloidal solution or jelly. [abbr. of foll.]

gelatine /ˈdʒeləti:n/ *n*. (also **gelatin** /-tɪn/) a transparent tasteless substance got from skins, tendons, etc., and used in cookery, photography, etc. [f. F f. It. (as JELLY)]

gelatinize /dʒɪˈlætɪnaɪz/ *v.t./i*. to make or become gelatinous; to coat or treat with gelatine. —**gelatinization** /-ˈzeɪʃ(ə)n/ *n*. [f. prec.]

gelatinous /dʒɪˈlætɪnəs/ *adj*. like jelly, especially in consistency. [f. GELATINE]

geld /geld/ *v.t*. to deprive (usu. a male animal) of reproductive ability, to castrate. [f. ON (*geldr* barren)]

gelding /ˈgeldɪŋ/ *n*. a gelded animal, especially a male horse. [as prec.]

gelignite /ˈdʒelɪgnaɪt/ *n*. a plastic high explosive (also known as gelatine dynamite) consisting of nitro-glycerine which is at least partially gelatinized by means of gun cotton. [f. GELATINE + L *ignis* fire]

gem *n*. **1** (also **gemstone**) a precious stone, especially cut and polished or engraved. **2** a thing of great beauty or worth. —*v.t*. (**-mm-**) to adorn with or as with gems. [f. OF f L *gemma* bud, jewel]

geminate /ˈdʒemɪneɪt/ *v.t*. to double, to repeat; to arrange in pairs. —/also -ət/ *adj*. combined in pairs. —**gemination** /-ˈneɪʃ(ə)n/ *n*. [f. L *geminare* (as foll.)]

Gemini /ˈdʒemɪnaɪ, -nɪ/ a constellation and the third sign of the zodiac, the Twins, which the sun enters about 21 May. [L, = twins]

gemma /ˈdʒemə/ *n*. (*pl*. **-ae**) (in cryptogams) the small cellular body that separates from the mother-plant and starts a new one. [L, = gem]

gemmation /dʒeˈmeɪʃ(ə)n/ *n*. reproduction by gemmae. [F (as prec.)]

gen /dʒen/ *n*. (*slang*) information. —*v.t./i*. (**-nn-**) (*slang*, with *up*) to gain or give information (to). [perh. f. *gen*eral information]

-gen /-dʒ(ə)n/ *suffix* forming nouns in the sense 'that which produces' (*hydrogen*). [f. F f. Gk *-genēs* -born, of a specified kind (as GENESIS)]

Gen. *abbr*. General.

gendarme /ˈʒɒndɑ:m/ *n*. a soldier employed in police duties, especially in France. [F, f. *gens d'arme* men of arms]

gender /ˈdʒendə(r)/ *n*. **1**. a grammatical classification of words, by which words are classed as masculine, feminine, and sometimes also neuter and common; any of these classes, the property of belonging to such a class; (of adjectives) the appropriate form for accompanying a noun of one such class. **2** (*colloq*.) a person's sex. [f. OF f. L GENUS]

gene /dʒi:n/ *n*. each of the units of heredity in an organism. [f. G *gen* (cf. -GEN)]

genealogy /dʒi:nɪˈælədʒɪ/ *n*. descent traced continuously from an ancestor, a pedigree; the study of pedigrees; a plant's or animal's line of development from earlier forms. —**genealogical** /-ˈlɒdʒɪk(ə)l/ *adj*., **genealogist** *n*. [f. OF f. L f. Gk (*genea* race, -LOGY)]

genera *pl*. of GENUS.

general /ˈdʒenər(ə)l/ *adj*. **1** including or affecting all or most parts, cases, or things; not partial or local or particular. **2** not restricted or specialized; applying to all or most cases. **3** involving only main features, not detailed. **4** usual, prevalent. **5** chief, head; with unrestricted authority. —*n*. **1** an army officer next below Field Marshal; a lieutenant-general or major-general; the commander of an army. **2** a strategist. **3** the chief of a religious order (e.g. of the Jesuits). —**general election,** an election of representatives to Parliament etc. from the whole country. **general practitioner,** a doctor treating cases of all kinds in the first instance. **general staff,** the officers assisting a military commander at headquarters. **general strike,** a strike of workers in all or most trades. **in general,** as a normal rule, usually, for the most part. —**generalship** *n.* [f. OF f. L (as GENUS)]

generalissimo /dʒenərəˈlɪsɪməʊ/ *n.* (*pl.* **-os**) a commander of combined military and naval and air forces, or of several armies. [It., superl. of *generale* (as prec.)]

generality /dʒenəˈrælɪtɪ/ *n.* **1** a general statement or rule. **2** general applicability, indefiniteness. **3** the majority or bulk of. [f. F f. L (as GENERAL)]

generalize /ˈdʒenərəlaɪz/ *v.t./i.* **1** to speak in general or indefinite terms; to form general notions; to reduce to a general statement. **2** to infer (a rule etc.) from particular cases. **3** to bring into general use. —**generalization** /-ˈzeɪʃ(ə)n/ *n.* [f. F (as GENERAL)]

generally *adv.* in a general sense, without regard to particulars or exceptions; in most respects or cases. [f. GENERAL]

generate /ˈdʒenəreɪt/ *v.t.* to bring into existence, to produce. [f. L *generare* beget (as GENUS)]

generation /dʒenəˈreɪʃ(ə)n/ *n.* **1** procreation. **2** production, especially of electricity. **3** a step in a pedigree; all persons born about the same time; the average time in which children are ready to take the place of their parents (about 30 years). —**generation gap,** differences of opinion or attitude between different generations. [f. OF f. L (as prec.)]

generative /ˈdʒenərətɪv/ *adj.* **1** of procreation. **2** productive. [f. OF or L (as prec.)]

generator /ˈdʒenəreɪtə(r)/ *n.* **1** a machine for converting mechanical into electrical energy. **2** an apparatus for producing gas, steam, etc. **3** an originator. [f. GENERATE]

generic /dʒɪˈnerɪk/ *adj.* characteristic of or applied to a genus or class; not specific or special. —**generically** *adv.* [f. F f. L (as GENUS)]

generous /ˈdʒenərəs/ *adj.* **1** giving freely. **2** not petty in feelings or conduct, free from prejudice. **3** given freely, plentiful. —**generosity** /-ˈrɒsɪtɪ/ *n.*, **generously** *adv.* [f. OF f. L *generosus* (as GENUS)]

genesis /ˈdʒenɪsɪs/ *n.* origin; mode of formation or generation. [L f. Gk, = origin]

genet /ˈdʒenɪt/ *n.* a kind of civet-cat (*Genetta vulgaris*); its fur. [f. OF f.Arab.]

genetic /dʒɪˈnetɪk/ *adj.* **1** of genetics or genes. **2** of or in origin. —**genetic code,** the system by which DNA and RNA molecules carry genetic information. **genetic engineering,** the deliberate modification of hereditary features by transferring fragments of DNA containing particular genes from one organism to another. —**genetically** *adv.* [f. GENESIS]

genetics *n.* the study of heredity and variation in animals and plants. —**geneticist** *n.* [f. prec.]

genial /ˈdʒi:nɪəl/ *adj.* **1** jovial, kindly, sociable. **2** (of climate etc.) mild, warm, conducive to growth; cheering. —**geniality** /-ˈælɪtɪ/ *n.*, **genially** *adv.* [f. L *genialis* (as GENIUS)]

-genic /-dʒenɪk/ *suffix* forming adjectives in the sense (1) 'producing' (*pathogenic*), (2) 'well suited to' (*photogenic*), (3) 'produced by' (*iatrogenic*). [f. -GEN]

genie /ˈdʒi:nɪ/ *n.* (*pl.* **genii** /-nɪaɪ/) a jinnee, a sprite or goblin of Arabian tales. [f. F *génie* f. L GENIUS]

genista /dʒɪˈnɪstə/ *n.* a kind of flowering shrub of the genus *Genista*, e.g. dyer's broom, *G. tinctoria*. [L]

genital /ˈdʒenɪt(ə)l/ *adj.* of animal reproduction. —*n.* (in *pl.*; also **genitalia** /-ˈteɪlɪə/) the external genital organs. [f. OF or L (*gignere genit-* beget)]

genitive /ˈdʒenɪtɪv/ *adj.* (*Gram.*, of a case) corresponding to *of*, *from*, etc., with a noun representing a possessor, source, etc. —*n.* the genitive case. [as prec.]

genius /ˈdʒi:nɪəs/ *n.* (*pl.* **geniuses**) **1** an exceptional intellectual or creative power or other natural ability or tendency; a person having this. **2** the tutelary spirit of a person, place, etc.; a person or spirit influencing a person powerfully for good or evil. **3** the prevalent feeling or association etc. (*of* a people, place, or age). [L, f. *gignere genit-* beget]

genizah /geˈni:zə/ *n.* a store-room or repository attached to a synagogue, housing damaged, discarded, or heretical books etc. and sacred relics; its contents. [Heb., = hiding-place (*gānaz* hide, set aside)]

genocide /ˈdʒenəsaɪd/ *n.* deliberate extermination of a people or nation. —**genocidal** /-ˈsaɪd(ə)l/ *adj.* [f. Gk *genos* race + -CIDE]

genotype /ˈdʒenəʊtaɪp/ *n.* the genetic constitution of an individual. [f. G *genotypus* (as GENE, TYPE)]

-genous /-dʒənəs/ *suffix* forming adjectives in the sense 'produced' (*endogenous*). [as -GEN]

genre /ʒɑ̃r/ *n.* **1** a kind or style of art, literature, etc. **2** (also **genre-painting**) portrayal of scenes etc. from ordinary life, especially the type of subject-matter favoured by Dutch artists of the 17th c. [F (as GENDER)]

gent *n.* (*colloq.*) gentleman; (in *pl.*, in shops) men. —**the Gents,** (*colloq.*) a men's public lavatory. [abbr. of GENTLEMAN]

genteel /dʒenˈtiːl/ *adj.* affectedly stylish or refined; upper-class. —**genteelly** *adv.* [f. F *gentil* (as GENTLE)]

genteelism *n.* a word used because thought to be less vulgar than the usual word (e.g. *perspire* for *sweat*). [f. prec.]

gentian /ˈdʒenʃ(ə)n/ *n.* a plant of the genus *Gentiana* or *Gentianella*, especially one of the blue-flowered mountain kinds. —**gentian violet,** a purple dye with various uses, e.g. as an antiseptic. [OE f. L (acc. to Pliny, f. *Gentius* king of Illyria)]

gentile /ˈdʒentaɪl/ *adj.* not Jewish; heathen. —*n.* a non-Jewish person. [f. L (*gens* race, family)]

gentility /dʒenˈtɪlɪtɪ/ *n.* social superiority; good manners and elegance, upper-class habits. [f. OF (as foll.)]

gentle *adj.* **1** not rough or severe; mild, moderate; quiet, requiring patience. **2** (of birth etc.) of good family. —**gently** *adv.*, **gentleness** *n.* [f. OF *gentil* (as GENTILE)]

gentlefolk *n.pl.* people of good family.

gentleman *n.* (*pl.* **-men**) **1** (in polite or formal use) a man. **2** a chivalrous well-bred man; a man of good social position or of wealth and leisure. **3** a man of gentle birth attached to a royal household. —**gentleman-at-arms** *n.* one of the sovereign's bodyguard. **gentleman's** (*or* **-men's**) **agreement,** an agreement binding in honour but not enforceable. —**gentlemanly** *adj.*

gentlewoman *n.* (*pl.* **-women**) (*archaic*) a woman of good birth or breeding.

gentry /ˈdʒentrɪ/ *n.pl.* **1** people next below the nobility. **2** (*derog.*) people. [f. OF (as GENTLE)]

genuflect /ˈdʒenjuːflekt/ *v.i.* to bend the knee, especially in worship. —**genuflexion** /-ˈflekʃ(ə)n/ *n.* [f. L (*genu* knee, *flectere* bend)]

genuine /ˈdʒenjuːɪn/ *adj.* **1** really coming from its reputed source etc.; not sham. **2** properly so called; pure-bred. —**genuinely** *adv.*, **genuineness** *n.* [f. L (*genu* knee, because a father acknowledged a new-born child by placing it on his knee)]

genus /ˈdʒiːnəs/ *n.* (*pl.* **genera** /ˈdʒenərə/) **1** a group of animals or plants with common structural characteristics, usually containing several species. **2** (in logic) kinds of things including subordinate kinds or species. **3** (*colloq.*) a kind, a class. [L, = race, stock]

geo- /dʒiːəʊ/ *in comb.* earth. [f. Gk (*gē* earth)]

geocentric /dʒiːəʊˈsentrɪk/ *adj.* **1** considered as viewed from the earth's centre. **2** having the earth as the centre. —**geocentrically** *adv.* [f. GEO- + CENTRIC]

geochemistry /dʒiːəʊˈkemɪstrɪ/ *n.* the study of the chemistry of the earth, especially the principles governing the geological distribution of individual elements.

geochronology /dʒiːəʊkrəˈnɒlədʒɪ/ *n.* the chronology of the earth; the measurement of geological time and the ordering of past geological events.

geode /ˈdʒiːəʊd/ *n.* a small cavity lined with crystals; a rock containing this. [f. Gk *geōdēs* earthy (*gē* earth)]

geodesic /dʒiːəʊˈdiːsɪk, -desɪk/ *adj.* (also **geodetic**) of geodesy. —**geodesic** (*or* **geodetic**) **dome,** a dome built of short struts holding flat triangular or polygonal pieces fitted together to form a rough hemisphere. **geodesic line,** the shortest possible line on a curved surface between two points.[f. foll.]

geodesy /dʒiːˈɒdɪsɪ/ *n.* the study of the shape and area of the earth. [f. Gk *geōdaisia* (GEO-, *daiō* divide)]

geographical /dʒiːəˈgræfɪk(ə)l/ *adj.* (also **geographic**) of geography. —**geographical mile**, 1 minute of latitude, about 1.85 km. —**geographically** *adv.* [as foll.]

geography /dʒɪˈɒgrəfɪ/ *n.* **1** the science of the earth's form, physical features, climate, population, etc. **2** the features or arrangement of a place. —**geographer** *n.* [f. F or L f. Gk (as GEO-, -GRAPHY)]

geology /dʒɪˈɒlədʒɪ/ *n.* **1** the study of the composition, structure, and history of the earth, and the processes occurring within it; the study of the rocks of the earth's crust; the corresponding study of other planets. **2** the geological features of a district. —**geological** /-ˈlɒdʒɪk(ə)l/ *adj.*, **geologically** *adv.*, **geologist** *n.* [f. GEO- + -LOGY.]

geomagnetism /dʒɪəʊˈmægnɪtɪz(ə)m/ *n.* study of the earth's magnetic properties. —**geomagnetic** /-ˈnetɪk/ *adj.*

geometric /dʒiːəˈmetrɪk/ *adj.* (also **geometrical**) of geometry. —**geometric progression,** a progression with a constant ratio between successive quantities, e.g. 1, 3, 9, 27. —**geometrically** *adv.* [f. F (as foll.)]

geometry /dʒɪˈɒmɪtrɪ/ *n.* the branch of mathematics that deals with space and the properties of such entities as points, lines, curves, planes, curved surfaces. —**geometer** *n.*, **geometrician** /-ˈtrɪʃ(ə)n/ *n.* [f. OF f. L f. Gk (as GEO-, METRY)]

geomorphology /dʒɪəʊmɔːˈfɒlədʒɪ/ *n.* the study of the physical features of the earth's (or other planet's) surface and their relation to its geological structures.

geophysics /dʒiːəʊˈfɪzɪks/ *n.* the study of the physical properties of the earth, especially of its crust; the application of the principles, methods, and techniques of physics to the study of the earth. —**geophysical** *adj.*, **geophysicist** *n.*

geopolitics /dʒi:əʊˈpɒlɪtɪks/ *n.* the influence of geographical features on the political character, history, and institutions etc. of States; the study of this.

Geordie /ˈdʒɔ:dɪ/ *n.* a native of Tyneside. [f. name *George*]

George Cross, George Medal decorations for gallantry, chiefly in civilian life, instituted in 1940 by King George VI.

georgette /dʒɔ:ˈdʒet/ *n.* a thin dress-material made from highly twisted yarn. [f. *Georgette* de la Plante, French dressmaker]

Georgian[1] /ˈdʒɔ:dʒɪən/ *adj.* belonging to the characteristic of the reigns of the first four Kings George (1714-1830) or of Kings George V and VI (1910-52), especially of literature of 1910-20. [f. GEORGE[1]]

Georgian[2] /ˈdʒɔ:dʒɪən/ *adj.* of Georgia in the Caucasus or its people or language. —*n.* **1** a native or inhabitant of Georgia. **2** the language of Georgia. [f. *Georgia*]

geranium /dʒəˈreɪnɪəm/ *n.* a herb or shrub of the genus *Geranium*, bearing fruit shaped like a crane's bill; (*pop.*) the cultivated pelargonium. [L f. Gk (*geranos* crane)]

gerbil /ˈdʒɜ:bɪl/ *n.* a mouselike rodent of the subfamily Gerbillinae, with long hind legs. [f. F (as JERBOA)]

geriatrics /dʒerɪˈætrɪks/ *n.pl.* (usu. treated as *sing.*) the branch of medical science dealing with old age and its diseases. —**geriatric** *adj.*, **geriatrician** /-ˈtrɪʃ(ə)n/ *n.* [f. Gk *gēras* old age + *iatros* physician]

germ *n.* **1** a micro-organism or microbe, especially one causing disease. **2** a portion of an organism capable of becoming a new one; a rudiment of an animal or plant; the embryo of a seed. **3** a thing that may develop, an elementary principle. —**germ warfare,** the use of germs to spread disease in war. [f. F f. L *germen* sprout]

German /ˈdʒɜ:mən/ *adj.* of Germany or its people or language. —*n.* **1** a native of Germany. **2** the language of Germany. —**German measles,** a disease like mild measles. **German shepherd dog,** an Alsatian. **High German,** the variety of Teutonic speech, originally confined to 'High' or southern Germany, now accepted as the literary language of the whole country. **Low German,** the general name for the dialects of Germany which are not High German. [f. L *Germanus*]

german /ˈdʒɜ:mən/ *adj.* (placed after *brother*, *sister*, *cousin*) having a full relationship, not a half-brother etc. [f. OF f. L *germanus* genuine, of same parents]

germander /dʒɜ:ˈmændə(r)/ *n.* a plant of the genus *Teucrium*. —**germander speedwell,** a speedwell with leaves like a germander. [f. L, ult. f Gk *chamaedrys* ground-oak]

germane /dʒɜ:ˈmeɪn/ *adj.* relevant *to* a subject. [var. of GERMAN]

Germanic /dʒɜ:ˈmænɪk/ *adj.* **1** of Germanic. **2** of the Scandinavians, Anglo-Saxons, or Germans. **3** having German characteristics. **4** (*hist.*) of the Germans. —*n.* the primitive (unrecorded) language of the Germanic peoples. [f. L (as GERMAN)]

germanium /dʒɜ:ˈmeɪnɪəm/ *n.* a brittle greyish-white semi-metallic element, symbol Ge, atomic number 32. [f. L *Germanus* German]

Germano- /dʒɜ:mənəʊ-/ *in comb.* German.

germicide /ˈdʒɜ:mɪsaɪd/ *n.* a substance that destroys germs. —**germicidal** *adj.* [f. GERM + -CIDE]

germinal /ˈdʒɜ:mɪn(ə)l/ *adj.* **1** of germs. **2** in the earliest stage of development. **3** productive of new ideas etc. —**germinally** *adv.* [as GERM]

germinate /ˈdʒɜ:mɪneɪt/ *v.t./i.* to sprout or bud (*lit.* or *fig.*); to cause to do this. —**germination** /-ˈneɪʃ(ə)n/ *n.*, **germinative** *adj.* [f. L *germinare* (as GERM)]

gerontology /dʒerɒnˈtɒlədʒɪ/ *n.* the study of old age and the process of ageing. [f. Gk *gerōn* old man + -LOGY]

gerrymander /dʒerɪˈmændə(r)/ *v.t./i.* to manipulate the boundaries of (a constituency etc.) so as to give undue influence to some party or class in an election. —*n.* this practice. [f. Governor *Gerry* of Massachusetts (who rearranged boundaries for this purpose in 1812), after *salamander*]

gerund /ˈdʒerənd/ *n.* a verbal noun, in English ending in *-ing*. —**gerundial** *adj.* [f. L (*gerundum* gerund of *gerere* carry on)]

gerundive /dʒəˈrʌndɪv/ *n.* a Latin form of the verb functioning as an adjective with the sense 'that should be done' etc. [as prec.]

gesso /ˈdʒesəʊ/ *n.* (*pl.* **-oes**) gypsum as used in painting or sculpture. [It., = GYPSUM]

Gestapo /geˈstɑ:pəʊ/ *n.* the Nazi secret police; any comparable organization. [G, = *Ge*heime *Sta*ats*po*lizei]

gestation /dʒeˈsteɪʃ(ə)n/ *n.* **1** carrying in the womb; the period of this, between conception and birth. **2** the development of an idea etc. [f. L (*gestare* carry)]

gesticulate /dʒeˈstɪkjʊleɪt/ *v.t./i.* to use gestures instead of or to reinforce speech; to express thus. —**gesticulation** /-ˈleɪʃ(ə)n/ *n.* [f. L *gesticulari* (*gesticulus* dim. of *gestus*, as foll.)]

gesture /ˈdʒestʃə(r)/ *n.* **1** a movement of a limb or the body conveying meaning; the use of such movements. **2** an action to evoke a response or convey an intention. —*v.t./i.* to gesticulate. —**gestural** *adj.* [f. L (*gerere* wield)]

get /get/ *v.t./i.* (**-tt-**; *past* **got**; *p.p.* **got** or (*archaic & US*) **gotten**) **1** to come into possession of, to obtain or receive. **2** to fetch or procure; to go to reach or catch (a train, bus, etc.). **3** to prepare (a meal). **4** to receive (a broadcast signal); to establish communication by telephone etc. with. **5** to experience or suffer; to contract (an illness); to establish (an idea etc.) in one's mind. **6** to bring or come into a specified condition; to induce. **7** to come or go or arrive; to cause to do this. **8** (in *perf.*) to possess, to have, to be bound *to do* or *be*. **9** (*colloq.*) to understand. **10** (*colloq.*) to attract, obsess, or irritate. **11** (*colloq.*) to harm, injure, or kill, especially in retaliation. **12** to develop an inclination (with *infin.*). **13** (usu. of animals) to beget. —**get across,** (*colloq.*) to be or make effective or acceptable; (*slang*) to annoy. **get along,** to get on. **get at,** to reach; (*colloq.*) to mean, to imply; (*slang*) to imply a criticism of; (*slang*) to tamper with, to bribe. **get away,** to escape; to depart on a journey etc. **get away with,** to escape blame, punishment, or misfortune deserved for (an action). **get by,** (*colloq.*) to manage; to be acceptable. **get down,** to record in writing; to swallow; to make dejected. **get down to,** to begin working on. **get going,** (*colloq.*) to begin moving or acting. **get off,** to be or cause to be acquitted; to escape with little or no punishment; to start; to alight from (a bus etc.); (*colloq.*) to achieve an amorous or sexual relationship *with*. **get on,** to manage; to make progress; to be on friendly or harmonious terms. **get on!** (*colloq.*) an expression of incredulity. **get one's own back,** (*colloq.*) to have one's revenge. **get-out** *n.* a means of avoiding something. **get out of,** to avoid or escape (a duty etc.). **get over,** to get across; to recover from (an illness or shock etc.); **get round,** to evade (a rule or law); to coax or cajole (a person), especially to secure a favour. **get round to,** to deal with (a task etc.) in due course. **get somewhere,** to make progress, to be successful. **get there,** to reach one's goal; (*slang*) to succeed, to understand what is meant. **get through,** to pass (an examination etc.); to finish or use up; to make contact by telephone. **get through to,** (*colloq.*) to succeed in making (a person) understand. **get-together** *n.* (*colloq.*) a social gathering. **get up,** to rise from sitting etc., or from bed after sleeping; to prepare or organize; to work up (anger etc., a subject for an examination etc.); to dress or arrange elaborately. **get-up** *n.* (*colloq.*) a style or arrangement of dress etc. **get up to,** to become involved in (mischief etc.). [f. ON *geta* obtain, beget, guess]

get-at-able /get'ætəb(ə)l/ *adj.* accessible.

getaway *n.* an escape, especially after a crime.

geum /'dji:əm/ *n.* a perennial rosaceous plant of the genus *Geum* (which includes herb bennet), with red, orange, yellow, or white flowers. [var. of L *gaeum*]

gewgaw /'gju:gɔ:/ *n.* a gaudy plaything or ornament; a showy trifle. [orig. unkn.]

geyser /'gaɪzə(r), 'gi:-, 'geɪ-/ *n.* **1** an intermittently erupting hot spring. **2** /'gi:zə(r)/ an apparatus for heating water for use in baths, sinks, etc. [f. Icel. *Geysir* name of a spring (*geysa* gush)]

ghastly /'gɑ:stlɪ/ *adj.* **1** horrible, frightful; (*colloq.*) objectionable. **2** deathlike, pallid. **3** (of a smile etc.) forced, grim. —*adv.* ghastlily (pale etc.). —**ghastlily** *adv.*, **ghastliness** *n.* [f. obs. *gast* terrify]

ghat /gɔ:t/ *n.* (also **ghaut**) (in India), steps leading to a river, a landing-place. —**burning-ghat** *n.* a level area at the top of a river ghat where Hindus burn their dead. [f. Hindi]

ghee /gi:/ *n.* Indian clarified butter made from the milk of a buffalo or cow. [f. Hindi f. Skr., = sprinkled]

gherkin /'gɜ:kɪn/ *n.* a small cucumber for pickling. [f. Du.]

ghetto /'getəʊ/ *n.* (*pl.* **-os**) a part of a city occupied by a minority group (*hist.*, the Jewish quarter in a city); a segregated group or area. [perh. f. It. *getto* foundry, as the first ghetto founded in Venice in 1516 was on the site of a foundry)]

ghost /gəʊst/ *n.* **1** an apparition of a dead person or animal, a disembodied spirit. **2** an emaciated or pale person. **3** a shadow or semblance. **4** a secondary or duplicated image in a defective telescope or television-picture. —*v.t./i.* to act as a ghost writer (of). —**ghost town,** a town with few or no remaining inhabitants. **ghost writer,** a writer doing work for which the employer takes credit. **give up the ghost,** to die. —**ghostliness** *n.*, **ghostly** *adj.* [OE]

ghoul /gu:l/ *n.* **1** a person morbidly interested in death etc. **2** (in Muslim folklore) a spirit preying on corpses. —**ghoulish** *adj.*, **ghoulishly** *adv.* [f. Arab., = protean desert demon]

GHQ *abbr.* General Headquarters.

ghyll var. of GILL[2].

GI /dʒi:'aɪ/ *n.* a private soldier in the US army. —*adj.* of or for US servicemen. [abbr. of *government* (or *general*) *issue*]

giant /'dʒaɪənt/ *n.* **1** an imaginary or mythical being of human form but superhuman size. **2** a person of great size, ability, strength, etc.; an abnormally tall animal or plant. **3** a star of relatively great luminosity arising from either high surface temperatures or very extended atmospheres. —*adj.* gigantic; of a very large kind. —**giantess** *n.fem.* [f. OF f. L f. Gk *gigas gigantos*]

gibber /ˈdʒɪbə(r)/ *v.i.* to jabber inarticulately. [imit.]

gibberish /ˈdʒɪbərɪʃ/ *n.* unintelligible speech, meaningless sounds. [perh. f. prec.]

gibbet /ˈdʒɪbɪt/ *n.* (*hist.*) a gallows, a post with an arm on which an executed criminal was hung. —*v.t.* **1** to put to death by hanging; to expose or hang up on a gibbet. **2** to hold up to contempt. [f. OF *gibet*, dim. of *gibe* club]

gibbon /ˈgɪbən/ *n.* a long-armed SE Asian anthropoid ape of the genus *Hylobates*. [F, f. aboriginal name]

gibbous /ˈgɪbəs/ *adj.* convex; (of the moon or a planet) having the bright part greater than a semicircle but less than a circle; hump-backed. [f. L (*gibbus* hump)]

gibe /dʒaɪb/ *v.t./i.* to jeer or mock (at). —*n.* a jeering remark, a taunt. [perh. f. OF *giber* handle roughly]

giblets /ˈdʒɪblɪts/ *n.pl.* the edible organs etc. of a bird, taken out and usually cooked separately. [f. OF *gibelet* game stew (*gibier* game)]

giddy /ˈgɪdɪ/ *adj.* **1** dizzy, tending to fall or stagger. **2** causing dizziness. **3** mentally intoxicated, frivolous; flighty. —**giddily** *adv.*, **giddiness** *n.* [OE, = insane, lit. 'possessed by a god' (f. GOD)]

gift /gɪft/ *n.* **1** a thing given, a present; a natural ability or talent. **2** giving. **3** (*colloq.*) an easy task. —*v.t.* to endow with gifts; to present *with* as a gift; to bestow as a gift. —**gift token** *or* **voucher,** a voucher used as a gift and exchangeable for goods. **gift-wrap** *v.t.* to wrap attractively (as a gift). **in a person's gift,** his to bestow. [f. ON (as GIVE)]

gifted *adj.* talented. [f. GIFT]

gig[1] /gɪg/ *n.* **1** a light two-wheeled one-horse carriage. **2** a light ship's-boat for rowing or sailing. **3** a rowing-boat chiefly used for racing. [prob. imit.]

gig[2] /gɪg/ *n.* (*colloq.*) an engagement to play jazz etc., especially for one night. [orig. unkn.]

giga- /gɪgə-, gaɪgə-/ *in comb.* one thousand million. [f. Gk *gigas* giant]

gigantic /dʒaɪˈgæntɪk/ *adj.* giant-like, huge. —**gigantically** *adv.* [f. L *gigas gigantis* giant]

giggle *v.i.* to laugh in small half-suppressed bursts. —*n.* such a laugh; (*colloq.*) an amusing person or thing, a joke. —**giggly** *adj.* [imit.]

gigolo /ˈʒɪgələʊ/ *n.* (*pl.* **-os**) a young man paid by an older woman to be an escort or lover. [F, as masc. of *gigole* dance-hall woman]

Gila /ˈhiːlə/ *n.* (in full **Gila monster**) a large venomous lizard, *Heloderma suspectum*, found in the southwestern USA. [name of river in New Mexico and Arizona]

gild[1] /gɪld/ *v.t.* (*p.p.* sometimes GILT[1] as adj. in lit. sense, otherwise **gilded**) to cover thinly with gold; to tinge with golden colour. —**gild the lily,** to try to improve what is already satisfactory. [OE (as GOLD)]

gild[2] var. of GUILD.

gill[1] /gɪl/ *n.* (usu. in *pl.*) **1** a respiratory organ in a fish etc. **2** a vertical radial plate on the underside of a mushroom etc. **3** the flesh below a person's jaws and ears. [f. ON]

gill[2] /dʒɪl/ *n.* a unit of liquid measure, equal to ¼ pint. In many districts the gill is equal to ½ pint, the ¼ pint being called a *jack*. [f. OF f. L *gillo* water-pot]

gill[3] /gɪl/ *n.* **1** a deep ravine, usually wooded. **2** a narrow mountain torrent. [f. ON]

gillie /ˈgɪlɪ/ *n.* a man or boy attending a sportsman in Scotland. [f. Gael. *gille* lad, servant]

gillyflower /ˈdʒɪlɪflaʊə(r)/ *n.* a clove-scented flower, e.g. the wallflower; the clove-scented pink (*Dianthus carophyllus*). [f. OF *gilofre, girofle* f. L f. Gk *karuophullon* clove-tree]

gilt[1] /gɪlt/ *adj.* covered thinly with gold; gold-coloured. —*n.* **1** gilding. **2** a gilt-edged security. —**gilt-edged** *adj.* (of securities, stocks, etc.) having a high degree of reliability. [f. GILD[1]]

gilt[2] /gɪlt/ *n.* a young sow. [f. ON]

gimbals /ˈdʒɪmb(ə)lz/ *n.pl.* a contrivance of rings and pivots for keeping instruments horizontal at sea. [f. OF *gemel* double finger-ring f. L *gemellus* twin]

gimcrack /ˈdʒɪmkræk/ *adj.* showy but flimsy and worthless. —*n.* a showy ornament etc., a knick-knack. [f. earlier *gibecrake* (?inlaid work), of unkn. orig.]

gimlet /ˈgɪmlɪt/ *n.* a small tool with a screw-tip for boring holes. —**gimlet eye,** an eye with a piercing glance. [f. OF *guimbelet*]

gimmick /ˈgɪmɪk/ *n.* a trick or device, especially to attract attention or publicity. —**gimmickry** *n.*, **gimmicky** *adj.* [orig. US; etym. unkn.]

gimp /gɪmp/ *n.* a twist of silk etc. with a cord or wire running through it; a fishing-line of silk etc. bound with wire. [f. Du.]

gin[1] /dʒɪn/ *n.* a spirit made from grain or malt and flavoured with juniper berries. —**gin rummy,** a form of the card-game rummy. **gin sling,** (*US*) a cold drink of gin flavoured and sweetened. [abbr. of *geneva* f. Du. f. OF *genevre*, = JUNIPER]

gin[2] /dʒɪn/ *n.* **1** a snare, a trap. **2** a machine separating cotton from its seeds. **3** a kind of crane and windlass. —*v.t.* (**-nn-**) **1** to treat (cotton) in a gin. **2** to trap. [f. OF *engin* engine]

ginger /ˈdʒɪndʒə(r)/ *n.* **1** a hot spicy root used in cooking and medicine and preserved in syrup or candied; the plant from which this comes (*Zingiber officinale*). **2** light reddish yellow. **3** mettle, spirit; stimulation. —*v.t.* **1** to flavour with ginger. **2** to liven *up*. —**ginger-ale, -beer** *ns.* kinds of aerated ginger-flavoured drink. **ginger group,** a group urging a party or movement to more decided action. **ginger-nut** *n.* a ginger-flavoured biscuit. **ginger-snap** *n.* a thin brittle ginger-flavoured biscuit. —**gingery** *adj.* [f. OE & OF f. L *zingiber* f. Gk f. Skr.]

gingerbread *n.* ginger-flavoured treacle cake. —*adj.* gaudy, tawdry.

gingerly /ˈdʒɪndʒəlɪ/ *adj.* showing great care or caution. —*adv.* in a gingerly manner. [perh. f. OF *gensor* delicate]

gingham /ˈgɪŋəm/ *n.* a plain-woven cotton cloth often striped or checked. [f. Du. f. Malay, = striped]

gingivitis /dʒɪndʒɪˈvaɪtɪs/ *n.* inflammation of the gums. [f. L *gingiva* gum + -ITIS]

ginkgo /ˈgɪŋkəʊ/ *n.* (*pl.* **-os**) a tree (*Gingko biloba*) with fan-shaped leaves and yellow flowers, originally from China and Japan. [f. Jap. f. Chin., = silver apricot]

ginseng /ˈdʒɪnseŋ/ *n.* a medicinal plant of the genus *Panax* found in eastern Asia and North America; the root of this. [f. Chin., perh. = man-image, alluding to forked root]

gippy tummy /ˈdʒɪpɪ/ (*colloq.*) diarrhoea affecting visitors to hot countries. [f. EGYPTIAN]

gipsy var. of GYPSY.

giraffe /dʒɪˈrɑːf/ *n.* a large four-legged African animal (*Giraffa camelopardalis*) with a long neck and forelegs. [f. F ult. f. Arab.]

gird /gɜːd/ *v.t.* (*past* & *p.p.* **girded** or **girt**) to encircle or attach or secure with a belt or band; to put (a cord) *round*; to enclose or encircle. —**gird up one's loins,** to prepare for action. [OE]

girder *n.* an iron or steel beam or compound structure for a bridge-span etc.; a beam supporting joists. [f. GIRD]

girdle[1] /ˈgɜːd(ə)l/ *n.* **1** a belt or cord used to gird the waist. **2** an elasticated corset not extending above the waist. **3** a thing that surrounds. **4** the bony support of a limb. —*v.t.* to surround with a girdle. [OE (as GIRD)]

girdle[2] /ˈgɜːd(ə)l/ *n.* (esp. *Sc.*) a round iron plate set over a fire or otherwise heated for baking etc. [var. of GRIDDLE]

girl /gɜːl/ *n.* **1** a female child. **2** a young woman. **3** a woman working in an office, factory, etc.; a female servant. **4**. a man's girl-friend. —**girl Friday,** see FRIDAY. **girl-friend** *n.* a regular female companion. —**girlhood** *n.*, **girlish** *adj.*, **girlishly** *adv.*, **girlishness** *n.* [perh. cogn. with LG *gör* child]

girlie *n.* a little girl (as a term of endearment). —*adj.* (of a publication etc.) depicting young women in erotic poses. [f. GIRL]

giro /ˈdʒaɪrəʊ/ *n.* (*pl.* **-os**) a system of credit transfer between banks, post offices, etc. [G f. It., = circulation (of money)]

girt see GIRD.

girth /gɜːθ/ *n.* **1** the distance round a thing. **2** a strap round the body of a horse etc. securing the saddle etc. [f. ON (as GIRD)]

gist /dʒɪst/ *n.* the main substance or essence *of* a matter. [OF (*gesir* lie f. L *jacēre*)]

git /gɪt/ *n.* (*slang*) a silly or contemptible person. [var. of *get* fool]

give /gɪv/ *v.t./i.* (*past* **gave**; *p.p.* **given** /ˈgɪv(ə)n/) **1** to transfer the possession of gratuitously; to cause to receive or have; to supply. **2** to deliver (a message); to render (a benefit); to assign; to pledge (one's word etc.); to cause to undergo or experience. **3** to make over in exchange or payment. **4** to devote, to dedicate. **5** to utter; to declare (judgement etc.) authoritatively; (*colloq.*) to tell what one knows. **6** to perform (an action or effort); to affect with this. **7** to provide (a meal etc.) as host. **8** to present or offer (news, a sign, etc.); to perform (a play or lecture etc.) in public; (usu. in *p.p.*) to grant or specify. **9** to yield as a product or result. **10** to be the source of. **11** (of a window or road etc.) to look or lead (*on to*, *into*, etc.). **12** to lose firmness, to be flexible, to yield when pressed or pulled. —**give and take,** exchange of talk or ideas; willingness to make concessions. **give away,** to transfer as a gift; to hand over (the bride) to the bridegroom at a wedding; to reveal (a secret etc.) unintentionally. **give-away** *n.* (*colloq.*) a thing given as a gift or at a low price; an unintentional disclosure. **give in,** to yield, to acknowledge defeat; to hand in (a document etc.) to the proper official. **give it to,** (*colloq.*) to scold or punish (a person). **give me,** (in *imper.*) I prefer or admire. **given name,** (*US*) a first or Christian name. **give off,** to emit (fumes etc.). **give or take,** (*colloq.*) to accept as a margin of error in estimating. **give out,** to distribute; to announce, to emit; to be exhausted, to run short. **give over,** to devote, to hand over; (*colloq.*) to stop or desist. **give tongue,** to speak one's thoughts; (of hounds) to bark, especially on tracing a scent. **give up,** to cease from effort or activity; to part with; to resign or surrender; to renounce hope (of); to pronounce incurable or insoluble; to deliver (a fugitive etc.) to pursuers etc.; to abandon or addict (*oneself to*). **give way,** to yield under pressure; to give precedence. —**giver** *n.* [OE]

gizzard /ˈgɪzəd/ *n.* a bird's second stomach for

grinding food; the muscular stomach of some fish, insects, molluscs, etc. [f. OF f. L *gigeria* cooked entrails of fowl]

glacé /ˈglæseɪ/ *adj.* **1** (of fruit) iced or sugared. **2** (of cloth etc.) smooth, polished. —**glacé icing,** icing made from icing sugar and water. [F, = iced (as foll.)]

glacial /ˈgleɪʃ(ə)l/ *adj.* **1** of ice; characterized or produced by ice. **2** cold and forbidding. —**glacial period,** a period when an unusually large area was covered by an ice-sheet. —**glacially** *adv.* [F, or f. L (*glacies* ice)]

glaciated /ˈgleɪsɪeɪtɪd/ *adj.* covered with glaciers or an ice-sheet; affected by the friction of moving ice. —**glaciation** /-ˈeɪʃ(ə)n/ *n.* [f. L *glaciare* freeze (as GLACIAL)]

glacier /ˈglæsɪə(r)/ *n.* a slowly moving river or mass of ice formed by an accumulation of snow on higher ground. [F (as GLACIAL)]

glad *adj.* **1** pleased (usu. *predic.*); expressing or causing pleasure. **2** ready and willing. —**be glad of,** to find useful. **glad eye,** (*slang*) an amorous glance. **glad hand,** (*colloq.*) a hearty welcome. **glad rags,** (*colloq.*) best clothes. —**gladly** *adv.*, **gladness** *n.* [OE]

gladden /ˈglæd(ə)n/ *v.t.* to make glad. [f. prec.]

glade *n.* an open space in a forest. [orig. unkn.]

gladiator /ˈglædɪeɪtə(r)/ *n.* a trained fighter in ancient Roman shows. —**gladiatorial** /-əˈtɔːrɪəl/ *adj.* [L (*gladius* sword)]

gladiolus /glædɪˈəʊləs/ *n.* (*pl.* **-li** /-laɪ/) a plant of the genus *Gladiolus*, with spikes of flowers and sword-shaped leaves. [L., dim. of *gladius* sword]

gladsome *adj.* (*poetic*) cheerful, joyous. [f. GLAD + -SOME]

Gladstone bag a case for clothes etc. hinged to open flat into two approximately equal compartments. [f. W. E. *Gladstone*, British statesman (d. 1898)]

glair *n.* white of egg; a viscous substance made from or resembling this. [f. OF, ult. f. L *clarus* clear]

glamorize /ˈglæməraɪz/ *v.t.* to make glamorous or attractive. [f. foll.]

glamour /ˈglæmə(r)/ *n.* **1** alluring beauty. **2** attractive and exciting qualities. —**glamorous** *adj.* [var. of GRAMMAR in obs. sense 'magic']

glance /glɑːns/ *v.t./i.* **1** to look briefly. **2** to strike at an angle and glide *off* an object. **3** (usu. with *at*) to refer briefly or indirectly to (a subject). **4** (of a light etc.) to flash or dart. —*n.* **1** a brief look. **2** a flash or gleam. **3** a glancing stroke in cricket. [prob. f. OF *glacier* to slip (as GLACIER)]

gland *n.* an organ secreting substances that are to be used in the body or expelled from it; a similar organ in a plant. [f. F f. L *glandulae* throat-glands]

glanders /ˈglændəz/ *n.pl.* a contagious disease of horses and related animals. [f. OF *glandre* (as GLAND)]

glandular /ˈglændjʊlə(r)/ *adj.* of a gland or glands. —**glandular fever,** an infectious disease with swelling of the lymph-glands. [f. F (as GLAND)]

glare /gleə(r)/ *v.i.* **1** to look fiercely or fixedly. **2** to shine oppressively. —*n.* **1** a fierce or fixed look. **2** an oppressive light; tawdry brilliance. [f. MDu. or MLG]

glaring *adj.* **1** shining oppressively. **2** obvious or conspicuous. —**glaringly** *adv.* [f. prec.]

glasnost /ˈglæznɒst/ *n.* openness as a policy (esp. since 1985) in the USSR in reporting news etc. [f. Russ., = publicity]

glass /glɑːs/ *n.* **1** a hard usually brittle and transparent substance made by fusing sand with soda or potash and other ingredients; a substance of similar properties, e.g. fibreglass. **2** glass utensils, ornaments, windows, greenhouses, etc. **3** an object made (partly) of glass; a glass drinking-vessel or its contents; a mirror; a lens; a barometer. **4** (in *pl.*) spectacles, binoculars. —*v.t.* to fit with glass. **glass-blowing** *n.* shaping semi-molten glass by blowing air into it through a tube. **glass-cloth** *n.* a cloth for drying glasses. **glass fibre,** a fabric made from or plastic reinforced by glass filaments. **glass-paper** *n.* paper coated with glass particles, for smoothing or polishing. **glass wool,** a mass of fine glass fibres for packing and insulation. [OE]

glasshouse *n.* **1** a greenhouse. **2** (*slang*) a military prison.

glassware *n.* articles made of glass.

glassy *adj.* **1** like glass. **2** (of the eye or expression) dull and fixed. —**glassily** *adv.*, **glassiness** *n.* [f. GLASS]

Glaswegian /glæzˈwiːdʒ(ə)n/ *adj.* of Glasgow, a city in western Scotland. —*n.* a native of Glasgow. [f. *Glasgow* after *Norwegian*]

glaucoma /glɔːˈkəʊmə/ *n.* a condition caused by increased pressure of the fluid within the eyeball, causing weakening or loss of sight. [L f. Gk (*glaukos* greyish-blue)]

glaze *v.t./i.* **1** to fit or cover with glass. **2** to coat with a glossy surface. **3** to cover (the eye) with a film. **4** to become glassy. —*n.* **1** a vitreous substance for glazing pottery. **2** a smooth shiny coating on materials or food. **3** a coat of transparent paint to modify an underlying tone. **4** a surface formed by glazing. [f. GLASS]

glazier /ˈgleɪzɪə(r)/ *n.* a person who glazes windows etc. professionally. [f. prec.]

GLC *abbr.* Greater London Council (1963–86).

gleam *n.* **1** a subdued or transient light. **2** a faint or momentary show (*of* humour, hope, etc.). —*v.i.* to emit gleams. [OE]

glean *v.t./i.* **1** to acquire (facts etc.) in small amounts. **2** to gather (corn left by reapers). —**gleaner** *n.* [f. OF *glener*, prob. f. Celtic]

gleanings *n.pl.* things gleaned. [f. prec.]

glebe /gli:b/ *n.* a portion of land going with a benefice and providing revenue. [f. L *gl(a)eba* clod, soil]

glee *n.* **1** lively or triumphant joy. **2** a part-song for three or more (usu. male) voices. —**glee club,** a society for singing part-songs. [OE]

gleeful *adj.* joyful. —**gleefully** *adv.* [f. GLEE + -FUL]

glen *n.* a narrow valley. [f. Gaelic & Ir.]

glengarry /glenˈgærɪ/ *n.* a kind of Highland cap with a pointed front. [f. *Glengarry* in Highland]

glib *adj.* fluent but insincere. —**glibly** *adv.*, **glibness** *n.* [rel. to obs. *glibbery* slippery, perh. imit.]

glide *v.t./i.* **1** to move smoothly and continuously; to pass gradually or imperceptibly. **2** to fly in a glider or (of aircraft) without engine-power. —*n.* a gliding movement. —**glide path,** an aircraft's line of descent to land, especially as indicated by ground radar. [OE]

glider /ˈglaɪdə(r)/ *n.* a fixed-wing aircraft that is not power-driven when in flight. [f. GLIDE]

glimmer *n.* **1.** a faint or intermittent light. **2.** (also **glimmering**) a gleam (*of* hope etc.). —*v.i.* to shine faintly or intermittently. [prob. f. Scand. (as GLEAM)]

glimpse *n.* a brief view (*of*); a faint transient appearance. —*v.t.* to have a brief view of. [corresp. to MHG *glimsen* (as prec.)]

glint *v.i.* to flash, to glitter. —*n.* a brief flash of light. [prob. f. Scand.]

glissade /glɪˈsɑ:d, -ˈseɪd/ *v.i.* **1** to make a controlled slide down a snow slope in mountaineering. **2** to make a gliding step in a dance. —*n.* a glissading movement or step. [F (*glisser* slide, slip)]

glisten /ˈglɪs(ə)n/ *v.i.* to shine like a wet or polished surface; to glitter, to sparkle. —*n.* glistening. [OE]

glitter *v.i.* **1** to sparkle. **2** to be showy or splendid. —*n.* a sparkle. [f. ON]

gloaming *n.* the evening twilight. [OE, rel. to GLOW]

gloat *v.i.* to look or ponder with greedy or malicious pleasure (*over* etc.). —*n.* the act of gloating. [perh. rel. to ON *glotta* grin]

global /ˈgləʊb(ə)l/ *adj.* **1** world-wide. **2** all-embracing. —**globally** *adv.* [F (as foll.)]

globe *n.* a spherical object, especially *the* earth, or a representation of it with a map on its surface; a thing shaped like this, e.g. a lamp-shade or a fish-bowl. —**globe-fish** *n.* a fish of the family Tetraodontidae, that inflates itself into a globe form. **globe-flower** *n.* a plant of the genus *Trollius*, with spherical usually yellow flowers. **globe-trotter** *n.* one who travels widely. **globe-trotting** *n.* such travel. [F, or f. L *globus*]

globular /ˈglɒbjʊlə(r)/ *adj.* **1** globe-shaped. **2** composed of globules. [f. foll.]

globule /ˈglɒbju:l/ *n.* a small globe or round particle, a drop. [F, or f. L *globulus* (as GLOBE)]

globulin /ˈglɒbjʊlɪn/ *n.* a protein found usually associated with albumin in animal and plant tissues. [f. prec.]

glockenspiel /ˈglɒkənspɪəl/ *n.* a percussion instrument formed from a set of tuned metal bars each supported at two points but with both ends free and struck in the centre with small hand-held hammers. [G, = bell-play]

gloom *n.* **1** semi-darkness. **2** a feeling of sadness and depression. —*v.t./i.* to make, look, or be gloomy. [orig. unkn.; cf. GLUM]

gloomy *adj.* **1** dark or dim. **2** depressed; depressing. —**gloomily** *adv.*, **gloominess** *n.* [f. obs. *gloom* a frown f. prec.]

glorify /ˈglɔ:rɪfaɪ/ *v.t.* **1** to praise highly. **2** to worship with adoration and praise. **3** to make seem more splendid than it is. —**glorification** /-ˈkeɪʃ(ə)n/ *n.* [f. OF f. L (as GLORY)]

glorious /ˈglɔ:rɪəs/ *adj.* **1** possessing or conferring glory. **2** splendid, illustrious; excellent (often *iron.*). —**gloriously** *adv.* [f. AF (as foll.)]

glory /ˈglɔ:rɪ/ *n.* **1** fame and honour. **2** adoration and praise in worship. **3** resplendent beauty, magnificence, etc.; an exalted or prosperous state. **4** a thing that brings renown, a special distinction. **5** the halo of a saint etc. —*v.i.* to take great pride (*in*). —**glory-hole** *n.* (*slang*) an untidy room or cupboard etc. **go to glory,** (*slang*) to die, to be destroyed. [f. OF f. L *gloria*]

Glos. *abbr.* Gloucestershire.

gloss[1] *n.* **1** the lustre of a surface. **2** a deceptively attractive appearance. —*v.t.* to make glossy. —**gloss over,** to seek to conceal. **gloss paint,** paint giving a glossy finish. [orig. unkn.]

gloss[2] *n.* an explanatory comment added to a text, e.g. in the margin; a comment or paraphrase. —*v.t./i.* to make such a comment; to add a comment to (a text or word etc.). [f. OF f. L *glossa* f. Gk (as GLOTTIS)]

glossary /ˈglɒsərɪ/ *n.* a dictionary or list of technical or special words; a collection of glosses. [f. L (as GLOSS[2])]

glossy *adj.* having a gloss, shiny. —**glossily** *adv.*, **glossiness** *n.* [f. GLOSS[1]]

glottal /ˈglɒt(ə)l/ *adj.* of the glottis. —**glottal stop,** the sound produced by the sudden opening or shutting of the glottis. [f. foll.]

glottis /ˈglɒtɪs/ *n.* the opening at the upper end of the windpipe between the vocal cords. [f. Gk *glōtta* var. of *glōssa* tongue]

Gloucester /ˈglɒstə(r)/ *n.* a cheese made in Gloucestershire (now usu. **double Gloucester**, originally a richer kind). [f. *Gloucester* city in SW England]

glove /glʌv/ *n.* a hand-covering, usually with separate fingers, for protection, warmth, etc.; a boxing-glove. *v.t.* to cover or provide with a glove or gloves. —**with the gloves off**, arguing or contending in earnest. [OE]

glover /ˈglʌvə(r)/ *n.* a glove-maker. [f. prec.]

glow /gləʊ/ *v.i.* **1** to emit light and heat without flame. **2** to shine like a thing intensely heated; to show a warm colour. **3** to burn *with* or indicate bodily heat or fervour. —*n.* a glowing state; warmth of colour; ardour. —**glow-worm** *n.* a beetle (*Lampyris noctiluca*) whose wingless female emits light from the end of the abdomen. [OE]

glower /ˈglaʊə(r)/ *v.i.* to look angrily (*at*). [orig. unkn.]

gloxinia /glɒkˈsɪnɪə/ *n.* an American tropical plant of the genus *Gloxinia*, with bell-shaped flowers. [f. B. P. *Gloxin*, 18th-c. German botanist]

glucose /ˈglu:kəʊs, -əʊz/ *n.* a sugar found in the blood or in fruit-juice etc. [F, f. Gk *gleukos* sweet wine (*glukus* sweet)]

glue /glu:/ *n.* a sticky substance used as an adhesive. —*v.t.* **1** to attach with glue. **2** to hold closely. —**glue-sniffer** *n.* one who inhales the fumes of plastic glue as a narcotic. **glue-sniffing** *n.* —**gluey** *adj.* [f. OF f. L *gluten*]

glum *adj.* dejected, sullen. —**glumly** *adv.*, **glumness** *n.* [rel. to dial. *glum* v. frown, var. of GLOOM]

glut *v.t.* (**-tt-**) **1** to satisfy fully with food; to sate. **2** to overstock (a market). —*n.* an excessive supply. [prob. f. OF *gloutir* swallow f. L (as GLUTTON)]

glutamate /ˈglu:təmeɪt/ *n.* a salt or ester of glutamic acid, especially the sodium salt used to flavour food. [f. foll.]

glutamic acid /glu:ˈtæmɪk/ an amino acid normally found in proteins. [f. foll. + AMINE]

gluten /ˈglu:t(ə)n/ *n.* **1** the viscous part of flour left when the starch is removed. **2** a viscous animal secretion. [F f. L, = glue]

glutinous /ˈglu:tɪnəs/ *adj.* sticky, gluelike, viscous. [f. F or L. (as prec.)]

glutton /ˈglʌt(ə)n/ *n.* **1** an excessive eater; a person insatiably eager (*for* work etc.). **2** the wolverine (see entry). —**gluttonous** *adj.* [f. OF f. L (*gluttire* swallow)]

gluttony /ˈglʌtənɪ/ *n.* the character or conduct of a glutton. [f. prec.]

glyceride /ˈglɪsəraɪd/ *n.* a compound ester of glycerine. [f. foll.]

glycerine /ˈglɪsəri:n/ *n.* (also **glycerol**) a colourless sweet viscous liquid obtained from fats, used as an ointment etc. and in explosives. [f. F f. Gk *glukeros* sweet]

gm *abbr.* gram(s).

G-man /ˈdʒi:mæn/ *n.* (*US slang*) a federal criminal-investigation officer. [f. *G*overnment + MAN]

GMT *abbr.* Greenwich Mean Time.

gnarled /nɑ:ld/ *adj.* (of a tree, hands, etc.) knobbly, rugged, twisted. [rel. to KNURL]

gnash /næʃ/ *v.t./i.* to grind (one's teeth); (of the teeth) to strike together. [f. ON (imit.)]

gnat /næt/ *n.* a small two-winged biting fly of the genus *Culex*. [OE]

gnaw /nɔ:/ *v.t./i.* (*p.t.* **gnawed** or **gnawn**) **1** to bite persistently. **2** (of a destructive agent) to corrode or consume. **3** (of pain etc.) to hurt continuously. [OE]

gneiss /naɪs, gnaɪs/ *n.* a coarse-grained metamorphic rock of quartz, feldspar, and mica. [G]

gnome /nəʊm/ *n.* **1** a kind of dwarf in fairy-tales, living underground and guarding the treasures of the earth. **2** a figure of such a dwarf as a garden ornament. **3** (in *pl.*) persons (esp. financiers) with secret influence. [F, f. L *gnomus* (word invented by Paracelsus)]

gnomic /ˈnəʊmɪk/ *adj.* of maxims, sententious. [f. Gk (*gnōmē* opinion)]

gnomon /ˈnəʊmən/ *n.* the rod or pin etc. of a sundial, showing the time by its shadow. [F, or f. L f. Gk, = indicator]

gnostic /ˈnɒstɪk/ *adj.* **1** of knowledge. **2** having special mystical knowledge. **3 Gnostic**, of the Gnostics or Gnosticism. —**Gnostic** *n.* an adherent of a heretical movement in the early Christian Church, claiming mystical knowledge. [f. L f. Gk (*gnōsis* knowledge)]

GNP *abbr.* gross national product.

gnu /nu:/ *n.* an oxlike antelope of the genus *Connochaetes*, also called a wildebeest. [ult. f. Kaffir]

go[1] /gəʊ/ *v.i.* (*past* **went**; *p.p.* **gone** /gɒn/; *partic.* **going**) **1** to begin to move, to be moving from one position or point in time to another; (with *partic.*) to make a trip for (a specified purpose). **2** to lie or extend in a certain direction. **3** to be functioning, moving, etc. **4** to make a specified motion or sound. **5** to be in a specified state, habitually or for a time; to pass into a specified condition, to escape *free*, *unnoticed*, etc. **6** (of time or a distance) to pass, to be traversed. **7** to be regularly kept or put, to belong; to fit, to be able to be put. **8** (of a number) to be contained in another, especially without a remainder. **9** to be current; to be on the average. **10** to fare, (of events) to turn out; to take a certain course or views. **11** to have a specified form or wording.

12 to be successful; (*colloq.*) to be acceptable or permitted, to be accepted without question. 13 to be sold. 14 (of money or supplies etc.) to be spent or used up. 15 to be relinquished or abolished. 16 to fail or decline; to give way, to collapse. 17 to die. 18 to be allotted or awarded. 19 to contribute, to tend, to extend, to reach. 20 to carry an action or commitment to a certain point. 21 (in *imper.*, *colloq.* or *US*) to proceed to. —*n.* 1 animation, dash. 2 a turn or try; an attack *of* an illness; a portion served at one time. 3 a success. 4 (*colloq.*) vigorous activity. 5 (*colloq.*) a state of affairs. —*adj.* (*colloq.*) functioning properly. —**go ahead,** to proceed immediately. **go-ahead** *n.* permission to proceed; (*adj.*) enterprising. **go along with,** to agree with. **go and,** (*colloq.*) to be so unwise etc. as to. **go back on,** to fail to keep (a promise etc.). **go-between** *n.* an intermediary. **go by,** to be dependent on; to be guided by. **go-cart** *n.* a simple four-wheeled structure for a child to play on. **go down,** to descend or sink; to be swallowed; to be written down; to leave university; to find acceptance (*with*); to become ill (*with* a disease). **go for,** to like, to prefer, to choose; to pass or be accounted as (*little* etc.); (*slang*) to attack. **go-getter** *n.* (*colloq.*) a pushful enterprising person. **go-go** *adj.* (*colloq.*) very active or energetic. **go-go dancer,** a performer of lively erotic dances at a night-club etc. **go in for,** to compete or engage in. **go into,** to become a member of (a profession etc.) or a patient in (a hospital etc.); to investigate (a matter). **go a long way,** to have much effect *towards*; (of supplies) to last long; (of money) to buy much. **go off,** to explode; to deteriorate; to fall asleep; (of an event) to proceed *well* etc.; to begin to dislike. **go on,** to continue (*doing*); to persevere (*with*); to talk at great length; to proceed next *to do*; (*colloq.*) to nag (*at*). **go on** *or* **upon,** to judge by, to base conclusions on. **go out,** to be extinguished; to go to social functions; to be broadcast; to cease to be fashionable; (*US colloq.*) to lose consciousness; (of the heart etc.) to feel sympathy. **go round,** to be large enough or sufficient. **go slow,** to work at a deliberately slow pace as an industrial protest. **go-slow** *n.* such action. **go through,** to examine or revise; to perform or undergo; to spend or use up (money or supplies). **go through with,** to complete (an undertaking). **go to,** to attend (a school, church, etc.). **go under,** to succumb, to fail. **go up,** to rise in price; to explode, to burn; to enter university. **go with,** to match or suit, to harmonize or belong with. **go without,** to abstain from, to tolerate the lack (of). **on the go,** (*colloq.*) in constant motion, active. [OE; *went* orig. past of WEND]

go[2] /gəʊ/ *n.* a Japanese board-game of territorial possession, played on a board of 18 × 18 squares, each player having about 200 pieces. [Jap.]

goad *n.* 1 a spiked stick for urging cattle. 2 a thing that torments or incites. —*v.t.* 1 to urge with a goad. 2 to irritate; to drive or stimulate (*into* action etc.). [OE]

goal *n.* 1 a structure into or through which a ball is to be driven in certain games. 2 a point or points scored thus. 3 an objective; a destination; the point where a race ends. —**goal-line** *n.* a line forming the end boundary of a field of play. **goal-post** *n.* either of the pair of posts marking the limits of a goal. [perh. = obs. *gol* boundary]

goalie /ˈgəʊlɪ/ *n.* (*colloq.*) a goalkeeper. [f. GOAL]

goalkeeper *n.* a player defending the goal.

goat *n.* 1 a small horned ruminant of the genus *Capra*. 2 **the Goat,** the constellation or sign of the zodiac Capricorn. 3 a licentious man. 4 (*colloq.*) a foolish person. —**get a person's goat,** (*slang*) to annoy him. [OE]

goatee /gəʊˈtiː/ *n.* a small pointed beard like a goat's. [f. prec.]

goatherd *n.* one who tends goats.

goatsucker *n.* the nightjar.

gob[1] *n.* (*slang*) the mouth. —**gob-stopper** *n.* a large hard sweet for sucking. [perh. f. Gael. & Ir., = beak, mouth]

gob[2] *n.* (*vulgar*) a clot of a slimy substance. [f. OF *go(u)be* mouthful]

gobbet /ˈgɒbɪt/ *n.* an extract from a text, set for translation or comment. [f. OF *gobet* (as prec.)]

gobble[1] *v.t./i.* to eat hurriedly and noisily. [prob. f. GOB[2]]

gobble[2] *v.i.* 1 (of a turkey-cock) to make a gurgling sound in the throat. 2 to speak thus. [imit.]

gobbledegook /ˈgɒb(ə)ldɪguːk/ *n.* (*slang*) pompous or unintelligible official or professional jargon. [imit. of turkey-cock]

goblet /ˈgɒblɪt/ *n.* a drinking-vessel, especially of glass, with a foot and stem. [f. OF (*gobel* cup)]

goblin /ˈgɒblɪn/ *n.* a mischievous ugly demon in folklore. [f. L *Gobelinus* name of spirit, rel. to G *kobold* demon in mines]

goby /ˈgəʊbɪ/ *n.* a small fish of the genus *Gobius*, with the ventral fins joined to form a disc or sucker. [f. L *gōbius* f. Gk *kōbios*, = GUDGEON]

god *n.* 1 a superhuman being worshipped as having power over nature and human affairs. 2 **God,** the supreme being, creator and ruler of the universe in the Christian and other monotheistic religions. 3 an image of a god, an idol. 4 a person or thing greatly admired or adored. —**the gods,** (*colloq.*) the gallery of a theatre. **God-fearing** *adj.* earnestly religious. **God forbid,** may it not be so. **God-forsaken** *adj.* dismal, wretched. **God knows,** we (or I) cannot know. **God Save the King** *or* **Queen,** the British national anthem. **God willing,** if circumstances allow. [OE]

godchild *n.* a child or person in relation to a godparent or godparents.

god-daughter *n.* a female godchild.

goddess /ˈgɒdɪs/ *n.fem.* **1** a female deity. **2** an adored woman. [f. GOD]

godetia /gəˈdiːʃə/ *n.* a showy-flowered hardy annual of the genus *Godetia*. [f. C. H. *Godet*, Swiss botanist (d. 1879)]

godfather *n.* **1** a male godparent. **2** a person directing an illegal organization.

godhead *n.* **1** divine nature, deity. **2 the Godhead,** God. [f. GOD + -HEAD]

godless *adj.* not believing in God or a god; impious, wicked. —**godlessly** *adv.*, **godlessness** *n.* [f. GOD + -LESS]

godlike *adj.* like God or a god.

godly *adj.* pious, devout. —**godliness** *n.* [f. GOD]

godmother *n.* a female godparent.

godown /gəˈdaʊn/ *n.* a warehouse in eastern Asia, especially in India. [f. Port. f. Malay]

godparent *n.* a person who sponsors another (especially a child) at baptism.

godsend *n.* a piece of unexpected good luck having a decisive effect, a useful or effective acquisition.

godson *n.* a male godchild.

Godspeed *n.* an expression of good wishes to a person starting a journey.

godwit *n.* a wading bird of the genus *Limosa*, like the curlew but with a straight or slightly upcurved bill. [orig. unkn.]

goer /ˈgəʊə(r)/ *n.* **1** a person or thing that goes. **2** a lively or persevering person. **3** (*in comb.*) a regular attender. [f. GO¹]

goggle *v.t./i.* **1** to look with wide-open eyes. **2** (of the eyes) to be rolled, to project. **3** to roll (the eyes). —*adj.* (of the eyes) protuberant, rolling. —*n.* (in *pl.*) enclosed transparent shields for protecting the eyes from glare, dust, etc. [prob. imit. (cf. JOG)]

going /ˈgəʊɪŋ/ *n.* **1** the state of the ground for walking or riding on. **2** rate of progress. —*adj.* in action; existing, functioning, available; currently valid. —**get going,** to begin, to start. **going on (for),** approaching (a time, age, etc.). **going-over** *n.* (*colloq.*) an inspection or overhaul, (*slang*) a beating. **goings-on** *n.pl.* strange behaviour or events. **going to,** about to, intending or likely to. **to be going on with,** to start with, for present needs. **while the going is good,** while circumstances are favourable. [f. GO¹]

goitre /ˈgɔɪtə(r)/ *n.* abnormal enlargement of the thyroid glands. [F, ult. f. L *guttur* throat]

go-kart *n.* = KART.

gold /gəʊld/ *n.* **1** a precious yellow malleable ductile metallic element of high density, symbol Au, atomic number 79. **2** its yellow colour. **3** coins or articles made of gold, wealth; a gold medal, usually given as a first prize. **4** the bull's-eye of an archery target; a shot that strikes this. **5** something very good or precious. —*adj.* of or coloured like gold. —**gold-digger** *n.* (*slang*) a woman who uses her attractions to wheedle money out of men. **gold-dust** *n.* gold in fine particles as often found naturally. **gold-field** *n.* an area where gold is found. **gold mine,** a place where gold is mined; a source of wealth. **gold plate,** vessels of gold; material plated with gold. **gold-plate** *v.t.* to plate with gold. **gold reserve,** gold held by a central bank to guarantee the value of a country's currency. **gold-rush** *n.* a rush to a newly discovered gold-field, especially the transcontinental journey to California after the discovery of gold there in 1848. **gold standard,** a system by which the value of money is based on that of gold. [OE]

goldcrest *n.* a very small bird (*Regulus regulus*) with a golden crest.

golden *adj.* **1** made of gold. **2** yielding gold. **3** coloured or shining like gold. **4** precious, excellent. —**golden age,** a period of great prosperity or cultural achievement. **golden eagle,** a large eagle (*Aquila chrysaetos*) with yellow-tipped head-feathers. **golden handshake,** a gratuity as compensation for dismissal or early retirement. **golden jubilee,** a 50th anniversary. **golden mean,** neither too much nor too little. **golden rod,** a plant of the genus *Solidago*, with yellow flower-spikes. **golden rule,** a basic principle of action. **golden section,** the name given in the 19th c. to the proportion (derived from a Euclidean line-division) in which the third term is the sum of the first and second (A : B = B : A + B). **golden syrup,** pale treacle. **golden wedding,** the 50th anniversary of a wedding. [f. GOLD]

goldfinch *n.* a songbird (*Carduelis carduelis*) with a yellow band across each wing.

goldfish *n.* a small reddish Chinese carp (*Carassius auratus*), often kept as an ornamental fish.

goldsmith *n.* one who works in gold.

golf /gɒlf/ *n.* a game in which a small hard ball is struck with various clubs into a series of small cylindrical holes (now usually 18 or 9) on smooth greens at varying distances apart and separated by fairways, rough ground, hazards, etc. —*v.i.* to play golf. —**golf ball,** a ball used in golf; a spherical unit carrying the type in some electric typewriters. —**golf-course** *or* **-links** *n.* an area of land on which golf is played. —**golfer** *n.* [Sc.; orig. unkn.]

golliwog /ˈgɒlɪwɒg/ *n.* a black-faced soft male doll with bright clothes and fuzzy hair. [perh. f. GOLLY[1] + dial. *polliwog* tadpole]

golly[1] *int.* expressing surprise. [euphem. for *God*]

golly[2] *n.* a golliwog. [abbr.]

golosh var. of GALOSH.

gonad /ˈgəʊnæd/ *n.* an animal organ producing gametes, e.g. a testis or ovary. [f. Gk *gonē*, *gonos*, generation, seed]

gondola /ˈgɒndələ/ *n.* **1** a light pleasure-boat, much ornamented, with a high rising and curving stem and stern-post, used on the canals of Venice and propelled by one man with a single oar, standing near the stern. **2** an elongated car attached to the under side of a dirigible balloon or airship. [It. f. dial., = rock, roll]

gondolier /gɒndəˈlɪə(r)/ *n.* a rower of a gondola. [F f. It. (as prec.)]

gone *p.p.* of GO[1].

goner /ˈgɒnə(r)/ *n.* (*slang*) a person or thing that is dead, ruined, or irretrievably lost. [f. prec.]

gonfalon /ˈgɒnfələn/ *n.* a banner, often with streamers, hung from a crossbar. [f. It. f. Gmc]

gong *n.* **1** a large metal disc with a turned rim giving a resonant note when struck, especially one used as a signal for meals. **2** a percussion instrument generally comprising a large hanging bronze disc with a bossed centre which is struck in the middle with a soft-headed drumstick. **3** a saucer-shaped bell. **4** (*slang*) a medal. [f. Malay (imit.)]

goniometer /gəʊnɪˈɒmɪtə(r)/ *n.* an instrument for measuring angles. [f. F f. Gk *gōnia* angle + -METER]

gonorrhoea /gɒnəˈriːə/ *n.* a venereal disease with an inflammatory discharge from the urethra or vagina. [L f. Gk (*gonos* semen, *rhoia* flux)]

goo *n.* (*slang*) **1** a viscous or sticky substance. **2** sickly sentiment. [perh. f. slang *burgoo* porridge]

good /gʊd/ *adj.* (*compar.* BETTER; *superl.* BEST) **1** having the right or desirable qualities, satisfactory. **2** right, proper, expedient. **3** commendable, worthy (esp. in *my good man* etc.). **4** morally correct, virtuous; (of a child) well-behaved. **5** agreeable, enjoyable. **6** suitable, efficient, competent. **7** thorough, considerable. **8** valid, genuine; financially sound. **9** not less than. **10** used in exclamations (*good God!*, *gracious!*, etc.). —*adv.* (*US colloq.*) well. —*n.* **1** a good quality or circumstance, especially what is beneficial or morally right. **2** (in *pl.*) movable property or merchandise; things to be transported or supplied. —**the good,** (*pl.*) good people. **all in good time,** in due course but without haste. **as good as,** practically. **for good (and all),** finally, permanently. **good afternoon, day,** etc., forms used in greeting or parting. **good faith,** an honest or sincere intention. **good for,** beneficial to, having a good effect on; able to undertake or pay. **good-for-nothing** *adj.* worthless; (*n.*) a worthless person. **Good Friday,** the Friday before Easter Sunday, commemorating the Crucifixion. **good-looking** *adj.* having a pleasing appearance. **in good time,** with no risk of being late. **good will,** an intention that good shall result (see also GOODWILL). **to the good,** having as a profit or benefit. [OE]

goodbye /gʊdˈbaɪ/, *int.* farewell (expressing good wishes on parting, ending a telephone conversation, etc.). —*n.* a parting, a farewell. [contr. of *God be with you*]

goodly /ˈgʊdlɪ/ *adj.* **1** handsome. **2** of imposing size etc. —**goodliness** *n.* [OE (as GOOD)]

goodness *n.* **1** virtue, excellence; kindness. **2** used instead of 'God' in exclamations. [OE (as GOOD)]

goodwill *n.* **1** kindly feeling. **2** the established reputation of a business etc. as enhancing its value.

goody *n.* **1** something good or attractive, especially to eat. **2** (*colloq.*) a good or favoured person. —*int.* expressing childish delight. [f. GOOD]

goody-goody *adj.* obtrusively or smugly virtuous. —*n.* a goody-goody person. [f. GOOD]

gooey *adj.* (*slang*) **1** viscous or sticky. **2** sentimental. [f. GOO]

goof *n.* (*slang*) **1** a foolish or stupid person. **2** a mistake. —*v.t./i.* (*slang*) **1** to blunder, to bungle. **2** to idle. —**goofy** *adj.* [f. F f. It. f. L *gufus* coarse]

googly /ˈguːglɪ/ *n.* a ball in cricket bowled so as to bounce in an unexpected direction. [orig. unkn.]

goon *n.* (*slang*) **1** a stupid person. **2** a hired ruffian. [perh. f. dial. *gooney* booby; influenced by subhuman cartoon character 'Alice the *Goon*']

goosander /guːˈsændə(r)/ *n.* a duck (*Mergus merganser*) with a sharp serrated bill. [app. f. foll.]

goose *n.* (*pl.* **geese**) **1** a web-footed bird of the genus *Anser* or subfamily Anserinae, between a duck and a swan in size; the female of this (cf. GANDER); the flesh of the goose as food. **2** a simpleton. **3** (*pl.* **gooses**) a tailor's smoothing-iron (with a handle like a goose's neck). —**goose-flesh** *or* **-pimples** *ns.* a bristling state of the skin due to cold or fright. **goose-neck** *n.* a thing shaped like the neck of a goose. **goose-step** *n.* a parade-step of marching soldiers with the legs kept straight. [OE]

gooseberry /ˈgʊzbərɪ/ *n.* a small green sour berry; the thorny shrub bearing it (*Ribes grossularia*). —**play gooseberry,** to be an unwanted extra person. [perh. f. prec.]

gopher /ˈgəʊfə(r)/ *n.* **1** an American burrowing rodent of the genus *Geomys* or *Thomomys.* **2** a ground-squirrel of the genus *Citellus.* **3** a burrowing tortoise (*Testudo carolina*). [perh. f. Canadian F *gaufre* honeycomb]

Gordian /ˈgɔːdɪən/ *adj.* **cut the Gordian knot,** to solve a problem forcefully. [f. *Gordius*, king of ancient Phrygia, who tied an intricate knot that was later cut, rather than untied, by Alexander the Great]

gore[1] *n.* blood shed and clotted. [OE, = dirt]

gore[2] *v.t.* to pierce with a horn, tusk, etc. [orig. unkn.]

gore[3] *n.* a wedge-shaped piece in a garment; a triangular or tapering piece in an umbrella etc. —*v.t.* to shape with a gore. [OE, = triangle of land]

gorge *n.* **1** a narrow opening between hills. **2** gorging, a surfeit. **3** the contents of the stomach. —*v.t./i.* **1** to feed or devour greedily. **2** to satiate; to choke up. —**one's gorge rises at,** one is sickened by. [f. OF, = throat]

gorgeous /ˈgɔːdʒəs/ *adj.* richly coloured, sumptuous; (*colloq.*) strikingly beautiful; (*colloq.*) very pleasant, splendid. —**gorgeously** *adv.*, **gorgeousness** *n.* [f. OF *gorgias* elegant]

gorgon /ˈgɔːgən/ *n.* **1** a frightening woman. **2 Gorgon,** (*Gk myth.*) any of three sisters with snakes for hair, whose look turned the beholder to stone. [f. L f. Gk *Gorgō* (*gorgos* terrible)]

Gorgonzola /gɔːgənˈzəʊlə/ *n.* a kind of rich blue-veined cheese. [f. *Gorgonzola* in N. Italy]

gorilla /gəˈrɪlə/ *n.* a large powerful anthropoid ape. [perh. Afr. = wild man, in Gk account of Hanno's voyage (5th or 6th c. BC), adapted as specific name 1847]

gormandize /ˈgɔːməndaɪz/ *v.t./i.* to eat greedily. —**gormandizer** *n.* [f. GOURMAND]

gormless /ˈgɔːmlɪs/ *adj.* (*colloq.*) foolish, lacking sense. [f. dial. *gaum* understanding]

gorse *n.* furze. —**gorsy** *adj.* [OE]

Gorsedd /ˈgɔːseð/ *n.* a meeting of Welsh etc. bards and druids (especially as the preliminary to an eisteddfod). [Welsh, lit. 'throne']

gory /ˈgɔːrɪ/ *adj.* covered with blood; involving bloodshed. —**gorily** *adv.*, **goriness** *n.* [f. GORE[1]]

gosh *int.* expressing surprise. [euphem. for *God*]

goshawk /ˈgɒshɔːk/ *n.* a large hawk (*Accipiter gentilis*) with short wings. [OE (as GOOSE, HAWK[1])]

gosling /ˈgɒzlɪŋ/ *n.* a young goose. [dim. of GOOSE]

gospel /ˈgɒspəl/ *n.* **1** the tidings of redemption preached by Christ. **2 Gospel,** each of the four books in which this was set forth, attributed to Matthew, Mark, Luke, and John. **3** a thing that may safely be believed; a principle one acts upon or advocates. [OE (as GOOD, SPELL[1] = news)]

gossamer /ˈgɒsəmə(r)/ *n.* **1** the filmy substance of small spiders' webs. **2** delicate flimsy material. —*adj.* light and flimsy as gossamer. [app. f. GOOSE + SUMMER, (*goose summer*, St Martin's summer, i.e. early November)]

gossip /ˈgɒsɪp/ *n.* **1** casual talk or writing, especially about persons or social incidents. **2** a person indulging in gossip. —*v.i.* to talk or write gossip. —**gossip column,** a section of a newspaper devoted to gossip about well-known people. —**gossipy** *adj.* [OE, orig. = godparent (GOD, SIB)]

got *past & p.p.* of GET.

Goth /gɒθ/ *n.* a member of a Germanic tribe which invaded the Roman Empire from the east between the 3rd and 5th centuries. [f. L *Gothi* f. Gk f. Gothic]

Gothic /ˈgɒθɪk/ *adj.* **1** of the Goths. **2** in the style of architecture prevalent in western Europe in the 12th-16th c., characterized by pointed arches. **3** (*Print.*) of an old-fashioned German style of type, also known as 'black letter'. —*n.* **1** Gothic architecture or type. **2** the Gothic language. **3** Gothic type. —**Gothic novel** etc., an English genre of fiction, popular in the 18th-early 19th c., characterized by an atmosphere of mystery and horror and with a pseudo-medieval ('Gothic') setting. **Gothic revival,** the reintroduction in England of Gothic architecture towards the middle of the 19th c. [f. F or L (as GOTH)]

gotten see GET.

Götterdämmerung /gɜːtəˈdemərʊŋ/ *n.* the twilight of the gods (see TWILIGHT), the complete downfall of a regime etc. [G, esp. as title of opera by Wagner]

gouache /guːˈɑːʃ/ *n.* painting with opaque pigments ground in water and thickened with gum and honey; these pigments. [F, f. It. *guazzo*]

Gouda /ˈgaʊdə/ *n.* a flat round cheese with yellow rind, originally made at Gouda in Holland.

gouge /gaʊdʒ/ *n.* a chisel with a concave blade. —*v.t.* **1** to cut with or as with a gouge. **2** to scoop or force *out*. [F, f. L. *gubia*, perh. f. Celtic]

goulash /ˈguːlæʃ/ *n.* a stew of meat and vegetables highly seasoned with paprika. [f. Magyar, = herdsman's meat]

gourd /gʊəd/ *n.* 1 the fleshy usually large fruit of a trailing or climbing plant of the family Cucurbitaceae. 2 the dried rind of this fruit used as a bottle. [f. AF, ult. f. L *cucurbita*]

gourmand /ˈgʊəmənd/ *n.* 1 a glutton. 2 a gourmet. [f. OF; orig. unkn.]

gourmandise /ˈgʊəmɑ̃diːz/ *n.* gluttony. [F (as prec.)]

gourmet /ˈgʊəmeɪ/ *n.* a connoisseur of good or delicate food. [F, = wine-taster]

gout *n.* a disease with inflammation of the joints, especially of the big toe. —**gouty** *adj.* [f. OF f. L *gutta* drop]

govern /ˈgʌv(ə)n/ *v.t.* 1 to rule or control with authority, to conduct the policy and affairs of. 2 to influence or determine (a person or course of action etc.). 3 to restrain or control. 4 (*Gram.*, esp. of a verb or preposition) to have (a noun or its case) depending on it. [f. OF f. L *gubernare* f. Gk *kubernaō* steer]

governance /ˈgʌvənəns/ *n.* the act, manner, or function of governing. [f. OF (as prec.)]

governess /ˈgʌv(ə)nɪs/ *n.fem.* a woman employed to teach children in a private household. [f. OF (as GOVERNOR)]

government /ˈgʌvənmənt/ *n.* 1 governing; the manner or system of this; the form of organization of a State. 2 the group of persons governing a State. 3 the State as an agent. —**governmental** /-ˈment(ə)l/ *adj.* [f. OF (as GOVERN)]

governor /ˈgʌv(ə)nə(r)/ *n.* 1 a ruler; an official governing a province, town, etc., or representing the Crown in a colony. 2 the executive head of each State of the USA. 3 an officer commanding a fortress etc. 4 the head, or a member of the governing body, of an institution; the official in charge of a prison; (*slang*) one's employer or father. 5 an automatic regulator controlling the speed of an engine, etc. —**Governor-General** *n.* a representative of the Crown in a Commonwealth country that regards the Queen as the Head of State. [f. AF f. L *gubernator* (as GOVERN)]

gown *n.* 1 a loose flowing garment, especially a long dress worn by a woman. 2 the loose flowing outer garment that is the official or uniform robe of a lawyer, judge, member of a university, etc. 3 a surgeon's overall. [f. OF f. L *gunna* fur garment]

goy *n.* (*pl.* **goyim** or **goys**) the Jewish name for a non-Jew. [f. Heb. *goy* people]

GP *abbr.* general practitioner.

GPO *abbr.* General Post Office.

gr. *abbr.* 1 gram(s). 2 grain(s). 3 gross.

Graafian follicle or **vesicle** /ˈgrɑːfiən/ each of the small sacs in the mammal ovary in which ova are matured. [f. R. de *Graaf*, Dutch anatomist (d. 1673)]

grab *v.t./i.* (**-bb-**) 1 to grasp suddenly; to snatch *at*. 2 to take greedily; to appropriate. 3 (of brakes) to act harshly or jerkily. 4 (*slang*) to attract the attention of, to impress. —*n.* 1 a sudden clutch or attempt to seize. 2 a mechanical device for gripping things and lifting them. [f. MLG or MDu.; cf. GRIP]

graben /ˈgrɑːbən/ *n.* a depression of the earth's surface between faults. [G, orig. = ditch]

grace *n.* 1 attractiveness, especially in design, manner, or movement. 2 becoming courtesy. 3 manner, bearing; an attractive feature, an accomplishment. 4 (in Christian theology) the supernatural assistance of God bestowed upon a rational being with a view to his salvation. 5 goodwill, favour; a delay granted as a favour. 6 a prayer of thanksgiving before or after a meal. 7 (in *pl.*, **Graces**) three sister goddesses in Greek mythology, personifying charm, grace, and beauty. —*v.t.* to add grace to; to bestow honour on. —**grace-and-favour house** etc., a house etc. occupied by permission of a sovereign. **grace-note** *n.* a note embellishing a melody or harmony but not essential to it. **His, Her, Your,** etc., **Grace,** a title used in addressing or referring to a duke, duchess, or archbishop. **in a person's good graces,** in his favour. **with a good** (*or* **bad**) **grace,** as if willingly (or reluctantly). **year of grace,** a year of the Christian era. [f. OF f. L *gratia* (*gratus* pleasing)]

graceful *adj.* having or showing grace or elegance. —**gracefully** *adv.*, **gracefulness.** *n.* [f. GRACE + -FUL]

graceless *adj.* lacking grace, inelegant, ungracious. [f. GRACE + -LESS]

gracious /ˈgreɪʃəs/ *adj.* kind, indulgent and beneficent to inferiors; (of God) merciful, benign. —*int.* expressing surprise. —**gracious living,** an elegant way of life. —**graciously** *adv.*, **graciousness** *n.* [f. OF f. L (as GRACE)]

gradate /grəˈdeɪt/ *v.t./i.* to pass or cause to pass by gradations from one shade to another; to arrange in gradations. [back-formation f. foll.]

gradation /grəˈdeɪʃ(ə)n/ *n.* 1 (usu. in *pl.*) a stage of transition or advance. 2 a degree in rank, merit, intensity, etc.; arrangement in such degrees. 3 gradual passing from one shade or tone etc. to another. —**gradational** *adj.* [f. L *gradatio* (as foll.)]

grade *n.* 1 a step, stage, or degree in rank, quality, proficiency, etc. 2 a class of persons or things of the same grade. 3 a mark indicating the quality of a student's work. 4 a slope. **5** (*US*) a class or form in a school. —*v.t./i.* **1** to arrange in grades. **2** to give a grade to (a student). **3** to reduce (a road etc.) to easy gradients. **4** to pass gradually between grades or *into* a grade. —**grade school,** (*US*) an elementary school. **make the grade,** to succeed. [F, or f. L *gradus* step]

gradient /ˈgreɪdɪənt/ *n.* the amount of slope in a road, railway, etc.; a sloping road etc. [prob. f. prec., after *salient*]

gradual /ˈgrædjʊəl/ *adj.* occurring by degrees, not rapid or steep or abrupt. —**gradually** *adv.* [f. L (as GRADE)]

gradualism *n.* a policy of gradual change. [f. prec.]

graduate /ˈgrædjʊət/ *n.* the holder of an academic degree. —/-eɪt/ *v.t./i.* **1** to take an academic degree. **2** to move up *to* (a higher grade of activity etc.). **3** to mark out in degrees or parts; to arrange in gradations; to apportion (tax) according to a scale. —**graduation** /-ˈeɪʃ(ə)n/ *n.* [f. L *graduari* take degree (as GRADE)]

Graeco-Roman /griːkəʊˈrəʊmən/ *adj.* of the Greeks and Romans. [f. L *Graecus* Greek + ROMAN]

graffito /grəˈfiːtəʊ/ *n.* (*pl.* **-ti** /-tiː/) writing or a drawing scribbled or scratched on a wall etc. [It. (*graffio* scratching)]

graft[1] /grɑːft/ *n.* **1** a shoot or scion from one plant or tree planted in a slit made in another. **2** a piece of living tissue transplanted surgically. **3** the process of grafting. **4** (*slang*) hard work. —*v.t./i.* **1** to insert (a graft) *in* or *on*; to transplant (living tissue). **2** to fix or join (a thing) permanently to another. **3** (*slang*) to work hard. [f. OF *grafe* f. L f. Gk *graphion* stylus]

graft[2] /grɑːft/ *n.* (*colloq.*) practices, especially bribery, used to secure illicit gains in politics or business; such gains. —*v.i.* to seek or make such gains. [orig. unkn.]

Grail /greɪl/ *n.* **the Holy Grail,** (in medieval legend) the cup or platter used by Christ at the Last Supper. [f. F f. L *gradalis* dish]

grain *n.* **1** the fruit or a seed of a cereal; (*collect.*) wheat or an allied food-grass, its fruit, corn. **2** a small hard particle of salt, sand, etc. **3** the smallest unit of weight in some systems, 0.0648 gram; the least possible amount. **4** granular texture, roughness of a surface; the texture produced by the particles in skin, wood, stone, etc.; the pattern of the lines of fibre in wood or paper, the lamination in stone, etc. —*v.t./i.* **1** to paint in imitation of the grain of wood etc. **2** to give a granular surface to. **3** to dye in the grain. **4** to form into grains. —**against the grain,** contrary to one's natural inclination or feeling. —**grainy** *adj.* [f. OF f. L *granum*]

grallatorial /grælәˈtɔːrɪəl/ *adj.* of the long-legged wading birds. [f. L *grallator* stilt-walker (*grallae* stilts)]

gram *n.* the metric unit of mass, 0.001 kilogram, originally defined as the mass of 1 cc of pure water at its maximum density. [f. F *gramme* f. Gk *gramma* small weight]

-gram *suffix* forming nouns denoting a thing (so) written or recorded (*diagram, monogram, telegram*); cf. -GRAPH. [f. Gk *gramma* thing written (*graphō* write)]

graminaceous /græmɪˈneɪʃəs/ *adj.* of or like grass. [f. L *gramen* grass]

graminivorous /græmɪˈnɪvərəs/ *adj.* feeding on grass, cereals, etc. [as prec. + L *vorare* devour]

grammar /ˈgræmə(r)/ *n.* **1** the study of the main elements of a language, including its sounds, inflections or other means of showing the relation between words as used in speech or writing, and the established rules for using these **2** the elements themselves. **3** a treatise or book on grammar. **4** a person's manner of using grammatical forms; speech or writing regarded as good or bad by the rules of grammar. **5** the elements of an art or science. **grammar school,** a secondary school with an academic curriculum (orig. a school for teaching Latin). [f. AF f. L f. Gk *grammatikē* (*tekhnē* art) of letters of the alphabet]

grammarian /grəˈmeərɪən/ *n.* an expert in grammar or linguistics. [f. OF (as prec.)]

grammatical /grəˈmætɪk(ə)l/ *adj.* of or according to grammar. —**grammatically** *adv.* [F, or f. L f. Gk (as GRAMMAR)]

gramme var. of GRAM.

gramophone /ˈgræməfəʊn/ *n.* an instrument for reproducing recorded sounds such as music or speech. [inversion of PHONOGRAM]

grampus /ˈgræmpəs/ *n.* a sea-animal (*Grampus griseus*) resembling the dolphin and famous for blowing. [f. OF f. L (*crassus piscis* fat fish)]

gran *n.* (*colloq.*) a grandmother. [abbr.]

granadilla /grænəˈdɪlə/ *n.* a passion-fruit. [Sp., dim. of *granada* pomegranate]

granary /ˈgrænərɪ/ *n.* **1** a storehouse for threshed grain. **2** a region producing, and especially exporting, much corn. [f. L *granarium* (as GRAIN)]

grand *adj.* **1** splendid, magnificent, imposing, dignified. **2** main, of chief importance; of the highest rank. **3** (*colloq.*) excellent, enjoyable. —*n.* **1** a grand piano. **2** (*slang*) a thousand pounds, dollars, etc. —**grand jury,** (*US*) a jury convened to decide whether the evidence against an accused justifies a trial. **Grand National,** an annual steeplechase at Aintree, Liverpool. **grand opera,** an opera on a serious theme, or in which the entire libretto is sung and there are no spoken parts. **grand piano,** a large full-toned piano with horizontal strings. **grand slam,** see SLAM[2]. **grand total,** the sum of other totals. **grand tour,** (*hist.*) a tour of the chief cities etc. of Europe, completing a person's education; an extensive tour. —**grandly** *adv.*, **grandness** *n.* [f. OF f. L *grandis* full-grown]

grand- *in comb.* denoting the second degree of ascent or descent in relationships. [= prec.]

grandad *n.* (*colloq.*) a grandfather; an elderly man. [f. GRAND- + DAD]

grandam /ˈgrændæm/ *n.* (*archaic*) a grandmother; an elderly woman. [f. AF (as GRAND, DAME)]

grandchild *n.* a person's child's child. [f. GRAND- + CHILD]

grand-dad var. of GRANDAD.

granddaughter *n.* a female grandchild. [f. GRAND- + DAUGHTER]

grandee /grænˈdiː/ *n.* a Spanish or Portuguese noble of high rank; a great personage. [f. Sp. & Port. *grande* (as GRAND)]

grandeur /ˈgrændjə(r), -ndʒə(r)/ *n.* splendour, magnificence, grandness; high rank, eminence; nobility of character. [F (as GRAND)]

grandfather *n.* a male grandparent. —**grandfather clock**, a clock in a tall wooden case, worked by weights. [f. GRAND- + FATHER]

grandiloquent /grænˈdɪləkwənt/ *adj.* pompous or inflated in language. —**grandiloquence** *n.*, **grandiloquently** *adv.* [f. L *grandiloquus* (as GRAND, *loqui* speak)]

grandiose /ˈgrændɪəʊs/ *adj.* producing or meant to produce an imposing effect; planned on a large scale. —**grandiosity** /-ˈɒsɪtɪ/ *n.* [F f. It. (as GRAND)]

grandma /ˈgrænmɑː/ *n.* (*colloq.*) a grandmother. [f. GRAND- + MA]

grand mal /grɑ̃ mæl/ epilepsy with loss of consciousness. [F, = great sickness]

grandmaster *n.* a chess-player of the highest class.

grandmother *n.* a female grandparent. [f. GRAND- + MOTHER]

Grand Prix /grɑ̃ ˈpriː/ **1** (in full **Grand Prix de Paris**) an international horse-race for three-year-olds, founded in 1863 and run annually in June at Longchamp near Paris. **2** any of various important motor-racing contests, governed by international rules. [F, = great or chief prize]

grandsire *n.* (*archaic*) a grandfather. [f. GRAND- + SIRE]

grandson *n.* a male grandchild. [f. GRAND- + SON]

grandstand *n.* the main stand for spectators at a racecourse etc. —**grandstand finish,** a close and exciting finish to a race, etc.

grange /greɪndʒ/ *n.* a country house with farm-buildings. [f. AF f. L *granica* (as GRAIN)]

graniferous /grəˈnɪfərəs/ *adj.* producing grain or grainlike seed. [as GRAIN + L *ferre* bear]

granite /ˈgrænɪt/ *n.* a granular crystalline plutonic rock consisting mainly of quartz, feldspar, and (commonly) mica, used for building. —**granitic** /-ˈnɪtɪk/ *adj.* [f. It. *granito* grained (L *granum* grain)]

granivorous /grəˈnɪvərəs/ *adj.* feeding on grains. [as GRAIN + L *vorare* devour]

granny *n.* (*colloq.*) (also **grannie**) a grandmother. —**granny flat,** a part of a house, made into self-contained accommodation for a relative. **granny knot,** a reef-knot crossed the wrong way and therefore insecure. [dim. of obs. *grannam* for GRANDAM]

grant /grɑːnt/ *v.t.* **1** to consent to fulfil (a request etc.). **2** to give formally, to transfer (property) legally. **3** to admit as true; to concede, to allow. —*n.* **1** something granted, especially a sum of money. **2** granting; formal conferment. —**take for granted,** to assume to be true or valid; to cease to appreciate through familiarity. [f. OF *gr(e)anter* ult. f. L *credere* entrust]

grantor /grɑːnˈtɔː(r)/ *n.* a person by whom property etc. is legally transferred. [f. GRANT]

granular /ˈgrænjʊlə(r)/ *adj.* of or like grains or granules. —**granularity** /-ˈlærɪtɪ/ *n.* [f. L (as GRANULE)]

granulate /ˈgrænjʊleɪt/ *v.t./i.* **1** to form into grains. **2** to roughen the surface of. **3** (of a wound etc.) to form small prominences as the beginning of healing or junction. —**granulation** /-ˈleɪʃ(ə)n/ *n.* [as prec.]

granule /ˈgrænjuːl/ *n.* a small grain. [f. L *granulum* dim. of *granum* grain]

grape *n.* a berry (usually green or purple) growing in clusters on a vine, used as a fruit and in making wine. —**grape hyacinth,** a small plant of the genus *Muscari* with a cluster of flowers, usually blue. (*hist.*) small balls as a scattering charge for cannon. **grape-vine** *n.* a vine; a means of transmission of rumour. [f. OF, = bunch of grapes]

grapefruit *n.* (*pl.* same) a large round yellow citrus fruit (that of *Citrus paradisi*) with an acid juicy pulp.

graph /grɑːf/ *n.* a diagram showing the relation of two variable quantities each measured along one of a pair of axes. —*v.t.* to plot or trace on a graph. —**graph paper,** paper ruled with a grid of lines as a help in drawing graphs. [abbr. of *graphic formula*]

-graph /grɑːf/ *suffix* forming nouns denoting a thing written or drawn etc. in a specified way (*holograph*, *photograph*), an instrument that records (*telegraph*), or the corresponding verbs. [f. F f. L f. Gk (*graphō* write)]

graphic /ˈgræfɪk/ *adj*. **1** of writing, drawing, etching, etc. **2** vividly descriptive. —**graphically** *adv*. [f. L f. Gk (*graphē* writing)]

-graphic /-græfɪk/ *suffix* (also **-graphical**) forming adjectives from nouns in *-graph* or *-graphy*. [f. Gk (as prec.)]

graphics /ˈgræfɪks/ *n.pl*. **1** the products of the graphic arts. **2** (usu. treated as *sing*.) the use of diagrams in calculation and design. [f. GRAPHIC]

graphite /ˈgræfaɪt/ *n*. a crystalline allotropic electrically-conducting form of carbon used in pencils (see LEAD² 2), as a lubricant, in various electrical devices, as a moderator in nuclear reactors, etc. —**graphitic** /-ˈɪtɪk/ *adj*. [f. G f. Gk *graphō* write]

graphology /grəˈfɒlədʒɪ/ *n*. the study of handwriting, especially as a guide to character. —**graphological** /-ˈlɒdʒɪk(ə)l/ *adj*., **graphologist** *n*. [as GRAPHIC + -LOGY]

-graphy *suffix* forming nouns denoting a descriptive science (*geography*) or a style or method of writing etc. (*calligraphy*, *stenography*). [ult. f. Gk *graphia* writing]

grapnel /ˈgræpn(ə)l/ *n*. an instrument with iron claws, for dragging or grasping things; a small anchor with several flukes. [f. OF *grapon*]

grapple *v.t./i*. **1** to seize or hold firmly. **2** to struggle at close quarters (*with*). **3** to try to deal *with* (a problem). **4** to seize (as) with a grapnel. —*n*. **1** a hold (as) in wrestling. **2** a close contest. **3** a clutching-instrument, a grapnel. —**grappling-iron** *n*. a grapnel. [f. OF f. Prov. (*grapa* hook, as GRAPNEL)]

grasp /grɑːsp/ *v.t./i*. **1** to seize or hold firmly, especially with the hands or arms; to seize eagerly or greedily. **2** to understand or realize. —*n*. **1** a firm hold, a grip. **2** mastery, control. **3** a mental hold, understanding. —**grasp at,** to try to seize; to accept eagerly. **grasp the nettle,** to tackle a difficulty boldly. [for earlier *grapse*, rel. to GROPE]

grasping *adj*. greedy for money or possessions. [f. GRASP]

grass /grɑːs/ *n*. **1** any of a group of wild low-lying plants with green blades that are eaten by animals; any species of this (*Bot*. including cereals, reeds, and bamboos). **2** pasture land; grass-covered ground, a lawn; grazing. **3** (*slang*) marijuana. **4** (*slang*) a person who 'grasses', an informer. —*v.t./i*. **1** to cover with turf. **2** (*US*) to provide with pasture. **3** (*slang*) to betray, to inform the police. —**grass roots,** the fundamental level or source; ordinary people; the rank and file of a political party etc. **grass snake,** a small non-poisonous snake (*Natrix natrix*). **grass widow,** a woman whose husband is away for a prolonged period. —**grassy** *adj*. [OE, rel. to GREEN]

grasshopper *n*. a jumping insect of the sub-order Saltatoria, with a loud chirping sound.

grassland *n*. a large open area covered with grass, especially used for grazing.

grate¹ *v.t./i*. **1** to reduce to small particles by rubbing on a rough surface. **2** to rub with a harsh noise; to grind (the teeth); to sound harshly. **3** to have an irritating effect (*on* a person or the nerves). —**grater** *n*. [f. OF *grater*]

grate² *n*. a metal framework that keeps fuel in a fireplace; the fireplace itself. [orig. = grating; f. OF f. L *cratis* hurdle]

grateful /ˈgreɪtful/ *adj*. **1** thankful, feeling or showing gratitude. **2** pleasant, acceptable. —**gratefully** *adv*. [f. obs. *grate* adj. f. L *gratus* thankful, pleasing]

gratify /ˈgrætɪfaɪ/ *v.t*. to please, to delight; to please by compliance; to yield to (a desire). —**gratification** /-fɪˈkeɪʃ(ə)n/ *n*. [f. F or L *gratificari* (as prec.)]

grating /ˈgreɪtɪŋ/ *n*. a framework of parallel or crossed bars, wires, lines ruled on glass, etc. [f. GRATE²]

gratis /ˈgreɪtɪs, ˈgrɑː-/ *adj*. & *adv*. free, without charge. [L (*gratia* thanks)]

gratitude /ˈgrætɪtjuːd/ *n*. being thankful, feeling or showing that one values a kindness or benefit received. [f. F or L (as GRATEFUL)]

gratuitous /grəˈtjuːɪtəs/ *adj*. **1** given or done gratis. **2** uncalled for, lacking good reason. —**gratuitously** *adv*. [f. L (as GRATIS)]

gratuity /grəˈtjuːɪtɪ/ *n*. money given in recognition of services. [f. OF or L (as GRATEFUL)]

gravamen /grəˈveɪmen/ *n*. (*pl*. **-s**) **1** the essence or most serious part (*of* an accusation). **2** a grievance. [L (*gravare* to load f. *gravis* heavy)]

grave¹ *n*. **1** a hole dug for the burial of a corpse; a mound or monument over this. **2** death. [OE (as GRAVE³)]

grave² *adj*. **1** serious, weighty, important; dignified, solemn; sombre. **2** (of a sound) low-pitched, not acute. —**gravely** *adv*. [F, or f. L *gravis* heavy]

grave³ *v.t*. (*p.p*. **graven, graved**) **1** to fix indelibly (*in* or *on* one's memory etc.). **2** (*archaic*) to engrave, to carve. —**graven image**, an idol. [OE]

grave⁴ /grɑːv, greɪv/ *n*. an accent (`) over a vowel to show its quality or length. [f. GRAVE²]

grave⁵ *v.t*. to clean (a ship's bottom) by burning and tarring. —**graving dock**, a dry dock. [perh. f. F *grave*, *grève* shore]

gravel /ˈgræv(ə)l/ *n*. **1** coarse sand and small stones, used for paths etc. **2** crystals formed in the bladder. —*v.t.* (-ll-) 1 to lay with gravel. 2 to perplex. [f. OF, dim. of *grave* (as GRAVE[5])]

gravelly *adj.* 1 like gravel; consisting of gravel. 2 (of the voice) deep and rough-sounding. [f. prec.]

graven see GRAVE[3].

Graves /grɑ:v/ *n.* a wine (esp. white) from the Graves district of the Bordeaux region in France.

gravestone *n.* a stone (usually inscribed) marking a grave.

graveyard *n.* a burial-ground.

gravid /ˈgrævɪd/ *adj.* pregnant. [f. L *gravidus* (*gravis* heavy)]

gravimeter /grəˈvɪmɪtə(r)/ *n.* an instrument measuring the difference in the force of gravity between two places. [f. F (L *gravis* heavy, -METER)]

gravitate /ˈgrævɪteɪt/ *v.t./i.* 1 to move or be attracted (*to* or *towards*). 2 to move or tend by the force of gravity (*towards*); to sink by or as by gravity. [as GRAVITY]

gravitation /grævɪˈteɪʃ(ə)n/ *n.* 1 gravitating. 2 the attraction exercised by every particle of matter on every other; the movement or tendency produced by this; the falling of bodies to earth. —**gravitational** *adj.* [as prec.]

gravity /ˈgrævɪtɪ/ *n.* 1 the force that attracts a body to the centre of the earth etc. (see prec.); the intensity of this. 2 weight. 3 importance, seriousness; solemnity. —**gravity feed,** the supply of material by its fall under gravity. [f. F or L *gravitas* heaviness (as GRAVE[2])]

gravy /ˈgreɪvɪ/ *n.* 1 the juices exuding from meat in and after cooking; a dressing for food, made of these. 2 (*slang*) unearned or unexpected money. —**gravy-boat** *n.* a boat-shaped vessel for gravy. [perh. f. OF *grané* (as GRAIN), misread as *gravé*]

grayling *n.* a silver-grey freshwater fish of the genus *Thymallus*. [f. GREY]

graze[1] *v.t./i.* to suffer or cause a slight abrasion of (a part of the body); to touch lightly in passing; to move (*against*, *along*, etc.) with such a contact. —*n.* an abrasion. [perh. by transference f. foll. 'take off the grass close to the ground']

graze[2] *v.t./i.* 1 (of cattle etc.) to eat growing grass; to feed on (grass). 2 to feed (cattle etc.) on growing grass; to pasture cattle. [OE (as GRASS)]

grazier /ˈgreɪzɪə(r)/ *n.* 1 one who feeds cattle for market. 2 (*Austral.*) a sheep-farmer. [f. GRASS]

grazing *n.* grassland suitable for pasturage. [f. GRAZE[2]]

grease /gri:s/ *n.* oily or fatty matter, especially as a lubricant; the melted fat of a dead animal. —/also gri:z/ *v.t.* to smear or lubricate with grease. —**grease-paint** *n.* the make-up used by actors etc. **grease the palm of,** (*colloq.*) to bribe. [f. OF *graisse* f. L *crassus* fat]

greasy *adj.* 1 of or like grease. 2 smeared or covered with grease; having much or too much grease; slippery. 3 (of a person or manner) too unctuous. —**greasily** *adv.*, **greasiness** *n.* [f. prec.]

great /greɪt/ *adj.* 1 of a size, amount, extent, or intensity much above the normal or average (also *contemptuously*). 2 important, pre-eminent. 3 remarkable in ability, character, etc. 4 (also **greater**) the larger of the name. 5 fully deserving the name of; doing a thing much or on a large scale. 6 (*colloq.*) very enjoyable or satisfactory. 7 competent *at*; well-informed *on*. —*n.* a great person or thing. —**great circle,** a circle whose plane passes through the centre of the sphere on which the circle lies. **Great Dane,** see DANE. **Great Russian,** a member of the principal ethnic group in the USSR; their language. **Greats,** the Oxford BA course in classics and philosophy; the final examinations in this. **Great Seal,** the official seal used on important State papers. **Great War,** the First World War (1914-18). —**greatness** *n.* [OE]

great- *in comb.* (of family relationships) one degree more remote (*great-aunt*, *great-grandfather*; *great-greatgrandfather*). [= prec.]

greatcoat *n.* a heavy overcoat.

greatly *adv.* by a considerable amount, much. [f. GREAT]

greave *n.* (usu. in *pl.*) armour for the shin. [f. OF, = shin]

grebe /gri:b/ *n.* any of various short-bodied almost tailless diving birds of the family Podicipedidae, especially of the genus *Podiceps*. [f. F]

Grecian /ˈgri:ʃ(ə)n/ *adj.* (of architecture or facial outline) Greek. —**Grecian nose,** a straight nose that continues the line of the forehead without a dip. [f. OF or L (*Graecia* Greece)]

greed *n.* an excessive desire especially for food or wealth. [back-formation f. foll.]

greedy *adj.* showing greed, wanting or taking in excess; gluttonous; very eager (*to do* a thing). —**greedily** *adv.*, **greediness** *n.* [OE]

Greek *adj.* of Greece or its people or language. —*n.* a native or the language of Greece. —**Greek cross,** a cross with four equal arms. **Greek fire,** a combustible composition for setting fire to an enemy's ships, works, etc., emitted by a flame-throwing weapon, so called from being first used by the Greeks besieged in Constantinople (673-8). **Greek to me,**

incomprehensible to me. [OE f. L *Graecus* f. Gk]

green *adj.* **1** of a colour between blue and yellow, like that of grass. **2** covered with leaves or grass. **3** (of fruit etc. or wood) unripe or unseasoned; not dried, smoked, or tanned. **4** inexperienced, gullible. **5** sickly-hued; jealous, envious. **6** young, flourishing; not withered or worn out. —*n.* **1** green colour or pigment; green clothes or material. **2** a piece of grassy public land; a grassy area for a special purpose. **3** (in *pl.*) green vegetables. **4** vigour, youth. —*v.t./i.* to make or become green. —**green belt,** an area of open land for preservation round a city. **green card,** a motorist's international insurance document. **green-eyed** *adj.* jealous. **green fingers,** skill in growing plants. **green light,** a signal to proceed on a road etc., (*colloq.*) permission to go ahead with a project. **Green Paper,** a preliminary report of government proposals, for discussion. **green party,** a political party of environmentalists and ecologists. **green pound,** the agreed value of the £ according to which payments to agricultural producers are reckoned in the EEC. **green revolution,** greatly increased crop production in the developing countries by improvement of soil fertility, pest control, increased mechanization, etc. **green-room** *n.* a room behind the stage, probably so called because it was originally painted green, for the use of actors and actresses when not required on stage. **Greens** *n.pl.* (*colloq.*) = green party. **green-stick fracture,** a fracture, especially in children, in which one side of a bone is broken and one only bent. **green tea,** tea made from steam-dried leaves. —**greenish** *adj.*, **greenly** *adv.*, **greenness** *n.* [OE]

greenery *n.* green foliage or growing plants. [f. GREEN]

greenfinch *n.* a finch (*Carduelis chloris*) with green and yellow plumage.

greenfly *n.* a green aphid; such insects collectively.

greengage *n.* a round green plum. [f. GREEN + Sir W. *Gage* (*c.* 1725)]

greengrocer *n.* a retailer of fruit and vegetables. —**greengrocery** *n.*

greenhorn *n.* an inexperienced person, a new recruit. [orig. of animals with 'green' or young horns]

greenhouse *n.* a light structure with the sides and roof mainly of glass, for rearing plants. —**greenhouse effect,** the phenomenon whereby the surface and the lower atmosphere of a planet are maintained at a relatively high temperature owing to the greater transparency of the atmosphere to visible radiation from the sun than to infra-red radiation from the planet.

greensand *n.* a green sandstone.

greenstone *n.* **1** a green eruptive rock containing feldspar and hornblende. **2** (*NZ*) a kind of jade.

greenstuff *n.* vegetation, green vegetables.

greensward *n.* an expanse of grassy turf.

Greenwich Mean Time /ˈgrenɪtʃ/ mean solar time on the meridian of Greenwich in London, used as the international basis of time reckoning.

greenwood *n.* woodlands in summer.

greet[1] *v.t.* **1** to address politely on meeting or arrival. **2** to salute, to receive (a person, news, etc., *with* a reaction). **3** (of a sight, sound, etc.) to meet (the eye, ear, etc.). [OE]

greet[2] *v.i.* (*Sc.*) to weep. [OE]

greeting *n.* words, gestures, etc., used to greet a person; (often in *pl.*) an expression of goodwill. —**greetings card,** a decorative card sent to convey greetings. [f. GREET[1]]

gregarious /grɪˈgeərɪəs/ *adj.* **1** fond of company. **2** living in flocks or communities. —**gregariously** *adv.*, **gregariousness** *n.* [f. L (*grex* flock)]

Gregorian /grɪˈgɔːrɪən/ *adj.* of the plainchant ritual music named after Gregory the Great (d. 604). [f. *Gregory*]

Gregorian calendar the modified calendar, also known as the 'New Style', introduced by Pope Gregory XIII in 1582, adopted in Great Britain in 1752, and now in use throughout most of the Christian world. [f. *Gregory*]

gremlin /ˈgremlɪn/ *n.* (*slang*) a mischievous sprite said to interfere with machinery etc. [orig. unkn., but prob. formed by analogy with GOBLIN]

grenade /grɪˈneɪd/ *n.* a small bomb thrown by hand or shot from a rifle. [F, f. OF & Sp., = pomegranate]

grenadier /grenəˈdɪə(r)/ *n.* (*hist.*) a soldier armed with grenades. —**Grenadiers** *or* **Grenadier Guards,** the first regiment of the royal household infantry. [F (as prec.)]

grew *past* of GROW.

grey /greɪ/ *adj.* **1** of a colour between black and white. **2** dull, dismal. **3** (of the hair) turning white; (of a person) with grey hair. **4** aged, experienced, mature, ancient. **5** anonymous, unidentifiable. —*n.* **1** grey colour or pigment; grey clothes or material. **2** a grey horse. —*v.t./i.* to become or make grey. —**grey area,** that part of a matter where there are no exact rules about right and wrong etc. **Grey Friars,** Franciscan friars, so called from their grey cloaks. **grey matter,** the parts of the brain, consisting of nerve-cell bodies, that are grey in appearance; (*colloq.*) intelligence. **grey**

squirrel, a common squirrel of the USA (*Sciurus carolinensis*) which was introduced into Europe in the late 19th c. —**greyish** *adj.*, **greyness** *n.* [OE]

greyhound *n.* a slender dog noted for swiftness and used in racing and coursing. [OE, = bitch-hound]

greylag *n.* the European wild goose, *Anser anser*. [f. GREY + *lag* (perh. = obs. *lag* goose, of imit. origin)]

grid *n.* **1** a grating. **2** a system of numbered squares printed on a map and forming the basis of map references. **3** a network of lines, electric-power connections, gas-supply lines, etc. **4** a pattern of lines marking the starting-places on a car-racing track. **5** a wire network between the filament and anode of a thermionic valve. **6** an arrangement of town streets in a rectangular pattern. **7** a gridiron. [f. GRIDIRON]

griddle *n.* = GIRDLE². [f. OF f. L *craticula* (*cratis* hurdle)]

gridiron /ˈgrɪdaɪən/ *n.* a cooking utensil of metal bars for broiling or grilling. [as GRIDDLE]

grief /gri:f/ *n.* deep or intense sorrow; a cause of this. —**come to grief,** to meet with disaster. [f. OF (as GRIEVE)]

grievance /ˈgri:v(ə)ns/ *n.* a real or fancied ground of complaint. [f. OF (as GRIEF)]

grieve /gri:v/ *v.t./i.* to cause grief to; to feel grief. [f. OF f. L *gravare* (*gravis* heavy)]

grievous /ˈgri:vəs/ *adj.* (of pain etc.) severe; causing grief; injurious; flagrant, heinous. —**grievous bodily harm,** (*Law*) serious injury. —**grievously** *adv.* [f. OF (as prec.)]

griffin /ˈgrɪfɪn/ *n.* a fabulous creature with an eagle's head and wings and a lion's body. [f. OF f. L *gryphus* f. Gk]

griffon /ˈgrɪf(ə)n/ *n.* **1** a terrier-like dog with coarse hair. **2** a large vulture of the genus *Gyps*. **3** a griffin. [var. of GRIFFIN]

grill *n.* **1** a device on a cooker for radiating heat downwards. **2** a gridiron. **3** grilled food. **4** a grill-room. **5** a grille. —*v.t.* **1** to cook on a gridiron or under a grill. **2** to subject to or undergo torture or great heat; to subject to severe questioning, especially by the police. —**grill-room** *n.* a small restaurant serving grills etc. [var. of foll.]

grille /grɪl/ *n.* **1** a grating or latticed screen, especially in a door. **2** a metal grid protecting the radiator of a motor vehicle. [F f. L (as GRIDDLE)]

grilse *n.* a young salmon that has been only once to the sea. [orig. unkn.]

grim *adj.* **1** of harsh or forbidding appearance; stern, merciless. **2** ghastly, joyless; unpleasant, unattractive. —**grimly** *adv.*, **grimness** *n.* [OE]

grimace /grɪˈmeɪs/ *n.* a distortion of the face in disgust etc., or to amuse. —*v.i.* to make a grimace. [F f. Sp. *grimazo* (*grima* fright)]

grime *n.* soot or dirt ingrained in a surface, especially the skin. —*v.t.* to blacken with grime. —**grimy** *adj.*, **griminess** *n.* [f. MLG or MDu.]

grin *v.t./i.* (**-nn-**) to smile broadly, showing the teeth; to make a forced, unrestrained or stupid smile; to express by grinning. —*n.* an act or the action of grinning. —**grin and bear it,** to take pain etc. stoically. [OE]

grind /graɪnd/ *v.t./i.* (*past* & *p.p.* **ground**) **1** to crush to small particles; to produce (flour) thus. **2** to oppress, to harass with exorbitant demands. **3** to sharpen or smooth by friction. **4** to rub together gratingly. **5** to study hard, to toil. **6** to produce or bring *out* with effort. **7** to turn the handle of (a barrel-organ). —*n.* **1** grinding. **2** hard dull work. **3** the size of ground particles. —**grind to a halt,** to stop laboriously with the sound of grating. **ground glass,** glass made opaque by grinding. [OE]

grinder /ˈgraɪndə(r)/ *n.* **1** a person or thing (especially a machine) that grinds. **2** a molar tooth. [f. prec.]

grindstone *n.* a thick revolving disc used for grinding, sharpening, and polishing; the kind of stone used for this. —**keep one's nose to the grindstone,** to work hard and continuously.

grip *v.t./i.* (**-pp-**) **1** to grasp tightly; to take a firm hold, especially by friction. **2** to compel the attention of. —*n.* **1** a firm hold, a grasp. **2** grasping power; way of clasping the hands or of grasping or holding. **3** mastery, intellectual hold. **4** a gripping part of a machine etc.; the part of a weapon etc. that is held. **5** a hair-grip. **6** (*US*) a suitcase, a travelling-bag. —**come** *or* **get to grips with,** to approach purposefully, to begin to deal with. [OE (as GRIPE)]

gripe *v.t./i.* **1** to cause colic; to affect with colic. **2** (*slang*) to complain. **3** to clutch, to grip. **4** to oppress. —*n.* **1** (usu. in *pl.*) colic. **2** (*slang*) a complaint. —**gripe-water** *n.* a medicine to cure colic in babies. [OE]

grisaille /grɪˈzeɪl, -ˈzaɪ/ *n.* a method of decorative painting in grey monochrome representing figures and objects in relief; a stained-glass window of this kind. [F (*gris* grey)]

grisly /ˈgrɪzlɪ/ *adj.* causing horror, disgust, or fear. —**grisliness** *n.* [OE]

grist *n.* corn to grind. —**grist to the mill,** a source of profit or advantage. [OE (as GRIND)]

gristle /ˈgrɪs(ə)l/ *n.* tough flexible tissue, cartilage, especially in meat. —**gristly** *adj.* [OE]

grit *n.* **1** particles of stone or sand, especially as causing discomfort, clogging machinery, etc. **2** coarse sandstone. **3** (*colloq.*) courage, endurance. —*v.t./i.* (**-tt-**) **1** to spread grit on (icy roads etc.). **2** to clench (the teeth), especially in enduring pain or trouble. **3** to make a grating sound. —**gritty** *adj.*, **grittiness** *n.* [OE]

grits *n.pl.* coarsely ground grain, especially oatmeal; oats that have been husked but not ground. [OE]

grizzle *v.i.* (*colloq.*, esp. of a child) to cry fretfully. —**grizzler** *n.* [orig. unkn.]

grizzled /'grɪz(ə)ld/ *adj.* grey-haired or partly so. [f. *grizzle* grey f. OF *grisel* (*gris* grey)]

grizzly *adj.* grey, grey-haired. —*n.* a grizzly bear. —**grizzly bear,** a large fierce bear (*Ursus horribilis*) of North America. [as prec.]

groan *v.t./i.* **1** to make a deep sound expressing pain, grief, or disapproval; to utter with groans. **2** to be loaded or oppressed. —*n.* the sound made in groaning. [OE]

groat *n.* **1** a silver coin recognized from the 13th c. in various countries of Europe; an English coin issued 1351-1662. **2** a fourpenny piece 1836-56. [f. MDu., = great]

groats *n.pl.* hulled or crushed grain, especially oats. [OE (rel. to GRIT, GRITS)]

grocer /'grəʊsə(r)/ *n.* a dealer in food and household provisions. [f. AF *grosser* f. L (as GROSS); orig. one who sells in the gross]

grocery *n.* a grocer's trade or shop; (in *pl.*) grocer's provisions. [f. prec.]

grog *n.* a drink of spirit (originally rum) and water. [perh. f. *Grogram* nickname of Admiral Vernon, who in 1740 first had grog served to sailors instead of neat rum]

groggy *adj.* unsteady, tottering. —**groggily** *adv.*, **grogginess** *n.* [f. prec.]

grogram /'grɒgrəm/ *n.* a coarse fabric of silk, mohair, etc. [f. F *gros grain* coarse grain]

groin *n.* **1** the depression between the belly and the thigh. **2** the edge formed by vaults intersecting in a roof; an arch supporting a vault. —*v.t.* to build with groins. [perh. f. OE *grynde* depression]

groom *n.* **1** a person employed to take care of horses. **2** a bridegroom. **3** any of certain officers of the Royal Household. —*v.t.* **1** to curry or tend (a horse). **2** to give a neat appearance to (a person etc.). **3** to prepare (a person) *as* a political candidate, *for* a career, etc. [orig. = 'boy', etym. unkn.]

groove *n.* **1** a channel or hollow, especially one made to guide motion or receive a ridge; a spiral cut in a gramophone record for the stylus. **2** a piece of routine, a habit. **3** (*slang*) something excellent. —*v.t./i.* to make a groove or grooves in. [f. Du.; cf. GRAVE[1]]

groovy *adj.* **1** of or like a groove. **2** (*slang*) excellent. [f. prec.]

grope *v.t./i.* to feel about as in the dark; to search blindly (*lit.* or *fig.*). —**grope one's way,** to proceed tentatively. [OE, rel. to GRIP]

grosbeak /'grəʊsbi:k/ *n.* any of various large finches, e.g. the pine grosbeak *Pinicola enucleator*. [f. F *grosbec*, = large beak]

grosgrain /'grəʊgreɪn/ *n.* a corded fabric of silk etc. [F, = coarse grain]

gros point /grəʊ 'pwæ̃/ cross-stitch embroidery on canvas. [F (as GROSS, POINT)]

gross /grəʊs/ *adj.* **1** flagrant, outrageous. **2** total, without deductions, not net. **3** not refined, indecent, vulgar. **4** thick, solid. **5** overfed, bloated, repulsively fat; (of vegetation) luxuriant, rank. **6** (of the senses etc.) dull. —*n.* (*pl.* same) twelve dozen. —*v.t.* to produce as gross profit. —**gross domestic product,** the total value of goods produced and services provided in a country in one year. **gross national product,** the gross domestic product plus the total of net income from abroad. —**grossly** *adv.* [f. OF f. L *grossus* big]

grotesque /grəʊ'tesk/ *adj.* comically or repulsively distorted; incongruous, absurd. —*n.* **1** a decoration interweaving human and animal forms with foliage. **2** a comically distorted figure or design. —**grotesquely** *adv.*, **grotesqueness** *n.* [f. F f. It. (as foll.)]

grotto /'grɒtəʊ/ *n.* (*pl.* **-oes**) a picturesque cave; an artificial or simulated cave. [f. It. *grotta* f. L (as CRYPT)]

grotty *adj.* (*slang*) unpleasant, dirty, ugly, useless. [f. GROTESQUE]

grouch *v.i.* (*colloq.*) to grumble. —*n.* (*colloq.*) a discontented person; a fit of grumbling or the sulks. —**groucher** *n.*, **grouchy** *adj.* [as GRUDGE]

ground[1] *n.* **1** the surface of the earth, especially as contrasted with the air around it; a part of this specified in some way; a position or area on the earth's surface. **2** a foundation or motive. **3** an area of a special kind or use. **4** the surface worked upon in painting etc.; the predominant colour. **5** (in *pl.*) enclosed land attached to a house. **6** (in *pl.*) dregs, especially of coffee. **7** an electrical earth. **8** the bottom of the sea. **9** the floor of a room etc. —*attrib.* (in the names of birds) terrestrial; (of animals) burrowing, living on the ground; (of plants) dwarfish, trailing. —*v.t./i.* **1** to run aground, to strand. **2** to refuse authority for (an airman or aircraft) to fly. **3** to instruct thoroughly (*in* a subject). **4** to base (a principle or conclusion *on* a fact etc.). **5** to connect with the earth as a conductor. **6** to alight on the ground. **7** to place or lay (esp. weapons) on the ground. —**break new ground,** to treat a subject previously not dealt with. **cover the ground,**

to deal adequately with a subject. **fall to the ground,** (of a plan etc.) to fail. **get off the ground,** to make a successful start. **give** *or* **lose ground,** to retreat, to decline. **go to ground,** (of a fox etc.) to enter an earth etc.; (of a person) to withdraw from public notice. **ground bass,** a short theme constantly repeated in the bass with the upper parts of the music varied. **ground frost,** frost on the surface of the ground or in the top layer of soil. **ground-nut** *n.* a peanut; a wild bean (*Apios tuberosa*), originally from North America, with an edible tuber. **ground-plan** *n.* a plan of a building at ground level, the general outline of a scheme. **ground-rent** *n.* the rent for land leased for building. **ground speed,** aircraft speed relative to the ground. **ground squirrel,** a burrowing rodent related to the squirrel. **ground swell,** a heavy sea due to a distant or past storm or earthquake. **ground water,** the water found in the surface soil. **hold one's ground,** not to retreat. [OE]

ground[2] *past* & *p.p.* of GRIND.

groundhog *n.* the North American marmot, the woodchuck.

grounding *n.* basic training or instruction in a subject. [f. GROUND[1]]

groundless *adj.* without motive or foundation. —**groundlessly** *adv.* [f. GROUND[1] + -LESS]

groundsel /ˈgraʊns(ə)l/ *n.* a plant of the genus *Senecio*, of which the commonest species, a garden weed, is used as a food for cage-birds. [OE]

groundsheet *n.* a waterproof sheet for spreading on the ground.

groundsman *n.* (*pl.* **-men**) a person who maintains a sports ground.

groundwork *n.* preliminary or basic work.

group /gru:p/ *n.* **1** a number of persons or things close together, or belonging or classed together. **2** a number of commercial companies under a single ownership. **3** a pop group. **4** a division of an air force. **5** (*Math.*) a set of elements with an operation for combining any pair to give another element in the set. —*v.t.* to form into a group; to place in a group or groups. —**group captain,** an RAF officer next below air commodore. **group therapy,** therapy in which similarly affected patients are brought together to assist one another. [f. F f. It. *gruppo*]

grouse[1] /graʊs/ *n.* (*pl.* same) a game-bird of the family Tetraonidae with feathered feet; its flesh as food. [orig. unkn.]

grouse[2] /graʊs/ *v.i.* (*colloq.*) to grumble, to complain. —*n.* (*colloq.*) a grumble. —**grouser** *n.* [orig. unkn.]

grout *n.* thin fluid mortar. —*v.t.* to apply grout to. [cf. dial. F *grouter* grout a wall.]

grove *n.* a small wood, a group of trees. [OE]

grovel /ˈgrɒv(ə)l/ *v.i.* (**-ll-**) to lie prone in abject humility; to humble oneself. [f. foll.]

grovelling *adj.* abject, base; prone. [f. obs. *grufe* face down f. ON]

grow /grəʊ/ *v.t./i.* (*past* **grew**; *p.p.* **grown**) **1** to increase in size, height, amount, intensity, etc. **2** to develop or exist as a living plant or natural product. **3** to become gradually. **4** to produce by cultivation; to let (a beard etc.) develop; (in *pass.*) to be covered (*over* etc.) with growth. —**growing pains,** neuralgic pain in children's legs due to fatigue etc.; early difficulties in the development of a project etc. **grown-up** *adj.* adult; (*n.*) an adult. **grow on,** to have an increasing charm etc. for. **grow out of,** to become too large to wear (a garment); to become too mature to retain (a habit etc.); to develop from. **grow up,** to advance to maturity; (of a custom) to arise. [OE]

grower *n.* **1** a person growing produce, especially fruit. **2** a plant that grows in a specified way. [f. GROW]

growl /graʊl/ *n.* a guttural sound of anger; a rumble; an angry murmur, a complaint. —*v.t./i.* to make a growl; to utter with a growl. [imit.]

grown *p.p.* of GROW.

growth /grəʊθ/ *n.* **1** growing, development. **2** increase in size or value. **3** what has grown or is growing. **4** a tumour. —**growth industry,** an industry developing faster than most others. [f. GROW]

groyne /grɔɪn/ *n.* a structure of wood, stone, or concrete projecting towards the sea, preventing sand and pebbles from being washed away by the current. —*v.t.* to protect with groynes. [f. dial. *groin* snout f. OF f. L (*grunnire* grunt)]

grub *n.* **1** the larva of an insect; a maggot. **2** (*slang*) food. —*v.t./i.* (**-bb-**) **1** to dig superficially. **2** to clear (ground) of roots etc.; to clear away (roots etc.); to fetch *up* or *out* by digging (*lit.* or *fig.* in books etc.); to rummage. —**grub-screw** *n.* a headless screw. [perh. as GRAVE[3]]

grubby *adj.* **1** dirty. **2** full of grubs. —**grubbily** *adv.*, **grubbiness** *n.* [f. GRUB]

grudge *v.t.* to be resentfully unwilling to give or allow. —*n.* a feeling of resentment or ill will. —**grudging** *adj.*, **grudgingly** *adv.* [f. OF *grouc(h)ier* murmur]

gruel /ˈgrʊəl/ *n.* a liquid food of oatmeal etc. boiled in milk or water. [f. OF]

gruelling /ˈgru:əlɪŋ/ *adj.* exhausting. [f. prec.]

gruesome /ˈgru:səm/ *adj.* horrible, grisly, disgusting. [f. Sc. *grue* to shudder]

gruff *adj.* (of the voice) low and harsh; having a gruff voice; surly. —**gruffly** *adv.*, **gruffness** *n.* [f. Du. or MLG *grof* coarse]

grumble *v.t./i.* **1** to complain peevishly; to be

discontented. **2** to make a rumbling sound. —*n*. an act or sound of grumbling. —**grumbler** *n*. [cf. MDu. *grommen*]

grummet /ˈgrʌmɪt/ *n*. **1** an insulating washer placed round an electric conductor where it passes through a hole in metal. **2** (*Naut.*) a ring usually of twisted rope as a fastening etc. [f. F (*gourmer* to curb)]

grumpy *adj*. morose and irritable, surly. —**grumpily** *adv*., **grumpiness** *n*. [imit.]

grunt *n*. the low guttural sound characteristic of the pig. —*v.t./i*. **1** to utter a grunt. **2** to speak or say with a grunt. **3** to grumble. [OE (imit.)]

gruyère /ˈgruːjeə(r)/ *n*. a kind of cheese, originally Swiss, with many holes. [f. *Gruyère* in Switzerland]

gryphon var. of GRIFFIN.

G-string /ˈdʒiːstrɪŋ/ *n*. **1** a narrow strip of cloth etc. covering the genitals, attached to a string round the waist. **2** the string on a violin etc. sounding the note G.

GT *n*. a high-performance car. [abbr. of It. *gran turismo* great touring]

guano /ˈgwɑːnəʊ/ *n*. (*pl*. **-os**) **1** excrement of sea-fowl, used as manure. **2** artificial manure, especially that made from fish. [Sp. f. Quechua]

Guarani /ˈgwɑːrənɪ/ *n*. a member or the language of a South American ethnic group. —*adj*. of this group or their language. [Sp.]

guarantee /gærənˈtiː/ *n*. **1** a formal promise or assurance, especially that a thing is of a specified quality and durability. **2** a guarantor. **3** a guaranty; a thing serving as a security. —*v.t*. to give or serve as a guarantee for; to provide with a guarantee; to give one's word; to secure (a thing *to* a person). [earlier *garante*, perh. f. Sp. and F (as WARRANT)]

guarantor /ˈgærəntə(r), -ˈtɔː(r)/ *n*. the giver of a guaranty or security. [f. prec.]

guaranty /ˈgærəntɪ/ *n*. an undertaking, usually written, to answer for the payment of a debt or the performance of an obligation by the person primarily liable; the ground of a security. [f. AF *guarantie*, var. of *warantie* warranty]

guard /gɑːd/ *v.t./i*. **1** to watch over and defend or protect. **2** to supervise (prisoners etc.) and prevent from escaping. **3** to keep (thoughts or speech) in check. **4** to take precautions (*against*). —*n*. **1** a state of vigilance or watchfulness. **2** a protector, a sentry; (*US*) a prison warder. **3** a railway official in charge of a train. **4** soldiers protecting a place or person; an escort; a separate portion of an army. **5** a device to prevent injury or accident. **6** a defensive posture or motion in boxing, fencing, etc. **7** (in *pl*., usu. **Guards**) the Household troops. —**on** (*or* **off**) **one's guard,** ready (or not ready) against an attack or challenge. **stand guard,** to act as a sentry or guard (*over*). [f. OF *garder* (as WARD)]

guardant /ˈgɑːd(ə)nt/ *adj*. (in heraldry) depicted with the body sideways but the face towards the spectator. [f. prec.]

guarded /ˈgɑːdɪd/ *adj*. (of remarks) cautious. [f. GUARD]

guardhouse *n*. a building accommodating a military guard or securing prisoners.

guardian /ˈgɑːdɪən/ *n*. **1** a protector, a keeper. **2** a person having legal custody of one incapable of managing his own affairs, or of his property. —**guardianship** *n*. [f. AF (as GUARD, WARDEN)]

guardroom *n*. a room accommodating a military guard or securing prisoners.

guardsman *n*. (*pl*. **-men**) a soldier belonging to a guard or the Guards.

guava /ˈgwɑːvə/ *n*. a tropical American tree (*Psidium guajava*,); its edible orange acid fruit. [f. Sp. *guayaba* prob. f. S. Amer. name]

gubernatorial /gjuːbənəˈtɔːrɪəl/ *adj*. (*US*) of a governor. [f. L *gubernator* governor]

gudgeon[1] /ˈgʌdʒ(ə)n/ *n*. **1** a small freshwater fish (*Gobio gobio*) used as bait. **2** a credulous person. [f. OF f. L *gobio* goby]

gudgeon[2] /ˈgʌdʒ(ə)n/ *n*. a kind of pivot or metal pin; a socket for a rudder. [f. OF *goujon* (as GOUGE)]

guelder rose /ˈgeldə(r)/ a shrub (*Viburnum opulus*) with bunches of round white flowers. [f. Du. (*Gelderland* in Holland)]

Guernsey /ˈgɜːnzɪ/ *n*. a breed of dairy cattle from Guernsey in the Channel Islands; an animal of this breed. —**Guernsey lily,** a kind of amaryllis (*Nerine sarniensis*).

guernsey /ˈgɜːnzɪ/ *n*. **1** a thick knitted woollen (usually blue) outer tunic or jersey. **2** (*Austral.*) a football shirt. [f. prec.]

guerrilla /gəˈrɪlə/ *n*. a person taking part in irregular fighting by small groups acting independently. [f. Sp. (dim. of *guerra* war)]

guess /ges/ *v.t./i*. **1** to estimate without measurement or detailed calculation. **2** to form an opinion; to form a hypothesis about; to think likely. **3** to conjecture (the answer to a riddle etc.) correctly. —*n*. a rough estimate; a conjecture. —**guess at,** to make a guess concerning. **I guess,** (*US*) I think it likely, I suppose. —**guesser** *n*. [orig. unkn.]

guesswork *n*. guessing; procedure based on this.

guest /gest/ *n*. **1** a person invited to visit one's house or have a meal etc. at one's expense. **2** a person lodging at a hotel etc. **3** a performer not belonging to the regular company. —**guest-house** *n*. a superior boarding-house. [f. ON]

guff *n.* (*slang*) empty talk. [imit.]

guffaw /gʌˈfɔː/ *n.* a boisterous laugh. —*v.i.* to utter a guffaw. [imit.]

guidance /ˈgaɪd(ə)ns/ *n.* guiding, being guided; advice on problems. [f. foll.]

guide /gaɪd/ *n.* **1** one who shows the way. **2** a hired conductor for tourists. **3** a person or thing by which others regulate their movements. **4** Guide (formerly **Girl Guide**) a member of a girls' organization corresponding to the Scout Association. **5** an adviser; a directing principle. **6** a book of rudiments; a guidebook. **7** a rod etc. directing motion. **8** a thing marking a position or guiding the eye. —*v.t.* **1** to act as a guide to. **2** to be the principle or motive of. **3** to arrange the course of (events). —**guided missile,** a missile under remote control or directed by equipment within itself. **guide-dog** *n.* a dog trained to guide a blind person. **guided tour,** a tour accompanied by a guide. **guide-line** *n.* a directing principle. [f. OF]

guidebook *n.* a book of information for tourists.

Guider *n.* an adult leader of Guides. [f. GUIDE]

guild /gɪld/ *n.* an association formed for the mutual aid and protection of its members, or for some common purpose. [prob. f. G and Du., rel. to OE *gi(e)ld* payment, guild]

guilder /ˈgɪldə(r)/ *n.* **1** a currency unit of the Netherlands, a florin. **2** (*hist.*) a gold coin of the Netherlands and Germany. [alt. of Du. *gulden*]

guild-hall *n.* **1** a hall in which a medieval guild met. **2** a town hall. —**Guildhall,** the hall of the Corporation of the City of London, used for State banquets etc.

guile /gaɪl/ *n.* treachery, deceit; cunning, craftiness. —**guileful** *adj.*, **guileless** *adj.*, **guilelessness** *n.* [f. OF]

guillemot /ˈgɪlɪmɒt/ *n.* an auk of the genus *Uria* or *Cepphus*. [F, f. *Guillaume* William]

guillotine /ˈgɪləti:n, -ˈti:n/ *n.* **1** a machine with a blade sliding in grooves, used for beheading criminals. **2** a machine for cutting paper, metal, etc. **3** a method of preventing a delay in Parliament by fixing the times for voting on parts of a bill. —*v.t.* to use a guillotine on. [F, f. J.-I. *Guillotin*, physician who suggested its use in 1789]

guilt /gɪlt/ *n.* the fact of having committed a specified or implied offence; culpability; a feeling that one is to blame. [OE]

guiltless *adj.* **1** innocent. **2** not having knowledge or possession *of*. [f. GUILT + -LESS]

guilty *adj.* **1** having, showing, or due to guilt. **2** having committed the offence (of). —**guiltily** *adv.*, **guiltiness** *n.* [f. GUILT]

guinea /ˈgɪnɪ/ *n.* **1** a former British gold coin worth 21 shillings (£1.05), first coined for the African trade (whence its name). **2** this sum of money, used in stating professional fees etc. —**guinea-fowl** *n.* a domestic fowl of the genus *Numida* (especially *N. meleagris*) with grey plumage spotted with white. **guinea-pig** *n.* a South American rodent of the genus *Cavia* kept as a pet or for research in biology; a person used as a subject for experiment. [f. *Guinea* in W. Africa]

guipure /ˈgi:pʊə(r)/ *n.* a heavy lace of linen pieces joined by embroidery. [F (*guiper* cover with silk etc.)]

guise /gaɪz/ *n.* an assumed appearance, a pretence; external appearance. [f. OF (as WISE[2])]

guitar /gɪˈtɑ:(r)/ *n.* a plucked string instrument with frets, played either with the fingers or with a plectrum or finger-pick. —**guitarist** *n.* [f. F or Sp. f. Gk *kithara*]

Gujarati /gu:dʒəˈrɑ:tɪ/ *n.* **1** a native of the State of Gujarat. **2** a language spoken in Gujarat. [Hindi]

gulch *n.* (*US*) a ravine, especially containing a torrent. [perh. f. dial. *gulch* to swallow]

gules /gju:lz/ *n.* & *adj.* (in heraldry) red. [f. OF *go(u)les* (pl. of *gole* throat) red-dyed fur neck-ornaments]

gulf *n.* **1** a large area of sea partly surrounded by land. **2** a deep hollow, a chasm. **3** a wide difference of opinion etc. —**Gulf Stream,** a warm ocean current flowing from the Gulf of Mexico to NW Europe. [f. OF f. It. f. Gk *kolpos* bosom, gulf]

gull[1] *n.* a large sea-bird of the family Laridae, with webbed feet and long wings. [prob. f. Welsh *gwylan*]

gull[2] *n.* (*archaic*) a fool, a dupe. —*v.t.* (*archaic*) to cheat, to fool. [perh. f. obs. *gull* yellow f. ON]

gullet /ˈgʌlɪt/ *n.* the passage for food, extending from the mouth to the stomach. [f. OF dim. (*goule* throat f. L *gula*)]

gullible /ˈgʌlɪb(ə)l/ *adj.* easily persuaded or deceived. —**gullibility** /-ˈbɪlɪtɪ/ *n.* [f. GULL[2]]

gully *n.* **1** a channel or ravine cut by water. **2** a gutter, a drain. **3** a fielding-position in cricket between point and slips. [f. F *goulet* bottle-neck (as GULLET)]

gulp *v.t./i.* **1** to swallow (*down*) hastily, greedily, or with effort. **2** to keep (sobs etc.) *back* or *down* with difficulty. **3** to make a swallowing action with effort, to choke. —*n.* **1** the act of gulping. **2** a large mouthful of liquid. [f. MDu. *gulpen* (imit.)]

gulper *n.* a deep-sea fish with a soft tapered body, long tail, and greatly expandable stomach that can accommodate large prey. [f. GULP]

gum[1] *n.* **1** a sticky substance secreted by some trees and shrubs, used especially for sticking paper etc. together. **2** chewing-gum. **3** a gum-drop. **4** gum arabic. **5** a gum tree. —*v.t.* (**-mm-**) to fasten with gum; to apply gum to. —**gum arabic,** a gum exuded by some kinds of acacia. **gum-drop** *n.* a hard transparent sweet made of gelatine etc. **gum-tree** *n.* a tree that exudes gum, especially a eucalyptus (*up a gum-tree,* in great difficulty). **gum up,** (*colloq.*) to interfere with, to spoil. [f. OF f. L *gummi, cummi* f. Gk f. Egyptian]

gum[2] *n.* (often in *pl.*) the firm flesh around the roots of the teeth. [OE]

gum[3] *n.* **by gum!,** (*slang*) by God! [corruption of *God*]

gumboil *n.* a small abscess on the gum.

gumboot *n.* a rubber boot.

gummy[1] *adj.* sticky, exuding gum. —**gumminess** *n.* [f. GUM[1]]

gummy[2] *adj.* toothless. [f. GUM[2]]

gumption /ˈgʌmpʃ(ə)n/ *n.* (*colloq.*) common sense; resource, initiative. [orig. unkn.]

gun *n.* **1** any kind of weapon consisting of a metal tube for throwing missiles with an explosive propellant. **2** a starting-pistol. **3** a device for discharging grease etc. on to a desired point. **4** a person using a sporting gun as a member of a shooting-party. **5** (*US*) a gunman. —*v.t./i.* (**-nn-**) **1** to shoot at or *down*. **2** (*colloq.*) to accelerate (an engine etc.). **3** to go shooting. —**at gunpoint,** threatened by a gun. **be gunning for,** to seek to attack or rebuke. **going great guns,** acting vigorously and near success. **gun-carriage** *n.* a wheeled support for a gun. **gun cotton,** an explosive of cellulose steeped in acid. **gun dog,** a dog trained to retrieve game in a shoot. **gun-fight** *n.* (*US*) a fight with firearms. **gun-metal** *n.* an alloy formerly used for guns; its bluish-grey colour. **gun-runner** *n.* a person involved in gun-running. **gun-running** *n.* the systematic smuggling of guns and ammunition into a country. **stick to one's guns,** to maintain one's position. [perh. f. Scand. *Gunnhildr* woman's name]

gunboat *n.* a small warship with relatively heavy guns. —**gunboat diplomacy,** diplomacy backed by the threat of force.

gunfire *n.* the firing of guns.

gunman *n.* (*pl.* **-men**) a man armed with a gun, especially in committing a crime.

gunnel var. of GUNWALE.

gunner *n.* **1** an artillery soldier especially as the official term for a private. **2** a naval warrant officer in charge of a battery, magazine, etc. **3** an airman who operates a gun. **4** a game-shooter. [f. GUN]

gunnery *n.* **1** the construction and management of large guns. **2** the firing of guns. [f. GUN]

gunny *n.* a coarse sacking usually of jute fibre; a sack made of this. [f. Hindi & Marathi f. Skr.]

gunpowder *n.* the earliest known propellant explosive, a mixture of potassium nitrate, charcoal, and sulphur.

gunroom *n.* **1** a room in a warship for junior officers. **2** a room for sporting-guns etc. in a house.

gunshot *n.* **1** a shot from a gun. **2** the range of a gun.

gunsmith *n.* a maker and repairer of small firearms.

gunwale /ˈgʌn(ə)l/ *n.* the upper edge of a ship's or boat's side. [f. GUN + WALE (because formerly used to support guns)]

guppy /ˈgʌpɪ/ *n.* a small West Indian fish (*Lebistes reticulatus*). [f. R. J. L. *Guppy,* who sent the first specimen to the British Museum]

gurdwara /gɜːˈdwɑːrə/ *n.* a Sikh place of worship, containing a copy of the Adi Granth. [Punjabi, f. Skr. *guru* teacher, *dvara* door]

gurgle *n.* a bubbling sound as of water from a bottle. —*v.t./i.* to make gurgles; to utter with gurgles. [prob. imit.]

Gurkha /ˈgɜːkə/ *n.* **1** a member of a military people of Nepal. **2** a member of one of the Gurkha regiments (orig. specifically for Nepalese soldiers) in the British Army. [native name, f. Skr. *gāus* cow, *raksh* protect]

gurnard /ˈgɜːnəd/ *n.* a sea-fish of the family Triglidae, with a large head, mailed cheeks, and finger-like pectoral rays. [f. OF]

guru /ˈgʊruː/ *n.* **1** a Hindu spiritual teacher or head of a religious sect. **2** an influential or revered teacher. [f. Hindi, f. Skr., = heavy]

gush *n.* **1** a sudden or copious stream. **2** effusiveness. —*v.t./i.* **1** to flow (*out* etc.) with a gush; to emit a gush of (water etc.). **2** to speak or behave effusively. [prob. imit.]

gusher *n.* **1** an oil-well emitting unpumped oil. **2** an effusive person. [f. GUSH]

gusset /ˈgʌsɪt/ *n.* **1** a piece let into a garment etc. to strengthen or enlarge it. **2** a strengthening iron bracket. [f. OF *gousset* flexible piece filling up a joint in armour]

gust *n.* a sudden violent rush of wind; a burst of rain, smoke, anger, etc. —*v.i.* to blow in gusts. —**gusty** *adj.*, **gustily** *adv.* [f. ON]

gustatory /ˈgʌstətərɪ/ *adj.* connected with the sense of taste. [f. L (*gustare* f. *gustus* taste)]

gusto /ˈgʌstəʊ/ *n.* zest, enjoyment in doing a thing. [It. f. L *gustus* taste]

gut *n.* **1** the intestine; (in *pl.*) the bowels or entrails. **2** (in *pl., colloq.*) pluck, force of character; staying power. **3** material for violin etc. strings or surgical use made from the intestines of animals; material for fishing-lines made from the intestines of the silk-worm. **4** (in *pl.*) the contents or fittings; a thing's essence. **5** a narrow passage or water-passage. —*adj*. instinctive; fundamental. —*v.t*. (**-tt-**) **1** to remove the guts of (a fish). **2** to remove or destroy the internal fittings of (a building). **3** to extract the essence of (a book etc.). —**hate a person's guts**, to dislike him intensely. [OE]

gutless *adj*. (*colloq*.) lacking energy or courage. [f. GUT + -LESS]

gutsy *adj*. **1** (*colloq*.) courageous. **2** (*slang*) greedy. [f. GUT]

gutta-percha /gʌtəˈpɜːtʃə/ *n*. a tough plastic substance from the latex of various Malayan trees. [f. Malay]

gutter *n*. a shallow trough below the eaves, or a channel at the side of a street, for carrying off rain-water; a channel, a groove. —*v.i*. (of a candle) to burn unsteadily and melt away rapidly. —**the gutter**, a place of low breeding or vulgar behaviour. **gutter press**, sensational journalism. [f. AF f. L *gutta* drop]

guttering *n*. material for gutters. [f. prec.]

guttersnipe *n*. a street urchin.

guttural /ˈgʌtər(ə)l/ *adj*. **1** throaty, harsh-sounding. **2** (of consonants) produced in the throat or by the back of the tongue and palate. **3** of the throat. —*n*. a guttural consonant (as *g*, *k*). —**gutturally** *adv*. [F, or f. L (*guttur* throat)]

guv *n*. an informal form of address to a superior. [abbr.]

guy[1] /gaɪ/ *n*. **1** an effigy of Guy Fawkes burnt on 5 Nov. **2** (*slang*) a man. **3** a grotesquely-dressed person. —*v.t*. to ridicule. [f. *Guy* Fawkes, conspirator in the Gunpowder Plot to blow up Parliament in 1605]

guy[2] /gaɪ/ *n*. a rope or chain to secure a tent or steady a crane-load etc. —*v.t*. to secure with guys. [prob. f. LG]

guzzle *v.t./i*. to eat or drink greedily. [prob. f. OF *gosiller* (*gosier* throat)]

gybe /dʒaɪb/ *v.t./i*. (of a fore-and-aft sail or boom) to swing to the other side; to make (a sail) gybe; (of a boat etc.) to change course thus. [f. obs. Du. *gibjen*]

gym /dʒɪm/ *n*. (*colloq*.) **1** a gymnasium. **2** gymnastics. —**gym-slip** *n*. a sleeveless tunic, usually belted, worn by schoolgirls. [abbr.]

gymkhana /dʒɪmˈkɑːnə/ *n*. a meeting for competition in a sport, especially horse-riding. [f. Hindi *gendkhāna* ball-house, assim. to foll.]

gymnasium /dʒɪmˈneɪzɪəm/ *n*. (*pl*. **-ums**) a room etc. equipped for gymnastics. [L f. Gk (*gumnos* naked)]

gymnast /ˈdʒɪmnæst/ *n*. an expert in gymnastics. [f. F or Gk (as prec.)]

gymnastic /dʒɪmˈnæstɪk/ *adj*. of gymnastics. —**gymnastically** *adv*. [f. L f. Gk (as GYMNASIUM)]

gymnastics *n.pl*. (occas. treated as *sing*.) exercises to develop the muscles or demonstrate agility (also *fig*.). [f. prec.]

gymnosperm /ˈdʒɪmnəspɜːm/ *n*. a member of the group of plants (mainly trees) that bear seeds 'naked', i.e. not enclosed in an ovary (opp. ANGIOSPERM). [f. Gk *gumnos* naked]

gymp var. of GIMP.

gynaecology /gaɪnɪˈkɒlədʒɪ/ *n*. the science of the physiological functions and diseases of women. —**gynaecological** /-kəˈlɒdʒɪk(ə)l/ *adj*., **gynaecologist** *n*. [f. Gk *gunē* woman + -LOGY]

gyp /dʒɪp/ *n*. **give a person gyp**, (*colloq*.) to punish severely or hurt him. [perh. f. *gee up* (GEE[2])]

gypsum /ˈdʒɪpsəm/ *n*. a mineral (calcium sulphate) used to make plaster of Paris or as a fertilizer. —**gypseous** *adj*. [L f. Gk *gupsos*]

gypsy /ˈdʒɪpsɪ/ *n*. a member of a travelling people with dark skin and hair, and usually living by seasonal work, itinerant trade, and fortune-telling. —**gypsy moth**, a kind of tussock-moth very destructive to foliage. **gypsy's warning**, a cryptic or sinister warning. [earlier *gipcyan*, *gipsen*, f. EGYPTIAN, reflecting their supposed origin when they appeared in England about the beginning of the 16th c.]

gyrate /dʒaɪˈreɪt/ *v.i*. to move in a circle or spiral. —**gyration** *n*., **gyratory** /ˈdʒaɪrətərɪ/ *adj*. [f. L *gyrare* (as GYRO-)]

gyrfalcon /ˈdʒɜːfɔːlkən/ *n*. a large northern falcon (*Falco rusticolus*). [f. OF f. ON]

gyro- /gaɪrəʊ-/ *in comb*. rotation; gyroscopic. [f. Gk *guros* ring]

gyro /ˈdʒaɪrəʊ/ *n*. (*colloq*.) a gyroscope. [abbr.]

gyrocompass *n*. a compass giving the true north and bearings from it relative to the earth's rotation and depending on the properties of a gyroscope, independent of earth's magnetism.

gyroscope /ˈdʒaɪrəskəʊp/ *n*. a rotating wheel whose axis is free to change its direction but maintains a fixed direction in the absence of perturbing forces. —**gyroscopic** /-ˈskɒpɪk/ *adj*. [F (as GYRO-, -SCOPE)]

Hh

H, h /eɪtʃ/ *n.* (*pl.* **Hs, H's**) the eighth letter of the alphabet.

H *abbr.* hard (pencil-lead).

H *symbol* hydrogen.

h. *abbr.* **1** hecto-. **2** hot. **3** hour(s).

Ha *symbol* hahnium.

ha /hɑː/ *int.* expressing surprise, suspicion, triumph, etc.

ha. *abbr.* hectare(s).

habeas corpus /ˈheɪbɪəs ˈkɔpəs/ a writ requiring a person under arrest to be brought before a judge or into court, especially to investigate the lawfulness of his restraint. [L, = you must have the body]

haberdasher /ˈhæbədæʃə(r)/ *n.* a dealer in accessories of dress and in sewing-goods. —**haberdashery** *n.* [orig. unkn.]

habiliments /həˈbɪlɪmənts/ *n.pl.* clothing, attire. [f. OF (*habiller* fit out, f. *habile* able)]

habit /ˈhæbɪt/ *n.* **1** a settled or regular tendency or practice; a practice that is hard to give up. **2** mental constitution. **3** dress, especially of a religious order. —**habit-forming** *adj.* causing addiction. [f. OF f. L *habitus* (*habēre* have)]

habitable *adj.* suitable for living in. —**habitability** /-ˈbɪlɪtɪ/ *n.* [f. OF f. L (*habitare* inhabit)]

habitat /ˈhæbɪtæt/ *n.* the natural home of an animal or plant. [L, = it inhabits]

habitation /hæbɪˈteɪʃ(ə)n/ *n.* **1** a house or home. **2** inhabiting. [f. OF f. L (as HABITABLE)]

habitual /həˈbɪtjʊəl/ *adj.* **1** done constantly or as a habit; regular, usual. **2** given to a habit. —**habitually** *adv.* [f. L (as HABIT)]

habituate /həˈbɪtjʊeɪt/ *v.t.* to accustom (to). —**habituation** /-ˈeɪʃ(ə)n/ *n.* [f. L (as HABIT)]

habitué /həˈbɪtjʊeɪ/ *n.* a resident or frequent visitor (*of*). [F (as prec.)]

hachures /hæˈʃʊə(r)z/ *n.pl.* parallel lines used on maps to indicate the degree of slope in hills. [F (as HATCH[3])]

hacienda /hæsɪˈendə/ *n.* (in a Spanish-speaking country) a large estate etc. with a dwelling-house. [Sp., f. L *facienda* things to be done]

hack[1] *v.t./i.* **1** to cut or chop roughly. **2** to kick the shin of (an opponent at football); to deal chopping blows (*at*). **3** (*colloq.*) to gain unauthorized access to (computer files); (in *partic.*) to use a computer for the satisfaction that it gives. —*n.* **1** a kick with the toe of a boot etc.; a wound from this. **2** a mattock. **3** a miner's pick. —**hacking cough,** a short dry frequent cough. **hack-saw** *n.* a saw with a narrow blade set in a frame, for cutting metal. —**hacker** *n.* [OE]

hack[2] *n.* **1** a horse for ordinary riding; a horse let out for hire. **2** a person hired to do dull routine work, especially as a writer. —*v.i.* to ride on horseback at an ordinary pace. —*adj.* used as a hack; commonplace. [abbr. of HACKNEY]

hackle *n.* **1** the long feather(s) on the neck of the domestic cock etc. **2** a steel comb for dressing flax etc. —**make a person's hackles rise,** to make him very angry. **with his hackles up,** angry, ready to fight. [rel. to HOOK]

hackney /ˈhæknɪ/ *n.* a horse for ordinary riding. —**hackney carriage,** a taxi. [perh. f. *Hackney* in London]

hackneyed /ˈhæknɪd/ *adj.* (of a phrase etc.) made commonplace or trite by long over-use. [f. prec.]

had *past* & *p.p.* of HAVE.

haddock /ˈhædək/ *n.* (*pl.* same) a sea-fish (*Melanogrammus aeglefinus*) related to the cod, used for food. [prob. f. AF]

Hades /ˈheɪdiːz/ *n.* hell. [Gk, = unseen]

hadj /hædʒ/ *n.* pilgrimage to Mecca, a duty of Muslims. [f. Arab., = pilgrimage]

hadji /ˈhædʒɪ/ *n.* (also **hajji**) a Muslim who has been to Mecca as a pilgrim. [f. Pers. & Turk., = pilgrim (as prec.)]

hadn't (*colloq.*) had not.

hadron /ˈhædrɒn/ *n.* any strongly interacting sub-atomic particle. [f. Gk *hadros* thick, bulky]

haemal /ˈhiːm(ə)l/ *adj.* of the blood. [f. Gk *haima* blood]

haematic /hiːˈmætɪk/ *adj.* of or containing blood. [as prec.]

haematite /ˈhiːmətaɪt/ *n.* ferric oxide as ore. [f. L f. Gk, = bloodlike stone (as HAEMAL)]

haematology /hiːməˈtɒlədʒɪ/ *n.* the study of the physiology of the blood. [as HAEMAL + -LOGY]

haemoglobin /hi:mə'gləubın/ *n.* the oxygen-carrying substance in the red blood-cells of vertebrates. [f. *haematin* constituent of haemoglobin (as HAEMAL) + GLOBULIN]

haemophilia /hi:mə'fılıə/ *n.* a constitutional, usually hereditary, tendency to bleed severely from even a slight injury, through failure of the blood to clot normally. —**haemophilic** *adj.* [f. Gk *haima* blood + *philia* loving]

haemophiliac /hi:mə'fılıæk/ *n.* a person suffering from haemophilia. [f. prec.]

haemorrhage /'hemərıdʒ/ *n.* an escape of blood from a blood-vessel, especially when profuse. —*v.i.* to undergo haemorrhage. [f. F f. L f. Gk (*haima* blood, *rhēgnumi* burst)]

haemorrhoid /'hemərɔıd/ *n.* (usu. in *pl.*) a swollen vein at or near the anus. [f. OF or L f. Gk (*haima* blood, *-rhoos* -flowing)]

hafnium /'hæfnıəm/ *n.* a metallic element with a silver lustre, symbol Hf, atomic number 72. [f. *Hafnia* Latinized name of Copenhagen (Da. *havn* harbour)]

haft /hɑ:ft/ *n.* a handle (of a dagger, knife, etc.). —*v.t.* to furnish with a haft. [OE]

hag *n.* an ugly old woman; a witch. —**haggish** *adj.* [OE]

haggard /'hægəd/ *adj.* looking exhausted and distraught from prolonged worry etc. —*n.* a hawk caught when full-grown. [f. F]

haggis /'hægıs/ *n.* a Scottish dish of offal boiled in a bag with suet, oatmeal, etc. [orig. unkn.]

haggle *v.i.* to dispute or argue (esp. *about* or *over* a price or terms). —*n.* haggling. [orig. = 'to hack', f. ON]

hagio- /hægıəυ-/ *in comb.* of saints. [f. Gk *hagios* holy]

hagiography /hægı'ɒgrəfı/ *n.* the writing of saints' lives. —**hagiographer** *n.* [f. HAGIO- + -GRAPHY]

hagiology /hægı'ɒlədʒı/ *n.* the literature of the lives and legends of saints. [f. HAGIO- + -LOGY]

hagridden *adj.* afflicted by nightmares or fears. [f. HAG + *ridden* p.p. of RIDE]

ha ha /hɑ: 'hɑ:/ repr. laughter. [OE]

ha-ha /'hɑ:hɑ:/ *n.* a ditch with a wall on the inner side, forming the boundary to a park or garden without interrupting the view. [F, perh. f. cry of surprise at discovering the obstacle]

hahnium /'hɑ:nıəm/ *n.* the US name for the chemical element of atomic number 105. [f. O. *Hahn*, German chemist (d. 1968)]

haiku /'haıkυ/ *n.* (*pl.* same) a Japanese lyric form of 17 syllables in lines of 5, 7, 5, syllables. [Jap.]

hail[1] *n.* **1** pellets of frozen rain falling in a shower. **2** a shower *of* blows, missiles, questions, etc. —*v.t./i.* to fall or send down as or like hail. [OE]

hail[2] *int.* of greeting. —*v.t./i.* **1** to salute; to greet *as*. **2** to call to (a person or ship) in order to attract attention; to signal to (a taxi etc.) to stop. **3** to originate, to have come. —*n.* hailing. —**be hail-fellow-well-met**, to be very friendly or too friendly (*with* strangers etc.). [f. ON *heill* whole, sound (cf. HALE)]

hailstone *n.* a pellet of hail.

hailstorm *n.* a prolonged period of heavy hail.

hair *n.* **1** any of the fine threadlike strands growing from the skin of animals, especially from the human head; these collectively; an elongated cell growing from the surface of a plant. **2** a thing resembling a hair. **3** a very small quantity. —**get in a person's hair**, to encumber or annoy him. **hair-do** *n.* (*pl.* **-dos**) (*colloq.*) a hair-style; the process of a woman's hairdressing. **hair-grip** *n.* a flat hairpin with the prongs closing tightly together. **hair-line** *n.* the edge of a person's hair on the forehead etc.; a very narrow crack or line. **hair-net** *n.* a net worn to hold the hair in place. **hair-piece** *n.* a quantity of false hair worn to augment a person's natural hair. **hair-raising** *adj.* terrifying. **hair's breadth**, a minute distance. **hair shirt**, a shirt of haircloth worn by penitents or ascetics. **hair-slide** *n.* a clip for keeping the hair in position. **hair-splitting** *adj.* splitting hairs (see below). **hair-style** *n.* a particular way of arranging the hair. **hair-trigger** *n.* a trigger set for release at the slightest pressure. **keep one's hair on,** (*slang*) to remain calm and not get angry. **let one's hair down,** (*colloq.*) to abandon restraint, to behave wildly; to become confidential. **make one's hair stand on end,** to horrify one. **not to turn a hair,** to remain unmoved or unaffected. **split hairs,** to make small and insignificant distinctions. [OE]

hairbrush *n.* a brush for arranging the hair.

haircloth *n.* cloth woven from hair.

haircut *n.* cutting the hair; a style of doing this.

hairdresser *n.* one whose business is to arrange and cut hair.

hairpin *n.* a U-shaped pin for fastening the hair. —**hairpin bend,** a sharp U-shaped bend in a road.

hairspring *n.* a fine-spring regulating the balance-wheel in a watch.

hairy *adj.* **1** having much hair; made of hair. **2** (*slang*) hair-raising, unpleasant, difficult. —**hairiness** *n.* [f. HAIR]

hake *n.* a sea-fish of the genus *Merluccius*, resembling the cod, used as food. [perh. f. dial. *hake* hook]

halal /hɑ:'lɑ:l/ *v.t.* to kill (an animal for meat) as prescribed by Muslim law. —*n.* meat prepared thus. [f. Arab., = lawful]

halberd /ˈhælbəd/ *n.* (*hist.*) a combined spear and battle-axe. [f. F f. It. f. MHG *helmbarde*]

halcyon /ˈhælsɪən/ *adj.* calm and peaceful; (of a period) happy, prosperous. [f. L f. Gk, = kingfisher, reputed to calm the sea at midwinter]

hale[1] *adj.* strong and healthy. [northern var. of WHOLE]

hale[2] *v.t.* (*archaic*) to drag or draw forcibly. [f. OF f. ON]

half /hɑːf/ *n.* (*pl.* **halves** /hɑːvz/) **1** either of two equal or corresponding parts into which a thing is or might be divided; either of two equal periods of play in sports. **2** a half-price ticket, especially for a child. **3** a school term. **4** (*colloq.*) a half-back. **5** (*colloq.*) a half-pint. —*adj.* amounting to half; forming a half. —*adv.* to the extent of half; (*loosely*) to some extent. —**at half cock,** when only half-ready. **by half,** excessively. **by halves,** without complete commitment (usu. after *neg.*). **go halves,** to share equally (*with*). **half-and-half** *adj.* being half one thing and half another. **half-back** *n.* a player between the forwards and the full-back in football, hockey, etc. **half-baked** *adj.* not thoroughly thought out, foolish. **half-binding** *n.* the binding of a book with leather on the spine and corners. **half-breed, -caste** *ns.* a person of mixed race. **half-brother, -sister** *ns.* a brother or sister with only one parent in common. **half-crown, half a crown,** (*hist.*) a coin or amount of 2*s.* 6*d.* **half-hearted** *adj.* lacking enthusiasm. **half hitch,** a knot formed by passing the end of a rope round its standing part and then through the bight. **half-landing** *n.* a landing half-way up a flight of stairs. **half-mast** *n.* the position of a flag half-way up a mast, as a mark of respect for a dead person. **half measures,** measures lacking thoroughness. **half moon,** the moon when only half its disc is illuminated; the time when this occurs; a semicircular object. **half nelson,** a hold in wrestling with the arm under an opponent's arm and behind his back. **half-term** *n.* the period about half-way through a school term, usually with a short holiday. **half-timbered** *adj.* having walls with a timber frame and brick or plaster filling, a structural style common in England in the 15th-16th c. **half-time** *n.* the time at which half of a game or contest is completed, the interval then occurring. **half-title** *n.* the title or short title of a book usually printed on the recto of the leaf preceding the title-leaf. **half-tone** *n.* a black-and-white photographic illustration in which the light and dark shades are reproduced by small and large dots. **half-track** *n.* a propulsion system with wheels at the front and an endless driven belt at the back; a vehicle having this. **half-truth** *n.* a statement conveying only part of the truth. **half-volley** *n.* a return of the ball in tennis as soon as it has touched the ground, a ball in cricket so pitched that the batsman may hit it as it bounces; a hit so made. **half-way** *adj.* & *adv.* at a point equidistant between two others (*half-way house*, a compromise). **not half,** by no means; (*colloq.*) not at all; (*slang*) extremely, violently. [OE]

half-life *n.* the time taken for half of any sample of a particular radioactive isotope to decay into other materials.

halfpenny /ˈheɪpnɪ/ *n.* (*pl.* as PENNY) (*hist.*) half a penny, a coin of this value (legal tender until 1984). —**halfpennyworth** *n.*

half-wit *n.* a stupid or foolish person —**half-witted** *adj.*

halibut /ˈhælɪbət/ *n.* a large flat-fish (*Hippoglossus vulgaris*) used for food. [f. *haly* holy + *butt* flat-fish, perh. because eaten on holy days]

halitosis /hælɪˈtəʊsɪs/ *n.* unpleasant-smelling breath. [f. L *halitus* breath]

hall /hɔl/ *n.* **1** a space or passage into which the front entrance of a house etc. opens. **2** a large room or building for meetings, meals, concerts, etc. **3** a large country house, especially with a landed estate; a university building used for the residence or instruction of students; (in college etc.) a common dining-room. **4** a large public room in a palace etc.; the principal living-room of a medieval house. **5** the building of a guild. [OE]

hallelujah var. of ALLELUIA.

halliard var. of HALYARD.

hallmark *n.* **1** a mark used at Goldsmiths' Hall (and by UK assay offices) for indicating the standard of gold, silver, and (since 1975) platinum. **2** a distinctive feature —*v.t.* to stamp with a hallmark.

hallo /həˈləʊ/ *int.* used in greeting, or to call attention or express surprise. —*n.* (*pl.* **-os**) the cry 'hallo'. [var. of earlier *hollo*]

halloo /həˈluː/ *int.* & *n.* a cry used to urge on hounds, or to attract attention. —*v.t./i.* to shout 'halloo' (to). [perh. f. *hallow* pursue with shouts f. OF (imit.)]

hallow /ˈhæləʊ/ *v.t.* to make or honour as holy. [OE (as HOLY]

Hallowe'en /hæləʊˈiːn/ *n.* 31 Oct., the eve of All Saints' Day. [f. *hallow* holy person + EVEN[2]]

hallucinate /həˈluːsɪneɪt/ *v.t./i.* to experience or cause to experience hallucinations. —**hallucinant** *adj.* & *n.* [f. L, = wander in mind f. Gk *alussō* be uneasy]

hallucination /həluːsɪˈneɪʃ(ə)n/ *n.* an illusion of seeing or hearing an external object not actually present. —**hallucinatory** /həˈluːsɪnətərɪ/ *adj.* [as prec.]

hallucinogen /həˈluːsɪnədʒen/ *n.* a drug causing hallucinations. —**hallucinogenic** /-ˈdʒenɪk/ *adj.* [f. prec. + -GEN]

halma /ˈhælmə/ *n.* a game for two or four persons, played on a board of 256 squares, with men that are moved by leaping over others into the vacant squares beyond, from one corner to the opposite corner. [Gk, = leap]

halo /ˈheɪləʊ/ *n.* (*pl.* **-oes**) **1** a disc or ring of light shown round the head of a sacred figure. **2** a glory round an idealized person etc. **3** a disc of light seen round a luminous body, especially the sun or moon, caused by the refraction of light through vapour. —*v.t.* to surround with a halo. [f. L f. Gk *halōs* threshing-floor, disc of sun or moon]

halogen /ˈhælədʒ(ə)n/ *n.* any of the five chemically related non-metallic elements fluorine, chlorine, bromine, iodine, and astatine. [f. Gk. *hals halos* salt + -GEN]

halt[1] /hɔlt, hɒlt/ *n.* **1** a stop (usually temporary); an interruption to progress. **2** a railway stopping-place for local services, without station buildings. —*v.t./i.* to come or bring to a halt, —**call a halt,** to decide to stop. [f. G (*halt* hold)]

halt[2] /hɔlt, hɒlt/ *v.i.* **1** to walk hesitatingly; (*archaic*) to be lame. **2** to waver. **3** (esp. of reasoning, verse, etc.) to falter, to be defective. —**the halt,** (*archaic*) lame or crippled people. [OE; orig. in phr. *make halt* f. G (*halt* hold)]

halter /ˈhɔltə(r), ˈhɒl-/ *n.* **1** a rope or strap with a headstall, used for leading or tying up a horse. **2** a style of dress-top held up by a strap passing round the back of the neck. —*v.t.* to put a halter on (a horse). [OE]

halve /hɑːv/ *v.t.* **1** to divide into two halves or parts. **2** to reduce by half. **3** (in golf) to draw (a hole or match) with an opponent. **4** to fit (crossing timbers) together by cutting out half the thickness of each. [f. HALF]

halves *pl.* of HALF.

halyard /ˈhæljəd/ *n.* a rope for raising or lowering a sail, yard, etc. [f. HALE[2]]

ham *n.* **1** the upper part of a pig's leg salted and dried or smoked for food; meat from this. **2** the back of the thigh, the thigh and buttock. **3** (*slang*) an inexpert performer or actor. **4** (*colloq.*) the operator of an amateur radio station. —*v.t./i.* (**-mm-**) to overact, to exaggerate one's actions. —**ham-fisted** *adj.*, **ham-handed** *adj.* (*slang*) clumsy. [OE]

hamburger /ˈhæmbɜːgə(r)/ *n.* a flat round cake of minced beef served fried, often eaten in a soft bread roll. [G (f. city of *Hamburg*)]

hamlet /ˈhæmlɪt/ *n.* a small village, especially one without a church. [f. AF dim. *hamelet* ult.f. MLG *hamm*]

hammer *n.* **1** a tool with a heavy metal head at right angles to the handle, used for breaking, driving nails, etc. **2** a similar contrivance, as for exploding the charge in a gun, striking the strings of a piano, etc.; an auctioneer's mallet indicating by a rap that an article is sold. **3** a metal ball attached to a wire for throwing as an athletic contest. —*v.t./i.* **1** to hit or beat (as) with a hammer; to strike loudly. **2** to defeat utterly. —**come under the hammer,** to be sold at an auction. **hammer and sickle,** the symbols of the industrial worker and the peasant, used as the emblem of the USSR. **hammer and tongs,** with great vigour and commotion. **hammer-beam** *n.* a beam that projects into a room etc. from the foot of one of the roof's principal rafters. **hammer-head** *n.* a shark of the family Sphyrnidae, with lateral extensions of the head bearing the eyes. **hammer out,** to devise (a plan) with great effort. **hammer-toe** *n.* a toe bent permanently downwards. [OE]

hammock /ˈhæmək/ *n.* a bed of canvas or rope network, suspended by cords at the ends, used especially on board ship. [f. earlier *hamaca* f. Sp. f. Carib]

hamper[1] *n.* a large basket usually with a hinged lid, especially with contents of food. [f. OF *hanapier* case for goblet (*hanap* goblet)]

hamper[2] *v.t.* to prevent the free movement or activity of; to hinder. [orig. unkn.]

hamster *n.* a small ratlike rodent of the genus *Cricetus* etc., with cheeck-pouches for carrying grain. [G]

hamstring *n.* any of the five tendons at the back of the human knee; the great tendon at the back of the quadruped's hock. —*v.t.* (*past & p.p.* **-stringed** or **-strung**) **1** to cripple (a person, an animal) by cutting the hamstring or hamstrings. **2** to impair the activity or efficiency of.

hand *n.* **1** the end part of the human arm beyond the wrist; the similar member of a monkey. **2** control, custody, disposal; a share in an action, active support; agency. **3** a thing like a hand, especially the pointer of a clock or watch. **4** the right or left side or direction relative to a person or thing. **5** a pledge of marriage. **6** skill; a person with reference to a skill. **7** style of writing; a signature. **8** a person who does or makes something; a person etc. as a source. **9** a manual worker in a factory, farm, etc. **10** the playing-cards dealt to a player; such a player; a round of play. **11** (*colloq.*) applause. **12** a forefoot of a quadruped; a forehock of pork. **13** the measure of a horse's height, = 4 in. —*attrib.* operated by hand; held or carried by hand; done by hand not by machine. —*v.t.* to deliver, to transfer by hand or otherwise (*down*, *in*, *over*, etc.); to serve or distribute *round*. —**all hands,** the entire crew of a ship. **at hand,** close by; about to happen. **by hand,** by a person not a machine; delivered by messenger not by post. **from hand to mouth,** with only one's immediate needs. **get** *or* **have** *or* **keep one's hand in,** to become or be in practice. **hand and** *or* **in glove,** in collusion or association (*with*). **hand-axe** *n.* a prehistoric stone implement, normally oval or pear-shaped and bifacially worked, used for cutting and scraping things as well as for chopping. **hand down,** to transmit (a decision) from a higher court etc. **hand it to,** (*colloq.*) to award deserved praise to. **hand-me-down** *n.* clothing etc. passed on from someone else. **hand-out** *n.* something given free to a needy person; a statement given to the press etc. **hand-over-fist,** (*colloq.*) with rapid progress. **hand-picked** *adj.* carefully chosen. **hands down,** with no difficulty. **hand to hand,** (of fighting) at close quarters. **have one's hands full,** to be fully occupied. **in hand,** at one's disposal, under one's control, receiving attention. **off one's hands,** no longer one's responsibility. **on hand,** available. **on one's hands,** resting on one as a responsibility. **on the one** (*or* **on the other**) **hand,** as one (or another) point of view. **out of hand,** out of control, peremptorily. **put** *or* **set** *or* **turn one's hand to,** to start work on, to engage in. **to hand,** within reach; available. [OE]

handbag *n.* a small bag for holding a purse and small personal articles, carried especially by women.

handball *n.* **1** a ball for throwing with the hand. **2** a game played with this.

handbell *n.* a small bell rung by hand.

handbill *n.* a printed notice circulated by hand.

handbook *n.* a short manual or guidebook.

handbrake *n.* a brake operated by hand.

h. & c. *abbr.* hot and cold (water).

handcart *n.* a small cart pushed or drawn by hand.

handclap *n.* a clapping of the hands.

handcuff *v.t.* to put handcuffs on. —*n.* (in *pl.*) a pair of lockable linked metal rings for securing a prisoner's wrists.

handful *n.* **1** a quantity that fills the hand. **2** a small number (*of* people or things). **3** (*colloq.*) a troublesome person or task. [f. HAND + -FUL]

handicap /ˈhændɪkɜːp/ *n.* **1** a disadvantage imposed on a superior competitor or competitors in order to make the chances more equal; a race or contest in which this is imposed. **2** the number of strokes by which a golfer normally exceeds par for the course. **3** a thing that makes progress or success difficult. **4** a physical or mental disability. —*v.t.* (**-pp-**) to impose a handicap on; to place (a person) at a disadvantage. [app. f. phr. *hand i'* (= in) *cap* describing a kind of sporting lottery]

handicapped *adj.* suffering from a physical or mental disability. [f. prec.]

handicraft /ˈhændɪkrɑːft/ *n.* work that requires both manual and artistic skill. [f. earlier *handcraft*]

handiwork /ˈhændɪwɜːk/ *n.* work done or a thing made by the hands, or by a particular person. [OE *handgeweore* (as HAND, WORK)]

handkerchief /ˈhæŋkətʃɪf, -tʃiːf/ *n.* (*pl.* **-chiefs, -chieves** /-tʃiːvz/) a square of linen, cotton, etc., usually carried in a pocket for wiping the nose etc. [f. HAND + KERCHIEF]

handle *n.* **1** the part by which a thing is held, carried, or controlled. **2** a fact that may be taken advantage of. **3** (*colloq.*) a personal title. —*v.t./i.* **1** to touch, to feel, or move with the hands. **2** to manage or deal with; to deal in (goods); to discuss or write about (a subject). —**fly off the handle,** (*colloq.*) to lose one's self-control. [OE (as HAND)]

handlebar *n.* (often in *pl.*) the steering-bar of a bicycle etc., with a hand-grip at each end. —**handlebar moustache,** a thick moustache with curved ends.

handler *n.* a person who handles things; a person who handles animals, especially one in charge of a trained police-dog etc. [f. HANDLE.]

handmade *adj.* made by hand not machine.

handmaid *n.* (also **-maiden**) (*archaic*) a female servant.

handrail *n.* a narrow rail for holding as a support on stairs etc.

handset *n.* a telephone mouthpiece and ear-piece as one unit.

handshake *n.* a shaking of a person's hand with one's own as a greeting etc.

handsome /ˈhænsəm/ *adj.* **1** good-looking. **2** generous; (of a price, fortune, etc.) considerable. —**handsomely** *adv.*, **handsomeness** *n.* [f. HAND; orig. = 'easily handled']

handspring *n.* a somersault in which one lands first on the hands and then on the feet.

handstand *n.* the acrobatic feat of supporting one's body on one's hands with feet in the air or against a wall.

handwriting *n.* writing with a pen, pencil, etc.; a person's particular style of this. —**handwritten** *adj.*

handy *adj.* **1** convenient to handle or use; ready to hand. **2** clever with the hands. —**handily** *adj.*, **handiness** *n.* [f. HAND]

handyman *n.* (*pl.* **-men**) a person who is good at doing household repairs etc. or who is employed to do odd jobs.

hang *v.t./i.* (*past* & *p.p.* **hung** except in sense 6) **1** to cause a thing to be supported from above, especially with the lower part free. **2** to set up (a door) on hinges. **3** to place (a picture) on a wall or in an exhibition. **4** to attach (wallpaper) to a wall. **5** to decorate (a room etc.) *with* pictures, ornaments, etc. **6** (*past & p.p.* **hanged**) to execute or kill by suspending from a rope round the neck. **7** (*colloq.*, as an imprecation) damn, be damned. **8** to let droop; to be or remain hung (in various senses); to be hanged. —*n.* the way a thing hangs. —**get the hang of,** (*colloq.*) to get the knack of, to understand. **hang about** *or* **around,** to loiter, not to move away. **hang back,** to show reluctance. **hang fire,** to be slow in taking action or in progressing. **hang heavily** *or* **heavy,** (of time) to pass slowly. **hang on,** to stick or hold closely (*to*); to depend on (a circumstance); to remain in office or doing one's duty etc.; to attend closely to; (*colloq.*) not to ring off in telephoning; (*slang*) to wait for a short time. **hang out,** to lean out (*of* a window etc.); to put on a clothes-line etc. **hang over,** to threaten. **hang together,** to be coherent; to remain associated. **hang up,** to hang from a hook etc.; to put aside; to end a telephone conversation; to cause delay to. **hang-up** *n.* (*slang*) an emotional inhibition or problem. **hung parliament,** one in which no party has a clear majority. **not care** *or* **give a hang,** (*colloq.*) not to care at all. [OE]

hangar /ˈhæŋə(r), -ŋgə(r)/ *n.* a shed for housing aircraft etc. [F]

hangdog *adj.* shame-faced.

hanger *n.* **1** a person or thing that hangs. **2** a shaped piece of wood etc. from which clothes may be hung. **3** a loop etc. by which a thing may be hung. —**hanger-on** *n.* (*pl.* **hangers-on**) a follower or dependant, especially an unwelcome one.

hang-glider *n.* the frame used in hang-gliding.

hang-gliding *n.* the sport of gliding while being suspended from an airborne frame controlled by one's movements.

hanging *n.* **1** execution by being hanged. **2** (in *pl.*) draperies hung on a wall etc. —*adj.* that hangs.

hangman *n.* (*pl.* **-men**) an executioner who hangs condemned persons.

hangnail *n.* an agnail. [corrupt.]

hangover *n.* **1** a severe headache or other after-effects caused by an excess of alcohol. **2** something left over from an earlier time.

hank *n.* a coil or length of wool or thread etc. [f. ON]

hanker *v.i.* to long *for*, to crave *after*. [f. obs. *hank*]

hanky *n.* (*colloq.*) a handkerchief. [abbr.]

hanky-panky *n.* (*slang*) dishonest dealing, trickery; naughtiness. [arbitrary]

Hanoverian /hænəʊˈvɪərɪən/ *adj.* of British sovereigns from George I to Victoria. [f. *Hanover* in Germany]

Hansard /ˈhænsɑːd/ the official reports of the proceedings of the Houses of Parliament. [f. *Hansard*, its orig. printer (19th c.)]

Hansen's disease /ˈhæns(ə)nz/ leprosy. [f. G. H. A. *Hansen*, Norwegian physician (d. 1912), discoverer of the leprosy bacillus]

hansom /ˈhænsəm/ *n.* (*hist.*) (in full **hansom cab**) a two-wheeled horse-drawn cab for two inside, with the driver seated behind. [f. J. A. *Hansom*, English architect (d. 1882)]

Hants *abbr.* Hampshire.

Hanukka /ˈhɑːnəkə/ *n.* an eight-day Jewish festival of lights, beginning in December, commemorating the re-dedication of the Temple in 165 BC after its desecration by the Syrian king. [f. Heb., = consecration]

hap *n.* (*archaic*) chance, luck; a chance occurrence. —*v.i.* (**-pp-**) (*archaic*) to come about by chance. [f. ON]

haphazard /hæpˈhæzəd/ *adj.* done etc. by chance, random. —*adv.* at random. —**haphazardly** *adv.* [f. HAP + HAZARD]

hapless *adj.* unlucky. [f. HAP + -LESS]

haploid /ˈhæplɔɪd/ *adj.* having a single set of unpaired chromosomes; having this in somatic cells. —*n.* a haploid cell or organism. [G, f. Gk *haplous* single + *eidos* form]

ha'p'orth /ˈheɪpəθ/ *n.* a halfpennyworth. [contr.]

happen *v.i.* **1** to occur (by chance or otherwise). **2** to have the (good or bad) fortune (*to do* a thing). **3** to be the fate or experience of. —**happen on** *or* **upon,** to find by chance. [f. HAP]

happening *n.* **1** an event. **2** an improvised or spontaneous theatrical etc. performance. [f. prec.]

happy *adj.* **1** feeling or showing pleasure or contentment. **2** fortunate. **3** (of words or behaviour) apt, pleasing. —**happy event,** the birth of a child. **happy-go-lucky** *adj.* cheerfully casual. **happy medium,** a means of satisfactory avoidance of extremes. —**happily** *adv.*, **happiness** *n.* [f. HAP]

hara-kiri /hærəˈkɪrɪ/ *n.* ritual suicide involving disembowelment with the sword, formerly practised by samurai to avoid dishonour. [Jap *hara* belly, *kiri* cutting)]

harangue /həˈræŋ/ *n.* a lengthy and earnest speech. —*v.t./i.* to make a harangue to. [f. OF f. L]

harass /ˈhærəs/ *v.t.* to trouble and annoy continually; to make repeated attacks on (an enemy). —**harassment** /ˈhærəsmənt/ *n.* [f. F f. OF *harer* set dog on]

harbinger /ˈhɑːbɪndʒə(r)/ *n.* a person or thing that announces or signals the approach of another; a forerunner. [f. OF (*herberge* lodging, as foll.), formerly = one sent on ahead to purvey lodgings for army etc.]

harbour /ˈhɑ:bə(r)/ *n.* a place of shelter for ships; shelter. —*v.t.* **1** to give shelter to (a criminal etc.). **2** to keep in one's mind (an unfriendly thought etc.). —**harbour-master** *n.* the officer in charge of a harbour. [OE or f. ON, = army shelter]

hard *adj.* **1** firm, not yielding to pressure; solid, not easily cut. **2** difficult to understand or do or answer. **3** causing unhappiness, difficult to bear; harsh, unpleasant; unsympathetic; (of a season or weather) severe, frosty; (of a bargain) without concessions. **4** strenuous, enthusiastic. **5** (of liquor) strongly alcoholic. **6** (of a drug) potent and addictive. **7** (of water) containing mineral salts that prevent soap from lathering freely and cause a hard coating to form inside kettles, water, tanks, etc. **8** (of facts etc.) established, not to be disputed. **9** (of currency or prices) not likely to fall suddenly in value. **10** (of pornography) highly obscene. **11** (of consonants) guttural (as *c* in *cat*, *g* in *go*). —*adv.* strenuously, intensively; copiously. —**hard and fast,** (of a rule or distinction) definite, unalterable. **hard-boiled** *adj.* (of an egg) boiled until the white and yolk are solid; (of a person) callous. **hard by,** close by. **hard case,** an intractable person; a case of hardship. **hard cash,** coins and banknotes, not cheques or credit. **hard copy,** printed material produced by computer, suitable for ordinary reading. **hard core,** an irreducible nucleus; heavy material as a road-foundation. **hard-headed** *adj.* practical, not sentimental. **hard-hearted** *adj.* unsympathetic. **hard labour,** heavy manual work (e.g. stone-breaking) formerly imposed on persons convicted of serious crimes. **hard line,** unyielding adherence to a firm policy. **hard of hearing,** somewhat deaf. **hard on** *or* **upon,** close to in pursuit or sequence. **hard pad,** a form of distemper in dogs etc. **hard palate,** the front part of the palate. **hard-pressed** *adj.* closely pursued; burdened with urgent business. **hard put to it,** in difficulty. **hard sell,** aggressive salesmanship. **hard shoulder,** a hardened strip alongside a motorway for stopping on in an emergency. **hard up,** short of money; at a loss *for*. **hard-wearing** *adj.* able to stand much wear. —**hardness** *n.* [OE]

hardback *adj.* bound in stiff covers. —*n.* a hardback book.

hardbitten *adj.* tough and tenacious.

hardboard *n.* stiff board made of compressed and treated wood-pulp.

harden *v.t./i.* to make or become hard or harder, or (of an attitude etc.) unyielding. [f. HARD]

hardihood /ˈhɑ:dɪhʊd/ *n.* boldness, daring. [f. HARDY]

hardly *adv.* **1** only with difficulty. **2** scarcely, only just. **3** harshly. [f. HARD]

hardship *n.* severe discomfort or lack of the necessaries of life; a circumstance causing this. [f. HARD + -SHIP]

hardware *n.* **1** tools and household articles of metal etc. **2** heavy machinery or weaponry. **3** the mechanical and electronic components of a computer etc.

hardwood *n.* the hard heavy wood from deciduous trees.

hardy /ˈhɑ:dɪ/ *adj.* robust, capable of enduring difficult conditions; (of a plant) able to grow in the open air all the year. —**hardy annual,** an annual plant that may be sown in the open; a subject that comes up at regular intervals. —**hardiness** *n.* [f. OF *hardi* (*hardir* become bold, as HARD)]

hare *n.* a field mammal of the genus *Lepus* like a rabbit, with long ears, a short tail, hind legs longer than the forelegs, and a divided upper lip. —*v.i.* to run rapidly. —**hare-brained** *adj.* wild and foolish, rash. [OE]

harebell *n.* a plant (*Campanula rotundifolia*) with pale-blue bell-shaped flowers.

harelip *n.* a congenital fissure of the upper lip.

harem /ˈhɑ:ri:m, -ˈri:m/ *n.* the women of a Muslim household, living in a separate part of the house; their quarters. [f. Arab., = prohibited]

haricot /ˈhærɪkəʊ/ *n.* (in full **haricot bean**) the white dried seed of a variety of bean (*Phaseolus vulgaris*). [F]

hark *v.i.* to listen attentively. —**hark back,** to revert *to* a subject. [as HEARKEN]

harlequin /ˈhɑ:lɪkwɪn/ *adj.* in varied colours. [F, f. *Harlequin*, character in Italian comedy]

harlequinade /hɑ:lɪkwɪˈneɪd/ *n.* **1** a play or section of a pantomime in which Harlequin plays the leading role (see prec.). **2** a piece of buffoonery. [f. F (as prec.)]

harlot /ˈhɑ:lət/ *n.* (*archaic*) a prostitute. —**harlotry** *n.* [f. OF, = lad, knave]

harm *n.* damage, injury. —*v.t.* to cause harm to. —**out of harm's way,** in safety. [OE]

harmattan /hɑ:məˈtæn/ *n.* a dry dusty wind that blows on the coast of West Africa from December to February. [f. Afr. dialect *haramata*]

harmful *adj.* causing harm. —**harmfully** *adv.* [f. HARM + -FUL]

harmless *adj.* not able or likely to cause harm; inoffensive. —**harmlessly** *adv.*, **harmlessness** *n.* [f. HARM + -LESS]

harmonic /hɑ:ˈmɒnɪk/ *adj.* **1** (*Mus.*) of or relating to harmony; (of tones) produced by the vibration of a string etc. in any of certain

fractions (half, third, quarter, fifth, etc.) of its length. **2** harmonious. —*n.* a harmonic tone, an overtone. —**harmonic series,** (*Mus.*) the series of overtones that make up the natural components of a single sound.
—**harmonically** *adv.* [f. L f. Gk (as HARMONY)]

harmonica *n.* a mouth-organ. [L (as prec.)]

harmonious /hɑːˈməʊnɪəs/ *adj.* **1** sweet-sounding. **2** forming a pleasing or consistent whole. **3** free from disagreement or dissent.
—**harmoniously** *adv.* [f. HARMONY]

harmonium /hɑːˈməʊnɪəm/ *n.* a keyboard musical instrument in which the notes are produced by air driven through metal reeds by bellows operated by the feet. [F f. L (as HARMONY)]

harmonize /ˈhɑːmənaɪz/ *v.t./i.* **1** to add notes to a melody to provide a harmonic accompaniment to it. **2** to bring into or be in harmony (*with*). —**harmonization** /-ˈzeɪʃ(ə)n/ *n.* [f. F (as foll.)]

harmony /ˈhɑːmənɪ/ *n.* **1** a combination of simultaneously sounded musical notes to form chords and chord progressions; the study of this. **2** a pleasing effect of the apt arrangement of parts. **3** agreement, concord. —**in harmony (with)**, in agreement (with). [f. OF f. L f. Gk *harmonia* joining (*harmos* joint)]

harness /ˈhɑːnɪs/ *n.* the equipment of straps and fittings by which a horse is fastened to a cart etc. and controlled; a similar arrangement for fastening a thing to a person. —*v.t.* **1** to put a harness on (a horse); to attach by a harness (*to*). **2** to utilize (a river or other natural force) to produce electrical power etc. —**in harness,** in the routine of daily work. [f. OF, = military equipment]

harp *n.* an instrument comprising a set of strings placed over an open frame so that they can be plucked or swept with the fingers from both sides. —*v.i.* to dwell tediously *on* (a subject). —**harpist** *n.* [OE]

harpoon /hɑːˈpuːn/ *n.* a barbed spear-like missile with a rope attached, for catching whales etc. —*v.t.* to spear with a harpoon. [f. F *harpoon* f. L f. Gk *harpē* sickle]

harp-seal *n.* a Greenland seal with a dark harp-shaped mark on its back.

harpsichord /ˈhɑːpsɪkɔːd/ *n.* a wing-shaped keyboard instrument which differs from clavichord and piano in that the strings are plucked by a small leather or quill plectrum. —**harpsichordist** *n.* [f. F f. L *harpa* harp + *chorda* string]

harpy /ˈhɑːpɪ/ *n.* **1** a mythical monster with a woman's head and body ad a bird's wings and claws. **2** a grasping unscrupulous person. [f. F or L f. Gk *harpuiai* snatchers (*harpazō* snatch)]

harridan /ˈhærɪd(ə)n/ *n.* a bad-tempered old woman. [perh. f. F *haridelle* old horse]

harrier /ˈhærɪə(r)/ *n.* **1** a hound used for hunting hares. **2** (in *pl.*) cross-country runners. **3** a falcon of the genus *Circus*. [f. HARE or HARROW]

harrow /ˈhærəʊ/ *n.* a heavy frame with iron teeth dragged over ploughed land to break up clods, cover seed, etc. —*v.t.* **1** to draw a harrow over (land). **2** to distress greatly. [f. ON]

harry /ˈhærɪ/ *v.t.* to ravage or despoil; to harass. [OE]

harsh *adj.* unpleasantly rough or sharp, especially to the senses; severe, cruel.
—**harshly** *adv.*, **harshness** *n.* [f. MLG (as HAIR]

hart *n.* the male of the (red) deer, especially after the 5th year. [OE]

hartebeest /ˈhɑːtɪbiːst/ *n.* a large African antelope of the genus *Alcelaphus*, with curving horns. [Afrik. f. Du. (as HART + BEAST)]

harum-scarum /heərəm ˈskeərəm/ *adj.* wild and reckless. —*n.* such a person. [rhyming formation on HARE, SCARE]

harvest /ˈhɑːvɪst/ *n.* the gathering in of crops etc., the season of this; the season's yield; the product of any action. —*v.t./i.* to gather as a harvest, to reap. —**harvest festival,** a thanksgiving festival in church for the harvest. **harvest moon,** the full moon nearest to the autumn equinox (22 or 23 Sept.). **harvest mouse,** a very small mouse (*Micromys minutus*) nesting in the stalks of standing corn. [OE]

harvester *n.* **1** a reaper. **2** a reaping-machine. [f. prec.]

has see HAVE. —**has-been** *n.* a person or thing that is no longer as famous or successful etc. as formerly.

hash[1] *n.* **1** a dish of cooked meat cut into small pieces and recooked. **2** a mixture, a jumble. **3** re-used material. —*v.t.* to make (meat) into a hash. —**make a hash of,** (*colloq.*) to make a mess of, to bungle. **settle a person's hash,** (*colloq.*) to deal with and subdue him. [f. F *hacher* (*hache* hatchet)]

hash[2] *n.* (*colloq.*) hashish. [abbr.]

Hashemite /ˈhæʃɪmaɪt/ *adj.* of an Arab princely family related to Muhammad. [f. *Hashim* great-grandfather of Muhammad]

hashish /ˈhæʃiːʃ/ *n.* the top leaves and tender parts of hemp, dried for smoking or chewing as a narcotic. [f. Arab.]

hasn't /ˈhæz(ə)nt/ (*colloq.*) has not.

hasp /hɑːsp/ *n.* a hinged metal clasp that fits over a staple and is secured by a padlock. [OE]

hassle *n.* (*colloq.*) a quarrel, a struggle; a difficulty. —*v.t./i.* (*colloq.*) to quarrel; to harass. [dial.]

hassock /ˈhæsək/ *n.* **1** a thick firm cushion for kneeling on. **2** a tuft of grass. [OE]

haste /heɪst/ *n.* urgency of movement or action, hurry. —*v.i.* to hasten. —**in haste,** quickly, hurriedly. **make haste,** to be quick. [f. OF]

hasten /ˈheɪs(ə)n/ *v.t./i.* **1** to make haste, to hurry. **2** to cause to occur or be ready or be done sooner. [f. prec.]

hasty /ˈheɪstɪ/ *adj.* **1** hurried, acting too quickly. **2** said, made, or done too quickly or too soon. —**hastily** *adv.*, **hastiness** *n.* [f. OF]

hat *n.* a covering for the head, especially worn out of doors. —**hat trick,** the taking of three wickets at cricket by the same bowler with three successive balls; the scoring of three goals or winning of three victories by one person. **keep it under one's hat,** to keep it secret. **out of a hat,** by random selection. **pass the hat round,** to collect contributions of money. **take off one's hat,** to applaud. **talk through one's hat,** (*slang*) to talk wildly or ignorantly. [OE]

hatband *n.* a band of ribbon etc. round a hat above the brim.

hatch[1] *n.* **1** an opening in a floor or wall etc.; an opening or door in an aircraft etc. **2** a cover for a hatchway. [OE]

hatch[2] *v.t./i.* **1** (of a young bird or fish etc.) to emerge from the egg; (of an egg) to produce a young animal; to incubate (an egg). **2** to devise (a plot etc.). —*n.* hatching; a brood hatched. [rel. to MHG *hecken* etc.]

hatch[3] *v.t.* to mark with close parallel lines. —**hatching** *n.* [f. F *hacher* (as HASH[1])]

hatchback *n.* a car with a sloping back hinged at the top to form a door.

hatchet /ˈhætʃɪt/ *n.* a light short-handled axe. —**hatchet man,** a hired killer, a person employed to make personal attacks. [f. OF *hachette* (*hache* axe)]

hatchway *n.* an opening in a ship's deck for lowering cargo.

hate *n.* **1** hatred. **2** (*colloq.*) a hated person or thing. —*v.t.* to feel hatred towards; to dislike greatly; (*colloq.*) to be reluctant. —**hater** *n.* [OE]

hateful *adj.* arousing hatred. [f. HATE + -FUL]

hatred /ˈheɪtrɪd/ *n.* intense dislike or ill will. [f. HATE + *-red* f. OE *rǣden* condition]

hatter *n.* a maker or seller of hats. [f. HAT]

haughty /ˈhɔːtɪ/ *adj.* arrogantly proud of oneself and looking down on others. —**haughtily** *adv.*, **haughtiness** *n.* [f. OF *haut* high f. L *altus*]

haul /hɔːl/ *v.t./i.* **1** to pull or drag forcibly. **2** to transport by lorry or cart etc. **3** to turn a ship's course. **4** (*colloq.*) to bring (*up*) for reprimand or trial. —*n.* **1** hauling. **2** an amount gained or acquired. **3** a distance to be traversed. [var. of HALE[2]]

haulage /ˈhɔːlɪdʒ/ *n.* transport of goods; the charge for this. [f. HAUL]

haulier /ˈhɔːlɪə(r)/ *n.* a firm or person engaged in the transport of goods by road. [f. HAUL]

haulm /hɔːm/ *n.* a stalk or stem; (*collect.*) the stems of potatoes, peas, beans, etc. [OE]

haunch /hɔːntʃ/ *n.* the fleshy part of the buttock and thigh; a leg and loin of deer etc. as food. [f. OF *hanche*]

haunt /hɔːnt/ *v.t.* **1** (of a ghost) to be frequently in (a place), especially with reputed manifestations of its presence. **2** to be persistently in (a place). **3** (of a memory etc.) to linger in the mind of. —*n.* a place frequented by a person. [f. OF *hanter* (rel. to HOME)]

hautboy /ˈəʊbɔɪ/ *n.* obs. name of the OBOE. [f. F, = high wood]

haute couture /əʊt kuːˈtjʊə(r)/ high fashion; the leading fashion houses collectively, or their products. [F]

haute cuisine /əʊt kwɪˈziːn/ high-class cookery. [F]

hauteur /əʊˈtɜː(r)/ *n.* haughtiness of manner. [F (*haut* high)]

have[1] /həv, *emphat.* hæv/ *v.t.* (3 sing. pres. **has** /həz, *emphat.* hæz/; *past* & *p.p.* **had** / həd, *emphat.* hæd/; *partic.* **having**) **1** to be in possession of; to possess in a certain relationship. **2** to contain as a part or quality. **3** to experience, to undergo. **4** to engage in (an activity). **5** to give birth to (a baby). **6** to form (an idea etc.) in the mind; to know (a language). **7** to receive; to eat or drink. **8** to be burdened with or committed to. **9** to be provided with. **10** to cause or instruct to be or do or be done etc.; to accept or tolerate; (usu. *neg.*) to permit to. **11** to let (a feeling etc.) be present in the mind; to be influenced by (a quality, as mercy etc). **12** (*colloq.*) to have sexual intercourse with. **13** (*colloq.*) to deceive; to get the better of. —*v.aux.* with p.p. of verbs forming past tenses (*I have, had, shall have, seen*; *had I known I would have gone*). **have had it,** (*colloq.*) to have missed one's chance, to have passed one's prime, to have been killed. **have it,** to express the view *that*; to win a discussion; (*colloq.*) to have found the answer; to possess an advantage. **have it in for,** (*colloq.*) to be hostile or ill-disposed to. **have it off,** (*slang*) to have sexual intercourse. **have it out,** to settle a dispute by argument (*with*). **have on,** to wear (clothes); to have (an engagement); to tease or hoax. **have to,** (*colloq.*) to have got to, to be obliged to, must. **have up,** to bring before a court of justice or to be interviewed. [OE]

have[2] /hæv/ *n.* **1** one who has (especially wealth or resources). **2** (*slang*) a swindle. **—haves and have-nots,** the rich and the poor. [= prec.]

haven /ˈheɪv(ə)n/ *n.* a refuge; a harbour; a port. [OE]

haven't /ˈhæv(ə)nt/ (*colloq.*) have not.

haver /ˈheɪvə(r)/ *v.i.* **1** to hesitate, to vacillate. **2** to talk foolishly. [orig. unkn.]

haversack /ˈhævəsæk/ *n.* a strong canvas etc. bag carried on the back or over the shoulder. [f. F f. G, = oats-sack]

havoc /ˈhævək/ *n.* widespread destruction, great disorder. [f. AF f. OF *havo(r)*]

haw[1] *n.* a hawthorn berry [OE; cf. HEDGE]

haw[2] see HUM.

hawfinch *n.* a large finch (*Coccothraustes coccothraustes*) with a powerful beak. [f. HAW[1] + FINCH]

hawk[1] *n.* **1** a bird of prey of the family Accipitridae, with rounded wings shorter than a falcon's. **2** a person who advocates an aggressive policy. *—v.t./i.* to hunt with a hawk **—hawk-eyed** *adj.* keen-sighted. **hawk-moth** *n.* a large hovering and darting moth of the family Sphingidae. [OE]

hawk[2] *v.t./i.* to clear the throat of phlegm noisily; to bring up (phlegm) thus. [prob. imit.]

hawk[3] *v.t.* to carry (goods) about for sale. [f. foll.]

hawker *n.* one who hawks goods about. [prob. f. LDu.; cf. HUCKSTER]

hawser /ˈhɔzə(r)/ *n.* a thick rope or cable for mooring or towing a ship. [f. OF *haucier* hoist f. L *altus* high]

hawthorn *n.* a thorny shrub of the genus *Crataegus* with small dark red berries. [f. HAW[1] and THORN]

hay *n.* grass mown and dried for fodder. **—hay fever,** an allergic disorder caused by pollen or dust. **hit the hay,** (*slang*) to go to bed. **make hay of,** to throw into confusion. **make hay while the sun shines,** to seize opportunities for profit. [OE]

haymaking *n.* mowing grass and spreading it to dry. **—haymaker** *n.*

haystack *n.* (also **hayrick**) a packed pile of hay with a pointed or ridged top.

haywire *adj.* (*colloq.*) badly disorganized, out of control. [f. use of hay-baling wire in makeshift repairs]

hazard /ˈhæzəd/ *n.* **1** a danger or risk; a source of this. **2** an obstacle on a golf-course. *—v.t.* to risk; to venture (an action or suggestion etc.). [f. F f. Sp. f. Arab., = chance, luck]

hazardous *adj.* risky. **—hazardously** *adv.* [f. prec.]

haze *n.* **1** thin atmospheric vapour. **2** mental confusion or obscurity. [f. HAZY]

hazel /ˈheɪz(ə)l/ *n.* **1** a bush or small tree of the genus *Corylus* bearing small edible nuts. **2** a light brown colour. **—hazel-nut** *n.* [OE]

hazy *adj.* **1** misty; vague, indistinct. **2** confused, uncertain. **—hazily** *adv.*, **haziness** *n.* [orig. unkn.]

HB *abbr.* hard black (pencil-lead).

H-bomb /ˈeɪtʃbɒm/ *n.* a hydrogen bomb. [f. H (for HYDROGEN) + BOMB]

HCF *abbr.* highest common factor.

HE *abbr.* **1** high explosive. **2** His Eminence. **3** His or Her Excellency.

He *symbol* helium.

he /hi:/ *pron.* (*obj.* HIM; *poss.* HIS; *pl.* THEY) **1** the man, boy, or male animal previously named or in question. **2** a person etc. of unspecified sex. *—n.* a male, a man. *—adj.* (usu. with hyphen) male (*he-goat*). **—he-man** *n.* a masterful or virile man. [OE]

head /hed/ *n.* **1** the upper part of the human body, or the foremost part of an animal's body, containing the mouth, sense-organs, and brain. **2** the seat of the intellect and the imagination; mental aptitude. **3** (*colloq.*) a headache. **4** a person, an individual; an individual animal; (*collect.*) animals. **5** an image of the head on one side of a coin; (usu. in *pl.*) this side turning up in the toss of a coin. **6** the height or length of the head as a measure. **7** a thing like a head in form or position, e.g. the striking part of a tool, the flattened top of a nail, the mass of leaves or flowers at the top of a stem, the flat end of a drum; the foam on top of beer etc.; the closed end of the cylinder in a pump or engine; the component on a tape-recorder that touches the moving tape in play and converts the signals. **8** the upper end (of a table, occupied by the host; of a lake, at which a river enters; of a bed etc., for one's head); the front (of a procession etc.); the bows of a ship. **9** the top or highest part (of stairs, a list, page, mast, etc.). **10** a chief person or ruler; a master etc. of a college; a headmaster or headmistress; (*attrib.*) highest in authority. **11** a position of command. **12** a confined body of water or steam; the pressure exerted by this. **13** a promontory (esp. in place-names). **14** a division in a discourse; a category. **15** a culmination, a climax or crisis. **16** the fully developed top of a boil etc. *—v.t./i.* **1** to be at the head of or in charge of. **2** to strike (the ball) with the head in football. **3** to provide with a head or heading. **4** to face or move (in a specified direction). **5** to direct the course (of). **—give a person his head,** to let him move or act freely. **go to one's head,** (of liquor) to make one dizzy or slightly drunk; (of success) to make one conceited. **head-dress** *n.* an ornamental covering or band for head. **head first,** (of a plunge etc.) with the head foremost; (*fig.*) precipitately. **head for,** to be moving towards (a place, or (*fig.*) trouble). **head off,** to get ahead so as to intercept; to forestall. **head-on** *adj.* & *adv.* (of a collision etc.) head to head or front to front. **head over heels,** rolling the body over in a forward direction; topsyturvy. **head-shrinker** *n.* (*slang*) a psychiatrist. **head start,** an advantage granted or gained at an early stage. **head wind,** a wind blowing from directly in front. **keep** (*or* **lose**) **one's head,** to keep (or lose) calm or self-control. **make head or tail of** (usu. *neg.*), to understand. **off one's head,** (*colloq.*) crazy. **off the top of one's head,** (*colloq.*) impromptu, at random. **on one's (own) head,** being one's responsibility. **over a person's head,** beyond his understanding; to a position or authority higher than his. **put heads together,** to consult together. **turn a person's head,** to make him conceited. [OE]

headache *n.* **1** a continuous pain in the head. **2** (*colloq.*) a worrying problem.

headboard *n.* an upright panel along the head of a bed.

header *n.* **1** a heading of the ball in football. **2** (*colloq.*) a dive or plunge with the head first. **3** a brick etc. laid at right angles to the face of a wall. [f. HEAD]

headgear *n.* a hat or head-dress.

heading *n.* **1** a title at the head of a page or section of a book etc. **2** a horizontal passage in a mine. [f. HEAD]

headlamp *n.* a headlight.

headland *n.* a promontory.

headlight *n.* a powerful light at the front of a motor vehicle or railway engine; the beam from this.

headline *n.* a heading at the top of an article or page, especially in a newspaper; (in *pl.*) a summary of the most important items in a broadcast news bulletin.

headlong *adj.* & *adv.* with the head foremost; in a rush.

headman *n.* (*pl.* **-men**) the chief man of a tribe etc.

headmaster *n.* the principal master of a school, responsible for organizing it. —**headmistress** *n.fem.*

headphones *n.pl.* earphones held in position by a band fitting over the head.

headquarters *n.* (as *sing.* or *pl.*) the place where a military or other organization is centred.

headroom *n.* the space or clearance above a vehicle etc.

headship *n.* the position of chief or leader, especially of a headmaster or headmistress.

headstall *n.* the part of a bridle or halter fitting round a horse's head.

headstone *n.* a stone set up at the head of a grave.

headstrong *adj.* self-willed and obstinate.

headwaters *n.pl.* the streams formed from the sources of a river.

headway *n.* **1** progress; the rate of progress of a ship. **2** headroom.

headword *n.* a word forming a heading.

heady *adj.* **1** (of liquor) strong, likely to cause intoxication. **2** (of success etc.) likely to cause conceit. **3** impetuous. —**headily** *adv.*, **headiness** *n.* [f. HEAD]

heal *v.t./i.* **1** (of sore or wounded parts) to form healthy flesh again; to unite after being cut or broken. **2** to cause to do this. **3** to put right (differences etc.); to alleviate (sorrow etc.). **4** (*archaic*) to cure. —**healer** *n.* [OE]

health /helθ/ *n.* the state of being well in body or mind; a person's mental or physical condition. —**health centre,** the headquarters of a group of local medical services. **health food,** natural food thought to have health-giving qualities. **health service,** a public service providing medical care. **health visitor,** a trained person visiting babies or sick or elderly people at their homes. [OE (as WHOLE)]

healthful *adj.* conducive to good health, beneficial. —**healthfully** *adv.*, **healthfulness** *n.* [f. prec. + -FUL]

healthy *adj.* **1** having, showing, or producing good health. **2** beneficial; functioning well. —**healthily** *adv.*, **healthiness** *n.* [f. HEALTH]

heap *n.* **1** a number of things or particles lying irregularly upon one another. **2** (*colloq.*, esp. in *pl.*) a large number or amount. —*v.t./i.* **1** to pile or become piled (*up*) in a heap. **2** to load with large quantities; to give large numbers of. [OE]

hear *v.t./i.* (*past* & *p.p.* **heard** /hɜːd/) **1** to perceive with the ear. **2** to listen or pay attention to; to listen to and try (a case) in a lawcourt. **3** to be informed (*that*); to be told (*about*). **4** to grant (a prayer); to obey (an order). —**hear from,** to receive a letter etc. from. **hear! hear!** an expression of agreement or applause. **hear of,** to be told about; (with *neg.*) to consider, to allow. [OE]

hearer *n.* one who hears, especially as a member of an audience. [f. HEAR]

hearing *n.* **1** the faculty of perceiving sounds by the response of the brain to the action of sound upon the ear. **2** the range within which sounds may be heard; presence. **3** an opportunity to be heard; trial of a case in a lawcourt, especially before a judge without a jury. —**hearing-aid** *n.* a small sound-amplifier worn by a deaf person. [f. HEAR]

hearken /ˈhɑːkən/ *v.i.* (*archaic*) to listen (*to*). [OE]

hearsay *n.* rumour, gossip [f. *hear say*]

hearse /hɜːs/ *n.* a vehicle for conveying the coffin at a funeral. [f. OF *herse* harrow f. L (*h*)*irpex* large rake f. Samnite (*h*)*irpus* wolf, w. ref. to its teeth]

heart /hɑːt/ *n.* **1** the hollow muscular organ maintaining the circulation of blood in the vascular system by rhythmic contraction and dilation. **2** the region of the heart, the breast. **3** the centre of thought, feeling, and emotion (especially love); capacity for feeling emotion; courage, enthusiasm. **4** the central or innermost part, the essence; the compact head of a cabbage etc. **5** a symmetrical figure conventionally representing a heart; a playing-card of the suit (**hearts**) marked with red designs of this shape. —**at heart,** in one's innermost feelings; basically. **break a person's heart,** to distress him or her overwhelmingly. **by heart,** in or from memory. **change of heart,** a change in one's feeling about something. **give** (*or* **lose**) **one's heart to,** to fall in love with. **have the heart to,** (usu. with *neg.*) to be insensitive or hard-hearted enough *to do* a thing. **heart attack,** a sudden occurrence of heart failure. **heart-break** *n.* overwhelming distress. **heartbreaking, -broken** *adjs.* causing or affected by this. **heart failure,** a failure of the heart to function properly. **heart-lung machine,** a machine which can temporarily take over the functions of the heart and lungs. **heart-rending** *adj.* very distressing. **heart-searching** *n.* an examination of one's own feelings and motives. **heart-strings** *n.* one's deepest feelings. **heart-throb** *n.* the beating of the heart; (*colloq.*) an object of romantic affections. **heart-to-heart** *adj.* frank and personal. **heart-warming** *adj.* emotionally rewarding or uplifting. **set one's heart on,** to want eagerly. **take to heart,** to be much affected by. **with all one's heart,** sincerely, with all goodwill. [OE]

heartache *n.* mental anguish.

heartbeat *n.* the pulsation of the heart.

heartburn *n.* a burning sensation in the chest.

hearten *v.t./i.* to make or become more cheerful. [f. HEART]

heartfelt *adj.* sincere, deeply felt.

hearth /hɑːθ/ *n.* **1** the floor of a fireplace; the area in front of this. **2** the fireside as the symbol of domestic comfort. **3** the bottom of a blast furnace; a fire for heating metal for forging etc. [OE]

heartily *adv.* in a hearty manner; very. [f. HEARTY]

heartland *n.* the central part of a homogeneous geographical, political, industrial, etc., area.

heartless *adj.* unfeeling, pitiless. —**heartlessly** *adv.*, **heartlessness** *n.* [f. HEART + -LESS]

heartsick *adj.* despondent.

heartwood *n.* the dense inner part of a tree-trunk, yielding the hardest timber.

hearty /ˈhɑːtɪ/ *adj.* **1** strong, vigorous. **2** (of a meal or appetite) copious. **3** showing warmth of feeling, enthusiastic. —**heartiness** *n.* [f. HEART]

heat *n.* **1** a form of energy arising from the random motion of the molecules of bodies, capable of transmission by conduction, convection, or radiation **2** being hot; the sensation or perception of this; temperature; a high temperature. **3** hot weather. **4** an intense feeling, especially of anger; tension; the most vigorous stage of a discussion etc. **5** a preliminary or trial round in a race or contest, of which winners take part in a further round or in the final. **6** the receptive period of the sexual cycle, especially in female mammals. **7** redness of the skin with a sensation of heat. —*v.t./i.* to make or become hot; to inflame. —**heat-shield** *n.* a device to protect (esp. a spacecraft) from excessive heat. **heat-stroke** *n.* an illness caused by excessive heat. **heat wave,** a period of very hot weather. [OE (as HOT)]

heated *adj.* (of a person or discussion etc.) angry, inflamed with passion or excitement. —**heatedly** *adj.* [f. HEAT]

heater *n.* a stove or other heating device. [f. HEAT]

heath *n.* **1** an area of flat uncultivated land covered with heather and related plants. **2** a plant growing on such land, especially of the genus *Erica* or *Calluna*. [OE]

heathen /ˈhiːð(ə)n/ *n.* one who is not a member of a widely-held religion, especially not a Christian, Jew, or Muslim. —*adj.* of heathens; having no religion. —**the heathen,** heathen people. [OE (as prec., perh. rendering L *paganus* pagan)]

heather /ˈheðə(r)/ *n.* a low shrub (*Calluna vulgaris*) with small usually purple bell-shaped flowers. [orig. unkn.]

Heath Robinson /hiːθ ˈrɒbɪns(ə)n/ absurdly ingenious and impracticable. [f. W. *Heath Robinson* English cartoonist (d. 1944)]

heave *v.t./i.* (*past* **heaved** or (*Naut.*) **hove**) **1** to lift or haul (a heavy thing) with great effort. **2** to utter with effort. **3** (*colloq.*) to throw. **4** (*Naut.*) to haul by rope. **5** to rise and fall alternately like waves at sea. **6** to pant, to retch. —*n*. heaving. —**heave in sight,** to come into view. **heave to,** to bring (a ship) or come to a standstill with the ship's head to the wind. —**heaver** *n*. [OE]

heaven /ˈhev(ə)n/ *n*. **1** (in Christian, Jewish, and Islamic theology) a place believed to be the abode of God and of the righteous after death. **2** (usu. **Heaven**) God, Providence. **3** a place or state of supreme bliss; something delightful. —**the heavens,** the sky as seen from the earth, in which the sun, moon, and stars appear. **heaven-sent** *adj*. providential. [OE]

heavenly *adj*. **1** of heaven, divine; **2** of the heavens or sky. **3** (*colloq*.) very pleasing. —**heavenly bodies,** the sun, stars, etc. [f. prec.]

heavy /ˈhevɪ/ *adj*. **1** of great weight or density, difficult to lift or carry or move; abundant; laden *with*; (of machinery, artillery, etc.) very large of its kind, large in calibre etc. **2** (*Phys*., esp. of isotopes and compounds containing them) having a greater than the usual mass. **3** severe, intense, extensive; doing a thing to excess; needing much physical effort. **4** striking or falling with force; (*colloq*.) using brutal methods. **5** (of ground) difficult to traverse, clinging; (of mist or fog) dense; (of bread etc.) dense from not having risen; (of food or *fig*. of writings) stodgy, hard to digest. **6** (of the sky) overcast, gloomy. **7** clumsy or ungraceful in appearance or effect; unwieldy; tedious; serious or sombre in attitude or tone; stern. **8** oppressive, hard to endure. —*n*. **1** a villainous or tragic role or actor in a play etc. **2** (usu. in *pl*.) a serious newspaper; a heavy vehicle. —*adv*. (esp. *in comb*.) heavily. —**heavier-than-air** *adj*. (of an aircraft) weighing more than the air it displaces. **heavy-duty** *adj*. intended to withstand hard use. **heavy going,** slow or difficult progress. **heavy-handed** *adj*. clumsy, oppressive. **heavy-hearted** *adj*. sad, doleful. **heavy hydrogen,** deuterium. **heavy industry,** that producing metal, machinery, etc. **heavy water,** deuterium oxide, used as a moderator and coolant in some nuclear reactors. **make heavy weather of,** to exaggerate a difficulty or burden presented by a problem etc. —**heavily** *adv*., **heaviness** *n*. [OE (rel. to HEAVE)]

heavyweight *n*. **1** the heaviest boxing-weight, with no upper limit (see BOXING-WEIGHT). **2** a person of above average weight. **3** a person of influence or importance —**light heavyweight,** the boxing-weight between middleweight and heavyweight.

hebdomadal /hebˈdɒməd(ə)l/ *adj*. weekly. [f. L f. Gk *hebdomas* week (*hepta* seven)]

Hebraic /hiːˈbreɪk/ *adj*. of Hebrew or the Hebrews. [f. L f. Gk (as HEBREW)]

Hebraist /ˈhiːbreɪɪst/ *n*. an expert in Hebrew. [f. foll.]

Hebrew /ˈhiːbruː/ *n*. **1** a member of a Semitic people living in ancient Palestine, an Israelite; a Jew. **2** their Semitic language or a modern form of this. —*adj*. **1** of Hebrew. **2** of the Hebrews or Jews. [f. OF, ult. f. Aramaic f. Heb., = one from the other side (of the river)]

heck *n*. (*colloq*.) (in oaths) hell. [alt. of HELL]

heckle *v.t*. to interrupt and harass (a public speaker). —**heckler** *n*. [var. of HACKLE]

hectare /ˈhektɑː(r)/ *n*. a metric unit of square measure, 100 ares (2.471 acres). —**hectarage** *n*. [f. (as HECTO- + ARE²)]

hectic *adj*. busy and confused, excited; feverish. —**hectically** *adv*. [f. OF f. L f. Gk (*hexis* habit)]

hecto- /hektə-/ *in comb*. one hundred. [F f. Gk *hekaton* a hundred]

hectogram /ˈhektəgræm/ *n*. a metric unit of mass, equal to 100 grams. [f. HECTO- + GRAM]

hector /ˈhektə(r)/ *v.t*. to bully, to intimidate. —*n*. a bully. [f. *Hector*, Trojan warrior]

hedge *n*. **1** a fence or boundary formed by closely planted bushes or shrubs. **2** a protection against possible loss. —*v.t./i*. **1** to surround or bound with a hedge; to surround and restrict the movement of. **2** to make or trim hedges. **3** to reduce one's risk of loss on (a bet etc.) by compensating transactions on the other side. **4** to avoid committing oneself. —**hedge-hop** *v.i*. to fly at a very low altitude. **hedge-sparrow** *n*. a common brown-backed bird, the dunnock (*Prunella modularis*). —**hedger** *n*. [OE]

hedgehog *n*. a small insect-eating mammal of the genus *Erinaceus* with a piglike snout and a thick coat of spines, rolling itself up into a ball when attacked.

hedgerow *n*. a row of bushes etc. forming a hedge.

hedonic /hiːˈdɒnɪk/ *adj*. of pleasure. [f. Gk (as foll.)]

hedonism /ˈhiːd(ə)nɪz(ə)m/ *n*. the theory that pleasure is the chief good or the proper aim; behaviour based on this. —**hedonist** *n*., **hedonistic** /-ˈnɪstɪk/ *adj*. [f. Gk *hēdonē* pleasure]

heebie-jeebies /ˈhiːbɪdʒiːbɪz/ *n.pl*. (*slang*) nervous depression or anxiety. [orig. unkn.]

heed *v.t./i*. to attend to, to take notice of. —*n*. careful attention. [OE]

heedless *adj*. not taking heed. —**heedlessly** *adv*., **heedlessness** *n*. [f. HEED + -LESS]

hee-haw *n*. the bray of a donkey. —*v.i*. to bray like a donkey. [imit.]

heel¹ *n*. **1** the back part of the human foot below the ankle; the corresponding part of the hind limb in a quadruped, often raised above the ground; the hinder part of a hoof; (in *pl.*) hind feet. **2** the part of a stocking or sock covering the heel; the part of a shoe etc. supporting the heel. **3** a thing like a heel in form or position, e.g. the part of the palm next to the wrist, the handle-end of a violin bow. **4** (*slang*) a dishonourable person. —*v.t./i.* **1** to fit or renew the heel on (a shoe etc.) **2** to touch the ground with the heel, as in dancing. **3** to pass the ball with the heel in Rugby football. —**at** *or* **to heel,** (of a dog or *fig.*) close behind, under control. **at** *or* **on the heels of,** following closely after. **cool** *or* **kick one's heels,** to be kept waiting. **down at heel,** (of a shoe) with the heel worn down; (of a person) shabby. **take to one's heels,** to run away. **well-heeled** *adj.* wealthy. [OE]

heel[2] *v.t./i.* (of a ship) to tilt temporarily to one side; to cause (a ship) to do this. —*n.* an act or the amount of heeling. [prob. f. obs. *heeld* incline, f. OE]

heel[3] var. of HELE.

heelball *n.* a mixture of hard wax and lampblack used by shoemakers for polishing; this or a similar mixture used in brass-rubbing.

hefty *adj.* (of a person) big and strong; (of thing) large, heavy, powerful. —**heftily** *adv.*, **heftiness** *n.* [f. dial. *heft* weight (as HEAVE)]

hegemony /hɪˈgemənɪ/ *n.* leadership, especially by one State of a confederacy. [f. Gk (*hēgemōn* leader)]

Hegira /ˈhedʒɪrə/ *n.* Muhammad's flight from Mecca to Medina in AD 622. [L f. Arab., = departure from one's country]

heifer /ˈhefə(r)/ *n.* a young cow, especially one that has not had a calf. [OE]

heigh /heɪ/ *int.* expressing surprise or curiosity. [var. of *heh*, imit.]

height /haɪt/ *n.* **1** the measurement from the base to the top or (of a standing person) from the head to the foot. **2** the distance (of an object or position) above ground or sea level. **3** a high place or area. **4** the top; the highest point, the utmost degree. [OE (as HIGH)]

heighten *v.t./i.* to make or become higher or more intense [f. prec.]

heinous /ˈheɪnəs/ *adj.* utterly odious or wicked. [f. OF (*haïne* hatred)]

heir /eə(r)/*n.* a person entitled to property or rank as the legal successor of its former owner. —**heir apparent,** an heir whose claim cannot be set aside by the birth of another heir. **heir presumptive,** one whose claim may be set aside thus. —**heiress** *n.fem.* [f. OF f. L *heres*]

heirloom *n.* a piece of personal property that has been in a family for several generations; a piece of property as part of an inheritance. [f. HEIR + LOOM[1] in sense 'tool']

held *past & p.p.* of HOLD.

hele *v.t.* to set (a plant) in the ground and cover its roots *in*. [OE, rel. to HELL]

heliacal /hɪˈlaɪək(ə)l/ *adj.* of or near the sun. —**heliacal rising** (*or* **setting**), the first rising of a star after (or its last setting before) a period of invisibility due to its conjunction with the sun. [f. L f. Gk (*hēlios* sun)]

helical /ˈhelɪk(ə)l/ *adj.* having the form of a helix. [as HELIX]

helicopter /ˈhelɪkɒptə(r)/ *n.* an aircraft which derives both its lift and its control from one or more powered rotors which rotate about a vertical or near-vertical axis [f. F f. Gk HELIX + *pteron* wing]

helio- /hiːlɪə-/ *in comb.* sun. [f. Gk *hēlios* sun]

heliocentric /hiːlɪəˈsentrɪk/ *adj.* **1** considered as viewed from the sun's centre. **2** regarding the sun as the centre.

heliograph /ˈhiːlɪəgrɑːf/ *n.* a signalling device reflecting the sun's rays in flashes; a message sent by this. —*v.t.* to send (a message) thus. [f. HELIO- + -GRAPH]

heliotrope /ˈhiːlɪətrəʊp/ *n.* **1** a plant of the genus *Heliotropium* with small fragrant purple flowers. **2** a light purple colour. [f. L f. Gk, = plant turning its flowers to the sun (as HELIO-, *trepō* turn)]

heliport /ˈhelɪpɔt/ *n.* a place where helicopters take off and land. [f. HELICOPTER, after *airport*]

helium /ˈhiːlɪəm/ *n.* a colourless odourless element, the lightest of the noble gases, symbol He, atomic number 2. [f. Gk. *hēlios* sun]

helix /ˈhiːlɪks/ *n.* (*pl.* **helices** /-lisiːz/) a spiral (like a corkscrew, or in one plane like a watch-spring). —**double helix,** a pair of parallel helices with a common axis, especially in the structure of the DNA molecule. [L f. Gk]

hell *n.* **1** the place or state of punishment for the wicked after death, the abode of devils. **2** a place or state of misery or wickedness. **3** (*colloq.*) an exclamation of surprise or annoyance. —**beat** *or* **knock hell out of,** to pound heavily. **come hell or high water,** no matter what the obstacles. **for the hell of it,** just for fun. **get hell,** (*colloq.*) to be scolded or punished. **give a person hell,** (*colloq.*) to scold or punish him. **hell-bent** *adj.* recklessly determined (*on*). **hell-fire** *n.* the fire(s) of hell. **hell for leather,** at full speed. **Hell's Angel,** a member of a gang of violent lawless youths, usu. with motor cycles. [OE f. Gmc, = cover, conceal]

hellebore /ˈhelɪbɔ(r)/ *n.* a plant with white or greenish flowers, of the genus *Helleborus* including the Christmas rose. [f. OF or L f. Gk]

Hellene /ˈheliːn/ *n.* a Greek person; an ancient

Greek of genuine Greek descent. —**Hellenic** /-ˈli:nɪk/ *adj.* [f. Gk *Hellēn* eponymous ancestor, son or brother of Deucalion]

Hellenism /ˈhelɪnɪz(ə)m/ *n.* Greek character or culture (especially of ancient Greece). —**Hellenist** *n.* [f. Gk (as prec.)]

Hellenistic /helɪˈnɪstɪk/ *adj.* of the Greek world from the death of Alexander the Great in 323 BC until the defeat of Mark Antony and Cleopatra by Roman forces under Octavian at the battle of Actium in 31 BC. [as prec.]

hellish *adj.* of or like hell; extremely unpleasant. [f. HELL]

hello var. of HALLO.

helm[1] *n.* the tiller or wheel by which a ship's rudder is controlled. —**at the helm,** at the head of an organization etc., in control. [OE, prob. rel. to HELVE]

helm[2] *n.* (*archaic*) a helmet. [OE, cf. foll.].

helmet *n.* a protective head-covering worn by a policeman, fireman, diver, motor-cyclist, etc., or as part of armour. [f. OF, dim. of *helme*, f. Gmc]

helmsman /ˈhelmzmən/ *n.* (*pl.* **-men**) one who steers a ship. [f. HELM[1]]

helot /ˈhelət/ *n.* a serf, esp. in ancient Sparta. [f. L f. Gk]

help *v.t.* **1** to make it easier for (a person) to do something or for (a thing) to happen, to do part of the work of (a person) for him. **2** to be of use or service; to do something for the benefit of (one in need); to contribute to alleviating (a pain or difficulty). **3** to prevent, to remedy. **4** (with *neg.*) to refrain from. —*n.* **1** the act of helping or being helped. **2** a person or thing that helps. **3** a domestic servant or servants; an employee or employees. **4** a remedy etc. —**cannot help oneself,** cannot avoid an undesired action. **help oneself (to),** to take without seeking help or permission. **help out,** to give help, especially in difficulty. **help a person to,** to serve him with (food at a meal). —**helper** *n.* [OE]

helpful *adj.* giving help, useful. —**helpfully** *adv.*, **helpfulness** *n.* [f. HELP + -FUL]

helping *n.* a portion of food at a meal. [f. HELP]

helpless *adj.* **1** lacking help, defenceless. **2** having or showing an inability to act without help; unable to help oneself. —**helplessly** *adv.*, **helplessness** *n.* [f. HELP + -LESS]

helpmate *n.* a helpful companion or partner.

helter-skelter /heltə ˈskeltə(r)/ *adv.* in disorderly haste. —*n.* a tall structure with an external spiral track for sliding down. [imit., perh. f. obs. *skelte* hasten]

helve *n.* the handle of a weapon or tool. [OE]

Helvetian /helˈvi:ʃ(ə)n/ *adj.* Swiss. —*n.* a Swiss person. [f. L *Helvetia* Switzerland (*Helvetii* Celtic tribe living there)].

hem[1] *n.* the border of cloth where the edge is turned under and sewn down. —*v.t.* (**-mm-**) to turn down and sew in the edge of (cloth etc.). —**hem in,** to surround and restrict the movement of. **hem-stitch** *n.* an ornamental stitch; (*v.t.*) to hem with this. —**hemmer** *n.* [OE]

hem[2] *int.* calling attention or expressing hesitation by a slight cough. —*n.* an utterance of this. —*v.i.* (**-mm-**) to say *hem*, to hesitate in speech. [imit.]

hemi- /hemɪ-/ *prefix* half. [f. Gk *hēmi-* = L *semi-*]

hemipterous /heˈmɪptərəs/ *adj.* of the insect order including aphids, bugs, and cicadas, with the base of the front wings thickened. [f. HEMI- + Gk *pteron* wing]

hemisphere /ˈhemɪsfɪə(r)/ *n.* half a sphere; any half of the earth, especially as divided by the equator or by a line passing through the poles. —**hemispherical** /-ˈsferɪk(ə)l/ *adj.* [f. OF & L f. Gk (as HEMI-, SPHERE)]

hemline *n.* the lower edge of a skirt or dress.

hemlock /ˈhemlɒk/ *n.* a poisonous plant (*Conium maculatum*) with small white flowers; the poison made from it. [OE]

hemp *n.* **1** an Asian herbaceous plant (*Cannabis sativa*); its fibre, used to make rope and coarse fabrics. **2** any of several narcotic drugs made from the hemp plant. —**hempen** *adj.* [OE]

hen *n.* the female bird, especially of the common domestic fowl. —**hen-party** *n.* (*colloq.*) a social gathering of women only. [OE]

henbane *n.* a poisonous plant (*Hyoscyamus niger*) with an unpleasant smell.

hence *adv.* **1** from this time. **2** for this reason. **3** (*archaic*) from here. [OE (f. root of HE)]

henceforth /hensˈfɔ:θ/ *adv.* (also **henceforward**) from this time onwards.

henchman *n.* (*pl.* **-men**) a trusty supporter. [f. OE *heng(e)st* male horse + MAN]

henge /hendʒ/ *n.* a monument of wood or stone resembling the circle of stones at Stonehenge in Wiltshire. [f. *Stonehenge*]

henna *n.* **1** a tropical shrub (*Lawsonia inermis*). **2** the reddish dye made from it, used especially on the hair. [f. Arab.]

henpeck *v.t.* (of a wife) to domineer over (a husband).

henry /ˈhenrɪ/ *n.* (*pl.* **-ries**) a unit of inductance which gives an e.m.f. of one volt in a closed circuit with rate of change of current one ampere per second. [f. J. *Henry*, American physicist (d. 1878)]

hep *adj.* (*slang*) aware of the latest trends and styles. [orig. unkn.]

hepatic /hɪˈpætɪk/ *adj.* of the liver [f. L f. Gk (*hēpar* liver)]

hepatitis /hepəˈtaɪtɪs/ *n.* inflammation of the liver. [as prec. + -ITIS]

hepta- *in comb.* seven. [f. Gk *hepta* seven]

heptagon /ˈheptəgən/ *n.* plane figure with seven sides and angles. —**heptagonal** /-ˈtægən(ə)l/ *adj.* [f. Gk (HEPTA-, *-gōnos* -angled]

her *pron.* obj. case of SHE; (*colloq.*) she. —*poss. adj.* **1** of or belonging to her. **2** (in titles) that she is (*Her Majesty*). [OE dat. & gen. of SHE]

herald /ˈher(ə)ld/ *n.* **1** a forerunner; a messenger, a bringer of news (often as the title of a newpaper). **2** an official concerned with pedigrees and coats of arms. **3** (*hist.*) an officer who made State proclamations, bore messages between princes, etc. **4** an official of the Heralds' College. —*v.t.* to proclaim the approach of, to usher in. —**Heralds' College,** the College of Arms (see entry). —**heraldic** /-ˈrældɪk/*adj.* [f. OF f. Gmc]

heraldry /ˈherəldrɪ/ *n.* the science or art of a herald, especially in blazoning armorial bearings and settling the right of persons to bear arms.

herb *n.* a plant whose stem is soft and dies to the ground after flowering; a plant whose leaves or seeds etc. are used for flavouring, food, medicine, scent, etc. —**herby** *adj.* [f. OF f. L *herba* grass, herb]

herbaceous /hɜːˈbeɪʃəs/ *adj.* of or like herbs. —**herbaceous border,** a garden border containing especially perennial flowering plants. [f. L (as prec.)]

herbage *n.* herb collectively, especially as pasture. [f. OF f. L (as HERB)]

herbal *adj.* of herbs in medicinal and culinary use. —*n.* a manual describing these. [f. L (as HERB)]

herbalist *n.* a dealer in medicinal herbs; a writer on herbs. [f. prec.]

herbarium /hɜːˈbeərɪəm/ *n.* (*pl.* **-ia**) a systematic collection of dried plants; a book, case, or room for these. [f. L (as HERB)]

herbicide /ˈhɜːbɪsaɪd/ *n.* a toxic substance used to destroy unwanted vegetation. [f. HERB + -CIDE]

herbivore /ˈhɜːbɪvɔː(r)/ *n.* a herbivorous animal. [as foll.]

herbivorous /hɜːˈbɪvərəs/ *adj.* feeding on plants. [as HERB + L *vorare* devour]

herculean /hɜːkjʊˈliːən/ *adj.* **1** extremely strong. **2** (of a task) requiring great strength. [f. *Hercules*, hero in Gk. myths]

herd *n.* **1** a number of cattle or other animals feeding or staying together. **2** a large number of people, a mob. —*v.t./i.* **1** to collect, go, or drive in a herd. **2** to tend (sheep or cattle). —**herd instinct,** the tendency to remain or conform with the majority. [OE]

herdsman *n.* (*pl.* **-men**) a person who tends a herd of animals.

here /hɪə(r)/ *adv.* **1** in, at, or to this place or position. **2** at this point (in a speech, performance, writing, etc.). —*int.* calling attention or as a command; as a reply (= I am present) in a roll-call. —*n.* this place. —**here and there,** in or to various places. **here goes,** I am ready to begin. **here's to,** I drink to the health of. **neither here nor there,** of no importance. [OE]

hereabouts /hɪərəˈbaʊts/ *adv.* (also **hereabout**) near this place.

hereafter /hɪərˈɑːftə(r)/ *adv.* in future, from now on. —*n.* the future; life after death.

hereby /hɪəˈbaɪ/ *adv.* by this means, as a result of this.

hereditable /hɪˈredɪtəb(ə)l/ *adj.* that may be inherited. [f. obs. F or L (*hereditare* inherit f. *heres* heir)]

hereditary /hɪˈredɪtərɪ/ *adj.* **1** descending by inheritance. **2** that may be transmitted from one generation to another. **3** holding a hereditary office. [f. L (as prec.)]

heredity /hɪˈredɪtɪ/ *n.* the property of organic beings by which offspring have the nature and characteristics of their parents or ancestors; the sum of these characteristics; genetic constitution. [f. F or L *hereditas* heirship (as HEIR)]

Hereford /ˈherɪfəd/ *n.* a breed of red and white beef cattle; an animal of this breed. [f. *Hereford* in England]

herein /hɪərˈɪn/ *adv.* (*formal*) in this place, document, etc.

hereinafter /hɪərɪnˈɑːftə(r)/ *adv.* (*formal*) in a later part of this document etc.

hereof /hɪərˈɒv/ *adv.* (*archaic*) of this.

heresy /ˈherɪsɪ/ *n.* an opinion contrary to the doctrine of the Christian Church, or to the accepted doctrine on any subject. [f. OF f. L *haeresis* school of thought f. Gk *hairesis* choice, sect (*haireomai* choose)]

heretic /ˈherɪtɪk/ *n.* one advocating a heresy (especially in religion). —**heretical** /hɪˈretɪk(ə)l/ *adj.* [f. OF f. L f. Gk *hairetikos* able to choose (as prec.)]

hereto /hɪəˈtuː/ *adv.* (*archaic*) to this.

heretofore /hɪətʊˈfɔː(r)/ *adv.* (*formal*) formerly.

hereupon /hɪərəˈpɒn/ *adv.* after or in consequence of this.

herewith /hɪəˈwɪð/ *adv.* with this (especially of an enclosure in a letter etc.).

heritable /ˈherɪtəb(ə)l/ *adj.* **1** that may be inherited; transmissible from parent to offspring. **2** capable of inheriting. [f. OF *heriter* (as HEREDITABLE)]

heritage /ˈherɪtɪdʒ/ *n.* what is or may be

inherited; inherited circumstances or benefits etc.; one's portion or lot. [f. OF (as prec.)]

hermaphrodite /hɜːˈmæfrədaɪt/ *n.* a person or animal having the characteristics or organs of both sexes; a plant in which the same flower has stamens and a pistil. —*adj.* having such characteristics. —**hermaphroditic** /-ˈdɪtɪk/ *adj.* [f. L f. Gk, orig. name of son of Hermes and Aphrodite, who became joined in one body with the nymph Salmacis]

hermetic /hɜːˈmetɪk/ *adj.* **1** with an airtight closure. **2** of alchemy or other occult science; esoteric. —**hermetically** *adv.* [f. *Hermes*, Gk god, identified with Thoth, regarded as founder of alchemy]

hermit /ˈhɜːmɪt/ *n.* a person (especially an early Christian) living in solitude. —**hermit-crab** *n.* a crab of the family Paguridae, that lives in a mollusc's cast-off shell. [f. OF or L f. Gk *erēmitēs* (*erēmos* solitary)]

hermitage /ˈhɜːmɪtɪdʒ/ *n.* the place of a hermit's retreat; a secluded dwelling. [as HERMIT]

hernia /ˈhɜːnɪə/ *n.* a protrusion of part of an organ through an aperture in the enclosing membrane etc., especially of the abdomen. [L]

hero /ˈhɪərəʊ/ *n.* (*pl.* **-oes**) **1** a man admired for great deeds and noble qualities. **2** the chief male character in a poem, play, or story. —**hero-worship** *n.* excessive devotion to an admired person. [f. L f. Gk *hērōs*]

heroic /hɪˈrəʊɪk/*adj.* having the characteristics of or suited to a hero, very brave. —*n.* (in *pl.*) **1** over-dramatic talk or behaviour. **2** heroic verse. —**heroic verse,** a form used in epic poetry, e.g. the iambic pentameter. —**heroically** *adv.* [f. F or L f. Gk (as prec.)]

heroin /ˈherəʊɪn/ *n.* a powerful sedative addictive drug prepared from morphine. [G, perh. as HERO (from its effects on the user's opinion of himself)]

heroine /ˈherəʊɪn/ *n.fem.* a female hero. [f. F or L f. Gk (as HERO)]

heroism /ˈherəʊɪz(ə)m/ *n.* heroic conduct or qualities. [f. F (as HERO)]

heron /ˈherən/ *n.* a wading bird of the genus *Ardea* with a long neck and long legs. [f. OF *hairon*]

heronry *n.* a place where herons breed. [f. prec.]

herpes /ˈhɜːpiːz/ *n.* a virus disease causing blisters on the skin. [f. L f. Gk, = shingles (*herpō* creep)]

herpetology /hɜːpɪˈtɒlədʒɪ/ *n.* the study of reptiles. —**herpetologist** *n.* [f. Gk *herpeton* reptile (*herpō* creep) + -LOGY]

Herr /heə(r)/ *n.* (*pl.* **Herren**) a German man; the title of a German man, = Mr. [G]

herring /ˈherɪŋ/ *n.* an Atlantic fish (*Clupea harengus*) used for food. —**herring-bone** *n.* a stitch or weave suggesting the bones of a herring; a zigzag pattern. **herring gull,** a large gull (*Larus argentatus*) with dark wing-tips. [OE]

hers /hɜːz/ *poss.pron.* of or belonging to her; the thing(s) belonging to her. [f. HER]

herself /hɜːˈself/ *pron.* emphat. & refl. form of SHE and HER. —**be herself,** to behave in her normal manner, to be in her normal health and spirits. [OE (as HER, SELF)]

Herts. *abbr.* Hertfordshire.

hertz *n.* (*pl.* same) a unit of frequency, equal to one cycle per second. [f. H. R. *Hertz*, German physicist (d. 1894)]

hesitant /ˈhezɪtənt/ *adj.* irresolute, hesitating. —**hesitancy** *n.*, **hesitantly** *adv.* [as foll.]

hesitate /ˈhezɪteɪt/ *v.i.* to feel or show uncertainty or reluctance, to pause in doubt; to be reluctant. —**hesitation** /-ˈteɪʃ(ə)n/ *n.*, **hesitater** *n.* [f. L *haesitare* (*haerēre* stick fast)]

hessian /ˈhesɪən/ *n.* a strong coarse fabric of hemp or jute, sack-cloth. [f. *Hesse* in Germany]

het *adj.* **het up,** (*slang*) excited, overwrought. [dial. *p.p.* of HEAT]

hetaera /hɪˈtɪərə/ *n.* (*pl.* **-rae**) a courtesan, especially in ancient Greece. [Gk, lit. = 'female companion']

hetero- /hetərə-/ *in comb.* other, different. [f. Gk *heteros* other]

heterodox /ˈhetərədɒks/ *adj.* not orthodox. —**heterodoxy** *n.* [f. HETERO- + Gk *doxa* opinion]

heterodyne /ˈhetərədaɪn/ *adj.* relating to the production of a lower radio frequency from a combination of two high frequencies.

heterogeneous /hetərəˈdʒiːnɪəs/ *adj.* diverse in character; varied in content. —**heterogeneity** /-dʒɪˈniːɪtɪ/ *n.* [f. L f. Gk (HETERO-, *genos* kind)]

heteromorphic /hetərəˈmɔːfɪk/ *adj.* of dissimilar forms. —**heteromorphism** *n.* [f. HETERO- + Gk *morphē* form]

heterosexual /hetərəˈseksjʊəl/ *adj.* characterized by attraction to the opposite sex. —*n.* a heterosexual person. —**heterosexuality** /-ˈælɪtɪ/ *n.*

heuristic /hjʊəˈrɪstɪk/ *adj.* serving or helping to find out or discover; proceeding by trial and error. [f. Gk *heuriskō* find]

hew *v.t./i.* (*p.p.* **hewed** or **hewn**) to chop or cut with an axe, sword, etc.; to cut into shape. [OE]

hexa- /heksə/ *in comb.* six. [f. Gk (*hex* six)]

hexagon /ˈheksəgən/ *n.* a plane figure with six sides and angles. —**hexagonal** /-ˈægən(ə)l/ *adj.* [f. L f. Gk (HEXA-, *-gōnos* -angled)]

hexagram /ˈheksəgræm/ *n.* a six-pointed star formed by two intersecting equilateral triangles. [f. HEXA- + -GRAM]

hexameter /hekˈsæmɪtə(r)/ *n.* a line of six

metrical feet, especially (**dactylic hexameter**) one with five dactyls and a trochee or spondee, any of the first four feet (and rarely the fifth) being replaceable by a spondee. [f. L f. Gk (HEXA-, *metron* measure)]

hey /heɪ/ *int.* calling attention or expressing surprise or inquiry. —**hey presto!** a conjuror's formula in performing a trick. [cf. OF *hay*, etc.]

heyday /ˈheɪdeɪ/ *n.* the time of greatest success or prosperity. [f. LG *heidi, heida* excl. of joy]

HF *abbr.* high frequency.

Hf *symbol* hafnium.

Hg *symbol* mercury.

hg *abbr.* hectogram(s).

HGV *abbr.* heavy goods vehicle.

HH *abbr.* double-hard (pencil-lead).

hi /haɪ/ *int.* calling attention or as a greeting. [parallel form to HEY]

hiatus /haɪˈeɪtəs/ *n.* a break or gap in a sequence or series; a break between two vowels coming together but not in the same syllable. [L, = gaping (*hiare* gape)]

hibernate /ˈhaɪbəneɪt/ *v.i.* (of an animal) to spend the winter in a dormant state. —**hibernation** /-ˈneɪʃ(ə)n/ *n.* [f. L *hibernare* (*hibernus* of winter)]

Hibernian /haɪˈbɜːnɪən/ *adj.* of Ireland. —*n.* a native of Ireland. [f. L *Hibernia* Ireland f. Gk *Iernē*]

hibiscus /hɪˈbɪskəs/ *n.* a cultivated shrub of the genus *Hibiscus*, with large bright-coloured flowers. [L f. Gk, = marsh-mallow]

hiccup /ˈhɪkʌp/ *n.* (also **hiccough**) an involuntary spasm of the respiratory organs with an abrupt cough-like sound —*v.i.* to make a hiccup. [imit.]

hick *n.* (*US colloq.*) a country bumpkin. [familiar form of *Richard*]

hickory /ˈhɪkərɪ/ *n.* a North American tree of the genus *Carya*, related to the walnut; its hard wood. [f. Virginian Indian *pohickery*]

hid *past* of HIDE[1].

hidalgo /hɪˈdælgəʊ/ *n.* (*pl.* **-os**) a member of the lower nobility in Spain. [Sp. (*hijo dalgo* son of something)]

hidden *p.p.* of HIDE[1].

hide[1] *v.t./i.* (*past* **hid**; *p.p.* **hidden**) **1** to put or keep out of sight; to prevent from being seen. **2** to keep (a fact etc.) secret (*from*). **3** to conceal oneself. —*n.* a concealed place for observing wildlife. —**hide-and-seek** *n.* a children's game in which a player hides and is sought by others. **hide-out** *n.* (*colloq.*) a hiding-place. [OE]

hide[2] *n.* an animal's skin, raw or dressed; (*colloq.*) the human skin. [OE]

hidebound *adj.* rigidly conventional, narrow-minded.

hideous /ˈhɪdɪəs/ *adj.* very ugly, revolting. —**hideously** *adv.*, **hideousness** *n.* [f. AF (OF *hisde* horror)]

hiding[1] /ˈhaɪdɪŋ/ *n.* the state of remaining hidden. —**hiding-place** *n.* a place in which one hides or where something is hidden. [f. HIDE[1]]

hiding[2] /ˈhaɪdɪŋ/ *n.* (*colloq.*) a thrashing. [f. HIDE[2]]

hie /haɪ/ *v.i.* & *refl.* (*archaic* or *poetic*) to go quickly. [OE *higian* strive, pant]

hierarchy /ˈhaɪərɑːkɪ/ *n.* a system in which grades of status or authority rank one above another. —**hierarchical** /-ˈrɑːkɪk(ə)l/ *adj.* [f. OF f. L f. Gk (*hieros* sacred, *arkhō* rule)]

hieratic /haɪəˈrætɪk/ *adj.* of the priests, priestly. —*n.* hieratic script, a form of cursive hieroglyphs used from early times in ancient Egypt, originally for religious texts. [f. L f. Gk (*hiereus* priest)]

hieroglyph /ˈhaɪərəglɪf/ *n.* **1** a picture of an object used to represent a word, sound, or syllable in any of the pictorial systems of writing, especially the ancient Egyptian. **2** a secret or enigmatic symbol. **3** (in *pl.*, *joc.*) writing that is difficult to make out. [f. foll.]

hieroglyphic /haɪərəˈglɪfɪk/ *adj.* of or written in hieroglyphs. —*n.* (in *pl.*) hieroglyphs, hieroglyphic writing. [f. F or L f. Gk (*hieros* sacred, *gluphē* carving)]

hi-fi /ˈhaɪfaɪ/ *adj.* (*colloq.*) high-fidelity. —/also -ˈfaɪ/ *n.* (*colloq.*) high-fidelity equipment. [abbr.]

higgledy-piggledy /hɪg(ə)ldɪˈpɪg(ə)ldɪ/ *adj.* & *adv.* disordered, in confusion. [rhyming jingle, perh. ref. to irregular herding together of pigs]

high /haɪ/ *adj.* **1** extending far upwards; extending above the normal or average level. **2** situated far above the ground or above sea level. **3** measuring a specified distance in upward extent. **4** ranking above others in importance or quality; luxurious. **5** extreme, intense, greater than the normal or average; (of opinion) very favourable. **6** (of time) far advanced; fully reached; (of a period) at its peak of development. **7** (of sound) having rapid vibrations, not deep or low. **8** (of meat etc.) beginning to go bad; (of game) hung until slightly decomposed and ready to cook. **9** (*colloq.*) intoxicated by or *on* alcohol or drugs. **10** (of animals or plants etc.) of complex structure, highly developed. —*n.* **1** a high or the highest level or number. **2** an area of high pressure. **3** (*slang*) a euphoric state caused by a drug. —*adv.* **1** far up, aloft. **2** in or to a high degree. **3** at a high price. **4** (of sound) at or to a high pitch. —**high and dry**, aground, stranded. **high and low**, everywhere. **high and mighty**, (*colloq.*) pompous, arrogant.

high chair, a young child's chair for meals, with long legs and usually an attached tray. **High Church,** the section of the Church of England which stresses historical continuity with Catholic Christianity and attaches 'high' importance to the authority of the episcopate and the saving grace of the Sacraments. **High Commission,** an embassy from one Commonwealth country to another. **High Commissioner,** the head of this. **High Court (of Justice),** the supreme court for civil cases. **higher education,** education at university etc. **high explosive,** an explosive with a violent shattering effect. **high-falutin(g)** *adj.* (*colloq.*) bombastic, pretentious. **high fidelity,** reproduction of sound with little distortion, giving a result very similar to the original. **high-flown** *adj.* (of language etc.) extravagant, bombastic. **high-flyer, high-flier** *n.* an ambitious person; a person or thing with the potential for great achievements. **high-flying** *adj.* ambitious. **high frequency,** (in radio) 3–30 megahertz. **high-handed** *adj.* overbearing. **high hat,** a tall hat; = HI-HAT. **high jump,** an athletic contest of jumping over a high horizontal bar; *be for the high jump,* to be likely to receive a severe punishment (the reference is to being hanged). **high-level** *adj.* (of discussions etc.) conducted by persons of the highest rank. **high-level language,** a computer language close to ordinary language and usually not machine-readable. **high-minded** *adj.* having high moral principles. **high-pitched** *adj.* (of a sound or voice) shrill; (of a roof) steep. **high-powered** *adj.* having or using great power, important or influential **high pressure,** a high degree of activity or exertion; a condition of the atmosphere with the pressure above average. **high priest,** a chief priest, a head of a cult. **high-rise** *adj* (of a building) having many storeys. **high road,** a main road. **high school,** a secondary (especially a grammar) school. **high seas,** the open seas not under any country's jurisdiction. **high season,** the regular period of the greatest number of visitors at a resort etc. **high-spirited** *adj.* in high spirits, cheerful. **high spot,** (*colloq.*) the most important place or feature. **high street,** the principal street of a town etc. **high table,** an elevated table at a public dinner or in a college etc., for the most important guests or members. **high tea,** an evening meal of tea and cooked food. **high-tech** *adj.* (*colloq.*) characterized by high technology; (of interior design etc.) imitating styles more usual in industry etc. **high technology,** a state of advanced technological development. **high tension,** high voltage. **high tide,** a tide at the highest level; the time of this. **high treason,** treason against one's ruler or country. **high-up** *n.* (*colloq.*) a person of high rank. **high water,** high tide. **high-water mark,** the level reached at high water; the highest recorded point or value. **high wire,** a high tightrope. **on high,** in or to a high place or heaven. [OE]

highball *n.* (*US*) a drink of spirits and soda etc. served with ice in a tall glass.

highbrow *adj.* (*colloq.*) intellectual or highly cultural in interest or appeal. —*n.* (*colloq.*) a highbrow person.

highland *n.* (usu. in *pl.*) mountainous country, especially (**Highlands**) of northern Scotland. —*adj.* of the highland or the Scottish Highlands. —**Highland cattle,** a breed with shaggy hair and long curved horns.

highlander *n.* a native or inhabitant of highlands or (**Highlander**) of the Scottish Highlands.

highlight *n.* **1** a moment or detail of vivid interest; an outstanding feature. **2** the bright part of a picture, etc. —*v.t.* to bring into prominence.

highly *adv.* in a high degree; favourably. —**highly-strung** *adj.* very sensitive and nervous. [f. HIGH]

highness *n.* **1** the title used in addressing or referring to a prince or princess. **2** the state of being high (esp. *fig.*).

highway *n.* **1** a public road. **2** a main route. **3** a conductor transmitting signals in a computer. —**Highway Code,** the set of rules issued officially for the guidance of road-users. **King's** *or* **Queen's highway,** a public road regarded as protected by royal power.

highwayman *n.* (*pl.* **-men**) (*hist.*) a man, usually on horseback, who held up and robbed travellers on the highway.

hi-hat /haɪˈhæt/ *n.* (also **high hat**) a pair of cymbals worked by the foot. [abbr. HIGH + HAT]

hijack /ˈhaɪdʒæk/ *v.t.* to seize control of (a vehicle or aircraft), especially to force it to a new destination; to seize (goods in transit). —*n.* a hijacking. —**hijacker** *n.* [orig. unkn.]

hike *n.* a long walk, especially across country. —*v.i.* to go for a hike; to walk laboriously. —**hiker** *n.* [dial.; orig. unkn.]

hilarious /hɪˈleərɪəs/ *adj.* **1** boisterously merry. **2**. extremely funny. —**hilariously** *adv.*, **hilarity** /hɪˈlærɪtɪ/ *n.* [f. L. f. Gk *hilaros* cheerful]

hill *n.* **1** a natural elevation of the ground, not as high as a mountain. **2** a sloping piece of road. **3** a heap or mound. [OE]

hill-billy /ˈhɪlbɪlɪ/ *n.* **1** folk music like that of the southern USA. **2** (*US colloq.*, often *derog.*) a person from a remote rural area in a southern State. [f. HILL + *billy* fellow]

hillock /ˈhɪlək/ *n.* a small hill, a mound. [f. HILL]

hillside *n.* the sloping side of a hill.

hilly *adj.* having many hills. —**hilliness** *n.* [f. HILL]

hilt *n.* the handle of a sword, dagger, etc. —**up to the hilt,** completely. [OE]

him *pron.* obj. case of HE; (*colloq.*) he. [OE, dat. of HE]

himself /hɪmˈself/ *pron.* emphat. & refl. form of HE and HIM (cf. HERSELF). [OE (as HIM, SELF)]

hind[1] /hamd/ *adj.* situated at the back. [perh. shortened f. OE *bihindan* behind]

hind[2] /hamd/ *n.* the female of the (esp. red) deer, especially in and after the third year. [OE]

hinder[1] /ˈhɪndə(r)/ *v.t.* to keep (a person or thing) back by delaying progress. [OE, rel. to HIND[1]]

hinder[2] /ˈhamdə(r)/ *adj.* hind (HIND[1]). [perh. f. OE (as HIND[1])]

Hindi /ˈhɪndɪ/ *n.* **1** a literary form of Hindustani **2** a group of spoken dialects of northern India, belonging to the Indo-European family of languages and related to Urdu. —*adj.* of Hindi. [f. Urdu (*hind* India)]

hindmost /ˈhamdməʊst/ *adj.* furthest behind. [f. HIND[1] + -MOST]

hindquarters /hamdˈkwɔːtəz/ *n.pl.* the hind legs and adjoining parts of a quadruped

hindrance /ˈhɪndrəns/ *n.* **1** a thing that hinders. **2** hindering, being hindered. [f. HINDER[1]]

hindsight /ˈhamdsaɪt/ *n.* wisdom after the event.

Hindu /hɪnˈduː, ˈhɪ-/ *n.* an adherent of Hinduism. —*adj.* of the Hindus. [Urdu, f. Pers. (*Hind* India)]

Hinduism /ˈhɪnduːɪz(ə)m/ *n.* a system of religious beliefs and social customs, with adherents especially in India. [f. prec.]

Hindustani /hɪndəˈstɑːnɪ)/ *n.* a language based on Hindi, used esp. in northern India and (as colloquial Urdu) Pakistan. —*adj.* of Hindustani. [f. HINDU + *-stan* country]

hinge /hɪndʒ/ *n.* **1** a movable joint on which a door, lid, etc. turns or swings. **2** a principle on which all depends. —*v.t./i.* **1** to attach or be attached by a hinge. **2** to depend *on*. [rel. to HANG]

hinny *n.* the offspring of a she-ass and a stallion. [f. L *hinnus* f. Gk]

hint *n.* **1** a slight or indirect indication or suggestion. **2** a small piece of practical information. **3** a small amount, a trace. —*v.t./i.* to suggest slightly or indirectly. —**hint at,** to refer indirectly to. **take a hint,** to act upon a hint. [f. obs. *hent* grasp]

hinterland /ˈhɪntəlænd/ *n.* the district behind a coast or a river's banks; an area served by a port or other centre. [G (*hinter* behind, as LAND)]

hip[1] *n.* **1** the projection formed by the pelvis and upper part of the thigh-bone. **2** the arris of a roof from ridge to eaves. —**hip-bath** *n.* a portable bath in which one sits immersed to the hips. **hip-bone** *n.* the bone forming the hip. **hip-flask** *n.* a flattish flask for spirits, carried in the hip-pocket. **hip-pocket** *n.* a trouser-pocket just behind the hip. [OE]

hip[2] *n.* the fruit of the (esp. wild) rose. [OE]

hip[3] *int.* used in cheering (*hip, hip, hurray*). [orig. unkn.]

hip[4] *adj.* (*slang*) var. of HEP.

hippeastrum /hɪpɪˈæstrəm/ *n.* a South American plant of the genus *Hippeastrum* with showy red or white flowers. [f. Gk *hippeus* horseman (the leaves appearing to ride on one another) + *astron* star (from the flower-shape)]

hippie /ˈhɪpɪ/ *n.* a young person who rejects conventional ideas and society and adopts an unusual style of dress, living habits, etc. [f. HIP[4]]

hippo /ˈhɪpəʊ/ *n.* (*pl.* **-os**) (*colloq.*) a hippopotamus. [abbr.]

Hippocratic oath /hɪpəˈkrætɪk/ an oath stating the obligations and proper conduct of physicians, formerly taken by those beginning medical practice. [f. *Hippocrates*, Gk physician (d. 357 BC)]

hippodrome /ˈhɪpədrəʊm/ *n.* **1** a music-hall or dance-hall. **2** (in classical antiquity) a course for chariot races etc. [F, or f. L f. Gk (*hippos* horse, *dromos* race-course)]

hippopotamus /hɪpəˈpɒtəməs/ *n.* (*pl.* **-muses**) a large African mammal (*Hippopotamus amphibius*) with short legs and a thick skin, inhabiting rivers etc. [f. L f. Gk (*hippos* horse, *potamos* river)]

hipster /ˈhɪpstə(r)/ *adj.* (of a garment) hanging from the hips rather than the waist. [f. HIP[1]]

hire *v.t.* to obtain the use of (a thing) or the services of (a person) temporarily, for payment; (often with *out*) to grant the use of thus. —**for** *or* **on hire,** ready to be hired. **hire-purchase** *n.* a system by which a thing becomes the hirer's after a number of payments. —**hirer** *n.* [OE]

hireable /ˈhaɪ(ə)rəb(ə)l/ *adj.* that may be hired. [f. HIRE]

hireling /ˈhaɪəlɪŋ/ *n.* (usu. *derog.*) a person who works for hire. [OE, as HIRE, -LING]

hirsute /ˈhɜːsjuːt/ *adj.* hairy, shaggy. [f. L *hirsutus*]

his /hɪz/ *poss. pron.* & *adj.* **1** of or belonging to him, the thing(s) belonging to him. **2** (in titles) that he is (*His Majesty*). [OE, gen. of HE]

Hispanic /hɪsˈpænɪk/ *adj.* of Spain (and

Portugal); of Spain and other Spanish-speaking countries. —*n.* a Hispanic person. [f. L (*Hispania* Spain)]

hiss *n.* a sharp sibilant sound, as of the letter *s.* —*v.t./i.* to make a hiss; to express disapproval (of) by hisses; to utter with an angry hiss. [OE]

histamine /ˈhɪstəmɪn, -iːn/ *n.* a chemical compound in the body tissues, causing some allergic reactions. [as HISTOLOGY + AMINE]

histogram /ˈhɪstəgræm/ *n.* a statistical diagram in which the frequency of the values of a quantity is shown by columns. [f. Gk. *histos* mast + -GRAM]

histology /hɪsˈtɒlədʒɪ/ *n.* the science of organic tissues. —**histological** /hɪstəˈlɒdʒɪk(ə)l/ *adj.* [f. Gk. *histos* web + -LOGY]

historian /hɪˈstɔːrɪən/ *n.* a writer of history; a person learned in history. [f. F f. L (as HISTORY)]

historic /hɪˈstɒrɪk/ *adj.* **1** famous or important in history or potentially so. **2** (*Gram.*, of a tense) normally used of past events. [f. L f. Gk (as HISTORY)]

historical *adj.* **1** of or concerning history or facts in history. **2** having occurred in fact not legend or rumour. **3** (of a novel etc.) dealing with a past period. **4** (of the study of a subject) showing the development over a period of time. —**historically** *adv.* [as prec.]

historicism /hɪˈstɒrɪsɪz(ə)m/ *n.* **1** the belief that historical events are governed by laws. **2** a tendency to stress historical development and the influence of the past etc. [f. HISTORIC]

historicity /hɪstəˈrɪsɪtɪ/ *n.* historical truth or authenticity. [as prec.]

historiography /hɪstɒrɪˈɒgrəfɪ/ *n.* the writing of history; the study of this. —**historiographer** *n.* [f. Gk (as foll.)]

history /ˈhɪstərɪ/ *n.* **1** a continuous record of important or public events. **2** the study of past events, especially of human affairs. **3** past events; those connected with a person or thing. **4** an interesting or eventful past. —**history painting,** pictorial representation of an event or series of events. **make history,** to do something memorable; to be the first to do something. [f. L f. Gk *historia* finding out by enquiry, narrative]

histrionic /hɪstrɪˈɒnɪk/ *adj.* of acting; dramatic or theatrical in manner. —*n.* (in *pl.*) theatricals; dramatic behaviour intended to impress others. [f. L (*histrio* actor)]

hit *v.t./i.* (**-tt-**; *past & p.p.* **hit**) **1** to strike with a blow or missile; to aim a blow *at*; to come against (a thing) with force. **2** to have an effect on (a person), to cause to suffer. **3** to propel (a ball etc.) with a bat or club; to score runs or points thus. **4** (*colloq.*) to encounter, to reach. **5** (*slang*) to attack, to raid. —*n.* **1** a blow, a stroke. **2** a shot that reaches its target. **3** a success, especially in popularity. —**hit-and-run** *adj.* causing damage or injury and fleeing immediately. **hit back,** to retaliate. **hit in the eye,** to be glaringly obviously to. **hit it off,** to get on well (*with* a person). **hit list,** (*slang*) a list of people to be killed or eliminated etc. **hit man,** (*slang*) a hired assassin. **hit the nail on the head,** to guess or explain precisely. **hit on,** to find (a solution etc., especially by chance). **hit-or-miss** *adj.* aimed or done carelessly. **hit out,** to deal vigorous blows (*lit.* or *fig.*). **hit parade,** a list of the best-selling records of popular music. **hit the road,** (*slang*) to depart. [OE f. ON, = meet with]

hitch *v.t./i.* **1** to move (a thing) with a slight jerk. **2** to fasten or be fastened with a loop or hook etc. **3** to hitch-hike; to obtain (a lift) in this way. —*n.* **1** a temporary difficulty, a snag. **2** a slight jerk. **3** any of various kinds of noose or knot. —**get hitched,** (*slang*) to get married. [orig. unkn.]

hitch-hike *v.i.* to travel by seeking free rides in passing vehicles. —**hitch-hiker** *n.*

hither /ˈhɪðə(r)/ *adv.* to or towards this place. —*adj.* situated on this side; the nearer (of two). —**hither and thither,** to and fro. [OE]

hitherto /hɪðəˈtuː/ *adv.* until this time, up to now.

Hittite /ˈhɪtaɪt/ *n.* **1** a member of a powerful and widespread ancient (non-Semitic) people in Asia Minor and Syria **2** their Indo-European language. **3** (in the Bible) a member of a Canaanite or Syrian tribe. [f. Heb.]

hive /haɪv/ *n.* **1** a box etc. for housing bees. **2** the bees occupying a hive. **3.** a scene of busy activity. —*v.t./i.* place (bees) in a hive; to store (as) in a hive. —**hive off,** to separate from a larger group. [OE]

hives *n.pl.* a skin eruption, especially nettle-rash. [orig. Sc.; etym. unkn.]

HM *abbr.* Her or His Majesty('s).

HMS *abbr.* Her or His Majesty's Ship.

HMSO *abbr.* Her or His Majesty's Stationery Office.

HNC *abbr.* Higher National Certificate.

HND *abbr.* Higher National Diploma.

Ho *symbol* holmium.

ho /həʊ/ *int.* expressing triumph or scorn, or calling attention. [natural excl.]

hoard *n.* a carefully kept store of money etc. —*v.t./i.* to amass and store in a hoard. —**hoarder** *n.* [OE]

hoarding *n.* a temporary fence of light boards round a building; a structure erected to carry advertisements etc. [f. obs. *hoard* f. AF, rel. to HURDLE]

hoar-frost *n.* frozen water vapour on lawns etc. [OE *hār* + FROST]

hoarse *adj.* **1** (of the voice) rough and deep-sounding, husky, croaking. **2** having a hoarse voice. —**hoarsely** *adv.*, **hoarseness** *n.* [f. ON & OE]

hoary *adj.* **1** (of the hair) white or grey with age; having such hair, aged. **2** (of a joke etc.) old. [f. HOAR]

hoax *v.t.* to deceive, especially by way of a joke. —*n.* a humorous or mischievous deception. —**hoaxer** *n.* [prob. contr. of *hocus* (HOCUS-POCUS)]

hob *n.* a flat metal shelf at the side of a fireplace, where a kettle, pan, etc., can be kept hot; a flat heating surface on a cooker. [perh. var. of HUB]

hobbit /ˈhɒbɪt/ *n.* any of the imaginary dwarfish creatures in stories by J. R. R. Tolkien. [invented by Tolkien and said by him to mean 'hole-builder']

hobble *v.t./i.* **1** to walk lamely; to cause to do this. **2** to tie the legs of (a horse etc.) to limit its movement. —*n.* **1** a hobbling walk. **2** a rope etc. for hobbling a horse. [prob. f. LG]

hobby *n.* an occupation or activity pursued for pleasure, not as a livelihood. [as foll.]

hobby-horse *n.* **1** a stick with a horse's head, used as a toy; a figure of a horse used in the morris dance etc. **2** a favourite subject or idea. [f. *Hobby* pet-form of name Robin + HORSE]

hobgoblin /ˈhɒbgɒblɪn/ *n.* a mischievous or evil spirit; a bugbear. [f. *Hob* pet-form of Robin (Goodfellow) + GOBLIN]

hobnail *n.* a heavy-headed nail for boot-soles.

hob-nob *v.i.* (**-bb-**) to associate or spend time (*with*). [f. *hob or nob* give or take, of alternate drinking]

hobo /ˈhəʊbəʊ/ *n.* (*pl.* **-os**) (*US*) a wandering workman or tramp. [orig. unkn.]

Hobson's choice /ˈhɒbs(ə)nz/ the option of taking what is offered or nothing. [f. T. *Hobson* (d. 1831) Cambridge carrier who hired horses on this basis, customers being obliged to take the one nearest to the stable door]

hock[1] *n.* the joint of a quadruped's hind leg between the knee and the fetlock. [f. obs. *hockshin* f. OE (as HOUGH)]

hock[2] *n.* a German white wine, properly that of Hochheim on the River Main. [abbr. of obs. *hockamore* f. G *Hochheimer* (German name of the wine)]

hock[3] *v.t.* (*slang*) to pawn. —**in hock,** in pawn; in prison; in debt. [f. Du. *hok* hutch, prison]

hockey[1] /ˈhɒkɪ/ *n.* a game played with a ball on a field or by skaters with a puck on ice (when it is also called **ice hockey**) with hooked sticks, between two goals. [orig. unkn.; the name probably belonged originally to the hooked stick]

hockey[2] /ˈhɒkɪ/ *n.* (in the game of darts) the line from which the player throws. [orig. unkn.]

hocus-pocus /həʊkəs ˈpəʊkəs/ *n.* trickery. [sham L]

hod *n.* **1** a builder's light trough on a pole for carrying bricks etc. **2** a container for shovelling and holding coal. [prob. f. OF *hotte* pannier]

hodgepodge /ˈhɒdʒpɒdʒ/ var. of HOTCHPOTCH.

hoe *n.* a long-handled tool with a blade, used for loosening the soil or scraping up weeds etc. —*v.t./i.* (*partic.* **hoeing**) to weed (crops), to loosen (ground), to dig up (weeds), with a hoe. [f. OF *houe* (as HEW)]

hog *n.* **1** a castrated male pig. **2** (*colloq.*) a greedy person. —*v.t./i.* (**-gg-**) to take greedily; to hoard selfishly.—**go the whole hog,** (*slang*) to do a thing thoroughly. **hog's back,** a steep-sided hill-ridge. —**hoggish** *adj.* [OE]

hogmanay /ˈhɒgməneɪ/ *n.* (*Sc.*) New Year's Eve. [cf. OF *aguillanneuf*]

hogshead *n.* a large cask; a liquid or dry measure, usually about 50 gallons.

hogwash *n.* nonsense, rubbish.

hogweed *n.* a tall plant of the genus *Heracleum*, with thick hollow stems and umbrella-like clusters of white or pinkish flowers, liable to be eaten by animals.

ho-ho /həʊˈhəʊ/ *int.* expressing surprise, triumph, or derision. [redupl. of HO]

hoick *v.t.* (*slang*) to lift or bring (*out*), especially with a jerk. [perh. var. of HIKE]

hoi polloi /hɔɪ pəˈlɔɪ/ the masses, the common people. [Gk, = the many]

hoist *v.t.* to raise or haul up; to lift with ropes and pulleys etc.—*n.* **1** an apparatus for hoisting things. **2** hoisting. —**hoist with one's own petard,** caught by one's own trick etc. [alt. of *hoise*, prob. f. LG]

hoity-toity /hɔɪtɪˈtɔɪtɪ/ *adj.* haughty. [f. obs. *hoit* indulge in riotous mirth]

hokum /ˈhəʊkəm/ *n.* (*slang*) **1** a speech, action, or properties etc. used in a play or film to make a sentimental or melodramatic appeal to an audience. **2** bunkum. [orig. unkn.]

hold[1] /həʊld/ *v.t./i.* (*past & p.p.* **held**) **1** to take and keep in one's hand(s), arms, teeth, etc.; to grasp. **2** to keep in a particular position or condition; to grasp so as to control; to detain in custody; to keep (a person) *to* (a promise etc.). **3** to be able to contain. **4** to have in one's possession; to have gained (a qualification or achievement); to have the position of, to occupy (a job or office). **5** to occupy militarily; to keep possession of (a place) against attack; to keep the attention of; to dominate (the stage etc.). **6** to conduct or celebrate (a conversation, meeting, festival, etc.). **7** to remain unbroken under pressure etc.; (of weather) to continue fine; (of a circumstance or condition) to remain. **8** to believe, to consider; to assert. **9** to restrain; (*colloq.*) to cause to cease action or movement. —*n.* **1** the act or manner of holding something; grasp (*lit.* or *fig.*). **2** a means of exerting influence. —**hold back,** to restrain; to hesitate, to refrain *from*. **hold down,** to repress; (*colloq.*) to be competent enough to keep (one's job). **hold forth,** to speak at length or tediously. **hold it!** cease action etc. **hold the line,** not to ring off (on the telephone). **hold off,** to delay; to keep one's distance; not to begin. **hold on,** to maintain one's grasp; to wait a moment; not to ring off (on the telephone). **hold one's own,** to maintain one's position, not to be beaten. **hold out,** to offer (an inducement etc.); (of supplies etc.) to last; to maintain resistance; to continue to make a demand *for*. **hold out on,** (*colloq.*) to refuse something to (a person). **hold over,** to postpone. **hold up,** to hinder or obstruct; to support or sustain; to stop with force and rob. **hold-up** *n.* a stoppage or delay; a robbery by force. **hold water,** (of reasoning) to be sound, to bear examination. **hold with** (usu. with *neg.*), to approve of. **no holds barred,** with all restrictions on methods etc. relaxed. **take hold,** (of a custom or habit) to become established. —**holder** *n.* [OE]

hold[2] /həʊld/ *n.* a cavity below the deck of a ship for cargo. [OE (rel. to HOLLOW)]

holdall *n.* a large soft travelling bag.

holdfast *n.* a clamp securing an object to a wall etc.

holding *n.* the tenure of land; land or stocks held. —**holding company**, one formed to hold the shares of other companies, which it then controls. [f. HOLD[1]]

hole *n.* **1** an empty place in a solid body or mass; a sunken place on a surface; an opening through something. **2** an animal's burrow. **3** a small or gloomy place. **4** (*slang*) an awkward situation. **5** a hollow or cavity into which the ball etc. must be got in various games; (in golf) a section of a course between the tee and the hole. —*v.t./i.* **1** to make a hole or holes in; to pierce the side of (a ship). **2** to put into a hole. —**hole-and-corner** *adj.* underhand. **hole in the heart,** a congenital defect in the heart membrane. **hole up,** (*US slang*) to hide oneself. **make a hole in,** to use a large amount of (one's supply). **pick holes in,** to find fault with. —**holey** *adj.* [OE]

Holi /ˈhəʊli:/ *n.* a Hindu spring festival celebrated in February or March in honour of Krishna the amorous cowherd. [Hindi f. Skr.]

holiday /ˈhɒlɪdeɪ/ *n.* **1** a day of break from one's normal work, especially for recreation or festivity; (also in *pl.*) a period of this, a period of recreation away from home. **2** a religious festival. —*v.i.* to spend a holiday. [OE (as HOLY, DAY)]

holiness /ˈhəʊlmɪs/ *n.* being holy or sacred. —**His Holiness**, the title of the Pope. [OE, as HOLY]

holistic /hɒˈlɪstɪk/ *adj.* of or involving the whole. —**holistic medicine**, a form of medical treatment that attempts to deal with the whole person and not merely with his or her physical condition. [f. Gk *holos* whole]

holland /ˈhɒlənd/ *n.* a smooth hard-wearing linen fabric. —**brown holland**, this fabric unbleached. [f. *Holland* = Netherlands]

holler *v.t./i.* (*US colloq.*) to shout. —*n.* a shout. [f. *hollo* (as HALLO)]

hollow /ˈhɒləʊ/ *adj.* **1** having a space or cavity inside, not solid. **2** having a sunken area. **3** hungry. **4** (of a sound) echoing, as if made in or on a hollow container. **5** without validity, worthless. **6** cynical, insincere. —*n.* a hollow or sunken place, a hole; a valley. —*adv.* completely. —*v.t./i.* (often with *out*) to make or become hollow. —**hollowly** *adv.* [f. OE *holh* cave (as HOLE)]

holly *n.* an evergreen shrub of the genus *Ilex* with prickly leaves and red berries. [OE]

hollyhock /ˈhɒlɪhɒk/ *n.* a tall plant (*Althaea rosea*) with showy flowers. [orig. = marsh mallow, f. HOLY + obs. *hock* mallow]

holmium /ˈhəʊlmɪəm/ *n.* a silvery soft metallic element of the lanthanide series, symbol Ho, atomic number 67. [f. *Holmia* Stockholm, native city of its discoverer (P. T. Cleve)]

holm-oak /ˈhəʊməʊk/ *n.* an evergreen oak (*Quercus ilex*) with holly-like leaves, the ilex. [f. dial. *holm* holly]

holocaust /ˈhɒləkɔ:st/ *n.* large-scale destruction, especially by fire. —**the Holocaust,** the mass murder of Jews by the Nazis in 1939–45. [f. OF f. L f. Gk (*holos* whole, *kaustos* burnt)]

hologram /ˈhɒləgræm/ *n.* a photographic pattern that gives a three-dimensional image when illuminated with coherent light. [f. Gk *holos* whole + -GRAM]

holograph[1] /ˈhɒləgrɑ:f/ *v.t.* to record as a hologram. —**holographic** /-ˈgræfɪk/ *adj.*, **holography** /-ˈlɒgrəfɪ/ *n.* [f. prec., after *telegraph*]

holograph[2] /ˈhɒləgrɑ:f/ *adj.* wholly written by the person named as the author. —*n.* a holograph document. [f. F or L f. Gk (*holos* whole, -GRAPH)]

holster /ˈhəʊlstə(r)/ *n.* a leather case for a pistol or revolver, usually fixed to a saddle or belt. [=Du. *holster*]

holy /ˈhəʊlɪ/ *adj.* **1** of God and therefore regarded with reverence; associated with God or religion. **2** consecrated, sacred. **3** devoted to the service of God. —**holier-than-thou** *adj.*

(*colloq.*) self-righteous. **Holy Communion,** see COMMUNION. **Holy Father,** the title of the pope. **Holy Ghost,** the Holy Spirit. **Holy Grail,** see GRAIL. **Holy Land,** western Palestine. **holy of holies,** the sacred inner chamber of a Jewish temple; any place or retreat regarded as most sacred. **holy orders,** see ORDER. **Holy See,** papacy or papal court. **Holy Spirit,** the third Person of the Trinity, God acting spiritually. **Holy Week,** the week before Easter Sunday. **Holy Writ,** holy writing especially the Bible. [OE (rel. to WHOLE)]

holystone /ˈhəʊlɪstəʊn/ *n.* a soft sandstone formerly used for scouring the decks of ships. —*v.t.* to scour with this. [prob. f. HOLY + STONE; the stones were called *bibles* etc., perh. because used while kneeling]

homage /ˈhɒmɪdʒ/ *n.* a tribute, an expression of reverence; (in feudal law) a formal expression of allegiance. [f. OF f. L *hominaticum* (*homo* man)]

Homburg /ˈhɒmbɜːg/ *n.* a man's hat with a curled brim and a lengthwise dent in the crown. [f. *Homburg* in West Germany, where first worn]

home *n.* **1** the place where one lives; the fixed residence of a family or household. **2** one's native land; the district where one was born or has lived for a long time, or to which one feels attached. **3** a dwelling-house or flat. **4** an institution where those needing care or rest etc. may live. **5** the place where a thing originates or is most common; the natural environment of a plant or animal. **6** the finishing point in a race etc. **7** (in games) a home match or win. —*adj.* **1** of or connected with one's home or country; carried on, done, or produced there. **2** (of a game or team) played or playing on one's own ground etc. —*adv.* **1** to or at one's home. **2** to the point aimed at; as far as possible. —*v.t./i.* **1** (of a pigeon etc.) to make its way home. **2** (of a vessel, missile, etc.), to be guided (*in*) to a destination or *on* a target. —**at home,** in one's own house etc.; at ease; familiar or well-informed (*in, on, with,* a subject); available to callers. **at-home** *n.* a reception of visitors within certain hours. **bring home to,** to cause to realize fully. **home and dry,** having achieved one's aim. **home-brew** *n.* beer brewed at home. **Home Counties,** the counties closest to London. **home economics,** the study of household management. **home farm,** a farm worked by the owner of an estate containing other farms. **Home Guard,** the British volunteer army organized for defence in 1940. **home help,** a person who helps with housework etc., especially in a service organized by a local authority. **home-made** *adj.* made at home. **Home Office,** the government department dealing with law and order etc. in England and Wales. **Home Secretary,** the government minister in charge of the Home Office. **home truth,** a (usu. unwelcome) truth about oneself heard from another. [OE]

homeland *n.* **1** one's native land. **2** (in the Republic of South Africa) an area reserved for African Blacks, 1948-

homeless *adj.* lacking a dwelling-place. [f. HOME + -LESS]

homely *adj.* **1** simple and informal, unpretentious. **2** (*US*, of a person's appearance) plain, not beautiful. —**homeliness** *n.* [f. HOME]

homer /ˈhəʊmə(r)/ *n.* a homing pigeon. [f. HOME]

Homeric /həʊˈmerɪk/ *adj.* of the writings of Homer; of Bronze Age Greece as described in them. [f. L f. Gk]

homesick *adj.* depressed by absence from home. —**homesickness** *n.*

homespun *adj.* **1** made of yarn spun at home. **2** plain, simple. —*n.* a homespun fabric.

homestead /ˈhəʊmsted/ *n.* **1** a house with its adjoining land and outbuildings, a farm. **2** (*Austral.* & *NZ*) the owner's residence on a sheep or cattle station. [OE, as HOME, STEAD]

homeward /ˈhəʊmwəd/ *adv.* (also **homewards**) towards home. —*adj.* going towards home. [OE (as HOME, -WARD)]

homework *n.* work to be done at home by a school pupil; preparatory work or study.

homicide /ˈhɒmɪsaɪd/ *n.* **1** the killing of one person by another. **2** a person who kills another. —**homicidal** /-ˈsaɪd(ə)l/ *adj.* [f. OF f. L (*homo* man, -CIDE)]

homily /ˈhɒmɪlɪ/ *n.* a sermon, a moralizing lecture. —**homiletic** /-ˈletɪk/ *adj.* [f. L f. Gk *homilia* (*homilos* crowd)]

homing *adj.* **1** (of a pigeon) trained to fly home from a distance. **2** (of a device) for guiding to a target etc. [f. HOME]

hominid /ˈhɒmɪnɪd/ *adj.* of the zoological family Hominidae that includes existing and fossil man. —*n.* a member of this family. [f. L *homo* man]

hominoid /ˈhɒmɪnɔɪd/ *adj.* manlike. —*n.* an animal resembling man. [as prec.]

homo /ˈhəʊməʊ/ *n.* (*pl.* **-os**) (*colloq.*) a homosexual. [abbr.]

homo- *in comb.* same. [f. Gk *homos* same]

homoeopathy /həʊmɪˈɒpəθɪ/ *n.* treatment of disease by substances, usually in minute doses, that in a healthy person would produce symptoms like those of the disease. —**homoeopathic** /-ˈpæθɪk/ *adj.*, **homoeopathist** *n.* [f. G f. Gk *homoios* like + -PATHY]

homogeneous /hɒməˈdʒiːnɪəs/ *adj.* of the same kind; consisting of parts all of the same kind.

—homogeneity /-dʒɪ'ni:ɪtɪ/ *n.* [f. L f. (HOMO-, *genos* kind)]

homogenize /hə'mɒdʒɪnaɪz/ *v.t.* **1** to make homogeneous. **2** to treat (milk) so that fat droplets are emulsified and cream does not separate. **—homogenization** /-'zeɪʃ(ə)n/ *n.* [f. prec.]

homograph /'hɒməgrɑ:f/ *n.* a word spelt like another, but of different meaning or origin, e.g. BAT[1], BAT[2]. [f. HOMO- + -GRAPH]

homologous /hə'mɒləgəs/ *adj.* having the same relation or relative position; corresponding; (*Biol.*) similar in position and structure but not necessarily in function; (*Chem.*) forming a series with constant successive differences of composition. [f. L f. Gk (HOMO-, *logos* ratio)]

homologue /'hɒməlɒg/ *n.* a homologous thing. [F f. Gk (as prec.)]

homology /hə'mɒlədʒɪ/ *n.* a homologous state or relation. **—homological** /-'lɒdʒɪk(ə)l/ *adj.* [f. HOMOLOGOUS]

homonym /'hɒmənɪm/ *n.* **1** a word of the same spelling or sound as another but with a different meaning, e.g. POLE[1], POLE[2]; THEIR, THERE. **2** a namesake. [f. L f. Gk (HOMO-, *onoma* name)]

homophone /'hɒməfəʊn/ *n.* a word having the same sound as another, but of different meaning or origin, e.g. SON, SUN. [f. Gk (HOMO-, *phōnē* sound)]

Homo sapiens /həʊməʊ 'sæpɪenz/ modern man regarded as a species. [L, = wise man]

homosexual /həʊməʊ'seksjʊəl, hɒm-/ *adj.* feeling sexually attracted to people of the same sex. *—n.* a homosexual person. **—homosexuality** /-'ælɪtɪ/ *n.* [f. HOMO- + SEXUAL]

Hon. *abbr.* **1** Honorary. **2** Honourable.

hone /həʊn/ *n.* a whetstone for sharpening razors and tools. *—v.t.* to sharpen (as) on a hone (*lit.* & *fig.*). [OE, = stone]

honest /'ɒnɪst/ *adj.* **1** truthful, trustworthy. **2** fairly earned. **3** sincere but undistinguished. [f. OF f. L *honestus* (*honos* honour)]

honestly *adv.* **1** in an honest way. **2** really. [f. prec.]

honesty *n.* **1** being honest; truthfulness. **2** a plant of the genus *Lunaria*, with purple flowers and flat round semi-transparent seed-pods. [f. OF f. L *honestas* (as HONEST)]

honey /'hʌnɪ/ *n.* **1** the sweet sticky fluid made by bees from nectar collected from flowers. **2** its yellowish colour. **3** sweetness; a sweet thing. **4** an excellent person or thing; darling (esp. as a form of address). **—honey-bee** *n.* the common hive-bee (*Apis mellifera*). **—honeyed** *adj.* [OE]

honeycomb *n.* **1** the bees' wax structure of hexagonal cells for honey and eggs. **2** a pattern arranged hexagonally. *—v.t.* to fill with cavities or tunnels; to mark with a honeycomb pattern.

honeydew *n.* **1** a sweet sticky substance found on leaves and stems, excreted by aphids. **2** a variety of melon with a smooth pale skin and green flesh.

honeymoon *n.* **1** the holiday spent together by a newly-married couple. **2** an initial period of enthusiasm or goodwill. *—v.i.* to spend a honeymoon. [f. HONEY + MOON, orig. with ref. to waning affection, not to period of a month]

honeysuckle *n.* a climbing shrub of the genus *Lonicera* with fragrant yellow and pink flowers.

honk *n.* **1** the hooting cry of the wild goose. **2** the sound of a vehicle's horn. *—v.t./i.* to make a honk; to sound (a horn). [imit.]

honky-tonk /'hɒŋkɪtɒŋk/ *n.* (*colloq.*) **1** ragtime piano music. **2** a cheap or disreputable night-club. [orig. unkn.]

honorarium /ɒnə'reərɪəm/ *n.* (*pl.* **-iums**) a voluntary payment for services without the normal fee. [L (as foll.)]

honorary /'ɒnərərɪ/ *adj.* **1** conferred as an honour. **2** (of an office or its holder) unpaid. [f. L *honorarius* (as HONOUR)]

honorific /ɒnə'rɪfɪk/ *adj.* conferring honour; implying respect. [f. L *honorificus* (as HONOUR + *-fic* f. *facere* make)]

honour /'ɒnə(r)/ *n.* **1** great respect, high public regard. **2** a mark of this; an official award for bravery or achievement; a privilege given or received. **3** a person or thing that brings honour. **4** adherence to what is right or to an accepted standard of conduct; (of a woman) chastity, a reputation for this. **5** exalted position; a title of respect to certain judges and other important persons. **6** (in *pl.*) a specialized degree-course or special distinction in an examination. **7** (in card-games) the four or five highest-ranking cards. *—v.t.* **1** to respect highly; to confer honour on. **2** to accept or pay (a bill or cheque) when due; to observe the terms of (an agreement). **—do the honours,** to perform the duties of a host to guests etc. **on one's honour,** under a moral obligation (*to do* a thing). [f. OF f. L *honor*]

honourable /'ɒnərəb(ə)l/ *adj.* **1** deserving, bringing, or showing honour. **2 Honourable,** the courtesy title of certain high officials and judges, also of the children of viscounts and barons, the younger sons of earls, and used during debates by MPs to one another. **—Right Honourable,** see RIGHT. **—honourably** *adv.* [f. OF f. L (as prec.)]

hooch /hu:tʃ/ *n.* (*US colloq.*) alcoholic liquor, especially inferior or illicit whisky. [abbr. of Alaskan *hoochinoo* liquor-making tribe]

hood[1] /hʊd/ *n.* **1** a covering for the head and neck, often forming part of a garment. **2** a separate hoodlike garment worn as a part of academic dress. **3** a thing resembling a hood, e.g. a folding soft roof over a car. **4** (*US*) the bonnet of a car. **5** a canopy to protect the user of machinery or to remove fumes etc. —*v.t.* to cover with a hood [OE]

hood[2] /hʊd/ *n.* (*US slang*) a gangster, a gunman. [abbr. of HOODLUM]

-hood /-hʊd/ *suffix* forming nouns of condition, quality, or grouping (*childhood, falsehood, sisterhood*). [OE (orig. a separate word *hād* person, condition, quality)]

hooded *adj.* having a hood; (of an animal) having a hoodlike part. [f. HOOD[1]]

hoodlum /ˈhu:dləm/ *n.* a hooligan, a young thug; a gangster. [orig. unkn.]

hoodoo /ˈhu:du:/ *n.* (*US*) **1** bad luck; a thing that brings or causes this. **2** voodoo. —*v.t.* (*US*) to make unlucky, to bewitch. [alt. of VOODOO]

hoodwink /ˈhʊdwɪŋk/ *v.t.* to deceive, to delude. [f. HOOD[1] + WINK]

hooey /ˈhu:ɪ/ *n.* & *int.* (*slang*) nonsense. [orig. unkn.]

hoof /hu:f/ *n.* (*pl.* **hoofs, hooves**) the horny part of the foot of a horse etc. —*v.i.* (usu. as **hoof it**) (*slang*) to go on foot. [OE]

hoo-ha /ˈhu:hɑ:/ *n.* (*slang*) a commotion. [orig. unkn.]

hook /hʊk/ *n.* **1** a bent or curved piece of wire or metal etc. for catching hold or for hanging things on. **2** a curved cutting instrument. **3** a hooklike thing or formation of land, a bend in a river etc. **4** a hooking stroke; a short swinging blow in boxing. —*v.t./i.* **1** to grasp or secure with a hook or hooks. **2** to catch with a hook or (*fig.*) as if with a hook; (*slang*) to steal. **3** (in sports) to send (the ball) in a curving or deviating path; (in a Rugby football scrum) to secure and pass (the ball) backward with the foot. —**be hooked on,** (*slang*) to be addicted to or captivated by. **by hook or by crook,** by one means or another. **hook and eye,** a small metal hook and loop as a dress-fastener. **hook, line, and sinker,** entirely. **hook it,** (*slang*) to make off. **hook-up** *n.* a connection, especially an interconnection in a broadcast transmission. **off the hook,** (*colloq.*) out of difficulty or trouble. [OE]

hookah /ˈhʊkə/ *n.* an oriental tobacco-pipe with a long tube passing through water for cooling the smoke as it is drawn through. [Urdu f. Arab., = casket]

hooked *adj.* in the shape of a hook. [f. HOOK]

hooker[1] *n.* **1** a player in the front row of the scrum in Rugby football, who tries to hook the ball. **2** (*US slang*) a prostitute. [f. HOOK]

hooker[2] *n.* a small Dutch or Irish fishing-vessel. [f. Du. *hoeker* (as HOOK)]

hookey *n.* **play hookey** (*US slang*) to play truant. [orig. unkn.]

hookworm *n.* a worm of the family Ancylostomatidae, the male of which has hooklike spines, infesting humans and animals.

hooligan /ˈhu:lɪgən/ *n.* a young ruffian. —**hooliganism** *n.* [perh. orig. name of Irish family of ruffians in SE London]

hoop /hu:p/ *n.* **1** a circular band of metal or wood etc. for binding a cask etc., or forming part of a framework. **2** a large ring of wood etc., bowled along by a child, or for circus performers to jump through. **3** an iron etc. arch used in croquet. —*v.t.* to bind or encircle with a hoop or hoops. —**be put** *or* **go through the hoop,** to undergo an ordeal. [OE]

hoop-la /ˈhu:plɑ:/ *n.* a game in which rings are thrown in an attempt to encircle a prize. [f. HOOP + *la* int.]

hoopoe /ˈhu:pu:/ *n.* a bird, especially *Upupa epops*, with a fanlike crest and striped wings and tail. [f. OF f. L *upupa*, imit. of its cry]

hooray /hʊˈreɪ/ var. of HURRAH.

hoot /hu:t/ *n.* **1** an owl's cry. **2** the sound made by a vehicle's horn or a steam whistle. **3** a shout expressing scorn or disapproval. **4** (*colloq.*) laughter; a cause of this. —*v.t./i.* to make a hoot or hoots; to sound (a horn). —**not care** *or* **give** etc. **a hoot,** (*slang*) not to care at all. [perh. imit.]

hooter /ˈhu:tə(r)/ *n.* **1** a siren, a steam whistle, especially as a signal for work to begin or cease. **2** a vehicle's horn. **3** (*slang*) the nose. [f. HOOT]

Hoover /ˈhu:və(r)/ *n.* [P] a type of vacuum cleaner. —**hoover** *v.t.* to clean with a vacuum cleaner.

hooves *pl.* of HOOF.

hop[1] *v.t./i.* (**-pp-**) **1** (of a bird or animal) to spring with two or all feet at once. **2** (of a person) to jump on one foot. **3** to cross (a ditch etc.) —*n.* **1** a hopping movement. **2** an informal dance. **3** a short flight in an aircraft. —**hop in** (*or* **out**), (*colloq.*) to get into (or out of) a car. **hop it!** (*slang*) go away! **hopping mad,** (*colloq.*) very angry. **on the hop,** unprepared. [OE]

hop[2] *n.* a climbing plant (*Humulus lupulus*) bearing cones; (in *pl.*) its ripe cones used to flavour beer. —*v.t.* (**-pp-**) to flavour with hops. —**hop-bind** *or* **hop-bine** *n.* the climbing stem of the hop. [f. MLG or MDu.]

hope *n.* **1** expectation and desire, e.g. for a certain event to occur. **2** a person, thing, or circumstance that encourages hope. **3** what is hoped for. —*v.t./i.* to feel hope; to expect and desire; to feel fairly confident. —**hope**

against hope, to cling to a mere possibility. [OE]

hopeful *adj.* feeling or causing hope; likely to succeed. —*n.* a person who hopes or seems likely to succeed. [f. HOPE + -FUL]

hopefully *adv.* **1** in a hopeful manner. **2** (D) it is to be hoped. [f. prec.]

hopeless *adj.* **1** feeling or admitting no hope. **2** inadequate, incompetent. —**hopelessly** *adv.*, **hopelessness** *n.* [f. HOPE + -LESS]

hoplite /ˈhɒplaɪt/ *n.* a heavy-armed infantry soldier in ancient Greece. [f. Gk (*hoplon* weapon)]

hopper[1] *n.* **1** one who hops; a hopping insect. **2** a container tapering to the base, with an opening at the base for discharging the contents. [f. HOP[1]]

hopper[2] *n.* a hop-picker. [f. HOP[2]]

hopsack *n.* a kind of loosely-woven fabric. [f. HOP[2] + SACK]

hopscotch *n.* a children's game of hopping over squares marked on the ground to retrieve a stone tossed into these. [f. HOP[1] + SCOTCH[2]]

horde /hɔːd/ *n.* **1** a large group, a gang. **2** a troop of Tartar or other nomads. [f. Pol. f. Turki *ordī, ordū* camp; cf. URDU]

horehound /ˈhɔːhaʊnd/ *n.* a herb (*Marrubium vulgare*) producing a bitter juice used against coughs. [OE (as HOAR, *hune* a plant)]

horizon /həˈraɪz(ə)n/ *n.* **1** the line at which earth and sky appear to meet. **2** the limit of mental perception, experience, interest, etc. —**on the horizon,** imminent, becoming apparent. [f. OF f. L f. Gk (*horizō* bound)]

horizontal /hɒrɪˈzɒnt(ə)l/ *adj.* **1** parallel to the plane of the horizon; at right angles to the vertical. **2** at or concerned with the same status, work, etc. —*n.* a horizontal line etc. —**horizontally** *adv.* [as prec.]

hormone /ˈhɔːməʊn/ *n.* any of numerous organic compounds secreted internally (esp. into the bloodstream) by a specific group of cells, and regulating a specific physiological activity of other cells, or produced by plants whose growth and other physiological activities they regulate; a similar synthetic substance. —**hormonal** /-ˈməʊn(ə)l/ *adj.* [f. Gk (*hormaō* impel)]

horn *n.* **1** a hard outgrowth, often curved and pointed, from the head of an animal; each of the two branched appendages on the head of (esp. male) deer. **2** a hornlike projection on other animals, e.g. a snail's tentacle. **3** the substance of which horns are made. **4** a wind instrument, originally made of horn, now usually brass. **5** an instrument for sounding a warning. **6** a receptacle or instrument made of horn. **7** a horn-shaped projection; an extremity of the moon or other crescent, an arm of a river etc. **8** either alternative of a dilemma. —*v.t.* **1** to furnish with horns. **2** to gore with the horns. —**horn in,** (*slang*) to intrude, to interfere. **horn of plenty,** a cornucopia. [OE, cogn. w. L *cornu*]

hornbeam *n.* a tree (*Carpinus betulus*) with hard tough wood.

hornbill *n.* a tropical bird of the family Bucerotidae with a hornlike excrescence on the bill.

hornblende /ˈhɔːnblend/ *n.* a black or green or dark brown mineral, a constituent of granite etc. [G (as HORN, BLENDE)]

hornet /ˈhɔːnɪt/ *n.* a large kind of wasp (especially *Vespa crabro*). —**hornet-moth** *n.* a kind of moth (*Sesia apiformis*) resembling the hornet. **stir up a hornet's nest,** to cause an angry outburst. [prob. f. MLG or MDu.]

hornpipe *n.* a lively dance, usually for one person; the music for this. Its traditional association with British seamen seems to date from the late 18th *c.*

horny *adj.* **1** of or like horn; hard like horn, calloused. **2** (*slang*) lecherous. [f. HORN]

horology /həˈrɒlədʒɪ/ *n.* the art of measuring time or making clocks, watches, etc. —**horological** /hɒrəˈlɒdʒɪk(ə)l/ *adj.* [f. Gk *hōra* time + -LOGY]

horoscope /ˈhɒrəskəʊp/ *n.* a forecast of a person's future from a diagram showing the relative positions of the planets etc. at a particular time; this diagram. [F f. L f. Gk (as prec., *skopos* observer)]

horrendous /həˈrendəs/ *adj.* horrifying. [f. gerundive of L *horrēre* (as foll.)]

horrible /ˈhɒrɪb(ə)l/ *adj.* causing or exciting horror; (*colloq.*) unpleasant. —**horribly** *adv.* [f. L *horribilis* (*horrēre* bristle, shudder)]

horrid /ˈhɒrɪd/ *adj.* horrible, revolting; (*colloq.*) unpleasant. —**horridly** *adv.* [f. L *horridus* (as prec.)]

horrific /həˈrɪfɪk/ *adj.* horrifying. —**horrifically** *adv.* [f. F or L (as HORRIBLE)]

horrify /ˈhɒrɪfaɪ/ *v.t.* to arouse horror in, to shock. [f. L (as prec.)]

horror /ˈhɒrə(r)/ *n.* **1** an intense feeling of loathing and fear; intense dislike or dismay. **2** a person or thing causing horror; (*colloq.*) a bad or mischievous person etc. —**the horrors,** a fit of depression or nervousness etc. [f. OF f. L (as HORRIBLE)]

hors d'œuvre /ɔːrˈdɜːvr/ *n.* an appetizer served at the beginning of a meal. [F, = outside the work]

horse *n.* **1** a large four-legged animal (*Equus caballus*) with a long mane and tail, used for riding or to carry or pull loads; an adult male horse, a stallion. **2** (*collect.*, as *sing.*) cavalry. **3** a gymnastic vaulting-block. **4** a supporting frame. —*v.i.* (*colloq.*) to fool *around*. —**from the horse's mouth,** (of information etc.) from the original or an authoritative source. **horse-box** *n.* a closed vehicle for transporting a horse or horses. **horse-chestnut** *n.* a tree of the genus *Aesculus* with conical clusters of white or pink flowers; its dark brown fruit. **horse-fly** *n.* any of various insects troublesome to horses and cattle. **Horse Guards,** a cavalry brigade of household troops; its headquarters in Whitehall, London. **horse latitudes,** a belt of calms at the northern edge of the NE trade winds. **horse laugh,** a loud coarse laugh. **horse-radish** *n.* a plant (*Armoracia rusticana*) with a pungent root used to make a sauce. **horse sense,** (*colloq.*) plain common sense. **horse-tail** *n.* the tail of a horse; a plant of the genus *Equisetum* resembling it. **horse-trading** *n.* (*US*) dealing in horses; shrewd bargaining. **on one's high horse,** (*colloq.*) acting haughtily. **on horseback,** mounted on a horse. [OE]

horseflesh *n.* **1** the flesh of the horse as food. **2** horses collectively.

horsehair *n.* hair from the mane or tail of a horse, used for padding etc.

horseman *n.* (*pl.* **-men**) a rider on horseback; a skilled rider. —**horsemanship** *n.*, **horsewoman** *n.fem.* (*pl.* **-women**).

horseplay *n.* boisterous play.

horsepower *n.* (*pl.* same) a unit for measuring the power of an engine, about 750 watts.

horse-racing *n.* the sport of conducting races between horses with riders.

horseshoe *n.* a U-shaped iron shoe for a horse; a thing of this shape.

horsewhip *n.* a whip for driving horses. —*v.t.* (**-pp-**) to beat (a person) with a horsewhip.

horst *n.* a long plateau with a geological fault on each side. [G = heap]

horsy *adj.* **1** of or like a horse. **2** concerned with or devoted to horses; showing this in dress, conversation, etc. [f. HORSE]

hortative /ˈhɔːtətɪv/ *adj.* (also **hortatory** /ˈhɔːtətərɪ/) tending or serving to exhort. [f. L (*hortari* exhort)]

horticulture /ˈhɔːtɪkʌltʃə(r)/ *n.* the art of garden cultivation. —**horticultural** /-ˈkʌltʃər(ə)l/ *adj.*, **horticulturist** *n.* [f. L *hortus* garden, after *agriculture*]

hosanna /həʊˈzænə/ *n.* a shout of adoration. [f. L f. Gk f. Heb., = save now]

hose /həʊz/ *n.* **1** (also **hose-pipe**) a flexible tube for conveying water. **2** (*collect.* as *pl.*, esp. in trade use) stockings and socks. **3** (*hist.*) breeches. —*v.t.* to water or spray with a hose. [OE]

hosier /ˈhəʊzɪə(r)/ *n.* a dealer in stockings and socks. [f. HOSE]

hosiery *n.* (esp. in trade use) stockings and socks; knitted or woven underwear. [f. prec.]

hospice /ˈhɒspɪs/ *n.* **1** a lodging for travellers, especially one kept by a religious order. **2** a home for destitute or (esp. terminally) ill people. [F, f. L *hospitium* (as HOST²)]

hospitable /hɒsˈpɪtəb(ə)l/ *adj.* giving or disposed to give hospitality. —**hospitably** *adv.* [F, f. L *hospitare* entertain (as HOST²)]

hospital /ˈhɒspɪt(ə)l *n.* **1** an institution providing medical and surgical treatment and nursing care for ill or injured people. **2** (*hist.*) a charitable institution, a hospice. [f. OF f. L *hospitale* (as HOST²)]

hospitality /hɒspɪˈtælɪtɪ/ *n.* friendly and generous reception and entertainment of guests or strangers. [as prec.]

hospitalize /ˈhɒspɪtəlaɪz/ *v.t.* to send or admit (a patient) to hospital. —**hospitalization** /-ˈzeɪʃ(ə)n/ *n.* [f. HOSPITAL]

hospitaller /ˈhɒspɪt(ə)lə(r)/ *n.* a member of certain charitable religious orders. [as HOSPITAL]

host¹ /həʊst/ *n.* a large number of people or things; (*archaic*) an army. [f. OF f. L *hostis* enemy, army]

host² /həʊst/ *n.* **1** one who receives or entertains another as his guest; the landlord of an inn. **2** an animal or plant having a parasite. —*v.t.* to act as host to (a person) or at (an event). [f. OF f. L *hospes* host, guest]

host³ /həʊst/ *n.* the bread consecrated in the Eucharist. [f. OF f. L *hostia* sacrificial victim]

hostage /ˈhɒstɪdʒ/ *n.* a person seized or held as security for the fulfilment of a condition or conditions. [f. OF f. L *obses*]

hostel /ˈhɒst(ə)l/ *n.* a house of residence or lodging for students or other special groups. [f. OF f. L (as HOSPITAL)]

hostelry /ˈhɒst(ə)lrɪ/ *n.* (*archaic*) an inn. [f. OF (*h*)*ostelier* innkeeper (as prec.)]

hostess /ˈhəʊstɪs/ *n.fem.* a woman host; a woman employed to entertain guests in a night-club etc. [f. HOST²]

hostile /ˈhɒstaɪl/ *adj.* **1** of an enemy. **2** unfriendly, opposed (*to*). —**hostilely** *adv.* [F, or f. L (as HOST¹)]

hostility /hɒˈstɪlɪtɪ/ *n.* being hostile, enmity; a state of warfare; (in *pl.*) acts of warfare. [f. F or L (as prec.)]

hot *adj.* **1** having a relatively or noticeably high temperature; causing a sensation of heat; feeling heat. **2** (of pepper, spices, etc.) producing a burning sensation to the taste. **3** eager, excited; having intense feeling, angry or upset. **4** (of news etc.) fresh, recent; (of a scent in hunting) strong. **5** (of a competitor, performer, feat) skilful, formidable. **6** (of music) strongly rhythmical and emotional.

7 (*slang*) (of goods) stolen, especially if difficult to dispose of. 8 (*slang*) radioactive. —*v.t./i.* (-tt-) (*colloq.*, often with *up*) 1 to make or become hot. 2 to become active or exciting. —**hot air,** (*slang*) empty or boastful talk. **hot-blooded** *adj.* ardent, passionate. **hot cross bun,** a bun marked with a cross and eaten on Good Friday. **hot dog,** (*colloq.*) a hot sausage sandwiched in a soft roll. **hot gospeller,** (*colloq.*) an eager preacher of the gospel. **hot line,** a direct exclusive line of communication especially for an emergency. **hot money,** capital frequently transferred. **hot potato,** (*colloq.*) a controversial or awkward matter or situation. **hot rod,** a motor vehicle modified to have extra power and speed. **hot seat,** (*slang*) a position of difficult responsibility; the electric chair. **hot stuff,** (*colloq.*) a formidably capable person; an important person or thing; a sexually attractive person. **hot-tempered** *adj.* impulsively angry. **hot water,** (*colloq.*) difficulty or trouble. **hot-water bottle,** a rubber, metal, or earthenware container filled with hot water to warm a bed etc. —**hotly** *adv.*, **hotness** *n.* [OE]

hotbed *n.* 1 a bed of earth heated by fermenting manure. 2 a place promoting the growth of something (esp. unwelcome).

hotchpotch /ˈhɒtʃpɒtʃ/ *n.* a confused mixture, a jumble; a mixed broth or stew. [f. OF *hochepot* (*hocher* shake, as POT)]

hotel /həʊˈtel/ *n.* an establishment providing meals and accommodation for payment. [f. F (as HOSTEL)]

hotelier /həʊˈtelɪə(r)/ *n.* a hotel-keeper. [f. F f. OF (see HOSTELRY)]

hotfoot *adv.* in eager haste. —*v.i.* (usu. with *it*) to hurry eagerly.

hothead *n.* an impetuous person. —**hotheaded** *adj.*

hothouse *n.* a heated building, usually largely of glass, for rearing plants.

hotplate *n.* a heated metal plate etc. (or a set of these) for cooking food or keeping it hot.

hotpot *n.* meat and vegetables cooked in an oven in a closed pot.

Hottentot /ˈhɒt(ə)ntɒt/ *n.* (*pl.* same or **-s**) 1 a member of a stocky Negroid people of SW Africa. 2 their language [Afrik., perh. = stutterer, from their mode of pronunciation]

hound *n.* 1 a dog used in hunting, a foxhound. 2 a contemptible man. —*v.t.* to harass or pursue; to urge or incite. [OE]

hour /aʊə(r)/ *n.* 1 a twenty-fourth part of a day and night, 60 minutes. 2 a time of day; a point in time; (in *pl.* with preceding numerals in the form *18.00*, *20.30*, etc.) this number of hours and minutes past midnight on the 24-hour clock. 3 a period set aside for some purpose; (in *pl.*) a fixed period of time for work, the use of a building, etc. 4 a short, indefinite period of time. 5 *the* present time; a time for action etc. 6 the distance traversed in an hour. 7 (in the RC Church) prayers said at one of seven fixed times of the day. —**the hour,** the time o'clock; the time of a whole number of hours. **after hours,** after normal business etc. hours. [f. AF f. L *hora* f. Gk]

hourglass *n.* a sand-glass that runs for an hour.

houri /ˈhʊərɪ/ *n.* a beautiful young woman of the Muslim paradise. [F f. Pers. f. Arab., = gazelle-like]

hourly /ˈaʊəlɪ/ *adj.* done or occurring every hour; frequent. —*adv.* every hour; frequently. [f. HOUR]

house /haʊs/ *n.* (*pl.* **houses** /ˈhaʊzɪz/) 1 a building for human habitation. 2 a building for a special purpose or for keeping animals or goods. 3 a residential establishment, especially of a religious order, university college, section of a boarding-school, etc. 4 a division of a day-school for games, competitions, etc. 5 a royal family or dynasty. 6 a firm or institution; its place of business. 7 a legislative etc. assembly; the building where it meets. 8 an audience or performance in a theatre etc. 9 a twelfth part of the heavens in astrology. —/haʊz/ *v.t.* 1 to provide a house or accommodation for; to store (goods etc.). 2 to enclose or encase (a part or fitting). —**house-agent** *n.* an agent for the sale and letting of houses. **house arrest,** detention in one's own house, not prison. **house-bound** *adj.* unable to leave one's house. **house-dog** *n.* a dog kept to guard a house. **house-fly** *n.* the common fly (*Musca domestica*) found in and around houses. **house martin,** a bird (*Delichon urbica*) that builds a mud nest on house walls. **house of cards,** an insecure scheme etc. **House of Commons,** the lower house of the British Parliament; its buildings. **House of Keys,** the elective branch of the legislature of the Isle of Man, with 24 members. **House of Lords,** the upper house of the British Parliament; its buildings. **house party,** a group of guests staying at a country house etc. **house-proud** *adj.* attentive to the care and appearance of the home. **house-room** *n.* space or provision in one's house (*would not give it house-room*, would not have it in any circumstances). **house-trained** *adj.* (of animals) trained to be clean in the house; (*colloq.*) well-mannered. **house-warming** *n.* a party celebrating a move to a new home. **keep house,** to provide for a household. **like a house on fire,** vigorously, successfully. **on the house,** at the management's expense, free. **put** *or* **set one's house in order,** to make needed reforms. [OE]

houseboat *n.* a boat fitted up for living in.

housebreaking *n.* the act of breaking into a building, especially in daytime, to commit a crime. (In 1968 the term was replaced, in English law, by *burglary*.)

housecoat *n.* a woman's long dresslike garment for informal wear in the house.

household *n.* **1** the occupants of a house regarded as a unit. **2** a house and its affairs. —**Household troops,** troops nominally employed to guard the sovereign. **household word,** a familiar saying or name.

householder *n.* **1** a person owning or renting a house. **2** the head of a household.

housekeeper *n.* a person employed to manage a household.

housekeeping *n.* **1** management of household affairs. **2** money allowed for this.

houseleek *n.* a plant (*Sempervivum tectorum*) with pink flowers, growing on walls and roofs.

housemaid *n.* a woman servant in a house. —**housemaid's knee,** inflammation of the kneecap.

houseman *n.* (*pl.* **-men**) a resident doctor at a hospital etc.

housemaster *n.* a teacher in charge of a house at a boarding-school. —**housemistress** *n.fem.*

housewife *n.* a woman managing a household. —**housewifely** *adj.* [f. HOUSE + WIFE = woman (not 'married woman')]

housework *n.* the cleaning and cooking etc. done in housekeeping.

housing /ˈhaʊzɪŋ/ *n.* **1** dwelling-houses collectively; provision of these; shelter, lodging. **2** a rigid casing enclosing machinery etc. **3** a shallow trench or groove cut across the grain in a piece of wood to receive an insertion. —**housing estate,** a residential area planned as a unit. [f. HOUSE]

hove see HEAVE.

hovel /ˈhɒv(ə)l/ *n.* a small miserable dwelling. [orig. unkn.]

hover /ˈhɒvə(r)/ *v.i.* **1** (of a bird etc.) to remain in one place in the air. **2** to wait (*about, round*); to wait close at hand. —*n.* **1** hovering. **2** a state of suspense. [f. obs. *hove* hover, linger]

hovercraft *n.* a vehicle that travels over land or water on a cushion of air provided by a downward blast.

how *adv.* **1** in what way, by what means. **2** in what condition (esp. of health); to what extent. **3** in whatever way, as. **4** (*colloq.*) = that. —**how about,** what do you think of; would you like. **how do you do,** a formal greeting. **how-do-you-do** *n.* (*colloq.*) an awkward situation. **how many,** what number of. **how much,** what amount; what price. **how's that?** how do you regard or explain that?; (said to an umpire in cricket) is the batsman out or not? [OE (as WHO)]

howbeit /haʊˈbiːɪt/ *adv.* (*archaic*) nevertheless.

howdah /ˈhaʊdə/ *n.* a seat, usually with a canopy, for riding on the back of an elephant or camel. [f. Urdu f. Arab., = litter]

however /haʊˈevə(r)/ *adv.* **1** in whatever way, to whatever extent. **2** nevertheless.

howitzer /ˈhaʊɪtsə(r)/ *n.* a short gun for the high-angle firing of shells. [f. Du. f. G f. Czech, = catapult]

howl *n.* **1** the long doleful cry of a dog etc.; a similar noise, e.g. that made by a strong wind. **2** a loud cry of pain, rage, derision, or laughter. —*v.t./i.* **1** to make a howl. **2** to weep loudly. **3** to utter with a howl. —**howl down,** to prevent (a speaker) from being heard by howling derision. [= MLG, MDu. *hulen* (imit.)]

howler *n.* **1** a South American monkey of the genus *Alouatta*, with a howling cry. **2** (*colloq.*) a glaring mistake. [f. HOWL]

howsoever /haʊsəʊˈevə(r)/ *adv.* in whatsoever way, to whatever extent.

hoy *int.* used to call attention. [natural cry]

hoyden /ˈhɔɪd(ə)n/ *n.* a girl who behaves boisterously. —**hoydenish** *adj.* [prob. f. MDu. *heiden* (as HEATHEN)]

HP *abbr.* **1** hire-purchase. **2** (also **hp**) horsepower. **3** (also **h.p.**) high pressure.

HQ *abbr.* headquarters.

HRH *abbr.* Her or His Royal Highness.

hr(s). *abbr.* hour(s).

HT *abbr.* high tension.

hub *n.* **1** the central part of a wheel, from which the spokes radiate. **2** a central point of interest, activity, etc. [orig. unkn.]

hubble-bubble /ˈhʌb(ə)l bʌb(ə)l/ *n.* **1** a simple form of hookah. **2** a bubbling sound; confused talk. [redupl. of BUBBLE; imit.]

hubbub /ˈhʌbʌb/ *n.* a confused noise; a disturbance. [perh. of Ir. orig.]

hubby *n.* (*colloq.*) a husband. [abbr.]

hubris /ˈhjuːbrɪs/ *n.* arrogant pride or presumption. —**hubristic** /hjuːˈbrɪstɪk/ *adj.* [Gk]

huckaback /ˈhʌkəbæk/ *n.* a strong linen or cotton fabric with a rough surface, used for towels. [orig. unkn.]

huckleberry /ˈhʌk(ə)lbərɪ/ *n.* a low shrub of the genus *Gaylussacia* common in North America; its blue or black fruit. [perh. alt. of *hurtleberry* = WHORTLEBERRY]

huckster *n.* **1** a hawker. **2** a mercenary person. —*v.i.* **1** to haggle. **2** to be a hawker. [prob. f. LG; rel. to HAWKER]

huddle *v.t./i.* **1** to heap or crowd together. **2** to nestle closely; to curl one's body into a small space. —*n.* a confused mass. —**go into a huddle,** to hold a close or secret conference. [perh. f. LG]

hue[1] /hju:/ *n.* a colour, a tint; a variety or shade of a colour. —**hued** *adj.* [OE]

hue[2] *n.* **hue and cry,** a loud outcry (*against*), a clamour. [f. OF, = outcry (imit.). There is some ground for thinking that *hue* (as distinct from *cry*) originally meant inarticulate sound, including that of a horn or trumpet as well as of the voice.]

huff *n.* a fit of petty annoyance. —*v.t./i.* **1** to blow. **2** to remove (an opponent's piece) as a forfeit in draughts. —**in a huff,** annoyed and offended. [imit. of blowing]

huffy *adj.* apt to take offence; offended. [f. HUFF]

hug *v.t.* (**-gg-**) **1** to squeeze tightly in one's arms, usually with affection. **2** (of a bear) to squeeze between the forelegs. **3** to keep close to. —*n.* a strong clasp with the arms; a grip in wrestling. [prob. f. Scand.]

huge /hju:dʒ/ *adj.* extremely large, enormous; (of an abstract thing) very great. —**hugeness** *n.* [f. OF *ahuge*]

hugely *adv.* very much. [f. HUGE]

hugger-mugger /ˈhʌgəmʌgə(r)/ *adj.* & *adv.* **1** secret(ly). **2**. confused, in confusion. —*n.* **1** confusion. **2** secrecy. [perh. rel. to obs. *hoder* huddle, *mokere* conceal]

Huguenot /ˈhju:gənəʊ/ *n.* (*hist.*) a Calvinist French Protestant [F, assim. of *eiguenot* (= confederate) to name of Geneva burgomaster Hugues]

huh /hʌ/ *int.* expressing disgust, surprise, etc. [imit.]

hula /ˈhu:lə/ *n.* a Hawaiian woman's dance with flowing movements of the arms. —**hula hoop,** a large hoop for spinning round the body. [Hawaiian]

hulk *n.* **1** the body of a dismantled ship; (*hist.*, in *pl.*) this used as a prison. **2** a large clumsy-looking person or thing. [OE]

hulking *adj.* (*colloq.*) bulky, clumsy. [f. HULK]

hull[1] *n.* the body of a ship, airship, etc. [perh. rel. to HOLD[2]]

hull[2] *n.* the pod of peas or beans, the husk of certain seeds or fruits, the calyx of a ripe strawberry, raspberry, etc. —*v.t.* to remove the hulls of (strawberries etc.). [OE]

hullabaloo /hʌləbəˈlu:/ *n.* an uproar. [redupl. of *hallo, hullo*, etc.]

hullo var. of HALLO.

hum *v.t./i.* (**-mm-**) **1** to make a low steady continuous sound like that of a bee. **2** to sing with closed lips and without words. **3** to utter a slight inarticulate sound, especially of hesitation. **4** (*colloq.*) to be in an active state. **5** (*slang*) to smell unpleasantly. —*n.* **1** a humming sound. **2** an exclamation of hesitation. **3** (*slang*) a bad smell. —**hum and ha** *or* **haw,** to hesitate. [imit.]

human /ˈhju:mən/ *adj.* **1** of or belonging to mankind. **2** having the qualities that distinguish mankind, not divine or animal or mechanical; showing mankind's better qualities (as kindness, pity, etc.). —*n.* a human being. —**human being,** see MAN[1]. **human rights,** the rights held to be claimable by any living person. [f. OF f. L *humanus* (*homo* man)]

humane /hjʊˈmeɪn/ *adj.* benevolent, compassionate, merciful; (of learning), tending to civilize. —**humane killer,** an implement for the painless slaughter of animals. —**humanely** *adv.* [var. of prec.]

humanism /ˈhju:mənɪz(ə)m/ *n.* **1** a belief or attitude emphasizing common human needs and seeking solely rational ways of solving human problems. **2** literary culture, esp. in the Renaissance. —**humanist** *n.*, **humanistic** /-ˈnɪstɪk/ *adj.* [f. F f. It. (as HUMAN)]

humanitarian /hju:mænɪˈteərɪən/ *adj.* concerned with promoting human welfare. —*n.* a humanitarian person. —**humanitarianism** *n.* [f. foll.]

humanity /hju:ˈmænɪtɪ/ *n.* **1** human nature or (in *pl.*) qualities. **2** the human race, people. **3** being humane, kind-heartedness. **4** (in *pl.*) learning or literature concerned with human culture, formerly especially the Greek and Latin classics. [as HUMAN]

humanize /ˈhju:mənaɪz/ *v.t.* to make human or humane. —**humanization** /-ˈzeɪʃ(ə)n/ *n.* [f. F (as HUMAN)]

humanly /ˈhju:mənlɪ/ *adv.* in a human manner; by human means, within human limitations. [f. HUMAN]

humble *adj.* **1** having or showing a low estimate of one's own importance. **2** of a low social or political rank. **3** (of a thing) not large or elaborate. —*v.t.* to make humble, to lower the rank or self-importance of. —**eat humble pie,** to make a humble apology [f. *umbles* edible offal of deer]. —**humbleness** *n.*, **humbly** *adv.* [f. OF f. L *humilis* lowly (*humus* ground)]

humbug /ˈhʌmbʌg/ *n.* **1** deceptive or false talk or behaviour. **2** an impostor. **3** a hard-boiled sweet usually flavoured with peppermint. —*v.t./i.* (**-gg-**) to be or behave like an impostor; to deceive. [orig. unkn.]

humdinger /ˈhʌmdɪŋə(r)/ *n.* (*slang*) a remarkable person or thing. [orig. unkn.]

humdrum /ˈhʌmdrʌm/ *adj.* dull, commonplace, monotonous. [prob. redupl. f. HUM]

humerus /ˈhju:mərəs/ *n.* the bone of the upper arm.—**humeral** *adj.* [L, = shoulder]

humid /ˈhju:mɪd/ *adj.* (of the air or a climate) damp. [f. F or L ((*h*)*umēre* be moist)]

humidifier /hjuːˈmɪdɪfaɪə(r)/ *n.* a device for keeping the air moist in a room etc. [f. foll.]

humidify /hjuːˈmɪdɪfaɪ/ *v.t.* to make humid. [f. HUMID]

humidity /hjuːˈmɪdɪtɪ/ *n.* dampness; degree of moisture, especially in the atmosphere. [f. OF or L (as HUMID)]

humiliate /hjuːˈmɪlɪeɪt/ *v.t.* to harm the dignity or self-respect of. —**humiliation** /-ˈeɪʃ(ə)n/ *n.* [f. L *humiliare* (as HUMBLE)]

humility /hjuːˈmɪlɪtɪ/ *n.* a humble attitude of mind; humbleness. [f. OF f. L (as HUMBLE)]

humming-bird *n.* a small tropical bird of the family Trochilidae, that makes a humming sound with its wings.

hummock /ˈhʌmək/ *n.* a low hill or hump. [orig. unkn.]

hummus /ˈhʊməs/ *n.* an hors d'œuvre made from ground chick-peas and sesame oil flavoured with lemon and garlic. [f. Turk.]

humoresque /hjuːməˈresk/ *n.* a light and lively musical composition. [f. G. *humoreske* (as HUMOUR)]

humorist /ˈhjuːmərɪst/ *n.* a writer or speaker noted for humour. [f. HUMOUR]

humorous /ˈhjuːmərəs/ *adj.* full of humour, amusing. —**humorously** *adv.* [f. foll.]

humour /ˈhjuːmə(r)/ *n.* **1** the quality of being amusing. **2** the ability to enjoy what is comic or amusing. **3** a state of mind. **4** each of the four fluids (blood, phlegm, choler, and melancholy) formerly held to determine a person's physical and mental qualities. —*v.t.* to keep (a person) contented by indulging his wishes. —**aqueous humour**, the transparent substance between the lens of the eye and the cornea. **vitreous humour**, that filling the eyeball. [f. OF f. L (*h*)*umor* moisture (as HUMID)]

hump *n.* **1** the rounded protuberance on the back of a camel etc., or as an abnormality on a person's back. **2** a rounded raised mass of earth etc. **3** (*slang*) a fit of depression or annoyance. —*v.t.* **1** to form into a hump. **2** to hoist or shoulder (one's pack etc.). [perh. f. LG or Du.]

humpback *n.* a deformed back with a hump; a person with this. —**humpback bridge**, a small bridge with a steep ascent and descent. —**humpbacked** *adj.*

humph /hʌmf/ *int.* & *n.* an inarticulate sound expressing doubt or dissatisfaction. [imit.]

humus /ˈhjuːməs/ *n.* a rich dark organic material formed by the decay of dead leaves and plants etc., and essential to the fertility of soil. [L, = ground]

Hun *n.* **1** (usu. *derog.*) a German. **2** a member of an Asiatic people who ravaged Europe in the 4th-5th c. [OE, ult. f. Turki *Hun-yü*]

hunch *v.t./i.* to bend or arch into a hump. —*n.* **1** a hump, a hunk. **2** an intuitive feeling. [orig. unkn.]

hunchback *n.* a humpback. —**hunchbacked** *adj.*

hundred /ˈhʌndrəd/ *adj.* & *n.* **1** (*sing.* form is used, with plural verb, when qualified by a preceding word) ten times ten; the symbol for this (100, c, C). **2** (in *pl.*) very many. **3** (*hist.*) a subdivision of a county or shire with its own court. —**hundreds and thousands**, tiny coloured sweets for decorating a cake etc. —**hundredth** *adj.* & *n.* [OE]

hundredfold *adj.* & *adv.* **1** a hundred times as much or as many. **2** consisting of a hundred parts. [f. prec. + -FOLD)]

hundredweight *n.* (*pl.* same) a measure of weight, 112 lb. —**metric hundredweight**, 50 kg. **short hundredweight**, (*US*) 100 lb.

hung see HANG.

Hungarian /hʌnˈgeərɪən/ *adj.* of Hungary or its people or language. —*n.* **1** a native or inhabitant of Hungary. **2** the language of Hungary. [f. L (*Hungari* Magyar nation)]

hunger /ˈhʌŋgə(r)/ *n.* **1** need for food, the discomfort felt when one has not eaten for some time. **2** strong desire. —*v.i.* to feel hunger. —**hunger strike**, refusal of food (esp. by a prisoner) as a form of protest. [OE]

hungry /ˈhʌŋgrɪ/ *adj.* feeling or showing hunger; inducing hunger. —**hungrily** *adv.* [OE (as prec.)]

hunk *n.* a large piece cut off. [prob. f. LDu.]

hunkers *n.pl.* the haunches. [orig. Sc. (*hunker* to squat)]

hunt *v.t./i.* **1** to pursue (wild animals or game, or *absol.*) for sport or food; (of an animal) to pursue its prey. **2** to pursue with hostility. **3** to search for; to make a search (*for*); to search (a district) for game. **4** to use (a horse or hounds) for hunting. **5** (of an engine) to run alternately too fast and too slow. —*n.* **1** hunting. **2** an association of people hunting; the district where they hunt. [OE (*hentan* seize)]

hunter *n.* **1** one who hunts. **2** a horse ridden for hunting. **3** a watch with a hinged metal cover protecting the glass. —**hunter's moon**, the first full moon after the harvest moon. [f. HUNT]

huntsman *n.* (*pl.* **-men**) a hunter; a person in charge of hounds.

hurdle *n.* **1** a portable rectangular frame with bars, for a temporary fence etc. **2** each of a series of upright frames to be jumped over in a race; (in *pl.*) a race with such jumps. **3** an obstacle; a difficulty. —*v.t./i.* **1** to fence off with hurdles. **2** to run in a hurdle-race. [OE]

hurdler *n.* **1** one who runs in hurdle-races. **2** one who makes hurdles. [f. prec.]

hurdy-gurdy /ˈhɜːdɪgɜːdɪ/ *n.* **1** a stringed instrument with strings that are brought into play by means of slide-keys projecting from a key-box. **2** (*colloq.*) a barrel-organ. [prob. imit.]

hurl *v.t.* **1** to throw with great force. **2** to utter vehemently. —*n.* a forceful throw. [prob. imit.; cf. LG *hurreln*]

hurling *n.* the game of **hurley,** an Irish form of hockey played with broad sticks. [f. HURL]

hurly-burly /ˈhɜːlɪbɜːlɪ/ *n.* boisterous activity, a commotion. [redupl. f. HURL]

hurrah /hʊˈrɑː/ *int.* & *n.* (also **hurray** /-ˈreɪ/) an exclamation of joy or approval. [alt. of earlier *huzza* (perh. orig. sailor's cry)]

hurricane /ˈhʌrɪkən/ *n.* a storm with a violent wind, especially a West Indian cyclone; a wind of 73 m.p.h. or more. —**hurricane lamp,** a lamp with the flame protected from violent wind. [f. Sp. & Port. f. Carib]

hurry /ˈhʌrɪ/ *n.* great haste; eagerness, urgency; the need for haste. —*v.t./i.* **1** to move or act with eager or excessive haste. **2** to cause to move or proceed in this way. **3** (in *p.p.*) hasty, done rapidly. —**hurry up,** (*colloq.*) to make haste. **in a hurry,** hurrying; easily or readily. [imit.]

hurry-scurry /hʌrɪˈskʌrɪ/ *n.* disorderly haste. —*adj.* & *adv.* in confusion. [redupl. f. prec.]

hurt *v.t./i.* (*past* & *p.p.* **hurt**) **1** to cause pain, injury, or damage to; to cause pain or harm. **2** to cause mental pain or distress to. **3** to feel pain. —*n.* an injury, harm. [f. OF *hurter*]

hurtful *adj.* causing (esp. mental) hurt. —**hurtfully** *adv.* [f. HURT + -FUL]

hurtle *v.t./i.* to move or hurl rapidly or with a clattering sound; to come with a crash. [f. HURT in obs. sense 'strike forcibly']

husband /ˈhʌzbənd/ *n.* a married man in relation to his wife. —*v.t.* to use economically. [OE f. ON, = house-dweller]

husbandry *n.* **1** farming. **2** the management of resources. [f. prec. in archaic use = manager of affairs]

hush *v.t./i.* to make or become silent or quiet. —*n.* silence. —**hush-hush** *adj.* (*colloq.*) highly confidential, very secret. **hush-money** *n.* money paid to prevent the disclosure of a discreditable affair. **hush up,** to suppress public mention of (an affair). [f. obs. *husht* imit. int. taken as *p.p.*]

husk *n.* **1** the dry outer covering of certain seeds and fruits. **2** the worthless outside part of anything. —*v.t.* to remove the husk(s) from. [f. LG, = sheath (as HOUSE)]

husky[1] *adj.* **1** full of or dry as husks. **2** (of a person or voice) dry in the throat, hoarse. **3** big and strong. —**huskily** *adv.*, **huskiness** *n.* [f. prec.]

husky[2] *n.* a dog of a powerful breed used in the Arctic for pulling sledges. [perh. contr. f. ESKIMO]

hussar /hʊˈzɑː(r)/ *n.* a soldier of a light cavalry regiment. [f. Magyar ult. f. It. (as CORSAIR)]

hussy *n.* a saucy girl; an immoral woman. [contr. of HOUSEWIFE]

hustings *n.* **1** parliamentary election proceedings. **2** (*hist.*) a platform from which (before 1872) candidates for Parliament were nominated and addressed electors. [pl. of *husting*, OE, f. ON, = house of assembly (as HOUSE, THING)]

hustle /ˈhʌs(ə)l/ *v.t./i.* **1** to jostle, to push roughly. **2** to hurry. **3** to bustle; to cause to act quickly and without time to consider things. **4** (*slang*) to swindle; to obtain by force —*n.* hustling, bustle. —**hustler.** *n.* [f. MDu *husselen* shake]

hut *n.* a small simple or crude house or shelter; a temporary housing for troops. —*v.t.* (**-tt-**) **1** to place (troops etc.) in huts. **2** to furnish with huts. [f. F *hutte* f. MHG]

hutch *n.* a boxlike pen for rabbits etc. [orig. = coffer, f. OF *huche* f. L]

hyacinth /ˈhaɪəsɪnθ/ *n.* **1** a plant of the genus *Hyacinthus* with fragrant bell-shaped (esp. purplish-blue) flowers. **2** purplish-blue. —**wild hyacinth,** the bluebell. [f. F f. L f. Gk *huakinthos* flower and gem, also name of youth loved by Apollo]

hybrid /ˈhaɪbrɪd/ *n.* **1** the offspring of two animals or plants of different species or varieties. **2** a thing composed of diverse elements; a word with parts from different languages. —*adj.* bred or produced as a hybrid; cross-bred. —**hybridism** *n.*, **hybridity** /-ˈbɪdɪtɪ/ *n.* [f. L *hybrida* orig. = offspring of tame sow and wild boar]

hybridize *v.t./i.* to subject (a species etc.) to cross-breeding; to produce hybrids; (of an animal or plant) to interbreed. —**hybridization** /-ˈzeɪʃ(ə)n/ *n.* [f. prec.]

hydra /ˈhaɪdrə/ *n.* **1** a thing hard to extirpate. **2** a water-snake. **3** a freshwater polyp of the genus *Hydra*, with a tubular body and tentacles around the mouth. [f. *Hydra*, snake in Gk myth., whose many heads grew again when cut off]

hydrangea /haɪˈdreɪndʒə/ *n.* a shrub of the genus *Hydrangea*, with globular clusters of white, pink, or blue flowers. [f. Gk *hudōr* water + *aggos* vessel (from shape of seed-capsules)]

hydrant /ˈhaɪdrənt/ *n.* a pipe (especially in a street) with a nozzle for a hose, for drawing water from a main. [as HYDRO-]

hydrate /ˈhaɪdreɪt/ *n.* a chemical compound of water with another compound or an element. -/also -ˈdreɪt/ *v.t.* to combine chemically with water; to cause to absorb water. —**hydration** /-ˈdreɪʃ(ə)n/ *n.* [F (as HYDRO-)]

hydraulic /haɪˈdrɔ:lɪk/ *adj.* **1** (of water etc.) conveyed through pipes or channels. **2** operated by the movement of liquid. —**hydraulically** *adj.* [f. L F. Gk (*hudōr* water, *aulos* pipe)]

hydraulics *n.pl.* (usu. treated as *sing.*) the science of the conveyance of liquids through pipes etc., especially as motive power. [f. prec.]

hydride /ˈhaɪdraɪd/ *n.* a compound of hydrogen especially with a metal. [f. HYDROGEN]

hydro /ˈhaɪdrəʊ/ *n.* (*pl.* **-os**) (*colloq.*) **1** a hotel etc. providing hydropathic treatment. **2** a hydroelectric power plant. [abbr.]

hydro- /ˈhaɪdrə(ʊ)-/ *in comb.* **1** water, liquid. **2** combined with hydrogen. [f. Gk (*hudōr* water)]

hydrocarbon /haɪdrəʊˈkɑ:bən/ *n.* a compound consisting only of hydrogen and carbon (e.g. methane, benzene).

hydrocephalus /haɪdrəʊˈsefələs/ *n.* a condition (especially in young children) with an accumulation of fluid in the cavity of the cranium, which can impair the mental faculties. —**hydrocephalic** /-sɪˈfælɪk/ *adj.* [f. HYDRO- + Gk *kephalē* head]

hydrochloric /haɪdrəʊˈklɔ:rɪk/ *adj.* containing hydrogen and chlorine.

hydrochloride /haɪdrəʊˈklɔ:raɪd/ *n.* a compound of an organic base with hydrochloric acid.

hydrocyanic /haɪdrəʊsaɪˈænɪk/ *adj.* containing hydrogen and cyanogen.

hydrodynamics /haɪdrəʊdaɪˈnæmɪks/ *n.pl.* (usu. treated as *sing.*) the science of the forces acting on or exerted by liquids (esp. water). —**hydrodynamic** *adj.*

hydroelectric /haɪdrəʊɪˈlektrɪk/ *adj.* developing electricity by the utilization of water-power; (of electricity) produced thus —**hydroelectricity** /-ˈtrɪsɪtɪ/ *n.*

hydrofoil /ˈhaɪdrəfɔɪl/ *n.* a boat equipped with a device for raising the hull out of the water to enable rapid motion; this device. [f. HYDRO-, after *aerofoil*]

hydrogen /ˈhaɪdrədʒ(ə)n/ *n.* a gaseous element, the lightest of all the elements, symbol H, atomic number 1—**hydrogen bomb,** an immensely powerful bomb utilizing the explosive fusion of hydrogen nuclei. **hydrogen sulphide,** an unpleasant-smelling poisonous gas formed by rotting animal matter. —**hydrogenous** /-ˈdrɒdʒɪnəs/ *adj.* [f. F (as HYDRO-, -GEN)]

hydrogenate /haɪˈdrɒdʒɪneɪt/ *v.t.* to charge with or cause to combine with hydrogen. —**hydrogenation** /-ˈneɪʃ(ə)n/ *n.* [f. prec.]

hydrography /haɪˈdrɒgrəfɪ/ *n.* the scientific study of seas, lakes, rivers, etc. —**hydrographer** *n.*, **hydrographic** /-ˈgræfɪk/ *adj.* [f. HYDRO- + -GRAPHY]

hydrology /haɪˈdrɒlədʒɪ/ *n.* the science of the properties of water, especially of its movement in relation to the land. —**hydrological** /haɪdrəˈlɒdʒɪk(ə)l/ *adj.* [f. HYDRO- + -LOGY]

hydrolyse /ˈhaɪdrəlaɪz/ *v.t.* to decompose by hydrolysis. [as foll.]

hydrolysis /haɪˈdrɒlɪsɪs/ *n.* the decomposition of a substance by the chemical action of water. [f. HYDRO- + Gk *lusis* dissolving]

hydrometer /haɪˈdrɒmɪtə(r)/ *n.* an instrument for measuring the density of liquids. [f. HYDRO- + -METER]

hydropathy /haɪˈdrɒpəθɪ/ *n.* medical treatment by external and internal application of water. —**hydropathic** /-ˈpæθɪk/ *adj.* [f. HYDRO-, after *homoeopathy* etc.]

hydrophilic /haɪdrəˈfɪlɪk/ *adj.* having an affinity for water; able to be wetted by water. [f. HYDRO- + Gk *philos* loving]

hydrophobia /haɪdrəˈfəʊbɪə/ *n.* aversion to water, especially as a symptom of rabies in man; rabies, especially in man. —**hydrophobic** *adj.* [f. L f. Gk (as HYDRO-, -PHOBIA)]

hydroplane /ˈhaɪdrəpleɪn/ *n.* **1** a light fast motor boat designed to skim over the surface of the water. **2** a finlike device on a submarine enabling it to rise or descend. [f. HYDRO-, after *aeroplane*]

hydroponics /haɪdrəˈpɒnɪks/ *n.* the art of growing plants without soil, in sand etc. or liquid with added nutrients. [f. HYDRO- + Gk *ponos* labour]

hydrosphere /ˈhaɪdrəsfɪə(r)/ *n.* the waters of the earth's surface.

hydrostatic /haɪdrəʊˈstætɪk/ *adj.* of the equilibrium of liquids and the pressure exerted by liquids at rest. [f. Gk *hudrostatēs* hydrostatic balance (as HYDRO-, STATIC)]

hydrostatics *n.pl.* (usu. treated as *sing.*) the branch of mechanics concerned with the hydrostatic properties of liquids. [f. prec.]

hydrous /ˈhaɪdrəs/ *adj.* (of substances) containing water. [as HYDRO-]

hydroxide /haɪˈdrɒksaɪd/ *n.* a compound of an element or radical with a hydroxyl. [f. HYDRO- + OXIDE]

hydroxyl /haɪˈdrɒksɪl/ *n.* a radical containing hydrogen and oxygen. [f. HYDRO- + OXYGEN]

hyena /haɪˈi:nə/ *n.* a carnivorous mammal of the order Hyaenidae of Africa and Asia, with a shrill cry resembling laughter. [f. OF & L f. Gk *huaina*]

hygiene /ˈhaɪdʒi:n/ *n.* the principles of maintaining health, especially by cleanliness;

sanitary science. —**hygienic** /-ˈdʒiːnɪk/ *adj.*, **hygienically** *adv.*, **hygienist** *n.* [f. F f. Gk *hugieine* (*tekhne*) (*hugies* healthy)]

hygrometer /haɪˈgrɒmɪtə(r)/ *n.* an instrument for measuring the humidity of the air or a gas. [f. Gk *hugros* wet + -METER]

hygroscope /ˈhaɪgrəskəʊp/ *n.* an instrument indicating but not measuring the humidity of the air. [as prec. + -SCOPE]

hygroscopic /haɪgrəˈskɒpɪk/ *adj.* **1** of the hygroscope. **2** (of a substance) tending to absorb moisture from the air. [as prec.]

hymen /ˈhaɪmen/ *n.* the membrane partially closing the external opening of the vagina of a virgin. [L f. Gk *humēn* membrane]

hymenopterous /haɪməˈnɒptərəs/ *adj.* of the order of insects including the ant, bee, wasp, etc., with four membranous wings. [f. Gk (as prec. + *pteron* wing)]

hymn /hɪm/ *n.* a song of praise, especially to God. —*v.t.* to praise or celebrate in hymns. [f. OF f. L f. Gk *humnos*]

hymnal /ˈhɪmn(ə)l/ *n.* a book of hymns. [f. L (as prec.)]

hymnology /hɪmˈnɒlədʒɪ/ *n.* the composition or study of hymns. —**hymnologist** *n.* [f. HYMN + -LOGY]

hyoscine /ˈhaɪəsiːn/ *n.* a poisonous alkaloid from which a sedative is made, found in plants of the nightshade family. [f. foll.]

hyoscyamine /haɪəˈsaɪəmiːn/ *n.* a poisonous alkaloid used as a sedative, got from henbane. [f. Gk *huoskuamos* henbane (*hus* pig, *kuamos* bean)]

hyper- /haɪpə(r)-/ *prefix* in the senses 'over', 'above', 'too'. [f. Gk (*huper* over)]

hyperactive /haɪpəˈræktɪv/ *adj.* (of a person) abnormally active.

hyperbola /haɪˈpɜːbələ/ *n.* the plane curve produced when a cone is cut by a plane that makes a larger angle with the base than the side of the cone makes. —**hyperbolic** /-ˈbɒlɪk/ *adj.* [as foll.]

hyperbole /haɪˈpɜːbəlɪ/ *n.* a statement exaggerated for special effect. —**hyperbolical** /-ˈbɒlɪk(ə)l/ *adj.* [L f. Gk, = excess (as HYPER-, *ballō* throw)]

hypercritical /haɪpəˈkrɪtɪk(ə)l/ *adj.* excessively critical. —**hypercritically** *adv.*

hypermarket /ˈhaɪpəmɑːkɪt/ *n.* a very large self-service store usually outside a town. [f. F *hypermarché* (as HYPER-, MARKET)]

hyperon /ˈhaɪpərɒn/ *n.* an unstable baryon. [f. HYPER-]

hypersensitive /haɪpəˈsensɪtɪv/ *adj.* excessively sensitive. —**hypersensitivity** /-ˈtɪvɪtɪ/ *n.*

hypersonic /haɪpəˈsɒnɪk/ *adj.* **1** of speeds more than about five times that of sound. **2** of sound frequencies above about 1,000 megahertz. [f. HYPER-, after *supersonic*]

hypertension /haɪpəˈtenʃ(ə)n/ *n.* **1** abnormally high blood pressure. **2** great emotional tension.

hypertrophy /ˈhaɪpɜːtrəfɪ/ *n.* enlargement of an organ etc. due to excessive nutrition. —**hypertrophic** /-pəˈtrɒːfɪk/ *adj.* [f. HYPER- + Gk *trophē* nourishment]

hyphen /ˈhaɪf(ə)n/ *n.* the sign (-) used to join words together (e.g. *fruit-tree*, *pick-me-up*), to mark the division of a word at the end of a line, to divide a word into parts, etc. —*v.t.* to join (words) with a hyphen; to write (a word or words) with a hyphen. [L f. Gk *huphen* together (as HYPO-, *hen* one)]

hyphenate /ˈhaɪfəneɪt/ *v.t.* to hyphen. —**hyphenation** /-ˈneɪʃ(ə)n/ *n.* [f. prec.]

hypnosis /hɪpˈnəʊsɪs/ *n.* (*pl.* **-oses** /-əʊsiːz/) a state like sleep in which the subject acts only on external suggestion; an artificially produced sleep. [f. Gk *hupnos* sleep]

hypnotic /hɪpˈnɒtɪk/ *adj.* of or producing hypnosis. —*n.* a hypnotic drug or influence. —**hypnotically** *adv.* [f. F f. L f. Gk (*hupnoō* put to sleep)]

hypnotism /ˈhɪpnətɪz(ə)m/ *n.* the production or process of hypnosis. —**hypnotist** *n.* [f. prec.]

hypnotize *v.t.* to produce hypnosis in; to fascinate, to capture the mind of (a person). [f. HYPNOTIC]

hypo[1] /ˈhaɪpəʊ/ *n.* sodium thiosulphate (incorrectly called hyposulphite) used in photographic fixing. [abbr.]

hypo[2] /ˈhaɪpəʊ/ *n.* (*pl.* **-os**) (*slang*) a hypodermic. [abbr.]

hypo- /haɪpə(ʊ)-/ *prefix* in the senses 'under', 'below', 'slightly'. [f. Gk (*hupo* under)]

hypocaust /ˈhaɪpəkɔːst/ *n.* a hollow space under a floor into which hot air from a furnace was sent for heating an ancient Roman house or baths. [f. L f. Gk (as HYPO-, *kaiō* burn)]

hypochondria /haɪpəˈkɒndrɪə/ *n.* abnormal anxiety about one's health. [L f. Gk, = parts of body below ribs (whence melancholy was thought to arise)]

hypochondriac *n.* a person suffering from hypochondria. —*adj.* of hypochondria. [f. prec.]

hypocrisy /hɪˈpɒkrɪsɪ/ *n.* simulation of virtue or goodness, insincerity. [f. OF f. L f. Gk, = acting of a part]

hypocrite /ˈhɪpəkrɪt/ *n.* a person guilty of hypocrisy. —**hypocritical** /-ˈkrɪtɪk(ə)l/ *adj.*, **hypocritically** *adv.* [as prec.]

hypodermic /haɪpəˈdɜːmɪk/ *adj.* **1** of the area beneath the skin. **2** injected there; used for such injection. —*n.* a hypodermic injection or syringe. —**hypodermic syringe**, a syringe with a hollow needle for injection beneath the skin. —**hypodermically** *adv.* [f. HYPO- + Gk *derma* skin]

hypostasis /haɪˈpɒstəsɪs/ *n.* (*pl.* **-ses** = /si:z/) **1** the underlying substance of a thing as distinct from its attributes. **2** any of the three persons of the Trinity. [L f. Gk (as HYPO-, *stasis* standing)]

hypostatic /haɪpəˈstætɪk/ *adj.* of or involving hypostasis. —**hypostatic union,** the union of divine and human natures in Christ, a doctrine formally accepted by the Church in 451. [as prec.]

hypotension /haɪpəˈtenʃ(ə)n/ *n.* abnormally low blood pressure.

hypotenuse /haɪˈpɒtənju:z/ *n.* the side opposite the right angle of a right-angled triangle. [f. L. f. Gk, = subtending line]

hypothalamus /haɪpəʊˈθæləməs/ *n.* a part of the brain, controlling body-temperature etc. [f. HYPO- + Gk *thalamos* room]

hypothecate /haɪˈpɒθɪkeɪt/ *v.t.* to pledge, to mortgage. —**hypothecation** /-ˈkeɪʃ(ə)n/ *n.* [f. L f. Gk *hupothēcē* deposit (as HYPO-, *tithēmi* place)]

hypothermia /haɪpəˈθɜ:mɪə/ *n.* the condition of having an abnormally low body-temperature. [f. HYPO- + Gk *thermē* heat]

hypothesis /haɪˈpɒθɪsɪs/ *n.* (*pl.* **-ses** /-si:z/) a proposition or supposition made from known facts as the basis for reasoning or investigation. [L f. Gk, = foundation]

hypothesize /haɪˈpɒθɪsaɪz/ *v.t./i.* to form a hypothesis; to assume as a hypothesis. [f. prec.]

hypothetical /haɪpəˈθetɪk(ə)l/ *adj.* of or based on a hypothesis; supposed but not necessarily real or true. —**hypothetically** *adv.* [f. HYPOTHESIS]

hyssop /ˈhɪsəp/ *n.* **1** a small bushy aromatic herb of the genus *Hyssopus* formerly used medicinally. **2** a plant used for sprinkling in ancient Jewish rites. [OE, ult. f. Gk f. Semitic]

hysterectomy /hɪstəˈrektəmɪ/ *n.* a surgical removal of the womb. [f. Gk *hustera* womb + -ECTOMY]

hysteresis /hɪstəˈri:sɪs/ *n.* (*pl.* **hystereses** /-si:z/) the lagging of an effect when the cause varies in amount, especially of magnetic induction lagging behind the magnetizing force. [f. Gk (*husteros* coming after)]

hysteria /hɪˈstɪərɪə/ *n.* **1** wild uncontrollable emotion or excitement. **2** a functional disturbance of the nervous system, of psychoneurotic origin. [as foll.]

hysteric /hɪˈsterɪk/ *n.* **1** a hysterical person. **2** (in *pl.*) a fit of hysteria. [f. L f. Gk (*hustera* womb), hysteria being thought to affect women more than men]

hysterical *adj.* of or caused by hysteria; suffering from hysteria. —**hysterically** *adv.* [f. prec.]

Hz *abbr.* hertz.

Ii

I, i /aɪ/ *n.* (*pl.* **Is, I's**) **1** the ninth letter of the alphabet. **2** (as a Roman numeral) 1.

I *symbol* iodine.

I /aɪ/ *pron.* (*obj.* ME¹; *poss.* MY, MINE¹; *pl.* WE etc.) the person who is speaking and referring to himself. [OE]

I. *abbr.* Island(s); Isle(s).

iambic /aɪˈæmbɪk/ *adj.* of or using iambuses. —*n.* (usu. in *pl.*) iambic verse. [f. F f. L f. Gk (as foll.)]

iambus /aɪˈæmbəs/ *n.* (*pl.* **-uses**) a metrical foot with one short or unstressed syllable followed by one long or stressed syllable. [L f. Gk (*iaptō* assail in words, f. its use in lampoons)]

IBA *abbr.* Independent Broadcasting Authority.

Iberian /aɪˈbɪərɪən/ *adj.* of Iberia, the peninsula comprising Spain and Portugal. —*n.* a native or the language of ancient Iberia. [f. L *Iberia*, f. Gk]

ibex /ˈaɪbeks/ *n.* a wild goat (genus *Capra*) of the Alps etc., with large recurved horns. [L]

ibid. *abbr.* in the same book or passage etc. [L *ibidem* in the same place]

ibis /ˈaɪbɪs/ *n.* a wading bird of the family Threskiornithidae, with a down-curved bill. [f. L f. Gk]

-ible *suffix* forming adjectives with senses as -ABLE (*terrible, defensible, forcible, possible*). [F, or f. L *-ibilis*]

ice /aɪs/ *n.* **1** frozen water; a sheet of this on the surface of water. **2** a portion of ice-cream or water-ice. —*v.t./i.* **1** to become covered with ice; to freeze. **2** to cover or mix with ice; to cool in ice. **3** to cover (a cake etc.) with icing. —**break the ice,** to make a start; to overcome formality. **ice age,** a glacial period (see GLACIAL), **ice-blue** *adj.* very pale blue. **ice-breaker** *n.* a ship designed to break through ice. **ice-cap** *n.* a permanent covering of ice, e.g. in polar lands. **ice-cream** *n.* a sweet creamy frozen food. **ice-field** *n.* a large expanse of floating ice. **ice hockey,** a form of hockey played on ice with a puck instead of a ball (see HOCKEY). **ice lolly,** a kind of water-ice on a stick. **on ice,** (*colloq.*) held in a state of temporary suspension, or in reserve; quite certain. **on thin ice,** in a risky situation. [OE]

iceberg /ˈaɪsbɜːg/ *n.* a huge floating mass of ice. [prob. f. Du.]

icebox *n.* a compartment in a refrigerator for making or storing ice; (*US*) a refrigerator.

Icelander /ˈaɪsləndə(r)/ *n*, a native of Iceland, an island country in the North Atlantic.

Icelandic /aɪsˈlændɪk/ *adj.* of Iceland or its language. —*n.* the language of Iceland.

ichneumon /ɪkˈnjuːmən/ *n.* **1** a mongoose (*Herpestes ichneumon*) of North Africa etc., noted for destroying crocodiles' eggs. **2** an ichneumon fly. —**ichneumon fly,** an insect of the family Ichneumonidae, that deposits its eggs in or on the larva of another egg. [L f. Gk (*ikhneuō* track)]

ichthyology /ɪkθɪˈɒlədʒɪ/ *n.* the study of fishes. [f. Gk *ikhthus* fish + -LOGY]

ichthyosaurus /ɪkθɪəˈsɔːrəs/ *n.* (*pl.* **-uses**) an extinct marine animal of the order Ichthyosauria, with a long head, tapering body, four paddles, and a large tail. [f. Gk *ikhthus* fish + *sauros* lizard]

ICI *abbr.* Imperial Chemical Industries.

icicle /ˈaɪsɪk(ə)l/ *n.* a tapering, hanging spike of ice formed from dripping water. [f. ICE + dial. *ickle* icicle]

icing /ˈaɪsɪŋ/ *n.* **1** a coating of sugar etc. on a cake or biscuit. **2** the formation of ice on an aircraft. —**icing sugar,** finely powdered sugar used for making icing. [f. ICE]

icon /ˈaɪkɒn/ *n.* an image or statue; (in the Orthodox Church) a painting or mosaic of a sacred person, itself regarded as sacred. [L f. Gk *eikōn* image]

iconoclast /aɪˈkɒnəklæst/ *n.* **1** a breaker of images, especially one who took part in a movement in the 8th-9th c. against the use of images in religious worship in churches in the Eastern Roman Empire, or a Puritan of the 16th-17th c. **2** one who attacks cherished beliefs. —**iconoclasm** *n.*, **iconoclastic** /-ˈklæstɪk/ *adj.* [f. L f. Gk (*eikōn* image, *klaō* break)]

iconography /aɪkəˈnɒgrəfɪ/ *n.* **1** the illustration of a subject by drawings etc. **2** the study of portraits especially of one person. [f. Gk, = sketch (as ICON, -GRAPHY)]

icosahedron /aɪkɒsəˈhiːdrən/ *n.* a solid figure with twenty faces. [f. L f. Gk (*eikosi* twenty, *hedra* base)]

ictus /ˈɪktəs/ *n.* a rhythmical or metrical stress. [L, = a blow (*icere* strike)]

icy /ˈaɪsɪ/ *adj.* **1** very cold. **2** covered with or abounding in ice. **3** (of tone or manner) unfriendly, hostile. —**icily** *adv.*, **iciness** *n.* [f. ICE]

id *n.* a person's inherited psychological impulses as part of the unconscious. [L, = that]

idea /aɪˈdɪə/ *n.* **1** a plan or scheme formed in the mind by thinking. **2** a mental impression or conception. **3** an opinion or belief; a vague notion, a fancy. **4** an ambition or aspiration. **5** an archetype, a pattern. —**have no idea,** (*colloq.*) to be ignorant or incompetent. [L f. Gk, = look, form, kind]

ideal /aɪˈdɪəl/ *adj.* **1** satisfying one's idea of what is perfect. **2** existing only in an idea, visionary. —*n.* a person or thing regarded as perfect or as a standard for attainment or imitation; a conception of this. [f. F f. L (as prec.)]

idealism /aɪˈdɪəlɪz(ə)m/ *n.* (usu. opp. REALISM) **1** the representation of things in an ideal or idealized form; imaginative treatment; the practice of forming or following after ideals. **2** a system of thought in which the object of external perception is held to consist of ideas. —**idealist** *n.*, **idealistic** /-ˈlɪstɪk/ *adj.* [f. F or G (as prec.)]

idealize /aɪˈdɪəlaɪz/ *v.t.* to regard or represent as ideal or perfect. —**idealization** /-ˈzeɪʃ(ə)n/ *n.* [f. IDEAL]

ideally /aɪˈdɪəlɪ/ *adv.* according to an ideal; in ideal circumstances. [f. IDEAL]

idée fixe /iːdeɪ ˈfiːks/ a recurrent or dominating idea. [F, = fixed idea]

identical /aɪˈdentɪk(ə)l/ *adj.* **1** one and the same. **2** agreeing in all details. **3** (of twins) developed from a single fertilized ovum and thus of the same sex and very similar in appearance. —**identically** *adv.* [f. L (as IDENTITY)]

identifiable /aɪˈdentɪfaɪəb(ə)l/ *adj.* that may be identified. [f. IDENTIFY]

identification /aɪdentɪfɪˈkeɪʃ(ə)n/ *n.* identifying; a means of identifying. —**identification parade,** an assembly of persons from whom a suspect is to be identified. [f. foll.]

identify /aɪˈdentɪfaɪ/ *v.t./i.* **1** to establish the identity of, to recognize. **2** to treat as identical (*with*). **3** to associate (a person, *oneself*) closely (*with* a party, policy, etc.); to associate oneself *with*; to regard oneself as sharing characteristics *with* another person. **4** to select by consideration. [f. L *identificare* (as IDENTITY)]

identikit /aɪˈdentɪkɪt/ *n.* [P] a composite picture made from drawings of separate features, assembled from descriptions, put together to form a likeness, especially of a person sought by the police. [f. foll. + KIT]

identity /aɪˈdentɪtɪ/ *n.* **1** the condition of being a specified person or thing. **2** the state of being identical, absolute sameness. **3** individuality, personality. **4** equality of two algebraic expressions for all values of quantities, the expression of this. [f. L *identitas* (*idem* same)]

ideogram /ˈɪdɪəgræm/ *n.* a character or symbol indicating the idea of a thing without expressing the sounds in its name. [f. IDEA + -GRAM]

ideograph /ˈɪdɪəgrɑːf/ *n.* an ideogram. —**ideographic** /-ˈgræfɪk/ *adj.*, **ideography** /-ˈɒgrəfɪ/ *n.* [f. IDEA + -GRAPH]

ideologue /ˈaɪdɪəlɒg/ *n.* an adherent of an ideology. [as foll.]

ideology /aɪdɪˈɒlədʒɪ/ *n.* the ideas at the basis of an economic or political theory or system, or characteristic of some class etc. —**ideological** /-ˈlɒdʒɪk(ə)l/ *adj.*, **ideologist** *n.* [f. F (as IDEA, -LOGY)]

ides /aɪdz/ *n.pl.* the 15th day of March, May, July, October, the 13th of other months, in the ancient Roman calendar. [f. OF f. L *idus*]

idiocy /ˈɪdɪəsɪ/ *n.* **1** the state of being an idiot. **2** extreme stupidity; stupid behaviour or action. [f. IDIOT]

idiom /ˈɪdɪəm/ *n.* **1** a form of expression or usage peculiar to a language, especially one whose meaning is not given by those of its separate words. **2** the language of a people. **3** a characteristic mode of expression in art etc. [f. F or L f. Gk *idiōma* (*idios* own, private)]

idiomatic /ɪdɪəˈmætɪk/ *adj.* relating or conforming to an idiom; characteristic of a language. —**idiomatically** *adv.* [f. Gk (as prec.)]

idiosyncrasy /ɪdɪəˈsɪŋkrəsɪ/ *n.* an attitude, form of behaviour, or mental or physical constitution, peculiar to a person. —**idiosyncratic** /-ˈkrætɪk/ *adj.* [f. Gk (*idios* own, *sun* together, *krasis* mixture)]

idiot /ˈɪdɪət/ *n.* **1** a mentally deficient person who is permanently incapable of rational conduct. **2** (*colloq.*) a stupid person. —**idiotic** /-ˈɒtɪk/ *adj.*, **idiotically** /-ˈɒtɪk(ə)l/ *adv.* [f. OF f. L f. Gk, = private citizen, layman]

idle /ˈaɪd(ə)l/ *adj.* **1** doing no work, not employed; not active or in use. **2** avoiding work, lazy. **3** (of time) unoccupied. **4** useless; having no special purpose; groundless. —*v.t./i.* **1** (of an engine) to run slowly without doing work. **2** to pass (time etc.) in idleness. —**idleness** *n.*, **idler** *n.*, **idly** *adv.* [OE]

idol /ˈaɪd(ə)l/ *n.* **1** an image of a deity as an object of worship. **2** an object of excessive or supreme devotion. [f. OF f. L f. Gk *eidōlon* (*eidos* form)]

idolater /aɪˈdɒlətə(r)/ *n.* one who worships idols; a devout admirer. —**idolatrous** *adj.*, **idolatry** *n.* [f. OF f. L f. Gk (as prec., *latreuō* worship)]

idolize /ˈaɪdəlaɪz/ *v.t.* to venerate or love excessively; to treat as an idol. —**idolization** /-ˈzeɪʃ(ə)n/ *n.* [f. IDOL]

idyll /ˈɪdɪl/ *n.* a short description usually in verse of a picturesque scene or incident especially in rustic life; such a scene or incident. [f. L f. Gk *eidullion* (*eidos* form)]

idyllic /ɪˈdɪlɪk/ *adj.* of or like an idyll; peaceful and happy. —**idyllically** *adv.* [f. prec.]

i.e. *abbr.* that is to say. [f. L *id est*]

if *conj.* **1** on the condition or supposition that; in the event that; supposing or granting that. **2** even though. **3** whenever. **4** whether. **5** expressing a wish or surprise. —*n.* a condition or supposition. —**as if,** as the case would be if. [OE]

igloo /ˈɪglu:/ *n.* an Eskimo dome-shaped hut, especially one built of snow. [Eskimo, = house]

igneous /ˈɪgnɪəs/ *adj.* **1** of fire, fiery. **2** (of rocks) formed by solidification of magma (cf. METAMORPHIC, SEDIMENTARY). [f. L *igneus* (*ignis* fire)]

ignite /ɪgˈnaɪt/ *v.t./i.* to set fire to; to catch fire; to make intensely hot. [f. L *ignire* (as prec.)]

ignition /ɪgˈnɪʃ(ə)n/ *n.* **1** igniting. **2** the mechanism for or act of starting combustion in the cylinder of an internal-combustion engine. [F or f. L (as prec.)]

ignoble /ɪgˈnəʊb(ə)l/ *adj.* **1** dishonourable, not noble in character, aims, or purpose. **2** of lowly birth or position. —**ignobly** *adv.* [F or f. L (as IN-², NOBLE)]

ignominious /ɪgnəˈmɪnɪəs/ *adj.* bringing contempt or disgrace, humiliating. —**ignominiously** *adv.* [f. F or L (as foll.)]

ignominy /ˈɪgnəmɪnɪ/ *n.* disgrace, humiliation. [f. F or L (as IN-², *nomen* name)]

ignoramus /ɪgnəˈreɪməs/ *n.* an ignorant person. [L, = we do not know (as IGNORE)]

ignorant /ˈɪgnərənt/ *adj.* lacking knowledge; uninformed; uncouth through lack of knowledge. —**ignorance** *n.*, **ignorantly** *adv.* [f. OF f. L (as foll.)]

ignore /ɪgˈnɔ:(r)/ *v.t.* to refuse to take notice of; to disregard intentionally. [f. F or L *ignorare* not know]

iguana /ɪgˈwɑ:nə/ *n.* a large tree lizard (of the family Iguanidae) of the West Indies and South America. [Sp. f. Carib]

iguanodon /ɪgˈwɑ:nədɒn/ *n.* a large herbivorous dinosaur. [f. prec., after *mastodon*]

il-¹·² see IN-¹·².

ileum /ˈɪlɪəm/ *n.* (*pl.* **ilea**) the third and last portion of the small intestine. [var. of L *ilium*]

ilex /ˈaɪleks/ *n.* **1** the holm-oak. **2** a plant of the genus *Ilex*, including holly. [f. L]

iliac /ˈɪlɪæk/ *adj.* of the flank. [f. L (*ilia* flanks)]

ilk *n.* **of that ilk,** (*Sc.*) of the ancestral estate with the same name as a family; (*colloq.*) of that kind. [OE, = same]

ill *adj.* **1** physically or mentally unwell; (of health) unsound, not good. **2** harmful. **3** wretched, disastrous; hostile, unfavourable. **4** irritable. **5** improper, deficient. —*adv.* **1** badly, wrongly. **2** unfavourably. **3** imperfectly, scarcely. —*n.* injury, harm, evil; (in *pl.*) misfortunes. —**ill-advised** *adj.* (of an action) unwise. **ill at ease,** embarrassed, uncomfortable. **ill-bred** *adj.* badly brought up, rude. **ill-fated** *adj.* unlucky. **ill-favoured** *adj.* unattractive. **ill-gotten** *adj.* acquired by evil or unlawful means. **ill-mannered** *adj.* having bad manners. **ill-natured** *adj.* churlish, unkind. **ill-starred** *adj.* unlucky. **ill-tempered** *adj.* morose, irritable. **ill-timed** *adj.* done or occurring at an unsuitable time. **ill-treat** *v.t.*, **ill-use** *v.t.* to treat badly or cruelly. **ill will,** hostility, unkind feeling. [f. ON]

illegal /ɪˈli:g(ə)l/ *adj.* not legal, contrary to the law. —**illegality** /ɪlɪˈgælɪtɪ/ *n.*, **illegally** *adv.* [f. F or L (as IL-², LEGAL)]

illegible /ɪˈledʒɪb(ə)l/ *adj.* not legible. —**illegibility** /-ˈbɪlɪtɪ/ *n.*, **illegibly** *adv.* [f. IL-² + LEGIBLE]

illegitimate /ɪlɪˈdʒɪtɪmət/ *adj.* **1** (of a child) born of parents who are not married to each other. **2** not authorized by the law or by rules. **3** illogical, wrongly inferred. —**illegitimacy** *n.*, **illegitimately** *adv.* [f. L (as IL-², LEGITIMATE)]

illiberal /ɪˈlɪbər(ə)l/ *adj.* **1** intolerant, narrow-minded. **2** without liberal culture, sordid. **3** stingy. —**illiberality** /-ˈrælɪtɪ/ *n.*, **illiberally** *adv.* [f. F (as IL-², LIBERAL)]

illicit /ɪˈlɪsɪt/ *adj.* unlawful, forbidden. —**illicitly** *adv.* [f. F or L (as IL-², LICIT)]

illiterate /ɪˈlɪtərət/ *adj.* unable to read; uneducated. —*n.* an illiterate person. —**illiteracy** *n.* [f. L (as IL-², LITERATE)]

illness *n.* **1** ill health, the state of being ill. **2** a disease. [f. ILL]

illogical /ɪˈlɒdʒɪk(ə)l/ *adj.* contrary to or devoid of logic. —**illogicality** /-kælɪtɪ/ *n.*, **illogically** *adv.* [f. IL-² + LOGICAL]

illuminant /ɪˈlu:mɪnənt/ *n.* a means of illumination. —*adj.* serving to illuminate. [f. L (as foll.)]

illuminate /ɪˈlu:mɪneɪt/ *v.t.* **1** to light up, to make bright. **2** to enlighten spiritually or intellectually; to help to explain (a subject); to shed lustre on. **3** to decorate with lights as a sign of festivity. **4** to decorate (a manuscript, initial letter, etc.) with gold or other bright colours. —**illumination** /-ˈneɪʃ(ə)n/ *n.*,

illuminative *adj.* [f. L *illuminare* (IL-[1], *lumen* light)]

illumine /ɪˈlju:mɪn/ *v.t.* (*literary*) to light up; to enlighten spiritually. [f. OF f. L (as prec.)]

illusion /ɪˈlu:ʒ(ə)n, ɪˈlju:-/ *n.* **1** a false belief; something wrongly believed to exist. **2** deceptive appearances. —**illusive** *adj.*, **illusory** *adj.* [f. F f. L (*illudere* mock)]

illusionist *n.* a producer of illusions, a conjuror. [f. prec.]

illustrate /ˈɪləstreɪt/ *v.t.* **1** to provide (a book, newspaper, etc.) with pictures. **2** to make clear, especially by examples or drawings. **3** to serve as an example of. —**illustrator** *n.* [f. L *illustrare* (IL-[1], *lustrare* light up)]

illustration /ɪləˈstreɪʃ(ə)n/ *n.* **1** illustrating. **2** a picture or drawing in a book etc. **3** an explanatory example. [f. OF f. L (as prec.)]

illustrative /ˈɪləstrətɪv/ *adj.* illustrating, explanatory (*of*). [f. ILLUSTRATE]

illustrious /ɪˈlʌstrɪəs/ *adj.* distinguished, renowned. [f. L *illustris* (cf. ILLUSTRATE)]

im-[1,2] see IN-[1,2].

image /ˈɪmɪdʒ/ *n.* **1** a representation of an object's external form, e.g. a statue (especially as an object of worship). **2** reputation, the general impression of a person or thing as perceived by the public. **3** a simile, a metaphor. **4** a mental representation. **5** an optical counterpart produced by rays of light reflected from a mirror etc. **6** a counterpart in appearance. **7** an idea, a conception. —*v.t.* **1** to describe or imagine vividly. **2** to make an image of, to portray. **3** to reflect, to mirror. [f. OF f. L *imago*]

imagery *n.* **1** figurative illustration; use of images in literature etc. **2** images, statuary; carving. [as prec.]

imaginable /ɪˈmædʒɪnəb(ə)l/ *adj.* able to be imagined. [f. foll.]

imaginary /ɪˈmædʒɪnərɪ/ *adj.* existing only in the imagination. [f. L (as IMAGE)]

imagination /ɪmædʒɪˈneɪʃ(ə)n/ *n.* the mental faculty forming images or concepts of objects not existent or present, the creative faculty of the mind. [f. OF f. L (as IMAGINE)]

imaginative /ɪˈmædʒɪnətɪv/ *adj.* having or showing a high degree of imagination. —**imaginatively** *adv.* [as foll.]

imagine /ɪˈmædʒɪn/ *v.t.* **1** to form a mental image of, to picture in one's mind. **2** to think or believe; to guess; (*colloq.*) to suppose. [f. OF f. L (as IMAGE)]

imago /ɪˈmeɪgəʊ/ *n.* (*pl.* **imagines** /-dʒɪni:z/) the fully developed stage of an insect, e.g. a butterfly. [L (as IMAGE)]

imam /ɪˈmɑ:m/ *n.* **1** the leader of prayers in a mosque. **2** the title of various Muslim leaders, especially of one succeeding Muhammad as leader of Islam. —**imamate** *n.* [f. Arab., = leader (*'amma* precede)]

imbalance /ɪmˈbæləns/ *n.* lack of balance; disproportion. [f. IM-[2] + BALANCE]

imbecile /ˈɪmbɪsi:l/ *n.* **1** a mentally deficient person; an adult whose intelligence is equal to that of an average five-year-old child. **2** a stupid person. —*adj.* idiotic. —**imbecility** /-ˈsɪlɪtɪ/ *n.* [f. F f. L *imbecillus* weak]

imbibe /ɪmˈbaɪb/ *v.t.* **1** to drink (esp. alcoholic liquor). **2** to absorb (ideas, moisture, etc.). **3** to inhale (air etc.). [f. L *imbibere* (IM-[1], *bibere* drink)]

imbroglio /ɪmˈbrəʊljəʊ/ *n.* (*pl.* **-os**) **1** a complicated or confused situation. **2** a confused heap. [It. (as EMBROIL)]

imbue /ɪmˈbju:/ *v.t.* **1** to inspire or permeate (*with* feelings, opinions, or qualities). **2** to saturate or dye (*with*). [f. F or L *imbuere* moisten]

IMF *abbr.* International Monetary Fund.

imitable /ˈɪmɪtəb(ə)l/ *adj.* able to be imitated. [f. foll.]

imitate /ˈɪmɪteɪt/ *v.t.* to follow the example of; to mimic; to make a copy of; to be like. —**imitator** *n.* [f. L (rel. to IMAGE)]

imitation /ɪmɪˈteɪʃ(ə)n/ *n.* **1** imitating. **2** a copy, a counterfeit (often *attrib.*). [F or f. L (as prec.)]

imitative /ˈɪmɪtətɪv/ *adj.* imitating. [f. L (as IMITATE)]

immaculate /ɪˈmækjʊlət/ *adj.* pure, spotless; faultless, innocent. —**Immaculate Conception,** the doctrine that the Virgin Mary was conceived, and remained, free from all stain of original sin. —**immaculacy** *n.*, **immaculately** *adv.* [f. L *immaculatus* (IM-[2], *macula* spot)]

immanent /ˈɪmənənt/ *adj.* inherent; (of God) permanently pervading the universe. —**immanence** *n.* [f. L *immanēre* (IM-[1], *manēre* remain)]

immaterial /ɪməˈtɪərɪəl/ *adj.* not material, not corporeal; unimportant, irrelevant. —**immateriality** /-ˈælɪtɪ/ *n.* [f. L (as IM-[2], MATERIAL)]

immature /ɪməˈtjʊə(r)/ *adj.* not mature; unripe. —**immaturity** *n.* [f. L (as IM-[2], MATURE)]

immeasurable /ɪˈmeʒərəb(ə)l/ *adj.* not measurable; immense. —**immeasurably** *adv.* [f. IM-[2] + MEASURABLE]

immediate /ɪˈmi:dɪət/ *adj.* **1** occurring at once. **2** without an intervening medium; direct, nearest; not separated by others. —**immediacy** *n.* [f. F or L (as IM-[2], MEDIATE)]

immediately *adv.* **1** without pause or delay. **2** without an intermediary. —*conj.* (*colloq.*) as soon as. [f. prec.]

immemorial /ɪmɪˈmɔ:rɪəl/ *adj.* ancient beyond

memory or record; very old. [f. L (as IM-[2], MEMORIAL)]

immense /ɪˈmens/ *adj.* exceedingly large; (*colloq.*) great. —**immensely** *adv.*, **immensity** *n.* [f. F f. L *immensus* (IM-[2], p.p. of *metiri* measure)]

immerse /ɪˈmɜ:s/ *v.t.* **1** to put completely *in* water or other liquid. **2** to absorb or involve deeply *in* thought, business, etc. **3** to embed. [f. L *immergere* (IM-[1], *mergere mers-* dip)]

immersion /ɪˈmɜ:ʃ(ə)n/ *n.* immersing, being immersed. —**immersion heater,** an electric heater designed to be immersed in the liquid to be heated, especially as a fixture in a hot-water tank. [as prec.]

immigrant /ˈɪmɪgrənt/ *n.* one who immigrates; a descendant of recent immigrants. —*adj.* immigrating; of immigrants. [as foll.]

immigrate /ˈɪmɪgreɪt/ *v.i.* to come into a foreign country as a settler. —**immigration** /-ˈgreɪʃ(ə)n/ *n.* [f. L *immigrare* (as IM-[1], MIGRATE)]

imminent /ˈɪmɪnənt/ *adj.* (of an event, esp. danger) about to happen. —**imminence** *n.* [f. L *imminēre* overhang]

immiscible /ɪˈmɪsɪb(ə)l/ *adj.* that cannot be mixed (*with* another substance). —**immiscibility** /-ˈbɪlɪtɪ/ *n.* [f. L (as IM-[2], MISCIBLE)]

immobile /ɪˈməʊbaɪl/ *adj.* immovable; not mobile; motionless. —**immobility** /ɪməˈbɪlɪtɪ/ *n.* [f. OF f. L (as IM-[2], MOBILE)]

immobilize /ɪˈməʊbɪlaɪz/ *v.t.* to make or keep immobile; to keep (a limb or patient) still for healing purposes. —**immobilization** /-ˈzeɪʃ(ə)n/ *n.* [f. F (as prec.)]

immoderate /ɪˈmɒdərət/ *adj.* excessive, lacking moderation. —**immoderately** *adv.* [f. L (as IM-[2], MODERATE)]

immodest /ɪˈmɒdɪst/ *adj.* **1** lacking in modesty, indecent. **2** conceited. —**immodestly** *adv.*, **immodesty** *n.* [f. F or L (as IM-[2], MODEST)]

immolate /ˈɪməleɪt/ *v.t.* to kill as a sacrifice. —**immolation** /-ˈleɪʃ(ə)n/ *n.* [f. L *immolare*, orig. = sprinkle with meal (*mola*)]

immoral /ɪˈmɒr(ə)l/ *adj.* not conforming to the accepted rules of morality, morally wrong (especially in sexual matters). —**immorality** /ɪməˈrælɪtɪ/ *n.*, **immorally** *adv.* [f. IM-[2] + MORAL]

immortal /ɪˈmɔ:t(ə)l/ *adj.* **1** not mortal, living for ever. **2** famous for all time. —*n.* an immortal being or person. —**immortality** /-ˈtælɪtɪ/ *n.*, **immortally** *adv.* [f. L (as IM-[2], MORTAL)]

immortalize /ɪˈmɔ:təlaɪz/ *v.t.* to make immortal. [f. prec.]

immovable /ɪˈmu:vəb(ə)l/ *adj.* **1** unable to be moved; motionless. **2** steadfast, unyielding, not changing in one's purpose; not moved emotionally. **3** (of property) consisting of land, houses, etc. —**immovability** /-ˈbɪlɪtɪ/ *n.*, **immovably** *adv.* [f. IM-[2] + MOVABLE]

immune /ɪˈmju:n/ *adj.* having immunity (*from* punishment or taxation; *against* infection or poison; *to* criticism). [f. L *immunis* exempt from public service]

immunity /ɪˈmju:nɪtɪ/ *n.* **1** the ability of an organism to resist and overcome infection. **2** freedom or exemption (*from*). [as prec.]

immunize /ˈɪmjʊnaɪz/ *v.t.* to make immune, especially against infection. —**immunization** /-ˈzeɪʃ(ə)n/ *n.* [f. IMMUNE]

immunology /ɪmjʊˈnɒlədʒɪ/ *n.* the study of resistance to infection. [f. IMMUNITY + -LOGY]

immure /ɪˈmjʊə(r)/ *v.t.* to imprison; to shut in. [f. F or L *immurare* (IM-[1], *murus* wall)]

immutable /ɪˈmju:təb(ə)l/ *adj.* unchangeable. —**immutability** /-ˈbɪlɪtɪ/ *n.*, **immutably** *adv.* [f. L (as IM-[2], MUTABLE)]

imp *n.* **1** a small devil. **2** a mischievous child. [OE, = young shoot]

impact /ˈɪmpækt/ *n.* **1** a collision; the force of a collision. **2** strong effect or influence, especially of something new. —/ɪmˈpækt/ *v.t.* **1** to press or fix firmly. **2** (in p.p., of a tooth) wedged between another tooth and the jaw, (of a fractured bone) with the parts pushed together. —**impaction** /-ˈpækʃ(ə)n/ *n.* [f. L (as IMPINGE)]

impair /ɪmˈpeə(r)/ *v.t.* to damage, to weaken. —**impairment** *n.* [f. OF f. L (IM-[1], *pejorare* f. *pejor* worse)]

impala /ɪmˈpɑ:lə/ *n.* (*pl.* same) a small African antelope (*Aepyceros melampus*). [Zulu]

impale /ɪmˈpeɪl/ *v.t.* **1** to fix or pierce with a pointed stake etc. **2** (in heraldry) to combine (two coats of arms) by placing side by side on one shield separated by a vertical line down the middle. —**impalement** *n.* [f. F or L *impalare* (IM-[1], *palus* stake)]

impalpable /ɪmˈpælpəb(ə)l/ *adj.* **1** not palpable. **2** not easily grasped by the mind, intangible. **3** (of a powder) very fine. —**impalpability** /-ˈbɪlɪtɪ/ *n.*, **impalpably** *adv.* [F or f. L (as IM-[2], PALPABLE)]

impart /ɪmˈpɑ:t/ *v.t.* **1** to give a share of. **2** to communicate (news etc. *to*). [f. OF f. L *impartire* (IM-[1], *pars* part)]

impartial /ɪmˈpɑ:ʃ(ə)l/ *adj.* not favouring one side more than another. —**impartiality** /-ʃɪˈælɪtɪ/ *n.*, **impartially** *adv.* [f. IM-[2] + PARTIAL]

impassable /ɪmˈpɑ:səb(ə)l/ *adj.* that cannot be traversed. —**impassability** /-ˈbɪlɪtɪ/ *n.*, **impassably** *adv.* [f. IM-[2] + PASSABLE]

impasse /ˈæmpɑ:s/ *n.* deadlock; a position from which there is no escape. [F (as IM-[2], PASS[1])]

impassible /ɪmˈpæsɪb(ə)l/ *adj.* not liable to pain or injury; impassive. —**impassibility** /-bɪlɪtɪ/ *n.*, **impassibly** *adv.* [f. OF f. L (IM-[2], *passibilis* capable of suffering, as PASSION)]

impassioned /ɪmˈpæʃ(ə)nd/ *adj.* deeply moved, ardent [f. It. *impassionato* (as IM-¹, PASSION)]

impassive /ɪmˈpæsɪv/ *adj.* not feeling or showing emotion; serene. —**impassively** *adv.*, **impassivity** /-ˈsɪvɪtɪ/ *n.* [f. IM-² + PASSIVE]

impasto /ɪmˈpæstəʊ/ *n.* the laying on of paint thickly so that it projects from the picture surface and gives a textured quality, catching and reflecting light and throwing its own shadow. [It. (as IM-¹, *pasta* paste)]

impatient /ɪmˈpeɪʃ(ə)nt/ *adj.* **1** unable to wait patiently; eager. **2** showing a lack of patience. **3** intolerant (*of*). —**impatience** *n.*, **impatiently** *adv.* [f. OF f. L (as IM-², PATIENT)]

impeach /ɪmˈpiːtʃ/ *v.t.* **1** to accuse of treason or other serious crime before a competent tribunal. **2** to call in question, to disparage. —**impeachment** *n.* [f. OF *empecher* f. L (IM-¹, *pedica* fetter)]

impeccable /ɪmˈpekəb(ə)l/ *adj.* faultless; not liable to sin. —**impeccability** /-ˈbɪlɪtɪ/ *n.*, **impeccably** *adv.* [f. L (IM-², *peccare* sin)]

impecunious /ɪmpɪˈkjuːnɪəs/ *adj.* having little or no money. —**impecuniosity** /-ˈɒsɪtɪ/ *n.* [f. IM-² + L *pecuniosus* (*pecunia* money)]

impedance /ɪmˈpiːdəns/ *n.* **1** the total effective resistance of an electric circuit etc. to the flow of alternating current. **2** a similar mechanical property. [f. foll.]

impede /ɪmˈpiːd/ *v.t.* to retard by obstructing, to hinder. [f. L *impedire*, lit. = shackle the feet of (IM-¹, *pes* foot)]

impediment /ɪmˈpedɪmənt/ *n.* **1** a hindrance. **2** a defect in speech, especially a lisp or stammer. [f. L (as prec.)]

impedimenta /ɪmpedɪˈmentə/ *n.pl.* encumbrances; baggage, especially of the army. [L, = prec.]

impel /ɪmˈpel/ *v.t.* (**-ll-**) **1** to urge or drive to do something. **2** to send or drive forward, to propel. [f. L *impellere* (IM-¹, *pellere puls-* drive)]

impend /ɪmˈpend/ *v.i.* (of an event or danger) to be imminent; to hang (*over*). [f. L *impendēre* (IM-¹, *pendēre* hang)]

impenetrable /ɪmˈpenɪtrəb(ə)l/ *adj.* **1** not penetrable. **2** inscrutable. **3** impervious (*to* or *by* ideas etc.). —**impenetrability** /-ˈbɪlɪtɪ/ *n.*, **impenetrably** *adv.* [f. F f. L (as IM-², PENETRABLE)]

impenitent /ɪmˈpenɪt(ə)nt/ *adj.* not penitent. —**impenitence** *n.* [f. L (as IM-², PENITENT)]

imperative /ɪmˈperətɪv/ *adj.* **1** essential, urgently needed. **2** (*Gram.*) of the mood expressing command. **3** peremptory. —*n.* (*Gram.*) the imperative mood. [f. L (*imperare* command)]

imperceptible /ɪmpəˈseptɪb(ə)l/ *adj.* not perceptible, very slight or gradual. —**imperceptibly** *adv.* [f. F or L (as IM-², PERCEPTIBLE)]

imperfect /ɪmˈpɜːfɪkt/ *adj.* **1** not perfect, incomplete, faulty. **2** (*Gram.*) of a tense denoting action going on but not completed (esp. in the past, e.g. *was doing*). —*n.* (*Gram.*) the imperfect tense. —**imperfectly** *adv.* [f. OF f. L (as IM-², PERFECT)]

imperfection /ɪmpəˈfekʃ(ə)n/ *n.* **1** being imperfect. **2** a fault, a blemish. [as prec.]

imperial /ɪmˈpɪərɪəl/ *adj.* **1** of or characteristic of an empire or similar sovereign State; of an emperor or empress. **2** majestic. **3** (of weights and measures) used (now or formerly) by statute in the UK. —**imperially** *adv.* [f. OF f. L (*imperium* supreme power)]

imperialism *n.* **1** imperial rule; an imperial system. **2** (usu. *derog.*) the policy of extending a country's influence over less powerful, less developed countries by acquiring dependencies or through trade, diplomacy, etc. —**imperialist** *n.*, **imperialistic** /-ˈlɪstɪk/ *adj.* [f. prec.]

imperil /ɪmˈperɪl/ *v.t.* (**-ll-**) to endanger. [f. IM-¹ + PERIL]

imperious /ɪmˈpɪərɪəs/ *adj.* **1** domineering. **2** urgent. —**imperiously** *adv.* [f. L (as IMPERIAL)]

imperishable /ɪmˈperɪʃəb(ə)l/ *adj.* that cannot perish. [f. IM-² + PERISHABLE]

impermanent /ɪmˈpɜːmənənt/ *adj.* not permanent. —**impermanence** *n.*, **impermanency** *n.* [f. IM-² + PERMANENT]

impermeable /ɪmˈpɜːmɪəb(ə)l/ *adj.* not permeable. —**impermeability** /-ˈbɪlɪtɪ/ *n.* [f. F or L (as IM-², PERMEABLE)]

impersonal (ɪmˈpɜːsən(ə)l/ *adj.* **1** not influenced by personal feeling; showing no emotion. **2** not referring to any particular person. **3** having no existence as a person. **4** (of a verb) used without a definite subject (e.g. *it is raining*); (of a pronoun) indefinite. —**impersonality** /-ˈnælɪtɪ/ *n.*, **impersonally** *adv.* [f. L (as IM-², PERSONAL)]

impersonate /ɪmˈpɜːsəneɪt/ *v.t.* to pretend to be (another person); to play the part of. —**impersonation** /-ˈneɪʃ(ə)n/ *n.*, **impersonator** *n.* [as IM-¹ + PERSONATE]

impertinent /ɪmˈpɜːtɪnənt/ *adj.* **1** insolent, not showing proper respect. **2** irrelevant. —**impertinence** *n.*, **impertinently** *adv.* [f. OF or L (as IM-², PERTINENT)]

imperturbable /ɪmpəˈtɜːbəb(ə)l/ *adj.* not excitable, calm. —**imperturbability** /-ˈbɪlɪtɪ/ *n.*, **imperturbably** *adv.* [f. L (as IM-², PERTURB)]

impervious /ɪmˈpɜːvɪəs/ *adj.* **1** not able to be penetrated, not affording passage *to* water etc. **2** not responsive (*to* an argument etc.). [f. L (as IM-², PERVIOUS)]

impetigo /ɪmpɪˈtaɪgəʊ/ *n.* a contagious skin disease causing blisters or pimples. [f. L (*impetere* assail)]

impetuous /ɪmˈpetjuːəs/ *adj.* acting or done rashly or on impulse or with sudden energy; moving violently or fast. —**impetuosity** /-ˈɒsɪtɪ/ *n.*, **impetuously** *adv.* [f. OF f. L (as foll.)]

impetus /ˈɪmpɪtəs/ *n.* the force or energy with which a body moves; an impulse, a driving force. [L, = assault (as IMPETIGO)]

impiety /ɪmˈpaɪətɪ/ *n.* lack of piety or reverence. [f. OF or L (as IMPIOUS)]

impinge /ɪmˈpɪndʒ/ *v.i.* to make an impact; to encroach. —**impingement** *n.* [f. L *impingere* (IM-¹, *pangere* fix, drive)]

impious /ˈɪmpɪəs/ *adj.* not pious; wicked. —**impiously** *adv.* [f. L (as IM-², PIOUS)]

impish *adj.* of or like an imp; mischievous. —**impishly** *adv.*, **impishness** *n.* [f. IMP]

implacable /ɪmˈplækəb(ə)l/ *adj.* not able to be placated, relentless. —**implacability** /-ˈbɪlɪtɪ/ *n.*, **implacably** *adv.* [f. F or L (as IM-², PLACABLE)]

implant /ɪmˈplɑːnt/ *v.t.* **1** to plant, to insert or fix (*in*). **2** to instil (an idea etc.) *in* a person's mind. **3** to insert (tissue etc.) in a living body. —/ˈɪmplɑːnt/ *n.* a thing implanted, especially a piece of tissue. —**implantation** /-ˈteɪʃ(ə)n/ *n.* [f. F or L (as IM-¹, PLANT)]

implausible /ɪmˈplɔːzɪb(ə)l/ *adj.* not plausible. —**implausibility** /-ˈbɪlɪtɪ/ *n.*, **implausibly** *adv.* [f. IM-² + PLAUSIBLE]

implement /ˈɪmplɪmənt/ *n.* a tool, an instrument, a utensil. —/also -ment/ *v.t.* to put (a contract, decision, promise, etc.) into effect. —**implementation** /-ˈteɪʃ(ə)n/ *n.* [f. L (*implēre* fill up)]

implicate /ˈɪmplɪkeɪt/ *v.t.* **1** to show (a person) to be concerned (*in* a charge, crime, etc.). **2** to lead to as a consequence or inference. [f. L *implicare* (IM-¹, *plicare* fold)]

implication /ɪmplɪˈkeɪʃ(ə)n/ *n.* **1** implying; implicating. **2** a thing implied. [f. prec.]

implicit /ɪmˈplɪsɪt/ *adj.* **1** implied though not expressed. **2** absolute, unquestioning. —**implicitly** *adv.* [f. F or L (as IMPLICATE)]

implode /ɪmˈpləʊd/ *v.t./i.* to burst or cause to burst inwards. —**implosion** /-ˈpləʊʒ(ə)n/ *n.* [f. IM-¹ + L *-plodere* (after EXPLODE)]

implore /ɪmˈplɔː(r)/ *v.t.* to entreat, to request earnestly. —**imploringly** *adv.* [f. F or L *implorare* (IM-¹, *plorare* lament)]

imply /ɪmˈplaɪ/ *v.t.* **1** to indicate or suggest without stating directly. **2** to involve the truth or existence of. **3** to mean. [f. OF f. L, = IMPLICATE]

impolite /ɪmpəˈlaɪt/ *adj.* not polite. —**impolitely** *adv.* [f. L (as IM-², POLITE)]

impolitic /ɪmˈpɒlɪtɪk/ *adj.* inexpedient, unwise. [f. IM-² + POLITIC]

imponderable /ɪmˈpɒndərəb(ə)l/ *adj.* **1** that cannot be estimated. **2** weightless, very light. —*n.* an imponderable thing. —**imponderably** *adv.* [f. IM-² + PONDERABLE]

import /ɪmˈpɔːt/ *v.t.* **1** to bring (goods etc.) into a country from abroad; to bring in from an outside source. **2** to imply, to indicate. —/ˈɪmpɔːt/ *n.* **1** the importing of goods etc. **2** something imported. **3** meaning. **4** importance. —**importation** /-ˈteɪʃ(ə)n/ *n.*, **importer** *n.* [f. L *importare* (IM-¹, *portare* carry)]

important /ɪmˈpɔːt(ə)nt/ *adj.* **1** having or able to have a great effect. **2** (of a person) having high rank or great authority or influence. **3** pompous. —**importance** *n.*, **importantly** *adv.* [F f. L (as prec.)]

importunate /ɪmˈpɔːtʊnət/ *adj.* making persistent or pressing requests. —**importunity** /ɪmpɔːˈtjuːnɪtɪ/ *n.* [f. L *importunus* inconvenient, orig. = harbourless (IM-², *portus* harbour)]

importune /ɪmˈpɔːtjuːn, -ˈtjuːn/ *v.t.* **1** to make insistent requests (to). **2** to solicit for an immoral purpose. [f. F or L (as prec.)]

impose /ɪmˈpəʊz/ *v.t./i.* **1** to lay (a tax, duty, etc., *on* or *upon*). **2** to enforce compliance with. **3** to inflict; to palm off (a thing *upon* a person). **4** to lay (pages of type) in proper order. —**impose on** *or* **upon,** to take advantage of (a person, his good nature etc.), to deceive, to impress, to overawe. [f. F f. L *imponere* (IM-¹, *ponere* put)]

imposing *adj.* impressive, formidable, especially in appearance. [f. prec.]

imposition /ɪmpəˈzɪʃ(ə)n/ *n.* **1** an unfair demand or burden. **2** a tax, a duty. **3** work set as a punishment at school. **4** the laying on of hands in blessing etc. **5** an act of deception or taking advantage. [f. OF or L (as IMPOSE)]

impossible /ɪmˈpɒsɪb(ə)l/ *adj.* **1** not possible, unable to be done or to exist; (*loosely*) not easy, inconvenient, incredible. **2** (*colloq.*) outrageous, intolerable. —**impossibility** /-ˈbɪlɪtɪ/ *n.*, **impossibly** *adv.* [f. OF or L (as IM-², POSSIBLE)]

impost¹ /ˈɪmpəʊst/ *n.* a tax or duty. [F f. L (as IMPOSE)]

impost² /ˈɪmpəʊst/ *n.* the upper course of a pillar, carrying the arch. [f. F or It. *imposta* f. L (as IMPOSE)]

impostor /ɪmˈpɒstə(r)/ *n.* one who assumes a false character or personality; a swindler. [f. F f. L (as IMPOSE)]

imposture /ɪmˈpɒstʃə(r)/ *n.* a deception, a sham. [F f. L (as IMPOST¹)]

impotent /ˈɪmpət(ə)nt/ *adj.* **1** powerless, unable to take action. **2** (of a male) unable to copulate or reach orgasm; unable to procreate. —**impotence** *n.*, **impotently** *adv.* [f. OF f. L (as IM-², POTENT)]

impound /ɪmˈpaʊnd/ *v.t.* **1** to confiscate; to take

legal possession of. **2** to shut up (cattle etc.) in a pound. [f. IM-[1] + POUND[3]]

impoverish /ɪmˈpɒvərɪʃ/ *v.t.* **1** to make poor. **2** to exhaust the vitality or fertility of. —**impoverishment** *n.* [f. OF (as IM-[1], *poverir* f. *povre* poor)]

impracticable /ɪmˈpræktɪkəb(ə)l/ *adj.* not practicable. —**impracticability** /-ˈbɪlɪtɪ/ *n.*, **impracticably** *adv.* [f. IM-[2] + PRACTICABLE]

impractical /ɪmˈpræktɪk(ə)l/ *adj.* **1** not practical. **2** not practicable. —**impracticality** /-ˈkælɪtɪ/ *n.* [f. IM-[2] + PRACTICAL]

imprecate /ˈɪmprɪkeɪt/ *v.t.* to invoke (evil *upon*). —**imprecation** /-ˈkeɪʃ(ə)n/ *n.* [f. L (IM-[1], *precari* pray)]

imprecatory /ˈɪmprɪkeɪtərɪ/ *adj.* making an imprecation. [f. prec.]

imprecise /ɪmprɪˈsaɪs/ *adj.* not precise. —**imprecision** /-ˈsɪʒ(ə)n/ *n.* [f. IM-[2] + PRECISE]

impregnable /ɪmˈpregnəb(ə)l/ *adj.* (of a fortress etc. or *fig.*) proof against attack. —**impregnability** /-ˈbɪlɪtɪ/ *n.*, **impregnably** *adv.* [f. OF *imprenable* (IM-[2], *prendre* take)]

impregnate /ˈɪmpregneɪt/ *v.t.* **1** to fill or saturate (*with*). **2** to imbue (*with*). **3** to make (a female) pregnant; to fertilize (an ovum). —**impregnatable** *adj.*, **impregnation** /-ˈneɪʃ(ə)n/ *n.* [f. L (IM-[1], *praegnare* be pregnant)]

impresario /ɪmprɪˈsɑːrɪəʊ/ *n.* (*pl.* **-os**) an organizer of public entertainment, especially an opera or concert. [It. (*impresa* undertaking)]

impress[1] /ɪmˈpres/ *v.t.* **1** to cause to form a strong (usually favourable) opinion. **2** to fix or imprint (an idea etc. *on* a person). **3** to imprint or stamp (a mark etc. *on* a thing, a thing with a mark). —/ˈɪmpres/ *n.* **1** a mark impressed. **2** a characteristic quality. —**impressible** *adj.* [f. OF (as IM-[1], PRESS[1])]

impress[2] /ɪmˈpres/ *v.t.* (*hist.*) to force to serve in the army or navy. —**impressment** *n.* [f. IM-[1] + PRESS[2]]

impression /ɪmˈpreʃ(ə)n/ *n.* **1** an effect, especially on the mind or feelings. **2** an uncertain idea, belief, or remembrance. **3** an imitation of a person or sound, done to entertain. **4** impressing; a mark impressed. **5** an unaltered reprint from standing type or plates; the copies forming one issue of a book, newspaper, etc. **6** a print made from type or from an engraving. [f. OF f. L (as IMPRESS[1])]

impressionable *adj.* easily influenced. —**impressionability** /-ˈbɪlɪtɪ/ *n.*, **impressionably** *adv.* [f. F (as prec.)]

impressionism *n.* a style of painting so as to give a general tone and effect without elaborate finish or detail; an analogous style in music or literature. —**impressionist** *n.*, **impressionistic** /-ˈnɪstɪk/ *adj.* [f. F (as IMPRESSION)]

impressive /ɪmˈpresɪv/ *adj.* able to excite deep feeling, especially of approval or admiration. —**impressively** *adv.* [f. IMPRESS[1]]

imprimatur /ɪmprɪˈmeɪtə(r)/ *n.* a licence to print, usually from the Roman Catholic Church; authoritative permission. [L, = let it be printed]

imprint /ɪmˈprɪnt/ *v.t.* **1** to set firmly (a mark *on*, an idea etc. *on* or *in* the mind). **2** to stamp (*with* a figure). **3** to make or become recognized by (a young bird or animal in the first hours of its life) as an object of trust etc. —/ˈɪmprɪnt/ *n.* **1** a mark made by pressing or stamping a surface. **2** a publisher's name etc. on the title-page of a book. [f. OF f. L (as IMPRESS[1])]

imprison /ɪmˈprɪz(ə)n/ *v.t.* to put into prison; to confine. —**imprisonment** *n.* [f. OF (as IM-[1], PRISON)]

improbable /ɪmˈprɒbəb(ə)l/ *adj.* not likely. —**improbability** /-ˈbɪlɪtɪ/ *n.*, **improbably** *adv.* [F or f. L (as IM-[2], PROBABLE)]

improbity /ɪmˈprəʊbɪtɪ/ *n.* wickedness, dishonesty. [f. L (as IM-[2], PROBITY)]

impromptu /ɪmˈprɒmptjuː/ *adj.* & *adv.* unrehearsed. —*n.* **1** a musical composition resembling an improvisation. **2** an extempore performance. [F f. L *in promptu* in readiness (as PROMPT)]

improper /ɪmˈprɒpə(r)/ *adj.* **1** not conforming to the rules of social or lawful conduct; indecent. **2** wrong, incorrect. —**improper fraction,** a fraction with the numerator greater than the denominator. —**improperly** *adv.* [f. F or L (as IM-[2], PROPER)]

impropriety /ɪmprəˈpraɪɪtɪ/ *n.* being improper; an improper act or remark etc. [as prec.]

improvable /ɪmˈpruːvəb(ə)l/ *adj.* able to be improved. [f. foll.]

improve /ɪmˈpruːv/ *v.t./i.* **1** to make or become better. **2** to make good use of (an occasion, opportunities). —**improve on** *or* **upon,** to produce something better than. —**improvement** *n.* [f. AF *emprower* (EM-, OF *prou* profit)]

improver *n.* **1** a person who works at a trade for little or no payment in order to improve his skill. **2** a substance added to food by a manufacturer or processor in order to improve its texture, keeping quality, etc. [f. prec.]

improvident /ɪmˈprɒvɪdənt/ *adj.* lacking foresight or care for the future, wasting one's resources. —**improvidence** *n.*, **improvidently** *adv.* [f. F (as IM-[2], PROVIDENT)]

improvise /ˈɪmprəvaɪz/ *v.t.* **1** to compose (verse, music, etc.) extempore. **2** to construct from materials not intended for the purpose.

—**improvisation** /-ˈzeɪʃ(ə)n/ *n.*, **improviser** *n.* [f. F or It. (*improvviso* extempore)]

imprudent /ɪmˈpru:dənt/ *adj.* unwise, rash. —**imprudence** *n.*, **imprudently** *adv.* [f. L (as IM-², PRUDENT)]

impudent /ˈɪmpjʊdənt/ *adj.* impertinent, cheeky. —**impudence** *n.*, **impudently** *adv.* [f. L *impudens* (IM-², *pudēre* be ashamed)]

impugn /ɪmˈpju:n/ *v.t.* to express doubts about the truth or honesty of, to try to discredit. —**impugnment** *n.* [f. L *impugnare* assail (IM-¹, *pugnare* fight)]

impulse /ˈɪmpʌls/ *n.* **1** impelling; a push or thrust, impetus; a sharp force producing change of momentum; this change. **2** a stimulating force in a nerve. **3** a sudden inclination to act, without thought for the consequences. [f. L (as IMPEL)]

impulsion /ɪmˈpʌlʃ(ə)n/ *n.* **1** impelling, a push; impetus. **2** a mental impulse. [f. OF f. L (as prec.)]

impulsive /ɪmˈpʌlsɪv/ *adj.* **1** tending to act on impulse; done on impulse. **2** tending to impel. —**impulsively** *adv.*, **impulsiveness** *n.* [f. F or L (as IMPEL)]

impunity /ɪmˈpju:nɪtɪ/ *n.* exemption from punishment or injurious consequences. [f. L (IM-², *poena* penalty)]

impure /ɪmˈpjʊə(r)/ *adj.* not pure. [f. L (as IM-², *purus* pure)]

impurity /ɪmˈpjʊərɪtɪ/ *n.* **1** being impure. **2** a substance that makes another impure by being present in it. [f. prec.]

impute /ɪmˈpju:t/ *v.t.* to attribute (a fault etc.) *to*. —**imputation** /-ˈteɪʃ(ə)n/ *n.* [f. OF f. L *imputare*, orig. = enter in an account]

In *symbol* indium.

in *prep.* **1** expressing inclusion or a position within the limits of space, time, circumstances, surroundings, etc. **2** expressing quantity, proportion (*packed in tens*), form or arrangement (*written in French*; *hanging in folds*), material, dress, or colour (*in shades of blue*), influence or respect (*spoke in anger*; *lacking in courage*). **3** expressing activity, occupation, or membership (*he is in the army*). **4** within the ability of. **5** (of a female animal) pregnant with (*in calf*). **6** (with verbs of motion or change) into (*put it in your pocket*). **7** introducing an indirect object after a verb (*believe in*; *share in*). **8** forming adverbial phrases (*in any case*; *in vain*). —*adv.* **1** expressing position bounded by certain limits, or to a point enclosed by these. **2** into a room, house, etc. **3** at home. **4** on or towards the inside. **5** in fashion, season, or office; elected; in effective or favourable action; (of the tide) high; (in cricket and baseball) batting. **6** (of a domestic fire) burning. **7** having arrived or been gathered or received. —*adj.* **1** internal; living etc. in, inside. **2** fashionable. —**in for**, about to undergo; competing in or for. **in on**, sharing in, privy to. **ins and outs**, all the details of an activity or procedure. **in shore**, on the water near or nearer to the shore. **in that**, because; in so far as. **in with**, on good terms with; sharing or co-operating with. **nothing** (*or* **not much**) **in it**, no (or little) advantage to be seen in one possibility over another. [OE]

in-¹ *prefix* (**il-** before *l*; **im-** before *b, m, p*; **ir-** before *r*) in, on, into, towards, within. [f. prec. or L *in* in, into]

in-² *prefix* (**il-** etc. as prec.) added to adjectives in sense 'not', and to nouns in sense 'without', 'lacking'. [L]

in. *abbr.* inch(es).

inability /ɪnəˈbɪlɪtɪ/ *n.* being unable [f. IN-² + ABILITY]

in absentia /ɪn æbˈsentɪə/ in (his or her or their) absence. [L]

inaccessible /ɪnəkˈsesɪb(ə)l/ *adj.* not accessible; (of a person) unapproachable. —**inaccessibility** /-ˈbɪlɪtɪ/ *n.*, **inaccessibly** *adv.* [f. F or L (as IN-², ACCESSIBLE)]

inaccurate /ɪnˈækjʊrət/ *adj.* not accurate. —**inaccuracy** *n.*, **inaccurately** *adv.* [f. IN-² + ACCURATE]

inaction /ɪnˈækʃ(ə)n/ *n.* lack of action, doing nothing. [f. IN-² + ACTION]

inactive /ɪnˈæktɪv/ *adj.* not active, showing no activity. —**inactively** *adv.*, **inactivity** /-ˈtɪvɪtɪ/ *n.* [f. IN-² + ACTIVE]

inadequate /ɪnˈædɪkwət/ *adj.* not adequate. **inadequately** *adv.*, **inadequacy** *n.* [f. IN-² + ADEQUATE]

inadmissible /ɪnədˈmɪsɪb(ə)l/ *adj.* not allowable. —**inadmissibility** /-ˈbɪlɪtɪ *n.*, **inadmissibly** *adv.* [f. IN-² + ADMISSIBLE]

inadvertent /ɪnədˈvɜ:tənt/ *adj.* **1** unintentional. **2** negligent, inattentive. —**inadvertence** *n.*, **inadvertency** *n.*, **inadvertently** *adv.* [f. IN-² + ADVERT²]

inadvisable /ɪnədˈvaɪzəb(ə)l/ *adj.* not advisable. [f. IN-² + ADVISABLE]

inalienable /ɪnˈeɪlɪənəb(ə)l/ *adj.* not able to be given or taken away. —**inalienability** /-ˈbɪlɪtɪ/ *n.*, **inalienably** *adv.* [f. IN-² + ALIENABLE]

inamorato /ɪnæməˈrɑ:təʊ/ *n.* (*fem.* **inamorata** /-tə/) a lover. [It. (as ENAMOUR)]

inane /ɪˈneɪn/ *adj.* silly, senseless; empty, void. —**inanely** *adv.*, **inanity** /ɪˈnænɪtɪ/ *n.* [f. L *inanis* empty]

inanimate /ɪnˈænɪmət/ *adj.* **1** not endowed with life; lacking animal life. **2** showing no sign of life. **3** spiritless, dull. —**inanimation** /-ˈmeɪʃ(ə)n/ *n.* [f. L (as IN-², ANIMATE)]

inanition /ɪnəˈnɪʃ(ə)n/ *n.* emptiness, especially

from lack of nourishment. [f. L (*inanire* make empty, as INANE)]

inapplicable /ɪnˈæplɪkəb(ə)l/ *adj*. not applicable. [f. IN-² + APPLICABLE]

inapposite /ɪnˈæpəzɪt/ *adj*. not apposite, out of place. [f. IN-² + APPOSITE]

inapprehensible /ɪnæprɪˈhensɪb(ə)l/ *adj*. that cannot be grasped by the mind or perceived by the senses. [f. IN-² + APPREHENSIBLE]

inappropriate /ɪnəˈprəʊprɪət/ *adj*. unsuitable. —**inappropriately** *adv*. [f. IN-² + APPROPRIATE]

inapt /ɪnˈæpt/ *adj*. **1** unsuitable. **2** unskilful. —**inaptitude** *n*., **inaptly** *adv*. **inaptness** *n*. [f. IN-² + APT]

inarticulate /ɪnɑːˈtɪkjʊlət/ *adj*. **1** unable to speak distinctly or express oneself clearly. **2** not expressed in words; indistinctly pronounced. **3** dumb. **4** not jointed. —**inarticulately** *adv*. [f. L (as IN-², ARTICULATE)]

inartistic /ɪnɑːˈtɪstɪk/ *adj*. not artistic. —**inartistically** *adv*. [f. IN-² + ARTISTIC]

inasmuch /ɪnəzˈmʌtʃ/ *adv*. **inasmuch as,** since, because; (*archaic*) in so far as. [f. *in as much*]

inattention /ɪnəˈtenʃ(ə)n/ *n*. lack of attention; neglect. [f. IN-² + ATTENTION]

inattentive /ɪnəˈtentɪv/ *adj*. not paying attention; neglecting to show courtesy. —**inattentively** *adv*., **inattentiveness** *n*. [f. IN-² + ATTENTIVE]

inaudible /ɪnˈɔːdɪb(ə)l/ *adj*. not audible, unable to be heard. —**inaudibility** /-ˈbɪlɪtɪ/ *n*., **inaudibly** *adv*. [f. IN-² + AUDIBLE]

inaugural /ɪˈnɔːgjʊr(ə)l/ *adj*. of an inauguration. —*n*. an inaugural speech or lecture. [F (as foll.)]

inaugurate /ɪˈnɔːgjʊreɪt/ *v.t*. **1** to admit formally to office. **2** to begin (an undertaking) ceremonially; to initiate the public use of (a building etc.) with a ceremony. **3** to begin, to introduce. —**inauguration** /-ˈreɪʃ(ə)n/ *n*., **inaugurator** *n*. [f. L (as IN-¹, AUGUR)]

inauspicious /ɪnɔːˈspɪʃəs/ *adj*. not auspicious. —**inauspiciously** *adv*., **inauspiciousness** *n*. [f. IN-² + AUSPICIOUS]

inboard /ˈɪnbɔːd/ *adv*. within the sides or towards the centre of a ship, aircraft, or vehicle. —*adj*. situated inboard. [f. IN + BOARD]

inborn *adj*. naturally inherent, innate. [f. IN + BORN]

inbred *adj*. **1** inborn. **2** produced by inbreeding. [f. IN + BRED]

inbreeding *n*. breeding from closely related animals or persons. [f. IN + BREEDING]

in-built *adj*. built-in.

Inc. *abbr*. (*US*) Incorporated.

Inca /ˈɪŋkə/ *n*. (*pl*. same or **-s**) a member of an American Indian people of the central Andes before the Spanish conquest. [Quechua, = lord, royal person]

incalculable /ɪnˈkælkjʊləb(ə)l/ *adj*. too great for calculation; not calculable beforehand, uncertain. —**incalculability** /-ˈbɪlɪtɪ/ *n*., **incalculably** *adv*. [f. IN-² + CALCULABLE]

incandesce /ɪnkænˈdes/ *v.t./i*. to glow with heat; to cause to do this [f. foll.]

incandescent /ɪnkænˈdes(ə)nt/ *adj*. glowing with heat; shining; (of artificial light) produced by a glowing filament etc. —**incandescence** *n*. [F f. L *incandescere* (IN-¹, *candēre* be white)]

incantation /ɪnkænˈteɪʃ(ə)n/ *n*. a magical formula, a spell or charm. —**incantatory** *adj*. [f. OF f. L (IN-¹, *cantare* sing)]

incapable /ɪnˈkeɪpəb(ə)l/ *adj*. not capable; not capable of rational conduct. —**incapability** /-ˈbɪlɪtɪ/ *n*., **incapably** *adv*. [F or f. L (as IN-², CAPABLE)]

incapacitate /ɪnkəˈpæsɪteɪt/ *v.t*. to make incapable or unfit. —**incapacitation** /-ˈteɪʃ(ə)n/ *n*. [f. foll.]

incapacity /ɪnkəˈpæsɪtɪ/ *n*. inability, lack of power; legal disqualification. [f. F or L (as IN-², CAPACITY)]

incarcerate /ɪnˈkɑːsəreɪt/ *v.t*. to imprison. —**incarceration** /-ˈreɪʃ(ə)n/ *n*. [f. L *incarcerare* (IN-¹, *carcer* prison)]

incarnate /ɪnˈkɑːneɪt/ *adj*. /also -ət/ embodied in flesh, especially in human form. —*v.t*. **1** to embody in flesh. **2** to put (an idea etc.) into concrete form. **3** to be a living embodiment of (a quality etc.) [f. L *incarnare* (IN-¹, *caro* flesh)]

incarnation /ɪnkɑːˈneɪʃ(ə)n/ *n*. **1** embodiment in flesh, especially in human form. **2** a living type (*of* a quality). —**the Incarnation,** the embodiment of God in human form as Jesus Christ. [f. OF f. L (as prec.)]

incautious /ɪnˈkɔːʃəs/ *adj*. not cautious, rash. —**incautiously** *adv*., **incautiousness** *n*. [f. IN-² + CAUTIOUS]

incendiarism /ɪnˈsendɪərɪz(ə)m/ *n*. an act or acts of arson. [f. foll.]

incendiary /ɪnˈsendɪərɪ/ *adj*. **1** (of a bomb) filled with material for causing fires. **2** tending to stir up strife, inflammatory. **3** of arson; guilty of arson. —*n*. **1** an incendiary bomb. **2** an arsonist. **3** a person who stirs up strife. [f. L (*incendere* set fire to)]

incense[1] /ˈɪnsens/ *n*. a gum or spice giving a sweet smell when burning; the smoke of this, especially in religious ceremonial. —*v.t*. to burn incense to; to perfume or fumigate (as) with incense. [f. OF f. L *incensum* (as prec.)]

incense[2] /ɪnˈsens/ *v.t*. to make angry. [f. OF f. L *incendere* (as INCENDIARY)]

incentive /ɪnˈsentɪv/ *n*. a motive or incitement; a payment or concession encouraging an effort in work. —*adj*. inciting. [f. L, = setting the tune (IN-¹, *canere* sing)]

inception /ɪnˈsepʃ(ə)n/ *n*. beginning. [f. OF or L (*incipere* begin)]

inceptive /ɪnˈseptɪv/ *adj*. beginning; initial; (of a verb) denoting the beginning of action. [f. L (as prec.)]

incertitude /ɪnˈsɜːtɪtjuːd/ *n*. uncertainty. [F or f. L (as IN-², CERTITUDE)]

incessant /ɪnˈses(ə)nt/ *adj*. continual, repeated; unceasing. —**incessantly** *adv*. [F or f. L (as IN-², CEASE)]

incest /ˈɪnsest/ *n*. sexual intercourse of near relations. [f. L (IN-², *castus* chaste)]

incestuous /ɪnˈsestjuːəs/ *adj*. of incest; guilty of incest. [as prec.]

inch *n*. **1** a twelfth of a (linear) foot, 2.54 cm; this used as a unit of rainfall (= 1 inch depth of water) or as a unit of map-scale (= 1 inch to 1 mile). **2** a small amount. —*v.t./i.* to move gradually. —**every inch,** thoroughly. **within an inch of his life,** almost to death. [OE, f. L *uncia* twelfth part]

inchoate /ˈɪnkəʊət/ *adj*. undeveloped; just begun. —**inchoation** /-ˈeɪʃ(ə)n/ *n*. [f. L *inchoare, incohare* begin]

incidence /ˈɪnsɪdəns/ *n*. **1** falling on or contact with a thing. **2** the range, scope, extent, or rate of occurrence or influence (*of* a disease, tax, etc.). **3** the falling of a line, ray, particles, etc., on a surface. [f. OF or L (as foll.)]

incident /ˈɪnsɪdənt/ *n*. **1** an event or occurrence, especially a minor one. **2** a clash of armed forces. **3** a public disturbance. **4** a distinct piece of action in a film, play, etc. —*adj*. **1** apt to occur; naturally attaching (*to*). **2** (of rays etc.) falling (*on* or *upon*). [f. F or L *incidere* fall on (IN-¹, *cadere* fall)]

incidental /ɪnsɪˈdent(ə)l/ *adj*. having a minor role in relation to a more important thing or event etc., not essential. —**incidental music,** music played during or between the scenes of a play, film, etc. [f. prec.]

incidentally *adv*. **1** as an unconnected remark. **2** in an incidental way. [f. prec.]

incinerate /ɪnˈsɪnəreɪt/ *v.t.* to consume by fire. —**incineration** /-ˈreɪʃ(ə)n/ *n*. [f. L *incinerare* (IN-¹, *cinis* ashes)]

incinerator /ɪnˈsɪnəreɪtə(r)/ *n*. a furnace or device for incinerating things. [f. prec.]

incipient /ɪnˈsɪpɪənt/ *adj*. beginning, in its early stages. [f. L (as INCEPTION)]

incise /ɪnˈsaɪz/ *v.t.* to make a cut in; to engrave. —**incision** /ɪnˈsɪʒ(ə)n/ *n*. [f. F f. L *incidere* (IN-¹, *caedere* cut)]

incisive /ɪnˈsaɪsɪv/ *adj*. sharp; clear and effective. —**incisively** *adv*., **incisiveness** *n*. [f. L (as prec.)]

incisor /ɪnˈsaɪzə(r)/ *n*. any of the teeth between the canine teeth. [L, = cutter (as INCISE)]

incite /ɪnˈsaɪt/ *v.t.* to urge or stir up (*to* action). —**incitement** *n*. [f. F f. L *incitare* (IN-¹, *citare* rouse)]

incivility /ɪnsɪˈvɪlɪtɪ/ *n*. rudeness; an impolite act. [f. F or L (as IN-², CIVILITY)]

inclement /ɪnˈklemənt/ *adj*. (of weather) severe or stormy. —**inclemency** *n*. [f. F or L (as IN-², CLEMENT)]

inclination /ɪnklɪˈneɪʃ(ə)n/ *n*. **1** a tendency. **2** a liking or preference. **3** the slope or slant (*of* a line from the vertical, *to* another line); the angle between the lines. **4** a leaning or bending movement; the dip of a magnetic needle. [f. OF or L (as foll.)]

incline /ɪnˈklaɪn/ *v.t./i.* **1** to lean or cause to lean, usually from the vertical; to bend forward or downward. **2** to dispose or influence. **3** to have a certain tendency. —/ˈɪnklaɪn/ *n*. a slope; an inclined plane. —**inclined plane,** a sloping plane used e.g. to raise a load with less force. **incline one's ear,** to listen favourably. [f. OF f. L *inclinare* bend]

include /ɪnˈkluːd/ *v.t.* **1** to have, regard, or treat as part of a whole. **2** to put into a certain category etc. —**inclusion** *n*. [f. L *includere* enclose (IN-¹, *claudere* shut)]

inclusive /ɪnˈkluːsɪv/ *adj*. including (with *of*); including the limits stated; including all or much. —**inclusively** *adv*. [f. L (as prec.)]

incognito /ɪnkɒgˈniːtəʊ, ɪnˈkɒgnɪtəʊ/ *adv*. under a false name, with one's identity concealed. —*adj*. acting incognito. —*n*. (*pl*. **-os**) a pretended identity; a person who is incognito. [It., = unknown (as foll.)]

incognizant /ɪnˈkɒgnɪz(ə)nt/ *adj*. unaware. —**incognizance** *n*. [f. IN-² + COGNIZANT]

incoherent /ɪnkəʊˈhɪərənt/ *adj*. rambling in speech or reasoning. —**incoherence** *n*., **incoherently** *adv*. [f. IN-² + COHERENT]

incombustible /ɪnkəmˈbʌstɪb(ə)l/ *adj*. not able to be burnt by fire. [f. L (as IN-², COMBUSTIBLE)]

income /ˈɪnkʌm/ *n*. money received, especially periodically or in a year, from one's work, lands, investments, etc. —**income tax,** a tax levied on income. [f. IN + COME]

incoming /ˈɪnkʌmɪng/ *adj*. coming in; succeeding another person or thing. [f. IN + *coming* (COME)]

incommensurable /ɪnkəˈmenʃərəb(ə)l/ *adj*. not commensurable; having no common measure integral or fractional (*with*). —**incommensurability** /-ˈbɪlɪtɪ/. [f. L (as IN-², COMMENSURABLE)]

incommensurate /ɪnkəˈmenʃərət/ *adj*. disproportionate, inadequate (*to*); incommensurable. [f. IN-² + COMMENSURATE]

incommode /ɪnkəˈməʊd/ *v.t.* to inconvenience; to annoy; to impede. [f. F or L *incommodare* (IN-², *commodus* convenient)]

incommodious /ɪnkəˈməʊdɪəs/ *adj.* not providing comfort, inconvenient. [f. IN-² + COMMODIOUS]

incommunicable /ɪnkəˈmjuːnɪkəb(ə)l/ *adj.* that cannot be shared or told. [f. L (as IN-², COMMUNICABLE)]

incommunicado /ɪnkəˈmjuːnɪkɑːdəʊ/ *adj.* without means of communication; (of a prisoner) in solitary confinement. [f. Sp. (*incomunicar* deprive of communication)]

incommunicative /ɪnkəˈmjuːnɪkətɪv/ *adj.* not communicative, taciturn. [f. IN-² + COMMUNICATIVE]

incomparable /ɪnˈkɒmpərəb(ə)l/ *adj.* without an equal, matchless. —**incomparability** /-ˈbɪlɪtɪ/ *n.*, **incomparably** *adv.* [f. OF f. L (as IN-², COMPARABLE)]

incompatible /ɪnkəmˈpætɪb(ə)l/ *adj.* not compatible; inconsistent. —**incompatibility** /-ˈbɪlɪtɪ/ *n.*, **incompatibly** *adv.* [f. L (as IN-², COMPATIBLE)]

incompetent /ɪnˈkɒmpɪt(ə)nt/ *adj.* not qualified or able; not able to function; not legally qualified. —*n.* an incompetent person. —**incompetence** *n.*, **incompetently** *adv.* [f. F or L (as IN-², COMPETENT)]

incomplete /ɪnkəmˈpliːt/ *adj.* not complete. —**incompletely** *adv.*, **incompleteness** *n.* [f. L (as IN-², COMPLETE)]

incomprehensible /ɪnkɒmprɪˈhensɪb(ə)l/ *adj.* not able to be understood. —**incomprehensibility** /-ˈbɪlɪtɪ/ *n.*, **incomprehensibly** *adv.* [f. L (as IN-², COMPREHENSIBLE)]

incomprehension /ɪnkɒmprɪˈhenʃ(ə)n/ *n.* failure to understand. [f. IN-² + COMPREHENSION]

inconceivable /ɪnkənˈsiːvəb(ə)l/ *adj.* that cannot be imagined; (*colloq.*) most unlikely. —**inconceivably** *adv.* [f. IN-² + CONCEIVABLE]

inconclusive /ɪnkənˈkluːsɪv/ *adj.* (of evidence or an argument etc.) not fully convincing, not decisive. —**inconclusively** *adv.* [f. IN-² + CONCLUSIVE]

incongruous /ɪnˈkɒŋgrʊəs/ *adj.* out of place, absurd; out of keeping (*with*). —**incongruity** /-ˈuːɪtɪ/ *n.*, **incongruously** *adv.* [f. L (as IN-², CONGRUOUS)]

inconsequent /ɪnˈkɒnsɪkwənt/ *adj.* irrelevant; disconnected; not following logically. —**inconsequence** *n.*, **inconsequently** *adv.* [f. L (as IN-², CONSEQUENT)]

inconsequential /ɪnkɒnsɪˈkwenʃ(ə)l/ *adj.* unimportant; inconsequent. —**inconsequentially** *adv.* [f. IN-² + CONSEQUENTIAL]

inconsiderable /ɪnkənˈsɪdərəb(ə)l/ *adj.* not worth considering; of small size, amount, or value. —**inconsiderably** *adv.* [f. obs. F or L (as IN-², CONSIDERABLE)]

inconsiderate /ɪnkənˈsɪdərət/ *adj.* (of a person or action) lacking in regard for others' feelings, thoughtless. —**inconsiderately** *adv.* [f. L (as IN-², CONSIDERATE)]

inconsistent /ɪnkənˈsɪstənt/ *adj.* not consistent. —**inconsistency** *n.*, **inconsistently** *adv.* [f. IN-² + CONSISTENT]

inconsolable /ɪnkənˈsəʊləb(ə)l/ *adj.* unable to be consoled. —**inconsolability** /-ˈbɪlɪtɪ/ *n.*, **inconsolably** *adv.* [F or f. L (as IN-², CONSOLE¹)]

inconsonant /ɪnˈkɒnsənənt/ *adj.* not consistent, not harmonious. [f. IN-² + CONSONANT]

inconspicuous /ɪnkənˈspɪkjʊəs/ *adj.* not conspicuous. —**inconspicuously** *adv.*, **inconspicuousness** *n.* [f. L (as IN-², CONSPICUOUS)]

inconstant /ɪnˈkɒnst(ə)nt/ *adj.* fickle; variable. —**inconstancy** *n.* [f. OF f. L (as IN-², CONSTANT)]

incontestable /ɪnkənˈtestəb(ə)l/ *adj.* that cannot be disputed. —**incontestably** *adv.* [F or f. L (as IN-², CONTEST)]

incontinent /ɪnˈkɒntɪnənt/ *adj.* unable to control excretions voluntarily; lacking self-restraint (especially in sexual desire). —**incontinence** *n.* [f. OF or L (as IN-², CONTINENT)]

incontrovertible /ɪnkɒntrəˈvɜːtɪb(ə)l/ *adj.* indisputable, undeniable. —**incontrovertibility** /-ˈbɪlɪtɪ/ *n.*, **incontrovertibly** *adv.* [f. IN-² + *controvertible* (f. CONTROVERT)]

inconvenience /ɪnkənˈviːnɪəns/ *n.* being inconvenient; a cause or instance of this. —*v.t.* to cause inconvenience to. [f. OF f. L (as foll.)]

inconvenient /ɪnkənˈviːnɪənt/ *adj.* not convenient, not suiting one's needs or requirements; slightly troublesome. —**inconveniently** *adv.* [f. OF f. L (as IN-², CONVENIENT)]

incorporate /ɪnˈkɔːpəreɪt/ *v.t./i.* **1** to include as a part or ingredient; to unite. **2** to form into a corporation; to admit as a member of a company etc. —/-ət/ *adj.* incorporated. —**incorporation** /-ˈreɪʃ(ə)n/ *n.* [f. L *incorporare* (IN-¹, *corpus* body)]

incorporeal /ɪnkɔːˈpɔːrɪəl/ *adj.* without substance or material existence. —**incorporeally** *adv.*, **incorporeity** /-ˈriːɪtɪ/ *n.* [f. L *incorporeus* (IN-², *corpus* body)]

incorrect /ɪnkəˈrekt/ *adj.* not correct. —**incorrectly** *adv.*, **incorrectness** *n.* [f. OF or L (as IN-², CORRECT)]

incorrigible /ɪnˈkɒrɪdʒɪb(ə)l/ *adj.* (of a person or habit) incurably bad. —**incorrigibility** /-ˈbɪlɪtɪ/ *n.*, **incorrigibly** *adv.* [f. OF or L (as IN-², CORRIGIBLE)]

incorruptible /ɪnkəˈrʌptɪb(ə)l/ *adj.* that cannot decay or be corrupted (especially by bribery).

—**incorruptibility** /-ˈbɪlɪtɪ/ *n.*, **incorruptibly** *adv.* [f. OF or L (as IN-², CORRUPTIBLE)]

increase /ɪnˈkri:s/ *v.t./i.* **1** to make or become greater or more numerous. **2** to advance (*in* power etc.). —/ˈɪnkri:s/ *n.* **1** growth, enlargement; the amount of this. **2** (of people, animals, or plants) multiplication. —**on the increase,** increasing. —**increasingly** *adv.* [f. OF f. L *increscere* (IN-¹, *crescere* grow)]

incredible /ɪnˈkredɪb(ə)l/ *adj.* that cannot be believed; (*colloq.*) surprising. —**incredibility** /-ˈbɪlɪtɪ/ *n.*, **incredibly** *adv.* [f. L (as IN-², CREDIBLE)]

incredulous /ɪnˈkredjʊləs/ *adj.* unwilling to believe. —**incredulity** /ɪnkrɪˈdju:lɪtɪ/ *n.*, **incredulously** *adv.* [f. L (as IN-², CREDULOUS)]

increment /ˈɪnkrɪmənt/ *n.* an increase, an added amount; profit. —**incremental** /-ˈment(ə)l/ *adj.* [f. L *incrementum* (as INCREASE)]

incriminate /ɪnˈkrɪmɪneɪt/ *v.t.* to indicate as involved in a crime. —**incrimination** /-ˈneɪʃ(ə)n/ *n.*, **incriminatory** *adj.* [f. L *incriminare* (IN-¹, *crimen* accusation)]

incrustation /ɪnkrʌsˈteɪʃ(ə)n/ *n.* **1** encrusting. **2** a crust, a hard coating; a deposit on a surface. [F or f. L (as ENCRUST)]

incubate /ˈɪnkjʊbeɪt/ *v.t./i.* **1** to hatch (eggs) by sitting on them or by artificial heat; to sit on eggs. **2** to cause (bacteria etc.) to develop. [f. L *incubare* (IN-¹, *cubare* lie)]

incubation /ɪnkjʊˈbeɪʃ(ə)n/ *n.* incubating; the development of disease germs before the first symptoms appear. [as prec.]

incubator /ˈɪnkjʊbeɪtə(r)/ *n.* **1** an apparatus with artificial warmth for hatching eggs or developing bacteria. **2** an apparatus in which babies born prematurely can be kept in a constant controlled heat and supplied with oxygen etc. [f. INCUBATE]

incubus /ˈɪŋkjʊbəs/ *n.* (*pl.* **-uses**) **1** an oppressive person or thing. **2** an evil spirit visiting a sleeper; a nightmare. [L, = nightmare (as INCUBATE)]

inculcate /ˈɪnkʌlkeɪt/ *v.t.* to implant (a habit or idea) by persistent urging. —**inculcation** /-ˈkeɪʃ(ə)n/ *n.* [f. L *inculcare* (IN-¹, *calcare* tread)]

inculpate /ˈɪnkʌlpeɪt/ *v.t.* to incriminate; to accuse, to blame. —**inculpation** /-ˈpeɪʃ(ə)n/ *n.*, **inculpatory** /ɪnˈkʌlpətərɪ/ *adj.* [f. L *inculpare* (IN-¹, *culpare* blame)]

incumbency /ɪnˈkʌmbənsɪ/ *n.* the office or tenure of an incumbent. [as foll.]

incumbent /ɪnˈkʌmbənt/ *adj.* **1** forming an obligation or duty. **2** lying or resting (*on*). —*n.* the holder of an office, especially a benefice. [f. L *incumbere* lie on]

incunabulum /ɪnkju:ˈnæbju:ləm/ *n.* (*pl.* **-la**) **1** an early printed book, especially from before 1501. **2** (in *pl.*) the early stages of a thing [L (in *pl.*), = swaddling-clothes]

incur /ɪnˈkɜ:(r)/ *v.t.* (**-rr-**) to bring on oneself (danger, blame, loss, etc.). [f. L *incurrere* (IN-¹, *currere* run)]

incurable /ɪnˈkjʊərəb(ə)l/ *adj.* that cannot be cured. —*n.* an incurable person. —**incurability** /-ˈbɪlɪtɪ/ *n.*, **incurably** *adv.* [f. OF or L (as IN-², CURABLE)]

incurious /ɪnˈkju:rɪəs/ *adj.* feeling or showing no curiosity about something. —**incuriously** *adv.* [f. L (as IN-², CURIOUS)]

incursion /ɪnˈkɜ:ʃ(ə)n/ *n.* an invasion or attack, especially sudden or brief. —**incursive** *adj.* [f. L (as INCUR)]

incurve /ɪnˈkɜ:v/ *v.t.* to bend into a curve; (esp. in *p.p.*) to curve inwards. —**incurvation** /-ˈveɪʃ(ə)n/ *n.* [f. L *incurvare* (as IN-¹, CURVE)]

indebted /ɪnˈdetɪd/ *adj.* under a debt or obligation (to). —**indebtedness** *n.* [f. OF *endetté* (as IN-¹, DEBT)]

indecent /ɪnˈdi:sənt/ *adj.* offending against decency; unseemly. —**indecent assault,** a sexual attack not involving rape. —**indecency** *n.*, **indecently** *adv.* [f. F or L (as IN-², DECENT)]

indecipherable /ɪndɪˈsaɪfərəb(ə)l/ *adj.* that cannot be deciphered. [f. IN-² + DECIPHERABLE]

indecision /ɪndɪˈsɪʒ(ə)n/ *n.* lack of decision, hesitation. [f. F (as IN-², DECISION)]

indecisive /ɪndɪˈsaɪsɪv/ *adj.* not decisive. —**indecisively** *adv.*, **indecisiveness** *n.* [f. IN-² + DECISIVE]

indeclinable /ɪndɪˈklaɪnəb(ə)l/ *adj.* (of words) having no inflexions. [f. F f. L (as IN-², DECLINE)]

indecorous /ɪnˈdekərəs/ *adj.* improper, not in good taste. —**indecorously** *adv.* [f. L (as IN-², DECOROUS)]

indeed /ɪnˈdi:d/ *adj.* **1** in truth, really. **2** admittedly. —*int.* expressing incredulity, surprise, etc. [f. IN + DEED]

indefatigable /ɪndɪˈfætɪgəb(ə)l/ *adj.* not becoming tired; unremitting. —**indefatigably** *adv.* [f. obs. F or L (as IN-², *defatigare* tire out)]

indefeasible /ɪndɪˈfi:zɪb(ə)l/ *adj.* (of a right, possession, etc.) that cannot be forfeited or annulled. —**indefeasibly** *adv.* [f. IN-² + *defeasible* (AF f. OF *defaire* undo)]

indefensible /ɪndɪˈfensɪb(ə)l/ *adj.* that cannot be defended or justified. —**indefensibility** /-ˈbɪlɪtɪ/ *n.*, **indefensibly** *adv.* [f. IN-² + DEFENSIBLE]

indefinable /ɪndɪˈfaɪnəb(ə)l/ *adj.* that cannot be defined or described clearly. —**indefinably** *adv.* [f. IN-² + DEFINABLE]

indefinite /ɪnˈdefɪnɪt/ *adj.* **1** not clearly defined, stated, or decided; unlimited. **2** (of adjectives, adverbs, and pronouns) not determining the person etc. referred to (e.g. *some*, *someone*, *anyhow*). —**indefinite article**, see ARTICLE. —**indefinitely** *adv*. [f. L (as IN-², DEFINITE)]

indelible /ɪnˈdelɪb(ə)l/ *adj*. that cannot be rubbed out; that makes indelible marks. —**indelibly** *adv*. [f. F or L (IN-², *delēre* efface)]

indelicate /ɪnˈdelɪkət/ *adj*. **1** slightly indecent; not refined. **2** tactless. —**indelicacy** *n*., **indelicately** *adv*. [f. IN-² + DELICATE]

indemnify /ɪnˈdemnɪfaɪ/ *v.t.* **1** to protect or insure (a person *from* or *against* loss); to exempt from a penalty (*for* actions). **2** to compensate. —**indemnification** /-ˈkeɪʃ(ə)n/ *n*. [f. L *indemnis* free from loss]

indemnity /ɪnˈdemnɪtɪ/ *n*. **1** protection or insurance against damage or loss; exemption from a penalty. **2** compensation for damage. [f. F f. L (as prec.)]

indent /ɪnˈdent/ *v.t./i.* **1** to make notches, dents, or recesses in. **2** to start (a line of print or writing) further from the margin than the others. **3** to place an indent for goods; to order (goods) by an indent. **4** to draw up (a document) in duplicate. —/ˈɪndent/ *n*. **1** an official order for goods. **2** an indentation. **3** an indenture. [f. AF f. L (IN-¹, *dens* tooth)]

indentation /ɪndenˈteɪʃ(ə)n/ *n*. **1** indenting. **2** a notch; a deep recess. [f. prec.]

indention /ɪnˈdenʃ(ə)n/ *n*. indenting, especially in printing; a notch. [f. INDENT]

indenture /ɪnˈdentʃə(r)/ *n*. **1** a formal sealed agreement, especially (usu. in *pl*.) one binding an apprentice to a master. **2** a formal list, certificate, etc. —*v.t.* to bind by indentures. [f. AF (as INDENT)]

independence /ɪndɪˈpend(ə)ns/ *n*. being independent. —**Independence Day**, 4 July, celebrated in the USA as the anniversary of the date in 1776 when the American colonies formally declared themselves free and independent of Britain; a similar festival elsewhere. [f. foll.]

independent /ɪndɪˈpend(ə)nt/ *adj*. **1** not depending on the authority or control (*of*, or abs.); self-governing. **2** not depending on another thing for validity etc., or on another person for one's opinion or livelihood. **3** (of broadcasting, a school, etc.) not supported from public funds. **4** (of an income or resources) making it unnecessary to earn one's living. **5** unwilling to be under obligation to others. **6** acting independently of any political party. —*n*. a person who is politically independent. —**independently** *adv*. [f. IN-² + DEPENDENT]

indescribable /ɪndɪˈskraɪbəb(ə)l/ *adj*. too unusual to be described; vague. —**indescribably** *adv*. [f. IN-² + *describable* (f. DESCRIBE)]

indestructible /ɪndɪˈstrʌktɪb(ə)l/ *adj*. that cannot be destroyed. —**indestructibility** /-ˈbɪlɪtɪ/ *n*., **indestructibly** *adv*. [f. IN-² + *destructible* (f. DESTROY)]

indeterminable /ɪndɪˈtɜːmɪnəb(ə)l/ *adj*. that cannot be ascertained or settled. —**indeterminably** *adv*. [f. L (as IN-², DETERMINE)]

indeterminate /ɪndɪˈtɜːmɪnət/ *adj*. not fixed in extent, character, etc.; left doubtful. —**indeterminate vowel**, the vowel /ə/ heard in '*a* moment *a*go'. —**indeterminacy** *n*., **indeterminately** *adv*., **indeterminateness** *n*. [f. L (as IN-², DETERMINATE)]

indetermination /ɪndɪtɜːmɪˈneɪʃ(ə)n/ *n*. lack of determination. [f. prec.]

index /ˈɪndeks/ *n*. (*pl*. **indexes** or **indices** /-ɪsiːz/) **1** an alphabetical list of subjects etc. with references, usually at the end of a book. **2** a number indicating the level of prices or wages as compared with some standard value. **3** the exponent of a number. **4** a pointer (*lit*. or *fig*.). —*v.t.* **1** to furnish (a book) with an index; to enter in an index. **2** to relate (wages etc.) to the value of a price index. —**index finger**, the forefinger. **index-linked** *adj*. related to the value of a price index. [L, = forefinger, informer]

indexation /ɪndekˈseɪʃ(ə)n/ *n*. making wages etc. index-linked. [f. prec.]

India ink (*US*) Indian ink.

Indiaman /ˈɪndɪəmən/ *n*. (*pl*. **-men**) (*hist*.) a ship engaged in trade with India or the East Indies.

Indian /ˈɪndɪən/ *adj*. **1** of India; of the subcontinent comprising India, Pakistan, and Bangladesh. **2** of the original inhabitants (other than Eskimo) of America and the West Indies. —*n*. **1** a native of India. **2** an original inhabitant (other than an Eskimo) of America or the West Indies; a Red Indian (see RED). —**Indian clubs**, a pair of bottle-shaped clubs swung to exercise the arms. **Indian corn**, maize. **Indian file**, single file. **Indian ink**, a black pigment. **Indian summer**, a calm dry period in late autumn; (*fig*.) a tranquil late period. [f. *India*]

indiarubber /ɪndɪəˈrʌbə(r)/ *n*. a rubber, especially for rubbing out pencil marks etc.

Indic /ˈɪndɪk/ *adj*. Indo-Aryan. [f. L f. Gk *Indikos* Indian]

indicate /ˈɪndɪkeɪt/ *v.t.* **1** to point out, to make known. **2** to be a sign of, to show the presence of. **3** to show the need of, to require. **4** to state briefly. —**indication** /-ˈkeɪʃ(ə)n/ *n*. [f. L *indicare* point out (as INDEX)]

indicative /ɪnˈdɪkətɪv/ *adj*. **1** suggestive *of*, giving an indication. **2** (*Gram*., of a mood) expressing a statement not a command, wish, etc. —*n*. (*Gram*.) the indicative mood or form. [f. F f. L (as prec.)]

indicator /ˈɪndɪkeɪtə(r)/ *n*. **1** a person or thing

that indicates or points to something. **2** a device indicating the condition of a machine etc. **3** a board giving current information. **4** a device to show the direction of an intended turn by a vehicle. [f. INDICATE]

indicatory /ɪnˈdɪkətərɪ/ *adj*. indicative (*of*). [as prec.]

indices see INDEX.

indict /ɪnˈdaɪt/ *v.t.* to accuse formally by legal process. [f. AF (as DICTATE)]

indictable /ɪnˈdaɪtəb(ə)l/ *adj*. (of an offence) making the doer liable to be charged with a crime; (of a person) so liable. [f. prec.]

indictment /ɪnˈdaɪtmənt/ *n*. a document stating alleged crimes; an accusation. [f. AF (as INDICT)]

indifference /ɪnˈdɪfərəns/ *n*. **1** lack of interest or attention. **2** unimportance. [f. L (as foll.)]

indifferent /ɪnˈdɪfərənt/ *adj*. **1** showing indifference or lack of interest. **2** neither good nor bad. **3** of poor quality or ability. **4** unimportant. —**indifferently** *adv*. [f. OF or L (as IN-², DIFFERENT)]

indigenous /ɪnˈdɪdʒɪnəs/ *adj*. native or belonging naturally (*to* a place). [f. L *indigena* (*indi-* = IN¹, *gen-* be born)]

indigent /ˈɪndɪdʒ(ə)nt/ *adj*. needy, poor. —**indigence** *n*. [f. OF f. L *indigēre* (*indi-* = IN-¹, *egēre* need)]

indigestible /ɪndɪˈdʒestɪb(ə)l/ *adj*. difficult or impossible to digest. —**indigestibility** /-ˈbɪlɪtɪ/ *n*. [F or f. L (as IN-², DIGESTIBLE)]

indigestion /ɪndɪˈdʒestʃ(ə)n/ *n*. difficulty in digesting food; pain caused by this. [f. OF or L (as IN-², DIGESTION)]

indignant /ɪnˈdɪgnənt/ *adj*. feeling or showing indignation. —**indignantly** *adv*. [f. L *indignari* regard as unworthy (IN-², *dignus* worthy)]

indignation /ɪndɪgˈneɪʃ(ə)n/ *n*. scornful anger at supposed injustice, wickedness, etc. [f. OF or L (as prec.)]

indignity /ɪnˈdɪgnɪtɪ/ *n*. humiliating treatment, an insult; humiliating quality. [f. F or L *indignitas* (as INDIGNANT)]

indigo /ˈɪndɪgəʊ/ *n*. (*pl*. **-os**) deep violet-blue; a dye of this colour. [Sp. or Port. f. L f. Gk, = Indian dye]

indirect /ɪndɪˈrekt, -daɪ-/ *adj*. not direct. —**indirect object**, a person or thing affected by verbal action but not primarily acted on (e.g. *him* in *give him the book*). **indirect question**, a question in indirect speech. **indirect speech**, reported speech. **indirect tax**, a tax paid in the form of an increased price for taxed goods. —**indirectly** *adv*. [f. OF or L (as IN-², DIRECT)]

indiscernible /ɪndɪˈsɜːnɪb(ə)l/ *adj*. that cannot be discerned. —**indiscernibly** *adv*. [f. IN-² + DISCERNIBLE]

indiscipline /ɪnˈdɪsɪplɪn/ *n*. lack of discipline. [f. IN-² + DISCIPLINE]

indiscreet /ɪndɪsˈkriːt/ *adj*. **1** not discreet, revealing secrets. **2** incautious, unwary. —**indiscreetly** *adv*. [f. L *indiscretus* (as IN-², DISCREET)]

indiscretion /ɪndɪsˈkreʃ(ə)n/ *n*. indiscreet conduct or action. [f. OF or L (as IN-², DISCRETION)]

indiscriminate /ɪndɪsˈkrɪmɪnət/ *adj*. done or acting without judgement or discrimination. —**indiscriminately** *adv*., **indiscrimination** /-ˈneɪʃ(ə)n/ *n*. [f. IN-² + *discriminate* adj. (as DISCRIMINATE)]

indispensable /ɪndɪˈspensəb(ə)l/ *adj*. that cannot be dispensed with, necessary *to* or *for*. —**indispensability** /-ˈbɪlɪtɪ/ *n*., **indispensably** *adv*. [f. L (as IN-², DISPENSABLE)]

indisposed /ɪndɪˈspəʊzd/ *adj*. **1** slightly unwell. **2** averse or unwilling. —**indisposition** /-spəˈzɪʃ(ə)n/ *n*. [f. IN-² + DISPOSE]

indisputable /ɪndɪˈspjuːtəb(ə)l/ *adj*. not able to be disputed, undeniable. —**indisputability** /-ˈbɪlɪtɪ/ *n*., **indisputably** *adv*. [f. L (as IN-², DISPUTE)]

indissoluble /ɪndɪˈsɒljʊb(ə)l/ *adj*. that cannot be dissolved or destroyed, firm and lasting. —**indissolubly** *adv*. [f. L (as IN-², DISSOLUBLE)]

indistinct /ɪndɪˈstɪŋkt/ *adj*. not distinct; confused, obscure. —**indistinctness** *n*. [f. L (as IN-², DISTINCT)]

indistinguishable /ɪndɪˈstɪŋgwɪʃəb(ə)l/ *adj*. that cannot be distinguished. —**indistinguishably** *adv*. [f. IN-² + DISTINGUISHABLE]

indite /ɪnˈdaɪt/ *v.t.* to put into words; to write (a letter etc.). [f. OF (as INDICT)]

indium /ˈɪndɪəm/ *n*. a rare silver-white soft metallic element, symbol In, atomic number 49. [f. L *indicum* indigo, with ref. to the two indigo lines which form its characteristic spectrum]

individual /ɪndɪˈvɪdjʊəl/ *adj*. **1** single, separate; of or for one person. **2** having a distinct character; characteristic of a particular person or thing. —*n*. a single member of a class; a single human being; (*colloq*.) a person. —**individually** *adv*. [orig. = indivisible, f. L *individuus* (as IN-², DIVIDE)]

individualism *n*. **1** self-reliant action by an individual. **2** a social theory favouring free action by individuals. **3** egotism. —**individualist** *n*., **individualistic** /-ˈlɪstɪk/ *adj*. [f. prec.]

individuality /ɪndɪvɪdjʊˈælɪtɪ/ *n*. **1** separate existence. **2** individual character, especially when strongly marked. [f. INDIVIDUAL]

individualize *v.t.* to give an individual character to. [as prec.]

indivisible /ɪndɪˈvɪzɪb(ə)l/ *adj*. not divisible.

—**indivisibility** /-ˈbɪlɪtɪ/ *n.*, **indivisibly** *adv.* [f. L (as IN-², DIVISIBLE)]

Indo- /ɪndəʊ-/ *in comb.* Indian (and).

Indo-Aryan *adj.* of the group of Indo-European languages comprising Sanskrit and the modern Indian languages which are its descendants. —*n.* **1** this language group. **2** its speakers.

indoctrinate /ɪnˈdɒktrɪneɪt/ *v.t.* to imbue with a doctrine or opinion; to teach, to instruct. —**indoctrination** /-ˈneɪʃ(ə)n/ *n.* [f. IN-¹ + DOCTRINE]

Indo-European *adj.* of the family of languages (also called *Indo-Germanic* or *Aryan*) spoken over the greater part of Europe and extending into Asia as far as northern India. —*n.* **1** this family of languages. **2** a speaker of any of these.

indolent /ˈɪndələnt/ *adj.* lazy, averse to exertion. —**indolence** *n.*, **indolently** *adv.* [f. L (IN-², *dolere* suffer pain)]

indomitable /ɪnˈdɒmɪtəb(ə)l/ *adj.* unyielding, stubbornly persistent. —**indomitably** *adv.* [f. L (IN-², *domitare* tame)]

indoor *adj.* of or done or for use in a building or under cover. [for earlier *within-door*]

indoors /ɪnˈdɔːz/ *adv.* in(to) a building; under a roof. [earlier *within doors*]

indrawn /ˈɪndrɔːn/ *adj.* **1** drawn in. **2** aloof. [f. IN + DRAW]

indubitable /ɪnˈdjuːbɪtəb(ə)l/ *adj.* that cannot be doubted. —**indubitably** *adv.* [F or f. L (IN-², *dubitare* doubt)]

induce /ɪnˈdjuːs/ *v.t.* **1** to persuade. **2** to produce or cause; to bring on (labour in childbirth) artificially. **3** to produce by induction; to infer as an induction. [f. L *inducere* (IN-¹, *ducere* lead)]

inducement *n.* a thing that induces; an attraction, a motive. [f. prec.]

inducible *adj.* that may be induced. [f. INDUCE]

induct /ɪnˈdʌkt/ *v.t.* to install or initiate (*into* a benefice or office etc.). [as INDUCE]

inductance /ɪnˈdʌkt(ə)ns/ *n.* the amount of induction of an electric current. [f. prec.]

induction /ɪnˈdʌkʃ(ə)n/ *n.* **1** inducting. **2** inducing. **3** the inferring of a general law from particular instances. **4** the production of an electric or magnetic state by the proximity (without contact) of an electrified or magnetized body; the quantity giving the measure of such an influence; the production of an electric current by a change of magnetic field. **5** the drawing of a fuel mixture into the cylinder(s) of an internal-combustion engine. [f. OF or L (as INDUCE)]

inductive /ɪnˈdʌktɪv/ *adj.* **1** (of reasoning etc.) based on or using induction. **2** of electric or magnetic induction. [f. L (as INDUCE)]

indulge /ɪnˈdʌldʒ/ *v.t./i.* **1** to take pleasure freely (*in* an activity etc.). **2** to yield freely to (a desire etc.). **3** to gratify by compliance with wishes. [f. L *indulgēre*]

indulgence /ɪnˈdʌldʒ(ə)ns/ *n.* **1** indulging. **2** a privilege granted. **3** remission of the temporal punishment still due for sins even after sacramental absolution. [f. OF f. L (as prec.)]

indulgent *adj.* indulging; lenient, willing to overlook faults etc.; too lenient. —**indulgently** *adv.* [F or f. L (as INDULGE)]

indurate /ˈɪndjʊəreɪt/ *v.t./i.* to make or become hard; to make callous. —**induration** /-ˈreɪʃ(ə)n/ *n.*, **indurative** *adj.* [f. L *indurare* (IN-¹, *durus* hard)]

industrial /ɪnˈdʌstrɪəl/ *adj.* of, engaged in, for use in, or serving the needs of industries; (of a nation etc.) having highly developed industries. —**industrial action,** a strike or other disruptive action used in an industrial dispute. **industrial relations,** the relations between management and workers in industries. —**industrially** *adv.* [f. INDUSTRY]

industrialism *n.* a system involving the prevalence of industries. [f. prec.]

industrialist *n.* a person engaged in the management of industry. [f. INDUSTRIAL]

industrialize *v.t.* to make (a nation or area etc.) industrial. —**industrialization** /-ˈzeɪʃ(ə)n/ *n.* [as prec.]

industrious /ɪnˈdʌstrɪəs/ *adj.* hard-working. —**industriously** *adv.* [f. F or L (as foll.)]

industry /ˈɪndəstrɪ/ *n.* **1** trade or manufacture; a branch of this; any business activity. **2** diligence. [f. F or L *industria*]

indwelling *adj.* permanently present in something. [f. IN-¹ + DWELL]

inebriate /ɪˈniːbrɪət/ *adj.* drunken. —*n.* a drunkard. —/-eɪt/ *v.t.* to make drunk. —**inebriation** /-ˈeɪʃ(ə)n/ *n.*, **inebriety** /-ˈbraɪətɪ/ *n.* [f. L *inebriare* (IN-¹, *ebrius* drunk)]

inedible /ɪnˈedɪb(ə)l/ *adj.* not edible (because of its nature). [f. IN-² + EDIBLE]

ineducable /ɪnˈedjʊkəb(ə)l/ *adj.* incapable of being educated, especially through mental retardation. [f. IN-² + EDUCABLE]

ineffable /ɪnˈefəb(ə)l/ *adj.* **1** too great for description in words. **2** that must not be uttered. —**ineffably** *adv.* [f. OF or L (IN-², *effari* speak out)]

ineffaceable /ɪnɪˈfeɪsəb(ə)l/ *adj.* not able to be effaced. [f. IN-² + EFFACE]

ineffective /ɪnɪˈfektɪv/ *adj.* not effective; (of a person) inefficient. —**ineffectively** *adv.* [f. IN-² + EFFECTIVE]

ineffectual /ɪnɪˈfektjʊəl/ *adj.* not effectual. —**ineffectually** *adv.* [f. L (as IN-², EFFECTUAL)]

inefficacious /ɪnefɪˈkeɪʃəs/ *adj.* (of a remedy etc.) not efficacious. [f. IN-² + EFFICACIOUS]

inefficient /ɪnɪˈfɪʃ(ə)nt/ *adj.* not efficient. —**inefficiency** *n.*, **inefficiently** *adv.* [f. IN-² + EFFICIENT]

inelastic /ɪnɪˈlæstɪk/ *adj.* not elastic, not adaptable. [f. IN-² + ELASTIC]

inelegant /ɪnˈelɪgənt/ *adj.* not elegant. —**inelegance** *n.*, **inelegantly** *adv.* [f. F f. L (as IN-², ELEGANT)]

ineluctable /ɪnɪˈlʌktəb(ə)l/ *adj.* against which it is useless to struggle. [f. L (IN-², *eluctari* struggle clear)]

inept /ɪˈnept/ *adj.* **1** unskilful. **2** unsuitable, absurd. —**ineptitude** *n.*, **ineptly** *adv.* [f. L *ineptus* (as IN-², APT)]

inequable /ɪnˈekwəb(ə)l/ *adj.* **1** unfair. **2** not uniform. [f. L (as IN-², EQUABLE)]

inequality /ɪnɪˈkwɒlɪtɪ/ *n.* lack of equality in any respect, variableness; unevenness of surface. [f. OF or L (as IN-², EQUALITY)]

inequitable /ɪnˈekwɪtəb(ə)l/ *adj.* unfair, unjust. [f. IN-² + EQUITABLE]

inequity /ɪnˈekwɪtɪ/ *n.* unfairness, bias. [f. IN-² + EQUITY]

ineradicable /ɪnɪˈrædɪkəb(ə)l/ *adj.* that cannot be eradicated. [f. IN-² + ERADICABLE]

inert /ɪˈnɜːt/ *adj.* **1** without an inherent power of action, reaction, motion, or resistance. **2** sluggish, slow. —**inert gas**, a noble gas (see NOBLE). —**inertly** *adv.*, **inertness** *n.* [f. L *iners* (as IN-², ART)]

inertia /ɪˈnɜːʃə/ *n.* **1** inertness. **2** the property by which matter continues in its existing state of rest or uniform motion in a straight line unless that state is changed by an external force. —**inertia reel**, a reel allowing the automatic adjustment of a safety-belt rolled round it. **inertia selling**, the sending of goods not ordered in the hope that they will not be refused. [L (as prec.)]

inertial /ɪˈnɜːʃ(ə)l/ *adj.* of or involving inertia; (of navigation) in which the course of a vehicle or vessel is calculated or controlled automatically, by a computer, from its acceleration at each successive moment. [f. prec.]

inescapable /ɪnɪˈskeɪpəb(ə)l/ *adj.* that cannot be escaped or avoided. —**inescapably** *adv.* [f. IN-² + ESCAPE]

inescutcheon /ɪnɪˈskʌtʃ(ə)n/ *n.* (in heraldry) a small escutcheon placed on a larger one. [f. IN-¹ + ESCUTCHEON]

inessential /ɪnɪˈsenʃ(ə)l/ *adj.* not essential. —*n.* an inessential thing. [f. IN-² + ESSENTIAL]

inestimable /ɪnˈestɪməb(ə)l/ *adj.* too good, great, etc. to be estimated. —**inestimably** *adv.* [f. OF f. L (as IN-², ESTIMABLE)]

inevitable /ɪnˈevɪtəb(ə)l/ *adj.* unavoidable, bound to happen or appear; (*colloq.*) tiresomely familiar. —**inevitability** /-ˈbɪlɪtɪ/ *n.*, **inevitably** *adv.* [f. L (IN-², *evitare* avoid)]

inexact /ɪnɪgˈzækt/ *adj.* not exact. —**inexactitude** *n.*, **inexactly** *adv.* [f. IN-² + EXACT]

inexcusable /ɪnɪkˈskjuːzəb(ə)l/ *adj.* that cannot be excused or justified. —**inexcusably** *adv.* [f. L (as IN-², EXCUSE)]

inexhaustible /ɪnɪgˈzɔːstɪb(ə)l/ *adj.* that cannot be totally used up, available in unlimited quantity. [f. IN-² + EXHAUSTIBLE]

inexorable /ɪnˈeksərəb(ə)l/ *adj.* relentless; that cannot be persuaded by entreaty. —**inexorably** *adv.* [F or f. L (IN-², *exorare* move by entreaty)]

inexpedient /ɪnɪkˈspiːdɪənt/ *adj.* not expedient. —**inexpediency** *n.* [f. IN-² + EXPEDIENT]

inexpensive /ɪnɪkˈspensɪv/ *adj.* not expensive, offering good value for the price. —**inexpensively** *adv.* [f. IN-² + EXPENSIVE]

inexperience /ɪnɪkˈspɪərɪəns/ *n.* lack of experience or of knowledge or skill arising from experience. —**inexperienced** *adj.* [f. F f. L (as IN-², EXPERIENCE)]

inexpert /ɪnˈekspɜːt/ *adj.* unskilful, lacking expertise. —**inexpertly** *adv.* [f. OF f. L (as IN-², EXPERT)]

inexpiable /ɪnˈekspɪəb(ə)l/ *adj.* that cannot be expiated or appeased. [f. L (as IN-², EXPIATE)]

inexplicable /ɪnˈeksplɪkəb(ə)l, ɪnɪkˈsplɪk-/ *adj.* that cannot be explained. —**inexplicably** *adv.* [F or f. L (as IN-², EXPLICABLE)]

inexpressible /ɪnɪkˈspresɪb(ə)l/ *adj.* that cannot be expressed in words. —**inexpressibly** *adv.* [f. IN-² + EXPRESSIBLE]

in extenso /ɪn eksˈtensəʊ/ at full length. [L]

in extremis /ɪn eksˈtriːmɪs/ **1** at the point of death. **2** in great difficulties. [L]

inextricable /ɪnˈekstrɪkəb(ə)l/ *adj.* **1** that cannot be resolved or escaped from. **2** that cannot be loosened. —**inextricably** *adv.* [f. L (as IN-², EXTRICATE)]

infallible /ɪnˈfælɪb(ə)l/ *adj.* **1** incapable of making a mistake or being wrong. **2** never failing in its effect. —**infallibility** /-ˈbɪlɪtɪ/ *n.*, **infallibly** *adv.* [f. F or L (as IN-², FALLIBLE)]

infamous /ˈɪnfəməs/ *adj.* having or deserving a very bad reputation, abominable. —**infamy** /ˈɪnfəmɪ/ *n.* [f. L (as IN-², FAME)]

infant /ˈɪnf(ə)nt/ *n.* **1** a child during the earliest period of life; (*Law*) a person under the age of 18. **2** a thing in an early stage of development. —**infancy** *n.* [f. OF f. L (IN-², *fari* speak), lit. = one unable to speak]

infanta /ɪnˈfæntə/ *n.* a daughter of the Spanish or (*hist.*) Portuguese king. [Sp. & Port. f. L (as prec.)]

infanticide /ɪnˈfæntɪsaɪd/ *n.* the killing of an infant soon after birth; one who is guilty of this. [F f. L (as INFANT, -CIDE)]

infantile /ˈɪnfəntaɪl/ *adj.*/ of or like infants.

—infantile paralysis, poliomyelitis. [F or f. L (as INFANT)]

infantry /ˈɪnfəntrɪ/ *n.* soldiers marching and fighting on foot. [f. F f. It. (*infante* youth, as INFANT)]

infantryman *n.* (*pl.* **-men**) a soldier of an infantry regiment.

infatuate /ɪnˈfætjʊeɪt/ *v.t.* to inspire with intense fondness and admiration. **—infatuation** /-ˈeɪʃ(ə)n/ *n.* [f. L *infatuare* (IN-¹, *fatuus* foolish)]

infect /ɪnˈfekt/ *v.t.* **1** to affect or contaminate with a germ or virus or the consequent disease. **2** to imbue with an opinion or feeling etc. [f. L *inficere* taint]

infection /ɪnˈfekʃ(ə)n/ *n.* infecting, being infected; an instance of this; a disease; the communication of disease, especially by the agency of air, water, etc. [f. OF or L (as prec.)]

infectious /ɪnˈfekʃəs/ *adj.* **1** infecting others. **2** able to be transmitted by infection. **—infectiousness** *n.* [f. prec.]

infelicitous /ɪnfɪˈlɪsɪtəs/ *adj.* not felicitous, unfortunate. **—infelicitously** *adv.* [f. IN-² + FELICITOUS]

infelicity /ɪnfɪˈlɪsɪtɪ/ *n.* **1** unhappiness. **2** an infelicitous expression or detail. [f. L (as IN-², FELICITY)]

infer /ɪnˈfɜː(r)/ *v.t.* (**-rr-**) **1** to deduce or conclude. **2** (**D**) to imply, to suggest. [f. L *inferre* (IN-¹, *ferre* bring)]

inferable *adj.* that may be inferred. [f. prec.]

inference /ˈɪnfərəns/ *n.* **1** inferring. **2** a thing inferred. **—inferential** /-ˈrenʃ(ə)l/ *adj.* [f. L (as INFER)]

inferior /ɪnˈfɪərɪə(r)/ *adj.* **1** lower in rank or quality etc. (*to*); of poor quality. **2** situated below; written or printed below the line. *—n.* a person inferior to another especially in rank. [f. compar. of L *inferus* that is below]

inferiority /ɪnfɪərɪˈɒrɪtɪ/ *n.* being inferior. **—inferiority complex,** an unconscious feeling of inferiority to others, sometimes manifested in aggressive behaviour; (*colloq.*) a feeling of inferiority. [f. prec.]

infernal /ɪnˈfɜːn(ə)l/ *adj.* **1** of hell; hellish. **2** (*colloq.*) detestable, annoying. **—infernally** *adv.* [f. OF f. L (*infernus* situated below)]

inferno /ɪnˈfɜːnəʊ/ *n.* (*pl.* **-os**) a raging fire; a scene of horror or distress; hell. [It., = hell (with reference to Dante's *Divine Comedy*), f. L (as prec.)]

infertile /ɪnˈfɜːtaɪl/ *adj.* not fertile. **—infertility** /-ˈtɪlɪtɪ/ *n.* [F or f. L (as IN-², FERTILE)]

infest /ɪnˈfest/ *v.t.* (of harmful persons or things, esp. vermin) to overrun (a place) in large numbers. **—infestation** /-ˈteɪʃ(ə)n/ *n.* [f. F or L *infestare* assail (*infestus* hostile)]

infibulation /ɪnfɪbjuːˈleɪʃ(ə)n/ *n.* fastening with a clasp; fastening of the genitals thus or surgically to prevent sexual intercourse. [f. L *infibulare* (IN-¹, FIBULA)]

infidel /ˈɪnfɪd(ə)l/ *n.* a disbeliever in religion or in a specified religion. *—adj.* unbelieving; of infidels. [f. F or L *infidelis* (IN-², *fidelis* faithful)]

infidelity /ɪnfɪˈdelɪtɪ/ *n.* disloyalty, especially to one's husband or wife. [f. F or L (as prec.)]

infield *n.* (in cricket) the part of the ground near the wicket.

infighting *n.* **1** hidden conflict in an organization. **2** boxing within arm's length.

infilling *n.* the placing of buildings in the gaps between others.

infiltrate /ˈɪnfɪltreɪt/ *v.t./i.* **1** to enter (a territory, political party, etc.) gradually and imperceptibly; to cause (troops etc.) to do this. **2** to pass (fluid) by filtration (*into*); to permeate by filtration. **—infiltration** /-ˈtreɪʃ(ə)n/ *n.*, **infiltrator** *n.* [f. IN-¹ + FILTRATE]

infinite /ˈɪnfɪnɪt/ *adj.* **1** having no limit, endless. **2** very great; very many. **3** (*Math.*) greater than any assignable quantity or countable number; (of a series) that may be continued indefinitely. **—the infinite,** God. **the infinite,** infinite space. **—infinitely** *adv.* [f. L (as IN-², FINITE)]

infinitesimal /ɪnfɪnɪˈtesɪm(ə)l/ *adj.* infinitely or very small. **—infinitesimal calculus,** that dealing with very small quantities. **—infinitesimally** *adv.* [f. prec.]

infinitive /ɪnˈfɪnɪtɪv/ *n.* a verb form expressing the verbal notion without a particular subject, tense, etc. (often with *to*; e.g. *see* in *we came to see, let him see*). *—adj.* having this form. **—infinitival** /-ˈtaɪv(ə)l/ *adj.* [f. L (IN-², *finitivus* definite)]

infinitude /ɪnˈfɪnɪtjuːd/ *n.* infinity, being infinite. [as INFINITE]

infinity /ɪnˈfɪnɪtɪ/ *n.* **1** an infinite number, extent, or time. **2** being infinite. [f. OF f. L (as INFINITE)]

infirm /ɪnˈfɜːm/ *adj.* **1** physically weak, especially from age. **2** weak, irresolute. [f. L (as IN-², FIRM¹)]

infirmary *n.* a hospital; the sick-quarters in a monastery, school, etc. [as prec.]

infirmity *n.* **1** being infirm. **2** a particular physical weakness. [f. INFIRM]

infix /ɪnˈfɪks/ *v.t.* to fasten or fix in. [f. IN-¹ + FIX]

in flagrante delicto /ɪn flæˈgræntɪ deˈlɪktəʊ/ in the very act of committing an offence. [L, = in blazing crime]

inflame /ɪnˈfleɪm/ *v.t./i.* **1** to provoke to strong feeling; to arouse anger in. **2** to cause inflammation in. **3** to catch fire, to cause to do this; to light up with or as with a flame; to make hot. [f. OF f. L *inflammare* (as IN-¹, FLAME)]

inflammable /ɪnˈflæməb(ə)l/ *adj.* easily set on fire or excited. —**inflammably** *adv.* [f. prec.]

inflammation /ɪnfləˈmeɪʃ(ə)n/ *n.* **1** inflaming (*lit.* or *fig.*). **2** a condition of a part of the body with heat, swelling, redness, and usually pain. [f. L (as INFLAME)]

inflammatory /ɪnˈflæmətərɪ/ *adj.* **1** tending to arouse anger or strong feeling. **2** of inflammation. [as prec.]

inflatable /ɪnˈfleɪtəb(ə)l/ *adj.* that may be inflated. [f. foll.]

inflate /ɪnˈfleɪt/ *v.t.* **1** to distend or become distended with air or gas. **2** to puff up (*with* pride etc.). **3** to increase (a price etc.) artificially. **4** to resort to the inflation of (currency). [f. L *inflare* (IN-¹, *flare* blow)]

inflation /ɪnˈfleɪʃ(ə)n/ *n.* **1** inflating, being inflated. **2** a general rise in prices and fall in the purchasing power of money; an increase in the supply of money, regarded as the cause of such a rise. [as prec.]

inflationary *adj.* causing inflation. [f. prec.]

inflect /ɪnˈflekt/ *v.t.* **1** to change the pitch of (the voice). **2** to modify (a word) to express grammatical relation. **3** to bend, to curve. [f. L *inflectere* (IN-¹, *flectere* bend)]

inflective /ɪnˈflektɪv/ *adj.* of grammatical inflexion. [f. prec.]

inflexible /ɪnˈfleksɪb(ə)l/ *adj.* **1** not flexible, that cannot be bent. **2** that cannot be altered. **3** refusing to alter one's demands etc., unyielding. —**inflexibility** /-ˈbɪlɪtɪ/ *n.*, **inflexibly** *adv.* [f. L (as IN-², FLEXIBLE)]

inflexion /ɪnˈflekʃ(ə)n/ *n.* **1** a modulation of the voice. **2** an inflected word; a suffix etc. used to inflect. **3** inflecting. —**inflexional** *adj.* [F or f. L (as INFLECT)]

inflict /ɪnˈflɪkt/ *v.t.* **1** to deal (a blow etc.) *on*. **2** to impose or deliver forcibly. —**infliction** *n.*, **inflictor** *n.* [f. L *infligere* (IN-¹, *fligere* strike)]

inflorescence /ɪnfləˈres(ə)ns/ *n.* **1** the arrangement of the flowers of a plant in relation to the axis and to each other. **2** the flower(s) of a plant. **3** flowering (*lit.* or *fig.*). [f. L *inflorescere* (as IN-¹, FLORESCENCE)]

inflow *n.* **1** flowing in. **2** that which flows in. [f. IN + FLOW]

influence /ˈɪnflʊəns/ *n.* **1** the power to produce an effect. **2** the ability to affect a person's character, beliefs, or actions. **3** a thing or person with this ability. —*v.t.* to exert an influence on, to affect. —**under the influence**, (*colloq.*) drunk. [f. OF or L *influentia* inflow (IN-¹, *fluere* flow)]

influential /ɪnflʊˈenʃ(ə)l/ *adj.* having great influence. —**influentially** *adv.* [f. L (as prec.)]

influenza /ɪnflʊˈenzə/ *n.* an acute virus disease usually with fever and severe aching and catarrh, occurring in epidemics. [It. f. L (as INFLUENCE)]

influx /ˈɪnflʌks/ *n.* a flowing in, especially of persons or things into a place. [F or f. L *influxus* (as INFLUENCE)]

inform /ɪnˈfɔːm/ *v.t./i.* **1** to give information to. **2** to bring a charge or complaint (*against* or *on*). **3** (in *p.p.*) knowing the facts, enlightened. [f. OF f. L, orig. = give shape to (as IN-¹, FORM)]

informal /ɪnˈfɔːm(ə)l/ *adj.* not formal; without formality. —**informality** /-ˈmælɪtɪ/ *n.*, **informally** *adv.* [f. IN-² + FORMAL]

informant /ɪnˈfɔːmənt/ *n.* a giver of information. [f. L (as INFORM)]

information /ɪnfəˈmeɪʃ(ə)n/ *n.* **1** facts told, heard, or discovered. **2** a charge or complaint lodged with a court etc. **3** facts fed into a computer etc. **4** the process of informing. —**information technology**, a wide range of modern technologies based on the widespread availability of computing power for recording, transmitting, and disseminating information, and including computing science, telecommunications, printing, and broadcasting. [f. OF f. L (as INFORM)]

informative /ɪnˈfɔːmətɪv/ *adj.* giving information, instructive. [f. L (as INFORM)]

informer *n.* one who informs against others. [f. INFORM]

infra /ˈɪnfrə/ *adv.* below or further on in a book etc. [L, = below]

infra- /ɪnfrə-/ *prefix* below. [L (as prec.)]

infraction /ɪnˈfrækʃ(ə)n/ *n.* infringement. [f. L (as INFRINGE)]

infra dig (*colloq.*) beneath one's dignity. [abbr. of L *infra dignitatem*]

infra-red /ɪnfrəˈred/ *adj.* of or using rays with a wavelength just below the red end of the visible spectrum.

infrastructure /ˈɪnfrəstrʌktʃə(r)/ *n.* the subordinate parts of an undertaking, especially permanent installations forming a basis of defence. [F (as INFRA-, STRUCTURE)]

infrequent /ɪnˈfriːkwənt/ *adj.* not frequent. —**infrequency** *n.*, **infrequently** *adv.* [f. L (as IN-², FREQUENT)]

infringe /ɪnˈfrɪndʒ/ *v.t./i.* **1** to act contrary to (a law, another's rights, etc.). **2** to encroach or trespass (*on*). —**infringement** *n.* [f. L *infringere* (IN-¹, *frangere* break)]

infuriate /ɪnˈfjʊərɪeɪt/ *v.t.* to make furious. [f. L *infuriare* (as IN-¹, FURY)]

infuse /ɪnˈfjuːz/ *v.t./i.* **1** to cause to be saturated or filled *with* a quality. **2** to instil (life, a quality, etc., *into*). **3** to steep (tea etc.) in a liquid to extract the constituents; (of tea etc.) to be steeped thus. [f. L *infundere* (IN-¹, *fundere* pour)]

infusible /ɪnˈfjuːzɪb(ə)l/ *adj.* that cannot be melted. —**infusibility** /-ˈbɪlɪtɪ/ *n.* [f. IN-² + FUSIBLE]

infusion /ɪnˈfjuːʒ(ə)n/ *n.* **1** infusing. **2** a liquid extract so obtained. **3** an infused element. [f. F or L (as INFUSE)]

ingenious /ɪnˈdʒiːnɪəs/ *adj.* **1** clever at inventing things or methods. **2** cleverly contrived. —**ingeniously** *adv.* [f. F or L *ingeniosus* (*ingenium* cleverness)]

ingénue /ˈæ̃ʒemjuː/ *n.* an artless young woman, especially as a stage role. [F (as INGENUOUS)]

ingenuity /ɪndʒɪˈnjuːɪtɪ/ *n.* ingeniousness. [f. L, = ingenuousness; assoc. in Eng. with INGENIOUS]

ingenuous /ɪnˈdʒenjʊəs/ *adj.* artless; frank. —**ingenuously** *adv.*, **ingenuousness** *n.* [f. L *ingenuus* free-born, frank (IN-[1], *gignere* beget)]

ingest /ɪnˈdʒest/ *v.t.* to take in by swallowing or absorbing. —**ingestion** *n.* [f. L *ingerere* (IN-[1], *gerere* carry)]

ingle-nook /ˈɪŋg(ə)lnʊk/ *n.* a nook providing a seat beside a recessed fireplace. [f. *ingle* fire in hearth (orig. Sc., perh. f. Gael.) + NOOK]

inglorious /ɪnˈglɔːrɪəs/ *adj.* **1** ignominious. **2** not famous. [f. L (as IN-[2], GLORY)]

ingoing *adj.* going in.

ingot /ˈɪŋgət/ *n.* a mass, usually oblong, of cast metal, especially gold, silver, or steel. [perh. f. IN + *p.p.* of OE *geotan* cast]

ingrained /ɪnˈgreɪnd, *attrib.* ˈɪn-/ *adj.* **1** (of habits, feelings, or tendencies) deeply rooted, inveterate. **2** (of dirt etc.) deeply embedded. [f. OF *engrainer* dye thoroughly (as EN-, GRAIN)]

ingratiate /ɪnˈgreɪʃɪeɪt/ *v.t.* to bring *oneself* into favour (*with*). [f. L *in gratiam* into favour]

ingratitude /ɪnˈgrætɪtjuːd/ *n.* lack of due gratitude. [f. OF or L (as IN-[2], GRATITUDE)]

ingredient /ɪnˈgriːdɪənt/ *n.* a component part in a mixture. [f. L *ingredi* enter into]

ingress /ˈɪngres/ *n.* going in; the right to go in. [f. L *ingressus* (as INGREDIENT)]

ingrowing *adj.* (of a nail) growing into the flesh.

inguinal /ˈɪŋgwɪn(ə)l/ *adj.* of the groin. [f. L (*inguen* groin)]

inhabit /ɪnˈhæbɪt/ *v.t.* to live in (a place) as one's home or dwelling-place. [f. OF or L *inhabitare* (IN-[1], *habitare* dwell)]

inhabitable *adj.* suitable for inhabiting. [f. prec.]

inhabitant *n.* a person etc. who inhabits a place. [f. OF f. L (as prec.)]

inhalant /ɪnˈheɪlənt/ *n.* a medicinal substance for inhaling. [f. L (as foll.)]

inhale /ɪnˈheɪl/ *v.t./i.* to breathe in (air, gas, etc.); to take (tobacco-smoke etc.) into the lungs. —**inhalation** /ɪnhəˈleɪʃ(ə)n/ *n.* [f. L *inhalare* (IN-[1], *halare* breathe)]

inhaler *n.* an inhaling-apparatus, especially a device for sending out vapour for inhaling. [f. prec.]

inharmonious /ɪnhɑːˈməʊnɪəs/ *adj.* not harmonious. [f. IN-[2] + HARMONIOUS]

inhere /ɪnˈhɪə(r)/ *v.i.* to be inherent. [f. L *inhaerēre* (IN-[1], *haerēre* stick)]

inherent /ɪnˈhɪərənt/ *adj.* existing or abiding in something as an essential quality or characteristic. —**inherence** *n.*, **inherently** *adv.* [f. L (as prec.)]

inherit /ɪnˈherɪt/ *v.t.* to receive (property or rank) as an heir; to derive (qualities, problems, etc.) from parents, a predecessor, etc. —**inheritor** *n.* [f. OF f. L *inhereditare* (IN-[1], *heres* heir)]

inheritance *n.* **1** what is inherited. **2** inheriting. [f. AF (as prec.)]

inhibit /ɪnˈhɪbɪt/ *v.t.* **1** to restrain, to prevent. **2** to hinder the impulses of; to cause inhibitions in. —**inhibitory** *adj.* [f. L *inhibēre* (IN-[1], *habēre* hold)]

inhibition /ɪnhɪˈbɪʃ(ə)n/ *n.* **1** inhibiting, being inhibited. **2** the restraint of a direct expression of instinct; (*colloq.*) an emotional resistance to a thought or action. [f. OF or L (as prec.)]

inhospitable /ɪnˈhɒspɪtəb(ə)l, -ˈpɪt-/ *adj.* not hospitable; (of a place or climate) not giving shelter or favourable conditions. —**inhospitably** *adv.* [f. obs. F (as IN-[2], HOSPITABLE)]

in-house *adv.* within an institution. —*adj.* done or existing in-house.

inhuman /ɪnˈhjuːmən/ *adj.* brutal, lacking the human qualities of kindness, pity, etc. —**inhumanity** /-ˈmænɪtɪ/ *n.* [f. L (as IN-[2], HUMAN)]

inhumane /ɪnhjuːˈmeɪn/ *adj.* not humane. [f. IN-[2] + HUMANE]

inimical /ɪˈnɪmɪk(ə)l/ *adj.* hostile, harmful. —**inimically** *adv.* [f. L *inimicus* enemy]

inimitable /ɪˈnɪmɪtəb(ə)l/ *adj.* that cannot be imitated. —**inimitably** *adv.* [F or f. L (as IN-[2], IMITABLE)]

iniquity /ɪˈnɪkwɪtɪ/ *n.* **1** wickedness. **2** gross injustice. —**iniquitous** *adj.* [f. OF f. L (as IN-[2], EQUITY)]

initial /ɪˈnɪʃ(ə)l/ *adj.* of or at the beginning; (of a letter) at the beginning of a word. —*n.* an initial letter, especially (in *pl.*) those of a person's names. —*v.t.* (**-ll-**) to mark or sign with initials. —**initially** *adv.* [f. L (*initium* beginning)]

initiate /ɪˈnɪʃɪeɪt/ *v.t.* **1** to originate, to begin, to set going. **2** to admit (a person) into a society, office, etc. **3** to instruct, especially in rites or forms. —/-ət/ *n.* an initiated person. —**initiation** /-ˈeɪʃ(ə)n/ *n.*, **initiator** *n.*, **initiatory** *adj.* [f. L *initiare* (as prec.)]

initiative /ɪˈnɪʃɪətɪv/ *n.* **1** the ability to initiate things, enterprise. **2** the first step. **3** the power or right to begin. [F (as prec.)]

inject /ɪnˈdʒekt/ *v.t.* **1** to force (a fluid, medicine, etc., *into* a cavity etc.) by or as by a syringe; to fill with fluid etc. thus; to administer medicine etc. to (a person) thus. **2** to introduce (a new element or quality etc.). —**injection** *n.*, **injector** *n.* [f. L *injicere* (IN-[1], *jacere* throw)]

injudicious /ɪndʒʊˈdɪʃəs/ *adj.* unwise, ill-judged. —**injudiciously** *adv.*, **injudiciousness** *n.* [f. IN-[2] + JUDICIOUS]

injunction /ɪnˈdʒʌŋkʃ(ə)n/ *n.* an authoritative order; a judicial process restraining a person from a specified act, compelling restitution, etc. [f. L (as ENJOIN)]

injure /ˈɪndʒə(r)/ *v.t.* to cause harm, damage, or hurt to; to do wrong to. [f. INJURY]

injurious /ɪnˈdʒʊərɪəs/ *adj.* causing or likely to cause injury. [f. F or L (as foll.)]

injury /ˈɪndʒərɪ/ *n.* **1** harm, damage; a particular form of this. **2** an unjust action. [f. AF f. L *injuria* (IN-[2], *jus* right)]

injustice /ɪnˈdʒʌstɪs/ *n.* lack of justice, unfairness; an unjust action. —**do a person an injustice**, to judge him unfairly. [f. OF f. L (as IN-[2], JUSTICE)]

ink *n.* **1** a black or coloured fluid used for writing, printing, etc. **2** a black liquid ejected by cuttlefish etc. —*v.t.* to mark (*in*, *over*, etc.) with ink. —**ink out**, to obliterate with ink. **ink-well** *n.* a pot for holding ink, fitted into a hole in a desk. [f. OF f. L f. Gk *egkauston* Roman emperors' purple ink (as ENCAUSTIC)]

inkling /ˈɪŋklɪŋ/ *n.* a hint, slight knowledge or suspicion (*of*). [f. obs. *inkle* utter in an undertone]

inkstand *n.* a stand for one or more ink-bottles.

inky *adj.* **1** of ink; stained with ink. **2** very black. —**inkiness** *n.* [f. INK]

inland /ˈɪnlənd, -lænd/ *adj.* **1** in the interior of a country, remote from the sea or a border. **2** within a country. —/usu. -ˈlænd/ *adv.* in or towards the interior of a country. —*n.* the interior of a country. —**inland revenue**, revenue from taxes and inland duties.

in-laws *n.pl.* (*colloq.*) relatives by marriage. [f. IN + LAW (as in *father-in-law*)]

inlay /ɪnˈleɪ/ *v.t.* (*past* & *p.p.* **inlaid**) to set or embed (pieces of wood or metal etc.) in another material so that the surfaces are level, forming a design; to decorate thus. —/ˈɪnleɪ/ *n.* **1** inlaid material or work. **2** a filling shaped to fit a tooth-cavity. [f. IN- + LAY[1]]

inlet /ˈɪnlet/ *n.* **1** a small arm of a sea, lake, or river. **2** a piece inserted. **3** a way in. [f. IN + LET[1]]

in loco parentis /ɪn ləʊkəʊ pəˈrentɪs/ in the place of a parent. [L]

inmate /ˈɪnmeɪt/ *n.* any of the occupants of a house, hospital, prison, etc. [prob. orig. f. INN + MATE[1]]

in memoriam /ɪn mɪˈmɔːrɪæm/ in memory of. [L]

inmost *adj.* most inward. [OE (as IN, -MOST)]

inn /ɪn/ *n.* a house providing lodgings etc. for payment, especially for travellers; a house providing alcoholic liquor. —**Inn of Court**, any of the four law societies in London with the exclusive right of admitting people to practise as barristers in England; a similar society in Ireland. [OE (as IN)]

innards /ˈɪnədz/ *n.pl.* (*colloq.*) inner parts, especially entrails. [f. dial. pronunc. of INWARD]

innate /ɪˈneɪt, ˈɪn-/ *adj.* inborn, natural. [f. L *innatus* (IN-[1], *nasci* be born)]

inner *adj.* nearer to the centre or inside, interior, internal. —*n.* the division of a target next outside the bull's-eye; a shot striking this. —**inner city**, the central area of a city, usually with overcrowding and poverty. **inner man** *or* **woman**, the soul, the mind; the stomach. **inner tube**, a separate inflatable tube in a pneumatic tyre. —**innermost** *adj.* [OE (compar. of IN)]

innings /ˈɪnɪŋz/ *n.* (*pl.* same) **1** the part of a game of cricket etc. in which one side or player is batting. **2** the time of power etc. of a political party etc.; the period of a person's chance to achieve something. [f. *in* v. go in]

innkeeper *n.* the keeper of an inn.

innocent /ˈɪnəs(ə)nt/ *adj.* **1** not guilty *of* a particular crime etc. **2** free of all evil or wrongdoing. **3** harmless, without guile; affectedly so. —*n.* an innocent person, especially a child. —**innocence** *n.*, **innocently** *adv.* [f. OF or L (IN-[2], *nocēre* do harm)]

innocuous /ɪˈnɒkjʊəs/ *adj.* harmless. [f. L *innocuus* (as prec.)]

innovate /ˈɪnəveɪt/ *v.i.* to bring in new methods, ideas, etc.; to make changes *in*. —**innovation** /-ˈveɪʃ(ə)n/ *n.*, **innovative** *adj.*, **innovator** *n.*, **innovatory** *adj.* [f. L *innovare* (IN-[1], *novus* new)]

innuendo /ɪnjuːˈendəʊ/ *n.* (*pl.* **-oes**) an allusive remark or hint, usually disparaging. [L, = by nodding at (IN-[1], *nuere* nod)]

innumerable /ɪˈnjuːmərəb(ə)l/ *adj.* too many to be counted. —**innumerably** *adv.* [f. L (IN-[2], *numerare* count)]

innumerate /ɪˈnjuːmərət/ *adj.* not knowing basic mathematics and science. —**innumeracy** *n.* [f. IN-[2] + NUMERATE]

inoculate /ɪˈnɒkjʊleɪt/ *v.t.* to treat (a person or animal) with a vaccine or serum, especially as a protection against disease. —**inoculation** /-ˈleɪʃ(ə)n/ *n.* [f. L *inoculare* engraft (IN-[1], *oculus* eye, bud)]

inoffensive /ɪnəˈfensɪv/ *adj.* not offensive, harmless, not objectionable. [f. IN-² + OFFENSIVE]

inoperable /ɪnˈɒpərəb(ə)l/ *adj.* that cannot be cured by surgical operation. [f. F (as IN-², OPERABLE)]

inoperative /ɪnˈɒpərətɪv/ *adj.* not working or taking effect. [f. IN-² + OPERATIVE]

inopportune /ɪnˈɒpətju:n/ *adj.* not opportune, coming or happening at an unsuitable time. —**inopportunely** *adv.* [f. L (as IN-², OPPORTUNE)]

inordinate /ɪˈnɔ:dɪnət/ *adj.* excessive. —**inordinately** *adv.* [f. L (as IN-², ORDAIN)]

inorganic /ɪnɔ:ˈgænɪk/ *adj.* **1** (of a chemical compound etc.) mineral not organic. **2** without an organized physical structure. **3** extraneous. —**inorganic chemistry**, the chemistry of inorganic substances. [f. IN-² + ORGANIC]

in-patient *n.* a patient residing in hospital during treatment.

input /ˈɪnpʊt/ *n.* **1** what is put in. **2** the place of entry of energy, information, etc. —*v.t.* (**-tt-**; *past & p.p.* **input, inputted**) to put in or *into*; to supply (data, programs, etc., *to* a computer).

inquest /ˈɪnkwest/ *n.* **1** an inquiry held by a coroner into the cause of death. **2** a prolonged discussion after misfortune, failure, etc. [as INQUIRE]

inquietude /ɪnˈkwaɪɪtju:d/ *n.* uneasiness. [f. OF or L (as IN-², QUIET)]

inquire /ɪnˈkwaɪə(r)/ *v.i.* to undertake a formal investigation (*into*). [f. OF f. L *inquirere* (*quaerere* seek)]

inquiry /ɪnˈkwaɪərɪ/ *n.* an investigation, especially an official one. [f. prec.]

inquisition /ɪŋkwɪˈzɪʃ(ə)n/ *n.* an intensive investigation or inquiry. —**Inquisition** *n.* (*hist.*) a court established for the detection and punishment of heretics. —**inquisitional** *adj.* [as INQUIRE]

inquisitive /ɪnˈkwɪzɪtɪv/ *adj.* seeking knowledge; unduly curious, prying. —**inquisitively** *adv.* [as INQUIRE]

inquisitor /ɪnˈkwɪzɪtə(r)/ *n.* one who questions searchingly; an official investigator; an officer of the Inquisition. [f. F f. L (as INQUIRE)]

inquisitorial /ɪnkwɪzɪˈtɔ:rɪəl/ *adj.* of or like an inquisitor; prying. —**inquisitorially** *adv.* [f. L (as prec.)]

in re /ɪn ri:/ = RE¹. [L, = in the matter (of)]

INRI *abbr.* Jesus of Nazareth, king of the Jews. [f. L *Iesus Nazarenus Rex Iudaeorum*]

inroad *n.* **1** a hostile incursion. **2** (often in *pl.*) an encroachment; the using up of resources etc. [f. IN + ROAD (in sense 'riding')]

inrush *n.* a violent influx.

insalubrious /ɪnsəˈlu:brɪəs/ *adj.* (of a place or climate etc.) unhealthy. [f. L (as IN-², SALUBRIOUS)]

insane /ɪnˈseɪn/ *adj.* **1** not sane, mad. **2** very foolish. —**insanely** *adv.*, **insanity** /-ˈsænɪtɪ/ *n.* [f. L (as IN-², SANE)]

insanitary /ɪnˈsænɪtərɪ/ *adj.* unclean and likely to be harmful to health. [f. IN-² + SANITARY]

insatiable /ɪnˈseɪʃəb(ə)l/ *adj.* that cannot be satisfied, very greedy. —**insatiability** /-ˈbɪlɪtɪ/ *n.*, **insatiably** *adv.* [f. OF or L (as IN-², SATIABLE)]

insatiate /ɪnˈseɪʃɪət/ *adj.* never satisfied. [f. L (as IN-², SATIATE)]

inscribe /ɪnˈskraɪb/ *v.t.* **1** to write (words etc. *in* or *on* a surface); to mark (a surface *with* characters). **2** to draw (a geometrical figure) within another so that points of it lie on the other's boundary. **3** to enter (a name) on a list or in a book. **4** to place an informal dedication in or on (a book etc.). [f. L *inscribere* (IN-¹, *scribere* write)]

inscription /ɪnˈskrɪpʃ(ə)n/ *n.* **1** words inscribed. **2** inscribing. —**inscriptional** *adj.* [f. L (as prec.)]

inscrutable /ɪnˈskru:təb(ə)l/ *adj.* baffling, impossible to understand or interpret. —**inscrutability** /-ˈbɪlɪtɪ/ *n.*, **inscrutably** *adv.* [f. L (IN-², *scrutari* search)]

insect /ˈɪnsekt/ *n.* any of a class of small invertebrate animals of the phylum Arthropoda, typically having six legs, two or four wings, and a body divided into three sections: head, thorax, and abdomen. [f. L *insectum* notched (animal) (IN-¹, *secare* cut)]

insecticide /ɪnˈsektɪsaɪd/ *n.* a substance for killing insects. [f. prec. + -CIDE]

insectivore /ɪnˈsektɪvɔ:(r)/ *n.* an animal that feeds on insects and other small creatures; a plant that traps and absorbs insects. —**insectivorous** /-ˈtɪvərəs/ *adj.* [F (as INSECT, L *vorare* devour)]

insecure /ɪnsɪˈkjʊə(r)/ *adj.* **1** not secure or safe or dependable. **2** feeling a lack of security, constantly anxious. —**insecurely** *adv.*, **insecurity** *n.* [f. L (as IN-², SECURE)]

inseminate /ɪnˈsemɪneɪt/ *v.t.* **1** to impregnate with semen. **2** to sow (a seed etc., *lit.* & *fig.*, *in*). —**insemination** /-ˈneɪʃ(ə)n/ *n.* [f. L *inseminare* (as IN-¹, SEMEN)]

insensate /ɪnˈsenseɪt/ *adj.* **1** without sensibility, unfeeling. **2** stupid. **3** without physical sensation. [f. L (as IN-², SENSE)]

insensible /ɪnˈsensɪb(ə)l/ *adj.* **1** unconscious. **2** unaware (*of*, *to*, *how*). **3** callous. **4** too small or gradual to be perceived. —**insensibility** /-ˈbɪlɪtɪ/ *n.*, **insensibly** *adv.* [f. OF or L (as IN-², SENSIBLE)]

insensitive /ɪnˈsensɪtɪv/ *adj.* not sensitive. —**insensitively** *adv.*, **insensitivity** /-ˈtɪvɪtɪ/ *n.* [f. IN-² + SENSITIVE]

insentient /ɪnˈsenʃ(ə)nt/ *adj.* not sentient. [f. IN-² + SENTIENT]

inseparable /ɪnˈsepərəb(ə)l/ *adj.* **1** that cannot be separated. **2** liking to be constantly together. —*n.* (usu. in *pl.*) an inseparable person or thing, especially a friend. —**inseparability** /-ˈbɪlɪtɪ/ *n.*, **inseparably** *adv.* [f. L (as IN-², SEPARABLE)]

insert /ɪnˈsɜːt/ *v.t.* to place or put (one thing into another). —/ˈɪnsɜːt/ *n.* the thing inserted. [f. L *inserere* (IN-¹, *serere* join)]

insertion /ɪnˈsɜːʃ(ə)n/ *n.* **1** inserting. **2** a thing inserted. [f. L (as prec.)]

inset /ˈɪnset/ *n.* an extra piece inserted in a book, garment, etc.; a small map etc. within the border of a larger one. —/ɪnˈset/ *v.t.* (**-tt-**; *past & p.p.* **inset** or **insetted**) to put in as an inset; to decorate with an inset.

inshore *adj.* & *adv.* near the shore.

inside *n.* **1** the inner side, surface, or part. **2** a position on the inner side. **3** (in *sing.* or *pl.*, *colloq.*) the stomach and bowels. **4** (of a path) the side away from the road. —*adj.* of or on or in the inside; nearer to the centre of a games field. —*adv.* **1** on, to, or in the inside. **2** (*slang*) in prison. —*prep.* **1** within, on the inside of. **2** in less than. —**inside information,** information not accessible to outsiders. **inside job,** (*colloq.*) a burglary etc. by one living or working on the premises. **inside out,** turned so that the inner side becomes the outer.

insider *n.* a person within a group or a society etc.; one who is in the secret. [f. prec.]

insidious /ɪnˈsɪdɪəs/ *adj.* **1** proceeding inconspicuously but harmfully. **2** crafty. —**insidiously** *adv.*, **insidiousness** *n.* [f. L, = cunning (*insidiae* ambush)]

insight *n.* **1** the ability to perceive and understand a thing's true nature; mental penetration. **2** a piece of knowledge obtained by this.

insignia /ɪnˈsɪgnɪə/ *n.pl.* badges or emblems of rank, office, etc. [L (*insignis* distinguished)]

insignificant /ɪnsɪgˈnɪfɪkənt/ *adj.* of no importance or meaning; worthless, trivial. —**insignificance** *n.*, **insignificantly** *adv.* [f. IN-² + SIGNIFICANT]

insincere /ɪnsɪnˈsɪə(r)/ *adj.* not sincere or candid. —**insincerely** *adv.*, **insincerity** /-ˈserɪtɪ/ *n.* [f. L (as IN-², SINCERE)]

insinuate /ɪnˈsɪnjʊeɪt/ *v.t.* **1** to hint obliquely or unpleasantly. **2** to insert gradually or stealthily. —**insinuation** /-ˈeɪʃ(ə)n/ *n.* [f. L *insinuare* (IN-¹, *sinuare* curve)]

insipid /ɪnˈsɪpɪd/ *adj.* **1** lacking in flavour. **2** dull, without liveliness. —**insipidity** /-ˈpɪdɪtɪ/ *n.*, **insipidly** *adv.* [f. F or L (as IN-², SAPID)]

insist /ɪnˈsɪst/ *v.t./i.* to demand or declare emphatically. [f. L *insistere* (IN-¹, *sistere* stand)]

insistent *adj.* **1** insisting. **2** forcing itself upon the attention. —**insistence** *n.*, **insistently** *adv.* [f. prec.]

in situ /ɪn ˈsɪtjuː/ in its original place. [L]

insobriety /ɪnsəˈbraɪətɪ/ *n.* intemperance, especially in drinking. [f. IN-² + SOBRIETY]

insofar /ɪnsəʊˈfɑː(r)/ *adv.* in so far (see FAR).

insolation /ɪnsəˈleɪʃ(ə)n/ *n.* exposure to the sun's rays. [f. L *insolare* (IN-¹, *sol* sun)]

insole /ˈɪnsəʊl/ *n.* the inner sole of a boot or shoe; a removable inner sole for use in a shoe. [f. IN + SOLE¹]

insolent /ˈɪnsələnt/ *adj.* impertinently insulting. —**insolence** *n.*, **insolently** *adv.* [f. L, = unaccustomed, immoderate (IN-², *solere* be accustomed)]

insoluble /ɪnˈsɒljʊb(ə)l/ *adj.* that cannot be dissolved or solved. —**insolubility** /-ˈbɪlɪtɪ/ *n.*, **insolubly** *adv.* [f. OF or L (as IN-², SOLUBLE)]

insolvent /ɪnˈsɒlv(ə)nt/ *adj.* unable to pay debts. —*n.* an insolvent debtor. —**insolvency** *n.* [f. IN-² + SOLVENT]

insomnia /ɪnˈsɒmnɪə/ *n.* habitual sleeplessness. [L (IN-², *somnus* sleep)]

insomniac /ɪnˈsɒmnɪæk/ *n.* a person suffering from insomnia. [f. prec.]

insomuch /ɪnsəʊˈmʌtʃ/ *adv.* to such an extent *that*; inasmuch *as*. [orig. *in so much*]

insouciant /ɪnˈsuːsɪənt/ *adj.* carefree, unconcerned. —**insouciance** *n.* [F (IN-², *soucier* care)]

inspan /ɪnˈspæn/ *v.t.* (**-nn-**) (*S.Afr.*) to yoke (oxen etc.) in a team to a vehicle; to harness animals to (a wagon). [f. Du. (as IN-¹, SPAN¹)]

inspect /ɪnˈspekt/ *v.t.* to examine carefully and critically, especially looking for faults; to examine officially; to visit in order to see that rules and standards are being observed. —**inspection** *n.* [f. L *inspicere* (IN-¹, *specere* look at)]

inspector *n.* **1** a person employed to inspect or supervise. **2** a police officer next above sergeant. —**inspector of taxes,** an official assessing income tax payable. [as prec.]

inspiration /ɪnspɪˈreɪʃ(ə)n/ *n.* **1** inspiring. **2** a sudden brilliant idea. **3** a source of inspiring influence. [as foll.]

inspire /ɪnˈspaɪə(r)/ *v.t.* **1** to stimulate (a person) to creative or other activity. **2** to animate (a person etc. *with* a feeling); to instil thought or feeling into (a person). **3** to breathe (air etc.) in. [f. OF f. L *inspirare* (IN-¹, *spirare* breathe)]

inspirit /ɪnˈspɪrɪt/ *v.t.* to put life into, to animate; to encourage. —**inspiriting** *adj.* [f. IN-¹ + SPIRIT]

inst. *abbr.* instant (= of the current month, *the 6th inst.*).

instability /ɪnˈstəbɪlɪtɪ/ *n.* lack of stability or firmness. [f. F f. L (as IN-², STABILITY)]

install /ɪnˈstɔːl/ *v.t.* **1** to place (a person) formally or ceremonially in office. **2** to fix or establish (a person, equipment, etc.). —**installation** /ɪnstəˈleɪʃ(ə)n/ *n.* [f. L *installare* (as IN-¹, STALL)]

instalment /ɪnˈstɔːlmənt/ *n.* any of the successive parts in which a sum is (to be) paid; any of the parts of a whole successively delivered, published, etc. [f. AF *estalement* (*estaler* fix)]

instance /ɪnst(ə)ns/ *n.* an example, an illustration of a general truth; a particular case. —*v.t.* to cite as an instance. —**in the first instance**, as the first stage (in a process). [f. OF f. L (as foll.)]

instant /ˈɪnst(ə)nt/ *adj.* **1** immediate. **2** (of food) that can be prepared easily for immediate use. **3** of the current month. —*n.* **1** a precise moment. **2** a short time, a moment. [f. F f. L *instare* be urgent]

instantaneous /ɪnstənˈteɪnɪəs/ *adj.* occurring or done in an instant. —**instantaneously** *adv.* [f. L (as prec.)]

instantly *adv.* immediately. [f. INSTANT]

instead /ɪnˈsted/ *adv.* as an alternative or substitute. [f. IN + STEAD]

instep /ˈɪnstep/ *n.* the top of the foot between the toes and the ankle; the part of a shoe etc. over or under this. [ult. as IN-¹ + STEP]

instigate /ˈɪnstɪgeɪt/ *v.t.* to incite or persuade; to bring about thus. —**instigation** /-ˈgeɪʃ(ə)n/ *n.*, **instigator** *n.* [f. L *instigare* (IN-¹, *stigare* prick)]

instil /ɪnˈstɪl/ *v.t.* (**-ll-**) **1** to put (ideas etc. *into* the mind etc.) gradually. **2** to put *into* by drops. —**instillation** /-ˈleɪʃ(ə)n/ *n.*, **instilment** *n.* [f. L *instillare* (IN-¹, *stilla* drop)]

instinct /ˈɪnstɪŋkt/ *n.* an innate propensity, especially in lower animals, to seemingly rational acts; an innate impulse or behaviour; intuition. —/ɪnˈstɪŋkt/ *adj.* filled or charged (*with* life, energy, etc.). —**instinctive** /ɪnˈstɪŋktɪv/ *adj.*, **instinctively** *adv.*, **instinctual** /ɪnˈstɪŋktjʊəl/ *adj.*, **instinctually** *adv.* [f. L *instinctus* (IN-¹, *stinguere* prick)]

institute /ˈɪnstɪtjuːt/ *n.* **1** an organized body for the promotion of an educational, scientific, or similar object. **2** its building. —*v.t.* **1** to establish, to found. **2** to initiate (an inquiry etc.). **3** to appoint (a person *to* or *into* a benefice). —**institutor** *n.* [f. L *instituere* (IN-¹, *statuere* set up)]

institution /ɪnstɪˈtjuːʃ(ə)n/ *n.* **1** instituting, being instituted. **2** an organized body, especially with a charitable purpose. **3** an established law, custom, or practice. **4** (*colloq.*) a person who has become a familiar figure in some activity. [f. OF f. L (as prec.)]

institutional *adj.* of or like an institution; typical of charitable institutions. —**institutionally** *adv.* [f. prec.]

institutionalize *v.t.* to make institutional; to place or keep (a person needing care) in an institution. [f. prec.]

instruct /ɪnˈstrʌkt/ *v.t.* **1** to give instruction to (a person *in* a subject or skill). **2** to inform. **3** to give instructions to. **4** to authorize (a solicitor or counsel) to act on one's behalf. —**instructor** *n.*, **instructress** *n.fem.* [f. L *instruere* furnish, teach (as IN-¹, STRUCTURE)]

instruction /ɪnˈstrʌkʃ(ə)n/ *n.* **1** the process of teaching. **2** knowledge or teaching imparted. **3** (usu. in *pl.*) statements making known to a person what he is required to do; orders. —**instructional** *adj.* [f. OF f. L (as prec.)]

instructive /ɪnˈstrʌktɪv/ *adj.* tending to instruct, enlightening. [f. INSTRUCT]

instrument /ˈɪnstrumənt/ *n.* **1** a tool or implement, especially for delicate or scientific work. **2** a device for measuring or controlling the function of a machine or aircraft etc. **3** a device for giving controlled musical sounds. **4** a thing used in an action; a person used and controlled by another to perform an action. **5** a formal or legal document. [f. OF or L (as INSTRUCT)]

instrumental /ɪnstruˈment(ə)l/ *adj.* **1** serving as an instrument or means. **2** (of music) performed on instruments. **3** of or due to an instrument. **4** (*Gram.*, of a case) denoting the means. [f. F f. L (as prec.)]

instrumentalist *n.* a performer on a musical instrument. [f. prec.]

instrumentality /ɪnstrumenˈtælɪtɪ/ *n.* agency or means. [f. INSTRUMENTAL]

instrumentation /ɪnstrumenˈteɪʃ(ə)n/ *n.* **1** the arrangement of music for instruments. **2** the provision or use of mechanical or scientific instruments. [F, as INSTRUMENT]

insubordinate /ɪnsəˈbɔːdɪnət/ *adj.* disobedient, rebellious. —**insubordination** /-ˈneɪʃ(ə)n/ *n.* [f. IN-² + SUBORDINATE]

insubstantial /ɪnsəbˈstænʃ(ə)l/ *adj.* **1** not existing in reality. **2** not strongly made, lacking solidity. [f. L (as IN-², SUBSTANTIAL)]

insufferable /ɪnˈsʌfərəb(ə)l/ *adj.* **1** intolerable. **2** unbearably conceited or arrogant. —**insufferably** *adv.* [f. IN-² + SUFFERABLE]

insufficient /ɪnsəˈfɪʃ(ə)nt/ *adj.* not sufficient. —**insufficiency** *n.*, **insufficiently** *adv.* [f. OF f. L (as IN-², SUFFICIENT)]

insufflate /ˈɪnsʌfleɪt/ *v.t.* to blow or breathe (air, gas, powder, etc.) into a cavity of the body; to treat thus. —**insufflation** /-ˈfleɪʃ(ə)n/ *n.*, **insufflator** *n.* [f. L *insufflare* (IN-¹, *sufflare* blow upon)]

insular /ˈɪnsjʊlə(r)/ *adj.* **1** of or on an island; forming an island. **2** of or like islanders; unable or unwilling to take a broad mental view. —**insularity** /-ˈlærɪtɪ/ *n.* [as foll.]

insulate /ˈɪnsjuleɪt/ *v.t.* to isolate, especially with a substance or device preventing the passage of electricity, heat, or sound. —**insulation** /-ˈleɪʃ(ə)n/ n., **insulator** *n.* [f. L *insula* island]

insulin /ˈɪnsjʊlɪn/ *n.* a hormone produced in the pancreas and having effects that include the removal of sugar from the blood (so that a deficiency of insulin causes diabetes mellitus). [f. L *insula* island (because it is produced by the islets of Langerhans)]

insult /ɪnˈsʌlt/ *v.t.* **1** to abuse scornfully. **2** to offend the self-respect or modesty of. **3** to affect and damage (an organ etc. of the body). —/ˈɪnsʌlt/ *n.* **1** an insulting remark or action. **2** damage to the body; a substance causing this. [f. L *insultare* leap upon, assail]

insuperable /ɪnˈsuːpərəb(ə)l/ *adj.* (of a barrier, difficulty, etc.) that cannot be surmounted or overcome. —**insuperability** /-ˈbɪlɪtɪ/ *n.*, **insuperably** *adv.* [f. OF or L (IN-², *superare* overcome)]

insupportable /ɪnsəˈpɔːtəb(ə)l/ *adj.* unbearable; unjustifiable. —**insupportably** *adv.* [F (as IN-², SUPPORT)]

insurable /ɪnˈʃʊərəb(ə)l/ *adj.* that may be insured. [f. INSURE]

insurance /ɪnˈʃʊərəns/ *n.* **1** a procedure or contract securing compensation for loss, damage, or injury, etc., especially in return for a premium paid in advance. **2** the business of providing this. **3** the sum paid to effect such a contract, a premium. **4** the amount paid in compensation. [f. OF (as ENSURE)]

insure /ɪnˈʃʊə(r)/ *v.t.* to effect insurance *against* or with respect to. —**insurer** *n.* [var. of ENSURE]

insurgent /ɪnˈsɜːdʒənt/ *n.* a rebel. —*adj.* in revolt, rebellious. —**insurgence** *n.*, **insurgency** *n.* [F f. L (IN-¹, *surgere* rise)]

insurmountable /ɪnsəˈmaʊntəb(ə)l/ *adj.* unable to be surmounted, insuperable. [f. IN-² + SURMOUNTABLE]

insurrection /ɪnsəˈrekʃ(ə)n/ *n.* a rising in open resistance to established authority, an incipient rebellion. —**insurrectionist** *n.* [f. OF f. L (as INSURGENT)]

insusceptible /ɪnsəˈseptɪb(ə)l/ *adj.* not susceptible. [f. IN-² + SUSCEPTIBLE]

intact /ɪnˈtækt/ *adj.* **1** undamaged, unimpaired. **2** entire. **3** untouched. [f. L (IN-², *tangere* touch)]

intaglio /ɪnˈtɑːlɪəʊ/ *n.* (*pl.* **-os**) an engraved design; a gem with an incised design. [It. (IN-¹, *tagliare* cut)]

intake /ˈɪnteɪk/ *n.* **1** the action of taking in. **2** the place where water is taken into a pipe, fuel or air into an engine etc. **3** the persons, things, or quantity taken in or received.

intangible /ɪnˈtændʒɪb(ə)l/ *adj.* that cannot be touched or mentally grasped. —**intangibly** *adv.* [F or f. L (as IN-², TANGIBLE)]

integer /ˈɪntɪdʒə(r)/ *n.* a whole number. [L, = untouched, whole]

integral /ˈɪntɪgr(ə)l/ *adj.* **1** of or necessary to a whole. **2** complete, forming a whole. **3** of or denoted by an integer. —*n.* (*Math.*) a quantity of which a given function is a derivative. —**integral calculus**, the branch of calculus concerned with finding integrals, their properties, etc. —**integrally** *adv.* [f. L (as prec.)]

integrate /ˈɪntɪgreɪt/ *v.t./i.* **1** to combine (parts) into a whole. **2** to bring or come into equal membership of a community; to end racial segregation (of or at). **3** to complete by the addition of parts. **4** (*Math.*) to find the integral of. —**integrated circuit**, a small piece of material replacing a conventional electric circuit of many components. —**integration** /-ˈreɪʃ(ə)n/ *n.* [f. L *integrare* make whole (as INTEGER)]

integrity /ɪnˈtegrɪtɪ/ *n.* **1** honesty. **2** wholeness; soundness. [f. F or L (as INTEGER)]

integument /ɪnˈtegjʊmənt/ *n.* a skin, husk, rind, or other covering. [f. L (*integere* cover)]

intellect /ˈɪntɪlekt/ *n.* **1** the faculty of knowing and reasoning. **2** ability to use this well; a person with such ability. [f. OF or L (as INTELLIGENT)]

intellectual /ɪntɪˈlektjʊəl/ *adj.* of, requiring, or using the intellect; having a highly developed intellect. —*n.* an intellectual person. —**intellectuality** /-ˈælɪtɪ/ *n.*, **intellectually** *adv.* [f. L (as prec.)]

intellectualism *n.* **1** (esp. excessive) exercise of the intellect alone. **2** the theory that knowledge is wholly or mainly derived from pure intellect. —**intellectualist** *n.* [f. prec.]

intelligence /ɪnˈtelɪdʒ(ə)ns/ *n.* **1** mental ability, the power of learning; quickness of understanding. **2** information, news; the collection of this, especially for military purposes; persons engaged in such collection. —**intelligence quotient**, the ratio of a given person's intelligence to the normal or average. **intelligence test**, a test designed to measure intelligence rather than acquired knowledge. [f. OF f. L (as foll.)]

intelligent /ɪnˈtelɪdʒ(ə)nt/ *adj.* having or showing great intelligence, clever. —**intelligently** *adv.* [f. L *intellegere* understand]

intelligentsia /ɪntelɪˈdʒentsɪə/ *n.* intellectuals as a class, especially those regarded as cultured and politically enterprising. [Russ. f. Polish f. L (as INTELLIGENCE)]

intelligible /ɪnˈtelɪdʒɪb(ə)l/ *adj.* that can be understood. —**intelligibility** /-ˈbɪlɪtɪ/ *n.*, **intelligibly** *adv.* [as INTELLIGENT]

intemperate /ɪnˈtempərət/ *adj.* **1** lacking moderation. **2** excessive in indulging the appetite; addicted to drinking. —**intemperance** *n.*, **intemperately** *adv.* [f. L (as IN-², TEMPERATE)]

intend /ɪnˈtend/ *v.t.* **1** to have as one's purpose or wish. **2** to plan or destine (a person or thing *for* a purpose, *as* something, *to do*). [f. L *intendere* (IN-¹, *tendere* stretch, tend)]

intended *adj.* done on purpose. —*n.* (*colloq.*) a fiancé(e). [f. prec.]

intense /ɪnˈtens/ *adj.* **1** strong in quality or degree, violent, vehement; having a quality strongly. **2** eager, ardent, strenuous. **3** feeling or apt to feel emotion strongly. —**intensely** *adv.*, **intenseness** *n.* [f. OF or L (as INTEND)]

intensify /ɪnˈtensɪfaɪ/ *v.t./i.* to make or become intense or more intense. —**intensification** /-fɪˈkeɪʃ(ə)n/ *n.* [f. prec.]

intensity /ɪnˈtensɪtɪ/ *n.* **1** intenseness. **2** amount of force, brightness, etc. [f. prec.]

intensive /ɪnˈtensɪv/ *adj.* **1** employing much effort, concentrated. **2** (of words) giving emphasis. **3** (as *suffix*) making much use of (*labour-intensive*). —**intensive care,** medical treatment with constant supervision of the patient. —**intensively** *adv.* [f. F or L (as INTEND)]

intent /ɪnˈtent/ *n.* intention. —*adj.* **1** with one's mind or intention fixed *on* a purpose. **2** with one's attention concentrated (*on*); earnest, eager. —**to all intents and purposes,** virtually, practically. —**intently** *adv.*, **intentness** *n.* [f. OF or L (as INTEND)]

intention /ɪnˈtenʃ(ə)n/ *n.* **1** a thing intended, a purpose. **2** intending. [f. OF f. L (as INTEND)]

intentional *adj.* done on purpose, intended. —**intentionally** *adv.* [f. prec.]

inter /ɪnˈtɜː(r)/ *v.t.* (**-rr-**) to place (a corpse etc.) in the earth or a tomb, to bury. [f. OF *enterrer* f. L *terra* earth]

inter- *prefix* between, among, mutually, reciprocally. [f. OF *entre-* or L *inter-*]

interact /ɪntərˈækt/ *v.i.* to act on each other. —**interaction** *n.*, **interactive** *adj.*

inter alia /ɪntə(r) ˈeɪlɪə/ among other things. [L]

interbreed /ɪntəˈbriːd/ *v.t./i.* to breed with each other; to cause animals to do this; to produce (a hybrid individual).

intercalary /ɪntəˈkælərɪ/ *adj.* (of a day or days or month) inserted to harmonize the calendar with the solar year; (of a year) having such additions; interpolated. [f. L (as foll.)]

intercalate /ɪnˈtɜːkəleɪt/ *v.t.* to interpose; to insert (an intercalary day etc.). —**intercalation** /-ˈleɪʃ(ə)n/ *n.* [f. L *intercalare* (INTER-, *calare* proclaim)]

intercede /ɪntəˈsiːd/ *v.i.* to interpose on another's behalf, to mediate; to plead (*with* a person *for* another). [f. F or L *intercedere* (INTER-, *cedere* go)]

intercept /ɪntəˈsept/ *v.t.* to seize, catch, or stop in transit or progress; to cut off (light etc. *from*). —/ˈɪntəsept/ *n.* **1** a message or conversation picked up by intercepting a letter or a telephone or radio conversation. **2** a device for performing such interception. —**interception** *n.*, **interceptive** *adj.*, **interceptor** *n.* [f. L *intercipere* (INTER-, *capere* catch)]

intercession /ɪntəˈseʃ(ə)n/ *n.* interceding. —**intercessor** *n.* [F or f. L (as INTERCEDE)]

interchange /ɪntəˈtʃeɪndʒ/ *v.t.* **1** to put (things) in each other's place. **2** (of two persons) to exchange (things) with each other. **3** to alternate. —/ˈɪntətʃeɪndʒ/ *n.* **1** an exchange (*of* things) between persons etc. **2** alternation. **3** a junction of roads on different levels. —**interchangeability** /-əˈbɪlɪtɪ/ *n.*, **interchangeable** *adj.*

inter-city /ɪntəˈsɪtɪ/ *adj.* existing or travelling between cities.

intercom /ˈɪntəkɒm/ *n.* (*colloq.*) a system of inter-communication operating like a telephone. [abbr.]

intercommunicate /ɪntəkəˈmjuːnɪkeɪt/ *v.i.* to communicate mutually; to have free passage into each other. —**intercommunication** /-ˈkeɪʃ(ə)n/ *n.*

intercommunion /ɪntəkəˈm- juːnɪən/ *n.* mutual communion, especially between Christian denominations.

interconnect /ɪntəkəˈnekt/ *v.t./i.* to connect with each other. —**interconnection** *n.*

intercontinental /ɪntəkɒntɪˈnent(ə)l/ *adj.* connecting or travelling between continents.

intercourse /ˈɪntəkɔːs/ *n.* **1** social communication between individuals. **2** communication between countries etc., especially in trade. **3** sexual intercourse (see SEXUAL).

interdenominational /ɪntədɪnɒmɪˈneɪʃən(ə)l/ *adj.* of or involving more than one Christian denomination.

interdepartmental /ɪntədiːpɑːtˈment(ə)l/ *adj.* of more than one department.

interdependent /ɪntədɪˈpend(ə)nt/ *adj.* dependent on each other. —**interdependence** *n.*, **interdependency** *n.*

interdict /ɪntəˈdɪkt/ *v.t.* to prohibit or forbid authoritatively. —/ˈɪntədɪkt/ *n.* an authoritative prohibition; (*RC Church*) a sentence debarring a person or place from ecclesiastical functions etc. —**interdiction** /-ˈdɪkʃ(ə)n/ *n.*, **interdictory** /-ˈdɪktərɪ/ *adj.* [f. OF f. L (INTER-, *dicere* say)]

interdisciplinary /ɪntədɪsɪˈplɪnərɪ/ *adj.* of or involving different branches of learning.

interest /ˈɪntrəst/ *n.* **1** a feeling of curiosity or concern; a quality causing this; the thing towards which one feels it. **2** advantage, benefit. **3** money paid for the use of a loan of money. **4** a legal concern, title, or right (*in* property); a money stake (*in* a business); a thing in which one has a stake or concern. —*v.t.* to arouse the interest of; to cause to be interested or involved (*in*). —**compound interest,** interest (on a loan) reckoned on the principal and accumulations of interest. **simple interest,** interest reckoned on the principal only and paid at fixed intervals. [f. AF f. L, = it matters]

interested *adj.* **1** feeling interest or curiosity. **2** having a private interest, not impartial. [f. prec.]

interesting *adj.* causing curiosity, holding the attention. [f. INTEREST]

interface *n.* **1** a surface forming the common boundary of two regions. **2** a place or piece of equipment where interaction occurs between two systems etc.

interfere /ɪntəˈfɪə(r)/ *v.i.* **1** to take part in dealing with others' affairs without right or invitation. **2** to obstruct wholly or partially. [f. OF, = strike one another (f. L INTER-, *ferire* strike)]

interference *n.* **1** interfering. **2** the fading of received radio signals because of atmospherics or unwanted signals. [f. prec.]

interferon /ɪntəˈfɪərɒn/ *n.* a protein released by an animal cell, usually in response to the entry of a virus, which has the property of inhibiting further development of viruses of any kind in the animal or in others of the same species. [f. INTERFERE]

interfuse /ɪntəˈfju:z/ *v.t./i.* to intersperse; to blend. —**interfusion** *n.* [f. L *interfundere* (INTER-, *fundere* pour)]

interglacial /ɪntəˈgleɪʃ(ə)l/ *n.* a period of milder climate between glacial periods.

interim /ˈɪntərɪm/ *n.* the intervening time. —*adj.* temporary, provisional. [L, = meanwhile]

interior /ɪnˈtɪərɪə(r)/ *n.* **1** the inner part, the inside. **2** an inland region. **3** the inside of a room etc.; a picture of this. **4** the home affairs of a country. —*adj.* **1** situated or coming from within. **2** further in. **3** inland. **4** internal, domestic. **5** existing in the mind. [L, compar. of *inter* among]

interject /ɪntəˈdʒekt/ *v.t.* to put in (words) abruptly or parenthetically. [f. L *interjicere* (INTER-, *jacere* throw)]

interjection /ɪntəˈdʒekʃ(ə)n/ *n.* an exclamation, especially as a part of speech (e.g. *ah, whew*). [f. OF f. L (as prec.)]

interlace /ɪntəˈleɪs/ *v.t./i.* to bind intricately together, to interweave; to cross each other intricately. —**interlacement** *n.*

interlard /ɪntəˈlɑ:d/ *v.t.* to mix (writing or speech *with* unusual words or phrases).

interleave /ɪntəˈli:v/ *v.t.* to insert leaves, usually blank, between the leaves of (a book). [f. INTER- + LEAF]

interlinear /ɪntəˈlɪnɪə(r)/ *adj.* written or printed between the lines of a text.

interlink /ɪntəˈlɪŋk/ *v.t./i.* to link together.

interlock /ɪntəˈlɒk/ *v.t./i.* to engage with each other by overlapping; to lock or clasp in each other. —*adj.* (of a fabric) knitted with closely interlocking stitches. —*n.* such a fabric. [f. INTER- + LOCK[1]]

interlocutor /ɪntəˈlɒkjʊtə(r)/ *n.* one who takes part in a conversation. [f. L (INTER-, *loqui* speak)]

interlocutory /ɪntəˈlɒkjʊtərɪ/ *adj.* **1** of dialogue. **2** (of a decree etc.) given in the course of a legal action. [f. L (as prec.)]

interloper /ˈɪntələʊpə(r)/ *n.* an intruder, one who thrusts himself into others' affairs, especially for profit. [f. INTER- + *loper* (as in *landloper* vagabond, f. Du.)]

interlude /ˈɪntəlu:d/ *n.* **1** a pause between the parts of a play etc.; something performed during this. **2** an intervening time or event of a different character. **3** a piece of music played between the verses of a hymn etc. [f. L *interludium* (INTER-, *ludus* play)]

intermarry /ɪntəˈmærɪ/ *v.i.* (of tribes, nations, families, etc.) to become connected by marriage. —**intermarriage** *n.*

intermediary /ɪntəˈmi:dɪərɪ/ *n.* **1** a mediator. **2** an intermediate thing. —*adj.* **1** acting as a mediator. **2** intermediate. [f. F ult. f. L *intermedius* (INTER-, *medius* middle)]

intermediate /ɪntəˈmi:dɪət/ *adj.* coming between two things in time, place, character, etc. —*n.* **1** an intermediate thing. **2** a chemical compound formed by one reaction and then taking part in another. [f. L (as prec.)]

interment /ɪnˈtɜ:mənt/ *n.* a burial. [f. INTER]

intermezzo /ɪntəˈmetsəʊ/ *n.* (*pl.* **-zzi** /-tsi:/) **1** a short connecting movement in a musical work, or a similar but independent piece. **2** a short light dramatic or other performance between the acts of a play or opera. [It. (as INTERMEDIARY)]

interminable /ɪnˈtɜ:mɪnəb(ə)l/ *adj.* tediously long; endless. —**interminably** *adv.* [f. L (as IN-[2], TERMINABLE)]

intermingle /ɪntəˈmɪŋg(ə)l/ *v.t./i.* to mix together, to mingle.

intermission /ɪntəˈmɪʃ(ə)n/ *n.* an interval, a pause in work or action. [F or f. L (as foll.)]

intermittent /ɪntəˈmɪt(ə)nt/ *adj.* occurring at intervals, not continuous. —**intermittently** *adv.* [f. L (INTER-, *mittere* let go)]

intermix /ɪntəˈmɪks/ *v.t./i.* to mix together.

intern /ɪnˈtɜ:n/ *v.t.* to oblige (a prisoner, alien, etc.) to live within prescribed limits.

—/ˈɪntɜːn/ *n.* (*US*) a recent graduate or advanced student living in a hospital and acting as an assistant physician or surgeon. —**internment** *n.* [f. F (as foll.)]

internal /ɪnˈtɜːn(ə)l/ *adj.* **1** of or in the inside or invisible part. **2** relating or applied to the interior of the body. **3** of a country's domestic affairs. **4** of students attending a university as well as taking its examinations. **5** used or applying within an organization. **6** intrinsic. **7** of the mind or soul. —**internal-combustion engine,** an engine in which motive power comes from an explosion of gas or vapour with air in the cylinder of an engine. —**internal evidence,** evidence derived from the contents of the thing discussed. —**internality** /-ˈnælɪtɪ/ *n.*, **internally** *adv.* [f. L *internus*]

international /ɪntəˈnæʃən(ə)l/ *adj.* existing or carried on between nations; agreed on or used by all or many nations. —*n.* **1** a contest, usually in sport, between representatives of different nations. **2** such a representative. —**International** *n.* an international Socialist organization. —**internationality** /-ˈnælɪtɪ/ *n.*, **internationally** *adv.*

internationalism *n.* **1** advocacy of the community of interests among nations. **2** support of an International. —**internationalist** *n.* [f. INTERNATIONAL]

internationalize *v.t.* to make international; to bring under the protection or control of two or more nations. [f. INTERNATIONAL]

internecine /ɪntəˈniːsaɪn/ *adj.* mutually destructive. [orig. = deadly, murderous; f. L (INTER-, *necare* kill)]

internee /ɪntɜːˈniː/ *n.* a person interned. [f. INTERN]

internist /ɪnˈtɜːnɪst/ *n.* a specialist in internal diseases; (*US*) a general practitioner. [f. INTERNAL]

interpenetrate /ɪntəˈpenɪtreɪt/ *v.t./i.* to penetrate each other; to pervade. —**interpenetration** /-ˈtreɪʃ(ə)n/ *n.*

interpersonal /ɪntəˈpɜːs(ə)n(ə)l/ *adj.* between persons.

interplanetary /ɪntəˈplænɪtərɪ/ *adj.* between planets; of travel between planets.

interplay /ˈɪntəpleɪ *n.* interaction.

Interpol /ˈɪntəpɒl/ *n.* International Criminal Police Commission, an organization (founded in 1923, with headquarters in Paris) that co-ordinates investigations made by the police forces of member countries into crimes with an international basis. [abbr. *Inter*national *pol*ice]

interpolate /ɪnˈtɜːpəleɪt/ *v.t.* **1** to interject. **2** to insert (new material) misleadingly into a book etc.; to make such insertions in (a book). **3** to insert (terms) in a mathematical series; to estimate (values) from known ones in the same range. —**interpolation** /-ˈleɪʃ(ə)n/ *n.*, **interpolator** *n.* [f. L *interpolare* furbish up (INTER-, *-polare* rel. to *polire* polish)]

interpose /ɪntəˈpəʊz/ *v.t./i.* **1** to insert (a thing *between* others). **2** to say (words) as an interruption; to speak thus. **3** to exercise or advance (a veto or objection) so as to interfere. **4** to intervene (*between* parties). —**interposition** /-pəˈzɪʃ(ə)n/ *n.* [f. F f. L *interponere* (INTER-, *ponere* put)]

interpret /ɪnˈtɜːprɪt/ *v.t./i.* **1** to explain the meaning of. **2** to understand in a specified way. **3** to act as interpreter. —**interpretation** /-ˈteɪʃ(ə)n/ *n.*, **interpretative** *adj.*, **interpretive** *adj.* [f. OF or L (*interpres* one who explains)]

interpreter *n.* one who interprets, especially one who orally translates the words of persons speaking different languages. [f. prec.]

interregnum /ɪntəˈregnəm/ *n.* (*pl.* **-ums**) **1** an interval when usual government is suspended, especially between successive reigns. **2** an interval, a pause. [L (INTER-, *regnum* reign)]

interrelated /ɪntərɪˈleɪtɪd/ *adj.* related to each other. —**interrelation** *n.*

interrogate /ɪnˈterəgeɪt/ *v.t.* to question closely or formally. —**interrogation** /-ˈgeɪʃ(ə)n/ *n.*, **interrogator** *n.* [f. L *interrogare* (INTER-, *rogare* ask)]

interrogative /ɪntəˈrɒgətɪv/ *adj.* of or like or used in questions. —*n.* an interrogative word (e.g. *who?*). —**interrogatively** *adv.* [as prec.]

interrogatory /ɪntəˈrɒgətərɪ/ *adj.* questioning. —*n.* a formal set of questions. [as INTERROGATE]

interrupt /ɪntəˈrʌpt/ *v.t.* **1** to break the continuity of. **2** to break the flow of (a speech or speaker etc.) by inserting a remark. **3** to obstruct (a view etc.). —**interrupter** *n.*, **interruption** *n.* [f. L *interrumpere* (INTER-, *rumpere* break)]

intersect /ɪntəˈsekt/ *v.t./i.* **1** to divide (a thing) by passing or lying across it. **2** (of lines, roads, etc.) to cross each other. [f. L *intersecare* (INTER-, *secare* cut)]

intersection *n.* **1** a place where two roads intersect. **2** the point or line common to lines or planes that intersect. **3** intersecting. [as prec.]

interspace /ˈɪntəspeɪs/ *n.* an intervening space. —/ɪntəˈspeɪs/ *v.t.* to put a space or spaces between.

intersperse /ɪntəˈspɜːs/ *v.t.* to insert contrasting material here and there in (a thing); to scatter (material) thus. [f. L *interspergere* (INTER-, *spargere* scatter)]

interstate /ˈɪntəsteɪt/ *adj.* existing or carried on between States especially of the USA.

interstellar /ɪntəˈstelə(r)/ *adj.* between stars. [f. INTER- + L *stella* star]

interstice /ɪnˈtɜːstɪs/ *n.* an intervening space; a chink, a crevice. [f. L *interstitium* (INTER-, *sistere* stand)]

interstitial /ɪntəˈstɪʃ(ə)l/ *adj.* of or in or forming interstices. —**interstitially** *adv.* [as prec.]

intertwine /ɪntəˈtwaɪn/ *v.t./i.* to twine closely together.

interval /ˈɪntəv(ə)l/ *n.* **1** an intervening time or space. **2** a pause, a break, especially between parts of a performance. **3** the difference of pitch between two sounds. —**at intervals,** here and there, now and then. [f. L, = space between ramparts (INTER-, *vallum* rampart)]

intervene /ɪntəˈviːn/ *v.i.* **1** to occur in time between events. **2** to cause hindrance by occurring; to enter a discussion or dispute etc. in order to change its course or resolve it. **3** to come in as an extraneous thing. **4** to be situated *between* others. [f. L *intervenire* (INTER-, *venire* come)]

intervention /ɪntəˈvenʃ(ə)n/ *n.* intervening, interference, especially by the State; mediation. [f. prec.]

interventionist *n.* one who favours intervention. [f. prec.]

interview /ˈɪntəvjuː/ *n.* **1** a conversation between a reporter and a person whose views he wishes to publish or broadcast. **2** an oral examination of an applicant. **3** a meeting of persons face to face, especially for consultation. —*v.t.* to have an interview with. —**interviewee** /-vjuːˈiː/ *n.*, **interviewer** *n.* [f. F *entrevue* (as INTER-, VIEW)]

inter-war /ɪntəˈwɔː(r)/ *adj.* existing in the period between two wars.

interweave /ɪntəˈwiːv/ *v.t.* to weave together; to blend intimately.

intestate /ɪnˈtesteɪt/ *adj.* not having made a will before death. —*n.* a person who has died intestate. —**intestacy** /ɪnˈtestəsɪ/ *n.* [f. L (IN-², *testari* make a will)]

intestine /ɪnˈtestɪn/ *n.* (in *sing.* or *pl.*) the lower part of the alimentary canal. —**intestinal** *adj.* [f. L (*intestinus* internal)]

intimacy /ˈɪntɪməsɪ/ *n.* **1** being intimate. **2** an intimate act; sexual intercourse. [f. foll.]

intimate /ˈɪntɪmət/ *adj.* **1** closely acquainted, familiar. **2** private and personal. **3** having sexual relations (*with*). **4** (of knowledge) detailed, thorough. **5** (of relations between things) close. —*n.* an intimate friend. —/-eɪt/ *v.t.* to state or make known; to imply, to hint. —**intimately** *adv.*, **intimation** /-ˈmeɪʃ(ə)n/ *n.* [f. L (*intimus* inmost)]

intimidate /ɪnˈtɪmɪdeɪt/ *v.t.* to frighten, especially in order to subdue or influence. —**intimidation** /-ˈdeɪʃ(ə)n/ *n.*, **intimidator** *n.* [f. L *intimidare* (IN-¹, *timidus* timid)]

into /ˈɪntʊ, -tə/ *prep.* **1** expressing motion or direction to a point on or within. **2** expressing a change of state. **3** (*colloq.*) interested and involved in. [OE (as IN, TO)]

intolerable /ɪnˈtɒlərəb(ə)l/ *adj.* that cannot be endured. —**intolerableness** *n.*, **intolerably** *adv.* [f. OF or L (as IN-², TOLERABLE)]

intolerant /ɪnˈtɒlərənt/ *adj.* not tolerant, especially of views or beliefs differing from one's own. —**intolerance** *n.*, **intolerantly** *adv.* [f. L (as IN-², TOLERANT)]

intonation /ɪntəˈneɪʃ(ə)n/ *n.* **1** intoning. **2** a modulation of the voice, a slight accent. [f. L (as foll.)]

intone /ɪnˈtəʊn/ *v.t.* **1** to recite (prayers etc.) with prolonged sounds, especially in a monotone. **2** to utter with a particular tone. [f. L *intonare* (IN-¹, *tonus* tone)]

in toto /ɪn ˈtəʊtəʊ/ completely. [L]

intoxicant /ɪnˈtɒksɪkənt/ *adj.* intoxicating. —*n.* an intoxicant drink or substance. [as foll.]

intoxicate /ɪnˈtɒksɪkeɪt/ *v.t.* to make drunk; to excite or elate beyond self-control. —**intoxication** /-ˈkeɪʃ(ə)n/ *n.* [f. L *intoxicare* poison (IN-¹, *toxicum* poison)]

intra- *prefix* within, on the inside. [f. L *intra* inside]

intractable /ɪnˈtræktəb(ə)l/ *adj.* hard to control or deal with; difficult, stubborn. —**intractability** /-ˈbɪlɪtɪ/ *n.*, **intractably** *adv.* [f. L (as IN-², TRACTABLE)]

intramural /ɪntrəˈmjʊər(ə)l/ *adj.* **1** situated or done within walls. **2** forming part of ordinary university work. —**intramurally** *adv.* [f. INTRA- + L *murus* wall]

intransigent /ɪnˈtrænsɪdʒ(ə)nt/ *adj.* uncompromising, stubborn. —*n.* an intransigent person. —**intransigence** *n.* [f. F f. Sp. *los intransigentes* extreme republicans (as IN-², TRANSACT)]

intransitive /ɪnˈtrænsɪtɪv/ *adj.* (of a verb) not taking a direct object. —**intransitively** *adv.* [f. L (as IN-², TRANSITIVE)]

intra-uterine /ɪntrəˈjuːtəraɪn, -rɪn/ *adj.* within the womb.

intravenous /ɪntrəˈviːnəs/ *adj.* in or into a vein or veins. —**intravenously** *adv.* [f. INTRA- + L *vena* vein]

in-tray *n.* a tray for incoming documents.

intrepid /ɪnˈtrepɪd/ *adj.* fearless, brave. —**intrepidity** /ɪntrɪˈpɪdɪtɪ/ *n.*, **intrepidly** *adv.* [f. F or L (IN-², *trepidus* alarmed)]

intricate /ˈɪntrɪkət/ *adj.* very complicated. —**intricacy** /ˈɪntrɪkəsɪ/ *n.*, **intricately** *adv.* [f. L (IN-¹, *tricae* tricks, perplexities)]

intrigue /ɪnˈtriːg/ *v.t./i.* **1** to plot in an underhand way; to use secret influence. **2** to rouse the interest or curiosity of. —/also ˈɪn-/

n. 1. underhand plotting or plot. 2 (*archaic*) a secret love affair. [f. F f. It. (as prec.)]

intrinsic /ɪnˈtrɪnsɪk/ *adj.* inherent, essential. —**intrinsically** *adv.* [f. F f. L *intrinsecus* inwardly]

intro- *prefix* into, inwards. [f. L, = to the inside]

introduce /ɪntrəˈdju:s/ *v.t.* 1 to make known by name *to* another. 2 to announce or present to an audience. 3 to bring (a bill) before Parliament. 4 to cause to become acquainted with a subject. 5 to bring (a custom or idea etc.) into use or into a system. 6 to bring or put in. [f. L *introducere* (INTRO-, *ducere* lead)]

introduction /ɪntrəˈdʌkʃ(ə)n/ *n.* 1 introducing. 2 a formal presentation of a person to another. 3 an explanatory section at the beginning of a book etc. 4 an introductory treatise. 5 a thing introduced. [f. OF or L (as prec.)]

introductory /ɪntrəˈdʌktərɪ/ *adj.* that introduces; preliminary. [f. L (as INTRODUCE)]

introit /ˈɪntrɔɪt/ *n.* a psalm or antiphon sung or said while a priest approaches the altar for Eucharist. [f. OF f. L *introitus* entrance]

introspection /ɪntrəˈspekʃ(ə)n/ *n.* examining one's own thoughts. —**introspective** *adj.* [f. L (INTRO-, *specere* look)]

introvert /ˈɪntrəvɜ:t/ *n.* an introverted person. [f. foll.]

introverted /ˈɪntrəvɜ:tɪd/ *adj.* principally interested in one's own thoughts; reserved, shy. —**introversion** /-ˈvɜ:ʃ(ə)n/ *n.* [f. INTRO- + L *vertere* turn]

intrude /ɪnˈtru:d/ *v.t./i.* to force or come uninvited or unwanted. [f. L *intrudere* (IN-[1], *trudere* thrust)]

intruder *n.* one who intrudes; a burglar; a raiding aircraft. [f. prec.]

intrusion /ɪnˈtru:ʒ(ə)n/ *n.* 1 intruding. 2 an influx of molten rock between strata etc. —**intrusive** *adj.* [f. OF or L (as prec.)]

intuition /ɪntju:ˈɪʃ(ə)n/ *n.* immediate apprehension by the mind without reasoning; immediate apprehension by a sense. —**intuitional** *adj.* [f. L (IN-[1], *tueri* look)]

intuitive /ɪnˈtju:ɪtɪv/ *adj.* of, having, or perceived by intuition. —**intuitively** *adv.* [f. L (as INTUITION)]

inundate /ˈɪnʌndeɪt/ *v.t.* to flood or overwhelm (*with*). —**inundation** /-ˈdeɪʃ(ə)n/ *n.* [f. L *inundare* flow (IN-[1], *unda* wave)]

inure /ɪˈnjʊə(r)/ *v.t./i.* 1 to accustom (*to* a difficulty etc.). 2 (*Law*) to take effect. —**inurement** *n.* [f. OF *euvre* work f. L *opera*]

in vacuo /ɪn ˈvækju:əʊ/ in a vacuum. [L]

invade /ɪnˈveɪd/ *v.t.* 1 to enter (a country) with armed forces to control or subdue it. 2 to swarm into. 3 (of a disease etc.) to attack. 4 to encroach on (rights, esp. privacy). —**invader** *n.* [f. L *invadere* (IN-[1], *vadere* go)]

invalid[1] /ˈɪnvəli:d/ *n.* a person enfeebled or disabled by illness or injury. —*adj.* of or for invalids; being an invalid. —*v.t.* 1 to remove from active service or send away (*home* etc.) as an invalid. 2 to disable by illness. —**invalidism** *n.* [f. L (IN-[2], *validus* strong); = INVALID[2], with F pronunc.]

invalid[2] /ɪnˈvælɪd/ *adj.* not valid. [f. L (as IN-[2], VALID)]

invalidate /ɪnˈvælɪdeɪt/ *v.t.* to make (an argument, contract, etc.) invalid. —**invalidation** /-ˈdeɪʃ(ə)n/ *n.* [f. L (as prec.)]

invalidity /ɪnvəˈlɪdɪtɪ/ *n.* 1 lack of validity. 2 being an invalid. [f. F or L (as INVALID[1,2])]

invaluable /ɪnˈvælju:əb(ə)l/ *adj.* having a value that is too great to be measured. —**invaluably** *adv.* [f. IN-[2] + VALUABLE]

invariable /ɪnˈveərɪəb(ə)l/ *adj.* not variable, always the same. —**invariably** *adv.* [F or f. L (as IN-[2], VARIABLE)]

invasion /ɪnˈveɪʒ(ə)n/ *n.* invading, being invaded. —**invasive** *adj.* [F or f. L (as INVADE)]

invected /ɪnˈvektɪd/ *adj.* (in heraldry) bordered by or consisting of a series of small convex lobes. [as INVEIGH]

invective /ɪnˈvektɪv/ *n.* a strong verbal attack; abusive language. [f. OF f. L (as foll.)]

inveigh /ɪnˈveɪ/ *v.i.* to speak or write with strong hostility (*against*). [f. L *invehi* ride into, assail]

inveigle /ɪnˈveɪg(ə)l/ *v.t.* to entice, to persuade by guile (*into*). —**inveiglement** *n.* [f. OF *aveugler* to blind]

invent /ɪnˈvent/ *v.t.* 1 to create by thought, to make or design (something that did not exist before). 2 to concoct (a false or fictional story). —**inventor** *n.* [f. L *invenire* discover]

invention /ɪnˈvenʃ(ə)n/ *n.* 1 inventing. 2 a thing invented; a fictitious story. 3 inventiveness. [f. L (as prec.)]

inventive /ɪnˈventɪv/ *adj.* able to invent. —**inventiveness** *n.* [f. F or L (as INVENT)]

inventory /ˈɪnvəntərɪ/ *n.* a detailed list (of goods etc.); goods in this. —*v.t.* to make an inventory of; to enter (goods) in an inventory. [f. L *inventorium* (as INVENT)]

inverse /ɪnˈvɜ:s, ˈɪn-/ *adj.* 1 inverted in position or order or relation. 2 (of a proportion or ratio) between two quantities one of which increases in proportion as the other decreases. —*n.* 1 an inverted state. 2 a thing that is the direct opposite (*of* another). —**inversely** *adv.* [f. L (as INVERT)]

inversion /ɪnˈvɜ:ʃ(ə)n/ *n.* turning upside down; reversal of normal order, position, or relation. —**inversive** *adj.* [as foll.]

invert /ɪnˈvɜːt/ *v.t.* to turn upside down; to reverse the position, order, or relation of. —/ˈɪnvɜːt/ *n.* a homosexual. —**inverted commas**, quotation marks. [f. L *invertere* (IN-[1], *vertere* turn)]

invertebrate /ɪnˈvɜːtɪbrət/ *adj.* without a backbone or spinal column. —*n.* an invertebrate animal. [f. IN-[2] + VERTEBRATE]

invest /ɪnˈvest/ *v.t./i.* **1** to use (money) to buy stocks, shares, or property, etc. so as to earn interest or bring profit; to spend money, time, or effort *in* obtaining stocks etc. or something useful. **2** to end *with* qualities, insignia, or rank. **3** to clothe, to cover (as) with a garment. **4** to lay siege to. [f. F or L *investire* (IN-[1], *vestire* clothe)]

investigate /ɪnˈvestɪgeɪt/ *v.t./i.* to make a careful study of (a thing) in order to discover the facts about it; to make a systematic inquiry. —**investigation** /-ˈgeɪʃ(ə)n/ *n.*, **investigative** *adj.*, **investigator** *n.*, **investigatory** *adj.* [f. L *investigare* (IN-[1], *vestigare* track)]

investiture /ɪnˈvestɪtʃə(r)/ *n.* the process of investing a person with rank or office, etc.; a ceremony at which the sovereign confers honours. [f. L (as INVEST)]

investment *n.* **1** investing. **2** money invested. **3** something in which money, time, or effort is invested. [f. INVEST]

investor *n.* one who invests money. [as prec.]

inveterate /ɪnˈvetərət/ *adj.* (of a habit etc.) deep-rooted; (of a person) confirmed in a habit etc. —**inveteracy** *n.* [f. L *inveterare* (IN-[1], *vetus* old)]

invidious /ɪnˈvɪdɪəs/ *adj.* likely to excite ill-will or indignation against the performer, possessor, etc. —**invidiously** *adv.* [f. L (*invidia* envy)]

invigilate /ɪnˈvɪdʒɪleɪt/ *v.i.* to supervise candidates at an examination. —**invigilation** /-ˈleɪʃ(ə)n/ *n.*, **invigilator** *n.* [f. L *invigilare* (IN-[1], *vigilare* keep watch)]

invigorate /ɪnˈvɪgəreɪt/ *v.t.* to give vigour or strength to. [f. L (IN-[1], *vigorare* make strong)]

invincible /ɪnˈvɪnsɪb(ə)l/ *adj.* unconquerable. —**invincibility** /-ˈbɪlɪtɪ/ *n.*, **invincibly** *adv.* [f. OF f. L (IN-[2], *vincere* conquer)]

inviolable /ɪnˈvaɪələb(ə)l/ *adj.* not to be violated or profaned. —**inviolability** /-ˈbɪlɪtɪ/ *n.*, **inviolably** *adv.* [F or f. L (as IN-[2], VIOLABLE)]

inviolate /ɪnˈvaɪələt/ *adj.* not violated. —**inviolacy** *n.* [f. L (as IN-[2], VIOLATE)]

invisible /ɪnˈvɪzɪb(ə)l/ *adj.* that cannot be seen. —**invisible exports, imports**, items for which payment is made by or to another country but which are not goods. —**invisibility** /-ˈbɪlɪtɪ/ *n.*, **invisibly** *adv.* [f. OF or L (as IN-[2], VISIBLE)]

invitation /ɪnvɪˈteɪʃ(ə)n/ *n.* **1** inviting, being invited. **2** a letter or card etc. used to invite someone. **3** a thing that invites (unintentional) consequences. [f. foll.]

invite /ɪnˈvaɪt/ *v.t.* **1** to ask courteously to come to one's house or to a function etc., or to do something). **2** to ask for (suggestions etc.). **3** to tend to call forth (criticism etc.), to act so as to be likely to cause (a thing) unintentionally. **4** to attract, to tempt. —/ˈɪnvaɪt/ *n.* (*colloq.*) an invitation. [f. F or L *invitare*]

inviting *adj.* attractive, tempting. [f. prec.]

invocation /ɪnvəˈkeɪʃ(ə)n/ *n.* **1** invoking. **2** an appeal to a Muse for inspiration. **3** a preacher's prefatory words 'In the name of the Father' etc. —**invocatory** /ɪnˈvɒkətərɪ/ *adj.* [f. OF f. L (as INVOKE)]

invoice /ˈɪnvɔɪs/ *n.* a list of goods shipped or sent, or services rendered, with prices. —*v.t.* to make an invoice of; to send an invoice to. [app. f. OF *envoy* dispatch of goods (*envoyer* send)]

invoke /ɪnˈvəʊk/ *v.t.* **1** to call on (a deity etc.) in prayer or as a witness. **2** to appeal to (a law, authority, etc.) for protection or help. **3** to summon (a spirit) by charms. **4** to ask earnestly for (vengeance etc.). [f. F f. L *invocare* (IN-[1], *vocare* call)]

involuntary /ɪnˈvɒləntərɪ/ *adj.* done without exercise of the will; not controlled by the will. —**involuntarily** *adv.*, **involuntariness** *n.* [f. L (as IN-[2], VOLUNTARY)]

involute /ˈɪnvəluːt, -ljuːt/ *adj.* **1** involved, intricate. **2** spirally curved. —*n.* the locus of a point fixed on a straight line that rolls without sliding on a curve and is in the plane of that curve (cf. EVOLUTE). [f. L (as INVOLVE)]

involuted /ˈɪnvəluːtɪd/ *adj.* complicated, abstruse. [f. prec.]

involution /ɪnvəˈluːʃ(ə)n/ *n.* **1** involving; intricacy; entanglement. **2** curling inwards; a part so curled. [as foll.]

involve /ɪnˈvɒlv/ *v.t.* **1** to cause to share (*in*) an experience or effect; to include or affect in its operation. **2** to contain within itself, to make necessary as a condition or result. **3** to implicate. **4** (in *p.p.*) concerned (*in*); complicated in thought or form. —**involvement** *n.* [f. L *involvere* (IN-[1], *volvere* roll)]

invulnerable /ɪnˈvʌlnərəb(ə)l/ *adj.* that cannot be wounded or hurt (esp. *fig.*). —**invulnerability** /-ˈbɪlɪtɪ/ *n.*, **invulnerably** *adv.* [f. L (as IN-[2], VULNERABLE)]

inward /ˈɪnwəd/ *adj.* **1** directed towards the inside, going in. **2** situated within. **3** mental, spiritual. —*adv.* (also **inwards**) **1** towards the inside. **2** within the mind or spirit. [OE (as IN, -WARD)]

inwardly *adv.* **1** on the inside. **2** not aloud. **3** in the mind or spirit. [OE (as prec.)]

inwardness *n.* inner nature; spirituality. [f. INWARD]

inwrought /ɪnˈrɔːt, *attrib.* ˈɪn-/ *adj.* (of fabric) decorated (*with* a pattern); (of a pattern) wrought (*in* or *on* fabric). [f. IN + WROUGHT]

iodide /ˈaɪədaɪd/ *n.* a binary compound of iodine. [f. foll.]

iodine /ˈaɪədiːn, -ɪn/ *n.* a non-metallic element of the halogen group, symbol I, atomic number 53. [f. F f. Gk *iōdēs* violet-like (*ion* violet)]

iodize /ˈaɪədaɪz/ *v.t.* to impregnate with iodine. [f. prec.]

IOM *abbr.* Isle of Man.

ion /ˈaɪən/ *n.* any of the electrically charged particles into which the atoms or molecules of certain substances are dissociated by solution in water, making the solution a conductor of electricity; a similarly charged molecule of gas e.g. in air exposed to X-rays. [Gk, partic. of *eimi* go]

Ionic /aɪˈɒnɪk/ *adj.* of an order of Greek architecture characterized by columns with scroll-shapes on either side of the capital. [f. L f. Gk]

ionic /aɪˈɒnɪk/ *adj.* of or using ions. —**ionically** *adv.* [f. ION]

ionize /ˈaɪənaɪz/ *v.t.* to convert or be converted into an ion or ions. —**ionization** /-ˈzeɪʃ(ə)n/ *n.* [f. ION]

ionosphere /aɪˈɒnəsfɪə(r)/ *n.* an ionized region of the upper atmosphere reflecting radio-waves. —**ionospheric** /-ˈferɪk/ *adj.* [f. ION + SPHERE]

iota /aɪˈəʊtə/ *n.* **1** the ninth letter of the Greek alphabet, = i. **2** the smallest possible amount, a jot. [Gk *iōta*]

IOU /aɪəʊˈjuː/ *n.* a signed document acknowledging a debt. [= *I owe you*]

IOW *abbr.* Isle of Wight.

IPA *abbr.* International Phonetic Alphabet.

ipecacuanha /ɪpɪkækuˈɑːnə/ *n.* the root of a South American plant (*Cephaëlis ipecacuanha*), used as an emetic or purgative. [f. Port. f. Tupi-Guarani, = emetic creeper]

ipso facto /ˈɪpsəʊ ˈfæktəʊ/ by that very fact. [L]

IQ *abbr.* intelligence quotient.

Ir *symbol* iridium.

ir-[1,2] see IN-[1,2].

IRA *abbr.* Irish Republican Army.

irascible /ɪˈræsɪb(ə)l/ *adj.* irritable, hot-tempered. —**irascibility** /-ˈbɪlɪtɪ/ *n.*, **irascibly** *adv.* [f. L (*irasci* grow angry, f. *ira* anger)]

irate /aɪˈreɪt/ *adj.* angry, enraged. [f. L *iratus* (as prec.)]

ire /ˈaɪə(r)/ *n.* (*literary*) anger. [f. OF f. L *ira* anger]

iridaceous /ɪrɪˈdeɪʃəs/ *adj.* of the iris family (Iridaceae). [as IRIS]

iridescent /ɪrɪˈdes(ə)nt/ *adj.* showing rainbow-like colours; changing colour with position. —**iridescence** *n.* [f. L *iris* (see IRIS)]

iridium /ɪˈrɪdɪəm/ *n.* a rare hard white metallic element, symbol Ir, atomic number 77. [f. L *iris* rainbow, from its highly coloured salts]

iris /ˈaɪərɪs/ *n.* **1** the circular coloured membrane behind the cornea of the eye, with a circular opening (the pupil) in the centre. **2** a perennial herbaceous plant of the genus *Iris* usually with tuberous roots, sword-shaped leaves, and showy flowers. **3** a diaphragm with a hole of variable size. [f. L f. Gk, = rainbow]

Irish /ˈaɪərɪʃ/ *adj.* of Ireland; of or like its people. —*n.* the Celtic language of Ireland. —**the Irish,** the people of Ireland. **Irish stew** a stew of mutton, potato, and onion. [f. OE]

Irishman *n.* (*pl.* **-men**) a man of Irish birth or descent. —**Irishwoman** *n.fem.* (*pl.* **-women**)

irk *v.t.* to annoy, to be tiresome to. [orig. unkn.]

irksome /ˈɜːksəm/ *adj.* tiresome, annoying. [f. IRK + -SOME]

iron /ˈaɪən/ *n.* **1** an abundant metallic element of great strength, atomic number 26, symbol Fe. **2** a tool or implement made of iron; an implement (orig. of iron) with a flat base that is heated for smoothing cloth or clothes etc.; a golf-club with an iron or steel head and a sloping face; (in *pl.*) fetters, stirrups; (often in *pl.*) a leg-support to rectify malformations etc. **3** a preparation of iron as a tonic. —*adj.* **1** of iron. **2** very robust. **3** unyielding, merciless. —*v.t.* to smooth (cloth or clothes etc.) with an iron. —**Iron Ages,** the period when weapons and tools were made of iron. **Iron Cross,** a German military decoration. **Iron Curtain,** a barrier to free passage of people and information between the Soviet bloc and the West. **iron-grey** *adj.* & *n.* grey like the colour of freshly broken iron. **ironing-board** *n.* a narrow flat stand on which clothes etc. are ironed. **iron lung,** a rigid case over a patient's body for prolonged artificial respiration. **iron out,** to remove (difficulties etc.). **iron ration,** a small supply of tinned food etc. for use in an emergency. **many irons in the fire,** many undertakings or resources. **strike while the iron is hot,** to act promptly at a good opportunity. [OE]

ironclad *adj.* covered in or protected with iron. —*n.* (*hist.*) a ship cased with plates of iron.

ironic /aɪˈrɒnɪk/ *adj.* (also **ironical**) using or displaying irony. —**ironically** *adv.* [f. F or L f. Gk *eirōnikos* dissembling (as IRONY)]

ironmaster *n.* a manufacturer of iron.

ironmonger /ˈaɪənmʌŋgə(r)/ *n.* a dealer in hardware etc. —**ironmongery** *n.*

ironsides /ˈaɪənsaɪdz/ *n.* **1** a man of great bravery. **2** (as *pl.*) Cromwell's cavalry troopers during the English Civil War, so called by their Royalist opponents in allusion to their hardiness in battle.

ironstone *n.* **1** hard iron-ore. **2** a kind of hard white pottery.

ironware *n.* things made of iron.

ironwork *n.* work in iron; things made of iron.

ironworks *n.pl.* (often treated as *sing.*) a place where iron is smelted or where heavy iron goods are made.

irony /ˈaɪərənɪ/ *n.* **1** the expression of one's meaning by language of the opposite or a different tendency, e.g. adoption of a laudatory tone for the purpose of ridicule. **2** the ill-timed or perverse occurrence of an event or circumstance that would in itself be desirable. —**dramatic** *or* **tragic irony,** (orig. in Greek tragedy) the use of statements etc. whose implications are understood by the audience but not by the person(s) addressed or concerned (occas. including the speaker). **Socratic irony,** a pose of ignorance assumed in order to confute others by enticing them into a display of supposed knowledge. [f. L f. Gk, = simulated ignorance (*eirōn* dissembler)]

irradiate /ɪˈreɪdɪeɪt/ *v.t.* **1** to subject to radiation; to shine upon, to light up. **2** to throw light on (a subject). —**irradiation** /-ˈeɪʃ(ə)n/ *n.* [f. L *irradiare* (IN-[1], *radius* ray)]

irrational /ɪˈræʃən(ə)l/ *adj.* **1** unreasonable, illogical. **2** not endowed with reason. **3** not commensurable with natural numbers. **irrationality** /-ˈnælɪtɪ/ *n.*, **irrationally** *adv.* [f. L (as IR-[2], RATIONAL)]

irreconcilable /ɪˈrekənsaɪləb(ə)l/ *adj.* **1** implacably hostile. **2** incompatible. —**irreconcilability** /-ˈbɪlɪtɪ/ *n.*, **irreconcilably** *adv.* [f. IR-[2] + RECONCILABLE]

irrecoverable /ɪrɪˈkʌvərəb(ə)l/ *adj.* that cannot be recovered or remedied. —**irrecoverably** *adv.* [f. IR-[2] + RECOVERABLE]

irredeemable /ɪrɪˈdi:məb(ə)l/ *adj.* that cannot be redeemed; hopeless. —**irredeemably** *adv.* [f. IR-[2] + REDEEMABLE]

irreducible /ɪrɪˈdju:sɪb(ə)l/ *adj.* that cannot be reduced or simplified. —**irreducibly** *adv.* [f. IR-[2] + REDUCIBLE]

irrefutable /ɪˈrefjʊtəb(ə)l, ɪrɪˈfju:-/ *adj.* that cannot be refuted. —**irrefutably** *adv.* [f. L (as IR-[2], REFUTABLE)]

irregular /ɪˈregjʊlə(r)/ *adj.* **1** not regular; unsymmetrical, uneven, varying. **2** contrary to a rule, principle, or custom. **3** (of troops) not in the regular army. **4** abnormal. **5** (of a verb, noun, etc.) not inflected normally. **6** disorderly. —*n.* (in *pl.*) irregular troops. —**irregularity** /-ˈlærɪtɪ/ *n.*, **irregularly** *adv.* [f. OF f. L (as IR-[2], REGULAR)]

irrelevant /ɪˈrelɪv(ə)nt/ *adj.* not relevant. —**irrelevance** *n.*, **irrelevancy** *n.*, **irrelevantly** *adv.* [f. IR-[2] + RELEVANT]

irreligious /ɪrɪˈlɪdʒəs/ *adj.* lacking or hostile to religion. [f. L (as IR-[2], RELIGIOUS)]

irremediable /ɪrɪˈmi:dɪəb(ə)l/ *adj.* that cannot be remedied. —**irremediably** *adv.* [f. L (as IR-[2], REMEDIABLE)]

irremovable /ɪrɪˈmu:vəb(ə)l/ *adj.* that cannot be removed, especially from office. —**irremovably** *adv.* [f. IR-[2] + REMOVABLE]

irreparable /ɪˈrepərəb(ə)l/ *adj.* that cannot be rectified or made good. —**irreparably** *adv.* [f. OF f. L (as IR-[2], REPARABLE)]

irreplaceable /ɪrɪˈpleɪsəb(ə)l/ *adj.* that cannot be replaced. —**irreplaceability** /-ˈbɪlɪtɪ/ *n.*, **irreplaceably** *adv.* [f. IR-[2] + REPLACEABLE]

irrepressible /ɪrɪˈpresɪb(ə)l/ *adj.* that cannot be repressed or restrained. —**irrepressibly** *adv.* [f. IR-[2] + REPRESS]

irreproachable /ɪrɪˈprəʊtʃəb(ə)l/ *adj.* faultless, blameless. —**irreproachably** *adv.* [f. F (as IR-[2], REPROACH)]

irresistible /ɪrɪˈzɪstɪb(ə)l/ *adj.* too strong or delightful or convincing to be resisted. —**irresistibly** *adv.* [f. L (as IR-[2], RESISTIBLE)]

irresolute /ɪˈrezəlu:t/ *adj.* feeling or showing uncertainty, hesitating. —**irresolutely** *adv.*, **irresoluteness** *n.*, **irresolution** /-ˈlu:ʃ(ə)n/ *n.* [f. IR-[2] + RESOLUTE]

irrespective /ɪrɪˈspektɪv/ *adj.* not taking account *of*, regardless *of*. [f. IR-[2] + RESPECTIVE]

irresponsible /ɪrɪˈspɒnsɪb(ə)l/ *adj.* acting or done without due sense of responsibility; not responsible for one's conduct. —**irresponsibility** /-ˈbɪlɪtɪ/ *n.*, **irresponsibly** *adv.* [f. IR-[2] + RESPONSIBLE]

irretrievable /ɪrɪˈtri:vəb(ə)l/ *adj.* that cannot be retrieved or recovered. —**irretrievably** *adv.* [f. IR-[2] + RETRIEVABLE]

irreverent /ɪˈrevərənt/ *adj.* lacking reverence. —**irreverence** *n.*, **irreverently** *adv.* [f. L (as IR-[2], REVERENT)]

irreversible /ɪrɪˈvɜ:sɪb(ə)l/ *adj.* not reversible or alterable. —**irreversibly** *adv.* [f. IR-[2] + REVERSIBLE]

irrevocable /ɪˈrevəkəb(ə)l/ *adj.* unable to be revoked, unalterable; gone beyond recall. —**irrevocably** *adv.* [f. L (as IR-[2], REVOCABLE)]

irrigate /ˈɪrɪgeɪt/ *v.t.* **1** to supply (land or crops) with water by means of streams, channels, pipes, etc. **2** to wash (a wound) with a constant flow of liquid. —**irrigation** /-ˈgeɪʃ(ə)n/ *n.*, **irrigator** *n.* [f. L *irrigare* (IR-[1], *rigare* moisten)]

irritable /ˈɪrɪtəb(ə)l/ *adj.* **1** easily annoyed, bad-tempered. **2** (of an organ etc.) sensitive. —**irritability** /-ˈbɪlɪtɪ/ *n.*, **irritably** *adv.* [f. L (as IRRITATE)]

irritant /ˈɪrɪt(ə)nt/ *adj.* causing irritation. —*n.* an irritant substance. [f. foll.]

irritate /ˈɪrɪteɪt/ *v.t.* **1** to annoy, to rouse slight anger or impatience in. **2** to cause itching in (a part of the body). **3** to stimulate (an organ) to action. —**irritation** /-ˈteɪʃ(ə)n/ *n.*, **irritative** *adj.* [f. L *irritare*]

irrupt /ɪˈrʌpt/ *v.i.* to enter forcibly or violently (*into*). —**irruption** *n.* [f. L *irrumpere* (IR-¹, *rumpere* break)]

is see BE.

-isation, -ise variants of -IZATION, -IZE.

ISBN *abbr.* international standard book number.

-ish *suffix* forming adjectives (1) from nouns, in the senses 'having the qualities of' (*knavish*), 'of the nationality of' (*Danish*); (2) from adjectives, in the sense of 'somewhat' (*thickish*); (3) (*colloq.*) of an approximate age or time (*fortyish*). [OE]

isinglass /ˈaɪzɪŋglɑːs/ *n.* **1** a kind of gelatin obtained from fish, especially the sturgeon, and used for jellies, glue, etc. **2** mica. [f. obs. Du. *huisenblas* sturgeon's bladder]

Islam /ˈɪzlɑːm, -ˈlɑːm/ *n.* the religion of Muslims, revealed through Muhammad as Prophet of Allah; the Muslim world. —**Islamic** /-ˈlæmɪk/ *adj.* [f. Arab., = submission (to God), f. *aslama* resign oneself]

island /ˈaɪlənd/ *n.* **1** a piece of land surrounded by water. **2** a detached or isolated thing; a traffic island. —**islands area**, an administrative area in Scotland, consisting of a number of islands. [OE, orig. *igland*; -*s*- from ISLE]

islander *n.* an inhabitant of an island. [f. prec.]

isle /aɪl/ *n.* (chiefly *poetic* and in names) an island, especially a small one. [f. OF f. L *insula*]

islet /ˈaɪlɪt/ *n.* **1** a small island. **2** a detached portion of tissue. —**islets of Langerhans**, groups of pancreatic cells secreting insulin. [OF, dim. of *isle* (as prec.)]

ism /ɪz(ə)m/ *n.* (usu. *derog.*) any distinctive doctrine or practice. [f. foll.]

-ism /-ɪz(ə)m/ *n. suffix* forming nouns, especially a system or principle (*Conservatism*, *jingoism*), a state or quality (*barbarism*, *heroism*), or a peculiarity in language (*Americanism*). [f. F f. L f. Gk (as -IZE)]

isn't /ˈɪz(ə)nt (*colloq.*) is not.

iso- /aɪsəʊ-/ *in comb.* equal. [f. Gk *isos* equal]

isobar /ˈaɪsəbɑː(r)/ *n.* a line on a map connecting places with the same atmospheric pressure. —**isobaric** /-ˈbærɪk/ *adj.* [f. Gk (ISO-, *baros* weight)]

isochronous /aɪˈsɒkrənəs/ *adj.* **1** occupying an equal time. **2** occurring at the same time. [f. Gk (ISO-, *khronos* time)]

isoclinal /aɪsəʊˈklaɪn(ə)l/ *adj.* **1** corresponding to equal values of magnetic dip. **2** (*Geol.*, of a fold) with the parts of each side parallel to each other. [f. ISO- + Gk *klinō* slope]

isolate /ˈaɪsəleɪt/ *v.t.* **1** to place apart or alone. **2** to separate (a patient with a contagious or infectious disease) from others. **3** to separate (a substance) from a compound. **4** to insulate (electrical apparatus). —**isolation** /-ˈleɪʃ(ə)n/ *n.* [f. F f. It. f. L *insulatus* (as ISLE)]

isolationism *n.* the policy of holding aloof from affairs of other countries or groups. —**isolationist** *n.* [f. ISOLATION]

isomer /ˈaɪsəmɜː(r)/ *n.* any of two or more substances whose molecules have the same atoms in different arrangements. —**isomeric** /-ˈmerɪk/ *adj.*, **isomerism** /aɪˈsɒmərɪz(ə)m/ *n.* [G f. Gk (ISO-, *meros* portion)]

isometric /aɪsəˈmetrɪk/ *adj.* **1** (of muscle action) developing tension while the muscle is prevented from contracting. **2** (of a drawing or projection) with the plane of projection at equal angles to the three principal axes of the object shown. **3** of equal measure. [f. Gk *isometria* equality of measure]

isometrics *n.pl.* a system of physical exercises in which muscles are caused to act against each other or against a fixed object. [f. prec.]

isomorph /ˈaɪsəmɔːf/ *n.* a substance having the same form as another. —**isomorphic** *adj.*, **isomorphous** *adj.* [f. ISO- + Gk *morphē* form]

isosceles /aɪˈsɒsɪliːz/ *adj.* (of a triangle) having two sides equal. [L f. Gk (ISO-, *skelos* leg)]

isotherm /ˈaɪsəθɜːm/ *n.* a line on a map connecting places with the same temperature. —**isothermal** /-ˈθɜːm(ə)l/ *adj.* [f. F (as ISO- + Gk *thermē* heat)]

isotope /ˈaɪsətəʊp/ *n.* any of two or more types of atom of the same element that contain equal numbers of protons but different numbers of neutrons in their nuclei, and hence differ in atomic weight but not in chemical properties. —**isotopic** /-ˈtɒpɪk/ *adj.* [f. ISO- + Gk *topos* place (i.e. in the periodic table of elements)]

isotropic /aɪsəˈtrɒpɪk/ *adj.* having the same physical properties in all directions. —**isotropy** /aɪˈsɒtrəpɪ/ *n.* [f. ISO- + Gk *tropos* turn]

Israeli /ɪzˈreɪlɪ/ *adj.* of the modern State of Israel in W. Asia. —*n.* an Israeli person. [f. *Israel*]

Israelite /ˈɪzrəlaɪt/ *adj.* of ancient Israel. —*n.* an Israelite person. [f. Heb. *Israel*]

issue /ˈɪʃuː, ˈɪsjuː/ *n.* **1** an outgoing or outflow. **2** the issuing of things for use or for sale; the number or quantity issued. **3** any set of publications in a series issued regularly. **4** a result, an outcome. **5** the point in question, an important topic of discussion or litigation. **6** a way out; a place of emergence of a stream etc. **7** (*Law*) progeny, children. —*v.t./i.* **1** to go or come or flow out. **2** to put out for sale or as information etc., to publish; to send out (orders etc.). **3** to supply or distribute for use. **4** to result; to originate. —**at issue,** in dispute, under discussion. **join** or **take issue,** to proceed to argue. [f. OF f. L *exitus* (as EXIT)]

-ist *suffix* forming personal nouns expressing an adherent of a creed etc. in *-ism* (*Marxist, fatalist*), a person concerned with something (*pathologist, tobacconist*), a person who uses a thing (*violinist, motorist*), or a person who does a thing expressed by a verb in *-ize* (*plagiarist*). [F & L f. Gk]

isthmus /ˈɪsməs/ *n.* a narrow piece of land connecting two larger bodies of land; a narrow connecting part. —**isthmian** *adj.* [L f. Gk]

it[1] *pron.* (*pl.* THEY) **1** the thing (or occas. animal or child) previously named or in question; the person in question. **2** as the subject of an impersonal verb making a general statement about the weather or about circumstances etc., or as an indefinite object. **3** as a substitute for a deferred subject or object; as the antecedent to a relative pronoun. **4** exactly what is needed. **5** the extreme limit of achievement etc. **6** (*colloq.*) sexual intercourse; sex appeal. **7** (in children's games) the player who has to catch others. [OE]

it[2] *n.* (*colloq.*) Italian vermouth. [abbr.]

Italian /ɪˈtælɪən/ *adj.* of Italy or its people or language. —*n.* **1** a native or inhabitant of Italy. **2** the language of Italy. —**Italian vermouth,** sweet vermouth. [f. It. (*Italia* Italy)]

Italianate /ɪˈtælɪəneɪt/ *adj.* of Italian style or appearance. [f. It. *Italianato*]

Italic /ɪˈtælɪk/ *adj.* of ancient Italy. [f. L f. Gk (as ITALIAN)]

italic /ɪˈtælɪk/ *adj.* **1** (of printed letters) of a sloping kind now used especially for emphasis and in foreign words. **2** (of handwriting) compact and pointed like early Italian handwriting. —*n.* **1** a letter in italic type; such type. **2** of a form of handwriting (developed in Italy) somewhat resembling this, or a modern adaptation of such a form. [= prec.]

italicize /ɪˈtælɪsaɪz/ *v.t.* to print in italics. [f. prec.]

itch *n.* **1** an irritation in the skin; a contagious disease accompanied by this. **2** an impatient desire. —*v.i.* to feel an itch. —**itching palm,** avarice. [OE]

itchy *adj.* having or causing an itch. —**itchiness** *n.* [f. ITCH]

item /ˈaɪtəm/ *n.* any one of enumerated things; a detached piece of news etc. [L, = in like manner, also]

itemize /ˈaɪtəmaɪz/ *v.t.* to state by items. —**itemization** /-ˈzeɪʃ(ə)n/ *n.* [f. ITEM]

iterate /ˈɪtəreɪt/ *v.t.* to repeat, to state repeatedly. —**iteration** /-ˈreɪʃ(ə)n/ *n.*, **iterative** /-rətɪv/ *adj.* [f. L *iterare* (*iterum* again)]

itinerant /aɪˈtɪnərənt, ɪ-/ *adj.* travelling from place to place. —*n.* an itinerant person. [f. L *itinerare* (*iter* journey)]

itinerary /aɪˈtɪnərərɪ, ɪ-/ *n.* a route, a list of places to be visited on a journey. [f. L (as prec.)]

-itis /-aɪtɪs/ *suffix* forming nouns, especially names of inflammatory diseases (*appendicitis*) or (*colloq.*) of mental states fancifully regarded as diseases (*electionitis*). [Gk]

its *poss. pron. & adj.* of it, of itself. [f. IT[1]]

it's (*colloq.*) it has, it is.

itself /ɪtˈself/ *pron.* emphat. and refl. form of IT[1]. —**by itself,** apart from its surroundings, automatically. **in itself,** viewed in its essential qualities. [OE (IT[1], SELF)]

ITV *abbr.* independent television.

IUD *abbr.* intra-uterine (contraceptive) device.

ivory /ˈaɪvərɪ/ *n.* **1** the hard substance of the tusks of the elephant etc. **2** the creamy-white colour of this. **3** (usu. in *pl.*) an article made of ivory. **4** (usu. in *pl.*, *slang*) a dice; a billiard-ball; a piano-key; a tooth. —**ivory tower,** seclusion or withdrawal from harsh realities. [f. OF f. L *ebur*]

ivy /ˈaɪvɪ/ *n.* a climbing evergreen (*Hedera helix*) with shining usually five-pointed leaves. [OE]

ixia /ˈɪksɪə/ *n.* a South African iridaceous plant of the genus *Ixia* with large showy flowers. [L f. Gk, = kind of thistle]

Jj

J, j /dʒeɪ/ *n.* (*pl.* **Js, J's**) the tenth letter of the alphabet.

J *abbr.* joule(s).

jab *v.t.* (**-bb-**) to poke roughly; to thrust abruptly (a thing *into*). —*n.* **1** an abrupt blow with a pointed thing or with the fist. **2** (*colloq.*) a hypodermic injection. [var. of *job* prod]

jabber *v.t./i.* to chatter volubly; to utter (words) fast and indistinctly. —*n.* chatter, gabble. [imit.]

jabot /ˈʒæbəʊ/ *n.* an ornamental frill or ruffle of lace etc. worn on the front of a shirt or blouse. [F, orig. = crop of bird]

jacaranda /dʒækəˈrændə/ *n.* a tropical American tree of the genus *Dalbergia* etc. with hard scented wood, or one of the genus *Jacaranda* with blue flowers. [Tupi-Guarani]

jacinth /ˈdʒæsɪnθ/ *n.* a reddish-orange gem, a variety of zircon. [f. OF or L, = HYACINTH]

jack *n.* **1** a device for lifting heavy objects, especially one for raising the axle of a motor vehicle so that a wheel may be changed. **2** a court-card with a picture of a soldier or page. **3** a ship's flag, especially one flown from the bow and showing nationality. **4** a device using a single plug to connect an electrical circuit. **5** a device for turning a spit. **6** a type of the common man. **7** (*slang*) a policeman, a detective. **8** a small white ball in bowls for the players to aim at. **9** a pike, especially a young one. **10** the male of various animals. —*v.t.* (often with *up*) to raise with or as with a jack. —**Jack Frost**, frost personified. **jack in** *or* **up**, (*slang*) to abandon (an attempt etc.). **jack-in-the-box** *n.* a toy figure that springs out of a box when the lid is lifted. **jack-in-office** *n.* a self-important official. **jack of all trades**, a person who can do many different kinds of work. **jack-rabbit**, (*US*) a large prairie hare (*Lepus townsendii*, etc.) with very long ears. **Jack tar**, a sailor. [f. *Jack*, pet-name for JOHN]

jackal /ˈdʒækɔl, -(ə)l/ *n.* **1** any of several members of the dog family found wild in Asia and Africa, living on carrion and small animals. **2** one who does the preliminary drudgery etc. for another. [f. Turk. f. Pers.]

jackanapes /ˈdʒækəneɪps/ *n.* a pert or insolent fellow. [f. *Jack Napes* nickname (1450) of Duke of Suffolk whose badge was an ape's clog and chain]

jackass /ˈdjækæs/ *n.* **1** a male ass. **2** a stupid person. —**laughing jackass**, the kookaburra. [f. JACK + ASS]

jackboot *n.* **1** a large boot reaching above the knee. **2** military oppression, bullying behaviour.

jackdaw *n.* a bird (*Corvus monedula*) of the crow family, with a chuckling call. [f. JACK + DAW]

jacket /ˈdʒækɪt/ *n.* **1** a short coat, usually reaching to the hips. **2** a thing worn similarly. **3** an outer covering round a boiler etc. to reduce loss of heat. **4** a dust jacket. **5** the skin of a potato. **6** an animal's coat. —**jacketed** *adj.* [f. OF *ja(c)quet*]

jackknife *n.* **1** a large clasp-knife. **2** a dive in which the body is first bent at the waist and then straightened. —*v.i.* (of an articulated vehicle) to fold against itself in an accidental skidding movement.

jackpot *n.* the accumulated prize or stakes in a lottery, the game of poker, etc. —**hit the jackpot**, to win remarkable luck or success.

Jacobean /dʒækəˈbiːən/ *adj.* of James I's reign (d. 1625). [f. L *Jacobus* James f. Gk *Iakōbos* Jacob]

Jacobite /ˈdʒækəbaɪt/ *n.* an adherent of the deposed James II, or of his descendants, or of the Stuarts after the Revolution of 1688, in their claim to the British throne. [as prec.]

Jacquard /ˈdʒækɑːd/ *n.* **1** an apparatus with perforated cards, fitted to a loom to facilitate the weaving of figured fabrics. **2** a fabric made thus. [f. J.M. *Jacquard* of Lyons (d.1834), the inventor]

Jacuzzi /dʒəˈkuːzɪ/ *n.* [P] a large bath with underwater jets of water to massage the body. [f. name of inventor and manufacturer]

jade[1] *n.* **1** a hard green, blue, or white stone, a silicate of calcium and magnesium. **2** its green colour. [F, f. Sp. (*piedra de*) *ijada* (stone of) the colic f. L. *ilia* flanks]

jade[2] *n.* **1** a poor worn-out horse. **2** a hussy. [orig. unkn.]

jaded /ˈdʒeɪdɪd/ *adj.* tired and bored; (of the appetite) dulled, lacking zest for food. [f. prec.]

jadeite /ˈdʒeɪdaɪt/ *n.* a jadelike silicate of sodium and aluminium. [f. JADE[1]]

Jaffa /ˈdʒæfə/ *n.* (also **Jaffa orange**) a large oval thick-skinned variety of orange. [f. *Jaffa* port in Israel, near which it was first grown]

jag[1] *n.* a sharp projection of rock etc. —*v.t.* (**-gg-**) to cut or tear unevenly; to make indentations in. [prob. imit.]

jag[2] *n.* (*slang*) a drinking bout; a period of indulgence in an activity, emotion, etc. [orig. = load for one horse; orig. unkn.]

jagged /ˈdʒægɪd/ *adj.* with an unevenly cut or torn edge. [f. JAG[1]]

jaguar /ˈdʒægjʊə(r)/ *n.* a large American carnivorous spotted animal (*Panthera onca*) of the cat family. [f. Tupi-Guarani]

jail, jailer var. of GAOL, GAOLER.

Jain /dʒaɪn/ *adj.* of an Indian religion with doctrines like those of Buddhism. —*n.* an adherent of Jainism. [Hindi f. Skr. *jainas* of the conquerors (*ji* conquer)]

jalap /ˈdʒæləp/ *n.* a purgative drug from the tubers of a Mexican plant (*Exogonium purga*). [F f. Sp. (*Jalapa*, *Xalapa* Mexican city)]

jalopy /dʒəˈlɒpɪ/ *n.* (*colloq.*) a dilapidated old motor vehicle. [orig. unkn.]

jalousie /ˈʒælu:zi:/ *n.* a slatted blind or shutter to admit air and light but not rain etc. [F, = JEALOUSY]

jam[1] *v.t./i.* (**-mm-**) **1** to squeeze or wedge (*into* a space); to become wedged. **2** to cause (machinery) to become wedged etc. so that it cannot work; to become thus wedged. **3** to force or thrust violently. **4** to push or cram together in a compact mass; to block (a passage, road, etc.) by crowding. **5** to make (a radio transmission) unintelligible by causing interference. **6** (*colloq.*, in jazz etc.) to extemporize with other musicians. —*n.* **1** a squeeze, a crush; a stoppage (of a machine etc.) due to jamming. **2** a crowded mass. **3** (*colloq.*) an awkward position, a fix. **4** (*colloq.*) improvised playing by a group of jazz musicians. —**jam-packed** *adj.* (*colloq.*) very full. [imit.]

jam[2] *n.* **1** a sweet substance made of fruit and sugar boiled until thick. **2** (*colloq.*) something easy or pleasant. —**jam tomorrow,** a pleasant thing continually promised but usually never produced. [perh. = prec.]

jamb /dʒæm/ *n.* a side post or side of a doorway, window, or fireplace. [f. OF *jambe* leg f. L]

jamboree /dʒæmbəˈri:/ *n.* **1** a celebration, merry-making. **2** a large rally of Scouts. [orig. unkn.]

jammy *adj.* **1** covered with jam. **2** (*colloq.*) lucky, profitable. [f. JAM[2]]

Jan. *abbr.* January.

jangle *v.t./i.* **1** to make or cause to make a harsh metallic sound. **2** to cause irritation to (nerves etc.). —*n.* a jangling sound. [OF *jangler*]

janitor /ˈdʒænɪtə(r)/ *n.* a door-keeper; the caretaker of a building. —**janitorial** /-ˈtɔ:rɪəl/ *adj.* [L (*janua* door)]

janissary /ˈdʒænɪsərɪ/ *n.* a Turkish soldier; (*hist.*) a member of an elite and powerful body of Turkish infantry forming the sultan's guard and the main fighting force of the Turkish army from the late 14th to early 19th c. [f. Turk., = new troops]

January /ˈdʒænjʊərɪ/ the first month of the year. [L (*mensis*) *Januarius* (month) of Janus god of doorways and beginnings]

Jap *adj.* & *n.* (*colloq.*) Japanese. [abbr.]

japan /dʒəˈpæn/ *n.* a hard usually black varnish, especially a kind brought originally from Japan. —*v.t.* (**-nn-**) to coat with japan. [f. *Japan*, country in E. Asia]

Japanese /dʒæpəˈni:z/ *adj.* of Japan or its people or language. —*n.* **1** a Japanese person. **2** the language of Japan. [as prec.]

japonica /dʒəˈpɒnɪkə/ *n.* an ornamental variety of quince bearing red flowers in spring. [L *Japonicus* Japanese]

jar[1] *v.t./i.* (**-rr-**) **1** to jolt. **2** to sound with a harsh or unpleasant effect. **3** to shock. —*n.* a jarring movement or effect. [prob. imit.]

jar[2] *n.* **1** a glass or ceramic container with or without handle(s) and usually cylindrical. **2** its contents. **3** (*colloq.*) a glass (of beer etc.). [f. F. f. Arab. *jarra*]

jardinière /ʒɑ:dɪˈnjeə(r)/ *n.* a large ornamental pot for holding indoor plants. [F]

jargon /ˈdʒɑ:gən/ *n.* words or expressions developed for use within a particular group or profession, sounding ugly and unintelligible to outsiders. [OF, = chatter]

jasmine /ˈdʒæzmɪn/ *n.* a shrub of the genus *Jasminum* with white or yellow flowers, especially **common** or **white jasmine,** a climbing shrub (*J. officinale*) with fragrant flowers. **red jasmine,** a red-flowered frangipani (*Plumeria rubra*). **winter jasmine,** (*J. nudiflorum*) with yellow flowers. [f. F, ult. f. Pers. *yasamın*]

jasper /ˈdʒæspə(r)/ *n* an opaque variety of quartz, usually red, yellow, or brown. [f. OF f. L f. Gk *iaspis*, of oriental orig.]

jaundice /ˈdʒɔ:ndɪs/ *n.* **1** a condition caused by obstruction of the bile or by infective hepatitis and other diseases, and marked by yellowness of the skin, fluids, and tissues and occasionally by disordered vision. **2** disordered mental vision; resentment, jealousy. —*v.t.* **1** to affect with jaundice. **2** to fill with resentment or jealousy. [f. OF *jaunice* yellowness (*jaune* yellow)]

jaunt *n.* an excursion or journey, especially for

pleasure. —*v.i.* to take a jaunt. —**jaunting car,** a two-wheeled horse-drawn vehicle formerly common in Ireland. [orig. unkn.]

jaunty *adj.* **1** cheerful and self-confident. **2** (of clothes) stylish and cheerful. —**jauntily** *adv.*, **jauntiness** *n.* [f. F *gentil* (see GENTLE)]

javelin /ˈdʒæv(ə)lɪn/ *n.* a light spear thrown by hand as a weapon or in athletics. [f. F]

jaw *n.* **1** the bone(s) forming the framework of the mouth and (in vertebrates) carrying the teeth; the lower of these, the part of the face covering it; (in *pl.*) the mouth, its bones and teeth. **2** (in *pl.*) something resembling or gripping like jaws. **3** (*colloq.*) talkativeness, a lecture, a gossiping talk. —*v.t./i.* (*slang*) to talk long and boringly, to gossip. —**jawbone** *n.* a bone of the jaws, especially the lower jaw. **jaw-breaker** *n.* a word that is very long, or hard to pronounce. [f. OF *joe* cheek, jaw]

jay *n.* a bird of the crow family, especially the noisy chattering European bird *Garrulus glandarius* which has pinkish-brown plumage, a black tail, and a small blue barred patch on each wing. [f. OF f. L *gaius*, perh. f. name *Gaius*]

jay-walk *v.i.* to cross or walk in a road carelessly without regard for traffic or signals. —**jay-walker** *n.* [f. JAY = stupid person]

jazz *n.* **1** a type of 20th-c. music with syncopation, improvisation, and strong rhythm. **2** pretentious talk or behaviour. —*adj.* of, in or like jazz. —*v.t./i.* **1** to play or arrange as jazz. **2** to brighten or liven *up*. [perh. orig. = copulation]

jazzy *adj.* **1** of or like jazz. **2** vividly coloured, showy. [f. JAZZ]

jealous /ˈdʒeləs/ *adj.* **1** resentful of a rival or a person's advantages etc. **2** watchfully tenacious (*of* rights etc.). **3** (of God) intolerant of disloyalty. —**jealously** *adv.*, **jealousy** *n.* [f. OF f. L *zelosus* (as ZEAL)]

jean /dʒiːn/ *n.* **1** a kind of twilled cotton cloth. **2** (in *pl.*) trousers made of jean or of denim. [f. OF f. L *Janua* Genoa]

Jeep *n.* [P] a small sturdy motor vehicle with four-wheel drive. [f. *GP* = general purposes, influenced by 'Eugene the *Jeep*', animal in a comic strip]

jeer *v.t./i.* to laugh or shout (*at*) rudely or scornfully. —*n.* a jeering remark or shout. [orig. unkn.]

Jehovah /dʒɪˈhəʊvə/ God, the name of God used in the Old Testament. —**Jehovah's Witness,** a member of a fundamentalist Christian sect. [f. Heb. *yahveh*]

jejune /dʒɪˈdʒuːn/ *adj.* **1** insipid, unsatisfying to the mind. **2** deficient in nourishing qualities, barren. [L *jejunus* fasting]

jejunum /dʒɪˈdʒuːnəm/ *n.* the part of the small intestine between the duodenum and the ileum. [L, as prec.]

jell *v.i.* (*colloq.*) **1** to set as jelly. **2** to take definite form. [f. JELLY]

jellaba /ˈdʒeləbə/ *n.* a loose hooded cloak worn by Arab men in some countries. [Arab.]

jelly[1] *n.* **1** a soft solid semitransparent food made of or with gelatine. **2** a substance of similar consistency. **3** a kind of jam made of strained fruit-juice and sugar. —*v.t./i.* **1** to set or cause to set as jelly, to congeal. **2** to set (food) in jelly. —**jelly baby,** a gelatinous sweet in the shape of a baby. [f. OF *gelee* frost, jelly, f. L *gelare* freeze (*gelu* frost)]

jelly[2] *n.* (*slang*) gelignite. [f. GELIGNITE]

jellyfish *n.* (*pl.* **-fish**) a coelenterate (usually marine) animal with a saucer-shaped gelatinous body and stinging tentacles, = MEDUSA.

jemmy *n.* a burglar's crowbar for forcing doors, windows, etc. [pet-form of *James*]

jeopardize /ˈdʒepədaɪz/ *v.t.* to endanger. [f. foll.]

jeopardy /ˈdʒepədɪ/ *n.* danger. [f. OF *ieu parti* divided (i.e. even) game f. L *jocus* game, *partiri* divide]

jerboa /dʒɜːˈbəʊə/ *n.* **1** a small African desert rodent of the family Dipodidae, with long hind legs and tail. **2** any of various Australian animals resembling this. [L, f. Arab. *yarbū'* flesh of loins, jerboa]

jeremiad /dʒerɪˈmaɪəd/ *n.* a long mournful complaint about one's troubles. [f. F f. foll.]

jerk[1] *n.* **1** a sudden sharp pull, push, twist, start, etc. **2** a movement caused by involuntary contraction of a muscle. —*v.t./i.* to move with a jerk; to throw with suddenly arrested motion. —**jerky** *adj.*, **jerkily** *adv.*, **jerkiness** *n.* [perh. imit.]

jerk[2] *v.t.* to cure (beef etc.) by cutting it into long slices and drying it in the sun. [f. Amer. Sp. f. Quechua *echarqui* dried flesh]

jerkin *n.* **1** a sleeveless jacket. **2** (*hist.*) a man's close-fitting jacket, often of leather. [orig. unkn.]

jeroboam /dʒerəˈbəʊəm/ *n.* a wine-bottle of 6-12 times the ordinary size. [named after *Jeroboam*, a 'mighty man of valour', king of Israel, 10th c. BC (1 Kings 11: 28)]

Jerry *n.* (*colloq.*) a German; Germans collectively. [f. GERMAN]

jerry *n.* (*slang*) a chamber-pot. [prob. f. *Jeroboam*]

jerry-built *adj.* built badly and with poor materials —**jerry-builder** *n.*, **jerry-building** *n.* [prob. orig. dial.]

jerrycan /ˈdʒerɪkæn/ *n.* a kind of 5-gallon can for petrol or water, used by the Germans and named and later adopted by the Allied forces in the war of 1939-45.

Jersey /ˈdʒɜːzɪ/ *n.* a breed of light-brown dairy cattle that originated in Jersey, producing milk with a high fat content; an animal of this breed. [f. *Jersey* in the Channel Islands]

jersey /ˈdʒɜːzɪ/ *n.* **1** a pullover with sleeves. **2** machine-knitted fabric used for making clothes. [as prec.]

jess *n.* a short strap put round the leg of a hawk used in falconry. [f. OF *ges*, f. L *jactus* throw]

jessamine /ˈdʒesəmɪn/ *n.* = JASMINE.

jest *n.* a joke. —*v.i.* to joke. —**in jest**, jokingly. [orig. = exploit, f. OF *geste* f. L *gesta* (*gerere* do)]

jester *n.* **1** a professional entertainer employed at a king's court or in a noble household in the Middle Ages. **2** a person who makes jests. [f. JEST]

Jesuit /ˈdʒezjʊɪt/ *n.* a member of the Society of Jesus, an order of priests founded in 1534 in Paris by Ignatius Loyola. [f. *Jesus*]

Jesuitical /dʒezjʊˈɪtɪk(ə)l/ *adj.* **1** of or like Jesuits. **2** (*derog.*) dissembling, equivocating. [f. prec.]

jet[1] *n.* **1** a stream of water, gas(es), or flame etc. ejected, usually from a small opening. **2** a spout or opening from which this comes; a burner on a gas cooker. **3** a jet-propelled aircraft; a jet engine. —*v.t./i.* (**-tt-**) **1** to spurt in jets. **2** to travel or convey by jet-propelled aircraft. **3** to jut. —**jet engine**, an engine utilizing jet propulsion to provide forward thrust. **jet-foil** *n.* a vessel that travels above the surface of the water on struts attached to underwater foils. **jet lag**, delayed physical effects of tiredness etc. felt after a long flight by jet aircraft, especially owing to the difference of local time. **jet-propelled** *adj.* using jet propulsion. **jet propulsion**, propulsion by backward ejection of a high-speed jet of gas etc. **jet set**, the wealthy élite making frequent air journeys between social or business events. [f. F *jeter* throw f. L *jactare* frequent. of *jacere* throw]

jet[2] *n.* **1** hard black lignite that takes a brilliant polish. **2** its colour, deep glossy black. —*adj.* of this colour. —**jet-black** *adj.* & *n.* [f. Gk *Gagai*, town in Asia Minor]

jetsam *n.* goods thrown overboard from a ship in distress to lighten it, especially those that are washed ashore. [f. foll.]

jettison /ˈdʒetɪs(ə)n/ *v.t.* **1** to throw (goods) overboard; to release or drop from an aircraft or spacecraft in flight. **2** to discard as unwanted. [f. AF & OF f. L (as JET[1])]

jetty *n.* a breakwater or landing-stage. [f. OF (as JET[1])]

Jew *n.* a person of Hebrew descent; one whose religion is Judaism. —**Jew's harp**, a musical instrument consisting of a small U-shaped metal frame held in the teeth while a springy metal clip joining its ends is twanged with a finger. [f. F, ult. f. Heb. *yehudi*, member of the tribe of Judah]

jewel /ˈdʒuːəl/ *n.* **1** a precious stone worn as an ornament, a jewelled ornament. **2** a highly valued person or thing. [f. AF, perh. f. L *jocus* jest]

jewelled /ˈdʒuːəld/ *adj.* **1** set with jewels. **2** (of a watch) fitted with jewels for the pivot-holes on account of their resistance to wear. [f. prec.]

jeweller /ˈdʒuːələ(r)/ *n.* a person who deals in or makes jewellery or jewels. [f. JEWEL]

jewellery /ˈdʒuːəlrɪ/ *n.* jewels or similar ornaments to be worn. [as prec.]

Jewess *n.* a female Jew. [f. JEW]

Jewish *adj.* of Jews. [f. JEW]

Jewry *n.* the Jewish people. [f. JEW]

jib[1] *n.* **1** a triangular stay-sail from the outer end of the jib-boom to the head of the fore-topmast in large ships or from bowsprit to masthead in smaller ones. **2** the projecting arm of a crane. —*v.t./i.* (**-bb-**) = GYBE 1,2. —**cut of a person's jib**, his general appearance or manner. **jib-boom** *n.* a spar run out from the end of a bowsprit. [orig. unkn.]

jib[2] *v.i.* (**-bb-**) **1** to refuse to proceed in some action. **2** (of a horse) to stop suddenly and refuse to go forwards. —**jib at**, to show unwillingness or dislike for. [orig. unkn.]

jibbah /ˈdʒɪbə/ *n.* a long coat worn by Muslim men in some countries. [Arab.]

jibe /dʒaɪb/ *v.t./i.* & *n.* = GIBE.

jiff *n.* (also **jiffy**) (*colloq.*) a short time. [orig. unkn.]

jig *n.* **1** a lively jumping dance; the music for this. **2** a device that holds a piece of work and guides the tools operating upon it. **3** a template. —*v.t./i.* (**-gg-**) to move up and down rapidly and jerkily. [orig. unkn.]

jigger[1] *n.* **1** a measure of spirits etc.; a small glass holding this amount. **2** (*slang*) a cue-rest used in billiards. [partly f. JIG]

jigger[2] *n.* **1** = CHIGGER. **2** = CHIGOE. [corrupt. of these words]

jiggered /ˈdʒɪgəd/ *adj.* (*colloq.*, in a mild oath) damned. [euphem.]

jiggery-pokery /ˈdʒɪgərɪ ˈpəʊkərɪ/ *n.* (*colloq.*) trickery, underhand dealing. [Sc. *jouk* dodge, skulk]

jiggle *v.t./i.* to rock or jerk lightly. [f. JIG or JOGGLE]

jigsaw /ˈdʒɪgsɔː/ *n.* **1** a mechanically operated fretsaw. **2** (also **jigsaw puzzle**) a picture on wood or cardboard etc. cut into irregular pieces which can be shuffled and reassembled for amusement. [f. JIG + SAW[1]]

jihad /dʒɪ'hɑ:d/ *n.* (in Islam) a holy war. [Arab., = fight, struggle]

jilt *v.t.* to reject or abandon (a person) after having courted or promised to marry him or her. [orig. unkn.]

jingle *v.t./i.* to make or cause to make a metallic ringing or clinking sound. —*n.* **1** a jingling sound. **2** verse or words with simple catchy rhymes or repetitive sounds. [imit.]

jingo *n.* (*pl.* **-oes**) an aggressive fanatical patriot. —**jingoism** *n.*, **jingoist** *n.*, **jingoistic** *adj.* [f. *by jingo* (= by God) in a popular music-hall refrain]

jink *v.i.* to move with sudden quick turns, especially in dodging —*n.* an act of jinking. —**high jinks**, boisterous fun. [orig. Sc., prob. imit. of nimble motion]

jinnee /dʒɪ'ni:/ *n.* (*pl.* **jinn** also used as *sing.*) (*Islamic myth.*) any of the supernatural beings, similar to but distinguished from angels, able to appear in human and animal form. [Arab.]

jinx *n.* (*colloq.*) a person or thing that seems to bring bad luck. [perh. var. of *jynx* the wryneck, a bird used in witchcraft]

jitter *v.i.* (*colloq.*) to be nervous, to behave nervously. —*n.* (in *pl.*, *colloq.*) nervousness. —**jittery** *adj.* [orig. unkn.]

jitterbug *n.* **1** a nervous person. **2** a dance performed chiefly to boogie-woogie and swing music, popular in the early 1940s. —*v.i.* (**-gg-**) to dance the jitterbug. [f. prec.]

jive *n.* a type of fast lively jazz music; a dance done to this. —*v.i.* to dance to or play jive. [orig. unkn.]

Jnr. *abbr.* Junior.

job *n.* **1** a piece of work. **2** a position in paid employment. **3** a difficult task. —*v.t./i.* (**-bb-**) **1** to do jobs, to do piece-work. **2** to hire or let out for a definite time or job. **3** to buy and sell (stock or goods) as a middleman. —**bad** (*or* **good**) **job**, an unsatisfactory (or satisfactory) state of affairs. **job lot**, a collection of miscellaneous articles. **just the job**, (*slang*) precisely what is wanted. **make a (good) job of**, to do thoroughly or successfully. [orig. unkn.]

jobber *n.* **1** a principal or wholesaler dealing on the Stock Exchange. **2** one who jobs. [f. JOB]

jobbery /'dʒɒbərɪ/ *n.* corrupt dealing. [f. JOB]

jobcentre *n.* a government office displaying information about available jobs.

jobless *adj.* unemployed. [f. JOB + -LESS]

Jock *n.* a nickname for a Scotsman. [Sc. form of *Jack*]

jockey *n.* a person who rides in horse-races, especially a professional. —*v.t./i.* to manœuvre in order to gain an advantage. [f. Sc. *Jock* Jack]

jock-strap *n.* a support or protection for the male genitals, worn especially by sportsmen. [f. vulg. *jock* genitals]

jocose /dʒə'kəʊs/ *adj.* joking. —**jocosely** *adv.*, **jocoseness** *n.*, **jocosity** /-'kɒsɪtɪ/ *n.* [f. L (*jocus* jest)]

jocular /'dʒɒkjʊlə(r)/ *adj.* joking, humorous. **jocularly** *adv.*, **jocularity** /-'lærɪtɪ/ *n.* [as prec.]

jocund /'dʒɒkənd/ *adj.* (*literary*) merry, cheerful. —**jocundity** /dʒə'kʌndɪtɪ/ *n.* [f. OF f. L *jocundus* pleasant]

jodhpurs /'dʒɒdpəz/ *n.pl.* riding-breeches reaching to the ankle, fitting closely below the knee and loosely above it. [f. *Jodhpur*, city and former State of India]

joey *n.* (*Austral.*) **1** a young kangaroo. **2** a young animal. [Aboriginal *joè*]

jog *v.t./i.* (**-gg-**) **1** to shake with a push or jerk, to nudge. **2** to rouse or stimulate (memory). **3** to move up and down with an unsteady motion. **4** to move at a jogtrot, to run at a leisurely pace with short strides as a form of exercise. —*n.* **1** a slight shake or push, a nudge. **2** a slow walk, run, or trot. —**jog on** *or* **along**, to proceed slowly or laboriously. —**jogger** *n.* [imit.]

joggle *v.t./i.* to shake slightly, to move by slight jerks. —*n.* a slight shake, a joggling movement. [f. JOG]

jogtrot *n.* a slow regular trot.

John Bull /bʊl/ a personification of the English nation, a typical Englishman, represented as a stout red-faced farmer-like man in a top hat and high boots. [orig. character in satire (1712)]

johnny /'dʒɒnɪ/ *n.* (*colloq.*) a fellow, a man. —**johnny-come-lately** *n.* a newcomer, an upstart. [dim. of forename *John*]

joie de vivre /ʒwɑ: də 'vi:vr/ a feeling of exuberant enjoyment of life; high spirits. [F, = joy of living]

join *v.t./i.* **1** to put together, to fasten, to unite. **2** to connect (points) by a line etc. **3** to become a member of (a club, army, etc.); to take one's place with or in (a company, procession, etc.); to take part with others (*in* an activity etc.). **4** to unite (persons, or one *with* or *to* another); to be united in marriage, an alliance, etc. **5** (of a river, road, etc.) to become continuous or connected with (another). —*n.* the point, line, or surface where things join. —**join battle**, to begin fighting. **join forces**, to combine efforts. **join up**, to enlist in an army etc. [f. OF *joindre* f. L *jungere*]

joiner *n.* a maker of furniture and light woodwork. —**joinery** *n.* [f. AF & OF (as JOIN)]

joint *n.* **1** a place where two things are joined.

2 a means or device for joining parts of a structure; a structure by which bones fit together. 3 a section of an animal's carcass used for food. 4 a fissure in a mass of rock. 5 (*slang*) a place of meeting for drinking etc. 6 (*slang*) a marijuana cigarette. —*adj.* belonging to or done by two or more persons etc. in common; sharing in possession etc. —*v.t.* 1 to connect by a joint or joints. 2 to divide (a carcass) into joints or at a joint. —**joint-stock company,** a company with the capital held jointly by the shareholders. **out of joint,** dislocated; (*fig.*) out of order. —**jointly** *adv.* [f. OF (as JOIN)]

jointure /ˈdʒɔɪntʃə(r)/ *n.* an estate settled on a wife for the period during which she survives her husband. —*v.t.* to provide with a jointure. [f. OF f. L (as JOIN)]

joist *n.* one of the parallel timbers stretched from wall to wall to carry floorboards or a ceiling. [f. OF *giste* f. L *jacēre* lie]

joke *n.* 1 a thing said or done to excite laughter. 2 a ridiculous circumstance, person, etc. —*v.i.* to make jokes. —**no joke,** a serious matter. [perh. f. L *jocus* jest]

joker *n.* 1 one who jokes. 2 an extra playing-card used in some games. 3 (*slang*) a person. [f. JOKE]

jokey /ˈdʒəʊkɪ/ *adj.* joking, not serious. [f. JOKE]

jollify /ˈdʒɒlɪfaɪ/ *v.t./i.* to make or be merry. —**jollification** /-fɪˈkeɪʃ(ə)n/ *n.* [f. JOLLY]

jollity /ˈdʒɒlɪtɪ/ *n.* being jolly; merry-making. [f. OF *joliveté* (as foll.)]

jolly *adj.* 1 full of high spirits, cheerful, merry. 2 slightly drunk. 3 (*colloq.*, of a person or thing) pleasant, delightful (also *iron.*). —*adv.* (*colloq.*) very. —*v.t.* to coax or humour (a person) in a friendly way. [f. OF *jolif* gay, pretty (perh. as YULE)]

jolly-boat *n.* a clinker-built ship's boat, smaller than a cutter. [orig. unkn.]

jolt /dʒəʊlt/ *v.t./i.* 1 to shake or dislodge with a jerk. 2 to move along jerkily, as on a rough road. 3 to give a mental shock to. —*n.* 1 a jolting movement. 2 a surprise or shock. [orig. unkn.]

jonquil /ˈdʒɒŋkwɪl/ *n.* a species of narcissus (*Narcissus jonquilla*) with white or yellow fragrant flowers. [f. F f. Sp. f. L *juncus* rush; so called f. its rushlike leaves]

josh *v.t./i.* (*US slang*) to make fun of; to hoax; to indulge in ridicule. —*n.* (*US slang*) a good-natured joke. [orig. unkn.]

joss *n.* a Chinese idol. —**joss-house** *n.* a temple. **joss-stick** *n.* a stick of fragrant tinder and clay for incense. [perh. ult. f. Port. *deos* f. L *deus* god]

jostle *v.t./i.* to push roughly, especially when in a crowd; to struggle. —*n.* jostling. [f. JOUST]

jot *n.* a small amount, a whit. —*v.t.* (**-tt-**) to write (usu. *down*) briefly. [f. L f. Gk IOTA]

jotter *n.* a small notebook or note-pad. [f. JOT]

jottings *n.pl.* jotted notes. [f. JOT]

joule /dʒuːl/ *n.* a unit of work or energy, the work done by a force of 1 newton when its point of application moves 1 metre in the direction of action of the force, work done or heat generated by a current of 1 ampere flowing for 1 second against a resistance of 1 ohm. [f. J. P. *Joule*, English physicist (d. 1889)]

jounce *v.t./i.* to bump, to bounce, to jolt. [orig. unkn.]

journal /ˈdʒɜːn(ə)l/ *n.* 1 a daily record of events or of business transactions and accounts. 2 a periodical (orig. a daily newspaper). 3 the part of a shaft or axle that rests on the bearings. [f. OF f. L, = DIURNAL]

journalese /dʒɜːnəˈliːz/ *n.* a hackneyed style of language characteristic of some newspaper writing. [f. prec.]

journalist /ˈdʒɜːn(ə)list/ *n.* a person employed to write for a journal or newspaper. —**journalism** *n.*, **journalistic** /-ˈlɪstɪk/ *adj.* [f. JOURNAL]

journey /ˈdʒɜːnɪ/ *n.* an act of going from one place to another, especially at a long distance; the distance travelled in a specified time. —*v.i.* to make a journey. [f. OF, = day's work or travel, f. L *diurnus* daily]

journeyman *n.* (*pl.* **-men**) 1 a qualified mechanic or artisan working for another. 2 a sound but undistinguished workman.

joust /dʒaʊst/ *n.* a combat with lances between two mounted knights or men-at-arms. —*v.i.* to engage in a joust. [f. OF *juster* bring together f. L *juxta* beside]

Jove /dʒəʊv/ Jupiter. —**by Jove!,** an exclamation of surprise or approval. —**Jovian** *adj.* [f. L *Jovis* used as genitive of *Jupiter*]

jovial /ˈdʒəʊvɪ(ə)l/ *adj.* full of cheerful good humour. —**joviality** /-ˈælɪtɪ/ *n.*, **jovially** *adv.* [F f. L (as prec.); orig. ref. to influence of planet Jupiter]

jowl *n.* 1 the jaw or jawbone; the cheek. 2 loose skin on the throat, a dewlap. [OE]

joy *n.* gladness, deep pleasure; a cause of this. —**no joy,** (*colloq.*) no satisfaction or success. —**joyous** *adj.*, **joyously** *adv.* [f. OF *joie* f. L *gaudia* (*gaudēre* rejoice)]

joyful *adj.* full of joy. —**joyfully** *adv.*, **joyfulness** *n.* [f. JOY + -FUL]

joyless *adj.* without joy. [f. JOY + -LESS]

joy-ride *n.* a ride taken for pleasure in a car etc., usually unauthorized. —**joy-rider** *n.*, **joy-riding** *n.*

joystick *n.* the control-lever of an aeroplane.

JP *abbr.* Justice of the Peace.

Jr. *abbr.* Junior.

jubilant /ˈdʒuːbɪlənt/ *adj.* exultant, rejoicing. —**jubilance** *n.*, **jubilantly** *adv.* [f. L (*jubilare* shout for joy)]

jubilation /dʒuːbɪˈleɪʃ(ə)n/ *n.* exultation, rejoicing. [as prec.]

jubilee /ˈdʒuːbɪliː/ *n.* **1** an anniversary (especially the 50th). **2** a time of rejoicing. [f. OF f. L ult. f. Heb. *yobel* ram's-horn trumpet; assoc. with L *jubilare* (see JUBILANT)]

Judaic /dʒuːˈdeɪɪk/ *adj.* of or characteristic of the Jews. [f. L f. Gk (as JEW)]

Judaism /ˈdʒuːdeɪɪz(ə)m/ *n.* **1** the religion of the Jews. **2** Jews collectively. [as prec.]

Judaize /ˈdʒuːdeɪaɪz/ *v.t./i.* to make Jewish; to follow Jewish customs. [as JUDAIC]

Judas /ˈdʒuːdəs/ *n.* an infamous traitor. [f. *Judas* Iscariot, disciple who betrayed]

judder *v.i.* to shake noisily or violently. —*n.* a juddering movement or sound. [imit., cf. *shudder*]

judge /dʒʌdʒ/ *n.* **1** a public officer appointed to try causes in a court of justice. **2** a person appointed to decide a dispute or contest. **3** a person fit to decide on the merits of a thing or question. **4** (in ancient Israel) any of the leaders with temporary authority in the period between Joshua and the kings (*c.*13th–11th c. BC). —*v.t./i.* **1** to try (a cause) in a court of justice **2** to pronounce sentence on. **3** to decide (a contest or question). **4** to form an opinion about; to estimate; to conclude or consider. **5** to act as judge (of). —**Judges' Rules,** a set of rules about the mode of questioning of suspects by police. [f. OF f. L *judex*]

judgement /ˈdʒʌdʒmənt/ *n.* (in Law also **judgment**) **1** judging, being judged. **2** ability to judge; good sense. **3** the decision of a judge etc. in a court of justice. **4** the judging of mankind by God. **5** a misfortune as a sign of divine displeasure. —**Judgement Day** *or* **Day of Judgement,** the day of the **Last Judgement** when God will judge all mankind. [as prec.]

judicature /ˈdʒuːdɪkətʃə(r)/ *n.* **1** the administration of justice. **2** a judge's office. **3** a body of judges. [f. L (*judicare* to judge)]

judicial /dʒuːˈdɪʃ(ə)l/ *adj.* **1** of or by a court of law. **2** having the function of judgement. **3** of or proper to a judge. **4** expressing a judgement. **5** able to judge wisely, impartial. —**judicially** *adv.* [f. L (*judicium* court, judgement)]

judiciary /dʒuːˈdɪʃɪərɪ/ *n.* the judges of a State collectively [as prec.]

judicious /dʒuːˈdɪʃəs/ *adj.* judging wisely, showing good sense —**judiciously** *adv.* [f. F f. L (as JUDICIAL)]

judo /ˈdʒuːdəʊ/ *n.* a sport of unarmed combat that developed from ju-jitsu primarily in Japan. [Jap. *jū* gentle, *dō* way]

judoist /ˈdʒuːdəʊɪst/ *n.* a student of or an expert in judo. [f. JUDO]

jug *n.* **1** a deep vessel for liquids, with a handle and often a shaped lip. **2** (*slang*) prison. —*v.t.* (**-gg-**) to stew (a hare) in a covered vessel. [perh. f. *Jug*, pet-form of *Joan*]

juggernaut /ˈdʒʌgənɔːt/ *n.* **1** a large heavy vehicle. **2** an overpowering force or object. [f. Hindi *Jagannath* lord of the world]

juggins /ˈdʒʌgɪnz/ *n.* (*slang*) a simpleton. [perh. f. surname *Juggins*]

juggle *v.t./i.* **1** to perform feats of dexterity (*with* objects), especially by tossing and catching them, keeping several in the air at once. **2** to manipulate or arrange (facts, figures, etc.) to suit a purpose. —*n.* a trick, a deception. [f. OF *jogler* f. L *joculari* jest (as JOKE)]

juggler *n.* one who juggles, especially to entertain. [f. OF f. L *joculator* (as prec.)]

jugular /ˈdʒʌgjʊlə(r)/ *adj.* of the neck or throat. —*n.* the jugular vein. —**jugular vein,** either of the two large veins in the neck, conveying the blood from the head. [f. L (*jugulum* collar-bone, throat)]

juice /dʒuːs/ *n.* **1** the liquid content of fruits, vegetables, or meat. **2** a liquid bodily secretion. **3** (*slang*) electricity. **4** (*slang*) petrol used in an engine etc. [f. OF f. L *jus* broth]

juicy *adj.* **1** full of juice. **2** (*colloq.*) interesting, especially because scandalous. —**juicily** *adv.*, **juiciness** *n.* [f. prec.]

ju-jitsu /dʒuːˈdʒɪtsuː/ *n.* a Japanese method of self-defence using throws, punches, kicks, arm-locks, etc. [f. Jap. (*jū* gentle, *jutsu* skill)]

ju-ju /ˈdʒuːdʒuː/ *n.* an object venerated in West Africa as a charm or fetish; the magic attributed to this. [perh. f. F *joujou* toy]

jujube /ˈdʒuːdʒuːb/ *n.* a sweet fruit-flavoured lozenge of gelatin etc. [F or f. L ult. f. Gk *zizuphon* edible fruit of species of plant *zizyphus*, orig. used to flavour jujubes]

juke-box /ˈdʒuːkbɒks/ *n.* a machine that automatically plays a selected gramophone record when a coin is inserted. [f. *juke* cheap roadhouse providing music for dancing, f. Negro dialect (of West African origin) in the south-western USA + BOX[1]]

Jul. *abbr.* July.

julep /ˈdʒuːlep/ *n.* **1** a sweet drink, especially as a vehicle for medicine; a medicated drink. **2** (*US*) iced and flavoured spirit and water, especially *mint julep*. [f. OF f. Arab. f. Pers., = rose-water]

Julian /ˈdʒuːlɪən/ *adj.* of Julius Caesar. —**Julian calendar,** the calendar introduced by him in 46 BC in which the ordinary year has 365 days, and every fourth year is a leap year of 366 days. [f. L *Julianus* f. JULIUS]

julienne /dʒu:lɪ'en/ *n.* a clear meat soup containing vegetables cut into thin strips; such vegetables. —*adj.* cut into thin strips. [F, f. names *Jules* or *Julien*]

Juliet cap /'dʒu:ljət/ a small network skull-cap, usually ornamented with pearls. [f. name of heroine of Shakespeare's romantic tragedy 'Romeo and Juliet']

July /dʒu:'laɪ/ *n.* the seventh month of the year. [f. AF f. L *Julius* (*mensis*), named after Julius Caesar]

jumble *v.t.* to mix *up*, to confuse. —*n.* **1** a confused pile etc., a muddle. **2** articles for a jumble sale. —**jumble sale,** a sale of miscellaneous articles, usually second-hand, to raise funds for charity etc. [prob. imit.]

jumbo /'dʒʌmbəʊ/ *n.* (*pl.* **-os**) **1** a person, animal, or thing that is very large of its kind. **2** an elephant. **3** a jumbo jet. —*adj.* very large of its kind. —**jumbo jet,** a very large jet aircraft able to carry several hundred passengers. [prob. f. MUMBO-JUMBO]

jump *v.t./i.* **1** to move up off the ground etc. by bending and then extending the legs or (of fish) by a movement of the tail. **2** to move suddenly with a jump or bound; to rise suddenly from a seat etc.; to give a sudden movement from shock or excitement etc. **3** to pass over by jumping; to cause (a horse etc.) to jump. **4** to pass over (a thing) to a point beyond; to skip (part of a book etc.) in reading or studying. **5** to come *to* (a conclusion) hastily. **6** (of a train etc.) to leave (the rails). **7** to ignore and pass (a red traffic-light etc.). **8** to abscond from. **9** to pounce upon or attack (a person etc.). **10** to take summary possession of (a claim allegedly forfeit etc.). —*n.* **1** an act of jumping. **2** an abrupt rise in a price etc. **3** an obstacle to be jumped, especially by a horse. **4** a sudden transition. **5** a sudden movement caused by shock, excitement, etc. —**have the jump on,** (*slang*) to have an advantage over. **jump at,** to accept eagerly. **jump down a person's throat,** to reprimand or contradict him severely. **jumped-up** *adj.* upstart. **jump the gun,** (*colloq.*) to begin before the signal is given, or prematurely. **jump-jet** *n.* a jet aircraft that can take off and land vertically. **jump-lead** *n.* a cable for conveying current from one battery through another. **jump-off** *n.* a deciding round in show-jumping. **jump on,** to attack or criticize crushingly. **jump the queue,** to take unfair precedence. **jump suit,** a one-piece garment for the whole body. **jump to it,** to act promptly and energetically. **one jump ahead,** one stage ahead of a rival etc. [prob. imit.]

jumper[1] *n.* **1** a person or animal that jumps. **2** a short wire used to make or break an electrical circuit. [f. JUMP]

jumper[2] *n.* **1** a woman's knitted garment for the upper part of the body. **2** a loose outer jacket worn by sailors. [perh. f. dial. *jump* short coat]

jumpy *adj.* nervous, easily startled; making sudden movements. —**jumpily** *adv.*, **jumpiness** *n.* [f. JUMP]

Jun. *abbr.* **1** Junior. **2** June.

junction /'dʒʌŋkʃ(ə)n/ *n.* **1** joining. **2** a place where things join. **3** a place where railway lines or roads meet. —**junction box,** a box containing a junction of electric cables etc. [f. L (as JOIN)]

juncture /'dʒʌŋktʃə(r)/ *n.* **1** a critical convergence of events; a point of time. **2** joining. **3** a place where things join. [f. L (as JOIN)]

June /dʒu:n/ *n.* the sixth month of the year. [f. OF & L *Junius* (goddess *Juno*)]

jungle *n.* **1** land overgrown with tangled vegetation, especially in the tropics; an area of such land. **2** a tangled mass. **3** a place of bewildering complexity or confusion, or of ruthless struggle. —**jungly** *adj.* [f. Hindi f. Skr.]

junior /'dʒu:nɪə(r)/ *adj.* **1** the younger (esp. appended to a name for distinction between two persons of the same name). **2** younger in age; lower in rank or authority. **3** of a low or the lowest position. **4** for younger children. —*n.* **1** a junior person. **2** a person acting or working in a junior capacity. [L, compar. of *juvenis* young]

juniper /'dʒu:nɪpə(r)/ *n.* an evergreen shrub or tree of the genus *Juniperus*, especially one with purple berrylike cones yielding an oil used for flavouring gin and in medicine. [f. L *juniperus*]

junk[1] *n.* **1** discarded articles, rubbish; anything regarded as of little value. **2** (*slang*) a narcotic drug, especially heroin. —**junk food,** food which is not nutritious. **junk shop,** a shop selling miscellaneous cheap second-hand goods. [orig. unkn.]

junk[2] *n.* a flat-bottomed sailing vessel in the China seas. [f. F, Port. or Du., f. Javanese]

junket /'dʒʌŋkɪt/ *n.* **1** a dish of milk curdled by rennet and sweetened and flavoured. **2** a feast. **3** (*US*) a pleasure outing. **4** (*US*) an official's tour at public expense. —*v.i.* **1** to feast, to make merry. **2** (*US*) to hold a picnic or outing. —**junketing** *n.* [f. OF *jonquette* rush-basket (used for junket) f. L *juncus* rush]

junkie /'dʒʌŋkɪ/ *n.* (*slang*) a drug addict. [f. JUNK[1]]

junta /'dʒʌntə/ *n.* a political clique or faction, especially one holding power after a revolution. [Sp. & Port. f. L (as JOIN)]

jural /'dʒʊər(ə)l/ *adj.* of the law; of (moral) rights and obligations. [f. L *jus* law, right]

Jurassic /dʒʊə'ræsɪk/ *adj.* of the second period

of the Mesozoic era. —*n.* this period. [f. F *jurassique* f. JURA]

juridical /dʒʊəˈrɪdɪk(ə)l/ *adj.* of judicial proceedings; relating to the law. —**juridically** *adv.* [f. L *juridicus* (*jus* law, *dicere* say)]

jurisdiction /dʒʊərɪsˈdɪkʃ(ə)n/ *n.* **1** authority to interpret and apply the law. **2** official power exercised within a particular sphere of activity. **3** the extent or territory over which legal or other power extends. [f. OF & L (as prec.)]

jurisprudence /dʒʊərɪsˈpru:d(ə)ns/ *n.* the science or philosophy of law. —**jurisprudential** /-ˈdenʃ(ə)l/ *adj.* [f. L (as prec. + PRUDENCE)]

jurist /ˈdʒʊərɪst/ *n.* one who is skilled in the law. —**juristic** /-ˈrɪstɪk/ *adj.*, **juristical** *adj.*, **juristically** *adv.* [f. F or L (*jus* law)]

juror /ˈdʒʊərə(r)/ *n.* **1** a member of a jury. **2** a person taking an oath. [f. AF f. L *jurator* (*jurare* swear)]

jury /ˈdʒʊərɪ/ *n.* **1** a body of persons sworn to render a verdict in a court of justice or a coroner's court. **2** a body of persons selected to award the prizes in a competition. —**jury-box** *n.* an enclosure for the jury in a court. **grand jury**, see GRAND. **petty** *or* **trial jury**, a jury of twelve persons who try the final issue of fact in civil or criminal cases and pronounce the verdict. —**juryman** *n.* (*pl.* **-men**), **jurywoman** *n.fem.* (*pl.* **-women**) [f. AF *jurée* oath, inquiry (as prec.)]

jury-mast /ˈdʒʊərɪmɑ:st/ *n.* a temporary mast replacing one broken or lost. [perh. f. OF *ajurie* aid + MAST[1]]

jury-rigged /ˈdʒʊərɪrɪgd/ *adj.* makeshift. [as prec.]

just *adj.* **1** giving proper consideration to the claims of everyone concerned. **2** deserved, right in amount etc. **3** well-grounded in fact. —*adv.* **1** exactly. **2** barely, no more than; by only a short distance etc. **3** at this or that moment, only a little time ago. **4** (*colloq.*) simply, merely. **5** positively, quite. **6** (*slang*) really, indeed. —**just about,** (*colloq.*) almost exactly; almost completely. **just in case,** as a precaution. **just now,** at this moment; only a little time ago. **just so,** exactly arranged; exactly as you say. —**justly** *adv.*, **justness** *n.* [f. OF f. L *justus* (*jus* law, right)]

justice /ˈdʒʌstɪs/ *n.* **1** justness, fairness; the exercise of authority in the maintenance of right. **2** judicial proceedings. **3** a judge or magistrate. —**do justice to,** to treat fairly; to appreciate duly. **do oneself justice,** to perform in a manner worthy of one's abilities. **Justice of the Peace,** an unpaid lay magistrate appointed to hear minor cases. **Mr** (*or* **Mrs**) **Justice —**, the title of a High Court judge. [f. OF f. L *justitia* (as prec.)]

justiciary /dʒʌˈstɪʃjərɪ/ *n.* an administrator of justice. —**Court of Justiciary,** the supreme criminal court in Scotland. [f. L (as prec.)]

justifiable /ˈdʒʌstɪfaɪəb(ə)l/ *adj.* that can be justified or defended. —**justifiably** *adv.* [F (as foll.)]

justify /ˈdʒʌstɪfaɪ/ *v.t.* **1** to show the justice or truth of. **2** (of circumstances) to be an adequate ground for, to warrant. **3** to adjust (a line of type) to fill the space evenly. —**justification** /-fɪˈkeɪʃ(ə)n/ *n.*, **justificatory** /-fɪˈkeɪtərɪ/ *adj.* [f. F f. L *justificare* (as JUST)]

jut *v.i.* (**-tt-**) to project. —*n.* a projection. [var. of JET[1]]

Jute /dʒu:t/ *n.* a member of a Low German tribe that invaded southern England in the 5th c. and set up a kingdom in Kent. [OE (cf. Icel. *Iatar* people of Jutland in Denmark)]

jute /dju:t/ *n.* fibre from the bark of tropical plants of the genus *Corchorus*, used for sacking, mats, etc. [f. Bengali f. Skr.]

juvenile /ˈdʒu:vənaɪl/ *adj.* youthful; of or for young persons. —*n.* a young person; an actor playing such a part. —**juvenile delinquency,** violation of the law by persons below the age of legal responsibility. **juvenile delinquent,** such an offender. [f. L (*juvenis* young person)]

juvenilia /dʒu:vəˈnɪlɪə/ *n.pl.* the works produced by an author or artist in his youth. [L (as prec.)]

juvenility /dʒu:vəˈnɪlɪtɪ/ *n.* youthfulness; a youthful manner etc. [f. JUVENILE]

juxtapose /dʒʌkstəˈpəʊz/ *v.t.* to put side by side. —**juxtaposition** /-pəˈzɪʃ(ə)n/ *n.* [f. F f. L (*juxta* next, *ponere* put)]

Kk

K, k /keɪ/ *n.* (*pl.* **Ks, K's**) the eleventh letter of the alphabet.

K *abbr.* **1** kelvin. **2** king (in chess). **3** the unit of core-memory size in computers, = 1,024 (often taken as 1,000) words.

K *symbol* potassium. [f. modern L *kalium* (as ALKALI)]

K. *abbr.* **1** carat. **2** King('s). **3** Köchel (catalogue of Mozart's works).

k *abbr.* kilo-.

Kaddish /ˈkædɪʃ/ *n.* a Jewish prayer recited as a doxology in the synagogue service and as a prayer of mourning. [f. Aram., = holy]

Kaffir /ˈkæfə(r)/ *n.* a member or language of a South African people of the Bantu family. [f. Arab., = infidel]

kaiser /ˈkaɪzə(r)/ *n.* (*hist.*) an emperor, especially of Germany, Austria, or the Holy Roman Empire. [f. G f. L, = CAESAR]

kakemono /kækɪˈməʊnəʊ/ *n.* (*pl.* **-os**) a Japanese wall-picture, usually painted or inscribed on paper or silk and mounted on rollers. [Jap.(*kake-* hang, *mono* thing)]

kale *n.* a hardy variety of cabbage with wrinkled leaves. [northern form of COLE]

kaleidoscope /kəˈlaɪdəskəʊp/ *n.* a tube containing mirrors and pieces of coloured glass whose reflections produce patterns when the tube is rotated. —**kaleidoscopic** /-ˈskɒpɪk/ *adj.*, **kaleidoscopically** /-ˈskɒpɪkəlɪ/ *adv.* [f. Gk *kalos* beautiful + *eidos* form + -SCOPE]

kaleyard /ˈkeɪljɑ:d/ *n.* (*Sc.*) a kitchen garden.

kamikaze /kæmɪˈkɑ:zɪ/ *n.* (in the Second World War) a Japanese aircraft laden with explosives and suicidally crashed on a target by the pilot; the pilot of this. [Jap. (*kami* divinity, *kaze* wind)]

kangaroo /kæŋgəˈru:/ *n.* an Australian marsupial of the genus *Macropus* with hindquarters strongly developed for jumping. —**kangaroo court**, an illegal court held by strikers, prisoners, etc. [perh. f. Aboriginal name]

kaolin /ˈkeɪəlɪn/ *n.* a fine white clay used for porcelain and in medicine. [F f. Chinese *kao-ling* name of mountain]

kapok /ˈkeɪpɒk/ *n.* a fine cotton-like material from a tropical tree (*Ceiba pentandra*) used as padding. [f. Malay]

kappa /ˈkæpə/ *n.* the tenth letter of the Greek alphabet, = k. [Gk]

kaput /kæˈpʊt/ *adj.* (*slang*) broken, ruined, done for. [f. G]

karakul /ˈkærəkʊl/ *n.* **1** an Asian sheep whose lambs have a dark curled fleece. **2** a fur made from or resembling this. [Russ.]

karate /kəˈrɑ:tɪ/ *n.* a Japanese system of unarmed combat using the hands, feet, etc., as weapons.[Jap. (*kara* empty, *te* hand)]

karma /ˈkɑ:mə/ *n.* (*Buddhism & Hinduism*) the law of action according to which good or appropriate acts give rise to good effects, bad or inappropriate ones to bad effects, impelling a chain of successive births by transmigration, each life's condition being explained by actions in a previous life. [Skr., = action, fate]

karoo /kəˈru:/ *n.* (also **karroo**) a high plateau in South Africa, waterless in the dry season. [Hottentot]

karst *n.* a limestone region with underground streams and many cavities caused by dissolution of the rock. [name of such a region in Yugoslavia]

kart *n.* a miniature wheeled vehicle usually consisting of a tubular frame with a small rear-mounted engine and a seat for the driver used for a motor-racing sport (**karting**). [commercial alteration of *cart*]

kasbah /ˈkæzbɑ:/ *n.* **1** the citadel of an Arab city in North Africa. **2** the old crowded part near this, especially in Algiers. [f. F f. Arab., = citadel]

katydid /ˈkeɪtɪdɪd/ *n.* a large green grasshopper (family Tettigoniidae) of the USA. [imit. of its sound]

kauri /ˈkaʊrɪ/ *n.* a coniferous New Zealand timber-tree (*Agathis australis*) yielding a gum. [Maori]

kayak /ˈkaɪæk/ *n.* **1** a light covered-in canoe-type boat consisting of a wooden framework covered with sealskins, in which the paddler sits facing forward and using a double-bladed paddle, used by the Eskimo for fishing. **2** a boat developed from this, used for touring and sport. [Eskimo]

KBE *abbr*. Knight Commander of the Order of the British Empire.

KCB *abbr*. Knight Commander of the Order of the Bath.

KCMG *abbr*. Knight Commander of the Order of St Michael and St George.

kc/s *abbr*. kilocycles per second.

kea /ˈkeɪə/ *n*. a green New Zealand parrot (*Nestor notabilis*) said to attack sheep. [Maori, imit.]

kebab /kɪˈbæb/ *n*. (usu. in *pl*.) small pieces of meat, vegetables, etc., grilled on a skewer. [f. Urdu f. Arab.]

kedge *v.t./i*. to move (a ship) by a hawser attached to a small anchor. —*n*. a small anchor for this purpose. [perh. var. of dial. *cadge* bind]

kedgeree /ˈkedʒərɪ, -ˈriː/ *n*. **1** a European dish of fish, rice, hard-boiled eggs, etc. **2** an Indian dish of rice, pulse, onions, eggs, etc. [f. Hindi]

keel *n*. **1** the lengthwise timber or steel structure along the base of a ship, from which the framework is built up. **2** a structure resembling this; a ridge along the breastbone of many birds. —*v.t./i*. to turn keel upwards. —**keel over**, to overturn; to fall or collapse. **on an even keel**, level, steady. [f. ON]

keelhaul *v.t*. **1** to haul (a person) under a keel as a punishment. **2** to rebuke severely.

keelson var. of KELSON.

keen[1] *adj*. **1** showing or feeling intense interest or desire; (of desire etc.) intense. **2** perceiving things very distinctly; intellectually acute. **3** sharp, having a sharp edge or point. **4** (of sound or light etc.) acute, penetrating; (of wind etc.) piercingly cold; (of pain) acute. **5** (of a price) competitively low. —**keen on**, (*colloq*.) much attracted by. —**keenly** *adv*., **keenness** *n*. [OE]

keen[2] *n*. an Irish funeral song accompanied by wailing. —*v.t./i*. to utter the keen; to bewail (a person) thus. [f. Ir. *caoine*]

keep *v.t./i*. (*past* & *p.p*. **kept**) **1** to have continuous charge of; to retain possession of; to reserve (*for* a future time etc.). **2** to remain or cause to remain in a specified condition, position, course, etc. **3** to restrain, to hold back *from*; to detain. **4** to observe, to pay due regard to (a law, promise, appointment, etc.). **5** to refrain from disclosing (a secret etc.). **6** to own and look after (animals etc.); to maintain in return for sexual favours. **7** to guard or protect (a person, place, goal at football, etc.). **8** to maintain (a house etc.) in proper order; to manage (a shop etc.); to maintain (a diary, account-books, etc.) by making the requisite entries. **9** to preserve in being; to continue to have or do. **10** (of food etc.) to remain in good condition; to be able to be put aside until later. **11** to have (a commodity) regularly on sale. **12** to celebrate (a feast or ceremony). —*n*. **1** maintenance, food. **2** the central tower or other strongly fortified structure in a castle etc. —**for keeps**, (*colloq*.) permanently. **keep on**, to continue; to nag *at*. **keep to oneself**, to avoid contact with others; to keep (a thing) a secret. **keep under**, to repress. **keep up**, to maintain; to prevent from sinking (especially one's spirits etc.). **keep up with**, to achieve the same pace as. **keep up with the Joneses**, to strive to remain on terms of obvious social equality with one's neighbours. [OE]

keeper *n*. a person who keeps or looks after something; a custodian of a museum or art gallery or forest; a wicketkeeper. [f. KEEP]

keeping *n*. **1** custody, charge. **2** harmony, conformity. [f. KEEP]

keepsake *n*. a thing kept in memory of its giver.

keg *n*. a small cask or barrel. —**keg beer**, beer supplied from a sealed metal container. [f. ON]

kelp *n*. a large brown seaweed; the calcined ashes of this yielding iodine etc. [orig. unkn.]

kelpie *n*. (*Sc*.) **1** a malevolent water-spirit usually in the form of a horse. **2** an Australian sheepdog of Scottish origin. [orig. unkn.]

kelson /ˈkels(ə)n/ *n*. the line of timber fixing a ship's floor-timbers to the keel. [perh. f. LG (as KEEL, SWINE as name of timber)]

kelt *n*. a salmon or sea trout after spawning. [orig. unkn.]

kelvin /ˈkelvɪn/ *n*. the base unit of thermodynamic temperature (symbol K), the fraction 1/273.16 of the thermodynamic temperature of the triple point of water; a degree (equal to a Celsius degree) of the Kelvin scale. —**Kelvin scale**, a scale of temperature with zero at absolute zero. [f. W. *Kelvin*, British physicist (d. 1907)]

ken *v.t*. (**-nn-**) (*Sc*.) to know. —*n*. the range of knowledge or sight. [OE (as CAN[1])]

kendo /ˈkendəʊ/ *n*. the Japanese sport of fencing with two-handed bamboo swords. [Jap., = sword-way]

kennel /ˈken(ə)l/ *n*. **1** a small shelter for a dog. **2** (in *pl*.) a place where dogs are bred or boarded. **3** a pack of dogs. —*v.t*. (**-ll-**) to put or keep in a kennel. [f. OF *chenil* f. L *canis* dog]

kepi /ˈkepɪ, ˈkeɪpɪ/ *n*. a French military cap with a horizontal peak. [f. F f. Swiss G]

kept *past* & *p.p*. of KEEP.

kerb *n*. a stone edging to a pavement or raised path. [var. of CURB]

kerbstone *n*. each of the stones forming a kerb.

kerchief /ˈkɜːtʃɪf/ *n*. **1** a square cloth used to

cover the head. **2** a handkerchief. [f. OF *couvrechief* (as COVER, *chief* head)]

kerfuffle /kəˈfʌf(ə)l/ *n.* (*colloq.*) a fuss, a commotion. [orig. Sc.]

kermes /ˈkɜːmɪz/ *n.* the female of an insect (*Kermes ilicis*), formerly taken to be a berry, that feeds on an evergreen oak (*Quercus coccinea*); a red dye made from the dried bodies of these. [f. F f. Arab. & Pers.; rel. to CRIMSON]

kernel /ˈkɜːn(ə)l/ *n.* **1** the softer part within the hard shell of a nut or stone-fruit. **2** a seed within a husk etc., e.g. a grain of wheat. **3** the central or essential part of a thing. [OE, dim. of CORN[1]]

kerosene /ˈkerəsiːn/ *n.* a fuel-oil distilled from petroleum or from coal or bituminous shale, paraffin oil. [f. Gk *kēros* wax]

kestrel /ˈkestr(ə)l/ *n.* a kind of small falcon (esp. *Falco tinnunculus*) that often hovers in the air with its head to the wind. [perh. f. F *casserelle, créc(er)elle*]

ketch *n.* a small sailing vessel with two masts. [prob. f. CATCH]

ketchup /ˈketʃəp/ *n.* a thick spicy sauce made from tomatoes, mushrooms, etc. [f. Chinese, = pickled-fish brine]

ketone /ˈkiːtəʊn/ *n.* one of a class of organic compounds including acetone. [f. G *keton* alt. of *aketon* acetone]

kettle *n.* a vessel, usually of metal with a spout and handle, for boiling water. —**a fine** *or* **pretty** etc. **kettle of fish,** an awkward state of affairs. [f. ON ult. f. L *catillus*]

kettledrum *n.* a large drum consisting of an inverted metal bowl over which an adjustable membrane is stretched, enabling it to be tuned to a definite note; (in *pl.*) the timpani of an orchestra.

key[1] /kiː/ *n.* **1** an instrument, usually of metal, for moving the bolt of a lock so that it locks or unlocks. **2** a similar implement for operating a switch in the form of a lock, winding a clock etc., or grasping a screw, nut, etc. **3** each of a set of levers or buttons pressed by the finger in a musical instrument, typewriter, etc. **4** (*Mus.*) a system of notes based on material in a particular scale; (*fig.*) the general tone or style of thought or expression. **5** a solution to a problem, an explanation, a word or system for solving a cipher or code. **6** a thing or factor governing an opportunity for or access to something; (*attrib.*) essential, of vital importance. **7** a piece of wood or metal inserted between others to secure them. **8** a mechanical device for making or breaking an electric circuit. **9** the winged fruit of the sycamore, ash, etc. **10.** roughness of surface to help adhesion of plaster etc. —*v.t./i.* **1** to fasten with a pin, wedge, bolt, etc. **2** to roughen (a surface) to help the adhesion of plaster etc. **3** to align or link (*to*). **key in,** to enter (data) by means of a keyboard. **key money,** a payment required from an incoming tenant nominally for the provision of the key to a premises. **key-pad** *n.* a miniature keyboard for holding in the hand. **key-ring** *n.* a ring for keeping keys on. **key up,** to stimulate or excite (a person). [OE]

key[2] /kiː/ *n.* a reef, a low island. [f. Sp. *cayo*]

keyboard *n.* a set of keys on a typewriter, piano, etc.

keyhole *n.* the hole by which a key is put into a lock.

keynote *n.* **1** the prevailing idea or tone in a speech etc. **2** the lowest note in a scale on which a musical key is based.

keystone *n.* **1** the central locking stone in an arch. **2** a central principle.

keyword *n.* the key to a cipher.

KG *abbr.* Knight of the Order of the Garter.

kg *abbr.* kilogram(s).

KGB *n.* the secret police of the USSR since 1953. [Russ. abbr., = State security committee]

khaki /ˈkɑːkɪ/ *adj.* dull brownish-yellow. —*n.* khaki cloth or uniform. [f. Urdu, = dust-coloured]

kHz *abbr.* kilohertz.

kibbutz /kɪˈbuːts/ *n.* (*pl.* **-tzim** /-ˈtsiːm/) a communal settlement in Israel. [f. Heb., = gathering]

kibosh /ˈkaɪbɒʃ/ *n.* (*slang*) nonsense. —**put the kibosh on,** (*slang*) to put an end to. [orig. unkn.]

kick *v.t./i.* **1** to thrust, strike, or propel forcibly with the foot or hoof. **2** to score (a goal) by a kick. **3** to protest, to show dislike. **4** (*slang*) to abandon (a habit). —*n.* **1** a kicking action or blow. **2** the recoil of a gun when fired. **3** (*colloq.*) resilience. **4** (*colloq.*) a temporary interest or enthusiasm; a sharp stimulant effect, (usu. in *pl.*) a thrill. —**kick about** *or* **around,** to treat roughly; to move idly from place to place; to be unused or unwanted. **kick off,** to begin a football match; (*colloq.*) to make a start. **kick-off** *n.* a start, especially of a football match. **kick out,** (*colloq.*) to expel forcibly, to dismiss. **kick up,** (*colloq.*) to create or cause (a fuss, trouble, etc.). **kick upstairs,** to promote (a person) to an ostensibly higher position to remove him from the scene of real influence. —**kicker** *n.* [orig. unkn.]

kickback *n.* **1** a recoil. **2** (*colloq.*) a payment for help in making a profit or for showing favour etc.

kick-start *n.* (also **kick-starter**) a device to start the engine of a motorcycle etc. by a downward thrust of a pedal. —*v.t.* to start (a motorcycle etc.) thus.

kid *n.* **1** a young goat. **2** the leather made from its skin. **3** (*slang*) a child. —*v.t./i* (**-dd-**) **1** to give birth to a young goat. **2** (*slang*) to deceive or hoax. —**handle** *or* **treat** etc. **with kid gloves,** to treat tactfully. [f. ON]

kidnap /ˈkɪdnæp/ *v.t.* (**-pp-**) to carry off (a person) illegally especially to obtain a ransom; to steal (a child). —**kidnapper** *n.* [f. KID + *nap* var. of NAB]

kidney /ˈkɪdnɪ/ *n.* **1** either of the pair of glandular organs in the abdominal cavity of mammals, birds, and reptiles, serving to remove waste products from the blood and secrete urine; an animal's kidney as food. **2** nature, kind, temperament. —**kidney bean,** a kidney-shaped dwarf French bean, a scarlet runner bean. **kidney dish,** an oval dish indented at one side. **kidney machine,** a machine able to take over the functions of a kidney. [orig. unkn.]

kill *v.t.* **1** to deprive of life or vitality, to cause the death of. **2** to put an end to; to render ineffective; to switch off (a light, engine, etc.). **3** (*colloq.*) to cause severe pain to; to overwhelm with amusement. **4** to spend (time) unprofitably while waiting for something. —*n.* **1** the act of killing. **2** the animal(s) killed, especially in sport. —**dressed to kill,** dressed showily or alluringly. **in at the kill,** present at the time of victory. **kill off,** to get rid of by killing. **make a killing,** to have a great financial success. —**killer** *n.* [perh. rel. to QUELL]

killjoy *n.* a person who spoils or questions others' enjoyment.

kiln *n.* a furnace or oven for burning, baking, or drying, especially for calcining lime or firing pottery etc. [OE f. L *culina* kitchen]

kilo /ˈkiːləʊ/ *n.* (*pl.* **-os**) **1** a kilogram. **2** a kilometre. [F, abbr.]

kilo- /kɪlə-/ *in comb.* thousand. [F f. Gk *khilioi*]

kilocycle /ˈkɪləsaɪk(ə)l/ *n.* a kilohertz.

kilogram /ˈkɪləgræm/ *n.* the base unit of mass (symbol kg) approx. 2.205 lb.

kilohertz /ˈkɪləhɜːts/ *n.* a unit of frequency of electromagnetic waves, = 1,000 cycles per second.

kilolitre /ˈkɪləliːtə(r)/ *n.* a metric unit of capacity, 1,000 litres or approx. 35.31 cu. ft.

kilometre /ˈkɪləmiːtə(r), (**D**) kɪˈlɒmɪtə(r)/ *n.* a metric unit of length, 1,000 metres or approx. 0.62 mile.

kiloton /ˈkɪlətʌn/ *n.* a unit of explosive force equal to 1,000 tons of TNT.

kilotonne /ˈkɪlətʌn/ *n.* a metric unit equivalent to the kiloton.

kilowatt /ˈkɪləwɒt/ *n.* a unit of electrical power, equal to 1,000 watts. —**kilowatt-hour** *n.* the energy equal to one kilowatt working for one hour.

kilt *n.* a pleated usually tartan skirt reaching from the waist to the knee, especially worn by a Highland man. —*v.t.* **1** to tuck up (skirts) round the body. **2** to gather in vertical pleats. [f. Scand., cf. Da. *kilte* tuck]

kilted *adj.* wearing a kilt. [f. KILT]

kimono /kɪˈməʊnəʊ/ *n.* (*pl.* **-os**) **1** a long loose Japanese robe with wide sleeves, worn with a sash. **2** a European dressing-gown modelled on this. [Jap.]

kin *n.* one's relatives or family. —*predic. adj.* related. —**kinship** *n.* [OE]

-kin *suffix* forming diminutive nouns (*catkin, lambkin*). [f. MDu. *-kijn, -ken,* OHG *-chin*]

kind[1] /kaɪnd/ *n.* a class of similar or related things or animals. —**a kind of,** something resembling or belonging approximately to (the class named). **in kind,** (of payment) in goods or produce, not money; (of repayment, esp. *fig.*) in the same form as that received. **kind of,** (*colloq.*) somewhat. [OE (as KIN)]

kind[2] /kaɪnd/ *adj.* gentle or considerate in conduct or manner towards others. —**kind-hearted** *adj.*, **kindness** *n.* [as prec.; orig. = natural, native]

kindergarten /ˈkɪndəgɑːt(ə)n/ *n.* a school for very young children. [G, = children's garden]

kindle *v.t./i.* **1** to set on fire; to cause (a fire) to begin burning. **2** to arouse or stimulate (a feeling etc.). **3** to become kindled. [f. ON, rel. to *kindill* candle, torch]

kindling /ˈkɪndlɪŋ/ *n.* small sticks etc. for lighting a fire. [f. prec.]

kindly /ˈkaɪndlɪ/ *adj.* **1** kind. **2** (of a climate) pleasant, genial. —*adv.* **1** in a kind way. **2** (in a polite request or iron. command) please. —**not take kindly to,** to be displeased by. —**kindliness** *n.* [f. KIND[2]]

kindred /ˈkɪndrɪd/ *n.* **1** blood relationship. **2** one's relatives. **3** resemblance in character. —*adj.* related, of similar kind. —**kindred spirit,** a person whose tastes are similar to one's own. [f. KIN + OE *ræden* condition]

kine /kaɪn/ *archaic pl.* of cow[1].

kinematic /kɪnɪˈmætɪk/ *adj.* of motion considered abstractly without reference to force or mass. [f. Gk *kinēma* motion (as KINETIC)]

kinematics /kɪnɪˈmætɪks/ *n.pl.* the science of pure motion. [f. prec.]

kinetic /kɪˈnetɪk, kaɪ-/ *adj.* of or due to motion. —**kinetic art,** a form of visual art depending on moving components for its effect. **kinetic energy,** a body's ability to do work by virtue of its motion. [f. Gk *kinētikos* (*kineō* move)]

kinetics /kɪˈnetɪks, kaɪ-/ *n.pl.* (usu. treated as *sing.*) **1** the science of the relations between the motions of bodies and the forces acting upon them. **2** the study of the mechanisms and rates of chemical reactions or other processes. [f. prec.]

king *n.* **1** a male sovereign (esp. hereditary) ruler of an independent State. **2** a male person or a thing regarded as pre-eminent in a specified field or class. **3** (*attrib.*) the large or largest kind of. **4** the piece in chess that has to be protected from checkmate. **5** a crowned piece in draughts. **6** a court-card with a picture of a king. —**King of Arms,** a chief herald (at the College of Arms, Garter, Clarenceaux, and Norroy & Ulster; in Scotland, Lyon). **king of beasts,** the lion. **king of birds,** the eagle. **king-post** *n.* an upright post from a tie-beam to the top of a rafter. **king's evil,** scrofula, formerly held to be curable by the royal touch. **king-size, king-sized** *adjs.* larger than normal, very large. —**kingly** *adj.*, **kingship** *n.* [OE]

kingcup *n.* the marsh marigold.

kingdom /ˈkɪŋdəm/ *n.* **1** a territory or State ruled by a king or queen; a domain. **2** the most inclusive taxonomic category, consisting of a number of phyla (in zoology) or divisions (in botany). —**kingdom-come** *n.* (*slang*) the next world. [OE, as KING]

kingfisher *n.* a small land-bird of the family Alcedinidae with brilliant plumage, which dives for fish.

kingpin *n.* **1** a vertical bolt used as a pivot. **2** an essential person or thing.

kink *n.* **1** a sudden bend or twist in something straight or smoothly curved. **2** a mental peculiarity or twist. —*v.t./i.* to form or cause to form a kink. [f. MLG]

kinky *adj.* **1** having kinks. **2** (*colloq.*) bizarre, perverted (esp. sexually). —**kinkily** *adv.*, **kinkiness** *n.* [f. prec.]

kinsfolk /ˈkɪnzfəʊk/ *n.* one's blood relations.

kinsman /ˈkɪnzmən/ *n.* (*pl.* **-men**) a (male) blood relation. —**kinswoman** *n.fem.* (*pl.* **-women**).

kiosk /ˈkiːɒsk/ *n.* **1** a light usually outdoor structure for the sale of newspapers, food, etc. **2** a box-like structure in the street etc. for a public telephone. [f. F f. Turk. f. Pers., = pavilion]

kip *n.* (*slang*) **1** a sleep. **2** a place to sleep, a bed. —*v.i.* (**-pp-**) (*slang*) to sleep. [cf. Da. *kippe* mean hut]

kipper *n.* **1** a kippered fish, especially a herring. **2** a male salmon in the spawning season. —*v.t.* to cure (a herring etc.) by splitting open, salting, drying, and smoking. [orig. unkn.]

kirk *n.* (*Sc. & N. Engl.*) a church. —**kirk-session** *n.* the lowest court in the Church of Scotland and (*hist.*) other Presbyterian Churches, composed of ministers and elders. [f. ON f. OE, = CHURCH]

kismet /ˈkɪsmet, ˈkɪz-/ *n.* destiny, fate. [Turk., f. Arab.]

kiss *n.* a touch given with the lips. —*v.t.* **1** to touch with the lips, especially as a sign of love, affection, greeting, or reverence; (absol., of two persons) to touch each other's lips thus. **2** to touch gently. —**kiss-curl** *n.* a small curl of hair arranged on the face or at the nape. **kiss hands,** to greet a sovereign thus. **kiss of death,** an apparently friendly act causing ruin. **kiss of life,** the mouth-to-mouth method of artificial respiration. [OE]

kisser *n.* (*slang*) the mouth or face. [f. KISS]

Kiswahili /kɪswɑːˈhiːlɪ/ *n.* the Swahili language. [native name, f. *ki-* object + SWAHILI]

kit *n.* **1** the equipment or clothing required for a particular activity or situation. **2** a soldier's or traveller's pack or equipment. **3** a set of parts sold together from which a whole thing can be made. —*v.t./i.* (**-tt-**) to equip, to fit *out* or *up* with a kit. [f. MDu., = wooden vessel]

kitbag *n.* a large usually cylindrical bag for a soldier's or traveller's kit.

kitchen /ˈkɪtʃɪn/ *n.* a place where food is prepared and cooked. —**kitchen cabinet,** a group of unofficial advisers (orig. of the President of the USA) popularly believed to have greater influence than the official Cabinet or other elected group. **kitchen garden,** a garden for growing fruit and vegetables. [OE, ult. f. L *coquina* (*coquere* cook)]

kitchenette /kɪtʃɪˈnet/ *n.* a small room or alcove used as a kitchen. [f. KITCHEN + -ETTE]

kite *n.* **1** a toy consisting of a light framework with paper etc. stretched over it and flown in the wind at the end of a long string. **2** a bird of prey of the hawk family (esp. *Milvus milvus*). —**fly a kite,** (*colloq.*) to sound out public opinion. [OE]

Kitemark *n.* the official kite-shaped mark on goods approved by the British Standards Institution.

kith /kɪθ/ *n.* **kith and kin,** friends and relations. [OE, orig. = knowledge (as UNCOUTH)]

kitsch /kɪtʃ/ *n.* worthless pretentiousness or bad taste in art; art of this type. —**kitschy** *adj.* [G]

kitten /ˈkɪt(ə)n/ *n.* the young of a cat, ferret, etc. —*v.t./i.* to give birth to (kittens). —**have kittens,** (*colloq.*) to be very upset or nervous. —**kittenish** *adj.* [f. OF *chitoun* dim. of *chat* cat]

kittiwake /ˈkɪtɪweɪk/ *n.* a kind of small seagull (*Rissa tridactyla*). [imit. of its cry]

kitty *n.* a fund of money for communal use; the pool in some card-games. [orig. unkn.]

kiwi /ˈkiːwiː/ *n.* **1** a flightless New Zealand bird of the genus *Apteryx*, with rudimentary wings and no tail. **2 Kiwi,** (*colloq.*) a New Zealander. —**kiwi fruit,** the fruit of a deciduous fruiting vine (*Actinidia chinensis*), also called Chinese gooseberry. [Maori]

kl *abbr.* kilolitre(s).

Klaxon /ˈklæks(ə)n/ *n.* [P] a powerful electric horn. [f. name of manufacturer]

kleptomania /kleptəˈmeɪnɪə/ *n.* a tendency to steal, without regard for need or profit. —**kleptomaniac** *n.* & *adj.* [f. Gk *kleptēs* thief + -MANIA]

kloof *n.* (*S.Afr.*) a ravine or valley. [Du., = cleft]

km *abbr.* kilometre(s).

knack /næk/ *n.* **1** an acquired or intuitive ability to do something skilfully. **2** a habit. [prob. = *knack* sharp blow, f. LG]

knacker /ˈnækə(r)/ *n.* a buyer of useless horses for slaughter, or of old houses etc. for their materials. —*v.t.* (esp. in *p.p.*) (*slang*) to exhaust, to wear out. [orig. unkn.]

knapsack /ˈnæpsæk/ *n.* a soldier's or traveller's bag, usually of canvas, strapped to the back. [MLG (prob. f. *knapp* food, SACK)]

knapweed /ˈnæpwi:d/ *n.* a plant of the genus *Centaurea*, with purple flowers in a globular head. [f. earlier *knopweed* (KNOP, WEED)]

knave /neɪv/ *n.* **1** an unprincipled or dishonest person, a rogue. **2** the jack in playing-cards. —**knavish** *adj.* [OE, = boy, servant]

knavery *n.* the conduct of a knave. [f. prec.]

knead /ni:d/ *v.t.* **1** to work (moist flour, clay, etc.) into dough by pressing with the hands; to make (bread, pottery) thus. **2** to operate on using such motions (in massaging etc.). [OE]

knee /ni:/ *n.* **1** the joint between the thigh and the lower leg in man. **2** the corresponding joint in an animal. **3** the upper surface of the thigh of a sitting person. **4** the part of a garment covering the knee. —*v.t.* to touch or strike with the knee. —**bring a person to his knees**, to reduce him to submission. **knee-breeches** *n.pl.* breeches reaching to or just below the knee. **knee-deep** *adj.* immersed up to the knees; deeply involved; so deep as to reach the knees. **knee-high** *adj.* so high as to reach the knees. **knee-hole** *n.* a space for the knees, especially between columns of drawers at each side of a desk etc. **knee-jerk** *n.* a sudden involuntary kick caused by a blow on the tendon below the knee. **knees-up** *n.* (*colloq.*) a lively party with dancing. [OE]

kneecap *n.* **1** the convex bone in the front of the knee-joint. **2** a protective covering for the knee.

kneecapping *n.* shooting in the legs to lame a person as a punishment.

kneel /ni:l/ *v.i.* (*past* & *p.p.* **knelt** or (*US*) **kneeled**) to take or be in a position where the body is supported on the knee(s) with the lower part of the leg(s) bent back, especially in prayer or reverence. [OE (as KNEE)]

kneeler *n.* a hassock etc. for kneeling on. [f. prec.]

knell /nel/ *n.* **1** the sound of a bell, especially after a death or at a funeral. **2** an omen of death or extinction. [OE]

knelt *past* & *p.p.* of KNEEL.

Knesset /ˈknesɪt/ *n.* the parliament of the State of Israel. [Heb., = gathering]

knew *past* of KNOW.

knickerbockers /ˈnɪkəbɒkəz/ *n.pl.* loose-fitting breeches gathered in at the knee. [f. Diedrich *Knickerbocker*, pretended author of Washington Irving's *History of New York* (1809)]

knickers /ˈnɪkəz/ *n.pl.* a woman's or girl's undergarment covering the body below the waist and having separate legs or leg-holes. [abbr. of prec.]

knick-knack /ˈnɪknæk/ *n.* a trinket or small ornament. [redupl. of *knack* in obs. sense 'trinket']

knife /naɪf/ *n.* (*pl.* **knives**) a cutting instrument or weapon consisting of a metal blade with a long sharpened edge fixed in a handle; a cutting-blade in a machine. —*v.t.* to cut or stab with a knife. —**at knife-point**, threatened by a knife. **the knife**, (*colloq.*) surgery. **have got one's knife into**, to be persistently malicious or vindictive towards. **knife-edge** *n.* the sharp edge of a knife, a position of tense uncertainty about an outcome. **knife-pleat** *n.* a narrow flat pleat in an overlapping series. [OE f. ON]

knight /naɪt/ *n.* **1** a man raised to the rank below the baronetcy as a reward for personal merit or services to Crown or country, entitling the holder to the prefix *Sir*. **2** (*hist.*) a man raised to an honourable military rank by a king etc. **3** (*hist.*) a military follower, especially one devoted to the service of a lady as her attendant or champion in a war or tournament. **4** a chess piece usually with the shape of a horse's head. —*v.t.* to confer a knighthood on. —**knight errant**, a medieval knight wandering in search of chivalrous adventures; a man of such a spirit. **knight-errantry** *n.* [OE, = boy, youth]

knighthood *n.* the rank or dignity of a knight. [f. prec. + -HOOD]

knightly *adj.* of or like a knight; chivalrous. [f. KNIGHT]

knit /nɪt/ *v.t./i.* (**-tt-**; *past* & *p.p.* **knitted** or (esp. *fig.*) **knit**) **1** to make (a garment etc. or *absol.*) by interlocking loops of yarn or thread. **2** to form (yarn) into a fabric etc. in this way. **3** to make (a plain stitch) in knitting. **4** to wrinkle (the brow). **5** to make or become close or compact, to grow together. —**knitter** *n.* [OE (as KNOT)]

knitting *n.* work being knitted.

—**knitting-needle** *n.* each of a pair of slender pointed rods used in knitting by hand. [f. KNIT]

knitwear *n.* knitted garments.

knob /nɒb/ *n.* **1** a rounded protuberance, especially at an end or on a surface of a thing, e.g. a handle of a door, drawer, etc. or for adjusting a radio etc. **2** a small lump (of butter etc.). —**with knobs on,** (*slang*) that and more (often as an emphatic or ironical agreement). —**knobbly** *adj.* [f. MLG; cf. KNOP]

knobkerrie /ˈnɒbkerɪ/ *n.* a short stick with a knob at the end as a weapon of South African tribes. [f. Afrik. *knopkierie*]

knobbly /ˈnɒblɪ/ *adj.* hard and lumpy. [f. *knobble* dim. of KNOB]

knock /nɒk/ *v.t./i.* **1** to strike with an audible sharp blow. **2** to make a noise by striking a door etc. to summon a person or gain admittance. **3** to drive or make by striking. **4** (of an engine) to make a thumping or rattling noise, to pink. **5** to criticize or insult. —*n.* an act or sound of knocking; a sharp blow. —**knock about** *or* **around,** to treat roughly, to strike repeatedly; to wander about aimlessly. **knock back,** (*slang*) to eat or drink, esp. hastily; to disconcert. **knock down,** to strike (a person) to the ground; to demolish; to dispose of (an article *to* a bidder) by the knock of the hammer at an auction. **knock-down** *adj.* (of a price) very low; (of furniture etc.) easily dismantled and reassembled; overwhelming. **knock-for-knock** *adj.* (of insurance terms) with each company paying its policy-holder in a claim, regardless of liability. **knocking-shop** *n.* (*slang*) a brothel. **knock knees,** an abnormal inward curving of the legs at the knees. **knock-kneed** *adj.* having this. **knock off,** (*colloq.*) to cease work; to complete (a piece of work etc.) quickly; to deduct (a sum from a total); (*slang*) to steal or kill. **knock-on effect,** the effect of an alteration that causes similar alterations elsewhere. **knock out,** to render unconscious, especially by a blow to the head; to disable (a boxer) so that he is unable to recover in the required time; to defeat in a knock-out competition; to exhaust or disable. **knock spots off,** (*colloq.*) to surpass easily. **knock up,** to make or arrange hastily; to arouse by knocking at the door; to score (runs) at cricket, (*US slang*) to make pregnant. **knock-up** *n.* a practice game etc. [OE]

knockabout *adj.* rough, boisterous.

knocker *n.* a hinged metal device on a door for knocking to call attention. [f. KNOCK]

knock-out *adj.* **1** that knocks a boxer etc. out. **2** (of a competition) in which the loser of each round is eliminated. —*n.* **1** a knock-out blow. **2** (*slang*) an outstanding person or thing.

knoll /nəʊl/ *n.* a hillock, a mound. [OE]

knop /nɒp/ *n.* **1** an ornamental knob. **2** a loop, a tuft in a yarn. [f. MLG or MDu.]

knot[1] /nɒt/ *n.* **1** an intertwining of one or more pieces of rope, string, etc., to fasten them together. **2** a tangle. **3** a ribbon etc. tied with a knot for ornament etc. **4** a group or cluster. **5** a hard mass formed in a tree-trunk where a branch once grew out; a corresponding cross-grained piece in a board. **6** a difficulty or problem. **7** that which forms or maintains a union, especially a marriage. **8** the unit of a ship's or aircraft's speed equal to one nautical mile per hour (1 knot = 1.85 k.p.h. = 1.15 m.p.h.). —*v.t./i.* (**-tt-**) **1** to tie in or with a knot or knots. **2** to make (a fringe) by knotting threads. **3** to entangle. **4** to unite closely or intricately. —**at a rate of knots,** (*colloq.*) very fast. **knot-grass** *n.* a weed (*Polygonum aviculare*) with intricate creeping stems and pink flowers. **knot-hole** *n.* a hole in a wooden board, where a knot has fallen out. **tie in knots,** to make (a person) confused or baffled. [OE]

knot[2] /nɒt/ *n.* a small wading bird (*Calidris canutus*) of the sandpiper family. [orig. unkn.; the conjecture that the bird was named after King Cnut (Canute), because believed to be a visitor from Denmark, is without foundation]

knotty *adj.* **1** full of knots. **2** puzzling, difficult. [f. KNOT[1]]

know /nəʊ/ *v.t./i.* (*past* **knew** /njuː/, *p.p.* **known** /nəʊn/) **1** to have in the mind or memory as the result of experience, learning, or information. **2** to feel certain. **3** to be acquainted or have regular social contact with (a person). **4** to recognize or identify. **5** to understand and be able to use (a language, subject, or skill). **6** to have personal experience of (fear etc.). **7** to be subject to (limits etc.). —*n.* (*colloq.*) **in the know,** knowing secret or inside information. —**know-all** *n.* (*derog.*) a person who claims to know much. **know-how** *n.* practical knowledge or skill. **know one's own mind,** to know one's intentions firmly. **you never know,** it is always possible. [OE]

knowable *adj.* that may be known. [f. KNOW]

knowing *adj.* having or showing knowledge or awareness; shrewd, clever. —**knowingly** *adv.* [f. KNOW]

knowledge /ˈnɒlɪdʒ/ *n.* **1** knowing. **2** all that a person knows. **3** the sum of what is known to mankind. —**to my knowledge,** as far as I know. [f. KNOW]

knowledgeable /ˈnɒlɪdʒəb(ə)l/ *adj.* having much knowledge, well-informed. [f. prec.]

known *p.p.* of KNOW.

knuckle /ˈnʌk(ə)l/ *n.* **1** the bone at the finger-joint, especially at the root of the finger. **2** the knee- or ankle-joint of an animal, especially with the adjacent parts as a joint of meat. —*v.t./i.* to strike, press, or rub with the knuckles. —**knuckle down,** to apply oneself earnestly (*to* work etc.). **knuckle-duster** *n.* a metal guard worn over the knuckles in fist-fighting especially to increase the violence of a blow. **knuckle under,** to give in, to submit. **near the knuckle,** (*colloq.*) verging on indecency. [f. MLG or MDu. (dim. of *knoke* bone)]

knurl /nɜːl/ *n.* a small projecting ridge etc. [cf. *knur* knot, swelling, f. MDu. or MLG]

KO *abbr.* knock-out.

koala /kəʊˈɑːlə/ *n.* an Australian arboreal marsupial (*Phascolarctos cinereus*) with thick grey fur and large ears. [f. Aboriginal *kūl(l)a*]

kohl /kəʊl/ *n.* a powder used (especially in eastern countries) to darken the eyelids etc. [f. Arab.]

kohlrabi /kəʊlˈrɑːbɪ/ *n.* a cabbage with a turnip-like edible stem. [G f. It. f. L *caulorapa* (as COLE, RAPE[2])]

koine /ˈkɔɪnɪ/ *n.* a common language shared by various peoples, a lingua franca. [f. Gk, = common (language)]

kolinsky /kɒˈlɪnskɪ/ *n.* the Siberian mink (*Mustela sibirica*); its fur. [f. Russ. (*Kola* in NW Russia)]

kolkhoz /ˈkɒlkɒz/ *n.* a collective farm in the USSR. [Russ.]

koodoo var. of KUDU.

kook /kuːk/ *n.* (*US slang*) a crazy or eccentric person. —**kooky** *adj.* [prob. f. CUCKOO]

kookaburra /ˈkʊkəbʌrə/ *n.* a large Australian kingfisher (*Dacelo novaeguineae*) with a loud discordant cry. [Abor.]

kopje /ˈkɒpɪ/ *n.* (also **koppie**) (*S. Afr.*) a small hill. [Du. & Afrik., dim. of *kop* head]

Koran /kɔːˈrɑːn, kə-/, **the** the holy book of Islam, composed of the revelations which came to the Prophet Muhammad during his lifetime, from *c.*610 to his death in AD 632. —**Koranic** /-ˈrɑːnɪk, -ˈræ-/ *adj.* [f. Arab., = recitation (*kara'a* read)]

kosher /ˈkəʊʃə(r)/ *adj.* **1** (of food or a foodshop) fulfilling the requirements of Jewish law. **2** (*colloq.*) correct, genuine, legitimate. —*n.* kosher food; a kosher shop. [f. Heb., = proper]

kowtow /kaʊˈtaʊ/ *v.i.* **1** to behave obsequiously. **2** to perform the kowtow. —*n.* the Chinese custom of touching the ground with the head as a sign of worship or submission. [f. Chin., = knock the head]

k.p.h. *abbr.* kilometres per hour.

Kr *symbol* krypton.

kraal /krɑːl/ *n.* (*S. Afr.*) **1** a village of huts enclosed by a fence. **2** an enclosure for sheep or cattle. [Afrik. f. Port. *curral*, of Hottentot orig.]

kraken /ˈkrɑːkən/ *n.* a mythical sea-monster said to appear off the coast of Norway. [Norw.]

Kraut /kraʊt/ *n.* (*slang, derog.*) a German. [f. SAUERKRAUT]

kremlin /ˈkremlɪn/ *n.* a citadel within a Russian town, especially that of Moscow, traditionally the centre of administration as well as the last bastion of defence. —**the Kremlin,** the government of the USSR. [F f. Russ.]

krill *n.* small shrimp-like crustaceans of the order Euphausiacea; a large group of these animals forming food for fishes and whales. [f. Norw. *krill* tiny fish]

kris /kriːs, krɪs/ *n.* a Malay dagger with a wavy blade. [ult. f. Malay]

kromesky /krəˈmeskɪ/ *n.* minced meat or fish rolled in bacon and fried. [app. f. Polish *kromeczka* small slice]

krona /ˈkrəʊnə/ *n.* the currency unit of Sweden (*pl.* **kronor**) and of Iceland (*pl.* **kronur**). [Sw. & Icel., = CROWN]

krone /ˈkrəʊnə/ *n.* (*pl.* **kroner**) the currency unit of Denmark and of Norway. [Da. & Norwegian, = CROWN]

krugerrand /ˈkruːgərɑːnt/ *n.* a South African gold coin bearing a portrait of Kruger. [f. *Kruger*, S. Afr. statesman (d. 1904) + RAND]

krypton /ˈkrɪptɒn/ *n.* a rare colourless odourless element of the noble gas group, symbol Kr, atomic number 36. [f. Gk *krupton* hidden]

Kt. *abbr.* Knight.

kudos /ˈkjuːdɒs/ *n.* (*colloq.*) renown, glory. [Gk]

kudu /ˈkuːduː/ *n.* a large white-striped, spiral-horned African antelope of the genus *Strepsiceros*. [f. Xhosa-Kaffir]

kukri /ˈkʊkrɪ/ *n.* a heavy curved knife, broadening towards the point, used by Gurkhas as a weapon. [f. Hindi]

kümmel /ˈkʊm(ə)l/ *n.* a liqueur flavoured with caraway and cumin seeds. [G (as CUMIN)]

kumquat /ˈkʌmkwɒt/ *n.* a plum-sized orange-like fruit of the genus *Fortunella* used in preserves. [dial. form of Chin. *kin kü* golden orange]

kung fu /kʌŋ ˈfuː/ a Chinese form of karate. [Chin.]

kurchatovium /kɜːʃəˈtəʊvɪəm/ *n.* the Russian name for the element of atomic number 104, a short-lived artificially produced radioactive transuranic element (cf. RUTHERFORDIUM). [f. I. G. *Kurchatov* (d. 1960), Russian nuclear physicist]

Kurd /kɜːd/ *n.* a member of a people of eastern Turkey and neighbouring regions. —**Kurdish** *adj.* & *n.* [native name]

kV *abbr.* kilovolt(s).

kW *abbr.* kilowatt(s).

kWh *abbr.* kilowatt-hour(s).

kyle /kaɪl/ *n.* a narrow channel between an island and the mainland (or another island) in western Scotland. [f. Gael.]

L, l /el/ *n.* (*pl.* **Ls, L's**) **1** the twelfth letter of the alphabet. **2** an L-shaped thing. **3** (as a Roman numeral) 50.

L *abbr.* learner (driver).

L. *abbr.* **1** Lake. **2** Liberal. **3** Licentiate of.

£ *abbr.* pound (money). [f. L *libra*]

l. *abbr.* **1** left. **2** line. **3** litre(s).

LA *abbr.* Los Angeles.

La *symbol* lanthanum.

la var. of LAH.

lab *n.* (*colloq.*) laboratory. [abbr.]

Lab. *abbr.* Labour.

label /ˈleɪb(ə)l/ *n.* **1** a slip of paper etc. attached to an object to give some information about it. **2** a general classifying phrase applied to persons etc. —*v.t.* (**-ll-**) **1** to attach a label to. **2** to assign to a category. **3** to make (a substance, molecule, or constituent atom) recognizable, for identification in an experiment. [f. OF, = ribbon]

labial /ˈleɪbɪəl/ *adj.* **1** of the lips. **2** of the nature of a lip. **3** pronounced with partially or completely closed lips. —*n.* a labial sound (e.g. *p, m, v*). [f. L (*labia* lips)]

labium /ˈleɪbɪəm/ *n.* (*pl.* **-ia**) **1** (usu. in *pl.*) the lip of the female genitals. **2** the lower part of the mouth of an insect, crustacean, etc. —**labia majora,** the outer folds of the genital labia. **labia minora,** the inner folds. [L, = lip]

laboratory /ləˈbɒrətərɪ/ *n.* a room or building used for scientific experiments and research. [f. L (*laborare* toil, as LABOUR)]

laborious /ləˈbɔːrɪəs/ *adj.* **1** needing much work or perseverance. **2** showing signs of effort. **3** hard-working. —**laboriously** *adv.* [f. OF f. L (as foll.)]

labour /ˈleɪbə(r)/ *n.* **1** bodily or mental work, exertion. **2** a task. **3** the body of those doing (esp. manual or non-managerial) work; such a body as a political force. **4** Labour, the Labour Party. **5** the pains of childbirth; the process of giving birth. —*v.t./i.* **1** to exert oneself, to work hard. **2** to have to make a great effort, to operate or progress only with difficulty. **3** to treat (a point etc.) at great length or in excessive detail. **4** to suffer *under* (a delusion etc.). —**labour camp,** a place where prisoners must work as labourers. **Labour Day,** a day celebrated in honour of workers (often 1 May); in the USA a public holiday on the first Monday in September. **Labour Exchange,** (*colloq.* or *hist.*) an employment exchange. **Labour Party,** a British political party representing the interests especially of workers. **labour-saving** *adj.* designed to reduce or eliminate work. [f. OF f. L *labor*]

laboured *adj.* showing signs of great effort, not spontaneous. [f. prec.]

labourer *n.* a person who labours, especially one employed to do unskilled manual work. [f. LABOUR]

Labrador /ˈlæbrədɔː(r)/ *n.* a retriever dog of a breed with a smooth black or golden coat. [f. *Labrador* in Canada]

labrum /ˈleɪbrəm/ *n.* (*pl.* **-a**) the upper lip of an insect. [L, = lip (cogn. w. LABIUM)]

laburnum /ləˈbɜːnəm/ *n.* an ornamental tree of the genus *Laburnum* (esp. *L. anagyroides*), with drooping yellow flowers. [L]

labyrinth /ˈlæbərɪnθ/ *n.* **1** a complicated or confusing network of passages. **2** a tangled or intricate arrangement. **3** the complex cavity of the inner ear. —**labyrinthine** /læbəˈrɪnθaɪn/ *adj.* [f. F or L f. Gk]

lac /læk/ *n.* a resinous substance secreted by a SE Asian insect as a protective covering. [ult. f. Hindi f. Skr.]

lace *n.* **1** a cord or narrow strip threaded through holes or hooks for fastening or tightening shoes etc. **2** a fabric or trimming in an ornamental openwork design. —*v.t.* **1** to fasten or tighten with a lace or laces; to pass (a cord etc.) *through*. **2** to trim with lace. **3** to add a dash of spirits etc. to (a drink). **4** to beat, to lash. [f. OF f. L *laqueus* noose]

lacerate /ˈlæsəreɪt/ *v.t.* to tear (flesh etc.) roughly; to wound (the feelings). —**laceration** /-ˈreɪʃ(ə)n/ *n.* [f. L *lacerare* (*lacer* torn)]

lacewing *n.* a neuropterous fly.

lachrymal /ˈlækrɪm(ə)l/ *adj.* of tears. [f. L (*lacrima* tear)]

lachrymose /ˈlækrɪməʊs/ *adj.* tearful, given to weeping. [as prec.]

lack *n.* the state or fact of not having something.—*v.t.* not to have when needed, to be without. —**be lacking,** to be undesirably absent or deficient. [rel. to MDu., MLG *lak* deficiency]

lackadaisical /lækəˈdeɪzɪk(ə)l/ *adj.* lacking vigour or determination, unenthusiastic. —**lackadaisically** *adv.* [f. archaic *lackaday*, *lackadaisy* int. (as ALACK)]

lackey /ˈlækɪ/ *n.* an obsequious follower; a humble servant. —*v.t.* to play lackey to. [f. F. f. Catalan, = Sp. *alcalde*]

lacklustre /ˈlæklʌstə(r)/ *adj.* without lustre, dull.

laconic /ləˈkɒnɪk/ *adj.* terse, using few words. —**laconically** *adv.* [f. L f. Gk (*Lakōn* Spartan), the Spartans being proverbially terse]

lacquer /ˈlækə(r)/ *n.* **1** a hard shiny shellac or synthetic varnish. **2** a substance sprayed on the hair to keep it in place. —*v.t.* to coat with lacquer. [f. obs. F *lacre* sealing-wax f. Port. (as LAC)]

lacrosse /ləˈkrɒs/ *n.* a field game played with a netted stick with which a ball is driven or thrown, caught, and carried. [F. (*la* the, *crosse* crozier)]

lactate /lækˈteɪt/ *v.i.* to secrete milk. —/ˈlækteɪt/ *n.* a salt or ester of lactic acid. [f. L. *lactare* suckle (*lac* milk)]

lactation /lækˈteɪʃ(ə)n/ *n.* suckling, the secretion of milk [as prec.]

lactic *adj.* of milk. —**lactic acid,** the acid found in sour milk. [f. L *lac* milk]

lactose /ˈlæktəʊs/ *n.* a sugar present in milk. [f. L *lac* milk]

lacuna /ləˈkju:nə/ *n.* (*pl.* **-as, -ae** /-i:/) a gap or missing part, especially in a manuscript. [L, orig. = pool (as LAKE¹)]

lacy /ˈleɪsɪ/ *adj.* like lace fabrics, especially in fineness. [f. LACE]

lad *n.* a boy, a young fellow; (*colloq.*) a man. [orig. unkn.]

ladder *n.* **1** a series of horizontal bars fixed between a pair of long uprights, used for climbing up or down. **2** a vertical ladderlike flaw in stockings etc. **3** a means of progress in a career etc. —*v.t./i.* to cause a ladder in (a stocking etc.); to develop a ladder. —**ladder-back** *n.* a chair with the back made of horizontal bars between uprights. [OE (as LEAN¹)]

lade *v.t.* (*p.p.* **laden**) to load (a ship), to ship (goods); (in *p.p.*) loaded or burdened (*with*). —**bill of lading,** a detailed list of a ship's cargo. [OE]

la-di-da /lɑ:dɪˈdɑ:/ *adj.* (*colloq.*) pretentious or affected in manner or speech. [imit. of pronunc. used]

ladle /leɪd(ə)l/ *n.* a deep long-handled spoon for transferring liquids. —*v.t.* to transfer with a ladle. [OE (as LADE)]

lady /ˈleɪdɪ/ *n.* **1** a woman of good social standing; (as a polite term) any woman; a woman of polite or refined disposition. **2** **Lady,** the titled used as a less formal prefix to the name of a peeress below a duchess, or to the Christian name of a daughter of a duke, marquis, or earl, or to the surname of the wife or widow of a baronet or knight. **3** the woman with the authority in a household. **4** (*archaic*) a wife. **5** (*attrib.*) female. —**the Ladies,** (as *sing.*) a women's public lavatory. **ladies' man,** a man fond of women's company. **Lady Chapel,** a chapel dedicated to the Virgin Mary. **Lady Day,** the feast of the Annunciation, 25 March. **lady-in-waiting** *n.* a lady attending a royal lady. **lady-killer** *n.* a man given to making amorous conquests of women. **lady's-maid** *n.* the personal maidservant of a lady. **lady's slipper,** a flower of the genus *Cypripedium* of the orchid family, with the flowers shaped like a slipper or pouch. **Our Lady,** the Virgin Mary. [OE, = loaf-kneader]

ladybird *n.* a small round beetle of the family Coccinellidae, often reddish-brown with black spots.

ladylike *adj.* like or appropriate to a lady.

ladyship *n.* the title used in addressing or referring to a woman with the rank of Lady. [f. LADY + -SHIP]

lag¹ *v.i.* (**-gg-**) to go too slow, to fail to keep up with the others. —*n.* lagging, a delay. —**lagger** *n.* [orig. = hindmost person; perh. f. distortion of LAST¹ in children's game]

lag² *v.t.* (**-gg-**) to enclose (a boiler etc.) with a heat-insulating material. —*n.* such a material; an insulating cover. —**lagger** *n.* [prob. f. Scand.]

lag³ *n.* a convict (esp. in *old lag*). [orig. unkn.]

lager /ˈlɑ:gə(r)/ *n.* a kind of light beer. [f. G *lager-bier* beer brewed for keeping (*lager* store)]

laggard /ˈlægəd/ *n.* a person who lags behind, a procrastinator. [f. LAG¹]

lagging¹ *n.* a material used to lag a boiler etc. [f. LAG²]

lagging² *n.* a term of imprisonment. [as LAG³]

lagoon /ləˈgu:n/ *n.* a salt-water lake separated from the sea by a sandbank or coral reef etc. [f. F or It. & Sp. f. L, = LACUNA]

lah /lɑ:/ *n.* (*Mus.*) the sixth note of the major scale in tonic sol-fa (see entry). [f. *labii* (see GAMUT)]

laicize /ˈleɪɪsaɪz/ *v.t.* to make secular. —**laicization** /-ˈzeɪʃ(ə)n/ *n.* [f. *laic* lay, f. L f. Gk (as LAY²)]

laid *past* & *p.p.* of LAY¹

lain *p.p.* of LIE¹.

lair *n.* **1** a sheltered place where a wild animal habitually rests or eats. **2** a person's hiding-place. [OE (rel. to LIE¹)]

laird *n.* a landowner in Scotland. [Sc. form of LORD]

laissez-faire /leɪseɪ'feə(r)/ *n.* (also **laisser-faire**) a policy of non-interference. [F, = let act]

laity /'leɪɪtɪ/ *n.* a body of laymen, especially in a Church. [f. LAY¹]

lake¹ *n.* a large expanse of water surrounded by land. —**Lake District** *or* **the Lakes,** the region round the lakes in Cumbria in NW England. **lake-dwelling** *n.* a prehistoric dwelling built on piles driven into the bed or shore of a lake. [f. OF f. L *lacus*]

lake² *n.* a pigment made from a dye and a mordant; a reddish pigment, originally made from lac. [var. of LAC]

lakh /læk/ *n.* (in India) 100,000 (esp. in *a lakh of rupees*). [f. Hindustani f. Skr.]

Lallan /'lælən/ *adj.* (*Sc.*) of the Lowlands of Scotland. —*n.* (*Sc.*; also **Lallans**) Lowland Scots dialect, especially as a literary language. [var. of LOWLAND]

lam *v.t.* (**-mm-**) (*slang*) to hit hard, to thrash. [perh. f. Scand., as LAME]

lama/ 'lɑːmə/ *n.* an honorific applied to a spiritual leader in Tibetan Buddhism; any Tibetan Buddhist monk. [f. Tibetan *blama* superior one]

lamaism /'lɑːməɪz(ə)m/ *n.* a common but (strictly) incorrect term for Tibetan Buddhism. [f. prec.]

lamasery /lə'mɑːsərɪ/ *n.* a common but strictly incorrect term for a Tibetan Buddhist monastery. [f. LAMA]

lamb /læm/ *n.* **1** a young sheep. **2** its flesh as food. **3** a gentle, endearing, or vulnerable person. —*v.t./i.* **1** to give birth to a lamb; (in *pass.*, of a lamb) to be born. **2** to tend (lambing ewes). —**Lamb (of God),** Christ. **lamb's-wool** *n.* soft fine wool. [OE]

lambaste /læm'beɪst/ *v.t.* (*colloq.*) to thrash, to beat. [f. LAM + BASTE¹]

lambda /'læmdə/ *n.* the eleventh letter of the Greek alphabet, = l. [Gk]

lambent /'læmbənt/ *adj.* (of a flame or light) playing about a surface; (of the eyes, wit, etc.) gently brilliant. —**lambency** *n.* [f. L *lambere* lick]

lame *adj.* **1** (of a person or limb) disabled or unable to walk normally, especially by an injury or defect in the foot or leg. **2** (of an excuse etc.) unconvincing. **3** (of a metre) halting. —*v.t.* to make lame, to disable. —**lame duck,** a person or firm unable to cope without help. —**lamely** *adv.*, **lameness** *n.* [OE]

lamé /'lɑːmeɪ/ *n.* a fabric with gold or silver thread interwoven. [F]

lament /lə'ment/ *n.* a passionate expression of grief; an elegy. —*v.t./i.* to feel or express grief for or about; to utter a lament; (in *p.p.*) mourned for. [f. L *lamentum*, F or L *lamentari*]

lamentable /'læməntəb(ə)l/ *adj.* deplorable, regrettable. —**lamentably** *adv.* [f. prec.]

lamentation/ læmen'teɪʃ(ə)n/ *n.* **1** a lament. **2** lamenting. [f. LAMENT]

lamina /'læmɪnə/ *n.* (*pl.* **-ae** /-iː/) a thin plate, scale, or layer. —**laminar** *adj.* [L]

laminate /'læmɪneɪt/ *v.t./i.* **1** to beat or roll into laminae; to split into layers. **2** to overlay with metal plates, a plastic layer, etc. —/-ət/ *n.* a laminated structure, especially of layers fixed together. —/-ət/ *adj.* in the form of a lamina or laminae. —**lamination** /-'neɪʃ(ə)n/ *n.* [f. prec.]

Lammas /'læməs/ *n.* 1 August, formerly observed as an English harvest festival at which loaves made from the first ripe corn were consecrated; in Scotland, one of the quarter-days. [f. OE *hlafmæsse* (LOAF¹, MASS²)]

lamp *n.* a device or vessel for giving light or rays by the use of electricity or gas or by burning oil or spirit. [f. OF f. L f. Gk *lampas* torch]

lampblack *n.* a pigment made from soot.

lamplight *n.* the light given by a lamp.

lamplighter *n.* (usu. *hist.*) a man who lights street lamps.

lampoon /læm'puːn/ *n.* a piece of virulent or scurrilous satire on a person. —*v.t.* to write a lampoon against. —**lampoonist** *n.* [f. F *lampon*]

lamppost *n.* a tall post supporting a street lamp.

lamprey/'læmprɪ/ *n.* an eel-like aquatic animal (genera *Lampetra* and *Petromyzon*) with a sucker mouth. [f. OF f. L *lampetra* (perh. *lambere* lick, *petra* stone)]

lampshade *n.* a shade placed over a lamp.

Lancastrian /læŋ'kæstrɪən/ *adj.* **1** of Lancashire or Lancaster. **2** of the family descended from John of Gaunt, Duke of Lancaster, or of the Red Rose party supporting it in the Wars of the Roses (cf. YORKIST). —*n.* **1** a native or inhabitant of Lancashire or Lancaster. **2** a member or adherent of the Lancastrian family. [f. *Lancaster*.]

lance /lɑːns/ *n.* a long spear, especially one used by a horseman. —*v.t.* **1** to pierce with a lance. **2** to prick or cut open with a surgical lancet. —**lance-corporal** *n.* an NCO below a corporal. [f. OF f. L *lancea*]

lanceolate /'lænsɪələt/ *adj.* shaped like a spearhead, tapering to each end. [f. L (*lanceola* dim. of *lancea* lance)]

lancer /'lɑːnsə(r)/ *n.* **1** a soldier of a cavalry regiment originally armed with lances. **2** (in *pl.*) a kind of quadrille; the music for this. [f. F (as LANCE)]

lancet /ˈlɑːnsɪt/ *n.* **1** a surgical instrument with a point and two edges for small incisions. **2** a narrow pointed arch or window. [f. OF (as LANCE)]

Lancs. *abbr*. Lancashire.

land *n.* **1** the solid part of the earth's surface, not covered by water. **2** the ground, the soil, an expanse of country; this as a basis for agriculture, building, etc. **3** landed property; (in *pl.*) estates. **4** a country or State. —*v.t./i.* **1** to set or go ashore from a ship etc. **2** to bring (an aircraft) to the ground or other surface; to come down thus. **3** to alight after a jump etc. **4** to reach or find oneself in a certain place or situation; to cause to do this. **5** to deliver (a person a blow etc.). **6** to present (a person *with* a problem etc.). **7** to bring (a fish) to land; to win (a prize); to secure (an appointment etc.). —**how the land lies,** what is the state of affairs. **land-agent** *n.* a steward of an estate; a dealer in estates. **land-girl** *n.* a woman doing farm work, especially in wartime. **land-line** *n.* a means of telegraphic communication over land. **land-locked** *adj.* almost or entirely surrounded by land. **land mass,** a large area of land. **land-mine** *n.* an explosive mine laid in or on the ground. [OE]

landau /ˈlændɔː/ *n.* a four-wheeled horse-drawn carriage with a top of which the front and back halves can be raised and lowered independently. [f. *Landau* near Karlsruhe in W. Germany, where first made]

landed *adj.* **1** owning much land. **2** consisting of land. [f. LAND]

landfall *n.* an approach to land after a sea or air journey.

landing *n.* **1** the process of coming or bringing to land. **2** a place for disembarking. **3** the area at the top of a flight of stairs or between flights. —**landing-craft** *n.* a naval craft for putting ashore troops and equipment. **landing-gear** *n.* the undercarriage of an aircraft. **landing-stage** *n.* a platform for disembarking passengers and goods. [f. LAND]

landlady *n.* a woman landlord.

landless *adj.* holding no land. [f. LAND + -LESS]

landlord *n.* a person who lets rooms or keeps a boarding house, a public-house, etc.

landlubber *n.* a person with little or no experience of ships and the sea.

landmark *n.* **1** a conspicuous and easily recognized feature of the landscape. **2** an event marking an important stage in a process or history.

landowner *n.* one who owns land, especially a large area.

landscape /ˈlændskeɪp/ *n.* **1** the features of a land area as seen in broad view. **2** a picture of this. —*v.t./i.* to lay out or enhance (an area of land) with natural features. —**landscape gardening,** the laying-out of grounds to imitate natural scenery. [f. Du. (as LAND, -SHIP)]

landslide *n.* **1** a landslip. **2** an overwhelming majority for one side in an election.

landslip *n.* the sliding down of a mass of land on a slope or mountain.

landward /ˈlændwəd/ *adv.* (also **landwards**) towards the land. —*adj.* going or facing towards the land. [f. LAND + -WARD]

lane *n.* **1** a narrow road or street. **2** a passage between rows of people. **3** a strip of road for one line of traffic. **4** a strip of track or water for a competitor in a race. **5** a regular course followed by or prescribed for ships or aircraft [OE]

language /ˈlæŋgwɪdʒ/ *n.* **1** words and their use; the faculty of speech. **2** a system of words prevalent in one or more countries or in a profession etc. **3** a method or style of expression. **4** a system of symbols and rules for computer programs. —**language laboratory,** a room with tape-recorders etc. for learning foreign languages. [f. OF f. L *lingua* tongue]

languid /ˈlæŋgwɪd/ *adj.* **1** lacking vigour, not inclined to exert oneself. **2** (of a stream etc., or *fig.*) slow-moving, slack. —**languidly** *adv.* [f. F or L (as foll.)]

languish /ˈlæŋgwɪʃ/ *v.i.* **1** to lose or lack vitality. **2** to live *under* depressing conditions; to be neglected. **3** to pine (*for*). [f. OF f. L *languēre*]

languor /ˈlæŋgə(r)/ *n.* **1** a languid state, listlessness. **2** a soft or tender mood or effect. **3** an oppressive stillness of the air. —**languorous** *adj.* [as prec.]

lank *adj.* **1** tall and lean. **2** (of grass, hair, etc.) long and limp. [OE]

lanky *adj.* ungracefully lean and tall or long. —**lankiness** *n.* [f. LANK]

lanolin /ˈlænəlɪn/ *n.* a fat extracted from sheep's wool and used in ointments. [G f. L (*lana* wool, *oleum* oil)]

lantern /ˈlæntən/ *n.* **1** a transparent case holding a light and shielding it from wind etc. **2** the light-chamber of a lighthouse. **3** an erection on top of a dome or room, with glazed sides. —**lantern jaws,** long thin jaws giving the face a hollow look. [f. OF f. L *lanterna* f. Gk]

lanthanide /ˈlænθənaɪd/ *n.* any of the series of 15 rare earth elements from lanthanum to lutetium (atomic numbers 57-71); the same series excluding lanthanum itself. [f. G. *lanthanid* (as foll.)]

lanthanum /ˈlænθənəm/ *n.* a soft silvery-white metallic element of the lanthanide series, symbol La, atomic number 57. [f. Gk *lanthanō* escape notice, from having remained undetected in cerium oxide]

lanyard /ˈlænjəd/ *n.* **1** a short rope used on a ship for securing or fastening. **2** a cord worn round the neck or on the shoulder to which a knife etc. may be attached. [f. OF *lanière*, assim. to YARD[1]]

lap[1] *n.* **1** the flat area formed by the front of the thighs of a seated person; the part of a dress etc. covering this. **2** one circuit of a race-track etc. **3** a section of a journey etc. **4** the amount of overlap; an overlapping part. **5** a single turn of thread etc. round a reel etc. —*v.t./i.* (**-pp-**) **1** to be ahead of (a competitor in a race) by one or more laps. **2** to fold or wrap (*about* or *round*); to enfold (*in* wraps); (esp. in *pass.*) to enfold caressingly. **3** to cause to overlap. —**in the lap of the gods,** beyond human control. **in the lap of luxury,** in great luxury. **in a person's lap,** as his responsibility. **lap-dog** *n.* a small pet dog. **lap of honour,** a ceremonial circuit of a race-track etc. by the winner(s). **lap over,** to extend beyond (a limit). [OE]

lap[2] *v.t./i.* (**-pp-**) **1** to drink by scooping liquid with movements of the tongue. **2** (usu. with *up*) to take in (facts etc.) eagerly. **3** to flow (against) in ripples making a gentle splashing sound. —*n.* an act or sound of lapping. [OE]

laparotomy /læpəˈrɒtəmɪ/ *n.* surgical cutting through the abdominal wall for access to the internal organs etc. in the abdomen. [f. Gk *lapara* flank (*laparos* soft) + -TOMY]

lapel /ləˈpel/ *n.* the part of either side of a coat-front etc. folded back against the outer surface. —**lapelled** *adj.* [f. LAP[1]]

lapidary /ˈlæpɪdərɪ/ *adj.* **1** concerned with stones. **2** engraved on stone. —*n.* a cutter, polisher, or engraver of gems. [f. L (*lapis* stone)]

lapis lazuli /ˈlæpɪs ˈlæzju:lɪ/ a bright blue gem, mineral, colour, and pigment. [f. L (*lapis* stone, *lazulum* f. Pers., as AZURE)]

Lapp *n.* **1** a member of the indigenous population of the extreme north of Scandinavia. **2** their language. —*adj.* of the Lapps or their language. —**Lappish** *adj.* [f. Sw. *Lapp*, perh. orig. a term of contempt; cf. MHG *lappe* simpleton]

lappet /ˈlæpɪt/ *n.* **1** a flap or fold of a garment etc. or of flesh. **2** a kind of large moth whose caterpillars have side lobes. [f. LAP[1]]

lapse *n.* **1** a slight mistake, a slip of the memory etc. **2** a weak or careless decline to an inferior state. **3** the passage *of* time. —*v.i.* **1** to fail to maintain a position or standard; to fall back (*into* an inferior or previous state). **2** (of a right etc.) to become no longer valid because not used or claimed or renewed. **3** (in *p.p.*) that has lapsed. [f. L *lapsus* (*labi* slip, fall)]

lapwing /ˈlæpwɪŋ/ *n.* the peewit. [OE (as LEAP, WINK), f. mode of flight]

larboard /ˈlɑ:bəd/ *n.* & *adj.* = PORT[3]. [orig. *ladboard*, perh. 'side on which cargo is taken in' (f. LADE + BOARD)]

larceny /ˈlɑ:sənɪ/ *n.* theft of personal goods. —**larcenous** *adj.* [f. OF f. L *latrocinium* (*latro* robber)]

larch *n.* a deciduous coniferous tree of the genus *Larix*, with bright foliage; its wood. [f. MHG f. L *larix*]

lard *n.* pig fat prepared for use in cooking etc. —*v.t.* **1** to insert strips of bacon in (meat etc.) before cooking. **2** to garnish (talk etc.) *with* strange terms etc. [f. OF, = bacon, f. L *lardum*]

larder *n.* a room or cupboard for storing food. [f. AF (as prec.)]

lardy *adj.* like lard. —**lardy-cake** *n.* cake made with lard, currants, etc. [f. LARD]

large /lɑ:dʒ/ *adj.* **1** of considerable or relatively great size or extent. **2** of the larger kind. **3** of wide range, comprehensive. **4** doing a thing on a large scale. —**at large,** at liberty; as a body or whole; with all details; without a specific aim. —**large-scale** *adj.* made or occurring on a large scale or in large amounts. —**largeness** *n.* [f. OF f. L *largus* copious]

largely *adv.* to a great or preponderating extent. [f. prec.]

largess/ lɑ:ˈdʒes/ *n.* (also **largesse**) money or gifts freely given, especially on an occasion of rejoicing. [f. OF f. L (as LARGE)]

largo /ˈlɑ:gəʊ/ *adv.* (*Mus.*) in a slow tempo with a broad dignified treatment. —*n.* (*pl.* **-os**) a movement to be played in this way. [It., = broad]

lariat /ˈlærɪət/ *n.* a lasso, a rope used to catch or tether a horse etc. [f. Sp. *la reata* (*reatar* tie again)]

lark[1] *n.* a kind of small songbird, of the family Alaudidae, especially the skylark. —**get up with the lark,** to get up early. [OE]

lark[2] *n.* (*colloq.*). **1** a frolic or spree; an amusing incident. **2** an affair, a type of activity etc. —*v.i.* (*colloq.*) to play (*about*). [orig. unkn.]

larkspur *n.* a plant of the genus *Delphinium* with a spur-shaped calyx.

larn *v.t./i. joc.* or *vulgar var.* of LEARN; (*colloq.*) to teach. [dial. form of LEARN]

larrikin /ˈlærɪkɪn/ *n.* (*Austral.*) a hooligan. [perh. f. *Larry* pet-form of name *Lawrence*]

larva *n.* (*pl.* **-vae** /-vi:/) an insect in the stage between egg and pupa (e.g. a caterpillar) —**larval** *adj.* [L, = ghost, mask]

laryngeal /ləˈrɪndʒɪəl/ *adj.* of the larynx. [f. LARYNX]

laryngitis /lærɪn'dʒaɪtɪs/ *n.* inflammation of the larynx. [f. foll. + -ITIS]

larynx /'lærɪŋks/ *n.* the cavity in the throat holding the vocal cords. [f. Gk]

lasagne /lə'sænjə/ *n.* pasta in a wide ribbon form, especially as served with minced meat and a sauce. [It. pl., f. L *lasanum* cooking-pot]

Lascar /'læskə(r)/ *n.* an East Indian seaman. [ult. f. Urdu & Pers., = army (Arab. *al-'askari* the soldier)]

lascivious /lə'sɪvɪəs/ *adj.* lustful; inciting to lust. —**lasciviously** *adv.*, **lasciviousness** *n.* [f. L (*lascivus* sportive, wanton)]

laser /'leɪzə(r)/ *n.* any device that is capable of emitting a very intense narrow parallel beam of highly monochromatic and coherent light (or other electromagnetic radiation), either continuously or in pulses, and operates by using light to stimulate the emission of more light of the same wavelength and phase by atoms or molecules that have been excited by some means. [f. *l*ight *a*mplification by *s*timulated *e*mission of *r*adiation]

lash *v.t./i.* **1** to move in a sudden whiplike movement. **2** to strike with a whip; to beat or strike violently. **3** to attack violently in words. **4** to urge as with a lash. **5** to fasten or secure with cord etc. —*n.* **1** a stroke with a whip etc. (*lit.* or *fig.*). **2** the flexible part of a whip. **3** an eyelash. —**lash out,** to hit or speak out angrily; to spend lavishly. [prob. imit.]

lashings *n.pl.* (*slang*) a lot (*of*). [f. LASH]

lass /læs/ *n.* (also dim. **lassie**) (esp. *Sc.*, *N.Engl.*, or *poetic*) a girl. [f. ON, = unmarried]

Lassa fever /'læsə/ an acute virus disease, with fever, of tropical Africa. [f. *Lassa* in Nigeria]

lassitude /'læsɪtju:d/ *n.* tiredness, listlessness. [F or f. L (*lassus* tired)]

lasso /læ'su:/ *n.* (*pl.* **-os**) a rope with a running noose, especially for catching cattle. —*v.t.* to catch with a lasso. [f. Sp. *lazo*, = LACE]

last[1] /lɑ:st/ *adj.* **1** after all the others in position or time, coming or belonging at the end. **2** most recent; next before a specified time. **3** only remaining. **4** least likely, least suitable. —*adv.* **1** (esp. *in comb.*) after all the others. **2** on the last occasion before the present. **3** lastly. —*n.* **1** a person or thing that is last. **2** the last mention or sight. **3** the last performance of certain actions; the end or last moment, death. —**at (long) last,** in the end, after much delay. **have the last laugh,** to be ultimately the victor. **last ditch,** a place of final desperate defence. **last minute** *or* **moment,** the time just before a decisive event. **last name,** a surname. **last rites,** rites for a dying person. **last straw,** an addition to a burden or difficulty that makes it finally unbearable. **last word,** a final or definitive statement; the latest fashion. [OE, = *latest* (LATE)]

last[2] /lɑ:st/ *v.t./i.* to remain unexhausted, adequate, or alive for a specified or long time; to continue for a specified time. —**last out,** to be strong enough or sufficient to last. [OE]

last[3] /lɑ:st/ *n.* a shoemaker's model for shaping a shoe etc. on. [OE]

lasting *adj.* permanent, durable. [f. LAST[2]]

lastly *adv.* finally, in the last place. [f. LAST[1]]

lat. *abbr.* latitude.

latch *n.* **1** a bar with a catch and lever as the fastening of a gate etc. **2** a spring-lock preventing a door from being opened from the outside without the key after being shut. —*v.t./i.* to fasten with a latch. —**latch on to,** (*colloq.*) to attach oneself to; to understand. **on the latch,** fastened by the latch only. [prob. f. dial. *latch* v. seize, f. OE]

latchkey *n.* a key of an outer door.

late *adj.* (*compar.* **later,** LATTER; *superl.* **latest,** LAST[1]) **1** after the due or usual time; occurring or done etc. thus. **2** far on in the day or night or in a time, period, or development. **3** flowering or ripening towards the end of the season. **4** no longer alive or having a specified status. **5** of recent date. —*adv.* **1** after the due or usual time. **2** far on in time, at or until a late hour. **3** at a late stage of development. **4** formerly but not now. —**late in the day,** (*colloq.*) at a late stage in the proceedings. **of late,** recently. —**lateness** *n.* [OE]

lateen /lə'ti:n/ *adj.* (of a sail) triangular and on a long yard at an angle of 45° to the mast. —**lateen-rigged** *adj.* rigged with such a sail. [f. F (*voile*) *latine* Latin sail (because common in the Mediterranean)]

lately *adv.* in recent times, not long ago. [OE (as LATE)]

latent /'leɪtənt/ *adj.* concealed, dormant, existing but not developed or manifest. —**latent heat,** the amount of heat lost or gained by a substance changing from a solid to a liquid or from a liquid to a vapour, without change of temperature. —**latency** *n.* [f. L *latēre* be hidden]

lateral /'lætər(ə)l/ *adj.* **1** of, at, towards, or from the side(s). **2** descended from a brother or sister of a person in the direct line. —*n.* a lateral shoot or branch. —**lateral line,** a longitudinal line of pores opening into sensory organs along each side of many fishes and amphibians. **lateral thinking,** seeking to solve problems by indirect or unexpected methods. —**laterally** *adv.* [f. L (*latus* side)]

latex /'leɪteks/ *n.* **1** a milky fluid exuded from the cut surface of certain plants, e.g. the rubber plant. **2** a synthetic substance resembling this. [L, = liquid]

lath /lɑ:θ/ *n.* (*pl.* /lɑ:ðz/) a thin narrow strip of wood. [OE]

lathe /leɪð/ *n.* a machine for shaping wood, metal, etc., by rotating the article against cutting tools. [prob. rel. to ODa. *lad* structure, frame]

lather /ˈlɑ:ðə(r)/ *n.* **1** the froth produced by soap etc. mixed with water. **2** frothy sweat, especially of a horse. **3** a state of agitation. —*v.t./i.* **1** to form a lather. **2** to cover with a lather. **3** to thrash. [OE]

Latin /ˈlætɪn/ *n.* the language of ancient Rome and its empire. — **1** of or in Latin. **2** of the countries or peoples (e.g. France, Spain) using the languages developed from Latin. **3** of the Roman Catholic Church. —**Latin America,** the parts of Central and South America where Spanish or Portuguese is the main language. [f. OF or L *Latinus* (*Latium* district of Italy including Rome)]

Latinate /ˈlætɪneɪt/ *adj.* like or having the character of Latin. [f. prec.]

latish /ˈleɪtɪʃ/ *adj.* fairly late. [f. LATE]

latitude /ˈlætɪtju:d/ *n.* **1** angular distance on a meridian; a place's angular distance north or south of the equator; (usu. in *pl.*) regions with reference to their distance from the equator. **2** freedom from restriction in action or opinion. [f. L, = breadth (*latus* broad)]

latitudinarian /lætɪtju:dɪˈneərɪən/ *adj.* liberal, especially in religion. —*n.* a latitudinarian person. [as prec.]

latrine /ləˈtri:n/ *n.* a lavatory in a camp or barracks etc.; a trench or pit for human excreta where there are no sewers. [F f. L (*lavare* wash)]

latter *adj.* **1** second-mentioned of two; last-mentioned of three or more. **2** nearer to the end; recent; belonging to the end of a period, the world, etc. —**the latter,** the latter person or thing. **latter-day** *adj.* modern, newfangled. **Latter-day Saints,** the Mormons' name for themselves. [OE = *later* (LATE)]

latterly *adv.* in the later part of life or of a period; of late. [f. prec.]

lattice /ˈlætɪs/ *n.* **1** a structure of crossed laths or bars with spaces between, used as a screen, fence, etc. **2** a regular arrangement of atoms or molecules. —**lattice window,** a window with small panes set in diagonally crossing strips of lead. [f. OF *lattis* (*latte* lath)]

Latvian /ˈlætvɪən/ *adj.* of Latvia or its people or language. —*n.* **1** a native or inhabitant of Latvia. **2** (also *Lettish*) the language of Latvia. [f. *Latvia* on the Baltic Sea]

laud /lɔ:d/ *v.t.* to praise. —*n.* **1** praise, a hymn of praise. **2** (in *pl.*) the first religious service of the day in the Western (Roman Catholic) Church. In the Book of Common Prayer parts of Lauds and Matins were combined to form the service of Morning Prayer. [f. L *laudare* (*laus* praise)]

laudable *adj.* commendable. —**laudability** /-ˈbɪlɪtɪ/ *n.*, **laudably** *adv.* [f. LAUD]

laudanum /ˈlɔ:dnəm, ˈlɒd-/ *n.* tincture of opium. [orig. name of a costly medicament prescribed by Paracelsus]

laudatory /ˈlɔ:dətərɪ/ *adj.* praising. [f. LAUD]

laugh /lɑ:f/ *v.t./i.* to make the sounds and movements usual in expressing lively amusement, scorn etc.; to utter with a laugh. —*n.* **1** a sound, act, or manner of laughing. **2** (*colloq.*) a comical thing. —**laugh at,** to ridicule. **laugh in** *or* **up one's sleeve,** to laugh secretly. **laugh off,** to get rid of (embarrassment or humiliation) with a jest. [OE (imit.)]

laughable *adj.* ridiculous, causing amusement. —**laughably** *adv.* [f. prec.]

laughing *n.* laughter. —**laughing-gas** *n.* nitrous oxide as an anaesthetic, with an exhilarating effect when inhaled. **laughing-stock** *n.* a person or thing generally ridiculed. **no laughing matter,** a serious thing. [f. LAUGH]

laughter /ˈlɑ:ftə(r)/ *n.* the act or sound of laughing. [OE (as LAUGH)]

launch[1] /lɔ:ntʃ/ *v.t./i.* **1** to cause (a ship) to move or slide from land into the water. **2** to send forth by hurling or thrusting; to send on its course. **3** to put into action; to enter boldly or freely on a course of action. —*n.* the launching of a ship or spacecraft etc., or of an enterprise. —**launch out,** to spend money freely; to burst out into strong language; to start on an ambitious enterprise. —**launcher** *n.* [f. AF *launcher* (as LANCE)]

launch[2] /lɔ:ntʃ/ *n.* **1** a large motor boat. **2** a warship's largest boat. [f. Sp. *lancha*, perh. f. Malay]

launder /ˈlɔ:ndə(r)/ **1** to wash and iron (clothes etc.). **2** to transfer (funds) so as to conceal their illegal origin. [f. OF *lavandier* washer of linen f. L *lavanda* things to be washed (*lavare* wash)]

launderette /lɔ:nˈdret/ *n.* an establishment with coin-operated automatic washing-machines for public use. [*f.* prec. + -ETTE]

laundress /ˈlɔ:ndrɪs/ *n.* a woman whose job is to launder things. [f. LAUNDER]

laundry *n.* **1** a place for washing clothes. **2** a batch of clothes to be laundered. [f. OF *lavanderie* (as LAUNDER)]

laureate /ˈlɒrɪət ˈlɔ:-/ *adj.* wreathed with laurel as an honour. —*n.* a Poet Laureate. —**laureateship** *n.* [f. L *laureatus* (*laurea* laurel-wreath, as foll.)]

laurel /ˈlɒr(ə)l/ *n.* **1** an evergreen shrub (*Prunus laurocerasus*) with dark glossy leaves. **2** (in *sing.* or *pl.*) a wreath of bay-leaves (*Laurus* *nobilis*) as an emblem of victory or poetic merit. —**look to one's laurels,** to take care not to lose pre-eminence. **rest on one's laurels,** not to seek further success. [f. OF f. Prov. f. L *laurus* bay-tree]

lav *n.* (*colloq.*) a lavatory. [abbr.]

lava /ˈlɑːvə/ *n.* matter flowing from a volcano and solidifying as it cools. [It. (*lavare* wash f. L)]

lavatory /ˈlævətərɪ, -trɪ/ *n.* a pan (usually a fixture) into which urine and faeces may be discharged for hygienic disposal; a room, building, or compartment with this. [f. L (*lavare* wash)]

lave *v.t.* (*literary*) to wash or bathe; (of water) to wash against, to flow along. [f. OF f. L *lavare* (as prec.)]

lavender /ˈlævɪndə(r)/ *n.* **1** a shrub of the genus *Lavandula* with fragrant light purple flowers; these dried and used to scent linen etc. **2** a light purple colour. —**lavender-water** *n.* a light perfume made from lavender. [f. AF f. L *lavandula*]

laver /ˈleɪvə(r), ˈlɑː-/ *n.* edible seaweed. [L (orig. an unidentified water-plant, not a seaweed)]

lavish /ˈlævɪʃ/ *v.t.* to bestow or spend (money, effort, praise etc.) abundantly. —*adj.* giving or producing in large quantities. —**lavishly** *adv.*, **lavishness** *n.* [orig. = profusion, f. OF *lavasse* deluge of rain (as LAVE)]

law *n.* **1** a rule established in a community by authority or custom; a body of such rules; the controlling influence of or obedience to this; the subject or study of such rules. **2** the legal profession. **3** (*colloq.*) the police. **4** a judicial remedy; the lawcourts providing it. **5** a divine commandment; **the Law,** the Jewish name for the Pentateuch. **6** something that must be obeyed. **7** a factual statement of what always happens in certain circumstances; a regularity in natural occurrences. —**be a law unto oneself,** to disregard custom. **law-abiding** *adj.* obedient to the laws. **Law Lord,** a member of the House of Lords qualified to perform its legal work. **take the law into one's own hands,** to redress a grievance by one's own means, especially by force. [OE f. ON *lag* something 'laid down' or fixed]

lawcourt *n.* a court of law (see COURT).

lawful *adj.* conforming with or recognized by law; not illegal; (of a child) legitimate. —**lawfully** *adv.*, **lawfulness** *n.* [f. LAW + -FUL]

lawgiver *n.* one who codifies a body of laws.

lawless *adj.* **1** having no laws or no enforcement of them. **2** disregarding laws, uncontrolled. —**lawlessly** *adv.*, **lawlessness** *n.* [f. LAW + -FUL]

lawmaker *n.* a legislator.

lawn[1] *n.* a piece of grass kept mown and smooth in a garden etc. —**lawn-mower** *n.* a machine for cutting the grass of lawns. **lawn tennis,** a game played by two persons (*singles*) or four (*doubles*) with a soft ball, over a net stretcjed across a grass or hard court without walls. [f. obs. *laund* glade f. OF (as LAND)]

lawn[2] *n.* fine woven cotton or synthetic material. [prob. f. *Laon* in France]

lawrencium /ləˈrensɪəm/ *n.* an artificially made transuranic radioactive metallic element, symbol Lr, atomic number 103. [f. E. O. *Lawrence*, Amer. physicist (d. 1958)]

lawsuit *n.* a prosecution of a claim in a lawcourt.

lawyer /ˈlɔjə(r), ˈlɔɪə(r)/ *n.* a person pursuing law as a profession; a solicitor; an expert at law. [f. LAW]

lax *adj.* not strict, careless, slack. —**laxity** *n.*, **laxly** *adv.* [f. L *laxus*, rel. to SLACK]

laxative /ˈlæksətɪv/ *adj.* tending to cause or facilitate evacuation of the bowels. —*n.* a medicine for this. [f. OF or L (*laxare* loosen, as prec.)]

lay[1] *v.t./i.* (*past & p.p.* **laid**) **1** to place on a surface or in a certain position; to place or arrange in a horizontal position, to put into place; to locate (a scene). **2** to apply or impose; to assign. **3** to present or put forward for consideration. **4** (of a hen bird) to produce (an egg, or *absol.*). **5** to cause to subside or lie flat. **6** to stake as a wager, to bet. **7** to prepare (a plan or trap). **8** to prepare (a table) for a meal; to arrange fuel for (a fire). **9** to coat or strew *with*. **10** (*slang*) to have sexual intercourse with (a woman). —*n.* **1** the way, position, or direction in which something lies. **2** (*slang*) a woman partner in sexual intercourse. —**in lay,** (of a hen) laying eggs regularly. **laid paper,** paper with the surface marked in fine ribs. **lay about one,** to hit out on all sides. **lay bare,** to reveal. **lay down,** to put on the ground etc.; to give up (office); to establish as a rule or instruction; to store (wine) in a cellar for future use; to sacrifice (one's life). **lay down the law,** to talk authoritatively or as if sure of being right. **lay hands on,** to seize or attack. **lay one's hands on,** to obtain; to be able to find. **lay hold of,** to seize or grasp. **lay in,** to provide oneself with a stock of. **lay into,** (*slang*) to punish or scold harshly. **lay it on thick** *or* **with a trowel,** (*slang*) to exaggerate greatly. **lay low,** to overthrow; to humble; to incapacitate. **lay off,** to discharge (workers) temporarily through shortage of work; (*colloq.*) to cease, especially from causing trouble or annoyance. **lay-off** *n.* a temporary discharge of workers. **lay on,** to inflict blows forcibly; to provide; to spread (paint etc.). **lay open,** to break the skin of; to expose *oneself* (to criticism etc.). **lay out,** to arrange according to a plan; to prepare (a body) for burial; to spend (money) for a purpose; (*colloq.*) to knock unconscious; to cause (oneself) to make every effort. **lay up,** to store or save; to cause (a person) to be confined to bed or unfit for work etc. **lay waste,** to destroy the crops and buildings of. [OE, (rel. to LIE¹)]

lay² *adj.* **1** non-clerical; not ordained into the clergy. **2** not professionally qualified, especially in law or medicine; of or done by such persons. —**lay reader,** a layman licensed to conduct some religious services. [f. F f. L f. Gk *laïkos* (*laos* people)]

lay³ *n.* a minstrel's song, a ballad. [f. OF or Prov.]

lay⁴ *past* of LIE¹.

layabout *n.* a habitual loafer or idler.

lay-by *n.* (*pl.* **lay-bys**) an extra strip at the side of the open road for vehicles to stop temporarily.

layer *n.* **1** a thickness of matter, especially one of several, spread over a surface. **2** a person etc. that lays. **3** a shoot fastened down to take root while attached to the parent plant. —*v.t.* **1** to arrange or cut (hair) in layers. **2** to propagate (a plant) by fastening down an attached shoot to take root. [f. LAY¹]

layette /leɪˈet/*n.* the clothes etc. prepared for a new-born child. [F, dim. of OF *laie* drawer f. MDu.]

lay figure **1** a jointed figure of the human body used by artists for arranging drapery on etc. **2** an unreal character in a novel etc. **3** a person lacking in individuality. [*lay* f. obs. *layman* lay figure f. Du. (*led* joint)]

layman *n.* (*pl.* **-men**) **1** a person not in holy orders. **2** a person without professional or special knowledge. [f. LAY² + MAN]

layout *n.* the disposing or arrangement of ground, printed matter, etc.; a thing arranged thus.

layshaft *n.* a second or intermediate transmission-shaft in a machine.

laze *v.i.* (*colloq.*) to spend time doing nothing or relaxing. —*n.* a spell of lazing. [back-formation f. LAZY]

lazy /ˈleɪzɪ/ *adj.* **1** disinclined to work, doing little work. **2** of or inducing idleness. —**lazy-bones** *n.* a lazy person. —**lazily** *adv.*, **laziness** *n.* [perh. f. LG]

lb *abbr.* pound(s) weight. [f. L *libra*]

l.b.w. *abbr.* leg before wicket.

l.c. *abbr.* **1** in the passage etc. cited. [f. L *loco citato*]. **2** lower case.

LCM *abbr.* lowest common multiple.

LEA *abbr.* Local Education Authority.

lea *n.* (*poetic*) a piece of meadow or pasture or arable land. [OE]

leach *v.t.* to make (liquid) percolate through some material; to subject (bark, ore, ash, soil) to the action of a percolating fluid; (with *away* or *out*) to remove or be removed thus. [prob. f. OE *leccan* to water]

lead¹ /li:d/ *v.t./i.* (*past & p.p.* **led**) **1** to cause to go with one, to guide or help to go, especially by going in front or by taking a person's hand or an animal's halter etc. **2** to influence the actions or opinions of, to guide by persuasion, example, or argument. **3** to provide access; (with *to*) to have as its result. **4** to make (a rope, water, etc.) go in a certain course. **5** to live or go through (a life etc. of a specified kind). **6** to have the first place in; to go first; to be first in a race or game. **7** to be in charge of; to be pre-eminent in some field. **8** (in card-games) to play as one's first card; to be the first player in a trick. —*n.* **1** guidance given by going in front; an example; a clue. **2** the leader's place; the amount by which a competitor is ahead of the others. **3** a strip of leather or cord for leading a dog etc. **4** a conductor (usually a wire) conveying an electric current to the place of use. **5** the chief part in a play etc.; its player. **6** (in card-games) the act or right of playing first; a card so played. —**lead by the nose,** to control the actions of (a person) completely. **lead off,** to begin. **lead on,** to entice. **lead up the garden path,** to mislead. **lead up to,** to form the preparation for or introduction to; to direct a conversation towards. [OE]

lead² /led/ *n.* **1** a heavy soft grey metallic element, symbol Pb, atomic number 82. **2** (also called 'black lead') the graphite used in pencils; a stick of this. **3** a lump of lead used for taking soundings in water. **4** (in *pl.*) strips of lead covering a roof; a piece of lead-covered roof; the lead frames holding the glass of a lattice etc. **5** a metal strip in printing to give a space between lines. **6** (*attrib.*) made of lead. —*v.t.* to cover, weight, frame, or space with lead(s). —**lead pencil,** a pencil of graphite enclosed in wood. —**leaded** *adj.* [OE]

leaden /ˈled(ə)n/ *adj.* **1** of or like lead, heavy or slow. **2** lead-coloured. [f. LEAD²]

leader /ˈli:də(r)/ *n.* **1** a person or thing that leads; a person followed by others. **2** the principal first violin in an orchestra, or the first violin in a quartet etc. **3** a leading article. —**Leader of the House,** a member of the government in the House of Commons or Lords who arranges and announces the business of the House. —**leadership** *n.* [f. LEAD¹]

leading¹ /ˈli:dɪŋ/ *adj.* direct, most important. —**leading aircraftman,** one ranking above aircraftman. **leading article,** a newspaper-article giving the editorial opinion. **leading light,** a prominent and influential person. **leading note,** the seventh note of the diatonic scale. **leading question,** one prompting the desired answer. [f. LEAD[1]]

leading[2] /ˈledɪŋ/ *n.* a covering or framework of lead. [f. LEAD[2]]

leaf *n.* (*pl.* **leaves**) **1** a broad flat usually green part of a plant, often on a stem; (*collect.*) leaves. **2** the state of having leaves out. **3** a single thickness of paper, especially in a book with each side forming a page. **4** a very thin sheet of metal etc. **5** a hinged flap of a table etc.; an extra section inserted to extend a table. —*v.i.* to put forth leaves. —**leaf-insect** *n.* an insect of the family Phyllidae with wings like a plant-leaf. **leaf-mould** *n.* soil chiefly of decaying leaves. **leaf through,** to turn over the pages of (a book etc.). —**leafy** *adj.* [OE]

leafage *n.* the leaves of plants. [f. LEAF]

leaflet *n.* **1** a division of a compound leaf; a young leaf. **2** a sheet of paper (sometimes folded but not stitched) giving information, especially for free distribution. [f. LEAF + -LET]

league[1] /liːg/ *n.* **1** a group of people or countries etc. combining for a particular purpose. **2** an agreement to combine in this way. **3** a group of sports clubs which compete against each other for a championship. **4** a class of contestants. —*v.t./i.* to join in a league. —**in league,** allied, conspiring. **league table,** a list of contestants etc. in order of merit. [f. F or It. (*legare* bind f. L, as LIGATURE)]

league[2] /liːg/ *n.* (*archaic*) a varying measure of travelling-distance, usually about 3 miles. [ult. f. L *leuga*, f. Gaulish]

leak *n.* **1** a hole or crack etc. through which liquid or gas passes wrongly in or out. **2** the liquid or gas passing through this. **3** a similar escape of an electric charge; the charge that escapes. **4** a disclosure of secret information. —*v.t./i.* **1** to escape wrongly through an opening. **2** (of a container) to allow such escape; to let out (liquid or gas) wrongly. **3** to disclose (a secret). —**leak out,** (of a secret) to become known. —**leaky** *adj.* [prob. f. LG]

leakage *n.* **1** leaking. **2** that which has leaked out. [f. LEAK]

lean[1] *v.t.* (*past & p.p.* **leaned** or **leant** /lent/) **1** to be or put in a sloping position; to incline from the perpendicular. **2** to rest *against*, *on*, or *upon* for support. **3** to rely *on* or *upon* for help. **4** to be inclined or have a leaning *to* or *towards*. —*n* a deviation from the perpendicular, an inclination. —**lean on,** (*slang*) to put pressure on (a person) to make him co-operate. **lean-to** *n.* a building with the roof resting against a larger building or wall. [OE]

lean[2] *adj.* **1** (of a person or animal) without much flesh, having no superfluous fat. **2** (of meat) containing little fat. **3** meagre. —*n.* the lean part of meat (opp. *fat*). —**lean years,** a period of scarcity. —**leanness** *n.* [OE]

leaning *n.* a tendency or partiality. [f. LEAN[1]]

leap *v.t./i.* (*past & p.p.* **leaped** /liːpt, lept/ or **leapt** /lept/) to jump or spring vigorously. —*n.* a vigorous jump. —**by leaps and bounds,** with startlingly rapid progress. **leap in the dark,** a rash step or enterprise. **leap year,** a year with 366 days (including 29 Feb. as an intercalary day). [OE]

leap-frog *n.* a game in which the players in turn vault with parted legs over another who is bending down. —*v.t./i.* (**-gg-**) **1** to perform such a vault (over). **2** to overtake alternately.

learn /lɜːn/ *v.t./i.* (*past & p.p.* **learned** /lɜːnt/, **learnt**) **1** to gain knowledge of or skill in by study, experience, or being taught. **2** to commit to memory. **3** to receive instruction; to become aware *of* by information or observation. **4** (*archaic*, *vulgar*, or *joc.*) to teach. [OE]

learned /ˈlɜːnɪd/ *adj.* **1** having much knowledge acquired by study; showing or requiring learning. **2** concerned with the interests of learned persons. —**learnedly** *adv.* [f. prec.]

learner *n.* one who is learning a subject or skill. —**learner driver,** one who is learning to drive a motor vehicle but has not yet passed a driving test. [f. LEARN]

learning *n.* knowledge acquired by study. [as prec.]

lease /liːs/ *n.* a contract by which the owner of a building or land allows another to use it for a specified time, usually in return for payment. —*v.t.* to grant or take on lease. —**a new lease of** or (*US*) **on life,** an improved prospect of living or of use after repair. [f. AF *les* (*lesser* let f. L *laxare* loosen)]

leasehold *n.* the holding of property by lease; property held thus. —**leaseholder** *n.*

leash *n.* a thong for holding hounds etc. under restraint; a dog's lead. —*v.t.* to put a leash on; to hold in a leash. —**straining at the leash,** eager to begin. [f. OF (*laisser* let run on slack lead, as LEASE)]

least *adj.* **1** smallest in amount or degree; of a very small species etc. **2** lowest in rank or importance. —*n.* the least amount. —*adv.* in the least degree. —**at least,** at all events, anyway; not less than. **(in) the least,** at all. **to say the least (of it),** putting the case moderately. [OE, superl. of LESS]

leather /ˈleðə(r)/ *n.* **1** material made from animal skins by tanning or a similar process. **2** the leather part(s) of something. **3** a piece of leather for polishing with. **4** (in *pl.*) leggings, breeches. —*v.t.* **1** to cover with leather. **2** to polish or wipe with a leather. **3** to beat, to thrash. —**leather-back** *n.* the largest existing turtle (*Sphargis coriacea*), with a flexible shell. **leather-jacket** *n.* a crane-fly grub, which has a tough skin. [OE]

leatherette /leðə'ret/ *n.* an imitation leather. [f. prec. + -ETTE]

leathery *adj.* like leather; tough. —**leatheriness** *n.* [f. LEATHER]

leave[1] *v.t./i.* (*past & p.p.* **left**) **1** to go away (from); to go away finally or permanently; to abandon, to desert. **2** to cease to reside at or belong to or work for. **3** to cause or allow to remain; to depart without taking. **4** to have remaining after one's death. **5** to give as a legacy. **6** to allow to stay or proceed without interference. **7** to commit or refer *to* another person; to depute (a person) to perform a function in one's absence. **8** to refrain from consuming or dealing with. **9** to deposit for collection or transmission. —**leave alone,** to refrain from disturbing; not to interfere with. **leave off,** to discontinue; to come to or make an end. **leave out,** to omit. **left luggage,** luggage deposited for later retrieval. **left-overs** *n.pl.* items (especially food) remaining after the rest has been used. [OE]

leave[2] *n.* **1** permission. **2** permission to be absent from duty; the period for which this lasts. —**on leave,** legitimately absent from duty. **take (one's) leave (of),** to bid farewell (to). **take leave of one's senses,** to go mad. [OE]

leaved *adj.* having leaves; having a specified number of leaves. [f. LEAF]

leaven /'lev(ə)n/ *n.* **1** a substance (esp. yeast) used to make dough ferment and rise. **2** a pervasive transforming influence; an admixture *of* some quality. —*v.t.* **1** to ferment (dough) with leaven. **2** to permeate and transform; to modify *with* a tempering element. [f. OF f. L *levamen* (*levare* lift)]

leaves *pl.* of LEAF.

leavings *n.pl.* things left over, especially as worthless. [f. LEAVE[1]]

lecher /'letʃə(r)/ *n.* a lecherous man, a debauchee. [f. OF (*lechier* live in debauchery or gluttony, rel. to LICK)]

lecherous /'letʃərəs/ *adj.* lustful, having strong or excessive sexual desire. [f. prec.]

lechery /'letʃərɪ/ *n.* unrestrained indulgence of sexual desire. [f. LECHER]

lectern /'lektɜ:n/ *n.* a desk for holding a bible or hymn-book in church; a similar desk for a lecturer etc. [f. OF f. L *lectrum* (*legere* read)]

lectionary /'lekʃənərɪ/ *n.* a list of portions of Scripture apppointed to be read in churches. [f. L (*lectio* reading, as prec.)]

lecture /'lektʃə(r)/ *n.* a discourse giving information about a subject to a class or other audience; a long serious speech, especially as a scolding or reprimand. —*v.t./i.* to deliver a lecture or lectures; to talk seriously or reprovingly to. —**lecturer** *n.* [f. OF or L (as prec.)]

lectureship *n.* the official position of lecturer, especially at a university etc.

led *past & p.p.* of LEAD[1].

ledge *n.* a narrow horizontal projection or shelf. [perh. rel. to LAY[1]]

ledger *n.* a tall narrow book in which a firm's accounts are kept. [=Du. *ligger*, *legger* (as LIE[1], LAY[1])]

lee *n.* **1** the shelter given by a neighbouring object. **2** (in full **lee side**) the sheltered side, the side away from the wind. —**lee shore,** the shore to leeward of a ship. [OE]

leech[1] *n.* **1** a blood-sucking worm (*Hirudo medicinalis*) formerly used medicinally for bleeding. **2** a person who sponges on another. [OE]

leech[2] *n.* a vertical side of a square sail; the after side of a fore-and-aft sail. [perh. rel. to ON *lík*, nautical term of uncertain meaning]

leek *n.* a vegetable (*Allium porrum*) of the onion family with a cylindrical white bulb; this as the Welsh national emblem. [OE]

leer *v.i.* to look slyly or lasciviously or maliciously. —*n.* a leering look. [perh. f. obs. *leer* cheek f. OE, as though 'to glance over one's cheek']

leery *adj.* knowing, sly, wary *of.* [perh. f. obs. *leer* looking askance (as prec.)]

lees /li:z/ *n.pl.* the sediment of wine etc.; the dregs. [f. OF *lie*]

leeward /'li:wəd, (*Naut.*) 'lu:əd/ *adj.* & *adv.* on or towards the sheltered side. —*n.* the leeward side or region. [f. LEE + -WARD]

leeway *n.* **1** a ship's sideways drift leeward of a desired course. **2** an allowable deviation or freedom of action.

left[1] *adj.* **1** on or towards the side of the human body which in the majority of persons has the less-used hand and on which the heart lies; on or towards the analogous part of a thing. **2** politically to the left (see sense 3 below). —*adv.* on or to the left side. —*n.* **1** the left-hand part, region, or direction. **2** the left hand; a blow with this; (in marching) the left foot. **3** (often **Left**) a political group or section favouring radical socialism; such radicals collectively; the more advanced or innovative section of any group. —**have two left feet,** to be clumsy. **left bank,** the bank of a river on the left as one faces downstream. **left-hand** *adj.* of, on, or towards the left side of a person or thing. **left-handed** *adj.* using the left hand by preference as more serviceable; made by or for the left hand; turning to the left; awkward or clumsy; (of a compliment) ambiguous, of doubtful sincerity. **left-hander** *n.* a left-handed person or blow. **left wing,** the left side of a football etc. team on the field; a player in this position; the left section of a political party (see sense 3 above). **left-winger** *n.* a person on the left wing. [orig. = weak, worthless; cf. OE *lyft-adl* paralysis]

left[2] *past & p.p.* of LEAVE[1].

leftism *n.* radical socialism. —**leftist** *n.* [f. LEFT[1]]

leftward /ˈleftwəd/ *adv.* (also **leftwards**) towards the left. —*adj.* going towards or facing the left. [f. LEFT[1] + -WARD]

lefty *n.* (*colloq.*) **1** a left-winger in politics. **2** a left-handed person. [f. LEFT[1]]

leg *n.* **1** each of the projecting parts of an animal's body, on which it stands or moves; either of the two lower limbs of the human body; an artificial replacement of this. **2** the part of a garment covering the leg. **3** any of the projecting supports beneath a chair or other piece of furniture. **4** the part of a cricket field on the side where the batsman places his feet. **5** one section of a journey. **6** each of several stages in a competition etc. **7** one branch of a forked object. **8** (*Naut.*) a run made on a single tack. —**give a person a leg up,** to help him to mount a horse etc. or get over an obstacle or difficulty. **leg before wicket,** (of a batsman) out because of an illegal obstruction of ball with a part of the body other than the hand. **leg it,** to walk or run hard. **leg-pull** *n.* a hoax. **not have a leg to stand on,** to be unable to support an argument by facts or sound reasons. **on one's last legs,** near death or the end of usefulness etc. —**legged** /legd, ˈlegɪd/ *adj.* [f. ON]

legacy /ˈlegəsɪ/ *n.* **1** money or an article given by will to a survivor. **2** something handed down by a predecessor. [f. OF f. L (*legare* bequeath, commit)]

legal /ˈliːg(ə)l/ *adj.* of or based on law; concerned with, appointed, required, or permitted by law. —**legal aid,** a payment from public funds for legal advice or proceedings. **legal tender,** currency that cannot legally be refused in payment of a debt. —**legality** /lɪˈgælɪtɪ/ *n.*, **legally** /ˈliːgəlɪ/ *adv.* [f. F or L (*lex* law)]

legalism *n.* excessive adherence to a law or formula. —**legalist** *n.*, **legalistic** /-ˈlɪstɪk/ *adj.* [f. prec.]

legalize *v.t.* to make lawful; to bring into harmony with the law. —**legalization** /-ˈzeɪʃ(ə)n/ *n.* [f. LEGAL]

legate /ˈlegət/ *n.* an ambassador (now only one representing the pope). [f. OF f. L (*legare* commission)]

legatee /legəˈtiː/ *n.* a recipient of a legacy. [f. L *legare* bequeath]

legation /lɪˈgeɪʃ(ə)n/ *n.* **1** a body of deputies. **2** a diplomatic minister (especially below ambassadorial rank) and his staff. **3** a diplomatic minister's residence. **4** a legateship. [f. OF or L (as LEGATE)]

legato /lɪˈgɑːtəʊ/ *adv.* & *adj.* (*Mus.*) in a smooth manner. —*n.* (*pl.* **-os**) (*Mus.*) smooth playing; a passage played smoothly. [It., = bound, f. L *ligare* bind]

legend /ˈledʒ(ə)nd/ *n.* **1** a story (true or invented) handed down from the past; such stories collectively. **2** an inscription on a coin or medal. **3** a caption. **4** an explanation on a map etc. of the symbols used. [f. OF f. L *legenda* what is to be read (*legere* read)]

legendary /ˈledʒ(ə)ndərɪ/ *adj.* **1** of or based on legends, described in a legend. **2** (*colloq.*) famous, often talked about. [f. L (as prec.)]

legerdemain /ledʒədəˈmeɪn/ *n.* sleight of hand, juggling; trickery, sophistry. [f. F, = light of hand]

leger line /ˈledʒə(r)/ a short line added in a musical score for notes above or below the range of the staff. [var. of LEDGER]

legging *n.* (usu. in *pl.*) a protective outer covering of leather etc. for the leg from the knee to the ankle. [f. LEG]

leggy *adj.* long-legged. —**legginess** *n.* [f. LEG]

leghorn /ˈleghɔːn, lɪˈgɔːn/ *n.* **1** fine plaited straw; a hat of this. **2** Leghorn, one of a small hardy breed of domestic fowl. [f. *Leghorn* (*Livorno*) in Italy]

legible /ˈledʒɪb(ə)l/ *adj.* clear enough to be deciphered, readable. —**legibility** /-ˈbɪlɪtɪ/ *n.*, **legibly** *adv.* [f. L (*legere* read)]

legion /ˈliːdʒ(ə)n/ *n.* **1** a division of 3,000–6,000 men in the ancient Roman army. **2** a vast group, a multitude. [f. OF f. L *legere* choose)]

legionary *adj.* of a legion or legions. —*n.* a member of a legion; a legionary soldier in the ancient Roman army. [f. L (as prec.)]

legionnaire /liːdʒəˈneə(r)/ *n.* a member of the foreign legion or of the American or Royal British Legion. —**legionnaires' disease,** a form of bacterial pneumonia first identified after an outbreak at an American Legion meeting in 1976. [f. F (as LEGION)]

legislate /ˈledʒɪsleɪt/ *v.i.* to make laws. —**legislator** *n.* [as foll.]

legislation /ledʒɪsˈleɪʃ(ə)n/ *n.* law-making; the laws made. [f. L (*lex legis* law, *latio* proposing)]

legislative /ˈledʒɪslətɪv/ of or empowered to make legislation. [f. prec.]

legislature /ˈledʒɪsleɪtʃə(r)/ *n.* the legislative body of a State. [f. prec.]

legitimate /lɪˈdʒɪtɪmət/ *adj.* **1** in accordance with the law or rules. **2** (of a child) born of parents married to each other. **3** logically acceptable, justifiable. —**legitimate drama** *or* **theatre,** plays of recognized merit, normal comedy and tragedy as distinct from musical comedy, farce, revue, etc. The term arose in the 18th c. —**legitimacy** *n.*, **legitimately** *adv.* [f. L (*legitimus* lawful, f. *lex legis* law)]

legitimatize /lɪˈdʒɪtɪmətaɪz/ *v.t.* to legitimize. [f. prec.]

legitimize /lɪˈdʒɪtɪmaɪz/ *v.t.* to make legitimate; to serve as a justification for. —**legitimization** /-ˈzeɪʃ(ə)n/ *n.* [as LEGITIMATE]

legume /legju:m/ *n.* a leguminous plant; a fruit or edible part or pod of this. [f. F f. L *legumen* (*legere* pick), because pickable by hand]

leguminous /lɪˈgju:mɪnəs/ *adj.* of the family of plants Leguminosae, with seeds in pods (e.g. peas, beans). [as prec.]

lei /ˈleɪi:/ *n.* a Polynesian garland of flowers. [Hawaiian]

Leics. *abbr.* Leicestershire.

leisure /ˈleʒə(r)/ *n.* free time, time at one's disposal; the enjoyment of this. —**at leisure,** not occupied; in an unhurried manner. **at one's leisure,** when one has time. [f. AF f. L *licēre* be allowed]

leisured *adj.* having ample leisure. [f. prec.]

leisurely *adj.* unhurried, relaxed. —*adv.* without hurry. —**leisureliness** *n.* [f. LEISURE]

leitmotiv /ˈlaɪtməʊti:f/ *n.* (also **leitmotif**) a theme associated throughout a musical etc. composition with a particular person or idea. [G (as LEAD[1], MOTIVE)]

lemming /ˈlemɪŋ/ *n.* a small arctic rodent of the genus *Lemmus* etc., of which one species migrates in large numbers and has been reputed to continue headlong into the sea and drown. [Norw.]

lemon[1] /ˈlemən/ *n.* **1** a pale-yellow oval fruit with acid juice; the tree bearing it (*Citrus limon*). **2** pale yellow colour. **3** (*slang*) a simpleton; something disappointing or unsuccessful. —**lemon cheese** *or* **curd,** a thick creamy spread made from lemons. —**lemony** *adj.* [f. OF f. Arab. (as LIME[2])]

lemon[2] /ˈlemən/ *n.* (in full **lemon sole**) a kind of plaice (*Microstomus kitt*). [f. F *limande*]

lemonade /leməˈneɪd/ *n.* a drink made from lemon-juice or a synthetic substitute with similar flavour. [f. LEMON[1]]

lemur /ˈli:mə(r)/ *n.* a nocturnal mammal of Madagascar of the genus *Lemur*, allied to the monkeys. [f. L *lemures* spirits of the dead, f. its spectre-like face]

lend *v.t.* (*past & p.p.* **lent**) **1** to give or allow the use of (a thing) temporarily on the understanding that it or its equivalent will be returned. **2** to provide (money) temporarily in return for payment of interest. **3** to contribute as a temporary help or effect etc. —**lend an ear,** to listen. **lend a hand,** to help. **lend itself to,** to be suitable for. **lend oneself to,** to accommodate oneself to. —**lender** *n.* [OE (as LOAN)]

length /leŋθ/ *n.* **1** measurement or extent from end to end, especially along a thing's greatest dimension. **2** the amount of time occupied by something. **3** the distance a thing extends used as a unit of measurement; the length of a horse, boat, etc., as a measure of the lead in a race. **4** the degree of thoroughness in an action. **5** a piece of cloth etc. cut from a longer one; a piece of a certain length. **6** the quantity of a vowel or syllable. **7** (in cricket) the distance from the batsman at which the ball pitches; the proper amount of this. —**at length,** after a long time; taking a long time, in detail. [OE (as LONG[1])]

lengthen /ˈleŋθ(ə)n/ *v.t./i.* to make or become longer. [f. prec.]

lengthways *adv.* (also **lengthwise**) in a direction parallel with a thing's length.

lengthy *adj.* of unusual length; long and tedious. —**lengthily** *adv.*, **lengthiness** *n.* [f. LENGTH]

lenient /ˈli:nɪənt/ *adj.* merciful, not severe, mild. —**lenience** *n.* **leniency** *n.*, **leniently** *adv.* [f. L *lenire* soothe (*lenis* gentle)]

lens /lenz/ *n.* **1** a piece of a transparent substance with one or both sides curved for concentrating or dispersing light-rays in optical instruments. **2** a combination of lenses in photography. **3** the transparent substance behind the iris of the eye. [L, = lentil (from its shape)]

Lent *n.* the period from Ash Wednesday to Easter Eve of which the 40 weekdays are devoted to fasting and penitence in commemoration of Christ's fasting in the wilderness. —**Lenten** *adj.* [f. *Lenten*, orig. as *n.* = spring, f. OE]

lent *past & p.p.* of LEND.

lentil /ˈlentɪl/ *n.* a kind of leguminous plant (*Lens esculenta*); its edible seed. [f. OF f. L *lenticula* (as LENS)]

lento /ˈlentəʊ/ *adj. & adv.* (*Mus.*) slow, slowly. [It.]

leonine /ˈli:ənaɪn/ *adj.* of or like a lion. [f. OF or L (*leo* lion)]

leopard /ˈlepəd/ *n.* **1** a large African and South Asian carnivorous animal (*Panthera pardus*) of the cat family, with a dark-spotted yellowish-fawn or black coat, a panther. **2** any of various similar animals. **3** (in heraldry) a lion passant guardant as in the arms of England. —**leopardess** *n. fem.* [f. OF f. L (as LEO, *pardus* panther)]

leotard /ˈli:ətɑ:d/ *n.* a close-fitting one-piece garment worn by dancers etc. [f. J. *Léotard*, French trapeze artist (d. 1870)]

leper /ˈlepə(r)/ *n.* **1** a person with leprosy. **2** a person shunned on moral grounds.

[orig. = leprosy, f. OF f. L f. Gk *lepra* (*lepros* scaly)]

lepidopterous /lepɪˈdɒptərəs/ *adj.* of the Lepidoptera or insects with four scale-covered wings, including moths and butterflies. —**lepidopterist** *n.* [f. Gk *lepis* scale + *pteron* wing]

leprechaun /ˈleprəkɔːn/ *n.* a small mischievous sprite in Irish folklore. [f. OIr. *luchorpán* (*lu* small, *corp* body)]

leprosy /ˈleprəsɪ/ *n.* a chronic infectious bacterial disease affecting the nerves, skin, and certain other tissues of the human body, resulting in mutilations and deformities. [f. foll.]

leprous /ˈleprəs/ *adj.* of leprosy; having or resembling leprosy. [f. OF f. L (as LEPER)]

lesbian /ˈlezbɪən/ *n.* a homosexual woman. —*adj.* of lesbians; of homosexuality in women. —**lesbianism** *n.* [f. *Lesbos*, Gk island, home of the reputedly homosexual Sappho]

lèse-majesté /leɪzˈmæʒesteɪ/ *n.* (also **lese-majesty** /liːzˈmædʒɪstɪ/) **1** treason; an insult to a sovereign or ruler. **2** presumptuous conduct. [f. F *lèse-majesté* f. L (as foll., MAJESTY)]

lesion /ˈliːʒ(ə)n/ *n.* **1** damage, injury. **2** a harmful change in the functioning or texture of an organ of the body. [f. OF f. L *laesio* (*laedere* injure)]

less *adj.* **1** smaller in size, degree, duration, number, etc. **2** of smaller quantity, not so much. **3** (D) fewer. —*adv.* to a smaller extent, in a lower degree. —*n.* a smaller amount, quantity, or number. —*prep.* minus, deducting. [OE]

-less /-lɪs/ *suffix* forming adjectives and adverbs from nouns, in the sense 'not having, without, free from' (*doubtless, powerless*), and from verbs, in the sense 'unable to be —ed', 'not —ing' (*fathomless, tireless*). [OE]

lessee /leˈsiː/ *n.* a person holding property by lease, a tenant. [f. AF (as LEASE)]

lessen *v.t./i.* to make or become less, to diminish. [f. LESS]

lesser *adj.* (usu. *attrib.*) not so great as the other or the rest. [compar. of LESS]

lesson /ˈles(ə)n/ *n.* **1** a spell of teaching. **2** (in *pl.*) systematic instruction in a subject. **3** a thing to be learnt by a pupil. **4** an experience that serves to warn or encourage. **5** a passage from the Bible read aloud during a church service. [f. OF *leçon* f. L *lectio* (*legere* read)]

lessor /leˈsɔː(r)/ *n.* a person who lets a property by lease. [AF (as LEASE)]

lest *conj.* **1** in order that not, for fear that. **2** that. [OE, = whereby less that]

let[1] *v.t./i.* (**-tt-**; *past & p.p.* **let**) **1** to allow, enable, or cause to, not to prevent or forbid. **2** to allow or cause to come, go, or pass. **3** to grant the use of (rooms, land, etc.) for rent or hire. **4** as an auxiliary verb (with 1st and 3rd persons) expressing commands, appeals, etc. —*n.* the letting of rooms, land, etc. —**let alone**, to refrain from interfering with or doing; apart from, far less or more than, let be, to refrain from interfering with or doing. **let down**, to lower; to let out air from (an inflated tyre etc.); to fail to support or satisfy, to disappoint; to lengthen (a garment); to treat (gently etc.). **let-down** *n.* a disappointment. **let go**, to release, to loose one's hold (*of*). **let oneself go**, to abandon self-restraint. **let in for**, to involve in (loss or difficulty). **let loose**, to release. **let off**, to fire (a gun), to explode (a bomb); to ignite (a firework); to excuse from (duties etc.); to give little or no punishment to. **let off steam**, to allow steam to escape; to release pent-up energy or feeling. **let on**, (*colloq.*) to reveal a secret. **let out**, to release from restraint or obligation; to reveal (a secret etc.), to make (a garment) looser; to put out to rent or to contract. **let-out** *n.* an opportunity to escape. **let up**, (*colloq.*) to become less intense or severe, to relax one's efforts. **let-up** *n.* a reduction in intensity, a relaxation of effort. **to let**, available to rent. [OE]

let[2] *n.* an obstruction of the ball or a player in tennis etc., requiring the ball to be served again. —*v.t.* (**-tt-**; *past & p.p.* **letted** or **let**) (*archaic*) to hinder, to obstruct. —**without let or hindrance** unimpeded. [OE]

-let /-lɪt/ *suffix* forming nouns usu. diminutive (*flatlet*) or denoting articles of ornament or dress (*anklet*). [orig. f. OF, wrongly understood as dim. suffix]

lethal /ˈliːθ(ə)l/ *adj.* causing or sufficient to cause death. —**lethality** /-ˈælɪtɪ/ *n.*, **lethally** *adv.* [f. L *let(h)alis* (*letum* death)]

lethargy /ˈleθədʒɪ/ *n.* lack of energy or vitality; abnormal drowsiness. —**lethargic** /lɪˈθɑːdʒɪk/ *adj.*, **lethargically** *adv.* [f. OF f. L f. Gk (*lēthargos* forgetful)]

Lett *n.* a member of a people living near the Baltic, mainly in Latvia. [f. G f. Lettish *Latvi*]

letter /ˈletə(r)/ *n.* **1** any of the characters, representing one or more of the simple or compound sounds used in speech, of which written words are composed; an alphabetic symbol. **2** a written or printed communication, usually sent by post or messenger; (in *pl.*) an addressed legal or formal document. **3** the precise terms of a statement, strict verbal interpretation. **4** (in *pl.*) literature; acquaintance with books; erudition. —*v.t.* **1** to inscribe letters on. **2** to classify with letters. —**letter-bomb** *n.* a terrorist explosive device in the form of a letter sent through the post. **letter-box** *n.* a slit in a door, with a hinged flap, through which letters are delivered; a post-box. **letter of credit,** a letter from a bank authorizing the bearer to draw money from another bank. **man of letters,** a scholar or author. **to the letter,** with adherence to every detail. [f. OF f. L *littera*]

lettered *adj.* well-read, well-educated. [f. prec.]

letterhead *n.* a printed heading on stationery; stationery with this.

letterpress *n.* **1** the printed words in an illustrated book. **2** printing from raised type.

Lettish /ˈletɪʃ/ *adj.* of the Letts. —*n.* the language of the Letts, Latvian. [f. LETT]

lettuce /ˈletɪs/ *n.* a garden plant (*Lactuca sativa*) with crisp leaves used as salad. [f. OF f. L *lactuca* (*lac* milk, f. its milky juice)]

leuco- /ˈlu:kəʊ-/ *in comb.* white. [f. Gk *leukos* white]

leucocyte /ˈlu:kəʊsaɪt/ *n.* a white or colourless corpuscle in the blood. [f. LEUCO- + -CYTE]

leucotomy /lu:ˈkɒtəmɪ/ *n.* surgical incision into the white tissue of the frontal lobe of the brain to relieve some cases of mental disorder. [f. LEUCO- + -TOMY]

leukaemia /lu:ˈki:mɪə/ *n.* a progressive disease with an abnormal accumulation of white corpuscles in the tissues and usually in the blood. [G f. Gk (*leukos* white, *haima* blood)]

Levant /lɪˈvænt/ the eastern part of the Mediterranean together with its islands and neighbouring countries. —**Levantine** /lɪˈvæntaɪn, ˈlev(ə)n-/ *adj.* & *n.* [F, = point of sunrise, east (*lever* rise)]

levee[1] /ˈlevɪ/ *n.* (*archaic*) an assembly of visitors or guests, especially at a formal reception; (*hist.*) a sovereign's assembly for men only. [f. F *levé* var. of *lever* rising (as LEVY)]

levee[2] /ˈlevɪ/ *n.* **1** an embankment against river floods; a river's natural embankment. **2** a landing-place. [f. F *levée* (*lever* raise, as LEVY)]

level /ˈlev(ə)l/ *n.* **1** a horizontal line or plane, one joining points of equal height. **2** a measured height or value etc., a position on a scale; a social, moral, or intellectual standard. **3** a plane of rank or authority. **4** an instrument for giving or testing a horizontal line or plane. **5** a more or less flat surface or area. —*adj.* **1** horizontal. **2** on a level or equality (with); at the same height, rank, or position on a scale. **3** (of ground) flat, without hills or hollows. **4** steady, even, uniform. **5** equable or well-balanced in quality, style, temper, judgement, etc. —*v.t./i.* (**-ll-**) **1** to make or become level, even, or uniform. **2** to place on the same level; to bring *up* or *down* to a standard. **3** to raze or demolish. **4** to aim (a missile or gun). **5** to direct (an accusation etc., or *absol.*, *at* or *against*). —**do one's level best,** (*colloq.*) to do one's utmost. **find one's level,** to reach the social or intellectual level etc. that is most suitable for oneself. **level crossing,** a crossing of a railway and road, or two railways, at the same level. **level-headed** *adj.* mentally well-balanced, sensible. **level pegging,** equality of scores or achievements. **on the level,** (*colloq.*) honest, honestly, without deception. **on a level with,** in the same horizontal plane, as, equal with. —**leveller** *n.* [f. OF f. L *libella* (*libra* scales, balance)]

lever /ˈli:və(r)/ *n.* **1** a bar resting on a pivot and used to raise a heavy or firmly fixed object. **2** a device consisting of a straight bar or other rigid structure of which one point (the *fulcrum*) is fixed, another is connected with the force (*weight*) to be resisted or acted upon, and a third is connected with the force (*power*) applied. **3** a projecting handle moved to operate mechanism. **4** a means of exerting moral pressure. —*v.t./i.* to use a lever; to lift or move etc. by means of a lever. [f. AF (*lever* raise f. L *levare*)]

leverage /ˈli:vərɪdʒ/ *n.* **1** the action or power of a lever. **2** the means of accomplishing a purpose; power, influence. [f. prec.]

leveret /ˈlevərɪt/ *n.* a young hare, especially in the first year. [f. AF dim. of *levre* hare f. L *lepus*]

leviathan /lɪˈvaɪəθ(ə)n/ *n.* **1** (in the Bible) a sea monster. **2** anything very large or powerful. [f. L f. Heb.]

Levis /ˈli:vaɪz/ *n.pl.* [P] a type of (usually blue) denim jeans or overalls reinforced with rivets. [f. *Levi* Strauss, orig. US manufacturer in 1860s]

levitate /ˈlevɪteɪt/ *v.t./i.* to rise and float in the air, to cause to do this (esp. with reference to spiritualism). —**levitation** /-ˈteɪʃ(ə)n/ *n.* [f. L *levis* light, after *gravitate*]

Levite /ˈli:vaɪt/ *n.* a member of the Hebrew tribe of Levi, from which priests were drawn until after the Exile, when Levites were allotted only inferior duties in the Temple. [f. L f. Gk f. *Levi*, son of Jacob]

levity /ˈlevɪtɪ/ *n.* a disposition to make light of weighty matters, frivolity, lack of serious thought. [f. L *levitas* (*levis* light)]

levy /ˈlevɪ/ *v.t.* **1** to impose or collect (a payment etc.) compulsorily. **2** to enrol (troops etc.). **3** to wage (war). —*n.* **1** levying. **2** a payment etc. levied. **3** (in *pl.*) troops levied. [f. OF *levée* (*lever* raise f. L *levare*)]

lewd /lju:d/ *adj.* lascivious; indecent, treating sexual matters in a vulgar way. —**lewdly** *adv.*, **lewdness** *n.* [OE, = lay (LAY[2])]

lexical /ˈleksɪk(ə)l/ *adj.* **1** of the words of a language. **2** of a lexicon or dictionary. [f. Gk (as LEXICON)]

lexicography /leksɪˈkɒgrəfɪ/ *n.* the compilation of dictionaries. —**lexicographer** *n.*, **lexicographical** /-ˈgræfɪk(ə)l/ *adj.* [f. LEXICON + -GRAPHY]

lexicology /leksɪˈkɒlədʒɪ/ *n.* the study of words and their form, history, and meaning. [f. foll. + -GRAPHY]

lexicon /ˈleksɪk(ə)n/ *n.* **1** a dictionary, especially of Greek, Hebrew, Syriac, or Arabic. **2** the vocabulary of a person, language, branch of knowledge, etc. [f. Gk *lexicon* (*biblion* book), f. *lexis* word (*legō* speak)]

lexis /ˈleksɪs/ *n.* words, vocabulary; a total stock of words. [Gk (see prec.)]

ley[1] /leɪ/ *n.* land temporarily under grass. [f. *ley*, *lea* adj. fallow (as LAY[1], LIE[1])]

ley[2] /li:, leɪ/ *n.* the supposed straight line of a prehistoric track, usually between hilltops, with identifying points such as ponds, mounds, etc., marking its route. [var. of LEA]

Leyden jar /ˈleɪd(ə)n/ a kind of electrical condenser with a glass jar as a dielectric between sheets of tin foil, invented in 1745 at Leyden University. [f. *Leyden* (now *Leiden*) in Holland]

LF *abbr.* low frequency.

l.h. *abbr.* left hand.

Li *symbol* lithium.

liability /laɪəˈbɪlɪtɪ/ *n.* **1** being liable. **2** a troublesome person, a handicap. **3** (in *pl.*) debts etc. for which one is liable. [f. foll.]

liable /ˈlaɪəb(ə)l/ *predic. adj.* **1** legally obliged; subject or under an obligation *to*. **2** exposed or open *to* (something undesirable); apt or likely *to*. **3** answerable (*for*). [perh. f. OF *lier* bind f. L *ligare*]

liaise /lɪˈeɪz/ *v.i.* (*colloq.*) to act as a liaison or go-between. [back-formation f. foll.]

liaison /lɪˈeɪz(ə)n/ *n.* **1** communication and co-operation between units of an organization; a person effecting this. **2** an illicit sexual relationship. [F (*lier* bind, as LIABLE)]

liana /lɪˈɑ:nə/ *n.* a climbing and twining plant in tropical forests. [f. F *liane*, *lierne* clematis]

liar /ˈlaɪə(r)/ *n.* a person who tells lies. [f. LIE[2]]

lias /ˈlaɪəs/ *n.* a blue limestone rich in fossils. —**liassic** /lɪˈæsɪk/ *adj.* [f. OF *liois*]

Lib. *abbr.* **1** Liberal. **2** (*colloq.*) liberation.

libation /laɪˈbeɪʃ(ə)n/ *n.* the pouring of a drink-offering to a god; such a drink-offering. [f. L (*libare* pour as an offering)]

libel /ˈlaɪb(ə)l/ *n.* **1** a published false statement that is damaging to a person's reputation; the act of publishing it. **2** a false defamatory statement or representation.—*v.t.* (**-ll-**) to utter or publish a libel against. —**be a libel on,** do injustice to. —**libellous** *adj.* [f. OF f. L *libellus* dim. of *liber* book]

liberal /ˈlɪbər(ə)l/ *adj.* **1** given or giving freely; abundant. **2** open-minded, not prejudiced; not strict or rigorous; (of studies etc.) for general broadening of the mind. **3** favouring moderate political and social reform; **Liberal,** of the Liberal Party. —*n.* **1** a person of liberal views. **2 Liberal,** a member or supporter of the Liberal Party. —**Liberal Party,** a political party favouring moderate reform. —**liberalism** *n.*, **liberality** /-ˈrælɪtɪ/ *n.*, **liberally** *adv.* [orig. = befitting a free man, f. OF f. L (*liber* free)]

liberalize /ˈlɪbərəlaɪz/ *v.t.* to make more liberal or less strict. —**liberalization** /-ˈzeɪʃ(ə)n/ *n.* [f. prec.]

liberate /ˈlɪbəreɪt/ *v.t.* **1** to set free. **2** to free (a country) from an oppressor or enemy occupation. **3** to free from rigid social conventions. —**liberation** /-ˈreɪʃ(ə)n/ *n.*, **liberator** *n.* [f. L *liberare* (as LIBERAL)]

libertine /ˈlɪbəti:n/ *n.* a dissolute or licentious man. —*adj.* licentious. [f. L, = freedman (*liber* free)]

liberty /ˈlɪbətɪ/ *n.* **1** freedom from captivity, slavery, imprisonment, or despotic control. **2** the right or power to do as one pleases. **3** a right or privilege granted by authority. —**at liberty,** free, not imprisoned; allowed. **take liberties,** to behave in an unduly familiar manner; to interpret facts etc. too freely. [f. OF f. L *libertas* (*liber* free)]

libidinous /lɪˈbɪdɪnəs/ *adj.* lustful. [f. L (as foll.)]

libido /lɪˈbi:dəʊ/ *n.* (*pl.* **-os**) a psychic impulse or drive, especially that associated with sexual desire. —**libidinal** /lɪˈbɪdɪn(ə)l/ *adj.* [L, = lust]

Libra /ˈlɪbrə/ a constellation and the seventh sign of the zodiac, the Scales, which the sun enters at the autumnal equinox. [L, = scales, balance]

librarian /laɪˈbreərɪən/ *n.* a person in charge of or assisting in a library. —**librarianship** *n.* [f. L (as foll.)]

library /ˈlaɪbrərɪ/ *n.* **1** a collection of books for reading or borrowing. **2** a room or building where these are kept. **3** a similar collection of films, records, computer routines, etc.; the place where they are kept. **4** a series of books issued in similar bindings as a set. [f. OF f. L (*liber* book)]

libretto /lɪˈbretəʊ/ *n.* (*pl.* **-ti** /-tɪ/, **-tos**) the text of an opera or other long musical vocal work. —**librettist** *n.* [It., dim. of *libro* book f. L *liber*]

lice *pl.* of LOUSE.

licence /ˈlaɪsəns/ *n.* **1** a permit from the government etc. to own or do something or carry on some trade. **2** leave, permission. **3** excessive liberty of action. **4** disregard of law, rules, or custom; a writer's or artist's transgression of established rules for effect. [f. OF f. L (*licēre* be allowed)]

license /ˈlaɪsəns/ *v.t.* **1** to grant a licence to or for. **2** to authorize the use of (premises) for a certain purpose, especially the sale of alcoholic liquor. [f. prec.]

licensee /laɪsən'si:/ *n.* a holder of a licence, especially to sell alcoholic liquor. [f. prec.]

licentiate /laɪ'senʃɪət/ *n.* a holder of a certificate of competence to practise a certain profession. [f. L (as LICENCE)]

licentious /laɪ'senʃəs/ *adj.* disregarding the rules of conduct, especially in sexual matters. —**licentiousness** *n.* [f. L (as LICENCE)]

lichee var. of LITCHI.

lichen /'laɪkən, 'lɪtʃən/ *n.* a plant organism of the group Lichenes, composed of a fungus and an alga in association, usually of grey green, or yellow tint growing on and colouring rocks, tree-trunks, walls, roofs, etc. —**lichenous** *adj.* [L, f. Gk *leikhēn*]

lich-gate *n.* a roofed gateway to a churchyard, where a coffin awaits the clergyman's arrival. [OE *lic* corpse + GATE]

licit /'lɪsɪt/ *adj.* not forbidden. —**licitly** *adv.* [f. L *licitus* (as LICENCE)]

lick *v.t./i.* **1** to pass the tongue over; to take *up* or *off* or make *clean* by doing this. **2** (of a flame or waves etc.) to move like a tongue, to touch lightly. **3** (*slang*) to thrash. **4** (*slang*) defeat; to excel. —*n.* **1** an act of licking with the tongue. **2** a blow with a stick etc. **3** (*slang*) a (fast) pace. —**a lick and a promise,** (*colloq.*) a slight and hasty wash. **lick into shape,** to make presentable or efficient. **lick one's chops** *or* **lips,** to look forward with relish. **lick one's wounds,** to be in retirement trying to recover after a defeat. **lick a person's boots,** to be servile towards him or her. [OE]

lid *n.* **1** a hinged or removable cover, especially at the top of a container. **2** an eyelid. **3** (*slang*) a hat. —**put the lid on,** (*slang*) to be the culmination of; to put a stop to. —**lidded** *adj.* [OE]

lido /'li:dəʊ/ *n.* (*pl.* **-os**) a public open-air swimming-pool or bathing-beach. [It., name of beach near Venice]

lie[1] /laɪ/ *v.i.* (*past* **lay**; *p.p.* **lain**; *partic.* **lying**) **1** to be in or assume a horizontal position on a supporting surface. **2** to be resting on a surface. **3** to be or be kept or remain in a specified state or place; to be situated; (of troops) to be encamped. **4** (of an abstract thing) to exist or be found. **5** to be spread out to view. **6** (*Law*) to be admissible or able to be upheld. —*n.* the way, direction, or position in which a thing lies. —**lie down,** to assume a lying position; to have a short rest. **lie-down** *n.* a short rest. **lie down under,** to accept (an insult etc.) without protest. **lie in,** to remain in bed in the morning; to be brought to bed in childbirth. **lie-in** *n.* remaining in bed in the morning. **lie low,** to keep quiet or unseen; to be discreet about one's intentions. **lie of the land,** the state of affairs. **lie with,** to be the responsibility of. **take lying down,** to accept (an insult etc.) without protest. [OE]

lie[2] *n.* **1** an intentionally false statement. **2** an imposture, a thing that deceives. —*v.i.* (*partic.* **lying**) to tell lies; (of a thing) to be deceptive. —**give the lie to,** to serve to show the falsity of (a supposition etc.). **lie-detector** *n.* an instrument for determining whether a person is telling the truth by measuring physiological changes. [OE]

lief /li:f/ *adv.* (*archaic*) gladly, willingly (usu. *had* or *would lief*). [orig. adj., f. OE, = dear]

liege /li:dʒ/ *adj.* (usu. *hist.*) entitled to receive or bound to give feudal service or allegiance. —*n.* **1** a liege lord. **2** (usu. in *pl.*) a vassal, a subject. —**liege lord,** a feudal superior, a sovereign. [f. OF f. L *laeticus*]

lien /'li:ən/ *n.* the right to hold another's property until a debt on it is paid. [f. OF f. L *ligamen* bond (*ligare* bind)]

lieu /lju:/ *n.* **in lieu,** instead or in the place (*of*). [f. F f. L *locus* place]

Lieut. *abbr.* Lieutenant.

lieutenant /lef'tenənt/ *n.* **1** a deputy or substitute acting for a superior. **2** an army officer of the rank next below captain. **3** a naval officer of the rank next below lieutenant-commander. —**lieutenant-colonel, commander, -general** *ns.* an officer ranking next below colonel etc. —**lieutenancy** *n.* [f. OF (as LIEU, TENANT).

life *n.* (*pl.* **lives**) **1** being alive, the functional activity and continual change that is peculiar to animals and plants (before their death) and is not found in rocks and synthetic substances; state of existence as a living individual. **2** a living person; living things and their activity. **3** the period during which life lasts; the period from birth to the present time or from the present time to death. **4** an individual's actions and fortunes; a manner of existence or a particular aspect etc. of this. **5** energy, liveliness, animation. **6** the active part of existence; the business, pleasures, and social activities of the world. **7** a biography. **8** the time for which a thing exists or continues to function; **9** spiritual salvation, regenerate condition. **10** (*colloq.*) a sentence of imprisonment for life. —**as large as life,** life-size; (*joc.*) in person. **for dear life,** to escape death or as if to do this. **for life,** for the rest of one's life. **life-blood** *n.* the blood necessary to life; a vital factor or influence. **life cycle,** the cyclic series of changes undergone by an organism. **life-guard** *n.* an expert swimmer employed to rescue bathers from drowning; a bodyguard of soldiers. **Life Guards,** a regiment of the Household cavalry. **life-jacket** *n.* a jacket of buoyant material for supporting a person in the water. **life peer,** a peer whose title lapses on his or her death. **life-preserver** *n.* a short stick with a heavily leaded end; a life-jacket etc. **life sciences,** biology and related subjects. **life-size(d)** *adj.* of the same size as the person or thing represented. **life-style** *n.* an individual's way of life. **matter of life and death,** an issue on which a person's living or dying depends; a matter of great importance. **this life,** earthly life. [OE (as LIVE[1])]

lifebelt *n.* a belt of buoyant or inflatable material for supporting a person in the water.

lifeboat *n.* a specially constructed boat for rescuing those in distress at sea, launched from the land; a ship's small boat for use in an emergency.

lifebuoy *n.* a buoyant support for a person in the water.

lifeless *adj.* **1** lacking life, dead. **2** lacking movement or vitality. —**lifelessness** *n.* [f. LIFE + -LESS]

lifelike *adj.* closely resembling the person or thing represented.

lifeline *n.* **1** a rope used for life-saving, e.g. that attached to a lifebuoy. **2** a diver's signalling line. **3** a sole means of communication or transport.

lifelong *adj.* lasting a lifetime.

lifer *n.* (*slang*) **1** a person sentenced to imprisonment for life. **2** such a sentence. [f. LIFE]

lifetime *n.* the duration of a person's life.

lift *v.t./i.* **1** to raise to a higher level or position; to give an upward direction to (the eyes or face). **2** to take up from the ground or from its resting-place; to dig up (potatoes at harvest, plants for storing etc.). **3** to go up, to rise; (of fog etc.) to disperse. **4** to steal; to copy from another source. **5** to remove (a barrier or restriction). —*n.* **1** lifting, being lifted. **2** a ride as a passenger in a vehicle without payment. **3** an apparatus for raising and lowering persons or things from one floor to another in a building; an apparatus for carrying persons up or down a mountain etc. **4** the upward pressure that air exerts on an aircraft in flight. **5** an air-lift of goods etc.; the quantity thus transported. **6** a supporting or elating influence; a feeling of elation. —**lift-off** *n.* the vertical take-off of a spacecraft or rocket. [f. ON]

ligament /ˈlɪgəmənt/ *n.* a band of tough fibrous tissue binding bones together. [f. L (*ligare* bind)]

ligature /ˈlɪgətʃə(r)/ *n.* **1** a thing used in tying, especially a band or cord used in surgery. **2** the process of tying. **3** (*Mus.*) a slur, a tie. **4** two or more letters joined (as æ). **5** a bond, a thing that unites. —*v.t.* to bind with a ligature. [f. L (as prec.)]

light[1] /laɪt/ *n.* **1** the natural agent that stimulates the sense of sight; visible or other electromagnetic radiation from the sun, a fire, a lamp, etc. **2** the medium or condition of space in which this is present and therefore sight is possible (opp. *darkness*). **3** an appearance of brightness; the amount of this. **4** an object from which brightness emanates; a lamp lighthouse, traffic-light, etc. **5** a flame or spark serving to ignite something; a device producing this. **6** a thing's aspect, the way it appears to the mind. **7** enlightenment, elucidation. **8** spiritual illumination by divine truth. **9** vivacity, enthusiasm, or inspiration in a person's face, especially in the eyes. **10** (in *pl.*) one's mental attitude. **11** an eminent person. **12** the bright parts of a picture etc. **13** a window or opening in a wall to let in light. **14** (in a crossword etc.) a word to be deduced from clues. —*adj.* **1** well provided with light, not dark. **2** pale. —*v.t./i.* (*past* **lit**; *p.p.* **lit** or (esp. as *attrib. adj.*) **lighted**) **1** to set burning; to begin to burn. **2** (often with *up*) to provide (a room etc.) with light; to show (a person) the way or the surroundings with a light. **3** to brighten with animation. —**bring** (*or* **come**) **to light,** to reveal (or be revealed). **in a good** (*or* **bad**) **light,** easily (or barely) visible; giving a favourable (or unfavourable) impression. **in the light of,** drawing information from; with the help given by. **lighting-up time,** the time after which vehicles on the road must show prescribed lights. **light meter,** an instrument for measuring the intensity of light, especially to assess the correct photographic exposure. **light pen,** a penlike photosensitive device held to the screen of a computer terminal for passing information on to it. **light up,** to begin to smoke a cigarette etc.; to switch on lights. **light-year** *n.* a unit of distance employed by astronomers, representing the distance travelled by a ray of light in a vacuum during one year, and equal to 9.46 million million km (5.9 million million miles). **lit up,** (*slang*) drunk. **strike a light,** to produce a spark or flame with matches etc. [OE]

light[2] /laɪt/ *adj.* **1** of little weight, not heavy; easy to lift, carry, or move. **2** relatively low in weight, amount, density, strength, etc.; deficient in weight. **3** carrying or suitable for small loads; (of a ship) unladen; carrying only light arms, armaments, etc. **4** (of food) easy to digest. **5** easily borne or done. **6** intended only as entertainment, not profound. **7** (of sleep) easily disturbed. **8** free from sorrow, cheerful. **9** giddy. **10** nimble, quick-moving. **11** unchaste, wanton. **12** (of a building) elegant, graceful. —*adv.* **1** in a light manner. **2** with a minimum load. —*v.i.* (*past* & *p.p.* **lit** or

lighted) to come by chance *on* or *upon*. —**lighter-than-air** *adj*. (of an aircraft) weighing less than the air it displaces. **light-fingered** *adj*. given to stealing. **light-headed** *adj*. giddy; frivolous; delirious. **light-hearted** *adj*. cheerful; (unduly) casual. **light industry**, that producing small or light articles. **light into**, to attack. **light out**, to depart. **make light of**, to treat as unimportant. —**lightly** *adv*., **lightness** *n*. [OE]

lighten[1] /ˈlaɪt(ə)n/ *v.t./i*. **1** to shed light on; to make or become brighter. **2** to emit lightning. [f. LIGHT[1]]

lighten[2] /ˈlaɪt(ə)n/ *v.t./i*. **1** to make or become lighter in weight. **2** to reduce the weight or load of. **3** to bring relief to (the heart, mind, etc.). **4** to mitigate (a penalty). [f. LIGHT[2]]

lighter[1] *n*. a device for lighting cigarettes etc. [f. LIGHT[1]]

lighter[2] *n*. a boat, usually flat-bottomed, for transporting goods between a ship and a wharf etc. [f. MDu. (as LIGHT[2] v. in sense 'unload')]

lighthouse *n*. a tower or other structure containing a powerful light to warn or guide ships at sea.

lighting *n*. the equipment in a room or street etc. for producing light; an arrangement or effect of lights. [f. LIGHT[1]]

lightning /ˈlaɪtnɪŋ/ *n*. a flash of bright light produced by an electric discharge between clouds or cloud and the ground. —*adj*. very quick. —**lightning conductor** *or* (*US*) **rod**, a metal rod or wire fixed to an exposed part of a building or to a mast to divert lightning into the earth or sea. **like (greased) lightning**, (*colloq*.) with great speed. [f. LIGHTEN[2]]

lights *n.pl*. the lungs of sheep, pigs, etc., used as food especially for pets. [f. LIGHT[2] used as noun]

lightship *n*. a moored or anchored ship with a beacon light.

lightsome /ˈlaɪtsəm/ *adj*. gracefully light, agile, merry. [f. LIGHT[2]]

lightweight *adj*. **1** below average weight. **2** of little importance or influence. —*n*. **1** a lightweight person or thing. **2** a boxing-weight between featherweight and welterweight (see BOXING-WEIGHT).

ligneous /ˈlɪgnɪəs/ *adj*. of the nature of wood; (of plants) woody. [f. L (*lignum* wood)]

lignite /ˈlɪgnaɪt/ *n*. a brown coal of woody texture. [as prec.]

lignum vitae /lɪgnəm ˈvaɪtiː, ˈviːtaɪ/ a hard-wooded tree of the genus *Guaiacum*. [L, = wood of life]

like[1] *adj*. **1** having some or all of the qualities or appearance etc. of; similar. **2** characteristic of. **3** such as, for example. **4** in a suitable state or mood for. **5** (*archaic* or *colloq*.) likely. —*prep*. in the manner of, to the same degree as. —*adv*. **1** (*archaic*) in the same manner *as*. **2** (*vulgar*) so to speak. —*conj*. **1** (*colloq*., **D**) as. **2** (*US*) as if. —*n*. one that is like another, a similar thing. —**like anything** *or* **blazes** etc., (*colloq*.) very much; vigorously. **like hell**, recklessly; (*iron*.) not at all. **like-minded** *adj*. having the same tastes, opinions, etc. **what is he** (*or* **it** etc.) **like?** what sort of person is he (or thing is it etc.)? [OE]

like[2] *v.t*. **1** to find agreeable or pleasant (also *iron*.). **2** to choose to have, to prefer; to wish or be inclined *to*. —*n*. (usu. in *pl*.) a thing one likes or prefers. [OE]

-like /-laɪk/ *suffix* forming adjectives from nouns in the sense 'similar to', 'characteristic of'. [f. LIKE[1]]

likeable *adj*. pleasant, easy to like. —**likeably** *adv*. [f. LIKE[2]]

likelihood /ˈlaɪklɪhʊd/ *n*. probability. —**in all likelihood**, very probably. [f. foll.]

likely /ˈlaɪklɪ/ *adj*. **1** such as may reasonably be expected to happen or be true etc. **2** apparently suitable. **3** showing promise of being successful. —*adv*. probably. —**not likely**, (*colloq*.) certainly not, I refuse. [f. ON (as LIKE[1])]

liken *v.t*. to indicate or find a resemblance of (one person or thing to another). [f. LIKE[1]]

likeness *n*. **1** being like, a resemblance. **2** a semblance or guise. **3** a portrait, a representation. [f. LIKE[1]]

likewise *adv*. **1** also, moreover. **2** similarly. [f. LIKE[1] + -WISE]

liking *n*. **1** what one likes, one's taste. **2** one's feeling that one likes something. [OE (as LIKE[2])]

lilac /ˈlaɪlək/ *n*. **1** a shrub of the genus *Syringa* (esp. *S. vulgaris*), with fragrant pale pinkish-violet or white blossoms. **2** a pale pinkish-violet colour. —*adj*. of lilac colour. [obs. F, ult. f. Pers. (*nīl* blue)]

liliaceous /lɪlɪˈeɪʃəs/ *adj*. of the lily family. [f. L (as LILY)]

lilliputian /lɪlɪˈpjuːʃ(ə)n/ *n*. a diminutive person or thing. —*adj*. diminutive. [f. *Lilliput*, place in Swift's 'Gulliver's Travels', inhabited by people 6 inches high]

lilt *n*. a light pleasant rhythm; a song or tune with this. —*v.t./i*. to move or utter with a lilt. [orig. unkn.]

lily /ˈlɪlɪ/ *n*. a plant of the genus *Lilium*, growing from a bulb, with white, yellow, orange, or purple flowers on a tall slender stem; its flowers; a heraldic figure of a lily. —*attrib*. delicately white. —**lily-livered** *adj*. cowardly. **lily of the valley**, a spring plant (*Convallaria majalis*) with fragrant white bell-shaped flowers. [OE f.L *lilium*]

limb[1] /lɪm/ *n*. **1** a projecting part of an animal

body, used in movement or in grasping things. **2** a main branch of a tree. **3** an arm of a cross. —**out on a limb,** isolated, stranded, at a disadvantage. [OE]

limb² /lɪm/ *n.* (*Astron.*) a specified edge of the sun etc. [f. F or L *limbus* border]

limber¹ /ˈlɪmbə(r)/ *adj.* flexible; lithe, agile. —*v.t./i.* to make limber. —**limber up,** to exercise in preparation for athletic activity etc. [perh. f. foll., with ref. to movement of shafts]

limber² *n.* the detachable front part of a gun-carriage. —*v.t.* to attach a limber to (a gun). [app. rel. to L *limonarius* (*limo* shaft)]

limbo¹ /ˈlɪmbəʊ/ *n.* **1** (in medieval Christian theology) a region on the border of hell, the supposed abode of pre-Christian righteous persons and of unbaptized infants. **2** an intermediate state or condition (e.g. of a plan awaiting decision); a condition of being neglected and forgotten. [f. L phr. *in limbo* (as LIMB²)]

limbo² /ˈlɪmbəʊ/ *n.* (*pl.* **-os**) a West Indian dance in which the dancer bends backwards to pass under a horizontal bar which is progressively lowered. [West Indian word]

lime¹ *n.* a white substance (calcium oxide) obtained by heating limestone and used for making mortar, as a fertilizer, etc. —*v.t.* to treat with lime. —**lime-kiln** *n.* a kiln for heating limestone. [OE]

lime² *n.* the round fruit of the tree *Citrus medica*, like a lemon but smaller and more acid. —**lime green,** the palegreen colour of the lime. [F f. Prov. or Sp. f. Arab. (as LEMON)]

lime³ *n.* an ornamental tree of the genus *Tilia*, with heart-shaped leaves and fragrant yellow blossom. [alt. of *line* = *lind* = LINDEN]

limelight *n.* an intense white light obtained by heating a cylinder of lime in an oxyhydrogen flame, formerly used to illuminate the stages of theatres. —**the limelight,** the full glare of publicity.

limerick /ˈlɪmərɪk/ *n.* a humorous (often bawdy) five-line stanza. [f. *Limerick* in Ireland]

limestone *n.* a rock composed mainly of calcium carbonate.

Limey /ˈlaɪmɪ/ *n.* (*US slang*) a British person (originally a sailor) or ship. [f. LIME², f. the former issue of lime-juice on British ships as a drink to prevent scurvy]

limit /ˈlɪmɪt/ *n.* **1** the point, line, or level beyond which something does not or may not extend or pass. **2** the greatest or smallest amount permitted. —*v.t.* to set or serve as a limit to; to restrict. —**be the limit,** (*slang*) to be intolerable. **within limits,** with some degree of freedom. [f. L *limes* boundary]

limitation /lɪmɪˈteɪʃ(ə)n/ *n.* **1** limiting, being limited. **2** a lack of ability. **3** a limiting rule or circumstance. [as prec.]

limited *adj.* **1** confined within limits. **2** not great in scope or talents. **3** (of a monarch etc.) subject to constitutional restrictions. —**limited edition,** the production of a limited number of copies. **limited (liability) company,** a company whose members are legally responsible only to a limited degree for the debts of a company. [f. LIMIT]

limn /lɪm/ *v.t.* to paint (a picture), to portray. [f. obs. *lumine* illuminate (MSS) f. OF f. L (as ILLUMINATE)]

limnology /lɪmˈnɒlədʒɪ/ *n.* the study of fresh waters and their inhabitants. —**limnological** /-ˈlɒdʒɪk(ə)l/ *adj.*, **limnologist** *n.* [f. Gk *limnē* lake + -LOGY]

limousine /lɪmʊˈziːn/ *n.* a motor car with a closed body and a partition behind the driver; a luxurious motor car. [F, orig. = caped cloak worn in province of *Limousin*]

limp¹ *v.i.* **1** to walk lamely. **2** (of a damaged ship etc.) to proceed with difficulty. **3** (of verse) to be defective. —*n.* a lame walk. [rel. to OE *lemphealt* lame (as HALT²)]

limp² *adj.* **1** not stiff or firm, easily bent. **2** without will or energy. —**limply** *adv.*, **limpness** *n.* [orig. unkn.]

limpet /ˈlɪmpɪt/ *n.* a marine shellfish that sticks tightly to rocks. —**limpet mine,** a mine attached to a ship's hull and exploding after a set time. [OE (as LAMPREY)]

limpid /ˈlɪmpɪd/ *adj.* clear, transparent. —**limpidity** /-ˈpɪdɪtɪ/ *n.* [f. F or L *limpidus*]

linchpin *n.* **1** a pin passed through the axle-end to keep a wheel in position. **2** a person or thing vital to an organization etc. [f. OE *lynis* + PIN]

Lincs. *abbr.* Lincolnshire.

linctus *n.* a medicine, especially a soothing syrupy cough-mixture. [L (*lingere* lick)]

linden /ˈlɪnd(ə)n/ *n.* = LIME³. [f. OE *lind*]

line¹ *n.* **1** a long narrow mark traced on a surface; its use in art; a thing resembling such a traced mark, a band of colour, a furrow or wrinkle. **2** a straight or curved continuous extent of length without breadth, the track of a moving point. **3** a curve connecting all points having a specified common property. **4** a straight line. **5** a limit, a boundary; a mark limiting the area of play in sports; the starting-point in a race. **6** a row of persons or things; a direction as indicated by them, a trend; (*US*) a queue. **7** a piece of cord, rope, etc., serving a specified purpose. **8** a wire or cable for a telephone or telegraph; a connection by this. **9** a contour, outline, or lineament; the shape to which a garment is designed. **10** a course of procedure, conduct, thought, etc.; (in *pl.*) a plan, a draft, a manner of procedure. **11** a row of printed or written words, a verse; (in *pl.*) a piece of poetry, the words of an actor's part, a specified amount of text etc. to be written out as a school punishment. **12** a single track of a railway; one branch of a railway system; the whole system under one management. **13** a regular succession of buses, ships, aircraft, etc., plying between certain places; a company conducting this. **14** a connected series of persons following one another in time (esp. several generations of a family); lineage, stock. **15** a direction, a course, a track. **16** a department of activity, a province, a branch of business; a class of commercial goods. **17** a connected series of military fieldworks; an arrangement of soldiers side by side, ships etc. drawn up in battle array. **18** each of the very narrow horizontal sections forming a television picture. —*v.t.* **1** to mark with lines. **2** to position or stand at intervals along. —**the line,** the equator. **all along the line,** at every point. **bring** (*or* **come**) **into line,** to make conform, to conform. **drop a person a line,** to send him a short letter etc. **get a line on,** (*colloq.*) to learn something about. **in line for,** likely to receive. **in line with,** in accordance with. **lay** *or* **put it on the line,** to speak frankly. **line-drawing** *n.* one done with pen or pencil. **line of fire,** the path of a bullet etc. about to be shot. **line of vision,** the straight line along which an observer looks. **line-out** *n.* (in Rugby football) parallel lines of opposing forwards at right angles to the touch-line for the throwing in of the ball. **line printer,** a machine that prints the output from a computer a line at a time. **line up,** to arrange or be arranged in line(s). **line-up** *n.* a line of people for inspection; an arrangement of persons in a team etc. **out of line,** not in alignment; discordant. [OE & f. OF f. L *linea* (*linum* flax)]

line[2] *v.t.* **1** to cover the inside surface of (a garment, box, etc.) with a layer of material. **2** to serve as a lining for. **3** to fill (a purse, stomach, etc.). [f. obs. *line* fine linen (used for linings), f. L *linum* flax]

lineage /ˈlɪnɪdʒ/ *n.* lineal descent, ancestry. [f. OF (as LINE[1])]

lineal /ˈlɪnɪəl/ *adj.* **1** in the direct line of descent or ancestry. **2** linear. —**lineally** *adv.* [as prec.]

lineament /ˈlɪnɪəmənt/ *n.* (usu. in *pl.*) a distinctive feature or characteristic, especially of the face. [f. L (as LINE[1])]

linear /ˈlɪnɪə(r)/ *adj.* **1** of or in lines. **2** long and narrow and of uniform breadth. —**linearity** /-ˈærɪtɪ/ *n.* [as prec.]

lineation /lɪnɪˈeɪʃ(ə)n/ *n.* marking with or an arrangement of lines. [as LINEAMENT]

linen /ˈlɪnɪn/ *n.* **1** cloth woven from flax. **2** (*collect.*) articles made (or originally made) of linen, e.g. sheets, shirts, undergarments —*adj.* made of linen. [OE (as LINE[2])]

liner[1] /ˈlaɪnə(r)/ *n.* a ship or aircraft etc. carrying passengers on a regular route. —**liner train,** a fast freight train with detachable containers on permanently coupled wagons. [f. LINE[1]]

liner[2] /ˈlaɪnə(r)/ *n.* a removable lining. [f. LINE[2]]

linesman *n.* (*pl.* **-men**) an umpire's or referee's assistant who decides whether a ball falls within the playing area or not.

ling[1] *n.* a long slender sea-fish (*Molva molva*). [prob. f. MDu.]

ling[2] *n.* a kind of heather, especially *Calluna vulgaris*. [f. ON]

-ling *suffix* forming nouns denoting a person or thing connected with (*hireling*) or having the property of being (*weakling*) or undergoing (*starveling*), or denoting a diminutive (*duckling*), often derog. (*lordling*). [OE]

linga /ˈlɪŋgə/ *n.* (also **lingam**) a phallus, especially as the symbol of the Hindu god Siva. [Skr., = mark, symbol]

linger /ˈlɪŋgə(r)/ *v.i.* **1** to stay a long time, especially as if reluctant to leave; to dawdle. **2** to remain alive although becoming weaker, to be slow in dying. [frequent. of obs. *long* remain (as LONG[1])]

lingerie /ˈlæʒərɪ/ *n.* women's underwear and night-clothes. [F (*linge* linen)]

lingo /ˈlɪŋgəʊ/ *n.* (*pl.* **-os**) (*colloq.*) **1** a foreign language. **2** the vocabulary of a special subject or class of people. [prob. f. Port. *lingoa* f. L *lingua* tongue]

lingua franca /lɪŋgwə ˈfræŋkə/ a language used by speakers whose native languages are different; a system for mutual understanding. [It., = Frankish tongue]

lingual /ˈlɪŋgw(ə)l/ *adj.* **1** of or formed by the tongue. **2** of speech or languages. —**lingually** *adv.* [f. L (*lingua* tongue, language)]

linguist /ˈlɪŋgwɪst/ *n.* a person skilled in languages or linguistics. [f. L *lingua* language]

linguistic /lɪŋˈgwɪstɪk/ *adj.* of language or linguistics. —**linguistically** *adv.* [as prec.]

linguistics /lɪŋˈgwɪstɪks/ *n.* the study of language or languages, especially as regards their nature and structure.[f. prec.]

liniment /ˈlɪnɪmənt/ *n.* an embrocation, usually made with an oil. [f. L (*linere* smear)]

lining /ˈlaɪnɪŋ/ *n.* a layer of material used to line a surface. [f. LINE[2]]

link *n* **1** one loop or ring of a chain etc. **2** a connecting part; a thing or person that unites or provides continuity, one in a series; the state or a means of connection. **3** a cuff-link. —*v.t./i.* **1** to make or be a connection between. **2** to be joined (to a system, company, etc.). [f. ON]

linkage *n.* a system of links; linking; a link. [f. LINK]

linkman *n.* (*pl.* **-men**) a person providing continuity in a broadcast programme.

links *n.* (treated as *sing.* or *pl.*) a golf-course. [pl. of *link* rising ground (OE, perh. rel. to LEAN[1])]

linnet /ˈlɪnɪt/ *n.* a songbird, the common brown or grey finch (*Carduelis cannabina*). [f. OF *linette* (*lin* flax, f. its food)]

lino /ˈlaɪnəʊ/ *n.* (*pl.* **-os**) linoleum. [abbr.]

linocut /ˈlaɪnəʊkʌt/ *n.* a design cut in relief on a block of linoleum; a print made from this.

linoleum /lɪˈnəʊlɪəm/ *n.* a floor-covering of canvas backing thickly coated with a preparation of linseed oil and powdered cork etc. [f. L *linum* flax + *oleum* oil]

Linotype /ˈlaɪnəʊtaɪp/ *n.* [P] a composing-machine producing lines of words as single strips of metal, used especially for newspapers. [= *line o' type*]

linseed /ˈlɪnsiːd/ *n.* **1** the seed of flax. **2** an oil extracted from it and used in paint and varnish. [OE *līne* flax (as LINE[2]) + SEED]

linsey-woolsey /lɪnzɪˈwʊlzɪ/ *n.* a fabric of coarse wool woven on a cotton warp. [prob. f. *Lindsey* in Suffolk + WOOL]

lint *n.* **1** linen with one side made fluffy by scraping, used for dressing wounds. **2** fluff. [perh. f. OF *linette* linseed (*lin* flax)]

lintel /ˈlɪnt(ə)l/ *n.* a horizontal timber or stone across the top of a door or window. [f. OF (as LIMIT)]

lion /ˈlaɪən/ *n.* **1** a large powerful tawny African and South Asian carnivorous animal (*Felis leo*) of the cat family. **2** a brave or celebrated person. **3 the Lion,** the sign or constellation Leo. **4 Lions,** the Rugby Union team representing Britain, so called from the symbol on their official tie. **—lion-heart** *n.* a courageous person. **lion-hearted** *adj.* courageous. **lion's share,** the largest or best portion. **—lioness** *n.fem.* [f. AF f. L *leo* f. Gk]

lionize *v.t.* to treat as a celebrity. [f. LION]

lip *n.* **1** either of the fleshy parts forming the edges of the mouth-opening. **2** the edge of a cup etc.; the edge of a vessel shaped for pouring from. **3** (*slang*) impudent speech. —*v.t.* (**-pp-**) **1** to touch with the lips; to apply the lips to. **2** to touch lightly. **—bite one's lip,** to repress emotion, laughter, etc. **curl one's lip,** to express scorn. **lip-read** *v.t./i.* (esp. of a deaf person) to understand speech (of) entirely from observing the speaker's lip-movements. **lip-service** *n.* an insincere expression of support. **smack one's lips,** to part the lips noisily in relish or anticipation, especially of food **—lipped, -lipped** *adj.* [OE]

lipid /ˈlɪpɪd/ *n.* any of a group of compounds that are esters of fatty acids or fatlike substances. [f. F f. Gk *lipos* fat]

Lippizaner /lɪpɪˈtsɑːnə(r)/ *n.* a horse of a fine white breed used especially in displays of dressage. [G, f. *Lippiza* in Yugoslavia, the home of the former Austrian Imperial Stud where such a strain of horses was orig. bred]

lipsalve *n.* an ointment for sore lips.

lipstick *n.* a small stick of cosmetic for colouring the lips.

liquefy /ˈlɪkwɪfaɪ/ *v.t./i.* to make or become liquid. **—liquefaction** /-ˈfækʃ(ə)n/ *n.* [f. F f. L *liquefacere* (as LIQUID)]

liqueur /lɪˈkjʊə(r)/ *n.* any of several strong sweet alcoholic spirits, variously flavoured. [F, = LIQUOR]

liquid /ˈlɪkwɪd/ *adj.* **1** having a consistency like that of water or oil, flowing freely but not gaseous; having the qualities of water in appearance. **2** (of sounds) clear and pure. **3** (of assets) easily converted into cash. —*n.* **1** a liquid substance. **2** the sound of *l* or *r*. [f. L (*liquere* be liquid)]

liquidate /ˈlɪkwɪdeɪt/ *v.t./i.* **1** to wind up the affairs of (a company or firm) by ascertaining liabilities and apportioning its assets. **2** to undergo liquidation. **3** to pay off (a debt). **4** to put an end to or get rid of (esp. by violent means). **—liquidator** *n.* [f. L (as prec.)]

liquidation /lɪkwɪˈdeɪʃ(ə)n/ *n.* the liquidating of a company etc. **—go into liquidation,** (of a company etc.) to be wound up and have the assets apportioned. [f. prec.]

liquidity /lɪˈkwɪdɪtɪ/ *n.* the state of being liquid or having liquid assets. [f. F or L (as LIQUID)]

liquidize /ˈlɪkwɪdaɪz/ *v.t.* to reduce to a liquid state. [f. LIQUID]

liquidizer *n.* a machine for making purées etc. [f. prec.]

liquor /ˈlɪkə(r)/ *n.* **1** alcoholic drink. **2** juice or other liquid (esp. produced in cooking). [f. OF f. L (as LIQUID)]

liquorice /ˈlɪkərɪs, -ɪʃ/ *n.* **1** a black substance used as a sweet and in medicine. **2** the plant (*Glycyrrhiza glabra*) from whose root it is obtained. [f. AF f. L f. Gk *glukurrhiza* (*glukus* sweet, *rhiza* root)]

lira /ˈlɪərə/ *n.* (*pl.* **-re** /-reɪ/, **-ras**) the currency unit in Italy and in Turkey. [It. f. Prov. f. L *libra* pound]

lisle /laɪl/ *n.* a fine smooth cotton thread for stockings etc. [f. *Lille* in France]

lisp *n.* a speech defection in which /s/ is pronounced /θ/ and /z/ is pronounced /ð/. —*v.t./i.* to speak or say with a lisp. [OE (imit.)]

lissom /ˈlɪsəm/ *adj.* lithe, agile. **—lissomness** *n.* [as LITHE, -SOME]

list[1] *n.* **1** a number of connected items, names,

etc., written or printed together as a record or to aid the memory. **2** (in *pl.*) palisades enclosing a tilt-yard; the scene of a contest. —*v.t.* **1** to make a list of, to enter in a list. **2** to include (a building) in a list of those considered to be of special architectural or historic interest, having official protection from demolition or from alteration or extension affecting its character. —**enter the lists,** to issue or accept a challenge. [OE, orig. = edging, strip]

list² *v.i.* (of a ship etc.) to lean over to one side. —*n.* a listing position, a tilt. [orig. unkn.]

listen /ˈlɪs(ə)n/ *v.i.* **1** to make an effort to hear something, to wait alertly for a sound. **2** to hear with attention as a person speaks; to pay attention. **3** to allow oneself to be persuaded by a suggestion or request. —**listen in,** to tap a communication made by telephone; to listen to a radio broadcast. [OE]

listener /ˈlɪsnə(r)/ *n.* one who listens; a person listening to a radio broadcast. [f. prec.]

listless *adj.* without energy or enthusiasm. —**listlessly** *adv.*, **listlessness** *n.* [f. obs. *list* inclination (as LUST) + -LESS]

lit *past* & *p.p.* of LIGHT¹ and LIGHT².

litany /ˈlɪtənɪ/*n.* a series of supplications to God recited by a priest etc. with set responses by the congregation; **the Litany,** that in the Book of Common Prayer. [f. OF f. L f. Gk (*litē* supplication)]

litchi /ˈliːtʃiː/ *n.* a sweetish pulpy fruit in a thin brown shell; the tree (orig. Chinese) bearing this (*Litchi chinensis*). [f. Chin.]

literacy /ˈlɪtərəsɪ/ *n.* the ability to read and write. [f. LITERATE]

literal /ˈlɪtər(ə)l/ *adj.* **1** taking words in their usual sense without metaphor or allegory. **2** exactly corresponding to the original words. **3** (of a person) tending to interpret things in a literal way, unimaginative. **4** so called without exaggeration. **5** of a letter or letters of the alphabet. —*n.* a misprint of a letter. —**literally** *adv.*, **literalness** *n.* [f. OF or L (as LETTER)]

literalism *n.* insistence on literal interpretation, adherence to the letter. —**literalist** *n.* [f. prec.]

literary /ˈlɪtərərɪ/ *adj.* **1** of, concerned with, or interested in literature or books or written composition. **2** (of a word or idiom) used chiefly by writers, not in ordinary speech. —**literariness** *n.* [f. L (as LETTER)]

literate /ˈlɪtərət/ *adj.* able to read and write. —*n.* a literate person. [f. L *litteratus* (as LETTER)]

literati /lɪtəˈrɑːtiː/ *n.pl.* men of letters, the learned class. [L (as prec.)]

literature /ˈlɪtərətʃə(r)/ *n.* **1** written works, especially those valued for their beauty of form and style. **2** the writings of a country, period, or particular subject. **3** a literary production. **4** (*colloq.*) printed matter, leaflets, etc. [f. L (as LITERATE)]

lithe /laɪð/ *adj.* flexible, supple [OE]

lithium /ˈlɪθɪəm/ *n.* a soft silver-white element of the alkali-metal group, symbol Li, atomic number 3. [f. Gk *litheios* made of stone (*lithos* stone)]

litho /ˈlaɪθəʊ/ *n.* (*colloq.*) (*pl.* **-os**) the lithographic process. —*adj.* lithographic. —*v.t.* (*colloq.*) to lithograph. [abbr.]

lithograph /ˈlɪθəgrɑːf/ *n.* a print produced by lithography. —*v.t.* to produce a lithographic print of. [f. foll.]

lithography /lɪˈθɒgrəfɪ/ *n.* the process of obtaining prints from a stone, metal, or other flat surface so treated that what is to be printed can be inked but the remaining area rejects ink. —**lithographer** *n.*, **lithographic** /-ˈgræfɪk/ *adj.*, **lithographically** *adv.* [f. G f. Gk *lithos* stone + -GRAPHY]

litigant /ˈlɪtɪgənt/ *n.* a party to a lawsuit. —*adj.* engaged in a lawsuit. [as foll.]

litigate /ˈlɪtɪgeɪt/ *v.t./i.* to go to law; to contest (a point) at law. —**litigation** /-ˈgeɪʃ(ə)n/ *n.* [f. L *litigare* (*lis* lawsuit)]

litigious /lɪˈtɪdʒəs/ *adj.* fond of litigation, contentious. —**litigiousness** *n.* [f. OF or L (as prec.)]

litmus /ˈlɪtməs/ *n.* a blue colouring matter got from lichens that is turned red by acid and restored to blue by alkali. —**litmus paper,** paper stained with litmus and used as a test for acids or alkalis. [f. ONorw., = dye-moss]

litotes /laɪˈtəʊtiːz/ *n.* an ironic understatement, especially using a negative of its contrary (e.g. *I shan't be sorry* = I shall be glad). [L f. Gk (*litos* meagre)]

litre /ˈliːtə(r)/ *n.* a metric unit of capacity, equal to 1 cubic decilitre or about 1¾ pints. [F (*litron* obs. measure of capacity f. L f. Gk *litra* Sicilian monetary unit)]

Litt. D. *abbr.* Doctor of Letters. [f. L. *Litterarum Doctor*]

litter *n.* **1** refuse, especially paper, discarded on streets etc.; odds and ends lying about. **2** a vehicle containing a couch and carried on men's shoulders or by beasts of burden. **3** a kind of stretcher for the sick and wounded. **4** the young animals brought forth at a birth. **5** straw etc. as bedding for animals. **6** straw and dung, of a farmyard etc. —*v.t.* **1** to make (a place) untidy by discarding rubbish. **2** to give birth to (whelps etc., or *absol.*). **3** to provide (a horse etc.) with litter as bedding; to spread straw etc. on (a stable-floor etc.). [f. AF f. L *lectaria* (*lectus* bed)]

litterbug *n.* (also **litter-lout**) a person who carelessly strews litter in a street etc.

little *adj.* (*compar.* LESS, LESSER, **littler**; *superl.* LEAST, **littlest**) **1** small in size, amount, degree, etc., not great or big; short in stature; of short distance or duration. **2** relatively unimportant; operating on a small scale. **3** young or younger; **4** smaller or smallest of the name. **5** trivial, paltry, mean. **6** not much; a certain though small amount of. —*n.* not much, only a small amount; a certain but no great amount; a short time or distance. —*adv.* (compar. LESS; superl. LEAST) **1** to a small extent only. **2** not at all. —**little by little,** gradually, by a small amount at a time. **little end,** the smaller end of a connecting-rod, attached to a piston. **Little Englander,** (*hist.*) one desiring to restrict the dimensions of the British Empire and Britain's responsibilities. **the little people,** the fairies. **Little Russian,** Ukrainian. **little theatre,** a small playhouse, especially one used for experimental productions. **the little woman,** (*colloq.*) one's wife. [OE]

littoral /ˈlɪtər(ə)l/ *adj.* of or on the shore. —*n.* a region lying along the shore. [f. L (*litus* shore)]

liturgy /ˈlɪtədʒɪ/ *n.* the fixed form of public worship used in churches; the Book of Common Prayer. —**liturgical** /lɪːˈtɜːdʒɪk(ə)l/ *adj.*, **liturgically** *adv.* [f. F or L f. Gk *leitourgia* public worship]

live[1] /lɪv/ *v.t./i.* **1** to have life, to be or remain alive. **2** to subsist or feed *on*; to depend for livelihood, subsistence, or position. **3** to have one's home. **4** to lead (one's life) or arrange one's habits in a specified way; to express in one's life. **5** to enjoy life to the full. **6** (of a thing) to survive or endure. —**live down,** to cause (past guilt or scandal etc.) to be forgotten by blameless conduct thereafter. **live it up,** (*colloq.*) to live gaily and extravagantly. **live off,** to derive support or sustenance from. **live together,** (esp. of a couple not married to each other) to share a home and have a sexual relationship. **live up to,** to live or behave in accordance with (principles etc.). [OE]

live[2] /laɪv/ *attrib. adj.* **1** that is alive, living. **2** actual, not pretended or toy. **3** burning or glowing. **4** (of a match, bomb, etc.) ready for use, not yet exploded or kindled. **5** (of a wire etc.) charged with or carrying electricity. **6** (also *predic.*, of a performance, broadcast, etc.) transmitted during the occurrence or undertaken with an audience present. **7** of current or intense interest or importance; moving or imparting motion. —**live wire,** a highly energetic and forceful person. [f. ALIVE]

liveable /ˈlɪvəb(ə)l/ *adj.* **1** (of life) worth living. **2** (of a house, person, etc.) fit to live *in* or *with*. [f. prec.]

livelihood /ˈlaɪvlɪhʊd/ *n.* a means of living, sustenance. [OE (as LIFE, *lād* course)]

livelong /ˈlɪvlɒŋ/ *adj.* in its entire length. [as LIEF + LONG[1], assim. to LIVE[1]]

lively /ˈlaɪvlɪ/ *adj.* full of life, vigorous, energetic; cheerful; keen. —**liveliness** *n.* [OE (as LIFE)]

liven /ˈlaɪv(ə)n/ *v.t./i.* to make or become lively, to cheer. [f. LIFE]

liver[1] /ˈlɪvə(r)/ *n.* **1** a large glandular organ in the abdomen of vertebrates, secreting bile. **2** the flesh of some animals' liver as food. **3** dark reddish-brown. —**liver salts,** salts for curing dyspepsia or biliousness. **liver sausage,** sausage of cooked liver etc. [OE]

liver[2] /ˈlɪvə(r)/ *n.* a person who lives in a specified way. [f. LIVE[1]]

liveried /ˈlɪvərɪd/ *adj.* wearing livery. [f. LIVERY]

liverish /ˈlɪvərɪʃ/ *adj.* suffering from a disorder of the liver; peevish, glum.[f. LIVER[1]]

Liverpudlian /lɪvəˈpʌdlɪən/ *n.* a native of Liverpool. —*adj.* of Liverpool. [f. *Liverpool* in NW England]

liverwort /ˈlɪvəwɜːt/ *n.* a round flat bryophyte of the class Hepaticae, without stems or leaves and sometimes with a lobed body; a mosslike plant of the same group. [f. LIVER[1], f. the shape of some species]

livery /ˈlɪvərɪ/ *n.* **1** a distinctive uniform worn by a male servant or by a member of a City Company. **2** a distinctive guise or marking. **3** an allowance of fodder for horses. —**at livery,** (of a horse) kept for the owner for a fixed charge. **livery company,** any of the London City Companies that formerly had a distinctive costume. **livery stable,** a stable where horses are kept at livery or let out for hire. [f. AF *liveré* (*livrer* deliver)]

lives *pl.* of LIFE.

livestock /ˈlaɪvstɒk/ *n.* animals kept or dealt in for use or profit. [f. LIVE[2] + STOCK]

livid /ˈlɪvɪd/ *adj.* **1** of a bluish leaden colour. **2** (*colloq.*) very angry. [f. F or L (*livēre* be bluish)]

living /ˈlɪvɪŋ/ *n.* **1** being alive. **2** a means of earning or providing enough food etc. to sustain life. **3** a position held by a clergyman, providing an income. —*adj.* **1** having life; now alive. **2** contemporary. **3** (of a likeness) lifelike, exact. **4** (of a language) still in vernacular use. —**living-room** *n.* a room for general use during the day. **living wage,** a wage on which one can live without privation. **within living memory,** within the memory of people still alive. [f. LIVE[1]]

lizard /ˈlɪzəd/ *n.* a reptile of the suborder Lacertilia, having usually a long body and tail, four legs, and a rough or scaly hide. [f. OF f. L *lacertus*]

LJ *abbr.* (*pl.* **LJJ**) Lord Justice.

'll *v.* (*colloq.*, usu. after pronouns) shall, will. [abbr.]

llama /ˈlɑːmə/ *n.* a South American ruminant (*Lama glabra*) kept as a beast of burden and for its soft woolly hair. [Sp., prob. f. Quechua]

lm *abbr.* lumen.

lo /ləʊ/ *int.* (*archaic*) look. —**lo and behold,** an introduction to the mentioning of a surprising fact. [OE, = int. of surprise, and f. obs. *lo* = *loke* (as LOOK)]

loach *n.* a small freshwater fish of the family Cobitidae. [f. OF *loche*]

load *n.* **1** what is carried or to be carried; the debris carried along by a river. **2** an amount usually or actually carried; this as a weight or measure of some substances. **3** a weight of care, responsibility, etc. **4** the amount of power carried by an electric circuit or supplied by a generating station. **5** a material object or force acting as a weight etc. **6** (in *pl.*, *colloq.*) plenty. —*v.t./i.* **1** to put a load on or aboard; to place (a load) aboard ship, on a vehicle, etc.; (of a ship, vehicle, or person) to take a load aboard. **2** to burden, to strain. **3** to supply or assail overwhelmingly. **4** to put ammunition in (a gun), a film in (a camera), a cassette in (a tape-recorder), etc.; to put (a program or data etc.) in a computer. —**get a load of,** (*slang*) to take note of. **loaded question,** one put in such a way as to evoke a required answer. **load line,** a Plimsoll line. —**loader** *n.*, **-loading** *adj.* (of a gun or machine). [OE, = way (as LEAD¹)]

loaded *adj.* (*slang*) **1** rich. **2** drunk. **3** (*US*) drugged. [f. LOAD]

loadstone *n.* **1** a magnetic oxide of iron. **2** a piece of it used as a magnet. **3** a thing that attracts. [= way stone, f. LOAD (in its orig. sense) + STONE]

loaf[1] *n.* (*pl.* **loaves**) **1** a quantity of bread baked alone or as a separate or separable part of a batch, usually of a standard weight. **2** minced or chopped meat made in the shape of a loaf and cooked. **3** (*slang*) the head. [OE]

loaf[2] *v.i.* to spend time idly, to hang about. —**loafer** *n.* [perh. f. G *landläufer* vagabond]

loam *n.* a rich soil of clay, sand, and decayed vegetable matter. —**loamy** *adj.*, **loaminess** *n.* [OE (rel. to LIME¹)]

loan *n.* **1** a thing lent, especially a sum of money to be returned with or without interest. **2** lending, being lent. —*v.t.* (**D**) to lend. —**loan-word** *n.* a word adopted by one language from another in a more or less modified form (e.g. *morale*, *naïve*). **on loan,** being lent. [f. ON]

loath /ləʊθ/ *predic. adj.* averse, disinclined. [OE]

loathe /ləʊð/ *v.t.* to regard with hatred and disgust. —**loathing** *n.* [OE (as prec.)]

loathsome /ˈləʊðsəm/ *adj.* arousing hatred and disgust; repulsive. [f. *loath* n. disgust (f. LOATHE) + -SOME]

loaves *pl.* of LOAF¹.

lob *v.t./i.* (**-bb-**) to send or strike (a ball) slowly or in a high arc in cricket or tennis etc. —*n.* a lobbed ball; a slow underarm delivery in cricket. [prob. f. LDu.]

lobar /ˈləʊbə(r)/ *adj.* of a lobe, especially of the lung. [f. LOBE]

lobate /ˈləʊbeɪt/ *adj.* having a lobe or lobes. [f. LOBE]

lobby *n.* **1** an entrance-hall, a porch; an ante-room, a corridor. **2** (in the House of Commons) a large hall open to the public used especially for interviews between MPs and others; (in full **division lobby**) each of two corridors to which members retire to vote. **3** a body of lobbyists. —*v.t./i.* to seek to influence (an MP etc.) to support one's cause; to get (a bill etc.) through by interviews etc. in a lobby. [f. L *lobia*, *lobium* lodge]

lobbyist *n.* a person who lobbies an MP etc. [f. prec.]

lobe *n.* a rounded flattish part or projection, especially of an organ of the body; the lower soft pendulous part of the outer ear. [f. L f. Gk *lobos* lobe, pod]

lobelia /ləˈbiːlɪə/ *n.* a herbaceous plant of the genus *Lobelia* with brightly coloured flowers. [f. M de *Lobel*, Flemish botanist in England (d. 1616)]

lobotomy /ləˈbɒtəmɪ/ *n.* an incision into the white tissue of the frontal lobe of the brain to relieve some cases of mental disorder. [f. LOBE + -TOMY]

lobscouse /ˈlɒbskaʊs/ *n.* a sailor's dish of meat stewed with vegetables and ship's biscuit. [orig. unkn.]

lobster *n.* a large edible sea crustacean of the family Homaridae, with stalked eyes and heavy pincer-like claws, that turns from bluish-black to scarlet when boiled; its flesh as food. —**lobster-pot** *n.* a basket for trapping lobsters. [OE, corrupt. of L *locusta* crustacean, = LOCUST]

lobworm /ˈlɒbwɜːm/ *n.* a large earthworm used as a fishing-bait. [f. LOB in obs. sense 'pendulous object']

local /ˈləʊk(ə)l/ *adj.* **1** in regard to place. **2** belonging to or affecting a particular place or a small area; of one's own neighbourhood. **3** (of a train or bus etc.) of the neighbourhood, not long-distance; stopping at all points on a route. —*n.* **1** an inhabitant of a particular district. **2** a local train, bus, etc. **3** (*colloq.*) the local public house. —**local authority,** a body charged with the administration of local government. **local colour,** details characteristic of the place in which a story etc. is set, added to make it seem more real. **local government,** a system of administration of a county or district etc. by elected representatives of those living there. —**locally** *adv.* [f. OF f. L (*locus* place)]

locale /ləʊˈkɑːl/ *n.* the scene or locality of operations or events. [f. F *local* (as prec.)]

locality /ləʊˈkælɪtɪ/ *n.* **1** a thing's position; the site or scene of something, especially in relation to the surroundings. **2** a district. [f. F or L (as LOCAL)]

localize /ˈləʊkəlaɪz/ *v.t.* **1** to assign or confine to a particular place. **2** to invest with the characteristics of a particular place. **3** to decentralize. [f. LOCAL]

locate /ləˈkeɪt/ *v.t.* **1** to discover the place where something is. **2** to establish in a place; to state the locality of. [f. L *locare* (as LOCAL)]

location /ləˈkeɪʃ(ə)n/ *n.* **1** a particular place. **2** locating. —**on location,** (of filming) in a natural setting rather than in a studio. [as prec.]

locative /ˈlɒkətɪv/ *n.* (*Gram.*) the case expressing location. —*adj.* (*Gram.*) of or in the locative. [as LOCATE]

loc. cit. *abbr.* in the place cited. [f. L *loco citato*]

loch /lɒx, lɒk/ *n.* a Scottish lake or land-locked arm of the sea. [f. Gael.]

loci *pl.* of LOCUS.

lock[1] *n.* **1** a mechanism for fastening a door, lid, etc., with a bolt that requires a key of a particular shape to work it. **2** a section of a canal or river confined within sluiced gates for moving boats from one level to another. **3** a mechanism for exploding the charge of a gun. **4** the turning of the front wheels of a vehicle; the maximum extent of this. **5** an interlocked or jammed state. **6** a wrestling-hold that keeps the opponent's arm etc. fixed. **7** (in full **lock forward**) a player in the second row of the scrum in Rugby football. —*v.t./i.* **1** to fasten with a lock. **2** to shut into or out of a place by locking. **3** to store away securely or inaccessibly. **4** to bring or come into a rigidly fixed position, to jam. —**lock-keeper** *n.* a person in charge of a lock on a canal or river. **lock-knit** *adj.* knitted with an interlocking stitch. **lock-out** *n.* an employer's procedure of refusing the entry of workers to their place of work until certain terms are agreed to. **lock-stitch** *n.* see separate entry. **lock, stock, and barrel,** the whole of a thing, completely. **lock-up** *n.* premises that can be locked up; the time or process of locking up; a house or room for the temporary detention of prisoners; (*adj.*) able to be locked up. [OE]

lock[2] *n.* a portion of hair that hangs together; (in *pl.*) the hair of the head. [OE]

locker *n.* a small lockable cupboard or compartment. [f. LOCK[1]]

locket /ˈlɒkɪt/ *n.* a small ornamental case containing a portrait or lock of hair and usually hung from the neck. [f. OF dim. of *loc* latch (as LOCK[1])]

lockjaw *n.* a form of tetanus in which the jaws become rigidly closed.

locksmith *n.* a maker and mender of locks.

loco[1] /ˈləʊkəʊ/ *n.* (*pl.* **-os**) (*colloq.*) a locomotive engine. [abbr.]

loco[2] /ˈləʊkəʊ/ *adj.* (*US slang*) crazy. [Sp.]

locomotion /ləʊkəˈməʊʃ(ə)n/ *n.* **1** motion or the power of motion from place to place. **2** travel, a way (esp. artificial) of travelling. [f. L *locus* place + MOTION]

locomotive /ˈləʊkəməʊtɪv/ *n.* (in full **locomotive engine**) an engine for drawing trains. —*adj.* of, having, or effecting locomotion, not stationary. [as prec.]

locum tenens /ləʊkəm ˈtiːnenz/ (also (*colloq.*) **locum**) a deputy, especially one acting for a doctor or clergyman in his absence. [L, = (one) holding place]

locus /ˈləʊkəs/ *n.* (*pl.* **loci** /ˈləʊsaɪ/) the line or curve etc. made by all points satisfying certain conditions, or by the defined motion of a point or line or surface. [L, = place]

locus classicus /ləʊkəs ˈklæsɪkəs/ the best known or most authoritative passage on a subject. [L, = classic place]

locust /ˈləʊkəst/ *n.* **1** an African or Asian grasshopper of the family Acrididae, migrating in swarms and consuming all vegetation. **2** a person of devouring or destructive propensities. **3** any of various kinds of tree and their fruit, especially the false acacia (*Robinia pseudoacacia*). [f. OF f. L *locusta* lobster, locust]

locution /ləˈkjuːʃ(ə)n/ *n.* **1** a word, phrase, or idiom. **2** style of speech. [f. OF or L (*loqui* speak)]

lode *n.* a vein of metal ore. [var. of LOAD, orig. = leading, way]

lodestar *n.* **1** a star used as a guide in navigation, especially the pole-star. **2** a guiding principle; an object of pursuit.

lodge *n.* **1** a small house at the entrance to a park or the grounds of a large house, occupied by a gate-keeper or other employee. **2** a small house used in sporting seasons. **3** a porter's room at the entrance or gateway of a factory, college, etc. **4** the members or meeting-place (orig. a mason's hut or workshop on a building site) of a branch of the Freemasons or other society. **5** a beaver's or otter's lair. —*v.t./i.* **1** to provide with temporary accommodation. **2** to live as a lodger. **3** to deposit (money etc.) for security. **4** to submit (a complaint etc.) for attention. **5** to place (power etc.) in or with a person. **6** to stick or become embedded in; to cause to do this. [f. OF *loge* f. L *lobia* (as LOBBY)]

lodger *n.* a person receiving accommodation in another's house for payment. [f. prec]

lodging *n.* accommodation in hired rooms, a dwelling-place; (in *pl.*) a room or rooms rented for lodging in. [f. LODGE]

loess /ˈləuɪs/ *n.* a layer of fine light-coloured soil, found in large areas of Asia, Europe, and America and very fertile when irrigated, thought to have been deposited by winds during the ice age. [f. G *löss* f. Swiss G *lösch* loose]

loft *n.* **1** a space (with a floor) under the roof of a house; a similar space under the roof of a stable or barn, used for storing hay etc. **2** a gallery in a church or hall. **3** a pigeon-house. **4** a backward slope on the face of a golf-club. **5** a lofting stroke. —*v.t.* to send (a ball) in a high arc. [f. ON, = air, upper room (as LIFT)]

lofty *adj.* **1** towering, of imposing height. **2** haughty, keeping aloof. **3** exalted, noble. —**loftily** *adv.*, **loftiness** *n.* [f. LOFT (as in *aloft*)]

log[1] *n.* **1** an unhewn piece of a felled tree; any large rough piece of wood, especially one cut for firewood. **2** a floating device used to ascertain a ship's speed. **3** a log-book. —*v.t.* (**-gg-**) **1** to enter in a ship's log-book. **2** to enter (data etc.) in a regular record; to attain (a cumulative total thus recorded). **3** to cut into logs. —**log-book** *n.* a book in which details of a voyage or journey or the registration of a vehicle are recorded. **log cabin**, a hut built of logs. **log in** (*or* **out**), to begin (or finish) operations at a terminal of a multi-access computer. **log-line** *n.* a line to which the float of a ship's log is attached. [orig. unkn.]

log[2] *n.* a logarithm. [abbr.]

logan /ˈləugən/ *n.* (in full **logan-stone**) a poised heavy stone rocking at a touch. [= *logging* (*log* to rock)]

loganberry /ˈləugənberɪ/ *n.* a dark-red fruit, a hybrid of the raspberry and an American blackberry. [f. J. H. *Logan*, American horticulturist (d.1928) + BERRY]

logarithm /ˈlɒgərɪð(ə)m/ *n.* any of a series of arithmetic exponents tabulated to simplify computation by making it possible to use addition and subtraction instead of multiplication and division (see NAPIER). —**logarithmic** /-ˈrɪðmɪk/ *adj.*, **logarithmically** *adv.* [f. Gk *logos* reckoning, ratio + *arithmos* number]

loggerhead /ˈlɒgəhed/ *n.* **at loggerheads,** disagreeing, disputing. [f. dial. *logger* block of wood + HEAD]

loggia /ˈləudʒə/ *n.* an open-sided gallery or arcade; an open-sided extension to a house. [It., = LODGE]

logic /ˈlɒdʒɪk/ *n.* **1** the science of reasoning; a particular system or method of reasoning; a chain of reasoning (regarded as sound or unsound); use of or ability in argument. **2** (in computers) the principles or circuitry involved in carrying out processes, on electrical or other signals, analogous to the processes of reasoning, deduction, etc. **3** necessity, the compulsive power of events etc. [f. OF f. L f. Gk (as LOGOS)]

logical /ˈlɒdʒɪk(ə)l/ *adj.* **1** of or according to logic; correctly reasoned; defensible or explicable on the ground of consistency. **2** using or capable of correct reasoning. —**logicality** /-ˈkælɪtɪ/ *n.*, **logically** *adv.* [f. L (as LOGIC)]

logician /lɒˈdʒɪʃ(ə)n/ *n.* a user of or expert in logic. [f. LOGIC]

logistics /ləˈdʒɪstɪks/ *n.pl.* the art of supplying and organizing (orig. military) services and equipment etc. —**logistic** *adj.*, **logistically** *adv.* [f. F (*loger* lodge)]

logo /ˈləugəu, ˈlɒ-/ *n.* (*pl.* **-os**) (*colloq.*) a logotype. [abbr.]

logotype /ˈlɒgəutaɪp/ *n.* a non-heraldic design or symbol as the badge of an organization; a piece of type with this. [as prec.+ TYPE]

logwood *n.* a West Indian tree (*Haematoxylon campechianum*); the wood of this used in dyeing.

-logy /-lədʒɪ/ *suffix* forming nouns denoting a subject of study (*biology*), or body of writings (*trilogy*, *martyrology*), or a character of speech or language (*tautology*). [f. F or L or Gk *-logia* (as LOGOS)]

loin *n.* **1** (in *pl.*) the side and back of the body between the ribs and hip-bones. **2** (in *sing.*) a joint of meat that includes the loin vertebrae. [f. OF *loigne* f. L *lumbus*]

loincloth *n.* a cloth worn round the hips, especially as the sole garment.

loiter *v.i.* to stand about idly, to linger; to move or proceed indolently with frequent pauses. —**loiterer** *n.* [f. MDu. *loteren* wag about]

loll *v.t./i.* **1** to recline, sit, or stand in a lazy attitude. **2** to rest (one's head or limbs) lazily on something. **3** to hang (one's tongue) out; (of the tongue) to hang out. [prob. imit.]

lollipop /ˈlɒlɪpɒp/ *n.* a large round usually flat boiled sweet on a small stick. —**lollipop lady** *or* **man,** (*colloq.*) an official using a circular sign on a stick to stop traffic for children to cross a road. [perh. f. dial. *lolly* tongue + POP[1]]

lollop *v.i.* (*colloq.*) to move in ungainly bounds; to flop about. [prob. f. LOLL, assoc. with TROLLOP]

lolly *n.* **1** (*colloq.*) a lollipop; an ice lolly. **2** (*slang*) money. [abbr. of LOLLIPOP]

lone *attrib. adj.* **1** solitary, without companions. **2** uninhabited, lonely. —**lone hand,** a hand played or a player playing against the rest at cards; a person or action without allies. **lone wolf,** a loner. [f. ALONE]

lonely *adj.* **1** lacking friends or companions; despondent because of this. **2** isolated, unfrequented, uninhabited. —**loneliness** *n.* [f. LONE]

loner /ˈləʊnə(r)/ *n.* a person or animal preferring to act alone or not to associate with others. [f. LONE]

lonesome /ˈləʊnsəm/ *adj.* lonely, causing loneliness. [f. LONE + -SOME]

long[1] *adj.* **1** having great length in space or time. **2** having a specified length or duration. **3** seeming to be longer than it really is, tedious. **4** lasting, reaching far into the past or future. **5** far-reaching, acting at a distance; involving a great interval or distance. **6** of elongated shape. **7** (of a vowel sound or a syllable) having the greater of two recognized durations. **8** (of stocks etc.) bought in large quantities in advance, with the expectation of a rise in price. —*n.* **1** a long interval or period. **2** a long syllable or vowel. —*adv.* for a long time; by a long time; throughout a specified duration; (in *compar.*) after an implied point of time. —**as** *or* **so long as,** provided that. **in the long run,** over a long period, eventually. **the long and the short of it,** all that need be said, the eventual outcome. **long-distance** *adj.* travelling or operating between distant places. **long division,** division of numbers with the details of the calculation written down. **long-drawn (-out)** *adj.* prolonged. **long face,** a dismal expression. **long-haired** *adj.* intellectual; hippie. **long-headed** *adj.* shrewd, far-seeing; sagacious. **long-house** *n.* a large communal village house in certain parts of Malaysia and Indonesia. **long in the tooth,** rather old. **long johns,** (*colloq.*) long underpants. **long jump,** an athletic contest of jumping as far as possible along the ground in one leap. **long leg,** the position of a fieldsman in cricket far behind the batsman on the leg side. **long-life** *adj.* (of milk etc) treated to prolong the period of usability. **long-lived** *adj.* having a long life, durable. **long odds,** very uneven odds. **long off, long on,** the position of fieldsmen in cricket far behind the bowler and towards the off (or on) side. **long on,** (*colloq.*) well supplied with. **long-playing** *adj.* (of a gramophone record) playing for 15-30 minutes on each side. **long-range** *adj.* having a long range; relating to a long period of future time. **long shot,** a wild guess or venture; a bet at long odds (*not by a long shot,* by no means). **long-sighted** *adj.* able to see clearly only what is at a distance; having imagination or foresight. **long-standing** *adj.* that has long existed. **long-suffering** *adj.* bearing provocation patiently. **long suit,** many cards of one suit in a hand; one's strong point. **long-term** *adj.* occurring in or relating to a long period of time. **long ton,** see TON. **long wave** a radio wave of frequency less than 300 kHz. **long-winded** *adj.* (of a speech or writing) tediously lengthy. [OE]

long[2] *v.i.* to feel a strong desire; to wish ardently. [OF, = seem long to (as LONG[1])]

long. *abbr.* longitude.

longboat *n.* the largest boat carried by a sailing-ship.

longbow *n.* a large bow drawn by hand and shooting a long feathered arrow. —**longbowman** *n.* (*pl.* **-men**)

longeron /ˈlɒndʒərən/ *n.* (usu. in *pl.*) a longitudinal member of an aeroplane's fuselage. [F, = girder]

longevity /lɒnˈdʒevɪtɪ/ *n.* long life. [f. L (*longaevus* aged)]

longhand *n.* ordinary writing as distinct from typing, shorthand, etc.

longhorn *n.* one of a breed of cattle with long horns.

longing /ˈlɒŋɪŋ/ *n.* an intense desire. [f. LONG[2]]

longitude /ˈlɒŋgɪtju:d, ˈlɒndʒ-/ *n.* **1** the angular distance east or west from the meridian of Greenwich or other standard meridian to that of any place. **2** (*Astron.*) a body's or point's angular distance especially along an ecliptic. [f. L *longitudo* (*longus* long)]

longitudinal /lɒŋgɪˈtju:dɪn(ə)l, lɒndʒ-/ *adj.* **1** of longitude. **2** of or in length. **3** lying longways. —**longitudinally** *adv.* [f. prec.]

long-shore *adj.* **1** found on the shore. **2** employed along the shore, especially near a port. —**long-shore drift,** the gradual movement of beach materials (such as sand and shingle) along a shore. [f. *along shore*]

longshoreman *n.* (*pl.* **-men**) a person employed in loading and unloading ships from the shore.

longways *adv.* (also **longwise**) lengthways.

loo *n.* (*colloq.*) a lavatory. [perh. f. *Waterloo,* but there are a number of other possible derivations]

loofah /ˈlu:fə/ *n.* the dried pod of a kind of gourd (*Luffa aegyptiaca*) used as a rough sponge while bathing. [f. Egyptian Arab.]

look /lʊk/ *v.t./i.* **1** to use or direct one's eyes in order to see, search, or examine. **2** to direct one's attention, to consider. **3** to have a specified appearance, to seem. **4** (of a thing) to face in a certain direction. **5** to indicate (an emotion etc.) by one's looks. —*n.* **1** the act of looking, a gaze or glance. **2** an inspection or search. **3** (in *sing.* or *pl.*) the appearance of the face, the expression, the personal aspect. **4** (of a thing) appearance. —*int.* (also **look here!**) of protest or demanding attention. —**look after,** to attend to, to take charge of. **look-alike** *n.* a person or thing closely resembling another. **look down on** *or* **down one's nose at,** to regard with contempt or a feeling of superiority. **look for,** to expect; to try to find. **look forward to,** to await (an expected event) eagerly or with specified feelings. **look in,** to make a short visit or call. **look-in** *n.* a brief visit; a chance of participation or success. **look into,** to investigate. **look on,** to regard (*as*); to be a spectator. **look out,** to be vigilant or prepared; to search for and produce; to have an outlook *on* or *over*. **look over,** to inspect. **look-see** *n.* (*slang*) an inspection. **look sharp,** to make haste. **look to,** to consider; to be careful about; to rely on. **look up,** to seek information about in a reference book etc.; to improve in prospect; (*colloq.*) to go to visit. **look up to,** to respect or admire (a senior or superior person). **not like the look of,** to find alarming or suspicious. [OE]

looker *n.* **1** a person of specified appearance. **2** (*colloq.*) an attractive woman. —**looker-on** *n.* a spectator. [f. LOOK]

looking-glass *n.* a glass mirror.

look-out *n.* **1** a careful watch. **2** an observation-post. **3** a person etc. stationed to keep watch. **4** a prospect. **5** a person's own concern.

loom[1] *n.* an apparatus for weaving cloth. [OE, = tool]

loom[2] *v.i.* to appear dimly, to be seen in vague and often magnified or threatening form (*lit.* or *fig.*). [prob. f. LDu.]

loon *n.* **1** a kind of diving bird with a wild cry, especially a grebe or large diver. **2** (*slang*) a crazy person (cf. foll.). [alt. f. *loom* f. ON]

loony *n.* (*slang*) a lunatic. —*adj.* (*slang*) crazy. —**loony-bin** *n.* (*slang*) a mental home or mental hospital. [abbr.]

loop[1] *n.* **1** the figure produced by a curve or doubled thread etc. that crosses itself. **2** a thing, path, or pattern forming roughly this figure; a length of cord or wire etc. that crosses itself and is fastened at the crossing; a fastening shaped thus. **3** a curved piece of metal serving as a handle etc. **4** a contraceptive coil. **5** a complete circuit for an electrical current. **6** an endless strip of tape or film allowing continuous repetition. **7** a sequence of computer operations repeated until some condition is satisfied. —*v.t./i.* **1** to form (into) a loop or loops. **2** to enclose with or as with a loop. **3** to fasten or join with a loop or loops. —**loop-line** *n.* a railway or telegraph line that diverges from the main line and joins it again. **loop the loop,** to perform an aerobatic loop, with the aircraft turning upside down between climb and dive. [orig. unkn.]

loop[2] *n.* a loophole in a fort etc. [orig. unkn.]

looper *n.* a caterpillar (of a kind of moth) that progresses by arching itself into loops. [f. LOOP[1]]

loophole *n.* **1** a means of evading a rule etc. without infringing the letter of it. **2** a narrow vertical slit in the wall of a fort etc. for shooting or looking through or to admit light or air. [f. LOOP[2] + HOLE]

loopy *adj.* (*slang*) crazy. [f. LOOP[1]]

loose *adj.* **1** not or no longer held by bonds or a restraint. **2** detached or detachable from its place, not held together or contained or fixed. **3** slack, relaxed. **4** inexact, indefinite, vague or incorrect. **5** not compact or dense. **6** morally lax. —*v.t.* **1** to free, untie, or detach. **2** to release. **3** to discharge (a missile). **4** to loosen, to relax. —**at a loose end,** without definite occupation. **loose box,** a stall in which a horse can move about. **loose cover,** a removable cover for an armchair etc. **loose-leaf** *adj.* (of a notebook etc.) with each leaf separately removable. **on the loose,** enjoying oneself freely. —**loosely** *adv.*, **looseness** *n.* [f. ON]

loosen /ˈluːs(ə)n/ *v.t./i.* to make or become loose or looser. —**loosen a person's tongue,** to make him talk freely. [f. prec.]

loot *n.* goods taken from an enemy or by theft. —*v.t./i.* to plunder, to take as loot; to steal from shops or houses left unprotected after a violent event. —**looter** *n.* [f. Hindi]

lop[1] *v.t.* (**-pp-**) to cut away the branches or twigs of; to cut off. [cf. obs. *lip* to prune]

lop[2] *v.i.* (**-pp-**) to hang limply. —**lop-eared** *adj.* having drooping ears. [rel. to LOB]

lope *v.i.* to run with a long bounding stride. —*n.* a long bounding stride. [f. ON (as LEAP)]

lopsided /lɒpˈsaɪdɪd/ *adj.* with one side lower etc., unbalanced. [f. LOP[2] + SIDE]

loquacious /lɒˈkweɪʃəs/ *adj.* talkative. —**loquaciously** *adv.*, **loquacity** /-ˈkwæsɪtɪ/ *n.* [f. L (*loqui* speak)]

lord *n.* **1** a master or ruler; (*hist.*) a feudal superior, especially of a manor. **2** a nobleman; **Lord,** the title of a marquis, earl, viscount, baron, or (before a Christian name) of the younger son of a duke or marquis, or in the titles of certain high officials. —*int.* expressing surprise or dismay etc. —*v.t.* (with *it*) to domineer. —**the Lord,** God or Christ. **the Lords,** the House of Lords. **Lord Chamberlain,** the head of management in the Royal Household. **Lord Chief Justice,** the president of the Queen's Bench Division. **Lord**

(High) Chancellor, the highest officer of the Crown, presiding in the House of Lords etc. **Lord Lieutenant,** the chief executive authority and head of magistrates in each county; (*hist.*) the viceroy of Ireland. **Lord Mayor,** the title of the mayor in some large cities. **Lord President of the Council,** the Cabinet minister presiding at the Privy Council. **Lord Privy Seal,** a senior Cabinet minister without official duties. **Lord's day,** Sunday. **Lord's Prayer,** the prayer taught by Christ to his disciples (Matt. 6 : 9-13), beginning 'Our Father'. **Lords Spiritual,** the bishops in the House of Lords. **Lord's Supper,** the Eucharist. **Lords Temporal,** the members of the House of Lords who are not bishops. **Our Lord,** Christ. [OE, orig. = bread-keeper (as LOAF[1], WARD)]

lordly *adj.* **1** haughty, imperious. **2** suitable for a lord. —**lordliness** *n.* [f. LORD]

lordship *n.* the title used in addressing or referring to a man with the rank of Lord. [f. LORD + -SHIP]

lore[1] *n.* the body of traditions and facts on a subject. [OE (as LEARN)]

lore[2] *n.* a straplike surface between the eye and upper mandible of birds or between the eye and nostril of snakes. [f. L *lorum* strap]

lorgnette /lɔːˈnjet/ *n.* a pair of eyeglasses or opera-glasses held to the eyes on a long handle. [F (*lorgner* squint)]

loris /ˈlɔːrɪs/ *n.* a small slender tailless nocturnal arboreal lemur, with very large dark eyes, especially the **slender loris** (*Loris gracilis*) of southern India etc. and the **slow loris** (*Bradicebus tardigradus*) of southern and SE Asia. [F, perh. f. obs. Du. *loeris* clown]

lorn *adj.* (*archaic*) desolate, forlorn. [OE, p.p. of obs. *leese* lose]

lorry *n.* a large strong motor vehicle for transporting goods etc. [orig. N. Engl., perh. f. name *Laurie*]

lose /luːz/ *v.t./i.* (*past* & *p.p.* **lost**) **1** to be deprived of; to cease to have or maintain. **2** to become unable to find; to fail to keep in sight or follow or grasp mentally. **3** to let or have pass from one's control or reach. **4** to get rid of. **5** to fail to obtain or catch or perceive. **6** to be defeated in (a contest, lawsuit, argument, etc.). **7** to have to forfeit. **8** to spend (time, efforts, etc.) to no purpose. **9** to suffer loss or detriment; to be the worse off. **10** to cause a person the loss of. **11** (of a clock etc.) to become slow (by a specified time). **12** (in *pass.*) to disappear, to perish, to die or be dead. —**be lost** *or* **lose oneself in,** to be engrossed in. **be lost on,** to be wasted on, not to be noticed or appreciated by. **be lost to,** to be no longer affected by or accessible to. **get lost,** (*slang*, usu. in *imper.*) to go away. **lose out,** (*colloq.*) to be unsuccessful, not to get a full chance or advantage. **losing battle,** (esp. *fig.*) a battle in which defeat seems certain. [OE, = perish]

loser /ˈluːzə(r)/ *n.* a person who loses, especially a contest or game; (*colloq.*) one who regularly fails. [f. LOSE]

loss *n.* **1** losing, being lost. **2** a thing or amount lost. **3** detriment resulting from losing. —**at a loss,** (sold etc.) for less than was paid for it. **be at a loss,** to be puzzled or uncertain. **loss-leader** *n.* an article sold at a loss so as to attract customers. [prob. back-formation f. LOST]

lost *past* & *p.p.* of LOSE.

lot *n.* **1** (*colloq.* often in *pl.*) a large number or amount; much. **2** each of a set of objects used in making a chance selection; this method of deciding; a share or office resulting from it. **3** a person's destiny or appointed task etc. **4** a piece of land; (*US*) an area for a particular purpose. **5** an article or set of articles for sale at an auction etc. **6** a number or quantity of associated persons or things. —**bad lot,** a person of bad character. **cast** *or* **draw lots,** to decide with lots. **throw in one's lot with,** to decide to share the fortunes of. **the (whole) lot,** the total number or quantity. [OE]

loth var. of LOATH.

Lothario /ləˈθeərɪəʊ/ *n.* (*pl.* **-os**) a libertine. [character in Rowe's *Fair Penitent* (1703)]

lotion /ˈləʊʃ(ə)n/ *n.* a medicinal or cosmetic liquid preparation applied to the skin. [f. OF or L [(*lavare* wash)]

lottery /ˈlɒtərɪ/ *n.* **1** a means of raising money by selling numbered tickets and giving prizes to the holders of numbers drawn at random. **2** a thing whose outcome is governed by chance. [prob. f. Du. (as LOT)]

lotto /ˈlɒtəʊ/ *n.* a game of chance similar to bingo but with the numbers drawn instead of called. [It.]

lotus /ˈləʊtəs/ *n.* **1** a legendary plant inducing luxurious languor when eaten. **2** a kind of water-lily etc., especially as used symbolically in Hinduism and Buddhism. —**lotus-eater** *n.* a person given to indolent enjoyment. **lotus position,** a cross-legged position of meditation with the feet resting on the thighs. [L f. Gk]

loud *adj.* **1** strongly audible, producing much noise. **2** (of colours etc.) gaudy, obtrusive. —*adv.* loudly. —**loud hailer,** an electronic device for amplifying the sound of the voice so that it can be heard at a distance. **out loud,** aloud. —**loudly** *adv.*, **loudness** *n.* [OE]

loudspeaker /laʊdˈspiːkə(r)/ *n.* an apparatus that converts electrical impulses into sound.

lough /lɒk, -x/ *n.* (*Ir.*) a lake, an arm of the sea. [f. Ir. (as LOCH)]

lounge /laʊndʒ/ *v.i.* to recline casually and comfortably; to loll; to stand or move about idly. —*n.* **1** a public room (e.g. in a hotel) for sitting in. **2** a waiting-room at an airport etc. with seats for waiting passengers. **3** a sitting-room in a house. **4** a spell of lounging. —**lounge-suit** *n.* a man's suit for ordinary wear. —**lounger** *n.* [perh. f. obs. *lungis* lout, laggard]

lour /ˈlaʊə(r)/ *v.i.* to frown, to look sullen or (of the sky etc.) dark and threatening. [orig. unkn.]

louse /laʊs/ *n.* **1** (*pl.* **lice**) any of various insects of the orders Anoplura (sucking-lice) and Mallophaga (biting-lice), parasitic on mammals, birds, fish, or plants; a parasitic insect (*Pediculus humanus*, order Anoplura) infesting human hair and skin and transmitting many diseases. **2** (*slang*, *pl.* **louses**) a contemptible person. —*v.t.* to remove lice from. —**louse up,** (*slang*) to spoil, to mess up. [OE]

lousy /ˈlaʊzɪ/ *adj.* **1** infected with lice. **2** (*slang*) disgusting, very bad. **3** (*slang*) swarming, well supplied. —**lousily** *adv.*, **lousiness** *n.* [f. prec.]

lout *n.* a hulking or rough-mannered fellow. —**loutish** *adj.* [perh. f. archaic *lout* v. to bow, stoop]

louvre /ˈluːvə(r)/ *n.* **1** any of a set of overlapping slats arranged to admit air and exclude light or rain. **2** a domed erection on a roof with side openings for ventilation etc. [f. OF *lov(i)er* skylight]

lovable /ˈlʌvəb(ə)l/. *adj.* inspiring love or affection. [f. LOVE]

lovage /ˈlʌvɪdʒ/ *n.* a herb (*Levisticum officinale*) used for flavouring. [f. OF *levesche* f. L *levisticum*]

love /lʌv/ *n.* **1** warm liking or affection for a person or thing. **2** sexual passion; sexual relations. **3** a beloved one, a sweetheart (often as a form of address); (*colloq.*) a person of whom one is fond. **4** affectionate greetings. **5** (often **Love**) a representation of Cupid. **6** (in games) no score, nil. —*v.t./i.* **1** to feel love for. **2** to like greatly, to delight in. **3** to be inclined, especially as a habit. —**for love,** because of affection; without receiving payment. **in love (with),** feeling (esp. sexual) love (for). **love-affair** *n.* a romantic or sexual relationship between two people who are in love. **love-bird** *n.* a parakeet (esp. of the genus Agapornis) seeming to show great affection for its mate. **love-child** *n.* an illegitimate child. **love game,** a game in which the loser makes no score. **love-hate relationship,** an intense emotional response involving ambivalent feelings of love and hate towards the same object. **love-in-a-mist** *n.* a blue-flowered garden plant (*Nigella damascena*). **love-letter** *n.* a letter between sweethearts, expressing their love. **love-lies-bleeding** *n.* a garden plant (*Amaranthus caudatus*) with drooping spikes of purple-red bloom. **love-match** *n.* a marriage between two people who are in love with each other. **love-song** *n.* a song expressing love. **love-story** *n.* a story in which the theme is romantic love. **make love,** to have sexual intercourse; to pay amorous attentions *to.* **not for love or money,** not in any circumstances. [OE, rel. to LIEF]

loveless *adj.* unloving or unloved or both. [f. LOVE + -LESS]

lovelorn *adj.* pining from unrequited love.

lovely *adj.* exquisitely beautiful; (*colloq.*) pleasing, delightful. —*n.* (*colloq.*) a pretty woman. —**loveliness** *n.* [OE (as LOVE)]

lover *n.* **1** a person (esp. a man) in love with another; a man with whom a woman is having sexual relations; (in *pl.*) a pair in love. **2** one who likes or enjoys something. [f. LOVE]

lovesick *adj.* languishing with love.

lovey-dovey /lʌvɪˈdʌvɪ/ *adj.* (*colloq.*) fondly affectionate and sentimental. [f. LOVE]

loving /ˈlʌvɪŋ/ *adj.* feeling or showing love. —**loving-cup** *n.* a large drinking-vessel with two or more handles, passed from hand to hand at a banquet etc. so that each person may drink from its contents. —**lovingly** *adv.* [as LOVE]

low[1] /ləʊ/ *adj.* **1** not high or tall, not extending far upwards; coming below the normal or average level. **2** not elevated in position. **3** ranking below others in importance or quality. **4** of a small or less than normal amount, extent, intensity, etc.; (of opinion) unfavourable. **5** dejected, lacking vigour. **6** unfavourable. **7** ignoble, vulgar. **8** (of a sound or voice) deep not shrill, having slow vibrations; not loud. **9** (in *compar.*) situated on less high land or to the south; (of a geological period) earlier (called 'lower' because of the position of the corresponding rock formations); (of animals or plants etc.) of relatively simple structure, not highly developed. —*n.* **1** a low or the lowest level or number. **2** an area of low pressure. —*adv.* **1** in or to a low position (*lit.* or *fig.*). **2** in a low tone; (of a sound) at or to a low pitch. **Low Church,** the section of the Church of England which gives a relatively unimportant or 'low' place to the claims of the episcopate, priesthood, and sacraments. **low comedy,** that in which the subject and its treatment border on farce. **Low Countries,** the district now forming the Netherlands, Belgium, and Luxemburg. **low-down** *adj.* ignoble, dishonourable. **low-down** *n.* (*slang*) the relevant information (*on*). **low frequency,** (in radio) 30-300 kilohertz. **low-key** *adj.* restrained, lacking intensity. **low-level language,** a computer language close in form to a machine-readable code. **low-pitched** *adj.* (of a sound) low; (of a roof) having only a slight slope. **low pressure,** a low degree of activity or exertion; a condition of the atmosphere with the pressure below average. **low season,** the period of fewest visitors at a resort etc. **Low Sunday,** the Sunday after Easter. **low tide,** a tide of the lowest level; the time of this. **low water,** low tide; *in low water*, short of money. [f. ON (as LIE[1])]

low[2] /ləʊ/ *n.* the deep sound made by cows, a moo. —*v.i.* to make this sound. [OE]

lowbrow *adj.* (*colloq.*) not intellectual or cultured. —*n.* (*colloq.*) a lowbrow person.

lower[1] /ˈləʊə(r)/ *adj.* **1** less high in place or position. **2** situated on lower ground or to the south. **3** ranking below others. **4** (of a geological or archaeological period) earlier (cf. UPPER). —*v.t.* **1** to let or haul down. **2** to make or become lower; to reduce in amount or quantity etc. **3** to direct (one's gaze) downwards. —**lower case,** see CASE[2]. **Lower Chamber** *or* **House,** the lower and usually elected body in a legislature, especially the House of Commons. [compar. of LOW[1]]

lower[2] var. of LOUR.

lowermost *adj.* lowest. [f. LOWER[1] + -MOST]

lowland *n.* a low-lying country. —*adj.* of or in a lowland. —**lowlander** *n.*

lowly /ˈləʊlɪ/ *adj.* of humble rank or condition. —**lowliness** *n.* [f. LOW[1]]

loyal /ˈlɔɪəl/ *adj.* faithful; steadfast in allegiance, devoted to the legitimate sovereign etc. —**loyal toast,** a toast to the sovereign. —**loyally** *adv.*, **loyalty** *n.* [f. OF f. L *legalis*, = LEGAL]

loyalist *n.* one who remains loyal to the legitimate sovereign etc., especially in the face of rebellion or usurpation; **Loyalist,** (in Northern Ireland) one who favours retaining Ulster's link with Britain. —**loyalism** *n.* [f. prec.]

lozenge /ˈlɒzɪndʒ/ *n.* **1** a small sweet or medicinal etc. tablet to be dissolved in the mouth. **2** a rhombus, a diamond figure. **3** a lozenge-shaped object. [f. OF]

LP *abbr.* long-playing (record).

L-plate /ˈelpleɪt/ *n.* a sign bearing the letter L, attached to the front and rear of a motor vehicle to indicate that it is being driven by a learner.

Lr *symbol* lawrencium.

LSD *abbr.* lysergic acid diethylamide, a powerful hallucinogenic drug.

£.s.d. /elesˈdiː/ *n.* pounds, shillings, and pence (in former British currency); money, riches. [f. L *librae, solidi, denarii*]

LT *abbr.* low tension.

Lt. *abbr.* **1** Lieutenant. **2** light.

Ltd. *abbr.* Limited.

Lu *symbol* lutetium.

lubber *n.* a clumsy fellow, a lout. —**lubberly** *adj.* [perh. f. OF, = swindler]

lubricant /ˈluːbrɪkənt/ *n.* an oil or grease etc. used to reduce friction in machinery etc. [as foll.]

lubricate /ˈluːbrɪkeɪt/ *v.t.* to apply a lubricant to; to make slippery. —**lubrication** /-ˈkeɪʃ(ə)n/ *n.*, **lubricator** *n.* [f. L *lubricare* (*lubricus* slippery)]

lubricity /luːˈbrɪsɪtɪ/ *n.* **1** slipperiness. **2** skill in evasion. **3** lewdness. [f. F or L (as prec.)]

lucerne /luːˈsɜːn/ *n.* a cloverlike plant (*Medicago sativa*) used for fodder. [f. F f. Prov. = glow-worm, f. its shiny seeds]

lucid /ˈluːsɪd/ *adj.* **1** expressed or expressing things clearly. **2** sane. —**lucidity** /-ˈsɪdɪtɪ/ *n.*, **lucidly** *adv.* [f. F or It. or L *lucidus* bright (*lucēre* shine)]

luck *n.* chance regarded as a bringer of good or bad fortune; the circumstances of life (beneficial or not) brought by this; good fortune, success due to chance. —**down on one's luck,** in a period of bad fortune. **hard luck,** worse fortune than one deserves. **push one's luck,** to take undue risks. **try one's luck,** to make a venture. **worse luck,** unfortunately. [f. LG]

luckless *adj.* **1** invariably having bad luck. **2** ending in failure. [f. LUCK + -LESS]

lucky *adj.* having or resulting from good luck, especially as distinct from skill or design or merit; bringing good luck. —**lucky dip,** a tub etc. containing articles of different value into which one may dip at random on payment of a small sum. —**luckily** *adv.* [f. LUCK]

lucrative /ˈluːkrətɪv/ *adj.* profitable, producing much money. —**lucrativeness** *n.* [f. L (*lucrari* to gain, as foll.)]

lucre /ˈluːkə(r)/ *n.* (*derog.*) money, money-making as a motive for action. [f. F or L *lucrum* profit]

Lucullan /lʊˈkʌlən, luː-/ *adj.* (esp. of a feast) very sumptuous or luxurious. [f. *Lucullus* (1st c. BC), Roman general, famous for his lavish banquets]

Luddite /ˈlʌdaɪt/ *n.* **1** a member of the bands of English craftsmen who, when their jobs were threatened by the progressive introduction of machinery into their trades in the early 19th c., attempted to reverse the trend towards mechanization by wrecking the offending machines. **2** a person similarly seeking to obstruct progress. —*adj.* of Luddites. [perh. f. Ned *Lud*, an insane person said to have destroyed two stocking-frames *c.*1779]

ludicrous /ˈluːdɪkrəs/ *adj.* absurd, ridiculous, laughable. —**ludicrously** *adv.* [f. L (*ludicrum* stage-play, as foll.)]

ludo /ˈluːdəʊ/ *n.* a simple game played with dice and counters on a special board. [L, = I play]

luff *n.* the side of a fore-and-aft sail next to the mast or stay. —*v.t./i.* **1** to bring a ship's head nearer the wind; to bring the head of (a ship) thus. **2** to raise or lower (a crane's jib). [f. OF *lof* prob. f. LG]

Luftwaffe /ˈlʊftvɑːfə/ *n.* the German air force before and during the Second World War. [G, = air weapon]

lug *v.t./i.* (**-gg-**) to drag or carry with great effort; to pull hard. —*n.* **1** a hard or rough pull. **2** a projection on an object by which it may be carried, fixed in place, etc. **3** (*colloq.*) an ear. [prob. f. Scand.]

luge /luːʒ/ *n.* a short raised toboggan for one person seated. —*v.i.* to ride on a luge. [Swiss F]

luggage /ˈlʌgɪdʒ/ *n.* suitcases, bags, etc., for containing a traveller's belongings. [f. prec.]

lugger *n.* a small ship with four-cornered sails. [f. foll.]

lugsail *n.* a four-cornered sail on a yard. [prob. f. LUG]

lugubrious /luːˈguːbrɪəs/ *adj.* doleful. —**lugubriously** *adv.* [f. L (*lugēre* mourn)]

lugworm *n.* a large marine worm (*Arenicola marina*) used as bait. [orig. unkn.]

lukewarm /ˈluːkwɔːm/ *adj.* **1** moderately warm, tepid. **2** not enthusiastic, indifferent. [f. dial. *luke* tepid + WARM]

lull *v.t./i.* **1** to soothe or send to sleep. **2** to calm (suspicions etc.), usually by deception. **3** (of a storm or noise) to lessen, to become quiet. —*n.* an intermission in a storm etc.; a temporary period of inactivity or quiet. [imit. of sounds used in lulling a child]

lullaby /ˈlʌləbaɪ/ *n.* a soothing song to send a child to sleep. [as prec.]

lumbago /lʌmˈbeɪgəʊ/ *n.* a rheumatic muscular pain in the lower part of the back. [L (*lumbus* loin)]

lumbar /ˈlʌmbə(r)/ *adj.* of the loins. [f. L (as prec.)]

lumber *n.* **1** disused and cumbersome articles; useless stuff. **2** partly prepared timber. —*v.t./i.* **1** to encumber. **2** to fill up space inconveniently; to obstruct (a place). **3** to move in a blundering noisy way. **4** to cut and prepare forest timber. —**lumber-jacket** *n.* a jacket of the kind worn by lumberjacks. **lumber-room** *n.* a room in which disused articles are kept. [v. perh. imit.; n. perh. in part assoc. with obs. *lumber* pawnbroker's shop]

lumberjack *n.* one who fells and removes lumber (= timber).

lumen /ˈluːmen/ *n.* a unit of luminous flux, the flux per unit solid angle from a uniform source of one candela. [L, = light]

luminary /ˈluːmɪnərɪ/ *n.* **1** a natural light-giving body, especially the sun or moon. **2** a person as a source of intellectual or spiritual light. [f. OF or L (*lumen* light)]

luminescent /luːmɪˈnes(ə)nt/ *adj.* emitting light without heat. —**luminescence** *n.* [as prec.]

luminous /ˈluːmɪnəs/ *adj.* shedding light, phosphorescent and so visible in darkness. —**luminosity** /-ˈnɒsɪtɪ/ *n.* [f. OF or L (as LUMINARY)]

lump[1] *n.* **1** a hard or compact mass of no particular or regular shape. **2** a protuberance or swelling on a surface. **3** (*slang*) a great quantity, a lot. **4** a heavy, dull, or ungainly person. —*v.t.* to put or consider together; to treat as all alike. —**the lump,** casual workers especially in the building trade who are paid in lump sums. **in the lump,** generally, taking things as a whole. **lump in one's throat,** a feeling of discomfort there due to anxiety or emotion. **lump sugar,** sugar in small lumps or cubes. **lump sum,** a sum covering a number of items; money paid down all at once. [perh. f. Scand.]

lump[2] *v.t.* (*colloq.*) to put up with ungraciously. [imit.]

lumpish *adj.* **1** heavy and clumsy. **2** stupid, lethargic. [f. LUMP[1]]

lumpy *adj.* full of or covered with lumps; (of water) choppy. —**lumpily** *adv.*, **lumpiness** *n.* [f. LUMP[1]]

lunacy /ˈluːnəsɪ/ *n.* **1** insanity. **2** great folly. [f. LUNATIC]

lunar /ˈluːnə(r)/ *adj.* of, like, or concerned with the moon. —**lunar (excursion) module,** a module for making a journey from an orbiting spacecraft to the moon's surface and back. **lunar month,** the period of the moon's revolution, especially a lunation; (*pop.*) a period of four weeks. [f. L (*luna* moon)]

lunate /ˈluːneɪt/ *adj.* crescent-shaped. [as prec.]

lunatic /ˈluːnətɪk/ *adj.* insane; extremely reckless or foolish. —*n.* a lunatic person. —**lunatic asylum,** (*hist.*) a mental home or mental hospital. **lunatic fringe,** a fanatical or eccentric or visionary minority of a party etc. [f. OF f. L (as prec.), because formerly believed to be affected by changes of moon]

lunation /luːˈneɪʃ(ə)n/ *n.* the interval between new moons, about 29½ days. [f. L (as LUNAR)]

lunch *n.* **1** the midday meal. **2** a light refreshment at mid-morning. —*v.t./i.* **1** to take lunch. **2** to provide lunch for. [f. foll.]

luncheon /ˈlʌntʃ(ə)n/ *n.* (*formal*) the midday meal. —**luncheon meat,** tinned meat loaf of pork etc. **luncheon voucher,** a voucher given to an employee as part of his pay and exchangeable for food at certain restaurants and shops. [orig. unkn.]

lung *n.* either of the pair of air-breathing organs in man and most vertebrates.

—**lung-fish** *n.* a freshwater bony fish of the order Dipnoi, with a sac-shaped air-breathing organ in addition to or in place of gills. [OE, rel. to LIGHT²]

lunge *n.* **1** a sudden forward movement of the body in thrusting, hitting, or kicking; a thrust. **2** a long rope on which a horse is held and made to move in a circle round its trainer. —*v.t./i.* **1** to deliver or make a lunge; to drive (a weapon etc.) violently in some direction. **2** to exercise (a horse) on a lunge. [f. F *allonger* lengthen (as LONG¹)]

lupin /ˈlu:pɪn/ *n.* a garden or fodder plant of the genus *Lupinus*, with long tapering spikes of flowers. [f. L]

lupine /ˈlu:paɪn/ *adj.* of or like wolves. [f. L *lupinus* (*lupus* wolf)]

lupus /ˈlu:pəs/ *n.* an ulcerous skin disease, especially tuberculosis of the skin. [L, = wolf]

lurch¹ *n.* a sudden lean or deviation to one side, a stagger. —*v.i.* to make a lurch, to stagger. [orig. Naut., f. *lee-lurch* alt. of *lee-latch* drifting to leeward]

lurch² *n.* **leave in the lurch,** to abandon (a friend or ally) to an awkward situation; to desert in difficulties. [f. F *lourche* game like backgammon, bad defeat in this]

lurcher *n.* a dog cross-bred between a collie or sheep-dog and a greyhound, often used by poachers for retrieving game. [f. obs. *lurch* var. of LURK]

lure /ljʊə(r)/ *v.t.* **1** to entice. **2** to recall with a lure. —*n.* **1** a thing used to entice; the enticing quality of a pursuit etc. **2** a falconer's apparatus for recalling a hawk. [f. OF *luere*]

lurid /ˈljʊərɪd/ *adj.* **1** strong and glaring in colour. **2** sensational, showy. **3** horrifying. **4** ghastly, wan. —**luridly** *adv.*, **luridness** *n.* [f. L (*luror* wan or yellow colour)]

lurk *v.i.* **1** to linger furtively or unobtrusively. **2** to lie hidden while waiting to attack. **3** to be latent. [perh. f. LOUR]

luscious /ˈlʌʃəs/ *adj.* **1** richly sweet in taste or smell. **2** (of style) over-rich. **3** voluptuously attractive. —**lusciously** *adv.*, **lusciousness** *n.* [perh. f. obs. *licious* f. DELICIOUS]

lush *adj.* **1** (of grass etc.) luxuriant and succulent. **2** luxurious. —**lushly** *adv.*, **lushness** *n.* [perh. f. obs. *lash* soft f. OF (as LAX)]

lust *n.* **1** strong sexual desire. **2** any passionate desire or enjoyment. **3** sensuous appetite regarded as sinful. —*v.i.* to have a strong or excessive (esp. sexual) desire. —**lustful** *adj.*, **lustfully** *adv.* [OE]

lustre /ˈlʌstə(r)/ *n.* **1** the soft brightness of a smooth or shining surface. **2** glory, distinction. **3** an iridescent metallic glaze on pottery and porcelain; pottery and porcelain with this. —**lustrous** *adj.* [F f. It. (L *lustrare* illuminate)]

lusty *adj.* healthy and strong; vigorous, lively. —**lustily** *adv.*, **lustiness** *n.* [f. LUST]

lute¹ /lu:t/ *n.* a plucked stringed instrument with frets and a round body, resembling a halved pear. [f. F, ult. f. Arab.]

lute² /lu:t/ *n.* clay or cement for making joints airtight etc. —*v.t.* to treat with lute. [f. OF f. L *lutum* mud]

lutenist /ˈlu:tənɪst/ *n.* a lute-player. [f. L (as LUTE¹)]

lutetium /lu:ˈti:ʃəm/ *n.* a metallic element, the heaviest and last of the lanthanide series, symbol Lu, atomic number 71. [f. F f. L *Lutetia* ancient name of Paris, native city of its discoverer (G. Urbain, d. 1938)]

Lutheran /ˈlu:θərən/ *adj.* of Martin Luther or the Lutheran Church. —*n.* a follower of Luther; a member of the Lutheran Church. —**Lutheran Church,** the Church accepting the Augsburg Confession of 1530, with justification by faith alone as its cardinal doctrine. —**Lutheranism** *n.* [f. M. *Luther*, German Protestant theologian (d. 1546)]

lux /lʌks/ *n.* (*pl.* same) a unit of illumination, one lumen per square metre. [L, = light]

luxe /lʌks,lʊks/*n.* luxury, cf. DE LUXE. [F f. L *luxus*]

luxuriant /lʌgˈzjʊərɪənt/ *adj.* growing profusely; exuberant, florid. —**luxuriance** *n.* [f. *luxuriare* grow rank (as LUXURY)]

luxuriate /lʌgˈzjʊərɪeɪt/ *v.i.* to revel or feel keen delight; to abandon oneself to enjoyment or ease. [as prec.]

luxurious /lʌgˈzjʊərɪəs/ *adj.* **1** supplied with luxuries, extremely comfortable. **2** fond of luxury. —**luxuriously** *adv.*, **luxuriousness** *n.* [f. OF f. L (as foll.)]

luxury /ˈlʌkʃərɪ/ *n.* **1** choice or costly surroundings, possessions, food, etc.; the habitual use or enjoyment of these. **2** a thing desirable for comfort or enjoyment but not essential. **3** (*attrib.*) comfortable and expensive. [f. OF f. L *luxuria* (*luxus* abundance)]

LV *abbr.* luncheon voucher.

lx *abbr.* lux.

LXX *abbr.* the Septuagint. [Latin numeral, = 70]

Lyceum /laɪˈsi:əm/ *n.* **1** the garden at Athens where Aristotle taught. **2** his followers, his philosophy. [L f. Gk (*Lukeios* epithet of Apollo, whose temple stood near by)]

lychee /ˈlaɪtʃi:/ var. of LITCHI.

lychgate var. of LICHGATE.

lye /laɪ/ *n.* water made alkaline with wood ashes; any alkaline solution for washing things. [OE]

lying *partic.* of LIE[1], LIE[2].

lymph /lɪmf/ *n.* the colourless fluid from the tissues or organs of the body, containing white blood-cells; this fluid used as a vaccine. [f. F or L *lympha* water]

lymphatic /lɪm'fætɪk/ *adj.* **1** of, secreting, or conveying lymph. **2** (of a person) flabby, pale, sluggish. [orig. = frenzied, now assoc. w. LYMPH]

lynch /lɪntʃ/ *v.t.* (of a mob) to execute or punish violently without lawful trial. —**lynch law,** such a procedure by a self-constituted illegal court. [app. f. Capt. W. *Lynch*, judge in Virginia *c.*1780]

lynchet /'lɪntʃɪt/ *n.* a ridge or ledge formed by prehistoric ploughing on a slope. [f. OE *hlinc*; cf. LINKS]

lynx /lɪŋks/ *n.* a wild animal of the subgenus *Lynx* of the cat genus, with a short tail, spotted fur, and proverbially keen sight. —**lynx-eyed** *adj.* keen-sighted. [f. L f. Gk]

lyre /laɪə(r)/ *n.* a plucked stringed instrument in which strings are fixed to a crossbar supported by two arms. —**lyre-bird** *n.* an Australian bird of the genus *Menura*, the male of which has a lyre-shaped tail display. [f. OF f. L f. Gk]

lyric /'lɪrɪk/ *adj.* **1** (of poetry) expressing the writer's emotions, usually briefly and in stanzas or groups of lines; (of a poet) writing in this manner. **2** of or for the lyre; meant to be sung; fit to be expressed in song; of the nature of song. —*n.* **1** a lyric poem. **2** (esp. in *pl.*) the words of a song. **3** (in *pl.*) lyric verses. [f. F f. L f. Gk (as prec.)]

lyrical /'lɪrɪk(ə)l/ *adj.* **1** resembling or using language appropriate to lyric poetry. **2** (*colloq.*) highly enthusiastic. —**lyrically** *adv.* [as prec.]

lyricist /'lɪrɪsɪst/ *n.* a writer of lyrics [f. LYRIC]

-lysis /-lɪsɪs/ *suffix* forming nouns denoting disintegration or decomposition (*electrolysis*). [L f. Gk *lusis* loosening (*luō* loosen)]

-lyte /-laɪt/ *suffix* forming nouns denoting substances that can be decomposed (*electrolyte*). [L f. Gk *lutos* loosed (as prec.)]

Mm

M,m /em/ *n.* (*pl.* **Ms, M's**) **1** the thirteenth letter of the alphabet. **2** (as a Roman numeral) 1,000.

M *abbr.* **1** mega-. **2** motorway.

M. *abbr.* **1** Master. **2** *Monsieur.*

m *abbr.* **1** metre(s). **2** mile(s). **3** million(s). **4** milli-. **5** minute(s). **6** (also **m.**) masculine; married; male.

'm (*colloq.*) = *am* in *I'm.*

MA *abbr.* Master of Arts.

ma /mɑː/ *n.* (*colloq.*) mother. [abbr. of MAMMA].

ma'am /mæm, mɑːm, məm/ *n.* madam (used esp. in addressing a royal lady or an officer in the WRAC etc.). [abbr.]

mac *n.* (*colloq.*) a mackintosh. [abbr.]

macabre /məˈkɑːbr/ *adj.* grim, gruesome. [f. OF, perh. f. *Macabé* Maccabee, with ref. to play containing slaughter of the Maccabees]

macadam /məˈkædəm/ *n.* a material for road-making with successive layers of broken stone compacted; tar macadam (see TAR[1]). [f. J. L. *McAdam,* Scottish engineer (d. 1836) who advocated this method]

macadamize /məˈkædəmaɪz/ *v.t.* to surface with macadam. [f. prec.]

macaque /məˈkɑːk/ *n.* a monkey of the genus *Macaca,* e.g. the rhesus monkey, of India and SE Asia. [F f. Port., = monkey]

macaroni /mækəˈrəʊnɪ/ *n.* **1** pasta formed into tubes. **2** (*pl.* **-ies**) an 18th-c. dandy. [f. It. f. Gk *makaria* barley food]

macaronic /mækəˈrɒnɪk/ *adj.* (of verse) of burlesque form containing Latin or other foreign words and vernacular words with Latin etc. terminations. [f. obs. It., joc. (as prec.)]

macaroon /mækəˈruːn/ *n.* a small cake or biscuit made with ground almonds or coconut. [f. F f. It. (as MACARONI)]

macaw /məˈkɔː/ *adj.* an American parrot of the genus *Ara* etc., with bright colours and a long tail. [f. Port. *Macao*]

McCoy /məˈkɔɪ/ *n.* **the real McCoy,** (*colloq.*) the real thing, the genuine article. [orig. unkn.]

mace[1] *n.* **1** a staff of office, especially the symbol of the Speaker's authority in the House of Commons. **2** (*hist.*) a heavy club usually having a metal head and spikes. [f. OF]

mace[2] *n.* the dried outer covering of the nutmeg as a spice. [f. OF f. L *macir* spicy bark]

macédoine /ˈmæsɪdwɑːn/ *n.* mixed fruit or vegetables, especially cut up small or in jelly. [F]

macerate /ˈmæsəreɪt/ *v.t./i.* **1** to make or become soft by soaking. **2** to waste away by fasting. —**maceration** /-ˈreɪʃ(ə)n/ *n.* [f. L *macerare*]

machete /məˈtʃetɪ, -ˈtʃeɪtɪ/ *n.* a broad heavy knife used in Central America and the West Indies. [Sp. (*macho* hammer, f. L)]

machiavellian /mækɪəˈvelɪən/ *adj.* elaborately cunning; deceitful, perfidious. [f. N. *Machiavelli,* Italian statesman (d. 1527)]

machicolation /məʃɪkəˈleɪʃ(ə)n/ *n.* an opening between the corbels of a projecting parapet, through which missiles etc. could be hurled down on attackers; a structure with such openings. [f. OF, ult. f. Prov. (*macar* crush, *col* neck)]

machinate /ˈmækɪneɪt, ˈmæʃ-/ *v.i.* to lay plots, to intrigue. —**machination** /-ˈneɪʃ(ə)n/ *n.*, **machinator** *n.* [f. L *machinari* contrive (as foll.)]

machine /məˈʃiːn/ *n.* **1** an apparatus for applying mechanical power, having several parts each with a definite function. **2** a bicycle, motor cycle, etc., an aircraft; a computer. **3** the controlling system of an organization. **4** a person who acts mechanically. —*v.t.* to make or operate on with a machine (esp. of sewing or printing). —**machine-readable** *adj.* in a form that a computer can process. **machine tool,** a mechanically operated tool for working on metal, wood, or plastics. [f. F f. L *machina* f. Gk (as MECHANIC)]

machine-gun *n.* a mounted automatic gun giving continuous fire. —*v.t.* (**-nn-**) to shoot at with a machine-gun.

machinery *n.* **1** machines; a mechanism. **2** an organized system; a means arranged. [f. prec.]

machinist *n.* **1** one who operates a machine, especially a sewing-machine or a machine tool. **2** one who makes machinery. [f. F & f. MACHINE]

machismo /məˈtʃɪzməʊ/ *n.* assertive manliness, masculine pride. [Sp. (as MACHO)]

Mach number /mɑːk, mæk/ the ratio of the speed of a body to the speed of sound in the surrounding medium. [f. E. *Mach*, Austrian physicist (d. 1916)]

macho /ˈmætʃəʊ/ *adj.* manly, virile. —*n.* (*pl.* **-os**) **1** a macho man. **2** machismo. [Sp., = male, f. L *masculus*]

mack var. of MAC.

mackerel /ˈmækər(ə)l/ *n.* (*pl.* same) a sea-fish (*Scomber scombrus*) used as food. —**mackerel sky,** a sky dappled with rows of small white fleecy clouds (cirrocumulus). [f. AF]

mackintosh /ˈmækɪntɒʃ/ *n.* **1** a waterproof coat or cloak. **2** cloth waterproofed with rubber. [f. C. *Macintosh*, Scottish inventor of the material (d. 1843)]

macramé /məˈkrɑːmɪ/ *n.* the art of knotting cord or string in patterns to make decorative articles; work so made. [f. Turk. *makrama* bedspread, f. Arab.]

macro- *in comb.* long, large, large-scale. [f. Gk (*makros* long)]

macrobiotic /mækrəʊbaɪˈɒtɪk/ *adj.* of or following a Zen Buddhist dietary system (comprising pure vegetable foods, brown rice, etc.) intended to prolong life. [f. Gk (MACRO-, *biotos* life)]

macrocosm /ˈmækrəʊkɒz(ə)m/ *n.* the universe; any great whole. [f. F f. L (MACRO-, Gk *kosmos* world)]

macroeconomics /mækrəʊiːkəˈnɒmɪks/ *n.* the study of the economy as a whole.

macromolecule /ˈmækrəʊmɒlɪkjuːl/ *n.* a molecule containing a very large number of atoms.

macron /ˈmækrɒn/ *n.* the written or printed mark (¯) over a long or stressed vowel. [Gk, neut. of *makros* long]

macroscopic /mækrəʊˈskɒpɪk/ *adj.* **1** visible to the naked eye. **2** regarded in terms of large units. —**macroscopically** *adv.* [f. MACRO- + -SCOPIC]

macula /ˈmækjʊlə/ *n.* (*pl.* **-lae** /-liː/) a dark spot; a spot, especially a permanent one, in the skin. —**maculation** /-ˈleɪʃ(ə)n/ *n.* [L]

mad *adj.* **1** having a disordered mind, insane. **2** extremely foolish. **3** wildly enthusiastic or infatuated. **4** frenzied. **5** (*colloq.*) angry. **6** wildly light-hearted. —**like mad,** (*colloq.*) with great energy or enthusiasm. **mad cow disease,** see BSE. —**madness** *n.* [OE]

madam /ˈmædəm/ *n.* **1** a polite or respectful formal address or mode of reference to a woman. **2** (*colloq.*) a conceited or precocious young woman. **3** a woman brothel-keeper. [f. OF (as foll.)]

Madame /ˈmædəm, mæˈdɑːm/ *n.* (*pl.* ***Mesdames*** /meɪˈdɑːm, -ˈdæm/) the title used of or to a French-speaking woman, corresponding to Mrs or madam. [F, = my lady]

madcap *n.* a wildly impulsive person. —*adj.* wildly impulsive.

madden *v.t./i.* to make or become mad; to irritate. [f. MAD]

madder *n.* **1** a herbaceous plant (*Rubia tinctoria*) with yellowish flowers. **2** the red dye obtained from its root; a synthetic substitute for this. [OE]

made *past & p.p.* of MAKE. —*adj.* (of a person) **1** built or formed (*well-made*; *loosely-made*). **2** successful. —**have it made,** (*slang*) to be sure of success. **made for,** ideally suited to. **made of,** consisting of. **made of money,** (*colloq.*) very rich.

Madeira /məˈdɪərə/ *n.* a fortified white wine from Madeira. —**Madeira cake,** a rich cake containing no fruit. [f. island of *Madeira*]

Mademoiselle /mædəmwəˈzel/ *n.* (*pl.* ***Mesdemoiselles*** /meɪdm-/) **1** the title used of or to an unmarried French-speaking woman, corresponding to Miss or madam. **2 mademoiselle,** a young Frenchwoman; a French governess. [F (*ma* my, *demoiselle* as DAMSEL]

madhouse *n.* **1** (*colloq.*) a mental home or mental hospital. **2** a scene of confused uproar.

madly *adv.* in a mad manner; (*colloq.*) passionately, extremely. [f. MAD]

madman *n.* (*pl.* **-men**) a man who is mad.

madonna /məˈdɒnə/ *n.* a picture or statue of the Virgin Mary. —**madonna lily,** a tall white lily (*Lilium candidum*) often depicted in pictures of the Annunciation. [It., = my lady]

madrigal /ˈmædrɪg(ə)l/ *n.* **1** a part-song for several voices. **2** a short amatory poem. The form was developed and perfected by Petrarch. [f. It. f. L *matricalis* mother (as MATRIX)]

madwoman *n.* (*pl.* **-women**) a woman who is mad.

maelstrom /ˈmeɪlstrɒm/ *n.* **1** a great whirlpool. **2** a confused state. [Du.]

maenad /ˈmiːnæd/ *n.* a bacchante. [f. L f. Gk (*mainomai* rave)]

maestro /ˈmaɪstrəʊ/ *n.* (*pl.* **-ri** /-riː/) **1** a great conductor, composer, or teacher of music. **2** a masterly performer in any sphere. [It., = master]

Mafia /ˈmæfɪə/ *n.* **1** a secret organization, opposed to legal authority and engaged in crime, that originated in Sicily in the 13th c. and later spread to North and South America. **2 mafia,** a network of persons regarded as exerting hidden influence. [It. dial., = bragging]

Mafioso /mæfɪ'əʊsəʊ, mɑ:-/ *n.* (*pl.* **-si** /-si:/) a member of the Mafia. [It. (as prec.)]

magazine /mægə'zi:n/ *n.* **1** a periodical publication (now usually illustrated) containing contributions by various writers. **2** a store for arms, ammunition, and provisions, for use in war; a store for explosives. **3** a chamber for holding the supply of cartridges to be fed automatically to the breech of a gun; a similar device in a camera, slide-projector, etc. [f. F f. It. f. Arab., = store-house]

magenta /mə'dʒentə/ *n.* a bluish-crimson colour; an aniline dye of this colour. —*adj.* of or coloured with magenta. [f. *Magenta* in N. Italy, town near which the Austrians were defeated by the French under Napoleon III in 1859, the year of the dye's discovery]

maggot /'mægət/ *n.* a larva, especially of the bluebottle or cheese-fly. —**maggoty** *adj.* [perh. alt. of *maddock* f. ON]

magi *pl.* of MAGUS.

magic /'mædʒɪk/ *n.* **1** the supposed art of influencing the course of events by the occult control of nature or of spirits, witchcraft. **2** conjuring tricks. **3** an inexplicable or remarkable influence; an enchanting quality or phenomenon. —*adj.* of magic; producing surprising results. —*v.t.* (**-ck-**) to change or make by or as if by magic. —**magic carpet,** a mythical carpet able to transport the person on it to any place. **magic eye,** a photoelectric device for automatic control. **magic lantern,** a simple form of image-projector using slides. —**magical** *adj.*, **magically** *adv.* [f. OF f. L f. Gk (as MAGUS)]

magician /mə'dʒɪʃ(ə)n/ *n.* **1** one skilled in magic. **2** a conjuror. [as prec.]

magisterial /mædʒɪ'stɪərɪəl/ *adj.* **1** imperious; having authority. **2** of a magistrate. —**magisterially** *adv.* [f. L (as MASTER)]

magistracy /'mædʒɪstrəsɪ/ *n.* magisterial office; magistrates collectively. [f. foll.]

magistrate /'mædʒɪstreɪt/ *n.* a civil officer with authority to administer the law; a person conducting a court for minor cases and preliminary hearings. [f. L *magistratus* (as MAGISTERIAL)]

magma *n.* (*pl.* **-as** or **magmata**) a fluid or semi-fluid material under the earth's crust, from which igneous rock is formed by cooling. [L f. Gk (*massō* knead)]

magnanimous /mæg'nænɪməs/ *adj.* noble and generous in feelings or conduct, not petty. —**magnanimity** /-nə'nɪmɪtɪ/ *n.*, **magnanimously** *adv.* [f. L (*magnus* great, *animus* mind)]

magnate /'mægneɪt/ *n.* a wealthy and influential person, especially in business. [f. L *magnas* (*magnus* great)]

magnesia /mæg'ni:ʃə/ *n.* **1** magnesium oxide. **2** hydrated magnesium carbonate, used as an antacid and laxative. [f. *Magnesia* in Asia Minor]

magnesium /mæg'ni:zɪəm/ *n.* a silver-white metallic element of the alkaline-earth metal group, symbol Mg, atomic number 12. [f. prec.]

magnet /'mægnɪt/ *n.* **1** a piece of iron, steel, alloy, ore, etc., having the properties of attracting iron and of pointing approximately north and south when suspended; a loadstone. **2** a person or thing that attracts. [f. L f. Gk, = stone of Magnesia (as MAGNESIA)]

magnetic /mæg'netɪk/ *adj.* **1** having the properties of a magnet. **2** produced or acting by magnetism; capable of acquiring the properties of or of being attracted by a magnet. **3** strongly attractive. —**magnetic compass,** one using a magnetic needle. **magnetic needle,** an indicator made of magnetized steel, pointing north and south on the dial of a compass. **magnetic north,** the direction indicated by a magnetic needle, close to the geographical north but not identical with it. **magnetic pole,** the point near the north or south pole where a magnetic needle dips vertically. **magnetic storm,** a disturbance of the earth's magnetic field by charged particles from the sun etc. **magnetic tape,** a plastic strip coated or impregnated with magnetic particles for the recording and reproduction of signals. —**magnetically** *adv.* [as prec.]

magnetism /'mægnɪtɪz(ə)m/ *n.* **1** magnetic phenomena; the science of these; the natural agency producing them. **2** great charm and attraction. [f. prec.].

magnetize /'mægnɪtaɪz/ *v.t.* **1** to give magnetic properties to; to make into a magnet. **2** to attract (*lit.* or *fig.*) as a magnet does. —**magnetization** /-'zeɪʃ(ə)n/ *n.* [f. MAGNET]

magneto /mæg'ni:təʊ/ *n.* (*pl.* **-os**) an electric generator using permanent magnets (esp. for ignition in an internal-combustion engine). [abbr. of *magneto-electric* (comb. form of MAGNET, ELECTRIC)]

Magnificat /mæg'nɪfɪkæt/ *n.* a canticle, the song of praise (so called from the first word of the Latin text) in Luke 1:46–55 sung when the Virgin Mary was greeted by her cousin Elizabeth as the mother of the Lord. [L, = magnifies (i.e. extols)]

magnification /mægnɪfɪ'keɪʃ(ə)n/ *n.* magnifying; the amount of this. [f. MAGNIFY]

magnificent /mæg'nɪfɪs(ə)nt/ *adj.* **1** splendid in appearance etc.; sumptuously constructed or adorned; splendidly lavish. **2** (*colloq.*) excellent. —**magnificence** *n.*, **magnificently** *adv.* [F or f. L *magnificus* (*magnus* great, *facere* make)]

magnify /ˈmægnɪfaɪ/ *v.t.* **1** to make (a thing) appear larger than it is, as with a lens. **2** to exaggerate; to intensify. **3** (*archaic*) to extol. —**magnifying glass,** a lens used to magnify things. —**magnifier** *n.* [f. OF or L *magnificare* (as prec.)]

magnitude /ˈmægnɪtju:d/ *n.* **1** largeness; size. **2** importance. **3** a measure of the relative brightness of stars and other celestial objects. —**absolute magnitude,** the magnitude that a star would seem to have if at a distance of 10 parsecs or 32.6 light-years. **apparent magnitude,** as seen from the earth. [f. L *magnitudo* (*magnus* great)]

magnolia /mægˈnəʊlɪə/ *n.* a tree of the genus *Magnolia*, with dark-green foliage and waxlike flowers. [f. P. *Magnol*, French botanist (d. 1715)]

magnum /ˈmægnəm/ *n.* a bottle containing two reputed quarts of wine or spirits. [L, neut. of *magnus* great]

magnum opus /mægnəm ˈəʊpəs/ a great work of literature etc.; an author's greatest work. [L]

magpie /ˈmægpaɪ/ *n.* **1** a kind of crow (*Pica pica*) with black-and-white plumage and a long tail, reputed to collect objects. **2** a random collector. **3** a chatterer. [f. *Mag* abbr. of woman's name *Margaret* + PIE²]

magus /ˈmeɪgəs/ *n.* (*pl.* **magi** /-dʒaɪ/) a poet of ancient Persia; a sorcerer. —**the Magi,** the 'wise men' from the East who brought offerings to the infant Christ (Matt. 2: 1-12). [f. L f. Gk f. Pers.]

Magyar /ˈmægjɑ:(r)/ *n.* **1** a member of the people now predominant in Hungary. **2** the Hungarian language. —*adj.* of this people or their language. [native name]

maharaja /mɑ:həˈrɑ:dʒə/ *n.* (also **maharajah**) (*hist.*) the title of some Indian princes. [f. Hindi, = great rajah]

maharanee /mɑ:həˈrɑ:nɪ/ *n.* (also **maharani**) (*hist.*) a maharaja's wife or widow. [f. Hindi, = great ranee]

maharishi /mɑ:həˈrɪʃɪ/ *n.* a great Hindu sage. [f. Hindi]

mahatma /məˈhætmə/ *n.* (in India etc.) **1** a title of respect for a person regarded with reverence. **2** a member of a class of persons supposed by some Buddhists to have preternatural powers. [f. Skr., = great soul]

mah-jong /mɑ:ˈdʒɒŋ/ *n.* an old Chinese game resembling certain card-games, played usually by four persons using 136 or 144 pieces called *tiles*. [f. Chin. dial. *ma-tsiang* sparrows]

mahlstick /ˈmɑ:lstɪk/ var. of MAULSTICK.

mahogany /məˈhɒgənɪ/ *n.* **1** a reddish-brown wood, especially of a tropical American tree (*Swietenia majogani*), used for furniture. **2** its colour. **3** a tree yielding mahogany. [orig. unkn.]

mahout /məˈhaʊt/ *n.* (in India etc.) an elephant-driver. [f. Hindi f. Skr.]

maid *n.* **1** a female servant. **2** (*archaic*) a girl; a young woman. —**maid of all work,** a female servant doing general housework; a person doing many jobs. **maid of honour,** an unmarried lady attending a queen or princess; a kind of small custard tart; (*US*) a principal bridesmaid. [abbr. of foll.]

maiden /ˈmeɪd(ə)n/ *n.* **1** a girl, a young unmarried woman. **2** a maiden over. **3** a maiden horse. —*adj.* **1** unmarried. **2** (of a female animal) unmated. **3** (of a horse) that has never won a prize; (of a race) open only to such horses. **4** (of a speech, voyage, etc.) first. —**maiden name,** a woman's surname before marriage. **maiden over,** an over in cricket in which no runs are scored. —**maidenhood** *n.*, **maidenly** *adj.* [OE]

maidenhair *n.* a fern of the genus *Adiantum* with fine hairlike stalks and delicate fronds.

maidenhead *n.* virginity; the hymen.

maidservant *n.* a female servant.

mail¹ *n.* **1** matter conveyed by post; this system of conveyance; letters, parcels, etc., sent, collected, or delivered at one place on one occasion. **2** a vehicle carrying post. —*v.t.* to send by post. —**mail-bag** *n.* a large bag for carrying mail. **mailing list,** a list of persons to whom mail (esp. advertising matter) is to be posted. **mail order,** purchase of goods by post. [f. OF *male* wallet]

mail² *n.* armour composed of metal rings or plates. —**coat of mail,** a jacket or tunic covered with mail. [f. OF f. L *macula* spot, mesh]

maim *v.t.* to cripple, to disable, to mutilate. [f. OF *mahaignier*]

main *adj.* **1** principal, most important. **2** greatest in size or extent; exerted to the full. —*n.* **1** a principal channel, duct, etc., for water or sewage etc.; (usu in *pl.*) a principal cable for the supply of electricity. **2** (*archaic*) the mainland; the high seas. —**have an eye to the main chance,** to consider one's own interests. **in the main,** for the most part. **main brace,** a brace attached to the main yard. **main line,** an important railway line linking large cities. **main-topmast** *n.* the mast above the maintop. **main yard,** the yard on which the mainsail is extended. [f. ON & OE]

mainframe *n.* **1** the central processing unit of a computer. **2** (often *attrib.*) a large computer as distinct from a microcomputer etc.

mainland /ˈmeɪnlənd/ *n.* a large continuous extent of land, excluding neighbouring islands etc.

mainly *adv.* for the most part, chiefly. [f. MAIN]

mainmast *n.* the principal mast of a ship.

mainsail /ˈmeɪnseɪl/, -s(ə)l/ *n.* (in a square-rigged vessel) the lowest sail on a mainmast; (in a fore-and-aft rigged vessel) a sail set on the after part of a mainmast.

mainspring *n.* **1** the principal spring of a watch, clock, etc. **2** a chief motivating force or initiative.

mainstay *n.* **1** the chief support. **2** the stay from the maintop to the foot of the foremast.

mainstream *n.* **1** the principal current of a river etc. **2** the prevailing trend of opinion, fashion, etc.

maintain /meɪnˈteɪn/ *v.t.* **1** to cause to continue; to continue one's action in; to keep in existence. **2** to take action to preserve (a machine, house, etc.) in good order. **3** to support, to provide sustenance for; to provide means for. **4** to assert as true. —**maintained school,** a school supported from public funds. [f. OF *maintenir* f. L *manu tenēre* hold in the hand]

maintenance /ˈmeɪntɪnəns/ *n.* **1** maintaining, being maintained. **2** keeping equipment etc. in repair. **3** provision of the means to support life; an allowance of money for this. [as prec.]

maintop *n.* a platform above the head of the lower mainmast.

maisonette /meɪzəˈnet/ *n.* **1** part of a house let or used separately (usually not all one one floor). **2** a small house. [f. F, dim. of *maison* house]

maize *n.* **1** a cereal plant (*Zea mays*) of North American origin. **2** the grain of this. **3** the yellow colour of its ripe cobs. [f. F or Sp., of Carib orig.]

majestic /məˈdʒestɪk/ *adj.* stately and dignified, imposing. —**majestically** *adv.* [f. foll.]

majesty /ˈmædʒɪstɪ/ *n.* **1** impressive stateliness. **2** sovereign power. —**Christ in Majesty,** a representation of Christ enthroned within an aureole. **His, Her, Your,** etc., **Majesty,** a title used in addressing or referring to a king or queen or a sovereign's wife or widow. [f. OF f. L *majestas* (as MAJOR)]

majolica /məˈjɒlɪkə, -ˈdʒɒl-/ *n.* Italian earthenware of the Renaissance period with coloured ornamentation on white enamel; a modern imitation of this. [f. It., f. former name of *Majorca*, ships of which brought Spanish wares to Italy]

major /ˈmeɪdʒə(r)/ *adj.* **1** greater or relatively great in size or importance. **2** of full legal age. **3** (*Mus.*, of a scale) having intervals of a semitone above its third and seventh notes; (of an interval) normal or perfect (cf. MINOR); (of a key) based on a major scale. —*n.* **1** an army officer next below lieutenant-colonel. **2** an officer in charge of a section of band instruments. **3** a person of full legal age. **4** (*US*) a student's special course or subject. —*v.i.* (*US*) to specialize (in a subject). —**major-general** *n.* an army officer next below lieutenant-general. [f. L, compar. of *magnus* great]

major-domo /meɪdʒəˈdəʊməʊ/ *n.* (*pl.* **-os**) the chief steward of a great household; a house-steward, a butler. [f. Sp. & It. f. L *major domus* highest official of household]

majority /məˈdʒɒrɪtɪ/ *n.* **1** the greater number or part of a group etc. **2** the number by which votes for the winning party etc. exceed those for the next or for all others combined; the party etc. receiving a majority of votes. **3** full legal age (in Britain, since 1970 the age of 18 years, formerly 21 years). **4** the rank of major. —**majority rule,** the principle that the greater number should exercise the greater power. [f. F f. L (as MAJOR)]

majuscule /ˈmædʒəskju:l/ *adj.* (of lettering) large; written in large lettering. —*n.* large lettering; a large letter, whether capital or uncial. [F f. L *majuscula* (*littera* letter), dim. of MAJOR]

make *v.t./i* (*past* & *p.p.* MADE) **1** to construct, create, or prepare from parts or other substances. **2** to bring about, to cause to exist, to give rise to. **3** to frame in the mind. **4** to draw up as a legal document etc. **5** to establish (a distinction, rule, or law). **6** to gain or acquire. **7** to secure the advancement or success of. **8** to cause to be or become or seem. **9** to cause or compel (to). **10** to proceed, to act as if intending (to). **11** to perform (an action etc.). **12** to consider to be, to estimate as. **13** to constitute, to amount to. **14** to serve for, to be adequate as; to form or be reckoned as; to bring to (a chosen value etc.). **15** to accomplish or achieve (a distance, speed, score, etc.); to achieve a place in (a team, prize-list, etc.); to arrive at, to come in sight of; (*slang*) to catch (a train etc.). —*n.* **1** the way a thing is made. **2** the origin of manufacture, a brand. —**make away with,** to get rid of; to kill; to squander. **make believe,** to pretend. **make-believe** *adj.* pretended; (*n.*) pretence. **make a day** *or* **night** etc. **of it,** to devote a whole day etc. to an activity or relaxation. **make do,** to manage with the limited or inadequate means available. **make for,** to conduce to; to proceed towards (a place); to attack. **make good,** to repay, repair, or compensate for; to achieve (a purpose), to be successful. **make the grade,** to succeed. **make it,** to achieve one's purpose, to be successful. **make much (***or* **little) of,** to treat as important (or unimportant). **make nothing of,** to treat as trifling; to be unable to understand or use or deal with. **make off,** to depart hastily. **make off with,** to carry away, to steal. **make or break,** to cause the success or ruin of; to be crucial for. **make out,** to discern or understand; to fare or progress; to write out (a document etc.) or fill in (a form); to prove or try to prove to be; to pretend or claim. **make over,** to transfer possession of; to refashion or convert to a new purpose. **make time,** to contrive to find time to do something. **make up,** to put or get together; to prepare, to invent (a story etc.); to compensate (for); to complete (an amount originally deficient); to form or constitute; to apply cosmetics (to). **make (it) up** to be reconciled. **make-up** *n.* cosmetics; the way a thing is made or composed; character or temperament. **make up to,** to court, to curry favour with. **on the make,** (*slang*) intent on gain. [OE]

maker *n.* **1** one who makes something. **2 our Maker,** God. [f. MAKE]

makeshift *n.* a temporary substitute or device. —*adj.* serving as this.

makeweight *n.* **1** a small quantity added to make up the weight. **2** a person or thing supplying a deficiency.

making *n.* **1** (in *pl.*) earnings, profits. **2** (in *pl.*) the essential qualities for becoming. —**be the making of,** to be the main factor in the success or favourable development of. **in the making,** in the course of being made or formed. [OE (as MAKE)]

mal- /mæl-/ *prefix* bad (*malpractice*); badly (*maltreat*); faulty (*malfunction*); not (*maladroit*). [f. F *mal* badly f. L *male*]

Malacca cane /məˈlækə/ a rich-brown cane from the stem of the palm-tree *Calamus rotang*, used for walking-sticks etc. [f. *Malacca* State and city of Malaysia]

malachite /ˈmæləkaɪt/ *n.* a green mineral used for ornament. [f. OF f. L f. Gk *molokhitis* (*molokhē* mallow)]

maladjusted /mæləˈdʒʌstɪd/ *adj.* (of a person) not satisfactorily adjusted to his or her environment and conditions of life. —**maladjustment** *n.*

maladminister /mælədˈmɪnɪstə(r)/ *v.t.* to manage badly or improperly. —**maladministration** /-ˈstreɪʃ(ə)n/ *n.*

maladroit /mæləˈdrɔɪt, ˈmæ-/ *adj.* clumsy, bungling. —**maladroitly** *adv.*, **maladroitness** *n.* [F (as MAL-, ADROIT)]

malady /ˈmælədɪ/ *n.* a disease or ailment (*lit.* or *fig.*). [f. OF (*malade* sick)]

Malagasy /mæləˈgæsɪ/ *adj.* of Madagascar or its people or language. —*n.* **1** a native or inhabitant of Madagascar. **2** the language of Madagascar. [orig. *Malegass*, f. *Madagascar*]

malaise /mæˈleɪz/ *n.* bodily discomfort, especially without the development of a specific disease; an uneasy feeling. [F (as MAL-, EASE)]

malapropism /ˈmæləprɒpɪz(ə)m/ *n.* a ludicrous misuse of a word especially in mistake for one resembling it (e.g. *it will percussion the blow* for *cushion the blow*). [f. Mrs *Malaprop* (f. foll.) in Sheridan's *The Rivals*]

malapropos /mælæprəˈpəʊ/ *adv.* & *adj.* inopportunely said, done, or happening. [f. F *mal à propos* (*mal* ill, *à propos* to the purpose)]

malaria /məˈleərɪə/ *n.* a recurrent fever caused by a protozoan parasite of the genus *Plasmodium*, transmitted from infected persons by the bite of a female *Anopheles* mosquito after developing in the body of this insect. —**malarial** *adj.* [f. It. *mala aria* bad air, the unwholesome condition of the atmosphere which results from the exhalations of marshy districts, to which the disease was formerly attributed]

malarkey /məˈlɑːkɪ/ *n.* (*slang*) humbug, nonsense. [orig. unkn.]

malathion /mæləˈθaɪən/ *n.* an insecticide containing phosphorous and relatively harmless to plants and animals. [f. chemical name]

malcontent /ˈmælkəntent/ *n.* a discontented person. —*adj.* discontented. [F (as MAL-, CONTENT[2])]

male *adj.* **1** of the sex that can beget offspring by performing the fertilizing function; (of plants or flowers) containing stamens but no pistil; of men or male animals or plants. **2** (of parts of machinery etc.) designed to enter or fill a corresponding hollow part. —*n.* a male person or animal. [f. OF *ma(s)le* f. L *masculus*]

malediction /mælɪˈdɪkʃ(ə)n/ *n.* a curse; the uttering of a curse. —**maledictory** *adj.* [f. L (*male* ill, *dicere* speak)]

malefactor /ˈmælɪfæktə(r)/ *n.* a criminal; an evil-doer. —**malefaction** /-ˈfækʃ(ə)n/ *n.* [f. L (*male* ill, *facere* do)]

malevolent /məˈlevələnt/ *adj.* wishing ill to others. —**malevolence** *adj.* [f. OF or L (*male* ill, *volens* willing)]

malfeasance /mælˈfiːzəns/ *n.* misconduct, especially in an official capacity. [f. AF (MAL-, *faire* do)]

malformation /mælfɔːˈmeɪʃ(ə)n/ *n.* faulty formation. —**malformed** /-ˈfɔːmd/ *adj.*

malfunction /mælˈfʌŋkʃ(ə)n/ *n.* a failure to function in the normal manner. —*v.i.* to function faultily.

malice /ˈmælɪs/ *n.* desire to harm or cause difficulty to others, ill-will; (*Law*) harmful intent. [f. OF f. L *malitia* (*malus* bad)]

malicious /məˈlɪʃəs/ *adj.* feeling, showing, or arising from malice. —**maliciously** *adv.*, **maliciousness** *n.* [f. prec.]

malign /məˈlaɪn/ *adj.* **1** harmful; (of a disease) malignant. **2** malevolent. —*v.t.* to slander, to speak ill of. —**malignity** /-ˈlɪgnɪtɪ/ *n.* [f. OF or L *malignus* (*malus* bad)]

malignant /məˈlɪgnənt/ *adj.* **1** (of a tumour) tending to spread and to recur after removal, cancerous. **2** (of a disease) very virulent. **3** feeling or showing intense ill-will. **4** harmful. —**malignancy** *n.*, **malignantly** *adv.* [f. L *malignare* (as prec.)]

malinger /məˈlɪŋgə(r)/ *v.i.* to pretend to be ill to escape a duty. —**malingerer** *n.* [f. F *malingre* sickly]

mall /mæl, mɔːl/ *n.* a sheltered walk or promenade. [var. of MAUL, used of the hammer in the croquet-like game of pall-mall; applied to *The Mall* in London, orig. an alley where this game was played]

mallard /ˈmælɑːd/ *n.* (*pl.* same) a kind of wild duck (*Anas boscas*) of which the male has a green head. [f. OF (prob. as MALE)]

malleable /ˈmælɪəb(ə)l/ *adj.* **1** (of a metal etc.) that can be shaped by hammering. **2** adaptable, pliable. —**malleability** /-ˈbɪlɪtɪ/ *n.* [f. OF f. L (*malleare* to hammer, as MALLET)]

mallet /ˈmælɪt/ *n.* **1** a hammer, usually of wood. **2** a similarly shaped implement with a long handle, for striking the ball in croquet or polo. [f. OF *maillet* (*mail* hammer f. L *malleus*)]

mallow /ˈmæləʊ/ *n.* a flowering plant of the genus *Malva*, with purple, pink, or white flowers and hairy stems and leaves. [OE f. L *malva*]

malmsey /ˈmɑːmzɪ/ *n.* a sweet fortified wine made in Madeira, Cyprus, the Canary Islands, etc., from a kind of grape which came originally from the eastern Mediterranean. [f. MDu. or MLG f. *Monemvasia* in Greece]

malnutrition /mælnjuːˈtrɪʃ(ə)n/ *n.* insufficient nutrition; a condition where the diet omits some foods that are necessary for health.

malodorous /mælˈəʊdərəs/ *adj.* evil-smelling.

malpractice /mælˈpræktɪs/ *n.* **1** wrong-doing; an illegal action for one's own benefit while in a position of trust. **2** the improper or negligent treatment of a patient by a physician.

malt /mɔːlt, mɒlt/ *n.* **1** grain (usually barley) prepared by steeping, germination, and drying, for brewing etc. **2** (*colloq.*) malt liquor; malt whisky. —*v.t.* to convert (grain) into malt. —**malted milk**, a drink made from dried milk and extract of malt. **malt whisky**, whisky made entirely of malted barley. [OE]

Maltese /mɔːlˈtiːz, mɒl-/ *adj.* of Malta or its people or language. —*n.* **1** a native or inhabitant of Malta. **2** the Semitic language of Malta. —**Maltese cross**, a cross with the arms broadening outwards, often indented at the ends. [f. MALTA]

maltreat /mælˈtriːt/ *v.t.* to ill-treat. —**maltreatment** *n.*

malversation /mælvəˈseɪʃ(ə)n/ *n.* corrupt behaviour in a position of trust; corrupt administration of public money etc. [F (*malverser* f. L *male* badly, *versari* behave)]

mama var. of MAMMA.

mamba /ˈmæmbə/ *n.* a kind of venomous African snake of the genus *Dendroaspis*. [f. Zulu *m'namba*]

mamma /məˈmɑː/ *n.* (*archaic*) mother. [imit. of child's *ma, ma*]

mammal /ˈmæm(ə)l/ *n.* a vertebrate of the class Mammalia, characterized by secretion of milk by the female to feed the young. —**mammalian** /məˈmeɪlɪən/ *adj.* & *n.* [f. L *mammalis* (*mamma* breast)]

mammary /ˈmæmərɪ/ *adj.* of the breasts. [as prec.]

Mammon /ˈmæmən/ *n.* wealth regarded as an idol or evil influence. [f. L f. Gk f. Aram.]

mammoth /ˈmæməθ/ *n.* a large extinct elephant of the genus *Mammuthus*, with a hairy coat and curved tusks. —*adj.* huge. [f. Russ.]

man *n.* (*pl.* **men**) **1** a creature of the genus *Homo*, distinguished from other animals by superior mental development, power of articulate speech, and upright stance; (*collect.*) the human race, mankind. **2** an adult human male. **3** a person of a particular type or historical period. **4** (in indefinite or general application, without specification of sex) a person. **5** an individual person, especially in the role of assistant, opponent, or expert, or considered in terms of suitability. **6** a husband. **7** (usu. in *pl.*) an employee, a workman. **8** (usu. in *pl.*) a member of the armed forces, especially of those not officers. **9** (*colloq.*) as a form of address. **10** one of a set of objects used in playing chess, draughts, etc. —*v.t.* (**-nn-**) to supply with a man or manpower for service or to operate something. —**as one man**, in unison. **be one's own man**, to be independent. **man about town**, a fashionable socializer. **man-at-arms** *n.* (*pl.* **men-at-arms**) (*archaic*) a soldier. **man-hour** *n.* the work done by one person in one hour. **man-hunt** *n.* an organized search for a person (especially a criminal). **man in the street**, an ordinary average man. **man-made** *adj.* artificially made. **man-of-war** *n.* (*pl.* **men-of-war**) an armed ship of a country's navy. **man of the world**, see WORLD. **man-sized** *adj.* of the size of a man; adequate to a man, large. **man to man**, candidly. **to a man**, without exception. —**mannish** *adj.* [OE]

-man /-mən/ *suffix* (*pl.* **-men**) denoting a man concerned with (*clergyman*), or skilful with (*oarsman*), or describable as (*Welshman*). [= prec.]

manacle /ˈmænək(ə)l/ *n.* (usu. in *pl.*) **1** a fetter for the hand, a handcuff. **2** a restraint. —*v.t.*

to fetter with manacles. [f. OF f. L *manicula* (*manus* hand)]

manage /ˈmænɪdʒ/ *v.t./i.* **1** to organize or regulate; to be the manager of (a business etc.). **2** to succeed in achieving, to contrive; to succeed with limited resources or means, to be able to cope (with). **3** to secure the co-operation of (a person) by tact, flattery, etc. **4** to have under effective control. **5** to use or wield (a tool etc.) effectively. [f. It. *maneggiare* f. L *manus* hand]

manageable /ˈmænɪdʒəb(ə)l/ *adj.* that may be managed. [f. prec.]

management *n.* **1** managing, being managed. **2** the administration of business concerns or public undertakings; persons engaged in this. [f. MANAGE]

manager *n.* **1** a person conducting a business, institution, etc.; a person controlling the activities of a person or team in sport, entertainment, etc. **2** a person who manages money, household affairs, etc., in a specified way. —**manageress** /-ˈres/ *n.fem.*, **managerial** /mænəˈdʒɪərɪəl/ *adj.* [as prec.]

mañana /mənˈjɑːnə/ *n.* & *adv.* tomorrow (as a symbol of easy-going procrastination); the indefinite future. [Sp.]

manatee /mænəˈtiː/ *n.* a large tropical aquatic mammal of the genus *Trichechus*, feeding on plants. [f. Sp. f. Carib.]

Mancunian /mæŋˈkjuːnɪən/ *adj.* of Manchester. —*n.* a native or inhabitant of Manchester. [f. L *Mancunium* Roman settlement on site of Manchester]

mandala /ˈmændələ/ *n.* a circular figure as a religious symbol of the universe. [f. Skr.]

mandamus /mænˈdeɪməs/ *n.* a judicial writ issued as a command to an inferior court, or ordering a person to perform a public or statutory duty. [L, = we command]

mandarin /ˈmændərɪn/ *n.* **1** an influential person, especially a reactionary or secretive bureaucrat. **2** (*hist.*) a Chinese official. **3** Mandarin, the language formerly used by officials and educated persons in China; any of the varieties of this spoken as a common language in China, especially the Northern variety. **4** a small flat orange with a loose skin. [f. Port. f. Malay ult. f. Skr. *mantrin* counsellor]

mandatary /ˈmændətərɪ/ *n.* a holder or receiver of a mandate. [f. L (as foll.)]

mandate /ˈmændeɪt/ *n.* **1** authority to act for another; the political authority supposed to be given by the electors to a government. **2** a judicial or legal command from a superior. —/mænˈdeɪt/ *v.t.* **1** to give authority to (a delegate). **2** to commit (a territory) to a mandatary. [f. L *mandatum* (*mandare* command, entrust)]

mandatory /ˈmændətərɪ/ *adj.* compulsory; of or conveying a command. —**mandatorily** *adv.* [f. L (as prec.)]

mandible /ˈmændɪb(ə)l/ *n.* a jaw, especially the lower jaw in mammals and fishes; the upper or lower part of a bird's beak; either half of the crushing organ in the mouth-parts of an insect etc. [f. OF or L *mandibula* (*mandere* chew)]

mandolin /ˈmænd(ə)lɪn/ *n.* a plucked stringed instrument of the lute family with metal strings tuned in pairs and a characteristic tremolo when sustaining long notes. [F f. It.]

mandorla /mænˈdɔːlə/ *n.* = VESICA. [It., = almond]

mandragora /mænˈdrægərə/ *n.* the mandrake, especially as a narcotic (Shakespeare *Othello* III. iii. 330). [f. L F. Gk (as foll.)]

mandrake /ˈmændreɪk/ *n.* a plant of the genus *Mandragora*, with white or purple flowers and a large yellow fruit, having emetic and narcotic properties. [prob. f. MDu., ult. f. Gk *mandragoras*, assoc. w. MAN, *drake* dragon]

mandrel /ˈmændr(ə)l/ *n.* **1** a lathe-shaft to which work is fixed while being turned. **2** a cylindrical rod round which metal or other material is forged or shaped. [orig. unkn.]

mandrill /ˈmændrɪl/ *n.* a kind of large baboon (*Mandrillus sphinx*) of West Africa, with highly coloured patches and callosities on its face and hindquarters. [prob. f. MAN + DRILL[4]]

mane *n.* **1** the long hair on the neck of an animal, especially a horse or lion. **2** the long hair of a person. [OE]

manège /məˈneɪʒ/ *n.* **1** a riding-school. **2** horsemanship. **3** the movements of a trained horse. [F f. It. (as MANAGE)]

manful *adj.* brave, resolute. —**manfully** *adv.* [f. MAN + -FUL]

manganese /ˈmæŋgəniːz/ *n.* **1** a hard grey metallic element, symbol Mn, atomic number 25. **2** an oxide of this, a black mineral used in glass-making etc. [f. F f. It., f. MAGNESIA]

mange /meɪndʒ/ *n.* a skin disease in hairy and woolly animals. [f. OF *mangeue* itch (*mangier* eat f. L *manducare* chew)]

mangel-wurzel /ˈmæŋg(ə)l wɜːz(ə)l/ *n.* a large beet used as cattle food. [G (*mangold* beet, *wurzel* root)]

manger /ˈmeɪndʒə(r)/ *n.* a long open box or trough for horses or cattle to eat from. [f. OF *mangeoire* f. L (as MANGE)]

mangle[1] /ˈmæŋg(ə)l/ *v.t.* **1** to hack or mutilate by blows; to cut roughly so as to disfigure. **2** to spoil (a text etc.) by gross blunders. [f. AF *ma(ha)ngler* (app. as MAIM)]

mangle[2] /ˈmæŋg(ə)l/ *n.* a machine of two or more cylinders for squeezing water from and pressing washed clothes etc. —*v.t.* to press (clothes) in a mangle. [f. Du., ult. f. Gk *magganon* pulley]

mango /ˈmæŋgəʊ/ *n.* (*pl.* **-oes**) a tropical fruit with yellowish flesh; the tree (*Mangifera indica*) bearing this. [f. Port. f. Malay f. Tamil]

mangold /ˈmæŋg(ə)ld/ *n.* = MANGEL-WURZEL. [G, = beet]

mangrove /ˈmæŋgrəʊv/ *n.* a tropical tree or shrub of the genus *Rhizophora*, growing in shore-mud with many tangled roots above ground. [orig. unkn.; assim. to GROVE]

mangy /ˈmeɪndʒɪ/ *adj.* **1** having mange. **2** squalid, shabby. [f. MANGE]

manhandle *v.t.* **1** to move by human effort alone. **2** to treat roughly.

manhole *n.* an opening (usually with a lid) through which a person can enter a sewer, conduit, etc., to inspect or repair it.

manhood *n.* **1** the state of being a man. **2** manliness, courage. **3** the men of a country. [f. MAN + -HOOD]

mania /ˈmeɪnɪə/ *n.* **1** violent madness. **2** extreme enthusiasm. [f. L f. Gk, = madness (*mainomai* be mad)]

-mania /-meɪnɪə/ *suffix* forming nouns denoting a special type of mental disorder (*megalomania*), or enthusiasm or admiration. [as prec.]

maniac /ˈmeɪnɪæk/ *n.* a person affected with mania. —*adj.* of or affected with mania. [as MANIA]

-maniac /-meɪnɪæk/ *suffix* forming nouns with the sense 'a person affected with -mania' and adjectives with the sense 'affected with -mania'. [as prec.]

maniacal /məˈnaɪək(ə)l/ *adj.* of or like a mania or a maniac. —**maniacally** *adv.* [as MANIA]

manic /ˈmænɪk/ *adj.* of or affected with mania. —**manic-depressive** *adj.* relating to a mental disorder with alternating periods of elation and depression; (*n.*) a person having such a disorder. [f. MANIA]

manicure /ˈmænɪkjʊə(r)/ *n.* cosmetic treatment of the hands and finger-nails. —*v.t.* to apply such treatment to. —**manicurist** *n.* [F f. L *manus* hand, *cura* care]

manifest /ˈmænɪfest/ *adj.* clear and unmistakable. —*v.t./i.* **1** to show clearly, to give signs of; to make or become apparent or visible. **2** to be evidence of, to prove. **3** to record in a manifest. —*n.* a list of cargo or passengers carried by a ship or aircraft etc. —**manifestation** /-ˈsteɪʃ(ə)n/ *n.*, **manifestly** *adv.* [f. OF or L *manifestus*]

manifesto /mænɪˈfestəʊ/ *n.* (*pl.* **-os**) a public declaration of policy, especially by a political party. [It. (as prec.)]

manifold /ˈmænɪfəʊld/ *adj.* **1** many and various. **2** having various forms, applications, component parts, etc. —*n.* **1** a pipe or chamber (in a piece of a mechanism) with several openings. **2** a manifold thing. [OE (as MANY, -FOLD)]

manikin /ˈmænɪkɪn/ *n.* a little man, a dwarf. [f. Du. dim. (as MAN)]

manila /məˈnɪlə/ *n.* (also **manilla**) **1** the strong fibre of a Philippine tree (*Musa textilis*). **2** a brown paper originally made from this, used esp. for envelopes. [f. *Manila*, capital of the Philippines]

manioc /ˈmænɪɒk/ *n.* cassava; flour made from this. [f. Tupi *mandioca*]

maniple /ˈmænɪp(ə)l/ *n.* **1** a strip of material worn over the left arm by a priest celebrating the Eucharist. **2** a subdivision of a legion in the army of ancient Rome. [OF, or f. L *manipulus* handful, troop (*manus* hand)]

manipulable /məˈnɪpjʊləb(ə)l/ *adj.* that may be manipulated. [f. foll.]

manipulate /məˈnɪpjʊleɪt/ *v.t.* **1** to handle, manage, or use (a thing) skilfully. **2** to examine manually and treat (a part of the body) for a fracture etc. **3** to arrange or influence cleverly or unfairly. —**manipulation** /—ˈleɪʃ(ə)n/ *n.*, **manipulator** *n.* [f. F. *manipuler* f. L *manipulus* (see MANIPLE)]

mankind /mænˈkaɪnd/ *n.* **1** human beings in general, the human species. **2** /ˈmæn-/ men in general.

manly *adj.* having the qualities associated with a man (e.g. strength and courage); befitting a man. —**manliness** *n.* [f. MAN]

manna /ˈmænə/ *n.* **1** a substance miraculously supplied as food to the Israelites in the wilderness (Exod. 16). **2** something unexpected and delightful. [OE ult. f. Heb., prob. = Arab. *mann* exudation of tamarisk]

manned *adj.* (of a spacecraft etc.) having a human crew. (f. MAN]

mannequin /ˈmænɪkɪn/ *n.* **1** a person, usually a woman, employed by a dress designer etc. to model clothes. **2** a dummy for the display of clothes in a shop. [F, = MANIKIN]

manner /ˈmænə(r)/ *n.* **1** the way a thing is done or happens. **2** a person's bearing or way of behaving towards others, style of speaking, etc. **3** (in *pl.*) modes of life, conditions of society. **4** (in *pl.*) social behaviour; polite social behaviour. **5** style in literature or art. **6** kind, sort. —**all manner of**, every kind of. **comedy of manners**, a comedy with satirical portrayal of the manners of society. **in a manner of speaking**, in some sense, to some extent, so to speak. [f. AF f. L *manuarius* (*manus* hand)]

mannered *adj.* **1** behaving in a specified way (*ill-*, *well-mannered*). **2** full of mannerisms. [f. prec.]

mannerism /ˈmænərɪz(ə)m/ *n.* **1** a distinctive

gesture or feature of style; excessive use of these in art etc. **2** a style of Italian art of the 16th c. —**mannerist** *n.* [f. MANNER]

mannerly *adj.* well-behaved, polite. [as prec.]

manœuvre /məˈnuːvə(r)/ *n.* **1** a planned and controlled movement of a vehicle or body of troops etc.; (in *pl.*) large-scale exercises of troops or ships. **2** a deceptive or elusive movement; a skilful plan. —*v.t./i.* **1** to move (a thing, esp. a vehicle) carefully. **2** to perform manœuvres; to cause (troops or ships) to do this. **3** to guide skilfully or craftily. [f. F f. L *man(u)operari* work by hand (*manus* hand, *operari* to work)]

manometer /məˈnɒmɪtə(r)/ *n.* a pressure-gauge for gases and liquids. [f. F f. Gk *manos* thin + -METER]

manor /ˈmænə(r)/ *n.* **1** a large landed estate or its house (also **manor-house**). **2** (*hist.*) a territorial unit under the feudal control of a lord. **3** (*slang*) an area for which a police unit is responsible. —**manorial** /məˈnɔːrɪəl/ *adj.* [f. AF f. L *manēre* remain]

manpower *n.* the number of persons available for work or military service.

manqué /ˈmɑ̃keɪ/ *adj.* (placed after a noun) that might have been but is not. [F (*manquer* lack)]

mansard /ˈmænsɑːd/ *n.* a roof with each face having two slopes, with the steeper one below. [f. F. *Mansart*, French architect (d. 1666)]

manse *n.* an ecclesiastical residence, especially a Scottish Presbyterian minister's house. [f. L (as MANOR)]

manservant *n.* (*pl.* **menservants**) a male servant.

mansion /ˈmænʃ(ə)n/ *n.* a large grand house. —**the Mansion House**, the official residence of the Lord Mayor in the City of London. [f. OF f. L (as MANOR)]

manslaughter *n.* the unlawful killing of a human being without intentional malice.

mantel /ˈmænt(ə)l/ *n.* **1** a structure of wood or marble etc. above and around a fireplace. **2** a mantelpiece. [var. of MANTLE]

mantelpiece *n.* a shelf over a fireplace.

mantilla /mænˈtɪlə/ *n.* a lace scarf worn esp. by Spanish women over the hair and shoulders. [Sp. (as MANTLE)]

mantis /ˈmæntɪs/ *n.* (in full **praying mantis**) a predacious insect (*Mantis religiosa*) that holds its forelegs in a position suggesting hands folded in prayer. [Gk, = prophet]

mantle *n.* **1** a loose sleeveless cloak; a covering. **2** a fragile tube fixed round a gas-jet to give an incandescent light. **3** a bird's back, scapulars, and wing-coverts, especially when these are of a distinctive colour. **4** the region between the earth's crust and its core. —*v.t.* to clothe in or as in a mantle; to conceal, to envelop. [f. OF f. L *mantellum*]

mantra /ˈmæntrə/ *n.* **1** a sacred syllable, word, or phrase (especially in Buddhism and Hinduism) believed to possess supernatural powers. **2** a Vedic hymn. [Skr., = instrument of thought (*man* think)]

mantrap *n.* a trap for catching trespassers etc.

manual /ˈmænjʊəl/ *adj.* of or done with the hands; worked by hand, not by automatic equipment. —*n.* **1** a handbook; a reference book. **2** an organ keyboard played with the hands not the feet. —**manually** *adv.* [f. OF f. L *manualis* (*manus* hand)]

manufacture /mænjʊˈfæktʃə(r)/ *v.t.* **1** to produce (articles) by labour, especially by machinery on a large scale. **2** to invent or fabricate (evidence or a story etc.). —*n.* the manufacturing of articles; a branch of such an industry. —**manufacturer** *n.* [F f. It. & L (*manu facere* make by hand)]

manure /məˈnjʊə(r)/ *n.* a fertilizer, especially dung. —*v.t.* to apply manure to (land). [f. AF (as MANŒUVRE)]

manuscript /ˈmænjʊskrɪpt/ *n.* **1** a book or document written by hand. **2** an author's copy, written by hand or typed (not printed). **3** manuscript state. —*adj.* written by hand. [f. L (*manu scribere* write by hand)]

Manx /mæŋks/ *adj.* of the Isle of Man or its people or language. —*n.* the Celtic language of the Isle of Man, a dialect of Gaelic. —**the Manx**, the Manx people. **Manx cat**, a cat of a tailless variety. **Manxman** *n.* (*pl.* **-men**), **Manxwoman** *n.fem.* (*pl.* **-women**) [f. ON f. OIr. *Manu* Isle of Man]

many /ˈmenɪ/ *adj.* (*compar.* MORE, *superl.* MOST) great in number, numerous. —*n.pl.* many people or things. —**the many**, the multitude of people. **a good many**, a fair number. **a great many**, a large number. [OE]

Maoism /ˈmaʊɪz(ə)m/ *n.* the Communist doctrines of Mao Tse-tung. —**Maoist** *n.* [f. *Mao* Tse-tung (d. 1976)]

Maori /ˈmaʊrɪ/ *n.* **1** a member or the Polynesian language of the brown aboriginal people of New Zealand. **2** their Polynesian language. —*adj.* of the Maoris or their language. [native name]

map *n.* **1** a representation (usually on a flat surface) of the earth's surface or a part of it; a similar representation of the sky (showing the positions of stars etc.) or of the moon etc. **2** a diagram showing an arrangement or the components of a thing. —*v.t.* (**-pp-**) to represent on a map. —**map out**, to plan in detail. [f. L *mappa* napkin]

maple /ˈmeɪp(ə)l/ *n.* a kind of tree or shrub of the genus *Acer* grown for wood, ornament, shade, or sugar; its wood. —**maple-leaf** *n.* the emblem of Canada. **maple sugar**, a sugar obtained by evaporating the sap of some kinds of maple. **maple syrup,** a syrup made by evaporating maple sap or dissolving maple sugar. [f. OE]

maquette /mə'ket/ *n.* a preliminary model or sketch. [F f. It. (*macchia* spot)]

Maquis /'mæki:, 'mɑ:-/ *n.* a secret army of patriots in France during the German occupation in 1940-5; a member of this. [F, = brushwood, scrub (traditionally used as a refuge by fugitives)]

mar *v.t.* (**-rr-**) to spoil, to disfigure, to impair the perfection of. [OE]

Mar. *abbr.* March.

marabou /'mærəbu:/ *n.* a kind of stork (*Leptoptilus crumeniferus*); its down as a trimming etc. [F, f. Arab. = holy man (the stork being regarded as holy)]

maraca /mə'rækə/ *n.* a clublike gourd containing beans, beads, etc., held in the hand and shaken (usually in pairs) as a musical instrument. [f. Port., prob. f. Tupi]

maraschino /mærə'ski:nəʊ/ *n.* (*pl.* **-os**) a sweet liqueur made from cherries. —**maraschino cherry,** a cherry preserved in this. [It. (*marasca* small black cherry f. *amaro* bitter)]

marathon /'mærəθən/ *n.* a long-distance foot-race over roads, especially of 26 miles 385 yards (42.195 km) as a principal event of modern Olympic Games. It is named after Marathon in Greece, where the Athenians in 490 BC successfully defeated an invading Persian army; news of the victory was announced in Athens by an unnamed courier who ran all the way from the field of battle and fell dead on arrival. **2** a feat of endurance; an undertaking of long duration.

maraud /mə'rɔ:d/ *v.t./i.* to make a plundering raid (on); to go about pilfering. —**marauder** *n.* [f. F *marauder* (*maraud* rogue)]

marble *n.* **1** a kind of limestone able to take a high polish, used in sculpture and architecture. **2** this as a type of hardness or durability or smoothness (often *attrib.*). **3** (in *pl.*) a collection of sculptures. **4** a small ball of glass etc. as a toy; (in *pl.*) a game using these. —*v.t.* to stain or colour to look like variegated marble. [f. OF f. L *marmor* f. Gk]

marbled *adj.* **1** looking like variegated marble. **2** (of meat) streaked with fat. [f. MARBLE]

marcasite /'mɑ:kəsaɪt/ *n.* crystalline iron sulphide; a piece of this as an ornament. [f. L f. Arab. f. Pers.]

March *n.* the third month of the year. —**mad as a March hare,** a proverb referring to the seemingly insane antics of male hares in the breeding season (March), when they are seen bucking on stiff legs, boxing each other standing on hind legs, etc. [f. OF f. L *Martius* (*mensis* month) of Mars]

march[1] *v.t./i.* **1** to walk in a military manner with a regular and measured tread; to advance thus. **2** to walk purposefully. **3** (of events) to proceed steadily. **4** to cause to march or walk. —*n.* **1** the marching of troops; the uniform step of troops etc.; the distance covered by marching troops etc. **2** a long toilsome walk. **3** a procession as a protest or demonstration. **4** a piece of music meant to accompany a march. —**marching orders,** a command to troops to depart for war etc.; a dismissal. **march past,** the marching of troops in line past a saluting-point at a review. —**marcher** *n.* [f. F *marcher* f. L *marcus* hammer]

march[2] *n.* (*hist.*) **1** a boundary or frontier (often in *pl.*, esp. of the borderland between England and Scotland or Wales). **2** a tract of land, often disputed, between two countries. —*v.i.* (of countries, estates, etc.) to have a common frontier, to border. [f. OF (as MARK)]

marchioness /'mɑ:ʃənɪs, -'nes/ *n.* a marquis's wife or widow; a woman holding the rank of a marquis in her own right. [f. L (*marchio* captain of the marches, as prec.)]

mare[1] /meə(r)/ *n.* the female of a horse or related animal. —**mare's nest,** an illusory discovery. **mare's tail,** a slender perennial marsh plant (*Hippuris vulgaris*); (in *pl.*) long straight streaks of cirrus cloud. [OE]

mare[2] /'mɑ:rɪ/ *n.* (*pl.* **maria** /'mɑ:rɪə/) a large flat area on the moon, once thought to be a sea. [L, = sea]

margarine /mɑ:dʒə'ri:n, mɑ:g-/ *n.* a substance used like butter, made from animal or vegetable fats. [F, ult. f. Gk *margaron* pearl]

marge *n.* (*colloq.*) margarine. [abbr.]

margin /'mɑ:dʒɪn/ *n.* **1** an edge or border of a surface. **2** a plain space beside the main body of print etc. on a page. **3** an extra amount (of time, money, etc.) over and above the necessary or minimum; a sum deposited with a stockbroker to cover the risk of loss on a transaction. **4** a condition near the limit below or beyond which a thing ceases to be possible. —*v.t.* to furnish with a margin or with marginal notes. —**margin of error,** the difference allowed for miscalculation or mischance. [f. L *margo*]

marginal /'mɑ:dʒɪn(ə)l/ *adj.* **1** written in a margin. **2** of or at an edge. **3** (of a constituency) having an elected MP with only a small majority that may be lost at the next election. **4** close to the limit, especially of no profit, barely adequate or provided for. —**marginal cost,** the cost of producing one extra item of output. —**marginally** *adv.* [f. L (as prec.)]

marginalia /mɑ:dʒɪ'neɪlɪə/ *n.pl.* marginal notes. [L (as prec.)]

marguerite /mɑːɡəˈriːt/ *n.* an ox-eye daisy or similar flower. [F, f. L *margarita* pearl f. Gk]

maria *pl.* of MARE².

marigold /ˈmærɪɡəʊld/ *n.* any of various plants, especially of the genus *Calendula* or *Tagetes*, with golden or bright yellow flowers. [f. *Mary* (prob. the Virgin) + dial. *gold* marigold]

marijuana /mærɪˈhwɑːnə/ *n.* (also **marihuana**) the dried leaves and flowers and stems of common hemp, smoked as an intoxicant. [Amer. Sp.]

marimba /məˈrɪmbə/ *n.* **1** a xylophone of Africa and Central America. **2** a modern orchestral instrument evolved from this. [of Congolese orig.]

marina /məˈriːnə/ *n.* a place with moorings for pleasure-yachts etc. [It. & Sp. f. L (as MARINE)]

marinade /mærɪˈneɪd/ *n.* a mixture of wine, vinegar, oil, herbs, etc., for steeping meat or fish; meat or fish so steeped. —*v.t.* to steep in a marinade. [F f. Sp. (*marinar* pickle in brine, as MARINE)]

marinate /ˈmærɪneɪt/ *v.t.* to marinade. [f. It. or F (as prec.)]

marine /məˈriːn/ *adj.* **1** of, found in, or produced by the sea. **2** of shipping or naval matters. **3** for use at sea. —*n.* **1** a member of a corps trained to serve on land or sea. **2** a country's shipping, fleet, or navy. [f. OF f. L *marinus* (*mare* sea)]

mariner /ˈmærɪnə(r)/ *n.* a seaman. [f. AF f. L *marinarius* (as MARINE)]

marionette /mærɪəˈnet/ *n.* a puppet worked by strings. [f. F (*Marion* dim. of *Marie* Mary)]

marital /ˈmærɪt(ə)l/ *adj.* of marriage; of or between a husband and wife. —**maritally** *adv.* [f. L (*maritus* husband)]

maritime /ˈmærɪtaɪm/ *adj.* **1** situated or living or found near the sea. **2** connected with the sea or seafaring. [f. L *maritimus* (*mare* sea)]

marjoram /ˈmɑːdʒərəm/ *n.* an aromatic herb of the genus *Origanum* or *Majorana*, used in cookery. [f. OF f. L *majorana*]

mark¹ *n.* **1** a line or area that visibly breaks the uniformity of a surface, especially one that spoils its appearance. **2** a written or printed symbol; this as an assessment of conduct or proficiency; a numerical unit awarded for merit in an examination etc. **3** something that indicates the presence of a quality or feeling. **4** a sign or symbol placed on a thing to identify it or indicate its origin. **5** a cross etc. made in place of a signature by an illiterate person. **6** a lasting effect or influence. **7** a target or other object to be aimed at; a desired object. **8** a line etc. serving to indicate a position; a standard; a runner's starting-point in a race. **9** (followed by a numeral) a particular type or design of equipment etc. —*v.t.* **1** to make a mark on. **2** to distinguish with a mark; to characterize. **3** to assign marks of merit to (a student's work etc.). **4** to attach figures indicating prices to (goods). **5** to notice, to watch carefully. **6** to keep close to (an opposing player) in football etc. so as to hamper him if he receives the ball. —**make one's mark**, to attain distinction. **mark down**, to make a written note of; to mark at a lower price. **mark-down** *n.* a reduction in price. **mark off**, to separate, to mark the limits of. **mark out**, to mark the boundaries of; to trace (a course); to destine; to single out. **mark time**, to move the feet as in marching but without advancing; to occupy time routinely while awaiting events or an opportunity. **mark up**, to mark at a higher price. **mark-up** *n.* an amount the seller adds to the cost-price of an article to cover his profit margin etc. **off the mark**, having made a start; irrelevant. **on the mark**, ready to start; relevant. [OE]

mark² *n.* the currency unit of Germany (Deutschmark) and of Finland. [G]

marked *adj.* clearly noticeable or evident. —**marked man**, one singled out, especially as an object of attack etc. —**markedly** /-ɪdlɪ/ *adv.* [f. MARK¹]

marker *n.* **1** a thing marking a position. **2** a person or thing that marks. **3** a scorer in a game etc. [f. MARK¹]

market /ˈmɑːkɪt/ *n.* **1** a gathering for the purchase and sale of provisions, livestock, etc.; a space or building used for this. **2** a demand for a commodity or service; a place or group providing such a demand; the conditions as regards buying or selling; the opportunity for this. **3** the rate of purchase and sale. —*v.t./i.* to sell; to offer for sale; to buy or sell goods in a market. —**in the market for**, wishing to buy. **market-day** *n.* a day on which markets are regularly held. **market garden**, a place where vegetables are grown for market. **market-place** *n.* an open space where a market is held in a town; the scene of actual dealings. **market price**, the price in current dealings. **market research**, study of consumers' needs and preferences. **market town**, a town where a market is held. **market value**, the value as a saleable thing. **on the market**, offered for sale. [f. Old Saxon f. L *mercatus* (*mercari* buy)]

marketable *adj.* able or fit to be sold. [f. prec.]

marking *n.* **1** an indentification mark. **2** the colouring of an animal's fur or feathers etc. [f. MARK¹]

marksman *n.* (*pl.* **-men**) a skilled shot, especially with a rifle. —**marksmanship** *n.*

marl *n.* a soil consisting of clay and lime, used as a fertilizer. —*v.t.* to apply marl to. —**marly** *adj.* [f. OF f. L *margila*]

marlinspike /ˈmɑːlɪnspaɪk/ *n.* a pointed tool

used to separate strands of rope or wire. [f. *marline* line of two strands, f. Du.]

marmalade /ˈmɑːməleɪd/ *n.* a preserve of citrus fruit (usually oranges) made like jam. [f. F f. Port. *marmelada* (*marmelo* quince)]

marmoreal /mɑːˈmɔːrɪəl/ *adj.* of or like marble. [f. L (as MARBLE)]

marmoset /ˈmɑːməzet/ *n.* a small monkey of the family Callithricidae, with a bushy tail. [f. OF *marmouset* grotesque image]

marmot /ˈmɑːmət/ *n.* a burrowing rodent of the genus *Arctomys*, of the squirrel family. [f. F prob. f. Romansch *murmont* f. L, = mouse of the mountain]

marocain /ˈmærəkeɪn/ *n.* a kind of crêpe dress-fabric. [F, = Moroccan]

maroon[1] /məˈruːn/ *adj.* brownish-crimson. —*n.* **1** brownish-crimson colour. **2** a kind of firework that explodes with a sound like a cannon, used as a warning signal. [f. F *marron* a chestnut [f. It. f. Gk]

maroon[2] /məˈruːn/ *v.t.* **1** to put (a person) ashore in a desolate place and abandon him there. **2** to make unable to leave a place safely. [orig. = fugitive slave living rough, f. F f. Sp. *cimarrón* wild (*cima* peak)]

marque /mɑːk/ *n.* a make of motor car, as opposed to a specific model. [F, = MARK[1]]

marquee /mɑːˈkiː/ *n.* a large tent used for a party or exhibition etc. [f. MARQUISE, taken as pl.]

marquess var. of MARQUIS.

marquetry /ˈmɑːkɪtrɪ/ *n.* inlaid work in wood, ivory, etc. [F (*marqueter* variegate f. MARQUE)]

marquis /ˈmɑːkwɪs/ *n.* a nobleman ranking between a duke and (in the UK) an earl or (elsewhere) a count. [f. OF *marchis* (as MARCH[2])]

marquise /mɑːˈkiːz/ *n.* (in foreign nobility) a marchioness. [F (as prec.)]

marram /ˈmærəm/ *n.* a shore grass that binds sand (*Ammophila arenaria*). [f. ON, = sea-haulm]

marriage /ˈmærɪdʒ/ *n.* **1** the condition of a man and woman legally united for the purpose of living together and usually procreating lawful offspring. **2** an act or ceremony etc. establishing this condition. **3** a particular matrimonial union. —**marriage bureau,** an establishment arranging introductions between persons wishing to marry. **marriage certificate,** a certificate stating that a marriage ceremony has taken place. **marriage guidance,** the counselling of married couples who have problems in living together harmoniously. **marriage lines,** a marriage certificate. **marriage of convenience,** a marriage not made primarily for love. **marriage settlement,** an arrangement securing property to the wife. [f. OF (as MARRY)]

marriageable *adj.* old enough to marry; (of an age) fit for marriage. [f. prec.]

marron glacé /mærɒn ˈglæseɪ/ a chestnut preserved in sugar as a sweet. [F, = iced chestnut]

marrow /ˈmærəʊ/ *n.* **1** a gourd (the fruit of *Cucurbita pepo*) with whitish flesh, cooked as a vegetable. **2** the fatty substance in the cavities of bones. —**to the marrow,** right through. [OE]

marrowbone *n.* a bone containing edible marrow.

marrowfat *n.* a kind of large pea.

marry /ˈmærɪ/ *v.t./i.* **1** to take, give, or join in marriage; to enter into a marriage. **2** to unite intimately, to correlate as a pair. [f. OF *marier* f. L (*maritus* husband)]

Marsala /mɑːˈsɑːlə/ *n.* a dark usually sweet fortified wine. [f. *Marsala* in Sicily]

marsh *n.* low-lying watery land. —**marsh gas,** methane. **marsh mallow,** a shrubby herb (*Althaea officinalis*). **marsh marigold,** a plant (*Caltha palustris*) with golden flowers, growing in moist meadows. —**marshy** *adj.* [OE]

marshal /ˈmɑːʃ(ə)l/ *n.* **1** a high-ranking officer of State or in the armed forces. **2** an official arranging ceremonies, controlling the procedure at races, etc. —*v.t.* **(-ll-) 1** to arrange in due order. **2** to conduct (a person) ceremoniously. —**marshalling yard,** a railway yard in which goods trains etc. are assembled. **Marshal of the RAF,** the highest rank in the RAF. [f. OF *mareschal* f. L]

marshmallow *n.* a soft sweet made from sugar, albumen, gelatine, etc.

marsupial /mɑːˈsuːpɪəl/ *n.* a mammal of the order Marsupialia, which includes the kangaroo and opossum. The young are born in a very undeveloped state and usually nourished in an external pouch on the mother's abdomen. —*adj.* of marsupials. [f. L f. Gk *marsupion* pouch]

mart *n.* a trade centre; an auction-room, a market. [f. obs. Du., = MARKET]

marten /ˈmɑːtɪn/ *n.* an animal of the genus *Martes*, like a weasel, with valuable fur. [f. MDu. f. OF]

martial /ˈmɑːʃ(ə)l/ *adj.* of or appropriate to warfare; warlike, brave, fond of fighting. —**martial arts,** fighting sports such as judo and karate. **martial law,** military government, by which ordinary law is suspended. [f. OF or L *martialis* of Mars, god of war]

Martian /ˈmɑːʃ(ə)n/ *adj.* of the planet Mars. —*n.* a hypothetical inhabitant of Mars. [f. OF or L (as prec.)]

martin /ˈmɑːtɪn/ *n.* a bird, especially the house-martin (see HOUSE) and sand-martin (see SAND), of the swallow family. [prob. f. prec.]

martinet /mɑːtɪˈnet/ *n.* a strict disciplinarian. [f. J. *Martinet*, 17th-c. French drill-master]

martingale /ˈmɑːtɪŋgeɪl/ *n.* a strap, or set of straps, fastened at one end to the nose-band and at the other end to the girth, to prevent a horse from rearing etc. [F; orig. unkn.]

Martini /mɑːˈtiːniː/ *n.* [P] vermouth; a cocktail made of gin and vermouth. [f. *Martini* & Rossi, firm selling vermouth]

martyr /ˈmɑːtə(r)/ *n.* one who undergoes the death penalty for persistence in the Christian faith or obedience to the law of the Church, or undergoes death or suffering for any great cause. —*v.t.* **1** to put to death as a martyr. **2** to torment. —**martyr to,** a constant sufferer from (an ailment). [OE f. L f. Gk, orig. = witness]

martyrdom *n.* the sufferings and death of a martyr; torment. [f. prec.]

martyrology /mɑːtəˈrɒlədʒɪ/ *n.* a list or history of martyrs. —**martyrologist** *n.* [f. L f. Gk (as MARTYR -LOGY)]

marvel /ˈmɑːv(ə)l/ *n.* a wonderful thing; a wonderful example. —*v.i.* (**-ll-**) to feel surprise or wonder. [f. OF *merveille* f. L *mirabilis* (*mirari* wonder at)]

marvellous /ˈmɑːvələs/ *adj.* astonishing; excellent. —**marvellously** *adv.* [f. OF (as MARVEL)]

Marxism /ˈmɑːksɪz(ə)m/ *n.* the political and economic theory of the German socialist philosopher Karl Marx, predicting the violent overthrow of the capitalist class and the taking over of the means of production by the proletariat. —**Marxist** *n.* [f. K. *Marx* (d. 1883)]

marzipan /ˈmɑːzɪpæn/ *n.* a paste of ground almonds, sugar, etc. [G f. It.]

mascara /mæˈskɑːrə/ *n.* a cosmetic for darkening the eyelashes etc. [It., = mask]

mascot /ˈmæskɒt/ *n.* a person or animal or thing supposed to bring luck. [f. F f. Prov. (*masco* witch)]

masculine /ˈmæskjʊlɪn/ *adj.* **1** of men; having the qualities appropriate to a man. **2** (*Gram.*) of the gender proper to men's names. **3** (of a rhyme or line-ending) having a final stressed syllable. —*n.* (*Gram.*) the masculine gender; a masculine word. —**masculinity** /-ˈlɪnɪtɪ/ *n.* [f. OF f. L (as MALE)]

maser /ˈmeɪzə(r)/ *n.* a device for amplifying microwaves. [f. *m*icrowave *a*mplification by *s*timulated *e*mission of *r*adiation]

mash *n.* **1** a soft or confused mixture; a mixture of boiled grain, bran, etc., used as animal food. **2** (*colloq.*) mashed potatoes. **3** a mixture of malt and hot water used in brewing. —*v.t.* **1** to reduce (potatoes etc.) to a uniform mass by crushing; to crush to a pulp. **2** to mix (malt) with hot water. [OE]

mask /mɑːsk/ *n.* **1** a covering for all or part of the face, worn as a disguise, for protection, or (by a surgeon etc.) to prevent infection of the patient. **2** a respirator used to filter inhaled air or to supply gas for inhalation. **3** a likeness of a person's face, especially (as *death-mask*) one made by taking a mould from the face. **4** a disguise or pretence. —*v.t.* to cover or disguise with a mask; to conceal or protect. —**masking tape,** adhesive tape used in painting to cover areas on which paint is not wanted. [f. F *masque* f. It. f. Arab., = buffoon]

masochism /ˈmæsəkɪz(ə)m/ *n.* **1** a form of (esp. sexual) perversion in which the sufferer derives pleasure from his own pain or humiliation. **2** (*colloq.*) enjoyment of what appears to be painful or tiresome. —**masochist** *n.*, **masochistic** /-ˈkɪstɪk/ *adj.* [f. L. von Sacher-*Masoch*, Austrian novelist (d. 1895)]

mason /ˈmeɪs(ə)n/ *n.* **1** one who builds with stone. **2 Mason,** a Freemason. [f. OF *masson*]

Masonic /məˈsɒnɪk/ *adj.* of Freemasons. [f. MASON]

masonry /ˈmeɪs(ə)nrɪ/ *n.* **1** a mason's work; stonework. **2 Masonry,** Freemasonry. [as prec.]

masque /mɑːsk/ *n.* an amateur dramatic and musical entertainment especially in the 16th–17th c., with scenery and elaborate costumes, originally in dumb show but later with metrical dialogue; a dramatic composition for this. [var. of MASK]

masquerade /mɑːskəˈreɪd/ *n.* **1** a false show, a pretence. **2** a ball at which the guests wear masks. —*v.i.* to appear in disguise, to assume a false appearance. [f. Sp. (*mascara* mask)]

mass[1] /mæs/ *n.* **1** a coherent body of matter of indefinite shape. **2** a dense aggregation of objects. **3** (in *sing.* or *pl.*) a large number or amount. **4** an unbroken expanse of colour etc. **5** the quantity of matter a body contains, measured in terms of resistance to acceleration by a force (i.e., its inertia). —*v.t./i.* to gather into a mass; to assemble into one body. —*adj.* of or relating to large numbers of persons or things, large-scale. —**the mass,** the majority. **the masses,** the ordinary people. **in the mass,** in the aggregate. **mass media,** means of communication (e.g. newspapers or broadcasting) to large numbers of people. **mass meeting,** a large assembly of people. **mass production,** the production of large quantities of a standardized article by mechanical processes. [f. OF f. L *massa* f. Gk *maza* barley-cake]

mass² /mæs, mɑːs/ *n.* a celebration of the Eucharist, now especially in the Roman Catholic and High Church; the liturgy used in this; a musical setting for parts of it. [OE f. L *missa* (*mittere* dismiss), perh. from the concluding words *Ite, missa est*]

massacre /ˈmæsəkə(r)/ *n.* **1** a general slaughter (of persons, occasionally of animals). **2** utter defeat or destruction. —*v.t.* to make a massacre of; to murder (a large number of people) cruelly or violently. [F]

massage /ˈmæsɑːʒ/ *n.* the rubbing, kneading, etc., of the muscles and joints of the body with the hands, to stimulate their action, cure strains, etc. —*v.t.* **1** to treat (a part or person) thus. **2** to manipulate the presentation of (figures, data, etc.) so as to give a more acceptable result. [F]

masseur /mæˈsɜː(r)/ *n.* one who provides massage professionally. —**masseuse** /-ˈsɜːz/ *n. fem.* [F (as prec.)]

massif /ˈmæsiːf, -ˈsiːf/ *n.* mountain heights forming a compact group. [F (as MASSIVE)]

massive /ˈmæsɪv/ *adj.* **1** large and heavy or solid. **2** substantial, unusually large. —**massiveness** *n.* [f. F *massif* (as MASS¹)]

mast¹ /mɑːst/ *n.* **1** a long upright post set up on a ship's keel to support the sails. **2** a post or lattice-work upright to support a radio or television aerial. **3** a flag-pole. —**before the mast,** as an ordinary sailor. —**masted** *adj.* [OE]

mast² /mɑːst/ *n.* the fruit of the beech, oak, etc., especially as food for pigs. [OE]

mastectomy /mæˈstektəmɪ/ *n.* surgical removal of a breast. [f. Gk *mastos* breast + -ECTOMY]

master /ˈmɑːstə(r)/ *n.* **1** a person having control of people or things, especially an employer; the male head of a household or of a college etc.; the male owner of an animal or slave; (in full **master mariner**) the captain of a merchant ship. **2** a male teacher or tutor, a schoolmaster. **3** one who has or gets the upper hand. **4** a skilled workman, or one in business on his own account. **5** a holder of a master's degree from a university, originally giving the holder authority to teach in a university; a revered teacher in philosophy etc. **6** a great artist; a picture by one. **7** a chess player of proved ability at international level. **8** a thing from which a series of copies (e.g. of a film or gramophone record) is made. **9 Master,** a title prefixed to the name of a boy not old enough to be called *Mr.* —*adj.* **1** commanding, superior. **2** main, principal. **3** controlling others. —*v.t.* **1** to overcome, to bring under control. **2** to acquire knowledge or skill in. —**master-key** *n.* a key that opens several locks, each also having its own key. **Master of Ceremonies,** a person in charge of a ceremonial or social occasion, a person introducing the speakers at a banquet or the performers at a variety show. **Master of the Rolls,** the Court of Appeal judge in charge of the Public Record Office. **master-stroke** *n.* an outstandingly skilful act of policy etc. **master-switch** *n.* a switch controlling the electricity etc. supply to an entire system. [OE f. L *magister*]

masterful *adj.* **1** imperious, domineering. **2** masterly. —**masterfully** *adv.* [f. prec. + -FUL]

masterly *adj.* worthy of a master; very skilful. [f. MASTER]

mastermind *n.* **1** a person with an outstanding intellect. **2** a person directing an intricate operation. —*v.t.* to plan and direct (a scheme).

masterpiece *n.* an outstanding piece of artistry; one's best work. [prob. f. Du. or G (as MASTER, PIECE), orig. denoting the piece of work by which a craftsman gained from his guild the recognized rank of 'master']

mastery /ˈmɑːstərɪ/ *n.* **1** complete control, supremacy. **2** masterly skill or knowledge. [f. OF (as MASTER)]

masthead *n.* **1** the highest part of a ship's mast. **2** the title details of a newspaper at the head of its front or editorial page.

mastic /ˈmæstɪk/ *n.* **1** a gum or resin exuded from certain trees (esp. *Pistacia lentiscus*). **2** a type of cement. [f. OF f. L f. Gk (perh. as foll.)]

masticate /ˈmæstɪkeɪt/ *v.t.* to grind (food) with the teeth, to chew. —**mastication** /-ˈkeɪʃ(ə)n/ *n.*, **masticatory** *adj.* [f. L f. Gk *mastikhaō* gnash the teeth]

mastiff /ˈmæstɪf/ *n.* a large strong kind of dog. [ult. f. OF *mastin* f. L *mansuetus* tame]

mastodon /ˈmæstədɒn/ *n.* a large extinct animal of the genus *Mammut*, resembling the elephant. [f. Gk *mastos* breast + *odous* tooth, f. the nipple-shaped tubercles on its molars]

mastoid /ˈmæstɔɪd/ *adj.* shaped like a woman's breast. —*n.* the conical prominence on the temporal bone behind the ear (also **mastoid process**); (*colloq.*, usu. in *pl.*) inflammation of this. [f. F f. Gk (*mastos* breast)]

masturbate /ˈmæstəbeɪt/ *v.t./i.* to produce sexual orgasm or arousal (of) by stimulation of the genitals other than by sexual intercourse. —**masturbation** /-ˈbeɪʃ(ə)n/ *n.*, **masturbatory** *adj.* [f. L]

mat¹ *n.* **1** a piece of coarse material as a floor-covering or for wiping shoes on, especially a doormat. **2** a piece of cork, rubber, plastic, etc., to protect a surface from the heat or moisture of an object placed on it. **3** a piece of resilient material for landing on in gymnastics or wrestling. —*v.t./i.* (**-tt-**) **1** to make or become entangled in a thick mass.

2 to cover or furnish with mats. —**on the mat,** (*slang*) being reprimanded. [OE, f. L *matta*]

mat[2] var. of MATT.

matador /ˈmætədɔː(r)/ *n.* a bullfighter whose task is to kill the bull. [Sp. (*matar* kill, f. Pers.)]

match[1] *n.* **1** a contest or game of skill etc. in which persons or teams compete against each other. **2** a competitor able to contend with another as an equal; a person equal to another in some quality. **3** a person or thing exactly like or corresponding to another. **4** a marriage. **5** a person viewed in regard to eligibility for marriage. —*v.t./i.* **1** to be equal; to correspond in some essential respect. **2** to place in competition or conflict. **3** to find a material etc. that matches (another). **4** to find a person or thing suitable for another. —**match point,** the state of a game when one side needs only one more point to win the match; this point. [OE, = companion (as MAKE)]

match[2] *n.* **1** a short thin piece of wood etc. tipped with a composition that bursts into flame when rubbed on a rough or specially prepared surface. **2** a fuse for firing a cannon etc. [f. OF *mesche*]

matchboard *n.* a board with a tongue cut along one edge and a groove along the other, so as to fit with similar boards. [f. MATCH[1] + BOARD]

matchbox *n.* a box for holding matches.

matchless *adj.* incomparable. [f. MATCH[2] + -LESS]

matchmaker *n.* a person fond of scheming to bring about marriages. —**matchmaking** *adj.* & *n.*

matchstick *n.* the stem of a match.

matchwood *n.* **1** wood suitable for making matches. **2** wood reduced to minute splinters.

mate[1] *n.* **1** a companion, a fellow worker; (*colloq.*) a general form of address to an equal. **2** one of a pair, especially of birds; (*colloq.*) a partner in marriage. **3** a subordinate officer on a merchant ship. **4** an assistant to a worker. —*in comb.* a fellow member or joint occupant of (*team-mate, room-mate*). —*v.t./i.* **1** to bring or come together in marriage or for breeding. **2** to put or come together as a pair or as corresponding. [f. MLG]

mate[2] *n.* a checkmate. —*v.t.* to checkmate. [f. F *mat(er)*; see CHECKMATE]

mater /ˈmeɪtə(r)/ *n.* (*archaic slang*) mother. [L]

material /məˈtɪərɪəl/ *n.* **1** the substance or things from which something is or can be made; (in *pl.*) the things needed for an activity. **2** a person or thing suitable for a specified purpose. **3** cloth, fabric. **4** information etc. to be used in writing a book etc. —*adj.* **1** of matter; consisting of matter; of the physical (opp. spiritual) world. **2** of bodily comfort etc. **3** important, significant, relevant. [f. OF f. L (as MATTER)]

materialism *n.* **1** the tendency to prefer material possessions and physical comfort to spiritual values. **2** the theory that nothing exists but matter and its movements and modifications. —**materialist** *n.*, **materialistic** /-ˈlɪstɪk/ *adj.* [f. prec.]

materialize *v.t./i.* **1** to become a fact, to happen. **2** to appear, to become visible. **3** to represent in or assume bodily form. —**materialization** /-ˈzeɪʃ(ə)n/ *n.* [f. MATERIAL]

materially *adv.* substantially, considerably. [as prec.]

maternal /məˈtɜːn(ə)l/ *adj.* **1** of or like a mother, motherly. **2** related through one's mother. **3** of the mother in pregnancy and childbirth. —**maternally** *adv.* [f. OF or L *maternus* (*mater* mother)]

maternity /məˈtɜːnɪtɪ/ *n.* **1** motherhood. **2** motherliness. **3** (*attrib.*) for women in pregnancy or childbirth. [f. F f. L (as prec.)]

matey /ˈmeɪtɪ/ *adj.* sociable, familiar and friendly. —*n.* (*colloq.*, as a form of address) mate. —**matily** *adv.*, **matiness** *n.* [f. MATE[1]]

mathematical /mæθɪˈmætɪk(ə)l/ *adj.* of or involving mathematics. —**mathematically** *adv.* [as MATHEMATICS]

mathematician /mæθɪməˈtɪʃ(ə)n/ *n.* one who is skilled in mathematics. [f. foll.]

mathematics /mæθɪˈmætɪks/ *n.pl.* (also treated as *sing.*) **1** the body of knowledge and reasoning about numbers, spatial forms, logic, and relationships between them, and applications to measurement and prediction in science and other areas. **2** (as *pl.*) the use of this in calculation etc. [f. F f. L f. Gk (*mathēma* science f. *manthanō* learn)]

maths /mæθs/ *n.* (*colloq.*) mathematics. [abbr.]

matinée /ˈmætɪneɪ/ *n.* an afternoon performance at a theatre or cinema. —**matinée coat,** a baby's short coat. [F, = what occupies a morning (as foll.)]

matins /ˈmætɪnz/ *n.pl.* the service of morning prayer, especially in the Church of England. [f. OF f. L (*matutinus* of morning)]

matriarch /ˈmeɪtrɪɑːk/ *n.* a woman who is head of a family or tribe. —**matriarchal** /-ˈɑːk(ə)l/ *adj.* [f. L *mater* mother, on false analogy of PATRIARCH]

matriarchy /ˈmeɪtrɪɑːkɪ/ *n.* a social organization in which the mother is head of the family and descent is reckoned through the female line. [f. prec.]

matricide /ˈmeɪtrɪsaɪd/ *n.* **1** the crime of killing one's own mother. **2** one who is guilty of this. —**matricidal** *adj.* [f. L (*mater* mother, -CIDE)]

matriculate /mə'trɪkjʊleɪt/ *v.t./i.* to admit (a student) to membership of a university; to be thus admitted. [f. L (*matricula* register, as MATRIX)]

matriculation /mətrɪkjʊ'leɪʃ(ə)n/ *n.* matriculating; an examination to qualify for this. [f. prec.]

matrilineal /mætrɪ'lɪnɪəl/ *adj.* of or based on kinship with the mother or the female line of ancestors. [f. L *mater* mother + LINEAL]

matrimony /'mætrɪmənɪ/ *n.* **1** the rite of marriage. **2** the state of being married. —**matrimonial** /-'məʊnɪəl/ *adj.*, **matrimonially** *adv.* [f. AF f. L *matrimonium* (as MATER)]

matrix /'meɪtrɪks/ *n.* (*pl.* **-ices** /-ɪsi:z/) **1** a mould in which a thing is cast or shaped. **2** a place in which a thing is developed. **3** a mass of rock enclosing gems etc. **4** a rectangular array of mathematical quantities treated as a single quantity. [L, = womb (as MATER)]

matron /'meɪtrən/ *n.* **1** a married woman, especially one who is middle-aged or elderly and dignified. **2** a woman managing the domestic arrangements of a school etc. **3** a woman in charge of nurses in a hospital (now usu. called *senior nursing officer*). —**matron of honour**, a married woman attending the bride at a wedding. —**matronly** *adj.* [f. OF f. L *matrona* (as MATER)]

matt *adj.* (of a colour etc.) dull, not lustrous. [f. F (as MATE²)]

matter *n.* **1** that which occupies space and possesses rest mass, including atoms, their major constituents, and substances made of atoms, but not light and other electromagnetic radiation; physical substance in general, as distinct from mind and spirit. **2** a particular substance or material. **3** a discharge from the body, pus. **4** material for thought or expression; the content of a book, speech, etc. **5** a thing or things of a specified kind. **6** a situation or business being considered. **7** (with *of*) a quantity or extent of; a thing that depends on. —*v.i.* to be important. —**the matter**, the thing that is amiss, the trouble or difficulty. **as a matter of fact**, in reality (esp. to correct a falsehood or misunderstanding). **for that matter**, as far as that is concerned; and indeed also. **a matter of course**, a thing to be expected. **matter-of-fact** *adj.* strictly factual and not imaginative or emotional. **no matter**, it is of no importance. [f. AF f. L *materia*]

matting *n.* fabric for mats. [f. MAT¹]

mattock /'mætək/ *n.* an agricultural tool like a pickaxe with an adze and a chisel edge as the ends of its head. [OE]

mattress /'mætrɪs/ *n.* a pad of soft or firm or springy material enclosed in a fabric case, used on or as a bed. [f. OF *materas* f. It. f. Arab.]

maturate /'mætjʊreɪt/ *v.i.* (of a boil etc.) to come to maturation. [f. L (as MATURE)]

maturation /mætjʊ'reɪʃ(ə)n/ *n.* maturing, development; (of a boil etc.) the formation of purulent matter. [f. F or L (as foll.)]

mature /mə'tjʊə(r)/ *adj.* **1** with fully developed powers of body and mind, adult. **2** complete in natural development, ripe. **3** (of thought, intentions, etc.) duly careful and adequate. **4** (of a bill etc.) due for payment. —*v.t./i.* to make or become mature. —**maturely** *adv.*, **maturity** *n.* [f. L *maturus*]

matutinal /mætju:'taɪn(ə)l/ *adj.* of or occurring in the morning; early. [f. L *matutinus* (as MATINS)]

maudlin /'mɔ:dlɪn/ *adj.* weakly or tearfully sentimental, especially from drunkenness. [orig. = St Mary Magdalen, f. OF *Madeleine* f. L]

maul /mɔ:l/ *v.t.* **1** to treat roughly; to injure by rough handling or clawing. **2** to make damaging criticisms of. —*n.* **1** a loose scrum in Rugby football. **2** a brawl. **3** a heavy hammer. [f. OF f. L *malleus* hammer]

maulstick /'mɔ:lstɪk/ *n.* a stick used to support the hand in painting. [f. Du. *maalstok* (*malen* to paint)]

maunder /'mɔ:ndə(r)/ *v.i.* **1** to talk in a dreamy or rambling manner. **2** to move or act listlessly or idly. [perh. f. obs. *maunder* beggar, to beg]

Maundy /'mɔ:ndɪ/ *n.* the ceremony of washing the feet of a number of poor people, performed by royal or other eminent persons, or by ecclesiastics, on the Thursday before Easter, and commonly followed by the distribution of clothing, food, or money. —**Maundy Thursday**, the Thursday before Easter, celebrated in memory of the Last Supper. [f. OF *mandé* f. L, = commandment (as MANDATE), ref. to John 13: 34]

mausoleum /mɔ:sə'li:əm/ *n.* a large magnificent tomb. [f. *Mausolos*, King of Caria (d. 353 BC), for whom a great tomb was built]

mauve /məʊv/ *adj.* pale purple. —*n.* mauve colour or dye. [F, = mallow, f. L *malva*]

maverick /'mævərɪk/ *n.* **1** an unorthodox or independent person. **2** an unbranded calf or yearling. [f. S. A. *Maverick*, Texan who did not brand his cattle (*c.*1850)]

maw *n.* **1** the stomach, especially of an animal. **2** the jaws or throat of a voracious animal. [OE]

mawkish *adj.* sentimental in a feeble or sickly way. —**mawkishly** *adv.*, **mawkishness** *n.* [f. obs. *mawk* maggot]

max. *abbr.* maximum.

maxi- /mæksɪ-/ *in comb.* very large or long (*maxi-coat*). [abbr. of MAXIMUM; cf. MINI-]

maxilla /mæk'sɪlə/ *n.* (*pl.* **-lae** /-li:/) **1** the jaw, especially (in vertebrates) the upper one. **2** a masticatory mouth-part of insects and other arthropods. —**maxillary** *n.* [L]

maxim /ˈmæksɪm/ *n.* the succinct expression of a general truth or rule of conduct. [f. F or L *maxima* (*propositio*) (as MAXIMUM)]

maximal /ˈmæksɪm(ə)l/ *adj.* being or related to a maximum. —**maximally** *adv.*

maximize /ˈmæksɪmaɪz/ *v.t.* to increase or enhance to the utmost. —**maximization** /-ˈzeɪʃ(ə)n/ *n.* [f. L (as foll.)]

maximum /ˈmæksɪməm/ *n.* (*pl.* **-ima**) the highest amount possible, attained, usual, etc. —*adj.* that is a maximum. [neut. of L *maximus* greatest]

May *n.* the fifth month of the year. —**May Day,** 1 May especially as a festival or (since 1889) as an international holiday in honour of workers. **May Queen** *or* **Queen of the May,** a girl chosen to be queen of the games on May Day. [f. OF f. L *Maius* (*mensis*) (month) of goddess Maia]

may¹ *n.* the hawthorn; its blossom [= prec.]

may² *v.aux.* (3 *sing. pres.* **may**; *past* MIGHT¹) expressing possibility, permission, wish, uncertainty. [OE]

maya /ˈmɑ:jə/ *n.* (*Hinduism*) illusion, magic, the supernatural power wielded by gods and demons; (in Hindu and Buddhist philosophy) the power by which the universe becomes manifest, the illusion or appearance of the phenomenal world. [f. Skr. (*mā* create)]

maybe /ˈmeɪbi:/ *adv.* perhaps, possibly. [f. *it may be*]

mayday /ˈmeɪdeɪ/ *n.* an international radio distress-signal used by ships and aircraft. [repr. pronunc. of F *m'aider* help me]

mayflower *n.* any of various flowers that bloom in May.

mayfly *n.* an insect of the order Ephemoptera, which lives briefly in spring.

mayhem /ˈmeɪhem/ *n.* **1** violent or damaging action. **2** (*hist.*) the crime of injuring a person so as to render him wholly or partly defenceless. [f. AF & OF (as MAIM)]

mayn't /meɪnt/ (*colloq.*) may not.

mayonnaise /meɪəˈneɪz/ *n.* a dressing made of egg-yolks, oil, vinegar, etc.; a dish dressed with this. [F, perh. = of Port *Mahon* in Minorca]

mayor /meə(r)/ *n.* the head of the municipal corporation of a city or borough; the head of a district council with the status of a borough. —**mayoral** *adj.* [f. OF *maire* f. L (as MAJOR)]

mayoralty /ˈmeərəltɪ/ *n.* the office of mayor; the period of this. [as prec.]

mayoress /ˈmeərɪs/ *n.* a mayor's wife; a lady fulfilling the ceremonial duties of a mayor's wife; a woman mayor. [f. MAYOR]

maypole *n.* a pole decked with ribbons, for dancing round in celebrations on May Day. [f. MAY + POLE]

maze *n.* **1** a complicated network of paths, a labyrinth; a network of paths and hedges designed as a puzzle in which to try and find one's way. **2** a state of bewilderment; a confused mass etc. [rel. to AMAZE]

mazurka /məˈzɜ:kə/ *n.* a lively Polish dance in triple time; the music for this. [F or f. G f. Polish, = woman of province *Mazovia*]

MB *abbr.* Bachelor of Medicine. [f. L *Medicinae Baccalaureus*]

MBE *abbr.* Member of the Order of the British Empire.

MC *abbr.* **1** Master of Ceremonies. **2** Military Cross.

MCC *abbr.* Marylebone Cricket Club.

MD *abbr.* Doctor of Medicine. [f. L *Medicinae Doctor*]

Md *symbol* mendelevium.

me¹ /mi:, mɪ/ *pron.* obj. case of I; (*colloq.*) = I. [OE, acc. & dat. of I²]

me² /mi:/ *n.* (*Mus.*) the third note of the major scale in tonic sol-fa. [f. *mira* (see GAMUT)]

mead *n.* an alcoholic drink made from fermented honey and water. [OE]

meadow /ˈmedəʊ/ *n.* a piece of grassland, especially one used for hay; low well-watered ground, especially near a river. —**meadowy** *adj.* [OE]

meadowsweet *n.* a plant (*Filipendula ulmaria*) with masses of fragrant creamy-white flowers, often growing in profusion in damp meadows.

meagre /ˈmi:gə(r)/ *adj.* of poor quality and scanty in amount; (of a person) lean. [f. OF *maigre* f. L *macer*]

meal¹ *n.* **1** an occasion when food is eaten. **2** the food eaten on one occasion. —**make a meal of,** to treat (a task etc.) too laboriously or fussily. **meals-on-wheels** *n.* a public service whereby meals are delivered to old people, invalids, etc. **meal ticket,** a source of food or income. [OE]

meal² *n.* **1** coarsely ground grain or pulse. **2** (*Sc.*) oatmeal. **3** (*US*) maize flour. [OE]

mealie /ˈmi:lɪ/ *n.* (in southern Africa) maize, a cob with the corn on it. [f. Afrik. f. Port. f. L *milium* millet]

mealtime *n.* the (usual) time of eating.

mealy *adj.* of, like, or containing meal; dry and powdery. —**mealy-mouthed** *adj.* trying excessively to avoid offending people. [f. MEAL²]

mean¹ *v.t.* (*past & p.p.* **meant** /ment/) **1** to have as one's purpose or intention. **2** to design or destine for a purpose. **3** to intend to convey (a specified sense) or indicate or refer to (a thing). **4** to signify; (of words) to have as an equivalent in the same or another language. **5** to entail, to involve; to be likely or certain to result in. **6** to be of specified importance to. —**mean it,** not to be joking or exaggerating. **mean well,** to have good intentions. [OE]

mean[2] *adj.* **1** miserly, niggardly, not generous. **2** poor in quality or capacity; poor in appearance, not imposing. **3** malicious, ill-tempered; (*US*) vicious, nastily behaved. **4** (*US slang*) skilful. —**no mean,** very good. —**meanly** *adv.*, **meanness** *n.* [OE]

mean[3] *n.* **1** a condition, quality, or course of action equally removed from two opposite extremes. **2** the quotient of the sum of several quantities and their number. **3** a term between the first and last of an arithmetical etc. progression, especially of three terms. —*adj.* (of a point or quantity) equally far from two extremes. —**in the mean time,** meanwhile. **mean sea level,** the level half-way between high and low water. [f. OF *meien, moien* f. L (as MEDIAN)]

meander /mi:ˈændə(r)/ *v.i.* **1** (of a stream) to wind about. **2** to wander at random. —*n.* **1** (in *pl.*) the sinuous windings of a river. **2** a circuitous journey. [f. L f. Gk *Maiandros*, winding river in western Turkey]

meaning *n.* what is meant, the significance. —*adj.* expressive, significant. —**meaningful** *adj.*, **meaningfully** *adv.*, **meaningless** *adj.*, **meaninglessly** *adv.* [f. MEAN[1]]

means *n.pl.* **1** (usu. treated as *sing.*) that by which a result is brought about. **2** money resources, wealth. —**by all means,** certainly. **by no means,** not at all; far from it; certainly not. **means test,** an official inquiry to establish need before financial assistance is given. [as MEAN[3]]

meant *past* & *p.p.* of MEAN[1].

meantime *adv.* meanwhile. [f. MEAN[3] + TIME]

meanwhile *adv.* **1** in the intervening period of time. **2** at the same time. [f. MEAN[3] + WHILE]

meany *n.* (*colloq.*) a niggardly or small-minded person. [f. MEAN[2]]

measles /ˈmi:z(ə)lz/ *n.* an infectious virus disease marked by a red rash. [f. MLG *masele* or MDu. *masel* pustule]

measly /ˈmi:zlɪ/ *adj.* **1** of or affected with measles. **2** (*slang*) meagre; inferior, contemptible. [f. prec.]

measure /ˈmeʒə(r)/ *n.* **1** the size or quantity of something, found by measuring. **2** a unit, standard, or system used in measuring. **3** a device used in measuring, especially a rod, tape, or vessel marked with standard units. **4** degree or extent. **5** (often in *pl.*) suitable action taken to achieve some end; a law or proposed law. **6** that by which a thing is computed. **7** a prescribed quantity or extent. **8** a poetical rhythm, a metre; the metrical group of a dactyl or two disyllabic feet; (*archaic*) a dance. **9** a stratum containing a mineral. —*v.t./i.* **1** to find the extent or quantity of (a thing) by comparison with a fixed unit or with an object of known size; to ascertain the size and proportions of (a person etc.) for fitting clothing etc. **2** to be of a specified size. **3** to mark out (a given length) or deal out as a specified quantity. **4** to estimate (a quality etc.) by comparing it with some standard. **5** to bring into competition. —**beyond measure,** very great, very much. **for good measure,** in addition to what is necessary. **in some measure,** partly, to some extent. **made to measure,** made from measurements specially taken. **measure up (to),** to reach the necessary standard (for). [f. OF f. L *mensura* (*metiri* to measure)]

measured *adj.* **1** rhythmical, regular in movement. **2** (of language) carefully considered. [f. prec.]

measurement *n.* an act or the result of measuring; (in *pl.*) detailed dimensions. [f. MEASURE]

meat *n.* **1** animal flesh as food (usually excluding fish and poultry). **2** the essence or chief part. —**meat and drink,** a source of great pleasure *to*. **meat-safe** *n.* a ventilated cupboard for storing meat. [OE, = food]

meatball *n.* a small ball of minced meat.

meatus /mɪˈeɪtəs/ *n.* (*pl.* same or **-uses**) a channel or passage in the body; its opening. —**auditory meatus,** a channel of the ear. [L, = passage (*meare* flow, run)]

meaty *adj.* **1** like meat. **2** full of meat, fleshy. **3** full of informative matter. —**meatiness** *n.* [f. MEAT]

mechanic /mɪˈkænɪk/ *n.* a skilled worker, especially one who makes or uses or repairs machinery. [f. OF or L f. Gk *mekhanē* contrivance]

mechanical /mɪˈkænɪk(ə)l/ *adj.* **1** of machines or a mechanism. **2** working or produced by machinery. **3** (of a person or action) like a machine, acting or done without conscious thought; lacking originality; (of work) needing little or no thought. **4** of or belonging to the science of mechanics. —**mechanically** *adv.* [f. prec.]

mechanics /mɪˈkænɪks/ *n.pl.* (usu. treated as *sing.*) **1** the branch of applied mathematics dealing with motion and tendencies to motion. **2** the science of machinery. **3** (as *pl.*) the processes by which something is done or functions. [f. MECHANIC]

mechanism /ˈmekənɪz(ə)m/ *n.* **1** the structure

or parts of a machine or other set of mutually adapted parts. **2** the mode of operation of a process or machine. [f. Gk (as MACHINE)]

mechanize /ˈmekənaɪz/ *v.t.* **1** to introduce or use machines in; to equip with machines. **2** to give a mechanical character to. —**mechanization** /-ˈzeɪʃ(ə)n/ *n.* [f. MECHANIC]

Med *n.* (*colloq.*) the Mediterranean Sea. [abbr.]

medal /ˈmed(ə)l/ *n.* a piece of metal, usually in the form of a coin, struck or cast with an inscription and device to commemorate an event etc., or awarded as a distinction. [f. F f. It. ult. f. L *metallum* (as METAL)]

medallion /mɪˈdæljən/ *n.* **1** a large medal. **2** a thing so shaped, e.g. a decorative panel, a portrait. [f. F f. It. (as prec.)]

medallist /ˈmedəlɪst/ *n.* a winner of a medal. [f. MEDAL]

meddle *v.i.* **1** to interfere in people's affairs. **2** to tinker. —**meddler** *n.* [f. OF var. of *mesler*, ult. f. L *miscēre* mix]

meddlesome *adj.* fond of meddling. [f. prec. + -SOME]

media *pl.* of MEDIUM.

mediaeval var. of MEDIEVAL.

medial /ˈmi:dɪ(ə)l/ *adj.* situated in the middle. —**medially** *adv.* [f. L (*medius* middle)]

median /ˈmi:dɪən/ *adj.* medial. —*n.* **1** the straight line drawn from any vertex of a triangle to the middle of the opposite side. **2** a medial number or point in a series. **3** (in statistics) the value of a quantity such that exactly half of a given population have greater values of that quantity. [f. F or L (as prec.)]

mediate /ˈmi:dɪeɪt/ *v.t./i.* **1** to act as negotiator or peacemaker between the two sides in a dispute. **2** to bring about (a result) thus. —/ˈmi:dɪət/ *adj.* connected not directly but through some other person or thing. —**mediation** /-ˈeɪʃ(ə)n/ *n.*, **mediator** *n.* [f. L *mediare* (as MEDIAL)]

medic /ˈmedɪk/ *n.* (*colloq.*) a medical practitioner or student. [f. L *medicus* physician (*medēri* heal)]

medical /ˈmedɪk(ə)l/ *adj.* of the science of medicine in general or as distinct from surgery. —*n.* (*colloq.*) a medical examination. —**medical certificate,** a certificate of fitness or unfitness to work etc. **medical examination,** an examination to determine a person's physical fitness. **medical officer,** a person in charge of the health services of a local authority or other organization. —**medically** *adv.* [f. F or L (as prec.)]

medicament /mɪˈdɪkəmənt/ *n.* a substance used in curative treatment. [f. F or L (as MEDICATE)]

medicate /ˈmedɪkeɪt/ *v.t.* **1** to treat medically. **2** to impregnate with a medicinal substance. —**medication** /-ˈkeɪʃ(ə)n/ *n.*, **medicative** *adj.* [f. L *medicare* (as MEDIC)]

medicinal /mɪˈdɪsɪn(ə)l/ *adj.* of medicine; having healing properties. —**medicinally** *adv.* [f. OF f. L (as foll.)]

medicine /ˈmedsɪn, -ɪsɪn/ *n.* **1** the art of restoring and preserving health, especially by means of remedial substances etc. as distinct from surgery. **2** a substance used in this, especially one taken internally. —**medicine-man** *n.* a witch-doctor. **take one's medicine,** to submit to rebuke or punishment etc. [f. OF f. L *medicina* (as MEDIC)]

medico /ˈmedɪkəʊ/ *n.* (*pl.* **-os**) (*colloq.*) a medical practitioner or student. [It. f. L, = MEDIC]

medieval /medɪˈi:v(ə)l/ *adj.* of or imitating the Middle Ages. [f. L *medius* middle + *aevum* age]

mediocre /mi:dɪˈəʊkə(r)/ *adj.* of middling quality; second-rate. [f. F or L *mediocris* (as MEDIAL)]

mediocrity /mi:dɪˈɒkrɪtɪ/ *n.* **1** mediocre quality. **2** a mediocre person. [f. F f. L (as prec.)]

meditate /ˈmedɪteɪt/ *v.t./i.* **1** to think deeply and quietly; to do this in religious contemplation. **2** to plan in one's mind. —**meditation** /-ˈteɪʃ(ə)n/ *n.*, **meditator** *n.* [f. L *meditari*]

meditative /ˈmedɪtətɪv/ *adj.* inclined to meditate; indicative of meditation. —**meditatively** *adv.* [f. prec.]

Mediterranean /medɪtəˈreɪnɪən/ *adj.* of or characteristic of the Mediterranean Sea or the countries in and round it. —**Mediterranean Sea,** an almost land-locked sea between southern Europe and Africa, connected with the Atlantic Ocean by the Strait of Gibraltar and with the Red Sea by the Suez Canal. [f. L, = inland (*medius* middle, *terra* land)]

medium /ˈmi:dɪəm/ *n.* (*pl.* **-ia,** in sense 6 **-iums**) **1** a middle quality or degree of intensiveness etc. **2** a substance or surroundings in which something exists, moves, or is transmitted; an environment. **3** an agency or means by which something is done. **4** (in *pl.*, sometimes treated erron. as *sing.*) the mass media (see MASS[1]). **5** the material or form used by an artist or composer etc. **6** (*pl.* **-iums**) a person claiming to be able to communicate with the spirits of the dead etc. —*adj.* intermediate between two degrees or amounts; average, moderate. —**medium wave,** a radio wave of frequency between 300 kHz and 3 MHz. [L, neut. of *medius* middle]

mediumistic /mi:dɪəˈmɪstɪk/ *adj.* of a spiritualist medium. [f. prec.]

medlar /ˈmedlə(r)/ *n.* a fruit like a small apple, eaten when decayed; the tree bearing this (*Mespilus germanica*). [f. OF f. L f. Gk *mespilē*]

medley /ˈmedlɪ/ *n.* a varied mixture, a

miscellany; a collection of musical items from various sources. [f. OF f. L (as MEDDLE)]

medulla /mɪˈdʌlə/ *n.* **1** the marrow within a bone; the substance of the spinal cord. **2** the hindmost section of the brain. **3** the central part of some organs, e.g. that of the kidneys. **4** the soft internal tissue of plants. —**medullary** *adj.* [L]

medusa /mɪˈdju:zə/ *n.* (*pl.* **-ae** or **-as**) a jellyfish. [f. *Medusa*, snake-haired Gorgon]

meek *adj.* quiet and obedient, making no protest. —**meekly** *adv.*, **meekness** *n.* [f. ON]

meerschaum /ˈmɪəʃəm/ *n.* a white substance resembling clay; a tobacco-pipe with the bowl made of this. [G, = sea-foam]

meet[1] *v.t./i.* (*past* & *p.p.* **met**) **1** to come by accident or design into the company of, to come face to face (with). **2** to go to a place to be present at the arrival of (a person, train, etc.). **3** to come together or into contact (with). **4** to make the acquaintance of, to be introduced (to). **5** (of people or a group) to assemble. **6** to deal with or answer (a demand, objection, etc.) effectively; to satisfy or conform with (a person's wishes). **7** to pay (the cost, a bill at maturity). **8** to experience or receive (one's death, fate, etc.). **9** to oppose or be in opposition in a contest etc. —*n.* a meeting of persons and hounds for a hunt. —**meet the case,** to be adequate. **meet the eye** (*or* **ear**), to be visible (or audible) (*more in it than meets the eye*, hidden qualities or complications). **meet a person's eye,** to look into the eyes of a person looking at one. **meet a person half-way,** to respond to his advances, to make a compromise with him. **meet up with,** (*colloq.*) to happen to meet (a person). [OE]

meet[2] *adj.* (*archaic*) fitting, proper. [OE (rel. to METE)]

meeting *n.* **1** coming together. **2** an assembly of people, e.g. for discussion or (especially of Quakers) worship. **3** a race-meeting. [f. MEET[1]]

mega- /megə-/ *in comb.* **1** large. **2** one million. [Gk (*megas* great)]

megadeath /ˈmegədeθ/ *n.* the death of one million people (especially as a unit in estimating casualties of war).

megahertz /ˈmegəhɜ:ts/ *n.* a unit of frequency, equal to one million cycles per second.

megalith /ˈmegəlɪθ/ *n.* a large stone, especially one forming (part of) a prehistoric monument. —**megalithic** /-ˈlɪθɪk/ *adj.* [f. MEGA- + Gk *lithos* stone]

megalomania /megələˈmeɪnɪə/ *n.* a mental disorder involving an exaggerated idea of one's own importance; a passion for grandiose schemes etc. —**megalomaniac** *n.* [f. Gk *megas* great + MANIA]

megaphone /ˈmegəfəʊn/ *n.* a large funnel-shaped device for sending the sound of the voice to a distance. [f. MEGA- + Gk *phōnē* voice, sound]

megaton /ˈmegətʌn/ *n.* a unit of explosive force equal to one million tons of TNT.

megavolt /ˈmegəvəʊlt/ *n.* a unit of electromotive force equal to one million volts.

megawatt /ˈmegəwɒt/ *n.* a unit of electrical power equal to one million watts.

megohm /ˈmegəʊm/ *n.* a unit of electrical resistance equal to one million ohms. [f. MEGA- + OHM]

meiosis /maɪˈəʊsɪs/ *n.* (*pl.* **-oses** /-si:z/) **1** litotes. **2** the process of division of cell nuclei forming gametes each containing half the normal number of chromosomes. [f. Gk (*meioō* make less)]

melamine /ˈmeləmi:n/ *n.* a tough resilient kind of plastic. [f. *melam* (arbitrary) + AMINE]

melancholia /melənˈkəʊlɪə/ *n.* a mental disorder marked by depression and ill-founded fears. [L (as MELANCHOLY)]

melancholic /melənˈkɒlɪk/ *adj.* melancholy; liable to melancholy. [f. OF f. L f. Gk (as foll.)]

melancholy /ˈmelənkəlɪ/ *n.* pensive sadness; mental depression; a habitual or constitutional tendency to this. —*adj.* **1** sad, gloomy. **2** saddening, depressing. **3** (of words etc.) expressing sadness. [f. OF f. L f. Gk (*melas* black, *kholē* bile)]

mélange /meɪˈlɑ̃ʒ/ *n.* a medley. [F (*mêler* mix)]

melanin /melənɪn/ *n.* a dark pigment in the hair, skin, etc. [f. Gk *melas* black]

Melba toast thin crisp toast. [f. Nellie *Melba*, Australian soprano (d. 1931)]

mêlée /ˈmeleɪ/ *n.* **1** a confused fight or struggle. **2** a muddle. [F (as MEDLEY)]

mellifluous /meˈlɪfluəs/ *adj.* sweet-sounding. —**mellifluously** *adv.*, **mellifluousness** *n.* [f. OF or L (*mel* honey, *fluere* flow)]

mellow /ˈmeləʊ/ *adj.* **1** (of fruit) sweet and rich in flavour from being fully ripe; (of wine) well-matured; (of soil) rich, loamy. **2** made kindly and sympathetic by age or experience. **3** genial, jovial. **4** (of sound, colour, or light) soft and rich, free from harshness or sharp contrast. —*v.t./i.* to make or become mellow. —**mellowly** *adv.*, **mellowness** *n.* [perh. rel. to MEAL[2]]

melodic /mɪˈlɒdɪk/ *adj.* of melody. [f. F f. L f. Gk (as MELODY)]

melodious /mɪˈləʊdɪəs/ *adj.* of or producing melody; sweet-sounding. —**melodiously** *adv.*, **melodiousness** *n.* [f. OF (as MELODY)]

melodrama /ˈmelədrɑ:mə/ *n.* **1** a play with a sensational plot and crude appeal to the emotions; such plays as a genre. **2** behaviour or an occurrence suggestive of this. —**melodramatic**/-drəˈmætɪk/*adj.*,

melodramatically *adv.* [f. F f. Gk *melos* music + F *drame* (as DRAMA)]

melody /ˈmelədɪ/ *n.* **1** sweet music. **2** a musical arrangement of words, a song or tune. **3** an arrangement of single notes in a musically expressive succession; the principal part in harmonized music. [f. OF f. L f. Gk *melōidia* (as prec., ODE)]

melon /ˈmelən/ *n.* the sweet fruit of various gourds; a gourd producing this, especially the musk-melon (see MUSK) and water-melon (see WATER). [f. OF f. L, abbr. of *melopepo* f. Gk, = apple-gourd]

melt *v.t./i.* (*p.p.* **melted**, or (as *adj.*, of substances not easily melted) MOLTEN) **1** to change from solid to liquid by heat. **2** to become softened or dissolved easily. **3** to make or become gentler through pity or love. **4** to dwindle or fade away; to pass slowly into another form. **5** (*colloq.*) to depart unobtrusively. —**melt down,** to melt (metal articles) in order to use the metal as a raw material; to become liquid and lose structure. **melting-point** *n.* the temperature at which a solid melts. **melting-pot** *n.* a container (e.g. a crucible) in which substances are melted; a place or situation where ideas etc. are being fused or reconstructed. **melt-water** *n.* water resulting from the melting of ice or snow, especially that of a glacier. [OE]

meltdown *n.* the melting of (and consequent damage to) a structure, e.g. the overheated core of a nuclear reactor.

member *n.* **1** a person or thing belonging to a particular society or group. **2 Member,** (in full **Member of Parliament** or (*US*) **of Congress**) a person formally elected to take part in the proceedings of a parliament (in the UK the House of Commons; in the USA Congress). **3** a part of a complex structure. **4** a part or organ of the body. [f. OF f. L *membrum* limb]

membership *n.* **1** being a member. **2** the number of members; the body of members. [f. prec. + -SHIP]

membrane /ˈmembreɪn/ *n.* a pliable sheetlike tissue connecting or lining structures in an animal or vegetable body. —**membranous** /ˈmembreɪnəs/ *adj.* [f. L *membrana* (as MEMBER)]

memento /mɪˈmentəʊ/ *n.* (*pl.* **-oes**) an object serving as a reminder or souvenir. [L, imper. of *meminisse* remember]

memo /ˈmeməʊ/ *n.* (*pl.* **-os**) (*colloq.*) a memorandum. [abbr.]

memoir /ˈmemwɑː(r)/ *n.* **1** a record of events, written from personal knowledge or special sources of information. **2** (usu. in *pl.*) an autobiography; a biography. **3** an essay on a learned subject specially studied by the writer. [f. F *mémoire* (as MEMORY)]

memorabilia /memərəˈbɪlɪə/ *n.pl.* noteworthy things. [L (as foll.)]

memorable /ˈmemərəb(ə)l/ *adj.* **1** worth remembering. **2** easily remembered. —**memorability** /-ˈbɪlɪtɪ/ *n.*, **memorably** *adv.* [f. F or L *memorabilis* (*memorare* bring to mind)]

memorandum /meməˈrændəm/ *n.* (*pl.* **memoranda** or **-ums**) **1** a note or record made for future use. **2** an informal written message, especially in business etc. [L, = to be remembered (as prec.)]

memorial /mɪˈmɔːrɪəl/ *n.* an object, institution, or custom established in memory of a person or event. —*adj.* serving as a memorial. [f. OF or L (as MEMORY)]

memorize /ˈmeməraɪz/ *v.t.* to learn by heart. [f. foll.]

memory /ˈmemərɪ/ *n.* **1** the faculty by which things are recalled to or kept in the mind; this in an individual. **2** remembering; a person or thing remembered. **3** posthumous repute. **4** the length of time over which memory extends. **5** the store for data in a computer. —**from memory,** without verification. **in memory of,** to keep alive the remembrance of. [f. OF f. L *memoria* (*memor* mindful)]

memsahib /ˈmemsɑːɪb, -sɑːb/ *n.* (*hist.*) a European married woman as spoken of or to by Indians. [f. MA'AM + SAHIB]

men *pl.* of MAN.

menace /ˈmenɪs/ *n.* **1** a threat. **2** a dangerous or obnoxious person or thing. —*v.t.* to threaten. —**menacing** *adj.*, **menacingly** *adv.* [f. AF f. L *minaciae* (*minax* threatening)]

ménage /meɪˈnɑːʒ/ *n.* a domestic establishment. —***ménage à trois*** /ɑː trwɑː/ a household consisting of a husband, wife, and the lover of one of these. [f. OF f. L (as MANSION)]

menagerie /mɪˈnædʒərɪ/ *n.* a collection of wild animals in captivity for exhibition etc. [f. F (as prec.)]

mend *v.t./i.* **1** to make whole (something that is damaged), to repair. **2** to regain health. **3** to improve. —*n.* a place where a material etc. has been repaired. —**mend one's fences,** to make peace with a person. **on the mend,** improving in health or condition. [f. AF (as AMEND)]

mendacious /menˈdeɪʃəs/ *adj.* untruthful, lying. —**mendaciously** *adv.*, **mendacity** /-ˈdæsɪtɪ/ *n.* [f. L *mendax*]

mendelevium /mend(ə)lˈiːvɪəm/ *n.* an artificially made transuranic radioactive metallic element, symbol Md, atomic number 101 [f. D. I. *Mendeleev*, Russian chemist (d. 1907)]

Mendelian /menˈdiːlɪən/ *adj.* of Mendel's

theory of heredity by genes. [f. G. J. *Mendel*, Moravian botanist (d. 1884)]

Mendelism /ˈmendəlɪz(ə)m/ *n.* that part of genetics concerned with the manner in which hereditary factors (genes) and the characteristics they control are inherited during the course of sexual reproduction. The main principles were first outlined by Mendel, although they have been modified by later discoveries. [as prec.]

mendicant /ˈmendɪkənt/ *adj.* begging; (of a friar) living solely on alms. —*n.* a beggar; a mendicant friar. [f. L *mendicare* (*mendicus* beggar)]

menfolk *n.* **1** men in general. **2** the men in a family.

menhir /ˈmenhɪə(r)/ *n.* a tall upright prehistoric monumental stone. [f. Breton *men* stone, *hir* long]

menial /ˈmi:nɪəl/ *adj.* (of work) lowly, degrading. —*n.* a lowly domestic servant; a person who does humble tasks. —**menially** *adv.* [f. AF (*meinie* retinue)]

meninges /mɪˈnɪndʒi:z/ *n.pl.* the membranes enclosing the brain and spinal cord. [f. Gk *mēnigx -iggos* membrane]

meningitis /menɪnˈdʒaɪtɪs/ *n.* inflammation of the meninges. [f. prec. + -ITIS]

meniscus /mɪˈnɪskəs/ *n.* (*pl.* **-sci** /-saɪ/) **1** the curved upper surface of a liquid in a tube, usually concave upwards when the walls are wetted and convex when they are dry, because of the effects of surface tension. **2** a lens that is convex on one side and concave on the other. [f. Gk, = crescent (*mēnē* moon)]

menopause /ˈmenəpɔ:z/ *n.* the final cessation of the menses; the period of a woman's life (usually 40–50) when this occurs. —**menopausal** *adj.* [f. Gk *mēn* month + PAUSE]

menorah /məˈnɔ:rə/ *n.* a holy seven-branched candelabrum used in the ancient Temple in Jerusalem; a candelabrum with any number of branches used in modern synagogues. [Heb., = candlestick]

menses /ˈmensi:z/ *n.pl.* the flow of blood etc. from the mucous lining of the human or primate womb, occurring in women at monthly intervals from puberty until middle age. [L, pl. of *mensis* month]

menstrual /ˈmenstrʊəl/ *adj.* of menstruation. [f. L (*menstruus* monthly f. *mensis* month)]

menstruate /ˈmenstrʊeɪt/ *v.i.* to discharge the menses. —**menstruation** /-ˈeɪʃ(ə)n/ *n.* [f. L. *menstruare* (as prec.)]

mensurable /ˈmensjʊrəb(ə)l/ *adj.* measurable; having fixed limits. [F or f. L (*mensurare* to measure)]

mensuration /mensjʊəˈreɪʃ(ə)n/ *n.* measuring; the mathematical rules for finding lengths, areas, and volumes. [f. L (as prec.)]

menswear *n.* clothes for men.

-ment /-mənt/ *suffix* forming nouns expressing the result or means of a verbal action (*fragment*, *ornament*, *treatment*); also forming nouns from adjectives (*merriment*, *oddment*). [f. F f. L *-mentum*]

mental /ˈment(ə)l/ *adj.* **1** of the mind; done by the mind. **2** caring for mental patients. **3** (*colloq.*) affected with mental disorder. —**mental age**, the degree of a person's mental development expressed as the age at which the same degree is attained by the average child. **mental deficiency**, imperfect mental development leading to abnormally low intelligence. **mental patient**, a sufferer from mental illness. —**mentally** *adv.* [f. OF or L (*mens* mind)]

mentality /menˈtælɪtɪ/ *n.* mental character or outlook; mental ability. [f. prec.]

menthol /ˈmenθɒl/ *n.* a camphor-like substance obtained from oil of peppermint etc., used as a flavouring or to relieve local pain etc. [G, f. L *mentha* mint]

mentholated /ˈmenθəleɪtɪd/ *adj.* treated with or containing menthol. [f. prec.]

mention /ˈmenʃ(ə)n/ *v.t.* to refer to briefly or by name. —*n.* **1** mentioning. **2** a formal acknowledgement of merit. —**don't mention it**, a polite reply to thanks or an apology. **not to mention**, and also. [f. OF f. L]

mentor /ˈmentɔ:(r)/ *n.* an experienced and trusted adviser. [F, f. *Mentor* adviser of young Telemachus, son of Odysseus]

menu /ˈmenju:/ *n.* **1** a list of the dishes available in a restaurant etc. or to be served at a meal. **2** a list of options, displayed on a screen, from which a user selects what he requires a computer to do. [F, = detailed list (as MINUTE²)]

MEP *abbr.* Member of the European Parliament.

mercantile /ˈmɜ:kəntaɪl/ *adj.* of trade, commercial; trading. —**mercantile marine**, the merchant navy. [F f. It. (as MERCHANT)]

mercantilism /ˈmɜ:kəntɪlɪz(ə)m/ *n.* an economic theory that money is the only form of wealth. [f. prec.]

mercenary /ˈmɜ:sɪnərɪ/ *adj.* working merely for money or other reward; hired. —*n.* a hired soldier in foreign service. —**mercenarily** *adv.* [f. L *mercenarius* (*merces* reward)]

mercer /ˈmɜ:sə(r)/ *n.* a dealer in textile fabrics. [f. AF f. L *merx* goods]

mercerize /ˈmɜ:səraɪz/ *v.t.* to treat (cotton fabric or thread) with caustic alkali to give greater strength and lustre. [f. J. *Mercer*, alleged inventor of process (d. 1866)]

merchandise /ˈmɜːtʃəndaɪz/ *n.* the commodities of commerce; goods for sale. —*v.t./i.* to promote the sales of (goods etc.); to trade. [f. OF *marchandise* (as foll.)]

merchant /ˈmɜːtʃ(ə)nt/ *n.* **1** a wholesale trader, especially with foreign countries. **2** (*US & Sc.*) a retail trader. **3** (*slang*) a person fond of an activity etc. —**merchant bank,** a bank whose main business is the providing of long-term credit and the financing of trading enterprises. **merchant navy,** shipping engaged in commerce. **merchant prince,** a wealthy merchant. **merchant ship,** a ship carrying merchandise. [f. OF *marchand* f. L *mercari* trade (as MERCER)]

merchantable *adj.* saleable. [f. prec.]

merchantman *n.* (*pl.* **-men**) a merchant ship.

merciful /ˈmɜːsɪful/ *adj.* **1** having, showing, or feeling mercy. **2** giving relief from pain etc. —**mercifully** *adv.*, **mercifulness** *n.* [f. MERCY + -FUL]

merciless /ˈmɜːsɪlɪs/ *adj.* showing no mercy. —**mercilessly** *adv.*, **mercilessness** *n.* [f. MERCY + -LESS]

mercurial /mɜːˈkjʊərɪəl/ *adj.* **1** (of a person) volatile, ready-witted. **2** of or containing mercury. [f. OF or L (as foll.)]

mercury /ˈmɜːkjʊrɪ/ *n.* a silvery-white heavy metallic element, symbol Hg, atomic number 80, liquid at room temperatures. —**mercuric** /-ˈkjʊerɪk/ *adj.*, **mercurous** *adj.* [f. *Mercury.* (planet)]

mercy /ˈmɜːsɪ/ *n.* **1** refraining from inflicting punishment or pain on an offender or enemy etc. who is in one's power. **2** a tendency to behave in this way. **3** a merciful act; a thing to be thankful for. —**at the mercy of,** wholly in the power of; liable to danger or harm from. **mercy killing,** euthanasia. [f. OF f. L *merces* reward, later = pity, thanks]

mere[1] /mɪə(r)/ *attrib. adj.* that is solely or no more or better than what is specified. [f. AF f. L *merus* unmixed]

mere[2] /mɪə(r)/ *n. poetic* a lake. [OE]

merely *adv.* only, just. [f. MERE[1]]

meretricious /merɪˈtrɪʃəs/ *adj.* showily attractive but cheap or insincere. —**meretriciously** *adv.*, **meretriciousness** *n.* [f. L (*meretrix* prostitute)]

merganser /mɜːˈgænsə(r)/ *n.* a diving duck of the genus *Mergus* etc. [f. L *mergus* diver + *anser* goose]

merge /mɜːdʒ/ *v.t./i.* **1** to unite or combine into a whole. **2** to pass slowly into something else; to blend or become blended. [f. L *mergere* dip]

merger /ˈmɜːdʒə(r)/ *n.* the combining of two commercial companies etc. into one. [f. AF (as prec.)]

meridian /məˈrɪdɪən/ *n.* **1** a circle of constant longitude, passing through a given place and the terrestrial poles; a corresponding line on a map or the sky. **2** prime, full splendour. [f. OF or L (*meridies* midday)]

meridional /məˈrɪdɪən(ə)l/ *adj.* **1** of the south, especially of Europe, or its inhabitants. **2** of a meridian. [f. OF f. L (as prec.)]

meringue /məˈræŋ/ *n.* a mixture of white of egg, sugar, etc., baked crisp. [F]

merino /məˈriːnəʊ/ *n.* (*pl.* **-os**) **1** a variety of sheep with fine wool. **2** a soft woollen yarn or fabric originally of merino wool. [Sp.]

merit /ˈmerɪt/ *n.* **1** the quality of deserving to be praised, excellence. **2** a feature or quality that deserves praise. —*v.t.* to deserve. —**Order of Merit,** an order, founded in 1902, for distinguished achievement. [f. L *meritum* (*merēri* deserve)]

meritocracy /merɪˈtɒkrəsɪ/ *n.* government by persons selected for their merit. [as prec. + -CRACY]

meritorious /merɪˈtɔːrɪəs/ *adj.* having merit, praiseworthy. —**meritoriously** *adv.*, **meritoriousness** *n.* [f. L (as MERIT)]

merlin /ˈmɜːlɪn/ *n.* a kind of small falcon (*Falco columbarius*). [f. AF]

merlon /ˈmɜːlən/ *n.* the solid part of an embattled parapet, between two embrasures. [F, f. It. *merlone* (*merlo* battlement)]

mermaid /ˈmɜːmeɪd/ *n.* a legendary sea-creature with a woman's head and trunk and a fish's tail. [f. MERE[2] in obs. sense 'sea' + MAID]

merry *adj.* joyous, full of laughter or gaiety; (*colloq.*) slightly tipsy. —**make merry,** to be festive. **merry-go-round** *n.* a revolving machine with horses, cars, etc., for riding on at a fair etc., a revolving device in a playground, a cycle of bustling activities. **merry-making** *n.* festivity. —**merrily** *adv.*, **merriment** *n.* [OE (as MIRTH)]

mesa /ˈmeɪsə/ *n.* (*US*) a high tableland with steep sides. [Sp., = table]

mésalliance /meɪˈzælɪɑ̃s/ *n.* marriage with a social inferior. [F., = MISALLIANCE]

mescal /ˈmeskæl/ *n.* the peyote cactus. —**mescal buttons,** its disc-shaped dried tops. [f. Sp. f. Nahuatl]

mescaline /ˈmeskəliːn/ *n.* a hallucinogenic alkaloid present in mescal buttons. [f. prec.]

Mesdames *pl.* of MADAME; also used as *pl.* of MRS.

Mesdemoiselles *pl.* of MADEMOISELLE.

mesembryanthemum /mɪzembrɪˈænθɪməm/ *n.* a plant of the genus *Mesembryanthemum*, with flowers that are open in the middle of the day. [f. Gk *mesēmbria* noon + *anthemon* flower]

mesh *n.* **1** the open spaces between the threads or wires in a net, sieve, wire screen, etc.

2 network fabric. 3 (in *pl.*) a network; a trap or snare. —*v.t./i.* 1 (of toothed wheels) to engage with another or others. 2 to be harmonious. 3 to catch in a net (*lit.* or *fig.*). —**in mesh,** (of the teeth of wheels) engaged. [f. MDu.]

mesmerize /ˈmezməraɪz/ *v.t.* to hypnotize (see HYPNOSIS); to fascinate, to dominate the attention or will of. —**mesmeric** /-ˈmerɪk/ *adj.*, **mesmerism** *n.* [f. A. *Mesmer*, Austrian physician (d. 1815)]

meso- /mesə-/ *in comb.* middle, intermediate. [f. Gk *mesos* middle]

mesolithic /mesəˈlɪθɪk/ *adj.* of the transitional period between the palaeolithic and neolithic, especially in Europe. [f. MESO- + Gk *lithos* stone]

mesomorph /ˈmesəmɔːf/ *n.* a person with a compact muscular build of body. [f. MESO- + Gk *morphē* form]

meson /ˈmiːzɒn/ *n.* an unstable elementary particle intermediate in mass between a proton and an electron. [alt. of earlier *mesotron* (MESO-)]

mesopause /ˈmesəpɔːz/ *n.* the boundary between the mesosphere and the thermosphere, where the temperature stops decreasing with height and starts to increase.

mesosphere /ˈmesəsfɪə(r)/ *n.* the region of the earth's atmosphere from the top of the stratosphere to an altitude of about 80 km.

Mesozoic /mesəˈzəʊɪk/ *adj.* of the geological era between the Palaeozoic and Cainozoic. —*n.* this era. [f. Gk *mesos* middle + *zōion* animal]

mess *n.* 1 a dirty or untidy state of things; an untidy collection of things; something spilt. 2 a difficult or confused situation, trouble. 3 a disagreeable substance or concoction; excreta. 4 (*colloq.*) a person who looks untidy, dirty, or slovenly. 5 a group of people who take meals together, especially in the armed services; the room where such meals are taken; a meal so taken. 6 a portion of liquid or pulpy food. —*v.t./i.* 1 to make untidy or dirty. 2 to muddle or bungle (often with *up*). 3 to potter or fool *about* or *around*; to tinker. 4 to take one's meals with a military or other group. —**make a mess of,** to bungle. **mess-jacket** *n.* a short close-fitting coat worn at mess. **mess-kit** *n.* a soldier's cooking and eating utensils. [f. OF f. L *missus* course at dinner (*mittere* send)]

message /ˈmesɪdʒ/ *n.* 1 a spoken or written communication sent or transmitted from one person to another. 2 an inspired or significant communication from a prophet, writer, preacher, etc. —**get the message,** (*colloq.*) to understand what is meant. [f. OF, ult. f. L *mittere* send]

messenger /ˈmesɪndʒə(r)/ *n.* one who carries a message. [as prec.]

Messiah /mɪˈsaɪə/ *n.* 1 the expected deliverer and ruler of the Jewish people, whose coming was prophesied in the Old Testament. 2 Christ, regarded by Christians as this. 3 a liberator of oppressed people. [f. OF, ult. f. Heb., = anointed]

Messianic /mesɪˈænɪk/ *adj.* of the Messiah; inspired by hope or belief in a Messiah. [f. F (as prec.)]

Messieurs *pl.* of MONSIEUR.

Messrs /ˈmesəz/ *n.* used as *pl.* of MR, especially as a prefix to the name of a firm or to a list of men's names. [abbr. of MESSIEURS]

messuage /ˈmeswɪdʒ/ *n.* (*Law*) a dwelling-house with outbuildings and land. [f. AF, perh. alt. of *mesnage* dwelling (as MÉNAGE)]

messy *adj.* 1 untidy or dirty. 2 causing or accompanied by a mess. 3 difficult to deal with. —**messily** *adv.*, **messiness** *n.* [f. MESS]

met[1] *adj.* (*colloq.*) 1 meteorological. 2 metropolitan. —**the Met,** the Meteorological Office; the Metropolitan Opera House (New York). [abbr.]

met[2] *past* & *p.p.* of MEET[1].

meta- /metə/ *prefix* denoting a position or condition behind, after, beyond or transcending (*metacarpus*), or a change of position or condition (*metabolism*). [Gk (*meta* with, after)]

metabolism /mɪˈtæbəlɪz(ə)m/ *n.* the sum total of the organized chemical reactions taking place in a living cell, tissue, or organism in order to maintain life. —**metabolic** /metəˈbɒlɪk/ *adj.* [f. Gk *metabolē* change (META-, *ballō* throw)]

metabolize /mɪˈtæbəlaɪz/ *v.t.* to process (food) in metabolism. [f. prec.]

metacarpus /metəˈkɑːpəs/ *n.* (*pl.* **-pi** /-paɪ/) the part of the hand between the wrist and the fingers; the set of bones in this. —**metacarpal** *adj.* [f. Gk (as META-, CARPUS)]

metal /met(ə)l/ *n.* 1 any of a large class of elements which in general can take the form of opaque solids having a characteristic lustre; an alloy of these. 2 (in *pl.*) the rails of a railway-line; road-metal (see ROAD). —*adj.* made of metal. —*v.t.* (**-ll-**) 1 to furnish or fit with metal. 2 to make or mend (a road) with road-metal. [f. OF or L f. Gk *metallon* mine]

metallic /mɪˈtælɪk/ *adj.* 1 of metal; characteristic of metals. 2 sounding like struck metal. —**metallically** *adv.* [f. F f. L f. Gk (as prec.)]

metalliferous /metəˈlɪfərəs/ *adj.* (of rocks etc.) containing metal. [f. L (as METAL, -FEROUS)]

metallize /ˈmetəlaɪz/ *v.t.* 1 to render metallic. 2 to coat with a thin layer of metal. —**metallization** /-ˈzeɪʃ(ə)n/ *n.* [f. METAL]

metallography /metəˈlɒgrəfɪ/ *n.* the descriptive science of metals. [f. METAL + -GRAPHY]

metallurgy /mɪˈtælədʒɪ, ˈmetəlɜːdʒɪ/ *n.* **1** the science of the properties of metals. **2** the art of working metals, especially of extracting metals from ores. —**metallurgical** /metəˈlɜːdʒɪk(ə)l/ *adj.*, **metallurgist** *n.* [f. Gk (as METAL, *-ourgia* working)]

metamorphic /metəˈmɔːfɪk/ *adj.* **1** of or characterized by metamorphism. **2** (of rock) that has undergone structural, chemical, or mineralogical change by natural agencies, especially heat and pressure (cf. IGNEOUS, SEDIMENTARY), as in the transformation of limestone into marble. [f. META- + Gk *morphē* form]

metamorphism /metəˈmɔːfɪz(ə)m/ *n.* the process of metamorphic change in rock. [f. prec. + -ISM]

metamorphose /metəˈmɔːfəʊz/ *v.t.* to change into a new form; to change the nature of. [f. F (as foll.)]

metamorphosis /metəˈmɔːfəsɪs, -ˈfəʊsɪs/ *n.* (*pl.* **-oses** /-siːz/) a change of form, especially by magic or natural development; a change of character, conditions, etc. [L f. Gk (as METAMORPHIC)]

metaphor /ˈmetəfə(r)/ *n.* an application of a name or descriptive term or phrase to an object or action where it is not literally applicable (e.g. *a glaring error*). —**metaphorical** /-ˈfɒrɪk(ə)l/ *adj.*, **metaphorically** *adv.* [f. F or L f. Gk (*metapherō* transfer)]

metaphysical /metəˈfɪzɪk(ə)l/ *adj.* **1** of or involving metaphysics. **2** based on abstract reasoning, over-subtle. [f. foll.]

metaphysics /metəˈfɪzɪks/ *n.pl.* (usu. treated as *sing.*) **1** the branch of speculative inquiry that deals with such concepts as being, knowing, substance, cause, identity, time, space, etc. **2** (*pop.*) abstract or subtle talk, mere theory. [f. OF ult. f. Gk *ta meta ta phusica*, the title applied, at least from the 1st c. AD, to the 13 books of Aristotle dealing with questions of ontology.

metastasis /meˈtæstəsɪs/ *n.* (*pl.* **-ases** /-əsiːz/) the transfer of disease etc. from one part of the body to another. [L f. Gk, = removal, change]

metatarsus /metəˈtɑːsəs/ *n.* (*pl.* **-si** /-saɪ/) the part of the foot between the ankle and the toes; the set of bones in this. —**metatarsal** *adj.* [as META- + TARSUS]

mete /miːt/ *v.t.* to allot or deal (a punishment, reward, etc.). [OE (as MEET[2])]

meteor /ˈmiːtɪə(r)/ *n.* a bright moving body formed by a small mass of matter from outer space rendered incandescent by friction with the air as it passes through the earth's atmosphere. [f. Gk (*meteōros* high in the air)]

meteoric /miːtɪˈɒrɪk/ *adj.* **1** of meteors. **2** like a meteor in brilliance, sudden appearance, or transience. —**meteorically** *adv.* [f. prec.]

meteorite /ˈmiːtɪəraɪt/ *n.* a fallen meteor, a fragment of rock or metal from outer space, of sufficient size to survive a fiery passage through the atmosphere and reach the surface of the earth. [f. METEOR]

meteoroid /ˈmiːtɪərɔɪd/ *n.* a body moving through space, of the same nature as those which become visible as meteors. [as prec.]

meteorological /miːtɪərəˈlɒdʒɪk(ə)l/ *adj.* of meteorology. —**Meteorological Office**, a government department providing weather forecasts etc. [as foll.]

meteorology /miːtɪəˈrɒlədʒɪ/ *n.* the study of the phenomena of the atmosphere, especially for weather forecasting. —**meteorologist** *n.* [f. Gk (as METEOR, -LOGY)]

meter /ˈmiːtə(r)/ *n.* an instrument for recording the amount of a substance supplied or used, time spent, distance travelled, etc. —*v.t.* to measure by a meter. [f. METE]

-meter /-mɪtə(r)/ *suffix* forming names of automatic measuring instruments (*thermometer*, *voltmeter*) or of lines of verse with a specified number of measures (*pentameter*). [f. Gk *metron* measure]

methane /ˈmiːθeɪn/ *n.* an inflammable hydrocarbon gas of the paraffin series. [f. METHYL]

methinks /mɪˈθɪŋks/ *v.i.* (*impers.*) (*past* **methought** /mɪˈθɔːt/) (*archaic*) it seems to me. [OE (as ME[1], THINK)]

method /ˈmeθəd/ *n.* **1** a procedure or way of doing something. **2** orderliness; the orderly arrangement of ideas. **3** a theory and practice of acting in which the actor seeks to achieve a true interpretation of his part by mentally identifying himself with the character he is playing. [f. F or L f. Gk *methodos* pursuit of knowledge (META-, *hodos* way)]

methodical /mɪˈθɒdɪk(ə)l/ *adj.* characterized by method or order. —**methodically** *adv.* [f. L f. Gk (as prec.)]

Methodist /ˈmeθədɪst/ *n.* a member of a Protestant denomination originating in an 18th-c. evangelistic movement which grew out of a religious society established within the Church of England (from which it formally separated in 1791) by John and Charles Wesley at Oxford. —**Methodism** *n.* [f. METHOD]

methodology /meθəˈdɒlədʒɪ/ *n.* **1** the science of method. **2** the body of methods used in an activity. [f. METHOD + -LOGY]

methought *past* of METHINKS.

meths *n.* (*colloq.*) methylated spirit. [abbr.]

methyl /ˈmeθɪl, ˈmi:θaɪl/ *n.* the chemical radical present in methane etc. —**methyl alcohol,** a colourless volatile inflammable liquid. [G or F, ult. f. Gk *methu* wine + *hulē* wood]

methylated /ˈmeθɪleɪtɪd/ *adj.* mixed or impregnated with methyl alcohol. —**methylated spirit(s),** alcohol so treated to make it unfit for drinking and so exempt from duty. [f. prec.]

meticulous /mɪˈtɪkjʊləs/ *adj.* giving great or excessive attention to details, very careful and precise. —**meticulously** *adv.*, **meticulousness** *n.* [f. L (*metus* fear)]

métier /ˈmeɪtjeɪ/ *n.* one's trade, profession, or field of activity; one's forte. [F (as MINISTRY)]

metonymy /mɪˈtɒnɪmɪ/ *n.* substitution of the name of an attribute or adjunct for that of the thing meant (e.g. *crown* for *king*). [f. L f. Gk (META-, *onoma* name)]

metope /ˈmetəʊp/ *n.* a square space between triglyphs in a Doric frieze. [f. L f. Gk (as META-, *opē* hole for beam-end)]

metre¹ /ˈmi:tə(r)/ *n.* any form of poetic rhythm, determined by the character and number of feet; a metrical group. [OE, ult. f. Gk *metron* measure]

metre² /ˈmi:tə(r)/ *n.* the base unit of length (symbol m), defined in 1983 as the length of the path travelled by light in a vacuum during a time interval of 1/299 792 458 of a second. [f. F *mètre* (as prec.)]

metric /ˈmetrɪk/ *adj.* **1** of or based on the metre as a unit. **2** metrical. —**metric system,** a decimal measuring-system with the metre, litre, and gram as the units of length, capacity, and weight or mass. —**metrically** *adv.* [f. F *métrique* (as prec.)]

-metric *suffix* (also **-metrical**) forming adjectives from nouns in *-meter* or *-metry*. [f. F f. L (as foll.)]

metrical /ˈmetrɪk(ə)l/ *adj.* **1** of or composed in metre. **2** of or involving measurement. —**metrically** *adv.* [f. L f. Gk (as METRE)]

metricate /ˈmetrɪkeɪt/ *v.t./i.* to change or adapt to the metric system. —**metrication** /-ˈkeɪʃ(ə)n/ *n.* [f. METRIC]

metronome /ˈmetrənəʊm/ *n.* an instrument that sounds a click at a selected interval, used to indicate tempo while practising music. [f. Gk *metron* measure + *nomos* law]

metropolis /mɪˈtrɒpəlɪs/ *n.* the chief city of a county or region, a capital. [L f. Gk (*mētēr* mother, *polis* city)]

metropolitan /metrəˈpɒlɪt(ə)n/ *adj.* **1** of a metropolis. **2** of or forming the mother country as distinct from colonies etc. —*n.* **1** a bishop with authority over the bishops of a province. **2** an inhabitant of a metropolis. —**metropolitan county,** each of the six conurbations (other than Greater London) established in England by the local government reorganization of 1974, with powers analogous to those of counties. **metropolitan district,** each of the areas into which a metropolitan county is divided.

-metry /-mɪtrɪ/ *suffix* forming names of procedures and systems involving measurement (*geometry*). [f. Gk *-metria* (as METRE)]

mettle *n.* quality or strength of character, courage. —**on one's mettle,** incited to do one's best. [var. of METAL]

mettlesome *adj.* spirited. [f. prec. + -SOME]

mew¹ *n.* the characteristic cry of a cat. —*v.i.* to utter a mew. [imit.]

mew² *n.* a gull. [OE]

mews /mju:z/ *n.pl.* (treated as *sing.*) a set of stables round an open yard or lane, now often converted into dwellings. [orig. sing. *mew* = cage for hawks while moulting, f. OF f. L *mutare* change; orig. of royal stables on site of hawks' cages at Charing Cross in London]

mezzanine /ˈmetsəni:n/ *n.* an extra storey between two others, usually between the ground and first floors. [F f. It. (*mezzano* middle, as MEDIAN)]

mezzo /ˈmetsəʊ/ *adv.* (esp. *Mus.*) half, moderately. —***mezzo forte,*** fairly loud. ***mezzo piano,*** fairly soft. ***mezzo-soprano,*** a voice between soprano and contralto, a singer with this voice. [It. f. L *medius* middle]

mezzotint /ˈmetsəʊtɪnt/ *n.* **1** a method of engraving using a uniformly roughened plate, on which the rough areas give shaded parts and the areas scraped smooth give light. **2** a print produced by this. [f. It. (as prec. + TINT)]

mf *abbr. mezzo forte.*

Mg *symbol* magnesium.

mg *abbr.* milligram(s).

Mgr. *abbr. Monsignor*; *Monseigneur*.

MHz *abbr.* megahertz.

mi var. of ME².

miaow /mɪˈaʊ/ *n.* the cry of a cat, a mew. —*v.i.* to make this cry. [imit.]

miasma /mɪˈæzmə, maɪ-/ *n.* (*pl.* **-mata**) an infectious or noxious escape of air etc. [Gk, = defilement (*miainō* pollute)]

mica /ˈmaɪkə/ *n.* a kind of mineral found as small glittering scales in granite etc. or in crystals separable into thin transparent plates. [L, = crumb]

Micawber /mɪˈkɔ:bə(r)/ *n.* a person who is perpetually hoping that something good will turn up while making no positive effort. —**Micawberish** *adj.*, **Micawberism** *n.* [character in Dickens's novel *David Copperfield*, for whom the model was Dickens's father]

mice *pl.* of MOUSE.

Michaelmas /ˈmɪkəlməs/ *n.* the feast of St Michael, 29 Sept. —**Michaelmas daisy,** an aster flowering in autumn. **Michaelmas term,** the university and law term beginning near Michaelmas. [f. St *Michael* + MASS²]

mickey *n.* (*slang*) **take the mickey (out of),** to tease or mock. [orig. unkn.]

mickle *adj.* much, great. —*n.* a large amount. (The proverb *many a mickle makes a muckle* is an error for *many a little* (or *pickle*) *makes a mickle.*) [f. ON]

micro- /maɪkrəʊ-/ *in comb.* **1** small. **2** one millionth of (*microgram, microsecond*). [f. Gk (*mikros* small)]

microbe /ˈmaɪkrəʊb/ *n.* a micro-organism, especially a bacterium causing disease or fermentation. —**microbial** /-ˈrəʊbɪ(ə)l/ *adj.*, **microbially** *adv.* [F f. Gk (as MICRO-, *bios* life)]

microbiology /maɪkrəʊbaɪˈɒlədʒɪ/ *n.* the study of micro-organisms.

microchip /ˈmaɪkrəʊtʃɪp/ *n.* a tiny piece of semiconductor carrying many electrical circuits.

microcircuit /ˈmaɪkrəʊsɜːkɪt/ *n.* an integrated circuit or other very small electrical circuit.

microclimate /ˈmaɪkrəʊklaɪmət/ *n.* the climate of a small area.

microcomputer /maɪkrəʊkəmˈpjuːtə(r)/ *n.* a small computer in which the central processor is a microprocessor.

microcosm /ˈmaɪkrəkɒz(ə)m/ *n.* **1** a complex thing, especially man, viewed as an epitome of the universe. **2** a miniature representation. —**microcosmic** /-ˈkɒsmɪk/ *adj.* [f. F or L f. Gk *mikros kosmos* little world]

microdot /ˈmaɪkrəʊdɒt/ *n.* a photograph of a document etc. reduced to the size of a dot.

microelectronics /maɪkrəʊiːlekˈtrɒnɪks/ *n.* the design, manufacture, and use of microcircuits.

microfiche /ˈmaɪkrəʊfiːʃ/ *n.* (*pl.* same) a small sheet of film bearing tiny photographs of pages of documents etc. [f. MICRO- + F *fiche* slip of paper]

microfilm /ˈmaɪkrəʊfɪlm/ *n.* a length of film bearing a microphotograph of a document etc. —*v.t.* to record on this.

microlight /ˈmaɪkrəʊlaɪt/ *n.* a kind of motorized hang-glider. [f. MICRO- + LIGHT²]

microlith /ˈmaɪkrəlɪθ/ *n.* a very small worked flint, usually mounted on a piece of bone, wood, or horn as part of a composite tool, characteristic especially of mesolithic industries in Europe. —**microlithic** *adj.* [f. MICRO- + Gk *lithos* stone]

micrometer /maɪˈkrɒmɪtə(r)/ *n.* an instrument for measuring small lengths or angles. [f. MICRO- + -METER]

micron /ˈmaɪkrɒn/ *n.* one millionth of a metre. [Gk, neut. of *mikros* small]

micro-organism /maɪkrəʊˈɔːgənɪz(ə)m/ *n.* an organism not visible to the naked eye, e.g. a bacterium or virus.

microphone /ˈmaɪkrəfəʊn/ *n.* an instrument for converting sound-waves into electrical energy which may be reconverted into sound elsewhere. [f. MICRO- + Gk *phōnē* sound]

microprocessor /ˈmaɪkrəʊprəʊsesə(r)/ *n.* a miniature computer, or a unit of this, consisting of one or more microchips.

microscope /ˈmaɪkrəskəʊp/ *n.* an instrument magnifying small objects by means of a lens or lenses so as to reveal details invisible to the naked eye. [f. MICRO- + -SCOPE]

microscopic /maɪkrəˈskɒpɪk/ *adj.* **1** too small to be visible without a microscope. **2** extremely small. **3** of or by means of a microscope. —**microscopically** *adv.* [f. prec.]

microscopy /maɪˈkrɒskəpɪ/ *n.* use of the microscope. [f. MICROSCOPE]

microsurgery /ˈmaɪkrəʊsɜːdʒərɪ/ *n.* surgery using a microscope to see the tissue and instruments involved.

microwave /ˈmaɪkrəʊweɪv/ *n.* **1** an electromagnetic wave having a wavelength of between about 30 cm and 1 mm. **2** an oven using microwaves, where the moisture present in food selectively absorbs these, converts the energy into heat, and quickly cooks the food.

micturition /mɪktjʊəˈrɪʃ(ə)n/ *n.* urination. [f. L, = desire to urinate (*mingere* urinate)]

mid *adj.* **1** in the middle of (usu. as comb.: *mid-air; mid-week*). **2** that is in the middle, medium, half. —**mid-off, mid-on** *ns.* the positions of fieldsmen in cricket near the bowler on the off or on side. **Mid West,** = Middle West. [OE]

midday /ˈmɪddeɪ/ *n.* noon; the time near noon.

midden /ˈmɪd(ə)n/ *n.* a dunghill, a refuse-heap. [cf. Da. *mødding* (as MUCK, *dynge* heap)]

middle *attrib. adj.* **1** at an equal distance from extremities. **2** (of a member of a group) so placed as to have the same number of members on each side. **3** intermediate in rank, quality, etc.; average. —*n.* **1** a middle point, position, or part. **2** the waist. —**in the middle of,** during or half-way through (an activity or process). **middle age,** the middle part of normal life. **middle-aged** *adj.* of middle age. **Middle Ages,** the period in Europe after the Dark Ages (*c.*1000–1400) or in a wider sense *c.*600–1500. **middle C,** the C near the middle of the piano keyboard, the note between the treble and bass staves. **middle class,** the social class between the upper and lower, including professional and business people. **middle ear,** the cavity behind the ear-drum. **Middle East,** the region comprising the countries lying between the Near and Far

East, especially Egypt, Iran, and the countries between them. **middle name,** a given name between the first name and the surname; a person's most characteristic quality. **middle-of-the-road** *adj.* (of a person or action) moderate, avoiding extremes. **middle school,** a school for children from about 9 to 13. **middle-sized** *adj.* of medium size. **Middle West,** that part of the USA occupying the northern half of the Mississippi River basin, including the States of Ohio, Indiana, Illinois, Michigan, Wisconsin, Iowa, and Minnesota.

middleman *n.* (*pl.* **-men**) **1** any of the traders who handle a commodity between its producer and its customer. **2** an intermediary.

middleweight *n.* the boxing-weight between welterweight and heavyweight (see BOXING-WEIGHT).

middling *adj.* moderately good; fairly well in health. —*adv.* fairly, moderately. [f. MID]

midfield *n.* the part of a football pitch away from the goals.

midge *n.* a gnatlike insect, specifically one of the family Chironomidae. [OE]

midget /ˈmɪdʒɪt/ *n.* an extremely small person or thing. —*adj.* extremely small. [f. prec.]

midland /ˈmɪdlənd/ *adj.* of the middle part of a country. —**the Midlands,** the inland counties of central England.

midnight /ˈmɪdnaɪt/ *n.* 12 o'clock at night; the time near this; the middle of the night. —**midnight blue,** very dark blue. **midnight sun,** the sun visible at midnight during summer in polar regions.

midriff /ˈmɪdrɪf/ *n.* the region of the front of the body just above the waist. [OE, = mid-belly]

midshipman /ˈmɪdʃɪpmən/ *n.* (*pl.* **-men**) a naval officer ranking next above cadet.

midst *n.* the middle part. —**in the midst of,** among; in the middle of. [earlier *middest* f. *in middes* (IN, MID)]

midsummer /mɪdˈsʌmə(r), ˈmɪ-/ *n.* the period of or near the summer solstice, about 21 June. —**Midsummer's Day,** 24 June.

midway *adv.* half-way between.

midwicket /mɪdˈwɪkɪt/ *n.* a position in cricket on the leg side opposite the middle of the pitch.

midwife *n.* (*pl.* **midwives** /-vz/) a person trained to assist women in childbirth. —**midwifery** /-wɪfrɪ/ *n.* [f. obs. *mid* with + WIFE, in sense 'one who is with the mother']

midwinter /mɪdˈwɪntə(r)/ *n.* the period of or near the winter solstice, about 22 Dec.

mien /mi:n/ *n.* a person's bearing or look. [f. obs. *demean* behave (as DEMEANOUR)]

might[1] /maɪt/ *v.aux.* used as *past tense* of MAY[1] esp. (1) in reported speech, (2) with a perfect infinitive expressing possibility based on a condition not fulfilled, or based on an obligation not fulfilled; also used (*loosely*) as = MAY[2]. —**might-have-been** *n.* an event etc. that might have happened but did not. [as MAY[1]]

might[2] /maɪt/ *n.* great strength or power. —**with might and main,** with all one's power. [OE (as MAY[1])]

mightn't /ˈmaɪt(ə)nt/ (*colloq.*) might not.

mighty /ˈmaɪtɪ/ *adj.* **1** powerful, strong. **2** massive, bulky; (*colloq.*) great, considerable. —*adv.* (*colloq.*) very. —**mightily** *adv.*, **mightiness** *n.* [as MIGHT[2]]

mignonette /mɪnjəˈnet/ *n.* an annual plant of the genus *Reseda* with small fragrant flowers. [f. F dim. of *mignon* small]

migraine /ˈmi:greɪn/ *n.* a severe recurring form of headache, often with nausea and disturbance of the vision. [F, f. L f. Gk *hēmikrania* (as HEMI-, CRANIUM)]

migrant /ˈmaɪgrənt/ *adj.* that migrates. —*n.* a migrant person or animal, especially a bird. [as foll.]

migrate /maɪˈgreɪt/ *v.i.* **1** to leave one place and settle in another. **2** (of animals) to go periodically from one area to another, living in each place for part of a year. —**migration** *n.*, **migratory** /ˈmaɪgrətərɪ/ *adj.* [f. L *migrare*]

mihrab /ˈmi:rɑ:b/ *n.* a niche or slab in a mosque, used to show the direction of Mecca. [f. Arab., = praying-place]

mikado /mɪˈkɑ:dəʊ/ *n.* (*pl.* **-os**) the emperor of Japan. [Jap., = august door]

mike *n.* (*colloq.*) a microphone. [abbr.]

milady /mɪˈleɪdɪ/ *n.* an English noblewoman. [F, f. *my lady*]

milch /mɪltʃ/ *adj.* giving milk. —**milch cow,** a cow kept for milk; a source of regular or easy profit. [as MILK]

mild /maɪld/ *adj.* **1** moderate in intensity, character, or effect, not severe or harsh or drastic; (of climate etc.) moderately warm. **2** gentle in manner. **3** not strongly flavoured, not sharp or bitter in taste. —*n.* mild ale. —**mild steel,** steel that is tough but not easily tempered. —**mildly** *adv.*, **mildness** *n.* [OE]

mildew /ˈmɪldju:/ *n.* a growth of minute fungi forming on surfaces exposed to damp. —*v.t./i.* to taint or be tainted with mildew. —**mildewed** *adj.*, **mildewy** *adj.* [OE, = honey dew]

mile *n.* **1** a unit of linear measure, equal to 1,760 yds. (1.609 km). The nautical mile, used in navigation, is a unit of 2,025 yds. (1.852 km). **2** a great distance or amount. **3** a race extending over a mile. [OE, ult. f. L *mille* thousand]

mileage *n.* **1** the number of miles travelled. **2** the advantage to be derived from something. [f. MILE]

miler /ˈmaɪlə(r)/ *n.* a person or horse specializing in races of one mile. [f. MILE]

milestone *n.* **1** a stone set up beside a road to mark the distance in miles. **2** a significant event or stage in life or history.

milfoil /ˈmɪlfɔɪl/ *n.* a plant (*Achillea millefolium*) with small white flowers and finely divided leaves, yarrow. [f. OF f. L *millefolium* (*mille* thousand, *folium* leaf)]

milieu /ˈmiːljɜː/ *n.* (*pl.* **-ieux** /-jɜːz/) an environment; a state of life; social surroundings. [F (*mi* mid, *lieu* place]

militant /ˈmɪlɪtənt/ *adj.* **1** prepared to take aggressive action in support of a cause. **2** engaged in warfare. —*n.* a militant person. —**Militant Tendency,** a movement dedicated to upholding Trotskyist principles within the Labour Party. —**militancy** *n.*, **militantly** *adv.* [f. OF f. L (as MILITATE)]

militarism /ˈmɪlɪtərɪz(ə)m/ *n.* military spirit; an aggressive policy of reliance on military strength and means. —**militarist** *n.*, **militaristic** /-ˈrɪstɪk/ *adj.* [f. F (as MILITARY)]

militarize /ˈmɪlɪtəraɪz/ *v.t.* **1** to make military or warlike. **2** to equip with military resources. **3** to imbue with militarism. —**militarization** /-ˈzeɪʃ(ə)n/ *n.* [f. foll.]

military /mɪlɪtərɪ/ *adj.* of or for or done by soldiers or the armed forces. —**the military** (as *sing.* or *pl.*), the army (as distinct from the police or civilians). —**militarily** *adv.* [f. F or L *militaris* (*miles* soldier)]

militate /ˈmɪlɪteɪt/ *v.i.* (of facts or evidence) to tell or serve as a strong influence (*against*, rarely *in favour of*, a conclusion etc.). [f. L *militare* (as prec.)]

militia /mɪˈlɪʃə/ *n.* a military force, especially one raised from the civil population and supplementing the regular army in an emergency. [L, = military service (as MILITARY)]

milk *n.* **1** an opaque white fluid secreted by female mammals for the nourishment of their young; milk, especially of the cow, as a food. **2** a milklike liquid, e.g. in a coconut. —*v.t.* **1** to draw milk from (an animal). **2** to exploit or extract money etc. from (a person). —**milk and honey,** abundant means of prosperity. **milk and water,** a feeble or insipid or mawkish discourse or sentiment. **milk float,** a light low vehicle used in delivering milk. **milk run,** a routine expedition or mission. **milk shake,** a drink of milk and a flavouring mixed or shaken until frothy. **milk-tooth** *n.* any of the first temporary teeth in young mammals. [OE]

milkmaid *n.* a woman who milks or works in a dairy.

milkman /ˈmɪlkmən/ *n.* (*pl.* **-men**) a man who sells or delivers milk.

milksop *n.* a weak or timid man or youth.

milkweed *n.* any of various wild plants with a milky juice, especially sowthistle (*Sonchus oleraceus*).

milky *adj.* of, like, or containing milk; (of a liquid) cloudy, unclear. —**milkiness** *n.* [f. MILK]

mill *n.* **1** a building fitted with mechanical apparatus for grinding corn; such apparatus. **2** an apparatus for grinding any solid substance to a powder or pulp. **3** a building fitted with machinery for manufacturing-processes etc.; such machinery. —*v.t./i.* **1** to grind (corn) in a mill; to produce (flour) in a mill. **2** to produce regular markings on the edge of (a coin). **3** to cut or shape (metal) with a rotating tool. **4** (of people or animals) to move in an aimless manner. —**go** (*or* **put**) **through the mill,** to undergo (or cause to undergo) training or experience or suffering. **mill-pond** *n.* a pond formed by damming a stream to use the water in a mill. **mill-race** *n.* a current of water that works a mill-wheel. **mill-wheel** *n.* a wheel used to drive a watermill. [OE ult. f. L *mola* millstone (*molere* grind)]

millennium /mɪˈlenɪəm/ *n.* (*pl.* **-iums** or **-ia**) **1** a period of 1,000 years. **2** Christ's prophesied reign of 1,000 years on earth (Rev. 20). **3** a coming time of justice and happiness. —**millennial** *adj.* [f. L *mille* thousand + *annus* year]

millepede /ˈmɪlɪpiːd/ *n.* a many-legged arthropod of the class Diplopoda, having two pairs of legs to each segment. (Cf. CENTIPEDE.) [f. L, = wood-louse (*mille* thousand, *pes pedis* foot)]

miller *n.* one who works or owns a mill, usually a corn-mill. —**miller's thumb,** a kind of small fish of the genus *Cottus*. [f. MILL]

millesimal /mɪˈlesɪm(ə)l/ *adj.* **1** thousandth. **2** consisting of thousandths. —*n.* a thousandth part. [f. L *millesimus* (*mille* thousand)]

millet /ˈmɪlɪt/ *n.* a cereal plant, especially *Panicum miliaceum*, with small nutritious seeds; these seeds. [f. F dim. f. L *milium*]

milli- /mɪlɪ-/ *in comb.* **1** thousand. **2** one thousandth. [f. L *mille* thousand]

milliard /ˈmɪljəd/ *n.* one thousand million. [F (*mille* thousand)]

millibar /ˈmɪlɪbɑː(r)/ *n.* a unit of pressure equal to one thousandth of a bar. [f. MILLI- + BAR[2]]

milligram /ˈmɪlɪgræm/ *n.* a metric unit of mass, equal to 0.001 gram.

millilitre /ˈmɪlɪliːtə(r)/ *n.* a metric unit of capacity, equal to 0.001 litre.

millimetre /ˈmɪlɪmiːtə(r)/ *n.* a metric unit of length, equal to 0.001 metre or about 0.04 in.

milliner /ˈmɪlɪnə(r)/ *n.* a person who makes or

sells women's hats. —**millinery** *n.* [f. *Milan* in Italy; orig. = vendor of goods from Milan]

million /ˈmɪljən/ *adj.* & *n.* (for plural usage, see HUNDRED). **1** one thousand thousand. **2** a million pounds or dollars. **3** (in *pl.*) very many. —**millionth** *adj. n.* [f. OF prob. f. It. (*mille* thousand)]

millionaire /mɪljəˈneə(r)/ *n.* a person possessing a million pounds, dollars, etc.; a very rich person. [f. F (as prec.)]

millipede var. of MILLEPEDE.

millstone *n.* **1** either of two circular stones for grinding corn. **2** a heavy burden or responsibility.

millwright /ˈmɪlraɪt/ *n.* one who designs or erects mills.

milometer /maɪˈlɒmɪtə(r)/ *n.* an instrument for measuring the number of miles travelled by a vehicle. [f. MILE + -METER]

milt *n.* **1** the reproductive gland or sperm of a male fish. **2** the spleen of mammals. [OE]

mimbar /ˈmɪmbɑ:(r)/ *n.* a pulpit in a mosque. [f. Arab.]

mime *n.* acting with gestures and without words; a performance involving this. —*v.t.*/*i.* to perform in the form of a mime. [f. L f. Gk *mimos*]

mimeograph /ˈmɪmɪəgrɑ:f/ *n.* an apparatus for making copies from stencils. —*v.t.* to reproduce by means of this. [f. Gk *mimeomai* imitate + -GRAPH]

mimetic /mɪˈmetɪk/ *adj.* of or given to imitation or mimicry. [f. Gk *mimētikos* (as prec.)]

mimic /ˈmɪmɪk/ *v.t.* (**-ck-**) **1** to copy the appearance or ways of (a person etc.) playfully or for entertainment. **2** to copy minutely or servilely. **3** (of a thing) to resemble closely. —*n.* a person skilled in imitation, especially for entertainment. —**mimicry** *n.* [f. L f. Gk (as MIME)]

mimosa /mɪˈməʊzə/ *n.* any of several usually tropical shrubs, especially those of the genus *Mimosa*, with small fragrant globular flower-heads. [app. f. L (as MIME), because the leaves imitate animals in their sensitivity]

Min. *abbr.* **1** Minister. **2** Ministry.

min. *abbr.* **1** minute(s). **2** minimum. **3** minim.

mina /ˈmaɪnə/ *n.* a talking bird (*Gracula religiosa*) of the starling family. [f. Hindi]

minaret /mɪnəˈret, ˈmɪ-/ *n.* a slender turret connected with a mosque, from which a muezzin calls at the hours of prayer. [F or Sp. f. Turk. f. Arab.]

minatory /ˈmɪnətərɪ/ *adj.* threatening, menacing. [f. L (*minari* threaten)]

mince *v.t.*/*i.* **1** to cut into very small pieces, especially in a machine. **2** to walk or speak in an affected way. —*n.* minced meat. —**mince pie,** a pie containing mincemeat. **not to mince matters** *or* **one's words,** to speak plainly. [f. OF f. L (as MINUTIAE)]

mincemeat *n.* a mixture of currants, sugar, spices, suet, etc. —**make mincemeat of,** to defeat or refute utterly.

mind /maɪnd/ *n.* **1** the seat of consciousness, thought, volition, and feeling. **2** intellectual powers as distinct from the will and emotions. **3** remembrance. **4** opinion; this as expressed. **5** a way of thinking or feeling; a direction of thought or desires. **6** the normal condition of the mental faculties. **7** a person as embodying mental faculties. —*v.t.*/*i.* **1** to object to (usu. with neg. or interrog.); **2** to remember and take care (about). **3** to have charge of for a while. **4** to apply oneself to; to concern oneself about. —**be in two minds,** to be undecided. **change one's mind,** to discard one's opinion etc. in favour of another. **do you mind?** (*iron.*) please stop that. **have a mind of one's own,** to be capable of an independent opinion. **have a (good) mind to,** to feel (much) inclined or tempted to. **have in mind,** to think of; to intend. **in one's mind's eye,** in one's imagination. **make up one's mind,** to decide, to resolve. **mind one's P's and Q's,** to be careful in speech or conduct. **mind out,** to be careful; (in *imper.*) let me pass. **mind-reader** *n.* one who claims to be able to become aware of another's thoughts. **mind (you),** please take note. **never mind,** do not be troubled (about); I prefer not to answer; you may ignore. **on one's mind,** in one's thoughts; worrying one. [OE]

minded *adj.* **1** inclined to think in a specified way or concern oneself with a specified thing. **2** having a mind of a specified kind. **3** inclined or disposed (to do something). [f. MIND]

minder *n.* **1** a person whose business it is to attend to something, especially a child or machinery. **2** a bodyguard. [f. MIND]

mindful *adj.* taking thought or care (of something). —**mindfully** *adv.*, **mindfulness** *n.* [f. MIND + -FUL]

mindless *adj.* **1** lacking intelligence, stupid. **2** heedless (of). —**mindlessly** *adv.*, **mindlessness** *n.* [f. MIND + -LESS]

mine[1] *poss. pron.* of or belonging to me; the thing(s) belonging to me. [OE (as ME[1])]

mine[2] *n.* **1** an excavation in the earth for extracting metal, coal, salt, etc. **2** an abundant source (*of* information etc.). **3** a receptacle filled with explosive placed in or on the ground or in the water for destroying enemy personnel, material, or ships. —*v.t.*/*i.* **1** to obtain (metal, coal, etc.) from a mine; to dig in the earth etc. for ore etc. **2** to lay explosive mines under or in. [f. OF]

minefield *n.* **1** an area where explosive mines have been laid. **2** a subject etc. presenting many unseen hazards.

minelayer *n.* a ship or aircraft for laying explosive mines.

miner *n.* one who works in a mine. [f. MINE²]

mineral /ˈmɪnər(ə)l/ *n.* **1** a substance obtained by mining. **2** a natural inorganic substance having a definite chemical composition and usually a characteristic crystalline structure. **3** an artificial mineral water or similar drink. —*adj.* **1** obtained by mining. **2** inorganic, not animal or vegetable. —**mineral water,** water found in nature impregnated with a mineral substance; an artificial imitation of this; a non-alcoholic effervescent drink. [f. OF f. L (*minera* ore, f. OF)]

mineralogy /mɪnəˈrælədʒɪ/ *n.* the science of minerals. —**mineralogical** /-rəˈlɒdʒɪk(ə)l/ *adj.*, **mineralogist** *n.* [f. prec. + -LOGY]

minestrone /mɪnɪˈstrəʊnɪ/ *n.* an Italian soup containing vegetables and pasta or rice. [It.]

minesweeper *n.* a ship for clearing explosive mines from the sea.

mineworker *n.* a miner.

mingle /ˈmɪŋg(ə)l/ *v.t./i.* to mix, to blend. —**mingle with,** to go about among. [f. obs. *meng* (OE, rel. to AMONG)]

mingy /ˈmɪndʒɪ/ *adj.* (*colloq.*) mean, stingy. —**mingily** *adv.* [prob. f. MEAN² + STINGY]

Mini /ˈmɪnɪ/ *n.* [P] a type of small car. [abbr.]

mini /ˈmɪnɪ/ *n.* (*colloq.*) a miniskirt. [abbr.]

mini- /mɪnɪ-/ *in comb.* miniature, small of its kind (*minicar*; *mini-budget*). [abbr.]

miniature /ˈmɪnɪtʃə(r)/ *adj.* **1** much smaller than normal. **2** represented on a small scale. —*n.* **1** a small minutely finished portrait. **2** miniature thing. —**in miniature,** on a small scale. [f. It. f. L *miniare* (*minium* red lead)]

miniaturist /ˈmɪnɪtʃərɪst/ *n.* a painter of miniatures. [f. prec.]

miniaturize /ˈmɪnɪtʃəraɪz/ *v.t.* **1** to make miniature. **2** to produce in a smaller version. [f. MINIATURE]

minibus /ˈmɪnɪbʌs/ *n.* a small bus for about twelve passengers.

minicab /ˈmɪnɪkæb/ *n.* a small car like a taxi, that can be booked but does not ply for hire.

minicomputer /mɪnɪkəmˈpju:tə(r)/ *n.* a computer that is smaller than a main-frame but larger than a microcomputer.

minim /ˈmɪnɪm/ *n.* **1** (*Mus.*) a note half as long as a semibreve. **2** (*hist.*) one sixtieth of a fluid drachm, about 1 drop. [f. L (as MINIMUM)]

minimal /ˈmɪnɪm(ə)l/ *adj.* being or related to a minimum; very small or slight. —**minimally** *adv.* [as prec.]

minimize /ˈmɪnɪmaɪz/ *v.t.* **1** to reduce to a minimum. **2** to estimate at the smallest possible amount or degree; to estimate or represent at less than the true value or importance. —**minimization** /-ˈzeɪʃ(ə)n/ *n.* [as MINIM]

minimum /ˈmɪnɪməm/ *n.* (*pl.* **-ma**) the least amount possible, attained, usual, etc. [L, neut. of *minimus* least]

minion /ˈmɪnjən/ *n.* (*derog.*) a subordinate, an assistant. [orig. = favourite child etc., f. F *mignon* dainty]

miniskirt /ˈmɪnɪskɜ:t/ *n.* a skirt ending well above the knees.

minister /ˈmɪnɪstə(r)/ *n.* **1** a person at the head of a government department or a main branch of this. **2** a clergyman, especially in the Presbyterian and Nonconformist Churches. **3** a diplomatic agent, usually ranking below ambassador. **4** a person employed in the execution of one's purpose, will, etc. —*v.t./i.* to render aid or service (to a person, cause, etc.). —**Minister of State,** a departmental senior minister between departmental head and junior minister. —**ministerial** /-ˈstɪərɪ(ə)l/ *adj.* [f. OF f. L *minister* servant]

ministration /mɪnɪˈstreɪʃ(ə)n/ *n.* giving aid or service; ministering, especially in religious matters. —**ministrant** /ˈmɪnɪstrənt/ *adj.* & *n.* [f. OF or L (as prec.)]

ministry /ˈmɪnɪstrɪ/ *n.* **1** a government department; the building occupied by it. **2** the body of ministers of the government; a period of government under one Prime Minister. **3** office as a minister in the Christian Church; the period of this. **4** ministering; ministration. —**the ministry,** the clerical profession. [f. L *ministerium* (as MINISTER)]

mink *n.* **1** a small stoatlike animal of the family Mustelidae, especially *Mustela vison*. **2** its fur. **3** a coat made from this. [cf. Sw. *mänk*]

minnow /ˈmɪnəʊ/ *n.* a small freshwater fish (esp. *Phoxinus phoxinus*). [OE, prob. infl. by F *menu* (*poisson*) small fish (as MINUTE²)]

Minoan /mɪˈnəʊən/ *adj.* of the Bronze Age civilization of Crete *c.*3000–1100 BC or its people, culture, or language. —*n.* **1** an inhabitant of Minoan Crete or other parts of the Minoan world. **2** the language or scripts associated with the Minoan civilization. [f. *Minos*, legendary king of Crete]

minor /ˈmaɪnə(r)/ *adj.* **1** lesser or relatively less in size or importance. **2** under full legal age. **3** (*Mus.*) (of a scale) having intervals of a semitone above its second and seventh notes; (of an interval) less by a semitone than a major interval; (of a key) based on a minor scale. —*n.* **1** a person under full legal age. **2** (*US*) a student's subsidiary subject or course.—*v.i.* (*US*) to undertake study (in a subject) as a subsidiary course. —**minor planets,** (also called *asteroids*) the small rocky bodies (less than a few kilometres across) orbiting the sun. [L, = smaller, lesser]

Minorite /ˈmaɪnəraɪt/ *n.* a Franciscan friar, so called because the Franciscans regarded themselves as of humbler rank than members of other orders. [f. MINOR]

minority /maɪˈnɒrɪtɪ, mɪ-/ *n.* **1** the smaller number or part of a group etc. **2** the state of having fewer than half the votes. **3** a small group of persons differing from others in race, religion, language, opinion on a topic, etc. **4** the state or period of being under full legal age (see MAJORITY). [f. F or L (as prec.)]

minster *n.* a large or important church; the church of a monastery. [OE (as MONASTERY)]

minstrel /ˈmɪnstr(ə)l/ *n.* **1** a medieval singer or musician, who sang or recited (often his own) poetry; (in earlier use) an entertainer of any kind. **2** (usu. in *pl.*) a member of a band of public entertainers, with blackened faces etc., performing songs and music ostensibly of Black origin. [f. OF *menestral* attendant f. L (as MINISTERIAL)]

minstrelsy /ˈmɪnstrəlsɪ/ *n.* a minstrel's art or poetry. [as prec.]

mint[1] *n.* **1** an aromatic herb of the genus *Mentha*, used in cooking. **2** peppermint; a small sweet flavoured with this. —**minty** *adj.* [OE f. L *ment(h)a* f. Gk]

mint[2] *n.* **1** a place where money is coined, usually under State authority. **2** a vast sum or amount. —*v.t.* **1** to make (a coin) by stamping metal. **2** to coin (a word or phrase). —**in mint condition,** as new, unsoiled. [OE f. L *moneta* (as MONEY)]

minuet /mɪnjʊˈet/ *n.* a slow stately dance in triple measure; music for this, or in the same rhythm and style (often as a movement in a suite, sonata, or symphony). [f. F *menuet* (as MENU)]

minus /ˈmaɪnəs/ *prep.* **1** with the subtraction of (symbol −). **2** below zero. **3** (*colloq.*) deprived of. —*adj.* **1** (of a number) less than zero, negative. **2** having a negative electrical charge. **3** (in evaluating) rather worse or lower than. —*n.* **1** a minus sign. **2** a disadvantage. **3** a negative quantity. —**minus sign,** the symbol −. [L, neut. of MINOR]

minuscule /ˈmɪnəskju:l/ *adj.* **1** extremely small. **2** lower-case. **3** (of a kind of cursive script developed in the 7th c.) small. —*n.* **1** a lower-case letter. **2** a letter in minuscule script. [F, f. L *minusculus* (dim. of MINOR)]

minute[1] /ˈmɪnɪt/ *n.* **1** a period of 60 seconds, a sixtieth part of an hour; the distance traversed in this. **2** a very brief portion of time. **3** a particular point of time. **4** a sixtieth part of a degree of measurement of angles. **5** (in *pl.*) a brief summary of the proceedings of an assembly, committee, etc. **6** an official memorandum authorizing or recommending a course of action. **7** a rough draft, a memorandum. —*v.t.* **1** to record in minutes; to make a note of. **2** to send a minute to (a person). —**in a minute,** very soon. **minute steak,** a thin slice of steak that can be cooked quickly. **up to the minute,** having the latest information; in the latest fashion. [f. OF f. L *minutus* (as foll.)]

minute[2] /maɪˈnju:t/ *adj.* **1** very small. **2** precise, detailed. —**minutely** *adv.*, **minuteness** *n.* [f. L *minutus* (*minuere* lessen)]

minutiae /maɪˈnju:ʃɪi:, mɪ-/ *n.pl.* very small or unimportant details. [L (as prec.)]

minx /mɪŋks/ *n.* a pert or mischievous or sly girl. [orig. unkn.]

miracle /ˈmɪrək(ə)l/ *n.* **1** a marvellous and welcome event that seems impossible to explain by means of the known laws of nature and is therefore attributed to a supernatural agency; a remarkable occurrence. **2** a remarkable specimen. [f. OF f. L *miraculum* object of wonder (*mirari* wonder at)]

miraculous /mɪˈrækjʊləs/ *adj.* **1** that is a miracle, supernatural. **2** remarkable. —**miraculously** *adv.* [f. F or L (as prec.)]

mirage /mɪˈrɑ:ʒ/ *n.* **1** an optical illusion caused by atmospheric conditions, especially the appearance of a sheet of water in the desert or on a hot road. **2** an illusory thing. [F (*se mirer* be reflected)]

mire *n.* **1** swampy ground, a bog. **2** mud. —*v.t.* **1** to plunge in mire. **2** to involve in difficulties. **3** to defile, to bespatter (*lit.* or *fig.*). —**in the mire,** in difficulties. —**miry** *adj.* [f. ON, rel. to MOSS]

mirror /ˈmɪrə(r)/ *n.* **1** a polished surface (usu. of amalgam-coated glass) reflecting an image. **2** what gives a faithful reflection or true description of a thing. —*v.t.* to reflect as in a mirror. —**mirror image,** a reflection or copy in which the left and right sides are reversed. [f. OF f. L *mirare* look at]

mirth *n.* merriment; laughter. —**mirthful** *adj.*, **mirthless** *adj.* [OE (as MERRY)]

mis- *prefix* **1** to verbs and verbal derivatives, in the sense 'amiss', 'badly', 'wrongly', 'unfavourably' (*mislead*, *misshapen*, *mistrust*). **2** to verbs, adjectives, and nouns, in the sense 'amiss', 'badly', 'wrongly', or negative (*misadventure*, *mischief*). [sense 1 OE; sense 2 f. OF *mes-* f. L (as MINUS)]

misadventure /mɪsədˈventʃə(r)/ *n.* **1** a piece of bad luck. **2** the killing of a person by a lawful act without negligence or any intention of hurt, for which there is no criminal responsibility.

misalliance /mɪsəˈlaɪəns/ *n.* an unsuitable alliance, especially a marriage with a social inferior.

misanthrope /ˈmɪsənθrəʊp, ˈmɪz-/ *n.* a hater of mankind; one who avoids human society. —**misanthropic** /-ˈθrɒpɪk/ *adj*., **misanthropically** /-ˈθrɒpɪkəlɪ/ *adv*. [F f. Gk (*misos* hatred, *anthrōpos* man)]

misanthropy /mɪˈsænθrəpɪ, mɪˈz-/ *n*. the condition or habits of a misanthrope. [f. prec.]

misapply /mɪsəˈplaɪ/ *v.t*. to apply (esp. funds) wrongly. —**misapplication** /-æplɪˈkeɪʃ(ə)n/ *n*.

misapprehend /mɪsæprɪˈhend/ *v.t*. to misunderstand. —**misapprehension** /-ʃ(ə)n/ *n*.

misappropriate /mɪsəˈprəʊprɪeɪt/ *v.t*. to take wrongly; to apply (another's money) wrongly to one's own use. —**misappropriation** /-ʃ(ə)n/ *n*.

misbegotten /mɪsbɪˈgɒt(ə)n/ *adj*. **1** contemptible, disreputable. **2** bastard.

misbehave /mɪsbɪˈheɪv/ *v.i*. to behave improperly. —**misbehaviour** *n*.

miscalculate /mɪsˈkælkjʊleɪt/ *v.t./i*. to calculate wrongly. —**miscalculation** /-ˈleɪʃ(ə)n/ *n*.

miscall /mɪsˈkɔːl/ *v.t*. to misname.

miscarriage /mɪsˈkærɪdʒ, ˈmɪs-/ *n*. **1** a spontaneous abortion; a delivery of the foetus in the 12th–28th week of pregnancy. **2** the miscarrying of a plan etc. —**miscarriage of justice**, the failure of a legal procedure to achieve justice. [f. foll.]

miscarry /mɪsˈkærɪ/ *v.i*. **1** (of a woman) to have a miscarriage. **2** (of a scheme etc.) to go wrong, to fail. **3** (of a letter etc.) to fail to reach its destination.

miscast /mɪsˈkɑːst/ *v.t*. (*past* & *p.p*. **miscast**) to allot an unsuitable part to (an actor).

miscegenation /mɪsɪdʒɪˈneɪʃ(ə)n/ *n*. interbreeding of races, especially of Whites with non-Whites. [f. L *miscēre* mix + *genus* race]

miscellaneous /mɪsəˈleɪmɪəs/ *adj*. **1** of various kinds. **2** of mixed composition or character. [f. L (*miscellus* mixed, as prec.)]

miscellany /mɪˈselənɪ/ *n*. **1** a mixture, a medley. **2** a book containing various literary compositions etc. [f. F (as prec.)]

mischance /mɪsˈtʃɑːns/ *n*. misfortune.

mischief /ˈmɪstʃɪf/ *n*. **1** troublesome but not malicious conduct, especially of children; playful malice or archness. **2** harm or injury, especially caused by a person. —**make mischief**, to create discord. [f. OF (MIS-, *chever* come to an end, as CHIEF)]

mischievous /ˈmɪstʃɪvəs/ *adj*. (of a person) disposed to mischief; (of conduct) playfully malicious, mildly troublesome; (of a thing) having harmful effects. —**mischievously** *adv*., **mischievousness** *n*. [f. AF (as prec.)]

miscible /ˈmɪsɪb(ə)l/ *adj*. that can be mixed. —**miscibility** /-ˈbɪlɪtɪ/ *n*. [f. L (*miscēre* mix)]

misconceive /mɪskənˈsiːv/ *v.t./i*. to have a wrong idea or conception (of). —**misconception** /-ˈsepʃ(ə)n/ *n*.

misconduct /mɪsˈkɒndʌkt/ *n*. **1** improper conduct, especially adultery. **2** bad management.

misconstrue /mɪskənˈstruː/ *v.t*. to misinterpret. —**misconstruction** *n*.

miscopy /mɪsˈkɒpɪ/ *v.t*. to copy wrongly.

miscount /mɪsˈkaʊnt/ *v.t./i*. to make a wrong count; to count (things) wrongly. —*n*. a wrong count, especially of votes.

miscreant /ˈmɪskrɪənt/ *n*. a wrongdoer, a villain. [f. OF (MIS-, *creant* believer)]

misdeal /mɪsˈdiːl/ *v.t./i*. (*past* & *p.p*. **misdealt** /-ˈdelt/) to make a mistake in dealing (cards). —*n*. such a mistake; a misdealt hand.

misdeed /mɪsˈdiːd/ *n*. a wrong or improper act, a crime.

misdemeanour /mɪsdɪˈmiːnə(r)/ *n*. a misdeed; (*Law*) an indictable offence, formerly (in the UK) one less heinous than a felony.

misdirect /mɪsdɪˈrekt, -daɪ-/ *v.t*. to direct wrongly. —**misdirection** *n*.

misdoing /mɪsˈduːɪŋ/ *n*. a misdeed.

mise en scène /miːz ɑ̃ ˈseɪn/ *n*. **1** the scenery and properties of an acted play. **2** the surroundings of an event. [F, p.p. of *mettre* put f. L *mittere miss-* send, put]

miser /ˈmaɪzə(r)/ *n*. a person who hoards wealth, especially one who lives miserably. —**miserliness** *n*., **miserly** *adj*. [L, = wretched]

miserable /ˈmɪzərəb(ə)l/ *adj*. **1** full of misery, wretchedly unhappy or uncomfortable. **2** wretchedly poor in quality etc., contemptible. **3** causing wretchedness. —**miserably** *adv*. [f. F f. L, = pitiable (*miserari* pity)]

misericord /mɪˈzerɪkɔːd/ *n*. a projection under a hinged seat in a choir stall serving (when the seat is turned up) to support a person standing. [f. OF f. L *misericordia* compassion]

misery /ˈmɪzərɪ/ *n*. **1** a condition or feeling of extreme unhappiness or discomfort. **2** a cause of this. **3** (*colloq*.) a constantly grumbling or doleful person. [f. OF or L *miseria* (as MISER)]

misfire /mɪsˈfaɪə(r)/ *v.i*. **1** (of a gun, motor, engine, etc.) to fail to go off or start its action or function regularly. **2** (of a plan etc.) to fail to have the intended effect. —*n*. such a failure.

misfit /ˈmɪsfɪt/ *n*. **1** a person unsuited to his environment or work. **2** a garment etc. that does not fit properly.

misfortune /mɪsˈfɔːtʃuːn/ *n*. bad luck; an instance of this.

misgive /mɪsˈgɪv/ *v.t*. (*past* **-gave**, *p.p*. **-given**) (of a person's mind, heart, etc.) to fill (him or her) with misgivings.

misgiving *n*. a feeling of doubt, mistrust, or apprehension. [f. prec.]

misgovern /mɪsˈɡʌvən/ *v.t.* to govern badly. —**misgovernment** *n.*

misguided /mɪsˈɡaɪdɪd/ *adj.* mistaken in thought or action. —**misguidedly** *adv.*

mishandle /mɪsˈhænd(ə)l/ *v.t.* **1** to deal with incorrectly or ineffectively. **2** to handle (a person or thing) roughly or rudely.

mishap /ˈmɪshæp/ *n.* an unlucky accident.

mishear /mɪsˈhɪə(r)/ *v.t.* (*past & p.p.* **-heard** /-hɜːd/) to hear incorrectly or imperfectly.

mishit /mɪsˈhɪt/ *v.t.* (**-tt-**; *past & p.p.* **-hit**) to hit (a ball) faultily or badly. —/ˈmɪshɪt/ *n.* a faulty or bad hit.

mishmash /ˈmɪʃmæʃ/ *n.* a confused mixture. [redupl. of MASH]

misinform /mɪsɪnˈfɔːm/ *v.t.* to give wrong information to. —**misinformation** /-fəˈmeɪʃ(ə)n/ *n.*

misinterpret /mɪsɪnˈtɜːprɪt/ *v.t.* to give a wrong interpretation to; to make a wrong inference from. —**misinterpretation** /-ˈteɪʃ(ə)n/ *n.*

misjudge /mɪsˈdʒʌdʒ/ *v.t./i.* **1** to have a wrong opinion of. **2** to judge wrongly. —**misjudgement** *n.*

mislay /mɪsˈleɪ/ *v.t.* (*past & p.p.* **-laid**) to put (a thing) in a place and be unable to remember where it is; to lose temporarily.

mislead /mɪsˈliːd/ *v.t.* (*past & p.p.* **-led**) to lead astray, to cause to go wrong in conduct or belief.

mismanage /mɪsˈmænɪdʒ/ *v.t.* to manage badly or wrongly. —**mismanagement** *n.*

mismatch /mɪsˈmætʃ/ *v.t.* to match unsuitably or incorrectly. —/ˈmɪsmætʃ/ *n.* a bad match.

misname /mɪsˈneɪm/ *v.t.* to name wrongly or unsuitably.

misnomer /mɪsˈnəʊmə(r)/ *n.* a name or term used wrongly; the use of a wrong name. [f. AF (MIS-, *nommer* name f. L *nominare*)]

misogynist /mɪˈsɒdʒɪnɪst/ *n.* one who hates all women. —**misogyny** *n.* [f. Gk (*misos* hatred, *gunē* woman)]

misplace /mɪsˈpleɪs/ *v.t.* **1** to put in the wrong place. **2** to bestow (affections or confidence) on the wrong object. **3** to time (words or an action) badly. —**misplacement** *n.*

misprint /ˈmɪsprɪnt/ *n.* a mistake in printing. —/mɪsˈprɪnt/ *v.t.* to print wrongly.

misprision /mɪsˈprɪʒ(ə)n/ *n.* (*Law*) a wrong act or an omission. —**misprision of treason** *or* **of felony**, concealment of one's knowledge of a treasonable or felonious intent. [f. AF (MIS-, *prendre* take)]

mispronounce /mɪsprəˈnaʊns/ *v.t.* to pronounce (a word etc.) wrongly. —**mispronunciation** /-nʌnsɪˈeɪʃ(ə)n/ *n.*

misquote /mɪsˈkwəʊt/ *v.t.* to quote inaccurately. —**misquotation** /-ˈteɪʃ(ə)n/ *n.*

misread /mɪsˈriːd/ *v.t.* (*past & p.p.* **-read** /-ˈred/) to read or interpret wrongly.

misrepresent /mɪsreprɪˈzent/ *v.t.* to give a false account of, to represent wrongly. —**misrepresentation** /-ˈteɪʃ(ə)n/ *n.*

misrule /mɪsˈruːl/ *n.* **1** bad government. **2** disorder. —*v.t.* to govern badly.

miss[1] *v.t./i.* **1** to fail to hit, reach, or catch (an object). **2** to fail to catch (a train etc.) or see (an event) or meet (a person); to fail to keep (an appointment) or seize (an opportunity). **3** to fail to hear or understand. **4** to notice or regret the loss or absence of. **5** to avoid. **6** (of an engine) to misfire; to fail. —*n.* a failure to hit or attain what is aimed at. —**miss out**, to omit, to leave out. **miss out (on)**, (*colloq.*) to fail to get benefit or enjoyment (from). [OE]

miss[2] *n.* **1** a girl or unmarried woman. **2** Miss, the title of an unmarried woman or girl; the title of a beauty queen from a specified region etc. [abbr. of MISTRESS]

missal /ˈmɪs(ə)l/ *n.* (in the RC Church) the book containing the service of the Mass for the whole year. [f. L (*missa* Mass)]

missel-thrush /ˈmɪs(ə)lθrʌʃ/ *n.* a large thrush (*Turdus viscivorus*) that feeds on mistletoe etc. berries. [f. OE *mistel* mistletoe]

misshapen /mɪsˈʃeɪpən/ *adj.* ill-shaped, deformed; distorted. [f. MIS- + *shapen*, old p.p. of SHAPE]

missile /ˈmɪsaɪl/ *n.* **1** an object or weapon suitable for throwing at a target or for discharge from a machine. **2** a weapon directed by remote control or automatically. [f. L *missilis* (*mittere* send)]

missing *adj.* **1** not in its place, lost. **2** (of a person) not yet traced or confirmed as alive but not known to be dead. **3** not present. —**missing link**, a thing lacking to complete a series; a hypothetical creature called upon to bridge the gap between man and his evolutionary non-human ancestors. [f. MISS[1]]

mission /ˈmɪʃ(ə)n/ *n.* **1** a body of persons sent to conduct negotiations or propagate a religious faith. **2** a missionary post. **3** a task to be performed; a journey for such a purpose; an operational sortie; the dispatch of an aircraft or spacecraft. **4** a person's vocation. [F or f. L (as MISSILE)]

missionary *adj.* of religious etc. missions. —*n.* a person doing missionary work. [as prec.]

missis /ˈmɪsɪz/ *n.* (*vulgar*) as a form of address to a woman. —**the missis**, my or your wife. [corrupt. of MISTRESS; cf. MRS]

missive /ˈmɪsɪv/ *n.* an official or long and serious letter. [f. L (as MISSILE)]

misspell /mɪsˈspel/ *v.t.* (*past & p.p.* **-spelt**, **-spelled**) to spell wrongly.

misspend /mɪsˈspend/ *v.t.* (*past* & *p.p.* **-spent**) to spend amiss or wastefully.

misstate /mɪsˈsteɪt/ *v.t.* to state wrongly. —**misstatement** *n.*

mist *n.* **1** water vapour near the ground in droplets smaller than raindrops and obscuring the atmosphere. **2** a condensed vapour obscuring windscreens etc. **3** a dimness or blurring of sight caused by tears etc. —*v.t./i.* to cover or become covered with or as with mist. [OE]

mistake /mɪˈsteɪk/ *n.* an incorrect idea or opinion; a thing incorrectly done or thought. —*v.t./i.* (*past* **mistook** /-ˈstʊk/, *p.p.* **mistaken**) **1** to misunderstand the meaning or intention of. **2** to choose or identify wrongly.

mistaken /mɪˈsteɪkən/ *adj.* wrong in opinion; ill-judged. —**mistakenly** *adv.* [f. prec.]

mister *n.* **1** a person without a title of nobility etc. **2** (*vulgar*) as a form of address to a man. [var. of MASTER; cf. MR]

mistime /mɪsˈtaɪm/ *v.t.* to say or do (a thing) at the wrong time.

mistletoe /ˈmɪs(ə)ltəʊ/ *n.* a parasitic plant (*Viscum album*) growing on apple and other trees and bearing white berries. [OE *misteltan* (as MISSEL-THRUSH, *tan* twig)]

mistook *past* of MISTAKE.

mistral /ˈmɪstr(ə)l, -ˈtrɑːl/ *n.* a cold north or north-west wind in southern France. [F f. Prov. f. L *magistralis* (as MAGISTRATE)]

mistreat /mɪsˈtriːt/ *v.t.* to treat badly. —**mistreatment** *n.*

mistress /ˈmɪstrɪs/ *n.* **1** a woman in authority or with power; the female head of a household or of a college etc.; the female owner of an animal or slave. **2** a female teacher or tutor, a schoolmistress. **3** a woman having an illicit sexual relationship with a (usu. married) man. [f. OF *maistresse* (*maistre* master)]

mistrial /mɪsˈtraɪəl/ *n.* a trial vitiated by an error.

mistrust /mɪsˈtrʌst/ *v.t.* to feel no confidence in; to be suspicious of. —*n.* lack of confidence, suspicion. —**mistrustful** *adj.*, **mistrustfully** *adv.*

misty *adj.* **1** of or covered with mist. **2** of dim outline; (*fig.*) obscure, vague. —**mistily** *adv.*, **mistiness** *n.* [OE (as MIST)]

misunderstand /mɪsʌndəˈstænd/ *v.t.* (*past* & *p.p.* **-stood** /-ˈstʊd/) to understand in a wrong sense; (esp. in *p.p.*) to misinterpret the words or action of.

misunderstanding *n.* **1** failure to understand correctly. **2** a slight disagreement or quarrel.

misusage /mɪsˈjuːsɪdʒ/ *n.* **1** a wrong or improper usage. **2** ill-treatment.

misuse /mɪsˈjuːz/ *v.t.* **1** to use wrongly, to apply to a wrong purpose. **2** to ill-treat. —/mɪsˈjuːs/ *n.* wrong or improper use or application.

mite *n.* **1** a small arachnid of the order Acari, especially of a kind found in cheese etc. **2** a modest contribution. **3** a small object or child. [OE]

mitigate /ˈmɪtɪgeɪt/ *v.t.* to make milder or less intense or severe; (of circumstances) to excuse (wrongdoing) partially. —**mitigation** /-ˈgeɪʃ(ə)n/ *n.* [f. L *mitigare* (*mitis* mild)]

mitosis /maɪˈtəʊsɪs, mɪt-/ *n.* (*pl.* **-oses** /-siːz/) a process of division of cell nuclei in which two new nuclei each with the full number of chromosomes are formed. —**mitotic** /-ˈtɒtɪk/ *adj.* [f. Gk *mitos* thread]

mitre /ˈmaɪtə(r)/ *n.* **1** a head-dress forming part of the insignia of a bishop in the Western Church, and worn also by abbots and other ecclesiastics as a mark of exceptional dignity. **2** a joint of two pieces of wood or other material at an angle of 90°, such that the line of junction bisects this angle. —*v.t.* **1** to bestow a mitre on. **2** to join with a mitre. [f. OF f. L f. Gk *mitra* turban; sense 2 of *n.* and *v.* perh. a different wd]

mitt *n.* **1** a mitten. **2** a baseball-player's glove. **3** (*slang*) a hand. [abbr. of foll.]

mitten /ˈmɪt(ə)n/ *n.* a kind of glove that leaves the fingers and thumb-tip bare, or that has no partitions between the fingers. [f. OF *mitaine* f. L *medietas* half (as MOIETY)]

mix *v.t./i.* **1** to combine or put together (two or more substances or things) so that the constituents of each are diffused among those of the other(s). **2** to prepare (a compound, cocktail, etc.) by mixing the ingredients. **3** to be capable of being blended. **4** to combine; (of things) to be compatible. **5** (of a person) to be harmonious or sociable; to have dealings. —*n.* a mixture; the proportion of materials in this; a mixture prepared commercially from suitable ingredients for making something. —**be mixed up in** *or* **with,** to be involved in or with. **mix it,** (*colloq.*) to start fighting. **mix up,** to mix thoroughly, to confuse. **mix-up** *n.* a confusion; a misunderstanding. [back-formation f. foll.]

mixed /mɪkst/ *adj.* **1** of diverse qualities or elements. **2** (of a group of persons) containing persons from various races or social classes. **3** for persons of both sexes. —**mixed bag,** a diverse assortment. **mixed blessing,** a thing having advantages but also disadvantages. **mixed doubles,** (in tennis) a doubles game with a man and woman as partners on each side. **mixed farming,** farming of both crops and livestock. **mixed feelings,** a mixture of pleasure and dismay. **mixed grill,** a dish of various grilled meats and vegetables. **mixed marriage,** a marriage between persons of different race or religion. **mixed metaphor,** a combination of inconsistent metaphors. **mixed-up** *adj.* (*colloq.*) mentally or emotionally confused, socially ill-adjusted. [f. earlier *mixt* f. OF f. L *mixtus*, p.p. of *miscēre* mix]

mixer *n.* **1** a device for mixing or blending foods etc. **2** a person who manages socially in a specified way. **3** a drink to be mixed with another. [f. MIX]

mixture /ˈmɪkstʃə(r)/ *n.* the process or result of mixing; a thing made by mixing; a combination of ingredients, qualities, characteristics, etc. —**the mixture as before,** the same treatment repeated. [f. F or L *mixtura* (as MIXED)]

mizen *n.* (also **mizen-sail**) the lowest fore-and-aft sail of a full-rigged ship's mizen-mast. —**mizen-mast** *n.* the mast next aft of the mainmast. [f. F *misaine* f. It. (as MEZZANINE)]

ml *abbr.* millilitre(s).

Mlle(s) *abbr. Mademoiselle, Mesdemoiselles.*

MM *abbr.* **1** *Messieurs.* **2** Military Medal.

mm *abbr.* millimetre(s).

Mme(s) *abbr. Madame, Mesdames.*

Mn *symbol* manganese.

mnemonic /nɪˈmɒnɪk/ *adj.* of or designed to aid the memory. —*n.* **1** a mnemonic device. **2** (in *pl.*) the art of or a system for improving the memory. —**mnemonically** *adv.* [f. Gk (*mnēmōn* mindful)]

MO *abbr.* **1** Medical Officer. **2** money order.

Mo *symbol* molybdenum.

mo /məʊ/ *n.* (*slang*) (*pl.* **mos**) a moment. [abbr.]

moa /ˈməʊə/ *n.* an extinct flightless New Zealand bird of the family Dinorthidae, resembling the ostrich. [Maori]

moan *n.* **1** a long murmur expressing physical or mental suffering; the low plaintive sound of wind etc. **2** a complaint, a grievance. —*v.t.*/*i.* to make a moan or moans; to utter with moans. [OE]

moat *n.* a defensive ditch round a castle, town, etc., usually filled with water. —**moated** *adj.* [f. OF *mot(t)e* mound]

mob *n.* **1** a disorderly crowd, a rabble. **2** the common people. **3** (*slang*) a gang; an associated group of persons. —*v.t.* (**-bb-**) to crowd round in order to attack or admire. [abbr. of *mobile* obs. n. = L *mobile vulgus* excitable crowd]

mob-cap *n.* (*hist.*) a woman's large indoor cap covering all the hair. [f. obs. *mob* slut + CAP]

mobile /ˈməʊbaɪl/ *adj.* **1** movable, not fixed; able to move or be moved easily. **2** (of the face etc.) readily changing its expression. **3** (of a shop etc.) accommodated in a vehicle so as to serve various places. **4** (of a person) able to change social status. —*n.* a light decorative structure that may be hung so as to turn freely. —**mobile home,** a caravan. —**mobility** /məˈbɪlɪtɪ/ *n.* [f. F f. L *mobilis* (*movēre* move)]

mobilize /ˈməʊbɪlaɪz/ *v.t.*/*i.* **1** to assemble (troops etc.) for service; to prepare for war or other emergency. **2** to assemble for a particular purpose. —**mobilization** /-ˈzeɪʃ(ə)n/ *n.* [as prec.]

Möbius strip /ˈməbɪəs/ a surface with only one side and one edge, formed by joining the ends of a rectangular strip after twisting one end through 180°. [f. A. F. *Möbius*, German mathematician (d. 1868)]

mobster *n.* (*slang*) a gangster. [f. MOB]

moccasin /ˈmɒkəsɪn/ *n.* a soft heelless shoe as originally worn by North American Indians. [f. Amer. Ind.]

mocha /ˈmɒkə, ˈməʊ-/ *n.* a kind of coffee; flavouring made with this. [f. *Mocha*, port on Red Sea]

mock *v.t.*/*i.* **1** to make fun of by imitating, to mimic. **2** to scoff or jeer; to defy contemptuously. —*attrib. adj.* sham, imitation (esp. without intent to deceive). —**mocking-bird** *n.* a bird (esp. the American songbird *Mimus polyglottus*) that mimics the notes of other birds. **mock orange,** a shrub (*Philadelphus coronarius*) with fragrant white flowers. **mock turtle soup,** a soup made from a calf's head etc., to resemble turtle soup. **mock-up** *n.* an experimental model or replica of a proposed structure etc. [f. OF *mo(c)quer*]

mockery /ˈmɒkərɪ/ *n.* **1** derision; the subject or occasion of this. **2** a counterfeit or absurdly inadequate representation. **3** a ludicrously or insultingly futile action etc. [as prec.]

mod *n.* (*colloq.*) a modification. —*adj.* modern. —**mod cons,** modern conveniences. [abbr.]

modal /ˈməʊd(ə)l/ *adj.* **1** of mode or form as opposed to substance. **2** (*Gram.*) of the mood of a verb; (of a verb, e.g. *would*) used to express the mood of another verb. [f. L (as MODE)]

mode *n.* **1** the way or manner in which a thing is done; a method of procedure. **2** the prevailing fashion or custom. **3** (*Mus.*) any of the scale systems or types of melody that make up the characteristic sound of the music of a country or tradition. [F & f. L *modus*]

model /ˈmɒd(ə)l/ *n.* **1** a representation in three dimensions of an existing person or thing or of a proposed structure, especially on a smaller scale. **2** a simplified description of a system for calculations etc. **3** a figure in clay, wax, etc., to be reproduced in another material. **4** a particular design or style of structure, especially of a motor vehicle. **5** a person or thing regarded as excellent of its kind and proposed for imitation. **6** a person employed to pose for an artist, or to display clothes etc. by wearing them. 7 a garment etc. by a well-known designer; a copy of this. —*adj*. exemplary, ideally perfect. —*v.t.*/*i*. (-ll-) 1 to fashion or shape (a figure) in clay, wax, etc. 2 to design or plan on or after the model of. 3 to act or pose as an artist's or fashion model; to display (clothes) thus. [f. F f. It. *modello* f. L (as MODULUS)]

modem /ˈməʊdem/ *n*. a combined device for modulation and demodulation, e.g. between a computer and a telephone line. [portmanteau word]

moderate /ˈmɒdərət/ *adj*. 1 medium in amount, intensity, or quality etc.; avoiding extremes. 2 temperate in conduct or expression; not holding extremist views. 3 fairly large or good, tolerably so. 4 (of prices) fairly low. —*n*. one who holds moderate views in politics etc. —/-eɪt/ *v.t.*/*i*. to make or become moderate or less intense etc.; to act as a moderator of. —**moderately** *adv*., **moderateness** *n*. [f. L (*moderare* reduce, control)]

moderation /mɒdəˈreɪʃ(ə)n/ *n*. 1 moderating. 2 moderateness. —**in moderation**, in moderate amounts or degree. [f. OF f. L (as prec.)]

moderator *n*. 1 an arbitrator, a mediator. 2 a presiding officer; a Presbyterian minister presiding over a church court or assembly. 3 a substance used in nuclear reactors to retard neutrons. [f. L (as MODERATE)]

modern /ˈmɒd(ə)n/ *adj*. of present and recent times; in current fashion, not antiquated. —*n*. a person living in modern times. —**modernity** /-ˈdɜːnɪtɪ/ *n*. [f. F or L (*modo* just now)]

modernism *n*. 1 modern views or methods. 2 a tendency in matters of religious belief to subordinate tradition to harmony with modern thought. 3 a modern term or usage. —**modernist** *n*., **modernistic** /-ˈnɪstɪk/ *adj*. [f. prec.]

modernize *v.t.*/*i*. to make modern, to adapt to modern needs or habits; to adopt modern ways or views. —**modernization** /-ˈzeɪʃ(ə)n/ *n*. [as prec.]

modest /ˈmɒdɪst/ *adj*. 1 having a humble or moderate estimate of one's own merits. 2 diffident, not putting oneself forward. 3 decorous in manner and conduct. 4 (of a demand, statement, etc.) not excessive or exaggerated. 5 unpretentious in appearance, amount, etc. —**modestly** *adv*., **modesty** *n*. [f. F f. L, = keeping due measure]

modicum /ˈmɒdɪkəm/ *n*. a small quantity. [L, neut. of *modicus* moderate]

modification /mɒdɪfɪˈkeɪʃ(ə)n/ *n*. 1 modifying, being modified. 2 a change made. —**modificatory** *adj*. [F or f. L (as foll.)]

modify /ˈmɒdɪfaɪ/ *v.t*. 1 to make less severe or decided, to tone down. 2 to make partial changes in. 3 (*Gram*.) to qualify the sense of (a word etc.). [f. OF f. L *modificare* (as MODE)]

modish /ˈməʊdɪʃ/ *adj*. fashionable. —**modishly** *adv*., **modishness** *n*. [f. MODE]

modiste /mɒˈdiːst/ *n*. a milliner, a dressmaker. [F (as MODE)]

modular /ˈmodjulə(r)/ *adj*. consisting of modules or moduli. [f. L MODULUS]

modulate /ˈmɒdjʊleɪt/ *v.t.*/*i*. 1 to regulate or adjust; to moderate. 2 to adjust or vary the tone or pitch of (the speaking voice); to alter the amplitude or frequency of (a wave) by a wave of lower frequency to convey a signal; (*Mus*.) to pass from one key to another. —**modulation** /ˈleɪʃ(ə)n/ *n*. [f. L *modulari* (as foll.)]

module /ˈmɒdjuːl/ *n*. a standardized part or independent unit in construction (esp. of furniture), buildings, spacecraft, etc., or in an academic course. [F or f. L (as foll.)]

modulus /ˈmɒdjʊləs/ *n*. (*pl*. -li /-laɪ/) a constant factor or ratio. [L, = measure (as foll.)]

modus operandi /ˈməʊdəs opəˈrændɪ/ the way a person goes about a task; the way a thing operates. [L, = mode of working]

modus vivendi /məʊdəs vɪˈvendɪ/ a way of living or coping; an arrangement whereby those in dispute can carry on pending a settlement. [L, = mode of living]

mog *n*. (also **moggie**) (*slang*) a cat. [dial.]

Mogul /ˈməʊg(ə)l/ *adj*. Mongolian; of the Moguls. —*n*. a Mongolian; a member of a Mongolian (Muslim) dynasty in India in the 16th–19th c. —**the (Great *or* Grand) Mogul**, the Mogul emperor. [f. Pers. & Arab., as MONGOL]

mogul /ˈməʊg(ə)l/ *n*. (*colloq*.) an important or influential person. [f. prec.]

mohair /ˈməʊheə(r)/ *n*. the hair of the Angora goat; a yarn or fabric from this. [ult. f. Arab.,= choice]

moiety /ˈmɔɪtɪ/ *n*. (*Law* or *literary*) a half; either of the two parts of a thing. [f. OF f. L *medietas* (*medius* middle)]

moil *v.i*. to drudge. [f. OF *moillier* paddle in mud]

moire /mwɑː(r)/ *n*. (also **moire antique**) a watered fabric, usually silk. [F, f. MOHAIR]

moiré /ˈmwɑːreɪ/ *adj*. 1 (of silk) watered. 2 (of metal) having a clouded appearance like watered silk. [F (as prec.)]

moist *adj*. slightly wet, damp; (of a season) rainy. —**moistness** *n*. [f. OF, perh. f. L *mucidus* (cf. MUCUS)]

moisten /ˈmɔɪs(ə)n/ *v.t.*/*i*. to make or become moist. [f. prec.]

moisture /ˈmɔɪstʃə(r)/ *n*. liquid diffused in a

small quantity as a vapour, within a solid, or condensed on a surface. [f. OF (as MOIST)]

moisturize *v.t.* to make less dry (esp. the skin by use of a cosmetic). —**moisturization** /-ˈzeɪʃ(ə)n/ *n.*, **moisturizer** *n.* [f. prec.]

moke *n.* (*slang*) a donkey. [perf. f. a proper name]

moksha /ˈmɒkʃə/ *n.* (*Hinduism & Jainism*) liberation from the chain of births impelled by the law of karma; the bliss attained by this liberation (cf. NIRVANA). [Skr., = release (*muc* to release)]

molar /ˈməʊlə(r)/ *adj.* (esp. of a mammal's back teeth) serving to grind. —*n.* a molar tooth. [f. L *molaris* (*mola* millstone)]

molasses /məˈlæsɪz/ *n.* uncrystallized syrup drained from raw sugar; (*US*) treacle. [f. Port. f. L *mellaceum* must (*mel* honey)]

mole[1] *n.* **1** a small burrowing mammal of the genus *Talpa*, with usually blackish velvety fur and very small eyes. **2** a person who secretly leaks confidential information, especially when placed in an organization etc. as a spy. [prob. f. MDu. or MLG]

mole[2] *n.* a small permanent dark spot on the human skin. [OE]

mole[3] *n.* a massive structure usually of stone, as a pier, breakwater, or causeway; an artificial harbour. [f. F f. L *moles* mass]

mole[4] *n.* the base unit of amount of substance (symbol mol), the amount of substance of a system which contains as many elementary entities as there are atoms in 0.012 kilogram of carbon 12. [f. G *mol* (*molekül*, as MOLECULE)]

molecular /məˈlekjʊlə(r)/ *adj.* of, relating to, or consisting of molecules. —**molecular weight**, the ratio between the mass of one molecule of a substance and one-twelfth of the mass of an atom of the isotope carbon 12. —**molecularity** /-ˈlærɪtɪ/ *n.* [f. foll.]

molecule /ˈmɒlɪkju:l/ *n.* the smallest particle (usually a group of atoms) to which a substance can be reduced by subdivision without losing its chemical identity. [f. F, as MOLE[3]]

molehill *n.* a small mound thrown up by a mole in burrowing. —**make a mountain out of a molehill**, to over-react to a small difficulty.

molest /məˈlest/ *v.t.* to annoy or pester (a person) in a hostile or injurious way. —**molestation** /-ˈsteɪʃ(ə)n/ *n.* [f. OF or L *molestare* (*molestus* troublesome)]

moll *n.* (*colloq.*) **1** a prostitute. **2** a gangster's female companion. [pet-form of *Mary*]

mollify /ˈmɒlɪfaɪ/ *v.t.* to appease; to soothe the anger of. —**mollification** /-fɪˈkeɪʃ(ə)n/ *n.* [f. F or L *mollificare* (*mollis* soft)]

mollusc /ˈmɒləsk/ *n.* an animal of the phylum Mollusca, of soft-bodied usually hard-shelled animals including snails, oysters, mussels, etc. [f. L *molluscus* (*mollis* soft)]

mollycoddle /ˈmɒlɪkɒd(ə)l/ *v.t.* to coddle excessively, to pamper. —*n.* an effeminate man or boy, a milksop. [as MOLL + CODDLE]

molten /ˈməʊlt(ə)n/ *adj.* melted, especially made liquid by heat. [f. MELT]

moly /ˈməʊlɪ/ *n.* (*Gk legend*) a magical plant with a white flower and black root, given by Hermes to Odysseus as a charm against the sorceries of Circe. [L, F. Gk *mōlu*]

molybdenum /məˈlɪbdɪnəm/ *n.* a hard silver-white metallic element, symbol Mo, atomic number 42. [f. L f. Gk, = plummet (*molubdos* lead)]

moment /ˈməʊmənt/ *n.* **1** a very brief portion of time. **2** an exact point of time. **3** importance. **4** the product of a force and the distance of its line of action from the centre of rotation. —**at the moment**, at this time, now. **in a moment**, very soon. **man** etc. **of the moment**, the one of importance at the time in question. **moment of truth**, a time of crisis or test. [f. OF f. L, = MOMENTUM]

momentary /ˈməʊməntərɪ/ *adj.* lasting only a moment. —**momentarily** *adj.* [f. L (as prec.)]

momentous /məˈmentəs/ *adj.* having great importance. [f. MOMENT]

momentum /məˈmentəm/ *n.* (*pl.* **-ta**) the quantity of motion of a moving body, the product of its mass and its velocity; impetus gained by movement (*lit.* or *fig.*). [L (*movimentum* f. *movēre* move)]

Mon. *abbr.* Monday.

monarch /ˈmɒnək/ *n.* a sovereign with the title of king, queen, emperor, empress, or the equivalent; a supreme ruler (*lit.* or *fig.*). —**monarchic** /məˈnɑ:kɪk/ *adj.*, **monarchical** /məˈnɑ:kɪk(ə)l/ *adj.* [f. F or L f Gk (*monos* alone, *arkhō* rule)]

monarchism /ˈmɒnəkɪz(ə)m/ *n.* the advocacy of or principles of monarchy. —**monarchist** *n.* [f. F (as foll.)]

monarchy /ˈmɒnəkɪ/ *n.* a form of government with a monarch at the head; a State governed in this way. [f. OF f. L f. Gk (as MONARCH)]

monastery /ˈmɒnəstərɪ/ *n.* the residence of a community of monks. [f. L f. Gk (*monazo* live alone, as MONO-)]

monastic /məˈnæstɪk/ *adj.* **1** of or like monks, nuns, friars, etc. **2** of monasteries. —**monastically** *adv.*, **monasticism** /məˈnæstɪsɪz(ə)m/ *n.* [f. F f. L f. Gk (as prec.)]

Monday /ˈmʌndeɪ, -dɪ/ *n.* the day of the week following Sunday. —*adv.* (*colloq.*) on Monday. [OE, = day of the moon]

monetarism /ˈmʌnɪtərɪz(ə)m/ *n.* advocacy of the control of money as the chief method of stabilizing the economy. —**monetarist** *n.* [f. foll.]

monetary /ˈmʌnɪtərɪ/ *adj.* of the currency in use; of or consisting of money. —**monetarily** *adv.* [f. F or L (as MONEY)]

money /ˈmʌnɪ/ *n.* **1** the current medium of exchange in the form of coins and banknotes. **2** (in *pl.* **moneys** or **monies**) sums of money. **3** wealth, property viewed as convertible into money. **4** a rich person or rich people. —**in the money,** having or winning plenty of money. **make money,** to acquire wealth. **money-bag** *n.* a bag for money; (in *pl.* treated as *sing.*, *colloq.*) a wealthy person. **money-box** *n.* a closed box for holding money dropped in through a slit. **money-changer** *n.* one whose business it is to change money, especially at an official rate. **money for jam,** (*slang*) a profit for little or no trouble. **money-grabber** *n.* a person greedily intent on amassing money. **money-grabbing** *adj.* given to this practice; (*n.*) this practice. **money-lender** *n.* one whose business it is to lend money at interest. **money-making** *adj.* producing wealth; (*n.*) the acquisition of wealth. **money-market** *n.* the sphere of operation of dealers in short-dated loans, stocks, etc. **money of account,** a unit of money used in accounting but not current as a coin or note. **money order,** an order for the payment of a specified sum, issued by a bank or the Post Office. **money-spider** *n.* a small spider supposed to bring good luck in money or other matters to the person over whom it crawls. **money-spinner** *n.* a thing that brings in much profit. **money's-worth** *n.* good value for one's money. **put money into,** to make an investment in. [f. OF f. L *moneta* mint]

moneyed /ˈmʌnɪd/ *adj.* wealthy; consisting of money. [f. prec.]

monger /ˈmʌŋgə(r)/ *n.* (chiefly *in comb.*) **1** a dealer or trader (*fishmonger*). **2** (usu. *derog.*) a spreader (*scandalmonger, scaremonger*). [OE f. L *mango*]

Mongol /ˈmɒŋg(ə)l/ *adj.* **1** of an Asian people now inhabiting Mongolia. **2** having Mongoloid characteristics. —*n.* a Mongol person. [native name, perh. f. *mong* brave]

mongol /ˈmɒŋg(ə)l/ *adj.* suffering from Down's syndrome. —*n.* a mongol person. —**mongolism** *n.* [f. prec.]

Mongolian /mɒŋˈgəʊlɪən/ *adj.* of Mongolia or its people or language. —*n.* **1** a native or inhabitant of Mongolia. **2** Mongol, Mongoloid. **3** the language of Mongolia. [f. prec.]

Mongoloid /ˈmɒŋgəlɔɪd/ *adj.* resembling the Mongolians in racial origin or in having a broad flat (yellowish) face. —*n.* a Mongoloid person. [f. MONGOL]

mongoose /ˈmɒŋgu:s/ *n.* (*pl.* **-gooses**) a small carnivorous tropical mammal of the genus *Herpestes*, especially a species common in India, able to kill venomous snakes unharmed. [f. Marathi]

mongrel /ˈmʌŋgr(ə)l/ *n.* **1** a dog of no definable breed. **2** an animal or plant resulting from the crossing of different breeds or types. —*adj.* of mixed origin, nature, or character. [rel. to MINGLE]

moniker /ˈmɒnɪkə(r)/ *n.* (*slang*) a name, a nickname. [orig. unkn.]

monism /ˈmɒnɪz(ə)m/ *n.* the theory that there is only a single ultimate principle or kind of being, not two or more (opp. DUALISM and PLURALISM); any of the theories that deny the duality of matter and mind. —**monist** *n.*, **monistic** /-ˈnɪstɪk/ *adj.* [f. Gk *monos* single]

monitor /ˈmɒnɪtə(r)/ *n.* **1** a pupil in a school with disciplinary or other duties. **2** a television receiver used in selecting or verifying the broadcast picture; a highly definitive screen used with a computer. **3** one who listens to and reports on foreign broadcasts etc. **4** a detector of radioactive contamination. —*v.t./i.* **1** to act as a monitor (of); to maintain regular surveillance (over). **2** to regulate the strength of (a recorded or transmitted signal). —**monitor lizard,** a lizard of the family Varanidae, found in tropical and subtropical regions. —**monitorial** /-ˈtɔ:rɪəl/ *adj.*, **monitress** *n.fem.* [L (*monēre* warn)]

monitory /ˈmɒnɪtərɪ/ *adj.* giving or serving as a warning. [f. L *monitorius* (as prec.)]

monk /mʌŋk/ *n.* a member of a community of men living apart under religious vows. —**monkish** *adj.* [OE, ult. f. Gk *monakhos* solitary]

monkey /ˈmʌŋkɪ/ *n.* **1** a mammal of a group closely allied to and resembling man, especially a small long-tailed member of the order Primates. **2** a mischievous person, especially a child. **3** (*slang*) £500; (*US*) $500. —*v.i.* **1** to play mischievously. **2** to tamper or play mischievous tricks. —**monkey business,** (*slang*) mischief. **monkey-nut** *n.* a peanut. **monkey-puzzle** *n.* a prickly tree of the genus *Araucaria* with interlaced branches, the Chile pine. **monkey-tricks** *n.pl.* (*slang*) mischief. **monkey-wrench** *n.* a wrench with an adjustable jaw. [orig. unkn.]

monkshood /ˈmʌŋkshʊd/ *n.* a poisonous plant (*Aconitum napellus*) with hood-shaped flowers.

mono /ˈmɒnəʊ/ *adj.* monophonic. —*n.* (*pl.* **-os**) a monophonic record, reproduction, etc. [abbr.]

mono- *in comb.* (before a vowel usu. **mon-**) one, alone, single. [Gk (*monos* alone)]

monochromatic /mɒnəkrəˈmætɪk/ *adj.* **1** (of light or other radiation) containing only one colour or wavelength. **2** executed in monochrome. —**monochromatically** *adv.*

monochrome /ˈmɒnəkrəʊm/ *n.* a picture done in one colour or different tints of this, or in black and white only. —*adj.* having or using only one colour. [f. Gk (MONO-, *khrōma* colour)]

monocle /ˈmɒnək(ə)l/ *n.* a single eyeglass. [F, orig. f. L *monoculus* one-eyed]

monocotyledon /mɒnəkɒtɪˈli:d(ə)n/ *n.* a flowering plant with a single cotyledon. —**monocotyledonous** *adj.*

monocular /məˈnɒkjʊlə(r)/ *adj.* with or for one eye. [f. L (as MONOCLE)]

monodrama /ˈmɒnədrɑ:mə/ *n.* a dramatic piece for one performer.

monody /ˈmɒnədɪ/ *n.* **1** an ode sung by a single actor in a Greek play. **2** a poem in which a mourner bewails someone's death. —**monodist** *n.* [f. L f. Gk *monōidia* (as MONO-, ODE)

monogamy /məˈnɒgəmɪ/ *n.* the practice or state of being married to one person at a time. —**monogamist** *n.*, **monogamous** *adj.* [f. F f. L f. Gk (MONO-, *gamos* marriage)]

monogram /ˈmɒnəgræm/ *n.* two or more letters, especially a person's initials, interwoven as a device. —**monogrammed** *adj.* [f. F f. L (as MONO-, -GRAM)]

monograph /ˈmɒnəgrɑ:f/ *n.* a separate treatise on a single subject or aspect of it. [f. MONO- + -GRAPH]

monolith /ˈmɒnəlɪθ/ *n.* **1** a single block of stone, especially shaped into a pillar etc. **2** a person or thing like a monolith in being massive, immovable, or solidly uniform. —**monolithic** /-ˈlɪθɪk/ *adj.* [f. F f. Gk (MONO-, *lithos* stone)]

monologue /ˈmɒnəlɒg/ *n.* **1** a scene in a drama where a person speaks alone; a dramatic composition for one performer. **2** a long speech by one person in a company. [F f. Gk *monologos* speaking alone]

monomania /mɒnəˈmeɪnɪə/ *n.* an obsession of the mind by one idea or interest. —**monomaniac** /-ɪæk/ *adj.* & *n.* [f. F (as MONO-, -MANIA)]

monophonic /mɒnəˈfɒnɪk/ *adj.* (of reproduction of sound) using only one channel of transmission. [f. MONO- + Gk *phōnē* sound]

Monophysite /məˈnɒfɪzaɪt/ *n.* an adherent of the doctrine that there was in the person of Christ only a single nature, part divine and part human, the human element being totally subordinate to the divine. [f. L f. Gk (*monos* one, *phusis* nature]

monoplane /ˈmɒnəpleɪn/ *n.* an aeroplane with one pair of wings.

monopolist /məˈnɒpəlɪst/ *n.* one who has or advocates a monopoly. —**monopolistic** /-ˈlɪstɪk/ *adj.* [f. MONOPOLY]

monopolize /məˈnɒpəlaɪz/ *v.t.* **1** to obtain exclusive possession or control of (a trade or commodity). **2** to dominate or prevent others from sharing in (a conversation etc.). —**monopolization** /-ˈzeɪʃ(ə)n/ *n.* [f. foll.]

monopoly /məˈnɒpəlɪ/ *n.* **1** exclusive possession of the trade in some commodity. **2** exclusive possession, control, or exercise (*of*, (*US*) *on*). **3** a thing of which one person or firm etc. has a monopoly. [f. L f. Gk (MONO-, *pōleō* sell)]

monorail /ˈmɒnəʊreɪl/ *n.* a railway in which the track consists of a single rail.

monosyllable /ˈmɒnəsɪləb(ə)l/ *n.* a word of one syllable. —**monosyllabic** /-ˈlæbɪk/ *adj.*

monotheism /ˈmɒnəθi:ɪz(ə)m/ *n.* the doctrine that there is only one god. —**monotheist** *n.*, **monotheistic** /-ˈɪstɪk/ *adj.* [f. MONO- + Gk *theos* god]

monotone /ˈmɒnətəʊn/ *n.* **1** a sound or utterance continuing or repeated on one note without change of pitch. **2** sameness in style of writing. —*adj.* without change of pitch. [f. Gk (as MONO-, TONE)]

monotonous /məˈnɒtənəs/ *adj.* lacking in variety, wearisome through sameness. —**monotonously** *adv.*, **monotony** *n.* [f. prec.]

monotreme /ˈmɒnətri:m/ *n.* a mammal of the subclass Monotremata of primitive egg-laying Australasian animals with a single vent. [f. MONO- + Gk *trēma* hole]

Monotype /ˈmɒnətaɪp/ *n.* [P] a composing-machine that casts and sets up pieces of type singly.

monovalent /ˈmɒnəveɪlənt/ *adj.* univalent. [f. MONO- + *-valent* (VALENCE[1])]

monoxide /məˈnɒksaɪd/ *n.* an oxide containing one oxygen atom.

Monseigneur /mɒnsenˈjɜ:(r)/ *n.* the title given to an eminent Frenchman, especially a prince, cardinal, archbishop, or bishop. [F (*mon* my, SEIGNEUR)]

Monsieur /məˈsjɜ:(r)/ *n.* (*pl.* ***Messieurs*** /meˈsjɜ:(r)/) the title used of or to a French-speaking man, corresponding to Mr or sir. [F (*mon* my, *sieur* lord)]

Monsignor /mɒnˈsi:njə(r)/ *n.* the title of various Roman Catholic prelates. [It., after MONSEIGNEUR]

monsoon /mɒnˈsu:n/ *n.* a wind in southern Asia, especially in the Indian Ocean, blowing from the south-west in summer and from the north-east in winter; the rainy season accompanying the south-west monsoon. [f. obs. Du. f. Port. f. Arab., = fixed season]

monster *n.* **1** an imaginary creature, usually large and frightening, compounded of incongruous elements. **2** a misshapen animal or plant. **3** an inhumanly cruel or wicked person. **4** an animal or thing of huge size.

—*adj.* huge. [f. OF f. L, = portent (*monēre* warn)]

monstrance /ˈmɒnstrəns/ *n.* (in the RC Church) a vessel in which the Host is exposed for veneration. [f. L *monstrantia* (*monstrare* show)]

monstrosity /mɒnˈstrɒsɪtɪ/ *n.* **1** a misshapen animal or plant; an outrageous thing. **2** monstrousness. [f. L (as foll.)]

monstrous /ˈmɒnstrəs/ *adj.* **1** like a monster; huge. **2** abnormally formed. **3** outrageously wrong or absurd, atrocious. —**monstrously** *adv.* [f. OF or L (as MONSTER)]

montage /mɒnˈtɑːʒ/ *n.* **1** a composite picture or piece of music etc. made of heterogeneous juxtaposed items, a pastiche; production of this. **2** (in cinematography) combination of images in quick succession to compress background information or provide atmosphere; a system of editing in which the narrative is modified or interrupted to include images that are not necessarily related to the dramatic development. [F (*monter* to mount)]

montbretia /mɒnˈbriːʃə/ *n.* a hybrid plant of the iris family (genus *Crocosmia*) with bright orange-coloured flowers. [f. A. F. E. Coquebert de *Montbret*, French botanist (d. 1801)]

month /mʌnθ/ *n.* **1** any of usually 12 periods of time into which the year is divided or any period between the same dates in successive such portions. **2** a period of 28 days. —**month of Sundays,** a very long period. [OE (as MOON)]

monthly *adj.* produced or occurring once every month. —*adv.* every month. —*n.* a monthly periodical. [f. prec.]

monument /ˈmɒnjʊmənt/ *n.* **1** anything enduring (especially a structure or building) designed or serving to celebrate or commemorate a person or event etc. **2** a structure preserved because of its historical importance. [f. F f. L (*monēre* remind)]

monumental /mɒnjʊˈment(ə)l/ *adj.* **1** of or serving as a monument. **2** (of a literary work) massive and of permanent importance. **3** extremely great. —**monumental mason,** a maker of tombstones etc. —**monumentally** *adv.* [f. prec.]

moo *n.* the characteristic vocal sound of the cow, a low. —*v.i.* to make this sound. [imit.]

mooch *v.t./i.* (*slang*) **1** to loiter, to walk slowly. **2** to steal. [prob. f OF *muchier* skulk]

mood[1] *n.* **1** a state of mind or feeling. **2** (in *pl.*) fits of melancholy or bad temper. —**in the mood,** disposed or inclined. [OE]

mood[2] *n.* (*Gram.*) a form or forms of a verb serving to indicate whether it is to express a fact, command, wish, etc.; a group of such forms, a distinction of meaning expressed by this. [var. of MODE]

moody *adj.* gloomy, sullen, subject to moods. —**moodily** *adv.*, **moodiness** *n.* [f. MOOD[1]]

moon *n.* **1** (also **Moon**) a satellite of Earth, revolving round it monthly, illuminated by the sun and reflecting some light to Earth; this when visible. **2** (*poet.*) a month. **3** any rocky or icy body orbiting a planet as a satellite. **4** something regarded as unlikely to be attained. —*v.i.* to move or look dreamily or listlessly. —**moon-daisy** *n.* an ox-eye daisy. **over the moon,** (*colloq.*) in raptures; highly excited. [OE]

moonbeam *n.* a ray of moonlight.

moonlight *n.* the light of the moon. —*adj.* lighted by the moon. —*v.i.* (*colloq.*) to have two paid occupations, especially one by day and one by night. —**moonlight flit,** a hurried removal by night to avoid paying rent.

moonlit *adj.* lighted by the moon.

moonshine *n.* **1** visionary talk or ideas. **2** illicitly distilled or smuggled alcoholic liquor.

moonstone *n.* a feldspar with a pearly appearance.

moonstruck *adj.* deranged in mind.

moony *adj.* **1** of or like the moon. **2** foolishly dreamy. —**moonily** *adv.* [f. MOON]

Moor /ˈmʊə(r)/ *n.* a member of a Muslim people of mixed Berber and Arab descent, inhabiting NW Africa. —**Moorish** *adj.* [f. OF f. L f. Gk *Mauros* inhabitant of Mauretania]

moor[1] /ˈmʊə(r)/ *n.* a stretch of open uncultivated land with low shrubs (e.g. heather); this used for preserving game for shooting. [OE]

moor[2] /ˈmʊə(r)/ *v.t.* to attach (a boat etc.) to a fixed object. [prob. f. MLG]

moorage *n.* a place or charge made for mooring. [f. MOOR[2]]

moorhen *n.* a small water-hen (*Gallinula chloropus*).

mooring *n.* (usu. in *pl.*) **1** permanent anchors and chains laid down for ships to be moored to. **2** a place where a vessel is moored.

moorland *n.* an area of moor.

moose *n.* (*pl.* same) a North American animal (*Alces americana*) closely allied to or the same as the European elk. [f. N. Amer. Indian *moos*]

moot *adj.* debatable. —*v.t.* to raise (a question) for discussion. —*n.* (*hist.*) an assembly. [OE, rel. to MEET[1]]

mop *n.* **1** a bundle of coarse yarn or cloth fastened at the end of a stick, for cleaning floors etc., a similarly shaped instrument for various purposes. **2** a thick head of hair like a mop. —*v.t.* (**-pp-**) **1** to wipe or clean (as) with a mop. **2** to wipe tears, sweat, etc., from (the face etc.); to wipe (tears etc.) thus. —**mop up,** to wipe up (as) with a mop; (*slang*) to absorb;

(*slang*) to dispatch or make an end of; to complete the military occupation of (a district etc.) by capturing or killing the troops left there; to capture or kill (stragglers). [perh. as MAP]

mope *v.i.* to be depressed and listless. —*n.* **1** one who mopes. **2** (in *pl.*) low spirits. —**mopy** *adj.* [orig. unkn.]

moped /ˈməʊped/ *n.* a motorized bicycle. [Sw. (*mo*tor, *ped*aler pedals)]

moppet /ˈmɒpɪt/ *n.* (as a term of endearment) a baby or small child. [f. obs. *moppe* baby, doll]

moquette /mɒˈket/ *n.* a material of wool on cotton with a looped pile, used for upholstery etc. [F, perh. f. obs. It. *mocaiardo* mohair]

moraine /mɒˈreɪn/ *n.* debris carried down and deposited by a glacier. —**morainic** *adj.* [F]

moral /ˈmɒr(ə)l/ *adj.* **1** concerned with goodness or badness of character or disposition or with the principles of what is right and what is wrong. **2** virtuous in general conduct. **3** (of rights or duties etc.) founded on moral law. **4** capable of moral action. —*n.* **1** the moral lesson of a fable, story, event, etc. **2** (in *pl.*) moral habits, e.g. sexual conduct. —**moral certainty,** a probability so great as to leave no reasonable doubt. **moral courage,** the courage to face disapproval rather than abandon the right course of action. **moral law,** the conditions to be fulfilled by any right course of action. **moral philosophy**, that concerned with ethics. **moral support,** that giving psychological rather than physical help. **moral victory,** a defeat that has some of the satisfactory elements of a victory. —**morally** *adv.* [f. L *moralis* (*mos* custom)]

morale /mɒˈrɑːl/ *n.* the mental attitude or bearing of a person or group, especially as regards confidence, discipline, etc. [respelling of F. *moral* (= prec.)]

moralist /ˈmɒrəlɪst/ *n.* one who practises or teaches morality; one who follows a natural system of ethics. —**moralistic** /-ˈlɪstɪk/ *adj.* [f. MORAL]

morality /mɒˈrælɪtɪ/ *n.* **1** degree of conformity to moral principles. **2** (esp. good) moral conduct. **3** moralizing. **4** the science of morals; a particular system of morals. —**morality play,** any of the medieval allegorical dramas, teaching a moral lesson, in which the main characters are personified human qualities. [f. OF or L (as MORAL)]

moralize /ˈmɒrəlaɪz/ *v.t./i.* **1** to indulge in moral reflection or talk. **2** to interpret morally. **3** to make (more) moral. —**moralization** /-ˈzeɪʃ(ə)n/ *n.* [f. F or L (as MORAL)]

morass /məˈræs/ *n.* **1** a marsh or bog. **2** an entanglement or confusion. [f. Du. f. OF (as MARSH)]

moratorium /mɒrəˈtɔːrɪəm/ *n.* (*pl.* **-s**) **1** a legal authorization to debtors to postpone payment; the period of this. **2** a temporary prohibition or suspension on an activity. [f. L *moratorius* (*morari* to delay)]

Moravian /məˈreɪvɪən/ *adj.* **1** of Moravia, a region of Czechoslovakia round the River Morava. **2** of a Protestant sect holding Hussite doctrines and a simple unworldly form of Christianity with the Bible as the only source of faith, founded in Saxony in 1722 by emigrants from Moravia. —*n.* **1** a native or inhabitant of Moravia. **2** a member of the Moravian Church. [f. *Moravia*]

morbid /ˈmɔːbɪd/ *adj.* **1** (of the mind, ideas, etc.) unwholesome, sickly. **2** given to morbid feelings; (*colloq.*) melancholy. **3** of the nature of or indicative of disease. —**morbidity** /-ˈbɪdɪtɪ/ *n.*, **morbidly** *adv.*, **morbidness** *n.* [f. L *morbidus* (*morbus* disease)]

mordant /ˈmɔːd(ə)nt/ *adj.* **1** (of sarcasm etc.) caustic, biting, pungent. **2** corrosive or cleansing. **3** serving to fix colouring matter. —*n.* a mordant acid or substance. —**mordancy** *n.* [f. F f. L *mordēre* bite]

more /mɔː(r)/ *adj.* **1** greater in quantity or degree. **2** additional, further. —*n.* a greater quantity or number. —*adv.* **1** in a greater degree. **2** again. **3** moreover. **4** forming the comparative of adjectives and adverbs (e.g. *more absurd*, *more easily*), especially those of more than one syllable. —**more or less,** in a greater or less degree, approximately. **what is more,** as an additional point, moreover. [OE]

moreish /ˈmɔːrɪʃ/ *adj.* (*colloq.*) pleasant to eat, causing a desire for more. [f. MORE]

morello /məˈreləʊ/ *n.* (pl. **-os**) a bitter kind of dark cherry. [f. It. = blackish, f. L (as MOOR)]

moreover /mɔːˈrəʊvə(r)/ *adv.* besides, in addition to that already said.

mores /ˈmɔːriːz/ *n.pl.* the customs or conventions regarded as characteristic of or essential to a community. [L, pl. of *mos* custom]

morganatic /mɔːgəˈnætɪk/ *adj.* (of a marriage) between a man of high rank and a woman of lower rank, the wife and children having no claim to the possessions or title of the father; (of a wife) so married. —**morganatically** *adv.* [f. F or G f. L, prob. f. Gmc, = morning gift, with ref. to husband's gift to wife on the morning after consummation (her sole claim on his possessions)]

morgue /mɔːg/ *n.* **1** a mortuary. **2** (in journalism) the repository where miscellaneous material for reference is kept. [F, orig. = building in Paris where those found dead were exposed for identification]

moribund /ˈmɒrɪbʌnd/ *adj.* at the point of death (*lit.* or *fig.*). [f. L (*mori* die)]

Mormon /ˈmɔːmən/ *n.* an adherent of the

Church of Jesus Christ of Latter-day Saints, based on revelation. [f. *Mormon*, name of supposed author of book on which Mormonism is founded]

morn *n.* (*poetic*) morning. [OE]

mornay /ˈmɔːneɪ/ *n.* a cheese-flavoured white sauce. [orig. unkn.]

morning *n.* the early part of the day, ending at noon or at the hour of the midday meal. —**morning after**, (*colloq.*) a time of hangover. **morning-after pill**, a contraceptive pill effective when taken some hours after intercourse. **morning coat**, a coat with the front cut away to form tails. **morning dress**, formal dress for a man of a morning coat and striped trousers. **morning glory**, a twining plant of the genus *Ipomoea* with trumpet-shaped flowers. **morning star**, a planet, especially Venus, seen in the east before sunrise. [as MORN]

morocco /məˈrɒkəʊ/ *n.* (*pl.* **-os**) a fine flexible leather of goatskin tanned with sumac. [f. *Morocco*, country in NW Africa]

moron /ˈmɔːrɒn/ *n.* **1** an adult with an intelligence equal to that of an average child of 8–12 years. **2** (*colloq.*) a very stupid person. —**moronic** /məˈrɒnɪk/ *adj.* [f. Gk, neut. of *mōros* foolish]

morose /məˈrəʊs/ *adj.* sullen, gloomy, and unsociable. —**morosely** *adv.*, **moroseness** *n.* [f. L (*mos* manner)]

morpheme /ˈmɔːfiːm/ *n.* a morphological element considered in respect of its functions in a linguistic system; the smallest morphological unit of a language (*farmer* consists of two morphemes, *farm* and *-er*; *farmers* of three, *farm*, *-er*, *-s*). [f. F (after *phoneme*), f. Gk *morphē* form]

morphia /ˈmɔːfiə/ *n.* morphine. [as foll.]

morphine /ˈmɔːfiːn/ *n.* the narcotic constituent of opium, used to alleviate pain. [f. G f. L *Morpheus*, Roman god of sleep]

morphology /mɔːˈfɒlədʒɪ/ *n.* the study of the forms of things, especially of plants and animals; the study of the forms of words, the system of forms in a language. —**morphological** /-əˈlɒdʒɪk(ə)l/ *adj.* [f. Gk *morphē* form + -LOGY]

morris dance /ˈmɒrɪs/ a vigorous (male) folk-dance of ancient date, characteristic of rural England. [f. *morys* var. of MOORISH (dance)]

morrow /ˈmɒrəʊ/ *n.* (*poetic*) the following day. [as MORN]

Morse *n.* (also **Morse code**) a signalling code in which letters are represented by various combinations of two signs, e.g. dot and dash, long and short flash. —*adj.* of this code. —*v.t./i.* to signal by Morse code. [f. S. F. B. *Morse*, American inventor (d. 1872)]

morse *n.* the clasp, often jewelled or ornamented, of a cope. [f. OF f. L *morsus* bite, catch (*mordēre* bite)]

morsel /ˈmɔːs(ə)l/ *n.* a small piece or quantity; a mouthful; a fragment. [f. OF (*mors* a bite, as MORDANT)]

mortal /ˈmɔːt(ə)l/ *adj.* **1** subject to death. **2** causing death, fatal; (of a combat) fought to the death. **3** accompanying death. **4** (of an enemy) implacable. **5** (of a pain, fear, affront, etc.) intense, very serious. **6** (*colloq.*) whatsoever. **7** (*colloq.*) long and tedious. —*n.* a mortal being; a human being. —**mortal sin**, a sin that causes the death of the soul or is fatal to salvation. —**mortally** *adv.* [f. OF or L (*mors* death)]

mortality /mɔːˈtælɪtɪ/ *n.* **1** being subject to death. **2** loss of life on a large scale. **3** the number of deaths in a given period etc. —**mortality rate**, the death rate. [f. OF f. L (as prec.)]

mortar /ˈmɔːtə(r)/ *n.* **1** a mixture of lime or cement, sand, and water, for joining stones or bricks in building. **2** a short large-bore cannon for throwing shells at high angles. **3** a vessel in which ingredients are pounded with a pestle. —*v.t.* **1** to plaster or join with mortar. **2** to attack or bombard with mortars. —**mortar-board** *n.* a board for holding mortar; an academic cap with a stiff square top. [f. AF f. L *mortarium*]

mortgage /ˈmɔːgɪdʒ/ *n.* conveyance of a property by a debtor to a creditor as security for a debt (especially one incurred by the purchase of the property), with the proviso that it shall be returned on payment of the debt within a certain period; the deed effecting this; a sum of money lent by this. —*v.t.* to convey (property) by a mortgage. [f. OF, = dead pledge (as GAGE[1])]

mortgagee /mɔːgɪˈdʒiː/ *n.* the creditor in a mortgage. [f. prec.]

mortgager /ˈmɔːgɪdʒə(r)/ *n.* (*Law* **mortgagor**) the debtor in a mortgage. [f. MORTGAGE]

mortician /mɔːˈtɪʃ(ə)n/ *n.* (*US*) an undertaker. [f. L *mors* death]

mortify /ˈmɔːtɪfaɪ/ *v.t./i.* **1** to humiliate greatly; to wound (feelings). **2** to subdue by discipline or self-denial. **3** (of flesh) to be affected by gangrene or necrosis. —**mortification** /-fɪˈkeɪʃ(ə)n/ *n.* [f. OF f. L *mortificare* kill (as prec.)]

mortise /ˈmɔːtɪs/ *n.* a hole in a framework to receive the end of another part, especially a tenon. —*v.t.* to join securely, especially by a mortise and tenon; to cut a mortise in. —**mortise lock**, a lock recessed in the edge of a door etc. [f. OF f. Arab., = fixed in]

mortuary /ˈmɔːtjʊərɪ/ *n.* a building in which dead bodies may be kept for a time. —*adj.* of death or burial. [f. AF f. L (*mortuus* dead)]

Mosaic /məʊ'zeɪɪk/ *adj.* of Moses. [f. F (*Moses* f. Heb.)]

mosaic /məʊ'zeɪɪk/ *n.* **1** a picture or pattern produced by juxtaposing small pieces of glass, stone, etc., of different colours; this form of art. **2** a thing consisting of divers elements in juxtaposition. [f. F, ult. f. Gk *mous(e)ion* (as MUSE)]

moselle /məʊ'zel/ *n.* a white wine produced in the valley of the Moselle and its tributaries in Germany.

Moslem /'mɒzləm/ var. of MUSLIM.

mosque /mɒsk/ *n.* a Muslim place of worship. [f. F, ult. f. Arab. *masjid*]

mosquito /mɒs'ki:təʊ/ *n.* (*pl.* **-oes**) a gnat especially of the genus *Culex* or *Anopheles*, of which the female punctures the skin of man and animals and sucks their blood. —**mosquito-net** *n.* a net to keep mosquitoes from a bed, room, etc. [Sp. & Port., dim. of *mosca* fly]

moss *n.* any of a class of small cryptogams of the class Musci, growing in dense clusters in bogs or on the surface of the ground, trees, stones, etc. —**moss-rose** *n.* a variety of rose with a mosslike growth on the calyx and stalk. —**mossy** *adj.* [OE]

most /məʊst/ *adj.* greatest in quantity or degree; the majority of. —*n.* the greatest quantity or degree; the majority. —*adv.* **1** in the highest degree. **2** forming the superlative of adjectives and adverbs (as *most absurd*, *most easily*), especially those of more than one syllable. —**at (the) most**, as the greatest amount. **for the most part**, in the main; usually. **make the most of**, to use or enjoy to the best advantage. **Most Reverend**, see REVEREND. [OE]

-most *suffix* forming adjectives with a superlative sense from prepositions and other words indicating relative position (*foremost*, *inmost*, *topmost*, *uttermost*). [OE]

mostly *adv.* for the most part. [f. MOST]

mot /məʊ/ *n.* a witty saying. —**mot juste** /ʒu:st/ an exactly appropriate expression. [F, = word]

MOT *abbr.* (hist.) **1** Ministry of Transport. **2** (in full **MOT test**) (*colloq.*) a compulsory annual test of motor vehicles of more than a specified age.

mote *n.* a particle of dust. [OE]

motel /məʊ'tel/ *n.* a roadside hotel often consisting of a group of furnished cabins accommodating motorists and their vehicles. [portmanteau word f. MOTOR + HOTEL]

motet /məʊ'tet/ *n.* a short usually unaccompanied anthem in the Roman Catholic or Lutheran Church. [f. OF (as MOT)]

moth *n.* a lepidopterous mainly nocturnal insect resembling a butterfly; an insect of this kind (of the family Tineidae) breeding in cloth etc., on which its larvae feed. —**moth-eaten** *adj.* damaged or destroyed by moths, antiquated, time-worn. [OE]

mothball *n.* a small ball of naphthalene etc. placed in stored clothes to keep away moths. —**in mothballs**, stored out of use for a considerable time.

mother /'mʌðə(r)/ *n.* **1** a female parent. **2** a quality or condition etc. that gives rise to something else. **3** the head of a female religious community. **4** (*colloq.*) a title used to or of an elderly woman. —*v.t.* **1** to give birth to; to be the origin of. **2** to look after in a motherly way. —**Mother Carey's chickens**, stormy petrels. **mother country**, a country in relation to its colonies. **mother earth**, the earth as the mother of its inhabitants. **mother goddess**, see separate entry. **Mother Goose rhyme**, (*US*) a nursery rhyme. **Mothering Sunday**, the fourth Sunday in Lent, with the old custom of giving one's mother a gift. **mother-in-law** *n.* (*pl.* **mothers-in-law**) a wife's or husband's mother. **mother-of-pearl** *n.* a smooth shining iridescent substance forming the inner layer of the oyster etc. shell. **Mother's Day**, Mothering Sunday. **mother tongue**, one's native language. —**motherhood** *n.* [OE]

mothercraft *n.* skill in looking after one's children as a mother.

motherland *n.* one's native land.

motherly *adj.* having or showing the good qualities of a mother. —**motherliness** *n.* [OE (as MOTHER)]

mothproof *adj.* (of clothes) treated so as to repel moths. —*v.t.* to treat (clothes) thus.

mothy /'mɒθɪ/ *adj.* infested with moths. [f. MOTH]

motif /məʊ'ti:f/ *n.* **1** a distinctive feature or dominant idea in an artistic, literary, or musical composition. **2** an ornament sewn separately on to a garment. **3** an ornament on a vehicle identifying the maker etc. [F (as MOTIVE)]

motion /'məʊʃ(ə)n/ *n.* **1** moving, change of position. **2** manner of movement. **3** change of posture; a particular movement; a gesture. **4** a formal proposal that is to be discussed and voted on at a meeting; an application for an order from a judge. **5** an evacuation of the bowels; (in *sing.* or *pl.*) faeces. —*v.t./i.* to direct by a gesture etc.; to make such a gesture. —**go through the motions**, to do a thing perfunctorily or superficially. **in motion**, not at rest, moving. **motion picture**, a film recording a story or events with movement as in real life. [f. OF f. L (as MOVE)]

motionless *adj.* not moving. —**motionlessly** *adv.* [f. prec. + -LESS]

motivate /ˈməʊtɪveɪt/ *v.t.* **1** to supply a motive to, to be the motive of; to cause (a person) to act in a particular way. **2** to stimulate the interest of (a person) in an activity. —**motivation** /-ˈveɪʃ(ə)n/ *n.* [f. foll.]

motive /ˈməʊtɪv/ *n.* **1** what induces a person to act in a particular way. **2** a motif. —*adj.* tending to initiate movement; concerned with movement. —**motive power,** moving or impelling power, especially the source of energy used to drive machinery. [f. OF f. L *motivus* (as MOVE)]

motley /ˈmɒtlɪ/ *adj.* **1** diversified in colour. **2** of varied character. —*n.* (*hist.*) a jester's particoloured dress. [perh. as MOTE]

moto-cross /ˈməʊtəʊkrɒs/ *n.* (also called *scrambling*) a form of motor-cycle racing held on a closed circuit consisting of a variety of cross-country terrain and natural obstacles. [f. MOTOR + CROSS]

motor *n.* **1** a machine (especially an internal-combustion engine) supplying the motive power for a vehicle etc. or for some other device with moving parts. **2** a motor car. —*adj.* **1** giving, imparting, or producing motion. **2** driven by a motor. **3** of or for motor vehicles. —*v.t./i.* to go or convey in a motor car. —**motor bicycle,** a motor cycle; a moped. **motor bike,** (*colloq.*) a motor cycle. **motor car,** a short-bodied motor-driven vehicle that can carry a driver and usually passengers. **motor cycle,** a two-wheeled motor-driven road vehicle. **motor-cyclist** *n.* the rider of a motor cycle. **motor nerve,** a nerve carrying impulses from the brain or spinal cord to a muscle. **motor vehicle,** a vehicle driven by a motor (esp. an internal-combustion engine). [L, = mover (as MOVE)]

motorcade /ˈməʊtəkeɪd/ *n.* a procession or parade of motor cars. [f. prec., after *cavalcade*]

motorist *n.* the driver of a motor car. [f. MOTOR]

motorize *v.t./i.* **1** to equip with motor transport. **2** to equip (a device etc.) with a motor. —**motorization** /-ˈzeɪʃ(ə)n/ *n.* [f. MOTOR]

motorway *n.* a road designed for fast traffic.

motte /mɒt/ *n.* a mound forming the site of an ancient castle, camp, etc., found in Britain and parts of northern France, dating from the Norman period onwards. [f. F (as MOAT)]

mottle *v.t.* (esp. in *p.p.*) to mark with spots or smears of colour. [back-formation f. MOTLEY]

motto /ˈmɒtəʊ/ *n.* (*pl.* **-oes**) **1** a maxim adopted as a rule of conduct or as expressing the aims and ideals of a family, country, institution, etc. **2** a sentence inscribed on an object. **3** a maxim, verse, or riddle etc. inside a paper cracker. [It., as MOT]

mould[1] /məʊld/ *n.* **1** a hollow container into which molten metal etc. is poured or soft material is pressed to harden in a required shape. **2** a vessel used to give a shape to puddings etc.; a pudding etc. so shaped. **3** form, shape. **4** a pattern or shape used in making mouldings. —*v.t.* **1** to bring into a particular shape or form. **2** to influence or control the development of. [f. OF *modle* f. L (as MODULUS)]

mould[2] /məʊld/ *n.* a furry growth of fungi on things of animal or vegetable origin that lie for some time in moist warm air. [prob. f. p.p. of *moul* grow mouldy, f. ON]

mould[3] /məʊld/ *n.* loose earth; the upper soil of cultivated land, especially when rich in organic matter. [OE, rel. to MEAL]

moulder /ˈməʊldə(r)/ *v.i.* to decay to dust, to rot or decline. [perh. f. prec.]

moulding *n.* **1** a moulded object, especially an ornamental strip of wood. **2** an ornamental variety of outline in the cornices etc. of a building; a similar shape in woodwork etc. [f. MOULD[1]]

mouldy *adj.* **1** covered with mould. **2** out-of-date, stale. **3** (*slang*) dull, miserable. —**mouldiness** *n.* [f. MOULD[2]]

moult /məʊlt/ *v.t./i.* to shed feathers, hair, skin, etc., before a new growth; to shed (feathers etc.) thus. —*n.* the process of moulting. [earlier *moute* ult. f. L *mutare* change]

mound *n.* **1** a mass of piled-up earth or stones. **2** a small hill. **3** a heap or pile. [orig. unkn.]

mount[1] *v.t./i.* **1** to ascend; to go upwards; to rise to a higher level or rank etc. **2** to get or put on (a horse etc.) in order to ride; to provide with a horse for riding. **3** to increase in amount or intensity. **4** to put into place on a support; to fix in position for use, display, or study. **5** to arrange and carry out (a programme, campaign, etc.). **6** to place on guard. **7** to put (a play) on the stage. —*n.* **1** a horse for riding. **2** something on which a thing is mounted for support or display etc. [f. OF f. L (as foll.)]

mount[2] *n.* a mountain or hill (*archaic* exc. before a name, as in *Mount Everest*). [OE & f. OF f. L *mons*]

mountain /ˈmaʊntɪn/ *n.* **1** a mass of land that rises to a great height, especially of over 1,000 ft. **2** a large heap or pile; a huge quantity. **3** a large surplus stock. —**mountain ash,** a tree (*Sorbus aucuparia*) bearing scarlet berries, rowan. **mountain dew,** (*colloq.*) whisky, especially that illicitly distilled. **mountain goat,** a white goatlike animal (*Oreamnos montanus*) of the Rocky Mountains etc. **mountain lion,** the puma. [f. OF *montaigne* (as prec.)]

mountaineer /maʊntɪˈnɪə(r)/ *n.* one skilled in mountain-climbing. —*v.i.* to climb mountains as a recreation. [f. prec.]

mountainous /ˈmaʊntɪnəs/ *adj*. **1** having many mountains. **2** huge. [f. MOUNTAIN]

mountainside *n*. the sloping side of a mountain.

mountebank /ˈmaʊntɪbæŋk/ *n*. **1** a swindler, a charlatan. **2** (*hist*.) an itinerant quack. [f. It., = mount on bench]

mounted *adj*. serving on horseback etc. [f. MOUNT¹]

Mountie /ˈmaʊntɪ/ *n*. (*colloq*.) a member of the Royal Canadian Mounted Police. [abbr.]

mourn /mɔːn/ *v.t./i*. to feel or show deep sorrow or regret for (a dead person, a lost or regretted thing); to grieve. [OE]

mourner *n*. one who mourns; one who attends a funeral. [f. prec.]

mournful *adj*. sorrowful, showing grief. —**mournfully** *adv*., **mournfulness** *n*. [f. MOURN + -FUL]

mourning *n*. **1** expression of sorrow at a death etc. **2** black or dark clothes worn as a conventional sign of bereavement. [f. MOURN]

mouse *n*. (*pl*. **mice**) **1** a small rodent, especially of the genus *Mus*; a species of this (*M. musculus*) infesting houses etc. **2** a shy or timid person. **3** a small hand-held device for controlling the position of the cursor on the visual display unit of a computer. —*v.i*. to hunt mice. —**mouser** *n*. [OE]

mousetrap *n*. **1** a trap for catching mice. **2** (*colloq*.) cheese of poor quality.

moussaka /mʊˈsɑːkə/ *n*. a Greek dish of minced meat, aubergines, eggs, etc. [Gk or Turk.]

mousse /muːs/ *n*. **1** a dish of cold whipped cream or a similar substance flavoured with fruit, chocolate, or meat or fish purée. **2** a substance of similar texture. [F, = moss, froth]

moustache /məˈstɑːʃ/ *n*. hair left to grow on a man's upper lip. [F, f. It. *mostaccio* f. Gk]

mousy /ˈmaʊsɪ/ *adj*. **1** greyish-brown. **2** shy, timid; quiet. [f. MOUSE]

mouth /maʊθ/ *n*. (*pl*. **-s** /maʊðz/) **1** the external opening in the head, with a cavity behind it, through which food is taken in and from which the voice is emitted; this cavity. **2** the opening of a bag, cave, cannon, trumpet, etc. **3** the place where a river enters the sea. **4** an individual as needing sustenance. —/maʊð/ *v.t./i*. **1** to utter or speak with affectation, to declaim. **2** to grimace; to move the lips silently. —**mouth-organ** *n*. a thin rectangular musical instrument played by blowing and sucking air through it. **keep one's mouth shut,** (*slang*) to refrain from revealing a secret. **mouth-watering** *adj*. making one's mouth water, appetizing. **put words into a person's mouth,** to tell him what to say; to represent him as having said such words. **take the words out of a person's mouth,** to say what he was about to say. [OE]

mouthful *n*. **1** an amount that fills the mouth. **2** a small quantity of food etc. **3** a lengthy word or phrase; something difficult to utter. [f. MOUTH + -FUL]

mouthpiece *n*. **1** the part of a pipe, musical instrument, telephone, etc., placed between or near the lips. **2** a person who speaks for another or others.

mouthwash *n*. a liquid for rinsing the mouth or gargling.

movable /ˈmuːvəb(ə)l/ *adj*. that can be moved; varying in date from year to year. [f. MOVE]

move /muːv/ *v.t./i*. **1** to change or cause to change position, place, or posture. **2** to be or cause to be in motion. **3** to change one's place of residence or business. **4** to live or be active in a specified group. **5** to provoke a reaction or emotion in, to stimulate; to prompt or incline, to motivate. **6** to cause (bowels) to empty; to be emptied thus. **7** (of goods etc.) to be sold. **8** to propose (a resolution) formally at a meeting. **9** to initiate action. —*n*. **1** the act or process of moving. **2** a change of residence, business premises, etc. **3** the moving of a piece in chess etc.; a player's turn to do this. **4** a calculated action done to achieve some purpose. —**get a move on,** (*colloq*.) to hurry. **move house,** to change one's place of residence. **move in,** to take possession of a new residence etc. **move over** *or* **up,** to adjust one's position to make room for another. **on the move,** progressing, moving about. —**mover** *n*. [f. AF f. L *movēre*]

movement /ˈmuːvmənt/ *n*. **1** moving, being moved. **2** action, activity. **3** the moving parts of a mechanism, especially of a clock or watch. **4** a campaign to achieve some purpose; a group undertaking this. **5** a trend. **6** market activity in some commodity. **7** any of the principal divisions in a long musical work. [f. OF f. L (as MOVE)]

movie /ˈmuːvɪ/ *n*. (*US slang*) a motion picture. [f. *moving* picture]

moving *adj*. emotionally affecting. —**movingly** *adv*. [f. MOVE]

mow /məʊ/ *v.t*. (*p.p*. **mowed** or **mown**) to cut (grass etc.) with a scythe or machine; to cut down the grass of (a lawn) or the produce of (a field) thus. —**mow down,** to kill or destroy randomly or in great numbers. [OE]

mower /ˈməʊə(r)/ *n*. **1** a mowing machine, especially a lawn-mower. **2** a person who mows. [f. MOW]

MP *abbr*. Member of Parliament.

mp *abbr*. *mezzo piano*.

m.p.g. *abbr*. miles per gallon.

m.p.h. *abbr*. miles per hour.

Mr /ˈmɪstə(r)/ *n*. (*pl*. MESSRS) the title of a man

without a higher title, or prefixed to a designation of an office etc. (*Mr Jones*; *Mr Speaker*). [abbr. of MISTER]

Mrs /ˈmɪsɪz/ *n.* (*pl.* same or **Mesdames**) the title of a married woman without a higher title. [abbr. of MISTRESS]

MS *abbr.* **1** manuscript. **2** multiple sclerosis.

Ms /mɪz/ *n.* the title of a woman without a higher title, whether or not married. [comb. of MRS, MISS]

M.Sc. *abbr.* Master of Science.

MSS /emˈesɪz/ *abbr.* manuscripts.

Mt *abbr.* Mount.

mu /mju:/ *n.* the twelfth letter of the Greek alphabet, = m. [Gk]

much *adj.* existing in great quantity. —*n.* a great quantity. —*adv.* **1** in a great degree. **2** often; for a large part of one's time. **3** approximately. —**as much,** that amount etc. **much of a muchness,** very alike, very nearly the same. **not much,** (*colloq.*) certainly not. **not much of a,** (*colloq.*) not a great or good example of. [f. *muchel* = MICKLE]

mucilage /ˈmju:sɪlɪdʒ/ *n.* a viscous substance extracted from plants; an adhesive gum. [f. F f. L *mucilago* musty juice (as MUCUS)]

muck *n.* farmyard manure; (*colloq.*) dirt, filth; (*colloq.*) mess. —*v.t./i.* **1** to manure. **2** to make dirty. —**make a muck of,** (*slang*) to bungle. **muck about** *or* **around,** (*slang*) to potter or fool about; to interfere. **muck in,** (*colloq.*) to share tasks etc. equally. **muck out,** to remove the manure from. **muck-raking** *n.* (*colloq.*) searching out and revealing scandal. **muck sweat,** (*colloq.*) a profuse sweat. **muck up,** (*slang*) to bungle, to spoil. [prob. f. Scand.]

muckle *adj.* & *n.* = MICKLE.

mucky *adj.* covered with muck, dirty. [f. MUCK]

mucous /ˈmju:kəs/ *adj.* of or covered with mucus. —**mucous membrane,** the skin lining the nose and other cavities of the body. —**mucosity** /-ˈkɒsɪtɪ/ *n.* [f. L *mucosus* (as foll.)]

mucus /ˈmju:kəs/ *n.* the slimy substance secreted by the mucous membrane. [L]

mud *n.* **1** wet soft earth. **2** a liquid (commonly a suspension of clay and other substances in water) used as a lubricant and sealant etc. of the drill pipe in the drilling of an oil or gas well. —**mud-flat** *n.* a stretch of muddy land uncovered at low tide. **mud pack,** a cosmetic paste applied thickly to the face. **one's name is mud,** one is in disgrace. **sling** *or* **throw mud,** to speak slanderously. [prob. f. MLG]

muddle *v.t./i.* **1** to bring into disorder. **2** to confuse (a person) mentally. **3** to confuse (one thing etc.) with another. **4** to act in a confused way. —*n.* disorder, a muddled condition. —**muddle-headed** *adj.* confused, stupid. **muddle through,** to succeed despite one's inefficiency etc. —**muddler** *n.* [perh. f. MDu., = dabble in mud (as prec.)]

muddy *adj.* **1** like mud. **2** covered in or full of mud. **3** confused, obscure. —*v.t.* to make muddy. —**muddiness** *n.* [f. MUD]

mudguard *n.* a curved strip or cover over the upper part of a wheel to protect a rider or another road-user from spray thrown up by the wheel.

muesli /ˈmju:zlɪ/ *n.* a food of crushed cereals, dried fruit, nuts etc. [Swiss G]

muezzin /mu:ˈezɪn/ *n.* a Muslim crier who proclaims the hours of prayer, usually from a minaret. [f. Arab.]

muff¹ *n.* a tubular covering, especially of fur, in which the hands are put to keep them warm. [f. Du. *mof* f. L]

muff² *v.t.* to bungle; to miss (a catch, ball, etc.); to blunder in (a theatrical part etc.). [orig. unkn.]

muffin /ˈmʌfɪn/ *n.* a light flat round spongy cake eaten toasted and buttered. [orig. unkn.]

muffle *v.t.* **1** to wrap or cover for warmth or protection, or to deaden sound. **2** (usu. in *p.p.*) to repress, to deaden the sound of. [perh. f. OF *enmoufler* (*moufle* thick glove, as MUFF¹)]

muffler *n.* **1** a scarf or wrap worn for warmth. **2** a thing used to deaden sound. [f. prec.]

mufti /ˈmʌftɪ/ *n.* plain clothes worn by one who normally wears uniform (esp. *in mufti*). [f. Arab., orig. = Muslim priest]

mug¹ *n.* **1** a drinking-vessel, usually cylindrical, with a handle, and used without a saucer; its contents. **2** (*slang*) the face or mouth. **3** (*slang*) a gullible person, a simpleton. —*v.t.* (**-gg-**) to attack and rob, especially in a public place. —**a mug's game,** an unprofitable or senseless occupation. —**mugger** *n.* [prob. f. Scand.]

mug² *v.t./i.* (**-gg-**) (with *up*) to learn (a subject) by concentrated study. [orig. unkn.]

muggins /ˈmʌgɪnz/ *n.* (*pl.* **-ses** or same) (*colloq.*) a person who allows himself to be outwitted. [perh. f. surname *Muggins*]

muggy *adj.* (of the weather etc.) oppressively humid and warm. —**mugginess** *n.* [f. dial. *mug* mist, f. ON]

Muhammadan /məˈhæmɪd(ə)n/ *adj.* of Muhammad; Muslim. —*n.* a Muslim. [f. *Muhammad*, founder of the Islamic faith (d. 632)]

mulatto /mju:ˈlætəʊ/ *n.* (*pl.* **-os**) a person of mixed White and Black parentage. [f. Sp. (as MULE¹)]

mulberry /ˈmʌlbərɪ/ *n.* **1** a tree of the genus *Morus*, bearing purple or white edible berries and with leaves which are used to feed silkworms. **2** its fruit. **3** dull purplish-red. [earlier *murberie*, f. L *morum* mulberry + BERRY]

mulch *n.* a mixture of wet organic material spread to protect the roots of newly planted trees etc. —*v.t.* to treat with mulch. [prob. f. obs. *mulsh* soft]

mulct *v.t.* to extract money from by fine, taxation, or fraudulent means. [f. F f. L *mulctare* to fine]

mule[1] /mju:l/ *n.* **1** an animal that is the offspring of a mare and a male ass, or (*loosely*) of a she-ass and a stallion (*properly* HINNY), known for its stubbornness. **2** a kind of spinning-machine invented in 1779 by Samuel Crompton (d. 1827) so called because it was a cross between Arkwright's 'water frame' and Hargreaves' spinning jenny. [f. OF f. L *mulus*]

mule[2] /mju:l/ *n.* a backless slipper. [F]

muleteer /mju:lɪ'tɪə(r)/ *n.* a mule-driver. [f. F *muletier* (as MULE[1])]

mulish *adj.* obstinate. [f. MULE[1]]

mull[1] *v.t./i.* to think (over), to ponder. [perh. f. *mull* grind to powder, f. MDu.]

mull[2] *v.t.* to make (wine or beer) into a hot drink with sugar, spices, etc. [orig. unkn.]

mull[3] *n.* (*Sc.*) a promontory. [cf. Gael. *maol*]

mullah /'mʌlə/ *n.* a Muslim learned in Islamic theology and sacred law. [f. Pers., Turk. & Urdu f. Arab.]

mullet[1] /'mʌlɪt/ *n.* a sea-fish of the families Mullidae or Mugilidae, valued for food. [f. OF f. L *mullus* f. Gk]

mullet[2] /'mʌlɪt/ *n.* (in heraldry) a star-shaped figure, usually with five points, given as a mark of cadency for a third son. [f. OF, = rowel]

mulligatawny /mʌlɪgə'tɔ:nɪ/ *n.* a highly seasoned soup, originally from India. [f. Tamil, = pepper-water]

mullion /'mʌljən/ *n.* a vertical bar dividing the lights in a window. [prob. alt. f. *monial*, f. OF *moinel* (as MEAN[3])]

multi- /mʌltɪ-/ *prefix* many. [L (*multus* much, many)]

multi-access /mʌltɪ'ækses/ *adj.* (of a computer system) allowing access to the central processor from several terminals at the same time.

multicoloured /'mʌltɪkʌləd/ *adj.* of many colours.

multifarious /mʌltɪ'feərɪəs/ *adj.* many and various; having a great variety. —**multifariously** *adv.* [f. L *multifarius*]

multiform /'mʌltɪfɔ:m/ *adj.* having many forms, of many kinds.

multilateral /mʌltɪ'lætər(ə)l/ *adj.* **1** (of an agreement, treaty, etc.) in which three or more parties participate. **2** having many sides.

multilingual /mʌltɪ'lɪŋgw(ə)l/ *adj.* in, using, or speaking many languages.

multimillionaire /mʌltɪmɪljə'neə(r)/ *n.* a person possessing several million pounds, dollars, etc.

multinational /mʌltɪ'næʃən(ə)l/ *adj.* operating in several countries. —*n.* a multinational company.

multiple /'mʌltɪp(ə)l/ *adj.* **1** having several parts, elements, or components. **2** many and various. —*n.* a quantity that contains another some number of times without a remainder. —**least** *or* **lowest common multiple,** the least quantity that is a multiple of two or more given quantities. **multiple-choice** *adj.* (of a question in an examination) accompanied by several possible answers from which the correct one is to be selected. **multiple sclerosis,** see SCLEROSIS. [F f. L *multiplus* (as foll.)]

multiplex /'mʌltɪpleks/ *adj.* of many elements, manifold. [L (MULTI-, *-plex* -fold)]

multiplicand /mʌltɪplɪ'kænd/ *n.* a quantity to be multiplied by another. [f. L, gerundive of *multiplicare* (as MULTIPLY)]

multiplication /mʌltɪplɪ'keɪʃ(ə)n/ *n.* multiplying, especially the arithmetical process. —**multiplication sign,** ×, as in 2×3. **multiplication table,** a table of the products of pairs of factors, especially from 1 to 12. [f. OF or L (as MULTIPLY)]

multiplicity /mʌltɪ'plɪsɪtɪ/ *n.* a great variety or number. [f. L (as MULTIPLEX)]

multiplier /'mʌltɪplaɪə(r)/ *n.* the quantity by which a multiplicand is multiplied. [f. foll.]

multiply /'mʌltɪplaɪ/ *v.t./i.* **1** to obtain from (a number) another that is a specified number of times its value. **2** to increase in number, as by breeding. **3** to produce a large number of (instances). **4** to breed (animals); to propagate (plants). [f. OF f. L *multiplicare* (as MULTIPLEX)]

multi-purpose /mʌltɪ'pɜ:pəs/ *adj.* serving many purposes.

multiracial /mʌltɪ'reɪʃ(ə)l/ *adj.* composed of or concerning people of several races.

multi-storey /'mʌltɪstɔ:rɪ/ *adj.* having several storeys.

multitude /'mʌltɪtju:d/ *n.* **1** a crowd of people. **2** a great number. —**the multitude,** the common people. [f. OF f. L *multitudo* (*multus* many)]

multitudinous /mʌltɪ'tju:dɪnəs/ *adj.* very numerous; consisting of many individuals. [f. L (as prec.)]

mum[1] *adj.* (*colloq.*) silent. —**mum's the word,** say nothing. [imit. of closed lips]

mum[2] *v.i.* (**-mm-**) to act in a mime. [cf. prec., and MLG *mummen*]

mum[3] *n.* (*colloq.*) = MUMMY[2]. [abbr.]

mumble *v.t./i.* to speak or utter indistinctly. —*n.* an indistinct utterance. —**mumbler** *n.* [f. MUM[1]; cf. LG *mummelen*]

mumbo-jumbo /mʌmbəʊˈdzʌmbəʊ/ *n.* **1** meaningless ritual. **2** language or action intended to mystify or confuse. **3** an object of senseless veneration. [f. *Mumbo Jumbo*, a supposed African idol]

mummer /ˈmʌmə(r)/ *n.* an actor in a traditional mime. [f. OF *momeur* (as MUM²)]

mummery /ˈmʌmərɪ/ *n.* **1** a performance by mummers. **2** a ridiculous (esp. religious) ceremonial. [f. OF *momerie* (as prec.)]

mummify /ˈmʌmɪfaɪ/ *v.t.* to preserve (a body) as a mummy. —**mummification** /-fɪˈkeɪʃ(ə)n/ *n.* [f. foll.]

mummy¹ *n.* (*colloq.*) mother. [imit. of child's pronunc.; cf. MAMMA]

mummy² /ˈmʌmɪ/ *n.* the body of a person or animal embalmed for burial, especially in ancient Egypt. [f. F, ult. f. Pers. *mūm* wax]

mumps *n.* an infectious disease with swelling of the neck and face. [f. obs. *mump* grimace]

munch *v.t./i.* to eat steadily with marked action of the jaws. [imit.]

mundane /mʌnˈdeɪn/ *adj.* **1** dull or routine. **2** of this world, worldly. [f. OF f. L (*mundus* world)]

municipal /mjuːˈnɪsɪp(ə)l/ *adj.* of or concerning a municipality or its self-government. —**municipally** *adv.* [f. L (*municipium* self-governing town of Italy or a Roman province)]

municipality /mjuːnɪsɪˈpælɪtɪ/ *n.* **1** a town or district having local self-government. **2** the governing body of this. [f. F (as prec.)]

munificent /mjuːˈnɪfɪs(ə)nt/ *adj.* splendidly generous. —**munificence** *n.*, **munificently** *adv.* [f. L *munificus* (*munus* gift)]

muniment /mjuːnɪmənt/ *n.* (usu. in *pl.*) a document kept as evidence of rights or privileges. [f. OF f. L *munimentum* title-deed, orig. = defence (as foll.)]

munition /mjuːˈnɪʃ(ə)n/ *n.pl.* military weapons, ammunition, equipment, and stores. [F f. L (*munire* fortify)]

muntjak /ˈmʌntjæk/ *n.* a small deer originally of SE Asia, of the genus *Muntiacus*, the male of which has small tusks and antlers. [f. native name]

mural /ˈmjʊər(ə)l/ *adj.* of or like a wall; on a wall. —*n.* a mural painting etc. [F f. L *muralis* (*murus* wall)]

murder *n.* **1** the intentional and unlawful killing of one person by another. **2** (*colloq.*) a highly troublesome or dangerous state of affairs. —*v.t.* **1** to kill (a person) unlawfully with malice aforethought; to kill wickedly or inhumanly. **2** (*colloq.*) to spoil by bad performance, mispronunciation, etc. **3** (*colloq.*) to defeat utterly. —**cry blue murder,** (*slang*) to make an extravagant outcry. **get away with murder,** (*colloq.*) to do whatever one wishes. —**murderer** *n.*, **murderess** *n.fem.* [OE]

murderous /ˈmɜːdərəs/ *adj.* capable of, intent on, or involving murder or great harm. [f. prec.]

murk *n.* darkness, poor visibility. [prob. f. Scand.]

murky *adj.* **1** dark, gloomy; (of liquid etc.) thick and dirty. **2** suspiciously obscure. —**murkily** *adv.*, **murkiness** *n.* [f. MURK]

murmur /ˈmɜːmə(r)/ *n.* **1** a subdued continuous sound. **2** softly spoken or nearly inarticulate speech. **3** a subdued expression of discontent. —*v.t./i.* to make a murmur; to utter (words) softly; to complain in low tones. —**murmurous** *adj.* [f. OF or L]

murphy /ˈmɜːfɪ/ *n.* (*slang*) a potato. [Irish surname, from the potato being regarded as the staple food of Ireland]

Murphy's law a name humorously given to various expressions of the apparent perverseness of things (roughly, 'anything that can go wrong will go wrong'). [Irish surname; orig. of phrase uncertain]

murrain /ˈmʌrɪn/ *n.* an infectious disease in cattle. [f. AF *moryn*]

muscadine /ˈmʌskədiːn, -daɪn/ *n.* a musk-flavoured kind of grape. [perh. f. MUSCAT]

muscat /ˈmʌskət/ *n.* **1** a muscadine. **2** wine made from muscadines. [F f. Prov. (as MUSK)]

muscatel /mʌskəˈtel/ *n.* **1** a muscadine. **2** wine or a raisin made from this. [f. OF (as prec.)]

muscle /ˈmʌs(ə)l/ *n.* **1** the contractile tissue that produces movement in an animal's body; a structure composed of such tissue, especially a skeletal muscle of a vertebrate. **2** that part of the animal body which is composed of muscles, the chief constituent of flesh. **3** power, strength. —*v.i.* (*slang*) to force one's way. —**muscle-bound** *adj.* with the muscles stiff and inelastic through excessive exercise or training. **muscle-man** *n.* a man with highly-developed muscles, especially as an intimidator. [F f. L *musculus*]

Muscovite /ˈmʌskəvaɪt/ *adj.* of Moscow. —*n.* a citizen of Moscow. [f. Russ, *Moskva* Moscow]

muscular /ˈmʌskjʊlə(r)/ *adj.* **1** of or affecting the muscles. **2** having well-developed muscles. —**muscularity** /-ˈlærɪtɪ/ *n.* [as MUSCLE]

Muse /mjuz/ *n.* **1** (*Gk & Rom. myth.*) any of the goddesses who presided over the arts and sciences. **2** muse, a poet's inspiring genius. [f. OF or L f. Gk *mousa*]

muse /mjuːz/ *v.t./i.* to ponder, to meditate; to say meditatively. [f. OF perh. f. L *musum* muzzle]

museum /mjuːˈziːəm/ *n.* a building used for the

exhibition and storage of objects illustrating antiquities, natural history, the arts, etc. —**museum piece,** a specimen of art, manufacture, etc., fit for a museum; an old-fashioned person or machine etc. [L f. Gk, = seat of the Muses]

mush[1] *n.* **1** soft pulp. **2** feeble sentimentality. **3** (*US*) maize porridge. [app. var. of MASH]

mush[2] *v.i.* (*N. Amer.*) **1** to travel across snow with a dog-sledge. **2** (as a command to sledge-dogs) get moving. [prob. corrupt. f. F *marchons* let us advance (as MARCH[2])]

mushroom /ˈmʌʃrum/ *n.* an edible fungus, especially *Agaricus campestris*, with a stem and domed cap. —*v.i.* **1** to spring up rapidly. **2** to expand and flatten like a mushroom cap. **3** to gather mushrooms. —**mushroom cloud,** a cloud of mushroom shape, especially from a nuclear explosion. [f. OF *mousseron* f. L]

mushy *adj.* **1** like mush, soft. **2** feebly sentimental. —**mushily** *adv.*, **mushiness** *n.* [f. MUSH[1]]

music /ˈmjuːzɪk/ *n.* **1** the art of combining vocal and/or instrumental sounds in harmonious and expressive ways; the sounds so produced. **2** a musical composition; a printed or written score of this. **3** a pleasant natural sound. —**face the music,** to face one's critics etc., not to shirk the consequences. **music centre,** equipment combining a radio, record-player, and tape-recorder. **music-hall** *n.* a variety entertainment with singing dancing, etc.; a theatre for this. **music-stool** *n.* a stool with adjustable height of the seat, for a pianist. **music to one's ears,** what one is pleased to hear. [f. OF f. L f. Gk, = of the Muses (as MUSE)]

musical /ˈmjuːzɪk(ə)l/ *adj.* **1** of music. **2** (of a sound etc.) melodious or harmonious. **3** fond of or skilled in music. **4** set to or accompanied by music. —*n.* a film or play etc. with music and song as the principal feature. —**musical box,** a box containing a mechanism (usually a revolving toothed cylinder striking a comblike metal plate) for playing a certain tune when set in motion. **musical chairs,** a party game in which players walk round chairs (one fewer than the number of players) until the music stops, when the player who finds no chair is eliminated and a chair is removed before the next round. **musical comedy,** an entertainment in which a story is told by a combination of spoken dialogue and songs. —**musicality** /-ˈkælɪtɪ/ *n.*, **musically** *adv.* [as prec.]

musician /mjuːˈzɪʃ(ə)n/ *n.* a person skilled in music, especially one practising it professionally. —**musicianship** *n.* [f. OF (as MUSIC)]

musicology /mjuːzɪˈkɒlədʒɪ/ *n.* the study of the history and forms of music as distinct from study to perform or compose it. —**musicologist** *n.* [f. F (as MUSIC, -LOGY)]

musique concrète /mjuːziːk kɔ̃ˈkret/ concrete music (see CONCRETE). [F]

musk *n.* **1** a substance secreted by the male musk-deer, used as the basis of perfumes. **2** a plant (esp. *Mimulus moschatus*) which has or used to have a musky smell. —**musk-deer** *n.* a small hornless ruminant of Central Asia, of the genus *Moschus*. **musk-melon** *n.* the common yellow melon (*Cucumis melo*). **musk-ox** *n.* a shaggy ruminant (*Ovibos moschatus*) with curved horns. **musk-rat** *n.* a large North American aquatic rodent (*Ondatra zibethica*) with a musky smell; its fur. **musk-rose** *n.* a rambling rose (*Rosa moschata* etc.) with a musky fragrance. [f. L f. Pers.]

musket /ˈmʌskɪt/ *n.* (*hist.*) an infantryman's (esp. smooth-bored) light gun. [f. F f. It. *moschetto* crossbow bolt]

musketeer /mʌskɪˈtɪə(r)/ *n.* a soldier armed with a musket. [f. prec.]

musky *adj.* smelling like musk. —**muskiness** *n.* [f. MUSK]

Muslim /ˈmuslɪm, -z-/ *n.* a believer in Islam. —*adj.* of Muslims. [f. Arab., = one who submits (as ISLAM)]

muslin /ˈmʌzlɪn/ *n.* a fine delicately woven cotton fabric. [f. F f. It. (*Mussolo* Mosul in Iraq, where it was made)]

musquash /ˈmʌskwɒʃ/ *n.* **1** the musk-rat. **2** its fur. [Algonquian]

mussel /ˈmʌs(ə)l/ *n.* a bivalve mollusc, especially the edible kind (genus *Mytilus*). [OE (ult. as MUSCLE)]

must[1] *v.aux.* (*pres. & past* **must;** no other parts used) expressing obligation, insistence, rightness or advisability, certainty or likelihood. —*n.* (*colloq.*) a thing that must be done, seen, etc. [OE]

must[2] *n.* grape-juice before the end of fermentation; new wine. [OE f. L *mustum*]

mustang /ˈmʌstæŋ/ *n.* a half-wild domestic horse of Mexico and California. [f. Sp. *mestengo & mostrenco*]

mustard /ˈmʌstəd/ *n.* **1** a plant (*Brassica nigra*) with yellow flowers. **2** a condiment made by grinding the seeds of this and making them into a paste with water or vinegar. **3** a fodder plant (*Sinapis alba*) the seed-leaves of which form part of 'mustard and cress'. **4** a brownish-yellow colour. —**mustard gas,** a colourless oily liquid or its vapour, a powerful irritant. **mustard plaster,** a plaster containing mustard, applied to the skin as a poultice. [f. OF f. L (as MUST[2]), the condiment being orig. prepared with must]

muster *v.t./i.* **1** to assemble or cause to assemble (orig. of soldiers assembled to check numbers etc. or for inspection). **2** to summon (courage, strength, etc.). —*n.* an assembly or gathering. —**pass muster,** to be accepted as adequate. [f. OF *mo(u)strer* f. L *monstrare* show]

mustn't /ˈmʌs(ə)nt/ (*colloq.*) must not.

musty *adj.* **1** mouldy, stale. **2** antiquated. —**mustily** *adv.*, **mustiness** *n.* [perh. alt. f. *moisty* (MOIST)]

mutable /ˈmju:təb(ə)l/ *adj.* liable to change; fickle. —**mutability** /-ˈbɪlɪtɪ/ *n.* [f. L *mutabilis* (*mutare* change)]

mutant /ˈmju:t(ə)nt/ *adj.* resulting from mutation. —*n.* a mutant form. [f. L (as MUTATION)]

mutate /mju:ˈteɪt/ *v.t./i.* to undergo mutation; to cause to do this. [f. foll.]

mutation /mju:ˈteɪʃ(ə)n/ *n.* **1** a change, an alteration. **2** a genetic change which when transmitted to an offspring gives rise to heritable variation. **3** a mutant. **4** umlaut. [f. L (*mutare* change)]

mutatis mutandis /mu:ˈtɑ:tɪs mu:ˈtændɪs/ with due alteration of details (in comparing cases). [L]

mute /mju:t/ *adj.* **1** silent, refraining from speech. **2** not emitting articulate sound; (of a person or animal) dumb. **3** (of a letter) not pronounced. **4** not expressed in speech. —*n.* **1** a dumb person. **2** an actor whose part is in dumb show. **3** a device to deaden the sound of a musical instrument. **4** a mute consonant. —*v.t.* **1** to deaden or soften the sound of (esp. a musical instrument). **2** to tone down, to make less intense. —**mute swan,** the common white swan (*Cygnus olor*). —**mutely** *adv.*, **muteness** *n.* [f. OF f. L *mutus*]

mutilate /ˈmju:tɪleɪt/ *v.t.* **1** to injure or disfigure by cutting off an important part. **2** to render (a book etc.) imperfect by excision etc. —**mutilation** /-ˈleɪʃ(ə)n/ *n.*, **mutilator** *n.* [f. L *mutilare* (*mutilus* maimed)]

mutineer /mju:tɪˈnɪə(r)/ *n.* one who mutinies. [f. F (*mutin* rebellious f. *muete* movement f. L *movere* move)]

mutinous /ˈmju:tɪnəs/ *adj.* rebellious, ready to mutiny. —**mutinously,** *adv.* [f. obs. *mutine* rebellion (as prec.)]

mutiny /ˈmju:tɪnɪ/ *n.* an open revolt against authority, especially by servicemen against officers. —*v.i.* to engage in a mutiny, to revolt. [as prec.]

mutt *n.* (*slang*) a stupid person. [abbr. of *mutton-head*]

mutter *v.t./i.* **1** to speak or utter in a low unclear tone. **2** to utter subdued grumbles. —*n.* muttering; muttered words. [as MUTE]

mutton *n.* the flesh of the sheep as food. —**mutton dressed as lamb,** a middle-aged or elderly woman dressed to look young.

mutton-head *n.* (*colloq.*) a stupid person. —**muttony** *adj.* [f. OF f. L *multo* sheep]

mutual /ˈmju:tjʊəl/ *adj.* **1** (of feeling, action, etc.) felt or done by each to or towards the other. **2** standing in (a specified) relation to each other. **3** (*colloq.*) (D) common to two or more persons. —**mutuality** /-ˈælɪtɪ/ *n.*, **mutually** *adv.* [f. OF f. L *mutuus*]

mutualism /ˈmju:tjʊəlɪz(ə)m/ *n.* mutually beneficial symbiosis. [f. prec.]

Muzak /ˈmju:zæk/ *n.* [P] a system of music transmission for playing in shops, factories, etc.; recorded light music as a background. [cf. MUSIC]

muzzle *n.* **1** the projecting part of an animal's head including the nose and mouth. **2** the open end of a firearm. **3** a contrivance of strap or wire etc. put over an animal's head to prevent it from biting or feeding. —*v.t.* **1** to put a muzzle on. **2** to impose silence on. [f. OF f. L *musum*]

muzzy *adj.* **1** dazed, feeling stupefied. **2** indistinct. —**muzzily** *adv.*, **muzziness** *n.* [orig. unkn.]

MW *abbr.* megawatt(s).

my /maɪ/ *poss. adj.* **1** of or belonging to me. **2** used in affectionate collocations and as an exclamation of surprise. [f. MINE[1]]

myalgia /maɪˈældʒɪə/ *n.* pain in muscle(s). [f. Gk *mus* muscle + *algos* pain]

myall /ˈmaɪəl/ *n.* an Australian acacia with hard scented wood used for fences etc. [f. Aboriginal *maial*]

Mycenaean /maɪsɪˈni:ən/ *adj.* of the culture developed in mainland Greece in the late Bronze Age, *c.*1580–1100 BC, illustrated by remains at Mycenae and other ancient cities of the Peloponnese. —*n.* a Mycenaean person. [f. L *Mycenaeus*]

mycology /maɪˈkɒlədʒɪ/ *n.* the study of fungi. —**mycologist** *n.* [f. Gk *mukēs* mushroom + -LOGY]

myna, mynah var. of MINA.

myopia /maɪˈəʊpɪə/ *n.* short-sightedness. —**myopic** /-ˈɒpɪk/ *adj.*, **myopically** /-ˈɒpɪkəlɪ/ *adv.* [f. Gk (*muō* shut, *ōps* eye)]

myriad /ˈmɪrɪəd/ *n.* (*literary*) **1** (in *pl.*) an indefinitely great number. **2** ten thousand. —*adj.* (*literary*) innumerable. [f. L f. Gk (*murioi* 10,000)]

myriapod /ˈmɪrɪəpɒd/ *n.* a small crawling arthropod with many legs, of the group Myriapoda comprising centipedes and millepedes. [as prec. + Gk *pous podos* foot]

myrmidon /ˈmɜ:mɪd(ə)n/ *n.* a hired ruffian, a base servant. [f. *Myrmidons*, Thessalians who followed Achilles to Troy]

myrrh /mɜ:(r)/ *n.* a gum resin from trees of the genus *Commiphora*, used in perfumes, medicine, and incense. [OE f. L f. Gk *murra*]

myrtle /ˈmɜːt(ə)l/ *n.* an evergreen shrub of the genus *Myrtus*, with shiny leaves and fragrant white flowers. [f. L dim. (*myrta*, *myrtus* f. Gk)]

myself /maɪˈself/ *pron.* emphat. & refl. form of I, ME[1]. [f. ME[1] + SELF]

mysterious /mɪˈstɪərɪəs/ *adj.* **1** full of or wrapped in mystery. **2** (of a person) enjoying mystery. —**mysteriously** *adv.* [f. F (as foll.)]

mystery /ˈmɪstərɪ/ *n.* **1** an inexplicable or secret matter. **2** secrecy, obscurity. **3** the practice of making a secret of things. **4** a fictional work dealing with a puzzling event, especially a crime. **5** a religious truth that is beyond human powers to understand. **6** (in *pl.*) secret cults in the ancient world, which generally included mystic ideas and involved initiation rites. **7** a mystery play, a vernacular medieval religious drama. —**mystery tour** *or* **trip,** a pleasure excursion to an unspecified destination. [f. OF or L f. Gk *musterion* (as MYSTIC)]

mystic /ˈmɪstɪk/ *n.* one who seeks by contemplation and self-surrender to obtain union with or absorption into the Deity, or who believes in the spiritual apprehension of truths beyond the understanding. —*adj.* **1** mysterious and awe-inspiring. **2** spiritually allegorical or symbolic. **3** occult, esoteric; of hidden meaning. [f. OF or L f. Gk (*mustēs* initiated person)]

mystical *adj.* **1** of mystics or mysticism. **2** having direct spiritual significance. —**mystically** *adv.* [as prec.]

mysticism /ˈmɪstɪsɪz(ə)m/ *n.* **1** mystical quality. **2** being a mystic. Mysticism is a widespread experience in Christianity and in many non-Christian religions, e.g. Buddhism, Taoism, Hinduism, and Islam. [f. MYSTIC]

mystify /ˈmɪstɪfaɪ/ *v.t.* to cause to feel puzzled. —**mystification** /-fɪˈkeɪʃ(ə)n/ *n.* [f. F (as MYSTIC or MYSTERY)]

mystique /mɪˈstiːk/ *n.* an atmosphere of mystery and veneration attending some activity or person; a skill or technique impressive to the layman. [F (as MYSTIC)]

myth /mɪθ/ *n.* **1** a traditional narrative usually involving supernatural or imaginary persons etc. and embodying popular ideas on natural or social phenomena etc.; such narratives collectively. **2** an imaginary person or thing. **3** a widely held but false notion. **4** an allegory. —**mythical** *adj.*, **mythically** *adv.* [f. L f. Gk *muthos*]

mythology /mɪˈθɒlədʒɪ/ *n.* **1** a body of myths. **2** the study of myths. —**mythological** /mɪθəˈlɒdʒɪk(ə)l/ *adj.*, **mythologically** *adv.*, **mythologist** *n.* [f. F or L f. Gk (as MYTH, -LOGY)]

myxomatosis /mɪksəməˈtəʊsɪs/ *n.* a virus disease in rabbits, with tumours in mucous tissue. [f. Gk *muxa* mucus]

Nn

N, n /en/ *n.* (*pl.* **Ns, N's**) **1** the fourteenth letter of the alphabet. **2** an indefinite number. —**to the nth degree,** to the utmost.

N *abbr.* **1** (in chess) knight. **2** newton(s).

N *symbol* nitrogen.

N. *abbr.* **1** New. **2** North, Northern.

n. *abbr.* **1** name. **2** neuter. **3** note.

Na *symbol* sodium. [f. L *natrium*]

NAAFI /ˈnæfɪ/ *abbr.* Navy, Army, and Air Force Institutes (a canteen for servicemen).

nab *v.t.* (**-bb-**) (*slang*) **1** to catch (a wrongdoer) in the act; to arrest. **2** to seize, to grab. [also *nap*, as in KIDNAP; orig. unkn.]

nabob /ˈneɪbɒb/ *n.* **1** (*hist.*) a Muslim official or governor under the Mogul empire. **2** (*archaic*) a wealthy luxury-loving person, especially one who has returned from India with a fortune. [f. Port. or Sp. f. Urdu (as NAWAB)]

nacre /ˈneɪkə(r)/ *n.* mother-of-pearl; the shellfish yielding this. —**nacreous** /-krɪəs/ *adj.* [F]

nadir /ˈneɪdɪə(r)/ *n.* **1** the point of the heavens directly under the observer (opp. ZENITH. **2** the lowest point, the state or time of greatest depression etc. [f. OF f. Arab., = opposite (to zenith)]

naevus /ˈni:vəs/ *n.* (*pl.* **-vi** /-vaɪ/) a birthmark in the form of a sharply-defined red mark in the skin; a mole (MOLE[2]). [L]

nag[1] *v.t./i.* (**-gg-**) **1** to find fault or scold persistently. **2** (of pain etc.) to be persistent. —**nagger** *n.* [perh. f. Scand. or LG]

nag[2] *n.* (*colloq.*) a horse. [orig. unkn.]

naiad /ˈnaɪæd/ *n.* a water-nymph. [f. L f. Gk]

nail *n.* **1** the horny covering of the upper surface of the tip of a finger or toe. **2** a small metal spike hammered in to hold things together or serve as a peg or ornament. —*v.t.* **1** to fasten with a nail or nails. **2** to secure, catch, or arrest (a person, thing, attention, etc.). **3** to identify precisely. —**nail down,** to bind to a promise etc.); to define precisely. **nail in a person's coffin,** a thing hastening a person's death. **nail-punch** *n.* a driving punch for nails. **on the nail,** (esp. of payment) without delay. [OE]

nainsook /ˈneɪnsʊk/ *n.* a fine soft cotton fabric, originally from India. [f. Hindi]

naïve /nɑ:ˈi:v/ *adj.* **1** simple, unaffected, unconsciously artless. **2** (of art etc.) straightforward in style, eschewing subtlety or conventional technique. —**naïvely** *adv.*, **naïveté** /-ˈi:vteɪ/ *n.*, **naïvety** /-ˈi:vtɪ/ *n.* [F, fem. of *naïf* f. L *nativus* native]

naked /ˈneɪkɪd/ *adj.* **1** unclothed, nude. **2** without the usual covering or furnishings; unsheathed or unprotected. **3** undisguised. **4** (of the eye) unassisted by a telescope or microscope etc. —**nakedly** *adv.*, **nakedness** *n.* [OE]

namby-pamby /næmbɪ ˈpæmbɪ/ *adj.* insipid, feeble, unmanly. —*n.* a person of this kind. [f. *Ambrose* Philips, English pastoral writer (d. 1749)]

name *n.* **1** the word by which an individual person, animal, place, or thing is spoken of or to. **2** the word denoting an object of thought, especially one applicable to many individuals. **3** a reputation. **4** a person as known, famed, etc. **5** a family, a clan.—*v.t.* **1** to give a name to. **2** to state the name of. **3** to mention, to specify, to cite. **4** to nominate or appoint. —**call a person names,** to address or speak of him abusively. **have to one's name,** to possess. **in the name of,** invoking; as representing. **in name only,** not in reality. **name-dropping** *n.* familiar mention of famous names as a form of boasting. **name-plate** *n.* a plate with a name inscribed on it, identifying the occupant etc. [OE, rel. to L *nomen*]

nameable *adj.* that may be named. [f. NAME]

nameless *adj.* **1** having no name or no known name. **2** left unnamed. **3** unmentionable, loathsome. [f. NAME + -LESS]

namely *adv.* that is to say, in other words, specifically. [f. NAME]

namesake *n.* a person or thing with the same name as another. [prob. f. *for the name's sake*]

nancy /ˈnænsɪ/ *n.* (*slang*) an effeminate or homosexual man or boy. [f. *Nancy*, pet-form of woman's name *Ann*]

nankeen /næŋˈki:n/ *n.* **1** a yellow cotton cloth. **2** the colour of this. [f. *Nankin(g)* in China]

nanny *n.* **1** a child's nurse or minder. **2** (*colloq.*) grandma. —**nanny-goat** *n.* a female goat. [as NANCY]

nano- /nænəʊ-, neməʊ-/ *in comb.* one thousand millionth. [f. L f. Gk *nanos* dwarf]

nap[1] *n.* a short period of light sleep, especially during the day.—*v.i.* (**-pp-**) to have a nap. —**catch a person napping,** to take him or her unawares; to find him or her remiss. [OE]

nap[2] *n.* a surface of cloth consisting of fibre-ends raised, cut even, and smoothed. [f. MDu. or MLG]

nap[3] *n.* **1** a card-game like whist, with bidding. **2** a racing tip claimed to be almost a certainty. —*v.t.* (**-pp-**) to name (a horse) as an almost certain winner. —**go nap,** to make the highest bid in nap; to risk everything. [abbr. of NAPOLEON]

napalm /ˈneɪpɑ:m/ *n.* a thickening agent made from naphthalene and coconut oil; jellied petrol made from this, used in bombs. —*v.t.* to attack with napalm bombs. [f. *na*phthenic acid (in petroleum) + *palm*itic acid (in coconut oil)]

nape *n.* the back of the neck. [orig. unkn.]

naphtha /ˈnæfθə/ *n.* an inflammable oil distilled from coal etc. [L f. Gk]

naphthalene /ˈnæfθəli:n/ *n.* a white crystalline substance obtained in distilling coal-tar. [f. prec.]

napkin *n.* **1** a piece of cloth or paper used at meals for wiping the lips and fingers or protecting the clothes. **2** a nappy. [f. OF *nappe* f. L *mappa* (as MAP)]

nappy *n.* a piece of material wrapped round the lower part of a baby's body and between its legs to hold or absorb excreta. [abbr. of NAPKIN]

narcissism /nɑ:ˈsɪsɪz(ə)m/ *n.* abnormal self-love or self-admiration. —**narcissistic** /-ˈsɪstɪk/ *adj.* [f. *Narkissos,* (Gk myth.) beautiful youth who fell in love with his reflection]

narcissus /nɑ:ˈsɪsəs/ *n.* (*pl.* **-si** /-saɪ/) a flowering bulb of the genus *Narcissus* (which includes the daffodil), especially the white-flowered *N. poeticus.* [as prec.]

narcosis /nɑ:ˈkəʊsɪs/ *n.* an insensible state; the induction of this. [f. Gk (*narkoō* benumb)]

narcotic /nɑ:ˈkɒtɪk/ *adj.* (of a substance) inducing sleep, drowsiness, or stupor, etc.; (of a drug) affecting the mind. —*n.* a narcotic substance, drug, or influence. [f. OF or L f. Gk (as prec.)]

nard *n.* spikenard; the plant (probably *Nardostachys jatamansi*) yielding this. [f. L f. Gk]

nark *v.t.* (*slang*) to annoy. —*n.* (*slang*) a police informer or spy. [f. Romany *nāk* nose]

narrate /nəˈreɪt/ *v.t./i.* to tell (a story), to give an account of; to write or speak a narrative. —**narration** *n.*, **narrator** *n.* [f. L *narrare*]

narrative /ˈnærətɪv/ *n.* a spoken or written account of connected events in order of happening. —*adj.* of or by narration. [f. F f. L (as prec.)]

narrow /ˈnærəʊ/ *adj.* **1** of small width in proportion to length, not broad. **2** with little scope or variety. **3** with little margin. **4** narrow-minded. —*n.* (usu. in *pl.*) the narrow part of a sound, strait, river, pass, or street. —*v.t./i.* to make or become narrower; to lessen, to contract. —**narrow boat,** a canal boat. **narrow-minded** *adj.* intolerant; rigid or restricted in one's views. **narrow seas,** the English Channel and the Irish Sea. —**narrowly** *adv.*, **narrowness** *n.* [OE]

narwhal /ˈnɑ:w(ə)l/ *n.* an Arctic mammal (*Monodon monoceros*) the male of which has a long tusk. [f. Du. f. Da.]

NASA /ˈnæsə/ (also **Nasa**) *abbr.* National Aeronautics and Space Administration, a body (set up in 1958) responsible for organizing research in extraterrestrial space conducted by the USA.

nasal /ˈneɪz(ə)l/ *adj.* **1** of the nose. **2** (of a letter or sound) pronounced with the nose passage open (e.g. *m, n, ng*). **3** (of a voice or speech) having many nasal sounds. —*n.* a nasal letter or sound. —**nasally** *adv.* [F or f. L (*nasus* nose)]

nasalize /ˈneɪzəlaɪz/ *v.t./i.* to speak nasally; to give a nasal sound to. [f. prec.]

nascent /ˈnæs(ə)nt, ˈneɪ-/ *adj.* in the process of birth, incipient, not mature. —**nascence** *n.*, **nascency** *n.* [f. L *nasci* be born]

nasturtium /nəˈstɜ:ʃ(ə)m/ *n.* a trailing garden plant of the genus *Tropaeolum,* with bright orange, yellow, or red flowers. [L, = a kind of cress]

nasty /ˈnɑ:stɪ/ *adj.* **1** unpleasant. **2** unkind, malicious. **3** difficult to deal with. —**nasty piece of work,** (*colloq.*) an unpleasant or undesirable person. —**nastily** *adv.*, **nastiness** *n.* [orig. unkn.]

Nat. *abbr.* **1** National; Nationalist. **2** Natural.

natal /ˈneɪt(ə)l/ *adj.* of or concerning birth. [f. L *natalis* (as foll.)]

nation /ˈneɪʃ(ə)n/ *n.* a community of people of mainly common descent, language, history, or political institutions and usually sharing one territory and government. —**nation-wide** *adj.* extending over the whole nation. [f. OF f. L *natio* (*nasci* be born)]

national /ˈnæʃ(ə)n(ə)l/ *adj.* of a nation; affecting or concerning a whole nation. —*n.* a citizen or subject of a specified country; one's fellow countryman. —**the National,** the Grand National. **national anthem,** a song of patriotism or loyalty adopted by a nation. **National Debt,** a debt incurred by a central government and secured against the national income. **National Front,** an extreme right-wing British political party holding extreme reactionary views on immigration etc. **national grid,** a network of high-voltage electric power-lines between major power-stations; a metric system of geographical co-ordinates used in maps of the British Isles. **National Guard,** (*US*) a reserve force partly maintained by individual States of the USA but available for federal use. **National Health Service,** a system of national medical service financed by taxation. **National Insurance,** a system of compulsory contribution from the employee and the employer to provide State assistance in sickness, unemployment, retirement, etc. **national park,** an area of countryside under State supervision to preserve its natural state for public enjoyment. **national service,** service by conscription in the armed services. **National Socialism,** the political creed of the National Socialist German Workers' Party, more commonly known as Nazism. —**nationally** *adv.* [F (as prec.)]

nationalism *n.* **1** patriotic feeling, principles, or efforts. **2** a policy of national independence. —**nationalist** *n.* [f. NATIONAL]

nationality /næʃəˈnælɪtɪ/ *n.* **1** the status of belonging to a particular nation. **2** distinctive national quality, being national. **3** an ethnic group forming part of one or more political nations. [f. NATIONAL]

nationalize /ˈnæʃ(ə)nəlaɪz/ *v.t.* to make national; to convert (an industry, institution, etc.) to public ownership. —**nationalization** /-ˈzeɪʃ(ə)n/ *n.* [as prec.]

native /ˈneɪtɪv/ *adj.* **1** inborn, innate, natural. **2** of one's birth; belonging to one by right of birth. **3** born in a particular place, indigenous; of the natives of a place. **4** (of metal etc.) found in a pure or uncombined state. —*n.* **1** one born in a particular place. **2** a local inhabitant. **3** a member of a non-European or less civilized indigenous people; (in South Africa) a Black. **4** an indigenous animal or plant. [f. OF or L *nativus* (as NATION)]

nativity /nəˈtɪvɪtɪ/ *n.* birth; **the Nativity,** that of Christ; a festival celebrating this. [f. OF f. L (as prec.)]

NATO /ˈneɪtəʊ/ *abbr.* (also **Nato**) North Atlantic Treaty Organization, an association of European and North American States, formed in 1949 for the defence of Europe and the North Atlantic against the perceived threat of Soviet aggression.

natter *v.i.* (*colloq.*) to chat, to chatter idly. —*n.* (*colloq.*) a chat, idle chatter. [orig. Sc., imit.]

natterjack /ˈnætədʒæk/ *n.* a kind of small toad (*Bufo calamita*), with a yellow stripe down its back, that runs instead of hopping. [perh. f. prec. (from its loud croak) + JACK]

natty *adj.* neat and trim, dapper. —**nattily** *adv.* [perh. rel. to NEAT]

natural /ˈnætʃər(ə)l/ *adj.* **1** of, existing in, or produced by nature. **2** conforming to the ordinary course of nature, normal. **3** suited to be such by nature. **4** not affected in manner etc. **5** not surprising, to be expected. **6** (of a child) illegitimate. **7** (*Mus.*, of a note) neither a sharp nor a flat. —*n.* **1** a person or thing that seems naturally suited (for a role, purpose, etc.). **2** (*Mus.*) a natural note; a sign denoting this. **3** pale fawn colour. —**natural gas,** gas found in the earth's crust, not manufactured. **natural history,** the study of animal and vegetable life. **natural law,** a correct statement of the invariable sequence between specified conditions and a specified phenomenon. **natural number,** any whole number greater than 0. **natural religion,** religion based on reason without accepting revelation (cf. DEISM). **natural science,** science dealing with natural or material phenomena. **natural selection,** the process favouring the survival of those organisms that are best adapted to their environment. **natural theology,** knowledge of God gained by reason and without the aid of revelation. —**naturalness** *n.* [f. OF f. L (as NATURE)]

naturalism /ˈnætʃər(ə)lɪz(ə)m/ *n.* **1** realistic method or adherence to nature in literature and art. **2** action based on natural instincts. **3** a theory of the world, and of man's relation to it, in which only the operation of natural (as opp. to supernatural or spiritual) laws and forces is assumed; the theory that moral concepts can be explained wholly in terms of concepts applicable to natural phenomena. —**naturalistic** /-ˈlɪstɪk/ *adj.* [f. prec.]

naturalist *n.* **1** an expert in natural history. **2** an adherent of naturalism. [f. F, & NATURAL]

naturalize *v.t.* **1** to admit (an alien) to citizenship. **2** to introduce and acclimatize (an animal or plant) into a country where it is not native. **3** to adopt (a foreign word or custom). **4** to cause to appear natural. —**naturalization** /-ˈzeɪʃ(ə)n/ *n.* [f. F (as NATURAL)]

naturally *adv.* **1** in a natural manner. **2** of course, as might be expected. [f. NATURAL]

nature /ˈneɪtʃə(r)/ *n.* **1** the phenomena of the physical world as a whole, the physical power causing these; **Nature,** these personified. **2** a thing's essential qualities; a person's or animal's innate character. **3** a kind or class. **4** vital force, functions, or needs. —**by nature,** innately. **by** *or* **in the nature of things,** inevitable, inevitably. **call of nature,** the need to urinate or defecate. **in a state of nature,** in an uncivilized or uncultivated state; totally naked. **nature trail,** a path through the countryside planned to show interesting natural objects. —**-natured** *adj.*

(*good-natured*). [f. OF f. L *natura* (*nasci nat-* be born)]

naturist *n.* a nudist. —**naturism** *n.* [f. prec.]

naught /nɔːt/ *n.* (*archaic*) nothing, nought. —*predic. adj.* (*archaic*) worthless, useless. —**come to naught,** not to succeed; to come to nothing. **set at naught,** to despise. [OE (as NO, WIGHT)]

naughty /ˈnɔːtɪ/ *adj.* **1** badly behaved, disobedient. **2** mildly indecent. —**naughtily** *adv.*, **naughtiness** *n.* [f. prec.]

nausea /ˈnɔːzɪə/ *n.* **1** inclination to vomit (orig. = seasickness). **2** loathing. —**nauseous** *adj.* [L f. Gk (*naus* ship)]

nauseate /ˈnɔːzɪeɪt/ *v.t./i.* **1** to affect with nausea, to disgust. **2** to loathe. **3** to feel nausea. [f. prec.]

nautch /nɔːtʃ/ *n.* a performance of Indian dancing girls. [f. Urdu f. Skr.]

nautical /nɔːtɪk(ə)l/ *adj.* of sailors or navigation. —**nautical mile,** see MILE. —**nautically** *adv.* [f. F or L f. Gk *nautikos* (*nautēs* sailor)]

nautilus /ˈnɔːtɪləs/ *n.* (*pl.* **-luses, -li** /-laɪ/) a mollusc of the genus *Nautilus*, with a spiral shell divided into compartments. [L f. Gk, = sailor (as prec.)]

naval /ˈneɪv(ə)l/ *adj.* of the or a navy; of ships. [f. L (*navis* ship)]

nave[1] *n.* the body of a church (apart from the choir or chancel, aisles, and transepts). [F. L *navis* ship]

nave[2] *n.* the hub of a wheel. [OE]

navel /ˈneɪv(ə)l/ *n.* **1** the hollow in the belly left by the detachment of the umbilical cord. **2** the central point of anything. —**navel orange,** an orange with a navel-like formation on the top. [OE (as prec.)]

navigable /ˈnævɪgəb(ə)l/ *adj.* **1** (of a river etc.) suitable for ships to sail in. **2** (of a ship etc.) seaworthy. **3** (of a balloon) steerable. —**navigability** /-ˈbɪlɪtɪ/ *n.*, **navigably** *adv.* [F or f. L (as foll.)]

navigate /ˈnævɪgeɪt/ *v.t./i.* **1** to sail in or through (a sea or river etc.). **2** to direct the course of (a ship, aircraft, or vehicle etc.). —**navigator** *n.* [f. L *navigare* (*navis* ship, *agere* drive)]

navigation /nævɪˈgeɪʃ(ə)n/ *n.* navigating; methods of determining a ship's or aircraft's position and course by geometry and astronomy or radio signals. —**navigational** *adj.* [F or f L (as prec.)] [F, or f. L *navigatio* (as prec.)]

navvy /ˈnævɪ/ *n.* a labourer employed in excavating for roads, railways, canals, etc. —*v.i.* to work as a navvy. [abbr. of *navigator*]

navy /ˈneɪvɪ/ *n.* **1** a State's warships with their crews and organization. **2** the officers and men of the navy. **3** (*poetic*) a fleet. —**navy (blue),** dark blue as of naval uniforms. [f. OF *navie* f. L (as NAVAL)]

nawab /nəˈwɑːb/ *n.* **1** the title of a distinguished Muslim in Pakistan. **2** (*hist.*) the title of a governor or nobleman in India. [f. Urdu f. Arab., = deputy; cf. NABOB]

nay *adv.* **1** (*archaic*) no. **2** or rather, and even, and more than that. —*n.* the word 'nay'. —**say nay,** to refuse, to contradict. [f. ON (*ne* not, as AYE²)]

Nazarene /næzəˈriːn, ˈnæ-/ *adj.* of Nazareth or the Nazarenes. —*n.* **1** a person of Nazareth, especially Christ. **2** (in Jewish or Muslim use) a Christian. [f. L f. Gk (*Nazaret* Nazareth)]

Nazarite /ˈnæzəraɪt/ *n.* (more correctly **Nazirite**) any of the Israelites specially consecrated to the service of God who were under vows to abstain from wine, let their hair grow, and avoid the defilement of contact with a dead body. [f. L f. Heb. (*nazar* consecrate oneself)]

Nazi /ˈnɑːtsɪ/ *n.* a member of the German National Socialist (Workers') Party in Germany, led by Adolf Hitler. —*adj.* of this party. —**Nazism** *n.* [repr. pronunc. of *Nati* in G *Nationalsozialist*]

NB *abbr.* note well. [f. L *nota bene*]

Nb *symbol* niobium.

NCO *abbr.* non-commissioned officer.

Nd *symbol* neodymium.

n.d. *abbr.* no date.

NE *abbr.* North-East, North-Eastern.

Ne *symbol* neon.

neap *n.* (in full **neap tide**) the tide at times of the month when there is least difference between high and low water. [OE *nēpflōd* (cf. FLOOD); orig. unkn.]

Neapolitan /nɪəˈpɒlɪt(ə)n/ *adj.* of Naples. —*n.* a native of Naples. [f. L (*Neapolis* Naples, f. Gk)]

near *adv.* **1** to, at, or within a short distance in space or time. **2** closely, nearly. —*prep.* **1** near to in space, time, condition, or semblance. **2** (*in comb.*) resembling, intended as a substitute for (*near-silk*), that is almost (*near-hysterical*). —*adj.* **1** with only a short distance or interval between. **2** closely related. **3** (of part of a vehicle, horse, or road) nearer to the side of the road when facing forward, usually left. **4** with little margin. **5** niggardly. —*v.t./i.* to draw near (to), to approach. —**near by,** not far off. **Near East,** the region comprising the countries of the eastern Mediterranean, sometimes also including those of the Balkan peninsula, SW Asia, or north Africa. **near miss,** something that misses its objective only narrowly; a narrowly avoided collision. **near-sighted** *adj.* short-sighted. **near thing,** a narrow escape. —**nearness** *n.* [f. ON, orig. = *nigher* (NIGH)]

nearby *adj.* close in position.

nearly *adv.* 1 almost. 2 closely. —**not nearly,** nothing like, far from. [f. NEAR]

neat *adj.* 1 simple, clean, and orderly in appearance. 2 done or doing things in a precise and skilful way. 3 (of alcoholic drink) undiluted. —**neatly** *adv.*, **neatness** *n.* [f. F, = NET²]

neaten *v.t.* to make neat. [f. prec.]

neath *prep.* (*poetic*) beneath. [f. BENEATH]

nebula /ˈnebjʊlə/ *n.* (*pl.* **-ae** /-iː/) a cloud of gas or dust situated within the interstellar space of a galaxy (usually our own) and appearing as either a bright or a dark cloud according to whether or not there are stars present to make it luminous. [L, = mist]

nebular /ˈnebjʊlə(r)/ *adj.* of a nebula or nebulae. —**nebular theory** *or* **hypothesis,** the theory that the solar and stellar systems were developed from nebulae. [f. prec.]

nebulous /ˈnebjʊləs/ *adj.* cloudlike, indistinct, having no definite form. [f. F or L (as NEBULA)]

necessary /ˈnesəsərɪ/ *adj.* 1 indispensable, required in order to achieve something. 2 inevitable, determined by natural laws or predestination and not by free will. —*n.* (usu. *pl.*) a thing without which life cannot be maintained or is unduly harsh. —**the necessary,** (*slang*) the money or action needed for a purpose. —**necessarily** *adv.* [f. OF f. L *necessarius* (*necesse* needful)]

necessitarianism /nɪsesɪˈteərɪənɪz(ə)m/ *n.* the denial of free will and the belief that all action is determined by causes. —**necessitarian** *adj.* & *n.* [f. NECESSITY]

necessitate /nɪˈsesɪteɪt/ *v.t.* to make necessary, to involve as a condition, accompaniment, or result. [f. L *necessitare* (as NECESSITY)]

necessitous /nɪˈsesɪtəs/ *adj.* needy. [f. F or f. foll.]

necessity /nɪˈsesɪtɪ/ *n.* 1 constraint or compulsion regarded as a law governing all human action. 2 the constraining power of circumstances. 3 an imperative need. 4 an indispensable thing. 5 poverty, hardship. —**of necessity,** unavoidably. [f. OF f. L *necessitas* (as NECESSARY)]

neck *n.* 1 the narrow part of the body connecting the head with the shoulders. 2 a narrow part, piece, or channel; the lower part of a capital, above the astragal terminating the shaft of a column. 3 the part of a garment around the neck. 4 the length of a horse's head and neck as a measure of its lead in a race. 5 the flesh of an animal's neck as food. 6 (*slang*) impudence. —*v.i.* (*slang*) to kiss and caress amorously. —**get it in the neck,** (*colloq.*) to suffer a heavy blow, to be severely reprimanded or punished. **neck and neck,** running level in a race. **risk** (*or* **save**) **one's neck,** to risk (or save) one's own life. **up to one's neck,** (*colloq.*) very deeply involved; very busy. [OE]

neckband *n.* a strip of material round the neck of a garment.

neckerchief /ˈnekətʃɪf/ *n.* a square of cloth worn round the neck. [f. NECK + KERCHIEF]

necklace /ˈneklɪs/ *n.* an ornament of beads, precious stones, etc., worn round the neck.

necklet /ˈneklɪt/ *n.* an ornament or fur garment for the neck. [f. NECK + -LET]

neckline *n.* the outline of a garment-opening at the neck.

necktie *n.* a band of material tied round a shirt-collar.

necro- /nekrəʊ-/ *in comb.* corpse. [f. Gk (*nekros* corpse)]

necromancy /ˈnekrəʊmænsɪ/ *n.* dealings with the dead as a means of divination; magic. —**necromancer** *n.* [f. OF f. L f. Gk (NECRO-, *mantis* seer)]

necrophilia /nekrəʊˈfɪlɪə/ *n.* abnormal (esp. erotic) attraction to corpses. [NECRO- + Gk *-philia* loving]

necropolis /neˈkrɒpəlɪs/ *n.* a cemetery, especially an ancient one. [Gk (NECRO-, *polis* city)]

necrosis /neˈkrəʊsɪs/ *n.* (*pl.* **necroses** /-siːz/) the death of a piece of bone or tissue. —**necrotic** /-ˈkrɒtɪk/ *adj.* [f. Gk (*nekroō* kill)]

nectar /ˈnektə(r)/ *n.* 1 a sweet fluid produced by plants and made into honey by bees. 2 (*Gk & Rom. myth.*) the drink of the gods. 3 any delicious drink. —**nectarous** *adj.* [f. L f. Gk]

nectarine /ˈnektərɪn, -iːn/ *n.* a kind of peach with a smooth downless skin. [f. prec.]

nectary /ˈnektərɪ/ *n.* a plant's nectar-secreting organ. [f. NECTAR]

NEDC *abbr.* (*colloq.* **Neddy**) National Economic Development Council.

neddy *n.* (*colloq.*) a donkey. [pet-form of man's name *Edward*]

née /neɪ/ *adj.* born (used in adding a married woman's maiden name after her surname: *Anne Hall, née Browne*). [F, fem. p.p. of *naître* be born]

need *n.* 1 circumstances requiring some course of action. 2 a requirement or want. 3 a time of difficulty or crisis. 4 destitution or poverty. —*v.t./i.* (in neg. interrog. *to* can be omitted, and 3 *sing. pres.* is **need**) 1 to be in need of, to require. 2 to be under a necessity or obligation. —**have need of,** to require. **need not have done,** did not need to do (but did). [OE]

needful *adj.* necessary. —**the needful,** (*slang*) money or action needed for a purpose. —**needfully** *adv.* [f. NEED + -FUL]

needle *n.* **1** a long slender piece of polished steel pointed at one end and with an eye for thread at the other, used in sewing. **2** a similar larger instrument of bone or plastic etc. without an eye, used in knitting or crocheting etc. **3** a piece of metal etc. transmitting the vibrations from a revolving gramophone record, a stylus. **4** the pointer of a compass or other instrument. **5** the pointed end of a hypodermic syringe. **6** the slender pointed leaf of a fir or pine. **7** a sharp rock or peak. **8** an obelisk. —*v.t.* (*colloq.*) to annoy or provoke. —**needle game** *or* **match,** a game or match closely contested or arousing exceptional personal feeling. **needle-point** *n.* embroidery on canvas; lace made with needles, not bobbins. [OE]

needlecord *n.* a finely ribbed corduroy fabric.

needless *adj.* unnecessary, uncalled for. —**needlessly** *adv.* [f. NEED + -LESS]

needlewoman *n.* (*pl.* **-women**) a seamstress; a woman or girl who sews.

needlework *n.* sewing or embroidery.

needn't (*colloq.*) need not.

needs *adv.* (*archaic*) of necessity (esp. in **must needs** or **needs must**). [as NEED]

needy *adj.* lacking the necessaries of life, extremely poor. —**neediness** *n.* [f. NEED]

ne'er /neə(r)/ *adv.* (*poetic*) never. [contr.]

ne'er-do-well *n.* a good-for-nothing person. —*adj.* good-for-nothing.

nefarious /nɪˈfeərɪəs/ *adj.* wicked. —**nefariously** *adv.* [f. L *nefarius* (*nefas* wrong)]

neg. *abbr.* negative.

negate /nɪˈgeɪt/ *v.t.* to nullify; to imply or involve the non-existence of. —**negation** *n.* [f. L *negare* deny]

negative /ˈnegətɪv/ *adj.* **1** expressing or implying denial, prohibition, or refusal. **2** not positive, lacking positive attributes; marked by an absence of qualities. **3** (of a quantity in algebra) less than zero; to be subtracted from others or from zero. **4** in the direction opposite that regarded as positive. **5** of or containing or producing the kind of electrical charge carried by electrons. **6** (of a photograph) having the lights and shades of the actual objects or scene reversed, or the colours replaced by complementary ones. —*n.* **1** a negative statement or word. **2** a developed photographic film etc. bearing a negative image from which positive pictures are obtained. —*v.t.* **1** to veto; to refuse consent to. **2** to serve to disprove. **3** to contradict (a statement). **4** to neutralize (an effect). —**in the negative,** with a refusal; with a negative statement or reply. —**negative sign,** the minus sign −. —**negatively** *adv.* [f. OF or L (as NEGATE)]

neglect /nɪˈglekt/ *v.t.* **1** to pay too little or no attention to. **2** to fail to take proper care of. **3** to omit to do, to be remiss about. —*n.* neglecting, being neglected; disregard. —**neglectful** *adj.* [f. L *neglegere* (*neg-* not, *legere* choose, pick up)]

negligé /ˈneglɪʒeɪ/ *n.* a woman's light flimsy dressing-gown. [F, p.p. of *négliger* = prec.]

negligence /ˈneglɪdʒ(ə)ns/ *n.* lack of proper care or attention, carelessness. —**negligent** *adj.*, **negligently** *adv.* [f. OF or L (as NEGLECT)]

negligible /ˈneglɪdʒɪb(ə)l/ *adj.* too small or unimportant to be considered. [obs. F (as NEGLECT)]

negotiable /nɪˈgəʊʃəb(ə)l/ *adj.* **1** that can be modified after discussion. **2** (of a cheque etc.) that can be converted into cash or transferred to another person. [f. foll.]

negotiate /nɪˈgəʊʃɪeɪt/ *v.t./i.* **1** to try to reach agreement by discussion; to arrange (an affair) or bring about (a result) thus. **2** to get or give the money value for (a cheque or bonds etc.). **3** to get over or through (an obstacle or difficulty). —**negotiation** /-ˈeɪʃ(ə)n/ *n.*, **negotiator** *n.* [f. L *negotiari* (*negotium* business)]

Negrillo /nɪˈgrɪləʊ/ *n.* (*pl.* **-os**) a member of a dwarf Negro people in central and southern Africa. [Sp., dim. of NEGRO]

Negrito /nɪˈgri:təʊ/ *n.* (*pl.* **-os**) a member of a small Negroid people in the Malayo-Polynesian region. [as prec.]

Negro /ˈni:grəʊ/ *n.* (*pl.* **-oes**) a member of the black- or dark-skinned group of human populations that exist or originated in Africa south of the Sahara. —*adj.* of Negroes, black- or dark-skinned. —**Negress** *n.fem.* [Sp. & Port., f. L *niger* black]

Negroid /ˈni:grɔɪd/ *adj.* of the group having physical characteristics resembling those of Negroes. —*n.* a Negroid person. [f. prec.]

negus /ˈni:gəs/ *n.* hot sweetened wine with water. [f. Col. F. *Negus* (d. 1732), its inventor]

neigh /neɪ/ *n.* the cry of a horse. —*v.i.* to utter a neigh. [OE (imit.)]

neighbour /ˈneɪbə(r)/ *n.* **1** a person who lives next door or near by. **2** a person or thing near or next to another. **3** a fellow human being. **4** (*attrib.*) neighbouring. —*v.t./i.* to adjoin, to border (on). [OE (as NIGH, BOOR)]

neighbourhood *n.* **1** a district. **2** the people of a district. **3** nearness, vicinity. —**in the neighbourhood of,** approximately. [f. prec. + -HOOD]

neighbourly *adj.* like a good neighbour, friendly, helpful. —**neighbourliness** *n.* [as prec.]

neither /ˈnaɪðə(r), ˈni:ðə(r)/ *adv.* not either, not on the one hand (introducing one of two negative statements, the other often introduced by *nor*). —*adj.* & *pron.* not either, not the one nor the other. —*conj.* (*archaic*) nor, not yet. [OE (as NO, WHETHER)]

nelly *n.* **not on your nelly,** (*slang*) certainly not. [perh. f. woman's name *Nelly*]

nelson /ˈnels(ə)n/ *n.* a wrestling hold in which the arm is passed under the opponent's arm from behind and the hand applied to his neck. [app. f. name *Nelson*]

nematode /ˈnemətəʊd/ *n.* a slender unsegmented worm of the phylum Nematoda. [f. Gk *nēma* thread]

nem. con. *abbr.* with no one dissenting. [f. L *nemine contradicente*]

nemesia /nɪˈmi:ʒə/ *n.* a South African plant of the genus *Nemesia*, cultivated for its variously coloured irregular flowers. [f. Gk *nemesion* name of a similar plant]

nemesis /ˈneməsɪs/ *n.* inevitable retribution. [f. *Nemesis*, Gk goddess of retribution]

neo- /ni:əʊ-/ *in comb.* new, modern; a new form of. [Gk (*neos* new)]

neoclassic /ni:əʊˈklæsɪk/ *adj.* neoclassical.

neoclassical /ni:əʊˈklæsɪk(ə)l/ *adj.* of a revival of classical style or treatment in the arts.

neoclassicism /ni:əʊˈklæsɪsɪz(ə)m/ *n.* neoclassical style etc.

neodymium /ni:əˈdɪmɪəm/ *n.* a metallic element of the lanthanide series, symbol Nd, atomic number 60. [f. NEO- + *didymium* (f. Gk. *didumos* twin, from being closely associated with lanthanum) substance orig. regarded as an element]

neolithic /nɪəˈlɪθɪk/ *adj.* of the later part of the Stone Age. —*n.* this period. [f. NEO- + Gk *lithos* stone]

neologism /ni:ˈɒlədʒɪz(ə)m/ *n.* **1** a newly-coined word. **2** the coining of words. [f. F (as NEO-, -LOGY)]

neon /ˈni:ɒn/ *n.* a colourless odourless element of the noble gas group, symbol Ne, atomic number 10. [Gk, neut. of *neos* new]

neophyte /ˈni:əʊfaɪt/ *n.* **1** a new convert. **2** a religious novice. **3** a beginner. [f. L f. Gk (NEO-, *phuton* plant)]

Neoplatonism /nɪəʊˈpleɪtənɪz(ə)m/ *n.* the revived Platonism which was the dominant philosophy of the pagan world from the mid-3rd c. AD down to the closing of the pagan schools by Justinian in 529, and strongly influenced medieval and Renaissance thought. —**Neoplatonist** *n.*

nephew /ˈnefju:, -v-/ *n.* one's brother's or sister's son. [f. OF f. L *nepos*]

nephritic /neˈfrɪtɪk/ *adj.* of or in the kidneys. [f. L f. Gk (*nephros* kidney)]

nephritis /neˈfraɪtɪs/ *n.* inflammation of the kidneys. [L f. Gk (as prec.)]

ne plus ultra /neɪ plʊs ˈʊltrɑ:/ **1** the furthest attainable point. **2** the acme, perfection. [L, = not further beyond (supposed inscription on Straits of Gibraltar)]

nepotism /ˈnepətɪz(ə)m/ *n.* favouritism shown to relatives in conferring offices (orig. by popes for their illegitimate sons, euphemistically called nephews). [f. F f. It. (*nepote* nephew)]

neptunium /nepˈtju:nɪəm/ *n.* a transuranic radioactive metallic element, symbol Np, atomic number 93. [f. *Neptune* (planet)]

Nereid /ˈnɪərɪɪd/ *n.* any of the sea-nymphs, daughters of the Greek sea-god Nereus. [f. *Nereus*]

nereid /ˈnɪərɪɪd/ *n.* a long sea-worm or centipede. [f. prec.]

nerve *n.* **1** a fibre or bundle of fibres conveying impulses of sensation or of movement between the brain or spinal cord and other parts of the body; the material constituting these. **2** courage, coolness in danger. **3** (*colloq.*) impudent boldness. **4** (*pl.*) nervousness; a condition of mental and physical stress. **5** (*Bot.*) the rib of a leaf. —*v.t.* to give strength, courage, or vigour to; to brace (oneself) to face danger etc. —**bundle of nerves,** a very nervous person. **get on a person's nerves,** to irritate him. **lose one's nerve,** to become timid or irresolute. **nerve-cell** *n.* a cell transmitting impulses in nerve tissue. **nerve-centre** *n.* a group of closely-connected ganglion-cells; a centre of control. **nerve gas,** a poison gas that affects the nervous system. **nerve-racking** *adj.* greatly taxing the nerves. **strain every nerve,** to do one's utmost. [f. L *nervus* sinew]

nerveless *adj.* lacking vigour or spirit; incapable of effort. [f. prec. + -LESS]

nervous /ˈnɜ:vəs/ *adj.* **1** timid and anxious, easily agitated; fearful. **2** of or affecting the nerves or nervous system; full of nerves. —**nervous breakdown,** loss of emotional and mental stability. **nervous system,** the nerves and nerve-centres as a whole. —**nervously** *adv.*, **nervousness** *n.* [f. L *nervosus* (as NERVE)]

nervure /ˈnɜ:vjə(r)/ *n.* **1** any of the tubes forming the framework of an insect's wing. **2** the principal vein of a leaf. [F (*nerf* nerve)]

nervy *adj.* nervous, easily excited. [f. NERVE]

nescient /ˈnesɪənt/ *adj.* not having knowledge (of). —**nescience** *n.* [f. L (*nescire* not know)]

ness *n.* a headland. [OE]

-ness /-nɪs/ *suffix* forming nouns from adjectives, expressing a state or condition (*happiness*) or an instance of this (*a kindness*). [OE]

nest *n.* **1** a structure or place where a bird lays eggs and shelters its young; an animal's or insect's building-place or lair. **2** a snug retreat or shelter. **3** a brood or swarm. **4** a group or set of similar objects, often of different sizes. —*v.t./i.* **1** to have or build a nest. **2** to take wild birds' nests or eggs. **3** (of objects) to fit together or one inside another. —**nest-egg** *n.* a sum of money saved for the future. [OE]

nestle /ˈnes(ə)l/ *v.t./i.* **1** to curl oneself up or press comfortably into a soft place. **2** to lie half-hidden or sheltered or embedded. [OE (as NEST)]

nestling /ˈnestlɪŋ/ *n.* a bird too young to leave the nest. [f. NEST or NESTLE]

net[1] *n.* **1** open-work material of thread, cord, or wire, etc. woven or jointed at intervals. **2** a piece of this for a particular purpose, e.g. catching fish, covering or protecting something, or enclosing a goal-space. —*v.t./i.* (**-tt-**) **1** to catch or procure (as) with a net. **2** to cover or confine with nets. **3** to put (a ball) into a net, especially of the goal. **4** to make cord etc. into a net. [OE]

net[2] *adj.* **1** remaining after necessary deductions. **2** (of a price) off which a discount is not allowed. **3** (of an effect, result, etc.) ultimate; excluding unimportant effects or those that cancel each other out. —*v.t.* (**-tt-**) to gain or yield (a sum) as net profit. —**net profit,** the actual profit after working expenses have been paid. **net weight,** that excluding the weight of wrappings etc. [F (as NEAT)]

netball *n.* a seven-a-side game in which a ball has to be thrown so as to fall through an elevated horizontal ring from which a net hangs.

nether /ˈneðə(r)/ *adj.* lower. —**nether regions** *or* **world,** hell, the underworld. —**nethermost** *adj.* [OE]

netsuke /ˈnetsʊkeɪ/ *n.* a carved button-like ornament formerly worn with Japanese dress to hang articles from a girdle. [Jap.]

nett var. of NET[2].

netting *n.* netted fabric; a piece of this. [f. NET[1]]

nettle *n.* a plant of the genus *Urtica* covered with stinging hairs; a plant resembling this. —*v.t.* to irritate or provoke. —**nettle-rash** *n.* a skin eruption like nettle-stings. [OE]

network *n.* **1** an arrangement or pattern with intersecting lines and interstices; a complex system of railways etc. **2** a chain of interconnected persons, operations, electrical conductors, etc.; a group of broadcasting stations connected for simultaneous broadcasts of the same programme. —*v.t.* to broadcast by this.

neural /ˈnjʊər(ə)l/ *adj.* of the nerves. —**neurally** *adv.* [f. Gk *neuron*]

neuralgia /njʊəˈrældʒə/ *n.* an intense intermittent pain in the nerves especially of the face and head. —**neuralgic** *adj.* [as prec. + Gk *algos* pain]

neurasthenia /njʊərəsˈθiːnɪə/ *n.* debility of the nerves causing fatigue etc. —**neurasthenic** *adj.* [as NEURAL + Gk *astheneia* weakness]

neuration /njʊəˈreɪʃ(ə)n/ *n.* the distribution of nervures. [as NEURAL]

neuritis /njʊəˈraɪtɪs/ *n.* inflammation of a nerve or the nerves. [as foll. + -ITIS]

neuro- /njʊərəʊ-/ *in comb.* nerve, nerves. [f. Gk *neuron* nerve]

neurology /njʊəˈrɒlədʒɪ/ *n.* the scientific study of nerve systems. —**neurological** /-ˈlɒdʒɪk(ə)l/ *adj.*, **neurologist** *n.* [as prec. + -LOGY]

neurone /ˈnjʊərəʊn/ *n.* (also **neuron** /-rɒn/) a nerve-cell and its appendages. [as NEURO-]

neuropterous /njʊəˈrɒptərəs/ *adj.* of the Neuroptera, an order of insects having four membranous transparent wings with a network of nervures. [f. NEURO- + Gk *pterux* wing]

neurosis /njʊəˈrəʊsɪs/ *n.* (*pl.* **-oses** /-siːz/) a disorder of the nervous system producing depression or irrational behaviour. [as NEURO- + -OSIS]

neurotic /njʊəˈrɒtɪk/ *adj.* caused by or suffering from neurosis; (*colloq.*) abnormally anxious or obsessive. —*n.* a neurotic person. —**neurotically** *adv.* [f. prec.]

neuter /ˈnjuːtə(r)/ *adj.* **1** (of a noun etc.) neither masculine nor feminine. **2** (of plants) having neither pistils nor stamens. **3** (of insects) sexually undeveloped, sterile. —*n.* **1** a neuter word; the neuter gender. **2** a sexually undeveloped female insect, especially a bee or ant. **3** a castrated animal. —*v.t.* to castrate. [f. OF or L, = neither]

neutral /ˈnjuːtr(ə)l/ *adj.* **1** not helping or supporting either of two opposing sides, impartial; belonging to a neutral State etc. **2** having no positive or distinctive characteristics, indeterminate; (of colours) not strong or positive, grey or fawn. **3** (of a gear) in which the engine is disconnected from the driven parts. **4** (*Chem.*) neither acid nor alkaline. **5** (*Electr.*) neither positive nor negative. **6** (*Biol.*) sexually undeveloped, asexual. —*n.* **1** a neutral State or person; a subject of a neutral State. **2** a neutral gear. —**neutrality** /-ˈtrælɪtɪ/ *n.*, **neutrally** *adv.* [f. obs. F or f. L, = of neuter gender (as prec.)]

neutralize *v.t.* **1** to make neutral, to make ineffective by an opposite force or effect. **2** to exempt or exclude (a place) from the sphere of hostilities. —**neutralization** /-ˈzeɪʃ(ə)n/ *n.* [f. F f. L (as prec.)]

neutrino /njuːˈtriːnəʊ/ *n.* (*pl.* **-os**) an elementary particle with zero electric charge and probably zero mass. [It., dim. of *neutro* neutral (as NEUTER)]

neutron /ˈnju:trɒn/ *n.* an elementary particle of about the same mass as a proton but without electric charge, present in all atomic nuclei except the common isotope of hydrogen. —**neutron bomb**, a nuclear bomb that kills by intense radiation but does little damage to buildings etc. [f. NEUTRAL]

névé /ˈneveɪ/ *n.* an expanse of granular snow not yet compressed into ice at the head of a glacier. [Swiss F, = glacier f. L *nix nivis* snow]

never /ˈnevə(r)/ *adv.* **1** at no time, on no occasion, not ever. **2** not at all. **3** (*colloq.*) surely not. —**never-never** *n.* (*colloq.*) hire-purchase. **well I never,** an exclamation of surprise. [OE (*ne* not, as EVER)]

nevermore *adv.* at no future time.

nevertheless /nevəðəˈles/ *adv.* for all that, notwithstanding.

new /nju:/ *adj.* **1** not existing before; of recent origin or arrival; made, invented, discovered, acquired, or experienced recently or now for the first time. **2** in the original condition, not worn or used. **3** renewed or reformed; now invigorated. **4** changed or different from a previous one; additional to another or others already existing. **5** unfamiliar or strange. **6** later, modern; (*derog.*) newfangled; advanced in method or doctrine; (in place-names) discovered or founded later than and named after. —*adv.* newly, recently (*new-born, new-found, new-laid*). —**the new mathematics,** the system using set theory (see SET²) in elementary teaching. **new moon,** the moon when first seen as a crescent after conjunction with the sun; the time of such an appearance. **new potatoes,** the earliest potatoes of the new crop. **new star,** a nova. **New Style,** (of a date) reckoned by the reformed or Gregorian Calendar. **New Testament,** the part of the Bible recording the life and teachings of Christ and some of his earliest followers. **new town,** a town established as a completely new settlement with government sponsorship. **New World,** North and South America. **new year,** the year about to begin or just begun; the first few days of the year. **New Year's Day,** 1 Jan. **New Year's Eve,** 31 Dec. —**newness** *n.* [OE]

newcomer *n.* a person recently arrived.

newel /ˈnju:əl/ *n.* the supporting central pillar of a winding stair; a post supporting a stair-handrail at the top or bottom of a flight of stairs. [f. OF *no(u)el* knob f. L (*nodus* knot)]

newfangled /nju:ˈfæŋg(ə)ld/ *adj.* objectionably new in method or style. [orig. = fond of novelty, f. NEW + *-fangle* (OE *fang* seize)]

newly *adv.* recently, afresh, new-; —**newly-weds** *n.pl.* a recently married couple (or couples). [f. NEW]

news /nju:z/ *n.pl.* (usu. treated as *sing.*) information about recent events, especially when published or broadcast; a broadcast report of news; new or interesting information. —**news-stand** *n.* a stall for the sale of newspapers. **news-vendor** *n.* a newspaper-seller. [f. NEW]

newsagent *n.* a dealer in newspapers.

newscast *n.* a radio or television broadcast of news reports.

newscaster *n.* a person who reads a newscast. [f. prec.]

newsletter *n.* an informal printed report issued to members of a club or some other group.

newspaper *n.* a printed publication (usu. daily or weekly) containing news, advertisements, correspondence, etc.; the sheets of paper forming this.

Newspeak /ˈnju:spi:k/ *n.* ambiguous euphemistic language used especially in political propaganda. [name of artificial official language in Orwell's *Nineteen Eighty-Four*]

newsprint *n.* the type of paper on which newspapers are printed.

newsreel *n.* a cinema film giving recent news.

newsworthy *adj.* topical, noteworthy as news.

newsy /ˈnju:zɪ/ *adj.* (*colloq.*) full of news.

newt /nju:t/ *n.* a small tailed amphibian especially of the genus *Triturus*, allied to the salamander. [*a newt* f. *an ewt* (var. of EFT)]

newton /ˈnju:t(ə)n/ *n.* a unit of force, the force that acting for 1 second on a mass of 1 kg gives it a velocity of 1 metre per second per second. [f. Sir Isaac *Newton*, English physicist (d. 1727)]

next *adj.* **1** being, lying, or living nearest (*to*). **2** nearest in order or time, soonest come to. —*adv.* **1** in the next place or degree. **2** on the next occasion. —*n.* the next person or thing. —*prep.* next to. —**next-best** *adj.* second-best. **next door,** in the next room or house. **next of kin,** one's closest living relative. **next to,** almost. **the next world,** life after death. [OE, superl. of NIGH]

nexus /ˈneksəs/ *n.* a connected group or series. [L (*nectere* bind)]

NHS *abbr.* National Health Service.

NI *abbr.* **1** National Insurance. **2** Northern Ireland.

Ni *symbol* nickel.

niacin /ˈnaɪəsɪn/ *n.* nicotinic acid. [f. *ni*cotinic *ac*id]

nib *n.* **1** a pen-point. **2** (in *pl.*) crushed coffee- or cocoa-beans. **3** a small projection on a tile. [prob. f. MDu. or MLG]

nibble *v.t./i.* **1** to take small quick or gentle bites at. **2** to eat in small amounts. **3** (with *at*) to show a cautious interest in (an offer etc.). —*n.* **1** an act of nibbling. **2** a very small amount of food. [prob. f. LDu.; cf. LG *nibbeln* gnaw]

nibs /nɪbz/ *n.* (*slang*) **his nibs,** a burlesque title of an important or self-important person. [f. earlier (cant) *nabs*]

nice *adj.* **1** pleasant, satisfactory, (of a person) kind, good-natured. **2** (*iron.*) bad, difficult, awkward. **3** needing precision and care; subtle. **4** fastidious, delicately sensitive. —**nice and,** satisfactorily. —**nicely** *adv.*, **niceness** *n.* [orig. = stupid, f. OF f. L *nescius* ignorant]

nicety /ˈnaɪsɪtɪ/ *n.* **1** precision. **2** a subtle distinction or detail. —**to a nicety,** exactly. [f. OF (as NICE)]

niche /nɪtʃ, niːʃ/ *n.* **1** a shallow recess, especially in a wall. **2** a comfortable or suitable position in life or employment. [F (*nicher* make a nest f. L *nidus* nest)]

nick *n.* **1** a small cut or notch. **2** (*slang*) prison; a police station. **3** (*slang*) condition. —*v.t.* **1** to make a nick or nicks in. **2** (*slang*) to steal. **3** (*slang*) to catch, to arrest. —**in the nick of time,** only just in time. [orig. unkn.]

nickel /ˈnɪk(ə)l/ *n.* **1** a hard silver-white metallic element, symbol Ni, atomic number 28. **2** (*US*) a five-cent piece. —**nickel silver,** an alloy of nickel, zinc, and copper. **nickel steel,** an alloy of nickel with steel. [abbr. of G *kupfernickel*, the ore whence it was first obtained]

nickelodeon /nɪkəˈləʊdɪən/ *n.* (*US colloq.*) a juke-box. [f. prec. + MELODEON]

nicker *n.* (*pl.* same) (*slang*) £1 sterling. [orig. unkn.]

nickname *n.* a familiar or humorous name given to a person or thing instead of or as well as the real name. —*v.t.* to give a nickname to. [*a nickname* f. *an eke-name* (*eke* addition, NAME)]

nicotine /ˈnɪkətiːn/ *n.* a poisonous alkaloid extracted as an oily liquid from tobacco. [F, f. generic name (*nicotiana herba*) of tobacco, f. J. *Nicot*, French diplomat who introduced tobacco into France 1560]

nicotinic acid /nɪkəˈtɪnɪk/ a vitamin of the B group, formed by oxidation of nicotine and acting to prevent pellagra. [f. prec.]

nictitate /ˈnɪktɪteɪt/ *v.i.* to blink, to wink. —**nictitating membrane,** the third or inner eyelid of many animals (including birds and fishes). —**nictitation** /-ˈteɪʃ(ə)n/ *n.* [f. L (*nictare* blink)]

niece /niːs/ *n.* one's brother's or sister's daughter. [f. OF f. L *neptis* grand-daughter]

nielsbohrium /niːlzˈbɔrɪəm/ *n.* the Russian name for the element of atomic number 105, a short-lived artificially produced radioactive transuranic element (cf. HAHNIUM). [f. Niels *Bohr*, Danish physicist (d. 1962)]

niff *n.* (*slang*) a smell, a stink. —*v.i.* (*slang*) to smell, to stink. —**niffy** *adj.* [orig. dial.]

nifty *adj.* (*slang*) **1** smart, stylish. **2** excellent, clever. [orig. unkn.]

niggard /ˈnɪgəd/ *n.* a stingy person. [prob. of Scand. orig.; cf. NIGGLE]

niggardly *adj.* stingy. —**niggardliness** *n.* [f. prec.]

nigger *n.* (*offensive*) a Black, a dark-skinned person. —**nigger in the woodpile,** a hidden cause of trouble or inconvenience. [f. F *nègre* f. Sp. (as NEGRO)]

niggle *v.t./i.* **1** to fuss over details, to find fault in a petty way. **2** to irritate, to nag. [app. of Scand. orig.]

niggling *adj.* petty, troublesome; nagging. [f. prec.]

nigh /naɪ/ *adv., prep., & adj.* (*archaic & dial.*) near. [OE]

night /naɪt/ *n.* **1** the period of darkness between one day and the next, the time from sunset to sunrise. **2** nightfall. **3** the darkness of night. **4** a night or evening appointed for some activity. —**make a night of it,** to spend most or all of the night enjoying oneself. **night-club** *n.* a club that is open at night and provides refreshment and entertainment. **night-dress** *n.* a woman's or girl's loose garment worn in bed. **night-gown** *n.* a night-dress or night-shirt. **night-life** *n.* the entertainment available at night in a town. **night-light** *n.* a short thick candle or dim bulb kept burning in a bedroom at night. **night-long** *adj.* & *adv.* throughout the night. **night safe,** a safe with an opening in the outer wall of a bank for the deposit of money etc. when the bank is closed. **night school,** a school providing evening classes for those working by day. **night-shirt** *n.* a man's or boy's long shirt for sleeping in. **night-time** *n.* the time of darkness. **night-watchman** *n.* a person employed to look after unoccupied premises at night; (in cricket) an inferior batsman sent in near the close of play to avoid the dismissal of a better one in adverse conditions. [OE]

nightcap *n.* **1** a cap worn in bed. **2** a hot or alcoholic drink taken at bedtime.

nightfall *n.* the end of daylight.

nightie *n.* (*colloq.*) a night-dress. [abbr.]

nightingale /ˈnaɪtɪŋgeɪl/ *n.* a small bird of the genus *Luscinia* of the thrush family, of which the male sings melodiously both by day and by night. [OE, = night-singer]

nightjar *n.* a nocturnal bird of the family Caprimulgidae with a harsh cry. [f. NIGHT + JAR[1]]

nightly *adj.* **1** happening, done, or existing in

the night. **2** recurring every night. —*adv.* every night. [f. NIGHT]

nightmare *n.* **1** a terrifying dream. **2** (*colloq.*) a terrifying or very unpleasant experience or situation; a haunting fear. —**nightmarish** *adj.* [orig. = monster supposed to sit on and suffocate sleepers, f. NIGHT + obs. *mare* goblin]

nightshade *n.* a plant of the genus *Solanum* with poisonous berries. —**deadly nightshade,** belladonna.

nihilism /ˈnaɪlɪz(ə)m/ *n.* **1** negative doctrines or total rejection of current beliefs in religion or morals, often involving a general sense of despair coupled with the belief that life is devoid of meaning. **2** philosophical scepticism that denies all existence. **3** the doctrine of a Russian extreme-revolutionary party in the 19th–20th c. finding nothing to approve of in the established order or social and political institutions. —**nihilist** *n.*, **nihilistic** /-ˈlɪstɪk/ *adj.* [f. L *nihil* nothing]

nil *n.* nothing, no number or amount, especially as a score in games. [L, = *nihil* nothing]

nimble *adj.* quick and light in movement or action, agile; (of the mind) quick, clever. —**nimbleness** *n.*, **nimbly** *adv.* [OE, = quick to seize]

nimbo-stratus /nɪmbəʊˈstreɪtəs, -ˈstrɑː-/ *n.* a low dark-grey layer of cloud. [f. foll. + STRATUS]

nimbus /ˈnɪmbəs/ *n.* (*pl.* **-bi** /-baɪ/, **-buses**) **1** a halo, an aureole. **2** a storm-cloud. [L]

nincompoop /ˈnɪnkəmpuːp/ *n.* a foolish person. [orig. unkn.]

nine *adj.* & *n.* **1** one more than eight; the symbol for this (9, ix, IX). **2** the size etc. denoted by nine. —**nine days' wonder,** a thing attracting interest for a short time. [OE]

ninefold *adj.* & *adv.* **1** nine times as much or as many. **2** consisting of nine parts. [f. NINE + -FOLD]

ninepins *n.pl.* a kind of skittles.

nineteen /naɪnˈtiːn/ *adj.* & *n.* **1** one more than eighteen; the symbol for this (19, xix, XIX). **2** the size etc. denoted by nineteen. —**nineteenth** *adj.* & *n.* [OE (as NINE, -TEEN)]

ninety *adj.* & *n.* **1** nine times ten; the symbol for this (90, xc, XC). **2** (in *pl.*) the numbers, years, or degrees of temperature from 90 to 99. —**ninetieth** *adj.* & *n.* [OE (as NINE)]

ninny *n.* a foolish person. [perh. for *innocent*]

ninth /naɪnθ/ *adj.* next after the eighth. —*n.* each of nine equal parts into which a thing may be divided. —**ninthly** *adv.* [f. NINE]

niobium /naɪˈəʊbɪəm/ *n.* a rare metallic element, symbol Nb, atomic number 41. [f. *Niobe* in Gk mythology]

nip[1] *v.t./i.* (**-pp-**) **1** to pinch or squeeze sharply; to bite quickly with the front teeth. **2** to pinch off. **3** to pain or harm with biting cold. **4** (*colloq.*) to go quickly or nimbly. —*n.* **1** a sharp pinch, squeeze, or bite. **2** biting coldness. —**nip in the bud,** to destroy at an early stage of development. [prob. f. L Du.]

nip[2] *n.* a small quantity of spirits. [abbr. of *nipperkin* small measure]

nipper *n.* **1** a crustacean's claw. **2** (in *pl.*) pincers or forceps for gripping things or cutting things off. **3** (*colloq.*) a young child. [f. NIP[1]]

nipple *n.* **1** a small projection in which the mammary ducts of either sex of mammals terminate and from which in females milk is secreted for the young. **2** the teat of a feeding-bottle. **3** a nipple-like protuberance. [perh. f. *neb* beak, tip]

Nipponese /nɪpɒˈniːz/ *adj.* & *n.* (*pl.* same) Japanese. [f. Jap. *Nippon* Japan]

nippy *adj.* (*colloq.*) **1** nimble, quick. **2** chilly, cold. [f. NIP[1]]

nirvana /nɜːˈvɑːnə/ *n.* the final goal of Buddhism, a transcendent state in which there is neither suffering, desire, nor sense of self (*atman*), with release from the effects of karma. [f. Skr., = extinction (i.e. the extinction of illusion, since suffering, desire, and self are all illusions)]

Nissen hut /ˈnɪs(ə)n/ a tunnel-shaped hut of corrugated iron with a cement floor. [f. P. N. *Nissen*, British engineer (d. 1930)]

nit *n.* **1** a louse or other parasite; its egg. **2** (*slang*) a stupid person. —**nit-picking** *n.* & *adj.* (*colloq.*) fault-finding in a petty way. [OE]

nitrate[1] /ˈnaɪtreɪt/ *n.* **1** a salt or ester of nitric acid. **2** potassium or sodium nitrate used as a fertilizer. [F (as NITRE)]

nitrate[2] /naɪˈtreɪt/ *v.t.* to treat, combine, or impregnate with nitric acid. [f. foll.]

nitre /ˈnaɪtə(r)/ *n.* saltpetre. [f. OF f. L f. Gk *nitron*]

nitric /ˈnaɪtrɪk/ *adj.* of or containing nitrogen. —**nitric acid,** a pungent corrosive caustic liquid. [f. F (as prec.)]

nitride /ˈnaɪtraɪd/ *n.* a binary compound of nitrogen. [f. NITRE]

nitrify /ˈnaɪtrɪfaɪ/ *v.t.* to turn into a nitrite or nitrate. —**nitrification** /-fɪˈkeɪʃ(ə)n/ *n.* [f. F (as NITRE)]

nitrite /ˈnaɪtraɪt/ *n.* a salt or ester of nitrous acid. [f. NITRE]

nitro- /naɪtrəʊ-/ *in comb.* of or made with nitric acid, nitre, or nitrogen. —**nitro-glycerine** *n.* a yellowish oily highly explosive liquid made by adding glycerine to nitric and sulphuric acids. [Gk (as NITRE)]

nitrogen /ˈnaɪtrədʒ(ə)n/ *n.* a colourless odourless gaseous element, symbol N, atomic number 7. —**nitrogenous** /-ˈtrɒdʒɪnəs/ *adj.* [f. F (as NITRO-, -GEN]

nitrous /ˈnaɪtrəs/ *adj.* of, like, or impregnated with nitre. —**nitrous acid,** a liquid resembling nitric acid but containing less oxygen. **nitrous oxide,** a colourless gas used as an anaesthetic, laughing-gas. [f. L (as NITRE)]

nitty-gritty *n.* (*slang*) the realities or basic facts of a matter. [orig. unkn.]

nitwit *n.* (*colloq.*) a stupid person. [perh. f. NIT + WIT]

nix *n.* (*slang*) nothing. [G, colloq. form of *nichts* nothing]

NNE *abbr.* north-north-east.

NNW *abbr.* north-north-west.

No *symbol* nobelium.

No. *abbr.* number. [f. L *numero* (*numerus* number)]

no /nəʊ/ *adj.* **1** not any. **2** not a, quite other than. **3** hardly any. —*adv.* **1** (as a negative answer to a question etc.) it is not so, I do not agree, I shall not, etc. **2** (with *compar.*) by no amount, not at all. **3** (after *or*) not. —*n.* (*pl.* **noes**) **1** the word or answer 'no'. **2** a denial or refusal; a negative vote. —**no-ball** *n.* an unlawfully delivered ball in cricket etc. **no-claim bonus,** a reduction of an insurance premium for a person who has not claimed payment under the insurance since a previous renewal. **no go,** it is hopeless or impossible. **no-go area,** one to which entry is forbidden or restricted. **no man's land,** the space between two opposing enemies; an area not assigned to any owner. **no one,** no person, nobody. **no way,** (*colloq.*) it is impossible; not at all. [f. NONE, orig. before consonants]

nob[1] *n.* (*slang*) a person of wealth or high social standing. —**nobby** *adj.* [orig. unkn.]

nob[2] *n.* (*slang*) the head. [perh. var. of KNOB]

nobble *v.t.* (*slang*) **1** to tamper with (a racehorse) to prevent its winning. **2** to influence (a person) by underhand means; to get possession of dishonestly. **3** to catch (a criminal). [prob. = dial. *knobble* beat (f. KNOB)]

nobelium /nəʊˈbiːlɪəm/ *n.* an artificially made transuranic radioactive metallic element, symbol No, atomic number 102. [as foll.]

Nobel Prize /ˈnəʊbel/ any of the (orig. five) prizes awarded annually for significant recent work in physics, chemistry, medicine, and literature, and to the person who is adjudged to have rendered the greatest service to the cause of peace. [f. A. B. *Nobel*, Swedish chemist (d. 1896), the original donor]

nobility /nəʊˈbɪlɪtɪ/ *n.* nobleness of character, mind, birth, or rank. —**the nobility,** the aristocracy. [f. OF or L *nobilitas* (as foll.)]

noble /ˈnəʊb(ə)l/ *adj.* **1** belonging to the aristocracy by birth or rank. **2** of excellent character, free from pettiness or meanness, magnanimous. **3** of imposing appearance, excellent. —*n.* a nobleman or noblewoman. —**noble gas,** any of the 6 chemically similar gaseous elements helium, neon, argon, krypton, xenon, and radon. **noble metal,** a metal (e.g. gold) that resists chemical attack. —**nobleness** *n.*, **nobly** *adv.* [f. OF f. L *nobilis*]

nobleman *n.* (*pl.* **-men**) a peer.

noblesse oblige /nəʊˈbles ɒˈbliːʒ/ privilege entails responsibility. [F]

noblewoman *n.* (*pl.* **-women**) a peeress.

nobody /ˈnəʊbədɪ/ *pron.* **1** no person. **2** a person of no importance.

nock *n.* a notch on a bow or arrow for the bowstring. [perh. = *hock* upper corner of sail, f. MDu.]

nocturnal /nɒkˈtɜːn(ə)l/ *adj.* **1** of or in the night. **2** done or active by night. —**nocturnally** *adv.* [f. L (*nocturnus* of night, f. *nox* night)]

nocturne /ˈnɒktɜːn/ *n.* **1** a dreamy musical piece. **2** a picture of a night scene. [F (as prec.)]

nod *v.t./i.* (**-dd-**) **1** to incline the head slightly and briefly in greeting, assent, or command. **2** to let the head droop in drowsiness; to be drowsy. **3** to incline (the head); to signify (assent etc.) by a nod. **4** (of flowers etc.) to bend downwards and sway. **5** to make a mistake due to a momentary lack of alertness or attention. —*n.* a nodding of the head. —**nod off,** to fall asleep. [orig. unkn.]

noddle *n.* (*colloq.*) the head. [orig. unkn.]

noddy *n.* **1** a simpleton. **2** a tropical sea-bird of the genus *Anous*, resembling the tern. [prob. f. obs. *noddy* foolish (as NOD)]

node *n.* **1** a knob-like swelling. **2** the point on the stem of a plant where a leaf or bud grows out. **3** a point at which a curve crosses itself. **4** the intersecting point of a planet's orbit and the ecliptic or of two great circles of the celestial sphere. —**nodal** *adj.* [f. L *nodus* knot]

nodule /ˈnɒdjuːl/ *n.* a small rounded lump; a small node. —**nodular** *adj.* [f. L *nodulus* dim. of *nodus* knot]

Noel /nəʊˈel/ *n.* (in carols etc.) Christmas. [F f. L (as NATAL)]

nog[1] *n.* a small block or peg of wood. [orig. unkn.]

nog[2] *n.* **1** strong beer. **2** an egg-nog. [orig. unkn.]

noggin /ˈnɒgɪn/ *n.* **1** a small mug. **2** a small (usually ¼-pint) measure. **3** (*slang*) the head. [orig. unkn.]

nogging *n.* brickwork in a wooden frame. [f. NOG[1]]

Noh /nəʊ/ *n.* a form of traditional Japanese drama. [Jap.]

noise /nɔɪz/ *n.* **1** a sound, especially a loud or

unpleasant one; a series of loud sounds. **2** irregular fluctuations accompanying a transmitted signal. **3** (in *pl.*) utterances, especially conventional remarks. —*v.t.* to make public, to make generally known. [f. OF = outcry, f. L (as NAUSEA)]

noiseless *adj.* without a sound. —**noiselessly** *adv.* [f. prec. + -LESS]

noisome /ˈnɔɪsəm/ *adj.* (*literary*) noxious, disgusting, especially to the smell. [f. obs. *noy* (f. ANNOY)]

noisy /ˈnɔɪzɪ/ *adj.* full of, making, or attended with noise; given to making a noise. —**noisily** *adv.*, **noisiness** *n.* [f. NOISE]

nomad /ˈnəʊmæd/ *n.* a member of a tribe roaming from place to place for pasture; a wanderer. —**nomadic** /-ˈmædɪk/ *adj.*, **nomadism** *n.* [f. F f. L f.Gk (*nemo* to pasture)]

nom de plume /nɒm də ˈpluːm/ *n.* (*pl.* ***noms pr.*** same) a writer's assumed name. [sham F, = pen-name]

nomen /ˈnəʊmen/ *n.* (in ancient Rome) the second or family name, e.g. Marcus *Tullius* Cicero. [L, = name]

nomenclature /nəʊˈmenklətʃə(r)/ *n.* a system of names or naming, terminology. [F f. L (as prec., *calare* call)]

nominal /ˈnɒmɪn(ə)l/ *adj.* **1** of, as, or like a noun. **2** of or in names. **3** existing in name only, not real or actual. **4** (of a sum of money etc.) virtually nothing, much below the actual value. —**nominal value,** face value. —**nominally** *adv.* [f. F or L (as NOMEN)]

nominalism /ˈnɒmɪnəlɪz(ə)m/ *n.* the theory that universals or general ideas (abstract concepts) are mere names (opp. REALISM). —**nominalist** *n.*, **nominalistic** /-ˈlɪstɪk/ *adj.* [as prec.]

nominate /ˈnɒmɪneɪt/ *v.t.* to appoint to or propose for election to an office; to name or appoint (a date etc.). —**nominator** *n.* [f. L *nominare* (as NOMEN)]

nomination /nɒmɪˈneɪʃ(ə)n/ *n.* **1** nominating, being nominated. **2** the right of nominating. [f. OF or L (as prec.)]

nominative /ˈnɒmɪnətɪv/ *n.* (*Gram.*) the case expressing the subject of a verb. —*adj.* (*Gram.*) of or in the nominative. [f. OF or L (as NOMINATE)]

nominee /nɒmɪˈniː/ *n.* a person who is nominated [as NOMINATE]

non- *prefix* not; (with *v.* to form *adj.*) not doing (*non-skid*), not behaving in a specified way (*non-stick*), not to be treated in a specified way (*non-iron*). [f. OF f. L *non* not]

nonage /ˈnəʊnɪdʒ, ˈnɒn-/ *n.* being under full legal age, minority; immaturity. [f. AF (as NON-, AGE)]

nonagenarian /nəʊnədʒɪˈneərɪən, ˈnɒn-/ *n.* a person from 90 to 99 years old. [f. L (*nonageni* ninety each)]

nonagon /ˈnɒnəgɒn/ *n.* a plane figure with nine sides and angles. [L (*nonus* ninth, Gk *-gōnos* angled)]

non-aligned *adj.* (of a State) not in alliance with any major bloc.

non-belligerent *adj.* taking no active or open part in a war. —*n.* a non-belligerent State.

nonce *n.* the time being, the present, esp. in **for the nonce,** for the occasion only. —**nonce-word** *n.* a word coined for one occasion. [f. obs. *than anes* the one (occasion), alt. by wrong division]

nonchalant /ˈnɒnʃələnt/ *adj.* not feeling or showing anxiety or excitement, calm and casual. —**nonchalance** *n.*, **nonchalantly** *adv.* [F (NON-, *chaloir* be concerned)]

non-com. *abbr.* non-commissioned (officer).

non-combatant *adj.* not fighting (esp. in war, as being a civilian, army chaplain, etc.). —*n.* such a person.

non-commissioned *adj.* (esp. of an officer) of a grade below those with commissions.

non-committal *adj.* not committing oneself to a definite opinion, course of action, etc. —**non-committally** *adv.*

non compos mentis /nɒn ˈkɒmpɒs ˈmentɪs/ *adj.* not in one's right mind, insane. [L, = not in control of one's mind]

non-conductor *n.* a substance that does not conduct heat or electricity.

nonconformist /nɒnkənˈfɔːmɪst/ *n.* **1** one who does not conform to the doctrine or discipline of an established Church; **Nonconformist,** a member of a (usu. Protestant) sect dissenting from the Anglican Church. **2** one who does not conform to a prevailing principle.

nonconformity /nɒnkənˈfɔːmɪtɪ/ *n.* **1** nonconformists or their principles etc. **2** failure to conform. **3** lack of correspondence between things.

non-contributory *adj.* not involving contributions.

non-co-operation *n.* failure or refusal to co-operate, especially as a protest.

nondescript /ˈnɒndɪskrɪpt/ *adj.* indeterminate, lacking distinctive characteristics. —*n.* a nondescript person or thing. [f. NON- + *descript* described (as DESCRIBE)]

none /nʌn/ *pron.* not any, no one; no person(s). —*adj.* not any (usu. with the reference supplied by an earlier or later noun). —*adv.* by no amount. —**none the less** nevertheless. [OE, = not one]

nonentity /nɒˈnentɪtɪ/ *n.* **1** a person or thing of no importance. **2** non-existence; a non-existent thing. [f. L (as NON-, ENTITY)]

nones /nəʊnz/ *n.pl.* the 7th day of March, May, July, Oct., the 5th of the other months, in the ancient Roman calendar. [f. OF f. L *nonae* (*nonus* ninth)]

nonesuch var. of NONSUCH.

non-event *n.* an event that turns out to be insignificant (usu. contrary to hopes or expectations).

non-existent *adj.* not existing.

non-ferrous *adj.* (of a metal) not iron or steel.

non-fiction *n.* a classification of literature that includes books in all subjects other than fiction.

non-intervention *n.* the principle or practice of not interfering in others' disputes.

non-moral *adj.* not concerned with morality.

non-nuclear *adj.* not involving nuclei or nuclear energy.

nonpareil /ˈnɒnpər(ə)l/ *adj.* unrivalled, unique. —*n.* such a person or thing. [F (NON-, *pareil* equal)]

non-party /nɒnˈpɑːtɪ/ *adj.* independent of political parties.

nonplus /nɒnˈplʌs/ *v.t.* (**-ss-**) to perplex completely. [f. L *non plus* not more]

non-profit-making *adj.* (of an enterprise) not conducted primarily with a view to making profits.

non-proliferation *n.* limitation of the number especially of nuclear weapons.

nonsense /ˈnɒnsəns/ *n.* **1** words put together in a way that does not make sense. **2** absurd or foolish talk, ideas, or behaviour. —*int.* you are talking nonsense. —**nonsensical** /-ˈsensɪk(ə)l/ *adj.*, **nonsensically** *adv.* [f. NON- + SENSE]

non sequitur /nɒn ˈsekwɪtə(r)/ *n.* a conclusion that does not logically follow from the premises. [L, = it does not follow]

non-skid *adj.* that does not, or is designed not to, skid.

non-smoker *n.* **1** a person who does not smoke. **2** a compartment in a train etc. where smoking is forbidden.

non-starter *n.* (*colloq.*) an idea or person not worth consideration.

non-stick *adj.* (of a saucepan etc.) to which food will not stick during cooking.

non-stop *adj.* **1** (of a train etc.) not stopping at intermediate stations. **2** not ceasing, done without pausing.—*adv.* without stopping.

nonsuch /ˈnʌnsʌtʃ/ *n.* **1** an unrivalled person or thing, a paragon. **2** a plant (*Medicago lupulina*) resembling lucerne with black pods. [f. NONE + SUCH]

non-U *adj.* (*colloq.*) not characteristic of upper-class speech or behaviour.

non-union *adj.* not belonging to or not made by members of a trade union.

non-voting *adj.* (of shares) not entitling the holder to a vote.

non-White *adj.* belonging to a race other than the White race. —*n.* a non-White person.

noodle *n.* **1** a simpleton. **2** (*slang*) the head. [orig. unkn.]

noodles /ˈnuːd(ə)lz/ *n.pl.* narrow strips of pasta used in soups etc. [f. G *nudel*]

nook /nʊk/ *n.* a secluded corner or recess. [orig. unkn.]

noon *n.* twelve o'clock in the day, midday. [OE, f. L *nona* (*hora*) ninth hour (as NONES)]

noonday *n.* midday.

noose *n.* a loop in a rope etc. with a running knot; a snare, a bond. —*v.t.* to catch with or enclose in a noose. [perh. f. OF *no*(*u*)*s* f. L *nodus* knot]

nor *conj.* and not; and not either. [contr. f. obs. *nother* (as NO[1], WHETHER)]

nor' *abbr.* north, esp. in compounds (*nor'ward*, *nor'wester*).

Nordic /ˈnɔːdɪk/ *adj.* **1** of or belonging to an extremely artificial sub-racial grouping of people who, as a population, are tall, with fair colouring, and dolichocephalic. **2** of Scandinavia, Finland, or Iceland. —*n.* a Nordic person. [f. F *nordique* (*nord* north)]

norm *n.* a standard, pattern, or type; a standard amount of work etc.; customary behaviour. [f. L *norma*, lit. = carpenter's square]

normal /ˈnɔːm(ə)l/ *adj.* **1** conforming to what is standard or usual; typical. **2** free from mental or emotional disorder. **3** (of a line) at right angles, perpendicular. —*n.* **1** the normal value of a temperature etc.; the usual state, level, etc. **2** a line at right angles. —**normalcy** *n.*, **normality** /-ˈmælɪtɪ/ *n.* [F or f. L *normalis* (as prec.)]

normalize *v.t./i.* to make or become normal; to cause to conform. —**normalization** /-ˈzeɪʃ(ə)n/ *n.* [f. prec.]

normally *adv.* **1** in a normal manner. **2** usually. [f. NORMAL]

Norman /ˈnɔːmən/ *n.* **1** a native or inhabitant of Normandy, a descendant of a mixed Scandinavian and Frankish people established there in early medieval times. **2** any of the kings of England from William I to Stephen. **3** the style of architecture developed by the Normans and employed in England after the Conquest, with rounded arches and heavy pillars. —*adj.* of the Normans or their style of architecture. —**Norman French**, the form of medieval French spoken by the Normans; the later form of this in English legal use. [f. OF f. ON (as NORTH, MAN)]

normative /ˈnɔːmətɪv/ *adj.* of or establishing a norm. [f. F f. L *norma* (as NORM)]

Norse *n.* **1** the Norwegian language. **2** the Scandinavian language group. —*adj.* of ancient Scandinavia, especially Norway. —**the Norse,** the Norwegians. **Old Norse,** the Germanic language of Norway and its colonies, or of Scandinavia, down to the 14th c. [f. Du. (*noord* north)]

Norseman /ˈnɔːsmæn/ *n.* (*pl.* **-men**) a Viking.

north *n.* **1** the point of the horizon corresponding to the compass point 90° anticlockwise from east; the direction in which this lies. **2** (usu. **North**) the part of a country or town lying to the north. —*adj.* **1** towards, at, near, or facing the north. **2** (of wind) blowing from the north. —*adv.* towards, at, or near the north. — **north country,** the northern part of England. **north-north-east** *n.*, *adj.*, & *adv.* midway between north and north-east. **north-north-west** *n.*, *adj.*, & *adv.* midway between north and north-west. **North Pole,** the northern end of the earth's axis of rotation. **North Star,** the pole-star. [OE]

Northants *abbr.* Northamptonshire.

north-east *n.* **1** the point midway between north and east; the direction in which this lies. **2** (usu. **North-East**) the part of a country or town lying to the north-east. —*adj.* of, towards, or coming from the north-east. —*adv.* towards, at, or near the north-east. —**North-east passage,** a passage for vessels along the northern coasts of Europe and Asia, formerly thought of as a possible course by which to make voyages to the East. —**north-easterly** *adj.* & *adv.*, **north-eastern** *adj.*

northeaster /nɔːθˈiːstə(r)/ *n.* a north-east wind. [f. prec.]

northerly /ˈnɔːðəlɪ/ *adj.* & *adv.* **1** in a northern position or direction. **2** (of wind) blowing from the north (approximately). [f. NORTH]

northern /ˈnɔːð(ə)n/ *adj.* of or in the north. —**northern lights,** the aurora borealis. —**northernmost** *adj.* [OE (as NORTH)]

northerner *n.* a native or inhabitant of the north. [f. NORTH]

northing /ˈnɔːθɪŋ/ *n.* (*Naut.* etc.) **1** a distance travelled or measured northward. **2** a northerly direction. [f. NORTH]

Northman *n.* (*pl.* **-men**) a native of Scandinavia, especially of Norway.

Northumb. *abbr.* Northumberland.

northward /ˈnɔːθwəd/ *adj.* & (also **northwards** /-z/) *adv.* towards the north. —*n.* a northward direction or region. [f. NORTH + -WARD]

north-west *n.* **1** the point midway between north and west; the direction in which this lies. **2** (usu. **North-West**) the part of a country or town lying to the north-west. —*adj.* of, towards, or coming from the north-west. —*adv.* towards, at, or near the north-west. —**north-westerly** *adj.* & *adv.*, **north-western** *adj.*

northwester /nɔːθˈwestə(r)/ *n.* a north-west wind. [f. prec.]

Norwegian /nɔːˈwiːdʒ(ə)n/ *adj.* of Norway or its people or language. —*n.* **1** a native or inhabitant of Norway. **2** the language of Norway. [f. L *Norvegia* Norway]

Nos. *abbr.* numbers. [cf. No.]

nose /nəʊz/ *n.* **1** the organ above the mouth on the face or head of a man or animal, used for smelling and breathing. **2** the sense of smell. **3** the ability to detect a particular thing. **4** an odour or perfume, e.g. of a wine. **5** the open end of a tube, pipe, etc.; the front end or projecting part of a thing, e.g. of a car or aircraft. **6** (*slang*) a police informer. —*v.t./i.* **1** to perceive a smell of; to discover by smell; to detect. **2** to thrust one's nose against or into. **3** to pry or search. **4** to make one's way cautiously forward. —**by a nose,** by a very narrow margin. **keep one's nose clean,** to stay out of trouble. **pay through the nose,** to have to pay an exorbitant price. **put a person's nose out of joint,** to embarrass or disconcert him. **rub a person's nose in it,** to remind him humiliatingly of an error etc. **turn up one's nose,** to show disdain. **under one's nose,** right before one. **with one's nose in the air,** haughtily. [OE]

nosebag *n.* a bag containing fodder, hung on a horse's head.

noseband *n.* the lower band of a bridle passing over the horse's nose and attached to the cheek-straps.

nosebleed *n.* bleeding from the nose.

nose-cone *n.* the cone-shaped nose of a rocket etc.

nosedive *n.* a steep downward plunge by an aeroplane; a sudden plunge or drop. —*v.i.* to make a nosedive.

nosegay /ˈnəʊzgeɪ/ *n.* a small bunch of flowers. [f. NOSE + obs. *gay* ornament]

nosh *v.t./i.* (*slang*) to eat. —*n.* (*slang*) food, especially a snack. —**nosh up** *n.* (*slang*) a large meal. [Yiddish]

nostalgia /nɒˈstældʒɪə/ *n.* **1** sentimental yearning for the past. **2** homesickness. —**nostalgic** *adj.*, **nostalgically** *adv.* [f. Gk *nostos* return home + *algos* pain]

nostril /ˈnɒstrɪl/ *n.* either of the openings in the nose. [OE, = nose-hole]

nostrum /ˈnɒstrəm/ *n.* **1** a quack remedy, a patent medicine. **2** a pet scheme, especially for political or social reform. [L, = of our own make]

nosy /ˈnəʊzɪ/ *adj.* inquisitive, prying. —**Nosy Parker,** a busybody. —**nosily** *adv.*, **nosiness** *n.* [f. NOSE]

not *adv*. expressing negation (also *colloq*. **-n't** as in *don't*, *haven't*); expressing denial or refusal, or used *ellipt*. for a negative phrase etc. —**not at all,** (in a polite reply to thanks) there is no need to thank me. [contr. of NOUGHT]

notable /ˈnəʊtəb(ə)l/ *adj*. worthy of notice, remarkable, eminent. —*n*. an eminent person. —**notability** /-ˈbɪlɪtɪ/ *n*., **notably** *adv*. [f. OF f. L *notabilis* (as NOTE)]

notary /ˈnəʊtərɪ/ *n*. (in full **notary public**) a person with the authority to draw up deeds and perform other legal formalities. —**notarial** /-ˈteərɪəl/ *adj*. [f. L, = secretary (as NOTE)]

notate /nəʊˈteɪt/ *v.t.* to write in notation. [back-formation f. foll.]

notation /nəʊˈteɪʃ(ə)n/ *n*. the representing of numbers, quantities, music sounds, etc., by symbols; any set of such symbols. [F or f. L (as NOTE)]

notch *n*. **1** a V-shaped cut or indentation. **2** a step in a graded system. —*v.t.* **1** to make a notch or notches in. **2** (often with *up*) to score (as) with notches. [f. AF]

note *n*. **1** a brief record of facts, topics, etc., written down to aid the memory. **2** a short or informal letter; a memorandum; a formal diplomatic communication. **3** a short comment on or explanation of a word or passage in a book etc. **4** a banknote. **5** a written promise of payment. **6** notice, attention; eminence. **7** a written sign representing the pitch and duration of a musical sound; a single tone of definite pitch made by a musical instrument, a voice, etc.; a key of a piano etc. **8** a significant sound or feature of expression. **9** a characteristic, a distinguishing feature. —*v.t.* **1** to notice, to give attention to. **2** (often with *down*) to record as a thing to be remembered or observed. **3** (in *p.p.*) celebrated, well known *for*. —**hit** *or* **strike the right note,** to speak or act in exactly the right manner. [f. OF f. L *nota* mark, *notare* to mark]

notebook *n*. a small book with blank pages in which to write memoranda.

notecase *n*. a wallet for holding bank-notes.

notelet /ˈnəʊtlɪt/ *n*. a small folded card or sheet for an informal letter.

notepaper *n*. paper for writing letters.

noteworthy *adj*. worthy of attention, remarkable.

nothing /ˈnʌθɪŋ/ *n*. **1** no thing; not anything. **2** a person or thing of no importance. **3** non-existence, what does not exist. **4** no amount, nought. —*adv*. not at all, in no way. —**for nothing,** at no cost, without payment; to no purpose. **have nothing on,** to be naked. **have nothing on (a person),** to possess no advantage over; to be much inferior to. **nothing doing,** (*colloq*.) no prospect of success or agreement. [OE (as NO[1], THING)]

nothingness *n*. **1** non-existence. **2** worthlessness, triviality. [f. prec.]

notice /ˈnəʊtɪs/ *n*. **1** attention, observation; heed. **2** news or information of what has happened or is about to happen; a warning. **3** written or printed information or instructions displayed publicly. **4** formal declaration of one's intention to end an agreement or leave employment at a specified time. **5** an account or review in a newspaper or magazine. —*v.t.* **1** to perceive, to become aware of. **2** to remark upon. —**at short notice,** with little warning. **notice-board** *n*. a board for displaying notices. **take (no) notice,** to show (no) signs of interest. **take notice of,** to observe; to act upon. [f. OF f. L *notitia* being known (*notus* known)]

noticeable *adj*. **1** noteworthy. **2** perceptible. —**noticeably** *adv*. [f. prec.]

notifiable /ˈnəʊtɪfaɪəb(ə)l/ *adj*. (of a disease or pest etc.) that must be notified to a public authority [f. foll.]

notify /ˈnəʊtɪfaɪ/ *v.t.* **1** to inform. **2** to report; to make (a thing) known. —**notification** /-fɪˈkeɪʃ(ə)n/ *n*. [f. OF f. L *notificare* (as NOTICE)]

notion /ˈnəʊʃ(ə)n/ *n*. **1** a concept or idea, a conception; a vague view or opinion. **2** an understanding; an inclination; an intention. **3** (in *pl*., *US*) small items used in sewing, haberdashery. [f. L *notion* (as NOTICE)]

notional *adj*. hypothetical; imaginary. —**notionally** *adv*. [obs. F, or f. L (as prec.)]

notochord /ˈnəʊtəʊkɔːd/ *n*. a flexible longitudinal rod found at some stage of the life cycle of all chordates. [f. Gk *nōton* back + CHORD[2]]

notorious /nəʊˈtɔːrɪəs/ *adj*. well known, especially for an unfavourable reason. —**notoriety** /-təˈraɪɪtɪ/ *n*., **notoriously** *adv*. [f. L (as NOTICE)]

Notts. *abbr*. Nottinghamshire.

notwithstanding /nɒtwɪθˈstændɪŋ, -wɪð-/ *prep*. in spite of, without prevention by. —*adv*. nevertheless. [f. NOT + WITHSTAND]

nougat /ˈnuːgɑː/ *n*. a sweet made from sugar or honey, nuts, and egg-white. [F f. Prov. (*noga* nut)]

nought /nɔːt/ *n*. **1** the figure 0. **2** (*poetic* or *archaic*) nothing. —**noughts and crosses,** a game in which two players seek to complete a row of three of either kind in a square array of usually nine spaces. [OE (*ne* not, AUGHT)]

noun /naʊn/ *n*. a word used as the name of a person, place, or thing. [f. AF f. L *nomen* name]

nourish /ˈnʌrɪʃ/ *v.t.* **1** to sustain with food (*lit.* or *fig*.).

2 to foster or cherish (a feeling etc.). [f. OF f. L (as NUTRIMENT)]

nourishing *adj*. containing much nourishment. [f. prec.]

nourishment *n*. **1** sustenance, food. **2** nourishing. [f. NOURISH]

nous /naus/ *n*. **1** (*Philos.*) the mind or intellect. **2** (*colloq.*) common sense. [Gk]

nouveau riche /nu:vəʊ 'ri:ʃ/ (*pl*. **-x -s,** pr. same) one who has acquired wealth only recently, especially one who displays this ostentatiously. [F, = new rich]

Nov. *abbr*. November.

nova /'nəʊvə/ *n*. (*pl*. **-ae, -as**) a star showing a sudden large increase in brightness and then subsiding. [L, fem. of *novus* new]

novel /'nɒv(ə)l/ *adj*. of a new kind, strange, hitherto unknown. —*n*. a fictitious prose story published as a complete book. [f. OF f. L *novellus* (as NOVA)]

novelette /nɒvə'let/ *n*. a short novel. [f. prec. + -ETTE]

novelist /'nɒvəlɪst/ *n*. a writer of novels. [f. NOVEL]

novella /nə'velə/ *n*. a short novel or narrative story. [It. (as NOVEL)]

novelty /'nɒvəltɪ/ *n*. **1** the quality of being novel. **2** a novel thing or occurrence. **3** a small unusual object. [f. OF (as NOVEL)]

November /nəʊ'vembə(r)/ *n*. the eleventh month of the year. [f. OF f. L (*novem* nine, because orig. the ninth month in the Roman calendar)]

novena /nə'vi:nə/ *n*. a Roman Catholic devotion consisting of special prayers or services on nine successive days. [L (*novem* nine)]

novice /'nɒvɪs/ *n*. **1** a probationary member of a religious order. **2** a new convert. **3** an inexperienced person, a beginner. [f. OF f. L *novicius* (as NOVA)]

noviciate /nə'vɪʃɪət/ *n*. (also **novitiate**) **1** the period of being a novice. **2** a religious novice. **3** novices' quarters. [f. F or L (as prec.)]

now *adv*. **1** at the present or mentioned time. **2** by this time. **3** immediately. **4** on this further occasion. **5** in the present circumstances. **6** (without reference to time, giving various tones to a sentence) surely, I insist, I wonder, etc. —*conj*. (also with *that*) as a consequence of the fact. —*n*. this time, the present. —**for now,** until a later time. **now and again** *or* **then,** from time to time, intermittently. [OE]

nowadays /'naʊədeɪz/ *adv*. at the present time or age, in these times. —*n*. the present time. [f. NOW + A[3] + DAY]

nowhere /'nəʊweə(r)/ *adv*. in or to no place. —*pron*. no place. —**get nowhere,** to make no progress. **nowhere near,** not nearly. [OE (as NO[1], WHERE)]

nowt *n*. (*colloq*. or *dial*.) nothing. [var. of NOUGHT]

noxious /'nɒkʃəs/ *adj*. harmful, unwholesome. [f. L *noxius* (*noxa* harm)]

nozzle *n*. the spout of a hose etc. for a jet to issue from. [dim. of NOSE]

Np *symbol* neptunium.

npn *abbr*. in which a p-type layer occurs between two n-type layers.

nr. *abbr*. near.

NS *abbr*. New Style. **2** new series. **3** Nova Scotia.

NSPCC *abbr*. National Society for the Prevention of Cruelty to Children.

NSW *abbr*. New South Wales.

n't see NOT.

NT *abbr*. **1** New Testament. **2** (*Austral.*) Northern Territory.

nu /nju:/ *n*. the thirteenth letter of the Greek alphabet, = n. [Gk]

nuance /'nju:ɑ̃s/ *n*. a subtle difference in or shade of meaning, feeling, colour, etc. [F (*nuer* to shade)]

nub *n*. **1** (also **nubble**) a small lump, especially of coal. **2** the central point or core of a matter or problem etc. —**nubbly** *adj*. [app. var. of *knub* knob]

nubile /'nju:baɪl/ *adj*. (of a woman) marriageable, sexually attractive. —**nubility** /-'bɪlɪtɪ/ *n*. [f. L (*nubere* become wife of)]

nuclear /'nju:klɪə(r)/ *adj*. **1** of or constituting a nucleus. **2** using nuclear energy. —**nuclear energy,** energy released or absorbed during reactions (nuclear fission or fusion) taking place in atomic nuclei. **nuclear family,** a father, mother, and their child or children. **nuclear fission,** the splitting of an atomic nucleus into smaller nuclei of roughly equal size, with consequent release of energy. **nuclear fuel,** a source of nuclear energy. **nuclear fusion,** the union of atomic nuclei to form heavier nuclei. **nuclear physics,** physics dealing with atomic nuclei and their reactions. **nuclear power,** power derived from nuclear energy; a country possessing nuclear weapons. **nuclear reactor,** an assembly of fissile and other materials (e.g. **moderators**) in which a controlled chain reaction can take place. **nuclear weapon,** a bomb or warhead deriving its destructive power from the rapid uncontrolled release of nuclear energy. **nuclear winter,** a conjectural period of changed climatic conditions following a nuclear war, characterized by extreme cold temperatures and other effects catastrophic to animal and vegetable life, caused by an atmospheric layer of smoke and dust particles blocking the sun's rays. [f. NUCLEUS]

nuclearize /ˈnju:klɪəraɪz/ *v.t.* to supply or equip (a nation) with nuclear weapons. —**nuclearization** /-ˈzeɪʃ(ə)n/ *n.* [f. NUCLEAR]

nucleate /ˈnju:klɪeɪt/ *v.t./i.* **1** to form (into) a nucleus. **2** (in *p.p.*) possessing a nucleus. [f. L (as NUCLEUS)]

nucleic acid /nju:ˈkli:ɪk/ either of two acids (DNA and RNA) present in all living cells. [f. NUCLEUS]

nucleon /ˈnju:klɪɒn/ *n.* a proton or neutron; a particle of which these are regarded as different states. [f. NUCLEUS]

nucleonic /nju:klɪˈɒnɪk/ *adj.* of nucleons or nucleonics. —**nucleonics** *n.pl.* (usu. treated as *sing.*) the branch of science and technology concerned with atomic nuclei and nucleons, especially the practical use of nuclear phenomena. [f. NUCLEAR & f. prec., after *electronics*]

nucleoprotein /nju:klɪəʊˈprəʊti:n/ *n.* a compound of a protein with nucleic acid. [f. NUCLEUS + PROTEIN]

nucleosynthesis /nju:klɪəʊˈsɪnθɪsɪs/ *n.* the formation of atoms more complicated than the hydrogen atom by cosmic processes. [f. NUCLEUS + SYNTHESIS]

nucleus /ˈnju:klɪəs/ *n.* (*pl.* **nuclei** /-ɪaɪ/) **1** the central part or thing around which others collect; the central part of an atom, of a seed, or of a plant or animal cell. **2** a kernel, an initial part meant to receive additions. [L, = kernel (*nux* nut)]

nude /nju:d/ *adj.* naked, bare, unclothed. —*n.* a picture or sculpture etc. of a nude human figure; a nude person. —**in the nude,** in an unclothed state, naked. —**nudity** *n.* [f. L *nudus*]

nudge *v.t./i.* **1** to prod gently with the elbow to attract attention. **2** to push gradually. —*n.* such a prod or push. [orig. unkn.]

nudist /ˈnju:dɪst/ *n.* a person who advocates or practises going unclothed. —**nudism** *n.* [f. NUDE]

Nuer /ˈnu:ə(r)/ *n.* (*pl.* same) a member or the language of an African people living in south-eastern Sudan. —*adj.* of this people or their language. [native name]

nugatory /ˈnju:gətərɪ/ *adj.* **1** futile, trifling. **2** inoperative, not valid. [f. L (*nugari* to trifle)]

nugget /ˈnʌgɪt/ *n.* **1** a lump of gold etc. as found in the earth. **2** something valuable. [f. dial. *nug* lump]

nuisance /ˈnju:s(ə)ns/ *n.* a source of trouble or annoyance; an annoying person, thing, or circumstance. [f. OF, = hurt (*nuire* to hurt)]

nuke /nju:k/ *n.* (*slang*, esp. *US*) a nuclear bomb, weapon, etc. [abbr. NUCLEAR]

null *adj.* **1** void, not valid. **2** characterless, expressionless. **3** non-existent. —**nullity** *n.* [f. F or L *nullus* none]

nullify /ˈnʌlɪfaɪ/ *v.t.* to neutralize, to invalidate. —**nullification** /-ˈkeɪʃ(ə)n/ *n.* [f. NULL]

numb /nʌm/ *adj.* deprived of feeling or the power of motion. —*v.t.* to make numb; to stupefy, to paralyse. —**numbly** *adv.*, **numbness** *n.* [f. *nome* p.p. of obs. *nim* take (as NIMBLE)]

numbat /ˈnʌmbæt/ *n.* the banded anteater *Myrmecobius fasciatus*, a small rare marsupial native to SW Australia. [Aboriginal]

number *n.* **1** a count, sum, or aggregate of persons, things, or abstract units. **2** an arithmetical value showing position in a series; a symbol or figure representing this. **3** a person or thing having a place in a series; a single issue of a magazine; an item in a programme etc. **4** numerical reckoning. **5** a company, a collection, a group. **6** (in *pl.*) numerical preponderance. **7** (*Gram.*) the class of word-forms including all singular, all plural, or all dual etc. forms. —*v.t.* **1** to count. **2** to assign a number or numbers to. **3** to have or amount to a specified number. **4** to include as a member of a class. **5** (in *pass.*) to be restricted in number. —**by numbers,** following simple instructions identified by numbers. **have a person's number,** (*slang*) to understand him or his motives. **one's number is up,** (*colloq.*) one is doomed to die. **number one,** (*colloq.*) oneself; the most important. **number-plate** *n.* a plate on a vehicle giving the registration number. **without number,** innumerable. [f. AF f. L *numerus*]

numberless *adj.* innumerable. [f. prec. + -LESS]

numerable /ˈnju:mərəb(ə)l/ *adj.* countable. [f. L (as NUMBER)]

numeral /ˈnju:mər(ə)l/ *n.* a symbol denoting a number. —*adj.* of or denoting a number. [f. L (as NUMBER)]

numerate /ˈnju:mərət/ *adj.* acquainted with the basic principles of mathematics and science. —**numeracy** *n.* [f. L *numerus* number, after *literate*]

numeration /nju:məˈreɪʃ(ə)n/ *n.* a method or process of numbering; calculation. [f. L (as NUMBER)]

numerator /ˈnju:məreɪtə(r)/ *n.* the number above the line in a vulgar fraction showing how many of the parts indicated by the denominator are taken. [f. F or L (as NUMBER)]

numerical /nju:ˈmerɪk(ə)l/ *adj.* of, in, or denoting a number or numbers. —**numerically** *adv.* [f. L (as NUMBER)]

numerology /nju:məˈrɒlədʒɪ/ *n.* the study of the occult significance of numbers. [f. L *numerus* number + -LOGY]

numerous /ˈnju:mərəs/ *adj.* many; consisting of many. [f. L *numerosus* (as prec.)]

numinous /ˈnju:mɪnəs/ *adj.* indicating the

presence of a divinity; spiritual, awe-inspiring. [f. L (*numen* deity)]

numismatic /nju:mɪz'mætɪk/ *adj*. of coins or coinage or medals. —**numismatist** /-'mɪzmətɪst/ *n*. [f. F f. L f. Gk *nomisma* current coin]

numismatics *n.pl*. (usu. treated as *sing*.) the study of coins or medals. [f. prec.]

numskull *n*. a stupid person. [f. NUMB + SKULL]

nun *n*. a member of a community of women living apart under religious vows. [OE & f. OF f. L *nonna*]

nuncio /'nʌnʃɪəʊ/ *n*. (*pl*. **-os**) an ambassador of the pope, accredited to a civil government. [It., f. L *nuntius* messenger]

nunnery *n*. a convent of nuns. [as NUN]

nuptial /'nʌpʃ(ə)l/ *adj*. of marriage or a wedding. —*n*. (usu. in *pl*.) a wedding. [F or f. L (*nuptiae* wedding)]

nurse *n*. **1** a person trained to care for the sick, injured, or infirm. **2** a woman employed to take charge of young children. —*v.t./i*. **1** to work as a nurse; to attend to (a sick person). **2** to feed or be fed at the breast. **3** to hold or treat carefully. **4** to foster, to promote the development of; to pay special attention to. —**nursing home**, a privately run hospital or home for invalids, old people, etc. [f. OF *norice* f. L (as NOURISH)]

nurseling *n*. (also **nursling**) an infant that is being suckled. [f. prec.]

nursemaid *n*. a young woman employed to take charge of a child or children.

nursery /'nɜ:sərɪ/ *n*. **1** a room or place equipped for young children; a day nursery. **2** a place where plants are reared for sale. —**nursery rhyme**, a simple traditional song or story in rhyme for children. **nursery school**, a school for children below normal school age. **nursery slopes**, slopes suitable for beginners at skiing. [as NURSE]

nurseryman *n*. (*pl*. **-men**) an owner of or a worker in a plant nursery.

nurture /'nɜ:tʃə(r)/ *n*. **1** bringing up, fostering care. **2** nourishment. —*v.t*. to bring up, to rear. [f. OF *nour(e)ture* (as NOURISH)]

nut *n*. **1** a fruit consisting of a hard or tough shell round an edible kernel; this kernel. **2** a pod containing hard seeds. **3** a small usually hexagonal piece of metal with a hole through it screwed on the end of a bolt to secure it. **4** (*slang*) the head. **5** (*slang*) a crazy person. **6** a small lump (of coal etc.). —*v.i*. (**-tt-**) to seek or gather nuts. —**do one's nut**, (*slang*) to be very angry. **nut-case** *n*. (*slang*) a crazy person. **nuts and bolts**, the practical details. **nut-tree** *n*. a tree bearing nuts, especially the hazel. [OE]

nutation /nju:'teɪʃ(ə)n/ *n*. **1** nodding. **2** the oscillation of the earth's axis. [f. L (*nutare* nod)]

nutcracker *n*. (usu. in *pl*.) an instrument for cracking nuts.

nuthatch /'nʌthætʃ/ *n*. a small climbing bird (*Sitta europaea*) feeding on nuts, insects, etc.

nutmeg *n*. the hard aromatic seed of an East Indian tree (*Myristica fragrans*), ground or grated as a spice. [partial transl. of OF *nois mug(u)ede* musky nut]

nutria /'nju:trɪə/ *n*. the skin or fur of the coypu. [Sp., = otter]

nutrient /'nju:trɪənt/ *adj*. serving as or providing nourishment. —*n*. a nutrient substance. [f. L *nutrire* nourish]

nutriment /'nju:trɪmənt/ *n*. nourishing food (*lit*. or *fig*.). [f. L *nutrimentum* (as prec.)]

nutrition /nju:'trɪʃ(ə)n/ *n*. food, nourishment. —**nutritional** *adj*., **nutritionally** *adv*. [F or f. L (as NUTRIENT)]

nutritious /nju:'trɪʃəs/ *adj*. efficient as food. —**nutritiously** *adv*., **nutritiousness** *n*. [f. L (as NURSE)]

nutritive /'nju:trɪtɪv/ *adj*. of nutrition; nutritious. [f. F f. L (as NUTRIENT)]

nuts *adj*. (*slang*) crazy, mad. —**nuts about** *or* **on**, (*slang*) very fond of or enthusiastic about. [pl. of NUT]

nutshell *n*. the hard exterior covering of a nut. —**in a nutshell**, in a few words.

nutter *n*. (*slang*) a crazy person. [f. NUT]

nutty *adj*. **1** full of nuts. **2** tasting like nuts. **3** (*slang*) crazy. —**nuttily** *adv*., **nuttiness** *n*. [f. NUT]

nux vomica /nʌks 'vɒmɪkə/ the seed of an East Indian tree (*Strychnos nux-vomica*), yielding strychnine. [L (*nux* nut, as VOMIT)]

nuzzle *v.t./i*. **1** to press or rub gently with the nose. **2** to nestle, to lie snug. [f. NOSE]

NW *abbr*. North-West, North-Western.

NY *abbr*. New York.

nylon /'naɪlɒn/ *n*. **1** a strong light synthetic polymer that may be produced as filaments, bristles, or sheets and as moulded objects. **2** fabric made from nylon yarn. **3** (in *pl*.) nylon stockings. [invented word, with *-on* suggested by *cotton* and *rayon*; there is no evidence to support the derivations frequently given for this word in popular sources]

nymph /nɪmf/ *n*. **1** a mythological semi-divine maiden of the sea, woods, etc. **2** (*poetic*) a maiden. **3** an immature insect which from the time of hatching has a general resemblance to the adult. [f. OF f. L f. Gk *numphē*]

nymphet /'nɪmfet, -'fet/ *n*. **1** a young nymph. **2** a nymphlike or sexually attractive girl. [f. prec.]

nympho /'nɪmfəʊ/ *n*. (*pl*. **-os**) (*colloq*.) a nymphomaniac. [abbr.]

nymphomania /nɪmfəʊˈmeɪnɪə/ *n.* excessive sexual desire in women. —**nymphomaniac** *n.* [NYMPH + -MANIA]

nystagmus /nɪˈstægməs/ *n.* continual rapid oscillation of the eyeballs; an eye-disease characterized by this. [f. Gk *nustagmos* nodding (*nustazō* nod)]

NZ *abbr.* New Zealand.

O[1], **o** /əʊ/ *n.* (*pl.* **Os, O's**) the fifteenth letter of the alphabet; (as a numeral, in telephone numbers etc.) nought, zero.

O[2] /əʊ/ *int.* prefixed to a name in the vocative or expressing a wish, entreaty, etc. [natural excl.]

O *symbol* oxygen.

o' /ə/ *prep.* of, on (esp. in phrases, e.g. *o'clock, will-o'-the-wisp*). [abbr.]

oaf *n.* (*pl.* **oafs**) an awkward lout. —**oafish** *adj.* [f. ON (as ELF)]

oak *n.* a forest tree (*Quercus robur* or *Q. petraea*) with hard wood, acorns, and lobed leaves; its wood; an allied or similar tree; (*attrib.*) of oak. —**oak-apple** *or* **oak-gall** *n.* = gall[3]. —**oaken** *adj.* [OE]

oakum /ˈəʊkəm/ *n.* loose fibre obtained by picking old rope to pieces. [OE, = off-combings]

OAP *abbr.* old-age pension(er).

oar /ɔ(r)/ *n.* **1** a pole with a blade used to propel a boat by leverage against the water. **2** a rower. —**put one's oar in,** to interfere. [OE]

oarsman *n.* (*pl.* **-men**) a rower. —**oarsmanship** *n.*, **oarswoman** *n.fem.*

oasis /əʊˈeɪsɪs/ *n.* (*pl.* **oases** /-iːz/) **1** a fertile spot in the desert, with a spring or well of water. **2** a thing or circumstance offering relief in difficulty. [L f. Gk, app. of Egyptian orig.]

oast *n.* a kiln for drying hops. —**oast-house** *n.* a building containing this. [OE]

oat *n.* **1** (in *pl.*) a hardy cereal (*Avena sativa*) grown as food; the grain yielded by this. **2** an oat-plant or a variety of it. —**off one's oats,** (*colloq.*) lacking appetite for food. —**oaten** *adj.* [OE]

oatcake *n.* a thin unleavened cake made of oatmeal.

oath *n.* (*pl.* /əʊðz/) **1** a solemn declaration or undertaking naming God or a revered object as witness. **2** casual use of the name of God etc. in anger or emphasis; an obscenity. —**on** *or* **under oath,** having made a solemn oath. [OE]

oatmeal *n.* meal made from oats.

ob- *prefix* (usu. **oc-** before *c*, **of-** before *f*, **op-** before *p*) esp. in words from Latin, expressing exposure, meeting, facing, direction, compliance, opposition, resistance, hindrance, concealment, finality, completeness. [L (*ob* towards, against, in the way of)]

ob. *abbr.* he or she died. [f. L *obiit*]

obbligato /ɒblɪˈgɑːtəʊ/ *n.* (*pl.* **-os**) (*Mus.*) a part or accompaniment forming an integral part of a composition. [It., = obligatory]

obdurate /ˈɒbdjʊrət/ *adj.* hardened, stubborn. —**obduracy** *n.* [f. L (OB-, *durare* harden f. *durus* hard)]

OBE *abbr.* Officer of the Order of the British Empire.

obedient /əʊˈbiːdɪənt/ *adj.* obeying, ready to obey; submissive to another's will. —**obedience** *n.*, **obediently** *adv.* [f. OF f. L (as OBEY)]

obeisance /əʊˈbeɪsəns/ *n.* a bow, curtsey, or other respectful gesture; homage. —**obeisant** *adj.* [f. OF (as OBEY)]

obelisk /ˈɒbəlɪsk/ *n.* a tapering usually four-sided stone pillar as a monument. [f. L f. Gk (dim. of foll.)]

obelus /ˈɒbələs/ *n.* (*pl.* **-li** /-laɪ/) a dagger-shaped mark of reference (†). [L f. Gk, = spit]

obese /əʊˈbiːs/ *adj.* very fat. —**obesity** *n.* [f. L, = having eaten oneself fat (OB-, *edere* eat)]

obey /əʊˈbeɪ/ *v.t./i.* **1** to do what is commanded by. **2** to be obedient. **3** to be actuated by (a force or impulse). [f. OF f. L *obedire* (OB-, *audire* hear)]

obfuscate /ˈɒbfʌskeɪt/ *v.t.* **1** to obscure or confuse (the mind, a topic, etc.). **2** to stupefy, to bewilder. —**obfuscation** /-ˈkeɪʃ(ə)n/ *n.* [f. L (OB-, *fuscus* dark)]

obituary /əˈbɪtjʊərɪ/ *n.* a notice of a person's death especially in a newspaper, often with an account of the life of the deceased person. —*adj.* of or serving as an obituary. [f. L (*obitus* death)]

object /ˈɒbdʒɪkt/ *n.* **1** a material thing that can be seen or touched. **2** a person or thing to which an action or feeling is directed. **3** a thing sought or aimed at. **4** (*Gram.*) a noun or its equivalent governed by an active transitive verb or by a preposition. **5** (*Philos.*) a thing external to the thinking mind or subject.

—/əbˈdʒekt/ *v.t./i.* 1 to express opposition; to feel or express dislike or reluctance. 2 to adduce as contrary or damaging. —**no object,** not forming an important or restricting factor. **object-glass** *n.* the lens in a telescope etc. nearest to the object observed. **object-lesson** *n.* a striking practical example of some principle. —**objector** /əbˈdʒektə(r)/ *n.* [f. L (OB-, *jacere* throw)]

objectify /ɒbˈdʒektɪfaɪ/ *v.t.* 1 to make objective. 2 to embody. [f. prec.]

objection /əbˈdʒekʃ(ə)n/ *n.* 1 a feeling of disapproval or opposition; a statement of this. 2 a reason for objecting; a drawback in a plan etc. [f. OF or L (as OBJECT)]

objectionable *adj.* open to objection; unpleasant, offensive. —**objectionably** *adv.* [f. prec.]

objective /əbˈdʒektɪv/ *adj.* 1 external to the mind, actually existing. 2 dealing with outward things or exhibiting facts uncoloured by feelings or opinions. 3 (*Gram.*, of a case or word) constructed as or appropriate to the object. 4 aimed at. —*n.* 1 something sought or aimed at. 2 (*Gram.*) the objective case. 3 an object-glass. —**objectively** *adv.*, **objectivity** /ɒbdʒekˈtɪvɪtɪ/ *n.* [f. L (as OBJECT)]

objet d'art /ɒbʒeɪ ˈdɑ:(r)/ (*pl.* ***objets d'art*** *pr.* same) a small decorative object. [F, = object of art]

objurgate /ˈɒbdʒɜ:geɪt/ *v.t.* (*literary*) to rebuke, to scold. —**objurgation** /-ˈgeɪʃ(ə)n/ *n.* [f. L *objurgare* quarrel (OB-, *jurgium* strife)]

oblate /ˈɒbleɪt, əˈbleɪt/ *adj.* (of a spheroid) flattened at the poles. [f. OB- + *-late* (as in PROLATE)]

oblation /əˈbleɪʃ(ə)n/ *n.* a thing offered to a divine being. [f. OF or L (as OFFER)]

obligate /ˈɒblɪgeɪt/ *v.t.* (usu. in *p.p.*) to oblige (a person legally or morally) to do a thing. [f. L (as OBLIGE)]

obligation /ɒblɪˈgeɪʃ(ə)n/ *n.* 1 being obliged to do something; the compelling power of a law, contract, duty, etc. 2 a duty, a task one must perform. 3 indebtedness for a service or benefit. —**under (an) obligation,** owing gratitude. [f. OF f. L (as OBLIGE)]

obligatory /əˈblɪgətərɪ/ *adj.* required by law, contract, or custom etc., not optional. —**obligatorily** *adv.* [f. L (as foll.)]

oblige /əˈblaɪdʒ/ *v.t./i.* 1 to compel by law, contract, custom etc., or necessity. 2 to help or gratify by performing a small service. —**be obliged to a person,** to be indebted or grateful to him. **much obliged,** thank you. [f. OF f. L *obligare* (OB-, *ligare* bind)]

obliging *adj.* courteous and helpful, accommodating. —**obligingly** *adv.* [f. prec.]

oblique /əˈbli:k/ *adj.* 1 declining from the vertical or horizontal, diverging from a straight line or course. 2 not going straight to the point, roundabout, indirect. 3 (*Gram.*, of a case) other than the nominative or vocative. —*n.* an oblique stroke (/). —**obliquely** *adv.*, **obliquity** /əˈblɪkwɪtɪ/ *n.* [f. F f. L *obliquus*]

obliterate /əˈblɪtəreɪt/ *v.t.* to blot out, to destroy and leave no clear traces of. —**obliteration** /-ˈreɪʃ(ə)n/ *n.*, **obliterator** *n.* [f. L *oblit(t)erare* erase (OB-, *litera* letter)]

oblivion /əˈblɪvɪən/ *n.* 1 the state of being forgotten. 2 the state of being oblivious. [f. OF f. L (*oblivisci* forget)]

oblivious /əˈblɪvɪəs/ *adj.* unaware or unconscious (with *of* or *to*). [f. L (as prec.)]

oblong /ˈɒblɒŋ/ *adj.* of a rectangular shape with adjacent sides unequal. —*n.* an oblong figure or object. [f. L, orig. = somewhat long]

obloquy /ˈɒbləkwɪ/ *n.* 1 abuse intended to damage a person's reputation. 2 discredit brought by this. [f. L *obloquium* contradiction (OB-, *loqui* speak)]

obnoxious /əbˈnɒkʃəs/ *adj.* offensive, objectionable, disliked. —**obnoxiously** *adv.* [f. L (OB-, *noxa* hard)]

oboe /ˈəʊbəʊ/ *n.* 1 a double-reed wood-wind instrument of treble pitch. 2 its player. 3 an organ reed-stop of similar quality. —**oboist** /-bəʊɪst/ *n.* [f. F *hautbois* (*haut* high, *bois* wood)]

obscene /əbˈsi:n/ *adj.* offensively indecent; (*Law*, of a publication) tending to deprave or corrupt; (*colloq.*) highly offensive. —**obscenely** *adv.*, **obscenity** /-ˈsenɪtɪ/ *n.* [f. F or L *obsc(a)enus*, orig. = ill-omened]

obscure /əbˈskjʊə(r)/ *adj.* 1 not clearly expressed, not easily understood. 2 dark, indistinct. 3 hidden, unnoticed; (of a person) undistinguished, hardly known. —*v.t.* to make obscure or unintelligible; to conceal. —**obscurely** *adv.*, **obscurity** *n.* [f. OF f. L *obscurus*]

obsequies /ˈɒbsɪkwɪz/ *n.pl.* funeral rites. [f. AF f. L *obsequiae*]

obsequious /əbˈsi:kwɪəs/ *adj.* excessively or sickeningly respectful. —**obsequiously** *adv.*, **obsequiousness** *n.* [f. L (*obsequium* compliance)]

observance /əbˈzɜ:vəns/ *n.* 1 the keeping or performance of a law, duty, etc. 2 a rite, a ceremonial act. [f. OF f. L *observantia* (as OBSERVE)]

observant *adj.* 1 quick at noticing things. 2 attentive in observance. —**observantly** *adv.* [F (as OBSERVE)]

observation /ɒbzəˈveɪʃ(ə)n/ *n.* 1 observing, being observed. 2 a comment or remark. 3 facts or data; the recording of these. —**observational** *adj.* [f. L (as OBSERVE)]

observatory /əbˈzɜ:vətərɪ/ *n.* a building designed and equipped for scientific observation of the stars or weather etc. [f. L (as foll.)]

observe /əbˈzɜːv/ *v.t./i.* **1** to see and notice; to watch carefully. **2** to keep or pay attention to (rules etc.). **3** to celebrate or perform (an occasion, rite, etc.). **4** to note and record (facts or data). **5** to remark. —**observable** *adj.* & *n.* [f. OF f. L *observare* (OB-, *servare* watch)]

observer *n.* one who observes; an interested spectator. [f. prec.]

obsess /əbˈses/ *v.t.* to occupy the thoughts of (a person) continually. [f. L *obsidere* besiege]

obsession /əbˈseʃ(ə)n/ *n.* **1** obsessing, being obsessed. **2** a persistent idea dominating a person's thoughts. —**obsessional** *adj.* [as prec.]

obsessive /əbˈsesɪv/ *adj.* of, causing, or showing obsession. —**obsessively** *adv.* [as OBSESS]

obsidian /əbˈsɪdɪən/ *n.* a dark vitreous lava or volcanic rock that looks like a coarse glass. [f. L f. *Obsius*, name of finder of a similar stone, mentioned by Pliny]

obsolescent /ɒbsəˈlesənt/ *adj.* becoming obsolete. —**obsolescence** *n.* [f. L *obsolescere* (OB-, *solēre* be accustomed)]

obsolete /ˈɒbsəliːt/ *adj.* no longer used, antiquated. [as prec.]

obstacle /ˈɒbstək(ə)l/ *n.* a thing obstructing progress. [f. OF f. L (*obstare* stand in the way)]

obstetrician /ɒbstɪˈtrɪʃ(ə)n/ *n.* a specialist in obstetrics. [f. foll.]

obstetrics /ɒbˈstetrɪks/ *n.pl.* (usu. treated as *sing.*) the branch of medicine and surgery dealing with childbirth. —**obstetric** *adj.*, **obstetrical** *adj.* [f. L *obstetricius* (*obstetrix* midwife)]

obstinate /ˈɒbstɪnət/ *n.* stubborn, intractable; firmly continuing in one's action or opinion and not yielding to persuasion. —**obstinacy** *n.*, **obstinately** *adv.* [f. L (*obstinare* persist)]

obstreperous /əbˈstrepərəs/ *adj.* noisy, unruly. —**obstreperously** *adv.* [f. L (*obstrepere* shout against)]

obstruct /əbˈstrʌkt/ *v.t.* **1** to prevent or hinder passage along (a path etc.) by means of an object etc. placed in it. **2** to prevent or hinder the movement, progress, or activities of. —**obstructor** *n.* [f. L *obstruere* (OB-, *struere* build)]

obstruction /əbˈstrʌkʃ(ə)n/ *n.* **1** obstructing, being obstructive. **2** a thing that obstructs, a blockage. [as prec.]

obstructive *adj.* causing or intended to cause obstruction. [f. OBSTRUCT]

obtain /əbˈteɪn/ *v.t./i.* **1** to get, to come into possession of (a thing) by effort or as a gift. **2** to be established or in use as a rule or customary practice. —**obtainment** *n.* [f. OF f. L *obtinēre* (OB-, *tenēre* hold)]

obtainable *adj.* that may be obtained. [f. prec.]

obtrude /əbˈtruːd/ *v.t./i.* to force (oneself or one's ideas) upon others; to be or become obtrusive. —**obtrusion** *n.* [f. L *obtrudere* (OB-, *trudere* thrust)]

obtrusive /əbˈtruːsɪv/ *adj.* obtruding oneself; unpleasantly noticeable. —**obtrusively** *adv.* [as prec.]

obtuse /əbˈtjuːs/ *adj.* **1** stupid, slow at understanding. **2** of blunt shape, not sharp-edged or pointed. **3** (of an angle) more than 90° but less than 180°. —**obtusely** *adv.*, **obtuseness** *n.* [f. L (OB-, *tundere* beat)]

obverse /ˈɒbvɜːs/ *n.* **1** the side of a coin or medal etc. that bears the head or principal design; the front or proper or top side of a thing. **2** the counterpart. [f. L *obvertere* turn towards]

obviate /ˈɒbvɪeɪt/ *v.t.* to make unnecessary; to get round (a danger or hindrance etc.). [f. L *obviare* withstand (OB-, *via* way)]

obvious /ˈɒbvɪəs/ *adj.* easily seen or recognized or understood. —**obviously** *adv.* [f. L (*ob viam* in the way)]

OC *abbr.* Officer Commanding.

oc- see OB-.

ocarina /ɒkəˈriːnə/ *n.* a small egg-shaped terracotta or metal wind instrument with holes for the fingers. [It. (*oca* goose, from its shape)]

occasion /əˈkeɪʒ(ə)n/ *n.* **1** a special event or happening; a particular time marked by this. **2** a reason, a need. **3** a suitable juncture, an opportunity. **4** an immediate but subordinate cause. **5** (in *pl.*) affairs, business. —*v.t.* to cause (esp. incidentally). —**on occasion**, now and then, when the need arises. [f. OF or L (*occidere* go down)]

occasional *adj.* **1** happening irregularly and infrequently. **2** made, intended for, or acting on a special occasion. —**occasionally** *adv.* [f. prec.]

Occident /ˈɒksɪdənt/ *n.* (*poetic* or *rhet.*) the West (especially Europe and America) as opposed to the Orient. [f. OF f. L, = sunset, west (as OCCASION)]

occidental /ɒksɪˈdent(ə)l/ *adj.* of the Occident, western. —*n.* a native or inhabitant of the Occident. [as prec.]

occiput /ˈɒksɪpʌt/ *n.* the back of the head. —**occipital** /ɒkˈsɪpɪt(ə)l/ *adj.* [f. L (OC-, *caput* head)]

occlude /ɒˈkluːd/ *v.t.* **1** to obstruct, to stop up. **2** to absorb and retain (gases). —**occluded front**, the atmospheric condition that occurs when a cold front overtakes a mass of warm air, and warm air is driven upwards, producing a long period of steady rain. —**occlusion** *n.* [f. L *occludere* (OC-, *claudere* shut)]

occult[1] /ɒˈkʌlt/ *adj.* **1** involving the supernatural, mystical, magical. **2** esoteric, recondite. —**the occult**, occult phenomena generally. [f. L *occulere* to hide]

occult[2] /ɒˈkʌlt/ *v.t.* to conceal, to cut off from view by passing in front (usu. *Astron.* of a concealing body much greater in apparent size than the concealed body). —**occultation** /-ˈteɪʃ(ə)n/ *n.* [f. L *occultare* frequent. of *occulere* (see prec.)]

occupant /ˈɒkjʊpənt/ *n.* a person occupying a dwelling, office, or position. —**occupancy** *n.* [f. OF f. L (as OCCUPY)]

occupation /ɒkjʊˈpeɪʃ(ə)n/ *n.* **1** an activity that keeps a person busy; one's employment. **2** occupying, being occupied; taking or holding possession of a country or district by military force. [f. OF f. L (as OCCUPY)]

occupational *adj.* of or connected with one's occupation. —**occupational disease** *or* **hazard**, a disease or hazard to which a particular occupation renders one especially liable. **occupational therapy**, mental or physical activity to assist recovery from a disease or injury. [f. prec.]

occupier /ˈɒkjʊpaɪə(r)/ *n.* a person residing in a house etc. as its owner or tenant. [f. foll.]

occupy /ˈɒkjʊpaɪ/ *v.t.* **1** to reside in, to be a tenant of. **2** to take up or fill (a space or time or place). **3** to hold (a position or office). **4** to take military possession of; to place oneself in (a building etc.) forcibly or without authority. **5** to keep (a person or his time) filled with activity. [f. OF f. L *occupare* seize]

occur /əˈkɜː(r)/ *v.i.* (**-rr-**) **1** to come into being as an event or process. **2** to be met with or found to exist in some place or condition. —**occur to**, to come into the mind of. [f. L *occurrere* present itself]

occurrence /əˈkʌrəns/ *n.* **1** occurring. **2** a thing that occurs, an event. [f. *occurrent* adj. f. F f. L (as prec.)]

ocean /ˈəʊʃ(ə)n/ *n.* **1** the sea surrounding the continents of the earth, especially one of five named divisions of this (*Atlantic*, *Pacific*, *Indian*, *Arctic*, and *Antarctic Oceans*). **2** an immense expanse or quantity. —**ocean-going** *adj.* (of a ship) able to cross the ocean. —**oceanic** /əʊʃɪˈænɪk/ *adj.* [f. OF f. L f. Gk, = stream encircling the earth]

oceanography /əʊʃəˈnɒgrəfɪ/ *n.* the study of oceans. —**oceanographer** *n.* [f. OCEAN + -GRAPHY]

ocellus /əˈseləs/ *n.* (*pl.* **ocelli** /-laɪ/) **1** any of the simple (as opp. compound) eyes of insects etc. **2** a facet of a compound eye. [L, dim. of *oculus* eye]

ocelot /ˈəʊsɪlɒt,ˈɒ-/ *n.* a leopard-like feline (*Felis pardalis*) of South and Central America. [F, abbr. by Buffon f. Nahuatl *tlalocelotl* jaguar of the field, and applied to a different animal]

och /ɒx/ *int.* (*Sc.* & *Ir.*) oh, ah. [Gael. & Ir.]

oche /ˈɒkɪ/ *n.* var. of HOCKEY[2].

ochre /ˈəʊkə(r)/ *n.* **1** an earth used as a yellow or brown or red pigment. **2** a pale brownish-yellow colour. —**ochrous** *adj.* [f. OF f. L f. Gk (*ōkhros* pale yellow)]

o'clock /əˈklɒk/ *adv.* = *of the clock*, used to specify an hour.

Oct. *abbr.* October.

oct-, octa- *in comb.* eight. [f. L or Gk (L *octo*, Gk *oktō* eight)]

octagon /ˈɒktəgən/ *n.* a plane figure with eight sides and angles. —**octagonal** /-ˈtægən(ə)l/ *adj.* [f. L f. Gk (OCTA-, *-gōnos* angled)]

octahedron /ɒktəˈhiːdrən/ *n.* (*pl.* **-s**) a solid figure contained by eight plane faces and usually by eight triangles. —**octahedral** *adj.* [f. Gk (OCTA-, *hedra* base)]

octane /ˈɒkteɪn/ *n.* a hydrocarbon compound of the paraffin series occurring in petrol. —**high-octane** *adj.* (of fuel used in internal-combustion engines) not detonating rapidly during the power stroke. **octane number**, a number indicating the anti-knock properties of fuel. [f. OCT-]

octave /ˈɒktɪv/ *n.* **1** (*Mus.*) a note seven diatonic degrees from a given note and having the same name; the interval between a given note and its octave; the series of notes filling this. **2** the seventh day after a religious festival; the period of eight days including the festival and its octave. **3** an eight-line stanza. [f. OF f. L (*octavus* eighth)]

octavo /ɒkˈteɪvəʊ/ *n.* (*pl.* **-os**) the size of a book or page given by folding a sheet of standard size three times to form eight leaves; a book or sheet of this size. [L (as OCTAVE)]

octet /ɒkˈtet/ *n.* (also **octette**) **1** a musical composition for eight performers; these performers. **2** any group of eight. **3** the set of eight lines beginning a sonnet. [f. It. or G (OCT-, after *duet*, *quartet*)]

octo- *in comb.* eight. [as OCT-, OCTA-]

October /ɒkˈtəʊbə(r)/ *n.* the tenth month of the year. [OE f. L (*octō* eight, because orig. the eighth month in the Roman calendar)]

octogenarian /ɒktəʊdʒɪˈneərɪən/ *n.* a person from 80 to 89 years old. [f. L (*octogeni* 80 each)]

octopus /ˈɒktəpəs/ *n.* (*pl.* **-uses**) a sea-mollusc of the family Octopodidae, with eight suckered tentacles. [f. Gk (OCTO-, *pous* foot)]

ocular /ˈɒkjʊlə(r)/ *adj.* of or connected with the eyes or sight, visual. [f. F f. L (*oculus* eye)]

oculist /ˈɒkjʊlɪst/ *n.* a specialist in the treatment of eye diseases and defects. [as prec.]

odalisque /ˈəʊdəlɪsk/ *n.* (*hist.*) an Oriental female slave or concubine, especially in the

Turkish sultan's seraglio. [F f. Turk. (*oda* chamber, *lik* function)]

odd *adj.* **1** unusual, strange, eccentric. **2** not regular, occasional; not normally noticed or considered; unconnected. **3** (of numbers such as 3 and 5) not integrally divisible by two; bearing such a number. **4** left over when the rest have been distributed or divided into pairs; detached from a set or series. **5** (appended to a number, sum, weight, etc.) something more than; by which a round number, given sum, etc., is exceeded. —**odd man out**, a person or thing differing from all others of a group in some respect. —**oddly** *adv.*, **oddness** *n.* [f. ON *odda-* in *odda-mathr* third man (*oddi* angle, triangle)]

oddball *n.* (*colloq.*) an eccentric person.

oddity /ˈɒdɪtɪ/ *n.* **1**. strangeness; a peculiar trait. **2** a strange person, thing, or event. [f. ODD]

oddment *n.* an odd article, something left over; (in *pl.*) odds and ends. [f. ODD]

odds *n.pl.* (sometimes treated as *sing.*). **1** the ratio between the amounts staked by the parties to a bet, based on the expected probability either way. **2** the balance of advantage or probability. **3** advantageous difference. —**at odds**, in conflict, at variance. **odds and ends**, remnants, stray articles. **odds-on** *n.* a state when success is expected to be more likely than failure. **over the odds**, above the generally agreed price etc. [app. pl. of ODD]

ode *n.* (in ancient literature) a poem intended or adapted to be sung; (in modern use) a rhymed (rarely unrhymed) lyric, often in the form of an address, generally dignified or exalted in subject, feeling, and style, but sometimes (in earlier use) simple and familiar (though less so than a song). [f. F f. L f. Gk *ōidē* song]

odious /ˈəʊdɪəs/ *adj.* hateful, repulsive. —**odiously** *adv.*, **odiousness** *n.* [f. OF f. L (as foll.)]

odium /ˈəʊdɪəm/ *n.* widespread dislike or disapproval felt towards a person or action. [L, = hatred]

odometer /əʊˈdɒmɪtə(r)/ *n.* an instrument for measuring the distance travelled by a wheeled vehicle. [f. F (Gk *hodos* way, -METER)]

odoriferous /əʊdəˈrɪfərəs/ *adj.* diffusing a (usu. agreeable) odour. [f. L (*odor* smell, *ferro* carry)]

odour /ˈəʊdə(r)/ *n.* **1** a smell. **2** a savour, a trace. **3** favour, repute. —**odorous** *adj.* [f. AF f. L *odor*]

odyssey /ˈɒdɪsɪ:/ *n.* a long adventurous journey. [f. *Odyssey*, Gk epic poem telling of the travels of Odysseus]

OECD *abbr.* Organization for Economic Co-operation and Development, an association of Western States founded in 1961 to assist the economy of member nations and to promote world trade.

OED *abbr.* Oxford English Dictionary.

oedema /i:ˈdi:mə, ɪˈd-/ *n.* a swollen state of tissue in the body. —**oedematous** *adj.* [L f. Gk (*oideō* swell)]

Oedipus complex /ˈi:dɪpəs/ the manifestation of a child's sexuality towards its parents, with attraction to the parent of the opposite sex (especially the mother) and jealousy of the other parent. —**Oedipal** *adj.* [f. *Oedipus* in Gk legend, who in ignorance married his mother]

o'er /ˈəʊə(r)/ *prep.* & *adv.* (chiefly *poetic*) = OVER. [contr.]

oesophagus /i:ˈsɒfəgəs/ *n.* (*pl.* **-gi** /-dʒaɪ/) the canal from the mouth to the stomach, the gullet. [f. Gk]

oestrogen /ˈi:strədʒ(ə)n/ *n.* a sex hormone maintaining or developing female bodily characteristics. [f. Gk *oistros* frenzy + -GEN]

œuvre /øvr/ *n.* **1** a work of art, music, or literature. **2** the corpus of work produced by an artist, composer, or writer, considered as a whole. [F, = work, f. L *opera*]

of /əv, emphat. ɒv/ *prep.* **1** belonging to; originating from. **2** concerning. **3** composed or made from. **4** with reference or regard to. **5** for, involving, directed towards. **6** so as to bring separation or relief from. **7** during; regularly on a specified day or time. —**of itself**, by or in itself. [OE]

of- see OB-.

off *adv.* **1** away, at, or to a distance. **2** out of position; not on or touching or attached, loose, separate; gone; so as to be rid of; incorrect, insufficient. **3** so as to break continuity or continuance; discontinued, stopped; not available on the menu etc. **4** to the end, entirely, so as to be clear. **5** situated as regards money, supplies, etc. **6** off-stage. **7** (of food etc.) beginning to decay. —*prep.* **1** from, away or down or up from, not on. **2** temporarily relieved of or abstaining from or not achieving. **3** using as a source or means of support. **4** leading from, not far from; at a short distance to sea from. —*adj.* far, further; (of a part of a vehicle, animal, or road) further from the side of a road when facing forward, usually the right; (in cricket) designating the half of the field (as divided lengthways through the pitch) to which the striker's feet are pointed. —*n.* **1** the off side in cricket. **2** the start of a race. —**a bit off,** (*slang*) rather annoying or unfair or unwell. **off and on,** intermittently, now and then. **off-beat** *adj.* eccentric, unconventional. **off chance,** a remote possibility. **off colour,** not in good health; (*US*) somewhat indecent. **off-day** *n.* a day when one is not at one's best. **off-key**

adj. out of tune; not quite suitable or fitting. **off-licence** *n.* a shop selling alcoholic drink for consumption elsewhere; a licence for this. **off-line** *adj.* (of computer equipment or a computer process) not directly controlled by or connected to a central processor. **off-load** *v.t.* to unload. **off-peak** *adj.* used or for use at times other than those of greatest demand. **off-putting** *adj.* (*colloq.*) disconcerting; repellent. **off-season** *n.* a time when business etc. is slack. **off-stage** *adj.* & *adv.* not on the stage and so not visible or audible to the audience. **off-white** *adj.* white with a grey or yellowish tinge. [var. of OF]

offal /ˈɒf(ə)l/ *n.* **1** the edible parts of a carcass (especially the heart, liver, etc.) cut off as less valuable. **2** refuse, scraps. [f. MDu. *afval* (as OFF, FALL)]

offcut *n.* a remnant of timber etc. after cutting.

offence /əˈfens/ *n.* **1** an illegal act, a transgression. **2** wounding of the feelings; annoyance or resentment caused thus. **3** an aggressive action. [f. F or OF f. L (as foll.)]

offend /əˈfend/ *v.t./i.* **1** to cause offence to; to displease or anger. **2** to do wrong. —**offender** *n.* [f. OF f. L *offendere*, orig. = strike against]

offensive /əˈfensɪv/ *adj.* **1** causing offence, insulting. **2** disgusting, repulsive. **3** aggressive, attacking; (of a weapon) meant for attacking. —*n.* an aggressive attitude, action, or campaign. —**offensively** *adv.*, **offensiveness** *n.* [f. F or L (as OFFENCE)]

offer *v.t./i.* **1** to present for acceptance or refusal or for consideration. **2** to express readiness or show intention to do, pay, or give. **3** to provide, to give opportunity for. **4** to make available for sale. **5** to present to sight or notice; to present itself, to occur. —*n.* **1** an expression of readiness to do or give if desired, or to buy or sell (for a certain amount); the amount offered; a bid. **2** a proposal, especially of marriage. —**on offer**, for sale at a certain (esp. reduced) price. [OE or f. OF f. L *offerre*]

offering *n.* a thing offered as a gift, contribution, sacrifice, etc. [f. prec.]

offertory /ˈɒfətərɪ/ *n.* **1** the offering of bread and wine at the Eucharist. **2** a collection of money at a religious service. [f. L (as OFFER)]

offhand *adj.* **1** curt or casual in manner. **2** without preparation etc. —*adv.* in an offhand way. —**offhanded** /-ˈhændɪd/ *adj.*, **offhandedly** *adv.*

office /ˈɒfɪs/ *n.* **1** a room or building used as a place of business, especially for clerical or administrative work; a room or department for a particular business. **2** a position with duties attached to it; tenure of an official position. **3** the quarters, staff, or collective authority of a government department. **4** a duty, a task, a function. **5** a piece of kindness, a service. **6** an authorized form of religious worship. **7** (in *pl.*) rooms in a house that are devoted to household work, storage, etc. [f. OF f. L *officium* (*opus* work, *facere* do)]

officer /ˈɒfɪsə(r)/ *n.* **1** a person holding a position of authority or trust, especially one with a commission in the armed services or mercantile marine, or on a passenger ship. **2** a policeman. **3** a holder of a post in a society (e.g. the president or secretary). —*v.t.* (usu. in *p.p.*) to provide with officers. [f. AF f. L *officiarius* (as prec.)]

official /əˈfɪʃ(ə)l/ *adj.* **1** of an office or its tenure. **2** characteristic of officials and bureaucracy. **3** properly authorized. —*n.* a person holding office or engaged in official duties. —**officialdom** *n.*, **officially** *adv.* [f. OF or L (as OFFICE)]

officiate /əˈfɪʃɪeɪt/ *v.i.* **1** to act in an official capacity. **2** to perform divine service. [f. L (as OFFICE)]

officious /əˈfɪʃəs/ *adj.* asserting one's authority, domineering; intrusively kind. —**officiously** *adv.* [f. L, = obliging (as OFFICE)]

offing *n.* the more distant part of the sea in view. —**in the offing**, not far away; likely to appear or happen. [perh. f. OFF]

offish *adj.* (*colloq.*) inclined to be aloof. [f. OFF]

offprint *n.* a printed copy of an article etc. originally forming part of a larger publication.

offset *n.* **1** a side-shoot from a plant serving for propagation. **2** compensation, a consideration or amount diminishing or neutralizing the effect of a contrary one. **3** a sloping ledge in a wall etc.; a bend in a pipe etc. to carry it past an obstacle. **4** (in full **offset process**) a method of printing with the transfer of ink from a plate or stone to a rubber or other surface and thence to paper. —/also -ˈset/ *v.t.* (**-tt-**; *p.p.* **offset**) **1** to counterbalance, to compensate. **2** to print by the offset process.

offshoot *n.* **1** a side-shoot or branch. **2** a derivative.

offshore *adj.* **1** at sea some distance from the shore. **2** (of a wind) blowing from the land towards the sea.

offside /ɒfˈsaɪd/ *adj.* (of a player in a field game) in a position where he may not play the ball.

offspring *n.* (*pl.* same) a person's child or children or descendants; an animal's young or descendants. [OE (as OF from, SPRING)]

oft /ɒft/ *adv.* (*archaic*) often. [OE]

often /ˈɒf(ə)n/ *adv.* **1** frequently, many times. **2** at short intervals. **3** in many instances. —**every so often**, from time to time. [extended f. prec.]

ogee /ˈəʊdʒiː, -ˈdʒiː/ *n.* a sinuous line of a double

continuous curve as in S; a moulding with such a section. [app. f. foll.]

ogham /ˈɒgəm/ *n.* **1** an ancient British and Irish alphabet of 20 characters, formed by parallel strokes on either side of or across a continuous line. **2** an inscription in this. **3** any of the characters. [OIr. *ogam*, referred to *Ogma* supposed inventor]

ogive /ˈəʊdʒaɪv, -ˈdʒaɪv/ *n.* **1** the diagonal rib of a vault. **2** a pointed arch. [f. F, ult. orig. unkn.]

ogle /ˈəʊg(ə)l/ *v.t./i.* to look amorously (at). —*n.* an amorous glance. [prob. f. LDu.]

ogre /ˈəʊgə(r)/ *n.* **1** a man-eating giant in folklore. **2** a terrifying person. —**ogress** *n.fem.*, **ogrish** *adj.* [f. F]

oh /əʊ/ *int.* expressing surprise, pain, entreaty, etc. [var. of O²]

ohm /əʊm/ *n.* a unit of electrical resistance, transmitting a current of one ampere when subjected to a potential difference of one volt. [f. G. S. *Ohm*, German physicist (d. 1854)]

OHMS *abbr.* On Her (or His) Majesty's Service.

oho /əʊˈhəʊ/ *int.* expressing surprise or exultation. [f. O² + HO]

oil *n.* **1** any of various liquid viscid unctuous, usually inflammable, chemically neutral substances lighter than and insoluble in water but soluble in alcohol and ether. **2** (*US*) petroleum. **3** (often in *pl.*) oil-colour. **4** an oil-painting. **5** (*colloq.*, usu. in *pl.*) oilskins. —*v.t.* **1** to apply oil to; to lubricate, impregnate, or treat with oil. **2** to supply oil to. —**oil-colour** *n.* (usu. in *pl.*) a paint made by mixing powdered pigment in oil. **oil-fired** *adj.* using oil as a fuel. **oil-paint** *n.* oil-colour. **oil-painting** *n.* the art of painting in oil-colours; a picture painted thus. **oil rig,** equipment for drilling an oil well. **oil-slick** *n.* a smooth patch of oil, especially on the sea. **oil well,** a well from which mineral oil is drawn. [f. AF f. L *oleum* olive oil]

oilcake *n.* compressed linseed from which oil has been expressed, used as cattle food or manure.

oilcloth *n.* a fabric, esp. canvas, water-proofed with oil.

oiled *adj.* (*slang*) drunk. [f. OIL]

oilfield *n.* a district yielding mineral oil.

oilskin *n.* cloth waterproofed with oil; a garment of this; (in *pl.*) a suit of this.

oily *adj.* **1** of or like oil. **2** covered or soaked with oil. **3** unpleasantly smooth in manner; ingratiating. —**oiliness** *n.* [f. OIL]

ointment /ˈɔɪntmənt/ *n.* a smooth greasy healing or beautifying preparation for the skin. [f. OF f. L (as UNGUENT)]

OK /əʊˈkeɪ/ (also **okay**) *adj.* & *adv.* all right, satisfactory; (as *int.*) I agree. —*n.* approval, agreement to a plan etc. —*v.t.* to give one's approval or agreement to. [orig. US, app. from the initials of *oll* (or *orl*) *korrect*, joc. spelling of *all correct*, and first used in 1839; it was used as a slogan for a candidate from Old Kinderhook in the American election of 1840; other suggestions about its origin are without acceptable foundation]

okapi /əˈkɑːpɪ/ *n.* a brightly coloured partially striped ruminant of Central Africa (*Okapia johnstoni*), discovered in 1900, resembling the giraffe but with a shorter neck and striped body. [Central Afr. native name]

okay var. of OK.

okra /ˈəʊkrə, ˈɒk-/ *n.* a tall originally African plant (*Hibiscus esculentus*) with seed-pods used for food. [W. Afr. native name]

old /əʊld/ *adj.* **1** having lived or existed for a long time. **2** made long ago; used, established, or known for a long time; shabby from age or wear. **3** having the characteristics, experience, feebleness, etc. of age; skilled through long experience. **4** not recent or modern; belonging chiefly to the past; former, original. **5** of a specified age (*ten years old*). **6** (*colloq.*) as a term of fondness or casual reference. —**the old,** old people. **of old,** of or in past times. **old age,** the later part of normal lifetime. **old-age pension,** a State pension paid to people above a certain age. **old-age pensioner,** a person receiving this. **old boy,** a former member of a school; (*colloq.*) an elderly man; (as a form of address) old man. **the old country,** one's mother country. **old-fashioned** *adj.* in or according to fashion or tastes no longer current, antiquated. **old girl,** a former member of a school; (*colloq.*) an elderly woman; (*colloq.*) as a fond form of address. **Old Glory,** (*US*) the Stars and Stripes. **old gold,** a dull brownish gold colour. **Old Guard,** the French Imperial Guard created by Napoleon I in 1804. **old guard,** the original or past or conservative members of a group. **old hat,** (*colloq.*) something tediously familiar. **old maid,** an elderly spinster; a prim and fussy person; a card game in which the object is to avoid the holding of an unpaired card. **old man,** (*colloq.*) one's father, husband, or employer etc.; (*colloq.*) as a fond form of address. **old man's beard,** a kind of clematis (*Clematis vitalba*) with grey fluffy hairs round the seeds. **old master,** a great painter of former times, especially of the 13th–17th c. in Europe, a painting by such a painter. **Old Nick,** the Devil. **Old Pals Act,** the doctrine that friends should always help one another. **Old Style,** (of a date) reckoned by the Julian calendar. **Old Testament,** the first 39 books of the Bible, the Hebrew scriptures containing an account of the creation and Jewish history. **old-time** *adj.* belonging to former times. **old-timer** *n.* a person with long experience or standing. **old wives' tale,** an old but foolish belief. **old woman,** (*colloq.*) a wife or mother; a fussy or timid man. **Old World,** Europe, Asia, and Africa, the part known by the ancients to exist. **old year,** the year just ended or about to end. —**oldness** *n.* [OE]

olden *adj.* (*archaic*) old; of old. [f. OLD]

oldie *n.* (*colloq.*) an old person or thing. [f. OLD]

oleaginous /əʊlɪ'ædʒɪnəs/ *adj.* **1** having the properties of or producing oil. **2** oily (*lit.* or *fig.*). [f. F f. L (as OIL)]

oleander /əʊlɪ'ændə(r)/ *n.* an evergreen flowering Mediterranean shrub (*Nerium oleander*). [L]

oleaster /əʊlɪ'æstə(r)/ *n.* a wild olive (*Olea oleaster*). [f. L (*olea* olive-tree)]

olefin /'əʊləfɪn/ *n.* a hydrocarbon of a type containing less than the maximum amount of hydrogen. [f. F *oléfiant* oil-forming]

O level ordinary level in the GCE examination. [abbr.]

olfactory /ɒl'fæktərɪ/ *adj.* concerned with smelling. [f. L *olfacere* to smell]

oligarch /'ɒlɪgɑːk/ *n.* a member of an oligarchy. [f. Gk (*oligoi* few, *arkhō* rule)]

oligarchy /'ɒlɪgɑːkɪ/ *n.* a form of government in which power is in the hands of a small group of people; this group; a State governed in this way. —**oligarchic** /-'gɑːkɪk/ *adj.*, **oligarchical** /-'gɑː-/ *adj.* [f. F or L f. Gk (as prec.)]

Oligocene /'ɒlɪgəsiːn/ *adj.* of the third epoch of the Tertiary period. —*n.* this epoch. [f. Gk *oligos* small + *kainos* new]

olive /'ɒlɪv/ *n.* **1** a small oval hard-stoned fruit, green when unripe and bluish-black when ripe. **2** the tree bearing it (*Olea europaea*); its wood. **3** leaves or a branch or wreath of olive as an emblem of peace. **4** the colour of an unripe olive. —*adj.* **1** of green colour like an unripe olive. **2** (of the complexion) yellowish-brown. —**olive-branch** *n.* something done or offered as the sign of a wish to make peace. **olive oil,** oil extracted from olives. [f. OF f. L *oliva* f. Gk]

olivine /'ɒlɪviːn/ *n.* a mineral, usually olive-green, composed of magnesium iron silicate. [f. L *oliva* olive]

Olympiad /ə'lɪmpɪæd/ *n.* **1** a period of four years between Olympic Games, used by the ancient Greeks in dating events. **2** a celebration of the modern Olympic Games. **3** a regular international contest in chess etc. [f. F or L f. Gk (as OLYMPIC)]

Olympian /ə'lɪmpɪən/ *adj.* **1** of Olympus, celestial. **2** (of manner etc.) magnificent, condescending, superior. **3** Olympic. —*n.* **1** a dweller in Olympus, a Greek god. **2** a person of great attainments or superhuman calm. [f. Mt. *Olympus* in Thessaly (where Greek gods were thought to dwell) or f. foll.]

Olympic /ə'lɪmpɪk/ *adj.* of the Olympic Games. —*n.* (in *pl.*) the Olympic Games. —**Olympic Games,** an ancient Greek athletic festival held at Olympia every four years; a modern international revival of this. [f. L f. Gk *Olumpikos* of Olympus or Olympia]

OM *abbr.* (Member of the) Order of Merit.

om (esp. in Buddhism and Hinduism) a mystic syllable, considered the most sacred mantra. It appears at the beginning and end of most Sanskrit recitations, prayers, and texts. [Skr., a universal affirmation]

ombudsman /'ɒmbʊdzmæn/ *n.* (*pl.* **-men**) an official appointed to investigate complaints by individuals against maladministration, esp. by public authorities.[Sw., = legal representative]

omega /'əʊmɪgə/ *n.* **1** the last letter of the Greek alphabet, = o. **2** the last of a series; the final development. [Gk, *ō mega* = great O]

omelette /'ɒmlɪt/ *n.* beaten eggs cooked in a frying pan and often served folded round a savoury or sweet filling. [F]

omen /'əʊmen/ *n.* an occurrence or thing regarded as a prophetic sign; prophetic significance. [L]

omicron /ə'maɪkrən/ *n.* the fifteenth letter of the Greek alphabet, = o. [Gk, *o micron* = small O]

ominous /'ɒmɪnəs/ *adj.* looking or seeming as if trouble is at hand, inauspicious. —**ominously** *adv.* [f. L (as OMEN)]

omission /ə'mɪʃ(ə)n/ *n.* **1** omitting, being omitted. **2** a thing omitted or not done. [f. OF or L (as foll.)]

omit /ə'mɪt/ *v.t.* (**-tt-**) **1** to leave out, not to insert or include. **2** to leave not done, to neglect or fail to do. [f. L *omittere* (OB-, *mittere* send)]

omni- *in comb.* all. [L (*omnis* all)]

omnibus /'ɒmnɪbəs/ *n.* **1** a bus. **2** a volume containing several novels etc. previously published separately. —*adj.* serving several objects at once; comprising several items. [F f. L, = for everybody]

omnifarious /ɒmnɪ'feərɪəs/ *adj.* of all sorts. [f. L (OMNI-; cf. MULTIFARIOUS)]

omnipotent /ɒm'nɪpət(ə)nt/ *adj.* all-powerful. —**omnipotence** *n.*, **omnipotently** *adv.* [f. OF f. L (as OMNI-, POTENT)]

omnipresent /ɒmnɪ'prez(ə)nt/ *adj.* ubiquitous. —**omnipresence** *n.* [f. L (as OMNI-, PRESENT)]

omniscient /ɒm'nɪsɪənt/ *adj.* knowing everything or much. —**omniscience** *n.* [f. L (OMNI-, *scire* know)]

omnivorous /ɒm'nɪvərəs/ *adj.* **1** feeding on many kinds of food, especially on both plants and flesh. **2** reading or observing etc.

whatever comes one's way. [f. L (OMNI-, *vorare* devour)]

on *prep.* **1** supported by, attached to, covering, enclosing; carried with. **2** during; exactly at; contemporaneously with; immediately after or before; as a result of. **3** having or so as to have membership of (a committee etc.). **4** supported financially by. **5** close to, just by; in the direction of, against, so as to threaten. **6** touching, striking. **7** having as a basis or motive; having as a standard, confirmation, or guarantee. **8** concerning; using, engaged with; so as to affect; to be paid by. **9** added to. **10** in a specified manner or state. —*adv.* **1** so as to be supported by, attached to, or covering something. **2** in an appropriate direction, towards something. **3** further toward; in an advanced position or state. **4** with continued movement or action. **5** in operation or activity; being shown or performed. —*adj.* (in cricket) being in, from, or towards the part of the field on the striker's side and in front of his wicket. —*n.* the on side in cricket. —**be on,** (of an event) to be due to take place; (*colloq.*) to be willing to participate or approve; to accept a proposition or wager; to be practicable or acceptable. **be on at,** (*colloq.*) to nag or grumble at. **be on to,** to realize the significance or intentions of. **on and off,** intermittently, now and then. **on and on,** continually, at tedious length. **on-line** *adj.* (of computer equipment or a computer process) directly controlled by or connected to a central processor. **on time,** punctual, punctually. **on to,** to a position on. [OE]

onager /ˈɒnəgə(r)/ *n.* a wild ass (esp. *Equus onager*). [f. L f. Gk (*onos* ass, *agrios* wild)]

onanism /ˈəʊnənɪz(ə)m/ *n.* masturbation. [f. F f. *Onan* (Gen. 38: 9)]

once /wʌns/ *adv.* **1** on one occasion only. **2** at some point or period in the past. **3** ever, at all. **4** multiplied by one; by one degree. —*conj.* as soon as. —*n.* one time or occasion. —**all at once,** without warning, suddenly; all together. **at once,** immediately; simultaneously. **(every) once in a while,** from time to time. **for once,** on this (or that) occasion, even if at no other. **once again** *or* **more,** another time. **once and for all,** in a final manner, esp. after much hesitation or uncertainty. **once or twice,** a few times. **once-over** *n.* (*colloq.*) a rapid preliminary inspection. **once upon a time,** at some vague time in the past. [orig. gen. of ONE]

oncology /ɒŋˈkɒlədʒɪ/ *n.* the study of tumours. [f. Gk *ogkos* mass + -LOGY]

oncoming *adj.* approaching from the front.

one /wʌn/ *adj.* **1** single and integral in number. **2** (with a noun implied) a single person or thing of a kind expressed or implied. **3** particular but undefined, especially as contrasted with another. **4** only such. **5** forming a unity. **6** identical, the same. —*n.* **1** the lowest cardinal numeral, a thing numbered with it (1, i, I); unity, a unit. **2** a single thing, person, or example (often referring to a noun previously expressed or implied). **3** a drink. **4** a story or joke. —*pron.* **1** a person of a specified kind. **2** any person, as representing people in general. **3** (*colloq.*) I. —**all one,** a matter of indifference (*to*). **at one,** in agreement. **one another,** each the other (as a formula of reciprocity). **one-armed bandit,** (*slang*) a fruit machine with a long handle. **one day,** on an unspecified day; at some unspecified future date. **one-horse,** *adj.* using a single horse; (*slang*) small, poorly equipped. **one-man** *adj.* involving or operated by only one man. **one-off** *adj.* (*colloq.*) made as the only one, not repeated. **one or two,** (*colloq.*) a few. **one-sided** *adj.* unfair, partial. **one-time** *adj.* former. **one-track mind,** a mind preoccupied with one subject. **one-up** *adj.* (*colloq.*) having a particular advantage. **one-upmanship** *n.* (*colloq.*) the art of maintaining a psychological advantage. **one-way** *adj.* allowing movement, travel, etc., in one direction only. [OE]

oneness *n.* **1** being one, singleness, uniqueness. **2** agreement. **3** sameness, changelessness. [f. ONE]

onerous /ˈɒnərəs, ˈəʊn-/ *adj.* burdensome. [f. OF f. L (*onus* burden)]

oneself /wʌnˈself/ *pron.* the reflexive and emphatic form of *one.*

ongoing *adj.* continuing, in progress.

onion /ˈʌnjən/ *n.* a vegetable (*Allium cepa*) with an edible bulb of pungent smell and flavour. —**oniony** *adj.* [f. AF f. L *unio*]

onlooker *n.* a spectator.

only /ˈəʊnlɪ/ *attrib. adj.* **1** existing alone of its or their kind. **2** best or alone worth knowing. —*adv.* **1** without anything or anyone else, and that is all. **2** no longer ago than; not until. **3** with no better result than. —*conj.* except that, but then. —**if only,** I wish that. **only too,** extremely. [OE (as ONE)]

o.n.o. *abbr.* or near offer.

onomatopoeia /ɒnəmætəˈpiːə/ *n.* formation of a word from a sound resembling that associated with the thing named (e.g. *cuckoo, sizzle*). —**onomatopoeic** *adj.* [L f. Gk (*onoma* name, *poieō* make)]

onrush *n.* an onward rush.

onset *n.* **1** an attack. **2** a beginning.

onshore *adj.* **1** on the shore. **2** (of a wind) blowing from the sea towards the land.

onside *adj.* (of a player in a field game) not offside.

onslaught /ˈɒnslɔːt/ *n.* a fierce attack. [f. MDu. (as ON, *slag* blow)]

ontology /ɒn'tɒlədʒɪ/ *n.* the branch of metaphysics dealing with the nature of being. —**ontological** /-'lɒdʒɪk(ə)l/ *adj.* [f. Gk *ont-* being + -LOGY]

onus /'əʊnəs/ *n.* a burden, a duty, a responsibility. [L]

onward /'ɒnwəd/ *adv.* (also **onwards**) further on; towards the front; with advancing motion. —*adj.* directed onwards. [f. ON + -WARD]

onyx /'ɒnɪks/ *n.* a kind of chalcedony with coloured layers. [f. OF f. L f. Gk, orig. = finger-nail]

oodles /'u:d(ə)lz/ *n. pl.* (*colloq.*) a very great amount. [orig. US; etym. unkn.]

ooh /u:/ *int.* expressing surprise, delight, pain, etc. [natural exclam.]

oolite /'əʊəlaɪt/ *n.* a granular limestone. —**oolitic** /-'lɪtɪk/ *adj.* [f. F (Gk *ōon* egg, *lithos* stone)]

oops /ʊps, u:ps/ *int.* on making an obvious mistake. [natural excl.]

ooze *v.t./i.* **1** (of a fluid) to trickle or leak slowly out. **2** to exude moisture. **3** to exude or exhibit (a feeling) freely. —*n.* **1** wet mud. **2** a sluggish flow. —**oozy** *adj.* [f. OE *wos* juice, sap]

op *n.* (*colloq.*) an operation. [abbr.]

op- see OB-.

op. *abbr.* opus.

opacity /əʊ'pæsɪtɪ/ *n.* opaqueness. [f. F f. L (as OPAQUE)]

opal /'əʊp(ə)l/ *n.* a precious stone usually of a milky or bluish colour with iridescent reflections. [f. F or L, prob. ult. f. Skr. *upalas* precious stone]

opalescent /əʊpə'les(ə)nt/ *adj.* iridescent. —**opalescence** *n.* [f. OPAL]

opaline /'əʊpəlaɪn/ *adj.* opal-like, opalescent. [f. OPAL]

opaque /əʊ'peɪk/ *adj.* **1** not transmitting light, impenetrable to sight. **2** unclear, obscure. [f. L *opacus*]

op art (*colloq.*) optical art (see OPTICAL). [abbr.]

op. cit. *abbr.* in the work already quoted. [f. L *opere citato*]

OPEC /'əʊpek/ *abbr.* Organization of Petroleum-Exporting Countries, an association of the eleven major oil-producing countries.

open /'əʊpən/ *adj.* **1** not closed or locked or blocked up; not sealed; giving access. **2** not covered or concealed or confined; not restricted. **3** spread out, unfolded, expanded. **4** with wide spaces between solid parts. **5** undisguised, public, manifest. **6** (of an exhibition, shop, etc.) admitting visitors or customers, ready for business. **7** (of a competition etc.) unrestricted as to who may compete. **8** not yet settled or decided; (of an offer or vacancy) still available; (with *to*) willing or liable to receive. **9** (of the bowels) not constipated. —*n.* **1** *the* open air; *the* country. **2** an open competition or championship. —*v.t./i.* **1** to make or become open or more open. **2** to begin or establish; to make a start. **3** to declare ceremonially to be open to the public. —**open air**, outdoors. **open-and-shut** *adj.* (*colloq.*) perfectly straightforward. **open book,** one who is easily understood; not having secrets. **open day,** a day when the public may visit a place normally closed to them. **open-ended** *adj.* without limit or restriction. **open a person's eyes,** to make him realize something unexpected. **open-handed** *adj.* generous. **open-hearted** *adj.* frank and kindly. **open-heart surgery,** surgery with the heart exposed and blood made to bypass it. **open letter,** a letter of protest etc. addressed to a person by name but printed in a newspaper etc. **open-minded** *adj.* accessible to new ideas, unprejudiced; undecided. **open-plan** *adj.* with few interior walls. **open prison,** a prison with few physical restraints on prisoners. **open question,** a matter on which no final verdict has yet been made or on which none is possible. **open sandwich,** a slice of bread covered with a layer of meat or cheese etc. **open sea,** the expanse of sea away from the land. **open secret,** one known to so many people that it is no longer a secret. **open society,** one without a rigid structure and with freedom of belief. **open verdict,** one affirming the commission of a crime but not specifying a criminal or (in the case of violent death) a cause. —**openness** *n.* [OE (as UP)]

opencast *adj.* (of a mine or mining) with removal of surface layers and working from above, not from shafts.

opener *n.* **1** a person or thing that opens something. **2** a device for opening tins or bottles etc. [f. OPEN]

opening *n.* **1** a space or gap; a place where something opens. **2** the beginning of something. **3** an opportunity. —**opening-time** *n.* the time at which public houses may legally open for custom. [f. OPEN]

openly *adv.* without concealment, publicly; frankly. [f. OPEN]

opera[1] /'ɒpərə/ *n.* a dramatic performance or composition of which music is an essential part; the branch of art concerned with this. —**opera-glasses** *n.pl.* small binoculars for use at the opera or theatre. **opera-hat** *n.* a man's collapsible hat. **opera-house** *n.* a theatre for operas. [It. f. L, = labour, work]

opera[2] *pl.* of OPUS.

operable /'ɒpərəb(ə)l/ *adj.* **1** that can be operated. **2** suitable for treatment by a surgical operation. [f. L (as foll.)]

operate /ˈɒpəreɪt/ *v.t./i.* 1 to be in action; to produce an effect. 2 to control the functioning of. 3 to perform a surgical operation. —**operating-theatre** *n.* a room for surgical operations. [f. L *operari* to work (as OPUS)]

operatic /ɒpəˈrætɪk/ *adj.* of or like an opera. —**operatically** *adv.* [f. OPERA¹]

operation /ɒpəˈreɪʃ(ə)n/ *n.* 1 operating, being operated; the way a thing works; validity, scope. 2 a piece of work, something to be done. 3 an act performed by a surgeon on any part of the body to remove or deal with a diseased, injured, or deformed part. 4 a piece of military activity. 5 a financial or other transaction. 6 (*Math.*) the subjection of a number, quantity, or function to a process affecting its value or form, e.g. multiplication, differentiation. [f. OF f. L (as OPERATE)]

operational *adj.* 1 of, engaged in, or used for operations. 2 able or ready to function. —**operational research**, the application of scientific principles to business etc. management. —**operationally** *adv.* [f. prec.]

operative /ˈɒpərətɪv/ *adj.* 1 in operation, having an effect; practical; having principal relevance. 2 of or by surgery. —*n.* a worker, especially in a factory. —**operatively** *adv.* [f. L (as OPERATE)]

operator /ˈɒpəreɪtə(r)/ *n.* 1 a person who operates a machine etc.; one who engages in business; (*colloq.*) a person acting in a specified way. 2 one who makes connections of lines at a telephone exchange. 3 (*Math.*) a symbol or function denoting an operation. [as OPERATE]

operculum /əˈpɜːkjʊləm/ *n.* (*pl.* **-ula**) a fish's gill-cover; a similar structure in a plant; the valve closing the mouth of a shell. [L (*operire* to cover)]

operetta /ɒpəˈretə/ *n.* a one-act or short opera; a light opera. [It. (dim. of OPERA)]

ophidian /əˈfɪdɪən/ *n.* a member of the Ophidia or Serpentes, a suborder of reptiles including the snakes; a snake. —*adj.* of this order; snakelike. [f. Gk *ophis* snake]

ophthalmia /ɒfˈθælmɪə/ *n.* inflammation of the eye, especially conjunctivitis. [L f. Gk (*ophthalmos* eye)]

ophthalmic /ɒfˈθælmɪk/ *adj.* 1 of or for the eye. 2 of, for, or affected with ophthalmia. —**ophthalmic optician**, an optician qualified to prescribe as well as dispense spectacles etc. [f. L (as prec.)]

ophthalmology /ɒfθælˈmɒlədʒɪ/ *n.* the study of the eye and its diseases. —**ophthalmologist** *n.* [f. Gk *ophthalmos* eye + -LOGY]

ophthalmoscope /ɒfˈθælməskəʊp/ *n.* an instrument for examining the eye. [as prec. + -SCOPE]

opiate /ˈəʊpɪət/ *adj.* 1 containing opium. 2 narcotic, soporific. —*n.* 1 a drug containing opium and easing pain or inducing sleep. 2 a soothing influence. [f. L (as OPIUM)]

opine /əʊˈpaɪn/ *v.t.* to express or hold as one's opinion. [f. L *opinari* believe]

opinion /əˈpɪnjən/ *n.* 1 a belief based on grounds short of proof, a view held as probable. 2 what one thinks about something. 3 a piece of professional advice. —**opinion poll**, an estimate of public opinion made by questioning a representative sample of people. [f. OF f. L *opinio* (as prec.)]

opinionated /əˈpɪnjəneɪtɪd/ *adj.* having strong opinions and holding them dogmatically. [f. prec.]

opium /ˈəʊpɪəm/ *n.* a drug made from the juice of the poppy *Papaver somniferum*, used especially as a narcotic or sedative. [f. L f. Gk *opion*]

opossum /əˈpɒsəm/ *n.* 1 an American marsupial of the family Didelphidae. 2 a similar Australian marsupial of the family Phalangeridae, living in trees. [f. Virginian Indian]

opp. *abbr.* opposite.

opponent /əˈpəʊnənt/ *n.* a person or group opposing another in a contest or war. [f. L *opponere* set against (OP-, *ponere* place)]

opportune /ˈɒpətjuːn/ *adj.* (of time) well-chosen, favourable; (of an action or event) well-timed. —**opportunely** *adv.* [f. OF f. L *opportunus* (OP-, *portus* harbour), orig. of wind driving ship towards harbour]

opportunism /ˈɒpətjuːnɪz(ə)m/ *n.* the grasping of opportunities, often in an unprincipled way. —**opportunist** *n.* [f. prec.]

opportunity /ɒpəˈtjuːnɪtɪ/ *n.* a time or set of circumstances suitable for a particular purpose. [f. OF f. L (as OPPORTUNE)]

oppose /əˈpəʊz/ *v.t.* 1 to place in opposition or contrast. 2 to set oneself against, to resist; to argue against. —**as opposed to**, in contrast with. [f. OF f. L (as OPPONENT)]

opposite /ˈɒpəzɪt/ *adj.* 1 (often with *to*) having a position on the other or further side, facing or back to back. 2 of a contrary kind, as different as possible. —*n.* an opposite thing, person, or term. —*adv.* in the opposite position. —*prep.* opposite to. —**opposite number**, a person holding the equivalent position in another group or organization. [as prec.]

opposition /ɒpəˈzɪʃ(ə)n/ *n.* 1 resistance, being hostile or in conflict or disagreement. 2 placing or being placed opposite, contrast; a diametrically opposite position, esp. of two heavenly bodies when their longitude differs by 180° (opp. *conjunction*). 3 the people who oppose a proposal etc.; a group of opponents or rivals. —**the Opposition**, the chief parliamentary party opposed to that in office. [f. OF f. L (as OB-, POSITION)]

oppress /əˈpres/ *v.t.* **1** to govern harshly, to treat with continual cruelty or injustice; to keep in subservience. **2** to weigh down with cares or unhappiness. —**oppression** *n.*, **oppressor** *n.* [f. OF f. L (as OP-, PRESS)]

oppressive *adj.* **1** oppressing. **2** difficult to endure. **3** (of weather) sultry and tiring. —**oppressively** *adv.*, **oppressiveness** *n.* [f. F f. L (as prec.)]

opprobrious /əˈprəʊbrɪəs/ *adj.* (of language) severely scornful, abusive. [f. L (as foll.)]

opprobrium /əˈprəʊbrɪəm/ *n.* great disgrace brought by shameful conduct. [L, f. *opprobrium* disgraceful act]

oppugn /əˈpju:n/ *v.t.* to controvert, to call in question. [f. L *oppugnare* attack (OP-, *pugnare* fight)]

opt *v.i.* to make a choice, to decide (*for* an alternative). —**opt out (of)**, to choose not to participate (in). [f. F f. L *optare* choose, wish]

optative /ɒpˈteɪtɪv, ˈɒptə-/ *adj.* (*Gram.*, esp. of a mood in Greek) expressing a wish. [f. F f. L (as prec.)]

optic /ˈɒptɪk/ *adj.* of the eye or sight. [f. F or L f. Gk (*optos* seen)]

optical /ˈɒptɪk(ə)l/ *adj.* **1** of sight, visual. **2** aiding sight. **3** of or according to optics. —**optical art**, a form of art using optical effects to provide illusions of movement etc. **optical fibre**, thin glass fibre used in fibre optics. **optical illusion**, an involuntary mental misinterpretation of a thing seen, due to its deceptive appearance (e.g. a mirage). —**optically** *adv.* [f. prec.]

optician/ɒpˈtɪʃ(ə)n/ *n.* a maker or seller of spectacles and other optical instruments; one trained to provide means to correct the defects of people's eyesight. [f. F f. L (as OPTIC)]

optics /ˈɒptɪks/ *n.pl.* (usu. treated as *sing.*) the science of light and vision. [f. OPTIC]

optimal /ˈɒptɪm(ə)l/ *adj.* the best or most favourable. [f. L *optimus* best]

optimism /ˈɒptɪmɪz(ə)m/ *n.* **1** a hopeful view or disposition; a tendency to expect a favourable outcome. **2** the belief that the actual world is the best possible. **3** the belief that good must ultimately prevail over evil. —**optimist** *n.* [f. F f. L (as OPTIMUM)]

optimistic /ɒptɪˈmɪstɪk/ *adj.* showing optimism; hopeful. —**optimistically** *adv.* [f. F f. L *optimum* best]

optimize /ˈɒptɪmaɪz/ *v.t.* to make optimum, to make the most of. [f. L *optimus* best]

optimum /ˈɒptɪməm/ *n.* (*pl.* **-ima**) the best or most favourable conditions or amount etc. —*adj.* optimal. [L, neut. of *optimus* best]

option /ˈɒpʃ(ə)n/ *n.* **1** a choice; a thing that is or may be chosen. **2** the liberty of choosing. **3** the right to buy or sell something at a certain price within a limited time. —**keep** *or* **leave one's options open**, to remain uncommitted. [F or f. L (as OPT)]

optional *adj.* open to choice, not obligatory. —**optionally** *adv.* [f. prec.]

opulent /ˈɒpjʊlənt/ *adj.* **1** wealthy. **2** abundant, luxuriant. **3** luxurious. —**opulence** *n.*, **opulently** *adv.* [f. L (*opes* wealth)]

opus /ˈəʊpəs, ˈɒp-/ *n.* (*pl.* **opera** /ˈɒpərə/) a musical composition numbered as one of a composer's works. [L, = work]

or[1] *conj.* introducing an alternative or another name for the same thing or an afterthought. [OE]

or[2] *n.* & *adj.* (usu. placed after *n.*) (in heraldry) gold, yellow. [F f. L *aurum*]

oracle /ˈɒrək(ə)l/ *n.* **1** (in classical antiquity) a place where deities were consulted through the medium of a priest etc. for advice or prophecy; the reply given. **2** a person or thing regarded as a source of wisdom etc. **3** Oracle [P], the teletext service provided by the IBA. —**oracular** /ɒˈrækjʊlə(r)/ *adj.* [f. OF f. L (*orare* speak)]

oral /ˈɔr(ə)l/ *adj.* **1** spoken, verbal, by word of mouth. **2** done or taken by mouth. —*n.* (*colloq.*) a spoken examination. —**orally** *adv.* [f. L (*os* mouth)]

orange /ˈɒrɪndʒ/ *n.* **1** a round juicy citrus fruit with reddish-yellow peel; the tree bearing it (*Citrus aurantium*). **2** reddish-yellow colour. —*adj.* orange-coloured. —**orangeblossom** *n.* the fragrant white flowers of the orange, traditionally worn by brides. [f. OF ult. f. Arab. *nāranj* f. Pers.]

orangeade /ɒrɪndʒˈeɪd/ *n.* a drink made from orange-juice or a synthetic substitute. [f. prec.]

Orangeman *n.* (*pl.* **-men**) a member of a political society formed in 1795 to support Protestantism in Ireland. [f. William of *Orange*]

orangery /ˈɒrɪndʒərɪ/ *n.* a building or hot-house for orange-trees. [f ORANGE]

orang-utan /ɔræŋu:ˈtæn/ *n.* a large long-armed anthropoid ape (*Pongo pygmaeus*) of the East Indies. [Malay, = wild man]

oration /ɔˈreɪʃ(ə)n/ *n.* a formal or ceremonial speech. [f. L *oratio* (*orare* speak, pray)]

orator /ˈɒrətə(r)/ *n.* a maker of a formal speech; a skilful speaker. [f. AF f. L (as prec.)]

oratorical /ɒrəˈtɒrɪk(ə)l/ *adj.* of or like oratory. [f. ORATORY]

oratorio /ɒrəˈtɔ:rɪəʊ/ *n.* (*pl.* **-os**) **1** a musical composition, usually on a sacred theme, for solo voices, chorus, and orchestra. **2** this as a musical form. [It. (as foll.), orig. of musical services held at Oratory of St Philip Neri in Rome]

oratory[1] /ˈɒrətərɪ/ *n.* the art of or skill in public speaking. [f. L *oratoria* (*ars* art) of speaking (as ORATION)]

oratory[2] /ˈɒrətərɪ/ *n.* a small chapel, a place for private worship. [f. AF f. L *oratorium* (as ORATOR)]

orb *n.* **1** a sphere, a globe. **2** a globe surmounted by a cross as part of the royal regalia; a heavenly body. **3** (*poetic*) the eye. [f. L *orbis* ring]

orbicular /ɔːˈbɪkjʊlə(r)/ *adj.* spherical, circular. [f. L (*orbiculus* dim. of *orbis*, as prec.)]

orbit /ˈɔːbɪt/ *n.* **1** the curved (usually closed) course of a planet, comet, satellite, spacecraft, etc., the closed path followed by an object constrained by a tangential velocity to remain bound to a massive body (a planet or star) while not falling directly towards the centre of attraction. **2** the path of an electron round an atomic nucleus. **3** a range or sphere of action. —*v.t./i.* **1** to move in an orbit (round). **2** to put into orbit. —**orbiter** *n.* [f. L, = track of wheel or moon (*orbis* ring)]

orbital /ˈɔːbɪt(ə)l/ *adj.* **1** of an orbit or orbits. **2** (of a road) passing round the outside of a city. —*n.* a state or function representing the possible motion of an electron round an atomic nucleus. —**orbitally** *adv.* [f. prec.]

Orcadian /ɔːˈkeɪdɪən/ *n.* a native or inhabitant of Orkney. —*adj.* of Orkney. [f. L *Orcades* Orkney Islands]

orchard /ˈɔːtʃəd/ *n.* an enclosed piece of land planted with fruit-trees. [OE (L *hortus* garden, YARD[2])]

orchestra /ˈɔːkɪstrə/ *n.* **1** a body of musicians playing together on stringed, wind, and percussion instruments according to an established scheme. **2** the area in a theatre etc. assigned to them (called orchestra-pit when on a lower level). **3** the semicircular space in front of the stage of an ancient Greek theatre, where the chorus danced and sang. —**orchestral** /ɔːˈkestr(ə)l/ *adj.* [L f. Gk (*orkheomai* to dance)]

orchestrate /ˈɔːkɪstreɪt/ *v.t.* **1** to compose, arrange, or score for an orchestral performance. **2** to arrange or combine (various elements) harmoniously or for maximum effect. —**orchestration** /-ˈstreɪʃ(ə)n/ *n.* [f. prec.]

orchid /ˈɔːkɪd/ *n.* any plant of the family Orchidaceae, often with brilliant flowers. [f. L *orchis* f. Gk, orig. = testicle (from shape of tuber in some species)]

ordain /ɔːˈdeɪn/ *v.t.* **1** to appoint ceremonially to perform religious duties in the Christian Church. **2** to destine. **3** to appoint or decree authoritatively. [f. AF f. L *ordinare* (*ordo -inis* order)]

ordeal /ɔːˈdiːl/ *n.* **1** a severe or testing trial or experience. **2** (*hist.*) a method of determining guilt by making a suspect undergo physical harm, the safe endurance of which betokened innocence. [OE]

order *n.* **1** a condition in which every part or unit is in its right place or in a normal or efficient state; the arrangement of things relative to one another; a proper or customary sequence. **2** the prevalence of constitutional authority and obedience to the law. **3** a system of rules or procedure. **4** a command, an authoritative instruction; a direction to supply something, the thing (to be) supplied; a written instruction to pay money or giving authority to do something. **5** a social class or rank. **6** a monastic organization or institution; a Masonic or similar fraternity; a company to which distinguished persons are admitted as an honour or reward; the insignia of this. **7** any of the ancient orders of architecture (see below). **8** a group of plants or animals classified as similar in many ways, below a class and above a family. —*v.t.* **1** to put in order, to arrange methodically. **2** to command; to prescribe. **3** to give an order for (goods etc.); to tell a waiter etc. to serve. —**holy orders,** the status of an ordained clergyman. **in order,** in correct sequence or position; according to rules etc.; in good condition. **in order to** *or* **that,** with the intention that; for the purpose of. **on order,** ordered but not yet received. **Order in Council,** a sovereign's order on an administrative matter given by the advice of the Privy Council. **order-paper** *n.* a written or printed order of a day's proceedings, especially in Parliament. **orders of architecture,** the styles of ancient architecture distinguished by the type of column used (Doric, Ionic, Corinthian, Tuscan, and Composite). **out of order,** not in order. **to order,** as specified by a customer. [f. OF *ordre* f. L *ordo*]

orderly /ˈɔːdəlɪ/ *adj.* **1** well arranged, in good order; tidy. **2** methodical. **3** obedient to discipline, well-behaved. —*n.* **1** a soldier in attendance on an officer to assist him or take messages etc. **2** an attendant in a hospital. —**orderly officer,** the officer on duty on a particular day. **orderly room,** a room where business is conducted in a military barracks. —**orderliness** *n.* [f. prec.]

ordinal /ˈɔːdɪn(ə)l/ *adj.* (of a number) defining a thing's position in a series (e.g. *first, tenth, hundredth*). —*n.* an ordinal number. [f. L (as ORDER)]

ordinance /ˈɔːdɪnəns/ *n.* **1** a decree. **2** a religious rite. [f. OF f. L (as ORDAIN)]

ordinand /ˈɔːdɪnænd/ *n.* a candidate for ordination. [f. L (as ORDAIN)]

ordinary /ˈɔːdɪnərɪ/ *adj.* usual, customary, not exceptional. —*n.* a rule or book laying down the order of divine service. —**in the ordinary way,** in normal circumstances, usually. **ordinary level,** the lowest level in the GCE examination. **ordinary seaman,** a seaman of a lower rating than an able seaman. **out of the ordinary,** unusual. —**ordinarily** *adv.* [f. L *ordinarius* (as ORDER)]

ordinate /ˈɔːdɪnət/ *n.* (*Math.*) a coordinate measured usually vertically. [f. L (as ORDAIN)]

ordination /ɔːdɪˈneɪʃ(ə)n/ *n.* ordaining, conferring of holy orders. [f. OF or L (as ORDAIN)]

ordnance /ˈɔːdnəns/ *n.* artillery and military supplies; the government department dealing with these. —**Ordnance Survey,** the government survey of the British Isles producing accurate and detailed maps of the whole country. [var. of ORDINANCE]

ordure /ˈɔːdjʊə(r)/ *n.* dung. [f. OF (*ord* foul f. L *horridus*)]

ore /ɔː(r)/ *n.* solid rock or mineral from which metal or other valuable substances may be extracted. [OE]

oregano /ɒrɪˈɡɑːnəʊ/ *n.* dried wild marjoram as a seasoning. [Sp., = ORIGAN]

organ /ˈɔːɡən/ *n.* **1** a musical instrument consisting of pipes that sound when air is forced through them, operated by keyboards and pedals; a similar electronic instrument without pipes; a harmonium. **2** a part of an animal or plant body serving a particular function. **3** a medium of communication (e.g. a newspaper) representing a party or interest. —**organ-grinder** *n.* the player of a barrel-organ. **organ-loft** *n.* a gallery for an organ. [OE & f. OF f. L f. Gk *organon* tool]

organdie /ˈɔːɡəndɪ, -ˈɡændɪ/ *n.* fine translucent muslin, usually stiffened. [f. F]

organic /ɔːˈɡænɪk/ *adj.* **1** of or affecting a bodily organ or organs. **2** (of plants or animals) having organs or an organized physical structure. **3** (of food etc.) produced without the use of artificial fertilizers or pesticides. **4** organized or arranged as a system of related parts. **5** (of a compound etc.) containing carbon in its molecules. **6** inherent, structural. —**organic chemistry,** the chemistry of carbon compounds, which are present in all living matter and in substances derived from it. —**organically** *adv.* [f. F f. L f. Gk *organikos* (as ORGAN)]

organism /ˈɔːɡənɪz(ə)m/ *n.* **1** an individual animal or plant. **2** an organized body. [f. F (as ORGANIZE)]

organist /ˈɔːɡənɪst/ *n.* the player of an organ. [f. ORGAN]

organization /ɔːɡənaɪˈzeɪʃ(ə)n/ *n.* **1** organizing, being organized. **2** an organized body of people; an organized system. —**organizational** *adj.* [f. foll.]

organize /ˈɔːɡənaɪz/ *v.t.* **1** to give an orderly structure to, to systematize. **2** to initiate or make arrangements for; to enlist (a person or group) in this. **3** to make organic, to make into living tissue. —**organizer** *n.* [f. OF f. L (as ORGAN)]

organza /ɔːˈɡænzə/ *n.* a thin stiff transparent dress-fabric of silk or synthetic fibre. [prob. f. *Lorganza* (US trade mark)]

orgasm /ˈɔːɡæz(ə)m/ *n.* the climax of sexual excitement. **orgasmic** /-ˈɡæzmɪk/ *adj.* [f. F f. Gk (*orgaō* swell)]

orgy /ˈɔːdʒɪ/ *n.* **1** a wild drunken or licentious party or revelry. **2** excessive indulgence in an activity. **3** (in ancient Greece and Rome) secret rites in the worship of various gods, especially Bacchus, with wild drinking etc. —**orgiastic** /-ˈæstɪk/ *adj.* [f. F f. L f. Gk *orgia* pl.]

oriel /ˈɔːrɪəl/ *n.* a polygonal recess with windows projecting from the wall of a house at an upper level. [f. OF *oriol* gallery]

Orient /ˈɔːrɪənt/ *n.* the East, the countries east of the Mediterranean, especially East Asia. [f. OF f. L *oriens* rising, sunrise (*oriri* rise)]

orient /ˈɔːrɪənt/ *v.t.* **1** to place or determine the position of with regard to the points of the compass. **2** to site (a building etc.) so that it faces east. **3** to face or turn (towards a specified direction); to bring into clearly understood relations, to direct. —**orient oneself,** to get one's bearings; to accustom oneself to a new situation etc. [= prec.]

oriental /ɔːrɪˈent(ə)l, ɒr-/ *adj.* of the Orient, of the eastern or East Asian world or its civilization. —*n.* a native or inhabitant of the Orient. [as ORIENT]

orientate /ˈɔːrɪenteɪt/ *v.t./i.* to orient. [f. foll.]

orientation /ɔːrɪənˈteɪʃ(ə)n/ *n.* **1** orienting, being oriented. **2** position relative to surroundings. [f. ORIENT]

orienteering /ɔːrɪənˈtɪərɪŋ/ *n.* the competitive sport of finding one's way on foot across rough country with map and compass. [f. Sw. *orientering*]

orifice /ˈɒrɪfɪs/ *n.* an aperture, the mouth of a cavity, a vent. [F f. L *orificium* (*os* mouth)]

origami /ɒrɪˈɡɑːmɪ/ *n.* the art of folding paper intricately into decorative shapes. [Jap.]

origan /ˈɒrɪɡən/ *n.* (also **origanum** /-ˈɡɑːnəm/) wild marjoram (*Origanum vulgare*). [f. L f. Gk]

origin /ˈɒrɪdʒɪn/ *n.* **1** the point, source, or cause from which a thing begins its existence. **2** parentage, ancestry. **3** (*Math.*) a point from which coordinates are measured. [f. F or L *origo* (*oriri* rise)]

original /əˈrɪdʒɪn(ə)l/ *adj.* 1 existing from the first, earliest; primitive; innate. 2 that has served as a pattern, of which a copy or translation has been made. 3 new in concept, not derived or imitative. 4 thinking or acting for oneself, inventive, creative. —*n.* the first form of something, the thing from which another is copied or translated. —**original sin,** (in Christian theology) the innate depravity held to be common to all human beings in consequence of the Fall. —**originality** /-ˈnælɪtɪ/ *n.*, **originally** *adv.* [f. OF or L (as prec.)]

originate /əˈrɪdʒɪneɪt/ *v.t./i.* 1 to have its origin, to begin. 2 to initiate or give origin to; to be the origin of. —**origination** /-ˈneɪʃ(ə)n/ *n.*, **originator** *n.* [f. L (as ORIGIN)]

oriole /ˈɔːrɪəʊl/ *n.* a bird of the genus *Oriolus*, especially (**golden oriole**) one with black and yellow plumage in the male. [f. OF f. L *aureolus* (*aureus* golden)]

ormolu /ˈɔːməluː/ *n.* 1 gilded bronze. 2 a gold-coloured alloy. 3 articles made of or decorated with ormolu. [f. F *or moulu* powdered gold]

ornament /ˈɔːnəmənt/ *n.* 1 a decorative object or detail. 2 decoration, adornment. 3 a person or quality that brings honour or adds distinction. —/-ment/ *v.t.* to decorate; to be an ornament to. —**ornamental** /-ˈment(ə)l/ *adj.*, **ornamentally** *adv.*, **ornamentation** /-ˈteɪʃ(ə)n/ *n.* [f. AF f. L (*ornare* adorn)]

ornate /ɔːˈneɪt/ *adj.* elaborately ornamented; (of literary style) embellished with flowery language. [f. L (as prec.)]

ornithology /ɔːnɪˈθɒlədʒɪ/ *n.* the study of birds. —**ornithological** /-ˈlɒdʒɪk(ə)l/ *adj.*, **ornithologist** *n.* [f. Gk (*ornis* bird, -LOGY)]

orogenesis /ɒrəˈdʒenɪsɪs/ *n.* the process of formation of mountains. —**orogenetic** /-dʒɪˈnetɪk/ *adj.* [f. Gk *oros* mountain + GENESIS]

orogeny /ɔˈrɒdʒənɪ/ *n.* 1 orogenesis. 2 a geological period of mountain-building. —**orogenic** /ɔrəˈdʒenɪk/ *adj.* [as prec.]

orotund /ˈɒrətʌnd/ *adj.* (of an utterance) dignified, imposing; pompous. [f. L *ore rotundo*, lit. 'with round mouth']

orphan /ˈɔːf(ə)n/ *n.* a child whose parents are dead. —*adj.* being an orphan; of or for orphans. —*v.t.* to make (a child) an orphan. [f. L f. Gk, = bereaved]

orphanage *n.* an institution where orphans are housed and cared for. [f. prec.]

Orphic /ˈɔːfɪk/ *adj.* of Orpheus or the mystic religion associated with him. —**Orphism** *n.* [f. *Orpheus*, legendary Gk poet and musician]

orpiment /ˈɔːpɪmənt/ *n.* arsenic trisulphide as a mineral, formerly used as a yellow dye and artists' pigment. [f. OF f. L *auripigmentum* (*aurum* gold, *pigmentum* pigment)]

orrery /ˈɒrərɪ/ *n.* a clockwork model of the planetary system. [f. 4th Earl of *Orrery*, for whom one was made]

orris /ˈɒrɪs/ *n.* a kind of iris, especially *Iris florentina*. —**orris-root** *n.* a violet-scented iris root used in perfumery etc. [app. alt. of IRIS]

ortho- *in comb.* right, straight, correct. [f. Gk *orthos* straight]

orthoclase /ˈɔːθəkleɪz/ *n.* common felspar in crystals with two cleavages at right angles. [f. ORTHO- + Gk *klasis* breaking]

orthodontics /ɔːθəˈdɒntɪks/ *n.* correction of irregularities in the teeth and jaws. —**orthodontic** *adj.*, **orthodontist** *n.* [f. ORTHO- + Gk *odous* tooth]

orthodox /ˈɔːθədɒks/ *adj.* holding the usual or currently accepted views, especially on religion; generally approved, conventional. —**Orthodox Church,** the Eastern or Greek Church, recognizing the Patriarch of Constantinople as its head, and the national Churches of Russia, Romania, etc., in communion with it. —**orthodoxy** *n.* [f. L f. Gk (ORTHO-, *doxa* opinion)]

orthography /ɔːˈθɒgrəfɪ/ *n.* spelling (esp. with reference to its correctness). —**orthographic** /-ˈgræfɪk/ *adj.*, **orthographical** *adj.* [f. OF f. L f. Gk (as ORTHO-, -GRAPHY)]

orthopaedics /ɔːθəˈpiːdɪks/ *n.* the branch of surgery dealing with the correction of deformities of the bones or muscles, originally in children. —**orthopaedic** *adj.*, **orthopaedist** *n.* [f. F (ORTHO-, Gk *paideia* rearing of children)]

orthoptic /ɔːˈθɒptɪk/ *adj.* relating to the correct or normal use of the eyes. [f. ORTHO- + OPTIC]

orthoptics /ɔːˈθɒptɪks/ *n.* remedial treatment of the eye muscles. —**orthoptist** *n.* [f. prec.]

ortolan /ˈɔtələn/ *n.* a European bunting (*Emberiza hortulana*) eaten as a delicacy. [F f. Prov., = gardener, f. L *hortulanus*]

oryx /ˈɒrɪks/ *n.* a large straight-horned African antelope of the genus *Oryx*. [f. L f. Gk *orux* stonemason's pickaxe, f. its pointed horns]

OS *abbr.* 1 old style. 2 ordinary seaman. 3 Ordnance Survey. 4 outsize.

Os *symbol* osmium.

Oscar /ˈɒskə(r)/ *n.* each of several gold statuettes awarded annually by the Academy of Motion Picture Arts and Sciences (Hollywood, USA) for excellence in film acting, directing, etc. [man's given name; the statuette is said to have reminded Margaret Herrick, then librarian of the Academy and later its Executive Director, of her Uncle Oscar (i.e. Oscar Pierce, American wheat and fruit grower)]

oscillate /ˈɒsɪleɪt/ *v.t./i.* 1 to swing to and fro; to cause to do this. 2 to vacillate, to vary between extremes. 3 (of an electric current) to reverse its direction with high frequency. —**oscillation** /-ˈleɪʃ(ə)n/ *n.* [f. L *oscillare* swing]

oscillator *n.* an instrument for producing oscillations. [f. prec.]

oscillograph /əˈsɪləgrɑ:f/ *n.* a device for recording oscillations. [as OSCILLATE + -GRAPH]

oscilloscope /əˈsɪləskəʊp/ *n.* a device for displaying oscillations, especially on the screen of a cathode-ray tube. [as OSCILLATE + -SCOPE]

osier /ˈəʊzɪə(r), ˈəʊʒə(r)/ *n.* a willow (*Salix viminalis* etc.) used in basketwork; a shoot of this. [f. OF]

-osis /-əʊsɪs/ *suffix* forming nouns denoting a process or condition (*metamorphosis*), especially a pathological state (*neurosis, thrombosis*). [f. L or Gk]

osmium /ˈɒzmɪəm/ *n.* a hard bluish-white metallic element, symbol Os, atomic number 76. [f. Gk *osmē* smell (from the pungent smell of its tetroxide)]

osmosis /ɒzˈməʊsɪs/ *n.* the tendency of a solvent to pass from a less concentrated into a more concentrated solution through a semipermeable membrane, permeable to the solvent but not to the solute. —**osmotic** /-ˈmɒtɪk/ *adj.* [ult. f. Gk *ōsmos* thrust]

osprey /ˈɒsprɪ/ *n.* a large raptorial bird (*Pandion haliaetus*) preying on fish in inland waters. [f. OF ult. f. L *ossifraga* (*os* bone, *frangere* break)]

osseous /ˈɒsɪəs/ *adj.* of bone; having bones, bony. [f. L *osseus* (*os* bone)]

ossicle /ˈɒsɪk(ə)l/ *n.* a small bone or piece of hard substance in an animal structure. [f. L *ossiculum* (as prec.)]

ossify /ˈɒsɪfaɪ/ *v.t./i.* 1 to turn into bone, to harden. 2 to make or become rigid and unprogressive. —**ossification** /-fɪˈkeɪʃ(ə)n/ *n.* [f. F (as OSSEOUS)]

ostensible /ɒˈstensɪbə)l/ *adj.* pretended, professed, put forward to conceal what is real. —**ostensibly** *adv.* [F f. L (*ostendere* show)]

ostensive /ɒˈstensɪv/ *adj.* directly showing. —**ostensively** *adv.* [f. L (as prec.)]

ostentation /ɒstenˈteɪʃ(ə)n/ *n.* pretentious display of wealth etc., showing off. —**ostentatious** *adj.*, **ostentatiously** *adv.* [f. OF f. L (as OSTENSIBLE)]

osteo- /ɒstɪə(ʊ)-/ *in comb.* bone. [f. Gk *osteon* bone]

osteopath /ˈɒstɪəpæθ/ *n.* a practitioner of osteopathy. [f. foll.]

osteopathy /ɒstɪˈɒpəθɪ/ *n.* treatment of disease by manipulation of bones (especially the spine) and muscles (their deformity being the supposed cause of problems). [f. OSTEO- + Gk *patheia* suffering]

ostler /ˈɒslə(r)/ *n.* a person in charge of stabling horses at an inn. [f. AF *hosteler* (as HOSTEL)]

Ostmark /ˈɒstmɑ:k/ *n.* the currency unit in the German Democratic Republic until 1990. [G, f. *Ost* east + MARK²]

Ostpolitik /ˈɒstpɒlɪti:k/ *n.* the policy of a West European country with regard to the Communist countries of East Europe. [G (*ost* east, *politik* politics)]

ostracize /ˈɒstrəsaɪz/ *v.t.* 1 (in ancient Athens) to banish (a dangerously powerful or unpopular citizen) by a voting-system in which the name of the person proposed for banishment was written on a potsherd. 2 to exclude from society, favour, or common privileges. —**ostracism** *n.* [f. Gk *ostrakon* potsherd]

ostrich /ˈɒstrɪtʃ/ *n.* 1 a large swift-running flightless African bird (*Struthio camelus*), that swallows hard substances to assist the working of its gizzard and is reputed to bury its head in the sand when pursued, believing that it cannot then be seen. 2 a person who refuses to acknowledge an awkward truth. [f. OF f. L *avis* bird, *struthio* ostrich f. Gk]

Ostrogoth /ˈɒstrəgɒθ/ *n.* a member of the eastern branch of the Goths, who conquered Italy in the 5th–6th c. —**Ostrogothic** /-ˈgɒθɪk/ *adj.* [f. L, = eastern Goth]

OT *abbr.* Old Testament.

other /ˈʌðə(r)/ *adj.* 1 not the same as one or some already mentioned or implied; separate in identity, distinct in kind. 2 alternative; additional; being the remaining one of a set of two or more. —*n.* or *pron.* another person or thing. —*adv.* otherwise. —**the other day** etc., a few days, nights, etc., ago. **other than**, different from. **other-worldly** *adj.* concerned or preoccupied with life after death or in some imagined world to the neglect of the present or real one. [OE]

otherwise *adv.* 1 in a different way. 2 in other respects. 3 in different circumstances. 4 or else. —*adj.* in a different state. [OE (as prec., WISE²)]

otiose /ˈəʊʃɪəʊs, ˈəʊt-/ *adj.* not required, serving no practical purpose. [f. L *otiosus* (*otium* leisure)]

otter /ˈɒtə(r)/ *n.* an aquatic fish-eating mammal of the genus *Lutra* etc. with webbed feet, thick brown fur, and a pointed tail somewhat flattened horizontally, feeding chiefly on fish; its fur. [OE]

Ottoman /ˈɒtəmən/ *adj.* of the dynasty of Osman or Othman I (13th c.), his branch of the Turks, or the empire ruled by his descendants. —*n.* an Ottoman person. [F f. Arab.]

ottoman /ˈɒtəmən/ *n.* **1** a long cushioned seat without back or arms. **2** a storage box with a padded top. [= prec.]

oubliette /u:blɪˈet/ *n.* a secret dungeon with a trapdoor entrance. [F (*oublier* forget)]

ouch *int.* expressing sharp or sudden pain. [natural excl.]

ought[1] /ɔ:t/ *v.aux.* (as present and past, the only form now in use; *neg.* **ought not**) expressing rightness or duty, advisability, or strong probability. [OE, past tense of OWE]

ought[2] /ɔ:t/ *n.* (*colloq.*) the figure 0, nought. [f. *an ought* for *a nought*]

oughtn't /ˈɔ:t(ə)nt/ (*colloq.*) = ought not.

Ouija /ˈwi:dʒə/ *n.* [P] (also **Ouija-board**) a board marked with the alphabet and other signs used with a movable pointer to obtain messages in spiritualistic seances. [f. F *oui* yes + G *ja* yes]

ounce[1] /aʊns/ *n.* **1** a unit of weight equal to one sixteenth of a pound (about 28 grams). **2** a very small quantity. [f. OF f. L *uncia* twelfth part of pound or foot]

ounce[2] /aʊns/ *n.* an Asian feline (*Panthera uncia*), the mountain panther or snow-leopard, smaller than the leopard but similarly marked. [f. OF *once* for earlier *lonce* (*l* mistaken for the definite article), ult. f. L LYNX]

our *poss. adj.* of or belonging to us; that we are concerned with or thinking of. —**Our Father,** the Lord's Prayer, beginning with these words (Matt. 6: 9-13). **Our Lady,** the Virgin Mary. [OE]

ours /ˈaʊəz/ *poss. pron.* of or belonging to us; the thing(s) belonging to us. [f. OUR]

ourself /aʊəˈself/ *pron.* corresponding to MYSELF when used by a sovereign etc.

ourselves /aʊəˈselvz/ *pron.* emphat. and refl. form of WE, US.

ousel var. of OUZEL.

oust /aʊst/ *v.t.* to eject, to drive out of office or power; to seize the place of. [f. AF f. L *obstare* oppose]

out *adv.* **1** expressing movement or position away from a centre or beyond or regardless of stated or implied limits, or a state other than the right or usual one; away from or not in a place; not at home, not in one's office etc.; not in its normal or usual state. **2** (so as to be) excluded. **3** not in effective or favourable action; no longer in fashion or season or office; (in cricket etc.) having had one's innings ended; (of workers) on strike; (of a light or fire etc.) no longer burning; no longer visible. **4** in or into the open; so as to be clear or perceptible; (of flowers) open, (of plants) in bloom; (of a secret) revealed; (of a book) published; (after a superlative) among known examples etc. **5** to or at an end, completely. **6** in error. **7** unconscious. **8** (of a jury) considering its verdict in private. **9** with attentiveness (*watch out*). —*prep.* out of. —*n.* a way of escape. —*int.* get out! —*v.t.* **1** to put out. **2** (*colloq.*) to eject forcibly. **3** (in boxing) to knock out. —**out and about,** active outdoors. **out and away,** by far. **out and out,** thoroughly, **out-and-out** *adj.* complete, thorough. **out for,** intent on, determined to get. **out of,** from within; from among; beyond the range of; because of; by the use of, (of an animal) having as its dam; so as to be without a supply of. **out of doors,** in or into the open air. **out to,** determined to. [OE]

out- *prefix* **1** out of, away from, outward. **2** external, separate. **3** so as to surpass or exceed. [= OUT]

outage /ˈaʊtɪdʒ/ *n.* a period of non-operation of a power-supply etc. [f. OUT]

outback *n.* the remote inland districts of Australia.

outbid /aʊtˈbɪd/ *v.t.* (**-dd-**) to bid higher than.

outboard *adj.* **1** towards the outside of a ship, aircraft, or vehicle. **2** (of a motor) attached externally to the stern of a boat; (of a boat) using such a motor.

outbreak *n.* a breaking out of anger, war, disease, fire, etc.

outbuilding *n.* an outhouse.

outburst *n.* a bursting out, especially of emotion in vehement words.

outcast *n.* a person cast out of his home or rejected by society. —*adj.* homeless, rejected.

outclass /aʊtˈklɑ:s/ *v.t.* to surpass in quality.

outcome *n.* the result or effect of an event etc.

outcrop *n.* **1** part of an underlying stratum, vein, or rock that emerges on the surface of the ground etc.; such emergence. **2** a breaking out, a noticeable manifestation.

outcry *n.* **1** a loud cry. **2** a strong protest.

outdated /aʊtˈdeɪtɪd/ *adj.* out of date, obsolete.

outdistance /aʊtˈdɪstəns/ *v.t.* to get far ahead of.

outdo /aʊtˈdu:/ *v.t.* (3 *sing. pres.* **outdoes** /-ˈdʌz/; *past* **outdid**; *p.p.* **outdone**) to do better than, to surpass.

outdoor *adj.* of, done, or for use out of doors; fond of the open air.

outdoors /aʊtˈdɔ:z/ *n.* the open air. —*adv.* in or into the open air.

outer *adj.* further from the centre or the inside; external, exterior. —**outer space,** the universe beyond the earth's atmosphere. —**outermost** *adj.* [f. OUT]

outface /aʊtˈfeɪs/ *v.t.* to disconcert by staring or by a display of confidence.

outfall *n.* an outlet of a river, drain, etc.

outfield *n.* the outer part of a cricket or baseball pitch.

outfit *n.* **1** a set of equipment or clothes. **2** (*colloq.*) a group of persons, an organization.

outfitter *n.* a supplier of equipment, especially men's clothes.

outflank /aʊtˈflæŋk/ *v.t.* to extend beyond or get round the flank of (an enemy); to outmanœuvre, outwit.

outflow *n.* an outward flow; what flows out.

outfox /aʊtˈfɒks/ *v.t.* to outwit.

outgoing *adj.* **1** going out; retiring from office. **2** sociable and friendly. —*n.* (in *pl.*) expenditure.

outgrow /aʊtˈgrəʊ/ *v.t.* (*past* **outgrew**; *p.p.* **outgrown**) **1** to grow faster or taller than. **2** to grow too big for; to be too old or developed for.

outgrowth *n.* **1** an offshoot. **2** a natural development or product.

outhouse *n.* a small building belonging to but separate from the main house.

outing *n.* a pleasure-trip or excursion. [f. OUT *v.*]

outlandish /aʊtˈlændɪʃ/ *adj.* looking or sounding very strange or foreign, bizarre. —**outlandishness** *n.* [OE (*ūtland* foreign country)]

outlast /aʊtˈlɑːst/ *v.t.* to last longer than.

outlaw *n.* a fugitive from the law (originally one placed beyond the protection of the law). —*v.t.* **1** to declare (a person) an outlaw. **2** to make illegal, to proscribe.

outlay *n.* expenditure.

outlet *n.* **1** a means of exit or escape. **2** a means of expressing feelings. **3** a market for goods.

outline *n.* **1** a line or lines showing the shape or boundary of something. **2** a summary; a statement of the chief facts. —*v.t.* to draw or describe in outline; to mark the outline of. —**in outline,** giving only an outline.

outlive /aʊtˈlɪv/ *v.t.* to live longer than (a person) or beyond (a period); to live through (an experience).

outlook *n.* **1** a view on which one looks out. **2** a mental attitude. **3** future prospects.

outlying *adj.* situated far from a centre, remote.

outmanœuvre /aʊtməˈnuːvə(r)/ *v.t.* to outdo in manœuvring.

outmatch /aʊtˈmætʃ/ *v.t.* to be more than a match for.

outmoded /aʊtˈməʊdɪd/ *adj.* out of fashion; obsolete.

outnumber /aʊtˈnʌmbə(r)/ *v.t.* to exceed in number.

outpace /aʊtˈpeɪs/ *v.t.* to go faster than; to outdo in a contest.

out-patient *n.* a patient not residing in hospital during treatment.

outpost *n.* **1** a detachment stationed at some distance from an army. **2** a distant branch or settlement.

output *n.* **1** the amount produced. **2** the electrical power etc. delivered by an apparatus. **3** the place where energy, information, etc., leaves a system. **4** the results etc. supplied by a computer. —*v.t./i.* (*past* & *p.p.* **output** or **outputted**) (of a computer) to supply (results etc.).

outrage *n.* **1** an extreme or shocking violation of others' rights, sentiments, etc.; a gross offence or indignity. **2** fierce resentment. —*v.t.* to subject to an outrage, to commit an outrage against; to shock and anger. [f. OF (*outrer* exceed f. L *ultra* beyond)]

outrageous /aʊtˈreɪdʒəs/ *adj.* greatly exceeding what is moderate or reasonable; grossly cruel, immoral, or offensive. —**outrageously** *adv.* [f. OF (as prec.)]

outrank /aʊtˈræŋk/ *v.t.* to be superior in rank to.

outré /ˈuːtreɪ/ *adj.* eccentric, violating decorum. [F, p.p. of *outrer* (as OUTRAGE)]

outrider *n.* a mounted attendant or motor-cyclist riding ahead of a procession etc.

outrigger *n.* **1** a spar or framework projecting from or over a ship's side. **2** a strip of wood fixed parallel to a canoe to stabilize it; a canoe with this. [perh. partly after obs. (Naut.) *outligger*]

outright /aʊtˈraɪt/ *adv.* altogether, entirely, not gradually; without reservation, openly. —/ˈaʊtraɪt/ *adj.* complete, thorough.

outrun /aʊtˈrʌn/ *v.t.* (**-nn-**; *past* **outran**; *p.p.* **outrun**) **1** to run faster or further than. **2** to go beyond (a point or limit).

outsell /aʊtˈsel/ *v.t.* (*past* & *p.p.* **outsold** /-ˈsəʊld/) to sell more than; to be sold in greater quantities than.

outset *n.* the beginning (usu. in **at** *or* **from the outset**).

outshine /aʊtˈʃaɪn/ *v.t.* (*past* & *p.p.* **outshone** /-ˈʃɒn/) to shine brighter than; to surpass in excellence etc.

outside /aʊtˈsaɪd, ˈaʊt-/ *n.* **1** the outer side of a surface or part. **2** the outer part(s). **3** outward appearance; all that is without. **4** a position on the outer side. —/ˈaʊtsaɪd/ *adj.* **1** of, on, or coming from the outside; outer. **2** not belonging to some circle or institution. **3** nearer to the outside of a games field. **4** the greatest existent or possible. —/aʊtˈsaɪd/ *adv.* on, at, or to the outside; in or into the open air. —/aʊtˈsaɪd/ *prep.* **1** on the outer side of; not in; at or to the outer side of. **2** other than.

3 not included in. —**at the outside,** (of amounts) at the most. **outside broadcast,** one not made from a studio. **outside chance,** a remote possibility.

outsider *n.* **1** a non-member of some circle, party, profession, etc. **2** a competitor thought to have little chance.

outsize *adj.* unusually large. —*n.* an outsize garment etc. or person.

outskirts *n.pl.* the outer area of a town etc.

outsmart /aʊtˈsmɑːt/ *v.t.* to outwit, to be cleverer than.

outspan /aʊtˈspæn/ *v.t.* (**-nn-**) (*S. Afr.*) to unyoke, to unharness. [f. Du. (as OUT, SPAN[1])]

outspoken /aʊtˈspəʊkən/ *adj.* speaking or spoken without reserve, frank.

outspread /aʊtˈspred/ *adj.* spread out. —*v.t.* to spread out.

outstanding /aʊtˈstændɪŋ/ *adj.* **1** conspicuous, especially from excellence. **2** still to be dealt with. —**outstandingly** *adv.*

outstay /aʊtˈsteɪ/ *v.t.* to stay longer than.

outstretched /aʊtˈstretʃt/ *adj.* stretched out.

outstrip /aʊtˈstrɪp/ *v.t.* (**-pp-**) **1** to go faster than. **2** to surpass.

out-tray *n.* a tray for outgoing documents.

outvote /aʊtˈvəʊt/ *v.t.* to defeat by a majority of votes.

outward /ˈaʊtwəd/ *adj.* **1** situated on or directed towards the outside. **2** going towards the outside. **3** external, material, apparent. —*adv.* (also **outwards**) in an outward direction, towards the outside. —**outward bound,** going away from home. [OE (as OUT, -WARD)]

outwardly *adv.* on the outside; in appearance.

outwardness *n.* external existence, objectivity.

outweigh /aʊtˈweɪ/ *v.t.* to exceed in weight, value, importance, or influence.

outwit /aʊtˈwɪt/ *v.t.* (**-tt-**) to be too clever for, to overcome by greater ingenuity.

outwork *n.* an advanced or detached part of a fortification.

outworn /aʊtˈwɔn/ *adj.* worn out, obsolete, exhausted.

ouzel /ˈuːz(ə)l/ *n.* **1** a small bird (*Turdus torquatus*) of the thrush family (**ring ouzel**). **2** a diving bird of the genus *Cinclus* (**water ouzel**), a dipper. [OE, = blackbird]

ouzo /ˈuːzəʊ/ *n.* a Greek drink of aniseed-flavoured spirits. [modern Gk]

ova *pl.* of OVUM.

oval /ˈəʊv(ə)l/ *adj.* having a rounded symmetrical shape longer than it is broad, elliptical or ellipsoidal. —*n.* a thing of oval shape or outline. [f. L (as OVUM)]

ovary /ˈəʊvərɪ/ *n.* **1** either of two reproductive organs in which ova are produced in female animals. **2** the lower part of the pistil in a plant, from which the fruit is formed. —**ovarian** /-ˈveərɪən/ *adj.* [f. OVUM]

ovate /ˈəʊveɪt/ *adj.* egg-shaped (as a solid or in outline), oval. [f. L (*ovum* egg)]

ovation /əˈveɪʃ(ə)n/ *n.* enthusiastic applause or reception. [f. L (*ovare* exult)]

oven /ˈʌv(ə)n/ *n.* an enclosed compartment for heating or cooking food etc. [OE]

ovenware *n.* dishes in which food can be cooked in an oven.

over /ˈəʊvə(r)/ *adv.* expressing movement or position or state above or beyond something stated or implied: **1** outward and downward from the brink or from an erect position. **2** so as to cover or touch a whole surface. **3** with movement from one side to the other or so that a different side is showing; upside down; across a street or other space; with transference or change from one hand, part, etc., to another. **4** with motion above something, so as to pass across. **5** from beginning to end, with repetition; thoroughly, with detailed consideration. **6** too, in excess, in addition, besides. **7** apart; until a later time. **8** at an end, settled. **9** (in a radio conversation) it is your turn to transmit. **10** (as an umpire's call in cricket) change ends for bowling etc. —*prep.* **1** in or to a position higher than. **2** out and down from; down from the edge of. **3** so as to clear; on or to the other side of. **4** so as to cover. **5** concerning. **6** while occupied with. **7** with or achieving superiority or preference to. **8** throughout the length or extent of; during. **9** beyond; more than. **10** transmitted by. **11** in comparison with. —*n.* a sequence of six (or eight) balls in cricket, bowled between two calls of 'over', play resulting from this. —*adj.* upper, outer, superior, extra (usu. as *prefix*; see OVER-). —**over and above,** besides. **over and over,** repeatedly. **over to you,** it is your turn to act. [OE]

overact /əʊvərˈækt/ *v.t./i.* to act with exaggeration.

overall *adj.* **1** from end to end. **2** total, inclusive of all. —/also -ˈɔl/ *adv.* in all parts, taken as a whole. —*n.* a protective outer garment; (in *pl.*) protective outer trousers or suit.

overarm *adj.* & *adv.* with the arm brought forward and down from above shoulder level.

overawe /əʊvərˈɔ/ *v.t.* to overcome with awe.

overbalance /əʊvəˈbæləns/ *v.t./i.* to lose one's balance and fall; to cause to do this.

overbear /əʊvəˈbeə(r)/ *v.t.* (*past* **-bore**; *p.p.* **-borne**) **1** to bear down by weight or force. **2** to repress by power or authority.

overbearing *adj.* domineering, bullying.

overblown /əʊvəˈbləʊn/ *adj*. **1** pretentious. **2** (of a flower) too fully open, past its prime.

overboard *adv*. from within a ship into the water. —**go overboard,** (*colloq*.) to show extreme enthusiasm.

overbook /əʊvəˈbʊk/ *v.t*. to make too many bookings for (an aircraft flight, hotel, etc., or *absol*.).

overcast /əʊvəˈkɑ:st/ *adv*. (of the sky) covered with cloud. —*v.t*. (*past* & *p.p*. **-cast**) to stitch over (an edge) to prevent fraying.

overcharge /əʊvəˈtʃɑ:dʒ/ *v.t*. **1** to charge too high a price to (a person) or for (a thing). **2** to put an excessive charge into; to overfill.

overcheck *n*. a check pattern superimposed on a pattern of smaller checks.

overcoat *n*. a warm outdoor coat.

overcome /əʊvəˈkʌm/ *v.t./i*. (*past* **-came**; *p.p*. **-come**) **1** to win a victory over, to succeed in subduing; to be victorious. **2** to make helpless, to deprive of proper self-control. **3** to find a way of dealing with (a problem etc.).

overcrowd /əʊvəˈkraʊd/ *v.t*. to crowd too many people into (a place or vehicle etc.).

overdevelop /əʊvədɪˈveləp/ *v.t*. to develop excessively.

overdo /əʊvəˈdu:/ *v.t*. (3 *sing*. *pres*. **-does** /-ˈdʌz/; *past* **-did**; *p.p*. **-done** /-ˈdʌn/) **1** to do (a thing) excessively, to go too far in. **2** to cook too much. **3** to exhaust. —**overdo it,** to work too hard; to exaggerate; to carry an action too far.

overdose *n*. an excessive dose, especially of a drug.

overdraft *n*. overdrawing of a bank account; the amount by which an account is overdrawn.

overdraw /əʊvəˈdrɔ/ *v.t*. (*past* **-drew**; *p.p*. **-drawn**) to draw more from (a bank account) than the amount in credit; (in *p.p*.) having overdrawn one's account.

overdress /əʊvəˈdres/ *v.t./i*. to dress ostentatiously or with too much formality.

overdrive *n*. a mechanism in a vehicle providing a gear ratio higher than that of the usual gears.

overdue /əʊvəˈdju:/ *adj*. past the due time for payment, arrival, etc.

overeat /əʊvərˈi:t/ *v.i*. (*past* **-ate**; *p.p*. **-eaten**) to eat too much.

over-emphasize /əʊvərˈemfəsaɪz/ *v.t*. to emphasize excessively. —**over-emphasis** *n*.

overestimate /əʊvərˈestɪmeɪt/ *v.t*. to form too high an estimate of. —/-ət/ *n*. too high an estimate.

over-expose /əʊvərɪkˈspəʊz/ *v.t*. to expose for too long. —**over-exposure** *n*.

overfeed /əʊvəˈfi:d/ *v.t./i*. (*past* & *p.p*. **-fed**) to feed too much.

overfish /əʊvəˈfɪʃ/ *v.t*. to fish (a river etc.) too much so that next season's supply is reduced.

overflow /əʊvəˈfləʊ/ *v.t./i*. **1** to flow over (a brim etc.); to flood (a surface or area). **2** (of a crowd etc.) to spread beyond the limits of (a room etc.). **3** (of a receptacle etc.) to be so full that the contents overflow; (of kindness, a harvest, etc.) to be very abundant. —/ˈəʊvə-/ *n*. **1** what overflows or is superfluous. **2** an outlet for excess liquid.

overfly /əʊvəˈflaɪ/ *v.t*. (*past* **-flew**; *p.p*. **-flown** /-ˈfləʊn/) to fly over or beyond (a place or territory).

overfull /əʊvəˈfʊl/ *adj*. filled too much, too full.

overgrown /əʊvəˈgrəʊn/ *adj*. **1** covered with plants, weeds, etc. **2** grown too big. —**overgrowth** *n*.

overhang /əʊvəˈhæŋ/ *v.t./i*. (*past* & *p.p*. **-hung**) to jut out (over). —/ˈəʊvə-/ *n*. overhanging; an overhanging part or amount.

overhaul /əʊvəˈhɔl/ *v.t*. **1** to check over thoroughly and make any necessary repairs to. **2** to overtake. —/ˈəʊvə-/ *n*. a thorough check with repairs if necessary.

overhead /əʊvəˈhed/ *adv*. above one's head, in the sky. —/ˈəʊvə-/ *adj*. placed overhead. —/ˈəʊvə-/ *n*. (in *pl*.) the routine administrative and maintenance expenses of a business.

overhear /əʊvəˈhɪə(r)/ *v.t*. (*past* & *p.p*. **-heard** /-ˈhɜ:d/) to hear unintentionally or without the speaker's knowledge.

overheat /əʊvəˈhi:t/ *v.t./i*. to make or become too hot.

overjoyed /əʊvəˈdʒɔɪd/ *adj*. filled with extreme joy.

overkill *n*. a surplus of capacity for destruction above what is needed to defeat or destroy an enemy.

overland /əʊvəˈlænd/ *adv*. by land. —/ˈəʊvə-/ *adj*. entirely or mainly by land.

Overlander /ˈəʊvəlændə(r) *n*. (*Austral. hist*.) one whose occupation was to drive large herds of livestock over a long distance or from one colony to another. [f. prec.]

overlap /əʊvəˈlæp/ *v.t./i*. (**-pp-**) **1** to extend beyond the edge of and partly cover. **2** to coincide partly. —/ˈəʊvə-/ *n*. overlapping; an overlapping part or amount.

overlay /əʊvəˈleɪ/ *v.t*. (*past* & *p.p*. **-laid**) **1** to lie on top of. **2** to cover the surface of with a coating etc. —/ˈəʊvə-/ *n*. a thing laid over another.

overleaf /əʊvəˈli:f/ *adv*. on the other side of a leaf of a book.

overlie /əʊvəˈlaɪ/ *v.t*. (*past* **-lay**; *p.p*. **-lain**; *partic*. **-lying**) to lie on top of; to smother thus.

overload /əʊvəˈləʊd/ *v.t*. to put too great a load on or into. —/ˈəʊvə-/ *n*. a load that is too great.

overlook /əʊvəˈlʊk/ *v.t.* **1** to fail to observe or consider. **2** to take no notice of, to allow (an offence) to go unpunished. **3** to have a view of from above. **4** to supervise.

overlord *n.* a supreme lord.

overly *adv.* (chiefly *Sc. & US*) excessively, too. [f. OVER]

overman /əʊvəˈmæn/ *v.t.* (**-nn-**) to provide with too many people as staff or crew.

overmantel *n.* ornamental shelves etc. over a mantelpiece.

overmuch /əʊvəˈmʌtʃ/ *adv.* too much.

overnight /əʊvəˈnaɪt/ *adv.* **1** during the course of a night. **2** on the preceding evening regarded from the next day. **3** (*colloq.*) instantly. —/ˈəʊvə-/ *adj.* done or for use etc. during a night.

overpass /ˈəʊvəpɑːs/ *n.* a road that passes over another by means of a bridge.

overpay /əʊvəˈpeɪ/ *v.t.* to pay too highly.

overplay /əʊvəˈpleɪ/ *v.t.* to give too much importance to. —**overplay one's hand,** to act with overestimation of one's strength.

overpower /əʊvəˈpaʊə(r)/ *v.t.* to overcome by greater strength or numbers.

overpowering *adj.* extreme, too intense.

overprint /əʊvəˈprɪnt/ *v.t.* to print over (something already printed). —/ˈəʊvə-/ *n.* a thing overprinted.

overrate /əʊvəˈreɪt/ *v.t.* to have too high an opinion of.

overreach /əʊvəˈriːtʃ/ *v.t.* to outwit, to circumvent. —**overreach oneself,** to fail through being too ambitious.

over-react /əʊvərɪˈækt/ *v.i.* to respond more strongly than is justified.

override /əʊvəˈraɪd/ *v.t.* (*past* **-rode**; *p.p.* **-ridden**) **1** to have or claim superior authority or precedence over; to set aside (an order etc.) thus. **2** to intervene and cancel the operation of. **3** to move so as to extend over or overlap.

overrider *n.* either of a pair of vertical attachments to the bumper of a car to prevent another bumper from becoming locked behind it.

overripe/əʊvəˈraɪp/ *adj.* too ripe.

overrule /əʊvəˈruːl/ *v.t.* to set aside (a decision etc.) by superior authority; to set aside a decision of (a person) thus.

overrun /əʊvəˈrʌn/ *v.t.* (**-nn-**; *past* **-ran**; *p.p.* **-run**) **1** to swarm or spread over. **2** to conquer (a territory) by force of numbers. **3** to exceed (a limit).

overseas *adj. & adv.* across or beyond the sea.

oversee /əʊvəˈsiː/ *v.t.* (*past* **-saw**; *p.p.* **-seen**) to superintend.

overseer /ˈəʊvəsɪə(r)/ *n.* a superintendent.

overset /əʊvəˈset/ *v.t.* (**-tt-**; *past & p.p.* **-set**) to overturn, to upset.

oversew /əʊvəˈsəʊ/ *v.t.* (*p.p.* **-sewn** or **-sewed**) to sew together (two edges) with stitches lying over them.

overshadow /əʊvəˈʃædəʊ/ *v.t.* **1** to appear much more prominent or important than. **2** to cast into the shade.

overshoe /ˈəʊvəʃuː/ *n.* an outer protective shoe worn over an ordinary shoe.

overshoot /əʊvəˈʃuːt/ *v.t.* (*past & p.p.* **-shot**) to pass or send beyond (a target or limit).

overshot *adj.* (of a water-wheel) turned by water falling on it from above.

oversight /ˈəʊvəsaɪt/ *n.* **1** failure to do or note something; an inadvertent mistake. **2** supervision.

over-simplify /əʊvəˈsɪmplɪfaɪ/ *v.t.* to distort or misrepresent by putting in too simple terms.

overskirt *n.* an outer skirt.

oversleep /əʊvəˈsliːp/ *v.i.* (*past & p.p.* **-slept**) to sleep beyond an intended time of waking.

overspend /əʊvəˈspend/ *v.i.* (*past & p.p.* **-spent**) to spend beyond one's means.

overspill *n.* **1** what spills over or overflows. **2** surplus population moving to a new area.

overstaff /əvəˈstɑːf/ *v.t.* (esp. in *p.p.*) to provide with too many staff.

overstate /əʊvəˈsteɪt/ *v.t.* to state too strongly, to exaggerate. —**overstatement** *n.*

overstay /əʊvəˈsteɪ/ *v.t.* to stay longer than.

oversteer *v.i.* (of a vehicle) to have a tendency to turn more sharply than was intended. —*n.* this tendency.

overstep /əʊvəˈstep/ *v.t.* (**-pp-**) to pass beyond (a limit).

overstock /əʊvəˈstɒk/ *v.t.* to stock too many of; to stock with too many items.

overstrung /əʊvəˈstrʌŋ/ *adj.* **1** (of a person or the nerves) too highly strung. **2** (of a piano) with strings arranged in sets crossing each other obliquely.

overstuffed /əʊvəˈstʌft/ *adj.* (of cushions etc.) filled with much or too much stuffing.

over-subscribed /əʊvəsəbˈskraɪbd/ *adj.* (esp. of shares for sale) not enough to meet the amount subscribed.

overt /əʊˈvɜːt, ˈəʊ-/ *adj.* done openly, unconcealed. — **overtly** *adv.* [f. OF, p.p. of *ovrir* open f. L]

overtake /əʊvəˈteɪk/ *v.t.* (*p.t.* **-took** /-tʊk/, *p.p.* **-taken**) **1** to pass (a person or vehicle travelling in the same direction); to come abreast or level with. **2** to exceed (a compared value or amount).

overtax /əʊvəˈtæks/ *v.t.* **1** to make excessive demands on. **2** to tax too highly.

overthrow /əʊvəˈθrəʊ/ *v.t.* (*past* **-threw** /-ˈθruː/;

p.p. **-thrown**) **1** to remove forcibly from power. **2** to conquer. **3** to knock down, to upset. —/ˈəʊvə-/ *n.* **1** defeat, downfall. **2** a fielder's throwing of a ball beyond an intended point.

overthrust *n.* a thrust of (esp. lower) strata on one side of a fault over those on the other side.

overtime *n.* time worked in addition to one's regular hours; payment for this. —*adv.* as or during overtime.

overtone *n.* **1** a subtle extra quality or implication. **2** (*Mus.*) any of the tones above the lowest in a harmonic series.

overtrick *n.* a trick taken in excess of one's contract in the game of bridge.

overture /ˈəʊvətjʊə(r)/ *n.* **1** an orchestral piece opening an opera etc.; a composition in this style. **2** (often in *pl.*) a friendly approach showing willingness to begin negotiations; a formal proposal or offer. [f. OF f. L (as APERTURE)]

overturn /əʊvəˈtɜːn/ *v.t./i.* **1** to turn over or fall down; to cause to do this. **2** to overthrow, to subvert.

over-use / əʊvəˈjuːz/ *v.t.* to use excessively. —/-ˈjuːs/ *n.* excessive use.

overview *n.* a general survey.

overweening /əʊvəˈwiːnɪŋ/ *adj.* arrogant, presumptuous. [f. OVER- + obs. *ween* think]

overweight /əʊvəˈweɪt/ *adj.* more than the allowed or normal or desired weight. —/ˈəʊvə-/ *n.* excess weight.

overwhelm /əʊvəˈwelm/ *v.t.* **1** to overpower, especially with an emotion or burden. **2** to overcome by force of numbers. **3** to bury or drown beneath a huge mass.

overwind /əʊvəˈwaɪnd/ *v.t.* (*past* & *p.p.* **-wound**) to wind (a watch etc.) beyond the proper stopping-point.

overwork /əʊvəˈwɜːk/ *v.t./i.* to work or cause to work too hard; to weary or exhaust with too much work. —*n.* excessive work.

overwrought /əʊvəˈrɔːt/ *adj.* suffering a nervous reaction from over-excitement.

ovi- /əʊvɪ-/ *in comb.* egg, ovum. [f. L (as OVUM)]

oviduct /ˈəʊvɪdʌkt/ *n.* a canal through which ova pass from the ovary, especially in oviparous animals. [f. OVI- + DUCT]

oviform /ˈəʊvɪfɔːm/ *adj.* egg-shaped. [f. OVI- + -FORM]

ovine /ˈəʊvaɪn/ *adj.* of or like sheep. [f. L (*ovis* sheep)]

oviparous /əʊˈvɪpərəs/ *adj.* producing young from eggs expelled from the body before being hatched (cf. VIVIPAROUS). [f. L (OVI-, *-parus* bearing)]

ovipositor /əʊvɪˈpɒzɪtə(r)/ *n.* a pointed tubular organ by which a female insect deposits eggs. [f. OVI- + POSIT]

ovoid /ˈəʊvɔɪd/ *adj.* (of a solid) egg-shaped. [f. F (as OVUM)]

ovulate /ˈɒvjʊleɪt/ *v.i.* to discharge an ovum or ova from an ovary; to produce ova. —**ovulation** /-ˈleɪʃ(ə)n/ *n.* [as foll.]

ovule /ˈəʊvjuːl/ *n.* **1** a germ-cell in a female plant. **2** an unfertilized ovum. [F f. L (dim. of foll.)]

ovum /ˈəʊvəm/ (*pl.* **ova**) **1** a female germ-cell in animals, from which by fertilization with male sperm the young is developed. **2** an egg, especially of a mammal or fish or insect. [L, = egg]

ow *int.* expressing sudden pain. [natural excl.]

owe /əʊ/ *v.t.* **1** to be under an obligation to pay or repay (money etc. to a person); to be in debt. **2** to have a duty to render. **3** to feel (gratitude etc. towards another) in return for a service. **4** to be indebted for (a thing) to a cause or to another's work etc. [OE]

owing *predic. adj.* owed, not yet paid. —**owing to,** caused by, because of. [f. OWE]

owl *n.* a nocturnal bird of prey of the order Strigiformes, with a large head and eyes and a hooked beak. [OE]

owlet /ˈaʊlɪt/ *n.* a small or young owl. [earlier *howlet*, dim. of OWL, assim. to HOWL]

owlish *adj.* like an owl; solemn and dull. —**owlishly** *adv.* [f. OWL]

own /əʊn/ *adj.* belonging to oneself or itself. —*v.t./i.* **1** to have as property, to possess. **2** to acknowledge paternity, authorship, or possession of. **3** to admit as existent, valid, true, etc. —**come into one's own,** to receive one's due, to achieve recognition. **of one's own,** belonging to oneself exclusively. **on one's own,** alone; independent, independently, without help. **own goal,** a goal scored by a member of a team against his own side. **own to,** to confess to. **own up (to),** to confess frankly. —**-owned** *adj.* [OE]

owner *n.* a possessor. **owner-occupier,** one who owns and occupies a house. —**ownership** *n.*

ox *n.* (*pl.* **oxen**) an animal of the kinds of large usually horned cloven-footed ruminant kept for draught, milk, and meat; a fully-grown bullock of the domesticated species (*Bos taurus*) of this. —**ox-bow** *n.* a horseshoe bend in a river; a lake formed from this when the river cuts across the narrow end. **ox-eye** *n.* any of several plants (esp. *Leucanthemum vulgare*) with flowers like the eye of an ox. [OE]

oxalic acid /ɒkˈsælɪk/ a highly poisonous and sour acid originally found in wood sorrel and other plants. [f. F f. L f. Gk *oxalis* wood sorrel]

Oxbridge /ˈɒksbrɪdʒ/ *n.* the universities of

Oxford and Cambridge, especially in contrast to newer universities. —*adj.* characteristic of these. [f. OX(FORD) + (CAM)BRIDGE]

oxen *pl.* of ox.

Oxfam *abbr.* Oxford Committee for Famine Relief.

oxherd *n.* a cowherd.

oxhide *n.* the hide of an ox; leather from this.

oxidant /ˈɒksɪdənt/ *n.* an oxidizing agent. [F, partic. of *oxider* (as OXIDE)]

oxidation /ɒksɪˈdeɪʃ(ə)n/ *n.* oxidizing, being oxidized. [F (as foll.)]

oxide /ˈɒksaɪd/ *n.* a binary compound of oxygen. [F (as OXYGEN)]

oxidize /ˈɒksɪdaɪz/ *v.t./i.* **1** to combine or cause to combine with oxygen. **2** to make or become rusty. **3** to coat (metal) with an oxide. —**oxidization** /-ˈzeɪʃ(ə)n/ *n.* [f. prec.]

Oxon. *abbr.* **1** Oxfordshire. **2** of Oxford University. [f. L *Oxoniensis* (as foll.)]

Oxonian /ɒkˈsəʊniən/ *adj.* of Oxford or Oxford University. —*n.* **1** a member of Oxford University. **2** a citizen of Oxford. [f. *Oxonia* Latinized form of *Ox(en)ford*]

oxtail *n.* the tail of an ox, much used for soup-making.

oxy-acetylene /ɒksɪəˈsetɪliːn/ *adj.* of or using a mixture of oxygen and acetylene, especially in the cutting or welding of metals. [f. foll. + ACETYLENE]

oxygen /ˈɒksɪdʒ(ə)n/ *n.* an odourless tasteless gaseous element, symbol O, atomic number 8. —**oxygen mask**, a mask placed over the nose and mouth to supply oxygen for breathing. **oxygen tent**, a tentlike enclosure supplying a patient with air having increased oxygen content. [f. F *oxygène* acidifying principle (Gk *oxus* sharp, -GEN), because it was at first held to be the essential principle in the formation of acids]

oxygenate /ˈɒksɪdʒəneɪt/ *v.t.* to supply, treat, or mix with oxygen, to oxidize. —**oxygenation** /-ˈneɪʃ(ə)n/ *n.* [f. F (as prec.)]

oxymoron /ɒksɪˈmɔːrɒn/ *n.* a figure of speech with pointed conjunction of apparent contradictions (e.g. *cheerful pessimist*). [f. Gk, = pointedly foolish (*oxus* sharp, *mōros* foolish)]

oxytocin /ɒksɪˈtəʊsɪn/ *n.* a pituitary hormone controlling uterine contraction and the release of milk, used in synthetic form to induce labour etc. [f. Gk *oxutokia* (as OXY-, *tokos* childbirth)]

oyez /əʊˈjes/ *int.* (also **oyes**) a cry uttered usually three times by a public crier or court officer to call for attention. [f. AF, imper. of *oïr* hear f. L *audire*]

oyster *n.* **1** a bivalve mollusc of the genus *Ostrea* or family Ostreidae, used as a food and in some types producing a pearl. **2** a symbol of all one desires. **3** white with a grey tinge. —**oyster-catcher** *n.* a shore-bird of the genus *Haematopus*. [f. OF f. L *ostrea*, *ostreum* f. Gk]

oz. *abbr.* ounce(s).

ozone /ˈəʊzəʊn/ *n.* **1** a form of oxygen with three atoms in the molecule, having a pungent smell. **2** (*pop.*) invigorating air at the seaside etc. [f. G f. Gk (*ozō* smell)]

Pp

P, p /pi:/ *n.* **(Ps, P's)** the sixteenth letter of the alphabet.

P *abbr.* pawn (in chess).

P *symbol* phosphorus.

p *abbr.* **1** penny, pence. **2** (*Mus.*) piano (= PIANO[2]).

p. *abbr.* page.

PA *abbr.* **1** personal assistant. **2** public address. **3** Press Association.

Pa *symbol* protactinium. —*abbr.* pascal.

pa /pɑ:/ *n.* (*colloq.*) father. [abbr. of PAPA]

p.a. *abbr.* per annum.

pace[1] *n.* **1** a single step in walking or running; the space traversed in this. **2** speed in walking or running. **3** any of the various gaits of (esp. a trained) horse etc. —*v.t./i.* **1** to walk with a slow or regular pace; to traverse by pacing. **2** to set the pace for (a rider, runner, etc.). **3** to measure (a distance) by pacing. **4** (of a horse) to amble. —**keep pace,** to advance at an equal rate. **put a person through his paces,** to test his qualities in action etc. **set the pace,** to set the speed, especially by leading. [f. OF *pas* f. L *passus*]

pace[2] /ˈpeɪsɪ, ˈpɑ:tʃeɪ/ *prep.* (in announcing a contrary opinion) with all due deference to (the person named). [L, abl. of *pax* peace]

pacemaker *n.* **1** a runner etc. who sets the pace in a race. **2** a structure or device for stimulating the heart muscle.

pachyderm /ˈpækɪdɜ:m/ *n.* a thick-skinned mammal, especially an elephant or rhinoceros. —**pachydermatous** /-ˈdɜ:mətəs/ *adj.* [f. F f. Gk (*pakhus* thick, *derma* skin)]

Pacific /pəˈsɪfɪk/ *adj.* of the Pacific Ocean. —*n.* the Pacific Ocean, separating Asia and Australia from North and South America. [= foll.]

pacific /pəˈsɪfɪk/ *adj.* peaceful; making or loving peace. —**pacifically** *adv.* [f. F or L (*pax* peace)]

pacifist /ˈpæsɪfɪst/ *n.* one who rejects war and violence and believes that disputes should be settled by peaceful means. —**pacifism** *n.* [f. F (as prec.)]

pacify /ˈpæsɪfaɪ/ *v.t.* **1** to calm and quieten, to appease. **2** to establish peace in. —**pacification** /-fɪˈkeɪʃ(ə)n/ *n.*, **pacificatory** /pəˈsɪfɪkətərɪ/ *adj.* [f. OF or L (as PACIFIC)]

pack[1] *n.* **1** a collection of things wrapped up or tied together for carrying. **2** (usu. *derog.*) a lot or set. **3** a set of playing-cards. **4** a group of wild animals, hounds, etc.; an organized group of Cub Scouts or Brownies. **5** a team's forwards in Rugby football. **6** a medicinal or cosmetic substance applied to the skin. **7** an area of pack-ice. **8** a method of packing. —*v.t./i.* **1** to put (things) together in a bundle, bag, etc. for transport, storing, or marketing, etc.; to fill with things thus; to fill a case etc. with one's belongings. **2** to be able to be packed. **3** to put closely together; to fill (a space) in this way; to fill (a theatre or meeting etc.) with persons. **4** to cover or protect with something pressed tightly round or inside. **5** to carry (a gun etc.); to be capable of delivering (a punch) with skill or force. **6** (of animals) to form a pack. —**pack-drill** *n.* a military punishment of drill in full marching equipment (*no names no pack-drill*, discretion will prevent punishment). **pack-horse** *n.* a horse for carrying packs. **pack-ice** *n.* large crowded floating pieces of ice in the sea. **pack it in,** (*slang*) to cease doing something. **pack off,** to send away. **pack-saddle** *n.* a saddle adapted for supporting packs. **pack up,** to put one's things together in readiness for departure or ceasing work; (*slang*, of machinery etc.) to break down. **send packing,** (*colloq.*) to dismiss summarily. —**packer** *n.* [f. MDu. or MLG]

pack[2] *v.t.* to select (a jury etc.) so as to secure a decision biased in one's favour. [prob. f. obs. v. *pact* f. PACT]

package *n.* **1** a bundle of things packed. **2** a parcel, a box, etc., in which things are packed. **3** a package deal. —*v.t.* to make up into or enclose in a package. —**package deal,** a transaction or proposals offered or agreed to as a whole. **package holiday** *or* **tour** etc., one with all arrangements made at an inclusive price. [f. PACK[1]]

packaging *n.* wrapping(s) or container(s) for goods. [f. prec.]

packet /ˈpækɪt/ *n.* **1** a small package. **2** (*colloq.*) a large sum of money won or lost. —**packet-boat** *n.* a mail-boat. [f. PACK[1]]

packing *n.* material used to pack and protect fragile articles etc. —**packing-case** *n.* a wooden case or framework for packing goods. [f. PACK[1]]

packthread *n.* stout thread for sewing or tying up packs.

pact *n.* an agreement, a treaty. [f. OF f. L *pactum* (*pacisci* agree)]

pad[1] *n.* **1** a piece of soft stuff used to reduce friction or jarring, rub things, fill out hollows, hold or absorb liquid, etc. **2** a number of sheets of blank paper fastened together at one edge. **3** the fleshy underpart of an animal's foot. **4** a guard for the leg and ankle in cricket etc. **5** a flat surface for a helicopter take-off and landing or a rocket launching. **6** (*slang*) a lodging. —*v.t.* (**-dd-**) **1** to provide with a pad or padding; to stuff. **2** to fill (a book etc.) with unnecessary material in order to lengthen it. —**padded cell,** a room with padded walls in a mental hospital. [prob. of Du. or LG orig.]

pad[2] *v.t./i.* (**-dd-**) **1** to walk with a soft dull steady sound of steps. **2** to travel (along) on foot. [f. LG *pad* path or *padden* tread]

padding *n.* **1** material used to pad things. **2** superfluous words in a book, sentence, etc.

paddle[1] *n.* **1** a short broad-bladed-oar used without a rowlock. **2** a paddle-shaped instrument or part. **3** a fin, a flipper. **4** any of the boards fitted round the circumference of a paddle-wheel or mill-wheel. **5** an act or spell of paddling. —*v.t./i.* to move on water or propel (a canoe) by means of paddles; to row gently. —**paddle-boat** *n.* a boat propelled by a paddle-wheel. **paddle-wheel** *n.* a wheel for propelling a ship, with boards round the circumference so as to press backward against the water as the wheel revolves. —**paddler,** *n.* [orig. unkn.]

paddle[2] *v.t./i.* to walk barefoot in shallow water; to dabble (the feet or hands) in shallow water. —*n.* an act or spell of paddling. [cf. LG *paddeln* tramp about]

paddock /ˈpædək/ *n.* **1** a small field, especially for keeping horses in. **2** a turf enclosure adjoining a racecourse where horses are assembled before a race; a similar enclosure at a motor-racing circuit. **3** (*Austral. & NZ*) a field, a plot of land. [app. var. of dial. *parrock* (as FARK)]

Paddy *n.* (*colloq.*) a nickname for an Irishman. [pet-form of Irish *Padraig* Patrick]

paddy[1] *n.* **1** (in full **paddy-field**) a field where rice is grown. **2** rice before threshing or in the husk. [f. Malay]

paddy[2] *n.* (*colloq.*) a rage, a fit of temper. [as PADDY]

padlock *n.* a detachable lock hanging by a pivoted hook from the object it fastens. —*v.t.* to secure with a padlock. [f. LOCK[1]; first element unkn.]

padre /ˈpɑːdrɪ/ *n.* (*colloq.*) a chaplain in an army etc. [It., Sp., & Port., = father]

paean /ˈpiːən/ *n.* a song of praise or triumph. [L f. Doric Gk *paian* hymn to Apollo]

paediatrics /piːdɪˈætrɪks/ *n.pl.* the branch of medicine dealing with children and their diseases. —**paediatric** *adj.*, **paediatrician** /piːdɪəˈtrɪʃ(ə)n/ *n.* [f. PAEDO- + Gk *iatros* physician]

paedo- /piːdə(ʊ)-/ *in comb.* child. [f. Gk *pais* boy, child]

paedophilia /piːdəˈfɪlɪə/ *n.* sexual love directed towards children. [f. prec. + -PHILIA]

paella /pɑːˈelə/ *n.* a Spanish dish of rice, saffron, chicken, seafood, etc., cooked and served in a large shallow pan. [Catalan, f. OF f. L *patella* pan]

pagan /ˈpeɪgən/ *adj.* **1** heathen; irreligious. **2** holding the belief that deity exists in natural forces; nature-worshipping, especially in contrast to believing in Christianity, Judaism, etc. —*n.* **1** a pagan person. **2** one with pagan beliefs. —**paganism** *n.* [f. L *paganus* (*pagus* village)]

page[1] *n.* a leaf of a book etc.; one side of this; what is written or printed on this; an episode that might fill a page in a written history etc. —*v.t.* to paginate. [F f. L *pagina*]

page[2] *n.* a boy or man, usually in livery, employed to run errands, attend to a door, etc.; a boy employed as a personal attendant of a person of rank, a bride, etc. —*v.t.* to summon (as) by a page. [f. OF perh. ult. f. Gk *paidion* small boy]

pageant /ˈpædʒ(ə)nt/ *n.* a brilliant spectacle, especially an elaborate parade; a spectacular procession, or play performed in the open, illustrating historical events; a tableau etc. on a fixed stage or moving vehicle. [orig. unkn.]

pageantry *n.* a spectacular show or display; what serves to make a pageant. [f. prec.]

paginate /ˈpædʒmeɪt/ *v.t.* to number the pages of (a book etc.). —**pagination** /-ˈneɪʃ(ə)n/ *n.* [f. F f. L (as PAGE[1])]

pagoda /pəˈgəʊdə/ *n.* a Hindu or Buddhist temple or sacred building, especially a tower, in India and the Far East; an ornamental imitation of this. [f. Port., prob. ult. f. Pers.]

pah /pɑː/ *int.* expressing disgust or contempt. [natural excl.]

paid *past & p.p.* of PAY.

pail *n.* a bucket. —**pailful** *n.* [OE]

pain *n.* **1** an unpleasant feeling caused by injury or disease of the body; mental suffering. **2** (in *pl.*) careful effort. **3** punishment, the threat of this. —*v.t.* to inflict pain on; (in *p.p.*) expressing pain. —**pain in the neck,** (*colloq.*) an annoying or tiresome person or thing. **pain-killer** *n.* a medicine for alleviating pain. [f. OF *peine* f. L *poena* punishment]

painful *adj.* 1 causing pain; (of a part of the body) suffering pain. 2 causing trouble or difficulty, laborious. —**painfully** *adv.*, **painfulness** *n.* [f. PAIN + -FUL]

painless *adj.* not causing pain. [f. PAIN + -LESS]

painstaking /ˈpeinzteɪkɪŋ/ *adj.* careful, industrious.

paint *n.* colouring-matter, especially in liquid form for applying to a surface; (in *pl.*) a collection of tubes or cakes of paint. —*v.t./i.* 1 to coat or decorate with paint; to colour thus. 2 to depict or portray with paint(s); to make pictures thus. 3 to describe. 4 to apply a liquid or cosmetic to (the skin or face); to apply (liquid etc.) thus. —**painted lady,** an orange-red butterfly (*Vanessa cardui*) with black and white spots. **paint the town red,** (*slang*) to enjoy oneself flamboyantly. [f. OF f. L *pingere*]

paintbox *n.* a box holding dry paints for use by an artist.

paintbrush *n.* a brush for applying paint.

painter[1] *n.* one who paints, especially as an artist or decorator. —**painterly** *adj.* [f. PAINT]

painter[2] *n.* a rope attached to the bow of a boat for tying it to a quay etc. [prob. f. OF *penteur* rope from mast-head]

painting *n.* a painted picture. [f. PAINT]

pair *n.* 1 a set of two persons or things used together or regarded as a unit. 2 an article consisting of two joined or corresponding parts. 3 an engaged or married couple; a mated couple of animals. 4 the other member of a pair. 5 two playing-cards of the same denomination. 6 either or both of two MPs of opposing parties who are absent from a division by mutual arrangement. —*v.t./i.* 1 to arrange or be arranged in couples. 2 (of animals) to mate. 3 to partner (a person) with a member of the opposite sex. 4 to make a pair in Parliament. —**pair off,** to form into pairs. [f. OF f. L *paria* (as PAR)]

Paisley /ˈpeɪzlɪ/ *adj.* having a distinctive pattern of curved abstract figures. [f. *Paisley* in Scotland]

pal *n.* (*colloq.*) a friend, a mate. —*v.i.* (**-ll-**) (with *up*) (*colloq.*) to become friends. [f. Romany, ult. as BROTHER]

palace /ˈpælɪs/ *n.* 1 an official residence of a sovereign, president, archbishop, or bishop. 2 a splendid mansion, a spacious building. —**palace revolution,** the overthrow of a sovereign etc. without a civil war. [f. OF f. L *Palatium* house of Augustus at Rome]

paladin /ˈpælədɪn/ *n.* 1 any of the Twelve Peers of Charlemagne's court, of whom the Count Palatine was the chief. 2 a knight errant, a champion. [f. F f. It. f. L (as PALATINE)]

palaeo- /pælɪə(ʊ)-/ *in comb.* ancient, of ancient times. [f. Gk *palaios*]

palaeography /pælɪˈɒgrəfɪ/ *n.* the study of ancient writing and documents. —**palaeographer** *n.*, **palaeographic** /-ˈgræfɪk/ *adj.* [f. F (as PALAEO-, -GRAPHY)]

palaeolithic /pælɪəˈlɪθɪk, peɪ-/ *adj.* of the earlier part of the Stone Age, when primitive stone implements were used. —*n.* this period. [f. PALAEO- + Gk *lithos* stone]

palaeontology /pælɪɒnˈtɒlədʒɪ/ *n.* the study of life in the geological past. —**palaeontologist** *n.* [f. PALAEO- + Gk *onta* beings (*eimi* be) + -LOGY]

Palaeozoic /pælɪəʊˈzəʊɪk/ *adj.* of the geological era beginning with the first appearance of fossils bearing hard shells and ending with the rise to dominance of the reptiles. —*n.* this era. [f. PALAEO- + Gk *zōē* life, *zōos* living]

palais /ˈpæleɪ/ *n.* a public hall for dancing. —**palais glide,** a type of ballroom dance in which large groups dance simultaneously. [F *palais* (*de danse*) public hall (for dancing), = PALACE]

palanquin /pælənˈkiːn/ *n.* (also **palankeen**) an eastern covered litter for one person. [f. Port.; cf. Hindi *palki*]

palatable /ˈpælətəb(ə)l/ *adj.* pleasant to the taste; agreeable to the mind. [f. PALATE]

palatal /ˈpælət(ə)l/ *adj.* of the palate; (of a sound) made by placing the tongue against the palate. —*n.* a palatal sound. —**palatally** *adv.* [F (as foll.)]

palate /ˈpælət/ *n.* 1 the structure forming the upper part of the mouth cavity in vertebrates. 2 the sense of taste. 3 mental taste, liking. [f. L *palatum*]

palatial /pəˈleɪʃ(ə)l/ *adj.* like a palace, spacious, splendid. —**palatially** *adv.* [f. L (as PALACE)]

palatinate /pəˈlætɪnert/ *n.* a territory under a Count Palatine. [f. foll.]

Palatine /ˈpælətaɪn/ *adj.* possessing royal privileges, having jurisdiction (within a territory) such as elsewhere belongs only to the sovereign, *Count Palatine*. [f. F f. L (as PALACE)]

palaver /pəˈlɑːvə(r)/ *n.* 1 fuss; profuse or idle talk. 2 (*slang*) an affair, a business. 3 (esp. *hist.*) a parley between African or other natives and traders etc. —*v.t./i.* to talk profusely; to wheedle. [f. Port. *palavra* word f. L (as PARABLE)]

pale[1] *adj.* 1 (of a person or complexion) having little colour, lighter than normal. 2 (of colour or light) faint, not bright or vivid; only faintly coloured. —*v.t./i.* 1 to make or become pale. 2 to become feeble in comparison. —**pale-face** *n.* a supposed North American

Indian name for a white man. —**palely** *adv.*, **paleness** *n.* [f. OF f. L *pallidus*]

pale[2] *n.* **1** a stake used in a fence etc.; a boundary. **2** (*hist.*) a district or territory within determined bounds or subject to a particular jurisdiction. **3** (in heraldry) a vertical stripe in the middle of a field. —**beyond the pale,** outside the bounds of civilized behaviour etc. [f. OF f. L *palus* stake]

palette /ˈpælət/ *n.* an artist's thin wooden slab etc. used for laying and mixing colours on. —**palette-knife** *n.* a thin steel blade with a handle for mixing colours or applying paint; a kitchen knife with a long blunt round-ended flexible blade. [F, dim. of *pale* shovel f. L]

palfrey /ˈpɔlfrɪ/ *n.* (*archaic*) a horse for ordinary riding, especially for ladies. [f. OF f. L *paraveredus* (Gk *para* beside, extra, L *veredus* light horse)]

palimpsest /ˈpælɪmpsest/ *n.* a writing-material or manuscript on which the original writing has been effaced to make room for other writing; a monumental brass turned and re-engraved on the reverse side. [f. L f. Gk (*palin* again, *psaō* rub smooth)]

palindrome /ˈpælɪndrəʊm/ *n.* a word or verse etc. that reads the same backwards as forwards (e.g. *rotator*, *nurses run*). —**palindromic** /-ˈdrɒmɪk/ *adj.* [f. L *palindromos* (*palin* back again, *drom-* run)]

paling /ˈpeɪlɪŋ/ *n.* **1** a fence of pales. **2** a pale. [f. PALE[2]]

palisade /pælɪˈseɪd/ *n.* **1** a fence of pales or of iron railings. **2** a strong pointed wooden stake. —*v.t.* to enclose or furnish with a palisade. [f. F f. Prov. f. L *palus* stake]

pall[1] /pɔl/ *n.* **1** a cloth spread over a coffin, hearse, or tomb. **2** a woollen shoulder-band with front and back pendants, worn by the pope and some metropolitans and archbishops. **3** something forming a dark heavy covering. [OE f. L *pallium* cloak]

pall[2] /pɔl/ *v.t./i.* to become uninteresting; to satiate, to cloy. —**pall on,** to cease to interest or attract. [f. APPAL]

palladium /pəˈleɪdɪəm/ *n.* a rare hard white metallic element, symbol Pd, atomic number 46. [f. *Pallas* (f. foll.) an asteroid discovered just previously]

pallbearer *n.* a person helping to carry the coffin at a funeral.

pallet[1] /ˈpælɪt/ *n.* a straw mattress; a mean or makeshift bed. [f. AF f. L *palea* straw]

pallet[2] /ˈpælɪt/ *n.* a portable platform for transporting and storing loads. [f. F, = PALETTE]

palliasse /ˈpælɪæs/ *n.* a straw mattress. [f. F *paillasse* f. It. f. L (as PALLET[1])]

palliate /ˈpælɪeɪt/ *v.t.* **1** to alleviate (a disease) without curing. **2** to excuse, to extenuate. —**palliative** *adj.* & *n.*, **palliation** /-ˈeɪʃ(ə)n/ *n.* [f. L *palliare* to cloak (as PALL[1])]

pallid /ˈpælɪd/ *adj.* pale, especially from illness. [f. L (as PALE[1])]

pallor /ˈpælə(r)/ *n.* pallidness, paleness. [L (*pallēre* be pale)]

pally *adj.* (*colloq.*) friendly. —**palliness** *n.* [f. PAL]

palm[1] /pɑːm/ *n.* **1** a chiefly tropical tree of the family Palmae, with no branches and a mass of large leaves at the top. **2** a leaf of this as the symbol of victory. **3** supreme excellence; the prize for this. —**palm-oil** *n.* the oil from various palms. **Palm Sunday,** the Sunday before Easter, on which Christ's entry into Jerusalem is celebrated by processions in which branches of palms are carried. [OE f. L *palma* (as foll.)]

palm[2] /pɑːm/ *n.* the inner surface of the hand between the wrist and the fingers; the part of a glove that covers this. —*v.t.* to conceal in the hand. —**palm off,** to impose or thrust fraudulently *on* a person; to put (a person) off *with*. —**palmar** /ˈpɑːmə(r)/ *adj.* [f. OF f. L *palma*]

palmate /ˈpælmeɪt/ *adj.* shaped like the palm of the hand, having lobes etc. like spread fingers. —**palmately** *adv.* [f. L (as prec.)]

palmetto /pælˈmetəʊ/ *n.* (*pl.* **-os**) a palm-tree, especially of small size. [f. Sp. *palmito* (as PALM[1])]

palmistry /ˈpɑːmɪstrɪ/ *n.* the pseudo-science of divination by the lines and swellings of the hand. —**palmist** *n.* [f. PALM[2]]

palmy /ˈpɑːmɪ/ *adj.* **1** of, like, or abounding in palms. **2** full of success, flourishing. [f. PALM[1]]

palomino /pæləˈmiːnəʊ/ *n.* (*pl.* **-os**) a golden or cream-coloured horse with a light-coloured mane and tail. [f. Sp., = young pigeon]

palp *n.* a segmented organ at or near the mouth of certain insects and crustaceans, used for feeling and tasting things. [f. L (*palpare* touch gently)]

palpable /ˈpælpəb(ə)l/ *adj.* that can be touched or felt; readily perceived by the senses or mind. —**palpability** /-ˈbɪlɪtɪ/ *n.*, **palpably** *adv.* [as PALP]

palpate /pælˈpeɪt/ *v.t.* to examine (esp. medically) by touch. —**palpation** /-ˈpeɪʃ(ə)n/ *n.* [as PALP]

palpitate /ˈpælpɪteɪt/ *v.i.* to pulsate, to throb; to tremble (with pleasure, fear, etc.). [f. L *palpitare* frequent. of *palpare* touch gently]

palpitation /pælpɪˈteɪʃ(ə)n/ *n.* throbbing, trembling; increased activity of the heart due to exertion, agitation, or disease. [f. prec.]

palsy /ˈpɔlzɪ/ *n.* paralysis, especially with involuntary tremors; a cause or state of powerlessness. —*v.t.* to affect with palsy. [f. OF f. L (as PARALYSIS)]

paltry /ˈpɔltrɪ/ *adj.* worthless, contemptible, trivial. —**paltriness** *n.* [f. dial. *palt* rubbish]

palynology /pælɪˈnɒlədʒɪ/ *n.* the study of pollen in connection with plant geography, the dating of fossils, allergies, etc. —**palynological** /-əˈlɒdʒɪk(ə)l *adj.* [f. Gk *palunō* sprinkle + -LOGY]

pampas /ˈpæmpəs/ *n.pl.* the large treeless plains in South America. —**pampas-grass** *n.* a large ornamental grass (*Cortaderia selloana*) originally from South America. [Sp. f. Quechua]

pamper *v.t.* to over-indulge (a person, taste, etc.); to spoil (a person) with luxury. [f. obs. *pamp* cram]

pamphlet /ˈpæmflɪt/ *n.* a small usually unbound booklet or leaflet containing information or a treatise. [f. *Pamphilet* pet-name of *Pamphilus* 12th-c. amatory poem]

pamphleteer /pæmflɪˈtɪə(r)/ *n.* a writer of (esp. political) pamphlets. [f. prec.]

pan[1] *n.* **1** a metal, earthenware, or plastic vessel used for cooking and other domestic purposes; a panlike vessel in which substances are heated etc. **2** the bowl of a pair of scales; the bowl of a lavatory. **3** the part of the lock that held the priming in obsolete types of gun. **4** a hollow in the ground. —*v.t.* (**-nn-**) to criticize severely. —**pan out,** (of gravel) to yield gold; (of an action etc.) to turn out (well etc.); to be successful. —**panful** *n.* [OE]

pan[2] *v.t./i.* (**-nn-**) to swing (a cine-camera) horizontally to give a panoramic effect or follow a moving object; (of a camera) to be moved thus. —*n.* a panning movement. [f. PANORAMA]

pan- *in comb.* all, relating to the whole of a continent, racial group, religion, etc. (*pan-American*). [Gk (*pan* neut. of *pas* all)]

panacea /pænəˈsɪə/ *n.* a universal remedy. [L f. Gk (PAN-, *akos* remedy)]

panache /pəˈnæʃ/ *n.* an assertively or flamboyantly confident style or manner. [F, = plume]

panama /ˈpænəmɑː/ *n.* a hat of strawlike material made from the leaves of a pine-tree. [f. prec.]

panatella /pænəˈtelə/ *n.* a long thin cigar. [f. Sp., = long thin biscuit]

pancake *n.* **1** a thin flat batter-cake usually fried in a pan. **2** a flat cake (e.g. of make-up). —**Pancake Day,** Shrove Tuesday (on which pancakes are traditionally eaten). **pancake landing,** a heavy landing of an aircraft descending too steeply in a level horizontal position.

panchromatic /pænkrəˈmætɪk/ *adj.* (of film etc.) sensitive to all visible colours of the spectrum.

pancreas /ˈpænkrɪəs/ *n.* a gland near the stomach discharging a digestive secretion into the duodenum and insulin into the blood. —**pancreatic** /-ˈætɪk/ *adj.* [f. Gk (PAN-, *kreas* flesh)]

panda /ˈpændə/ *n.* **1** (also **giant panda**) a large black-and-white bearlike mammal (*Ailuropoda melanoleuca*), native to limited mountainous forested areas in China. —**panda car,** a police patrol car (originally white with black stripes on the doors). [Nepali name]

pandemic /pænˈdemɪk/ *adj.* (of a disease) prevalent over a whole region or the world. [f. Gk (PAN-, *dēmos* people)]

pandemonium /pændɪˈməʊnɪəm/ *n.* uproar, utter confusion; a scene of this. [name of capital of hell in Milton, f. PAN- + DEMON]

pander *v.i.* (with *to*) to gratify or indulge a person or weakness etc. —*n.* **1** a go-between in illicit love-affairs; a procurer. **2** one who panders. [f. *Pandarus*, name of Cressida's uncle in the medieval legend of Troilus and Cressida, who acted as go-between for the lovers]

P. & O. *abbr.* Peninsular and Oriental Steamship Company.

p. & p. *abbr.* postage and packing.

pane *n.* a single sheet of glass in a window or door. [f. OF *pan* f. L *pannus* piece of cloth]

panegyric /pænɪˈdʒɪrɪk/ *n.* a laudatory discourse, a eulogy. —**panegyrical** *adj.* [f. F f. L f. Gk (PAN-, *agora* assembly)]

panel /ˈpæn(ə)l/ *n.* **1** a distinct usually rectangular section of a surface (e.g. of a wall, door, vehicle). **2** a strip of material as part of a garment. **3** a team in a broadcast or public quiz programme etc.; a body of experts assembled for discussion or consultation. **4** a list of jurors, a jury. —*v.t.* (**-ll-**) to cover or decorate with panels. —**panel game,** a quiz etc. played by a panel. **panel-saw** *n.* a saw with small teeth for cutting thin wood for panels. [f. OF, = piece of cloth (as PANE)]

panelling *n.* panelled work; wood for making panels. [f. prec.]

panellist *n.* a member of a panel. [f. PANEL]

pang *n.* a sudden sharp pain or painful emotion. [var. of earlier *pronge*, cf. MLG *prange* pinching]

pangolin /pæŋˈgəʊlɪn/ *n.* the scaly ant-eater, a large mammal of the genus *Manis*. [f. Malay, = roller (because it rolls itself up)]

panic /ˈpænɪk/ *n.* a sudden uncontrollable fear or alarm; infectious fright. —*adj.* of, connected with, or resulting from panic. —*v.t./i.* (**-ck-**) to affect or be affected with panic. —**panic-stricken** *or* **-struck** *adj.* affected with panic. —**panicky** *adj.* [f. F f. Gk (see PAN)]

panicle /ˈpænɪk(ə)l/ *n.* a loose branching cluster

of flowers. [f. L *paniculum*, dim. of *panus* thread]

panjandrum /pæn'dʒændrəm/ *n.* a mock title of an exalted personage. [invented by S. Foote in nonsense verse (1755)]

pannier /'pænɪə/ *n.* **1** a basket, especially one of a pair carried by a beast of burden or on a bicycle, motor cycle, etc. **2** (*hist.*) a part of a skirt looped up round the hips; a frame supporting this. [f. OF f. L *panarium* bread-basket (*panis* bread)]

panoply /'pænəplɪ/ *n.* **1** a complete suit of armour. **2** a complete or splendid array. [f. F f. Gk (PAN-, *hopla* arms)]

panorama /pænə'rɑ:mə/ *n.* **1** a view of a wide area; a picture or photograph of this. **2** a view of a constantly changing scene or series of events etc. —**panoramic** /-'ræmɪk/ *adj.* [f. PAN- + Gk *horama* view (*horaō* see)]

pan-pipe *n.* (in *sing.* or *pl.*) a musical instrument formed from three or more tubes of different lengths joined in a row (or in some areas of a block of wood with tubes drilled down into it) with mouthpieces in line, and sounded by blowing across the top. [f. *Pan*, Gk god + PIPE]

pansy /'pænzɪ/ *n.* **1** a garden plant (hybrids of *Viola tricolor*) with flowers of various rich colours. **2** (*colloq.*) an effeminate man; a male homosexual. [f. F *pensée* thought, pansy (*penser* think f. L *pensare* frequent. of *pendere* weigh)]

pant *v.t./i.* to breathe with short quick breaths; to utter breathlessly; to yearn; (of the heart etc.) to throb violently. —*n.* a panting breath; a throb. [f. OF *pantaisier* ult. f. Gk (as FANTASY)]

pantaloons /pæntə'lu:nz/ *n.pl.* (esp. *US*) trousers. [f. F f. It.]

pantechnicon /pæn'teknɪkən/ *n.* a large van for transporting furniture etc. [short for *pantechnicon van* (*pantechnicon* furniture warehouse, orig. a bazaar, as PAN-, TECHNIQUE)]

pantheism /'pænθɪɪz(ə)m/ *n.* the belief that God is everything and everything God. -**pantheist** *n.*, **pantheistic** /-'ɪstɪk/ *adj.* [f. PAN- + Gk *theos* god]

pantheon /'pænθɪən/ *n.* **1** a temple dedicated to all the gods. **2** the deities of a people collectively. **3 Pantheon,** a building in which the illustrious dead are buried or have memorials. [f. L f. Gk (PAN-, *theios* divine)]

panther /'pænθə(r)/ *n.* a leopard (see entry). [f. OF f. L f. Gk]

panties /'pæntɪz/ *n.pl.* (*colloq.*) short-legged or legless knickers worn by women and girls. [dim. of PANTS]

pantihose /'pæntɪhəʊz/ *n.* women's tights. [f. prec. + HOSE]

pantile /'pæntaɪl/ *n.* a curved roof-tile. [f. PAN[1] + TILE]

panto /'pæntəʊ/ *n.* (*colloq.*) a pantomime. [abbr.]

pantograph /'pæntəgrɑ:f/ *n.* **1** an instrument with jointed rods for enlarging or reducing a plan etc. **2** a jointed framework conveying current to an electric vehicle from overhead wires. [f. *panto-* all (as PAN-) + -GRAPH]

pantomime /'pæntəmaɪm/ *n.* **1** a dramatic entertainment usually produced about Christmas and based on a fairy-tale. **2** gestures and facial expression used to convey meaning. —**pantomimic** /-'mɪmɪk/ *adj.* [F or f. L f. Gk (*panto-* as PAN- + MIME)]

pantry /'pæntrɪ/ *n.* **1** a room or cupboard in which crockery, cutlery, table-linen, etc. are kept. **2** a larder. [f. OF (*panetier* baker f. L *panis* bread)]

pants *n.pl.* **1** (*colloq.*) underpants, panties. **2** (*US*) trousers. [abbr. of PANTALOONS]

pap[1] *n.* **1** soft or semi-liquid food for infants or invalids. **2** undemanding reading matter. [prob. f. MLG or MDu. f. L *pappare* eat]

pap[2] *n.* (*archaic* or *dial.*) a nipple of the breast. [f. Scand., imit. of sucking]

papa /pə'pɑ:/ *n.* (*archaic*; esp. as child's word) father. [F f. L f. Gk *pap(p)as*]

papacy /'peɪpəsɪ/ *n.* **1** the pope's office or tenure. **2** the papal system. [f. L *papatia* (*papa* pope)]

papal /'peɪp(ə)l/ *adj.* of the pope or his office. —**papally** *adv.* [f. OF f. L (as prec.)]

papaw /pə'pɔ, 'pɔ:pɔ:/ *n.* **1** an oblong orange fruit with a thick fleshy rind, and numerous black seeds embedded in its pulp, used as food. **2** the palmlike tropical American tree (*Carica papaya*) bearing this. **3** (*US*) a North American tree (*Asimina triloba*) bearing purple flowers and an oblong edible fruit. [earlier *papay(a)* f. Sp. & Port. f. Carib]

paper /'peɪpə(r)/ *n.* **1** a substance in thin sheets made from pulp of wood or other fibrous material, used for writing or drawing or printing on, as a wrapping material, etc. **2** a document; documents attesting identity or credentials; the documents belonging to a person or relating to a matter. **3** a newspaper. **4** wallpaper. **5** a piece of paper, especially as a wrapper etc. **6** a set of questions to be answered at one session in an examination; the written answers to these. **7** an essay or dissertation, especially one read to a learned society. —*adj.* made of or flimsy like paper; existing only in theory. —*v.t.* to decorate (a wall etc.) with paper. —**on paper,** in writing; in theory; to judge from written or printed evidence. **paper-boy, paper-girl** *ns.* one who delivers or sells newspapers. **paper-clip** *n.* a clip of bent wire or of plastic for holding a few sheets of paper together. **paper-knife** *n.* a blunt knife for opening letters etc. **paper money,** money in the form of banknotes. **paper tiger,** a threatening but ineffectual person or thing. [f. AF f. L, = PAPYRUS]

paperback *adj*. bound in stiff paper, not boards. —*n*. a paperback book.

paperweight *n*. a small heavy object for keeping loose papers in place.

paperwork *n*. routine clerical or administrative work.

papery *adj*. like paper in thinness or texture. [f. PAPER]

papier mâché /pæpjeɪˈmæʃeɪ/ moulded paper pulp used for boxes, trays, etc. [F, = chewed paper]

papilla /pəˈpɪlə/ *n*. (*pl*. **-lae** /-liː/) a small nipple-like protuberance in or on the body. [L, = nipple]

papillary /pəˈpɪlərɪ/ *adj*. papilla-shaped. [f. prec.]

papillon /ˈpæpɪjɔ̃/ *n*. a dog of a toy breed related to the spaniel, having a white coat with a few darker patches and erect ears resembling the shape of a butterfly's wings. [F, = butterfly]

papist /ˈpeɪpɪst/ *n*. an advocate of papal supremacy; (usu. *derog*.) a Roman Catholic. [f. F f. L *papa* pope]

papoose /pəˈpuːs/ *n*. a North American Indian baby. [Algonquin]

paprika /ˈpæprɪkə/ *n*. a ripe red pepper; the red condiment made from it. [Magyar]

papyrology /pæpɪˈrɒlədʒɪ/ *n*. the study of ancient papyri. —**papyrologist** *n*. [f. foll. + -LOGY]

papyrus /pəˈpaɪrəs/ *n*. (*pl*. **-ri** /-riː/) **1** an aquatic plant (*Cyperus papyrus*) of the sedge family. **2** an ancient writing material made from the stem of this; a manuscript written on it. [f. L f. Gk]

par *n*. **1** an average or normal amount, degree, condition, etc. **2** equality, an equal status or footing. **3** (in golf) the number of strokes a scratch player should normally require for a hole or course. **4** the face value of stocks and shares etc. **5** (in full **par of exchange**) the recognized value of one country's currency in terms of another's. [L, = equal]

para /ˈpærə/ *n* (*colloq*.) a paratrooper. [abbr.]

para-[1] /pærə-/ *prefix* **1** beside (*parabola, paramilitary*). **2** beyond (*paradox, paranormal*). [f. Gk]

para-[2] /pærə-, *in comb*. to protect, to ward off (*parachute, parasol*). [F f. It. (*parare* defend)]

para. *abbr*. paragraph.

parable /ˈpærəb(ə)l/ *n*. a narrative of imagined events used to illustrate a moral or spiritual lesson; an allegory. [f. OF f. L *parabola* comparison (as foll.)]

parabola /pəˈræbələ/ *n*. an open plane curve formed by the intersection of a cone with a plane parallel to its slanting side. [f. Gk *parabolē* placing side by side]

parabolic /pærəˈbɒlɪk/ *adj*. **1** of or expressed in a parable. **2** of or like a parabola. —**parabolically** *adv*. [f. L f. Gk (as prec.)]

paracetamol /pærəˈsiːtəmɒl, -set-/ *n*. a compound forming a white powder, used to relieve pain and reduce fever; a tablet of this. [f. its chemical name]

parachute /ˈpærəʃuːt/ *n*. an umbrella-shaped or rectangular apparatus of silk, nylon, etc. allowing a person or heavy object to descend safely from a height, especially from an aircraft; (*attrib*.) (to be) dropped by parachute. —*v.t./i*. to descend or convey by parachute. —**parachutist** *n*. [F (as PARA-[2], CHUTE)]

Paraclete /ˈpærəkliːt/ *n*. the Holy Spirit as an advocate or counsellor. [f. OF f. L f. Gk, = called in aid (PARA-[1], *kaleō* call)]

parade /pəˈreɪd/ *n*. **1** a muster of troops for inspection. **2** a public procession. **3** an ostentatious display. **4** a public square or promenade. **5** a parade-ground. —*v.t./i*. **1** to assemble for a parade. **2** to march through (streets etc.) in procession, to march ceremonially. **3** to display ostentatiously. —**parade-ground** *n*. a place for the muster of troops. [F, = show, f. It. & Sp. f. L *parare* prepare]

paradigm /ˈpærədaɪm/ *n*. an example or pattern, especially of the inflexions of a noun, verb, etc. —**paradigmatic** /-dɪgˈmætɪk/ *adj*. [f. L f. Gk (PARA-[1], *deiknumi* show)]

paradise /ˈpærədaɪs/ *n*. **1** the abode of God and of the righteous after death, heaven. **2** a region or state of supreme bliss. **3** (in Gen. 2, 3) the garden of Eden. —**paradisiac** /-ˈdaɪsɪæk/ *adj*., **paradisiacal** /-dɪˈsaɪək(ə)l/ *adj*., **paradisal** *adj*. [f. OF ult. f. Avestan *pairidaēza* park]

paradox /ˈpærədɒks/ *n*. **1** a seemingly absurd though perhaps actually well-founded statement. **2** a self-contradictory or essentially absurd statement. **3** a person or thing conflicting with a preconceived notion of what is reasonable or possible. **4** paradoxical nature. —**paradoxical** /-ˈdɒksɪk(ə)l/ *adj*., **paradoxically** *adj*. [f. L f. Gk (PARA-[1], *doxa* opinion)]

paraffin /ˈpærəfɪn/ *n*. **1** an inflammable waxy or oily substance obtained by distillation from petroleum and shale and used especially as a fuel. **2** a hydrocarbon of the methane series, containing the maximum amount of hydrogen. —**liquid paraffin,** a tasteless mild laxative. **paraffin wax,** paraffin in a solid form. [G, f. L *parum* little + *affinis* related]

paragon /ˈpærəgən/ *n*. a model of excellence, a supremely excellent person or thing; a model (*of* virtue etc.). [obs. F f. It. *paragone* touchstone f. Gk]

paragraph /ˈpærəgrɑːf/ *n.* one or more sentences on a single theme, forming a distinct section of a piece of writing and beginning on a new (usually indented) line. —*v.t.* to arrange in paragraphs. —**paragraphic** /-ˈgræfɪk/ *adj.* [f. F or L f. Gk *paragraphos* short stroke marking break in sense (PARA-[1], *graphō* write)]

parakeet /ˈpærəkiːt/ *n.* any of various small usually long-tailed species of parrot. [f. OF, perh. ult. f. dim. of *Pierre* Peter]

parallax /ˈpærəlæks/ *n.* the apparent difference in position or direction of an object caused by a change of the point of observation; the angular amount of this. —**parallactic** /-ˈlæktɪk/ *adj.* [f. F f. Gk *parallaxis* change, alternation]

parallel /ˈpærəlel/ *adj.* **1** (of lines or planes) continuously equidistant; (of a line or plane) having this relation. **2** analogous, having features that correspond. —*n.* **1** a person or thing that is analogous to another. **2** a comparison. **3** (in full **parallel of latitude**) each of the imaginary parallel circles of constant latitude on the earth's surface; a corresponding line on a map. **3** two parallel lines (||) as a reference mark. —*v.t.* (*p.t.* **paralleled**) **1** to be parallel to, to correspond to. **2** to represent as similar, to compare. **3** to adduce a parallel instance to. —**in parallel,** (of an electric circuit) arranged so as to join at common points at each end. **parallel bars,** a pair of parallel rails on posts for gymnastics. [f. F f. L f. Gk, = alongside each other (PARA-[1], *allēlos* one another)]

parallelepiped /pærəleˈlepɪped, -əˈpaɪped/ *n.* a solid body of which each face is a parallelogram. [f. Gk (as prec., *epipedon* plane surface, EPI-, *pedon* ground)]

parallelism *n.* being parallel; correspondence. [f. PARALLEL]

parallelogram /pærəˈleləgræm/ *n.* a four-sided plane rectilinear figure with the opposite sides parallel. [f. F f. L f. Gk (as PARALLEL, *grammē* line)]

paralyse /ˈpærəlaɪz/ *v.t.* **1** to affect with paralysis. **2** to render powerless; to bring to a standstill. [f. F (as foll.)]

paralysis /pəˈrælɪsɪs/ *n.* **1** impairment or loss of the power of movement, caused by disease or injury to nerves. **2** a state of powerlessness; inability to move or operate normally. [L f. Gk (PARA-[1], *luō* loosen)]

paralytic /pærəˈlɪtɪk/ *adj.* **1** affected by paralysis. **2** (*slang*) very drunk. —*n.* a person affected by paralysis. [f. OF f. L f. Gk (as prec.)]

paramedical /pærəˈmedɪk(ə)l/ *adj.* (of services etc.) supplementing and supporting medical work.

parameter /pəˈræmɪtə(r)/ *n.* **1** a quantity that is constant in the case considered but which varies in different cases. **2** a variable quantity or quality that restricts or gives a particular form to the thing it characterizes. [f. Gk *para* beside + *metron* measure]

paramilitary /pærəˈmɪlɪtərɪ/ *adj.* organized like a military force but not part of the armed services. —*n.* a member of a paramilitary organization.

paramount /ˈpærəmaʊnt/ *adj.* supreme; in supreme authority. [f. AF (OF *par* by, *amont* above; see AMOUNT)]

paramour /ˈpærəmʊə(r)/ *n.* (*archaic*) a married person's illicit lover. [f. OF *par amour* by love]

parang /ˈpɑːræŋ/ *n.* a heavy Malayan sheath-knife. [Malay]

paranoia /pærəˈnɔɪə/ *n.* **1** a mental disorder with delusions of grandeur, persecution, etc. **2** an abnormal tendency to suspect and mistrust others. [f. Gk (PARA-[1], *noos* mind)]

paranoiac /pærəˈnɔɪæk/ *adj.* (also **paranoic** /pærəˈnəʊɪk/) paranoid. —*n.* a paranoid person. [f. prec.]

paranoid /ˈpærənɔɪd/ *adj.* affected by paranoia. —*n.* a paranoid person. [f. PARANOIA]

paranormal /pærəˈnɔːm(ə)l/ *adj.* (of phenomena or powers) presumed to operate according to natural laws beyond or outside those considered normal or known.

parapet /ˈpærəpɪt/ *n.* a low wall at the edge of a roof, balcony, etc., or along the sides of a bridge etc.; a defence of earth or stone to conceal and protect troops. [F or f. It., = breast-high wall (PARA-[2], *petto* breast)]

paraphernalia /pærəfəˈneɪlɪə/ *n.pl.* miscellaneous belongings, accessories, etc. [L f. Gk, = personal articles which a woman could keep after marriage, as opp. to her dowry which went to her husband (PARA-[1], *phernē* dowry)]

paraphrase /ˈpærəfreɪz/ *n.* expression of the meaning of a passage in other words. —*v.t.* to express the meaning of (a passage) in other words. [F or f. L f. Gk (PARA-, *phrazō* tell)]

paraplegia /pærəˈpliːdʒə/ *n.* paralysis of the legs and part or the whole of the trunk. [f. Gk (PARA-[1], *plēssō* strike)]

paraplegic /pærəˈpliːdʒɪk/ *adj.* of paraplegia. —*n.* one who suffers from paraplegia. [f. prec.]

parapsychology /pærəsaɪˈkɒlədʒɪ/ *n.* the study of mental phenomena outside the sphere of ordinary psychology (hypnosis, telepathy, etc.).

paraquat /ˈpærəkwɒt/ *n.* an extremely

poisonous quick-acting herbicide that becomes inactive on contact with the soil. [f. PARA-[1] + QUATERNARY (with ref. to its chemical composition)]

parasite /ˈpærəsaɪt/ *n.* **1** an animal or plant living in or on another and drawing nutriment directly from it. **2** a person who lives off or exploits another or others. —**parasitic** /-ˈsɪtɪk/ *adj.*, **parasitically** /-ˈsɪtɪkəlɪ/ *adv.*, **parasitism** *n.* [f. L f. Gk, = one who eats at another's table (PARA-[1], *sitos* food)]

parasol /ˈpærəsɒl/ *n.* a light umbrella used to give shade from the sun. [F f. It. (PARA-[2], *sole* sun)]

paratrooper /ˈpærətru:pə(r)/ *n.* a member of the paratroops. [f. foll.]

paratroops /ˈpærətru:ps/ *n.pl.* parachute troops. [f. PARACHUTE + TROOPS]

paratyphoid /pærəˈtaɪfɔɪd/ *n.* a fever resembling typhoid but caused by a different bacterium.

parboil /ˈpɑ:bɔɪl/ *v.t.* **1** to boil (food) until it is partly cooked. **2** to subject (a person) to great heat. [f. OF f. L *perbullire* (*per-* thoroughly, confused with PART)]

parcel /ˈpɑ:s(ə)l/ *n.* **1** a thing or things wrapped as a single package for carrying or for sending by post. **2** a piece of land. **3** the quantity dealt with in one commercial transaction. —*v.t.* (**-ll-**) **1** to wrap up as a parcel. **2** to divide (*out*) into portions. [f. OF dim. of L *particula* (as PARTICLE)]

parch *v.t./i.* **1** to make or become hot and dry. **2** to roast (peas, corn, etc.) slightly. [orig. unkn.]

parchment /ˈpɑ:tʃmənt/ *n.* **1** a heavy paper-like material made from animal skins. **2** a manuscript written on this. **3** a high-grade paper made to resemble parchment. [f. OF f. L *pergamina* f. PERGAMUM which from the 2nd c. BC was noted for the production of parchment]

pardon /ˈpɑ:d(ə)n/ *n.* **1** forgiveness. **2** remission of the legal consequences of a crime or conviction. **3** courteous forbearance. —*v.t.* **1** to forgive. **2** to make courteous allowances for, to excuse. —**I beg your pardon,** (*colloq.*) **pardon (me),** a formula of apology or disagreement, or a request to repeat something said. [f. OF f. L *perdonare* concede]

pardonable *adj.* that may be pardoned, easily excused. —**pardonably** *adv.* [f. prec.]

pare *v.t.* **1** to trim or shave by cutting away the surface or edge. **2** to diminish little by little. [f. OF f. L *parare* prepare]

paregoric /pærɪˈgɒrɪk/ *n.* a camphorated tincture of opium used as an analgesic; an anodyne. —*adj.* soothing. [f. L f. Gk (PARA-[1], *-agoros* speaking f. *agora* assembly)]

parent /ˈpeərənt/ *n.* **1** one who has begotten or borne offspring, a father or mother. **2** a forefather. **3** a person who has adopted a child. **4** an animal or plant from which others are derived. **5** a source from which other things are derived. —*v.t./i.* to be a parent (of). —**parent-teacher association,** an organization consisting of, and promoting good relations between, teachers and the parents of their pupils. —**parental** /pəˈrent(ə)l/ *adj.*, **parentally** *adv.*, **parenthood** *n.* [f. OF f. L (*parere* bring forth)]

parentage *n.* lineage, descent from parents.

parenthesis /pəˈrenθəsɪs/ *n.* (*pl.* **-eses** /-əsi:z/) **1** a word, clause, or sentence inserted as an explanation or afterthought into a passage which is grammatically complete without it, and usually marked off by brackets, dashes, or commas. **2** (in *pl.*) a pair of round brackets ( ) used for this. —**in parenthesis,** as a parenthesis; as an aside or digression. [L f. Gk (*parentithēmi* put in beside (as PARA-[1], EN-, *tithēmi* place)]

parenthesize /pəˈrenθəsaɪz/ *v.t.* to insert as a parenthesis; to put (words) between parentheses. [f. prec.]

parenthetic /pærənˈθetɪk/ *adj.* of or inserted as a parenthesis. —**parenthetical** *adj.*, **parenthetically** *adv.* [f. PARENTHESIS]

par excellence /pɑ:r eksəˈlɑ̃ns/ *adv.* above all others that may be so called. [F, = by virtue of special excellence]

parfait /ˈpɑ:feɪ/ *n.* **1** a rich iced pudding of whipped cream, eggs, etc. **2** layers of ice-cream, fruit, etc., served in a tall glass. [F, = PERFECT]

parget /ˈpɑ:dʒɪt/ *v.t.* to plaster (a wall etc.) especially with an ornamental pattern; to roughcast. —*n.* plaster; roughcast. [f. OF *pargeter* (*par* all over, *jeter* throw)]

pariah /pəˈraɪə/ *n.* **1** a member of a low or no caste. **2** a social outcast. [f. Tamil]

parietal /pəˈraɪət(ə)l/ *adj.* of the wall of the body or any of its cavities. —**parietal bone,** either of a pair of bones forming part of the skull. [f. F or L (*paries* wall)]

paring /ˈpeərɪŋ/ *n.* a strip or piece cut off. [f. PARE]

parish /ˈpærɪʃ/ *n.* **1** an area having its own church and clergyman. **2** a district constituted for the purposes of local government. **3** the inhabitants of a parish. —**parish clerk,** an official performing various duties concerned with a church. **parish council,** the administrative body in a civil parish. **parish register,** a book recording christenings, marriages, and burials, at a parish church. [f. OF f. L *parochia* f. Gk, = sojourning (PARA-[1], *oikeō* dwell)]

parishioner /pəˈrɪʃənə(r)/ *n.* an inhabitant of a parish. [f. obs. *parishen* in same sense (as prec.)]

Parisian /pəˈrɪzɪən/ *adj.* of the city of Paris. —*n.* a native or inhabitant of Paris. [f. *Paris*, capital of France]

parity /ˈpærɪtɪ/ *n.* **1** equality, equal status or pay etc. **2** the equivalence of one currency in another; being at par. [f. F or L *paritas* (as PAR)]

park *n.* **1** a large public garden in a town, for recreation. **2** a large enclosed piece of ground, usually with woodland and pasture, attached to a country house etc. **3** a large tract of land in its natural state for public enjoyment. **4** an area for motor cars etc. to be left in. **5** (*US*) a sports ground. —*v.t.* **1** to place and leave (a vehicle, or *absol.*) temporarily. **2** (*colloq.*) to deposit temporarily. —**park oneself**, (*colloq.*) to sit down. **parking-lot** *n.* (*US*) an outdoor area for parking vehicles. **parking-meter** *n.* a coin-operated meter which receives the fees for vehicles parked in a street and indicates the time available. **parking-ticket** *n.* a notice of a fine etc. imposed for parking a vehicle illegally. [f. OF *parc*]

parka /ˈpɑːkə/ *n.* a skin jacket with a hood, worn by Eskimos; a similar windproof fabric garment worn by mountaineers etc. [Aleutian]

Parkinson's disease /ˈpɑːkɪns(ə)nz/ (also **Parkinsonism**) a progressive disease of the nervous system with tremor, muscular rigidity, and emaciation. [f. J. *Parkinson*, English surgeon, who described it in 1817 under the names 'shaking palsy' and 'paralysis agitans']

Parkinson's law /ˈpɑːkɪns(ə)nz/ the notion that 'work expands so as to fill the time available for its completion'. [f. C. N. *Parkinson*, English writer (1909–)]

parkland *n.* open grassland with clumps of trees etc.

parky *adj.* (*slang*) chilly. [orig. unkn.]

parlance *n.* way of speaking, phraseology. [OF (*parler* speak, ult. f. L *parabola*, as PARABLE)]

parley /ˈpɑːlɪ/ *n.* a conference for debating points in dispute, especially a discussion of the terms for an armistice etc. —*v.i.* to hold a parley. [perh. f. OF *parlee*, fem. p.p. of *parler* (as prec.)]

parliament /ˈpɑːləmənt/ *n.* the legislative assembly of a country; **Parliament**, that of the UK. —**Houses of Parliament**, the House of Commons and House of Lords. [f. OF *parlement* speaking (as PARLANCE)]

parliamentarian /pɑːləmenˈteərɪən/ *n.* a skilled debater in parliament. [f. prec.]

parliamentary /pɑːləˈmentərɪ/ *adj.* **1** of parliament; enacted or established by a parliament. **2** (of language) admissible in Parliament, (*colloq.*) polite. [f. PARLIAMENT]

parlour /ˈpɑːlə(r)/ *n.* **1** a sitting-room in a private house. **2** a room in a hotel, convent, etc., for private conversation. **3** a shop providing specified goods or services. —**parlour game**, an indoor game, especially a word-game. [f. AF (as PARLANCE)]

parlous /ˈpɑːləs/ *adj.* (*archaic*) perilous, hard to deal with. —*adv.* (*archaic*) extremely. [= PERILOUS]

Parmesan /pɑːmɪˈzæn, (*attrib.*) ˈpɑː-/ *n.* a kind of hard cheese made originally at Parma and used especially in a grated form. [F f. It. *parmegiano* (*Parma* in Italy)]

parochial /pəˈrəʊkɪəl/ *adj.* **1** of a parish. **2** (of affairs, views, etc.) merely local, confined to a narrow area. —**parochialism** *n.*, **parochially** *adv.* [f. AF f. L (as PARISH)]

parody /ˈpærədɪ/ *n.* **1** a humorous exaggerated imitation of an author, literary work, style, etc. **2** a grotesque imitation, a travesty. —*v.t.* to compose a parody of, to mimic humorously. —**parodist** *n.* [f. L or Gk *parōidia* burlesque poem (PARA-[1], *ōidē* song)]

parole /pəˈrəʊl/ *n.* **1** release of a prisoner (temporarily for a special purpose, or completely) before expiry of the sentence, on promise of good behaviour; such a promise. **2** a person's word of honour. —*v.t.* to release on parole. [F, = word, f. L *parabola* (as PARABLE)]

parotid /pəˈrɒtɪd/ *adj.* situated near the ear. —*n.* the parotid gland. —**parotid gland**, the salivary gland in front of the ear. [f. F or L f. Gk *parōtis* (PARA-[1], *ous* ear)]

paroxysm /ˈpærəksɪz(ə)m/ *n.* a sudden attack or outburst of rage, laughter, etc.; a spasm. —**paroxysmal** /-ˈsɪzm(ə)l/ *adj.* [f. F f. L f. Gk (*paroxunō* exasperate)]

parquet /ˈpɑːkeɪ, -kɪ/ *n.* flooring of wooden blocks arranged in a pattern. —*v.t.* to floor (a room) thus. —**parquetry** /-kɪtrɪ/ *n.* [F, = small compartment (as PARK)]

parr /pɑː(r)/ *n.* a young salmon. [orig. unkn.]

parricide /ˈpærɪsaɪd/ *n.* **1** the crime of killing one's own parent or other near relative. **2** one who is guilty of this. —**parricidal** *adj.* [F, or f. L (assoc. with *pater* father, *parens* parent, -CIDE)]

parrot /ˈpærət/ *n.* **1** a mainly tropical bird with a short hooked bill of the order Psittaciformes, of which many species have vivid plumage and some can imitate words. **2** a person who mechanically repeats another's words or imitates his actions. —*v.t.* to repeat mechanically. [prob. f. dial. F (dim. of *Pierre* Peter)]

parry /ˈpærɪ/ *v.t.* **1** to ward off (a weapon or blow) by using one's own weapon etc. to block the thrust. **2** to evade (an awkward question) by an adroit reply. —*n.* parrying. [prob. f. F *parer* f. It. *parare* ward off]

parse /pɑːz/ *v.t.* to describe (a word in context)

grammatically, stating its inflexion, relation to the sentence, etc.; to resolve (a sentence) into its component parts and describe them grammatically. [perh. f. obs. *pars* parts of speech f. OF (as PART)]

parsec /ˈpɑːsek/ *n.* a unit of distance used in astronomy, about 3.26 light-years, the distance at which a star would have a parallax of one second of an arc, i.e. at which the mean radius of the earth's orbit subtends this angle. [f. PARALLAX + SECOND²]

Parsee /pɑːˈsiː/ *n.* an adherent of Zoroastrianism in India, a descendant of the Persians who fled to India from Muslim persecution in the 7th–8th c. [f. Pers. *Parsi* Persian]

parsimony /ˈpɑːsɪmənɪ/ *n.* carefulness in the use of money or resources; meanness, stinginess. —**parsimonious** /-ˈməʊnɪəs/ *adj.*, **parsimoniously** *adv.* [f. L (*parcere* spare)]

parsley /ˈpɑːslɪ/ *n.* a herb (*Petroselinum crispum*) used for seasoning and garnishing dishes. [f. OF f. L f. Gk *petroselinon* (*petra* rock, *selinon* parsley)]

parsnip /ˈpɑːsnɪp/ *n.* a plant (*Pastinaca sativa*) with a pale yellow tapering root used as a culinary vegetable; its root. [f. OF *pasnaie* f. L *pastinaca*, assim. to *nep* turnip]

parson /ˈpɑːs(ə)n/ *n.* a rector; a vicar or any beneficed clergyman; (*colloq.*) any (esp. Protestant) clergyman. —**parson's nose,** the rump of a (cooked) fowl. [f. OF f. L, = PERSON]

parsonage *n.* the house provided for a parson. [f. prec.]

part *n.* **1** some but not all of a thing or number of things. **2** an integral member or component. **3** a division of a book, broadcast serial, etc., especially as much as is issued etc. at one time. **4** each of several equal portions of a whole. **5** a portion allotted, a share; a person's share in an action, his duty. **6** a character assigned to an actor on the stage; the words spoken by an actor on the stage; a copy of these. **7** (*Mus.*) a melody or other constituent of harmony assigned to a particular voice or instrument. **8** a side in an agreement or dispute. **9** (in *pl.*) a region, a district. **10** (in *pl.*) abilities. —*v.t./i.* **1** to divide or separate into parts; to cause to do this. **2** to separate (the hair of the head on either side of a parting) with a comb. **3** to quit one another's company. **4** (*colloq.*) to part with one's money, to pay. —*adv.* in part, partly. —**for my part,** so far as I am concerned. **in part,** partly. **on the part of,** proceeding from, done etc. by. **part and parcel,** an essential part *of*. **part-exchange** *n.* a transaction in which an article is given as part of the payment for a more expensive one. **part of speech,** each of the grammatical classes of words (in English usually noun, adjective, pronoun, verb, adverb, preposition, conjunction, interjection). **part-song** *n.* a song for several voice-parts, often unaccompanied. **part time,** less than full time. **part-time** *adj.* occupying or using only part of the available working time. **part-timer** *n.* one employed in part-time work. **part with,** to give up possession of, to hand over. **take in good part,** not to be offended by. **take part,** to assist or have a share (*in*). **take the part of,** to support, to back up. [f. OF f. L *pars*]

partake /pɑːˈteɪk/ *v.i.* (*past* **partook** /-ˈtʊk/, *p.p.* **partaken**) **1** to participate. **2** to take a share, especially of food or drink. —**partaker** *n.* [back-formation f. *partaker* = part-taker]

parterre /pɑːˈteə(r)/ *n.* **1** a level space in a garden occupied by flower-beds. **2** the pit of a theatre. [F, = *par terre* on the ground]

parthenogenesis /pɑːθɪnəʊˈdʒenəsɪs/ *n.* reproduction from gametes without fertilization. —**parthenogenetic** /-dʒɪˈnetɪk/ *adj.* [f. Gk *parthenos* virgin + GENESIS]

Parthian /ˈpɑːθɪən/ *adj.* of the ancient Asian kingdom of Parthia, SE of the Caspian Sea. —**Parthian shot,** a telling remark reserved for the moment of departure, so called from the trick used by Parthians of shooting arrows while in real or pretended flight. [f. *Parthia*]

partial /ˈpɑːʃ(ə)l/ *adj.* **1** not complete, forming only a part. **2** biased, unfair. —**partial eclipse,** an eclipse in which only part of the luminary is covered or darkened. **partial to,** having a liking for. —**partially** *adv.* [f. OF f. L (as PART)]

partiality /pɑːʃɪˈælɪtɪ/ *n.* **1** bias, favouritism. **2** a strong liking. [f. OF f. L (as prec.)]

participant /pɑːˈtɪsɪpənt/ *n.* a participator. [as foll.]

participate /pɑːˈtɪsɪpeɪt/ *v.i.* to have a share, to take part. —**participation** /-ˈpeɪʃ(ə)n/ *n.*, **participator** *n.* [f. L (*particeps* taking part f. *pars* part + *-cip-* f. *capere* take)]

participle /ˈpɑːtɪsɪp(ə)l/ *n.* a word formed from a verb (e.g. *going, gone, being, been*) and used in compound verb-forms (e.g. *is being, has been*) or as an adjective (*going concern, painted wall*). —**participial** /-ˈsɪpɪəl/ *adj.* [f. OF f. L *participium* (as prec.)]

particle /ˈpɑːtɪk(ə)l/ *n.* **1** a minute portion of matter. **2** the least possible amount. **3** a minor part of speech, especially a short indeclinable one; a common prefix or suffix such as *un-*, *-ship*. [f. L *particula* (as PART)]

particoloured /ˈpɑːtɪkʌləd/ *adj.* partly in one colour and partly in another. [f. OF *parti* divided (as PARTY) + COLOURED]

particular /pəˈtɪkjʊlə(r)/ *adj.* **1** relating to one person or thing as distinct from others, individual. **2** more than usual, special.

3 scrupulously exact, fastidious; detailed. —*n.* 1 a detail, an item. 2 (in *pl.*) information, a detailed account. —**in particular,** especially; specifically. [f. OF f. L (as PARTICLE)]

particularity /pətɪkjʊ'lærɪtɪ/ *n.* 1 the quality of being individual or particular. 2 fullness or minuteness of detail in description. [f. prec.]

particularize /pə'tɪkjʊləraɪz/ *v.t.* to name specially or one by one; to specify (items). —**particularization** /-'zeɪʃ(ə)n/ *n.* [f. F (as PARTICULAR)]

particularly *adv.* especially, very. [f. PARTICULAR]

parting *n.* 1 leave-taking; departure. 2 the dividing line where hair is combed in different directions. 3 division, separating. [f. PART]

partisan /pɑ:tɪ'zæn, 'pɑ:-/ *n.* 1 a strong (often uncritical) supporter of a party, cause, etc. 2 a guerrilla. —**partisanship** *n.* [F f. It. dial. *partigiano* (as PART)]

partition /pɑ:'tɪʃ(ə)n/ *n.* 1 division into parts. 2 a part formed thus. 3 a structure separating two such parts, a thin wall. —*v.t.* 1 to divide into parts; to share out thus. 2 to divide, to separate (part of a room etc.) by means of a partition. [f. OF f. L (*partiri* divide, as PART)]

partitive /'pɑ:tɪtɪv/ *adj.* (*Gram.*, of a word, form, etc.) denoting a part of a group or quantity. —*n.* a partitive word (e.g. *some, any*) or form. —**partitively** *adv.* [f. F or L (as prec.)]

partly *adv.* with respect to a part, in some degree. [f. PART]

partner /'pɑ:tnə(r)/ *n.* 1 one who shares or takes part with another or others, especially in a business firm with shared risks and profits. 2 either of two people dancing together or playing tennis or cards etc. on the same side and scoring jointly. 3 a husband or wife; a person with whom one lives as if married. —*v.t.* to be a partner of; to associate as partners. —**partnership** *n.* [alt. of *parcener* joint heir]

partridge /'pɑ:trɪdʒ/ *n.* a game-bird of the genus *Perdix* etc., especially the brown and grey varieties. [f. OF f. L f. Gk *perdix*]

parturient /pɑ:'tjʊərɪənt/ *adj.* about to give birth. [f. L *parturire* to be in labour (*parere* bring forth)]

parturition /pɑ:tjʊə'rɪʃ(ə)n/ *n.* the act of bringing forth young, childbirth. [as prec.]

party *n.* 1 a social gathering, usually of invited guests. 2 a body of persons working or travelling together. 3 a group of people united in a cause, opinion, etc., especially a political group organized on a national basis. 4 a person or persons forming one side in an agreement or dispute. 5 an accessory (*to* an action etc.) 6 (*colloq.*) a person. —**party line,** the policy adopted by a political party; a telephone line shared by two or more subscribers. **party-wall** *n.* a wall common to the two buildings or rooms that it divides. [f. OF *partie* (as PARTITION)]

pas /pɑ:/ *n.* (*pl.* same) a step in dancing. —***pas de deux*** /də'dɜ:/, a dance for two persons. [F, = step]

Pascal /pæ'skɑ:l/ *n.* a computer language used esp. in training. [f. B. *Pascal*, French mathematician (d. 1662)]

pascal /'pæsk(ə)l/ *n.* a unit of pressure, one newton per square metre. [as prec.]

paschal /'pæsk(ə)l, 'pɑ:-/ *adj.* 1 of the Jewish Passover. 2 of Easter. —**paschal lamb,** a lamb sacrificed at Passover; (*fig.*) Christ. [f. OF f. L (*pascha* Passover f. Gk f. Aram.)]

pasha /'pɑ:ʃə/ *n.* (*hist.*) the title (placed after the name) of a Turkish officer of high rank. [f. Turk.]

Pashto /'pʌʃtəʊ/ *n.* the Iranian language of the Pathans. —*adj.* of or in this language. [Pashto]

pass[1] /pɑ:s/ *v.t./i.* (*p.p.* **passed** /pɑ:st/ or as *adj.* PAST) 1 to go or move onward or past something, to proceed; to leave (a thing) on one side or behind, to disregard. 2 to go from one person or place etc. to another, to be transferred. 3 to surpass, to be too great for. 4 to cause to move across, over, or past; (in football etc.) to send (the ball, or *absol.*) to a player of one's own side. 5 to discharge from the body as or with excreta. 6 to change from one state or condition etc. into another; to cease or come to an end; (of time) to go by. 7 to happen, to be done or said. 8 to occupy (time). 9 to circulate or cause to circulate; to be accepted or currently known in a certain way. 10 to be tolerated, to go uncensured. 11 to examine and declare satisfactory; to approve (a law etc.), especially by vote. 12 to achieve the required standard in performing (a test); to be accepted as satisfactory. 13 to go beyond. 14 to utter; to pronounce as a decision. 15 (in cards etc.) to refuse one's turn, e.g. in bidding. —*n.* 1 passing, especially of a test or at cards; a status of degree etc. without honours. 2 a permit to go into or out of a place or be absent from one's quarters. 3 (in football etc.) transference of the ball to a player of one's own side. 4 a movement made with the hand(s) or with something held. 5 a critical state of affairs. —**bring to pass,** to cause to happen. **come to pass,** to happen, to occur. **in passing,** by the way, in the course of speech. **make a pass at,** (*colloq.*) to try to attract sexually. **pass away,** (euphem.) to die. **pass for,** to be accepted as. **pass off,** to cease gradually; (of an event) to take place and be completed (in a specified way); to offer or dispose of (a thing) under false pretences; to evade or dismiss (an awkward remark etc.) lightly. **pass out,** to become unconscious; to complete one's military training. **pass over,** to omit, ignore, or disregard; to ignore the claims of (a person) to promotion etc. **pass up,** (*colloq.*) to refuse or neglect (an opportunity etc.). [f. OF *passer* f. L *passus* (as PACE[1])]

pass[2] /pɑːs/ *n.* a narrow route through mountains. [var. of PACE[1]]

passable /ˈpɑːsəb(ə)l/ *adj.* **1** (barely) satisfactory, adequate. **2** that can be passed. —**passably** *adv.* [f. PASS[1]]

passage /ˈpæsɪdʒ/ *n.* **1** passing; transition from one state to another; a journey by sea or air. **2** (also **passageway**) a narrow way for passing along, especially with walls on either side. **3** a tubelike structure through which air or secretions etc. pass in the body. **4** the liberty or right to pass through; the right of conveyance as a passenger by sea or air. **5** a short section of a book etc. or of a piece of music. **6** (in *pl.*) an interchange of words etc. —**passage of arms,** a fight; a dispute. [f. OF (as PASS[1])]

passbook *n.* a book issued by a bank or building society to an account-holder, recording the sums deposited and withdrawn.

passant /ˈpæs(ə)nt/ *adj.* (in heraldry, of an animal) walking and looking to the dexter side, with three paws on the ground and the right fore-paw raised. [f. OF f. *passer* pass]

passé /ˈpæseɪ/ *adj.* **1** behind the times. **2** past the prime. [F, p.p. of *passer* (as PASS[1])]

passenger /ˈpæsɪndʒə(r)/ *n.* **1** a traveller in or on a public or private conveyance (other than the driver, pilot, crew, etc.). **2** (*colloq.*) a member of a team, crew, etc. who does no effective work. [f. OF *passager* (as PASSAGE)]

passer-by *n.* one who goes past especially by chance. [f. PASS[1]]

passerine /ˈpæsəraɪn/ *adj.* of the order Passeriformes, the perching birds, whose feet are adapted for gripping branches and stems. —*n.* a passerine bird. [f. L *passer* sparrow]

passim /ˈpæsɪm/ *adv.* throughout or at many points in a book or article etc. [L (*passus* spread out)]

passion /ˈpæʃ(ə)n/ *n.* **1** strong emotion. **2** an outburst of anger. **3** sexual love. **4** great enthusiasm. **5** Passion, the sufferings of Christ on the Cross; a narrative of this from the Gospels; a musical setting of this narrative. —**passion-flower** *n.* a plant of the genus *Passiflora* with a flower thought to resemble the crown of thorns and other things associated with the Passion of Christ. **passion-fruit** *n.* the edible fruit of some species of passion-flower. **passion-play** *n.* a medieval religious drama in the vernacular. **Passion Sunday,** the fifth Sunday in Lent. [f. OF f. L (*pati* suffer)]

passionate /ˈpæʃənət/ *adj.* **1** full of passion; showing or moved by strong emotion. **2** (of emotion) intense. —**passionately** *adv.* [f. L (as prec.)]

passive /ˈpæsɪv/ *adj.* **1** suffering an action, acted upon. **2** not resisting, submissive. **3** (of substances) not active, inert. **4** (*Gram.*) indicating that the subject undergoes the action of the verb (e.g. in *he was seen*). —**passive resistance,** resistance by non-violent refusal to co-operate. **passive voice,** (*Gram.*) that comprising the passive forms of verbs. —**passively** *adv.*, **passiveness** *n.*, **passivity** /-ˈsɪvɪtɪ/ *n.* [f. OF or L (as PASSION)]

passkey *n.* **1** a private key to a door or gate etc. **2** a master-key.

Passover *n.* **1** (Heb. *Pesach*) the Jewish festival celebrated each spring, held from 14 to 21 Nisan and commemorating the liberation of the Israelites from slavery in Egypt. **2** the Paschal lamb. [f. *pass over*, with reference to the exemption of the Israelites from the death of the first-born which afflicted the Egyptians (Exod. 12)]

passport /ˈpɑːspɔːt/ *n.* **1** an official document issued by a government certifying the holder's identity and citizenship, and entitling him to travel under its protection to and from a foreign country. **2** a thing that secures admission to or attainment of something. [f. F (as PASS[1], PORT[1])]

password *n.* a selected word or phrase known only to one's own side, enabling sentries to distinguish friend from enemy.

past /pɑːst/ *adj.* **1** belonging to the time before the present; (of time) gone by. **2** (*Gram.*) expressing a past action or state. —*n.* **1** (esp. **the past**) past time; past events. **2** a person's past life or career, esp. one that is discreditable. **3** the past tense. —*prep.* **1** beyond in time or place. **2** beyond the range, limits, powers, or stage of. —*adv.* so as to pass by. —**not put it past,** (*colloq.*) to believe it possible of (a person). **past it,** (*slang*) incompetent or unusable through age. **past master,** an expert; a former master of a Freemason's lodge etc. [f. PASS[1]]

pasta /ˈpæstə/ *n.* dried paste made with flour and produced in various shapes (e.g. lasagne, macaroni); a cooked dish made with this. [It. (as foll.)]

paste /peɪst/ *n.* **1** any moist fairly stiff mixture, especially of a powder and liquid. **2** a dough of flour with fat, water, etc. **3** a liquid adhesive for paper etc. **4** an easily spread preparation of ground meat, fish, etc. **5** a hard vitreous composition used in making imitation gems. —*v.t.* 1 to fasten or coat with paste. 2 (*slang*) to beat, thrash, bomb, etc. heavily. —**paste-up** *n.* a document prepared for copying etc. by pasting sections on a backing. [f. OF f. L *pasta* lozenge f. Gk *pastē* (*pastos* sprinkled)]

pasteboard *n.* a kind of thin board made of layers of paper or wood fibres pasted together.

pastel /ˈpæst(ə)l/ *n.* 1 a crayon made of dried paste compounded of pigments with gum solution. 2 a drawing made with this. 3 a light delicate shade of colour. [F or f. It. (as PASTE)]

pastern /ˈpæstɜːn/ *n.* the part of a horse's foot between fetlock and hoof. [f. OF *pasturon* (*pasture* cord used to tether, f. L, ult. as PASTOR)]

pasteurize /ˈpɑːstʃəraɪz/ *v.t.* to subject (milk etc.) to a process of partial sterilization by heating. —**pasteurization** /-ˈzeɪʃ(ə)n/ *n.* [f. L. *Pasteur*, French chemist (d. 1895)]

pastiche /pæˈstiːʃ/ *n.* 1 a picture or musical or literary composition made up of selections from various sources. 2 a literary or other work composed in the style of a well-known author. [F, f. It. *pasticcio* f. L *pasta* paste]

pastille /ˈpæstɪl, -stiːl/ *n.* 1 a small medicinal or flavoured lozenge. 2 a small roll of aromatic paste burnt as a fumigator etc. [F f. L, = little loaf, lozenge (*panis* loaf)]

pastime /ˈpɑːstaɪm/ *n.* something done to pass time pleasantly, a recreation. [f. PASS[1] + TIME]

pastor /ˈpɑːstə(r)/ *n.* a minister in charge of a church or congregation; a person exercising spiritual guidance. [f. OF f. L, = shepherd (*pascere* feed)]

pastoral /ˈpɑːstər(ə)l/ *adj.* 1 of or portraying shepherds or country life. 2 (of land) used for pasture. 3 of a pastor; concerned with Christian spiritual guidance. —*n.* 1 a pastoral poem, play, picture, etc. 2 a letter from a pastor (esp. a bishop) to the clergy or people. —**pastorally** *adv.* [f. L (as prec.)]

pastoralist /ˈpɑːstərəlɪst/ *n.* (*Austral.*) a sheep- or cattle-farmer. [f. prec.]

pastorate /ˈpɑːstərət/ *n.* 1 a pastor's office or tenure. 2 a body of pastors. [f. PASTOR]

pastrami /pæˈstrɑːmɪ/ *n.* seasoned smoked beef. [Yiddish]

pastry /ˈpeɪstrɪ/ *n.* 1 a dough made of flour, fat, and water, used for covering pies or holding filling. 2 food made with this. 3 a cake made wholly or partly of pastry. —**pastry-cook** *n.* a cook who makes pastry, especially for public sale. [f. PASTE]

pasturage /ˈpɑːstʃərɪdʒ/ *n.* 1 pasture-land. 2 pasturing. [as foll.]

pasture /ˈpɑːstʃə(r)/ *n.* 1 land covered with grass etc. suitable for grazing animals; a piece of such land. 2 grass etc. on this. —*v.t./i.* to put (animals) to graze in a pasture; (of animals) to graze. [f. OF f. L *pastura* (as PASTOR)]

pasty[1] /ˈpæstɪ/ *n.* pastry with a sweet or savoury filling baked without a dish. [f. OF *pasté(e)* f. L *pasta* paste]

pasty[2] /ˈpeɪstɪ/ *adj.* 1 of, like, or covered in paste. 2 unhealthily pale. —**pastily** *adv.*, **pastiness** *n.* [f. PASTE]

pat *v.t.* (**-tt-**) to strike gently with the hand or a flat surface; to flatten or mould thus. —*n.* 1 a light stroke or tap; the sound made by this. 2 a small mass of butter or other soft substance. —*adj.* 1 apposite, opportune. 2 known thoroughly and ready for any occasion. —*adv.* in a pat manner, appositely. —**have off pat**, to know or have memorized perfectly. **pat on the back**, a congratulatory acknowledgement. [prob. imit.]

Pat. *abbr.* Patent.

patch *n.* 1 a piece of material or metal etc. put on to mend a hole or as a reinforcement. 2 a piece of plaster or a pad put over a wound; a shield worn to protect an injured eye. 3 a distinguishable area on a surface; an isolated area or period of time. 4 a piece of ground; this covered by specified plants; (*colloq.*) an area assigned to a particular policeman etc. 5 a scrap, a remnant. —*v.t.* 1 to put a patch or patches on; (of a material) to serve as a patch to. 2 to piece together (*lit.* or *fig.*). —**not a patch on**, (*colloq.*) greatly inferior to. **patch-pocket** *n.* one made of a piece of cloth sewn on a garment. **patch up**, to repair with patches; to settle (a quarrel etc.) esp. hastily or temporarily; to put together hastily. [perh. f. OF *pieche*, = PIECE]

patchouli /ˈpætʃʊlɪ/ *n.* a fragrant plant of the genus *Pogostemon*, grown in the Far East, the leaves of which yield an essential oil; perfume made from this. [native name in Madras]

patchwork *n.* 1 needlework in which assorted small pieces of cloth are joined edge to edge, often in a pattern. 2 a thing made of assorted pieces.

patchy *adj.* 1 uneven in quality. 2 having or existing in patches. —**patchily** *adv.*, **patchiness** *n.* [f. PATCH]

pate *n.* (*archaic* or *colloq.*) the head, often as the seat of the intellect. [orig. unkn.]

pâté /ˈpæteɪ/ *n.* 1 a paste of meat etc. 2 a pie, a patty. —**pâté de foie gras**, /də fwɑː grɑː/ a paste of fatted goose liver. [F (as PASTY)]

patella /pəˈtelə/ *n.* (*pl.* **-lae** /-liː/) the kneecap. —**patellar** *adj.* [L, = small pan (as foll.)]

paten /ˈpæt(ə)n/ *n.* a shallow dish used for the bread at the Eucharist. [f. OF or L *patina*]

patent /ˈpeɪtənt, ˈpæ-/ *n.* 1 an official document (orig. **letters patent**) conferring a right or title etc., especially the sole right to make, use, or sell some invention; the right granted by this.

2 an invention or process so protected. —*adj.* 1 conferred or protected by a patent; (of a food, medicine, etc.) proprietary. 2 obvious, plain. 3 (*colloq.*) ingenious, well-contrived. —*v.t.* to obtain a patent for (an invention). —**patent leather,** leather with a glossy varnished surface. **Patent Office,** the government office from which patents are issued. —**patently** *adv.* [f. OF or L (*patēre* lie open)]

patentee /peɪtən'ti:/ *n.* one who takes out or holds a patent; a person for the time being entitled to the benefit of a patent. [f. prec.]

pater /'peɪtə(r)/ *n.* (*archaic, slang*) father. [L]

paternal /pə'tɜ:n(ə)l/ *adj.* 1 of or like a father. 2 related through the father. 3 (of a government etc.) limiting freedom and responsibility by well-meant regulations. —**paternally** *adv.* [f. L *paternalis* (*pater* father)]

paternalism *n.* the policy of governing in a paternal way. —**paternalistic** /-'lɪstɪk/ *adj.* [f. prec.]

paternity /pə'tɜ:nɪtɪ/ *n.* 1 fatherhood. 2 one's paternal origin. 3 authorship, source. [f. OF or L (as PATERNAL)]

paternoster /pætə'nɒstə(r)/ *n.* the Lord's Prayer, especially in Latin. [OE f. L, = our father]

path /pɑ:θ/ *n.* (*pl.* /pɑ:ðz/) 1 a way or track laid down for walking or made by walking. 2 a line along which a person or thing moves. 3 a course of action. [OE]

Pathan /pə'tɑ:n/ *n.* a member of a people inhabiting NW Pakistan and SE Afghanistan. —*adj.* of this people. [Hindi]

pathetic /pə'θetɪk/ *adj.* arousing pity or sadness; arousing contempt; miserably inadequate. —**pathetic fallacy,** crediting inanimate things with human emotions. —**pathetically** *adv.* [f. F f. L f. Gk (as PATHOS)]

pathfinder *n.* an explorer. [OE]

pathogen /'pæθədʒ(ə)n/ *n.* an agent causing disease. —**pathogenic** /-'dʒenɪk/ *adj.* [f. Gk *pathos* suffering (as PATHOS) + -GEN]

pathological /pæθə'lɒdʒɪk(ə)l/ *adj.* 1 of pathology. 2 of or caused by a physical or mental disorder. —**pathologically** *adv.* [f. foll.]

pathology /pə'θɒlədʒɪ/ *n.* 1 the science of bodily diseases. 2 abnormal changes in body tissue, caused by disease. —**pathologist** *n.* [f. F (as PATHOGEN + -LOGY)]

pathos /'peɪθɒs/ *n.* a quality in speech, writing, events, etc., that arouses pity or sadness. [f. Gk, = suffering (*paskhō* suffer)]

pathway *n.* a footway or track, especially one made by walking.

patience /'peɪʃ(ə)ns/ *n.* 1 calm endurance of hardship, annoyance, inconvenience, delay, etc. 2 perseverance. 3 a card-game (usually for one player) in which cards are brought into a specified arrangement. [f. OF f. L (as foll.)]

patient /'peɪʃ(ə)nt/ *adj.* having or showing patience. —*n.* a person receiving (or registered to receive) medical or dental treatment. —**patiently** *adv.* [f. OF f. L (*pati* suffer)]

patina /'pætɪnə/ *n.* 1 an incrustation, usually green, on the surface of old bronze; a similar alteration on other surfaces. 2 the gloss produced by age on woodwork. [It. f. L (as PATEN)]

patio /'pætɪəʊ/ *n.* (*pl.* **-os**) 1 a paved, usually roofless area adjoining a house. 2 an inner court open to the sky in a Spanish or Spanish-American house. [Sp.]

patisserie /pə'ti:sərɪ/ *n.* a pastry-cook's shop or wares. [f. F f. L *pasticium* pastry (as PASTE)]

patois /'pætwɑ:/ *n.* (*pl.* same /-ɑ:z/) 1 the dialect of the common people of a region, differing fundamentally from the literary language. 2 jargon. [F, = rough speech]

patriarch /'peɪtrɪɑ:k/ *n.* 1 the male head of a family or tribe. 2 (in the Orthodox and RC Churches) a bishop of high rank. 3 a venerable old man. —**the Patriarchs,** the men named in Genesis as the ancestors of mankind or of the tribes of Israel. —**patriarchal** /-'ɑ:k(ə)l/ *adj.* [f. OF f. L f. Gk (*patria* family, *-arkhēs* -ruler)]

patriarchate /'peɪtrɪɑ:kət/ *n.* the office, see, or residence of an ecclesiastical patriarch. [f. L (as prec.)]

patriarchy /'peɪtrɪɑ:kɪ/ *n.* a patriarchal system of society, government, etc. [f. L f. Gk (as PATRIARCH)]

patrician /pə'trɪʃ(ə)n/ *n.* an ancient Roman noble. —*adj.* 1 noble, aristocratic. 2 of the ancient Roman nobility. [f. OF f. L, = having a noble father (*pater* father)]

patricide /'pætrɪsaɪd/ *n.* 1 the crime of killing one's own father. 2 one who is guilty of this. —**patricidal** *adj.* [f. L, alt. of *parricida* (see PARRICIDE)]

patrilineal /pætrɪ'lɪnɪəl/ *adj.* of or based on kinship with the father or the male line of ancestors. [f. L *pater* father + LINEAL]

patrimony /'pætrɪmənɪ/ *n.* property inherited from one's father or ancestors; a heritage (*lit.* or *fig.*). —**patrimonial** /-'məʊnɪəl/ *adj.* [f. OF f. L (as PATER)]

patriot /'pætrɪət, 'peɪ-/ *n.* one who is devoted to and ready to defend his country. —**patriotic** /-'ɒtɪk/ *adj.*, **patriotically** /-'ɒtɪkəlɪ/ *adv.*, **patriotism** *n.* [f. F f. L f. Gk (*patrios* of one's father)]

patristic /pə'trɪstɪk/ *adj.* of the early Christian

writers (the Church Fathers) or their work. [f. G f. L (as PATER)]

patrol /pəˈtrəul/ *v.t./i.* (-ll-) to walk or travel round (an area, or *absol.*) in order to protect or supervise it; to act as a patrol. —*n.* 1 patrolling. 2 a person or persons or vehicle(s) assigned or sent out to patrol. 2 a unit of usually six in a Scout troop or Guide company. [f. F *patrouiller* paddle in mud]

patrolman *n.* (*pl.* **-men**) (*US*) a policeman of the lowest rank.

patron /ˈpeɪtrən/ *n.* 1 one who gives financial or other support to a person, activity, or cause. 2 a customer of a shop, restaurant, etc. —**patron saint**, a saint regarded as protecting a person or place etc. —**patroness** *n. fem.* [f. OF f. L *patronus* protector of clients (as PATER)]

patronage /ˈpætrənɪdʒ/ *n.* 1 a patron's or customer's support. 2 the right of bestowing or recommending for an appointment. 3 patronizing airs. [f. OF (as prec.)]

patronize /ˈpætrənaɪz/ *v.t.* 1 to act as a patron towards, to support. 2 to treat condescendingly. —**patronizing** *adj.*, **patronizingly** *adv.* [f. obs. F or L (as PATRON)]

patronymic /pætrəˈnɪmɪk/ *n.* a name derived from that of a father or male ancestor. [f. L f. Gk (*pater* father, *onoma* name)]

patten /ˈpæt(ə)n/ *n.* a shoe with the sole set on an iron ring etc. to raise the wearer's foot above the level of surface mud etc. [f. OF *patin* (*patte* paw)]

patter[1] *v.i.* 1 to make a rapid succession of taps, as rain on a window-pane. 2 to run with short quick steps. —*n.* a series of taps or short light steps. [f. PAT]

patter[2] *n.* rapid and often glib or deceptive speech, e.g. that used by a salesman or conjuror. —*v.t./i.* to repeat (prayers etc.) in a rapid mechanical way; to talk glibly. [f. *pater* = PATERNOSTER]

pattern /ˈpætən/ *n.* 1 a decorative design as executed on a carpet, wallpaper, cloth, etc. 2 a model, design, or instructions from which a thing is to be made. 3 an excellent example or model. 4 a regular form or order. 5 a sample of cloth etc. —*v.t.* 1 to model (a thing *after* or *on* a design etc.). 2 to decorate with a pattern. [f. PATRON]

patty *n.* 1 a small pie or pasty. 2 (*US*) a small flat cake of minced meat etc. [f. F *pâté* (as PASTY[1])]

paucity /ˈpɔːsɪtɪ/ *n.* smallness of quantity or supply. [f. OF or L *paucitas* (*paucus* few)]

Pauline /ˈpɔːlaɪn/ *adj.* of St Paul. [f. *Paul*]

Paul Pry /ˈpraɪ/ an inquisitive person. [character in US song (1820)]

paunch /pɔːntʃ/ *n.* 1 the stomach or belly. 2 a protruding abdomen. —*v.t.* to disembowel (an animal). —**paunchy** *adj.* [f. AF f. L *pantex* bowels]

pauper /ˈpɔːpə(r)/ *n.* a very poor person; (*hist.*) a recipient of poor-law relief. —**pauperism** *n.* [L, = poor]

pauperize /ˈpɔːpəraɪz/ *v.t.* to make into a pauper; to impoverish greatly. [f. prec.]

pause /pɔːz/ *n.* 1 a temporary stop in action, sound, speech, etc. 2 (*Mus.*) a character placed over a note or rest indicating that it is to be lengthened at the performer's discretion. —*v.i.* to make a pause. —**give pause to**, to cause to hesitate. [f. OF or L *pausa* f. Gk (*pauō* stop)]

pavan /pəˈvæn/ *n.* (also **pavane**) a stately dance in slow duple time; the music for this. [f. F f. Sp. (*pavon* peacock)]

pave *v.t.* to cover (a street, floor, etc.) with a durable surface. —**pave the way**, to make preparations. [f. OF *paver* (as foll.)]

pavement *n.* a paved surface or path, especially (for pedestrians) at the side of a road. [f. OF f. L *pavimentum* (*pavire* ram)]

pavilion /pəˈvɪljən/ *n.* 1 a light building in a park etc. used as a shelter. 2 a building on a sports ground for players and spectators. 3 an ornamental building for public entertainment. 4 a large tent. [f. OF f. L *papilio*, orig. = butterfly]

paving /ˈpeɪvɪŋ/ *n.* a paved surface; the material for this. [f. PAVE]

pavlova /pævˈləuvə/ *n.* a meringue cake served with cream and fruit. [f. Anna *Pavlova*, Russian dancer (d. 1931)]

paw *n.* 1 the foot of an animal having claws or nails. 2 (*colloq.*) a person's hand. —*v.t./i.* 1 to strike with a paw. 2 to scrape (the ground) with a hoof. 3 (*colloq.*) to touch awkwardly or rudely with the hand(s). [f. OF *poue*]

pawky *adj.* (*Sc.* & *dial.*) drily humorous. —**pawkily** *adv.*, **pawkiness** *n.* [f. Sc. & N. Engl. dial. *pawk* trick]

pawl *n.* 1 a lever with a catch for the teeth of a wheel or bar. 2 (*Naut.*) a short bar to prevent a capstan etc. from recoiling. [perh. f. LG & Du. *pal*]

pawn[1] *n.* 1 a chess-man of the smallest size and value. 2 an unimportant person subservient to others' plans. [f. AF *poun* f. L *pedo* foot-soldier]

pawn[2] *v.t.* 1 to deposit (a thing) with a pawnbroker as security for money borrowed. 2 to pledge in the hope of receiving something in return. —*n.* the state of being pawned. [f. OF *pan*, *pand*, etc. pledge]

pawnbroker *n.* one who lends money at interest on the security of personal property deposited. —**pawnbroking** *n.* the business of a pawnbroker.

pawnshop *n.* a pawnbroker's place of business.

pawpaw var. of PAPAW.

pay *v.t./i.* (*past & p.p.* **paid**) **1** to hand over (money) in return for goods or services or in discharge of a debt; to give (a person) what is owed; to hand over the amount of (wages, a debt, ransom, etc.). **2** to bear the cost of something. **3** to be profitable, beneficial, or worth while (to). **4** to bestow, render, or express. **5** to suffer (a penalty etc.) **6** to let out (a rope) by slackening it. —*n.* payment; wages. —**in the pay of,** employed by. **pay-as-you-earn** *n.* a method of collecting income tax by deducting it at source from wages etc. **pay for,** to suffer or be punished because of. **pay in,** to pay into a bank account etc. **paying guest,** one who pays for his board and lodging. **pay its way,** to make enough profit to cover expenses. **pay off,** to pay in full and be free from (a debt) or discharge (an employee); (*colloq.*) to yield good results. **pay-off** *n.* (*slang*) payment; reward or retribution; a climax, especially of a joke or story. **pay one's way,** not get into debt. **pay out,** to punish or be revenged on. **pay-packet** *n.* a packet containing an employee's wages. **pay phone,** a telephone with a coin-box for prepayment of calls. **pay up,** to pay in full; to pay what is demanded. —**payer** *n.* [f. OF f. L *pacare* appease (*pax* peace)]

payable *adj.* that must or may be paid. [f. PAY]

PAYE *abbr.* pay-as-you-earn.

payee /peɪˈiː/ *n.* a person to whom money is (to be) paid. [f. PAY]

payload *n.* the part of an aircraft's load from which revenue is derived; the total weight of bombs or instruments carried by an aircraft or rocket etc.; goods etc. carried on a road vehicle.

paymaster *n.* an official who pays troops, workers, etc. —**Paymaster General,** the minister at the head of the department of the Treasury through which payments are made.

payment *n.* **1** paying. **2** an amount paid. **3** reward, recompense.

payola /peɪˈəʊlə/ *n.* a bribe or bribery offered in return for illicit or unfair help in promoting a commercial product. [f. PAY + *-ola* after *Pianola* etc.]

payroll *n.* a list of employees receiving regular pay.

Pb *symbol* lead. [f. L *plumbum*]

PC *abbr.* **1** police constable. **2** Privy Counsellor. **3** personal computer.

p.c. *abbr.* **1** per cent. **2** postcard.

Pd *symbol* palladium.

pd. *abbr.* paid.

PE *abbr.* physical education.

pea *n.* **1** a hardy climbing plant (*Pisum sativum*) whose seeds grow in pods and are used for food. **2** its seed. **3** any of various similar plants. —**pea-green** *adj.* & *n.* bright green. **pea-shooter** *n.* a toy tube from which dried peas are shot by blowing. **pea-souper** *n.* (*colloq.*) a thick yellow fog. [f. PEASE taken as pl.]

peace /piːs/ *n.* **1** quiet, tranquillity; mental calm. **2** freedom from or cessation of war. **3** a treaty ending a war. **4** freedom from civil disorder. —**at peace,** in a state of peace, not in strife. **hold one's peace,** to keep quiet. **keep the peace,** to prevent or refrain from strife. **make one's peace,** to bring oneself back into friendly relations (*with*). **peace offering,** something offered to show that one is willing to make peace. **peace-pipe** a tobacco-pipe as a token of peace among North American Indians. **peace-time** *n.* a period when a country is not at war. [f. AF f. L *pax*]

peaceable /ˈpiːsəb(ə)l/ *adj.* **1** desiring to be at peace with others, not quarrelsome. **2** peaceful. —**peaceably** *adv.* [f. OF f. L *placabilis* pleasing (as PLEASE)]

peaceful *adj.* characterized by or concerned with peace; not violating or infringing peace. —**peacefully** *adv.*, **peacefulness** *n.* [f. PEACE + -FUL]

peacemaker *n.* one who brings about peace.

peach *n.* **1** a round juicy fruit with a downy yellowish or reddish skin. **2** the tree (*Prunus persica*) bearing it. **3** its yellowish-pink colour. **4** (*slang*) a person or thing of superlative merit; an attractive young woman. —**peach Melba,** a dish of ice-cream and peaches with a raspberry sauce. —**peachy** *adj.* [f. OF *peche* f. L *persicum* (*malum*) peach (lit. 'Persian apple')]

peacock *n.* the male peafowl, a bird with brilliant plumage and a tail that can be spread upright like a fan. —**peacock blue,** the lustrous blue of the peacock's neck. **peacock butterfly,** a butterfly (*Inachis io*) with conspicuous 'eyes' on its wings. [*pea* (OE f. L *pavo* peacock) + COCK[1]]

peafowl *n.* a kind of pheasant of the genus *Pavo*, a peacock or peahen. [as prec. + FOWL]

peahen *n.* the female of the peafowl.

pea-jacket /ˈpiːdʒækɪt/ *n.* a sailor's short double-breasted overcoat of coarse woollen cloth. [prob. f. Du. *pijjakker*]

peak[1] *n.* **1** a pointed top, especially of a mountain. **2** any shape, edge, or part that tapers to form a point. **3** the projecting part (usually at the front) of the brim of a cap. **4** the highest point of achievement, intensity, etc. **5** (*attrib.*) maximum, most busy or intense etc. —*v.i.* to reach the highest value, quality, etc. —**Peak District,** an area in

Derbyshire where there are many peaks. [f. dial. *picked* pointed (as PICK)]

peak² *v.i.* **1** to waste away. **2** (in *p.p.*) pinched, drawn. [orig. unkn.]

peaky *adj.* sickly, peaked. —**peakiness** *n.* [f. PEAK²]

peal *n.* **1** the loud ringing of a bell or bells, especially a series of changes on a set of bells. **2** a set of bells with different notes. **3** a loud outburst of sound, especially of thunder or laughter. —*v.t./i.* to sound or cause to sound in a peal. [f. APPEAL]

peanut *n.* **1** a plant (*Arachis hypogaea*) bearing pods that ripen underground, containing seeds used as food and yielding oil. **2** its seed. **3** (in *pl.*, *slang*) a paltry or trivial thing or amount, especially of money. —**peanut butter,** a paste of ground roasted peanuts.

pear /peə(r)/ *n.* **1** a rounded fleshy fruit tapering towards the stalk. **2** the tree bearing it (*Pyrus communis*). [OE, ult. f. L *pirum*]

pearl /pɜːl/ *n.* **1** a smooth lustrous mass, usually white or bluish-grey, formed within the shell of certain oysters and used as a gem; an imitation of this. **2** a thing like a pearl in form. **3** a precious thing, the finest example. —*adj.* like a pearl in form or colour. —*v.t./i.* **1** to fish for pearls. **2** to reduce (barley etc.) to small rounded grains. **3** to form pearl-like drops. **4** to sprinkle with pearly drops. —**pearl barley,** barley rubbed into small rounded grains. **pearl button,** a button of real or imitation mother-of-pearl. **pearl-diver,** *n.* one who dives for oysters containing pearls. [f. OF *perle* prob. ult. f. L *perna* leg (applied to a kind of bivalve)]

pearly *adj.* like or adorned with pearls. —*n.* (in *pl.*) costermongers' clothes decorated with pearl buttons. —**Pearly Gates,** the gates of heaven. **pearly king** (*or* **queen**), a leading London costermonger (or his wife) wearing pearlies.

peasant /ˈpez(ə)nt/ *n.* (in some rural or agricultural countries) a worker on the land, a farm labourer; a small farmer. —**peasantry** *n.* [f. AF *paisant* (*païs* country f. L *pagus* village)]

pease /piːz/ *n.* (*archaic*) peas. —**pease-pudding** *n.* a pudding of boiled peas, eggs, etc. [OE *pise* pea f. L *pisum*]

peat *n.* vegetable matter decomposed in water and partly carbonized, used for fuel, in horticulture, etc.; a cut piece of this. —**peaty** *adj.* [perh. rel. to PIECE]

peatbog *n.* a bog composed of peat.

pebble *n.* a small stone worn and rounded by the action of water. —**pebble-dash** *n.* mortar with pebbles in it as a coating for a wall. —**pebbly** *adj.* [OE]

pecan /ˈpiːkən, pɪˈkæn/ *n.* the pinkish-brown smooth nut of a hickory (*Carya illinoensis*) of the Mississippi region; this tree. [f. Algonquian]

peccadillo /pekəˈdɪləʊ/ *n.* (*pl.* **-oes**) a trivial offence. [f. Sp. (dim. of *pecado* sin f. L *peccare* to sin)]

peccary /ˈpekərɪ/ *n.* a wild pig of the genus *Tayassu* of tropical America. [f. Carib]

peck¹ *v.t./i.* **1** to strike, nip, or pick up with the beak; to make (a hole) with the beak. **2** to kiss hastily or perfunctorily. **3** (*colloq.*) to eat in a nibbling or listless fashion. **4** to carp *at*. **5** to mark with short strokes. —*n.* **1** a stroke, nip, or mark made by a beak. **2** a hasty or perfunctory kiss. —**pecking order,** a social hierarchy, originally as observed among domestic fowls, where aggressive behaviour towards those of inferior status took the form of pecking. [prob. f. MLG]

peck² *n.* **1** a measure of capacity for dry goods, = 2 gallons or 8 quarts. **2** a lot. [f. AF]

pecker *n.* (*in comb.*) a bird that pecks. —**keep your pecker up,** (*slang*) stay cheerful. [f. PECK¹]

peckish *adj.* (*colloq.*) hungry. [f. PECK¹]

pectin /ˈpektɪn/ *n.* a soluble gelatinous carbohydrate found in ripe fruits etc. and used as a setting agent in jams and jellies. [f. Gk *pēktos* congealed]

pectoral /ˈpektər(ə)l/ *adj.* of or for the breast or chest; worn on the breast. —*n.* a pectoral fin or muscle. [f. OF f. L (*pectus* breast)]

peculate /ˈpekjʊleɪt/ *v.t./i.* to embezzle (money). —**peculation** /-ˈleɪʃ(ə)n/ *n.*, **peculator** *n.* [f. L (rel. to foll.)]

peculiar /pɪˈkjuːlɪə(r)/ *adj.* **1** strange, eccentric. **2** belonging exclusively *to*; belonging to the individual. **3** particular, special. —**peculiarly** *adv.* [f. L (*peculium* private property, as PECUNIARY)]

peculiarity /pɪkjuːlɪˈærɪtɪ/ *n.* **1** being peculiar. **2** a characteristic. **3** an oddity, an eccentricity. [f. prec.]

pecuniary /pɪˈkjuːnɪərɪ/ *adj.* of or consisting of money. [f. L (*pecunia* money f. *pecu* cattle, because in early Rome wealth consisted in cattle and sheep)]

pedagogue /ˈpedəgɒg/ *n.* (*archaic*) a schoolmaster; (*derog.*) one who teaches in a pedantic way. [f. L f. Gk *paidagōgos* (*pais* boy, *agōgos* guide)]

pedagogy /ˈpedəgɒdʒɪ/ *n.* the science of teaching. —**pedagogic** /-ˈgɒdʒɪk/ *adj.*, **pedagogical** /-ˈgɒdʒɪk(ə)l/ *adj.* [f. F f. Gk (as prec.)]

pedal /ˈped(ə)l/ *n.* a lever or key operated by the foot, especially in a bicycle or motor vehicle or some musical instruments (e.g. the organ and the harp). —*v.t./i.* (**-ll-**) **1** to move or operate by means of pedals. **2** to ride a bicycle. —/also ˈpiː-/ *adj.* of the foot or feet. [f. L or f. F f. It. f. L (*pes* foot)]

pedalo /ˈpedələʊ/ *n.* (*pl.* **-os**) a small pedal-operated pleasure-boat. [f. prec.]

pedant /ˈped(ə)nt/ *n.* one who lays excessive emphasis on detailed points of learning or procedure. —**pedantic** /pɪˈdæntɪk/ *adj.*, **pedantically** /pɪˈdæntɪkəlɪ/ *adv.*, **pedantry** *n.* [f. F f. It., app. as PEDAGOGUE]

peddle *v.t.* to sell (goods) as a pedlar; to carry about and offer for sale (*lit.* & *fig.*). [f. PEDLAR]

pederast /ˈpedəræst/ *n.* one who commits pederasty. [as foll.]

pederasty *n.* a homosexual act with a boy. [f. Gk (*pais* boy, *erastēs* lover)]

pedestal /ˈpedɪst(ə)l/ *n.* **1** a base supporting a column, pillar, or statue etc. **2** each of the two supporting columns of a knee-hole desk etc. —**put on a pedestal,** to admire or respect greatly. [f. F *piédestal* f. It. (*piede* foot, as STALL[1])]

pedestrian /pɪˈdestrɪən/ *n.* a person who is walking, especially in a street. —*adj.* **1** prosaic, dull. **2** of walking; going or performed on foot. **3** for walkers. —**pedestrian crossing,** a part of a road where crossing pedestrians have priority over the traffic. —**pedestrianism** *n.* [f. F or L *pedester* (*pes* foot)]

pedicure /ˈpedɪkjʊə(r)/ *n.* **1** care or treatment of the feet and toe-nails. **2** a person who practises this professionally. [f. F (L *pes* foot, *curare* care for)]

pedigree /ˈpedɪgriː/ *n.* **1** a genealogical table. **2** ancestral line (especially a distinguished one) of a person or animal. **3** derivation. **4** (*attrib.*) having a recorded line of descent, especially one showing pure breeding. [f. earlier *pedegru* f. AF & OF, = crane's foot, mark denoting succession in pedigrees]

pediment /ˈpedɪmənt/ *n.* a triangular part crowning the front of a building, especially over a portico. [earlier *periment*, perh. corrupt. of PYRAMID]

pedlar /ˈpedlə(r)/ *n.* **1** a travelling vendor of small articles that are usually carried in a pack. **2** a seller of illegal drugs. **3** a retailer *of* gossip etc. [alt. of obs. *pedder* (*ped* pannier)]

pedology /pɪˈdɒlədʒɪ/ *n.* the science of natural soils. —**pedological** /-dəˈlɒdʒɪk(ə)l/ *adj.*, **pedologist** *n.* [f. Russ. f. Gk *pedon* ground + -LOGY]

pedometer /pɪˈdɒmɪtə(r)/ *n.* an instrument for estimating the distance travelled on foot by recording the number of steps taken. [f. F (as PEDESTRIAN, -METER)]

peduncle /pɪˈdʌŋk(ə)l/ *n.* the stalk of a flower, fruit, or cluster, especially the main stalk bearing a solitary flower or subordinate stalks. —**peduncular** /pɪˈdʌŋkjʊlə(r)/ *adj.* [f. L *pes* foot]

pee *v.i.* (*colloq.*) to urinate. —*n.* (*colloq.*) **1** urination. **2** urine. [f. *piss*]

peek *v.i.* to peep, to glance. —*n.* a peep, a glance. [orig. unkn.]

peel *n.* the outer skin of certain fruits and vegetables; the outer coating of prawns etc. —*v.t./i.* **1** to remove the peel from; to take *off* (peel etc.); to be able to be peeled. **2** to come *off* in strips or layers; to lose skin or bark etc. thus. **3** (*slang*) to strip off one's clothes before exercise. —**peel off,** to veer away from a formation of which one formed part. —**peeler** *n.* [f. earlier *pill*, perh. f. L *pilare* remove hair from (*pilus* hair)]

peeling *n.* a piece peeled off, especially the skin of a fruit or vegetable. [f. PEEL]

peep[1] *v.i.* **1** to look quickly or surreptitiously; to look through a narrow opening or from a concealed place. **2** to come briefly or partially into view; to emerge slightly. —*n.* **1** a brief or surreptitious look. **2** the first appearance (of dawn, day, etc.). —**peep-hole** *n.* a small hole to peep through. **Peeping Tom,** a furtive voyeur (from the name of a Coventry tailor said to have peeped at Lady Godiva when she rode naked through Coventry). **peep-of-day boys,** a Protestant organization in Ireland (1784–95) searching opponents' houses at daybreak for arms. **peep-show** *n.* a device, usually in the form of a box, with a small eyepiece, inside which are arranged the receding elements of a perspective view. **peep-toe(d)** *adj.* (of shoes) with a small opening at the tip of the toe. [rel. to PEEK, PEER[1]]

peep[2] *n.* a weak high chirping sound like that made by young birds. —*v.i.* to make this sound. [imit.]

peer[1] *v.i.* **1** to look searchingly or with difficulty. **2** (*archaic*) to appear, to come into view. [var. of earlier *pire* f. LG; perh. partly f. APPEAR]

peer[2] *n.* **1** one who is equal to another in rank, standing, merit, etc.; a member of the same age-group or social set. **2** a member of one of the degrees (duke, marquis, earl, viscount, baron) of nobility in the United Kingdom; a noble of any country. —**peer group,** a person's associates who are of the same age or social status as himself. [f. AF f. L *par* equal]

peerage *n.* **1** peers, the nobility. **2** the rank of peer or peeress. **3** a book containing a list of peers. [f. PEER[2]]

peeress /ˈpɪərɪs/ *n.* a female holder of a peerage; a peer's wife. [f. PEER[2]]

peerless *adj.* unrivalled, superb. [f. PEER[2] + -LESS]

peeve *v.t./i.* (*slang*) **1** to irritate, to annoy. **2** to grumble. —*n.* (*slang*) **1** a cause of annoyance. **2** a mood of vexation. [back-formation f. PEEVISH]

peeved /pi:vd/ *adj.* (*slang*) annoyed, vexed. [f. foll.]

peevish /ˈpi:vɪʃ/ *adj.* irritable, querulous. —**peevishly** *adv.*, **peevishness** *n.* [earlier = silly, mad, spiteful; orig. unkn.]

peewit /ˈpi:wɪt/ *n.* a kind of plover (*Vanellus vanellus*) named from its cry. [imit.]

peg *n.* **1** a pin or bolt of wood, metal, etc., for holding things together, hanging things on, holding a tent-rope taut, marking a position, or as a stopper. **2** a clothes-peg. **3** any of a series of pins or screws for adjusting the tension in a string of a violin etc. **4** an occasion or opportunity, a pretext. **5** a drink or measure of spirits. —*v.t./i.* (**-gg-**) **1** to fix or mark with a peg or pegs. **2** to maintain (prices or wages) at a certain level. —**off the peg,** (of clothes) ready-made. **peg away,** to work diligently, to be persistent. **peg-board** *n.* a board with holes and pegs for displaying or hanging things on. **peg-leg** *n.* an artificial leg; a person with this. **peg out,** to mark out the boundaries of; (*slang*) to die. **square peg in a round hole,** a person not suited to his surroundings, position, etc. **take a person down a peg (or two),** to humble or humiliate him or her. [prob. f. LDu.]

PEI *abbr.* Prince Edward Island.

pejorative /pɪˈdʒɒrətɪv, ˈpi:dʒə-/ *adj.* derogatory, disparaging. —*n.* a pejorative word. —**pejoratively** *adv.* [f. F f. L *pejorare* (*pejor* worse)]

peke /pi:k/ *n.* (*colloq.*) a Pekingese dog. [abbr.]

Pekingese /pi:kɪˈni:z/ *n.* (*pl.* same) **1** a native or inhabitant of Peking. **2** a dog of a short-legged snub-nosed breed with long silky hair, originally brought to Europe from the Summer Palace at Peking in 1860. [f. *Peking*, capital of China]

pekoe /ˈpi:kəʊ/ *n.* a superior kind of black tea. [f. Chin. dial. *pek-ho* white down (leaves being picked young with down on them)]

pelargonium /pelɑ:ˈgəʊnɪəm/ *n.* a plant of the genus *Pelargonium*, with showy flowers. [f. Gk *pelargos* stork; cf. GERANIUM]

pelf *n.* (usu. *derog.* or *joc.*) money, wealth. [rel. to OF *pelfre* spoils (as PILFER)]

pelican /ˈpelɪkən/ *n.* a large water-bird of the genus *Pelicanus*, with a pouch in the bill for storing fish. —**pelican crossing,** a pedestrian crossing with traffic lights operated by pedestrians. [OE & f. OF f. L f. Gk (*pelekus* axe, with ref. to its bill)]

pelisse /peˈli:s/ *n.* **1** a woman's cloaklike garment with armholes or sleeves, reaching to the ankles. **2** a fur-lined mantle or cloak, especially as part of a hussar's uniform. [F f. L *pellicia* fur garment (*pellis* skin)]

pellagra /pɪˈlægrə, -ˈleɪgrə/ *n.* a deficiency disease with cracking of the skin, often ending in insanity. [It. (*pelle* skin)]

pellet /ˈpelɪt/ *n.* **1** a small rounded closely packed mass of a soft substance. **2** a slug of small shot. [f. OF f. L *pila* ball]

pellicle /ˈpelɪk(ə)l/ *n.* a thin skin; a membrane; a thin layer. [f. F f. L *pellicula* dim. of *pellis* skin]

pell-mell /pelˈmel/ *adv.* & *adj.* in a hurrying disorderly manner; headlong. [f. F f. OF *pesle-mesle* redupl. of *mesle* (*mesler* mix)]

pellucid /pɪˈlju:sɪd, -ˈlu:-/ *adj.* **1** transparent, not distorting images or diffusing the light. **2** clear in style, expression, or thought. [f. L (as PER-, LUCID)]

pelmet /ˈpelmɪt/ *n.* a valance or pendent border, especially over a window or door to conceal curtain rods. [prob. f. F *palmette* palm-leaf ornament (as PALM¹)]

pelt¹ *v.t./i.* **1** to attack or strike repeatedly with missiles. **2** (of rain etc.) to beat down fast. **3** to run fast. —*n.* pelting. —**at full pelt,** as fast as possible. [orig. unkn.]

pelt² *n.* an animal skin, especially with the hair or fur still on it. [f. OF, ult. f. L *pellis* skin]

pelvis /ˈpelvɪs/ *n.* the basin-shaped cavity formed by the bones of the haunch with the sacrum and other vertebrae. —**pelvic** *adj.* [L, = basin]

pemmican /ˈpemɪkən/ *n.* a North American Indian cake of dried and pounded meat mixed with melted fat; beef so treated and flavoured with currants etc. for Arctic and other travellers. [f. Cree *pimecan* (*pime* fat)]

pen¹ *n.* **1** an instrument for writing in ink (orig. a sharpened quill, now usu. a device with a metal nib). **2** writing, especially as a profession. —*v.t.* (**-nn-**) to write (a letter etc.). —**pen-friend** *n.* a friend acquired and known mainly or only from correspondence. **pen-name** *n.* a literary pseudonym. **pen-pushing** *n.* (*colloq.*) clerical work. [f. OF f. L *penna* feather]

pen² *n.* a small enclosure for cows, sheep, poultry, etc. —*v.t.* (**-nn-**) to enclose, to shut in or as if in a pen. [OE *penn* (orig. unkn.)]

pen³ *n.* a female swan. [orig. unkn.]

penal /ˈpi:n(ə)l/ *adj.* of or involving punishment, especially by law; (of an offence) punishable. —**penally** *adv.* [f. OF or L (*poena* punishment)]

penalize /ˈpi:nəlaɪz/ *v.t.* **1** to inflict a penalty on. **2** to place at a comparative disadvantage. **3** to make or declare (an action) penal. [f. prec.]

penalty /ˈpenəltɪ/ *n.* **1** a punishment for

breaking a law, rule, or contract; a fine or loss etc. incurred by this. **2** a disadvantage imposed by an action or circumstances. **3** a disadvantage to which a player or team in a sport must submit for breach of a rule. —**penalty area,** the area in front of the goal on a football field in which a foul by the defenders involves the award of a penalty kick. [f. F f. L *penalitas* (as PENAL)]

penance /ˈpenəns/ *n.* **1** an act of self-mortification as an expression of repentance. **2** (in the RC and Orthodox Churches) a sacrament involving confession, absolution, and an act of repentance imposed by a priest. —**do penance,** to perform such an act. [f. OF f. L *poenitentia* (as PENITENT)]

pence *pl.* of PENNY.

penchant /ˈpɑ̃ʃɑ̃/ *n.* an inclination or liking. [F (*pencher* incline)]

pencil /ˈpens(ə)l/ *n.* **1** an instrument for drawing or writing, especially of graphite, chalk, etc., enclosed in a cylinder of wood or a metal etc. case with a tapering end. **2** something used or shaped like this. —*v.t.* (**-ll-**) to write, draw, or mark with a pencil. [f. OF f. L *penicillum* paintbrush (ult. as PENIS)]

pendant /ˈpend(ə)nt/ *n.* a hanging ornament, especially one attached to a necklace, bracelet, etc. [f. OF f. L *pendēre* hang]

pendent /ˈpend(ə)nt/ *adj.* **1** hanging, overhanging. **2** undecided, pending. —**pendency** *n.* [var. of prec.]

pendentive /penˈdentɪv/ *n.* a spherical triangle formed by the intersection of a dome with two adjacent arches springing from supporting columns. [f. F (as PENDANT)]

pending *adj.* **1** waiting to be decided or settled. **2** about to come into existence. —*prep.* **1** until. **2** during. [after F *pendant* (as PENDANT)]

pendulous /ˈpendjʊləs/ *adj.* hanging down, hanging so as to swing freely. [f. L (*pendēre* hang)]

pendulum /ˈpendjʊləm/ *n.* **1** a body suspended so that it can swing freely or oscillate. **2** an instrument consisting of a rod with a weight or 'bob' at the end, so suspended as to swing to and fro by the action of gravity. [as prec.]

peneplain /ˈpenɪpleɪn/ *n.* a region that has become almost a plain as a result of erosion. [f. L *paene* almost + PLAIN]

penetrable /ˈpenɪtrəb(ə)l/ *adj.* that can be penetrated. —**penetrability** /-ˈbɪlɪtɪ/ *n.* [as foll.]

penetrate /ˈpenɪtreɪt/ *v.t./i.* **1** to make a way into or through. **2** to enter and permeate. **3** to see into or through (darkness etc.). **4** to explore or comprehend mentally. **5** to be absorbed by the mind. —**penetration** /-ˈtreɪʃ(ə)n/ *n.* [f. L *penetrare* (*penitus* inmost)]

penetrating *adj.* **1** having or showing great insight. **2** (of a voice or sound) easily heard through or above other sounds, carrying. —**penetratingly** *adv.* [f. prec.]

penguin /ˈpeŋgwɪn/ *n.* a flightless sea-bird of the family Spheniscidae of the southern hemisphere, with the wings developed into flippers for swimming under water. [orig. = great auk; etym. unkn.]

penicillin /penɪˈsɪlɪn/ *n.* an antibiotic of the group produced naturally on moulds. [f. *Penicillium* genus of moulds f. L (as PENCIL)]

peninsula /pɪˈnɪnsjʊlə/ *n.* a piece of land almost surrounded by water or projecting far into the sea. —**peninsular** *adj.* [f. L *paeninsula* (*paene* almost, *insula* island)]

penis /ˈpiːnɪs/ *n.* the sexual and (in mammals) urinatory organ of a male animal. [L, orig. = tail]

penitent /ˈpenɪt(ə)nt/ *adj.* repentant. —*n.* a repentant sinner; a person doing penance under the direction of a confessor. —**penitence** *n.*, **penitently** *adv.* [f. OF f. L (*paenitēre* repent)]

penitential /penɪˈtenʃ(ə)l/ *adj.* of penitence or penance. [as prec.]

penitentiary /penɪˈtenʃərɪ/ *n.* (*US*) a prison for offenders convicted of serious crimes. —*adj.* **1** of penance. **2** of reformatory treatment. [f. L (as PENITENCE)]

penknife *n.* a small folding knife, especially for carrying in the pocket.

penmanship *n.* **1** skill or style in writing or handwriting. **2** the process of literary composition.

pennant /ˈpenənt/ *n.* a tapering flag, especially that flown at the mast-head of a vessel in commission; a pennon. [blend of PENDANT and PENNON]

penniless /ˈpenɪlɪs/ *adj.* having no money; poor, destitute. [f. PENNY + -LESS]

pennon /ˈpenən/ *n.* **1** a long narrow flag, triangular or swallow-tailed. **2** a long pointed streamer of a ship. [f. OF f. L *penna* feather]

penny *n.* (*pl.* **pennies** for separate coins, **pence** for a sum of money) **1** a British bronze coin worth $\frac{1}{100}$ of a pound, or formerly a coin worth $\frac{1}{12}$ of a shilling; the monetary unit represented by this. **2** (*US colloq.*) a cent. —**in for a penny, in for a pound,** a thing once begun should be concluded at all costs. **in penny numbers,** in small quantities at a time. **pennies from heaven,** unexpected benefits. **penny black,** the first adhesive postage stamp (1840), printed in black. **the penny drops,** understanding dawns (from the use of a coin to operate slot-machines etc.). **penny farthing,** a former type of bicycle with a large front wheel and a small rear one. **penny-pinching** *adj.* niggardly; (*n.*) niggardliness. **penny whistle,** one with six holes for the different notes. **penny wise (and pound foolish),** careful or thrifty in small matters (but wasteful in large ones). **a pretty penny,** a large sum of money. **two a penny,** commonly found and of little value. [OE]

pennyweight *n.* a unit of weight equal to 24 grains, $\frac{1}{20}$ ounce troy.

pennyroyal /penɪˈrɔɪəl/ *n.* a creeping species of mint (*Pulegium vulgare*). [f. AF *puliol real* royal thyme]

pennywort *n.* a plant with rounded leaves, **wall pennywort** (*Umbilicus rupestris*) or **marsh pennywort** (*Hydrocotyle vulgaris*).

pennyworth *n.* as much as can be bought for a penny.

penology /piːˈnɒlədʒɪ/ *n.* the study of punishment and prison management. —**penological** /-ˈlɒdʒɪk(ə)l/ *adj.*, **penologist** *n.* [f. L *poena* penalty + -LOGY]

pension[1] /ˈpenʃ(ə)n/ *n.* a periodic payment made by the State to a person above a specified age or to a widowed or disabled person, or by an employer to a retired employee. —*v.t.* to grant a pension to. —**pension off,** to dismiss with a pension; to cease to employ (a person) or use (a thing). [f. OF f. L, = payment (*pendere* pay)]

pension[2] /ˈpɑ̃sɪɔ̃/ *n.* a continental boarding-house. [F, = prec.]

pensionable *adj.* entitled or entitling one to a pension. [f. PENSION[1]]

pensionary *adj.* of a pension. —*n.* a recipient of a pension. [f. L (as PENSION[1])]

pensioner *n.* a recipient of a retirement or other pension. [f. PENSION[1]]

pensive /ˈpensɪv/ *adj.* deep in thought. —**pensively** *adv.*, **pensiveness** *n.* [f. OF (*penser* think f. L *pensare*)]

penstock /ˈpenstɒk/ *n.* a sluice, a flood-gate. [f. PEN[2] in sense 'mill-dam' + STOCK]

pent *adj.* shut in a confined space. [p.p. of *pend* var. of PEN[2]]

penta- *in comb.* five. [Gk (*pente* five)]

pentacle /ˈpentək(ə)l/ *n.* a figure used as a symbol, especially in magic, e.g. a pentagram. [f. L *pentaculum* (as PENTA-)]

pentagon /ˈpentəgən/ *n.* a plane figure with five sides and angles. —**the Pentagon,** the headquarters of the US Department of Defense, Washington, built in the form of a pentagon. —**pentagonal** /-ˈtægən(ə)l/ *adj.* [f. F or L f. Gk (PENTA-, *-gōnos* -angled)]

pentagram /ˈpentəgræm/ *n.* a five-pointed star. [f. Gk (as PENTA-, -GRAM)]

pentameter /penˈtæmɪtə(r)/ *n.* a line of five metrical feet. [L f. Gk (as PENTA-, -METER)]

Pentateuch /ˈpentətjuːk/ *n.* the first five books of the Old Testament. [f. L f. Gk *pente* five, *teuchos* implement, book]

pentathlon /penˈtæθlən/ *n.* an athletic contest in which each competitor takes part in the five different events which it comprises. [f. Gk *pente* five, *athlon* contest]

pentatonic /pentəˈtɒnɪk/ *adj.* of a five-note musical scale. [f. PENTA- + TONE]

Pentecost /ˈpentɪkɒst/ *n.* **1** the Jewish harvest festival on the fiftieth day after the second day of Passover. **2** Whit Sunday. —**pentecostal** /-ˈkɒst(ə)l/ *adj.* [OE & OF f. L f. Gk, = fiftieth day]

penthouse /ˈpenthaus/ *n.* **1** a separate apartment or flat etc. on the roof of a tall building. **2** a sloping roof, especially as a subsidiary structure attached to the wall of a main building. [f. OF *apentis* f. L *appendicium* (as APPEND)]

penult /pɪˈnʌlt, ˈpiː-/ *adj.* & *n.* (esp. of a syllable) penultimate. [abbr. of foll.]

penultimate /pɪˈnʌltɪmət/ *adj.* & *n.* last but one. [f. L *paenultimus* (*paene* almost, as ULTIMATE)]

penumbra /pɪˈnʌmbrə/ *n.* (*pl.* **-ae** /-iː/ or **-as**) a partly shaded region round the shadow of an opaque body, especially of the moon or earth in eclipse; partial shadow. —**penumbral** *adj.* [f. L *paene* almost + UMBRA]

penurious /pɪˈnjuərɪəs/ *adj.* **1** poverty-stricken. **2** scanty. **3** grudging, stingy. [f. L (as foll.)]

penury /ˈpenjurɪ/ *n.* **1** extreme poverty. **2** lack, scarcity. [f. L *penuria*]

peony /ˈpiːənɪ/ *n.* a garden plant of the genus *Paeonia* with large round red, pink, or white flowers. [OE f. L f. Gk (*Paean* physician of the gods)]

people /ˈpiːp(ə)l/ *n.* **1** human beings in general. **2** the persons belonging to a place or forming a group or social class; the subjects or citizens of a State. **3** ordinary persons, those not having high rank or office etc. **4** a person's parents or other relatives. —*v.t.* to fill with people, to populate. [f. AF f. L *populus*]

pep *n.* (*slang*) vigour, spirit. —*v.t.* (**-pp-**) (*slang*) to fill with vigour, to enliven. —**pep pill,** a pill containing a stimulant drug. **pep talk,** a talk urging the listener to greater effort or courage. —**peppy** *adj.* [abbr. of foll.]

pepper *n.* **1** a pungent aromatic condiment obtained from the dried berries of certain plants, especially *Piper nigrum*. **2** a capsicum plant grown as a vegetable; its fruit. —*v.t.* **1** to sprinkle with or as with pepper. **2** to pelt with missiles. —**pepper-and-salt** *adj.* (of cloth) woven so as to show small dots of dark and light colour intermingled. **pepper-mill** *n.* a mill for grinding peppercorns by hand. **pepper-pot** *n.* a small container with a perforated lid for sprinkling pepper. [OE f. L *piper* f. Gk f. Skr.]

peppercorn *n.* a dried pepper-berry.

—peppercorn rent, a nominal or very low rent.

peppermint *n.* **1** a kind of mint (*Mentha* × *piperita*) grown for its strong fragrant oil. **2** a lozenge or sweet flavoured with this. **3** the oil itself.

peppery *adj.* **1** of, like, or abounding in pepper; hot and spicy. **2** (of persons) irascible; (of remarks etc.) pungent. [f. PEPPER]

pepsin /ˈpepsɪn/ *n.* an enzyme contained in gastric juice. [G, f. Gk *pepsis* digestion (as foll.)]

peptic /ˈpeptɪk/ *adj.* digestive. **—peptic ulcer,** an ulcer in the stomach or duodenum. **—peptically** *adv.* [f. Gk (*peptos* cooked)]

peptide /ˈpeptaɪd/ *n.* a compound consisting of a chain of amino acids, chemically linked. [f. G (as prec.)]

per *prep.* **1** for each. **2** through, by, by means of. **—as per,** in accordance with. **as per usual,** (*colloq.*) as usual. [L, = through]

per- *prefix.* **1** through or all over (*pervade*). **2** completely, very (*perturb*). **3** to destruction (*perdition*); to the bad (*pervert*). [f. L (as prec.)]

peradventure /pərədˈventʃə(r)/ (*archaic* or *joc.*) *adv.* perhaps; by chance. **—***n.* uncertainty, chance, conjecture; doubt. [f. OF, = by chance (as PER, ADVENTURE)]

perambulate /pəˈræmbjʊleɪt/ *v.t./i.* to walk through, over, or about (a place); to walk about or from place to place. **—perambulation** /-ˈleɪʃ(ə)n/ *n.* [f. L (PER-, *ambulare* walk)]

perambulator /pəˈræmbjʊleɪtə(r)/ *n.* a pram. [f. prec.]

per annum /pɜːr ˈænəm/ *adv.* for each year. [L]

percale /pəˈkeɪl/ *n.* a closely-woven cotton fabric. [F]

per caput /pɜː ˈkæpʊt/ *adv.* & *adj.* (also **per capita** /pɜː ˈkæpɪtə/) for each person. [L, = by head(s)]

perceive /pəˈsiːv/ *v.t.* to become aware of with the mind or through one of the senses; to see or notice. [f. OF f. L *percipere* orig. = seize (PER-, *capere* take)]

per cent /pəˈsent/ *adv.* in every hundred. **—***n.* a percentage; one part in every hundred. [f. PER + *cent* f. L *centum* hundred]

percentage /pəˈsentɪdʒ/ *n.* a rate or proportion per cent; a proportion. [f. prec.]

perceptible /pəˈseptɪb(ə)l/ *adj.* that can be perceived. **—perceptibility** /-ˈbɪlɪtɪ/ *n.*, **perceptibly** *adv.* [OF or f. L (as PERCEIVE)]

perception /pəˈsepʃ(ə)n/ *n.* perceiving; the ability to perceive. [f. L (as PERCEIVE)]

perceptive /pəˈseptɪv/ *adj.* **1** of perception. **2** having or showing insight and sensitive understanding. **—perceptively** *adv.*, **perceptiveness** *n.*, **perceptivity** /-ˈtɪvɪtɪ/ *n.* [f. L (as PERCEIVE)]

perceptual /pəˈseptjʊəl/ *adj.* of or involving perception. [as prec.]

perch[1] *n.* **1** a branch or bar etc. serving as a bird's resting-place. **2** an elevated position. **3** a former measure of length (esp. for land) equal to $5\frac{1}{2}$ yards. **—***v.t./i.* to rest or place on or as if on a perch. **—percher** *n.* [f. OF f. L *pertica* pole]

perch[2] *n.* (*pl.* same) a spiny-finned freshwater food-fish of the genus *Perca*. [f. OF f. L *perca* f. Gk]

perchance /pəˈtʃɑːns/ *adv.* (*archaic*) **1** by chance. **2** possibly, maybe. [f. AF *par chance* (*par* by, CHANCE)]

percipient /pəˈsɪpɪənt/ *adj.* perceiving, perceptive. **—percipience** *n.* [f. L (as PERCEIVE)]

percolate /ˈpɜːkəleɪt/ *v.t./i.* **1** to filter or cause to filter, especially through small holes. **2** to permeate. **3** to prepare (coffee) in a percolator. **—percolation** /-ˈleɪʃ(ə)n/ *n.* [f. L *percolare* (PER-, *colum* strainer)]

percolator /ˈpɜːkəleɪtə(r)/ *n.* a pot for making and serving coffee, in which boiling water is made to rise up a central tube and down through a perforated drum of ground coffee. [f. prec.]

percussion /pəˈkʌʃ(ə)n/ *n.* **1** the forcible striking of one object against another. **2** the group of percussion instruments in an orchestra. **3** a gentle tapping of the body in medical diagnosis. **—percussion cap,** a small metal or paper device containing explosive powder and exploded by the fall of a hammer, used as a detonator or in a toy pistol. **percussion instrument,** a musical instrument played by striking a resonating surface **—percussive** *adj.* [F or f. L (*percutere* strike)]

perdition /pəˈdɪʃ(ə)n/ *n.* damnation; eternal death. [f. OF or L (*perdere* destroy)]

peregrination /perɪgrɪˈneɪʃ(ə)n/ *n.* travelling; a journey. [f. L *peregrinare* (as foll.)]

peregrine /ˈperɪgrɪn/ *n.* a kind of falcon (*Falco peregrinus*) used for hawking. [f. L *peregrinus* foreign (*peregre* abroad)]

peremptory /pəˈremptərɪ, ˈperɪm-/ *adj.* imperious, insisting on obedience. **—peremptorily** *adv.*, **peremptoriness** *n.* [f. AF f. L (*perimere* destroy, put an end to)]

perennial /pəˈrenɪəl/ *adj.* lasting through the year; lasting long or for ever; (of a plant) living for several years. **—***n.* a perennial plant. **—perennially** *adv.* [f. L *perennis* (PER-, *annus* year)]

perestroika /pereˈstrɔɪkə/ *n.* restructuring, esp. of the economy of the USSR since 1985. [f. Russ.]

perfect /ˈpɜːfɪkt/ *adj.* **1** complete and with all

necessary qualities; faultless, not deficient. 2 exact, precise. 3 (*colloq.*) excellent, most satisfactory. 4 entire, unqualified. 5 (*Gram.*, of a tense) denoting a completed event or action viewed in relation to the present (e.g. *he has gone*). —*n.* (*Gram.*) the perfect tense. —/pəˈfekt/ *v.t.* to make perfect. —**perfect interval,** (*Mus.*) an interval between the tonic and the fourth or fifth or octave in a major or minor scale. —**perfectly** *adv.* [f. OF f. L (*perficere* complete)]

perfectible /pəˈfektɪb(ə)l/ *adj.* that can be perfected. —**perfectibility** /-ˈbɪlɪtɪ/ *n.* [f. prec.]

perfection /pəˈfekʃ(ə)n/ *n.* 1 making or being perfect; faultlessness. 2 a perfect person or thing. —**to perfection,** perfectly. [f. OF f. L (as PERFECT)]

perfectionist *n.* one who is satisfied with nothing less than what he thinks is perfect. —**perfectionism** *n.* [f. prec.]

perfidy /ˈpɜːfɪdɪ/ *n.* a breach of faith, treachery. —**perfidious** /pəˈfɪdɪəs/ *adj.*, **perfidiously** *adv.* [f. L *perfidia* (*perfidus* treacherous)]

perforate /ˈpɜːfəreɪt/ *v.t.* to make a hole or holes through, to pierce; to make a row of small holes in (paper etc.) so that part may be torn off easily. —**perforation** /-ˈreɪʃ(ə)n/ *n.* [f. L *perforare* (PER-, *forare* bore through)]

perforce /pəˈfɔːs/ *adv.* unavoidably, necessarily. [f. OF *par force* (*par* by, FORCE)]

perform /pəˈfɔːm/ *v.t./i.* 1 to carry into effect, to be the agent of, to do. 2 to go through (some process), to execute (a function, piece of music, etc.). 3 to act in a play etc., to play an instrument or sing etc. before an audience. 4 to function. —**performing arts,** those (such as drama) that require public performance. —**performer** *n.* [f. AF f. OF *parfournir* (as PER-, FURNISH)]

performance /pəˈfɔːməns/ *n.* 1 the process or manner of performing. 2 a notable or (*colloq.*) a ridiculous action. 3 the performing of or in a play etc. [f. prec.]

perfume /ˈpɜːfjuːm/ *n.* 1 a sweet smell. 2 a fragrant liquid for giving a pleasant smell, especially to the body. —*v.t.* to give a sweet smell to; to apply perfume to. [f. F *parfumer* f. obs. It. (as PER-, FUME); orig. of smoke from burning substance]

perfumery /pəˈfjuːmərɪ/ *n.* perfumes; the making or selling of these. [f. prec.]

perfunctory /pəˈfʌŋktərɪ/ *adj.* done superficially or without much care or interest, as a duty or routine; (of a person) acting thus. —**perfunctorily** *adv.*, **perfunctoriness** *n.* [f. L (PER-, *fungi* perform)]

pergola /ˈpɜːgələ/ *n.* an arbour or covered walk formed of growing plants trained over trellis-work. [It. f. L *pergula* projecting roof]

perhaps /pəˈhæps, præps/ *adv.* it may be, possibly. [f. PER + HAP]

peri /ˈpɪərɪ/ (*Persian myth.*) a fairy, a good (orig. evil) genius; a beautiful or graceful being. [f. Pers.]

peri- /perɪ-/ *prefix* round, about. [f. Gk]

perianth /ˈperɪænθ/ *n.* the outer part of a flower. [f. F (PERI-, Gk *anthos* flower)]

pericardium /perɪˈkɑːdɪəm/ *n.* (*pl.* **-ia**) the membranous sac enclosing the heart. [f. Gk (PERI-, *kardia* heart)]

pericarp /ˈperɪkɑːp/ *n.* a vessel containing the seed, with the pulp if present, formed from the wall of the ripened ovary. [f. F (PERI-, Gk *karpos* fruit, shell)]

perigee /ˈperɪdʒiː/ *n.* the point in the orbit of the moon, a planet, or an artificial satellite when it is nearest to the earth. [f. F f. Gk (PERI-, *gē* earth)]

perihelion /perɪˈhiːlɪən/ *n.* (*pl.* **-ia**) the point of closest approach to the sun by an orbiting planet or satellite. [f. PERI- + Gk *hēlios* sun]

peril /ˈperɪl/ *n.* serious danger. —**perilous** *adj.*, **perilously** *adv.* [f. OF f. L *peric(u)lum*]

perimeter /pəˈrɪmɪtə(r)/ *n.* 1 the circumference or outline of a closed figure; the length of this. 2 the outer boundary of an enclosed area. [f. F or L f. Gk (PERI-, *metron* measure)]

perineum /perɪˈniːəm/ *n.* the region of the body between the anus and the scrotum or vulva. —**perineal** *adj.* [f. L f. Gk *perinaion*]

period /ˈpɪərɪəd/ *n.* 1 a length or portion of time; a distinct portion of history, life, etc.; a time forming part of a geological era. 2 the interval between recurrences of an astronomical or other phenomenon. 3 the time allocated for a lesson in school. 4 an occurrence of menstruation; the time of this. 5 a complete sentence, especially one consisting of several clauses. 6 a full stop in punctuation. —*adj.* belonging to or characteristic of some past period. [f. OF f. L f. Gk *periodos* (PERI-, *hodos* way)]

periodic /pɪərɪˈɒdɪk/ *adj.* appearing or occurring at intervals. —**periodic table,** a tabular arrangement of the elements in order of atomic numbers, which also brings together those whose atoms have a similar pattern of orbiting electrons. [as prec.]

periodical /pɪərɪˈɒdɪk(ə)l/ *adj.* periodic. —*n.* a magazine etc. published at regular intervals. —**periodically** *adv.* [f. prec.]

periodicity /pɪərɪəˈdɪsɪtɪ/ *n.* being periodic; the tendency to recur at intervals. [f. PERIODIC]

periodontal /perɪəˈdɒnt(ə)l/ *adj.* of the tissues surrounding the teeth. [f. PERI- + Gk *odous odontos* tooth]

peripatetic perɪpəˈtetɪk/ *adj.* going from place to place, itinerant; **Peripatetic,** of the Greek philosopher Aristotle (d. 322 BC) or his ideas (so called from Aristotle's custom of walking in the Lyceum while teaching). —*n.* a traveller, an itinerant; **Peripatetic,** an adherent of Aristotle. [f. OF or L f. Gk (PERI-, *pateō* walk)]

peripheral /pəˈrɪfər(ə)l/ *adj.* **1** of minor but not central importance. **2** of a periphery. —*n.* (in a computer system) any input, output, or storage device that can be controlled by the central processing unit. [f. foll.]

periphery /pəˈrɪfərɪ/ *n.* the boundary of a surface, area, or subject etc.; the region just outside or inside this. [f. L f. Gk, = circumference (PERI-, *pherō* bear)]

periphrasis /pəˈrɪfrəsɪs/ *n.* (*pl.* **-ases** /-əsi:z/) a roundabout phrase or way of speaking, a circumlocution. —**periphrastic** /perɪˈfræstɪk/ *adj.* [L f. Gk (PERI-, *phrazō* declare)]

periscope /ˈperɪskəʊp/ *n.* an apparatus with a tube and mirrors by which an observer in a submerged submarine, a trench, the rear of a crowd, etc., can see things otherwise out of sight. —**periscopic** /-ˈskɒpɪk/ *adj.* [f. PERI- + -SCOPE]

perish /ˈperɪʃ/ *v.t./i.* **1** to be destroyed, to suffer death or ruin. **2** to lose or cause (a fabric etc.) to lose its normal qualities, to rot. **3** to distress or wither by cold or exposure; to suffer thus. [f. OF f. L *perire*]

perishable *adj.* liable to perish, subject to speedy decay. —*n.* (usu. in *pl.*) perishable goods (esp. foods). [f. prec.]

perisher *n.* (*slang*) an annoying person, especially a child. [f. PERISH]

perishing *adj.* **1** (*colloq.*) intensely cold. **2** (*colloq.*) confounded. [as prec.]

peristyle /ˈperɪstaɪl/ *n.* a row of columns surrounding a temple, court, cloister, etc.; the space surrounded by these. [f. F f. L f. Gk (PERI-, *stulon* pillar)]

peritoneum /perɪtəˈnɪəm/ *n.* (*pl.* **-ums**) the membrane lining the cavity of the abdomen. —**peritoneal** *adj.* [L f. Gk (PERI-, *-tonos* stretched)]

peritonitis /perɪtəˈnaɪtɪs/ *n.* inflammation of the peritoneum. [f. prec. + -ITIS]

periwig /ˈperɪwɪg/ *n.* (esp. *hist.*) a wig. [alt. of PERUKE]

periwinkle[1] /ˈperɪwɪŋk(ə)l/ *n.* an evergreen trailing plant of the genus *Vinca*, with blue or white flowers. [f. AF *pervenke* f. L *pervinca*, assim. to foll.]

periwinkle[2] /ˈperɪwɪŋk(ə)l/ *n.* a winkle. [orig. unkn.]

perjure /ˈpɜ:dʒə(r)/ *v.refl.* to cause *oneself* to be guilty of perjury; (in *p.p.*) guilty of or involving perjury. [f. OF f. L *perjurare* (PER-, *jurare* swear)]

perjury /ˈpɜ:dʒərɪ/ *n.* wilful utterance of a false statement while on oath. —**perjurious** /-ˈdʒʊərɪəs/ *adj.* [f. AF f. L *perjurium* (as prec.)]

perk[1] *v.t./i.* (*colloq.*, usu. with *up*) **1** to regain or cause to regain courage, confidence, or liveliness. **2** to smarten. **3** to raise (the head etc.) briskly. [perh. f. var. of PERCH[1]]

perk[2] *n.* (*colloq.*) a perquisite. [abbr.]

perky *adj.* lively and cheerful. —**perkily** *adv.*, **perkiness** *n.* [f. PERK[1]]

perm[1] *n.* (*colloq.*) a permanent wave. —*v.t.* (*colloq.*) to give a permanent wave to. [abbr.]

perm[2] *n.* (*colloq.*) a permutation. —*v.t.* (*colloq.*) to make a permutation of. [abbr.]

permafrost /ˈpɜ:məfrɒst/ *n.* permanently frozen subsoil, especially in polar regions. [f. PERMANENT + FROST]

permanency /ˈpɜ:mənənsɪ/ *n.* a permanent thing or arrangement. [f. foll.]

permanent /ˈpɜ:mənənt/ *adj.* lasting or intended to last or function indefinitely. —**permanent wave,** a long-lasting artificial wave in the hair. **permanent way,** the finished road-bed of a railway. —**permanence** *n.*, **permanently** *adv.* [f. OF or L (PER-, *manēre* remain)]

permeable /ˈpɜ:mɪəb(ə)l/ *adj.* admitting the passage of liquid etc. —**permeability** /-ˈbɪlɪtɪ/ *n.* [f. foll.]

permeate /ˈpɜ:mɪeɪt/ *v.t./i.* to pass, flow, or spread into every part of; to diffuse itself. —**permeation** /-ˈeɪʃ(ə)n/ *n.* [f. L *permeare* (PER-, *meare* pass)]

Permian /ˈpɜ:mɪən/ *adj.* of the final period of the Palaeozoic era, following the Carboniferous. —*n.* this period. [f. *Perm* in the USSR]

permissible /pəˈmɪsɪb(ə)l/ *adj.* that can be permitted. —**permissibility** /-ˈbɪlɪtɪ/ *n.*, **permissibly** *adv.* [f. F or L (as PERMIT)]

permission /pəˈmɪʃ(ə)n/ *n.* consent or authorization to do something. [f. OF or L (as PERMIT)]

permissive /pəˈmɪsɪv/ *adj.* **1** tolerant, allowing much freedom especially in social conduct and sexual matters. **2** giving permission. —**permissively** *adv.*, **permissiveness** *n.* [f. OF or L (as foll.)]

permit /pəˈmɪt/ *v.t./i.* (**-tt-**) **1** to give permission or consent to; to authorize, to allow. **2** to give an opportunity; to make possible; to admit *of* (alteration, delay, etc.). —/ˈpɜ:mɪt/ *n.* a written order giving permission to act, especially for entry into a place; permission. [f. L *permittere* (PER-, *mittere* let go, send)]

permittivity /pəmɪˈtɪvɪtɪ/ *n.* a quantity measuring a substance's ability to store energy in an electric field. [f. prec.]

permutation /pɜ:mju:ˈteɪʃ(ə)n/ *n.* **1** variation of

the order of a set of things. **2** any one such arrangement. **3** a combination or selection of a specified number of items from a larger group (especially of matches in a football pool). [f. OF or L (PER-, *mutare* change)]

pernicious /pəˈnɪʃəs/ *adj*. having a very harmful effect. —**pernicious anaemia**, a severe (formerly often fatal) form of anaemia. [f. L (*pernicies* ruin)]

pernickety /pəˈnɪkɪtɪ/ *adj*. (*colloq*.) fastidious; over-precise. [orig. Sc.; etym. unkn.]

peroration /perəˈreɪʃ(ə)n/ *n*. a lengthy speech; the concluding part of a speech. [f. L (PER-, *orare* speak)]

peroxide /pəˈrɒksaɪd/ *n*. a compound of oxygen with another element containing the maximum proportion of oxygen; (in full **hydrogen peroxide**) a colourless liquid used in a water solution, especially to bleach the hair. —*v.t.* to bleach (hair) with peroxide. [f. PER- + OXIDE]

perpendicular /pɜːpənˈdɪkjʊlə(r)/ *adj*. **1** at right angles to a given line, plane, or surface. **2** upright, at right angles to the horizontal. **3** (of a cliff etc.) having a vertical face; very steep. **4 Perpendicular**, of the style of English Gothic architecture (14th–15th c.) characterized by vertical tracery in large windows. —*n*. a perpendicular line; a perpendicular position or direction. —**perpendicularity** /-ˈlærɪtɪ/ *n*., **perpendicularly** *adv*. [f. L (*perpendiculum* plumb-line)]

perpetrate /ˈpɜːpɪtreɪt/ *v.t*. to commit or perform (a blunder, crime, hoax, thing regarded as outrageous). —**perpetration** /-ˈtreɪʃ(ə)n/ *n*., **perpetrator** *n*. [f. L (PER-, *patrare* effect)]

perpetual /pəˈpetjʊəl/ *adj*. lasting for ever or indefinitely; unceasing; continuous; (*colloq*.) frequent, much repeated. —**perpetual motion**, the motion of a hypothetical machine running for ever unless subject to external forces or wear. —**perpetually** *adv*. [f. OF f. L (*perpetuus* f. *perpes* continuous)]

perpetuate /pəˈpetjʊeɪt/ *v.t*. to make perpetual, to cause to be always remembered. —**perpetuation** /-ˈeɪʃ(ə)n/ *n*., **perpetuator** *n*. [f. L (as prec.)]

perpetuity /pɜːpɪˈtjuːɪtɪ/ *n*. **1** the state or quality of being perpetual. **2** a perpetual possession, or position, or annuity. —**in perpetuity**, for ever. [f. OF f. L (as PERPETUAL)]

perplex /pəˈpleks/ *v.t*. **1** to bewilder, to puzzle greatly. **2** to complicate or confuse (a matter). [f. OF or L *perplexus* involved (PER-, *plectere* plait)]

perplexedly /pəˈpleksɪdlɪ/ *adv*. in a perplexed manner. [f. prec.]

perplexity /pəˈpleksɪtɪ/ *n*. **1** perplexing, being perplexed. **2** a thing that perplexes. [as PERPLEX]

per pro. *abbr*. by proxy, through an agent. [f. L *per procurationem*]

perquisite /ˈpɜːkwɪzɪt/ *n*. a profit, allowance, or privilege etc. given or looked upon as one's right in addition to wages or salary etc. [f. L *perquirere* search diligently for (PER-, *quaerere* seek)]

perry /ˈperɪ/ *n*. a drink made from fermented pear-juice. [f. OF *peré* f. L *pirum* pear]

per se /pɜː ˈseɪ/ by or in itself, intrinsically. [L]

persecute /ˈpɜːsɪkjuːt/ *v.t*. to subject to constant hostility and ill-treatment, especially because of religious or political beliefs; to harass. —**persecution** /-ˈkjuːʃ(ə)n/ *n*., **persecutor** *n*. [f. OF f. L (*persequi* pursue)]

persevere /pɜːsɪˈvɪə(r)/ *v.i*. to continue steadfastly, especially in something that is difficult or tedious. —**perseverance** *n*., **persevering** *adj*. & *n*. [f. OF f. L *perseverare* (PER-, *severus* strict)]

Persian /ˈpɜːʃ(ə)n/ *n*. **1** a native or inhabitant of (esp. ancient) Persia. **2** the language of Persia. —*adj*. of Persia or its people or language. —**Persian cat**, a cat of a breed with long silky hair. **Persian lamb**, the silky tightly-curled fur of karacul lambs. [f. OF f. L]

persiflage /ˈpɜːsɪflɑːʒ/ *n*. banter. [F (PER-, *siffler* whistle)]

persimmon /pɜːˈsɪmən/ *n*. an American or East Asian tree of the genus *Diospyros*; its edible orange plumlike fruit. [corrupt. of Algonquian word]

persist /pəˈsɪst/ *v.i*. **1** to continue firmly or obstinately. **2** to continue in existence, to survive. —**persistence** *n*., **persistency** *n*., **persistent** *adj*., **persistently** *adv*. [f. L *persistere* (PER-, *sistere* stand)]

person /ˈpɜːs(ə)n/ *n*. **1** an individual human being. **2** the living body of a human being. **3** (*Gram*.) each of the three classes of personal pronouns, verb-forms, etc., denoting respectively the person etc. speaking (**first person**), spoken to (**second person**), or spoken of (**third person**). **4** God as Father, Son, or Holy Ghost. —**in person**, physically present. [f. OF f. L *persona* (as foll.)]

persona /pɜːˈsəʊnə/ *n*. (*pl*. **-ae** /-iː/) an aspect of one's personality as perceived by others. [L, orig. = actor's mask]

personable *adj*. pleasing in appearance or behaviour. [f. PERSON]

personage /ˈpɜːsənɪdʒ/ *n*. a person, especially an important one. [as prec.]

persona grata /pɜːˈsəʊnə ˈgrɑːtə/ a person acceptable to certain others, especially a diplomat acceptable to a foreign government. —***persona non grata***, one who is not acceptable. [L]

personal /ˈpɜːsənəl/ *adj.* **1** of one's own or a particular person's own. **2** done or made etc. in person. **3** directed to or concerning an individual; of one's own or another's private life; referring (esp. in a hostile way) to an individual's private life or concerns. **4** of the body. **5** of or existing as a person; (*Gram.*) of or denoting one of the three persons. —**personal column,** a column of private advertisements or messages in a newspaper. **personal property,** all property except land and those interests in land that pass to one's heirs. [as PERSON]

personality /pɜːsəˈnælɪtɪ/ *n.* **1** the distinctive character or qualities of a person. **2** personal existence or identity, being a person. **3** a famous person, a celebrity. **4** (in *pl.*) personal remarks. [as prec.]

personalize /ˈpɜːsənəlaɪz/ *v.t.* **1** to make personal, especially by marking with the owner's name etc. **2** to personify. [f. prec.]

personally *adv.* **1** in person. **2** for one's own part. [f. PERSONAL]

personate /ˈpɜːsəneɪt/ *v.t.* **1** to play the part of (a character in a drama etc.). **2** to impersonate for fraudulent purposes. —**personation** /-ˈneɪʃ(ə)n/ *n.*, **personator** *n.* [f. L *personare* (as PERSON)]

personify /pɜːˈsɒnɪfaɪ/ *v.t.* **1** to represent (a thing or abstraction) as having a personal nature. **2** to symbolize (a quality) by a figure in human form. **3** (esp. in *p.p.*) to embody in one's own person or exemplify (a quality). —**personification** /-fɪˈkeɪʃ(ə)n/ *n.* [f. F (as PERSON)]

personnel /pɜːsəˈnel/ *n.* the body of employees, the staff (in a public undertaking, armed forces, an office, etc.). —**personnel department,** the department of a firm etc. dealing with the appointment and welfare of employees. [F, = personal]

perspective /pəˈspektɪv/ *n.* **1** the art of drawing solid objects on a plane surface so as to give the right impression of their relative positions, size, etc.; a picture so drawn. **2** the apparent relation between visible objects as to position, distance, etc. **3** a mental view of the relative importance of things. **4** a view or prospect (*lit.* or *fig.*). —*adj.* of or in perspective. —**in perspective,** drawn or viewed according to the rules of perspective; correctly regarded as to relative importance. [f. L (*ars*) *perspectiva* (*perspicere* look through, examine)]

Perspex /ˈpɜːspeks/ *n.* [P] a tough light transparent plastic. [as prec.]

perspicacious /pɜːspɪˈkeɪʃəs/ *adj.* having or showing great insight. —**perspicaciously** *adv.*, **perspicacity** /-ˈkæsɪtɪ/ *n.* [f. L *perspicax* (as PERSPECTIVE)]

perspicuous /pəˈspɪkjuəs/ *adj.* **1** easily understood, clearly expressed. **2** expressing things clearly. —**perspicuity** /pɜːspɪˈkjuːɪtɪ/ *n.*, **perspicuously** *adv.*, **perspicuousness** *n.* [f. L orig. = transparent (as PERSPECTIVE)]

perspiration /pɜːspɪˈreɪʃ(ə)n/ *n.* sweat, sweating. [F (as foll.)]

perspire /pəˈspaɪə(r)/ *v.t./i* to sweat. [f. F f. L (PER-, *spirare* breathe)]

persuade /pəˈsweɪd/ *v.t.* to cause (a person) to do or believe something, especially by reasoning, to induce. —**persuadable** *adj.*, **persuasible** *adj.* [f. L (PER-, *suadēre* induce)]

persuasion /pəˈsweɪʒ(ə)n/ *n.* **1** persuading. **2** persuasiveness. **3** a belief or conviction; a sect holding a particular religious belief. [f. L (as prec.)]

persuasive /pəˈsweɪsɪv/ *adj.* able or tending to persuade. —**persuasively** *adv.*, **persuasiveness** *n.* [f. F or L (as PERSUADE)]

pert *adj.* **1** cheeky. **2** jaunty, lively. —**pertly** *adv.*, **pertness** *n.* [f. OF *apert* f. L *apertus* open, & f. OF *aspert* f. L *expertus* (as EXPERT)]

pertain /pəˈteɪn/ *v.i.* **1** to be relevant or appropriate. **2** to belong as a part, appendage, or accessory. [f. OF f. L *pertinēre* belong]

pertinacious /pɜːtɪˈneɪʃəs/ *adj.* holding firmly to an opinion or course of action; persistent, determined. —**pertinaciously** *adv.*, **pertinacity** /-ˈnæsɪtɪ/ *n.* [f. L *pertinax* (as PER-, TENACIOUS)]

pertinent /ˈpɜːtɪnənt/ *adj.* relevant to the matter in hand; to the point. —**pertinence** *n.*, **pertinency** *n.*, **pertinently** *adv.* [f. OF or L (as PERTAIN)]

perturb /pəˈtɜːb/ *v.t.* to disturb greatly, to make anxious or uneasy. —**perturbation** /pɜːtɜːˈbeɪʃ(ə)n/ *n.* [f. OF f. L *perturbare* (PER-, *turbare* disturb)]

peruke /pəˈruːk/ *n.* (esp. *hist.*) a wig. [f. F f. It.]

peruse /pəˈruːz/ *v.t.* to read or study (a document etc.) thoroughly or carefully. —**perusal** *n.* [prob. as PER- + USE]

pervade /pəˈveɪd/ *v.t.* to spread or be present throughout, to permeate. —**pervasion** *n.* [f. L *pervadere* (PER-, *vadere* go)]

pervasive /pəˈveɪsɪv/ *adj.* pervading. —**pervasiveness** *n.* [as prec.]

perverse /pəˈvɜːs/ *adj.* deliberately or stubbornly doing something different from what is reasonable or required; having this tendency, intractable. —**perversely** *adv.*, **perverseness** *n.*, **perversity** *n.* [f. OF f. L (as PERVERT)]

perversion /pəˈvɜːʃ(ə)n/ *n.* **1** perverting, being perverted. **2** preference for a form of sexual activity that is considered abnormal or unacceptable. [f. L (as foll.)]

pervert /pəˈvɜːt/ *v.t.* **1** to turn (a thing) from its proper use or nature; to misapply (words etc.). **2** to lead astray from right behaviour or beliefs. **3** (in *p.p.*) showing perversion. —/ˈpɜ:vɜ:t/ *n.* a perverted person; one showing perversion of sexual instincts. [f. OF or L *pervertere* (PER-, *vertere* turn)]

pervious /ˈpɜ:vɪəs/ *adj.* **1** permeable, allowing passage. **2** accessible (*to* reason etc.). [f. L *pervius* (PER-, *via* way)]

peseta /pəˈseɪtə/ *n.* the currency unit of Spain. [Sp., dim. of *pesa* weight]

pesky /ˈpeskɪ/ *adj.* (*US colloq.*) troublesome, annoying. [perh. f. PEST]

peso /ˈpeɪsəʊ/ *n.* (*pl.* **-os**) the currency unit of Chile, several Latin-American countries, and the Philippines. [Sp., = weight, f. L *pensum* (as POISE)]

pessary /ˈpesərɪ/ *n.* a device worn in the vagina to prevent uterine displacement or as a contraceptive; a vaginal suppository. [f. L f. Gk *pessos* oval stone]

pessimism /ˈpesɪmɪz(ə)m/ *n.* **1** a gloomy view or disposition; a tendency to expect an unfavourable outcome. **2** the belief that the actual world is the worst possible, or that all things tend to be evil. —**pessimist** *n.* [f. L *pessimus* worst]

pessimistic /pesɪˈmɪstɪk/ *adj.* showing pessimism; gloomy. —**pessimistically** *adv.* [f. prec.]

pest *n.* **1** a troublesome or annoying person or thing. **2** an insect or animal that is destructive to plants, food, etc. [f. F or L *pestis* plague]

pester *v.t.* to trouble or annoy, especially with frequent or persistent requests. [prob. f. F *empestrer* encumber; infl. by prec.]

pesticide /ˈpestɪsaɪd/ a substance for destroying harmful insects etc. [f. PEST + -CIDE]

pestiferous /peˈstɪfərəs/ *adj.* troublesome, harmful. [f. L (as PEST, *ferre* bear)]

pestilence /ˈpestɪləns/ *n.* a fatal epidemic disease, especially bubonic plague. [f. OF f. L (as foll.)]

pestilent /ˈpestɪlənt/ *adj.* **1** destructive to life, deadly; harmful. **2** (*colloq.*) troublesome, annoying. [f. L (*pestis* plague)]

pestilential /pestɪˈlenʃ(ə)l/ *adj.* of a pestilence, pestilent. [f. L (as prec.)]

pestle /ˈpes(ə)l/ *n.* a club-shaped instrument for pounding substances in a mortar. [f. OF f. L *pistillum* (*pinsere* pound)]

pestology /peˈstɒlədʒɪ/ *n.* the scientific study of harmful insects and of the methods of dealing with them. [f. PEST + -LOGY]

pet[1] *n.* **1** a domesticated animal treated with affection and kept for pleasure or companionship. **2** a darling, a favourite. —*adj.* **1** of, for, or in the nature of a pet. **2** favourite, particular. **3** expressing fondness or familiarity. —*v.t.* (**-tt-**) **1** to fondle (esp. erotically). **2** to treat with affection. [orig. unkn.]

pet[2] *n.* offence at being slighted, ill-humour. [orig. unkn.]

peta- /petə-/ *in comb.* denoting a factor of 10^{15}. [perh. f. PENTA-]

petal /ˈpet(ə)l/ *n.* each division of the corolla of a flower. —**petalled** *adj.* [f. L f. Gk *petalon* leaf]

petard /pɪˈtɑ:d/ *n.* (*hist.*) a small bomb used to blast down a door etc. —**hoist with his own petard,** injured by his own devices against others. [f. F (*péter* break wind)]

peter /ˈpi:tə(r)/ *v.i.* **peter out,** to diminish gradually and come to an end. [orig. unkn.]

petersham /ˈpi:təʃəm/ *n.* a thick ribbed silk ribbon. [f. Lord *Petersham*, English army officer (d. 1851)]

petiole /ˈpetɪəʊl/ *n.* a slender stalk joining a leaf to a stem. [f. F f. L *petiolus* little foot, stalk]

petit bourgeois /pəti: ˈbʊəʒwɑ:/ a member of the lower middle classes. [F]

petite /pəˈti:t/ *adj.* (of a woman) small and dainty in build. [F, fem. of *petit* small]

petit four /pəti: ˈfʊə(r)/ (*pl.* ***petits fours*** *pr.* same) a very small fancy cake. [F, = little oven]

petition /pəˈtɪʃ(ə)n/ *n.* **1** asking, supplication. **2** a formal written request, especially one signed by many people, appealing to an authority for a right or benefit etc. **3** an application to a court for a writ, order, etc. —*v.t./i.* **1** to make or address a petition to. **2** to ask earnestly or humbly. —**petitioner** *n.* [f. OF f. L (*petere* seek)]

petit mal /pəti: ˈmæl/ a mild form of epilepsy without loss of consciousness. [F, = small sickness]

petit point /pəti: ˈpwæ̃/ embroidery on canvas using small stitches. [F]

petrel /ˈpetr(ə)l/ *n.* a kind of sea-bird, of the family Procellariidae or Hydrobatidae, that flies far from land. [orig. unkn.]

petrify /ˈpetrɪfaɪ/ *v.t./i.* **1** to paralyse with fear, astonishment, etc. **2** to turn or be turned into stone. —**petrification** /-fɪˈkeɪʃ(ə)n/ *n.* [f. F f. L *petrificare* (*petra* rock f. Gk)]

petrochemical /petrəʊˈkemɪk(ə)l/ *n.* a substance industrially obtained from petroleum or natural gas. [f. PETROLEUM + CHEMICAL]

petrodollar /ˈpetrəʊdɒlə(r)/ *n.* a dollar held by a petroleum-exporting country. [f. PETROLEUM + DOLLAR]

petrography /pɪˈtrɒgrəfɪ/ *n.* the scientific description of the composition and formation of rocks. —**petrographic** /petrəˈgræfɪk/ *adj.* [f. Gk *petra* rock + -GRAPHY]

petrol /ˈpetr(ə)l/ *n.* refined petroleum used as

fuel in motor vehicles, aircraft, etc. —**petrol station,** a filling station. [f. F f. L (as foll.)]

petroleum /pɪˈtrəʊlɪəm/ *n.* a hydrocarbon oil found in the upper strata of the earth, refined for use as a fuel etc. —**petroleum jelly,** a translucent solid mixture of hydrocarbons obtained from petroleum and used as a lubricant etc. [L (*petra* rock f. Gk, *oleum* oil)]

petrology /pɪˈtrɒlədʒɪ/ *n.* the study of the origin, structure, etc., of rocks. —**petrological** /-ˈlɒdʒɪk(ə)l/ *adj.* [f. Gk *petra* rock + -LOGY]

petticoat /ˈpetɪkəʊt/ *n.* **1** a woman's or girl's dress-length undergarment hanging from the waist or shoulders. **2** (*attrib.*) feminine, of or by women. [f. *petty coat*]

pettifogging /ˈpetɪfɒgɪŋ/ *adj.* **1** quibbling or wrangling about unimportant details. **2** practising legal chicanery. [f. *pettifogger* inferior legal practitioner (PETTY, *fogger* underhand dealer)]

pettish *adj.* peevish, petulant, irritable. —**pettishly** *adv.*, **pettishness** *n.* [f. PET²]

petty *adj.* **1** unimportant, trivial. **2** small-minded. **3** minor; inferior; on a small scale. —**petty cash,** money kept for small cash items of expenditure. **petty officer,** a naval NCO. **petty sessions,** a meeting of two or more magistrates for the summary trial of certain offences. —**pettily** *adv.*, **pettiness** *n.* [f. OF *petit* small]

petulant /ˈpetjʊlənt/ *adj.* peevishly impatient or irritable. —**petulance** *n.*, **petulantly** *adv.* [f. F f. L (*petere* seek)]

petunia /pɪˈtjuːnɪə/ *n.* a plant of the genus *Petunia* with funnel-shaped flowers of vivid purple, red, white, etc. [f. F f. Guarani, = tobacco]

pew *n.* **1** a long backed bench or enclosed compartment in a church. **2** (*colloq.*) a seat. [f. OF *puye* balcony f. L (as PODIUM)]

pewter /ˈpjuːtə(r)/ *n.* **1** a grey alloy of tin with lead or other metal. **2** articles made of this. [f. OF *peutre*]

peyote /peɪˈəʊtɪ/ *n.* **1** a Mexican cactus of the genus *Lophophora*. **2** a hallucinogenic drug prepared from it. [Amer. Sp., f. Nahuatl]

pfennig /ˈpfenɪg/ *n.* a small German coin worth $\frac{1}{100}$ of a mark. [G (as PENNY)]

PG *abbr.* paying guest.

pH /piːˈeɪtʃ/ *n.* a measure of the acidity or alkaline level of a solution. [G (*potenz* power, *H* (symbol for hydrogen) dissolved hydrogen ions)]

phagocyte /ˈfægəsaɪt/ *n.* a leucocyte etc. capable of absorbing foreign matter (esp. bacteria) in the body. [f. Gk *phag-* eat + -CYTE]

phalanger /fəˈlændʒə(r)/ *n.* (in Australia & New Zealand) a tree-dwelling marsupial of the family Phalangeridae, with webbed hind feet. [f. Gk *phalaggion* spider's web, f. its webbed toes]

phalanx /ˈfælæŋks/ *n.* (*pl.* **phalanxes**) **1** (in ancient Greece) a line of battle, especially a body of infantry drawn up in close order. **2** a set of persons etc. forming a compact mass or banded together for a common purpose. **3** (*pl.* **phalanges**) a bone of the finger or toe. [L f. Gk]

phallus /ˈfæləs/ *n.* (*pl.* **-uses**) an image of the penis (usu. in erection) as a symbol of generative power. —**phallic** *adj.* [L f. Gk]

phantasm /ˈfæntæz(ə)m/ *n.* an illusion, a phantom. —**phantasmal** /-ˈtæzm(ə)l/ *adj.* [f. OF f. L f. Gk (*phantazō* make visible)]

phantasmagoria /fæntæzməˈgɒrɪə/ *n.* a shifting scene of real or imagined figures. —**phantasmagoric** /-ˈgɒrɪk/ *adj.* [prob. f. F *fantasmagorie* (as prec., with fanciful ending)]

phantom /ˈfæntəm/ *n.* **1** a ghost, an apparition. **2** something without substance or reality, a mental illusion. —*adj.* merely apparent, illusory. [f. OF *fantosme* f. Gk (as PHANTASM)]

Pharaoh /ˈfeərəʊ/ *n.* the title of the ruler of ancient Egypt. [f. L f. Gk f. Heb. f. Egyptian, = great house]

Pharisee /ˈfærɪsiː/ *n.* **1** a member of an ancient Jewish sect. **2** a self-righteous person, a hypocrite. —**Pharisaic** /-ˈseɪɪk/ *adj.* [OE, ult. f. Aram., f. Heb. *parush* separated]

pharmaceutical /fɑːməˈsjuːtɪk(ə)l/ *adj.* of or engaged in pharmacy; of the use or sale of medicinal drugs. [f. L f. Gk (*pharmakeutēs* druggist f. *pharmakon* drug)]

pharmaceutics *n.pl.* (usu. treated as *sing.*) pharmacy (PHARMACY sense 1). [f. prec.]

pharmacist /ˈfɑːməsɪst/ *n.* a person engaged in pharmacy. [f. PHARMACY]

pharmacology /fɑːməˈkɒlədʒɪ/ *n.* the science of the action of drugs on the body. —**pharmacological** /-ˈlɒdʒɪk(ə)l/ *adj.*, **pharmacologist** *n.* [f. Gk *pharmakon* drug + -LOGY]

pharmacopoeia /fɑːməkəˈpiːə/ *n.* **1** a book (especially one published officially) containing a list of drugs with directions for their use. **2** a stock of drugs. [f. Gk (*pharmakopoios* drug-maker, as prec. + *-poios* making)]

pharmacy /ˈfɑːməsɪ/ *n.* **1** the preparation and dispensing of drugs. **2** a pharmacist's shop; a dispensary. [f. OF f. L f. Gk (*pharmakeus* druggist, as PHARMACEUTICAL)]

pharyngitis /færɪnˈdʒaɪtɪs/ *n.* inflammation of the pharynx. [f. PHARYNX + -ITIS]

pharynx /ˈfærɪŋks/ *n.* the cavity behind the mouth and nose. —**pharyngeal** /-mˈdʒiːəl/ *adj.* [f. Gk *pharugx*]

phase /feɪz/ *n.* **1** a stage of change or development. **2** an aspect of the moon or a planet, according to the amount of illumination. **3** a stage in a periodically recurring sequence of changes, e.g. of alternating current or light-vibrations. —*v.t.* to carry out (a programme etc.) in phases or stages. —**phase in** *or* **out**, to bring gradually into (or out of) use. [f. F f. Gk *phasis* appearance]

Ph.D. *abbr.* Doctor of Philosophy. [f. L *philosophiae doctor*]

pheasant /ˈfez(ə)nt/ *n.* a long-tailed game-bird with bright plumage, especially *Phasianus colchicus*, originally Asian but long naturalized in Europe. [f. AF f. Gk *phasianus* (*Phasis* river in Asia Minor)]

phenol /ˈfi:nɒl/ *n.* a hydroxyl derivative of aromatic hydrocarbons. [f. F (*phène* benzene)]

phenomenal /fɪˈnɒmɪn(ə)l/ *adj.* of the nature of a phenomenon; extraordinary, remarkable. —**phenomenally** *adv.* [f. PHENOMENON.]

phenomenon /fɪˈnɒmɪnən/ *n.* (*pl.* **-ena**) **1** a fact or occurrence that appears or is perceived, especially a thing the cause of which is in question. **2** a remarkable person or thing. [f. L f. Gk (*phainomai* appear)]

pheromone /ˈferəməʊn/ *n.* a substance secreted and released by an animal for detection and response by another of the same (or a closely related) species. [f. Gk *pherō* convey + HORMONE]

phew /fju:/ *int.* expressing relief, weariness, surprise, etc. [imit. of puffing]

phi /faɪ/ *n.* the twenty-first letter of the Greek alphabet, = ph. [Gk]

phial /ˈfaɪəl/ *n.* a small glass bottle, especially for liquid medicine. [f. OF f. L f. Gk (as VIAL)]

phil- see PHILO-.

philander /fɪˈlændə(r)/ *v.i.* (of a man) to flirt. —**philanderer** *n.* [f. Gk *philandros* fond of men, taken as name of lover]

philanthropy /fɪˈlænθrəpɪ/ *n.* concern for the welfare of mankind, especially as shown by acts of benevolence. —**philanthropic** /-ˈθrɒpɪk/ *adj.*, **philanthropically** /-ˈθrɒpɪkəlɪ/ *adv.*, **philanthropist** *n.* [f. L f. Gk (PHIL-, *anthrōpos* human being)]

philately /fɪˈlætəlɪ/ *n.* the collecting and study of postage-stamps. —**philatelic** /-ˈtelɪk/ *adj.*, **philatelist** *n.* [f. F f. Gk PHIL-, *ateleia* exemption from payment (*a-* not, *telos* tax).

-phile /-faɪl/ *suffix* (also **-phil**) forming nouns and adjectives in the sense 'one who is fond of' (*bibliophile*). [f. Gk *philos* loving]

philharmonic /fɪlɑ:ˈmɒnɪk/ *adj.* (in the names of orchestras and music societies) fond of music. [f. F f. It. (as PHIL-, HARMONIC)]

philippic /fɪˈlɪpɪk/ *n.* a bitter invective. [f. L f. Gk (*Philippos* Philip); orig. applied to the orations of Demosthenes against Philip II of Macedon]

Philistine /ˈfɪlɪstaɪn/ *n.* a member of an ancient non-Semitic people who settled in the coastal region of Canaan. —*adj.* of the Philistines. [ult. f. Heb.]

philistine /ˈfɪlɪstaɪn/ *n.* one who is hostile or indifferent to culture, or whose interests are material or commonplace. —*adj.* having such characteristics. —**philistinism** /-ɪnɪz(ə)m/ *n.* [= prec.]

philo- /-fɪlə(ʊ)-/ *in comb.* (**phil-** before a vowel or *h*) liking, fond of. [f. Gk (*phileō* to love)]

philology /fɪˈlɒlədʒɪ/ *n.* **1** the study (esp. historical and comparative) of language(s). **2** (*US*) the study of literature. **3** (*archaic*) love of learning and literature. —**philologian** /-ˈləʊdʒɪən/ *n.*, **philological** /-ˈlɒdʒɪk(ə)l/ *adj.*, **philologist** *n.* [f. F, ult. f. Gk, = love of learning]

philosopher /fɪˈlɒsəfə(r)/ *n.* **1** one engaged or learned in philosophy or a branch of it. **2** one who lives by philosophy or acts philosophically. —**philosopher's stone** an object sought by alchemists as a means of turning other metals into gold or silver. [f. AF f. L f. Gk (as PHILOSOPHY)]

philosophical /fɪləˈsɒfɪk(ə)l/ *adj.* (also **philosophic**) **1** of or according to philosophy. **2** skilled in or devoted to philosophy. **3** calmly reasonable; bearing unavoidable misfortune unemotionally. —**philosophically** *adv.* [f. L (as PHILOSOPHY)]

philosophize /fɪˈlɒsəfaɪz/ *v.i.* to reason like a philosopher; to speculate, to theorize; to moralize. [app. f. F *philosopher* (as foll.)]

philosophy /fɪˈlɒsəfɪ/ *n.* **1** the use of reason and argument in the search for truth and the knowledge of reality, especially of the causes and nature of things, and of the principles governing existence, perception, human behaviour, and the material universe. **2** a particular system or set of beliefs preached by this. **3** a system of conduct in life. **4** a philosophical attitude to misfortune etc. **5** advanced learning in general. [f. OF, ult. f. Gk, = love of wisdom]

philtre /ˈfɪltə(r)/ *n.* a drink supposed to be able to excite sexual love. [f. F f. L f. Gk *philtron* (*phileō* love)]

phlebitis /flɪˈbaɪtɪs/ *n.* inflammation of the walls of a vein. —**phlebitic** /-ˈbɪtɪk/ *adj.* [f. Gk *phleps* vein + -ITIS]

phlegm /flem/ *n.* **1** a thick viscous substance secreted by the mucous membranes of the respiratory passages, discharged by coughing. **2** (*archaic*) this substance regarded as a humour (see HUMOUR *n.* 4). **3** calmness; sluggishness. [f. OF f. L f. Gk, = inflammation]

phlegmatic /flegˈmætɪk/ *adj.* calm, not easily

agitated; sluggish. —**phlegmatically** *adv.* [f. prec.]

phloem /ˈfləʊem/ *n.* the soft tissue of stems (opp. XYLEM) that carries the food materials made by photosynthesis to all parts of the plant. [f. Gk *phloos* bark]

phlogiston /flɒˈdʒɪst(ə)n/ *n.* a substance formerly supposed to cause combustion. [f. Gk (*phlogizō* set on fire, f. *phlox* flame)]

phlox /flɒks/ *n.* a plant of the genus *Phlox*, with clusters of reddish or purple or white flowers. [L f. Gk name of a plant (lit. 'flame')]

-phobe /-fəʊb/ *suffix* forming nouns and adjectives in the sense '(a person) disliking or fearing' (*Anglophobe*). [F f. L f. Gk (*phobos* fear)]

phobia /ˈfəʊbɪə/ *n.* a persistent abnormal fear or dislike of something. [as foll.]

-phobia /-fəʊbɪə/ *suffix* forming abstract nouns corresponding to adjectives in *-phobe* (*xenophobia*). —**-phobic** *adj.* [L f. Gk (*phobos* fear)]

Phoenician /fɪˈnɪʃ(ə)n/ *adj.* of Phoenicia, the ancient name for the area on the east coast of the Mediterranean, occupied by the Phoenicians, or its people or colonies. —*n.* a Phoenician person. [f. F f. L f. Gk]

phoenix /ˈfiːnɪks/ *n.* a mythical bird of the Arabian desert, the only one of its kind, said to live for five or six centuries and then burn itself on a funeral pyre, rising from its ashes with renewed youth to live through another cycle. [OE, ult. f. Gk *phoinix* Phoenician, purple, phoenix]

phone /fəʊn/ *n.* (*colloq.*) a telephone. —*v.t./i.* (*colloq.*) to telephone. —**phone-in** *n.* a broadcast programme in which listeners participate by telephoning the studio. [abbr.]

phoneme /ˈfəʊniːm/ *n.* a unit of significant sound in a specified language (e.g. the sound of *c* in *cat*, which differs from the *b* in *bat* and distinguishes the two words). —**phonemic** /-ˈniːmɪk/ *adj.*, **phonemics** *n.pl.* (also as *sing.*) [f. F f. Gk, = sound, speech (as foll.)]

phonetic /fəˈnetɪk/ *adj.* of or representing vocal sounds; (of a spelling) corresponding to the pronunciation. —**phonetically** *adv.* [f. Gk (*phōneō* speak)]

phonetician /fəʊnɪˈtɪʃ(ə)n/ *n.* an expert in phonetics. [f. foll.]

phonetics /fəˈnetɪks/ *n.pl.* phonetic phenomena; (as *sing.*) the study of these. [f. PHONETIC]

phoney /ˈfəʊnɪ/ *adj.* (*slang*) sham, counterfeit, fictitious. —*n.* (*slang*) a phoney person or thing. [orig. unkn.]

phonic /ˈfəʊnɪk, ˈfɒ-/ *adj.* of sound; of vocal sound. —**phonically** *adv.* [f. Gk *phōnē* voice, sound]

phono- /fəʊnə(ʊ)-/ *in comb.* sound. [f. Gk *phōnē* (as prec.)]

phonograph /ˈfəʊnəgrɑːf/ *n.* an early form of gramophone; (*US*) a gramophone. [f. PHONO- + -GRAPH]

phonology /fəˈnɒlədʒɪ/ *n.* the study of the sounds in a language. —**phonological** /-ˈlɒdʒɪk(ə)l/ *adj.* [f. PHONO- + -LOGY]

phosphate /ˈfɒsfeɪt/ *n.* a salt or ester of phosphoric acid; an artificial fertilizer composed of or containing this. [F (as PHOSPHORUS)]

phosphor /ˈfɒsfə(r)/ *n.* a synthetic fluorescent or phosphorescent substance. [G f. L, = PHOSPHORUS]

phosphoresce /fɒsfəˈres/ *v.i.* to show phosphorescence. [f. foll.]

phosphorescence /fɒsfəˈres(ə)ns/ *n.* radiation similar to fluorescence but detectable after the excitation ceases; emission of light without combustion or perceptible heat. —**phosphorescent** *adj.* [f. PHOSPHORUS]

phosphorus /ˈfɒsfərəs/ *n.* a non-metallic element, symbol P, atomic number 15. —**phosphoric** /-ˈfɒrɪk/ *adj.*, **phosphorous** *adj.* [L, = morning star, f. Gk (*phōs* light, *-phoros* bringing)]

photo *n.* (*pl.* **-os**) a photograph. —**photo finish**, a close finish of a race with the winner determined by scrutiny of a photograph; any close-run thing. [abbr.]

photo- /fəʊtə(ʊ)-/ *in comb.* **1** light. **2** photography. [f. Gk *phōs* light, or as prec.]

photocopier /ˈfəʊtəʊkɒpɪə(r)/ *n.* a machine for photocopying documents etc.

photocopy /ˈfəʊtəʊkɒpɪ/ *n.* a copy of a document etc. made on a machine employing a light-sensitive process. —*v.t.* to make a photocopy of.

photoelectric /fəʊtəʊɪˈlektrɪk/ *adj.* with or using the emission of electrons from substances exposed to light. —**photoelectric cell**, a device using this effect to generate current. —**photoelectricity** /-ˈtrɪsɪtɪ/ *n.*

photofit /ˈfəʊtəʊfɪt/ *n.* a composite picture made from photographs of separate features assembled from descriptions put together to form a likeness, especially of a person sought by the police.

photogenic /fəʊtəʊˈdʒenɪk, -dʒiːnɪk/ *adj.* **1** apt to be a good subject for photography, coming out well in photographs. **2** producing, or emitting light. —**photogenically** *adv.* [f. PHOTO- + Gk *-genēs* born]

photograph /ˈfəʊtəgrɑːf/ *n.* a picture formed by the chemical action of light or other radiation on a sensitive film. —*v.t.* **1** to take a photograph of. **2** to come out in a specified way when photographed. [f. PHOTO- + -GRAPH]

photographer /fəˈtɒgrəfə(r)/ *n.* one who takes photographs. [f. prec.]

photographic /fəʊtəˈgræfɪk/ *adj*. **1** of or produced by photography. **2** (of the memory) recalling in detail from a single sight. —**photographically** *adv*. [f. PHOTOGRAPH]

photography /fəˈtɒgrəfɪ/ *n*. the taking and processing of photographs. [f. PHOTO- + -GRAPHY]

photogravure /fəʊtəgrəˈvjʊə(r)/ *n*. a picture produced from a photographic negative transferred to a metal plate and etched in. [F (PHOTO-, *gravure* etching)]

photolithography /fəʊtəʊlɪˈθɒgrəfɪ/ *n*. lithography with the plates made by photography.

photometer /fəʊˈtɒmɪtə(r)/ *n*. an instrument for measuring light. —**photometric** /fəʊtəˈmetrɪk/ *adj*., **photometry** *n*. [f. PHOTO- + -METER]

photon /ˈfəʊtɒn/ *n*. a quantum of electromagnetic radiation energy, proportional to the frequency. [f. Gk *phōs* light, after *electron*]

photosensitive /fəʊtəʊˈsensɪtɪv/ *adj*. reacting chemically etc. to light.

Photostat /ˈfəʊtəʊstæt/ *n*. [P] a photographic copy of a document etc. made by the Photostat process. —*v.t*. (-**tt**-) to make a Photostat of. [f. PHOTO- + *-stat* (as in *thermostat* etc.)]

photosynthesis /fəʊtəʊˈsɪnθɪsɪs/ *n*. the process by which carbon dioxide is converted into organic matter in the presence of the chlorophyll of plants under the influence of light, which in all plants except some bacteria involves the production of oxygen from water.

phrase /freɪz/ *n*. **1** a group of words forming a conceptual unit and usually without a predicate, grammatically equivalent to a noun, adjective, or adverb. **2** an idiomatic or short pithy expression; a mode of expression. **3** (*Mus*.) a group of notes forming a distinct unit within a longer melody. —*v.t*. **1** to express in words. **2** to divide (music) into phrases, especially in performance. —**phrase-book** *n*. a book for travellers, listing phrases and their foreign equivalents. —**phrasal** *adj*. [f. L *phrasis* f. Gk (*phrazō* declare)]

phraseology /freɪzɪˈɒlədʒɪ/ *n*. choice or arrangement of words; mode of expression. —**phraseological** /-ˈlɒdʒɪk(ə)l/ *adj*. [as prec. + -LOGY]

phrenology /frɪˈnɒlədʒɪ/ *n*. the study of the external form of the cranium as a supposed indication of a person's character and mental faculties. —**phrenological** /frenəˈlɒdʒɪk(ə)l/ *adj*., **phrenologist** *n*. [f. Gk *phrēn* mind + -LOGY]

phthisis /ˈθaɪsɪs/ *n*. a progressive wasting disease, now especially pulmonary tuberculosis. [L f. Gk (*phthinō* decay)]

phut /fʌt/ *n*. a dull sound of impact, the collapse of an inflated object, etc. —**go phut**, to explode or collapse with this sound; (*colloq*.) to collapse; to come to nothing. [f. Hindi, = to burst]

phylactery /fɪˈlæktərɪ/ *n*. **1** a small leather box containing Hebrew texts, worn by Jews at morning weekday prayer to remind them to keep their law. **2** an amulet or charm. [f. L f. Gk, = amulet (*phulassō* guard)]

phylum /ˈfaɪləm/ *n*. (*pl*. **phyla**) a major division of the animal or plant kingdom. [f. Gk *phulon* race]

physic /ˈfɪzɪk/ *n*. (*archaic*) **1** the art of healing, medicine (excluding surgery). **2** a medicine. [f. OF f. L f. Gk (*phusis* nature)]

physical /ˈfɪzɪk(ə)l/ *adj*. **1** of matter, material (opp. moral, spiritual, or imaginary). **2** of the body. **3** of nature, according to its laws. **4** of physics. —**physical chemistry**, the branch of chemistry in which physics is applied to the study of substances and their reactions. **physical geography**, that dealing with natural features. **physical jerks**, (*colloq*.) physical exercises. **physical science**, the study of inanimate natural objects. —**physically** *adv*. [f. L f. Gk (as prec.)]

physician /fɪˈzɪʃ(ə)n/ *n*. a doctor, especially a specialist in medical diagnosis and treatment. [f. OF (as PHYSIC)]

physicist /ˈfɪzɪsɪst/ *n*. an expert in physics. [f. foll.]

physics /ˈfɪzɪks/ *n.pl*. (usu. treated as *sing*.) the science dealing with the properties and interactions of matter and energy; (as *pl*.) these properties. [as PHYSIC]

physiognomy /fɪzɪˈɒnəmɪ/ *n*. **1** the features of the face; a type of face. **2** the art of judging character from facial or bodily features. **3** the external features of a country etc. —**physiognomist** *n*. [f. OF f. L f. Gk (as PHYSIC, GNOMON)]

physiography /fɪzɪˈɒgrəfɪ/ *n*. **1** the description of nature or natural phenomena, or of a class of objects. **2** physical geography. —**physiographer** *n*. [f. F (as PHYSIC, -GRAPHY)]

physiology /fɪzɪˈɒlədʒɪ/ *n*. the science of the functions and phenomena of living organisms and their parts; these functions. —**physiological** /-ˈlɒdʒɪk(ə)l/ *adj*., **physiologist** *n*. [f. F or L f. Gk (as PHYSIC, -LOGY)]

physiotherapy /fɪzɪəʊˈθerəpɪ/ *n*. the treatment of disease or injury or deformity by massage, exercises, heat, etc., not by drugs. —**physiotherapist** *n*. [as PHYSIC + THERAPY]

physique /fɪˈzi:k/ *n*. bodily structure and development. [F (as PHYSIC)]

pi /paɪ/ *n*. **1** the sixteenth letter of the Greek alphabet, = p. **2** (π) the symbol of the ratio of the circumference of a circle to the diameter (approx. 3.14159). [Gk]

pianissimo /pɪæˈnɪsɪməʊ/ *adv.* (*Mus.*) very softly. —*n.* (*Mus.*) a passage to be played very softly. [It., superl. of PIANO²]

pianist /ˈpɪənɪst/ *n.* a player of the piano. [f. F (as foll.)]

piano¹ /pɪˈænəʊ/ *n.* (*pl.* **-os**) a musical instrument with metal strings struck by hammers worked by levers from a keyboard (vibration being stopped by dampers when keys are released), and with pedals regulating the quality of the tone. —**piano-accordion** *n.* an accordion with the melody played on a small piano-like keyboard. [It., abbr. of PIANOFORTE]

piano² /pɪˈɑːnəʊ/ *adv.* (*Mus.*) softly. —*n.* (*Mus.*) a passage to be played softly. [It. f. L *planus* flat, (of sound) soft]

pianoforte /pɪænəˈfɔːtɪ/ *n.* (*formal* or *archaic*) a piano. [f. It. *piano e forte* soft and loud]

Pianola /pɪəˈnəʊlə/ *n.* [P] a kind of automatic mechanical piano. [dim. of PIANO¹]

pibroch /ˈpiːbrɒk/ *n.* a series of variations for the bagpipe. [f. Gael., = art of piping]

pica /ˈpaɪkə/ *n.* **1** a unit of type-size (⅙ inch). **2** a size of letters in typewriting (ten per inch). [f. L, = 15th-c. book of rules about church feasts (perh. as PIE²)]

picador /ˈpɪkədɔː(r)/ *n.* a mounted man with a lance in a bullfight. [Sp. (*picar* prick)]

picaresque /pɪkəˈresk/ *adj.* (of a style of fiction) dealing with the adventures of rogues. [F f. Sp. (*picaro* rogue)]

picayune /pɪkəˈjuːn/ *n.* (*US*) **1** a small coin. **2** (*colloq.*) an insignificant person or thing. —*adj.* (*US colloq.*) mean, contemptible; petty. [f. F *picaillon* Piedmontese coin]

piccalilli /pɪkəˈlɪlɪ/ *n.* a pickle of chopped vegetables, mustard, and spices. [perh. f. PICKLE + CHILLI]

piccaninny /pɪkəˈnɪnɪ/ *n.* a small Black or Australian Aboriginal child. [W. Ind. Negro f. Sp. *pequeño* little]

piccolo /ˈpɪkələʊ/ *n.* (*pl.* **-os**) a small flute, sounding an octave higher than the ordinary. [It., = small]

pick *v.t./i.* **1** to select (esp. carefully or thoughtfully). **2** to detach (a flower, fruit, etc.) from the plant bearing it. **3** to make a hole in or break the surface of with the fingers or a sharp instrument; to make (a hole) thus. **4** to open (a lock) with a pointed instrument, especially to force entry. **5** to probe or dig at to remove unwanted matter. **6** to eat (food) desultorily or in small bits. **7** to clear (a bone or carcass) of its flesh. —*n.* **1** picking, selection; the right to select. **2** the best or most wanted part. **3** a pickaxe. **4** an instrument for picking; a plectrum. —**pick and choose,** to select fastidiously. **pick at,** to find fault with; to eat desultorily. **pick a person's brains,** to extract ideas or information from him for one's own use. **pick holes in,** to find fault with. **pick-me-up,** *n.* a tonic (*lit.* or *fig.*) to restore health or revive the spirits. **pick off,** to pluck off; to select and shoot (a target or succession of targets) with care. **pick on,** to find fault with, to nag at; to select. **pick out,** to take from a large number; to identify or recognize; to distinguish from the surrounding objects; to play (a tune) by ear on a piano etc. **pick over,** to look over item by item; to choose the best from. **pick a person's pocket,** to steal its contents from him. **pick a quarrel,** to provoke or seize an opportunity for one. **pick to pieces,** to criticize harshly. **pick up,** to take hold of and lift; to learn routinely; to stop for and take with one; to take (cargo etc.) on board; (of the police) to catch and take into custody; to acquire by chance or casually; to encounter and get to know (a person); to manage to receive (a broadcast signal etc.); to improve, to recover health, (of an engine) to recover speed. **pickup** *n.* picking-up; a person met casually; the part of a record-player carrying the stylus; a small open motor truck. —**picker** *n.* [orig. unkn.]

pick-a-back /ˈpɪkəbæk/ var. of PIGGY-BACK.

pickaxe /ˈpɪkæks/ *n.* a heavy iron tool with a point at one end and a wooden handle at right angles to it, for breaking up hard ground etc. [f. OF *picois*, rel. to PIKE]

picket /ˈpɪkɪt/ *n.* **1** one or more persons stationed by strikers outside a place of work to dissuade others from entering. **2** a small body of troops acting as a patrol, a party of sentries. **3** a pointed stake driven into the ground. —*v.t./i.* **1** to place or act as a picket outside (a place of work). **2** to post as a military picket. **3** to tether (an animal). **4** to secure (a place) with stakes. [f. F *piquet* pointed stake (*piquer* prick)]

pickings *n.pl.* **1** casual profits or perquisites. **2** gains from pilfering. **3** the remaining scraps, gleanings. [f. PICK]

pickle *n.* **1** a food, especially a vegetable, preserved in brine, vinegar, or a similar liquor; the liquor used. **2** (*colloq.*) a plight. —*v.t.* **1** to preserve in or treat with pickle. **2** (in *p.p.*, *slang*) drunk. [f. MDu. or MLG *pekel*]

pickpocket *n.* one who steals from people's pockets.

Pickwickian /pɪkˈwɪkɪən/ *adj.* (of words or their sense) not in accordance with the usual meaning, conveniently interpreted so as to avoid offence etc. [f. *Pickwick*, character in Dickens's *Pickwick Papers* (1836-7)]

picky *adj.* (*colloq.*) excessively fastidious. [f. PICK]

picnic /ˈpɪknɪk/ *n.* **1** a pleasure outing including

an informal outdoor meal; the meal itself. **2** (*colloq.*) something readily or easily accomplished. —*v.i.* (**-ck-**) to take part in a picnic. —**picnicker** *n.* [f. F *pique-nique*, orig. unkn.]

pico- /paɪkəʊ-, pi:-/ *in comb.* denoting a factor of 10^{-12} one billionth (*picometre*). [f. Sp. *pico* beak, peak, little bit]

picot /ˈpi:kəʊ/ *n.* a small loop of twisted thread in an edging to lace etc. [F, dim. of *pic* peak, point]

picric acid /ˈpɪkrɪk/ a yellow bitter substance used in dyeing and explosives. [f. Gk *pikros* bitter]

Pict *n.* a member of an ancient people who formerly inhabited parts of northern Britain. —**Pictish** *adj.* [f. L *Picti*, perh. = painted people, or perh. assim. to native name]

pictograph /ˈpɪktəgrɑ:f/ *n.* (also **pictogram**) **1** a pictorial symbol used as a form of writing. **2** a pictorial representation of statistics. —**pictographic** /-ˈgræfɪk/ *adj.* [f. L *pingere* paint + -GRAPH, -GRAM]

pictorial /pɪkˈtɔ:rɪəl/ *adj.* of or expressed in a picture or pictures: illustrated. —*n.* a periodical with pictures as the main feature. —**pictorially** *adv.* [f. L *pictorius* (*pictor* painter)]

picture /ˈpɪktʃə(r)/ *n.* **1** a likeness or representation of a subject produced by painting, drawing, or photography; a portrait. **2** a beautiful object or person. **3** a scene, a total visual or mental impression produced. **4** an image on a television screen. **5** a cinema film; (in *pl.*) a performance at a cinema. —*v.t.* **1** to form a mental picture of, to imagine. **2** to represent in a picture. **3** to describe graphically. —**in the picture,** fully informed; noticed. **picture postcard,** a postcard with a picture on one side. **picture window,** a large window facing an attractive view. [f. L (*pingere* paint)]

picturesque /pɪktʃəˈresk/ *adj.* **1** striking and pleasant to look at. **2** (of language) graphic, expressive. —**picturesquely** *adv.*, **picturesqueness** *n.* [f. F *pittoresque* f. It. (as PICTORIAL)]

piddle *v.i.* **1** to work or act in a trifling way. **2** (*colloq.*) to urinate. [sense 1 perh. f. PEDDLE; sense 2 prob. f. PISS + PUDDLE]

piddling *adj.* (*colloq.*) trifling, trivial. [f. prec.]

pidgin /ˈpɪdʒɪn/ *n.* a simplified form of a language, used for communication between persons of different nationality etc. —**pidgin English,** a jargon, chiefly of English words, used originally between Chinese and Europeans. [corrupt. of *business*]

pi-dog var. of PYE-DOG.

pie[1] *n.* **1** a dish of meat, fish, or fruit, etc. enclosed in or covered with pastry or other crust and baked. **2** a confused mass of printers' type; chaos. —**easy as pie,** very easy. **pie chart,** a diagram representing various quantities as sectors of a circle. **pie in the sky,** a delusive prospect of future happiness, especially as a reward in heaven for virtue or suffering on earth. [perh. = foll.]

pie[2] *n.* a magpie. [f. OF f. L *pica*]

piebald /ˈpaɪbɔld/ *adj.* (of a horse etc.) with irregular patches of white and black or other dark colour. —*n.* a piebald animal. [f. PIE[2] + BALD]

piece /pi:s/ *n.* **1** any of the distinct portions of which a thing is composed or into which it is divided or broken; a detached portion. **2** a single example or specimen, an item. **3** a distinct section or area (of land etc.). **4** any of the things of which a set is composed. **5** a definite quantity in which a thing is made up for sale etc. **6** a fixed unit of work. **7** a (usu. short) literary, dramatic, or musical composition. **8** a coin. **9** a man in board-games, especially a chess-man (usu. other than a pawn). **10** a firearm; an artillery weapon. **11** (*derog.*) a person, especially a woman. —*v.t.* to form into a whole, to join the pieces of. —**go to pieces,** to lose self-control; to collapse. **in one piece,** not broken, unharmed. **of a piece,** uniform, consistent. **piece-goods** *n.pl.* textile fabrics woven in standard lengths. **pieces of eight,** (*hist.*) Spanish dollars. **piecework** *n.* work paid at a rate per piece. **say one's piece,** to give one's opinion; to make a prepared statement. **take to pieces,** to separate the parts of; to be divisible thus. [f. AF, prob. f. Celtic]

pièce de résistance /pɪes də reˈzɪstɑ̃s/ the most important or remarkable item; the main dish at a meal. [F]

piecemeal /ˈpi:smi:l/ *adv.* piece by piece or part at a time. —*adj.* done etc. piecemeal. [f. PIECE + MEAL]

pied /paɪd/ *adj.* particoloured. [f. PIE[2]]

pied-à-terre /pjeɪdɑ:ˈteə(r)/ *n.* (*pl.* ***pieds-à-terre*** *pr.* same) a place kept available as temporary quarters when needed. [F, lit. 'foot to earth']

pie-dog var. of PYE-DOG.

pier /pɪə(r)/ *n.* **1** a structure running out into the sea and serving as a promenade, or landing-stage, or breakwater. **2** a support of an arch or of a span of a bridge; a pillar. **3** the solid masonry between windows etc. —**pier-glass** *n.* a large mirror of a kind originally placed between windows. [f. L *pera*]

pierce /pɪəs/ *v.t./i.* **1** to penetrate (*lit.* & *fig.*). **2** to prick with or like a sharp instrument; to make (a hole) thus. **3** to force one's way through or into. [f. OF ult. f. L *pertundere* bore through (PER-, *tundere* thrust)]

piercing *adj.* **1** (of pain or cold etc.) intense, penetrating sharply. **2** (of a look or sound) sharp or shrill, fierce. [f. prec.]

pierrot /ˈpɪərəʊ/ *n.* a stock character in the French and English theatres (*fem.* **Pierrette**), with whitened face and loose white costume. [F, dim. of *Pierre* Peter]

pietà /pɪeɪˈtɑ:/ *n.* a picture or sculpture of the Virgin Mary holding the dead body of Christ on her lap. [It. f. L (as PIETY)]

pietism /ˈpaɪətɪz(ə)m/ *n.* pious sentiment; exaggeration or affectation of this. [f. G (as foll.)]

piety /ˈpaɪətɪ/ *n.* piousness; an act etc. showing this. [f. OF f. L (as PIOUS)]

piezoelectricity /paɪi:zəʊɪlekˈtrɪsɪtɪ, pi:zəʊ-/ *n.* the phenomenon, exhibited especially by certain crystals such as quartz, in which a substance becomes electrically polarized when subjected to pressure. —**piezoelectric** *adj.* [f. Gk *piezō* press + ELECTRIC]

piffle *n.* (*slang*) nonsense, worthless talk. —*v.i.* (*slang*) to talk or act feebly or frivolously. [imit.]

piffling *adj.* (*slang*) trivial, worthless. [f. prec.]

pig *n.* **1** a wild or domesticated animal of the family Suidae with a broad snout, stout bristly body, and short legs. **2** pork. **3** (*colloq.*) a greedy, dirty, or unpleasant person. **4** (*slang, derog.*) a policeman. **5** an oblong mass of metal (especially iron or lead) from a smelting-furnace. —*v.t./i.* to live or behave like a pig (esp. *pig it*). —**pig in a poke**, a thing acquired or offered without previous sight or knowledge of it. **pig-iron** *n.* crude iron from a smelting-furnace (see IRON). [f. OE]

pigeon /ˈpɪdʒ(ə)n/ *n.* a bird of the dove family. [f. OF f. L *pipio*]

pigeon-hole *n.* **1** a small recess for a pigeon to rest in. **2** each of a set of small compartments in a cabinet or on a wall for papers, letters, etc. —*v.t.* **1** to put in a pigeon-hole. **2** to put aside for future consideration or indefinitely. **3** to classify mentally.

piggery *n.* a place where pigs are bred; a pigsty. [f. PIG]

piggish *adj.* like a pig, greedy or dirty. [f. PIG]

piggy *n.* a little pig. —**piggy bank**, a money-box in the form of a hollow pig. [f. PIG]

piggy-back *n.* a ride on the shoulders and back of another. —*adv.* by means of a piggy-back. [for earlier *pick-a-back*; orig. unkn.]

pigheaded *adj.* obstinate, stubborn.

piglet /ˈpɪglɪt/ *n.* a young pig. [f. PIG + -LET]

pigment /ˈpɪgmənt/ *n.* colouring-matter. —*v.t.* to colour (skin or other tissue) with natural pigment. —**pigmentation** /-ˈteɪʃ(ə)n/ *n.* [f. L *pigmentum* (*pingere* paint)]

pigskin *n.* a pig's skin; leather made from this.

pigsty *n.* **1** a partly-covered pen for pigs. **2** a very dirty or untidy place.

pigswill *n.* the swill of a kitchen or brewery fed to pigs.

pigtail *n.* a plait of hair hanging from the back of the head.

pike *n.* **1** (*pl.* same) a large voracious freshwater fish with a long narrow snout. **2** a peaked top of a hill. **3** (*hist.*) an infantry weapon consisting of a long wooden shaft with a pointed metal head. [OE, = point]

piked /paɪkt/ *adj.* (in diving and gymnastics) with the legs straight and forming an angle with the body at the hips. [orig. unkn.]

pikelet /ˈpaɪklɪt/ *n.* a crumpet. [f. Welsh (*bara*) *pyglyd* pitchy (bread)]

pikestaff *n.* the wooden shaft of a pike. —**plain as a pikestaff**, quite plain or obvious.

pilaff /ˈpɪlæf/ *n.* an oriental dish of rice with meat, spices, etc. [f. Turk.]

pilaster /pɪˈlæstə(r)/ *n.* a rectangular column, especially one fastened into a wall. [f. F f. It. f. L (*pila* pillar)]

pilau /pɪˈlaʊ/ var of PILAFF.

pilchard /ˈpɪltʃəd/ *n.* a small sea-fish (*Sardinia pilchardus*) related to the herring. [orig. unkn.]

pile[1] *n.* **1** a number of things lying one upon another. **2** (*colloq.*) a large quantity, especially of money. **3** a grand or lofty building. **4** (in full **funeral pile**) a heap of wood etc. on which a corpse is burnt. **5** a series of plates of dissimilar metals laid alternately to produce an electric current. **6** (in full **atomic pile**) a nuclear reactor. —*v.t./i.* **1** to heap, stack, or load. **2** to crowd. —**pile it on**, (*colloq.*) to exaggerate. **pile up**, to accumulate, to cause (a vehicle or aircraft) to crash. **pile-up** *n.* a collision of several motor vehicles. [f. OF f. L *pila* pillar]

pile[2] *n.* **1** a pointed stake or post. **2** a heavy beam of metal, concrete, or timber driven vertically into the ground as a foundation or support for a building or bridge. —**pile-driver** *n.* a machine for driving piles into the ground. **pile-dwelling** *n.* a lake-dwelling (see LAKE[1]). [OE f. L *pilum* javelin]

pile[3] *n.* the soft surface of a fabric with a tangible depth formed by cut or uncut loops. [prob. f. AF f. L *pilus* hair]

pile[4] *n.* (usu. in *pl.*) a haemorrhoid. [prob. f. L *pila* ball]

pilfer *v.t./i.* to steal, especially in small quantities. —**pilferer** *n.* [f. AF *pelfrer* pillage]

pilgrim /ˈpɪlgrɪm/ *n.* one who journeys to a sacred or revered place as an act of religious devotion. [f. Prov. f. L, = PEREGRINE]

pilgrimage *n.* a pilgrim's journey. [f. prec.]

pill *n.* **1** a small ball or flat piece of medicinal substance for swallowing whole. **2** something that has to be endured, a humiliation. —**the pill,** (*colloq.*) the contraceptive pill. [f. MDu. or MLG (prob. as PILULE)]

pillage /ˈpɪlɪdʒ/ *n.* plundering, especially in war. —*v.t.* to plunder. —**pillager** *n.* [f. OF (*piller* plunder)]

pillar /ˈpɪlə(r)/ *n.* **1** a slender vertical structure of stone etc. used as a support or ornament. **2** an upright mass of air, water, rock, etc. **3** a person regarded as a main supporter of a cause or principle. —**from pillar to post,** rapidly from one place or situation to another. **pillar-box** *n.* a hollow pillar in which letters may be posted. [f. AF *piler* ult. f. L *pila* pillar]

pillbox *n.* **1** a shallow cylindrical box for holding pills. **2** a small concrete shelter for a gun emplacement.

pillion /ˈpɪljən/ *n.* a seat for a passenger behind a motor-cyclist etc. —**ride pillion,** to ride on this as a passenger. [f. Gaelic, = small cushion, f. L *pellis* skin]

pillory /ˈpɪlərɪ/ *n.* a wooden framework with holes for the head and hands, into which offenders were formerly locked for exposure to public ridicule. —*v.t.* **1** to put in a pillory. **2** to expose to ridicule. [f. OF]

pillow /ˈpɪləʊ/ *n.* **1** a cushion used as a support for the head, especially in a bed. **2** a pillow-shaped block or support. —*v.t.* to rest or prop up on a pillow. [OE, ult. f. L *pulvinus* cushion]

pillowcase *n.* (also **pillowslip**) a washable cover of cotton etc. for a pillow.

pilot /ˈpaɪlət/ *n.* **1** a person who operates the controls of an aircraft. **2** a person qualified to take charge of ships entering or leaving a harbour or travelling through certain waters. **3** a guide. —*v.t.* **1** to act as the pilot of. **2** to guide. —*adj.* experimental, testing (on a small scale) how a scheme etc. will work. —**pilot-light** a small gas-burner kept alight and lighting a larger burner when this is turned on; an electric indicator light or control light. **pilot officer,** the lowest commissioned rank in the RAF. [f. F f. L ult. f. Gk *pēdon* oar]

Pilsener /ˈpɪlznə(r), -s-/ *n.* a pale-coloured lager beer with a strong hop flavour, of the type brewed at Pilsen (Plzeň) in Czechoslovakia.

pilule /ˈpɪlju:l/ *n.* a small pill. [F f. L *pilula* dim. of *pila* ball]

pimento /pɪˈmentəʊ/ *n.* (*pl.* **-os** **1** a West Indian tree (*Pimenta officinalis*) the ground berry of which produces allspice. **2** this spice. **3** a sweet pepper. [f. Sp. f. L (as PIGMENT)]

pimp *n.* one who solicits clients for a prostitute or brothel. —*v.i.* to act as a pimp. [orig. unkn.]

pimpernel /ˈpɪmpənel/ *n.* an annual plant (*Anagallis arvensis*) with small scarlet, blue, or white flowers that close in cloudy or rainy weather. [f. OF, ult. f. L *piper* pepper]

pimple *n.* a small hard inflamed spot on the skin; a similar slight swelling on a surface. —**pimply** *adj.* [OE, = break out in pustules]

pin *n.* **1** a thin usually cylindrical piece of metal with a sharp point and round broadened head for fastening together papers, fabrics, etc. or (with an ornamental head) as a decoration. **2** a larger similar object of wood or metal for various purposes. **3** the projecting part of a dovetail joint. **4** (in golf) a stick with a flag on it marking the position of a hole. **5** (in *pl.*, *colloq.*) the legs. —*v.t.* (**-nn-**) **1** to fasten with a pin or pins. **2** to fix the responsibility for (a deed *on* a person). **3** to seize and hold fast (against a wall etc.). **4** to transfix with a pin, lance, etc. —**pin-ball** *n.* a game in which small metal balls are shot across a sloping board and strike against pins. **pin down,** to make (a person) declare his intentions etc. clearly; to restrict the actions of (an enemy etc.); to specify (a thing) precisely. **pin one's faith** *or* **hopes on,** to rely absolutely on. **pin-money** *n.* a small sum of money, originally that allowed to a woman or earned by her for private expenses. **pins and needles,** a tingling sensation in a limb recovering from numbness. **pin-stripe** *n.* a very narrow stripe in cloth. **pin-table** *n.* a table used in pin-ball. **pin-tuck** *n.* a very narrow ornamental tuck. **pin-up** *n.* a picture of an attractive or famous person, pinned up on a wall etc.; such a person. **pin-wheel** *n.* a small Catherine wheel. [OE f. L *pinna* point etc.]

pinafore /ˈpɪnəfɔ:(r)/ *n.* a full-length apron. —**pinafore dress,** a dress without a collar and sleeves, worn over a blouse or jumper. [f. PIN + AFORE]

pince-nez /ˈpæ̃snei/ *n.* (*pl.* same) a pair of eyeglasses with a spring that clips on the nose. [F, = pinch-nose]

pincers /ˈpɪnsəz/ *n.pl.* **1** (also **pair of pincers**) a gripping-tool of two pivoted limbs forming jaws. **2** a similar organ of crustaceans etc. —**pincer movement,** a military movement in which forces converge from each side on an enemy position. [f. AF (OF *pincier* pinch)]

pinch *v.t./i.* **1** to squeeze tightly between two surfaces, especially between finger and thumb. **2** (of cold, hunger, etc.) to affect painfully; to cause to shrivel. **3** to stint, to be niggardly. **4** (*slang*) to steal. **5** (*slang*) to arrest. —*n.* **1** pinching, squeezing. **2** the stress of circumstances. **3** as much as can be taken up with the tips of the finger and thumb. —**at a pinch,** in an emergency, if necessary. **pinch off** *or* **out,** to shorten or remove (buds etc.) by pinching. [f. OF *pincier* ult. f. L *pungere* prick]

pinchbeck *n.* a goldlike alloy of copper and zinc used in cheap jewellery etc. —*adj.* counterfeit, sham. [f. C. *Pinchbeck*, English watchmaker (d. 1732)]

pincushion *n.* a small cushion or pad into which pins are stuck to keep them ready for use.

pine[1] *n.* an evergreen coniferous tree of the genus *Pinus* with needle-shaped leaves growing in clusters; its wood. —**pine-cone** *n.* the seed-head of the pine. [OE & f. OF f. L *pinus*]

pine[2] *v.i.* **1** to waste away through grief or yearning. **2** to feel an intense longing. [OE]

pineal /ˈpɪnɪəl/ *adj.* shaped like a pine-cone. [f. F f. L *pinea* pine-cone]

pineapple /ˈpaɪnæp(ə)l/ *n.* **1** a large juicy tropical fruit with a yellow flesh and tough segmented skin. **2** the plant (*Ananas comosus*) bearing this. [f. PINE[1] + APPLE (f. the resemblance of the fruit to a pine-cone)]

ping *n.* an abrupt single ringing sound. —*v.t./i.* to make or cause to make this sound. —**pinger** *n.* [imit.]

ping-pong *n.* table tennis. [imit., f. sound of bat striking ball]

pinion[1] /ˈpɪnjən/ *n.* a small cog-wheel engaging with a larger one; a cogged spindle engaging with a wheel. [f. F *pignon* f. L (as PINEAL)]

pinion[2] /ˈpɪnjən/ *n.* **1** the outer segment of a bird's wing. **2** (*poetic*) a wing. **3** a flight-feather. —*v.t.* **1** to clip the wings of (a bird) to prevent it from flying. **2** to restrain (a person) by holding or binding his arms; to bind (arms) thus. [f. OF, ult. f. L *pinna* feather]

pink[1] *n.* **1** pale red colour. **2** pink clothes or material. **3** a garden plant of the genus *Dianthus* with fragrant flowers. **4** the best or most perfect condition. —*adj.* **1** of pale red colour. **2** (*slang*) mildly communist. —**in the pink,** (*slang*) in very good health. **pink gin,** gin flavoured with angostura bitters. —**pinkness** *n.* [perh. f. obs. *pink-eyed* small-eyed]

pink[2] *v.t.* **1** to pierce slightly. **2** to cut a scalloped or zigzag edge on. —**pinking shears,** a dressmaker's serrated scissors for cutting a zigzag edge. [perh. f. L Du.; cf. LF *pinken* strike, peck]

pink[3] *v.i.* (of a vehicle engine) to emit high-pitched explosive sounds when running faultily. [imit.]

pinnace /ˈpɪnɪs/ *n.* a warship's or other ship's small boat. [f. F]

pinnacle /ˈpɪnək(ə)l/ *n.* **1** a small ornamental turret crowning a buttress, roof, etc. **2** a natural peak. **3** the highest point (of fame, success, etc.). [f. OF f. L *pinnaculum* (*pinna* wing, point)]

pinnate /ˈpɪnɪt/ *adj.* (of a compound leaf) with leaflets on each side of the leaf-stalk. —**pinnately** *adv.* [f. L *pinnatus* feathered]

pinny *n.* (*colloq.*) a pinafore. [abbr.]

pin-point *n.* **1** the point of a pin. **2** something very small or sharp. —*v.t.* to locate or designate with high precision. —*adj.* **1** seeming as small or sharp as the point of a pin. **2** performed with or exhibiting high precision.

pinprick *n.* a trifling irritation.

pint /paɪnt/ *n.* **1** a measure of capacity of liquids etc., ⅛ of a gallon (in Britain 4546 cc, in the USA 3785 cc). **2** this quantity of liquid, especially milk or beer. —**pint-sized** *adj.* (*colloq.*) diminutive. [f. OF]

pinta /ˈpaɪntə/ *n.* (*colloq.*) a pint of milk etc. [corrupt. (orig. in advertising slogan) of *pint of*]

pintail *n.* a duck or grouse with a pointed tail.

pintle /ˈpɪnt(ə)l/ *n.* a bolt or pin, especially one on which some other part turns. [OE, = penis]

pioneer /paɪəˈnɪə(r)/ *n.* an original explorer or settler or investigator of a subject etc.; an initiator of an enterprise. —*v.t./i.* to be a pioneer; to originate (a course of action etc. followed later by others). [f. F *pionnier* foot-soldier (as PEON)]

pious /ˈpaɪəs/ *adj.* **1** devout in religion. **2** ostentatiously virtuous. **3** dutiful. —**piously** *adv.*, **piousness** *n.* [f. L *pius*]

pip[1] *n.* a seed of an apple, orange, grape, etc. [abbr. of PIPPIN]

pip[2] *n.* **1** each spot on playing-cards, dice, or dominoes. **2** a star (up to three according to rank) on the shoulder of an army officer's uniform. [earlier *peep* (orig. unkn.)]

pip[3] *v.t.* (**-pp-**) **1** (*colloq.*) to hit with a shot. **2** (also **pip at the post**) to forestall; to defeat narrowly or at the last moment. [f. prec. or PIP[1]]

pip[4] *n.* a short high-pitched sound, especially one produced electronically e.g. as a time-signal. [imit.]

pip[5] *n.* **1** a disease of poultry, hawks, etc. **2** (*slang*) a fit of disgust, depression, or bad temper. [f. MDu. or MLG, perh. ult. f. L *pituita* slime]

pipe *n.* **1** a tube of metal, plastic, etc., especially for conveying water, gas, etc. **2** a narrow tube with a bowl at one end containing tobacco for smoking; the quantity of tobacco held by this. **3** a wind-instrument of a single tube; each tube by which the sound is produced in an organ; (in *pl.*) bagpipes. **4** a tubular organ, vessel, etc., in an animal body.

5 a boatswain's whistle; the sounding of this. **6** a cask for wine, especially as a measure (usu. = 105 gal.). —*v.t./i.* **1** to convey (oil, water, gas, etc.) by pipes. **2** to transmit (recorded music etc.) by wire or cable for hearing elsewhere. **3** to play on a pipe or pipes. **4** to utter in a shrill voice. **5** to lead or bring (a person etc.) by the sound of a pipe; to summon by sounding a whistle. **6** to decorate or trim with piping. **7** to furnish with pipes. —**pipe-cleaner** *n.* a piece of flexible tuft-covered wire to clean inside a tobacco-pipe. **pipe down,** (*colloq.*) to be quiet or less insistent. **pipe-dream** *n.* an unattainable or fanciful hope or scheme, as indulged in when smoking a pipe (orig. of opium). **pipe up,** to begin to sing, play a tune, etc.; to interject a remark. [OE, ult. f. L *pipare* chirp]

pipeclay *n.* a fine white clay for tobacco-pipes or for whitening leather etc.

pipeline *n.* **1** a series of pipes conveying oil etc. to a distance. **2** a channel of supply or information. —**in the pipeline,** being considered, prepared, etc.

pip emma /pɪp 'emə/ (*colloq.*) p.m. [former signallers' names for letters *P.M.*]

piper *n.* one who plays on a pipe, especially the bagpipes. [f. PIPE]

pipette /pɪ'pet/ *n.* a slender tube for transferring or measuring small quantities of liquids. [F dim. (as PIPE)]

piping /'paɪpɪŋ/ *n.* **1** a length of pipe; a system of pipes. **2** a pipelike fold enclosing a cord as a decoration for the edges or seams of upholstery etc. **3** ornamental cordlike lines of icing on a cake. —*adj.* **piping hot,** (of food or water) very hot.

pipistrelle /pɪpɪ'strel/ *n.* a small bat of the genus *Pipistrellus.* [f. F f. It. f. L *vespertilio* bat (*vesper* evening)]

pipit /'pɪpɪt/ *n.* a small bird of the family Motacillidae, resembling a lark. [prob. imit.]

pippin /'pɪpɪn/ *n.* an apple grown from seed; any of various red and yellow desert apples. [f. OF *pepin*]

pip-squeak *n.* (*slang*) a small or unimportant but self-assertive fellow.

piquant /'pi:kənt/ *adj.* **1** pleasantly sharp in its taste or smell, appetizing. **2** pleasantly stimulating or exciting to the mind. —**piquancy** *n.*, **piquantly** *adv.* [F (*piquer* prick)]

pique /pi:k/ *v.t.* **1** to wound the pride or self-respect of. **2** to irritate to arouse (curiosity or interest). —*n.* a feeling of resentment or hurt pride. [f. F (as prec.)]

piquet /pɪ'ket/ *n.* a card-game for two players with a pack of 32 cards (omitting the low cards two to six). [F]

piranha /pɪ'rɑ:nə, -njə/ *n.* a voracious South American freshwater fish of the genus *Serrasalmus.* [Port. f. Tupi]

pirate /'paɪərət/ *n.* **1** a seafaring robber attacking other ships etc.; a ship used by a pirate. **2** one who infringes another's copyright or business rights or who broadcasts without authorization. —*v.t.* **1** to plunder. **2** to reproduce (a book etc.) or trade (goods) without due authorization. —**piracy** *n.*, **piratical** /paɪ'rætɪk(ə)l/ *adj.* [f. L f. Gk (*peiraō* attempt, assault)]

pirouette /pɪru:'et/ *n.* a ballet-dancer's spin on one foot or the point of the toe. —*v.i.* to perform a pirouette. [F, = spinning-top]

piscatorial /pɪskə'tɔrɪəl/ *adj.* of fishermen or fishing. [f. L (*piscator* fisherman)]

Pisces /'paɪsi:z/ *n.* a constellation and the twelfth sign of the zodiac, the Fishes, which the sun enters about 20 Feb. —**Piscean** *adj.* & *n.* [L, = fishes]

piscina /pɪ'si:nə/ *n.* **1** a perforated stone basin near the altar in a church for carrying away water used in rinsing the chalice etc. **2** a fish-pond. [L (as prec.)]

piss *v.t./i.* (*vulgar*) **1** to urinate. **2** (in *p.p.*) drunk. —*n.* (*vulgar*) urine; urination. [f. OF *pisser* (imit.)]

pistachio /pɪ'stæʃɪəʊ/ *n.* (*pl.* **-os**) a nut with a greenish edible kernel; the tree (*Pistacia vera*) bearing this. [f. It. & Sp., ult. f. Pers. *pistah*]

piste /pi:st/ *n.* a ski-track of compacted snow. [F, = racetrack]

pistil *n.* the female organ of a flower, comprising the ovary, style, and stigma. —**pistillate** *adj.* [f. F or L (as PESTLE)]

pistol /'pɪst(ə)l/ *n.* a small gun. —*v.t.* (**-ll-**) to shoot with a pistol. —**pistol-grip** *n.* a handle shaped like the butt of a pistol. **pistol-whip** *v.t.* to beat with a pistol. [f. F f. G f. Czech]

piston /'pɪst(ə)n/ *n.* **1** a sliding cylinder fitting closely in a tube and moving up and down in it, used in steam and internal-combustion engines to impart motion, or in a pump to receive motion. **2** a sliding valve in a trumpet etc. —**piston-rod** *n.* the rod by which a piston imparts motion. [F f. It. (as PESTLE)]

pit *n.* **1** a large hole in the ground, especially one made in digging for a mineral etc. or for industrial purposes. **2** a coal-mine. **3** a covered hole as a trap for animals. **4** a hollow on a surface. **5** a part of the auditorium of a theatre on the floor of the house; the sunken part before the stage, accommodating the orchestra. **6** a sunken area in a workshop floor for access to the underside of motor vehicles. **7** an area of the side of the track at a racecourse, where racing cars are serviced etc. during a race. —*v.t.* **1** to match or set in competition. **2** (esp. in *p.p.*) to make pits or scars in. **3** to put into a pit. —**pit-head** *n.* the top of the shaft of a coal-mine; the area surrounding this. **pit of the stomach,** the depression below the breastbone. [OE f. L *puteus* well]

pita /ˈpiːtə/ *n.* (also **pitta**) a flat bread originating in Greece and the Middle East. [modern Gk, = cake]

pit-a-pat /ˈpɪtəpæt/ *n.* a sound as of quick light steps or quick tapping. —*adv.* with this sound. [imit.]

pitch[1] *v.t./i.* **1** to erect and fix (a tent or camp); to fix in a definite position. **2** to throw or fling. **3** to cause (a bowled ball in cricket) to strike the ground at a particular point; (of a ball) to strike the ground thus. **4** to express in a particular style or at a particular level. **5** to fall heavily; (of a ship or aircraft) to plunge alternately backwards and forwards in a lengthwise direction. **6** (*Mus.*) to set at a particular pitch. **7** (*slang*) to tell (a tale, a yarn). —*n.* **1** the act or process of pitching. **2** an area marked out for play in outdoor games; (in cricket) the area between or near the wickets. **3** (*Mus.*) the relative sound of a note, governed by the rate of vibration of a string etc.; the degree of highness or lowness of tone. **4** the place at which a street vendor etc. is stationed. **5** an approach taken in advertising or sales-talk. **6** the intensity of a quality etc. **7** the distance between successive ridges of a screw, teeth of a cog, etc.; the steepness of a slope. —**absolute pitch,** ability to recognize or reproduce the pitch of a note (also **perfect pitch**); a fixed standard of pitch. **pitched battle,** a battle fought between armies in prepared positions and formations; a fierce argument. **pitched roof,** one that slopes. **pitch in,** (*colloq.*) to set to work vigorously. **pitch into,** (*colloq.*) to attack forcefully. [perh. rel. to OE *picung* stigmata]

pitch[2] *n.* a dark resinous substance from the distillation of tar or turpentine, used for caulking the seams of ships etc. —*v.t.* to coat with pitch. —**pitch-black** *or* **pitch-dark** *adj.* dark with no light at all. **pitch-pine** *n.* a pine-tree (*Pinus rigida*) yielding much resin. —**pitchy** *adj.* [OE f. L *pix*]

pitchblende /ˈpɪtʃblend/ *n.* uranium oxide found in pitchlike masses and yielding radium. [f. G (as prec., BLENDE)]

pitcher[1] *n.* a large jug with a handle or two ears and usually a lip, for holding liquids. —**pitcher-plant** *n.* a plant, especially of the genus *Sarracenia*, with pitcher-shaped leaves holding a secretion in which insects become trapped. [f. OF (as BEAKER)]

pitcher[2] *n.* the player who delivers the ball in baseball. [f. PITCH[1]]

pitchfork *n.* a long-handled fork with two prongs, used for pitching hay. —*v.t.* **1** to throw (as) with a pitchfork. **2** to thrust (a person) forcibly into a position, office, etc.

piteous /ˈpɪtɪəs/ *adj.* deserving or arousing pity. —**piteously** *adv.* [f. AF (as PITY)]

pitfall *n.* **1** an unsuspected danger or difficulty. **2** a covered hole as a trap for animals.

pith *n.* **1** the spongy tissue in plant stems and branches or lining the rind of an orange etc. **2** the essential part. **3** physical strength, vigour. [OE]

pithy *adj.* **1** terse, condensed, and forcible. **2** of or like pith. —**pithiness** *n.* [f. PITH]

pitiable /ˈpɪtɪəb(ə)l/ *adj.* deserving or arousing pity or contempt. —**pitiably** *adv.* [f. OF (as PITY)]

pitiful /ˈpɪtɪfʊl/ *adj.* **1** causing pity. **2** contemptible. —**pitifully** *adv.* [f. PITY + -FUL]

pitiless /ˈpɪtɪlɪs/ *adj.* showing no pity. —**pitilessly** *adv.* [f. PITY + -LESS]

piton /ˈpiːtɒn/ *n.* a spike or peg with a hole through which a rope can be passed, driven into rock or crack as a support in rock-climbing. [F, = eye-bolt]

pittance /ˈpɪt(ə)ns/ *n.* a very small allowance or remuneration. [f. OF f. L (as PITY)]

pitter-patter /ˈpɪtəpætə(r)/ *n.* & *adv.* pit-a-pat. [imit.]

pituitary /pɪˈtjuːɪtərɪ/ *n.* the pituitary gland. —**pituitary gland** *or* **body,** a pea-sized endocrine gland at the base of the brain. [f. L (*pituita* slime, phlegm, referring to the fact that the gland was once thought to secrete nasal mucus)]

pity /ˈpɪtɪ/ *n.* **1** a feeling of sorrow for another's suffering. **2** a cause for regret. —*v.t.* to feel pity (often with contempt) for. —**take pity on,** to feel or act compassionately towards. [f. OF *pité* f. L (as PIETY)]

pivot /ˈpɪvət/ *n.* **1** a short pin or shaft on which something turns or oscillates. **2** a person or point that is crucial. —*v.t./i.* **1** to turn (as) on a pivot. **2** to provide with a pivot. **3** to depend crucially, to hinge. —**pivotal** *adj.* [F]

pixie /ˈpɪksɪ/ *n.* (*also* **pixy**) a supernatural being akin to a fairy. —**pixie hood,** a hood with a pointed crown. [orig. unkn.]

pizza /ˈpiːtsə/ *n.* an Italian dish of a layer of dough baked with a savoury topping. [It., = pie]

pizzicato /pɪtsɪˈkɑːtəʊ/ *adv.* (*Mus.*) with a string of the violin etc. plucked instead of played with the bow. —*n.* (*pl.* **-os**) a note or passage to be played in this way. [It.]

pl. *abbr.* plural.

placable /ˈplækəb(ə)l/ *adj.* easily appeased, forgiving. —**placability** /-ˈbɪlɪtɪ/ *n.* [f. OF or L (*placare* appease)]

placard /ˈplækɑːd/ *n.* a large notice for public display. —*v.t.* **1** to put placards on (a wall etc.). **2** to advertise by placards. **3** to display as a placard. [f. OF (*plaquier* to plaster f. MDu.)]

placate /plə'keɪt/ *v.t.* to conciliate, to pacify. —**placatory** *adj.* [f. L *placare*]

place *n.* **1** a particular part of space or of an area on a surface. **2** a particular town, district, building, etc. **3** (in names) a short street; a square or the buildings round it; a country mansion. **4** a passage or part in a book etc.; the point one has reached in reading. **5** a proper space for a thing; position in a series. **6** rank, position in a community, etc.; a duty appropriate to this. **7** a position of employment. **8** a space, seat, or accommodation for a person; one's home or dwelling. **9** (in racing) a position among placed competitors, especially other than the winner. **10** a step in the progression of an argument or statement etc. **11** the position of a figure in a series as indicating its value in decimal or other notation. —*v.t.* **1** to put into a particular or proper place, state, rank, order, etc.; to find a place for. **2** to locate; to identify in relation to circumstances etc. **3** to put or give (goods, an order for these) into the hands of a firm etc.; to invest (money). —**be placed,** to be among the first three in a race. **give place to,** to make room for; to yield precedence to; to be succeeded by. **go places,** (*colloq.*) to be successful. **in place,** in the right place; suitable. **in place of,** in exchange for, instead of. **in places,** at some places but not others. **out of place,** in the wrong place; unsuitable. **place-kick** *n.* a kick in football with the ball placed on the ground. **place-mat** *n.* a table-mat for a person's place at table. **place-setting** *n.* a set of cutlery or dishes for one person at table. **put a person in his place,** to snub a presumptious person. **take place,** to occur. **take the place of,** to be substituted for. —**placement** *n.* [f. OF f. L *platea* broad way f. Gk]

placebo /plə'si:bəʊ/ *n.* (*pl.* **-os**) a medicine intended to cure by reassuring the patient rather than by its physiological effect; a dummy pill etc. used in a controlled trial. [L, = I shall be acceptable (*placēre* please), first word of Ps. 114: 9 in Vulgate]

placenta /plə'sentə/ *n.* (*pl.* **-ae** /-i:/ or **-as**) **1** a flattened circular spongy vascular structure that develops in the uterus of pregnant mammals through which the developing foetus is supplied with nutriment and rid of waste products, and to which it is attached by the umbilical cord. **2** (in plants) the part of the carpel to which ovules are attached. —**placental** *adj.* [L f. Gk, = flat cake]

placer /'pleɪsə(r), 'plæ-/ *n.* a deposit of sand or gravel etc. containing valuable minerals in particles. [Amer. Sp.]

placid /'plæsɪd/ *adj.* calm and peaceful; not easily made anxious or upset. —**placidity** /plə'sɪdɪtɪ/ *n.*, **placidly** *adv.* [f. F or L *placidus* (*placēre* please)]

placket /'plækɪt/ *n.* an opening or slit in a woman's skirt, for fastenings or access to a pocket. [var. of PLACARD]

plagiarize /'pleɪdʒəraɪz/ *v.t.* to pass off (another's ideas, writings, or inventions) as one's own. —**plagiarism** *n.*, **plagiarist** *n.* [f. L *plagiarius* kidnapper]

plague /pleɪg/ *n.* **1** a deadly contagious disease transmitted to man by rats' fleas, especially bubonic plague. **2** an infestation of a pest. **3** a great trouble or affliction; (*colloq.*) a nuisance. —*v.t.* **1** to afflict with plague. **2** (*colloq.*) to pester, to annoy. [f. L *plaga* stroke]

plaice *n.* (*pl.* same) a kind of edible marine flat-fish (*Pleuronectes platessa*). [f. OF f. L *platessa*]

plaid /plæd/ *n.* a long piece of twilled woollen cloth with a chequered or tartan pattern, the outer article of Highland costume; the cloth used for this. —*adj.* made of or having a plaidlike pattern. [Gaelic]

Plaid Cymru /plaɪd 'kʌmrɪ/ the Welsh nationalist party, founded in 1925 and dedicated to seeking autonomy for Wales. [Welsh, = party of Wales]

plain *adj.* **1** clear and unmistakable, easily perceived or understood. **2** not elaborate or intricate; not luxurious; (of food) not rich or highly seasoned. **3** straightforward, candid. **4** undistinguished in appearance, not beautiful or good-looking. **5** homely in manner, without affectation. —*n.* **1** a large level tract of country. **2** the ordinary stitch in knitting, producing a smooth surface towards the knitter. —*adv.* plainly, simply. —**plain chocolate,** chocolate made without milk. **plain clothes,** civilian clothes as distinct from uniform or official dress. **plain flour,** flour that does not contain a raising agent. **plain sailing,** a simple situation or course of action. **plain-spoken** *adj.* frank. —**plainly** *adv.*, **plainness** *n.* [f. OF f. L *planus*]

plainsong *n.* (also **plainchant**) traditional church music in medieval modes and in free rhythm depending on accentuation of the words, sung in unison, with a single line of vocal melody to words taken from the liturgy.

plaint *n.* **1** (*Law*) an accusation, a charge. **2** (*poetic*) a lamentation, a complaint. [f. OF f. L (*plangere* lament)]

plaintiff /'pleɪntɪf/ *n.* the party who brings a suit into a lawcourt. [f. OF, = foll.]

plaintive /'pleɪntɪv/ *adj.* mournful-sounding. —**plaintively** *adv.* [f. OF (as PLAINT)]

plait /plæt/ *n.* an interlacing of three or more strands of hair or ribbon or straw etc.;

material thus interlaced. —*v.t.* to form into a plait. [f. OF f. L *plicare* fold]

plan *n.* **1** a method or procedure, thought out in advance, by which a thing is to be done. **2** a map of a town or district. **3** a drawing showing the relative position and size of the parts of a building or structure. **4** a scheme of arrangement. —*v.t./i.* (**-nn-**) **1** to arrange or work out the details of (a procedure, enterprise, etc.) beforehand; to make plans. **2** to make a plan of or design for. **3** (in *p.p.*) done in accordance with a plan. —**plan on,** (*colloq.*) to aim at or envisage. —**planner** *n.* [F f. It. *pianta* plan of building (as PLANT)]

planchette /plænˈʃet/ *n.* a small board supported on castors and a pencil, said to trace letters etc. at spiritualist seances without conscious direction when one or more persons rest their fingers lightly on the board. [F dim. (as PLANK)]

plane[1] *n.* **1** a surface such that a straight line joining any two points in it lies wholly in it; a level surface. **2** a level of attainment or knowledge etc. **3** an aeroplane; a main aerofoil. —*adj.* level as or lying in a plane. [f. L *planus* (as PLAIN)]

plane[2] *n.* a tool for smoothing the surface of wood by paring shavings from it. —*v.t.* to pare or make smooth with a plane. [OF f. L (as prec.)]

plane[3] *n.* a tall spreading broad-leaved tree of the genus *Platanus.* [f. OF f. L *platanus* f. Gk]

planet /ˈplænɪt/ *n.* any of the heavenly bodies in orbit round the sun. —**planetary** *adj.* [f. OF f. L f. Gk, lit. = wanderer (*planaomai* wander), orig. distinguished from fixed stars by apparently having a motion of its own, and including the sun and moon]

planetarium /plænɪˈteərɪəm/ *n.* (*pl.* **-ums**) a device for projecting an image of the night sky as seen at various times and places; a building containing this. [as prec.]

plangent /ˈplændʒənt/ *adj.* **1** loud and reverberating. **2** loud and plaintive. —**plangency** *n.* [f. L (as PLAINT)]

plank *n.* **1** a long flat piece of timber. **2** an item of a political or other programme. —*v.t.* **1** to furnish or cover with planks. **2** (*colloq.*) to put down roughly or violently; to pay (money) on the spot. —**walk the plank,** (*hist.*) to be made to walk blindfold into the sea along a plank laid over the side of a ship. [f. OF f. L *planca*]

planking *n.* planks collectively; a structure or surface of planks. [f. PLANK]

plankton /ˈplæŋkt(ə)n/ *n.* the forms of organic life (chiefly microscopic) that drift or float in the sea or fresh water. —**planktonic** /-ˈtɒnɪk/ *adj.* [G f. Gk, = wandering]

plano- /pleɪnəʊ-/ *in comb.* level, flat; having one surface plane. [f. L *planus* flat]

planographic /pleɪnəˈgræfɪk/ *adj.* printing from a flat surface. [f. prec. + -GRAPHIC]

plant /plɑːnt/ *n.* **1** an organism that obtains its food by photosynthesis or by absorption, and that has neither power of locomotion nor special organs of sensation or digestion; a small organism of this kind as distinguished from a tree or shrub. **2** the machinery and implements etc. used in industrial processes; a factory and its equipment. **3** (*slang*) a thing deliberately placed for discovery by others; a hoax or trap. —*v.t.* **1** to place in the ground or soil for growing; to put plants or seeds into (the ground or soil). **2** to put or fix firmly in position. **3** to station (a person), especially as a look-out or spy. **4** to cause (an idea etc.) to be established in the mind. **5** to deliver (a blow or thrust) with deliberate aim. **6** (*slang*) to conceal, especially with a view to misleading a later discoverer. **7** to settle or establish (a colony, community, etc.). [f. OE & F f. L *planta* sprout, cutting]

plantain[1] /ˈplæntɪn/ *n.* a herb of the genus *Plantago* with broad flat leaves spread close to the ground and seeds used for food for cage-birds. [f. OF f. L *plantago* (*planta* sole of foot)]

plantain[2] /ˈplæntɪn/ *n.* a tropical banana-like fruit; the treelike plant (*Musca paradisiaca*) bearing this. [f. Sp. *pla(n)tano* plane-tree (as PLANE[3])]

plantation /plɑːnˈteɪʃ(ə)n/ *n.* **1** an extensive collection or area of cultivated trees or plants. **2** an estate for the cultivation of cotton, tobacco, rubber, etc. **3** (*hist.*) colonization; a settlement in a new or conquered country, a colony. [f. OF or L (as PLANT)]

planter *n.* **1** the owner or manager of a plantation. **2** a container for house plants. [f. PLANT]

plaque /plɑːk, plæk/ *n.* **1** a flat tablet or plate of metal or porcelain etc. fixed on a wall as an ornament or memorial. **2** film on teeth, where bacteria can proliferate. [F f. Du. *plak* (as PLACARD)]

plasma /ˈplæzmə/ *n.* **1** the colourless coagulable part of blood, lymph, or milk, in which corpuscles or fat-globules float. **2** a gas in which there are positive ions and free negative electrons, usually in approximately equal numbers throughout and therefore electrically neutral; any analogous collection of charged particles in which one or both kinds are mobile, as the conduction electrons in a metal or the ions in a salt solution. [L, = mould, f. Gk (*plassō* to shape)]

plasmid /ˈplæzmɪd/ *n.* any genetic structure in a cell that can replicate independently of the chromosomes. [as prec.]

plaster /ˈplɑːstə(r)/ *n.* **1** a soft mixture of lime, sand, and water, for spreading on walls etc. to form a smooth surface and harden by drying. **2** a medicinal or protective substance spread on fabric and applied to the body. **3** sticking-plaster. **4** plaster of Paris. —*v.t.* **1** to cover (a wall etc.) with plaster or a similar substance. **2** to coat or daub, to cover thickly. **3** to stick or fix (a thing) like plaster on a surface; to make (hair) smooth with a fixative etc. **4** (*slang*) to bomb or shell heavily. **5** (in *p.p.*, *slang*) drunk. —**plaster of Paris,** a fine white plaster of gypsum for making moulds or casts. —**plasterer** *n.* [OE & OF f. L f. Gk *emplastron*]

plasterboard *n.* board with a core of plaster used for partitions, walls, etc.

plastic /ˈplæstɪk/ *n.* a synthetic polymeric organic substance that can be given any permanent shape; a material formed from such a substance together with fillers, colouring agents, etc. —*adj.* **1** made of plastic. **2** capable of being moulded; pliant, supple. **3** giving form to clay or wax etc. —**plastic arts,** the arts concerned with modelling or with the representation of solid objects. **plastic bomb,** one containing putty-like explosive. **plastic surgeon,** a specialist in plastic surgery. **plastic surgery,** the repair or replacement of injured or defective tissue. —**plasticity** /plæˈstɪsɪtɪ/ *n.* [f. F or L f. Gk (as PLASMA)]

Plasticine /ˈplæstɪsi:n/ *n.* [P] a plastic substance used for modelling. [f. prec.]

plasticize /ˈplæstɪsaɪz/ *v.t./i.* to make or become plastic. —**plasticizer** *n.* [f. prec.]

plastron /ˈplæstrən/ *n.* (*hist.*) **1** a steel breastplate. **2** an ornamental front on a woman's bodice. [F, f. It. *piastra* f. L *emplastrum* plaster]

plate *n.* **1** a shallow usually circular vessel from which food is eaten or served; the contents of this. **2** a similar vessel used for the collection of money in churches etc. **3** (*collect.*) utensils of silver, gold, or other metal; objects of plated metal. **4** a piece of metal with a name or inscription for affixing to something. **5** an illustration on special paper in a book. **6** a thin sheet of metal, glass, etc., coated with a sensitive film for use in photography etc. **7** a flat thin usually rigid sheet of metal etc. **8** each of a number of nearly rigid pieces of the earth's crust which each cover a large area, some of them including whole continents, and which together constitute the surface of the earth. **9** a smooth piece of metal etc. for engraving; an impression from this. **10** a silver or gold cup as a prize for a horse-race etc.; such a race. **11** a thin piece of plastic material, moulded to the shape of the gums etc., to which artificial teeth are attached; (*colloq.*) a denture. —*v.t.* **1** to cover (another metal) with a thin coat especially of silver, gold, or tin. **2** to cover with plates of metal. —**on a plate,** (*colloq.*) available with little trouble to the recipient. **on one's plate,** for one to deal with or consider. [f. OF f. L *plata* plate armour]

plateau /ˈplætəʊ/ *n.* (*pl.* **-eaux** /-əʊz/) **1** an area of fairly level high ground. **2** a state of little variation after an increase. [F f. OF *platel* (*plat* flat)]

plateful *n.* **1** as much as a plate will hold. **2** (*colloq.*) a great deal (of work etc.). [f. PLATE + -FUL]

platelayer *n.* a person employed in fixing and repairing railway rails.

platelet /ˈpleɪtlɪt/ *n.* a small colourless disc found in the blood and involved in clotting. [f. PLATE + -LET]

platen /ˈplæt(ə)n/ *n.* a plate in a printing-press by which the paper is pressed against the type; the roller in a typewriter against which the paper rests as it is struck by the letters. [f. OF *platine* flat piece (as PLATEAU)]

plateresque /plætəˈresk/ *adj.* richly ornamented in a style suggesting silverware. [f. Sp. (*platero* silversmith f. *plata* silver)]

platform *n.* **1** a raised level surface, especially one from which a speaker addresses an audience. **2** a raised area along the side of a line at a railway station, where passengers board or alight from trains. **3** the floor area at the entrance to a bus. **4** a thick sole of a shoe. **5** the declared policy of a political party. [f. F, = ground-plan (as PLATEAU, FORM)]

platinum /ˈplætɪnəm/ *n.* a rare white heavy metallic element, symbol Pt, atomic number 78. —**platinum blonde,** a woman with silvery-blonde hair; this colour. [f. earlier *platina* f. Sp., dim. of *plata* silver]

platitude /ˈplætɪtju:d/ *n.* a commonplace remark, especially one solemnly delivered. —**platitudinous** /-ˈtju:dɪnəs/ *adj.* [F (*plat* flat), after *certitude* etc.]

Platonic /pləˈtɒnɪk/ *adj.* **1** of Plato or his philosophy. **2 platonic,** confined to words or theory, not leading to action, harmless; (of love or friendship) purely spiritual, not sexual. [f. L f. Gk (*Platōn* Plato, Gk philospher, d. 347 BC)]

Platonism /ˈpleɪtənɪz(ə)m/ *n.* **1** the doctrines of Plato or his followers. **2** any of various revivals of these doctrines or related ideas, especially Neoplatonism (3rd-5th c. AD), and Cambridge Platonism (17th c.) centred on Cambridge. —**Platonist** *n.* [as prec.]

platoon /pləˈtu:n/ *n.* **1** a subdivision of a military company. **2** a group of persons acting together. [f. F *peloton* small ball (as PELLET)]

platter *n.* a flat dish or plate, especially for food. [AF *plater* (as PLATE)]

platypus /ˈplætɪpəs/ *n.* an Australian egg-laying aquatic and burrowing mammal (*Ornithorhynchus anatinus*) with a ducklike beak and flat tail. [f. Gk (*platus* broad, flat, *pous* foot)]

plaudit /ˈplɔːdɪt/ *n.* (usu. in *pl.*) a round of applause; an emphatic expression of approval. [f. L *plaudite*, imper. of *plaudere* clap (said by Roman actors at end of play)]

plausible /ˈplɔːzɪb(ə)l/ *adj.* (of a statement etc.) seeming reasonable or probable; (of a person) persuasive but deceptive. —**plausibility** /-ˈbɪlɪtɪ/ *n.*, **plausibly** *adv.* [f. L (as prec.)]

play *v.t./i.* **1** to occupy oneself in a game or other recreational activity; to act light-heartedly or flippantly. **2** to take part in (a game). **3** to compete against in a game. **4** to occupy (a specified position) in a team for a game; to assign (a player) to a position. **5** to move (a piece) or put (a card) on the table or strike (a ball etc.) in a game. **6** to perform on (a musical instrument); to perform (a piece of music etc.); to cause (a record or record-player etc.) to produce sound. **7** to act in a drama etc.; to act the part of; to perform (a drama or role) on stage. **8** to move about lightly or irregularly; to allow (light or water etc.) to fall on something; (of a fountain or hosepipe) to discharge water. **9** to allow (a fish) to exhaust itself pulling against the line. —*n.* **1** playing; recreation, amusement, especially as the spontaneous activity of children. **2** the playing of a game; the action or manner of this. **3** a literary work written for performance on the stage; a similar work for broadcasting. **4** activity, operation. **5** free movement; space or scope for this. **6** a brisk, light, or fitful movement. **7** gambling. —**in** (*or* **out of**) **play,** (of the ball etc. in a game) in (or not in) position for continued play according to the rules. **make a play for,** (*slang*) to seek to acquire. **make play with,** to use effectively or ostentatiously. **play about** *or* **around,** to behave irresponsibly. **play along,** to pretend to co-operate. **play at,** to perform or engage in half-heartedly. **play back,** to play (sounds recently recorded). **play-back** *n.* the playing back of sound. **play by ear,** to perform (music) without having seen a score; to proceed step by step going by one's instinct or by results. **play down,** to minimize the importance of. **played out,** exhausted of energy or usefulness. **play fast and loose,** to act unreliably. **play for time,** to seek to gain time by delaying. **play the game,** to observe the rules, to behave honourably. **play havoc** *or* **hell with,** (*colloq.*) to produce great disorder in. **play into a person's hands,** to act so as unwittingly to give him an advantage. **play the market,** to speculate in stocks etc. **play off,** to oppose (a person *against* another) especially for one's own advantage; to play an extra match to decide a draw or tie. **play-off** *n.* a match so played. **play on,** to take advantage of (a person's feelings etc.). **play on words,** to pun; a pun. **play-pen** *n.* a portable enclosure for a young child to play in. **play safe** *or* **for safety,** to avoid risks. **play up,** to behave mischievously; to annoy thus, to put all one's energy into a game. **play up to,** to flatter so as to win favour etc. **play with fire,** to take foolish risks. [OE]

playbill *n.* a poster announcing a theatre programme.

playboy *n.* a pleasure-seeking usually wealthy man.

player *n.* **1** a person taking part in a game. **2** a performer on a musical instrument. **3** an actor. **4** a record-player. [f. PLAY]

playfellow *n.* a playmate.

playful *adj.* **1** full of fun. **2** in a mood for play, not serious; done in fun. —**playfully** *adv.*, **playfulness** *n.* [f. PLAY + -FUL]

playgoer *n.* one who goes to the theatre.

playground *n.* an outdoor area for children to play on.

playgroup *n.* a group of pre-school children who play regularly together under supervision.

playhouse *n.* a theatre.

playing-card *n.* a small oblong card with rounded corners used in games; one of a set of usually 52 divided into four suits.

playing-field *n.* a field used for outdoor games.

playmate *n.* a child's companion in play.

plaything *n.* a toy or other thing to play with.

playtime *n.* time for play or recreation.

playwright *n.* a dramatist.

PLC *abbr.* Public Limited Company.

plea *n.* **1** an appeal, an entreaty. **2** (*Law*) a formal statement by or on behalf of a defendant. **3** a pleading argument, an excuse. [f. AF f. L *placitum* decree (as PLEASE)]

pleach *v.t.* to entwine or interlace (esp. branches to form a hedge). [f. OF f. L *plectere* plait]

plead *v.t./i.* **1** to address a lawcourt as an advocate; to put forward (a case) in a lawcourt. **2** to declare oneself to be (guilty or not guilty) to a charge; to allege formally as a plea. **3** to offer as an excuse. **4** to make an appeal or entreaty. —**plead with,** to entreat earnestly. [f. AF (as PLEA)]

pleasant /ˈplez(ə)nt/ *adj.* pleasing to the mind, feelings, or senses. —**pleasantly** *adv.*, **pleasantness** *n.* [f. OF (as PLEASE)]

pleasantry *n.* **1** jocularity. **2** humorous speech; a joking or polite remark. [f. F (as prec.)]

please /pli:z/ *v.t./i.* **1** to give pleasure (to); to make satisfied or glad. **2** to think fit; to have the desire; to be the wish of. **3** (short for *may it please you*) used in polite requests. **—if you please,** if you are willing, esp. (*iron.*) to indicate unreasonableness. **please oneself,** to do as one likes. [f. OF *plaisir* f. L *placēre*]

pleasurable /ˈpleʒərəb(ə)l/ *adj.* causing pleasure. **—pleasurably** *adv.* [f. foll.]

pleasure /ˈpleʒə(r)/ *n.* **1** a feeling of satisfaction or joy, enjoyment. **2** a source of pleasure or gratification. **3** one's will or desire. **4** (*attrib.*) done or used for pleasure. [OF (as PLEASE)]

pleat *n.* a fold or crease, especially a flattened fold in cloth doubled upon itself. *—v.t.* to make a pleat or pleats in. [var. of PLAIT]

pleb *n.* (*slang*) a person of the lower classes. [abbr. of foll.]

plebeian /plɪˈbi:ən/ *n.* a commoner, especially in ancient Rome. *—adj.* of low birth, of the common people; uncultured; coarse, ignoble. [f. L (*plebs* common people)]

plebiscite /ˈplebɪsɪt/ *n.* a direct vote of all the electors of a State on an important public question. [f. F f. L (as prec., *scitum* decree)]

plectrum *n.* (*pl.* **-tra**) a small thin piece of horn or metal etc. for plucking the strings of a guitar etc. [L f. Gk (*plēssō* strike)]

pledge *n.* **1** a thing given as security for the fulfilment of a contract, payment of a debt, etc., and liable to forfeiture in case of failure; a thing put in pawn. **2** a thing given as a token of favour etc. or of something to come. **3** a solemn promise. **4** the drinking of a health, a toast. *—v.t.* **1** to deposit as a security, to pawn. **2** to promise solemnly by pledge of (one's honour, word, etc.); to bind by a solemn promise. **3** to drink to the health of. [OF (rel. to PLIGHT[2])]

plein air /plen ˈeə(r)/ (in painting) representing effects of atmosphere and light that are not observable in a studio. **—plein-airism** *n.* [F, = open air, orig. of French impressionists *c.*1870]

Pleistocene /ˈplaɪstəsi:n/ *adj.* of the first of the two epochs forming the Quaternary period. *—n.* this epoch. [f. Gk *pleistos* most + *kainos* new]

plenary /ˈpli:nərɪ/ *adj.* **1** entire, unqualified. **2** (of an assembly) to be attended by all members. [f. L (*plenus* full)]

plenipotentiary /plenɪpəˈtenʃərɪ/ *n.* a person (especially a diplomat) invested with full power of independent action. *—adj.* having this power. [f. L (as prec., *potentia* power)]

plenitude /ˈplenɪtju:d/ *n.* fullness, completeness; abundance. [f. OF f. L (as PLENARY)]

plenteous /ˈplentɪəs/ *adj.* (*literary*) plentiful. [f. OF (as PLENTY)]

plentiful /ˈplentɪfʊl/ *adj.* existing in ample quantity. **—plentifully** *adv.* [f. foll. + -FUL]

plenty *n.* quite enough, as much as one could need or desire. *—adv.* (*colloq.*) quite, fully. [f. OF f. L *plenitas* (as PLENARY)]

pleonasm /ˈpli:ənæz(ə)m/ *n.* the use of extra words not needed to give the sense (e.g. *hear with one's ears*). **—pleonastic** /-ˈnæstɪk/ *adj.* [f. L f. Gk (*pleonazō* be superfluous)]

plesiosaurus /pli:sɪəˈsɔ:rəs/ *n.* an extinct marine reptile with a long neck, short tail, and four large paddles. [f. Gk *plēsios* near + *sauros* lizard]

plethora /ˈpleθərə/ *n.* an over-abundance. [L f. Gk *plēthōrē* (*plēthō* be full)]

pleura /ˈplʊərə/ *n.* (*pl.* **-ae** /-i:/) the membrane enveloping the lungs. [L f. Gk, = rib]

pleurisy /ˈplʊərɪsɪ/ *n.* inflammation of the pleura. **—pleuritic** /-ˈrɪtɪk/ *adj.* [f. OF f. L f. Gk *pleuritis* (as prec.)]

plexus /ˈpleksəs/ *n.* the network of nerves or vessels in an animal body. [L (*plectere* plait)]

pliable /ˈplaɪəb(ə)l/ *adj.* **1** bending easily, flexible. **2** easily influenced; compliant. **—pliability** /-ˈbɪlɪtɪ/ *n.*, **pliably** *adv.* [F (*plier* bend f. L *plicare*)]

pliant /ˈplaɪənt/ *adj.* pliable. **—pliancy** *n.*, **pliantly** *adv.* [f. OF (as prec.)]

pliers /ˈplaɪəz/ *n.pl.* pincers with parallel flat surfaces for holding small objects, bending wire, etc. [f. dial. *ply* bend (as PLY[1])]

plight[1] /plaɪt/ *n.* a condition or state, especially an unfortunate one. [AF *plit* (as PLAIT)]

plight[2] /plaɪt/ *v.t.* (*archaic*) to pledge. [f. OE, = danger; cf. PLEDGE]

plimsoll /ˈplɪms(ə)l/ *n.* a rubber-soled canvas sports shoe. [as foll.]

Plimsoll line /ˈplɪms(ə)l/ (also **Plimsoll mark**) a marking on a ship's side showing the limit of legal submersion in summer or under various conditions. [f. S. *Plimsoll*, English politician (d. 1898)]

plinth *n.* the lower square member of the base of a column; a base supporting a vase or statue etc. [f. F or L f. Gk, = tile]

Pliocene /ˈplaɪəsi:n/ *adj.* of the final epoch of the Tertiary period. *—n.* this epoch. [f. Gk *pleiōn* more + *kainos* new]

PLO *abbr.* Palestine Liberation Organization.

plod *v.i.* (**-dd-**) **1** to walk doggedly or laboriously, to trudge. **2** to work slowly and steadily. *—n.* a spell of plodding. **—plodder** *n.* [prob. imit.]

plonk[1] *n.* a heavy thud. *—v.t.* to set down hurriedly or clumsily; to put firmly. [imit.]

plonk[2] *n.* (*slang*) cheap or inferior wine. [perh. f. prec. or F *vin blanc* white wine]

plop *n.* a sound as of an object dropping into water without a splash. —*v.t./i.* (**-pp-**) to fall or cause to fall with a plop. —*adv.* with a plop. [imit.]

plosive /ˈpləʊsɪv/ *adj.* (of a consonant, e.g. p, d, k) pronounced with a sudden release of the breath. —*n.* a consonant of this kind. [f. EXPLOSIVE]

plot *n.* **1** a defined and usually small piece of ground. **2** the interrelationship of main events in a play, novel, film, etc. **3** a conspiracy, a secret plan. —*v.t.* (**-tt-**) **1** to make a plan or map of. **2** to mark on a chart or diagram; to make (a curve etc.) by marking out a number of points. **3** to plan or contrive (a crime etc.); to plan secretly. —**plotter** *n.* [OE & f. OF *complot* secret plan]

plough /plaʊ/ *n.* **1** an implement for cutting furrows in soil and turning it up. **2** an implement resembling this (e.g. a snow-plough). **3 the Plough,** a constellation also known as the Great Bear. —*v.t.* **1** to turn up (earth, or *absol.*) or cast out (roots etc.) with a plough; to cut (a furrow). **2** to make one's way or advance laboriously (through snow, a book, etc.). **3** to advance with irresistible penetration and damage. **4** (*slang*) to fail in (an examination); to declare that (a candidate) has failed. —**plough back,** to turn (growing grass etc.) into the soil to enrich it; to reinvest (profits) in the business producing them. [OE f. ON]

ploughman *n.* (*pl.* **-men**) a man who guides a plough. —**ploughman's lunch,** a meal of bread and cheese etc.

ploughshare *n.* the cutting-blade of a plough.

plover /ˈplʌvə(r)/ *n.* a medium-sized wading bird of the family Charadriidae, e.g. the peewit. [AF, ult. f. L *pluvia* rain]

ploy *n.* (*colloq.*) a cunning manœuvre used to gain an advantage. [orig. Sc.; etym. unkn.]

PLR *abbr.* Public Lending Right.

pluck *v.t./i.* **1** to pick or pull out or away. **2** to strip (a bird) of feathers. **3** to pull at, to twitch. **4** to sound (the string of a musical instrument) with the finger or a plectrum. **5** to plunder, to swindle. —*n.* **1** courage, spirit. **2** plucking, a twitch. **3** an animal's heart and liver and lungs as food. —**pluck up courage,** to summon up one's courage. [OE]

plucky *adj.* brave, spirited. —**pluckily** *adv.*, **pluckiness** *n.* [f. prec.]

plug *n.* **1** a piece of solid material fitting tightly into a hole, used to fill a gap or cavity or act as a wedge or stopper. **2** a device of metal pins in an insulated casing fitting into holes in a socket for making an electrical connection; (*colloq.*) the socket. **3** a sparking-plug. **4** (*colloq.*) favourable publicity for a commercial product etc. **5** (*colloq.*) the release-mechanism of a water-closet flushing-apparatus. **6** a cake or stick of tobacco; a piece of this for chewing. —*v.t./i.* (**-gg-**) **1** to put a plug into; to stop with a plug. **2** (*slang*) to shoot or strike (a person etc.). **3** (*colloq.*) to mention favourably; to seek to popularize (a song, product, policy, etc.) by constant recommendation. **4** (*colloq.*) to work steadily. —**plug in,** to connect electrically by inserting a plug into a socket. **plug-in** *adj.* able to be connected thus. [f. MDu. & MLG *plugge*]

plum *n.* **1** a roundish fleshy fruit with sweet pulp and a flattish pointed stone; the tree (*Prunus domestica*) bearing it; the dried fruit used in cooking. **2** a thing that is highly prized or the best of its kind. —**plum pudding,** a boiled pudding containing raisins etc. [OE, ult. f. L *prunum*]

plumage /ˈpluːmɪdʒ/ *n.* a bird's feathers. [f. OF (as PLUME)]

plumb[1] /plʌm/ *n.* a ball of lead, especially attached to the end of a line for finding the depth of water or testing whether a wall etc. is vertical. —*adj.* vertical. —*adv.* **1** exactly; vertically. **2** (*US slang*) quite, utterly. —*v.t.* **1** to measure or test with a plumb-line. **2** to reach or experience (depths of feeling etc.). **3** to get to the bottom of (a matter). —**out of plumb,** not vertical. **plumb-line** *n.* a line with a plumb attached. [f. L *plumbum* lead]

plumb[2] /plʌm/ *v.t./i.* **1** to work as a plumber. **2** to provide with a plumbing system; to fit (a thing) as part of this. [back-formation f. PLUMBER]

plumbago /plʌmˈbeɪgəʊ/ *n.* **1** graphite. **2** a herbaceous plant of the genus *Plumbago* with spikes of tubular white, blue, or purplish flowers. [L (as PLUMB[1])]

plumber /ˈplʌmə(r)/ *n.* a person who fits and repairs the domestic apparatus of a water-supply. [as PLUMB[1]]

plumbing /ˈplʌmɪŋ/ *n.* **1** the system or apparatus of a water-supply. **2** the work of a plumber. **3** (*colloq.*) lavatory installations. [f. prec.]

plume /pluːm/ *n.* a feather, especially a large one used for ornament; an ornament of feathers etc. attached to a helmet or hat or worn in the hair; something resembling this. —*v.t.* **1** to furnish with a plume or plumes. **2** to pride (oneself). **3** (of a bird) to preen (itself or its feathers). [f. OF f. L *pluma*]

plummet /ˈplʌmɪt/ *n.* **1** a plumb; a plumb-line; a sounding-lead. **2** a weight attached to a fishing-line to keep a float upright. —*v.i.* to fall or plunge rapidly. [f. OF *plommet* (as PLUMB[1])]

plummy *adj.* **1** of plums; full of plums.

2 (*colloq.*) good, desirable. 3 (of a voice) sounding affectedly rich in tone. [f. PLUM]

plump[1] *adj.* having a full rounded shape, fleshy. —*v.t./i.* to make or become plump; to fatten. —**plumpness** *n.* [f. MDu. or MLG, = blunt, shapeless]

plump[2] *v.t./i.* to drop or plunge with an abrupt descent. —*n.* an abrupt or heavy fall. —*adv.* with a plump. —**plump for,** to choose; to decide on. [f. MLG or MDu. (imit.)]

plumy /ˈplu:mɪ/ *adj.* 1 plumelike, feathery. 2 adorned with plumes. [f. PLUME]

plunder *v.t.* to rob (a place or person) forcibly of goods, especially (as) in war; to rob systematically; to steal or embezzle. —*n.* the violent or dishonest acquisition of property; the property so acquired; (*slang*) profit, gain. —**plunderer** *n.* [f. LG *plündern*]

plunge /plʌnj/ *v.t./i.* 1 to thrust or go suddenly or violently into something; to jump or dive into water; to immerse completely. 2 to enter or cause to enter a condition, course, or set of circumstances. 3 to descend suddenly; to move with a rush. 4 (*slang*) to gamble heavily; to run deeply into debt. —*n.* a plunging action or movement, a dive. —**take the plunge,** to take a bold decisive step. [f. OF, ult. f. L *plumbum* lead]

plunger *n.* 1 a part of a mechanism that works with a plunging or thrusting movement. 2 a rubber cup on a handle for the removal of blockages from pipes by a plunging action. 3 (*slang*) a reckless gambler. [f. prec.]

pluperfect /plu:ˈpɜ:fɪkt/ *adj.* (*Gram.*, of a tense) denoting action completed prior to some past point of time (e.g. *he had said*). —*n.* (*Gram.*) the pluperfect tense. [f. L *plus quam perfectum* more than perfect]

plural /ˈplʊər(ə)l/ *adj.* 1 more than one in number. 2 (*Gram.*, of a word or form) denoting more than one. —*n.* (*Gram.*) a plural word or form; the plural number. [f. OF f. L (*plus* more)]

pluralism /ˈplʊərəlɪz(ə)m/ *n.* 1 a form of society in which members of minority groups maintain independent traditions. 2 the holding of more than one office at a time. —**pluralist** *n.*, **pluralistic** /-ˈlɪstɪk/ *adj.* [f. prec.]

plurality /plʊəˈrælɪtɪ/ *n.* 1 the state of being plural. 2 pluralism, a benefice or office held with another. 3 (*US*) a majority that is not absolute. [as PLURAL]

plus *prep.* 1 with addition of (symbol +). 2 (of a temperature) above zero. 3 (*colloq.*) with, having gained; possessing. —*adj.* 1 additional, extra. 2 (after a number) at least, rather better than. 3 (*Math.*) positive. 4 having positive electrical charge. —*n.* 1 the symbol +. 2 an additional quantity; a positive quantity. 3 an advantage. [L, = more]

plus-fours /plʌsˈfɔːz/ *n.pl.* long wide knickerbockers. [so named because, to produce the overhang, four inches are added to ordinary knickerbockers]

plush *n.* a cloth of silk or cotton etc. with a long soft nap. —*adj.* 1 made of plush. 2 plushy. [f. F *peluche* f. It., ult. f. L *pilus* hair]

plushy *adj.* luxurious. —**plushiness** *n.* [f. prec.]

plutocracy /plu:ˈtɒkrəsɪ/ *n.* 1 government by the wealthy; a State so governed. 2 a wealthy élite. [f. Gk (*ploutos* wealth, -CRACY)]

plutocrat /ˈplu:təkræt/ *n.* 1 a member of a plutocracy. 2 a wealthy man. —**plutocratic** /-ˈkrætɪk/ *adj.* [f. prec.]

plutonic /plu:ˈtɒnɪk/ *adj.* 1 (of igneous rocks) formed by crystallization of molten material at a great depth underground. 2 attributing most geological phenomena to the action of internal heat (opp. *Neptunian*). [f. L *Pluto* god of the underworld, f. Gk]

plutonium /plu:ˈtəʊnɪəm/ *n.* a fissile transuranic radioactive metallic element, symbol Pu, atomic number 94. [f. *Pluto*, planet next beyond Neptune]

pluvial /ˈplu:vɪəl/ *adj.* 1 of rain, rainy. 2 (*Geol.*) caused by rain. [f. L (*pluvia* rain)]

ply[1] /plaɪ/ *n.* 1 a thickness or layer of cloth or wood etc. 2 a strand of rope or yarn etc. [f. F *pli* (as PLIABLE)]

ply[2] /plaɪ/ *v.t./i.* 1 to use or wield (a tool or weapon). 2 to work steadily (at). 3 to supply continuously with food or drink etc.; to approach repeatedly with questions etc. 4 (of a vehicle etc.) to travel regularly to and fro between; to work (a route) thus. 5 (of a taxi-driver etc.) to attend regularly for custom. [f. APPLY]

Plymouth Brethren /ˈplɪməθ/ a Calvinistic denomination with no formal creed and no official order of ministers. [f. *Plymouth* in Devon]

plywood /ˈplaɪwʊd/ *n.* a strong thin board made by gluing layers with the direction of the grain alternating through 90°. [f. PLY[1] + WOOD]

PM *abbr.* 1 Prime Minister. 2 post-mortem.

Pm *symbol* promethium.

p.m. *abbr.* after noon. [f. L *post meridiem*]

pneumatic /nju:ˈmætɪk/ *adj.* 1 filled with wind or air. 2 working by means of compressed air. —**pneumatic drill,** a machine for breaking up the hard surface of a road etc., driven by compressed air. **pneumatic tyre,** a tyre inflated with air. —**pneumatically** *adv.* [f. F or L f. Gk (*pneuma* wind)]

pneumonia /nju:ˈməʊnɪə/ *n.* inflammation of one or both lungs. [L f. Gk (*pneumōn* lung)]

pnp *abbr.* in which an n-type layer occurs between two p-type layers.

PO *abbr.* **1** Post Office. **2** postal order. **3** Petty Officer. **4** Pilot Officer.

Po *symbol* polonium.

po /pəʊ/ *n.* (*pl.* **pos**) (*colloq.*) a chamber-pot. —**po-faced** *adj.* (*colloq.*) solemn-faced, humourless. [F pronunc. of POT]

poach[1] *v.t./i.* **1** to catch (game or fish, or *absol.*) illegally. **2** to trespass or encroach (on the property or idea etc. of another). [perh. f. F *pocher* (as foll.)]

poach[2] *v.t./i.* **1** to cook (an egg) without the shell in boiling water or in a poacher. **2** to cook by simmering in a small amount of liquid. [f. OF *pochier* (*poche* bag; cf. POKE[2])]

poacher[1] *n.* one who poaches (see POACH[1]). [f. POACH[1]]

poacher[2] *n.* a pan with one or more cup-shaped containers in which eggs (without the shells) are placed for cooking over boiling water. [f. POACH[2]]

pock *n.* an eruptive spot on the skin, especially in smallpox. —**pock-marked** *adj.* bearing the scars left by such spots. [OE]

pocket /ˈpɒkɪt/ *n.* **1** a small bag sewn into or on clothing, for carrying small articles. **2** a pouchlike compartment in a suitcase, car door, etc. **3** money resources. **4** an isolated group or area. **5** a cavity in the earth filled with gold or other ore. **6** a pouch at the corner or on the side of a billiard-table into which balls are driven. **7** an air pocket. —*adj.* **1** of suitable size or shape for carrying in a pocket. **2** smaller than the usual size. —*v.t.* **1** to put into one's pocket. **2** to appropriate (esp. dishonestly). **3** to confine as in a pocket. **4** to submit to (an injury or affront). **5** to conceal or suppress (feelings). **6** to drive (a billiard ball) into a pocket. —**in a person's pocket,** close to or intimate with him, under his control. **in pocket,** having gained in a transaction. **out of pocket,** having lost. **pocket-book** *n.* a notebook; a booklike case for papers or money carried in the pocket. **pocket-knife** *n.* a knife with a folding blade or blades, for carrying in the pocket. **pocket-money** *n.* money for minor expenses, especially that allowed to children. [f. AF dim. (as POKE[1])]

pocketful *n.* (*pl.* **-fuls**) as much as a pocket will hold. [f. prec. + -FUL]

pod *n.* a long seed-vessel, especially of the pea or bean. —*v.t./i.* (**-dd-**) **1** to bear or form pods. **2** to remove (seeds etc.) from pods. [f. dial. *podware*, *podder* field crops]

podgy /ˈpɒdʒɪ/ *adj.* short and fat; plump, fleshy. —**podgily** *adv.*, **podginess** *n.* [f. *podge* short fat person]

podium /ˈpəʊdɪəm/ *n.* (*pl.* **-ia**) **1** a continuous projecting base or pedestal round a room or house etc. **2** a rostrum. [L f. Gk *podion* (dim. of *pous* foot)]

poem /ˈpəʊɪm/ *n.* **1** a metrical composition, especially one concerned with feeling or imaginative description; an elevated composition in verse or prose. **2** something with poetic qualities. [f. F or L f. Gk *poēma* (*poieō* make)]

poesy /ˈpəʊɪsɪ/ *n.* (*archaic*) poetry. [f. OF f. L f. Gk *poēsis* (as prec.)]

poet /ˈpəʊɪt/ *n.* a writer of poems; one possessing high powers of imagination or expression etc. —**Poet Laureate,** see LAUREATE. —**poetess** *n.fem.* [f. OF f. L f. Gk *poētēs* (as POEM)]

poetaster /pəʊɪˈtæstə(r)/ *n.* a paltry or inferior poet. [as prec. + L *-aster* derog. suffix]

poetic /pəʊˈetɪk/ *adj.* of or like poetry or poets. —**poetic justice,** well-deserved punishment or reward. **poetic licence,** a writer's or artist's exaggeration or disregard of rules, for effect. —**poetically** *adv.* [f. F f. L f. Gk (as POET)]

poetical /pəʊˈetik(ə)l/ *adj.* poetic; written in verse. —**poetically** *adv.* [as prec.]

poetry /ˈpəʊɪtrɪ/ *n.* **1** the art or work of a poet. **2** poems collectively. **3** a quality that pleases the mind as poetry does. [f. L *poetria* (as POET)]

pogo /ˈpəʊgəʊ/ *n.* (*pl.* **-os**) (also **pogo stick**) a stiltlike toy with a spring, used for jumping about on. [orig. unkn.]

pogrom /ˈpɒgrəm/ *n.* an organized massacre (originally of Jews in Russia 1905–6). [Russ., = devastation]

poignant /ˈpɔɪnjənt/ *adj.* **1** painfully sharp to the senses or feelings, deeply moving. **2** sharp or pungent in taste or smell; pleasantly piquant. **3** arousing sympathy. —**poignancy** *n.*, **poignantly** *adv.* [f. OF f. L (as POINT)]

poinsettia /pɔɪnˈsetɪə/ *n.* a plant (*Euphorbia pulcherrima*) with large scarlet bracts surrounding small yellowish flowers. [f. J. R. *Poinsett*, American ambassador to Mexico (d. 1851)]

point *n.* **1** the sharp or tapered end of something; the tip or extremity. **2** (in geometry) that which has position but no magnitude (e.g. the intersection of two lines). **3** a dot; this used as a punctuation-mark; a dot or small stroke used in Semitic languages to indicate vowels or distinguish consonants; a decimal point. **4** a particular place or spot; an exact moment; a stage or degree of progress or increase; the level of temperature at which a change occurs. **5** each of the 32 directions marked on the compass; a corresponding direction towards the horizon. **6** a unit of measurement or value or scoring. **7** a separate item or detail. **8** a distinctive or significant feature; the essential thing; the thing intended or under discussion; the salient feature of a story, joke, remark, etc. **9** effectiveness, purpose, value. **10** (usu. in *pl.*) a tapering movable rail by which a train may pass from one line to another. **11** an electrical socket, a power point. **12** (usu. in *pl.*) an electrical contact device in the distributor of an internal-combustion engine. **13** (in cricket) a fieldsman on the off side near the batsman; his position. —*v.t./i.* **1** to direct or aim; to be directed or aimed; to direct attention, to indicate. **2** to provide with a point or points. **3** to give force to (words or actions). **4** to fill the joints of (brickwork etc.) with smoothed mortar or cement. —**at** *or* **on the point of,** on the verge of. **beside the point,** irrelevant, irrelevantly. **in point of,** as a matter of (fact etc.). **make a point of,** to indicate the necessity of; to call particular attention to (an action). **point-duty** *n.* (of a policeman etc.) being stationed at a particular point to control traffic. **point of no return,** the point in a journey or enterprise at which it becomes essential or more practical to continue to the end. **point of view,** a position from which a thing is viewed; a way of considering a matter. **point out,** to indicate, to draw attention to. **point-to-point** *n.* a horse-race over a course defined only by certain landmarks. **point up,** to emphasize. **to the point,** relevant, relevantly. **up to a point,** to some extent but not completely. [f. F f. L *punctum, puncta* (*pungere* prick)]

point-blank *adj.* **1** (of a shot) aimed or fired at a range very close to the target; (of range) very close. **2** (of a remark etc.) blunt, direct. —*adv.* **1** at point-blank range. **2** bluntly, directly.

pointed *adj.* **1** sharpened or tapering to a point. **2** (of a remark or manner etc.) clearly aimed at a particular person or thing; emphasized. —**pointedly** *adv.* [f. POINT]

pointer *n.* **1** a thing that points, e.g. the index hand of a gauge etc.; a rod for pointing to the features on a chart etc. **2** (*colloq.*) a hint. **3** a dog of a breed that on scenting game stands rigid looking towards it. [f. POINT]

pointillism /ˈpwæntɪlɪz(ə)m/ *n.* a technique of impressionist painting in which pigment is applied in small spots of various pure colours which are blended by the spectator's eye. —**pointillist** *n.* [f. F (*pointiller* mark with dots, as POINT)]

pointing *n.* the cement filling the joints of brickwork; the facing produced by this. [f. POINT]

pointless *adj.* without point or force; lacking purpose or meaning. —**pointlessly** *adv.* [f. POINT + -LESS]

poise /pɔɪz/ *v.t./i.* **1** to balance or be balanced. **2** to hold suspended or supported. **3** to carry (one's head etc.) in a specified way. —*n.* **1** balance, the way something is poised. **2** a dignified and self-assured manner. [f. OF f. L *pensare* (*pendere* weigh)]

poison /ˈpɔɪz(ə)n/ *n.* **1** a substance that when introduced into or absorbed by a living organism causes death or injury, especially one that kills by rapid action even in a small quantity. **2** a harmful influence. —*v.t.* **1** to administer poison to; to kill, injure, or infect with poison; (esp. in *p.p.*) to smear (a weapon) with poison. **2** to corrupt or pervert (a person or the mind). **3** to spoil or destroy (a person's pleasure etc.). —**poison ivy,** a North American climbing plant (*Rhus toxicodendron*) secreting an irritant oil from the leaves. **poison pen,** an anonymous writer of libellous or scurrilous letters; the practice of writing these. —**poisoner** *n.*, **poisonous** *adj.* [f. OF (as POTION)]

poke[1] *v.t./i.* **1** to thrust with the end of a finger or a stick etc. **2** to stir (a fire) with a poker. **3** to produce (a hole etc.) by poking. **4** to thrust or be thrust forward, to protrude. **5** to pry or search. **6** to potter. —*n.* the act of poking; a thrust or nudge. —**poke fun at,** to ridicule. **poke one's nose into,** to pry or intrude into. [f. MDu. & MLG *poken*]

poke[2] *n.* a bag, a sack (*dial.* exc. in *a pig in a poke*). [f. OF (cf. POUCH)]

poker[1] *n.* a stiff metal rod with a handle, for stirring a fire. [f. POKE[1]]

poker[2] *n.* a card-game in which players bet on the value of their hands. —**poker-face** *n.* an impassive countenance appropriate to a poker-player; a person with this. [cf. G *pochen* to brag]

poky /ˈpəʊkɪ/ *adj.* (of a room etc.) small and cramped. —**pokiness** *n.* [f. POKE[1]]

polar /ˈpəʊlə(r)/ *adj.* **1** of or near either pole of the earth or the celestial sphere. **2** having electric or magnetic polarity. **3** directly opposite in character. —**polar bear,** a large white bear (*Thalarctos maritimus*) living in Arctic regions. **polar circles,** the parallels at 23° 27′ from the poles. [f. F (as POLE[2])]

polariscope /pəˈlærɪskəʊp/ *n.* an instrument for showing the polarization of light or for viewing objects in polarized light. [f. POLAR + -SCOPE]

polarity /pəʊˈlærɪtɪ/ *n.* **1** the tendency of a magnet etc. to point with its extremities to the earth's magnetic poles, or of a body to lie with its axis in a particular direction. **2** the possession of two poles having contrary qualities. **3** the electrical condition of a body as positive or negative. [f. POLAR]

polarize /ˈpəʊləraɪz/ *v.t./i.* **1** to restrict the vibrations of (light-waves etc.) so that they have different amplitudes in different planes.

2 to give electric or magnetic polarity to. 3 to set or become set at opposite extremes of opinion. —**polarization** /-ˈzeɪʃ(ə)n/ *n.* [f. POLAR]

Polaroid /ˈpəʊlərɔɪd/ *n.* [P] a material in thin sheets polarizing light passing through it; a camera able to develop a negative and produce a print within a short time of exposure.

polder /ˈpəʊldə(r)/ *n.* a piece of low-lying land reclaimed from the sea or a river, especially in the Netherlands. [f. MDu.]

Pole *n.* a native or inhabitant of Poland. [G f. Polish]

pole[1] *n.* 1 a long slender rounded piece of wood or metal, especially one used as part of a supporting structure or in propelling a barge etc. 2 (as a measure) a perch (PERCH[1] sense 3). —**pole-jump** *or* **pole-vault** *n.* a vault over a high bar with the help of a pole held in the hands. **up the pole,** (*slang*) in a difficulty; crazy. [OE f. L *palus* stake]

pole[2] *n.* 1 either of the ends of the earth's axis of rotation; either of two points in the celestial sphere about which the stars appear to revolve; the North Pole or South Pole. 2 each of the two opposite points on the surface of a magnet at which the magnetic forces are concentrated. 3 each of the two terminals (positive and negative) of an electric cell or battery etc. 4 each of two opposed principles. —**be poles apart,** to differ greatly. **pole-star** *n.* a star near the North Pole in the sky. [f. L f. Gk *polos* axis]

pole-axe *n.* 1 a battleaxe with a long handle. 2 a butcher's axe with a hammer at the back. —*v.t.* to slaughter or strike with a pole-axe. [f. MDu. or MLG (as POLL, AXE)]

polecat /ˈpəʊlkæt/ *n.* 1 a small dark-brown mammal of the weasel family, especially *Mustela putorius.* 2 (*US*) a skunk. [f. CAT; first element unkn.]

polemic /pəˈlemɪk/ *n.* a verbal attack; a controversial discussion. —*adj.* (also **polemical**) controversial, involving dispute. —**polemically** *adv.* [f. L f. Gk (*polemos* war)]

polemics /pəˈlemɪks/ *n.pl.* the art or practice of controversial discussion. [f. prec.]

police /pəˈliːs/ *n.* 1 a civil force responsible for maintaining public order; (as *pl.*) its members. 2 a force with a similar function of enforcing the regulations of an organization etc. —*v.t.* 1 to maintain order in (a place) by means of police; to provide with police. 2 to keep order in, to control. —**police state,** a totalitarian State regulated by means of a national police force controlling citizens' activities. **police station,** an office of a local police force. [F f. L (as POLITY)]

policeman *n.* (*pl.* **-men**) a man who is a member of a police force. —**policewoman** *n.fem.* (*pl.* **-women**)

policy[1] /ˈpɒlɪsɪ/ *n.* 1 a course of action adopted by a government or party or person. 2 prudent conduct, sagacity. [f. OF f. L f. Gk (as POLITY)]

policy[2] /ˈpɒlɪsɪ/ *n.* a contract of insurance; a document containing this. [f. F, = bill of lading, ult. f. Gk *apodeixis* evidence]

polio /ˈpəʊlɪəʊ/ *n.* (*colloq.*) poliomyelitis. [abbr.]

poliomyelitis /pəʊlɪəʊmaɪəˈlaɪtɪs/ *n.* an infectious viral disease which may cause temporary or permanent localized paralysis as a result of the infection and death of nerve cells in the spinal cord or brain stem. [f. Gk *polios* grey + *muelos* marrow]

Polish /ˈpəʊlɪʃ/ *adj.* of Poland or the Poles or their language. —*n.* the Slavonic language of Poland. [f. POLE]

polish /ˈpɒlɪʃ/ *v.t./i.* 1 to make or become smooth and glossy by rubbing. 2 (esp. in *p.p.*) to refine or improve, to add finishing touches to. —*n.* 1 a substance used for polishing things. 2 smoothness or glossiness produced by friction. 3 refinement, elegance. —**polish off,** to finish off quickly. —**polisher** *n.* [f. OF f. L *polire*]

Politbureau /ˈpɒlɪtbjʊərəʊ/ *n.* the highest policy-making committee of the USSR or of some other Communist countries. [f. Russ., = political bureau]

polite /pəˈlaɪt/ *adj.* 1 having good manners, socially correct. 2 cultivated, cultured; refined, elegant. —**politely** *adv.*, **politeness** *n.* [f. L *politus* (as POLISH)]

politic /ˈpɒlɪtɪk/ *adj.* (of an action) judicious, expedient; (of a person) prudent, sagacious. —*v.i.* (**-ck-**) to engage in politics. [f. OF f. L f. Gk (*politēs* citizen)]

political /pəˈlɪtɪk(ə)l/ *adj.* 1 of or engaged in politics. 2 of or affecting the State or its government; of public affairs. 3 relating to a person's or organization's status or influence. —**political economy,** the study of the economic problems of government. **political geography,** that dealing with the boundaries and possessions of States. **political prisoner,** a person imprisoned for a political offence. **political science,** the study of the factors involved in politics; the scientific analysis of political activity and behaviour. —**politically** *adv.* [f. L (as prec.)]

politician /pɒlɪˈtɪʃ(ə)n/ *n.* one who is engaged in politics, especially as a profession; one who is skilled in political affairs. [as POLITIC]

politicize /pəˈlɪtɪsaɪz/ *v.t./i.* 1 to engage in or talk politics. 2 to give a political character to. —**politicization** /-ˈzeɪʃ(ə)n/ *n.* [as POLITIC]

politics /ˈpɒlɪtɪks/ *n.pl.* 1 (also treated as *sing.*) the science and art of government; political affairs or life. **2** political principles or practice. [f. POLITIC]

polity /ˈpɒlɪtɪ/ *n.* **1** the form or process of civil government. **2** an organized society, a State. [f. L f. Gk *politeia* (*politēs* citizen f. *polis* city)]

polka /ˈpɒlkə/ *n.* a lively dance originating in Bohemia; music for this. —*v.i.* to dance the polka. —**polka dot,** a round dot as one of many forming a regular pattern on a textile fabric etc. [F & G f. Czech, = half-step]

poll /pəʊl/ *n.* **1** voting at an election; the result of voting; the number of persons voting or of votes recorded. **2** an opinion poll (see OPINION). **3** the head; the crown or top of the head. —*v.t./i.* **1** to vote at an election. **2** (of a candidate) to receive as votes. **3** to cut off the horns of (cattle) or the top of (a tree etc.). —**poll tax** a tax levied on every adult; the community charge (see COMMUNITY). [perph f. LDu.]

pollack /ˈpɒlæk/ *n.* a marine food-fish (*Pollachius pollachius*) related to the cod. [f. earlier *podlock*; orig. unkn.]

pollard /ˈpɒləd/ *n.* **1** an animal that has cast or lost its horns; an ox, sheep, or goat of a hornless breed. **2** a tree polled so as to produce a close rounded head of young branches. —*v.t.* to make (a tree) into a pollard. [f. POLL]

pollen /ˈpɒlən/ *n.* a fine powdery substance discharged from a flower's anther, containing the fertilizing element. —**pollen analysis,** palynology. **pollen count,** an index of the amount of pollen in the air, published as a warning to those allergic to it. [L, = fine flour]

pollinate /ˈpɒlɪneɪt/ *v.t.* to sprinkle the stigma of (a flower) with pollen. —**pollination** /-ˈneɪʃ(ə)n/ *n.*, **pollinator** *n.* [as prec.]

pollock var. of POLLACK.

pollster /ˈpəʊlstə(r)/ *n.* a person who organizes an opinion poll. [f. POLL]

pollute /pəˈlu:t/ *v.t.* **1** to make foul or impure. **2** to corrupt. —**pollutant** *adj.* & *n.*, **pollution** *n.* [f. L *polluere*]

polo /ˈpəʊləʊ/ *n.* a four-a-side game resembling hockey, played on horseback with a long-handled mallet (polo-stick). —**polo neck,** a high round turned-over collar on a jumper etc. [Kashmir dialect, = ball]

polonaise /pɒləˈneɪz/ *n.* a slow processional dance of Polish origin; music for this. [F, = Polish (as foll.)]

polonium /pəˈləʊnɪəm/ *n.* a rare radioactive metallic element, symbol Po, atomic number 84. [f. L *Polonia* Poland (discoverer's native country)]

polony /pəˈləʊnɪ/ *n.* a sausage of partly cooked pork etc. [app. for *Bologna* sausage]

poltergeist /ˈpɒltəgaɪst/ *n.* a mischievous ghost or spirit manifesting itself by making a noisy disturbance. [G (*poltern* create disturbance, *geist* ghost)]

poltroon /pɒlˈtru:n/ *n.* (*archaic*) a spiritless coward. —**poltroonery** *n.* [f. F f. It. (*poltro* sluggard)]

poly /ˈpɒlɪ/ *n.* (*pl.* **polys**) (*colloq.*) a polytechnic. [abbr.]

poly- /pɒlɪ-/ *prefix* **1** many (*polygamy*). **2** polymerized (*polyester*). [f. Gk (*polus* much)]

polyandry /ˈpɒlɪændrɪ/ *n.* polygamy in which one woman has more than one husband. —**polyandrous** /-ˈændrəs/ *adj.* [f. Gk (as POLY-, *anēr* man, husband)]

polyanthus /pɒlɪˈænθəs/ *n.* a cultivated primrose produced from hybridized primulas. [f. POLY- + Gk *anthos* flower]

polychromatic /pɒlɪkrəˈmætɪk/ *adj.* **1** many-coloured. **2** (of radiation) consisting of more than one wavelength. —**polychromatically** *adv.*

polychrome /ˈpɒlɪkrəʊm/ *adj.* in many colours. —*n.* a polychrome work of art. [F f. Gk (as POLY-, *khrōma* colour)]

polyester /pɒlɪˈestə(r)/ *n.* a synthetic resin or fibre.

polyethylene /pɒlɪˈeθɪli:n/ *n.* polythene.

polygamy /pəˈlɪgəmɪ/ *n.* the practice of having more than one wife or (less usually) husband at once. —**polygamist** *n.*, **polygamous** *adj.* [f. F f. Gk (as POLY-, *gamos* marriage)]

polyglot /ˈpɒlɪglɒt/ *adj.* knowing or using or written in several languages. —*n.* a polyglot person. [f. F f. Gk (as POLY-, *glōtta* tongue)]

polygon /ˈpɒlɪgɒn/ *n.* a figure with many (usually five or more) sides and angles. —**polygonal** /pəˈlɪgən(ə)l/ *adj.* [f. L f. Gk (as POLY-, *-gōnos* angled)]

polygraph /ˈpɒlɪgrɑ:f/ *n.* a machine for reading physiological characteristics (e.g. the pulse-rate), and made to serve as a lie-detector. [f. Gk (as POLY-, -GRAPH)]

polygyny /pəˈlɪdʒɪnɪ/ *n.* polygamy in which one man has more than one wife. —**polygynous** *adj.* [f. POLY- + Gk *gunē* woman, wife]

polyhedron /pɒlɪˈhi:drən/ *n.* (*pl.* **-dra**) a solid figure with many (usually seven or more) faces. —**polyhedral** *adj.* [f. Gk (as POLY-, *hedra* base)]

polymath /ˈpɒlɪmæθ/ *n.* a person with wide knowledge of many subjects. [f. Gk (as POLY-, *manthanō* learn)]

polymer /ˈpɒlɪmə(r)/ *n.* a compound whose molecule is formed from many repeated units of one or more compounds. —**polymeric** /-ˈmerɪk/ *adj.* [G f. Gk *polumeros* having many parts]

polymerize /ˈpɒlɪməraɪz/ *v.t./i.* to combine or

become combined into a polymer. —**polymerization** /-ˈzeɪʃ(ə)n/ *n.* [f. prec.]

polymorphic /pɒlɪˈmɔːfɪk/ *adj.* (also **polymorphous** /-əs/) varying in individuals, passing through successive variations. [f. Gk (as POLY-, *morphē* form)]

polynomial /pɒlɪˈnəʊmɪəl/ *adj.* (of an algebraic expression) consisting of three or more terms. —*n.* a polynomial expression. [f. POLY-, after BINOMIAL]

polyp /ˈpɒlɪp/ *n.* **1** a simple organism with a tube-shaped body, e.g. an individual coelenterate. **2** a small growth of mucous membrane. [f. F f. L f. Gk (as POLY-, + *pous* = foot)]

polypeptide /pɒlɪˈpeptaɪd/ *n.* a peptide formed by combination of many amino acids.

polyphonic /pɒlɪˈfɒnɪk/ *adj.* **1** having many voices. **2** contrapuntal. **3** (of a letter or symbol) representing more than one sound. —**polyphony** /pəˈlɪfənɪ/ *n.* [f. Gk (as POLY-, *phōnē* voice, sound)]

polyploid /ˈpɒlɪplɔɪd/ *adj.* having more than two haploid sets of chromosomes. —*n.* a polyploid cell or organism. [G (as POLY-, after HAPLOID)]

polystyrene /pɒlɪˈstaɪriːn/ *n.* a kind of plastic, a polymer of styrene.

polysyllabic /pɒlɪsɪˈlæbɪk/ *adj.* **1** having many syllables. **2** characterized by polysyllables.

polysyllable /ˈpɒlɪsɪləb(ə)l/ *n.* a polysyllabic word.

polytechnic /pɒlɪˈteknɪk/ *adj.* giving instruction in many (including vocational) subjects at an advanced level. —*n.* a polytechnic institution, especially a college. [f. F f. Gk (as POLY-, *tekhnē* art)]

polytheism /ˈpɒlɪθiːɪz(ə)m/ *n.* the belief in or worship of more than one god. —**polytheist** *n.*, **polytheistic** /-ˈɪstɪk/ *adj.* [f. F f. Gk (as POLY-, *theos* god)]

polythene /ˈpɒlɪθiːn/ *n.* a tough light plastic. [f. POLYETHYLENE]

polyunsaturated /pɒlɪʌnˈsætʃəreɪtɪd/ *adj.* of those kinds of fat or oil that are not associated with the formation of cholesterol in the blood.

polyurethane /pɒlɪˈjʊərɪθeɪn/ *n.* a synthetic resin or plastic used especially as foam, as an electrical insulator, and in varnish. [f. POLY- + UREA + ETHANE]

polyvinyl chloride /pɒlɪˈvaɪnɪl/ a vinyl plastic used as an insulation or as a fabric.

pom *n.* **1** a Pomeranian. **2** (*Austral. & NZ slang*) a pommy. [abbr.]

pomace /ˈpʌmɪs/ *n.* the mass of crushed apples in cider-making. [f. L, = cider (*pomum* apple)]

pomade /pəˈmɑːd/ *n.* a scented ointment for the hair and the skin of the head. [f. F f. It. (as prec.)]

pomander /pəˈmændə(r)/ *n.* a ball of mixed aromatic substances; a round container for this. [f. OF f. L, = apple of ambergris]

pomegranate /ˈpɒmɪgrænɪt/ *n.* a tropical fruit with a tough rind and reddish pulp enclosing many seeds; the tree (*Punica granatum*) bearing it. [f. OF f. L, lit. = many-seeded apple]

pomelo /ˈpʊmɪləʊ/ *n.* (*pl.* **-os**) a shaddock or grapefruit. [orig. unkn.]

Pomeranian /pɒməˈreɪmɪən/ *n.* a small dog of a breed with long silky hair. [f. *Pomerania* region in Germany and Poland]

pomfret-cake /ˈpʌmfrɪt, ˈpɒ-/ *n.* a small round flat liquorice sweet. [f. Pontefract (earlier *Pomfret*) in West Yorkshire.]

pommel /ˈpʌm(ə)l/ *n.* **1** a knob, especially at the end of a sword-hilt. **2** the upward projecting front of a saddle. **3** either of pair of handgrips fitted to a vaulting-horse. —*v.t.* (**-ll-**) to pummel. [f. OF *pomel* dim. f. L *pomum* apple]

pommy *n.* (also **pommie**) (*Austral. & NZ slang*) a British person, especially a recent immigrant. [orig. unkn.]

pomp *n.* **1** a stately and splendid display. **2** specious glory. [f. OF f. L f. Gk, = procession]

pom-pom[1] /ˈpɒmpɒm/ *n.* an automatic quick-firing gun. [imit.]

pom-pom[2] var. of POMPON.

pompon /ˈpɒmpɒn/ *n.* **1** a decorative tuft or ball on a hat or shoe etc. **2** a dahlia etc. with small tightly clustered petals. [F]

pompous /ˈpɒmpəs/ *adj.* ostentatiously or affectedly grand or solemn; (of language) pretentious, unduly grand. —**pomposity** /-ˈpɒsɪtɪ/ *n.*, **pompously** *adv.* [f. OF f. L (as POMP)]

ponce *n.* **1** a man who lives off a prostitute's earnings. **2** (*slang*) an effeminate or homosexual man. —*v.i.* **1** to act as a ponce. **2** (*slang*) to move in an effeminate way; to potter. [perh. f. POUNCE]

poncho /ˈpɒntʃəʊ/ *n.* (*pl.* **-os**) a blanket-like piece of cloth with a slit in the middle for the head, worn as a cloak; a garment shaped like this. [S. Amer. Sp.]

pond *n.* a small area of still water. [var. of POUND[3]]

ponder *v.t./i.* **1** to think over, to consider. **2** to muse, to be deep in thought. [f. OF f. L *ponderare* weigh]

ponderable *adj.* having appreciable weight or significance. [f. L (as prec.)]

ponderous /ˈpɒndərəs/ *adj.* **1** heavy, unwieldy. **2** (of a style) dull, tedious. —**ponderously** *adv.* [f. L (*pondus* weight)]

pondweed *n.* an aquatic herb especially of the genus *Potamogeton*, growing in still water.

pong *n.* (*slang*) a stink. —*v.i.* (*slang*) to stink. [orig. unkn.]

poniard /ˈpɒnjəd/ *n.* (*hist.*) a dagger. [f. F f. L *pugnale* (*pugnus* fist)]

Pontefract-cake /ˈpɒntɪfrækt/ *n.* a small round flat cake of liquorice, made at Pontefract in West Yorkshire.

pontiff *n.* a bishop, a chief priest; the pope. [f. F f. L *pontifex*]

pontifical /pɒnˈtɪfɪk(ə)l/ *adj.* **1** of or befitting a pontiff. **2** pompously dogmatic. —**pontifically** *adv.* [f. F or L (as PONTIFF)]

pontificate /pɒnˈtɪfɪkeɪt/ *v.i.* **1** to speak in a pontifical way. **2** to play the pontiff. —/pɒnˈtɪfɪkət/ *n.* the office of bishop or pope; the period of this. [f. L (as PONTIFF)]

pontoon[1] /pɒnˈtu:n/ *n.* a card-game in which players try to acquire cards with a face-value totalling 21 and no more. [prob. corrupt. of *vingt-un* vingt-et-un]

pontoon[2] /pɒnˈtu:n/ *n.* **1** a flat-bottomed boat used as a ferry-boat or to carry lifting-gear etc. **2** each of several boats etc. used to support a temporary bridge (**pontoon bridge**). [f. F f. L *ponto* (*pons* bridge)]

pony /ˈpəʊnɪ/ *n.* a horse of any small breed. —**pony-tail** *n.* hair drawn back, tied, and hanging down behind the head. **pony-trekking** *n.* travelling across country on ponies for pleasure. [perh. f. F *poulenet* dim. of *poulain* foal]

poodle *n.* a dog of a breed with thick curling hair often elaborately clipped and shaved. [f. G *pudel*(*hund*), as PUDDLE]

poof /pu:f/ *n.* (*slang*) an effeminate or homosexual man. [cf. PUFF]

pooh /pu:/ *int.* expressing contempt or impatience. [imit.]

Pooh-Bah /pu:ˈbɑ:/ *n.* a holder of many offices at once. [character in W. S. Gilbert's *The Mikado* (1885)]

pooh-pooh /pu:ˈpu:/ *v.t.* to express contempt for, to ridicule. [redupl. of POOH]

pool[1] *n.* **1** a small body of still water, usually of natural formation. **2** a small shallow body of any liquid. **3** a deep place in a river. **4** a swimming-pool. [OE]

pool[2] *n.* **1** a common fund, e.g. of the profits of separate firms or of players' stakes in gambling. **2** a common supply of persons, vehicles, commodities, etc., for sharing by a group of people; a group of persons sharing duties etc. **3** an arrangement between competing parties to fix prices and share business. **4** (*US*) a game played on a billiard-table with usually 16 balls. —*v.t.* to put into a common fund; to share in common. —**the pools,** football pools, especially as conducted on a weekly basis. [f. F *poule*, orig. = hen]

poop *n.* **1** the stern of a ship. **2** the aftermost and highest deck. [f. OF f. L *puppis*]

poor /pʊə(r)/ *adj.* **1** having little money or means. **2** deficient in a specified quality or possession. **3** scanty, inadequate; less good than is usual or expected. **4** deserving pity or sympathy, unfortunate. **5** spiritless, despicable. **6** humble, insignificant. —**Poor Law,** (*hist.*) law relating to the support of the poor in England. **poor man's,** an inferior or cheaper substitute for. **poor white,** (*US derog.*) a member of a socially inferior group of white people. —**poorness** *n.* [f. OF *povre* f. L *pauper*]

poorhouse *n.* (*hist.*) the workhouse.

poorly *adv.* in a poor manner, badly. —*predic. adj.* unwell. [f. POOR]

pop[1] *n.* **1** a sudden sharp explosive sound, as of a cork when drawn. **2** an effervescing drink. —*v.t.*/*i.* **1** to make or cause to make a pop. **2** to go, move, or put abruptly. **3** (*slang*) to pawn. —*adv.* with the sound of a pop. —**pop-eyed** *adj.* with eyes bulging or wide open. **pop off,** (*slang*) to die. **pop the question,** (*colloq.*) to propose marriage. **pop-shop** *n.* (*slang*) a pawnbroker's shop. **pop-up** *adj.* involving parts that pop up automatically. [imit.]

pop[2] *adj.* (*colloq.*) **1** in a popular modern style. **2** performing popular music. —*n.* (*colloq.*) pop music or records. —**pop art,** art that uses themes drawn from popular culture. **pop music,** modern popular music (e.g. rock music) appealing particularly to younger people. [abbr. POPULAR]

pop[3] *n.* (*colloq.*) father; any older man. [f. PAPA]

popcorn *n.* maize which when heated bursts open to form fluffy balls.

pope[1] *n.* **1** the Bishop of Rome as head of the Roman Catholic Church. **2** the head of the Coptic Church. [OE f. L *papa* f. Gk, = father]

pope[2] *n.* a parish priest of the Orthodox Church in Russia etc. [f. Russ. *pop* (as prec.)]

popery /ˈpəʊpərɪ/ *n.* (*derog.*) the papal system; the Roman Catholic religion. [f. POPE[1]]

popgun *n.* a child's toy gun firing a cork etc. by the action of compressed air.

popinjay /ˈpɒpɪndʒeɪ/ *n.* a fop; a conceited person. [f. OF *papingay* f. Sp. f. Arab.]

popish /ˈpəʊpɪʃ/ *adj.* (*derog.*) of popery. [f. POPE[1]]

poplar /ˈpɒplə(r)/ *n.* a tall slender tree of the genus *Populus*, with a straight trunk and often tremulous leaves. [f. AF *popler* (*pople* f. L *populus*)]

poplin /ˈpɒplɪn/ *n.* a plain-woven fabric usually of cotton. [f. obs. F *papeline* perh. f. It. (as PAPAL)]

poppadam /ˈpɒpədəm/ *n.* a thin crisp biscuit made with lentil-flour. [f. Tamil]

popper *n.* (*colloq.*) a press-stud. [f. POP¹]

poppet /ˈpɒpɪt/ *n.* (*colloq.*) (esp. as a term of endearment) a small or dainty person. [ult. f. L *pu(p)pa* doll]

popping-crease *n.* (in cricket) the line in front of and parallel to the wicket within which a batsman stands. [f. POP¹]

poppy *n.* a plant of the genus *Papaver* with showy (esp. scarlet) flowers and milky juice. —**Poppy Day,** Remembrance Sunday, on which artificial poppies are worn. [OE f. L *papaver*]

poppycock *n.* (*slang*) nonsense. [OE f. Du. dial. *pappekak*]

populace /ˈpɒpjʊləs/ *n.* the common people. [F f. It. *popolaccio* (*popolo* people)]

popular /ˈpɒpjʊlə(r)/ *adj.* **1** liked or admired by many people. **2** of, for, or prevalent among the general public. —**popular music,** music that appeals to general taste, not highbrow or classical. —**popularity** /-ˈlærɪtɪ/ *n.*, **popularly** *adv.* [f. AF or L (*populus* people)]

popularize *v.t.* **1** to make generally liked. **2** to present (a subject) in a readily understandable form. —**popularization** /-ˈzeɪʃ(ə)n/ *n.*, **popularizer** *n.* [f. prec.]

populate /ˈpɒpjʊleɪt/ *v.t.* **1** to inhabit, to form the population of. **2** to supply with inhabitants. [f. L *populare* (as PEOPLE)]

population /pɒpjʊˈleɪʃ(ə)n/ *n.* **1** the inhabitants of a place or country etc.; the total number of these. **2** the extent to which a place is populated. —**population explosion,** a sudden large increase of population. [f. L (as PEOPLE)]

populist /ˈpɒpjʊlɪst/ *n.* an adherent of a political party claiming to support the interests of ordinary people. [f. L *populus* people]

populous /ˈpɒpjʊləs/ *adj.* thickly inhabited. [f. L *populosus* (as PEOPLE)]

porcelain /ˈpɔːslɪn/ *n.* fine earthenware with a translucent body and a transparent glaze; articles made of this. [F f. It. *porcellana* cowrie shell, china ware resembling this polished substance, f. *porcella* dim. of *porca* sow (perh. from resemblance of shells to a sow's vulva)]

porch *n.* a covered approach to the entrance of a building. [f. OF f. L *porticus*]

porcine /ˈpɔːsaɪn/ *adj.* of or like a pig. [f. F or L (as PORK)]

porcupine /ˈpɔːkjʊpaɪn/ *n.* a rodent of the family Hystricidae with a body and tail covered with erectile spines. [f. OF *porcespin* (as PORK, SPINE)]

pore¹ *n.* a minute opening in the surface of a skin or leaf etc. through which fluids may pass. [f. OF f. L f. Gk *poros*]

pore² *v.i.* (with *over*) to be absorbed in studying (a book etc.); to meditate or think intently about. [perh. rel. to PEER¹]

pork *n.* the flesh (esp. unsalted) of a pig used as food. —**pork pie,** a raised pie of minced pork etc., eaten cold. **pork-pie hat,** a hat with a flat rimmed crown and the brim turned up all round. [OF *porc* f. L *porcus* pig]

porker *n.* a pig raised for pork. [f. PORK]

porky *adj.* **1** of or like pork. **2** (*colloq.*) fleshy. —**porkiness** *n.* [f. PORK]

porn *n.* (*colloq.*) pornography. [abbr.]

pornography /pɔːˈnɒgrəfɪ/ *n.* the explicit representation of sexual activity visually or descriptively to stimulate erotic rather than aesthetic feelings; pictures or literature etc. containing this. —**pornographer** *n.*, **pornographic** /-ˈgræfɪk/ *adj.* [f. Gk (*pornē* prostitute, -GRAPHY)]

porous /ˈpɔːrəs/ *adj.* **1** containing pores. **2** able to be permeated by fluid or air. —**porosity** /-ˈrɒsɪtɪ/ *n.* [f. OF f. L (as PORE¹)]

porphyry /ˈpɔːfɪrɪ/ *n.* a hard rock composed of crystals of red or white feldspar in a red matrix. —**porphyritic** /-ˈrɪtɪk/ *adj.* [f. L *porphyreum* ult. f. Gk *porphura* purple dye]

porpoise /ˈpɔːpəs/ *n.* a sea mammal of the genus *Phocaena* related to the whale, with a blunt rounded snout. [f. OF f. L *porcus* pig + *piscis* fish]

porridge /ˈpɒrɪdʒ/ *n.* a food made by boiling oatmeal or other meal or cereal in water or milk. [alt. f. POTTAGE]

porringer /ˈpɒrɪndʒə(r)/ *n.* (*archaic*) a small soup-basin, especially for a child. [alt. f. earlier *pottinger* f. OF *potager* (as POTTAGE)]

port¹ *n.* a harbour; a town or place possessing a harbour; a place where customs officers are stationed to supervise the entry of goods into a country. —**port of call,** a place where a ship or person stops during a journey. [OE f. L *portus*]

port² *n.* a strong sweet usually dark-red fortified win. [f. *Oporto* in Portugal, whence shipped]

port³ *n.* the left-hand side (when facing forward) of a ship or aircraft. —*v.t.* to turn (the helm) to port. —**port tack,** a tack with the wind on the port side. [prob. orig. the side turned towards port (PORT¹)]

port⁴ *n.* **1** an opening in a ship's side for entrance or loading etc. **2** a porthole. [OF f. L *porta* gate]

port⁵ *v.t.* to carry (a rifle) diagonally across and close to the body. [f. F f. L *portare* carry]

portable /ˈpɔːtəb(ə)l/ *adj.* easily movable, convenient for carrying. —*n.* a portable form of typewriter, television set, etc. —**portability** /-ˈbɪlɪtɪ/ *n.* [f. OF or L (as prec.)]

portage /ˈpɔːtɪdʒ/ *n.* the carrying of boats or goods between two navigable waters; a place at which this is necessary; the charge for it.

-*v.t.* to convey (a boat or goods) over a portage. [f. OF (as PORT[5])]

portal /ˈpɔːt(ə)l/ *n.* a gate or doorway etc., especially an elaborate one. —**portal vein,** a vein conveying blood to the liver or some other organ except the heart. [f. OF f. L *portale* (as PORT[4])]

portcullis /pɔːtˈkʌlɪs/ *n.* a strong heavy grating sliding up and down in vertical grooves, lowered to block a gateway in a fortress etc. [f. OF, = sliding door]

portend /pɔːˈtend/ *v.t.* to foreshadow, as an omen, to give warning of. [f. L *portendere* (as PRO-, TEND[1])]

portent /ˈpɔːtent/ *n.* **1** an omen; a significant sign of something to come. **2** a prodigy, a marvellous thing. [f. L *portentum* (as prec.)]

portentous /pɔːˈtentəs/ *adj.* **1** being or like a portent. **2** pompously solemn. [f. prec.]

porter[1] *n.* **1** a person employed to carry luggage etc. **2** a dark beer brewed from charred or browned malt. [f. OF f. L *portator* (as PORT[5])]

porter[2] *n.* a doorman or gate-keeper, especially of a large building. [AF f. L *portarius* (as PORT[4])]

porterage *n.* the hire of porters. [f. PORTER[1]]

porterhouse steak a thick choice steak of beef. [said to derive its name from a porter-house, i.e. one selling porter (= dark beer; PORTER[1]), in New York]

portfolio /pɔːtˈfəʊlɪəʊ/ *n.* (*pl.* **-os**) **1** a case for loose drawings, sheets of paper, etc. **2** a list of investments held by a person or company etc. **3** the office of a minister of State. —**Minister without portfolio,** a minister not in charge of any department of State. [f. It. *portafogli* (*portare* carry, *foglio* sheet of paper)]

porthole *n.* an aperture, usually glazed, in a ship's or aircraft's side for the admission of light and air to a ship or light to an aircraft. [f. PORT[4] + HOLE]

portico /ˈpɔːtɪkəʊ/ *n.* (*pl.* **-oes**) a colonnade, a roof supported by columns at regular intervals, usually attached as a porch to a building. [It. f. L, = PORCH]

portion /ˈpɔːʃ(ə)n/ *n.* **1** a part or share. **2** the amount of food allotted to one person. **3** a dowry. **4** one's destiny or lot. —*v.t./i.* **1** to divide into portions; to distribute. **2** to give a dowry to. [f. OF f. L *portio*]

Portland cement /ˈpɔːtlənd/ cement manufactured from chalk and clay. [f. Isle of *Portland*, Dorset]

Portland stone a valuable building limestone. [cf. prec.]

portly *adj.* corpulent and dignified. —**portliness** *n.* [f. OF *port* deportment (as PORT[5])]

portmanteau /pɔːtˈmæntəʊ/ *n.* (*pl.* **-eaus**) a trunk for clothes etc., opening into two equal parts. —**portmanteau word,** a factitious word blending the sounds and combining the meanings of two others. (e.g. CHORTLE). [f. F (as PORT[5], MANTLE)]

portrait /ˈpɔːtrɪt/ *n.* **1** a likeness of a person or animal made by drawing, painting, or photography. **2** a description in words. —**portraitist** *n.* [F (as PORTRAY)]

portraiture /ˈpɔːtrɪtʃə(r)/ *n.* **1** portraying. **2** a portrait. **3** a description in words. [as foll.]

portray /pɔːˈtreɪ/ *v.t.* **1** to make a picture of. **2** to describe in words. —**portrayal** *n.* [f. OF *portraire*]

Portuguese /pɔːtjʊˈgiːz/ *adj.* of Portugal or its people or language. —*n.* (*pl.* same) **1** a native or inhabitant of Portugal. **2** the language of Portugal and its territories and of Brazil. —**Portuguese man-of-war,** a tropical or subtropical hydrozoan of the genus *Physalia*, with a sail-shaped crest and a poisonous sting. [f. Port. f. L *portugalensis*]

pose /pəʊz/ *v.t./i.* **1** to put into or assume a desired position for a portrait or photograph etc. **2** to take a particular attitude for effect or to impress others. **3** (with *as*) to pretend to be. **4** to present (a question or problem). —*n.* **1** an attitude in which a person etc. is posed. **2** an affectation, a pretence. [f. F f. L *pausare* pause; confused in part with L *ponere* place]

poser *n.* a puzzling question or problem. [f. POSE]

poseur /pəʊˈzɜː(r)/ *n.* a person who poses for effect or behaves affectedly. [F (as POSE)]

posh *adj.* (*slang*) high-class, smart. —*v.t.* (*slang*) to smarten. [perh. f. slang *posh* money, a dandy.

posit /ˈpɒzɪt/ *v.t.* to assume as a fact, to postulate. [f. L (as foll.)]

position /pəˈzɪʃ(ə)n/ *n.* **1** the place occupied by a person or thing. **2** the proper place. **3** being advantageously placed. **4** the way in which a thing or its parts are placed or arranged. **5** a mental attitude; a way of looking at a question. **6** a situation in relation to others. **7** rank or status; high social standing. **8** paid (official or domestic) employment. **9** a place where troops are posted for strategic purposes. **10** a configuration of chess-men etc during a game. —*v.t.* to place in a position. —**positional** *adj.* [f. OF or L (*ponere* place)]

positive /ˈpɒzɪtɪv/ *adj.* **1** formally or explicitly stated. **2** definite, unquestionable. **3** (of a person) convinced, confident or over-confident in an opinion. **4** absolute, not relative. **5** (*colloq.*) downright, out-and-out. **6** constructive. **7** marked by the presence and not absence of qualities. **8** dealing only with matters of fact, practical. **9** tending in the direction naturally or arbitrarily taken as that of increase or progress. **10** (of a quantity in algebra) greater than zero. **11** of, containing, or producing the kind of electrical charge produced by rubbing glass with silk. **12** (of a photograph) showing the lights and shades or colours as in the original image cast on a film etc. **13** (*Gram.*, of an adjective or adverb) in the primary form expressing a simple quality without comparison. —*n.* a positive adjective, photograph, quantity, etc. —**positive vetting,** an intensive inquiry into the background and character of a candidate for a senior post in the civil service etc. —**positively** *adv.*, **positiveness** *n.* [f. OF or L (as prec.)]

positivism /ˈpɒsɪtɪvɪz(ə)m/ *n.* the theory that every rationally justifiable assertion can be scientifically verified or is capable of logical or mathematical proof. —**logical positivism,** a form of positivism in which symbolic logic is used and linguistic problems are emphasized. —**positivist** *n.*, **positivistic** /-ˈvɪstɪk/ *adj* [f. F (as prec.)]

positron /ˈpɒzɪtrɒn/ *n.* an elementary particle with the mass of an electron and a charge the same as an electron's but positive. [f. POSITIVE]

posse /ˈpɒsɪ/ *n.* a body (of constables); a strong force or company. [L, = to be able]

possess /pəˈzes/ *v.t.* **1** to hold as belonging to oneself, to have or own. **2** to have (a faculty or quality etc.). **3** to occupy or dominate the mind of. —**like one possessed,** with great energy. —**possessor** *n.* [f. OF f. L *possidere*]

possession /pəˈzeʃ(ə)n/ *n.* **1** possessing, being possessed. **2** a thing possessed. **3** occupancy. **4** (in *pl.*) property, wealth. **5** a subject territory. —**take possession of,** to become the owner or possessor of. [f. OF or L (as prec.)]

possessive /pəˈzesɪv/ *adj.* **1** showing a desire to possess or to retain what one possesses. **2** (*Gram.*, of a word or form) indicating possession (e.g. *Anne's*, *my*, *mine*). —*n.* (*Gram.*) a possessive case or word. —**possessively** *adv.*, **possessiveness** *n.* [f. L (as POSSESS)]

possibility /pɒsɪˈbɪlɪtɪ/ *n.* **1** the fact or condition of being possible. **2** something that may exist or happen. **3** capability of being used or of producing good results. [as foll.]

possible /ˈpɒsɪb(ə)l/ *adj.* capable of existing, happening, being done, etc. —*n.* **1** a possible candidate, member of a team, etc. **2** the highest possible score, especially in shooting. [f. OF or L (as POSSE)]

possibly /ˈpɒsɪblɪ/ *adv.* **1** in accordance with possibility. **2** perhaps, for all one knows to the contrary. [f. prec.]

possum /ˈpɒsəm/ *n.* **1** (*colloq.*) an opossum. **2** (*Austral.* & *NZ*) a member of a large family of arboreal phalangers, some of which have a prehensile tail. —**play possum,** (*colloq.*) to pretend to be unconscious or unaware of something (from the opossum's habit of seeming to feign death if attacked). [abbr. OPOSSUM]

post[1] /pəust/ *n.* **1** a long stout piece of timber or metal set upright in the ground etc. to support something, mark a position or boundary, etc. **2** the pole marking the start or finish of a race. —*v.t.* (also with *up*) **1** to attach (a paper etc.) in a prominent place. **2** to announce or advertise by a placard or in a published list. [OE f. L *postis*]

post[2] /pəust/ *n.* **1** the official conveying of parcels, letters, etc. **2** the letters etc. conveyed; a single collection or delivery of these. **3** a place where letters etc. are dealt with. —*v.t.* **1** to put (a letter etc.) into the post. **2** (esp. in *p.p.*) to supply (a person) with information. **3** to enter (an item) in a ledger; to complete (a ledger) thus. —**post-bag** *n.* a mail-bag. **post-box** *n.* a box into which letters are inserted for dispatch or are delivered. **post-code** *n.* a group of letters and numerals in a postal address to assist sorting. **post-free** *adj.* & *adv.* carried by post without charge to the recipient. **post-haste** *adv.* with great speed. **post-office,** a building or room where postal business is carried on. **Post Office,** the public department or corporation responsible for postal services. **post-paid** *adj.* on which postage has been paid. [f. F f. It. *posta* f. L (as POSITION)]

post[3] /pəust/ *n.* **1** a situation of paid employment. **2** the appointed place of a soldier etc. on watch; a place of duty. **3** a place (especially a frontier fort) manned by soldiers; the soldiers there. **4** a trading station. —*v.t.* **1** to place (a soldier etc.) at his post. **2** to appoint to a post or command. —**last post,** a military bugle-call at the time of retiring for the night or at a funeral. [f. F f. It. *posto* (as prec.)]

post- /pəust-/ *prefix* after, behind. [f. L *post* adv. & prep.]

postage /ˈpəustɪdʒ/ *n.* the amount charged for sending a letter etc. by post. —**postage stamp,** an official adhesive stamp for sticking on a letter etc. indicating the amount of postage paid. [f. POST[2]]

postal /ˈpəust(ə)l/ *adj.* of or by post. —**postal code,** a post-code. **postal order,** a kind of money order issued by the Post Office. —**postally** *adv.* [F (as POST[2])]

postcard *n.* a card for sending by post without an envelope.

postdate /pəustˈdeɪt/ *v.t.* **1** to follow in time. **2** to give a date later than the true date to.

poster /ˈpəustə(r)/ *n.* **1** a placard in a public place. **2** a large printed picture. [f. POST[1]]

poste restante /pəʊst re'stɑ̃t/ a department in a post office where letters are kept until called for. [F, = letters remaining]

posterior /pɒ'stɪərɪə(r)/ *adj.* **1** later, coming after in a series or in order of time. **2** situated behind or at the back. —*n.* the buttocks. [L, compar. of *posterus* following (as POST-)]

posterity /pɒ'sterɪtɪ/ *n.* **1** future generations. **2** a person's descendants. [f. OF f. L (as prec.)]

postern /'pɒstɜːn/ *n.* a small entrance at the back or side of a fortress etc. [f. OF f. L *posterula* dim. f. *posterus* (see POSTERIOR)]

postgraduate /pəʊst'grædjʊət/ *adj.* (of studies) carried on after taking a first degree; (of a student) engaged in such studies. —*n.* a postgraduate student.

posthumous /'pɒstjʊməs/ *adj.* **1** occurring after death. **2** published after the author's death. **3** born after the father's death. —**posthumously** *adv.* [f. L *postumus* last (as POSTERIOR), assoc. with *humus* ground]

postilion /pə'stɪljən/ *n.* a rider on the near horse drawing a coach etc. where there is no coachman. [f. F f. It., = post-boy (as POST²)]

Post-Impressionism *n.* the theory or practice of the Post-Impressionist school in art, an extension of impressionism. —**Post-Impressionist** *n.* a member of a movement in French painting in the late 19th and early 20th c. who sought to reveal the subject's structural form without strict fidelity to its natural appearance.

postman *n.* (*pl.* **-men**) one who delivers or collects letters etc.

postmark *n.* an official mark on a letter etc. cancelling the stamp and giving the place and date. —*v.t.* to stamp with a postmark.

postmaster *n.* the official in charge of certain post offices. —**postmistress** *n.fem.*

post-mortem /pəʊst'mɔːtəm/ *n.* **1** an examination made after death, especially to determine its cause. **2** (*colloq.*) a discussion after the conclusion of a game, election, etc. —*adv.* & *adj.* after death. [L]

post-natal /pəʊst'neɪt(ə)l/ *adj.* of or concerning the period after childbirth.

postpone /pəʊst'pəʊn/ *v.t.* to cause or arrange to take place at a later time. —**postponement** *n.* [f. L *postponere* (POST-, *ponere* place)]

postprandial /pəʊst'prændɪəl/ *adj.* (usu. *joc.*) after lunch or dinner. [f. POST- + L *prandium* dinner]

postscript /'pəʊstskrɪpt/ *n.* an additional paragraph, especially at the end of a letter after the signature. [f. L (POST-, *scribere* write)]

postulant /'pɒstjʊlənt/ *n.* a candidate, especially for admission to a religious order. [F or f. L (as foll.)]

postulate /'pɒstjʊleɪt/ *v.t.* to assume or require to be true, especially as a basis for reasoning; to claim; to take for granted. —/'pɒstjʊlət/ *n.* a thing postulated. —**postulation** /-'leɪʃ(ə)n/ *n.* [f. L *postulare* demand]

posture /'pɒstʃə(r)/ *n.* **1** an attitude of the body or mind; the relative position of parts, especially of the body. **2** a condition or state (of affairs etc.). —*v.t./i.* **1** to assume a posture, especially for effect. **2** to dispose the limbs of (a person) in a particular way. —**postural** *adj.*, **posturer** *n.* [F f. It. f. L (as POSITION)]

post-war /pəʊst'wɔ(r), *attrib.* 'pəʊst-/ *adj.* occurring or existing after a war.

posy /'pəʊzɪ/ *n.* a small bunch of flowers. [contr. of POESY]

pot[1] *n.* **1** a rounded vessel of earthenware, metal, or glass, for holding liquids or solids or for cooking in. **2** a chamber-pot, teapot, etc. **3** the contents of a pot. **4** the total amount bet in a game etc.; (*colloq.*) a large sum. **5** (*slang*) a prize in an athletic contest, especially a silver cup. **6** (*slang*) a pot-belly. —*v.t./i.* (**-tt-**) **1** to plant in a pot. **2** to sit (a child) on a chamber-pot. **3** to send (a ball) into the pocket in billiards etc. **4** to shoot, to hit or kill (an animal) by a pot-shot. **5** to seize or secure. **6** to abridge or epitomize. **7** (esp. in *p.p.*) to preserve (food) in a sealed pot etc. —**go to pot**, (*colloq.*) to deteriorate, to be ruined. **pot-belly** *n.* a protruding belly; a person with this. **pot-boiler** *n.* a piece of art, writing, etc., done merely to earn money. **pot-herb** *n.* a herb used in cooking. **pot-hole** *n.* a deep hole in rock; a rough hole worn in a road surface. **pot-holing** *n.* exploring pot-holes in rock. **pot-hook** *n.* a hook over a fireplace for hanging or lifting a pot; a curved stroke in handwriting. **pot-hunter** *n.* a sportsman who shoots at random; a person who takes part in a contest merely for the sake of the prize. **pot luck**, whatever is available for a meal etc. **pot plant**, a plant grown in a flower-pot. **pot-roast** *n.* a piece of meat cooked slowly in a covered dish; (*v.t.*) to cook thus. **pot-shot** *n.* a random shot; a casual attempt. **potting-shed** *n.* a shed in which plants are grown in pots for planting out later. [OE]

pot[2] *n.* (*slang*) marijuana. [prob. f. Mex. Sp. *potiguaya*]

potable /'pəʊtəb(ə)l/ *adj.* drinkable. [F or f. L (*potare* drink)]

potage /pɒ'tɑːʒ/ *n.* thick soup. [F, = POTTAGE]

potash /'pɒtæʃ/ *n.* any of various salts of potassium, especially potassium carbonate. [f. Du. (as POT¹, ASH¹)]

potassium /pə'tæsɪəm/ *n.* a soft silver-white metallic element, symbol K, atomic number 19. [f. prec.]

potation /pə'teɪʃ(ə)n/ *n.* drinking; a drink. [f. OF or L (as POTABLE)]

potato /pə'teɪtəʊ/ *n.* (*pl.* **-oes**) a plant (*Solanum tuberosum*) with starchy tubers used as food; its tuber. [f. Sp. *patata* f. S.Amer. Indian name]

poteen /pɒ'ti:n/ *n.* (in Ireland) whisky from an illicit still. [f. Ir. *poitín* dim. (as POT¹)]

potent /'pəʊt(ə)nt/ *adj.* **1** powerful, strong; (of a reason) forceful, cogent. **2** (of a man) not sexually impotent. —**potency** *n.* [f. L *potens* (*posse* be able)]

potentate /'pəʊtənteɪt/ *n.* a monarch or ruler with great power. [f. OF or L (as prec.)]

potential /pə'tenʃ(ə)l/ *adj.* capable of coming into being or of being developed or used etc. —*n.* **1** ability or capacity available for use or development; usable resources. **2** a quantity determining the energy of a mass in a gravitational field, of a charge in an electric field, etc. —**potentiality** /-ʃɪ'ælɪtɪ/ *n.*, **potentially** *adv.* [f. OF or L (*potentia* power, as POTENT)]

pother /'pɒðə(r)/ *n.* (*literary*) a commotion, fuss. [orig. unkn.]

potion /'pəʊʃ(ə)n/ *n.* a liquid for drinking as a medicine or drug. [f. OF f. L (*potus* having drunk)]

pot-pourri /pəʊ'pʊrɪ/ *n.* **1** a scented mixture of dried petals and spices. **2** a musical or literary medley. [F, = rotten pot]

potsherd /'pɒtʃɜ:d/ *n.* a broken piece of earthenware (esp. in archaeology).

pottage *n.* (*archaic*) a soup, a stew. [f. OF *potage* (as POT¹)]

potter¹ *v.i.* to work on trivial tasks in a leisurely relaxed way. —**potterer** *n.* [frequent. of dial. *pote* push]

potter² *n.* a maker of earthenware vessels. [OE (as POT¹)]

pottery *n.* **1** vessels etc. made of baked clay. **2** a potter's work or workshop. —**the Potteries**, a district in north Staffordshire, seat of the English pottery industry. [f. OF (as prec.)]

potty¹ *adj.* (*slang*) **1** crazy, foolish. **2** insignificant, trivial. [orig. unkn.]

potty² *n.* (*colloq.*) a chamber-pot, especially for a child. [f. POT¹]

pouch *n.* **1** a small bag or detachable outside pocket. **2** a baglike formation. —*v.t.* **1** to put into a pouch; to pocket. **2** to make (part of a dress etc.) hang like a pouch. [f. OF (cf. POKE²)]

pouffe /pu:f/ *n.* a padded stool without legs, large enough to be used as a seat. [F]

poult /pəʊlt/ *n.* a young domestic fowl, turkey, or game-bird. [contr. of PULLET]

poulterer /'pəʊltərə(r)/ *n.* a dealer in poultry and usually game. [f. earlier *poulter* f. OF *pouletier* (as PULLET)]

poultice /'pəʊltɪs/ *n.* a soft heated mass of bread or kaolin etc. applied to a sore part of the body. —*v.t.* to apply a poultice to. [orig. *pultes* pl. f. L *puls* pottage, pap]

poultry /'pəʊltrɪ/ *n.* domestic fowls, ducks, geese, turkeys, etc., especially as a source of food. [f. OF (as POULTERER)]

pounce *v.i.* **1** to spring or swoop down in a sudden attack. **2** to seize *on* (an opportunity, mistake, etc.) eagerly. —*n.* a pouncing movement. [perh. as PUNCH¹]

pound¹ *n.* **1** a unit of weight, equal to 16 oz. avoirdupois (454 g), 12 oz. troy (373 g). **2** (*pl.* **pounds** or **pound**) the currency unit of the UK (in full **pound sterling**); the currency unit of some other countries. —**pound note**, a banknote for one pound. **pound of flesh**, any legal but morally offensive demand (with allusion to Shylock's demand for a pound of Antonio's flesh, pledged as security for a loan, in Shakespeare's *Merchant of Venice*). [OE f. L *pondo* Roman pound weight]

pound² *v.t./i.* **1** to crush or beat with heavy repeated strokes. **2** to deliver heavy blows or gunfire etc. **3** to make one's way heavily. **4** (of the heart) to beat heavily. [OE]

pound³ *n.* an enclosure where stray animals or officially removed vehicles are kept until claimed. [f. OE (cf. POND)]

poundage *n.* a commission or fee of so much per pound in money or weight. [f. POUND¹]

pounder *n.* a thing that weighs a pound or (**-pounder**) so many pounds; a gun carrying a shell of such weight.

pour /pɔ:(r)/ *v.t./i.* **1** to flow or cause to flow especially downwards in a stream or shower; to serve by pouring. **2** to rain heavily. **3** to come or go in profusion or rapid succession. **4** to discharge or send freely. **5** to utter at length or in a rush. —**pourer** *n.* [orig. unkn.]

pout *v.t./i.* to push forward one's lips as a sign of displeasure or sulking; to protrude (the lips); (of the lips) to be pushed forward thus. —*n.* a pouting expression. [orig. unkn.]

pouter *n.* a kind of pigeon that can inflate its crop greatly. [f. POUT]

poverty /'pɒvətɪ/ *n.* **1** being poor, great lack of money or resources. **2** scarcity, lack. **3** inferiority, poorness. —**poverty line**, the minimum income level needed to secure the necessities of life. **poverty-stricken** *adj.* greatly affected by poverty. **poverty trap**, a situation in which an increase of income incurs loss of State benefits so that the recipient is no better off than before. [f. OF f. L *paupertas* (as PAUPER)]

POW *abbr.* prisoner of war.

powder *n.* **1** a mass of fine dry particles. **2** a medicine or cosmetic in this form. **3** gunpowder. —*v.t.* **1** to apply a powder to. **2** to reduce to a fine powder. —**powder blue**, pale blue. **powder-puff** *n.* a soft pad for applying powder to the skin. **powder-room** *n.* a ladies' lavatory in a public building. —**powdery** *adj.*, **powderiness** *n.* [f. OF *poudre* f. L *pulvis*]

power *n.* **1** the ability to do something; a particular faculty of the body or mind. **2** vigour, energy. **3** an active property or function. **4** (*colloq.*) a large amount. **5** control, influence; ascendancy. **6** authorization. **7** an influential person or organization etc.; a State having international influence. **8** a deity. **9** capacity for exerting mechanical force. **10** mechanical or electrical energy as opposed to hand labour; (*attrib.*) operated by this. **11** the electricity supply. **12** the product obtained by multiplying a number by a given number of factors equal to it. **13** the magnifying capacity of a lens. —*v.t.* to supply with mechanical or electrical energy. —**power-point** *n.* a socket in a wall etc. for connecting an electrical device to the mains. **power-station** *n.* a building where electrical power is generated for distribution. **the powers that be,** those in authority. [AF *poer* f. L (as POTENT)]

powerful *adj.* having great power or influence. —**powerfully** *adv.*, **powerfulness** *n.* [f. prec. + -FUL]

powerhouse *n.* **1** a power-station. **2** a person etc. of great energy.

powerless *adj.* without power; wholly unable. —**powerlessly** *adv.*, **powerlessness** *n.* [f. POWER + -LESS]

powwow /ˈpaʊwaʊ/ *n.* a conference or meeting for discussion (originally among North American Indians). —*v.i.* to hold a powwow. [f. Algonquian, = magician]

pox *n.* a virus disease with pocks; (*colloq.*) syphilis. [alt. spelling of *pocks* pl. of POCK]

pp. *abbr.* pages.

p.p. *abbr. per pro.*

pp *abbr.* pianissimo.

p.p.m. *abbr.* parts per million.

PPS *abbr.* **1** Parliamentary Private Secretary. **2** additional postscript (*postpostscript*).

PR *abbr.* **1** proportional representation. **2** public relations.

Pr *symbol* praseodymium.

practicable /ˈpræktɪkəb(ə)l/ *adj.* that can be done or used; possible in practice. —**practicability** /-ˈbɪlɪtɪ/ *n.* [f. F (as foll.)]

practical /ˈpræktɪk(ə)l/ *adj.* **1** involving activity as distinct from study or theory. **2** suited to use or action. **3** (of a person) inclined to action; able to do or make functional things well. **4** virtual. —*n.* a practical examination or lesson. —**practical joke,** a humorous trick played on a person. —**practicality** /-ˈkælɪtɪ/ *n.* [f. obs. F or L f. Gk (*prattō* do)]

practically *adv.* **1** virtually, almost. **2** in a practical way. [f. prec.]

practice /ˈpræktɪs/ *n.* **1** a habitual action, a custom. **2** repeated exercise to improve a skill; a spell of this. **3** action as opposed to theory. **4** the professional work of a doctor, lawyer, etc.; this as a business; the patients or clients regularly consulting these. —**out of practice,** temporarily lacking a former skill etc. [f. foll.]

practise /ˈpræktɪs/ *v.t./i.* **1** to do habitually; to carry out in action. **2** to do repeatedly as an exercise to improve a skill. **3** to pursue (a profession, religion, etc.; also *absol.*). **4** (in *p.p.*) experienced, expert. [f. OF or L f. Gk (as PRACTICAL)]

practitioner /prækˈtɪʃənə(r)/ *n.* a person practising a profession, especially medicine. [f. prec.]

praenomen /priːˈnəʊmen/ *n.* an ancient Roman's first or personal name (e.g. *Marcus* Tullius Cicero). [L (*prae* before, *nomen* name)]

praetor /ˈpriːtə(r)/ *n.* a magistrate in ancient Rome, ranking below a consul and performing some of his duties. [f. F or L, perh. f. *prae* before, *ire* go]

praetorian /prɪˈtɔːrɪən/ *adj.* of a praetor. —**Praetorian Guard,** (in ancient Rome) soldiers who formed the bodyguard of a general or of the emperor. [f. L (as prec.)]

pragmatic /prægˈmætɪk/ *adj.* **1** dealing with matters from a practical point of view. **2** treating the facts of history with reference to their practical lessons. —**pragmatically** *adv.* [f. L f. Gk (*pragma* deed)]

pragmatism /ˈprægmətɪz(ə)m/ *n.* **1** the matter-of-fact treatment of things. **2** a philosophy that evaluates assertions solely by their practical consequences and bearing on human interests. **pragmatist** *n.* [f. Gk *pragma* (as prec.)]

prairie /ˈpreərɪ/ *n.* a large treeless area of grassland, especially in North America. —**prairie-dog** *n.* a North American rodent of the genus *Cynomys* with a bark like a dog's. **prairie oyster,** a raw egg seasoned and swallowed whole. [f. OF, ult. f. L *pratum* meadow]

praise /preɪz/ *v.t.* **1** to express warm approval or admiration of. **2** to glorify (God) in words. —*n.* praising; approval expressed in words. [f. OF *preisier* f. L *pretiare* (*pretium* price)]

praiseworthy *adj.* worthy of praise.

praline /ˈprɑːliːn/ *n.* a sweet made by browning nuts in boiling sugar. [F, f. Marshal de Plessis-*Pralin* (d. 1675), whose cook invented it]

pram *n.* a four-wheeled carriage for a baby, pushed by a person walking. The invention dates from the mid-19th c. [abbr. of PERAMBULATOR]

prance /prɑ:ns/ *v.i.* **1** to walk or behave in an elated or arrogant manner. **2** (of a horse) to raise the forelegs and spring from the hind legs. —*n.* prancing; a prancing movement. [orig. unkn.]

prang *v.t.* (*slang*) **1** to crash (an aircraft or vehicle); to damage by impact. **2** to bomb (a target) successfully. —*n.* (*slang*) a crash; damage by impact. [imit.]

prank *n.* a practical joke, a piece of mischief. [orig. unkn.]

prankster *n.* a person fond of playing pranks. [f. prec.]

praseodymium /preɪsɪəˈdɪmɪəm/ *n.* a metallic element of the lanthanide series, symbol Pr, atomic number 59. [f. G f. Gk *prasios* leek-green (from its green salts), as NEODYMIUM]

prat *n.* (*slang*) **1** a fool. **2** the buttocks. [orig. unkn.]

prate *v.i.* to chatter, to talk too much; to talk foolishly or irrelevantly. —*n.* prating, idle talk. [f. MDu. or MLG, prob. imit.]

prattle *v.i.* to chatter or say in a childish way. —*n.* childish chatter; inconsequential talk. [as prec.]

prawn *n.* an edible shellfish of the genus *Palaemon*, *Penaeus*, etc., like a large shrimp. [orig. unkn.]

pray *v.t./i.* **1** to say prayers. **2** to make a devout supplication; to entreat; to ask earnestly (for). **3** (*archaic*, before an imperative) = please. —**praying mantis**, see MANTIS. [f. OF *preier* f. L *precari*]

prayer[1] /ˈpreə(r)/ *n.* **1** a solemn request or thanksgiving to God or to an object of worship; a formula used in praying. **2** the act of praying; a religious service consisting largely of prayers. **3** an entreaty to a person. —**prayer-book** *n.* a book of set prayers. **prayer-mat** *n.* a small rug on which Muslims kneel to pray. **prayer-wheel** *n.* a revolving cylindrical box inscribed with or containing prayers, used especially by the Buddhists of Tibet. [f. OF f. L (as PRECARIOUS)]

prayer[2] /ˈpreɪə(r)/ *n.* one who prays. [f. PRAY]

pre- *prefix* before (in time, place, order, degree, or importance). [f. L *prae* before]

preach *v.t./i.* **1** to deliver a sermon or religious address; to deliver (a sermon); to make (the Gospel) known by preaching. **2** to give moral advice in an obtrusive way. **3** to advocate or urge people to (a quality or practice etc.). —**preacher** *n.* [f. OF f. L *praedicare* proclaim]

preamble /pri:ˈæmb(ə)l/ *n.* a preliminary statement; the introductory part of a statute or document etc. [f. OF f. L (as PRE-, AMBLE)]

pre-arrange /pri:əˈreɪndʒ/ *v.t.* to arrange beforehand. —**pre-arrangement** *n.*

prebend /ˈprebənd/ *n.* the stipend of a canon or member of a chapter; the portion of land or tithe from which this is drawn. —**prebendal** *adj.* [f. OF f. L *praebenda* pension (*praebēre* grant)]

prebendary /ˈprebəndərɪ/ *n.* a holder of a prebend; an honorary canon. [f. L (as prec.)]

Precambrian /pri:ˈkæmbrɪən/ *adj.* of the geological era preceding the Cambrian period and Palaeozoic era. —*n.* this era.

precarious /prɪˈkeərɪəs/ *adj.* uncertain, dependent on chance; insecure. —**precariously** *adv.*, **precariousness** *n.* [f. L, = obtained by entreaty (*prex* prayer)]

pre-cast /pri:ˈkɑ:st/ *adj.* (of concrete) cast in blocks before use.

precaution /prɪˈkɔʃ(ə)n/ *n.* an action taken beforehand to avoid a risk or ensure a good result. —**precautionary** *adj.* [f. F f. L (as PRE-, CAUTION)]

precede /prɪˈsi:d/ *v.t.* to come, go, or place before in time, order, importance, etc. [f. OF f. L *praecedere* (*prae* before, *cedere* go)]

precedence /ˈpresɪdəns/ *n.* priority in time or order etc.; the right of preceding others. [f. foll.]

precedent /ˈpresɪdənt/ *n.* a previous case taken as an example for subsequent cases or as a justification. —*adj.* preceding in time or order etc. [f. OF (as PRECEDE)]

precentor /prɪˈsentə(r)/ *n.* one who leads the singing or (in a synagogue) the prayers of a congregation. [f. F or L *praecentor* (*prae* before, *canere* sing)]

precept /ˈpri:sept/ *n.* **1** a command, a rule of conduct. **2** a writ, a warrant. [f. L *praeceptum* f. *praecipere* warn, instruct]

preceptor /prɪˈseptə(r)/ *n.* a teacher, an instructor. —**preceptorial** /-ˈtɔrɪ(ə)l/ *adj.*, **preceptress** *n.fem.* [as prec.]

precession /prɪˈseʃ(ə)n/ *n.* the slow movement of the axis of a spinning body round another axis (e.g. that of a spinning-top, initially vertical but describing a cone round its original position as the top slows down). —**precession of the equinoxes**, the apparent slow retrograde motion of the equinoctial points along the ecliptic; the resulting earlier occurrence of the equinoxes in each successive sidereal year. [f. L (as PRECEDE)]

pre-Christian /pri:ˈkrɪstjən/ *adj.* before Christianity.

precinct /ˈpri:sɪŋkt/ *n.* **1** an enclosed area, especially round a place of worship. **2** (in full **pedestrian precinct**) an area in a town where traffic is prohibited. **3** (in *pl.*) environs. **4** (*US*) a subdivision of a county, city, or ward for election and police purposes. [f. L (*praecingere* encircle)]

preciosity /preʃɪˈɒsɪtɪ/ *n.* over-refinement,

especially in choice of words. [f. OF f. L (as foll.)]

precious /ˈpreʃəs/ *adj.* **1** of great value or worth. **2** beloved; much prized. **3** affectedly refined. **4** (*colloq.*, often *iron.*) considerable. —*adv.* (*colloq.*) extremely, very. —**precious metals,** gold, silver, and platinum. **precious stone,** a piece of mineral having great value, especially as used in jewellery. —**preciously** *adv.*, **preciousness** *n.* [f. OF f. L *pretiosus* (*pretium* price)]

precipice /ˈpresɪpɪs/ *n.* a vertical or steep face of a rock, cliff, mountain, etc. [f. F f. L (as PRECIPITATE)]

precipitance /prɪˈsɪpɪt(ə)ns/ *n.* (also **precipitancy**) rash haste. [f. obs. F (as foll.)]

precipitate /prɪˈsɪpɪteɪt/ *v.t.* **1** to cause to happen suddenly or soon; to make occur prematurely. **2** to send rapidly into a certain state or condition. **3** to throw down headlong. **4** to cause (a substance) to be deposited in solid form from a solution. **5** to condense (a vapour) into drops which fall as rain etc. —/-tət/ *adj.* headlong, violently hurried; (of a person or act) hasty, rash, inconsiderate. —/-tət/ *n.* a substance precipitated from a solution; moisture condensed from vapour and falling as rain etc. —**precipitately** *adv.* [f. L *praecipitare* (*praeceps* headlong)]

precipitation /prɪsɪpɪˈteɪʃ(ə)n/ *n.* **1** precipitating, being precipitated. **2** rash haste. **3** rain or snow etc. falling to the ground; the quantity of this. [f. F or L (as prec.)]

precipitous /prɪˈsɪpɪtəs/ *adj.* of or like a precipice, dangerously steep; precipitate. —**precipitously** *adv.* [f. obs. F f. L (as PRECIPITATE)]

précis /ˈpreɪsi:/ *n.* (*pl.* same /-i:z/) a summary, an abstract. —*v.t.* to make a précis of. [F, = foll.]

precise /prɪˈsaɪs/ *adj.* **1** accurately expressed. **2** exact, definite. **3** scrupulous in being exact. [f. F f. L (*praecidere* cut short)]

precisely *adv.* **1** in a precise manner, exactly. **2** in exact terms. **3** (as a reply) quite so, as you say. [f. prec.]

precision /prɪˈsɪʒ(ə)n/ *n.* **1** accuracy. **2** (*attrib.*) characterized by or adapted for precision. [f. F or L (as PRECISE)]

preclude /prɪˈklu:d/ *v.t.* to exclude the possibility of, to prevent. [f. L *praecludere* (*prae* before, *claudere* shut)]

precocious /prɪˈkəʊʃəs/ *adj.* (of a person) having developed certain abilities or characteristics earlier than is usual; (of abilities etc.) showing such development. —**precocity** /prɪˈkɒsɪtɪ/ *n.*, **precociously** *adv.* [f. L *praecox* prematurely ripe]

precognition /pri:kɒgˈnɪʃ(ə)n/ *n.* (supposed) foreknowledge, especially of a supernatural kind.

Pre-Columbian /prɪkəˈlʌmbɪən/ *adj.* of the period before the discovery of America by Columbus.

preconceive /pri:kənˈsi:v/ *v.t.* to form (an idea or opinion etc.) beforehand.

preconception /pri:kənˈsepʃ(ə)n/ *n.* a preconceived idea; a prejudice.

pre-condition /pri:kənˈdɪʃ(ə)n/ *n.* a condition that must be fulfilled before something else can happen.

precursor /pri:ˈkɜ:sə(r)/ *n.* **1** a forerunner, a harbinger. **2** a thing that precedes a later and more developed form. [f. L (*praecurrere* run before)]

predacious /prɪˈdeɪʃəs/ *adj.* (of an animal) predatory. [f. L *praeda* plunder]

pre-date /pri:ˈdeɪt/ *v.t.* to antedate.

predator /ˈpredətə(r)/ *n.* a predatory animal. [f. L (*praedari* seize as plunder)]

predatory *adj.* **1** (of an animal) preying naturally upon others. **2** plundering or exploiting others. [as prec.]

predecease /pri:dɪˈsi:s/ *v.t.* to die earlier than (another person).

predecessor /ˈpri:dɪsesə(r)/ *n.* **1** a former holder of an office or position with respect to a later holder. **2** an ancestor. **3** a thing to which something else has succeeded. [f. OF f. L (as PRE-, DECEASE)]

predella /prɪˈdelə/ *n.* **1** an altar-step; a painting on the vertical face of this. **2** a raised shelf at the back of an altar; a painting or sculpture on this. [It., = stool]

predestination /prɪdestɪˈneɪʃ(ə)n/ *n.* God's foreordaining of all that happens, or that certain souls are destined for salvation and eternal life and others are not. [f. L *praedestinare* (*prae* before, *destinare* destine)]

predestine /pri:ˈdestɪn/ *v.t.* to determine beforehand; to ordain by divine will or as if by fate. [as prec.]

predetermine /pri:dɪˈtɜ:mɪn/ *v.t.* to decide beforehand, to predestine. —**predetermination** /-ˈneɪʃ(ə)n/ *n.*

predicable /ˈpredɪkəb(ə)l/ *adj.* that may be predicated or affirmed. [as PREDICATE]

predicament /prɪˈdɪkəmənt/ *n.* a difficult or unpleasant situation. [as PREDICATE]

predicate /ˈpredɪkeɪt/ *v.t.* to assert or affirm as true or existent. —/-kət/ *n.* **1** (in logic) what is predicated (e.g. *mortal* in *all men are mortal*). **2** (*Gram.*) what is said about the subject of a sentence etc. (e.g. *went home* in *John went home*). —**predication** /-ˈkeɪʃ(ə)n/ *n.* [f. L *praedicare* proclaim]

predicative /prɪˈdɪkətɪv/ *adj.* forming part or all of the predicate (e.g. *old* in *the dog is old* but not in *the old dog*). —**predicatively** *adv.* [as prec.]

predict /prɪˈdɪkt/ *v.t.* to foretell, to prophesy. —**predictor** *n.* [f. L *praedicere* (*prae* before, *dicere* say)]

predictable *adj.* that can be predicted or is to be expected. —**predictability** /-ˈbɪlɪtɪ/ *n.*, **predictably** *adv.* [f. prec.]

prediction /prɪˈdɪkʃ(ə)n/ *n.* **1** predicting, being predicted. **2** a thing predicted. [f. PREDICT]

predilection /priːdɪˈlekʃ(ə)n/ *n.* a preference or special liking. [f. F f. L *praediligere* prefer]

predispose /priːdɪˈspəʊz/ *v.t.* **1** to influence favourably in advance. **2** to render liable or inclined. —**predisposition** /-pəˈzɪʃ(ə)n/ *n.*

predominant /prɪˈdɒmɪnənt/ *adj.* predominating; being the strongest or main element. —**predominance** *n.*, **predominantly** *adv.* [as foll.]

predominate /prɪˈdɒmɪneɪt/ *v.i.* **1** to have or exert control, to be superior. **2** to be the stronger or main element. [f. L (*prae* before, *dominari* dominate)]

pre-dynastic /priːdaɪˈnæstɪk/ *adj.* of the period before dynasties, especially in ancient Egypt.

pre-eminent /priːˈemɪnənt/ *adj.* excelling others, outstanding. —**pre-eminence** *n.*, **pre-eminently** *adv.*

pre-empt /priːˈempt/ *v.t.* to obtain by pre-emption; to appropriate beforehand; to forestall. [back-formation f. foll.]

pre-emption /priːˈempʃ(ə)n/ *n.* the purchase or taking of a thing by one person or party before an opportunity is offered to others. [f. L (*prae* before, *emere* buy)]

pre-emptive /priːˈemptɪv/ *adj.* pre-empting; (of a military action) intended to prevent an attack by disabling the enemy. [as prec.]

preen *v.t.* (of a bird) to tidy (the feathers) with the beak; (of a person) to smarten (oneself or one's clothes etc). —**preen oneself,** to congratulate oneself, to show self-satisfaction. [var. of obs. *prune* v., assoc. with dial. *preen* pierce]

pre-exist /priːɪgˈzɪst/ *v.t./i.* to exist beforehand or prior to. —**pre-existence** *n.*

prefab /ˈpriːfæb/ *n.* (*colloq.*) a prefabricated building. [abbr.]

prefabricate /priːˈfæbrɪkeɪt/ *v.t.* to manufacture in sections that are ready for assembly on a site. —**prefabrication** /-ˈkeɪʃ(ə)n/ *n.*

preface /ˈprefəs/ *n.* **1** an introduction to a book, stating its subject, scope, etc. **2** the preliminary part of a speech. —*v.t.* **1** to provide or introduce with a preface. **2** to lead up to (an event). [f. OF f. L (*prae* before, *fari* speak)]

prefatory /ˈprefətərɪ/ *adj.* of or serving as a preface, introductory. [as prec.]

prefect /ˈpriːfekt/ *n.* **1** the chief administrative officer of certain departments in France, Japan, etc. **2** a senior pupil in a school etc. authorized to maintain discipline. [f. OF f. L (*praeficere* set in authority)]

prefecture /ˈpriːfektjʊə(r)/ *n.* a district under the government of a prefect; a prefect's office or tenure. [f. F or L (as prec.)]

prefer /prɪˈfɜː(r)/ *v.t.* (**-rr-**) **1** to choose as more desirable, to like better. **2** to submit (information, an accusation, etc.) for consideration. **3** to promote (a person to an office). [f. OF f. L *praeferre* (*prae* before, *ferre* bear)]

preferable /ˈprefərəb(ə)l/ *adj.* to be preferred; more desirable. —**preferably** *adv.* [f. prec.]

preference /ˈprefərəns/ *n.* **1** preferring, being preferred. **2** a thing preferred. **3** the favouring of one person etc. before others. **4** a prior right. —**in preference to,** as a thing preferred over (another). **preference shares** *or* **stock,** shares or stock on which a dividend is paid before profits are distributed to holders of ordinary shares etc. [f. F f. L (as PREFER)]

preferential /prefəˈrenʃ(ə)l/ *adj.* of or involving preference; giving or receiving favour. —**preferentially** *adv.* [as prec.]

preferment /prɪˈfɜːmənt/ *n.* promotion to an office. [f. PREFER]

prefigure /priːˈfɪgə(r)/ *v.t.* to represent or imagine beforehand.

prefix /ˈpriːfɪks/ *n.* **1** a verbal element placed at the beginning of a word to qualify the meaning (e.g. *ex-*, *non-*). **2** a title placed before a name (e.g. *Mr*). —*v.t.* **1** to put as an introduction. **2** to join as a prefix (to a word).

preform /priːˈfɔːm/ *v.t.* to form beforehand.

pregnant /ˈpregnənt/ *adj.* **1** (of a woman or female animal) having a child or young developing in the womb. **2** full of meaning, significant or suggestive. **3** (with *with*) full of. **4** fruitful in results. —**pregnancy** *n.* [f. F or L, prob. f. *prae* before, (*g*)*nasci* be born]

prehensile /prɪˈhensaɪl/ *adj.* (of a tail or limb) capable of grasping things. [f. F f. L (*prehendere* seize)]

prehistoric /priːhɪˈstɒrɪk/ *adj.* **1** of the period before written records. **2** (*derog.*) antiquated, long out of date. —**prehistorically** *adv.*, **prehistory** /-ˈhɪstərɪ/ *n.* [f. F (as PRE-, HISTORIC)]

pre-ignition /priːɪgˈnɪʃ(ə)n/ *n.* the premature firing of an explosive mixture in an internal combustion engine.

prejudge /priːˈdʒʌdʒ/ *v.t.* to pass judgement on (a person) before a trial or proper enquiry; to form a premature judgement on.

prejudice /ˈpredʒʊdɪs/ *n.* **1** a preconceived opinion, like, or dislike. **2** injury to someone's rights etc. —*v.t.* **1** (esp. in *p.p.*) to cause to have a prejudice. **2** to injure (a person's right etc.). —**without prejudice,** without detriment to an existing right or claim. [f. OF f. L (*prae* before, *judicium* judgement)]

prejudicial /predʒʊ'dɪʃ(ə)l/ *adj.* causing prejudice; detrimental (to rights, interests, etc.). —**prejudicially** *adv.*

prelacy /'preləsɪ/ *n.* **1** church government by prelates. **2** prelates collectively. **3** the office or rank of prelate. [f. AF f. L (as foll.)]

prelate /'prelət/ *n.* a high ecclesiastical dignitary, e.g. a bishop. —**prelatical** /prɪ'lætɪk(ə)l/ *adj.* [f. OF f. L *praelatus* (as PREFER)]

prelim /prɪ'lɪm/ *n.* **1** (*colloq.*) a preliminary examination. **2** (in *pl.*; also /'pri:lɪmz/) the front matter of a book, the pages preceding the text. [abbr.]

preliminary /prɪ'lɪmɪnərɪ/ *adj.* introductory, preparatory. —*n.* (usu. in *pl.*) a preliminary action or arrangement. —*adv.* preparatory. —**preliminarily** *adv.* [f. F (as PRE-, L *limen* threshold)]

prelude /'prelju:d/ *n.* **1** an action, event, or situation that precedes another and leads up to it. **2** the introductory part of a poem etc. **3** (*Mus.*) the introductory movement or first part of a suite; a short piece of music of a similar type. —*v.t./i.* to serve as a prelude to; to introduce with a prelude. [f. F or L *praeludium* (*prae* before, *ludere* play)]

pre-marital /pri:'mærɪt(ə)l/ *adj.* of the time before marriage; occurring before marriage.

premature /'premətjʊə(r)/ *adj.* occurring or done before the usual or proper time, too early; hasty; (of a baby) born at least three weeks before the expected time. —**prematurely** *adv.*, **prematureness** *n.*, **prematurity** /-'tjʊərɪtɪ/ *n.* [f. L, = very early (*prae* early, *maturus* mature)]

premedication /pri:medɪ'keɪʃ(ə)n/ *n.* (also (*colloq.*) **premed**) medication in preparation for an operation etc.

premeditate /pri:'medɪteɪt/ *v.t.* (esp. in *p.p.*) to plan beforehand. —**premeditation** /-'teɪʃ(ə)n/ *n.*

pre-menstrual /pri:'menstrʊəl/ *adj.* of the time immediately before each menstruation.

premier /'premɪə(r)/ *adj.* first in importance, order, or time. —*n.* **1** (orig. short for *premier minister*) a Prime Minister. **2** the head of the government of a province of Canada or State of Australia. —**premiership** *n.* [f. OF, = first, f. L (as PRIMARY)]

première /'premɪeə(r)/ *n.* the first performance or showing of a play or film. —*v.t.* to give a première of. [F, fem. of *premier* adj. (as prec.)]

premise /'premɪs/ *n.* **1** a premiss. **2** (in *pl.*) a house or building with its grounds and appurtenances. **3** (*Law*) the houses, lands, or tenements previously specified in a document etc. —**on the premises,** in the house etc. concerned. [f. OF f. L *praemissa* (*praemittere* send in front)]

premiss /'premɪs/ *n.* a statement from which another is inferred. [var. of prec.]

premium /'pri:mɪəm/ *n.* **1** an amount to be paid for a contract of insurance. **2** a sum added to interest, wages, etc. **3** a reward or prize. —**at a premium,** above the usual or nominal price, highly valued. **Premium (Savings) Bond,** a British government security without interest but with chances of cash prizes. **put a premium on,** to provide or act as an incentive to; to attach special value to. [f. L *praemium* reward]

premolar /pri:'məʊlə(r)/ *n.* a tooth nearer the front of the mouth than the molars. —*adj.* of these teeth.

premonition /pri:mə'nɪʃ(ə)n, pre-/ *n.* a forewarning, a presentiment. —**premonitory** /prɪ'mɒnɪtərɪ/ *adj.* [f. F or L (*praemonēre* warn)]

pre-natal /pri:'neɪt(ə)l/ *adj.* of the period before being born or before childbirth.

preoccupation /pri:ɒkjʊ'peɪʃ(ə)n/ *n.* **1** the state of being preoccupied. **2** a thing that engrosses one's mind.

preoccupy /pri:'ɒkjʊpaɪ/ *v.t.* **1** (of a thought etc.) to dominate or engross the mind of so as to exclude other thoughts; (in *p.p.*) inattentive because of this. **2** to appropriate beforehand.

pre-ordain /pri:ɔ:'deɪn/ *v.t.* to decree or determine beforehand.

prep *n.* school work that a pupil is required to do outside lessons; a school period when this is done. —**prep school,** a preparatory school. [abbr.]

preparation /prepə'reɪʃ(ə)n/ *n.* **1** preparing, being prepared. **2** a specially prepared substance. **3** = prep. **4** (usu. in *pl.*) a thing done to make ready. [f. OF f. L (as PREPARE)]

preparatory /prɪ'pærətərɪ/ *adj.* serving to prepare, introductory. —*adv.* in a preparatory way. —**preparatory school,** a school preparing pupils for a higher school or (*US*) for a college or university. [f. L (as foll.)]

prepare /prɪ'peə(r)/ *v.t.* **1** to make or get ready. **2** to make (food or other substances) ready for use; to assemble (a meal etc.) for eating. —**be prepared to,** to be disposed or willing to. [f. F or L *praeparare* (*prae* before, *parare* make ready)]

prepay /pri:'peɪ/ *v.t.* to pay (a charge) beforehand; to pay the postage on (a letter or parcel etc.) beforehand, e.g. by buying and affixing a stamp. —**prepayment** *n.*

preponderate /prɪ'pɒndəreɪt/ *v.i.* to be greater in influence, quantity, or number; to weigh more; to predominate. —**preponderance** *n.*,

preponderant *adj*., **preponderantly** *adv*. [f. L *praeponderare* (*prae* before, *pondus* weight)]

preposition /prepəˈzɪʃ(ə)n/ *n*. a word governing (and usually preceding) a noun or pronoun and expressing the relation to another word or element (e.g. the man *on* the platform, came *after* dinner, went *by* train). —**prepositional** *adj*. [f. L (*praeponere* place in front)]

prepossess /pri:pəˈzes/ *v.t.* **1** (usu. in *pass*., of an idea etc.) to take possession of (a person). **2** to prejudice (usu. favourably and at first sight). —**prepossession** *n*.

prepossessing *adj*. attractive, making a good impression on others. [f. prec.]

preposterous /prɪˈpɒstərəs/ *adj*. utterly absurd, outrageous; contrary to nature, reason, or common sense. —**preposterously** *adv*. [f. L, lit. = back to front (*prae* before, *posterus* coming after)]

prepuce /ˈpri:pju:s/ *n*. the foreskin; a similar structure at the tip of the clitoris. [f. L *praeputium*]

Pre-Raphaelite /pri:ˈræfɪəlaɪt/ *n*. an artist or writer in the mid-19th c. who aimed at producing work in the spirit that prevailed before the time of Raphael.

prerequisite /pri:ˈrekwɪzɪt/ *adj*. required as a pre-condition. —*n*. a prerequisite thing.

prerogative /prɪˈrɒgətɪv/ *n*. a right or privilege exclusive to an individual or class. [f. OF or L *praerogativa*, orig. = tribe voting first (*praerogare* ask first)]

presage /ˈpresɪdʒ/ *n*. **1** an omen, a portent. **2** a presentiment. —/ also prɪˈseɪdʒ/ *v.t.* **1** to portend, to be an advance sign of. **2** to predict, to have a presentiment of. [f. F f. L *praesagium* (*prae* before, *sagire* perceive keenly)]

presbyter /ˈprezbɪtə(r)/ *n*. (in the Episcopal Church) a minister of the second order, a priest; (in the Presbyterian Church) an elder. [L f. Gk, = elder]

Presbyterian /prezbɪˈtɪərɪən/ *adj*. (of a Church) governed by elders all of equal rank, especially the national Church of Scotland. —*n*. a member of the Presbyterian Church; an adherent of the Presbyterian system. —**Presbyterianism** *n*. [f. L *presbyterium* (as foll.)]

presbytery /ˈprezbɪtərɪ/ *n*. **1** a body of presbyters, especially the court next above the kirk-session. **2** the eastern part of a chancel. **3** the house of a Roman Catholic priest. [f. OF f. L f. Gk (as PRESBYTER)]

preschool /ˈpri:sku:l/ *adj*. of the time before a child is old enough to attend school.

prescient /ˈpresɪənt/ *adj*. having foreknowledge or foresight. —**prescience** *n*. [f. L *praescire* (*prae* before, *scire* know)]

prescribe /prɪˈskraɪb/ *v.t.* **1** to lay down as a course or rule to be followed. **2** to advise the use of (a medicine etc.). [f. L *praescribere* direct in writing]

prescript /ˈpri:skrɪpt/ *n*. an ordinance, a law, a command. [f. L *praescriptum* (as prec.)]

prescription /prɪˈskrɪpʃ(ə)n/ *n*. **1** prescribing. **2** a doctor's (usually written) instruction for the composition and use of a medicine; a medicine thus prescribed. [f. OF f. L (as PRESCRIBE)]

prescriptive /prɪˈskrɪptɪv/ *adj*. **1** prescribing; laying down rules. **2** based on prescription; prescribed by custom. [as PRESCRIBE]

presence /ˈprezəns/ *n*. **1** being present in a place; the place where a person is. **2** a person's appearance or bearing, especially when imposing. **3** a person or thing that is present. —**presence of mind**, calmness and self-command in a sudden difficulty etc. [f. OF f. L (as foll.)]

present[1] /ˈprez(ə)nt/ *adj*. **1** being in the place in question. **2** now existing, occurring, or being such. **3** now being considered etc. **4** (*Gram*.) expressing an action etc. now going on or habitually performed. —*n*. **1** the time now passing. **2** (*Gram*.) the present tense. —**at present**, now. **by these presents**, (*Law*) by this document. **for the present**, just now, as far as the present is concerned. **present-day** *adj*. of this time, modern. [f. OF f. L (*praeesse* be at hand)]

present[2] /ˈprez(ə)nt/ *n*. a thing given. [as prec.]

present[3] /prɪˈzent/ *v.t.* **1** to introduce (a person) to another or others. **2** to give as a gift or award; to offer for acceptance, attention, consideration, etc. **3** to show, to reveal (a quality etc.). **4** to level or aim (a weapon). —**present arms**, to hold a rifle etc. vertically in front of the body as a salute. —**presenter** *n*. [f. OF f. L *praesentare* (as PRESENT[1])]

presentable /prɪˈzentəb(ə)l/ *adj*. of good appearance, fit to be presented. —**presentability** /-ˈbɪlɪtɪ/ *n*., **presentably** *adv*. [f. prec.]

presentation /prezənˈteɪʃ(ə)n/ *n*. **1** presenting, being presented. **2** a thing presented. [as PRESENT[3]]

presentiment /prɪˈzentɪmənt/ *n*. a vague expectation, a foreboding (esp. of evil). [f. obs. F (as PRE-, SENTIMENT)]

presently *adv*. **1** soon, after a short time. **2** (esp. *US* & *Sc*.) at the present time, now. [f. PRESENT[1]]

preservative /prɪˈzɜ:vətɪv/ *n*. a substance for preserving perishable foodstuffs etc. —*adj*. tending to preserve. [as foll.]

preserve /prɪˈzɜ:v/ *v.t.* **1** to keep safe; to keep in an unchanged condition; to retain (a quality or condition). **2** to keep from decay; to treat (food etc.) so as to prevent decomposition or fermentation. **3** to protect (game, or a river etc.) for private use. —*n.* **1** (also in *pl.*) preserved fruit, jam. **2** a place where game etc. is preserved. **3** a sphere regarded by a person as being for him alone. —**preservation** /prezə'veɪʃ(ə)n/ *n.*, **preserver** *n.* [f. OF f. L *praeservare* (*prae* before, *servare* keep)]

preside /prɪ'zaɪd/ *v.i.* to be chairman or president; to have the position of authority or control. [f. F f. L *praesidēre* (*prae* before, *sedēre* sit)]

presidency /'prezɪdənsɪ/ *n.* the office of president; the period of this. [f. Sp. or It. f. L (as prec.)]

president /'prezɪdənt/ *n.* **1** the head of a republican State. **2** a person who is head of a society or council etc.; the head of some colleges; (*US*) the head of a university or company etc.; the person in charge of a meeting. —**presidential** /-'denʃ(ə)l/ *adj.* [f. OF f. L (as PRESIDE)]

presidium /prɪ'sɪdɪəm/ *n.* a standing committee in a Communist organization, especially that of the Supreme Soviet in the Soviet Union which functions as the ultimate legislative authority when the Soviet itself is not sitting. [f. Russ. f. L *praesidium* garrison (as PRESIDE)]

press[1] *v.t./i.* **1** to apply steady force to (a thing in contact). **2** to compress or squeeze (a thing) so as to flatten, shape, or smooth it or extract juice etc.; to make by pressing; to squeeze out (juice etc.); to iron (clothes etc.). **3** to be urgent, to require immediate action. **4** to throng closely; to push one's way; to hasten. **5** to exert pressure on (an enemy etc.); to oppress. **6** to urge or entreat; to make an insistent demand (upon). **7** to force the acceptance of; to insist upon. **8** (in golf) to strike the ball imperfectly by trying too hard for a long hit. —*n.* **1** pressing. **2** a device or machinery for compressing, flattening, or shaping something, or for extracting juice. **3** a printing-press; a printing or publishing firm. **4** newspapers and periodicals generally; journalists and photographers etc. involved in these; publicity in newspapers etc. **5** crowding; a throng of people. **6** haste; the pressure of affairs. **7** a large usually shelved cupboard for clothes, books, etc. —**be pressed for**, to have barely enough (time etc.). **go** *or* **send to press**, to go or send to be printed. **press agent**, a person employed to attend to advertising and press publicity. **press conference**, an interview given to a body of journalists. **press-gallery** *n.* a gallery for reporters especially in a legislative assembly. **press-stud** *n.* a small fastening device engaged by pressing the two parts together. **press-up** *n.* (usu. in *pl.*) an exercise in which a person lying prone presses down on the hands to straighten the arms so that head, shoulders, and trunk are raised. [f. OF f. L *pressare* frequent. of *premere* press]

press[2] *v.t.* (*hist.*) to force to serve in the army or navy. —**press-gang** *n.* (*hist.*) a body of men employed to force men to serve in the army or navy; a group using coercive methods; (*v.t.*) to force into service. **press into service**, to bring into use as a makeshift. [alt. of obs. *prest* f. OF, = loan, advance pay, f. L *praestare* furnish]

pressing *adj.* urgent; urging strongly. —*n.* a thing made by pressing, especially a gramophone record; a series of such made at one time. [f. PRESS[1]]

pressure /'preʃə(r)/ *n.* **1** the exertion of continuous force on or against a body by another in contact with it; the force so exerted; the amount of this (expressed by the force on a unit area), especially that of the atmosphere. **2** urgency. **3** an affliction or difficulty. **4** a constraining influence. —*v.t.* to apply pressure to; to coerce, to persuade. —**pressure-cooker** *n.* a sealed pan for cooking food in a short time under steam pressure. —**pressure group**, a group seeking to influence a policy by concerted action and propaganda. [f. L (as PRESS[1])]

pressurize *v.t.* **1** to raise to a high pressure; (esp. in *p.p.*) to maintain normal atmospheric pressure in (an aircraft cabin etc.) at high altitude. **2** coerce. —**pressurized water reactor**, a nuclear reactor in which the coolant is water at high pressure. —**pressurization** *n.* [f. prec.]

prestidigitator /prestɪ'dɪdʒɪteɪtə(r)/ *n.* a conjuror. —**prestidigitation** /-'teɪʃ(ə)n/ *n.* [f. F (as PRESTO, DIGIT)]

prestige /pre'sti:ʒ/ *n.* influence or good reputation derived from past achievements, associations, etc. —*adj.* having or conferring prestige. [F, = illusion, glamour (as foll.)]

prestigious /pre'stɪdʒəs/ *adj.* having or showing prestige. [orig. = deceptive, f. L (*praestigiae* juggler's tricks)]

presto /'prestəʊ/ *adv.* (*Mus.*) in quick tempo. —*n.* (*pl.* **-os**) (*Mus.*) a movement to be played this way. [It. f. L *praestus* (*praesto* ready)]

pre-stressed /pri:'strest/ *adj.* (of concrete) strengthened by means of stretched wires within it (see CONCRETE).

presumably /prɪ'zju:məblɪ/ *adv.* it is or may be reasonably presumed. [f. foll.]

presume /prɪ'zju:m/ *v.t./i.* **1** to suppose to be true, to take for granted. **2** to take the liberty, to be impudent enough, to venture; to be presumptuous. —**presume on** *or* **upon**, to take advantage of or make unscrupulous use of (a person's good nature etc.). [f. OF f. L *praesumere* anticipate]

presumption /prɪˈzʌmpʃ(ə)n/ *n.* **1** presumptuous behaviour. **2** presuming a thing to be true; a thing that is, or may be, presumed to be true; a ground for presuming something. [as prec.]

presumptive /prɪˈzʌmptɪv/ *adj.* giving grounds for presumption. —**presumptively** *adv.* [as PRESUME]

presumptuous /prɪˈzʌmptjʊəs/ *adj.* behaving with impudent boldness; acting without due authority. —**presumptuously** *adv.*, **presumptuousness** *n.* [as PRESUME]

presuppose /priːsəˈpəʊz/ *v.t.* **1** to assume beforehand. **2** to imply the existence of. —**presupposition** /-sʌpəˈzɪʃ(ə)n/ *n.* [f. OF (as PRE-, SUPPOSE)]

pre-tax /priːˈtæks/ *adj.* (of income) before the deduction of taxes.

pretence /prɪˈtens/ *n.* **1** pretending, make-believe. **2** a claim, e.g. to merit or knowledge. **3** false profession of purpose, a pretext. **4** ostentation, show. —**in pretence,** (in heraldry) borne on an inescutcheon to indicate pretension or claim. [f. AF (as foll.)]

pretend /prɪˈtend/ *v.t./i.* **1** to claim or assert falsely so as to deceive. **2** to imagine to oneself in play. **3** (in *p.p.*) falsely claimed to be such. —**pretend to,** to lay claim to (a right or title); to profess to have. —**pretendedly** *adv.* [f. F or L *praetendere* (*prae* before, *tendere* stretch)]

pretender *n.* **1** one who pretends. **2** one who claims a throne or title. —**Old Pretender, Young Pretender,** the son and grandson of James II, claimants to the British throne. [f. prec.]

pretension /prɪˈtenʃ(ə)n/ *n.* **1** the assertion of a claim; a justifiable claim. **2** pretentiousness. [f. L (as PRETEND)]

pretentious /prɪˈtenʃəs/ *adj.* making an excessive claim to great merit or importance; ostentatious. —**pretentiously** *adv.*, **pretentiousness** *n.* [f. F (as prec.)]

preterite /ˈpretərɪt/ *adj.* (*Gram.*) expressing a past action or state. —*n.* (*Gram.*) the preterite tense of a verb. [f. OF or L (*praeterire* pass)]

preternatural /priːtəˈnætʃr(ə)l/ *adj.* outside the ordinary course of nature, unusual. —**preternaturally** *adv.* [f. L (*praeter naturam* beyond nature)]

pretext /ˈpriːtekst/ *n.* an ostensible reason, an excuse offered. [f. L *praetextus* outward display (*prae* before, *texere* weave)]

pretty /ˈprɪtɪ/ *adj.* **1** attractive in a delicate way. **2** fine or good of its kind. **3** (*iron.*) considerable. —*adv.* fairly, moderately. —**pretty much,** *or* **nearly** *or* **well,** almost, very nearly. **pretty-pretty** *adj.* with the prettiness overdone. —**prettily** *adv.*, **prettiness** *n.* [OE]

prevail /prɪˈveɪl/ *v.i.* **1** to be victorious, to gain the mastery. **2** to be more usual or prominent; to exist or occur in general use or experience. —**prevail on** *or* **upon,** to persuade. [f. L *praevalere* (*prae* before, *valere* have power)]

prevalent /ˈprevələnt/ *adj.* generally existing or occurring, predominant. —**prevalence** *n.*, **prevalently** *adv.* [as prec.]

prevaricate /prɪˈværɪkeɪt/ *v.i.* to speak or act evasively or misleadingly; to quibble, to equivocate. —**prevarication** /-ˈkeɪʃ(ə)n/ *n.*, **prevaricator** *n.* [f. L, orig. = walk crookedly]

prevent /prɪˈvent/ *v.t.* to keep from happening or doing something; to hinder, to make impossible. —**prevention** *n.* [orig. = anticipate, f. L *praevenire* come before]

preventable *adj.* that may be prevented. [f. prec.]

preventative /prɪˈventətɪv/ *adj.* & *n.* preventive. [as foll.]

preventive /prɪˈventɪv/ *adj.* serving to prevent, especially preventing a disease. —*n.* a preventive agent, measure, drug, etc. —**preventive detention,** the imprisonment of a person thought likely to commit a crime. [f. PREVENT]

preview /ˈpriːvjuː/ *n.* a showing of a film or play etc. before it is seen by the general public. —*v.t.* to view or show in advance of public presentation.

previous /ˈpriːvɪəs/ *adj.* **1** coming before in time or order; prior. **2** done or acting hastily. —**previous to,** before. —**previously** *adv.* [f. L *praevius* (*prae* before, *via* way)]

pre-war /priːˈwɔː(r), *attrib.* ˈpriː-/ *adj.* occurring or existing before a war.

prey /preɪ/ *n.* **1** an animal that is hunted or killed by another for food. **2** a person or thing that falls victim to an enemy, disease, fear, etc. —*v.i.* **prey on** *or* **upon,** to seek or take as prey; (of a disease or emotion etc.) to exert a harmful influence on. —**beast** *or* **bird of prey,** one that kills and devours other animals. [f. OF f. L *praeda* plunder]

price *n.* **1** the amount of money for which a thing is bought or sold. **2** what must be given or done etc. to obtain or achieve something. **3** the odds in betting. —*v.t.* to fix or find the price of (a thing for sale); to estimate the value of. —**at a price,** at a high cost. **price-fixing** *n.* the maintaining of prices at a certain level by agreement between competing sellers. **price on a person's head,** a reward for his capture or death. **price-tag** *n.* a label on an item showing its price, the cost of an undertaking etc. **what price . . . ?** (*colloq.*) what is the chance of . . . ?; the vaunted . . . has failed. [f. OF *pris* f. L *pretium*]

priceless *adj.* **1** invaluable. **2** (*colloq.*) very amusing or absurd. [f. PRICE + -LESS]

pricey *adj.* (*compar.* **pricier;** *superl.* **priciest**) (*colloq.*) expensive. [f. PRICE]

prick *v.t./i.* **1** to pierce slightly, to make a small hole in. **2** to mark with pricks or dots. **3** to trouble mentally. **4** to feel a pricking sensation. —*n.* **1** a small hole or mark made by pricking. **2** a pain caused (as) by pricking. **3** (*vulgar*) the penis; (*derog.*) a man. —**prick out,** to plant out (seedlings) in small holes pricked in soil. **prick up one's ears,** (of a dog) to make the ears erect when on the alert; (of a person) to become suddenly attentive. —**pricker** *n.* [OE]

prickle *n.* **1** a small thorn. **2** the hard-pointed spine of a hedgehog etc. **3** a prickling sensation. —*v.t./i.* to affect or be affected with a sensation as of pricking. [OE]

prickly *adj.* **1** having prickles. **2** (of a person) irritable. **3** tingling. —**prickly heat,** inflammation of the skin near the sweat glands with an eruption of vesicles and a prickly sensation, common in hot countries. **prickly pear,** a cactus of the genus *Opuntia* with a pear-shaped edible fruit; this fruit. —**prickliness** *n.* [f. prec.]

pride *n.* **1** a feeling of elation or satisfaction at one's achievements, qualities, or possessions etc. **2** an object of this feeling. **3** unduly high opinion of one's own importance or merits etc. **4** a proper sense of what befits one's position, self-respect. **5** the best condition, the prime. **6** a group or company (of lions etc.). —*v.refl.* (with *on* or *upon*) to be proud of. —**pride of place,** the most important or prominent position. **take pride in,** to be proud of. [OE (as PROUD)]

prie-dieu /priː'djɜː/ *n.* a desk at which one kneels for prayer. [F, = pray God]

priest /priːst/ *n.* an ordained minister of the Roman Catholic or Orthodox Church, or of the Anglican Church (above a deacon and below a bishop); an official minister of a non-Christian religion. —*v.t.* to make (a deacon) into a priest. —**priesthood** *n.* [OE (ult. as PRESBYTER)]

priestess /'priːstɪs/ *n.* a female priest of a non-Christian religion. [f. prec.]

priestly *adj.* of, like, or befitting a priest. —**priestliness** *n.* [f. PRIEST]

prig *n.* a self-righteously correct or moralistic person. —**priggery** *n.*, **priggish** *adj.* [orig. unkn.]

prim *adj.* (of a person or manner) stiffly formal and precise, demure; disliking what is rough or improper, prudish. —**primly** *adv.*, **primness** *n.* [prob. f. OF *prin* fine, delicate (as PRIME)]

prima ballerina /'priːmə/ a ballerina of the highest rank; the leading ballerina of a ballet company. [It., = first female dancer]

primacy /'praɪməsɪ/ *n.* **1** pre-eminence. **2** the office of primate. [as PRIMATE]

prima donna /priːmə 'dɒnə/ **1** the chief female singer in an opera. **2** a temperamentally self-important person. [It., = first lady]

prima facie /praɪmə 'feɪʃiː/ at first sight; (of evidence) based on the first impression. [L]

primal /'praɪm(ə)l/ *adj.* **1** primitive, primeval. **2** chief, fundamental. —**primally** *adv.* [f. L (as PRIME[1])]

primary /'praɪmərɪ/ *adj.* **1** earliest in time or order; first in a series, not derived. **2** of the first importance, chief. —*n.* a thing that is primary; a primary feather etc.; (*US*) a primary election. —**primary battery,** a battery producing electricity by an irreversible chemical action. **primary education,** the first stage of education in which the rudiments of knowledge are taught. **primary election,** (*US*) an election to appoint party conference delegates or to select candidates for a principal election. **primary feather,** any of the large flight-feathers of a bird's wing. **primary school,** a school where primary education is given. —**primarily** *adv.* [f. L *primarius* (as PRIME[1])]

primate /'praɪmət, -eɪt/ *n.* **1** an archbishop. **2** a member of the order Primates, the highest order of mammals, including man, apes, monkeys, tarsiers, and lemurs. —**Primate of England,** the Archbishop of York. **Primate of all England,** the Archbishop of Canterbury. [f. OF f. L, = of first rank (*primus* first)]

prime[1] *adj.* **1** chief, most important. **2** first-rate, excellent. **3** primary, fundamental. —*n.* **1** the state of highest perfection; the best part. **2** a beginning. **3** the second canonical hour of prayer. **4** a prime number. —**prime minister,** the chief minister of a government. **prime number,** a natural number other than 1 that can be divided exactly only by itself and unity. **prime time,** the time at which a television etc. audience is expected to be largest. [f. OF f. L *primus* first]

prime[2] *v.t.* **1** to prepare (a thing) for use or action; to prepare (a gun) for firing or (an explosive) for detonation. **2** to pour (liquid) into a pump to make it start working. **3** to prepare (wood etc.) for painting by applying a substance that prevents the paint from being absorbed. **4** to equip (a person) with information. **5** to ply (a person) with food or drink in preparation for something. [orig. unkn.]

primer[1] *n.* a substance used to prime wood etc. [f. PRIME[2]]

primer[2] *n.* **1** an elementary school-book for

teaching children to read. **2** a small book introducing a subject. [f. AF f. L (as PRIMARY)]

primeval /praɪˈmiːv(ə)l/ *adj.* of the first age of the world; ancient, primitive. —**primevally** *adv.* [f. L (*primus* first, *aevum* age)]

primitive /ˈprɪmɪtɪv/ *adj.* **1** ancient, at an early stage of civilization. **2** undeveloped, crude, simple. —*n.* an untutored painter with a direct naïve style; a picture by such a painter. —**primitively** *adv.*, **primitiveness** *n.* [f. OF or L *primitivus* first of its kind (as PRIME¹)]

primogeniture /praɪməʊˈdʒenɪtʃə(r)/ *n.* **1** the fact of being the first-born child. **2** the right of succession or inheritance belonging to the eldest son. [f. L (*primo* first, *genitura* begetting)]

primordial /praɪˈmɔːdɪ(ə)l/ *adj.* existing at or from the beginning, primeval. —**primordially** *adv.* [f. L (as PRIME¹, *ordiri* begin)]

primp *v.t.* to make (the hair etc.) tidy; to smarten. [dial. var. of PRIM]

primrose /ˈprɪmrəʊz/ *n.* **1** a plant (*Primula vulgaris*) bearing a pale yellow flower in spring; its flower. **2** the colour of this flower. **primrose path,** the unjustified pursuit of ease or pleasure (with ref. to Shakespeare *Hamlet* I. iii. 50). [f. OF f. L, = first rose]

primula /ˈprɪmjʊlə/ *n.* a herbaceous perennial of the genus *Primula* with flowers of various colours. [L, dim. of *primus* first]

Primus /ˈpraɪməs/ *n.* [P] a brand of portable stove burning vaporized paraffin for cooking etc. [L, = first]

prince *n.* **1** a male member of a royal family who is not a reigning king; (in Britain) a son or grandson of the sovereign. **2** a ruler, especially of a small State. **3** a nobleman of some countries. **4** a person who is outstanding of his kind. —**prince consort,** the husband of a reigning queen who is himself a prince. **Prince of Wales,** a title usually conferred on the heir apparent to the British throne. **Prince Regent,** a prince acting as regent, especially the future George IV who was regent 1811-20. [f. OF f. L *princeps* chieftain]

princeling /ˈprɪnslɪŋ/ *n.* a young or petty prince. [f. prec. + -LING]

princely *adj.* **1** of or worthy of a prince. **2** sumptuous, splendid, generous. [f. PRINCE]

princess /prɪnˈses, *attrib.* ˈprɪn-/ *n.* **1** the wife of a prince. **2** a female member of a royal family who is not a reigning queen; (in Britain) a daughter or granddaughter of the sovereign. —**princess royal,** a title that may be conferred on the sovereign's eldest daughter. [as PRINCE]

principal /ˈprɪnsɪp(ə)l/ *adj.* (usu. *attrib.*) first in rank or importance, chief; main, leading. —*n.* **1** the person with highest authority in an organization etc.; the head of some schools, colleges, and universities. **2** a person who takes a leading part in an activity or in a play etc. **3** a capital sum as distinct from interest or income. **4** a person for whom another is agent. **5** a civil servant of the grade below Secretaries. —**principal boy,** the leading male part in a pantomime, usually played by a woman. **principal parts,** the parts of a verb from which all the other parts can be deduced. —**principally** *adv.* [as PRINCE]

principality /prɪnsɪˈpælɪtɪ/ *n.* a State ruled by a prince. —**the Principality,** Wales. [as prec.]

principle /ˈprɪnsɪp(ə)l/ *n.* **1** a fundamental truth or a general law or doctrine that is used as a basis of reasoning or action. **2** a personal code of right conduct; (in *pl.*) such rules of conduct. **3** a general law in physics. **4** a law of nature forming the basis for the construction or working of a machine. **5** (*Chem.*) a constituent of a substance, especially one giving rise to some quality etc. **6** a fundamental source, a primary element. —**in principle,** as regards fundamentals but not necessarily in detail. **on principle,** from a settled moral motive. [f. OF f. L *principium* source]

prink *v.t.* **1** to make (oneself) smart. **2** (of a bird) to preen. **3** to walk daintily. [cf. *prank* in similar sense, rel. to Du. *pronk* finery]

print *n.* **1** an indentation or mark left on a surface by the pressure of a thing in contact. **2** printed lettering or writing; words in printed form. **3** a picture or design printed from a block or plate. **4** a photograph produced from a negative. **5** a printed cotton fabric. —*v.t.* **1** to produce (a book, picture, etc., or *absol.*) by applying inked types, blocks, or plates to paper etc.; to express or publish in print. **2** to impress or stamp (a surface, or a mark or design in or on a surface). **3** to write (words, letters, or *absol.*) without joining, in imitation of typography. **4** to produce (a photograph) from a negative. **5** to mark (a textile fabric) with a coloured design. **6** to impress (an idea or scene etc. on the mind or memory). **7** to make (a printed circuit or component). —**in** *or* **out of print,** (of a book etc.) available (or no longer available) from a publisher. **printed circuit,** an electric circuit with lines of conducting material printed on a flat insulating sheet (instead of using wires). [f. OF f. L *premere* (as PRESS)]

printer *n.* **1** one whose job or business is the printing of books, newspapers, etc. **2** a device that prints. [f. prec.]

printing *n.* **1** the production of printed books etc. **2** a single impression of a book. **3** printed letters or writing imitating them. —**printing-press** *n.* a machine for printing from types or plates etc. [f. PRINT]

printout *n.* computer output in printed form.

prior /ˈpraɪə(r)/ *adj.* earlier; coming before in

time, order, or importance. —*n.* a superior of a religious house or order; (in an abbey) the deputy of the abbot. —**prior to,** before. —**prioress** *n.fem.* [f. OF or L, = former (*prae* before)]

priority /praɪˈɒrɪtɪ/ *n.* **1** being earlier or more important; precedence in rank etc.; the right to be first. **2** an interest having a prior claim to attention. [as prec.]

priory /ˈpraɪərɪ/ *n.* a monastery governed by a prior; a nunnery governed by a prioress. [f. AF (as PRIOR)]

prise /praɪz/ *v.t.* to force open or out by leverage. [OF, = levering instrument (as PRIZE²)]

prism /ˈprɪz(ə)m/ *n.* **1** a solid figure whose two ends are equal parallel rectilinear figures, and whose sides are parallelograms. **2** a transparent body of this form, usually triangular, with refracting surfaces at an acute angle with each other. —**prism binoculars,** binoculars in which triangular prisms are used to shorten the instrument. [f. L f. Gk *prisma* thing sawn (*prizō* saw)]

prismatic /prɪzˈmætɪk/ *adj.* of or like a prism; (of colours) formed or distributed (as if) by a transparent prism. —**prismatically** *adv.* [f. F f. Gk (as prec.)]

prison /ˈprɪz(ə)n/ *n.* **1** a place where people are confined after being convicted (or in certain cases accused) of crimes. **2** any place of custody or confinement. **3** imprisonment, confinement. —**prison-camp** *n.* a camp serving as a prison for prisoners of war etc. [f. OF f. L *prensio* (*prehendere* seize)]

prisoner /ˈprɪz(ə)nə(r)/ *n.* **1** a person kept in prison. **2** (also **prisoner at the bar**) a person in custody on a criminal charge and on trial. **3** a captive. **4** a person or thing held in confinement or in another's grasp etc. —**prisoner of conscience,** a person in prison for an act of conscientious protest etc. **prisoner of war,** one who has been captured in a war. **take prisoner,** to seize and hold as a prisoner. [f. AF (as prec.)]

prissy *adj.* prim. —**prissily** *adv.*, **prissiness** *n.* [perh. f. PRIM + SISSY]

pristine /ˈprɪsti:n, -aɪn/ *adj.* **1** in the original condition, unspoilt. **2** (D) spotless, fresh as if new. **3** ancient, primitive. [f. L *pristinus* former]

privacy /ˈprɪvəsɪ, ˈpraɪ-/ *n.* being alone or undisturbed; the right to this; freedom from intrusion or public attention. [f. foll.]

private /ˈpraɪvɪt/ *adj.* **1** belonging to an individual, one's own, personal. **2** confidential, not to be disclosed to others. **3** kept from public knowledge or observation; (of a place) secluded. **4** not open to the public. **5** (of a person) not holding a public office or official position. **6** (of medical treatment) conducted outside the State system, at the patient's expense. —*n.* **1** a private soldier. **2** (in *pl.*) the genitals. —**in private,** privately, not in public. **private bill,** a parliamentary bill affecting an individual or corporation only. **private company,** one with restricted membership and no issue of shares. **private detective,** one engaged privately, outside the official police force. **private enterprise,** a business or businesses privately owned and free of direct State control. **private eye,** (*colloq.*) a private detective. **private hotel,** one not obliged to take all comers. **private means,** income from investments etc., apart from earned income. **private member,** an MP not holding a government appointment. **private parts,** the genitals. **private school,** a school supported wholly by pupils' fees and by endowments. **private sector,** the part of the economy free of direct State control. **private soldier,** an ordinary soldier, not an officer. —**privately** *adv.* [f. L *privatus* (*privare* deprive)]

privateer /praɪvəˈtɪə(r)/ *n.* **1** an armed vessel owned and officered by private persons holding a commission from the government and authorized to use it against a hostile nation, especially in the capture of merchant shipping. **2** its commander. —**privateering** *n.* [f. prec.]

privation /praɪˈveɪʃ(ə)n/ *n.* a lack of the comforts or necessaries of life. [as PRIVATE]

privative /ˈprɪvətɪv/ *adj.* consisting in or showing loss or absence; (*Gram.*) indicating lack or absence. [f. F or L (as prec.)]

privatize /ˈpraɪvətaɪz/ *v.t.* to assign to private enterprise, to denationalize. —**privatization** /-ˈzeɪʃ(ə)n/ *n.* [f. PRIVATE]

privet /ˈprɪvɪt/ *n.* a bushy evergreen shrub of the genus *Ligustrum*, with smooth dark-green leaves, used for hedges. [orig. unkn.]

privilege /ˈprɪvɪlɪdʒ/ *n.* a special right, advantage, or immunity belonging or granted to a person, group, or office; a special benefit or honour. —*v.t.* to invest with a privilege. [f. OF f. L, = law affecting an individual (*privus* private, *lex legis* law)]

privileged *adj.* having a privilege or privileges. [f. prec.]

privy /ˈprɪvɪ/ *adj.* hidden, secluded, secret. —*n.* (*archaic* or *US*) a lavatory. —**Privy Council,** a sovereign's or governor-general's private counsellors; (in the USA) an advisory council consisting of the heads of executive departments. **Privy Counsellor,** a member of the Privy Council of the UK. **privy purse,** an allowance from public revenue for the sovereign's private expenses. **privy seal,** a State seal formerly attached to documents that were afterwards to pass the Great Seal, or to ones of lesser importance not requiring the Great Seal. **Lord Privy Seal,** a senior Cabinet minister without official duties (formerly keeper of the privy seal). **privy to,** sharing in the secret of (a person's plans etc.). —**privily** *adv.* [f. OF *privé* f. L, = PRIVATE]

prize[1] *n.* **1** something that can be won in a competition or lottery etc. **2** an award given as a symbol of victory or superiority. **3** something striven for or worth striving for. —*adj.* **1.** to which a prize is awarded. **2** excellent of its kind. —*v.t.* to value highly. —**prize-fighter** *n.* a professional boxer; (*hist.*) one who fought to the finish (in bare fists) for a prize or stake, before the introduction of Queensberry Rules. [var. of PRICE]

prize[2] *n.* a ship or property captured in naval warfare. [f. OF *prise* f. L *prehendere* seize]

prize[3] var. of PRISE.

PRO *abbr.* public relations officer.

pro[1] /prəʊ/ *n.* (*pl.* **pros**) (*colloq.*) a professional. [abbr.]

pro[2] /prəʊ/ *adj.* & *prep.* (of an argument or reason) for, in favour (of). —*n.* (*pl.* **pros**) a reason for or in favour (esp. in **pros and cons**). [L, = for, on behalf of]

pro-[1] *prefix* **1** as a substitute or deputy for, substituted for. **2** favouring, siding with. **3** forwards (*produce*). **4** forwards and downwards (*prostrate*). **5** onwards (*proceed*). **6** in front of (*protect*). [f. L (as prec.)]

pro-[2] *prefix* before (in time, place, or order). [f. Gk *pro* before]

probability /prɒbəˈbɪlɪtɪ/ *n.* **1** being probable; likelihood. **2** something that is probable, the most probable event. **3** the extent to which an event is likely to occur, measured by the ratio of favourable cases to all possible cases. —**in all probability,** most probably. [f. F or L (as foll.)]

probable /ˈprɒbəb(ə)l/ *adj.* that may be expected to happen or prove true; likely. —*n.* a probable candidate, member of a team, etc. —**probably** *adv.* [f. OF or L (as PROVE)]

probate /ˈprəʊbeɪt/ *n.* **1** the official proving of a will. **2** a verified copy of a will with a certificate as handed to the executors. [f. L (as PROVE)]

probation /prəˈbeɪʃ(ə)n/ *n.* **1** the testing of the character or abilities of a person, especially of a candidate for employment or membership. **2** a system whereby certain offenders are supervised by an official as an alternative to imprisonment. —**on probation,** undergoing probation before full admission to employment or membership, or as a criminal offender. **probation officer,** an official supervising offenders on probation. —**probationary** *adj.* [as PROVE]

probationer *n.* a person undergoing a probationary period of testing, e.g. a hospital nurse at an early stage of training. [f. prec.]

probative /ˈprəʊbətɪv/ *adj.* affording proof. [as PROVE]

probe *n.* **1** a device for exploring an otherwise inaccessible place or object etc.; a blunt-ended surgical instrument for exploring a wound. **2** an unmanned exploratory spacecraft transmitting information about its environment. **3** a penetrating investigation. —*v.t.* **1** to explore with a probe. **2** to penetrate (a thing) with a sharp instrument. **3** to examine or enquire into closely. [f. L *proba* (as PROVE)]

probity /ˈprəʊbɪtɪ/ *n.* uprightness, honesty. [f. F or L (*probus* good)]

problem /ˈprɒbləm/ *n.* **1** a doubtful or difficult matter requiring solution. **2** something hard to understand, accomplish, or deal with. **3** an exercise in mathematics or chess etc. [f. OF or L f. Gk. *problēma* (PRO-², *ballō* throw)]

problematic /prɒbləˈmætɪk/ *adj.* (also **problematical**) **1** hard to understand, accomplish, or deal with. **2** doubtful, questionable. —**problematically** *adv.* [f. F or L f. Gk (as prec.)]

proboscis /prəˈbɒsɪs/ *n.* (*pl.* **-ises**) **1** an elephant's trunk; the long flexible snout of the tapir etc. **2** an elongated part of the mouth of some insects, used for sucking things. [L f. Gk (PRO-², *boskō* feed)]

procedure /prəˈsi:djə(r), -dʒə(r)/ *n.* **1** a mode of conducting business or a legal action. **2** a series of actions conducted in a certain order or manner. —**procedural** *adj.* [f. F (as foll.)]

proceed /prəˈsi:d/ *v.i.* **1** to go forward or onward; to make one's way. **2** to continue in an activity; (of an action) to be carried on or continued. **3** to adopt a course of action. **4** to go on to say. **5** to start a lawsuit (against a person). **6** to come forth, to originate. [f. OF f. L (PRO-¹, *cedere* go)]

proceeding *n.* **1** an action, a piece of conduct. **2** (in *pl.*) a legal action. **3** (in *pl.*) a published report of discussions or a conference. [f. prec.]

proceeds /ˈprəʊsi:dz/ *n.pl.* money produced by a sale or performance etc. [pl. of obs. *proceed* n. f. PROCEED]

process[1] /ˈprəʊses/ *n.* **1** a series of actions or proceedings used in making, manufacturing, or achieving something. **2** progress, course. **3** a natural or involuntary operation or series of changes. **4** a lawsuit; a summons or writ. **5** a natural appendage or outgrowth on an organism. —*v.t.* to put through a manufacturing or other process; to treat, especially so as to prevent decay. [as PROCEED]

process[2] /prəˈses/ *v.i.* (*colloq.*) to walk in procession. [back-formation f. foll.]

procession /prəˈseʃ(ə)n/ *n.* a number of persons or vehicles etc. going along in orderly succession, especially as a ceremony or demonstration or festivity; the action of this. [as PROCEED]

processional *adj.* of processions; used, carried, or sung in processions. —*n.* a processional hymn. [f. L (as prec.)]

processor /ˈprəusesə(r)/ *n.* a machine that processes things. —**central processor,** the part of a computer that controls and co-ordinates the activities of the other units and performs the actions specified in the program. [f. PROCESS¹]

proclaim /prəˈkleɪm/ *v.t.* **1** to announce publicly or officially, to declare; to declare (a person) to be (a king, traitor, etc.). **2** to reveal as being. [f. L *proclamare* cry out (PRO-¹, *clamare* cry)]

proclamation /prɒkləˈmeɪʃ(ə)n/ *n.* **1** proclaiming. **2** a thing proclaimed. [f. prec.]

proclivity /prəˈklɪvɪtɪ/ *n.* a tendency or natural inclination. [f. L (*proclivis* inclined f. PRO-¹, *clivus* slope)]

procrastinate /prəˈkræstɪneɪt/ *v.i.* to defer action; to be dilatory. —**procrastination** /-ˈneɪʃ(ə)n/ *n.*, **procrastinator** *n.* [f. L (PRO-¹, *crastinus* of tomorrow)]

procreate /ˈprəukrɪeɪt/ *v.t.* to bring (offspring) into existence by the natural process of reproduction. —**procreation** /-ˈeɪʃ(ə)n/ *n.*, **procreative** *adj.* [f. L (as PRO-¹, CREATE)]

Procrustean /prəˈkrʌstɪən/ *adj.* seeking to enforce uniformity by violent methods. [f. *Procrustes*, robber in Gk legend, who made travellers fit a bed by lopping or stretching them]

proctor /ˈprɒktə(r)/ *n.* each of two university officers at Oxford and Cambridge, appointed annually and having mainly disciplinary functions. —**Queen's** *or* **King's Proctor,** an official who has the right to intervene in probate, divorce, and nullity cases when collusion or suppression of facts is alleged. —**proctorial** /-ˈtɔːrɪəl/ *adj.*, **proctorship** *n.* [syncopation of PROCURATOR]

procuration /prɒkjʊəˈreɪʃ(ə)n/ *n.* **1** procuring. **2** the function or an authorized action of an attorney. [as PROCURE]

procurator /ˈprɒkjʊəreɪtə(r)/ *n.* an agent or proxy, especially with power of attorney. —**procurator fiscal,** an officer of a sheriff's court in Scotland, acting as public prosecutor of a district and with other duties similar to those of a coroner. **procurator general,** the head of the Treasury law department. [as foll.]

procure /prəˈkjʊə(r)/ *v.t./i.* **1** to obtain by care or effort, to acquire. **2** to bring about. **3** to act as a procurer or procuress (of). —**procurement** *n.* [f. OF f. L (PRO-¹, *curare* look after)]

procurer *n.* one who obtains women for prostitution. —**procuress** *n.fem.* [f. OF f. L, = PROCURATOR]

prod *v.t./i.* (**-dd-**) **1** to poke. **2** to urge or stimulate to action. —*n.* **1** a poke. **2** a stimulus to action. **3** a pointed instrument for prodding things. [perh. imit.]

prodigal /ˈprɒdɪg(ə)l/ *adj.* **1** recklessly wasteful or extravagant. **2** lavish. —*n.* a prodigal person. —**prodigal son,** a repentant wastrel, a returned wanderer (Luke 15: 11-32). —**prodigality** /-ˈgælɪtɪ/ *n.*, **prodigally** *adv.* [f. L *prodigus* lavish]

prodigious /prəˈdɪdʒəs/ *adj.* **1** marvellous. **2** enormous. **3** abnormal. —**prodigiously** *adv.* [f. L (as foll.)]

prodigy /ˈprɒdɪdʒɪ/ *n.* **1** a person with exceptional qualities or abilities, especially a precocious child. **2** a marvellous thing; a wonderful example of something. [f. L *prodigium* portent]

produce /prəˈdjuːs/ *v.t.* **1** to bring forward for consideration, inspection, or use. **2** to bring (a play or performance etc.) before the public; to be the producer of. **3** to manufacture (goods) from raw materials etc. **4** to bear or yield (offspring, fruit, a harvest, etc.); to bring into existence; to cause or bring about (a reaction etc.). **5** to extend or continue (a line). —/ˈprɒdjuːs/ *n.* what is produced, especially agricultural and natural products generally; the amount of this. [f. L *producere* (PRO-¹, *ducere* lead)]

producer /prəˈdjuːsə(r)/ *n.* **1** one who produces articles or agricultural products etc. (opp. *consumer*). **2** a person who directs the acting of a play. **3** a person in charge of the expenditure, schedule, and quality of a film or a broadcast programme. [f. prec.]

product /ˈprɒdʌkt/ *n.* **1** a thing or substance produced by a natural process or by manufacture. **2** a result. **3** a quantity obtained by multiplying. [as PRODUCE]

productive /prəˈdʌktɪv/ *adj.* **1** of or engaged in the production of goods; producing commodities of exchangeable value. **2** producing much. **3** (with *of*) producing, giving rise to. —**productively** *adv.*, **productiveness** *n.* [f. F or L (as PRODUCE)]

production /prəˈdʌkʃ(ə)n/ *n.* **1** producing; being produced or manufactured, especially in large quantities. **2** the total yield. **3** a thing produced, especially a literary or artistic work, a play or film, etc. [f. OF f. L (as prec.)]

productivity /prɒdʌkˈtɪvɪtɪ/ *n.* capacity to produce; effectiveness of productive effort, especially in industry. [f. prec.]

proem /ˈprəʊem/ *n.* an introductory discourse. [f. OF or L f. Gk *prooimion* (PRO-², *oimē* song)]

Prof. *abbr.* Professor.

profane /prəˈfeɪn/ *adj.* **1** not sacred, secular. **2** irreverent, blasphemous. —*v.t.* to treat (a sacred thing) with irreverence or disregard; to violate or pollute (what is entitled to respect). —**profanation** /-ˈneɪʃ(ə)n/ *n.*, **profanely** *adv.* [f. OF f. L, = before (i.e. outside) the temple]

profanity /prəˈfænɪtɪ/ *n.* a profane act or profane language, blasphemy. [f. prec.]

profess /prəˈfes/ *v.t.* **1** to claim openly to have (a quality or feeling); to pretend, to allege. **2** to declare. **3** to affirm one's faith in or allegiance to. [f. L *profitēri* declare publicly (PRO-¹, *fatēri* confess)]

professed /prəˈfest/ *adj.* **1** avowed, openly acknowledged by oneself. **2** pretended, alleged. **3** having taken the vows of a religious order. —**professedly** *adv.* [f. prec.]

profession /prəˈfeʃ(ə)n/ *n.* **1** an occupation, especially in some branch of advanced learning or science. **2** the body of persons engaged in this. **3** a declaration, an avowal. [f. OF f. L (as PROFESS)]

professional *adj.* **1** of, belonging to, or connected with a profession. **2** having or showing the skill of a professional. **3** engaged in a specified activity as one's main paid occupation (often as distinct from *amateur*). —*n.* a professional person. —**professionalism** *n.*, **professionally** *adv.* [f. prec.]

professor /prəˈfesə(r)/ *n.* **1** a university teacher of the highest (in the USA, of high) rank. **2** one who makes a profession (of a religion etc.). —**professorial** /-ˈsɔːrɪəl/ *adj.*, **professorship** *n.* [f. OF or L (as PROFESS)]

proffer *v.t.* to offer. [f. AF (as PRO-¹, OFFER)]

proficient /prəˈfɪʃənt/ *adj.* able to do something correctly or competently through training or practice, skilled. —**proficiency** *n.*, **proficiently** *adv.* [f. L *proficere* make progress]

profile /ˈprəʊfaɪl/ *n.* **1** an outline (especially of a human face) as seen from one side; a representation of this. **2** a short biographical or character sketch. **3** a vertical cross-section of a structure or of layers of soil etc. —*v.t.* to represent in profile. —**keep a low profile,** to remain inconspicuous. [f. obs. It. *profilare* draw in outline]

profit /ˈprɒfɪt/ *n.* **1** an advantage or benefit obtained from doing something. **2** money gained in a business transaction; the excess of returns over outlay. —*v.t./i.* **1** to be beneficial (to). **2** to obtain an advantage or benefit. —**profit-sharing** *n.* the practice of allowing the employees of a company to share directly in its profits. [f. OF f. L *profectus* (as PROFICIENT)]

profitable *adj.* bringing profit or benefits. —**profitability** /-ˈbɪlɪtɪ/ *n.*, **profitably** *adv.* [f. prec.]

profiteer /prɒfɪˈtɪə(r)/ *v.t./i.* to make or seek excessive profits out of others' needs, especially in times of scarcity. —*n.* a person who profiteers. [f. PROFIT]

profiterole /prəˈfɪtərəʊl/ *n.* a small hollow cake of choux pastry with sweet or savoury filling. [F, dim. of *profit* (as PROFIT)]

profligate /ˈprɒflɪgət/ *adj.* **1** licentious, dissolute. **2** recklessly wasteful or extravagant. —*n.* a profligate person. —**profligacy** *n.* [f. L (*profligare* overthrow, ruin)]

pro forma /prəʊˈfɔːmə/ **1** for form's sake. **2** (in full **pro forma invoice**) an invoice sent to a purchaser in advance of the goods for the completion of business formalities. [L]

profound /prəˈfaʊnd/ *adj.* **1** having or showing great knowledge or insight into a subject. **2** requiring much study or thought. **3** deep, intense; far-reaching. —**profoundly** *adv.*, **profundity** /-ˈfʌndɪtɪ/ *n.* [f. OF f. L *profundus* deep]

profuse /prəˈfjuːs/ *adj.* **1** lavish, extravagant. **2** plentiful. —**profusely** *adv.*, **profuseness** *n.*, **profusion** /-ˈfjuːʒ(ə)n/ *n.* [f. L *profusus* (PRO-¹, *fundere* pour)]

progenitor /prəˈdʒenɪtə(r)/ *n.* an ancestor; a predecessor, an original. [f. OF f. L (PRO-¹, *gignere* beget)]

progeny /ˈprɒdʒənɪ/ *n.* **1** offspring. **2** an outcome. [f. OF f. L *progenies* (as prec.)]

progesterone /prəʊˈdʒestərəʊn/ *n.* a sex hormone causing uterine changes in the latter part of the menstrual cycle and maintaining pregnancy. [f. G (as PRO-², GESTATION, STEROID)]

prognosis /prɒgˈnəʊsɪs/ *n.* (*pl.* **-oses** /-iːz/) a forecast or advance indication, especially of the course of a disease. [L f. Gk (PRO-², *gignōskō* know)]

prognostic /prɒgˈnɒstɪk/ *n.* an advance indication or omen; a prediction. —*adj.* foretelling, predictive. [f. OF f. L f. Gk (as prec.)]

prognosticate /prɒgˈnɒstɪkeɪt/ *v.t.* to foretell or foresee; (of a thing) to betoken. —**prognostication** /-ˈkeɪʃ(ə)n/ *n.*, **prognosticator** *n.* [f. L (as PROGNOSIS)]

programmable *adj.* that may be programmed. [f. foll.]

programme /ˈprəʊgræm/ *n.* (*US* & in computing **program**) *n.* **1** a plan of intended procedure. **2** a descriptive list or notice of a series of events; these events. **3** a broadcast performance or entertainment. **4 program,** a series of instructions to control the operation of a computer. —*v.t.* (**-mm-**) **1** to make a programme of. **2** program, to express (a problem) or instruct (a computer etc.) by means of a program. —**programmatic** /-ˈmætɪk/ *adj*., **programmer** *n*. [f. L f. Gk (*programphō* write publicly)]

progress /ˈprəugres/ *n*. **1** forward or onward movement. **2** an advance or development, especially to a better state. **3** (*archaic*) a State journey, especially by a royal person. —/prəˈgres/ *v.t./i*. **1** to move forward or onward. **2** to advance or develop, especially to a better state. **3** to deal with at successive stages. —**in progress**, taking place, in the course of occurrence. [f. L *progressus* (*progredi* go forward)]

progression /prəˈgreʃ(ə)n/ *n*. **1** progressing. **2** a succession or series. [f. OF or L (as prec.)]

progressive /prəˈgresɪv/ *adj*. **1** making continuous forward movement. **2** proceeding steadily or in regular degrees. **3** favouring political or social reform; advancing in social conditions, efficiency, etc. **4** (of a disease etc.) continuously increasing in severity or extent. **5** (of a card-game, dance, etc.) with a periodic change of partners. **6** (of taxation) at rates increasing with the sum taxed. **7** (*Gram*., of a tense) expressing an action in progress. —*n*. an advocate of a progressive policy. —**progressively** *adv*., **progressiveness** *n*. [f. F or L (as PROGRESS)]

prohibit /prəˈhɪbɪt/ *v.t*. to forbid or prevent. —**prohibited degrees**, see DEGREE. —**prohibitor** *n*., **prohibitory** *adj*. [f. L *prohibēre*]

prohibition /prəuhɪˈbɪʃ(ə)n, prəuɪ-/ *n*. **1** forbidding, being forbidden. **2** an edict or order that forbids something. **3** the forbidding by law of the manufacture and sale of intoxicants, especially (**Prohibition**) that established in the USA in 1919 and repealed in 1933. [f. OF or L (as prec.)]

prohibitionist *n*. an advocate of legal prohibition. [f. prec.]

prohibitive /prəˈhɪbɪtɪv/ *adj*. prohibiting; (of prices, costs, taxes, etc.) extremely high. —**prohibitively** *adv*. [f. F or L (as PROHIBIT)]

project /ˈprɒdʒekt/ *n*. **1** a plan or scheme; a planned undertaking. **2** a task set as an educational exercise, requiring students to do their own research and present the results. —/prəˈdʒekt/ *v.t./i*. **1** to plan or contrive (a scheme etc.). **2** to cause (a light, shadow, or image) to fall on a surface. **3** to send or throw outward or forward. **4** to extend outwards from a surface. **5** to imagine (a thing or person or oneself) as having another's feelings, being in another situation or in the future, etc.; to attribute (one's own feelings) to another person or thing, esp. unconsciously. **6** to extrapolate (results to a future time etc.). **7** to make a projection of (the earth or sky etc.). [f. L *projicere* throw forward (PRO-¹, *jacere* throw)]

projectile /prəˈdʒektaɪl/ *n*. an object to be hurled or projected forcibly, especially from a gun. —*adj*. of or serving as a projectile. [as prec.]

projection /prəˈdʒekʃ(ə)n/ *n*. **1** projecting, being projected. **2** a thing that projects from a surface. **3** a representation on a plane surface of (any part of) the surface of the earth or of a celestial sphere. **4** a mental image viewed as objective reality. [as PROJECT]

projectionist *n*. a person who operates a projector. [f. prec.]

projector /prəˈdʒektə(r)/ *n*. an apparatus for projecting the image of a film etc. on a screen. [f. PROJECT]

prolapse /ˈprəulæps/ *n*. (also **prolapsus**) the slipping forward or downward of a part or organ, especially of the womb or rectum. —/prəˈlæps/ *v.i*. to undergo a prolapse. [f. L (PRO-¹, *labi* slip)]

prolate /ˈprəuleɪt/ *adj*. (of a spheroid) lengthened along the polar diameter. [f. L, = brought forward, prolonged]

prolegomena /prəulɪˈgɒmɪnə/ *n.pl*. a preliminary discourse or matter prefixed to a book etc. [L f. Gk, neut. pass. partic. of *prolegō* say beforehand]

proletarian /prəulɪˈteərɪən/ *adj*. of the proletariat. —*n*. a member of the proletariat. [f. L, = one who served the State not with property but with offspring (*proles*)]

proletariat /prəulɪˈteərɪət/ *n*. the working class (contrasted with the bourgeoisie). [f. F (as prec.)]

proliferate /prəˈlɪfəreɪt/ *v.t./i*. **1** to reproduce itself or grow by the multiplication of elementary parts; to produce (cells) thus. **2** to increase rapidly in numbers etc. —**proliferation** /-ˈreɪʃ(ə)n/ *n*. [f. F f. L *proles* offspring, *ferre* bear]

prolific /prəˈlɪfɪk/ *adj*. producing much offspring or output; abundantly productive. —**prolifically** *adv*. [f. L (as prec.)]

prolix /ˈprəulɪks/ *adj*. lengthy, tediously wordy. —**prolixity** /prəˈlɪksɪtɪ/ *n*. [f. OF or L *prolixus* long, extended]

prologue /ˈprəulɒg/ *n*. **1** an introduction to a poem or play etc. **2** an act or event serving as an introduction. [f. OF f. L f. Gk (as PRO-², *logos* speech)]

prolong /prəˈlɒŋ/ *v.t*. to extend in duration or spatial length. —**prolongation** /prəulɒŋˈgeɪʃ(ə)n/ *n*. [f. OF & L *prolongare* (PRO-¹, *longus* long)]

prom *n*. (*colloq*.) **1** a promenade. **2** a promenade concert. [abbr.]

promenade /prɒməˈnɑ:d/ *n*. **1** a public place for

walking, especially a paved area along the sea front in a seaside town. **2** a leisurely walk, especially for pleasure. —*v.t./i.* **1** to take a leisurely walk (through). **2** to lead (a person) about a place, especially for display. —**promenade concert,** a concert with an area for a part of the audience to stand and move about. **promenade deck,** the upper deck on a passenger ship. [F (*se promener* walk)]

promethium /prəˈmiːθɪəm/ *n.* a radioactive metallic element of the lanthanide series, symbol Pm, atomic number 61. [f. *Prometheus* in Gk mythology]

prominence /ˈprɒmɪnəns/ *n.* **1** being prominent. **2** a prominent thing. [obs. F f. L (as foll.)]

prominent *adj.* **1** jutting out, projecting. **2** conspicuous. **3** distinguished, well-known. —**prominently** *adv.* [f. L *prominēre* project (cf. EMINENT)]

promiscuous /prəˈmɪskjʊəs/ *adj.* **1** having casual sexual relations with many people. **2** casual, indiscriminate. **3** of mixed and indiscriminate composition or kinds. —**promiscuity** /prɒmɪˈskjuːɪtɪ/ *n.*, **promiscuously** *adv.* [f. L *promiscuus* (PRO-[1], *miscēre* mix)]

promise /ˈprɒmɪs/ *n.* **1** an assurance as to what one will or will not do, or of help or giving something. **2** an indication of something that may be expected to come or occur. **3** an indication of future achievement or good result. —*v.t./i.* **1** to make a promise, to give an assurance; to give (a person) a promise of (a thing); (*colloq.*) to assure. **2** to seem likely. —**promised land,** Canaan, promised by God to Abraham and his descendants (Gen. 17: 8); any place of expected happiness. [f. L *promissum* (*promittere* send forth, promise)]

promising *adj.* likely to turn out well or produce good results. —**promisingly** *adv.* [f. prec.]

promissory /ˈprɒmɪsərɪ/ *adj.* conveying or implying a promise. —**promissory note,** a signed document containing a written promise to pay a stated sum. [as PROMISE]

promontory /ˈprɒməntərɪ/ *n.* a point of high land jutting out into the sea etc., a headland. [f. L *promunturium* (perh. f. PRO-[1], *mons* mountain)]

promote /prəˈməʊt/ *v.t.* **1** to raise (a person) to a higher rank or office. **2** to help forward or encourage (an enterprise or result). **3** to publicize (a product) in order to sell it. **4** to initiate (a project). **5** to take the necessary steps for the passing of (a private bill in Parliament). —**promotion** *n.*, **promotional** *adj.* [f. L *promovēre* (as PRO-[1], *movēre* move)]

promoter *n.* one who promotes an enterprise financially, especially the formation of a joint-stock company or the holding of a sporting event etc. [f. prec.]

prompt *adj.* **1** acting or done without delay or at once. **2** punctual. —*adv.* punctually. —*v.t.* **1** to incite or stimulate (a person) to action. **2** to inspire or give rise to (a feeling or action). **3** to help (an actor etc., or *absol.*) by supplying the words that come next; to assist (a hesitant person) with a suggestion etc. —*n.* a thing said to help the memory, especially of an actor. —**prompt side,** the side of a stage (usually to the actors' left) where the prompter is placed. —**promptitude** *n.*, **promptly** *adv.*, **promptness** *n.* [f. OF or L (*promere* produce)]

prompter *n.* a person (placed out of sight of the audience) who prompts the actors on a stage. [f. prec.]

promulgate /ˈprɒməlgeɪt/ *v.t.* to make known to the public, to disseminate; to proclaim (a decree or news). —**promulgation** /-ˈgeɪʃ(ə)n/ *n.*, **promulgator** *n.* [f. L *promulgare* (PRO-[1], *mulgēre* milk, cause to come forth)]

prone *adj.* **1** lying face downwards (opp. *supine*); lying flat, prostrate. **2** disposed (*to*), liable or likely (*to*). —**proneness** *n.* [f. L *pronus* (*pro* forwards)]

prong *n.* each of the two or more projecting pointed parts at the end of a fork etc. [perh. rel. to MLG *prange* pinching instrument]

pronged *adj.* having a specified number or kind of prongs. [f. prec.]

pronominal /prəˈnɒmɪn(ə)l/ *adj.* of or of the nature of a pronoun. [f. L (as foll.)]

pronoun /ˈprəʊnaʊn/ *n.* **1** a word used instead of a noun to designate (without naming) a person or thing. **2** a pronominal adjective. [f. PRO-[1] + NOUN, after L *pronomen*]

pronounce /prəˈnaʊns/ *v.t./i.* **1** to utter (a word or speech-sound) distinctly or correctly or in a specified way. **2** to utter or declare formally. **3** to declare as one's opinion; to pass judgement. [f. OF f. L *pronuntiare* (PRO-[1], *nuntiare* announce)]

pronounceable *adj.* (of a word etc.) that may be pronounced. [f. prec.]

pronounced *adj.* noticeable, strongly marked. [f. PRONOUNCE]

pronouncement *n.* a formal statement, a declaration. [as prec.]

pronto /ˈprɒntəʊ/ *adv.* (*slang*) promptly, quickly. [Sp. f. L, = prompt]

pronunciation /prənʌnsɪˈeɪʃ(ə)n/ *n.* the way in which a word is pronounced; a person's way of pronouncing words. [f. OF or L (as PRONOUNCE)]

proof *n.* **1** a fact or thing that shows or helps to show that something is true or exists. **2** a demonstration of the truth of something. **3** the process of testing whether something is true, good, or valid. **4** a standard of strength for distilled alcoholic liquors. **5** a trial impression of printed matter, produced for correction. **6** a trial print of a photograph. —*adj*. impervious to penetration, damage, or undesired action. —*v.t.* **1** to make a proof of (printed matter). **2** to make (a thing) proof, against something; to make (a fabric etc.) waterproof. — **-proof** *in comb*. in the sense 'impervious', 'resistant', forming adjectives (*bullet-proof*; *waterproof*) and verbs (*soundproof*). —**proof-read** *v.t.* to read and correct (printed proofs). **proof-reader** *n*. a person who does this. **proof spirit,** a mixture of alcohol and water having a standard strength. [f. OF f. L *proba* (as PROVE)]

prop[1] *n*. **1** a rigid support, especially not a structural part of the thing supported. **2** a person etc. depended on for help or support. —*v.t.* (**-pp-**) to support (as) with a prop (often with *up*). [prob. f. MDu.]

prop[2] *n*. (*colloq*.) an aircraft propeller. [abbr.]

prop[3] *n*. (*colloq*.) a stage property in a theatre. [abbr.]

propaganda /prɒpəˈgændə/ *n*. publicity intended to spread ideas or information; (usu. *derog*.) the ideas etc. thus propagated. —**propagandist** *n*. [It. f. L *congregatio de propaganda fide*, title of RC committee in charge of foreign missions (as foll.)]

propagate /ˈprɒpəgeɪt/ *v.t./i.* **1** to breed or reproduce from parent stock. **2** to disseminate (news or ideas etc.). **3** to transmit (a vibration, earthquake, etc.). **4** to be propagated. —**propagation** /-ˈgeɪʃ(ə)n/ *n*., **propagator** *n*. [f. L *propagare* multiply plants from layers (PRO-[1], *pangere* fix, layer)]

propane /ˈprəʊpeɪn/ *n*. a hydrocarbon of the paraffin series. [f. *propionic acid* (PRO-[2], Gk *piōn* fat)]

propel /prəˈpel/ *v.t.* (**-ll-**) to drive or push forward, to give onward motion to. —**propellent** *adj*. [f. L *propellere* (PRO-[1], *pellere* drive)]

propellant *n*. a propelling agent. [f. prec.]

propeller *n*. (in full **screw-propeller**) a device with blades on a revolving shaft for propelling a ship or aircraft to which it is fitted. [f. PROPEL]

propensity /prəˈpensɪtɪ/ *n*. an inclination or tendency. [f. L *propensus* inclined]

proper /ˈprɒpə(r)/ *adj*. **1** suitable, appropriate. **2** correct, according to rules. **3** respectable, in conformity with social standards or conventions. **4** real or genuine; rightly so called; (usu. placed after the noun) strictly so called. **5** belonging or relating exclusively or distinctively (*to*). **6** (*colloq*.) thorough, complete. —**proper fraction,** a fraction less than unity, with the numerator less than the denominator. **proper name** *or* **noun,** the name of an individual person, place, or thing. —**properly** *adv*. [f. OF f. L *proprius* one's own]

propertied /ˈprɒpətɪd/ *adj*. having property, especially of real estate. [f. foll.]

property /ˈprɒpətɪ/ *n*. **1** a thing or things owned. **2** real estate, a person's land or house etc. **3** a movable object used on a theatre stage or in a film etc. [f. OF f. L *proprietas* (as PROPER)]

prophecy /ˈprɒfɪsɪ/ *n*. **1** the power of prophesying. **2** a prophetic utterance. **3** the foretelling of future events. [as PROPHET]

prophesy /ˈprɒfɪsaɪ/ *v.t./i.* to speak as a prophet; to foretell future events; to foretell. [f. OF *profecier* (as foll.)]

prophet /ˈprɒfɪt/ *n*. **1** an inspired teacher, a person regarded as revealing or interpreting divine will. **2** any of the prophetical writers in the Old Testament; **the Prophets,** their writings. **3** one who foretells events. **4** a spokesman or advocate of a principle etc. **the Prophet,** Muhammad. —**prophetess** *n.fem*. [f. OF f. L f. Gk, orig. = spokesman (PRO-[2], *phēmi* speak)]

prophetic /prəˈfetɪk/ *adj*. (also **prophetical**) **1** of a prophet. **2** predicting or containing a prediction of (an event etc.). —**prophetically** *adv*. [f. F or L f. Gk (as prec.)]

prophylactic /prɒfɪˈlæktɪk/ *adj*. tending to prevent a disease or other misfortune. —*n*. a prophylactic medicine or course of action. —**prophylactically** *adv*. [f. F f. Gk (PRO-[2], *phulassō* guard)]

prophylaxis /prɒfɪˈlæksɪs/ *n*. preventive treatment against a disease etc. [f. PRO-[2] + Gk *phulaxis* guarding]

propinquity /prəˈpɪŋkwɪtɪ/ *n*. **1** nearness in place. **2** close kinship. [f. OF or L (*propinquus* near)]

propitiate /prəˈpɪʃɪeɪt/ *v.t.* to win the favour or forgiveness of, to placate. —**propitiation** /-ˈeɪʃ(ə)n/ *n*. [f. L *propitiare* (as PROPITIOUS)]

propitiatory /prəˈpɪʃətərɪ/ *adj*. serving or intended to propitiate. [as prec.]

propitious /prəˈpɪʃəs/ *adj*. favourable, giving a good omen or a suitable opportunity. —**propitiously** *adv*. [f. OF or L *propitius*]

proponent /prəˈpəʊnənt/ *n*. a person who puts forward a proposal; a person who supports a cause etc. [f. L *proponere* (as PROPOUND)]

proportion /prəˈpɔːʃ(ə)n/ *n*. **1** a fraction or comparative share of a whole. **2** a ratio. **3** the correct relation in size, amount, or degree between one thing and another or between a thing's parts. **4** (in *pl*.) dimensions, size. —*v.t.* to give correct proportions to; to make (one thing) proportionate to another.

—**proportionment** *n.* [f. OF or L (as PRO-¹, PORTION)]

proportional *adj.* in correct proportion; corresponding in size, amount, or degree. —**proportional representation,** an electoral system in which each party is allocated a number of seats in proportion to the number of votes for its candidates. —**proportionally** *adv.* [f. L (as prec.)]

proportionate /prəˈpɔːʃənət/ *adj.* in due proportion. —**proportionately** *adv.* [f. prec.]

proposal /prəˈpəʊz(ə)l/ *n.* **1** the proposing of something. **2** a course of action etc. proposed. **3** an offer of marriage. [f. foll.]

propose /prəˈpəʊz/ *v.t./i.* **1** to put forward for consideration. **2** to have and declare as one's plan or intention; to make a proposal. **3** to make an offer of marriage. **4** to offer (a person or a person's health) as the subject for the drinking of a toast. **5** to nominate (a person) as a member of a society etc. [f. OF f. L (as PROPOUND)]

proposition /prɒpəˈzɪʃ(ə)n/ *n.* **1** a proposal, a scheme proposed. **2** a statement, an assertion. **3** (*colloq.*) a thing to be considered, dealt with, or undertaken. **4** a formal statement of a theorem or problem, often including a demonstration. —*v.t.* (*colloq.*) to put a proposal to; to suggest extramarital sexual intercourse to. [f. OF or L (as foll.)]

propound /prəˈpaʊnd/ *v.t.* to put forward for consideration. —**propounder** *n.* [f. L *proponere*, lit. = place in front]

proprietary /prəˈpraɪətərɪ/ *adj.* **1** of a proprietor. **2** holding property. **3** held in private ownership. **4** manufactured and sold by one particular firm, usually under a patent. [f. L *proprietarius* (as PROPERTY)]

proprietor /prəˈpraɪətə(r)/ *n.* the holder of a property; the owner of a business. —**proprietorial** /-ˈtɔːrɪəl/ *adj.*, **proprietress** *n.fem.* [f. prec.]

propriety /prəˈpraɪɪtɪ/ *n.* **1** being proper or suitable. **2** correctness of behaviour or morals. **3** (in *pl.*) the details of correct conduct. [f. OF, = PROPERTY]

propulsion /prəˈpʌlʃ(ə)n/ *n.* driving or pushing forward. —**propulsive** *adj.* [f. obs. *propulse* v. f. L *propulsare* frequent. of *propellere* propel]

propulsor /prəˈpʌlsə(r)/ *n.* a ducted propeller which can be swivelled to give forward, upward, or downward flight to an airship. [as prec.]

pro rata /prəʊ ˈrɑːtə/ proportional; in proportion. [L, = according to the rate]

prorogue /prəˈrəʊg/ *v.t./i.* to discontinue the meetings of (a parliament etc.) without dissolving it; (of a parliament etc.) to be prorogued. —**prorogation** /prəʊrəˈgeɪʃ(ə)n/ *n.* [f. OF f. L *prorogare* prolong (PRO-¹, *rogare* ask)]

prosaic /prəˈzeɪɪk/ *adj.* **1** like prose, lacking in poetic beauty. **2** unromantic, commonplace, dull. —**prosaically** *adv.* [f. F or L (as PROSE)]

proscenium /prəʊˈsiːnɪəm/ *n.* (*pl.* **-s**) the part of a theatre stage in front of a drop or curtain, especially with the enclosing arch. [L f. Gk (as PRO-², SCENE)]

proscribe /prəˈskraɪb/ *v.t.* **1** to forbid by law. **2** to denounce as dangerous etc. **3** to put (a person) outside the protection of the law; to banish, to exile. —**proscription** /-ˈskrɪpʃ(ə)n/ *n.*, **proscriptive** /-ˈskrɪptɪv/ *adj.* [f. L *proscribere* (PRO-¹, *scribere* write)]

prose /prəʊz/ *n.* **1** written or spoken language not in verse form. **2** dull or matter-of-fact quality. —*v.i.* to talk tediously. —**prose poem,** an elevated prose composition. [f. OF f. L *prosa* (*oratio*) straightforward discourse (*prorsus* direct)]

prosecute /ˈprɒsɪkjuːt/ *v.t.* **1** to institute legal proceedings against (a person, or *absol.*) or with reference to (a crime or claim etc.). **2** to carry on or be occupied with. [f. L *prosequi* (PRO-¹, *sequi* follow)]

prosecution /prɒsɪˈkjuːʃ(ə)n/ *n.* **1** the institution and carrying on of legal proceedings. **2** the prosecuting party. **3** prosecuting, being prosecuted. [f. OF or L (as prec.)]

prosecutor /ˈprɒsɪkjuːtə(r)/ *n.* one who prosecutes, especially in a criminal court. [f. PROSECUTE]

proselyte /ˈprɒsɪlaɪt/ *n.* **1** a person converted from one opinion or belief etc. to another. **2** a Gentile convert to the Jewish faith. [f. L f. Gk (*proserkhomai* come to a place)]

proselytism /ˈprɒsɪlɪtɪz(ə)m/ *n.* **1** being a proselyte. **2** the practice of proselytizing. [f. prec.]

proselytize /ˈprɒsɪlɪtaɪz/ *v.t.* to seek to make a proselyte of (a person, or *absol.*). [f. PROSELYTE]

prosody /ˈprɒsədɪ/ *n.* the science of versification; the study of speech-rhythms. —**prosodic** /prəˈsɒdɪk/ *adj.*, **prosodically** /prəˈsɒdɪkəlɪ/ *adv.*, **prosodist** *n.* [f. L f. Gk (*pros* to, as ODE)]

prospect /ˈprɒspekt/ *n.* **1** what one is to expect; a chance (of success etc.). **2** an extensive view of a landscape etc.; a mental scene or view of matters. **3** (*colloq.*) a possible or likely customer etc. —/prəˈspekt/ *v.t./i.* to explore or search (for gold etc.); to look out *for*. —**prospector** /prəˈspektə(r)/ *n.* [f. L, = PROSPECTUS]

prospective /prəˈspektɪv/ *adj.* expected to be or occur; future, possible. [f. obs. F or L (as prec.)]

prospectus /prəˈspektəs/ *n.* a printed document describing the chief features of a school or business etc. [L, = prospect (*prospicere* look forward)]

prosper /ˈprɒspə(r)/ *v.i.* to be successful, to thrive. [f. obs. F or L *prosperare* (as PROSPEROUS)]

prosperity /prɒˈsperɪtɪ/ *n.* prosperous state or condition, wealth. [f. foll.]

prosperous /ˈprɒspərəs/ *adj.* **1** financially successful, thriving. **2** auspicious. —**prosperously** *adv.* [f. obs. F f. L *prosperus*]

prostate /ˈprɒsteɪt/ *n.* (in full **prostate gland**) the large gland round the neck of the bladder, accessory to the male genital organs. —**prostatic** /-ˈtætɪk/ *adj.* [F f. Gk *prostatēs* one who stands before]

prosthesis /ˈprɒsθɪsɪs/ *n.* (*pl.* **-theses** /-iːz/) **1** the making up of bodily deficiencies, e.g. by an artificial limb. **2** a part supplied for this. —**prosthetic** /-ˈθetɪk/ *adj.* [L f. Gk, = placing in addition]

prostitute /ˈprɒstɪtjuːt/ *n.* a woman who engages in sexual intercourse for payment; a man who engages in homosexual acts for payment. —*v.t.* to make a prostitute of (esp. *oneself*); to sell or make use of (one's honour or abilities etc.) unworthily. —**prostitution** /-ˈtjuːʃ(ə)n/ *n.* [f. L *prostituere* offer for sale (PRO-¹, *statuere* set up)]

prostrate /ˈprɒstreɪt/ *adj.* **1** lying with one's face to the ground, especially in submission or humility. **2** lying in a horizontal position. **3** overcome, overthrown. **4** physically exhausted. —/prɒˈstreɪt/ *v.t.* **1** to throw (oneself) down prostrate. **2** to overcome, to make submissive. **3** (of fatigue etc.) to reduce to extreme physical weakness. —**prostration** /prɒˈstreɪʃ(ə)n/ *n.* [f. L *prosternere* (PRO-¹, *sternere* lay flat)]

prosy /ˈprəʊzɪ/ *adj.* prosaic, dull. —**prosily** *adv.*, **prosiness** *n.* [f. PROSE]

protactinium /prəʊtækˈtɪnɪəm/ *n.* a naturally-occurring radioactive metallic element, symbol Pa, atomic number 91. [G (as PROTO- + ACTINIUM)]

protagonist /prəʊˈtægənɪst/ *n.* **1** the chief person in a drama or the plot of a story; the principal performer. **2** (**D**) a champion or advocate of a course or method etc. [f. Gk (PROTO-, *agonistēs* actor)]

protean /ˈprəʊtɪən, -ˈtiːən/ *adj.* variable, versatile; taking many forms. [f. PROTEUS]

protect /prəˈtekt/ *v.t.* **1** to keep from harm or injury. **2** to guard (a home industry) against competition by import duties on foreign goods. [f. L *protegere* (PRO-¹, *tegere* cover)]

protection /prəˈtekʃ(ə)n/ *n.* **1** protecting, being protected. **2** a person or thing that protects. **3** the system of protecting home industries. **4** immunity from molestation obtained by payment under threat of violence; money so paid. [f. OF or L (as prec.)]

protectionism *n.* the principle or practice of economic protection. —**protectionist** *n.* [f. prec.]

protective *adj.* protecting; giving or intended for protection. —**protective custody**, the detention of a person actually or allegedly for his own protection. —**protectively** *adv.* [f. PROTECT]

protector *n.* **1** a person or thing that protects. **2** a regent in charge of a kingdom during the minority or absence of a sovereign. —**protectorship** *n.*, **protectress** *n.fem.* [f. OF f. L (as PROTECT)]

protectorate /prəˈtektərət/ *n.* **1** the office of protector of a kingdom or State, especially that under the Cromwells in 1653-9. **2** protectorship of a weak or underdeveloped State by a stronger one; a State thus protected. [f. prec.]

protégé /ˈprɒteʒeɪ/ *n.* a person to whom another is protector or patron. —**protégée** *n.fem.* [F (as PROTECT)]

protein /ˈprəʊtiːn/ *n.* any of a class of large molecules which form an essential part of all living things. [f. F & G f. Gk *prōteios* primary]

pro tem /prəʊ ˈtem/ (*colloq.*) *pro tempore*. [abbr.]

pro tempore /prəʊ ˈtempərɪ/ for the time being. [L]

protest /prəˈtest/ *v.t./i.* **1** to express disapproval or dissent; (*US*) to object to (a decision etc.). **2** to declare solemnly or firmly, especially in reply to an accusation etc. **3** to write or obtain a protest in regard to (a bill). —/ˈprəʊtest/ *n.* **1** a formal statement or action of disapproval or dissent. **2** a written declaration that a bill has been presented and payment or acceptance refused. —**under protest**, unwillingly and after making protests. —**protestor** /prəˈtestə(r)/ *n.* [f. OF f. L *protestari* (PRO-¹, *testari* assert on oath)]

Protestant /ˈprɒtɪst(ə)nt/ *n.* a member or adherent of any of the Christian bodies that separated from the Roman communion in the Reformation (16th c.), or their offshoots. —**Protestantism** *n.* [f. L (as prec.)]

protestation /prɒteˈsteɪʃ(ə)n/ *n.* a solemn affirmation; a protest. [as PROTEST]

Protista /prəˈtɪstə/ *n.pl.* a kingdom of organisms (bacteria, protozoa, etc.) not distinguished as animals or plants. [f. Gk (*prōtos* first)]

proto- /prəʊtə(ʊ)-/ *in comb.* first. [f. Gk (*prōtos* first)]

protocol /ˈprəʊtəkɒl/ *n.* **1** official formality and etiquette; observance of this. **2** the original draft of a diplomatic document, especially of the agreed terms of a treaty. —*v.t./i.* (**-ll-**) to draw up a protocol or protocols; to record in a protocol. [f. OF f. L f. Gk, = flyleaf (PROTO-, *kolla* glue)]

proton /ˈprəʊtɒn/ *n.* a positively charged elementary particle found in the nuclei of all atoms. [f. Gk *prōtos* first, reflecting their character as primitive constituents of all atomic nuclei; also perhaps suggested by the name of William *Prout* (d. 1850), English chemist and physician, who suggested that hydrogen was a constituent of all the elements]

protoplasm /ˈprəʊtəplæz(ə)m/ *n.* the contents of a living cell. —**protoplasmic** /-ˈplæzmɪk/ *adj.* [f. Gk (as PROTO-, PLASMA)]

protoplast /ˈprəʊtəplæst/ *n.* (*Biol.*) the contents of a cell after the cell wall has been removed. [f. F or L f. Gk (PROTO-, *plastos* moulded; cf. PLASMA)]

prototype /ˈprəʊtətaɪp/ *n.* an original thing or person in relation to a copy or imitation or developed form; a trial model, a preliminary version (e.g. of an aeroplane). [F or f. L f. Gk (as PROTO-, TYPE)]

protozoon /prəʊtəˈzəʊən/ *n.* (*pl.* **-zoa**) an animal of the subkingdom or phylum Protozoa, usually unicellular and microscopic. —**protozoan** *adj.* & *n.* [as PROTO- + Gk *zōion* animal]

protract /prəˈtrækt/ *v.t.* to prolong in duration. —**protraction** *n.* [f. L *protrahere* (PRO-¹, *trahere* draw)]

protractor *n.* an instrument for measuring angles, usually a semicircle marked off in degrees. [f. prec.]

protrude /prəˈtruːd/ *v.t./i.* to project or cause to project from a surface; to thrust forward. —**protrusion** *n.*, **protrusive** /-ˈtruːsɪv/ *adj.* [f. L *protrudere* (PRO-¹, *trudere* thrust)]

protuberant /prəˈtjuːbərənt/ *adj.* bulging out, prominent. —**protuberance** *n.* [f. L (PRO-¹, *tuber* bump)]

proud *adj.* **1** feeling or showing justifiable pride; marked by or causing such feeling. **2** feeling oneself greatly honoured. **3** full of self-respect and independence. **4** having an unduly high opinion of one's own qualities or merits. **5** (of a thing) imposing, splendid. **6** slightly projecting; (of flesh) overgrown round a healing wound. —**do a person proud,** to treat him with great generosity or honour. —**proudly** *adv.* [OE f. OF *prud* valiant]

provable /ˈpruːvəb(ə)l/ *adj.* that may be proved. —**provability** /-ˈbɪlɪtɪ/ *n.* [f. foll.]

prove /pruːv/ *v.t./i.* **1** to give or be proof of. **2** to be found to be, to emerge as. **3** to establish the validity of (a will). **4** to rise or cause (dough) to rise. **5** (*archaic*) to test the qualities of. —**not proven,** (*Sc. Law*) the evidence is insufficient to establish guilt or innocence. **prove oneself,** to demonstrate one's abilities etc. [f. OF f. L *probare* test, demonstrate (*probus* good)]

provenance /ˈprɒvənəns/ *n.* origin, place of origin. [F, f. L *provenire* come forth (PRO-¹, *venire* come)]

Provençal /prɒvɑ̃ˈsɑːl/ *adj.* of Provence or its people or language. —*n.* **1** a native or inhabitant of Provence. **2** its dialect of French; a Romance language of this region. [f. *Provence* f. L *provincia* province]

provender /ˈprɒvɪndə(r)/ *n.* fodder; (*colloq.*) food for humans. [f. OF f. L *praebenda* (as PREBEND)]

proverb /ˈprɒvɜːb/ *n.* **1** a short pithy saying in general use, stating a truth or giving advice. **2** a person or thing that is widely known as exemplifying something. [f. OF or L *proverbium* (PRO-¹, *verbum* word)]

proverbial /prəˈvɜːbɪəl/ *adj.* **1** of or expressed in proverbs. **2** well-known, notorious. —**proverbially** *adv.* [f. L (as prec.)]

provide /prəˈvaɪd/ *v.t./i.* **1** to cause (a person) to have possession or use of something; to supply, to make available. **2** to supply the necessities of life. **3** to make due preparation (for or against a contingency). **4** to stipulate, to give as a condition. —**provided** *or* **providing (that),** on the condition or understanding that. [f. L *providēre* foresee (PRO-¹, *vidēre* see]

providence /ˈprɒvɪd(ə)ns/ *n.* **1** being provident; foresight, timely care. **2** the beneficent care of God or nature. **3** Providence, God in this aspect. [f. OF or L (as prec.)]

provident /ˈprɒvɪd(ə)nt/ *adj.* having or showing wise foresight for future needs or events; thrifty. —**Provident Society,** a Friendly Society. [as PROVIDE]

providential /prɒvɪˈdenʃ(ə)l/ *adj.* **1** of or by divine foresight or intervention. **2** opportune, lucky. —**providentially** *adv.* [f. PROVIDENCE]

provider /prəˈvaɪdə(r)/ *n.* one who provides; the breadwinner of a family etc. [f. PROVIDE]

province /ˈprɒvɪns/ *n.* **1** each of the principal administrative divisions of certain countries. **2** a district consisting of a group of adjacent dioceses, under the charge of an archbishop. **3** a sphere of responsibility or concern or of knowledge; a branch of learning. **4** (in Roman history) a territory under Roman rule, outside Italy. —**the Province,** (in recent use) Northern Ireland. **the provinces,** the whole of a country outside its capital city. [f. OF f. L *provincia*]

provincial /prəˈvɪnʃ(ə)l/ *adj.* **1** of a province or provinces. **2** having restricted views or the interests or manners etc. attributed to inhabitants of the provinces. —*n.* an inhabitant of a province or the provinces. —**provincialism** *n.* [as prec.]

provision /prəˈvɪʒ(ə)n/ *n.* **1** providing; preparation for a future contingency. **2** a provided amount of something; (in *pl.*) a supply of food and drink. **3** a formally stated condition or stipulation. —*v.t.* to supply with provisions. [f. OF f. L (as PROVIDE)]

provisional /prəˈvɪʒən(ə)l/ *adj.* arranged or agreed upon temporarily but possibly to be altered later. —**Provisional** *n.* a member of the Provisional wing of the IRA. The name is taken from the 'Provisional Government of the Republic of Ireland' which was declared in 1916. —**provisionally** *adv.* [f. prec.]

proviso /prəˈvaɪzəʊ/ *n.* (*pl.* **-os**) a stipulation, a clause giving a stipulation in a document. [f. F or L (as PROVIDE)]

provisory /prəˈvaɪzərɪ/ *adj.* **1** conditional. **2** making provision. [f. F or L (as PROVIDE)]

provocation /prɒvəˈkeɪʃ(ə)n/ *n.* **1** provoking, being provoked. **2** something that provokes anger or retaliation. [f. OF or L (as PROVOKE)]

provocative /prəˈvɒkətɪv/ *adj.* **1** tending or intended to arouse anger, interest, or sexual desire. **2** deliberately annoying. —**provocatively** *adv.* [f. obs. F f. L (as foll.)]

provoke /prəˈvəʊk/ *v.t.* **1** to rouse or incite (a person) to a feeling or action. **2** to annoy or irritate. **3** to cause or give rise to (a feeling or reaction etc.). **4** to tempt, to allure. [f. OF f. L *provocare* (PRO-¹, *vocare* summon)]

provost /ˈprɒvəst/ *n.* **1** the head of some colleges. **2** the head of a Scottish municipal corporation or burgh. **3** (in full **provost marshal** /prəʊˈvəʊ/) the head of the military police in a camp or on active service. [OE & f. OF f. L *propositus* for *praepositus* placed in charge)]

prow /praʊ/ *n.* the projecting front part of a ship or boat. [f. F, ult. f. Gk *prōira*]

prowess /ˈpraʊɪs/ *n.* great ability or daring. [f. OF (as PROUD)]

prowl *v.t./i.* to go about stealthily in search of prey or to catch others unawares; to traverse (a place) thus; to pace or wander restlessly. —*n.* prowling. —**prowler** *n.* [orig. unkn.]

prox. *abbr.* proximo.

proximate /ˈprɒksɪmət/ *adj.* **1** nearest, next before or after (in time or order, in causation etc.). **2** approximate. [f. L (*proximus* nearest)]

proximity /prokˈsɪmɪtɪ/ *n.* **1** nearness in space or time. **2** neighbourhood. [f. F or L (as prec.)]

proximo /ˈprɒksɪməʊ/ *adj.* (in commerce) of the next month. [L, = in the next (*mense* month)]

proxy /ˈprɒksɪ/ *n.* **1** a person authorized to act for another; the agency of such a person. **2** a document authorizing a person to vote on behalf of another; a vote so given. [f. obs. *procuracy* f. L (as PROCURATION)]

prude /pru:d/ *n.* a person of extreme or exaggerated propriety in conduct or speech, one who is easily shocked by sexual matters. —**prudery** *n.*, **prudish** *adj.*, **prudishly** *adv.*, **prudishness** *n.* [F, f. *prudefemme* fem. of *prud'homme* good man and true (as PROUD)]

prudent /ˈpru:dənt/ *adj.* showing care and foresight, avoiding rashness. —**prudence** *n.*, **prudently** *adv.* [f. OF or L (as PROVIDENT)]

prudential /pru:ˈdenʃ(ə)l/ *adj.* of, involving, or characterized by prudence. —**prudentially** *adv.* [f. prec.]

prune¹ *v.t.* **1** to trim by cutting away dead or overgrown branches or shoots, especially to promote growth. **2** to remove or reduce (what is regarded as superfluous or excessive); to remove items thus from. [f. OF *pr(o)ignier*]

prune² *n.* a dried plum. [f. OF f. L *prunum* plum]

prurient /ˈprʊərɪənt/ *adj.* given to or arising from the indulgence of lewd thoughts. —**prurience** *n.*, **pruriently** *adv.* [f. L *prurire* itch]

Prussian /ˈprʌʃ(ə)n/ *adj.* of Prussia. —*n.* a native of Prussia. —**Prussian blue**, a deep blue pigment. [f. *Prussia*, former German kingdom]

prussic /ˈprʌsɪk/ *adj.* of or obtained from Prussian blue. —**prussic acid**, a highly poisonous aqueous solution of hydrogen cyanide. [f. F (as prec.)]

pry /praɪ/ *v.i.* to inquire impertinently (into a person's affairs etc.); to look or peer inquisitively and often furtively. [orig. unkn.]

PS *abbr.* postscript.

psalm /sɑ:m/ *n.* a sacred song, especially one of those in the Book of Psalms in the Old Testament. [OE f. L f. Gk *psalmos* song sung to the harp (*psallō* pluck the strings)]

psalmist *n.* an author of psalms. [f. L (as prec.)]

psalmody /ˈsɑ:mədɪ, ˈsælmədɪ/ *n.* the practice or art of singing psalms etc., especially in public worship. [f. L f. Gk (as PSALM, *ōidē* singing)]

Psalter /ˈsɔ:ltə(r), ˈsɒ-/ *n.* **1** the Book of Psalms. **2 psalter**, a copy or version of this. [f. L f. Gk *psaltērion* stringed instrument (as PSALM)]

psaltery /ˈsɔ:ltərɪ, ˈsɒ-/ *n.* an ancient and medieval instrument like a dulcimer but played by plucking the strings. [f. OF f. L (as prec.)]

psephology /pseˈfɒlədʒɪ, se-/ *n.* the study of trends in elections and voting. —**psephologist** *n.* [f. Gk *psēphos* pebble used in voting + -LOGY]

pseudo- /sju:dəʊ-/ *in comb.* false, apparent, supposed but not real. [Gk (*pseudēs* false)]

pseudonym /ˈsju:dənɪm/ *n.* a fictitious name, especially one assumed by an author.

—**pseudonymity** /-ˈnɪmɪtɪ/ *n.*, **pseudonymous** /-ˈdɒnɪməs/ *adj.* [f. F f. Gk (PSEUDO-, *onoma* name)]

pseudopodium /sju:dəˈpəʊdɪəm/ *n.* (*pl.* **-ia**) a temporary footlike protrusion of cell tissue, used for movement, feeding, etc., by some protozoa and other animals. [f. PSEUDO + Gk *podion* dim. of *pous podos* foot]

psi /psaɪ/ *n.* the twenty-third letter of the Greek alphabet, = ps. [Gk]

psoriasis /sɔ:ˈraɪəsɪs/ *n.* a skin disease with red scaly patches. [f. Gk (*psōriaō* have itch)]

psst *int.* to attract the attention surreptitiously. [imit.]

PSV *abbr.* public service vehicle.

psyche /ˈsaɪkɪ/ *n.* the human soul or spirit; the human mind. [L f. Gk]

psychedelic /saɪkɪˈdelɪk/ *adj.* **1** hallucinatory, expanding the mind's awareness. **2** having intensely vivid colours or sounds etc. [as prec. + Gk *dēlos* clear]

psychiatric /saɪkɪˈætrɪk/ *adj.* (also **psychiatrical**) of or concerning psychiatry. —**psychiatrically** *adv.* [f. foll.]

psychiatry /saɪˈkaɪətrɪ/ *n.* the study and treatment of mental disease. —**psychiatrist** *n.* [PSYCHO- + Gk *iatreia* healing]

psychic /ˈsaɪkɪk/ *adj.* psychical, able to exercise psychical or occult powers. —*n.* **1** a person susceptible to psychical influence, a medium. **2** (in *pl.*) the study of psychical phenomena. —**psychically** *adv.* [f. Gk (as PSYCHE)]

psychical /ˈsaɪkɪk(ə)l/ *adj.* of the soul or mind, of phenomena and conditions apparently outside the domain of physical law. —**psychically** *adv.* [as prec.]

psycho- /saɪkəʊ-/ *in comb.* mind, soul. [f. Gk (as PSYCHE)]

psychoanalyse /saɪkəʊˈænəlaɪz/ *v.t.* to treat by psychoanalysis. —**psychoanalyst** *n.* [f. foll.]

psychoanalysis /saɪkəʊəˈnælɪsɪs/ *n.* **1** a therapeutic method originated by Freud for treating disorders of the personality or behaviour by bringing into a patient's consciousness his unconscious conflicts and fantasies. —**psychoanalytic** /-ænəˈlɪtɪk/ *adj.*, **psychoanalytical** /-ænəˈlɪtɪk(ə)l/ *adj.*

psychological /saɪkəˈlɒdʒɪk(ə)l/ *adj.* of the mind; of psychology. —**psychological moment**, the psychologically appropriate moment; (*colloq.*) the most appropriate time. **psychological warfare**, warfare achieving its aims by weakening the enemy's morale. [f. foll.]

psychology /saɪˈkɒlədʒɪ/ *n.* **1** the science of the human mind; a treatise on or system of this. **2** (*colloq.*) mental characteristics. —**psychologist** *n.* [as PSYCHO- + -LOGY]

psychometry /saɪˈkɒmɪtrɪ/ *n.* **1** divination of facts concerning an object (e.g. its source, ownership) from contact with it. **2** measurement of mental abilities. —**psychometric** /-kəˈmetrɪk/ *adj.* [f. PSYCHO- + -METRY]

psychoneurosis /saɪkəʊnjʊəˈrəʊsɪs/ *n.* a neurosis, especially with indirect expression of emotional feelings. —**psychoneurotic** /-ˈrɒtɪk/ *adj.*

psychopath /ˈsaɪkəpæθ/ *n.* a person suffering from chronic mental disorder especially with aggressive antisocial behaviour; a mentally or emotionally unstable person. —**psychopathic** /-ˈpæθɪk/ *adj.*, **psychopathy** /-ˈkɒpəθɪ/ *n.* [f. PSYCHO- + Gk *-pathēs* sufferer]

psychopathology /saɪkəʊpəˈθɒlədʒɪ/ *n.* the science of mental disorders.

psychosis /saɪˈkəʊsɪs/ *n.* (*pl.* **-oses** /-i:z/) a severe mental derangement involving the whole personality. [f. Gk, = principle of life (as PSYCHE)]

psychosomatic /saɪkəʊsəˈmætɪk/ *adj.* of the mind and the body; (of a disease etc.) caused or aggravated by mental stress. —**psychosomatically** *adv.*

psychosurgery /saɪkəʊˈsɜ:dʒərɪ/ *n.* brain surgery as a means of treating mental disorder.

psychotherapy /saɪkəʊˈθerəpɪ/ *n.* treatment of mental disorders by psychological means.—**psychotherapeutic** /-ˈpju:tɪk/ *adj.*, **psychotherapist** *n.*

psychotic /saɪˈkɒtɪk/ *adj.* of or suffering from psychosis. —*n.* a psychotic person. [as PSYCHOSIS]

PT *abbr.* physical training.

Pt *symbol* platinum.

pt. *abbr.* **1** part. **2** pint. **3** point. **4** port.

PTA *abbr.* parent-teacher association.

ptarmigan /ˈtɑ:mɪgən/ *n.* a bird of the grouse family (*Lagopus mutus*). [f. Gaelic]

Pte *abbr.* Private (soldier).

pteridophyte /ˈterɪdəfaɪt/ *n.* a fern or similar plant. [f. Gk *pteris* fern + *phuton* plant]

pterodactyl /terəˈdæktɪl/ *n.* an extinct winged reptile. [f. Gk *pteron* wing + *daktulos* finger]

PTO *abbr.* please turn over.

ptomaine /ˈtəʊmeɪn/ *n.* any of various amines (some toxic) in putrefying animal and vegetable matter. [f. F f. It. f. Gk *ptōma* corpse]

p-type *adj.* (of a semiconductor device or a region in this) having positive carriers of electricity.

Pu *symbol* plutonium.

pub *n.* (*colloq.*) a public house. —**pub crawl**, a series of visits to several pubs with drinking at each. [abbr.]

puberty /ˈpju:bətɪ/ *n.* the stage at which a

person becomes capable of procreation through the natural development of the reproductive organs. —**pubertal** *adj.* [f. F or L (*puber* adult)]

pubes /ˈpjuːbiːz/ *n.* the lower part of the abdomen. [L]

pubescence /pjuːˈbes(ə)ns/ *n.* **1** arrival at puberty. **2** soft down on a plant or animal. —**pubescent** *adj.* [F or f. L (*pubescere* reach puberty)]

pubic /ˈpjuːbɪk/ *adj.* of the pubes or pubis. [f. PUBES]

pubis /ˈpjuːbɪs/ *n.* (*pl.* **pubes** /-iːz/) the bone forming the front of each half of the pelvis. [f. L *os pubis* bone of the pubes]

public /ˈpʌblɪk/ *adj.* **1** of, concerning, or for the use of the people as a whole. **2** representing the people; done by or for the people. **3** open to general observation or knowledge, openly done or existing. **4** of or engaged in the people's affairs or service. —*n.* the community in general; members of it; a section of the community. —**in public,** openly, for all to see or know. **public-address system,** a system of loud-speakers etc. for a speaker at a large gathering. **public company,** one with shares available to all buyers. **public house,** a place licensed for and mainly concerned with selling alcoholic drink for consumption on the premises. **Public Lending Right,** the right of authors to payment when their books are lent by public libraries. **public relations,** the promotion of good relations between a business etc. and the public. **public school,** (in England) an endowed secondary school for fee-paying pupils; (in Scotland, USA, etc.) a school managed by public authorities. **public servant,** a State official. **public-spirited** *adj.* ready to do things for the benefit of people in general. **public transport,** buses, trains, etc., available to the public and having fixed routes. **public utility,** an organization supplying gas or electricity or water, etc., and regarded as a public service. **public works,** building operations undertaken by the State. —**publicly** *adv.* [f. OF or L *publicus* (*populus* people, infl. by *pubes* adult population)]

publican /ˈpʌblɪkən/ *n.* **1** the keeper of a public house. **2** (*Rom. hist.* & in the New Testament) a tax-collector. [f. OF f. L, = tax-collector]

publication /pʌblɪˈkeɪʃ(ə)n/ *n.* **1** the issuing of a book or periodical etc. to the public. **2** a book etc. so issued. **3** making publicly known. [f. OF f. L (as PUBLISH)]

publicist /ˈpʌblɪsɪst/ *n.* **1** a writer on or a person skilled in current public affairs. **2** an expert in publicity. [f. F f. L (*jus*) *publicum* public (law)]

publicity /pʌbˈlɪsɪtɪ/ *n.* **1** public attention; the means of attracting it, the business of advertising. **2** being open to general observation; notoriety. [f. F (as PUBLIC)]

publicize /ˈpʌblɪsaɪz/ *v.t.* to make publicly known, especially by advertisement. [f. PUBLIC]

publish /ˈpʌblɪʃ/ *v.t.* **1** to issue copies of (a book, or periodical, newspaper, etc., or *absol.*) for sale to the public. **2** to make generally known, to announce formally. [f. OF f. L *publicare* (as PUBLIC)]

publisher *n.* a person or firm that issues and distributes copies of a book, periodical, newspaper, etc. [f. prec.]

puce *adj.* & *n.* brownish-purple. [F, = flea, flea-colour, f. L *pulex*]

puck *n.* a rubber disc used in ice hockey. [orig. unkn.]

pucker *v.t./i.* to gather or cause to gather into wrinkles, folds, or bulges, intentionally or as a fault. —*n.* such a wrinkle or bulge. [prob. frequent. (as POKE², POCKET)]

pud /pʊd/ *n.* (*colloq.*) pudding. [abbr.]

pudding /ˈpʊdɪŋ/ *n.* **1** any sweet food made with sugar, eggs, etc.; a dessert. **2** food of various kinds containing or enclosed in a mixture of flour (or a similar substance) and other ingredients and cooked by baking, boiling, or steaming. **3** a kind of sausage. **4** a dumpy slow-witted person. —**puddingy** *adj.* [f. OF *boudin* black pudding, ult. f. L *botellus* sausage]

puddle *n.* **1** a small pool especially of rain on a road etc. **2** clay made into a watertight coating. —*v.t.* **1** to make muddy. **2** to knead (clay and sand) with water into a muddy mixture. **3** to stir (molten iron) to produce wrought iron by expelling the carbon. —**puddly** *adj.* [dim. of OE *pudd* ditch]

pudenda /pjuːˈdendə/ *n.pl.* the genitals, especially of a woman. [L, = things to be ashamed of]

pueblo /ˈpwebləʊ/ *n.* (*pl.* **-os**) a type of settlement in the southwestern USA and Latin America, especially of Indians, with multistorey adobe dwellings occupied by a number of families. [Sp., = people, village, f. L *populus*]

puerile /ˈpjʊəraɪl/ *adj.* suitable only for children, silly and immature. —**puerility** /-ˈrɪlɪtɪ/ *n.* [f. F or L (*puer* boy)]

puerperal /pjuːˈɜːpər(ə)l/ *adj.* of or due to childbirth. —**puerperal fever,** a fever following childbirth and caused by uterine infection. [f. L *puerperus* (*puer* child, *-parus* bearing)]

puff *n.* **1** a short quick blowing of breath or wind etc.; its sound; a small quantity of smoke or vapour etc. emitted at a puff. **2** the act of smoking a pipe etc. **3** a powder-puff. **4** a cake of light pastry. **5** a piece of extravagant praise as a review or advertisement etc. —*v.t./i.* **1** to emit a puff or puffs; to emit (smoke etc.) in puffs; to smoke (a pipe etc.) in puffs. **2** to come (out or up) in puffs. **3** to blow (dust etc.) away with a puff. **4** to breathe hard, to pant; to put out of breath. **5** to make or become inflated; to swell. **6** to advertise (goods etc.) with extravagant praise. —**puff-adder** *n.* a large venomous African viper (esp. *Bitis arietans*) that inflates the upper part of its body when excited. **puff-ball** *n.* a fungus of the genus *Lycoperdon* with a ball-shaped sporecase. **puff pastry,** light flaky pastry. **puff** *or* **puffed sleeve,** a short sleeve that is very full at the shoulder. **puff up,** (esp. in *p.p.*) to elate, to make proud. [prob. imit.]

puffin /ˈpʌfɪn/ *n.* a North Atlantic auk (*Fratercula arctica*) with a short striped bill. [orig. unkn.]

puffy *adj.* **1** puffed out, swollen. **2** short-winded. —**puffily** *adv.*, **puffiness** *n.* [f. PUFF]

pug *n.* a dog of a dwarf breed with a broad flat nose and wrinkled face. —**pug-nosed** *adj.* having a short flattish nose. [perh. f. L Du.]

pugilist /ˈpju:dʒɪlɪst/ *n.* a professional boxer. —**pugilism** *n.*, **pugilistic** /-ˈlɪstɪk/ *adj.* [f. L *pugil*]

pugnacious /pʌgˈneɪʃəs/ *adj.* disposed to fight, aggressive. —**pugnaciously** *adv.*, **pugnacity** /-ˈnæsɪtɪ/ *n.* [f. L *pugnax* (*pugnare* fight)]

puisne /ˈpju:nɪ/ *n.* a judge of a superior court who is inferior in rank to a chief justice. [F (*puis* after (f. L *postea*), *né* born f. L *natus*)]

puissance /ˈpwi:sɑ:ns/ *n.* (in show-jumping) a test of a horse's ability to jump high obstacles. [F (as foll.)]

puissant /ˈpju:ɪs(ə)nt, ˈpwi:-/ *adj.* (*literary*) having great power or influence, mighty. [f. OF f. L *posse* be able (cf. POTENT)]

puke *v.t./i.* to vomit. —*n.* vomit. [prob. imit.]

pukka /ˈpʌkə/ *adj.* (*colloq.*) genuine; of good quality. [f. Hindi, = cooked]

pulchritude /ˈpʌlkrɪtju:d/ *n.* (*literary*) beauty. —**pulchritudinous** /-ˈtju:dɪnəs/ *adj.* [f. L (*pulcher* beautiful)]

pule *v.i.* to whimper, to cry querulously or weakly. [prob. imit.]

pull /pʊl/ *v.t./i.* **1** to exert force on (a thing) so as to move it towards oneself or towards the origin of the force; to cause to move thus; to exert such a force. **2** to remove (a cork or tooth) by pulling. **3** to damage (a muscle etc.) by abnormal strain. **4** to move (a boat) by pulling on its oars; (of a boat etc.) to be caused to move, especially in a specified direction. **5** to proceed with effort. **6** to bring out (a weapon) for use. **7** to restrain the speed of (a horse). **8** to attract (customers). **9** to draw (liquor) from a barrel etc. **10** (in cricket) to strike (a ball) to the leg side; (in golf) to strike (a ball) widely to the left. **11** to print (a proof etc.). —*n.* **1** the act of pulling; the force thus exerted. **2** a means of exerting influence, an advantage. **3** a deep draught of liquor. **4** a prolonged effort, e.g. in going up a hill. **5** a handle etc. for applying pull. **6** a printer's rough proof. **7** a pulling stroke in cricket or golf. —**pull apart** *or* **to pieces,** to separate the parts of forcibly; to criticize severely. **pull back,** to retreat or cause to retreat. **pull down,** to demolish; to humiliate. **pull a fast one,** (*slang*) to gain an advantage by unfair or deceitful means. **pull in,** to earn or acquire; (of a train etc.) to enter a station; (of a vehicle) to move to the side of or off a road; (*colloq.*) to arrest. **pull-in** *n.* a place for a vehicle to pull in off the road. **pull a person's leg,** to deceive him playfully. **pull off,** to remove by pulling; to succeed in achieving or winning. **pull oneself together,** to recover control of oneself. **pull out,** to depart; to withdraw from an undertaking; (of a train etc.) to leave a station; (of a vehicle) to move from the side of a road, or into position to overtake another. **pull one's punches,** to avoid using one's full force. **pull rank,** to take unfair advantage of seniority. **pull round** *or* **through,** to recover from an illness. **pull strings,** to exert (esp. clandestine) influence. **pull up,** to stop or cause to stop moving; to reprimand; to pull out of the ground; to check oneself. **pull one's weight,** to do one's fair share of work. [OE]

pullet /ˈpʊlɪt/ *n.* a young domestic fowl, especially a hen that has begun to lay but not yet moulted. [f. OF dim. of *poule* f. L *pullus*]

pulley /ˈpʊlɪ/ *n.* **1** a grooved wheel for a cord etc. to pass over, set in a block and used for changing the direction of a force. **2** a wheel or drum fixed on a shaft and turned by a belt, used especially to increase speed or power. [f. OF *polie* prob. ult. f. Gk (as POLE²)]

Pullman /ˈpʊlmən/ *n.* **1** a type of railway carriage with luxurious furnishings and without compartments; a luxurious motor coach. **2** a sleeping-car. [f. G. M. *Pullman*, American designer (d. 1897)]

pullover *n.* a knitted garment (with no fastenings) for the upper part of the body, put on over the head.

pullulate /ˈpʌljʊleɪt/ *v.i.* **1** to sprout; to develop. **2** to abound *with*. —**pullulation** /-ˈleɪʃ(ə)n/ *n.* [f. L *pullulare* sprout (as PULLET)]

pulmonary /ˈpʌlmənərɪ/ *adj.* **1** of, in, or affecting the lungs. **2** affected with or subject to lung-disease. [f. L (*pulmo* lung)]

pulp *n.* **1** the fleshy part of a fruit, animal body, etc. **2** a soft shapeless mass, especially that of rags or wood etc., from which paper is made. **3** (*attrib.*, of a magazine etc.) of a kind originally printed on rough paper made from wood pulp, often with sensational or poor-quality writing. —*v.t./i.* to reduce to or become pulp. —**pulpy** *adj.*, **pulpiness** *n.* [f. L *pulpa*]

pulpit /ˈpʊlpɪt/ *n.* a raised enclosed platform in a church etc. from which a preacher delivers a sermon. [f. L *pulpitum*]

pulsar /ˈpʌlsɑ:(r)/ *n.* a cosmic source from which light or radio waves are emitted in short bursts with great regularity. [f. *puls*ating *star*]

pulsate /pʌlˈseɪt, ˈpʌl-/ *v.i.* to expand and contract rhythmically, to throb; to vibrate, to quiver. —**pulsation** /-ˈseɪʃ(ə)n/ *n.*, **pulsator** /-ˈseɪtə(r)/ *n.*, **pulsatory** /ˈpʌlsətərɪ/ *adj.* [f. L *pulsare* (as foll.)]

pulse[1] *n.* **1** the rhythmical throbbing of the arteries as blood is propelled along them; each successive beat of the arteries or heart; the rate of this beat. **2** a single vibration of sound or light or electric current etc., especially as a signal. **3** a throb or thrill of life or emotion; a latent feeling. —*v.i.* to pulsate. [f. L *pulsus* (*pellere* drive, beat)]

pulse[2] *n.* **1** (as *sing.* or *pl.*) the edible seeds of leguminous plants, e.g. peas, beans, lentils. **2** any kind of these. [f. OF f. L *puls* meal porridge]

pulverize /ˈpʌlvəraɪz/ *v.t./i.* **1** to reduce or crumble to powder or dust; to demolish. **2** to defeat utterly. —**pulverization** /-ˈzeɪʃ(ə)n/ *n.* [f. L (*pulvis* dust)]

puma /ˈpju:mə/ *n.* a large tawny American feline (*Felis concolor*). [Sp., f. Quechua]

pumice /ˈpʌmɪs/ *n.* (also **pumice-stone**) a light porous lava used for removing stains from the skin etc. or as a powder for polishing; a piece of this. [f. OF f. L *pumex*]

pummel /ˈpʌm(ə)l/ *v.t.* (**-ll-**) to strike repeatedly, especially with the fist. [alt. f. POMMEL]

pump[1] *n.* a machine or device of various kinds for raising or moving liquids or gases; a machine for raising water for domestic use. —*v.t./i.* **1** to raise, move, or inflate by using a pump; to use a pump; to empty by using a pump. **2** to pour or cause to pour forth as if by pumping. **3** to move vigorously up and down like a pump-handle. **4** to question (a person) persistently to obtain information. [orig. naut.; prob. imit.]

pump[2] *n.* **1** a plimsoll. **2** a light shoe for dancing etc. **3** (*US*) a court shoe. [orig. unkn.]

pumpernickel /ˈpʌmpənɪk(ə)l, ˈpʊ-/ *n.* German wholemeal rye bread. [G, orig. = lout, stinker (*pumpe(r)n* break wind, *Nickel* Nicholas)]

pumpkin *n.* **1** the large round orange-coloured fruit of a trailing vine, *Cucurbita pepo*, used as a vegetable and (in the USA) a filling for pies. **2** this vine. [f. earlier *pompon*, ult. f. Gk *pepōn* large melon]

pun *n.* humorous use of a word to suggest different meanings, or of words of the same sound with a different meaning (e.g. 'the sole has no feet and therefore no sole, poor soul'). —*v.i.* (**-nn-**) to make a pun or puns. [perh. f. obs. *pundigrion*]

Punch *n.* a grotesque hook-nosed hump-backed in a puppet-show called 'Punch and Judy'. —**as pleased** *or* **proud as Punch,** showing great pleasure or pride. [abbr. *Punchinello*, perh. dim. of It. *pollecena* young turkey-cock (with hooked beak which the nose of Punch's mask resembles)]

punch[1] *v.t.* **1** to strike with the fist. **2** to pierce a hole in (metal, paper, a ticket, etc.) as or with a punch; to pierce (a hole) thus. —*n.* **1** a blow with the fist; the ability to deliver this. **2** (*slang*) vigour, effective force. **3** an instrument or machine for cutting holes or impressing a design in leather, metal, paper, etc. —**punch-ball** *n.* an inflated ball held on a stand etc. and punched as a form of exercise. **punch-drunk** *adj.* stupefied through having been severely punched (*lit.* or *fig.*). **punch-line** *n.* the words giving the point of a joke or story. **punch-up** *n.* a fist-fight, a brawl. [var. of *pounce* emboss]

punch[2] *n.* a drink usually of wine or spirits mixed with hot or cold water, spice, etc. —**punch-bowl** *n.* a bowl in which punch is mixed; a round deep hollow in a hill. [orig. unkn.]

punch[3] *n.* (in full **Suffolk punch**) a short-legged thickset draught horse. [prob. as PUNCH]

punchy *adj.* having vigour, forceful. [f. PUNCH[1]]

punctilio /pʌŋkˈtɪlɪəʊ/ *n.* (*pl.* **-os**) **1** a delicate point of ceremony or honour; the etiquette of such points. **2** petty formality. [f. It. & Sp. dim. (as POINT)]

punctilious /pʌŋkˈtɪlɪəs/ *adj.* attentive to formality or etiquette; precise in behaviour. —**punctiliously** *adv.*, **punctiliousness** *n.* [f. F (as prec.)]

punctual /ˈpʌŋktjʊəl/ *adj.* observant of the appointed time; neither early nor late. —**punctuality** /-ˈælɪtɪ/ *n.*, **punctually** *adv.* [f. L (as POINT)]

punctuate /ˈpʌŋktjʊeɪt/ *v.t.* **1** to insert punctuation marks in. **2** to interrupt at intervals. **3** to emphasize, to accentuate. [f. L *punctuare* (as prec.)]

punctuation /pʌŋktjʊˈeɪʃ(ə)n/ *n.* punctuating; the system used for this. —**punctuation mark,** any of the marks (e.g. full stop and comma) used in writing to separate sentences and phrases etc. and clarify meaning. [as prec.]

puncture /ˈpʌŋktʃə(r)/ *n.* a prick or pricking,

especially an accidental piercing of a pneumatic tyre; a hole thus made. —*v.t./i.* to make a puncture in; to undergo a puncture; to prick or pierce. [f. L *punctura* (*pungere* prick)]

pundit /ˈpʌndɪt/ *n.* **1** a learned Hindu. **2** a learned expert or teacher. —**punditry** *n.* [f. Hind. f. Skr., = learned]

pungent /ˈpʌndʒ(ə)nt/ *adj.* **1** having a sharp or strong taste or smell. **2** (of remarks) penetrating, biting, caustic. **3** mentally stimulating. —**pungency** *n.*, **pungently** *adv.* [as PUNCTURE]

punish /ˈpʌnɪʃ/ *v.t.* **1** to cause (an offender) to suffer for an offence; to inflict a penalty for (an offence). **2** (*colloq.*) to inflict severe blows on (an opponent). **3** to tax severely, to subject to severe treatment. [f. OF f. L *punire* (*poena* penalty)]

punishable *adj.* liable to be punished, especially by law. [f. prec.]

punishment *n.* **1** punishing, being punished. **2** that which an offender is made to suffer for his offence. **3** severe treatment or suffering. [f. PUNISH]

punitive /ˈpju:nɪtɪv/ *adj.* inflicting or intended to inflict punishment. [f. F or L (as PUNISH)]

punk *n.* (*colloq.*) **1** a worthless person or thing. **2** punk rock; a devotee of this or of the bizarre dress, hair-style, etc., associated with it. —**punk rock,** a type of pop music using aggressive and outrageous effects. [orig. unkn.]

punnet /ˈpʌnɪt/ *n.* a small basket or container for fruit etc. [perh. dim. of dial. *pun* pound (POUND¹)]

punster *n.* a habitual maker of puns. [f. PUN]

punt¹ *n.* a flat-bottomed shallow boat propelled by a long pole thrust against the bottom of a river etc. —*v.t./i.* to propel (a punt) with a pole in this way; to travel or convey in a punt. —**punter**¹ *n.* [f. MLG or MDu. f. L *ponto* Gaulish transport vessel]

punt² *v.t.* to kick (a football) after it has dropped from the hands and before it reaches the ground. —*n.* such a kick. —**punter**² *n.* [prob. f. dial. *punt* push forcibly]

punt³ *v.i.* **1** (in some card-games) to lay a stake against the bank. **2** (*colloq.*) to bet on a horse etc.; to speculate in shares etc. [f. F *ponter* (*ponte* player against bank f. Sp., as POINT)]

punter³ *n.* **1** one who punts (PUNT³). **2** (*colloq.*) the victim of a swindler or confidence trickster; a customer or client etc., a spectator. [f. PUNT³]

puny /ˈpju:nɪ/ *adj.* undersized, weak, feeble. —**puniness** *n.* [phonetic spelling of PUISNE]

pup *n.* a young dog; a young wolf, rat, seal, etc. —*v.t.* (**-pp-**) (of a bitch etc.) to bring forth (young, or *absol.*). —**in pup,** (of a bitch) pregnant. **sell a person a pup,** to swindle him or her, especially by selling a thing on its prospective value. [f. PUPPY]

pupa /ˈpju:pə/ *n.* (*pl.* **-ae**) an insect in its passive phase of development between larva and imago. —**pupal** *adj.* [L, = doll]

pupate /pju:ˈpeɪt/ *v.t.* to become a pupa. —**pupation** /-ˈpeɪʃ(ə)n/ *n.* [f. prec.]

pupil /ˈpju:pɪl/ *n.* **1** one who is taught by another; a schoolchild; a disciple. **2** the circular opening in the centre of the iris of the eye. [f. OF f. L *pupillus, pupilla*, dim. of *pupus* boy, *pupa* girl]

puppet /ˈpʌpɪt/ *n.* **1** an inanimate figure representing a human being or an animal etc., ranging in size from a few inches to larger than life, moved by various means as an entertainment. **2** a person whose acts are controlled by another. —**puppet state,** a country that is apparently independent but actually under the control of another power. —**puppetry** *n.* [var. of POPPET]

puppy *n.* **1** a young dog. **2** a vain empty-headed young man. —**puppy-fat** *n.* temporary fatness of a child or adolescent. [perh. f. OF *po(u)pee* doll (as POPPET)]

purblind /ˈpɜ:blaɪnd/ *adj.* **1** partly blind, dim-sighted. **2** stupid, dim-witted. [orig. *pur(e)* (= utterly) *blind*]

purchase /ˈpɜ:tʃəs/ *v.t.* **1** to buy. **2** to obtain or achieve with a specified cost or sacrifice. —*n.* **1** buying. **2** a thing bought. **3** an annual rent or return from land. **4** a firm hold on a thing to move it or prevent it slipping, leverage. —**purchaser** *n.* [f. AF (as PRO-¹, CHASE¹)]

purdah /ˈpɜ:də/ *n.* a system of screening Muslim or Hindu women from strangers by means of a veil or curtain. [f. Urdu & Pers., = veil, curtain]

pure *adj.* **1** not mixed with any other substance; free from impurities; of unmixed origin. **2** morally or sexually undefiled; chaste. **3** mere, nothing but. **4** (of sound) not discordant, perfectly in tune. **5** dealing with theory only, not with practical applications. —**pureness** *n.* [f. OF f. L *purus*]

purée /ˈpjʊəreɪ/ *n.* a pulp of vegetables or fruit etc. reduced to a smooth cream. [F]

purely *adv.* in a pure manner; merely; solely, exclusively; entirely. [f. PURE]

purgative /ˈpɜ:gətɪv/ *adj.* **1** serving to purify. **2** strongly laxative. —*n.* a purgative thing; a laxative. [f. OF or L (as PURGE)]

purgatory /ˈpɜ:gətərɪ/ *n.* **1** the condition or a place of spiritual cleansing, especially (in the RC and Orthodox Church) of souls departing this life in the grace of God but having to expiate venial sins etc. **2** a place or state of temporary suffering or expiation. —**purgatorial** /-ˈtɔ:rɪəl/ *adj.* [f. AF f. L (as foll.)]

purge *v.t.* **1** to make physically or spiritually

clean; to remove by a cleansing process. **2** to rid of persons regarded as undesirable. **3** to empty (the bowels); to empty the bowels of (a person). **4** (*Law*) to atone for or wipe out (an offence, esp. contempt of court). —*n.* **1** the act or process of purging. **2** a purgative. [f. OF f. L *purgare* (as PURE)]

purify /ˈpjʊərɪfaɪ/ *v.t.* to cleanse or make pure; to make ceremonially clean; to clear of extraneous elements. —**purification** /-fɪˈkeɪʃ(ə)n/ *n.*, **purificatory** *adj.*, **purifier** *n.* [f. OF f. L (as PURE)]

purist /ˈpjʊərɪst/ *n.* a stickler for or affecter of scrupulous purity, especially in language. —**purism** *n.*, **puristic** /-ˈrɪstɪk/ *adj.* [f. F (as PURE)]

Puritan /ˈpjʊərɪt(ə)n/ *n.* **1** a member of the more extreme English Protestants who sought a further purification of the Church from supposedly unscriptural forms. **2 puritan,** a person practising or affecting extreme strictness in religion or morals. —*adj.* **1** of the Puritans. **2 puritan,** scrupulous in religion or morals. —**puritanical** /-ˈtænɪk(ə)l/ *adj.*, **puritanism** *n.* [f. L *puritas* purity (*purus* pure)]

purity /ˈpjʊərɪtɪ/ *n.* pureness, cleanness; freedom from physical or moral pollution. [f. OF (as PURE)]

purl[1] *n.* **1** a knitting-stitch with the needle put into the stitch in an opposite to the normal direction, producing a ridge towards the knitter. **2** a chain of minute loops, a picot. —*v.t.* to make (a stitch, or *absol.*) purl. [f. Sc. *pirl* twist]

purl[2] *v.i.* (of a brook etc.) to flow with a swirling motion and babbling sound. [prob. imit.]

purler *n.* (*colloq.*) a headlong fall. [f. *purl* overturn (prob. as PURL¹)]

purlieu /ˈpɜːljuː/ *n.* **1** one's bounds or limits or usual haunts. **2** (*hist.*) a tract on the border of a forest. **3** (in *pl.*) outskirts, an outlying region. [prob. alt. of AF *purale(e)* perambulation to settle boundaries]

purlin /ˈpɜːlɪn/ *n.* a horizontal beam along a roof. [f. L *perlio*]

purloin /pɜːˈlɔɪn/ *v.t.* to steal, to pilfer. [f. AF (as PRO-, *loign* far f. L *longe*)]

purple *n.* **1** a colour between red and blue. **2** (in full **Tyrian purple**) a crimson colour obtained from some molluscs. **3** a purple robe, especially as the dress of an emperor etc. **4** the scarlet official dress of a cardinal. —*adj.* of a purple or Tyrian purple colour. —*v.t./i.* to make or become purple. —**born in the purple,** born to a reigning family; belonging to the most privileged class. [tr. L *porphyrogenitus*, orig. used of one born of the imperial family at Constantinople and (it is said) in a chamber called the *Porphyra*] **purple passage** *or* **patch,** an over-ornate passage in a literary composition. —**purplish** *adj.* [OE f. L *purpura* f. Gk *porphura* (shellfish yielding) purple]

purport /pəˈpɔːt/ *v.t.* **1** to profess, to be intended to seem. **2** (of a document or speech) to have as its meaning, to state. —/ˈpɜːpɔːt/ *n.* an ostensible meaning; the sense or tenor of a document or statement. —**purportedly** *adv.* [f. AF f. L *proportare* (PRO-¹, *portare* carry)]

purpose /ˈpɜːpəs/ *n.* **1** an intended result, something for which effort is being made. **2** intention to act, determination. —*v.t.* to have as one's purpose, to intend. —**on purpose,** intentionally. **purpose-built** *or* **purpose-made** etc. *adj.* built etc. for a specific purpose. **to little** *or* **no purpose,** with little or no result or effect. **to the purpose,** relevant, useful. [f. AF f. L, =PROPOSE]

purposeful *adj.* having or indicating a (conscious) purpose; intentional; acting or done with determination. —**purposefully** *adv.*, **purposefulness** *n.* [f. prec. + -FUL]

purposely *adv.* on purpose. [f. PURPOSE]

purposive /ˈpɜːpəsɪv/ *adj.* having, serving, or done with a purpose; purposeful. [as prec.]

purr /pɜː(r)/ *v.i.* (of a cat etc.) to make a low vibratory sound expressing pleasure; (of machinery etc.) to make a similar sound. —*n.* such a sound. [imit.]

purse *n.* **1** a small pouch of leather etc. for carrying money on the person. **2** (*US*) a handbag. **3** money, funds. **4** a sum given as a present or prize for a contest. —*v.t./i.* to pucker or contract (the lips or brow) in wrinkles; to become wrinkled. —**hold the purse-strings,** to have control of expenditure. [OE f. L *bursa* f. Gk, = leather]

purser *n.* an officer on a ship who keeps the accounts, especially the head steward in a passenger vessel. [f. prec.]

pursuance /pəˈsjuːəns/ *n.* carrying out or observance (of a plan, rules, etc.). [as foll.]

pursuant /pəˈsjuːənt/ *adj.* (with *to*) in accordance with. [f. OF (as foll.)]

pursue /pəˈsjuː/ *v.t./i.* **1** to follow with intent to overtake, capture, or do harm to. **2** to continue, to proceed along or with (a route, course of action, topic, etc.). **3** to engage in (a study or other activity). **4** to seek to attain. **5** (of misfortune etc.) to assail persistently. —**pursuer** *n.* [f. AF f. L (as PRO-¹ or PER-, SUE)]

pursuit /pəˈsjuːt/ *n.* **1** pursuing. **2** an occupation or activity pursued. [f. OF (as PRO-¹ or PER-, SUIT)]

pursuivant /ˈpɜːsɪv(ə)nt/ *n.* an officer of the College of Arms below a herald. [f. OF (as PURSUE)]

purulent /ˈpjʊərʊlənt/ *adj.* of, containing, or

discharging pus. —**purulence** *n.* [F or f. L (as PUS)]

purvey /pəˈveɪ/ *v.t.* to provide or supply (articles of food) as one's business. —**purveyor** *n.* [f. AF f. L *providēre* provide]

purview /ˈpɜːvjuː/ *n.* **1** the scope or range of a document or scheme etc. **2** the range of physical or mental vision. [as prec.]

pus /pʌs/ *n.* yellowish viscous matter produced from inflamed or infected tissue. [L *pus puris*]

push /pʊʃ/ *v.t./i.* **1** to exert force on (a thing) so as to move it away from oneself or from the origin of the force; to cause to move thus; to exert such a force. **2** to thrust outwards; to cause to project. **3** to move forward or extend by effort. **4** to make a vigorous effort in order to succeed to surpass others. **5** to urge or impel; to put a strain on the abilities or tolerance of. **6** to promote the use or sale or adoption of (e.g. by advertising); to sell (a drug) illegally. —*n.* **1** the act of pushing; the force thus exerted. **2** a vigorous effort; a military attack in force. **3** enterprise, determination to succeed; use of influence to advance a person. **4** the pressure of affairs, a crisis. —**be pushed for,** (*colloq.*) to have very little of. **push around,** to bully. **push-bike** *n.* (*colloq.*) a pedal cycle. **push-button** *n.* a button to be pushed especially to operate an electrical device; (*adj.*) operated thus. **push-chair** *n.* a folding chair on wheels, in which a child can be pushed along. **push for,** to demand. **push one's luck,** see LUCK. **push off,** to push with an oar etc. against the bank etc. in order to get a boat out into a stream; (*slang*) to go away. **push-over** *n.* (*colloq.*) something easily done; a person who is easily convinced or charmed. **push-start** *n.* the starting of a motor vehicle by pushing it to turn the engine; (*v.t.*) to start (a vehicle) thus. **push through,** to get completed or accepted quickly. —**pusher** *n.* [f. OF *pousser* f. L *pulsare* (as PULSATE)]

pushful *adj.* self-assertive, determined to succeed. —**pushfully** *adv.*, **pushfulness** *n.* [f. PUSH + -FUL]

pushing *adj.* **1** (of a person) pushful. **2** (*colloq.*) having nearly reached (a specified age). [f. PUSH]

Pushtu /ˈpʌʃtuː/ *n.* & *adj.* Pashto. [f. Pers.]

pushy *adj.* (*colloq.*) pushful. [f. PUSH]

pusillanimous /pjuːsɪˈlænɪməs/ *adj.* lacking courage, timid. —**pusillanimity** /-ˈnɪmɪtɪ/ *n.*, **pusillanimously** *adv.* [f. L (*pusillus* small, *animus* mind)]

puss /pʊs/ *n.* **1** a cat (esp. as a form of address). **2** (*colloq.*) a playful or coquettish girl. [prob. f. MLG or Du.]

pussy /ˈpʊsɪ/ *n.* **1** (also **pussy-cat**) a cat. **2** (*vulgar*) the vulva. —**pussy willow,** a willow with furry catkins. [f. PUSS]

pussyfoot *v.i.* (*colloq.*) **1** to move stealthily. **2** to shirk dealing with or referring directly to a problem etc.

pustulate /ˈpʌstjʊleɪt/ *v.t./i.* to form into pustules. [f. L *pustulare* (as foll.)]

pustule /ˈpʌstjuːl/ *n.* a pimple or blister, especially one containing pus. —**pustular** *adj.* [f. OF or L *pustula*]

put /pʊt/ *v.t./i.* (**-tt-**; *past* & *p.p.* **put**) **1** to move to or cause to be in a specified place or position. **2** to bring into a specified condition or state. **3** to impose as a tax etc. **4** to submit for consideration or attention. **5** to express or state. **6** to estimate. **7** to place as an investment; to stake (money) in a bet. **8** to lay (blame). **9** (of a ship) to proceed. **10** to hurl (the shot or weight) as an athletic exercise. —*n.* a throw of a shot or weight. —**put across,** to succeed in communicating (an idea etc.); to cause to seem acceptable. **put away,** (*colloq.*) to put into prison or into a mental home; (*colloq.*) to consume as food or drink. **put back,** to restore to a former place; to move back the hands of (a clock or watch). **put by,** to save for future use. **put down,** to suppress by force or authority; to snub; to have (an animal) destroyed; to record or enter in writing; to enter (a person's name) as one who will subscribe; to reckon or consider; to attribute. **put-down** *n.* a snub. **put in,** to make (an appearance); to enter (a claim etc.); to spend (time) in working etc. **put in for,** to apply for. **put it across,** (*slang*) to trick or get the better of. **put it to a person,** to challenge him to deny. **put off,** to postpone; to postpone an engagement with (a person); to make excuses and try to avoid; to dissuade, to repel; to put (an electrical device or light etc.) out. **put on,** to stage (a play etc.); to cause (an electrical device or light etc.) to function; to advance the hands of (a clock or watch); to feign (an emotion); to increase one's weight by (so much). **put oneself in a person's place,** to imagine oneself in his or her situation etc. **put out,** to disconcert, to annoy, to inconvenience; to cause (a fire or light etc.) to cease to burn or function. **put over,** to put across. **put through,** to carry out or complete; to connect by telephone. **put under,** to make unconscious. **put up,** to build, to erect; to raise (a price etc.), to provide with or receive accommodation; to engage in (a fight, struggle, etc.) as a form of resistance; to present (a proposal); to present oneself as a candidate; to provide (money as a backer); to offer for sale or competition; to concoct. **put-up** *adj.* fraudulently concocted. **put upon,** (*colloq.*) unfairly burdened or deceived. **put a**

person up to, to instigate him in. **put up with**, to tolerate, to submit to. [f. OE]

putative /ˈpju:tətɪv/ *adj*. reputed, supposed. [f. OF or L (*putare* think)]

putlog /ˈpʌtlɒg/ *n*. each of the short horizontal timbers projecting from a wall, on which scaffold floor-boards rest. [orig. unkn.]

putrefy /ˈpju:trɪfaɪ/ *v.i.* to rot, to decay; to fester or suppurate. —**putrefaction** /-ˈfækʃ(ə)n/ *n*. [f. L *putrefacere* (*puter* rotten, *facere* make)]

putrescent /pju:ˈtres(ə)nt/ *adj*. decaying, rotting; of or accompanying this process. —**putrescence** *n*. [f. L *putrescere* (as foll.)]

putrid /ˈpju:trɪd/ *adj*. **1** decomposed, rotten. **2** foul, noxious. **3** (*slang*) of poor quality; very unpleasant. —**putridity** /-ˈtrɪdɪtɪ/ *n*. [f. L (*putrēre* rot)]

putsch /pʊtʃ/ *n*. an attempt at a political revolution. [Swiss G, = thrust]

putt /pʌt/ *v.t./i.* to strike (a golf-ball) gently to get it into or nearer to a hole on a putting-green. —*n*. such a stroke. —**putting-green** *n*. (in golf) the smooth area of grass round a hole. [var. of PUT]

puttee /ˈpʌtɪ/ *n*. a long strip of cloth wound spirally round the leg from the ankle to the knee for protection and support. [f. Hindi, = bandage]

putter /ˈpʌtə(r)/ *n*. a golf-club used in putting. [f. PUTT]

putty /ˈpʌtɪ/ *n*. a soft hard-setting paste of chalk powder and linseed oil for fixing glass in a frame, filling up holes in woodwork, etc. —*v.t.* to fix or fill with putty. [f. F *potée* (as POT)]

puzzle *n*. **1** a difficult or confusing problem. **2** a problem or toy designed to test knowledge or ingenuity. —*v.t./i.* to confound or disconcert mentally; to require much thought to comprehend. —**puzzle about** *or* **over**, to be confused about; to ponder about. **puzzle out**, to solve or understand by hard thought. —**puzzlement** *n*. [orig. unkn.]

puzzler *n*. a difficult question or problem. [f. prec.]

PVC *abbr*. polyvinyl chloride.

PW *abbr*. Policewoman.

PWR *abbr*. pressurized water reactor.

pyaemia /paɪˈi:mɪə/ *n*. blood-poisoning with formation of abscesses in the viscera. [f. Gk *puon* pus + *haima* blood]

pye-dog /ˈpaɪdɒg/ *n*. a vagrant mongrel of the East. [f. Hindi *pahi* outsider + DOG]

pygmy /ˈpɪgmɪ/ *n*. **1** a member of a population whose average male height is not greater than 150 cm (4 ft. 11 in.), e.g. the Bambuti of tropical central Africa (the term 'Negrito' is used of similar populations of SE Asia). **2** a very small person or thing. **3** an insignificant person or thing. —*adj*. **1** of pygmies. **2** very small. [f. L f. Gk (*pugmē* length from elbow to knuckles)]

pyjamas /pɪˈdʒɑ:məz/ *n.pl.* a suit of loose trousers and jacket for sleeping in; a similar garment for beach or evening wear by women. [f. Urdu, = leg-clothing]

pylon /ˈpaɪlən/ *n*. **1** a tall lattice-work structure used as a support for overhead electricity cables or as a boundary. **2** a structure marking a path for aircraft. **3** a structure supporting the engine of an aircraft. **4** a gateway or gate-tower, especially the monumental gateway to an Egyptian temple, usually formed by two truncated pyramidal towers connected by a lower architectural member containing the gate. [f. Gk *pulōn* (*pulē* gate)]

pyorrhoea /paɪəˈrɪə/ *n*. discharge of pus, especially in disease of the tooth-sockets. [f. Gk *puon* pus + *rhoia* flux]

pyracantha /paɪərəˈkænθə/ *n*. an evergreen thorny shrub of the genus *Pyracantha* with white flowers and scarlet or orange berries. [L f. Gk]

pyramid /ˈpɪrəmɪd/ *n*. **1** a monumental structure, especially in ancient Egypt, usually with a square base and with four equal triangular sides meeting at an apex. **2** a solid of this shape with a base of three or more sides. **3** a thing or pile of things shaped like this. —**pyramid selling**, a system of selling goods in which agency rights are sold to an increasing number of distributors at successively lower levels. —**pyramidal** /-ˈræmɪd(ə)l/ *adj*. [f. L f. Gk *puramis*]

pyre /ˈpaɪə(r)/ *n*. a heap of combustible material, especially a funeral pile for burning a corpse. [f. L f. Gk *pura* (as PYRO-)]

pyrethrum /paɪˈri:θrəm/ *n*. **1** a chrysanthemum with finely divided leaves (esp. *Chrysanthemum coccineum* and *C. cinerariifolium*). **2** an insecticide made from its dried flowers. [L f. Gk, = feverfew]

pyretic /paɪˈretɪk, pɪ-/ *adj*. of or producing fever. [f. Gk *puretos* fever]

Pyrex /ˈpaɪreks/ *n*. [P] a hard heat-resistant glass. [invented word]

pyrexia /paɪˈreksɪə/ *n*. fever. [f. Gk *purexis* (*puressō* be feverish, as PYRO-)]

pyrites /paɪˈraɪti:z/ *n*. a mineral that is a sulphide of iron (*iron pyrites*) or of copper and iron (*copper pyrites*). [L f. Gk (as PYRO-)]

pyro- /ˈpaɪrəʊ-/ *in comb*. fire. [f. Gk (*pur* fire)]

pyromania /paɪrəʊˈmeɪnɪə/ *n*. an uncontrollable impulse to start fires. —**pyromaniac** *n*. & *adj*. [f. PYRO- + -MANIA]

pyrotechnics /paɪrəʊˈteknɪks/ *n.pl.* **1** the art of making fireworks. **2** a display of fireworks.

3 any loud or brilliant display. —**pyrotechnic** *adj*. [f. PYRO- + Gk *tekhnē* art]

pyrrhic /ˈpɪrɪk/ *adj*. (of a victory) won at too great a cost. [f. *Pyrrhus* king of Epirus, who defeated the Romans thus in 279 BC]

python /ˈpaɪθ(ə)n/ *n*. a large snake (esp. of the genus *Python*) that kills its prey by compressing and asphyxiating it. [L f. Gk *Puthōn* huge serpent or monster slain near Delphi by Apollo in myth]

pyx /pɪks/ *n*. **1** a vessel in which bread consecrated for the Eucharist is kept. **2** a box in which specimen coins are deposited at the Royal Mint. —**trial of the pyx,** an annual test of specimen coins at the Royal Mint by a group of members (called a *jury*) of the Goldsmith's Company. [f. L f. Gk *puxis* (*puxos* box)]

Qq

Q, q /kju:/ *n.* (*pl.* **Qs, Q's**) the seventeenth letter of the alphabet.

Q. *abbr.* **1** Queen('s). **2** question.

QC *abbr.* Queen's Counsel.

QED *abbr.* which was the thing to be proved. [initials of L *quod erat demonstrandum*]

Qld. *abbr.* Queensland.

qr. *abbr.* quarter(s).

qt. *abbr.* quart(s).

q.t. *abbr.* (*slang*) quiet (*on the q.t.*).

qua /kweɪ/ *conj.* in the capacity of. [L, = in the manner in which]

quack[1] *n.* the harsh cry of a duck. —*v.i.* **1** to utter a quack. **2** to talk loudly. [imit.]

quack[2] *n.* a person who falsely claims to have medical skill or to provide remedies which will cure disease, a charlatan. —*adj.* **1** being a quack. **2** characteristic of or used by a quack. —**quackery** *n.* [abbr. of Du. *quacksalver*, f. *quacken* boast, *salf* salve, ointment]

quad[1] /kwɒd/ *n.* (*colloq.*) **1** a quadruplet. **2** a quadrangle. **3** quadraphony. —*adj.* quadraphonic. [abbr.]

quad[2] /kwɒd/ *n.* a small metal block used by printers in spacing. [abbr. of *quadrat*, f. L *quadratus* made square]

Quadragesima /kwɒdrəˈdʒesɪmə/ *n.* the first Sunday in Lent. [f. L, = fortieth (day), Lent having 40 days]

quadrangle /ˈkwɒdræŋg(ə)l/ *n.* **1** a four-cornered figure, especially a square or rectangle. **2** a four-sided court bordered by large buildings, especially in colleges. —**quadrangular** /-ˈræŋgjʊlə(r)/ *adj.* [f. OF f. L (as QUADRI-, ANGLE)]

quadrant /ˈkwɒdrənt/ *n.* **1** a quarter of a circle's circumference; a quarter of a circle as cut by two diameters at right angles; a quarter of a sphere as cut by two planes intersecting at right angles at the centre. **2** a thing shaped like a quarter-circle, especially a graduated strip of metal etc.; an instrument including this for taking angular measurements. [f. L *quadrans* quarter (*quattuor* four)]

quadraphonic /kwɒdrəˈfɒnɪk/ *adj.* (of sound-reproduction) using four transmission channels. —**quadraphonically** *adv.*, **quadraphony** /-ˈrɒfənɪ/ *n.* [f. QUADRI- + (STEREO)PHONIC]

quadrat /ˈkwɒdræt/ *n.* a small area marked out for study of the plants and animals it contains. [f. L *quadratus* made square]

quadrate /ˈkwɒdreɪt/ *adj.* square, rectangular. [as prec.]

quadratic equation /kwɒdˈrætɪk/ an equation involving the square and no higher power of an unknown quantity or variable. [f. F or L (as QUADRAT)]

quadrennial /kwɒdˈrenɪəl/ *adj.* **1** lasting for four years. **2** recurring every four years. —**quadrennially** *adv.* [as foll.]

quadrennium /kwɒdˈrenɪəm/ *n.* (*pl.* **-s**) a period of four years. [f. L *quadriennium* (QUADRI-, *annus* year)]

quadri- /kwɒdrɪ/ *in comb.* four. [L (*quattuor* four)]

quadrilateral /kwɒdrɪˈlætər(ə)l/ *adj.* having four sides. —*n.* a quadrilateral figure. [f. L (QUADRI-, *latus* side)]

quadrille[1] /kwəˈdrɪl/ *n.* a square dance usually containing five figures; music for this. [F f. Sp. *cuadrilla* squadron (*cuadra* square)]

quadrille[2] /kwəˈdrɪl/ *n.* a card-game fashionable in the 18th c., played by four persons with 40 cards (i.e. an ordinary pack without the 8s, 9s, and 10s). [F, perh. f. Sp. (*cuarto* fourth)]

quadrillion /kwəˈdrɪljən/ *n.* (for *pl.* usage see HUNDRED) **1** a million raised to the fourth power (1 followed by 24 ciphers). **2** (*Amer.*) a thousand raised to the fifth power (1 followed by 15 ciphers). [QUADRI- + MILLION]

quadriplegia /kwɒdrɪˈpli:dʒɪə/ *n.* paralysis of all four limbs. —**quadriplegic** *adj.* and *n.* [f. QUADRI- + Gk *plēgē* blow]

quadroon /kwəˈdru:n/ *n.* the offspring of a White and a mulatto, a person of one-quarter Negro blood. [f. Sp. *cuarterón* (*cuarto* fourth)]

quadruped /ˈkwɒdrʊped/ *n.* a four-footed animal, especially a mammal. [f. F or L (QUADRI-, *pes* foot)]

quadruple /ˈkwɒdrʊp(ə)l/ *adj.* **1** fourfold; having four parts; being four times as many or as much. **2** (of time in music) having four beats in a bar. —*n.* a fourfold number or amount. —*v.t./i.* to multiply by four. —**quadruply** *adv.* [f. F f. L *quadruplus* (as QUADRI-)]

quadruplet /ˈkwɒdrʊplɪt, -ˈru:p-/ *n.* each of four children born at one birth. [f. prec., after *triplet*]

quadruplicate /kwɒˈdru:plɪkət/ *adj.* **1** fourfold. **2** of which four copies are made. —/-eɪt/ *v.t.* **1** to multiply by four. **2** to make four copies of. —**in quadruplicate,** in four copies. [f. L (*quadruplex* fourfold)]

quaestor /ˈkwi:stə(r)/ *n.* a magistrate in ancient Rome who acted as the State treasurer, paymaster, etc. [f. L (*quaerere* seek)]

quaff /kwɒf, kwɑ:f/ *v.t./i.* (*literary*) to drain (a cup etc.) in copious draughts; to drink deeply. [perh. imit.]

quagmire /ˈkwægmaɪə(r), ˈkwɒg-/ *n.* a quaking bog, a marsh, a slough. [f. *quag* marsh, or dial. *quag* to shake + MIRE]

quail[1] *n.* (*pl.* same or **-s**) a bird of the genus *Coturnix* related to the partridge. [f. OF f. L *coacula* (prob. imit.)]

quail[2] *v.i.* to flinch, to show fear. [orig. unkn.]

quaint *adj.* piquantly or attractively unfamiliar or old-fashioned, daintily odd. —**quaintly** *adv.*, **quaintness** *n.* [orig. = cunning, f. OF f. L *cognitus* (*cognoscere* ascertain)]

quake *v.i.* to shake or tremble from unsteadiness; (of a person) to shake with fear etc. —*n.* (*colloq.*) an earthquake. [OE]

Quaker /ˈkweɪkə(r)/ *n.* a member of the Society of Friends (see SOCIETY). —**Quakerism** *n.* [f. prec.; the reason for the name is disputed]

qualification /kwɒlɪfɪˈkeɪʃ(ə)n/ *n.* **1** qualifying. **2** an accomplishment fitting a person for a position or purpose. **3** a thing that modifies or limits a meaning etc. —**qualificatory** *adj.* [F or f. L (as foll.)]

qualify /ˈkwɒlɪfaɪ/ *v.t./i.* **1** to make competent or fit for a position or purpose; to make legally entitled. **2** (of a person) to satisfy the conditions or requirements. **3** to modify or make (a statement etc.) less absolute. **4** to moderate, to mitigate, to make less extreme. **5** to attribute a quality to, to describe as. —**qualifier** *n.* [f. F. f. L *qualificare* (*qualis* such as, of what kind)]

qualitative /ˈkwɒlɪtətɪv/ *adj.* concerned with or depending on quality. [f. L (as foll.)]

quality /ˈkwɒlɪtɪ/ *n.* **1** degree or level of excellence. **2** general excellence. **3** an attribute or faculty. **4** (of a voice or sound) timbre. **5** (*archaic*) high social standing. [f. OF f. L (as QUALIFY)]

qualm /kwɑ:m/ *n.* **1** a misgiving, an uneasy doubt, a scruple of conscience. **2** a momentary faint or sick feeling. [orig. unkn.]

quandary /ˈkwɒndərɪ/ *n.* a perplexed state, a practical dilemma. [orig. unkn.]

quango /ˈkwæŋgəʊ/ *n.* (*pl.* **-os**) a semi-public body with financial support from and senior appointments made by the government. [abbr. of *qua*si-*a*utonomous *n*on-*g*overnmental *o*rganization]

quanta *pl.* of QUANTUM.

quantifiable /ˈkwɒntɪfaɪəb(ə)l/ *adj.* that may be quantified. [f. foll.]

quantify /ˈkwɒntɪfaɪ/ *v.t.* to express as a quantity; to determine the quantity of. —**quantification** /-fɪˈkeɪʃ(ə)n/ *n.* [f. L *quantificare* (*quantus* how much)]

quantitative /ˈkwɒntɪtətɪv/ *adj.* concerned with quantity; measured or measurable by quantity. [f. L (as foll.)]

quantity /ˈkwɒntɪtɪ/ *n.* **1** ability to be measured through having size, weight, amount, or number. **2** an amount or number of things; a specified or considerable amount or number. **3** length or shortness of vowel sounds or syllables. **4** a thing having quantity. —**quantity surveyor,** a person who measures and prices the work of builders. [f. OF f. L (as QUANTIFY)]

quantum /ˈkwɒntəm/ *n.* (*pl.* **quanta**) **1** a minimum amount of a physical quantity (such as energy or momentum) which can exist in a given situation and by multiples of which changes in the quantity occur. **2** a required, desired, or allowed amount. —**quantum mechanics,** a mathematical form of quantum theory dealing with the motion and interaction of (esp. subatomic) particles and incorporating the concept that these particles can also be regarded as waves. **quantum theory,** the body of theory based on the existence of quanta of energy. [L, neut. of *quantus* how much]

quarantine /ˈkwɒrənti:n/ *n.* isolation imposed on a ship, persons, or animals to prevent infection or contagion; the period of this. —*v.t.* to put into quarantine. [f. It., = forty days (*quaranta* forty)]

quark /kwɑ:k, kwɔk/ *n.* any of a group of (originally three) hypothetical components of elementary particles. [from phrase 'Three quarks for Muster Mark!' in James Joyce's *Finnegans Wake* (1939)]

quarrel /ˈkwɒr(ə)l/ *n.* **1** a violent disagreement; a break in friendly relations. **2** a cause for complaint. —*v.i.* (**-ll-**) **1** to engage in a quarrel; to break off friendly relations. **2** to find fault. [f. OF f. L *querel(l)a* complaint (*queri* complain)]

quarrelsome *adj.* given to quarrelling. —**quarrelsomeness** *n.* [f. prec. + -SOME]

quarry[1] /ˈkwɒrɪ/ *n.* a place from which stone is extracted for building etc. —*v.t./i.* to extract (stone) from a quarry. —**quarry tile,** an unglazed floor-tile. [f. L f. OF *quarriere* f. L *quadrum* square]

quarry[2] /ˈkwɒrɪ/ *n.* an intended prey or victim being hunted; something sought or pursued. [f. OF *cuiree*, ult. f. L *cor* heart; orig. = parts of deer given to hounds]

quart /kwɔt/ *n.* a liquid measure equal to one quarter of a gallon. [f. OF f. L (*quartus* fourth)]

quarter /ˈkwɔtə(r)/ *n.* **1** each of four equal parts into which a thing is divided. **2** a period of three months, especially one ending on a quarter-day. **3** a point of time 15 minutes before or after any hour. **4** 25 US or Canadian cents; a coin for this. **5** a division of a town, especially as occupied by a particular class. **6** a point of the compass; the region at this; a direction; a district; a person or group regarded as a possible source of supply. **7** (in *pl.*) lodgings; an abode, a station of troops. **8** one fourth of a lunar month; the moon's position between the first two (**first quarter**) and the last two (**last quarter**) of these. **9** each of the four parts into which a carcass is divided. **10** (in *pl.*) the hind legs and adjoining parts of a quadruped; the hindquarters. **11** exemption from being put to death, on condition of surrender. **12**a grain-measure of 8 bushels, one quarter of a hundredweight. —*v.t.* **1** to divide into quarters; (*hist.*) to divide (the body of an executed person) thus. **2** to put (troops etc.) into quarters; to provide with lodgings. **3** to place (coats of arms) on four parts of a shield's surface. —**cry quarter,** to ask for mercy. **quarter-day** *n.* any of the four days beginning an official quarter of the year for fiscal purposes (in England 25 March, 24 June, 29 Sept., 25 Dec.; in Scotland 2 Feb., 15 May, 1 August, 11 Nov.). **quarter-final** *n.* a match or round preceding a semi-final. **quarter-light** *n.* a small vertically opening window in a motor vehicle. **quarter sessions,** (*hist.*) a court with limited criminal and civil jurisdiction, usually held quarterly. [f. AF f. L *quartarius* (as prec.)]

quarterdeck *n.* the part of a ship's upper deck near the stern, usually reserved for officers.

quartering *n.* (often in *pl.*) coats of arms arranged on one shield to denote alliances of families. [f. QUARTER]

quarterly *adv.* **1** once in each quarter of a year. **2** (in heraldry) in the four, or in two diagonally opposite, quarters of a shield. —*adj.* **1** done, published, or due quarterly. **2** (in heraldry, of a shield) quartered. —*n.* a quarterly publication. [as prec.]

quartermaster *n.* **1** a regimental officer in charge of quartering, rations, etc. **2** a naval petty officer in charge of steering, signals, etc.

quarterstaff *n.* a stout pole, six to eight feet long, formerly used by peasantry as a weapon.

quartet /kwɔˈtet/ *n.* (also **quartette**) **1** a musical composition for four performers; these performers. **2** any group of four. [f. F f. It. (*quarto* fourth, f. L *quartus* four)]

quarto /ˈkwɔtəʊ/ *n.* (*pl.* **-os**) the size of a book or page given by twice folding a sheet of standard size to form four leaves; a book or sheet of this size. [f. L (*in*) *quarto* (in) fourth (of sheet)]

quartz /kwɔts/ *n.* silica in various forms. —**quartz clock** *or* **watch,** one operated by electric vibrations of a quartz crystal. **quartz lamp,** a quartz tube with mercury vapour as the light-source. [f. G f. Slavonic]

quasar /ˈkweɪsɑː(r)/ *n.* any of a class of point-like sources of light visible in large telescopes, often associated with intense radio emission. [f. *quas*i + stell*ar*]

quash /kwɒʃ/ *v.t.* **1** annul, regard as not valid, esp. by legal procedure. **2** suppress, crush. [f. OF *quasser* f. L *quassare* shake violently]

quasi- /ˈkweɪzaɪ/ *prefix* seeming(ly), not real(ly); almost. [f. L *quasi* as if]

quassia /ˈkwɒʃə/ *n.* **1** a South American tree (*Quassia amara*); its wood, bark, or root. **2** a bitter tonic from these. [f. G. *Quassi*, 18th-c. Surinam Negro, who discovered its medicinal properties]

quaternary /kwəˈtɜːnərɪ/ *adj.* **1** having four parts. **2 Quaternary,** of the second period of the Cainozoic era. —**Quaternary** *n.* this period. [f. L (*quaterni* four each)]

quatrain /ˈkwɒtreɪn/ *n.* a four-line stanza. [F (*quatre* four)]

quatrefoil /ˈkætrəfɔɪl/ *n.* **1** a four-cusped figure. **2** a four-lobed leaf or flower. [f. AF (*quatre* four, *foil* leaf)]

quattrocento /kwɑːtrəʊˈtʃentəʊ/ *n.* Italian art of the 15th c. [It., = 1400, used of years 14—]

quaver /ˈkweɪvə(r)/ *v.t./i.* **1** to tremble, to vibrate. **2** to say or speak in a trembling voice; to sing with trembling. —*n.* **1** a quavering sound; quavering speech. **2** a trill. **3** (*Mus.*) a note half as long as a crotchet. —**quavery** *adj.* [frequent. of obs. *quave* (imit.)]

quay /kiː/ *n.* an artificial landing-place for loading and unloading ships. [f. OF *kay*]

queasy /ˈkwiːzɪ/ *adj.* **1** feeling slight nausea; having an easily upset digestion. **2** (of food) causing nausea. **3** (of a conscience or person) over-scrupulous. —**queasily** *adv.*, **queasiness** *n.* [perh. rel. to OF *coisier* hurt]

queen *n.* **1** a female sovereign (esp. hereditary) ruler of an independent State. **2** a king's wife. **3** a woman, country, or thing regarded as pre-eminent in a specified field, area, or class. **4** a perfect fertile female of the bee, ant, etc.

5 the most powerful piece in chess. 6 a court-card with a picture of a queen. 7 (*slang*) a male homosexual. —*v.t.* to convert (a pawn in chess) to a queen when it reaches the opponent's end of the board; (of a pawn) to be thus converted. —**Queen-Anne** *adj.* in the style of English design characteristic of the early 18th c. **queen consort,** a king's wife. **queen it,** to act the queen. **queen mother,** a king's widow who is the mother of a sovereign. **queen-post** *n.* either of the two upright posts between the tie-beam and the main rafters. —**queenly** *adj.*, **queenliness** *n.* [OE]

Queensberry Rules /ˈkwi:nzbərɪ/ the standard rules of boxing, drafted in 1867 under the name and patronage of the Marquess of Queensberry.

queer *adj.* 1 strange, odd, eccentric. 2 suspect, of questionable character. 3 slightly ill, faint. 4 (*slang*, esp. of a man) homosexual. —*n.* (*slang*) a homosexual (esp. male) person. —*v.t.* (*slang*) to spoil, to put out of order. —**in Queer Street,** (*slang*) in debt or trouble or disrepute. **queer the pitch for,** to spoil the chances of (a person) beforehand. —**queerly** *adv.*, **queerness** *n.* [perh. f. G *quer* oblique]

quell *v.t.* to suppress; to reduce to submission. [OE, = kill]

quench *v.t.* 1 to satisfy (one's thirst) by drinking. 2 to extinguish (a fire or light). 3 to cool, especially with water. 4 to stifle or suppress (a desire etc.). [OE]

quern /kwɜ:n/ *n.* 1 a simple apparatus for grinding corn, consisting of two hard stones, the upper of which is rubbed to and fro, or rotated, on the lower one. 2 a small hand-mill for pepper etc. [OE]

querulous /ˈkwerʊləs/ *adj.* complaining peevishly. —**querulously** *adv.*, **querulousness** *n.* [f. L (*queri* complain)]

query /ˈkwɪərɪ/ *n.* 1 a question. 2 a question mark or the word *query* spoken or written as a mark of interrogation. —*v.t.* 1 to ask or inquire. 2 to call in question, to dispute the accuracy of. [anglicized form of L *quaere* (imper. of *quaerere* ask)]

quest *n.* 1 seeking, a search. 2 a thing sought. —*v.i.* to seek or search for something. —**in quest of,** seeking. [f. OF f. L *quaerere* seek]

question /ˈkwestʃ(ə)n/ *n.* 1 a sentence so worded or expressed as to seek information. 2 a doubt or dispute about a matter; the raising of such doubt etc. 3 the matters to be discussed or decided. 4 a problem for solution. 5 a thing depending on the conditions *of*. —*v.t.* 1 to ask questions of; to subject to examination. 2 to call in question; to throw doubt on. —**beyond (all) question,** certainly. **call in question,** to express doubts about, to dispute. **in question,** being mentioned or discussed. **out of the question,** impracticable, not worth considering. **question mark,** the punctuation mark (?) indicating a question. **question-master** *n.* the person who puts the questions to people taking part in a quiz game or similar entertainment. **question time,** a period in Parliament when MPs may question ministers. —**questioner** *n.* [as prec.]

questionable *adj.* of doubtful truth, validity, or advisability; suspect. —**questionably** *adv.* [f. prec.]

questionnaire /kwestʃəˈneə(r)/ *n.* a formulated series of questions put to a number of people, especially as part of a survey. [F (as QUEST)]

queue /kju:/ *n.* 1 a line or sequence of persons or vehicles etc. awaiting their turn. 2 a pigtail. —*v.i.* (often with *up*) to stand in or join a queue. [F f. L *cauda* tail]

quibble *n.* 1 a petty objection, a trivial point of criticism. 2 a play on words, a pun. 3 an equivocation, an evasion; an argument depending on the ambiguity of a word or phrase. —*v.i.* to use quibbles. —**quibbler** *n.* [dim. of obs. *quib* prob. f. L *quibus* dat. and abl. pl. of *qui* who (used in legal documents)]

quiche /ki:ʃ/ *n.* an open tart, usually with a savoury filling. [F]

quick *adj.* 1 taking only a short time to do something or to traverse a distance or to be done or obtained etc. 2 able to notice or learn or think quickly; alert. 3 (of temper) easily roused. 4 (*archaic*) living, alive. —*adv.* quickly, at a rapid rate; in a fairly short time. —*n.* 1 the sensitive flesh below the nails or skin or a sore. 2 the seat of feeling or emotion. —**quick-freeze** *v.t.* to freeze (food) rapidly for storing, so that it keeps its natural qualities. **quick-witted** *adj.* alert; quick to understand a situation; quick at making jokes. —**quickly** *adv.* **quickness** *n.* [OE, orig. = alive]

quicken *v.t./i.* 1 to make or become quicker, to accelerate. 2 to make or become livelier, to stimulate. 3 (of a woman or foetus) to reach the stage of pregnancy when the foetus makes movements that can be felt by the mother. [f. prec.]

quickie *n.* (*colloq.*) a thing made or done quickly. [f. QUICK]

quicklime *n.* unslaked lime.

quicksand *n.* an area of loose wet sand into which heavy objects readily sink.

quickset *adj.* formed of live plants set to grow in a hedge. —*n.* a hedge formed thus.

quicksilver *n.* 1 mercury. 2 a mercurial temperament.

quickstep *n.* a ballroom dance with quick steps; the music for this.

quid[1] *n.* (*pl.* same) (*slang*) one pound sterling.

—quids in, able to profit. [prob. f. *quid* nature of a thing, f. L what, something]

quid[2] *n.* a lump of tobacco for chewing. [dial. var. of CUD]

quiddity /ˈkwɪdɪtɪ/ *n.* **1** the essence of a thing. **2** a quibble, a captious subtlety. [f. L *quidditas* (*quid* what)]

quid pro quo /kwɪd prəʊ ˈkwəʊ/ a thing given as compensation. [L, = something for something]

quiescent /kwɪˈesənt/ *adj.* inactive, dormant. **—quiescence** *n.* [as foll.]

quiet /ˈkwaɪət/ *adj.* **1** with little or no sound or motion. **2** of gentle or peaceful disposition. **3** unobtrusive, not showy. **4** not overt, private, disguised. **5** undisturbed, uninterrupted; free or far from vigorous action; informal. **6** enjoyed in quiet; not anxious or remorseful. —*n.* an undisturbed state, tranquillity; repose; stillness, silence. —*v.t./i.* to make or become quiet or calm. **—be quiet,** (*colloq.*) to cease talking etc. **keep quiet,** to say nothing. **on the quiet,** unobtrusively, secretly. **—quietly** *adv.*, **quietness** *n.* [f. OF f. L (*quiescere* become calm)]

quieten *v.t./i.* to make or become quiet. [f. prec.]

quietism /ˈkwaɪətɪz(ə)m/ *n.* a passive contemplative attitude to life, as a form of religious mysticism. **—quietist** *n.* & *adj.* [f. It. (as QUIET)]

quietude /ˈkwaɪɪtju:d/ *n.* quietness. [f. QUIET]

quietus /kwaɪˈi:təs/ *n.* release from life, final riddance. [f. L *quietus* (*est* he is) quit, used in receipts]

quiff *n.* a lock of hair plastered down or brushed up on the forehead. [orig. unkn.]

quill *n.* **1** a large feather of a bird's wing or tail; a pen made from this. **2** the hollow stem of a feather; a plectrum or other device made from this. **3** one of a porcupine's spines. [prob. f. MLG]

quilt *n.* a coverlet, especially of quilted material. —*v.t.* to line (a coverlet or garment) with padding held between two layers of cloth etc. by cross-lines of stitching. [f. OF *coilte* f. L *culcita* cushion]

quin *n.* (*colloq.*) a quintuplet. [abbr.]

quince *n.* an acid pear-shaped fruit used in jams etc.; the tree (*Cydonia oblonga*) bearing it. [orig. pl. of obs. *quoyn* f. OF f. L *cotoneum, cydoneum* (*Cydonia* in Crete)]

quincentenary /kwɪnsenˈti:nərɪ/ *n.* a 500th anniversary; a celebration of this. —*adj.* of a quincentenary. [f. L *quinque* five + CENTENARY]

quincunx /ˈkwɪnkʌŋks/ *n.* **1** the centre and four corner points of a square or rectangle. **2** five trees etc. so placed. [L, = five-twelfths (*quinque* five, *uncia* twelfth part; see OUNCE[1])]

quinine /ˈkwɪni:n/ *n.* a bitter drug obtained from the bark of the cinchona tree, used to reduce fever and as a tonic. [f. *quina* cinchona bark (Sp. f. Quechua *kina* bark)]

Quinquagesima /kwɪŋkwəˈdʒesɪmə/ *n.* the Sunday before Lent (50 days before Easter). [L (*quinquagesimus* fiftieth; cf. QUADRIGESIMA)]

quinquennial /kwɪŋˈkwenɪəl/ *adj.* lasting or recurring every five years. **—quinquennially** *adv.* [f. L *quinquennis* (as foll.)]

quinquennium /kwɪŋˈkwenɪəm/ *n.* (*pl.* **-iums**) a period of five years. [L (*quinque* five, *annus* year)]

quinquereme /ˈkwɪŋkwɪri:m/ *n.* an ancient galley (see entry), probably with five men at each oar. [f. L (*quinque* five, *remus* oar)]

quinsy /ˈkwɪnzɪ/ *n.* inflammation of the throat, especially with an abscess on the tonsil(s). [f. OF f. L *quinancia* f. Gk]

quintessence /kwɪnˈtes(ə)ns/ *n.* **1** the purest and most perfect form or manifestation or embodiment of a quality etc. **2** a highly refined extract. **—quintessential** /-tɪˈsenʃ(ə)l/ *adj.*, **quintessentially** *adv.* [f. F f. L *quinta essentia* fifth essence (underlying the four elements)]

quintet /kwɪnˈtet/ *n.* **1** a musical composition for five performers; these performers. **2** any group of five. [f. F f. It. (*quinto* fifth, f. L)]

quintuple /ˈkwɪntjʊp(ə)l/ *adj.* fivefold; having five parts; being five times as many or as much. —*n.* a fivefold number or amount. —*v.t./i.* to multiply by five. [f. F f. L *quintus* fifth]

quintuplet /ˈkwɪntjʊplɪt, -ˈtju:-/ *n.* each of five children born at one birth. [f. prec., after *triplet* etc.]

quintuplicate /kwɪnˈtju:plɪkət/ *adj.* **1** fivefold. **2** of which five copies are made. [as QUINTUPLE, after QUADRUPLICATE]

quip *n.* a clever saying, an epigram. —*v.i.* (**-pp-**) to make quips. [perh. f. L *quippe* forsooth]

quire *n.* **1** 25 (formerly 24) sheets of writing paper. **2** each of the folded sheets that are sewn together in book-binding. **—in quires,** unbound. [f. OF f. L *quaterni* (as QUATERNARY)]

quirk *n.* **1** a peculiarity of behaviour. **2** a trick of fate. **3** a flourish in writing. **—quirky** *adj.* [orig. unkn.]

quisling /ˈkwɪzlɪŋ/ *n.* a traitor, especially one who collaborates with an enemy occupying his country. [f. V. *Quisling* Norwegian collaborator (d. 1945)]

quit *v.t.* (**-tt-**) **1** to give up, to abandon. **2** to cease. **3** to leave or depart (from). —*predic. adj.* rid. [earlier = release, f. OF f. L *quittus, quietus* (as QUIET)]

quitch *n.* a weed with long creeping roots, couch-grass (*Elymus repens*). [OE]

quite *adv.* **1** completely, entirely, wholly. **2** really, actually. **3** somewhat, to some extent. —**quite a few,** a fair number. **quite (so),** I grant the truth of that. **quite something,** remarkable. [var. of *quit* adj. (QUIT)]

quits *predic. adj.* on even terms by retaliation or repayment. —**call it** *or* **cry quits,** to acknowledge that things are now even, to agree to stop quarrelling etc. [perh. abbr. of L *quittus* (as QUIT)]

quittance /ˈkwɪt(ə)ns/ *n.* (*archaic*) **1** release from an obligation. **2** an acknowledgement of payment. [f. OF (as QUIT)]

quitter *n.* a deserter, a shirker. [f. QUIT]

quiver[1] /ˈkwɪvə(r)/ *v.i.* to tremble or vibrate with a slight rapid motion. —*n.* a quivering motion or sound. [f. obs. *quiver* nimble]

quiver[2] /ˈkwɪvə(r)/ *n.* a case for holding arrows. [f. OF *quivre* f. WG]

qui vive /kiː ˈviːv/ **on the qui vive,** on the alert. [F, = (long) live who? (as sentry's challenge)]

quixotic /kwɪkˈsɒtɪk/ *adj.* chivalrous and unselfish to an extravagant or impractical extent. —**quixotically** *adv.*, **quixotry** /ˈkwɪksətrɪ/ *n.* [f. prec.]

quiz *n.* (*pl.* **quizzes**) a series of questions testing people's knowledge, especially as a form of entertainment. —*v.t.* (**-zz-**) **1** to interrogate. **2** (*archaic*) to stare at curiously or critically. **3** (*archaic*) to make fun of. [orig. unkn.]

quizzical /ˈkwɪzɪk(ə)l/ *adj.* **1** expressing or done with mild or amused perplexity. **2** strange, comical. —**quizzically** *adv.* [f. QUIZ]

quod *n.* (*slang*) prison. [orig. unkn.]

quoin /kɔɪn/ *n.* **1** an outside corner of a building. **2** a corner-stone. **3** an inside corner of a room. **4** a wedge used for various purposes. [var. of COIN]

quoit /kɔɪt/ *n.* **1** a ring thrown at a mark or to encircle a peg. **2** (in *pl.*) a game using these. [orig. unkn.]

quondam /ˈkwɒndæm/ *adj.* that once was, sometime, former. [L, = formerly]

quorum /ˈkwɔːrəm/ *n.* the number of members that must be present to constitute a valid meeting. —**quorate** *adj.* [L, = of which people]

quota /ˈkwəʊtə/ *n.* **1** the share to be contributed to or received from a total by one of the parties concerned. **2** the total number or amount required or permitted. [f. L *quota* (*pars*) how great (a part) (*quot* how many)]

quotable /ˈkwəʊtəb(ə)l/ *adj.* worth quoting. [f. foll.]

quotation /kwəʊˈteɪʃ(ə)n/ *n.* **1** quoting. **2** a passage or price quoted. —**quotation-marks** *n.pl.* inverted commas (' ' or " ") used at the beginning and end of quoted passages or words. [f. L (as foll.)]

quote *v.t./i.* **1** to cite or appeal to (an author or book) in confirmation of some view. **2** to repeat or copy out a passage from; to repeat or copy out (a passage). **3** to enclose (words) in quotation marks. **4** to state the price of (usu. *at* a figure). —*n.* (*colloq.*) **1** a passage or price quoted. **2** (usu. in *pl.*) a quotation-mark. [f. L *quotare* mark with numbers (as QUOTA)]

quoth /kwəʊθ/ *v.t.* (*archaic*) (only with *I* or *he* or *she* placed after) said. [OE]

quotidian /kwəˈtɪdɪən/ *adj.* **1** daily; (of a fever) recurring every day. **2** everyday, commonplace. [f. OF f. L (*quotidie* daily)]

quotient /ˈkwəʊʃənt/ *n.* the result of a division sum. [f. L *quotiens* how many times]

q.v. *abbr.* which see (in references). [f. L *quod vide*]

qy. *abbr.* query.

R, r /ɑ:(r)/ *n.* (*pl.* **Rs, R's**) the eighteenth letter of the alphabet. —**the three Rs,** reading, (w)riting, (a)rithmetic.

R *abbr.* (in chess) rook.

® *symbol* registered as a trademark.

R. *abbr.* **1** *Regina.* **2** *Rex.* **3** River.

r. *abbr.* right.

RA *abbr.* **1** Royal Academician; Royal Academy. **2** Royal Artillery.

Ra *symbol* radium.

rabbet /ˈræbɪt/ *n.* & *v.t.* = REBATE². [f. OF *rab(b)at* recess (as REBATE¹)]

rabbi /ˈræbaɪ/ *n.* a Jewish religious leader; a Jewish scholar or teacher, especially of the law. —**rabbinical** /-ˈbɪnɪk(ə)l/ *adj.* [ult. f. Heb., = my master]

rabbit /ˈræbɪt/ *n.* **1** a herbivorous mammal (*Oryctolagus cuniculus*), native to western Europe, allied to the hare but with shorter legs and smaller ears, brownish-grey in the natural state, also black, white, or pied in domestication. **2** (*US*) a hare. **3** (*colloq.*) a poor performer at a game. —*v.i.* **1** to hunt rabbits. **2** (*slang*) to talk lengthily or in a rambling way. —**rabbit punch,** a short chop with the edge of the hand to an opponent's nape, such as is used for breaking a rabbit's neck. —**rabbity** *adj.* [perh. f. OF]

rabble *n.* a disorderly crowd, a mob; a contemptible or inferior set of people; the lower or disorderly classes of the populace. [orig. unkn.]

rabid /ˈræbɪd/ *adj.* **1** furious, raging. **2** fanatical. **3** of or affected with rabies. —**rabidity** /rəˈbɪdɪtɪ/ *n.*, **rabidly** *adv.* [f. L (*rabere* rave)]

rabies /ˈreɪbi:z, -ɪz/ *n.* a contagious virus disease of dogs and other warm-blooded animals, which produces paralysis or a vicious excitability and in man causes a fatal encephalitis with convulsions and with throat spasm on swallowing. [L (as prec.)]

race¹ *n.* **1** a contest of speed in reaching a certain point or in doing or achieving something; (in *pl.*) a series of these for horses or dogs at a fixed time on a regular course. **2** a strong fast current of water. **3** a channel for the balls in a ball-bearing. —*v.t./i.* **1** to compete in a race; to have a race with; to cause to race. **2** to move or cause to move or operate at full or excessive speed. **3** to take part in horse-racing. —**race-meeting** *n.* a series of horse-races at one venue at fixed times. **race-track** *n.* a course for racing horses, vehicles, etc. —**racer** *n.* [orig. = running, f. ON]

race² *n.* **1** each of the major divisions of mankind with distinct inherited physical characteristics; the fact or concept of division into races. **2** a group of persons, animals, or plants connected by common descent; a genus, species, breed, or variety of animals or plants. —**the human race,** mankind. **race relations,** relations between members of different races in the same country or community. **race riot,** an outbreak of violence due to racial antagonism. [F f. It. *razza*]

racecourse *n.* a ground for horse-racing.

racegoer *n.* one who frequents horse-races.

racehorse *n.* a horse bred or kept for racing.

raceme /rəˈsi:m/ *n.* a flower-cluster with flowers attached by short stalks at intervals along a stem. [f. L *racemus* grape-bunch]

rachel /rəˈʃel/ *n.* a light tannish colour of face-powder. [f. *Rachel*, stage-name of Elisa Félix (1820–58), French actress]

racial /ˈreɪʃ(ə)l/ *adj.* of or characteristic of a race; concerning or caused by race. —**racially** *adv.* [f. RACE²]

racialism *n.* **1** belief in the superiority of a particular race. **2** antagonism towards a particular race. —**racialist** *n.* & *adj.* [f. prec.]

racism /ˈreɪsɪz(ə)m/ *n.* **1** racialism. **2** the theory that human abilities etc. are determined by race. —**racist** *n.* & *adj.* [f. RACE²]

rack¹ *n.* **1** a framework, usually with bars or pegs etc., for holding things or hanging things on. **2** a cogged or toothed bar or rail engaging with a wheel or pinion etc. **3** (*hist.*) an instrument of torture, a frame with a roller at each end to which the victim's wrists and ankles were tied so that his joints were stretched when the rollers were turned. —*v.t.* **1** (of a disease or pain) to inflict suffering on. **2** (*hist.*) to torture (a person) on a rack. **3** to place on or in a rack. **4** to shake violently; to injure by straining. —**on the rack,** in pain or distress. **rack one's brains,** to try hard to remember or think of something. **rack-railway** *n.* a mountain railway with a cogged rail in which a pinion on the locomotive engages. **rack-rent** *n.* an exorbitant rent. [f. Du or MLG]

rack[2] *n.* destruction (esp. in *rack and ruin*). [var. of WRACK]

racket[1] /ˈrækɪt/ *n.* **1** a bat having a round or oval frame strung with catgut or nylon etc., used in ball-games such as tennis and rackets. **2** (in *pl.*) a ball-game for two or four persons, played with rackets in a plain four-walled court. [f. F, ult. f. Arab., = palm of the hand]

racket[2] /ˈrækɪt/ *n.* **1** a din, a noisy fuss. **2** a business or other scheme in which dishonest means are used. **3** (*slang*) a line of business; a dodge. —*v.i.* to move about noisily; to engage in wild social activities. —**stand the racket,** (*colloq.*) to bear the costs or consequences. [perh. imit.]

racketeer /rækɪˈtɪə(r)/ *n.* one who operates a dishonest scheme. —**racketeering** *n.* [f. prec.]

rackety *adj.* noisy, rowdy. [f. RACKET[2]]

raconteur /rækɒnˈtɜː(r)/ *n.* a teller of anecdotes. —**raconteuse** /-ˈtɜːz/ *n.fem.* [F (*raconter* relate)]

racoon /rəˈkuːn/ *n.* a North American mammal (*Procyon lotor*) with a bushy tail, sharp snout, and greyish-brown fur. [American Indian]

racy /ˈreɪsɪ/ *adj.* **1** lively and vigorous in style. **2** (*US*) *risqué.* **3** of a distinctive quality; retaining traces of its origin. —**racily** *adv.*, **raciness** *n.* [f. RACE[2]]

rad *abbr.* **1** radian(s). **2** radical.

radar /ˈreɪdɑː(r)/ *n.* **1** a system for detecting the presence of objects at a distance, or ascertaining their position and motion, by transmitting short radio waves and detecting or measuring their return after they are reflected; a similar system in which the return signal consists of radio waves that a suitably equipped target automatically transmits when it receives the outgoing waves. **2** an apparatus or installation used for this system. —**radar trap,** an arrangement using radar to detect vehicles etc. travelling faster than the speed limit. [f. *ra*dio *d*etection *a*nd *r*anging]

raddle *n.* red ochre. —*v.t.* to colour with raddle, or with much rouge crudely used. [var. of RUDDLE]

raddled *adj.* worn out. [f. prec.]

radial /ˈreɪdɪəl/ *adj.* **1** of or arranged like rays or radii; having spokes or lines radiating from a centre. **2** acting or moving along lines that diverge from a centre. **3** (of a tyre; also **radial-ply**) having fabric layers with cords lying radial to the hub of the wheel (not crossing each other). —*n.* a radial-ply tyre. —**radially** *adv.* [f. L (as RADIUS)]

radian /ˈreɪdɪən/ *n.* a unit of plane angle; the angle at the centre of a circle formed by the radii of an arc with a length equal to the radius. [f. RADIUS]

radiant /ˈreɪdɪənt/ *adj.* **1** emitting rays of light. **2** looking very bright and happy; (of beauty) splendid, dazzling. **3** (of light) issuing in rays. —*n.* a point or object from which light or heat radiates. —**radiant heat,** heat transmitted by radiation. —**radiance** *n.*, **radiancy** *n.*, **radiantly** *adv.* [f. L *radiare* (as RADIUS)]

radiate /ˈreɪdɪeɪt/ *v.t./i.* **1** to emit rays of light, heat or other radiation; to emit from a centre; (of light or heat) to issue in rays. **2** to diverge or spread from a central point; to cause to do this. **3** to exude or show (a feeling etc.) clearly. —/ˈreɪdɪət/ *adj.* having the parts radially arranged. [as prec.]

radiation /reɪdɪˈeɪʃ(ə)n/ *n.* **1** radiating, being radiated. **2** the emission of energy as electromagnetic waves or as moving particles. **3** energy thus transmitted. —**radiation sickness,** sickness caused by exposure to excessive amounts of radioactivity. [as RADIATE]

radiator /ˈreɪdɪeɪtə(r)/ *n.* **1** an apparatus for heating a room etc. by the radiation of heat, especially a metal structure through which steam or hot water circulates, or one heated electrically. **2** an engine-cooling apparatus in a motor vehicle or aeroplane, with a large surface for cooling circulating water. [f. prec.]

radical /ˈrædɪk(ə)l/ *adj.* **1** fundamental, far-reaching, thorough. **2** advocating radical reforms; holding extreme views, revolutionary. **3** forming the basis, primary. **4** of the root of a number or quantity. **5** of the roots of words. —*n.* **1** a person holding radical views or belonging to a radical party. **2** a group of atoms forming part of a compound and remaining unaltered during its ordinary chemical changes. **3** the root of a word. **4** a mathematical quantity forming or expressed as the root of another. —**radicalism** *n.*, **radically** *adv.* [f. L (*radix* root)]

radicle /ˈrædɪk(ə)l/ *n.* the part of a plant embryo that develops into the primary root; a rootlet. [f. L *radicula* dim. of *radix* root]

radii *pl.* of RADIUS.

radio /ˈreɪdɪəʊ/ *n.* (*pl.* **-os**) **1** the transmission and reception of messages etc. by electromagnetic waves of radio-frequency, without a connecting wire. **2** an apparatus for transmitting or receiving signals by radio. **3** sound broadcasting; a station engaged in this. —*adj.* **1** of, using, or sent by radio; equipped with radio. **2** of or concerned with stars or other celestial bodies from which radio waves are received or reflected. —*v.t./i.* to send (a message) by radio; to communicate (with) or broadcast by radio. —**radio star,** a small celestial object emitting strong radio waves. [short for *radio-telegraphy* etc.]

radio- /reɪdɪəʊ-/ *in comb.* of or connected with rays, radiation, radioactivity, or radio. [f. RADIUS]

radioactive /reɪdɪəʊ'æktɪv/ *adj.* of or exhibiting radioactivity.

radioactivity /reɪdɪəʊæk'tɪvɪtɪ/ *n.* the property of spontaneous disintegration of atomic nuclei, usually with emission of penetrating radiation or particles.

radio-carbon *n.* a radioactive isotope of carbon, especially carbon 14 which has been used in a technique of assigning absolute dates to ancient organic material.

radio-controlled *adj.* controlled from a distance by radio.

radio-frequency *n.* frequency of radio waves, between about 10 kilohertz and 0.1 terahertz.

radiogram /'reɪdɪəʊgræm/ *n.* **1** a combined radio and gramophone. **2** a telegram sent by radio. **3** a picture obtained by X-rays etc. [f. RADIO- + -GRAM]

radiograph /'reɪdɪəgrɑ:f/ *n.* **1** a picture obtained by X-rays etc. **2** an instrument for recording the intensity of radiation. —*v.t.* to obtain a picture of by X-rays etc. —**radiographer** /-'ɒgrəfə(r)/ *n.*, **radiography** /-'ɒgrəfɪ/ *n.* [f. RADIO- + -GRAPH]

radio-isotope *n.* a radioactive isotope.

radiolarian /reɪdɪə'leərɪən/ *n.* a protozoan of the order Radiolaria, with a silicious skeleton and radiating pseudopodia. [f. L *radiolus* dim. of RADIUS]

radiology /reɪdɪ'ɒlədʒɪ/ *n.* the study of X-rays and other high-energy radiation, especially for use in medicine. —**radiologist** *n.* [f. RADIO- + -LOGY]

radiometry /reɪdɪ'ɒmətrɪ/ *n.* measurement of radioactivity or ionizing radiation. —**radiometric** /-ə'metrɪk/ *adj.* [f. RADIO + -METRY]

radioscopy /reɪdɪ'ɒskəpɪ/ *n.* the examination by X-rays etc. of objects opaque to light. [f. RADIO- + -SCOPY]

radio-telegraphy *n.* telegraphy using radio.

radio-telephony *n.* telephony using radio.

radio-therapy *n.* the treatment of disease by radiation, especially X-rays.

radish /'rædɪʃ/ *n.* a plant (*Raphanus sativus*) with a crisp pungent root eaten raw; this root. [OE f. L *radix* root]

radium /'reɪdɪəm/ *n.* a radioactive element, the heaviest member of the alkaline-earth metal group, symbol Ra, atomic number 88. [f. L *radius* ray]

radius /'reɪdɪəs/ *n.* (*pl.* **radii** /-ɪaɪ/) **1** a straight line from the centre to the circumference of a circle or sphere; the length of this; distance from a centre. **2** any of a set of lines diverging from a point like the radii of a circle. **3** the thicker and shorter bone in the forearm on the same side as the thumb; the corresponding bone in an animal's foreleg or bird's wing. [L, = spoke, ray]

radix /'reɪdɪks/ *n.* (*pl.* **-ices** /-si:z/) a number or symbol used as the basis of a numeration scale. [L, = root]

radon /'reɪdɒn/ *n.* a radioactive gaseous element, the heaviest of the noble gases, symbol Rn, atomic number 86. [f. RADIUM, after *argon* etc.]

RAF *abbr.* Royal Air Force.

raffia /'ræfɪə/ *n.* a fibre from the leaves of a kind of palm-tree, used for tying up plants and making mats and baskets etc.; this tree (*Raphia ruffia*). [Malagasy]

raffish *adj.* disreputable, rakish; tawdry. —**raffishness** *n.* [f. *raff* rubbish]

raffle *n.* a sale of articles by lottery, especially for charity. —*v.t.* to sell by a raffle. [orig. = dice-game, f. OF *raf(f)le*]

raft /rɑ:ft/ *n.* a flat floating structure of wood or fastened logs etc., used in water for transport or as an emergency boat. [f. ON, rel. to foll.]

rafter /'rɑ:ftə(r)/ *n.* any of the sloping beams forming the framework of a roof. [OE]

rag[1] *n.* **1** a torn, frayed or worn piece of woven material. **2** (in *pl.*) old or torn or worn clothes. **3** (*collect.*) rags used as a material for making paper, stuffing, etc. **4** (*derog.*) a newspaper. —**in rags,** much torn. **rag-and-bone man,** *n.* an itinerant dealer in old clothes, furniture, etc. **rag-bag** *n.* a bag for old rags; a miscellaneous collection. **rags to riches,** poverty to affluence. **rag trade,** (*colloq.*) the clothing business. [prob. back-formation f. RAGGED]

rag[2] *n.* **1** a programme of stunts, parades, and entertainment, staged by students to collect money for charity. **2** (*colloq.*) a prank. **3** (*slang*) a rowdy celebration; a noisy disorderly scene. —*v.t./i.* (**-gg-**) (*slang*) **1** to tease, to play rough jokes on. **2** to engage in rough play, to be riotous. [orig. unkn.]

rag[3] *n.* a piece of ragtime. [perh. f. RAGGED]

ragamuffin /'rægəmʌfɪn/ *n.* a person in ragged dirty clothes. [f. RAG[1] with fanciful ending]

rage *n.* **1** fierce or violent anger; a fit of this. **2** the violent operation of a natural force. —*v.i.* **1** to be fiercely angry; to speak furiously or madly. **2** (of a wind or battle etc.) to be violent, to be at its height. —**be all the rage,** to be temporarily very popular or fashionable. [f. OF f. L, = RABIES]

ragged /'rægɪd/ *adj.* **1** torn, frayed. **2** wearing ragged clothes. **3** having a broken jagged outline or surface. **4** faulty, lacking finish or smoothness or uniformity. —**run a person ragged,** to exhaust or debilitate him or her. —**raggedly** *adv.*, **raggedness** *n.* [f. ON, = tufted]

raglan /ˈræglən/ *n.* (usu. *attrib.*) a garment, especially an overcoat, with sleeves that continue to the neck and are joined to the body of the garment by sloping seams. —**raglan sleeve,** a sleeve of this kind. [f. Lord *Raglan*, British commander in Crimea (d. 1855)]

ragout /ˈrægu:/ *n.* a highly-seasoned stew of meat and vegetables. [f. F (*ragoûter* revive taste of)]

ragtag (and bobtail) riff-raff, disreputable people. [f. RAG[1]]

ragtime *n.* music with a syncopated melodic line and regularly-accented accompaniment. [prob. f. RAG[3] + TIME]

ragwort /ˈrægwɜ:t/ *n.* a wild plant of the genus *Senecio* with yellow flowers and ragged leaves.

raid *n.* **1** a sudden attack and withdrawal made by a military party or by ships or aircraft. **2** an attack made in order to steal or do harm. **3** a surprise visit by police etc. to arrest suspected persons or to seize illicit goods. —*v.t./i.* to make a raid (on). —**raider** *n.* [Sc. form of ROAD]

rail[1] *n.* **1** a level or sloping bar or series of bars used to hang things on, as the top of banisters, as part of a fence, as a protection against contact or falling over etc. **2** a horizontal piece (cf. STILE[2]) in the frame of a panelled door etc. **3** a steel bar or continuous line of bars laid on the ground usually as one of two forming a railway track. **3** railways as a means of transport. —*v.t.* **1** to furnish with a rail. **2** to enclose with rails. —**off the rails,** disorganized, out of order or control; crazy. [f. OF *reille* f. L *regula* rule]

rail[2] *v.i.* to complain or protest fiercely or abusively. [f. F *railler*]

rail[3] *n.* a small wading bird of the family Rallidae. [f. OF *raille* (perh. imit.)]

railcar *n.* a self-propelled railway coach.

railhead *n.* **1** the furthest point reached by a railway under construction. **2** the point on a railway at which the road transport of goods begins or ends.

railing *n.* a fence or barrier made of rails. [f. RAIL[1]]

raillery /ˈreɪlərɪ/ *n.* good-humoured ridicule. [f. F *raillerie* (as RAIL[2])]

railman *n.* (*pl.* **-men**) a railway-man.

railroad *n.* (*US*) a railway. —*v.t.* to rush or force into hasty action.

railway *n.* **1** a track or set of tracks of steel rails for the passage of trains conveying passengers and goods. **2** a system of transport using these; the organization and personnel required for its working. **3** a track on which wheeled equipment is run.

railwayman *n.* (*pl.* **-men**) a railway employee.

raiment /ˈreɪmənt/ *n.* (*archaic*) clothing. [f. obs. *arrayment* (as ARRAY)]

rain *n.* **1** condensed moisture of the atmosphere falling in drops; a fall of these; (in *pl.*) falls of rain, the season of these. **2** falling liquid or solid particles or objects (*lit.* or *fig.*); a rainlike descent of these. —*v.t./i.* **1** to fall or send down as or like rain; to send down rain. **2** to supply in large quantities. —**it rains** *or* **is raining,** rain falls or is falling. **rain forest,** luxuriant tropical forest with heavy rainfall. **rain off,** (esp. in *pass.*) to cause to be cancelled because of rain. **rain-shadow** *n.* a region in the lee of mountains where rainfall is low because it is sheltered from the prevailing winds. **rain-water** *n.* water that has fallen as rain, not obtained from wells etc. [OE]

rainbow /ˈreɪnbəʊ/ *n.* an arch of colours formed in the sky by the refraction and dispersion of the sun's rays in falling rain or in spray or mist. —*adj.* many-coloured. —**rainbow trout,** a large trout (*Salmo gairdnerii*) originally of the Pacific coast of North America. [OE (as RAIN, BOW[1])]

raincoat *n.* a waterproof or water-resistant coat.

raindrop *n.* a single drop of rain.

rainfall *n.* a fall of rain; the quantity of rain falling within a given area in a given time.

rainy *adj.* (of the weather, a day, region, etc.) in or on which rain is falling or much rain usually falls. —**rainy day,** a time of special need in the future. [OE (as RAIN)]

raise /reɪz/ *v.t.* **1** to put or take into a higher position; to cause to rise or stand up or be vertical. **2** to construct or build up. **3** to levy, to collect, to manage to obtain. **3** to cause to be heard or considered. **4** to set going or bring into being; to breed (animals) or grow (crops). **5** to bring up, to educate. **6** to increase the amount, value, or strength of. **7** to promote to a higher rank. **8** to multiply (a quantity to a power). **9** to cause (bread) to rise. **10** (in a card-game) to bet more than (another player). **11** to abandon or force an enemy to abandon (a siege etc.). **12** to remove (a barrier). **13** to cause (a ghost etc.) to appear. **14** (*colloq.*) to find (a person etc. who is wanted). —*n.* an increase in a stake or bid; (*US*) an increase in salary. —**raise from the dead,** to restore to life. **raise a laugh,** to cause others to laugh. **raise one's eyebrows,** to look supercilious or shocked. **raise the wind,** to procure money for a purpose. [f. ON]

raisin /ˈreɪz(ə)n/ *n.* a partially dried grape. [f. OF f. L *racemus* grape-bunch]

raison d'être /reɪzɔ̃ ˈdetr/ the purpose or reason that accounts for or justifies or originally caused a thing's existence. [F]

raj /rɑːdʒ/ *n.* British sovereignty in India. [Hindi, = reign]

raja /ˈrɑːdʒə/ *n.* (also **rajah**) (*hist.*) an Indian king or prince; a noble or petty dignitary. [f. Hindi f. Skr. *rājan* king]

rake[1] *n.* an implement of a pole with a toothed cross-bar at the end for drawing together hay etc. or smoothing loose soil or gravel; an implement like this, e.g. to draw in money at a gaming-table. —*v.t./i.* **1** to collect or gather (as) with a rake; to make tidy or smooth with a rake; to use a rake. **2** to search thoroughly, to ransack. **3** to direct gunfire along (a line) from end to end; to direct one's eyes or a camera thus. **4** to scratch or scrape. —**rake in,** (*colloq.*) to amass (profits etc.). **rake-off** *n.* (*colloq.*) a commission or share, especially in a disreputable deal. **rake up,** to revive (unwelcome memories etc.). [OE]

rake[2] *n.* a dissipated or immoral man of fashion. [f. *rakehell* (as RAKE[1], HELL)]

rake[3] *v.t./i.* to set or be set at a sloping angle; (of a mast or funnel) to incline from the perpendicular towards the stern. —*n.* a raking position or build; the amount by which a thing rakes. [prob. rel. to G *ragen* project]

rakish /ˈreɪkɪʃ/ *adj.* like a rake (RAKE[2]); dashing, jaunty. —**rakishly** *adv.*, **rakishness** *n.* [f. RAKE[2]]

rallentando /rælənˈtændəʊ/ *adv.* (*Mus.*) with a gradual decrease of speed. —*n.* (*pl.* **-os**) (*Mus.*) a passage to be played this way. [It.]

rally[1] /ˈrælɪ/ *v.t./i.* **1** to bring or come together as support or for united effort. **2** to bring or come together again after a rout or dispersion. **3** to rouse or revive (courage etc.); to recover after an illness; (of share-prices etc.) to increase after a fall. —*n.* **1** rallying, being rallied. **2** a mass meeting of supporters or persons having a common interest. **3** a competition for motor vehicles, usually over public roads. **4** a series of strokes in tennis etc. before a point is decided. [f. F *rallier* (as RE-, ALLY)]

rally[2] *v.t.* to subject to good-humoured ridicule. [f. F *railler* (as RAIL[2])]

RAM *abbr.* random-access memory (see RANDOM).

ram *n.* **1** an uncastrated male sheep. **2** the Ram, the constellation or sign of the zodiac Aries. **3** a battering-ram. **4** the falling weight of a pile-driving machine. **5** a hydraulic water-raising or lifting machine. —*v.t.* (**-mm-**) **1** to force or squeeze into place by pressure; to beat or drive (*down* or *in* etc.) by heavy blows. **2** to strike and push heavily, to crash against. —**ram-jet** *n.* a simple form of jet engine in which the air used for combustion is compressed solely by the forward motion of the engine. —**rammer** *n.* [OE]

Ramadan /ræməˈdɑːn/ *n.* the ninth month of the lunar calendar of Islam, which Muslims are obligated to spend in fasting and ritual prayer. [f. Arab. (*ramada* be hot); reason for name uncertain]

ramble *v.i.* **1** to walk for pleasure, with or without a definite route. **2** to talk or write disconnectedly. —*n.* a walk taken for pleasure. [prob. f. MDu. *rammelen* (of an animal) wander about in sexual excitement, frequent. of *rammen* copulate with (rel. to RAM)]

rambler *n.* **1** one who rambles. **2** a vigorously growing and straggling climbing rose. [f. prec.]

rambling *adj.* that rambles; (of a house, street, etc.) irregularly arranged; (of a plant) straggling, climbing. [f. RAMBLE]

ramekin /ˈræmɪkɪn/ *n.* a small dish for baking and serving an individual portion of food; food served in this. [f. F *ramequin*]

ramify /ˈræmɪfaɪ/ *v.t./i.* **1** to form branches or subdivisions or offshoots, to branch out. **2** (usu. in *pass.*) to cause to branch out; to arrange in a branching manner. —**ramification** /-fɪˈkeɪʃ(ə)n/ *n.* [f. F f. L *ramificare* (*ramus* branch)]

ramp[1] *n.* **1** a slope joining two levels of ground or floor etc. **2** movable stairs for entering or leaving an aircraft. —*v.t./i.* **1** to furnish or build with a ramp. **2** to take a threatening posture. **3** to rampage. [f. F *rampe* (OF *ramper* creep)]

ramp[2] *n.* (*slang*) a swindle, a racket, especially one involving exorbitant prices. —*v.t./i.* (*slang*), to engage in a ramp; to subject (a person etc.) to a ramp. [orig. unkn.]

rampage /ræmˈpeɪdʒ/ *v.i.* to rush wildly or violently about; to rage, to storm. —/ˈræmpeɪdʒ/ *n.* wild or violent behaviour. —**on the rampage,** rampaging. —**rampageous** /ræmˈpeɪdʒəs/ *adj.* [perh. f. RAMP[1]]

rampant /ˈræmpənt/ *adj.* **1** (in heraldy, esp. of a lion) standing on the left hind foot with forefeet raised, right higher than left, facing dexter. **2** unrestrained, flourishing excessively. **3** violent or extravagant in action or opinion. —**rampancy** *n.* [f. OF (as RAMP[1])]

rampart /ˈræmpɑːt/ *n.* **1** a defensive wall with a broad top and usually a stone parapet; a walkway on this. **2** a defence, a protection. [f. F (*remparer* fortify)]

ramrod /ˈræmrɒd/ *n.* **1** a rod for ramming down the charge of a muzzle-loaded firearm. **2** a thing that is very straight or rigid.

ramshackle /ˈræmʃæk(ə)l/ *adj.* tumbledown, rickety. [f. p.p. of obs. *ransackle* (as RANSACK)]

ran *past* of RUN.

ranch /rɑːntʃ/ *n.* **1** a cattle-breeding establishment especially in the USA and Canada. **2** a farm where certain other animals are bred. —*v.i.* to farm on a ranch. —**rancher** *n.* [f. Sp. *rancho* persons eating together]

rancid /ˈrænsɪd/ *adj.* smelling or tasting like rank stale fat. —**rancidity** /-ˈsɪdɪtɪ/ *n.* [f. L *rancidus*]

rancour /ˈræŋkə(r)/ *n.* inveterate bitterness, malignant hate. —**rancorous** *adj.*, **rancorously** *adv.* [f. OF f. L (as prec.)]

rand /rænd, rɑːnt/ *n.* the currency unit of South African countries. [f. the *Rand*, gold-field near Johannesburg]

R & D *abbr.* research and development.

random /ˈrændəm/ *adj.* made or done etc. without method or conscious choice. —**at random**, without aim or purpose or principle. **random access**, (in computers, usu. *attrib.*) a memory or file all parts of which are directly accessible so that it need not be processed sequentially. —**randomly** *adv.* [f. OF *randon* great speed (*randir* gallop)]

randy *adj.* lustful, eager for sexual gratification; —**randily** *adv.*, **randiness** *n.* [perh. f. obs. Du. *randen* rant]

ranee /ˈrɑːnɪ/ *n.* a raja's wife or widow. [f. Hindi f. Skr. *rājnī* fem. of *rājan* king]

rang *past* of RING².

range /reɪndʒ/ *n.* **1** the area over which a thing is found or has effect or relevance, scope. **2** the region between limits of variation; such limits. **3** the distance attainable or to be covered by a gun or missile etc.; the distance that can be covered by a vehicle or aircraft without refuelling; the distance between a camera and the subject to be photographed. **4** a row or series, especially of mountains. **5** an open or enclosed area with targets for shooting. **6** a fireplace with ovens and hotplates for cooking. **7** a large open area for grazing or hunting. —*v.t./i.* **1** to place in a row or rows or in a specified arrangement. **2** to rove or wander. **3** to reach; to lie; to spread out; to be found over a specified area; to vary between limits. **4** to traverse in all directions. —**range-finder** *n.* an instrument to determine the distance of an object for shooting or photography. [f. OF, = row (as RANK¹)]

ranger /ˈreɪndʒə(r)/ *n.* **1** a keeper of a royal or national park or forest. **2** a member of a body of mounted troops. **3 Ranger**, a senior Guide. [f. prec.]

rangy /ˈreɪndʒɪ/ *adj.* tall and lanky. [f. RANGE]

rank¹ *n.* **1** a place in a scale of quality or value etc.; a position or grade. **2** high social position. **3** a line of people or things. **4** a place where taxis stand to await hire. —*v.t./i.* **1** to have a specified rank or place. **2** to assign a rank to, to classify. **3** to arrange in a rank. —**close ranks**, to maintain solidarity. **rank and file**, ordinary undistinguished people. **the ranks**, common soldiers. [f. OF, as RING¹]

rank² *adj.* **1** too luxuriant, coarse; choked with or apt to produce weeds or excessive foliage. **2** foul-smelling; loathsome, corrupt. **3** flagrant, unmistakably bad, complete. —**rankly** *adv.*, **rankness** *n.* [OE]

rankle *v.i.* (of envy or disappointment etc. or their cause) to cause persistent annoyance or resentment. [f. OF, = festering sore, f. L *dra(cu)nculus* dim. of *draco* serpent]

ransack /ˈrænsæk/ *v.t.* **1** to pillage or plunder. **2** to search thoroughly. [f. ON (*rann* house, *-saka* seek)]

ransom /ˈrænsəm/ *n.* a sum of money or other payment demanded or paid for the release of a prisoner; liberation of a prisoner in return for this. —*v.t.* **1** to buy the freedom or restoration of, to redeem. **2** to hold to ransom. **3** to release for a ransom. —**hold to ransom**, to hold (a captive) and demand a ransom for his release; to demand concessions from (a person etc.) by threatening some damaging action. [f. OF f. L, = redemption (as REDEEM)]

rant *v.t./i.* to use bombastic language; to declaim, to recite theatrically; to preach noisily. —*n.* a piece of ranting. [f. Du.]

ranunculus /rəˈnʌŋkjʊləs/ *n.* (*pl.* **-uses**) a plant of the genus *Ranunculus*, including the buttercup. [L, orig. dim. of *rana* frog]

rap¹ *n.* **1** a quick sharp blow. **2** a knock, a sharp tapping sound. **3** (*slang*) blame, punishment. **4** a rhythmic recitation to music; rock music with words recited. —*v.t./i.* (**-pp-**) **1** to strike quickly and sharply. **2** to knock, to make the sound of a rap. **3** to criticize adversely. —**rap out**, to utter abruptly; to express by raps. [prob. imit.]

rap² *n.* a small amount, the least bit. [orig. = counterfeit halfpenny, abbr. of Ir. *ropaire*]

rapacious /rəˈpeɪʃəs/ *adj.* grasping, extortionate; predatory. —**rapaciously** *adv.*, **rapacity** /rəːˈpæsɪtɪ/ *n.* [f. L *rapax* (*rapere* snatch)]

rape¹ *n.* **1** the act or crime of having sexual intercourse with a person (usually a woman) without freely given consent. **2** violent assault or interference. —*v.t.* to commit rape on. [f. AF f. L (as prec.)]

rape² *n.* a plant (*Brassica napus*) grown as fodder and for its seed from which oil is made. [f. L *rapum*, *rapa* turnip]

rape³ *n.* the refuse of grapes that is left after wine-making. [f. F f. L *raspa*]

rapid /ˈræpɪd/ *adj.* **1** quick, swift; acting or completed in a short time. **2** (of a slope) descending steeply. —*n.* (usu. in *pl.*) a steep descent in a river-bed with a swift current. —**rapidity** /rəˈpɪdɪtɪ/ *n.*, **rapidly** *adv.* [f. L *rapidus* (*rapere* seize)]

rapier /ˈreɪpɪə(r)/ *n.* a light slender double-edged sword used for thrusting. [prob. f. Du. or LG, f. F *rapière* (orig. unkn.)]

rapine /ˈræpaɪn/ *n.* plundering. [f. OF or L *rapina* (*rapere* seize)]

rapist /ˈreɪpɪst/ *n.* one who commits rape. [f. RAPE[1]]

rapport /ræˈpɔː(r)/ *n.* an understanding relationship or communication between people. [F (*rapporter*, as RE-, AP-, *porter* f. L *portare* carry)]

rapprochement /ræˈprɒʃmɑ̃/ *n.* resumption of harmonious relations, especially between States. [F (as RE-, APPROACH)]

rapscallion /ræpˈskæljən/ *n.* a rascal. [earlier *rascallion*, perh. f. RASCAL]

rapt *adj.* fully intent or absorbed, enraptured; carried away with emotion or lofty thought. [f. L *raptus* p.p. of *rapere* seize]

raptorial /ræpˈtɔːrɪəl/ *adj.* predatory. —*n.* a predatory animal or bird. [f. L *raptor* ravisher, plunderer (as prec.)]

rapture /ˈræptʃə(r)/ *n.* ecstatic delight; (in *pl.*) great pleasure or enthusiasm, the expression of this. —**rapturous** *adj.*, **rapturously** *adv.* [obs. F, or f. L *raptura* (as RAPT)]

rare[1] *adj.* **1** seldom done or found or occurring, very uncommon, unusual. **2** exceptionally good. **3** of less than usual density. —**rare earth,** any of a class of 17 chemically similar metallic elements or their oxides, including scandium, yttrium, and the lanthanides (the term is sometimes applied to the lanthanides alone). —**rareness** *n.* [f. L *rarus*]

rare[2] *adj.* (of meat) underdone. [OE]

rarebit /ˈreəbɪt/ *n.* a Welsh rarebit (see WELSH). [alt. of (*Welsh*) *rabbit*]

rarefy /ˈreərɪfaɪ/ *v.t./i.* **1** to make or become less solid or dense. **2** to refine. **3** to make (an idea etc.) subtle. —**rarefaction** /-ˈfækʃ(ə)n/ *n.* [f. OF or L *rarefacere* (*rarus* rare, *facere* make)]

rarely *adv.* seldom, not often; exceptionally. [f. RARE[1]]

raring /ˈreərɪŋ/ *adj.* (*colloq.*) enthusiastic, eager (*to go* etc.). [partic. of *rare*, dial. var. of REAR[2]]

rarity /ˈreərɪtɪ/ *n.* **1** rareness. **2** an uncommon thing. [f. F or L (as RARE[1])]

rascal /ˈrɑːsk(ə)l/ *n.* a dishonest or mischievous person. —**rascally** *adj.* [f. OF *rascaille* rabble]

rash[1] *adj.* acting or done without due consideration of the possible consequences or risks. —**rashly** *adv.*, **rashness** *n.* [f. OE, = MDu. *rasch*]

rash[2] *n.* **1** an eruption of spots or patches on the skin. **2** a sudden widespread onset. [cf. OF *ra(s)che* eruptive sores]

rasher *n.* a thin slice of bacon or ham. [orig. unkn.]

rasp /rɑːsp/ *n.* **1** a coarse kind of file having separate teeth. **2** a grating sound. —*v.t./i.* **1** to scrape with a rasp; to scrape roughly. **2** to make a grating sound; to say gratingly. **3** to grate upon (a person or his feelings). [f. OF *raspe, rasper*]

raspberry /ˈrɑːzbərɪ/ *n.* **1** an edible sweet usually red conical berry; the plant (*Rubus idaeus*) bearing this. **2** (*slang*) a sound expressing derision or dislike. —**raspberry-cane** *n.* a raspberry plant. [f. obs. *raspis* (orig. unkn.) + BERRY]

Rasta /ˈræstə/ *n.* a Rastafarian. [abbr.]

Rastafarian /ræstəˈfeərɪən/ *adj.* of the Rastafari sect, of Jamaican origin, which believes that Blacks are the chosen people, that the late Emperor Haile Selassie of Ethiopia was God Incarnate, and that he will secure their repatriation to their homeland in Africa. —*n.* a member of this sect. [f. the title and name *Ras Tafari* (Amharic, *ras* chief) by which Haile Selassie was known from 1916 until his accession in 1930]

rat *n.* **1** a rodent of the genus *Rattus* like a large mouse; a similar rodent. **2** (*colloq.*) an unpleasant or treacherous person. —*v.i.* (**-tt-**) **1** to hunt or kill rats. **2** to act as an informer. —**rat on,** to desert or betray (a person). **rat race,** a fiercely competitive struggle, especially to maintain one's position in work or life. **smell a rat,** to begin to suspect treachery etc. [OE & OF]

ratafia /rætəˈfiːə/ *n.* **1** a liqueur flavoured with almonds or fruit-kernels. **2** a kind of small almond biscuit. [F, prob. rel. to *tafia* kind of rum]

ratatouille /rɑːtɑːˈtuːɪ/ *n.* a Provençal dish of vegetables (chiefly aubergines, tomatoes, onions, and peppers) stewed in oil. [F dial.]

ratchet /ˈrætʃɪt/ *n.* **1** a set of teeth on the edge of a bar or wheel with a catch allowing motion in one direction only. **2** (in full **ratchet-wheel**) a wheel with a rim so toothed. [f. F *rochet* lance-head]

rate[1] *n.* **1** a stated numerical proportion between two sets of things (the second usually expressed as unity), especially as a measure of amount or degree or as the basis of calculating an amount or value. **2** a fixed or appropriate charge, cost, or value; a measure of this. **3** rapidity of movement or change. **4** class, rank. **5** (until 1989-90) an assessment by a local authority levied on the value of buildings and land owned or leased; (in *pl.*) the amount payable. See COMMUNITY CHARGE.

—*v.t./i.* 1 to estimate or assign the worth or value of. 2 to consider, to regard as; to rank or be regarded in a specified way. 3 to subject to the payment of a local rate; to value for the assessment of rates. 4 (*US*) to be worthy of, to deserve. —**at any rate,** in any case, whatever happens. **at this rate,** if this example is typical. [f. OF f. L *rata* (*rēri* reckon)]

rate[2] *v.t./i.* to scold angrily. [orig. unkn.]

rateable /ˈreɪtəb(ə)l/ *adj.* liable to rates. —**rateable value,** the value at which a house etc. is assessed for rates. [f. RATE[1]]

ratepayer *n.* a person liable to pay rates.

rath /rɑːθ/ *n.* (in Ireland & SW Wales) a small circular hill-fort. [Ir.]

rather /ˈrɑːðə(r)/ *adv.* 1 by preference, more willingly. 2 more truly; as the more likely alternative. 3 more precisely. 4 slightly, to some extent. 5 (*colloq.*, in an answer) most certainly. —**had rather,** would rather. [f. OE, = earlier]

ratify /ˈrætɪfaɪ/ *v.t.* to confirm or accept (an agreement made in one's name) by formal consent, signature, etc. —**ratification** /-fɪˈkeɪʃ(ə)n/ *n.* [f. OF f. L *ratificare* (as RATE[1], *facere* make)]

rating[1] /ˈreɪtɪŋ/ *n.* 1 a place in a rank or class. 2 the estimated standing of a person as regards credit etc. 3 a non-commissioned sailor. 4 the amount fixed as a local rate. 5 the relative popularity of a broadcast programme as determined by the estimated size of the audience. [f. RATE[1]]

rating[2] /ˈreɪtɪŋ/ *n.* an angry reprimand. [f. RATE[2]]

ratio /ˈreɪʃɪəʊ/ *n.* (*pl.* **-os**) the quantitative relation between two similar magnitudes determined by the number of times one contains the other. [L (as RATE[1])]

ratiocinate /rætɪˈɒsɪneɪt/ *v.i.* to reason, especially using syllogisms. —**ratiocination** /-ˈneɪʃ(ə)n/ *n.* [f. L (as prec.)]

ration /ˈræʃ(ə)n/ *n.* an allowance or portion of food or clothing etc., especially an official allowance in time of shortage; (usu. in *pl.*) a fixed daily allowance of food in the armed forces etc. —*v.t.* to limit (persons or provisions) to a fixed ration; to share (food etc.) in fixed quantities. [F, f. It. or Sp. f. L *ratio* reckoning, ratio]

rational /ˈræʃən(ə)l/ *adj.* 1 of or based on reason; sane, sensible. 2 endowed with reason. 3 rejecting what is unreasonable or cannot be tested by reason in religion or custom. 4 (of a quantity or ratio) expressible as a ratio of integers. —**rationality** /-ˈnælɪtɪ/ *n.*, **rationally** *adv.* [f. L (as prec.)]

rationale /ræʃəˈnɑːl/ *n.* a fundamental reason; a logical basis. [neut. of L *rationalis* (as RATION)]

rationalism /ˈræʃ(ə)nəlɪz(ə)m/ *n.* 1 the practice of explaining the supernatural in religion in a way that is consonant with reason, or of treating reason as the ultimate authority in religion as elsewhere. 2 the theory that reason is the foundation of certainty in knowledge (opp. EMPIRICISM, SENSATIONALISM). —**rationalist** *n.*, **rationalistic** /-ˈlɪstɪk/ *adj.* [f. RATIONAL]

rationalize *v.t.* 1 to offer a reasoned but specious explanation of (behaviour or an attitude). 2 to make logical and consistent. 3 to make (an industry) more efficient by reorganizing it to reduce or eliminate waste. 4 to explain by rationalism. —**rationalization** /-ˈzeɪʃ(ə)n/ *n.* [as prec.]

ratline /ˈrætlɪn/ *n.* (also **ratlin**) any of the small lines fastened across a sailing-ship's shrouds like ladder-rungs. [orig. unkn.]

rattan /rəˈtæn/ *n.* 1 a palm of the genus *Calamus* etc. with long thin many-jointed pliable stems. 2 a piece of rattan stem used as a cane etc. [f. Malay]

rat-tat /rætˈtæt/ *n.* a rapping sound, especially of a knocker. [imit.]

rattle *v.t./i.* 1 to make or cause to make a rapid succession of short sharp hard sounds; to cause such sounds by shaking something. 2 to move or travel with a rattling noise. 3 (usu. with *off*) to say or recite rapidly; (usu. with *on*) to talk in a lively thoughtless way. 4 (*slang*) to disconcert, to alarm. —*n.* 1 a rattling sound. 2 a device or toy etc. for making a rattling sound. [prob. f. MDu. or LG (imit.)]

rattlesnake *n.* a poisonous American snake of the genus *Crotalus* with a rattling structure of horny rings in its tail.

rattletrap *n.* a rickety old vehicle etc.

rattling *adj.* brisk, vigorous. —*adv.* remarkably. [f. RATTLE]

ratty *adj.* 1 relating to or infested with rats. 2 (*slang*) irritable, angry. [f. RAT]

raucous /ˈrɔːkəs/ *adj.* harsh-sounding, loud and hoarse. —**raucously** *adv.*, **raucousness** *n.* [f. L *raucus*]

raunchy /ˈrɔːntʃɪ/ *adj.* coarse, earthy; boisterous. [orig. unkn.]

ravage /ˈrævɪdʒ/ *v.t./i.* to devastate, to plunder, to make havoc (in). —*n.* 1 devastation; 2 (usu. in *pl.*) destructive effect. [f. F, alt. of *ravine* rush of water (as RAVINE)]

rave *v.i.* 1 to talk wildly or furiously (as) in delirium. 2 to speak with rapturous admiration. —*n.* 1 (*colloq.*) a highly enthusiastic review (of a film or play etc.). 2 (*slang*) an infatuation. —**rave-up** *n.* (*slang*) a lively party. **raving beauty,** an excitingly beautiful person. **raving mad,** completely mad. [prob. f. OF *raver*]

ravel /ˈrævəl/ *v.t./i.* (**-ll-**) 1 to entangle or

become entangled. **2** to confuse or complicate (a question or problem). **3** to fray out; **4** to disentangle, to unravel; to distinguish the separate threads or subdivisions of. —*n.* a tangle, a knot; a complication. [perh. f. Du. *ravelen*]

raven[1] /ˈreɪv(ə)n/ *n.* a large crow (*Corvus corax*) with glossy blue-black feathers and a hoarse cry. —*adj.* (usu. of hair) glossy black. [OE]

raven[2] /ˈræv(ə)n/ *v.t./i.* **1** to plunder, to seek prey or booty. **2** to devour voraciously. [f. OF *raviner* ravage f. L (as RAPINE)]

ravenous /ˈrævənəs/ *adj.* very hungry; voracious; rapacious. —**ravenously** *adv.* [f. OF (as prec.)]

ravine /rəˈviːn/ *n.* a deep narrow gorge. [F f. L, = RAPINE]

ravioli /rævɪˈəʊlɪ/ *n.* small pasta cases containing meat etc. [It.]

ravish /ˈrævɪʃ/ *v.t.* **1** to commit rape on. **2** to enrapture, to fill with delight. —**ravishment** *n.* [f. OF f. L *rapere* seize]

raw *adj.* **1** uncooked. **2** in its natural state, not yet or not fully processed or manufactured. **3** inexperienced; untrained. **4** stripped of skin and having the underlying flesh exposed; sensitive to the touch from being so exposed. **5** (of atmosphere or a day etc.) damp and chilly. **6** crude in artistic quality, lacking finish. **7** (of an edge of cloth) not a selvage and not hemmed. —**in the raw,** in its natural state without mitigation; naked. **raw-boned** *adj.* gaunt. **raw deal,** see DEAL[1]. **raw material,** that from which a process of manufacture makes articles. **touch a person on the raw,** to wound his feelings on a point where he is sensitive. —**rawness** *n.* [OE]

rawhide *n.* untanned leather; a rope or whip of this.

Rawlplug /ˈrɔːlplʌg/ *n.* [P] a thin cylindrical plug for holding a screw or nail in masonry. [f. J. J. & W. R. *Rawl*ings, English electrical engineers + PLUG]

ray[1] *n.* **1** a single line or narrow beam of light or other radiation. **2** a straight line in which radiation is propagated to a given point; (in *pl.*) radiation of a specified type. **3** a remnant or beginning of an enlightening or cheering influence. **4** any of a set of radiating lines, parts, or things. **5** the marginal part of a composite flower (e.g. a daisy). [f. OF *rai* f. L, = RADIUS]

ray[2] *n.* a large sea-fish of the order *Hypotremata*, related to the shark and used as food. [f. OF f. L *raia*]

ray[3] *n.* (*Mus.*) the second note of the major scale in tonic sol-fa (see entry). [f. *resonare* (see GAMUT)]

rayon /ˈreɪɒn/ *n.* an artificial textile fibre or fabric made from cellulose. [f. RAY[1]]

raze *v.t.* to destroy completely, to tear down (usu. *to the ground*). [f. OF, = shave close, ult. f. L *radere* scrape]

razor /ˈreɪzə(r)/ *n.* an instrument with a sharp blade used in cutting hair especially from the skin. —**razor-bill** *n.* an auk (*Alca torda*) with a sharp-edged bill. **razor-blade** *n.* a blade used in a razor, especially a flat piece of metal with two sharp edges used in a safety razor. **razor-edge** *n.* a keen edge; a sharp mountain ridge; a critical situation; a sharp line of division. [f. OF (as prec.)]

razzle *n.* (*slang*) a spree, a lively outing. [f. foll.]

razzle-dazzle /ˈræz(ə)ldæz(ə)l/ *n.* (*slang*) **1** excitement, bustle, a spree. **2** (*slang*) noisy advertising. [redupl. of DAZZLE]

razzmatazz /ræzməˈtæz/ *n.* (*colloq.*) **1** excitement, bustle. **2** noisy advertising. **3** insincere actions, humbug. [prob. alt. f. prec.]

Rb *symbol* rubidium.

RC *abbr.* Roman Catholic.

Rd. *abbr.* road.

Re *symbol* rhenium.

re[1] /riː/ *prep.* in the matter of (as the first word in a heading, especially of a legal document; (*colloq.*) about, concerning. [L, abl. of *res* thing]

re[2] /reɪ/ var. of RAY[3].

're *abbr.* are.

re-[1] *prefix* (sometimes **red-** before vowels: *redolent*) in verbs and verbal derivatives denoting: in return, mutually (*react, resemble*), opposition (*repel, resist*), behind or after (*relic, remain*), retirement or secrecy (*recluse, reticence*), off, away, down (*recede, relegate, repress*), frequentative or intensive force (*redouble, refine, resplendent*), negative force (*recant, reveal*). [f. L]

re-[2] *prefix* attachable to almost any verb or its derivative in senses (1) once more, afresh, anew; (2) back, with return to a previous state. A hyphen is normally used when the word begins in *e-* (*re-enact*) or to distinguish the compound from a more familiar one-word form (*re-form* = form again). [as prec.]

reach *v.t./i.* **1** to stretch out or extend. **2** to stretch out the hand etc. in order to touch or grasp or take something; to make a reaching motion or effort (*lit.* or *fig.*). **3** to get as far as, to arrive at, to attain. **4** to make contact by hand etc. or by telephone etc. **5** to sail with the wind abeam or abaft the beam.. —*n.* **1** an act of reaching. **2** the extent to which a hand etc. can be reached out, an influence exerted, or a mental power used. **3** a continuous extent, especially the part of a river that can be looked along at once between two bends, or part of a canal between locks. **4** (in sailing) the distance traversed in reaching (**broad reach,** with the wind aft the beam but not so far aft that the vessel is running. **close reach,** with the wind forward of the beam but not so far forward that the vessel is close-hauled. —**reach-me-down** *adj*. (*colloq*.) ready-made. [OE]

reachable *adj*. that may be reached.

react /riːˈækt/ *v.i.* **1** to respond *to* a stimulus, to undergo a change or show behaviour that is due to some influence. **2** to be actuated by repulsion *against*, to tend in a reverse or backward direction.

reaction /riːˈækʃ(ə)n/ *n*. **1** reacting; a responsive feeling. **2** an occurrence of a condition after its opposite. **3** tendency to oppose change or to return to a former system, especially in politics. **4** the interaction of substances undergoing chemical change. [f. prec.]

reactionary /riːˈækʃənərɪ/ *adj*. showing reaction; opposed to progress or reform. —*n*. a reactionary person. [f. prec.]

reactivate /riːˈæktɪveɪt/ *v.t.* to restore to a state of activity. —**reactivation** /-ˈveɪʃ(ə)n/ *n*.

reactive /riːˈæktɪv/ *adj*. showing reaction. —**reactivity** /-ˈtɪvɪtɪ/ *n*. [f. REACT]

reactor /riːˈæktə(r)/ *n*. a nuclear reactor (see entry). [f. REACT]

read /riːd/ *v.t./i.* (*past* & *p.p.* **read** /red/) **1** to reproduce mentally or vocally the words of (an author, book, letter, etc.) while following their symbols with the eyes or fingers. **2** to be able to understand the meaning of (written or printed words or symbols). **3** to interpret mentally, to find implications; to declare the interpretation of. **4** (of a measuring instrument) to show (a figure etc.). **5** to have a specified wording. **6** to study or discover by reading; to study (a subject at university); to carry out a course of study. **7** (of a computer) to copy or transfer (data). —*n*. a spell of reading. —**read between the lines,** to look for and find a hidden or implicit meaning. **read-only memory,** (in computers) a memory whose contents can usually be read at high speed but cannot be changed by program instructions. **read up,** to make a special study of (a subject). **take as read,** to dispense with actual reading or discussion of. **well read,** (of a person) having knowledge of a subject or good general acquaintance with literature through reading. [OE]

readable *adj*. able to be read; interesting to read. [f. READ]

readdress /riːəˈdres/ *v.t.* to alter the address on (a letter).

reader *n*. **1** one who reads. **2** a book containing passages for practice in reading by students learning a language. **3** a device to produce an image that can be read from a microfilm etc. **4** a university lecturer of a higher grade. **5** a publisher's employee who reports on submitted manuscripts; a printer's proof-corrector. [f. READ]

readership *n*. the readers of a newspaper etc. [f. prec.]

readily /ˈredɪlɪ/ *adv*. **1** without showing reluctance, willingly. **2** without difficulty. [f. READY]

readiness *n*. **1** a ready or prepared state. **2** willingness. **3** facility, quickness in argument or action. [f. READY]

reading *n*. **1** the act of one who reads. **2** an entertainment at which a thing is read. **3** matter to be read; its specified quality. **4** literary knowledge. **5** a figure etc. given by a measuring instrument. **6** an interpretation. **7** each of the three occasions on which a Bill must be presented to a legislature for acceptance. —**reading-room** *n*. a room in a club, library, etc., for those wishing to read. [f. READ]

readjust /riːəˈdʒʌst/ *v.t./i.* to adjust (a thing) again; to adapt oneself again. —**readjustment** *n*.

ready /ˈredɪ/ *adj*. **1** with preparations complete; in a fit state for immediate use or action. **2** willing; about or inclined to do something. **3** easily available; within reach. **4** prompt, quick, facile. —*adv*. beforehand, so as to be ready when the time comes. —*n*. (*slang*) ready money. —*v.t.* to make ready, to prepare. —**at the ready,** ready for action. **ready-made** *adj*. (esp. of clothes) made for immediate wear, not to measure. **ready money,** actual coin or notes; payment on the spot. **ready reckoner,** a book or table of the results of arithmetical computations of the kind commonly wanted in business etc. [OE]

reagent /riːˈeɪdʒ(ə)nt/ *n*. a substance used to cause a chemical reaction, especially to detect another substance.

real[1] /ˈrɪəl/ *adj*. **1** existing as a thing or occurring in fact, not imaginary. **2** genuine, rightly so called; not artificial or imitation. **3** (*Law*) consisting of immovable property such as land or houses. **4** (of income or value etc.) appraised by purchasing power. —*adv*. (*Sc. & US colloq.*) really, very. —**real money,** coin, cash. **real time,** the actual time of a process analysed by a computer. [AF & f. L *realis* (*res* thing)]

real[2] /reɪˈɑːl/ *n*. (*hist.*) a silver coin in Spanish-speaking countries. [Sp. (as ROYAL)]

realgar /rɪˈælgə(r)/ *n*. a mineral consisting of arsenic sulphide, used as a pigment and in fireworks. [f. L f. Arab., = dust of the cave]

realign /riːəˈlaɪn/ *v.t./i.* **1** to align again. **2** to regroup in politics etc. —**realignment** *n*.

realism /ˈrɪəlɪz(ə)m/ *n*. (usu. opp. IDEALISM)

1 the practice of regarding things in their true nature, and dealing with them as they are; practical views and policy. 2 fidelity of representation, truth to nature, insistence upon details; the showing of life as it is without glossing over what is ugly or painful. 3 the medieval theory that universals or general ideas have objective existence. 4 belief that matter as an object of perception has real existence. —**realist** *n.* [f. REAL[1]]

realistic /rɪəˈlɪstɪk/ *adj.* 1 regarding things as they are, following a policy of realism. 2 based on facts rather than ideals. 3 (of wages or prices) high enough to pay the worker or seller adequately. —**realistically** *adv.* [f. prec.]

reality /rɪˈælɪtɪ/ *n.* 1 what is real or existent or underlies appearances. 2 real existence, being real. 3 resemblance to an original. [f. L or F (as REAL[1])]

realize /ˈriːəlaɪz/ *v.t.* 1 to be fully aware of; to present or conceive as real; to understand clearly. 2 (usu. in *pass.*) to convert (a hope or plan) into a fact. 3 to convert (securities or profit) into money by selling. 4 to acquire (a profit); to be sold for (a specified price). —**realization** /-ˈzeɪʃ(ə)n/ *n.* [f. REAL[1]]

really /ˈriːəlɪ/ *adv.* 1 in reality, in fact. 2 indeed, I assure you. 3 as an expression of interest, surprise, or mild protest. [f. REAL[1]]

realm /relm/ *n.* 1 a kingdom. 2 a field of activity or interest. [f. OF f. L, = REGIMEN]

realty /ˈrɪəltɪ/ *n.* real estate. [f. REAL[1]]

ream[1] *n.* 1 twenty quires of paper (about 500 sheets). 2 (usu. in *pl.*) a large quantity of writing. [f. OF ult. f. Arab., = bundle]

ream[2] *v.t.* to enlarge or give a smooth finish to (a hole drilled in metal etc.) by a borer. —**reamer** *n.* [orig. unkn.]

reap *v.t.* 1 to cut or gather (a crop, esp. grain) as harvest; to harvest the crop of (a field etc.). 2 to receive as the consequence of one's own or another's actions. [OE]

reaper *n.* 1 a person who reaps. 2 a machine for reaping crops. 3 death personified. [f. REAP]

reappear /riːəˈpɪə(r)/ *v.i.* to appear again. —**reappearance** *n.*

reappraise /riːəˈpreɪz/ *v.t.* to appraise again, to reconsider. —**reappraisal** *n.*

rear[1] *n.* 1 the back part, the space behind, position at the back of something. 2 (*colloq.*) the buttocks. —*adj.* at the back, in the rear. —**bring up the rear,** to come last. **Rear Admiral,** see ADMIRAL. **rear-lamp** *or* **rear-light** *n.* a light, usually red, on the back of a vehicle. [prob. f. REARWARD or REARGUARD (cf. VAN[2])]

rear[2] *v.t./i.* 1 to bring up and educate (children); to breed and care for (animals); to cultivate (crops). 2 (of a horse etc.) to raise itself on its hind legs. 3 to set upright, to build; to hold upwards. 4 to extend to a great height. [OE]

rearguard *n.* a body of troops detached to protect the rear of the main force; especially in retreats. —**rearguard action,** an engagement between the rearguard and the enemy (*lit.* or *fig.*). [f. OF *rereguarde* (as RETRO-, GUARD)]

rearm /riːˈɑːm/ *v.t./i.* to arm again, especially with improved weapons. —**rearmament** *n.*

rearmost *adj.* furthest back. [f. REAR[1]]

rearrange /riːəˈreɪndʒ/ *v.t.* to arrange in a different way. —**rearrangement** *n.*

rearward /ˈrɪəwəd/ *n.* the rear (esp. in prepositional phrases: *to the rearward of, in the rearward*). —*adj.* to the rear. —*adv.* (also **rearwards**) towards the rear. [f. AF *rerewarde* (as REARGUARD)]

reason /ˈriːz(ə)n/ *n.* 1 a motive, cause, or justification; a fact adduced or serving as this. 2 the intellectual faculty by which conclusions are drawn from premisses. 3 sanity. 4 good sense, sensible conduct; what is right or practical or practicable; moderation. —*v.t./i.* 1 to form or try to reach conclusions by connected thought, to state as a step in this. 2 to try to persuade a person by giving reasons. —**by reason of,** owing to. **in** *or* **within reason,** within the bounds of moderation. **with reason,** not unjustifiably. [f. OF f. L, = RATIO]

reasonable *adj.* 1 having or based on sound judgement or moderation; sensible, not expecting too much. 2 not excessive, not expensive or extortionate. 3 ready to listen to reason. —**reasonableness** *n.*, **reasonably** *adv.* [as prec.]

reassemble /riːəˈsemb(ə)l/ *v.t./i.* to assemble again.

reassure /riːəˈʃʊə(r)/ *v.t.* to restore confidence to, to dispel the apprehensions of. —**reassurance** *n.*

reave *v.t.* (*past* & *p.p.* **reft**) (*archaic*) to deprive forcibly; to take by force or carry off. [OE]

rebarbative /rɪˈbɑːbətɪv/ *adj.* (*literary*) repellent, unattractive. [f. F (*barbe* beard)]

rebate[1] /ˈriːbeɪt/ *n.* a deduction from a sum to be paid, a discount; a partial refund. [f. OF *rebattre* (as RE-[1], ABATE)]

rebate[2] /ˈriːbeɪt/ *n.* a step-shaped channel etc. cut along the edge or face of wood etc., usually to receive the edge or tongue of another piece. —*v.t.* to join or fix with a rebate; to make a rebate in. [as RABBET, after prec.]

rebel /ˈreb(ə)l/ *n.* 1 a person who fights against, resists, or refuses allegiance to the established government; a person or thing that resists authority or control. **2** (*attrib.*) rebellious; of rebels; in rebellion. —/rɪˈbel/ *v.i.* (**-ll-**) **1** to act as a rebel. **2** to feel or display repugnance (against a custom etc.). [f. OF f. L *rebellare* (RE-[1], *bellum* war)]

rebellion /rɪˈbeljən/ *n.* open resistance to authority, especially organized armed resistance to the established government. [f. OF f. L (as prec.)]

rebellious /rɪˈbeljəs/ *adj.* **1** in rebellion. **2** disposed to rebel, defying lawful authority. **3** (of a thing) unmanageable, refractory. —**rebelliously** *adv.*, **rebelliousness** *n.* [f. prec.]

rebirth /riːˈbɜːθ/ *n.* **1** a new incarnation; a return to life or activity, a revival. **2** spiritual enlightenment.

rebound /rɪˈbaʊnd/ *v.i.* **1** to spring back after impact. **2** (of an action) to have an adverse effect upon the originator. —/ˈriːbaʊnd/ *n.* **1** an act of rebounding, a recoil. **2** reaction after disappointment or other emotion. [f. OF (as RE-[1], BOUND[1])]

rebuff /rɪˈbʌf/ *n.* an unkind or contemptuous rejection; snub. —*v.t.* to give a rebuff to. [f. F f. It. (as RE-[1], *buffo* puff)]

rebuild /riːˈbɪld/ *v.t.* (*past* & *p.p.* **rebuilt**) to build again after destruction or demolition.

rebuke /rɪˈbjuːk/ *v.t.* to reprove sharply or severely. —*n.* a sharp or severe reproof. [f. AF *rebuker* (RE-[1] + OF *buchier* beat)]

rebus /ˈriːbəs/ *n.* a representation of a word (especially a name) by pictures etc. suggesting its syllables. [f. F f. L *rebus*, abl. pl. of *res* thing]

rebut /rɪˈbʌt/ *v.t.* (**-tt-**) **1** to refute or disprove (evidence or an accusation). **2** to force or turn back. —**rebutment** *n.* **rebuttal** *n.* [f. AF (as RE-[2], BUTT[1])]

recalcitrant /rɪˈkælsɪtrənt/ *adj.* obstinately disobedient, resisting authority or discipline. —**recalcitrance** *n.* [f. L *recalcitrare* kick out (*calx* heel)]

recall /rɪˈkɔːl/ *v.t.* **1** to summon to return. **2** to bring back to the attention or memory etc. **3** to recollect, to remember. **4** to revoke or annul (an action or decision). —*n.* **1** a summons to come back. **2** the act of remembering; ability to remember. **3** the possiblity of revoking or annulling.

recant /rɪˈkænt/ *v.t./i.* to withdraw and renounce (a former belief or statement etc.) as erroneous or heretical; to disavow a former opinion, especially with a public confession of error. —**recantation** /riːkænˈteɪʃ(ə)n/ *n.* [f. L *recantare* (RE-[1], *cantare* sing)]

recap /ˈriːkæp/ *v.t.* (*colloq.*) (**-pp-**) to recapitulate. —*n.* (*colloq.*) recapitulation. [abbr.]

recapitulate /riːkəˈpɪtjʌleɪt/ *v.t./i.* to state again briefly; to repeat the main points of. [f. L *recapitulare* (RE-[2], *capitulum* chapter)]

recapitulation /riːkəpɪtjʌˈleɪʃ(ə)n/ *n.* **1** recapitulating. **2** (*Mus.*) the part of a movement in which the themes from the exposition are restated. [f. OF or L (as prec.)]

recapture /riːˈkæptʃə(r)/ *v.t.* **1** to capture again (a person or thing that has escaped or been lost to an enemy). **2** to re-experience (a past emotion etc.). —*n.* recapturing.

recast /riːˈkɑːst/ *v.t.* (*past* & *p.p.* **recast**) to put into a new form, to improve the arrangement of. —*n.* **1** recasting. **2** a recast form.

recce /ˈrekɪ/ *n.* (*slang*) a reconnaissance. —*v.t./i.* (*slang*) to reconnoitre. [abbr.]

recede /rɪˈsiːd/ *v.i.* **1** to go or shrink back or further off; to be left at an increasing distance by the observer's motion. **2** to slope backwards. **3** to decline in force or value etc. [f. L *recedere* (RE-[1], *cedere* go)]

receipt /rɪˈsiːt/ *n.* **1** receiving, being received. **2** a written acknowledgement that something has been received or that money has been paid. **3** (*archaic*) a recipe. —*v.t.* to put a written receipt on (a bill). [f. AF *receite* (as foll.)]

receive /rɪˈsiːv/ *v.t.* **1** to acquire, accept, or take in (something offered, sent, or given). **2** to have conferred or inflicted upon one, to experience; to be treated with. **3** to take the force, weight, or impact of. **4** to consent to hear (a confession or an oath) or consider (a petition). **5** to accept (stolen goods knowingly; also *absol.*). **6** to serve as a receptacle for; to be able to hold or accommodate. **7** to allow to enter as a member or guest; to greet or welcome in a specified manner. **8** to be marked (*lit.* or *fig.*) more or less permanently with (an impression etc.). **9** to convert (broadcast signals) into sound or a picture. **10** (esp. in *p.p.*) to give credit to, to accept as authoritative or true. —**be at** *or* **on the receiving end**, (*colloq.*) to bear the brunt of something unpleasant. **received pronunciation**, the form of English speech used (with local variations) by the majority of educated English-speaking people. [f. OF f. L *recipere* recover (RE-[2], *capere* take)]

receiver *n.* **1** a person or thing that receives something. **2** an official who administers property under a receiving-order. **3** a person who accepts stolen goods while knowing them to be stolen. **4** the part of a telephone that receives incoming sound and is held to the ear. **5** a radio or television receiving apparatus. [f. prec.]

receiving-order *n.* a lawcourt's order to an official (the *receiver*) to take charge of the property of a bankrupt or insane person or of property that is the subject of litigation. [f. RECEIVE]

recent /ˈri:s(ə)nt/ *adj.* not long past, that happened or began to exist or existed shortly before the present. —**recency** *n.*, **recently** *adv.* [f. F or L *recens recentis*]

receptacle /rɪˈseptək(ə)l/ *n.* a container, something for holding or containing what is put into it. [as foll.]

reception /rɪˈsepʃ(ə)n/ *n.* **1** receiving, being received. **2** the way in which a person or thing is received. **3** a social occasion for receiving guests, especially after a wedding. **4** the place where guests or clients are registered or welcomed on arrival at a hotel or office etc. **5** the receiving of broadcast signals; the quality of this. —**reception room**, a room available or suitable for receiving company or visitors. [f. OF or L (as RECEIVE)]

receptionist *n.* a person employed to receive guests or clients etc. [f. prec.]

receptive /rɪˈseptɪv/ *adj.* able or quick to receive knowledge, impressions, ideas, etc. —**receptiveness** *n.*, **receptivity** /ri:sepˈtɪvɪtɪ/ *n.* [f. F or L (as RECEIVE)]

receptor /rɪˈseptə(r)/ *n.* an organ able to respond to light, heat, a drug, etc., and transmit a signal to a sensory nerve. [f. OF or L (as prec.)]

recess /rɪˈses/ *n.* **1** a part or space set back from the line of a wall etc.; a small hollow place inside something; a remote or secret place. **2** temporary cessation from business (esp. of Parliament); a time of this. —*v.t./i.* **1** to make a recess in or of (a wall etc.). **2** (*US*) to take a recess, to adjourn. [f. L *recessus* (as RECEDE)]

recession /rɪˈseʃ(ə)n/ *n.* **1** a temporary decline in economic activity or prosperity. **2** receding or withdrawal from a place or point. [as prec.]

recessional /rɪˈseʃən(ə)l/ *adj.* sung while the clergy and choir withdraw after a service. —*n.* a recessional hymn. [f. prec.]

recessive /rɪˈsesɪv/ *adj.* **1** tending to recede. **2** (of an inherited characteristic) remaining latent when a dominant characteristic is present. —**recessively** *adv.* [f. RECESS]

recharge /ri:ˈtʃɑ:dʒ/ *v.t.* to charge (a battery or gun) again. —**recharge one's batteries**, to have a period of rest and recovery.

rechargeable /ri:ˈtʃɑ:dʒəb(ə)l/ *adj.* that may be recharged. [f. prec.]

recherché /rəˈʃeəʃeɪ/ *adj.* devised or selected with care or difficulty; far-fetched. [F (RE-[1], *chercher* seek)]

rechristen /ri:ˈkrɪs(ə)n/ *v.t.* to christen again; to give a new name to.

recidivist /rɪˈsɪdɪvɪst/ *n.* one who relapses into crime. —**recidivism** *n.* [f. F f. L *recidivus* falling back (RE-[2], *cadere* fall)]

recipe /ˈresɪpɪ/ *n.* **1** a statement of the ingredients and procedure for preparing a dish etc. in cookery. **2** a procedure to be followed in order to achieve something. [L, imper. of *recipere* receive (RE-[2], *capere* take)]

recipient /rɪˈsɪpɪənt/ *n.* a person who receives something. [f. F f. It. or L (as prec.)]

reciprocal /rɪsɪprək(ə)l/ *adj.* **1** given or received in return. **2** mutual; (*Gram.*) (of a pronoun) expressing mutual relation (e.g. *each other*). **3** corresponding but the other way round. —*n.* a mathematical expression or function so related to another that their product is unity. —**reciprocally** *adv.* [f. L *reciprocus*, orig. = moving backwards and forwards (*re-* back, *pro* forward)]

reciprocate /rɪˈsɪprəkeɪt/ *v.t./i.* **1** to give and receive mutually; to make a return for something done, given or felt. **2** (of a machine part) to go with alternate backward and forward motion. —**reciprocation** /-ˈkeɪʃ(ə)n/ *n.* [f. L *reciprocare* (as prec.)]

reciprocity /resɪˈprɒsɪtɪ/ *n.* **1** the condition of being reciprocal. **2** a mutual action. **3** give-and-take, especially the interchange of privileges. [f. F (as RECIPROCAL)]

recital /rɪˈsaɪt(ə)l/ *n.* **1** reciting. **2** a long account of a series of facts or events. **3** a musical entertainment given by one performer or group; a similar entertainment of any kind (e.g. by a dancer). [f. RECITE]

recitation /resɪˈteɪʃ(ə)n/ *n.* **1** reciting. **2** a thing recited. [f. F or L (as RECITE)]

recitative /resɪtəˈti:v/ *n.* musical declamation of the kind usual in the narrative and dialogue parts of opera and oratorio. [f. It. *recitativo* (as foll.)]

recite /rɪˈsaɪt/ *v.t./i.* **1** to repeat aloud or declaim (a poem or passage) from memory; to give a recitation. **2** to state (facts) in order. [f. OF or L *recitare* (RE-[2], CITE)]

reckless /ˈreklɪs/ *adj.* regardless of consequences or danger etc. —**recklessly** *adv.*, **recklessness** *n.* [OE (*reck* concern oneself)]

reckon /ˈrekən/ *v.t/i.* **1** to count up; to compute by calculation. **2** to include in a total or as a member of a particular class. **3** to have as one's opinion; to consider or regard; to feel confident. —**day of reckoning**, the time when something must be atoned for or avenged. **reckon on**, to rely or count or base plans on. **reckon with**, to take into account; to settle accounts with (a person). [OE]

reckoner *n.* an aid to reckoning, a ready reckoner (see READY). [f. prec.]

reclaim /rɪˈkleɪm/ *v.t.* **1** to seek the return of (one's property); to take action so as to recover possession of. **2** to bring (flooded or waste land) under cultivation. **3** to win back or away from vice, error, or waste condition. —**reclamation** /rekləˈmeɪʃ(ə)n/ *n.* [f. OF f. L *reclamare* cry out against (RE-², *clamare* shout)]

recline /rɪˈklaɪn/ *v.t./i.* to assume or be in a horizontal or leaning position, to put in this position. [f. OF or L *reclinare* (RE-², *clinare* bend)]

recluse /rɪˈklu:s/ *n.* a person given to or living in seclusion or isolation. [f. OF f. L *recludere* shut away (RE-¹, *claudere* shut)]

recognition /rekəgˈnɪʃ(ə)n/ *n.* recognizing, being recognized. [f. L (as RECOGNIZE)]

recognizable /ˈrekəgnaɪzəb(ə)l/ *adj.* that can be identified or detected. —**recognizably** *adv.* [f. RECOGNIZE]

recognizance /rɪˈkɒgnɪz(ə)ns/ *n.* a bond by which a person undertakes before a court or magistrate to observe some condition, e.g. to appear when summoned; a sum pledged as surety for such an observance. [f. OF (as RE-¹, COGNIZANCE)]

recognize /ˈrekəgnaɪz/ *v.t.* **1** to identify as known before. **2** to realize or discover the nature of. **3** to realize or admit (a fact). **4** to acknowledge the existence, validity, character, or claims of. **5** to show appreciation of, to reward. [f. OF f. L *recognoscere* (RE-², *cognoscere* learn)]

recoil /rɪˈkɔɪl/ *v.i.* **1** to move suddenly or spring back, or shrink mentally, in horror, disgust, or fear. **2** to rebound after impact. **3** to have an adverse reactive effect upon the originator. **4** (of a gun) to be driven backwards by a discharge. —/also ˈri:kɔɪl/ *n.* the act or sensation of recoiling. [f. OF *reculer* f. L *culus* buttocks]

recollect /rekəˈlekt/ *v.t.* to remember; to succeed in remembering, to call to mind. [f. L *recolligere* (RE-², *colligere* collect)]

recollection /rekəˈlekʃ(ə)n/ *n.* **1** recollecting. **2** a thing recollected. **3** a person's memory; the time over which it extends. [F or f. L (as prec.)]

recommence /ri:kəˈmens/ *v.t./i.* to begin again. —**recommencement** *n.*

recommend /rekəˈmend/ *v.t.* **1** to suggest as fit for employment or favour or trial. **2** to advise (a course of action etc.). **3** (of qualities or conduct etc.) to make acceptable or desirable. **4** to commend or entrust (to a person or his care). —**recommendation** /-ˈdeɪʃ(ə)n/ *n.* [f. L *recommendare* (RE-¹, *commendare* commend)]

recompense /ˈrekəmpens/ *v.t.* **1** to make amends to (a person) or for (a loss etc.). **2** to requite, reward, or punish (a person or action). —*n.* a reward, a requital; retribution. [f. OF f. L *recompensare* (RE-¹, *compensare* compensate)]

reconcilable /ˈrekənsaɪləb(ə)l/ *adj.* that may be reconciled. [f. foll.]

reconcile /ˈrekənsaɪl/ *v.t.* **1** to make friendly again after an estrangement or quarrel. **2** to induce to accept or be submissive (to an unwelcome fact or situation). **3** to harmonize (facts), to show the compatibility of. —**reconciliation** /-sɪlɪˈeɪʃ(ə)n/ *n.* [f. OF or L *reconciliare* (RE-², *conciliare* conciliate)]

recondite /ˈrekəndaɪt/ *adj.* (of a subject or knowledge) abstruse, out of the way, little known; (of an author or style) dealing in recondite knowledge or allusion, obscure. [f. L *reconditus* (RE-¹, *condere* hide)]

recondition /ri:kənˈdɪʃ(ə)n/ *v.t.* to overhaul, to renovate to make usable again.

reconnaissance /rɪˈkɒnɪs(ə)ns/ *n.* a survey of a region, especially a military examination to locate an enemy or ascertain strategic features; a preliminary survey. [F (as foll.)]

reconnoitre /rekəˈnɔɪtə(r)/ *v.t./i.* to make a reconnaissance (of). [f. obs. F f. L, = RECOGNIZE]

reconquer /ri:ˈkɒŋkə(r)/ *v.t.* to conquer again. —**reconquest** /ri:ˈkɒŋkwest/ *n.*

reconsider /ri:kənˈsɪdə(r)/ *v.t.* to consider again, especially for a possible change of decision. —**reconsideration** /-ˈreɪʃ(ə)n/ *n.*

reconstitute /ri:ˈkɒnstɪtju:t/ *v.t.* **1** to reconstruct, to reorganize. **2** to restore the previous constitution of (dried food etc.) by adding water. —**reconstitution** /-ˈtju:ʃ(ə)n/ *n.*

reconstruct /ri:kənˈstrʌkt/ *v.t.* **1** to construct or build again. **2** to piece together (past events) into an intelligible whole, by imagination or by re-enacting them. **3** to reorganize. —**reconstruction** *n.*

recopy /ri:ˈkɒpɪ/ *v.t.* to make a fresh copy of.

record /rɪˈkɔ:d/ *v.t.* **1** to set down for remembrance or reference, to put in writing or other permanent form. **2** to convert (sound or visual scenes, esp. television pictures) to a permanent form for later reproduction. **3** (of a measuring instrument) to register. —/ˈrekɔ:d/ *n.* **1** the state of being recorded or preserved in writing etc. **2** a piece of recorded evidence or information; an account of a fact preserved in a permanent form; a document or monument preserving it. **3** an official report of public or legal proceedings. **4** the known facts about a person's past; a list and the details of previous offences. **5** a disc (formerly a cylinder) from which recorded sound can be reproduced. **6** an object serving as a memorial, portrait, etc. **7** (often *attrib.*) the best performance or most remarkable event of its kind on record. —**for the record,** so that facts may be recorded officially. **go on record,** to state an opinion openly so that it is published. **have a record,** to have been convicted on a previous occasion. **off the record,** unofficially, confidentially. **on record,** officially recorded, publicly known. **recorded**

delivery, a Post Office service whereby safe delivery is recorded by the signature of the recipient. **record-player** *n.* a gramophone (see entry). [f. OF f. L *recordari* remember (RE-², *cor* heart)]

recorder /rɪˈkɔːdə(r)/ *n.* **1** a keeper of records. **2** a barrister or solicitor appointed to act for a period as a part-time judge of a Crown Court; (*hist.*) a judge in certain courts. **3** an apparatus for recording things, especially a tape-recorder. **4** a vertical instrument like a flute. [f. prec.]

recording /rɪˈkɔːdɪŋ/ *n.* **1** a process by which audio or video signals are recorded for later reproduction. **2** the material or programme thus recorded. [f. RECORD]

recordist /rɪˈkɔːdɪst/ *n.* a person who records sound. [as prec.]

recount /rɪˈkaʊnt/ *v.t.* to narrate, to tell in detail. [f. AF *reconter* (as RE-², COUNT)]

re-count /riːˈkaʊnt/ *v.t.* to count again. —/ˈriː kaʊnt/ *n.* re-counting, especially of election votes.

recoup /rɪˈkuːp/ *v.t.* **1** to recover or regain (a loss). **2** to compensate or reimburse for loss. —**recoup oneself,** to recover a loss. —**recoupment** *n.* [f. F (RE-¹, *couper* cut)]

recourse /rɪˈkɔːs/ *n.* **1** resorting to a possible source of help. **2** person or thing forming such a source. —**have recourse to,** to adopt as an adviser or helper or as an expedient. [f. OF f. L (as RE-², COURSE)]

recover /rɪˈkʌvə(r)/ *v.t./i.* **1** to regain possession, use, or control of. **2** to come back to health or consciousness or to a normal state or position. **3** to obtain or secure by legal process. **4** to retrieve or make up for (a loss or setback etc.). —**recover oneself,** to regain calmness or consciousness or control of one's limbs. [f. AF *recoverer* f. L (as RECUPERATE)]

recoverable *adj.* that may be recovered. [f. prec.]

recovery *n.* the act or process of recovering or being recovered. [f. AF *recoverie* (*as* RECOVER)]

recreant /ˈrekrɪənt/ *adj.* (*literary*) craven, cowardly. —*n.* a coward. [f. OF (*recroire* yield in trial by combat, f. L (*se*) *recredere*)]

re-create /riːkrɪˈeɪt/ *v.t.* to create again.

recreation /rekrɪˈeɪʃ(ə)n/ *n.* the process or a means of refreshing or entertaining oneself after work by some pleasurable activity. —**recreational** *adj.* [f. OF f. L (as RE-², CREATION)]

recriminate /rɪˈkrɪmɪneɪt/ *v.i.* to make mutual or counter accusations. —**recrimination** /-ˈneɪʃ(ə)n/ *n.*, **recriminatory** *adj.* [f. L *recriminare* accuse (RE-¹, *crimen* accusation)]

recross /riːˈkrɒs/ *v.t./i.* to cross again, to go back across.

recrudesce /riːkruːˈdes, rek-/ *v.i.* (of a disease or sore or discontent etc.) to break out again. —**recrudescence** *n.*, **recrudescent** *adj.* [f. L *recrudescere* (RE-², *crudus* raw)]

recruit /rɪˈkruːt/ *n.* a serviceman newly enlisted and not yet fully trained; a new member of a society etc.; a beginner. —*v.t./i.* **1** to enlist (a person) as a recruit; to enlist recruits for (an army etc.); to get or seek recruits. **2** to replenish or reinvigorate (numbers or strength etc.). —**recruitment** *n.* [f. obs. F dial. *recrute* f. L *recrescere* grow again]

rectal /ˈrekt(ə)l/ *adj.* of or by means of the rectum. [f. RECTUM]

rectangle /ˈrektæŋg(ə)l/ *n.* a four-sided plane rectilinear figure with four right angles, especially one with adjacent sides unequal. —**rectangular** /-ˈtæŋgʊlə(r)/ *adj.* [F or f. L *rectangulum* (*rectus* straight, *angulus* angle)]

rectifiable /ˈrektɪfaɪəb(ə)l/ *adj.* that may be rectified. [f. foll.]

rectify /ˈrektɪfaɪ/ *v.t.* **1** to put right, to correct. **2** to purify or refine, especially by repeated distillation. **3** to convert (alternating current) to direct current. —**rectification** /-fɪˈkeɪʃ(ə)n/ *n.*, **rectifier** *n.* [f. OF f. L *rectificare* (*rectus*) straight, right, *facere* make)]

rectilinear /rektɪˈlɪnɪə(r)/ *adj.* **1** bounded or characterized by straight lines. **2** in or forming a straight line. [f. L *rectilineus* (*rectus* straight, *linea* line)]

rectitude /ˈrektɪtjuːd/ *n.* moral goodness; correctness of behaviour or procedure. [f. OF or L *rectitudo* (as RECTIFY)]

recto /ˈrektəʊ/ *n.* (*pl.* **-os**) the right-hand page of an open book; the front of a leaf of a manuscript etc. (opp. *verso*). [f. L *recto* (*folio*) on the right leaf]

rector /ˈrektə(r)/ *n.* **1** an incumbent of a Church of England parish where all the tithes formerly passed to the incumbent; the head priest of a Roman Catholic church. **2** the head of a university, college, or religious institution. —**rectorship** *n.* [f. OF or L, = ruler (*regere* rule)]

rectory *n.* the house provided for a rector. [f. AF or L (as prec.)]

rectrix /ˈrektrɪks/ *n.* (*pl.* **rectrices** /-ɪsiːz/) any of a bird's strong tail-feathers, directing its flight. [L, fem. of RECTOR]

rectum /ˈrektəm/ *n.* (*pl.* **-ums**) the final section of the large intestine, terminating at the anus. [f. L, = straight (intestine)]

recumbent /rɪˈkʌmbənt/ *adj.* lying down, reclining. [f. L *recumbere* (RE-², *cumbere* lie)]

recuperate /rɪˈkjuːpəreɪt, -ˈkuː-/ *v.t./i.* to recover from illness, exhaustion, or loss etc.; to regain (health or losses etc.). —**recuperation** /-ˈreɪʃ(ə)n/ *n.* **recuperative** *adj.* [f. L *recuperare*]

recur /rɪˈkɜː(r)/ *v.i.* (**-rr-**) **1** to occur again, to be repeated. **2** to go back in thought or speech. —**recurring decimal,** a decimal fraction in which the same figures are repeated indefinitely. [f. L *recurrere* run back (RE-², *currere* run)]

recurrent /rɪˈkʌrənt/ *adj.* recurring, happening repeatedly. —**recurrence** *n.* [as prec.]

recusant /ˈrekjuz(ə)nt/ *n.* one who refuses submission to authority or compliance with a regulation. —**recusancy** *n.* [f. L *recusare* refuse]

recycle /ri:ˈsaɪk(ə)l/ *v.t.* to return (a material) to a previous stage of a cyclic process; to convert (waste) into a form in which it can be reused.

red *adj.* **1** of the colour of blood or a colour approaching this (ranging to pink or orange); flushed in the face with shame, anger, etc.; (of the eyes) sore, bloodshot; (of the hair) reddish-brown, tawny. **2** having to do with bloodshed, burning, violence, or revolution. **3 Red,** Russian, Soviet; socialist, communist. —*n.* **1** red colour or pigment. **2** red clothes or material. **3** a socialist or communist. —**in the red,** in debt. **red admiral,** see ADMIRAL. **red-blooded** *adj.* virile, vigorous. **red card,** such a card shown by the referee at a football match to a player whom he is sending off the field. **red carpet,** privileged treatment of an important visitor. **red cent,** (*US*) the smallest (orig. copper) coin. **Red Crescent,** the equivalent of the Red Cross in Muslim countries. **Red Cross,** an organization for the treatment of the sick and wounded in war and those suffering by large-scale natural disasters. **red flag,** a symbol of danger or of revolution. **red-handed** *adj.* in the act of committing a crime or doing wrong etc. **red hat,** a cardinal's hat, the symbol of his office. **red herring,** an irrelevant distraction. **red-hot** *adj.* heated to redness; highly exciting or excited; angry; (of news) fresh, completely new. **red-hot poker,** a garden plant of the genus *Kniphofia* with spikes of red or yellow flowers. **Red Indian,** a North American Indian, with reddish skin. **red lead,** a pigment made from red oxide of lead. **red-letter day,** one that is pleasantly noteworthy or memorable (originally a festival marked in red on a calendar). **red light,** a signal to stop on a road or railway; a warning. **red-light district,** one containing many brothels. **red pepper,** cayenne pepper; the ripe fruit of a capsicum plant. **red rag,** a thing that excites a person's rage. **red rose,** the emblem of Lancashire or Lancastrians. **red squirrel,** a squirrel of the native English species (*Sciurus leucouros*) with reddish fur. **red tape,** excessive use of or adherence to formalities especially in public business. —**reddish** *adj.*, **redly** *adv.*, **redness** *n.* [OE]

red- see RE-¹.

redbreast *n.* a robin.

redbrick *adj.* (of English universities) founded in the 19th c. or early 20th c., as distinct from Oxford and Cambridge (*Oxbridge*).

redcap *n.* a member of the military police.

redcoat *n.* (*hist.*) a British soldier.

redcurrant *n.* a small round red edible berry; the shrub (*Ribes sylvestre*) bearing it.

redden /ˈred(ə)n/ *v.t./i.* to make or become red. [f. RED]

redecorate /ri:ˈdekəreɪt/ *v.t.* to decorate freshly. —**redecoration** /-ˈreɪʃ(ə)n/ *n.*

redeem /rɪˈdi:m/ *v.t.* **1** to buy back, recover by expenditure of effort or by a stipulated payment. **2** to make a single payment to cancel (a regular charge or obligation). **3** to convert (tokens or bonds) into goods or cash. **4** to save, rescue, or reclaim; to deliver from damnation or from the consequences of sin. **5** to make amends for, to serve as a compensating factor; to save from a defect or from blame. **6** to purchase the freedom of (a person); to save (a person's life) by a ransom. **7** to fulfil (a promise). [f. OF or L *redimere* (RE-², *emere* buy)]

redeemable *adj.* that may be redeemed. [f. prec.]

redeemer *n.* one who redeems. —**the Redeemer,** Christ, who redeemed mankind. [f. REDEEM]

redemption /rɪˈdempʃ(ə)n/ *n.* **1** redeeming, being redeemed. **2** a thing that redeems. [as REDEEM]

redeploy /ri:dɪˈplɔɪ/ *v.t.* to send (troops or workers etc.) to a new place or task. —**redeployment** *n.*

redevelop /ri:dɪˈveləp/ *v.t.* to develop (esp. land) afresh. —**redevelopment** *n.*

rediffusion /ri:dɪˈfju:ʒ(ə)n/ *n.* the relaying of broadcast programmes, especially by wire from a central receiver.

redirect /ri:dɪˈrekt/ *v.t.* to direct or send to another place, to readdress. —**redirection** *n.*

rediscover /ri:dɪˈskʌvə(r)/ *v.t.* to discover again (what has been lost).

redo /ri:ˈdu:/ *v.t.* (*past* **redid**; *p.p.* **redone** /-ˈdʌn/) **1** to do again. **2** to redecorate.

redolent /ˈredələnt/ *adj.* strongly smelling or suggestive or reminiscent *of*; fragrant. —**redolence** *n.* [f. L *redolēre* (RE-¹, *olēre* smell)]

redouble /ri:ˈdʌb(ə)l/ *v.t./i.* **1** to make or grow greater or more intense or numerous. **2** to double again a bid in bridge already doubled by an opponent. —*n.* redoubling of a bid in bridge.

redoubt /rɪˈdaʊt/ *n.* an outwork or fieldwork without flanking defences. [f. F f. It. f. L *reductus* refuge (as REDUCE)]

redoubtable /rɪˈdaʊtəb(ə)l/ *adj.* formidable, especially as an opponent. [f. OF (*redouter* fear)]

redound /rɪˈdaʊnd/ *v.i.* to come back as an advantage or disadvantage, to accrue. [f. OF f. L *redundare* overflow (RE-[1], *unda* wave)]

redpoll *n.* **1** a bird with a red forehead (esp. *Carduelis flammea*) similar to a linnet. **2** an animal of a red breed of polled cattle.

redress /rɪˈdres/ *v.t.* to set right; to rectify (a wrong or grievance etc.). —*n.* reparation, amends for a wrong done; redressing of a grievance etc. —**redress the balance,** to restore equality. [f. OF (as RE-[2], DRESS)]

redshank *n.* a large kind of sandpiper (*Tringa totanus*).

redskin *n.* a Red Indian.

redstart *n.* a small red-tailed songbird of the genus *Phoenicurus*. [RED + OE *steort* tail]

reduce /rɪˈdju:s/ *v.t./i.* **1** to make or become smaller or less. **2** to bring by force or necessity to some state or action. **3** to convert to another (esp. simpler) form; to convert (a fraction) to the form with the lowest terms; to bring, simplify, or adapt by classification or analysis to its components etc. **4** to subdue, to bring back to obedience. **5** to make lower in status or rank. **6** to slim. **7** to weaken; to impoverish. **8** to convert (an oxide etc.) to a metal; to remove oxygen from or add hydrogen or electrons to. **9** to restore (a broken or dislocated part) to its original or proper position; to remedy (a dislocation) thus. —**reducer** *n.* [f. L *reducere* (RE-[2], *ducere* bring)]

reducible *adj.* that may be reduced. [f. prec.]

reductio ad absurdum /rɪdʌktɪəʊ æd əbˈsɜ:dəm/ *n.* proof of falsity by showing the absurd logical consequence; the carrying of a principle to unpractical lengths. [L, = reduction to the absurd]

reduction /rɪˈdʌkʃ(ə)n/ *n.* **1** reducing, being reduced; an instance of this. **2** the amount by which something is reduced, especially in price. **3** a reduced copy of a picture or version of a musical score etc. [f. OF or L (as REDUCE)]

reductive /rɪˈdʌktɪv/ *adj.* causing reduction. [as prec.]

redundant /rɪˈdʌnd(ə)nt/ *adj.* **1** superfluous; that can be omitted without loss of significance. **2** (of a worker) no longer needed for any available job and therefore liable to dismissal. —**redundancy** *n.* [f. L (as REDOUND)]

reduplicate /rɪˈdju:plɪkeɪt/ *v.t.* to make double, to repeat; to repeat (a word or syllable) exactly or with a slight change (e.g. *hurly-burly, see-saw*). —**reduplication** /-ˈkeɪʃ(ə)n/ *n.*, **reduplicative** /-kətɪv/ *adj.* [f. L *reduplicare* (RE-[2], *duplicare* duplicate)]

redwing *n.* a thrush (*Turdus iliacus*) with red flanks.

redwood *n.* a very large North American tree (*Sequoia sempervirens*) yielding reddish wood.

re-echo /ri:ˈekəʊ/ *v.t./i.* to echo repeatedly, to resound.

reed *n.* **1** a water or marsh plant of the genus *Phragmites* with a firm stem; a tall straight stalk of this. **2** the vibrating part of some wind instruments. **3** (usu. in *pl.*) such an instrument. —**reed-stop** *n.* a reeded organ-stop. [OE]

reeded *adj.* with a vibrating reed. [f. REED]

reedy *adj.* **1** full of reeds. **2** like a reed in slenderness or (of grass) thickness. **3** like a reed instrument in tone. —**reediness** *n.* [f. REED]

reef[1] *n.* **1** a ridge of rock or sand etc. at or near the surface of the sea etc. **2** a lode of ore; the bedrock surrounding this. [f. MDu. or MLG f. ON (as foll.)]

reef[2] *n.* each of several strips along the top or bottom of a sail that can be taken in or rolled up to reduce the sail's surface in high wind. —*v.t.* to take in the reef(s) of (a sail). —**reef-knot** *n.* a double knot made symmetrically. [f. Du. f. ON, = RIB]

reefer *n.* **1** a marijuana cigarette. **2** a thick double-breasted jacket. [f. prec.]

reek *v.i.* to smell strongly or unpleasantly; to have unpleasant or suspicious associations. —*n.* **1** a foul or stale smell. **2** (esp. *Sc.*) smoke, vapour, a visible exhalation. [OE]

reel *n.* **1** a cylindrical device on which thread, silk, yarn, paper, film, wire, etc., are wound; a quantity of thread etc. wound on a reel; a device for winding and unwinding a line as required, especially in fishing. **2** a revolving part in various machines. **3** a lively folk-dance or Scottish dance; the music for this. —*v.t./i.* **1** to wind (thread, a fishing-line, etc.) on or off reel. **2** to draw (a fish etc.) in by using a reel. **3** to stand, walk, or run unsteadily; to be shaken physically or mentally; to rock from side to side, to swing violently. **4** to dance a reel. —**reel off,** to say or recite very rapidly and without apparent effort. [OE]

re-elect /ri:ɪˈlekt/ *v.t.* to elect again. —**re-election** *n.*

re-enter /ri:ˈentə(r)/ *v.t./i.* to enter again. —**re-entry** *n.*

re-entrant /ri:ˈentrənt/ *adj.* (of an angle) pointing inwards, reflex.

re-establish /ri:ɪˈstæblɪʃ/ *v.t.* to establish again. —**re-establishment** *n.*

reeve[1] *n.* (*hist.*) the chief magistrate of a town or district. [OE]

reeve[2] *v.t.* (*past* **rove**) (*Naut.*) to thread (a rope or rod etc.) through a ring or other aperture;

to fasten (a rope or block etc.) thus. [prob. f. Du. *reven* (as REEF²)]

reeve³ *n.* a female ruff. [orig. unkn.]

re-examine /riːɪgˈzæmɪn/ *v.t.* to examine again. —**re-examination** /-ˈneɪʃ(ə)n/ *n.*

ref *n.* (*colloq.*) a referee in sports. [abbr.]

reface /riːˈfeɪs/ *v.t.* to put a new facing on (a building).

refectory /rɪˈfektərɪ, ˈrefɪk-/ *n.* a room for communal meals, especially in a monastery or college. —**refectory table,** a long narrow table. [f. L *refectorium* (*reficere* refresh)]

refer /rɪˈfɜː(r)/ *v.t./i.* **(-rr-) 1** to ascribe; to consider as belonging to a specified date, place or class. **2** to send on or direct (a person, a question for discussion) to an authority or source of information; to make an appeal or have recourse thus. **3** to make an allusion; to direct attention by words; to interpret (a statement) as being directed, (of a statement) to have relation or be directed (to what is specified). —**referred pain,** pain felt in a part of the body other than its true source. —**referral** *n.* [f. OF f. L *referre* carry back (RE-², *ferre* carry)]

referable /rɪˈfɜːrəb(ə)l, ˈrefər-/ *adj.* that may be referred. [f. prec.]

referee /refəˈriː/ *n.* **1** a person to whom a dispute is or may be referred for decision. **2** an umpire, especially in football or boxing. **3** a person willing to testify to the character of an applicant for employment etc. —*v.t./i.* to act as a referee (for). [f. REFER]

reference /ˈrefərəns/ *n.* **1** the referring of a matter for decision, settlement, or consideration to some authority. **2** the scope given to such an authority. **3** relation, respect, or correspondence *to*. **4** allusion. **5** a direction to a book etc. (or a passage in it) where information may be found; a book or passage so cited. **6** the act of looking up a passage etc. or of referring to a person etc. for information. **7** a written testimonial supporting an applicant for employment etc.; a person giving this. —**in** *or* **with reference to,** regarding, as regards, about. **reference book,** a book for occasional consultation, providing information for reference but not designed to be read straight through. **reference library** *or* **room,** one providing books that may be consulted but not taken away. —**referential** /-ˈrenʃ(ə)l/ *adj.* [as prec.]

referendum /refəˈrendəm/ *n.* (*pl.* **-ums**) the referring of a political question to the electorate for a direct decision by a general vote. [L, gerund of *referre* refer]

refill /riːˈfɪl/ *v.t.* to fill again. —/ˈriːfɪl/ *n.* a new filling; the material for this.

refine /rɪˈfaɪn/ *v.t./i.* **1** to free from impurities or defects. **2** to make or become more polished or elegant or cultured. [f. RE-¹, + FINE¹, & F *raffiner*]

refined *adj.* characterized by polish, elegance, or subtlety. [f. prec.]

refinement *n.* **1** refining, being refined. **2** fineness of feeling or taste; polish or elegance in behaviour or manners. **3** an added development or improvement. **4** a piece of subtle reasoning, a fine distinction. [f. REFINE]

refiner *n.* one who refines, especially one whose business is to refine crude oil or sugar or metal etc. [as prec.]

refinery *n.* a place where oil etc. is refined. [f. REFINE]

refit /riːˈfɪt/ *v.t./i.* **(-tt-)** to make or become fit again (especially of a ship undergoing renewal and repairs). —/ˈriːfɪt/ *n.* refitting. —**refitment** *n.*

reflate /riːˈfleɪt/ *v.t.* to cause the reflation of (a currency or economy etc.). [f. RE-², after *deflate, inflate*]

reflation /riːˈfleɪʃ(ə)n/ *n.* the inflation of a financial system to restore the previous condition after deflation. —**reflationary** *adj.* [f. RE-², after *deflation, inflation*]

reflect /rɪˈflekt/ *v.t./i.* **1** (of a surface or body) to throw back (heat, light, or sound). **2** (of a mirror etc.) to show an image of; to reproduce to the eye or mind; to correspond in appearance or effect to. **3** (of an action or result etc.) to show or bring (credit etc.) on the person or method responsible; (*absol.*) to bring discredit on the person etc. responsible. **4** to think deeply, to consider; to remind oneself of past events. [f. OF or L *reflectere* (RE-², *flectere* bend)]

reflection /rɪˈflekʃ(ə)n/ *n.* (also **reflexion**) **1** reflecting, being reflected. **2** reflected light or heat etc; a reflected image. **3** discredit; a thing bringing this. **4** reconsideration. **5** deep thought; an idea or statement produced by this. [as prec.]

reflective *adj.* **1** (of a surface etc.) giving back a reflection or image. **2** (of mental faculties) concerned in reflection or thought; (of a person or mood etc.) thoughtful, given to meditation. [f. REFLECT]

reflector *n.* **1** a piece of glass or metal etc. for reflecting light in a required direction, e.g. a red one on the back of a motor vehicle. **2** a mirror producing images; a telescope equipped with this. [as prec.]

reflex /ˈriːfleks/ *adj.* **1** (of an action) independent of the will, as an automatic response to nerve-stimulation (e.g. a sneeze). **2** (of an angle) exceeding 180°. —*n.* **1** a reflex action. **2** a secondary manifestation, a corresponding result. **3** reflected light; a reflected image. —**reflex camera,** a camera in which the image is reflected by a mirror to allow focusing up to the moment of exposure. [f. L *reflexus* (as REFLECT)]

reflexive /rɪˈfleksɪv/ *adj.* (*Gram.*) (of a word or form) implying the subject's action on himself or itself. —*n.* a reflexive word or form, especially a pronoun (e.g. *myself*). [as prec.]

refloat /riːˈfləʊt/ *v.t.* to set (a stranded ship) afloat again.

reflux /ˈriːflʌks/ *n.* backward flow; (*Chem.*) a method of boiling in which vapour is liquefied and returned to the boiler.

reform /rɪˈfɔːm/ *v.t./i.* to make or become better by the removal of faults or errors; to abolish or cure (an abuse or malpractice). —*n.* the removal of faults or abuses, especially of a moral or political or social kind; an improvement made or suggested. **Reformed Church,** any of the Protestant Churches which have accepted the principles of the Reformation, especially of those following Calvinist rather than Lutheran doctrines. —**reformer** *n.* [f. OF or L *reformare* (RE-[2], *formare* form)]

re-form /riːˈfɔːm/ *v.t./i.* to form again.

reformation /refəˈmeɪʃ(ə)n/ *n.* reforming, being reformed, especially a radical change for the better in public affairs. —**the Reformation,** the movement for reform of abuses in the Church, that led to the division of Western Christendom in the 16th c. [as REFORM]

reformative /rɪˈfɔːmətɪv/ *adj.* tending or intended to produce reform. [f. OF or L (as REFORM)]

reformatory /rɪˈfɔːmətərɪ/ *adj.* reformative. —*n.* (*US* & *hist.*) an institution to which young offenders are sent to be reformed. [f. REFORMATION]

refract /rɪˈfrækt/ *v.t.* (of water, air, glass, etc.) to deflect (a ray of light etc.) at a certain angle when it enters obliquely from another medium of different density. —**refraction** *n.*, **refractive** *adj.* [f. L *refringere* (RE-[1], *frangere* break)]

refractor *n.* a refracting medium or lens; a telescope using a lens to produce an image. [f. prec.]

refractory /rɪˈfræktərɪ/ *adj.* **1** resisting control or discipline, stubborn. **2** (of a disease or wound etc.) not yielding to treatment. **3** (of a substance) resistant to heat; hard to fuse or work. [f. L *refractarius* (as REFRACT)]

refrain[1] /rɪˈfreɪn/ *v.i.* to abstain or keep oneself (*from* a thing or action). [f. OF f. L *refrenare* (RE-[2], *frenum* bridle)]

refrain[2] /rɪˈfreɪn/ *n.* a recurring phrase or lines especially at the end of stanzas; the music accompanying this. [f. OF ult. f. L (as REFRACT)]

refrangible /rɪˈfrændʒɪb(ə)l/ *adj.* that can be refracted. [as REFRACT]

refresh /rɪˈfreʃ/ *v.t.* to give fresh spirit or vigour to; to stimulate (one's memory). [f. OF (as RE-[2], FRESH)]

refresher *n.* **1** an extra fee to counsel in a prolonged lawsuit. **2** (*colloq.*) a drink. —**refresher course,** a course reviewing previous studies, or giving instruction in modern methods etc. [f. prec.]

refreshment *n.* **1** refreshing, being refreshed. **2** a thing that refreshes, especially food and drink, (usu. in *pl.*) this when not regarded as constituting a meal. [as REFRESH]

refrigerant /rɪˈfrɪdʒərənt/ *n.* a substance used for refrigeration. —*adj.* refrigerating. [f. F or L (as foll.)]

refrigerate /rɪˈfrɪdʒəreɪt/ *v.t./i.* to make or become cool or cold; to subject (food etc.) to cold in order to freeze or preserve it. —**refrigeration** /-ˈreɪʃ(ə)n/ *n.* [f. L *refrigerare* (RE-[2], *frigus* cold)]

refrigerator *n.* a cabinet or room in which food etc. is refrigerated. [f. prec.]

reft see REAVE.

refuel /riːˈfjuːəl/ *v.t./i.* (**-ll-**) to replenish the fuel supply (of).

refuge /ˈrefjuːdʒ/ *n.* shelter from pursuit or danger or trouble; a person or place etc. offering this. [f. OF f. L *refugium* (RE-[1], *fugere* flee)]

refugee /refjʊˈdʒiː/ *n.* a person taking refuge, especially in a foreign country from war or persecution or natural disaster. [f. F *réfugié* (as prec.)]

refulgent /rɪˈfʌldʒ(ə)nt/ *adj.* shining, gloriously bright. —**refulgence** *n.* [f. L (RE-[1], *fulgēre* shine)]

refund /riːˈfʌnd/ *v.t./i.* to pay back (money or expenses); to reimburse (a person); to make repayment. —/ˈriːfʌnd/ *n.* refunding, repayment. [orig. = pour back, f. OF or L *refundere* (RE-[2], *fundere* poor)]

refurbish /riːˈfɜːbɪʃ/ *v.t.* to brighten up, to redecorate.

refusal /rɪˈfjuːz(ə)l/ *n.* **1** refusing, being refused. **2** the right or privilege of deciding to accept or refuse a thing before it is offered to others. [f. foll.]

refuse[1] /rɪˈfjuːz/ *v.t./i.* **1** to say or show that one is unwilling to accept, give, or do (what is requested); to indicate unwillingness; not to grant a request made by (a person). **2** (of a horse) to be unwilling to jump (a fence etc.). [f. OF prob. f. L *recusare* refuse after *refutare* refute]

refuse[2] /ˈrefjuːs/ *n.* what is rejected as worthless, waste. [perh. f. OF (as prec.)]

refutable /rɪˈfjuːtəb(ə)l/ *adj.* that may be refuted. [f. foll.]

refute /rɪˈfjuːt/ *v.t.* to prove the falsity or error

of (a statement etc. or a person advancing it); to rebut by argument. —**refutation** /refju:ˈteɪʃ(ə)n/ *n.* [f. L *refutare*; cf. CONFUTE]

regain /rɪˈgeɪn/ *v.t.* **1** to obtain possession, use, or control of after loss. **2** to reach (a place) again.

regal /ˈri:g(ə)l/ *adj.* of or by a king or kings; fit for a king, magnificent. —**regality** /rɪˈgælɪtɪ/ *n.*, **regally** *adv.* [f. OF or L *regalis* (*rex* king)]

regale /rɪˈgeɪl/ *v.t.* to entertain lavishly with feasting or talk etc.; (of beauty, flowers, etc.) to give delight to. [f. F *régaler* (OF *gale* pleasure)]

regalia /rɪˈgeɪljə/ *n.pl.* the insignia of royalty used at coronations; the insignia of an order or civic dignity. [L (as REGAL)]

regard /rɪˈgɑ:d/ *v.t.* **1** to gaze steadily at (usu. in a specified way). **2** to give heed to, to take into account. **3** to look upon or contemplate mentally in a specified way, to consider to be. —*n.* **1** a steady gaze. **2** heed, consideration. **3** respectful or kindly feeling. **4** reference, a point attended to. **5** (in *pl.*) an expression of friendliness in a letter etc., compliments. —**as regards,** about, concerning, in respect of. **in** *or* **with regard to,** regarding, in respect of. [f. F *regarder* (as RE-[1], GUARD)]

regardant /rɪˈgɑ:dənt/ *adj.* (in heraldry) looking backwards. [f. AF & OF (as REGARD)]

regardful *adj.* mindful *of.* [f. REGARD + -FUL]

regarding *prep.* about, concerning, with reference to. [f. REGARD]

regardless *adj.* without regard or consideration (*of*). —*adv.* without paying attention. [f. REGARD + -LESS]

regatta /rɪˈgætə/ *n.* a meeting for boat or yacht races. [It. (Venetian dialect)]

regency /ˈri:dʒ(ə)nsɪ/ *n.* the office of a regent; a commission acting as regent; a regent's or regency commission's period of office. —**the Regency,** the period of 1810-20 in Britain when George, Prince of Wales, acted as regent, or 1715-23 in France with Philip, Duke of Orleans, as regent. [f. L (as REGENT)]

regenerate /rɪˈdʒenəreɪt/ *v.t./i.* **1** to generate again; to form afresh. **2** to give new life or vigour to. **3** to reform spiritually or morally. —/rɪˈdʒenərət/ *adj.* spiritually born again, reformed. —**regeneration** /-ˈreɪʃ(ə)n/ *n.*, **regenerative** *adj.* [f. L *regenerare* (as RE-[2], GENERATE)]

regent /ˈri:dʒ(ə)nt/ *n.* a person appointed to administer a State during the minority, absence, or incapacity of a monarch. —*adj.* (placed after a noun) acting as regent. [f. OF or L *regere* rule]

reggae /ˈregeɪ/ *n.* a kind of music, of Jamaican origin, characterized by a strongly accentuated subsidiary beat and often a prominent bass. [orig. unkn.; perh. rel. to Jamaican English *rege-rege* quarrel, row]

regicide /ˈredʒɪsaɪd/ *n.* **1** the killing of a king. **2** a person guilty of or involved in this. —**regicidal** /-ˈsaɪd(ə)l/ *adj.* [f. L *rex regis* king + -CIDE]

regime /reɪˈʒi:m/ *n.* a method or system of government; the prevailing order or system of things. [f. F (as foll.)]

regimen /ˈredʒɪmen/ *n.* a prescribed course of exercise, way of life, and especially diet. [L (*regere* rule)]

regiment /ˈredʒɪmənt/ *n.* **1** a permanent unit of the army usually commanded by a colonel and divided into several companies, troops, or batteries and often into two or more battalions. **2** an operational unit of artillery etc. **3** a large array or number of things. —/also -ment/ *v.t.* to organize rigidly into groups or according to a system; to form into regiment(s). —**regimentation** /-ˈteɪʃ(ə)n/ *n.* [f. OF f. L (as prec.)]

regimental /redʒɪˈment(ə)l/ *adj.* of a regiment. —*n.* (in *pl.*) military uniform, especially of a particular regiment. —**regimentally** *adv.* [f. prec.]

Regina /rɪˈdʒaɪnə/ *n.* the reigning queen (in the titles of lawsuits, e.g. *Regina* v. *Jones*, the Crown versus Jones). [L, = queen]

region /ˈri:dʒ(ə)n/ *n.* **1** a continuous part of a surface, space, or body, with or without definite boundaries or with certain characteristics. **2** an administrative division of a country, especially in Scotland. **3** the sphere or realm of a subject etc. —**in the region of,** approximately. —**regional** *adj.*, **regionally** *adv.* [f. OF f. L *regio* direction, district (*regere* direct)]

register /ˈredʒɪst(ə)r/ *n.* **1** an official list of names, items, attendances, etc.; the book or other document(s) in which this is kept. **2** a mechanical device for indicating or recording speed, force, numbers, etc., automatically. **3** an adjustable plate for widening or narrowing an opening and regulating draught, especially in a fire-grate. **4** the compass of a voice or instrument; a part of the voice-compass. **5** a set of organ-pipes; a sliding device controlling this. **6** exact correspondence of position in printing etc. —*v.t./i.* **1** to enter or cause to be entered in a register. **2** to set down formally in writing; to present for consideration. **3** to entrust (a letter etc.) to a post office for transmission by registered post. **4** (of an instrument) to indicate or record automatically. **5** to notice and remember. **6** to express (an emotion) facially or by a gesture. **7** to make an impression on a person's mind. —**registered post,** a procedure with special precautions for safety and for compensation in case of loss.

register office, a place where records of births, marriages, and deaths are made and where civil marriages are performed. [f. OF or L (*regesta* things recorded, RE-², *gerere* carry)]

registrar /redʒɪˈstrɑː(r)/ *n.* **1** a person charged with keeping a register; the senior administrative officer in a university etc. **2** a doctor undergoing hospital training as a specialist. [f. L (as prec.)]

registration /redʒɪˈstreɪʃ(ə)n/ *n.* registering, being registered. —**registration mark** *or* **number,** a combination of letters and figures uniquely identifying a motor vehicle. [f. obs. F or L (as REGISTER)]

registry /ˈredʒɪstrɪ/ *n.* a place or office where registers are kept. —**registry office,** a register office. [f. L *registerium* (as REGISTER)]

Regius professor /ˈriːdʒɪəs/ the holder of a chair founded by a sovereign (especially one at Oxford or Cambridge instituted by Henry VIII) or filled by Crown appointment. [L, = royal (*rex regis* king)]

regnant /ˈregnənt/ *adj.* reigning. [f. L *regnare* reign]

regress /rɪˈgres/ *v.i.* **1** to move backwards. **2** to go back to an earlier or more primitive state. —/ˈriːgres/ *n.* regressing; relapse, backward tendency. —**regression** *n.*, **regressive** *adj.* [f. L *regredi* (RE-², *gradi* to step)]

regret /rɪˈgret/ *v.t.* (**-tt-**) to feel or express sorrow, repentance, or distress over (an action or loss etc.); to say with sorrow or remorse. —*n.* a feeling of sorrow or repentance etc. over an action or loss etc. —**give** *or* **send** etc. **one's regrets,** to decline an invitation. [f. OF *regreter* bewail, perh. rel. to GREET²]

regretful *adj.* feeling or showing regret. —**regretfully** *adv.* [f. prec. + -FUL]

regrettable *adj.* (of events or conduct) undesirable, unwelcome, deserving censure. —**regrettably** *adv.* [f. REGRET]

regroup /riːˈgruːp/ *v.t./i.* to form into new groups.

regular /ˈregjʊlə(r)/ *adj.* **1** conforming to a rule or principle or to a standard of procedure; consistent; symmetrical. **2** acting, done, or recurring uniformly or calculably in time or manner; habitual, constant, orderly. **3** conforming to a standard of etiquette or procedure. **4** properly constituted or qualified; devoted exclusively or primarily to its nominal function. **5** (*Gram.*, of a noun, verb, etc.) following the normal type of inflexion. **6** (*colloq.*) thorough, indubitable. **7** bound by a religious rule; belonging to a religious or monastic order. —*n.* **1** a regular soldier. **2** (*colloq.*) a regular customer, visitor, etc. **3** a member of the regular clergy. —**regularity** /-ˈlærɪtɪ/ *n.* **regularly** *adv.* [f. OF & L (*regula* rule)]

regularize /ˈregjʊləraɪz/ *v.t.* to make regular. [f. prec.]

regulate /ˈregjʊleɪt/ *v.t.* **1** to control or direct by rule(s); to subject to restrictions. **2** to adapt to requirements; to alter the speed of (a machine or clock) so that it will work accurately. —**regulator** *n.* [f. L *regulare* (as prec.)]

regulation /regjʊˈleɪʃ(ə)n/ *n.* **1** regulating, being regulated. **2** a prescribed rule. —*adj.* in accordance with regulations, of the correct type etc.; usual. —**the Queen's Regulations,** those applying to the armed forces. [f. prec.]

regurgitate /riːˈgɜːdʒɪteɪt/ *v.t./i.* **1** to bring (swallowed food) up again to the mouth. **2** to cast or pour out again; to gush back. —**regurgitation** /-ˈteɪʃ(ə)n/ *n.* [f. L *regurgitare* (RE-², *gurges* whirlpool)]

rehabilitate /riːhəˈbɪlɪteɪt/ *v.t.* **1** to restore to effectiveness or normal life by training, especially after imprisonment or illness. **2** to restore to privileges, reputation, or proper condition. —**rehabilitation** /-ˈteɪʃ(ə)n/ *n.*

rehash /riːˈhæʃ/ *v.t.* to put (old material) into a new form without significant change or improvement. —/ˈriːhæʃ/ *n.* rehashing; material rehashed.

rehearsal /rɪˈhɜːs(ə)l/ *n.* rehearsing; a trial performance or practice. [f. foll.]

rehearse /rɪˈhɜːs/ *v.t./i.* **1** to practise before performing in public. **2** to train by rehearsal. **3** to recite, to say over; to give a list of, to enumerate. [f. AF & OF, perh. as RE-², *hercer* harrow]

reheat /riːˈhiːt/ *v.t.* to heat again. —**reheater** *n.*

rehoboam /riːhəˈbəʊəm/ *n.* a large winebottle, twice the size of a jeroboam. [f. *Rehoboam*, king of Isreal (10th c. BC)]

rehouse /riːˈhaʊz/ *v.t.* to provide with new accommodation.

Reich /raɪx, -k/ *n.* the German State or commonwealth, especially during the period 1871-1945. —**Third Reich,** the regime under the rule of Hitler and the Nazi party, 1933-45. [G, = kingdom, realm, State]

reign /reɪn/ *n.* sovereignty, rule; the period during which a sovereign reigns. —*v.i.* **1** to be king or queen. **2** to prevail. [f. OF f. L *regnum* kingdom (*rex* king)]

reimburse /riːɪmˈbɜːs/ *v.t.* to repay (a person who has expended money, a person's expenses). —**reimbursement** *n.* [f. RE-² + obs. *imburse* f. L (as IM-¹, PURSE)]

rein /reɪn/ *n.* (in *sing.* or *pl.*) **1** a long narrow strap with each end attached to a bit, used to guide or check a horse etc. in riding or driving; a similar device to restrain a child etc. **2** a means of control. —*v.t.* **1** to check or control with reins; to pull or hold (as) with reins. 2 to restrain, to control. —**give free rein to,** to allow free scope to. **keep a tight rein on,** to allow little freedom to. [f. OF f. L *retinēre* (see RETAIN)]

reincarnation /riːmkɑːˈneɪʃ(ə)n/ *n.* the rebirth of a soul in a new body. —**reincarnate** /-ɪnˈkɑːnɪt/ *adj.*

reindeer /ˈreɪndɪə(r)/ *n.* (*pl.* usu. same) a subarctic deer (*Rangifer tarandus*) with large antlers. [f. ON]

reinforce /riːɪnˈfɔːs/ *v.t.* to strengthen or support, especially by additional men or material or by an increase of numbers, quantity, size, etc. [f. F *renforcer* (as RE-¹, ENFORCE)]

reinforcement *n.* 1 reinforcing, being reinforced. 2 a thing that reinforces; (in *pl.*) additional personnel, ships, etc. sent to reinforce armed forces etc. [f. prec.]

reinstate /riːɪnˈsteɪt/ *v.t.* to restore to or replace in a lost position or privileges etc. —**reinstatement** *n.* [f. RE-² + *instate* establish in office (IN-¹, STATE)]

reinsure /riːɪnˈʃʊə(r)/ *v.t./i.* to insure again (esp. of an insurer securing himself by transferring risk to another insurer). —**reinsurance** *n.*

reissue /riːˈɪsjuː/ *v.t.* to issue (a thing) again. —*n.* a thing reissued.

reiterate /riːˈɪtəreɪt/ *v.t.* to say or do again or repeatedly. —**reiteration** /-ˈreɪʃ(ə)n/ *n.*, **reiterative** /-ˈɪtərətɪv/ *adj.*

reject /rɪˈdʒekt/ *v.t.* 1 to refuse to accept or believe in. 2 to put aside or send back as not to be used or done or complied with etc. —/ˈriːdʒekt/ *n.* a person or thing rejected. —**rejection** /rɪˈdʒekʃ(ə)n/ *n.*, **rejector** *n.* [f. L *rejicere* (RE-², *jacere* throw)]

rejig /riːˈdʒɪg/ *v.t.* (**-gg-**) to re-equip (a factory etc.) for a new kind of work; (*colloq.*) to rearrange.

rejoice /rɪˈdʒɔɪs/ *v.t./i.* 1 to feel or show great joy; to take delight. 2 to cause joy to. —**rejoicing** *n.* [f. OF *rejoir* (as RE-¹, JOY)]

rejoin¹ /riːˈdʒɔɪn/ *v.t./i.* to join together again, to reunite.

rejoin² /rɪˈdʒɔɪn/ *v.t./i.* to say in answer, to retort; to reply to a charge or pleading in a lawsuit. [f. OF *rejoindre* (as RE-², JOIN)]

rejoinder /rɪˈdʒɔɪndə(r)/ *n.* what is said in reply or rejoined, a retort. [as prec.]

rejuvenate /rɪˈdʒuːvəneɪt/ *v.t.* to make (as if) young again. —**rejuvenation** /-ˈneɪʃ(ə)n/ *n.*, **rejuvenator** *n.* [f. RE-² + L *juvenis* young]

relapse /rɪˈlæps/ *v.i.* to fall back into a previous condition, or into a worse state after improvement. —*n.* relapsing, especially after partial recovery from illness. [f. L (RE-², *labi* slip)]

relate /rɪˈleɪt/ *v.t./i.* 1 to narrate, to tell in detail. 2 to bring into relation. 3 to have reference. 4 to bring oneself into a sympathetic or successful relationship (to a person or thing). [f. L (as REFER)]

related *adj.* connected, especially by blood or marriage; having a common descent or origin. [f. prec.]

relation /rɪˈleɪʃ(ə)n/ *n.* 1 the way in which one person or thing is related to another; a similarity, correspondence, or contrast between people or things or events. 2 (in *pl.*) dealings with others; sexual intercourse. 3 a person who is a relative. 4 being related. 5 narration, a narrative. —**in relation to,** as regards. —**relationship** *n.* [f. OF or L (as REFER)]

relative /ˈrelətɪv/ *adj.* 1 considered in relation to something else. 2 proportionate; comparative. 3 corresponding in some way, related to each other; having reference or relating *to*. 4 (*Gram.*, of a word) referring to an expressed or implied antecedent and attaching a subordinate clause to it; (of a clause) attached to an antecedent by a relative word. —*n.* 1 a person who is related to another by parentage, descent, or marriage. 2 a species related to another by a common origin. 3 (*Gram.*) a relative word, especially a pronoun. —**relatively** *adv.*, **relativeness** *n.* [f. OF or L (as REFER)]

relativity /reləˈtɪvɪtɪ/ *n.* 1 being relative. 2 a theory based on the principle that all motion is relative and that light travels with a constant maximum speed in a vacuum (also **special relativity**); a theory extending this to gravitation and accelerated motion (**general relativity**). [f. prec.]

relax /rɪˈlæks/ *v.t./i.* 1 to make or become less stiff, rigid, or tense. 2 to make or become less formal or strict. 3 to reduce or abate (one's attention or efforts etc.). 4 to cease work or effort; to indulge in recreation. —**relaxation** /-ˈseɪʃ(ə)n/ *n.* [f. L *relaxare* (RE-², *laxus* lax)]

relay /ˈriːleɪ/ *n.* 1 a fresh set of people or animals taking the place of others who have completed a spell of work. 2 a fresh supply of material to be used or worked on. 3 a relay race. 4 a device activating an electric circuit; a device that receives and transmits a telegraph message or broadcast etc. 5 a relayed message or transmission. —/also riːˈleɪ/ *v.t.* to receive (a message, broadcast etc.) and transmit to others. —**relay race,** a race between teams of which each member in turn covers part of the distance. [f. OF *relai* (as RE-¹, L *laxare*; cf. RELAX)]

re-lay /riːˈleɪ/ *v.t.* (*past* & *p.p.* **re-laid**) to lay again.

release /rɪˈliːs/ *v.t.* 1 to set free (*lit.* or *fig.*); to unfasten. 2 to remove or allow to move from a fixed position; to allow to fall or fly etc. 3 to make (information or a recording etc.) public; to issue (a film etc.) for general exhibition. —*n.* 1 releasing, being released. 2 a handle or catch etc. that unfastens a device or machine-part. 3 a document etc. made available for publication; a film or record etc. that is released; the releasing of a document or film etc. thus. [f. OF *relesser* f. L *relaxare* relax]

relegate /ˈrelɪgeɪt/ *v.t.* to consign or dismiss to an inferior position; to transfer (a sports team) to a lower division of a league etc.; to banish. —**relegation** /-ˈgeɪʃ(ə)n/ *n.* [f. L *relegare* (RE-[1], *legare* send)]

relent /rɪˈlent/ *v.i.* to relax one's severity, to abandon a harsh intention, to yield to compassion. [f. RE-[2] + L *lentare* bend]

relentless *adj.* unrelenting. —**relentlessly** *adv.*, **relentlessness** *n.* [f. prec. + -LESS]

relevant /ˈrelɪv(ə)nt/ *adj.* related to the matter in hand. —**relevance** *n.* [f. L *relevare* (as RELIEVE)]

reliable /rɪˈlaɪəb(ə)l/ *adj.* that may be relied on. —**reliability** /-ˈbɪlɪtɪ/ *n.*, **reliably** *adv.* [f. RELY]

reliance /rɪˈlaɪəns/ *n.* relying; trust, confidence. [f. RELY]

relic /ˈrelɪk/ *n.* 1 something that survives from an earlier age; a surviving custom or belief etc. from a past age; an object that is interesting because of its age or associations. 2 a part of a holy person's body or belongings kept after his or her death as an object of reverence. 3 (in *pl.*) residue, surviving scraps; the dead body or remains of a person. [f. OF f. L *reliquiae* (as RELINQUISH)]

relict /ˈrelɪkt/ *n.* 1 a person's widow. 2 a geological or other object surviving in a primitive form. [f. L *relinquere* (see RELINQUISH)]

relief /rɪˈli:f/ *n.* 1 alleviation of or deliverance from pain, distress, anxiety, etc. 2 a feature etc. that breaks up monotony or relaxes tension. 3 assistance given to persons in special danger, need, or difficulty. 4 the replacing of a person or persons on duty by another or others; the person(s) thus taking over. 5 a thing supplementing another in some service. 6 a method of moulding, carving, or stamping in which the design stands out from the surface; a piece of sculpture etc. in relief; representation of relief given by the arrangement of line, colour, or shading. 7 deliverance of a beseiged place, especially by raising the siege. 8 redress of a hardship or grievance. —**relief map,** a map showing hills and valleys by shading or colouring etc. rather than by contour lines alone. **relief road,** a road by which traffic can avoid a congested area. [f. AF & F f. It. (as foll.)]

relieve /rɪˈli:v/ *v.t.* 1 to give relief, bring or be a relief to. 2 to mitigate the tedium or monotony of. 3 to release (a person) from duty by taking his place or providing a substitute. —**relieve one's feelings,** to use strong language or vigorous behaviour when annoyed. **relieve oneself,** to urinate or defecate. **relieve a person of,** to take (a burden or responsibility etc.) from him. [f. OF *relever* f. L *relevare* lift (RE-[2], *levis* light)]

relievo /rɪˈli:vəʊ/ *n.* (*pl.* **-os**) relief in sculpture etc. [f. It. (as RELIEF)]

religion /rɪˈlɪdʒ(ə)n/ *n.* 1 belief in a superhuman controlling power, especially in a personal God or gods entitled to obedience and worship; the expression of this in worship. 2 a particular system of faith. 3 a thing that one is devoted to. 4 life under monastic vows. [f. AF f. L *religio* obligation, bond, reverence]

religious /rɪˈlɪdʒəs/ *adj.* 1 believing firmly in a religion and paying attention to its practices. 2 of or concerned with religion. 3 of or belonging to a monastic order. 4 scrupulous, conscientious. —*n.* (*pl.* same) a person bound by monastic vows. —**religiously** *adv.* [f. AF f. L *religiosus* (as prec.)]

relinquish /rɪˈlɪŋkwɪʃ/ *v.t.* 1 to give up or cease from (a habit, plan, or belief etc.). 2 to resign or surrender (a right or possession). 3 to relax one's hold of. —**relinquishment** *n.* [f. OF f. L *relinquere* leave behind (RE-[1], *linquere* leave)]

reliquary /ˈrelɪkwərɪ/ *n.* a receptacle for relics. [f. F *reliquaire* (as RELIC)]

relish /ˈrelɪʃ/ *n.* 1 great liking or enjoyment. 2 appetizing flavour, attractive quality. 3 a thing eaten with plainer food to add flavour. 4 a distinctive taste or tinge *of*. —*v.t.* to get pleasure from, to enjoy greatly. [f. OF, = remainder (as RELEASE)]

relive /ri:ˈlɪv/ *v.t.* to live (an experience etc.) over again, especially in the imagination.

reload /ri:ˈləʊd/ *v.t./i.* to load again.

relocate /ri:ləʊˈkeɪt/ *v.t./i.* to locate in or move to a new place. —**relocation** /-ˈkeɪʃ(ə)n/ *n.*

reluctant /rɪˈlʌkt(ə)nt/ *adj.* unwilling, with consent grudgingly given. —**reluctance** *n.*, **reluctantly** *adv.* [f. L *reluctari* (RE-[1], *luctari* struggle)]

rely /rɪˈlaɪ/ *v.i.* (with *on* or *upon*) to trust confidently, to depend on for help. [orig. = rally, be vassal of, f. OF *relier* bind together f. L *religare* (RE-[2], *ligare* bind)]

remain /rɪˈmeɪn/ *v.i.* 1 to be left after other parts have been removed, used, or dealt with. 2 to be in the same place or condition during further time; to continue to be. [f. OF f. L *remanēre* (RE-[1], *manēre* stay)]

remainder /rɪˈmeɪndə(r)/ *n.* 1 the remaining persons, things, or part. 2 the number left after subtraction or division. 3 the copies of a book left unsold when demand has almost ceased. —*v.t.* to dispose of (the remainder of the copies of a book) at a reduced price. [f. AF (as prec.)]

remains *n.pl.* **1** what remains after other parts have been removed or used etc. **2** relics of antiquity, especially of buildings. **3** a dead body. [f. OF (as REMAIN)]

remand /rɪˈmɑːnd/ *v.t.* to send back (a prisoner) into custody while further evidence is sought. —*n.* remanding, being remanded. —**on remand,** held in custody after being remanded. **remand centre** *or* **home,** an institution to which young offenders may be sent. [f. L *remandare* (RE-², *mandare* commit)]

remanent /ˈremənənt/ *adj.* remaining, residual. —**remanent magnetism,** magnetization remaining after the source of excitation has been removed. [f. L (as REMAIN)]

remark /rɪˈmɑːk/ *v.t./i.* to say by way of comment. **2** to take notice of, to regard with attention. —*n.* **1** a written or spoken comment, anything said. **2** noticing. [f. F *remarquer* (as RE-¹, MARK¹)]

remarkable *adj.* worth notice, exceptional, unusual. —**remarkably** *adv.* [f. F (as prec.)]

remarry /riːˈmærɪ/ *v.t./i.* to marry again. —**remarriage** *n.*

remediable /rɪˈmiːdɪəb(ə)l/ *adj.* that may be remedied. [f. REMEDY]

remedial /rɪˈmiːdɪəl/ *adj.* providing a remedy for a disease or deficiency; (of teaching) for slow or backward children. —**remedially** *adv.* [f. L (as foll.)]

remedy /ˈremɪdɪ/ *n.* **1** something that cures or relieves a disease or that puts right a matter. **2** redress, legal or other reparation. —*v.t.* to be a remedy for; to put right. [f. AF f. L *remedium* (RE-¹, *medēri* heal)]

remember /rɪˈmembə(r)/ *v.t.* **1** to keep in one's mind, not to forget. **2** to recall (knowledge or an experience etc.) to one's mind; to be able to do this. **3** to think of (a person), especially in making a gift etc. **4** to convey greetings from. [f. OF f. L *rememorari* (RE-², *memor* mindful)]

remembrance /rɪˈmembrəns/ **1** remembering, being remembered; memory. **2** a memento; a memorial. **3** (in *pl.*) greetings conveyed through a third person. —**Remembrance Sunday,** the Sunday nearest 11 Nov., when those who were killed in the First and Second World Wars are commemorated. [f. OF (as prec.)]

remind /rɪˈmaɪnd/ *v.t.* to cause (a person) to remember or think *of.* [f. RE-² + MIND]

reminder *n.* a thing that reminds or is a momento. [f. prec.]

reminisce /remɪˈnɪs/ *v.i.* to indulge in reminiscences. [back-formation f. foll.]

reminiscence /remɪˈnɪs(ə)ns/ *n.* **1** remembering of things past. **2** (in *pl.*) an account of facts and incidents remembered, especially in literary form. **3** a thing that is reminiscent of something else. [f. L (*reminisci* remember)]

reminiscent *adj.* **1** inclined to reminisce. **2** reminding or suggestive *of.* —**reminiscently** *adv.* [as prec.]

remiss /rɪˈmɪs/ *adj.* careless of one's duty, lax, negligent. [f. L *remissus* (as REMIT)]

remission /rɪˈmɪʃ(ə)n/ *n.* **1** shortening of a prison sentence on account of good behaviour; the remitting of a debt or penalty etc. **2** diminution of force or intensity especially of a disease or pain. **3** God's pardon or forgiveness of sins. [f. OF or L (as foll.)]

remit /rɪˈmɪt/ *v.t./i.* (-tt-) **1** to cancel (a debt etc.); to refrain from inflicting (a punishment). **2** to make or become less intense; to cease. **3** to send (money etc.) in payment. **4** to refer (a matter for decision etc.) to some authority. **5** to postpone. **6** (of God) to pardon or forgive (sins). —/also ˈriːmɪt/ *n.* **1** an item remitted for consideration. **2** the terms of reference of a committee etc. [f. L *remittere* (RE-², *mittere* send)]

remittance /rɪˈmɪtəns/ *n.* the sending of money to a person; the money sent. [f. prec.]

remittent *adj.* that abates at intervals. [as REMIT]

remnant /ˈremnənt/ *n.* **1** a small remaining quantity, part, or number of people or things; a surviving trace. **2** a piece of cloth etc. left when the greater part has been used or sold. [f. OF *remenant* (as REMAIN)]

remodel /riːˈmɒd(ə)l/ *v.t.* to model again or differently; to reconstruct or reorganize.

remonstrance /rɪˈmɒnstrəns/ *n.* **1** (*hist.*) a formal statement of public grievances. **2** remonstrating, a protest. [as foll.]

remonstrate /ˈremənstreɪt/ *v.t./i.* to make a protest (*with* a person). [f. L *remonstrare* (RE-¹, *monstrare* show)]

remorse /rɪˈmɔːs/ *n.* deep regret for a wrong committed; compunction. [f. OF f. L (*remordēre* vex, RE-¹, *mordēre* bite)]

remorseful *adj.* filled with remorse. —**remorsefully** *adv.* [f. prec. + -FUL]

remorseless *adj.* relentless, without compassion. —**remorselessly** *adv.* [f. REMORSE + -LESS]

remote /rɪˈməʊt/ *adj.* **1** far apart; far away in place or time. **2** far from civilization etc.; secluded. **3** not closely related. **4** slight. **5** aloof, not friendly. —**remote control,** control of apparatus etc. from a distance, usually by means of an electrically operated device, radio, etc. —**remotely** *adv.*, **remoteness** *n.* [f. L *remotus* (as REMOVE)]

remould /riːˈməʊld/ *v.t.* to mould again, to

refashion; to reconstruct the tread of (a tyre). —/ˈriːməʊld/ *n.* a remoulded tyre.

removable /rɪˈmuːvəb(ə)l/ *adj.* that may be removed. [f. REMOVE]

removal /rɪˈmuːv(ə)l/ *n.* removing, being removed; transfer of furniture etc. to a different house. [f. foll.]

remove /rɪˈmuːv/ *v.t./i.* **1** to take off or away from the place occupied; to convey to another place. **2** to get rid of. **3** to dismiss from office. **4** to take off (clothing). **5** (in *p.p.*) distant, remote. —*n.* **1** distance, degree of remoteness. **2** a stage in gradation. **3** a form or division in some schools. —**cousin once, twice, etc., removed,** see COUSIN. —**remover** *n.* [f. OF f. L (as RE-¹, MOVE)]

remunerate /rɪˈmjuːnəreɪt/ *v.t.* to pay or reward (a person) for a service rendered; to pay for or reward (work etc.). —**remuneration** /-ˈreɪʃ(ə)n/ *n.*, **remunerative** *adj.* [f. L *remunerari* (RE-¹, *munus* gift)]

Renaissance /rɪˈneɪs(ə)ns, -sɑ̃s/ *n.* **1** the revival of art and learning under the influence of classical models which began in Italy in the late Middle Ages and reached its peak at the end of the 15th c. before spreading northwards into the rest of Europe; the period of this; the style of art and architecture developed by it. **2** **renaissance,** any similar revival. [F, = rebirth (as RENASCENT)]

renal /ˈriːn(ə)l/ *adj.* of the kidneys. [f. F f. L (*renes* kidneys)]

rename /riːˈneɪm/ *v.t.* to give a fresh name to.

renascent /rɪˈnæs(ə)nt/ *adj.* springing up anew, being reborn. —**renascence** *n.* [f. L (RE-², *nasci* be born)]

rend *v.t./i.* (*past* & *p.p.* **rent**) (*archaic*) to tear or wrench forcibly. [OE]

render *v.t.* **1** to cause to be or become. **2** to give or pay (money, a service, etc.) especially in return or as a thing due; to give (assistance). **3** to present, to send in. **4** to represent or portray; to act (a role); to perform (music). **5** to translate. **6** to melt down (fat). **7** to cover (stone or brick) with a first coat of plaster. [f. AF *rendre* f. L *reddere* (RE-¹, *dare* give)]

rendezvous /ˈrɒndeɪvuː/ *n.* (*pl.* same /-uːz/) an agreed or regular meeting-place; a meeting by agreement. —*v.i.* (3 *sing. pres.* **-vouses** /-vuːz/, *past* **-voused** /-vuːd/, *partic.* **-vousing** /-vuːɪŋ) to meet at a rendezvous. [f. F *rendez-vous* present yourselves]

rendition /renˈdɪʃ(ə)n/ *n.* the rendering or interpretation of a dramatic role, musical piece, etc. [obs. F (as RENDER)]

renegade /ˈrenɪgeɪd/ *n.* one who deserts his or her party or principles. [f. Sp. *renegado* f. L (as foll.)]

renege /rɪˈniːg, -ˈneɪg/ *v.t/i.* **1** to deny, to renounce. **2** (*US*, in cards) to revoke. —**renege on,** to fail to keep (a promise etc.); to disappoint (a person). [f. L *renegare* (RE-¹, *negare* deny)]

renew /rɪˈnjuː/ *v.t.* **1** to restore to its original state; to revive, to regenerate. **2** to replace with a fresh supply etc. **3** to repeat, to re-establish; to make, get, or give again; to arrange for a continuation or continued validity of (a licence, subscription, lease, etc.). —**renewal** *n.*

rennet /ˈrenɪt/ *n.* curdled milk found in the stomach of an unweaned calf, or a preparation of a bovine stomach-membrane or of a plant, used in curdling milk for cheese or junket. [prob. rel. to RUN]

renounce /rɪˈnaʊns/ *v.t.* **1** to give up (a claim or right etc.) formally. **2** to repudiate, to refuse to recognize any longer; to decline further association or disclaim a relationship with. [f. OF *renoncer* f. L *renuntiare* (RE-¹, *nuntiare* announce)]

renovate /ˈrenəveɪt/ *v.t.* to restore to a good condition, to repair. —**renovation** /-ˈveɪʃ(ə)n/ *n.*, **renovator** *n.* [f. L *renovare* (RE-², *novus* new)]

renown /rɪˈnaʊn/ *n.* fame, high distinction. [f. AF & OF (*renomer* make famous (as RE-², NOMINATE)]

renowned *adj.* famous, celebrated. [f. prec.]

rent¹ *n.* a tenant's periodical payment to an owner or landlord for the use of land or premises; payment for the use of equipment etc. —*v.t./i.* **1** to pay rent for occupation or use of. **2** to let or hire for rent; to be let at a specified rent. [f. OF *rente* (as RENDER)]

rent² *n.* a large tear in a garment etc.; an opening in clouds etc. [as REND]

rent³ *past* & *p.p.* of REND.

rentable /ˈrentəb(ə)l/ *adj.* that may be rented. [f. RENT¹]

rental /ˈrent(ə)l/ *n.* **1** the amount paid or received as rent. **2** renting. [f. AF or L (as RENT¹)]

rentier /ˈrɑ̃tɪeɪ/ *n.* a person living on income from property or investments. [F (*rente* dividend)]

renumber /riːˈnʌmbə(r)/ *v.t.* to change the numbering of.

renunciation /rɪnʌnsɪˈeɪʃ(ə)n/ *n.* renouncing; the giving up of things. [as RENOUNCE]

reopen /riːˈəʊpən/ *v.t./i.* to open again.

reorder /riːˈɔːdə(r)/ *v.t.* **1** to order again. **2** to put into a new order.

reorganize /riːˈɔːgənaɪz/ *v.t.* to organize again in a different way. —**reorganization** /-ˈzeɪʃ(ə)n/ *n.*

rep¹ *n.* a textile fabric with a corded surface, used in curtains and upholstery. [f. F *reps*]

rep[2] *n.* (*colloq.*) a representative, especially a commercial traveller. [abbr.]

rep[3] *n.* (*colloq.*) a repertory theatre or company. [abbr.]

repaint /ri:ˈpeɪnt/ *v.t.* to paint again or differently. —/ˈri:peɪnt/ *n.* **1** repainting. **2** a repainted thing.

repair[1] /rɪˈpeə(r)/ *v.t.* **1** to restore to a good condition after damage or wear. **2** to set right or make amends for (a loss or wrong etc.). —*n.* **1** restoring to a sound condition; the act or result of doing this. **2** condition as regards being repaired. —**repairer** *n.* [f. OF *reparer* f. L *reparare* (RE-², *parare* make ready)]

repair[2] /rɪˈpeə(r)/ *v.i.* to go, resort, or have recourse *to*. [f. OF f. L *repatriare* (as REPATRIATE)]

reparable /ˈrepərəb(ə)l/ *adj.* (of a loss etc.) that can be made good. [F f. L (as REPAIR²)]

reparation /repəˈreɪʃ(ə)n/ *n.* making amends; compensation. [f. OF f. L (as REPAIR²)]

repartee /repɑ:ˈti:/ *n.* a witty retort; the making of witty retorts. [f. F *repartie* (*repartir* reply promptly)]

repast /rɪˈpɑ:st/ *n.* a meal; the food and drink for a meal. [f. OF f. L *repascere* feed]

repatriate /ri:ˈpætrɪeɪt/ *v.t./i.* to restore (a person) to his native land; to return thus. —/-ət/ *n.* a repatriated person. —**repatriation** /-ˈeɪʃ(ə)n/ *n.* [f. L *repatriare* (RE-², *patria* native land)]

repay /ri:ˈpeɪ/ *v.t./i.* **1** to pay back (money) ; to pay back money to (a person). **2** to give in return or recompense; to make recompense for (a service etc.); to requite (an action). —**repayment** *n.*

repayable *adj.* that can or must be repaid. [f. prec.]

repeal /rɪˈpi:l/ *v.t.* to annul or revoke (a law etc.). —*n.* repealing. [f. AF & OF (as RE-², APPEAL)]

repeat /rɪˈpi:t/ *v.t./i.* **1** to say, do, or provide again. **2** to say, recite, or report (something heard or learnt). **3** to recur, to appear again or repeatedly. **4** (of food) to be tasted intermittently for some time after being swallowed. —*n.* **1** repeating. **2** a thing repeated; a repeated broacast programme; (*Mus.*) a passage intended to be repeated, a mark indicating this; each occurrence of a pattern repeated in wallpaper etc. —**repeat itself,** to recur in the same form. **repeat oneself,** to say or do the same thing over again. [f. OF f. L *repetere* (RE-², *petere* seek)]

repeatable *adj.* that may be repeated; suitable for being repeated. [f. prec.]

repeatedly *adv.* many times over. [f. REPEAT]

repeater *n.* a person or thing that repeats, especially a firearm that fires several shots without reloading, or a watch etc. that strikes the last quarter etc. again when required; a device that repeats a signal. [as prec.]

repel /rɪˈpel/ *v.t.* (-ll-) **1** to drive back, to ward off; to refuse admission, approach, or acceptance to. **2** to be impenetrable by. **3** to be repulsive or distasteful to. [f. L *repellere* (RE-¹, *pellere* drive)]

repellent *adj.* that repels. —*n.* a substance that repels something (esp. insects). [f. prec.]

repent /rɪˈpent/ *v.t./i.* to feel deep sorrow or regret about (one's wrongdoing or omission etc.). —**repentance** *n.*, **repentant** *adj.* [f. OF *repentir* (as RE-¹, PENITENT)]

repercussion /ri:pəˈkʌʃ(ə)n/ *n.* **1** an indirect effect or reaction of an event or act. **2** a recoil after impact. **3** an echo. [f. OF or L (as RE-¹, PERCUSSION)]

repertoire /ˈrepətwɑ:(r)/ *n.* a stock of pieces etc. that a performer or company knows or is prepared to give; a stock of regularly performed pieces, regularly used techniques, etc. [f. F f. L (as foll.)]

repertory /ˈrepətərɪ/ *n.* **1** a repertoire. **2** theatrical performance of various plays for short periods by one company. **3** a store or collection, especially of information or instances etc. [f. L *repertorium* (*reperire* find)]

repetition /repɪˈtɪʃ(ə)n/ *n.* **1** repeating, being repeated. **2** a thing repeated; a copy. —**repetitious** *adj.*, **repetitive** /rɪˈpetɪtɪv/ *adj.*, **repetitively** *adv.* [f. F or L (as REPEAT)]

repine /rɪˈpaɪn/ *v.i.* to fret, to be discontented. [f. RE-¹ + PINE², after *repent*]

replace /rɪˈpleɪs/ *v.t.* **1** to put back in place. **2** to take the place of. **3** to find or provide a substitute for.

replaceable *adj.* that may be replaced. [f. prec.]

replacement *n.* **1** replacing, being replaced. **2** a person or thing that takes the place of another. [f. REPLACE]

replant /ri:ˈplɑ:nt/ *v.t.* to plant again or differently.

replantation /ri:plɑ:nˈteɪʃ(e)n/ *n.* **1** replanting. **2** permanent reattachment to the body of a part which has been removed or severed. [f. prec.]

replay /ri:ˈpleɪ/ *v.t.* to play (a match, recording, etc.) over again. —/ˈri:pleɪ/ *n.* the replaying (of a match, a recording of an incident in a game, etc.).

replenish /rɪˈplenɪʃ/ *v.t.* to fill up again (*with*); to renew (a supply etc.). —**replenishment** *n.* [f. OF *replenir* (RE-², *plein* full f. L *plenus*)]

replete /rɪˈpli:t/ *adj.* filled or well supplied; full, gorged, sated. —**repletion** *n.* [f. OF or L *replēre* (RE-¹, *plēre* fill)]

replica /ˈreplɪkə/ *n.* an exact copy, especially a

duplicate made by an original artist of his picture etc.; a model, especially on a smaller scale. [It. (*replicare*, as REPLY)]

reply /rɪˈplaɪ/ *v.t./i.* to make an answer; to say in answer. —*n.* **1** replying. **2** what is replied, an answer. [f. OF f. L *replicare*, lit. = fold again (RE-², *plicare* fold)]

report /rɪˈpɔːt/ *v.t./i.* **1** to bring back or give an account of; to state as a fact or news; to narrate, describe, or repeat, especially as an eye-witness or hearer etc.; to describe (an event etc.) for publication or broadcasting; to make an official or formal statement about. **2** to make a formal accusation about (an offence or offender). **3** to present oneself as having returned or arrived. **4** to be responsible to a specified person as one's superior or supervisor. —*n.* **1** a spoken or written account of something seen, done, or studied. **2** a description for publication or broadcasting. **3** a periodical statement on a pupil's work, conduct, etc. **4** rumour, a piece of gossip. **5** the sound of an explosion or firing of a gun. —**reported speech,** a speaker's words as given in a report of them, with person and tense etc. adapted. [f. OF f. L *reportare* (RE-², *portare* carry)]

reporter *n.* a person employed to gather and report news for a newspaper or broadcast. [f. prec.]

repose¹ /rɪˈpəʊz/ *n.* **1** cessation of activity, excitement, or toil; sleep. **2** a peaceful or quiescent state, tranquillity. —*v.t./i.* to rest, to lie; to be supported. [f. OF f. L *repausare* (RE-¹, *pausare* pause)]

repose² /rɪˈpəʊz/ *v.t.* to place (trust etc.) *in*. [f. RE-¹ + POSE]

reposeful *adj.* inducing or exhibiting repose. —**reposefully** *adv.* [f. REPOSE¹ + -FUL]

repository /rɪˈpɒzɪtərɪ/ *n.* a place where things are stored, especially a warehouse or museum; a receptacle; a recipient of secrets etc. [f. obs. F or L (as REPOSE²)]

repossess /riːpəˈzes/ *v.t.* to regain possession of (esp. goods on which hire-purchase payments are in arrears). —**repossession** *n.*

repp var. of REP¹.

reprehend /reprɪˈhend/ *v.t.* to rebuke, to blame. [f. L *reprehendere* (RE-¹, *prehendere* seize)]

reprehensible /reprɪˈhensɪb(ə)l/ *adj.* deserving rebuke. —**reprehensibly** *adv.* [f. prec.]

represent /reprɪˈzent/ *v.t.* **1** to be an example or embodiment of. **2** to symbolize. **3** to present a likeness or description of to the mind or senses. **4** to describe or depict, *as*, to declare *to be*; to declare. **5** to show or play the part of in a picture or stage play etc. **6** to be a deputy, agent, or spokesman for; to be the elected representative of (the people of an area) in a legislative assembly. [f. OF or L *repraesentare* (RE-², *praesentare* present)]

representation /reprɪzenˈteɪʃ(ə)n/ *n.* **1** representing, being represented. **2** a thing that represents something. **3** (esp. in *pl.*) a statement made by way of an allegation or to convey an opinion. —**representational** *adj.* [as prec.]

representative /reprɪˈzentətɪv/ *adj.* **1** typical of a group or class. **2** containing examples of all or many types. **3** consisting of elected deputies or representatives; based on the representation of a nation etc. by such deputies. **4** serving as a portrayal or symbol *of*. —*n.* **1** a sample, or specimen, or typical embodiment. **2** an agent of a person, or firm, or society; a firm's travelling salesman. **3** a delegate, a person chosen to represent another or others, or to take part in a legislative assembly on their behalf. —**House of Representatives,** the lower and larger branch of the legislative assembly in the USA. [f. OF or L (as REPRESENT)]

repress /rɪˈpres/ *v.t.* to keep down, to suppress; to keep (emotions etc.) from finding an outlet; (in *p.p.*) suffering from repression of the emotions. —**repression** *n.*, **repressive** *adj.*, **repressively** *adv.* [f. L *reprimere* (RE-¹, *premere* press)]

reprieve /rɪˈpriːv/ *v.t.* **1** to postpone or remit the execution of (a condemned person). **2** to give a respite to. —*n.* **1** reprieving, being reprieved; remission or commutation of a capital sentence; a warrant for this. **2** a respite. [f. AF *repris* (*reprendre* take back)]

reprimand /ˈreprɪmɑːnd/ *n.* a formal or offical rebuke. —*v.t.* to administer a reprimand to. [f. F f. Sp. f. L *reprimenda* (as REPRESS)]

reprint /riːˈprɪnt/ *v.t.* to print again. —/ˈriːprɪnt/ *n.* the reprinting of a book etc.; a book etc. reprinted.

reprisal /rɪˈpraɪz(ə)l/ *n.* an act of retaliation. [f. AF (as REPREHEND)]

reprise /rɪˈpriːz/ *n.* a repeated passage in music; a repeated song etc. in a musical programme. [F (as REPRIEVE)]

reproach /rɪˈprəʊtʃ/ *v.t.* to express disapproval to (a person) for a fault or offence. —*n.* **1** reproaching; an instance of this. **2** a thing that brings disgrace or discredit. **3** disgraced or discredited state. —**beyond reproach,** deserving no blame, perfect. [f. OF *reprocher* f. L (RE-¹, *prope* near)]

reproachful *adj.* inclined to or expressing reproach. —**reproachfully** *adv.* [f. prec + -FUL]

reprobate /ˈreprəbeɪt/ *n.* an unprincipled or immoral person. [f. L (as REPROVE)]

reprobation /reprəˈbeɪʃ(ə)n/ *n.* strong condemnation. [as prec.]

reproduce /ri:prəˈdju:s/ *v.t./i.* **1** to produce a copy or representation of. **2** to cause to be seen or heard etc. again or to occur again. **3** to produce further members of the same species by natural means; to produce offspring of.

reproducible *adj.* that may be reproduced. [f. prec.]

reproduction /ri:prəˈdʌkʃ(ə)n/ *n.* **1** reproducing, being reproduced. **2** a copy of a painting etc. **3** (*attrib.*, of furniture etc.) made in imitation of an earlier style. [f. REPRODUCE]

reproductive /ri:prəˈdʌktɪv/ *adj.* of or concerning reproduction. [as prec.]

reprography /rɪˈprɒgrəfɪ/ *n.* the science and practice of copying documents by photography, xerography, etc. —**reprographic** /ri:prəˈgræfɪk/ *adj.* [f. REPRODUCE + -GRAPHY]

reproof /rɪˈpru:f/ *n.* an expression of condemnation for a fault or offence. [f. OF *reprove* (as foll.)]

reprove /rɪˈpru:v/ *v.t.* to give a reproof to (a person) or for (conduct etc.). [f. OF *reprover* f. L *reprobare* disapprove]

reptile /ˈreptaɪl/ *n.* a vertebrate animal of the class Reptilia, which includes snakes, lizards, crocodiles, turtles, and tortoises. [f. L *reptilis* (*repere* crawl)]

reptilian /repˈtɪlɪən/ *adj.* **1** of reptiles. **2** (of animals) creeping. —*n.* a reptile. [f. prec.]

republic /rɪˈpʌblɪk/ *n.* a State in which supreme power is held by the people or its elected representatives or by an elected or nominated president, not by a monarch etc. [f. F f. L *respublica* (*res* concern, *publicus* public)]

republican *adj.* **1** of or constituted as a republic; characteristic of republics. **2** advocating or supporting republican government. —*n.* **1** a person advocating or supporting republican government. **2 Republican,** a member of the **Republican Party,** one of the two chief political parties in the USA (the other being the Democratic Party). —**republicanism** *n.* [f. prec.]

repudiate /rɪˈpju:dɪeɪt/ *v.t.* to reject or disown utterly; to deny; to refuse to recognize or obey (an authority or treaty) or discharge (an obligation or debt). —**repudiation** /-ˈeɪʃ(ə)n/ *n.*, **repudiator** *n.* [f. L *repudiare* (*repudium* divorce)]

repugnant /rɪˈpʌgnənt/ *adj.* **1** strongly distasteful or objectionable. **2** (of ideas etc.) inconsistent, incompatible. —**repugnance** *n.* [f. F or L (*repugnare* fight against)]

repulse /rɪˈpʌls/ *v.t.* **1** to drive back (an attack or attacking enemy) by force of arms. **2** to rebuff. **3** to refuse (a request or offer, or its maker). —*n.* **1** repulsing, being repulsed. **2** a rebuff. [f. L (as REPEL)]

repulsion /rɪˈpʌlʃ(ə)n/ *n.* **1** repelling, being repelled. **2** a feeling of strong distaste, revulsion. [as REPEL]

repulsive /rɪˈpʌlsɪv/ *adj.* **1** arousing strong distaste, loathsome. **2** causing repulsion. —**repulsively** *adv.*, **repulsiveness** *n.* [f. F *répulsif* or REPULSE]

reputable /ˈrepjʊtəb(ə)l/ *adj.* of good repute, respected. —**reputably** *adv.* [obs. F or f. L (as REPUTE)]

reputation /repjʊˈteɪʃ(ə)n/ *n.* **1** what is generally said or believed about a person or thing. **2** the state of being well thought of. [f. L (as foll.)]

repute /rɪˈpju:t/ *n.* reputation. —*v.t.* (in *pass.*) to be generally considered. [f. OF or L *reputare* (RE-[1], *putare* think)]

reputed /rɪˈpju:tɪd/ *adj.* said or thought to be but possibly not. —**reputed pint** etc., a bottle of wine or spirits etc. sold as a pint etc. but not guaranteed as an imperial measure. —**reputedly** *adv.* [f. prec.]

request /rɪˈkwest/ *n.* **1** asking for something. **2** a thing asked for. **3** the state of being sought after, demand. —*v.t.* to make a request for (a thing) or of (a person); to seek permission. —**by** *or* **on request,** in response to an expressed wish. **request stop,** a place where a bus etc. stops only on a passenger's (or intended passenger's) request. [f. OF f. L *requaerere* (as REQUIRE)]

requiem /ˈrekwɪem/ *n.* a form of Mass for the repose of souls of the dead; the music for this. [f. L (accusative of *requies* repose)]

require /rɪˈkwaɪə(r)/ *v.t.* **1** to be unable to do without, to depend on for success, fulfilment, growth, etc. **2** to lay down as imperative; to order or oblige. **3** to wish to have. [f. OF f. L *requirere* (RE-[1], *quaerere* seek)]

requirement *n.* a thing required; a need. [f. prec.]

requisite /ˈrekwɪzɪt/ *adj.* required by circumstances, necessary to success. —*n.* a thing needed for some purpose. [f. L *requisitus* (as prec.)]

requisition /rekwɪˈzɪʃ(ə)n/ *n.* **1** an official order laying claim to the use of property or materials; a formal written demand that some duty should be performed. **2** being called or put into service. —*v.t.* to demand use or supply of, especially by a formal requisition. [f. F or L (as REQUIRE)]

requite /rɪˈkwaɪt/ *v.t.* to make a return for (a service) to avenge (a wrong or injury etc.); to make a return to (a person); to repay with good or evil. —**requital** *n.* [f. RE-[1] + *quite* var. of QUIT]

reredos /ˈrɪədɒs/ *n.* an ornamental screen covering the wall above the back of an altar.

[f. OF *areredos* (*arere* behind, *dos* back; cf. ARREAR)]

re-route /riːˈruːt/ *v.t.* to send or carry by a different route.

rerun /riːˈrʌn/ *v.t.* (**-nn-**) to run again. —/ˈriːrʌn/ *n.* an act of rerunning; a repeat of a film etc.

resale /riːˈseɪl/ *n.* sale to another person of something one has bought.

rescind /rɪˈsɪnd/ *v.t.* to abrogate, to revoke, to cancel. —**rescission** /-ʒ(ə)n/ *n.* [f. L *rescindere* (RE-¹, *scindere* cut)]

rescript /ˈriːskrɪpt/ *n.* **1** a Roman emperor's or pope's written reply to an appeal for a decision; any papal decision. **2** an official edict or announcement. [f. L *rescriptum* (*rescribere* write back)]

rescue /ˈreskjuː/ *v.t.* to save or bring away from capture, danger, harm, etc. —*n.* rescuing, being rescued. —**rescuer** *n.* [f. OF *rescoure* (RE-¹, L *executere* shake out)]

research /rɪˈsɜːtʃ, (D) ˈriː-/ *n.* systematic investigation and study in order to establish facts and reach new conclusions. —*v.t./i.* to do research (into). —**researcher** *n.* [f. obs. F (as RE-¹, SEARCH)]

resell /riːˈsel/ *v.t.* (*past* & *p.p.* **resold** /-ˈsəʊld/) to sell (what one has bought) to another person.

resemble /rɪˈzemb(ə)l/ *v.t.* to be like (another person or thing). —**resemblance** *n.* [f. OF *resembler* f. L (RE-¹, *similis* like)]

resent /rɪˈzent/ *v.t.* to feel indignation at or retain bitter feelings about (an action or injury etc.); to feel offended by (a person). [f. obs. F *resentir* (RE-¹, L *sentire* feel)]

resentful *adj.* feeling resentment. —**resentfully** *adv.* [f. prec. + -FUL]

resentment *n.* indignant or bitter feelings. [f. F or It. (as RESENT)]

reservation /rezəˈveɪʃ(ə)n/ *n.* **1** reserving, being reserved. **2** a reserved seat or hotel accommodation etc.; a record of this. **3** a limitation on one's agreement or acceptance of an idea etc. **4** a strip of land between the carriageways of a road. **5** a tract of land set apart by a government for some special purpose or for the exclusive use of certain persons, e.g. American or Canadian Indians, African Blacks, Australian Aborigines. [as foll.]

reserve /rɪˈzɜːv/ *v.t.* **1** to put aside or keep back for a later occasion or special use. **2** to order to be specially retained or allocated for a particular person at a particular time. **3** to retain (a right etc.). **4** to postpone delivery of (a judgement). —*n.* **1** a thing reserved for future use; an extra amount or stock kept available for use when needed. **2** a limitation or exception attached to something. **3** self-restraint, reticence; coolness of manner. **4** a company's profit added to the capital. **5** (in *sing.* or *pl.*) troops withheld from action to reinforce or protect others; forces outside the regular ones but available in an emergency. **6** a member of a military reserve. **7** an extra player chosen in case a substitute should be needed in a team. **8** a place reserved for special use, especially as a habitat. —**in reserve**, unused and available if needed. **reserve price**, the lowest acceptable price stipulated for an item sold at an auction. [f. OF f. L *reservare* (RE-¹, *servare* keep)]

reserved *adj.* reticent, uncommunicative; tending not to reveal emotions or opinions. [f. prec.]

reservist *n.* a member of a military reserve. [f. RESERVE]

reservoir /ˈrezəvwɑː(r)/ *n.* **1** a large natural or artificial lake as the source of an area's water supply. **2** a container for a supply of fuel or other liquid. **3** a supply of information etc. [f. F (as RESERVE)]

reshuffle /riːˈʃʌf(ə)l/ *v.t.* to shuffle (cards) again; to interchange the posts or responsibilities of (a group of people). —*n.* reshuffling.

reside /rɪˈzaɪd/ *v.i.* **1** to have one's home or dwell permanently (in a specified place). **2** (of power, right, or quality etc.) to be vested or present (in a specified person etc.). [prob. back-formation f. RESIDENT]

residence /ˈrezɪd(ə)ns/ *n.* **1** residing. **2** a place where one resides. **3** a house, especially of considerable pretension. —**in residence**, dwelling at a specified place especially for the performance of duties or work. [as foll.]

resident /ˈrezɪd(ə)nt/ *n.* a permanent inhabitant, not a visitor; (in a hotel) a person staying overnight. —*adj.* having quarters on the spot; residing; in residence; located. [f. OF or L *residēre* (RE-¹, *sedēre* sit)]

residential /rezɪˈdenʃ(ə)l/ *adj.* **1** suitable for or occupied by private houses. **2** used as a residence. **3** based on or connected with residence. —**residentially** *adv.* [f. RESIDENCE]

residual /rɪˈzɪdjʊəl/ *adj.* left as a residue or residuum. —*n.* a residual quantity. —**residually** *adv.* [f. RESIDUE]

residuary /rɪˈzɪdjʊərɪ/ *adj.* **1** of the residue of an estate. **2** residual. [f. RESIDUUM]

residue /ˈrezɪdjuː/ *n.* **1** the remainder, what is left or remains over. **2** what remains of an estate after the payment of charges, debts, and bequests. [f. OF f. L, = foll.]

residuum /rɪˈzɪdjuːəm/ *n.* (*pl.* **-ua**) what remains, especially a substance left after combustion or evaporation. [L (*residuus* remaining, as RESIDENT)]

resign /rɪˈzaɪn/ *v.t./i.* to give up or surrender (one's job, property, claim, etc.); to give up one's job. —**resign oneself to**, to come to accept or tolerate; to regard as inevitable. [f.

OF f. L *resignare* unseal, cancel (RE-[1], *signare* sign, seal)]

resignation /rezɪg'neɪʃ(ə)n/ *n.* **1** resigning, especially of a job. **2** a letter etc. conveying that one wishes to resign. **3** a resigned attitude or expression. [as prec.]

resigned /rɪ'zaɪnd/ *adj.* having resigned oneself; content to endure, showing patient acceptance of an unwelcome task or situation. —**resignedly** /-nɪdlɪ/ *adv.* [f. RESIGN]

resilient /rɪ'zɪlɪənt/ *adj.* **1** springing back to its original form after compression etc. **2** (of a person) readily recovering from shock or depression etc. —**resilience** *n.*, **resiliently** *adv.* [f. L *resilire* spring back (RE-[2], *salire* jump)]

resin /'rezɪn/ *n.* **1** a sticky substance secreted by many plants and trees, used in making varnish etc. **2** a similar synthetic substance, especially an organic compound made by polymerization and used as a plastic or in plastics. —*v.t.* to rub or treat with resin. —**resinous** *adj.* [f. L *resina*]

resist /rɪ'zɪst/ *v.t./i.* **1** to be undamaged or unaffected by; to stop the course of. **2** to refrain from accepting or yielding to (a pleasure or temptation etc.). **3** to oppose, to strive against, to try to impede; to refuse to comply (with). [f. OF or L *resistere* stop (RE-[1], *stare* stand)]

resistance /rɪ'zɪstəns/ *n.* **1** resisting, refusal to comply; the power to resist; ability to resist harsh or bad conditions. **2** an influence that hinders or stops something. **3** the property of failing to conduct electricity or heat etc.; the measure of this; a resistor. **4** (also **Resistance**) a secret organization resisting the authorities, especially in a conquered or enemy-occupied country. —**line of least resistance,** the easiest method or course. —**resistant** *adj.* [f. F f. L (as prec.)]

resistivity /rezɪs'tɪvɪtɪ/ *n.* the power of a specified material to resist the passage of an electric current. [f. RESIST]

resistor /rɪ'zɪstə(r)/ *n.* a device having resistance to the passage of an electric current. [as prec.]

resit /ri:'sɪt/ *v.t.* (**-tt-**) to take (an examination) again, usually after failing.

resoluble /rɪ'zɒljʊb(ə)l/ *adj.* that can be resolved; analysable. [f. F or L (as RESOLVE)]

resolute /'rezəlu:t, -lju:t/ *adj.* showing great determination, not vacillating or shrinking. —**resolutely** *adv.*, **resoluteness** *n.* [as RESOLVE]

resolution /rezə'lu:ʃ(ə)n, -'lju:-/ *n.* **1** the quality of being resolute, great determination. **2** a thing resolved on, an intention. **3** a formal expression of opinion agreed on by a committee or assembly. **4** the solving of a doubt, problem, or question. **5** separation into constituent parts; conversion into another form; causing musical discord to pass into concord; the smallest interval measurable by a scientific instrument. [as foll.]

resolve /rɪ'zɒlv/ *v.t./i.* **1** to decide firmly; to cause to do this. **2** (of an assembly or meeting) to pass a resolution. **3** to separate into constituent parts; to analyse mentally. **4** to solve or settle (a doubt, argument, etc.). **5** (*Mus.*) to convert (discord) or be converted into concord. —*n.* **1** a firm decision or intention. **2** determination. —**resolving power,** the ability of a lens etc. to distinguish very small or very close objects. [f. L *resolvere* (RE-[1], *solvere* solve)]

resolved *adj.* resolute, determined. [f. prec.]

resonant /'rezənənt/ *adj.* resounding, echoing. —**resonance** *n.* [f. F or L *resonare* (RE-[1], *sonare* sound)]

resonate /'rezəneɪt/ *v.i.* to produce or show resonance, to resound. [f. L (as prec.)]

resonator /'rezəneɪtə(r)/ *n.* **1** an instrument responding to a single note and used for detecting it in combinations. **2** an appliance for giving resonance to sounds or other vibrations. [f. prec.]

resort /rɪ'zɔ:t/ *n.* **1** a place frequented especially for holidays or for a specified purpose. **2** a thing to which recourse is had, an expedient; recourse. **3** frequenting, or being frequented. —*v.i.* **1** to turn for aid or as an expedient. **2** to go in large numbers or as a frequent or customary practice. —**in the last resort,** when all else has failed, as a final attempt. [f. OF (RE-[2], *sortir* go out)]

resound /rɪ'zaʊnd/ *v.t./i.* **1** (of a place) to be filled with sound, to echo; to re-echo (a sound). **2** (of a voice, instrument, sound, etc.) to produce echoes; to go on sounding; to fill a place with sound. **3** (of a reputation etc.) to be much talked of, to produce a sensation.

resounding *adj.* **1** that resounds. **2** notable, decisive. —**resoundingly** *adv.* [f. prec.]

resource /rɪ'sɔ:s, -'zɔ:s/ *n.* **1** something to which one can turn for help or support or to achieve one's purpose. **2** (usu. in *pl.*) available assets, a stock that can be drawn on; (in *pl.*) a country's sources of wealth or means for defence. **3** ingenuity; quick wit. [f. F (RE-[1], L *surgere* rise)]

resourceful *adj.* good at devising expedients. —**resourcefully** *adv.*, **resourcefulness** *n.* [f. prec. + -FUL]

respect /rɪ'spekt/ *n.* **1** admiration felt or shown towards a person or thing that has good qualities or achievements; politeness arising from this. **2** heed, consideration for something. **3** an aspect or detail. **4** reference, relation. **5** (in *pl.*) polite greetings. —*v.t.* **1** to feel or show respect for. **2** to avoid interfering with or harming; to refrain from offending. —**in respect of,** as concerns, with reference to. **pay one's respects,** to make a polite visit. **pay one's last respects,** to show respect for a dead person, especially by attending the funeral. [f. OF or L *respectus* (*respicere* look back at)]

respectable /rɪˈspektəb(ə)l/ *adj*. **1** deserving respect. **2** of moderately good social standing; honest and decent; proper in appearance or behaviour. **3** of a moderately good standard or size etc.; not bringing disgrace or embarrassment. —**respectability** /-ˈbɪlɪtɪ/ *n*., **respectably** *adv*. [f. prec.]

respecter *n*. one who respects. —**be no respecter of persons,** to treat everyone in the same way without being influenced by their importance etc. [f. RESPECT]

respectful *adj*. showing respect. —**respectfully** *adv*., **respectfulness** *n*. [as prec. + -FUL]

respecting *prep*. in respect of, concerning. [f. RESPECT]

respective *adj*. concerning or appropriate to each of several individually; comparative. [f. F or L (as RESPECT)]

respectively *adv*. for each separately or in turn, and in the order mentioned. [f. prec.]

respiration /respəˈreɪʃ(ə)n/ *n*. **1** breathing. **2** a plant's absorption of oxygen and emission of carbon dioxide. **3** the biochemical processes within living cells by which carbon compounds are broken down to obtain energy, usually involving as a final step the combining of carbon with atmospheric oxygen to form carbon dioxide. **4** a single inspiration and expiration, a breath. [F or f. L (as RESPIRE)]

respirator /ˈrespəreɪtə(r)/ *n*. **1** an apparatus worn over the mouth and nose to warm, filter, or purify inhaled air or to prevent inhalation of a poison, gas, etc. **2** an apparatus for maintaining artificial respiration. [as RESPIRE]

respiratory /ˈrespəreɪtərɪ, rɪˈspaɪərət-/ *adj*. of respiration. [as foll.]

respire /rɪˈspaɪə(r)/ *v.t./i*. to breathe; (of plants) to perform the process of respiration. [f. OF or L *respirare* (RE-², *spirare* breathe)]

respite /ˈrespaɪt, -ɪt/ *n*. **1** an interval of rest or relief. **2** a delay permitted before an obligation must be discharged or a penalty suffered. —*v.t*. to grant or bring respite to. [f. OF *respit* f. L, = RESPECT]

resplendent /rɪˈsplendənt/ *adj*. brilliant with colour or decorations. —**resplendence** *n*., **resplendency** *n*., **resplendently** *adv*. [f. L *resplendēre* (RE-¹, *splendēre* glitter)]

respond /rɪˈspɒnd/ *v.i*. **1** to make an answer; to act or behave in an answering or corresponding manner. **2** to show sensitiveness to a stimulus or action etc., by behaviour or change. [f. L *respondēre* (RE-¹, *spondēre* pledge)]

respondent *n*. a defendant, especially in an appeal or divorce case. —*adj*. in the position of a defendant. [as prec.]

response /rɪˈspɒns/ *n*. **1** an answer given in word or act. **2** a feeling, movement, or change etc. caused by a stimulus or influence. **3** any part of the liturgy said or sung in answer to a priest etc. [f. OF or L *responsum* (as RESPOND)]

responsibility /rɪspɒnsɪˈbɪlɪtɪ/ *n*. **1** being responsible. **2** something for which one is responsible. **3** responsible quality. [f. foll.]

responsible /rɪˈspɒnsɪb(ə)l/ *adj*. **1** legally or morally obliged to take care of something or to carry out a duty, liable to be blamed for loss or favour etc.; having to account for one's actions *to* a specified person. **2** capable of rational conduct. **3** evidently trustworthy, of good credit or repute. **4** being the primary cause. **5** involving important duties. —**responsibly** *adv*. [obs. F, f. L (as RESPOND)]

responsive /rɪˈspɒnsɪv/ *adj*. **1** responding readily to a stimulus; responding warmly and favourably. **2** answering; by way of answer. —**responsively** *adv*., **responsiveness** *n*. [f. F or L (as RESPOND)]

respray /riːˈspreɪ/ *v.t*. to spray again, especially to change the colour of paint on a vehicle. —/ˈriːspreɪ/ *n*. the act or process of respraying.

rest[1] *v.t./i*. **1** to cease from work, exertion, or action etc.; to be still or asleep, especially in order to regain one's vigour; to cause or allow to do this. **2** to place or be placed for support. **3** to rely. **4** (of a look etc.) to alight, to be directed. **5** (of a subject) to be left without further investigation or discussion. **6** to lie buried. **7** (in *p.p.*) refreshed or invigorated by resting. —*n*. **1** inactivity or sleep as a way of regaining vigour; a period of this. **2** a support for holding or steadying something. **3** (*Mus.*) an interval of silence between notes; a sign indicating this. —**at rest,** not moving; no longer anxious; (of the dead) free from trouble or anxiety. **be resting,** (of an actor) to be out of work. **rest mass,** the mass of a body when at rest. **rest one's case,** to conclude presentation of it. **rest-cure** *n*. a prolonged period of rest (usually in bed) as medical treatment. **rest on one's oars,** to relax one's efforts. **rest-room** *n*. a lavatory and other facilities for employees or customers. [OE]

rest[2] *n*. **the rest,** the remaining part(s) or individuals, the others; the remaining quantity etc. —*v.i*. to remain in a specified state. —**rest with,** to be left in the hands or charge of. [f. OF *reste* (*rester* remain behind, f. L *restare*, RE-¹, *stare* stand)]

restaurant /ˈrestərɒnt/ *n.* a place where meals can be bought and eaten. —**restaurant car,** a dining car. [F (*restaure* restore)]

restaurateur /restərəˈtɜ:(r)/ *n.* a restaurant-keeper. [as prec.]

restful *adj.* inducing rest or a feeling of rest. —**restfully** *adv.*, **restfulness** *n.* [f. REST[1] + -FUL]

restitution /restɪˈtju:ʃ(ə)n/ *n.* **1** restoration of a thing to its proper owner or to its original state. **2** reparation for injury or damage. [f. OF or L *restituere* restore (RE-[2], *statuere* establish)]

restive /ˈrestɪv/ *adj.* restless, resisting control because made impatient by delay or restraint. —**restively** *adv.*, **restiveness** *n.* [f. OF (as REST[2])]

restless *adj.* **1** unable to rest or to be still; constantly in motion or fidgeting. **2** without rest or sleep. —**restlessly** *adv.*, **restlessness** *n.* [f. REST[1] + -LESS]

restock /ri:ˈstɒk/ *v.t.*/*i.* to stock again, to replenish one's stock.

restoration /restəˈreɪʃ(ə)n/ *n.* **1** restoring, being restored. **2** a model, drawing, or reconstruction representing the supposed original form of an extinct animal, ruined building, etc. —**the Restoration,** the restoration of the Stuart monarchy in Britain with the return of Charles II to the throne in 1660. [as RESTORE]

restorative /rɪˈstɒrətɪv/ *adj.* that tends to restore health or strength. —*n.* a restorative food or medicine etc. [as foll.]

restore /rɪˈstɔ:(r)/ *v.t.* **1** to bring back to its original state, e.g. by rebuilding or repairing. **2** to bring back to good health or vigour. **3** to put back in its former position; to reinstate; to give back to its original owner. **4** to make a representation of the supposed original form of (an extinct animal, a ruin, etc.). —**restorer** *n.* [f. OF f. L *restaurare*]

restrain /rɪˈstreɪn/ *v.t.* to hold back from movement or action; to keep under control or within bounds. [f. OF f. L *restringere* (RE-[1], *stringere* tie)]

restraint /rɪˈstreɪnt/ *n.* **1** restraining, being restrained. **2** an agency or influence that restrains. **3** self-control; avoidance of excess or exaggeration; reserve of manner. **4** confinement, especially because of insanity. [as prec.]

restrict /rɪˈstrɪkt/ *v.t.* to put a limit on, to subject to limitations. —**restriction** *n.* [f. L *restringere* (as RESTRAIN)]

restrictive /rɪˈstrɪktɪv/ *adj.* restricting. —**restrictive practice,** an agreement or practice that limits efficiency or output in industry. [f. OF or L (as prec.)]

restructure /ri:ˈstrʌktʃə(r)/ *v.t.* to give a new structure to; to rebuild, to rearrange.

result /rɪˈzʌlt/ *n.* **1** that which is produced by an activity or operation, an effect, a consequence; a satisfactory outcome. **2** a quantity or formula etc. obtained by calculation. **3** a statement of the score, marks, or name of the winner in a sporting event, competition, or examination; (in *pl.*) a list of these. —*v.i.* **1** to occur as a result. **2** to have a specified result. [f. L *resultare* spring back (RE-[2], *saltare* frequent. of *salire* jump)]

resultant /rɪˈzʌltənt/ *adj.* occurring as a result, especially as the total outcome of more or less opposed forces. —*n.* a force etc. equivalent to two or more acting in different directions at the same point. [as prec.]

resume /rɪˈzju:m/ *v.t.*/*i.* **1** to begin again or go on after interruption, to begin to speak, work, or use again. **2** to get or take again or back. [f. OF or L *resumere* (RE-[2], *sumere* take up)]

résumé /ˈrezju:meɪ/ *n.* a summary. [F (as prec.)]

resumption /rɪˈzʌmpʃ(ə)n/ *n.* resuming. —**resumptive** *adj.* [as RESUME]

resurface /ri:ˈsɜ:fɪs/ *v.t.*/*i.* **1** to put a new surface on. **2** to return to the surface.

resurgent /rɪˈsɜ:dʒ(ə)nt/ *adj.* rising or arising again after defeat, destruction, or disappearance. —**resurgence** *n.* [f. L (RE-[2], *surgere* rise)]

resurrect /rezəˈrekt/ *v.t.* **1** to revive the practice or memory of. **2** to take from the grave, to exhume. **3** to dig up. [back-formation f. foll.]

resurrection /rezəˈrekʃ(ə)n/ *n.* **1** rising from the dead, especially (**Resurrection**) that of Christ. **2** revival after disuse, inactivity, or decay. [f. OF f. L (as RESURGENT)]

resuscitate /rɪˈsʌsɪteɪt/ *v.t.*/*i.* **1** to revive from unconsciousness or apparent death. **2** to revive (an old custom or institution etc.); to return or restore to vogue, vigour, or vividness. —**resuscitation** /-ˈteɪʃ(ə)n/ *n.* [f. L *resuscitare* (RE-[2], *suscitare* rouse)]

retable /rɪˈteɪb(ə)l/ *n.* a shelf, or frame enclosing decorative panels, above the back of an altar. [f. F f. L *retrotabulum* rear table (as RETRO-, TABLE)]

retail /ˈri:teɪl/ *n.* the selling of things in small quantities to the general public and usually not for resale. —*adj.* of retail. —*adv.* by retail. —*v.t.*/*i.* **1** to sell or be sold by retail. **2** /also ri:ˈteɪl/ to recount, to relate details of. —**retailer** *n.* [f. OF *retaille* piece cut off (as RE-[1], TAIL[2])]

retain /rɪˈteɪn/ *v.t.* **1** to keep possession of, not to lose; to continue to have, practise, or recognize. **2** to keep in one's memory. **3** to keep in place, to hold fixed. **4** to secure the services of (a person, especially a barrister) with a preliminary payment. [f. AF f. L *retinēre* (RE-¹, *tenēre* hold)]

retainer *n.* **1** a person or thing that retains. **2** a fee for retaining a barrister etc. **3** (*hist.*) a dependant or follower of a person of rank. —**old retainer,** (*joc.*) a faithful old servant. [f. prec.]

retake /riːˈteɪk/ *v.t.* (*past* **retook**; *p.p.* **retaken**) to take again; to recapture.

retaliate /rɪˈtælɪeɪt/ *v.t./i.* to repay (an injury or insult etc.) in kind; to make a counter-attack. —**retaliation** /-ˈeɪʃ(ə)n/ *n.*, **retaliatory** /-ljətərɪ/ *adj.* [f. L *retaliare* (RE-¹, *talis* such)]

retard /rɪˈtɑːd/ *v.t.* to make slow or late, to delay the progress or accomplishment of. —**retardation** /riːtɑːˈdeɪʃ(ə)n/ *n.* [f. F f. L *retardare* (RE-¹, *tardus* slow)]

retarded *adj.* backward in mental or physical development. [f. prec.]

retch *v.i.* to make a motion as in vomiting, esp. involuntarily and without effect. [OE, = spit (imit.)]

retell /riːˈtel/ *v.t.* (*past* & *p.p.* **retold** /-ˈtəʊld/) to tell (a story etc.) again.

retention /rɪˈtenʃ(ə)n/ *n.* retaining, being retained. [f. OF or L (as RETAIN)]

retentive /rɪˈtentɪv/ *adj.* tending to retain; (of the memory) not forgetful. —**retentiveness** *n.* [as prec.]

rethink /riːˈθɪŋk/ *v.t.* (*past* & *p.p.* **rethought** /-θɔːt/) to consider afresh, especially with a view to making changes. —/ˈriːθɪŋk/ *n.* rethinking, a reassessment.

reticence /ˈretɪsəns/ *n.* avoidance of expressing all one knows or feels or more than is necessary; disposition to silence, taciturnity. —**reticent** *adj.*, **reticently** *adv.* [f. L *reticentia* (RE-¹, *tacēre* be silent)]

reticle /ˈretɪk(ə)l/ *n.* a network of fine threads or lines in the focal plane of an optical instrument to help accurate observation. [f. L *reticulum* dim. of *rete* net]

reticulate /rɪˈtɪkjʊleɪt/ *v.t./i.* to divide or be divided in fact or appearance into a network. —/rɪˈtɪkjʊlət/ *adj.* reticulated. [f. L (as RETICULE)]

reticulation /rɪtɪkjʊˈleɪʃ(ə)n/ *n.* (usu. in *pl.*) a netlike marking or arrangement. [as prec.]

reticule /ˈretɪkjuːl/ *n.* **1** a reticle. **2** a woman's bag of woven or other material, carried or worn to serve the purpose of a pocket. [f. F f. L (as foll.)]

reticulum /rɪˈtɪkjʊləm/ *n.* (*pl.* **-la**) **1** a ruminant's second stomach. **2** a netlike structure, a fine network in cytoplasm etc., a reticulated membrane etc. [L, dim. of *rete* net]

retina /ˈretɪnə/ *n.* (*pl.* **-as**) the layer at the back of the eyeball sensitive to light. —**retinal** *adj.* [f. L (*rete* net)]

retinue /ˈretɪnjuː/ *n.* a body of attendants accompanying an important person. [f. OF (as RETAIN)]

retire /rɪˈtaɪə(r)/ *v.t./i.* **1** to give up one's regular work because of advancing age; to cause (an employee) to do this. **2** to withdraw; to go away; to retreat. **3** to seek seclusion or shelter; to go to bed. **4** (of a batsman at cricket) to terminate voluntarily or be compelled to suspend one's innings. —**retire into oneself,** to become uncommunicative or unsociable. —**retirement** *n.* [f. F *retirer* (RE-², *tirer* draw)]

retired *adj.* **1** who has retired. **2** withdrawn from society or observation, secluded. [f. prec.]

retiring *adj.* shy, avoiding society, fond of seclusion. [f. RETIRE]

retort¹ /rɪˈtɔːt/ *n.* an incisive, witty, or angry reply. —*v.t./i.* **1** to say by way of retort; to make a retort. **2** to repay (an insult or attack) in kind. [f. L *retorquēre* (RE-², *torquēre* twist)]

retort² /rɪˈtɔːt/ *n.* **1** a vessel (usually of glass) with a long downward-bent neck, used in distilling liquids. **2** a vessel for heating mercury for purification, coal to generate gas, or iron and carbon to make steel. [f. F f. L (as prec.)]

retouch /riːˈtʌtʃ/ *v.t.* to improve (a picture or photograph etc.) by fresh touches or alterations. [f. F *retoucher* (as RE-², TOUCH)]

retrace /rɪˈtreɪs/ *v.t.* to go back over; to trace back to the source or beginning; to recall the course of in memory. [f. F (as RE-², TRACE¹)]

retraceable *adj.* that may be retraced. [f. prec.]

retract /rɪˈtrækt/ *v.t./i.* **1** to draw or be drawn back or in. **2** to withdraw (a statement or opinion etc.); to refuse to keep (an agreement). —**retraction** *n.*, **retractor** *n.* [f. OF or L *retractare* (RE-², *tractare* frequent. of *trahere* draw)]

retractable *adj.* that may be retracted. [f. prec.]

retractile /rɪˈtræktaɪl/ *adj.* (esp. of a bodily part) retractable. [f. RETRACT]

retread /riːˈtred/ *v.t.* to put a fresh tread on (a tyre). —/ˈriːtred/ *n.* a retreaded tyre.

retreat /rɪˈtriːt/ *v.i.* **1** to withdraw after defeat or when faced with danger or difficulty; to go away to a place of shelter. **2** to recede. —*n.* **1** retreating; the military signal for this; a military bugle-call at sunset. **2** withdrawal into privacy or security; a place of shelter or seclusion. **3** a period of withdrawal from worldly activities for prayer and meditation. —**beat a retreat,** to retreat, to abandon an undertaking. [f. OF f. L *retrahere* (RE-², *trahere* draw)]

retrench /rɪˈtrentʃ/ *v.t./i.* to reduce the amount

of (expense or its cause); to reduce one's expenditure or operations. —**retrenchment** *n.* [f. obs. F *retrencher* cut back] (as RE-[1], TRENCH)]

retrial /ri:ˈtraɪəl/ *n.* the retrying of a lawsuit. [f. RETRY]

retribution /retrɪˈbju:ʃ(ə)n/ *n.* a deserved punishment, requital, usually for evil done. —**retributive** /rɪˈtrɪbjʊtɪv/ *adj.* [f. L (RE-[1], *tribuere* assign)]

retrievable /rɪˈtri:vəb(ə)l/ *adj.* that may be retrieved. [f. foll.]

retrieve /rɪˈtri:v/ *v.t.* **1** to regain possession of; to recover by investigation or effort of memory. **2** to find again (stored information etc.). **3** (of a dog) to find and bring in (killed or wounded game etc.). **4** to rescue, to restore to a flourishing state. **5** to repair or set right (a loss or error etc.). —*n.* possiblity of recovery. —**retrieval** *n.* [f. OF (RE-[2], *trover* find)]

retriever *n.* a dog of a breed used for retrieving game. [f. prec.]

retro- /retrəʊ-/ *prefix.* **1** backwards; back again; in return. **2** behind. [f. L *retro* backwards]

retroactive /retrəʊˈæktɪv/ *adj.* having a retrospective effect. —**retroactively** *adv.*

retrograde /ˈretrəgreɪd/ *adj.* **1** directed backwards. **2** reverting, especially to an inferior state; declining. **3** reversed. —*v.i.* to move backwards, to recede; to decline, to revert. [f. L *retrogradus* (*retrogradi* move backwards)]

retrogress /retrəˈgres/ *v.i.* to move backwards, to deteriorate. —**retrogression** /-eʃ(ə)n/ *n.*, **retrogressive** *adj.* [f. RETRO-, after PROGRESS]

retro-rocket /ˈretrəʊrɒkɪt/ *n.* an auxiliary rocket for slowing down a spacecraft etc.

retrospect /ˈretrəspekt/ *n.* a survey of or reference to past time or events etc. —**in retrospect,** when one looks back on a past event or situation. [f. RETRO-, after PROSPECT]

retrospection /retrəˈspekʃ(ə)n/ *n.* looking back, especially on the past. [as prec.]

retrospective /retrəˈspektɪv/ *adj.* **1** looking back on or dealing with the past. **2** (of a statute etc.) applying to the past as well as the future. —**retrospectively** *adv.* [f. RETROSPECT]

retroussé /rəˈtru:seɪ/ *adj.* (of the nose) turned up at the tip. [F, p.p. of *retrousser* tuck up (as RE-[2], TRUSS)]

retroverted /ˈretrəvɜ:tɪd/ *adj.* (esp. of the womb) turned backwards. [f. L (RETRO-, *vertere* turn)]

retry /ri:ˈtraɪ/ *v.t.* to try (a defendant or lawsuit) again.

retsina /retˈsi:nə/ *n.* a resin-flavoured Greek wine. [modern Gk]

return /rɪˈtɜ:n/ *v.t./i.* **1** to come or go back. **2** to bring, give, put, or send back; to pay back or reciprocate, to give in response; to yield (a profit). **3** to say in reply, to retort. **4** to send (a ball) back in cricket or tennis etc. **5** to state or describe officially, especially in answer to a writ or formal demand. **6** (of a constituency) to elect as an MP etc. —*n.* **1** coming or going back. **2** bringing, giving, putting, or sending back; paying back. **3** a thing given etc. back. **4** a return ticket. **5** (in *sing.* or *pl.*) the proceeds or profit of an undertaking; the coming in of these. **6** a formal report compiled or submitted by order. —**by return (of post),** by the next available post in the return direction. **in return,** as an exchange or reciprocal action. **many happy returns (of the day),** a birthday or festival greeting. **return crease,** (in cricket) each of two lines joining the popping-crease and bowling-crease and extending beyond the latter. In his delivery stride the bowler's back foot must land within the return crease. **returning officer,** an official conducting an election in a constituency and announcing the name of the person elected. **return ticket,** a ticket for the journey to a place and back to the starting point. [f. OF *retorner* (as RE-[2], TURN)]

retype /ri:ˈtaɪp/ *v.t.* to type again.

reunion /ri:ˈju:njən/ *n.* **1** reuniting, being reunited. **2** a social gathering of people who were formerly associated. [f. F (as RE-[2], UNION)]

reunite /ri:ju:ˈnaɪt/ *v.t./i.* to unite again after separation.

reuse /ri:ˈju:z/ *v.t.* to use again. —/-ˈju:s/ *n.* using or being used again.

rev *n.* (*colloq.*) a revolution (of an engine). —*v.t./i.* (**-vv-**) (*colloq.*) **1** (of an engine) to cause the crankshaft to rotate. **2** to rev up. —**rev up,** to cause (an engine) to run quickly, to increase the speed of its revolution. [abbr.]

Rev. *abbr.* Reverend.

revalue /ri:ˈvælju:/ *v.t.* to reassess the value of; to give a new (higher) value to a currency etc. —**revaluation** /-ˈeɪʃ(ə)n/ *n.*

revamp /ri:ˈvæmp/ *v.t.* to renovate, to give a new appearance to.

Revd *abbr.* Reverend.

reveal /rɪˈvi:l/ *v.t.* to make known (a secret etc.); to uncover and allow to be seen. —*n.* the internal side surface of an opening or recess, especially of the aperture of a door or window. [f. OF or L *revelare* (RE-[1], *velum* veil]

reveille /rɪˈvælɪ/ *n.* a military waking-signal. [f. F *réveillez* imper. of *réveiller* wake up]

revel /ˈrev(ə)l/ *v.i.* (**-ll-**) **1** to make merry, to be riotously festive. **2** to take keen delight. —*n.* (in *sing.* or *pl.*) revelling, merry-making; an instance of this. —**reveller** *n.* [f. OF *reveler* riot f. L, = REBEL]

revelation /revəˈleɪʃ(ə)n/ *n.* 1 the revealing of a fact. 2 the disclosing of knowledge, or knowledge disclosed, to man by a divine or supernatural agency; **the Revelation (of St John the Divine),** the last book of the New Testament (see APOCALYPSE). 3 something revealed, a startling disclosure. [as REVEAL]

revelry /ˈrevəlrɪ/ *n.* revelling, revels. [f. REVEL]

revenge /rɪˈvendʒ/ *n.* 1 punishment or injury inflicted in return for what one has suffered; desire to inflict this; the act of retaliation. 2 opportunity to defeat in a return game an opponent who won an earlier game etc. —*v.t.* to avenge. —**be revenged** *or* **revenge oneself,** to obtain revenge. [f. OF f. L *revindicare* (as RE-[1], VINDICATE)]

revengeful *adj.* eager for revenge. —**revengefully** *adv.* [f. prec. + -FUL]

revenue /ˈrevənju:, -vɪn-/ *n.* 1 income, especially of a large amount, from any source; (in *pl.*) items constituting this. 2 a State's annual income from which public expenses are met; the department of the Civil Service collecting this. [f. OF (*revenir* come back)]

reverberate /rɪˈvɜ:bəreɪt/ *v.t./i.* (of sound, light, or heat) to be returned or reflected; to return (a sound etc.) thus. —**reverberant** *adj.*, **reverberation** /-ˈreɪʃ(ə)n/ *n.*, **reverberative** *adj.* [f. L *reverberare* (RE-[2], *verberare* lash f. *verbera* scourge)]

revere /rɪˈvɪə(r)/ *v.t.* to feel deep respect or religious veneration for. [f. F or L *reverēri* (RE-[1], *verēri* fear)]

reverence /ˈrevərəns/ *n.* 1 revering, being revered. 2 a feeling of awe and respect or veneration. —*v.t.* to regard or treat with reverence. —**His, Your,** etc. **Reverence,** (*archaic* or *joc.*) a title used in addressing or referring to a clergyman. [f. OF f. L (as prec.)]

reverend /ˈrevərənd/ *adj.* deserving reverence. —**the Reverend,** the title of a clergyman (**Very Reverend,** of a dean; **Right Reverend,** of a bishop; **Most Reverend,** of an archbishop). **Reverend Mother,** the Mother Superior of a convent. [f. OF or L *reverendus* (as REVERE)]

reverent /ˈrevərənt/ *adj.* feeling or showing reverence. —**reverently** *adv.* [f. L *reverens* (as REVERE)]

reverential /revəˈrenʃ(ə)l/ *adj.* of the nature of, due to, or characterized by reverence. —**reverentially** *adv.* [as REVERENCE]

reverie /ˈrevərɪ/ *n.* a fit of abstracted musing, a day-dream; being engaged in this. [f. OF, = rejoicing, revelry (*rever* be delirious)]

revers /rɪˈvɪə(r)/ *n.* (*pl.* same /-ɪəz/) a turned-back edge of a garment revealing the under-surface; the material on this surface. [F (as REVERSE)]

reversal /rɪˈvɜ:s(ə)l/ *n.* reversing, being reversed. [f. foll]

reverse /rɪˈvɜ:s/ *v.t./i.* 1 to turn the other way round or up or inside out. 2 to change to the opposite character or effect. 3 to travel or cause to travel backwards; to make (an engine etc.) work in the contrary direction. 4 to revoke or annul (a decree, act, etc.). —*adj.* 1 facing or moving in the opposite direction. 2 opposite in character or order. 3 upside down. —*n.* 1 the opposite; the opposite of the usual manner. 2 a piece of misfortune; a defeat in battle. 3 reverse gear or motion. 4 the reverse side; the back of a coin etc. bearing a secondary design; the verso of a leaf. —**reverse arms,** to hold rifles butt upwards. **reverse the charges,** to make the recipient of a telephone call responsible for payment. **reverse gear,** the gear used to make a vehicle etc. travel backwards. **the reverse of,** far from, not at all. **reversing light,** a white light at the rear of a vehicle, operated when a vehicle travels backwards. —**reversely** *adv.* [f. OF f. L *reversare* (RE-[2], *versare* frequent. of *vertere* turn)]

reversible *adj.* that may be reversed. [f. REVERSE]

reversion /rɪˈvɜ:ʃ(ə)n/ *n.* 1 the legal right (esp. of an original owner or his or her heirs) to possess or succeed to property on the death of the present possessor. 2 return to a previous state, esp. (*Biol.*) to an earlier type. [as prec.]

revert /rɪˈvɜ:t/ *v.i.* 1 to return to a former state, practice, subject, etc. 2 (of property, an office, etc.) to return by reversion. [as REVERSE]

revetment /rɪˈvetmənt/ *n.* a facing of masonry on a rampart or wall; a retaining wall. [f. F (*revêtir* f. L, as RE-[2], VEST)]

review /rɪˈvju:/ *n.* 1 a general survey or assessment of a subject or thing; a survey of past events. 2 re-examination, reconsideration. 3 a display and formal inspection of troops etc. 4 a published report assessing the merits of a book or play etc.; a periodical publication with critical articles on current events, the arts, etc. —*v.t.* 1 to survey or look back on. 2 to re-examine, to reconsider. 3 to hold a review of (troops etc.). 4 to write a review of (a book or play etc.). —**reviewer** *n.* [f. obs. F (*revoir* see again (RE-[2], *voir* see)]

revile /rɪˈvaɪl/ *v.t.* to criticize abusively. —**revilement** *n.* [f. OF *reviler* (as RE-[1], VILE)]

revise /rɪˈvaɪz/ *v.t.* 1 to re-examine and alter or correct. 2 to go over (work learnt or done) in preparation for an examination. —*n.* a printer's proof-sheet embodying corrections made in an earlier proof. —**Revised Version,** the revision made in 1870-84 of the Authorized Version of the Bible. **Revised Standard Version,** the revision made in 1946-57 of the

American Standard Version (the latter was based on the English RV and published in 1901). [f. F or L *revisere* (RE-², *visere* intensive of *vidēre* see)]

revision /rɪˈvɪʒ(ə)n/ *n.* **1** revising, being revised. **2** a revised edition or form. [f. L (as prec.)]

revisit /riːˈvɪzɪt/ *v.t.* to pay another visit to (a place).

revisory /rɪˈvaɪzərɪ/ *adj.* of revision. [f. REVISE]

revival /rɪˈvaɪv(ə)l/ *n.* **1** reviving, being revived. **2** something brought back into use or fashion; a new production of an old play etc. **3** a reawakening of religious fervour; a campaign to promote this. [f. REVIVE]

revivalist *n.* one who promotes a religious revival. —**revivalism** *n.* [f. prec.]

revive /rɪˈvaɪv/ *v.t./i.* **1** to come or bring back to consciousness, life, or strength. **2** to come or bring back to existence, use, notice, etc. —**reviver** *n.* [f. OF or L *revivere* (RE-², *vivere* live)]

revivify /riːˈvɪvɪfaɪ/ *v.t.* to restore to life or strength or activity. —**revivification** /-fɪˈkeɪʃ(ə)n/ *n.* [f. F or L *revivificare* (as RE-², VIVIFY)]

revocable /ˈrevəkəb(ə)l/ *adj.* that may be revoked. [OF or f. L (as foll.)]

revoke /rɪˈvəʊk/ *v.t./i.* **1** to withdraw or cancel (a decree or promise etc.). **2** to fail to follow suit in a card-game when able to do so. —*n.* revoking in a card-game. [f. OF or L *revocare* (RE-², *vocare* call)]

revolt /rɪˈvəʊlt/ *v.t./i.* **1** to rise in rebellion; to be in a mood of protest or defiance. **2** to affect with strong disgust. **3** to feel or turn away in strong disgust. —*n.* **1** an act or state of rebelling or defying authority. **2** a sense of strong disgust. [f. F, ult. as REVOLVE]

revolting *adj.* disgusting. [f. prec.]

revolution /revəˈluːʃ(ə)n/ *n.* **1** the forcible overthrow of a government or social order, in favour of a new system. **2** any fundamental change or reversal of conditions or ideas. **3** revolving; a single completion of an orbit or rotation; the time taken for this; cyclic recurrence. [f. OF or L (as REVOLVE)]

revolutionary *adj.* **1** involving great change. **2** of or causing political revolution. —*n.* an instigator or supporter of political revolution. [f. prec.]

revolutionize *v.t.* to introduce fundamental change to. [f. REVOLUTION]

revolve /rɪˈvɒlv/ *v.t./i.* **1** to turn or cause to turn round, especially on an axis. **2** to move in orbit. **3** to ponder (a problem etc.) in one's mind. —**revolving door,** a door with several radial partitions turning round a central axis. [f. L *revolvere* (RE-², *volvere* roll)]

revolver /rɪˈvɒlvə(r)/ *n.* a pistol with revolving chambers enabling several shots to be fired without reloading. The Colt revolver was patented in 1835. [f. prec.]

revue /rɪˈvjuː/ *n.* **1** a theatrical entertainment consisting of a number of short items which are normally unrelated. **2** an elaborate musical show consisting of numerous unrelated scenes. [F, = review]

revulsion /rɪˈvʌlʃ(ə)n/ *n.* **1** a feeling of strong disgust. **2** a sudden violent change of feeling. [F or f. L (RE-², *vellere* pluck)]

reward /rɪˈwɔːd/ *n.* **1** something given or received in return for what was done, or for a service or merit. **2** a sum of money offered for the detection of a criminal, recovery of lost property, etc. —*v.t.* to give a reward to (a person) or for (a service etc.). [f. AF, = REGARD]

rewarding *adj.* (of an activity etc.) well worth doing. [f. prec.]

rewind /riːˈwaɪnd/ *v.t.* (*past & p.p.* **rewound**) to wind (a film or tape etc.) back to the beginning.

rewire /riːˈwaɪə(r)/ *v.t.* to renew the wiring of (a house etc.).

reword /riːˈwɜːd/ *v.t.* to change the wording of.

rewrite /riːˈraɪt/ *v.t.* (*past* **rewrote**; *p.p.* **rewritten**) to write again or differently. —/ˈriːraɪt/ *n.* a thing rewritten.

Rex *n.* the reigning king (in use as REGINA). [L, = king]

Rf *symbol* rutherfordium.

Rh *symbol* rhodium.

r.h. *abbr.* right hand.

rhapsodize /ˈræpsədaɪz/ *v.i.* to utter or write rhapsodies. [f. foll.]

rhapsody /ˈræpsədɪ/ *n.* **1** an ecstatic spoken or written statement. **2** a romantic musical composition in an irregular form. —**rhapsodic** /-ˈsɒdɪk/ *adj.*, **rhapsodical** /-ˈsɒdɪk(ə)l/ *adj.* [f. Gk *rhapsōidos* (*rhaptō* stitch, *ōdē* song)]

Rhenish /ˈriːnɪʃ, ˈren-/ *adj.* (*archaic*) of the Rhine or neighbouring regions. [f. AF f. L (*Rhenus* Rhine)]

rhenium /ˈriːnɪəm/ *n.* a rare hard heavy metallic element, symbol Re, atomic number 75. [f. L *Rhenus* Rhine]

rhesus /riːsəs/ *n.* a small Indian monkey (*Macaca mulatta*). —**rhesus factor,** an antigen occurring in the red blood cells of most persons and some animals. **rhesus negative,** not having this factor. **rhesus positive,** having this factor. [f. *Rhesus* mythical king of Thrace (the use of the name is arbitrary)]

rhetoric /ˈretərɪk/ *n.* **1** the art of speaking or writing impressively. **2** language used for its impressive sound (often with an implication of insincerity, exaggeration, etc.). [f. OF f. L f. Gk (*rhētōr* orator)]

rhetorical /rɪˈtɒrɪk(ə)l/ *adj.* expressed with a view to impressive effect; the nature of rhetoric. —**rhetorical question,** a question asked not for information but to produce an effect (e.g. *who cares?*). —**rhetorically** *adv.* [f. L f. Gk (as prec.)]

rheumatic /ru:ˈmætɪk/ *adj.* of, caused by, or suffering from rheumatism. —*n.* (in *pl.*, *colloq.*) rheumatism. —**rheumatic fever,** a serious form of rheumatism with fever, especially in children. —**rheumatically** *adv.*, **rheumaticky** *adj.* [f. OF or L f. Gk (*rheuma* watery secretion)]

rheumatism /ˈru:mətɪz(ə)m/ *n.* any of several diseases causing pain in the joints, muscles, or fibrous tissue, especially rheumatoid arthritis. [as prec.]

rheumatoid /ˈrumətɔɪd/ *adj.* having the character of rheumatism. —**rheumatoid arthritis,** a chronic progressive disease causing inflammation and stiffening of the joints. [f. prec.]

rheumatology /ru:məˈtɒlədʒɪ/ *n.* the study of rheumatic diseases. —**rheumatologist** *n.* [f. RHEUMATISM + -LOGY]

rhinestone /ˈraɪnstəʊn/ *n.* an imitation diamond. [f. RHINE + STONE]

rhino /ˈraɪnəʊ/ *n.* (*pl.* same or **-os**) (*colloq.*) a rhinoceros. [abbr.]

rhinoceros /raɪˈnɒsərəs/ *n.* (*pl.* **-oses** or same) a large thick-skinned quadruped of Africa and southern Asia, with a horn or two horns on the nose. [f. L f. Gk *rhino-* nostril, nose, *keras* horn]

rhizome /ˈraɪzəʊm/ *n.* a rootlike stem growing along or under the ground and emitting both roots and shoots. [f. Gk *rhizōma* (*rhizoō* take root)]

rho /rəʊ/ *n.* the seventeenth letter of the Greek alphabet, = rh. [Gk]

rhodium /ˈrəʊdɪəm/ *n.* a hard white metallic element, symbol Rh, atomic number 45. [f. Gk *rhodon* rose (from colour of solution of its salts)]

rhododendron /rəʊdəˈdendrən/ *n.* an evergreen shrub of the genus *Rhododendron*, with large clusters of trumpet-shaped flowers. [L, = oleander, f. Gk (*rhodon* rose, *dendron* tree)]

rhomboid /ˈrɒmbɔɪd/ *adj.* like a rhombus. —*n.* a quadrilateral of which only the opposite sides and angles are equal. —**rhomboidal** *adj.* [f. F or L f. Gk (as foll.)]

rhombus /ˈrɒmbəs/ *n.* (*pl.* **-uses**) an oblique equilateral parallelogram, such as the diamond on playing-cards. [L f. Gk *rhombos*]

rhubarb /ˈru:bɑ:b/ *n.* **1** a garden plant of the genus *Rheum* with fleshy leaf-stalks used like fruit; these stalks. **2** the root of a Chinese plant of the genus *Rheum*; a purgative made from this. [f. OF f. L *rhabarbarum* foreign rha (*rha* f. Gk, perh. f. *Rha* ancient name of river Volga)]

rhumb /rʌm/ *n.* **1** any of the 32 points of the compass. **2** the angle between the directions of any two successive compass-points. **3** a rhumb-line. —**rhumb-line** *n.* a line cutting all meridians at the same angle; the line followed by a ship sailing according to a fixed compass-bearing. [f. F prob. f. Du. *ruim* room, assoc. with L *rhombus*]

rhyme /raɪm/ *n.* **1** identity of sound between the endings of words or of verse-lines. **2** (in *sing.* or *pl.*) a verse having rhymes. **3** the use of rhyme. **4** a word providing a rhyme to another. —*v.t./i.* **1** to form a rhyme; to have rhymes. **2** to write rhymes; to put or make (a story etc.) into rhyme. **3** to treat (a word) as rhyming with another. —**rhyming slang,** slang which replaces words by words or phrases that rhyme with them (e.g. *stairs* by *apples and pears*). **without rhyme or reason,** lacking discernible sense or logic. [f. OF *rime* f. L f. Gk (as RHYTHM)]

rhymester /ˈraɪmstə(r)/ *n.* a writer of (esp. simple) rhymes. [f. prec.]

rhythm /ˈrɪð(ə)m/ *n.* **1** the pattern produced by various relations of emphasis and duration of notes in music or by long and short or accented and unaccented syllables; the aspect of composition concerned with this. **2** a movement with a regular succession of strong and weak elements. **3** a regularly recurring sequence of events. —**rhythm and blues,** popular music with blues themes and a strong rhythm. **rhythm method,** contraception by avoiding sexual intercourse near the time of ovulation (which recurs regularly). —**rhythmic** *adj.*, **rhythmical** *adj.*, **rhythmically** *adv.* [f. F or L f. Gk *rhuthmos* (cf. *rheō* flow)]

rib *n.* **1** each of the bones articulated in pairs to the spine and curving round to protect the thoracic cavity and its organs. **2** a joint of meat from this part of an animal. **3** a ridge or long raised piece often of stronger or thicker material across a surface or through a structure, serving to support or strengthen; any of the hinged rods forming the framework of an umbrella. **4** a combination of plain and purl stitches in knitting, producing a ribbed somewhat elastic fabric. —*v.t.* (**-bb-**) **1** to provide with ribs. **2** to knit as rib. **3** (*colloq.*) to tease. —**rib-cage** *n.* the framework of ribs round the thoracic cavity. [OE]

ribald /ˈrɪbəld/ *adj.* (of language or its user) coarsely or disrespectfully humorous. [orig. = low-born retainer, f. OF *ribault* (*riber* pursue licentious pleasures)]

ribaldry /ˈrɪbəldrɪ/ *n.* ribald talk. [f. prec.]

riband /ˈrɪbənd/ *n.* a ribbon. [f. OF *riban*]

ribbed /rɪbd/ *adj.* **1** having ribs or riblike markings. **2** knitted in rib. [f. RIB]

ribbon /ˈrɪbən/ *n.* **1** a narrow strip or band of silk or other ornamental material, used for decoration or for tying something; material in this form. **2** a ribbon of a special colour or pattern worn to indicate some honour or membership of a sports team etc. **3** a long narrow strip of anything, e.g. inked material used in a typewriter. **4** (in *pl.*) ragged strips. —**ribbon development,** the building of houses in a narrow strip along a road outwards from a town or village. [var. of RIBAND]

ribonucleic acid /raɪbəʊnjuːˈkliːɪk/ a nucleic acid yielding ribose on hydrolysis (see RNA). [f. *ribose* a sugar + NUCLEIC]

rice *n.* a kind of grass (*Oryza sativa*) grown in marshes, especially in Asia, producing seeds that are used as food; these seeds. —**rice-paper** *n.* paper made from the pith of an oriental tree (*Tetrapanax papyriferum*) and used for painting and in cookery. [f. OF *ris* f. It. f. L f. Gk *oruza*]

rich *adj.* **1** having much wealth. **2** having a large supply of something; having great natural resources; (of soil) full of nutrients, fertile. **3** splendid, made of costly materials, elaborate. **4** producing or produced abundantly. **5** (of food or diet) containing a large proportion of fat, oil, eggs, spice, etc. **6** (of a mixture in an internal-combustion engine) containing a high proportion of fuel. **7** (of colour, sound, or smell) pleasantly deep or strong. **8** (of an incident or assertion etc.) highly amusing or ludicrous. —**richness** *n.* [OE & f. OF *riche*]

riches /ˈrɪtʃɪz/ *n.pl.* a great quantity of money, property, valuable possessions, natural resources, etc. [as RICH]

richly *adv.* **1** in a rich way. **2** fully, thoroughly. [f. RICH]

Richter scale /ˈrɪktə(r), ˈrɪx-/ a scale for stating the strength of an earthquake. [f. C. F. *Richter*, American seismologist (1900–85)]

rick[1] *n.* a stack of hay etc. [OE]

rick[2] *v.t.* to sprain or strain slightly. —*n.* a slight sprain or strain. [f. MLG *wricken*]

rickets /ˈrɪkɪts/ *n.* (as *sing.* or *pl.*) a children's deficiency disease with softening of the bones. —**rickettsial** /rɪˈketsɪəl/ *adj.* [orig. unkn.]

rickety /ˈrɪkɪtɪ/ *adj.* **1** shaky, weak-jointed, insecure. **2** suffering from rickets. —**ricketiness** *n.* [f. prec.]

rickrack var. of RICRAC.

rickshaw /ˈrɪkʃɔː/ *n.* (also **ricksha**) a light two-wheeled hooded vehicle drawn by one or more persons. [abbr. of *jinricksha(w)* f. Jap. (*jin* person, *riki* power, *sha* vehicle)]

ricochet /ˈrɪkəʃeɪ, -ʃet/ *v.i.* (*past* **ricocheted** /-eɪd/; *partic.* **ricocheting** /-eɪɪŋ/) to rebound from a surface as a missile does when it strikes with a glancing blow. —*n.* a rebound of this kind; a hit made after it. [F; orig. unkn.]

ricrac /ˈrɪkræk/ *n.* a zigzag braided trimming for garments. [redupl. of RACK[1]]

rid *v.t.* (**-dd-**; *past* & *p.p.* **rid**) to free from something unpleasant or unwanted. —**get rid of,** to cause to go away; (*colloq.*) to succeed in selling. [orig. = clear (land etc.), f. ON]

riddance /ˈrɪd(ə)ns/ *n.* ridding. —**good riddance,** welcome deliverance from an unwanted person or thing. [f. RID]

ridden *p.p.* of RIDE.

riddle[1] *n.* **1** a question or statement testing ingenuity in finding its answer or meaning. **2** a puzzling fact, thing, or person. —*v.i.* to speak in or propound riddles. [OE, rel. to READ]

riddle[2] *v.t.* **1** to pierce with many holes. **2** (in *p.p.*) thoroughly permeated (with faults etc.). **3** to pass through a riddle. —*n.* a coarse sieve for gravel or cinders etc. [OE]

ride *v.t./i.* (*past* **rode**; *p.p.* **ridden** /ˈrɪd(ə)n/) **1** to sit on and control or be carried by (a horse etc.). **2** to travel on horseback, a bicycle, train, or other conveyance; to travel thus over or through. **3** to be carried on or conveyed by, to be supported on; to float or seem to float. **4** to yield to (a blow) so as to reduce its impact. **5** to give a ride to. —*n.* **1** a spell of riding; a journey on a horse etc. or in a vehicle. **2** a track for riding on, especially through woods. **3** a roundabout or other device on which people ride at a fairground etc. **4** the quality of sensations felt when riding. —**let a thing ride,** to leave it undisturbed. **ride down,** to overtake or trample on horseback. **ride out,** to come safely through (a storm etc., or a danger or difficulty). **ride up,** (of a garment) to work upwards when worn. **riding-light** *n.* a light shown by a ship at anchor. **take for a ride,** (*slang*) to hoax or deceive. [OE]

rider *n.* **1** one who rides a horse or bicycle etc. **2** an additional clause amending or supplementing a document, a corollary; a recommendation etc. added to a verdict; (*Math.*) a problem arising as a corollary of a theorem etc. [f. RIDE]

riderless *adj.* without a rider. [f. prec. + -LESS]

ridge /rɪdʒ/ *n.* **1** the line of junction of two surfaces sloping upwards towards each other; a long narrow hill-top, a mountain range, a watershed; any narrow elevation across a surface. **2** an elongated region of high barometric pressure. **3** a raised strip of arable land, usually one of a set separated by furrows. —**ridge-piece** *n.* a beam along the ridge of a roof. **ridge-pole** *n.* a horizontal pole of a long tent. —**ridgy** *adj.* [OE]

ridgeway /ˈrɪdʒweɪ/ *n.* a road along a ridge, sometimes dating back to medieval or perhaps even prehistoric times.

ridicule /ˈrɪdɪkjuːl/ *n.* making or being made an object of derision. —*v.t.* to make fun of, to subject to ridicule. [F or f. L *ridiculum* (*ridēre* laugh)]

ridiculous /rɪˈdɪkjʊləs/ *adj.* **1** deserving to be laughed at, especially in a malicious or scornful way. **2** not worth serious consideration, preposterous. —**ridiculously** *adv.* [as prec. or f. L *ridiculosus*]

riding /ˈraɪdɪŋ/ *n.* a former administrative division of Yorkshire (*East, North*, and *West Riding*). [OE f. ON, = third part]

Riesling /ˈriːslɪŋ/ *n.* a kind of dry white wine made from a European variety of grape; this grape. [G]

rife *predic. adj.* **1** of common occurrence, widespread. **2** well provided, full. [OE prob. f. ON, = acceptable]

riffle *v.t./i.* to turn (pages) in quick succession; to leaf quickly (through a book); to thumb (a block of paper or pack of cards etc.), releasing the edges in (rapid) sucession. [perh. var. of RUFFLE]

riff-raff /ˈrɪfræf/ *n.* a rabble, disreputable or undesirable persons. [f. OF *rif et raf*]

rifle /ˈraɪf(ə)l/ *n.* **1** a gun with a long rifled barrel, especially one fired from shoulder level. **2** (in *pl.*) riflemen. —*v.t.* **1** to search and rob. **2** to make spiral grooves in (a gun or its barrel or bore) to make the bullet spin and so travel more accurately when fired. [f. OF *rifler* scratch, plunder, f. ODu.]

rifleman *n.* (*pl.* **-men**) a soldier armed with a rifle.

rifling /ˈraɪflɪŋ/ *n.* the arrangement of grooves in a rifle. [f. RIFLE]

rift *n.* **1** a crack or split in an object. **2** a cleft in the earth or a rock. **3** a disagreement, a breach in friendly relations. —**rift-valley** *n.* a steep-sided valley formed by subsidence of the earth's crust. [Scand., rel. to RIVEN]

rig[1] *v.t.* (**-gg-**) **1** to provide (a ship) with spars and ropes etc. **2** (often with *out* or *up*) to provide with clothes or other equipment. **3** to set up hastily or as a makeshift. **4** to assemble and adjust the parts of (an aircraft). —*n.* **1** the arrangement of a ship's masts and sails etc. **2** equipment for a special purpose, e.g. a radio transmitter. **3** an oil-rig. —**rig-out** *n.* (*colloq.*) an outfit of clothes. [perh. Scand. (cf. Norw. *rigga* bind)]

rig[2] *v.t.* (**-gg-**) to manage or conduct fraudulently. —**rig the market,** to cause an artificial rise or fall in prices. [orig. unkn.]

rigging *n.* a ship's spars and ropes etc. used to support masts and set or work the sails. [f. RIG[1]]

right /raɪt/ *adj.* **1** (of conduct etc.) morally good, in accordance with justice, equity, or duty. **2** proper, correct, true; preferable, most suitable; (of a side of a fabric) meant for show or use. **3** in a good or normal condition; sane; well-advised, not mistaken. **4** on or towards the right-hand side. **5** politically to the right (see sense 4 below). **6** (*archaic* or *colloq.*) real, properly so called. —*n.* **1** what is just; a fair claim or treatment. **2** being entitled to a privilege or immunity; a thing one is entitled to. **3** the right-hand part, region, or direction; the right hand; a blow with this; (in marching) the right foot. **4** (often **Right**) the right wing of a political party or other group; conservatives collectively. —*v.t.* **1** to restore to a proper, correct, or vertical position. **2** to set right, to make amends or take vengeance for; to vindicate, to justify; to rehabilitate. **3** to correct. —*adv.* **1** straight. **2** (*colloq.*) immediately. **3** all the way, completely. **4** exactly, quite. **5** on or to the right-hand side. **6** rightly. **7** all right; what you say is correct; I agree. **8** (*archaic*) very, to the full. —**by right(s),** if right were done. **in one's own right,** through one's own position or effort etc. **in the right,** having justice or truth on one's side. **on the right side of,** in the favour of (a person); somewhat less than (a stated age). **put** *or* **set to rights,** to arrange in proper order. **right and left,** on all sides. **right angle,** an angle of 90°, made by lines meeting with equal angles on either side (**at right angles,** placed to form a right angle). **right ascension,** the celestial co-ordinate corresponding to longitude, measured eastwards on the celestial sphere from the point known as the First Point of Aries, where the ecliptic intersects the celestial equator. **right bank,** the bank of a river on the right as one faces downstream. **right hand,** the hand that in most people is used more than the left, on the side opposite the left hand; a right-hand man. **right-hand** *adj.* of, on, or towards this side of a person or the corresponding side of a thing. **right-handed** *adj.* using the right hand by preference as more serviceable; made by or for the right hand; turning to the right. **right-hander** *n.* a right-handed person or blow. **right-hand man,** an indispensable or chief assistant. **Right Honourable,** the title of earls, viscounts, barons, Privy Counsellors, and certain others. **right-minded** *adj.* having proper or honest principles. **right of way,** the right to pass over another's ground; a path that is subject to such a right; the right to proceed while another vehicle etc. must wait. **right-oh!** (*colloq.*) an expression of agreement to what is suggested. **Right Reverend,** see

REVEREND. **rights issue,** an issue of shares offered by a company at a special price to its existing shareholders. **rights of man,** = human rights (see HUMAN). **right wing,** the right-hand side of a football team etc. on the field; a player in this position; the supporters of more conservative or traditional policies than others in their group. **right-winger** *n.* a person on the right wing. —**rightly** *adv.*, **rightness** *n.* [OE]

righteous /ˈraɪtʃəs/ *adj.* doing what is morally right; making a show of this; morally justifiable. —**righteously** *adv.*, **righteousness** *n.* [OE (as prec. + -WISE), after *bounteous* etc.]

rightful *adj.* in accordance with what is just, proper, or legal; (of property etc.) to which one is entitled. —**rightfully** *adv.* [OE (as RIGHT, -FUL)]

rightism *n.* political conservatism. —**rightist** *n.* [f. RIGHT]

rightward /ˈraɪtwəd/ *adv.* (also **rightwards**) towards the right. —*adj.* going towards or facing the right. [f. RIGHT + -WARD]

rigid /ˈrɪdʒɪd/ *adj.* **1** not flexible, that cannot be bent. **2** inflexible, strict. —**rigidity** /-ˈdʒɪdɪtɪ/ *n.*, **rigidly** *adv.* [f. F or L *rigidus* (as RIGOR)]

rigmarole /ˈrɪgmərəʊl/ *n.* **1** a rambling statement; meaningless talk. **2** a lengthy procedure. [alt. f. obs. *ragman roll* = catalogue]

rigor /ˈraɪgɔː(r), ˈrɪgə(r)/ *n.* a sudden chill with shivering. —**rigor mortis,** stiffening of the body after death. [f. L (*rigēre* be stiff)]

rigour /ˈrɪgə(r)/ *n.* **1** severity, strictness. **2** (in *pl.*) harshness of weather or conditions. **3** logical exactitude. —**rigorous** *adj.*, **rigorously** *adv.* [f. OF f. L, = prec.]

rile *v.t. colloq.* to anger, to irritate. [var. of *roil* make turbid, perh. f. OF, = mix mortar, f. L *regulare*]

rill *n.* a small stream. [cf. LG *ril(le)*]

rim *n.* a raised edge or border; the outer edge of a wheel, on which a tyre is fitted. [OE]

rime *n.* frost; (*poetic*) hoar-frost. —*v.t.* to cover with rime. [OE]

rimmed *adj.* edged, bordered. [f. RIM]

rind /raɪnd/ *n.* a tough outer layer or skin on fruit, vegetables, cheese, bacon, etc. [OE]

rinderpest /ˈrɪndəpest/ *n.* a disease of ruminants (esp. cattle). [G (*rinder* cattle, as PEST)]

ring[1] *n.* **1** a circlet, usually of precious metal, worn on a finger. **2** a circular band of any material; (in *pl.*) a pair of metal or wooden rings 236 mm in diameter suspended 500 mm apart and 2,500 mm (approx. 8 ft.) above the ground, used in gymnastics competitions in which swinging and balancing movements are performed. **3** a line or band round, or the rim of, a cylindrical or circular object. **4** a mark or part etc. having the form of a circular band. **5** a circular or other enclosure for a circus, boxing, betting at races, the showing of cattle, etc. **6** persons or things arranged in a circle; such an arrangement; a combination of traders, politicians, spies, etc., acting together for the control of operations. **7** a circular or spiral course. —*v.t.* **1** to enclose with a ring, to encircle, to put a ring on (a bird etc.) to identify it. **3** to cut a ring in the bark of (a tree), especially to retard its growth and improve fruit-production. —**the ring,** bookmakers. **make** *or* **run rings round,** to do things much better than (another person). **ring-dove** *n.* a large species of pigeon (*Columba palumbus*). **ring-finger** *n.* the third finger especially of the left hand, on which a wedding ring is usually worn. **ring main** *or* **circuit,** an electrical circuit serving many sockets in a continuous ring. **ring road,** a bypass encircling a town. [OE]

ring[2] *v.t./i.* (*past* **rang**; *p.p.* **rung**) **1** to give out a clear resonant sound of or like that of a bell when struck. **2** to make (a bell) ring; to sound (a peal etc.) on bells; to sound a bell as a summons; to signal by ringing. **3** to make a telephone call (to). **4** to resound. **5** (of the ears) to be filled with a sensation of ringing. **6** (*colloq.*) to alter and sell (a stolen vehicle). —*n.* **1** a ringing sound or tone. **2** the act of ringing a bell; the sound caused by this. **3** a specified feeling conveyed by an utterance. **4** (*colloq.*) a telephone call. **5** a set of (church) bells. —**ring a bell,** (*colloq.*) to begin to revive a memory. **ring down** (or **up**) **the curtain,** to cause it to be lowered (or raised). **ring off,** to end a telephone call. **ring up,** to call by telephone; to record (an amount) on a cash register. [OE]

ringer *n.* **1** a person who rings bells. **2** (*US*) a racehorse etc. fraudulently substituted for another. **3** a person's double. [f. RING²]

ringleader *n.* a leading instigator in crime, mischief etc.

ringlet /ˈrɪŋlɪt/ *n.* a long tubular curl of hair. —**ringleted** *adj.* [f. RING¹ + -LET]

ringmaster *n.* a person directing a circus performance.

ringside *n.* the area immediately beside a boxing or circus ring. —*adj.* (of a seat etc.) close to the scene of action.

ringworm *n.* a contagious fungus skin-disease forming circular patches, especially on a child's scalp.

rink *n.* **1** an area of natural or artificial ice for skating or a game of curling etc.; a floor for roller-skating; a building containing either of these. **2** a strip of bowling green. **3** a team in bowls or curling. [perh. f. OF *renc,* = RANK¹]

rinse *v.t.* to wash out with clean water; to wash

lightly; to put (clothes etc.) through clean water to remove soap etc.; to remove (impurities) by rinsing. —*n.* **1** rinsing. **2** a solution washed through hair to tint or condition it. [f. OF *rincer*]

riot /ˈraɪət/ *n.* **1** a wild disturbance by a crowd of people. **2** loud revelry; a lavish display or enjoyment. **3** (*colloq.*) a very amusing thing or person. —*v.i.* to make or take part in a riot. —**riot helmet, riot shield,** a helmet or shield for use by police or soldiers dealing with riots. **run riot,** to behave in an unruly way; (of plants) to grow or spread uncontrolled. —**rioter** *n.* [f. OF *riote, rioter*]

riotous /ˈraɪətəs/ *adj.* **1** disorderly, unruly. **2** boisterous, unrestrained. —**riotously** *adv.* [f. RIOT]

RIP *abbr.* may he, she or they rest in peace. [f. L *requiesca(n)t in pace*]

rip[1] *v.t./i.* (**-pp-**) **1** to tear or cut (a thing) quickly or forcibly away or apart; to make (a hole etc.) thus; to make a long tear or cut in. **2** to come violently apart, to split. **3** to rush along. —*n.* **1** a long tear or cut. **2** an act of ripping. **3** a stretch of rough water. —**let rip,** (*colloq.*) to refrain from holding back the speed of or from interfering with (a person or thing); to speak violently. **rip-cord** *n.* a cord for releasing a parachute from its pack. **rip off,** (*slang*) to defraud; to steal. **rip-off** *n.* (*slang*) a fraud; a theft. **rip-roaring** *adj.* wildly noisy. **rip-saw** *n.* a saw for sawing wood along the grain. —**ripper** *n.* [orig. unkn.]

rip[2] *n.* **1** a dissolute person. **2** a worthless horse. [perh. var. of *rep* = REPROBATE]

riparian /raɪˈpeərɪən/ *adj.* of or on a river-bank. [f. L *riparius* (*ripa* bank)]

ripe *adj.* **1** (of grain or fruit etc.) ready to be gathered and used; (of cheese or wine etc.) matured and ready to be eaten or drunk. **2** mature, fully developed; (of a person's age) advanced. **3** ready, in a fit state. —**ripely** *adv.*, **ripeness** *n.* [OE]

ripen *v.t./i.* to make or become ripe. [f. RIPE]

riposte /rɪˈpɒst/ *n.* **1** a quick counterstroke; a retort. **2** a quick return thrust in fencing. —*v.i.* to deliver a riposte. [f. F f. It. (as RESPONSE)]

ripple *n.* **1** a ruffling of the surface of water, a small wave or series of waves. **2** a gentle lively sound that rises and falls. **3** a wavy appearance in hair etc. —*v.t./i.* **1** to form or flow in ripples; to cause to do this. **2** to show or sound like ripples. —**ripply** *adj.* [orig. unkn.]

rise /raɪz/ *v.i.* (*past* **rose** /rəʊz/; *p.p.* **risen** /ˈrɪz(ə)n/) **1** to come or go up; to grow, project, swell, or incline upwards; to become higher; to reach a higher position, level, intensity, or amount; to come to the surface; to become or be visible above the surroundings or horizon; (of bread or cake etc.) to swell by the action of yeast etc.; (of fish) to come to the surface to feed; (of a person's spirits) to become more cheerful. **2** to get up from lying, sitting, or kneeling, or from a bed; (of a meeting etc.) to cease to sit for business, to recover a standing or vertical position, to become erect; to leave the ground; to come to life again. **3** to cease to be quiet or submissive, to rebel; (of the wind) to begin to blow, to strengthen. **4** (of a river etc.) to have its origin, to begin or begin to flow. —*n.* **1** the act, manner, or amount of rising. **2** an upward slope, a small hill. **3** social advancement, upward progress; an increase in power, rank, price, amount, height, wages, etc. **4** a movement of fish to the surface. **5** origin. —**get a rise out of,** to cause to display temper or characteristic behaviour. **give rise to,** to cause. **rise to,** to develop powers equal to dealing with (an occasion). [OE]

riser *n.* the vertical piece between the treads of a staircase. [f. RISE]

risible /ˈrɪzɪb(ə)l/ *adj.* **1** laughable, ludicrous. **2** inclined to laugh. [f. L *risibilis* (*ridēre* laugh)]

rising /ˈraɪzɪŋ/ *adj.* **1** advancing to maturity or high standing. **2** approaching (a specified age). **3** (of ground) sloping upwards. —*n.* a revolt. [f. RISE]

risk *n.* **1** the possibility of meeting danger or suffering harm or loss; exposure to this. **2** a person or thing causing risk or regarded in relation to risk. —*v.t.* to expose to risk; to accept the risk of; to venture on. —**at risk,** exposed to danger. **run a** *or* **the risk,** to expose oneself to danger or loss etc. [f. F *risque, risquer* f. It.]

risky *adj.* **1** full of risk. **2** risqué. —**riskily** *adv.*, **riskiness** *n.* [f. RISK]

risotto /rɪˈzɒtəʊ/ *n.* (*pl.* **-os**) an Italian dish of rice containing chopped meat or cheese and vegetables. [It.]

risqué /ˈrɪskeɪ/ *adj.* (of a story etc.) slightly indecent. [F (as RISK)]

rissole /ˈrɪsəʊl/ *n.* a ball or cake of minced meat mixed with potato or breadcrumbs etc. and usually fried. [F, ult. f. L *russeolus* reddish]

ritardando /riːtɑːˈdændəʊ/ *adv.* & *n.* (*pl.* **-os**) rallentando. [It.]

rite *n.* a religious or other solemn ceremony; an action required or usual in this; the body of usage characteristic of a Church. [f. OF or L *ritus*]

ritual /ˈrɪtjʊəl/ *n.* **1** the series of actions used in a religious or other rite; a particular form of this. **2** a procedure regularly followed. —*adj.* of or done as a ritual. —**ritually** *adv.* [f. L (as prec.)]

ritualism *n.* regular or excessive practice of ritual. —**ritualist** *n.*, **ritualistic** /-ˈlɪstɪk/ *adj.*, **ritualistically** /-ˈlɪstɪkəlɪ/ *adv.* [f. prec.]

ritzy /ˈrɪtsɪ/ *adj.* (*colloq.*) high-class, luxurious, ostentatiously smart. [f. *Ritz*, name of luxurious hotels, f. C. *Ritz* (d.1918) Swiss hotel-owner]

rival /ˈraɪv(ə)l/ *n.* **1** a person or thing competing with another. **2** a person or thing that equals another in quality. —*attrib. adj.* being a rival or rivals. —*v.t.* (**-ll-**) to be a rival of or comparable to; to seem or claim to be as good as. —**rivalry** *n.* [f. L (*rivus* stream); orig. = one using the same stream]

riven /ˈrɪv(ə)n/ *adj.* split, torn violently. [*p.p.* of archaic *rive* f. ON]

river /ˈrɪvə(r)/ *n.* **1** a copious natural stream of water flowing in a channel to the sea etc. **2** a copious flow. —**sell down the river,** (*colloq.*) to defraud or betray. [f. AF *river(e)* river (bank) f. L (as RIPARIAN)]

riverside *n.* the ground along a river-bank.

rivet /ˈrɪvɪt/ *n.* a nail or bolt for holding metal plates etc. together, its headless end being beaten out or pressed down when in place. —*v.t.* **1** to join or fasten with a rivet or rivets. **2** to beat out or press down the end of (a nail or bolt). **3** to fix, to make immovable; to direct (the eyes or attention etc.) intently; to engross (a person or his attention). —**riveter** *n.* [f. OF (*river* clench)]

Riviera /rɪvɪˈeərə/ that part of the Mediterranean coastal region of southern France and northern Italy extending from Nice to La Spezia, famous for its scenic beauty, fertility, and mild climate, and with many fashionable resorts; a region resembling this. [It., = sea-shore]

rivulet /ˈrɪvjʊlɪt/ *n.* a small stream. [alt. f. obs. *riveret* (F, dim. of RIVER)]

RM *abbr.* Royal Marines.

RN *abbr.* Royal Navy.

Rn *symbol* radon.

RNA *abbr.* ribonucleic acid, a substance similar to DNA, found in all cells.

roach *n.* a small freshwater fish (esp. *Rutilus rutilus*) of the carp family. [f. OF *roc(h)e*]

road *n.* **1** a way by which people, animals, or vehicles may pass between places, especially one with a prepared surface. **2** a way of getting to or achieving something. **3** one's way or route. **4** (usu. in *pl.*; also **roadstead**) a piece of water near a shore in which ships can ride at anchor. —**one for the road,** (*colloq.*) a final drink before departure. **on the road,** travelling, especially as a commercial traveller, itinerant performer, or vagrant. **road-block** *n.* a barricade set up by police etc. on a road to enable them to stop and search traffic. **road-hog** *n.* a reckless or inconsiderate motorist or cyclist. **road-holding** *n.* the stability of a moving vehicle. **road show,** a theatrical performance by a company on tour. **road test,** a test of a vehicle by use on the road. **road train,** (*Austral.*) a very large lorry hauling two or three trailers. **road-works** *n.pl.* construction or repair of roads. [OE (as RIDE)]

roadie /ˈrəʊdɪ/ *n.* (*colloq.*) an assistant of a touring band, responsible for equipment. [f. ROAD]

roadside *n.* the border of a road.

roadstead *n.* see ROAD 4.

roadster *n.* an open car without rear seats. [f. ROAD]

roadway *n.* a road; the part of a road intended for vehicles.

roadworthy *adj.* (of a vehicle) fit for use on a road. —**roadworthiness** *n.*

roam *v.t./i.* to wander (through). —*n.* a wander. [orig. unkn.]

roan *adj.* (of an animal) with a coat of which the prevailing colour is thickly interspersed with another, esp. bay, sorrel, or chestnut mixed with white or grey. —*n.* a roan animal, esp. a horse. [OE]

roar *n.* **1** a long loud deep sound like that made by a lion. **2** loud laughter. —*v.t./i.* **1** to utter a roar; to express in this way. **2** to function with the sound of a roar; to travel in a vehicle at high speed with the engine roaring. —**roarer** *n.* [OE (imit.)]

roaring *adj.* **1** noisy. **2** briskly active. —*adv.* **roaring drunk,** very or noisily drunk. —**roaring forties,** stormy ocean tracts between latitudes 40° and 50° S. [f. ROAR]

roast *v.t./i.* **1** to cook (food, esp. meat) by exposure to heat or in an oven. **2** to heat (coffee-beans) before grinding. **3** to expose to fire or great heat. **4** (*US*) to censure. **5** to undergo roasting. —*attrib. adj.* (of meat, a potato, chestnut, etc.) roasted. —*n.* **1** roast meat; a joint of meat for roasting. **2** the operation of roasting. [f. OF *rostir*]

roaster *n.* **1** a fowl etc. suitable for roasting. **2** an apparatus that will roast meat etc. [f. prec.]

roasting *adj.* very hot. [f. ROAST]

rob *v.t.* (**-bb-**) to steal from, to deprive unlawfully. **2** to deprive of what is due or normal. —**robber** *n.*, **robbery** *n.* [f. OF *rob(b)er*]

robe *n.* **1** a long loose garment. **2** (often in *pl.*) a long outer garment worn as an indication of the wearer's rank or office etc. **3** a dressing-gown. —*v.t./i.* to put on robes; to clothe in a robe; to dress. [f. OF (as ROB, orig. sense 'booty')]

robin /ˈrɒbɪn/ *n.* a small brown red-breasted European bird (*Erithacus rubecula*); (*US*) a red-breasted thrush (*Turdus migratorius*); a bird of similar appearance etc. to either of these. [f. OF, pet-form of man's name *Robert*]

robot /ˈrəʊbɒt/ *n.* **1** a machine designed to function in place of a living agent. **2** an apparently human automaton; a machine like person. **3** (*S.Afr.*) an automatic traffic-signal. [Czech, f. *robota* forced labour; used by K. Čapek in his play *R.U.R.* (Rossum's Universal Robots), 1920]

robotic /rəˈbɒtɪk/ *adj.* of robots; resembling a robot. —**robotics** *n.pl.* the design, construction, operation, and application of robots; the study of robots. [f. prec.]

robust /rəʊˈbʌst/ *adj.* strong, vigorous. —**robustly** *adv.*, **robustness** *n.* [f. F or L *robustus* (*robur* strength)]

roc /rɒk/ *n.* a gigantic bird of Eastern legend. [f. Sp. f. Arab.]

rochet /ˈrɒtʃɪt/ *n.* a surplice-like vestment used chiefly by bishops and abbots. [f. OF]

rock[1] *n.* **1** the hard part of the earth's crust underlying the soil; the hard compact material of which rock consists. **2** a large detached stone. **3** a mass of rock projecting and forming a hill, cliff, etc., or standing up into or out of water from the bottom. **4** a hard sweet made in a cylindrical stick, usually flavoured with peppermint. —**on the rocks,** (*colloq.*) short of money, (of a drink) served neat with ice. **rock-bottom** *adj.* & *n.* (*colloq.* of prices etc.) the very lowest. **rock-bound** *adj.* (of a coast) rocky, very rugged. **rock-cake** *n.* a small fruit cake with a rugged surface. **rock-crystal** *n.* transparent colourless quartz usually in hexagonal prisms. **rock-garden** *n.* a rockery; a garden in which rockeries are the chief feature. **rock-plant** *n.* a plant growing on or among rocks. **rock salmon,** dogfish as sold for food. **rock-salt** *n.* common salt as a solid mineral. [f. OF *ro(c)que, roche*]

rock[2] *v.t./i.* **1** to move or be moved gently to and fro while supported on something. **2** to sway or shake violently. **3** to disturb greatly by shock. —*n.* **1** a rocking motion. **2** a kind of modern popular music, usually with a strong beat; rock 'n' roll. —**rocking-chair** *n.* a chair mounted on rockers or springs so that it can be rocked by the sitter. **rocking-horse** *n.* a wooden horse mounted on rockers or springs so that it can be rocked by a child sitting on it. **rock 'n' roll,** a kind of popular music with a strong beat, containing elements of blues. [OE]

rocker *n.* **1** a device for rocking or being rocked. **2** each of the curved bars on which a rocking-chair etc. is mounted. —**off one's rocker,** (*slang*) crazy. [f. ROCK[2]]

rockery /ˈrɒkərɪ/ *n.* an artificial mound or bank containing large stones and planted with rock-plants. [f. ROCK[1]]

rocket /ˈrɒkɪt/ *n.* **1** a firework or similar device (e.g. as a signal) that rises into the air when ignited and then explodes. **2** a projectile operating by the reaction of a continuous jet of gases released in the combustion of a propellant within it; a device propelled by this, especially a bomb or spacecraft. **3** (*slang*) a reprimand. —*v.t./i.* **1** to move rapidly upwards or away. **2** to bombard with rockets. [f. F *roquette* f. It. (*rocca* distaff)]

rocketry *n.* the science or practice of rocket propulsion. [f. prec.]

rocky[1] *adj.* of or like a rock; abounding in rocks. [f. ROCK[1]]

rocky[2] *adj.* (*colloq.*) unsteady, tottering. —**rockily** *adv.*, **rockiness** *n.* [f. ROCK[2]]

rococo /rəˈkəʊkəʊ/ *adj.* of an ornate style of art, music, and literature in Europe in the 18th c. —*n.* this style. [F, joc. alt. of *rocaille* fancy shell- and rock-work for fountains and grottoes, f. *roc* rock]

rod *n.* **1** a slender straight round stick or metal bar. **2** a cane or birch for use in flogging people. **3** a fishing rod; an angler with the right to use this on a specified stretch of water. **4** (as a measure) a perch (PERCH[1]; see GUNTER). —**make a rod for one's own back,** to cause future trouble or effort for oneself. [OE]

rode *past* of RIDE.

rodent /ˈrəʊd(ə)nt/ *n.* an animal with strong incisors for gnawing things and no canine teeth (e.g. a rat, squirrel, beaver). —*adj.* gnawing; (of an ulcer) spreading slowly. —**rodent officer,** an official rat-catcher. [f. L *rodere* gnaw]

rodeo /rəʊˈdeɪəʊ/ *n.* (*pl.* **-os**) **1** an exhibition of cowboys' skill in handling animals. **2** a round-up of cattle on a ranch for branding etc. [Sp. (*rodear* go round)]

roe[1] /rəʊ/ *n.* a mass of eggs in a female fish's ovary (**hard roe**); a male fish's milt (**soft roe**). [f. MLG or MDu.]

roe[2] /rəʊ/ *n.* (*pl.* **roes** or **roe**) (also **roe-deer**) a small kind of deer (*Capreolus capreolus*). [OE]

roebuck *n.* a male roe-deer.

roentgen /ˈrʌntjən/ *n.* a former unit of ionizing radiation. [f. W. C. RÖNTGEN]

rogation /rəˈgeɪʃ(ə)n/ *n.* (usu. in *pl.*) the litany of the saints chanted on the three Rogation days before Ascension Day. —**Rogation days,** certain days prescribed in the Western Church for prayer and fasting, on which intercession is made especially for the harvest. **Rogation Sunday,** the Sunday before Ascension Day. [f. L (*rogare* ask)]

roger /ˈrɒdʒə(r)/ (in telegraphy etc.) your message has been received and understood; (*slang*) I agree. [man's name *Roger*, used in signalling code for letter *R*]

rogue /rəʊg/ *n.* **1** a dishonest or unprincipled person. **2** a mischievous person, especially a child. **3** a wild animal driven away or living apart from the herd and of savage temper. **4** an inferior or defective specimen among many acceptable ones. —**rogue's gallery,** a collection of photographs of known criminals etc. —**roguery** *n.*, **roguish** *adj.*, **roguishly** *adv.*, **roguishness** *n.* [orig. unkn.]

roister *v.i.* to revel noisily, to be uproarious. [f. F *rustre* ruffian, f. L (as RUSTIC)]

role /rəʊl/ *n.* **1** an actor's part. **2** a person's or thing's function. [f. F, = foll.]

roll /rəʊl/ *n.* **1** a cylinder formed by turning a flexible material over and over on itself without folding; a thing of similar form. **2** a small individual portion of bread separately baked. **3** an official list or register. **4** a rolling motion or gait; a spell of rolling. **5** a continuous rhythmic sound of thunder or a drum. **6** a complete revolution of an aircraft about its longitudinal axis. —*v.t./i.* **1** to move, send, or go in some direction by turning on an axis. **2** (of a vehicle) to advance or convey on wheels; (of a person) to be so conveyed. **3** to turn over and over into a cylindrical or spherical shape; to make thus. **4** to flatten by passing under or between rollers. **5** to walk with a swaying gait; (of a ship or vehicle) to sway to and fro sideways; (of an aircraft) to turn (partially or completely) on its horizontal axis. **6** to undulate; to show an undulating surface or motion; to go, propel, or carry with such a motion. **7** to sound with a vibration or trill. —**be rolling in,** to have a large supply of. **Master of the Rolls,** one of the judges of the Court of Appeal, and Keeper of the Records at the Public Record Office. **roll by** *or* **on,** (of time) to pass steadily. **roll-call** *n.* the calling of a list of names to establish presence. **rolled gold,** a thin coating of gold applied to a base metal. **rolled into one,** combined in one person etc. **roll-film** *n.* a length of photographic film backed with opaque paper and rolled on a spool. **roll one's eyes,** to show the whites in various directions. **roll in,** to arrive in great numbers. **rolling-mill** *n.* a machine or factory for rolling metal into shape. **rolling-pin** *n.* a roller for pastry. **rolling-stock** *n.* stock of railway (or (*US*) road) vehicles. **rolling stone,** a person unwilling to settle for long in one place. **roll of honour,** a list of those honoured, especially the dead in a war. **roll-on** *n.* a light elastic corset; (*adj.*) (of a ship) on to which motor vehicles can be driven; (of a cosmetic) applied from a container with a rotating ball in its neck. **roll-top desk,** a desk with a flexible cover sliding in curved grooves. **roll up,** to make into or form a roll; (*colloq.*) to arrive in a vehicle or on the scene. **strike off the rolls,** to debar from practising as a solicitor. [f. OF f. L *rotulus* (*rota* wheel)]

roller /ˈrəʊlə(r)/ *n.* **1** a hard cylinder for smoothing, spreading, or crushing things etc. **2** a small cylinder on which the hair is rolled for setting. **3** a long swelling wave. —**roller-coaster** *n.* a switchback at a fair etc. **roller-skate** *n.* see SKATE[1]. **roller towel,** a towel with the ends joined, hung on a roller. [f. ROLL]

rollicking /ˈrɒlɪkɪŋ/ *adj.* jovial and boisterous. [f. *rollick* (perh. f. ROMP + FROLIC)]

rollmops /ˈrəʊlmɒps/ *n.* (sometimes erroneously treated as *pl.*) a rolled fillet of herring, flavoured with sliced onions, spices, etc., and pickled in brine. [G]

roly-poly /rəʊlɪˈpəʊlɪ/ *n.* a pudding made of a sheet of suet pastry covered with jam etc., formed into a roll, and boiled or baked. —*adj.* (usu. of a child) podgy, plump. [prob. formed on ROLL]

ROM *abbr.* read-only memory (see READ).

rom. *abbr.* roman (type).

Roman /ˈrəʊmən/ *adj.* **1** of ancient or modern Rome or the Roman republic or Empire. **2** of the Roman Catholic Church. **3** (of the nose) having a prominent upper part or bridge like those seen in portraits of ancient Romans. **4** **roman,** of the plain upright lettering or type used in ordinary print (opp. *Gothic* or *black letter*, and *italic*). **5** (of the alphabet) based on the ancient Roman system with letters A–Z. —*n.* **1** a native or inhabitant of ancient or modern Rome, a citizen of the Roman republic or Empire. **2** a Roman Catholic. **3** **roman,** roman type. —**Roman candle,** a tubular firework discharging a shower of sparks with coloured balls of flame. **Roman Catholic,** of the Roman Catholic Church, the Church that acknowledges the pope as its head; a member of this Church. **Roman Catholicism,** the beliefs and practice of this Church. **Roman numerals,** Roman letters representing numbers (I = 1, V = 5, X = 10, L = 50, C = 100, D = 500, M = 1,000). [f. OF f. L *Romanus* (*Roma* Rome)]

Romance /rəˈmæns/ *adj.* of the group of European languages descended from Latin. —*n.* this group, of which the main languages are French, Spanish, Portuguese, Italian, and Romanian. [f. OF f. L (as ROMANIC)]

romance /rəˈmæns/ *n.* **1** an episode or story centred on highly imaginative and emotive scenes of love or heroism etc., originally a long verse narrative written in a Romance language; such stories as a genre; the atmosphere characterizing them; a mental tendency to be influenced by it, sympathetic imaginativeness. **2** a love affair viewed as resembling a tale of romance; a love-story. **3** a picturesque exaggeration or falsehood; an instance of this. —*v.i.* to exaggerate or distort the truth in an imaginative way. [f. prec.]

Romanesque /rəʊmə'nesk/ *n.* a style of art and architecture prevalent in Europe *c.*1050–1200, with massive vaulting and round arches. —*adj.* of this style. [F (as ROMANCE)]

roman-fleuve /rəʊmɑ̃'flɜːv/ *n.* (*pl.* **-ns- -es,** pr. same) a sequence of self-contained novels [F, = river novel]

romanize /'rəʊmənaɪz/ *v.t.* **1** to make Roman or Roman Catholic in character. **2** to put into the Roman alphabet or roman type. —**romanization** /-'zeɪʃ(ə)n/ *n.* [f. ROMAN]

Romano- /rəmeɪnəʊ-/ *in comb.* Roman. [f. ROMAN]

romantic /rə'mæntɪk/ *adj.* **1** of, characterized by, or suggestive of romance; (of a person) enjoying romance and situations etc. characterized by this. **2** (freq. **Romantic**; of music, literature, painting, or the composers etc. involved) imaginative, charged with feeling and emotion and not conforming to classical conventions. **3** (of an idea etc.) characterized by fantasy, unpractical. —*n.* **1** a romantic person. **2** (freq. **Romantic**) a composer etc. in the Romantic style. —**romantically** *adv.* [f. *romaunt* tale of chivalry, f. OF (as ROMANCE)]

romanticism /rə'mæntɪsɪz(ə)m/ *n.* **1** a tendency towards romance or romantic views. **2** (freq. **Romanticism**) the distinctive qualities or spirit of the Romantic movement in music, literature, and painting. —**romanticist** *n.* [f. prec.]

romanticize *v.t./i.* **1** to make romantic. **2** to indulge in romantic ideas etc. [f. ROMANTIC]

Romany /'rəʊmənɪ/ *adj.* of the gypsies or their language. —*n.* **1** a gypsy. **2** the distinctive language of gypsies. [f. Romany *Rom* man]

Romeo /'rəʊmɪəʊ/ *n.* a romantic lover. [hero of Shakespeare's romantic tragedy *Romeo and Juliet*]

romer /'rəʊmə(r)/ *n.* a small piece of plastic or card marked with scales along two edges meeting at a right angle, or (if transparent) bearing a grid, used for measuring grid references on a map. [f. C. *Romer* (d.1951), British barrister, its inventor]

romp *v.i.* **1** to play about roughly and energetically. **2** to succeed easily. —*n.* a spell of romping. [perh. var. of RAMP¹]

rompers *n.pl.* a young child's play-garment, usually covering the trunk only. [f. prec.]

rondeau /'rɒndəʊ/ *n.* a short poem with only two rhymes throughout and the opening words used twice as a refrain. [F (as foll.)]

rondel /'rɒnd(ə)l/ *n.* a rondeau, esp. of a special form. [f. OF (as ROUND); cf. ROUNDEL]

rondo /'rɒndəʊ/ *n.* (*pl.* **-os**) a piece of music with a leading theme which recurs several times. [It. f. F, = RONDEAU]

rood *n.* **1** a crucifix, especially one raised on the middle of a rood-screen. **2** a quarter-acre. —**rood-loft** *n.* a gallery above a rood-screen. **rood-screen** *n.* a carved wooden or stone screen separating the nave from the chancel in a church, found in England and on the Continent especially in the 14th–mid-16th c. [OE]

roof *n.* the upper covering of a building; the top of a covered vehicle; the overhead rock in a cave or mine etc. —*v.t.* to cover with a roof; to be the roof of. —**hit** *or* **raise the roof,** (*colloq.*) to become very angry. **roof-garden** *n.* a garden on the flat roof of a building. **roof of the mouth,** the palate. **roof-rack** *n.* a framework to carry luggage etc. on the roof of a car. **roof-top** *n.* the outer surface of a roof. **roof-tree** *n.* the ridge-piece of a roof. [OE]

roofing *n.* material used for a roof. [f. ROOF]

rook¹ /rʊk/ *n.* a black bird (*Corvus frugilegus*) of the crow family, nesting in colonies. —*v.t.* **1** to win money from at cards etc., especially by swindling. **2** to charge (a customer) extortionately. [OE]

rook² /rʊk/ *n.* a chess piece with a battlement-shaped top. [f. OF f. Arab. (orig. sense uncertain)]

rookery /'rʊkərɪ/ *n.* **1** a colony of rooks, penguins, or seals. **2** (*archaic*) a crowded cluster of mean houses or tenements. [f. ROOK¹]

rookie /'rʊkɪ/ *n.* (*slang*) a recruit. [corruption of *recruit*]

room /ruːm, rʊm/ *n.* **1** space that is or could be occupied by something. **2** a part of a house enclosed by walls or partitions; the people in this; (in *pl.*) apartments, lodgings. **3** opportunity, scope. —*v.i.* (*US*) to have a room or rooms, to lodge. —**rooming-house** *n.* a lodging-house. **room-mate** *n.* a person sharing a room. **room service,** provision of food etc. in a hotel bedroom. [OE]

roomy /'ruːmɪ/ *adj.* having much room, spacious. —**roominess** *n.* [f. ROOM]

roost *n.* a bird's perching or resting place, especially a place where fowls sleep. —*v.i.* (of a bird or person) to settle for sleep; to be perched or lodged for the night. —**come home to roost,** to recoil upon the originator. [OE]

rooster *n.* (*US*) a domestic cock. [f. prec.]

root¹ *n.* **1** the part of a plant that attaches it to the earth and conveys water and nourishment from the soil; (in *pl.*) fibres or branches of this. **2** a small plant with a root for transplanting. **3** a plant with an edible root, such a root. **4** the embedded part of a hair, tooth, etc. **5** (in *pl.*) what causes close emotional attachment to a place etc. **6** a source or origin; a basis; a means of continuance. **7** a number that when multiplied by itself a given number of times yields a given number, especially a square root (see SQUARE); the value of a quantity such that a given equation is satisfied. **8** an ultimate element of a language from which words have been made by addition or modification. —*v.t./i.* **1** to take root; to cause to do this. **2** (esp. in *p.p.*) to fix or establish firmly. **3** to drag or dig up by the roots. —**root and branch,** thoroughly, radically. **root out,** to find and get rid of. **root-stock** *n.* a rhizome; a plant into which a graft is inserted; a source from which offshoots have arisen. **take root,** to begin to draw nourishment from the soil; to become established. [OE]

root[2] *v.t./i.* **1** to dig or turn up (the ground etc.) with the snout or beak in search of food. **2** to rummage; to find or extract by rummaging —**root for,** (*US slang*) to encourage by applause or support. [OE]

rope *n.* **1** stout cord made by twisting together strands of fibre or wire etc.; a piece of this. **2** a quantity of similar things strung together. —*v.t.* **1** to fasten, secure, or catch with a rope. **2** to enclose with rope. **3** to connect with rope. —**the rope,** a halter for hanging a person. **know** (*or* **learn**) **the ropes,** to know (or learn) the procedure for doing something. **rope in,** to persuade to take part. **rope-ladder** *n.* a ladder made of two long ropes connected by rungs. **rope-walk** *n.* a long piece of ground where ropes are made. **rope-walker** *n.* a performer on a tightrope. [OE]

ropy /ˈrəupɪ/ *adj.* **1** like a rope; forming viscous or gelatinous threads. **2** (*colloq.*) poor in quality. [f. ROPE]

Roquefort /ˈrɒkfɔ:(r)/ *n.* [P] blue cheese originally made at Roquefort, a town in southern France, usually from ewes' milk and ripened in limestone caves, with a strong characteristic flavour.

rorqual /ˈrɔ:kw(ə)l/ *n.* a whale of the genus *Balaenoptera*, with a dorsal fin. [F f. Norw. f. OIcel. *reythr* the specific name + *hvalr* whale]

rosaceous /rəuˈzeɪʃəs/ *adj.* of the Rosaceae, the large family of plants of which the rose is the type. [f. L (as ROSE¹)]

rosary /ˈrəuzərɪ/ *n.* **1** (in the RC Church) a form of devotion in which five or fifteen decades of Aves are repeated, each decade preceded by the Paternoster and followed by the Gloria; a book containing this; a string of 55 or 165 beads for keeping count of these prayers. **2** a similar form of bead-string used in other religions. [f. L *rosarium* rose-garden (*rosa* rose)]

rose[1] /rəuz/ *n.* **1** a prickly bush or shrub of the genus *Rosa*, bearing ornamental usually fragrant flowers; its flower; a flowering plant resembling this. **2** deep pink colour. **3** a representation of the flower; a design based on it. **4** the sprinkling-nozzle of a hose or watering-can. —*adj.* deep pink. —**rose-bay** *n.* a willow-herb (*Epilobium angustifolium*). **rose-bud** *n.* the bud of a rose. **rose-water** *n.* a fragrant liquid perfumed with roses. **rose-window** *n.* a circular window with a roselike pattern of tracery. **see things through rose-coloured spectacles,** to take an unduly cheerful view of things. [f. OE f. L *rosa*]

rose[2] *p.p.* of RISE.

rosé /ˈrəuzeɪ/ *n.* a light pink wine, coloured by only brief contact with the grape-skins. [F, = pink]

roseate /ˈrəuzɪət/ *adj.* **1** deep pink. **2** unduly cheerful. [f. L *roseus* (as ROSE¹)]

rosemary /ˈrəuzmərɪ/ *n.* an evergreen fragrant shrub (*Rosmarinus officinalis*) with leaves used as a culinary herb, in perfume, etc., and regarded as an emblem of remembrance. [f. OF or MDu. or L *ros marinus* dew of the sea]

rosery /ˈrəuzərɪ/ *n.* a rose-garden. [f. ROSE¹]

rosette /rəˈzet/ *n.* a roselike object, symbol, or arrangement of parts; a rose-shaped ornament of ribbons etc., especially as a supporter's badge, or as an award or a symbol of an award in a competition; a rose-shaped carving. [F dim. (as ROSE¹)]

rosewood *n.* any of several fragrant close-grained woods used in making furniture.

Rosicrucian /rəuzɪˈkru:ʃ(ə)n/ *n.* **1** a member of certain secret societies who venerated the emblems of the Rose and the Cross as twin symbols of Christ's Resurrection and Redemption. Early in the 17th c. **2** a member of various present-day societies that claim to continue the Rosicrucian tradition. —*adj.* of the Rosicrucians. [f. L *rosa crucis* (or *crux*, lit. rose cross) as Latinization of Rosenkreutz]

rosin /ˈrɒzɪn/ *n.* resin, esp. in a solid form. —*v.t.* to rub (esp. the bow of a violin etc.) with rosin. [alt. f. RESIN]

roster /ˈrɒstə(r)/ *n.* a list or plan showing turns of duty etc. —*v.t.* to put on a roster. [f. Du., orig. = grid-iron, with ref. to parallel lines]

rostrum /ˈrɒstrəm/ *n.* (*pl.* **-tra**) a platform for public speaking or for an orchestral conductor. [L, = beak (orig. *rostra* in Roman forum adorned with beaks of captured galleys)]

rosy /ˈrəuzɪ/ *adj.* **1** rose-coloured, deep pink. **2** promising, cheerful, helpful. —**rosily** *adv.*, **rosiness** *n.* [f. ROSE¹]

rot *v.t./i.* (**-tt-**) **1** (of animal or vegetable matter) to lose its original form by chemical action caused by bacteria or fungi etc. **2** to perish or become weak through lack of use or activity.

3 to cause to rot. —*n.* 1 rotting; rottenness. 2 (*slang*) nonsense, an absurd statement or argument. 3 a series of failures, a rapid decline. —*int.* expressing incredulity or ridicule. —**rot-gut** *n.* (*slang*) inferior or harmful liquor. [OE]

rota /ˈrəʊtə/ *n.* a list of persons acting, or duties to be done, in rotation; a roster. [L, = wheel]

Rotarian /rəʊˈteərɪən/ *n.* a member of Rotary. —*adj.* of Rotary. [f. foll.]

Rotary /ˈrəʊtərɪ/ *n.* (in full **Rotary International**) a world-wide society for business and professional men having as its aim the promotion of unselfish service and international goodwill. Its name derives from the fact that the first local group, formed at Chicago in 1905, met at each member's premises in rotation. —**Rotary Club**, a local branch of Rotary. [f. foll.]

rotary /ˈrəʊtərɪ/ *adj.* acting by rotation. [f. L *rotarius* (as ROTA)]

rotate /rəʊˈteɪt/ *v.t./i.* 1 to move round an axis or centre, to revolve or cause to revolve. 2 to arrange or deal with in rotation. —**rotator** *n.* [f. L *rotare* (as ROTA)]

rotation /rəʊˈteɪʃ(ə)n/ *n.* 1 rotating, being rotated. 2 recurrence; a recurrent series or period; a regular succession of various members of a group. 3 the practice of growing a different crop each year on a plot of land in a regular order, to avoid exhausting the soil. —**rotational** *adj.* [as prec.]

rotatory /ˈrəʊtətərɪ/ *adj.* rotating; of rotation. [f. ROTATE]

rote *n.* **by rote**, by memory without thought of the meaning; by a fixed procedure. [orig. unkn.]

rotisserie /rəˈtɪsərɪ/ *n.* a cooking-device for roasting food on a revolving spit. [f. F (as ROAST)]

rotor /ˈrəʊtə(r)/ *n.* 1 a rotary part of a machine. 2 a horizontally-rotating vane of a helicopter. [irreg. for ROTATOR]

rotten /ˈrɒt(ə)n/ *adj.* 1 rotting, rotted; falling to pieces or liable to break or tear from age or use. 2 morally or politically corrupt; effete. 3 contemptible, worthless. 4 (*colloq.*) unpleasant. —**rotten borough**, see BOROUGH. —**rottenly** *adv.*, **rottenness** *n.* [f. ON (as ROT)]

rotter *n.* (*slang*) an objectionable or contemptible person. [f. ROT]

rotund /rəʊˈtʌnd/ *adj.* 1 (of a person) rounded, plump. 2 (of speech or literary style etc.) sonorous, grandiloquent. —**rotundity** *n.* [f. L *rotundus* (as ROTATE)]

rotunda /rəʊˈtʌndə/ *n.* a circular building or hall, especially one with a dome. [f. It. *rotonda* (as prec.)]

rouble /ˈruːb(ə)l/ *n.* the currency unit of the USSR. [F. f. Russ.]

roué /ˈruːeɪ/ *n.* a dissolute person, esp. an elderly one. [F (*rouer* break on wheel, = one deserving this)]

rouge /ruːʒ/ *n.* a red cosmetic used to colour the cheeks. —*v.t.* to colour with rouge. [F, = red, f. L *rubeus*]

rough /rʌf/ *adj.* 1 having an uneven or irregular surface, not smooth or level. 2 not gentle or restrained or careful; violent, boisterous, harsh; severe, unpleasant, demanding. 3 lacking finish or delicacy; not perfected or detailed; approximate. —*adv.* in a rough manner. —*n.* 1 hardship. 2 a hooligan, a ruffian. 3 something rough, rough ground etc. 4 an unfinished or natural state; a rough drawing or design etc. —*v.t.* 1 to make rough. 2 to shape, plan, or sketch *out* roughly. —**rough-and-ready** *adj.* rough or crude but effective; not elaborate or over-particular. **rough-and-tumble** *adj.* disorderly, irregular; (*n.*) a disorderly fight. **rough deal**, see DEAL[1]. **rough diamond**, an uncut diamond; a person of good nature but rough manners. **rough-dry** *v.t.* to dry (clothes) without ironing. **rough house**, (*slang*) a disturbance, violent behaviour. **rough it**, do without basic comforts. **rough justice**, treatment that is approximately fair. **rough-rider** *n.* one who rides unbroken horses. **rough shooting**, shooting (as a sport) without the help of beaters. **rough up**, (*slang*) to attack (a person) violently. —**roughly** *adv.*, **roughness** *n.* [OE]

roughage /ˈrʌfɪdʒ/ *n.* indigestible fibrous material in plants which are used as food (e.g. bran, green vegetables, and certain fruits) that stimulates the action of the intestines. [f. prec.]

roughcast *n.* a plaster of lime and gravel, used on outside walls. —*v.t.* to coat with this.

roughen /ˈrʌf(ə)n/ *v.t./i.* to make or become rough. [f. ROUGH]

roughneck *n.* 1 (*colloq.*) a driller on an oil rig. 2 (*US slang*) a rough person.

roughshod *adj.* (of a horse) having shoes with nail-heads projecting to prevent slipping. —**ride roughshod over**, to treat inconsiderately or arrogantly.

roulette /ruːˈlet/ *n.* a gambling game played with a revolving compartmented wheel in which a ball rolls randomly. [F f. L (dim. of *rota* wheel)]

round *adj.* 1 having a curved shape or outline; shaped like a circle, sphere, or cylinder. 2 done with a circular motion. 3 full, complete; candid. —*n.* 1 a round object; a rung of a ladder; a slice of bread cut across the loaf; a sandwich made from whole slices of bread. 2 a revolving motion; a circular or recurring course or series; a route on which things are to be delivered or inspected. 3 a single provision of drinks etc. to each member of a group. **4** one spell of play in a game etc.; one stage in a competition or struggle; one section of a boxing-match. **5** the playing of all the holes in a golf-course once. **6** a single shot or volley of shots from one or more firearms; ammunition for this. **7** a solid form of sculpture etc. **8** a musical composition for two or more voices in which each sings the same melody but starts at a different time. —*adv.* **1** with a circular motion; in a circle or curve; with return to the starting-point or an earlier state; into consciousness after unconsciousness; so as to change to an opposite position (*lit.* or *fig.*). **2** to, at, or affecting all or many points of a circumference or area or members of a company etc.; in every direction from a centre or within a radius. **3** by a circuitous route; to a person's house etc. **4** measuring (a specified distance) in girth. —*prep.* **1** so as to encircle or enclose. **2** with successive visits to; to all points of interest in. **3** having as an axis or central point; coming close from various sides but not into contact (*lit.* or *fig.*). **4** so as to pass in a curved course; having thus passed; in a position thus reached. —*v.t./i.* **1** to give or take a round shape. **2** (with *up* or *down*) to make (a number etc.) round by omitting units or fractions. **3** to travel round (a cape, corner, etc.). —**go the rounds,** to go from person to person. **in the round,** with all features shown or considered; (of a sculpture) with all sides shown, not in relief; (of a theatre) with the audience all round the stage. **round about,** all round, on all sides (of); approximately. **round and round,** several times round. **round dance,** a dance with a circular movement or in which the dancers form a ring. **round figure,** *or* **number,** a figure or number without odd units or fractions. **round off,** to bring to a complete state. **round on,** to make an unexpected retort to or retaliation against. **round robin,** a petition with signatures in a circle to conceal the order of signing. **round shoulders,** shoulders bent forward so that the back is rounded. **round-table conference,** one with discussion by members round a table. **round trip,** a trip to one or more places and back again. **round up,** to gather or bring together. **round-up** *n.* a rounding up; a summary. [f. OF f. L (as ROTUND)]

roundabout *n.* **1** a road junction with traffic passing in one direction round a central island. **2** a merry-go-round or other revolving structure at a funfair. —*adj.* circuitous.

roundel /ˈraʊnd(ə)l/ *n.* **1** a small disc, a medallion. **2** a circular identifying mark. **3** a rondeau. [f. OF *rondel(le)* (as ROUND)]

roundelay /ˈraʊndɪleɪ/ *n.* a short simple song with a refrain. [f. F *rondelet* (as RONDEL)]

rounders /ˈraʊndəz/ *n.* an outdoor game played with a bat and ball between teams of 9 players, having features in common with baseball (its original name). [f. ROUND]

Roundhead *n.* a member of the party (also known as *Parliamentarians*) opposing the king (Charles I) in the English Civil War, so called because of the style in which the Puritans, who were an important element in the forces, wore their hair.

roundly *adv.* **1** thoroughly, severely. **2** in a rounded shape. [f. ROUND]

roundsman *n.* (*pl.* **-men**) a tradesman's employee delivering goods on a regular round.

roundworm *n.* a worm with a rounded body, especially one of the genus *Ascaris.*

rouse /raʊz/ *v.t./i.* **1** to wake; to cause to wake. **2** to make active or excited. [orig. unkn.]

rousing *adj.* vigorous, stirring. [f. prec.]

roustabout /ˈraʊstəbaʊt/ *n.* **1** a labourer on an oil rig. **2** an unskilled or casual labourer. [f. dial. *roust* rout out + ABOUT]

rout[1] *n.* a disorderly retreat of defeated troops; utter defeat. —*v.t.* to put to flight, to defeat utterly. [f. AF *rute*]

rout[2] var. of ROOT[2].

route /ru:t/ *n.* the way taken in getting from a starting-point to a destination. —*v.t.* (*partic.* **routeing**) to send by a particular route. —**route march,** a training-march for troops. [f. OF, = road, ult. f. L *rumpere* break]

router /ˈraʊtə(r)/ *n.* a type of two-handled plane for cutting grooves etc. [f. ROUT[2]]

routine /ru:ˈti:n/ *n.* **1** a regular course of procedure; the unvarying performance of certain acts. **2** a set sequence of movements in a dance or other performance. **3** a sequence of instructions to a computer. —*adj.* performed as a routine. —**routinely** *adv.* [F (as prec.)]

roux /ru:/ *n.* (*pl.* same) a mixture of fat and flour used as a basis for making a sauce etc. [F, = browned]

rove[1] *v.i.* to wander. —**rove-beetle** *n.* a long-bodied beetle of the family Staphylinidae. **roving commission,** authority to travel as may be necessary in conducting an inquiry or other work. **roving eye,** a tendency to flirt. [orig. archery term, = shoot at casual mark with range not determined, perh. f. dial. *rave* stray, prob. of Scand. orig.]

rove[2] *past* of REEVE[2].

rover[1] /ˈrəʊvə(r)/ *n.* a roving person, a wanderer. [f. ROVE[1]]

rover[2] /rəʊvə(r)/ *n.* a pirate. [f. MLG or MDu. (*roven* rob)]

row[1] /rəʊ/ *n.* **1** a number of persons or things in a more or less straight line. **2** a line of seats across a theatre etc. **3** a street with houses along one or each side. —**in a row,** (*colloq.*) in succession. [OE]

row[2] /rəʊ/ *v.t./i.* to propel (a boat) with oars; to convey (a passenger) in a boat thus. —*n.* a spell of rowing. —**rowing-boat** *or* **row-boat** *n.* a boat propelled by oars. [OE]

row[3] /raʊ/ *n.* (*colloq.*) **1** a loud noise or commotion. **2** a fierce quarrel or dispute. —*v.i.* (*colloq.*) to make or engage in a row. [orig. unkn.]

rowan /ˈrəʊən, ˈraʊ-/ *n.* the mountain ash (*Sorbus aucuparia*) its scarlet berry. [f. Scand.]

rowdy /ˈraʊdɪ/ *adj.* noisy and disorderly. —*n.* a rowdy person. —**rowdily** *adv.*, **rowdiness** *n.*, **rowdyism** *n.* [orig. unkn.]

rowel /ˈraʊəl/ *n.* a spiked revolving disc at the end of a spur. [f. OF *roel(e)* f. L (as ROULETTE)]

rowlock /ˈrɒlək/ *n.* a device for holding an oar in place and serving as a fulcrum. [alt. of earlier *oarlock* (OAR, LOCK[1])]

royal /ˈrɔɪəl/ *adj.* **1** of, suited to, or worthy of a king or queen. **2** in the service or under the patronage of royalty; belonging to a king or queen or their family. **3** splendid; on a great scale, of exceptional size etc. —*n.* **1** (*colloq.*) a member of a royal family. **2** a royal mast or sail (that above the topgallant). —**royal blue,** deep vivid blue. **Royal Commission,** a commission of inquiry appointed by the Crown at the request of the government. **Royal Family,** the family to which the sovereign belongs. **royal flush,** see FLUSH[3]. **royal icing,** hard icing for cakes, made with icing sugar and egg-white. **royal jelly,** a substance secreted by worker-bees and fed by them to future queen bees. **royal oak,** a sprig of oak worn on 29 May to commemorate the restoration of Charles II (1660) who hid in an oak-tree after the battle of Worcester (1651). **royal warrant,** a warrant authorizing a tradesman to supply goods to a specified royal person. —**royally** *adv.* [f. OF *roial* f. L, = REGAL]

royalist /ˈrɔɪəlɪst/ *n.* a monarchist, a supporter of a monarchy or the royal side in a civil war etc.; **Royalist,** a supporter of the Stuarts in the English Civil War. [f. prec.]

royalty *n.* **1** being royal. **2** a royal person or persons. **3** the sum paid to a patentee for the use of a patent or to an author etc. for each copy of his book etc. sold or for each public performance of his work. **4** a royal right (now especially over minerals) granted by a sovereign to an individual or a corporation. [f. OF (as ROYAL)]

r.p.m. *abbr.* revolutions per minute.

RSFSR *abbr.* Russian Soviet Federative Socialist Republic.

RSM *abbr.* Regimental Sergeant-Major.

RSPCA *abbr.* Royal Society for the Prevention of Cruelty to Animals (founded in 1824).

RSV *abbr.* Revised Standard Version (of the Bible).

RSVP *abbr.* (in an invitation etc.) please reply. [f. F *répondez s'il vous plaît*]

rt. *abbr.* right.

Rt. Hon. *abbr.* Right Honourable.

Rt. Revd *abbr.* Right Reverend.

Ru *symbol* ruthenium.

rub *v.t./i.* (**-bb-**) **1** to press one's hand or an object etc. against (a surface) and slide it to and fro; to apply thus. **2** to clean or polish by rubbing; to make or become dry, smooth, or sore etc. in this way; to remove by rubbing. **3** to move or slide (objects) against each other. —*n.* **1** the act or process of rubbing. **2** an impediment or difficulty. —**rub along,** (*colloq.*) to manage to get on without undue difficulty. **rub down,** to dry, smooth, or clean by rubbing. **rub it in,** to emphasize or repeat an embarrassing fact etc. **rub off on,** to be transferred to by contact (*lit.* or *fig.*). **rub shoulders with,** to associate with. **rub up,** to polish; to brush up (a subject etc.). **rub up the wrong way,** to irritate or repel. [perh. f. LG]

rubato /ruːˈbɑːtəʊ/ *n.* (*pl.* **-os**) (*Mus.*) a temporary relaxation of strict tempo. [It., = robbed]

rubber[1] *n.* **1** a tough elastic substance made from the latex of tropical plants or synthetically. **2** a piece of this or some other substance for erasing pencil or ink marks. **3** a device for rubbing things. **4** (*slang*) a condom. **5** (in *pl.*, *US*) galoshes. —**rubber band,** a loop of rubber to hold papers etc. together. **rubber plant,** a plant yielding rubber, especially *Ficus elastica* grown as a house-plant. **rubber stamp,** a device for inking and imprinting on a surface; one who mechanically agrees to others' actions; an indication of such agreement. **rubber-stamp** *v.t.* to approve (an action) automatically without proper consideration. —**rubbery** *adj.* [f. RUB]

rubber[2] *n.* a match of usually three successive games between the same sides or persons at bridge etc. or cricket. [orig. unkn.]

rubberneck *n.* (*US colloq.*) an inquisitive person; a gaping sightseer. —*v.i.* (*US colloq.*) to behave as a rubberneck.

rubbing *n.* a reproduction or impression made of a memorial brass or other relief design by placing paper over it and rubbing with pigment.

rubbish *n.* **1** waste or worthless matter. **2** absurd ideas or suggestions, nonsense (often as an exclamation of contempt). —**rubbishy** *adj.* [f. AF *rubbous*]

rubble *n.* waste or rough fragments of stone or

brick etc. —**rubbly** *adj*. [perh. f. OF *robe* spoils]

rubella /ru'belə/ *n*. German measles. [f. L *rubellus* reddish]

rubicund /'ru:bɪkʌnd/ *adj*. (of a person or complexion) ruddy, high-coloured. [f. F or L *rubicundus* (*rubēre* be red)]

rubidium /ru:'bɪdɪəm/ *n*. a soft silvery metallic element of the alkali-metal group, symbol Rb, atomic number 37. [f. L *rubidus* reddish (with ref. to its spectrum lines)]

rubric /'ru:brɪk/ *n*. **1** a direction for the conduct of divine service inserted in a liturgical book. **2** explanatory words. **3** a heading or passage in red or special lettering. [f. OF or L *rubrica* red ochre]

ruby /'ru:bɪ/ *n*. **1** a rare precious stone with a colour varying from deep crimson to pale rose. **2** a deep red colour. —*adj*. deep red. —**ruby wedding,** the 40th anniversary of a wedding. [f. OF *rubi* f. L (*rubeus* red)]

ruche /ru:ʃ/ *n*. a frill or gathering of lace etc. [F, f. L *rusca* tree-bark]

ruck[1] *n*. **1** the main body of competitors not likely to overtake the leaders. **2** the undistinguished crowd of persons or things. **3** (in Rugby football) a loose scrum with the ball on the ground. [orig. = stack of fuel; app. Scand.]

ruck[2] *v.t./i*. to crease or wrinkle. [f. ON]

rucksack /'rʌksæk, 'rʊk-/ *n*. a bag slung by straps from both shoulders and resting on the back. [G (*rucken* back, SACK[1])]

ruction /'rʌkʃ(ə)n/ *n*. (esp. in *pl*., *colloq*.) protests and noisy argument, a row; a disturbance. [orig. unkn.]

rudder *n*. a flat piece hinged vertically to the stern of a vessel or the rear of an aircraft for steering. [OE]

ruddy *adj*. **1** (of a person or complexion) freshly or healthily red. **2** reddish. **3** (*colloq*.) bloody, damnable. —**ruddily** *adv*., **ruddiness** *n*. [OE]

rude *adj*. **1** impolite, showing no respect or consideration; coarse. **2** roughly made or done; primitive, uneducated. **3** abrupt, sudden. **4** vigorous, hearty. —**rudely** *adv*., **rudeness** *n*. [f. OF f. L *rudis* unwrought]

rudiment /'ru:dɪmənt/ *n*. **1** (in *pl*.) the elements or first principles of knowledge or some subject. **2** (in *pl*.) the imperfect beginnings of something undeveloped. **3** a part or organ imperfectly developed because it is vestigial or has no function (e.g. the breast in males). —**rudimentary** /-'mentərɪ/ *adj*. [F or f. L (as prec.)]

rue[1] *v.t*. (*partic*. **ruing**) to repent of, to regret; to wish undone or non-existent. [OE]

rue[2] *n*. an evergreen shrub (*Ruta graveolens*) with bitter leaves. [f. OF f. L *ruta* f. Gk]

rueful /'ru:f(ə)l/ *adj*. expressing good-humoured regret. —**ruefully** *adv*. [f. RUE[1] + -FUL]

ruff[1] *n*. **1** a projecting starched frill worn round the neck especially in the 16th c. **2** a projecting or conspicuously coloured ring of feathers or hair round a bird's or animal's neck. **3** a bird of the sandpiper family (*Philomachus pugnax*). **4** a kind of pigeon. [perh. = ROUGH]

ruff[2] *v.t./i*. to trump at cards. —*n*. trumping. [orig. name of card-game f. OF *ro(u)ffle*]

ruffian /'rʌfɪən/ *n*. a violent lawless person. —**ruffianism** *n*., **ruffianly** *adj*. [f. F f. It. *ruffiano*]

ruffle *v.t./i*. **1** to disturb the smoothness or evenness of. **2** to upset the calmness or even temper of (a person). **3** to undergo ruffling. —*n*. a frill of lace etc. worn especially round the wrist or neck. [orig. unkn.]

rufous /'ru:fəs/ *adj*. (esp. of animals) reddish-brown. [f. L *rufus*]

rug *n*. **1** a thick floor-mat. **2** a piece of thick material used as a blanket or coverlet. —**pull the rug from under,** to deprive of support, to weaken, to unsettle. [prob. f. Scand.]

Rugby /'rʌgbɪ/ *n*. (in full **Rugby football**) a form of football played with an oval ball which may be carried as well as kicked. —**Rugby League,** a partly professional form of the game with teams of 13. **Rugby Union,** an amateur form with teams of 15. [f. *Rugby School*, Warwicks, where it developed]

rugged /'rʌgɪd/ *adj*. **1** having a rough uneven surface or outline; (of the features) irregular and strongly marked. **2** (of manner etc.) rough but kindly and sincere. **3** harsh-sounding. **4** sturdy. —**ruggedly** *adv*., **ruggedness** *n*. [prob. f. Scand.]

rugger /'rʌgə(r)/ *n*. (*colloq*.) Rugby football. [f. RUGBY]

ruin /'ru:ɪn/ *n*. **1** severe damage or destruction; a destroyed or wrecked state. **2** complete loss of fortune, resources, or prospects. **3** (in *sing*. or *pl*.) the remains of something that has suffered ruin. **4** a cause of ruin. —*v.t*. to bring into a state of ruin; to damage so severely that it is in ruins; (in *p.p*.) reduced to ruins. —**ruination** /-'neɪʃ(ə)n/ *n*. [f. OF f. L *ruina* (*ruere* fall)]

ruinous /'ru:ɪnəs/ *adj*. **1** bringing or likely to bring ruin, disastrous. **2** in ruins, dilapidated. —**ruinously** *adv*. [f. L *ruinosus* (as RUIN)]

rule *n*. **1** a statement of what can, must, or should be done in a certain set of circumstances or in playing a game; the customary or normal state of things or course of action. **2** government, exercise of authority, control. **3** a graduated straight often jointed measuring device used by carpenters etc. **4** a thin line or dash in printing. **5** the code of discipline of a religious order. **6** (*Law*) an order made by a judge or court with reference to a particular case only. —*v.t./i.* **1** to have authoritative control over, to govern. **2** to keep under control; to exercise a decisive influence over. **3** to give a decision as judge or other authority. **4** to mark parallel lines across (paper); to make (a straight line) with a ruler etc. —**as a rule,** usually, more often than not. **rule of thumb,** a rule based on experience or practice, not on theory. **rule out,** to exclude, to pronounce irrelevant or ineligible. **rule the roost,** to be in control, to dominate. [f. OF f. L *regula*]

ruler *n.* **1** a person who rules by authority, especially over a country etc. **2** a straight strip of wood or metal etc. used for measuring or for drawing straight lines. [f. RULE]

ruling *n.* an authoritative pronouncement. [f. RULE]

rum[1] *n.* a spirit distilled from sugar-cane or molasses. [perh. abbr. of 17th-c. forms *rumbullion, rumbustion*]

rum[2] *adj.* (*colloq.*) strange, odd. [16th-c. slang, orig. = excellent]

rumba /ˈrʌmbə/ *n.* a ballroom dance of Cuban origin, danced on the spot with a pronounced movement of the hips; the music for this. [Amer. Sp.]

rumble[1] *v.i.* to make a continuous deep sound as of distant thunder; (of a person or vehicle) to go along making such a sound. —*n.* a rumbling sound. [prob. f. MDu. *rommelen* (imit.)]

rumble[2] *v.t.* (*slang*) to see through (a deception), to detect the true character of. [orig. unkn.]

rumbustious /rʌmˈbʌstʃəs/ *adj.* (*colloq.*) boisterous, uproarious. [prob. var. of *robustious* robust]

ruminant /ˈruːmɪnənt/ *n.* an animal that chews the cud. —*adj.* **1** belonging to the ruminants. **2** meditative. [as foll.]

ruminate /ˈruːmɪneɪt/ *v.i.* **1** to chew the cud. **2** to ponder, to meditate. —**rumination** /-ˈneɪʃ(ə)n/ *n.*, **ruminative** *adj.* [f. L *ruminari* (*rumen* throat)]

rummage /ˈrʌmɪdʒ/ *v.t./i.* **1** to search by turning things over or disarranging them. **2** to discover thus. —*n.* a search of this kind. —**rummage sale,** a jumble sale. [orig. = arranging of casks in hold, f. OF *arrumage* (*arrumer* stow)]

rummy *n.* a card-game played usually with two packs, each player seeking to dispose of his cards by forming sequences or sets. [20th c.; orig. unkn.]

rumour /ˈruːmə(r)/ *n.* information spread by word of mouth, of doubtful accuracy. —*v.t.* (usu. in *pass.*) to spread as a rumour. [f. OF f. L *rumor* noise]

rump *n.* **1** the tail-end or buttocks of an animal, person, or bird. **2** a cut of meat from an animal's hindquarters. **3** an unimportant remnant. —**rump steak,** a steak cut from a rump of beef. [prob. f. Scand.]

rumple *v.t./i.* to make or become crumpled; to make (something smooth) untidy. [f. MDu. (*rompe* wrinkle)]

rumpus /ˈrʌmpəs/ *n.* (*colloq.*) an uproar; an angry dispute. [prob. fanciful]

run *v.t./i.* (**-nn-**; *past* **ran**; *p.p.* **run**) **1** to move with quick steps, never having both or all feet on the ground at once; (in cricket) to traverse the pitch to score a run. **2** to flee. **3** to go or travel hurriedly or swiftly; (of a ship) to go straight and fast; (of salmon) to go up river in large numbers from the sea. **4** to compete in a race or contest; to seek election. **5** to advance (as) by rolling or on wheels, or smoothly or easily. **6** to be in action or operation; to be current or valid. **7** (of a bus, train, etc.) to travel from point to point; to convey (a person) in a vehicle; to smuggle (guns etc.). **8** to extend; to have a course, order, or tendency. **9** to flow or cause to flow; to fill (a bath etc.) thus; to exude liquid; to be wet. **10** to spread rapidly or beyond the intended limit. **11** to make one's way through or over (a course, race, distance, etc.); to perform (an errand). **12** to own and use (a vehicle etc.); to operate (a business). **13** to cause to run, go, extend, or function. **14** (of a newspaper) to print as an item. **15** to sew (fabric) with running stitches. —*n.* **1** an act or spell of running. **2** a short excursion; a distance travelled. **3** a general tendency of development; a regular route. **4** a continuous or long stretch, spell, or course; a high general demand; a quantity produced in one period of operation. **5** the general or average type or class. **6** a point scored in cricket or baseball. **7** permission to make unrestricted use of something. **8** an animal's regular track; an enclosure where domestic animals can range; a track for some purpose. **9** a large number of salmon going up river from the sea. **10** a ladder in a stocking etc. —**on the run,** fleeing from pursuit or capture. **run across,** to happen to meet or find. **run away,** to leave secretly or hastily. **run away with,** to elope with; to win (a prize etc.) easily; to accept (an idea) too hastily; to require (much money) in expense. **run down,** to knock down with a moving vehicle or ship; to reduce the numbers of; (of a clock) to stop because not rewound; to discover after searching; to disparage; (in *pass.*) to be weak or exhausted from overwork or undernourishment. **run-down** *n.* a reduction in numbers; a detailed analysis; (*adj.*) decayed after being prosperous. **run dry,** to cease to flow. **run for it,** to seek safety by fleeing. **run for one's money,** some return for outlay or effort. **run in,** to run (a new engine or vehicle) carefully in the early stages; (*colloq.*) to arrest. **run into,** to collide with; to encounter; to reach as many as. **run off,** to run away; to produce (copies etc.) on a machine; to decide (a race) after a tie or heats; to flow or cause to flow away; to write or recite fluently. **run-of-the-mill** *adj.* ordinary, undistinguished. **run out,** to come to an end, to become used up; to exhaust one's stock; to jut out; to put down the wicket of (a batsman who is running). **run out on,** (*colloq.*) to desert (a person). **run over,** to overflow; to study or repeat quickly; (of a vehicle or driver) to pass over, to knock down or crush. **run through,** to examine or rehearse briefly; to deal successively with. **run to,** to have the money or ability for; to reach (an amount or number; to show a tendency to (fat etc.). **run up,** to accumulate (a debt etc.) quickly; to build hurriedly; to make quickly by sewing; to add up (a column of figures); to raise (a flag). **run-up** *n.* the period preceeding an important event. **run up against,** to meet with (a difficulty). [OE]

runaway *n.* a fugitive. —*adj.* **1** fugitive. **2** (of a victory) won easily.

rune /ru:n/ *n.* **1** any letter of the earliest Germanic alphabet, used especially by the Scandinavians and Anglo-Saxons from *c.* 3rd c. and formed by modifying Roman or Greek characters to suit carving. **2** a letter of a similar alphabet of 8th-c. Mongolian Turks. **3** a similar mark of mysterious or magical significance. **4** a Finnish poem; a division of this. —**runic** *adj.* [f. ON, = magic signs]

rung[1] *n.* **1** a cross-piece of a ladder (*lit.* or *fig.*). **2** a short stick fixed as a cross bar in a chair etc. [OE]

rung[2] *p.p.* of RING[2].

runnel /ˈrʌn(ə)l/ *n.* **1** a brook. **2** a gutter. [OE (as RUN)]

runner *n.* **1** one who or that which runs; a person or animal that runs in a race. **2** a messenger. **3** a creeping plant-stem that can take root. **4** a rod, groove, or roller for a thing to move on; each of the long strips on which a sledge etc. slides. **5** a long narrow strip of carpet, or of ornamental cloth for a table etc. —**runner bean,** a kind of climbing bean (*Phaseolus multiflorus*). **runner-up** *n.* a person or team finishing second in a competition. [f. RUN]

running *n.* the action of runners in a race etc.; the way a race proceeds. —*adj.* **1** performed while running. **2** continuous. **3** consecutive. —**in** (*or* **out of**) **the running,** with a good (or no) chance of succeeding. **make the running,** to set the pace (*lit.* or *fig.*). **running commentary,** a spoken description of events as they occur. **running knot,** a knot that slips along a rope etc. so that the size of the loop is changed. **running repairs,** minor repairs and replacements. **running-stitch** *n.* a line of evenly-spaced stitches made by a straight thread passing in and out of the material. [f. RUN]

runny *adj.* **1** tending to flow or exude fluid. **2** semi-liquid; excessively fluid. [f. RUN]

runt *n.* an undersized person or animal; the smallest of a litter. [orig. unkn.]

runway *n.* a specially prepared surface for the taking off and landing of aircraft.

rupee /ru:ˈpi:/ *n.* the currency unit of India, Pakistan, etc. [f. Hind. f. Skr., = wrought silver]

rupture /ˈrʌptʃə(r)/ *n.* **1** breaking, breach. **2** a breach of harmonious relations, disagreement and parting. **3** an abdominal hernia. —*v.t./i.* **1** to burst or break (tissue etc.); to become burst or broken. **2** to sever (a connection). **3** to affect with or suffer a hernia. [f. OF or f. L (*rumpere* break)]

rural /ˈrʊər(ə)l/ *adj.* in, of, or suggesting the countryside. —**rural dean,** see DEAN[1]. **rural district,** (*hist.*) a group of country parishes governed by an elected council. [f. OF or L (*rus* the country)]

ruse /ru:z/ *n.* a stratagem, a trick. [f. OF (*ruser* drive back)]

rush[1] *v.t./i.* **1** to go, move, or pass precipitately or with great speed. **2** to impel or carry along rapidly. **3** to act hastily; to force into hasty action. **4** to attack or capture with a sudden assault. —*n.* **1** rushing; an instance of this. **2** a period of great activity. **3** a sudden migration of large numbers. **4** a sudden great demand for goods etc. **5** (in *pl.*, *colloq.*) the first print or showing of a film after shooting, before it is cut and edited. —**rush one's fences,** to act with undue haste. **rush-hour** *n.* the time each morning and evening when traffic or business is heaviest. [F. AF *russher* = OF *ruser* (as prec.)]

rush[2] *n.* a marsh plant of the genus *Juncus* with slender pith-filled stems, used for making chair-seats or baskets etc.; a stem of this. —**rush candle,** a candle made by dipping the pith of a rush in tallow. —**rushy** *adj.* [OE]

rusk *n.* a slice of bread rebaked as a light biscuit, especially for feeding infants. [f. Sp. or Port. *rosca* twist, roll of bread]

russet /ˈrʌsɪt/ *adj.* reddish-brown —*n.* **1** russet colour. **2** an apple with a rough skin of this colour. [f. AF, ult. f. L *russus* red]

Russian /ˈrʌʃ(ə)n/ *adj.* of Russia (the largest republic in the USSR) or its people or language; (*loosely*) of the USSR. —*n.* **1** a native or inhabitant of Russia or (*loosely*) of the USSR. **2** the official language of the USSR. —**Russian roulette,** the firing of a revolver held to one's head after spinning the cylinder with one chamber loaded. **Russian salad,** a salad of mixed diced vegetables coated with mayonnaise. [f. prec.]

rust *n.* **1** a reddish or yellowish-brown corrosive coating formed on iron or steel by oxidation. **2** reddish-brown. **3** a plant-disease with rust-coloured spots. **4** an impaired state due to disuse or inactivity. —*v.t./i.* **1** to make or become rusty. **2** to lose quality or efficiency by disuse or inactivity. [OE, rel. to RED]

rustic /ˈrʌstɪk/ *adj.* **1** having the appearance or qualities ascribed to country people or peasants, simple and unsophisticated, rough and unrefined. **2** made of untrimmed branches or rough timber. —*n.* a countryman, a peasant. —**rustically** *adv.*, **rusticity** /-ˈtɪsɪtɪ/ *n.* [f. L *rusticus* (*rus* the country)]

rusticate /ˈrʌstɪkeɪt/ *v.t./i.* **1** to send down temporarily from a university as a punishment. **2** to retire to or live in the country. **3** to mark (masonry) with sunk joints or a roughened surface. —**rustication** /-ˈkeɪʃ(ə)n/ *n.* [f. L *rusticare* live in the country (as prec.)]

rustle /ˈrʌs(ə)l/ *v.t./i.* **1** to make or cause to make a gentle sound as of dry leaves blown in a breeze. **2** to steal (cattle or horses). —*n.* a rustling sound. —**rustle up,** (*colloq.*) to produce when needed. —**rustler** *n.* [imit.]

rustless *adj.* not liable to rust. [f. RUST + -LESS]

rusty *adj.* **1** rusted, affected by rust. **2** stiff with age or disuse; (of knowledge etc.) faded or impaired by neglect. **3** rust-coloured; (of black clothes) discoloured by age. —**rustily** *adv.* **rustiness** *n.* [OE (as RUST)]

rut[1] *n.* **1** a deep track made by the passage of wheels. **2** a fixed pattern of behaviour difficult to change; a habitual usually dull course of life. [prob. f. OF (as ROUTE)]

rut[2] *n.* the periodic sexual excitement of male deer etc. —*v.i.* (**-tt-**) to be affected with rut. [f. OF f. L *rugitus* (*rugire* roar)]

ruthenium /ru:ˈθi:nɪəm/ *n.* a rare hard white metallic element, symbol Ru, atomic number 44, chemically related to platinum. [f. L *Ruthenia* Russia (from its discovery in ores from the Urals)]

rutherfordium /rʌðəˈfɔ:dɪəm/ *n.* the American name for the element of atomic number 104, a short-lived artificially produced radioactive transuranic element (cf. KURCHATOVIUM). [f. Sir E. *Rutherford* (1871-1937), British physicist]

ruthless /ˈru:θlɪs/ *adj.* having no pity or compassion. —**ruthlessly** *adv.*, **ruthlessness** *n.* [f. *ruth* pity, f. RUE[1]]

rutted /ˈrʌtɪd/ *adj.* marked with ruts. [f. RUT[1]]

RV *abbr.* Revised Version (of the Bible).

rye /raɪ/ *n.* **1** a cereal plant (*Secale cereale*); the grain of this, used for bread and fodder. **2** (in full **rye whisky**) whisky distilled from rye. [OE]

rye-grass /ˈraɪgrɑ:s/ *n.* a fodder grass of the genus *Lolium*. [alt. of earlier *ray-grass*]

Ss

S, s /es/ *n.* (*pl.* **Ss, S's** /ˈesɪz/) **1** the nineteenth letter of the alphabet. **2** an S-shaped thing.

S *abbr.* siemens.

S *symbol* sulphur.

S. *abbr.* **1** Saint. **2** south, southern:

s. *abbr.* **1** second(s). **2** shilling(s) [f. L *solidus*, orig = gold coin of the Roman Empire]. **3** singular. **4** son.

's *abbr.* has, is, us.

SA *abbr.* **1** Salvation Army. **2** South Africa. **3** South Australia.

Sabbatarian /sæbəˈteərɪən/ *n.* a person who observes the sabbath strictly. —**Sabbatarianism** *n.* [f. L (as foll.)]

sabbath /ˈsæbəθ/ *n.* **1** a religious rest-day appointed for Jews on the last day of the week (Saturday). **2** Sunday as a Christian day of abstinence from work and play. [OE, ult. f. Heb., = rest]

sabbatical /səˈbætɪk(ə)l/ *adj.* **1** of the sabbath. **2** (of leave) granted at intervals to a university professor etc. for study or travel etc. —*n.* a period of sabbatical leave. [f. L f. Gk (as prec.)]

sable /ˈseɪb(ə)l/ *n.* **1** a small dark-furred arctic mammal (*Martes zibellina* or *M. americana*); its fur or skin. **2** (in heraldry) the colour black. —*adj.* black, gloomy. [f. OF, ult. f. Slav.]

sabot /ˈsæbəʊ/ *n.* a heavy wooden or wooden-soled shoe. [F]

sabotage /ˈsæbətɑːʒ/ *n.* malicious or wanton damage or destruction, especially for an industrial or political purpose. —*v.t.* to commit sabotage on; to destroy or render useless, to spoil. [F, f. *saboter* make a noise with sabots, perform or execute badly, destroy (tools, machinery, etc.) wilfully]

saboteur /sæbəˈtɜː(r)/ *n.* one who commits sabotage. [F]

sabre /ˈseɪbə(r)/ *n.* **1** a cavalry sword with a curved blade. **2** a light fencing-sword with a tapering blade. —**sabre-rattling** *n.* a display or threats of military force. [F, earlier *sable*, ult. f. Polish or Magyar]

sac /sæk/ *n.* a membranous bag in an animal or vegetable organism. [F or f. L (as SACK[1])]

saccharin /ˈsækərɪn/ *n.* a very sweet substance used as a substitute for sugar. [G f. L *saccharum* sugar]

saccharine /ˈsækəriːn/ *adj.* intensely sweet, cloying. [as prec.]

sacerdotal /sækəˈdəʊt(ə)l/ *adj.* of priests or priestly office. [f. OF or L (*sacerdos* priest)]

sachet /ˈsæʃeɪ/ *n.* a small bag or packet containing a small portion of a substance or filled with a perfumed substance for laying among clothes etc. [F, dim. of *sac* f. L *saccus* f. Gk]

sack[1] *n.* **1** a large strong bag for storing or conveying goods. **2** the quantity contained in a sack. **3** a woman's loose-fitting dress. **4** (*slang*) a bed. —*v.t.* **1** to put into a sack or sacks. **2** (*colloq.*) to dismiss from a job etc. —**the sack,** (*colloq.*) dismissal from a job etc. **hit the sack,** (*slang*) to go to bed. —**sackful** *n.* [OE f. L *saccus* f. Gk]

sack[2] *v.t.* to plunder and destroy (a captured town etc.). —*n.* the sacking of a town etc. [f. F *sac* (in phr. *mettre à sac*), f. It. *sacco* (as prec.)]

sack[3] *n.* (*hist.*) a white wine formerly imported from Spain and the Canary Islands. [orig. *wyne seck*, f. F *vin sec* dry wine]

sackbut /ˈsækbʌt/ *n.* an early form of trombone. [f. F *saqueboute* hook for pulling man off horse]

sackcloth *n.* **1** a coarse fabric of flax or hemp. **2** mourning or penitential garb (esp. in *sackcloth and ashes*).

sacking *n.* material for making sacks, sackcloth. [f. SACK[1]]

sacral /ˈseɪkr(ə)l/ *adj.* **1** of the sacrum. **2** of or for sacred rites. [f. SACRUM or f. L *sacrum* sacred rite (as foll.)]

sacrament /ˈsækrəmənt/ *n.* **1** a religious ceremony or act regarded as an outward and visible sign of inward and spiritual grace. **2** (in full **Blessed** or **Holy Sacrament**) the Eucharist. **3** a sacred thing, influence, etc. —**sacramental** /-ˈment(ə)l/ *adj.* [f. OF f. L (*sacrare* hallow, f. *sacer* holy)]

sacred /ˈseɪkrɪd/ *adj.* **1** associated with or dedicated to God or a god; regarded with reverence because of this. **2** connected with religion, not secular. **3** dedicated to some person or purpose. **4** safeguarded or required by religion or tradition, inviolable. —**sacred cow,** the cow as an object of veneration amongst Hindus; an idea or institution unreasonably held to be above criticism. **Sacred Heart,** the heart of Jesus (or *of Mary*) as an object of devotion. [p.p. of obs. *sacre* consecrate f. OF *sacrer* f. L *sacrare* (as prec.)]

sacrifice /ˈsækrɪfaɪs/ *n.* **1** the giving up of a valued thing for the sake of something else that is more important, worthy, or urgent. **2** the slaughter of a victim or presenting of a gift to win the favour of a deity. **3** the thing thus given up or offered. **4** (in games) a loss deliberately incurred to avoid greater loss or obtain a compensating advantage. —*v.t./i.* **1** to give up or offer as a sacrifice. **2** to devote *to*. —**sacrificial** /-ˈfɪʃ(ə)l/ *adj.* [f. OF f. L (as prec.)]

sacrilege /ˈsækrɪlɪdʒ/ *n.* disrespect or damage to something regarded as sacred. —**sacrilegious** /-ˈlɪdʒəs/ *adj.* [f. OF f. L (*sacrilegus* stealer of sacred things, f. *sacer* sacred + *legere* take possession of)]

sacristan /ˈsækrɪstən/ *n.* the person in charge of the sacristy and church contents. [f. L (as SACRED)]

sacristy /ˈsækrɪstɪ/ *n.* the repository for a church's vestments, vessels, etc. [f. F or It. or L *sacristia* (as prec.)]

sacro- /seɪkrəʊ-/ *in comb.* of the sacrum and. [f. SACRUM]

sacrosanct /ˈsækrəʊsæŋkt/ *adj.* reverenced or respected and therefore not to be violated or damaged. —**sacrosanctity** /-ˈsæŋkt-/ *n.* [f. L (as SACRED, SAINT)]

sacrum /ˈseɪkrəm/ *n.* the composite triangular bone forming the back of the pelvis. [f. L *os sacrum* sacred bone (from sacrificial use)]

sad *adj.* **1** showing or causing sorrow, unhappy. **2** regrettable; deplorably bad. **3** (of cake or pastry) dense from not having risen. —**sadly** *adv.*, **sadness** *n.* [OE]

sadden *v.t./i.* to make or become sad. [f. prec.]

saddle *n.* **1** a seat of leather etc., usually raised at the front and rear, fastened on a horse etc. for riding. **2** the seat for the rider of a bicycle etc. **3** a joint of meat consisting of the two loins. **4** a ridge rising to a summit at each end. —*v.t.* **1** to put a saddle on (a horse etc.). **2** to burden (a person) with a task etc.; to put (a burden etc.) on a person. —**saddle-bag** *n.* one of a pair of bags laid across the back of a horse etc.; a bag attached behind the saddle of a bicycle etc. —**in the saddle,** on horseback; in office or control. [OE]

saddleback *n.* **1** a saddlebacked hill or roof. **2** a black pig with a white stripe across its back.

saddlebacked *adj.* with a concave upper outline.

saddler *n.* a maker of or dealer in saddles etc. [f. SADDLE]

saddlery *n.* a saddler's trade or goods. [as prec.]

Sadducee /ˈsædjusi:/ *n.* a member of a Jewish sect at the time of Christ emphasizing traditional law and denying the resurrection of the dead. [OE ult. f. Heb., prob. = descendant of Zadok (2 Sam. 8: 17)]

sadhu /ˈsɑ:du:/ *n.* a Hindu or Jain ascetic and religious mendicant. [Skr., = holy man]

sadism /ˈseɪdɪz(ə)m/ *n.* enjoyment of cruelty to others; a sexual perversion characterized by this. —**sadist** *n.*, **sadistic** /səˈdɪstɪk/ *adj.*, **sadistically** *adv.* [f. F f. 'Marquis' de *Sade*, French author (d. 1814)]

s.a.e. *abbr.* stamped addressed envelope.

safari /səˈfɑ:rɪ/ *n.* an overland expedition, especially in Africa. —**safari park,** an area where wild animals are kept in the open for viewing from vehicles. [Swahili, f. Arab. *safara* travel]

safe *adj.* **1** free from risk or danger; not dangerous. **2** providing security or protection. —*n.* **1** a strong lockable cupboard or cabinet for valuables. **2** a ventilated cabinet for storing food. —**on the safe side,** having a margin of security against risks. **safe conduct,** the right to pass through a district on a particular occasion without risk of arrest or harm; a document granting this. **safe deposit,** a building containing safes and strong-rooms that are let separately. **safe period,** the time during and near a menstrual period when sexual intercourse is least likely to result in conception. —**safely** *adv.*, **safeness** *n.* [f. AF *saf* f. L *salvus* uninjured]

safeguard *n.* a stipulation, circumstance, etc., that tends to prevent something undesirable. —*v.t.* to protect by a stipulation or precaution.

safety *n.* being safe, freedom from risk or danger. —**safety-belt** *n.* a strap securing a person safely, especially a seat-belt. **safety-catch** *n.* a device for locking a gun-trigger or preventing the accidental or dangerous operation of machinery. **safety curtain,** a fireproof curtain in a theatre to divide the auditorium from the stage in case of fire etc. **safety lamp,** a miner's lamp so protected as not to ignite firedamp. **safety match,** a match that ignites only on a specially prepared surface. **safety net,** a net placed to catch an acrobat etc. in case of a fall from a height. **safety-pin** *n.* see separate entry. **safety razor,** one with a guard to prevent the blade cutting the skin. Its invention dates from the mid-19th c. **safety valve,** a valve that opens automatically to relieve excessive pressure in a boiler etc.; a means of harmlessly releasing excitement, anger, etc. [f. OF f. L (as SAFE)]

safety-pin *n.* a pin with a point that is bent back to the head and can be held in a guard so that the user may not be pricked nor the pin come out unintentionally.

saffron /ˈsæfrən/ *n.* the orange-coloured stigmas of a crocus (*Crocus sativus*) used for colouring and flavouring; the colour of this. —*adj.* saffron-coloured. [f. OF f. Arab.]

sag *v.i.* (**-gg-**) **1** to hang or subside loosely and unevenly; to sink or curve downwards in the middle under weight or pressure. **2** (of prices) to fall. —*n.* the state or amount of sagging. [f. MLG or Du., = subside]

saga /ˈsɑːgə/ *n.* a long story of heroic achievement, especially of medieval tale of Scandinavian heroes; a series of connected books telling the story of a family etc. [ON, = narrative (rel. to SAW²)]

sagacious /səˈgeɪʃəs/ *adj.* having or showing insight or good judgement. —**sagaciously** *adv.*, **sagacity** /-ˈgæsɪtɪ/ *n.* [f. L *sagax*]

sage¹ *n.* a kitchen herb (*Salvia officinalis*) with greyish-green leaves. —**sage-brush** *n.* the growth of plants (esp. of the genus *Artemisia*) in some sterile alkaline regions of the USA. [f. OF f. L *salvia* healing plant (as SAFE)]

sage² *adj.* profoundly wise, having wisdom gained from experience. —*n.* a profoundly wise man. —**sagely** *adv.* [f. OF f. L *sapere* be wise]

saggar /ˈsægə(r)/ *n.* a case of baked fireproof clay enclosing pottery while it is baked. [prob. contr. of SAFEGUARD]

Sagittarius /sædʒɪˈteərɪəs/ the ninth sign of the zodiac, the Archer. —**Sagittarian** *adj.* & *n.* [L, = archer]

sago /ˈseɪgəʊ/ *n.* (*pl.* **-os**) **1** a starch used in puddings etc. **2** a palm (esp. of the genus *Metroxylon*) with a pith yielding this. [f. Malay]

sahib /sɑːb, ˈsɑːɪb/ *n.* (*hist.*) a form of address to European men in India. [Urdu f. Arab., = lord]

said *past* & *p.p.* of SAY.

sail *n.* **1** a piece of canvas or other material extended on rigging to catch the wind and propel a vessel; a ship's sails collectively. **2** a voyage or excursion in a sailing-vessel. **3** a ship, especially as discerned from its sails. **4** the wind-catching apparatus on a windmill. —*v.t./i.* **1** to travel on water by the use of sails or engine-power. **2** to navigate (the sea, a ship, etc.); to set (a toy boat) afloat. **3** to start on a voyage. **4** to glide or move smoothly or in a stately manner. —**sail close to the wind,** to sail as nearly against the wind as possible; to come close to indecency or dishonesty. **sailing-boat** *or* **-ship** *n.* one moved by sails. **sail into,** to attack with blows or words. **under sail,** with the sails set. [OE]

sailboard *n.* a kind of surfboard with a sail, a windsurfer.

sailboarding *n.* the sport of riding on a sailboard, windsurfing. —**sailboarder** *n.*

sailcloth *n.* **1** canvas for sails. **2** a canvas-like dress material.

sailor *n.* **1** a seaman or mariner, especially one below the rank of officer. **2** a person considered as liable or not liable to sea-sickness (*bad* or *good sailor*). [var. of *sailer*, f. SAIL]

sailplane *n.* a glider designed for soaring.

sainfoin /ˈsænfɔɪn/ *n.* a pink-flowered fodder plant (*Onobrychis sativa*). [f. obs. F *saintfoin*, orig. = lucerne, f. L *sanctum foenum* holy hay]

saint /seɪnt, or often before a name sənt/ (abbr. **St** or **S.**, in *pl.* **Sts** or **SS**) *n.* **1** a holy person, one declared (in the Roman Catholic or Orthodox Church) worthy of veneration, whose intercession may be publicly sought. **2** the title of such a person or of one receiving veneration, or used in the name of a church not named after a saint (e.g. St Saviour's, St Cross). **3** each of the souls of the dead in paradise. **4** a member of the Christian Church or (in certain religious bodies) of one's own branch of it. **5** a very good, patient, or unselfish person. —*v.t.* to canonize; to call or regard as a saint; (in *p.p.*) sacred, worthy of sainthood. —**sainthood** *n.* [f. OF f. L *sanctus* holy (*sancire* consecrate)]

sake¹ *n.* **for the sake of, for (a person's) sake,** out of consideration for, in the interest of; in order to please, honour, get, or keep. **for heaven's** *or* **God's** etc. **sake,** an exclamation of dismay, annoyance, or supplication. [OE, = contention, charge]

sake² /ˈsɑːkɪ/ *n.* a Japanese fermented liquor made from rice. [Jap.]

salaam /səˈlɑːm/ *n.* **1** an oriental salutation 'Peace'; an Indian obeisance with or without this, a bow with the right palm on the forehead. **2** (in *pl.*) respectful compliments. —*v.t./i.* to make a salaam (to). [f. Arab.]

salacious /səˈleɪʃəs/ *adj.* indecently erotic, lewd. —**salaciously** *adv.*, **salaciousness** *n.*, **salacity** /-ˈlæsɪtɪ/ *n.* [f. L *salax* (*salire* leap)]

salad /ˈsæləd/ *n.* a mixture of raw or cold vegetables, herbs, etc., usually seasoned with oil, vinegar, etc., and often eaten with or including cold meat, cheese, etc.; a vegetable or herb suitable for eating raw. —**salad days,** one's period of youthful inexperience. **salad-dressing** *n.* a mixture of oil, vinegar, etc., used with a salad. [f. OF f. Prov., ult. f. L *sal* salt]

salamander /sæləˈmændə(r)/ *n.* **1** (in

mythology) a lizard-like animal living in fire. **2** a kind of tailed amphibian of the family Salamandridae. [f. OF f. L f. Gk]

salami /səˈlɑːmɪ/ *n.* a highly seasoned sausage, originally from Italy. [It., ult. f. L *sal* salt]

sal ammoniac /sæl əˈməʊnɪæk/ ammonium chloride, a hard white crystalline salt, said to have been made from camels' dung near the temple of Jupiter Ammon. [f. L (*sal* salt, *ammoniacus* of Jupiter Ammon)]

salary /ˈsælərɪ/ *n.* a fixed regular payment, usually calculated on an annual basis and paid monthly, made by an employer to an employee. —*v.t.* (esp. in *p.p.*) to pay a salary to. [f. AF f. L *salarium* orig. soldier's salt-money (*sal* salt)]

sale *n.* **1** selling, being sold. **2** an instance of this; the amount sold. **3** an event at which goods are sold, especially by public auction or for charity. **4** disposal of a shop's stock at reduced prices, e.g. at the end of a season. **5** (in *pl.*) the department of a firm concerned with selling its products. —**for** *or* **on sale**, offered for purchase. **sale of work**, a sale for charity etc. of goods provided by supporters. **sale or return**, an arrangement by which a retailer can return to a wholesaler without payment any goods left unsold. **sale-room** *n.* a room in which auctions are held. **sales talk**, persuasive talk to promote the sale of goods or the acceptance of an idea etc. [OE f. ON (as SELL)]

saleable *adj.* fit for sale; likely to find a purchaser. —**saleability** /-ˈbɪlɪtɪ/ *n.* [f. prec.]

Salesian /səˈliːʒ(ə)n/ *adj.* of a Roman Catholic educational religious order named after St Francis de Sales (d. 1622), French bishop of Geneva. —*n.* a member of this order. [f. *Sales*]

salesman *n.* (*pl.* **-men**) a man employed to sell goods in a shop etc. or as a middleman between producer and retailer.

salesmanship *n.* skill in selling. [f. prec. + -SHIP]

salesperson *n.* a salesman or saleswoman.

saleswoman *n.* (*pl.* **-women**) a woman employed to sell goods.

salicylic acid /sælɪˈsɪlɪk/ a benzene derivative used as an antiseptic and pain-killing substance. [f. F *salicyle* f. L *salix* willow]

salient /ˈseɪlɪənt/ *adj.* prominent, conspicuous; standing or pointing outwards. —*n.* a salient angle; a bulge in the line of a military attack or defence. [f. L *salire* leap]

saline /ˈseɪlaɪn/ *adj.* of salt or salts; containing or tasting of salt(s). —*n.* **1** a saline substance, especially a medicine. **2** a salt lake, spring, etc. —**salinity** /səˈlɪnɪtɪ/ *n.* [f. L *salinus* (*sal* salt)]

saliva /səˈlaɪvə/ *n.* the colourless liquid produced by glands in the mouth, assisting in chewing and digestion. —**salivary** *adj.* [L]

salivate /ˈsælɪveɪt/ *v.i.* to secrete or discharge saliva, especially in excess. —**salivation** /-ˈveɪʃ(ə)n/ *n.* [f. L *salivare* (as prec.)]

sallow[1] /ˈsæləʊ/ *adj.* (esp. of the complexion) of sickly yellow or pale brown. —*v.t./i.* to make or become sallow. —**sallowness** *n.* [OE, = dusky]

sallow[2] /ˈsæləʊ/ *n.* a low-growing willow; a shoot or the wood of this. [OE]

sally /ˈsælɪ/ *n.* **1** a rush from a besieged place upon the besiegers, a sortie. **2** an excursion. **3** a lively or witty remark. —*v.i.* to make a sally. —**sally forth** *or* **out**, to go on a journey or walk etc. [f. F *saillie* f. L (as SALIENT)]

Sally Lunn /sælɪ ˈlʌn/ a kind of sweet light teacake served hot. [perh. f. name of girl hawking them at Bath *c.*1800]

salmagundi /sælməˈgʌndɪ/ *n.* **1** a dish of chopped meat, anchovies, eggs, onions, etc., and seasoning. **2** a miscellaneous collection. [f. F *salmigondis*, orig. unkn.]

salmi /ˈsælmɪ/ *n.* a ragout or casserole, especially of game-birds. [F, abbr. f. as prec.]

salmon /ˈsæmən/ *n.* (*pl.* usu. same) **1** a large fish of the genus *Salmo* etc. with orange-pink flesh, highly valued for food and sport. **2** the colour of its flesh. —*adj.* orangepink. —**salmon-trout** *n.* a sea trout. [f. AF f. L *salmo*]

salmonella /sælməˈnelə/ *n.* a bacterium of the genus *Salmonella*, especially of a species causing food poisoning. [f. D. E. *Salmon*, American veterinary surgeon (d. 1914)]

salon /ˈsælɒn/ *n.* **1** the reception-room of a large continental house. **2** a meeting there of eminent people. **3** a room or establishment where a hairdresser or couturier etc. receives clients. [F f. It. *salone* (*sala* hall)]

saloon /səˈluːn/ *n.* **1** a large public room for a specified purpose. **2** a public room on a ship. **3** (*US*) a place where alcoholic drinks may be bought and drunk. **4** a saloon car. —**saloon-bar** *n.* a first-class bar in a public house. **saloon car**, a motor car with a closed body for driver and passengers. [f. F *salon* (as prec.)]

salsify /ˈsælsɪfɪ/ *n.* a plant (*Tragopogon porrifolius*) with a long fleshy root cooked as a vegetable. [f. F f. It. *salsefica*, orig. unkn.]

SALT /sɒlt/ *abbr.* Strategic Arms Limitation Talks, involving especially the USA and the Soviet Union, aimed at the limitation or reduction of nuclear armaments. (The last element is also understood as *Treaty*.)

salt /sɔlt, sɒlt/ *n.* **1** (also **common salt**) sodium chloride, a substance found in sea-water and obtained in crystalline forms by mining or by evaporation of sea-water etc., and used especially to season or preserve food. **2** a chemical compound of basic and acid radicals, the acid with the whole or part of its hydrogen replaced by a metal or metal-like radical. **3** (often in *pl.*) a substance resembling common salt in taste, form, etc.; (in *pl.*) such a substance used as a laxative. **4** piquancy, pungency, wit. **5** a salt-cellar. **6** (also **old salt**) an experienced sailor. —*adj.* containing or tasting of salt; cured, preserved, or seasoned with salt. —*v.t.* **1** to cure, preserve, or season with salt or brine. **2** to sprinkle with salt. **3** (*slang*) to make (a mine) appear rich by fraudulently inserting precious metal into it before it is viewed (also *fig.*); to make fraudulent entries in (accounts etc.). —**salt away** *or* **down,** (*colloq.*) to save or put aside for the future. **salt-cellar** *n.* a container for salt at table. **salt-lick** *n.* a place where animals lick earth impregnated with salt. **salt-mine** *n.* a mine yielding rock-salt; a place of unremitting toil. **the salt of the earth,** the finest people, those who keep society wholesome. **salt-pan** *n.* a hollow near the sea where salt is got by evaporation. **take with a grain** *or* **pinch of salt,** to regard sceptically. **worth one's salt,** deserving one's position, competent. [OE]

salting /ˈsɔltɪŋ, ˈsɒ-/ *n.* a marsh overflowed by the sea. [f. SALT]

saltire /ˈsæltaɪə(r)/ *n.* an X-shaped cross; this dividing a shield etc. into four sections. [f. OF *sau(l)toir* stirrup-cord, stile, f. L (*saltare* leap)]

saltpetre /sɒltˈpiːtə(r)/ *n.* potassium nitrate, a white crystalline salty substance used as a constituent of gunpowder, in preserving meat, and medicinally. [f. OF f. L *salpetra*, prob. = salt of the rock]

salty /ˈsɔltɪ, ˈsɒ-/ *adj.* **1** containing or tasting of salt. **2** piquant, pungent. —**saltiness** *n.* [f. SALT]

salubrious /səˈluːbrɪəs/ *adj.* health-giving, healthy. —**salubrity** *n.* [f. L *salubris* (*salus* health)]

saluki /səˈluːkɪ/ *n.* a tall slender silky-coated dog. [f. Arab.]

salutary /ˈsæljʊtərɪ/ *adj.* producing good effects. —**salutarily** *adv.* [f. F or L *salutaris* (*salus* health)]

salutation /sæljuːˈteɪʃ(ə)n/ *n.* a sign or expression of greeting or respect; the use of these. —**salutatory** /səˈljuːtətərɪ/ *adj.* [as foll.]

salute /səˈluːt, -ˈljuːt/ *n.* **1** a gesture of respect or courteous recognition. **2** a prescribed military movement of the hand or the firing of a gun or guns etc. as a formal or ceremonial sign of respect. —*v.t.* **1** to greet with a polite gesture. **2** to perform a military salute; to greet with this. **3** to express respect for, to commend. [f. OF or L *salutare* (*salus* health)]

salvage /ˈsælvɪdʒ/ *n.* **1** the rescue of property from loss at sea or from fire etc.; payment made or due for this; property so saved. **2** the saving and utilization of waste materials; materials salvaged. —*v.t.* **1** to save from a wreck etc. **2** to make salvage of. [F f. L *salvagium* (*salvare* save)]

salvation /sælˈveɪʃ(ə)n/ *n.* **1** the saving of the soul from sin and its consequences; the state of being saved. **2** preservation from loss or calamity; a thing that preserves from these. —**Salvation Army** an international organization for evangelistic and social work. —**salvationist** *n.* [f. OF f. L (*salvare* save)]

salve[1] *n.* **1** a healing ointment. **2** a thing that soothes or consoles. —*v.t.* to soothe. [OE]

salve[2] *v.t.* to save from a wreck or fire etc. —**salvor** *n.* [back-formation f. SALVAGE]

salver /ˈsælvə(r)/ *n.* a tray, usually metal, on which letters or refreshments etc. are handed. [f. F f. Sp. *salva* assaying of food (as SAVE)]

salvia /ˈsælvɪə/ *n.* a garden plant of the genus *Salvia*, especially a species with red flowers (*S. splendens*). [L, = SAGE[1]]

salvo /ˈsælvəʊ/ *n.* (*pl.* **-oes**) **1** a simultaneous discharge of guns or bombs. **2** a round of applause. [f. F f. It. *salva* salutation (as SAVE)]

sal volatile /sæl vəˈlætɪlɪ/ a solution of ammonium carbonate, used as a restorative in fainting etc. [L, = volatile salt]

Samaritan[1] /səˈmærɪt(ə)n/ *n.* **1** (also **good Samaritan**) a person who readily gives help to one in distress who has no claim upon him (with ref. to Luke 10: 30 ff.). **2** a member of an organization that gives comfort and help (esp. through the telephone service) to people in destress. [f. L f. Gk (*Samareia* Samaria)]

samarium /səˈmeərɪəm/ *n.* a metallic element of the lanthanide series, symbol Sm, atomic number 62. [f. *samarskite*, mineral in which its spectrum was first observed, f. *Samarski*, 19th-c. Russian official]

samba /ˈsæmbə/ *n.* a ballroom dance of Brazilian origin; the music for this. —*v.i.* to dance the samba. [Port., of Afr. orig.]

same *adj.* **1** being of one kind, not different; unchanged, unvarying. **2** just mentioned. —*pron.* (**the same**) the same person or thing; the person or thing just mentioned. —*adv.* (**the same**) in the same way, similarly. —**all** *or* **just the same,** nevertheless. **be all** *or* **just the same,** to make no difference (to a person). **same here,** (*colloq.*) the same applies to me, I agree. —**sameness** *n.* [f. ON]

samizdat /ˈsæmɪzdæt/ *n.* a system of clandestine publication of banned literature in the USSR. [Russ., = self-publishing (i.e. illegal)]

samovar /ˈsæməvɑː(r)/ *n.* a Russian tea-urn. [Russ., = self-boiler]

sampan /ˈsæmpæn/ *n.* a small boat used on the

rivers and coasts of China, Japan, and neighbouring islands, rowed with a scull (or two sculls) from the stern and usually having a sail of matting and an awning. [f. Chin. *san ban* (*san* three, *ban* board)]

samphire /ˈsæmfaɪə(r)/ *n.* a coastal plant (*Crithmum maritimum*) used in pickles. [f. F (*herbe de*) *Saint Pierre*, = St Peter's herb]

sample /ˈsɑːmp(ə)l/ *n.* a small separated part or quantity intended to show what the whole is like; a specimen; an illustrative or typical example. —*v.t.* to take or give a sample of; to try the qualities of; to get representative experience of. [f. AF *assample*, = EXAMPLE]

sampler *n.* a piece of embroidery worked in various stitches as a specimen of proficiency. [f. OF *essamplaire* (as EXEMPLAR)]

samurai /ˈsæmʊraɪ/ *n.* (*pl.* same) **1** a Japanese army officer. **2** (*hist.*) a member of the feudal warrior class of Japan which was bound by the code of bushido, emphasizing qualities of loyalty, bravery, and endurance. The samurai dominated Japanese society until the demise of the feudal order in the 19th c. [Jap.]

sanatorium /sænəˈtɔːrɪəm/ *n.* (*pl.* **-ums**) **1** an establishment for treating chronic diseases (e.g. tuberculosis) or convalescents. **2** accommodation for sick persons in a school etc. [f. L (*sanare* heal)]

sanctify /ˈsæŋktɪfaɪ/ *v.t.* **1** to make holy or sacred. **2** to justify. —**sanctification** /-fɪˈkeɪʃ(ə)n/ *n.* [f. OF f. L (*sanctus* holy)]

sanctimonious /sæŋktɪˈməʊnɪəs/ *adj.* making a show of righteousness or piety. —**sanctimoniously** *adv.*, **sanctimoniousness** *n.* [f. L *sanctimonia* sanctity (as SAINT)]

sanction /ˈsæŋkʃ(ə)n/ *n.* **1** permission or approval for an action or behaviour etc. **2** confirmation or ratification of a law etc. **3** a penalty for disobeying a law or a reward for obeying it; (esp. in *pl.*) action taken by a country etc. to penalize and coerce a country or organization that is considered to have violated a law, code of practice, or basic human rights. —*v.t.* **1** to give sanction or approval to, to authorize. **2** to ratify. **3** to attach a penalty or reward to (a law). [F f. L (*sancire* make holy)]

sanctity /ˈsæŋktɪtɪ/ *n.* holiness, sacredness. [f. OF or L *sanctitas* (as SAINT)]

sanctuary /ˈsæŋktjʊərɪ/ *n.* **1** a sacred place. **2** the holiest part of a temple; the part of the chancel containing the altar. **3** a place where birds or wild animals etc. are protected and encouraged to breed. **4** (esp. *hist.*) a sacred place where a fugitive from the law, or a debtor, was secured by medieval Church law against arrest or violence; a place in which similar immunity was established by custom or law. **5** a place of refuge. [f. AF f. L (as SAINT)]

sanctum /ˈsæŋktəm/ *n.* **1** a holy place. **2** a person's private room or study. [L (as SAINT)]

Sanctus /ˈsæŋktəs/ *n.* the hymn (from Isa. 6: 3) beginning 'Sanctus, sanctus, sanctus' or 'Holy, holy, holy', forming the conclusion of the Eucharistic preface; the music for this. —**Sanctus bell,** a bell in the turret at the junction of nave and chancel, or a handbell, rung at the sanctus or at the elevation of the host. [L, = holy]

sand *n.* the loose granular substance resulting from the wearing down of siliceous and other rocks and found on the sea-shore, river-beds, deserts, etc.; (in *pl.*) grains of sand, an expanse of sand, a sandbank. —*v.t.* **1** to smooth or polish with sandpaper. **2** to sprinkle, cover, or treat with sand. —**sand-blast** *n.* a jet of sand driven by compressed air or steam for cleaning a glass or stone etc. surface; (*v.t.*) to treat with this. **sand-castle** *n.* a structure of sand made by or for a child on the sea-shore. **sand-dune** *or* **-hill** *n.* a dune. **sand-glass** *n.* a wasp-waisted reversible glass with two bulbs containing enough sand to take a definite time in passing from the upper to the lower bulb. **sand-martin** *n.* a bird (*Riparia riparia*) nesting in sandy banks. **sand-pit** *n.* a pit etc. containing sand for children to play in. **sand-wasp** *n.* a wasp of the family Sphecidae that makes its nest in sand. **sand-yacht** *n.* a yachtlike vehicle on wheels for use on sand. [OE]

sandal[1] /sænd(ə)l/ *n.* a shoe with an open-work upper or no upper, usually fastened with straps. [f. L f. Gk *sandalion*]

sandal[2] /ˈsænd(ə)l/ *n.* (in full **sandal-wood**) a scented wood; a tree with this, especially one of the genus *Santalum*. [f. L ult. f. Skr.]

sandbag *n.* a bag filled with sand, used to protect a wall or building (e.g. in war) or to make temporary defences, or as a ruffian's weapon. —*v.t.* (**-gg-**) **1** to protect with sandbags. **2** to hit with a sandbag.

sandbank *n.* a deposit of sand forming a shallow place in a sea or river.

sander *n.* a device for sanding things. [f. SAND]

sandman *n.* an imaginary person causing sleepiness in children, the personification of tiredness causing children's eyes to smart towards bedtime.

sandpaper *n.* paper with a coating of sand or other abrasive for smoothing or polishing things. —*v.t.* to smooth or polish with sandpaper.

sandpiper *n.* a bird of the family Scolopacidae inhabiting wet sandy places.

sandstone *n.* a sedimentary rock of compressed sand.

sandstorm *n.* a storm with clouds of sand raised by the wind.

sandwich /ˈsænwɪdʒ/ *n.* **1** two or more slices of bread with a filling between. **2** a cake of two or more layers with jam or cream etc. between. —*v.t.* to put (a thing, statement, etc.) between two others of a different kind. —**sandwich-board** *n.* each of the two advertisement boards carried by a sandwich-man. **sandwich course,** a course of training with alternate periods of practical and theoretical work. **sandwich-man** *n.* a man walking in the street with advertisement boards hung one before and one behind him. [f. 4th Earl of *Sandwich* (d. 1792), said to have eaten only slices of bread and meat while gaming for 24 hours]

sandy *adj.* **1** having much sand. **2** sand-coloured. **3** (of hair) yellowish-red; (of a person) having hair of this colour. —**sandiness** *n.* [f. SAND]

sane *adj.* **1** having a sound mind, not mad. **2** showing good judgement, sensible and practical. —**sanely** *adv.* [f. L *sanus* healthy]

sang *past* of SING.

sang-froid /sɑ̃ˈfrwɑ:/ *n.* calmness in danger or difficulty. [F, = cold blood]

sangha /ˈsɑ:ŋə/ *n.* the Buddhist monastic order, including monks, nuns, and novices. [f. Skr., = community (*sam* together, *lan* come in contact)]

sangria /sæŋˈgri:ə/ *n.* a Spanish drink of red wine with lemonade etc. [Sp., = bleeding]

sanguinary /ˈsæŋgwɪnərɪ/ *adj.* accompanied by or delighting in bloodshed; bloody, bloodthirsty. [f. L (*sanguis* blood)]

sanguine /ˈsæŋgwɪn/ *adj.* **1** optimistic. **2** (of the complexion) bright and florid. [f. OF f. L *sanguineus* (as prec.)]

Sanhedrin /ˈsænɪdrɪn/ *n.* the supreme Jewish council and highest court of justice at Jerusalem in New Testament times. It pronounced sentence of death on Christ. [f. Heb. f. Gk *sunedrion* (*sun* with, *hedra* seat)]

sanitarium /sænɪˈteərɪəm/ *n.* (*US*) a sanatorium. [as foll.]

sanitary /ˈsænɪtərɪ/ *adj.* **1** of or assisting hygiene, hygienic. **2** of sanitation. —**sanitary towel,** an absorbent pad used during menstruation. [f. F f. L *sanitas* (as SANITY)]

sanitation /sænɪˈteɪʃ(ə)n/ *n.* sanitary conditions, the maintenance or improvement of these; the disposal of sewage and refuse etc. [irreg. f. prec.]

sanitize /ˈsænɪtaɪz/ *v.t.* to make sanitary. [f. SANITARY]

sanity /ˈsænɪtɪ/ *n.* being sane. [f. L *sanitas* (as SANE)]

sank *past* of SINK.

sanserif /sænˈserɪf/ *adj.* without serifs. —*n.* a form of typeface without serifs. [app. f. F *sans* without, SERIF]

Sanskrit /ˈsænskrɪt/ *n.* the ancient language of Hindus in India, belonging to a branch of the Indo-European family of languages. —*adj.* of or in Sanskrit. —**Sanskritic** /-ˈkrɪtɪk/ *adj.* [f. Skr., = composed (*sam* together, *kr* make)]

sap[1] *n.* **1** the vital juice circulating in plants, carrying nutriment to all parts. **2** vigour, vitality. **3** sapwood. **4** (*slang*) a foolish person. —*v.t.* (**-pp-**) **1** to drain or dry (wood) of sap. **2** to exhaust the vigour of, to weaken. [OE]

sap[2] *n.* **1** a tunnel or trench to conceal assailants' approach to a fortified place. **2** the insidious undermining of belief etc. —*v.t./i.* (**-pp-**) **1** to dig saps; to undermine (a wall etc.). **2** to destroy insidiously, to weaken. [f. F or It. *zappa* spade, spadework, prob. of Arab. orig.]

sapid /ˈsæpɪd/ *adj.* **1** savoury, palatable. **2** (of writings etc.) not insipid or vapid. —**sapidity** /səˈpɪdɪtɪ/ *n.* [f. L *sapidus* (*sapere* have flavour)]

sapient /ˈseɪpɪənt/ *adj.* (*literary*) wise, pretending to be wise. —**sapience** *n.* [f. OF or L *sapiens* (*sapere* be wise)]

sapling *n.* a young tree. [f. SAP[1]]

sapper *n.* **1** one who digs saps. **2** a soldier of the Royal Engineers (esp. as the official term for a private). [f. SAP[2]]

Sapphic /ˈsæfɪk/ *adj.* of the Greek poetess Sappho (7th c. BC) or her poetry, esp. (of a stanza or verse) in four-line form with a short fourth line. [f. F f. L f. Gk, = of Sappho]

sapphire /ˈsæfaɪə(r)/ *n.* **1** a transparent blue precious stone. **2** its bright blue colour. —*adj.* of sapphire blue. [f. OF f. L f. Gk, = lapis lazuli]

sappy *adj.* **1** full of sap. **2** young and vigorous. [f. SAP[1]]

saprophyte /ˈsæprəfait/ *n.* a vegetable organism living on dead organic matter. —**saprophytic** /-ˈfɪtɪk/ *adj.* [f. Gk *sapros* putrid + *phuō* grow]

sapwood *n.* the soft outer layers of recently formed wood between the heartwood and the bark.

saraband /ˈsærəbænd/ *n.* a slow Spanish dance; the music for this. [f. F f. Sp. & It. *zarabanda*]

Saracen /ˈsærəs(ə)n/ *n.* an Arab or Muslim of the time of the Crusades. [f. OF, perh. ult. f. Arab., = eastern]

sarcasm /ˈsɑ:kæz(ə)m/ *n.* an ironical remark or comment; the use of such remarks. [f. F or L f. Gk (*sarkazō* speak bitterly; orig. = tear flesh, f. *sarx* flesh)]

sarcastic /sɑ:ˈkæstɪk/ *adj.* using or showing sarcasm. —**sarcastically** *adv.* [as prec.]

sarcoma /sɑ:ˈkəʊmə/ *n.* (*pl.* **-mata**) a malignant tumour of connective tissue. [f. Gk (*sarkoō* become fleshy f. *sarx* flesh)]

sarcophagus /sɑːˈkɒfəgəs/ *n.* (*pl.* **-gi** /-gaɪ) a stone coffin. [L f. Gk, = flesh-consuming (*sarx* flesh, *-phagos* eating)]

sardine /sɑːˈdiːn/ *n.* a young pilchard or similar small fish, often tinned tightly packed in oil. —**like sardines,** crowded close together. [f. OF f. L *sardina*, perh. f. Gk *Sardô* Sardinia]

sardonic /sɑːˈdɒnɪk/ *adj.* humorous in a grim or sarcastic way; full of bitter mockery; cynical. —**sardonically** *adv.* [f. F f. L f. Gk *Sardonios* (= Sardinian), substituted for Homeric *sardanios* (epithet of bitter or scornful laughter) because of belief that eating a Sardinian plant could result in convulsive laughter ending in death]

sardonyx /ˈsɑːdənɪks/ *n.* an onyx in which white layers alternate with yellow or orange ones. [f. L f. Gk (*sardios* a precious stone, as ONYX)]

sargasso /sɑːˈgæsəʊ/ *n.* (*pl.* **-os**) a seaweed of the genus *Sargassum*, with berry-like air-vessels, found floating in island-like masses. [f. Port.; orig. unkn.]

sarge *n.* (*slang*) a sergeant. [abbr.]

sari /ˈsɑːrɪ/ *n.* a length of material draped around the body, worn as the main garment by Hindu women. [f. Hindi]

sarong /səˈrɒŋ/ *n.* a Malay and Javanese garment worn by both sexes, consisting of a long strip of cloth tucked round the waist or under the armpits. [Malay, lit. = sheath]

sarsaparilla /sɑːsəpəˈrɪlə/ *n.* a tropical American smilax especially *Smilax ornata*; its dried roots; a tonic made from these. [f. Sp. *zarzaparilla* (*zarza* bramble)]

sarsen /ˈsɑːs(ə)n/ *n.* a sandstone etc. boulder, a relict carried by ice in the glacial period. [prob. var. of SARACEN]

sarsenet /ˈsɑːsnɪt/ *n.* a soft silk fabric used especially as a lining. [f. AF *sarzinett* (perh. *sarzin* Saracen)]

sartorial /sɑːˈtɔːrɪ(ə)l/ *adj.* of clothes or tailoring. —**sartorially** *adv.* [f. L *sartor* tailor]

sash[1] *n.* a long strip or loop of cloth etc. worn over one shoulder or round the waist as part of a uniform or insignia, or (by a woman or child) round the waist for ornament. [f. Arab., = muslin, turban]

sash[2] *n.* a frame holding the glass in a sash-window. —**sash cord,** a strong cord attaching sash-weights to a sash. **sash-weight** *n.* a weight attached to each end of a sash to balance it at any height. **sash-window** *n.* a window usually made to slide up and down in grooves. [f. *sashes*, corrupt. of CHASSIS]

sassafras /ˈsæsəfræs/ *n.* **1** a small tree of the genus *Sassafras*, especially a North American species yielding bark that is used medicinally and in perfumes. **2** this bark. [f. Sp. or Port.; orig. unkn.]

Sassenach /ˈsæsənæx, -æk/ *n.* (*Sc.* & *Ir.*, usu. *derog.*) an Englishman. [f. Gael. or Ir. f. L (as SAXON)]

sat *past* & *p.p.* of SIT.

Sat. *abbr.* Saturday.

Satan /ˈseɪt(ə)n/ *n.* the Devil. [OE, ult. f. Heb. = adversary]

satanic /səˈtænɪk/ *adj.* of or like Satan; devilish, evil. —**satanically** *adv.* [f. prec.]

Satanism /ˈseɪtənɪz(ə)m/ *n.* **1** the worship of Satan, with a travesty of Christian forms. **2** the pursuit of evil. —**Satanist** *n.* [f. SATAN]

satchel /ˈsætʃ(ə)l/ *n.* a small bag usually with a shoulder-strap, especially for carrying school-books. [f. OF f. L *saccellus* (as SACK[1])]

sate *v.t.* to satiate. [prob. f. dial. *sade* (as SAD)]

sateen /sæˈtiːn/ *n.* a glossy cotton fabric woven like satin. [f. *satin* after *velveteen*]

satellite /ˈsætəlaɪt/ *n.* **1** a heavenly body revolving round a planet. **2** an artificial body placed in orbit round the Earth or other planet for purposes of observation, research, navigation or communications. **3** a follower, a hanger-on; a member of a retinue. **4** a small country etc. controlled by or dependent on another and following its lead. [F or f. L *satelles* guard]

satiable /ˈseɪʃəb(ə)l/ *adj.* that may be satiated. [f. foll.]

satiate /ˈseɪʃɪeɪt/ *v.t.* to gratify fully, to surfeit. —**satiation** /-ˈeɪʃ(ə)n/ *n.* [f. L *satiare* (*satis* enough)]

satiety /səˈtaɪətɪ/ *n.* the state or feeling of being satiated. [as SATIATE]

satin /ˈsætɪn/ *n.* a silky fabric so woven that it has a glossy surface on one side. —*adj.* smooth as satin. —*v.t.* to give a glossy surface to (paper). —**satiny** *adj.* [f. OF f. Arab., = of Tseutung in China]

satinwood *n.* a kind of choice glossy timber of any of various trees.

satire /ˈsætaɪə(r)/ *n.* **1** the use of ridicule, irony, or sarcasm to expose folly or vice etc. **2** a work or composition using satire. —**satirical** /səˈtɪrɪk(ə)l/ *adj.*, **satirically** *adv.* [F or f. L, orig. = medley)]

satirist /ˈsætɪrɪst/ *n.* a writer or performer of satires. [f. prec.]

satirize /ˈsætɪraɪz/ *v.t.* to attack with satire; to describe satirically. [f. F (as SATIRE)]

satisfaction /sætɪsˈfækʃ(ə)n/ *n.* **1** satisfying, being satisfied. **2** a thing that satisfies a desire or gratifies a feeling. **3** a thing that settles an obligation or debt, or compensates for an injury or loss. [as SATISFY]

satisfactory /sætɪsˈfæktərɪ/ *adj.* satisfying expectations or needs; adequate. —**satisfactorily** *adv.*, **satisfactoriness** *n.* [f. F or L (as foll.)]

satisfy /ˈsætɪsfaɪ/ *v.t./i.* **1** to give (a person) what he wants, demands, or needs; to make pleased or contented; to be adequate. **2** to deal adequately with (an obligation, debt, etc.); to pay (a creditor). **3** to put an end to (a demand or craving etc.) by giving what is required. **4** to provide with sufficient information or proof; to convince. [f. OF f. L *satisfacere* (*satis* enough, *facere* make)]

satrap /ˈsætræp/ *n.* a provincial governor in the ancient Persian empire. [f. OF or L f. Gk f. OPers., = country-protector]

satsuma /sætˈsu:mə/ *n.* a kind of mandarin orange originally grown in Japan. [f. *Satsuma*, province of Japan]

saturate /ˈsætʃəreɪt, -tjʊr-/ *v.t.* **1** to make thoroughly wet, to soak. **2** to cause to absorb or accept as much as possible. [f. L *saturare* (*satur* full)]

saturation /sætʃəˈreɪʃ(ə)n, -tjʊr-/ *n.* the act or result of being saturated. —**saturation point,** the point beyond which no more can be absorbed or accepted. [f. prec.]

Saturday /ˈsætədeɪ, -dɪ/ *n.* the day of the week following Friday. —*adv.* (*colloq.*) on Saturday. [OE, = day of Saturn]

Saturnalia /sætəˈneɪlɪə/ *n.* **1** the ancient Roman festival of Saturn, observed as a time of unrestrained merry-making. **2 saturnalia,** a scene or time of wild revelry or tumult. [f. prec.]

saturnine /ˈsætənaɪn/ *adj.* of gloomy forbidding temperament or appearance. [f. OF f. L (as prec.)]

satyr /ˈsætə(r)/ *n.* **1** (*Gk myth.*) a half-human half-animal woodland spirit. **2** a grossly lustful man. [f. OF or L f. Gk]

sauce /sɔ:s/ *n.* **1** a liquid or soft preparation served with food to add flavour or richness. **2** impudence. —*v.t.* (*colloq.*) to be impudent to (a person). [f. OF ult. f. L *salsus* salted]

saucepan *n.* a metal cooking-vessel, usually round and with a long handle at the side, for use on top of a cooker etc.

saucer /ˈsɔ:sə(r)/ *n.* **1** a small shallow dish, especially for standing a cup on. **2** a thing of this shape. [f. OF (as SAUCE)]

saucy /ˈsɔ:sɪ/ *adj.* **1** impudent. **2** (*colloq.*) stylish, smart-looking. —**saucily** *adv.*, **sauciness** *n.* [f. SAUCE]

Saudi /ˈsaʊdɪ/ *n.* **1** a native or inhabitant of Saudi Arabia. **2** a member of the dynasty founded by Saud. —*adj.* of the Saudis or Saudi Arabia. [f. A. Ibn-*Saud* (d. 1953), Arab. king]

sauerkraut /ˈsaʊəkraʊt/ *n.* a German dish of chopped pickled cabbage. [G (*sauer* sour, *kraut* vegetable)]

sauna /ˈsɔ:nə/ *n.* a Finnish-style steam-bath; a building or room for this. [Finnish]

saunter /ˈsɔ:ntə(r)/ *v.i.* to walk in a leisurely way. —*n.* a leisurely walk or walking-pace. [orig. unkn.]

saurian /ˈsɔ:rɪən/ *n.* an animal of the lizard family. —*adj.* of or like a lizard. [f. Gk *saura* lizard]

sausage /ˈsɒsɪdʒ/ *n.* **1** minced meat seasoned and enclosed in a cylindrical case of thin membrane; a length of this. **2** a sausage-shaped object. —**not a sausage,** (*slang*) nothing at all. **sausage roll,** sausage meat baked in a cylindrical pastry-case. [f. OF *saussiche* f. L *salsicia* (as SAUCE)]

sauté /ˈsəʊteɪ/ *adj.* quickly and lightly fried in a little fat. —*n.* food cooked thus. —*v.t.* (*past & p.p.* **sautéd**) to cook thus. [F (*sauter* jump)]

Sauternes /səʊˈtɜ:n/ *n.* a sweet white French wine. [f. *Sauternes* district of SW France]

savage /ˈsævɪdʒ/ *adj.* **1** in a primitive or uncivilized state. **2** wild and fierce. **3** cruel and hostile. **4** (*colloq.*) very angry. —*n.* **1** a member of a savage tribe. **2** a brutal or barbarous person. —*v.t.* **1** (of an animal) to attack savagely, to maul. **2** (of a critic etc.) to attack fiercely. —**savagely** *adv.*, **savageness** *n.* [f. OF *sauvage* f. L *silvaticus* (*silva* forest)]

savagery /ˈsævɪdʒrɪ/ *n.* savage behaviour or state. [f. prec.]

savannah /səˈvænə/ *n.* a grassy plain in a tropical or subtropical region, with few or no trees. [f. Sp. *zavana*, perh. of Carib. orig.]

savant /ˈsæv(ə)nt/ *n.* a learned person. [F (*savoir* know)]

save *v.t./i.* **1** to rescue, to keep from danger, harm, or capture. **2** to keep for future use or enjoyment; to put aside (money) for future use. **3** to make unnecessary (for); to avoid wasting. **4** to effect the spiritual salvation of. **5** to avoid losing (a match or game etc.); (in football etc.) to prevent an opponent from scoring. —*n.* (in football etc.) the act of preventing an opponent from scoring. —*prep.* except, but. —*conj.* (*archaic*) unless, except. —**save-as-you-earn** *n.* a method of saving by regular deduction from earnings. —**saver** *n.* [f. AF *sa(u)ver* f. L *salvare* (*salvus* safe)]

saveloy /ˈsævəlɔɪ/ *n.* a highly seasoned dried sausage. [corrupt. of F *cervelas* f. It. (*cervello* brain)]

saving /ˈseɪvɪŋ/ *n.* **1** the act of rescuing or keeping from danger etc. **2** (usu. in *pl.*) money put aside for future use. —*adj.* **1** that saves or redeems. **2** that makes economical use of (labour etc.). **3** (of a clause etc.) stipulating an exception or reservation. —*prep.* **1** except; with the exception of. **2** without offence to. —**savings bank,** a bank paying interest on small deposits. **savings certificate,** an interest-bearing document issued by the government for savers. [f. SAVE]

saviour /ˈseɪvjə(r)/ *n.* a person who saves others from harm or danger. —**our** *or* **the Saviour,** Christ. [f. OF f. L *salvator* (as SAVE)]

savoir faire /sævwɑːˈfeə(r)/ knowledge of how to behave in any situation that may arise, tact. [F, = know how to do]

savory /ˈseɪvərɪ/ *n.* an aromatic herb of the genus *Satureia*, used in cookery. [perh. OE f. L *satureia*]

savour /ˈseɪvə(r)/ *n.* **1** a characteristic taste or smell (*lit.* or *fig.*). **2** the power to arouse enjoyment. —*v.t./i.* **1** to taste or smell (a thing) with enjoyment or deliberation (*lit.* or *fig.*). **2** to have a certain taste or smell. **3** to give a specified impression. [f. OF f. L *sapor* (*sapere* taste)]

savoury /ˈseɪvərɪ/ *adj.* **1** having an appetizing taste or smell. **2** having a salt or piquant and not a sweet taste. —*n.* a savoury dish, especially at the end of a meal or as an appetizer. —**savouriness** *n.* [as prec.]

savoy /səˈvɔɪ/ *n.* a cabbage with wrinkled leaves. [f. prec.]

savvy /ˈsævɪ/ *v.t./i.* (*slang*) to know. —*n.* (*slang*) knowingness, understanding. —*adj.* (*US*) knowing, wise. [orig. Negro & Pidgin f. Sp. *sabe usted* you know]

saw[1] *n.* a tool with a toothed metal blade or edge for cutting wood, metal, stone, etc., by a to-and-fro or rotary motion. —*v.t./i.* (*p.p.* **sawn** or **sawed**) **1** to cut (wood etc.) with a saw; to make (boards etc.) with a saw. **2** to move to and fro, to divide (the air etc.) with the motion as of a saw or a person sawing. —**saw off,** to remove or reduce by sawing. **saw-tooth** or **-toothed** *adj.* shaped like the teeth of a saw, serrated. [OE]

saw[2] *n.* an old saying, a maxim. [OE (rel. to SAY)]

saw[3] *past* of SEE[1].

sawdust *n.* powdery fragments of wood produced in sawing.

sawfish *n.* a large sea-fish of the family Pristidae, having a blade-like snout with jagged edges that it uses as a weapon.

sawmill *n.* a mill for the mechanical sawing of wood.

sawn *p.p.* of SAW[1].

sawyer *n.* a workman who saws timber. [f. SAW[1]]

sax *n.* (*colloq.*) a saxophone. [abbr.]

saxe /sæks/ *n.* (also **saxe blue**) light blue with a greyish tinge. [F, = Saxony]

saxhorn /ˈsækshɔːn/ *n.* a brass wind instrument of the trumpet family made in several sizes, usually held with its mouth upwards. [f. A. *Sax*, Belgian instrument-maker (d. 1894) + HORN]

saxifrage /ˈsæksɪfrɪdʒ/ *n.* a rock plant of the genus *Saxifraga* with tufted foliage. [f. OF or L *saxifraga* (*saxum* rock, *frangere* break)]

Saxon /ˈsæks(ə)n/ *n.* **1** a member of a north German tribe, one branch of which, along with the Angles and the Jutes, conquered and colonized much of southern Britain in the 5th and 6th centuries. **2** (also **Old Saxon**) the language of this tribe. **3** Anglo-Saxon. **4** a native of modern Saxony. **5** the Germanic (as opposed to Latin or Romance) elements of English. —*adj.* of the Saxons or their language. [f. F f. L *Saxo*]

saxophone /ˈsæksəfəʊn/ *n.* a keyed brass wind instrument with a reed. —**saxophonist** /-ˈsɒfənɪst/ *n.* [f. *Sax* (see SAXHORN) + -PHONE]

say *v.t./i.* (*past & p.p.* **said** /sed/; 3 sing. pres. **says** /sez/) **1** to utter or recite in a speaking voice. **2** to state; to have a specified wording. **3** to put into words; to convey information; to indicate or show. **4** to give as an argument or excuse. **5** to give as an opinion or decision. **6** to suppose as a possibility; to select as an example etc.; to take (a specified amount etc.) as being near enough. —*n.* **1** what one wishes to say; an opportunity of saying this. **2** a share in a discussion or decision; the power of final decision. —**go without saying,** to be obvious. **I'll say,** (*colloq.*) yes indeed. **I say,** an exclamation drawing attention, opening a conversation, or expressing surprise. **say-so** *n.* the power of decision; mere assertion. **says you,** (*slang*) I disagree. **that is to say,** in other words. [OE]

SAYE *abbr.* save-as-you-earn.

saying *n.* a frequent or proverbial remark. [f. SAY]

Sb *symbol* antimony. [f. L *stibium*]

Sc *symbol* scandium.

sc. *abbr.* scilicet.

scab *n.* **1** a crust formed over a sore in healing. **2** a kind of skin-disease or plant-disease with scabs or scablike roughness. **3** (*derog.*) a blackleg in a strike. —*v.i.* (**-bb-**) **1** to form a scab; to heal over thus. **2** (*derog.*) act as a blackleg. —**scabby** *adj.* [rel. to SHABBY]

scabbard /ˈskæbəd/ *n.* the sheath of a sword etc. [f. AF]

scabies /ˈskeɪbiːz/ *n.* a contagious skin-disease causing itching [L (*scabere* scratch)]

scabious /ˈskeɪbɪəs/ *n.* a wild or garden flower of the genus *Scabiosa* (or allied genera). [f. L *scabiosa* (*herba*) plant curing itch (as prec.)]

scabrous /ˈskeɪbrəs/ *adj.* **1** (of the skin etc.) rough and scaly. **2** indecent. [f. F or L (*scaber* rough)]

scaffold /ˈskæf(ə)ld/ *n.* **1** a platform on which criminals are executed. **2** scaffolding. [f. OF; cf. CATAFALQUE]

scaffolding *n.* **1** a temporary structure of poles or tubes and planks providing platforms for building work; the materials for this. **2** any temporary framework. [f. prec.]

scalar /ˈskeɪlə(r)/ *adj.* (*Math.*) having magnitude but not direction. —*n.* a scalar quantity. [f. L (as SCALE[1])]

scald[1] /skɔld, skɒld/ *v.t.* **1** to injure or pain with hot liquid or vapour. **2** to heat (esp. milk or cream) to near boiling-point. **3** to cleanse (a vessel) with boiling water. —*n.* an injury to the skin by scalding. [f. AF f. L *excaldare* (*calidus* hot)]

scald[2] var. of SKALD.

scale[1] *n.* **1** a set of marks at fixed distances on a line for use in measuring etc.; a rule determining the intervals between these; a piece of metal etc. on which they are marked. **2** relative dimensions or extent; the ratio of reduction or enlargement in a map, drawing, etc. **3** a series of degrees; a ladder-like arrangement, a graded system. **4** (*Mus.*) a set of sounds belonging to a key, arranged in order of pitch. —*v.t.* **1** to climb (a wall, precipice, etc.) with a ladder or by clambering. **2** to represent in dimensions different from but proportional to the actual ones. —**in scale,** in proportion. **on a large** (*or* **small) scale,** to a large (or small) extent. **scale down** (*or* **up**), to make smaller (or larger) in proportion; to reduce (or increase) in size. **to scale,** with uniform reduction or enlargement. [f. L *scala* ladder]

scale[2] *n.* **1** any of the small thin horny overlapping plates protecting the skin of many fishes and reptiles. **2** a thin plate or flake resembling this. **3** an incrustation inside a boiler or kettle etc. in which hard water is regularly used; tartar on teeth. —*v.t./i.* **1** to remove scale(s) from. **2** to form or drop off in scales. —**scaly** *adj.* [f. OF *escale* (cf. foll.)]

scale[3] *n.* **1** the pan of a weighing-balance. **2** (in *pl.*) a weighing instrument; **the Scales,** the constellation or sign of the zodiac Libra. —*v.t.* to be found to weigh (a specified amount). —**pair of scales,** a simple balance. **tip** *or* **turn the scale(s),** to outweigh the opposite scale; to be the decisive factor. [f. ON, = bowl]

scalene /ˈskeɪliːn/ *adj.* (of a triangle etc.) having unequal sides. [f. L f. Gk *skalēnos* unequal]

scallion /ˈskæljən/ *n.* a shallot; a long-necked bulbless onion. [f. AF f. L, = onion of *Ascalon* in Palestine]

scallop /ˈskɒləp/ *n.* **1** a shellfish of the genus *Pecten*, with two fan-shaped ridged shells. **2** one shell of this used as a container in which food is cooked and served. **3** each of a series of ornamental semi-circular curves edging a fabric etc. —*v.t.* **1** to cook in a scallop. **2** to ornament (material etc.) with scallops. **3** (usu. in *p.p.*) to bake (slices of potato) overlapping in a scallop-like arrangement. [f. OF, = ESCALOPE]

scalloping *n.* a scallop-edging. [f. prec.]

scallywag /ˈskælɪwæg/ *n.* a rascal. [orig. US slang; etym. unkn.]

scalp *n.* the skin and hair of the top of the head; this formerly cut off as a trophy by an American Indian. —*v.t.* **1** to remove the scalp of. **2** to criticize savagely. **3** (*US colloq.*) to resell at a high or quick profit. [prob. f. Scand.]

scalpel /ˈskælp(ə)l/ *n.* a small surgical knife. [F or f. L dim. of *scalprum* chisel (*scalpere* scratch, carve)]

scamp *n.* a rascal. —*v.t.* to do (work etc.) perfunctorily or inadequately. [f. *scamp* rob on highway, prob. f. MDu. = decamp]

scamper *v.i.* to move or run hastily or impulsively, to run about playfully. —*n.* an act of scampering. [prob. as prec.]

scampi /ˈskæmpɪ/ *n.pl.* large prawns; these as food. [It.]

scan *v.t./i.* (**-nn-**) **1** to look at all parts of (a thing) successively. **2** to look over quickly or cursorily. **3** to traverse with a controlled electronic or radar beam. **4** to resolve (a picture) into its elements of light and shade for television transmission. **5** to test the metre of (a line etc. of verse) by examining the nature and number of its feet and syllables; (of a line etc.) to be metrically correct. —*n.* an act or process of scanning. —**scanner** *n.* [f. L *scandere*, orig. = climb]

scandal /ˈskænd(ə)l/ *n.* **1** a general feeling of (esp. moral) outrage or indignation; a thing causing this. **2** malicious gossip about people's faults and wrongdoing. [f. OF f. L f. Gk, = stumbling-block]

scandalize /ˈskændəlaɪz/ *v.t.* to offend the moral feelings or sense of propriety of. [as prec.]

scandalmonger /ˈskændəlmʌŋgə(r)/ *n.* a person who disseminates scandal.

scandalous /ˈskændələs/ *adj.* containing or arousing scandal, outrageous, shocking. —**scandalously** *adv.* [f. SCANDAL]

Scandinavian *adj.* of Scandinavia (Denmark, Norway, Sweden, Iceland) or its people or languages. —*n.* **1** a native of Scandinavia. **2** the languages of Scandinavia. [f. *Scandinavia*]

scandium /ˈskændɪəm/ *n.* a metallic element, symbol Sc, atomic number 21. [f. L *Scandia* Scandinavia (source of minerals containing it)]

scansion /ˈskænʃ(ə)n/ *n.* metrical scanning. [f. L (as SCAN)]

scant *adj.* scanty, insufficient. —*v.t.* (*archaic*) to skimp, to stint. [f. ON (*skammr* short)]

scantling *n.* **1** a timber beam of small cross-section. **2** the size to which stone or timber is to be cut. **3** a set of standard dimensions for parts of a structure, especially in shipbuilding. [f. obs. *scantlon* f. OF, = sample]

scanty *adj.* **1** of small amount or extent. **2** barely sufficient. —**scantily** *adv.*, **scantiness** *n.* [as SCANT]

scapegoat /ˈskeɪpgəʊt/ *n.* **1** a goat allowed to escape when the Jewish chief priest had symbolically laid the sins of the people upon it (Lev. 16). **2** a person who is made to bear blame or punishment that should rightly fall on others. [f. archaic *scape* escape + GOAT]

scapegrace /ˈskeɪpgreɪs/ *n.* a wild and foolish or rash person, especially a child or young person who constantly gets into trouble. [as prec. + GRACE, = one who escapes the grace of God]

scapula /ˈskæpjʊlə/ *n.* (*pl.* **-lae** /-li:/) the shoulder-blade. [L]

scapular /ˈskæpjʊlə(r)/ *adj.* of the scapula. —*n.* **1** a monastic short cloak. **2** a scapular feather. [as prec.]

scar[1] *n.* **1** a mark left by damage, especially on the skin by a healed wound or on a plant by the loss of a leaf etc. **2** the lasting effect of grief etc. —*v.t./i.* (**-rr-**) to mark with a scar; to form a scar or scars. [f. OF f. L f. Gk *eskhara* scab]

scar[2] *n.* a precipitous craggy part of a mountain-side or cliff. [f. ON, = reef]

scarab /ˈskærəb/ *n.* **1** a beetle of the family Scarabaeidae. **2** the sacred dung-beetle of ancient Egypt. **3** a carving of a beetle, engraved with symbols on the flat side and used in ancient Egypt as a charm. [f. L *scarabaeus* f. Gk]

scarce /skeəs/ *adj.* **1** (usu. *predic.*) not plentiful, insufficient for demand or need. **2** seldom found, rare. —*adv.* (*literary*) scarcely. —**make oneself scarce**, to go away; to keep out of the way. [f. AF ult. f. L *excerpere* (as EXCERPT)]

scarcely *adv.* **1** almost not; not quite; only just. **2** not; surely not; probably not. [f. prec.]

scarcity /ˈskeəsɪtɪ/ *n.* being scarce; a shortage. [f. SCARCE]

scare *v.t./i.* to strike or be struck with sudden fear, to startle and frighten; to drive (away, off, etc.) by fright; (in *p.p.*) frightened. —*n.* a sudden outbreak of fear; alarm caused by a rumour. [f. ON *skirra* frighten]

scarecrow *n.* **1** a figure of a man dressed in old clothes and set up in a field to scare birds away from crops. **2** a badly dressed or grotesque person.

scaremonger *n.* a person who raises unnecessary or excessive alarm. —**scaremongering** *n.*

scarf[1] *n.* (*pl.* **scarves** /skɑ:vz/) **1** a long narrow strip of material worn for warmth or ornament round the neck. **2** a square piece of material worn round the neck or over a woman's hair. [prob. f. OF *escarpe* sash]

scarf[2] *n.* a joint made by thinning the ends of two pieces of timber etc. so that they overlap without an increase of thickness and fastening them with bolts etc. —*v.t.* to join with a scarf. [rel. to F *écarver*]

scarify[1] /ˈskeərɪfaɪ, ˈskɪ-/ *v.t.* **1** to loosen the surface of (soil etc.). **2** to make slight incisions in (skin etc.); to cut off skin from. **3** to criticize etc. mercilessly. —**scarification** /-fɪˈkeɪʃ(ə)n/ *n.* [f. F f. L f. Gk (*skariphos* stylus)]

scarify[2] /ˈskeərɪfaɪ/ *v.t.* (*colloq.*) to scare, to terrify. [f. SCARE]

scarlatina /skɑ:ləˈti:nə/ *n.* scarlet fever. [It. (as SCARLET)]

scarlet /ˈskɑ:lɪt/ *adj.* of brilliant red colour. —*n.* **1** scarlet colour or pigment. **2** scarlet clothes or material. —**scarlet fever**, an infectious fever with a scarlet rash. **scarlet runner**, a kind of bean; the scarlet-flowered climbing plant (*Phaseolus multiflorus*) bearing this. [f. OF *escarlate*]

scarp *n.* a steep slope, especially the inner side of a ditch in a fortification. —*v.t.* to make steep or perpendicular. [f. It. *scarpa*]

scarper *v.i.* (*slang*) to escape, to run away. [prob. f. It. *scappare* escape, infl. by rhyming slang *Scapa Flow* go]

scary /ˈskeərɪ/ *adj.* (*colloq.*) frightening. [f. SCARE]

scat[1] *v.i.* (**-tt-**) (*colloq.*) to depart quickly. —*int.* (*colloq.*) depart quickly. [perh. abbr. of SCATTER]

scat[2] *n.* wordless jazz singing using the voice as an instrument. —*v.i.* to sing in this style. [prob. imit.]

scathe /skeɪð/ *v.t.* (*archaic*) to harm or injure. —*n.* (*archaic*) harm, injury. [f. ON; cf. OE *sceatha* malefactor, injury]

scathing /ˈskeɪðɪŋ/ *adj.* (of a look, criticism, etc.) harsh, severe. [f. prec.]

scatology /skæˈtɒlədʒɪ/ *n.* preoccupation with obscene literature or with excrement. —**scatological** /skætəˈlɒdʒɪk(ə)l/ *adj.* [f. Gk *skōr* dung + -LOGY]

scatter *v.t./i.* **1** to throw or put here and there; to cover thus. **2** to go or send in different directions. **3** to deflect or diffuse (light or particles etc.). **4** (in *p.p.*) not situated together, wide apart. —*n.* **1** scattering. **2** a small amount scattered. **3** the extent of distribution, especially of shot. —**scatter-brain** *n.* a scatter-brained person. **scatter-brained** *adj.*

lacking concentration; disorganized; flighty. [prob. var. of SHATTER]

scatty *adj.* (*slang*) scatter-brained, crazy. —**scattily** *adv.*, **scattiness** *n.* [f. *scatter-brained*]

scaup *n.* a diving duck of the genus *Aythya*, frequenting northern coasts. [f. *scaup*, Sc. var. of *scalp* mussel-bed, which it frequents]

scaur var. of SCAR[2].

scavenge /ˈskævɪndʒ/ *v.t./i.* **1** to be or act as a scavenger (of). **2** to remove dirt, waste, or impurities etc. from. [back-formation f. foll.]

scavenger /ˈskævɪndʒə(r)/ *n.* **1** a person who searches among or collects things unwanted by others. **2** an animal or bird that feeds on carrion. [orig. = inspector of imports, f. AF (rel. to SHOW)]

Sc.D. *abbr.* Doctor of Science. [f. L *scientiae doctor*]

scenario /sɪˈnɑːrɪəʊ/ *n.* (*pl.* **-os**) **1** the script or synopsis of a film, play, etc. **2** an imagined sequence of future events. [It. (as SCENE)]

scene /siːn/ *n.* **1** the place in which an event or series of events takes or took place. **2** a portion of a play during which the action is continuous; a subdivision of an act; a similar portion of a film, book, etc. **3** an incident thought of as resembling this. **4** a dramatic outburst of temper or emotion; a stormy interview. **5** a landscape or view as seen by a spectator. **6** stage scenery. **7** (*slang*) an area or subject of activity or interest; a way of life. —**behind the scenes,** behind stage, out of sight of the audience; not known to the public, working secretly. **come on the scene,** to arrive. **set the scene,** to describe the location of events etc. **scene-shifter** *n.* a person engaged in changing the scenery in a theatre. [f. L f. Gk *skēnē* tent, stage]

scenery /ˈsiːnərɪ/ *n.* **1** structures used on a theatre stage to represent features in the scene of the action. **2** the general appearance of a landscape; its picturesque features. [earlier *scenary* f. It. SCENARIO]

scenic /ˈsiːnɪk/ *adj.* **1** having fine natural scenery. **2** of scenery. **3** of or on the stage. —**scenic railway,** a miniature railway running through artificial picturesque scenery as an amusement at a fair. —**scenically** *adv.* [as SCENE]

scent /sent/ *n.* **1** a characteristic odour, especially a pleasant one. **2** liquid perfume. **3** the smell or trail left by an animal; a line of investigation or pursuit. **4** the power of detecting or distinguishing smells or discovering the presence of something. —*v.t.* **1** to discern by sense of smell. **2** to sniff out. **3** to begin to suspect the presence or existence of. **4** to make fragrant, to apply perfume to. —**off the scent,** misled by false information etc. —**scented** *adj.* [f. OF *sentir* perceive, smell, f. L *sentire* feel, sense]

sceptic /ˈskeptɪk/ *n.* **1** a sceptical person; one who doubts the truth of religious doctrines. **2** a philosopher who questions the possibility of knowledge. —**scepticism** /-sɪz(ə)m/ *n.* [f. F or L f. Gk (*skeptomai* consider)]

sceptical /ˈskeptɪk(ə)l/ *adj.* inclined to disbelieve things; doubting or questioning the truth of claims or statements etc. —**sceptically** *adv.* [as prec.]

sceptre /ˈseptə(r)/ *n.* a staff borne as a symbol of sovereignty. [f. OF f. L f. Gk *skēptron* (*skēptō* lean on)]

schadenfreude /ˈʃɑːdənfrɔɪdə/ *n.* malicious enjoyment of others' misfortunes. [G (*schaden* harm, *freude* joy)]

schedule /ˈʃedjuːl/ *n.* **1** a timetable or programme of planned events or work etc. **2** a table of details or items, especially as an appendix to a document. —*v.t.* **1** to make a schedule of; to include in a schedule; to appoint a time for. **2** to include (an ancient monument) in a list of those considered to be of national importance and so to be preserved. —**on schedule,** to time, not late. **scheduled flight,** one operated on a regular timetable. [f. OF f. L *schedula* slip of paper, dim. of *scheda* f. Gk *skhēdē* papyrus-leaf]

schematic /skɪˈmætɪk/ *adj.* in the form of a diagram or chart. —*n.* a schematic diagram. —**schematically** *adv.* [as SCHEME]

schematize /ˈskiːmətaɪz/ *v.t.* to put into schematic form; to formulate in regular order. —**schematization** /-ˈzeɪʃ(ə)n/ *n.* [f. Gk, = assume a form (or as foll.)]

scheme /skiːm/ *n.* **1** a plan of work or action. **2** an orderly planned arrangement. **3** a secret or underhand plan. —*v.t./i.* to make plans; to plan, especially in secret or in an underhand way. —**schemer** *n.* [f. L f. Gk *skhēma* form, figure]

scherzo /ˈskeətsəʊ/ *n.* (*pl.* **-os**) a vigorous often playful movement in a symphony or sonata etc.; a lively vigorous musical composition. [It., = jest]

schism /ˈsɪz(ə)m, ˈskɪ-/ *n.* division into opposing groups because of a difference in belief or opinion, especially in a religious body. —**schismatic** /-ˈmætɪk/ *adj.*, **schismatically** *adv.* [f. OF f. L f. Gk *skhisma* cleft (*skhizō* split)]

schist /ʃɪst/ *n.* a layered crystalline rock. [f. F f. L f. Gk *skhistos* split (as prec.)]

schizo /ˈskɪtsəʊ/ *n.* (*pl.* **-os**) (*colloq.*) a schizophrenic. [abbr.]

schizoid /ˈskɪtsɔɪd/ *adj.* of or resembling schizophrenia or a schizophrenic. —*n.* a schizoid person. [f. foll.]

schizophrenia /skɪtsəˈfriːnɪə/ *n.* a mental

disease marked by disconnection between thought, feelings, and actions, often with delusions and withdrawal from social relationships. —**schizophrenic** /-ˈfrenɪk/ *adj.* & *n.* [f. Gk *skhizō* split + *phrēn* mind]

schmaltz /ʃmɔlts/ *n.* sugary sentimentalism, especially in music or literature. [Yiddish f. G, = dripping]

schnapps /ʃnæps/ *n.* a kind of strong gin. [G, = dram of liquor, f. LG & Du. *snaps* mouthful (as SNAP)]

schnitzel /ˈʃnɪts(ə)l/ *n.* a veal cutlet. [G]

scholar /ˈskɒlə(r)/ *n.* **1** a person with great learning in a particular subject; one who is skilled in academic work. **2** a person who learns. **3** a person who holds a scholarship. —**scholarly** *adj.* [f. OF f. L *scholaris* (as SCHOOL¹)]

scholarship *n.* **1** an award of money towards education, usually gained by means of a competitive examination. **2** learning or knowledge in a particular subject. **3** the methods and achievements characteristic of scholars and academic work. [f. prec. + -SHIP]

scholastic /skɒˈlæstɪk/ *adj.* of schools or education, academic. —**scholastically** *adv.* [f. L f. Gk (as SCHOOL¹)]

scholasticism /skəˈlæstɪsɪz(ə)m/ *n.* the educational tradition of the medieval 'schools' (i.e. universities), especially a method of philosophical and theological speculation which aimed at a better understanding of the revealed truths of Christianity by defining, systematizing, and reasoning. [f. prec.]

school¹ /sku:l/ *n.* **1** an institution for educating children or giving instruction. **2** (*US*) a university; a department of this. **3** the buildings or pupils of such an institution; the time during which teaching is done. **4** the process of being educated in a school; circumstances or an occupation serving to educate or discipline. **5** a branch of study at a university. **6** a group of thinkers, artists, etc., sharing the same principles, methods, characteristics, or inspirations. **7** a group of card-players or gamblers. **8** a medieval lecture-room. —*v.t.* **1** to educate; to send to school. **2** to discipline; to train or accustom. —**school-leaver** *n.* a person who has just left school. **school year,** the period when schools are in session, reckoned from the autumn term. [f. OE, ult. f. L *schola* school f. Gk *skholē* leisure, disputation, philosophy, lecture-place]

school² /sku:l/ *n.* a shoal of fish, whales, etc. [f. MLG or MDu., = OE *scolu* troop]

schoolchild *n.* (*pl.* **-children**) (also **schoolboy, schoolgirl**) a child who attends school.

schoolhouse *n.* the building of a school, especially that of a village.

schooling *n.* education, especially in a school.

schoolman *n.* (*pl.* **-men**) **1** a teacher in a medieval European university. **2** a theologian seeking to deal with religious doctrines by the rules of Aristotelian logic.

schoolmaster *n.* a male teacher in a school. —**schoolmistress** *n.fem.*

schoolroom *n.* a room used for lessons in a school or private house.

schoolteacher *n.* a teacher in a school.

schooner /ˈsku:nə(r)/ *n.* **1** a fore-and-aft-rigged ship with more than one mast. **2** a large glass of sherry etc. [orig. unkn.]

schottische /ʃɒˈti:ʃ/ *n.* a kind of slow polka; the music for this. [f. G *der schottische tanz* the Scottish dance]

schwa /ʃwɑ:, ʃvɑ:/ *n.* an indeterminate vowel sound (as in *another*); the symbol (ə) representing this. [G f. Heb., app. = emptiness]

sciatic /saɪˈætɪk/ *adj.* **1** of the hip; affecting the hip or sciatic nerve. **2** suffering from or liable to sciatica. —**sciatic nerve,** the large nerve from the pelvis to the thigh. [f. F f. L f. Gk *iskhiadikos* (*iskhion* hip-joint)]

sciatica /saɪˈætɪkə/ *n.* neuralgia affecting the sciatic nerve. [L (as prec.)]

science /ˈsaɪəns/ *n.* **1** the branch of knowledge involving systematized observation and experiment, especially one dealing with substances, or animal and vegetable life, and natural laws. **2** systematic and formulated knowledge; the pursuit or principles of this. **3** an organized body of knowledge on a subject. **4** skilful technique. —**science fiction** a class of prose narrative which assumes an imaginary technological or scientific advance, portrays space travel or life on other planets, or depends upon a spectacular change in the human environment. [f. OF f. L *scientia* knowledge (*scire* know)]

scientific /saɪənˈtɪfɪk/ *adj.* **1** of science; used or engaged in science. **2** following the systematic methods of science. **3** having, using, or requiring trained skill. —**scientifically** *adv.* [f. F or L (as SCIENCE)]

scientist /ˈsaɪəntɪst/ *n.* a student of or expert in one or more of the natural or physical sciences. [f. SCIENCE or prec.]

Scientology /saɪənˈtɒlədʒɪ/ *n.* a religious system based on the study of knowledge and seeking to develop the highest potentialities of its members, founded in 1951 by American science-fiction writer L. Ron Hubbard (1911–86). —**Scientologist** *n.* [f. L *scientia* (as SCIENCE)]

sci-fi /ˈsaɪfaɪ/ *n.* (*colloq.*) science fiction. [abbr.]

scilicet /ˈsaɪlɪset/ *adv.* that is to say (introducing a word to be supplied or an explanation of an ambiguous word). [L]

scimitar /ˈsɪmɪtə(r)/ *n.* a curved oriental sword. [f. F or It.]

scintilla /sɪnˈtɪlə/ *n.* a sign or trace. [L, = spark]

scintillate /ˈsɪntɪleɪt/ *v.i.* **1** to sparkle; to give off sparks. **2** to talk or act with brilliance. —**scintillation** /-ˈleɪʃ(ə)n/ *n.* [f. L *scintillare* (as prec.)]

sciolism /ˈsaɪəlɪz(ə)m/ *n.* superficial knowledge; a display of this. —**sciolist** *n.*, **sciolistic** /-ˈlɪstɪk/ *adj.* [f. L *sciolus* smatterer, dim. of *scius* knowing]

scion /ˈsaɪən/ *n.* **1** a shoot of a plant, especially one cut for grafting. **2** a descendant; a young member of a family. [f. OF, = shoot, twig]

scissors /ˈsɪzəz/ *n. pl.* (also **pair of scissors**) a cutting instrument made of two blades so pivoted that their cutting edges close on what is to be cut. [f. OF f. L *cisorium* cutting instrument (as CHISEL), rel. to *scindere* cut]

sclerosis /sklɪəˈrəʊsɪs/ *n.* abnormal hardening of body tissue. —**disseminated** *or* **multiple sclerosis**, sclerosis spreading to all or many parts of the body. —**sclerotic** /-ˈrɒtɪk/ *adj.* [f. L f. Gk (*sklēroō* harden)]

scoff[1] *v.i.* to speak derisively; to jeer. —*n.* a scoffing remark, a jeer. —**scoffer** *n.* [perh. f. Scand.]

scoff[2] *v.t./i.* (*slang*) to eat greedily. —*n.* (*slang*) food, a meal. [f. Afrik. *schoff* quarter of a day]

scold /skəʊld/ *v.t./i.* to rebuke (esp. a child). —*n.* a nagging woman. [prob. f. ON (as SKALD)]

scolding *n.* a lengthy rebuke (esp. to a child). [f. SCOLD]

scollop var. of SCALLOP.

sconce[1] *n.* a wall-bracket holding a candlestick or light-fitting. [f. OF f. L *absconsa* covered light (as ABSCOND)]

sconce[2] *n.* a small fort or earthwork. [f. Du. *schans* brushwood]

scone /skɒn, skəʊn/ *n.* a small soft cake of flour, oatmeal, or barley-meal baked quickly and eaten buttered. [perh. f. MDu. or MLG, = fine (bread)]

scoop *n.* **1** a deep shovel-like tool for taking up and moving grain, sugar, coal, etc. **2** a ladle; a device with a small round bowl and a handle, for serving portions of ice-cream etc. **3** the quantity taken with a scoop. **4** a scooping movement. **5** a large profit made quickly or by anticipating one's competitors. **6** an exclusive item in a newspaper etc. —*v.t.* **1** to lift or hollow with or as with a scoop. **2** to secure (a large profit etc.) by sudden action or luck. **3** to forestall (a rival newspaper etc.) with a news scoop. [f. MDu. or MLG, = bucket etc. (rel. to SHAPE)]

scoot *v.i.* (*colloq.*) to run or dart; to go away hastily. [for earlier *scout* (orig. unkn.)]

scooter *n.* **1** a child's toy vehicle consisting of a footboard with a wheel at front and back and a long steering-handle, propelled by thrusting one foot against the ground while the other rests on the footboard. **2** (also **motor scooter**) a kind of lightweight motor cycle with a protective shield extending from below the handles to where the rider's feet rest. —**scooterist** *n.* [f. prec.]

scope *n.* **1** the reach or sphere of observation or action; the extent to which it is possible or permissible to range or develop etc. **2** opportunity, outlet. [f. It. f. Gk, = target]

-scope *suffix* forming nouns denoting a thing looked at or through (*telescope*) or an instrument for observing or showing (*oscilloscope*). [f. Gk *skopeō* look at]

scorbutic /skɔːˈbjuːtɪk/ *adj.* of, like, or affected with scurvy. [f. L *scorbutus* scurvy]

scorch *v.t./i.* **1** to burn or discolour the surface of with dry heat; to become burnt or discoloured thus. **2** (*slang*) to go at a very high speed. —*n.* a mark made by scorching. —**scorched earth policy**, the policy of burning one's crops etc. and removing or destroying anything that might be useful to an occupying enemy. [perh. rel. to *skorkle* in same sense]

scorcher *n.* (*colloq.*) a very hot day. [f. prec.]

score *n.* **1** the number of points or goals etc. made by a player or side in a game, or gained in a competition etc.; a list or total of these, a reckoning. **2** (for plural usage see HUNDRED) a set of twenty; (in *pl.*) very many. **3** a copy of a musical composition with the parts on a series of staves. **4** the music for a musical comedy, film, etc. **5** a reason or motive; a topic. **6** (*colloq.*) a remark or act by which a person scores off another. **7** a line or mark cut into a surface. **8** a record of money owing. —*v.t./i.* **1** to gain (a point or points) in a game etc.; to make a score; to achieve (a success, victory, etc.). **2** to keep a record of the score; to record in a score. **3** to have an advantage; to be successful, to have good luck; to make a clever retort that puts an opponent at a disadvantage. **4** to cut a line or mark(s) into. **5** to write out as a musical score; to arrange (a piece of music) for specified instruments. —**know the score**, to be aware of essential facts. **on that score**, so far as that matter is concerned. **pay off old scores**, to get one's revenge. **score-board** *or* **-book, -card, -sheet** *n.* a board etc. on which a score is entered or displayed. **score off**, (*colloq.*) to humiliate; to defeat in argument or repartee. **score out**, to delete. —**scorer** *n.* [f. ON = notch, tally, twenty (as SHEAR)]

scoria /ˈskɔːrɪə/ *n.* (*pl.* **-ae** /-iː/) slag, a clinker-like mass of lava. —**scoriaceous** /-ˈeɪʃəs/ *adj.* [L f. Gk, = refuse (*skōr* dung)]

scorn *n.* **1** strong contempt. **2** an object of this. —*v.t.* **1** to feel or show strong contempt for. **2** to reject as unworthy, to refuse scornfully. [f. OF; cf. OS *skern* mockery]

scornful *adj.* feeling or showing scorn. —**scornfully** *adv.*, **scornfulness** *n.* [f. SCORN + -FUL]

Scorpio /ˈskɔːpɪəʊ/ a constellation and the eighth sign of the zodiac, the Scorpion, which the sun enters about 23 Oct. —**Scorpian** *adj.* & *n.* [L f. Gk, = scorpion]

scorpion /ˈskɔːpɪən/ *n.* **1** a lobster-like arachnid of the order Scorpionida, with a jointed stinging tail. **2 the Scorpion,** the constellation or sign of the zodiac Scorpio. [f. OF f. L (as prec.)]

Scot *n.* **1** a native of Scotland. **2** (*hist.*) a member of a Gaelic tribe that migrated from Ireland to Scotland about the 6th c. [OE f. L *Scottus*]

Scotch /skɒtʃ/ *adj.* of Scotland or Scottish people or their form of English. —*n.* **1** the form of English used (especially in the Lowlands) in Scotland. **2** Scotch whisky. —**Scotch broth,** soup made from beef or mutton with vegetables, pearl barley, etc. **Scotch cap,** a man's wide beret, like that worn as part of Highland dress. **Scotch egg,** a hard-boiled egg enclosed in sausage-meat. **Scotch fir** *or* **pine,** a type of pine-tree (*Pinus sylvestris*). **Scotch mist,** thick mist and drizzle. **Scotch terrier,** a small rough-haired short-legged kind of terrier. **Scotch whisky,** whisky distilled in Scotland. **Scotch woodcock,** scrambled eggs on toast, garnished with anchovies. [contr. of SCOTTISH]

scotch /ˈskɒtʃ/ *v.t.* **1** to put an end to decisively; to frustrate (a plan etc.). **2** (*archaic*) to wound without killing. —*n.* a line on the ground for hopscotch. [orig. unkn.]

scot-free *adj.* unharmed, unpunished. [f. obs. *scot* tax, f. ON *skot* + FREE]

Scots *adj.* & *n.* Scottish (see note at SCOTCH). [orig. *Scottis*, northern var. of SCOTTISH]

Scotsman *n.* (*pl.* **-men**) a native of Scotland. —**Scotswoman** *n.fem.* (*pl.* **-women**)

Scottie /ˈskɒtɪ/ *n.* (*colloq.*) **1** a Scotsman. **2** a Scotch terrier. [f. SCOT]

Scottish /ˈskɒtɪʃ/ *adj.* of Scotland or its inhabitants. —**Scottish National Party,** a political party formed in 1934 by an amalgamation of the National Party of Scotland and the Scottish Party, which seeks autonomous government for Scotland. **Scottish Nationalist,** a member of this party. [f. SCOT]

scoundrel /ˈskaʊndr(ə)l/ *n.* an unscrupulous person, a villain. —**scoundrelly** *adj.* [orig. unkn.]

scour[1] *v.t.* **1** to clean or brighten by rubbing; to rub away (rust or a stain etc.). **2** to clear (a channel or pipe etc.) by the force of water flowing over or through it. **3** to purge drastically. —*n.* **1** scouring. **2** the action of water on a channel etc. [f. MDu. & MLG f. L *excurare* clean off (EX-[1], *curare* clean)]

scour[2] *v.t./i.* to search rapidly or thoroughly. [orig. unkn.]

scourer *n.* an abrasive pad or powder for scouring things. [f. SCOUR[1]]

scourge /skɜːdʒ/ *n.* **1** a person or thing regarded as a bringer of vengeance or punishment. **2** a whip for flogging people. —*v.t.* **1** to chastise, to afflict greatly. **2** to whip. [f. OF f. L *corrigia* whip]

scouse /skaʊs/ *adj.* (*slang*) of Liverpool. —*n.* (*slang*) **1** a native of Liverpool. **2** Liverpool dialect. [f. LOBSCOUSE]

scout[1] *n.* **1** a person, especially a soldier, sent out to get information about an enemy etc. **2** an act of seeking information. **3** a talent-scout. **4** Scout, a member of the Scout Association. **5** a college servant at Oxford. **6** (*colloq.*) a fellow, a person. —*v.i.* to act as a scout. —**scout about** *or* **around,** to search. **Scout Association** an organization (originally called the Boy Scouts) founded in 1908 by Lord Baden-Powell for helping boys to develop character by training them in open-air activities. [f. OF *escoute(r)* f. L *auscultare* listen]

scout[2] *v.t.* to reject (an idea etc.) with scorn. [f. Scand.; cf. ON *skúta* taunt]

Scouter *n.* an adult leader in the Scout Association. [f. SCOUT[1]]

scow /skaʊ/ *n.* a flat-bottomed boat. [f. Du., = ferry-boat]

scowl *n.* a sullen or bad-tempered look on a person's face. —*v.i.* to make a scowl. [prob. f. Scand.; cf. Da. *skule* look down or sidelong]

Scrabble *n.* [P] a game in which players use small square blocks displaying individual letters to form words on a special board. [f. foll.]

scrabble *v.i.* **1** to make a scratching movement or sound with the hands or feet. **2** to grope busily; to struggle to find or obtain something. —*n.* scrabbling. [f. MDu., frequent. of *schrabben* scrape]

scrag *n.* **1** (also **scrag-end**) the bony part of an animal's carcass as food; neck of mutton; the less meaty end of this. **2** a skinny person or animal. —*v.t.* (**-gg-**) to seize roughly by the neck; to handle roughly, to beat up. [perh. alt. f. dial. *crag* neck]

scraggy *adj.* thin and bony. —**scraggily** *adv.*, **scragginess** *n.* [f. SCRAG]

scram *v.i.* (**-mm-**) (*slang*, esp. in *imper.*) to go away. [perh. f. foll.]

scramble *v.t./i.* **1** to move as best one can over

rough ground or by clambering; to move hastily and awkwardly. **2** to struggle eagerly to do or obtain something. **3** (of aircraft or their crew) to hurry and take off quickly in an emergency. **4** to mix together indiscriminately; to cook (egg) by mixing its contents and heating the mixture in a pan until it thickens. **5** to make (a telephone conversation etc.) unintelligible except to a person with a special receiver by altering the frequencies on which it is transmitted. —*n.* **1** a climb or walk over rough ground. **2** an eager struggle to do or obtain something. **3** a motor-cycle race over rough ground (see MOTO-CROSS). —**scrambled egg,** (*colloq.*) gold braid on an officer's cap. [imit.]

scrambler *n.* a device for scrambling telephone conversations. [f. prec.]

scrap[1] *n.* **1** a small detached piece, a fragment. **2** rubbish, waste material; discarded metal suitable for reprocessing. **3** (with neg.) the smallest piece or amount. **4** (in *pl.*) odds and ends, bits of uneaten food. —*v.t.* (**-pp-**) to discard as useless. —**scrap-book** *n.* a book in which newspaper cuttings or similar souvenirs are mounted. **scrap-merchant** *n.* a dealer in scrap. **scrap-yard** *n.* a place where scrap is collected. [f. ON, rel. to SCRAPE]

scrap[2] *n.* (*colloq.*) a fight or rough quarrel. —*v.i.* (**-pp-**) to have a scrap. [perh. f. foll.]

scrape *v.t./i.* **1** to make (a thing) level, clean, or smooth by causing a hard edge to move across the surface; to apply (a hard edge) thus; to remove by scraping. **2** to scratch or damage by scraping. **3** to dig (a hollow etc.) by scraping. **4** to draw or move with a sound (as) of scraping; to produce such a sound. **5** to pass along or through something with difficulty, with or without touching it. **6** to obtain or amass with effort or by parsimony. **7** to be very economical. **8** to draw back the foot in making a clumsy bow. —*n.* **1** a scraping movement or sound. **2** a scraped place or mark. **3** a thinly applied layer of butter etc. on bread. **4** an awkward situation resulting from an escapade. —**scrape acquaintance,** to contrive to become acquainted. **scrape the barrel,** to be driven to using one's last and inferior resources because the better ones are finished. **scrape through** etc., to get through a difficult situation or pass an examination by only a very narrow margin. [f. ON or MDu.]

scraper *n.* a device used for scraping things. [f. prec.]

scrapie /ˈskreɪpɪ/ *n.* a virus disease of sheep that affects the central nervous system, causing lack of co-ordination so that affected animals rub against trees etc. for support.

scraping *n.* (esp. in *pl.*) a fragment produced by scraping. [f. SCRAPE]

scrappy *adj.* consisting of scraps or disconnected elements. —**scrappily** *adv.*, **scrappiness** *n.* [f. SCRAP[1]]

scratch /skrætʃ/ *v.t.* **1** to make a shallow mark or wound on (a surface) with something sharp. **2** to make or form by scratching. **3** to scrape with the finger-nail(s) in order to relieve itching. **4** to make a thin scraping sound. **5** to obtain with difficulty. **6** (with *off*, *out*, or *through*) to delete by drawing a line through; to withdraw from a race, competition, or (*US*) election. —*n.* **1** a mark, wound, or sound made by scratching; (*colloq.*) a trifling wound. **2** a spell of scratching oneself. **3** a line from which competitors start in a race, especially those receiving no handicap. —*adj.* **1** collected by chance or from whatever is available. **2** with no handicap given. —**from scratch,** from the beginning; without help or advantage. **scratch one's head,** to be perplexed. **scratch the surface,** to deal with a matter only superficially. **up to scratch,** up to the required standard. [prob. f. earlier *scrat* & *cratch*; orig. unkn.]

scratchy *adj.* **1** tending to make scratches or a scratching noise. **2** tending to cause itchiness. **3** (of a drawing etc.) done in scratches or carelessly. —**scratchily** *adv.*, **scratchiness** *n.* [f. prec.]

scrawl *v.t./i.* **1** to write in a hurried untidy way. **2** to cross *out* thus. —*n.* hurried writing; a scrawled note. [perh. f. obs. *scrawl* sprawl]

scrawny *adj.* lean, scraggy. [var. of dial. *scranny*]

scream *v.t./i.* **1** to emit a piercing cry of pain, terror, annoyance, or excitement. **2** to speak or sing (words etc.) in such a tone. **3** to make or move with a shrill sound like a scream. **4** to laugh uncontrollably. **5** to be blatantly obvious. —*n.* **1** a screaming cry or sound. **2** (*colloq.*) an irresistibly funny occurrence or person. [OE]

scree *n.* (in *sing.* or *pl.*) a mass of small loose stones, sliding when trodden on; a mountain slope covered with these. [f. ON, = landslip]

screech *n.* a harsh high-pitched scream. —*v.t./i.* to utter with or make a screech. —**screech-owl** *n.* an owl that screeches instead of hooting, especially a barn-owl. [var. of earlier *scritch* (imit.)]

screed *n.* **1** a tiresomely long letter or other document. **2** a level strip of material formed or placed on a floor, road, etc., as a guide for the accurate finishing of it. **3** a levelled layer of material forming part of a floor etc. —*v.t.* to level by means of a screed; to apply (material) as a screed. [prob. var. of SHRED]

screen *n.* **1** an upright structure used to conceal, protect, or divide something.

2 anything serving a similar purpose; an expression or measure etc. adopted for concealment; the protection given by this. 3 a blank surface on which a film, televised picture, radar image, etc., is projected; the cinema industry. 4 a sight-screen; a windscreen. 5 a large sieve or riddle. 6 a frame with fine wire netting to keep out flies, mosquitoes, etc. 7 a system for showing the presence or absence of a disease, quality, etc. 8 (*Printing*) a transparent finely-ruled plate or film used in half-tone reproduction. —*v.t.* 1 to shelter, conceal, or protect. 2 to protect from discovery or deserved blame by diverting suspicion. 3 to show (images or a film etc.) on a screen. 4 to prevent from causing electrical interference. 5 to sieve. 6 to test for the presence or absence of a disease, quality (esp. reliability or loyalty), etc. —**screen-printing** *n.* a process like stencilling with ink forced through a prepared sheet of fine material. [f. OF *escren* f. OHG *skrank* barrier]

screenplay *n.* the script of a film.

screw /skru:/ *n.* 1 a cylinder or cone with a spiral ridge round the outside (**male screw**) or the inside (**female screw**); a metal male screw with a slotted head and a sharp point for fastening things (esp. of wood) together. 2 a wooden or metal screw used to exert pressure; (in *sing.* or *pl.*) an instrument of torture operating thus. 3 a propeller or other device acting like a screw. 4 one turn of a screw. 5 a small twisted-up paper of tobacco etc. 6 (in billiards etc.) an oblique curling motion of the ball. 7 (*slang*) a prison warder. 8 (*slang*) the amount of one's salary or wages. 9 (*vulgar*) sexual intercourse; a partner in this. —*v.t./i.* 1 to fasten or tighten with a screw or screws. 2 to turn (a screw); to twist or turn round like a screw. 3 (of a ball etc.) to swerve. 4 to put the screws on, to oppress; to extort (consent, money, etc.). 5 to contort or contract (one's face etc.). 6 (*vulgar*) to have sexual intercourse (with). —**have a screw loose,** (*colloq.*) to be slightly crazy. **put the screws on,** to exert pressure (on), to intimidate or extort money. **screw-cap** *or* **-top** *n.* a cap or top that screws on to a bottle etc. **screw up,** to contort or contract (one's eyes, face, etc.); to summon up (one's courage); (*slang*) to bungle or mismanage. [f. OF *escroue* female screw, nut, f. L *scrofa* female pig used for breeding]

screwball *n.* (*US slang*) a crazy or eccentric person.

screwdriver *n.* a tool with a shaped tip fitting into the slot of a screw to turn it.

screwed *adj.* (*slang*) drunk. [f. SCREW]

screwy *adj.* (*slang*) crazy, eccentric; absurd. [f. SCREW]

scribble *v.t./i.* 1 to write carelessly or hurriedly. 2 to make meaningless marks. —*n.* something scribbled; hurried or careless writing; scribbled meaningless marks. —**scribbler** *n.* [f. L *scribillare* dim. of L *scribere* write]

scribe *n.* 1 an ancient or medieval copyist of manuscripts. 2 a professional Jewish religious scholar in New Testament times. 3 a pointed instrument for making marks on wood etc. —*v.t.* to mark with a scribe. —**scribal** *adj.* [f. L *scriba* (*scribere* write)]

scrim *n.* an open-weave fabric for lining or upholstery etc. [orig. unkn.]

scrimmage /ˈskrɪmɪdʒ/ *n.* a confused struggle; a skirmish. —*v.i.* to engage in a scrimmage. [var. of SKIRMISH]

scrimp *v.t./i.* to skimp. [perh. rel. to SHRIMP]

scrimshank /ˈskrɪmʃæŋk/ *v.i.* (*slang*) to shirk work, to malinger. [orig. unkn.]

scrip *n.* 1 a provisional certificate of money subscribed entitling the holder to dividends; (*collect.*) such certificates. 2 an extra share or shares issued instead of a dividend. [abbr. of *subscription receipt*]

script *n.* 1 handwriting, written characters. 2 type imitating handwriting. 3 an alphabet or system of writing. 4 the text of a play, film, broadcast talk, etc. 5 an examinee's written answer. —*v.t.* to write the script for (a film etc.). —**script-writer** *n.* a writer for broadcasting or films etc. [f. OF f. L *scriptum* (*scribere* write)]

scripture /ˈskrɪptʃə(r)/ *n.* 1 sacred writings. 2 **Scripture** *or* **the Scriptures,** the sacred writings of the Christians (the Old and New Testaments) or the Jews (the Old Testament). —**scriptural** *adj.* [f. L (as prec.)]

scrivener /ˈskrɪvənə(r)/ *n.* (*hist.*) a drafter of documents, a copyist, a notary. [f. OF *escrivein* f. L (as SCRIBE)]

scrofula /ˈskrɒfjʊlə/ *n.* a disease with glandular swellings, probably a form of tuberculosis. —**scrofulous** *adj.* [L dim. of *scrofulae* (*pl.*) scrofulous swelling f. *scrofa* (see SCREW)]

scroll /skrəʊl/ *n.* 1 a roll of parchment or paper, especially with writing; a book of the ancient roll form. 2 an ornamental design imitating a roll of parchment. —*v.t.* to move (the display on a VDU screen) up or down as new material appears. [orig. *scrowle* alt. f. *rowle* roll]

scrolled /skrəʊld/ *adj.* having a scroll ornament. [f. prec.]

Scrooge /skru:dʒ/ *n.* a miser. [character in Dickens's *Christmas Carol*]

scrotum /ˈskrəʊtəm/ *n.* (*pl.* **scrota**) the pouch of skin containing the testicles. —**scrotal** *adj.* [L]

scrounge *v.t./i.* (*slang*) to cadge; to collect by

foraging. —**scrounger** *n.* [var. of dial. *scrunge* steal]

scrub[1] *v.t./i.* (**-bb-**) **1** to rub hard so as to clean or brighten, especially with a hard brush; to use a brush thus. **2** to remove impurities from (gas) in a scrubber. **3** (*slang*) to scrap or cancel (a plan, order, etc.) —*n.* scrubbing, being scrubbed. —**scrub up,** (of a surgeon etc.) to clean the hands and arms by scrubbing before an operation. [prob. f. MLG or MDu.]

scrub[2] *n.* **1** brushwood or stunted forest growth; land covered with this. **2** a stunted or insignificant person etc. —**scrubby** *adj.* [var. of SHRUB]

scrubber[1] *n.* **1** an apparatus for cleaning gases. **2** (*slang*) an immoral or sluttish woman. [f. SCRUB[1]]

scrubber[2] *n.* (*Austral.*) an inferior animal, especially a bullock, living in scrub country. [f. SCRUB[2]]

scruff *n.* the back of the neck. [alt. of *scuff*, perh. f. ON, = soft hair]

scruffy *adj.* (*colloq.*) shabby and untidy. —**scruffily** *adv.*, **scruffiness** *n.* [f. *scruff* var. of SCURF]

scrum *n.* a scrummage. —**scrum-half** *n.* the half-back who puts the ball into the scrum. [abbr.]

scrummage /ˈskrʌmɪdʒ/ *n.* (in Rugby football) the grouping of all forwards on each side to push against those of the other and seek possession of the ball thrown on the ground between them. [as SCRIMMAGE]

scrump *v.t./i.* (*dial.* or *slang*) to steal (apples), especially from orchards. [f. dial. *scrump* small apple]

scrumptious /ˈskrʌmpʃəs/ *adj.* (*colloq.*) delicious, delightful. [orig. unkn.]

scrumpy *n.* (*colloq.*, orig. *dial.*) rough cider. [as SCRUMP]

scrunch *n.* a crunch. —*v.t.* to crunch. [var. of CRUNCH]

scruple /ˈskruːp(ə)l/ *n.* **1** due regard to the morality or propriety of an action etc.; doubt or hesitation caused by this. **2** (*hist.*) a unit of weight of 20 grains. —*v.i.* to feel or be influenced by scruples; (esp. with neg.) to be reluctant because of scruples. [f. F or L *scrupulus* (*scrupus* rough pebble)]

scrupulous /ˈskruːpjʊləs/ *adj.* **1** careful to avoid doing wrong. **2** conscientious or thorough even in small matters; painstakingly careful and thorough. —**scrupulosity** /-ˈlɒsɪtɪ/ *n.*, **scrupulously** *adv.*, **scrupulousness** *n.* [as prec.]

scrutineer /ˌskruːtɪˈnɪə(r)/ *n.* a person who scrutinizes ballot-papers. [f. SCRUTINY]

scrutinize /ˈskruːtɪnaɪz/ *v.t.* to subject to scrutiny. [f. foll.]

scrutiny /ˈskruːtɪnɪ/ *n.* a careful look or examination; an official examination of ballot-papers to check their validity or the accuracy of counting. [f. L *scrutinium* (*scrutari* search)]

scuba /ˈskuːbə/ *n.* self-contained underwater breathing apparatus, designed to enable a swimmer to breathe while under the water. [acronym]

scud *v.i.* (**-dd-**) **1** to run or fly straight and fast, to skim along. **2** (*Naut.*) to run before the wind. —*n.* **1** a spell of scudding; a scudding motion. **2** vapoury driving clouds; a driving shower. [perh. alt. of SCUT]

scuff *v.t./i.* **1** to walk with dragging feet, to shuffle. **2** to graze or brush against; to mark or wear out (shoes etc.) thus. —*n.* a mark of scuffing. [imit.]

scuffle *n.* a confused struggle or fight at close quarters. —*v.i.* to engage in a scuffle. [prob. f. Scand. (cf. SHOVE)]

scull *n.* **1** each of a pair of small oars used by a single rower. **2** an oar that rests on the stern of a boat, used with a screwlike motion. **3** (in *pl.*) a sculling race. —*v.t.* to propel (a boat, or *absol.*) with sculls. [orig. unkn.]

sculler *n.* **1** a user of a scull or sculls. **2** a boat for sculling. [f. SCULL]

scullery /ˈskʌlərɪ/ *n.* a back kitchen; a room in which dishes etc. are washed. [f. OF *escuelerie* (*escuele* dish f. L *scutella* salver dim. of *scutra* wooden platter)]

scullion /ˈskʌljən/ *n.* (*archaic*) a cook's boy, one who washes dishes. [orig. unkn.]

sculpt *v.t./i.* (*colloq.*) to sculpture. [abbr.]

sculptor /ˈskʌlptə(r)/ *n.* one who sculptures. —**sculptress** *n. fem.* [L (as foll.)]

sculpture /ˈskʌlptʃə(r)/ *n.* **1** the art of forming representations in the round or in relief by chiselling stone, carving wood, modelling clay, casting metal, etc. **2** a work of sculpture. —*v.t./i.* to represent in or adorn with sculpture; to practise sculpture. —**sculptural** *adj.*, **sculpturally** *adv.* [f. L *sculptura* (*sculpere* carve)]

scum *n.* **1** a layer of dirt, froth, or impurities etc. that rises to the top of a liquid. **2** a worthless part; a worthless person or persons. —*v.t./i.* (**-mm-**) to remove the scum from; to form a scum (*on*). —**scummy** *adj.* [f. MLG or MDu.]

scuncheon /ˈskʌntʃ(ə)n/ *n.* the inside face of a door-jamb, window-frame, etc. [f. OF *escoinson* (as EX-, COIN)]

scupper *n.* a hole in a ship's side to carry off water from the deck. —*v.t.* (*slang*) **1** to sink (a ship) deliberately. **2** to defeat or ruin (a plan etc.). **3** to kill. [perh. f. AF deriv. of OF *escopir* spit, orig. imit.]

scurf *n.* flakes of dead skin, especially on the

scalp. —**scurfy** *adj.* [OE, prob. rel. to *sceorfian* cut to shreds]

scurrilous /ˈskʌrɪləs/ *adj.* **1** abusive and insulting. **2** coarsely humorous. —**scurrility** /-ˈrɪlɪtɪ/ *n.*, **scurrilously** *adv.* [f. L *scurrilis* (*scurra* buffoon)]

scurry /ˈskʌrɪ/ *v.i.* to run or move hurriedly, especially with short quick steps; to scamper. —*n.* **1** an act or sound of scurrying; a rush. **2** a flurry of rain or snow. [abbr. of *hurry-scurry* redupl. of HURRY]

scurvy /ˈskɜːvɪ/ *n.* a deficiency disease caused by lack of vitamin C in the diet. —*adj.* paltry, dishonourable, contemptible. —**scurvily** *adv.*, **scurviness** *n.* [f. SCURF; the n. infl. by F *scorbut* (cf. SCORBUTIC)]

scut *n.* a short tail, especially of a rabbit, hare, or deer. [orig. unkn.]

scutter *v.i.* (*colloq.*) to scurry. —*n.* (*colloq.*) a scurry. [perh. alt. of SCUTTLE³]

scuttle[1] *n.* **1** a receptacle for carrying and holding a small supply of coal. **2** the part of a motor-car body between the windscreen and bonnet. [f. ON or OHG f. L *scutella* dish]

scuttle[2] *n.* a hole with a lid in a ship's deck or side. —*v.t.* to let water into (a ship), especially to sink it. [perh. f. obs. F f. Sp. *escotilla* hatchway (*escota* cutting out cloth)]

scuttle[3] *v.i.* to scurry, to flee from danger or difficulty. —*n.* **1** a scuttling run. **2** a precipitate flight or departure. [cf. dial. *scuddle* (as SCUD)]

scythe /saɪð/ *n.* a mowing and reaping instrument with a long curved blade swung over the ground. —*v.t.* to cut with a scythe. [OE]

SDLP *abbr.* Social Democratic and Labour Party, a political party in Northern Ireland, founded in 1970.

SE *abbr.* south-east, south-eastern.

Se *symbol* selenium.

sea *n.* **1** the expanse of salt water that covers most of the earth's surface and surrounds the continents; any part of this as opposed to land or fresh water. **2** a named tract of salt water partly or wholly enclosed by land; a large freshwater inland lake. **3** the waves of the sea; their motion or state. **4** a vast quantity or expanse. —(*attrib.*) living or used in, on, or near the sea (often prefixed to the name of a marine animal, plant, etc., having a superficial resemblance to what it is named after). —**at sea,** in a ship on the sea; perplexed, confused. **by sea,** in a ship or ships. **go to sea,** to become a sailor. **on the sea,** in a ship at sea; situated on the coast. **sea anchor,** a bag to retard the drifting of a ship. **sea anemone,** a large polyp of the order Actiniaria, with petal-like tentacles. **sea-bird** *n.* a bird frequenting the sea or land near the sea. **sea-borne** *adj.* conveyed by the sea. **sea change,** a notable or unexpected transformation. **sea-cow** *n.* a sirenian; a walrus; a hippopotamus. **sea-dog** *n.* an old sailor, especially an Elizabethan captain. **sea-girt** *adj.* surrounded by sea. **sea-green** *adj.* & *n.* bluish green. **sea-horse** *n.* a small fish of the genus *Hippocampus* with a head suggestive of a horse's at right angles to its body, and a tail that can be wrapped round a support; a mythical creature with a horse's head and a fish's tail. **sea-kale** *n.* a herb (*Crambe maritima*) with young shoots used as a vegetable. **sea-legs** *n. pl.* the ability to walk on the deck of a rolling ship. **sea-level** *n.* the mean level of the sea's surface, used in reckoning the height of hills etc. and as a barometric standard. **sea-lion** *n.* a large eared seal especially of the genus *Zalophus* or *Otaria*. **Sea Lord,** a naval member of the Admiralty Board. **sea mile,** a nautical mile (see MILE). —**sea-room** *n.* space for a ship to turn etc. at sea. **sea-salt** *n.* salt produced by evaporating sea-water. **Sea Scout,** a member of the maritime branch of the Scout Association. **sea-shell,** the shell of a salt-water mollusc. **sea-shore** *n.* land close to the sea. **sea-urchin** *n.* a small sea-animal of the order Echinoidea with a prickly shell. **sea-way** *n.* a ship's progress; a place where a ship lies in open water; an inland waterway open to seagoing ships. [OE]

seaboard *n.* the seashore or line of a coast; a coastal region.

seafarer *n.* a sailor, a traveller by sea.

seafaring *adj.* & *n.* travelling by sea, especially as one's regular occupation.

seafood *n.* edible marine fish or shellfish.

seagoing *adj.* **1** (of ships) fit for crossing the sea. **2** (of a person) seafaring.

seagull *n.* a gull (GULL¹).

seal[1] *n.* **1** a piece of wax, lead, paper, etc., with a stamped design, attached to a document as a guarantee of authenticity or to a receptacle, room, envelope, etc., as a sign that (while the seal is unbroken) the contents have not been tampered with since it was affixed. **2** an engraved piece of metal etc. for stamping such a design. **3** a substance or device to close an aperture etc. **4** an act, gesture, or event regarded as a confirmation or guarantee. **5** a decorative adhesive stamp. —*v.t.* **1** to stamp or fasten with a seal; to fix a seal to; to certify as correct with a seal or stamp. **2** to close securely or hermetically. **3** to confine securely. **4** to settle or decide. —**sealing-wax** *n.* a mixture of shellac and rosin softened by heating and used for seals. **seal off,** to prevent entry to and exit from (an area). **seals of office,** those held during tenure of office, especially by a Lord Chancellor or Secretary of State. **set one's seal to,** to authorize or confirm. [f. AF f. L *sigillum* dim. of *signum* sign]

seal[2] *n.* **1** a fish-eating amphibious sea mammal of the family Phocidae, with flippers. **2** sealskin. —*v i.* to hunt seals. [OE]

sealant *n.* material for sealing things, especially to make them airtight or watertight. [f. SEAL[1]]

sealer *n.* a ship or person engaged in hunting seals. [f. SEAL[2]]

sealskin *n.* the skin or prepared fur of a seal; a garment made from this.

Sealyham /ˈsiːlɪəm/ *n.* a wire-haired short-legged terrier. [f. *Sealyham* in Dyfed, Wales]

seam *n.* **1** the line where two edges join, especially of cloth or leather etc. or boards. **2** a fissure between parallel edges. **3** a wrinkle. **4** a stratum of coal etc. —*v.t.* **1** to join by a seam. **2** (esp. in *p.p.*) to mark or score with a seam, fissure, or scar. —**seam bowler,** a bowler in cricket who makes the ball spin by bouncing it off its seam. [OE]

seaman *n.* (*pl.* **-men**) one whose occupation is on the sea; a sailor, especially below the rank of officer.

seamanship *n.* skill in managing a ship or boat. [f. prec. + -SHIP]

seamstress /ˈsemstrɪs/ *n.* a woman who sews, especially as a job. [OE (as SEAM)]

seamy *adj.* marked with or showing seams. —**seamy side,** the disreputable or unattractive side. [f. SEAM]

Seanad /ˈʃænəð/ *n.* the upper house of parliament in the Republic of Ireland. [Ir., = senate]

seance /ˈseɪɑ̃s/ *n.* a meeting for the exhibition or investigation of spiritualistic phenomena. [f. F, = a sitting]

seaplane *n.* an aircraft that can land on and take off from water using floats instead of an undercarriage. It differs from a flying boat in that its hull does not support it in the water.

seaport *n.* a port on the coast.

sear *v.t.* **1** to scorch, to cauterize. **2** to make (the conscience or feelings etc.) callous. [OE]

search /sɜːtʃ/ *v.t./i.* **1** to look through or go over thoroughly in order to find something. **2** to examine the clothes and body of (a person) to see if anything is concealed there. **3** to examine thoroughly (*lit.* or *fig.*). —*n.* an act of searching; an investigation. —**in search of,** trying to find. **search me,** (*colloq.*) I do not know. **search out,** to look for, to seek out. **search-party** *n.* a group of people organized to look for a lost person or thing. **search-warrant** *n.* an official authority to enter and search a building. —**searcher** *n.* [f. AF f. L *circare* go round (as CIRCUS)]

searchlight *n.* an electric lamp with a powerful concentrated beam that can be turned in any direction; the light or beam from this.

seascape *n.* a picture or view of the sea. [f. SEA, after *landscape*]

seasick *adj.* suffering from sickness or nausea from the motion of a ship etc. —**seasickness** *n.*

seaside *n.* the sea-coast, especially as a holiday resort.

season /ˈsiːz(ə)n/ *n.* **1** each of the divisions of the year (spring, summer, autumn, winter) associated with a type of weather and a stage of vegetation. **2** a proper or suitable time; the time when something is plentiful, active, or in vogue; the high season. **3** the time of year regularly devoted to an activity, or to social life generally. **4** an indefinite period. **5** (*colloq.*) a season ticket. —*v.t./i.* **1** to flavour or make palatable with salt, herbs, etc.; to enhance with wit etc.; to temper or moderate. **2** to make or become suitable or in a desired condition, especially by exposure to air or weather. —**in season,** (of food) available in good condition and plentifully; (of an animal) on heat. **season-ticket** *n.* a ticket entitling the holder to any number of journeys, admittances, etc., in a given period. [f. OF *saison* f. L *satio* sowing]

seasonable *adj.* **1** suitable or usual to the season. **2** opportune; meeting the needs of the occasion. —**seasonably** *adv.* [f. prec.]

seasonal *adj.* of, depending on, or varying with the season. —**seasonally** *adv.* [f. SEASON]

seasoning *n.* flavouring added to food. [as prec.]

seat *n.* **1** a thing made or used for sitting on; a place for one person in a theatre, vehicle, etc. **2** occupation of a seat; the right to this, e.g. as a member of a board or of the House of Commons. **3** the buttocks; the part of the trousers etc. covering them. **4** the part of a chair etc. on which the sitter's weight directly rests; the part of a machine that supports or guides another part. **5** a site or location. **6** a country mansion, especially with large grounds. **7** a person's manner of sitting on a horse etc. —*v.t.* **1** to cause to sit. **2** to provide sitting accommodation for. **3** (in *p.p.*) sitting. **4** to put or fit in position. —**be seated,** to sit down. **by the seat of one's pants,** by instinct rather than knowledge or logic. **seat-belt** *n.* a belt securing a person in the seat of a car or aircraft. **take a seat,** to sit down. **take one's seat,** to sit down, especially in one's appointed place; to assume one's official position, to be formally admitted to Parliament or to Congress. [f. ON (as SIT)]

-seater *in comb.* having a specified number of seats. [f. SEAT]

seating *n.* seats collectively, sitting accommodation. [f. SEAT]

seaward /ˈsiːwəd/ *adv.* (also **seawards**) towards the sea. —*adj.* going or facing towards the sea. —*n.* such a direction or position. [f. SEA + -WARD]

seaweed *n.* any alga growing in the sea or in rocks on the shore.

seaworthy *adj.* fit to put to sea.

sebaceous /sɪˈbeɪʃəs/ *adj.* fatty, secreting or conveying oily matter. [f. L (*sebum* tallow)]

sec *adj.* (of wine) dry. [F f. L *siccus* dry]

Sec. *abbr.* Secretary.

sec. *abbr.* second(s).

secant /ˈsiːkənt/ *n.* a straight line that cuts a curve, especially a circle, at two points; the radius of a circle produced through one end of an arc to meet the tangent to the other end; the ratio of this to the radius. —**secant of an angle,** the ratio of the length of the hypotenuse to the length of the side adjacent to that angle in a right-angled triangle. [f. F f. L *secare* cut]

secateurs /sekəˈtɜːz/ *n.* pruning-clippers used with one hand. [f. F f. L *secare* cut]

secede /sɪˈsiːd/ *v.i.* to withdraw formally from an organization, e.g. a political federation. [f. L *secedere* (*se-* aside, *cedere* go)]

secession /sɪˈseʃ(ə)n/ *n.* seceding. —**secessionist** *n.* [f. F or L (as prec.)]

seclude /sɪˈkluːd/ *v.t.* to keep (a person) apart from others; to keep (a place) screened or sheltered from view. [f. L *secludere* (*se-* aside, *claudere* shut)]

seclusion /sɪˈkluːʒ(ə)n/ *n.* **1** secluding, being secluded; privacy. **2** a secluded place. [as prec.]

second[1] /ˈsekənd/ *adj.* **1** next after first. **2** another besides one or the first, additional. **3** of subordinate importance or position etc., inferior. **4** (*Mus.*) performing a lower or subordinate part. **5** metaphorical, such as to be comparable to. —*n.* **1** the person or thing that is second; the second day of a month. **2** another person or thing besides the previously mentioned or principal one. **3** second-class honours in a university degree. **4** an assistant to a combatant in a duel, boxing match, etc. **5** (in *pl.*) a second helping of food; a second course of a meal. —*v.t.* **1** to back up, to assist. **2** to support, (a resolution etc. or its proposer) formally so as to show that the proposer is not isolated or as a means of bringing it to a vote. —**second-best** *adj.* & *n.* next after the best; inferior in quality (*come off second-best*, to fail to win). **second chamber,** the upper house of a parliament. **second class,** the second-best group or category or accommodation etc.; the class of mail that does not have priority in delivery. **second-class** *adj.* & *adv.* of or by the second or inferior class. **second fiddle,** a subordinate position or role. **second-guess** *v.t./i.* (*US*) to anticipate the action of; to predict; to criticize by hindsight. **second-hand** *adj.* having had a previous owner, not new; (of a shop etc.) supplying such goods; (*adv.*) from a secondary source (*at second hand*, indirectly). **second lieutenant,** an army officer next below lieutenant. **second nature,** an acquired tendency that has become instinctive. **second officer,** an assistant mate on a merchant ship. **second person,** see PERSON. **second-rate** *adj.* in the second class, inferior. **second sight,** the supposed power of perceiving future events. **second teeth,** adults' permanent teeth. **second thoughts,** a new opinion or resolution reached after further consideration. **second wind,** recovery of regular breathing during continued exertion after breathlessness; renewed capacity for effort after tiredness. —**seconder** *n.* [f. OF f. L *secundus* (*sequi* follow)]

second[2] /sɪˈkɒnd/ *v.t.* to transfer (an officer or official) temporarily to another appointment or department. —**secondment** *n.* [= prec.]

second[3] /ˈsekənd/ *n.* **1** the base unit of time (symbol s), the duration of 9,192,631,770 periods of the radiation of a certain transition of the caesium-133 atom. **2** one sixtieth part of an angle. **3** (*colloq.*) a very short time. [f. OF f. L *secunda* (*minuta*) secondary minute, i.e. minute of a minute]

secondary /ˈsekəndərɪ/ *adj.* **1** coming after or next below what is primary; derived from, depending on, or supplementing what is primary; of lesser importance or rank etc. than the first. **2** (of education, a school etc.) for those who have received primary education but have not yet proceeded to a university or occupation. —*n.* a thing that is secondary. —**secondary colours,** see COLOUR. **secondary picketing,** furtherance of an industrial dispute by picketing the premises of a firm not directly involved in it. —**secondarily** *adv.* [f. L (as SECOND[1])]

secondly *adv.* in the second place, furthermore. [f. SECOND[1]]

secrecy /ˈsiːkrəsɪ/ *n.* keeping things secret; being kept secret. —**sworn to secrecy,** having promised to keep a secret. [f. foll.]

secret /ˈsiːkrɪt/ *adj.* **1** kept or meant to be kept from the knowledge or view of others or of all but a few; to be known only by specified people. **2** acting or operating secretly. **3** fond of secrecy. —*n.* **1** a thing kept or meant to be kept secret. **2** a mystery, a thing for which an explanation is unknown or not widely known. **3** a valid but not generally known method for achieving something. —**in secret,** in a secret manner. **secret agent,** a spy acting for a country. **secret ballot,** one in which individual voters' choices are not made public. **secret police,** a police force operating in secret for political ends. **secret service,** a government department concerned with espionage. **secret society,** one whose members are sworn to secrecy about it. —**secretly** *adv.* [f. OF f. L *secretus* f. *secernere* separate, set apart (*se-* aside, *cernere* sift)]

secretaire /sekrɪˈteə(r)/ *n.* an escritoire. [F (as SECRETARY)]

secretariat /sekrəˈteərɪət/ *n.* an administrative office or department; its members or premises. [f. F f. L (as foll.)]

secretary /ˈsekrətərɪ/ *n.* **1** a person employed to assist with correspondence, keep records, make appointments, etc. **2** an official appointed by a society etc. to conduct its correspondence, keep its records, etc. **3** the principal assistant of a government minister, ambassador, etc. —**secretary-bird** *n.* a long-legged African bird (*Sagittarius serpentarius*) with a crest likened to quill pens placed behind a writer's ear. **Secretary-General** *n.* the principal administrator of an organization. **Secretary of State,** the head of a major government department; (*US*) the Foreign Secretary. —**secretarial** /-ˈteərɪəl/ *adj.*, **secretaryship** *n.* [f. L *secretarius* (as SECRET)]

secrete /sɪˈkri:t/ *v.t.* **1** to put into a place of concealment. **2** to separate (a substance) in a gland etc. from blood or sap for a function in the organism or for excretion. —**secretor** *n.* [f. SECRET or as back-formation f. foll.]

secretion /sɪˈkri:ʃ(ə)n/ *n.* **1** secreting, being secreted. **2** a secreted substance. [f. F or L *secretio* (as SECRET)]

secretive /ˈsi:krətɪv/ *adj.* making a secret of things unnecessarily, uncommunicative. —**secretively** *adv.*, **secretiveness** *n.* [back-formation f. *secretiveness* after F *secrétivité* (as SECRET)]

secretory /sɪˈkri:tərɪ/ *adj.* of physiological secretion. [f. SECRETE]

sect *n.* a group of people with religious or other beliefs that differ from those more generally accepted; the followers of a particular philosophy or school of thought. [f. OF or L *secta* (*sequi* follow)]

sectarian /sekˈteərɪən/ *adj.* of or concerning a sect; bigoted or narrow-minded in following one's sect. —*n.* a member of a sect. —**sectarianism** *n.* [f. L *sectarius* adherent (as prec.)]

section /ˈsekʃ(ə)n/ *n.* **1** a part cut off; one of the parts into which a thing is divided or divisible or out of which a structure can be fitted together; a subdivision of a book, statute, group of people, etc.; (*US*) an area of land, a district of a town; a subdivision of an army platoon. **2** separation by cutting. **3** the cutting of a solid by a plane; the resulting figure or area of this. —*v.t.* to arrange in or divide into sections. —**section-mark** *n.* a sign (§) used to indicate the start of a section of a book etc. [F or f. L (*secare* cut)]

sectional *adj.* **1** of a section; **2** made in sections. **3** local rather than general; partisan. —**sectionally** *adv.* [f. prec.]

sector /ˈsektə(r)/ *n.* **1** a distinct part or branch of an enterprise, of society or the economy, etc. **2** the plane figure enclosed between two radii of a circle, ellipse, etc., and the arc cut off by them. **3** any of the parts into which a battle area is divided for control of operations. [L, orig. = cutter (as SECTION)]

secular /ˈsekjʊlə(r)/ *adj.* **1** concerned with the affairs of this world, not spiritual or sacred. **2** not ecclesiastical or monastic. **3** occurring once in an age or century. —**secularity** /-ˈlærɪtɪ/ *n.* [f. F or L *saecularis* (*saeculum* an age)]

secularism *n.* the belief that morality or education should not be based on religion. —**secularist** *n.* [f. prec.]

secure /sɪˈkjʊə(r)/ *adj.* **1** safe, especially against attack. **2** certain not to slip or fail; reliable. —*v.t.* **1** to make secure; to fasten or close securely. **2** to succeed in obtaining. **3** to guarantee, to make safe against loss. —**securely** *adv.* [f. L *securus*, orig. = free from worry (*se-* aside, *cura* care)]

security /sɪˈkjʊərɪtɪ/ *n.* **1** the state or feeling of being secure; a thing that gives this. **2** the safety of a State, organization, etc., against espionage, theft, or other danger; an organization for ensuring this. **3** a thing deposited or pledged as a guarantee of the fulfilment of an undertaking or payment of a loan, to be forfeited in case of failure. **4** (often in *pl.*) a document as evidence of a loan; a certificate of stock, a bond, etc. —**security risk,** a person whose presence may threaten security. [f. OF or L (as prec.)]

sedan /sɪˈdæn/ *n.* **1** (also **sedan-chair**) an enclosed chair as a vehicle for one person (17th–18th c.), mounted on two horizontal poles and carried by two men. **2** (*US*) an enclosed motor car for four or more persons. [perh. f. It. dial., ult. f. L *sella* saddle (*sedēre* sit)]

sedate[1] /sɪˈdeɪt/ *adj.* tranquil and dignified, not lively. —**sedately** *adv.*, **sedateness** *n.* [f. L *sedare* make calm (*sedēre* sit)]

sedate[2] /sɪˈdeɪt/ *v.t.* to treat with sedatives. —**sedation** /-ˈdeɪʃ(ə)n/ *n.* [back-formation f. *sedation* f. F or L (as prec.)]

sedative /ˈsedətɪv/ *adj.* tending to calm or

soothe. —*n.* a sedative medicine or influence. [f. OF or L (as SEDATE)]

sedentary /ˈsedəntərɪ/ *adj.* sitting; (of work etc.) characterized by much sitting and little physical exercise; (of a person) having or inclined to work etc. of this kind. [f. F or L (*sedère* sit)]

sedge *n.* a waterside or marsh plant of the genus *Carex*, resembling coarse grass. —**sedgy** *adj.* [OE]

sediment /ˈsedɪmənt/ *n.* **1** very fine particles of solid matter suspended in a liquid or settling to the bottom of it. **2** solid matter (e.g. sand, gravel) carried by water or wind and deposited on the surface of the land. —**sedimentation** /-ˈteɪʃ(ə)n/ *n.* [f. F or L (*sedēre* sit)]

sedimentary /sedɪˈmentərɪ/ *adj.* **1** of or like sediment. **2** (of rock) formed from sediment. [f. prec.]

sedition /sɪˈdɪʃ(ə)n/ *n.* conduct or speech inciting people to rebellion. —**seditious** *adj.* [f. OF or L *seditio* (*se-* aside, *ire* go)]

seduce /sɪˈdju:s/ *v.t.* to tempt into (esp. extramarital) sexual intercourse; to persuade (esp. into wrongdoing) by offering temptations. —**seducer** *n.*, **seductress** /-ˈdʌktrɪs/ *n.fem.* [f. L (*se-* aside, *ducere* lead)]

seduction /sɪˈdʌkʃ(ə)n/ *n.* **1** seducing, being seduced. **2** a tempting or attractive thing or quality. [f. F or L (as prec.)]

seductive /sɪˈdʌktɪv/ *adj.* tending to seduce, alluring, enticing. —**seductively** *adv.*, **seductiveness** *n.* [f. prec.]

sedulous /ˈsedjʊləs/ *adj.* diligent and persevering. —**sedulity** /sɪˈdju:lɪtɪ/ *n.*, **sedulously** *adv.*, **sedulousness** *n.* [f. L *sedulus* zealous]

sedum /ˈsi:dəm/ *n.* a fleshy-leaved plant of the genus *Sedum*, with pink, white, or yellow flowers. [L, = houseleek]

see[1] *v.t./i.* (*past* **saw**; *p.p.* **seen**) **1** to perceive with the eyes; to have or use the power of doing this. **2** to perceive with the mind, to understand; to ascertain; to consider, to take time to do this; to foresee; to find attractive qualities (in a person etc.). **3** to watch, to be a spectator of. **4** to look at for information; to learn (a fact) from a newspaper or other visual source. **5** to meet; to be near and recognize. **6** to grant or obtain an interview (with); to visit in order to consult. **7** to interpret, to have an opinion of. **8** to supervise, to ensure. **9** to experience; to have presented to one's attention. **10** to call up a mental picture of, to imagine. **11** to escort or conduct. **12** (in gambling, esp. poker) to equal (a bet); to equal the bet of (a player). —**see about,** to attend to. **see after,** to take care of. **see the back of,** to be rid of (an unwanted person or thing). **see into,** to investigate. **see the light,** to realize one's mistakes etc.; to undergo a religious conversion. **see off,** to accompany to a place of departure; to ensure the departure of (a person). **see out,** to accompany out of a building etc.; to finish (a project etc.) completely; to wait until the end of (a period). **see over,** to inspect, to tour and examine. **see red,** to become suddenly enraged. **see stars,** to see lights before one's eyes as a result of a blow on the head. **see through,** not to be deceived by, to detect the nature of. **see a person through,** to support him during a difficult time. **see a thing through,** to finish it completely. **see-through** *adj.* (esp. of clothing) transparent, diaphanous. **see to,** to attend to; to organize; to put right. [OE]

see[2] *n.* the area under the authority of a bishop or archbishop; his office or jurisdiction. [f. AF f. L *sedes* seat]

seed *n.* **1** the unit of reproduction of a plant, a fertilized ovule capable of developing into another such plant; (*collect.*) seeds in any quantity, especially as collected for sowing. **2** semen, milt. **3** something from which a tendency or feeling etc. can develop. **4** offspring, descendants. **5** (in tennis etc.) a seeded player. —*v.t./i.* **1** to plant seeds (in); to sprinkle (as) with seed. **2** to produce or drop seed. **3** to remove seeds from (fruit etc.). **4** to place crystal etc. in (a cloud) to produce rain. **5** to name (a strong player) as not to be matched against another named in this way in the early rounds of a knock-out tournament, so as to increase the interest of later rounds; to arrange (the order of play) thus. —**go** *or* **run to seed,** to cease flowering as the seed develops; to become degenerate or unkempt etc. **seed-bed** *n.* a bed of fine soil in which to sow seeds; a place of development. **seed-pearl** *n.* a very small pearl. **seed-potato** *n.* a potato kept for seed. [OE (as SOW[1])]

seedling *n.* a young plant, especially one raised from seed and not from a cutting etc. [f. SEED + -LING]

seedsman *n.* (*pl.* **-men**) a dealer in seeds.

seedy *adj.* **1** full of seed; going to seed. **2** shabby-looking. **3** (*colloq.*) unwell. —**seedily** *adv.*, **seediness** *n.* [f. SEED]

seeing *n.* use of the eyes. —*conj.* (also **seeing that**) considering that, inasmuch as, because. [f. SEE]

seek *v.t./i.* (*past & p.p.* **sought** /sɔt/) **1** to make a search or inquiry (for); to try or want to find, obtain, or reach or do. **2** (*archaic*) to aim at, to attempt. —**seek out,** to seek specially, to single out for companionship etc. [OE]

seem *v.i.* to have the air, appearance, or feeling of being; to give a certain impression as to an action or state. —**it seems,** it appears to be true or the fact. [f. ON, = honour]

seeming *adj.* apparent but perhaps not real. [f. SEEM]

seemly *adj.* conforming to accepted standards of good taste; proper; suitable. —**seemliness** *n.* [as SEEM]

seen *p.p.* of SEE¹.

seep *v.i.* to ooze slowly out of or through; to percolate slowly. [perh. dial. form of OE, = soak]

seepage *n.* seeping; the quantity that seeps out. [f. SEEP]

seer *n.* **1** one who sees. **2** a person who sees visions, a prophet. [f. SEE¹]

seersucker /ˈsɪəsʌkə(r)/ *n.* a striped material of linen or cotton etc. woven with a puckered surface. [f. Pers., lit. = milk and sugar]

see-saw *n.* **1** a device for children, with a long plank balanced on a central support and a child sitting at each end moving up and down alternately; a game played on this. **2** an up-and-down or to-and-fro motion. **3** a contest in which the advantage repeatedly changes from one side to the other. —*v.i.* **1** to play on a see-saw; to move up and down as on a see-saw. **2** to vacillate in policy etc. —*adj.* & *adv.* with an up-and-down or backward-and-forward motion. [redupl. of SAW¹]

seethe /siːð/ *v.i.* **1** to bubble or surge as in boiling. **2** to be very agitated (esp. with anger) or excited. [OE]

segment /ˈsegmənt/ *n.* a part cut off or separable or marked off as though separable from the other parts of a thing; part of a circle or sphere etc. cut off by a line or plane intersecting it. —/also -ˈment/ *v.t./i.* to divide into segments. —**segmental** /-ˈment(ə)l/ *adj.*, **segmentation** /-ˈteɪʃ(ə)n/ *n.* [f. L *segmentum* (*secare* cut)]

segregate /ˈsegrɪgeɪt/ *v.t./i.* to put or come apart from the rest, to isolate; to separate (esp. a racial group) from the rest of the community. —**segregation** /-ˈgeɪʃ(ə)n/ *n.* [f. L *segregare* (*se-* apart, *grex* flock)]

segregationist /segrɪˈgeɪʃənɪst/ *n.* a person who is in favour of racial segregation. [f. prec.]

seigneur /seɪnˈjɜː(r)/ *n.* a feudal lord. —**seigneurial** *adj.* [f. OF f. L, = SENIOR]

seine /seɪn/ *n.* a fishing-net for encircling fish, with floats at the top and weights at the bottom edge. —*v.t./i.* to fish or catch with a seine. [f. OF & OE, ult. f. Gk *sagēnē*]

seise see SEIZE 5.

seismic /ˈsaɪzmɪk/ *adj.* of earthquakes; of earth vibrations produced artificially by explosions. —**seismic survey,** a survey of an area that is being explored for oil and gas, employing seismic methods. —**seismically** *adv.* [f. Gk *seismos* earthquake (*seiō* shake)]

seismogram /ˈsaɪzməgræm/ *n.* the record given by a seismograph. [as prec. + -GRAM]

seismograph /ˈsaɪzməgrɑːf/ *n.* an instrument for detecting, recording, and measuring the force and direction etc. of earthquakes. [as SEISMIC + -GRAPH]

seismography /saɪzˈmɒgrəfɪ/ *n.* the study or recording of natural or artificially produced seismic phenomena. —**seismographer** *n.*, **seismographic** /-məˈgræfɪk/ *adj.* [as SEISMIC + -GRAPHY]

seismology /saɪzˈmɒlədʒɪ/ *n.* seismography. —**seismological** /-ˈlɒdʒɪk(ə)l/ *adj.*, **seismologist** *n.* [as SEISMIC + -LOGY]

seize /siːz/ *v.t./i.* **1** to take hold of (a thing) forcibly, suddenly, or eagerly. **2** to take possession of forcibly or by legal power. **3** to affect suddenly. **4** to grasp with the mind quickly or clearly. **5** (*Law* also **seise** /siːz/) to put in possession of. **6** (*Naut.*) to fasten by binding with turns of yarn etc. **seize on** *or* **upon,** to seize eagerly. **seize up,** (of a mechanism) to become stuck or jammed from undue heat or friction. [f. OF]

seizure /ˈsiːʒə(r)/ *n.* **1** seizing, being seized. **2** a sudden attack of apoplexy etc., a stroke. [f. prec.]

sejant /ˈsiːʒ(ə)nt/ *adj.* (in heraldry, of an animal) sitting upright on its haunches. [f. OF, = sitting f. L *sedēre* sit]

seldom /ˈseldəm/ *adv.* rarely, not often. [OE]

select /sɪˈlekt/ *v.t.* to pick out as the best or most suitable. —*adj.* **1** chosen for excellence or fitness. **2** (of a society etc.) exclusive, cautious in admitting members. —**select committee,** a small parliamentary committee appointed to conduct a special inquiry. [f. L *seligere* (*se-* apart, *legere* pick)]

selection /sɪˈlekʃ(ə)n/ *n.* **1** selecting, being selected. **2** the selected person(s) or thing(s). **3** a collection of things from which a choice may be made. **4** the process by which some animals or plants thrive more than others, as a factor in evolution. [f. L *selectio* (as prec.)]

selective *adj.* **1** chosen or choosing carefully. **2** able to select. —**selectively** *adv.*, **selectivity** /-ˈtɪvɪtɪ/ *n.* [f. SELECT]

selector *n.* **1** a person who selects; a member of a committee selecting a national sports team. **2** a device in machinery making the required selection of gear etc. [as prec.]

selenium /sɪˈliːnɪəm/ *n.* a semi-metallic element, symbol Se, atomic number 34, chemically related to sulphur. [f. Gk *selēnē* moon]

self *n.* (*pl.* **selves**) /selvz/) **1** a person's or thing's own individuality or essence. **2** a person or thing as the object of introspection or reflexive action. **3** one's own interests or pleasure; concentration on these. **4** (in commerce, or *colloq.*) myself, yourself, herself, etc. —*adj.* of the same colour as the rest or throughout. [OE]

self- *prefix* expressing a reflexive action in the senses 'of or by oneself or itself', 'on, in, for, or relating to oneself or itself'. [f. prec.]

self-abnegation *n.* self-sacrifice.

self-abuse *n.* masturbation.

self-addressed *adj.* addressed to oneself.

self-appointed *adj.* appointed by himself or herself, especially in an officious or self-righteous way, and not necessarily recognized by others.

self-assertive /selfəˈsɜːtɪv/ *adj.* asserting onself, one's rights, etc., confidently. —**self-assertion** *n.*

self-assured /selfəˈʃʊəd/ *adj.* self-confident. —**self-assurance** *n.*

self-catering *adj.* catering for oneself, providing one's own meals, especially while on holiday.

self-centred /selfˈsentəd/ *adj.* preoccupied with oneself or one's own affairs.

self-confessed *adj.* openly confessing oneself to be.

self-confident *adj.* having confidence in one's own abilities. —**self-confidence** *n.*

self-conscious *adj.* embarrassed or unnatural in manner from knowing that one is observed by others. —**self-consciousness** *n.*

self-contained *adj.* **1** complete in itself; (of accommodation) having all the necessary facilities and not sharing these. **2** (of a person) independent, able to do without the company of others; not communicating freely.

self-control *n.* ability to control one's behaviour and not act emotionally. —**self-controlled** *adj.*

self-deception *n.* deceiving oneself, especially about one's feelings etc.

self-defeating *adj.* (of a course of action etc.) frustrating the purpose it was intended to serve.

self-defence *n.* defence of oneself or of one's rights or good reputation etc.

self-denial *n.* deliberately going without the pleasures etc. that one would like to have.

self-determination *n.* **1** determination of one's own fate or course of action, free will. **2** a nation's determination of its own form of government or its allegiance.

self-discipline *n.* discipline and training of oneself.

self-drive *adj.* (of a hired vehicle) driven by the hirer.

self-educated *adj.* educated by oneself, with little or no help from schools etc.

self-effacing *adj.* keeping oneself in the background. —**self-effacement** *n.*

self-employed *adj.* working independently and not for an employer.

self-esteem *n.* good opinion of oneself.

self-evident *adj.* evident without proof, explanation, or further evidence.

self-explanatory *adj.* that needs no (further) explanation.

self-fertilizing *adj.* (of a plant) fertilizing itself by its own pollen, not from others. —**self-fertilization** *n.*

self-fulfilment *n.* fulfilment of one's own hopes and ambitions etc.

self-governing *adj.* governing itself. —**self-government** *n.*

self-help *n.* use of one's own abilities or resources to achieve success, without dependence on others.

self-important *adj.* having a high opinion of one's own importance, pompous. —**self-importance** *n.*

self-imposed *adj.* (of a task etc.) imposed by oneself on oneself.

self-induced *adj.* induced by oneself or itself.

self-indulgent *adj.* greatly indulging one's own desires for comfort and pleasure. —**self-indulgence** *n.*

self-inflicted *adj.* inflicted by oneself on oneself.

self-interest *n.* one's personal interest or advantage. —**self-interested** *adj.*

selfish *adj.* acting or done according to one's own interests and needs without regard for those of others; keeping good things for oneself and not sharing. —**selfishly** *adv.*, **selfishness** *n.* [f. SELF]

selfless *adj.* disregarding oneself or one's own interests, unselfish. —**selflessly** *adv.*, **selflessness** *n.* [f. SELF + -LESS]

self-loading *adj.* (of a firearm) reloading itself after firing, automatic.

self-locking *adj.* locking automatically when closed.

self-made *adj.* having risen from poverty or obscurity and achieved success by one's own efforts.

self-opinionated *adj.* stubbornly adhering to one's own opinions.

self-pity *n.* pity for oneself.

self-portrait *n.* a portrait of himself by an artist; an account of himself by a writer.

self-possessed *adj.* feeling or remaining calm and dignified, especially in difficulty. —**self-possession** *n.*

self-preservation *n.* protection of oneself from death, harm, or injury etc.; the instinct to ensure one's own survival.

self-propelled *adj.* propelled by itself or its own motor etc., not drawn or pushed. —**self-propulsion** *n.*

self-raising *adj.* (of flour) containing a raising agent and for use without additional baking-powder.

self-recording *adj.* (of a scientific instrument) recording measurements or changes etc. automatically.

self-regard *n.* regard for oneself.

self-reliant *adj.* reliant on or confident in one's own abilities and resources. —**self-reliance** *n.*

self-reproach *n.* reproach or blame directed by oneself at oneself.

self-respect *n.* respect for oneself, the feeling that one is behaving with honour, dignity, etc. —**self-respecting** *adj.*

self-restrained *adj.* able to restrain one's own emotions. —**self-restraint** *n.*

self-righteous *adj.* conceitedly aware of or asserting one's own righteousness. —**self-righteously** *adv.*

self-sacrifice *n.* sacrifice of one's own interests and wishes so that others may benefit. —**self-sacrificing** *adj.*

selfsame *adj.* the very same, identical.

self-satisfied *adj.* pleased or unduly satisfied with oneself or one's own achievements, conceited. —**self-satisfaction** *n.*

self-sealing *adj.* sealing automatically; (of a tyre etc.) having the means of automatically sealing small punctures.

self-seeking *adj.* & *n.* seeking to promote one's own interests rather than those of others.

self-service *n.* (often *attrib.*) the system in a shop or restaurant etc. by which customers serve themselves and pay for what they have taken.

self-sown *adj.* grown from seed that has dropped naturally from the plant.

self-starter *n.* an electric device for starting an internal-combustion engine.

self-styled *adj.* using a title or name etc. that one has given oneself, especially without authorization or right.

self-sufficient *adj.* able to supply one's own needs without outside help. —**self-sufficiency** *n.*

self-supporting *adj.* that supports oneself or itself without help; self-sufficient.

self-taught *adj.* having taught oneself without formal help from a teacher etc.

self-willed *adj.* obstinately determined to follow one's own wishes, intentions, etc.; stubborn. —**self-will** *n.*

self-winding *adj.* (of a watch or clock) having a mechanism that winds it automatically.

sell *v.t./i.* (*past* & *p.p.* **sold** /səʊld/) **1** to make over or dispose of in exchange for money. **2** to keep a stock of (goods) for sale. **3** (of goods) to find purchasers; to have a specified price. **4** to betray or offer dishonourably for money or other reward. **5** to promote sales of; to inspire with a desire to buy, acquire, or agree to. —*n.* (*colloq.*) **1** the manner of selling. **2** a deception, a disappointment. —**be sold on,** to be enthusiastic about. **selling-point** *n.* an advantage recommending a thing. **sell off,** to sell the remainder of (goods) at reduced prices. **sell out,** to sell (all one's stock, shares, etc., or *absol.*); to betray; to be treacherous or disloyal to. **sell-out** *n.* the selling of all tickets for a show etc., a commercial success; a betrayal. **sell short,** to disparage; to underestimate. **sell up,** to sell one's business, house, etc. [OE]

sellable *adj.* that may be sold, able to find purchasers. [f. SELL]

seller *n.* one who sells. —**seller's market,** a situation in which a commodity is scarce and therefore expensive. [f. SELL]

Sellotape /ˈseləʊteɪp/ *n.* [P] an adhesive usually transparent cellulose or plastic tape. —**sellotape** *v.t.* to fix or seal with tape of this kind. [f. CELL(ULOSE) + TAPE]

selvage /ˈselvɪdʒ/ *n.* **1** an edge of cloth so woven that it does not unravel. **2** a tape-like border along the edge of cloth, intended to be removed or hidden. [f. SELF + EDGE]

selves *pl.* of SELF.

semantic /sɪˈmæntɪk/ *adj.* of meaning in language; of connotation. —**semantically** *adv.* [f. F f. Gk (*sēmainō* signify)]

semantics *n.pl.* (usu. treated as *sing.*) **1** the branch of philology concerned with meaning. **2** meaning, connotation. **3** interpretation of symbols (e.g. road signs) other than words. [f. prec.]

semaphore /ˈseməfɔː(r)/ *n.* **1** a system of signalling by holding the arms or two flags in certain positions to indicate letters of the alphabet. **2** a signalling apparatus consisting of a post with movable arm(s) etc. used on railways etc. —*v.t./i.* to signal or send by semaphore. [f. F f. Gk *sēma* sign, *pherō* bear]

semblance /ˈsembləns/ *n.* **1** an outward appearance (either real or pretended), a show. **2** a resemblance or likeness. [f. OF f. L (as SIMULATE)]

semen /ˈsiːmen/ *n.* the whitish reproductive fluid produced by male animals, containing spermatozoa. [L, = seed]

semester /sɪˈmestə(r)/ *n.* a half-year course or term in (esp. German and US) universities. [G f. L *semestris* six-monthly (*sex* six, *mensis* month)]

semi /ˈsemɪ/ *n.* (*colloq.*) a semi-detached house. [abbr.]

semi- *prefix* **1** half, partly. **2** occurring or appearing twice in a specified period (*semi-annual*). [F or L, = half (corresp. to Gk HEMI-)]

semibreve /ˈsemɪbriːv/ *n.* (*Mus.*) the longest note in common use.

semicircle /ˈsemɪsɜːk(ə)l/ *n.* half of a circle or of its circumference.

semicircular /semɪˈsɜːkjuːlə(r)/ *adj.* arranged in or shaped like a semicircle. —**semicircular canal,** each of three fluid-filled channels in the ear giving information to the brain to help to maintain balance.

semicolon /semɪˈkəulən/ *n.* a punctuation mark (;) used where there is a more distinct break than that indicated by a comma but less than that indicated by a full stop.

semiconductor /semɪkənˈdʌktə(r)/ *n.* a substance that has an electrical conductivity intermediate between insulators and metals. —**semiconducting** *adj.*

semi-detached *adj.* (of a house) joined to another on one side only.

semifinal /semɪˈfaɪn(ə)l/ *n.* the match or round preceding the final. —**semifinalist** *n.*

seminal /ˈsemɪn(ə)l/ *adj.* **1** of seed or semen; of reproduction. **2** (of ideas etc.) providing a basis for future development. —**seminal fluid,** semen. [f. OF or L (as SEMEN)]

seminar /ˈsemɪnɑː(r)/ *n.* **1** a small class at a university etc. for discussion and research. **2** a short intensive course of study. [G (as foll.)]

seminary /ˈsemɪnərɪ/ *n.* a training-college for priests or rabbis etc. —**seminarist** *n.* [f. L, = seed-plot (*semen* seed)]

semiology /siːmɪˈɒlədʒɪ/ *n.* the branch of linguistics concerned with signs and symbols. —**semiotic** *adj.* [f. Gk *sēmeion* sign (*sēma* mark) + -LOGY]

semi-permeable *adj.* (of a membrane etc.) allowing small molecules to pass through but not large ones; permeable to molecules of water but not to those of any dissolved substance.

semiprecious /semɪˈpreʃəs/ *adj.* (of a gem) less valuable than the stones called precious.

semiquaver /ˈsemɪkweɪvə(r)/ *n.* (*Mus.*) a note equal to half a quaver.

semi-rigid *adj.* (of an airship) having a flexible gas-container to which is attached a stiffened keel or framework.

semi-skilled *adj.* (of work or a worker) having or needing some training but less than for a skilled worker.

Semite /ˈsiːmaɪt/ *n.* a member of any of the races supposedly descended from Shem, son of Noah (Gen. 10: 21 ff.), including the Jews, Phoenicians, Arabs, and Assyrians. —*adj.* of the Semites. [f. L f. Gk *Sēm* Shem]

Semitic /sɪˈmɪtɪk/ *adj.* **1** of the family of languages that includes Hebrew, Arabic, and Aramaic, and certain ancient languages such as Phoenician, Assyrian, and Babylonian. **2** of Semites; of the Jews. [f. prec.]

semitone /ˈsemɪtəun/ *n.* half a tone in the musical scale.

semi-trailer /semɪˈtreɪlə(r)/ *n.* a trailer having wheels at the back and supported at the front by a towing vehicle.

semitropical /semɪˈtrɒpɪk(ə)l/ *adj.* subtropical.

semivowel /ˈsemɪvauəl/ *n.* a sound intermediate between a vowel and a consonant (e.g. *w*, *y*); a letter representing this.

semolina /seməˈliːnə/ *n.* the hard grains left after the milling of flour, used in milk puddings etc.; a pudding made of this. [f. It. *semolino* (*semola* bran)]

sempstress var. of SEAMSTRESS.

SEN *abbr.* State Enrolled Nurse.

sen. *abbr.* **1** Senator. **2** Senior.

senate /ˈsenət/ *n.* **1** the State council of the ancient Roman republic and empire, composed (after the early period) of ex-magistrates and having a variety of administrative, legislative, and judicial functions. **2** the upper and smaller branch of the legislative assembly in the USA, France, States of the USA, etc. **3** the governing (academic) body of certain universities or (*US*) colleges. [f. OF f. L *senatus* (*senex* old man)]

senator /ˈsenətə(r)/ *n.* a member of a senate. —**senatorial** /-ˈtɔrɪəl/ *adj.* [as prec.]

send *v.t./i.* (*past* & *p.p.* **sent**) **1** to order, cause, or enable to go to a certain destination; to have (a thing) conveyed. **2** to send a message or letter. **3** (of God, Providence, etc.) to grant, bestow, or inflict. **4** to cause to move or go. **5** to cause to become. **6** (*slang*) to affect emotionally, to put into ecstasy. —**send away for,** to order (goods etc.) by post from a dealer. **send down,** to rusticate or expel from a university; to put in prison. **send for,** to order (a person) to come to one's presence; to order (a thing) to be brought or delivered from elsewhere. **send off,** to dispatch (a letter etc.); to attend the departure of (a person) as a sign of respect etc.; (of a referee) to order (a player) to leave the field and take no further part in the game. **send-off** *n.* a demonstration of goodwill etc. at the departure of a person, the start of a project, etc. **send on,** to transmit to a further destination or in advance of one's own arrival. **send up,** to cause to go up; to transmit to higher authority; (*colloq.*) to satirize, to ridicule by comic imitation. **send-up** *n.* (*colloq.*) a satire or parody. **send word,** to send information. —**sender** *n.* [OE]

senescent /sɪˈnes(ə)nt/ *adj.* growing old. —**senescence** *n.* [f. L *senescere* (*senex* old)]

seneschal /ˈsenɪʃ(ə)l/ *n.* the steward of a medieval great house. [f. OF f. L *seniscalus*]

senile /ˈsiːnaɪl/ *adj.* of or characteristic of old age; having the symptoms and weaknesses of old age. —**senility** /sɪˈnɪlɪtɪ/ *n.* [f. F or L *senilis* (as SENESCENT)]

senior /ˈsiːnɪə(r)/ *adj.* **1** older or oldest in age; (placed after a name) older than another of the same name. **2** higher in rank or authority. **3** for older children. —*n.* **1** a senior person; one's senior in age or rank etc. **2** a member of a senior school. —**senior citizen,** an elderly person, especially an old-age pensioner. **senior nursing officer,** a person in charge of nurses in a hospital. **senior school,** a school for older children (especially those over 11). **senior service,** the Royal Navy. [L, compar. of *senex* old]

seniority /siːnɪˈɒrɪtɪ/ *n.* the state of being senior. [f. prec.]

senna /ˈsenə/ *n.* cassia; a laxative prepared from this. [f. L f. Arab.]

señor /senˈjɔː(r)/ *n.* (*pl.* ***señores*** /-rez/) a title used of or to a Spanish-speaking man. [Sp. f. L, = SENIOR]

señora /senˈjɔːrə/ *n.* a title used of or to a Spanish-speaking married woman. [fem., as prec.]

señorita /senjəˈriːtə/ *n.* a title used of or to a Spanish-speaking unmarried woman. [as prec.]

sensation /senˈseɪʃ(ə)n/ *n.* **1** an awareness or feeling produced by stimulation of a sense-organ or of the mind, emotions, etc. **2** ability to feel such stimulation. **3** a condition of eager interest, excitement, or admiration aroused in a community or group of people; a person or thing arousing this. [f. L *sensatio* f. *sensus* sense]

sensational *adj.* **1** arousing eager interest, excitement, or admiration in a community or group of people. **2** (*colloq.*) extraordinary. —**sensationally** *adv.* [f. prec.]

sensationalism *n.* **1** pursuit of the sensational; use of subject-matter, words, or style etc. in order to produce excessive emotional excitement in people. **2** the theory that ideas are derived solely from sensation (opp. RATIONALISM). —**sensationalist** *n.* [f. prec.]

sense *n.* **1** any of the special powers (usually reckoned as sight, hearing, smell, taste, touch) by which a living thing becomes aware of external objects and of changes in the condition of its own body. **2** ability to perceive, feel, or be conscious of a thing; awareness or recognition of something. **3** practical wisdom or judgement; conformity to this; common sense. **4** the meaning of a word etc.; possession of a meaning or of reasonableness. **5** the prevailing opinion. **6** (in *pl.*) a person's sanity or normal state of mind. —*v.t.* **1** to perceive by one or more of the senses. **2** to become aware of by receiving a mental impression; to realize. **3** (of a machine etc.) to detect. —**come to one's senses,** to regain consciousness; to be sensible after acting foolishly. **in a** *or* **one sense,** if the statement is understood in a particular way. **make sense,** to be intelligible or practicable. **make sense of,** to show or find the meaning of. **sense-datum** *n.* whatever is the immediate object of any of the senses, usually (but not always) with the implication that it is not a material object. **sense-organ** *n.* a bodily organ conveying external stimuli to the sensory system. [f. L *sensus* (*sentire* feel)]

senseless *adj.* **1** unconscious. **2** not showing good sense, wildly foolish; without meaning or purpose. —**senselessness** *n.* [f. prec. + -LESS]

sensibility /sensɪˈbɪlɪtɪ/ *n.* **1** the capacity to feel physically or emotionally. **2** exceptional or excessive sensitiveness; delicacy of feeling, susceptibility. **3** (in *pl.*) a tendency to feel offended etc. [f. L (as foll.)]

sensible /ˈsensɪb(ə)l/ *adj.* **1** having or showing good sense. **2** aware. **3** perceptible by the senses; great enough to be perceived. **4** (of clothing etc.) practical and functional rather than fashionable. —**sensibly** *adv.* [f. OF or L *sensibilis* (as SENSE)]

sensitive /ˈsensɪtɪv/ *adj.* **1** affected by stimuli or mental impressions; receiving impressions quickly and easily. **2** alert and considerate about the feelings of others. **3** easily hurt or offended. **4** (of an instrument etc.) readily responsive to or recording slight changes; (of photographic materials etc.) prepared so as to respond to the action of light. **5** (of a topic) requiring tactful treatment so as to avoid embarrassment, ensure security, etc. —**sensitive plant,** a mimosa (*Mimosa pudica*) or other plant that droops or closes when touched; a sensitive person. —**sensitively** *adv.* [f. OF or L (as SENSE)]

sensitivity /sensɪˈtɪvɪtɪ/ *n.* the quality or degree of being sensitive. [f. prec.]

sensitize /ˈsensɪtaɪz/ *v.t.* to make sensitive. —**sensitization** /-ˈzeɪʃ(ə)n/ *n.* [f. SENSITIVE]

sensor /ˈsensə(r)/ *n.* a device to detect, record, or measure a physical property. [f. foll.]

sensory /ˈsensərɪ/ *adj.* of sensation or the senses; receiving or transmitting sensation. [f. L *sensorium* seat of feeling (as SENSE)]

sensual /ˈsensjʊəl/ *adj.* **1** physical, gratifying to the body. **2** indulging oneself with physical pleasures; showing that one does this. —**sensualism** *n.*, **sensuality** /-ˈælɪtɪ/ *n.*, **sensually** *adv.* [f. L (as SENSE)]

sensuous /ˈsensjʊəs/ *adj.* of, affecting, or appealing to the senses, esp. aesthetically. —**sensuously** *adv.* [as SENSE]

sent *past & p.p.* of SEND.

sentence /ˈsentəns/ *n.* **1** a set of words (or occasionally one word) that is complete in itself as an expression of thought, containing or implying a subject and a predicate and expressing a statement, question, exclamation, or command. **2** the decision of a lawcourt, especially the punishment allotted to a person convicted in a criminal trial; the declaration of this. —*v.t.* to pass sentence upon (a convicted person); to condemn to a specified punishment. —**sentential** /-ˈtenʃ(ə)l/ *adj.* (in *Gram.* sense). [f. OF f. L *sententia* opinion]

sententious /senˈtenʃəs/ *adj.* affectedly or pompously formal or moralizing; aphoristic. —**sententiously** *adv.*, **sententiousness** *n.* [f. L (as prec.)]

sentient /ˈsenʃənt/ *adj.* perceiving or capable of perceiving things by means of the senses. —**sentience** *n.*, **sentiency** *n.* [f. L *sentire* feel]

sentiment /ˈsentɪmənt/ *n.* **1** a mental attitude produced by one's feeling about something; a verbal expression of this; an opinion. **2** emotion as opposed to reason; sentimentality. [f. OF f. L (as prec.)]

sentimental /sentɪˈment(ə)l/ *adj.* **1** of or characterized by romantic or nostalgic feeling. **2** showing or affected by emotion rather than reason. —**sentimental value,** the value of a thing to a particular person because of its associations. —**sentimentalism** *n.*, **sentimentalist** *n.*, **sentimentality** /-ˈtælɪtɪ/ *n.*, **sentimentally** *adv.* [f. prec.]

sentimentalize /sentɪˈmentəlaɪz/ *v.t.* to show sentimentality. [f. prec.]

sentinel /ˈsentɪn(ə)l/ *n.* a look-out, a sentry. [f. F f. It.; orig. unkn.]

sentry /ˈsentrɪ/ *n.* a soldier etc. stationed to keep guard. —**sentry-box** *n.* a wooden cabin large enough to shelter a standing sentry. **sentry-go** *n.* the duty of pacing up and down as a sentry. [perh. f. obs. *centrinel*, var. of prec.]

sepal /ˈsep(ə)l/ *n.* a division or leaf of the calyx. [f. F (coined 1790), perh. as SEPARATE + PETAL]

separable /ˈsepərəb(ə)l/ *adj.* that may be separated. —**separability** /-ˈbɪlɪtɪ/ *n.* **separably** *adv.* [f. F or L (as foll.)]

separate /ˈsepərət/ *adj.* not joined or united with others; forming a unit that is or may be regarded as apart or by itself, distinct, individual. —*n.* (in *pl.*) separate articles of dress suitable for wearing together in various combinations. —/-eɪt/ *v.t./i.* **1** to make separate, to divide, to keep apart; to prevent the union or contact of; to be between. **2** to become separate; to go different ways; to withdraw oneself from a union; to cease to live together as a married couple. **3** to divide into sorts or sizes etc.; to extract (an item or set of items etc.) thus. —**separately** *adv.* [f. L *separare* (*se-* apart, *parare* make ready)]

separation /sepəˈreɪʃ(ə)n/ *n.* **1** separating, being separate. **2** (in full **judicial** or **legal separation**) an arrangement by which a husband and wife remain married but live apart. [f. OF f. L (as prec.)]

separatism /ˈsepərətɪz(ə)m/ *n.* a policy of separation, especially for political or ecclesiastical independence. —**separatist** *n.* [f. SEPARATE]

separative /ˈsepərətɪv/ *adj.* tending to cause separation. [as prec.]

separator /ˈsepəreɪtə(r)/ *n.* a machine for separating things, e.g. cream from milk. [f. SEPARATE]

Sephardi /seˈfɑːdɪ/ *n.* (*pl.* **-im**) a Jew of Spanish or Portuguese descent (cf. ASHKENAZI). —**Sephardic** *adj.* [Heb., f. name of country (*Sepharad*) mentioned in Obad. 20 and held in late Jewish tradition to be Spain]

sepia /ˈsiːpɪə/ *n.* a dark reddish-brown colour or paint. [L f. Gk, = cuttlefish]

sepoy /ˈsiːpɔɪ/ *n.* (*hist.*) a native Indian soldier under British or other European discipline. [f. Urdu & Pers. *sipāhī* soldier]

sepsis /ˈsepsɪs/ *n.* a septic condition. [Gk (as SEPTIC)]

sept *n.* a clan, especially in Ireland. [prob. alt. of SECT]

Sept. *abbr.* September.

September /sepˈtembə(r)/ *n.* the ninth month of the year. [f. L (*septem* seven, because orig. the seventh month in the Roman calendar)]

septennial /sepˈtenɪəl/ *adj.* lasting or recurring every seven years. —**septennially** *adv.* [f. L *septennium* (*septem* seven, *annus* year)]

septet /sepˈtet/ *n.* **1** a musical composition for seven performers; these performers. **2** any group of seven. [f. G f. L *septem* seven]

septic /ˈseptɪk/ *adj.* infected with harmful micro-organisms that cause pus to form. —**septic tank,** a tank into which sewage is conveyed and in which it remains until the activity of bacteria makes it liquid enough to drain away. —**septically** *adv.* [f. L f. Gk *sēptikos* (*sēpō* make rotten)]

septicaemia /septɪˈsiːmɪə/ *n.* blood-poisoning. —**septicaemic** *adj.* [as prec. + Gk *haima* blood]

septuagenarian /septjʊədʒɪˈneərɪən/ *adj.* from

70 to 79 years old. —*n.* a septuagenarian person. [f. L (*septuageni* seventy each)]

Septuagesima /septjʊə'dʒesɪmə/ *n.* the Sunday before Sexagesima. [L. = seventieth (day) (as foll.), with ref. to period of 70 days from Septuagesima to Saturday after Easter]

septum /'septəm/ *n.* (*pl.* **septa**) a partition such as that between the nostrils or the chambers of a poppy-fruit or a shell. [f. L (*saepire* fence off)]

septuple /'septjʊp(ə)l/ *adj.* sevenfold; having seven parts; being seven times as many or as much. —*n.* a sevenfold number or amount. [f. L *septuplus* (*septem* seven)]

sepulchral /sɪ'pʌlkr(ə)l/ *adj.* **1** of a sepulchre or interment. **2** gloomy, funereal. [f. F or L (as foll.)]

sepulchre /'sepəlkə(r)/ *n.* a tomb, especially one cut in rock or built of stone or brick. —*v.t.* to place in a sepulchre; to serve as a sepulchre for. [f. OF f. L *sepulc(h)rum* (*sepelire* bury)]

sepulture /'sepəltʃə(r)/ *n.* burying, placing in a grave. [f. OF f. L *sepultura* (as prec.)]

sequel /'si:kw(ə)l/ *n.* **1** what follows or arises out of an earlier event. **2** a novel or film etc. that continues the story of an earlier one. [f. OF or L *sequela* (*sequi* follow)]

sequence /'si:kwəns/ *n.* **1** a succession; the order of succession. **2** a set of things belonging next to one another, an unbroken series. **3** a section of a cinema film, dealing with one scene or topic [f. L *sequentia* (as prec.)]

sequential /sɪ'kwenʃ(ə)l/ *adj.* forming a sequence or consequence. —**sequentially** *adv.* [f. prec.]

sequester /sɪ'kwestə(r)/ *v.t.* **1** to seclude, to isolate. **2** to sequestrate. [f. OF or L *sequestrare* (*sequester* person with whom a contested thing is deposited)]

sequestrate /sɪ'kwestreɪt, 'si:-/ *v.t.* to confiscate; to take temporary possession of (a debtor's estate etc.). —**sequestration** /si:kwe'streɪʃ(ə)n/ *n.*, **sequestrator** *n.* [f. L (as prec.)]

sequin /'si:kwɪn/ *n.* a circular spangle on a dress etc. —**sequinned** *adj.* [F f. It. *zecchino* gold coin]

sequoia /sɪ'kwɔɪə/ *n.* a Californian coniferous tree of the genus *Sequoia*, growing to a great height. [f. *Sequoiah*, name of a Cherokee]

serac /se'ræk/ *n.* each of the castellated masses into which a glacier is divided at steep points by the crossing of crevasses. [f. Swiss F *sérac*, originally the name of a compact white cheese]

seraglio /se'rɑ:lɪəʊ/ *n.* (*pl.* **-os**) **1** a harem. **2** (*hist.*) a Turkish palace. [f. It. f. Turk. f. Pers. *sarāy* palace]

seraph /'serəf/ *n.* (*pl.* **seraphim** or **seraphs**) an angelic being of the highest order of the celestial hierarchy. —**seraphic** /sə'ræfɪk/ *adj.*, **seraphically** *adv.* [backformation f. *seraphim* (ult. f. Heb.)]

serenade /serə'neɪd/ *n.* **1** a piece of music sung or played by a lover to his lady, or suitable for this. **2** an orchestral suite for a small ensemble. —*v.t.* to sing or play a serenade to. [f. F or It. *serenata* (as SERENE)]

serendipity /serən'dɪpɪtɪ/ *n.* the faculty of making happy discoveries by accident. —**serendipitous** *adj.* [coined by Horace Walpole (1754) f. *The Three Princes of Serendip* (Sri Lanka), a fairy-tale]

serene /sɪ'ri:n/ *adj.* **1** (of the sky, air, etc.) clear and calm; (of the sea) unruffled. **2** tranquil, calm and unperturbed. —**His, Her, Your Serene Highness,** titles used of or to members of some European royal families. —**serenely** *adv.*, **serenity** /-'renɪtɪ/ *n.* [f. L *serenus*]

serf *n.* **1** a labourer who could not be removed (except by manumission) from his lord's land on which he worked, and was transferred with it when it passed to another owner. **2** an oppressed labourer, a drudge. —**serfdom** *n.* [OF f. L *servus* slave]

serge *n.* a durable twilled worsted etc. fabric used for making clothes. [f. OF f. L *serica* (*lana*) (as SILK)]

sergeant /'sɑ:dʒ(ə)nt/ *n.* **1** a non-commissioned Army or RAF officer next below warrant officer. **2** a police officer below inspector. —**(regimental) sergeant-major** *n.* a warrant officer assisting the adjutant of a regiment or battalion. [f. OF f. L *serviens* servant (as SERVE)]

serial /'sɪərɪəl/ *n.* a story published or broadcast etc. in regular instalments. —*adj.* **1** of, in or forming a series. **2** (of a story etc.) in the form of a serial. **3** (of music) using serial composition. —**serial composition,** a technique used in composing music whereby the twelve notes of the chromatic scale are arranged in a fixed order and form the basic core of a piece. **serial number,** a number identifying an item in a series. —**serialism** *n.*, **serially** *adv.* [f. SERIES]

serialize /'sɪərɪəlaɪz/ *v.t.* to publish or produce in instalments. —**serialization** /-'zeɪʃ(ə)n/ *n.* [f. SERIAL]

series /'sɪəri:z, -ɪz/ *n.* (*pl.* same) **1** a number of things of the same kind, or related to each other in a similar way, occurring, arranged, or produced in order. **2** a set of geological strata with a common characteristic. **3** a set of stamps or coins etc. issued at one time or in one reign. **4** an arrangement of the twelve notes of the chromatic scale as the basis for serial composition (see SERIAL). —**in series,** in an ordered succession; (of a set of electrical circuits) arranged so that the same current passes through each circuit. [L, = row, chain (*serere* join)]

serif /ˈserɪf/ *n.* a slight projection finishing off the stroke of a printed letter (as in T, contrasted with sanserif T). [perh. f. Du. *schreef* line]

serio-comic /sɪərɪəʊˈkɒmɪk/ *adj.* combining the serious and the comic. —**serio-comically** *adv.* [f. foll. + COMIC]

serious /ˈsɪərɪəs/ *adj.* **1** solemn and thoughtful, not smiling. **2** sincere, in earnest, not casual or lighthearted. **3** important, demanding thought. **4** causing great concern, not slight. —**seriously** *adv.*, **seriousness** *n.* [f. OF or L *seriosus*]

serjeant /ˈsɑːdʒ(ə)nt/ *n.* (also **serjeant-at-law**) (*hist.*) a barrister of the highest rank. —**serjeant-at-arms** *n.* an official of a court, city, or parliament, with ceremonial duties; an officer of each House of Parliament with the duty of enforcing the commands of the house, arresting offenders, etc. [var. of SERGEANT]

sermon /ˈsɜːmən/ *n.* **1** a spoken or written discourse on religion or morals etc., especially one delivered by a clergyman during a religious service. **2** a long moralizing talk. [f. AF f. L *sermo* discourse]

sermonize *v.t./i.* to deliver a moral lecture (to). [f. prec.]

serous /ˈsɪərəs/ *adj.* **1** of or like serum, watery. **2** (of a gland etc.) having a serous secretion. —**serosity** /-ˈrɒsɪtɪ/ *n.* [f. F or L (as SERUM)]

serpent /ˈsɜːpənt/ *n.* **1** a snake, especially of a large kind. **2** a sly or treacherous person. [f. OF f. L *serpens* (*serpere* creep)]

serpentine /ˈsɜːpəntaɪn/ *adj.* of or like a serpent, twisting and turning; cunning, treacherous. —*n.* a soft usually dark green rock, sometimes mottled. [as prec.]

serrated /seˈreɪtɪd/ *adj.* with a toothed edge like a saw. —**serration** *n.* [f. L *serrare* (*serra* saw)]

serried /ˈserɪd/ *adj.* (of ranks of soldiers) close together. [f. *serry* press close f. F *serrer* to close]

serum /ˈsɪərəm/ *n.* (*pl.* **sera** or **serums**) **1** the thin amber-coloured fluid that remains from blood when the rest has clotted; this taken from an immunized animal and used for inoculation. **2** any watery fluid from animal tissue (e.g. in a blister). [L, = whey]

servant /ˈsɜːv(ə)nt/ *n.* **1** a person employed to do domestic work in a household or as a personal attendant. **2** an employee considered as performing services for his employer. **3** a devoted follower, a person willing to serve another. [f. OF (as foll.)]

serve *v.t./i.* **1** to perform services for; to be a servant to; to work for. **2** to be employed or performing a spell of duty; to be a member of the armed forces. **3** to be useful to or serviceable for; to do what is required; to provide a facility for. **4** to go through a due period of (office, apprenticeship, a prison sentence, etc.). **5** to set out or present (food) for those about to eat it; to act as a waiter; to attend to (a customer in a shop). **6** (of a quantity of food) to be enough for. **7** to treat or act towards (a person) in a specified way. **8** to assist (the officiating priest) in a religious service. **9** to make legal delivery of (a writ etc.). **10** (in tennis etc.) to set the ball in play. **11** (of an animal) to copulate with (a female). —*n.* a service in tennis etc.; a person's turn for this. —**serve a person right,** to be his deserved punishment or misfortune. **serve up,** to offer for acceptance. —**server** *n.* [f. OF *servir* f. L (*servus* slave)]

servery /ˈsɜːvərɪ/ *n.* **1** a room from which meals are served and in which utensils are kept. **2** a serving-hatch. [f. prec.]

service /ˈsɜːvɪs/ *n.* **1** the doing of work for another or for a community etc.; the work done; assistance or benefit given to someone; readiness to perform this. **2** a provision or system of supplying some public need, e.g. transport or (in *pl.*) a supply of water, gas, electricity, etc. **3** being a servant; employment or position as a servant. **4** employment in a public organization or Crown department; such an organization or department; a branch of the armed forces; (*attrib.*) of the kind issued to the armed forces. **5** a ceremony of worship; a form of liturgy for this. **6** maintenance and repair of a vehicle, machine, appliance, etc., at intervals. **7** assistance or advice given to customers after the sale of goods. **8** the serving of food etc.; an extra charge nominally made for this. **9** a set of dishes, plates, etc., required for serving a meal. **10** the act or manner of serving in tennis etc.; a game in which one serves. —*v.t.* **1** to maintain or repair (machinery etc.). **2** to provide with service(s), to repair (a car or machine etc.). —**at a person's service,** ready to serve him. **in service,** employed as a servant; in use. **of service,** useful, helpful. **on active service,** serving in the armed forces in wartime. **see service,** to have experience of serving, especially in the armed forces; (of a thing) to be much used. **service area,** an area beside a major road for the supply of petrol, refreshments, etc.; an area served by a broadcasting station. **service-box** *n.* the marked area of a squash court within which a validly served ball must fall. **service charge,** an additional charge for service. **service-court** *n.* (in tennis etc.) the marked area within which a validly served ball must fall. **service flat,** a flat in which domestic service and sometimes meals are provided by the management. **service industry,** one providing services not goods. **service line,** (in tennis) the line bounding a service-court. **service road,** a road serving houses lying back from a main road. **service station,** a place beside a road selling petrol and oil etc. to motorists. [f. OF or L *servitium* (as SERVE)]

serviceable *adj.* useful or usable, able to render service; durable, suited for use rather than ornament. —**serviceability** /-ˈbɪlɪtɪ/ *n.*, **serviceably** *adv.* [f. prec.]

serviceman *n.* (*pl.* **-men**) **1** a man in the armed forces. **2** a man providing service or maintenance.

servicewoman *n.* (*pl.* **-women**) a woman in the armed forces.

serviette /sɜːvɪˈet/ *n.* a table-napkin. [f. OF (as SERVE)]

servile /ˈsɜːvaɪl/ *adj.* **1** of or like a slave; suitable for a servant, menial. **2** excessively submissive, lacking independence. —**servilely** *adv.*, **servility** /-ˈvɪlɪtɪ/ *n.* [f. L *servilis* (as SERVE)]

serving *n.* a quantity of food for one person. —**serving-hatch** *n.* an aperture through which food is served. [f. SERVE]

servitor /ˈsɜːvɪtə(r)/ *n.* (*archaic*) a servant, an attendant. [f. OF or L (as SERVE)]

servitude /ˈsɜːvɪtjuːd/ *n.* slavery, subjection. [f. OF f. L (as SERVE)]

servo /ˈsɜːvəʊ/ *n.* (*pl.* **-os**) a servo-motor or -mechanism. [abbr.]

servo- /sɜːvəʊ-/ *in comb.* a means of powered automatic control of a larger system (*servo-assisted*, *-mechanism*, *-motor*). [f. F f. L *servus* slave]

sesame /ˈsesəmɪ/ *n.* an annual East Indian plant (*Sesamum indicum*) with oil-yielding seeds; its seeds. —**open sesame,** a magic formula used in an Arabian-Nights tale to cause a door to open; a magical or mysterious means of access to what is usually inaccessible. [f. L f. Gk, of Oriental origin]

sesqui- /seskwɪ/ *prefix* denoting one and a half (*sesquicentenary*). [L]

sessile /ˈsesaɪl/ *adj.* **1** (of a flower or leaf or an eye etc.) attached directly by the base without a stalk or peduncle. **2** fixed in one position, immobile. [f. L *sessilis* (*sedēre* sit)]

session /ˈseʃ(ə)n/ *n.* **1** an assembly for deliberative or judicial business; a single meeting for such a purpose; a period during which such meetings are regularly held. **2** an academic year; (*US*) a university term. **3** a period devoted to an activity. —**in session,** assembled for business, not on vacation. —**sessional** *adj.* [f. OF or L *sessio* (as prec.)]

sestet /sesˈtet/ *n.* **1** the set of six lines ending a sonnet. **2** a sextet. [f. It. (*sesto* f. L *sextus* sixth)]

set[1] *v.t./i.* (**-tt-**; *past & p.p.* **set**) **1** to put or place; to cause to stand in position. **2** to put in contact with, to apply (one thing) to another. **3** to fix ready or in position; to adjust the hands of (a clock or watch); to adjust (an alarm-clock) to sound at the required time; to adjust the mechanism of (a trap etc.); to lay (a table) for a meal. **4** to fix, decide, or appoint. **5** to arrange and protect (a broken bone, limb, etc.) into the right relative position so that it will heal after fracture or dislocation; to arrange (the hair) while damp so that it will dry in the required style; to insert (a jewel) in a ring, framework, etc.; to decorate or provide (a surface etc.) with jewels, ornaments, etc. **6** to put into a specified state, to cause to be or to do or begin doing. **7** to represent (a story etc.) as happening at a certain time or place. **8** to present or assign as work to be done. **9** to exhibit as a type or model; to initiate (a fashion etc.); to establish (a record). **10** to make or become hard, firm, or established. **11** to provide a tune for (words). **12** to arrange (type) or type for (a book etc.). **13** to cause (a hen) to sit on eggs; to place (eggs) for a hen to sit on. **14** (of the sun, moon, etc.) to be brought towards or below the horizon by the earth's movement. **15** (of a tide or current etc.) to have a specified motion or direction. **16** (in certain dances) to face another dancer and make certain steps. **17** (*vulgar* or *dial.*) to sit. —**set about,** to begin (a task); to attack with blows or words. **set back,** to place further back in space or time; to impede the progress of; to cause a change for the worse; to cost (a person) a specified sum. **set-back** *n.* impeding of progress; a change for the worse. **set foot in** *or* **on,** to enter or arrive at (a place etc.). **set forth,** to set out. **set in,** to begin and become established. **set off,** to begin a journey; to cause to begin; to ignite (a firework etc.) or cause to explode; to serve as an adornment or foil to, to enhance; to use as a compensating item. **set on** *or* **upon,** to attack violently; to cause or urge to attack. **set out,** to begin a journey; to have a specified aim or intention; to arrange or exhibit; to declare, to make known. **set sail,** to hoist sail; to begin a voyage. **set to,** to begin doing something vigorously; to begin fighting, arguing, or eating; to begin making (a loud sound); to cause; to supply adequately; to restore or enhance the health of; to establish (a record). **set-up** *n.* an arrangement or organization; the structure of this. **set up house,** to establish a household. [OE]

set[2] *n.* **1** a number of things or persons that are grouped together as similar or forming a unit; a section of society whose members consort together or have similar interests etc. **2** a collection of implements, vessels, etc., needed for a specified purpose. **3** a radio or television receiver. **4** (in tennis etc.) a group of games forming a unit or part of a match. **5** the way something sets or is set, placed, or arranged; the process or style of setting hair. **6** the scenery in use for a play or film; the stage etc. where this is performed. **7** (also **sett**) a badger's burrow; a granite paving-block; a slip, shoot, bulb, or tuber for planting. —**dead set,** a determined attack or initiative. **set theory,** the branch of mathematics which deals with sets (i.e. things grouped together as forming a unit) without regard to the nature of their individual constituents. [sense 1 f. OF *sette* f. L (as SECT); senses 2-3 f. SET[1]]

set[3] *adj.* **1** prescribed or determined in advance; unchanging, unmoving; (of a phrase or speech etc.) having an invariable or predetermined wording, not extempore. **2** prepared for action. —**set on** *or* **upon,** determined to get or achieve etc. **set piece,** a formal or elaborate arrangement especially in art or literature; fireworks arranged on scaffolding etc. **set square,** a draughtsman's right-angled triangular plate for drawing lines in a certain relation to each other, especially at 90°, 45°, or 30°. [p.p. of SET[1]]

sett *n.* var. of SET[2] sense 7.

settee /se'ti:/ *n.* a long seat, with a back and usually arms, for more than one person. [perh. fanciful var. of SETTLE[2]]

setter *n.* a dog of a long-haired breed trained to stand rigid when it scents game. [f. SET[1]]

setting *n.* **1** the position, place, or manner etc. in which something is set. **2** music for the words of a song etc. **3** a set of cutlery or crockery for one person at table. [f. SET[1]]

settle[1] *v.t./i.* **1** to place (a thing etc.) so that it stays in position. **2** to establish or be established more or less permanently; to make one's home; to occupy as settlers. **3** to sink or come to rest; to cause to do this; to become compact in this way. **4** to make or become calm or orderly; to stop being restless. **5** to arrange as desired; to end or arrange conclusively; to deal with; to pay (a debt etc., or *absol.*). **6** to bestow by legal process. **7** (in *p.p.*) not soon changing. —**settle down,** to become settled after disturbance or movement etc.; to adopt a regular or secure style of life; to apply oneself (to work etc.). **settle up,** to pay what is owing. **settle with,** to pay all or part of the amount due to (a creditor); to get revenge on. [OE (as foll.)]

settle[2] *n.* a wooden seat for two or more people, with a high back and arms and often with a box below the seat. [OE, = place to sit]

settlement *n.* **1** settling, being settled. **2** a place occupied by settlers. **3** a political or financial etc. agreement; an arrangement ending a dispute; the terms on which property is settled on a person by legal process; a deed stating these; the amount of property given. [f. SETTLE[1]]

settler *n.* one who goes to live permanently in a previously unoccupied land, a colonist. [as prec.]

seven /'sev(ə)n/ *adj.* & *n.* **1** one more than six; the symbol for this (7, vii, VII). **2** the size etc. denoted by seven. [OE]

sevenfold *adj.* & *adv.* seven times as much or as many; consisting of seven parts. [f. prec. + -FOLD]

seventeen /sevən'ti:n/ *adj.* & *n.* **1** one more than sixteen; the symbol for this (17, xvii, XVII). **2** the size etc. denoted by seventeen. —**seventeenth** *adj.* & *n.* [OE (as SEVEN, -TEEN)]

seventh *adj.* next after the sixth. —*n.* each of seven equal parts of a thing. —**Seventh-day Adventist,** a member of a sect of Adventists who originally expected the second coming of Christ in 1844 and still preach that his return is imminent. **seventh heaven,** a state of intense joy; the highest of seven heavens in Muslim and some Jewish systems. —**seventhly** *adv.* [f. SEVEN]

seventy /'sevəntɪ/ *adj.* & *n.* **1** seven times ten; the symbol for this (70, lxx, LXX). **2** (in *pl.*) the numbers, years, or degrees of temperature from 70 to 79. —**seventieth** *adj.* & *n.* [OE (as SEVEN)]

sever /'sevə(r)/ *v.t./i.* **1** to divide, break, or make separate, especially by cutting. **2** to terminate the employment contract of (a person). [f. AF f. L (as SEPARATE)]

several /'sevr(ə)l/ *adj.* & *pron.* **1** a few, more than two but not many. **2** separate, respective. —**severally** *adv.* [as prec.]

severance /'sevərəns/ *n.* severing, being severed; a severed state. —**severance pay,** the amount paid to an employee on the termination of his contract. [f. SEVER]

severe /sɪ'vɪə(r)/ *adj.* **1** strict; without sympathy; imposing harsh treatment. **2** intense, forceful. **3** making great demands on endurance, energy, ability, etc. **4** plain and without decoration. —**severely** *adv.*, **severity** /sɪ'verɪtɪ/ *n.* [f. F or L *severus*]

sew /səʊ/ *v.t./i.* (*p.p.* **sewn** or **sewed**) to fasten by passing thread again and again through material, using a threaded needle or an awl etc. or a sewing-machine; to make or attach by sewing; to use a needle and thread or a sewing-machine thus. —**sew up,** to join or enclose by sewing; (*colloq.*, esp. in *p.p.*) to arrange or finish dealing with (a project etc.). [OE]

sewage /ˈsju:ɪdʒ, ˈsu:-/ *n.* liquid waste matter drained away from houses, towns, factories, etc., for disposal. —**sewage farm,** a farm on which a town's sewage is treated and used for manure. **sewage works,** a place where sewage is purified so that it can safely be discharged into a river etc. [f. foll.]

sewer /ˈsju:ə(r), ˈsu:-/ *n.* a public drain for carrying away sewage and drainage water. —*v.t.* to provide or drain with sewers. [f. AF, orig. = channel to carry off overflow from a fish-pond, ult. f. L *aqua* water (rel. to EWER)]

sewerage /ˈsju:ərɪdʒ, ˈsu:-/ *n.* a system of sewers; drainage by sewers. [f. prec.]

sewing-machine *n.* a machine for sewing or stitching things.

sewn *p.p.* of SEW.

sex *n.* **1** either of the two main divisions (male and female) into which living things are placed on the basis of their reproductive functions; the fact of belonging to one of these. **2** sexual instincts, desires, etc., or their manifestation. **3** (*colloq.*) sexual intercourse. —*adj.* of sex; arising from the difference or consciousness of sex. —*v.t.* **1** to determine the sex of (a young animal etc.). **2** (in *p.p.*) having sexual characteristics or instincts etc. —**sex appeal,** sexual attractiveness. **sex life,** a person's sexual activities. **sex-starved** *adj.* lacking sexual gratification. **sex symbol,** a person who is for many the epitome of sexual attraction and glamour. —**sexer** *n.* [f. OF or L *sexus*]

sexagenarian /seksədʒɪˈneərɪən/ *adj.* from 60 to 69 years old. —*n.* a sexagenarian person. [f. L (*sexageni* sixty each)]

Sexagesima /seksəˈdʒesɪmə/ *n.* the Sunday before Quinquagesima. [L, = sixtieth (day), prob. named loosely as preceding Quinquagesima]

sexagesimal *adj.* of sixtieths or sixty; reckoning or reckoned by sixtieths. [f. L *sexagesimus* sixtieth]

sexism *n.* **1** prejudice or discrimination against people (esp. women) because of their sex. **2** the assumption that a person's abilities and social functions are predetermined because of his or her sex. —**sexist** *adj.* & *n.* [f. SEX]

sexless *adj.* **1** lacking sex, neuter. **2** not involving sexual feelings or attraction. —**sexlessly** *adv.* [f. SEX + -LESS]

sexology /sekˈsɒlədʒɪ/ *n.* the study of human sexual life or relationships. —**sexological** /-ˈlɒdʒɪk(ə)l/ *adj.*, **sexologist** *n.* [f. SEX + -LOGY]

sextant /ˈsekst(ə)nt/ *n.* an instrument with a graduated arc of 60 used in navigation and surveying for measuring the angular distance of objects by means of mirrors. [f. L *sextans* sixth part (*sexus* sixth), because early sextants all contained 60 i.e. one sixth of a circle]

sextet /sekˈstet/ *n.* **1** a musical composition for six performers; these performers. **2** any group of six. [alt. of SESTET]

sexton /ˈsekst(ə)n/ *n.* a person who looks after a church and churchyard, often acting as bell-ringer and grave-digger. [f. AF f. L (as SACRISTAN)]

sextuple /ˈsekstjʊp(ə)l/ *adj.* sixfold, having six parts; being six times as many or as much. —*n.* a sixfold number or amount. [f. L *sextuplus* (*sex* six)]

sextuplet /ˈsekstju:plɪt/ *n.* each of six children born at one birth. [f. prec. after *triplet* etc.]

sexual /ˈseksjʊəl, ˈsekʃ-/ *adj.* **1** of sex or the sexes or the relationship or feelings etc. between them. **2** (of reproduction) occurring by fusion of male and female gametes. —**sexual intercourse,** copulation (esp. of a man and a woman); insertion of the penis into the vagina, usually followed by the ejaculation of semen. —**sexuality** /-ˈælɪtɪ/ *n.* **sexually** *adv.* [f. L *sexualis* (as SEX)]

sexy *adj.* sexually attractive or stimulating. —**sexily** *adv.* **sexiness** *n.* [f. SEX]

sez (*slang*) says.

SF *abbr.* science fiction.

sf *abbr.* sforzando.

sforzando /sfɔtˈsændəʊ/ *adj.* & *adv.* (*Mus.*) with sudden emphasis. [It. (*sforzare* use force)]

sh *int.* hush.

shabby *adj.* **1** worn and faded; not kept in good condition; (of a person) poorly dressed. **2** contemptible, dishonourable. —**shabbily** *adj.*, **shabbiness** *n.* [f. *shab* scab f. OE]

shack *n.* a roughly built hut or shed. —**shack up,** (*slang*) to cohabit. [perh. f. Mexican *jacal* wooden hut]

shackle *n.* **1** a metal loop or link, closed by a bolt, to connect chains etc. **2** a fetter enclosing an ankle or wrist. **3** a restraint, an impediment. —*v.t.* **1** to put shackles on. **2** to impede, to restrict. [OE]

shad *n.* (*pl.* **shads** or **shad**) a large edible fish of the genus *Alosa*. [f. OE]

shade *n.* **1** comparative darkness (and usually coolness) caused by shelter from direct light and heat; a place or area sheltered from the sun. **2** the darker part of a picture etc. **3** a colour, especially with regard to its depth or as distinguished from one nearly like it. **4** a slight amount or difference. **5** a translucent cover for a lamp etc.; a screen excluding or moderating light; (*US*) a window-blind; (*US*, in *pl.*) sun-glasses. **6** a ghost; (in *pl.*) reminders of some person or thing. —*v.t.*/*i.* **1** to screen from light. **2** to cover, moderate, or exclude the light of. **3** to darken (parts of a drawing etc.), especially with parallel lines to represent shadow etc. **4** to change or pass gradually into another colour or variety. —**in the shade,** in comparative obscurity. [OE]

shadoof /ʃæˈdu:f/ *n.* a pole with a bucket at one end and a counterweight at the other, used for drawing water from a river etc., especially in Egypt. [f. Egyptian Arab.]

shadow /ˈʃædəʊ/ *n.* **1** shade; a patch of shade; a dark figure projected by a body intercepting rays of light. **2** one's inseparable attendant or companion; a person secretly following another; **3** a very slight trace. **4** a weak or insubstantial thing, a remnant. **5** the shaded part of a picture. **6** gloom, sadness. —*v.t.* **1** to cast a shadow over. **2** to follow and watch secretly. —**shadow-boxing** *n.* boxing against an imaginary opponent as a form of training. **Shadow Cabinet, Chancellor,** etc., members of the opposition party serving as spokesmen for affairs for which Cabinet ministers have responsibility. —**shadower** *n.* [OE (as SHADE)]

shadowy *adj.* like a shadow; full of shadows; vague, indistinct. [f. SHADOW]

shady /ˈʃeɪdɪ/ *adj.* **1** giving shade. **2** situated in the shade. **3** disreputable, of doubtful honesty. —**shadily** *adv.*, **shadiness** *n.* [f. SHADE]

shaft /ʃɑ:ft/ *n.* **1** an arrow, spear, or similar device; its long slender stem. **2** a remark intended to hurt or stimulate. **3** a ray (of light); a bolt (of lightning). **4** a stem or stalk; the central stem of a feather; the stem or long handle of a tool, implement, etc.; a long narrow part supporting, connecting, or driving a part or parts of greater thickness etc.; a column, especially between the base and the capital. **5** a long narrow vertical or sloping passage or opening giving access to a mine, or as an outlet for air or smoke; a vertical passage for movement of a lift etc. **6** each of a pair of poles between which a horse is harnessed to a vehicle. **7** (*US slang*) harsh or unjust treatment. —*v.t.* to treat harshly or unjustly. [OE]

shag *n.* **1** a rough growth or mass of hair or fibre. **2** a strong coarse kind of tobacco. **3** a cormorant, especially the crested cormorant (*Phalacrocorax aristotelis*). [OE]

shaggy *adj.* **1** having long rough hair or fibre. **2** (of hair etc.) rough, thick, and untidy. —**shaggy-dog story,** a long inconsequential narrative or joke. —**shaggily** *adv.*, **shagginess** *n.* [f. SHAG]

shagreen /ʃæˈgri:n/ *n.* a kind of untanned leather with a granulated surface; sharkskin (rough with natural papillae) used for rasping and polishing things. [var. of CHAGRIN in sense 'rough skin']

shah /ʃɑ:/ *n.* the former ruler of Iran. [f. Pers., = king]

shake *v.t./i.* (*past* **shook** /ʃʊk/; *p.p.* **shaken**) **1** to move violently or quickly up and down or to and fro; to tremble or vibrate, to cause to do this. **2** to agitate or shock; (*colloq.*) to upset the composure of. **3** to weaken or impair; to make less convincing or firm or courageous. **4** (of a voice etc.) to make tremulous or rapidly alternating sounds, to trill. **5** to make a threatening gesture with (one's fist, stick, etc.). **6** (*colloq.*) to shake hands. —*n.* **1** shaking, being shaken; a jerk or shock. **2** a milk shake. **3** (*Mus.*) a trill. **4** (*colloq.*) a moment. —**the shakes,** a fit of trembling. **no great shakes,** (*colloq.*) not very good or significant. **shake down,** to settle or cause to fall by shaking; to settle down, to become established. **shake hands,** to clasp hands (with another person), especially when meeting or parting, in reconciliation or congratulation, or as a sign of a bargain. **shake one's head,** to move one's head from side to side in refusal, denial, disapproval, or concern. **shake off,** to get rid of (an unwanted thing, bad habit, illness, undesirable companion, worry, etc.). **shake out,** to empty by shaking; to spread or open (a sail, flag, etc.) by shaking. **shake up,** to mix (ingredients) by shaking; to restore to shape by shaking; to disturb or make uncomfortable; to rouse from lethargy, apathy, conventionality, etc. **shake-up** *n.* an upheaval, a reorganization. [OE]

shaker *n.* **1** a person or thing that shakes. **2** a container for shaking together the ingredients of cocktails etc. **3** Shaker, a member of an American religious sect (named from their religious dances) with a simple life in celibate mixed communities. [f. SHAKE]

Shakespearian /ʃeɪksˈpɪərɪən/ *adj.* of Shakespeare. [f. *Shakespeare*, English dramatist (d. 1616)]

shako /ˈʃækəʊ/ *n.* (*pl.* **-os**) a cylindrical peaked military hat with an upright plume or tuft. [f. F f. Magyar, = peaked (cap)]

shaky *adj.* **1** unsteady, apt to shake, trembling. **2** unsound, infirm; unreliable, wavering. —**shakily** *adv.*, **shakiness** *n.* [f. SHAKE]

shale *n.* a soft rock that splits easily, resembling slate. —**shaly** *adj.* [prob. f. G, rel. to SCALE[2]]

shall /ʃ(ə)l, *emphat.* ʃæl/ *v. aux.* (3 *sing.* **shall,** *archaic* 2 *sing.* (with *thou*) **shalt**; *past* SHOULD) expressing (1) (in the first person) a future action or state, (2) (in other persons) a strong assertion, promise, or command. —**shall I?** do you want me to? [OE]

shallot /ʃəˈlɒt/ *n.* an onion-like plant (*Allium ascalonicum*) with cloves like those of garlic. [f. F (as SCALLION)]

shallow /ˈʃæləʊ/ *adj.* **1** of little depth. **2** not thinking deeply; not thought out deeply. **3** not capable of deep feelings. —*n.* (often in *pl.*) a shallow place. —*v.t./i.* to make or become shallow. —**shallowly** *adv.*, **shallowness** *n.* [rel. to SHOAL]

shalom /ʃəˈləʊm/ *n.* & *int.* a Jewish salutation at a meeting or parting. [f. Heb., = peace]

shalt see SHALL.

shalwar /ˈʃʌlvɑː(r)/ *n.* loose trousers worn by both sexes in some South Asian countries. [f. Pers.]

sham *v.t./i.* (**-mm-**) to pretend; to pretend to be. —*n.* a pretence; a thing or feeling that is not genuine; a person pretending to be something that he or she is not. —*adj.* pretended, not genuine. —**shammer** *n.* [perh. dial. var. of SHAME]

shaman /ˈʃæmən/ *n.* (in primitive religions) a person regarded as having direct access to, and influence in, the spiritual world which is usually manifested during a trance and empowers him or her to guide souls, cure illnesses, etc. —**shamanism** *n.* [f. G & Russ. f. Tungusian]

shamateur /ˈʃæmətə(r)/ *n.* a sports player classed as an amateur though often profiting like a professional. —**shamateurism** *n.* [f. SHAM + AMATEUR]

shamble *v.i.* to walk or run with a shuffling, awkward, or lazy gait. —*n.* a shambling gait. [perh. f. *shamble legs* with ref. to straddling trestles (as foll.)]

shambles /ˈʃæmb(ə)lz/ *n. pl.* (usu. treated as *sing.*) (*colloq.*) **1** a butcher's slaughter-house. **2** a scene or condition of great bloodshed or disorder. [pl. of *shamble* stall, OE f. L *scamellum* dim. of *scamnum* bench]

shambolic /ʃæmˈbɒlɪk/ *adj.* (*colloq.*) chaotic, disorganized. [f. prec., after SYMBOLIC]

shame *n.* **1** a feeling of distress or humiliation caused by consciousness of one's guilt or folly etc.; capacity for experiencing this feeling. **2** a state of disgrace or discredit. **3** a person or thing that brings disgrace etc.; a thing that is wrong or regrettable, a pity. —*v.t.* to bring shame on, to make ashamed; to put to shame; to force by shame. —**for shame!** a reproof to a person for not showing shame. **put to shame,** to disgrace or humiliate by revealing superior qualities etc. [OE]

shamefaced *adj.* **1** showing shame. **2** bashful, shy.

shameful *adj* causing shame, disgraceful. —**shamefully** *adv.* [f. SHAME + -FUL]

shameless *adj.* having or showing no feeling of shame; impudent. —**shamelessly** *adv.* [f. SHAME + -LESS]

shammy *n.* a chamois-leather. [corrupt pronunc. of CHAMOIS]

shampoo /ʃæmˈpuː/ *n.* **1** a liquid or cream used to lather and wash the hair. **2** a liquid or chemical for washing a car or carpet etc. **3** the act or process of shampooing. —*v.t.* to wash with shampoo. [f. Hind. imper. of *chāmpnā* to press]

shamrock /ˈʃæmrɒk/ *n.* a trefoil (esp. *Trifolium minus*) used as the national emblem of Ireland. [f. Ir., dim. of *seamar* clover]

shandy /ˈʃændɪ/ *n.* beer mixed with lemonade or ginger-beer. [f. earlier *shandygaff* (orig. unkn.)]

shanghai /ʃæŋˈhaɪ/ *v.t.* **1** (*hist.*) to force (a person) aboard a ship to serve as a sailor, usually after stupefying him by drugs etc. **2** to transfer forcibly, to abduct; to compel. [f. *Shanghai* seaport in China]

shank *n.* **1** the leg; the lower part of the leg; a shin-bone. **2** a shaft or stem; the long narrow part of an implement etc. —**Shank's mare** *or* **pony,** one's own legs as a means of conveyance. [OE, rel. to MHG *schenkel* thigh]

shan't /ʃɑːnt/ (*colloq.*) = shall not.

shantung /ʃænˈtʌŋ/ *n.* a soft undressed Chinese silk, usually undyed; fabric resembling this. [f. *Shantung*, Chinese province]

shanty[1] /ˈʃæntɪ/ *n.* a shack. —**shanty town,** a town consisting of shanties. [orig. N. Amer.; etym. unkn.]

shanty[2] /ˈʃɛntɪ/ *n.* a song traditionally sung by sailors while hauling ropes etc. [prob. F *chantez*, imper. of *chanter* sing]

shape *n.* **1** an external form or appearance, the total effect produced by a thing's outlines. **2** a specific form or guise in which something appears. **3** a kind, sort, or way. **4** a definite or proper arrangement; condition, good condition. **5** a person or thing as seen, especially as indistinctly seen or imagined. **6** a mould or pattern; a jelly etc. shaped in a mould; a piece of material, paper, etc., made or cut in a particular form. —*v.t./i.* **1** to give a certain shape or form to. **2** to adapt or modify (one's ideas etc.); to frame mentally, to imagine. **3** to assume or develop into a certain shape or condition; to give signs of future development. —**shape up,** to take (a specified form); to show promise; to make good progress. —**shaper** *n.* [OE, = creation]

shapeless *adj.* lacking proper shape or shapeliness. —**shapelessly** *adv.*, **shapelessness** *n.* [f. SHAPE + -LESS]

shapely *adj.* well formed or proportioned; of an elegant or pleasing shape or appearance. —**shapeliness** *n.* [f. SHAPE]

shard *n.* var of SHERD. [OE, = crack]

share[1] *n.* **1** a part given to an individual out of a larger amount which is being divided or of a commitment or achievement; the part one is entitled to have or obliged to give or do. **2** each of the equal parts forming a business company's capital and entitling the holder to a proportion of the profits. —*v.t./i.* **1** to give portions of (a thing) to two or more people; to give away part of. **2** to have a share of; to use, possess, endure, or benefit from (a thing) jointly with others. —**go shares,** to share. **share-cropper** *n.* a tenant farmer who pays part of his crop as rent to the owner. **share-cropping** *n.* this process. **share-out** *n.* a division and distribution, especially of profits or proceeds. —**sharer** *n.* [OE, rel. to SHEAR]

share[2] *n.* a ploughshare. [OE (as SHEAR)]

shareholder *n.* an owner of shares in a company.

shariah /ʃæ'ri:ə/ *n.* the sacred law of Islam, including the teachings of the Koran and the traditional sayings of Muhammad, prescribing religious and other duties. [f. Arab.]

shark *n.* **1** a large voracious sea-fish of the order Selachii. **2** a rapacious person; a swindler. [orig. unkn.]

sharkskin *n.* **1** the skin of a shark. **2** a wool, silk, or rayon fabric with a smooth slightly lustrous finish.

sharp *adj.* **1** having an edge or point able to cut or pierce; tapering to a point or edge; abrupt, not gradual; steep, angular. **2** well-defined, clean-cut, distinct. **3** intense, forceful; loud and shrill; irritable, speaking harshly and angrily; (of tastes or smells) producing a smarting sensation. **4** quick to see, hear, or notice things, intelligent. **5** quick to take advantage; artful, unscrupulous, dishonest. **6** vigorous, brisk. **7** (*Mus.*, of a note) above the correct or normal pitch; a semitone higher than the corresponding note or key of natural pitch. —*adv.* **1** punctually. **2** suddenly. **3** at a sharp angle. **4** (*Mus.*) above the correct pitch. —*n.* **1** (*Mus.*) a note that is a semitone higher than the corresponding one of natural pitch; the sign indicating this. **2** (*colloq.*) a swindler, a cheat. —**sharp end,** (*colloq.*) the bow of a ship; the place where decisions are made and correct action is taken. **sharp-eyed** *adj.* quick at noticing things. —**sharp practice,** dishonest or barely honest dealings. —**sharply** *adv.*, **sharpness** *n.* [OE]

sharpen *v.t./i.* to make or become sharp. —**sharpener** *n.* [f. prec.]

sharper *n.* a swindler, especially at cards. [f. SHARP]

sharpish *adj.* (*colloq.*) fairly sharp. —*adv.* (*colloq.*) fairly sharply, quite quickly. [f. SHARP]

sharpshooter *n.* a skilled marksman.

shatter *v.t./i.* **1** to break or become broken violently into small pieces. **2** to destroy utterly. **3** to disturb or upset the calmness of. [rel. to SCATTER]

shave *v.t./i.* (*p.p.* **shaved** or (esp. as *adj.*) **shaven** /'ʃeɪv(ə)n/) **1** to cut (growing hair) from the chin etc. with a razor; to remove hair from the chin etc. (of). **2** to cut thin slices from the surface of (wood etc.) to shape it. **3** to graze gently in passing. **4** to reduce or remove. —*n.* **1** shaving, being shaved. **2** (esp. **close shave**) a narrow miss or escape. **3** a tool for shaving wood etc. [OE]

shaver *n.* **1** a thing that shaves, especially an electric razor. **2** (*colloq.*) a young lad. [f. SHAVE]

shaving *n.* (esp. in *pl.*) a thin strip shaved from the surface of wood etc. [f. SHAVE]

shawl *n.* a large piece of fabric, usually rectangular and often folded into a triangle, worn over the shoulders or head or wrapped round a baby. —*v.t.* (esp. in *p.p.*) to put a shawl on (a person). [f. Urdu f. Pers., prob. f. *Shaliat* in India]

shawm *n.* an obsolete musical instrument of the oboe type. [f. OF, ult. f. Gk *kalamos* reed]

she /ʃi:/ *pron.* (*obj.* HER; *poss.* HER, HERS; *pl.* THEY) the woman, girl, or female animal (or thing regarded as female, e.g. a ship) previously named or in question. —*n.* a female animal. —*adj.* (usu. with hyphen) female (*she-ass*). [OE]

sheaf *n.* (*pl.* **sheaves**) **1** a bundle of stalks of corn etc. tied together after reaping. **2** a bundle of arrows, papers, etc., laid lengthways together. —*v.t.* to make into sheaves. [OE (as SHOVE)]

shear *v.t./i.* (*past* **sheared**; *p.p.* **shorn** or **sheared**). **1** to cut or trim with scissors, shears, etc.; to remove or take off by cutting; to clip wool off (a sheep etc.). **2** to strip bare, to deprive. **3** to break or distort by shear; to be broken or distorted by shear. —*n.* **1** a type of distortion or fracture produced by pressure, in which each successive layer (e.g. of a mass of rock) slides over the next; transformation of a geometrical figure or solid in which one line or plane remains fixed and those parallel to it move sideways. **2** (in *pl.*; also **pair of shears**) a clipping or cutting instrument working like scissors but much larger and usually operated with both hands. [OE]

sheath /ʃi:θ/ *n.* (*pl.* /ʃi:ðz/) **1** a covering into which a blade is thrust when not in use; a protective covering. **2** a sheath-like covering in various animal and vegetable structures; the tubular fold of skin into which the penis of a horse, bull, dog, etc., is retracted. **3** a condom. **4** a woman's close-fitting dress. —**sheath-knife** *n.* a dagger-like knife carried in a sheath. [OE]

sheathe /ʃi:ð/ *v.t.* to put into a sheath; to encase or protect with a sheath. [f. prec.]

sheave *v.t.* to make into sheaves. [f. SHEAF]

sheaves *pl.* of SHEAF.

shebeen /ʃɪˈbiːn/ *n.* (*Ir.*) an unlicensed house selling alcoholic liquor. [f. Anglo-Ir. (*séibe* mugful)]

shed[1] *n.* a one-storied building for storing things or as a shelter for livestock etc., or for use as a workshop. [app. var. of SHADE]

shed[2] *v.t.* (**-dd-**; *past & p.p.* **shed**) **1** to lose (a thing) by a natural falling off. **2** to take off (clothes etc.). **3** to reduce (an electrical power load) by disconnection etc. **4** to allow to pour forth. **5** to send forth, to diffuse, to radiate. —**shed light on,** to help to explain. [OE]

sheen *n.* gloss, lustre. —**sheeny** *adj.* [f. obs. *sheen* beautiful f. OE; sense assim. to SHINE]

sheep *n.* (*pl.* **sheep**) **1** a grass-eating animal of the genus *Ovis* with a thick woolly coat, esp. kept in flocks for its wool or meat. **2** a bashful, timid, or silly person. **3** (usu. in *pl.*) a member of a minister's congregation. —**separate the sheep from the goats,** to separate the good from the wicked (cf. Matt. 25: 33). **sheep-dip** *n.* a preparation for cleansing sheep of vermin etc.; a place where sheep are dipped in this. **sheep-dog** *n.* a dog trained to guard and herd sheep; a dog of a breed suitable for this. **sheep-fold** *n.* an enclosure for sheep. [OE]

sheepish *adj.* bashful; embarrassed through shame. —**sheepishly** *adv.*, **sheepishness** *n.* [f. per.]

sheepshank *n.* a knot used to shorten a rope temporarily.

sheepskin *n.* **1** a garment or rug of sheep's skin with the wool on. **2** leather of sheep's skin used in bookbinding etc.

sheer[1] *adj.* **1** mere, pure, not mixed or qualified. **2** (of a cliff or ascent etc.) with little or no slope, perpendicular. **3** (of a textile) very thin, diaphanous. —*adv.* perpendicularly, directly. [prob. f. dial. *shire* clear, f. OE]

sheer[2] *v.i.* to swerve or change course. —**sheer off,** to go away, to leave a person or topic that one dislikes or fears. [perh. f. MLG, = SHEAR]

sheer-legs *n.* (also **sheers**) a hoisting-apparatus of two (or more) poles attached at or near the top and separated at the bottom, used for fitting masts to ships or putting in engines etc. [var. of SHEAR]

sheet[1] *n.* **1** a large rectangular piece of cotton or other fabric, used esp. in pairs as inner bedclothes. **2** a thin broad usually flat piece of material (e.g. paper or glass). **3** a wide expanse of water, ice, flame, falling rain, etc. **4** a newspaper. —*v.t./i.* **1** to provide or cover with sheets. **2** to form into sheets. **3** (of rain etc.) to fall in sheets. —**sheet lightning,** lightning that looks like a sheet of light across the sky. **sheet metal,** metal formed into thin sheets by rolling, hammering, etc. **sheet music,** music published in separate sheets. [OE]

sheet[2] *n.* a rope or chain attached to the lower corner of a sail for securing or controlling it. —**sheet anchor,** a second anchor for use in emergencies; a person or thing depended on for security or stability. [OE (rel. to prec.)]

sheeting *n.* material for making sheets. [f. SHEET[1]]

sheikh /ʃeɪk, ʃiːk/ *n.* a chief, the head of an Arab tribe, family, or village; a Muslim leader. —**sheikhdom** *n.* [ult. f. Arab., = old man]

sheila /ˈʃiːlə/ *n.* (*Austral. & NZ slang*) a young woman, a girl. [orig. *shaler* (etym. unkn.)]

shekel /ˈʃek(ə)l/ *n.* **1** the currency unit of Israel. **2** an ancient Jewish etc. weight and silver coin. **3** (in *pl.*, *colloq.*) money, riches. [f. Heb. (*shākal* weigh)]

sheldrake /ˈʃeldreɪk/ *n.* (*pl.* **shelduck**) a bright-plumaged wild duck of the genus *Tadorna*. [prob. f. dial. *sheld* pied + DRAKE]

shelduck *n.* **1** a female sheldrake. **2** (as *pl.*) see prec. [as prec. + DUCK]

shelf *n.* (*pl.* **shelves**) **1** a horizontal board or slab etc. projecting from a wall or forming one tier of a bookcase or cupboard. **2** something resembling this; a ledge, a horizontal steplike projection in a cliff face etc.; a reef or sandbank. —**on the shelf,** (esp. of a person) no longer active or of use; (of a woman) past the age when she might expect to get married. **shelf-life** *n.* the time for which a stored thing remains usable. **shelf-mark** *n.* a mark on a book to show its place in a library. [f. MLG, rel. to OE *scylfe* partition, *scylf* crag]

shell *n.* **1** the hard outer covering of a nut-kernel, egg, seed, or fruit, or of an animal such as a crab, snail, or tortoise. **2** a structure that forms a firm framework or covering. **3** the walls or framework of an unfinished or gutted building or ship etc. **4** an explosive projectile for firing from a large gun etc.; the hollow case containing explosives for a cartridge, firework, etc. **5** a light rowing-boat for racing. **6** a group of electrons in an atom, with almost equal energy. —*v.t.* **1** to take out of a shell, to remove the shell or pod from. **2** to fire shells at. —**come out of one's shell,** to become more communicative and less shy. **shell out,** (*slang*) to pay out (money). **shell-shock** *n.* a nervous breakdown resulting from prolonged exposure to battle conditions. —**shell-less** *adj.*, **shelly** *adj.* [OE]

shellac /ʃəˈlæk/ *n.* a resinous substance used for making varnish etc. —*v.t.* (**-ck-**) to varnish with shellac. [f. SHELL + LAC]

shelled *adj.* **1** having a shell. **2** deprived of its shell. [f. SHELL]

shellfish *n.* (*pl.* same) a water animal with a shell, especially an edible mollusc or a crustacean.

shelter *n.* **1** something that serves as a shield or barrier against attack, danger, heat, wind, etc.; a structure providing this. **2** refuge, a shielded condition. —*v.t./i.* **1** to provide with shelter. **2** to protect from blame, trouble, or competition. **3** to find or take shelter. —**sheltered housing** etc., that provided for people who are old or handicapped, with special facilities or services. [perh. as SHIELD]

shelve *v.t./i.* **1** to arrange on a shelf or shelves. **2** to fit with shelves. **3** to defer consideration of (a plan etc.); to remove (a person) from active work etc. **4** (of ground) to slope away. [f. SHELF]

shelves *pl.* of SHELF.

shelving *n.* shelves collectively; material for shelves. [f. SHELVE]

shemozzle /ʃɪ'mɒz(ə)l/ *n.* (*slang*) a rumpus, a brawl; a muddle. [f. Yiddish after Heb., = of no luck]

shenanigan /ʃɪ'nænɪgən/ *n.* (*colloq.*) nonsense; trickery; high-spirited behaviour. [orig. unkn.]

shepherd /'ʃepəd/ *n.* **1** a man who tends a flock of sheep at pasture. **2** a spiritual leader, a priest. —*v.t.* **1** to tend (sheep). **2** to lead spiritually. **3** to marshal, conduct, or drive (a crowd etc.) like sheep. —**shepherd's pie,** cottage pie. —**shepherdess** *n.fem.* [OE (as SHEEP, HERD)]

Sheraton /'ʃerət(ə)n/ *n.* a style of furniture introduced in England *c.*1790, with delicate and graceful forms. [f. T. *Sheraton*, English furniture-maker (d. 1806)]

sherbet /'ʃɜ:bət/ *n.* **1** an oriental drink of sweetened diluted fruit-juice. **2** a fizzy flavoured drink; the powder for this. [f. Turk. or Pers. f. Arab., = drink (as SYRUP)]

sherd *n.* a potsherd. [var. of SHARD]

sheriff /'ʃerɪf/ *n.* **1** (also **High Sheriff**) the chief executive officer of the Crown in a county, nominally charged with keeping the peace, administering justice through the courts, executing writs by deputy, presiding over elections, etc. **2** an honorary officer elected annually in some towns. **3** (*Sc.*; also **sheriff-depute**) the chief judge of a county or district. **4** (*US*) the chief law-enforcement officer of a county. [OE (as SHIRE, REEVE[1])]

Sherlock /'ʃɜ:lɒk/ *n.* a person who investigates mysteries or shows great perceptiveness; a private detective. [f. *Sherlock* HOLMES]

Sherpa /'ʃɜ:pə/ *n.* a member of a Himalayan people living on the borders of Nepal and Tibet. [native name]

sherry *n.* a white usually fortified wine originally from southern Spain; a glass of this. [f. *Xeres* (now Jerez de la Frontera) in Spain]

Shetland /'ʃetlənd/ *adj.* of the Shetland Islands, NNE of Scotland. —**Shetland pony,** a small hardy rough-coated pony. **Shetland wool,** fine loosely-twisted wool from Shetland sheep. —**Shetlander** *n.*

shew (*archaic*) var. of SHOW.

Shiah /'ʃi:ə/ *n.* the group of the Shiites. [f. Arab., = party (of Ali, Muhammad's cousin and son-in-law)]

shibboleth /'ʃɪbəleθ) *n.* an old-fashioned doctrine or formula of a party or sect; a catchword; a word, custom, or principle etc. regarded as revealing a person's orthodoxy etc. [f. Heb., = ear of corn, from the story in Judg. 12: 6 where it was a kind of password distinguishing those who could pronounce it from those who could not]

shield *n.* **1** a piece of defensive armour carried in the hand or on the arm to protect the body against missiles or thrusts. **2** an object, structure, or layer of material that protects something; a person giving protection; a shieldlike part in an animal or plant. **3** a mass of ancient rock under a land area, a flat or gently convex platform usually forming the nucleus of a continent. **4** a representation of a shield as a heraldic device displaying a coat of arms. **5** a trophy in the form of a shield. —*v.t.* to protect or screen; to protect from discovery. [OE, prob. rel. to SCALE[2]]

shift *v.t./i.* **1** to change or move from one position to another. **2** to change form or character. **3** to pass (responsibility etc.) on to someone else. **4** (*slang*) to move quickly; to consume (food or drink). **5** (*US*) to change gear in a motor vehicle. —*n.* **1** a change of place, position, form, or character. **2** a set of workers who start work as another set finishes; the period for which they work. **3** a scheme for achieving something, an expedient. **4** a trick, a piece of evasion. **5** a woman's straight-cut dress. **6** a change of position of typewriter type-bars to type capitals etc. **7** a displacement of the lines of the spectrum. **8** (*US*) a gear-change in a motor vehicle. —**make shift,** to manage in less than ideal circumstances. **shift for oneself,** to depend on one's own efforts. **shift one's ground,** to take a new position in an argument etc. —**shifter** *n.* [OE, = arrange, divide]

shiftless *adj.* lazy and inefficient; lacking resourcefulness. —**shiftlessly** *adv.*, **shiftlessness** *n.* [f. SHIFT]

shifty *adj.* evasive, deceitful, untrustworthy. —**shiftily** *adv.*, **shiftiness** *n.* [f. SHIFT]

Shiite /'ʃi:aɪt/ *n.* a member of the Shiah, one of the two major groups in Islam (opp. *Sunnite*), centred chiefly in Iran. [as SHIAH]

shillelagh /ʃɪˈleɪlə, -lɪ/ *n.* an Irish cudgel. [f. *Shillelagh* in Co. Wicklow, Ireland]

shilling *n.* a former British currency unit and coin worth one-twentieth of a pound (i.e. 5p); a monetary unit in East African countries. [OE]

shilly-shally /ˈʃɪlɪʃælɪ/ *v.i.* to vacillate, to hesitate or be undecided. [redupl. of *shall I?* (SHALL)]

shim *n.* a thin wedge used in machinery etc. to make parts fit. —*v.t.* (**-mm-**) to fit or fill up thus. [orig. unkn.]

shimmer *v.i.* to shine with a tremulous or faint diffused light. —*n.* such a light. [OE (cf. SHINE)]

shin *n.* **1** the front of the leg below the knee. **2** (in full **shin of beef**) an ox's (esp. fore-)shank as a cut of meat. —*v.t./i.* (**-nn-**) to climb by clinging with arms and legs. —**shin-bone** *n.* the inner and usually larger of the two bones from knee to ankle. [OE]

shindig /ˈʃɪndɪg/ *n.* (also **shindy**) (*colloq.*) **1** a festive gathering, especially a boisterous one. **2** a din, a brawl. [perh. alt. of SHINTY]

shine *v.t./i.* (*past* & *p.p.* **shone** /ʃɒn/) **1** to emit or reflect light, to be bright, to glow. **2** (of the sun, a star, etc.) to be clearly visible. **3** to be brilliant, to excel. **4** to cause to shine (in a certain direction etc.). **5** (*p.p.* **shined**) to polish so as to produce a shine. —*n.* brightness, a lustre, a polish; light, sunshine. —**take a shine to,** (*colloq.*) to take a liking to. [OE]

shiner /ˈʃaɪnə(r)/ *n.* (*colloq.*) a black eye. [f. SHINE]

shingle[1] /ˈʃɪŋg(ə)l/ *n.* (in *sing.* or *pl.*) pebbles in a mass, as on a sea-shore. —**shingly** *adj.* [orig. unkn.]

shingle[2] /ˈʃɪŋg(ə)l/ *n.* **1** a rectangular piece of wood used as a roof-tile. **2** shingled hair; shingling the hair. —*v.t.* **1** to roof with shingles. **2** to cut (a woman's hair) short so that it tapers from the back of the head to the nape of the neck so that all ends are exposed like roof-shingles. [app. f. L *scindula*]

shingles /ˈʃɪŋg(ə)lz/ *n.pl.* (usu. treated as *sing.*) an acute painful viral inflammation of nerve ganglia, with a skin eruption often forming a girdle around the middle of the body. [f. L *cingulus* girdle (*cingere* gird)]

Shinto /ˈʃɪntəʊ/ *n.* (also **Shintoism**) a Japanese religion revering ancestors and nature-spirits. —**Shintoist** *n.* [Jap. f. Chin., = way of the gods]

shinty /ˈʃɪntɪ/ *n.* **1** a game like hockey, brought to Scotland by the invading Irish Gaels and sharing its history with hurling until the mid-14th c. **2** the stick or ball used in this. [earlier *shinny*, app. f. cry (*shin ye*) used in the game]

shiny /ˈʃaɪnɪ/ *adj.* having a shine; (of clothes) with the nap worn off. —**shinily** *adv.*, **shininess** *n.* [f. SHINE]

ship *n.* **1** a large seagoing vessel. **2** (*colloq.*) a spacecraft; (*US*) an aircraft. —*v.t./i.* (**-pp-**) **1** to put, send, or take on board a ship for conveyance to a destination. **2** to transport. **3** to fix (a mast, rudder, etc.) in its place on a ship. **4** to embark; (of a sailor) to take service on a ship. **5** to take (oars) from the rowlocks and lay them inside the boat. **6** to have (water, a sea) come into a boat etc. over the gunwale. **take ship,** to go on board a ship for a journey. **when one's ship comes home** *or* **in,** when one's fortune is made. [OE]

-ship *suffix* forming nouns denoting quality or condition (*friendship, hardship*), status, office, or honour (*authorship, lordship*), tenure of an office (*chairmanship*), skill in a certain capacity (*workmanship*), the collective individuals of a group (*membership*). [OE]

shipboard *n.* esp. in **on shipboard,** on board a ship.

shipbuilder *n.* a person engaged in the business of building ships. —**shipbuilding** *n.*

shipload *n.* the quantity of cargo or passengers that a ship can carry.

shipmate *n.* a person belonging to or sailing on the same ship as another.

shipment *n.* the placing of goods on a ship; the amount shipped. [f. SHIP]

shipowner *n.* a person owning or having shares in a ship or ships.

shipper *n.* one who ships goods, especially in import or export. [f. SHIP]

shipping *n.* ships collectively; transport of goods by ship. [f. SHIP]

shipshape *adv.* & *predic. adj.* in good order, neat and tidy.

shipwreck *n.* **1** destruction of a ship at sea by storm or by striking rocks etc. **2** the remains of a ship destroyed thus. **3** the ruin of plans etc. —*v.t.* to cause to suffer a shipwreck.

shipwright *n.* **1** a shipbuilder. **2** a ship's carpenter.

shipyard a place where ships are built.

shire *n.* **1** a county. **2** (*Austral.*) a rural area with its own elected council. —**shire-horse** *n.* a draught-horse of a heavy powerful breed, with long white hair covering the lower part of the legs. **the shires,** the band of English counties with names (formerly) ending in *-shire*, extending NE from Hampshire and Devon; the midland counties of England; the fox-hunting district of England, comprising mainly Leicestershire and Northamptonshire. [OE, rel. to OHG, = care, official charge; orig. unkn.]

shirk *v.t.* to avoid (a duty or work etc., or *absol.*) from laziness, cowardice, etc. —**shirker** *n.* [perh. f. G *schurke* scoundrel]

shirr *v.t.* to gather (fabric), especially with elastic or parallel threads run through it. [orig. unkn.]

shirt *n.* a loose sleeved garment of cotton or silk etc. for the upper part of the body. **—keep one's shirt on,** (*slang*) to keep one's temper. **put one's shirt on,** (*slang*) to bet all one's money on (a horse etc.). **shirt dress** a woman's dress with a bodice like a shirt. [OE]

shirting *n.* material for shirts. [f. SHIRT]

shirtwaister *n.* a shirt dress.

shirty *adj.* (*slang*) angry, annoyed. **—shirtily** *adv.*, **shirtiness** *n.* [f. SHIRT]

shish kebab /ʃɪʃ kɪˈbæb/ pieces of meat and vegetable grilled on skewers. [f. Turk. (*shish* skewer, *kebab* roast meat)]

shit *v.t./i.* (**-tt-**; *past* & *p.p.* **shit**) (*vulgar*) to defecate; to get rid of as excrement. *—n.* (*vulgar*) **1** faeces. **2** an act of defecating. **3** nonsense. **4** a despicable person. *—int.* (*vulgar*) expressing anger or annoyance. [OE]

shiver[1] /ˈʃɪvə(r)/ *v.i.* to tremble slightly, especially with cold or fear. *—n.* a shivering movement. **—the shivers,** an attack of shivering; a feeling or fear or horror. **—shivery** *adj.* [perh. f. obs. *chavele* chatter (as JOWL)]

shiver[2] /ˈʃɪvə(r)/ *n.* (usu. in *pl.*) a small fragment, a splinter. *—v.t./i.* to break into shivers. [rel. to OHG *scivaro* splinter]

shoal[1] *n.* a multitude, a great number, especially of fish swimming together. *—v.i.* (of fish) to form a shoal or shoals. [prob. f. MDu., = SCHOOL[2]]

shoal[2] *n.* **1** a shallow place in the sea; a submerged sandbank, especially one that shows at low water. **2** (usu. in *pl.*) hidden danger. *—v.i.* to become shallow. [OE, rel. to SHALLOW]

shock[1] *n.* **1** the effect of a violent impact or shake; a violent shake or tremor of the earth's crust in an earthquake. **2** a sudden violent effect upon the mind or emotions; an acute state of prostration caused by physical injury or pain or by mental shock; an electric shock. **3** great disturbance of or injury to an organization, stability, etc. *—v.t./i.* **1** to affect with an electrical or mental shock. **2** to appear horrifying or outrageous to. **—shock absorber,** a device on a vehicle etc. for absorbing vibration and shock. **shock therapy** *or* **treatment,** psychiatric treatment by means of a shock induced artificially by electricity or drugs. **shock troops,** troops specially trained for violent assaults. **shock wave,** an air-wave caused by an explosion or by a body moving faster than sound. [f. F *choc, choquer*]

shock[2] *n.* a group of corn-sheaves propped up together in a field. *—v.t.* to arrange (corn) in shocks. [= MDu. & MLG *schok*]

shock[3] *n.* an unkempt or shaggy mass of hair. [cf. obs. *shock(-dog)* shaggy-haired poodle]

shocker *n.* (*colloq.*) a person or thing that shocks; a very bad specimen of something; a sordid or sensational novel, film, etc. [f. SHOCK]

shocking *adj.* causing shock; scandalous; (*colloq.*) very bad. **—shockingly** *adv.* [f. SHOCK]

shod *past* & *p.p.* of SHOE.

shoddy *n.* fibre made from old cloth shredded; cloth made partly from this. *—adj.* of poor quality or workmanship. **—shoddily** *adv.*, **shoddiness** *n.* [orig. unkn.]

shoe /ʃu:/ *n.* **1** an outer foot-covering of leather etc., especially one not reaching above the ankle. **2** a thing like a shoe in shape or use. **3** a metal rim nailed to a horse's hoof. **4** a brake-shoe (see BRAKE[1]). *—v.t.* (*past* & *p.p.* **shod**; *partic.* **shoeing**) **1** to fit (a horse etc.) with a shoe or shoes. **2** (in *p.p.*) having shoes etc. of a specified kind. **—in a person's shoes,** in his position or predicament. **shoe-lace** *n.* a cord for lacing a shoe. **shoe-string** *n.* a shoe-lace; (*colloq.*) a small or inadequate amount of money (especially as capital). **shoe-tree** *n.* a shaped block for keeping a shoe in shape. [OE]

shoehorn *n.* a curved piece of horn or metal etc. for easing the heel into a shoe.

shoemaker *n.* a person whose business is making and repairing boots and shoes. **—shoemaking** *n.*

shoeshine *n.* (*US*) the polishing of shoes.

shogun /ˈʃəʊgʊn/ *n.* the hereditary commander of the army in feudal Japan. **—shogunate** *n.* [Jap., = general, f. Chinese *jiang jung*]

shone *past* & *p.p.* of SHINE.

shoo *int.* a sound used to frighten animals away. *—v.t./i.* to utter such a sound; to drive away thus. [imit.]

shook *past* of SHAKE.

shoot *v.t./i.* (*past* & *p.p.* **shot**) **1** to cause (a weapon, or *absol.*) to discharge a missile; to kill or wound with a missile from a weapon. **2** to hunt with a gun for sport. **3** to come, go, or send swiftly or violently. **4** to pass swiftly over (rapids etc.) or under (a bridge). **5** (in football etc.) to take a shot at goal; to score (a goal). **6** to photograph; to film. **7** (of a plant) to put forth buds; (of a bud) to appear. **8** (as *int.*, *US*) say what you have to say. *—n.* **1** a young branch or sucker; the new growth of a plant. **2** an expedition or party for shooting game; land in which game is shot. **3** a chute. **—be** *or* **get shot of,** to be rid of. **shoot down,** to kill (a person) cold-bloodedly by shooting; to cause (an aircraft or its pilot) to fall to the ground by shooting; to argue effectively against (a proposal etc.). **shooting-brake** *n.* an estate car. **shooting-gallery** *n.* a place for shooting at targets with rifles etc. **shooting star,** a small meteor moving rapidly. **shooting-stick** *n.* a walking-stick with a handle folding out to form a small seat. **shoot one's mouth off,** (*slang*) to talk freely or indiscreetly. **shoot up,** to rise or grow rapidly; to destroy or terrorize by shooting. **the whole shoot,** (*slang*) everything. —**shooter** *n.* [OE]

shop *n.* **1** a building or room where goods or services are on sale to the public. **2** a place where manufacturing or repairing is done. **3** one's work or profession as a subject of conversation (*to talk shop*). **4** (*slang*) an institution, an establishment, a place of business etc. —*v.t./i.* (**-pp-**) **1** to go to shops to make purchases etc. **2** (*slang*) to inform against, especially to the police. —**all over the shop,** (*slang*) in great disorder, scattered everywhere. **shop around,** to look for the best bargain. **shop-assistant,** an employee in a retail shop. **shop-floor** *n.* the production area in a factory etc.; workers as distinct from management. **shop-soiled** *adj.* soiled or faded by having been on display in a shop. **shop-steward** *n.* an official of a trade union elected by fellow-workers as their spokesman. [f. AF & OF *eschoppe* booth, f. MLG]

shopkeeper *n.* the owner or manager of a shop.

shoplifter *n.* a person who steals goods from a shop after entering as a customer. —**shoplifting** *n.*

shopper *n.* **1** a person who shops. **2** a shopping-bag. [f. SHOP]

shopping *n.* **1** buying goods from shops. **2** the goods bought. —**shopping-bag** *n.* a bag for holding shopping. **shopping centre,** an area or complex of buildings where shops are concentrated. **shopping-trolley** *n.* a trolley with a large shopping-bag mounted on it. [f. SHOP]

shopwalker *n.* a supervisor in a large shop.

shore[1] *n.* the land that adjoins the sea or a large body of water. —**on shore,** ashore. [f. MDu. or MLG, perh. rel. to SHEAR]

shore[2] *n.* a prop, a beam set obliquely against a wall or ship etc. as a support. —*v.t.* to prop or support with shores. [f. MDu. or MLG = prop (orig. unkn.)]

shoreline *n.* the line of a shore.

shorn *p.p.* of SHEAR.

short *adj.* **1** measuring little from end to end in space or time; soon traversed or finished. **2** of small stature, not tall. **3** not lasting, not reaching far into the past or future. **4** not far-reaching, acting near at hand; insufficient, having an insufficient supply; (seemingly) less than the stated or usual amount etc. **5** concise, brief; curt; (of temper) easily lost. **6** (of an alcoholic drink) small and concentrated, made with spirits. **7** (of a vowel sound or a syllable) relatively brief or light (cf. LONG[1] 7). **8** (of pastry) rich and crumbly through containing much fat. **9** (of a sale in stocks etc.) effected with borrowed stock in expectation of acquiring stock later at a lower price. **10** (of a fielding position in cricket) close to the batsman. —*adv.* **1** abruptly, suddenly. **2** before the natural or expected time or place. **3** in a short manner. —*n.* **1** a short thing, especially a short syllable or vowel; a short film. **2** (*colloq.*) a short circuit. **3** (*colloq.*) a short drink. —*v.t./i.* (*colloq.*) to short-circuit. —**be caught** *or* **taken short,** to be put at a disadvantage; (*colloq.*) to have a sudden need to go to the lavatory. **come** *or* **fall short of,** to fail to reach or amount to. **for short,** as a short name. **in short,** briefly. **short-change** *v.t.* to rob or cheat, especially by giving insufficient change. **short circuit,** a connection (usually a fault) in an electrical circuit in which current flows through small resistance. **short-circuit** *v.t./i.* to cause a short circuit in; to have a short circuit; to shorten or avoid by taking a short cut. **short cut,** a shorter way or method than that usually followed. **short division,** division of numbers without writing down details of the calculation. **short for,** serving as an abbreviation of. **short-handed** *adj.* undermanned, with insufficient help. **short list,** a list of selected candidates from which the final choice will be made. **short-list** *v.t.* to put on a short list. **short-lived** *adj.* having a short life, ephemeral. **short of,** not having enough of; less than; distant from; without going so far as. **short on,** (*colloq.*) deficient in. **short-range** *adj.* having a short range; relating to a short period of future time. **short shrift,** curt attention or treatment. **short sight,** the ability to see clearly only what is comparatively near. **short-sighted** *adj.* having short sight; lacking imagination or foresight. **short-term** *adj.* occurring in or relating to a short period of time. **short-wave,** a radio wave of frequency greater than 3 MHz. **short-winded** *adj.* easily becoming breathless. —**shortness** *n.* [OE]

shortage *n.* a deficiency; the amount of this. [f. prec.]

shortbread *n.* a rich crumbly biscuit made with flour, butter, and sugar.

shortcake n. **1** shortbread. **2** a cake of short pastry, usually served with fruit.

shortcoming *n.* failure to reach a required standard, a deficiency.

shorten *v.t./i.* to make or become short or shorter. [f. SHORT]

shortening *n.* fat used for making short pastry. [f. prec.]

shortfall *n.* a deficit.

shorthand *n.* **1** a method of rapid writing used in dictation etc. **2** an abbreviated or symbolic mode of expression.

shorthorn *n.* one of a breed of cattle with short horns.

shortly *adv.* **1** soon, not long, in a short time. **2** in a few words. **3** curtly. [f. SHORT]

shorts *n.pl.* **1** trousers that do not reach to the knee. **2** (*US*) underpants. [f. SHORT]

shorty *n.* (also **shortie**) (*colloq.*) a person or garment shorter than average. [f. SHORT]

shot[1] *n.* **1** the discharge of a gun etc.; the sound of this; an attempt to hit something by shooting or throwing etc. **2** a stroke or kick in a ball-game. **3** an attempt to do something. **4** a possessor of a specified skill in shooting. **5** a single missile for a gun etc., especially a non-explosive projectile; a small lead pellet of which several are used for a single charge; (as *pl.*) these collectively. **6** the heavy metal ball used in shot-put. **7** a photograph; the scene photographed; a film sequence taken by one camera. **8** the launch of a space-rocket. **9** the injection of a drug etc. **10** (*colloq.*) a dram of spirits. —**like a shot,** very quickly; without hesitation, willingly. **shot in the arm,** a stimulus or encouragement. **shot in the dark,** a mere guess. **shot-put** *or* **putting the shot,** an athletic contest of throwing a heavy metal ball. [OE (as SHOOT)]

shot[2] *past* & *p.p.* of SHOOT. —*adj.* **1** that has been shot. **2** (of fabric) woven or dyed so as to show different colours at different angles. —**shot through,** permeated, suffused.

shotgun *n.* a gun for firing small shot at short range. —**shotgun wedding,** one that is enforced, especially because of the bride's pregnancy.

should /ʃəd, *emphat.* ʃʊd/ *v.aux.* (*3 sing.* **should**) past tense of SHALL, used esp. in reported speech or to express obligation, condition, likelihood, or a tentative suggestion. [f. SHALL]

shoulder /ˈʃəʊldə(r)/ *n.* **1** the part of the body to which the arm, wing, or foreleg is attached; either lateral projection below or behind the neck. **2** the part of a garment covering the shoulder. **3** an animal's upper foreleg as a joint of meat. **4** (in *pl.*) the body regarded as bearing a burden, blame, etc. **5** a part or projection resembling a human shoulder; a strip of land adjoining a metalled road-surface. —*v.t./i.* **1** to push with one's shoulder; to make one's way thus. **2** to take a burden on one's shoulders; to assume the responsibility or blame for. —**put one's shoulder to the wheel,** to make a strong effort. **shoulder arms,** to move a rifle to a position with the barrel against the shoulder and the butt in the hand. **shoulder-blade** *n.* either large flat bone of the upper back. **shoulder-strap** *n.* a strap passing over the shoulder to support something; a strap from the shoulder to the collar of a garment, especially with indication of military rank. **shoulder to shoulder,** side by side; with a united effort. **straight from the shoulder,** (of a blow) well delivered; (of criticism etc.) frank, direct. [OE]

shouldn't /ˈʃʊd(ə)nt/ (*colloq.*) = should not.

shout *n.* **1** a loud utterance or vocal sound calling attention or expressing joy, excitement, disapproval, etc. **2** (*Austral. & NZ colloq.*) one's turn to buy a round of drinks. —*v.t./i.* **1** to emit a shout; to speak, say, or call loudly. **2** (*Austral. & NZ colloq.*) to buy drinks etc. for. —**shout down,** to reduce to silence by shouting. [perh. rel. to SHOOT]

shove /ʃʌv/ *v.t./i.* to push vigorously; (*colloq.*) to put casually. —*n.* an act of shoving. —**shove-halfpenny** *n.* a game in which coins etc. are pushed along a marked board. **shove off,** to start from the shore in a boat; (*colloq.*) to depart. [OE]

shovel /ˈʃʌv(ə)l/ *n.* an implement shaped like a spade with the side edges turned up, used for scooping up earth, snow, coal, etc.; a machine or part of a machine with a similar function. —*v.t.* (**-ll-**) **1** to move with or as with a shovel. **2** to scoop or thrust roughly. —**shovel hat,** a broad-brimmed hat. —**shovelful** *n.* [OE (rel. to SHOVE)]

shovelboard *n.* a game played especially on a ship's deck by pushing discs over a marked surface.

shoveller /ˈʃʌvələ(r)/ *n.* a duck (*Anas clypeata*) with a shovel-like beak. [f. SHOVEL]

show /ʃəʊ/ *v.t./i.* **1** to allow or cause to be seen; to offer for inspection or viewing; to exhibit in a show. **2** to demonstrate, to point out, to prove; to cause to understand. **3** to conduct. **4** to give (specified treatment to a person or thing). **5** to be visible or noticeable. —*n.* **1** showing, being shown. **2** a display; a public exhibition for competition, entertainment, or advertisement etc.; a pageant; (*colloq.*) any public entertainment or performance. **3** (*slang*) a concern or undertaking; a business. **4** an outward appearance; the impression produced; ostentation, mere display. **5** a discharge of blood from the vagina in menstruation or at the start of childbirth. —**show business,** the entertainment industry. **show-case** *n.* a glazed case for displaying exhibits. **show-down** *n.* a final test or battle etc.; a disclosure of achievements or possibilities. **show one's hand,** to reveal one's intentions. **show house,** one house in an estate etc. furnished and prepared for inspection. **show-jumping** *n.* competitive jumping on horseback. **show off,** to display to advantage; to act in a flamboyant way in order to impress. **show-off** *n.* a person who shows off. **show of hands,** the raising of hands to vote for or against a proposal etc. **show-piece** *n.* an excellent specimen suitable for display. **show-place** *n.* an attractive or much visited place. **show trial,** a judicial trial regarded as intended mainly to impress public opinion. **show up,** to make or be visible or conspicuous; to expose or humiliate; (*colloq.*) to appear or arrive. [OE]

shower /ˈʃaʊə(r)/ *n.* **1** a brief fall of rain or snow etc., or of bullets, stones, dust, etc.; a sudden copious arrival of gifts or honours etc. **2** (in full **shower-bath**) a bath in which water is sprayed from above; a room or device for this. **3** (*slang*) a contemptible or unpleasant person or group. **4** (*US*) a party for giving gifts, especially to a prospective bride. —*v.t./i.* **1** to descend in a shower. **2** to discharge (water or missiles etc.) in a shower; to bestow (gifts etc.) lavishly. **3** to use a shower-bath. [OE]

showery /ˈʃaʊərɪ/ *adj.* (of weather) with many showers. [f. prec.]

showing /ˈʃəʊɪŋ/ *n.* a display or performance; the quality or appearance of a performance or achievement etc.; the evidence or putting of a case. [f. SHOW]

showman *n.* (*pl.* **-men**) **1** a proprietor or organizer of public entertainment. **2** a person skilled in showmanship.

showmanship *n.* capacity for exhibiting one's goods or capabilities to the best advantage.

shown *p.p.* of SHOW.

showroom *n.* a room where goods are displayed or kept for inspection.

showy /ˈʃəʊɪ/ *adj.* making a good or conspicuous display; gaudy. —**showily** *adv.*, **showiness** *n.* [f. SHOW]

shrank *past* of SHRINK.

shrapnel /ʃræpn(ə)l/ *n.* **1** fragments of exploded bombs or shells. **2** an artillery shell containing metal pieces which it scatters on explosion. [f. Gen. H. *Shrapnel*, who invented this shell *c.*1806]

shred *n.* **1** a piece torn, scraped, or broken off; a scrap or fragment. **2** the least amount. —*v.t.* (**-dd-**) to tear or cut into shreds. —**shredder** *n.* [OE]

shrew /ʃru:/ *n.* **1** a small mouselike animal of the family Soricidae, with a long snout. **2** a bad-tempered or scolding woman. [OE]

shrewd /ʃru:d/ *adj.* showing astute powers of judgement, clever and judicious. —**shrewdly** *adv.*, **shrewdness** *n.* [perh. f. prec. in sense 'evil person']

shrewish *adj.* scolding, bad-tempered. [f. SHREW]

shriek /ʃri:k/ *n.* a shrill scream or sound. —*v.t./i.* to make a shriek; to say in shrill tones. [imit.]

shrift *n.* (*archaic*) confession and absolution. —**short shrift,** see SHORT. [OE (as SHRIVE)]

shrike *n.* a bird of the family Laniidae, with a strong hooked and toothed bill. [perh. rel. to OE *scric* thrush (imit.)]

shrill *adj.* piercing and high-pitched in sound. —*v.t./i.* to sound or utter shrilly. —**shrilly** *adv.*, **shrillness** *n.* [rel. to LG *schrell* sharp in tone]

shrimp *n.* **1** a small edible crustacean especially of the genus *Crangon*, pink when boiled. **2** (*colloq.*) a very small person. —*v.i.* to go in search of shrimps. [prob. rel. to SCRIMP]

shrine *n.* **1** a place for special worship or devotion. **2** a tomb or casket containing sacred relics. **3** a place hallowed by some memory or association etc. [OE f. L *scrinium* book-case]

shrink *v.t./i.* (*past* **shrank**; *p.p.* **shrunk** or (esp. as *adj.*) **shrunken**) **1** to make or become smaller, especially by the action of moisture, heat, or cold; **2** to draw back so as to avoid something; to withdraw; to be averse (from an action). —*n.* **1** the act of shrinking. **2** (*slang*, short for *head-shrinker*) a psychiatrist. —**shrink-wrap** *v.t.* to enclose (an article) in material that shrinks tightly round it. [OE]

shrinkage *n.* **1** the process or amount of shrinking. **2** (in commerce) loss by theft or wastage etc.

shrive *v.t.* (*past* **shrove**; *p.p.* **shriven** /ˈʃrɪv(ə)n/) (*archaic*) to hear the confession of and give absolution to; to submit (oneself) for this. [OE, = impose as penance f. L *scribere* write]

shrivel /ˈʃrɪv(ə)l/ *v.t./i.* (**-ll-**) to contract into a wrinkled or curled-up state. [perh. f. ON; cf. Sw. dial. *skryvla* to wrinkle]

shroud *n.* **1** a winding-sheet. **2** something that conceals. **3** (in *pl.*) the ropes supporting a ship's mast. —*v.t.* **1** to clothe (a corpse) for burial. **2** to cover and conceal or disguise. [OE (rel. to SHRED)]

shrove *past* of SHRIVE. —**Shrove Tuesday,** the day before Ash Wednesday, on which it was customary to be shriven. [f. SHRIVE]

Shrovetide *n.* Shrove Tuesday and the two preceding days. [f. prec. + TIDE]

shrub *n.* a woody plant smaller than a tree and usually with separate stems from or near the root. —**shrubby** *adj.* [f. OE, = shrubbery (rel. to SCRUB[2])]

shrubbery *n.* an area planted with shrubs. [f. prec.]

shrug *v.t./i.* (**-gg-**) to raise (one's shoulders) slightly and momentarily to express indifference, helplessness, doubt, etc. —*n.* a shrugging movement. —**shrug off,** to dismiss as unimportant. [orig. unkn.]

shrunk *p.p.* of SHRINK.

shrunken see SHRINK.

shudder *n.* a sudden or convulsive shivering or quivering; a vibrating motion. —*v.i.* **1** to experience a shudder; to feel strong repugnance or fear etc. **2** to vibrate strongly. [f. MDu. or MLG]

shuffle *v.t./i.* **1** to walk without lifting the feet clear of the ground; to move (one's feet) thus. **2** to slide (cards) over one another so as to change their order; to rearrange, to jumble. **3** to keep shifting one's position; to prevaricate, to be evasive. —*n.* **1** a shuffling movement or walk; a shuffling dance. **2** shuffling of cards etc. **3** a general rearrangement. —**shuffle off,** to remove or get rid of. —**shuffler** *n.* [f. LG, = walk clumsily]

shun *v.t.* (**-nn-**) to avoid, to keep away from; to abstain from. [OE]

shunt *v.t./i.* **1** to move (a train etc.) to another track; (of a train) to be shunted. **2** to move or put aside; to redirect. —*n.* **1** shunting, being shunted. **2** a conductor joining two points of an electrical circuit for the diversion of current. **3** (in surgery) an alternative path for the circulation of blood. **4** (*slang*) a collision of vehicles, especially nose-to-tail. —**shunter** *n.* [perh. f. SHUN]

shush *int.* hush! —*v.t./i.* to call for silence (from); to be silent. [imit.]

shut *v.t./i.* (**-tt-**; *past* & *p.p.* **shut**) **1** to move (a door, window, lid, etc.) into position to block an opening; (of a door etc.) to move or admit of being moved thus; to shut the door or lid etc. of (a room, box, eye, etc.). **2** to bring (a book, telescope, etc.) into a folded-up or contracted state. **3** to catch or pinch (a finger, dress, etc.) by shutting something on it. **4** to bar access to (a place). —**be shut of,** (*slang*) to be rid of. **shut down,** to cease working or business, either at the end of a day or permanently; to cause to do this. **shut-down** *n.* this process. **shut-eye** *n.* (*slang*) sleep. **shut off,** to stop the flow of (water, gas, etc.); to separate from society etc. **shut up,** to shut securely or permanently; to imprison; to put away in a box etc.; (*colloq.*, esp. in *imper.*) to stop talking. **shut up shop,** to cease business or work at the end of the day or permanently. [OE]

shutter *n.* **1** a movable hinged cover for a window. **2** a device that opens and closes the lens aperture of a camera to allow light to fall on the film. —*v.t.* to provide with shutters. —**put up the shutters,** to cease business at the end of the day or permanently. [f. SHUT]

shuttle *n.* **1** a holder carrying the weft-thread to and fro between the threads of the warp in weaving. **2** a moving holder carrying the lower thread in a sewing-machine. **3** a vehicle used in a shuttle service; a space-shuttle. **4** a shuttlecock. —*v.t./i.* to move, travel, or send to and fro. —**shuttle diplomacy,** negotiations conducted by a mediator who travels to several countries at brief intervals. **shuttle service,** a transport system operating to and fro over a relatively short distance. [OE, = a dart (as SHOOT)]

shuttlecock *n.* a small rounded piece of cork etc. with a ring of feathers attached, or of other material made in this shape, struck to and fro with a battledore in the old game of battledore and shuttlecock, and with a racket in badminton. [f. prec. + COCK, prob. f. flying motion]

shy[1] /ʃaɪ/ *adj.* **1** timid and lacking self-confidence in the presence of others; avoiding company; reserved; (of behaviour) showing shyness. **2** (of an animal) timid and avoiding observation. **3** (as *suffix*) showing fear or distaste of (*workshy*). —*v.i.* to jump or move suddenly in alarm. —*n.* an act of shying. —**shy of,** wary of. [OE]

shy[2] /ʃaɪ/ *v.t.* (*colloq.*) to fling or throw. —*n.* (*colloq.*) a throw. [orig. unkn.]

shyster /ˈʃaɪstə(r)/ *n.* (*colloq.*) a person who acts unscrupulously or unprofessionally. [orig. unkn.]

SI *abbr.* International System of Units (tr. F *Système international d'unités*), a system of physical units (together with a set of prefixes indicating multiplication or division by a power of ten) based on the metre, kilogram, second, ampere, kelvin, candela, and mole as independent basic units, with each of the derived units defined in terms of these without any multiplying factor.

Si *symbol* silicon.

si /siː/ *n.* (*Mus.*) te. [perh. f. initials of *Sancte Iohannes* (see GAMUT)]

Siamese /saɪəˈmiːz/ *adj.* of Siam or its people or language. —*n.* **1** a native or the language (also called Thai) of Siam. **2** a Siamese cat. —**Siamese cat,** a cat of a breed with short pale fur and dark markings. **Siamese twins,** identical twins that are physically conjoined at birth. [f. *Siam*, former name of Thailand]

sib *n.* a sibling. [OE]

sibilant /ˈsɪbɪlənt/ *adj.* sounded with a hiss; hissing. —*n.* a sibilant letter or sound. —**sibilance** *n.*, **sibilancy** *n.* [f. L *sibilare* hiss]

sibling *n.* each of two or more children having one or both parents in common. [f. SIB]

sibyl /ˈsɪbɪl/ *n.* any of the women who in ancient times acted as the reputed mouthpiece of a god, uttering prophecies and oracles. [f. OF or L f. Gk *Sibulla*]

sibylline /ˈsɪbɪlaɪn/ *adj.* issuing from a sibyl; oracular, mysteriously prophetic. [f. L (as prec.)]

sic /sɪk/ *adv.* thus used, spelt, etc. (used in brackets to confirm or call attention to the form of quoted words). [L, = thus]

sick *adj.* **1** physically or mentally unwell, feeling the effects of a disease. **2** vomiting, tending to vomit. **3** of or for those who are sick (*sick-bed*, *-leave*, *-pay*, *-room*, etc.). **4** greatly distressed or disgusted. **5** (of humour) finding amusement in misfortune or in morbid subjects. —*v.t.* (*colloq.*) to vomit (esp. with *up*). —**be sick,** to vomit. **sick-bay** *n.* a room or rooms for sick people in an institution or on a ship etc. **sick of,** tired of, bored with through having already had too much of. [OE]

sicken *v.t./i.* to make or become sick or disgusted etc. —**sicken for,** to be in the first stages of (an illness). [f. SICK]

sickle *n.* **1** an implement with a curved blade and a short handle, used for reaping or lopping etc. **2** something shaped like this. —**sickle cell,** a sickle-shaped red blood-corpuscle, especially as found in a severe hereditary form of anaemia. [OE, f. L *sicula* (*secare* cut)]

sickly *adj.* **1** liable to be ill, of weak health. **2** unhealthy-looking, faint, pale. **3** causing ill-health. **4** inducing or connected with nausea; mawkish, weakly sentimental. —**sickliness** *n.* [f. SICK]

sickness *n.* **1** being ill, disease. **2** a specified disease. **3** vomiting. [f. SICK]

side *n.* **1** any of the surfaces bounding an object, especially the vertical inner or outer surface or one of those distinguished from the top and bottom or front and back or ends. **2** (*Math.*) each of the lines bounding a triangle, rectangle, etc.; each of the two quantities stated to be equal in an equation. **3** either surface of a thing regarded as having only two; the amount of writing filling one side of a sheet of paper. **4** the right or left part of a person's or animal's body; the corresponding half of a carcass. **5** a direction; the part of an object or place etc. that faces a specified direction or is on an observer's right or left. **6** the region to the right or left of (or nearer or further than) a real or imaginary dividing line; the part or area near the edge or away from the centre. **7** a partial aspect of a thing; an aspect differing from or opposed to other aspects. **8** each of two sets of opponents at war or competing in some way; the cause represented by these. **9** the line of descent through one parent. **10** (in billiards etc.) the spinning motion given to a ball by striking it on one side. **11** (*slang*) assumption of superiority, swagger. —*in comb.* **1** situated at or directed to or from a side (*side-door*, *-table*; *sideglance*). **2** secondary, minor, incidental (*side-effect*, *-issue*, *-road*, *-street*). —*v.i.* to take part or be on the same side. —**-sided** *adj.* having a specified number or type of sides. —**by the side of,** close to; compared with. **on one side,** not in the main or central position; aside. **on the side,** as a sideline. **on the — side,** somewhat. **side by side,** standing close together, especially for mutual encouragement. **side-car** *n.* a passenger car attachable to the side of a motor cycle. **side-drum** *n.* a small double-headed drum. **side-saddle** *n.* a saddle enabling a rider to have both feet on the same side of a horse; (*adv.*) sitting thus on a horse. **side-show** *n.* a small show at a fair or exhibition; a minor or subsidiary activity or affair. **side-slip** *n.* a skid, a movement sideways; (*v.i.*) to move sideways. **side-splitting** *adj.* causing hearty laughter. **side-step** *n.* a step sideways; (*v.t.*) to avoid by stepping sideways; to evade (an issue etc.). **side-swipe** *n.* a glancing blow along the side; an indirect or incidental criticism etc.; (*v.t.*) to hit with a side-swipe. **side-track** *v.t.* to divert (a person) from the main course or issue. **side-whiskers** *n.pl.* those growing on the cheek. **side wind,** a wind coming from one side. [OE]

sideboard *n.* a table or flat-topped chest with drawers and cupboards for china etc.

sideburns *n.pl.* short side-whiskers. [f. Amer. General *Burnside* (d. 1881), who sported a moustache, whiskers, and clean-shaven chin]

sidekick *n.* (*US colloq.*) a close associate; a subordinate member of a pair or group.

sidelight *n.* **1** light from the side. **2** a piece of incidental information about a subject etc. **3** each of a pair of small lights at the front of a vehicle. **4** a light at the side of a moving ship.

sideline *n.* **1** work etc. carried on in addition to one's main activity. **2** (in *pl.*) the lines bounding the sides of a football pitch etc.; the space just outside these. **3** a place for spectators as distinct from participants.

sidelong *adj.* directed to the side, oblique. —*adv.* to the side.

sidereal /saɪˈdɪərɪəl/ *adj.* of or determined by means of the stars. —**sidereal day,** the time between successive passages of any given star over a meridian. [f. L *sidereus* (*sidus* star)]

sidesman *n.* (*pl.* **-men**) an assistant churchwarden who takes the collection etc.

sidewalk *n.* (*US*) a pavement at the side of a road.

sideways *adj.* & *adv.* **1** with the side foremost. **2** to or from one side.

siding /ˈsaɪdɪŋ/ *n.* a short railway track to the side of a railway line, used for shunting.

sidle /ˈsaɪd(ə)l/ *v.i.* to walk obliquely; to move

timidly or furtively. [back-formation f. *sideling* sidelong]

siege /si:dʒ/ *n.* the surrounding and blockading of a fortified place; the surrounding by the police etc. of a house occupied by a gunman etc. —**lay siege to,** to conduct a siege of. **raise a siege,** to end it. [f. OF *sege* seat]

siemens /ˈsi:mənz/ *n.* the unit of electrical conductance, the reciprocal of the ohm. [f. E. W. von *Siemens*, German electrical engineer (d. 1892)]

sienna /sɪˈenə/ *n.* a kind of clay used as a pigment; its colour of reddish-brown (**burnt sienna**) or yellowish-brown (**raw sienna**). [f. *Siena* in Italy]

sierra /sɪˈerə/ *n.* a long jagged mountain-chain in Spain or Spanish America. [Sp., f. L *serra* saw]

siesta /sɪˈestə/ *n.* an afternoon nap or rest, especially in hot countries. [Sp., f. L *sexta* (*hora*) sixth hour]

sieve /sɪv/ *n.* a utensil with a network or perforated bottom through which liquids or fine particles can pass while solid or coarser matter is retained, or used for reducing a soft mixture pressed through it to a uniform pulp. —*v.t.* to put through a sieve. [OE]

sift *v.t./i.* **1** to separate with or cause to pass through a sieve. **2** to sprinkle (flour etc.) from a sieve or perforated container. **3** to subject (information etc.) to close scrutiny or analysis. **4** (of snow etc.) to fall as if from a sieve. —**sifter** *n.* [OE (as prec.)]

sigh /saɪ/ *n.* a long deep audible breath expressing sadness, weariness, longing, relief, etc.; an act of making this; a sound resembling it. —*v.t./i.* **1** to make a sigh; to express with sighs. **2** to yearn *for* a person or thing desired or lost. [OE]

sight /saɪt/ *n.* **1** the faculty of perception through the response of the brain to the action of light on the eye. **2** seeing, being seen. **3** the range of vision; the region open to vision. **4** the way of regarding something, opinion. **5** a thing seen or visible or worth seeing; (in *pl.*) the noteworthy or attractive features of a town etc. **6** a person or thing regarded as unsightly or ridiculous-looking. **7** a precise aim with a gun or observation with an optical instrument; a device for assisting this. **8** (*colloq.*) a great quantity. —*v.t.* **1** to get a sight of, to observe the presence of. **2** to aim (a gun etc.) by using the sights. —**at first sight,** on the first glimpse or impression. **at** *or* **on sight,** as soon as a person or thing is seen. **catch sight of,** to begin to see or be aware of. **in sight,** visible, imminent. **set one's sights on,** to be determined to acquire or achieve etc. **a sight for sore eyes,** a person or thing one is delighted to see. **sight-read** *v.t.* to read (music) at sight, without preliminary practice or study of the score. **sight-screen** *n.* (in cricket) a large white screen placed near the boundary in line with the wicket to help the batsman see the ball. **sight unseen,** without previous inspection. [OE (as SEE[1])]

sighted *adj.* having sight, not blind. [f. prec.]

sightless *adj.* blind. [f. SIGHT + -LESS]

sightly *adj.* attractive to look at. —**sightliness** *n.* [f. SIGHT]

sightseer *n.* a person visiting the sights of a place. —**sightseeing** *n.*

sigma /ˈsɪgmə/ *n.* the eighteenth letter of the Greek alphabet, = s. [L f. Gk]

sign /saɪn/ *n.* **1** a thing perceived that suggests the existence of a fact, quality, or condition, either past, present, or future. **2** a mark or device with a special meaning, a symbol. **3** a motion or gesture used instead of words to convey information, a demand, etc. **4** each of the twelve divisions of the zodiac. **5** a publicly displayed symbol or device giving information; a signboard. —*v.t./i.* **1** to write one's name on (a document) to show its authenticity or one's agreement or acceptance; to write (one's name) thus. **2** to engage or be engaged by signing a contract. **3** to indicate or communicate by a gesture. —**sign away,** to relinquish a right to by signing. **sign-language** *n.* a series of signs used by deaf or dumb people for communication. **sign off,** to end work or a contract etc.; to indicate the end of a broadcast etc. **sign on,** to sign a contract of employment etc.; to register oneself (e.g. as available for employment); to indicate the start of a broadcast etc. [f. OF f. L *signum* mark, token]

signal /ˈsɪgn(ə)l/ *n.* **1** a sign (especially a pre-arranged one) conveying information or giving an instruction; a message made up of such signs. **2** a device on a railway giving instructions or warnings to train-drivers etc. **3** an event which causes immediate activity. **4** transmitted electrical impulses or radio waves; a sequence of these. —*v.t./i.* (**-ll-**) to make a signal or signals (to); to transmit or announce by a signal; to direct by a signal. —*adj.* remarkably good or bad, noteworthy. —**signal-box** *n.* a building from which railway signals are controlled. —**signaller** *n.* [f. OF f. L *signalis* (as prec.)]

signalize *v.t.* to make noteworthy or remarkable. [f. prec.]

signally *adv.* remarkably, notably. [f. SIGNAL]

signalman *n.* (*pl.* **-men**) a person responsible for displaying or operating signals.

signatory /ˈsɪgnətərɪ/ *adj.* that has signed an

agreement, especially a treaty. —*n.* a signatory party, especially a State. [as foll.]

signature /ˈsɪgnətʃə(r)/ *n.* **1** a person's name or initials used in signing. **2** the act of signing. **3** (*Mus.*) a sign put after the clef to indicate the key or time. **4** a section of a book made from one sheet folded and cut; a letter or figure indicating a sequence of these. —**signature tune,** a tune used, especially in broadcasting, to announce a particular programme or performer etc. [f. L *signatura* (*signare* to mark, as SIGN)]

signboard *n.* a board with a name or symbol etc. displayed outside a shop or hotel etc.

signet /ˈsɪgnɪt/ *n.* a small seal used with or instead of a person's signature. —**signet ring,** a finger-ring with a signet set in it. [f. OF or L (as SIGN)]

significance /sɪgˈnɪfɪkəns/ *n.* **1** signifying. **2** what is meant. **3** importance. —**significancy** *n.* [OF or f. L (as SIGNIFY)]

significant /sɪgˈnɪfɪkənt/ *adj.* **1** having or conveying a meaning, especially an important or noteworthy one. **2** important. —**significant figure,** (*Math.*) a digit conveying information about a number containing it, and not a zero used simply to fill a vacant place at the beginning or end. —**significantly** *adv.* [f. L (as foll.)]

signify /ˈsɪgnɪfaɪ/ *v.t./i.* **1** to be a sign, symbol, or indication of. **2** to mean, to have as a meaning. **3** to make known. **4** to be of importance. —**signification** /-fɪˈkeɪʃ(ə)n/ *n.* [f. OF f. L *significare* (as SIGN, *facere* make)]

signor /ˈsiːnjɔː(r)/ *n.* (*pl.* ***signori*** /-ˈnjɔːrɪ/) the title used of or to an Italian man. [It. f. L, = SENIOR]

signora /siːnˈjɔːrə/ *n.* the title used of or to an Italian married woman. [fem. of prec.]

signorina /siːnjəˈriːnə/ *n.* the title used of or to an Italian unmarried woman. [as prec.]

signpost *n.* a post bearing a sign, especially one indicating direction. —*v.t.* to provide with a post or posts of this kind.

Sikh /siːk, sɪk/ *n.* an adherent of Sikhism. [Hindi, = disciple, f. Skr.]

Sikhism /ˈsiːkɪz(ə)m, ˈsɪ-/ *n.* a monotheistic religion founded in the Punjab in the 15th c. by Guru Nanak, which combines elements of Hinduism and Islam. [f. prec.]

silage /ˈsaɪlɪdʒ/ *n.* **1** storage in a silo. **2** green fodder so stored. [alt. f. ENSILAGE after SILO]

silence /ˈsaɪləns/ *n.* **1** absence of sound. **2** avoidance of or abstinence from speech or making a noise. **3** avoidance of mentioning a thing or of betraying a secret etc. —*v.t.* to make silent by coercion or superior argument; to stop the sound of. —**in silence,** without speech or other sound. [f. OF or L *silentium* (as SILENT)]

silencer *n.* a device for reducing the noise made by a gun or a vehicle's exhaust etc. [f. prec.]

silent /ˈsaɪlənt/ *adj.* not speaking; not making or accompanied by a sound; saying little. —**silent majority,** people of moderate opinions who rarely make themselves heard. —**silently** *adv.* [f. L *silēre* be silent]

silhouette /sɪluːˈet/ *n.* **1** a picture of a person in profile or of a thing in outline only, either dark against a light background or vice versa, or cut out in pages. **2** an appearance of a person or thing against the light so that only the outline is distinguishable. —*v.t.* to represent or (usu. in *pass.*) show in silhouette. [f. Étienne de *Silhouette*, Fr. author and politician (d. 1767), amateur maker of paper cut-outs]

silica /ˈsɪlɪkə/ *n.* a mineral (silicon dioxide) occurring as quartz and as the main constituent of sandstone and other rocks. —**siliceous** /sɪˈlɪʃəs/ *adj.* [f. L *silex* flint]

silicate /ˈsɪlɪkeɪt/ *n.* a compound of a metal or metals, silicon and oxygen. [f. prec.]

silicon /ˈsɪlɪkən/ *n.* a non-metallic element, symbol Si, atomic number 14. —**silicon chip,** a microchip made of silicon. **Silicon Valley,** the Santa Clara valley SE of San Francisco, where many leading US microelectronic firms are situated. [as SILICA, replacing earlier *silicium*]

silicone /ˈsɪlɪkəʊn/ *n.* one of many polymeric organic compounds of silicon with high resistance to cold, heat, water, and the passage of electricity, used in polishes, paints, lubricants, etc. [f. prec.]

silicosis /sɪlɪˈkəʊsɪs/ *n.* a lung disease caused by inhaling dust containing silica. [as SILICA]

silk *n.* **1** the fine soft strong fibre produced by a silkworm in making its cocoon; thread or cloth made from or resembling this; (in *pl.*) clothing made from silk. **2** a similar fibre produced by spiders or some insects. **3** (*colloq.*) a King's or Queen's Counsel, as having the right to wear a silk gown. **4** fine soft strands like threads of silk. **5** (*attrib.*) made of silk. —**silk hat,** a tall cylindrical hat covered with silk plush. **silk-screen printing,** screen-printing. **take silk,** to become a King's or Queen's Counsel. [OE f. L *sericum* (*seres* f. Gk *Seres* the Chinese or neighbouring peoples)]

silken *adj.* of or resembling silk; soft, smooth, or lustrous. [as prec.]

silkworm *n.* a caterpillar of a kind of moth, which feeds on mulberry leaves and spins its cocoon of silk.

silky *adj.* **1** soft and smooth like silk. **2** suave. —**silkily** *adv.*, **silkiness** *n.* [f. SILK]

sill *n.* **1** a slab of wood or stone etc. at the base of a window or doorway etc. **2** a sheet of igneous rock intruded between other rocks. [OE]

sillabub var. of SYLLABUB.

silly *adj.* **1** lacking good sense, foolish, unwise. **2** weak-minded. **3** (of a fielding position in cricket) very close to the batsman. —*n.* (*colloq.*) a foolish person. —**silly-billy** *n.* (*colloq.*) a foolish person. —**silliness** *n.* [OE, = happy]

silo /ˈsaɪləʊ/ *n.* (*pl.* **silos**) **1** a pit or airtight structure in which green crops are stored for fodder. **2** a tower or pit for the storage of cement or grain etc. **3** an underground place where a guided missile is kept ready for firing. [Sp. f. L f. Gk *siros* pit for corn]

silt *n.* sediment deposited by water in a channel or harbour etc. —*v.t./i.* to block or be blocked with silt. —**siltation** /-ˈteɪʃ(ə)n/ *n.* [perh. rel. to Da. *sylt* salt-marsh (as SALT)]

silvan /ˈsɪlv(ə)n/ *adj.* of the woods; having woods, rural. [f. F or L (*silva* wood)]

silver *n.* **1** a white lustrous precious metallic element, symbol Ag, atomic number 47. **2** coins or articles made of or looking like silver. **3** the colour of silver. **4** a silver medal. —*adj.* of or coloured like silver. —*v.t./i.* **1** to coat or plate with silver. **2** to give a silvery appearance to. **3** to provide (a mirror-glass) with a backing of tin amalgam etc. **4** (of hair) to turn grey or white. —**silver birch,** the common birch (*Betula pendula*) with a silver-coloured bark. **silver-fish** *n.* a silver-coloured fish; a silvery bristletail (*Lepisma saccharina*) found in books and damp places. **silver jubilee,** a 25th anniversary. **silver lining,** a consolation or hopeful feature in misfortune. **silver medal,** a medal of silver awarded as second prize. **silver paper,** tin foil. **silver plate,** articles plated with silver. **silver-plated** *adj.* plated with silver. **silver sand,** fine pure sand used in gardening. **silver wedding,** the 25th anniversary of a wedding. [OE]

silverside *n.* the upper (and usually best) side of a round of beef.

silversmith *n.* one who makes articles in silver.

silverware *n.* articles made of or plated with silver.

silvery *adj.* **1** like silver in colour or appearance. **2** having a clear gentle ringing sound. [f. SILVER]

silviculture /ˈsɪlvɪkʌltʃə(r)/ *n.* cultivation of forest trees. [F (as SILVAN, CULTURE)]

simian /ˈsɪmɪən/ *adj.* resembling an ape or monkey. —*n.* an ape or monkey. [f. L *simia* monkey]

similar /ˈsɪmɪlə(r)/ *adv.* **1** like, alike; having a resemblance but not quite the same. **2** of the same kind, nature, shape, or amount. —**similarity** /-ˈlærɪtɪ/ *n.*, **similarly** *adv.* [f. F or L (*similis* like)]

simile /ˈsɪmɪlɪ/ *n.* a figure of speech in which one thing is compared to another; the use of such a comparison. [L, neut. of *similis* like]

similitude /sɪˈmɪlɪtju:d/ *n.* **1** similarity, outward appearance. **2** comparison; expression of comparison. [f. OF or L (as prec.)]

simmer *v.t./i.* **1** to keep or be kept bubbling or boiling gently. **2** to be in a state of anger or laughter which is only just suppressed. —*n.* a simmering condition. —**simmer down,** to become less agitated. [alt. f. earlier *simper* (perh. imit.)]

simnel /ˈsɪmn(ə)l/ *n.* a rich cake, especially for Mothering Sunday or Easter, covered with marzipan and decorated. [f. OF, ult. f. L *simila* fine flour]

simony /ˈsaɪmənɪ/ *n.* the buying or selling of ecclesiastical offices. [f. OF f. L (*Simon* Magus (Acts 8: 18), with allusion to his offer of money to the Apostles to purchase the power of giving the Holy Ghost by the laying on of hands)]

simoom /sɪˈmu:m/ *n.* a hot dry dust-laden desert wind. [f. Arab. (*samma* to poison)]

simper *v.t./i.* to smile in a silly or affected way; to express by or with simpering. —*n.* such a smile. [cf. Da. & Norw. *semper* delicate]

simple *adj.* **1** easily understood or done, presenting no difficulty. **2** not complicated or elaborate; without luxury or sophistication. **3** not compound, consisting of or involving only one element or operation etc. **4** absolute, unqualified; straightforward; **5** foolish, ignorant; gullible; feeble-minded. —**simple fracture,** a fracture of the bone only. **simple interest,** see INTEREST. **simple-minded** *adj.* unsophisticated, without cunning; feeble-minded. **simple time,** (*Mus.*) that with a binary subdivision of the unit (e.g. into two, four, eight). [f. OF f. L *simplus*]

simpleton /ˈsɪmp(ə)lt(ə)n/ *n.* a stupid or gullible person. [f. prec., after surnames from place-names in *-ton* (town)]

simplicity /sɪmˈplɪsɪtɪ/ *n.* the fact or quality of being simple. [f. L *simplex* (as SIMPLE)]

simplify /ˈsɪmplɪfaɪ/ *v.t.* to make simple or less difficult. —**simplification** /-fɪˈkeɪʃ(ə)n/ *n.* [f. F f. L *simplificare* make simple]

simplistic /sɪmˈplɪstɪk/ *adj.* excessively or affectedly simple or simplified. —**simplistically** *adv.* [f. SIMPLE]

simply *adv.* **1** in a simple manner. **2** absolutely, without doubt. **3** merely. [f. SIMPLE]

simulate /ˈsɪmjʊleɪt/ *v.t.* **1** to pretend to be, have, or feel. **2** to imitate or counterfeit; to imitate the conditions of (a situation etc.), e.g.

for training. —**simulation** /-ˈleɪʃ(ə)n/ *n.*, **simulator** *n.* [f. L *simulare* (*similis* like)]

simultaneous /sɪməlˈteɪnɪəs/ *adj.* occurring or operating at the same time. —**simultaneity** /-təˈneɪɪtɪ/ *n.*, **simultaneously** *adv.* [f. L (*simul* at the same time)]

sin[1] *n.* **1** the breaking of a religious or moral law, especially by a conscious act; an act that does this. **2** a serious fault or offence. **3** an act that is contrary to common sense. —*v.i.* (**-nn-**) to commit a sin. [OE]

sin[2] /saɪn/ *abbr.* sine.

since *prep.* after (a specified past event or time); between (a past event or time) and now. —*conj.* **1** during or in the time after. **2** for the reason that, because. —*adv.* **1** from that time or event until now. **2** ago. [OE, = after that]

sincere /sɪnˈsɪə(r)/ *adj.* free from pretence or deceit. —**sincerity** /sɪnˈserɪtɪ/ *n.* [f. L *sincerus* clean, pure]

sincerely *adv.* in a sincere manner. —**yours sincerely,** a formula for ending a letter. [f. prec.]

sine /saɪn/ *n.* the ratio of the side of the opposite acute angle (in a right-angled triangle) to the hypotenuse. [f. L *sinus* curve, fold of toga, tr. Arab. *jayb* bosom, sine]

sinecure /ˈsaɪnɪkjʊə(r)/ *n.* a position that requires little or no work but yields profit or honour. [f. L *sine cura* without care]

sine die /saɪnɪ ˈdaɪiː, sɪneɪ ˈdiːeɪ/ *adv.* (of business adjourned indefinitely) with no appointed date. [L, = without a day]

sine qua non /sɪneɪ kwɑː ˈnəʊn, saɪnɪ kweɪ ˈnɒn/ an indispensable condition or qualification. [L, = without which not]

sinew /ˈsɪnjuː/ *n.* **1** tough fibrous tissue joining a muscle to a bone; a piece of this. **2** (in *pl.*) muscles, bodily strength. **3** a thing that strengthens or sustains. [OE]

sinewy *adj.* having strong sinews. [f. prec.]

sinful *adj.* committing or involving sin; wicked. —**sinfully** *adv.*, **sinfulness** *n.* [f. SIN + -FUL]

sing *v.t./i.* (*past* **sang**; *p.p.* **sung**) **1** to utter musical sounds with the voice, especially with a set tune; to utter or produce by singing. **2** (of the wind, a kettle, etc.) to make a humming, buzzing, or ringing sound; (of the ears) to be affected with a ringing or buzzing sound. **3** (*slang*) to act as an informer. —**sing-along** *n.* a song or recording to which one can sing in accompaniment; a sing-song to the accompaniment of a leader or tune. **sing out,** to shout. **sing the praises of,** to praise enthusiastically or continually. —**singer** *n.* [OE]

singe /sɪndʒ/ *v.t./i.* (*partic.* **singeing**) to burn superficially or lightly; to burn off the tips or ends of. —*n.* **1** a superficial burn. **2** an act of singeing. [OE]

Singhalese var. of SINHALESE.

single /ˈsɪŋg(ə)l/ *adj.* **1** one only, not double or multiple; united, undivided; designed for or used or done by one person etc. **2** one by itself; regarded separately; not married. **3** (of a ticket) valid for the outward journey only, not a return. **4** (with neg. or interrog.) even one. **5** (of a flower) having only one set of petals. —*n.* **1** a thing that is single, a single item in a series. **2** a single ticket. **3** a pop record with one piece of music on each side. **4** a hit for one run in cricket. **5** (usu. in *pl.*) a game with one player on each side. —*v.t.* (with *out*) to choose for special attention etc.; to distinguish from others. —**single-breasted** *adj.* (of a coat etc.) having only one set of buttons and overlapping little across the breast. **single combat,** a duel. **single file,** a file of persons in one line. **single-handed** *adv.* without help from another; (*adj.*) done single-handed. **single-minded** *adj.* having or intent on only one purpose. —**singly** *adv.* [f. OF f. L *singulus* (rel. to SIMPLE)]

singlet /ˈsɪŋglɪt/ *n.* a man's sleeveless garment worn under or instead of a shirt. [f. prec., after *doublet*]

singleton /ˈsɪŋgəlt(ə)n/ *n.* a single person or thing, especially a player's only card of a suit. [f. SINGLE, after *simpleton*]

singsong *adj.* uttered with a monotonous rhythm or cadence. —*n.* **1** a singsong manner. **2** an informal gathering for singing in chorus.

singular /ˈsɪŋgjʊlə(r)/ *adj.* **1** unique; much beyond the average; extraordinary; eccentric, strange. **2** (*Gram.* of a word or form) denoting one person or thing. —*n.* (*Gram.*) a singular word or form, the singular number. —**singularity** /-ˈlærɪtɪ/ *n.*, **singularly** *adv.* [f. OF f. L *singularis* (as SINGLE)]

Sinhala /ˈsɪnhələ/ *adj.* & *n.* = foll. [Sinh.]

Sinhalese /sɪnhəˈliːz/ *adj.* of the Sinhalese or their language. —*n.* (*pl.* same) **1** a member of an Aryan people deriving from northern India and forming the majority of the population in Sri Lanka. **2** their language. [f. Skr. *Sinhalam* Sri Lanka]

sinister /ˈsɪnɪstə(r)/ *adj.* **1** suggestive of evil, looking malignant or villainous; wicked, criminal; of evil omen. **2** (in heraldry) of or on the left-hand side (the observer's right) of a shield etc. [f. OF or L, = left]

sink *v.t./i.* (*past* **sank**; *p.p.* **sunk** or (as *adj.*) SUNKEN) **1** to fall slowly downwards; to come gradually to a lower level or pitch; to disappear below the horizon; to go or penetrate below the surface, especially of a liquid; (of a ship) to go to the bottom of the sea etc. **2** to pass into a less active condition; to lose value or strength etc. gradually. **3** to cause or allow to sink; to overlook or forget (one's differences etc.) to cause the failure or discomfiture of. **4** to dig (a well); to bore (a shaft). **5** to engrave (a die). **6** to invest (money). **7** to cause (a ball) to enter a pocket in billiards, a hole in golf, etc. —*n.* **1** a fixed basin with a drainage pipe and usually with a water-supply. **2** a place where foul liquid collects; a place of rampant vice etc. —**sink in,** to penetrate; to become understood. **sinking feeling,** a feeling of hunger or fear. **sinking fund,** a fund for the gradual repayment of a debt. **sunk fence,** a fence formed by or built along the bottom of a ditch. [OE]

sinker *n.* a weight used to sink a fishing-line or sounding-line. [f. SINK]

sinner *n.* one who sins. [f. SIN]

Sino- /saməʊ-/ *in comb.* Chinese (and) (*Sino-American*; *Sinophobia*). [f. Gk *Sinai* the Chinese]

sinology /sɪˈnɒlədʒɪ, saɪ-/ *n.* the study of the Chinese language and history etc. —**sinologist** *n.* [f. SINO- + -LOGY]

sinter *n.* a solid coalesced by heating. —*v.t./i.* to form into a sinter. [G, = CINDER]

sinuate /ˈsɪnju:ət/ *adj.* wavy-edged, with distinct inward and outward bends along the edge. [f. L, p.p. of *sinuare* to bend]

sinuous /ˈsɪnjʊəs/ *adj.* with many curves, undulating, meandering. —**sinuosity** /-ˈɒsɪtɪ/ *n.*, **sinuously** *adv.* [f. F or L (as foll.)]

sinus /ˈsaɪnəs/ *n.* a cavity of bone or tissue, especially in the skull communicating with the nostrils. [L, = bosom, recess]

sinusitis /saɪnəˈsaɪtɪs/ *n.* inflammation of the sinus. [f. prec. + -ITIS]

Sioux /su:/ *n.* (*pl.* same) a member or the language of a group of North American Indian tribes. —*adj.* of the Sioux or their language. —**Siouan** /ˈsu:ən/ *adj.* [F, f. native name]

sip *v.t./i.* (**-pp-**) to drink in repeated small mouthfuls or spoonfuls. —*n.* a small mouthful of liquid; an act of taking this. [perh. modification of SUP]

siphon /ˈsaɪf(ə)n/ *n.* **1** a pipe or tube shaped like an inverted V or U with unequal legs, to convey liquid from a container to a lower level of atmospheric pressure. **2** a bottle from which aerated water is forced out by the pressure of a gas. **3** the sucking-tube of some insects or small animals. —*v.t./i.* to conduct or flow (as) through a siphon. [F or f. L f. Gk *siphōn* pipe]

sir /sɜ:(r)/ *n.* **1** a polite or respectful form of address or reference to a man. **2** Sir, the title prefixed to the Christian name of a knight or baronet. [reduced form of SIRE]

sire *n.* **1** the male parent of an animal, especially a stallion kept for breeding. **2** (*archaic*) a form of address to a king **3** (*archaic*) a father or male ancestor. —*v.t* (esp. of a stallion) to beget. [f. OF f. L *senior* (see SENIOR)]

siren /ˈsaɪrən/ *n.* **1** (*Gk myth.*) any of the creatures (two or three in number) who had the power of luring seafarers to destruction by their song. **2** a dangerously fascinating woman, a temptress; (*attrib.*) irresistibly tempting. **3** a device for making a loud prolonged signal or warning sound; the sound made. [f. OF f. L f. Gk]

sirenian /saɪˈri:nɪən/ *adj.* of the order Sirenia of large aquatic plant-eating mammals that includes the dugong and the manatee. —*n.* a member of this order. [as prec.]

sirloin /ˈsɜ:lɔɪn/ *n.* **1** the upper and choicer part of a loin of beef. **2** (*US*) a rump steak. [f. OF (as SUR-², LOIN)]

sirocco /sɪˈrɒkəʊ/ *n.* (*pl.* **-os**) a hot moist wind in southern Europe. [F f. It. ult. f. Arab., = east wind]

sis *n.* (*colloq.*) sister. [abbr.]

sisal /ˈsaɪs(ə)l/ *n.* fibre from the leaves of an agave. [f. *Sisal*, port of Yucatan]

siskin /ˈsɪskɪn/ *n.* a small songbird (*Spinus spinus*). [f. MDu.]

sissy *n.* an effeminate or cowardly person. —*adj.* characteristic of a sissy. [f. SIS]

sister *n.* **1** a woman or girl in relation to the other sons and daughters of her parents. **2** a close woman friend or associate; a female fellow member of the same church, trade union, or other association, or of the human race. **3** a member of a sisterhood, especially a nun. **4** a female hospital nurse in authority over others; (*colloq.*) any female nurse. **5** (*attrib.*) of the same type, design, origin, etc. —**sister-in-law** *n.* (*pl.* **sisters-in-law**) the sister of one's husband or wife; one's brother's wife. —**sisterly** *adj.* [f. ON]

sisterhood *n.* **1** the relationship (as) of sisters. **2** a society of women bound by monastic views or devoting themselves to religious or charitable work. [f. prec. + -HOOD]

Sisyphean /sɪsɪˈfi:ən/ *adj.* endlessly laborious, as of Sisyphus (*Gk myth.*), condemned for his misdeeds to Hades where his eternal task was to roll a large stone to the top of a hill from which it always rolled down again.

sit *v.t./i.* (**-tt-**; *past* & *p.p.* **sat**) **1** to take or be in a position in which the body is supported more or less upright by the buttocks resting on the ground or a raised seat etc. **2** to cause to sit, to place in a sitting position. **3** (of a bird) to perch; (of an animal) to rest with the hind legs bent and the body close to the ground. **4** (of a bird) to remain on the nest to hatch eggs. **5** to be engaged in an occupation in which the sitting position is usual; to pose for a portrait; to be a Member of Parliament *for* a constituency; to be a candidate *for* an examination etc.; to undergo (an examination). **6** (of a parliament or court etc.) to be in session. **7** to be in a more or less permanent position or condition. **8** (of clothes etc.) to fit or hang in a certain way. **9** to keep or have one's seat on (a horse etc.). —**be sitting pretty,** to be comfortably or advantageously placed. **sit at a person's feet,** to be his or her pupil. **sit back,** to relax one's efforts. **sit down,** to sit after standing; to cause to sit; to suffer tamely (under humiliation etc.). **sit-down** *adj.* (of a meal) eaten sitting **sit-down strike,** a strike in which workers refuse to leave their place of work. **sit in,** to occupy a place as a protest. **sit-in** *n.* such a protest. **sit in judgement,** to assume the right of judging others; to be censorious. **sit in on,** to be present as a guest or observer at (a meeting). **sit on,** to be a member of (a committee etc.); to hold a session or inquiry concerning; (*colloq.*) to delay action about; (*slang*) to repress, rebuke, or snub. **sit on the fence,** to remain neutral or undecided. **sit out,** to take no part in (a dance etc.); to stay until the end of (an ordeal etc.). **sit tight,** (*colloq.*) to remain firmly in one's place; not to yield. **sit up,** to rise from a lying to a sitting position; to sit firmly upright; not to go to bed (until later than the usual time); (*colloq.*) to have one's interest or attention suddenly aroused. **sit-upon** *n.* (*colloq.*) the buttocks. [f. OE]

sitar/ sɪˈtɑ:(r)/ *n.* an Indian long-necked lute. [f. Hindi f. Pers.]

sitcom /ˈsɪtkɒm/ *n.* (*colloq.*) a situation comedy. [abbr.]

site *n.* **1** the ground on which a town or building stood, stands, or is to stand. **2** the place where some activity or event takes place or took place. —*v.t.* to locate; to provide with a site. [f. AF or L *situs* local position]

sitter *n.* **1** one who sits, especially for a portrait. **2** a baby-sitter. **3** (*slang*) an easy catch or shot; something easy to do. [f. SIT]

sitting *n.* **1** the time during which a person or assembly etc sits continuously. **2** a clutch of eggs. —*adj.* **1** having sat down. **2** (of an animal or bird) not running or flying. —**sitting duck** *or* **target,** a person or thing that is a helpless victim of attack. **sitting-room** *n.* a room for sitting in; space enough to accommodate seated persons. **sitting tenant,** one already occupying a house etc. [f. SIT]

situate /ˈsɪtju:eɪt/ *v.t.* **1** to place or put in a specified position, situation, etc.; (in *p.p.*) in specified circumstances. **2** to establish or indicate the place of; to put in a context. —/-ət/ *adj.* (*archaic* or *Law*) situated. [f. L *situare* f. *situs* site]

situation /sɪtju:ˈeɪʃ(ə)n/ *n.* **1** a place (with its surroundings) that is occupied by something. **2** a set of circumstances; a state of affairs; a condition. **3** an employee's position or job. —**situation comedy,** a comedy (especially a serial) in which the humour derives largely from the particular conjunction of characters and circumstances. —**situational** *adj.* [f. F or L (as prec.)]

six *adj.* & *n.* **1** one more than five; the symbol for this (6, vi, VI). **2** the size etc. denoted by six. —**at sixes and sevens,** in confusion or disagreement. **hit** *or* **knock for six,** (*colloq.*) to surprise utterly or overwhelm. **six-gun** *or* **-shooter** *n.* (*US*) a revolver with six chambers. [OE]

sixfold *adj.* & *adv.* six times as much or as many; consisting of six parts. [f. SIX + -FOLD]

sixpence *n.* the sum of 6p; (*formerly*) the sum of 6d., a silver coin worth this.

sixpenny *adj.* costing or worth sixpence.

sixteen /sɪksˈti:n/ *adj.* & *n.* **1** one more than fifteen; the symbol for this (16, xvi, XVI). **2** the size etc. denoted by sixteen. —**sixteenth** *adj.* & *n.* [OE (as SIX, -TEEN)]

sixth *adj.* next after the fifth. —*n.* each of six equal parts of a thing. —**sixth form,** a form in a secondary school for pupils over 16. **sixth-form college,** a college with special courses for such pupils. **sixth sense,** a supposed faculty giving intuitive or extra-sensory knowledge. —**sixthly** *adv.* [f. SIX]

sixty /ˈsɪkstɪ/ *adj.* & *n.* **1** six times ten; the symbol for this (60, lx, LX). **2** (in *pl.*) the numbers, years, or degrees of temperature from 60 to 69. —**sixtieth** *adj.* & *n.* [OE (as SIX)]

size[1] *n.* **1** the extent of a thing; dimensions, magnitude. **2** each of the series of standard measurements in which things of the same kind are made, grouped, sold, etc. —*v.t.* to group or sort according to size. —**size up,** to estimate the size of; (*colloq.*) to form a judgement of. **that is the size of it,** (*colloq.*) that is the truth of the matter. —**-sized** *adj.* of a specific size (*large-sized*). [f. OF (as ASSIZE)]

size[2] *n.* a gelatinous solution used in glazing paper, stiffening textiles, etc. —*v.t.* to treat with size. [perh. = prec.]

sizeable *adj.* fairly large. [f. SIZE[1]]

sizzle *v.i.* **1** to make a spluttering or hissing noise as of frying. **2** (*colloq.*) to be in a state of great heat or excitement etc. —*n.* a sizzling sound. [imit.]

SJ *abbr.* Society of Jesus.

sjambok /ˈʃæmbɒk/ *n.* (in South Africa) a rhinoceros-hide whip. [Afrik. f. Malay f. Urdu]

skald /skɔld, skɒld/ *n.* an ancient-Scandinavian poet. [f. ON]

skate[1] *n.* each of a pair of blades, or (**roller-skate**) metal frames with four small wheels, fitted to the soles of boots or shoes so that the wearer can glide over ice or a hard surface. —*v.t./i.* to move on skates, to perform (a specified figure) on skates. —**get one's skates on,** (*slang*) to make haste. **skate on thin ice,** to behave rashly, to risk danger etc. **skate over,** to make only a passing reference (or no reference) to. —**skater** *n.* [f. Du. *schaats* f. OF *eschasse* stilt]

skate[2] *n.* (*pl.* **skate**) a fish that is a kind of ray (especially *Raja batis*). [f. ON]

skate[3] *n.* (*slang*) (also **cheap skate**) a contemptible or dishonest person. [orig. unkn.]

skateboard *n.* a short narrow board on roller-skate wheels for riding on while standing. —**skateboarder** *n.*, **skateboarding** *n.*

skedaddle /skɪˈdæd(ə)l/ *colloq. v.i.* to depart hurriedly. —*n.* a hurried departure. [orig. unkn.]

skein /skeɪn/ *n.* **1** a loosely coiled bundle of yarn or thread. **2** a flock of wild geese etc. in flight. [f. OF *escaigne*; orig. unkn.]

skeleton /ˈskelɪt(ə)n/ *n.* **1** the hard framework of bones of an animal body; the shell or other hard structure covering or supporting an invertebrate animal. **2** any supporting framework or structure. **3** a very thin person or animal. **4** the remaining part of something after its life or usefulness is gone. **5** an outline sketch, an epitome. **6** (*attrib.*) having only the essential or minimum number of persons or parts etc. —**skeleton in the cupboard,** a discreditable or embarrassing fact kept secret. **skeleton key,** a key fitting many locks. —**skeletal** *adj.* [Gk, neut. of *skeletos* dried-up]

skep *n.* **1** a wooden or wicker basket, the quantity contained in this. **2** a straw or wicker beehive. [f. ON]

skerry *n.* a reef, a rocky island. [Orkney dial. f. ON, rel. to SCAR]

sketch *n.* **1** a rough drawing or painting. **2** a brief account of something. **3** a short usually humorous play. **4** a short descriptive piece of writing. **5** a musical composition of a single movement. —*v.t./i.* to make a sketch or sketches (of). —**sketch-book** *n.* sheets of drawing-paper made up in the form of a book. **sketch in,** to indicate briefly or in outline. **sketch-map** *n.* a roughly drawn map with few details. —**sketcher** *n.* [f. Du. f. It. ult. f. Gk *skhedios* extempore]

sketchy *adj.* like a sketch, rough and not detailed; unsubstantial or imperfect, especially through haste. —**sketchily** *adv.*, **sketchiness** *n.* [f. prec.]

skew *adj.* set askew, slanting, oblique; distorted. —*n.* a skewed position, a slant. —*v.t./i.* **1** to make skew; to distort. **2** to move obliquely. —**on the skew,** askew. **skew-whiff** *adj.* (*colloq.*) askew. [f. OF as ESCHEW]

skewbald /ˈskju:bɔld/ *adj.* (of an animal) with irregular patches of white and another colour. —*n.* a skewbald animal, especially a horse. [f. obs. *skued* (orig. unkn.), after PIEBALD]

skewer *n.* a long pin designed for holding meat compactly together while it is cooking. —*v.t.* to fasten together or pierce (as) with a skewer. [var. of dial. *skiver* (orig. unkn.)]

ski /ski:/ *n.* (*pl.* **skis**) each of a pair of long narrow pieces of wood etc. fastened under the feet for travelling over snow; a similar device under a vehicle. —*v.i.* (*past* & *p.p.* **ski'd** or **skied** /ski:d/; *partic.* **skiing**) to travel on skis. —**ski-jump** *n.* a steep slope levelling off before a sharp drop to allow a skier to leap through the air. **ski-lift** *n.* a device for carrying skiers up a slope, usually on seats hung from an overhead cable. **ski-run** *n.* a slope suitable for skiing. —**skier** *n.* [Norw., f. ON *skíth* billet, snow-shoe]

skid *v.t./i.* (**-dd-**) (of a vehicle etc.) to slide (esp. sideways or obliquely) on a slippery road etc.; to cause (a vehicle) to skid. —*n.* **1** an act of skidding. **2** a piece of wood etc. serving as a support or fender etc. **3** a braking device, especially a wooden or metal shoe on a wheel. **4** a runner on an aircraft for use when landing. —**on the skids,** (*colloq.*) about to be discarded or defeated. **put the skids under,** to hasten the downfall or failure of. **skid-pan** *n.* a slippery surface prepared for vehicle-drivers to practise control of skidding. **skid row,** (*US*) a district frequented by vagrants. [orig. unkn.]

skiff *n.* a light rowing or sailing boat. [f. F *esquif* (as SHIP)]

skilful *adj.* having or showing skill. —**skilfully** *adv.* [f. SKILL + -FUL]

skill *n.* the ability to do something well. [f. ON, = distinction. (*skilja* distinguish)]

skilled *adj.* **1** skilful. **2** (of a worker) highly trained or experienced; (of work) requiring skill or special training. [f. SKILL]

skillet /ˈskɪlɪt/ *n.* **1** a small metal cooking-pot with a long handle and usually legs. **2** (*US*) a frying-pan. [perh. f. OF *escuelete* dim. of *escuela* platter f. pop. L *scutella*]

skim *v.t./i.* (**-mm-**) **1** to take floating matter or cream etc. from the surface of a liquid; to clear (a liquid) thus. **2** to pass over (a surface) almost touching it or touching it lightly; to glide along. **3** to read or look at cursorily. —**skim milk,** milk from which the cream has been skimmed. —**skimmer** *n.* [back-formation f. foll.]

skimmer *n.* **1** a ladle etc. for skimming liquids. **2** a long-winged marine bird of the genus *Rynchops* that feeds by skimming over water with its knifelike lower mandible immersed. [f. OF f. *escume* scum]

skimp *v.t./i.* to supply or use a meagre amount or rather less than what is needed (of); to be parsimonious. [orig. unkn. (cf. SCRIMP)]

skimpy *adj.* meagre, not ample; scanty. —**skimpily** *adv.*, **skimpiness** *n.* [as prec.]

skin *n.* **1** the flexible continuous covering of the human or animal body. **2** a skin (with or without hair) removed from an animal; material made from this; a container for water or wine, made from an animal's whole skin. **3** the colour or complexion of a person's skin. **4** outer layer or covering; a film like a skin on the surface of a liquid. **5** a ship's planking or plating. —*v.t./i.* (**-nn-**) **1** to strip or scrape the skin from. **2** to cover or become covered (as) with skin. **3** (*slang*) to fleece, to swindle. —**be (all) skin and bone,** to be very thin. **by the skin of one's teeth,** by a very narrow margin. **get under a person's skin,** (*colloq.*) to interest or annoy him intensely. **have a thick** (*or* **thin**) **skin,** to be insensitive (or sensitive) to criticism etc. **no skin off one's nose,** (*colloq.*) of no consequence to one. **save one's skin,** to avoid death or harm etc. **skin-deep** *adj.* superficial, not deep or lasting. **skin-diver** *n.* one who swims underwater without a diving-suit, usually with an aqualung and flippers. **skin-diving** *n.* such swimming. **skin-flick** *n.* (*slang*) a pornographic film. **skin-graft** *n.* a surgical transplanting of skin; the skin thus transferred. **skin-tight** *adj.* very close-fitting. [OE f. ON; cf. OHG *scinden* flay]

skinflint *n.* a miserly person.

skinful *n.* (*colloq.*) enough alcoholic liquor to make one drunk. [f. SKIN + -FUL]

skinhead *n.* a youth with hair shaved off or cut very short, especially one of a group adopting this style.

skinny *adj.* thin or emaciated. —**skinniness** *n.* [f. SKIN]

skint *adj.* (*slang*) having no money. [= *skinned* (SKIN)]

skip[1] *v.t./i.* (**-pp-**) **1** to move along lightly, especially by taking two steps with each foot in turn. **2** to jump lightly from the ground; to jump using a skipping-rope. **3** to pass quickly from one subject or point to another. **4** to omit in reading or dealing with; (*colloq.*) not to participate in. **5** (*colloq.*) to leave hurriedly. —*n.* a skipping movement or action. —**skip bail,** to jump bail. **skip it!** (*slang*) abandon the topic etc. **skipping-rope** *n.* a length of rope (usually with two handles) revolved over the head and under the feet while jumping as a game or exercise. [prob. f. Scand.]

skip[2] *n.* **1** a large container for refuse etc. **2** a cage or bucket etc. in which men or materials are raised or lowered in mines etc. [var. of SKEP]

skipper *n.* the captain of a ship, especially of a small trading or fishing vessel; the captain of an aircraft; the captain of a side in games. —*v.t.* to act as captain of. [f. MDu. or MLG *schipper* (as SHIP)]

skirl *n.* the shrill sound characteristic of bagpipes. —*v.i.* to make a skirl. [prob. Scand. (imit.)]

skirmish *n.* a minor fight especially between small or outlying parts of armies or fleets; a short argument or contest of wit etc. —*v.i.* to engage in a skirmish. [f. OF *eskirmir*]

skirt *n.* **1** a woman's outer garment hanging from the waist; the part of a coat etc. that hangs below the waist. **2** the hanging part round the base of a hovercraft. **3** an edge, a border, an extreme part; skirt of beef (see below). —*v.t./i.* **1** to go or lie along or round the edge of. **2** to avoid dealing with (an issue etc.). —**skirting-board** *n.* a narrow board etc. along the bottom of a room-wall. **skirt of beef,** the diaphragm etc. as food; meat from the lower flank. [f. ON, = SHIRT]

skit *n.* a light usually short piece of satire or burlesque. [rel. to *skit* move lightly (perh. as SHOOT)]

skittish /ˈskɪtɪʃ/ *adj.* lively, playful; (of a horse etc.) nervous, inclined to shy. —**skittishly** *adv.*, **skittishness** *n.* [perh. as prec.]

skittle *n.* **1** (in *pl.*) a game played with usually nine wooden pins set up at the end of an alley to be bowled down usually with a wooden ball or disc; a game played with similar pins set up on a board to be knocked down by a swinging suspended ball. **2** a pin used in these games. —*v.t.* (with *out*) to get (batsmen in cricket) out in rapid succession. [orig. also *kittle-pins*; orig. unkn.]

skive *v.t./i.* (*slang*) to evade (a duty). —**skive off,** to depart evasively. —**skiver** *n.* [orig. = split (leather), f. ON]

skivvy /ˈskɪvɪ/ *n.* (*colloq.*, *derog.*) a female domestic servant. [orig. unkn.]

skua /ˈskuːə/ *n.* a large predatory sea-bird of the genus *Stercorarius* etc. [f. Faeroese & ON]

skulduggery /skʌlˈdʌgərɪ/ *n.* trickery; unscrupulous behaviour. [orig. Sc. = unchastity; etym. unkn.]

skulk *v.i.* to loiter, move, or conceal oneself stealthily, especially in cowardice, evasion of duty, or because intending mischief. [f. Scand.; cf. Norw. *skulka* lurk]

skull *n.* **1** the bony case of the brain of a

vertebrate. **2** the bony framework of the head; a representation of this. **3** the head as the site of the intelligence. —**skull and cross-bones,** a representation of a skull with two thigh-bones crossed below it as an emblem of piracy or death. **skull-cap** *n.* a small close-fitting peakless cap. [orig. unkn.]

skunk *n.* **1** a black white-striped bushy-tailed American animal of the genus *Mephitis* etc., about the size of a cat and able to emit a powerful stench from liquid secreted by its anal glands when attacked; its fur. **2** a contemptible person. [f. Amer. Ind.]

sky /skaɪ/ *n.* (in *sing.* or *pl.*) the region of the clouds, atmosphere, and outer space seen from the earth. —*v.t.* to hit (a cricket ball) high into the air. —**sky-blue** *adj.* & *n.* bright clear blue. **sky-diving** *n.* parachuting in which the parachute is opened only at the last safe moment. **sky-high** *adv.* & *adj.* reaching the sky; very high. **sky-rocket** *n.* a rocket exploding high in the air; (*v.i.*) to rise very steeply or rapidly. **sky-writing** *n.* legible smoke-trails emitted by an aeroplane. **to the skies,** without reserve. [orig. = cloud(s), f. ON]

skyjack *v.t.* (*slang*) to hijack (an aircraft). [f. SKY + HIJACK]

skylark *n.* a lark (*Alauda arvensis*) that soars while singing. —*v.i.* to play tricks and practical jokes.

skylight *n.* a window in a roof.

skyline *n.* the outline of hills, buildings, etc., defined against the sky.

skyscraper *n.* a very tall building with many storeys, especially the type of office building that dominates Manhattan Island, New York, and the centres of other large American cities.

skyward /ˈskaɪwəd/ *adv.* (also **skywards**) & *adj.* towards the sky. [f. SKY + -WARD]

slab *n.* a flat thick usually square or rectangular piece of solid matter. [orig. unkn.]

slack[1] *adj.* **1** lacking firmness or tautness. **2** lacking energy or activity; sluggish; negligent. **3** (of the tide etc.) neither ebbing nor flowing. —*n.* **1** a slack period, slack part of a rope, etc.; (*colloq.*) a spell of inactivity. **2** (in *pl.*) informal trousers. —*v.t.*/*i.* **1** to slacken. **2** (*colloq.*) to take a rest; to be lazy. —**slack off,** to loosen, to lose or cause to lose vigour. **slack up,** to reduce speed. —**slackly** *adv.*, **slackness** *n.* [OE]

slack[2] *n.* coal-dust. [prob. f. LDu.]

slacken *v.t.*/*i.* to make or become slack. [f. SLACK]

slacker *n.* a shirker, an indolent person. [f. SLACK]

slag *n.* solid non-metallic waste matter left when metal has been separated from ore by smelting. —*v.i.* (**-gg-**) to form slag. —**slag-heap** *n.* a hill of refuse from a mine etc. —**slaggy** *adj.* [f. MLG]

slain *p.p.* of SLAY.

slake *v.t.* **1** to assuage or satisfy (one's thirst, revenge, etc.). **2** to disintegrate (lime) by combination with water. [OE (as SLACK)]

slalom /ˈslɑːləm/ *n.* a ski-race down a zigzag course with artificial obstacles; an obstacle race in canoes. [Norw., = sloping track]

slam[1] *v.t.*/*i.* (**-mm-**) **1** to shut forcefully with a loud bang; to put, knock, or move with a similar sound or violently. **2** (*slang*) to criticize severely; to hit, to beat; to gain an easy victory over. —*n.* the sound or action of slamming. [prob. f. Scand.]

slam[2] *n.* the gaining of every trick at cards. —**grand slam,** the winning of 13 tricks in bridge; the winning of all of a group of championships in a sport. [perh. f. obs. *slampant* trickery]

slander /ˈslɑːndə(r)/ *n.* a false statement maliciously uttered that is damaging to a person's reputation; the uttering of this. —*v.t.* to utter a slander about. —**slanderous** *adj.*, **slanderously** *adv.* [f. AF & OF f. L (as SCANDAL)]

slang *n.* words and phrases, or particular meanings of these, that are found only in very informal language or in that of restricted groups of people. —*v.t.*/*i.* to use abusive language (to). —**slanging-match** *n.* a prolonged exchange of insults. —**slangy** *adj.* [orig. unkn.]

slant /slɑːnt/ *v.t.*/*i.* **1** to slope, to lie or go at an angle from the vertical or horizontal; to cause to do this. **2** to present (information etc.) from a particular point of view or unfairly. —*n.* **1** a slope, an oblique position. **2** the way information etc. is presented; an attitude or bias. —*adj.* sloping, oblique. —**on a** *or* **the slant,** aslant. [var. of dial. *slent*, f. ON *sletta* dash]

slantwise *adv.* aslant. [f. prec. + -WISE]

slap *v.t.*/*i.* (**-pp-**) **1** to strike with the palm of the hand or a flat object, or so as to make a similar noise. **2** to lay forcefully. **3** to put hastily or carelessly. —*n.* a blow with the palm of the hand or a flat object; a slapping sound. —*adv.* with a slap; directly, suddenly; exactly. —**slap and tickle,** (*colloq.*) lively (esp. amorous) amusement. **slap-bang** *adv.* violently, noisily, headlong. **slap down,** (*colloq.*) to snub; to reprimand. **slap-happy** *adj.* (*colloq.*) cheerfully casual or flippant. **slap in the face,** a rebuff or insult. **slap on the back,** congratulations. **slap-up** *adj.* lavish, first-class. [f. LG (imit.)]

slapdash *adj.* hasty and careless. —*adv.* in a slapdash manner.

slapstick *n.* boisterous knockabout comedy.

slash *v.t./i.* **1** to make a sweeping stroke or strokes with a sword, knife, whip, etc.; to strike or cut thus. **2** to make an ornamental slit in (a garment), especially so as to show underlying fabric. **3** to reduce (prices etc.) drastically. **4** (in *partic.*) vigorously incisive or effective. **5** to censure vigorously. —*n.* a slashing cut or stroke. [perh. f. OF, = break in pieces]

slat *n.* a thin narrow piece of wood or plastic etc., especially used in an overlapping series as in a fence or Venetian blind. [f. OF *esclat* splinter]

slate *n.* **1** a kind of metamorphic rock easily split into flat smooth plates. **2** a piece of such a plate used as a roofing-material or for writing on. **3** the dull blue or grey colour of slate. —*v.t.* **1** to cover with slates. **2** (*colloq.*) to criticize severely. **3** (*US*) to make arrangements for (an event etc.). **4** (*US*) to nominate for office etc. —**clean slate,** no discreditable history. **clean the slate,** to remove obligations, grievances, etc. —**slaty** *adj.* [f. OF *esclate* fem. of *esclat* (see prec.)]

slattern /ˈslætɜːn/ *n.* a slovenly woman. —**slatternliness** *n.*, **slatternly** *adj.* [rel. to dial. *slatter* spill, slop]

slaughter /ˈslɔːtə(r)/ *n.* **1** the killing of animals for food etc. **2** the ruthless killing of many persons or animals. —*v.t.* **1** to kill (animals) for food etc. **2** to kill ruthlessly in great numbers. **3** (*colloq.*) to defeat utterly. —**slaughterer** *n.* [f. ON (as SLAY)]

slaughterhouse *n.* a place for the slaughter of animals as food.

Slav /slɑːv/ *n.* a member of a group of peoples in central and eastern Europe, including the Russians, Poles, Czechs, Bulgarians, Serbo-Croats, etc., speaking languages of the Slavonic group. —*adj.* of the Slavs. [f. L *Sclavus*]

slave *n.* **1** a person who is owned by another and has to serve him. **2** a drudge, a person working very hard. **3** a helpless victim of some dominating influence. **4** a part of a machine directly controlled by another.—*v.i.* to work very hard. —**slave-driver** *n.* an overseer of slaves at work; a hard taskmaster. **slave labour,** forced labour. **slave-trade** *n.* the procuring, transporting, and selling of slaves, especially African Blacks. [f. OF *esclave* f. L (as prec.), the Slavonic peoples in parts of Central Europe having been reduced to bondage by conquest]

slaver[1] /ˈsleɪvə(r)/ *n.* a ship or person engaged in the slave-trade. [f. prec.]

slaver[2] /ˈslævə(r)/ *n.* **1** saliva running from the mouth. **2** flattery; drivel. —*v.i.* to let saliva run from the mouth, to dribble. [prob. f. LDu.; cf. SLOBBER]

slavery /ˈsleɪvərɪ/ *n.* **1** the condition or work of a slave. **2** very hard work, drudgery. **3** the custom of having slaves. [f. SLAVE]

slavish /ˈsleɪvɪʃ/ *adj.* **1** of or like slaves; excessively submissive. **2** showing no independence or originality. —**slavishly** *adv.*, **slavishness** *n.* [f. SLAVE]

Slavonic /sləˈvɒnɪk/ *adj.* **1** of the group of languages including Russian and Polish and Czech. **2** of the Slavs. —*n.* the Slavonic group of languages. [f. L *S(c)lavonia* country of the Slavs]

slay *v.t.* (*past* **slew** /sluː/; *p.p.* **slain**) to kill. [OE]

sleazy *adj.* squalid, tawdry; slatternly. —**sleazily** *adv.*, **sleaziness** *n.* [orig. unkn.]

sled *n.* (*US*) a sledge. —*v.t./i.* (**-dd-**) (*US*) to sledge. [f. MLG (rel. to SLIDE)]

sledge *n.* a vehicle on runners instead of wheels for conveying loads or passengers, especially over snow. —*v.t./i.* to travel or convey by sledge. [f. MDu. *sleedse*, rel. to prec.]

sledge-hammer *n.* **1** a large heavy hammer. **2** (*attrib.*) heavy and powerful. [OE *slecg* (as SLAY) + HAMMER]

sleek *adj.* **1** (of hair or skin etc.) smooth and glossy. **2** looking well-fed and comfortable. **3** ingratiating. —*v.t.* to make sleek. —**sleekly** *adv.*, **sleekness** *n.* [var. of SLICK]

sleep *n.* **1** the naturally recurring condition of rest in animals, in which the eyes are closed, postural muscles relaxed, and consciousness suspended; a sleep-like state. **2** a spell of sleeping. **3** the inert condition of hibernating animals. —*v.t./i.* **1** to be in a state of sleep; to fall asleep. **2** to stay for a night's sleep. **3** to have sexual intercourse in bed *together* or *with*. **4** to spend (time) in sleeping. **5** to provide sleeping accommodation for. **6** to be inactive or dead. —**go to sleep,** to enter the state of sleep; (of a limb etc.) to become numbed. **last sleep,** death. **put to sleep,** to anaesthetize; to kill (an animal) painlessly. **sleep around,** (*colloq.*) to be sexually promiscuous. **sleep in,** to remain asleep later than usual. **sleeping-bag** *n.* a lined or padded bag to sleep in, especially when camping etc. **sleeping-car** *or* **-carriage** *n.* a railway coach with beds or berths. **sleeping partner,** one not sharing in the actual work of a firm. **sleeping-pill** *n.* a pill to induce sleep. **sleeping sickness,** a tropical disease causing extreme lethargy. **sleep off,** to get rid of (a headache etc.) by sleeping. **sleep on it,** to refrain from deciding (a question etc.) until the next day. **sleep-walker** *n.* a person who walks about while asleep. **sleep-walking** *n.* this condition. [OE]

sleeper *n.* **1** one who sleeps. **2** each of the beams on which railway rails run. **3** a sleeping-car; a berth in this. **4** a ring or stud worn in a pierced ear to keep the hole from closing. [f. SLEEP]

sleepless *adj.* **1** lacking sleep; unable to sleep. **2** continually active. —**sleeplessly** *adv.*, **sleeplessness** *n.* [f. SLEEP + -LESS]

sleepy *adj.* **1** ready for sleep, about to fall asleep. **2** lacking activity or bustle. —**sleepily** *adv.*, **sleepiness** *n.* [f. SLEEP]

sleet *n.* snow and rain together; hail or snow melting as it falls. —*v.i.* to fall as sleet. —**it sleets** *or* **is sleeting,** sleet is falling. —**sleety** *adj.* [rel. to MLG *sloten* hail]

sleeve *n.* **1** the part of a garment that encloses the arm or a part of it. **2** the cover of a gramophone record. **3** a tube enclosing a rod or smaller tube. **4** a wind-sock. —**up one's sleeve,** concealed but ready for use. —**sleeved** *adj.* [OE]

sleeveless *adj.* without sleeves. [f. prec. + -LESS]

sleigh /sleɪ/ *n.* a sledge, especially one for riding on. —*v.i.* to travel on a sleigh. [f. Du. *slee* (as SLED)]

sleight /slaɪt/ *n.* (*archaic*) dexterity, cunning. —**sleight-of-hand** *n.* a display of dexterity; conjuring. [f. ON (as SLY)]

slender *adj.* **1** of small girth or breadth; slim and graceful. **2** relatively small in amount etc.; scanty. —**slenderness** *n.* [orig. unkn.]

slept *past* & *p.p.* of SLEEP.

sleuth /slu:θ/ *n.* a detective. —**sleuth-hound** *n.* a bloodhound; a detective. [orig. *sleuth-hound*, f. ON *slóth* track (cf. SLOT) + HOUND]

slew[1] /slu:/ *v.t./i.* to turn or swing forcibly or with effort to a new position. —*n.* such a turn. [orig. unkn.]

slew[2] *past* of SLAY.

slice *n.* **1** a thin broad or wedge-shaped piece cut from something. **2** a share or portion. **3** an implement with a broad flat blade for lifting or serving fish etc. or for scraping or chipping things. **4** (in golf) a slicing stroke. —*v.t./i.* **1** to cut into slices; to cut from a larger piece. **2** to cut cleanly or easily with or like a knife. **3** (in golf) to strike (a ball) badly so that it deviates from the direction intended, going to the right of a right-handed player. —**sliced bread,** bread that is sliced and wrapped before being sold. —**slicer** *n.* [f. OF *esclice* splinter (cf. SPLIT)]

slick *adj.* **1** skilful or efficient, especially in a superficial or pretentious way or with some trickery. **2** smooth in manner or speech. **3** shrewd, wily. **4** smooth and slippery. —*n.* a slippery place or patch; a thick patch of oil floating on the sea. —*v.t.* to make sleek. —**slickness** *n.* [prob. f. OE, = polish; cf. SLEEK]

slide *v.t./i.* (*past* & *p.p.* **slid**) **1** to move or cause to move along a smooth surface with constant friction on the same part of the thing moving. **2** to move or go smoothly or quietly. **3** to pass gradually or imperceptibly into a condition or habit. **4** to glide more or less erect over ice or other smooth surface without using skates. —*n.* **1** an act of sliding. **2** a smooth surface for sliding on; an inclined plane down which goods etc. are slid or for children to play on. **3** a sliding part of a machine or instrument. **4** a thing slid into place; a mounted picture or transparency for showing by means of a projector; a small glass plate holding an object for examination under a microscope. **5** a hair-slide. —**let things slide,** to fail to give them proper attention or control; to allow deterioration. **slide over,** to skate over (a delicate subject etc.). **slide-rule** *n.* a ruler with a sliding central strip, graduated logarithmically for use in making rapid calculations. **sliding scale,** a scale of fees, taxes, wages, etc., that varies as a whole according to changes in some standard. —**slider** *n.* [OE]

slight /slaɪt/ *adj.* **1** not much, not great, not thorough; inconsiderable. **2** slender and frail-looking, not heavily built. —*v.t.* to treat or speak of (a person etc.) with disrespect or as not worth attention.—*n.* an act of slighting. —**slightly** *adv.*, **slightness** *n.* [f. ON, = level, smooth]

slim *adj.* **1** of small girth or thickness, not heavily built. **2** relatively small. —*v.t./i.* **(-mm-) 1** to make oneself slimmer by dieting, exercise, etc. **2** to reduce (a work-force etc.) in size. —**slimly** *adv.*, **slimmer** *n.*, **slimness** *n.* [Du. or LG, = MLG *slim(m)* slanting]

slime *n.* an unpleasant slippery thick liquid substance. [OE, rel. to L *limus* mud, Gk *limnē* marsh]

slimline *adj.* of slender design.

slimy /ˈslaɪmɪ/ *adj.* **1** like slime; covered with or full of slime. **2** disgustingly obsequious, meek, or dishonest. —**slimily** *adv.*, **sliminess** *n.* [f. SLIME]

sling[1] *n.* **1** a belt, strap, or chain(s) etc. looped round an object to lift it or support it as it hangs. **2** a bandage etc. looped round the neck to support an injured arm. **3** a looped strap used to throw a stone or other missile. —*v.t.* (*past* & *p.p.* **slung**) **1** to suspend or lift with a sling; to arrange so as to be held or moved from above. **2** to hurl with a sling; (*colloq.*) to throw. —**sling-back** *n.* a shoe held in place by a strap above and behind the heel. **sling one's hook,** (*slang*) to make off. [prob. f. ON & LDu.]

sling[2] *n.* (*US*) a sweetened drink of gin or other spirits and water. [orig. unkn.]

slink *v.i.* (*past* & *p.p.* **slunk**) to move in a

stealthy, guilty, or shamefaced manner. [OE, = crawl]

slinky *adj.* **1** moving in a slinking manner; stealthy. **2** smooth and sinuous; (of clothes) close-fitting and sinuous. —**slinkily** *adv.*, **slinkiness** *n.* [f. SLINK]

slip[1] *v.t./i.* (**-pp-**) **1** to slide unintentionally or momentarily; to lose one's footing or one's balance thus. **2** to go or put with a smooth movement or stealthily. **3** to escape restraint or capture by being slippery or not grasped firmly. **4** to make one's way quietly or unobserved. **5** to make a careless or casual error; to fall below one's normal standard. **6** to release from restraint or connection. **7** (in knitting) to move (a stitch) to the other needle without looping the yarn through it. **8** to escape from; to evade. —*n.* **1** an act of slipping. **2** an accidental or slight error. **3** a loose covering or garment; a petticoat. **4** a reduction in the movement or speed of a pulley or propeller etc. **5** (in *sing.* or *pl.*) a slipway. **6** (in cricket) a fieldsman close behind the wicket; (in *sing.* or *pl.*) this part of the ground. —**give a person the slip,** to escape from or evade him. **let slip,** to release accidentally or deliberately; to miss (an opportunity); to utter inadvertently. **slip-case** *or* **-cover** *n.* a fitted cover for a book or furniture etc. **slip-knot** *n.* a knot that can be undone at a pull, a running knot. **slip of the pen** (*or* **tongue**), a small mistake in which something is written (or said) unintentionally. **slip-on** *adj.* (of shoes or clothes) that can be easily slipped on or off. **slipped disc,** a disc between the vertebrae that has become displaced and causes lumbar pain. **slip-road** *n.* a road for entering or leaving a motorway etc. **slip-stream** *n.* a current of air or water driven back by a propeller or moving vehicle. **slip up,** (*colloq.*) to make a mistake. **slip-up** *n.* (*colloq.*) a mistake, a blunder. [prob. f. MLG]

slip[2] *n.* **1** a small piece of paper, especially for writing on. **2** a cutting taken from a plant for grafting or planting. —**slip of a girl** etc., a small slim girl etc. [prob. f. MDu. or MLG]

slip[3] *n.* finely ground clay mixed with water for coating or decorating earthenware. [OE, = slime]

slipper *n.* a light loose shoe for indoor wear. [f. SLIP[1]]

slippery *adj.* **1** difficult to grasp because of smoothness or wetness etc. **2** (of a surface) on which slipping is likely. **3** (of a person) unreliable, unscrupulous. —**slipperiness** *n.* [prob. made by Coverdale (1535) after Luther's *schlipfferig*; partly f. dial. *slipper* adj., f. OE]

slippy *adj.* (*colloq.*) slippery. —**look slippy,** to make haste. [f. SLIP[1]]

slipshod *adj.* **1** slovenly, careless. **2** having shoes that are down at heel.

slipway *n.* a sloping structure used for building ships or as a landing-stage.

slit *n.* a straight narrow incision or opening. —*v.t.* (**-tt-**; *past & p.p.* **slit**) to make a slit in; to cut into strips. [f. OE]

slither /ˈslɪðə(r)/ *v.i.* to slip or slide unsteadily. —*n.* an act of slithering. —**slithery** *adj.* [OE (frequent. of SLIDE)]

sliver /ˈslɪvə(r)/ *n.* a thin strip or piece of wood etc. —*v.t./i.* to break off as a sliver; to break or form into slivers. [rel. to dial. *slive* cleave]

slob *n.* (*colloq.*) a large and coarse or stupid person. [f. Ir. *slab* mud]

slobber *v.t./i.* **1** to slaver or dribble. **2** to show excessive sentiment over a person etc. —*n.* slaver. —**slobbery** *adj.* [= Du. *slobbern* (imit.)]

sloe /sləʊ/ *n.* the blackthorn (*Prunus spinosa*); its small bluish-black fruit. [OE]

slog *v.t./i.* (**-gg-**) **1** to hit hard. **2** to work or walk doggedly. —*n.* **1** a hard hit. **2** hard steady work; a spell of this. —**slogger** *n.* [orig. unkn.; cf. SLUG[2]]

slogan /ˈsləʊgən/ *n.* a short catchy phrase used in advertising etc.; a party cry, a watchword. [f. Gael., = war-cry]

sloop *n.* a small one-masted fore-and-aft-rigged vessel. [f. Du. *sloep*]

slop *v.t./i.* (**-pp-**) **1** to spill (liquid); to be spilt; to splash liquid on. **2** to behave effusively. **3** to plod clumsily through mud or puddles etc.; to move in a slovenly way. —*n.* **1** slopped liquid. **2** weak sentimentality. **3** (in *pl.*) household liquid refuse; the contents of chamber-pots; dregs from teacups etc. **4** (in *sing.* or *pl.*) unappetizing liquid food. —**slop-basin** *n.* a basin for the dregs of cups at table. **slop out,** (in prison) to carry slops out from cells. **slop-pail** *n.* a pail for removing bedroom or kitchen slops. [earlier = slush, rel. to OE *slyppe* slimy substance]

slope *n.* **1** a position, direction, or state at an angle from the horizontal or vertical; a state in which one end or side is at a higher level than the other; the difference in level between two ends or sides of a thing. **2** a piece of rising or falling ground; a place for skiing on the side of a mountain. —*v.t./i.* **1** to have or take a slope. **2** to cause to do this. —**slope arms,** to place a rifle in a sloping position against the shoulder. **slope off,** (*slang*) to go away. [f. *aslope* crosswise]

sloppy *adj.* **1** having a liquid consistency and splashing easily; excessively liquid. **2** unsystematic, careless. **3** untidy and ill-fitting; loose-fitting. **4** weakly sentimental. —**sloppily** *adv.*, **sloppiness** *n.* [f. SLOP]

slosh *v.t./i.* **1** to splash; to move with a splashing sound. **2** to hit heavily. **3** to pour (liquid) clumsily (on). —*n.* **1** slush. **2** an act or sound of splashing. **3** (*slang*) a heavy blow. [var. of SLUSH]

sloshed *adj.* (*slang*) drunk. [f. SLOSH]

slot *n.* **1** a slit or other narrow aperture in a machine etc. for something (especially a coin) to be inserted. **2** a groove, channel, or slit into which something fits or in which something works. **3** an allotted place in an arrangement or scheme. —*v.t./i.* (**-tt-**) **1** to put into or be placed in a slot. **2** to make a slot or slots in. —**slot-machine** *n.* a machine worked by the insertion of a coin, especially delivering small purchased articles or providing amusement. [orig. = hollow of the breast, f. OF *esclot*; orig. unkn.]

sloth /sləʊθ/ *n.* **1** laziness, indolence. **2** a South and Central American slow-moving arboreal mammal of the genera *Choloepus* and *Bradypus*. [f. SLOW]

slothful *adj.* lazy. —**slothfully** *adv.* [f. SLOTH + -FUL]

slouch *v.i.* to stand, move, or sit in a drooping ungainly fashion. —*n.* **1** a slouching posture or movement. **2** the downward bend of a hat-brim. **3** (*slang*) a lazy, incompetent, or slovenly worker etc. —**slouch hat,** a hat with a wide flexible brim. —**sloucher** *n.* [orig. unkn.]

slough[1] /slaʊ/ *n.* a swamp, a miry place. [OE]

slough[2] /slʌf/ *n.* a snake's cast skin; dead tissue that drops away. —*v.t./i.* to cast or drop as slough. [perh. rel. to LG *slu*(*we*) husk]

Slovak /ˈsləʊvæk/ *n.* a native or the language of Slovakia (formerly part of Hungary, now the Slovak Socialist Republic, a part of Czechoslovakia). —*adj.* of the Slovaks. [f. Slovak etc. *Slovák*]

sloven /ˈslʌv(ə)n/ *n.* a slovenly person. [perh. f. Flemish *sloef* dirty]

slovenly /ˈslʌvənlɪ/ *adj.* careless and untidy, unmethodical. —*adv.* in a slovenly manner. —**slovenliness** *n.* [f. SLOVEN]

slow /sləʊ/ *adj.* **1** not quick or fast; acting, moving, or done without haste or rapidity. **2** tending to cause slowness. **3** (of a clock etc.) showing a time earlier than the correct one. **4** dull-witted, stupid; not understanding readily. **5** lacking liveliness, slack or sluggish. **6** (of a fire or oven) giving low heat. **7** (of photographic film) not very sensitive to light, needing a long exposure; (of a lens) having only a small aperture. **8** lacking the inclination. —*adv.* slowly (used when *slow* gives the essential point, as in *go slow*). —*v.t./i.* (with *down* or *up*) to reduce the speed of; to go more slowly. —**slow-down** *n.* the action of slowing down. **slow motion,** a speed of cinema film in which movements appear much slower than in real life; a simulation of this. —**slowly** *adv.*, **slowness** *n.* [OE]

slowcoach *n.* a person who is slow in his actions, understanding, or work etc.

slow-worm *n.* a small European legless lizard (*Anguis fragilis*). [OE, first element of uncertain origin but not f. SLOW]

sludge *n.* **1** thick greasy mud; muddy or slushy sediment. **2** sewage. —**sludgy** *adj.* [cf. SLUSH]

slug[1] *n.* **1** a small gastropod especially of the families Limacidae and Arionidae, like a snail but without a shell. **2** a piece of metal; a bullet of irregular shape; a missile for an airgun. **3** (*US*) a tot of liquor. [f. earlier *slugg*(*e*) sluggard, prob. f. Scand.]

slug[2] *v.t./i.* (*US*) (**-gg-**) to hit hard. —*n.* (*US*) a hard hit. [orig. unkn.; cf. SLOG]

sluggard /ˈslʌgəd/ *n.* a lazy person. [f. *slug* be slothful (as SLUG[1])]

sluggish *adj.* inert, slow-moving. —**sluggishly** *adv.*, **sluggishness** *n.* [f. SLUG[1]]

sluice /slu:s/ *n.* **1** (also **sluice-gate**) a sliding gate or other contrivance for regulating the flow or level of water. **2** the water regulated by this. **3** (also **sluice-way**) an artificial channel for carrying off water. **4** a place for rinsing things. —*v.t./i.* **1** to let out (water) by means of a sluice; (of water) to rush out freely (as) from a sluice. **2** to flood, scour, or rinse with a flow of water. [f. OF *escluse* f. L (as EXCLUDE)]

slum *n.* a dirty overcrowded district inhabited by poor people. —*v.i.* (**-mm-**) **1** to live in slumlike conditions. **2** to visit a slum for curiosity or for charitable purposes. —**slummy** *adj.* [19th-c. slang]

slumber *v.t./i.* to sleep (*lit.* or *fig.*). —*n.* sleep (*lit.* or *fig.*). —**slumberer** *n.*, **slumberous** *adj.*, **slumbrous** *adj.* [f. OE]

slump *n.* a sudden severe or prolonged fall in prices and values and in demand for goods etc. —*v.i.* **1** to undergo a slump. **2** to sit or fall down limply. [orig. = sink in bog (imit.)]

slung *past* & *p.p.* of SLING[1].

slunk *past* & *p.p.* of SLINK.

slur *v.t./i.* (**-rr-**) **1** to sound or write (words, musical notes, etc.) so that they run into one another. **2** to put a slur upon (a person or character). **3** to pass lightly or deceptively (over a fact etc.). —*n.* **1** an imputation; discredit. **2** an act of slurring. **3** (*Mus.*) a curved line joining notes to be slurred. [orig. unkn.]

slurp *v.t.* (*colloq.*) to eat or drink with a noisy sucking sound. —*n.* (*colloq.*) this sound. [f. Du.]

slurry /ˈslʌrɪ/ *n.* thin mud; a suspension of fine solid material in water or other liquid; thin liquid cement. [rel. to dial. *slur* thin mud]

slush *n.* **1** thawing snow; watery mud. **2** silly sentimental talk or writing. —**slush fund,**

money used to bribe officials etc., e.g. by illicit commission. —**slushy** *adj*. [orig. unkn.; cf. SLUDGE]

slut *n*. a slovenly woman. —**sluttish** *adj*. [orig. unkn.]

sly /slaɪ/ *adj*. **1** done or doing things in an unpleasantly cunning and secret way. **2** mischievous and knowing. —**on the sly,** secretly. —**slyly** *adv*., **slyness** *n*. [f. ON, orig. = able to strike (as SLAY)]

Sm *symbol* samarium.

smack[1] *n*. **1** a sharp slap or blow; a hard hit. **2** a sharp sound as of a surface struck by a flat object; a loud kiss. —*v.t.* to slap; to move with a smack. —*adv*. (*colloq*.) with a smack; suddenly, directly, violently. —**smack in the eye,** a rebuff. [f. MDu. (imit.)]

smack[2] *v.t./i.* to have a slight flavour or trace of something. —*n*. a slight flavour or trace. [OE]

smack[3] *n*. a boat with a single mast, used for sailing or fishing. [f. Du.]

smacker *n*. (*slang*) **1** a loud kiss, a sounding blow. **2** £1; (*US*) $1. [f. SMACK[1]]

small /smɔːl/ *adj*. **1** not large or big. **2** not great in importance, amount, power, etc.; not much, insignificant. **3** consisting of small particles. **4** doing things on a small scale. **5** socially undistinguished, poor or humble. **6** mean, ungenerous; paltry. —*n*. **1** the slenderest part of something (esp. *small of the back*). **2** (in *pl*., *colloq*.) small articles of laundry, especially underwear. —*adv*. into small pieces. —**feel** *or* **look small,** to be humiliated or ashamed. **small arms,** portable firearms. **small beer,** an insignificant thing. **small change,** coins, especially low denominations as opposed to notes. **small fry,** see FRY[2]. **small hours,** the period soon after midnight. **small-minded** *adj*. narrow or selfish in outlook. **small-scale** *adj*. made or occurring on a small scale. **small talk,** social conversation on unimportant matters. **small-time** *adj*. unimportant, petty. —**smallness** *n*. [OE]

smallholder *n*. an owner or user of a smallholding.

smallholding *n*. a piece of agricultural land smaller than a farm.

smallpox /ˈsmɔːlpɒks/ *n*. an acute contagious virus disease with fever and pustules usually leaving permanent scars.

smarm *v.t.* (*colloq*.) **1** to smooth, to slick. **2** to flatter fulsomely. [orig. dial.; etym. unkn.]

smarmy *adj*. (*colloq*.) ingratiating. —**smarminess** *n*. [f. SMARM]

smart *adj*. **1** clever, ingenious; quick-witted. **2** neat and elegant; fashionable. **3** forceful; brisk. —*v.i.* to feel acute pain or distress. —*n*. a stinging sensation or mental feeling. —**look smart,** to make haste. **smart alec,** a know-all. —**smartly** *adv*., **smartness** *n*. [OE]

smarten *v.t./i.* (usu. with *up*) to make or become smart. [f. SMART]

smash *v.t./i.* **1** to break or become broken suddenly and noisily into pieces. **2** to destroy, defeat, or overthrow suddenly and completely; to suffer such destruction etc. **3** to strike or move with great force; to strike (a ball) forcefully downwards in tennis etc. —*n*. **1** an act or sound of smashing; a collision; a disaster, financial ruin. **2** (also **smash hit**) a very successful play or song etc. —*adv*. with a smash. —**smash-and-grab** *adj*. (of a robbery) in which a thief smashes a window and seizes goods. [imit.]

smasher *n*. (*colloq*.) a very pleasing or beautiful person or thing. [f. SMASH]

smashing *adj*. (*colloq*.) excellent, wonderful; beautiful. [f. SMASH]

smattering /ˈsmætərɪŋ/ *n*. a slight knowledge of something. [f. *smatter* talk ignorantly; orig. unkn.]

smear *v.t.* **1** to daub or stain with a greasy or sticky substance. **2** to smudge. **3** to discredit or defame; to seek to do this. —*n*. **1** the action or result of smearing. **2** material smeared on a microscope slide etc. for examination; a specimen of this. **3** discrediting, defaming; an attempt at this. —**smeary** *adj*. [OE]

smell *n*. **1** the faculty of perception through the response of the brain to the action of odour on the nose. **2** the quality in substances that affects this sense. **3** an unpleasant odour. **4** an act of inhaling to ascertain a smell. —*v.t./i.* (*past* & *p.p.* **smelt** or **smelled**) **1** to perceive, detect, or examine by smell; to have or use the sense of smell. **2** to give off a smell; to seem by smell to be; to be redolent *of* something specified. —**smelling-salts** *n.pl.* sharp-smelling solid substances sniffed to relieve faintness etc. **smell out,** to seek or discover by smelling or investigation. [prob. f. OE]

smelly *adj*. having a strong or unpleasant smell. —**smelliness** *n*. [f. SMELL]

smelt[1] *v.t.* to extract metal from (ore) by melting; to extract (metal) thus. [f. MDu. or MLG, rel. to MELT]

smelt[2] *n*. a small edible green and silver fish of the genus *Osmerus* etc. [OE]

smelt[3] *past* & *p.p.* of SMELL.

smidgen /ˈsmɪdʒ(ə)n/ *n*. (*colloq*.) a small bit or amount. [perh. f. synonymous *smitch*]

smilax /ˈsmaɪlæks/ *n*. **1** a climbing plant, often with a prickly stem, of the genus *Smilax*, some tropical species of which yield sarsaparilla from tuberous root-stocks. **2** a South African climbing asparagus (*Asparagus* *asparagoides*) much used in decoration. [L f. Gk, = bindweed]

smile *v.t./i.* to make or have a facial expression indicating pleasure or amusement, with the lips stretched and turning upwards at their ends; to express by smiling; to give (a smile) of a specified kind. —*n.* an act of smiling; a smiling expression or aspect. —**smile on** *or* **at,** to look encouragingly on; (of a circumstance etc.) to favour. —**smiler** *n.* [perh. f. Scand. (rel. to SMIRK)]

smirch *v.t.* to besmirch. —*n.* **1** a smear or stain. **2** discredit. [orig. unkn.]

smirk *n.* a silly or self-satisfied smile. —*v.i.* to give a smirk. [OE (*smerian* laugh at)]

smite *v.t./i.* (*past* **smote**; *p.p.* **smitten** /ˈsmɪt(ə)n/) **1** (*archaic*) to hit hard; to chastise, to defeat. **2** to have a sudden effect on. **3** (esp. in *p.p.*) to strike with a disease, desire, emotion, or fascination. [OE *smītan* smear]

smith *n.* **1** a worker in metal. **2** a blacksmith. **3** one who creates something (*song-smith*). [OE]

smithereens /smɪðəˈri:nz/ *n.pl.* small fragments. [f. dial. *smithers* (orig. unkn.)]

smithy /ˈsmɪðɪ/ *n.* a blacksmith's workshop, a forge. [f. SMITH]

smitten *p.p.* of SMITE.

smock *n.* **1** a loose overall. **2** (also **smock-frock**) a loose shirtlike garment often ornamented with smocking. —*v.t.* to decorate with smocking. [OE]

smocking *n.* ornamentation on cloth made by gathering it tightly with stitches into a honeycomb pattern. [f. SMOCK]

smog *n.* fog intensified by smoke. —**smoggy** *adj.* [portmanteau word]

smoke *n.* **1** the visible vapour given off by a burning substance. **2** an act or period of smoking tobacco. **3** (*colloq.*) a cigarette or cigar. —*v.t./i.* **1** to emit smoke or other visible vapour. **2** to inhale and exhale the smoke of a cigarette, cigar, or pipe; to do this habitually; to use (a cigarette etc.) thus. **3** to darken or preserve by the action of smoke. —**go up in smoke,** to come to nothing. **smoke-bomb** *n.* a bomb that emits dense smoke on exploding. **smoke out,** to drive out by means of smoke; to drive out of hiding or secrecy etc. —**smoke-stack** *n.* a chimney or funnel for discharging the smoke of a locomotive or steamer. [OE]

smokeless *adj.* having or producing little or no smoke. [f. SMOKE + -LESS]

smoker *n.* **1** a person who smokes tobacco habitually. **2** a part of a railway coach in which smoking is allowed. [f. SMOKE]

smokescreen *n.* **1** a cloud of smoke concealing military or other operations. **2** a device or ruse for disguising activities.

smoky *adj.* **1** producing or emitting much smoke. **2** covered or filled with smoke; obscured (as) with smoke. **3** suggestive of or having the greyish colour of smoke. —**smokily** *adv.*, **smokiness** *n.* [f. SMOKE]

smolt /sməʊlt/ *n.* a young salmon at the stage between parr and grilse, when it is covered with silvery scales and migrates to the sea for the first time. [orig. Sc. & N. Engl.; orig. unkn.]

smooch *v.i.* (*colloq.*) to kiss and caress; to dance slowly and closely to a lazy romantic melody. —*n.* a spell of smooching; music for this. [imit.]

smooth /smu:ð/ *adj.* **1** having an even surface; without roughness, projections, or indentations; not hairy; (of water) without waves. **2** having an even texture, without lumps. **3** not harsh in sound or taste; moving evenly without jolts or bumping; progressing without hindrance. **4** pleasantly polite but perhaps insincere. —*v.t./i.* **1** to make or become smooth. **2** to remove problems or dangers from. —*adv.* smoothly. —*n.* a smoothing touch or stroke. —**smoothly** *adv.*, **smoothness** *n.* [OE]

smorgasbord /ˈsmɔ:gəsbɔ:d/ *n.* Swedish hors d'œuvres typically consisting of open sandwiches with an assortment of delicacies; a buffet meal with a variety of dishes. [Sw. (*smörgås* (slice of) bread and butter, *bord* table)]

smote *past* of SMITE.

smother /ˈsmʌðə(r)/ *v.t./i.* **1** to suffocate or stifle; to be suffocated. **2** to cover thickly; to overwhelm (with gifts, kindness, etc.). **3** to put out or keep down (a fire) by heaping ashes etc. on it. **4** to repress or conceal. —*n.* a cloud of smoke or dust etc.; obscurity caused by this. [f. OE *smorian* suffocate]

smoulder /ˈsməʊldə(r)/ *v.i.* **1** to burn slowly without flame or in a suppressed way. **2** to burn inwardly with concealed anger or jealousy etc. **3** (of feelings) to exist in a suppressed state. [rel. to LG *smöln*]

smudge *n.* a blurred or smeared mark. —*v.t./i.* **1** to make a smudge on or of. **2** to become smeared or blurred. —**smudgy** *adj.* [orig. unkn.]

smug *adj.* self-satisfied, complacent; consciously respectable. —**smugly** *adv.*, **smugness** *n.* [f. LG *smuk* pretty]

smuggle *v.t.* to import or export (goods) illegally, especially without paying customs duties; to convey secretly. —**smuggler** *n.* [f. LG]

smut *n.* **1** a small flake of soot; a small black mark made (as) by this. **2** obscene talk, pictures, or stories. **3** a cereal-disease turning parts of the plant to black powder. —*v.t./i.*

(**-tt-**) **1** to mark with smuts. **2** to infect with or contract smut disease. —**smutty** *adj.*, **smuttiness** *n.* [rel. to LG *smutt* (cf. SMUDGE)]

Sn *symbol* tin. [f. L *stannum* tin]

snack *n.* a small, casual, or hurried meal. —**snack bar,** a place where snacks are served. [orig. = a snap or bite, f. MDu. (*snacken* v., var. of *snappen* snap)]

snaffle *n.* a simple bridle-bit without a curb. —*v.t.* **1** to put a snaffle on. **2** (*slang*) to take, to steal. [prob. f. LDu.; cf. MLG *snavel* beak, mouth]

snag *n.* **1** an unexpected or hidden difficulty. **2** a jagged projection. **3** a tear in fabric caused by a snag. —*v.t./i.* (**-gg-**) to catch, tear, or be caught on a snag. —**snaggy** *adj.* [prob. f. Scand.; cf. Norw. dial. *snag*(*e*) sharp point]

snail *n.* a slow-moving gastropod mollusc, especially of the family Helicidae, with a spiral shell. —**snail's pace,** very slow movement. [OE]

snake *n.* **1** a long limbless reptile of the suborder Ophidia. **2** (also **snake in the grass**) a treacherous person; a secret enemy. —*v.i.* to move or twist etc. like a snake. —**snake-charmer** *n.* a person appearing to make snakes move to music etc. **snakes and ladders,** a game with counters moved, according to the throw of the dice, along a board with sudden advances up 'ladders' or returns down 'snakes' depicted on the board. [OE]

snaky /ˈsneɪkɪ/ *adj.* **1** infested with snakes; (of the hair of the Furies) composed of snakes. **2** snakelike in appearance or movements or in cunning, treachery, etc. —**snakily** *adv.* [f. prec.]

snap *v.t./i.* (**-pp-**) **1** to make or cause to make a sharp cracking sound; to open or close thus. **2** to break suddenly or with a cracking sound. **3** to speak or say with sudden irritation. **4** to make a sudden audible bite. **5** to move quickly. **6** to take a snapshot of. —*n.* **1** an act or sound of snapping. **2** a catch that fastens with a snap. **3** a crisp brittle cake or biscuit. **4** a snapshot. **5** (also **cold snap**) a sudden brief spell of cold weather. **6** a card-game in which players call 'Snap' when two similar cards are exposed (also as *int.* at the unexpected similarity of two things). **7** vigour, liveliness. —*adv.* with a snapping sound. —*adj.* sudden; done or arranged etc. quickly or at short notice. —**snap fastener,** a press-stud. **snap one's fingers at,** to defy; to regard with contempt. **snap out of,** (*slang*) to throw off (a mood etc.) by a sudden effort. **snap up,** to pick up or buy hastily or eagerly. [prob. f. MDu. or MLG (imit.)]

snapdragon *n.* a plant of the genus *Antirrhinum* with a bag-shaped flower like a dragon's mouth.

snapper *n.* any of several food-fish, especially of the family Lutianidae. [f. SNAP]

snappish *adj.* inclined to snap; irritable, petulant. —**snappishly** *adv.* [f. SNAP]

snappy *adj.* (*colloq.*) **1** brisk, full of zest. **2** neat and elegant. —**make it snappy,** (*colloq.*) to be quick. —**snappily** *adv.* [f. SNAP]

snapshot *n.* a photograph taken informally or casually.

snare *n.* **1** a trap, especially with a noose, for catching birds or animals. **2** a thing that tempts or exposes one to danger or failure etc. **3** (often in *pl.*) an arrangement of twisted gut or wire etc. stretched across the lower head of a side-drum to produce a rattling sound; (also **snare-drum**) a drum fitted with snares. —*v.t.* to catch in a snare; to ensnare. [OE f. ON]

snarl[1] *v.t./i.* **1** to growl angrily with bared teeth. **2** to speak irritably or cynically. —*n.* an act or sound of snarling. [f. earlier *snar*, f. LG]

snarl[2] *v.t./i.* (often with *up*) to tangle; to become entangled; to confuse and hamper the movement of (traffic etc.). —*n.* a tangle. —**snarl-up** *n.* a confusion or jam of traffic etc. [f. SNARE]

snatch *v.t./i.* to seize quickly, eagerly, or unexpectedly; to take quickly or when a chance occurs. —*n.* **1** an act of snatching. **2** a fragment of song or talk etc. **3** a short spell of activity etc. [perh. rel. to SNACK]

snazzy /ˈsnæzɪ/ *adj.* (*slang*) smart, stylish; excellent. —**snazzily** *adv.*, **snazziness** *n.* [orig. unkn.]

sneak *v.t./i.* **1** to go or convey furtively. **2** (*slang*) to steal unobserved. **3** (*slang*) to tell tales, especially at school. —*n.* a cowardly underhand person; (*slang*) a tell-tale, especially at school. —*adj.* acting or done without warning; secret. —**sneak-thief** *n.* a petty thief; a person who steals from open rooms etc. —**sneaky** *adj.* [perh. rel. to obs. *snike* creep]

sneakers *n.pl.* soft-soled shoes. [f. SNEAK]

sneaking *adj.* (of a feeling or suspicion etc.) persistent but not openly acknowledged. [f. SNEAK]

sneer *n.* a scornful smile or remark. —*v.t./i.* to show scorn by a sneer; to utter thus. [perh. f. LDu.]

sneeze *n.* a sudden involuntary expulsion of air from the nose and mouth caused by irritation in the nostrils. —*v.i.* to make a sneeze. —**not to be sneezed at,** (*colloq.*) not contemptible, worth having. [earlier *snese*, *nese*, *fnese*, f. ON]

snick *v.t.* **1** to make a small notch or incision in. **2** (in cricket) to hit (the ball) with a light glancing stroke. —*n.* such a notch or stroke. [suggested by *snickersnee* large knife]

snicker *v.i.* to snigger. —*n.* a snigger. [imit.]

snide *adj.* (*colloq.*) **1** sneering, slyly derogatory. **2** counterfeit. **3** (*US*) mean, underhand. [19th c. slang]

sniff *v.t./i.* to draw up air audibly through the nose; to smell thus. —*n.* an act or sound of sniffing. —**sniff at,** to try the smell of; to show contempt for or disapproval of. [imit.]

sniffle *v.i.* to sniff repeatedly or slightly. —*n.* an act of sniffling; (in *pl.*) a cold in the head causing sniffling. [imit.; cf. SNIVEL]

sniffy *adj.* (*colloq.*) disdainful. —**sniffily** *adv.*, **sniffiness** *n.* [f. SNIFF]

snifter *n.* (*slang*) a small drink of alcoholic liquor. [f. dial. *snift* sniff]

snigger *n.* a sly giggle. —*v.i.* to utter a snigger. [var. of SNICKER]

snip *v.t./i.* (**-pp-**) to cut with scissors or shears, especially in small quick strokes. —*n.* **1** an act of snipping. **2** a piece snipped off. **3** (*slang*) something cheaply acquired or easily done. [f. LG or Du. (imit.)]

snipe *n.* (*pl.* **snipes** or (*collect.*) **snipe**) a wading bird of the genus *Gallinago* with a long straight bill. —*v.i.* **1** to fire shots from a hiding-place, usually at long range. **2** to make a sly critical remark attacking a person or thing. —**sniper** *n.* [prob. f. Scand.]

snippet /ˈsnɪpɪt/ *n.* **1** a small piece cut off. **2** (usu. in *pl.*) a scrap or fragment of information or knowledge etc.; a short extract from a book etc. [f. SNIP]

snitch *v.t.* (*slang*) to steal. [orig. = fillip on the nose; etym. unkn.]

snivel /ˈsnɪv(ə)l/ *v.i.* (**-ll-**) **1** to cry or complain in a miserable whining way; to weep with sniffling. **2** to run at the nose. —*n.* **1** an act of snivelling. **2** running mucus. —**sniveller** *n.* [f. OE (*snofl* mucus); cf. SNUFFLE]

snob *n.* a person who has an exaggerated respect for social position or wealth, or attainments or tastes, and despises those he considers inferior. —**snobbery** *n.*, **snobbish** *adj.*, **snobbishly** *adv.*, **snobbishness** *n.* [orig. = cobbler; etym. unkn.]

snoek /snu:k/ *n.* (in S. Afr.) a barracouta. [Afrik., f. Du. = pike; prob. rel. to SNACK]

snog *v.i.* (**-gg-**) (*slang*) to engage in kissing and caressing. —*n.* (*slang*) a spell of snogging. [orig. unkn.]

snood *n.* a loose baglike ornamental net in which a woman's hair is held at the back. [OE *snōd*; orig. unkn.]

snook /snu:k/ *n.* (*colloq.*) a contemptuous gesture with the thumb to the nose and the fingers spread. —**cock a snook at,** to make this gesture at; to show cheeky contempt for. [orig. unkn.]

snooker /ˈsnu:kə(r)/ *n.* **1** a form of pool played with 15 red and 6 other coloured balls on a billiard table. **2** a position in this game where a direct shot would lose points. —*v.t.* to subject to a snooker; (*slang*, esp. in *pass.*) to thwart, to defeat. [19th c.; orig. unkn.]

snoop *v.i.* to pry inquisitively. —*n.* an act of snooping. —**snooper** *n.*, **snoopy** *adj.* [f. Du., = eat on the sly]

snoot *n.* (*slang*) the nose. [var. of SNOUT]

snooty *adj.* (*colloq.*) supercilious, haughty, snobbish. —**snootily** *adv.* [orig. unkn.]

snooze *n.* a short sleep, especially in the daytime. —*v.i.* to take a snooze. [orig. unkn.]

snore *n.* a snorting or grunting sound in breathing during sleep. —*v.i.* to make such sounds. —**snorer** *n.* [prob. imit.]

Snorkel /ˈsnɔ:k(ə)l/ *n.* [P] a piece of apparatus consisting of a platform which may be elevated and extended, used in fighting fires in tall buildings.

snorkel *n.* **1** a breathing-tube for supplying air to an underwater swimmer. **2** a device by which a submerged submarine can take in and expel air. —*v.i.* (**-ll-**) to swim with a snorkel. [f. G *schnorchel*]

snort *n.* **1** an explosive sound made by the sudden forcing of breath through the nose, especially expressing indignation or incredulity; a similar sound made by an engine etc. **2** (*colloq.*) a small drink of liquor. —*v.t./i.* to make a snort; to express or utter with a snort. [prob. imit.]

snorter *n.* (*slang*) something notably vigorous or difficult etc. [f. SNORT]

snot *n.* (*slang*) **1** nasal mucus. **2** a contemptible person. [prob. f. MDu. or MLG; rel. to SNOUT]

snotty *adj.* (*slang*) **1** running or foul with nasal mucus. **2** contemptible, bad-tempered. **3** supercilious. —**snottily** *adv.*, **snottiness** *n.* [f. SNOT]

snout *n.* the projecting nose (and mouth) of an animal; (*derog.*) the human nose; the pointed front of a thing. [f. MDu. or MLG]

snow /snəʊ/ *n.* **1** frozen atmospheric vapour falling to earth in light white flakes; a fall of this; a layer of it on the ground. **2** a thing resembling snow in whiteness or texture etc.; (*slang*) cocaine. —*v.i.* to fall as or like snow; to come in large numbers or quantities. —**it snows** *or* **is snowing,** snow falls or is falling. **snow-berry** *n.* a garden shrub (*Symphoricarpos rivularis*) with white berries. **snow-blind** *adj.* temporarily blinded by the glare from snow. **snow-bound** *adj.* prevented by snow from going out or travelling. **snow-capped** *adj.* (of a mountain) covered at the top with snow. **snow-drift** *n.* a bank of snow heaped by the wind. **snowed in** *or* **up,** snow-bound. **snowed under,** covered (as) with snow; overwhelmed with a quantity of letters, work, etc. **snow goose,** the arctic white goose (*Anser caerulescens*). **snow-line** *n.* the level above which snow never melts entirely. **snow-plough** *n.* a device for clearing a road or railway of snow; a skiing movement turning the points of the skis inwards so as to stop. **snow-shoe** *n.* a flat device like a racket attached to the foot for walking on snow without sinking in. **snow-white** *adj.* pure white. [OE]

snowball *n.* snow pressed together into a ball for throwing in play. —*v.t./i.* **1** to throw or pelt with snowballs. **2** to increase rapidly. —**snowball-tree** *n.* a variety of guelder rose (*Viburnum opulus* var. *roseum*).

snowdrop *n.* a spring-flowering plant (*Galanthus nivalis*) with white drooping flowers.

snowfall *n.* the amount of fallen snow.

snowflake *n.* each of the small collections of crystals in which snow falls.

snowman *n.* (*pl.* **-men**) a figure made of compressed snow roughly in the shape of a man.

snowmobile /ˈsnəʊməbiːl/ *n.* a motor vehicle, especially with runners or Caterpillar tracks, for travel over snow.

snowstorm *n.* a heavy fall of snow, especially with a high wind.

snowy *adj.* **1** with snow falling; with much snow. **2** covered with snow. **3** as white as snow. —**snowy owl,** a large white owl (*Nyctea nyctea*). [f. SNOW]

SNP *abbr.* Scottish National Party.

Snr. *abbr.* Senior.

snub[1] *v.t.* (**-bb-**) to rebuff or humiliate with sharp words or a marked lack of cordiality. —*n.* an act of snubbing. [f. ON, = chide]

snub[2] *adj.* (of the nose) short and stumpy. **snub-nosed** *adj.* [f. prec. in sense 'check growth of']

snuff[1] *n.* the charred part of a candle-wick. —*v.t./i.* to remove the snuff from (a candle). —**snuff it,** (*slang*) to die. **snuff out,** to extinguish (a candle) by snuffing; to kill or put an end to (hopes etc.); (*slang*) to die. [orig. unkn.]

snuff[2] *n.* **1** powdered tobacco or medicine taken by sniffing it up the nostrils. **2** a sniff. —*v.t./i.* **1** to take snuff. **2** to sniff. —**snuff-box** *n.* a small box for holding snuff. **snuff-coloured** *adj.* dark yellowish-brown. [f. MDu., = snuffle]

snuffer *n.* a device for snuffing or extinguishing a candle. [f. SNUFF[1]]

snuffle *v.t./i.* **1** to sniff in a noisy way; to breathe noisily (as) through a partly blocked nose. **2** to speak or say with snuffles. —*n.* a snuffling sound. [prob. f. LG & Du. (as SNUFF[2]); cf. SNIVEL]

snug *adj.* cosy, sheltered and comfortable; (of a garment) close-fitting. —*n.* a small bar in a public house, with comfortable seating for a few people. —**snugly** *adv.* [orig. Naut.; prob. f. LDu.]

snuggery *n.* a snug place, especially a person's private room. [f. SNUG]

snuggle *v.t./i.* to settle or draw into a warm comfortable position. [f. SNUG]

so /səʊ/ *adv.* & *conj.* **1** in this or that way; in the manner, position, or state described or implied; to that or to such an extent. **2** to a great or notable degree. **3** (with verbs of saying or thinking etc.) thus, this, that. **4** consequently, therefore; indeed, in actual fact. **5** also. —**and so on** *or* **forth,** and others of the same kind; and in other similar ways. **or so,** approximately. **so as to,** in order to, in such a way as to. **so be it,** an expression of acceptance of or resignation to an event etc. **so-called** *adj.* called or named thus (but perhaps wrongly or inaccurately). **so long,** (*colloq.*) goodbye. **so many** (*or* **much**), a definite number (or amount); nothing but. **so much for,** that is all that need be said or done about. **so-so** *adj.* & *adv.* only moderately good or well. **so that,** in order that. **so to say** *or* **speak,** an expression of reserve or apology for an exaggeration or neologism etc. **so what?** that is irrelevant or of no importance. [OE]

soak *v.t./i.* **1** to place or lie in a liquid so as to become thoroughly wet. **2** (of liquid) to penetrate gradually; (of rain) to drench. **3** to absorb (lit. or fig.). **4** (*slang*) to extort money from. —*n.* **1** the act or process of soaking. **2** (*colloq.*) a hard drinker. —**soak-away** *n.* an arrangement for the disposal of water by percolation through the soil. **soak oneself in,** to absorb (a liquid or knowledge etc.). **soak through,** (of moisture) to penetrate, to make thoroughly wet. [OE (as SUCK)]

so-and-so /ˈsəʊənsəʊ/ *n.* (*pl.* **so-and-so's**) **1** a particular person or thing not needing to be specified. **2** (*colloq.*, to avoid use of a vulgar word) an unpleasant or objectionable person. [f. SO]

soap *n.* a cleansing substance made of fat or oil combined with an alkali, yielding lather when rubbed in water. —*v.t.* to apply soap to; to rub with soap. —**soap-box** *n.* a makeshift stand for a street orator. **soap-flakes** *n.pl.* flakes of soap prepared for washing clothes etc. **soap opera,** a sentimental domestic broadcast serial. **soap powder,** a powder, especially with additives, for washing clothes etc. [OE]

soapstone *n.* steatite.

soapsuds *n.pl.* suds.

soapy *adj.* **1** of or like soap. **2** containing or smeared with soap. **3** unctuous, flattering. —**soapily** *adv.*, **soapiness** *n.* [f. SOAP]

soar *v.i.* **1** to rise high in flight. **2** to reach a high level or standard. [f. OF *essorer*, ult. f. L *aura* breeze]

sob *v.t./i.* (**-bb-**) to draw the breath in convulsive gasps usually with weeping; to utter with sobs. —*n.* the act or sound of sobbing. —**sob-story** *n.* (*colloq.*) a narrative meant to evoke sympathy. **sob-stuff** *n.* (*colloq.*) pathos, sentimental writing or behaviour. [prob. imit.]

sober /ˈsəʊbə(r)/ *adj.* **1** not intoxicated; not given to heavy drinking. **2** serious, sedate, not frivolous. **3** moderate, well-balanced. **4** (of colour etc.) quiet and inconspicuous. —*v.t./i.* to make or become sober. —**soberly** *adv.*, **sobriety** /səˈbraɪətɪ/ *n.* [f. OF f. L]

sobriquet /ˈsəʊbrɪkeɪ/ *n.* a nickname. [F, orig. = tap under chin]

Soc. *abbr.* **1** Socialist. **2** Society.

soccer /ˈsɒkə(r)/ *n.* (*colloq.*) Association football. [abbr. of *Association*]

sociable /ˈsəʊʃəb(ə)l/ *adj.* fond of company; characterized by friendly companionship. —**sociability** /-ˈbɪlɪtɪ/ *n.*, **sociably** *adv.* [F, or f. L (*sociare* unite, as foll.)]

social /ˈsəʊʃ(ə)l/ *adj.* **1** of society or its organization; concerned with the mutual relationships of people or classes living in association. **2** living in organized communities, not solitary. **3** sociable. **4** of or designed for companionship and sociability. —*n.* a social gathering, especially one organized by a club etc. —**social climber,** a person seeking to gain a higher rank in society. **social contract,** an agreement to co-operate for social benefits, especially involving submission to restrictions on individual liberty. **social science,** the study of human society and social relationships. **social security,** State assistance to those lacking adequate means or welfare. **social services,** the welfare services provided by the State, including education, health, housing, pensions, etc. **social work,** organized work to alleviate social problems. **social worker,** a person engaged in this. —**socially** *adv.* [F of f. L (*socius* companion)]

socialism /ˈsəʊʃ(ə)lɪz(ə)m/ *n.* a political and economic theory of social organization which advocates that the community as a whole should own and control the means of production, distribution, and exchange; a policy or practice based on this theory. —**socialist** *n.*, **socialistic** /-ˈlɪstɪk/ *adj.* [f. F (as prec.)]

socialite /ˈsəʊʃ(ə)laɪt/ *n.* a person prominent in fashionable society. [f. SOCIAL]

socialize /ˈsəʊʃ(ə)laɪz/ *v.t./i.* **1** to behave sociably; to make social. **2** to organize in a socialistic manner. —**socialization** *n.* [f. SOCIAL]

society /səˈsaɪətɪ/ *n.* **1** an organized and interdependent community; the system of living in this. **2** people of the higher social classes. **3** company, companionship. **4** an association of persons sharing a common aim or interest etc. —**Society of Friends,** a Christian sect, founded *c.*1668, with no written creed or ordained ministers, formerly noted for plain dress and simple living. **Society of Jesus,** the Jesuits. [f. F f. L (as SOCIAL)]

socio- /səʊsɪəʊ-, -ʃɪəʊ-/ *in comb.* of society or sociology (and). [f. L *socius* companion]

sociobiology /səʊʃɪəʊbaɪˈɒlədʒɪ/ *n.* the study of the biological (esp. ecological and evolutionary) bases of human and animal social behaviour. [f. SOCIO- + BIOLOGY]

sociology /səʊsɪˈɒlədʒɪ/ *n.* the study of society and social problems. —**sociological** /-sɪəˈlɒdʒɪk(ə)l/ *adj.* **sociologist** *n.* [f. F, as SOCIO- + -LOGY)]

sock[1] *n.* **1** a short stocking, usually not reaching the knee. **2** a loose insole. —**pull one's socks up,** (*colloq.*) to make an effort to improve. **put a sock in it,** (*slang*) to be quiet. [OE f. L *soccus* actor's shoe]

sock[2] *v.t.* (*slang*) to hit (a person) hard —*n.* (*slang*) a hard blow. —**sock it to,** to attack or address (a person) vigorously. [orig. unkn.]

socket /ˈsɒkɪt/ *n.* a natural or artificial hollow for something to fit into or stand firm or revolve in, especially a device receiving a plug or light-bulb etc. to make an electrical connection. [f. AF, dim. of OF *soc* ploughshare]

Socratic /səˈkrætɪk/ *adj.* of Socrates or his philosophy. —**Socratic irony,** see IRONY. **Socratic method,** dialectic, procedure by question and answer. [f. *Socrates*, Gk philosopher (5th c. BC)]

sod[1] *n.* turf, a piece of turf; the surface of the ground. —**under the sod,** in the grave. [f. MDu. or MLG; orig. unkn.]

sod[2] *n.* (*vulgar*) an unpleasant or despicable person; a fellow. —*v.t.* (**-dd-**) (*vulgar*) to damn. [abbr. of SODOMITE]

soda /ˈsəʊdə/ *n.* **1** a compound of sodium in common use, especially sodium carbonate (**washing-soda**), bicarbonate (**baking-soda**), or hydroxide (**caustic soda**). **2** (also **soda-water**) water made effervescent with carbon dioxide and used as a drink alone or with spirits etc. —**soda-bread** *n.* bread leavened with baking-soda. **soda-fountain** *n.* a device supplying soda-water; a shop equipped with this. [L, perh. f. *sodanum* glasswort]

sodden /ˈsɒd(ə)n/ *adj.* **1** saturated with liquid, soaked through. **2** rendered stupid or dull etc. with drunkenness. [p.p. of SEETHE]

sodium /ˈsəʊdɪəm/ *n.* a soft silver-white metallic element of the alkali metal group, symbol Na, atomic number 11. —**sodium bicarbonate,** a white crystalline compound used in baking-powder. **sodium carbonate,** = washing-soda. **sodium chloride,** common salt. **sodium hydroxide,** a compound of sodium with hydroxyl. **sodium lamp,** a lamp giving a yellow light from an electrical discharge in sodium vapour. [f. SODA]

sodomite /ˈsɒdəmaɪt/ *n.* a person practising sodomy. [f. OF f. L f. Gk (as foll.)]

sodomy /ˈsɒdəmɪ/ *n.* an anal or other copulation-like act, especially between males or between a person and an animal. [f. L f. *Sodom*, town in ancient Palestine, destroyed for its wickedness (Gen. 18-19)]

soever /səʊˈevə(r)/ *adv.* (*literary*) of any possible kind or extent.

sofa /ˈsəʊfə/ *n.* a long upholstered seat with a back and raised ends or arms. [F, ult. f. Arab.]

soffit *n.* an under-surface of an arch or lintel etc. [f. F or It. (as SUFFIX)]

soft *adj.* **1** not hard or firm, yielding to pressure; malleable, plastic, easily cut. **2** (of cloth etc.) smooth or fine in texture, not rough or stiff. **3** (of air etc.) mild, balmy. **4** (of water) free from mineral salts that prevent soap from lathering. **5** (of light or colour etc.) not brilliant or glaring; (of sound) not loud or strident. **6** (of a consonant) sibilant (as *c* in *ice*, *g* in *age*). **7** (of an outline etc.) not sharply defined. **8** (of an action or manner etc.) gentle, conciliatory; complimentary, amorous; (of the heart or feelings etc.) compassionate, sympathetic. **9** (of character etc.) feeble, effeminate, silly, sentimental. **10** (*slang*) (of a job etc.) easy. **11** (of drugs) not likely to cause addiction. **12** (of currency, prices, etc.) likely to depreciate. **13** (of pornography) not highly obscene. —*adv.* softly. —**be soft on,** (*colloq.*) to be lenient towards; to be infatuated with. **soft-boiled** *adj.* (of an egg) boiled so as to leave the yolk still soft. **soft drink,** a non-alcoholic drink. **soft fruit,** small stoneless fruits such as strawberries and currants. **soft furnishings,** curtains and rugs etc. **soft-hearted** *adj.* compassionate. **soft landing,** one made with little or no damage. **soft option,** the easier alternative. **soft palate,** the back part of the palate, which is not bony. **soft pedal,** the pedal on a piano making the tone softer. **soft-pedal** *v.t./i.* to refrain from emphasizing. **soft roe,** see ROE¹. **soft sell,** restrained salesmanship. **soft-soap** *v.t.* (*colloq.*) to persuade (a person) with flattery. **soft-spoken** *adj.* speaking with a soft voice. **soft spot,** a feeling of affection for a person or thing. **soft touch,** (*slang*) a person readily parting with money when asked. —**softly** *adv.*, **softness** *n.* [OE *sōfte* agreeable]

softball *n.* a modified form of baseball using a softer and larger ball, originally devised (*c.*1887) as an indoor game.

soften /ˈsɒf(ə)n/ *v.t./i.* to make or become soft or softer. —**soften up,** to make weaker by a preliminary attack; to make more persuasible by preliminary approaches etc. —**softener** *n.* [f. SOFT]

softie /ˈsɒftɪ/ *n.* (*colloq.*) a person who is physically weak or not hardy, or who is soft-hearted. [f. SOFT]

software *n.* the programs and procedures required for computer operation, as opposed to the physical components of the system (*hardware*); other interchangeable material for performing operations.

softwood *n.* the wood of a coniferous tree.

soggy *adj.* **1** sodden. **2** moist and heavy in texture. —**soggily** *adv.*, **sogginess** *n.* [f. dial. *sog* a swamp]

soh /səʊ/ *n.* (*Mus.*) the fifth note of the major scale in tonic sol-fa. [f. *solve* (see GAMUT)]

soigné /swɑːˈnjeɪ/ *adj.* (*fem.* ***soignée***) carefully finished or arranged; well-groomed and sophisticated. [p.p. of F *soigner* take care of]

soil¹ *n.* **1** the upper layer of earth in which plants grow. **2** the ground belonging to a nation, territory. [f. AF, perh. f. L *solium* seat]

soil² *v.t./i.* **1** to make or become dirty. **2** to defile, to bring discredit to. —*n.* **1** a dirty mark; defilement. **2** filth; refuse matter. —**soil-pipe** *n.* the discharge-pipe of a water-closet. [f. OF *suill(i)er* ult. f. L *sus* pig]

soirée /ˈswɑːreɪ/ *n.* an evening party, especially for conversation or music. [F (*soir* evening)]

sojourn /ˈsɒdʒɜːn/ *n.* a temporary stay. —*v.i.* to make a sojourn. [f. OF *so(r)jorn(er)* f. L SUB-, *diurnum* day]

sol¹ *n.* a liquid solution or suspension of a colloid. [abbr. of SOLUTION]

sol² *n.* var. of SOH.

sola /ˈsəʊlə/ *n.* a pithy-stemmed East Indian swamp plant (*Aeschynomene aspera*). —**sola topi,** a sun-helmet made from its pith. [f. Urdu or Bengali]

solace /ˈsɒləs/ *n.* comfort in distress or disappointment or in tedium. —*v.t.* to give solace to. [f. OF f. L *solatium* (*solari* console)]

solan /ˈsəʊlən/ *n.* a large gooselike gannet (*Sula bassana*). [prob. f. ON, = gannet-duck]

solar /ˈsəʊlə(r)/ *adj.* of or reckoned by the sun. —*n.* **1** a solarium. **2** the upper chamber in a medieval house —**solar battery** *or* **cell,** a device converting solar radiation into electricity. **solar day,** the interval between meridian transits of the sun. **solar plexus,** the complex of radiating nerves at the pit of the stomach. **solar system,** the collection of nine planets and their moons in orbit round the sun, together with smaller bodies in the form of asteroids, meteors, and comets. **solar year,** see YEAR. [f. L *solaris* (*sol* sun)]

solarium /sə'leərɪəm/ *n.* (*pl.* **-ia**) a place for the enjoyment or medical use of sunshine. [L (as prec.)]

sold *past* & *p.p.* of SELL.

solder /'səʊldə(r), 'sɒ-/ *n.* a fusible alloy used to join less fusible metals or wires etc. —*v.t.* to join with solder. —**soldering-iron** *n.* a tool to melt and apply solder. [f. OF *soudure* (*souder* f. L *solidare* fasten, as SOLID)]

soldier /'səʊldʒə(r)/ *n.* **1** a member of an army; (also **common soldier**) a private or NCO in an army. **2** a military commander of specified ability. —*v.i.* to serve as a soldier. —**soldier of fortune,** an adventurous person ready to serve any State or person, a mercenary. **soldier on,** (*colloq.*) to persevere doggedly. —**soldierly** *adj.* [f. OF (*sou(l)de* soldier's pay, f. L, as SOLID)]

soldiery *n.* soldiers, especially of a specified character. [f. prec.]

sole[1] *n.* **1** the under-surface of the foot; the part of a shoe or sock etc. below the foot, especially the part other than the heel. **2** the lower surface or base of a plough, golf-club head, etc. —*v.t.* to provide (a shoe etc.) with a sole. [OE f. L *solea* sandal]

sole[2] *n.* a flat-fish of the genus *Solea* used as food. [f. OF f. L (as prec., from its shape)]

sole[3] *adj.* one and only, single, exclusive. —**solely** *adv.* [f. OF f. L *solus* alone]

solecism /'sɒlɪsɪz(ə)m/ *n.* an offence against grammar, idiom, or etiquette. —**solecistic** /-'sɪstɪk/ *adj.* [f. F or L f. Gk (*soloikos* speaking incorrectly)]

solemn /'sɒləm/ *adj.* **1** not smiling or cheerful. **2** dignified and impressive. **3** formal, accompanied by ceremony. —**solemnly** *adv.*, **solemnness** *n.* [f. OF f. L *sollemnis* customary (*sollus* entire)]

solemnity /sə'lemnɪtɪ/ *n.* **1** being solemn. **2** a solemn rite. [as prec.]

solemnize /'sɒləmnaɪz/ *v.t.* **1** to perform (a ceremony, especially of marriage) with formal rites. **2** to make solemn. —**solemnization** /-'zeɪʃ(ə)n/ *n.* [as SOLEMN]

solenoid /'səʊlənɔɪd/ *n.* a cylindrical coil of wire acting as a magnet when carrying an electric current. [f. F f. Gk *sōlēn* tube]

sol-fa /sɒl'fɑ:/ *n.* see TONIC SOL-FA. [f. *sol* var. of SOH + FA]

soli see SOLO.

solicit /sə'lɪsɪt/ *v.t./i.* **1** to ask repeatedly or earnestly for; to seek to obtain. **2** to make an immoral sexual offer; to accost and offer one's services as a prostitute. —**solicitation** /-'teɪʃ(ə)n/ *n.* [f. OF f. L *sollicitare* agitate (*sollicitus* anxious f. *sollus* entire + *citus* set in motion)]

solicitor *n.* a member of the legal profession, formerly one competent to advise clients and instruct barristers but not appearing as an advocate except in certain lower courts. —**Solicitor-General** *n.* a law officer below the Attorney-General or Lord Advocate. [as prec.]

solicitous /sə'lɪsɪtəs/ *adj.* anxious and concerned, especially about a person's welfare or comfort. —**solicitously** *adv.* [f. L *sollicitus* (see SOLICIT)]

solicitude /sə'lɪsɪtju:d/ *n.* solicitous concern. [as SOLICIT]

solid /'sɒlɪd/ *adj.* **1** firm and stable in shape, not liquid or fluid. **2** of solid material throughout, not hollow; of the same substance throughout. **3** of strong material, construction, or build, not flimsy or slender etc. **4** having three dimensions; concerned with solids. **5** sound and reliable; sound but without special flair etc.; financially sound. **6** (*colloq.*) (of time) uninterrupted. **7** (*colloq.*) unanimous, undivided. —*n.* **1** a solid substance or body. **2** (in *pl.*) solid food. —**solid state,** a state of matter in which the constituent atoms or molecules occupy fixed positions with respect to each other and cannot move freely. **solid-state** *adj.* of or relating to the solid state; using the electronic properties of solids, especially semiconductors, to replace those of valves. —**solidly** *adv.* [f. OF or L *solidus* (rel. to *salvus* safe, *sollus* entire)]

solidarity /sɒlɪ'dærɪtɪ/ *n.* unity or agreement of feeling or action, especially among individuals with a common interest; mutual dependence. [f. F (as prec.)]

solidify /sə'lɪdɪfaɪ/ *v.t./i.* to make or become solid. —**solidification** /-fɪ'keɪʃ(ə)n/ *n.* [f. F (as SOLID)]

solidity /sə'lɪdɪtɪ/ *n.* the state of being solid, firmness. [f. SOLID]

soliloquize /sə'lɪləkwaɪz/ *v.i.* to utter a soliloquy. [f. foll.]

soliloquy /sə'lɪləkwɪ/ *n.* a speech in which a person expresses his thoughts aloud without addressing any specific person, especially in a play; a period of this. [f. L (*solus* alone, *loqui* speak)]

solipsism /'sɒlɪpsɪz(ə)m/ *n.* the view that the self is all that exists or can be known. —**solipsist** *n.* [f. L *solus* alone + *ipse* self]

solitaire /sɒlɪ'teə(r)/ *n.* **1** a jewel set by itself; a piece of jewellery containing this. **2** a game played on a special board by one person with marbles etc. removed one at a time after another has been jumped over each. **3** (*US*) the card-game of patience, which is played by one person. [F f. L (= foll.)]

solitary /'sɒlɪtərɪ/ *adj.* **1** alone, without

companions, living alone, not gregarious. **2** single, sole. **3** (of a place) unfrequented, lonely. —*n.* **1** a recluse. **2** (*slang*) solitary confinement. —**solitary confinement,** isolation in a separate cell as a punishment. —**solitarily** *adv.*, **solitariness** *n.* [f. L (*solus* alone)]

solitude /ˈsɒlɪtju:d/ *n.* **1** being solitary. **2** a solitary place. [f. OF or L (as prec.)]

solmization /sɒlmɪˈzeɪʃ(ə)n/ *n.* the system of associating each note of the musical scale with a particular syllable (e.g. *do, re, mi*, etc., or doh, ray, me, etc.; see TONIC SOL-FA). [f. F (*sol* var. of SOH, *mi* var. of ME[2])]

solo /ˈsəʊləʊ/ *n.* (*pl.* **-os**) **1** (*pl.* also **-li** /-li:/) a musical composition or passage for a single voice or instrument, with or without accompaniment. **2** a performance by one person; a pilot's flight in an aircraft without an instructor or companion. **3** (in full **solo whist**) a card-game like whist in which one player may oppose the others. —*adj.* & *adv.* performed as a solo; unaccompanied, alone. [It. f. L (as SOLE[1])]

soloist /ˈsəʊləʊɪst/ *n.* a performer of a solo, especially in music. [f. SOLO]

solstice /ˈsɒlstɪs/ *n.* each of two occasions during the year when the sun is at its highest or lowest point above the celestial equator (and appears to pause before returning) and the number of hours of daylight greatest (at the **summer solstice,** about 21 June) or smallest (**winter solstice,** about 22 Dec.). [f. OF f. L (*sol* sun, *sistere* stand still)]

soluble /ˈsɒlju:b(ə)l/ *adj.* that can be dissolved (especially in water) or solved. —**solubility** /-ˈbɪlɪtɪ/ *n.*, **solubly** *adv.* [f. OF f. L (as SOLVE)]

solute /ˈsɒlju:t/ *n.* a dissolved substance. [as SOLVE]

solution /səˈlu:ʃ(ə)n, -ˈlju:-/ *n.* **1** solving or the means of solving a problem or difficulty. **2** the conversion of a solid or gas into a liquid by mixture with a liquid; the state resulting from this. **3** dissolving, being dissolved. [f. OF f. L (as SOLVE)]

solvable *adj.* that may be solved. [f. SOLVE]

Solvay process /ˈsɒlveɪ/ a manufacturing process for obtaining sodium carbonate (= washing-soda) from limestone, ammonia, and brine. [f. E. *Solvay* (d. 1922), Belgian chemist, who developed the process]

solve *v.t.* to find the answer to (a problem or puzzle); to find an action or course that removes or effectively deals with (a problem or difficulty). —**solver** *n.* [f. L *solvere* unfasten, release]

solvent /ˈsɒlvənt/ *adj.* **1** able to dissolve or form a solution with something. **2** having enough money to meet one's liabilities. —*n.* a solvent liquid etc. —**solvency** *n.* [as prec.]

Som. *abbr.* Somerset.

soma /ˈsəʊmə/ *n.* the intoxicating juice of a plant, used in Vedic ritual and religion. [f. Skr. *sōma*]

somatic /səˈmætɪk/ *adj.* of the body, not of the mind. —**somatically** *adv.* [f. Gk (*sōma* body)]

sombre /ˈsɒmbə(r)/ *adj.* dark, gloomy, dismal. —**sombrely** *adv.* [F f. L SUB-, *umbra* shade]

sombrero /sɒmˈbreərəʊ/ *n.* (*pl.* **-os**) a broad-brimmed hat worn especially in Latin American countries. [Sp. (*sombra* shade, as prec.)]

some /səm, *emphat.* sʌm/ *adj.* **1** an unspecified amount or number of. **2** that is unknown or unnamed. **3** approximately. **4** a considerable amount or number of; at least a small amount of. **5** such to a certain extent; (*slang*) notably such. —*pron.* some people or things; some number or amount. —*adv.* (*colloq.*) to some extent. [OE]

-some /-səm/ *suffix* forming (1) adjectives in the senses 'adapted to, productive of' (*cuddlesome, fearsome*), 'characterized by being' (*fulsome*), 'apt to' (*tiresome, meddlesome*); (2) nouns from numerals in the sense 'a group of' (*foursome*). [OE]

somebody *n.* & *pron.* **1** some person. **2** a person of importance.

somehow *adv.* **1** in some unspecified or unexplained manner. **2** for some reason or other.

someone *n.* & *pron.* somebody.

someplace *adv.* (*US*) somewhere.

somersault /ˈsʌməsɒlt/ *n.* an acrobatic movement in which the body rolls head over heels either on the ground or in the air; a similar overturning movement. —*v.i.* to perform a somersault. [f. OF f. L *supra* above, *saltus* leap]

something *n.* & *pron.* **1** some unspecified or unknown thing. **2** a known or understood but unexpressed quantity or quality or extent. **3** an important or notable person or thing. —**see something of,** to meet (a person) occasionally or for a short time. [OE]

sometime *adv.* **1** at some time. **2** formerly. —*adj.* former.

sometimes *adv.* at some times.

somewhat *adv.* to some extent.

somewhere *adv.* in or to some place.

somnambulism /sɒmˈnæmbju:lɪz(ə)m/ *n.* sleep-walking. —**somnambulant** *adj.*, **somnambulist** *n.* [f. L *somnus* sleep + *ambulare* walk]

somnolent /ˈsɒmnələnt/ *adj.* sleepy, asleep; inducing drowsiness. —**somnolence** *n.* [f. OF or L (*somnus* sleep)]

son /sʌn/ *n.* **1** a male child in relation to his parent(s). **2** a male descendant, a male member of a family etc. **3** a person regarded as inheriting an occupation or quality etc. **4** a form of address to a boy. —**son-in-law** *n.* (*pl.* **sons-in-law**) a daughter's husband. **the Son of God** *or* **of Man,** Christ. [OE]

sonar /ˈsəʊnɑː(r)/ *n.* a system of detecting objects under water by reflected or emitted sound; the apparatus for this. [f. *so*und *na*vigation and *r*anging]

sonata /s(ə)ˈnɑːtə/ *n.* a composition for one instrument or two, normally with three or four movements contrasted in rhythm and speed but related in key. —**sonata form,** a type of composition in which two themes ('subjects') are successively set forth, developed, and restated. [It., f. *sonare* sound (i.e. a piece to be played rather than sung)]

son et lumière /sɒn eɪ luːˈmjeə(r)/ an entertainment by night at a historic building etc. with recorded sound and lighting effects to give a dramatic narrative of its history. [F, = sound and light]

song *n.* **1** singing, vocal music. **2** a piece of music for singing, a short poem etc. set to music or meant to be sung; a musical composition suggestive of a song. —**for a song,** very cheaply. **song and dance,** an outcry, a commotion. **song thrush,** a common thrush (*Turdus philomelos*) noted for its singing. [f. OE *sang* (as SING)]

songbird *n.* a bird with a melodious cry.

Song of Solomon see SOLOMON.

songster *n.* a singer, a songbird. —**songstress** *n. fem.* [OE, as SONG]

sonic /ˈsɒnɪk/ *adj.* of or involving sound or sound-waves. —**sonic bang** *or* **boom,** the noise made when an aircraft passes the speed of sound. **sonic barrier,** the sound barrier (see SOUND[1]). [f. L. *sonus* sound]

sonnet /ˈsɒnɪt/ *n.* a poem of 14 lines with lengths and rhymes in accordance with one of several schemes, in English usually having 10 syllables per line. [F or f. It. *sonetto* dim. of *suono* sound]

sonny /ˈsʌnɪ/ *n.* (*colloq.*) a familiar form of address to a young boy. [f. SON]

sonorous /ˈsɒnərəs, səˈnɔːrəs/ *adj.* resonant, having a loud, full, or deep sound; (of speech etc.) sounding imposing. —**sonority** /səˈnɒrɪtɪ/ *n.*, **sonorously** *adv.* [f. L (*sonor* sound)]

soon *adv.* **1** after no long interval of time. **2** relatively early, quickly. **3** (after *as* or in compar.) readily, willingly. —**as** *or* **so soon as,** at the moment that; not later than, as early as. **sooner or later,** at some future time, eventually. [OE]

soot /sʊt/ *n.* a black powdery substance rising in smoke and deposited by it on surfaces. —*v.t.* to cover with soot. [OE]

sooth *n.* (*archaic*) truth. [OE *sōth* (orig. adj., = true)]

soothe /suːð/ *v.t.* to calm (a person or feelings etc.); to soften or mitigate (a pain etc.). —**soothing** *adj.* [OE, = verify (as prec.)]

soothsayer /ˈsuːθseɪə(r)/ *n.* one who foretells the future, a diviner. [f. SOOTH + *sayer* (SAY)]

sooty /ˈsʊtɪ/ *adj.* **1** covered with soot. **2** like soot; black or brownish-black. [f. SOOT]

sop *n.* **1** a piece of bread etc. dipped in liquid before being eaten or cooked. **2** a concession made in order to pacify or bribe a troublesome person. **3** a milksop. —*v.t./i.* (**-pp-**) **1** to dip in liquid. **2** to soak up (liquid) with something absorbent. [OE (rel. to SUP)]

sophism /ˈsɒfɪz(ə)m/ *n.* a false argument, especially one intended to deceive. [f. OF f. L f. Gk *sophisma* clever device (*sophizomai* become wise f. *sophos* wise)]

sophist /ˈsɒfɪst/ *n.* a captious or fallacious reasoner, a quibbler (see prec.). —**sophistic** /-ˈfɪstɪk/ *adj.* [f. *Sophists*, Gk philosophers, 5th c. BC (as prec.)]

sophisticate /səˈfɪstɪkeɪt/ *v.t.* (esp. in *p.p.*) **1** to make (a person etc.) worldly-wise, cultured, or refined. **2** to make (equipment or techniques etc.) highly developed or complex. —/-kət/ *adj.* sophisticated. —/-kət/ *n.* a sophisticated person. —**sophistication** /-ˈkeɪʃ(ə)n/ *n.* [f. L, = tamper with (as SOPHIST)]

sophistry /ˈsɒfɪstrɪ/ *n.* the use of sophisms; a sophism. [f. SOPHIST]

sophomore /ˈsɒfəmɔː(r)/ *n.* (*US*) a second-year student at a university or high school. [app. f. *sophom* obs. var. of SOPHISM]

soporific /sɒpəˈrɪfɪk/ *adj.* tending to produce sleep. —*n.* a soporific drug or influence. —**soporifically** *adv.* [f. L *sopor* sleep, *facere* make]

sopping *adj.* drenched. [f. SOP]

soppy *adj.* **1** very wet. **2** (*colloq.*) mawkishly sentimental; silly. —**soppily** *adv.*, **soppiness** *n.* [f. SOP]

soprano /səˈprɑːnəʊ/ *n.* (*pl.* **-os**) **1** the highest female or boy's singing-voice. **2** a singer with such a voice; the part written for it. **3** an instrument of the higher or highest pitch in its family. [It. (*sopra* above f. L *supra*]

sorbet /ˈsɔːbət/ *n.* a water-ice; a sherbet. [F f. It., ult. f. Arab. (as SHERBET)]

sorcerer /ˈsɔːsərə(r)/ *n.* a magician, a wizard.—**sorceress** *n. fem.*, **sorcery** *n.* [f. OF *sorcier* f. L *sors* lot]

sordid *adj.* **1** dirty, squalid. **2** ignoble, not honourable; mercenary. —**sordidly** *adv.*, **sordidness** *n.* [f. F or L *sordidus* (*sordēre* be dirty)]

sore *adj.* **1** causing or feeling pain from injury or disease. **2** causing or feeling mental distress or annoyance. **3** (*archaic*) serious, severe. —*n.* **1** a sore place on the body. **2** a source of distress or annoyance. —*adv.* (*archaic*) sorely. —**soreness** *n.* [OE]

sorely *adv.* very much; severely. [f. SORE]

sorghum /ˈsɔːgəm/ *n.* a tropical cereal grass of the genus *Sorghum*. [f. It. *sorgo*]

Soroptimist /səˈrɒptɪmɪst/ *n.* a member of the Soroptimist Club, an international club for professional and business women, with the aim of providing service to the community. [app. f. L *soror* sister + OPTIMIST]

sorority /səˈrɒrɪtɪ/ *n.* **1** a devotional sisterhood. **2** (*US*) a women's society in a university or college. [f. L (*soror* sister)]

sorrel[1] /ˈsɒr(ə)l/ *n.* a sour-leaved herb (*Rumex acetosa*). [f. OF (as SOUR)]

sorrel[2] /ˈsɒr(ə)l/ *adj.* of a light reddish-brown colour. —*n.* **1** this colour. **2** a sorrel animal, especially a horse. [f. OF *sorel* (*sor* yellowish)]

sorrow /ˈsɒrəʊ/ *n.* **1** mental distress caused by loss or disappointment etc. **2** a thing causing sorrow. —*v.i.* to feel sorrow, to grieve. [OE]

sorrowful *adj.* feeling or showing sorrow; distressing. —**sorrowfully** *adv.* [f. prec. + -FUL]

sorry /ˈsɒrɪ/ *adj.* **1** (*predic.*) feeling pity, regret, or sympathy. **2** an expression of apology. **3** (*attrib.*) wretched; paltry. —**sorry for oneself,** (*colloq.*) dejected. [OE (as SORE)]

sort *n.* **1** a particular kind or variety. **2** (*colloq.*) a person with regard to his (specified) character. —*v.t.* to arrange according to sort, size, destination, etc. —**of a sort** *or* **of sorts,** not fully deserving the name given. **out of sorts,** slightly unwell; in low spirits. **sort of,** (*colloq.*) as it were, to some extent. **sort out,** to separate into sorts; to select (things of one or more sorts) from a miscellaneous group; to disentangle; to put into order; to solve; (*slang*) to deal with or punish. —**sorter** *n.* [f. OF f. L *sors* lot, condition]

sortie /ˈsɔːtiː/ *n.* **1** a sally, especially from a besieged garrison. **2** an operational flight by a military aircraft. [F. (*sortir* go out)]

SOS /esəʊˈes/ *n.* (*pl.* **SOSs**) the international code-signal of extreme distress; an urgent appeal for help etc. [letters chosen as easily recognized in Morse code]

sostenuto /sɒstəˈnuːtəʊ/ *adv.* (*Mus.*) in a sustained manner. —*n.* (*pl.* **-os**) a passage to be played in this way. [It. (as SUSTAIN)]

sot *n.* a habitual drunkard. —**sottish** *adj.* [OE & f. OF, = foolish]

sotto voce /ˈsɒtəʊ ˈvəʊtʃɪ/ in an undertone. [It., = under the voice]

sou /suː/ *n.* **1** a former French coin of low value. **2** (*colloq.*) a very small amount of money. —**not a sou,** no money at all. [F f. OF f. L *solidus* Roman gold coin]

soubrette /suːˈbret/ *n.* a pert maidservant etc. in comedy; an actress taking this part. [F f. Prov. (*soubret* coy)]

soubriquet var. of SOBRIQUET.

soufflé /ˈsuːfleɪ/ *n.* a light spongy dish usually made with stiffly beaten egg-whites. [F, = blown]

sough /sʌf, saʊ/ *n.* a moaning or whispering sound as of the wind in trees. —*v.i.* to make this sound. [f. OE, = resound]

sought *past* & *p.p.* of SEEK.

souk /suːk/ *n.* a market-place in Muslim countries. [f. Arab.]

soul /səʊl/ *n.* **1** the spiritual or immaterial element in a person, often regarded as immortal. **2** the moral, emotional, or intellectual nature of a person or animal. **3** a personification or pattern. **4** an individual; a person regarded with familiarity or pity etc. **5** a person regarded as the animating or essential part. **6** emotional or intellectual energy or intensity, especially as revealed in a work of art. **7** the emotional or spiritual quality of Black American life and culture; soul music. —**soul-destroying** *adj.* deadeningly monotonous or depressing. **soul mate,** a person ideally suited to another. **soul music,** a kind of jazz played in a strong emotional style. **soul-searching** *adj.* examining one's own emotions or motives. **upon my soul,** an exclamation of surprise. [OE]

soulful *adj.* having, expressing, or evoking deep feeling. —**soulfully** *adv.* [f. SOUL + -FUL]

soulless *adj.* **1** lacking sensitivity or noble qualities. **2** undistinguished, uninteresting. [f. SOUL + -LESS]

sound[1] *n.* **1** waves of pressure that travel through the air or other elastic medium (such as water) and are detectable at certain frequencies by the ear. **2** the sensation produced by these; a particular kind of it. **3** a sound made in speech. **4** sound reproduced in a film etc. **5** the mental impression produced by a statement or description etc. —*v.t./i.* **1** to emit or cause to emit sound. **2** to utter, to pronounce. **3** to convey an impression when heard. **4** to give an audible signal for (an alarm etc.). **5** to test (the lungs etc.) by noting the sound produced. —**sound barrier,** the high resistance of the air to objects moving at speeds near that of sound. **sound effects,** sounds other than speech or music produced artificially for use in a play or film etc. **sounding-board** *n.* a canopy projecting sound towards an audience; a means of disseminating opinions etc. **sound off,** (*colloq.*) to talk loudly, to express one's opinions forcefully. **sound-wave** *n.* a wave of condensation and rarefaction, by which sound is transmitted in the air etc. —**sounder** *n.* [f. AF f. L *sonus*]

sound[2] *adj.* **1** healthy, not diseased or injured or rotten. **2** (of an opinion or policy etc.) correct, orthodox, well-founded. **3** financially secure; **4** undisturbed. **5** thorough. —*adv.* soundly. —**soundly** *adv.*, **soundness** *n.* [f. OE]

sound[3] *v.t.* **1** to test the depth or quality of the bottom of (the sea or a river etc.). **2** (also with *out*) to inquire into the opinions or feelings of. —**sounder** *n.* [f. OF *sonder* f. L *sub* under, *unda* wave]

sound[4] *n.* a strait (of water). [OE, = swimming]

sounding *n.* **1** measurement of the depth of water. **2** (in *pl.*) the region near enough to the shore to allow sounding. [f. SOUND[3]]

soundproof *adj.* impervious to sound. —*v.t.* to make soundproof.

soundtrack *n.* a strip on cinema film or videotape for recording sound; the sound itself.

soup /su:p/ *n.* a liquid food made by stewing bones, vegetables, etc. —*v.t.* (usu. with *up*) (*colloq.*) **1** to increase the power of (an engine etc.). **2** to enliven. —**in the soup,** (*slang*) in difficulties or trouble. **soup-kitchen** *n.* an establishment supplying free soup etc. to the poor or in times of distress. **soup-plate** *n.* a large deep plate for soup. —**soupy** *adj.* [f. F *soupe* f. L (cf. SUP)]

soupçon /ˈsu:psɔ̃/ *n.* a very small quantity, a trace or tinge. [F f. L, = SUSPICION]

sour *adj.* **1** tasting or smelling sharp like unripe fruit; not fresh, tasting or smelling sharp or unpleasant from fermentation or staleness. **2** (of soil) excessively acid; deficient in lime. **3** bad-tempered, disagreeable in manner.—*n.* an acid drink, especially of whisky with lemon-juice or lime-juice. —*v.t./i.* to make or become sour. —**go** *or* **turn sour,** to turn out badly; to lose one's keenness. **sour grapes,** said when a person disparages what he desires but cannot attain. (From the fable of the fox who wanted some grapes but found that they were out of reach and so pretended that they were sour and undesirable anyway.) —**sourly** *adv.*, **sourness** *n.* [OE]

source /sɔ:s/ *n.* **1** the place from which a thing comes or is obtained. **2** a person or book etc. providing information. **3** the starting-point of a river or stream. —**at source,** at the point of origin or issue. [f. OF *sors, sourse* f. *sourdre* rise f. L *surgere*]

sourpuss *n.* (*slang*) a bad-tempered person.

souse /saʊs/ *v.t./i.* **1** to steep in pickle. **2** to plunge or soak in liquid; to drench; to throw (liquid) over a thing. **3** (in *p.p.*, *slang*) drunk. —*n.* **1** pickle made with salt. **2** (*US*) food in pickle. **3** a plunge or soaking. [f. OF *sous* pickle f. OHG *sulza* brine (as SALT)]

soutane /su:ˈtɑ:n/ *n.* the cassock of a Roman Catholic priest. [F f. It. *sottana* (*sotto* under)]

south *n.* **1** the point of the horizon opposite north; the compass point corresponding to this; the direction in which this lies. **2** (usu. **South**) the part of a country or town lying to the south. —*adj.* **1** towards, at, near, or facing the south. **2** (of wind) blowing from the south. —*adv.* towards, at, or near the south. —**South Pole,** the southern end of the earth's axis of rotation. **south-south-east** *n.*, *adj.*, & *adv.* midway between south and south-east. **south-south-west** *n.*, *adj.*, & *adv.* midway between south and south-west. [OE]

south-east *n.* **1** the point midway between south and east; the direction in which this lies. **2** (usu. **South-East**) the part of a country or town lying to the south-east. —*adj.* of, towards, or coming from the south-east. —*adv.* towards, at, or near the south-east. —**south-easterly** *adj.* & *adv.*, **south-eastern** *adj.*

southeaster *n.* a south-east wind.

southerly /ˈsʌðəlɪ/ *adj.* & *adv.* **1** in a southern position or direction. **2** (of wind) blowing from the south (approximately). [f. SOUTH]

southern /ˈsʌðən/ *adj.* of or in the south. —**southern lights,** the aurora australis. **Southern States,** those in the south (esp. south-east) of the USA. [OE (as SOUTH)]

southerner *n.* a native or inhabitant of the south. [as SOUTHERN.]

southing /ˈsaʊθɪŋ/ *n.* (*Naut.* etc.) **1** a distance travelled or measured southward. **2** a southerly direction. [f. SOUTH]

southpaw *adj.* (*colloq.*) left-handed. —*n.* (*colloq.*) a left-handed person, especially a boxer.

southward /ˈsaʊθwəd/ *adj.* & (also **southwards**) *adv.* towards the south. —*n.* a southward direction or region. [f. SOUTH + -WARD]

south-west *n.* **1** the point midway between south and west; the direction in which this lies. **2** (usu. **South-West**) the part of a country or town lying to the south-west. —*adj.* of, towards, or coming from the south-west. —*adv.* towards, at, or near the south-west. —**south-westerly** *adj.* & *adv.*, **south-western** *adj.*

southwester *n.* a south-west wind.

souvenir /su:vəˈnɪə(r)/ *n.* a thing kept as a reminder of a place, person, or event. [F f. L *subvenire* occur to the mind (SUB-, *venire* come)]

sou'wester /saʊˈwestə(r)/ *n.* **1** a waterproof hat with a broad flap at the back. **2** a south-west wind. [f. SOUTHWESTER]

sovereign /ˈsɒvrɪn/ *n.* **1** a supreme ruler,

especially a monarch. **2** a British gold coin (now rarely used) nominally worth £1. —*adj.* **1** supreme; unmitigated. **2** possessing sovereign power; independent; royal. **3** very good or effective. —**sovereignty** *n.* [f. OF *so(u)verain* ult. f. L *super* over]

Soviet /ˈsəʊvɪət, ˈsɒv-/ *adj.* of the USSR. —*n.* a citizen of the USSR. —**soviet** *n.* an elected council in a district of the USSR. —**Supreme Soviet,** the governing council of the USSR or of any of its constituent republics. [f. Russ. *sovet* council]

sow[1] /səʊ/ *v.t.* (*past* **sowed**; *p.p.* **sown** or **sowed**) **1** to put (seed) on or in the earth for the purpose of growth; to plant (land) with seed. **2** to implant or spread (feelings or ideas). —**sower** *n.* [OE]

sow[2] /saʊ/ *n.* an adult female pig. [OE]

soy *n.* **1** a sauce made from pickled soya beans. **2** (also **soy bean**) a soya bean. [Jap. f. Chin. *shi-you* (*shi* salted beans, *you* oil)]

soya /ˈsɔɪə/ *n.* a leguminous plant (*Soja hispida*) yielding edible flour and oil. —**soya bean,** the seed of this plant. [f. Du. f. Malay (as prec.)]

sozzled /ˈsɒz(ə)ld/ *adj.* (*slang*) very drunk. [f. dial. *sozzle* mix sloppily (imit.)]

spa /spɑː/ *n.* a curative mineral spring; a place with this. [f. *Spa* in Belgium, celebrated since medieval times for the curative properties of its mineral springs]

space *n.* **1** the continuous expanse in which things exist and move; a portion of this; the amount of this taken by a particular thing or available for a particular purpose. **2** the interval between points or objects; an empty area. **3** an interval of time. **4** the area of paper used in writing or printing something. **5** outer space. **6** a large area. —*attrib.* of or used for travel etc. in outer space. —*v.t.* to set or arrange at intervals; to put spaces between. —**space age,** the era of space travel. **space shuttle,** a spacecraft travelling repeatedly e.g. between earth and a space station. **space station,** an artificial satellite as a base for operations in outer space. **space-time** *n.* the fusion of the concepts of space and time as a four-dimensional continuum. [f. OF *espace* f. L *spatium*]

spacecraft *n.* a vehicle for travelling in outer space.

spaceman *n.* (*pl.* **-men**) a space traveller.

spaceship *n.* a spacecraft.

spacesuit *n.* a sealed pressurized suit allowing the wearer to survive in outer space.

spacious /ˈspeɪʃəs/ *adj.* providing much space, roomy. —**spaciousness** *n.* [f. OF or L (as SPACE)]

spade[1] *n.* a digging-tool with a sharp-edged broad usually metal blade; a similar tool for various purposes. —**call a spade a spade,** to speak plainly or bluntly. —**spadeful** *n.* [OE]

spade[2] *n.* a playing-card of the suit (**spades**) marked with black figures shaped like an inverted heart with a short stem. [f. It. *spada* sword f. L f. Gk; assoc. with shape of prec.]

spadework *n.* hard preparatory work.

spadix /ˈspeɪdɪks/ *n.* a spike of flowers closely arranged round a fleshy axis and usually enclosed in a spathe. [L f. Gk, = palm-branch]

spaghetti /spəˈgetɪ/ *n.* pasta made in solid strings, between macaroni and vermicelli in thickness. [It., pl. of dim. of *spago* string]

Spam *n.* [P] a tinned meat made mainly from ham. [arbitrary formation or f. *sp*iced *ham*]

span[1] *n.* **1** the full extent from end to end or across; the maximum lateral extent of an aeroplane or its wing. **2** each part of a bridge between the supports. **3** the maximum distance between the tips of the thumb and little finger, especially as a measure = 9 in. **4** length in time from beginning to end. —*v.t.* (**-nn-**) to extend from side to side or end to end of; to bridge (a river etc.). [OE]

span[2] see SPICK.

spandrel /ˈspændr(ə)l/ *n.* the space between the curve of an arch and the surrounding rectangular moulding or framework or between the curves of adjoining arches and the moulding above. [perh. f. AF (*espaundre* expand)]

spangle *n.* a small piece of glittering material, especially one of many as an ornament of a dress etc. —*v.t.* (esp. in *p.p.*) to cover (as) with spangles. [f. *spang* f. MDu. & OHG, ON *spöng* brooch]

Spaniard /ˈspænjəd/ *n.* a native of Spain. [f. OF (*Espaigne* Spain)]

spaniel /ˈspænj(ə)l/ *n.* a dog of a breed with a long silky coat and drooping ears. [f. OF, = Spanish dog (as prec.)]

Spanish /ˈspænɪʃ/ *adj.* of Spain or its people or language. —*n.* the Spanish language. —**the Spanish,** the people of Spain. **Spanish fly,** a dried insect (*Lytta vesicatoria*) used in medicine and as an aphrodisiac. [f. SPAIN]

spank *v.t./i.* **1** to slap on the buttocks. **2** (of a horse etc.) to move briskly. —*n.* a slap given in spanking. [perh. imit.]

spanker *n.* a fore-and-aft sail on the after side of the mizen-mast. [f. SPANK]

spanking *n.* the process of spanking or being spanked. —*adj.* (*colloq.*) brisk, lively; excellent. —*adv.* (*colloq.*) briskly; excellently. [f. SPANK]

spanner *n.* a tool for turning a nut on a bolt etc. —**spanner in the works,** an upsetting element or influence. [G (*spannen* draw tight)]

spar[1] *n.* **1** a stout pole as used for a ship's mast etc. **2** the main longitudinal beam of an aeroplane wing. [f. OF *esparre* or ON *sperra*]

spar[2] *v.i.* (**-rr-**) **1** to make the motions of attack and defence with closed fists; to use the hands (as) in boxing. **2** to engage in argument etc. —*n.* a sparring motion; a boxingmatch. —**sparring-partner** *n.* a boxer employed to practise with another in training; a person with whom one enjoys arguing. [OE, orig. unkn.; cf. ON *sperrask* kick out]

spar[3] *n.* an easily split crystalline mineral. [MLG, rel. to OE *spæren* of plaster, *spærstān* gypsum]

spare *v.t.* **1** to refrain from hurting, harming, or destroying; to be merciful towards. **2** to use with great restraint; to refrain from using. **3** to part with, to be able to afford to give; to do without; to allow to have (a thing etc., especially that one does not need). —*adj.* **1** additional to what is usually needed or used; reserved for occasional or emergency use. **2** (of a person etc.) thin; lean. **3** small in quantity; frugal. —*n.* a spare part. —**go spare,** (*slang*) to become very angry. **not spare oneself,** to exert one's utmost efforts. **spare part,** a duplicate to replace a lost or damaged part. **spare-rib** *n.* a cut of pork from the lower ribs. **spare time,** leisure. **spare tyre,** (*colloq.*) a circle of fatness round or above the waist. —**sparely** *adv.*, **spareness** *n.* [OE]

sparing /ˈspeərɪŋ/ *adj.* economical, not generous or wasteful; restrained. —**sparingly** *adv.* [f. SPARE]

spark *n.* **1** a fiery particle, e.g. one thrown off by a burning substance or caused by friction. **2** a flash of light produced by an electrical discharge; such a discharge serving to fire an explosive mixture in an internal-combustion engine. **3** a flash of wit etc. **4** a minute amount of a quality etc. **5** a lively person. —*v.t./i.* **1** to emit a spark or sparks. **2** (also with *off*) to stir into activity, to initiate. —**spark-plug** or **sparking-plug** *n.* a device for making a spark in an internal combustion engine. [OE; orig. unkn.]

sparkle *v.i.* **1** to shine brightly with flashes of light. **2** to show brilliant wit or liveliness. **3** (of wine) to effervesce. —*n.* sparkling light or brightness. [f. SPARK]

sparkler *n.* **1** a sparking firework. **2** (in *pl.*, *slang*) diamonds. [f. prec.]

sparrow /ˈspærəʊ/ *n.* a small brownish-grey bird of the genus *Passer*. —**sparrow-hawk** *n.* a small hawk (*Accipiter nisus*). [OE]

sparse *adj.* thinly scattered, not dense; infrequent. —**sparsely** *adv.*, **sparseness** *n.*, **sparsity** *n.* [f. L *sparsus* (*spargere* scatter)]

Spartan /ˈspɑːtən/ *adj.* **1** of Sparta or its inhabitants. **2** (of conditions) simple and sometimes harsh, without comfort or luxuries (with allusion to the hardy and austere life of Spartans). —*n.* **1** a native of Sparta. **2** an austere person. [f. *Sparta*, ancient Greek city]

spasm /ˈspæz(ə)m/ *n.* **1** a sudden involuntary muscular contraction. **2** a sudden convulsive movement or emotion etc.; a brief spell of activity. [f. OF or L f. Gk (*spaō* pull)]

spasmodic /spæzˈmɒdɪk/ *adj.* of or occurring in spasms, intermittent. —**spasmodically** *adv.* [f. Gk *spasmōdēs* (as prec.)]

spastic /ˈspæstɪk/ *adj.* suffering from cerebral palsy with spasm of the muscles. —*n.* a spastic person. —**spastically** *adv.* [f. L f. Gk (as SPASM)]

spat[1] *n.* (usu. in *pl.*) a short gaiter covering the instep and reaching a little above the ankle. [abbr. of *spatterdash* (SPATTER)]

spat[2] *n.* the spawn of a shellfish, especially of the oyster. [AF; orig. unkn.]

spat[3] *n.* (*US colloq.*) a petty or brief quarrel. [prob. imit.]

spat[4] *past* & *p.p.* of SPIT[1].

spate *n.* **1** a sudden flood. **2** a large or excessive amount. —**in spate,** (of a river) flowing strongly at an abnormally high level. [orig. Sc. & N. Engl.; orig. unkn.]

spathe /speɪð/ *n.* a large bract or bracts enveloping a spadix or a flower-cluster. [f. L f. Gk, = broad blade]

spatial /ˈspeɪʃ(ə)l/ *adj.* of space. —**spatially** *adv.* [f. L *spatium* space]

spatter *v.t./i.* to splash or scatter in small drops. —*n.* a splash or splashes; the sound of spattering. [cf. Du. & LG *spatten* spout]

spatula /ˈspætjʊlə/ *n.* **1** a tool like a knife with a broad blunt flexible blade, used especially by artists and in cookery. **2** a strip of stiff material used by a doctor for pressing down the tongue etc. [L, f. dim. of *spatha* spathe]

spavin /ˈspævɪn/ *n.* a disease of a horse's hock with a hard bony swelling. —**spavined** *adj.* [f. OF *espavin*]

spawn *v.t./i.* **1** (of fish, frogs, molluscs, etc.) to deposit spawn; to produce (spawn); to be produced as spawn or young. **2** (*derog.*) to produce as offspring. **3** to produce or generate in large numbers. —*n.* **1** the eggs of fish, frogs, etc. **2** (*derog.*) human or other offspring. **3** the white fibrous matter from which fungi grow. [f. AF *espaundre* (as EXPAND)]

spay *v.t.* to remove the ovaries of (a female animal). [f. AF, = cut with sword (as ÉPÉE)]

speak *v.t./i.* (*past* **spoke**; *p.p.* **spoken**) **1** to utter words in an ordinary voice (not singing). **2** to hold a conversation; to make a speech; **3** to utter or pronounce (words); to use (a specified language) in speaking; to make known in words. **4** to convey an idea, to be evidence of something. —**generally** (*or* **strictly** etc.) **speaking,** in the general (or strict etc.) sense of the words. **not** (*or* **nothing**) **to speak of,** not (or nothing) worth mentioning. **on speaking terms,** sufficiently friendly or acquainted to hold a conversation. **speak for,** to act as a spokesman for; to speak in defence of; to bespeak. **speak for itself,** to be sufficient evidence. **speak out** *or* **up,** to speak loudly or freely; to give one's opinion etc. without hesitation or fear. **speak volumes (for),** to be very significant (in terms of). [OE]

speakeasy *n.* (*US slang*) a place where alcoholic liquor is sold illicitly.

speaker *n.* **1** one who speaks, especially in public; a person of a specified skill in speech-making; one who speaks a specified language. **2** a loudspeaker. **3 Speaker,** the presiding officer of a legislative assembly. [f. SPEAK]

spear *n.* a thrusting or hurling weapon consisting of a stout staff with a pointed tip of metal etc. —*v.t.* to pierce or strike (as) with a spear. [OE]

spearhead *n.* **1** the pointed tip of a spear. **2** a person or group leading an attack or challenge etc. —*v.t.* to act as the spearhead of (an attack etc.).

spearmint *n.* a common garden mint (*Mentha spicata*) used in cookery and to flavour chewing-gum.

spec *n.* (*colloq.*) a speculation. —**on spec,** as a speculation. [abbr.]

special /ˈspeʃ(ə)l/ *adj.* **1** of a particular or peculiar kind, not general; for a particular purpose. **2** exceptional in amount or degree etc. —*n.* a special constable, edition of a newspaper, dish on a menu, etc. —**Special Branch,** a section of the CID which deals with police matters involving political security. **special constable,** one assisting the police in routine duties or in emergencies. **special correspondent,** one appointed by a newspaper to report on a special event or facts. **special delivery,** a delivery of mail separately from the regular delivery. **special edition,** an edition of a newspaper including later news than the ordinary edition. **special licence,** a licence allowing a marriage to take place within a short time without banns. **special pleading,** (*Law*) pleading with particular reference to the circumstances of a case, as opposed to general pleading; (*pop.*) persuasive but unfair reasoning. —**specially** *adv.* [f. OF (= especial) or L *specialis* (as SPECIES)]

specialist *n.* one who specializes in a particular branch of a profession, especially medicine. [f. prec.]

speciality /speʃɪˈælɪtɪ/ *n.* **1** a special feature. **2** a special thing or activity; a special product; a subject in which one specializes. [as SPECIAL]

specialize /ˈspeʃəlaɪz/ *v.t./i.* **1** to be or become a specialist. **2** to make or become individual; to adapt for a particular purpose. —**specialization** /-ˈzeɪʃ(ə)n/ *n.* [f. F (as SPECIAL)]

specialty /ˈspeʃəltɪ/ *n.* a speciality. [f. OF (as SPECIAL)]

specie /ˈspi:ʃi:, -ʃɪ/ *n.* coin as opposed to paper money. [L, abl. of foll.]

species /ˈspi:ʃi:z, -ʃɪz/ *n.* (*pl.* same) **1** a class of things having some common characteristics. **2** a group of animals or plants within a genus. **3** a kind or sort. [L, orig. = appearance (*specere* look)]

specific /spɪˈsɪfɪk/ *adj.* **1** particular, clearly distinguished from others. **2** exact, giving full details. **3** peculiar, relating to a particular thing; (of a medicine etc.) having a distinct effect in curing a certain disease. —*n.* a specific detail or aspect; a specific medicine. —**specific gravity,** the ratio between the weight of a substance and that of the same volume of a substance used as a standard (usually water or air). —**specifically** *adv.*, **specificity** /-ˈfɪsɪtɪ/ *n.* [f. L (as prec. + *facere* make)]

specification /spesɪfɪˈkeɪʃ(ə)n/ *n.* (usu. in *pl.*) a detail of the design and materials etc. (to be) used in a machine or project etc. [f. L (as foll.)]

specify /ˈspesɪfaɪ/ *v.t.* to name expressly, to mention definitely; to include in specifications. [f. OF or L (as SPECIFIC)]

specimen /ˈspesɪmɪn/ *n.* an individual or part taken as an example of a class or whole, especially when used for investigation; (*colloq.*, usu. *derog.*) a person of a specified sort. [L. (*specere* look)]

specious /ˈspi:ʃəs/ *adj.* apparently good or sound but not really so; superficially plausible. —**speciously** *adv.* [f. L *speciosus* attractive (as SPECIES)]

speck *n.* a small spot or stain; a particle. —*v.t.* (esp. in *p.p.*) to mark with specks. [OE]

speckle *n.* a speck, especially one of many markings on the skin etc. —*v.t.* (esp. in *p.p.*) to mark with speckles. [f. MDu.]

specs *n.pl.* (*colloq.*) spectacles. [abbr.]

spectacle /ˈspektək(ə)l/ *n.* **1** an object of sight, especially of public attention; a striking, impressive, or ridiculous sight. **2** a public show. **3** (in *pl.*) a pair of lenses to correct or assist defective sight, set in a frame to rest on the nose and ears. —**spectacled** *adj.* [f. OF f. L *spectaculum* (*spectare* look)]

spectacular /spekˈtækjʊlə(r)/ *adj.* striking, impressive, amazing. —*n.* a spectacular performance; a lavishly produced film etc. —**spectacularly** *adv.*

spectator /spek'teɪtə(r)/ *n.* one who watches a show, game, or incident etc. —**spectator sport,** a sport which attracts many spectators. [f. F or L (as SPECTACLE)]

spectra *pl.* of SPECTRUM.

spectral /'spektr(ə)l/ *adj.* **1** of a spectre or spectres; ghostlike. **2** of the spectrum or spectra. —**spectrally** *adv.* [f. foll.]

spectre /'spektə(r)/ *n.* **1** a ghost. **2** a haunting presentiment. [F or f. L, = SPECTRUM]

spectrograph /'spektrəgrɑ:f/ *n.* an apparatus for photographing or otherwise reproducing spectra. —**spectrographic** /-'græfɪk/ *adj.* [f. SPECTRUM + -GRAPH]

spectrometer /spek'trɒmɪtə(r)/ *n.* a spectroscope that can be used for measuring observed spectra. [f. G or F (as SPECTRUM + -METER)]

spectroscope /'spektrəskəʊp/ *n.* an instrument for producing and examining spectra. —**spectroscopic** /-'skɒpɪk/ *adj.*, **spectroscopically** /-'skɒpɪkəlɪ/ *adv.* [f. G or F (as foll. + -SCOPE)]

spectroscopy /spek'trɒskəpɪ/ *n.* the examination and investigation of spectra (see SPECTRUM). [f. prec.]

spectrum /'spektrəm/ *n.* (*pl.* **-tra**) **1** the range of colours as seen in a rainbow or when white light is passed through a prism or a diffraction grating. **2** the whole range of other radiation or of sound in which the parts are arranged according to wavelength. **3** such a range characteristic of a body or substance when emitting or absorbing radiation. **4** a similar range of component parts of anything, arranged by degree, quality, etc. [L, = image, apparition (*specere* look)]

speculate /'spekjʊleɪt/ *v.i.* **1** to form or put forward opinions by conjecture, without definite knowledge. **2** to engage in risky financial transactions. —**speculation** /-'leɪʃ(ə)n/ *n.*, **speculator** *n.* [f. L *speculari* spy out (*specere* look)]

speculative /'spekjʊlətɪv/ *adj.* involving speculation. —**speculatively** *adv.*, **speculativeness** *n.* [f. prec.]

sped *past* & *p.p.* of SPEED.

speech *n.* **1** the act, faculty, or manner of speaking. **2** words spoken; a spoken communication to an audience. **3** the language of a nation or group etc. —**speech-day** *n.* an annual celebration at school when speeches are made. **speech therapy,** treatment to improve defective speech. [OE (as SPEAK)]

speechify /'spi:tʃɪfaɪ/ *v.i.* (*colloq.*) to make a speech or speeches. [f. prec.]

speechless *adj.* silent, temporarily unable to speak through emotion or surprise etc. —**speechlessly** *adv.*, **speechlessness** *n.* [f. SPEECH + -LESS]

speed *n.* **1** rapidity of movement or operation; quick motion. **2** the rate of motion or action. **3** the gear appropriate to a range of speeds on a bicycle etc. **4** the relative sensitivity of a photographic film to light; the lightgathering power of a lens. **5** (*archaic*) success, prosperity. —*v.t./i.* (*past* & *p.p.* **sped**) **1** to go or send quickly. **2** (of a motorist etc.; *past* & *p.p.* **speeded**) to travel at an illegal or dangerous speed. **3** (*archaic*) to be or make prosperous or successful. —**at full speed,** as fast as one can go or work. **at speed,** moving quickly. **speed limit,** the maximum permitted speed of a vehicle on a road etc. **speed up,** to move or work faster; to cause to do this. **speed-up** *n.* [OE]

speedboat *n.* a motor boat designed for high speed.

speedo /'spi:dəʊ/ *n.* (*pl.* **-os**) (*colloq.*) a speedometer.

speedometer /spi:'dɒmɪtə(r)/ *n.* a device indicating the speed of a vehicle. [f. SPEED + -METER]

speedway *n.* **1** motor-cycle racing; an arena for this. **2** (*US*) a road or track for fast traffic.

speedwell *n.* a small plant of the genus *Veronica* with usually bright-blue flowers. [f. SPEED + WELL[1]]

speedy *adj.* **1** moving quickly, rapid. **2** done or coming etc. without delay. —**speedily** *adv.*, **speediness** *n.* [f. SPEED]

speleology /spelɪ'ɒlədʒɪ, spi:-/ *n.* the study of caves. —**speleological** /-'lɒdʒɪk(ə)l/ *adj.*, **speleologist** *n.* [f. F f. L f. Gk *spēlaion* cave + -LOGY)]

spell[1] *n.* **1** words supposed to have magic power; the effect of these. **2** the fascination exercised by a person or activity etc. [OE]

spell[2] *v.t./i.* (*past* & *p.p.* **spelt** or **spelled**) **1** to write or name in their correct sequence the letters of (a word). **2** (of letters) to make up (a word). **3** (of circumstances etc.) to have as a consequence, to involve. —**spell out,** to make out (words etc.) laboriously or slowly; to spell aloud; to explain in detail. —**speller** *n.* [f. OF *espel(l)er*, rel. to prec.]

spell[3] *n.* a period of time or work; a period of some activity; a period of a certain type of weather. —*v.t.* to relieve (a person) in work etc. by taking one's turn. [var. of dial. *spele* take place of f. OE *spelian*; orig. unkn.]

spellbound *adj.* held as if by a spell, fascinated.

spelling *n.* **1** the way a word is spelt. **2** ability to spell. [f. SPELL[2]]

spelt[1] *n.* a kind of wheat (*Triticum spelta*) giving very fine flour. [OE]

spelt[2] see SPELL[2].

spend *v.t./i.* (*past & p.p.* **spent**) **1** to pay out (money) in buying something. **2** to use up, to consume (material or energy etc.). **3** to pass or occupy (time etc.). **4** (in *p.p.*) having lost its original force or strength. —**spend a penny,** (*colloq.*) to urinate or defecate. —**spender** *n.* [OE f. L (as EXPEND)]

spendthrift *n.* an extravagant person.

sperm *n.* (*pl.* **sperms** or **sperm**) semen; a spermatozoon. —**sperm whale,** a large whale (*Physeter catodon*) yielding spermaceti. —**spermatic** /-ˈmætɪk/ *adj.* [f. L f. Gk *sperma* seed]

spermaceti /spɜːməˈsetɪ/ *n.* a white waxy substance used for ointments etc. [f. L *sperma* sperm, *ceti* of whale, it being regarded as whale-spawn]

spermatozoon /spɜːmətəˈzəʊən/ *n.* (*pl.* **-zoa**) each of the male fertilizing elements in semen. [as SPERM + Gk *zōion* living creature]

spermicide /ˈspɜːmɪsaɪd/ *n.* a substance killing spermatozoa. —**spermicidal** *adj.* [f. SPERM + -CIDE]

spew *v.t./i.* **1** to vomit. **2** to gush out; to cause to do this. [OE (imit.)]

sphagnum /ˈsfægnəm/ *n.* (*pl.* **-na**) a moss of the genus *Sphagnum* growing in bogs and peat. [f. Gk *sphagnos* a moss]

sphenoid /ˈsfiːnɔɪd/ *adj.* wedge-shaped. —**sphenoid bone,** a compound bone between the temporal bone and the eye. [f. Gk (*sphēn* wedge)]

sphere /sfɪə(r)/ *n.* **1** a solid figure with every point on its surface equidistant from the centre; the surface of this. **2** a globe, a ball. **3** a field of action, influence, or existence; one's place in society. **4** each of the revolving shells in which the heavenly bodies were formerly thought to be set. [f. OF f. L f. Gk *sphaira* ball]

spherical /ˈsferɪk(ə)l/ *adj.* **1** shaped like a sphere. **2** of spheres. **3** (of a triangle etc.) bounded by the arcs of the great circles of a sphere. —**spherically** *adv.*, **sphericity** /-ˈrɪsɪtɪ/ *n.* [f. L f. Gk (as prec.)]

spheroid /ˈsfɪərɔɪd/ *n.* a spherelike but not perfectly spherical body. —**spheroidal** /-ˈrɔɪd(ə)l/ *adj.* [f. L f. Gk (as SPHERE)]

sphincter /ˈsfɪŋktə(r)/ *n.* a ring of muscle closing and opening an orifice. [L f. Gk (*sphiggō* bind tight)]

sphinx /sfɪŋks/ *n.* **1** a mythological monster with a human head and the body of a lion. **2** (in Egypt) a figure with a couchant lion's body and a man's or animal's head. **3** an enigmatic or inscrutable person. [L f. Gk, app. f. *sphiggō* draw tight]

spice *n.* **1** an aromatic or pungent vegetable substance used to flavour food; spices collectively. **2** an interesting or piquant quality. **3** a trace. —*v.t.* **1** to flavour with spice. **2** to enhance (with wit etc.). [f. OF *espice* f. L, = SPECIES]

spick and span /spɪk ənd ˈspæn/ clean and tidy; new-looking. [f. earlier *spick and span new*, extension of obs. *span new* (ON, f. *spann* chip)]

spicy /ˈspaɪsɪ/ *adj.* **1** of or flavoured with spice. **2** piquant; slightly scandalous or improper. —**spicily** *adv.*, **spiciness** *n.* [f. SPICE]

spider /ˈspaɪdə(r)/ *n.* **1** an eight-legged arthropod of the order Araneida, many species of which spin webs, especially to capture insects as food. **2** a thing resembling a spider. —**spider-crab** *n.* a crab of the superfamily Oxyrhyncha, with long thin legs. **spider-man** *n.* a man working at a great height on a building. **spider monkey,** a monkey of the genus *Ateles* with long limbs and a long prehensile tail. [OE (as SPIN)]

spidery *adj.* of or like a spider; very thin or long. [f. prec.]

spiel /spiːl/ *n.* (*slang*) a speech or story, especially a glib or long one. —*v.t./i.* (*slang*) to speak lengthily or glibly. [G, = game]

spigot /ˈspɪgət/ *n.* a small peg or plug; a device for controlling the flow of liquor from a cask etc. [perh. f. Prov. *espigou(n)* f. L (as foll.)]

spike[1] *n.* **1** a sharp projecting point; a pointed piece of metal, e.g. one of a set forming the top of an iron fence or worn on the bottom of a running-shoe to prevent slipping. **2** (in *pl.*) running-shoes fitted with spikes. **3** a large nail. **4** a pointed metal rod standing upright on a base and used e.g. to hold unused matter in a newspaper office. —*v.t.* **1** to put spikes on or into; to fix on a spike. **2** (*colloq.*) to add alcohol to (a drink). **3** (*hist.*) to plug the vent of (a gun) with a spike. —**spike a person's guns,** to spoil his plans. [perh. f. MLG or MDu., rel. to SPOKE[1]]

spike[2] *n.* a cluster of sessile flowers arranged closely on a long common axis; a separate sprig of any plant in which flowers form a spikelike cluster; an ear of corn. [f. L *spica* ear of corn]

spikenard /ˈspaɪknɑːd/ *n.* **1** a tall sweet-smelling plant (*Nardostachys jatamansi*). **2** an aromatic ointment formerly made from this. [f. L (as SPIKE[2], NARD)]

spiky *adj.* **1** like a spike; having a spike or spikes. **2** (*colloq.*) dogmatic; bad-tempered. —**spikily** *adv.*, **spikiness** *n.* [f. SPIKE[1]]

spill[1] *v.t./i.* (*past & p.p.* **spilt** or **spilled**) **1** to cause or allow (a liquid or powder etc.) to run over the edge of its container. **2** to become spilt. **3** to shed (others' blood). **4** to throw accidentally from a saddle or vehicle. **5** (*slang*) to disclose (information etc.). —*n.*

1 spilling, being spilt. 2 being thrown from a saddle etc.; a tumble, a fall. —**spill the beans,** see BEAN. [OE, = kill]

spill[2] *n.* a thin strip of wood or paper used for transferring flame, e.g. for lighting a fire or pipe. [rel. to *spile* wooden peg, f. MDu. or MLG]

spillage *n.* 1 the action of spilling. 2 the amount spilt. [f. SPILL[1]]

spillikin /ˈspɪlɪkɪn/ *n.* a splinter of wood etc.; (in *pl.*) a game in which a heap of these is removed by taking one at a time without disturbing the others. [f. SPILL[2]]

spillway *n.* a passage for surplus water from a dam.

spin *v.t./i.* (-nn-; *past* & *p.p.* **spun**) 1 to turn or cause to turn rapidly on its own axis. 2 to draw out and twist (raw cotton or wool etc.) into threads; to make (yarn) thus. 3 (of a spider or silkworm) to make (a web or cocoon) by emitting a viscous thread. 4 (of a person's head etc.) to be in a whirl through dizziness or astonishment; to toss (a coin). 5 to spin-dry. 6 to tell or compose (a story etc.). —*n.* 1 a spinning movement. 2 a short drive in a motor vehicle. 3 a rotating dive of an aircraft. 4 the intrinsic angular momentum of an elementary particle. —**spin bowler,** (in cricket) a bowler who imparts spin to a ball. **spin-drier** *n.* a machine for drying clothes by spinning them in a rotating drum so that moisture is squeezed out by centrifugal force. **spin-dry** *v.t.* to dry thus. **spin-off** *n.* an incidental or secondary result or benefit, especially in technology. **spin out,** to prolong (a speech or discussion etc.). **spun silk,** a cheap material of short-fibred and waste silk, often mixed with cotton. [OE]

spina bifida /ˈspaɪnə ˈbɪfɪdə/ a congenital defect of the spine in which certain bones are not properly developed and allow the meninges or spinal cord to protrude. [L, = cleft spine]

spinach /ˈspɪnɪdʒ/ *n.* a vegetable (*Spinacia oleracea*) with succulent leaves cooked as food. [prob. f. MDu. f. OF, ult. f. Pers.]

spinal /ˈspaɪn(ə)l/ *adj.* of the spine. —**spinal column,** the spine. **spinal cord,** the cylindrical nervous structure within the spine. [f. L (as SPINE)]

spindle *n.* 1 a slender rod or bar, often with tapered ends, to twist and wind thread. 2 a pin or axis that revolves or on which a thing revolves. —**spindle-shanks** *n.* a person with long thin legs. **spindle-tree** *n.* a tree of the genus *Euonymus*, especially *E. europaeus* with a hard wood used for spindles. [OE (as SPIN)]

spindly *adj.* long or tall or thin. [f. prec.]

spindrift /ˈspɪndrɪft/ *n.* spray blown along the surface of the sea. [Sc. var. of *spoondrift* (*spoon* run before the wind + DRIFT)]

spine *n.* 1 the column of small bones (vertebrae) extending from the skull down the centre of the back. 2 a sharp needle-like outgrowth of an animal or plant. 3 the part of a book's cover or jacket that encloses its page-fastening. 4 a sharp ridge or projection. —**spine-chiller** *n.* a spine-chilling book or film etc. **spine-chilling** *adj.* frighteningly thrilling or exciting. [f. OF *espine* or L *spina* thorn]

spineless *adj.* 1 lacking a backbone. 2 lacking resoluteness or strength of character, feeble. —**spinelessness** *n.* [f. SPINE + -LESS]

spinet /spɪˈnet/ *n.* (*hist.*) a small early keyboard instrument of the harpsichord family. [f. F f. It. *spinetta* (as SPINE)]

spinnaker /ˈspɪnəkə(r)/ *n.* a large triangular sail carried opposite the mainsail of a racing-yacht running before the wind. [f. *Sphinx*, name of first yacht to use it]

spinner *n.* 1 a person or thing that spins, especially a manufacturer engaged in cotton-spinning. 2 a spin bowler. 3 (in fishing) a revolving bait as a lure. [f. SPIN]

spinneret /ˈspɪnəret/ *n.* 1 the spinning-organ of a spider etc. 2 a device for forming synthetic fibre. [f. prec.]

spinney /ˈspɪnɪ/ *n.* a small wood, a thicket. [f. OF f. L *spinetum* (as SPINE)]

spinning-jenny *n.* a machine for spinning fibres with more than one spindle at a time.

spinning-top *n.* = TOP[2].

spinning-wheel *n.* a household device for spinning yarn or thread, with a spindle driven by a wheel operated originally by hand, later by a crank or treadle.

spinster *n.* an unmarried woman; an (elderly) woman thought unlikely to marry. [orig. = woman who spins, f. SPIN]

spiny /ˈspaɪnɪ/ *adj.* having (many) spines. —**spininess** *n.* [f. SPINE]

spiracle /ˈspaɪərək(ə)l/ *n.* an external respiratory orifice in insects; the blow-hole of a whale etc. [f. L (*spirare* breathe)]

spiraea /spaɪˈriːə/ *n.* a garden plant of the genus *Spiraea*, related to meadowsweet. [L f. Gk (*speira* coil)]

spiral /ˈspaɪər(ə)l/ *adj.* coiled in a plane or as round a cylinder or cone; having this shape. —*n.* 1 a spiral curve; a thing of spiral form. 2 a continuous increase or decrease in two or more quantities alternately or in succession, because of their dependence on each other. —*v.i.* (-ll-) to move in a spiral course. —**spiral staircase,** a staircase rising round a central axis. —**spirally** *adv.* [F or f. L (*spira* coil f. Gk)]

spirant /ˈspaɪərənt/ *adj.* uttered with a continuous expulsion of the breath. —*n.* a spirant consonant. [f. L *spirare* breathe]

spire *n.* a tapering structure like a tall cone or pyramid rising above a tower; any tapering body. [OE]

spirit /ˈspɪrɪt/ *n.* **1** a person's animating principle or intelligence. **2** a person's soul. **3** a person from an intellectual or moral viewpoint. **4** a disembodied person or incorporeal being. **5** a person's mental or moral nature. **6** an attitude or mood. **7** courage, self-assertion, vivacity. **8** (in *pl.*) a state of mind. **9** a tendency prevailing at a particular time etc. **10** a principle or purpose underlying the form of a law etc. **11** a volatile liquid produced by distillation; purified alcohol; (usu. in *pl.*) a strong distilled alcoholic liquor, e.g. whisky or gin. —*v.t.* to convey rapidly or mysteriously. —**in spirit,** inwardly. **spirit gum,** a quick-drying gum for attaching false hair. **spirit lamp,** a lamp burning methylated or other volatile spirit instead of oil. **spirit-level** *n.* a device consisting of a sealed glass tube nearly filled with liquid and containing an air-bubble, used to test levelness by the position of this bubble. [f. AF f. L *spiritus* breath (as SPIRANT)]

spirited *adj.* **1** full of spirit, lively, courageous. **2** having a specified spirit or disposition (*poor-spirited*). —**spiritedly** *adv.* [f. prec.]

spiritless *adj.* lacking vigour or courage. [f. SPIRIT + -LESS]

spiritual /ˈspɪrɪtjʊəl/ *adj.* of or concerned with the spirit, not physical or worldly; of the Church or religion. —*n.* a religious song especially of American Blacks. —**spirituality** /-ˈælɪtɪ/ *n.*, **spiritually** *adv.* [f. OF f. L (as SPIRIT)]

spiritualism /ˈspɪrɪtjʊəlɪz(ə)m/ *n.* the belief that the spirits of the dead communicate with the living, especially through mediums. —**spiritualist** *n.*, **spiritualistic** /-ˈlɪstɪk/ *adj.* [f. prec.]

spirituous /ˈspɪrɪtjʊəs/ *adj.* alcoholic, distilled and not only fermented. [f. SPIRIT]

spit[1] *v.t./i.* (**-tt-**; *past* & *p.p.* **spat** or **spit**) **1** to eject from the mouth; to eject saliva from the mouth; to do this as a gesture of contempt. **2** to utter (oaths or threats etc.) vehemently. **3** to make a noise as of spitting. **4** (of a fire or gun etc.) to throw out with an explosion. **5** (of rain) to fall lightly. —*n.* **1** spittle. **2** spitting. —**the (dead** *or* **very) spit,** a spitting image. **spit and polish,** a soldier's cleaning and polishing work. **spit it out,** (*colloq.*) to speak candidly or louder. **spitting image,** an exact counterpart or likeness. [OE, orig. imit.]

spit[2] *n.* **1** a rod on which meat is fixed for roasting over a fire etc. **2** a long narrow strip of land projecting into the sea. —*v.t.* (**-tt-**) to pierce (as) with a spit. [OE]

spit[3] *n.* a spade's depth of earth. [f. OE *spittan* dig with spade, prob. rel. to SPIT[2]]

spite *n.* malicious desire to hurt, annoy, or frustrate another person. —*v.t.* to hurt or annoy etc. through spite. —**in spite of,** not being prevented by, regardless of. [f. OF (as DESPITE)]

spiteful *adj.* full of spite; showing or caused by spite. —**spitefully** *adv.*, **spitefulness** *n.* [f. SPITE + -FUL]

spitfire *n.* a person of fiery temper.

spittle /ˈspɪt(ə)l/ *n.* saliva, especially as ejected from the mouth. [f. SPIT[1]]

spittoon /spɪˈtuːn/ *n.* a vessel for spitting into. [f. SPIT[1]]

spiv *n.* a man, especially a flashily-dressed one, living from shady dealings rather than regular work. —**spivvish** *adj.* [perh. f. dial. *spiff, spiffy* smartly dressed]

splash *v.t./i.* **1** to cause (liquid) to fly about in drops; to wet with such drops; (of liquid) to be splashed. **2** to move or fall with splashing. **3** to decorate with scattered patches of colour etc. **4** to display (news) prominently. **5** to spend (money) freely and ostentatiously. —*n.* **1** the act or sound of splashing. **2** a quantity of liquid splashed; a mark etc. made by splashing. **3** a patch of colour or light. **4** a striking or ostentatious display. **5** (*colloq.*) a small quantity of soda-water etc. (in a drink). —**make a splash,** to attract much attention. **splash-down** *n.* the alighting of a spacecraft on the sea. **splash out,** (*colloq.*) to spend money freely. —**splashy** *adj.* [alt. f. *plash* (prob. imit.)]

splashback *n.* a panel behind a sink etc. to protect a wall from splashes.

splatter *v.t./i.* to splash noisily; to spatter. —*n.* a noisy splashing sound. [imit.]

splay *v.t./i.* to spread apart; (of an opening) to have the sides diverging; to make (an opening) have divergent sides. —*n.* a surface at an oblique angle to another. —*adj.* splayed. [f. DISPLAY]

spleen *n.* **1** an abdominal organ maintaining the proper condition of the blood. **2** moroseness, irritability. [f. OF *esplen* f. L f. Gk *splēn*]

spleenwort /ˈspliːnwət/ *n.* a fern of the genus *Asplenium*, formerly used as a remedy for disorders of the spleen.

splendid /ˈsplendɪd/ *adj.* **1** magnificent, displaying splendour. **2** (*colloq.*) excellent. —**splendidly** *adv.* [f. F or L (*splendēre* shine)]

splendiferous /splenˈdɪfərəs/ *adj.* (*colloq.*) splendid. [f. foll. + L *ferre* bear]

splendour /ˈsplendə(r)/ *n.* brilliance, magnificent display or appearance; grandeur. [f. AF or L (as SPLENDID)]

splenetic /splɪˈnetɪk/ *adj.* bad-tempered, peevish. —**splenetically** *adv.* [f. L (as SPLEEN)]

splenic /ˈspliːnɪk, ˈsple-/ *adj.* of or in the spleen. [f. F or L f. Gk (as SPLEEN)]

splice *v.t.* **1** to join pieces of (ropes) by interweaving strands. **2** to join (pieces of wood or tape etc.) in an overlapping position. **3** (*colloq.*, esp. in *pass.*) to join in marriage. —*n.* a junction made by splicing. —**splice the main brace,** (*Naut.*) to serve a free drink of spirits. [prob. f. MDu. *splissen*; orig. unkn.]

splint *n.* **1** a strip of wood etc. bound to a limb, especially to keep a broken bone in the right position while it heals. **2** a tumour or bony excrescence on the inside of a horse's leg. **3** (also **splint-bone**) either of two small bones in a horse's foreleg lying behind and close to the cannon-bone; the human fibula. —*v.t.* to secure with a splint. [f. MDu. or MLG, = metal plate or pin (rel. to foll.)]

splinter *n.* a small sharp piece broken off wood or glass etc. —*v.t./i.* to break or become broken into splinters. —**splinter group,** a small (esp. political) group that has broken away from a larger one. —**splintery** *adj.* [f. MDu., rel. to prec.]

split *v.t./i.* (**-tt-**; *past* & *p.p.* **split**) **1** to break or become broken into parts, especially lengthwise or with the grain or the plane of cleavage. **2** to divide into parts; to divide and share. **3** to remove or be removed by breaking or dividing. **4** to divide or become divided into disagreeing or hostile parties. **5** to cause fission of (an atom). **6** (*slang*) to betray secrets, to inform (on a person). —*n.* **1** an act or the result of splitting. **2** a disagreement or schism. **3** a dish made of bananas etc. split open, with ice-cream etc. **4** (in *pl.*) the feat of sitting down or leaping with the legs widely spread out at right angles to the body. **5** a half bottle of mineral water; a half glass of liquor. —**be splitting,** (of the head) to feel acute pain from a headache. **split hairs,** see HAIR. **split infinitive,** one with an adverb etc. inserted between *to* and the verb. **split-level** *adj.* built or having components at more than one level. **split pea,** a pea dried and split for cooking. **split personality,** a change of personality as in schizophrenia. **split pin,** a pin or bolt etc. held in place by the splaying of its split end. **split second,** a very brief moment. **split one's sides,** to laugh heartily. **splitting headache,** a very severe headache. **split up,** to separate; (of a married couple etc.) to cease living together. [orig. Naut., f. MDu.]

splodge var. of SPLOTCH.

splosh *v.t./i.* (*colloq.*) to splash. —*n.* (*colloq.*) a splash. [imit.]

splotch *n.* a daub, blot, or smear. —*v.t.* to daub, to blot, to smear. [perh. f. SPOT + obs. *plotch* blotch]

splurge *n.* an ostentatious display or effort. —*v.i.* to make a splurge. [prob. imit.]

splutter *v.t./i.* **1** to make a rapid series of spitting sounds. **2** to speak or utter rapidly or incoherently. —*n.* a spluttering sound. [f. SPUTTER by assoc. with *splash*]

Spode /spəʊd/ *n.* a kind of fine pottery or porcelain named after the English potter Josiah Spode (1754-1827), its original maker.

spoil *v.t./i.* (*past* & *p.p.* **spoilt** or **spoiled**) **1** to make or become useless or unsatisfactory. **2** to diminish a person's enjoyment of. **3** to harm the character of (a person) by indulgence. **4** (of food etc.) to go bad. —*n.* (in *sing.* or *pl.*) **1** plunder, stolen goods, especially those taken by a victor. **2** profits; advantages accruing from success or an official position. —**be spoiling for,** to seek eagerly or aggressively. **spoil-sport** *n.* one who spoils other's enjoyment. **spoils system,** (*US*) the practice of giving public offices to adherents of the successful party. [f. OF f. L *spoliare* (*spolium* plunder)]

spoiler *n.* a device on an aircraft to retard it by interrupting the air-flow; a similar device on a vehicle to prevent it from being lifted off the ground at speed. [f. SPOIL]

spoke[1] *n.* **1** each of the bars or rods running from the hub to the rim of a wheel. **2** a rung of a ladder. —*v.t.* **1** to provide with spokes. **2** to obstruct (a wheel etc.) by thrusting a spoke in. —**put a spoke in a person's wheel,** to hinder or thwart his purpose. [OE (of SPIKE[1])]

spoke[2] *past* of SPEAK.

spoken *p.p.* of SPEAK. —*adj.* speaking in a specified way (*soft-*, *well-spoken*). [as SPEAK]

spokeshave /ˈspəʊkʃeɪv/ *n.* a tool for planing curved surfaces.

spokesman /ˈspəʊksmən/ *n.* (*pl.* **-men**) one who speaks on behalf of a group. —**spokeswoman** *n.fem.* [f. SPOKE[2] after *craftsman* etc.]

spoliation /spəʊlɪˈeɪʃ(ə)n/ *n.* plundering, pillage. [f. L (as SPOIL)]

spondee /ˈspɒndiː/ *n.* a metrical foot with two long or stressed syllables. —**spondaic** /-ˈdeɪɪk/ *adj.* [f. OF or L f. Gk (*spondē* libation, as being characteristic of music accompanying libations)]

sponge /spʌndʒ/ *n.* **1** a water animal of the phylum Porifera, with a porous body-wall and a tough elastic skeleton. **2** this skeleton, or a piece of a substance of similar texture, used for washing, cleaning, or padding things. **3** a thing of spongelike absorbency or consistency. **4** a sponge-cake. **5** the act of sponging; a wash with a sponge. —*v.t./i.* **1** to wipe or wash with a sponge. **2** to live parasitically on others, to scrounge. —**sponge-bag** *n.* a waterproof bag for toilet articles. **sponge-cake** (*or* **-pudding**) *n.* a light cake (or pudding) of spongelike consistency.

sponge rubber, rubber made porous like a sponge. **throw in** *or* **up the sponge,** to abandon a contest, to admit defeat. [OE f. L f. Gk *spoggia*]

spongeable /ˈspʌndʒəb(ə)l/ *adj.* that may be sponged. [f. prec.]

sponger /ˈspʌndʒə(r)/ *n.* a person who habitually sponges on others. [f. SPONGE]

spongy /ˈspʌndʒɪ/ *adj.* like sponge in texture or absorbency, soft and springy. —**spongily** *adv.*, **sponginess** *n.* [f. SPONGE]

sponson /ˈspɒns(ə)n/ *n.* **1** a projection from the side of a warship or tank to enable a gun to be trained forward and aft. **2** an air-filled structure fitted along the gunwale of a canoe to make it more stable and buoyant. **3** a short winglike projection from the hull of a seaplane, to stabilize it on water. [orig. unkn.]

sponsor /ˈspɒnsə(r)/ *n.* **1** a person who makes himself responsible for another, presents a candidate for baptism, introduces legislation, or contributes to a charity in return for a specified activity by another. **2** an advertiser who pays for a sporting event or a broadcast which includes an advertisement of his goods. —*v.t.* to be a sponsor for. —**sponsorial** /spɒnˈsɔːrɪəl/ *adj.*, **sponsorship** *n.* [L (*spondēre* promise solemnly)]

spontaneous /spɒnˈteɪnɪəs/ *adj.* acting, done, or occurring without external cause or incitement; resulting from natural impulse; (of a style or manner) gracefully natural and unconstrained. —**spontaneous combustion,** ignition of a substance by chemical changes within it, not by flame etc. from an external source. **spontaneity** /spɒntəˈniːɪtɪ/ *n.*, **spontaneously** *adv.* [f. L (*sponte* of one's own accord)]

spoof *n.* (*colloq.*) a parody; a hoax, a swindle. —*v.t.* (*colloq.*) to parody; to hoax, to swindle. [invented by A. Roberts, English comedian (d. 1933)]

spook *n.* (*colloq.*) a ghost. [Du.; orig. unkn.]

spooky *adj.* (*colloq.*) ghostly, eerie. —**spookiness** *n.* [f. SPOOK]

spool *n.* a reel on which something is wound, e.g. yarn or magnetic tape; the revolving cylinder of an angler's reel. —*v.t.* to wind on a spool. [f. OF *espole* or MLG or MDu.; orig. unkn.]

spoon *n.* **1** a utensil with an oval or round bowl and a handle, for conveying food (especially liquid) to the mouth or for stirring or measuring things. **2** a spoon-shaped thing. **3** (in full **spoon-bait**) a revolving spoon-shaped metal fish-lure. —*v.t./i.* **1** to take or lift with a spoon. **2** to hit (a ball) feebly upwards. **3** (*colloq.*) to behave in an amorous way. —**spoon-feed** *v.t.* to feed (a baby etc.) with a spoon; to give such extensive help etc. to (a person) that he need make no effort for himself. —**spoonful** *n.* [OE, = chip of wood]

spoonbill *n.* a wading-bird of the family Plataleidae with a broad flat tip of the bill.

spoonerism /ˈspuːnərɪz(ə)m/ *n.* a transposition, usually accidental, of the initial letter etc. of two or more words. [f. W. A. *Spooner*, English scholar (d. 1930), reputed to have made such errors in speaking]

spoor *n.* an animal's track or scent. [Afrik. f. MDu.]

sporadic /spəˈrædɪk/ *adj.* occurring only here and there or occasionally. —**sporadically** *adv.* [f. L f. Gk (*sporas* scattered)]

spore *n.* each of the minute structures that are the reproductive cell of cryptogamous plants; a resistant form of bacterium etc. [f. Gk *spora* sowing, seed]

sporran /ˈspɒrən/ *n.* a pouch worn in front of a kilt. [f. Gael. f. L (as PURSE)]

sport *n.* **1** an athletic (especially outdoor) activity; any game or pastime; an outdoor pastime such as hunting or fishing. **2** such activities or pastimes collectively; the world of sport; (in *pl.*) a meeting for competing in sports, especially athletics. **3** amusement, diversion, fun. **4** (*colloq.*) a good fellow, a sportsmanlike person. **5** an animal or plant differing from the normal type. —*v.t./i.* **1** to play, to amuse oneself. **2** to wear or display ostentatiously. —**in sport,** jestingly. **make sport of,** to ridicule. **sports car,** a low-built fast car. **sports coat** *or* **jacket,** a man's jacket for informal wear. [f. DISPORT]

sporting *adj.* **1** interested or concerned in sport. **2** sportsmanlike. —**a sporting chance,** some possibility of success. [f. SPORT]

sportive *adj.* playful. —**sportively** *adv.* [f. SPORT]

sportsman *n.* (*pl.* **-men**) **1** a person fond of sport. **2** a person who behaves fairly and generously. —**sportsmanlike** *adj.*, **sportsmanship** *n.*, **sportswoman** *n.fem.*

sporty *adj.* (*colloq.*) **1** fond of sport. **2** rakish, showy. —**sportily** *adv.*, **sportiness** *n.* [f. SPORT]

spot *n.* **1** a small roundish area or mark differing in colour or texture etc. from the surface it is on; a blemish or stain; a pimple. **2** a particular place, a definite locality. **3** (*colloq.*) one's (regular) position in an organization or programme etc. **4** a small quantity of something; a drop (of liquid). **5** a spotlight. —*v.t./i.* (**-tt-**) **1** to mark with a spot or spots; to become marked thus. **2** to make spots, to rain slightly. **3** (*colloq.*) to pick out, to recognize, to catch sight of; to watch for and take note of (trains, talent, etc.). **4** (in *p.p.*) marked or decorated with spots. —**in a**

(**tight** etc.) **spot,** (*colloq.*) in difficulty. **on the spot,** at the scene of an action or event; (*colloq.*) in a position such that a response or action is required. **spot cash,** money paid immediately on a sale. **spot check,** a sudden or random check. **spot-on** *adj.* (*colloq.*) precise, on target. **spotted dick,** a suet pudding containing currants. **spot welding,** welding between points of metal surfaces in contact. —**spotter** *n.* [perh. f. MDu. or LG, = small piece]

spotless *adj.* free from stain or blemish, perfectly clean. [f. SPOT + -LESS]

spotlight *n.* **1** a beam of light directed on a small area; a lamp projecting this. **2** full attention or publicity. —*v.t.* **1** to direct a spotlight on. **2** to make conspicuous, to draw attention to.

spotty *adj.* **1** marked with spots. **2** patchy, irregular. —**spottily** *adv.*, **spottiness** *n.* [f. SPOT]

spouse /spaʊs/ *n.* a husband or wife. [f. OF f. L *sponsus, sponsa* p.p. of *spondēre* betroth]

spout *n.* **1** a projecting tube or lip through which liquid etc. is poured or issues from a teapot, jug, roof-gutter, fountain, etc. **2** a jet or column of liquid etc. —*v.t./i.* **1** to discharge or issue forcefully or in a jet. **2** to utter in a declamatory manner. —**up the spout,** (*slang*) useless, ruined; in trouble; pawned. [f. MDu. (imit.)]

sprain *v.t.* to injure (a joint or its muscles or ligaments) by wrenching it violently. —*n.* such an injury [orig. unkn.]

sprang *past* of SPRING.

sprat *n.* a small sea-fish (*Sprattus sprattus*). [OE]

sprawl *v.t./i.* **1** to sit, lie, or fall with the limbs flung out or in an ungainly way; to spread (one's limbs) thus. **2** to be of an irregular or straggling form. —*n.* a sprawling position, movement, or mass. [OE]

spray[1] *n.* **1** water or other liquid flying in very small drops. **2** a liquid preparation to be applied in this way with an atomizer etc.; a device for such an application. —*v.t.* to send out (a liquid) in very small drops; to sprinkle thus; to sprinkle (plants etc.) thus with insecticides. —**spray-gun** *n.* a gunlike device for spraying paint etc. —**sprayer** *n.* [perh. rel. to MDu. *spra(e)yen* sprinkle]

spray[2] *n.* **1** a single shoot or branch with its leaves, twigs, and flowers. **2** a bunch of cut flowers etc. arranged decoratively. **3** an ornament in similar form. [orig. unkn.]

spread /spred/ *v.t./i.* (*past* & *p.p.* **spread**) **1** to open out, to extend the surface of, to unroll or unfold; to cause to cover a larger surface, to display thus. **2** to have a wide or specified extent; to become longer or wider. **3** to cover the surface of, to apply as a layer; to be able to be spread. **4** to make or become widely known or felt. **5** to distribute or become distributed over an area or period. —*n.* **1** spreading, being spread. **2** a thing's extent, expanse, or breadth. **3** expansion; increased bodily girth. **4** the range of prices, rates, etc. **5** (*colloq.*) a lavish meal. **6** a sweet or savoury paste for spreading on bread etc. **7** a bedspread. **8** printed matter spread across more than one column. —**spread eagle,** a figure of an eagle with the legs and wings extended, as an emblem. **spread-eagle** *v.t.* to place (a person) in a position with the arms and legs spread out; to defeat utterly. **spread oneself,** to be lavish or discursive. [OE]

spree *n.* a lively outing, especially where one spends money freely; a bout of fun or drinking etc. [orig unkn.]

sprig *n.* **1** a small branch, a shoot. **2** an ornament resembling this, especially on fabric. **3** (usu. *derog.*) a young man. —*v.t.* (**-gg-**) to ornament (fabric etc.) with sprigs. [f. or rel. to LG *sprick*]

sprightly /ˈspraɪtlɪ/ *adj.* lively, full of energy; brisk. —**sprightliness** *n.* [f. SPRITE]

spring *v.t./i.* (*past* **sprang**; *p.p.* **sprung**) **1** to jump, to move rapidly or suddenly, especially in a single movement. **2** to originate or arise (from ancestors or a source etc.). **3** to produce, develop, or operate suddenly or unexpectedly. **4** to rouse (game) from an earth or covert; to contrive the escape of (a prisoner etc.). **5** (of wood etc.) to become warped or split. **6** (usu. in *p.p.*) to provide with springs. —*n.* **1** the act of springing, a jump. **2** elasticity. **3** a device (usually of bent or coiled metal) that reverts to its original position after being compressed, tightened, or stretched, used especially to drive clockwork or (in groups) to make a seat etc. more comfortable. **4** the season in which vegetation begins to appear, from March to May in the northern hemisphere. **5** a place where water or oil comes up naturally from the ground; a basin or flow so formed. **6** a motive or origin of an action or custom etc. —**spring balance,** one that measures weight by the tension of a spring. **spring chicken,** a young fowl for eating; a youthful person. **spring-clean** *n.* a thorough cleaning of a house, especially in spring; (*v.t.*) to clean thus. **spring onion,** a young onion eaten raw. **spring roll,** a Chinese snack consisting of a pancake filled with vegetables and fried in the shape of a roll. **spring tide,** a tide of maximum height. **spring up,** to come into being, to appear. **sprung rhythm,** a poetic rhythm approximating to speech, each foot having one stressed syllable followed by a varying number of unstressed. [OE]

springboard *n.* a springy board giving an impetus in leaping or diving etc.; a source of impetus.

springbok /ˈsprɪŋbɒk/ *n.* **1** a South African gazelle (*Antidorcas marsupialis*) with the habit of springing in play or when alarmed. **2 Springboks,** a South African national sporting team or touring party. [Afrik., f. Du. *springen* spring, *bok* antelope]

springer *n.* **1** a small spaniel of a breed used to spring game. **2** the part of an arch where the curve begins; the lowest stone of this. [f. SPRING]

springtail *n.* a wingless insect of the order Collembola, leaping by means of a springlike caudal part.

springtime *n.* the season of spring.

springy *adj.* elastic, springing back quickly when squeezed or stretched. —**springily** *adv.*, **springiness** *n.* [f. SPRING]

sprinkle *v.t.* **1** to scatter in small drops or particles. **2** to scatter small drops etc. on (a surface). **3** to distribute in small amounts. —*n.* sprinkling; a light shower. [perh. f. MDu. *sprenkelen*]

sprinkler *n.* a device for sprinkling water. [f. prec.]

sprinkling *n.* a small thinly distributed number or amount. [as prec.]

sprint *v.t./i.* to run at full speed, especially over a short distance. —*n.* such a run; a similar spell of maximum effort in swimming, cycling, etc. —**sprinter** *n.* [f. ON & Icel. *spretta;* orig. unkn.]

sprit *n.* a small diagonal spar from a mast to the upper outer corner of a sail. [OE *sprēot* pole; rel. to SPROUT]

sprite *n.* an elf, fairy, or goblin. [f. *sprit*, var. of SPIRIT]

spritely /ˈspraɪtlɪ/ *adj.* (*US*) = SPRIGHTLY.

spritsail /ˈsprɪts(ə)l/ *n.* a sail extended by a sprit; a sail extended by a yard set under the bowsprit.

sprocket /ˈsprɒkɪt/ *n.* each of the several teeth on a wheel engaging with the links of a chain. [orig. unkn.]

sprout *v.t./i.* to begin to grow or appear, to put forth shoots; to produce thus. —*n.* **1** shoot of a plant. **2** a Brussels sprout (see BRUSSELS). [OE]

spruce[1] /spru:s/ *adj.* neat in dress and appearance, smart. —*v.t./i.* to make or become spruce. —**sprucely** *adv.*, **spruceness** *n.* [perh. f. foll. in sense 'Prussian']

spruce[2] /spru:s/ *n.* a conifer of the genus *Picea* with dense conical foliage; its wood. [alt. f. obs. *Pruce* Prussia]

sprung *p.p.* of SPRING.

spry /spraɪ/ *adj.* (*compar.* **spryer**; *superl.* **spryest**) lively, nimble. —**spryly** *adv.*, **spryness** *n.* [orig. unkn.]

spud *n.* **1** a small narrow spade for weeding. **2** (*slang*) a potato. —*v.t.* (**-dd-**) to dig with a spud. [orig. unkn.]

spume *n.* froth, foam. —*v.i.* to foam. —**spumy** *adj.* [f. OF or L *spuma*]

spun *p.p.* of SPIN.

spunk *n.* **1** touchwood. **2** (*colloq.*) mettle, spirit. **3** (*slang*) semen. —**spunky** *adj.* [orig. unkn.]

spur *n.* **1** a device with a small spike or spiked wheel attached to a rider's heel for urging a horse forward. **2** a stimulus, an incentive. **3** a spur-shaped thing, especially the hard projection on a cock's leg; a projection from a mountain or mountain range; a branch road or railway. —*v.t./i.* (**-rr-**) **1** to prick (a horse) with a spur. **2** to incite or stimulate; to urge on. **3** (esp. in *p.p.*) to provide with spurs. —**on the spur of the moment** on a momentary impulse. [OE]

spurge *n.* a plant of the genus *Euphorbia*, with an acrid milky juice. [f. OF *espurge* (*espurgier* f. L, as EXPURGATE)]

spurious /ˈspjʊərɪəs/ *adj.* not genuine, not what it purports to be. —**spuriously** *adv.* [f. L *spurius*, orig. = illegitimate]

spurn *v.t.* to reject with disdain, to treat with contempt; to repel with one's foot. [OE, cf. SPUR]

spurt *v.t./i.* **1** to gush, to send out (liquid) suddenly. **2** to increase speed suddenly. —*n.* **1** a sudden gush. **2** a sudden increase in speed; a short burst of activity. [orig. unkn.]

sputnik /ˈspʊtnɪk, ˈspʌ-/ *n.* a Russian artificial satellite orbiting the Earth. [Russ., = travelling companion]

sputter *v.t./i.* to splutter, to make a series of quick explosive sounds. —*n.* a sputtering sound. [f. Du. *sputteren* (imit.)]

sputum /ˈspju:təm/ *n.* (*pl.* **sputa**) saliva; expectorated matter, especially as used to diagnose disease. [L, p.p. of *spuere* spit]

spy /spaɪ/ *n.* a person secretly collecting and reporting information on the activities or movements of an enemy or competitor etc.; a person keeping a secret watch on others. —*v.t./i.* **1** to discern, especially by careful observation. **2** to act as a spy; to keep watch secretly. **3** to pry. [f. OF *espier* espy]

spyglass *n.* a small telescope.

spyhole *n.* a peep-hole.

sq. *abbr.* square.

squab /skwɒb/ *n.* **1** a short fat person. **2** a young (unfledged) pigeon or other bird. **3** a stuffed seat or cushion, especially as part (usually the back) of a seat in a motor car. —*adj.* short and fat, squat. [orig. unkn.; cf. obs. *quab* shapeless thing]

squabble /ˈskwɒb(ə)l/ *n.* a petty or noisy quarrel. —*v.i.* to engage in a squabble. [prob. imit.]

squad /skwɒd/ *n.* a small group of people sharing a task etc., especially a small number of soldiers. [f. F *escouade* f. It. *squadra* (as SQUARE)]

squadron /ˈskwɒdrən/ *n.* an organized body of persons etc., especially a cavalry division of two troops; a detachment of warships employed on a particular service; a unit of the RAF with 10 to 18 aircraft. —**squadron leader,** an officer commanding an RAF squadron, next below wing commander. [f. It. *squadrone* (as prec.)]

squalid /ˈskwɒlɪd/ *adj.* **1** dirty and unpleasant, especially because of neglect or poverty. **2** morally degrading. —**squalidly** *adv.* [f. L (*squalēre* be rough or dirty)]

squall /skwɔːl/ *n.* **1** a sudden or violent wind-storm, especially with rain or snow or sleet. **2** a discordant cry, a scream (especially of a baby). —*v.t./i.* to utter (with) a squall; to scream. —**squally** *adj.* [prob. f. SQUEAL, assoc. with *bawl*]

squalor /ˈskwɒlə(r)/ *n.* a squalid state. [L (as SQUALID)]

squander /ˈskwɒndə(r)/ *v.t.* to spend wastefully. [orig. unkn.]

square *n.* **1** a rectangle with four equal sides. **2** an object or arrangement of (approximately) this shape. **3** an open usually four-sided area surrounded by buildings. **4** (in astrology) the aspect of two planets 90° apart, regarded as having an unfavourable influence. **5** the product obtained when a number is multiplied by itself. **6** an L- or T-shaped instrument for obtaining or testing right angles. **7** (*slang*) a conventional or old-fashioned person. —*adj.* **1** having the shape of a square. **2** having or in the form of a right angle; at right angles, 90° apart; angular, not round. **3** of or using units that express the measure of an area; (of a unit of measure) equal to the area of a square having each side one specified unit in length. **4** level, parallel. **5** properly arranged, settled; (also **all square**) not in debt, with no money owed; (of scores etc.) balanced, equal. **6** fair and honest. **7** direct, uncompromising. **8** (*slang*) conventional, or old-fashioned. —*adv.* squarely; directly; fairly, honestly. —*v.t./i.* **1** to make right-angled. **2** to mark with squares. **3** to multiply (a number) by itself. **4** to place evenly or squarely. **5** to make or be consistent. **6** to settle or pay (a bill etc.); (*colloq.*) to pay or bribe (a person); to make the scores of (a match etc.) equal. —**back to square one,** (*colloq.*) back to the starting-point with no progress made. **on the square,** (*colloq.*) honest, honestly; fair, fairly. **out of square,** not at right angles. **square-bashing** *n.* (*slang*) military drill on a barrack-square. **square the circle,** to construct a square equal in area to a given circle; to do what is impossible. **square dance,** a dance with usually four couples facing inwards from four sides. **square deal,** a fair bargain or treatment. **square leg,** (in cricket) the position of the fieldsman at some distance on the batsman's leg-side and nearly opposite the stumps. **square meal,** a substantial and satisfying meal. **square-rigged** *adj.* with the principal sails at right angles to the length of the ship. **square root,** a number that multiplied by itself gives a specified number. **square up,** to settle an account etc. **square up to,** to move towards (a person) in a fighting attitude; to face and tackle (a difficulty) resolutely. —**squarely** *adv.*, **squareness** *n.* [f. OF *esquar(r)e* ult. f. L *quadra* square]

squash[1] /skwɒʃ/ *v.t./i.* **1** to crush, to squeeze or become squeezed flat or into pulp. **2** to pack tightly, to crowd, to squeeze into a small space. **3** to suppress. **4** to silence (a person) with a crushing reply, etc. —*n.* **1** a crowd of people squashed together; a crowded state. **2** a sound (as) of something being squashed. **3** a drink made of crushed fruit. **4** squash rackets. —**squash rackets,** a game played with rackets and a small soft ball in a closed court. —**squashy** *adj.* [alt. f. QUASH]

squash[2] /skwɒʃ/ *n.* a trailing annual plant of the genus *Cucurbita;* a gourd of this. [f. Narraganset]

squat /skwɒt/ *v.t./i.* (**-tt-**) **1** to sit on one's heels, or on the ground with the knees drawn up, or in a hunched position. **2** to put into a squatting position. **3** (*colloq.*) to sit down. **4** to act as a squatter. —*adj.* **1** short and thick, dumpy. **2** squatting. —*n.* **1** a squatting posture. **2** a place occupied by squatters. **3** being a squatter. [f. OF *esquatir* flatten]

squatter /ˈskwɒtə(r)/ *n.* **1** a person who takes unauthorized possession of unoccupied premises etc. **2** an Australian sheep-farmer. [f. SQUAT]

squaw *n.* a North American Indian woman or wife. [f. Narraganset]

squawk *n.* **1** a loud harsh cry especially of a bird. **2** a complaint. —*v.i.* to utter a squawk. [imit.]

squeak *n.* **1** a short high-pitched cry or sound **2** (also **narrow squeak**) a narrow escape; a success barely attained. —*v.t./i.* **1** to make a squeak. **2** to utter shrilly. **3** (with *through* or *by* etc.; *colloq.*) to pass or succeed narrowly. **4** (*slang*) to turn informer. —**squeaker** *n.* [imit., of *squeal*, *shriek*]

squeaky *adj.* making a squeaking sound. —**squeakily** *adv.*, **squeakiness** *n.* [f. prec.]

squeal *n.* a prolonged shrill sound or cry.

—*v.t./i.* **1** to make a squeal. **2** to utter with a squeal. **3** (*slang*) to turn informer. **4** (*slang*) to protest vociferously. [imit.]

squeamish /ˈskwi:mɪʃ/ *adj.* **1** easily nauseated, disgusted, or shocked. **2** over-scrupulous about principles. —**squeamishly** *adv.*, **squeamishness** *n.* [f. AF *escoymos*; orig. unkn.]

squeegee /skwi:ˈdʒi:/ *n.* an instrument with a rubber edge or roller on a long handle, used to remove liquid from surfaces. —*v.t.* to treat with a squeegee. [f. *squeege*, strengthened form of foll.]

squeeze *v.t./i.* **1** to exert pressure on from opposite or all sides. **2** to treat this so as to extract moisture or juice; to extract (juice) by squeezing; to reduce the size of or alter the shape of by squeezing. **3** to force into or through; to force one's way; to crowd. **4** to produce by pressure or effort. **5** to obtain by compulsion or strong urging; to extort money from; to harass thus. —*n.* **1** squeezing, being squeezed. **2** an affectionate clasp or hug. **3** a small amount of liquid produced by squeezing. **4** a crowd or crush; the pressure of this. **5** hardship or difficulty caused by a shortage of money or time etc. **6** restrictions on borrowing and investment during a financial crisis. [earlier *squise*, intensive of obs. *queise* (orig. unkn.)]

squelch *v.t./i.* **1** to make a sucking sound as of treading in thick mud; to move with a squelching sound. **2** to disconcert, to silence. —*n.* an act or sound of squelching. [imit.]

squib *n.* a small firework burning with a hissing sound and usually with a final explosion. —**damp squib**, an unsuccessful attempt to impress etc. [perh. imit.]

squid *n.* a ten-armed marine cephalopod especially of the genus *Loligo*. [orig. unkn.]

squiffy /ˈskwɪfɪ/ *adj* (*slang*) slightly drunk. [orig. unkn.]

squiggle *n.* a short curling line, especially in handwriting —**squiggly** *adj.* [imit.]

squill *n.* **1** a plant of the genus *Scilla*, growing from a bulb, resembling a bluebell. **2** a crustacean of the genus *Squilla*. [f. L f. Gk *skilla*]

squinch *n.* a straight or arched structure across the interior angle of a square tower to carry a dome etc. [var. of obs. *scunch* abbr. of SCUNCHEON]

squint *v.i.* **1** to have the eyes turned in different directions; to have a squint. **2** to look obliquely or with half-shut eyes or through a narrow opening. —*n.* **1** the abnormality of an eye which does not turn to match the other's direction. **2** a stealthy or sidelong glance; (*colloq.*) a glance, a look. **3** a narrow opening in a church wall giving a view of the altar. —*adj.* (*colloq.*) askew. [f. *asquint* adv. (cf. Du. *schuinte* slant)]

squire *n.* **1** a country gentleman, especially the chief landowner in a country district. **2** a woman's escort or gallant. **3** (*hist.*) a knight's attendant. **4** (*joc.*, as a form of address to a man) sir. —*v.t.* (of a man) to attend or escort (a woman). [f. OF, = ESQUIRE]

squirearchy /ˈskwaɪərɑ:kɪ/ *n.* landowners collectively, especially as having political or social influence. [f. prec., after *hierarchy* etc.]

squirm *v.i.* **1** to wriggle, to writhe. **2** to show or feel embarrassment or discomfiture. —*n.* a squirming movement. [imit.]

squirrel /ˈskwɪr(ə)l/ *n.* a bushy-tailed usually arboreal rodent of the family Sciuridae; its fur. —*v.t.* (**-ll-**) (with *away*) to hoard. [f. AF ult. f. Gk *skiouros* (*skia* shade, *oura* tail)]

squirt *v.t./i.* to eject (liquid etc.) in a jet; to be ejected thus. —*n.* **1** a jet of water etc. **2** a device for ejecting this. **3** (*colloq.*) an insignificant self-assertive person. [imit.]

squish *n.* a slight squelching sound. —*v.i.* to move with a squish. —**squishy** *adj.* [imit.]

Sr *symbol* strontium.

Sr. *abbr.* **1** Senior. **2** Señor.

sr *abbr.* steradian.

SRN *abbr.* State Registered Nurse.

SS *abbr.* **1** Saints. **2** steamship. **3** (*hist.*) the Nazi special police force (G *Schutz-Staffel*).

SSE *abbr.* south-south-east.

SSR *abbr.* Soviet Socialist Republic.

SSW *abbr.* south-south-west.

St *abbr.* Saint.

St. *abbr.* Street.

st. *abbr.* stone.

stab *v.t./i.* (**-bb-**) **1** to pierce or wound with a pointed tool or weapon; to aim a blow with such a weapon. **2** to cause a sensation like being stabbed. **3** to hurt or distress (a person or feelings etc.). —*n.* **1** an act or the result of stabbing; a wound or harm. **2** (*colloq.*) an attempt. —**stab in the back**, a treacherous or slanderous attack. [orig. unkn.]

stability /stəˈbɪlɪtɪ/ *n.* being stable. [as STABLE[1]]

stabilize /ˈsteɪbɪlaɪz/ *v.t./i.* to make or become stable. —**stabilization** /-ˈzeɪʃ(ə)n/ *n.* [f. STABLE[1]]

stabilizer *n.* a device to keep a ship, aircraft, or child's bicycle steady. [f. prec.]

stable[1] /ˈsteɪb(ə)l/ *adj.* firmly fixed or established, not easily moved or changed or destroyed or decomposed; resolute, constant. [f. AF f. L *stabilis* (*stare* stand)]

stable[2] /ˈsteɪb(ə)l/ *n.* **1** a building in which horses are kept. **2** a place where racehorses are kept and trained; the racehorses of a particular stable. **3** persons or products etc.

having a common origin or affiliation; such an origin or affiliation. —*v.t.* to put or keep (a horse) in a stable. —**stable-companion** *or* **-mate** *n.* a horse of the same stable; a member of the same organization. —**stably** *adv.* [f. OF f. L *stabulum* n. (*stare* stand)]

stabling /ˈsteɪb(ə)lɪŋ/ *n.* accommodation for horses. [f. prec.]

staccato /stəˈkɑːtəʊ/ *adj.* & *adv.* (esp. *Mus.*) in a sharp disconnected manner, not running on smoothly. [It., p.p. of *staccare* (as DETACH)]

stack *n.* **1** a pile or heap, especially in an orderly arrangement. **2** a haystack. **3** (*colloq.*) a large quantity. **4** a chimney-stack; a tall factory chimney; a chimney or funnel for smoke on a steamer etc.; a tall steel structure from which unwanted gas produced in association with oil is burnt off. **5** a stacked group of aircraft. **6** a library's store of books to which readers do not usually have direct access. **7** a high detached rock, especially off the coast of Scotland. —*v.t.* **1** to pile in a stack or stacks. **2** to arrange (cards) secretly for cheating; to manipulate (circumstances etc.) to one's advantage. **3** to cause (aircraft) to fly round the same point at different levels while waiting to land. [f. ON *stakkr* haystack]

stadium /ˈsteɪdɪəm/ *n.* an enclosed athletic or sports ground with tiers of seats for spectators. [L f. Gk *stadion*]

staff *n.* **1** a stick or pole used as a weapon, support, or measuring-stick, or as a symbol of office. **2** a body of officers assisting a commanding officer and concerned with an army, regiment, or fleet etc. as a whole. **3** a group of persons by whom a business is carried on; those responsible to a manager or other person in authority. **4** persons in authority within an organization (as distinct from pupils etc.); those engaged in administrative as distinct from manual work. **5** (*pl.* also **staves**) (*Mus.*) the set of usually five parallel lines to indicate the pitch of notes by position —*v.t.* to provide (an institution etc.) with a staff. —**staff college,** a college where officers are trained for staff duties. **staff nurse,** a nurse ranking just below a sister. **staff officer,** a member of a military staff. [OE]

Staffs. *abbr.* Staffordshire.

stag *n.* **1** a male deer. **2** a person who seeks to buy new shares and sell at once for profit. —**stag-beetle** *n.* a beetle of the family Lucanidae with branched mandibles like antlers. **stag-party** *n.* a party for men only. [perh. orig. = male animal in its prime (cf. ON *staggr* male bird)]

stage *n.* **1** a point or period in the course of a development or process. **2** a platform, especially a raised one on which plays etc. are performed before an audience. **3** the acting or theatrical profession; dramatic art or literature. **4** a scene of action. **5** a regular stopping-place on a route; the distance between two of these. **6** a section of a space-rocket with a separate means of propulsion. —*v.t.* **1** to present (a play etc.) on the stage. **2** to organize and carry out. —**stage direction,** an instruction in a play about an actor's movement, the sounds to be heard, etc. **stage fright,** nervousness on facing an audience, especially for the first time. **stage-hand** *n.* a person handling scenery etc. in a theatre. **stage-manage** *v.t.* to be the stage-manager of; to arrange and control for effect. **stage-manager** *n.* the person responsible for lighting and mechanical arrangements etc. on a stage. **stage-struck** *adj.* strongly wishing to be an actor or actress. **stage whisper,** an aside, a loud whisper meant to be heard by others than the person addressed. [f. OF *estage* ult. f. L *stare* stand]

stage-coach *n.* a large horse-drawn closed coach that formerly ran regularly by stages between two places.

stagecraft *n.* skill or experience in writing or staging plays.

stager *n.* (esp. **old stager**) an experienced person. [f. STAGE]

stagflation /stægˈfleɪʃ(ə)n/ *n.* a state of inflation without a corresponding increase of demand and employment. [f. STAGNATION + INFLATION]

stagger *v.t./i.* **1** to walk or move unsteadily; to cause to do this. **2** (of news etc.) to shock or confuse (a person). **3** to arrange (events or hours of work etc.) so that they do not coincide. **4** to arrange (objects) so that they are not in line. —*n.* a staggering movement; (in *pl.*) a disease, especially of horses and cattle, causing staggering. [f. ON (*staka* push, stagger)]

staggering *adj.* astonishing, bewildering. [f. prec.]

staghound *n.* a large hound used in hunting deer.

staging /ˈsteɪdʒɪŋ/ *n.* **1** the presentation of a play etc. **2** a platform or support, especially a temporary one; shelves for plants in a greenhouse. —**staging post,** a regular stopping-place, especially on an air route. [f. STAGE]

stagnant /ˈstægnənt/ *adj.* **1** (of water etc.) motionless, not flowing, still and stale. **2** showing no activity. —**stagnancy** *n.* [as foll.]

stagnate /stægˈneɪt/ *v.i.* to be or become stagnant. —**stagnation** *n.* [f. L *stagnare* (*stagnum* pool)]

stagy /ˈsteɪdʒɪ/ *adj.* theatrical in style or manner. [f. STAGE]

staid *adj*. of quiet and sober character or demeanour, sedate. [= *stayed*, p.p. of STAY[1]]

stain *v.t.* **1** to discolour or be discoloured by the action of a liquid sinking in. **2** to spoil or damage (a reputation or character etc.). **3** to colour (wood or glass etc.) with a substance that penetrates the material; to treat (a microscopic specimen) with a colouring agent. —*n*. **1** an act or the result of staining. **2** a blot or blemish. **3** damage to a reputation etc. **4** a substance used in staining. —**stained glass,** pieces of glass, either dyed or superficially coloured, set in a framework (usually of lead) to form decorative or pictorial designs. [f. earlier *distain* f. OF *desteindre* (as DIS-, TINGE)]

stainless *adj*. **1** without stains. **2** not liable to stain. —**stainless steel,** steel containing much chromium, that does not rust or tarnish under oxidizing conditions because it is protected by the film of oxide which forms on its surface. [f. STAIN + -LESS]

stair *n*. each of a set of fixed indoor steps; (in *pl*.) a set of these. —**stair-rod** *n*. a rod for securing a carpet in the angle between two steps. [OE]

staircase *n*. a flight of stairs and the supporting structure; the part of a building containing this.

stairway *n*. a flight of stairs; the way up this.

stake *n*. **1** a stout stick pointed at one end for driving into the ground as a support or marker etc.; (*hist*.) a post to which a person was tied to be burnt alive; this death as a punishment. **2** the money etc. wagered on an event. **3** an interest or concern, especially financial. **4** (in *pl*.) the money offered as the prize in a horse-race; the race itself. —*v.t.* **1** to secure or support with stakes. **2** to mark (an area) with stakes. **3** to establish (a claim). **4** to wager (money etc. *on* an event). **5** (*US colloq*.) to give financial or other support to. —**at stake,** wagered, risked, to be won or lost. **stake out,** to place under surveillance. [OE]

stakeholder *n*. a third party with whom money etc. wagered is deposited.

Stakhanovite /stəˈkɑːnəvaɪt/ *n*. one who is exceptionally hard-working and productive. —**Stakhanovism** *n*. [f. A. G. *Stakhanov*, Russian coal-miner (d. 1977), who in 1935 produced a phenomenal amount of coal by a combination of new methods and great energy]

stalactite /ˈstæləktaɪt/ *n*. an icicle-like deposit of calcium carbonate hanging from the roof of a cave etc. [f. Gk *stalaktos* dripping (*stalassō* drip)]

stalagmite /ˈstæləgmaɪt/ *n*. a deposit like a stalactite rising like a spike from the floor of a cave etc. [f. Gk *stalagma* a dripping (as prec.)]

stale *adj*. **1** not fresh; musty, insipid, or otherwise the worse for age or use; trite or unoriginal. **2** (of an athlete or musician etc.) having his ability impaired by excessive exertion or practice. —*v.t./i.* to make or become stale. —**stalely** *adv*., **staleness** *n*. [perh. f. AF *estaler* come to a standstill]

stalemate *n*. **1** the state of a chess-game counting as a draw, in which one player cannot move without going into check. **2** a deadlock in proceedings. —*v.t.* **1** to bring (a player) to a stalemate. **2** to bring a deadlock. [f. obs. *stale* in same sense (prob. f. AF *estale* position) + MATE[2]]

stalk[1] /stɔːk/ *n*. a stem, especially the main stem of a herbaceous plant or the slender stem supporting a leaf or flower or fruit etc.; a similar support of an organ etc. in animals. [prob. dim. of *stale* rung of ladder (OE)]

stalk[2] /stɔːk/ *v.t./i.* **1** to pursue or approach (a wild animal or an enemy etc.) stealthily. **2** to stride, to walk in a stately or imposing manner. —*n*. **1** a stalking of game. **2** an imposing gait. —**stalking-horse** *n*. a horse behind which a hunter hides; a pretext concealing one's real intentions or actions. —**stalker** *n*. [f. OE prob. rel. to STEAL]

stall[1] /stɔːl/ *n*. **1** a stable or cowhouse; a compartment for one animal in this. **2** a trader's booth in a market etc. **3** a fixed seat in a choir or chancel, more or less enclosed at the back and sides. **4** (usu. in *pl*.) each of the seats on the ground floor of a theatre. **5** a compartment for one person in a shower-bath, one horse at the start of a race, etc. **6** the stalling of an engine or aircraft; the condition resulting from this. —*v.t./i.* **1** (of a motor vehicle or its engine) to stop because of inadequate fuel-supply or overloading of the engine etc.; (of an aircraft) to get out of control because its speed is insufficient. **2** to cause (an engine etc.) to stall. **3** to put or keep (cattle etc.) in a stall or stalls. [OE]

stall[2] /stɔːl/ *v.t./i.* to play for time when being questioned etc.; to delay or obstruct (a person). [f. *stall* pickpocket's confederate, orig. = decoy, f. AF *estale* (as STALEMATE)]

stallion /ˈstæljən/ *n*. an uncastrated male horse. [f. OF *estalon* (as STALL[1])]

stalwart /ˈstɔːlwət/ *adj*. **1** strongly built, sturdy. **2** courageous; strong and faithful; resolute. —*n*. a stalwart person, especially a loyal uncompromising partisan. [OE, = place-worthy]

stamen /ˈsteɪmen/ *n*. the male fertilizing organ of a flowering plant. [L, lit. = warp-thread]

stamina /ˈstæmɪnə/ *n*. ability to endure prolonged physical or mental strain. [L, pl. of prec.]

stammer *v.t./i.* to speak with halting articulation, especially with pauses or rapid repetitions of the same syllable; to utter (words) thus. —*n.* an act or the habit of stammering. —**stammerer** *n.* [OE]

stamp *v.t./i.* **1** to bring down (one's foot) heavily on the ground etc.; to crush or flatten thus; to walk with heavy steps. **2** to impress (a pattern or mark etc.) on a surface; to impress (a surface) with a pattern or mark etc. **3** to affix a postage or other stamp to. **4** to assign a specific character to; to mark out. —*n.* **1** an instrument for stamping things. **2** a mark or design made by this. **3** (in full **postage stamp**) a small adhesive piece of paper showing the amount paid, affixed to letters etc. to be posted; a piece of paper impressed with an official mark as evidence of payment of a tax or fee, for affixing to a licence or deed etc.; a similar decorative device sold in aid of a charity. **4** a mark impressed on or a label etc. fixed to a commodity as evidence of its quality etc. **5** an act or sound of stamping of the foot. **6** a characteristic mark or quality. —**stamp-collector**, *n.* one who collects postage stamps as a hobby. **stamp-duty** *n.* a duty imposed on certain kinds of legal document. **stamping-ground** *n.* a favourite place of resort or action. **stamp on,** to impress on (the memory etc.); to suppress. **stamp out,** to produce by cutting out with a die etc.; to put an end to, to destroy. [= OHG *stampfōn* to pound (rel. to STEP)]

stampede /stæm'pi:d/ *n.* a sudden hurried rush of cattle or people etc., especially in fright; an uncontrolled or unreasoning action by a large number of people. —*v.t./i.* to take part in a stampede; to cause to do this. [f. Sp. *estampida* (rel. to prec.)]

stance /stɑ:ns, stæns/ *n.* **1** an attitude or position of the body. **2** a standpoint, an attitude. [F f. It., = STANZA]

stanch /stɑ:ntʃ/ *v.t.* to stop the flow of (blood) etc.); to stop the flow from (a wound). [f. OF *estanchier*]

stanchion /'stɑ:nʃ(ə)n/ *n.* an upright post or support; a device for confining cattle in a stall etc. [f. AF (as STANCE)]

stand *v.t./i.* (*past* & *p.p.* **stood** /stʊd/) **1** to have, take, or maintain an upright position, especially on the feet or a base. **2** to be situated. **3** to place, to set upright. **4** to be of a specified height. **5** to remain firm or valid, or in a specified condition. **6** to move to and remain in a specified position; to take a specified attitude (*lit.* or *fig.*); (of ships) to hold a specified course. **7** to maintain a position; to avoid falling, moving, or being moved; to remain stationary or unused. **8** to undergo; to endure or tolerate. **9** to provide at one's own expense. **10** to act as. —*n.* **1** a standing or stationary condition. **2** a position taken up, an attitude adopted (*lit.* or *fig.*). **3** resistance to attack or compulsion. **4** a rack or pedestal etc. on which something may be placed. **5** a table, booth, or other (often temporary) structure on which things are exhibited or sold. **6** a standing-place for vehicles. **7** a raised structure for persons to sit or stand on, e.g. at a sports ground. **8** (*US*) a witness-box. **9** a halt made by a touring-company etc. to give a performance or performances. **10** (in cricket) a prolonged stay at the wicket by two batsmen. **11** a group of growing trees etc. —**as it stands,** in its present condition; in the present circumstances. **stand by,** to stand ready for action; to stand near; to look without interfering; to uphold or support (a person); to adhere to (a promise etc.). **stand-by** *n.* (*pl.* **-bys**) a person or thing ready if needed in an emergency etc.; (esp. *attrib.*) a system of allocating spare seats on an aircraft to passengers who have not booked in advance. **stand corrected,** to accept that one was wrong. **stand down,** to withdraw from a position or candidacy. **stand for,** to represent; to be a candidate for (esp. public office); (*colloq.*) to tolerate. **stand one's ground,** not to yield. **stand in,** to deputize. **stand-in** *n.* a deputy or substitute, especially for a principal film actor or actress while the cameras and lighting for a scene are set. **stand off,** to move or keep away; to dispense temporarily with the services of (an employee). **stand-off half,** a half-back in Rugby football who forms a link between the scrum-half and the three-quarters. **stand-offish** *adj.* cold or distant in manner. **stand on,** to insist on, to observe scrupulously. **stand on one's own (two) feet,** to be self-reliant or independent. **stand out,** to be prominent or outstanding; to persist in resistance or support. **stand to,** to stand ready for action; to abide by; to be likely or certain to. **stand to reason,** to be obvious or logical. **stand up,** to come to or remain in or place in a standing position; to be valid; (*colloq.*) to fail to keep an appointment with. **stand-up** *adj.* (of a meal) eaten standing; (of a fight) violent and thorough; (of a collar) upright, not turned down. **stand up for,** to defend or support, to side with. **stand up to,** to face (an opponent) courageously; to be resistant to the harmful effects of (use or wear etc.). **take one's stand,** to base an argument or reliance (*on*). [OE]

standard /'stændəd/ *n.* **1** an object, quality, or specification serving as an example or principle to which others should conform or by which others are judged. **2** a required or specified level of excellence etc. **3** the average quality; the ordinary design or procedure etc. without added or novel features. **4** a distinctive flag. **5** an upright support or pipe.

6 a treelike shrub with (or grafted on) an upright stem. —*adj.* **1** serving or used as a standard. **2** having a recognized and permanent value, authoritative. **3** of normal or prescribed quality or size etc.; (of language) conforming to established educated usage. —**standard-bearer** *n.* a person who carries a distinctive flag; a prominent leader in a cause. **standard lamp,** a domestic lamp on a tall upright with a base. **standard of living,** the degree of material comfort enjoyed by a person or group. **standard time,** that established in a country or region by law or custom and based on the longitude. [f. AF (as EXTEND), in some senses infl. by prec.]

standardize *v.t.* to cause to conform to a standard. —**standardization** /-ˈzeɪʃ(ə)n/ *n.* [f. prec.]

standee /stænˈdiː/ *n.* (*colloq.*) one who stands, especially when all seats are occupied. [f. STAND]

standing *n.* **1** status; esteem, high repute. **2** past duration. —*adj.* **1** that stands, upright; (of corn) not yet harvested. **2** (of a jump or start) performed from rest without a run-up. **3** permanent, remaining effective or valid. **4** (of water) not flowing. —**standing joke,** an object of permanent ridicule. **standing order,** an instruction to a banker to make regular payments, or to a newsagent etc. for the regular supply of a periodical etc. **standing orders,** the rules governing procedure in Parliament or a council etc. **standing room,** space to stand in. [f. STAND]

standpipe *n.* a vertical pipe for fluid to rise in, e.g. to provide a water supply outside or at a distance from buildings.

standpoint *n.* a point of view.

standstill *n.* a stoppage, inability to proceed.

stank *past* of STINK.

Stannaries /ˈstænərɪz/ *n.pl.* the tin-mining district of Cornwall and Devon. —**Stannary court,** a lawcourt for the regulation of tin-mines in the Stannaries. [f. L (*stannum* tin)]

stanza /ˈstænzə/ *n.* a group of lines (usually four or more rhymed) as a repeated metrical unit. [It., orig. = standing-place, f. L *stare* stand]

staphylococcus /stæfɪləˈkɒkəs/ *n.* (*pl.* **-cocci** /-iː/) a form of pus-producing bacterium. —**staphylococcal** *adj.* [f. Gk *staphulē* bunch of grapes + *kokkos* berry]

staple[1] /ˈsteɪp(ə)l/ *n.* **1** a U-shaped metal bar or piece of wire with pointed ends, driven into wood etc. to hold something in place. **2** a piece of metal or wire driven into sheets of paper etc. and clenched to fasten them together. —*v.t.* to fasten or furnish with a staple.—**stapler** *n.* [OE, = OHG *staffal* foundation, ON *stöpull* pillar]

staple[2] /ˈsteɪp(ə)l/ *adj.* principal, standard; important as a product or export. —*n.* **1** an important (usually principal) article of commerce in a district or country. **2** a chief element or material. **3** the fibre of cotton or wool etc. as determining its quality. [f. OF *estaple* market f. MLG or MDu. (as prec.)]

star *n.* **1** a celestial body appearing as a luminous point in the night sky; a large self-luminous gaseous ball such as the sun; a celestial body regarded as influencing a person's fortunes etc. **2** a thing resembling a star in shape or appearance; a figure or object with radiating points, e.g. as a decoration or mark of rank, or showing a category of excellence. **3** a famous or brilliant person, especially an actor, actress, or other performer; a principal performer in a play or film etc. —*v.t./i.* **(-rr-) 1** to mark or adorn (as) with a star or stars. **2** to present or perform as a star actor etc. —**star-dust** *n.* a multitude of stars looking like dust. **star-gazer** *n.* (*colloq.*) an astronomer or astrologer. **Star of David,** a six-pointed star made of two interlaced equilateral triangles, used as the symbol of Judaism and of the State of Israel. **star-studded** *adj.* covered with stars; including many famous actors etc. **star turn,** the main item in an entertainment etc. [OE]

starboard /ˈstɑːbəd/ *n.* the right-hand side of a ship or aircraft looking forward. —*v.t.* to turn (the helm) to starboard. —**starboard tack,** a tack with the wind on the starboard side. [OE (as STEER[1], BOARD)]

starch *n.* **1** a white carbohydrate that is an important element in human food, found in cereals, potatoes, and all other plants except fungi. **2** a preparation of this for stiffening linen etc. **3** stiffness of manner, formality. —*v.t.* to stiffen (as) with starch. [cf. OHG *sterken* stiffen (as STARK)]

starchy *adj.* **1** of or like starch; containing much starch. **2** stiff and formal in manner. —**starchily** *adv.*, **starchiness** *n.* [f. STARCH]

stardom *n.* the position or fame of a star actor etc. [f. STAR]

stare *v.t./i.* to look fixedly with the eyes wide open, especially with curiosity, surprise, or horror; to reduce (a person) to a specified condition by staring. —*n.* a staring gaze. —**stare a person in the face,** to be clearly evident or imminent. [OE]

starfish *n.* a star-shaped sea creature of the class Asteroidea.

stark *adj.* **1** desolate, bare; cheerless. **2** sharply evident. **3** downright, complete. **4** completely naked. **5** (*archaic*) stiff, rigid. —*adv.* completely, wholly. —**starkly** *adv.*, **starkness** *n.* [OE]

starlet /ˈstɑ:lɪt/ *n*. a young film actress likely to become a star. [f. STAR + -LET]

starlight *n*. light from the stars.

starling /ˈstɑ:lɪŋ/ *n*. a noisy bird (*Sturnus vulgaris*) with glossy blackish speckled feathers, that forms large flocks. [OE]

starlit *adj*. lighted by stars; with stars visible.

starry *adj*. full of or bright with stars. —**starry-eyed** *adj*. (*colloq*.) bright-eyed, romantic but unpractical. [f. STAR]

start *v.t./i*. **1** to set in motion or action; to begin or cause to begin operating. **2** to cause or enable to begin; to establish or found; to conceive (a baby). **3** to begin a journey etc. **4** to make a sudden movement from pain or surprise etc. **5** to spring suddenly. **6** to rouse (game etc.) from a lair. **7** (of timber etc.) to become loose or displaced; to cause (timber) to do this. —*n*. **1** the beginning; the place where a race is begun. **2** an advantage granted in beginning a race; an advantageous initial position in life or business etc. **3** a sudden movement of pain or surprise etc. —**for a start**, as a thing to start with. **starting-block** *n*. a shaped block against which a runner braces his feet at the start of a race. **starting-price** *n*. the final odds before the start of a horse-race etc. **start off**, to begin; to start to move. **start out**, to begin; to begin a journey. **start up**, to rise suddenly; to come or bring into existence or action. [cf. OHG *sturzen* overthrow, rush]

starter *n*. **1** a device for starting the engine of a motor vehicle etc. **2** a person giving the signal for the start of a race. **3** a horse or competitor starting in a race. **4** the first course of a meal. [f. START]

startle *v.t*. to give a shock or surprise to. [OE (as START)]

starve *v.t./i*. **1** to die of hunger or suffer acutely from lack of food, to cause to do this; (*colloq*.) to feel very hungry or very cold. **2** to be deprived or short of something needed or wanted; to cause to be in this position. **3** to compel by starving. —**starvation** /-ˈveɪʃ(ə)n/ *n*. [OE, = die]

starveling /ˈstɑ:vlɪŋ/ *n*. a starving person or animal. [f. prec.]

stash *v.t*. (*slang*) to conceal, to stow. —*n*. (*slang*) **1** a hiding-place. **2** a thing hidden. [orig. unkn.]

stasis /ˈsteɪsɪs, ˈstæ-/ *n*. (*pl*. **stases** /-i:z/) a stoppage of flow or circulation. [Gk, = standing]

state *n*. **1** the quality of a person's or thing's characteristics or circumstances. **2** (*colloq*.) an excited or agitated condition of mind. **3** (often **State**) an organized community under one government or forming part of a federal republic; civil government. **4** pomp. —*adj*. of or concerned with the State or its ceremonial occasions. —*v.t*. **1** to express in speech or writing. **2** to fix or specify. **3** (*Mus*.) to play (a theme etc.), especially for the first time. —**in** *or* **into a fixed state**, in or into an excited or anxious or untidy condition. **lie in state**, to be laid in a public place of honour before burial. **State Department**, the department of foreign affairs in the government of the USA. **State Enrolled Nurse**, a nurse enrolled on a State register and having a qualification lower than that of a State Registered Nurse. **state of play**, the position in which a matter or business stands at a particular time. **State Registered Nurse**, a nurse enrolled on a State register and more highly qualified than a State Enrolled Nurse. **the States**, the USA. [f. ESTATE and f. L *status* standing]

statehood *n*. the condition of being a State. [f. STATE + -HOOD]

stateless *adj*. having no nationality or citizenship. [f. STATE + -LESS]

stately *adj*. dignified, imposing. —**stately home**, a large grand house, especially one of historical interest. —**stateliness** *n*. [f. STATE]

statement /ˈsteɪtmənt/ *n*. **1** stating, being stated. **2** expression in words; a thing stated. **3** a formal account of facts, especially of transactions in a bank account or of the amount due to a tradesman. [f. STATE]

stateroom *n*. **1** a state apartment. **2** a private compartment in a passenger ship.

statesman *n*. (*pl*. **-men**) a person skilled in affairs of State; a sagacious far-sighted politician. —**statesmanlike** *adj*., **statesmanship** *n*., **stateswoman** *n.fem*.

static /ˈstætɪk/ *adj*. **1** stationary; not movable; not acting, not changing. **2** concerned with bodies at rest or forces in equilibrium; of force acting by weight without motion (opp. *dynamic*). —*n*. **1** static electricity. **2** atmospherics. —**static electricity**, electricity present in a body and not flowing as current. —**statically** *adv*. [f. Gk *statikos* (*sta-* stand)]

statics *n.pl*. (usu. treated as *sing*.) **1** the science of static bodies or forces. **2** static. [f. prec.]

station /ˈsteɪʃ(ə)n/ *n*. **1** a place or building etc. where a person or thing stands or is placed or where a particular activity, especially a public service, is based or organized. **2** a regular stopping-place on a railway line; the buildings at this. **3** an establishment engaged in broadcasting. **4** a military or naval base; the inhabitants of this. **5** position in life, rank or status. **6** (*Austral*.) a large sheep-farm or cattle-farm. —*v.t*. to assign a station to; to put in position. —**station manager** *or* **-master** *n*. the official in charge of a railway station. **station-wagon** *n*. (*US*) an estate car. [f. OF f. L *statio* (*stare* stand)]

stationary /ˈsteɪʃənərɪ/ *adj.* not moving; not intended to be moved; not changing in amount or quantity. [f. L (as prec.)]

stationer /ˈsteɪʃənə(r)/ *n.* a dealer in stationery. [as prec. in L sense 'shopkeeper' as opp. pedlar]

stationery /ˈsteɪʃənərɪ/ *n.* writing materials, office supplies, etc. —**Stationery Office,** the government publishing-house in the UK. [f. prec.]

statistic /stəˈtɪstɪk/ *n.* a statistical fact or item. [f. G (as STATE)]

statistical /stəˈtɪstɪk(ə)l/ *adj.* of or concerned with statistics. —**statistical inference,** the science of drawing reliable conclusions from apparently random collections of numerical data, and of estimating the probability of the truth of those conclusions. —**statistically** *adv.* [f. prec.]

statistics /stəˈtɪstɪks/ *n.pl.* **1** numerical data systematically collected. **2** (usu. treated as *sing.*) the art of organizing numerical data so as to exhibit what is significant, especially the norm and deviations from it. —**statistician** /stætɪˈstɪʃ(ə)n/ *n.* [f. STATISTIC]

statuary /ˈstætjʊərɪ/ *adj.* of or for statues. —*n.* **1** statues; the making of these. **2** a maker of statues. [f. L (as foll.)]

statue /ˈstætju:, -tʃu:/ *n.* a sculptured, moulded, or cast figure of a person or animal etc., usually of life size or larger. [f. OF f. L *statua* (*stare* stand)]

statuesque /stætjʊˈesk, stætʃ-/ *adj.* like a statue in size, dignity, or stillness. —**statuesquely** *adv.*, **statuesqueness** *n.* [f. prec.]

statuette /stætjʊˈet, stætʃ-/ *n.* a small statue. [f. STATUE + -ETTE]

stature /ˈstætjə(r), -tʃə(r)/ *n.* **1** the natural height of the body. **2** greatness gained by ability or achievement. [f. OF f. L *statura* (as STATUE)]

status /ˈsteɪtəs/ *n.* **1** a person's position or rank in relation to others; a person's or thing's legal position. **2** high rank or prestige. —**status quo,** the state of affairs as it is or as it was before a recent change. **status symbol,** a possession or activity etc. regarded as evidence of a person's high status. [L, = standing (as STATION]

statute /ˈstætju:t/ *n.* **1** a law passed by a legislative body. **2** a rule of an institution. —**statute-book** *n.* the statute law; a book or books containing this. **statute law,** a statute; statutes collectively. **statute mile,** 1760 yds., about 1.6 km. [f. OF f. L (*statuere* set up, as prec.)]

statutory /ˈstætjʊtərɪ/ *adj.* enacted or required by statute. —**statutorily** *adv.* [f. prec.]

staunch /stɔ:ntʃ/ *adj.* **1** firm in attitude, opinion, or loyalty. **2** (of a ship or joint etc.) watertight, airtight. —**staunchly** *adv.* [f. OF *estanche*]

stave *n.* **1** each of the curved pieces of wood forming the sides of a cask or pail etc. **2** (*Mus.*) a staff. **3** a stanza, a verse. —*v.t.* (*past* & *p.p.* **stove** or **staved**) to break a hole in; to knock out of shape. —**stave in,** to crush by forcing inwards. **stave off,** to avert or defer (danger or misfortune etc.). [var. of STAFF]

staves see STAFF.

stay[1] *v.t./i.* **1** to continue to be in the same place or condition, not to depart or change. **2** to dwell temporarily, especially as a guest or visitor. **3** to stop or pause in movement, action, or speech; to cause to do this. **4** to postpone (judgement etc.). **5** to assuage (hunger etc.) especially for a short time. **6** to show endurance. —*n.* **1** an action or period of staying. **2** suspension or postponement of the execution of a sentence etc. —**stay-at-home** *adj.* remaining habitually at home; (*n.*) a person who does this. **stay the course,** to endure a struggle etc. to the end. **stay in,** to remain indoors. **staying-power** *n.* endurance. **stay the night,** to remain until the next day. **stay put,** (*colloq.*) to remain where it is placed or where one is. [f. AF *estai-* f. L *stare* stand]

stay[2] *n.* **1** a prop or support. **2** a rope etc. supporting a mast or flagstaff etc. **3** a tie-piece in an aircraft. **4** (in *pl.*) a corset. [OE]

stayer *n.* a person or animal with great endurance. [f. STAY[1]]

staysail /ˈsteɪseɪl, -s(ə)l/ *n.* a sail extended on a stay.

STD *abbr.* subscriber trunk dialling.

stead /sted/ *n.* **in a person's** *or* **thing's stead,** instead of him or her or it; as a substitute. **stand in good stead,** to be advantageous or serviceable to (a person). [OE (as STAND)]

steadfast /ˈstedfɑ:st/ *adj.* firm and not changing or yielding. —**steadfastly** *adv.*, **steadfastness** *n.* [OE (as prec. + FAST[1])]

steady /ˈstedɪ/ *adj.* **1** firmly in position, not tottering or rocking or wavering. **2** done, operating, or happening in a uniform and regular manner. **3** constant in mind or conduct. **4** serious and dependable in character. —*v.t./i.* to make or become steady. —*adv.* steadily. —*n.* (*colloq.*) a regular boy-friend or girl-friend. —**go steady with,** (*colloq.*) to have as a regular boy-friend or girl-friend. **steady on!** be careful! —**steadily** *adv.*, **steadiness** *n.* [f. STEAD]

steak /steɪk/ *n.* **1** a thick slice of meat (especially beef) or fish, cut for grilling or frying. **2** beef from the front of the animal, cut for stewing or braising. —**steak-house,** *n.* a restaurant specializing in beef-steaks. [f. ON, rel. to *stikna* be roasted]

steal *v.t./i.* (*past* **stole**; *p.p.* **stolen**) **1** to take (another's property) illegally or without permission, esp. secretly. **2** to obtain surreptitiously or by surprise; to gain insidiously or artfully etc. **3** to move or come silently or gradually. —*n.* (*US colloq.*) **1** stealing, theft. **2** an (unexpectedly) easy task or good bargain. —**steal a march on,** to gain an advantage over by acting surreptitiously or anticipating. **steal a person's thunder,** see THUNDER. **steal the show,** to outshine the other performers unexpectedly. [OE]

stealth /stelθ/ *n.* secrecy, secret or surreptitious behaviour. [as prec.]

stealthy /ˈstelθɪ/ *adj.* acting or done by stealth. —**stealthily** *adv.*, **stealthiness** *n.* [f. prec.]

steam *n.* **1** the invisible gas into which water is changed by boiling, used as motive power. **2** the visible vapour that forms when steam condenses in the air. **3** (*colloq.*) energy, power. —*v.t./i.* **1** to give out steam. **2** to cook or treat by steam. **3** to move by the power of steam; (*colloq.*) to work or move vigorously or rapidly. **steam-engine** *n.* a locomotive or stationary engine driven by steam. —**steam-hammer** *n.* a forging-hammer worked by steam. **steam iron,** an electric iron emitting steam from its flat surface. **steam radio,** (*colloq.*) radio broadcasting regarded as antiquated by comparison with television. **steam train,** a train pulled by a steam-engine. **steam up,** to cover or become covered with condensed steam. **be** *or* **get steamed up,** to be or become excited or agitated. [OE]

steamboat *n.* a steam-driven boat, especially a paddle-wheel craft used widely on rivers in the 19th c.

steamer *n.* **1** a steamship. **2** a container for steaming food etc. [f. STEAM]

steamroller *n.* **1** a heavy slow-moving locomotive with a roller, used in road-making. **2** a crushing power or force. —*v.t.* to crush or move along (as) with a steamroller.

steamship *n.* a steam-driven ship.

steamy *adj.* **1** of, like, or full of steam. **2** (*colloq.*) erotic. —**steamily** *adv.*, **steaminess** *n.* [f. STEAM]

steatite /ˈstiːətaɪt/ *n.* a kind of usually grey talc with a greasy feel. [f. L f. Gk (*stear* tallow)]

steed *n.* (*literary*) a horse. [OE *stēda* stallion, rel. to STUD²]

steel *n.* **1** a malleable alloy of iron and carbon capable of being tempered to many different degrees of hardness. **2** a steel rod for sharpening knives. **3** (*literary;* not in *pl.*) a sword. **4** great strength or firmness. —*adj.* of or like steel. —*v.t.* to harden or make resolute. —**steel band,** a band of musicians who play music (chiefly calypso-style) on steel drums. **steel wool,** fine shavings of steel massed together for use as an abrasive. [OE]

steely *adj.* of or like steel; inflexibly severe. —**steeliness** *n.* [f. STEEL]

steelyard *n.* a weighing-apparatus with a graduated arm along which a weight slides.

steep¹ *adj.* **1** sloping sharply, hard to climb. **2** (of a rise or fall) rapid; **3** (*colloq.*) exorbitant, unreasonable; exaggerated, incredible. —*n.* a steep slope, a precipice. —**steeply** *adv.*, **steepness** *n.* [OE, rel. to STOOP¹]

steep² *v.t.* to soak or bathe in a liquid. —*n.* **1** the action of steeping. **2** a liquid for steeping things in. —**steep in,** to pervade or imbue with; to make deeply acquainted with (a subject etc.). [rel. to STOUP]

steepen *v.t./i.* to make or become steep. [f. STEEP¹]

steeple *n.* a tall tower, especially one surmounted by a spire, above the roof of a church. [OE (as STEEP¹)]

steeplechase *n.* **1** a horse-race across a tract of country or on a racecourse with hedges, ditches, etc., to jump. **2** a cross-country foot-race. —**steeplechasing** *n.* the sport of riding in steeplechases. —**steeplechaser** *n.*

steeplejack *n.* a person who climbs steeples, tall chimneys, etc., to repair them.

steer¹ *v.t./i.* **1** to direct the course of; to guide (a vehicle or boat etc.) by means of its mechanism. **2** to be able to be steered. —**steer clear of,** to take care to avoid. **steering-column** *n.* the column on which a steering-wheel is mounted. **steering committee,** a committee deciding the order of business, the general course of operations, etc. **steering-wheel** *n.* the wheel by which a vehicle, vessel, etc., is steered. —**steerer** *n.* [OE]

steer² *n.* a young male ox, especially a bullock. [OE]

steerage *n.* **1** steering. **2** (*obs.*) the part of a ship assigned to passengers travelling at the cheapest rate. [f. STEER¹]

steersman *n.* (*pl.* **-men**) one who steers a ship.

stein /staɪn/ *n.* a large earthenware mug, especially for beer. [G, = stone]

stela /ˈstiːlə/ *n.* (also **stele** /-iː/; *pl.* **stelae** /-iː/) an ancient upright slab or pillar, usually inscribed and sculptured, especially as a gravestone. [L f. Gk *stēlē* standing block]

stellar /ˈstelə(r)/ *adj.* of a star or stars. [f. L (*stella* star)]

stem¹ *n.* **1** the main central part (usually above the ground) of a tree, shrub, or plant; a slender part supporting a fruit, flower, or leaf. **2** any stem-shaped part, e.g. the slender part of a wineglass between bowl and foot. **3** the root or main part of a noun or verb etc., to which case-endings etc. are added. **4** the curved upright timber or metal piece at the fore end of a ship; a ship's bows. —*v.i.* (**-mm-**)

1 (with *from*) to originate. **2** to make headway against (the tide etc.). [OE]

stem[2] *v.t./i.* **(-mm-) 1** to restrain the flow of (*lit.* or *fig.*), to dam. **2** (in skiing) to retard oneself by forcing the heel outwards. —*n.* (in skiing) the act of stemming. —**stem-turn** *n.* a turn made by stemming with one ski. [f. ON; cf. STAMMER]

stench *n.* a foul smell. [OE *stenc* (any) smell (cf. STINK)]

stencil /ˈstens(ə)l/ *n.* a thin sheet in which a pattern is cut, used to produce a corresponding pattern on the surface beneath it by applying ink or paint etc.; a pattern so produced. —*v.t.* **(-ll-)** to produce (a pattern) with a stencil; to mark (a surface) thus. [orig. = ornament, f. OF *estanceler* cover with stars f. L *scintilla* spark]

stenography /steˈnɒgrəfɪ/ *n.* the writing of shorthand. —**stenographer** *n.* [f. Gk *stenos* narrow + -GRAPHY]

stentorian /stenˈtɔːrɪən/ *adj.* (of a voice etc.) loud and powerful. [f. Gk *Stentōr*, herald in Trojan War]

step *n.* **1** a complete action of moving and placing one leg in walking or running; the distance covered by this; a unit of movement in dancing. **2** a measure taken, especially one of several in a course of action. **3** a surface on which the foot is placed in ascending or descending, a stair or tread; (in *pl.*) a step-ladder. **4** a short distance. **5** a mark or sound made by a foot in walking etc.; a manner of stepping. **6** a stage in a scale of promotion or precedence etc. —*v.t./i.* **(-pp-) 1** to lift and set down the foot or alternate feet as in walking. **2** to go a short distance or progress (as) by stepping. **3** to measure (a distance) by stepping. —**break step,** to get out of step. **in step,** putting the foot to the ground at the same time as others, especially in marching; conforming to the actions etc. of others. **keep step,** to remain in step. **mind** *or* **watch one's step,** to take care. **out of step,** not in step. **step by step,** gradually, cautiously. **step down,** to resign. **step in,** to enter; to intervene. **step-ladder** *n.* a short self-supporting ladder with flat steps. **step on it,** (*slang*) to go or act faster. **step out,** to take long brisk steps; to go out to enjoy oneself socially. **stepping-stone** *n.* a raised stone (usually one of a series) as a means of crossing a stream etc.; a means of progress towards achieving something. **step up,** to come up or forward; to increase the rate or volume of. [OE]

step- *prefix* denoting a relationship like the one specified but resulting from a parent's remarriage. [OE (rel. to OHG, = bereave)]

stepbrother *n.* a male child of one's step-parent's previous marriage.

stepchild *n.* a spouse's child by a previous marriage.

stepdaughter *n.* a female stepchild.

stepfather *n.* a male step-parent.

stephanotis /stefəˈnəʊtɪs/ *n.* a fragrant tropical climbing plant of the genus *Stephanotis*. [f. Gk, = fit for a wreath (*stephanos*)]

stepmother *n.* a female step-parent.

step-parent *n.* a mother's or father's later spouse.

steppe /step/ *n.* a level treeless plain. [f. Russ.]

stepsister *n.* a female child of one's step-parent's previous marriage.

stepson *n.* a male stepchild.

steradian /stəˈreɪdɪən/ *n.* the unit of solid angle, equal to the angle at the centre of a sphere subtended by part of the surface whose area is equal to the square of the radius. [as STEREO- + RADIAN]

stereo /ˈsterɪəʊ, ˈstɪər-/ *n.* (*pl.* **-os**) **1** a stereophonic record-player etc. **2** stereophony. **3** a stereoscope. **4** a stereotype. —*adj.* **1** stereophonic. **2** stereoscopic. [abbr.]

stereo- /sterɪəʊ-, stɪərɪəʊ-/ *in comb.* having three dimensions. [f. Gk *stereos* solid]

stereochemistry /sterɪəʊˈkemɪstrɪ, ˈstɪər-/ *n.* the branch of chemistry dealing with the composition of matter as affected by the relations of atoms in space. [f. STEREO- + CHEMISTRY]

stereophonic /sterɪəˈfɒnɪk, stɪər-/ *adj.* (of sound-reproduction) using two or more channels of transmission and reproduction so that the sound may seem to reach the listener from more than one direction and thus seems more realistic. —**stereophonically** *adv.*, **stereophony** /-ˈɒfənɪ/ *n.* [f. STEREO- + PHONIC]

stereoscope /ˈsterɪəskəʊp, ˈstɪər-/ *n.* a device by which two slightly different photographs etc. are viewed together, giving the impression of depth and solidity. —**stereoscopic** /-ˈskɒpɪk/ *adj.*, **stereoscopically** /-ˈskɒpɪkəlɪ/ *adv.* [f. STEREO- + -SCOPE]

stereotype /ˈsterɪətaɪp, ˈstɪər-/ *n.* **1** an unduly fixed mental impression; a conventional idea or opinion or character etc. **2** a printing-plate cast from a mould of composed type. —*v.t.* **1** (usu. in *p.p.*) to formalize, to make typical or conventional. **2** to print from a stereotype; to make a stereotype of. [f. F (as STEREO-, TYPE)]

sterile /ˈsteraɪl/ *adj.* **1** not able to produce seed or offspring, barren. **2** free from living micro-organisms. **3** without result, unproductive. —**sterility** /-ˈrɪlɪtɪ/ *n.* [f. F or L *sterilis*]

sterilize /ˈsterɪlaɪz/ *v.t.* **1** to make sterile or free from living micro-organisms. **2** to deprive of the power of reproduction, especially by removal or obstruction of reproductive organs. —**sterilization** /-ˈzeɪʃ(ə)n/ *n.* [f. prec.]

sterling /ˈstɜ:lɪŋ/ *adj.* **1** of or in British money. **2** (of coin or precious metal) genuine, of standard value or purity. **3** (of a person or qualities etc.) of solid worth, genuine, reliable. —*n.* British money. —**sterling silver,** silver of 92.5% purity. [prob. f. OE, = coin with a star (*steorra*), some of the early Norman pennies having on them a small star]

stern[1] *adj.* strict and severe, not lenient or cheerful or kindly. —**sternly** *adv.*, **sternness** *n.* [OE]

stern[2] *n.* the rear part of a ship or boat; any rear part. —**stern-post** *n.* the central upright timber etc. of the stern, usually bearing the rudder. [prob. f. ON, = steering (as STEER[1])]

sternum *n.* (*pl.* **sternums** or **sterna**) the breastbone. —**sternal** *adj.* [f. Gk *sternon* chest]

steroid /ˈstɪərɔɪd, ˈste-/ *n.* any of a large group of fat-soluble organic compounds whose molecules all have a basic structure that consists of four fused rings of carbon atoms. [f. foll.]

sterol /ˈstɪərɒl, ˈste-/ *n.* a complex solid alcohol important in vitamin synthesis. [f. CHOLESTEROL etc.]

stertorous /ˈstɜ:tərəs/ *adj.* (of breathing etc.) laboured and noisy. —**stertorously** *adv.* [f. L *stertere* snore]

stet *v. imper.* (placed beside a deleted word on a proof-sheet etc.) let it stand as printed or written. [L, 3 sing. pres. subjunctive of *stare* stand]

stethoscope /ˈsteθəskəʊp/ *n.* an instrument used for listening to sounds within the body, e.g. those of the heart and lungs. —**stethoscopic** /-ˈskɒpɪk/ *adj.* [f. F f. Gk *stēthos* breast + -SCOPE]

stetson /ˈstets(ə)n/ *n.* a slouch hat with a very wide brim and a high crown. [f. J. B. *Stetson*, American hat-maker (d. 1906)]

stevedore /ˈsti:vədɔ:(r)/ *n.* a man employed in loading and unloading ships. [f. Sp. (*estivar* stow a cargo f. L *stipare* pack tight)]

stew *v.t./i.* **1** to cook or be cooked by long simmering in a closed vessel with a liquid. **2** (*colloq.*) to swelter. —*n.* **1** a dish of stewed meat etc. **2** (*colloq.*) an agitated or angry state. —**stew in one's own juice,** to be obliged to suffer the consequences of one's own actions without help or intervention from others. [f. OF *estuver* prob. ult. f. Gk *tuphos* steam]

steward /ˈstju:əd/ *n.* **1** a person employed to manage another's property, especially a great house or estate. **2** a person responsible for supplies of food etc. for a college or club etc. **3** a passengers' attendant on a ship, aircraft, or train. **4** an official in charge of a race-meeting or show etc. —*v.t./i.* to act as a steward (of). —**Lord High Steward of England,** a high officer of State presiding at coronations. [OE f. *stig* house, *weard* ward]

stewardess *n.* a female steward, especially on a ship or aircraft. [f. prec.]

stewardship *n.* **1** the position or work of a steward. **2** the organized pledging of specific amounts of money etc. to be given regularly to the Church. [f. STEWARD + -SHIP]

stewed *adj.* **1** cooked by stewing. **2** (of tea) bitter or strong from infusing for too long. **3** (*slang*) drunk. [f. STEW]

stick[1] *n.* **1** a short slender branch or piece of wood, especially one trimmed for use as a support or weapon, or as firewood. **2** a thin rod of wood etc. for a particular purpose; a thing resembling this in shape; the implement used to propel the ball in hockey or polo etc.; a gear-lever; a conductor's baton; a more or less cylindrical piece of a substance, e.g. celery or dynamite; (*colloq.*) an item of furniture etc. **3** punishment, especially by beating; adverse criticism. **4** (*colloq.*) a person, especially one who is dull or unsociable. —**stick-insect** *n.* an insect of the family Phasmidae, with a slender sticklike body resembling the twigs of the trees in which it lives. [OE]

stick[2] *v.t./i.* (*past & p.p.* **stuck**) **1** to insert or thrust (a thing or its point) into something; to stab. **2** to fix on or upon a pointed object; (*colloq.*) to put. **3** to fix or be fixed (as) by glue or solution etc.; (*colloq.*) to remain in the same place; (*colloq.* of an accusation etc.) to be convincing or regarded as valid. **4** to lose or deprive of the power of motion or action through friction, jamming, or some other impediment or difficulty. **5** (*slang*) to endure, to tolerate. **6** (*colloq.*) to impose a difficult or unpleasant task upon. **7** to provide (a plant) with a stick as a support. —**be stuck for,** (*colloq.*) to be at a loss for or in need of. **be stuck on,** (*slang*) to be captivated by. **be stuck with,** (*colloq.*) to be unable to get rid of. **get stuck in** *or* **into,** (*slang*) to begin in earnest. **stick around,** (*slang*) to linger, to remain at the same place. **stick at,** (*colloq.*) to persevere with. **stick at nothing,** to allow nothing, especially no scruples, to deter one. **stick by** *or* **with,** to stay close or faithful to. **sticking-plaster** *n.* an adhesive plaster for wounds etc. **stick-in-the-mud** *n.* (*colloq.*) an unprogressive or old-fashioned person. **stick in one's throat,** to be against one's principles. **stick it out,** (*colloq.*) to endure something unpleasant. **stick one's neck out,** to expose oneself to danger etc. by acting boldly. **stick out,** to protrude or cause to protrude. **stick out for,** to persist in demanding. **stick to,** to remain fixed on or to, to remain faithful to, to keep to (a subject etc.). **stick together,** (*colloq.*) to remain united or mutually loyal.

stick up, to protrude or cause to protrude; to be or make erect; to fasten to an upright surface; (*slang*) to rob or threaten with a gun. **stick-up** *n.* (*slang*) a robbery with a gun. **stick up for,** to support or defend (a person or cause). [OE]

sticker *n.* **1** an adhesive label. **2** a persistent person. [f. prec.]

stickleback /ˈstɪk(ə)lbæk/ *n.* a small spiny-backed fish of the family Gasterosteidae. [OE, = thorn-back]

stickler *n.* a person who insists on something. [f. obs. *stickle* be umpire]

stickpin *n.* (*US*) a tie-pin.

sticky *adj.* **1** sticking or tending to stick to what is touched. **2** (of weather) humid. **3** (*colloq.*) making or likely to make objections. **4** (*slang*) very unpleasant or difficult. —**sticky wicket,** (*colloq.*) a pitch that is drying after rain and is difficult for batsmen; difficult circumstances. —**stickily** *adv.*, **stickiness** *n.* [f. STICK²]

stiction /ˈstɪkʃ(ə)n/ *n.* static friction, the friction which tends to prevent surfaces at rest from being set in motion. [f. *st*atic + f*riction*]

stiff *adj.* **1** not flexible; not moving or changing its shape easily. **2** not fluid, thick and hard to stir. **3** difficult to move or deal with; (of a breeze) blowing strongly; (of a price or penalty) high, severe; (of a drink or dose) strong. **4** formal in manner, not pleasantly sociable or friendly. **5** (*colloq.*) to an extreme degree. —*n.* (*slang*) **1** a corpse. **2** a foolish or useless person. —**stiff-necked** *adj.* obstinate; haughty. **stiff upper lip,** fortitude in enduring grief etc. **stiff with,** (*slang*) abundantly provided with. —**stiffly** *adv.*, **stiffness** *n.* [OE]

stiffen *v.t./i.* to make or become stiff. —**stiffener** *n.* [f. STIFF]

stifle¹ /ˈstaɪf(ə)l/ *v.t./i.* **1** to suffocate; to be or feel unable to breathe for lack of air. **2** to restrain, to suppress. —**stifling** *adj.* [perh. f. OF *estouffer*]

stifle² /ˈstaɪf(ə)l/ *n.* the joint of a dog's or horse's etc. leg between hip and hock. [orig. unkn.]

stigma /ˈstɪgmə/ *n.* (*pl.* **-as**) **1** a mark or sign of disgrace or discredit. **2** the part of a pistil that receives the pollen in pollination. **3** (in *pl.* **stigmata** /ˈstɪgmətə/) marks corresponding to those left on Christ's body by the nails and spear at his Crucifixion. [L f. Gk, = mark made by pointed instrument]

stigmatize /ˈstɪgmətaɪz/ *v.t.* to brand as unworthy or disgraceful. —**stigmatization** /-ˈzeɪʃ(ə)n/ *n.* [f. F or L f. Gk (as prec.)]

stile¹ *n.* an arrangement of steps allowing people but not animals to climb over a fence or wall. [OE]

stile² *n.* a vertical piece (cf. RAIL¹) in the frame of a panelled door, wainscot, etc. [prob. f. Du. *stijl* pillar, door-post]

stiletto /stɪˈletəʊ/ *n.* (*pl.* **-os**) **1** a short dagger. **2** a pointed instrument for making eyelets etc. —**stiletto heel,** a high tapering heel of a shoe. [It., dim. of *stilo* dagger (as STYLUS)]

still¹ *adj.* **1** without or almost without motion or sound. **2** (of drinks) not effervescing. —*n.* **1** silence and calm. **2** an ordinary static photograph (as opposed to a motion picture), especially a single shot from a cinema film. —*adv.* **1** without moving. **2** even until or at a particular time. **3** nevertheless, all the same. **4** even, yet, increasingly. —*v.t./i.* to make or become still, to quieten. —**still birth,** a birth in which the child is born dead. **still life** (*pl.* **still lifes**), a painting of inanimate objects, e.g. fruits. —**stillness** *n.* [OE]

still² *n.* an apparatus for distilling spirituous liquors etc. —**still-room** *n.* a room for distilling, a housekeeper's store-room in a large house. [f. *still* v. f. DISTIL]

stillborn *adj.* **1** born dead. **2** (of an idea or plan etc.) not developing.

stilt *n.* **1** each of a pair of poles with supports for the feet enabling the user to walk at a distance above the ground. **2** each of a set of piles or posts supporting a building etc. [f. LG]

stilted *adj.* **1** (of literary style etc.) stiff and unnaturally formal. **2** standing on stilts. —**stiltedly** *adv.* [f. STILT]

Stilton /ˈstɪltən/ *n.* a rich blue-veined cheese originally made at various places in Leicestershire and formerly sold to travellers at a coaching inn at Stilton (now in Cambridgeshire) on the Great North Road from London.

stimulant /ˈstɪmjʊlənt/ *adj.* that stimulates, especially that increases bodily or mental activity. —*n.* a stimulant substance or influence. [f. L (as foll.)]

stimulate /ˈstɪmjʊleɪt/ *v.t.* **1** to make more vigorous or active. **2** to apply a stimulus to. —**stimulation** /-ˈleɪʃ(ə)n/ *n.*, **stimulative** *adj.*, **stimulator** *n.* [f. L *stimulare* (as foll.)]

stimulus /ˈstɪmjʊləs/ *n.* (*pl.* **-li** /-laɪ/) a stimulating thing or effect; something that produces a reaction in an organ or tissue. [L, = goad]

sting *n.* **1** a sharp-pointed part or organ of an insect etc., used for wounding and often injecting poison. **2** a stiff sharp-pointed hair on certain plants, causing inflammation if touched. **3** infliction of a wound by a sting; the wound so inflicted. **4** any sharp bodily or mental pain; a wounding quality or effect. **5** (*slang*) a swindle. —*v.t./i.* (*past* & *p.p.* **stung**) **1** to wound or affect with a sting; to be able to do this. **2** to cause to feel sharp bodily or mental pain. **3** to stimulate sharply as if by a sting. **4** (*slang*) to swindle, especially by overcharging; to extort money from. —**stinging-nettle** *n.* a nettle that stings (opp. *dead-nettle*), a plant of the genus *Urtica*. **sting in the tail,** an unexpected pain or difficulty at the end. **sting-ray** *n.* a broad flat-fish, especially of the family Dasyatidae, with a stinging tail. [OE]

stinger *n.* a thing that stings, especially a sharp painful blow. [f. STING]

stingy /ˈstɪndʒɪ/ *adj.* spending, giving, or given grudgingly or in small amounts. —**stingily** *adv.*, **stinginess** *n.* [perh. f. dial. *stinge* sting]

stink *v.t./i.* (*past* **stank** or **stunk**; *p.p.* **stunk**) **1** to give off an offensive smell. **2** (*colloq.*) to be or seem very unpleasant, unsavoury, or dishonest. —*n.* **1** an offensive smell. **2** (*colloq.*) an offensive complaint or fuss. —**stink-bomb** *n.* a device emitting a stink when exploded. **stink out,** to drive out by a stink; to fill (a place) with a stink. [OE]

stinker *n.* **1** a person or thing that stinks. **2** (*slang*) a very objectionable person or thing; a difficult task; a letter etc. conveying strong disapproval. [f. STINK]

stinking *adj.* that stinks; (*slang*) very objectionable. —*adv.* (*slang*) extremely and usually objectionably. [f. STINK]

stint *v.t.* to restrict to a small allowance (of); to be niggardly with. —*n.* **1** a limitation of supply or effort. **2** a fixed or allotted amount of work. **3** a small sandpiper of the genus *Calidris*. [OE, = to blunt]

stipend /ˈstaɪpend/ *n.* a salary, especially of a clergyman. [f. OF or L *stipendium* (*stips* wages, *pendere* to pay)]

stipendiary /staɪˈpendjərɪ, stɪ-/ *adj.* receiving a stipend. —*n.* a person receiving a stipend. —**stipendiary magistrate,** a paid professional magistrate. [f. L (as prec.)]

stipple *v.t./i.* **1** to paint, draw, or engrave with small dots (not with lines or strokes). **2** to roughen the surface of (paint or cement etc.). —*n.* stippling; this effect. [f. Du. *stippelen* frequent. of *stippen* to prick (*stip* point)]

stipulate /ˈstɪpjʊleɪt/ *v.t./i.* to demand or specify as part of a bargain or agreement. —**stipulate for,** to mention or insist upon as essential. —**stipulation** /-ˈleɪʃ(ə)n/ *n.* [f. L *stipulari*]

stir[1] *v.t./i.* (**-rr-**) **1** to move a spoon etc. round and round in (a liquid etc.) so as to mix the ingredients. **2** to move or cause to move slightly; to be or begin to be in motion; to rise after sleeping. **3** to arouse, inspire, or excite (emotions etc., or a person as regards these). —*n.* **1** the act or process of stirring. **2** a commotion or disturbance; excitement, a sensation. —**stir one's stumps,** (*colloq.*) to begin to move; to hurry. **stir up,** to mix thoroughly by stirring; to stimulate. [OE]

stir[2] *n.* (*slang*) prison. [orig. unkn.]

stirrup /ˈstɪrəp/ *n.* a metal or leather support for a horse-rider's foot, hanging from the saddle. —**stirrup-cup** *n.* a drink offered to a person about to depart, originally on horseback. **stirrup-leather** *n.* a strap attaching a stirrup to a saddle. **stirrup-pump** *n.* a hand-operated water-pump with a stump-shaped foot-rest, used to extinguish small fires. [OE (*stigan* climb + ROPE)]

stitch *n.* **1** a single pass of a threaded needle in and out of fabric in sewing or tissue in surgery; a thread etc. between two needle-holes. **2** a single complete movement of a needle or hook in knitting or crochet; the loop of thread made thus. **3** a particular method of arranging the thread(s). **4** the least bit of clothing. **5** an acute pain in the side induced by running etc. —*v.t./i.* to sew, to make stitches (in). —**in stitches,** (*colloq.*) laughing uncontrollably. **stitch in time,** a timely remedy. **stitch up,** to join or mend by sewing. [OE]

stoa /ˈstəʊə/ *n.* (in ancient Greek architecture) a portico or roofed colonnade. [Gk]

stoat *n.* an ermine, especially when the fur is brown. [orig. unkn.]

stock *n.* **1** a store of goods etc. ready for sale or distribution etc.; a supply of things available for use. **2** livestock. **3** the capital of a business company; a portion of this held by an investor (differing from *shares* in that it is not issued in fixed amounts). **4** one's reputation or popularity. **5** money lent to a government at fixed interest. **6** a line of ancestry. **7** liquid made by stewing bones, vegetables, etc., as a basis for soup, sauce, etc. **8** a base, support, or handle for an implement or machine etc.; the butt of a rifle etc. **9** a plant into which a graft is inserted; the main trunk of a tree etc. **10** a fragrant-flowered cruciferous plant of the genus *Matthiola*. **11** (in *pl.*) supports for a ship during building. **12** (in *pl.*, *hist.*) a timber frame with holes for the legs of a seated person, used like the pillory. **13** a cravat worn e.g. as part of riding-kit; a piece of black or purple fabric worn over the shirt front by a clergyman, hanging from a clerical collar. —*adj.* **1** kept in stock and readily available. **2** commonly used, conventional; hackneyed. —*v.t./i.* **1** to have (goods) in stock. **2** to provide with goods, equipment, or livestock. **3** to fit (a gun etc.) with a stock. —**in** (*or* **out of**) **stock,** available (or not available) immediately for sale etc. **on the stocks,** in construction or preparation. **stock-car** *n.* a specially strengthened car for use in racing in which deliberate bumping is allowed. **stock exchange,** a place where stocks and shares are publicly bought and sold. **stock-in-trade** *n.* all the requisites of a trade or profession.

stock-market *n.* a stock exchange; the transactions on this. **stock-pot** *n.* a pot for making soup stock. **stock-room** *n.* a room for storing goods. **stock-still** *adj.* motionless. **stock-taking** *n.* making the inventory of the stock in a shop etc.; a review of one's position and resources. **stock up,** to provide with or get stocks or supplies. **stock up with,** to gather a stock of. **take stock,** to make an inventory of one's stock; to make a review or estimate of a situation etc. [OE (ON *stokkr* trunk)]

stockade /stɒˈkeɪd/ *n.* a line or enclosure of upright stakes. —*v.t.* to fortify with a stockade. [f. obs. F f. Sp. *estacada* (rel. to STAKE)]

stockbreeder *n.* a farmer who raises livestock.

stockbroker *n.* a broker on the Stock Exchange. —**stockbroking** *n.*

stockholder *n.* an owner of stocks or shares.

stockinet /stɒkɪˈnet/ *n.* (also **stockinette**) fine stretchable machine-knitted fabric used for underwear etc. [prob. f. *stocking-net*]

stocking *n.* **1** a close-fitting covering for the foot and all or part of the leg, usually knitted or woven of wool or nylon etc. **2** a differently-coloured lower part of the leg of a horse etc. —**in one's stocking** *or* **stockinged feet,** wearing stockings but no shoes. **stocking mask,** a nylon stocking worn over the head as a criminal's disguise. **stocking-stitch** *n.* alternate rows of plain and purl in knitting, giving a plain smooth surface on one side. [f. STOCK in dial. sense 'stocking']

stockist *n.* one who stocks (certain) goods for sale. [f. STOCK]

stockjobber *n.* a jobber on the Stock Exchange, until 1986 dealing with stockbrokers but not with the general public.

stockman *n.* (*pl.* **-men**) (*Austral.*) a man in charge of livestock.

stockpile *n.* an accumulated stock of goods etc. held in reserve. —*v.t.* to accumulate a stockpile of.

stockrider *n.* (*Austral.*) a herdsman on an unfenced station.

stocky *adj.* short and strongly built. —**stockily** *adv.*, **stockiness** *n.* [f. STOCK]

stockyard *n.* an enclosure for sorting or temporary keeping of cattle.

stodge /stɒdʒ/ *n.* (*colloq.*) **1** food of a thick heavy kind. **2** an unimaginative person or work. —*v.t./i.* (*colloq.*) **1** to stuff (oneself) with food etc. **2** to trudge through mud etc.; to work laboriously. [imit., after *stuff* and *podge*]

stodgy /ˈstɒdʒɪ/ *adj.* **1** (of food) heavy and thick, indigestible. **2** dull and uninteresting. —**stodgily** *adv.*, **stodginess** *n.* [f. prec.]

Stoic /ˈstəʊɪk/ *n.* a member of an ancient Greek school of philosophy that sought virtue as the highest good and control of one's feelings and passions. —**Stoicism** /-sɪz(ə)m/ *n.* [f. L f. Gk]

stoic /ˈstəʊɪk/ *n.* a stoical person. —*adj.* stoical. —**stoicism** *n.* [= prec.]

stoical /ˈstəʊɪk(ə)l *adj.* having or showing great self-control in adversity. —**stoically** *adv.* [f. STOIC]

stoke *v.t./i.* (often with *up*) **1** to tend and put fuel on (a fire or furnace etc.). **2** (*colloq.*) to consume food steadily and in large quantities. [back-formation f. STOKER]

stokehold *n.* a compartment in which a steamer's fires are tended.

stokehole *n.* a space for stokers in front of a furnace.

stoker /ˈstəʊkə(r)/ *n.* **1** a person who stokes a furnace etc., especially on a ship. **2** a mechanical device for doing this. [Du., f. *stoken* stoke f. MDu. *stoken* push (rel. to STICK²)]

STOL *abbr.* short take-off and landing.

stole¹ *n.* **1** a woman's long garment like a scarf, worn over the shoulders. **2** a strip of silk etc. worn similarly as a vestment by a priest. [OE f. L f. Gk *stolē* equipment]

stole² *past* of STEAL.

stolen *p.p.* of STEAL.

stolid /ˈstɒlɪd/ *adj.* not feeling or showing emotion or animation; not easily excited or moved. —**stolidity** /-ˈlɪdɪtɪ/ *n.*, **stolidly** *adv.* [f. obs. F or L *stolidus*]

stomach /ˈstʌmək/ *n.* **1** the internal organ in which the first part of digestion occurs; one of the several digestive organs of an animal. **2** the lower front of the body. **3** an appetite or inclination. —*v.t.* to endure, to put up with. —**stomach-ache** *n.* a pain in the belly, especially in the bowels. **stomach-pump** *n.* a syringe for emptying the stomach or forcing liquid into it. **stomach upset,** a temporary slight digestive disorder. [f. OF f. L f. Gk, orig. = gullet (*stoma* mouth)]

stomacher /ˈstʌməkə(r)/ *n.* (*hist.*) a pointed front-piece of a woman's dress, often jewelled or embroidered. [prob. f. OF *estomachier* (as prec.)]

stomp *n.* a lively jazz dance with heavy stamping. —*v.t./i.* to tread heavily (on); to dance a stomp. [US dial. var of STAMP]

stone *n.* **1** the solid non-metallic mineral matter of which rock is made. **2** a small piece of this; a piece of stone of a definite shape or for a particular purpose. **3** a thing resembling a stone in hardness or form, e.g. a hard morbid concretion in the body or a hard case of the kernel in some fruits. **4** a precious stone. **5** (*pl.* same) the weight of 14 lb. —*adj.* made of stone. —*v.t.* **1** to pelt with stones.

2 to remove the stones from (fruit). **3** (in *p.p.*, *slang*) very drunk; incapacitated or stimulated by drugs. —**cast** *or* **throw stones,** to make aspersions on the character etc. **leave no stone unturned,** to try every possible means. **Stone Age,** the period when certain tools and weapons etc. were made of stone. **stone-cold** *adj.* completely cold. **stone-dead** *adj.* completely dead. **stone-deaf** *adj.* completely deaf. **stone-fly** *n.* an insect of the order Plecoptera, with aquatic larvae found under stones, used as bait. **stone-fruit** *n.* a fruit with flesh or pulp enclosing a stone. **a stone's throw,** a short distance. [OE]

stonechat *n.* a small black and white bird (*Saxicola torquata*) with an alarm-note like the knocking of pebbles.

stonecrop *n.* a creeping rock-plant of the genus *Sedum*, especially *S. acre*.

stonemason *n.* a dresser of or builder in stone.

stonewall *v.i.* **1** to obstruct discussion etc. with non-committal answers. **2** (in cricket) to bat without attempting to score runs.

stoneware *n.* pottery made from very siliceous clay or from clay and flint.

stonework *n.* work built of stone, masonry.

stony /ˈstəʊnɪ/ *adj.* **1** full of stones. **2** like stone in texture, hard. **3** unfeeling, uncompromising, unresponsive. **4** (*slang*) = stony-broke. —**stony-broke** *adj.* (*slang*) = broke. —**stonily** *adv.*, **stoniness** *n.* [f. STONE]

stood *past* & *p.p.* of STAND.

stooge *n.* (*colloq.*) **1** a comedian's assistant, used as a target for jokes. **2** a subordinate who does routine work. **3** a person who's actions are entirely controlled by another. —*v.i.* (*colloq.*) **1** to act as a stooge. **2** to move or wander aimlessly. [orig. unkn.; perh. f. STUDENT (students having frequently been employed as stage assistants)]

stool *n.* **1** a movable seat without a back or arms, usually for one person; a footstool. **2** (usu. in *pl.*) faeces. **3** a root or stump of a tree or plant from which shoots spring. —**stool-pigeon** *n.* a pigeon as a decoy; a police informer. [OE]

stoop[1] *n.* **1** to bend (one's shoulders or body) forwards and downwards; to carry one's head and shoulders thus. **2** to condescend; to lower oneself morally. —*n.* a stooping posture. [OE, prob. rel. to STEEP[1]]

stoop[2] *n.* (*US*) a porch or small veranda or the steps in front of a house. [f. Du. *stoep* (rel. to STEP)]

stop *v.t./i.* (**-pp-**) **1** to put an end to the movement, progress, or operation etc. of; to cause to halt or pause. **2** to refrain from continuing, to cease motion or working. **3** (*slang*) to receive (a blow etc.) on one's body. **4** to remain, to stay for a short time. **5** to close by plugging or obstructing; to put a filling in (a tooth). **6** to keep back, to refuse to give or allow; to instruct a bank to withhold payment on (a cheque). **7** to obtain the desired pitch in a musical instrument by pressing (a string) or blocking (a hole). —*n.* **1** stopping, being stopped; a pause or check. **2** a place where a bus or train etc. regularly stops. **3** a sign to show a pause in written matter, especially a full stop. **4** a device for stopping motion at a particular point. **5** (*Mus.*) a change of pitch effected by stopping a string; (in an organ) a row of pipes of one character; a knob etc. operating these. **6** (in optics and photography) a diaphragm; the effective diameter of a lens; a device reducing this. **7** a plosive sound. —**pull out all the stops,** to make an extreme effort. **stop at nothing,** to be ruthless or unscrupulous. **stop-go** *n.* the alternate suppression and stimulation of progress. **stop off** *or* **over,** to break one's journey. **stopping train,** a train stopping at many intermediate stations. **stop-press** *n.* late news inserted in a newspaper after printing has begun. **stop-watch** *n.* a watch with a mechanism for instantly starting and stopping it, used in timing races etc. [OE]

stopcock *n.* an externally operated valve to regulate the flow in a pipe etc.

stopgap *n.* a temporary substitute.

stopoff *n.* (also **stopover**) a break in one's journey.

stoppage *n.* the condition of being blocked or stopped. [f. STOP]

stopper *n.* a plug for closing a bottle etc. —*v.t.* to close with a stopper. —**put a stopper on,** to cause to cease. [f. STOP]

stopping *n.* a filling for a tooth. [f. STOP]

storage /ˈstɔːrɪdʒ/ *n.* **1** the storing of goods etc. **2** a method of storing the space available for this. **3** the cost of storing. **4** the storing of data. —**storage battery** *or* **cell,** a battery or cell for storing electricity. **storage heater,** an electric heater accumulating heat outside peak hours for later release. [f. foll.]

store *n.* **1** a quantity of something or (also in *pl.*) articles accumulated so as to be available for use. **2** a large shop selling goods of many kinds; (*US*) a shop. **3** a storehouse, a warehouse where things are stored. **4** a device in a computer for storing data. —*v.t.* **1** to accumulate for future use. **2** to put (furniture etc.) into a warehouse for temporary keeping. **3** to stock with something useful. **4** (in computers) to enter or retain (data) for future retrieval. —**in store,** being stored; kept available for use; destined to happen, imminent. **set store by,** to consider important, to value greatly. **store-cattle** *n.* cattle kept for breeding or for future fattening. **store-room** *n.* a room used for storing things. [f. OF *estore, estorer* f. L *instaurare* renew]

storehouse *n.* a place where things are stored.

storekeeper *n.* **1** a person in charge of a store or stores. **2** (*US*) a shopkeeper.

storey /ˈstɔːrɪ/ *n.* **1** each of the parts into which a building is divided horizontally; the whole of the rooms etc. having a continuous floor. **2** a thing forming a horizontal division. —**storeyed** *adj.* [f. L *historia* history (perh. orig. a tier of painted windows)]

storied /ˈstɔːrɪd/ *adj.* celebrated in or associated with stories or legends. [f. STORY]

stork *n.* a tall usually white wading bird of the family Ciconiidae, with long legs and a long straight bill, sometimes nesting on buildings and humorously pretended to be the bringer of babies. [OE]

storm *n.* **1** a violent disturbance of the atmosphere with thunder, strong wind, heavy rain or snow, or hail. **2** a violent disturbance or commotion in human affairs; a violent dispute etc. **3** a violent shower of missiles or blows; a violent outbreak of applause, abuse, etc. **4** a direct military assault upon (and the capture of) a defended place. —*v.t./i.* **1** (of wind or rain) to rage, to be violent. **2** to move or behave violently or very angrily. **3** to attract or capture by storm. —**storm-centre** *n.* the centre of a storm or cyclone; a subject etc. upon which agitation is concentrated. **storm-cloud** *n.* a heavy rain-cloud; something threatening. **storm-door** *n.* an additional outer door. **storm in a teacup,** great excitement over a trivial matter. **storm petrel,** a small black and white petrel (*Hydrobates pelagicus*) of the North Atlantic, said to be active before storms. **storm-trooper** *n.* a member of storm-troops. **storm-troops** *n.pl.* shock-troops; the Nazi political militia. **take by storm,** to capture by storm; to captivate quickly. [OE]

stormy *adj.* **1** full of storms; affected by storms. **2** (of wind etc.) violent as in a storm. **3** full of violent anger or outbursts. —**stormy petrel,** the storm petrel (see STORM); a person whose arrival seems to foreshadow or attract trouble. —**stormily** *adv.*, **storminess** *n.* [f. STORM]

story *n.* **1** an account of an incident or of a series of incidents, either true or invented. **2** the past course of a person's or institution's life. **3** a report of an item of news; material suitable for this. **4** (also **story-line**) the plot of a novel or play etc. **5** (*colloq.*) a fib. [f. AF *estorie* f. L (as HISTORY)]

stoup /stuːp/ *n.* **1** a basin for holy water, especially in the wall of a church. **2** (*archaic*) a flagon, a beaker. [f. ON (rel. to STEEP[2])]

stout *adj.* **1** (of a person) solidly built and rather fat. **2** of considerable thickness or strength. **3** brave and resolute. —*n.* a strong dark beer brewed with roasted malt or barley. —**stoutly** *adv.*, **stoutness** *n.* [f. AF (*e*)*stout*]

stove[1] *n.* **1** an apparatus containing an oven or ovens. **2** a closed apparatus used for heating rooms etc. **3** a hothouse with artificial heat. —**stove-enamel** *n.* a heat-proof enamel produced by treating enamelled objects in a stove. **stove-enamelled** *adj.* [orig. = sweating-room, f. MDu. (perh. rel. to STEW)]

stove[2] see STAVE.

stow /stəʊ/ *v.t.* **1** to place in a receptacle for storage. **2** (*slang*, esp. in *imper.*) to cease from. —**stow away,** to put away in storage or in reserve; to conceal oneself as a stowaway. [f. BESTOW]

stowage *n.* stowing, being stowed; the space available for this; the charge for it. [f. STOW]

stowaway *n.* a person who hides on board a ship or aircraft etc. so as to travel without charge or unseen.

strabismus /strəˈbɪzməs/ *n.* squinting; a squint. [f. Gk (*strabizō* squint)]

straddle *v.t./i.* **1** to sit or stand (across) with the legs wide apart; to part (one's legs) widely. **2** to drop shots or bombs short of and beyond (a specified point). —*n.* the act of straddling. [f. *striddlings* astride (as STRIDE)]

strafe /strɑːf, streɪf/ *v.t.* to harass with gunfire or bombs. —*n.* an act of strafing. [adaptation of G 1914 catchword *Gott strafe* (God punish) *England*]

straggle *v.i.* **1** to lack or lose compactness, to grow or spread in an irregular or untidy way. **2** to go or wander separately, not in a group; to drop behind others. —*n.* a straggling group. —**straggler** *n.*, **straggly** *adj.* [perh. f. dial. *strake* go (rel. to STRETCH)]

straight /streɪt/ *adj.* **1** extending or moving uniformly in the same direction, without a curve or bend etc. **2** direct. **3** in unbroken succession. **4** level, tidy; in the proper order, place, or condition. **5** honest; candid; not evasive. **6** not modified or elaborate, without additions; (of a drink) undiluted. **7** conventional, respectable; heterosexual. —*n.* **1** the straight part of something, especially the concluding stretch of a racecourse. **2** a straight condition. **3** a sequence of five cards in poker. **4** (*slang*) a heterosexual person. —*adv.* in a straight line, direct; in the right direction, correctly. —**go straight,** to live an honest life after being a criminal. **on the straight,** not on the bias. **straight away,** immediately. **straight eye,** the ability to draw or cut etc. in a straight line or to detect deviation from the straight. **straight face,** an expression concealing or not showing one's amusement etc. **straight fight,** a contest between two candidates only. **straight-man** *n.* the member of a comic act who makes remarks for the comedian to joke about. **straight off,** (*colloq.*) immediately; without hesitation. —**straightly** *adv.*, **straightness** *n.* [*p.p.* of STRETCH]

straighten /ˈstreɪt(ə)n/ *v.t./i.* to make or become straight. —**straighten up,** to stand erect after bending. [f. prec.]

straightforward /streɪtˈfɔːwəd/ *adj.* **1** honest, frank. **2** (of a task etc.) uncomplicated. —**straightforwardly** *adv.*, **straightforwardness** *n.*

strain[1] *v.t./i.* **1** to stretch tightly, to make or become taut or tense. **2** to injure or weaken by excessive stretching or by over-exertion. **3** to make an intensive effort; to use in this. **4** to apply (a rule or meaning etc.) beyond its true application. **5** to hold in a tight embrace. **6** to pass (liquid) through a sieve or similar device in order to separate solids from the liquid in which they are dispersed; to filter out (solids) thus. —*n.* **1** straining, being strained; the force exerted in straining. **2** an injury caused by straining a muscle etc. **3** a severe demand on mental or physical strength or on resources; distress caused by this. **4** a passage from a piece of music or poetry. **5** a tone or tendency in speech or writing. [f. OF *estreindre* f. L *stringere* draw tight]

strain[2] *n.* **1** a line of descent of animals, plants, or micro-organisms; a variety or breed of these. **2** a slight or inherited tendency as part of character. [OE, = progeny]

strained *adj.* **1** (of behaviour or manner) produced by effort, not arising from genuine feeling. **2** (of a relationship) characterized by unpleasant tension. [f. STRAIN[1]]

strainer *n.* a device for straining liquids. [f. STRAIN[1]]

strait *n.* **1** (in *sing.* or *pl.*) a narrow passage of water connecting two large bodies of water. **2** (usu. in *pl.*) a difficult state of affairs. —*adj.* (*archaic*) narrow, limited, strict. —**strait-laced** *adj.* very prim and proper, puritanical. [f. OF *estreit* tight f. L (as STRICT)]

straiten /ˈstreɪt(ə)n/ *v.t.* to restrict; (in *p.p.*) of or characterized by poverty. [f. prec.]

strait-jacket *n.* **1** a strong garment put on a violent person to confine his arms. **2** restrictive measures. —*v.t.* **1** to restrain with a strait-jacket. **2** to restrict severely.

strake *n.* a continuous line of planking or plates from stem to stern of a ship. [rel. to OE *streccan* stretch]

stramonium /strəˈməʊnɪəm/ *n.* a drug used to treat asthma; the plant yielding it (*Datura stramonium*). [perh. f. Tartar *turman* horse-medicine]

strand[1] *v.t./i.* **1** to run or cause to run aground **2** (in *p.p.*) in difficulties, especially without money or means of transport. —*n.* a shore. [OE]

strand[2] *n.* **1** each of the threads or wires twisted round each other to make a rope or cable etc. **2** a single thread or strip of fibre; a lock of hair. **3** an element or strain in any composite whole. [orig. unkn.]

strange /streɪndʒ/ *adj.* **1** unusual, surprising; eccentric. **2** unfamiliar, not one's own, alien. **3** unaccustomed; not at one's ease. —**strangely** *adv.*, **strangeness** *n.* [f. OF *estrange* f. L (as EXTRANEOUS)]

stranger /ˈstreɪndʒə(r)/ *n.* a person in a place or company that he does not know or belong to or where he is unknown; a person one does not know. —**a** (*or* **no**) **stranger to,** unaccustomed (or accustomed) to. [f. OF *estrangier* f. L (as prec.)]

strangle *v.t.* **1** to squeeze the windpipe or neck of, especially so as to kill. **2** to restrict or prevent the proper growth, operation, or utterance of. —**strangler** *n.* [f. OF f. L *strangulare* f. Gk (*straggalē* halter)]

stranglehold *n.* **1** a strangling or deadly grip. **2** firm or exclusive control.

strangulate /ˈstræŋgjʊleɪt/ *v.t.* to compress (a vein or intestine etc.) so that nothing can pass through. [f. L (as STRANGLE)]

strangulation /stræŋgjʊˈleɪʃ(ə)n/ *n.* **1** strangling **2** strangulating. [as prec.]

strap *n.* **1** a strip of leather or other flexible material often with a buckle, for holding things together or in place. **2** a shoulder-strap. **3** a loop for grasping to steady oneself in a moving vehicle. —*v.t.* **(-pp-) 1** to secure with a strap or straps. **2** to beat with a strap. —**strapped for,** (*slang*) short of (cash etc.). [dial. form of STROP]

strapping *adj.* tall and healthy-looking. —*n.* **1** straps; material for these. **2** sticking-plaster etc. used for binding wounds or injuries. [f. STRAP]

strata *pl.* of STRATUM.

stratagem /ˈstrætədʒəm/ *n.* a cunning plan or scheme; trickery. [f. F f. L f. Gk *stratēgēma* (*stratēgos* a general)]

strategic /strəˈtiːdʒɪk/ *adj.* **1** of strategy. **2** giving an advantage. **3** (of materials) essential in war. **4** (of bombing) designed to disorganize or demoralize the enemy. —**strategic weapons,** missiles etc. that can reach the enemy's home territory (opp. *tactical weapons* which are for use at close quarters or in battle). —**strategically** *adv.* [f. F f. Gk (as prec.)]

strategy /ˈstrætɪdʒɪ/ *n.* **1** the art of war, especially the planning of the movements of troops into favourable positions. **2** a plan of action or policy in business or politics etc. —**strategist** *n.* [f. F f. Gk, = generalship (as STRATAGEM)]

strath *n.* (*Sc.*) a broad valley. [f. Gael *srath*]

strathspey /stræθˈspeɪ/ *n.* a slow Scottish dance; music for this. [f. *Strathspey* valley of the river Spey]

stratify /ˈstrætɪfaɪ/ *v.t.* (esp. in *p.p.*) to arrange in strata or grades etc. —**stratification** /-fɪˈkeɪʃ(ə)n/ *n.* [f. F (as STRATUM)]

stratigraphy /strəˈtɪgrəfɪ/ *n.* the order and relative positions of strata; the study of these. —**stratigraphic** /-ˈgræfɪk/ *adj.*, **stratigraphically** /-ˈgræfɪkəlɪ/ *adv.* [f. STRATUM + -GRAPHY]

stratocumulus /strætəʊˈkju:mju:ləs/ *n.* dark masses of low cloud, frequently merging to cover the whole sky. [f. STRATUS + CUMULUS]

stratopause /ˈstrætəʊpɔ:z/ *n.* the interface between the stratosphere and the ionosphere. [f. STRATOSPHERE + PAUSE]

stratosphere /ˈstrætəsfɪə(r)/ *n.* the layer of the atmosphere lying above the troposphere, in which the temperature does not decrease with increasing height. —**stratospheric** /-ˈsferɪk/ *adj.* [f. foll. + SPHERE]

stratum /ˈstrɑ:təm, ˈstreɪ-/ *n.* (*pl.* **strata**) **1** each of a series of layers, especially of rocks in the earth's crust. **2** a social level or class. [L, = something spread or laid down]

stratus /ˈstrɑ:təs, ˈstreɪ-/ *n.* (*pl.* **-ti** /-ti:/) a continuous horizontal sheet of cloud. [as prec.]

straw *n.* **1** dry cut stalks of grain used as material for bedding, packing, fodder, etc. **2** a single stalk or piece of straw. **3** a thin hollow tube for sucking drink through. **4** an insignificant thing. **5** the pale yellow colour of straw. —**clutch at straws,** to try a hopeless expedient in desperation. **straw in the wind,** a slight hint of future developments. **straw poll** *or* **vote,** an unofficial ballot as a test of opinion. [OE (rel. to STREW)]

strawberry /ˈstrɔ:bərɪ/ *n.* a pulpy red fruit having the surface studded with yellow seeds; the plant of the genus *Fragaria* bearing this. —**strawberry-mark** *n.* a reddish birthmark. [OE (as prec. + BERRY); reason for name unknown]

stray *v.i.* **1** to leave one's group or proper place with no settled destination or purpose; to roam. **2** to deviate from a direct course or from a subject. —*n.* a person or domestic animal that has strayed; a stray thing. —*adj.* **1** that has strayed, lost. **2** isolated, found or occurring occasionally or unexpectedly. **3** unwanted, unintentional. [f. AF *estrayer* (as ASTRAY)]

streak *n.* **1** a long thin usually irregular line or band, especially distinguished by its colour. **2** a flash of lightning. **3** a strain or element in a character. **4** a spell or series. —*v.t./i.* **1** to mark with streaks. **2** to move very rapidly; (*colloq.*) to run naked through a public place. —**streaker** *n.* [OE, = pen-stroke (as STRIKE)]

streaky *adj.* full of streaks; (of bacon) with alternate streaks of fat and lean. —**streakily** *adv.*, **streakiness** *n.* [f. prec.]

stream *n.* **1** a body of water flowing in its bed, a brook or river. **2** a flow of fluid or of a mass of things or people. **3** the current or direction of something flowing or moving. **4** (in some schools) a section into which children with the same level of ability are placed. —*v.t./i.* **1** to flow or move as a stream. **2** to emit a stream of; to run with liquid. **3** to float or wave at full length. **4** to arrange (schoolchildren) in streams. —**on stream,** in active operation or production. **stream of consciousness,** the continuous flow of a person's thoughts and reactions to events; a literary style depicting this, as in James Joyce's novel *Ulysses*. [OE]

streamer *n.* **1** a long narrow flag. **2** a long narrow ribbon or strip of paper attached at one or both ends. **3** a banner headline. [f. prec.]

streamline *v.t.* **1** to give a smooth even shape to (a vehicle, boat, etc.) so as to offer the least possible resistance to motion through air or water. **2** to make more efficient by simplifying, removing superfluities, etc.

street *n.* a public road in a city, town, or village; this with the houses or buildings on each side; the persons who live or work in a particular street. —**on the streets,** working as a prostitute. **streets ahead (of),** (*colloq.*) much superior (to). **street-walker** *n.* a prostitute seeking customers in the street. **up one's street,** (*colloq.*) within one's range of interest or knowledge, to one's liking. [OE f. L *strata* (*via*) paved (way)]

streetcar *n.* (*US*) a tram.

strength *n.* **1** the quality, extent, or manner of being strong. **2** what makes one strong. **3** the number of persons present or available; the full complement. —**from strength to strength,** with ever-increasing success. **in strength,** in large numbers. **on the strength of,** relying on, on the basis of. [OE (as STRONG)]

strengthen /ˈstreŋθ(ə)n/ *v.t./i.* to make or become stronger. —**strengthener** *n.* [f. prec.]

strenuous /ˈstrenjʊəs/ *adj.* making or requiring great exertions, energetic. —**strenuously** *adv.*, **strenuousness** *n.* [f. L *strenuus*]

streptococcus /streptəˈkɒkəs/ *n.* (*pl.* **-cocci** /-aɪ/) a bacterium causing serious infections. —**streptococcal** *adj.* [f. Gk *streptos* twisted + *kokkos* berry]

streptomycin /streptəˈmaɪsɪn/ *n.* an antibiotic effective against some disease-producing bacteria. [f. Gk *streptos* (as prec.) + *mukēs* fungus]

stress *n.* **1** pressure, tension; the measure of this. **2** a demand on physical or mental strength; distress caused by this. **3** emphasis; the extra force used on a syllable or on word(s) in speaking, or on a note or notes in music. —*v.t.* **1** to lay stress on. **2** to subject to stress. —**lay stress on,** to indicate as important. [f. DISTRESS or partly f. OF *estresse* narrowness, f. L (as STRICT)]

stressful *adj.* causing stress. —**stressfully** *adv.* [f. prec. + -FUL]

stretch *v.t./i.* **1** to pull out tightly or into a greater length, extent, or size; to be able to be stretched without breaking; to tend to become stretched. **2** to place or lie at full length or spread out; to extend one's limbs and tighten the muscles after being relaxed. **3** to be continuous from a point or between points; to have a specified length or extension. **4** to make great demands on the abilities of; to strain to the utmost or beyond a reasonable limit; to exaggerate (the truth). —*n.* **1** stretching, being stretched; the ability to be stretched. **2** a continuous expanse or tract; a continuous period of time. **3** (*slang*) a period of imprisonment. **4** (*US*) the straight part of a race-track. —*adj.* able to be stretched, elastic. —**stretch one's legs,** to exercise oneself by walking. **stretch out,** to extend (a hand or foot etc.); to last for a longer period; to prolong. **stretch a point,** to agree to something not normally allowed. [OE]

stretcher *n.* **1** a framework of two poles with canvas etc. between for carrying a sick or injured person in a lying position. **2** any of various devices for stretching things. **3** a brick etc. placed lengthwise in the face of a wall. [f. prec.]

stretchy *adj.* (*colloq.*) able or tending to stretch. —**stretchiness** *n.* [f. STRETCH]

strew /struː/ *v.t.* (*p.p.* **strewn** or **strewed**) to scatter or spread about over a surface; to cover or partly cover with scattered things. [OE]

stria /ˈstraɪə/ *n.* (*pl.* **striae** /-iː/) a slight furrow or ridge on a surface. [L]

striated /straɪˈeɪtɪd/ *adj.* marked with striae. —**striation** *n.* [f. STRIA]

stricken see STRIKE.

strict *adj.* **1** precisely limited or defined, without exception or deviation. **2** requiring or giving complete obedience or exact performance. —**strictly speaking,** if one uses words in their strict sense. —**strictly** *adv.*, **strictness** *n.* [f. L *strictus* (*stringere* draw tight)]

stricture /ˈstrɪktʃ(ə(r)/ *n.* **1** (usu. in *pl.*) a critical or censorious remark. **2** abnormal constriction of a tubelike part of the body. [as prec.]

stride *v.t./i.* (*past* **strode**; *p.p.* **stridden** /ˈstrɪd(ə)n/) **1** to walk with long steps. **2** to cross with one step. **3** to bestride. —*n.* **1** a single long step; the length of this; gait as determined by the length of the stride. **2** (usu. in *pl.*) progress. —**get into one's stride,** to settle into an efficient rate of work. **take in one's stride,** to manage without difficulty. [OE, rel. to MLG *strîden* straddle]

strident /ˈstraɪdənt/ *adj.* loud and harsh. —**stridency** *n.*, **stridently** *adv.* [f. L *stridere* creak]

strife *n.* quarrelling, a state of conflict; a struggle between opposed persons or things. [f. OF *estrif* (as STRIVE)]

strike *v.t./i.* (*past* & *p.p.* **struck**) **1** to subject to an impact; to bring or come into sudden hard contact (with); to inflict (a blow), to knock or propel with a blow or stroke. **2** to attack suddenly; (of a disease) to afflict. **3** (of lightning) to descend upon and blast. **4** to produce (sparks or a sound etc.) by striking something; to produce (a musical note) by pressing a key; to make (a coin or medal) by stamping metal etc.; to ignite (a match) by friction. **5** (of a clock) to indicate (time) by a sound; (of time) to be indicated thus. **6** to bring suddenly into a specified state as if at one stroke. **7** to reach (gold or mineral oil etc.) by digging or drilling. **8** to agree on (a bargain). **9** to put oneself theatrically into (an attitude). **10** to occur to the mind of; to produce a mental impression on. **11** to penetrate; to cause to penetrate; to fill with sudden fear etc. **12** to insert (a plant cutting) in the soil to take root; (of a cutting) to take root. **13** to cease work in protest about a grievance. **14** to lower or take down (a flag or tent etc.). **15** to take a specified direction. **16** to arrive at (an average or balance) by balancing or equalizing the items. —*n.* **1** an act or instance of striking. **2** employees' concerted refusal to work unless a grievance is remedied; a similar concerted abstention from activity by persons attempting to obtain a concession or register a grievance. **3** a sudden find or success. **4** an attack, especially from the air. —**be struck on,** (*slang*) to be infatuated with. **on strike,** taking part in an industrial strike. **strike-breaker** *n.* a person working or brought in in place of a striker. **strike home,** to deal an effective blow, to have an intended effect. **strike off,** to remove with a stroke; to delete (a name etc.) from a list. **strike out,** to hit out; to act vigorously; to delete (an item or name etc.). **strike pay,** an allowance paid by a trade union to members on strike. **strike up,** to start (an acquaintance, conversation, etc.) rapidly or casually; to begin playing (a tune etc.). [OE, = go, stroke]

striker *n.* **1** a person or thing that strikes. **2** an employee who is on strike. **3** (in football) a player whose main function is to try to score goals. [f. prec.]

striking *adj.* sure to be noticed; attractive and impressive. —**strikingly** *adv.* [f. STRIKE]

Strine *n.* a comic transliteration of Australian speech; Australian English, especially of the uneducated type. [alleged pronunc. of 'Australian' in such speech]

string *n.* **1** narrow cord, twine; a piece of this or a similar material used for tying or holding things together, for pulling, or interwoven in a frame to form the head of a racket. **2** a piece of catgut, cord, or wire stretched and caused to vibrate so as to produce notes in a musical instrument; (in *pl.*) the stringed instruments played with a bow in an orchestra etc.; (*attrib.*) relating to or consisting of these. **3** (in *pl.*) an awkward stipulation or complication. **4** a set of things strung together; a series of people or events; a group of racehorses trained at one stable. **5** a strip of tough fibre connecting two halves of a bean-pod etc. —*v.t./i.* (*past* & *p.p.* **strung**) **1** to fit or fasten with string(s). **2** to thread (beads etc.) on a string. **3** to arrange in or as a string. **4** to trim the tough fibre from (beans). **5** (esp. in *p.p.*) to make (the nerves or resolution etc.) tense and ready for action. —**on a string,** under one's control or influence. **string along,** (*colloq.*) to deceive. **string along with,** (*colloq.*) to accompany. **string-course** *n.* a raised horizontal band of bricks etc. on a building. **string up,** to hang up on strings etc.; to kill by hanging. **string vest,** a vest of a material with large mesh. [OE]

stringed *adj.* (of musical instruments) having strings. [f. prec.]

stringent /ˈstrɪndʒ(ə)nt/ *adj.* (of rules etc.) strict, severe, leaving no loophole for discretion. —**stringency** *n.*, **stringently** *adv.* [as STRICT]

stringer /ˈstrɪŋə(r)/ *n.* **1** a longitudinal structural member in a framework especially of a ship o[illegible]craft. **2** a newspaper correspond[illegible] not on the regular staff. [f. STRING]

stringy /ˈstrɪŋɪ/ *adj.* like a string, fibrous.— **stringiness** *n.* [f. STRING]

strip[1] *v.t./i.* (**-pp-**) **1** to remove the clothes or covering from; to undress oneself. **2** to deprive of property or titles. **3** to leave bare of accessories or fittings. **4** to remove the old paint from. **5** to damage the thread of (a screw) or the teeth of (a gear). —*n.* **1** an act of stripping, especially of undressing in a strip-tease. **2** (*colloq.*) the clothes worn by the members of a sports team. —**strip club,** a club where strip-tease is performed. **strip down,** to remove the accessory fittings of or take apart (a machine etc.). **strip-tease** *n.* an entertainment in which a woman (or occasionally a man) gradually undresses before an audience. [f. OE, = despoil]

strip[2] *n.* a long narrow piece or area. —**strip cartoon,** a comic strip. **strip light,** a tubular fluorescent lamp. **tear a person off a strip,** (*slang*) to rebuke him or her. [f. or rel. to MLG *strippe* strap, prob. rel. to foll.]

stripe *n.* **1** a long narrow band or strip differing in colour or texture from the surface on either side of it. **2** a chevron etc. denoting military rank. **3** (*archaic*, usu. in *pl.*) a blow with a scourge or lash. [perh. back-formation f. foll.]

striped /straɪpt/ *adj.* marked with stripes. [orig. unkn.]

stripling *n.* a youth not fully grown. [prob. f. STRIP[2]]

stripper *n.* **1** a person or thing that strips something. **2** a device or solvent for removing paint etc. **3** a strip-tease performer. [f. STRIP[1]]

stripy /ˈstraɪpɪ/ *adj.* striped. [f. STRIPE]

strive *v.i.* (*past* **strove**; *p.p.* **striven** /ˈstrɪv(ə)n/) **1** to make great efforts. **2** to carry on a conflict. [f. OF *estriver*]

strobe *n.* (*colloq.*) a stroboscope. [abbr.]

stroboscope /ˈstrəʊbəskəʊp/ *n.* a lamp made to flash intermittently; a device using this to determine speeds of rotation etc. —**stroboscopic** /-ˈskɒpɪk/ *adj.* [f. Gk *strobos* whirling + -SCOPE]

strode *past* of STRIDE.

stroganoff /ˈstrɒgənɒf/ *n.* (in full **beef stroganoff**) a dish of strips of beef cooked in a sauce containing sour cream. [f. Count Paul *Stroganov*, 19th-c. Russian diplomat]

stroke *n.* **1** an act of striking. **2** a sudden disabling attack, especially of apoplexy. **3** an action or movement, especially as one of a series or in a game etc.; the slightest such action; a highly effective effort, action, or occurrence of a specified kind. **4** the sound made by a striking clock. **5** a movement in one direction of a pen or paintbrush etc.; a detail contributing to a general effect. **6** a mode or action of moving an oar in rowing; a mode of moving the limbs in swimming. **7** (in full **stroke oar**) the oarsman nearest the stern, who sets the time of the stroke. **8** an act or spell of stroking. —*v.t.* **1** to pass the hand gently along the surface of (hair or fur etc.). **2** to act as stroke of (a boat or crew). —**at a stroke,** by a single action. **on the stroke (of),** punctually (at). [rel. to STRIKE]

stroll /strəʊl/ *v.i.* to walk in a leisurely way. —*n.* a short leisurely walk. —**strolling**

players, actors etc. going from place to place performing. [prob. f. G (*strolch* vagabond)]

strong *adj.* 1 having the power of resistance to being broken, damaged, disturbed, overcome, etc. 2 capable of exerting great force or of doing much; physically powerful; powerful through numbers, resources, or quality; powerful in effect; (of an argument etc.) convincing. 3 concentrated, having a large proportion of a flavouring or colouring element, or of a substance in water or other solvent; (of a drink) containing much alcohol. 4 (placed after a noun) having a specified number of members. —*adv.* strongly, vigorously. —**strong-arm** *adj.* using force. **strong-box** *n.* a strongly made small chest for valuables. **strong language,** forceful language, swearing. **strong-minded** *adj.* having a determined mind. **strong point,** a fortified position; a thing at which one excels. **strong-room** *n.* a strongly built room for the storage and protection of valuables. **strong suit,** a suit at cards in which one can take tricks; a thing at which one excels. **strong verb,** a verb forming inflexions by vowel-change within the stem rather than by the addition of a suffix. —**strongly** *adv.* [OE]

stronghold *n.* 1 a fortified place; a secure refuge. 2 a centre of support for a cause etc.

strontium /ˈstrɒntɪəm/ *n.* a soft silver-white metallic element of the alkaline-earth metal series, symbol Sr, atomic number 38. [f. *Strontian* town in Scotland where the carbonate was discovered]

strop *n.* a device, especially a strip of leather, for sharpening razors. —*v.t.* (**-pp-**) to sharpen on or with a strop. [f. MDu. or MLG; cf. L *stroppus*]

stroppy /ˈstrɒpɪ/ *adj.* (*slang*) bad-tempered, awkward to deal with. [orig. unkn.]

strove *past* of STRIVE.

struck *past* & *p.p.* of STRIKE.

structural /ˈstrʌktʃər(ə)l/ *adj.* 1 of a structure or framework. 2 used in the construction of buildings etc. —**structural linguistics,** the study of a language viewed as a system made up of interrelated elements without regard to their historical development. —**structurally** *adv.* [f. STRUCTURE]

structuralism /ˈstrʌktʃərəlɪz(ə)m/ *n.* 1 (*Psychol.*) a method of investigating the structure of consciousness through the introspective analysis of simple forms of sensation, thought, images, etc. 2 any theory or method in which a discipline or field of study is envisaged as comprising elements interrelated in systems and structures at various levels, being regarded as more significant than the elements considered in isolation. 3 any of the theories of linguistics in which language is considered as a system or structure comprising elements at various phonological, grammatical, and semantic levels, especially after the work of F. de Saussure (d. 1913). —**structuralist** *n.* [f. prec.]

structure /ˈstrʌktʃə(r)/ *n.* 1 the way in which a thing is constructed or organized. 2 a supporting framework or the essential parts of a thing. 3 a constructed thing, a complex whole; a building. —*v.t.* to give a structure to, to organize. [f. OF or L *structura* (*struere* build)]

strudel /ˈstru:d(ə)l/ *n.* a confection of thin pastry filled especially with apple. [G]

struggle *v.i.* 1 to throw one's limbs or body about in a vigorous effort to get free. 2 to make a vigorous or determined effort under difficulties; to make one's way or a living etc. with difficulty. 3 (with *with* or *against*) to try to overcome (an opponent) or deal with (a problem). —*n.* an act or period of struggling, a vigorous effort; a hard contest. [perh. imit.]

strum *v.t./i.* (**-mm-**) to play unskilfully or monotonously on (a stringed or keyboard instrument). —*n.* the act or sound of strumming. [imit.; cf. THRUM²]

strumpet /ˈstrʌmpɪt/ *n.* (*archaic*) a prostitute. [orig. unkn.]

strung *past* & *p.p.* of STRING.

strut *n.* 1 a bar forming part of a framework and designed to strengthen and brace it. 2 a strutting gait. —*v.t./i.* (**-tt-**) to walk in a stiff pompous way. 3 to brace with struts. [OE, ? = be rigid]

'struth /stru:θ/ *int.* (*colloq.*) an exclamation of surprise. [*God's truth*]

strychnine /ˈstrɪkni:n/ *n.* a highly poisonous alkaloid used in small doses as a stimulant. [f. L f. Gk *strukhnos* nightshade]

stub *n.* 1 a short stump; a remnant of a pencil or cigarette etc. after use. 2 the counterfoil of a cheque or receipt etc. —*v.t.* (**-bb-**) to strike (one's toe) against a hard object; (usu. with *out*) to extinguish (a cigarette etc.) by pressing the lighted end against something. [OE]

stubble *n.* 1 the lower ends of the stalks of cereal plants left sticking up from the ground after the harvest is cut. 2 a short stiff growth of hair or beard, especially that growing after shaving. —**stubbly** *adj.* [f. AF f. L, var. of *stipula* straw]

stubborn /ˈstʌbən/ *adj.* obstinate, not docile; not easy to control or deal with. —**stubbornly** *adv.*, **stubbornness** *n.* [orig. unkn.]

stubby *adj.* short and thick. —**stubbiness** *n.* [f. STUB]

stucco /ˈskʌkəʊ/ *n.* (*pl.* **-oes**) plaster or cement for coating walls or for moulding to form architectural decorations. —*v.t.* to coat with stucco. [It.]

stuck *past* & *p.p.* of STICK².

stuck-up *adj.* conceited, snobbish.

stud¹ *n.* **1** a short large-headed nail, a rivet; a small knob projecting from a surface, especially for ornament. **2** a device like a button on a shank, used e.g. to fasten a detachable shirt-collar. —*v.t.* (**-dd-**) to set (as) with stud. [OE]

stud² *n.* **1** a number of horses kept for breeding etc.; the place where these are kept. **2** a stallion. —**at stud,** (of a stallion) available for breeding on payment of a fee. **stud-book** *n.* a book containing pedigrees of horses. **stud-farm** *n.* a farm where horses are bred. **stud poker,** poker with betting after the dealing of successive cards face up. [OE]

studding *n.* the woodwork of a lath-and-plaster wall. [f. STUD¹]

studding-sail /ˈstʌns(ə)l/ *n.* an extra sail set at the side of a square sail in light winds. [perh. f. MLG or MDu. *stotinge* a thrusting]

student /ˈstju:dənt/ *n.* a person who is studying, especially at a university or other place of higher education; (*attrib.*) studying in order to become. [f. L *studēre* (as STUDY)]

studio /ˈstju:dɪəʊ/ *n.* (*pl.* **-os**) **1** the workroom of a painter, sculptor, photographer, etc. **2** a room or premises where cinema films are made. **3** a room from which radio or television programmes are regularly broadcast or in which recordings are made. —**studio couch,** a divan-like couch that can be converted into a bed. [It. f. L (as STUDY)]

studious /ˈstju:dɪəs/ *adj.* **1** assiduous in study or reading. **2** painstaking; careful and deliberate. —**studiously** *adv.*, **studiousness** *n.* [f. L *studiosus* (as foll.)]

study /ˈstʌdɪ/ *n.* **1** giving one's attention to acquiring information or knowledge, especially from books. **2** the object of this; a thing worth studying. **3** a work presenting the result of investigations into a particular subject; a preliminary drawing; a written or other portrayal of an aspect of behaviour or character etc. **4** a musical composition designed to develop a player's skill. **5** a room used by a person for reading, writing, etc. —*v.t./i.* **1** to make a study of; to examine attentively; to apply oneself to study. **2** to give care and consideration to. **3** (in *p.p.*) deliberate, carefully and intentionally contrived. [f. OF f. L *studium* zeal, study]

stuff *n.* **1** the material that a thing is made of or that may be used for some purpose. **2** a substance, things, or belongings of an indeterminate kind or quality or not needing to be specified; a particular knowledge or activity. **3** (*slang*) valueless matter, trash. **4** woollen fabric (as distinct from silk, cotton, or linen). —*v.t./i.* **1** to pack or cram; to fill tightly; to stop up. **2** to fill the empty skin of (an animal or bird etc.) with material to restore its original shape, e.g. for exhibition in a museum; to fill with padding; to fill (a fowl or rolled meat etc.) with minced seasoning etc. before cooking. **3** to fill (a person or oneself) with food; to eat greedily. **4** to push hastily or clumsily. **5** (*slang*) to dispose of as unwanted. —**get stuffed!** (*slang*) go away; stop annoying me. **stuff and nonsense,** an exclamation of incredulity or ridicule. **stuffed shirt,** (*colloq.*) a pompous person. [f. OF *estoffe* (*estoffer* equip f. Gk *stuphō* draw together)]

stuffing *n.* **1** padding used to stuff cushions etc. **2** a savoury mixture used to stuff fowl etc. [f. STUFF]

stuffy *adj.* **1** (of a room etc.) lacking ventilation or fresh air. **2** (of the nose) blocked with secretions so that breathing is difficult. **3** (*colloq.*) prim and pompous, old-fashioned or narrow-minded. **4** (*colloq.*) showing annoyance. —**stuffily** *adv.*, **stuffiness** *n.* [f. STUFF]

stultify /ˈstʌltɪfaɪ/ *v.t.* to make ineffective or useless, to impair. —**stultification** /-fɪˈkeɪʃ(ə)n/ *n.* [f. L *stultificare* (*stultus* foolish, *facere* make)]

stum *n.* unfermented grape-juice, must. —*v.t.* (**-mm-**) **1** to prevent from fermenting, or from continuing to ferment, by using sulphur etc. **2** to renew the fermentation of (wine) by adding stum. [f. Du. *stom* f. *stom* (adj.) dumb]

stumble *v.i.* **1** to lurch forward or have a partial fall from catching or striking or misplacing the foot; to walk with repeated stumbling. **2** to make a mistake or repeated mistakes in speaking or in playing music. —*n.* an act of stumbling. —**stumble across** *or* **on,** to discover accidentally. **stumbling-block** *n.* an obstacle or circumstance etc. causing difficulty or hesitation. [rel. to STAMMER]

stump *n.* **1** the projecting remnant of a tree remaining in the ground after the rest has fallen or been cut down; a corresponding remnant of a broken tooth, amputated limb, or of something worn down. **2** each of the three uprights of a wicket in cricket. —*v.t./i.* **1** to walk stiffly or noisily. **2** to put (a batsman in cricket) out by touching the stumps with the ball while he is outside his crease. **3** (*colloq.*) to be too difficult for, to baffle. —**stump up,** (*slang*) to pay or produce (money required); to pay what is owed. [f. MDu. or OHG]

stumpy *adj.* short and thick. —**stumpiness** *n.* [f. STUMP]

stun *v.t.* (**-nn-**) **1** to knock senseless. **2** to daze or shock by the impact of strong emotion. [f. OF, = ASTONISH]

stung *past* & *p.p.* of STING.

stunk see STINK.

stunner *n.* (*colloq.*) a stunning person or thing. [f. STUN]

stunning *adj.* (*colloq.*) extremely good or attractive. —**stunningly** *adv.* [f. STUN]

stunt[1] *v.t.* to retard the growth or development of. [*stunt* foolish, ON *stuttr* short]

stunt[2] *n.* (*colloq.*) something unusual or difficult done as a performance or to attract attention. —*v.i.* (*colloq.*) to perform stunts. —**stunt man,** a man employed to take an actor's place in performing dangerous stunts. [orig. unkn.]

stupa /ˈstjuːpə/ *n.* a round usually domed Buddhist monument, usually containing a sacred relic. [f. Skr., = heap, pile]

stupefy /ˈstjuːpɪfaɪ/ *v.t.* **1** to dull the wits or senses of. **2** to stun with astonishment. —**stupefaction** /-ˈfækʃ(ə)n/ *n.* [f. F f. L *stupefacere* (*stupēre* be amazed, *facere* make)]

stupendous /stjuːˈpendəs/ *adj.* amazing or prodigious, especially by its size or degree. —**stupendously** *adv.* [f. L (as prec.)]

stupid /ˈstjuːpɪd/ *adj.* **1** not intelligent or clever, slow at learning or understanding things; typical of stupid persons. **2** uninteresting, boring. **3** in a state of stupor. —**stupidity** /-ˈpɪdɪtɪ/ *n.*, **stupidly** *adv.* [f. F or L (as prec.)]

stupor /ˈstjuːpə(r)n/ *n.* a dazed or torpid or helplessly amazed state. [L (as STUPEFY)]

sturdy /ˈstɜːdɪ/ *adj.* strongly built, hardy, vigorous.—**sturdily** *adv.*, **sturdiness** *n.* [orig. = recklessly violent, f. OF *est(o)urdi* dazed]

sturgeon /ˈstɜːdʒ(ə)n/ *n.* a large edible fish of the genus *Acipenser* etc. yielding caviare. [f. AF]

stutter *v.t./i.* to stammer, especially by involuntarily repeating the first consonants of words; to utter (words) thus. —*n.* an act or habit of stuttering. —**stutterer** *n.* [frequent. of dial. *stut*]

sty[1] /staɪ/ *n.* a pigsty. [OE, prob. = *stig* hall]

sty[2] /staɪ/ *n.* an inflamed swelling on the edge of an eyelid. [shortened f. dial. *styany* = *styan eye* f. OE *stigend* sty, lit. riser + EYE, shortened as though = *sty on eye*]

Stygian /ˈstɪdʒɪən/ *adj.* of or like the Styx or Hades; gloomy, murky. [f. L f. Gk *Stugios* Styx, river of Hades]

style /staɪl/ *n.* **1** a kind or sort, especially in regard to appearance and form. **2** the manner of writing, speaking, or doing something; the distinctive manner of a person, school, or period. **3** the correct way of designating a person or thing. **4** elegance, distinction. **5** shape; pattern; fashion (in dress etc.). **6** a pointed implement for scratching or engraving things. **7** a narrow extension of a plant's ovary, supporting the stigma. —*v.t./i.* **1** to design or make etc. in a particular (especially a fashionable) style. **2** to designate in a specified way. [f. OF f. L (as STYLUS)]

stylish *adj.* in fashionable style; elegant. —**stylishly** *adv.*, **stylishness** *n.* [f. STYLE]

stylist *n.* **1** a person concerned with style, especially a writer having or aiming at a good literary style, or a designer of fashionable styles. **2** a hairdresser who styles hair. [f. STYLE]

stylistic /staɪˈlɪstɪk/ *adj.* of literary or artistic style. —*n.* (in *pl.*) the study of literary style. —**stylistically** *adv.* [f. prec.]

stylite /ˈstaɪlaɪt/ *n.* any of the ascetics who lived on a platform on top of a pillar, especially in Syria in the 5th c. [f. Gk (*stulos* pillar)]

stylized /ˈstaɪlaɪzd/ *adj.* (of a work of art etc.) made to conform to a conventional style. [f. STYLE]

stylus *n.* (*pl.* **styluses**) **1** a needle-like point for producing or following a groove in a gramophone record. **2** a pointed writing-implement. [erron. spelling of L *stilus*]

stymie /ˈstaɪmɪ/ *n.* **1** the situation in golf when an opponent's ball is between one's own ball and the hole. **2** a difficult situation that blocks or thwarts one's activities. —*v.t.* **1** to subject to a stymie. **2** to block or thwart the activities of. [orig. unkn.]

styptic /ˈstɪptɪk/ *adj.* checking the flow of blood by causing blood-vessels to contract. [f. L f. Gk *stuphō* contract]

styrene /ˈstaɪriːn/ *n.* a liquid hydrocarbon easily polymerized and used in making plastics. [f. Gk *sturax* a resin]

suasion /ˈsweɪʒ(ə)n/ *n.* persuasion. —**moral suasion,** a strong recommendation appealing to the moral sense. [f. OF or L (*suadēre* urge)]

suave /swɑːv/ *adj.* smooth-mannered. —**suavely** *adv.*, **suavity** *n.* [F or f. L *suavis* agreeable]

sub *n.* (*colloq.*) **1** a submarine. **2** a subscription. **3** a substitute. **4** a sub-editor. —*v.t./i.* (**-bb-**) (*colloq.*) **1** to substitute. **2** to sub-edit. [abbr.]

sub- *prefix* (in some Latin-derived words **suc-** before *c*, **suf-** before *f*, **sug-** before *g*, **sup-** before *p*, **sur-** before *r*, **sus-** before *s*) denoting **1** under, at, to, or from a lower position (*subordinate*, *submerge*, *subtract*). **2** secondary or inferior position (*subclass*, *sub-lieutenant*, *subtotal*). **3** nearly, more or less (*subarctic*). [f. L *sub* under]

subaltern /ˈsʌbəltən/ *n.* an officer of the rank next below a captain. [f. L (as SUB-, ALTERNATE)]

subaqua /sʌbˈækwə/ *adj.* (of a sport etc.) taking place underwater. [f. L *sub aqua* under the water]

subaquatic /sʌbəˈkwætɪk/ *adj.* underwater.

subaqueous /sʌbˈeɪkwɪəs/ *adj.* subaquatic.

subarctic /sʌbˈɑ:ktɪk/ *adj.* of or like the regions somewhat south of the Arctic Circle.

subatomic /sʌbəˈtɒmɪk/ *adj.* occurring in an atom; smaller than an atom.

subcommittee /ˈsʌbkəmɪtɪ/ *n.* a committee formed for a special purpose from some members of the main committee.

subconscious /sʌbˈkɒnʃəs/ *n.* the part of the mind that is considered to be not fully conscious but able to influence actions etc. —*adj.* of the subconscious. —**subconsciously** *adv.*

subcontinent /sʌbˈkɒntɪnənt/ *n.* a land-mass of great extent not classed as a continent.

subcontract /sʌbˈkɒntrækt/ *n.* an arrangement by which one who has contracted to do work arranges for it to be done by others. —/sʌbkənˈtrækt/ *v.t./i.* to make a subcontract (for). —**subcontractor** /-ˈtræktə(r)/ *n.*

subculture /ˈsʌbkʌltʃə(r)/ *n.* a social group or its culture within a larger culture.

subcutaneous /sʌbkju:ˈteɪmɪəs/ *adj.* under the skin.

subdivide /sʌbdɪˈvaɪd/ *v.t./i.* to divide again after the first division.

subdivision /ˈsʌbdɪvɪʒ(ə)n/ *n.* **1** sub-dividing. **2** a subordinate division.

subdue /səbˈdju:/ *v.t.* **1** to overcome, to bring under control. **2** (esp. in *p.p.*) to make softer, gentler, or less intense. [f. OF *souduire* seduce f. L *subducere* withdraw, used with sense of L *subdere* conquer]

sub-edit *v.t.* to act as sub-editor of.

sub-editor *n.* **1** an assistant editor. **2** one who prepares material for printing in a newspaper or book etc. —**sub-editorial** /-ˈtɔrɪ(ə)l/ *adj.*

subfusc /sʌbˈfʌsk/ *n.* the dull-coloured clothing worn in some universities on formal occasions. [f. L (SUB-, *fuscus* dark brown)]

subheading /ˈsʌbhedɪŋ/ *n.* a subordinate heading.

subhuman /sʌbˈhju:mən/ *adj.* less than human; not fully human.

subject[1] /ˈsʌbdʒɪkt/ *n.* **1** the person or thing being discussed, described, represented, or studied. **2** a person under a particular political rule; any member of a State except the supreme ruler; a person owing obedience to another. **3** a circumstance, person, or thing that gives occasion for a specified feeling or action. **4** a branch of study. **5** (*logic* & *Gram.*) the term about which something is predicated in a proposition; the word(s) in a sentence that name who or what does the action or undergoes what is stated in the verb. **6** (*Philos.*) the conscious self as opposed to all that is external to the mind; the substance as opposed to the attributes of something. **7** a principal theme in a piece of music. **8** (esp. in medicine) a person with a specified (usually undesirable) bodily or mental tendency. —*adj.* not politically independent, owing obedience to another State etc. —*adv.* (with *to*) provided that (a specified condition is fulfilled). —**subject to,** owing obedience to; liable to. [f. OF f. L *subjicere* place beneath (SUB-, *jacere* throw)]

subject[2] /səbˈdʒekt/ *v.t.* **1** (with *to*) to cause to undergo or experience. **2** to bring (a country etc.) under one's control. —**subjection** *n.* [as prec.]

subjective /səbˈdʒektɪv/ *adj.* **1** of or due to the consciousness or thinking or the percipient subject as opposed to real or external things, not objective; imaginary. **2** giving prominence to or depending on personal opinions or idiosyncrasy. **3** (*Gram.*) of the subject. —**subjectively** *adv.*, **subjectivity** /-ˈtɪvɪtɪ/ *n.* [f. L (as SUBJECT[1])]

subjoin /səbˈdʒɔɪn/ *v.t.* to add (an anecdote or illustration etc.) at the end.

sub judice /sʌb ˈdʒu:dɪsɪ/ under judicial consideration, not yet decided (and in the UK therefore not to be commented on). [L, = under a judge]

subjugate /ˈsʌbdʒʊgeɪt/ *v.t.* to conquer, to bring into subjection or bondage. —**subjugation** /-ˈgeɪʃ(ə)n/ *n.*, **subjugator** *n.* [f. L *subjugare* (SUB-, *jugum* yoke)]

subjunctive /səbˈdʒʌŋktɪv/ *adj.* (*Gram.*, of a word) expressing a wish, supposition, or possibility (e.g. *if I were you; suffice it to say*). —*n.* a subjunctive mood or form. [f. F or L (as SUBJOIN)]

subkingdom /ˈsʌbkɪŋdəm/ *n.* a taxonomic category below a kingdom.

sublease /ˈsʌbli:s/ *n.* a lease granted to a subtenant. —/sʌbˈli:s/ *v.t.* to lease by a sublease.

sublet /sʌbˈlet/ *v.t.* (**-tt-**; *past* & *p.p.* **sublet**) to let to a subtenant.

sublimate /ˈsʌblɪmeɪt/ *v.t.* **1** to divert the energy of (a primitive impulse etc.) into a culturally higher activity. **2** to sublime (a substance); to refine, to purify. —/ˈsʌblɪmət/ *n.* a sublimed substance. —**sublimation** /-ˈmeɪʃ(ə)n/ *n.* [f. L *sublimare* (as foll.)]

sublime /səˈblaɪm/ *adj.* **1** of the highest or most exalted sort, awe-inspiring. **2** characteristic of one who has no fear of the consequences. —*v.t./i.* to convert (a substance) from a solid into a vapour by heat (and usually allow to solidify again); (of a substance) to undergo this process; to purify or make sublime. —**sublimely** *adv.*, **sublimity** /-ˈlɪmɪtɪ/ *n.* [f. L *sublimis*]

subliminal /sʌbˈlɪmɪn(ə)l/ *adj.* below the threshold of consciousness; too faint or rapid to be consciously perceived. —**subliminally** *adv.* [f. SUB- + L *limen* threshold]

sublunar /sʌbˈluːnə(r)/ *adj.* (also **sublunary**) existing or situated beneath the moon or between its orbit and that of Earth; subject to the moon's influence.

sub-machine-gun *n.* a lightweight machine-gun held in the hand.

submarine /sʌbməˈriːn, ˈsʌb-/ *n.* a ship, especially an armed warship, equipped to operate below the surface of the sea. —*adj.* existing or occurring or done below the surface of the sea.

submerge /səbˈmɜːdʒ/ *v.t./i.* **1** to place below the surface of water or other liquid; to flood. **2** (of a submarine) to dive, to go below the surface. —**submergence** *n.*, **submersion** *n.* [f. L *submergere* (SUB-, *mergere* dip)]

submersible /səbˈmɜːsɪb(ə)l/ *adj.* capable of submerging. —*n.* a submersible vessel. [f. *submerse* v. = prec.]

submicroscopic /sʌbmaɪkrəˈskɒpɪk/ *adj.* too small to be seen by an ordinary microscope.

submission /səbˈmɪʃ(ə)n/ *n.* **1** submitting, being submitted. **2** a thing submitted; a theory etc. submitted by counsel to a judge or jury. [f. OF or L (as SUBMIT)]

submissive /səbˈmɪsɪv/ *adj.* submitting to power or authority; meek, willing to obey. —**submissively** *adv.*, **submissiveness** *n.* [f. prec.]

submit /səbˈmɪt/ *v.t./i.* (**-tt-**) **1** to surrender (oneself) to the control or authority of another; to cease to resist or oppose. **2** to present for consideration or decision. **3** to subject (a person or thing) to a process or treatment. [f. L *submittere* (SUB-, *mittere* send)]

subnormal /ˈsʌbnɔːm(ə)l/ *adj.* **1** less than normal. **2** below the normal standard of intelligence. —**subnormality** /-ˈmælɪtɪ/ *n.*

suborder /ˈsʌbɔːdə(r)/ *n.* a taxonomic category between order and family.

subordinate /səˈbɔːdɪnət/ *adj.* **1** of lesser importance or rank. **2** working under the control or authority of another. —*n.* a person in a subordinate position. —/-eɪt/ *v.t.* to make or treat as subordinate. —**subordinate clause**, a clause serving as a noun, adjective, or adverb within a sentence. —**subordination** /-ˈneɪʃ(ə)n/ *n.* [f. L (SUB-, *ordinare* ordain)]

suborn /səˈbɔːn/ *v.t.* to induce (especially by bribery) to commit perjury or some other crime. —**subornation** /-ˈneɪʃ(ə)n/ *n.* [f. L *subornare* incite secretly (SUB-, *ornare* equip)]

sub-plot *n.* a subordinate plot in a play.

subpoena /səbˈpiːnə/ *n.* a writ commanding a person's attendance in a law-court. —*v.t.* (*past & p.p.* **subpoenaed** /-nəd/) to serve a subpoena on. [f. L *sub poena* under penalty]

sub rosa /sʌb ˈrəʊzə/ in confidence or secretly. [L, = under the rose, as emblem of secrecy]

subscribe /səbˈskraɪb/ *v.t./i.* **1** to contribute (a sum of money); to pay regularly for membership of an organization, receipt of a publication, etc. **2** to sign (one's name) at the foot of a document; to sign (a document) thus. **3** (with *to*) to express one's agreement with (an opinion or resolution). [f. L *subscribere* (SUB-, *scribere* write)]

subscriber *n.* **1** one who subscribes. **2** a person paying a regular sum for the hire of a telephone. —**subscriber trunk dialling**, the making of trunk calls by a subscriber without the assistance of an operator. [f. prec.]

subscript /ˈsʌbskrɪpt/ *adj.* written or printed below. —*n.* a subscript number or symbol. [f. L (as SUBSCRIBE)]

subscription /səbˈskrɪpʃ(ə)n/ *n.* **1** subscribing. **2** money subscribed; a fee for membership of an organization etc. —**subscription concert**, a concert (usually one of a series) paid for mainly by those who subscribe in advance. [as SUBSCRIBE]

subsection /ˈsʌbsekʃ(ə)n/ *n.* a division of a section.

subsequent /ˈsʌbsɪkwənt/ *adj.* following a specified or implied event. —**subsequent to**, later than, after. —**subsequently** *adv.* [f. OF or L *subsequi* (SUB-, *sequi* follow)]

subservient /səbˈsɜːvɪənt/ *adj.* **1** subordinate. **2** servile, obsequious. **3** of use in a minor role. —**subservience** *n.*, **subserviently** *adv.* [f. L *subservire* (SUB-, *servire* serve)]

subside /səbˈsaɪd/ *v.i.* **1** to sink or settle to a lower level or to the bottom. **2** (of ground) to cave in, to sink. **3** to become less active or intense or prominent. **4** (of a person) to sink into a chair etc. —**subsidence** /səbˈsaɪdəns, ˈsʌbsɪdəns/ *n.* [f. L *subsidere* (SUB-, *sidere* settle, rel. to *sedēre* sit)]

subsidiary /səbˈsɪdɪərɪ/ *adj.* **1** of secondary (not primary) importance. **2** (of a company) controlled by another. —*n.* a subsidiary company, thing, or person. [f. L (as SUBSIDY)]

subsidize /ˈsʌbsɪdaɪz/ *v.t.* to provide with a subsidy; to reduce the cost of with a subsidy. [f. foll.]

subsidy /ˈsʌbsɪdɪ/ *n.* money contributed by the State or a public body etc. to keep prices at a desired level or to assist in meeting expenses etc. [f. AF f. L *subsidium* assistance]

subsist /səbˈsɪst/ *v.i.* to exist, to continue to exist, to get sustenance or a livelihood. [f. L *subsistere* stand firm (SUB-, *sistere* set, stand)]

subsistence /səbˈsɪst(ə)ns/ *n.* subsisting; a means of this. —**subsistence farming**, farming in which almost all the crops are consumed by the farmer's household.

subsistence level *or* **wage,** merely enough to provide the bare necessities of life. [as prec.]

subsoil /ˈsʌbsɔɪl/ *n.* the soil immediately below the surface soil.

subsonic /sʌbˈsɒnɪk/ *adj.* relating to speeds less than that of sound. —**subsonically** *adv.*

subspecies /ˈsʌbspiːʃiːz/ *n.* a taxonomic category below a species, usually a more or less permanent variety geographically isolated.

substance /ˈsʌbst(ə)ns/ *n.* **1** a particular kind of matter having more or less uniform properties. **2** the essence of what is spoken or written. **3** reality, solidity. **4** wealth and possessions. **5** content as distinct from form. —**in substance,** in the main points. [f. OF f. L, = essence (SUB-, *stare* stand)]

substandard /sʌbˈstændəd/ *adj.* below the usual or required standard.

substantial /səbˈstænʃ(ə)l/ *adj.* **1** of real importance or value; considerable in amount. **2** of solid structure. **3** having substance, actually existing. **4** well-to-do. **5** essential, virtual. —**substantially** *adv.* [as SUBSTANCE]

substantiate /səbˈstænʃɪeɪt/ *v.t.* to support with evidence, to prove the truth of. —**substantiation** /-ˈeɪʃ(ə)n/ *n.* [f. L *substantiare* give substance to (as prec.)]

substantive /ˈsʌbstəntɪv, səbˈstæntɪv/ *adj.* **1** having independent existence, not subordinate. **2** actual, real, permanent. —/ˈsʌb-/ *n.* a noun. —**substantival** /-ˈtaɪv(ə)l/ *adj.* [as SUBSTANCE)]

substation /ˈsʌbsteɪʃ(ə)n/ *n.* a subordinate station; a station at which electrical current is switched, transformed, or converted, intermediate between a generating station and a low-tension distribution network.

substitute /ˈsʌbstɪtjuːt/ *n.* a person or thing acting or serving in place of another. —*v.t.* to put, use, or serve as a substitute. —*adj.* acting as a substitute. —**substitution** /-ˈtjuːʃ(ə)n/ *n.* [f. L *substituere* (SUB-, *statuere* set up)]

substratum /ˈsʌbstrɑːtəm, -streɪ-/ *n.* (*pl.* **-ta**) an underlying layer or substance. [p.p. of L *substernere* (SUB-, *sternere* strew)]

subsume /səbˈsjuːm/ *v.t.* to include (an instance etc.) under a particular rule or class. —**subsumption** /-ˈsʌmpʃ(ə)n/ *n.* [f. L *subsumere* (SUB-, *sumere* take)]

subtenant /ˈsʌbtenənt/ *n.* a person renting a room or house etc. from one who is a tenant of it. —**subtenancy** *n.*

subtend /səbˈtend/ *v.t.* (of a line or arc) to form (an angle) at a point where lines drawn from each end of it meet; (of an angle or chord) to have bounding lines or points that meet or coincide with those of (a line or arc). [f. L *subtendere* (SUB-, *tendere* stretch)]

subterfuge /ˈsʌbtəfjuːdʒ/ *n.* a piece of trickery or deceit etc. used to escape blame or defeat etc.; the use of this. [F, or f. L *subterfugere* escape secretly (*subter* beneath, *fugere* flee)]

subterranean /sʌbtəˈreɪnɪən/ *adj.* underground. [f. L (SUB-, *terra* earth)]

subtitle /ˈsʌbtaɪt(ə)l/ *n.* **1** a subordinate or additional title of a book etc. **2** a caption of a cinema film, especially translating foreign dialogue. —*v.t.* to provide with a subtitle or subtitles.

subtle /ˈsʌt(ə)l/ *adj.* **1** slight and difficult to detect or describe. **2** making or able to make fine distinctions. **3** ingenious, crafty. —**subtlety** *n.*, **subtly** *adv.* [f. OF f. L *subtilis*]

subtopia /sʌbˈtəʊpɪə/ *n.* unsightly suburbs, especially those disfiguring a rural area. [f. SUB(URB) + (U)TOPIA]

subtotal /ˈsʌbtəʊt(ə)l/ *n.* the total of part of a group of figures to be added.

subtract /səbˈtrækt/ *v.t.* to deduct, to remove (a part, quantity, or number) from a greater one. —**subtraction** *n.* [f. L (SUB-, *trahere* draw)]

subtropical /sʌbˈtrɒpɪk(ə)l/ *adj.* **1** bordering on the tropics. **2** characteristic of subtropical regions.

suburb /ˈsʌbɜːb/ *n.* an outlying district of a city. [f. OF or L *suburbium* (SUB-, *urbs* city)]

suburban /səˈbɜːbən/ *adj.* of or characteristic of suburbs; having only limited interests and narrow-minded views. —**suburbanite** *n.* [f. L (as prec.)]

Suburbia /səˈbɜːbɪə/ *n.* (usu. *derog.*) the suburbs and their inhabitants. [f. SUBURB]

subvention /səbˈvenʃ(ə)n/ *n.* a subsidy. [f. OF f. L (*subvenire* come to a person's aid f. SUB-, *venire* come)]

subversive /səbˈvɜːsɪv/ *adj.* attempting subversion. —*n.* a subversive person. [f. L (as foll.)]

subvert /səbˈvɜːt/ *v.t.* to weaken or overthrow the authority of (a government etc.); to attempt to do this. —**subversion** *n.* [f. OF or L *subvertere* overturn (SUB-, *vertere* turn)]

subway /ˈsʌbweɪ/ *n.* **1** an underground passage, especially for pedestrians. **2** (*US*) an underground railway.

suc- *prefix* see SUB-.

succeed /səkˈsiːd/ *v.t./i.* **1** to be successful. **2** to come next in time or order, to follow. **3** to come by inheritance or due order (to an office or title). [f. OF or L *succedere* (SUC-, *cedere* go)]

success /səkˈses/ *n.* **1** a favourable outcome, the accomplishment of what was aimed at; the attainment of wealth, fame, or position. **2** a thing or person that turns out well. [f. L *successus* (as prec.)]

successful *adj.* having success, prosperous. —**successfully** *adv.* [f. prec. + -FUL]

succession /səkˈseʃ(ə)n/ *n.* **1** following in

order; a series of people or things one after another. **2** succeeding to the throne or to an office or inheritance; the right of doing this; a series of persons having such a right. —**in succession,** one after another. **in succession to,** as the successor of. [as SUCCEED]

successive /sək'sesɪv/ *adj.* following in succession; in an unbroken series. —**successively** *adv.* [f. L (as SUCCEED)]

successor /sək'sesə(r)/ *n.* a person or thing that succeeds another. [as SUCCEED]

succinct /sək'sɪŋkt/ *adj.* concise, expressed briefly and clearly. —**succinctly** *adv.*, **succinctness** *n.* [f. L *succingere* tuck up (SUC-, *cingere* gird)]

succour /'sʌkə(r)/ *n.* (*literary*) help given in time of need. —*v.t.* (*literary*) to give succour to. [f. OF f. L *succurrere* (SUC-, *currere* run)]

succulent /'sʌkjʊlənt/ *adj.* **1** juicy (*lit.* or *fig.*). **2** (of a plant) having thick fleshy leaves or stems. —*n.* a succulent plant. —**succulence** *n.* [f. L (*succus* juice)]

succumb /sə'kʌm/ *v.i.* to give way to something overpowering; to die. [f. OF or L *succumbere* (SUC-, *cumbere* lie)]

such *adj.* **1** of the kind or degree indicated or suggested. **2** of the same kind. **3** so great or extreme. —*pron.* such a person or persons or thing(s). —**as such,** as being what has been specified; in itself. **such-and-such** *adj.* (a person or thing) of a particular kind but not needing to be specified. **such as,** for example. [OE]

suchlike *adj.* of the same kind. —*pron.* (usu. *pl.*) things of this kind.

suck *v.t./i.* **1** to draw (liquid) into the mouth by using the lip muscles; to draw liquid from (a thing) thus. **2** to squeeze and extract the flavour from (a sweet etc.) in the mouth by using the tongue. **3** to use a sucking action or make a sucking sound. **4** to draw in; to obtain. —*n.* an act or period of sucking. —**suck dry,** to exhaust the contents of by sucking. **suck in** *or* **up,** to absorb; to engulf, to draw into itself. **suck up to,** (*slang*) to toady to. [OE]

sucker *n.* **1** a shoot springing from a plant's root or its stem below ground. **2** an organ in animals or a part of an apparatus for adhering by suction to surfaces. **3** (*slang*) a gullible or easily deceived person. [f. SUCK]

sucking-pig *n.* a pig that is not yet weaned, especially one suitable for roasting whole.

suckle *v.t.* **1** to feed (young) from the breast or udder. **2** (of young) to take milk thus. [prob. back-formation f. foll.]

suckling *n.* an unweaned child or animal. [f. SUCK]

sucrose /'sju:krəʊz, 'su:-/ *n.* sugar obtained from sugar-cane, sugar-beet, etc. [f. F *sucre* sugar]

suction /'sʌkʃ(ə)n/ *n.* **1** sucking. **2** production of a partial vacuum causing adhesion of surfaces or enabling external atmospheric pressure to force a liquid etc. into the vacant space. [f. L *suctio* (*sugere* suck)]

sudden /'sʌd(ə)n/ *adj.* done or occurring etc. abruptly or unexpectedly. —**all of a sudden,** suddenly. **sudden death,** (*colloq.*) a decision (especially in a drawn contest) by the result of a single event. —**suddenly** *adv.*, **suddenness** *n.* [f. AF f. L (*subitus* sudden)]

sudorific /sju:də'rɪfɪk, su:-/ *adj.* causing sweating. —*n.* a sudorific drug. [f. L *sudor* sweat, *facere* make]

Sudra /'su:drə/ *n.* a member of the lowest of the four great Hindu classes (the labourer class), whose function is to serve the other three varnas; this class. [f. Skr.]

suds /sʌdz/ *n.pl.* froth of soap and water. —**sudsy** *adj.* [cf. MDu. & MLG *sudde* marsh]

sue /sju:, su:/ *v.t./i.* **1** to begin a lawsuit against (a person). **2** to make an application. [f. AF, ult. f. L *sequi* follow]

suede /sweɪd/ *n.* **1** kid or other skin with the flesh side rubbed to a nap. **2** a cloth imitating this. [f. F (*gants de*) *Suède* (gloves of) Sweden]

suedette /sweɪ'det/ *n.* a material designed to imitate the texture of suede, especially a type of cotton or rayon fabric with a suede-like nap. [f. SUEDE + -ETTE]

suet /'sju:ɪt, 'su:-/ *n.* the hard fat of the kidneys and loins of oxen or sheep etc. —**suety** *adj.* [f. OF f. L *sebum* tallow]

suf- *prefix* see SUB-.

suffer *v.t./i.* **1** to experience the effects of (something unpleasant); to feel pain or grief; to be subjected to damage. **2** to undergo (a change). **3** to tolerate; (*archaic*) to permit. —**sufferer** *n.*, **suffering** *n.* [f. AF f. L *sufferre* (SUF-, *ferre* bear)]

sufferable *adj.* bearable. [f. prec.]

sufferance *n.* tacit consent, abstention from an objection. —**on sufferance,** tolerated but not supported. [as SUFFER]

suffice /sə'faɪs/ *v.t./i.* to be enough or adequate; to meet the needs of (a person etc.). —**suffice it to say,** I will content myself with saying. [f. OF f. L *sufficere* (SUF-, *facere* make)]

sufficiency /sə'fɪʃ(ə)nsɪ/ *n.* a sufficient amount. [f. L (as foll.)]

sufficient /sə'fɪʃ(ə)nt/ *adj.* enough. —**sufficiently** *adv.* [f. OF or L (as SUFFICE)]

suffix /'sʌfɪks/ *n.* a letter or letters added at the end of a word to form a derivative. —*v.t.* to append, especially as a suffix. [f. L (as SUF-, FIX)]

suffocate /'sʌfəkeɪt/ *v.t./i.* **1** to impede or stop the breathing of (a person etc.); to choke or kill thus. **2** to be or feel suffocated.

—**suffocation** /-ˈkeɪʃ(ə)n/ *n.* [f. L *suffocare* (SUF-, *fauces* throat)]

suffragan /ˈsʌfrəgən/ *n.* **1** a bishop appointed to assist a diocesan bishop. **2** a bishop in relation to his archbishop. [f. AF f. L (as foll.); orig. of bishop summoned to vote in synod]

suffrage /ˈsʌfrɪdʒ/ *n.* **1** the right of voting in political elections. **2** a short prayer or petition. [f. L *suffragium*]

suffragette /sʌfrəˈdʒet/ *n.* (*hist.*) a woman who agitated, especially with violence, for women's suffrage. [f. prec. + -ETTE]

suffuse /səˈfju:z/ *v.t.* (of a colour or moisture etc.) to spread throughout or over. —**suffusion** *n.* [f. L *suffundere* (SUF-, *fundere* pour)]

Sufi /ˈsu:fɪ/ *n.* a Muslim ascetic mystic; a member of any of several orders of Islamic mystics. —**Sufic** *adj.*, **Sufism** *n.* [f. Arab. *suf* wool (which was used for clothing by religious persons from pre-Islamic times)]

sug- *prefix* see SUB-.

sugar /ˈʃʊgə(r)/ *n.* **1** a sweet crystalline substance from sugar-cane, sugar-beet, and other plants, used in cookery, confectionery, etc. **2** a soluble usually sweet crystalline carbohydrate, e.g. glucose. **3** (*US colloq.*, as a term of address) darling. —*v.t.* to sweeten or coat with sugar. —**sugar-beet** *n.* a beet from whose roots sugar is made. **sugar-cane** *n.* a perennial tropical grass (*Saccharum officinarum*) with very tall stems from which sugar is made. **sugar-daddy** *n.* (*slang*) an elderly man who lavishes gifts on a young woman. **sugar-loaf** *n.* a conical moulded mass of sugar. **sugar soap,** an alkaline compound for cleaning or removing paint. [f. OF, ult. f. Arab. *sūkkar*]

sugary *n.* **1** containing or resembling sugar. **2** attractively or excessively sweet or pleasant. —**sugariness** *n.* [f. prec.]

suggest /səˈdʒest/ *v.t.* **1** to put forward for consideration or as a possibility; to propose tentatively. **2** to cause (an idea) to present itself; to bring (an idea) into the mind. —**suggest itself,** to come into the mind. [f. L *suggerere* (SUG-, *gerere* bring)]

suggestible /səˈdʒestɪb(ə)l/ *adj.* **1** easily influenced by suggestions. **2** that may be suggested. —**suggestibility** /-ˈbɪlɪtɪ/ *n.* [f. prec.]

suggestion /səˈdʒestʃ(ə)n/ *n.* **1** suggesting. **2** a thing suggested. **3** the insinuation of a belief or impulse into the mind. **4** a hint or slight trace. [f. OF f. L (as SUGGEST)]

suggestive /səˈdʒestɪv/ *adj.* **1** conveying a suggestion. **2** tending to convey an indecent or improper meaning etc. —**suggestively** *adv.*, **suggestiveness** *n.* [f. SUGGEST]

suicidal /ˈsu:ɪsaɪd(ə)l, ˈsju:-, -ˈsaɪ-/ *adj.* **1** of or tending to suicide; (of a person) liable to commit suicide. **2** extremely foolhardy, destructive to one's own interests etc. —**suicidally** *adv.* [f. foll.]

suicide /ˈsu:ɪsaɪd, sju:-/ *n.* **1** the intentional killing of oneself; an instance of this; a person who does this. **2** an action destructive to one's own interests or reputation etc. [f. L *sui* of oneself + -CIDE]

sui generis /sju:aɪ ˈdʒenərɪs, su:i:/ of its own kind, unique. [L]

suit /su:t, sju:t/ *n.* **1** a set of clothes for wearing together, especially of the same cloth and consisting of a jacket and trousers or skirt. **2** clothing for a particular purpose. **3** a set of pyjamas, armour, etc. **4** any of the four sets (spades, hearts, diamonds, clubs) into which a pack of cards is divided. **5** a lawsuit. **6** (*archaic*) suing; the seeking of a woman's hand in marriage. —*v.t./i.* **1** to satisfy, to meet the demands or needs of. **2** to be convenient or right for. **3** to give a pleasing appearance or effect upon. **4** (of a climate, food, etc.) to improve or not impair the health of, to agree with. **5** to adapt, to make suitable. —**suit oneself,** to do as one chooses; to find something that satisfies one. [f. AF *suite*; as SUE]

suitable *adj.* right or appropriate for the purpose or occasion etc. —**suitability** /-ˈbɪlɪtɪ/ *n.*, **suitably** *adv.* [f. prec.]

suitcase *n.* a rectangular case for carrying clothes etc., usually with a handle and a hinged lid.

suite /swi:t/ *n.* **1** a set of rooms or furniture. **2** a set of attendants, a retinue. **3** (*Mus.*) a set of instrumental pieces. [F (as SUIT)]

suitor /ˈsu:tə(r), ˈsju:-/ *n.* **1** a man wooing a woman. **2** a plaintiff or petitioner. [f. AF f. L *secutor* (*sequi* follow)]

sulfa var. of SULPHA.

sulk *v.i.* to be sulky. —*n.* (usu. in *pl.*) a sulky fit. [perh. back-formation f. foll.]

sulky *adj.* sullen and unsociable from resentment or bad temper. —*n.* a light two-wheeled one-horse vehicle for a single person, especially as used in trotting-races (see TROTTING), so called because it admits only one person. —**sulkily** *adv.*, **sulkiness** *n.* [perh. f. obs. *sulke* hard to dispose of]

sullen /ˈsʌlən/ *adj.* passively resentful, stubbornly ill-humoured, unresponsive. —**sullenly** *adv.*, **sullenness** *n.* [alt. f. earlier *solein* (as SOLE[3])]

sully /ˈsʌlɪ/ *v.t.* to stain or blemish; to diminish the purity or splendour of (a reputation etc.). [perh. f. F *souiller* (as SOIL[2])]

sulpha /ˈsʌlfə/ *adj.* sulphonamide. [abbr.]

sulphate /ˈsʌlfeɪt/ *n.* a salt of sulphuric acid. [f. F f. L *sulphur*]

sulphide /ˈsʌlfaɪd/ *n.* a binary compound of sulphur. [f. SULPHUR]

sulphite /ˈsʌlfaɪt/ *n.* a salt of sulphurous acid. [as SULPHATE]

sulphonamide /sʌlˈfɒnəmaɪd/ *n.* a type of antibiotic drug. [f. G *sulfon* (as SULPHUR) + AMIDE]

sulphur /ˈsʌlfə(r)/ *n.* **1** a pale-yellow non-metallic element, symbol S, atomic number 16 (see below). **2** a pale slightly greenish yellow colour. **3** a yellow butterfly of the family Pieridae. [f. AF f. L]

sulphureous /sʌlˈfjʊərɪəs/ *adj.* of or like sulphur. [f. L, = sulphur]

sulphuric /sʌlˈfjʊərɪk/ *adj.* containing sulphur in a higher valency. —**sulphuric acid,** a dense oily highly acid and corrosive fluid. [f. F (as SULPHUR)]

sulphurous /ˈsʌlfərəs/ *adj.* **1** of or like sulphur. **2** containing sulphur in a lower valency. —**sulphurous acid,** an unstable weak acid used as a reducing and bleaching agent. [f. SULPHUR]

sultan /ˈsʌlt(ə)n/ *n.* **1** a Muslim sovereign. **2** (also **sweet sultan**) a sweet-scented plant (*Centaurea moschata* or *C. suaveolens*) [F or f. L f. Arab. = power, ruler]

sultana /sʌlˈtɑːnə/ *n.* **1** a kind of seedless raisin. **2** a sultan's wife, mother, concubine, or daughter. [It. (as prec.)]

sultanate /ˈsʌlt(ə)nət/ *n* the position of or territory ruled by a sultan. [f. SULTAN]

sultry /ˈsʌltrɪ/ *adj.* **1** (of weather etc.) hot and humid. **2** of dark mysterious beauty, passionate, sensual. —**sultrily** *adv.*, **sultriness** *n.* [f. obs. *sulter* v ; rel. to SWELTER]

sum *n.* **1** a total resulting from the addition of items. **2** a particular amount of money. **3** a problem in arithmetic; the working out of this. **4** the whole amount. **5** the substance, a summary (of facts etc.) —*v.t.* (**-mm-**) to find the sum of. —**in sum,** briefly, in summary. **sum up,** to find or give the total of; to express briefly, to summarize; to form or express a judgement or opinion of; (esp. of a judge) to recapitulate the evidence or argument. [f. OF f. L *summa* (*summus* highest)]

sumac /ˈʃuːmæk/ *n.* a shrub of the genus *Rhus* yielding leaves which are dried and ground for use in tanning and dyeing; these leaves. [f. OF or L f. Arab.]

summarize /ˈsʌməraɪz/ *v.t.* to make or be a summary of. [f. foll.]

summary /ˈsʌmərɪ/ *n.* a statement giving the main points of something. —*adj.* **1** brief, giving the main points only. **2** done or given without delay, details, or formalities. —**summarily** *adv.* [f. L (as SUM)]

summation /sʌˈmeɪʃ(ə)n/ *n.* **1** the finding of a total. **2** summarizing. [f. SUM]

summer *n.* **1** the warmest season of the year, from June to August in the northern hemisphere. **2** the mature stage of life etc. —*adj.* characteristic of or suitable for summer. —**summer-house** *n.* a light building in a garden or park, providing shade in summer. **Summer Palace,** a palace (now in ruins) of the Chinese emperors near Peking. **summer pudding,** a dish made by pressing soft fruits into a bowl lined and covered with bread or sponge-cake. **summer school,** a series of lectures etc. in summer, especially at a university. **summer-time** *n.* the season or weather of summer. **summer time,** the time shown by clocks advanced in summer to give long light evenings during the summer months. —**summery** *adj.* [OE]

summit /ˈsʌmɪt/ *n.* **1** the highest point, the top. **2** the highest level of achievement or status. **3** (in full **summit meeting**) a discussion between heads of governments. [f. OF *somet* (*som* top f. L, as SUM)]

summon /ˈsʌmən/ *v.t.* **1** to demand the presence of, to call together. **2** to command (a person) to appear in a lawcourt. **3** to call upon (a person etc.) to do something. **4** to gather (one's strength, courage, or energy etc.) in order to do something). [f. OF *summonēre* (SUB-, *monēre* warn)]

summons /ˈsʌmənz/ *n.* an authoritative call to attend or do something, especially to appear before a judge or magistrate. —*v.t.* to serve with a summons. [as prec.]

sumo /ˈsuːməʊ/ *n.* (*pl.* **-os**) **1** a kind of Japanese wrestling in which a person is considered defeated if he touches the ground except with his feet, or fails to keep within a marked area. **2** a person who takes part in this. [Jap.]

sump *n.* **1** a casing holding lubricating oil in an internal-combustion engine. **2** a pit, well, or low area into which waste or superfluous liquid drains. [orig. = marsh, rel. to SWAMP]

sumptuary /ˈsʌmptʊərɪ/ *adj.* regulating expenditure. [f. L (*sumptus* cost f. *sumere* take)]

sumptuous /ˈsʌmptʊəs/ *adj.* splendid and costlylooking. —**sumptuously** *adv.*, **sumptuousness** *n.* [f. OF f. L (as prec.)]

sun *n.* **1** (also **Sun**) the star that Earth travels round and receives warmth and light from. **2** such warmth or light or both. **3** any fixed star with or without planets. **4** (*poet.*) a day or year. —*v.t./i.* (**-nn-**) to expose (oneself etc.) to the sun. —**a place in the sun,** a favourable situation or condition. **sun-glasses** *n.pl.* spectacles with tinted lenses to protect the eyes from sunlight or glare. **sun-god** *n.* the sun worshipped as a deity **Sun King,** Louis XIV of France, so called from the magnificence of his reign. **sun-lamp** *n.* a lamp giving ultraviolet rays for therapy or an artificial sun-tan. **sun lounge,** a room designed to receive much sunlight. **sun-roof** *n.* a roof with a sliding section in a saloon car. **sun-tan** *n.* tanning of the skin by exposure to the sun. **sun-tanned** *adj.* tanned by the sun. **sun-trap** *n.* a sunny place, especially one sheltered from the wind. **sun-up** *n.* (*US*) sunrise. **under the sun,** anywhere in the world. [OE]

Sun. *abbr.* Sunday.

sunbathe *v.i.* to expose one's body to the sun.

sunbeam *n.* a ray of sun.

sunburn *n.* tanning or inflammation of the skin caused by exposure to the sun. —**sunburnt** *adj.*

sundae /ˈsʌndeɪ/ *n.* a confection of ice-cream with fruit, syrup, etc. [perh. f. foll., either because the dish orig. included left-over ice-cream sold cheaply on Monday, or because it was at first sold only on Sunday, having been devised (according to some accounts) to circumvent Sunday legislation. The spelling is sometimes said to have been altered from *Sunday* out of deference to religious people's feelings]

Sunday /ˈsʌndeɪ/ *n.* **1** the day of the week following Saturday, the Christian day of rest and worship. **2** a newspaper published on Sundays. —*adv.* (*colloq.*) on Sunday. —**Sunday best,** one's best clothes (kept for use on Sundays). **Sunday painter,** an amateur painter, one who paints solely for pleasure. **Sunday school,** a school held on Sundays for children, now only for religious instruction. [OE. = day of the sun]

sunder *v.t.* to break or tear apart, to sever. [OE; cf. ASUNDER]

sundial *n.* an instrument showing the time by the shadow of a rod or plate cast by the sun on a scaled dial.

sundown *n.* sunset.

sundry /ˈsʌndrɪ/ *adj.* various, several. —*n.* (in *pl.*) oddments, accessories, items not needed to be specified. —**all and sundry,** everyone. [OE, rel. to SUNDER]

sunfish *n.* a large globular fish, especially the ocean fish *Mola mola*.

sunflower *n.* a tall garden-plant of the genus *Helianthus* with large golden-rayed flowers.

sung *p.p.* of SING.

sunk *past* & *p.p.* of SINK.

sunken *adj.* lying below the level of a surrounding area; (of cheeks etc.) shrunken, hollow. [p.p. of SINK]

sunless *adj.* without sunshine. [f. SUN + -LESS]

sunlight *n.* light from the sun.

sunlit *adj.* illuminated by sunlight.

Sunna /ˈsʌnə/ *n.* the traditional portion of Islamic law, based on Muhammad's words or acts but not written by him. [Arab., = form, way, rule]

Sunnite /ˈsʌnaɪt/ *n.* a member of one of the two major groups in Islam (opp. SHIITE), comprising the main community in most Muslim countries other than Iran. [f. SUNNA]

sunny *adj.* **1** bright with or as sunlight; exposed to or warm with the sun. **2** happy, cheerful. —**sunnily** *adv.*, **sunniness** *n.* [f. SUN]

sunrise *n.* the sun's rising; the moment of this; the eastern sky with the colours of the sunrise.

sunset *n.* the sun's setting; the moment of this; the western sky with the colours of the sunset.

sunshade *n.* a parasol or awning, giving shade from the sun.

sunshine *n.* **1** the light of the sun; the area illuminated by it. **2** fair weather. **3** cheerfulness, bright influence.

sunspot *n.* a dark patch on the sun's surface.

sunstroke *n.* illness caused by excessive exposure to sun.

sunwise *adv.* in the direction of the sun's course (and hence lucky; opp. *widdershins*).

sup *v.t./i.* (**-pp-**) **1** to drink by sips or spoonfuls. **2** to take supper. **3** (*colloq.*) to drink (beer etc.). —*n.* a mouthful of liquid; (*colloq.*) a drink of beer etc. [OE; in second sense of v. f. OF (as SOUP)]

sup- *prefix* see SUB-.

super /ˈsu:pə(r), ˈsju:-/ *adj.* (*slang*) excellent, superb. —*n.* (*colloq.*) **1** a supernumerary. **2** a superintendent. [abbr.]

super- /su:pə(r)-, sju:-/ *prefix* above or beyond or over (*superstructure, supernormal*); to a great or extreme degree (*superabundant, supertanker*); higher in status (*superintendent*). [f. L *super* over]

superabundant /su:pərəˈbʌnd(ə)nt, sju:-/ *adj.* very abundant, more than enough. —**superabundance** *n.*

superannuate /su:pəˈrænjʊeɪt, sju:-/ *v.t.* **1** to discharge (an employee) into retirement with a pension. **2** to discard as too old for use. [f. L (SUPER-, *annus* year)]

superannuation /su:pərænjʊˈeɪʃ(ə)n, sju:-/ *n.* **1** superannuating. **2** a pension granted to an employee on retirement; payment(s) contributed towards this during his or her employment. [f. prec.]

superb /su:ˈpɜ:b, sju:-/ *adj.* of the most impressive or splendid kind, excellent. —**superbly** *adv.* [f. F or L *superbus* proud]

supercargo *n.* (*pl.* **-oes**) a person in a merchant ship managing the sales etc. of cargo. [f. Sp. *sobrecargo* (*sobre* over, CARGO)]

supercharge *v.t.* **1** to charge to extreme or

excess (with energy etc.). **2** to use a supercharger on.

supercharger *n.* a device forcing extra air or fuel into an internal-combustion engine so as to increase its power.

superciliary /su:pəˈsɪlɪərɪ, sju:-/ *adj.* of the eybrow; over the eye. [f. L *supercilium* eyebrow (SUPER-, *cilium* eyelid)]

supercilious /su:pəˈsɪlɪəs, sju:-/ *adj.* with an air of superiority, haughty and scornful. —**superciliously** *adv.*, **superciliousness** *n.* [f. L (as prec.)]

superconductivity /su:pəkɒndʌkˈtɪvɪtɪ, sju:-/ *n.* absence of electrical resistance in some substances at temperatures near absolute zero. —**superconductive** /-kənˈdʌktɪv/ *adj.*

supercool *v.t.* to cool (a liquid) below its freezing-point without its becoming solid or crystalline.

super-ego /su:pərˈi:gəʊ, -ˈegəʊ, sju:-/ *n.* a person's ideals for himself, acting like a conscience in directing his behaviour.

supererogation /su:pərerəˈgeɪʃ(ə)n, sju:-/ *n.* the doing of more than duty requires. [f. L *supererogare* pay out in addition, orig. public money after formal request for permission (SUPER-, *rogare* ask)]

superfamily *n.* a taxonomic category between family and order.

superficial /su:pəˈfɪʃ(ə)l, sju:-/ *adj.* **1** of or on the surface only. **2** without depth of knowledge or feeling etc. **3** (of measure) square. —**superficiality** /-ʃɪˈælɪtɪ/ *n.*, **superficially** *adv.* [f. L (*superficies* surface f. SUPER-, *facies* face)]

superfine *adj.* extremely fine or refined.

superfluity /su:pəˈflu:ɪtɪ, sju:-/ *n.* **1** a superfluous amount or thing. **2** being superfluous. [f. OF f. L (as foll.)]

superfluous /su:ˈpɜ:flʊəs, sju:-/ *adj.* more than is needed or required; not needed. —**superfluously** *adv.*, **superfluousness** *n.* [f. L (SUPER-, *fluere* flow)]

supergrass *n.* (*slang*) one who informs against a large number of persons.

superheat *v.t.* to heat (liquid) above its boiling-point without allowing it to vaporize; to heat (vapour) above its boiling-point. —**superheater** *n.*

superhighway *n.* (*US*) a broad main road for fast traffic.

superhuman /su:pəˈhju:mən, sju:-/ *adj.* **1** exceeding the normal human capacity or power. **2** higher than humanity, divine.

superimpose /su:pərɪmˈpəʊz, sju:-/ *v.t.* to lay or place (a thing) on top of something else. —**superimposition** /-pəˈzɪʃ(ə)n/ *n.*

superintend /su:pərɪnˈtend, sju:-/ *v.t./i.* to supervise. —**superintendence** *n.* [f. L *superintendere* (SUPER-, INTEND)]

superintendent *n.* **1** one who superintends. **2** the director of an institution etc. **3** a police officer above the rank of inspector. [f. prec.]

superior /su:ˈpɪərɪə(r), sju:-/ *adj.* **1** higher in position or rank; (of figures etc.) written or printed above the line. **2** better or greater in some way; of high or higher quality. **3** showing that one feels oneself to be better or wiser etc. than others; conceited, supercilious. **4** (with *to*) not influenced by; not yielding or resorting to. —*n.* **1** a person or thing of higher rank, ability, or quality. **2** the head of a monastery or other religious community. —**superiority** /-ˈɒrɪtɪ/ *n.* [f. OF f. L, compar. of *superus* situated above (*super* above)]

superlative /su:ˈpɜ:lətɪv, sju:-/ *adj.* of the highest degree or quality, excellent. —*n.* (*Gram.*) the superlative degree; a superlative form. —**superlative adjective** (*or* **adverb**), an adjective (or adverb) in the superlative degree. **superlative degree,** the form expressing the highest or a very high degree of a quality (e.g. *bravest, most quickly*). —**superlatively** *adv.*, **superlativeness** *n.* [f. OF f. L (*superlatus* carried above f. SUPER-, p.p. of *ferre* bear)]

superman *n.* (*pl.* **-men**) a man of superhuman powers or achievement.

supermarket *n.* a large self-service store usually selling food and some household goods.

supernatural /su:əˈnætʃər(ə)l, sju:-/ *adj.* of or manifesting phenomena not explicable by natural or physical laws. —**supernaturally** *adv.*

supernova /su:pəˈnəʊvə, sju:-/ *n.* (*pl.* **-ae** or **-as**) a star that suddenly increases very greatly in brightness because of an explosion disrupting its structure.

supernumerary /su:pəˈnju:mərərɪ, sju:-/ *adj.* in excess of the normal number, extra. —*n.* a supernumerary person or thing. [f. L (*super numerum* beyond the number)]

superphosphate /su:pəˈfɒsfeɪt, sju:-/ *n.* a fertilizer made from phosphate rock.

superpose /su:pəˈpəʊz, sju:-/ *v.t.* to place (a geometrical figure) upon another so that their outlines coincide. —**superposition** /-pəˈzɪʃ(ə)n/ *n.*

superpower *n.* a nation or State having a dominant position in world politics, one with the power to act decisively in pursuit of interests affecting the whole world; the USA and USSR.

superscribe /ˈsu:pəskraɪb, ˈsju:-/ *v.t.* to write (an inscription) at the top of or outside a document etc. [f. L *superscribere* (SUPER-, *scribere* write)]

superscript /ˈsuːpəskrɪpt, ˈsjuː-/ *adj.* written or printed just above and to the right of a word, figure, or symbol. —*n.* a superscript figure or symbol. [as prec.]

superscription /suːpəˈskrɪpʃ(ə)n, sjuː-/ *n.* superscribed words. [as SUPERSCRIBE]

supersede /suːpəˈsiːd, sjuː-/ *v.t.* to take the place of; to put or use another in place of. —**supercession** /-ˈseʃ(ə)n/ *n.* [f. OF f. L *supersedēre* be superior to (SUPER-, *sedēre* sit)]

supersonic /suːpəˈsɒnɪk, sjuː-/ *adj.* of or having a speed greater than that of sound. —**supersonically** *adv.*

superstar *n.* a great star in entertainment etc.

superstition /suːpəˈstɪʃ(ə)n, sjuː-/ *n.* **1** belief in the existence or power of the supernatural; irrational fear of the unknown or mysterious; misdirected reverence. **2** a religion, or practice, or opinion based on such tendencies. **3** a widely held but wrong idea. —**superstitious** *adj.*, **superstitiously** *adv.*, **superstitiousness** *n.* [f. OF or L *superstitio* f. *superstare* (SUPER-, *stare* stand)]

superstore *n.* a large supermarket, especially one with a sales area of at least 2,500 sq. metres.

superstructure *n.* a structure built on top of something else; a building as distinct from its foundations.

supertanker *n.* a very large tanker.

supervene /suːpəˈviːn, sjuː-/ *v.i.* to occur as an interruption in or change from some state or process. —**supervention** *n.* [f. L *supervenire* (SUPER-, *venire* come)]

supervise /ˈsuːpəvaɪz, ˈsjuː-/ *v.t.* to direct and inspect (work, workers, or the operation of an organization). —**supervision** /-ˈvɪʒ(ə)n/ *n.*, **supervisor** *n.*, **supervisory** *adj.* [f. L *supervidēre* (SUPER-, *vidēre* see)]

supine /ˈsuːpaɪn, ˈsjuː-/ *adj.* **1** lying face upwards. **2** inactive, indolent. —*n.* a Latin verbal noun used only in the accusative and ablative cases. —**supinely** *adv.* [f. L *supinus* (*super* above)]

supper *n.* a light evening meal, the last meal of the day. [f. OF *soper*, *super* (as SUP)]

supplant /səˈplɑːnt/ *v.t.* to oust and take the place of. —**supplanter** *n.* [f. OF or L *supplantare* trip up (SUP-, *planta* sole)]

supple *adj.* bending easily, flexible, not stiff. —**supplely** *adv.*, **suppleness** *n.* [f. OF f. L *supplex* submissive (as SUPPLICATE)]

supplement /ˈsʌplɪmənt/ *n.* **1** a thing added as an extra or to make up for a deficiency. **2** a part added to a book etc. to give further information or to treat a particular subject; a set of special pages issued with a newspaper. —/also -ˈment/ *v.t.* to provide or be a supplement to. —**supplemental** /-ˈment(ə)l/ *adj.*, **supplementary** /-ˈmentərɪ/ *adj.*, **supplementation** /-ˈteɪʃ(ə)n/ *n.* [f. L (as SUPPLY)]

suppliant /ˈsʌplɪənt/ *n.* a humble petitioner. —*adj.* supplicating [f. F (*supplier* f. L, as foll.)]

supplicate /ˈsʌplɪkeɪt/ *v.t./i.* to petition humbly. —**supplication** /-ˈkeɪʃ(ə)n/ *n.*, **supplicatory** *adj.* [f. L *supplicare* (SUP-, *plicare* bend)]

supply /səˈplaɪ/ *v.t.* **1** to give or provide with (something needed or useful); to make available for use. **2** to make up for (a deficiency or need). —*n.* **1** provision of what is needed. **2** a stock or store, an amount of something provided or obtainable. **3** (in *pl.*) the collected necessaries for an army, expedition, etc. **4** a person, especially a schoolteacher or clergyman, acting as a temporary substitute for another. —**on supply**, (of a schoolteacher etc.) acting as a supply. **supply and demand**, the quantities available and required, as factors regulating the price of commodities. —**supplier** *n.* [f. OF f. L *supplēre* (SUP-, *plēre* fill)]

support /səˈpɔːt/ *v.t.* **1** to keep from falling or sinking; to hold in position; to bear all or part of the weight of. **2** to give strength to; to enable to last or continue; to supply with necessaries. **3** to assist by one's approval or presence or by subscription to funds; to speak in favour of (a resolution etc.); to be actively interested in (a particular sport or team). **4** to take a secondary part to (another performer). **5** to bring facts to confirm (a statement etc.); to corroborate. **6** to endure, to tolerate. —*n.* **1** supporting, being supported. **2** a person or thing that supports. —**in support of**, so as to support. **supporting film**, a less important film in a cinema programme. [f. OF f. L *supportare* (SUP-, *portare* carry)]

supporter *n.* **1** a person or thing that supports; a person supporting a team or sport. **2** (in heraldry) a representation of a living creature holding up or standing beside an escutcheon, usually as one of a pair on either side. [f. prec.]

supportive /səˈpɔːtɪv/ *adj.* providing support or encouragement. [f. SUPPORT]

suppose /səˈpəʊz/ *v.t.* **1** to accept as true or probable, to be inclined to think. **2** to take as a possiblity or hypothesis for the purpose of arguments; (in *imper.*) as a formula of proposal. **3** (of a theory or result etc.) to require as a condition; to presuppose. **4** (in *p.p.*) generally accepted as being so. —**be supposed to**, to be expected or required to; (*colloq.*, with *neg.*) ought not to, not to be allowed to. [f. OF (as SUP-, POSE)]

supposedly /səˈpəʊzɪdlɪ/ *adv.* as is generally supposed. [f. prec.]

supposition /sʌpəˈzɪʃ(ə)n/ *n.* **1** a thing supposed. **2** supposing. [f. SUPPOSE]

suppositious /sʌpəˈzɪʃəs/ *adj.* hypothetical.

—**suppositiously** *adv.*, **suppositiousness** *n.* [f. prec.]

supposititious /sʌpɒzɪˈtɪʃəs/ *adj.* substituted for the real person or thing, spurious. —**supposititiously** *adv.*, **supposititiousness** *n.* [f. L *supponere* substitute (SUP-, *ponere* place)]

suppository /səˈpɒzɪtərɪ/ *n.* a medical preparation for insertion into the rectum or vagina, where it is left to melt. [f. L (as prec.)]

suppress /səˈpres/ *v.t.* **1** to put an end to the activity or existence of, especially by force or authority. **2** to prevent from being seen, heard, or known. **3** to eliminate (electrical interference etc.) partially; to equip (a device) to reduce such interference as it produces. —**suppression** *n.*, **suppressor** *n.* [f. L *supprimere* (SUP-, *premere* press)]

suppressible *adj.* that may be suppressed. [f. prec]

suppurate /ˈsʌpjʊreɪt/ *v.i.* to form pus, to fester. —**suppuration** /-ˈreɪʃ(ə)n/ *n.* [f. L *suppurare* (SUP-, *pus puris* pus)]

supra /ˈsu:prə/ *adv.* above or further back in the book etc. [L, = above]

supra- /su:prə-/ *prefix* above. [as prec.]

supranational /su:prəˈnæʃən(ə)l/ *adj.* transcending national limits.

supremacy /su:ˈpreməsɪ, sju:-/ *n.* being supreme; the highest authority. [f. foll.]

supreme /su:ˈpri:m/ *adj.* **1** highest in rank or authority. **2** highest in importance, intensity, or quality; most outstanding; (of a penalty or sacrifice) involving death. —**Supreme Being,** God. **Supreme Court,** the highest judicial court in a State etc. [f. L *supremus*, superl. of *superus* (as SUPERIOR)]

supremo /su:ˈpri:məʊ, sju:-/ *n.* (*pl.* **-os**) a supreme leader or ruler. [Sp., = prec.]

sur-[1] *prefix* see SUB-.

sur-[2] *prefix* = SUPER- (*surcharge*, *surface*, *surrealism*). [OF]

surcease /sɜ:ˈsi:s/ *n.* (*archaic*) cessation. —*v.i.* (*archaic*) to cease. [f. OF *sursis* (*surseoir* refrain f. L, as SUPERSEDE)]

surcharge /ˈsɜ:tʃɑ:dʒ/ *n.* **1** an additional charge or payment. **2** a mark printed on a postage stamp, especially one changing its value. **3** an additional or excessive load. —/also -ˈtʃɑ:dʒ/ *v.t.* **1** to exact a surcharge from; to exact (a sum) as a surcharge. **2** to mark (a postage stamp) with a surcharge. **3** to overload. [f. OF (as SUR-[2], CHARGE)]

surd *adj.* **1** (of a number) irrational. **2** (of a sound) uttered with breath and not voice (e.g. *f, k, p, s, t*). —*n.* **1** a surd number, especially the root of an integer. **2** a surd sound. [f. L *surdus* deaf]

sure /ʃʊə(r), ʃɔ(r)/ *adj.* **1** having or seeming to have adequate reasons for one's belief; free from doubts; having satisfactory knowledge or trust. **2** certain to do something or to happen. **3** reliable, secure, unfailing. **4** undoubtedly true or truthful. —*adv.* (*colloq.*) certainly. —**be sure to,** to take care to, not to fail to. **for sure,** (*colloq.*) without doubt. **make sure,** to make or become certain, to ensure. **sure enough,** (*colloq.*) in fact, certainly. **sure-fire** *adj.* (*colloq.*) certain to succeed. **sure-footed** *adj.* never stumbling or making a mistake. **to be sure,** it is undeniable or admitted. —**sureness** *n.* [f. OF *sur* f. L, = SECURE]

surely /ˈʃʊəlɪ, ˈʃɔ-/ *adv.* **1** in a sure manner; with certainty; securely. **2** used for emphasis, or (in questions) as an appeal to likelihood or reason. **3** (as an answer) certainly, yes. [f. SURE]

surety /ˈʃʊərətɪ/ *n.* **1** a person who makes himself responsible for another's performance of an undertaking or payment of a debt. **2** (*archaic*) certainty. [f. OF f. L *securitas* security]

surf *n.* the foam of the sea breaking on the shore or on reefs. —*v.i.* to go surf-riding. —**surf-riding** *n.* the sport of being carried over the surf to the shore on a board etc. —**surfer** *n.* [f. earlier *suff*; orig. unkn.]

surface /ˈsɜ:fɪs/ *n.* **1** the outside of a thing; any of the limits terminating a solid. **2** the top of a liquid or of soil etc. **3** the outward aspect, what is perceived on a casual view or consideration. **4** (*Geom.*) that which has length and breadth but no thickness. —(*attrib.*) *adj.* of the surface; superficial. —*v.t./i.* **1** to give a (special) surface to (a road, paper, etc.). **2** to rise to the surface; to become visible or known; (*colloq.*) to become conscious. **3** to bring (a submarine) to the surface. —**surface mail,** mail carried overland and by sea. **surface tension,** tension of the surface of a liquid, tending to minimize its surface area. [F (as SUR-[2], FACE)]

surfboard *n.* a long narrow board used in surf-riding.

surfeit /ˈsɜ:fɪt/ *n.* an excess, especially in eating or drinking; the resulting satiety. —*v.t./i.* to over-feed; to be or cause to be wearied through excess. [f. OF; cf. L *superficiens* excessive (SUPER-, *facere* do)]

surge *v.i.* **1** to move to and fro (as) in waves. **2** to move suddenly and powerfully; to increase in volume or intensity. —*n.* **1** a powerful wave. **2** a surging motion; an impetuous onset. [f. OF f. L *surgere* rise]

surgeon /ˈsɜ:dʒ(ə)n/ *n.* a person skilled in surgery; a naval or military medical officer. [f. AF (OF *sirurgie* f. L *chirurgia* f. Gk, lit. = handiwork)]

surgery /ˈsɜ:dʒərɪ/ *n.* **1** the treatment of bodily injuries, disorders, and disease by cutting or manipulation of the affected parts. **2** the place where or time when a doctor or dentist etc. gives advice and treatment, or an MP or lawyer etc. is available for consultation. [f. OF (as prec.)]

surgical /ˈsɜːdʒɪk(ə)l/ *adj.* of or by surgeons or surgery; (of an appliance) used for surgery or in conditions suitable for surgery. **—surgical spirit,** methylated spirits used for cleansing etc. **—surgically** *adv.* [f. earlier *chirurgical* (*chirurgy* f. OF, as SURGEON)]

surly /ˈsɜːlɪ/ *adj.* bad-tempered and unfriendly. **—surlily** *adv.*, **surliness** *n.* [alt. of obs. *sirly* haughty f. SIR]

surmise /səˈmaɪz/ *n.* a conjecture. *—v.t./i.* to conjecture. [f. AF & OF p.p. of *surmettre* accuse f. L *supermittere* (SUPER-, *mittere* send)]

surmount /səˈmaʊnt/ *v.t.* **1** to overcome (a difficulty); to get over (an obstacle). **2** (in *p.p.*) capped or crowned by a specified thing. [f. OF (SUR-², *monter* mount)]

surmountable *adj.* that may be surmounted. [f. prec.]

surname /ˈsɜːneɪm/ *n.* the name common to all members of a family, a person's hereditary name. *—v.t.* to give a surname to. [alt. of *surnoun* f. AF (as SUR-², NOUN name)]

surpass /səˈpɑːs/ *v.t.* to do or be greater or better than, to excel; (in *partic.*) excelling or exceeding others. **—surpassingly** *adv.* [f. F (as SUR-², PASS¹)]

surplice /ˈsɜːplɪs/ *n.* a loose white linen vestment worn by clergy and choristers. [f. AF f. L *superpellicium* (SUPER-, *pellicia* PELISSE)]

surplus /ˈsɜːpləs/ *n.* an amount left over when requirements have been met; the excess of revenue over expenditure. *—adj.* exceeding what is needed or used. [f. AF f. L (as SUR-², PLUS)]

surprise /səˈpraɪz/ *n.* **1** the emotion aroused by something sudden or unexpected. **2** an event or thing arousing such emotion. **3** the catching of a person etc. unprepared. **4** (*attrib.*) made or done etc. unexpectedly, without warning. *—v.t.* **1** to affect with surprise, to turn out contrary to the expectations of; to shock, to scandalize. **2** to capture or attack by surprise; to come upon (a person) off his guard. **3** to startle into action by surprise. **4** to discover (a secret etc.) by unexpected action. **—by surprise,** unexpectedly **—surprising** *adj.*, **surprisingly** *adv.* [OF, p.p. of *surprendre* (SUR-², L *praehendere* seize)]

surrealism /səˈriːəlɪz(ə)m/ *n.* a 20th-c. movement in art and literature purporting to express the unconscious mind by depicting the phenomena of dreams etc. **—surrealist** *adj.* & *n.*, **surrealistic** /-ˈlɪstɪk/ *adj.*, **surrealistically** /-ˈlɪstɪkəlɪ/ *adv.* [f. F (as SUR-², REALISM)]

surrender /səˈrendə(r)/ *v.t./i.* **1** to hand over, to give into another's power or control, especially on demand or under compulsion. **2** to give oneself up; to accept an enemy's demand for submission. **3** to give up one's rights under (an insurance policy) in return for a small sum received immediately. *—n.* surrendering. **—surrender oneself to,** to give way to (an emotion). **surrender to one's bail,** to appear duly in a lawcourt after release on bail. [f. AF (as SUR-², RENDER)]

surreptitious /sʌrəpˈtɪʃəs/ *adj.* acting or done by stealth. **—surreptitiously** *adv.* [f. L *surripere* seize secretly. (SUR-¹, *rapere* seize)]

surrogate /ˈsʌrəgət/ *n.* a deputy, especially of a bishop; a substitute. **—surrogacy** *n.* [f. L, p.p. of *surrogare* elect as substitute (SUR-¹, *rogare* ask)]

surround /səˈraʊnd/ *v.t.* to come to be all round; to enclose on all sides; to encircle with enemy forces. *—n.* a border or edging, especially between walls and carpet; a floor-covering for this. **—surrounded by** *or* **with,** having on all sides. [orig. = overflow, f. AF f. L *superundare* (SUPER-, *unda* wave)]

surroundings *n.pl.* the things or conditions around and liable to affect a person or thing. [f. prec.]

surtax /ˈsɜːtæks/ *n.* an additional tax, especially on incomes over a certain amount. *—v.t.* to impose a surtax on. [f. F (as SUR-², TAX)]

surveillance /sɜːˈveɪləns/ *n.* close observation, especially of a suspected person. [F, f. *surveiller* keep watch on (SUR-², L *vigilare* keep watch)]

survey /səˈveɪ/ *v.t.* **1** to look at and take a general view of. **2** to make or present a survey of. **3** to examine the condition of (a building etc.). **4** to measure and map out the size, shape, position, elevation, etc. of (an area). —/ˈsɜːveɪ/ *n.* **1** the act of surveying. **2** a general examination of a situation or subject; an account of this. **3** the surveying of land etc.; a map or plan produced by this. [f. AF f. L *supervidēre* (SUPER-, *vidēre* see)]

surveyor /səˈveɪə(r)/ *n.* one who surveys land or buildings professionally. [f. prec.]

survival /səˈvaɪv(ə)l/ *n.* **1** surviving. **2** something that has survived from earlier times. [f. foll.]

survive /səˈvaɪv/ *v.t./i.* **1** to continue to live or exist. **2** to live or exist longer than. **3** to come alive through or continue to exist in spite of (a danger or accident etc.). **—survivor** *n.* [f. AF *survivre* f. L *supervivere* (SUPER-, *vivere* live)]

sus *n.* (*slang*) **1** suspicion. **2** a suspect. *—v.t.*

(**-ss-**) (*slang*, often with *out*) to investigate, to reconnoitre. [abbr.]

sus- *prefix* see SUB-.

susceptibility /səseptɪ'bɪlɪtɪ/ *n.* **1** being susceptible. **2** (in *pl.*) a person's sensitive feelings. [f. foll.]

susceptible /sə'septɪb(ə)l/ *adj.* **1** impressionable; falling in love easily. **2** (*predic.*, with *to*) liable to be affected by, sensitive to; (with *of*) able to undergo, admitting. —**susceptibly** *adv.* [f. L *suscipere* take up (SUS-, *capere* take)]

susceptive /sə'septɪv/ *adj* susceptible. [as prec.]

suspect /sə'spekt/ *v.t.* **1** to have an impression of the existence or presence of; to have a partial or unconfirmed belief. **2** to have suspicions or doubts about, to mistrust. —/'sʌspekt/ *n.* a suspected person. —/'sʌspekt/ *adj.* subject to suspicion or distrust. [f. L *suspicere* (SUS-, *specere* look)]

suspend /sə'spend/ *v.t.* **1** to hang up; (in *p.p.*, of solid particles etc. in a fluid) sustained somewhere between top and bottom, kept from falling or sinking. **2** to keep inoperative or undecided for a time, to postpone. **3** to put a temporary stop to; to deprive temporarily of a position or right. —**suspended sentence**, a sentence of imprisonment that is not enforced, on condition of good behaviour. [f. OF or L *suspendere* (SUS-, *pendere* hang)]

suspender *n.* **1** an attachment to hold up a stocking or sock by its top. **2** (in *pl.*, *US*) a pair of braces. —**suspender belt**, a woman's undergarment with suspenders. [f. prec.]

suspense /sə'spens/ *n.* a state of anxious uncertainty or expectation. [f. AF f. L (as SUSPEND)]

suspension /sə'spenʃ(ə)n/ *n.* **1** suspending, being suspended. **2** the means by which a vehicle is supported on its axles. **3** a substance consisting of particles suspended in a fluid. —**suspension bridge**, a bridge with a roadway suspended from cables supported by towers. [F or f. L (as SUSPEND)]

suspicion /sə'spɪʃ(ə)n/ *n.* **1** the feeling of one who suspects; a partial or unconfirmed belief. **2** suspecting, being suspected. **3** a slight trace. —**above suspicion**, too obviously good etc. to be suspected. **under suspicion**, suspected. [f. AF f. L (as SUSPECT)]

suspicious /sə'spɪʃəs/ *adj* **1** prone to or feeling suspicion. **2** indicating or justifying suspicion. —**suspiciously** *adv* [as prec.]

suss var. of SUS

sustain /sə'steɪn/ *v.t.* **1** to bear the weight of, to support, especially for a long period **2** to endure without giving way. **3** to undergo, to suffer (a defeat or injury etc.) **4** to confirm or uphold the validity of **5** to keep (a sound or effort etc.) going continuously. [f. AF f. L *sustinēre* (SUS-, *tenēre* hold)]

sustenance /'sʌstɪnəns/ *n.* **1** the process of sustaining life by food. **2** the food itself, nourishment. [as prec.]

sutler *n.* (*hist.*) a camp-follower selling food etc. [f. obs. Du. *soeteler* (*soetelen* perform mean duties)]

suttee /sʌ'ti:/ *n.* the former act or custom of a Hindu widow sacrificing herself on her husband's funeral pyre; a Hindu widow doing this. [Hindi & Urdu, f. Skr. = faithful wife]

suture /'su:tʃə(r)/ *n.* **1** surgical stitching of a wound; a stitch or thread etc. used in this. **2** a seamlike line of junction of two bones at their edges, especially in the skull; a similar junction or parts in a plant or animal body. —*v.t.* to stitch (a wound). [F, or f. L *sutura* (*suere* sew)]

suzerain /'su:zəreɪn/ *n.* **1** a feudal overlord. **2** a sovereign or State having some control over another State that is internally autonomous. —**suzerainty** *n.* [F, app. f. *sus* above]

svelte /svelt/ *adj.* slender and graceful. [F, f. It. *svelto*]

SW *abbr.* south-west, south-western.

swab /swɒb/ *n.* **1** a mop or other absorbent device for cleansing, drying, or absorbing things. **2** an absorbent pad used in surgery. **3** a specimen of a secretion taken for examination. —*v.t.* (**-bb-**) to clean with a swab; to take up (moisture) with a swab. [f. Du. *zwabber* f. Gmc = splash, sway]

swaddle /'swɒd(ə)l/ *v.t.* to swathe in wraps, clothes, or warm garments. —**swaddling-clothes** *n.pl.* the narrow bandages formerly wrapped round a new-born child to restrain its movements. [f. SWATHE]

swag *n.* **1** loot. **2** a carved ornamental festoon of fruit, flowers, etc., hung by its ends. **3** (*Austral.*) a bundle of personal belongings carried by a tramp etc. [f. *swag* sway, prob. f. Scand.]

swage *n.* **1** a die or stamp for shaping wrought iron. **2** a tool for bending metal etc. —*v.t.* to shape with a swage. [f. F *s(o)uage* decorative groove; orig. unkn.]

swagger *v.i.* to walk or behave with arrogance or self-importance. —*n.* a swaggering gait or behaviour; smartness. —*adj.* **1** (*colloq.*) smart, fashionable. **2** (of a coat) cut with a loose flare from the shoulders. —**swagger-stick** *n.* a short cane carried by a military officer. [app. f. SWAG]

Swahili /swɑ:'hi:lɪ/ *n.* **1** a Bantu people of Zanzibar and the adjacent coasts. **2** their Bantu language. [f. Arab., pl. of *sāhil* coast]

swain *n.* **1** (*archaic*) a country youth. **2** (*poetic*) a young lover or suitor. [f. ON *sveinn* lad = OE *swān* swine-herd]

swallow[1] /ˈswɒləʊ/ *v.t./i.* **1** to cause or allow (food etc.) to pass down one's throat; to perform the muscular movement (as) of swallowing something. **2** to accept (a statement) with ready credulity; to accept (an insult) meekly. **3** to repress (a sound or emotion etc.). **4** to take in so as to engulf or absorb. —*n.* **1** the act of swallowing. **2** the amount swallowed in one movement. [OE]

swallow[2] /ˈswɒləʊ/ *n.* a migratory swift-flying bird of the genus *Hirundo* etc. with a forked tail. —**swallow-dive** *n.* a dive with the arms outspread until close to the water. —**swallow-tail** *n.* a deeply forked tail; a butterfly or humming-bird with a forked tail. [OE]

swam *past* of SWIM.

swami /ˈswɑːmɪ/ *n.* a Hindu religious teacher. [f. Hindi, = master]

swamp /swɒmp/ *n.* a piece of wet spongy ground. —*v.t.* to overwhelm, flood, or soak with water; to overwhelm or make invisible etc. with an excess or large amount of something. —**swampy** *adj.* [prob. f. Gmc, = sponge, fungus]

swan /swɒn/ *n.* a large web-footed swimming bird usually of the genus *Cygnus*, with a long gracefully-curved neck, especially *C. olor*, with pure white plumage in the adult, black legs and feet, and a red bill with a black knob. —*v.i.* (**-nn-**) (*slang*) to go in a leisurely majestic way, like a swan. —**Swan of Avon,** Shakespeare. **swan-song** *n.* a person's final composition or performance etc. (from the old belief that a swan sang sweetly when about to die). **swan-upping** *n.* the annual taking up and marking (by the appropriate authorities) of swans on the Thames. [OE]

swank *n.* (*colloq.*) **1** boastful behaviour, ostentation. **2** a person who swanks. —*v.i.* (*colloq.*) to behave with swank. —**swanky** *adj.*, **swankily** *adv.*, **swankiness** *n.* [orig. Midland dial.]

swannery /ˈswɒnərɪ/ *n.* a place where swans are kept. [f. SWAN]

swansdown /ˈswɒnzdaʊn/ *n.* **1** the down of the swan used in trimmings etc. **2** thick cotton cloth with soft nap on one side.

swap /swɒp/ *v.t./i.* (**-pp-**) to exchange or barter. —*n.* **1** an act of swapping. **2** a thing suitable for swapping. [orig. = hit (prob. imit.)]

sward /swɔːd/ *n.* an expanse of short grass. [OE, = skin]

swarm[1] /swɔːm/ *n.* **1** a large number of insects, birds, small animals, or persons moving in a cluster. **2** a cluster of bees leaving the hive with a queen bee, to form a new home. —*v.i.* **1** to move in or form a swarm. **2** (of a place) to be crowded or overrun. [OE]

swarm[2] /swɔːm/ *v.i.* (with *up*) to climb by gripping with the hands or arms and legs. [orig. unkn.]

swarthy /ˈswɔːðɪ/ *adj.* dark, dark-complexioned. —**swarthily** *adv.*, **swarthiness** *n.* [var. of earlier *swarty* (*swart*, f. OE)]

swashbuckler /ˈswɒʃbʌklə(r)/ *n.* a person who swaggers aggressively. —**swashbuckling** *adj.* & *n.* [f. *swash* strike noisily + BUCKLER]

swastika /ˈswɒstɪkə/ *n.* a symbol formed by a cross with equal arms each continued as far again at right angles and all in the same direction, especially as the symbol of the Nazis. [f. Skr. *svastika* (*svasti* well-being f. *sú* good + *asti* being)]

swat /swɒt/ *v.t.* (**-tt-**) to hit hard; to crush (a fly etc.) with a blow. —*n.* an act of swatting. [earlier = sit down, dial. var. of SQUAT]

swatch /swɒtʃ/ *n.* a sample, especially of cloth; a collection of samples. [orig. unkn.]

swath /swɔːθ/ *n.* (*pl.* /swɔːθs, swɔːðz/) a ridge of grass or corn etc. lying after being cut; the space left clear after one passage of a mower etc.; a broad strip. [OE]

swathe[1] /sweɪð/ *v.t.* to wrap in layers of bandage, wrappings, or warm garments etc. [OE]

swathe[2] /sweɪð/ *n.* = SWATH.

swatter /ˈswɒtə(r)/ *n.* an implement for swatting flies. [f. SWAT]

sway *v.t./i.* **1** to swing or cause to swing gently; to lean from side to side or to one side. **2** to influence the opinions, sympathy, or action of. **3** to waver in one's opinion or attitude. —*n.* **1** a swaying movement. **2** influence, power; rule. [cf. LG *swajen* be blown to and fro, Du. *zwaaien* swing, wave]

swear /sweə(r)/ *v.t./i.* (*past* **swore**; *p.p.* **sworn**) **1** to state or promise solemnly or on oath; (*colloq.*) to state emphatically. **2** to cause to take an oath. **3** to use profane or obscene language in anger or surprise etc. —**swear by,** to appeal to as a witness in taking an oath; (*colloq.*) to have great confidence in. **swear in,** to induct into an office etc. by administering an oath. **swear off,** (*colloq.*) to promise to abstain from (drink etc.). **swear to,** (*colloq.*) to say that one is certain of. **swear-word** *n.* a profane or obscene word. —**swearer** *n.* [OE]

sweat /swet/ *n.* **1** moisture exuded through the pores of the skin, especially from heat or nervousness. **2** a state or period of sweating; (*colloq.*) a state of anxiety. **3** (*colloq.*) drudgery, an effort, a laborious task or undertaking. **4** condensed moisture on a surface. —*v.t./i.* (*past* & *p.p.* **sweated,** *US* **sweat**) **1** to exude sweat. **2** to be terrified, suffering, etc. **3** (of a wall etc.) to exhibit surface moisture. **4** to emit like sweat. **5** to make (a horse or athlete etc.) sweat by exercise. **6** to drudge or toil, to cause to do this. —**sweat-band** *n.* a band of absorbent material inside a hat or round the wrist etc. to soak up sweat. **sweat blood,** to work strenuously; to be extremely anxious. **sweated labour,** labour employed for long hours at low wages. **sweat out,** (*colloq.*) to endure to the end. **sweat-shirt** *n.* a sleeved cotton sweater. **sweat-shop** *n.* a place in which sweated labour is used. —**sweaty** *adj.* [OE]

sweater /ˈswetə(r)/ *n.* a jumper or pullover. [f. SWEAT]

Swede /swi:d/ *n.* a native of Sweden. [MLG & MDu., prob f. ON]

swede /swi:d/ *n.* a large yellow-fleshed turnip, brought from Sweden to Scotland in the 18th c. [= prec.]

Swedish /ˈswi:dɪʃ/ *adj.* of Sweden or its people or language. —*n.* the official language of Sweden. [f. SWEDE]

sweep *v.t./i.* (*past & p.p.* **swept**) **1** to clear away (dust or litter etc.) with or as with a broom or brush; to clean or clear (a surface or area) thus. **2** to move or remove by pushing; to carry in an impetuous course; to clear forcefully. **3** to go smoothly and swiftly or majestically. **4** to pass or cause to pass quickly over or along; to touch lightly; to affect swiftly. **5** to extend in a continuous line or slope. **6** to make (a bow or curtsy) with a smooth movement. —*n.* **1** a sweeping movement. **2** a sweeping line or slope. **3** the act of sweeping with a broom etc. **4** a chimney-sweep. **5** a sortie by aircraft. **6** (*colloq.*) a sweepstake. **7** a long oar. **8** the movement of a beam across the screen of a cathode-ray tube. —**make a clean sweep of,** to abolish or expel completely; to win all the prizes etc. in. **sweep the board,** to win all the money in a gambling-game; to win all the possible prizes etc. **sweep (-second) hand,** an extra hand on a clock or watch, indicating seconds. **swept-wing** *adj.* (of an aircraft) having the wing placed at an acute angle to the axis. [OE]

sweeper *n.* **1** one who cleans by sweeping. **2** a device for sweeping a carpet etc. **3** (in football) a defensive player positioned close to the goalkeeper. [f. SWEEP]

sweeping *adj.* **1** wide in range or effect. **2** taking no account of particular cases or exceptions. —*n.* (in *pl.*) dirt etc. collected by sweeping. —**sweepingly** *adv.* [f. SWEEP]

sweepstake *n.* a form of gambling on horse-races etc. in which all the competitors' stakes are paid to the winners; a race with betting of this kind; a prize or the prizes won in a sweepstake.

sweet *adj.* **1** tasting as if containing sugar, not bitter. **2** fragrant. **3** melodious. **4** fresh, (of food) not stale, (of water) not salt. **5** pleasant, gratifying; (*colloq.*) pretty, charming. —*n.* **1** a small shaped piece of sweet substance, usually made with sugar or chocolate. **2** a sweet dish forming one course of a meal. **3** (in *pl.*) delights, gratifications. **4** (esp. as a form of address) darling, sweetheart. —**be sweet on,** (*colloq.*) to be fond of or in love with. **sweet-and-sour** *adj.* cooked in a sauce with both sweet and sour ingredients. **sweet-brier** *n.* a small wild rose (*Rosa rubiginosa*) with fragrant leaves. **sweet corn,** a sweet-flavoured maize. **sweet pea,** a climbing garden plant (*Lathyrus odoratus*) with fragrant flowers in many colours. **sweet talk,** (*US*) flattery. **sweet-talk** *v.t.* (*US*) to persuade by flattery. **sweet tooth,** a liking for sweet-tasting things. **sweet-william** *n.* a garden plant (*Dianthus barbatus*) with clustered fragrant flowers. —**sweetly** *adv.*, **sweetness** *n.* [OE]

sweetbread *n.* the pancreas or thymus gland of an animal, especially as food.

sweeten *v.t./i.* to make or become sweet or sweeter. [f. SWEET]

sweetener *n.* **1** (also **sweetening**) a substance used to sweeten food or drink. **2** (*colloq.*) a bribe. [f. prec.]

sweetheart *n.* each of a pair of persons who are in love with each other (also as a term of endearment).

sweetie *n.* (*colloq.*) **1** a sweet. **2** a sweetheart. [f. SWEET]

sweetmeal *adj.* (of biscuits) sweetened with wholemeal.

sweetmeat *n.* a sweet; a small fancy cake.

swell *v.t./i.* (*p.p.* **swollen** /ˈswəulən/ or **swelled**) **1** to make or become larger because of pressure from within; to curve or cause to curve outwards. **2** to make or become larger in amount, volume, numbers, or intensity. **1** an act or the state of swelling. **2** a heaving of the sea with waves that do not break. **3** a crescendo; a mechanism in an organ etc. for obtaining a crescendo or diminuendo. **4** (*colloq.*) a person of distinction or of dashing or fashionable appearance. **5** a protuberant part. —*adj.* (*US colloq.*) smart, excellent. —**swelled** *or* **swollen head,** (*colloq.*) conceit. [OE]

swelling *n.* a part raised up from the surrounding surface; an abnormal protuberance. [f. SWELL]

swelter *v.i.* to be uncomfortably hot. —*n.* a sweltering condition. [f. OE, = perish]

swept *past & p.p.* of SWEEP.

swerve *v.t./i.* to turn or cause to turn aside from a straight course, especially in a sudden movement. —*n.* a swerving movement or course. [OE, = scour]

swift *adj.* quick, rapid. —*n.* a swift-flying bird of the family Apodidae with long wings. —**swiftly** *adv.*, **swiftness** *n.* [OE]

swig *v.t./i.* (**-gg-**) (*colloq.*) to take a drink or drinks (of). —*n.* (*colloq.*) a drink or swallow. [orig. unkn.]

swill *v.t./i.* **1** to pour water over or through; to wash or rinse. **2** (of water etc.) to pour. **3** to drink greedily. —*n.* **1** a rinse. **2** a sloppy mixture of waste food fed to pigs. **3** inferior liquor. [OE]

swim *v.t./i.* (**-mm-**; *past* **swam**; *p.p.* **swum**) **1** to propel the body through water by movements of the limbs or fins, tail, etc.; to traverse thus; to cause to swim. **2** to float. **3** to be covered or flooded with a liquid. **4** to seem to be whirling or undulating; to have a dizzy sensation. —*n.* **1** an act or spell of swimming. **2** a deep pool frequented by fish in a river. **3** the main current of affairs. —**in the swim,** active in or knowing what is going on. **swim-bladder** *n.* a gas-filled bladder, found in most types of fish, whose size can be adjusted to control buoyancy. **swimming-bath** *or* **-pool** *n.* a pool constructed for swimming. **swim-suit** a bathing-suit. —**swimmer** *n.* [OE]

swimmingly *adv.* with easy and unobstructed progress. [f. SWIM]

swindle *v.t./i.* to cheat (a person) in a business transaction; to obtain (money etc.) by fraud. —*n.* **1** a piece of swindling. **2** a fraudulent person or thing. —**swindler** *n.* [back-formation f. *swindler* f. G, = extravagant maker of schemes (*schwindeln* be dizzy)]

swine *n.* (*pl.* same) **1** a pig. **2** (*colloq.*) a disgusting or contemptible person or thing. [OE]

swing *v.t./i.* (*past* & *p.p.* **swung**) **1** to move to and fro while hanging or supported; to cause to do this; (*slang*) to be executed by hanging. **2** to suspend by its end(s). **3** to lift with a swinging movement; to move by gripping something and leaping; to walk or run with an easy rhythmical gait. **4** to turn (a wheel etc.) smoothly; to turn to one side or in a curve. **5** to change from one opinion or mood etc. to another; to influence (voters or voting etc.) decisively; (*slang*) to deal with, to arrange satisfactorily. **6** to play (music) with a swing rhythm. **7** (in *partic.*, *slang*) lively. —*n.* **1** a swinging motion or action. **2** a seat slung by ropes or chains for swinging in; a swing-boat; a spell of swinging in this. **3** the extent to which a thing swings; the amount by which votes, opinions, points scored, etc., change from one side to another. **4** a kind of jazz with the time of the melody varied while the accompaniment is in strict time. —**in full swing,** with activity at its greatest. **swing-boat** *n.* a boat-shaped swing at fairs. **swing bridge,** a bridge that can be swung aside to let ships pass. **swing-door** *n.* a door able to open in either direction and close itself when released. **swing the lead,** (*slang*) to malinger. **swing-wing** *n.* an aircraft wing that can move from a right-angled to a rear-slanting position. —**swinger** *n.* [OE *swingan* to beat]

swingeing /ˈswɪndʒɪŋ/ *adj.* **1** (of a blow) forcible. **2** huge in amount, number, or scope. [f. OE *swengan* shake, shatter]

swinish /ˈswaɪnɪʃ/ *adj.* bestial; filthy. [f. SWINE]

swipe *v.t./i.* **1** (*colloq.*) to hit hard and recklessly. **2** (*slang*) to steal. —*n.* (*colloq.*) a reckless hard hit or attempt to hit. [perh. var. of SWEEP]

swirl *v.t./i.* to move, flow, or carry along with a whirling motion. —*n.* a swirling motion; a twist, a curl. [orig. Sc., perh. f. LDu.]

swish *v.t./i.* to strike, move, or cause to move with a hissing sound. —*n.* a swishing action or sound. —*adj.* (*colloq.*) smart, fashionable. [imit.]

Swiss *adj.* of Switzerland or its people. —*n.* (*pl.* same) a native of Switzerland. —**Swiss guards,** Swiss mercenary troops employed formerly by sovereigns of France etc. and still at the Vatican. **Swiss roll,** a thin flat sponge-cake spread with jam etc. and rolled up. [f. F *Suisse* f. MHG]

switch *n.* **1** a device for making and breaking a connection in an electric circuit. **2** a transfer, a change-over; a deviation. **3** a flexible shoot cut from a tree; a light tapering rod. **4** a device at a junction of railway tracks for transferring a train from one track to another. —*v.t./i.* **1** to turn (an electrical or other appliance) on or off by means of a switch; to control (an electric current) by means of a switch. **2** to divert (thoughts or talk etc.) to another subject; to change or exchange (positions, methods, policy, etc.). **3** to transfer (a train) to another track. **4** to swing round quickly; to snatch suddenly. **5** to whip or flick with a switch. [prob. f. LG (*swukse* long thin stick)]

switchback *n.* **1** a railway used for amusement at fairs etc. in which a train's ascents are effected by the momentum of previous descents. **2** a road or railway with alternate ascents and descents, or zigzagging on a slope.

switchboard *n.* a panel with a set of switches for making telephone connections or operating electric circuits.

swivel /ˈswɪv(ə)l/ *n.* a coupling between two parts enabling one to revolve without the other. —*v.t./i.* (**-ll-**) to turn (as) on a swivel. —**swivel chair,** a chair with a seat turning horizontally. [f. OE, = sweep]

swizz *n.* (*slang*) a swindle, a disappointment. [orig. unkn.]

swizzle *n.* (*colloq.*) **1** a compounded intoxicating drink especially of rum or gin and bitters made frothy. **2** (*slang*) a swizz. —**swizzle-stick** *n.* a stick used for frothing or flattening drinks. [orig. unkn.]

swollen see SWELL.

swoon *v.i.* to faint. —*n.* a faint. [perh. f. OE *geswogen* overcome]

swoop *v.i.* to descend with a rushing movement like a bird upon its prey; to make a sudden attack. —*n.* a swooping or snatching movement or action. [perh. rel. to SWEEP]

swop var. of SWAP.

sword /sɔːd/ *n.* a weapon with a long blade and a hilt with a hand-guard. —**the sword,** war, military power. **cross swords,** to have a fight or dispute. **put to the sword,** to kill, especially in war. **sword-dance** *n.* a dance in which the performer brandishes swords or steps about swords laid on the ground. **sword-play** *n.* fencing, repartee or lively arguing. **sword-stick** *n.* a hollow walking-stick containing a blade that can be used as a sword. [OE]

swordfish *n.* a large sea-fish (*Xiphias gladius*) with the upper jaw prolonged into a sharp sword-like weapon.

swordsman *n.* (*pl.* **-men**) a person of good or specified skill with a sword. —**swordsmanship** *n.*

swore *past* of SWEAR.

sworn *p.p.* of SWEAR. —*adj.* bound (as) by an oath.

swot *v.t./i.* (*slang*) (**-tt-**) to study hard. —*n.* (*slang*) **1** a person who swots. **2** hard study. —**swot up,** to study (a subject) hard or hurriedly. [dial. var of SWEAT]

swum *p.p.* of SWIM.

swung *past* & *p.p.* of SWING.

sybarite /ˈsɪbəraɪt/ *n.* a person who is extremely fond of comfort and luxury. —**sybaritic** /-ˈrɪtɪk/ *adj.* [f. *Sybaris*, ancient city in southern Italy, noted for its luxury]

sycamore /ˈsɪkəmɔ(r)/ *n.* **1** a large maple (*Acer pseudoplatanus*). **2** (*US*) a plane-tree. **3** the wood of either of these. [var. of *sycomore* kind of fig-tree, f. OF f. L f. Gk]

sycophant /ˈsɪkəfænt/ *n.* a person who tries to win favour by flattery. —**sycophancy** *n.*, **sycophantic** /-ˈfæntɪk/ *adj.*, **sycophantically** *adv.* [f. F or L f. Gk, = informer]

syl- see SYN-.

syllabary /ˈsɪləbərɪ/ *n.* a list of characters representing syllables and serving the purpose, in some languages or stages of writing, of an alphabet. [as SYLLABLE]

syllabic /sɪˈlæbɪk/ *adj.* of or in syllables. —**syllabically** *adv.* [f. F or L f. Gk (as SYLLABLE)]

syllabification /sɪlæbɪfɪˈkeɪʃ(ə)n/ *n.* a division into or utterance in syllables. [f. L (as foll.)]

syllable /ˈsɪləb(ə)l/ *n.* **1** a unit of pronunciation forming the whole or a part of a word and usually having one vowel-sound often with a consonant or consonants before or after. **2** a character or characters representing a syllable. **3** the least amount of speech or writing. —**in words of one syllable,** simply, plainly. [f. AF f. L f. Gk *sullabē* (as SYL-, *lambanō* take)]

syllabub /ˈsɪləbʌb/ *n.* a dish of sweetened whipped cream flavoured with wine etc. [orig. unkn.]

syllabus /ˈsɪləbəs/ *n.* (*pl.* **-uses**) a programme or conspectus of a course of study, teaching, etc. [misreading of L *sittybas* f. Gk, = title-slips]

syllepsis /sɪˈlepsɪs/ *n.* (*pl.* **-pses** /-iːz/) a figure of speech applying a word to two others in different senses (e.g. *took the oath and his seat*), or to two others of which it grammatically suits one only (e.g. *neither you nor he knows*). [L f. Gk, = taking together (as SYLLABLE)]

syllogism /ˈsɪlədʒɪz(ə)m/ *n.* a form of reasoning in which from two given or assumed propositions (the *premisses*) which have a common or middle term a third is deduced (the *conclusion*) from which the middle term is absent, as in 'All As are Bs, all Bs are Cs, therefore all As are Cs'; 'Some As are Bs, all Bs are not Cs, therefore some As are not Cs'. —**syllogistic** /-ˈdʒɪstɪk/ *adj.* [f. OF f. L f. Gk f. *sullogizomai* (as SYN-, *logizomai* to reason)]

sylph /sɪlf/ *n.* **1** an elemental spirit of the air. **2** a slender graceful woman or girl. [perh. formed by Paracelsus f. L *sylvestris* of woodland + *nympha* nymph]

sylvan var. of SILVAN.

sym- see SYN-.

symbiosis /sɪmbɪˈəʊsɪs, -baɪ-/ *n.* (*pl.* **-oses** /-iːz/) **1** an association of two different organisms living attached to each other or one within the other, usually to their mutual advantage. **2** an association of co-operating persons. —**symbiotic** /-ˈɒtɪk/ *adj.* [f. Gk, = living together (as SYM-, *bios* life)]

symbol /ˈsɪmb(ə)l/ *n.* **1** a thing regarded as suggesting something or embodying certain characteristics. **2** a mark or sign with a special meaning, indicating an idea, object, process, etc. [f. L f. Gk *sumbolon* mark, token (as SYM-, *ballō* throw)]

symbolic /sɪmˈbɒlɪk/ *adj.* (also **symbolical**) of, using, or used as a symbol. [as prec.]

symbolism /ˈsɪmbəlɪz(ə)m/ *n.* **1** use of symbols to represent things; symbols collectively. **2** a school of painters and of (especially French) poets seeking special symbols to express the essence of things by suggestion. —**symbolist** *n.* [f. SYMBOL]

symbolize *v.t.* to be a symbol of; to represent by means of symbols. —**symbolization** /-ˈzeɪʃ(ə)n/ *n.* [f. F (as SYMBOL)]

symmetry /ˈsɪmɪtrɪ/ *n.* **1** correct proportion of parts; beauty resulting from this. **2** a structure that allows an object to be divided into parts of equal shape and size; possession of such a structure; the repetition of exactly similar parts facing each other or a centre. —**symmetric** /-ˈmetrɪk/ *adj.*, **symmetrical** /-ˈmetrɪk(ə)l/ *adj.*, **symmetrically** /-ˈmetrɪkəlɪ/ *adv.* [f. obs. F or L f. Gk (as SYM-, *metron* measure)]

sympathetic /sɪmpəˈθetɪk/ *adj.* **1** of, showing, or expressing sympathy; due to sympathy. **2** likeable. **3** not antagonistic. —**sympathetic magic,** magic seeking to affect an event etc. by imitating the effect desired. **sympathetic string,** (*Mus.*) a string which vibrates with sympathetic resonance, enriching the tone. —**sympathetically** *adv.* [f. SYMPATHY]

sympathize /ˈsɪmpəθaɪz/ *v.i.* to feel or express sympathy. —**sympathizer** *n.* [f. F (as foll.)]

sympathy /ˈsɪmpəθɪ/ *n.* **1** sharing or the ability to share another's emotions or sensations. **2** a feeling of pity or tenderness towards one suffering pain, grief, or trouble. **3** liking for each other produced in people who have similar opinions or tastes. **4** (in *sing.* or *pl.*) agreement with another person etc. in an opinion or desire. [f. L f. Gk (as SYM-, *pathos* feeling)]

symphonic /sɪmˈfɒnɪk/ *adj.* of or like a symphony or symphonies.—**symphonic poem,** an orchestral piece usually in one movement and usually descriptive or rhapsodic. —**symphonically** *adv.* [f. foll.]

symphony /ˈsɪmfənɪ/ *n.* **1** an elaborate composition for a full orchestra, usually with several movements. **2** (*US*) a symphony orchestra. —**symphony orchestra,** a large orchestra playing symphonies etc. [orig. = harmony of sound, f. OF f. L f. Gk (as SYM-, *phōnē* sound)]

symposium /sɪmˈpəʊzɪəm/ *n.* (*pl.* **-ia**) a conference or collection of essays etc. on a particular subject; a philosophical or other friendly discussion. [f. L f. Gk, = drinking-party (as SYM-, *potēs* drinker)]

symptom /ˈsɪmptəm/ *n.* a sign of the existence of a condition, especially a perceptible change from what is normal in the body, indicating disease or injury. [f. L f. Gk (*sumpiptō* happen, as SYM-, *piptō* fall)]

symptomatic /sɪmptəˈmætɪk/ *adj.* serving as a symptom. —**symptomatically** *adv.* [f. prec.]

syn- *prefix* (**syl-** before *l*, **sym-** before *b, m, p*) in senses 'together', 'at the same time', 'alike', etc. [f. Gk (*sun* with)]

synagogue /ˈsɪnəgɒg/ *n.* a meeting-place of a Jewish assembly for religious observance and instruction; the assembly itself. —**synagogal** *adj.*, **synagogical** /-ˈgɒgɪk(ə)l, -ˈgɒdʒɪk(ə)l/ *adj.* [f. OF f. L f. Gk, = assembly (as SYN-, *agō* bring]

sync /sɪŋk/ *n.* (also **synch**) (*colloq.*) synchronization. —*v.t.* (*colloq.*) to synchronize. [abbr.]

synchromesh /ˈsɪŋkrəʊmeʃ/ *n.* a system of gear-changing, especially in motor vehicles, in which the gear-wheels revolve at the same speed while they are being brought into engagement. —*adj.* of this system. [abbr. of *synchronized mesh*]

synchronic /sɪŋˈkrɒnɪk/ *adj.* concerned with a subject as it exists at a particular time. —**synchronic linguistics,** = descriptive linguistics. —**synchronically** *adv.* [as SYNCHRONOUS]

synchronism /ˈsɪŋkrənɪz(ə)m/ *n.* **1** being or treated as synchronous or synchronic. **2** synchronizing. [f. Gk (as SYNCHRONOUS)]

synchronize /ˈsɪŋkrənaɪz/ *v.t./i.* to make or be synchronous with. —**synchronization** /-ˈzeɪʃ(ə)n/ *n.*, **synchronizer** *n.* [f. prec.]

synchronous /ˈsɪŋkrənəs/ *adj.* **1** existing or occurring at the same time. **2** having the same or a proportional speed and operating simultaneously. [f. L f. Gk (as SYN-, *khronos* time)]

synchrotron /ˈsɪŋkrətrɒn/ *n.* a cyclotron in which the strength of the magnetic field increases with the energy of the particles, keeping their orbital radius constant. [f. SYNCHRONOUS + -TRON]

syncline /ˈsɪŋklaɪn/ *n.* a land formation in which strata are folded so that they slope up on opposite sides of a trough. —**synclinal** /-ˈklaɪn(ə)l/ *adj.* [f. SYN- + Gk *klinō* lean]

syncopate /ˈsɪŋkəpeɪt/ *v.t.* **1** to displace the beats or accents in (music). **2** to shorten (a word) by dropping an interior letter or letters. —**syncopation** /-ˈpeɪʃ(ə)n/ *n.* [f. L (as foll.)]

syncope /ˈsɪŋkəpɪ/ *n.* **1** syncopation. **2** temporary unconsciousness through a fall in blood-pressure; a faint, fainting. [f. L f. Gk (as SYN-, *koptō* cut off)]

syncretize /ˈsɪŋkrɪtaɪz/ *v.t./i.* to combine (different beliefs or principles). [f. Gk *sugkrētizō* combine as two parties against a third]

syndic /ˈsɪndɪk/ *n.* any of various university or government officials. [F f. L f. Gk, = advocate (as SYN-, *dikē* justice)]

syndicalism /ˈsɪndɪk(ə)lɪz(ə)m/ *n.* a movement among industrial workers (especially in France) aiming at the transfer of the means of production and distribution from their present owners to unions of workers. —**syndicalist** *n.* [f F (*syndicat* trade union), as prec.]

syndicate /ˈsɪndɪkət/ *n.* **1** a combination of persons or commercial firms to promote some common interest **2** an association supplying material simultaneously to a number of periodicals. **3** a committee of syndics. —/-keɪt/ *v.t.* **1** to form into a syndicate **2** to publish (material) through a syndicate. —**syndication** /-ˈkeɪʃ(ə)n/ *n.* [as SYNDIC]

syndrome /ˈsɪndrəʊm/ *n.* **1** a set of signs and symptoms that together indicate the presence of a disease or abnormal condition. **2** a combination of opinions, behaviour, etc., characteristic of a particular condition. [f. Gk (as SYN-, *dram-* run)]

synecdoche /sɪˈnekdəkɪ/ *n.* a figure of speech in which a part is named but the whole is understood, or conversely (e.g. *several new faces in the team* for *new persons*, or *England beat Australia at cricket*) [f. L f. Gk (as SYN-, *ekdekhomai* take up)]

synod /ˈsɪnəd/ *n.* a council of clergy and church officials (and sometimes laity) convened for discussing ecclesiastical affairs. [f. L f. Gk, = meeting (as SYN-, *hodos* way)]

synonym /ˈsɪnənɪm/ *n.* a word or phrase that means exactly or nearly the same as another in the same language. [f. L f. Gk (as SYN-, *onoma* name)]

synonymous /sɪˈnɒnɪməs/ *adj.* having the same meaning. [f. prec.]

synopsis /sɪˈnɒpsɪs/ *n.* (*pl.* **synopses** /-iːz/) a summary, a brief general survey. [L f. Gk (as SYN-, *opsis* seeing)]

synoptic /sɪˈnɒptɪk/ *adj.* of or giving a synopsis. —**Synoptic Gospels,** those of Matthew, Mark, and Luke, which have many similarities (whereas that of John differs greatly). —**synoptically** *adv.* [f. Gk (as prec.)]

synovia /saɪˈnəʊvɪə/ *n.* a thick sticky fluid lubricating the body joints etc. —**synovial** *adj.* [L]

syntax /ˈsɪntæks/ *n.* the arrangement of words and phrases to form sentences; the rules or analysis of this. —**syntactic** /-ˈtæktɪk/ *adj.*, **syntactically** /-ˈtæktɪkəlɪ/ *adv.* [f. F or L f. Gk, = marshalling (as SYN-, *tassō* arrange)]

synthesis /ˈsɪnθɪsɪs/ *n.* (*pl.* **syntheses** /-siːz/) **1** the combination of separate parts or elements into a complex whole. **2** the artificial production of a substance by a chemical process; the process itself. [L f. Gk (as SYN-, THESIS)]

synthesize /ˈsɪnθɪsaɪz/ *v.t.* to make by synthesis. [f. prec.]

synthesizer /ˈsɪnθɪsaɪzə(r)/ *n.* an electronic device for combining sounds so as to reproduce the musical tones of conventional instruments or produce a variety of artificial ones [f. prec]

synthetic /sɪnˈθetɪk/ *adj.* **1** produced by synthesis; manufactured (opp. produced naturally). **2** (*colloq.*) affected, insincere. —*n.* a synthetic substance or fabric. —**synthetically** *adv.* [f. F f. Gk (as prec.)]

syphilis /ˈsɪfɪlɪs/ *n.* a contagious venereal disease. —**syphilitic** /-ˈlɪtɪk/ *adj.* [f. title of a Latin poem (1530), by a physician of Verona in Italy, about a shepherd *Syphilus*, the supposed first sufferer from the disease]

Syriac /ˈsɪrɪæk/ *n.* the language of ancient Syria. —*adj.* of this language. [f. L f. Gk (*Suria* Syria)]

syringa /sɪˈrɪŋgə/ *n.* **1** the mock orange (*Philadelphus coronarius*). **2** the botanical name for lilac (*Syringa vulgaris*). [as foll., from stems of mock orange being used for pipestems]

syringe /ˈsɪrɪndʒ, -ˈrɪndʒ/ *n.* a device for drawing in liquid by suction and then ejecting it in a fine stream. —*v.t.* to sluice or spray with a syringe. [f. L *syringa* f. Gk *surigx* pipe]

syrup /ˈsɪrəp/ *n.* **1** a thick liquid of water (nearly) saturated with sugar; this flavoured or medicated. **2** condensed sugar-cane juice, molasses, treacle. **3** excessive sweetness of manner. —**syrupy** *adj.* [f. OF or L f. Arab. cf. SHERBERT]

system /ˈsɪstəm/ *n.* **1** a set of connected things or parts that form a whole or work together; a set of organs in the body with a common function. **2** an animal body as a whole. **3** a set of rules, principles, or practices forming a particular philosophy or form of government. **4** a major group of layers of rock that were deposited during a particular geological period and contain similar fossils. **5** a method of classification, notation, measurement, etc. **6** being systematic, orderliness. —**get a thing out of one's system,** to be rid of its effects. **systems analysis,** the analysis of an operation in order to use a computer to improve its efficiency. [f. F or L f. Gk *sustēma* (as SYN-, *histēmi* set up)]

systematic /sɪstəˈmætɪk/ *adj.* methodical, according to a system, not casually or at random. —**systematically** *adv.* [as prec.]

systematize /ˈsɪstəmətaɪz/ *v.t.* to make systematic. —**systematization** /-ˈzeɪʃ(ə)n/ *n.* [f. prec.]

Système International /sɪstem æteərnæsjɔ̃ˈnɑːl/ the international system (of units): see SI. [F]

systemic /sɪˈstemɪk/ *adj.* **1** of the bodily system as a whole. **2** (of an insecticide etc.) entering plant tissues via the roots and shoots. —**systemically** *adv.* [f. SYSTEM]

systole /ˈsɪstəlɪ/ *n.* the rhythmical contraction of the chambers of the heart, alternating with diastole to form the pulse. —**systolic** /sɪˈstɒlɪk/ *adj.* [L f. Gk (*sustellō* contract)]

Tt

T, t /tiː/ *n.* (*pl.* **Ts, T's**) **1** the twentieth letter of the alphabet. **2** a T-shaped thing. —**cross the t's**, to be minutely accurate. **to a T**, exactly, to a nicety.

T *abbr.* tesla.

T *symbol* tritium.

t. *abbr.* ton(s); tonne(s).

TA *abbr.* Territorial Army.

Ta *symbol* tantalum.

ta /tɑː/ *int.* (*colloq.*) thank you. [infantile form]

TAB *abbr.* typhoid-paratyphoid A and B vaccine.

tab *n.* **1** a small projecting flap or attached strip, especially one by which a thing can be hung, fastened, or identified. **2** (*colloq.*) an account, a tally; (*US colloq.*) a bill; a price. —*v.t.* (**-bb-**) to provide with tabs. —**keep a tab** *or* **tabs on**, to keep account of; to have under observation or in check. [prob. f. dial.; cf. TAG]

tabard /ˈtæbəd/ *n.* **1** a short-sleeved or sleeveless jerkin emblazoned with the arms of the sovereign and forming the official dress of a herald or pursuivant. **2** (*hist.*) a short surcoat open at the sides and with short sleeves, worn by a knight over armour and emblazoned with armorial bearings. **3** a woman's or girl's garment of similar shape. [f. OF *tabart*; orig. unkn.]

tabby /ˈtæbɪ/ *n.* **1** a grey or brownish cat with dark stripes. **2** a kind of watered silk. [f. F f. Arab., = quarter of Baghdad where tabby silk was produced; connection of sense 1. uncertain]

tabernacle /ˈtæbənæk(ə)l/ *n.* **1** (in the Bible) a fixed or movable habitation, usually of light construction; a tent containing the Ark of the Covenant, used as a portable shrine by the Israelites during their wanderings in the wilderness. **2** a meeting-place for worship used by non-Conformists (e.g. Baptists) or by Mormons; (*hist.*) any of the temporary structures used during the rebuilding of churches after the Fire of London (1666). **3** a canopied niche or recess in the wall of a church etc.; an ornamental receptacle for the pyx or consecrated elements of the Eucharist. [f. OF or L *tabernaculum* tent dim. of *taberna* hut]

tabla /ˈtæblə, ˈtɑːblə/ *n.* a pair of small Indian drums played with the hands, often to accompany the sitar. [Urdu f. Arab. *tabla* drum]

table /ˈteɪb(ə)l/ *n.* **1** a piece of furniture with a flat top supported on one or more legs, providing a level surface for putting things on. **2** the food provided at table. **3** a set of facts or figures systematically arranged, especially in columns; the matter contained in such a set. **4** a flat surface for working on or for machinery etc. **5** a slab of wood or stone etc.; the matter inscribed on it. —*v.t.* **1** to bring forward for discussion or consideration. **2** to postpone consideration of (a matter). —**at table,** taking a meal at a table. **on the table,** submitted for discussion or consideration. **table-cloth** *n.* a cloth spread on a table, especially for meals. **table licence,** a licence to serve alcoholic drinks with meals only. **table-linen** *n.* table-cloths, napkins, etc. **Table of the House,** the central table in either of the Houses of Parliament. **table tennis,** an indoor game played with small bats and a ball bouncing on a table divided by a net. **turn the tables on,** to reverse one's relations (with), especially to pass from a weaker to a stronger position. **under the table,** drunk. [f. OF f. L *tabula* plank, tablet]

tableau /ˈtæbləʊ/ *n.* (*pl.* **-eaux** /-əʊz/) **1** a picturesque presentation; a group of silent motionless persons arranged to represent a scene. **2** a dramatic or effective situation suddenly brought about. [F, dim. of *table* (see prec.)]

table d'hôte /tɑːbl ˈdəʊt/ a meal at a fixed time and price in a hotel etc., with less choice of dishes than à la carte. [F, = host's table]

tableland *n.* a plateau of land.

tablespoon *n.* a large spoon for serving food; the amount held by this. —**tablespoonful** *n.* (*pl.* **-fuls**)

tablet /ˈtæblɪt/ *n.* **1** a small measured and compressed amount of a substance, especially of a medicine or drug. **2** a small flat piece of soap etc. **3** a small slab or panel, especially for the display of an inscription. [f. OF f. L (as TABLE)]

tabloid /ˈtæblɔɪd/ *n.* a newspaper, usually

popular in style, printed on sheets that are half the size of larger newspapers. [orig. name of compressed drug-preparation (as prec.)]

taboo /tə'bu:/ *n.* the system or an act of setting a person or thing apart as sacred or accursed; a prohibition or restriction imposed by social custom. —*adj.* avoided or prohibited, especially by social custom —*v.t.* to put under a taboo; to exclude or prohibit by authority or social influence. [f. Tongan]

tabor /'teɪbə(r)/ *n.* (*hist.*) a small drum, especially used to accompany a pipe. [f. OF, cf. TABLA; Pers. *tabīra* drum]

tabular /'tæbjʊlə(r)/ *adj.* of or arranged in tables or lists. [f. L (as TABLE)]

tabulate /'tæbjʊleɪt/ *v.t.* to arrange (figures or facts) in tabular form. —**tabulation** /-'leɪʃ(ə)n/ *n.* [f. L *tabulare* (*tabula* table)]

tabulator *n.* **1** a person or thing that tabulates. **2** a device on a typewriter for advancing to a sequence of set positions in tabular work. [f. prec.]

tachisme /'tæʃɪz(ə)m/ *n.* action painting. [F (*tache* stain)]

tacho /'tækəʊ/ *n.* (*pl.* **-os**) (*colloq.*) a tachometer. [abbr.]

tachograph /'tækəgrɑ:f/ *n.* a device in a motor vehicle for recording the speed and travel-time. [f. Gk *takhos* speed + -GRAPH]

tachometer /tæ'kɒmɪtə(r)/ *n.* an instrument for measuring velócity or speed of rotation (especially of a vehicle engine). [as prec. + -METER]

tacit /'tæsɪt/ *adj.* understood or implied without being stated. —**tacitly** *adv.* [f. L *tacitus* (*tacēre* be silent)]

taciturn /'tæsɪtɜ:n/ *adj.* habitually saying very little, uncommunicative. —**taciturnity** /-'tɜ:nɪtɪ/ *n.* [f. F or L *taciturnus* (as prec.)]

tack[1] *n.* **1** a small sharp broad-headed nail; (*US*) a drawing-pin. **2** a long stitch used in fastening fabric in position lightly or temporarily. **3** the direction in which a ship moves as determined by the position of its sails; a temporary change of direction in sailing to take advantage of a side wind etc.; a rope for securing the corner of some sails; the corner to which this is fastened. **4** a course of action or policy. **5** sticky condition of varnish etc. —*v.t./i.* **1** to fasten with a tack or tacks. **2** to stitch with tacks. **3** to add as an extra thing. **4** to change a ship's course by turning its head to the wind; to make a series of such tacks. **5** to change one's conduct or policy etc. [cf. OF *tache* clasp]

tack[2] *n.* riding-harness, saddles etc. [f. TACKLE]

tackle *n.* **1** the equipment for a task or sport. **2** a mechanism, especially of ropes, pulley-blocks, hooks, etc., for lifting weights, managing sails, etc.; a windlass with its ropes and hooks. **3** the act of tackling in football etc. —*v.t.* **1** to try to deal with (a problem or difficulty); to grapple with or try to overcome (an opponent); to enter into a discussion with (a person, especially about an awkward matter). **2** (in football etc.) to intercept or stop (a player running with the ball). —**tackler** *n.* [prob. f. MLG (*taken* lay hold of)]

tacky *adj.* (of glue or varnish etc.) in the sticky stage before complete dryness. —**tackiness** *n.* [f. TACK[1]]

tact *n.* skill in avoiding giving offence or in winning goodwill by saying or doing the right thing. [F. f. L *tactus* (sense of) touch (*tangere* to touch)]

tactful *adj.* having or showing tact. —**tactfully** *adv.*, **tactfulness** *n.* [f. TACT + -FUL]

tactic /'tæktɪk/ *n.* a piece of tactics. [as TACTICS]

tactical /'tæktɪk(ə)l/ *adj.* **1** of tactics. **2** (of bombing) done in immediate support of military or naval operations. **3** adroitly planning or planned. —**tactical weapons**, see STRATEGIC WEAPONS. —**tactically** *adv.* [as TACTICS]

tactician /tæk'tɪʃ(ə)n/ *n.* an expert in tactics. [f. foll.]

tactics *n.pl.* (also treated as *sing.*) **1** the art of placing and manœuvring armed forces skilfully in a battle (dist. from *strategy*). **2** the procedure adopted in carrying out a scheme or achieving some end. [f. Gk *taktika* (*tassō* arrange)]

tactile /'tæktaɪl/ *adj.* of or connected with the sense of touch; perceived by touch. —**tactility** /-'tɪlɪtɪ/ *n.* [f. L *tactilis* (*tangere* touch)]

tactless *adj.* having or showing no tact. —**tactlessly** *adv.*, **tactlessness** *n.* [f. TACT + -LESS]

tadpole *n.* the larva of a frog or toad etc. at the stage when it lives in water and has gills and a tail. [as TOAD + POLL, f. size of head]

taffeta /'tæfɪtə/ *n.* a fine lustrous silk or silklike fabric. [f. OF or L ult. f. Pers., p.p. of *tāftan* twist]

taffrail /'tæfreɪl/ *n.* a rail round a ship's stern. [f. Du. *tafferel* panel (as TABLE); assim. to RAIL[1]]

Taffy /'tæfɪ/ *n.* (*colloq.*) a nickname for a Welshman. [supposed Welsh pronunc. of *Davy* = *David*]

tag[1] *n.* **1** a loop, flap, or label for handling, hanging, or marking a thing. **2** a metal or plastic point of a shoelace etc. used to assist insertion. **3** a loose or ragged end. **4** a trite quotation, a stock phrase. —*v.t./i.* (**-gg-**) **1** to attach a tag to. **2** to attach, to add as an extra thing. **3** (*colloq.*) to follow; to trail behind. —**tag along**, (*colloq.*) to go along with another or others. [orig. unkn.]

tag[2] *n.* a children's game of chasing and

touching. —*v.t.* (**-gg-**) to touch in a game of tag. [orig. unkn.]

Tagalog /ˈtæɡəlɒɡ/ *n.* **1** a member of the principal people of the Philippine Islands. **2** their language. [Tagalog (*taga* native, *ilog* river)]

tagliatelle /tɑːljɑːˈtelɪ/ *n.* a ribbon-shaped form of pasta. [It.]

tail[1] *n.* **1** the hindmost part of an animal, especially when prolonged beyond the rest of the body. **2** a thing like a tail in form or position, e.g. the part of a shirt below the waist, the hanging part of the back of a coat, the end of a procession; the part of a dovetail joint that is shaped like a dove's spread tail. **3** the rear part of an aeroplane or rocket. **4** the luminous train of a comet. **5** the inferior or weaker part of anything. **6** (in *pl.*, *colloq.*) a tailcoat; evening dress including this. **7** (usu. in *pl.*) the reverse of a coin turning up in a toss. **8** (*slang*) a person following or shadowing another. —*v.t./i.* **1** to remove the stalks of (fruit etc.). **2** (*slang*) to shadow, to follow closely. —**on a person's tail,** closely following him. **tail away** *or* **off,** to become fewer or smaller or slighter; to fall behind or away in a scattered line; to end inconclusively. **tail-back** *n.* a long line of traffic extending back from an obstruction. **tail-board** *n.* a hinged or removable back of a lorry etc. **tail-end** *n.* the hindmost, lowest, or last part. **tail-gate** *n.* a tail-board; a door at the back of a motor vehicle. **tail-light** *or* **-lamp** *n.* a light at the rear of a motor vehicle or bicycle. **tail-spin** *n.* the spin of an aircraft. **tail wind,** a wind blowing in the direction of travel of a vehicle or aircraft etc. **turn tail,** to turn one's back; to run away. **with one's tail between one's legs,** humiliated or dejected by defeat etc. [OE]

tail[2] *n.* limitation of ownership, especially of an estate limited to a person and his heirs. —*adj.* so limited. —**in tail,** under such limitation. [f. OF *taille* (*taillier* cut f. L *talea* twig)]

tailcoat *n.* a man's coat with a long skirt divided at the back into tails and cut away in front, worn as part of formal dress.

tailless *adj.* having no tail. [f. TAIL[1] + -LESS]

tailor /ˈteɪlə(r)/ *n.* a maker of men's clothes, especially to order. —*v.t.* **1** to make (clothes) as a tailor; to make in a simple smoothly-fitting design. **2** to make or adapt for a special purpose. —**tailor-bird** *n.* a small Asian bird, especially of the genus *Orthotomus*, sewing leaves together to form a nest. **tailor-made** *adj.* made by a tailor; entirely suited to a purpose. [f. AF *taillour* (as TAIL[2])]

tailpiece *n.* **1** the final part of a thing. **2** a decoration in the blank space at the end of a chapter etc.

tailpipe *n.* the rear section of the exhaust pipe of a motor vehicle.

tailplane *n.* the horizontal aerofoil at the tail of an aircraft.

tailstock *n.* the adjustable part of a lathe, with a fixed spindle to support one end of the workpiece.

taint *n.* a trace of some bad quality or of decay or infection. —*v.t./i.* to affect or become affected with a taint. [f. OF f. L (*tingere* dye)]

take *v.t./i.* (*past* **took** /tʊk; *p.p.* **taken**) **1** to get into one's hands; to get possession of, to win. **2** to obtain after fulfilling the necessary conditions; to obtain the use of by payment; to buy (a specified newspaper etc.) regularly. **3** to assume possession of; to occupy (a position), especially as one's right; to avail oneself of; to indulge in; to use as a means of transport. **4** to consume (food or medicine). **5** to be successful or effective. **6** to require; to use up. **7** to cause to come or go with one; to carry; to remove from its place; to dispossess a person of. **8** to catch or be infected with (fire, fever, etc.); to experience or be affected by; to exert (a feeling or effort). **9** to find out and note (a name, measurements, temperature, etc.). **10** to grasp mentally, to understand; to deal with or interpret in a specified way. **11** to accept, to endure. **12** to perform; to move round or over; to teach or be taught (a subject); to sit for (an examination). **13** to make by photography; to photograph. **14** to use as an instance. **15** (*Gram.*) to have or require as part of a construction. **16** to copulate with (a woman). —*n.* **1** the amount taken or caught. **2** a scene or sequence of a film photographed at one time without stopping the camera. —**take after,** to resemble (a parent etc.). **take against,** to begin to dislike. **take away,** to remove or carry elsewhere; to subtract. **take-away** *adj.* (of food) bought at a restaurant for eating elsewhere; (*n.*) a restaurant selling this. **take back,** to retract (a statement); to carry (a person) in thought to a past time. **take down,** to write down (spoken words); to remove (a structure) by separating it into pieces. **take for,** to regard as being. **take-home pay,** that received by an employee after deduction of tax etc. **take in,** to receive as a lodger etc.; to undertake (work) at home; to include; to visit (a place) en route; to make (a garment etc.) smaller; to understand; to cheat. **take in hand,** to undertake; to start doing or dealing with; to undertake the control or reform of. **take in vain,** to use (a person's name) lightly or profanely. **take it,** to assume; (*colloq.*) to endure punishment etc. bravely. **take it or leave it,** to accept it or not.

take it out of, to exhaust the strength of; to have revenge on. **take it out on,** to relieve frustration by attacking or treating harshly. **take it on** *or* **upon oneself,** to venture or presume to do a thing. **taken by** *or* **with,** attracted or charmed by. **taken ill,** suddenly affected by illness. **take off,** to remove (clothing) from the body; to deduct; to mimic humorously; to jump from the ground; to become airborne; to have (a day) as a holiday. **take-off** *n.* an act of becoming airborne; an act of mimicking; a place from which one jumps. **take oneself off,** to depart. **take on,** to undertake (work); to engage (an employee); to agree to oppose at a game; to acquire (a new meaning etc.); (*colloq.*) to show strong emotion. **take out,** to remove, to escort on an outing, to get (a licence or summons etc.) issued. **take a person out of himself,** to make him forget his worries etc. **take over,** to succeed to the management or ownership of; to assume control. **take-over** *n.* an assumption of control (especially of a business). **take one's time,** not to hurry. **take to,** to begin or fall into the habit of; to have recourse to; to adapt oneself to; to form a liking for. **take up,** to become interested or engaged in (a pursuit); to adopt as a protégé; to occupy (time or space); to begin (residence etc.); to resume after an interruption; to interrupt or question (a speaker); to accept (an offer etc.); to shorten (a garment). **take a person up on,** to accept (his offer etc.). **take up with,** to begin to associate with. [OE]

taker *n.* one who takes bets or accepts an offer etc. [f. TAKE]

taking *adj.* attractive, captivating. —*n.* (in *pl.*) the amount of money taken in a business. [f. TAKE]

talc *n.* **1** a translucent mineral often found in thin glasslike plates. **2** talcum powder. [F or f. L *talcum* f. Arab. f. Pers.]

talcum *n.* talc. —**talcum powder,** powdered talc for toilet use, usually perfumed. [L (as prec.)]

tale *n.* **1** a narrative or story, especially a fictitious one. **2** a report of an alleged fact, often malicious or in breach of a confidence. [OE (as TELL)]

talebearer *n.* a person who maliciously gossips or reveals secrets.

talent /ˈtælənt/ *n.* **1** a special or very great ability; high mental ability. **2** persons who have this. **3** an ancient weight and unit of currency, especially among the Greeks. —**talent-scout** *n.* a seeker-out of talent, especially for the entertainment industries. [OE, ult. f. Gk *talanton* balance, weight, sum of money]

talented /ˈtæləntɪd/ *adj.* having great ability. [f. prec.]

talisman /ˈtælɪzmən/ *n.* an object supposed to be endowed with magic powers, especially of averting evil from or bringing good luck to its holder. —**talismanic** /-ˈmænɪk/ *adj.* [F & Sp. f. Gk *telesma* completion, religious rite (*telos* end)]

talk /tɔːk/ *v.t./i.* **1** to convey or exchange ideas by spoken words. **2** to have the power of speech. **3** to express, utter, or discuss in words. **4** to use (a specified language) in speech. **5** to affect or influence by talking. **6** to betray secrets; to gossip. **7** to have influence. —*n.* **1** talking, conversation, discussion. **2** style of speech. **3** an informal lecture. **4** rumour, gossip; its theme. **5** talking or promises etc. without action or results. —**now you're talking,** (*colloq.*) I welcome that offer or suggestion. **talk back,** to reply defiantly. **talk down,** to silence by greater loudness or persistence; to speak patronizingly; to bring (a pilot or aircraft) to a landing by radio instructions from the ground. **talking book,** a recorded reading of a book, especially for the blind. **talk out,** to block the course of (a bill in Parliament) by prolonging the discussion to the time of adjournment. **talk over,** to discuss at length. **talk a person over** *or* **round,** to win him over by talking. **you can** *or* **can't talk,** (*colloq.*) you are just as bad yourself. —**talker** *n.* [f. TALE or TELL]

talkative /ˈtɔːkətɪv/ *adj.* talking very much. [f. TALK]

talkie /ˈtɔːkɪ/ *n.* (*colloq.*) a sound-film. [f. *talking film*, after MOVIE]

talking-to *n.* (*colloq.*) a reproof. [f. TALK]

tall /tɔːl/ *adj.* **1** of more than average height. **2** having a specified height. —**talk tall,** to talk extravagantly or boastfully. **tall order,** a difficult task. **tall story,** (*colloq.*) one that is difficult to believe. **walk tall,** to feel justifiable pride. —**tallness** *n.* [f. OE, = swift]

tallboy *n.* a tall chest of drawers.

tallow /ˈtæləʊ/ *n.* the harder kinds of (esp. animal) fat melted down for use in making candles, soap, etc. —**tallowy** *adj.* [f. MLG; orig. unkn.]

tally /ˈtælɪ/ *v.i.* to correspond. —*n.* **1** the reckoning of a debt or score. **2** a mark registering a fixed number of objects delivered or received; such a number as a unit. **3** (*hist.*) a piece of wood scored across with notches for the items of an account. **4** a ticket or label for identification. **5** a corresponding thing, a counterpart, a duplicate. [f. AF f. L *talea* twig]

tally-ho /tælɪˈhəʊ/ *int.* a huntsman's cry to the hounds on seeing a fox. —*n.* (*pl.* **tally-hos**) an utterance of this. —*v.t./i.* to utter the cry of 'tally-ho'; to indicate (a fox) or urge (hounds) with this. [cf. F *taïaut*]

Talmud /ˈtælmʊd/ *n.* a body of Jewish ceremonial law and legend comprising the Mishnah and the Gemara. —**Talmudic** /-ˈmʊdɪk/ *adj.* [f. Heb., = instruction (*lamad* learn)]

talon /ˈtælən/ *n.* a claw, especially of a bird of prey. [f. OF, = heel, f. L *talus* ankle]

TAM *abbr.* (usu. *attrib.*) television audience measurement, denoting a measure of the number of people watching a particular television programme as estimated by the company Television Audience Measurement Ltd.

tamarind /ˈtæmərɪnd/ *n.* a tropical tree (*Tamarindus indica*) with a fruit whose acid pulp is used for cooling or medicinal drinks; this fruit. [f. L f. Arab., = date of India]

tamarisk /ˈtæmərɪsk/ *n.* an evergreen shrub of the genus *Tamarix* with feathery branches. [f. L *tamarix*]

tambour /ˈtæmbʊə(r)/ *n.* **1** a drum. **2** a circular frame for holding a fabric taut while it is being embroidered. **3** a sloping buttress or projection in a fives-court or real-tennis court etc. [F, f. *tabour* tabor]

tambourine /tæmbəˈri:n/ *n.* a percussion instrument of a hoop with a parchment stretched over one side and jingling discs in slots round the hoop. [f. F *tambourin* (as prec.)]

tame *adj.* **1** (of an animal) gentle and not afraid of human beings, not wild or fierce. **2** insipid, not exciting or interesting. **3** (of a person) docile and available. —*v.t.* to make tame or manageable; to subdue. —**tamely** *adv.*, **tameness** *n.* [f. OE]

tameable *adj.* that may be tamed. [f. TAME]

Tamil /ˈtæmɪl/ *n.* **1** a member of a Dravidian people inhabiting southern India and Sri Lanka. **2** their language. —*adj.* of the Tamils or their language. [f. native name *Tamil*, rel. to DRAVIDIAN]

tam-o'-shanter /tæməˈʃæntə(r)/ *n.* a round Scottish cap, usually woollen. [f. hero of Burns's *Tam o' Shanter*]

tamp *v.t.* to pack or ram down tightly. [perh. f. *tampion* stopper for gun-muzzle (as TAMPON)]

tamper *v.i.* **tamper with**, to meddle with, to make unauthorized changes in; to exert a secret or corrupt influence upon, to bribe. [var. of TEMPER]

tampon /ˈtæmpən/ *n.* a plug of cotton-wool etc. used to absorb natural secretions or stop a haemorrhage. —*v.t.* to plug with a tampon. [F (as TAP[1])]

tan[1] *n.* **1** yellowish-brown colour. **2** the brown colour in skin exposed to sun. **3** tree-bark used in tanning hides. —*adj.* yellowish-brown. —*v.t./i.* (**-nn-**) **1** to make or become brown by exposure to sun. **2** to convert (raw hide) into leather by soaking in a liquid containing tannic acid or by the use of mineral salts etc. **3** (*slang*) to thrash. [OE, perh. f. Celt.]

tan[2] *abbr.* tangent.

tandem /ˈtændəm/ *n.* **1** a bicycle with seats and pedals for two or more persons one behind another. **2** a group of two persons or machines etc. with one behind or following the other. **3** a carriage driven tandem. —*adv.* with two or more horses harnessed one behind another. —**in tandem**, one behind another. [L, = at length]

tandoor /ˈtændʊə(r)/ *n.* a clay oven. [Hind.]

tandoori /tænˈdʊərɪ/ *n.* food cooked over charcoal in a tandoor. [f. prec.]

tang *n.* **1** a strong taste, flavour, or smell; a characteristic quality. **2** a projection on the blade of a tool by which the blade is held firm in the handle. [f. ON *tange* point]

tangent /ˈtændʒ(ə)nt/ *n.* **1** a straight line that meets a curve or curved surface at a point, but if extended does not intersect it at that point. **2** the ratio of the sides opposite and adjacent to the angle in a right-angled triangle. —**at a tangent**, diverging from a previous course of action or thought etc. [f. L *tangere* touch]

tangential /tænˈdʒenʃ(ə)l/ *adj.* **1** of or along a tangent. **2** divergent. **3** peripheral. —**tangentially** *adv.* [f. prec.]

tangerine /tændʒəˈri:n/ *n.* **1** a kind of small flattened orange from Tangier. **2** its deep orange-yellow colour. [f. *Tangier*, seaport of Morocco]

tangible /ˈtændʒɪb(ə)l/ *adj.* **1** perceptible by touch. **2** definite, clearly intelligible; not elusive or visionary. —**tangibility** /-ˈbɪlɪtɪ/ *n.*, **tangibly** *adv.* [F or f. L (as TANGENT)]

tangle *v.t./i.* **1** to twist or become twisted into a confused mass. **2** to entangle. **3** to become involved in conflict. **4** to complicate. —*n.* a tangled mass or condition. [orig. unkn.]

tangly *adj.* tangled. [f. prec.]

tango /ˈtæŋgəʊ/ *n.* (*pl.* **-os**) a slow South American ballroom dance; the music for this. —*v.i.* to dance the tango. [Amer. Sp.]

tangram /ˈtæŋgræm/ *n.* a Chinese puzzle square cut into seven pieces to be combined into various figures. [orig. unkn.]

tangy /ˈtæŋɪ/ *adj.* having a strong taste or flavour or smell. [f. TANG]

tank *n.* **1** a large receptacle for liquid or gas. **2** an armoured motor vehicle carrying guns and moving on Caterpillar tracks. —**tank up**, to fill the tank of a vehicle etc.; (*slang*) to drink heavily. [f. Gujarati, perh. f. Skr. *tadaga* pond]

tankard /ˈtæŋkəd/ *n.* a tall mug, especially a

silver or pewter mug for beer. [orig. unkn., cf. MDu *tanckaert*]

tanker *n.* a ship, aircraft, or road vehicle for carrying liquids (especially mineral oils) in bulk. [f. TANK]

tanner[1] *n.* one who tans hides. [f. TAN[1]]

tanner[2] *n.* (*hist.*) a sixpence. [orig. unkn.]

tannery /ˈtænərɪ/ *n.* a place where hides are tanned. [as TANNER[1]]

tannic /ˈtænɪk/ *adj.* of tan. —**tannic acid,** tannin. [f. F (as foll.)]

tannin /ˈtænɪn/ *n.* any of several astringent substances obtained from oak-galls and various tree-barks, used in preparing leather and in making ink etc. [f. F *tanin* (as TAN[1])]

Tannoy /ˈtænɔɪ/ *n.* [P] a type of public-address system. [orig. unkn.]

tansy /ˈtænzɪ/ *n.* an aromatic herb (*Chrysanthemum vulgare*) with yellow flowers. [f. OF f. L f. Gk *athanasia* immortality (*a* not, *thanatos* death)]

tantalize /ˈtæntəlaɪz/ *v.t.* to tease or torment by the sight of something that is desired but kept out of reach or withheld. —**tantalization** /-ˈzeɪʃ(ə)n/ *n.* [as TANTALUS]

tantalum /ˈtæntələm/ *n.* a rare hard white metallic element, symbol Ta, atomic number 73. [f. foll., with ref. to its non-absorbent quality]

tantalus /ˈtæntələs/ *n.* a stand in which decanters of spirits are locked up but visible. [f. *Tantalus*, mythical king punished in Hades by sight of unattainable water and fruit]

tantamount /ˈtæntəmaʊnt/ *predic. adj.* equivalent. [f. It. *tanto montare* to amount to so much]

tantra /ˈtæntrə/ *n.* each of a class of Hindu, Buddhist, or Jain sacred texts that deal with mystical and magical practices. —**tantric** *adj.* [Skr., = loom (*tan* stretch, weave)]

tantrum /ˈtæntrəm/ *n.* an outburst of bad temper or petulance, especially in a child. [orig. unkn.]

Taoiseach /ˈtiːʃəx, -k/ *n.* the prime minister of the Irish Republic. [Ir., = chief, leader]

Taoism /ˈtɑːəʊɪz(ə)m, ˈtaʊ-/ *n.* a Chinese philosophy advocating humility and religious piety. —**Taoist** *n.* [f. Chin. *dao* right way]

tap[1] *n.* **1** a device for drawing liquid from a cask or for allowing liquid or gas to come from a pipe or vessel in a controlled flow. **2** a device for cutting a screw-thread inside a cavity. **3** a connection for tapping a telephone. —*v.t.* (**-pp-**) **1** to fit a tap into (a cask); to let out (liquid) thus. **2** to draw sap from (a tree) or fluid from (the body) by incision; to draw (fluid etc.) thus. **3** to extract or obtain supplies or information from; to establish communication or trade with. **4** to cut a screw-thread inside (a cavity). **5** to make a connection in (a circuit etc.) so as to divert electricity or fit a listening-device for overhearing telephone conversations. —**on tap,** ready to be drawn off by tap; (*colloq.*) ready for immediate use. **tap-root** *n.* a tapering root growing vertically downwards. [OE]

tap[2] *v.t./i.* (**-pp-**) **1** to strike with a quick light but audible blow; to knock gently on (a door etc.). **2** to strike (a thing) lightly against something. —*n.* a quick light blow; the sound of this. —**tap-dance** *n.* a dance with a sharp rhythmical tapping of the feet; (*v.i.*) to perform this dance. [imit.]

tape *n.* **1** a narrow strip of woven cotton etc. used for tying, fastening, or labelling things; such a strip stretched across a race-track at the finishing-line. **2** a strip of paper or of transparent film etc. coated with adhesive for fastening packages etc. **3** a magnetic tape; a tape-recording. **4** a long strip of paper printed or punched to convey messages. **5** a tape measure. —*v.t.* **1** to tie or fasten with tape. **2** to record on magnetic tape. **3** to measure with a tape. —**have a person** *or* **thing taped,** (*slang*) to understand him or it fully. **tape-machine** *n.* a machine for receiving and recording telegraph messages. **tape-measure** *n.* a strip of tape or thin flexible metal marked for measuring length. **tape-record** *v.t.* to record (sounds) on magnetic tape. **tape-recorder** *n.* an apparatus for recording sounds on magnetic tape and afterwards reproducing them. **tape-recording** *n.* such a record or reproduction. [OE; orig. unkn.]

taper /ˈteɪpə(r)/ *n.* a wick coated thinly with wax, burnt to give a light or to light candles etc. —*v.t./i.* to make or become gradually narrower. —**taper off,** to make or become gradually less in amount etc.; to cease gradually. [OE f. L *papyrus*, whose pith was used for candle-wicks]

tapestry /ˈtæpɪstrɪ/ *n.* a thick textile fabric in which coloured weft threads are woven (originally by hand) to form pictures or designs; embroidery imitating this, usually in wools on canvas; a piece of such embroidery. —**tapestried** *adj.* [f. OF *tapisserie* (*tapissier* to carpet f. *tapis* carpet)]

tapeworm *n.* a tapelike worm of the genus *Taenia* etc. living as a parasite in the intestines.

tapioca /tæpɪˈəʊkə/ *n.* a starchy substance in hard white grains obtained from cassava and used for puddings etc. [f. Tupi & Guarani *tipioca* (*tipi* dregs, *og*, *ok* squeeze out)]

tapir /ˈteɪpə(r), -pɪə(r)/ *n.* a piglike mammal of the genus *Tapirus* of tropical America and Malaya, with a short flexible snout. [f. Tupi]

tappet /ˈtæpɪt/ *n.* a cam or other projecting part used in machinery to give intermittent motion. [app. f. TAP²]

taproom *n.* a room in which alcoholic drinks are available on tap.

tar¹ *n.* a dark thick inflammable liquid distilled from wood, coal, or peat etc. and used as a preservative of wood and iron, an antiseptic, etc.; a similar substance formed in the combustion of tobacco etc. —*v.t.* (**-rr-**) to cover with tar. —**tar and feather,** to smear with tar and then cover with feathers as a punishment. **tarred with the same brush,** having the same faults. **tar-seal** *v.t.* (*Austr.*) to surface (a road) with a mixture of tar and broken stone; (*n.*) a road surfaced thus. [OE]

tar² *n.* (*colloq.*) a sailor. [abbr. of TARPAULIN]

taradiddle /ˈtærədɪd(ə)l/ *n.* (*colloq.*) a petty lie; nonsense. [cf. DIDDLE]

tarantella /tærənˈtelə/ *n.* a rapid whirling South Italian dance; the music for this. [It. (as foll., because said to cure the dancing mania thought to affect those bitten by tarantulas)]

tarantula /təˈræntjʊlə/ *n.* **1** a large black spider of the genus *Lycosa* of southern Europe. **2** a large hairy tropical spider. [L f. It. (*Taranto* in S. Italy)]

tarboosh /tɑːˈbuːʃ/ *n.* a cap like a fez, worn alone or as part of a turban. [f. Arab., ult. f. Pers., = head cover]

tardy /ˈtɑːdɪ/ *adj.* slow to act, move, or happen; delaying or delayed beyond the right or expected time. —**tardily** *adv.*, **tardiness** *n.* [f. F *tardif* f. L *tardus* slow]

tare¹ *n.* **1** a kind of vetch, especially as a cornfield weed (*Vicia hirsuta*) or fodder (*V. sativa*). **2** (in *pl.*, in the Bible) an injurious cornfield weed, thought to be darnel. [orig. unkn.]

tare² *n.* an allowance made to the purchaser for the weight of the container in which goods are packed, or for the vehicle transporting them, in instances where the goods are weighed together with their container or vehicle. [f. F, = deficiency, ult. f. Arab., = what is rejected]

target /ˈtɑːgɪt/ *n.* **1** an object or mark that a person tries to hit in shooting etc.; a round or rectangular object painted with concentric circles for this purpose, especially in archery. **2** a person or thing against which criticism or scorn is directed. **3** an objective, a minimum result aimed at. —*v.t.* **1** to aim (a weapon etc.) at a target. **2** to plan or schedule (a thing) to attain an objective. [dim. of *targe* shield, f. OF]

Targum /ˈtɑːgəm/ *n.* any of various ancient Aramaic paraphrases or interpretations of the Hebrew scriptures. [f. Chaldee, = interpretation]

tariff /ˈtærɪf/ *n.* **1** a list of fixed charges. **2** the duty on a particular class of imports or exports; a list of duties or customs to be paid. [f. F ult. f. Arab., = notification]

tarlatan /ˈtɑːlət(ə)n/ *n.* a thin stiff open kind of muslin. [f. F; prob. of Indian orig.]

Tarmac /ˈtɑːmæk/ *n.* [P] tarmacadam; a runway etc. made of this. —**tarmac** *v.t.* (**-ck-**) to surface with tarmacadam. [abbr.]

tarmacadam /tɑːməˈkædəm/ *n.* road materials of stone or slag bound with tar. [f. TAR¹ + MACADAM]

tarn *n.* a small mountain lake. [f. ON]

tarnish /ˈtɑːnɪʃ/ *v.t./i.* **1** to lessen or destroy the lustre of (metal etc.). **2** to stain or blemish (a reputation etc.). **3** (of metal etc.) to lose its lustre. —*n.* **1** loss of lustre. **2** a blemish, a stain. [f. F *ternir* (*terne* dark)]

taro /ˈtɑːrəʊ/ *n.* (*pl.* **-os**) a tropical plant (*Colocasia esculenta*) of the arum family with a tuberous root used as a food especially in the Pacific islands. [Polynesian]

tarot /ˈtærət/ *n.* **1** a card (especially one of 22 trumps) in a pack of 78 cards used in a game or for fortune-telling. **2** (also in *pl.*) this game. [f. It & F; orig. unkn.]

tarpaulin /tɑːˈpɔːlɪn/ *n.* a waterproof cloth especially of tarred canvas; a sheet or covering of this. [prob. f. TAR¹ + PALL¹]

tarradiddle var. of TARADIDDLE.

tarragon /ˈtærəgən/ *n.* a plant (*Artemisia dracunculus*) related to wormwood, used to flavour salads and vinegar. [L f. Gk *tarkhōn*, perh. through Arab. f. Gk *drakōn* dragon]

tarry¹ /ˈtɑːrɪ/ *adj.* of or smeared with tar. —**tarriness** *n.* [f. TAR¹]

tarry² /ˈtærɪ/ *v.i.* (*archaic*) to delay in coming or going, to linger. [orig. unkn.]

tarsal /ˈtɑːs(ə)l/ *adj.* of the tarsus. [f. TARSUS]

tarsier /ˈtɑːsɪə(r)/ *n.* a small nocturnal tree-climbing animal of SE Asia, with soft fur and large prominent eyes (especially *Tarsius spectrum*), a primate related to the lemurs. [F (as TARSUS, from the structure of its foot)]

tarsus /ˈtɑːsəs/ *n.* (*pl.* **tarsi** /-siː/) **1** the small bones (seven in man) that make up the ankle. **2** the shank of a bird's leg. [f. Gk *tarsos* flat of the foot]

tart¹ *n.* **1** a small round of pastry with jam etc. on top. **2** a pie with a fruit or sweet filling. [f. OF *tarte*]

tart² *n.* (*slang*) a prostitute, an immoral woman. —*v.t./i.* (*colloq.*) to dress or decorate gaudily or with cheap finery; to smarten. [prob. abbr. of SWEETHEART]

tart³ *adj.* **1** sharp-tasting, acid. **2** sharp in manner, biting. —**tartly** *adv.*, **tartness** *n.* [OE; orig. unkn.]

tartan /ˈtɑːt(ə)n/ *n.* a pattern of coloured stripes

crossing at right angles, especially a distinctive pattern worn by Scottish Highlanders to denote their clan; cloth woven in such a pattern. [perh. f. OF *tertaine, tiretaine*]

Tartar /ˈtɑːtə(r)/ *n.* **1** a member of a group of Central Asian peoples, including Mongols and Turks. **2** their Turkic language. **3** a violent-tempered or intractable person. —*adj.* of the Tartars or their language. [f. OF or L *Tartarus*]

tartar /ˈtɑːtə(r)/ *n.* **1** a hard chalky deposit that forms on the teeth. **2** a reddish deposit that forms on the side of a cask in which wine is fermented. [f. L f. Gk *tartaron*]

tartaric /tɑːˈtærɪk/ *adj.* of tartar or tartaric acid. —**tartaric acid,** an organic acid present in many plants, especially unripe grapes. [f. F f. L (as prec.)]

tartar sauce /ˈtɑːtə(r)/ a sauce of mayonnaise containing chopped gherkins etc. [f. TARTAR]

tartlet /ˈtɑːtlɪt/ *n.* a small tart. [f. F (as TART¹ + -LET)]

Tarzan /ˈtɑːz(ə)n/ *n.* a man of powerful physique and great agility. [character in novels by E. R. Burroughs]

task /tɑːsk/ *n.* a piece of work to be done. —*v.t.* to make great demands on (a person's powers etc.). —**take to task,** to rebuke. **task force,** a unit specially organized for a task. [f. OF *tasque* f. L *tasca* (perh. as TAX)]

taskmaster *n.* one who imposes a task or burden.

tassel /ˈtæs(ə)l/ *n.* **1** a bunch of threads or cords tied at one end and hanging loosely, attached as an ornament to a cushion, scarf, etc. **2** a tassel-like catkin or head of certain plants (e.g. maize). [f. OF, = clasp; orig. unkn.]

tasset /ˈtæsɪt/ *n.* (in *pl.*) a series of overlapping plates in medieval armour, hanging from the corslet and protecting the thighs. [f. OF *tasse* purse, holster; connection of sense not clear]

taste /ˈteɪst/ *n.* **1** the sensation caused in the tongue by a soluble substance placed on it. **2** the faculty of perceiving this sensation. **3** a small portion of food or drink taken as a sample; a slight experience of something. **4** a liking. **5** aesthetic discernment in art, literature, or conduct; conformity to its dictates. —*v.t./i.* **1** to discern or test the flavour of (food etc., or *absol.*) by taking it into the mouth. **2** to eat or drink a small portion of. **3** to perceive the flavour of. **4** to have experience of. **5** to have a specified flavour. —**taste-bud** *n.* any of the cells on the surface of the tongue by which things are tasted. **to one's taste,** pleasing, suitable. [f. OF *tast* f. *taster* touch, try, perh. f. L *tangere* touch + *gustare* taste]

tasteful *adj.* having or showing good taste. —**tastefully** *adv.*, **tastefulness** *n.* [f. TASTE + -FUL]

tasteless *adj.* **1** lacking flavour. **2** having or showing bad taste. —**tastelessly** *adv.*, **tastelessness** *n.* [f. TASTE -LESS]

taster /ˈteɪstə(r)/ *n.* a person employed to judge teas or wines etc. by tasting them. [f. TASTE]

tasty /ˈteɪstɪ/ *adj.* having a strong flavour; appetizing. —**tastily** *adv.*, **tastiness** *n.* [f. TASTE]

tat¹ *n.* tatty things; a tatty person; tattiness. [back-formation f. TATTY]

tat² *v.t./i.* (**-tt-**) to do tatting; to make by tatting. [orig. unkn.]

ta-ta /tæˈtɑː/ *int.* (*colloq.*) goodbye. [orig. unkn.]

Tatar /ˈtɑːtə(r)/ var. of TARTAR.

tattered /ˈtætəd/ *adj.* in tatters. [f. foll.]

tatters *n.pl.* rags, irregularly torn pieces of cloth or paper etc. —**in tatters,** (of an argument etc.) ruined, demolished. [f. ON *tötrar* rags]

tatting /ˈtætɪŋ/ *n.* **1** a kind of knotted lace made by hand with a small shuttle and used for trimming etc. **2** the process of making this. [orig. unkn.]

tattle *v.i.* to chatter or gossip idly; to reveal information thus. —*n.* idle chatter or gossip. [f. Flem. *tatelen* (imit.)]

tattoo¹ /təˈtuː/ *n.* **1** an evening drum or bugle signal recalling soldiers to quarters. **2** an elaboration of this with music and marching as an entertainment. **3** a rapping or drumming sound. [f. earlier *tap-too* f. Du., = close the tap (of the cask)]

tattoo² /təˈtuː/ *v.t.* to mark (the skin) with an indelible pattern by puncturing and inserting pigment; to make (a design) thus. —*n.* such a design. —**tattooist** *n.* [f. Polynesian]

tatty /ˈtætɪ/ *adj.* (*colloq.*) **1** tattered, shabby and untidy. **2** tawdry, fussily ornate. —**tattily** *adv.*, **tattiness** *n.* [orig. Sc., = shaggy (app. as TATTER)]

tau /taʊ, tɔː/ *n.* the nineteenth letter of the Greek alphabet, = t. —**tau cross,** a T-shaped cross. [f. Gk]

taught *past & p.p.* of TEACH.

taunt *n.* a thing said to anger or wound a person. —*v.t.* to assail with taunts; to reproach (a person with conduct etc.) contemptuously. [f. F *tant pour tant* tit for tat, smart rejoinder]

taupe /təʊp/ *n.* grey with a tinge of another colour, usually brown. [F, = mole (MOLE¹)]

Taurus /ˈtɔːrəs/ a constellation and the second sign of the zodiac, the Bull, which the sun enters about 21 April. —**Taurean** *adj.* & *n.* [L, = bull]

taut *adj.* **1** (of a rope etc.) tight, not slack; (of the nerves) tense. **2** (of a ship etc.) in good condition. — **tautly** *adv.* [perh. as TOUGH]

tauten /ˈtɔːt(ə)n/ *v.t./i.* to make or become taut. [f. TAUT]

tautology /tɔːˈtɒlədʒɪ/ *n.* the saying of the same thing twice over in different words, especially as a fault of style (e.g. *arrived one after the other in succession*). —**tautological** /tɔːtəˈlɒdʒɪk(ə)l/ *adj.*, **tautologous** /-ləgəs/ *adj.* [f. L f. Gk *tautologia* (*tauto* the same, -LOGY)]

tavern /ˈtæv(ə)n/ *n.* (*literary*) an inn, a public house. [f. OF f. L *taberna* hut, tavern]

tawdry /ˈtɔːdrɪ/ *adj.* showy but worthless, gaudy. —**tawdrily**, *adv.*, **tawdriness** *n.* [short for *tawdry lace* f. *St Audrey's lace* (*Audrey* = Etheldrida, patron saint of Ely, d. 679) from the cheap finery sold at St Audrey's fair]

tawny /ˈtɔːnɪ/ *adj.* brownish-yellow, brownish-orange. —**tawniness** *n.* [f. AF *tauné* (as TAN)]

tawse /tɔːz/ *n.* (*Sc.*) a leather strap with a slit end, used for punishing children. [pl. of obs. *taw* leather made without tannin]

tax *n.* **1** a contribution to State revenue legally levied on persons, property, or business. **2** a heavy demand made upon a person, resources, etc. —*v.t.* **1** to impose a tax on; to require to pay tax. **2** to pay the tax on. **3** to make heavy demands on. **4** to accuse in a challenging way. —**tax-deductible** *adj.* (of expenses) that may be paid out of income before the deduction of income tax. **tax-free** *adj.* exempt from taxes. **tax haven,** a place where income tax is low. **tax return,** a declaration of income for taxation purposes. [f. OF f. L *taxare* censure, compute, perh. f. Gk *tassō* fix]

taxable *adj.* that may be taxed. [f. TAX]

taxation /tækˈseɪʃ(ə)n/ *n.* the imposition or payment of tax. [as TAX]

taxi /ˈtæksɪ/ *n.* (in full **taxi-cab**) a motor car plying for hire and usually fitted with a taximeter. — *v.t./i.* (*partic.* **taxiing**) **1** (of an aircraft or pilot) to go along the ground or surface of the water under the machine's own power before or after flying. **2** to go or convey in a taxi. [abbr. of *taximeter cab*]

taxidermy /ˈtæksɪdɜːmɪ/ *n.* the art of preparing, stuffing, and mounting the skins of animals with lifelike effect. —**taxidermist** *n.* [f. Gk *taxis* arrangement + *derma* skin]

taximeter /ˈtæksɪmiːtə(r)/ *n.* an automatic fare-indicator fitted to a taxi. [f. F (as TAX, -METER)]

taxman *n.* (*pl.* **-men**) an inspector or collector of taxes.

taxonomic /tæksəˈnɒmɪk/ *adj.* (also **taxonomical**) of or using taxonomy. —**taxonomically** *adv.* [f. foll.]

taxonomy /tækˈsɒnəmɪ/ *n.* classification, especially in biology; the principles of this. —**taxonomist** *n.* [f. F f. Gk *taxis* arrangement, *-nomia* distribution]

taxpayer *n.* one who pays taxes.

TB *abbr.* tubercle bacillus; (*colloq.*) tuberculosis.

Tb *symbol* terbium.

T-bone /ˈtiːbəʊn/ *n.* a T-shaped bone, especially in a steak from the thin end of the loin.

te /tiː/ *n.* (*Mus.*) the seventh note of the major scale in tonic sol-fa. [alt. f. *si*, perh. f. *S*ancte *I*ohannes (see GAMUT)]

tea *n.* **1** an evergreen shrub or small tree (*Camellia sinensis*) grown in India, China, etc. **2** its dried leaves. **3** a drink made by infusing tea-leaves in boiling water; a similar drink made from the leaves of other plants or from some other substance. **4** a meal at which tea is a main feature. —**tea-bag** *n.* a small porous bag of tea for infusion. **tea-chest** *n.* a light metal-lined wooden box in which tea is exported. **tea-cloth** *n.* a cloth for a tea-table. **tea-leaf** *n.* a leaf of tea especially (in *pl.*) after infusion or as dregs; (*rhyming slang*) a thief. **tea-room** *or* **-shop** *n.* a place where tea and light refreshments are served to the public. **tea-rose** *n.* a rose (*Rosa odorata*) with a scent like tea. **tea-towel** *n.* a towel for drying washed crockery etc. [orig. *tay* ult. f. Chin. *t'e*]

teacake *n.* a light usually sweet bun eaten at tea, usually served toasted and buttered.

teach *v.t./i.* (*past & p.p.* **taught** /tɔːt/) **1** to impart information or skill to (a person) or about (a subject) systematically; to do this as a profession. **2** to put forward as a fact or principle. **3** to induce to adopt a practice etc. by example or experience; (*colloq.*) to deter by punishment etc. —**teach-in** *n.* a lecture and discussion, or a series of these, on a subject of public interest. [OE]

teachable *adj.* **1** apt at learning. **2** (of a subject) that can be taught. [f. TEACH]

teacher *n.* one who teaches, especially in a school. [f. TEACH]

teaching *n.* **1** what is taught, a doctrine. **2** the teachers' profession. [f. TEACH]

teacup *n.* a cup from which tea and other hot drinks are drunk.

teak *n.* a heavy durable timber; the Asian tree (*Tectona grandis*) yielding this. [f. Port. f. Malayalam]

teal *n.* (*pl.* same) a small freshwater duck of the genus *Anas* etc. [rel. to MDu. *teling*; orig. unkn.]

team *n.* **1** a set of players forming one side in certain games and sports. **2** a set of persons working together. **3** two or more animals harnessed together to draw a vehicle or farm implement. —*v.t./i.* to combine into a team or set or for a common purpose. —**team-mate** *n.* a fellow member of a team. **team spirit,**

willingness to act for the benefit of one's group rather than oneself. **team-work** *n.* combined effort, co-operation. [OE, = offspring]

teamster *n.* **1** a driver of a team of animals. **2** (*US*) a lorry-driver. [f. TEAM]

teapot *n.* a pot with a handle, spout, and lid, in which tea is brewed and from which it is poured.

tear[1] /teə(r)/ *v.t./i.* (*past* **tore**; *p.p.* **torn**) **1** to pull forcibly apart, away, or to pieces; to make (a hole or rent) thus. **2** to become torn; to be capable of being torn. **3** to subject to conflicting desires or demands; to disrupt violently. **4** to run, walk, or travel hurriedly or impetuously. —*n.* a hole or rent caused by tearing. —**tear fault,** a geological fault in which the fracture is approximately vertical and movement is horizontal. **tear oneself away,** leave in spite of a strong desire to stay. **tear one's hair,** to pull it in anger or frustration or despair. [OE]

tear[2] /tɪə(r)/ *n.* a drop of clear salty liquid serving to moisten and wash the eye and falling from it in sorrow or distress etc. —**in tears,** weeping. **tear-drop** *n.* a single tear. **tear-gas** *n.* a gas that disables by causing severe irritation to the eyes. **tear-jerker** *n.* (*colloq.*) a story etc. calculated to evoke sadness or sympathy. **without tears,** presented so as to be learned or done easily. [OE]

tearaway /ˈteərəweɪ/ *n.* a reckless hooligan. [f. TEAR[1] + AWAY]

tearful /ˈtɪəfəl/ *adj.* shedding or ready to shed tears; sad. —**tearfully** *adv.* [f. TEAR[2] + -FUL]

tearing /ˈteərɪŋ/ *adj.* extreme, overwhelming. [f. TEAR[1]]

tease /ti:z/ *v.t.* **1** to try playfully or maliciously to provoke (a person) by jokes, questions, or petty annoyances. **2** to pick (wool etc.) into separate strands. **3** to brush up the nap on (cloth). —*n.* (*colloq.*) a person who is fond of teasing others. —**tease out,** to separate by disentangling. [OE]

teasel /ˈti:z(ə)l/ *n.* **1** a plant of the genus *Dipsacus* with prickly flower-heads. **2** such a head dried and used for raising the nap on cloth; a device used thus. [OE, rel. to prec.]

teaser /ˈti:zə(r)/ *n.* (*colloq.*) a hard question or task. [f. TEASE]

teaspoon *n.* a small spoon for stirring tea; the amount held by this. —**teaspoonful** *n.* (*pl.* **-fuls**)

teat *n.* **1** a mammary nipple, especially of an animal. **2** a device, especially of rubber, for sucking milk from a bottle. [f. OF *tete,* replacing TIT[3]]

tec *n.* (*slang*) a detective. [abbr.]

Tech /tek/ *n.* (*colloq.*) a technical college or school. [abbr.]

technetium /tekˈni:ʃəm/ *n.* an artificially produced radioactive metallic element, symbol Tc, atomic number 43. [f. Gk *tekhnētos* artificial (*tekhnē* art)]

technical /ˈteknɪk(ə)l/ *adj.* **1** of or involving the mechanical arts and applied sciences. **2** of or relating to a particular subject or craft etc. or its techniques. **3** (of a book or discourse etc.) using technical language, requiring special knowledge to be understood. **4** such in strict interpretation. —**technically** *adv.* [f. L f. Gk *tekhnikos* (*tekhnē* art)]

technicality /teknɪˈkælɪtɪ/ *n.* **1** being technical. **2** a technical expression. **3** a technical point or detail. [f. prec.]

technician /tekˈnɪʃ(ə)n/ *n.* **1** an expert in the techniques of a particular skill or craft. **2** a mechanic; a person employed to look after technical equipment in a laboratory etc. [as TECHNICAL]

Technicolor /ˈteknɪkʌlə(r)/ *n.* **1** [P] a process of colour cinematography. **2** vivid colour, artificial brilliance. [f. TECHNICAL + COLOUR]

technique /tekˈni:k/ *n.* the method of doing or performing something, especially in an art or science; skill in this. [F (as TECHNICAL)]

technocracy /tekˈnɒkrəsɪ/ *n.* government or control of a society or industry by technical experts. [f. Gk *tekhnē* art + -CRACY]

technocrat /ˈteknəkræt/ *n.* an exponent or advocate of technocracy. [f. prec.]

technological /teknəˈlɒdʒɪk(ə)l/ *adj.* of or using technology. —**technologically** *adv.* [f. foll.]

technology /tekˈnɒlədʒɪ/ *n.* the study or use of the mechanical arts and applied sciences; these subjects collectively. —**technologist** *n.* [f. Gk (as TECHNICAL, -LOGY)]

tectonics /tekˈtɒnɪks/ *n.pl.* (usu. treated as *sing.*) the study of the earth's structural features as a whole. [f. L f. Gk (*tektōn* carpenter)]

Ted *n.* (*colloq.*) a Teddy boy. [abbr.]

tedder *n.* a machine for drying hay. [f. ON *tethja* spread manure]

teddy bear a soft furry toy bear. [f. *Teddy* pet-name of *Theodore* Roosevelt (d. 1919)]

Teddy boy /ˈtedɪ/ (*colloq.*) a youth with a supposedly Edwardian style of dress, especially in the 1950s. [f. *Teddy,* pet-form of *Edward*]

tedious /ˈti:dɪəs/ *adj.* tiresomely long, wearisome. —**tediously** *adv.*, **tediousness** *n.* [f. OF or L (as foll.)]

tedium /ˈti:dɪəm/ *n.* tediousness. [f. L *taedium* (*taedēre* to weary)]

tee[1] *n.* the letter T. [phonetic spelling]

tee[2] *n.* **1** a cleared space from which a golf ball is struck at the beginning of play for each hole. **2** a small support of wood or plastic from which a ball is thus struck. **3** the mark aimed at in bowls, quoits, etc. —*v.t.* to place (a ball) on a golf tee. —**tee off,** to play a ball from a tee, to start, to begin. [f. earlier *teaz* (orig. unkn.); in last sense of n. perh. = TEE[1]]

teem[1] *v.i.* **1** to be abundant. **2** to be full, to swarm (*with*). [OE (as TEAM)]

teem[2] *v.i.* (of water etc.) to flow copiously. [f. ON]

-teen *suffix* forming the numerals 13-19. [OE (as TEN)]

teenage /ˈti:neɪdʒ/ *adj.* of or characteristic of teenagers. [f. TEENS + AGE]

teenager /ˈti:neɪdʒə(r)/ *n.* a person in his or her teens. [f. prec.]

teens /ti:nz/ *n.pl.* the years of one's age from 13 to 19. [f. -TEEN]

teeny /ˈti:nɪ/ *adj.* (*colloq.*) tiny. [var. of TINY]

teeny-bopper *n.*a girl in her teens or younger who is a fan of pop music and follows the latest fashions. [f. TEENS + BOPPER]

teeter *v.i.* to totter, to move unsteadily. [var. of dial. *titter*]

teeth *pl.* of TOOTH.

teethe /ti:ð/ *v.i.* to grow or cut teeth, especially the milk-teeth. —**teething-ring** *n.* a small ring for an infant to bite on while teething. **teething troubles**, initial troubles in an enterprise etc. [f. prec.]

teetotal /ti:ˈtəʊt(ə)l/ *adj* abstaining completely from alcoholic drinks. —**teetotalism** *n.*, **teetotaller** *n.* [redupl of TOTAL]

tektite /ˈtektaɪt/ *n.* a small roundish glassy solid body of unknown origin occurring in various parts of the earth. [f. G f. Gk *tēktos* molten (*tēkō* melt)]

telamon /ˈteləmən/ *n.* (*pl.* **telamones** /-ˈməʊni:z/) a sculptured male figure used as a pillar to support an entablature. [f. L f. Gk *Telamōn*, name of a mythical hero]

tele- /telɪ-/ *in comb.* **1** far, at a distance. **2** television. [in first sense f. Gk (*tēle* far off); in second sense f. TELEVISION]

telecommunication /telɪkəmju:nɪˈkeɪʃ(ə)n/ *n.* communication over long distances by cable, telegraph, telephone, or broadcasting; (usu. in *pl.*) this branch of technology.

telegram /ˈtelɪgræm/ *n.* a message sent by telegraph and then usually delivered in printed form. [f. TELE- + -GRAM]

telegraph /ˈtelɪgrɑ:f/ *n.* transmitting messages or signals to a distance, especially by making and breaking an electrical connection; an apparatus for this. —*v.t./i.* to send a message by telegraph (to); to send (a message) thus; to send an instruction to by telegraph. [f. F (as TELE-, -GRAPH)]

telegraphic /telɪˈgræfɪk/ *adj.* **1** of telegraphs or telegrams. **2** worded economically like telegrams. —**telegraphically** *adv.* [f. prec.]

telegraphist /tɪˈlegrəfɪst/ *n.* a person skilled or employed in telegraphy. [f. TELEGRAPH]

telegraphy /tɪˈlegrəfɪ/ *n.* the process of communication by telegraph. [as prec.]

telekinesis /telɪkaɪˈni:sɪs, -kɪ-/ *n.* movement of or in a body alleged to occur at a distance from, and without material connection with, the motive cause or agent. [f. TELE- + Gk *kinēsis* motion]

telemeter /ˈtelɪmi:tə(r)/ *n.* an apparatus for recording the readings of an instrument and transmitting it by radio. [f. TELE- + -METER]

telemetry /tɪˈlemɪtrɪ/ *n.* the process of obtaining measurements at a point removed from the place where they are made; transmission of these, usually by radio. [f. TELE- + -METRY]

teleology /telɪˈɒlədʒɪ/ *n.* the doctrine of final causes, especially as related to the evidence of design or purpose in nature. —**teleological** /-əˈlɒdʒɪk(ə)l/ *adj.* [f. Gk *telos* end + -LOGY]

telepath /ˈtelɪpæθ/ *n.* a person able to communicate by telepathy. [f. foll.]

telepathy /tɪˈlepəθɪ/ *n.* communication between minds otherwise than by the known senses. —**telepathic** /telɪˈpæθɪk/ *adj.*, **telepathist** *n.* [f. TELE- + Gk *pathos* feeling]

telephone /ˈtelɪfəʊn/ *n.* **1** an apparatus for transmitting sound (especially speech) to a distance by wire, cord, or radio, usually by converting acoustic vibrations into electrical signals for transmission. **2** the transmitting and receiving instrument used in this. **3** the system of communication by a network of telephones. —*v.t./i.* to speak to (a person) by telephone; to send (a message) by telephone; to make a telephone call. —**telephone box, booth,** *or* **kiosk,** a box-like kiosk containing a telephone for public use. **telephone directory** *or* **book,** a book listing the names and telephone numbers of people who are connected to a particular telephone system. **telephone number,** a number assigned to a particular telephone and used in making connections to it. —**telephonic** /-ˈfɒnɪk/ *adj.*, **telephonically** /-ˈfɒnɪkəlɪ/ *adv.* [f. TELE- + Gk *phōnē* voice]

telephonist /tɪˈlefənɪst/ *n.* an operator in a telephone exchange or at a switchboard. [f. prec.]

telephony /tɪˈlefənɪ/ *n.* the use or system of telephones. [f. TELEPHONE]

telephoto /telɪˈfəʊtəʊ/ *adj.* telephotographic. [abbr.]

telephotography /telɪfəˈtɒgrəfɪ/ *n.* the photographing of distant objects with combined lenses giving a large image. —**telephotographic** /-fəʊtəˈgræfɪk/ *adj.*

teleprinter /ˈtelɪprɪntə(r)/ *n.* a device for typing and transmitting telegraph messages and for receiving and typing them.

telescope /ˈtelɪskəʊp/ *n.* **1** an optical instrument using lenses or mirrors or both to make distant objects appear nearer and larger. **2** a radio telescope (see separate entry). —*v.t./i.* **1** to press or drive (sections of tube, colliding vehicles, etc.) together so that one slides into another like the sections of a telescope; to close or be driven or be capable of closing thus. **2** to compress so as to occupy less space or time. [f. It. (as TELE-, -SCOPE)]

telescopic /telɪˈskɒpɪk/ *adj.* **1** of or made with a telescope. **2** consisting of sections which telescope. —**telescopic sight**, a telescope used for sighting on a rifle etc. —**telescopically** *adv.* [f. prec.]

teletext /ˈtelɪtekst/ *n.* a news and information service from a computer source transmitted to the television screens of subcribers.

Teletype /ˈtelɪtaɪp/ *n.* [P] a kind of teleprinter.

televise /ˈtelɪvaɪz/ *v.t.* to transmit by television. [back-formation f. foll.]

television /ˈtelɪvɪʒ(ə)n, -ˈvɪʒ(ə)n/ *n.* **1** a system for reproducing on a screen visual images transmitted (with sound) by radio signals. **2** (in full **television set**) a device for receiving these signals. **3** television broadcasting generally. —**televisual** /-ˈvɪzjʊəl/ *adj.*

telex /ˈteleks/ *n.* a system of telegraphy using teleprinters and the public telecommunication network. A telex service opened in London in 1932. —*v.t.* to send by telex; to communicate with by telex. [f. TELEPRINTER + EXCHANGE]

tell[1] *v.t./i.* (*past & p.p.* **told** /təʊld/) **1** to make known, especially in spoken or written words; to utter. **2** to give information to; to assure; to reveal a secret. **3** to direct or order. **4** to decide, to determine; to distinguish. **5** to produce a noticeable effect. **6** to count. —**tell off**, (*colloq.*) to reprimand, to scold; to count off or detach for duty. **tell on**, to reveal the activities of (a person) by telling others. **tell tales**, to report a discreditable fact about another. **tell the time**, to read it from the face of a clock or watch. **you're telling me**, (*slang*) I am well aware of what you say. [OE]

tell[2] *n.* an artificial mound in the Middle East etc. formed by accumulated remains of ancient settlements superimposed on earlier ones. [f. Arab., = hillock]

teller *n.* **1** a person employed to receive and pay out money in a bank etc. **2** a person appointed to count votes. [f. TELL[1]]

telling *adj.* having a noticeable effect, striking. [f. TELL[1]]

tell-tale *n.* **1** a person who discloses another's private affairs or misdeeds. **2** an automatic registering device. **3** a metal sheet extending across the front wall of a squash court, above which the ball must strike the wall. —*adj.* that reveals or betrays.

tellurium /teˈljʊərɪəm/ *n.* a rare semi-metallic element, symbol Te, atomic number 52, chemically related to sulphur and selenium. [f. L *tellus -uris* earth, prob. named in contrast to uranium]

telly /ˈtelɪ/ *n.* (*colloq.*) television; a television set. [abbr.]

temerity /tɪˈmerɪtɪ/ *n.* audacity, rashness. [f. L *temeritas* (*temere* rashly)]

temp *n.* (*colloq.*) a temporary employee, especially a secretary. [abbr.]

temper *n.* **1** the state of the mind as regards calmness or anger. **2** a fit of anger; a tendency to have such fits. **3** calmness under provocation. **4** the condition of tempered metal as regards hardness and elasticity. —*v.t.* **1** to bring (metal or clay) to the proper hardness or consistency. **2** to moderate or mitigate. [OE f. L *temperare* mingle]

tempera /ˈtempərə/ *n.* a method of painting with powdered colours mixed with egg or size. It was used in Europe from the 12th or early 13th c. until the 15th c., when it began to give way to oil painting. [It., f. L *temperare* mix]

temperament /ˈtemprəmənt/ *n.* **1** a person's distinct nature and character, especially as determined by physical constitution and permanently affecting his or her behaviour. **2** (*Mus.*) the adjustment of intervals in the tuning of a piano etc. so as to fit the scale for use in all keys, especially (**equal temperament**) in which the twelve semitones are at equal intervals. [f. L (as TEMPER)]

temperamental /temprəˈment(ə)l/ *adj.* **1** of the temperament. **2** liable to erratic or moody behaviour —**temperamentally** *adv.* [f. prec.]

temperance /ˈtempərəns/ *n.* **1** moderation or self-restraint, especially in eating and drinking. **2** abstinence or partial abstinence from alcoholic drink. [f. AF f. L (as TEMPER)]

temperate /ˈtempərət/ *adj.* **1** avoiding excess; moderate. **2** of mild temperature. —**temperately** *adv.* [f. L (as TEMPER)]

temperature /ˈtemprɪtʃə(r)/ *n.* **1** the degree or intensity of the heat of a body in relation to others, especially as shown by a thermometer or perceived by touch; (*colloq.*) a body temperature above normal. **2** a degree of excitement in a discussion etc. [f. F or L (as TEMPER)]

tempest /ˈtempɪst/ *n.* a violent storm. [f. OF f. L *tempestas* season, storm (*tempus* time)]

tempestuous /temˈpestjʊəs/ *adj.* stormy, turbulent. [f. L (as prec.)]

Templar /ˈtemplə(r)/ *n.* a member of the Knights Templars, a military and religious order (1118-1312) for protecting pilgrims to the Holy Land. [f. AF (as TEMPLE¹)]

template /ˈtemplɪt/ *n.* a thin board or metal plate used as a guide in cutting, shaping, or drilling. [orig. *templet*, prob. dim. of *temple* device in loom for keeping cloth stretched, f. OF, orig. same word as TEMPLE²]

temple¹ /ˈtemp(ə)l/ *n.* a building devoted to the worship, or treated as a dwelling-place, of a god or gods. —**Inner** and **Middle Temple,** two Inns of Court in London. [OE & f. OF f. L *templum* open or consecrated space]

temple² /ˈtemp(ə)l/ *n.* the flat part of either side of the head between the forehead and the ear. [f. OF f. L *tempus*]

tempo *n.* (*pl.* **tempos** or **tempi** /-i:/) **1** the speed at which music is or should be played, especially as characteristic. **2** a rate of motion or activity. [It., f. L *tempus* time]

temporal /ˈtempər(ə)l/ *adj.* **1** of worldly as opposed to spiritual affairs, secular. **2** of or denoting time. **3** of the temple(s) of the head (*temporal bone*). [f. OF or L (as TEMPORARY, TEMPLE²)]

temporary /ˈtempərərɪ/ *adj.* lasting or meant to last only for a limited time. —*n.* a person employed temporarily. —**temporarily** *adv.*, **temporariness** *n.* [f. L (*tempus* time)]

temporize /ˈtempəraɪz/ *v.i.* to avoid committing oneself, to act so as to gain time; to comply temporarily with the requirements of an occasion. —**temporization** /-ˈzeɪʃ(ə)n/ *n.*, **temporizer** *n.* [f. F f. L (as prec.)]

tempt *v.t.* **1** to entice or incite to do a wrong or forbidden thing. **2** to arouse a desire in, to attract. **3** to risk provoking (fate or Providence) by deliberate rashness. —**be tempted to,** to be strongly disposed to. —**tempter** *n.*, **temptress** *n. fem.* [f. OF f. L *temptare* test]

temptation /tempˈteɪʃ(ə)n/ *n.* **1** tempting, being tempted; an incitement, especially to wrongdoing. **2** an attractive thing or course of action. **3** (*archaic*) putting to the test. [as prec.]

tempting *adj.* attractive, inviting. [f. TEMPT]

ten *adj.* & *n.* **1** one more than nine. **2** the symbol for this (10, x, X). **3** a size etc. denoted by ten. [OE]

tenable /ˈtenəb(ə)l/ *adj.* **1** that can be maintained against attack or objection. **2** (of an office etc.) that can be held for a specified period or by a specified class of person. —**tenability** /-ˈbɪlɪtɪ/ *n.* [F (*tenir* hold f. L *tenēre*)]

tenacious /tɪˈneɪʃəs/ *adj.* **1** keeping a firm hold (*of* property, principles, life, etc.). **2** (of memory) retentive. **3** holding tightly, not easily separable; tough. —**tenaciously** *adv.*, **tenacity** /tɪˈnæsɪtɪ/ *n.* [f. L *tenax* (*tenēre* hold)]

tenancy *n.* occupancy as a tenant. [f. foll.]

tenant /ˈtenənt/ *n.* a person who rents land or property from a landlord; the occupant of a place. —**tenant farmer,** one farming hired land. [f. OF (as TENABLE)]

tenantry *n.* the tenants of an estate etc. [f. prec.]

tench *n.* (*pl.* same) a European freshwater fish (*Tinca tinca*) of the carp family. [f. OF f. L *tinca*]

tend¹ *v.i.* **1** to be likely to behave in a specified way or to have a specified characteristic or influence. **2** to take a specified direction (*lit.* or *fig.*). [f. OF f. L *tendere* stretch]

tend² *v.t.* to take care of, to look after. [f. ATTEND]

tendency /ˈtendənsɪ/ *n.* **1** the way a person or thing tends to be or behave. **2** the direction in which something moves or changes, a trend. [f. L (as TEND¹)]

tendentious /tenˈdenʃəs/ *adj.* (*derog.*, of a speech or piece of writing etc.) designed to advance a cause, not impartial. —**tendentiously** *adv.*, **tendentiousness** *n.* [as prec.]

tender¹ *adj.* **1** easily cut or chewed, not tough. **2** easily hurt or wounded, susceptible to pain or grief; delicate, fragile, sensitive. **3** loving, gentle. **4** requiring tact. **5** (of age) early, immature. —**tender spot,** a subject on which one is touchy. —**tenderly** *adv.*, **tenderness** *n.* [f. OF f. L *tener*]

tender² *v.t./i.* **1** to make an offer of or present for acceptance. **2** to send in a tender for the execution of work etc. —*n.* an offer, especially in writing, to execute work or supply goods at a stated price. —**put out to tender,** to seek offers in respect of (work etc.). [f. OF *tendre* (as TEND¹)]

tender³ *n.* **1** one who looks after people or things. **2** a vessel attending a larger one and carrying stores etc. **3** a truck attached to a steam locomotive and carrying coal etc. [f. TEND²]

tenderfoot *n.* a newcomer who is unused to hardships, an inexperienced person.

tenderize *v.t.* to make tender; to make (meat) tender by beating etc. —**tenderizer** *n.* [f. TENDER¹]

tenderloin *n.* **1** the middle part of pork loin. **2** (*US*) the undercut of a sirloin.

tendon /ˈtend(ə)n/ *n.* a band or cord of strong tissue attaching a muscle to a bone etc. [F or f. L f. Gk *tenōn* sinew (*teinō* stretch)]

tendril /ˈtendrɪl/ *n.* any of the slender leafless shoots by which some climbing plants cling. [prob. f. obs. F *tendrillon* (*tendron* young shoot f. L, as TENDER¹)]

tenement /ˈtenɪmənt/ *n.* **1** a piece of land held

by an owner; (*Law*) any kind of permanent property held by a tenant. **2** a flat or room rented as a dwelling-place. **3** (*Sc.*) a house divided into and let in tenements. [f. OF f. L (*tenēre* hold)]

tenet /ˈtenɪt/ *n.* a doctrine held by a group or person. [L, = he holds (as prec.)]

tenfold /ˈtenfəʊld/ *adj.* & *adv.* ten times as much or as many; consisting of ten parts. [f. TEN + -FOLD]

tenner *n.* (*colloq.*) a £10 note. [f. TEN]

tennis /ˈtenɪs/ *n.* **1** lawn tennis (see LAWN). **2** (also **real, royal,** *or* (*US*) **court tennis**) an indoor game for two or four persons in which a small solid ball is struck with rackets over a net, or rebounds from side walls, in a walled court. [f. F *tenez* take, receive, called by server to his opponent]

tenon /ˈtenən/ *n.* a projection shaped to fit into a mortise. —**tenon-saw** *n.* a small saw with a strong brass or steel back, used for fine work. [f. F (*tenir* hold f. L *tenēre*)]

tenor /ˈtenə(r)/ *n.* **1** the highest ordinary adult male singing-voice; a singer with this; a part written for it. **2** a musical instrument with approximately the range of a tenor voice. **3** the general routine or course of something. **4** the general meaning or drift. [f. AF f. L *tenor* (*tenēre* hold)]

tenpin bowling a form of skittles similar to ninepins.

tense[1] *adj.* **1** stretched tightly. **2** with muscles tight in attentiveness for what may happen; unable to relax, edgy. **3** causing tenseness. —*v.t./i.* to make or become tense. —**tensely** *adv.*, **tenseness** *n.* [f.L *tensus* (as TEND[1])]

tense[2] *n.* the form taken by a word to indicate the time (also continuance or completeness) of an action; a set of such forms. [f. OF f. L *tempus* time]

tensile /ˈtensaɪl/ *adj.* **1** of tension. **2** capable of being stretched. —**tensile strength,** resistance to breaking under tension. —**tensility** /-ˈsɪlɪtɪ/ *n.* [f. L *tensilis* (as TEND[1])]

tension /ˈtenʃ(ə)n/ *n.* **1** stretching, being stretched. **2** tenseness, the condition when feelings are tense. **3** the effect produced by forces pulling against each other. **4** electromotive force. **5** (in knitting) the number of stitches and rows to a unit of measurement. [F or f. L (as TEND[1])]

tent *n.* **1** a portable shelter or dwelling of canvas or cloth etc. supported by poles and by ropes attached to pegs driven into the ground. **2** a cover etc. resembling a tent. [as TEND[1]]

tentacle /ˈtentək(ə)l/ *n.* **1** a long slender flexible appendage of an animal, used for feeling or grasping things or for moving. **2** a thing compared to a tentacle in use. —**tentacled** *adj.* [f. L *tentare* = *temptare* (as TEMPT)]

tentative /ˈtentətɪv/ *adj.* done as a trial, hesitant, not definite. —**tentatively** *adv.* [as prec.]

tenter *n.* a machine for stretching cloth to dry in shape. [f. L *tentorium* (as TEND[1]).

tenterhooks *n.pl.* hooks to which cloth is fastened on a tenter. —**on tenterhooks,** in a state of suspense or strain because of uncertainty.

tenth *adj.* next after the ninth. —*n.* each of ten equal parts of a thing. —**tenthly** *adv.* [f. TEN]

tenuous /ˈtenjʊəs/ *adj.* **1** having little substance or validity, very slight. **2** very thin in form or consistency. —**tenuity** /-ˈjuːɪtɪ/ *n.*, **tenuously** *adv.*, **tenuousness** *n.* [f. L *tenuis*]

tenure /ˈtenjə(r)/ *n.* the holding of office or of land or other permanent property or of accommodation etc.; the period or condition of this. [f. OF (as TENABLE)]

tepee /ˈtiːpiː/ *n.* a North American Indian conical tent. [f. Dakota *tīpī*]

tepid /ˈtepɪd/ *adj.* **1** slightly warm, lukewarm. **2** unenthusiastic. —**tepidity** /tɪˈpɪdɪtɪ/ *n.*, **tepidly** *adv.* [f. L *tepidus* (*tepēre* be lukewarm)]

tequila /teˈkiːlə/ *n.* a Mexican liquor made from agave. [f. *Tequila* in Mexico]

tera- /terə-/ *in comb.* one million million. [f. Gk *teras* monster]

terbium /ˈtɜːbɪəm/ *n.* a metallic element of the lanthanide series, symbol Tb, atomic number 65. [as YTTERBIUM]

tercel /ˈtɜːs(ə)l/ *n.* a male hawk. [f. OF, ult. f. L *tertius* third, because believed to come from third egg of clutch]

tercentenary /tɜːsenˈtiːnərɪ/ *n.* a three-hundredth anniversary; a celebration of this. [f. L *ter* thrice + CENTENARY]

terebinth /ˈterɪbɪnθ/ *n.* a South European tree (*Pistacia terebinthus*) yielding turpentine. [f. OF or L f. Gk *terebinthos*]

teredo /təˈriːdəʊ/ *n.* (*pl.* **-os**) a mollusc of the genus *Teredo* that bores into submerged timber. [L f. Gk *terēdōn* (*teirō* rub hard, bore)]

tergiversation /tɜːdʒɪvɜːˈseɪʃ(ə)n/ *n.* a change of party or principles, apostasy; the making of conflicting statements. [f. L (*tergum* the back, *vertere* turn)]

term *n.* **1** a word used to express a definite concept, especially in a branch of study etc. **2** (in *pl.*) language used, a mode of expression. **3** (in *pl.*) a relation between people. **4** (in *pl.*) conditions offered or accepted; stipulations. **5** (in *pl.*) the charge or price. **6** a limited period of some state or activity; a period of action or of contemplated results; a period during which instruction is given in a school or university, or during which a lawcourt holds sessions. **7** a word or words that may be the subject or predicate of a logical proposition. **8** (*Math.*) each quantity in a ratio or series; an item of a compound algebraic expression. **9** (*archaic*) an appointed limit. —*v.t.* to call by a specified term or expression. —**come to terms,** to reach agreement; to reconcile oneself (with a difficulty etc.). **in terms of,** in the language peculiar to; using as a basis of expression or thought. **terms of reference,** the points referred to an individual or body of persons for decision or report; the scope of an inquiry etc.; the definition of this. [f. OF f. L, = TERMINUS]

termagant /ˈtɜːməgənt/ *n.* an overbearing woman, a virago. [f. OF *Tervagan* f. It. *Trivigante* imaginary deity of violent character in morality plays]

terminable /ˈtɜːmɪnəb(ə)l/ *adj.* that may be terminated. [f. TERMINATE]

terminal /ˈtɜːmɪn(ə)l/ *adj.* **1** of or forming the last part or terminus. **2** forming or undergoing the last stage of a fatal disease. **3** of or done etc. each term. —*n.* **1** a terminating thing, an extremity. **2** a terminus for trains or long-distance buses; an air terminal (see AIR). **3** a point of connection for closing an electric circuit. **4** an apparatus for the transmission of messages to and from a computer or communications system etc —**terminally** *adv.* [f. L (as TERMINUS)]

terminate /ˈtɜːmɪneɪt/ *v.t./i.* to bring or come to an end. —**terminator** *n.* [f. L *terminare* (as TERMINUS)]

termination /tɜːmɪˈneɪʃ(ə)n/ *n.* an ending; the way something ends; a word's final letter(s). [f. OF or L (as prec.)]

terminology /tɜːmɪˈnɒlədʒɪ/ *n.* **1** the system of terms used in a particular subject **2** the science of the proper use of terms. —**terminological** /-nəˈlɒdʒɪk(ə)l/ *adj* [f. G (as foll., -LOGY)]

terminus /ˈtɜːmɪnəs/ *n.* (*pl.* **-ni** /-naɪ/) **1** a station at the end of a railway or bus route **2** a point at the end of a pipeline etc [L, = end, boundary]

termite /ˈtɜːmaɪt/ *n.* a small antlike insect of the order Isoptera, destructive to timber. [f. L *termes, tarmes* (*terere* rub)]

tern *n.* a sea-bird of the genus *Sterna*, like a gull but usually smaller and with a forked tail. [of Scand. orig.]

ternary /ˈtɜːnərɪ/ *adj.* composed of three parts. [f. L *ternarius* (*terni* three each)]

terotechnology /tɪərəʊtekˈnɒlədʒɪ, terəʊ-/ *n.* the branch of technology and engineering concerned with the installation, maintenance, and replacement of industrial plant and equipment and with related subjects and practices. [f Gk *tērō* watch over, take care of + -LOGY]

terrace /ˈterəs/ *n.* **1** a raised level space, natural or artificial, especially for walking, standing, or cultivation. **2** a row of houses on a raised level or built in one block of uniform style. **3** a flight of wide shallow steps as for spectators at a sports ground. [OF f. L *terra* earth]

terraced *adj.* formed into or having a terrace or terraces. —**terraced roof,** a flat roof especially of an Eastern house. [f. prec.]

terracotta /terəˈkɒtə/ *n.* **1** an unglazed usually brownish-red pottery used as an ornamental building-material and in statuary. **2** a statuette of this. **3** its colour. [It., = baked earth]

terra firma /terə ˈfɜːmə/ dry land, firm ground. [L]

terrain /teˈreɪn/ *n.* a tract of land as regards its natural features. [F f. L *terrenus* (as TERRENE)]

terrapin /ˈterəpɪn/ *n.* an edible freshwater tortoise of the family Emydidae of North America. [Algonquian]

terrarium /teˈreərɪəm/ *n.* (*pl.* **-ums**) **1** a place for keeping small land animals. **2** a sealed transparent globe etc. containing growing plants. [f. L *terra* earth, after *aquarium*]

terrazzo /tɪˈrætsəʊ/ *n.* (*pl.* **-os**) a flooring-material of stone chips set in concrete and given a smooth surface. [It., = terrace]

terrene /teˈriːn/ *adj.* of the earth, earthly; terrestrial. [f. AF f. L *terrenus* (*terra* earth)]

terrestrial /təˈrestrɪəl/ *adj.* of or on the earth; of or on dry land. [f. L *terrestris* (as prec.)]

terrible /ˈterɪb(ə)l/ *adj.* **1** appalling, distressing; causing or fit to cause terror. **2** (*colloq.*) extreme, hard to bear. **3** (*colloq.*) very bad or incompetent. —**terribly** *adv.* [f. F f. L (*terrēre* frighten)]

terrier /ˈterɪə(r)/ *n.* a small hardy active dog bred originally for turning out foxes etc. from their earths. [f. OF f. L *terrarius* (as TERRENE)]

terrific /təˈrɪfɪk/ *adj.* **1** (*colloq.*) of great size or intensity. **2** (*colloq.*) excellent. **3** causing terror. —**terrifically** *adv.* [f. L (*terrēre* frighten, *facere* make)]

terrify /ˈterɪfaɪ/ *v.t.* to frighten severely. [as prec.]

terrine /təˈriːn/ *n.* **1** a pâté or similar food. **2** an earthenware vessel holding this. [orig. form of TUREEN]

Territorial /terɪˈtɔːrɪəl/ *n.* a member of the Territorial Army. —*adj.* of a Territory or Territories. —**Territorial Army,** a trained reserve force organized by localities, for use in an emergency. [= foll.]

territorial /terɪˈtɔːrɪəl/ *adj.* of a territory or districts. —**territorial waters,** the waters under a State's jurisdiction, especially the part of the sea within a stated distance of the shore. —**territorially** *adv.* [as foll.]

territory /ˈterɪtərɪ/ *n.* **1** the land under the jurisdiction of a ruler, State, or city etc. **2 Territory,** a country or area forming part of the USA, Australia, or Canada, but not ranking as a State or province. **3** an area for which a person has responsibility or over which a salesman etc. operates. **4** a sphere of action or thought, a province. **5** an area claimed or dominated by one person or group and defended against others; an area defended by an animal against others of the same species. [f. L (*terra* land)]

terror /ˈterə(r)/ *n.* **1** extreme fear. **2** a person or thing causing terror; (*colloq.*) a formidable person, a troublesome person or thing. —**the Terror** *or* **Reign of Terror,** the period of the French Revolution between mid-1793 and July 1794 when the ruling Jacobin faction, dominated by Robespierre, ruthlessly executed opponents and anyone else considered a threat to their regime. **terror-stricken** *or* **-struck** *adj.* affected with terror. [f. OF f. L *terrēre* frighten]

terrorism *n.* the practice of using violent and intimidating methods, especially to achieve political ends. —**terrorist** *n.* [f. F (as prec.)]

terrorize *v.t.* to fill with terror; to coerce by terrorism. —**terrorization** /-ˈzeɪʃ(ə)n/ *n.* [f. TERROR]

terry /ˈterɪ/ *n.* a pile fabric with the loops uncut, used especially for towels. [orig. unkn.]

terse *adj.* concise, brief and forcible in style; curt. —**tersely** *adv.*, **terseness** *n.* [f. L *tersus* (*tergēre* wipe)]

tertiary /ˈtɜːʃərɪ/ *adj.* **1** coming after secondary, of the third order or rank etc. **2 Tertiary,** of the first period of the Cainozoic era (so called because it follows the Mesozoic, which was formerly also called *Secondary*), lasting from about 65 to 2 million years ago. —*n.* **1** a bird's flight feather of the third row. **2** a member of the third order of a monastic body. **3 Tertiary,** the Tertiary period. [f. L *tertiarius* (*tertius* third)]

Terylene /ˈterɪliːn/ *n.* [P] a synthetic polyester used as a textile fibre. [f. *terephthalic* acid + ETHYLENE]

tesla /ˈteslə/ *n.* the unit of magnetic flux density, = 10,000 gauss. [f. N. *Tesla* Amer. scientist (d. 1943)]

tessellated /ˈtesəleɪtɪd/ *adj.* of or resembling a mosaic; having a finely chequered surface. [f. L (*tessella* dim. of TESSERA)]

tessellation /tesəˈleɪʃ(ə)n/ *n.* an arrangement of polygons without gaps or overlapping, especially in a repeating pattern. [f. L *tessellare* (*tessella* dim. of foll.)]

tessera /ˈtesərə/ *n.* (*pl.* **-ae** /-iː/) each of the small cubes or blocks of which a mosaic consists. [L, f Gk *tessares* four]

test[1] *n.* **1** a critical examination or trial of a person's or thing's qualities. **2** the means, standard, or circumstances suitable for or serving such an examination. **3** a minor examination, especially in a school. **4** (*colloq.*) a test match. —*v.t.* **1** to subject to a test. **2** to try severely, to tax. **3** (*Chem.*) to examine by means of a reagent. —**put to the test,** to cause to undergo a test. **stand the test,** not to fail or incur rejection. **test case,** a case whose decision is taken as settling other cases involving the same question of law. **test match,** a cricket or Rugby match between the teams of certain countries, usually one of a series in a tour. **test paper,** an examination paper used in a test; (*Chem.*) a paper impregnated with a substance changing colour under known conditions. **test pilot,** a pilot who tests the performance of newly designed aircraft. **test-tube** *n.* a thin glass tube closed at one end used for chemical tests etc. **test-tube baby,** (*colloq.*) a baby developed from an ovum fertilized outside the mother's body. —**tester** *n.* [f. OF f. L *testu*(*m*) earthen pot (as foll.)]

test[2] *n.* the hard continuous shell of some invertebrates. [f. L *testa* tile, shell, etc.; cf. prec.]

testa /ˈtestə/ *n.* (*pl.* **testae** /-iː) a seed-coat. [L (as prec.)]

testaceous /teˈsteɪʃəs/ *adj.* having a hard continuous shell. [as prec.]

testacy /ˈtestəsɪ/ *n.* being testate. [f. TESTATE]

testament /ˈtestəmənt/ *n.* **1** (usu. **last will and testament**) a will. **2** (*colloq.*) a written statement of one's beliefs etc. **3** a covenant, a dispensation; **Testament,** a portion of the Bible. [f. L *testamentum* will (as TESTATE); in early Christian Latin rendering Gk *diathēkē* covenant]

testamentary /testəˈmentərɪ/ *adj.* of, by, or in a will. [as prec.]

testate /ˈtesteɪt/ *adj.* having left a valid will at death. —*n.* a testate person. [f. L (*testari* testify f. *testis* witness)]

testator /teˈsteɪtə(r)/ *n.* a person who has made a will, especially one who dies testate. —**testatrix** *n.fem.* [f. AF f. L (as prec.)]

tester *n.* a canopy, especially over a four-poster bed. [f. L (*testa* file)]

testicle /ˈtestɪk(ə)l/ *n.* the male organ that secretes spermatozoa etc., especially one of the pair in the scrotum behind the penis of man and most mammals. [f. L *testiculus* dim. of *testis* witness (of virility)]

testify /ˈtestɪfaɪ/ *v.t./i.* to bear witness; to give evidence; to declare; to be evidence of. [f. L (*testis* witness, *facere* make)]

testimonial /testɪˈməʊnɪəl/ *n.* **1** a certificate of character, conduct, or qualifications. **2** a gift presented to a person (esp. in public) as a mark of esteem. [f. OF or L (as foll.)]

testimony /ˈtestɪmənɪ/ *n.* **1** a declaration of statement (written or spoken), especially one made under oath. **2** evidence in support of something. [f. L (*testis* witness)]

testis *n.* (*pl.* **testes**/-i:z/) a testicle. [L, prob. = *testis* witness (cf. TESTICLE)]

testosterone /teˈstɒstərəʊn/ *n.* a male sex hormone produced in the testicles and (in very much smaller quantities) in the ovaries and adrenal cortex. [f. prec. + STEROL]

testy *adj.* irascible, short-tempered —**testily** *adv.*, **testiness** *n.* [f. AF *testif* (*teste* head, as TEST[2])]

tetanus /ˈtetənəs/ *n.* a bacterial disease with a continuous painful contraction of some or all voluntary muscles. [L f. Gk *tetanos* (*teinō* stretch)]

tetchy /ˈtetʃɪ/ *adj.* peevish, irritable, touchy. —**tetchily** *adv.*, **tetchiness** *n.* [prob. f. obs. *tecche, tache* blemish, fault, f. OF]

tête-à-tête /teɪtɑːˈteɪt/ *n.* a private conversation or interview, usually between two persons. —*adv.* & *adj.* together in private. [F, lit. head-to-head]

tether /ˈteðə(r)/ *n.* a rope or chain by which an animal is tied while grazing. —*v.t.* to tie with a tether. —**at the end of one's tether**, having reached the limit of one's patience or endurance etc. [f. ON]

tetra /tetrə-/ *in comb.* four. [Gk (*tessares* four)]

tetrad /ˈtetræd/ *n.* a group of four. [f. Gk (as prec.)]

tetragon /ˈtetrəgən/ *n.* a plane figure with four sides and angles. —**tetragonal** /-ˈrægən(ə)l/ *adj.* [f. Gk (TETRA-, *-gōnos* -angled)]

tetrahedron /tetrəˈhi:drən/ *n.* a four-sided solid, a triangular pyramid. —**tetrahedral** *adj.* [f. Gk (TETRA-, *hedra* base)]

tetralogy /teˈtrælədʒɪ/ *n.* a group of four related literary or dramatic works. [f. Gk (as TETRA-, -LOGY)]

tetrameter /teˈtræmɪtə(r)/ *n.* a line of verse of four measures. [f. L f. Gk (TETRA-, *metron* measure)]

Teuton /ˈtju:t(ə)n/ *n.* **1** a member of a Teutonic nation, especially a German. **2** a member of a north-European tribe combining with others to carry out raids on NE and southern France during the Roman period. [f. L f. Indo-European, = people, country]

Teutonic /tju:ˈtɒnɪk/ *adj.* **1** of the Teutons. **2** of the Germanic peoples or their languages. **3** German. [as prec.]

text *n.* **1** the main body of a book or page etc. as distinct from the notes, illustrations, appendices, etc. **2** the original words of an author or document, especially as distinct from a paraphrase or commentary. **3** a passage of Scripture quoted or used as the subject of a sermon etc.; a subject, a theme. **4** (in *pl.*) books prescribed for study. [f. OF f. L *textus* (*texere* weave)]

textbook *n.* a book of information for use in studying a subject. —*adj.* exemplary, accurate; instructively typical.

textile /ˈtekstaɪl/ *n.* a woven or machine-knitted fabric. —*adj.* of weaving; woven. [f. L *textilis* (as TEXT)]

textual /ˈtekstjʊəl/ *adj.* of, in, or concerning a text. —**textually** *adv.* [f. L (as TEXT)]

texture /ˈtekstʃə(r)/ *n.* the quality of a surface or substance when felt or looked at; the arrangement of threads in a textile fabric. —**textural** *adj.*, **texturally** *adv.* [f. L *textura* (as TEXT)]

textured *adj.* **1** having a specified texture. **2** provided with a texture, not smooth or plain. [f. prec.]

Thai /taɪ/ *adj.* of Thailand or its people or language. —*n.* **1** a native or inhabitant of Thailand. **2** the language of Thailand. [Thai, = free]

thalamus /ˈθæləməs/ *n.* (*pl.* **-mi** /-maɪ/) the interior region of the brain where the sensory nerves originate. [L f. Gk, = inner room]

thalidomide /θəˈlɪdəmaɪd/ *n.* a sedative drug found in 1961 to have caused malformation of the limbs of the embryo when taken by the mother early in pregnancy. [f. ph*thali*mido glutar*imide*]

thallium /ˈθælɪəm/ *n.* a rare soft white metallic element, symbol Tl, atomic number 81. [f. Gk *thallos* green shoot (from the green line in its spectrum)]

than /ðən, *emphat.* ðæn/ *conj.* introducing the second element in a comparison (*you are taller than he* (*is*); *we like you better than her*), or a statement of difference (*anyone other than me*). [OE, orig. = THEN]

thane *n.* **1** (in Anglo-Saxon England) one who held land from the king or other superior in return for performing military service. **2** (in Scotland until the 15th c.) one who held land from a Scottish king and ranked below an earl, a clan-chief. [OE, = servant, soldier]

thank *v.t.* **1** to express gratitude to. **2** to hold responsible. —*n.* (in *pl.*) gratitude, an expression of gratitude; (as a formula) thank you. —**thank goodness** *or* **heavens** etc., (*colloq.*) expressions of relief etc. **thank you**, a polite formula acknowledging a gift or service etc. [OE (rel. to THINK)]

thankful *adj.* feeling or expressing gratitude. —**thankfully** *adv.*, **thankfulness** *n.* [f. THANK + -FUL]

thankless *adj.* not likely to win thanks, giving

no pleasure or profit. —**thanklessly** *adv.*, **thanklessness** *n.* [f. THANK + -LESS]

thanksgiving *n.* the expression of gratitude, especially to God. —**Thanksgiving (Day),** an annual holiday for giving thanks to God, the fourth Thursday in November in the USA, usually the second Monday in October in Canada.

that /ðət, *emphat.* ðæt/ *pron.* (*pl.* **those** /ðəuz/) **1** the person or thing indicated, named, or understood. **2** the further or less obvious one of two (opp. *this*). **3** (as *relative pron.*) used instead of *which* or *who* to introduce a defining clause. —*adj.* (*pl.* **those**) designating the person or thing indicated etc. —*adv.* to that degree or extent, so. —*conj.* introducing a dependent clause, especially a statement or hypothesis, purpose, or result. —**all that,** very. **that's that,** that is settled or finished. [OE]

thatch *n.* **1** roofing of straw, or reeds, or similar material. **2** (*colloq.*) the hair of the head. —*v.t.* to roof with thatch. —**thatcher** *n.* [OE, = OHG *dach* roof]

thaw *v.t./i.* **1** to pass into a liquid or unfrozen state after being frozen. **2** to become warm enough to melt ice etc. or to lose numbness. **3** to become less cool or less formal in manner. **4** to cause to thaw. —*n.* thawing; warmth of weather that thaws ice etc. [OE]

the /*before a vowel* ðɪ; *before a consonant* ðə; *emphat.* ði:/ —*adj.* serving to particularize as needing no further identification (*have you seen the newspaper?*), to describe as unique (*the Queen; the Thames*), to assist in defining with an adjective (*Alfred the Great*) or (stressed) distinguish as the best-known (*do you mean* the *Kipling?*), to indicate a following defining clause or phrase (*the horse you mention*); to confer generic or representative or distributive value on (*diseases of the eye*; *the stage*; *5p in the pound*); or to precede an adjective used *absol.* (*nothing but the best*). —*adv.* (preceding comparatives in expressions of proportional variation) in or by that (or such) degree, on that account (*the more the merrier*; *am not the more inclined to help him because he is poor*). [OE (as THAT)]

theatre /ˈθɪətə(r)/ *n.* **1** a building or outdoor area for the performance of plays and similar entertainments. **2** the writing and production of plays. **3** a room or hall for lectures etc. with seats in tiers. **4** an operating theatre. —**theatre-in-the-round** *n.* a form of play presentation in which the audience is seated all round the acting area. **theatre weapons,** weapons intermediate between tactical and strategic (see STRATEGIC). [f. OF or L f. Gk *theatron* (*theaomai* behold)]

theatrical /θɪˈætrɪk(ə)l/ *adj.* **1** of or for the theatre or acting. **2** (of a person or manner etc.) calculated for effect, showy. —*n.* (in *pl.*) dramatic performances (esp. amateur) or behaviour —**theatricality** /-ˈkælɪtɪ/ *n.*, **theatrically** *adv.* [f. L f. Gk (as prec.)]

thee /ði:/ *pron.* the objective case of THOU.

theft *n.* stealing; an act or instance of this. [OE (as THIEF)]

their /ðeə(r)/ *poss. adj.* of or belonging to them. [f. ON]

theirs /ðeəz/ *poss. pron.* of or belonging to them; the thing(s) belonging to them. [f. THEIR]

theism /ˈθi:ɪz(ə)m/ *n.* belief in the existence of gods or a god, especially a God supernaturally revealed to man (*deism* denies such revelation) and maintaining a personal relation to his creatures. —**theist** *n.*, **theistic** /-ˈɪstɪk/ *adj.* [f. Gk *theos* god]

them /ð(ə)m, *emphat.* ðem/ *pron.* the objective case of THEY; (*colloq.*) they. —*adj.* (*vulgar*) those. [f. ON]

theme /θi:m/ *n.* **1** the subject or topic of talk, writing, or thought. **2** (*Mus.*) the leading melody in a composition. **3** (*US*) a school exercise on a given subject. —**theme song** *or* **tune,** a recurrent melody in a musical play or film; a signature tune. —**thematic** /θɪˈmætɪk/ *adj.*, **thematically** /θɪˈmætɪkəlɪ/ *adv.* [f. L f. Gk *thema* (*tithēmi* place)]

themselves /ðəmˈselvz/ *pron.* emphat. & refl. form of THEY and THEM. [f. THEM + pl. of SELF]

then /ðen/ *adv.* **1** at that time. **2** next, after that, and also. **3** in that case, therefore. **4** used to imply grudging or impatient concession, or to resume a narrative etc. —*adj.* existing at that time. —*n.* that time. —**then and there,** immediately and on the spot. [OE]

thence /ðens/ *adv.* **1** from that place. **2** for that reason. [OE]

thenceforth /ðensˈfɔθ/ *adv.* (also **thenceforward**) from that time on.

theo- *in comb.* God or a god. [Gk (*theos* god)]

theocracy /θɪˈɒkrəsɪ/ *n.* a form of government by God or a god directly or through a priestly order etc. —**theocratic** /θɪəˈkrætɪk/ *adj.*, **theocratically** /θɪəˈkrætɪkəlɪ/ *adv.* [f. Gk (as THEO-, -CRACY)]

theodolite /θɪˈɒdəlaɪt/ *n.* a surveying-instrument for measuring horizontal and vertical angles, with a rotating telescope. [orig. unkn.]

theogony /θɪˈɒgənɪ/ *n.* the genealogy of the gods; an account of this. [f. THEO- + Gk *-gonia* begetting]

theologian /θi:əˈləudʒɪən/ *n.* an expert in theology. [as foll.]

theology /θɪˈɒlədʒɪ/ *n.* the study or system of (esp. the Christian) religion. —**theological** /θi:əˈlɒdʒɪk(ə)l/ *adj.*, **theologically** *adv.* [f. OF f. L f. Gk (as THEO-, -LOGY)]

theorem /ˈθɪərəm/ *n.* **1** a general proposition not self-evident but demonstrable by argument, especially in mathematics. **2** a rule in algebra etc., especially one expressed by symbols or formulae. [f. F or L f. Gk (*theōreō* behold)]

theoretical /θɪəˈretɪk(ə)l/ *adj.* **1** concerned with knowledge but not with its practical application. **2** based on theory rather than experience. —**theoretically** *adv.* [as THEORY]

theoretician /θɪərɪˈtɪʃ(ə)n/ *n.* a person concerned with the theoretical part of a subject. [as THEORY]

theorist /ˈθɪərɪst/ *n.* a holder or inventor of a theory. [f. THEORY]

theorize /ˈθɪəraɪz/ *v.i.* to evolve or indulge in theories. [f. foll.]

theory /ˈθɪərɪ/ *n.* **1** a system of ideas formulated (by reasoning from known facts) to explain something. **2** an opinion, a supposition; ideas or suppositions in general (opp. *practice*). **3** an exposition of the principles on which a subject is based. [f. L f. Gk (as THEOREM)]

theosophy /θɪˈɒsəfɪ/ *n.* any of various philosophies professing to achieve a knowledge of God by spiritual ecstasy, direct intuition, or special individual relations, especially a modern movement following Hindu and Buddhist teachings and seeking universal brotherhood. —**theosophist** *n.*, **theosophical** /-əˈsɒfɪk(ə)l/ *adj.* [f. L f. Gk, = wise concerning God]

therapeutic /θerəˈpju:tɪk/ *adj.* of, for, or contributing to the cure of a disease. —**therapeutically** *adv.* [f. F or L f. Gk (*therapeuō* wait on, cure)]

therapeutics *n.pl.* (usu. treated as *sing.*) the branch of medicine concerned with the treatment and remedying of ill health. [f. prec.]

therapy /ˈθerəpɪ/ *n.* **1** curative medical treatment. **2** physiotherapy, psychotherapy. —**therapist** *n.* [f. Gk *therapeia* healing]

there /ðeə(r)/ *adv.* **1** in, at, or to that place or position; at that point (in a speech, performance, writing, etc.); in that respect; used for emphasis in calling attention. **2** used as an introductory word, usually with the verb *to be*, in a sentence where the verb precedes its subject, indicating a fact or the existence of something. —*n.* that place. —*int.* expressing confirmation, satisfaction, reassurance, etc. [OE]

thereabouts /ˈðeərəbaʊts/ *adv.* (also **thereabout**) near that place; near that number, quantity, time, etc.

thereafter /ðeərˈɑ:ftə(r)/ *adv.* (*formal*) after that.

thereby /ðeəˈbaɪ, ˈðeə-/ *adv.* by that means, as a result of that. —**thereby hangs a tale,** much could be said about that.

therefore /ˈðeəfɔ(r)/ *adv.* for that reason.

therein /ðeərˈɪn/ *adv.* (*formal*) in that place etc.; in that respect.

thereof /ðeərˈɒv/ *adv.* (*formal*) of that or it.

thereto /ðeəˈtu:/ *adv.* (*formal*) to that or it; in addition.

thereupon /ðeərəˈpɒn/ *adv.* in consequence of that; soon or immediately after that.

therm *n.* a unit of heat, in Britain especially the statutory unit of calorific value in a gas-supply (100,000 British thermal units). [f. Gk *thermē* heat]

thermal *adj.* of, for, or producing heat. —*n.* a rising current of heated air, used by gliders to gain height. —**thermal capacity,** the number of heat units needed to raise the temperature of a body by one degree. **thermal unit,** a unit for measuring heat (**British thermal unit,** the amount of heat needed to raise 1lb of water 1 F). —**thermally** *adv.* [F (as prec.)]

thermionic valve /θɜ:mɪˈɒnɪk/ a device consisting of a sealed tube containing two or more electrodes, one of which is heated to produce a flow of electrons in one direction. [f. THERMO- + ION]

thermo- /θɜ:məʊ-/ *in comb.* heat. [Gk (*thermos* hot, *thermē* heat)]

thermocouple /ˈθɜ:məʊkʌp(ə)l/ *n.* a device for measuring temperatures by means of the thermoelectric voltage developing between two pieces of wire of different metals joined to each other at each end.

thermodynamics /θɜ:məʊdaɪˈnæmɪks/ *n.pl.* (usu. treated as *sing.*) the science of the relations between heat and other forms of energy, and, by extension, of the relationships and interconvertibility of all forms of energy. —**thermodynamic** *adj.*, **thermodynamical** *adj.*, **thermodynamically** *adv.*

thermoelectric /θɜ:məʊɪˈlektrɪk/ *adj.* producing electricity by difference of temperatures.

thermometer /θəˈmɒmɪtə(r)/ *n.* an instrument for measuring temperature by means of a substance whose expansion and contraction under different degrees of heat and cold are capable of accurate measurement. [f. F (as THERMO-, -METER)]

thermonuclear /θɜ:məʊˈnju:klɪə(r)/ *adj.* relating to nuclear reactions that occur only at very high temperatures; (of a bomb etc.) using such reactions.

thermoplastic /θɜ:məʊˈplæstɪk/ *adj.* becoming plastic on heating and hardening on cooling —*n.* a thermoplastic substance.

Thermos /ˈθɜ:mɒs/ *n.* [P] a kind of vacuum flask. [f. Gk *thermos* hot]

thermosetting /θɜ:məʊˈsetɪŋ/ *adj.* (of plastics) setting permanently when heated.

thermosphere /ˈθɜ:məsfɪə(r)/ *n.* the part of the

atmosphere between the mesopause and the height at which it ceases to have the properties of a continuous medium, characterized throughout by an increase in temperature with height.

thermostat /ˈθɜːməstæt/ *n.* a device for the automatic regulation of temperature. —**thermostatic** /-ˈstætɪk/ *adj.*, **thermostatically** /-ˈstætɪkəlɪ/ *adv.* [f. THERMO- + Gk *statos* standing]

thesaurus /θɪˈsɔːrəs/ *n.* (*pl.* **-ri** /-raɪ/) a dictionary or encyclopaedia; a list of words or concepts arranged according to sense. [L f. Gk, = treasury]

these *pl.* of THIS.

thesis /ˈθiːsɪs/ *n.* (*pl.* **theses** /-siːz/) **1** a proposition to be maintained or proved. **2** a dissertation, especially by a candidate for a degree. [L f. Gk, = putting (as THEME)]

Thespian /ˈθespɪən/ *adj.* of tragedy or the drama. —*n.* an actor or actress. [f. *Thespis*, Gk dramatic poet (6th c. BC)]

theta /ˈθiːtə/ *n.* the eighth letter of the Greek alphabet, = th. [Gk]

thews /θjuːz/ *n.pl.* (*literary*) a person's muscular strength. [OE, = usage, conduct]

they /ðeɪ/ *pron.* (*obj.* THEM; *poss.* THEIR, THEIRS) *pl.* of HE, SHE, IT[1]; people in general; those in authority. [f. ON]

thick *adj.* **1** of great or specified distance in diameter or between opposite surfaces; (of a line etc.) broad, not fine. **2** arranged closely, crowded together, dense; densely covered or filled; firm in consistency, containing much solid matter; made of thick material; muddy, cloudy, impenetrable by the sight. **3** (*colloq.*) stupid, dull. **4** (of the voice) indistinct. **5** (*colloq.*) intimate, very friendly. —*n.* the thick part of anything. —*adv.* thickly. —**a bit thick,** (*slang*) unreasonable, intolerable. **in the thick of it,** in the busiest part of an activity or fight etc. **thick-headed** *adj.* stupid. **thick-skinned** *adj.* not sensitive to reproach or criticism. **through thick and thin,** under all conditions, in spite of all difficulties. —**thickly** *adv.* [OE]

thicken *v.t./i.* **1** to make or become thick or thicker. **2** to become more complicated. —**thickener** *n.* [f. THICK]

thicket /ˈθɪkɪt/ *n.* a tangle of shrubs or trees. [OE (as THICK)]

thickness *n.* **1** being thick; the extent to which a thing is thick. **2** a layer of material of known thickness. **3** the part between opposite surfaces. [f. THICK]

thickset *adj.* **1** set or growing closely together. **2** having a stocky or burly body.

thief *n.* (*pl.* **thieves** /θiːvz/) one who steals, esp. stealthily and without violence. [OE]

thieve *v.t./i.* to be a thief; to steal. [OE (as prec.)]

thievery *n.* stealing. [f. THIEF]

thievish *adj.* given to stealing. [f. THIEF]

thigh /θaɪ/ *n.* the part of the leg between the hip and the knee. [OE]

thimble *n.* a metal or plastic cap, usually with a closed end, worn on the end of the finger to protect the finger-tip and push the needle in sewing. [OE (as THUMB)]

thimbleful *n.* (*pl.* **-fuls**) a small quantity, especially of a liquid to drink. [f. prec. + -FUL]

thin *adj.* **1** having the opposite surfaces close together, of small thickness. **2** (of a line) narrow, not broad. **3** made of thin material. **4** lean, not plump. **5** not dense or copious; not of thick consistency, (of liquid) flowing easily. **6** lacking strength or substance or an important ingredient; (of an excuse etc.) feeble, transparent. —*adv.* thinly. —*v.t./i.* to make or become thin or thinner. —**have a thin time,** (*slang*) to have a wretched or uncomfortable time. **thin on the ground,** few in number, rare. **thin on top,** balding. **thin out,** to make or become fewer or less crowded. **thin-skinned** *adj.* sensitive to reproach or criticism. —**thinly** *adv.*, **thinness** *n.* [OE]

thine /ðaɪn/ *poss. pron.* (*archaic*) of or belonging to thee; the thing(s) belonging to thee. —*poss. adj.* (*archaic*) the form of THY before a vowel. [OE (as THOU)]

thing *n.* **1** whatever is or may be thought about or perceived. **2** an inanimate object as distinct from a living creature. **3** an unspecified object or item. **4** (expressing pity, contempt, or affection) a creature. **5** an act, fact, idea, quality, task, etc. **6** a specimen or type of something. **7** (*colloq.*) something remarkable. **8** (in *pl.*) personal belongings, clothing; implement, utensils. **9** (in *pl.*) affairs in general; circumstances, conditions. —**the thing,** what is conventionally proper or fashionable, what is needed or required, what is most important. **do one's own thing,** (*colloq.*) to pursue one's own interests or inclinations. **have a thing about,** (*colloq.*) to be obsessed or prejudiced about. **make a thing of,** to regard as essential; to cause a fuss about. [OE]

thingummy /ˈθɪŋəmɪ/ *n.* (also **thingumajig** etc.) (*colloq.*) a person or thing whose name one has forgotten or does not know. [f. THING, with meaningless suffix]

think *v.t./i.* (*past* & *p.p.* **thought** /θɔːt/) **1** to exercise the mind in an active way, to form connected ideas. **2** to have as an idea or opinion. **3** to form as an intention or plan. **4** to take into consideration. **5** to call to mind, to remember. —*n.* (*colloq.*) an act of thinking. —**think again,** to revise one's plans or opinions. **think aloud,** to utter one's thoughts as soon as they occur. **think better of,** to change one's mind about (an intention) after reconsideration. **think little** *or* **nothing of,** to consider insignificant. **think much** *or* **well** *or* **highly** etc. **of,** to have a high opinion of. **think out,** to consider carefully; to produce (an idea etc.) by thinking. **think over,** to reflect upon in order to reach a decision. **think through,** to reflect fully upon (a problem etc.). **think twice,** to use careful consideration, to avoid a hasty action etc. **think up,** (*colloq.*) to devise, to produce by thought. [OE]

thinker *n.* one who thinks, especially in a specified way; a person with a skilled or powerful mind. [f. THINK]

thinking *adj.* using thought or rational judgement. —*n.* opinion or judgement. [f. THINK]

think-tank *n.* an organization providing advice and ideas on national and commercial problems; an interdisciplinary group of specialist consultants.

thinner *n.* a volatile liquid used to make paint etc. thinner. [f. THIN]

thiosulphate /θaɪəˈsʌlfeɪt/ *n.* a sulphate in which some oxygen is replaced by sulphur. [f. Gk *theion* sulphur + SULPHATE]

third *adj.* & *n.* **1** next after second. **2** each of three equal parts of a thing. —**third degree,** a long and severe questioning, especially by the police to obtain information or a confession. **third man,** a fielder in cricket near the boundary behind the slips. **third party,** another party besides the two principals; a bystander etc. **third-party** *adj.* (of insurance) covering damage or injury suffered by a person other than the insured. **third person,** a third party; (*Gram.*) see PERSON. **third-rate** *adj.* inferior, very poor. **Third World,** the underdeveloped countries of the world; (orig.) countries considered as not politically aligned with Communist or Western nations. —**thirdly** *adv.* [OE (as THREE)]

thirst *n.* **1** the feeling caused by a desire or need to drink. **2** a strong desire. —*v.i.* to feel a thirst. [OE]

thirsty *adj.* **1** feeling thirst. **2** (of a country or season) in need of water, dry. **3** eager. **4** (*colloq.*) causing thirst. —**thirstily** *adv.*, **thirstiness** *n.* [OE (as prec)]

thirteen /θɜːˈtiːn/ *adj.* & *n.* **1** one more than twelve; the symbol for this (13, xiii, XIII). **2** the size etc. denoted by thirteen. —**thirteenth** *adj.* & *n.* [OE (as THREE, -TEEN)]

thirty /ˈθɜːtɪ/ *adj.* & *n.* **1** three times ten; the symbol for this (30, xxx, XXX). **2** (in *pl.*) the numbers, years, or degrees of temperature from 30 to 39. —**thirtieth** *adj.* & *n.* [OE (as THREE)]

this /ðɪs/ *pron.* (*pl.* **these** /ðiːz/) **1** the person or thing close at hand or indicated or already named or understood. **2** the nearer or more obvious one of two (opp. *that*). **3** the present day or time. —*adj.* (*pl.* **these**) designating the person or thing close at hand etc. —*adv.* to this degree or extent. —**this and that,** various things. [OE]

thistle /ˈθɪs(ə)l/ *n.* **1** a prickly herbaceous plant of the genus *Carduus, Cirsium*, etc., usually with globular heads of purple flowers. **2** a figure of this as the heraldic emblem of Scotland. [OE]

thistledown *n.* light fluffy stuff containing thistle-seeds and blown about in the wind.

thistly *adj.* overgrown with thistles [f. THISTLE]

thither /ˈðɪðə(r)/ *adv.* (*archaic*) to or towards that place. [OE]

thixotropy /θɪkˈsɒtrəpɪ/ *n.* the property of becoming temporarily liquid when shaken, stirred, etc., and returning to a gel state on standing. —**thixotropic** / əˈtrɒpɪk/ *adj.* [f. Gk *thixis* touching + *tropē* turning]

thole *n.* (in full **thole-pin**) a pin in the gunwale of a boat as a fulcrum for an oar; each of two such pins forming a rowlock. [OE, = ON *thollr* fir-tree, peg]

thong *n.* a narrow strip of hide or leather. [OE]

thorax /ˈθɔːræks/ *n.* (*pl.* **-races** /-rəsiːz/) the part of the body between the neck or head and the abdomen; the second segment of an insect body. —**thoracic** /-ˈræsɪk/ *adj.* [L f. Gk, orig. = cuirass]

thorium /ˈθɔːrɪəm/ *n.* a radioactive metallic element, symbol Th, atomic number 90, first discovered in 1828. [f. *Thor*, Norse god]

thorn *n.* **1** a stiff sharp-pointed projection on a plant. **2** a thorn-bearing shrub or tree. —**a thorn in one's flesh** *or* **side,** a constant source of annoyance. [OE]

thorny *adj.* **1** full of thorns. **2** like a thorn. **3** (of a subject) hard to handle without offence. —**thornily** *adv.*, **thorniness** *n.* [OE (as THORN)]

thorough /ˈθʌrə/ *adj.* complete and unqualified, not merely superficial; acting or done with great attention to detail; absolute. —**thoroughly** *adv.*, **thoroughness** *n.* [as THROUGH]

thoroughbred *adj.* bred of pure or pedigree stock. —*n.* a thoroughbred animal, especially a horse.

thoroughfare *n.* a road or path open at both ends, especially for traffic.

thoroughgoing *adj.* thorough; extreme.

those *pl.* of THAT.

thou /ðaʊ/ *pron.* of the second person singular (now replaced by YOU except in some formal, liturgical, and poetic uses). [OE]

though /ðəʊ/ *conj.* despite the fact that; even

supposing that; and yet, nevertheless. —*adv.* however, all the same. [f. ON]

thought[1] /θɔːt/ *n.* **1** the process, power, or manner of thinking; the faculty of reason. **2** the way of thinking associated with a particular time or people etc. **3** sober reflection, consideration. **4** an idea or chain of reasoning produced by thinking. **5** an intention. **6** (usu. in *pl.*) what one is thinking, one's opinion. —**a thought,** somewhat. **in thought,** meditating. **thought-reader** *n.* a person supposedly able to perceive another's thoughts without their being spoken. [OE (as THINK)]

thought[2] *past* & *p.p.* of THINK.

thoughtful *adj.* **1** thinking deeply; often absorbed in thought. **2** (of a book or writer etc.) showing signs of careful thought. **3** showing thought for the needs of others, considerate. —**thoughtfully** *adv.*, **thoughtfulness** *n.* [f. THOUGHT[1] + -FUL]

thoughtless *adj.* careless of consequences or of others' feelings; caused by lack of thought. —**thoughtlessly** *adv.*, **thoughtlessness** *n.* [f. THOUGHT[1] + -LESS]

thousand /ˈθaʊzənd/ *adj.* & *n.* (for plural usage see HUNDRED) **1** ten hundred; the symbol for this (1,000, m, M) **2** (in *pl.*) very many. —**thousandth** *adj.* & *n.* [OE]

thousandfold *adj.* & *adv.* a thousand times as much or as many; consisting of a thousand parts. [f. prec. + -FOLD]

thrall /θrɔːl/ *n.* (*literary*) **1** a slave (of or to a person or thing). **2** slavery. —**thraldom** *n.* [OE f. ON]

thrash *v.t./i.* **1** to beat severely with a stick or whip. **2** to defeat thoroughly in a contest. **3** to thresh (corn etc.). **4** to act like a flail, to deliver repeated blows; to move violently. —**thrash out,** to discuss to a conclusion. [OE]

thread /θred/ *n.* **1** a thin length of any substance. **2** a length of spun cotton or wool etc. used in weaving or in sewing or knitting. **3** anything regarded as threadlike with reference to its continuity or connectedness. **4** the spiral ridge of a screw. —*v.t.* **1** to pass a thread through the eye of (a needle). **2** to put (beads) on a thread. **3** to arrange (material in strip form, e.g. film) in the proper position on equipment. **4** to pick one's way through (a maze, a crowded place, etc.); to make (one's way) thus. —**threader** *n.* [OE (as THROW)]

threadbare *adj.* **1** (of cloth) so worn that the nap is lost and the threads are visible; (of a person) wearing such clothes. **2** hackneyed.

threadworm *n.* a small threadlike worm (*Strongyloides stercoralis*) infesting the intestines.

threat /θret/ *n.* **1** a declaration of intention to punish, hurt, or harm a person or thing. **2** an indication of something undesirable coming. **3** a person or thing as a likely cause of harm etc. [OE]

threaten /ˈθret(ə)n/ *v.t.* **1** to make a threat or threats against. **2** to be a sign or indication of (something undesirable). **3** to announce one's intention to do an undesirable or unexpected thing. **4** to give warning of the infliction of (harm etc.; or *absol.*). [OE (as prec.)]

three *adj.* & *n.* **1** one more than two; the symbol for this (3, iii, III). **2** the size etc. denoted by three. —**threecornered** *adj.* triangular; (of a contest etc.) between three parties each for himself. **three-decker** *n.* a warship with three gun-decks; a sandwich with three slices of bread; a three-volume novel. **three-dimensional** *adj.* having or appearing to have length, breadth, and depth. **three-legged race,** a race between pairs with the right leg of one tied to the other's left leg. **three-ply** *adj.* having three strands or layers; (*n.*) wool etc. having three strands; plywood having three layers. **three-point turn,** a method of turning a vehicle round in a narrow space by driving forwards, backwards, and forwards. **three-quarter** *n.* any of the three or four players just behind the half-backs in Rugby football. **three-quarters** *n.* three parts out of four. **the three Rs,** see R. **three-way** *adj.* involving three ways or participants. [OE]

threefold *adj.* & *adv.* three times as much or as many; consisting of three parts. [f. THREE + -FOLD]

threepence /ˈθrepəns/ *n.* the sum of three pence.

threepenny /ˈθrepənɪ/ *adj.* costing or worth three pence. —**threepenny bit,** a former coin worth 3d.

threescore *n.* (*archaic*) sixty.

threesome /ˈθriːsəm/ *n.* a group of three persons. [f. THREE + -SOME]

threnody /ˈθrenədɪ/ *n.* a song of lamentation, especially on a person's death. [f. Gk (*thrēnos* wailing, *ōidē* ode)]

thresh *v.t./i.* **1** to beat out or separate grain from (husks of corn etc.). **2** to make violent movements. —**threshing-floor** *n.* a hard level floor for threshing, especially with flails. [var. of THRASH]

threshold /ˈθreʃəuld/ *n.* **1** a strip of wood or stone forming the bottom of a doorway and crossed in entering a house etc. **2** the point of entry or beginning of something. **3** the limit below which a stimulus causes no reaction; the magnitude or intensity that must be exceeded for a certain reaction or phenomenon to occur. [OE, rel. to THRASH in sense 'tread']

threw *past* of THROW.

thrice *adv.* (*archaic*) **1** three times, on three occasions. **2** (esp. in *comb.*) highly. [OE (as THREE)]

thrift *n.* **1** economical management of money or resources. **2** the sea-pink (*Armeria maritima*). [f. ON (as THRIVE)]

thriftless *adj.* wasteful. [f. prec. + -LESS]

thrifty *adj.* practising thrift, economical. —**thriftily** *adv.*, **thriftiness** *n.* [f. THRIFT]

thrill *n.* a nervous tremor of emotion or sensation; a slight throb or pulsation. —*v.t./i.* to feel or cause to feel a thrill; to throb or pulsate slightly. [OE, = pierce (rel. to THROUGH)]

thriller *n.* an exciting or sensational story or play etc., especially one involving crime or espionage. [f. prec.]

thrips *n.* (*pl.* same) an insect of the order Thysanoptera, many of which injure plants by feeding on their juices. [L f. Gk, = woodworm]

thrive *v.i.* (*past* **throve** or **thrived**; *p.p.* **thriven** /ˈθrɪv(ə)n/ or **thrived**) **1** to prosper, to be successful. **2** to grow or develop well and vigorously. [f. ON]

throat *n.* **1** the windpipe, the gullet; the front part of the neck containing this. **2** a narrow passage entrance or exit. **3** the forward upper corner of a fore-and-aft sail. —**cut one's own throat,** to bring about one's own downfall. **ram** *or* **thrust down a person's throat,** to force (a thing) on his attention. **throat latch** *or* **lash,** the strap of a bridle passing under a horse's throat. [OE]

throaty *adj.* **1** uttered deep in the throat. **2** hoarsely resonant. —**throatily** *adv.*, **throatiness** *n.* [f. prec.]

throb *v.i.* (**-bb-**) **1** (of the heart or pulse etc.) to beat with more than usual force or rapidity. **2** to vibrate or sound with a persistent rhythm; to vibrate with emotion. —*n.* throbbing. [app. imit.]

throe *n.* (usu. in *pl.*) a violent pang, especially of childbirth or death. —**in the throes of,** (*colloq.*) struggling with the task of. [alt. f. earlier *throwe*, perh. f. OE *thrēa* calamity]

thrombosis /θrɒmˈbəʊsɪs/ *n.* (*pl.* **-oses** /-iːz/) a coagulation of blood in a blood-vessel or organ during life. —**thrombotic** /-ˈbɒtɪk/ *adj.* [f. Gk, = curdling (*thrombos* lump, blood-clot)]

throne *n.* **1** a chair of State for a sovereign or bishop etc. **2** sovereign power. —*v.t.* to enthrone. [f. OF f. L f. Gk *thronos* high seat]

throng *n.* a crowded mass of people. —*v.t./i.* to come, go, or press in a throng; to fill with a throng. [OE]

throstle /ˈθrɒs(ə)l/ *n.* a song-thrush. [OE (rel. to THRUSH)]

throttle *n.* **1** a valve controlling the flow of fuel or steam etc. in an engine; a lever or pedal operating this valve. **2** the throat, the gullet, the windpipe. —*v.t.* **1** to choke, to strangle. **2** to prevent the utterance etc. of. **3** to control (an engine or steam etc.) with a throttle. —**throttle back** *or* **down,** to reduce the speed of (an engine or vehicle) by throttling. [perh. f. THROAT]

through /θruː/ *prep.* **1** from end to end or side to side of; entering at one side or end and coming out at the other. **2** between, among. **3** from beginning to end of. **4** by reason of; by the agency, means, or fault of. **5** (*US*) up to and including. —*adv.* **1** through a thing; from side to side or end to end; from beginning to end. **2** so as to be connected by telephone. —*adj.* going through, especially of travel where the whole journey is made without change of line or vehicle etc. or with one ticket; (of traffic) going through a place to its destination. —**be through,** to have finished; to cease to have dealings; to have no further prospects. **through and through,** through again and again; thoroughly, completely. [OE]

throughout /θruːˈaʊt/ *prep.* right through, from end to end of. —*adv.* in every part or respect.

throughput *n.* the amount of material put through a process, especially in manufacturing or computing.

throve see THRIVE.

throw /θrəʊ/ *v.t./i.* (*past* **threw** /θruː/; *p.p.* **thrown**) **1** to propel with some force through the air or in a particular direction. **2** to force violently into a specified position or state; to compel to be in a specified condition. **3** to turn or move (a part of the body) quickly or suddenly. **4** to project or cast (a light, shadow, spell, etc.). **5** to bring to the ground in wrestling; (of a horse) to unseat (a rider); (*colloq.*) to disconcert. **6** to put (clothes etc.) on or off carelessly or hastily. **7** to cause (dice) to fall on a table; to obtain (a specified number) thus. **8** to cause to pass or extend suddenly. **9** to move (a switch or lever) so as to operate it. **10** to shape (round pottery) on a wheel. **11** to have (a fit or tantrum etc.). **12** (*slang*) to give (a party). **13** (*US*) to lose (a contest or race etc.) intentionally. —*n.* **1** an act of throwing. **2** the distance a thing is or may be thrown. **3** being thrown in wrestling. —**throw away,** to part with as useless or unwanted; to fail to make use of (an opportunity etc.). **throw-away** *adj.* meant to be thrown away after use. **throw back,** to revert to ancestral character; (usu. in *pass.*) to compel to rely *on*. **throw-back** *n.* reversion to ancestral character; an instance of this. **throw in,** to interpose (a word or remark); to include with no extra charge; to throw (a football) from the edge of a pitch where it has gone out of play. **throw off,** to discard; to contrive to get rid of or free oneself from; to write or utter easily, as if without effort, or in an offhand way. **throw oneself at,** to seek energetically to win the friendship or love of. **throw oneself into,** to engage vigorously in. **throw oneself on** *or* **upon,** to rely completely on. **throw open,** to cause to be suddenly or widely open; to make accessible. **throw out,** to put out forcibly or suddenly; to throw away; to reject (a proposal etc.); to confuse or distract (a person). **throw over,** to desert, to abandon. **throw together,** to assemble hastily; to bring into casual contact. **throw up,** to abandon; to resign from; to vomit; to erect hastily; to bring to notice. —**thrower** *n.* [OE, = twist]

thrum[1] *v.t./i.* (**-mm-**) to play (a stringed instrument) monotonously or unskilfully; to drum or tap idly (on). —*n.* such playing; the resulting sound. [imit.]

thrum[2] *n.* an unwoven end of a warp-thread, or the whole of such ends, left when the finished web is cut away; any short loose thread. [OE, = OHG *drum* remnant, end-piece]

thrush[1] *n.* a small bird of the family Turdidae, e.g. the blackbird, nightingale, or especially the song-thrush (*Turdus philomelos*) or missel-thrush. [OE]

thrush[2] *n.* a fungoid infection of the throat (esp. in children) or of the vagina. [orig. unkn.]

thrust *v.t./i.* (*past* & *p.p.* **thrust**) **1** to push forcibly. **2** to put forcibly into a specified position or condition; to force the acceptance of. **3** to make a forward stroke with a sword etc. —*n.* **1** a thrusting movement or force; the forward force exerted by a propeller or jet etc.; the stress between parts of an arch etc.; (*Geol.*) a compressive strain in the earth's crust. **2** a strong attempt to penetrate an enemy's line or territory. **3** a hostile remark aimed at a person. **4** the chief theme or gist of remarks etc. —**thruster** *n.*[f. ON]

thud *n.* a low dull sound as of a blow on a non-resonant thing. —*v.i.* (**-dd-**) to make a thud; to fall with a thud. [prob. OE, = thrust]

Thug *n.* a member of an association of professional robbers and murderers in India, who strangled their victims. [f. Hindi & Marathi, = swindler]

thug *n.* a vicious or brutal ruffian. —**thuggery** *n.* [f. THUG]

thulium /ˈθuːlɪəm/ *n.* a metallic element of the lanthanide series, symbol Tm, atomic number 69. [f. *Thule*, ancient name for a region in the remote north]

thumb /θʌm/ *n.* **1** the short thick finger set apart from the other four. **2** the part of a glove covering the thumb. —*v.t./i.* **1** to wear or soil (pages etc.) with the thumb. **2** to turn over pages (as) with the thumb. **3** to request or get (a lift in a passing vehicle) by indicating the desired direction with the thumb. **4** to use the thumb (on) in a gesture. —**thumb-index** *n.* a set of lettered grooves cut down the side of a book's leaves to enable the user to open the book directly at a particular section. **thumb-nail sketch,** a brief verbal description. **thumb one's nose,** to cock a snook. **thumbs down,** a gesture of rejection. **thumbs up,** a gesture or exclamation of satisfaction. **under a person's thumb,** completely dominated by him. [OE]

thumbscrew *n.* an instrument of torture for compressing the thumb(s).

thump *v.t./i.* to beat, or strike, or knock heavily, especially with the fist. **2** to thud. —*n.* a heavy blow; the sound of this. [imit.]

thumping *adj.* (*colloq.*) big. [f. THUMP]

thunder *n.* **1** a loud noise heard after lightning and due to disturbance of the air by a discharge of electricity. **2** a resounding loud deep noise. **3** (in *sing.* or *pl.*) authoritative censure or threats. —*v.t./i.* **1** to give forth thunder (esp. *it thunders, is thundering*). **2** to make a noise like thunder; to move with a loud noise. **3** to utter loudly; to make a forceful verbal attack. —**steal a person's thunder,** to forestall him by using his ideas or words etc. before he can do so himself. [from the remark of John Dennis, English dramatist (*c.* 1710), when the stage thunder he had intended for his own play was used for another] **thunder-cloud** *n.* a storm-cloud charged with electricity and producing thunder and lightning. —**thunderer** *n.*, **thundery** *adj.* [OE]

thunderbolt *n.* **1** a flash of lightning with a crash of thunder. **2** an imaginary destructive missile thought of as sent to earth with a lighting-flash. **3** a very startling and formidable event or statement.

thunderclap *n.* **1** a crash of thunder. **2** a sudden terrible event or news.

thundering *adj.* (*colloq.*) very big or great. [f. THUNDER]

thunderous *adj.* like thunder; very loud. [as prec.]

thunderstorm *n.* a storm with thunder and lightning and usually heavy rain or hail.

thunderstruck *adj.* amazed.

Thur. *abbr.* Thursday.

thurible /ˈθjʊərɪb(ə)l/ *n.* a censer. [f. OF or L *t(h)uribulum* (*t(h)us* incense)]

Thursday /ˈθɜːzdeɪ/ *n.* the day of the week following Wednesday. —*adv.* (*colloq.*) on Thursday. [OE, = day of Thor (Norse god), representing L *Jovis dies* day of Jupiter]

thus /ðʌs/ *adv.* (*formal*) **1** in this way, like this.

2 as a result or inference. **3** to this extent, so. [OE; orig. unkn.]

thwack *v.t.* to hit with a heavy blow. —*n.* a heavy blow. [imit.]

thwart /θwɔt/ *v.t.* to frustrate (a person or purpose etc.) —*n.* a rower's seat, placed across the boat. [f. ON = transverse]

thy /ðaɪ/ *poss. adj.* of or belonging to thee; now replaced by YOUR except in some formal, liturgical, and poetic uses. [as THINE]

thyme /taɪm/ *n.* any of several herbs of the genus *Thymus* with fragrant aromatic leaves. [f. OF f. L f. Gk *thumon* (*thuō* burn sacrifice)]

thymol /'θaɪmɒl/ *n.* an antiseptic made from oil of thyme. [f. THYME]

thymus /'θaɪməs/ *n.* a lymphoid organ near the base of the neck (in man becoming much smaller at puberty). [f. Gk *thumos*]

thyristor /θaɪ'rɪstə(r)/ *n.* a switch in the form of a semiconductor device in which a small electric current is used to start the flow of a large current. [f. Gk *thura* door + TRANSISTOR]

thyroid /'θaɪrɔɪd/ *n.* **1** the thyroid gland. **2** an extract from the thyroid gland of animals used in treating goitre etc. —**thyroid cartilage,** a large cartilage of the larynx, the projection of which in man forms the Adam's apple. **thyroid gland,** a large ductless gland near the larynx secreting a hormone which regulates growth and development. [f. obs. F f. Gk (*thureos* oblong shield)]

thyself *pron.* the emphat. & refl. form of THOU and THEE: now replaced in general use by YOURSELF (cf at THOU).

Ti *symbol* titanium.

tiara /tɪ'ɑ:rə/ *n* **1** a woman's ornamental crescent-shaped head-dress, worn on ceremonial occasions. **2** a head-dress worn by the pope, pointed at the top and surrounded by three crowns. [L f. Gk; orig. unkn.]

tibia /'tɪbɪə/ *n.* (*pl.* **-ae** /-i:/) the inner and usually larger of the two bones from knee to ankle; the corresponding bone in a bird. —**tibial** *adj.* [L, = shin-bone, flute]

tic *n.* a habitual spasmodic contraction of the muscles especially of the face; a kind of neuralgia. [F f. It. *ticchio*]

tick[1] *n.* **1** a slight recurring click, especially that of a watch or clock. **2** (*colloq.*) a moment, an instant. **3** a small mark set against items in a list etc. in checking. —*v.t./i.* **1** (of a clock etc.) to make ticks. **2** to mark (an item) with a tick. —**tick off,** (*slang*) to reprimand: **tick over,** (of an engine or *fig.*) to idle. **tick-tack** *n.* a kind of manual semaphore signalling used by bookmakers on a racecourse. **tick-tock** *n.* the ticking of a large clock etc. *what makes a person tick,* his motivation, what makes him behave as he does. [cf. Du. *tik* touch, tick]

tick[2] *n.* an arachnid of the order Acarina or a similar insect (e.g. *Melophagus*) parasitic on animals. [cf. M Du. or MLG *teke*]

tick[3] *n.* (*colloq.*) credit. [app. abbr. of TICKET in phr. *on the ticket*]

tick[4] *n.* the cover of a mattress or pillow; ticking. [f. MDu. or MLG, ult. f. Gk *thēkē* case]

ticker *n.* (*colloq.*) the heart; a watch; a tape-machine. —**ticker-tape** *n.* (*US*) a paper strip from a tape-machine; this or similar material thrown in long strips from windows to greet a celebrity. [f. TICK[1]]

ticket /'tɪkɪt/ *n.* **1** a written or printed piece of paper or card entitling the holder to enter a place, participate in an event, travel by public transport, etc. **2** a certificate of discharge from the army or of qualification as a ship's master, pilot, etc. **3** a label attached to a thing and giving its price etc. **4** an official notification of a traffic offence etc. **5** a list of candidates put forward by one group, especially a political party. —*v.t.* to attach a ticket to. —**the ticket,** (*slang*) the correct or desirable thing. [f. obs. F *étiquet* (OF *estiquier* fix, f. MDu.)]

ticking *n.* a stout usually striped linen or cotton material used for covering mattresses etc. [f. TICK[4]]

tickle /'tɪk(ə)l/ *v.t./i.* **1** to apply light touches or stroking to (a person or part of his body) so as to excite the nerves and usually produce laughter and spasmodic movement. **2** to feel this sensation. **3** to excite agreeably, to amuse, to divert. —*n.* an act or sensation of tickling. —**tickled pink** *or* **to death,** (*colloq.*) extremely amused or pleased. [prob. f. *tick* touch lightly (as TICK[1])]

ticklish *adj.* **1** sensitive to tickling. **2** (of a matter or person to be dealt with) difficult, requiring careful handling. —**ticklishness** *n.* [f. prec.]

tidal /'taɪd(ə)l/ *adj.* of or affected by a tide or tides. —**tidal wave,** an exceptionally large ocean wave (e.g. one caused by an earthquake); a widespread manifestation of feeling etc. —**tidally** *adv.* [f. TIDE]

tidbit *US* var. of TITBIT.

tiddler *n.* (*colloq.*) **1** a small fish, especially a stickleback or minnow. **2** an unusually small thing. [perh. rel. to *tiddly* little]

tiddly[1] *adj.* (*colloq.*) very small. [var. of *tiddy* (nursery wd); orig. unkn.]

tiddly[2] *adj.* (*slang*) slightly drunk. [orig. unkn.]

tiddly-winks *n.* a game in which small counters are caused to spring from the table into a cup-shaped or cylindrical receptacle by pressing upon their edges with a larger counter. —**tiddly-wink** *n.* a counter used in this game. [orig. unkn.]

tide *n.* **1** the regular rise and fall of the sea due to the attraction of the moon and sun; water as moved by this. **2** a trend of opinion, fortune, or events. **3** a time or season (*archaic* except in *noontide*, *Christmastide*, etc.). —*v.i.* to be carried by the tide. —**tide-mark** *n.* the mark made by the tide at high water; (*colloq.*) a line of dirt round a bath showing the level of the water that has been used, or on the body of a person showing the extent of his washing. **tide a person over,** to help him through a temporary need or difficulty. **tide-table** *n.* a list of the times of high tide at a place. **turn the tide,** to reverse the trend of events. [OE, = time]

tideway *n.* the tidal part of a river.

tidings /ˈtaɪdɪŋz/ *n.* (as *sing.* or *pl.*) news. [OE, prob. f. ON, = events]

tidy /ˈtaɪdɪ/ *adj.* **1** neat and orderly, methodically arranged or inclined. **2** (*colloq.*) considerable. —*n.* **1** a receptacle for odds and ends. **2** a cover for a chair-back etc. —*v.t.* to make tidy. —**tidily** *adv.*, **tidiness** *n.* [orig. = timely, f. TIDE]

tie /taɪ/ *v.t./i.* (*partic.* **tying**) **1** to attach or fasten with a string or cord etc. **2** to form (a string, ribbon, shoe-lace, necktie, etc.) into a knot or bow; to form (a knot or bow) thus. **3** to restrict or limit (a person) in some way. **4** to make the same score as another competitor. **5** to bind (rafters etc.) by a cross-piece etc. **6** (*Mus.*) to unite notes by a tie. —*n.* **1** a cord or chain etc. used for fastening. **2** a necktie. **3** a thing that unites or restricts persons. **4** equality of score or a draw or dead heat among competitors. **5** a match between any pair of players or teams. **6** a rod or beam holding parts of a structure together. **7** (*Mus.*) a curved line above or below two notes of the same pitch that are to be joined as one. —**tie-beam** *n.* a horizontal beam connecting rafters. **tie-break** *n.* a means of deciding the winner when competitors have tied. **tied cottage,** a dwelling occupied subject to the tenant's working for the owner. **tied house,** a public house bound to supply only a particular brewer's beer. **tie-dyeing** *n.* a method of producing dyed patterns by tying parts of the fabric so that they are protected from the dye. **tie in** *or* **up,** to agree or be closely associated; to cause to do this. **tie-pin** *n.* an ornamental pin holding a tie in place. **tie up,** to bind or fasten with cord etc.; to invest or reserve (capital etc.) so that it is not immediately available for use; to obstruct; (usu. in *pass.*) to occupy (a person) fully. [OE]

tier /tɪə(r)/ *n.* a row, rank, or unit of a structure as one of several placed one above another. —**tiered** *adj.* [f. F *tire* (*tirer* draw, elongate)]

tiff *n.* a petty quarrel. [orig. unkn.]

tiffin /ˈtɪfɪn/ *n.* (in India) lunch. [app. f. *tiffing* taking slight drink]

tiger /ˈtaɪgə(r)/ *n.* **1** a large Asian animal (*Panthera tigris*) of the cat family, with yellowish and black stripes. **2** a fierce, energetic, or formidable person. —**tiger-cat** *n.* any moderate-sized feline resembling a tiger, e.g. an ocelot. **tiger-lily** *n.* a tall garden lily (*Lilium tigrinum*) with dark-spotted orange flowers. **tiger-moth** *n.* a moth of the family Arctiidae, especially *Arctia caja*, with richly spotted and streaked wings. [f. OF f. L f. Gk *tigris*]

tight /taɪt/ *adj.* **1** fixed, fastened, or drawn together firmly and hard to move or undo. **2** fitting closely, made impermeable to a specified thing. **3** with things or people arranged closely together. **4** tense, stretched so as to leave no slack. **5** (*colloq.*) drunk. **6** (of money or materials) not easily obtainable. **7** produced by or requiring great exertion or pressure; (of precautions, a programme, etc.) stringent, demanding; (*colloq.*) presenting difficulties. **8** (*colloq.*) stingy. —*adv.* tightly. —**tight-fisted** *adj.* stingy. **tight-lipped** *adj.* with the lips compressed to restrain emotion or speech. —**tightly** *adv.*, **tightness** *n.* [prob. f. ON]

tighten *v.t./i.* to make or become tighter. [f. TIGHT]

tightrope *n.* a rope stretched tightly high above the ground, on which acrobats perform.

tights *n.pl.* a thin close-fitting elastic garment covering the legs and the lower part of the body, worn by women in place of stockings; a similar garment worn by a dancer, acrobat, etc. [f. TIGHT]

tigress /ˈtaɪgrɪs/ *n.* a female tiger. [f. TIGER]

tilbury /ˈtɪlbərɪ/ *n.* a light open two-wheeled carriage fashionable in the first half of the 19th c. [f. inventor's name]

tilde /ˈtɪldə/ *n.* the mark (˜) put over a letter, e.g. Spanish *n* when pronounced /nj/ (as in señor). [Sp. f. L (as TITLE)]

tile *n.* **1** a thin slab of glazed or unglazed baked clay or other material used in series for covering a roof, wall, or floor. **2** a thin flat piece used in a game (especially mah-jong). —*v.t.* to cover with tiles. —**on the tiles,** (*slang*) on a nocturnal spree. [OE f. L *tegula*]

tiling /ˈtaɪlɪŋ/ *n.* **1** the process of fixing tiles. **2** an area of tiles. [f. TILE]

till[1] *prep.* & *conj.* until. [f. OE & ON, = to]

till[2] *n.* a drawer for money in a shop or bank etc., especially with a device recording the amount of each purchase. [orig. unkn.]

till[3] *v.t.* to cultivate (land). [OE, = strive for]

tillage *n.* **1** preparation of land for crop-bearing. **2** tilled land. [f. TILL[3]]

tiller *n.* a bar by which the rudder is turned. [f. AF *telier* weaver's beam]

tilt *v.t./i.* **1** to move or cause to move into a sloping position. **2** to run or thrust with a lance in jousting. —*n.* **1** tilting. **2** a sloping position. **3** an attack, especially with argument or satire. —**(at) full tilt,** at full speed; with full force. [perh. f. OE *tealt* unsteady]

timber *n.* **1** wood prepared for use in building, carpentry, etc. **2** a piece of wood, a beam, especially as a rib of a vessel. **3** large standing trees. **4** (esp. as *int.*) a tree about to fall. —**timber-line** *n.* (on a mountain) the line or level above which no trees grow. [OE, = building]

timbered *adj.* **1** made wholly or partly of timber. **2** (of country) wooded. [f. prec.]

timbre /tæ̃br, 'tæmbə(r)/ *n.* the distinctive character of a musical sound or a voice apart from its pitch and intensity. [F, ult. f. Gk *tumpanon* drum]

timbrel /'tɪmbr(ə)l/ *n.* (*archaic*) a tambourine. [f. OF (as prec.)]

time *n.* **1** the indefinite continued existence of the universe in the past, present, and future regarded as a whole; the progress of this as affecting persons or things; (also **Father Time**) time personified as an aged man, bald but having a forelock, carrying a scythe and an hourglass. **2** the portion of time belonging to particular events or circumstances. **3** a portion of time between two points; the point or period allotted, available, or suitable for something; a prison sentence; an apprenticeship; a period of gestation; the date of childbirth or of death. **4** a point of time stated in hours and minutes of the day. **5** any of the standard systems by which time is reckoned. **6** an occasion or instance; (in *pl.*, expressing multiplication) a specified number of times. **7** (in *sing.* or *pl.*) the conditions of life or of a period. **8** measured time spent in work etc. **9** (*Mus.*) the duration of a note; a style depending on the number and accentuation of beats in the bar; a rate of performance. —*v.t.* **1** to choose the time or moment for; to arrange the time of. **2** to measure the time taken by. —**against time,** with the utmost speed so as to finish by a specified time. **at the same time,** in spite of this, however. **at times,** sometimes, intermittently. **behind the times,** old-fashioned. **for the time being,** until some other arrangement is made. **from time to time,** occasionally, at intervals. **half the time,** (*colloq.*) as often as not. **have a time of it,** to undergo trouble or difficulty. **have no time for,** to be unable or unwilling to spend time on; to dislike. **in no time,** very soon or quickly. **in time,** not late, punctual; sooner or later; in accordance with the time of music etc. **keep time,** to move or sing etc. in time. **lose time,** to waste time. **on time,** in accordance with the timetable; punctual, punctually. **pass the time of day,** (*colloq.*) to exchange a greeting or casual remarks. **time after time,** on many occasions; in many instances. **time and (time) again,** on many occasions. **time and a half,** a rate of payment for work at one-and-a-half times the normal rate. **time-and-motion** *adj.* concerned with measuring the efficiency of industrial and other operations. **time bomb,** a bomb designed to explode at a pre-set time. **time-clock** *n.* a clock with a device for recording workers' hours of work. **time exposure,** exposure of a photographic film for longer than an instant. **time-honoured** *adj.* esteemed by tradition or custom. **time-lag** *n.* an interval of time between cause and effect. **time-limit** *n.* a limit of time within which a thing must be done. **time of one's life,** a period of exceptional enjoyment. **time out of mind,** from before anyone can remember. **time-sharing** *n.* the use of a computer by several persons for different operations at one time; the ownership or right to the use of a property for a fixed limited time each year. **time-signal** *n.* an audible indication of the exact time of day. **time signature,** (*Mus.*) see SIGNATURE 3. **time-switch** *n.* a switch acting automatically at a pre-set time. **time was,** there was a time. **time zone,** a range of longitudes where a common standard time is used. [OE]

timekeeper *n.* **1** one who records the time, especially of workers or in a game. **2** a watch or clock etc. as regards its accuracy.

timeless *adj.* not affected by the passage of time; not to be thought of as having duration. [f. TIME + -LESS]

timely *adj.* opportune, coming at the right time. —**timeliness** *n.* [f. TIME]

timepiece *n.* a clock or watch.

timer /'taɪmə(r)/ *n.* a person or device that measures the time taken. [f. TIME]

timetable *n.* a list of the times at which events will take place, especially the arrival of buses or trains etc., or the series of lessons in a school etc.

timid /'tɪmɪd/ *adj.* easily frightened, not bold; shy. —**timidity** /tɪ'mɪdɪtɪ/ *n.*, **timidly** *adv.* [f. F or L *timidus* (*timēre* fear)]

timing /'taɪmɪŋ/ *n.* the way a thing is timed. [f. TIME]

timorous /'tɪmərəs/ *adj.* timid; frightened. —**timorously** *adv.*, **timorousness** *n.* [f. OF f. L (as TIMID)]

timpano /'tɪmpənəʊ/ *n.* (obs. exc. in *pl.*, **timpani**) a kettledrum. —**timpanist** *n.* [It., = TYMPANUM]

tin *n.* **1** a silvery-white malleable metallic element, symbol Sn, atomic number 50. **2** a container made of tin or tin plate, or of aluminium, especially one hermetically sealed for preserving food. **3** tin plate. —*v.t.* (**-nn-**) **1** to pack (food) in a tin for preservation. **2** to cover or coat with tin. —**tin foil,** foil made of tin, aluminium, or tin alloy, and used to wrap food for cooking, keeping fresh, etc. **tin god,** an object of unjustified veneration. **tin-opener** *n.* a tool for opening tins of food. **tin plate,** sheet iron or sheet steel coated with tin. **tin-tack** *n.* a tin-coated iron tack. **tin whistle,** a penny whistle. [OE]

tincture /ˈtɪŋktʃə(r)/ *n.* **1** a tinge or trace of some element or quality. **2** a medicinal solution of a drug in alcohol. —*v.t.* to tinge. [as TINGE]

tinder *n.* a dry substance that readily catches fire from a spark. —**tinder-box** *n.* a box containing tinder, flint, and steel, for kindling fires. —**tindery** *adj.* [OE]

tine *n.* each of the points or prongs of a fork, harrow, antler, etc. [OE]

tinge *v.t.* to colour slightly; to give a slight trace of some element or quality to. —*n.* a slight colouring or trace. [f. L *tingere* stain]

tingle *v.i.* to feel a slight pricking, stinging, or throbbing sensation, especially in the ears or hands; to cause this. —*n.* a tingling sensation. [perh. var. of TINKLE]

tinker *n.* **1** an itinerant mender of kettles and pans etc. **2** (*Sc. & Ir.*) a gypsy. **3** (*colloq.*) a mischievous person or animal. **4** a spell of tinkering. —*v.i.* **1** to work at something casually trying to improve or repair it. **2** to work as a tinker. [orig. unkn.]

tinkle *n.* **1** a series of short light ringing sounds. **2** (*colloq.*) a telephone call. —*v.t./i.* to make or cause to make a tinkle. [f. obs. *tink* to chink (imit.)]

tinny *adj.* **1** of or like tin. **2** (of a metal object) flimsy, insubstantial. **3** having a metallic taste or a thin metallic sound. —**tinnily** *adv.*, **tinniness** *n.* [f. TIN]

tinpot *adj.* (*colloq., derog.*) cheap, inferior.

tinsel /ˈtɪns(ə)l/ *n.* a glittering metallic substance used in strips or threads to give an inexpensive sparkling effect. —*adj.* superficially showy, gaudy. [prob. f. AF, ult. f. L, = SCINTILLA]

tinsmith *n.* a worker in tin and tin plate.

tint *n.* **1** a variety of a colour, especially made by adding white. **2** a slight trace of a different colour. **3** a faint colour spread over a surface. —*v.t.* to apply a tint to; to colour. —**tinted** *adj.* [f. L *tinctus* (as TINGE)]

tintinnabulation /tɪntɪnæbjʊˈleɪʃ(ə)n/ *n.* a ringing or tinkling of bells. [f. L *tintinnabulum* bell]

tiny /ˈtaɪnɪ/ *adj.* very small or slight. —**tinily** *adv.*, **tininess** *n.* [orig. unkn.]

tip[1] *n.* **1** the very end, especially of a small or tapering thing. **2** a small piece or part attached to an end of a thing. **3** a leaf-bud of tea. —*v.t.* (**-pp-**) to provide with a tip. —**on the tip of one's tongue,** just about to be said, or remembered and spoken. **tip of the iceberg,** the small evident part of something much larger. [f. ON (as TOP[1])]

tip[2] *v.t./i.* (**-pp-**) **1** to tilt or topple; to cause to do this. **2** to overturn, to cause to overbalance; to discharge (the contents of a truck or jug etc.) thus. **3** to make a small present of money to, especially for service given. **4** to name as the likely winner of a race or contest etc. **5** to strike or touch lightly. —*n.* **1** a small money present, especially for service given. **2** private or special information (e.g. about a horse-race or stock-market); a small or casual piece of advice. **3** a slight push or tilt. **4** a place where material (esp. rubbish) is tipped. **5** a light stroke. —**tip a person off,** to give him a hint or special information, or a warning. **tip-off** *n.* such information etc. **tip-up** *adj.* able to be tipped, e.g. of a seat in a theatre to allow passage past. **tip a person the wink,** to give him private information. [perh. f. Scand.; partly f. TIP[1]]

tippet /ˈtɪpɪt/ *n.* a small cape or collar of fur etc. with the ends hanging down in front. [prob. f. TIP[1]]

tipple *v.t./i.* to drink (wine or spirits etc.); to be a habitual drinker. —*n.* (*colloq.*) alcoholic or other drink. —**tippler** *n.* [back-formation f. *tippler*; orig. unkn.]

tipstaff *n.* **1** a sheriff's officer. **2** the metal-tipped staff carried by him as a badge of office.

tipster *n.* one who gives tips about horse-races etc. [f. TIP[2]]

tipsy /ˈtɪpsɪ/ *adj.* slightly intoxicated; caused by or showing slight intoxication. —**tipsy-cake** *n.* a sponge-cake soaked in wine or spirits and served with custard. —**tipsily** *adv.*, **tipsiness** *n.* [prob. f. TIP[2]]

tiptoe *n.* the tips of the toes. —*v.i.* to walk on tiptoe or very stealthily. —*adv.* on tiptoe, with the heels off the ground.

tiptop /ˈtɪptɒp, -ˈtɒp/ *adj.* (*colloq.*) excellent. —*n.* (*colloq.*) the highest point of excellence. —*adv.* (*colloq.*) excellently.

TIR *abbr.* Transport International Routier. [F, = international road transport]

tirade /taɪˈreɪd, tɪ-/ *n.* a long vehement denunciation or declamation. [F f. It., = volley]

tire[1] *v.t./i.* to make or become tired. [OE]

tire[2] *n.* **1** a band of metal placed round the rim of a wheel to strengthen it. **2** (*US*) a tyre. [perh. f. ATTIRE]

tired /ˈtaɪəd/ *adj.* **1** feeling that one would like to sleep or rest. **2** (of an idea etc.) hackneyed.

—tired of, having had enough of (a thing or activity) and feeling impatient or bored. [f. TIRE¹]

tireless *adj.* not tiring easily, having inexhaustible energy. **—tirelessly** *adv.* [f. TIRE¹ + -LESS]

tiresome *adj.* wearisome, tedious; (*colloq.*) annoying. [f. TIRE¹ + -SOME]

tiro /ˈtaɪərəʊ/ *n.* (*pl.* **tiros**) a beginner, a novice. [L, = recruit]

'tis /tɪz/ (*archaic*) it is.

tissue /ˈtɪʃuː, ˈtɪsjuː/ *n.* **1** any of the coherent substances of which animal or plant bodies are made. **2** tissue-paper. **3** a disposable piece of thin soft absorbent paper for wiping or drying things. **4** a fine gauzy fabric. **5** a connected series (of lies etc.). **—tissue-paper** *n.* thin soft unsized paper for wrapping or packing things. [f. OF *tissu* f. L *texere* weave]

tit[1] *n.* any of various small birds (e.g. *blue tit, coal-tit*). [prob. f. Scand.]

tit[2] *n.* **tit for tat,** blow for blow, retaliation. [= earlier *tip* (TIP²) *for tat*]

tit[3] *n.* (*vulgar*) a nipple; (in *pl.*) a woman's breasts. [OE]

titanic /taɪˈtænɪk/ *adj.* gigantic, colossal. **—titanically** *adv.* [f. Gk *Titan* member of giant race]

titanium /taɪˈteɪnɪəm, tɪ-/ *n.* a grey metallic element, symbol Ti, atomic number 22. [f. as prec., after *uranium*]

titbit *n.* a dainty morsel; a piquant item of news etc. [prob. f. dial. *tid* tender + BIT¹]

titfer *n.* (*slang*) a hat. [abbr. of *tit* (TIT²) *fer tat,* rhyming slang = hat]

tithe /taɪð/ *n.* (*hist.*) a tax of one tenth, especially a tenth part of the annual produce of land or labour formerly levied to support clergy and the Church. *—v.t./i.* to subject to tithes; to pay tithes. **—tithe barn,** a barn built to hold tithes paid in kind. [OE, = tenth]

titillate /ˈtɪtɪleɪt/ *v.t.* to excite pleasantly; to tickle. **—titillation** /-ˈleɪʃ(ə)n/ *n.* [f. L *titillare*]

titivate /ˈtɪtɪveɪt/ *v.t.* (*colloq.*) to smarten, to put the finishing touches to. **—titivation** /-veɪʃ(ə)n/ *n.* [earlier *tid-*, perh. f. TIDY after *cultivate*]

title /ˈtaɪt(ə)l/ *n.* **1** the name of a book, poem, or work of art etc. **2** the heading of a chapter or legal document etc.; a caption or credit title of a film. **3** a form of nomenclature indicating a person's status (e.g. *professor, queen*) or used as a form of address or reference (e.g. *Lord, Mr, Your Grace*). **4** a championship in sport. **5** the right to the ownership of property with or without possession; the facts constituting this; a just or recognized claim. **—title-deed** *n.* a legal instrument as evidence of a right. **title-page** *n.* a page at the beginning of a book giving the title and particulars of authorship etc. **title-role** *n.* the part in a play etc. that gives it its name (e.g. *Othello*). [f. OF f. L *titulus* placard, title]

titled /ˈtaɪt(ə)ld/ *adj.* having a title of nobility or rank. [f. TITLE]

titmouse *n.* (*pl.* **titmice**) a tit (TIT¹). [f. TIT¹ + obs. *mose* titmouse]

titrate /taɪˈtreɪt/ *v.t.* to ascertain the amount of a constituent in (a substance) by using a standard reagent. **—titration** /-ˈtreɪʃ(ə)n/ *n.* [f. F *titrer* (*titre* title)]

titter *v.i.* to laugh covertly, to giggle. *—n.* such a laugh. [imit.]

tittle /ˈtɪt(ə)l/ *n.* a small written or printed stroke or dot; a particle, a whit (esp. *not one jot or tittle*). [f. L (as TITLE)]

tittle-tattle *v.i.* to tattle. *—n.* tattle. [redupl. of TATTLE]

tittup /ˈtɪtəp/ *v.i.* to move in a lively or frisky way, to bob up and down. *—n.* such a movement. [perh. imit. of hoof-beats]

titular /ˈtɪtjʊlə(r)/ *adj.* **1** of or relating to a title. **2** existing or being such in title only. [f. F (as TITLE)]

tizzy /ˈtɪzɪ/ *n.* (*slang*) a state of nervous agitation or confusion. [orig. unkn.]

Tl *symbol* thallium.

Tm *symbol* thulium.

TNT *abbr.* trinitrotoluene.

to /tə, *before a vowel* tʊ, *emphat.* tuː/ *prep.* **1** in the direction of; so as to approach, reach, or be in (a place, position, or state etc.). **2** as far as, not falling far short of. **3** as compared with; in respect of. **4** for (a person or thing) to hold, possess, or be affected etc. by. **5** (with a verb) introducing an infinitive; expressing purpose, consequence, or cause; used alone when an infinitive is understood (*I meant to call but forgot to*). *—adv.* to or in a normal or required position or condition; to a standstill; (of a door) into a nearly closed position. **—to and fro,** backwards and forwards; repeatedly between the same places. [OE]

toad *n.* **1** a froglike amphibian of the genus *Bufo*. **2** a repulsive person. **—toad-in-the-hole** *n.* sausages or other meat baked in batter. [OE]

toadflax *n.* a plant of the genus *Linaria* or allied genera with spurred yellow or purple flowers.

toadstool *n.* a fungus, usually poisonous, with a round top and a slender stalk.

toady *n.* a sycophant, an obsequious hanger-on. *—v.t./i.* to behave as a toady (to). [f. *toad-eater* orig. the attendant of a charlatan, employed to eat or pretend to eat toads (held to be poisonous) to enable his master to exhibit his skill in expelling poison]

toast *n.* **1** a toasted slice of bread. **2** a person or thing in whose honour a company is requested to drink; the call to drink or an instance of drinking in this way. —*v.t.* **1** to brown the surface of (bread, a teacake, cheese, etc.) by placing it before a fire or other source of heat. **2** to warm (one's feet or oneself) thus. **3** to honour or pledge good wishes by drinking. —**have a person on toast,** (*slang*) to have him at one's mercy. **toasting-fork** *n.* a long-handled fork for holding a slice of bread before a fire to toast it. **toast-master** *n.* a person announcing the toasts at a public dinner. **toast-rack** *n.* a rack for holding slices of toast at table. [f. OF *toster* f. L *torrēre* parch]

toaster *n.* an electrical device for making toast. [f. TOAST]

tobacco /təˈbækəʊ/ *n.* (*pl.* **-os**) a plant of the genus *Nicotiana*, native to Central America, with narcotic leaves used for smoking, chewing, or snuff; its leaves, especially as prepared for smoking. [f. Sp. *tobaco*, of Amer. Indian origin]

tobacconist /təˈbækənɪst/ *n.* a shopkeeper who sells tobacco and cigarettes etc. [f. prec.]

toboggan /təˈbɒgən/ *n.* a long light narrow sledge curved upwards at the front, used for sliding downhill especially over snow or ice. —*v.i.* to ride on a toboggan. [f. Canadian F f. Algonquian]

toby jug a jug or mug in the form of a stout old man wearing a long full-skirted coat and a three-cornered hat (18th-c. costume). [f. *Toby*, man's name]

toccata /təˈkɑːtə/ *n.* a musical composition for a piano, organ, etc., designed to exhibit a performer's touch and technique. [It., p.p. of *toccare* touch]

tocsin /ˈtɒksɪn/ *n.* an alarm-signal; a bell used to sound an alarm. [F f. *touquesain*, *toquassen* f. Prov. (ult. as TOUCH, SIGN)]

tod *n.* (*slang*) **on one's tod,** alone, on one's own. [perh. f. *on one's Tod Sloan* (jockey, d. 1933), rhyming slang]

today /təˈdeɪ/ *adv.* on this present day; nowadays, in modern times. —*n.* this present day; modern times. [OE (as TO[1], DAY)]

toddle *v.i.* to walk with a young child's short unsteady steps; (*colloq.*, usu. with *off*) to depart. —*n.* a toddling walk. [orig. unkn.]

toddler *n.* a child who has only recently learnt to walk. [f. prec.]

toddy /ˈtɒdɪ/ *n.* a drink of spirits with hot water and sugar. [f. Hind. (*tar* palm)]

to-do /təˈduː/ *n.* a commotion, a fuss. [f. *to do* as in *What's to do*?]

toe *n.* **1** any of the terminal members (five in man) of the front part of the foot; the corresponding part of an animal or bird. **2** the part of footwear that covers the toes. **3** the lower end or tip of an implement etc. —*v.t.* to touch with the toes. —**on one's toes,** alert, eager. **toe-cap** *n.* the reinforced toe of a boot or shoe. **toe-hold** *n.* a slight foothold (*lit.* & *fig.*). **toe the line,** to conform (especially under compulsion) to the requirement of one's group or party. [OE]

toff *n.* (*slang*) a distinguished or well-dressed person. [perh. f. TUFT in archaic sense 'titled undergraduate', who formerly at Oxford and Cambridge Universities wore a gold tassel on the academic cap]

toffee /ˈtɒfɪ/ *n.* a kind of firm or hard sweet made by boiling sugar, butter, etc.; a small piece of this. —**can't do a thing for toffee,** (*slang*) is incompetent at it. **toffee-apple** *n.* a toffee-coated apple on a stick. **toffee-nosed** *adj.* (*slang*) snobbish, pretentious. [f. earlier *taffy* (orig. unkn.)]

tofu /ˈtəʊfuː/ *n.* (esp. in China and Japan) a curd made from mashed soya beans. [f. Jap. f. Chin., = rotten beans]

tog *n.* **1** (usu. in *pl.*, *slang*) a garment. **2** a unit expressing the insulating properties of clothes and quilts. —*v.t.* (**-gg-**) (with *out* or *up*) (*slang*) to dress. [abbr. of 16th-c. slang *togman* f. F *toge* or L *toga* (see foll.); sense 2 modelled on earlier US term *clo* (*clothes*)]

toga /ˈtəʊgə/ *n.* an ancient Roman citizen's loose flowing outer garment. —**toga'd** *adj.* [L (rel. to *tegere* cover)]

together /təˈgeðə(r)/ *adv.* **1** in or into company or conjunction; towards each other; so as to unite. **2** one with another. **3** simultaneously. **4** in an unbroken succession. **5** (*colloq.*) well organized or controlled. —**together with,** as well as, and also. [OE, (as TO[1], GATHER)]

togetherness *n.* being together; feeling or belonging together. [f. prec.]

toggle *n.* a fastening device consisting of a short piece of wood or metal etc. secured by its centre and passed through a loop or hole etc. —**toggle-switch** *n.* a switch operated by a projecting lever. [orig. unkn.]

toil *v.i.* to work long or laboriously; to move laboriously. —*n.* hard or laborious work. —**toiler** *n.* [f. AF, = dispute, f. L *tudiculare* stir about (*tudicula* machine for bruising olives, rel. to *tundere* beat)]

toilet /ˈtɔɪlɪt/ *n.* **1** a lavatory. **2** the process of washing oneself, dressing, etc. —**toilet-paper** *n.* paper for cleaning oneself after excreting. **toilet-roll** *n.* a roll of toilet-paper. **toilet soap,** soap for washing oneself. **toilet-training** *n.* the training of a young child to use the lavatory. **toilet water,** a scented liquid used in or after cleansing the skin. [f. F *toilette* (as TOILS)]

toiletries /ˈtɔɪlɪtrɪz/ *n.pl.* articles used in making one's toilet. [f. prec.]

tolls /tɒɪlz/ *n.pl.* a snare. [f. OF *toile* cloth f. L *tela* web]

toilsome /ˈtɔɪlsəm/ *adj.* involving toil. [f. TOIL + -SOME]

Tokay /təˈkeɪ/ *n.* a sweet Hungarian wine; a similar wine from elsewhere. [f. *Tokaj* in Hungary]

token /ˈtəʊkən/ *n.* **1** an indication; a thing serving as a symbol, reminder, keepsake, distinctive mark, or guarantee. **2** a voucher exchangeable for goods. **3** a thing used to represent something else; a device resembling a coin, bought for use in slot-machines etc. or for making certain payments. —*adj.* serving as a token or pledge but often on a small scale. —**by this** *or* **the same token,** similarly; moreover; in corroboration of what I say. [OE (rel. to TEACH)]

tokenism /ˈtəʊkənɪz(ə)m/ *n.* making only a token effort or granting only minimum concessions, especially to minority or suppressed groups. [f. TOKEN]

tolbooth /ˈtɒlbu:θ/ var. of TOLL-BOOTH.

told /təʊld/ *past* & *p.p.* of TELL.

tolerable /ˈtɒlərəb(ə)l/ *adj.* **1** able to be tolerated, endurable. **2** fairly good, passable. —**tolerableness** *n.*, **tolerably** *adv.* [f. OF f. L (as TOLERATE)]

tolerance /ˈtɒlərəns/ *n.* **1** willingness or ability to tolerate a person or thing. **2** permissible variation in dimension or weight. [as prec.]

tolerant /ˈtɒlərənt/ *adj.* having or showing tolerance. —**tolerantly** *adv.* [as prec.]

tolerate /ˈtɒləreɪt/ *v.t.* **1** to permit without protest or interference. **2** to find or treat as endurable. **3** to be able to take (a medicine) or undergo (a process etc.) without harm. —**toleration** /-ˈreɪʃ(ə)n/ *n.* [f. L *tolerare*]

toll[1] /təʊl/ *n.* **1** a charge payable for permission to pass a barrier or for the use of a bridge or road etc. **2** the cost or damage caused by a disaster or incurred in an achievement. —**take its toll,** to be accompanied by loss or injury etc. **toll-booth** *n.* (*archaic, Sc.*) a town hall or town gaol. **toll-bridge** *n.* a bridge at which a toll is charged. **toll-gate** *n.* a gate preventing passage until a toll is paid. **toll-house** *n.* (*hist.*) a small house built near a toll-gate for the use of the keeper, usually hexagonal in shape so that the windows commanded a view in all directions. **toll-road** *n.* a road maintained by the tolls collected on it. [OE f. L *toloneum* f. Gk (*telos* tax)]

toll[2] /təʊl/ *v.t./i.* **1** (of a bell) to sound with a slow uniform succession of strokes. **2** to ring (a bell or knell) or strike (an hour) or announce or mark (a death etc.) thus. —*n.* the tolling or stroke of a bell. [spec. use of obs. or dial. *toll* pull]

tolu /təˈlju:, ˈtəʊlju:/ *n.* a fragrant brown balsam from a South American tree (*Myroxylon balsamum*). [f. (Santiago de) *Tolu* in Colombia]

toluene /ˈtɒljʊi:n/ *n.* a colourless aromatic liquid hydrocarbon derivative of benzene, originally obtained from tolu, used in the manufacture of explosives etc. [f. TOLU]

toluol /ˈtɒljʊɒl/ *n.* a commercial grade of toluene. [f. TOLU]

tom *n.* (in full **tom-cat**) a male cat. —**Tom, Dick, and Harry,** (usu. *derog.*) persons taken at random, ordinary people (usu. preceded by *any* or *every*). [abbr. of man's name *Thomas*]

tomahawk /ˈtɒməhɔ:k/ *n.* a North American Indian war-axe. [f. Algonquian (*tämäham* he cuts)]

tomato /təˈmɑ:təʊ/ *n.* (*pl.* **-oes**) the glossy red or yellow fruit of a plant, *Lycopersicon esculentum*, native to tropical America; this plant. [f. F or Sp. & Port. f. Mex. *tomatl*]

tomb /tu:m/ *n.* a grave or other place of burial; a burial-vault; a sepulchral monument. [f. AF, ult. f. Gk *tumbos*]

tombola /tɒmˈbəʊlə/ *n.* a kind of lottery with tickets and prizes. [F or f. It. (*tombolare* tumble)]

tomboy *n.* a rough boyish girl.

tombstone *n.* a stone standing or laid over a grave, usually with an epitaph.

tome *n.* a large book or volume. [F f. L f. Gk *tomos*, orig. = section (*temnō* cut)]

tomfool /tɒmˈfu:l/ *adj.* extremely foolish. —*n.* a fool.

tomfoolery *n.* foolish behaviour. [f. prec.]

Tommy /ˈtɒmɪ/ *n.* a British private soldier. [f. *Tommy* (*Thomas*) *Atkins*, name used in specimens of completed official forms]

tommy-gun /ˈtɒmɪgʌn/ *n.* a sub-machine-gun. [f. co-inventor J. T. *Thompson* (US officer, d. 1940)]

tommy-rot /ˈtɒmɪrɒt/ *n.* (*slang*) nonsense. [f. *Tommy* (as TOM) + ROT]

tomography /təˈmɒgrəfɪ/ *n.* radiography in which an image of a selected plane in the body or other object is obtained by rotating the detector and the source of radiation in such a way that points outside the plane give a blurred image. —**tomographic** /-ˈgræfɪk/ *adj.* [f. Gk *tomē* cutting + -GRAPHY]

tomorrow /təˈmɒrəʊ/ *adv.* on the day after today; at some future time. —*n.* the day after today; the near future. [f. TO + MORROW]

tomtit *n.* a tit, especially a blue tit. [f. TOM + TIT[1]]

tom-tom /ˈtɒmtɒm/ *n.* a primitive drum beaten with the hands; a tall drum used in jazz bands etc. [f. Hindi *tamtam* (imit.)]

-tomy /-təmɪ/ *suffix* forming nouns with sense 'cutting', especially in names of surgical operations or incision (*laparotomy*). [f. Gk -*tomia* cutting (*temnō* cut)]

ton /tʌn/ *n.* **1** a measure of weight, 2,240 lb. (**long ton**) or 2,000 lb. (**short ton**). **2** a unit of measurement for a ship's tonnage. **3** (usu. in *pl.*) (*colloq.*) a large number or amount. **4** (*slang*) a speed of 100 m.p.h. **5** (*slang*) £100. —**ton-up boys,** motor-cyclists who travel at high speed. **weighs a ton,** is very heavy. [different spelling of TUN]

tonal /ˈtəʊn(ə)l/ *adj.* of or relating to tone or tonality. —**tonal language,** a tone language (see TONE). —**tonally** *adv.* [f. L (as TONE)]

tonality /təˈnælɪtɪ/ *n.* **1** the relationship between the notes of a musical scale; the observance of a single tonic key as the basis of a composition. **2** the colour-scheme of a picture. [f. TONAL]

tone *n.* **1** a musical or vocal sound, especially with reference to its pitch, quality, and strength. **2** the modulation of the voice to express a particular feeling or mood. **3** a manner of expression in writing. **4** (*Mus.*) a musical sound, especially of a definite pitch and character; an interval of a major second, e.g. C-D. **5** the general effect of colour or of light and shade in a picture; a tint or shade of colour. **6** the prevailing character of morals and sentiments etc. in a group. **7** proper firmness of bodily organs and tissues; a state of good or specified health. —*v.t./i.* **1** to give a desired tone to; to modify the tone of; to attune. **2** to harmonize in colour. —**tone-deaf** *adj.* unable to perceive differences of musical pitch accurately. **tone down,** to make or become softer in the tone of sound or colour; to make (a statement etc.) less harsh or emphatic. **tone language,** a language which uses variations in pitch to distinguish words which would otherwise sound identical. **tone poem,** an orchestral composition illustrating a poetic idea. **tone up,** to make or become brighter or more vigorous or intense. —**toner** *n.* [f. OF f. L f. Gk, orig. = tension (*teinō* stretch)]

tongs /tɒŋz/ *n.pl.* an instrument with two arms joined at one end, used for grasping and holding things. [OE]

tongue /tʌŋ/ *n.* **1** the fleshy muscular organ in the mouth used in tasting, licking, swallowing, and (in man) speech. **2** the tongue of an ox etc. as food. **3** the faculty of or a tendency in speech. **4** the language of a nation etc. **5** a thing like a tongue in shape, e.g. a long low promontory, a strip of leather under the laces in a shoe, the clapper of a bell, the pin of a buckle; the projecting strip on a wooden etc. board fitting into the groove of another. —**find** (*or* **lose**) **one's tongue,** to be able (or unable) to express oneself after a shock etc. **hold one's tongue,** to remain silent. **tongue-tie** *n.* a speech impediment due to a malformation of the tongue. **tongue-tied** *adj.* too shy or embarrassed to speak; having a tongue-tie. **tongue-twister** *n.* a sequence of words difficult to pronounce quickly and correctly. **with one's tongue in one's cheek,** insincerely or ironically; with sly humour. [OE]

tonguing *n.* (*Mus.*) the use of the tongue to articulate certain notes in playing a wind instrument. [f. prec.]

tonic /ˈtɒnɪk/ *n.* **1** an invigorating medicine; anything serving to invigorate. **2** tonic water. **3** a keynote in music. —*adj.* **1** serving as a tonic, invigorating. **2** of the tonic or keynote in music. —**tonic water,** a carbonated drink flavoured with quinine or another bitter. [f. F f. Gk (as TONE)]

tonic sol-fa /sɒlˈfɑː/ a system of musical notation used especially in teaching the notes in singing.

tonight /təˈnaɪt/ *adv.* on the present or approaching evening or night. —*n.* the present evening or night, the evening or night of today. [f. TO + NIGHT]

tonnage /ˈtʌnɪdʒ/ *n.* **1** a ship's internal cubic capacity or freight-carrying capacity. **2** the charge per ton on cargo or freight. [f. TON]

tonne /tʌn, ˈtʌnɪ/ *n.* a metric ton of 1000 kg. [F (as TON)]

tonsil /ˈtɒns(ə)l/ *n.* either of two small organs, one on each side of the root of the tongue. —**tonsillar** /ˈtɒnsɪlə(r)/ *adj.* [f. F or L *tonsillae*]

tonsillectomy /tɒnsɪˈlektəmɪ/ *n.* surgical removal of the tonsils. [f. prec. + -ECTOMY]

tonsillitis /tɒnsɪˈlaɪtɪs/ *n.* inflammation of the tonsils. [f. TONSIL + -ITIS]

tonsorial /tɒnˈsɔːrɪəl/ *adj.* of a barber or his work. [f. L *tonsor* (*tondēre* shave)]

tonsure /ˈtɒnʃə(r)/ *n.* the rite of shaving the crown of the head (in the RC Church until 1972) or the whole head (in the Orthodox Church), especially of a person entering the priesthood or a monastic order; the part shaved thus. —*v.t.* to give a tonsure to. [f. OF or L (as prec.)]

too *adv.* **1** to a greater extent than is desirable or permissible. **2** (*colloq.*) extremely. **3** in addition, moreover. —**none too,** rather less than. **too much,** intolerable. **too much for,** more than a match for; more than can be endured by. [stressed form of TO]

took *past* of TAKE.

tool *n.* **1** a thing (usually something held in the hand) for working upon something. **2** a simple machine, e.g. a lathe. **3** a thing used in an occupation or pursuit. **4** a person used as a mere instrument by another. —*v.t./i.* **1** to dress (stone) with a chisel. **2** to impress a design on (a leather book-cover etc.). **3** (*slang*) to drive or ride in a casual or leisurely manner. —**tool-pusher** *n.* a worker directing drilling on an oil-rig. [OE]

toot *n.* a short sharp sound (as) of a horn or trumpet. —*v.t./i.* to sound (a horn etc.) thus; to give out such a sound. [prob. f. MLG, or imit.]

tooth *n.* (*pl.* **teeth**) **1** each of the set of hard bony structures in the jaws of most vertebrates, used for biting and chewing things. **2** a toothlike part or projection, e.g. a cog of a gear-wheel, a point of a saw or comb etc. **3** sense of taste, an appetite. **4** (in *pl.*) force or effectiveness. —**armed to the teeth,** completely and elaborately armed or equipped. **fight tooth and nail,** to fight very fiercely. **get one's teeth into,** to devote oneself seriously to. **in the teeth of,** in spite of (opposition or difficulty etc.), in opposition to (instructions etc.); directly against (the wind etc.). **tooth-comb** *n.* a comb with fine close-set teeth (properly a fine-tooth comb; see FINE[1]). **tooth-powder** *n.* a powder for cleaning the teeth. [OE]

toothache *n.* pain in a tooth or the teeth.

toothbrush *n.* a brush for cleaning the teeth.

toothless *adj.* having no teeth. [f. TOOTH + -LESS]

toothpaste *n.* paste for cleaning the teeth.

toothpick *n.* a small sharp instrument for removing food etc. lodged between the teeth.

toothsome *adj.* (of food) delicious. [f. TOOTH + -SOME]

toothy *adj.* having large, numerous, or prominent teeth. [f. TOOTH]

tootle *v.i.* **1** to toot gently or repeatedly. **2** (*colloq.*) to go in a casual or leisurely way. [f. TOOT]

top[1] *n.* **1** the highest point or part; **2** the upper surface; a thing forming the upper part; the cover or cap of a container etc. **3** the highest rank; the foremost place or position; a person holding such a rank etc. **4** a garment for the upper part of the body. **5** (usu. in *pl.*) the leaves etc. of a plant grown chiefly for its root. **6** the utmost degree or intensity. **7** top gear. **8** a platform round the head of the lower mast of a ship. **9** (*predic.*, in *pl.*) a person or thing of the very best quality. —*adj.* highest in position, degree, or importance. —*v.t.* (**-pp-**) **1** to furnish with a top or cap. **2** to be higher than; to be superior to, to surpass. **3** to be at the top of; to reach the top of (a hill etc.) **4** to hit (a ball in golf) above its centre. —**at the top,** in the highest rank of a profession etc. **on top,** above, in a superior position. **on top of,** fully in control of; in close proximity to; in addition to. **on top of the world,** exuberant. **over the top,** over the parapet of a trench; into a final or decisive state or a state of excess. **top brass,** (*colloq.*) high-ranking officers. **top dog,** (*colloq.*) the victor, the master. **top drawer,** a high social position or origin. **top-dress** *v.t.* to apply manure or fertilizer on the top of (the earth), not dig it in. **top-flight** *adj.* in the highest rank of achievement. **top gear,** the highest gear. **top hat,** a tall silk hat. **top-heavy** *adj.* overweighted at the top and so in danger of falling. **top-hole** *adj.* (*slang*) first-rate. **top-level** *adj.* of or at the highest rank or level. **top-notch** *adj.* (*colloq.*) first-rate. **top off,** to put an end or finishing touch to. **top out,** to put the highest stone on (a building). **top secret,** of the highest secrecy. **top up,** to fill up (a partly empty container); to add extra money or items to. [OE]

top[2] *n.* a toy, usually conical or pear-shaped, with a sharp point at the bottom on which it rotates when set in motion. [OE]

topaz /ˈtəʊpæz/ *n.* a gem of various colours, especially yellow. [f. OF f. L f. Gk *topazos*]

topcoat *n.* **1** an overcoat. **2** an outer coat of paint etc.

tope[1] *n.* a small shark of the genus *Galeorhinus.* [perh. f. Cornish]

tope[2] *v.i.* (*archaic*) to drink intoxicating liquor to excess, esp. habitually. —**toper** *n.* [perh. f. obs. *top* quaff]

topgallant /tɒpˈgælənt/ *n.* the mast, sail, yard, or rigging immediately above the topmast and topsail.

topi /ˈtəʊpɪ/ *n.* (also **topee**) a sun-helmet, especially a sola topi. [f. Hindi]

topiary /ˈtəʊpɪərɪ/ *n.* the art of clipping shrubs etc. into ornamental shapes. —*adj.* of this art. [f. F f. L *topiarius* landscape-gardener ult. f. Gk *topos* place]

topic /ˈtɒpɪk/ *n.* a theme for discussion, a subject of conversation or discourse. [f. L f. Gk (*topos* place, a commonplace)]

topical *adj.* dealing with current topics. —**topicality** /-ˈkælɪtɪ/ *n.*, **topically** *adv.* [f. TOPIC]

topknot *n.* a tuft or crest or bow of ribbon etc. worn or growing on the head.

topless *adj.* without a top; (of a woman's clothing) leaving the breasts bare, (of a woman) so clothed. [f. TOP[1] + -LESS]

topmast *n.* the part of a mast next above the lower mast.

topmost *adj.* uppermost, highest. [f. TOP[1] + -MOST]

topography /təˈpɒgrəfɪ/ *n.* the natural and artificial features of a district; the knowledge or description of these. —**topographer** *n.*, **topographical** /tɒpəˈgræfɪk(ə)l/ *adj.* [f. L f. Gk (*topos* place + -GRAPHY)]

topology /təˈpɒlədʒɪ/ *n.* **1** the study of geometrical properties and spatial relations unaffected by continuous change of shape or size of the figures involved. **2** the branch of mathematics concerned with the abstract theory of continuity. —**topological** /tɒpəˈlɒdʒɪk(ə)l/ *adj.* [f. G f. Gk *topos* place + -LOGY]

topper *n.* (*colloq.*) a top hat. [f. TOP¹]

topping *n.* decorative cream etc. on top of a cake etc. [f. TOP¹]

topple *v.t./i.* **1** to fall headlong or as if top-heavy; to cause to do this. **2** to overthrow, to cause to fall from a position of authority. [f. TOP¹]

topsail /ˈtɒps(ə)l/ *n.* **1** a square sail next above the lowest. **2** a fore-and-aft sail on a gaff.

topside *n.* **1** the outer side of a round of beef. **2** the side of a ship above the water-line.

topsoil *n.* the top layer of soil.

topsy-turvy /tɒpsɪˈtɜːvɪ/ *adv.* & *adj.* **1** upside-down. **2** in or into utter confusion. [app. f. TOP¹ + obs. *turve* overturn]

toque /təʊk/ *n.* a woman's close-fitting brimless hat with a high crown. [F; orig. unkn.]

tor *n.* a rocky hill-top. [OE *torr*; cf. Gael. *tòrr* bulging hill]

Torah /ˈtɔːrə/ *n.* the Pentateuch, the Mosaic law; a scroll containing this. [f. Heb., = instruction]

torch *n.* **1** a small hand-held electric lamp powered by a battery or an electric power cell contained in a case. **2** a burning piece of resinous wood, or combustible material fixed on a stick and ignited, used as a light for carrying in the hand. —**carry a torch for,** to feel (unreturned) love for. [f. OF f. L *torqua* (*torquēre* twist)]

tore *past* of TEAR¹.

toreador /ˈtɒrɪədɔː(r)/ *n.* a bullfighter, especially on horseback. [Sp. (*toro* bull f. L *taurus*)]

torment /ˈtɔːment/ *n.* severe bodily or mental suffering; a cause of this. —/tɔːˈment/ *v.t.* to subject to torment; to tease or worry excessively. —**tormentor** /-ˈmentə(r)/ *n.* [f. OF f. L *tormentum* (as TORT)]

tormentil /ˈtɔːməntɪl/ *n.* a low-growing herb (*Potentilla erecta*) with yellow flowers. [f. OF f. L]

torn *p.p.* of TEAR¹.

tornado /tɔːˈneɪdəʊ/ *n.* (*pl.* **-oes**) **1** a violent storm over a small area, especially a rotatory one travelling in a narrow path. **2** a loud outburst. [app. assim. of Sp. *tronada* thunderstorm]

torpedo /tɔːˈpiːdəʊ/ *n.* (*pl.* **-oes**) a cigar-shaped self-propelled underwater missile fired at a ship from a submarine or surface ship or from an aircraft and exploding on impact. —*v.t.* **1** to destroy or attack with a torpedo. **2** to ruin (a policy or institution etc.) suddenly. —**torpedo-boat** *n.* a small fast warship armed with torpedoes. [L, = electric ray (*torpēre* be numb)]

torpid /ˈtɔːpɪd/ *adj.* sluggish, inactive, apathetic; (of a hibernating animal) dormant. —**torpidity** /-ˈpɪdɪtɪ/ *n.*, **torpidly** *adv.* [f. L *torpidus* (as foll.)]

torpor /ˈtɔːpə(r)/ *n.* a torpid condition. [L (*torpēre* be numb)]

torque /tɔːk/ *n.* **1** a twisting or rotary force especially in a machine. **2** a necklace or collar usually of twisted metal, worn by the ancient Britons, Gauls, etc. [f. L *torquēre* twist]

torrent /ˈtɒrənt/ *n.* **1** a rushing stream of water or lava etc. **2** (usu. in *pl.*) a great downpour of rain. **3** a violent flow (of abuse, questions, etc.). —**torrential** /təˈrenʃ(ə)l/ *adj.* [F f. It. f. L (as TORRID)]

torrid /ˈtɒrɪd/ *adj.* **1** (of land etc.) parched by the sun, very hot. **2** intense, passionate. —**torrid zone,** the tropics. [f. F or L *torridus* (*torrēre* scorch)]

torsion /ˈtɔːʃ(ə)n/ *n.* twisting, especially of one end of a thing while the other is held fixed. —**torsional** *adj.* [f. OF f. L (as TORT)]

torso /ˈtɔːsəʊ/ *n.* (*pl.* **-os**) **1** the trunk of the human body or of a statue. **2** a statue lacking the head and limbs. [It., = stalk, stump, f. L *thyrsus*]

tort *n.* a breach of a legal duty, other than under contract, with liability for damages. —**tortious** /ˈtɔːʃəs/ *adj.* [f. OF f. L *tortum* wrong (*torquēre* twist)]

tortilla /tɔːˈtɪlə/ *n.* a Latin American flat maize cake eaten hot. [Sp. dim. (*torta* cake f. L)]

tortoise /ˈtɔːtəs/ *n.* a slow-moving reptile of the order Chelonia of land or fresh water, with the body encased in a horny shell. [OF f. L *tortuca*; orig. unkn.]

tortoiseshell /ˈtɔːtəʃel/ *n.* **1** the yellowish-brown mottled and clouded shell of certain turtles. **2** a cat or butterfly with markings suggesting tortoiseshell. —*adj.* having such markings.

tortuous /ˈtɔːtjʊəs/ *adj.* **1** full of twists and turns. **2** devious, not straightforward. —**tortuosity** /-ˈɒsɪtɪ/ *n.*, **tortuously** *adv.* [f. OF f. L (*tortus* a twist, as TORT)]

torture /ˈtɔːtʃə(r)/ *n.* **1** the infliction of severe bodily pain especially as a punishment or means of coercion; a method of this. **2** severe physical or mental pain. —*v.t.* **1** to subject to torture. **2** to force out of its natural shape or meaning, to distort. —**torturer** *n.* [F f. L (as TORT)]

Tory /ˈtɔːrɪ/ *n.* **1** (*colloq.* or *derog.*) a member of the Conservative party. **2** (*hist.*) a British political party traditionally opposed to the Whigs. **3** (*US derog.*) a colonist loyal to the British during the American Revolution.

—*adj.* of Tories or the Tory party. —**Toryism** *n.* [orig. = Irish outlaw (Ir. *tóir* pursue)]

tosh *n.* (*slang*) nonsense, rubbish. [orig. unkn.]

toss *v.t./i.* **1** to move with an uneven or restless to-and-fro motion. **2** to throw lightly, carelessly, or easily; to throw back (the head), especially in contempt or impatience. **3** to send (a coin) spinning in the air to decide a choice etc. by the way it falls; to settle a dispute with (a person) thus. **4** to coat (food) by gently shaking it in a dressing etc. —*n.* **1** a tossing action or movement. **2** the result obtained by tossing a coin. —**argue the toss,** to dispute a choice already made. **take a toss,** to be thrown by a horse etc. **toss off,** to compose or finish rapidly and effortlessly; to drink (liquor) in one draught. **toss up,** to toss a coin. **toss-up** *n.* the tossing of a coin; (*colloq.*) an even chance. [orig. unkn.]

tot[1] *n.* **1** a small child. **2** a dram of liquor. [of dial. orig.]

tot[2] *v.t./i.* (**-tt-**) (usu. with *up*) to add up; (of items) to mount up. —**totting-up** *n.* the adding of separate items, especially of convictions towards disqualification from driving. **tot up to,** to amount to. [abbr. of TOTAL or of L *totum* the whole]

total /ˈtəʊt(ə)l/ *adj.* **1** including everything or everyone; comprising the whole. **2** absolute, unqualified. —*n.* the total number or quantity. —*v.t./i.* (**-ll-**) to reckon the total of; to amount in number (to). —**total internal reflection,** reflection without refraction, of a light-ray meeting the interface between two media at more than a certain critical angle to the normal. **total war,** war in which all available weapons and resources are employed. [f. OF f. L (*totus* entire)]

totalitarian /təʊtælɪˈteərɪən/ *adj.* relating to a form of government permitting no rival loyalties or parties, usually demanding total submission of the individual to the requirement of the State. —**totalitarianism** *n.* [f. foll.]

totality /təʊˈtælɪtɪ/ *n.* **1** the total number or amount. **2** being total. [f. L (as TOTAL)]

totalizator /ˈtəʊtəlaɪzeɪtə(r)/ *n.* a device showing the number and amount of the bets staked on a race to enable the total to be divided among those betting on the winner; this betting system. [f. foll.]

totalize *v.t.* to combine into a total. [f. TOTAL]

totally *adv.* completely. [f. TOTAL]

tote[1] *n.* (*slang*) a totalizator. [abbr.]

tote[2] *v.t.* (*colloq.*) to carry. —**tote bag,** a large bag for parcels etc. [17th-c. US, prob. of dial. orig.]

totem /ˈtəʊtəm/ *n.* a natural object, especially an animal, adopted as the emblem of a clan or individual, especially among North American Indians; an image of this. —**totem-pole** *n.* a pole on which totems are carved, painted, or hung. —**totemic** /-ˈtemɪk/ *adj.* [Algonquian]

totemism /ˈtəʊtəmɪz(ə)m/ *n.* the stage of cultural development of which totems are characteristic. —**totemistic** /-ˈmɪstɪk/ *adj.* [f. TOTEM]

t'other /ˈtʌðə(r)/ *adj.* & *pron.* the other. [f. *the tother*, for earlier *that other* 'the other']

totter *v.i.* **1** to walk unsteadily or feebly. **2** to rock or shake as if about to collapse; (of a State or system) to be shaken, to be on the point of collapse. —*n.* an unsteady or shaky movement or gait. —**tottery** *adj.* [f. MDu., = swing]

toucan /ˈtu:kən/ *n.* a tropical American bird of the family Ramphastidae, with a large bill. [f. Tupi or Guarani]

touch /tʌtʃ/ *v.t./i.* **1** to be or come together so that there is no space between; to meet or cause to meet thus. **2** to put one's hand etc. lightly upon; to press or strike lightly. **3** to reach as far as; to reach momentarily; to approach in excellence. **4** (with *neg.*) to move, harm, affect, or attempt in any degree; to have any dealings with; to eat or drink even a little of. **5** to arouse sympathy or other emotion in. **6** to modify; to draw or paint with light strokes. **7** (*slang*) to persuade to give money as a loan or gift. **8** (in *p.p.*) slightly crazy. —*n.* **1** an act or the fact of touching. **2** the faculty of perception through the response of the brain to touching things especially with the fingers. **3** small things done in producing a piece of work. **4** a small amount, a tinge or trace. **5** the manner of touching the keys or strings, of an instrument; the response of the keys etc. to this; a distinctive manner of workmanship or procedure. **6** a relationship of communication or knowledge. **7** the part of a football field beyond the side limits. **8** (*slang*) an act of obtaining money from a person; a person from whom money may be obtained. —**finishing touch(es),** the final details completing and enhancing a piece of work etc. **touch-and-go** *adj.* uncertain as regards the result, risky. **touch at,** (of a ship) to call at (a port etc.) **touch bottom,** to reach the bottom of the water with the feet; to reach the lowest or worst point. **touch down,** (of an aircraft) to reach the ground in landing. **touch-judge** *n.* a linesman in Rugby football. **touch-line** *n.* the side limit of a football field. **touch off,** to explode by touching with a match etc.; to initiate (a process) suddenly. **touch on** *or* **upon,** to refer to or mention briefly or casually; to verge on. **touch-paper** *n.* a paper impregnated with nitre to burn slowly and ignite a firework etc. **touch-type** *v.t./i.* to use a typewriter without looking at the keys. **touch**

up, to correct or improve with minor additions. **touch wood,** to put the hand on something wooden in the superstitious belief of averting bad luck (also used as a phrase implying such action). [f. OF *tochier* (prob. imit.)]

touchdown *n.* the act of touching down by an aircraft.

touché /ˈtuːʃeɪ/ *int.* acknowledging a hit by a fencing-opponent or a justified retort by another in a discussion. [F, = touched (as TOUCH)]

touching /ˈtʌtʃɪŋ/ *adj.* raising sympathy or tender feelings. —*prep.* concerning. —**touchingly** *adv.* [f. TOUCH]

touchstone *n.* **1** dark schist or jasper for testing alloys by the marks they make on it. **2** a criterion.

touchwood *n.* readily inflammable rotten wood or similar substance.

touchy /ˈtʌtʃɪ/ *adj.* apt to take offence, over-sensitive. —**touchily** *adv.*, **touchiness** *n.* [f. TOUCH]

tough /tʌf/ *adj.* **1** difficult to break, cut, tear, or chew. **2** able to endure hardship; not easily hurt, damaged, or injured. **3** unyielding, stubborn; resolute; (*colloq.*) acting sternly or viciously. **4** (*colloq.*, of luck etc.) hard. **5** (*US slang*) vicious, rough and violent. **6** (of clay etc.) stiff, tenacious. —*n.* a tough person, especially a ruffian. —**toughly** *adv.*, **toughness** *n.* [OE]

toughen /ˈtʌf(ə)n/ *v.t./i.* to make or become tough or tougher. [f. TOUGH]

toupee /ˈtuːpeɪ/ *n.* a wig; an artifical patch of hair worn to cover a bald part of the head. [f. *toupet* hair-tuft (as TOP¹)]

tour /tʊə(r)/ *n.* **1** a journey through a country, town, or building etc. visiting various places or things of interest or giving performances. **2** a spell of duty on military or diplomatic service. —*v.t./i.* to make a tour (of). —**on tour,** touring. [f. OF f. L f. Gk *tornos* lathe (cf. TURN)]

tour de force /tʊə də ˈfɔːs/ a great feat of strength or skill. [F]

tourism /ˈtʊərɪz(ə)m/ *n.* **1** visiting places as a tourist. **2** the business of providing accommodation and services for tourists. [f. TOUR]

tourist /ˈtʊərɪst/ *n.* a person who is travelling or visiting a place for recreation. —**tourist class,** a class of passenger accommodation in a ship or aircraft etc. lower than first class. **tourist trap,** a place that exploits tourists. **Tourist Trophy,** motor-cycle races held annually on the Isle of Man. [f. TOUR]

touristy *adj.* (*derog.*) suitable for tourists; frequented by tourists. [f. prec.]

tourmaline /ˈtʊəməlɪn, -iːn/ *n.* a mineral with unusual electric properties and used as a gem. [F f. Sinhalese (it was orig. found in Sri Lanka)]

tournament /ˈtʊənəmənt/ *n.* **1** a contest of skill between a number of competitors, involving a series of matches. **2** a medieval spectacle in which two sides contended with usually blunted weapons. **3** a modern display of military exercises, contests, etc. [f. OF (as TOURNEY)]

tournedos /ˈtʊənədəʊ/ *n.* (*pl.* same) a small round thick slice of fillet for one person, cooked with a strip of fat round it. [F]

tourney /ˈtʊənɪ/ *n.* a tournament. —*v.i.* to take part in a tournament. [f. OF *tornei*, *torneier* (as TURN)]

tourniquet /ˈtʊənɪkeɪ/ *n.* a device or strip of material drawn tightly round a limb to stop the flow of blood through an artery by compression. [F, prob. f. OF *tournicle* coat of mail, infl. by *tourner* turn]

tousle /taʊz(ə)l/ *v.t.* to pull about roughly, to make (the hair or clothes) untidy. [f. dial. *touse*]

tout *v.t./i.* **1** to pester possible customers with requests for orders; to solicit the custom of (a person) or for (a thing). **2** to spy out the movements and condition of racehorses in training. —*n.* a person who touts; a tipster touting information about racehorses etc. [orig. = look out, = obs. or dial. *toot*]

tow¹ /təʊ/ *v.t.* to pull along behind, especially with a rope etc. —*n.* towing, being towed. —**in tow,** being towed; (*colloq.*) accompanying or under the charge of a person. **on tow,** being towed. **tow-bar** *n.* the bar by which a caravan is attached to the vehicle towing it. **tow-path** *or* **towing-path** *n.* a path beside a river or canal for use when a horse is towing a barge etc. [OE; cf. TUG]

tow² /təʊ/ *n.* fibres of flax or hemp prepared for spinning. —**tow-headed** *adj.* having a head of very light-coloured or tousled hair. [f. MLG *touw*]

towards /təˈwɔːdz/ *prep.* (also **toward**) **1** in the direction of. **2** as regards, in relation to. **3** for the purpose of achieving or promoting; as a contribution to. **4** near, approaching. [OE, = future (as TO¹, -WARD)]

towel /ˈtaʊəl/ *n.* an absorbent cloth or paper etc. for drying with after washing. —*v.t./i.* (**-ll-**) to wipe or dry with a towel. —**throw in the towel,** to admit defeat. [f. OF *toail(l)e*]

towelling *n.* material for towels. [f. prec.]

tower *n.* **1** a tall usually square or circular structure, either standing alone (e.g. as a fort) or forming part of a castle, church, or other large building; a similar structure housing machinery etc. **2** a tower block. —*v.i.* to be of great height; to be taller or more eminent than others. —**the Tower,** the Tower of London. **tower block,** a very tall building containing flats or offices. **tower of strength,** a person who gives strong and reliable support. [OE f. L *turris*]

towering *adj.* **1** high, lofty. **2** (of rage etc.) violent. [f. prec.]

town *n.* **1** a collection of dwellings and other buildings, larger than a village, especially one not created a city; its inhabitants. **2** a town or city as distinct from country. **3** the central business and shopping area of a neighbourhood. **4** London. —**go to town,** to act or work with energy and enthusiasm. **on the town,** (*colloq.*) on a spree in town. **town clerk,** an officer of a town corporation, in charge of records etc. **town crier,** a person making official announcements in public places. **town gas,** manufactured inflammable gas for domestic use. **town hall,** a building for a town's official business, often with a hall that may be used for public events. **town house,** a residence in town as distinct from the country; a terrace house or a house in a compact group in a town. **town planning,** planning for the regulated growth and improvement of towns. [OE *tūn* enclosure]

townee /taʊˈniː/ *n.* (also **townie** /ˈtaʊnɪ/) (*derog.*) an inhabitant of a town. [f. TOWN]

townscape *n.* **1** a picture of a town. **2** the visual appearance of a town or towns. [f. TOWN, after *landscape*]

townsfolk *n.* the inhabitants of a town or towns.

township *n.* (formerly in the UK) a small town or village that formed part of a large parish. **2** (*US* & *Canada*) an administrative division of a county, or a district six miles square. **3** (in some other countries) a small town or settlement; (in South Africa) an area set aside for non-White occupation. [f. TOWN + -SHIP]

townsman *n.* (*pl.* **-men**) an inhabitant of a town. —**townswoman** *n.fem.* (*pl.* **-women**)

townspeople *n.pl.* the inhabitants of a town.

toxaemia /tɒkˈsiːmɪə/ *n.* **1** blood-poisoning. **2** the condition of abnormally high blood-pressure in pregnancy. —**toxaemic** *adj.* [as foll. + Gk *haima* blood]

toxic *adj.* of, caused by, or acting as a poison. —**toxicity** /tɒkˈsɪsɪtɪ/ *n.* [f. L f. Gk *toxikon pharmakon* poison for arrows (*toxa* arrows)]

toxicology /tɒksɪˈkɒlədʒɪ/ *n.* the study of poisons. —**toxicological** /-ˈlɒdʒɪk(ə)l/ *adj.*, **toxicologist** *n.* [f. TOXIC + -LOGY]

toxin /ˈtɒksɪn/ *n.* a poison, especially of animal or vegetable origin; a poison secreted by a micro-organism and causing a particular disease. [f. TOXIC]

toxophilite /tɒkˈsɒfɪlaɪt/ *n.* a student or lover of archery. —*adj.* of archery. —**toxophily** *n.* [f. Ascham's *Toxophilus* (1545) f. Gk *toxon* bow + -PHIL]

toy *n.* **1** a thing to play with, especially for a child. **2** a trinket or curiosity; a thing intended for amusement rather than for serious use. —*adj.* **1** that is a toy. **2** (of a dog) of a diminutive breed or variety, kept as a pet. —*v.i.* (with *with*) to handle or finger idly; to deal with or consider without great seriousness. [orig. unkn.]

trace[1] *n.* **1** a mark left behind, as the track of an animal, a footprint, or the line made by a moving pen. **2** a perceptible sign of what has existed or happened. **3** a very small quantity. —*v.t.* **1** to follow or discover by observing marks, tracks, pieces of evidence, etc. **2** to go along (a path etc.). **3** to mark out, to sketch the outline of; to form (letters etc.) laboriously. **4** to copy (a drawing etc.) by marking its lines on a piece of transparent paper placed over it. —**trace element,** a substance occurring or required (especially in soil) only in minute amounts. [f. OF *tracier* f. L *tractus* drawing (see TRACT)]

trace[2] *n.* each of the two side-straps, chains, or ropes by which a horse draws a vehicle. —**kick over the traces,** to become insubordinate or reckless. [f. OF *trais*, pl. of TRAIT]

traceable *adj.* that may be traced. [f. TRACE[1]]

tracer /ˈtreɪsə(r)/ *n.* **1** a bullet that when ignited by the propellant emits light or a trail of smoke etc. by which its course may be observed, enabling the gunner to correct his aim. **2** an artificial radioisotope whose course in the human body etc. can be followed by the radiation it produces. [f. TRACE[1]]

tracery /ˈtreɪsərɪ/ *n.* stone ornamental open-work especially in the head of a Gothic window; a decorative lacelike pattern suggesting this. [f. TRACE[1]]

trachea /trəˈkiːə, ˈtreɪkɪə/ *n.* the windpipe. [f. L f. Gk, = rough artery (*trakhus* rough)]

tracheotomy /treɪkɪˈɒtəmɪ, træk-/ *n.* surgical incision of the trachea. [f. prec. + Gk *-tomia* cutting]

trachoma /trəˈkəʊmə/ *n.* a contagious disease of the eye with inflamed granulation on the inner surface of the eyelids. [f. Gk (*trakhus*) rough)]

tracing /ˈtreɪsɪŋ/ *n.* a traced copy of a map or drawing etc.; the process of making this. —**tracing paper,** transparent paper for making tracings. [f. TRACE[1]]

track *n.* **1** a mark or series of marks left by a person, or animal, or vehicle etc. in passing along. **2** a path or rough road, especially one established by use. **3** the course taken. **4** a course, action, or procedure. **5** a prepared course for racing etc. **6** a continuous line of railway. **7** a continuous band round the wheels of a tank or tractor etc. **8** a sound-track; a groove on a gramophone record; a particular recorded section of a gramophone record or magnetic tape. —*v.t./i.* **1** to follow the track or course of; to find or observe by doing this. **2** (of wheels) to run so that the hinder wheel is exactly in the first wheel's track. **3** (of a stylus) to follow a groove. **4** (of a cine-camera) to move along a set path while taking a picture. —**in one's tracks,** (*colloq.*) where one stands, then and there. **keep** (*or* **lose**) **track of,** to follow (or fail to follow) the course or development of. **make tracks,** (*slang*) to go away. **make tracks for,** (*slang*) to go in pursuit of or towards. **off the track,** away from the subject in hand. **track down,** to reach or capture by tracking. **track event,** (in athletics) an event taking place on a track, e.g. running. **track record,** a person's past achievements. **track suit,** a suit worn by athletes etc. while training or before or after competing. [f. OF *trac*, perh. f. L Du. *tre(c)k* draught etc.]

tracker *n.* a person or thing that tracks. —**tracker dog,** a police dog tracing by scent. [f. TRACK]

tracklement /ˈtræk(ə)lmənt/ *n.* an article of food, especially a jelly, for eating with meat. [orig. unkn.]

tract[1] *n.* **1** a region or area of indefinite (usually large) extent. **2** a system of connected parts in an animal body, along which something passes. [f. L *tractus* (*trahere* draw, pull)]

tract[2] *n.* an essay or pamphlet, especially on a religious subject. [app. abbr. of L *tractatus* treatise (as foll.)]

tractable /ˈtræktəb(ə)l/ *adj.* easy to manage or deal with; docile. —**tractability** /-ˈbɪlɪtɪ/ *n.* [f. L (*tractare* handle)]

Tractarian /trækˈteərɪən/ *n.* an adherent or promoter of Tractarianism. —**Tractarianism** *n.* a name for the earlier stages of the Oxford Movement, derived from the *Tracts for the Times*, the series of ninety pamphlets issued under its aegis. [f. TRACT]

traction /ˈtrækʃ(ə)n/ *n.* **1** pulling or drawing a load along a surface. **2** a therapeutic sustained pull on a limb etc. —**traction-engine** *n.* a steam or diesel engine for drawing a heavy load on a road or across fields etc. [F or f. L (as TRACT[1])

tractor /ˈtræktə(r)/ *n.* **1** a powerful motor vehicle for pulling farm machinery or other heavy equipment. **2** a traction-engine. [as prec.]

trad *adj.* (*colloq.*) traditional. —*n.* (*colloq.*) traditional jazz. [abbr.]

trade *n.* **1** the exchange of goods for money or other goods. **2** business done with a specified class or at a specified time. **3** business carried on for earnings or profit (especially as distinct from a profession); a skilled handicraft. **4** the persons engaged in a particular trade. **5** (usu. in *pl.*) a trade wind. —*v.t./i.* **1** to engage in trade, to buy and sell. **2** to exchange (goods) in trade; to have a transaction (*with* a person). —**trade in,** to give (a used article) in part payment for another. **trade-in** *n.* an article given in this way. **trade mark,** a device or word(s) legally registered or established by use to distinguish the goods of a particular manufacturer etc. **trade name,** a name by which a thing is known in the trade, or given by a manufacturer to a proprietary article, or under which a business is carried on. **trade off,** to exchange as a compromise. **trade-off** *n.* a thing given in this way. **trade on** *or* **upon,** to make great use of for one's own advantage. **trade secret,** a technique used in a trade and giving an advantage because it is not generally known.**Trades Union Congress,** the official representative body of British trade unions. **trade union** (also **trades union**) an organized association of workers in a trade or group of allied trades or a profession, formed for protection and promotion of their common interests. —**trade-unionism** *n.* this style of association. **trade-unionist** *n.* an advocate of trade-unionism; a member of a trade union. **trade wind** a constant wind blowing towards the equator from the north-east or south-east. [f. MLG, = track (as TREAD)]

trader /ˈtreɪdə(r)/ *n.* a person or ship engaged in trade. [f. TRADE]

tradescantia /trædɪˈskæntɪə/ *n.* a perennial plant of the genus *Tradescantia* with large blue, white, or pink flowers. [f. J. *Tradescant*, English naturalist (d. 1638)]

tradesman *n.* (*pl.* **-men**) a person engaged in trade, especially a shopkeeper.

trading /ˈtreɪdɪŋ/ *n.* engaging in trade, buying and selling. —**trading estate,** an area designed to be occupied by industrial and commercial firms. **trading stamp,** a stamp given by a tradesman to a customer and exchangeable in quantity for various articles or for cash. [f. TRADE]

tradition /trəˈdɪʃ(ə)n/ *n.* an opinion, belief, or custom handed down from one generation to another, especially orally; this process of handing down; an artistic or literary principle based on usage or experience. [f. OF or L (*tradere* hand on)]

traditional *adj.* of, based on, or obtained by tradition; (of jazz) based on an early style. —**traditionally** *adv.* [f. prec.]

traditionalism *n.* great or excessive respect for tradition. —**traditionalist** *n.* [f. F or prec.]

traduce /trəˈdjuːs/ *v.t.* to misrepresent in an

unfavourable way, to slander. —**traducement** *n.* [f. L, = disgrace (as TRANS-, *ducere* lead)]

traffic /'træfɪk/ *n.* **1** vehicles, ships, or aircraft moving along a route. **2** trade, especially in illicit goods. **3** the number of persons or amount of goods conveyed. **4** the use of a service, the amount of this. **5** dealings between persons etc. —*v.t./i.* (**-ck-**) to trade; to deal in. —**traffic island,** a paved etc. area in a road to direct the traffic and provide a refuge for pedestrians. **traffic-light** *n.* a signal controlling road traffic by coloured lights (see below). **traffic warden,** a person employed to assist the police in controlling the movement and parking of road vehicles. —**trafficker** *n.* [f. F or Sp. f. It.]

tragacanth /'trægəkænθ/ *n.* a white or reddish gum from plants of the genus *Astragalus*, used in pharmacy etc. [f. F f. L f. Gk *tragacantha*, name of shrub (*tragos* goat, *acantha* thorn)]

tragedian /trə'dʒi:dɪən/ *n.* **1** a writer of tragedies. **2** an actor in tragedy. [as TRAGEDY]

tragedienne /trədʒi:dɪ'en/ *n.* an actress in tragedy. [F (as prec.)]

tragedy /'trædʒɪdɪ/ *n.* **1** a serious drama with unhappy events or a sad ending. **2** the branch of drama consisting of such plays. **3** a sad event; a serious accident; a calamity. [f. OF f. L f. Gk *tragōidia*, app. = goat-song (*tragos* goat, *ōidē* song).]

tragic /'trædʒɪk/ *adj.* **1** of or in the style of tragedy. **2** sorrowful. **3** causing great sadness; calamitous. [f. F f. L f. Gk (*tragos* goat)]

tragical /'trædʒɪk(ə)l/ *adj.* **1** sorrowful. **2** causing great sadness. —**tragically** *adv.* [as prec.]

tragicomedy /trædʒɪ'kɒmɪdɪ/ *n.* a drama of mixed tragic and comic events. —**tragicomic** *adj.*, **tragicomically** *adv.* [f. F or It. f. L (as TRAGIC, COMEDY)]

trail *v.t./i.* **1** to drag or be dragged along behind, especially on the ground. **2** to move wearily; to lag or straggle. **3** to hang or float loosely; (of a plant) to hang or spread downwards. **4** to be losing in a contest; to be losing to (a specified team etc.). **5** to diminish, to become fainter. **6** to follow the trail of, to track. —*n.* **1** a mark left where something has passed; a track or scent followed in hunting. **2** a beaten path, especially through a wild region. **3** a thing that trails or hangs trailing. **4** a line of people or things following behind something. —**trailing edge,** the rear edge of a moving body. [f. OF or MLG f. L *tragula* drag-net]

trailer *n.* **1** a truck etc. drawn by a vehicle and used to carry a load. **2** a set of short extracts from a film, shown in advance to advertise it. **3** a person or thing that trails. **4** (*US*) a caravan. [f. TRAIL]

train *n.* **1** a series of railway carriages or trucks drawn by a locomotive. **2** a succession or series of persons or things; a set of parts in machinery, actuating one another in a series. **3** a body of followers, a retinue. **4** a thing drawn along behind or forming the hinder part, especially the elongated part of a long dress or robe that trails on the ground behind the wearer. **5** a line of combustible material placed to lead fire to an explosive. —*v.t./i.* **1** to bring to a desired standard of performance or behaviour by instruction and practice; to undergo such a process; to teach and accustom (a person or animal) to do something. **2** to bring or come to physical efficiency by exercise and diet. **3** to cause (a plant) to grow in the required direction. **4** to aim (a gun or camera etc.). —**in train,** in preparation; arranged. **train-bearer** *n.* an attendant holding up the train of a person's robe. **train-spotter** *n.* a collector of the identification-numbers of railway engines seen. [f. OF ult. f. L *trahere* draw]

trainable *adj.* that may be trained. [f. TRAIN]

trainee /treɪ'ni:/ *n.* a person being trained, especially for an occupation. [f. TRAIN]

trainer *n.* **1** a person who trains horses or athletes etc. **2** an aircraft or device simulating it to train pilots. **3** a training shoe. [f. TRAIN]

training *n.* the process by which one is trained for a sport or contest or for an occupation. —**training shoe,** a soft running-shoe without spikes. [f. TRAIN]

traipse *v.i.* (*colloq.*) to trudge; to go about on errands etc. [orig. unkn.]

trait /treɪ/ *n.* a distinguishing feature in a character, appearance, habit, or portrayal. [F, f. L *tractus* (as TRACT[1])]

traitor /'treɪtə(r)/ *n.* a person who behaves disloyally; one who betrays his country. —**traitorous** *adj.*, **traitress** *n.fem.* [f. OF f. L *traditor* (as TRADITION)]

trajectory /'trædʒɪktərɪ, trə'dʒek-/ *n.* the path of a body (e.g. a comet or bullet) moving under given forces. [f. L (*traicere* throw across, TRANS-, *jacere* throw)]

tram *n.* **1** (also **tramcar**) a passenger vehicle running on rails laid in a public road. **2** a four-wheeled truck used in coal-mines. [f. MLG & MDu. *trame* beam]

tramlines *n.pl.* **1** the rails for a tram. **2** (*colloq.*) the pair of parallel lines at the edge of a tennis or badminton court.

trammel /'træm(ə)l/ *n.* **1** a kind of drag-net in which a fine net is hung loosely between vertical walls of coarser net, so that fish passing through carry some of the fine net through the coarser and are trapped in the pocket thus formed. **2** (usu. in *pl.*) things that hamper one's activities. —*v.t.* (**-ll-**) to hamper.

[f. OF f. L *tramaculum*, perh. as TRI- + *macula* mail]

tramp *v.t./i.* **1** to walk with a firm heavy tread; to walk laboriously; to travel on foot across (an area or distance) thus. **2** to trample. **3** to live as a tramp. —*n.* **1** a person who goes from place to place as a vagrant. **2** the sound of heavy footsteps. **3** a long walk. **4** (*slang*) a dissolute woman. **5** a freight-vessel, especially a steamer, that does not travel on a regular route. [prob. f. Gmc]

trample *v.t./i.* to tread repeatedly with heavy or crushing steps; to crush or harm thus. [f. prec.]

trampoline /ˈtræmpəliːn/ *n.* a stretched canvas sheet connected by springs to a horizontal frame, used for jumping on in acrobatic leaps. —*v.i.* to use a trampoline. [f. It. *trampolino* (*trampoli* stilts)]

tramway *n.* the rails for a tram.

trance /trɑːns/ *n.* a sleeplike state without response to stimuli; a hypnotic or cataleptic state; mental abstraction from external things, rapture, ecstasy. [f. OF *transe* (*transir* depart f. L, as TRANSIT)]

tranche /trɑːnʃ/ *n.* a portion, especially of income or of a block of shares. [F, = slice (as TRENCH)]

tranny /ˈtrænɪ/ *n.* (*slang*) a transistor radio. [abbr.]

tranquil /ˈtræŋkwɪl/ *adj.* calm and undisturbed, not agitated. —**tranquillity** /-ˈkwɪlɪtɪ/ *n.*, **tranquilly** *adv.* [f. F or L *tranquillus*]

tranquillize /ˈtræŋkwɪlaɪz/ *v.t.* to make tranquil, to calm, especially by a drug. [f. prec.]

tranquillizer *n.* a drug used to diminish anxiety and induce calmness. [f. prec.]

trans- /trænz-, trɑːnz-/ *prefix* across, through, beyond; to or on the farther side of. [f. L *trans* across]

transact /trænˈzækt, trɑː-/ *v.t.* to perform or carry out (business). —**transactor** *n.* [f. L (as TRANS-, ACT)]

transaction /trænˈzækʃ(ə)n, trɑː-/ *n.* **1** transacting. **2** business transacted. **3** (in *pl.*) the reports of discussions and lectures at the meetings of a learned society. [as prec.]

transalpine /trænzˈælpaɪn, trɑː-/ *adj.* on the north side of the Alps. [f. L (as TRANS-, ALPINE)]

transatlantic /trænsətˈlæntɪk, trɑː-/ *adj.* **1** crossing the Atlantic. **2** on or from the other side of the Atlantic; American; (*US*) European.

transceiver /trænˈsiːvə(r), trɑː-/ *n.* a combined radio transmitter and receiver. [f. TRANSMITTER + RECEIVER]

transcend /trænˈsend, trɑː-/ *v.t.* **1** to go or be beyond the range or grasp of (human experience, belief, description, etc.). **2** to surpass. [f. OF or L *transcendere* (TRANS-, *scandere* climb)]

transcendent *adj.* **1** transcending human experience. **2** of supreme merit or quality, surpassing. **3** (of God) existing apart from, or not subject to the limitations of, the material universe. —**transcendence** *n.*, **transcendency** *n.*, **transcendently** *adv.* [as prec.]

transcendental /trænsenˈdent(ə)l, trɑː-/ *adj.* **1** not based on experience, intuitively accepted, innate in the mind. **2** consisting of, dealing in, or inspired by abstraction, visionary. —**Transcendental Meditation**, a technique of meditation and relaxation based on yoga. —**transcendentally** *adv.* [f. L (as prec.)]

transcendentalism *n.* a philosophy or belief taking account of transcendental things. —**transcendentalist** *n.* [f. prec.]

transcontinental /trænzkɒntɪˈnent(ə)l, trɑː-/ *adj.* extending or travelling across a continent.

transcribe /trænˈskraɪb, trɑː-/ *v.t.* **1** to copy in writing. **2** to write out (shorthand etc.) in ordinary characters. **3** (*Mus.*) to adapt (a composition) for a voice or instrument other than that for which it was originally written. —**transcriber** *n.* [f. L *transcribere* (TRANS-, *scribere* write)]

transcript /ˈtrænskrɪpt, ˈtrɑː-/ *n.* a written copy. [f. OF f. L (as prec.)]

transcription /trænˈskrɪpʃ(ə)n, trɑː-/ *n.* **1** transcribing, the written representation of sounds. **2** a transcript; something transcribed. [F or f. L (as TRANSCRIBE)]

transducer /trænzˈdjuːsə(r), trɑː-/ *n.* any device which produces an output signal (e.g. a voltage) in response to a different sort of input signal (e.g. pressure). [f. L *transducere* lead across (TRANS-, *ducere* lead)]

transept /ˈtrænsept, ˈtrɑː-/ *n.* the part of a cruciform church at right angles to the nave; either arm of this. [as TRANS- + SEPTUM]

transfer /trænsˈfɜː(r), trɑː-/ *v.t./i.* (**-rr-**) **1** to convey, move, or hand over from one person, group, or place to another; to make over possession of (property or rights etc.). **2** to convey (a design etc.) from one surface to another. **3** to change or be moved to another group or occupation. **4** to go from one station or route or conveyance to another in order to continue a journey. **5** to change (a meaning) by extension or metaphor. —/ˈtrænsfɜː(r), ˈtrɑː-/ *n.* **1** transferring, being transferred. **2** a document effecting the conveyance of property or a right. **3** a design or picture that is or can be conveyed from one surface to another. —**transference** /ˈtræ-, ˈtrɑː-/ *n.* [f. F or L *transferre* (TRANS-, *ferre* bear)]

transferable /træns'fɜ:rəb(ə)l, trɑ:-/ *adj.* that may be transferred. [f. prec.]

transfiguration /trænsfɪgə'reɪʃ(ə)n, trɑ:-/ *n.* transfiguring, being transfigured; **Transfiguration,** that of Christ (Matt. 17: 2), celebrated on 6 Aug. [as foll.]

transfigure /træns'fɪgə(r), trɑ:-/ *v.t.* to change the appearance of, especially to something nobler or more beautiful. [f. OF or L (as TRANS-, FIGURE)]

transfinite /træns'faɪnaɪt/ *adj.* beyond or surpassing what is finite; (*Math.*, of a number) exceeding all finite numbers.

transfix /træns'fɪks, trɑ:-/ *v.t.* **1** to pierce with or impale on something sharp-pointed. **2** to make motionless with fear or astonishment etc. [f. L (as TRANS-, FIX)]

transform /træns'fɔ:m, trɑ:-/ *v.t.* **1** to make a considerable change in the form, appearance, or character of. **2** to change the voltage of (an electric current). —**transformation** /-fə'meɪʃ(ə)n/ *n.*, **transformational** /-fə'meɪʃən(ə)l/ *adj.* [f. OF or L (as TRANS-, FORM)]

transformer *n.* an apparatus for reducing or increasing the voltage of an alternating current. [f. prec.]

transfuse /træns'fju:z, trɑ:-/ *v.t.* **1** to cause (a fluid, colour, influence, etc.) to permeate; to imbue thus. **2** to inject (blood or other liquid) into a blood-vessel to replace that lost. —**transfusion** /-'fju:ʒ(ə)n/ *n.* [f. L *transfundere* (TRANS-, *fundere* pour)]

transgress /træns'gres, trɑ:-/ *v.t./i.* **1** to break (a rule or law etc.); to go beyond (a limitation). **2** to sin. —**transgression** *n.*, **transgressor** *n.* [f. F or L *transgredi* (TRANS-, *gradi* step, go)]

transient /'trænsɪənt, 'trɑ:-/ *adj.* quickly passing away, fleeting. —**transience** *n.* [f. L *transire* (as TRANSIT)]

transistor /træn'sɪstə(r), trɑ:-/ *n.* **1** a semiconductor device, usually having three terminals and two junctions, in which the load current can be made to be proportional to a small input current, so that it is functionally equivalent to a valve but is much smaller and more robust, operates at lower voltages, and consumes less power and produces less heat. **2** (in full **transistor radio**) a portable radio set equipped with transistors. [f. TRANSFER + RESISTOR]

transistorize *v.t.* to equip with transistors (rather than valves). [f. prec.]

transit /'trænsɪt, 'trɑ:-/ *n.* **1** the process of going, conveying, or being conveyed across, over, or through. **2** a passage or route. **3** the apparent passage of a heavenly body across the disc of another or across the meridian of a place. —**transit camp,** a camp for the temporary accommodation of soldiers, refugees, etc. [f. L *transitus* (*transire* go across)]

transition /træn'sɪʃ(ə)n, trɑ:-/ *n.* **1** the process of changing from one state or subject etc. to another. **2** a period during which one style of art develops into another, especially of architecture between Norman and Early English. —**transitional** *adj.*, **transitionally** *adv.* [F or f. L (as prec.)]

transitive /'trænsɪtɪv, 'trɑ:-/ *adj.* (of a verb) taking a direct object expressed or understood. —**transitively** *adv.* [as TRANSIT]

transitory /'trænsɪtərɪ, 'trɑ:-/ *adj.* existing for a time but not long-lasting, merely temporary. —**transitorily** *adv.*, **transitoriness** *n.* [f. AF f. L (as TRANSIT)]

translate /træns'leɪt, trɑ:-/ *v.t.* **1** to express the sense of (a word or text etc.) in another language, in plainer words, or in another form of representation. **2** to infer or declare the significance of, to interpret. **3** to move from one person, place, or condition to another; to remove (a bishop) to another see; to move (a saint's relics etc.) to another place; (in the Bible) to convey to heaven without death. —**translation** *n.*, **translator** *n.* [f. L *translatus* p.p. of *transferre* (see TRANSFER)]

transliterate /træns'lɪtəreɪt, trɑ:-/ *v.t.* to represent (a letter or word) in the corresponding character(s) of another alphabet or language. —**transliteration** *n.*, **transliterator** *n.* [f. TRANS- + L *littera* letter]

translucent /træns'lu:sənt, trɑ:-/ *adj.* allowing light to pass through, especially without being transparent. —**translucence** *n.*, **translucency** *n.* [f. L *translucēre* (TRANS-, *lucēre* shine)]

transmigrate /trænsmaɪ'greɪt, trɑ:-/ *v.i.* **1** (of a soul) to pass into a different body. **2** to migrate. —**transmigration** *n.* [f. L (as TRANS-, MIGRATE)]

transmissible /træns'mɪsɪb(ə)l, trɑ:-/ *adj.* transmittable. [as TRANSMIT]

transmission /træns'mɪʃ(ə)n, trɑ:-/ *n.* **1** transmitting, being transmitted. **2** a broadcast programme. **3** the gear transmitting power from the engine to the axle in a motor vehicle. [f. L (as TRANS-, MISSION)]

transmit /træns'mɪt, trɑ:-/ *v.t.* (**-tt-**) **1** to send or pass on from one person, place, or thing to another. **2** to allow to pass through or along, to be a medium for. **3** to send out (a message, signal, or programme etc.) by telegraph wire or radio waves. [f. L *transmittere* (TRANS-, *mittere* send)]

transmittable /træns'mɪtəb(ə)l/ *adj.* that may be transmitted. [f. prec.]

transmitter *n.* **1** the equipment used to transmit a message, signal, etc. **2** a person or thing that transmits. [f. TRANSMIT]

transmogrify /træns'mɒgrɪfaɪ, trɑ:-/ *v.t.* to

transform, especially in a magical or surprising manner. —**transmogrification** /-fɪˈkeɪʃ(ə)n/ *n.* [orig. unkn.]

transmutation /trænsmjuːˈteɪʃ(ə)n, trɑː-/ *n.* transmuting, being transmuted. —**transmutation of metals,** the turning of other metals into gold as the alchemists' aim. [f. OF or L (as foll.)]

transmute /trænsˈmjuːt, trɑː-/ *v.t.* to change the form, nature, or substance of, to convert into a different thing. [f. L *transmutare* (TRANS-, *mutare* change)]

transoceanic /trænsəʊʃɪˈænɪk, trɑː-/ *adj.* 1 crossing the ocean. 2 on or from the other side of the ocean.

transom /ˈtrænsəm/ *n.* a cross-beam, especially a horizontal bar of wood or stone above a door or above or in a window; a window above this. [f. OF *traversin* (as TRAVERSE)]

transparency /trænsˈpærənsɪ, trɑː-/ *n.* 1 being transparent. 2 a picture (especially a photographic slide) to be viewed by light passing through it. [f. L (as foll.)]

transparent /trænsˈpærənt, trɑː-/ *adj.* 1 transmitting rays of light without diffusion so that bodies behind can be distinctly seen (cf. *translucent*). 2 (of a disguise or pretext etc.) easily seen through. 3 clear and unmistakable; easily understood; free from affectation or disguise. —**transparently** *adv.* [f. OF f. L *transparēre* shine through (TRANS-, *parēre* appear)]

transpire /trænsˈpaɪə(r), trɑː-/ *v.t./i.* 1 (of a secret or fact etc.) to become known. 2 (D) to happen. 3 to emit (vapour or moisture) through leaves or the pores of the skin etc.; to be emitted thus. —**transpiration** /-pɪˈreɪʃ(ə)n/ *n.* [f. F or L *transpirare* (TRANS-, *spirare* breathe)]

transplant /trænsˈplɑːnt, trɑː-/ *v.t.* 1 to uproot and replant or establish elsewhere (often *fig.*). 2 to transfer (living tissue or an organ) and implant in another part of the body or in another (human or animal) body. —/ˈtræ-, ˈtrɑː-/ *n.* transplanting of tissue or an organ; a thing transplanted. —**transplantation** /-plɑːnˈteɪʃ(ə)n/ *n.* [f. L *transplantare* (as TRANS-, PLANT)]

transport /trænsˈpɔːt, trɑː-/ *v.t.* 1 to take (a person or goods etc.) from one place to another. 2 (*hist.*) to deport (a criminal) to a penal colony. 3 (esp. in *p.p.*) to affect with strong emotion. —/ˈtræ-, trɑː-/ *n.* 1 transporting. 2 means of conveyance; a ship or aircraft employed to carry soldiers, stores, etc. 3 vehement emotion. —**transport café,** a café catering chiefly for long-distance lorry drivers. —**transportation** /-ˈteɪʃ(ə)n/ *n.* [f. OF or L *transportare* (TRANS-, *portare* carry)]

transportable /trænsˈpɔːtəb(ə)l, trɑː-/ *adj.* that may be transported. [f. prec.]

transporter /trænsˈpɔːtə(r), trɑː-/ *n.* a vehicle used to transport other vehicles, heavy machinery, etc. —**transporter bridge,** a bridge carrying vehicles across water on a suspended platform. [f. TRANSPORT]

transpose /trænsˈpəʊz, trɑː-/ *v.t.* 1 to cause (two or more things) to change places; to change the position of (a thing) in a series; to change the natural or existing order or position of (a word or words) in a sentence. 2 to put (music) into a different key. —**transposition** /-pəˈzɪʃ(ə)n/ *n.* [f. OF (as TRANS-, POSE)]

transsexual /trænzˈseksjʊəl, trɑː-/ *adj.* having the physical characteristics of one sex and the psychological characteristics of the other. —*n.* a transsexual person. —**transsexualism** *n.*

trans-ship /trænsˈʃɪp, trɑː-/ *v.t.* (-pp-) to transfer from one ship or conveyance to another. —**trans-shipment** *n.*

transubstantiation /trænsəbstænʃɪˈeɪʃ(ə)n/ *n.* the Roman Catholic doctrine that in the Eucharist the whole substance of the bread and wine, after consecration, is converted into the body and blood of Christ, only the 'accidents' (i.e. appearances) of bread and wine remaining. (Cf. CONSUBSTANTIATION.) [f. L *transubstantiare* (as TRANS-, SUBSTANCE)]

transuranic /trænsjʊˈrænɪk, ˈtrɑː-/ *adj.* (of an element) having a higher atomic number than uranium.

transverse /ˈtrænzvɜːs, ˈtrɑː-, -ˈvɜːs/ *adj.* situated, arranged, or acting in a crosswise direction. —**transversely** *adv.* [f. L (TRANS-, *vertere* turn)]

transvestism /trænzˈvestɪz(ə)m, trɑː-/ *n.* clothing oneself in the garments of the opposite sex as a form of psychological abnormality. [f. TRANS- + L *vestire* clothe]

transvestite /trænzˈvestaɪt, trɑː-/ *n.* a person who indulges in transvestism. [as prec.]

trap[1] *n.* 1 a device, often baited, for catching and holding animals. 2 a trick betraying a person into speech or an act. 3 an arrangement to catch an unsuspecting person, e.g. a speeding motorist. 4 a device for effecting the sudden release e.g. of a greyhound in a race, of a ball to be struck at, of a clay pigeon to be shot at. 5 a curve in a drainpipe etc. serving when filled with liquid to seal it against the return of a gas. 6 a two-wheeled carriage. 7 a trapdoor. 8 (*slang*) the mouth. —*v.t.* (-pp-) 1 to catch in a trap to stop and retain (as) in a trap. 2 to furnish (a place) with traps. [OE]

trap[2] *n.* a kind of dark volcanic rock. [f. Sw. *trapp* (*trappa* stair, from its stairlike appearance)]

trapdoor *n.* a door in a floor, ceiling, or roof.

trapeze /trəˈpiːz/ *n.* a crossbar suspended by cords as a swing for acrobatics etc. [f. F f. L (as foll.)]

trapezium /trəˈpiːzɪəm/ *n.* (*pl.* **-ia** or **-iums**) **1** a quadrilateral with only one pair of sides parallel. **2** (*US*) a trapezoid. [L f. Gk *trapezion* (*trapeza* table)]

trapezoid /ˈtræpɪzɔɪd/ *n.* **1** a quadrilateral with no sides parallel (the term *quadrilateral* is preferred). **2** (*US*) a trapezium. —**trapezoidal** /-ˈzɔɪd(ə)l/ *adj.* [f. Gk (as prec.)]

trapper *n.* a person who traps wild animals, especially for furs. [f. TRAP[1]]

trappings /ˈtræpɪŋz/ *n.pl.* ornamental accessories; the harness of a horse, especially when ornamental. [f. obs. *trap* f. OF *drap* cloth (as DRAPE)]

Trappist /ˈtræpɪst/ *n.* a member of the branch of the Cistercian order founded in 1664 at La Trappe in Normandy, following an austere rule and noted (at least until recently) for abstinence from meat and for practice of perpetual silence. —**Trappistine** /-tɪn/ *n.* a member of an affiliated order of nuns. [f. F f. La *Trappe*]

traps *n.pl.* (*colloq.*) baggage, belongings. [perh. f. TRAPPINGS]

trash *n.* **1** worthless or waste stuff, rubbish. **2** a worthless person; worthless people. —**trash-can** *n.* a dustbin. —**trashy** *adj.* [orig. unkn.]

trattoria /trætəˈriːə/ *n.* an Italian eating-house. [It.]

trauma /ˈtrɔːmə/ *n.* (*pl.* **-as**) **1** an emotional shock producing a lasting effect. **2** a wound or injury; the condition caused by this. [Gk, = wound]

traumatic /trɔːˈmætɪk/ *adj.* **1** of or causing trauma. **2** (*colloq.*) very unpleasant. [f. L f. Gk (as prec.)]

travail /ˈtræveɪl/ *n.* **1** (*literary*) painful or laborious effort. **2** (*archaic*) the pains of childbirth. —*v.i.* **1** (*literary*) to make a painful or laborious effort. **2** (*archaic*) to suffer the pains of childbirth. [f. OF f. L *trepalium* instrument of torture]

travel /ˈtræv(ə)l/ *v.t./i.* (**-ll-**) **1** to go from one place or point to another; to make a journey, especially of some length or abroad. **2** to journey along or through (a country); to cover (a distance) in travelling. **3** (*colloq.*) to withstand a long journey. **4** to go from place to place as a salesman. **5** to move or proceed in a specified manner or at a specified rate. **6** (*colloq.*) to move quickly. **7** (of a machine part) to move. —*n.* **1** travelling, especially in foreign countries. **2** the range, rate, or mode of movement of a machine part. —**travel agency** (*or* **agent**), an agency (or agent) making arrangements for travellers. **travelling crane**, a crane able to move along an overhead support. [orig. = prec.]

travelled *adj.* experienced in travelling. [f. prec.]

traveller *n.* **1** a person who travels or is travelling. **2** a commercial traveller. **3** a gypsy. —**traveller's cheque**, a cheque for a fixed amount, encashable on a signature usually in many countries. **traveller's joy**, wild clematis (*Clematis vitalba*). **traveller's tale**, an incredible and probably untrue story. [f. TRAVEL]

travelogue /ˈtrævəlɒg/ *n.* a film or illustrated lecture with a narrative of travel. [f. TRAVEL, after *monologue* etc.]

traverse /trəˈvɜːs/ *v.t./i.* **1** to travel or lie across. **2** to consider or discuss the whole extent of (a subject). **3** to turn (a large gun) horizontally. —/ˈtrævəs/ *n.* **1** a sideways movement or course; traversing. **2** a thing that crosses another. —**traversal** /trəˈvɜːs(ə)l/ *n.* [f. OF f. L (as TRANSVERSE)]

travesty /ˈtrævɪstɪ/ *n.* a grotesque misrepresentation or imitation. —*v.t.* to make or be a travesty of. [f. F *travestir* change clothes of, f. It. (as TRANSVESTISM)]

trawl *n.* a large wide-mouthed fishing-net dragged by a boat along the bottom of the sea etc. —*v.t./i.* to catch with a trawl or seine; to catch by trawling. [prob. f. MDu. *tragelen* drag]

trawler *n.* a boat for use with a trawl. [f. TRAWL]

tray *n.* **1** a flat utensil, usually with a raised edge, on which small articles are placed for display or carrying. **2** a meal on a tray. **3** an open receptacle for holding a person's correspondence etc. in an office. **4** a tray-like (often removable) receptacle forming a compartment in a trunk, cabinet, or other container. [OE]

treacherous /ˈtretʃərəs/ *adj.* **1** guilty of or involving treachery. **2** (of the weather, ice, memory, etc.) not to be relied on, likely to fail or give way. —**treacherously** *adv.*, **treacherousness** *n.* [f. OF (*trechier*, *trichier* deceive, as TRICK)]

treachery /ˈtretʃərɪ/ *n.* violation of faith or trust, especially by secret desertion of the cause to which one professes allegiance. [as prec.]

treacle /ˈtriːk(ə)l/ *n.* the syrup produced in refining sugar; molasses. —**treacly** *adj.* [orig. = antidote for snake-bite, f. OF f. L *theriaca* f. Gk]

tread /tred/ *v.t./i.* (*past* **trod**; *p.p.* **trodden** or **trod**) **1** to set one's foot down; to walk or step; (of a foot) to be set down. **2** to walk on; to press or crush with the feet; to perform (steps etc.) by walking; to make (a path or hole etc.) by treading. **3** (of a male bird) to copulate with (a hen, or *absol.*). —*n.* **1** the manner or sound of walking. **2** the top surface of a step or stair. **3** the part of a wheel that touches the ground or rails; the part of a rail that the wheels touch; a thick moulded part of a vehicle tyre for gripping the road; a part of the sole of a boot etc. similarly moulded. —**tread the boards,** to be an actor. **tread on air,** to feel elated. **tread on a person's corns** *or* **toes,** to offend his feelings or encroach upon his privileges. **tread water,** to maintain an upright position in water by making treading movements with the feet and hands. [OE]

treadle /ˈtred(ə)l/ *n.* a lever worked by the foot and imparting motion to a machine. [OE (as prec.)]

treadmill *n.* **1** a wide mill-wheel turned by people treading on steps fixed along the length of its circumference, formerly worked by prisoners as a punishment. **2** a similar device used for exercise. **3** tiring monotonous routine work.

treason /ˈtri:z(ə)n/ *n.* violation by a subject of his allegiance to a sovereign or the State; a breach of faith, disloyalty. —**treasonous** *adj.* [f. AF *treisoun* f. L (as TRADITION)]

treasonable *adj.* involving or guilty of treason. —**treasonableness** *n.*, **treasonably** *adv.* [f. prec.]

treasure /ˈtreʒə(r)/ *n.* **1** precious metals or gems; a hoard of these, accumulated wealth. **2** a thing valued for its rarity, workmanship, associations, etc. **3** (*colloq.*) a beloved or highly valued person. —*v.t.* to store as valuable (*lit.*, or *fig.* in the memory); to value highly. —**treasure-hunt** *n.* a search for treasure; a game in which the players seek a hidden object. **treasure trove,** gold or silver coins, plate, or bullion found hidden and of unknown ownership; something very useful or desirable that a person finds. [f. OF f. L *thesaurus* f. Gk]

treasurer *n.* a person in charge of the funds of a society or municipality etc. [f. AF & OF (as prec.)]

treasury *n.* **1** a place where treasure is kept. **2** the funds or revenue of a State, or institution, or society. **3 Treasury,** the department managing the public revenue of a country; the offices and officers of this. —**Treasury bench,** the front bench in Parliament occupied by the Prime Minister, the Chancellor of the Exchequer, etc. **treasury bill,** a bill of exchange issued by a government to raise money for temporary needs. [as TREASURE]

treat *v.t./i.* **1** to act or behave towards (a person or thing) in a specified way. **2** to deal with or act upon (a person or thing) with a view to obtaining a particular result; to subject to a chemical or other process; to give medical or surgical treatment to. **3** to present or deal with (a subject). **4** to provide with food or entertainment at one's own expense. **5** to negotiate terms. —*n.* **1** a thing that gives pleasure, especially something unexpected or unusual; an entertainment designed to do this. **2** the treating of others to something at one's own expense. —**stand treat,** to bear the expense of an entertainment etc. [f. AF *treter* f. L *tractare* handle]

treatise /ˈtri:tɪs, -ɪz/ *n.* a written work dealing formally and systematically with a subject. [as prec.]

treatment *n.* **1** the process or manner of behaving towards or dealing with a person or thing. **2** something done to relieve or cure an illness or abnormality etc. [f. TREAT]

treaty /ˈtri:tɪ/ *n.* **1** a formally concluded and ratified agreement between States. **2** an agreement between persons, especially for the purchase of property. [f. AF f. L *tractatus* (as TREAT)]

treble /ˈtreb(ə)l/ *adj.* **1** threefold; triple; three times as much or many. **2** (of the voice) high-pitched; (*Mus.*) soprano (esp. of a boy or boy's voice; or of an instrument). —*n.* **1** a treble quantity or thing. **2** a hit at darts on the narrow ring between the two middle circles on the board, scoring treble. **3** a soprano, especially a boy or boy's voice; a high-pitched voice. —*v.t./i.* to multiply or be multiplied by three. —**trebly** *adv.* [f. OF f. L, = TRIPLE]

tree *n.* **1** a perennial plant with a single woody self-supporting stem (*trunk*) usually unbranched for some distance above the ground. **2** a Christmas tree. **3** a piece or frame of wood for various purposes. **4** a family tree. —*v.t.* to force (an animal, or (also *fig.*) a person) to take refuge up a tree. —**grow on trees,** to be plentifully available without effort. **tree-creeper** *n.* a small creeping bird of the family Certhiidae feeding on insects in the tree-bark. **tree-fern** *n.* a large fern with an upright woody stem. **tree-house** *n.* a structure in a tree for children to play in. **tree-ring** *n.* a ring in the cross-section of a tree, from one year's growth. **tree surgeon,** one who specializes in the care of trees. [OE]

trefoil /ˈtrefɔɪl, ˈtri:-/ *n.* **1** a kind of plant with leaves of three leaflets (clover, shamrock, etc.). **2** a three-lobed thing, especially an ornamentation in tracery. [f. AF f. L (TRI-, *folium* leaf)]

trek *v.i.* (**-kk-**) (orig. *S.Afr.*) **1** to travel arduously. **2** to migrate or journey with one's belongings in ox-wagons. —*n.* (orig. *S.Afr.*) **1** such a journey; each stage of it. **2** an organized migration of a body of persons. [f. S.Afr. Du. *trekken* draw, pull]

trellis /ˈtrelɪs/ *n.* a lattice or grating of light wooden or metal bars used especially as a support for fruit-trees or creepers and often fastened against a wall. [f. OF f. L *trilix* three-ply]

trematode /ˈtremətəʊd/ *n.* a parasitic flatworm of the class Trematoda. [f. Gk, = perforated (*trēma* hole)]

tremble *v.i.* to shake involuntarily with fear, excitement, weakness, etc.; to be in a state of apprehension; to move in a quivering manner. —*n.* trembling, a quiver. [f. OF f. L *tremulare* (as TREMULOUS)]

trembler *n.* an automatic vibrator for making and breaking an electric circuit. [f. prec.]

trembly *adj.* (*colloq.*) trembling. [f. TREMBLE]

tremendous /trɪˈmendəs/ *adj.* **1** immense. **2** (*colloq.*) remarkable, excellent. —**tremendously** *adv.*, **tremendousness** *n.* [f. L, = to be trembled at (as TREMOR)]

tremolo /ˈtreməlәʊ/ *n.* (*pl.* **-os**) a tremulous effect in playing music or in singing. [It. (as TREMULOUS)]

tremor /ˈtremə(r)/ *n.* **1** a slight shaking or trembling movement, a vibration; a slight earthquake. **2** a thrill of fear or other emotion. [f. OF & L (*tremere* tremble)]

tremulous /ˈtremjʊləs/ *adj.* **1** trembling from nervousness or weakness. **2** easily made to quiver. —**tremulously** *adv.* [f. L *tremulus* (as TREMOR)]

trench *n.* a long narrow usually deep ditch, especially one dug by troops to stand in and be sheltered from an enemy's fire. —*v.t.* to dig a trench or trenches in (the ground); to dig (soil or a garden) thus so as to bring the subsoil to the top. —**trench coat,** a belted coat or raincoat with pockets and flaps like those of a military uniform coat. [f. OF, = cut, f. L (as TRUNCATE)]

trenchant /ˈtrentʃənt/ *adj.* (of style or language etc.) incisive, strong and effective. —**trenchancy** *n.*, **trenchantly** *adv.* [as prec.]

trencher *n.* (*hist.*) a wooden platter for serving food. [f. AF *trenchour* (as TRENCH)]

trencherman *n.* (*pl.* **-men**) a person with regard to the amount he usually eats.

trend *n.* the general direction that something takes; a continuing tendency.—*v.i.* to have a specified trend. —**trend-setter** *n.* a person who leads the way in a fashion etc. [OE, = revolve]

trendy *adj.* (*colloq.*) up to date, following the latest trends of fashion. —*n.* (*colloq.*) a trendy person. —**trendily** *adv.*, **trendiness** *n.* [f. TREND]

trepan /trɪˈpæn/ *n.* a surgeon's cylindrical saw for removing part of the skull. —*v.t.* (**-nn-**) to perforate (a skull) with a trepan. [f. L f. Gk *trupanon* auger (*trupē* hole)]

trephine /trɪˈfiːn/ *n.* an improved form of trepan with a guiding centre-pin. —*v.t.* to operate on with this. [orig. *trafine*, f. L *tres fines* three ends, app. after TREPAN]

trepidation /trepɪˈdeɪʃ(ə)n/ *n.* a state of fear and anxiety, nervous agitation. [f. L (*trepidare* be agitated)]

trespass /ˈtrespəs/ *v.i.* **1** to enter a person's land or property unlawfully. **2** to intrude or make use of unreasonably. **3** (*archaic*) to sin, to do wrong. —*n.* **1** an act of trespassing. **2** a sin, wrongdoing. —**trespasser** *n.* [f. OF f. L (as TRANS-, PASS)]

tress *n.* a lock of human (especially female) hair; (in *pl.*) a head of such hair. [f. OF, perh. ult. f. Gk *trikha* threefold]

trestle /ˈtres(ə)l/ *n.* **1** each of a pair or set of supports on which a board is rested to form a table. **2** a trestle-work. —**trestle-table** *n.* a table consisting of a board or boards laid on trestles or other supports. **trestle-work** *n.* an open braced framework to support a bridge etc. [f. OF ult. f. L *transtrum* cross-beam]

trews /truːz/ *n.pl.* close-fitting usually tartan trousers. [f. Ir. or Gael.; cf. TROUSERS]

TRH *abbr.* Their Royal Highnesses.

tri- *in comb.* three, three times. [L & Gk (L *tres* & Gk *treis* three)]

triad /ˈtraɪæd, -əd/ *n.* **1** a group of three (especially notes in a chord). **2** the number three. **3** a Chinese secret usually criminal organization. —**triadic** /-ˈædɪk/ *adj.*, **triadically** *adv.* [f. F or L f. Gk (as TRI-)]

trial /ˈtraɪəl/ *n.* **1** a judicial examination and determination of issues between parties by a judge with or without a jury. **2** the process of testing qualities or performance by use and experience. **3** a sports match to test the ability of players who may be selected for an important team. **4** a test of individual ability on a motor cycle over rough ground or on a road. **5** a trying thing, experience, or person. —**on trial,** undergoing a trial; to be chosen or retained only if suitable. **trial and error,** the process of trying repeatedly and learning from one's errors until one succeeds. **trial run,** a preliminary testing of a vehicle or vessel etc. [AF (as TRY)]

triangle /ˈtraɪæŋg(ə)l/ *n.* **1** a plane figure with three sides and angles. **2** any three things not in a straight line, with the imaginary lines joining them. **3** an implement etc. of this shape; a musical instrument of a steel rod bent into a triangle sounded by striking with a small steel rod. **4** a situation etc. involving three persons. [f. OF or L (as TRI-, ANGLE[1])]

triangular /traɪˈæŋgjʊlə(r)/ *adj.* **1** triangle-shaped, three-cornered. **2** (of a contest or treaty etc.) between three persons or parties. **3** (of a pyramid) having a three-sided base. [f. L (as prec.)]

triangulate /traɪˈæŋgjʊleɪt/ *v.t.* to divide (an area) into triangles for surveying purposes. —**triangulation** /-ˈleɪʃ(ə)n/ *n.* [as prec.]

tribe *n.* **1** a group of families (especially in a primitive or nomadic culture) living as a community under one or more chiefs and usually claiming descent from a common ancestor; any similar natural or political division; any of the twelve divisions of the people of ancient Israel, each traditionally descended from one of the patriarchs. **2** (usu. *derog.*) a set or number of persons, especially of one profession etc. or family. —**tribal** *adj.*, **tribally** *adv.* [f. OF or L *tribus*]

tribesman *n.* (*pl.* **-men**) a member of a tribe or one's own tribe.

tribology /trɪˈbɒlədʒɪ, traɪ-/ *n.* the study of the friction, wear, lubrication, and design of bearings. [f. Gk *tribos* rubbing + -LOGY]

tribulation /trɪbjʊˈleɪʃ(ə)n/ *n.* great affliction. [f. OF f. L (*tribulare* oppress f. *tribulum* threshing-sledge)]

tribunal /traɪˈbju:n(ə)l, trɪ-/ *n.* **1** a board appointed to adjudicate in or to investigate some matter. **2** a seat or bench for a judge or judges. [F or f. L (as foll.)]

tribune[1] /ˈtrɪbju:n/ *n.* **1** a popular leader or demagogue. **2** (in ancient Rome) an official chosen by the people to protect their liberties; an officer commanding a legion for two-month periods. —**tribunate** *n.* [f. L *tribunus* (prob. as TRIBE)]

tribune[2] /ˈtrɪbju:n/ *n.* **1** a bishop's throne in a basilica; an apse containing this. **2** a dais, a rostrum. [F f. It. f. L (as TRIBUNAL)]

tributary /ˈtrɪbjʊtərɪ/ *n.* **1** a river or stream flowing into a larger river or lake. **2** a person or State paying or subject to tribute. —*adj.* **1** that is a tributary. **2** contributory. [as foll.]

tribute /ˈtrɪbju:t/ *n.* **1** a thing said, done, or given as a mark of respect or affection etc. **2** a payment formerly made periodically by one State or ruler to another as a sign of dependence. [f. L *tributum* (*tribuere* assign, orig. divide between tribes)]

trice *n.* **in a trice,** in an instant. [f. *trice* haul up, f. MDu. & MLG]

triceps /ˈtraɪseps/ *n.* a muscle (especially in the upper arm) with three points of attachment. [L (TRI-, *caput* head)]

trichinosis /trɪkɪˈnəʊsɪs/ *n.* a disease caused by hairlike worms in the muscles. [f. *trichina* hairlike worm f. Gk *trikhinos* hairlike]

trichology /trɪˈkɒlədʒɪ/ *n.* the study of hair. —**trichologist** *n.* [f. Gk *thrix* hair + -LOGY]

trichromatic /traɪkrəˈmætɪk/ *adj.* **1** three-coloured. **2** (of vision) having the normal three colour-sensations (red, green, purple). [f. TRI- + CHROMATIC]

trick *n.* **1** a thing done to fool, outwit, or deceive someone. **2** an optical or other illusion. **3** a special technique; the exact or best way to do something. **4** a feat of skill done for entertainment. **5** a mischievous, foolish, or discreditable act; a practical joke. **6** a peculiar or characteristic habit. **7** the cards played in one round of a card-game; the winning of a round. **8** (*attrib.*) done to deceive or mystify. —*v.t.* to deceive or persuade by a trick. —**do the trick,** (*colloq.*) to achieve what is required. **how's tricks?** (*slang*) how are things? **trick or treat?** (*US*) a phrase said by children who call at houses at Hallowe'en seeking to be given sweets etc. and threatening to do mischief if these are not provided. **trick out** *or* **up,** to deck, to decorate. [f. OF *trique*, *triche* (*trichier* deceive; orig. unkn.)]

trickery *n.* deception, the use of tricks. [f. TRICK]

trickle *v.t./i.* **1** to flow in drops or in a small stream; to cause to do this. **2** to come or go slowly or gradually. —*n.* a trickling flow. —**trickle charger,** an accumulator-charger that works at a steady slow rate from the mains. [prob. imit.]

trickster *n.* a person who tricks or cheats people. [f. TRICK]

tricksy *adj.* full of tricks, playful. [f. TRICK]

tricky *adj.* **1** requiring skilful handling. **2** crafty, deceitful. —**trickily** *adv.*, **trickiness** *n.* [f. TRICK]

tricolour /ˈtrɪkələ(r)/ *n.* a flag of three colours, especially the French national flag of blue, white, and red. [f. F f. L (as TRI-, COLOUR)]

tricorne /ˈtraɪkɔ:n/ *adj.* (of a hat) with the brim turned up to give a three-cornered appearance. —*n.* such a hat. [f. F or L (TRI-, *cornu* horn)]

tricot /ˈtrɪkəʊ, ˈtri:-/ *n.* a fine jersey fabric. [F, = knitting]

tricycle /ˈtraɪsɪk(ə)l/ *n.* **1** a three-wheeled pedal-driven vehicle. **2** a three-wheeled motor vehicle for a disabled driver. —*v.i.* to ride on a tricycle. —**tricyclist** *n.* [f. TRI- + CYCLE]

trident /ˈtraɪd(ə)nt/ *n.* a three-pronged spear; the three-pronged fish-spear carried by Neptune and by Britannia as a symbol of power over the sea. [f. L (TRI-, *dens* tooth)]

triennial /traɪˈenɪəl/ *adj.* **1** lasting for three years. **2** recurring every third year. —**triennially** *adv.* [f. L (TRI-, *annus* year)]

trier /ˈtraɪə(r)/ *n.* **1** one who perseveres in his attempts. **2** a tester. [f. TRY]

trifle /ˈtraɪf(ə)l/ *n.* **1** a thing of only slight value or importance. **2** a very small amount, especially of money. **3** a sweet dish made of sponge-cake soaked in wine or jelly with fruit and topped with custard and cream. —*v.i.* to talk or behave frivolously. —**trifle with,** to treat with flippancy or derision; to toy with. —**trifler** *n.* [f. OF *truf(f)le* = *truf(f)e* deceit]

trifling /ˈtraɪf(ə)lɪŋ/ *adj.* trivial. [f. prec.]

triforium /traɪˈfɔrɪəm/ *n.* (*pl.* **-ia**) an arcade or gallery above the nave and choir arches. [L; orig. unkn.]

trigeminal /traɪˈdʒemɪn(ə)l/ *adj.* of the fifth and (in man) largest pair of cranial nerves, dividing into three main branches (ophthalmic, maxillary, and mandibular nerves). [f. L, = born as a triplet (TRI-, *geminus* born at same birth)]

trigger *n.* **1** a movable device for releasing a spring or catch and so setting a mechanism (especially that of a gun) in motion. **2** an agent that sets off a chain reaction. —*v.t.* (often with *off*) to set (an action or process) in motion; to be the immediate cause of. —**quick on the trigger,** quick to respond. **trigger-happy** *adj.* apt to shoot on slight provocation. [f. Du. *trekker* (as TREK)]

triglyph /ˈtrɪglɪf/ *n.* an ornament of a frieze in the Doric order, consisting of a block or tablet with two vertical grooves and a half-groove on each side of these, alternating with metopes. [f. L f. Gk (TRI-, *gluphē* carving)]

trigonometry /trɪgəˈnɒmɪtrɪ/ *n.* the part of geometry that deals primarily with angles and their functions (e.g. sine, cosine, tangent); (formerly) the study of triangles. —**spherical trigonometry,** the theory of triangles that are formed by segments of great circles on a spherical surface, important in navigation and astronomy. —**trigonometric** /-nəˈmetrɪk/ *adj.*, **trigonometrical** /-nəˈmetrɪk(ə)l/ *adj.*, **trigonometrically** /-nəˈmetrɪkəlɪ/ *adv.* [f. Gk *trigōnon* triangle (TRI-, *-gōnos* cornered) + -METRY]

trike *n.* (*colloq.*) a tricycle. [abbr.]

trilateral /traɪˈlætər(ə)l/ *adj.* **1** of, on, or having three sides. **2** affecting or between three parties. [f. L (TRI-, *latus* side)]

trilby /ˈtrɪlbɪ/ *n.* a soft felt hat with a narrow brim and a lengthwise dent in the crown. [f. name of heroine of G. du Maurier's novel *Trilby* (1894), in the stage version of which such a hat was worn]

trilingual /traɪˈlɪŋgw(ə)l/ *adj.* **1** speaking or able to speak three languages. **2** written in three languages. [f. TRI- + L *lingua* tongue]

trill *n.* a quavering or vibratory sound (e.g. a rapid alternation of the main note and the note above in music, a bird's warbling, a pronunciation of *r* with vibration of the tongue). —*v.t./i.* to produce a trill; to warble (a song) or pronounce (*r* etc.) with a trill. [f. It. *trillo, trillare*]

trillion /ˈtrɪljən/ *n.* (for plural usage see HUNDRED) **1** a million million million. **2** (*US* and increasingly in British use) a million million. **3** (in *pl.*) very many. —**trillionth** *adj.* & *n.* [F or f. It. (as TRI-, MILLION)]

trilobite /ˈtraɪləbaɪt/ *n.* a kind of fossil marine arthropod of Palaeozoic times, characterized by a three-lobed body. [f. TRI- + Gk *lobos* lobe]

trilogy /ˈtrɪlədʒɪ/ *n.* a group of three related items, especially literary or operatic works. [f. Gk (as TRI-, -LOGY)]

trim *v.t./i.* (**-mm-**) **1** to set in good order; to make neat or of the required size and form, especially by cutting away irregular or unwanted parts; (with *off* or *away*) to remove (such parts). **2** to ornament. **3** to adjust the balance of (a ship or aircraft) by the arrangement of its cargo etc. **4** to arrange (sails) to suit the wind. **5** (*colloq.*) to rebuke sharply; to thrash. **6** (*colloq.*) to get the better of in a bargain etc. —*n.* **1** a state of readiness or fitness. **2** the trimming on a dress or furniture etc.; the colour or type of upholstery and other fittings in a vehicle. **3** the trimming of hair etc. **4** the balance or the even horizontal position of a boat or aircraft etc. —*adj.* neat and orderly; having a smooth outline or compact structure. —**trimly** *adv.*, **trimmer** *n.*, **trimness** *n.* [OE, = make firm]

trimaran /ˈtraɪməræn/ *n.* a vessel like a catamaran, with three hulls side by side. [f. TRI- + CATAMARAN]

trimeter /ˈtrɪmɪtə(r)/ *n.* a line of verse of three measures. [f. L f. Gk (as TRI-, METRE)]

trimming *n.* **1** an ornamentation, a decoration. **2** (in *pl.*, *colloq.*) the usual accompaniments, especially of the main course of a meal. **3** (in *pl.*) pieces cut off when something is trimmed. [f. TRIM]

trine *n.* (in astrology) the aspect of two planets one third of the zodiac (= 120°) apart, regarded as having a favourable influence. —*adj.* having this aspect. [f. OF f. L *trinus* threefold (*tres* three)]

Trinitarian /trɪnɪˈteərɪən/ *n.* a person who believes in the doctrine of the Trinity, as contrasted with a Unitarian. —**Trinitarianism** *n.* [f. TRINITY]

trinitrotoluene /traɪnaɪtrəʊˈtɒljʊiːn/ *n.* (also **trinitrotoluol**) a high explosive. [f. TRI- + NITRO- + TOLUENE]

trinity /ˈtrɪnɪtɪ/ *n.* being three; a group of three. —**the (Holy) Trinity,** the union of three persons (Father, Son, Holy Spirit) in one Godhead; the doctrine of this. **Trinity Sunday,** the Sunday next after Whit Sunday, celebrated in honour of the Holy Trinity. **Trinity term,** the university and law term beginning after Easter. [f. OF f. L (*trinus* threefold)]

trinket /ˈtrɪŋkɪt/ *n.* a small fancy article or piece of jewellery. [orig. unkn.]

trio /ˈtriːəʊ/ *n.* **1** a musical composition for three performers; these performers. **2** any group of three. [F & It. f. L *tres* three, after *duo*]

triode /ˈtraɪəʊd/ *n.* **1** a thermionic valve having three electrodes. **2** a semiconductor rectifier having three terminals. [f. TRI- + ELECTRODE]

triolet /ˈtriːəlɪt, ˈtraɪ-/ *n.* a poem of eight (usually eight-syllabled) lines, rhyming *abaaabab*, in which the first line recurs as the fourth and seventh and the second as the eighth. [F (as TRIO + -LET)]

trip *v.t./i.* **(-pp-)** **1** to walk, run, or dance with quick light steps; (of rhythm) to run lightly. **2** to stumble, to catch one's foot in something and fall; to cause to do this. **3** (often with *up*) to make a slip or blunder; to cause to do this; to detect in a blunder. **4** to take a trip to a place. **5** (*colloq.*) to have a visionary experience caused by a drug. **6** to release (a switch or catch) so as to operate a machine etc. —*n.* **1** a journey or excursion, especially for pleasure. **2** a stumble or blunder, tripping or being tripped up. **3** a nimble step. **4** (*colloq.*) a visionary experience caused by a drug; a device for tripping a mechanism. —**trip-hammer** *n.* a large hammer mounted on a pivot and operated by releasing a catch, used in metal forging. **trip-wire** *n.* a wire stretched close to the ground, operating a trap or alarm etc. when tripped against. [f. OF f. MDu. *trippen* skip, hop]

tripartite /traɪˈpɑːtaɪt/ *adj.* **1** consisting of three parts. **2** shared by or involving three parties. [f. L (TRI-, *partiri* divide)]

tripe *n.* **1** the first or second stomach of a ruminant, especially an ox, as food. **2** (*slang*) nonsense; a worthless thing. [f. OF]

triple *adj.* **1** threefold, consisting of three parts or involving three parties. **2** being three times as many or as much. **3** (of time in music) having three beats in the bar. —*n.* **1** a threefold number or amount. **2** a set of three. —*v.t./i.* to make or become three times as many or as much. —**triple jump,** an athletic contest comprising a hop, a step, and a jump. **triple point,** the temperature and pressure at which the solid, liquid, and vapour phases of a pure substance can coexist in equilibrium. —**triply** *adv.* [OF or f. L *triplus* f. Gk]

triplet /ˈtrɪplɪt/ *n.* **1** each of three children or animals born at a birth. **2** a set of three things, especially of notes played in the time of two, or of three lines of verse rhyming together. [f. TRIPLE, after *doublet*]

triplex *adj.* triple, threefold. [L, (TRI-, *plex* f. *plic-* fold)]

triplicate /ˈtrɪplɪkət/ *adj.* **1** existing in three examples. **2** having three corresponding parts. **3** tripled. —*n.* each of three things exactly alike. —/-keɪt/ *v.t.* to make in three copies; to multiply by three. —**triplication** /-ˈkeɪʃ(ə)n/ *n.* [f. L *triplicare* (as prec.)]

tripod /ˈtraɪpɒd/ *n.* **1** a three-legged stand for a camera etc. **2** a stool, table, or utensil resting on three feet or legs. [f. L f. Gk (TRI-, *pous* foot)]

tripos /ˈtraɪpɒs/ *n.* the honours examination for the BA degree at Cambridge University. [as prec., with ref. to stool on which a BA sat to deliver satirical speech].

tripper *n.* a person who goes on a pleasure trip or excursion. —**trippery** *adj.* [f. TRIP]

triptych /ˈtrɪptɪk/ *n.* a picture or carving on three panels, usually hinged vertically together. [f. TRI- after *diptych*]

trireme /ˈtraɪriːm/ *n.* an ancient warship, with three banks of oars. [f. F or L (TRI-, *remus* oar)]

trisect /traɪˈsekt/ *v.t.* to divide into three (usually equal) parts. —**trisection** *n.* [f. TRI- + L *secare* cut]

trite *adj.* (of a phrase, opinion, etc.) hackneyed, worn out by constant repetition. [f. L *tritus* (*terere* rub)]

tritium /ˈtrɪtɪəm/ *n.* a heavy radioactive isotope of hydrogen with a mass about three times that of ordinary hydrogen. [f. Gk *tritos* third]

triumph /ˈtraɪəmf/ *n.* **1** the state of being victorious; a great success or achievement. **2** a supreme example. **3** joy at a success, exultation. **4** the processional entry of a victorious general into ancient Rome. —*v.i.* **1** to gain a victory, to be successful; to prevail. **2** to exult. **3** (of a Roman general) to ride in a triumph. [f. OF f. L *triump(h)us*, prob. f. Gk *thriambos* hymn to Bacchus]

triumphal /traɪˈʌmf(ə)l/ *adj.* of, used in, or celebrating a triumph. [f. OF or L (as prec.)]

triumphant /traɪˈʌmfənt/ *adj.* **1** victorious, successful. **2** rejoicing at success etc. —**triumphantly** *adv.* [as prec.]

triumvir /ˈtraɪəmvɪə(r), -ˈʌmvə(r)/ *n.* a member of a triumvirate. [L (*tres viri* three men)]

triumvirate /traɪˈʌmvərət/ *n.* a board or ruling group of three men, especially in ancient Rome. [f. L (as prec.)]

trivalent /traɪˈveɪlənt/ *adj.* having a valence of three. [f. TRI- + VALENCE]

trivet /ˈtrɪvɪt/ *n.* an iron tripod or bracket for a cooking-pot or kettle to stand on. —**as right as a trivet,** (*colloq.*) in a perfectly good state. [app. f. L *tripes* three-footed (TRI-, *pes* foot)]

trivia /ˈtrɪvɪə/ *n.pl.* trivial things. [as foll.]

trivial /ˈtrɪvɪəl/ *adj.* of only small value or importance, trifling; (of a person) concerned only with trivial things. —**triviality** /-ˈælɪtɪ/ *n.*, **trivially** *adv.* [f. L, = commonplace (*trivium* place where three roads meet f. TRI-, *via* road)]

trochee /ˈtrəʊki:/ *n.* a metrical foot consisting of one long or stressed syllable followed by one short or unstressed syllable. —**trochaic** /trəˈkeɪɪk/ *adj.* [f. L f. Gk, = running (*trekhō* run)]

trod, trodden see TREAD.

troglodyte /ˈtrɒglədaɪt/ *n.* a cave-dweller, especially in prehistoric times. [f. L f. Gk f. name of Ethiopian people, after *troglē* hole]

troika /ˈtrɔɪkə/ *n.* **1** a Russian vehicle with a team of three horses abreast; such a team. **2** a group of three persons especially as an administrative council. [Russ. (*troe* three)]

Trojan /ˈtrəʊdʒ(ə)n/ *adj.* of Troy or its people. —*n.* **1** an inhabitant of Troy. **2** a person who works, fights, or endures courageously. —**Trojan horse,** the hollow wooden horse used by the Greeks to enter Troy; a person or device insinuated to bring about an enemy's downfall. **Trojan War,** the ten-year siege of Troy by the Greeks in Greek legend. [f. L *Troianus*]

troll[1] /ˈtrəʊl/ *n.* (*Scand. myth.*) a member of a race of supernatural beings formerly conceived as giants but now (in Denmark and Sweden) as friendly but mischievous dwarfs. [f. ON & Sw. *troll*, Da. *trold*]

troll[2] /trəʊl/ *v.t./i.* **1** to sing out in a carefree jovial manner. **2** to fish by drawing bait along in the water. [orig. = stroll, roll; cf. OF *troller* to quest]

trolley /ˈtrɒlɪ/ *n.* **1** a platform on wheels for transporting goods; a small cart or truck. **2** a small table on wheels or castors for transporting food or small articles. **3** a trolley-wheel. —**trolley-bus** *n.* a bus powered by electricity from an overhead wire to which it is linked by a trolley-wheel. **trolley-wheel** *n.* a wheel attached to a pole etc. for collecting current from an overhead electric wire to drive a vehicle. [dial., perh. f. prec.]

trollop /ˈtrɒləp/ *n.* a disreputable girl or woman. [perh. rel. to archaic *trull* prostitute]

trombone /trɒmˈbəʊn/ *n.* a brass wind instrument with a forward-pointing extendable slide. [F or f. It. (*tromba* trumpet, as TRUMP[2])]

trompe l'œil /trɔ̃p ˈlʌi:/ *adj.* (of a still-life painting etc.) designed to make a spectator think the objects represented are real. —*n.* such a painting etc. [F, lit. 'deceives the eye']

-tron *suffix* forming nouns denoting elementary particles or particle accelerators. [f. ELECTRON]

troop *n.* **1** an assemblage of persons or animals, especially when moving. **2** (in *pl.*) soldiers, armed forces. **3** a cavalry unit commanded by a captain; a unit of artillery. **4** a unit of three or more Scout patrols. —*v.i.* to assemble or go as a troop or in great numbers. —**troop the colour,** to show the regimental flag ceremonially along ranks of soldiers. [f. F *troupe* ult. f. L *troppus* flock]

trooper *n.* **1** a private soldier in a cavalry or armoured unit. **2** (*Austral. hist.* & *US*) a mounted or motor-borne policeman. **3** a cavalry horse. **4** a troop-ship. —**swear like a trooper,** to swear extensively or forcefully. [f. TROOP]

trophy /ˈtrəʊfɪ/ *n.* **1** a thing taken in war or hunting etc. as a souvenir of success. **2** an object awarded as a prize or token of victory. [f. F f. L f. Gk *tropaion* (*tropē* rout f. *trepō* turn)]

tropic /ˈtrɒpɪk/ *n.* the parallel of latitude 23 27′ north (**tropic of Cancer**) or south (**tropic of Capricorn**) of the equator; the corresponding circle on the celestial sphere where the sun appears to turn after reaching its greatest declination. —*adj.* **1** tropical. **2** of or showing tropism. —**the tropics,** the region between the tropics of Cancer and Capricorn, with a hot climate. [f. L f. Gk (*tropē* turning)]

tropical /ˈtrɒpɪk(ə)l/ *adj.* of, peculiar to, or suggestive of the tropics. —**tropically** *adv.* [as prec.]

tropism /ˈtrəʊpɪz(ə)m/ *n.* the turning or movement of an organism in response to an eternal stimulus, e.g. that of plant leaves etc. in response to light. [f. Gk *-tropos* turning (*trepō* turn)]

troposphere /ˈtrɒpəsfɪə(r)/ *n.* the layer of atmospheric air extending about seven miles upwards from the earth's surface, in which the temperature falls with increasing height. [f. Gk *tropos* turning + SPHERE]

trot *v.t./i.* (**-tt-**) **1** (of a quadruped) to proceed at a steady pace faster than a walk lifting each diagonal pair of legs alternately, often with brief intervals during which the body is unsupported. **2** (of a person) to run at a moderate pace, especially with short strides; (*colloq.*) to walk, to go. **3** to cause to trot. **4** to traverse (a distance) at a trot. —*n.* the action or exercise of trotting. —**on the trot,** (*colloq.*) continually busy; in succession. **trot out,** to produce, to bring out for inspection or approval etc. [f. OF f. L *trottare*]

troth /trəʊθ/ *n.* (*archaic*) faith, loyalty; truth. —**pledge** *or* **plight one's troth,** to pledge one's word, especially in marriage or betrothal. [as TRUTH]

Trotskyist /ˈtrɒtskɪɪst/ *n.* a radical left-wing Communist. —**Trotskyism** *n.* [f. Leon *Trotsky*, Russian revolutionary (d. 1940)]

trotter *n.* **1** a horse bred or trained for trotting-races. **2** (usu. in *pl.*) an animal's foot as food. [f. TROT]

trotting *n.* a form of horse-racing (also called *harness-racing*) in which a horse pulls a two-wheeled vehicle (a *sulky*) and its driver. [f. TROT]

troubadour /ˈtru:bədʊə(r)/ *n.* a member of a class of lyric poets composing in Provençal during the 12th and early 13th c. [F f. Prov. *trovador* (*trovar* find, compose)]

trouble /ˈtrʌb(ə)l/ *n.* **1** difficulty, inconvenience, distress, vexation, misfortune; a cause of any of these; unpleasant exertion. **2** faulty functioning of mechanism or of the body or mind. **3** conflict; (in *pl.*) public disturbances; **the Troubles,** any of various rebellions, civil wars, and unrest in Ireland, especially in 1919-23 and (in Northern Ireland) from 1968. **4** unpleasantness involving punishment or rebuke. —*v.t./i.* **1** to cause trouble or pain to; to distress. **2** to be disturbed or worried; to be subjected to inconvenience or unpleasant exertion. —**ask** *or* **look for trouble,** (*colloq.*) to behave rashly, incautiously, indiscreetly, etc. **in trouble,** involved in a matter likely to bring censure or punishment; (*colloq.*) pregnant while unmarried. **trouble-maker** *n.* a person who habitually causes trouble. **trouble-shooter** *n.* a person who traces and corrects faults in machinery etc.; a mediator in a dispute. [f. OF, ult. as TURBID]

troublesome *adj.* causing trouble, annoying. [f. prec. + -SOME]

troublous /ˈtrʌbləs/ *adj.* (*literary*) full of troubles, agitated, disturbed. [as TROUBLE]

trough /trɒf/ *n.* **1** a long narrow open receptacle for water, animal feed, etc. **2** a channel or hollow comparable to this. **3** an elongated region of low barometric pressure. [OE]

trounce *v.t.* **1** to defeat heavily. **2** to beat, to thrash; to punish severely. [orig. unkn.]

troupe /tru:p/ *n.* a company of actors or acrobats etc. [F, = TROOP]

trouper /ˈtru:pə(r)/ *n.* **1** a member of a theatrical troupe. **2** a staunch colleague. [f. prec.]

trousers /ˈtraʊzəz/ *n.pl.* a two-legged outer garment reaching from the waist usually to the ankles. —**trouser-suit** *n.* a woman's suit of trousers and jacket. —**trousered** *adj.* [extended form of archaic *trouse*, f. Ir. & Gael. (as TREWS)]

trousseau /ˈtru:səʊ/ *n.* (*pl.* **-eaus**) a bride's collection of clothes etc. [F, = bundle (as TRUSS)]

trout *n.* (*pl.* usu. same) a small fish of the genus *Salmo* in northern rivers and lakes, valued as food and game; a similar fish of the family Salmonidae (**salmon** or **sea trout**). —**old trout,** (*slang, derog.*) an old woman. [OE]

trove *n.* treasure trove. [f. AF *trové* (*trover* find)]

trow /traʊ, trəʊ/ *v.t.* (*archaic*) to think, to believe. [OE, rel. to TRUCE]

trowel /ˈtraʊ(ə)l/ *n.* **1** a small tool with a flat blade for spreading mortar or splitting bricks. **2** a small garden tool with a curved blade for lifting small plants or scooping earth etc. [f. OF f. L *trulla* scoop, dim. of *trua* ladle]

troy *n.* (in full **troy weight**) a system of weights used for precious metals and gems, with a pound of 12 ounces or 5760 grains. [prob. f. *Troyes* in France]

truant /ˈtru:ənt/ *n.* a child who absents himself from school; a person missing from work etc. —*adj.* (of a person or his conduct etc.) shirking, idle, wandering. —**play truant,** to stay away as a truant. —**truancy** *n.* [f. OF prob. f. Celt. (Welsh *truan*, Gael. *truaghan* wretched)]

truce /ˈtru:s/ *n.* a temporary cessation of hostilities; an agreement for this. [orig. pl.; OE, = covenant]

truck[1] *n.* **1** an open container on wheels for transporting heavy loads; an open railway wagon; a hand-cart. **2** a lorry. [perh. short for TRUCKLE]

truck[2] *n.* dealings; barter, exchange. —*v.t./i.* (*archaic*) to barter, to exchange. [f. F *troquer* f. L *trocare*; orig. unkn.]

truckle *v.i.* to submit obsequiously. —**truckle-bed** *n.* a low bed on wheels so that it may be pushed under another, especially as formerly used by servants etc. [f. AF *trocle* f. L *trochlea* pulley]

truculent /ˈtrʌkjʊlənt/ *adj.* defiant and aggressive. —**truculence** *n.*, **truculency** *n.*, **truculently** *adv.* [f. L *truculentus* (*trux* fierce)]

trudge /trʌdʒ/ *v.t./i.* to walk laboriously; to traverse (a distance) thus. —*n.* a trudging walk. [orig. unkn.]

true /tru:/ *adj.* **1** in accordance with fact. **2** in accordance with correct principles or an accepted standard; rightly or strictly so called; genuine, not false. **3** exact, accurate; (of the voice etc.) in good tune. **4** accurately placed, balanced, or shaped; upright; level. **5** loyal, faithful. —**come true,** to happen in the way that was prophesied or hoped. **true-blue** *adj.* completely true to one's principles; firmly loyal; (*n.*) such a person. **true north,** north according to the earth's axis, not the magnetic north. —**trueness** *n.* [OE]

truffle *n.* **1** an edible subterranean fungus of the genus *Tuber*, with a rich flavour. **2** a round soft sweet made of a chocolate mixture covered with cocoa etc. [prob. f. Du. f. obs. F, perh. f. L *tubera* pl. of TUBER]

trug *n.* a shallow oblong basket usually of wood

strips, used by gardeners. [perh. dial. var. of TROUGH]

truism /ˈtru:ɪz(ə)m/ *n.* **1** a statement too obviously true or too hackneyed to be worth making. **2** a statement that repeats an idea already implied in one of its terms (e.g. *there is no need to be unnecessarily careful*). [f. TRUE]

truly /ˈtru:lɪ/ *adv.* **1** sincerely, genuinely. **2** faithfully, loyally. **3** accurately, truthfully. [OE (as TRUE)]

trump[1] *n.* **1** a playing-card of a suit temporarily ranking above the others. **2** an advantage, especially involving surprise. **3** (*colloq.*) a helpful or excellent person. —*v.t.* to defeat (a card or its player) with a trump. —**trump card,** a card belonging to, or turned up to determine, the trump suit; a valuable resource. **trump up,** to invent (an accusation or excuse etc.) fraudulently. **turn up trumps** (*colloq.*) to turn out better than expected; to be greatly successful or helpful. [corruption of TRIUMPH in same (now obs.) sense]

trump[2] *n.* (*archaic*) a trumpet-blast. —**the last trump,** a trumpet-blast to wake the dead on Judgement Day. [f. OF *trompe* (prob. imit.)]

trumpery /ˈtrʌmpərɪ/ *adj.* showy but worthless. —*n.* worthless finery etc. [f. OF *tromperie* (*tromper* deceive)]

trumpet /ˈtrʌmpɪt/ *n.* **1** a metal tubular or conical wind instrument with a flared mouth and a bright penetrating tone. **2** a trumpet-shaped thing. **3** a sound (as) of a trumpet. —*v.t./i.* **1** to blow a trumpet. **2** (of an elephant etc.) to make a loud sound as of a trumpet. **3** to proclaim (a person's or thing's merit) loudly. —**trumpet-call** *n.* an urgent summons to action. **trumpet-major** *n.* the chief trumpeter of a cavalry regiment. [f. OF *trompette* (as TRUMP[2])]

trumpeter *n.* one who sounds a trumpet, especially a cavalry soldier giving signals. [f. prec.]

truncate /trʌŋˈkeɪt/ *v.t.* to cut the top or end from. —**truncation** /-ˈkeɪʃ(ə)n/ *n.* [f. L *truncare* maim (as TRUNK)]

truncheon /ˈtrʌntʃ(ə)n/ *n.* **1** a short club carried by a policeman. **2** a staff or baton as a symbol of authority. [f. OF *tronchon* stump f. L (as TRUNK)]

trundle *v.t./i.* to roll along; to move heavily on a wheel or wheels. [var. of obs. or dial. *trendle* f. OE *trendel* circle (as TREND)]

trunk *n.* **1** the main stem of a tree as distinct from the branches and roots. **2** a person's or animal's body apart from the limbs and head. **3** a large box with a hinged lid, used for transporting or storing clothes etc. **4** (*US*) the boot of a motor car. **5** an elephant's elongated prehensile nose. **6** (in *pl.*) men's close-fitting shorts worn for swimming, boxing, etc. —**trunk-call** *n.* a telephone call on a trunk-line with charges according to distance. **trunk-line** *n.* a main line of a railway, telephone system, etc. **trunk-road** *n.* an important main road. [f. OF *tronc* f. L *truncus*]

trunnion /ˈtrʌnjən/ *n.* **1** a supporting cylindrical projection on each side of a cannon or mortar. **2** a hollow gudgeon supporting the cylinder in a steam-engine and giving passage to steam. [f. F *trognon* core, tree-trunk; orig. unkn.]

truss *n.* **1** a framework of beams or bars supporting a roof or bridge etc. **2** a padded belt or other device worn to support a hernia. **3** a bundle of hay or straw. **4** a compact cluster of flowers or fruit. —*v.t.* **1** to tie or bind securely; to tie (a fowl) compactly for cooking. **2** to support (a roof or bridge etc.) with a truss or trusses. [f. OF *trusser* v., *trusse* n. (orig. unkn.)]

trust *n.* **1** firm belief in the reliability, truth, strength, etc., of a person or thing; the state of being relied on. **2** confident expectation. **3** a thing or person committed to one's care; the resulting obligation. **4** (*Law*) trusteeship; a board of trustees; property committed to a trustee or trustees. **5** an association of several companies for the purpose of united action to reduce or defeat competition. —*v.t./i.* **1** to have or place trust in; to treat as reliable. **2** to entrust. **3** to hope earnestly. —**in trust,** held as a trust (see sense 4). **on trust,** accepted without investigation. **trust to,** to place reliance on. [f. ON (*traustr* strong)]

trustee /trʌsˈti:/ *n.* **1** a person or a member of a board given possession of property with a legal obligation to administer it solely for the purposes specified. **2** a State made responsible for the government of an area. —**trusteeship** *n.* [f. TRUST]

trustful *adj.* full of trust or confidence, not feeling or showing suspicion. —**trustfully** *adv.*, **trustfulness** *n.* [f. TRUST + -FUL]

trusting *adj.* having trust, trustful. [f. TRUST]

trustworthy *adj.* deserving of trust, reliable. —**trustworthiness** *n.*

trusty *adj.* (*archaic*) trustworthy. —*n.* a prisoner who is given special privileges or responsibilities because of continuous good behaviour. —**trustily** *adv.*, **trustiness** *n.* [f. TRUST]

truth /tru:θ/ *n.* (*pl.* /-ðz, -θs/) **1** the quality or state of being true or truthful. **2** what is true. —**in truth,** (*literary*) truly, really. [OE (as TRUE)]

truthful *adj.* **1** habitually telling the truth. **2** (of a story etc.) true. —**truthfully** *adv.*, **truthfulness** *n.* [f. TRUTH + -FUL]

try /ˈtraɪ/ *v.t./i.* **1** to make an effort with a view to success; to use effort to achieve or perform. **2** to test (the quality of a thing) by use or experiment; to test the qualities of (a person or thing); to examine the effectiveness or usefulness of for a purpose. **3** to make severe demands on. **4** to investigate and decide (a case or issue) judicially; to subject (a person) to trial.—*n.* **1** an effort to accomplish something. **2** (in Rugby football) a touching-down of the ball by a player behind the goal-line, scoring points and entitling his side to a kick at goal. —**try and,** (*colloq.*) try to. **try for,** to apply or compete for; to seek to reach or attain. **try one's hand,** to see how skilful one is, especially at a first attempt. **try it on,** (*colloq.*) to test another's patience. **try on,** to put on (clothes etc.) to see if they are suitable. **try-on** *n.* (*colloq.*) an act of 'trying it on', an attempt to deceive or outwit. **try out,** to put to the test, to test thoroughly. **try-out** *n.* an experimental test. [orig. = separate, distinguish, f. OF *trier* sift]

trying *adj.* putting a strain on one's temper, patience, or endurance; annoying. [f. TRY]

trypanosome /ˈtrɪpənəsəʊm/ *n.* a flagellate protozoan parasite infesting the blood etc. and causing diseases of a group that includes sleeping sickness. [f. Gk *trupanon* borer, *sōma* body]

tryst /trɪst, traɪst/ *n.* (*archaic*) a time and place for a meeting, especially of lovers. [f. OF *triste* appointed station in hunting]

tsar /zɑː(r)/ *n.* the title of the former emperor of Russia. It was formally assumed as a title by Ivan the Terrible in 1547; some earlier uses exist. [f. Russ., ult. f. L *Caesar*]

tsetse /ˈtsetsɪ, ˈtetsɪ/ *n.* a fly of the genus *Glossina*, found only in tropical Africa, carrying disease (especially sleeping sickness) to man and animals by biting. [Tswana]

T-shirt /ˈtiːʃɜːt/ *n.* a short-sleeved shirt for casual wear, having the form of T when spread out.

T-square /ˈtiːskweə(r)/ *n.* a T-shaped instrument for drawing or testing right angles.

tsunami /tsʊˈnɑːmɪ/ *n.* **1** a series of long high sea-waves caused by disturbance of the ocean floor or seismic movement. **2** an exceptionally large tidal wave. [Jap. (*tsu* harbour, *nami* wave)]

Tswana /ˈtswɑːnə/ *n.* **1** a member of a Negroid people living in Africa between the Orange and Zambezi rivers. **2** their Bantu language (also called *Sechuana*). [native name]

TT *abbr.* **1** Tourist Trophy. **2** tuberculin-tested. **3** teetotal; teetotaller.

Tuareg /ˈtwɑːreg/ *n.* (*pl.* same or **-s**) **1** a member of a Berber group of nomadic pastoralists of North Africa. **2** their Berber dialect. —*adj.* of this people or their language. [native name]

tub *n.* **1** an open flat-bottomed usually round vessel used for washing or for holding liquids or containing soil for plants etc. **2** (*colloq.*) a bath. **3** (*colloq.*) a clumsy slow boat. —*v.t./i.* (**-bb-**) to plant, bath, or wash in a tub. —**tub-thumper** *n.* a ranting preacher or orator. [prob. f. LDu.]

tuba /ˈtjuːbə/ *n.* a low-pitched brass wind instrument. [It. f. L, = trumpet]

tubal /ˈtjuːb(ə)l/ *adj.* of a tube or tubes, especially the bronchial or Fallopian tubes. [f. TUBE]

tubby *adj.* tub-shaped; (of a person) short and fat. —**tubbiness** *n.* [f. TUB]

tube *n.* **1** a long hollow cylinder; a natural or artificial structure having approximately this shape with open or closed ends and serving for the passage of fluid etc. or as a receptacle. **2** (*colloq.*) the London underground railway. **3** an inner tube. **4** a cathode-ray tube, e.g. in a television set. **5** (*US*) a thermionic valve. —*v.t.* **1** to equip with a tube or tubes. **2** to enclose in a tube. —**the tube,** (*US*) television. [F or f. L *tubus*]

tuber /ˈtjuːbə(r)/ *n.* a thick round root (e.g. of a dahlia) or underground stem (e.g. of a potato), frequently bearing buds. [L, = hump, swelling]

tubercle /ˈtjuːbək(ə)l/ *n.* a small rounded swelling in a plant or organ of the body, especially as characteristic of tuberculosis in the lungs. —**tubercle bacillus,** the bacillus causing tuberculosis. [f. L *tuberculum*, dim. of prec.]

tubercular /tjuːˈbɜːkjʊlə(r)/ *adj.* of or affected with tuberculosis. [as prec.]

tuberculin /tjuːbɜːkjʊlɪn/ *n.* a preparation from cultures of the tubercle bacillus used for the treatment and diagnosis of tuberculosis. —**tuberculin-tested** *adj.* (of milk) from cows shown by a tuberculin test to be free of tuberculosis. [as foll.]

tuberculosis /tjuːbɜːkjʊˈləʊsɪs/ *n.* an infectious bacterial wasting disease affecting various parts of the body, in which tubercles appear on body tissue; (in full **pulmonary tuberculosis**) this disease of the lungs.) [f. TUBERCLE + -OSIS]

tuberculous /tjuːˈbɜːkjʊləs/ *adj.* of, having, or caused by tubercles or tuberculosis. [as prec.]

tuberose /ˈtjuːbərəʊz/ *n.* a plant (*Polianthes tuberosa*) with fragrant creamy-white flowers. [f. L (as TUBER)]

tuberous *adj.* having tubers; of or like a tuber. [f. F or L (as prec.)]

tubing /ˈtjuːbɪŋ/ *n.* a length of tube; a quantity of tubes. [f. TUBE]

tubular /ˈtjuːbjʊlə(r) *adj.* tube-shaped; having or consisting of tubes; (of furniture etc.) made of tubular pieces. [as foll.]

tubule /ˈtju:bju:l/ *n.* a small tube. [f. L *tubulus* dim. of *tubus* tube]

TUC *abbr.* Trades Union Congress.

tuck *v.t.* **1** to turn (edges or ends) or fold (a part) in, into, or under something so as to be concealed or held in place. **2** to cover snugly and compactly. **3** to put away compactly. **4** to put a tuck or tucks in (a garment etc.). **5** (in *p.p.*, of a dive or somersault etc.) with the knees drawn up to the chest. —*n.* **1** a flattened usually stitched fold in material or a garment etc. to make it smaller or as an ornament. **2** (*slang*) food, especially sweets, cakes, and pastry etc. that children enjoy. —**tuck in,** (*slang*) to eat food heartily. **tuck-in** *n.* (*slang*) a large meal. **tuck into,** (*slang*) to eat (food) heartily. **tuck-shop** *n.* a shop selling sweets etc. to schoolchildren. [f. MDu. and MLG *tucken* (rel. to TUG)]

tucker *n.* **1** a piece of lace or linen etc. in or on a woman's bodice (*hist.* exc. in **best bib and tucker,** one's best clothes). **2** (*Austral. colloq.*) food. —*v.t.* (*US colloq.*) to tire. [f. TUCK]

Tudor /ˈtju:də(r)/ *adj.* **1** of the royal family of England ruling 1485–1603. **2** of the architectural style of this period, esp. with half-timbering and elaborately decorated design of houses. [f. Owen *Tudor*]

Tue. *abbr.* Tuesday.

Tuesday /ˈtju:zdeɪ, -dɪ/ *n.* the day of the week following Monday. —*adv.* (*colloq.*) on Tuesday. [OE, = day of Tiw (Teutonic god of war)]

tufa /ˈtju:fə/ *n.* **1** porous rock formed round springs of mineral water. **2** tuff. [It. (as foll.)]

tuff *n.* rock formed from volcanic ashes. [f. F f. It. f. L *tofus* loose porous stones]

tuffet /ˈtʌfɪt/ *n.* a small mound; a tussock. [var. of TUFT]

tuft *n.* a bunch or collection of threads, grass, feathers, or hair etc. held or growing together at the base. —**tufty** *adj.* [prob. f. OF *tof(f)e*]

tufted *adj.* having or forming a tuft or tufts; (of a bird) with a tuft of feathers on its head; (of a mattress or cushion) with depressions formed by stitching tightly through it at intervals to hold the filling in place. [f. TUFT]

tug *v.t./i.* (**-gg-**) **1** to pull vigorously or with great effort. **2** to tow by means of a tugboat. —*n.* **1** a vigorous pull (*lit.* or *fig.*). **2** a tugboat. —**tug of love,** (*colloq.*) a dispute over the custody of a child. **tug of war,** a contest in which two teams hold a rope at opposite ends and pull until one team hauls the other over a central point; a struggle between two persons etc. for power. [rel. to TOW¹]

tugboat *n.* a small powerful steam-vessel for towing others.

tuition /tju:ˈɪʃ(ə)n/ *n.* teaching instruction, especially as a thing to be paid for. [f. OF f. L (*tuēri* look after)]

tulip /ˈtju:lɪp/ *n.* a spring-flowering plant of the genus *Tulipa*, growing from a bulb, with showy cup-shaped flowers; its flower. —**tulip-tree** *n.* a tree (*Liriodendron tulipifera*) with tulip-like flowers. [f. Turk. *tul(i)band* f. Pers., = TURBAN (from the shape of the flowers)]

tulle /tju:l/ *n.* a soft fine silk net for veils and dresses. [f. *Tulle* in SW France]

tum *n.* (*colloq.*) the stomach. [abbr. of TUMMY]

tumble *v.t./i.* **1** to fall helplessly or headlong; to cause to do this. **2** to fall in value or amount. **3** to roll or toss over and over in a disorderly way. **4** to move or rush in a hasty careless way. **5** to throw or push carelessly in a confused mass. **6** to rumple, to disarrange. **7** to perform somersaults or other acrobatic feats. **8** (of a pigeon) to throw itself over backwards in flight. —*n.* **1** a tumbling fall. **2** an untidy state. —**tumble-drier** *n.* a machine for drying washing in a heated rotating drum. **tumble to,** (*colloq.*) to realize or grasp the meaning of. [f. MLG *tummelen*, frequent. of *tūmōn*]

tumbledown *adj.* falling or fallen into ruin, dilapidated.

tumbler *n.* **1** a drinking-glass with no handle or foot. **2** an acrobat. **3** a pivoted piece in a lock that holds the bolt until lifted by a key; any of various kinds of pivoted or swivelling parts in a mechanism. **4** a pigeon that tumbles in its flight. [f. TUMBLE]

tumbrel /ˈtʌmbr(ə)l/ *n.* (also **tumbril**) an open cart in which condemned persons were conveyed to the guillotine during the French Revolution. [f. OF *tomberel* (*tomber* fall)]

tumescent /tjʊˈmesənt/ *adj.* swelling. —**tumescence** *n.* [f. L *tumescere* (as TUMOUR)]

tumid /ˈtju:mɪd/ *adj.* swollen, inflated; (of style etc.) bombastic. —**tumidity** /-ˈmɪdɪtɪ/ *n.* [f. L *tumidus* (as TUMOUR)]

tummy /ˈtʌmɪ/ *n.* (*colloq.*) the stomach. —**tummy-button** *n.* (*colloq.*) the navel. [childish pronunc.]

tumour /ˈtju:mə(r)/ *n.* an abnormal mass of new tissue growing on or in the body. —**tumorous** *adj.* [f. L *tumor* (*tumēre* swell)]

tumult /ˈtju:mʌlt/ *n.* **1** an uproar, a public disturbance. **2** a state of confusion and agitation. [f. OF or L *tumultus*]

tumultuous /tjʊˈmʌltjʊəs/ *adj.* making a tumult. —**tumultuously** *adv.* [as prec.]

tumulus /ˈtju:mjʊləs/ *n.* (*pl.* **-li** /-laɪ/) an ancient burial mound. [L, = mound]

tun *n.* **1** a large cask for wine; a brewer's fermenting-vat. **2** a measure of capacity (usually about 210 gallons). [OE f. L *tunna*, prob. of Gaulish origin]

tuna /ˈtju:nə/ *n.* (*pl.* same) the tunny; (also **tuna-fish**) the flesh of the tunny as food. [Amer. Sp.]

tundra /ˈtʌndrə/ *n.* a vast level treeless Arctic region where the subsoil is frozen. [Lappish]

tune *n.* **1** a melody with or without harmony. **2** the correct pitch or intonation in singing or playing; an adjustment of a musical instrument to obtain this. —*v.t.* **1** to put (a musical instrument) in tune. **2** to adjust (a radio receiver etc.) to a particular wavelength of signals. **3** to adjust (an engine etc.) to run smoothly and efficiently. **4** to adjust or adapt (a thing to a purpose etc.). —**call the tune,** to have control of events. **change one's tune,** to change one's style of language or manner, especially from an insolent to a respectful tone. **in** (*or* **out of**) **tune with,** harmonizing (or clashing) with. **to the tune of,** to the considerable sum or amount of. **tune in,** to set a radio receiver to the right wavelength to receive a certain signal. **tune up,** (of an orchestra) to bring the instruments to the proper or a uniform pitch; to bring to the most efficient condition; to begin to play or sing. **tuning-fork** *n.* a two-pronged steel fork giving a particular note when struck. [var. of TONE]

tuneful *adj.* melodious, having a pleasing tune. —**tunefully** *adv.*, **tunefulness** *n.* [f. TUNE + -FUL]

tuneless *adj.* not melodious; without a tune. [f. TUNE + -LESS]

tuner /ˈtju:nə(r)/ *n.* a person who tunes instruments, especially pianos. [f. TUNE]

tungsten /ˈtʌŋst(ə)n/ *n.* a heavy metallic element (also known as wolfram), symbol W, atomic number 74. [Swedish (*tung* heavy, *sten* stone)]

tunic /ˈtju:nɪk/ *n.* **1** the close-fitting short coat of a police or military uniform. **2** a loose garment, often sleeveless, reaching to the hips or knees. [f. F or L *tunica*]

tunicate /ˈtju:nɪkət/ *n.* a member of the subphylum Urochorda of marine animals with a hard outer coat. [f. L *tunicare* clothe with a tunic (as prec.)]

tunnel /ˈtʌn(ə)l/ *n.* an underground passage; a passage dug through a hill or under a road etc., especially for a railway or road; a passage made by a burrowing animal. —*v.t./i.* (**-ll-**) to make a tunnel through (a hill etc.); to make one's way thus. [f. OF *tonel* dim. of *tonne* tun]

tunny /ˈtʌnɪ/ *n.* a large edible sea-fish, especially of the genus *Thunnus.* [f. F *thon* f. L f. Gk *thunnos*]

tup *n.* a male sheep, a ram. —*v.t.* (**-pp-**) (of a ram) to copulate with (a ewe). [orig. unkn.]

tuppence /ˈtʌpəns/ *n.* = TWOPENCE. [phonetic spelling]

tuppenny /ˈtʌpənɪ/ *adj.* = TWOPENNY. [phonetic spelling]

turban /ˈtɜ:bən/ *n.* **1** a man's head-dress of cotton or silk wound round a cap, worn especially by Muslims and Sikhs. **2** a woman's head-dress or hat resembling this. [ult. f. Turk. f. Pers. (as TULIP)]

turbid /ˈtɜ:bɪd/ *adj.* **1** (of a liquid or colour) muddy, not clear. **2** (of style etc.) not lucid. —**turbidity** /-ˈbɪdɪtɪ/ *n.*, **turbidly** *adv.* [f. L (*turba* crowd, disturbance)]

turbine /ˈtɜ:baɪn/ *n.* a device for producing continuous mechanical power, in which a fluid (water, steam, air, or a gas) is accelerated to a high speed in a channel or nozzle and the resulting jet(s) directed at a rotating wheel with vanes or scoop-shaped buckets round its rim. [F f. L *turbo* spinning-top, whirlwind]

turbo- /ˈtɜ:bəʊ/ *in comb.* turbine.

turbofan *n.* a jet engine with additional thrust from cold air drawn in by a fan. [f. TURBO- + FAN]

turbo-jet *n.* a jet engine in which jet gases also operate a turbine-driven compressor for supplying compressed air to the combustion chamber; an aircraft with such an engine. [f. TURBO- + JET[1]]

turbo-prop *n.* a jet engine in which a turbine is used as in a turbo-jet and also to drive a propeller; an aircraft with such an engine. [f. TURBO- + PROP[2]]

turbot /ˈtɜ:bət/ *n.* a large European flat-fish (*Scopthalmus maximus*) valued as food. [f. OF]

turbulent /ˈtɜ:bjʊlənt/ *adj.* **1** in a state of commotion or unrest; (of air or water) moving violently and unevenly. **2** unruly. —**turbulence** *n.*, **turbulently** *adv.* [as TURBID]

Turco- /ˈtɜ:kəʊ-/ *in comb.* Turkish. [f. L (as TURK)]

turd *n.* (*vulgar*) a ball or lump of excrement. [OE]

tureen /tjʊəˈri:n/ *n.* a deep covered dish from which soup is served. [f. F *terrine* earthenware dish f. L *terra* earth]

turf *n.* (*pl.* **turfs** or **turves**) **1** the layer of grass etc. with earth and matted roots as the surface of grassland. **2** a piece of this cut from the ground. **3** a slab of peat for fuel. —*v.t.* to plant (ground) with turf. —**the turf,** the racecourse, horse-racing. **turf-accountant** *n.* a bookmaker. **turf out,** (*slang*) to throw out. —**turfy** *adj.* [OE]

turgescent /tɜ:ˈdʒesənt/ *adj.* becoming turgid. —**turgescence** *n.* [f. L *turgescere* (as foll.)]

turgid /ˈtɜ:dʒɪd/ *adj.* **1** swollen or distended and not flexible. **2** (of language or style) pompous, not flowing easily. —**turgidity** /-ˈdʒɪdɪtɪ/ *n.* [f. L *turgidus* (*turgēre* swell)]

Turk *n.* **1** a native of Turkey. **2** a member of the Central Asian people from whom the Ottomans derived, speaking Turkic languages. **3** (esp. **young Turk**) a ferocious, wild, or unmanageable person. —**Turk's head,** a turban-like ornamental knot. [= F *Turc* etc., Pers. & Arab. *Turk*]

turkey /ˈtɜːkɪ/ *n.* **1** a large American bird of the genus *Meleagris*, especially *M. gallopavo*. **2** its flesh as food. —**talk turkey,** (*US colloq.*) to talk in a frank and businesslike way. **turkey-cock** *n.* a male turkey. [short for *turkey-cock*, orig. applied to the guinea-fowl (with which the American turkey was confused) because imported into Europe through Turkey]

Turki /ˈtɜːkɪ/ *adj.* of the Turkic languages or the peoples who speak these. —**Turkic** *adj. & n.* [f. Pers. *Turkī* (as TURK)]

Turkish /ˈtɜːkɪʃ/ *adj.* of Turkey or the Turks or their language. —*n.* the language of Turkey. —**Turkish bath,** a hot air or steam bath followed by washing, massage, etc.; (in *sing.* or *pl.*) a building for this. **Turkish carpet,** a Turkey carpet. **Turkish coffee,** strong usually sweet black coffee made from very finely ground beans and boiled so that it becomes very thick. **Turkish delight,** a sweet consisting of lumps of flavoured gelatine coated in powdered sugar. **Turkish towel,** a towel made of cotton terry. [f. TURK]

Turko- var. of TURCO-.

turmeric /ˈtɜːmərɪk/ *n.* **1** an East Indian plant (*Curcuma longa*) of the ginger family. **2** its aromatic root powdered and used as a flavouring, stimulant, or dye. [perh. f. F *terre mérite*]

turmoil /ˈtɜːmɔɪl/ *n.* great disturbance or confusion. [orig. unkn.]

turn *v.t./i.* **1** to move or cause to move round a point or axis; to perform (a somersault) with a rotary motion. **2** to change or cause to change in position so that a different side becomes uppermost or faces a certain direction. **3** to give a new direction to; to take a new direction; to aim or become aimed in a certain way; to seek help, to have recourse. **4** to move to the other side of, to go round. **5** to pass (a certain hour or age). **6** to cause to go, to send or put. **7** to change or become changed in form, nature, appearance, colour, etc.; to translate. **8** to make or become sour. **9** to make or become nauseated. **10** to shape in a lathe; to give an elegant form to. —*n.* **1** turning, being turned; a turning movement. **2** a change of direction or condition etc.; the point at which this occurs. **3** an angle; a bend or corner in a road. **4** character, tendency of mind etc. **5** an opportunity or obligation etc. that comes successively to each of a number of people or things. **6** a short performance in an entertainment. **7** a service of a specified kind; a purpose. **8** (*colloq.*) an attack of illness; a momentary nervous shock. **9** (*Mus.*) an ornament consisting of the principal note with those above and below it, in various sequences. **10** each round in a coil of rope, wire, etc. —**at every turn,** in every place; continually. **by turns,** in rotation of individuals or groups; alternately. **in turn,** in succession. **in one's turn,** when one's turn comes. **out of turn,** before or after one's turn; at an inappropriate moment; presumptuously. **take turns,** to act etc. alternately. **to a turn,** so as to be cooked perfectly. **turn-about** *n.* turning to face a new direction; an abrupt change of policy etc. **turn against,** to make or become hostile to. **turn and turn about,** alternately. **turn away,** to send away; to reject. **turn-buckle** *n.* a device for tightly connecting parts of metal rod or wire. **turn down,** to reject; to reduce the volume or strength of (sound or heat etc.) by turning a knob etc.; to fold down. **turn in,** to hand in or return; to register (a score etc.); (*colloq.*) to go to bed; (*colloq.*) to abandon (a plan etc.). **turn in his grave,** (of a dead person) to be disturbed in his eternal rest if he knew of a specified fact which would have shocked or distressed him while he was alive. **turn off,** to stop the flow or operation of by means of a tap or switch etc.; to move (a tap etc.) thus; to enter a side-road; (*colloq.*) to cause to lose interest. **turn on,** to start the flow or operation of by means of a tap or switch etc.; to move (a tap etc.) thus; to be suddenly hostile to; (*colloq.*) to arouse the interest or emotion of, to excite sexually or with drugs etc.; to depend on. **turn out,** to expel; to extinguish (an electric light etc.); to dress or equip; to produce (goods etc.); to empty or clean out (a room etc.); to empty (a pocket); (*colloq.*) to get out of bed; (*colloq.*) to go out of doors; to prove to be the case, to result. **turn-out** *n.* the number of people at a meeting etc.; a set of clothes or equipment. **turn over,** to reverse the position of; to hand over; to transfer; to consider carefully; to start the running of (an engine etc.); (of an engine) to start running. **turn over a new leaf,** to improve one's conduct. **turn round,** to face in a new direction; to unload and reload (a ship etc.), to process and return (a piece of work etc.). **turn-round** *n.* the process or time taken in unloading and reloading etc. **turn to,** to set about one's work. **turn up,** to increase the volume or strength of (sound or heat etc.) by turning a knob etc.; to discover or reveal; to be found; to happen or present itself; to fold over or upwards. **turn-up** *n.* the lower turned-up end of a trouser leg; (*colloq.*) an unexpected happening. [OE & f. OF f. L *tornare* turn on lathe (*tornus* lathe)]

turncoat *n.* one who changes his allegiance or principles.

turner *n.* a lathe-worker. [f. TURN]

turnery *n.* **1** objects made on a lathe. **2** work with a lathe. [f. TURN]

turning *n.* **1** a place where one road meets another, forming a corner. **2** the use of a lathe. **3** (in *pl.*) chips or shavings from a lathe. —**turning-circle** *n.* the smallest circle in which a vehicle can turn. **turning-point** *n.* the point at which a decisive change occurs. [f. TURN]

turnip /ˈtɜːnɪp/ *n.* a plant (*Brassica rapa*) with a globular root used as a vegetable and as fodder; its root. —**turnip-tops** *n.pl.* its leaves used as a vegetable. —**turnipy** *adj.* [first element of uncertain origin; second element f. dial. *neep* (OE f. L *napus*)]

turnkey *n.* a gaoler.

turnover *n.* **1** turning over. **2** the amount of money taken in a business; the amount of business done. **3** a pie or tart made by folding half the pastry over so as to enclose the filling. **4** the number of persons entering or leaving employment etc.

turnpike /ˈtɜːnpaɪk/ *n.* **1** (*hist.*) a toll-gate. **2** (*hist.* & *US*) [orig. = defensive frame of spikes]

turnstile *n.* an admission-gate with arms revolving on a post.

turntable *n.* a circular revolving platform or support, e.g. for a gramophone record being played or to turn a locomotive to face in the opposite direction.

turpentine /ˈtɜːpəntaɪn/ *n.* **1** a resin obtained from various trees (originally the terebinth). **2** (in full **oil of turpentine**) a volatile pungent oil distilled from this resin, used in mixing paints and varnishes and in medicine. [f. OF *ter(e)-bentine* f. L (as TEREBINTH)]

turpitude /ˈtɜːpɪtjuːd/ *n.* wickedness. [F or f. L (*turpis* shameful)]

turps *n.* (*colloq.*) oil of turpentine. [abbr.]

turquoise /ˈtɜːkwɔɪz, -kwɑːz/ *n.* **1** a precious stone, usually opaque and greenish-blue. **2** greenish-blue colour. —*adj.* greenish-blue. [f. OF, = Turkish (stone) (as TURK)]

turret /ˈtʌrɪt/ *n.* **1** a small tower, especially as a decorative addition to a building. **2** a low flat usually revolving armoured tower for a gun and gunners in a ship, aircraft, fort, or tank. **3** a rotating holder for tools in a lathe etc. —**turreted** *adj.* [f. OF *to(u)rete* dim. of *to(u)r* tower]

turtle /ˈtɜːt(ə)l/ *n.* **1** a marine or (*US*) freshwater reptile of the order Chelonia with flippers and a horny shell. **2** its flesh used for soup. —**turn turtle**, to capsize. **turtle-neck** *n.* a high close-fitting neck of a knitted garment. [alt. of OF *tortue* as (TORTOISE)]

turtle-dove *n.* a wild dove of the genus *Streptopelia*, especially *S. turtur*, noted for its soft cooing and its affection for its mate. [f. *turtle* (OE f. L *turtur*) + DOVE]

Tuscan /ˈtʌskən/ *adj.* **1** of Tuscany, a region of west central Italy. **2** (*Archit.*) of a simple unornamented order. —*n.* an inhabitant or the classical Italian language of Tuscany. [f. L (*Tuscus* Etruscan)]

tusk *n.* a long pointed tooth, especially one projecting from the mouth as in the elephant, walrus, or boar. [alt. of OE *tux*]

tussle *n.* a struggle, a scuffle. —*v.i.* to engage in a tussle. [orig. Sc. & N.Engl., perh. dim. of *touse* (as TOUSLE)]

tussock /ˈtʌsək/ *n.* a clump of grass etc. —**tussocky** *adj.* [perh. f. dial. *tusk* tuft]

tut *int.*, *n.*, & *v.i.* = TUT-TUT. [imit. of click of tongue]

tutelage /ˈtjuːtɪlɪdʒ/ *n.* **1** guardianship, being under this. **2** instruction, tuition. [f. L *tutela* (*tuēri* watch over)]

tutelary /ˈtjuːtɪlərɪ/ *adj.* serving as a guardian, giving protection. [as prec.]

tutor /ˈtjuːtə(r)/ *n.* **1** a private teacher, especially one in general charge of a person's education. **2** a university teacher supervising the studies or welfare of assigned undergraduates. **3** a book of instruction in a subject. —*v.t./i.* **1** to act as tutor to; to work as a tutor. **2** to restrain, to discipline. —**tutorship** *n.* [f. AF or L (as TUTELARY)]

tutorial /tjuːˈtɔrɪəl/ *adj.* of or as a tutor. —*n.* a period of individual tuition given by a college tutor. —**tutorially** *adv.* [f. L (as prec.)]

tutti /ˈtʊtiː/ *adv.* (*Mus.*) with all voices or instruments together. —*n.* a passage to be performed this way. [It., pl. of *tutto* all]

tutti-frutti /tʊtɪˈfrʊtɪ/ *n.* ice-cream containing or flavoured with mixed fruits. [It., = all fruits]

tut-tut *int.* expressing rebuke, impatience, or contempt. —*n.* such an exclamation. —*v.i.* (**-tt-**) to exclaim thus. [as TUT]

tutu /ˈtuːtuː/ *n.* a ballet dancer's short skirt made of layers of stiffened frills. [F]

tu-whit, tu-whoo /tʊˈwɪt tʊˈwuː/ *n.* the cry of an owl. [imit.]

tuxedo /tʌkˈsiːdəʊ/ *n.* (*pl.* **-os**) (*US*) a dinner-jacket. [f. *Tuxedo* Park, New York]

TV *abbr.* television.

twaddle /ˈtwɒd(ə)l/ *n.* useless or dull writing or talk. —*v.i.* to indulge in this. [f. earlier *twattle*, alt. of TATTLE]

twain *adj.* & *n.* (*archaic*) two. [OE, masc. nom. & acc. (as TWO)]

twang *n.* the sound made by a plucked string of

a musical instrument or by a bowstring; a quality of voice compared to this (esp. *nasal twang*). —*v.t./i.* to emit a twang; to cause to twang. [imit.]

'twas /twɒz, twəz/ (*archaic*) it was. [contr.]

tweak *v.t.* to pinch and twist or jerk. —*n.* such an action. [prob. f. dial. *twick* & TWITCH]

twee *adj.* affectedly dainty or quaint. [childish pronunc. of SWEET]

tweed *n.* a rough-surfaced woollen cloth, frequently of mixed colours; (in *pl.*) a suit of tweed. —**tweedy** *adj.* [orig. misreading of *tweel*, Sc. form of TWILL]

'tween *prep.* between. [f. BETWEEN]

tweet *n.* the chirp of a small bird. —*v.i.* to utter a tweet. [imit.]

tweeter *n.* a loudspeaker for accurately reproducing high-frequency signals. [f. TWEET]

tweezers /ˈtwi:zəz/ *n.pl.* a small pair of pincers for taking up small objects, plucking out hairs, etc. [f. *tweezes* pl. of obs. *tweeze* case for small instruments, f. F *étui*]

twelfth *adj.* next after the eleventh. —*n.* each of twelve equal parts of a thing. —**the Twelfth,** 12 August, on which grouse-shooting legally begins. **Twelfth-day** *n.* 6 January, the twelfth day after Christmas, the feast of Epiphany. **Twelfth-night** *n.* the night before this, formerly the last day of Christmas festivities and observed as a time of merrymaking. —**twelfthly** *adv.* [OE (as foll.)]

twelve *adj.* & *n.* **1** one more than eleven; the symbol for this (12, xii, XII). **2** a size etc. denoted by twelve. **twelve-note** *adj.* (*Mus.*) using the twelve chromatic notes of the octave arranged in a chosen order without a conventional key. [OE]

twelvefold *adj.* & *adv.* twelve times as much or as many; consisting of twelve parts. [f. prec. + -FOLD]

twelvemonth *n.* a year.

twenty *adj.* & *n.* **1** twice ten; the symbol for this (20, xx, XX). **2** (in *pl.*) the numbers, years, or degrees of temperature from 20 to 29. —**twentieth** *adj.* & *n.* [OE]

'twere /twɜ:(r), twə(r)/ (*archaic*) it were. [contr.]

twerp *n.* (*slang*) a stupid or objectionable person. [orig. unkn.]

Twi /twi:/ *n.* **1** the chief language spoken in Ghana, consisting of several mutually intelligible dialects. **2** its speakers.

twice *adv.* **1** two times, on two occasions. **2** in double degree or quantity. [OE (as TWO)]

twiddle *v.t.* to twirl or handle aimlessly; to twist quickly to and fro. —*n.* **1** an act of twiddling. **2** a twirled mark or sign. —**twiddle one's thumbs,** to make them rotate round each other, especially for want of anything to do. —**twiddler** *n.*, **twiddly** *adj.* [app. imit., after *twirl*, *fiddle*]

twig[1] *n.* a small branch or shoot of a tree or shrub. —**twiggy** *adj.* [OE]

twig[2] *v.t.* (**-gg-**) (*colloq.*) to understand, to realize or grasp the meaning or nature (of). [orig. unkn.]

twilight /ˈtwaɪlaɪt/ *n.* **1** the light from the sky when the sun is below the horizon, especially in the evening; the period of this. **2** a faint light. **3** a state of imperfect understanding. **4** a period of decline or destruction. —**twilight of the gods,** (*Scand. myth.*) the destruction of the gods and of the world in conflict with the powers of evil. **twilight zone,** a decrepit urban area; an area between others in position and character. [f. *twi-* (as TWO) + LIGHT[1]]

twilit /ˈtwaɪlɪt/ *adj.* dimly illuminated (as) by twilight. [f. prec.]

twill *n.* a fabric so woven as to have a surface of parallel ridges. —**twilled** *adj.* [f. OE *twili* two-thread]

'twill (*archaic*) it will. [contr.]

twin *n.* **1** each of a closely related or associated pair, especially of children or animals born at a birth; **the Twins,** the constellation or sign of the zodiac Gemini. **2** an exact counterpart of a person or thing. —*adj.* forming or being one of such a pair. —*v.t./i.* (**-nn-**) **1** to join intimately together; to pair (with). **2** to bear twins. —**twin bed,** each of a pair of single beds. **twin-engined** *adj.* having two engines. **twin set,** a woman's matching cardigan and jumper. **twin towns,** two towns, usually in different countries, establishing special cultural and social links. [OE, = double (as TWO)]

twine *n.* **1** strong thread or string made of two or more strands twisted together. **2** a coil, a twist. —*v.t./i.* to twist; to wind or coil. [OE]

twinge /twɪndʒ/ *n.* a slight or brief pang. [f. *twinge* v. = pinch, wring, f. OE]

twinkle *v.i.* **1** to shine with a light that flickers rapidly; to sparkle. **2** (of the eyes) to sparkle with amusement. **3** (of the feet in dancing etc.) to move rapidly. —*n.* a twinkling light, look, or movement. —**in the twinkling of an eye** *or* **in a twinkling,** in an instant. [OE]

twirl *v.t./i.* to twist lightly or rapidly. —*n.* **1** a twirling movement. **2** a twirled mark or sign. —**twirly** *adj.* [prob. alt. (after *whirl*) f. obs. *tirl* trill]

twist *v.t./i.* **1** to change the form of by rotating one end and not the other or the two ends in opposite ways; to undergo such a change; to make or become spiral; to distort, to warp; to wrench; (with *off*) to break off by twisting. **2** to wind (strands) about each other; to make (a rope etc.) thus. **3** to take a curved course; to make one's way in a winding manner. **4** to distort or misrepresent the meaning of (words). **5** (*colloq.*) to swindle. —*n.* **1** twisting; a twisted state. **2** a thing formed by twisting. **3** the point at which a thing twists or bends. **4** a peculiar tendency of mind or character. **5** (*colloq.*) a swindle. —**round the twist,** (*slang*) crazy. **twist a person's arm,** (*colloq.*) to coerce him. **twist a person round one's little finger,** to persuade or manage him very easily. [rel. to TWIN, TWINE]

twister *n.* (*colloq.*) an untrustworthy person, a swindler. [f. TWIST]

twisty *adj.* full of twists. —**twistily** *adv.*, **twistiness** *n.* [f. TWIST]

twit[1] *n.* (*slang*) a foolish person. [dial., perh. f. foll.]

twit[2] *v.t.* (**-tt-**) to taunt, usually good-humouredly. [OE]

twitch *v.t./i.* **1** to pull with a light jerk. **2** to quiver or contract spasmodically. —*n.* **1** a twitching movement. **2** (*colloq.*) a state of nervousness. [= LG *twikken*]

twitter *v.t./i.* **1** to make a series of light chirping or tremulous sounds. **2** to talk or utter rapidly in an anxious or nervous way. —*n.* **1** twittering. **2** (*colloq.*) an excited or nervous state. [imit.]

'twixt *prep.* (*archaic*) betwixt. [abbr.]

two /tu:/ *adj.* & *n.* **1** one more than one; the symbol for this (2, ii, II). **2** a size etc. denoted by two. —**in two,** in or into two pieces. **put two and two together,** to make an inference from known facts. **two-dimensional** *adj.* having or appearing to have length and breadth but no depth. **two-edged** *adj.* having two cutting edges. **two-faced** *adj.* insincere. **two-handed** *adj.* used with both hands or by two persons. **two-piece** *n.* a suit of clothes or a woman's bathing-suit comprising two separate parts. **two-ply** *adj.* (of wool etc.) of two strands, layers, or thicknesses. **two-step** *n.* a ballroom dance in march or polka time. **two-stroke** *adj.* (of an internal-combustion engine) having its power cycle completed in one up-and-down movement (i.e. two strokes) of the piston. **two-time** *v.t.* (*slang*) to swindle; to deceive, especially by infidelity. **two-up** *n.* (*Austral.* & *NZ*) a gambling game played by tossing two coins, bets being laid on the showing of two heads or two tails. [OE]

twofold *adj.* & *adv.* **1** twice as much or as many. **2** consisting of two parts. [f. TWO + -FOLD]

twopence /ˈtʌpəns/ *n.* the sum of two pence.

twopenny /ˈtʌpənɪ/ *adj.* **1** costing two pence. **2** cheap, worthless. —**twopenny-halfpenny** *adj.* insignificant, contemptible.

twosome /ˈtu:səm/ *n.* two people together, a pair or couple of persons. [f. TWO + -SOME]

'twould /twʊd/ (*archaic*) it would. [contr.]

tycoon /taɪˈku:n/ *n.* a business magnate. [f. Jap., = great prince]

tying *partic.* of TIE.

tyke /taɪk/ *n.* a low or objectionable fellow. [f. ON, = bitch]

tympanum /ˈtɪmpənəm/ *n.* (*pl.* **-a**) **1** the ear-drum; the middle-ear. **2** the space enclosed in a pediment or between a lintel and the arch above. [L, f. Gk *tumpanon* drum]

Tynwald /ˈtɪnwɒld/ *n.* the legislative assembly of the Isle of Man, which meets annually to proclaim newly enacted laws. [f. ON *thing-völlr* place of assembly]

type /taɪp/ *n.* **1** a class of people or things that have characteristics in common, a kind. **2** a typical example or instance. **3** (*colloq.*) a person of specified character. **4** a piece of metal etc. with a raised letter or character on its upper surface for use in printing; a kind or size of such pieces; a set or supply of these. —*v.t./i.* **1** to write with a typewriter. **2** to classify according to type. **3** to be a type or example of. —**type-cast** *v.t.* to cast (an actor) in the kind of part which he has the reputation of playing successfully or which seems to fit his personality. **type site,** an archaeological site where objects regarded as defining the characteristics of an industry etc. are found. [f. F or L f. Gk *tupos* impression (*tuptō* strike)]

typeface *n.* **1** a set of printing types in one design. **2** an inked surface of such types.

typescript *n.* a typewritten text or document.

typesetter *n.* **1** a compositor. **2** a machine for setting type. —**typesetting** *n.*

typewriter *n.* a machine for producing characters similar to those of print, with keys that are pressed to cause raised metal characters to strike the paper, usually through inked ribbon.

typewritten *adj.* produced with a typewriter.

typhoid /ˈtaɪfɔɪd/ *adj.* like typhus. —*n.* (also **typhoid fever**) an infectious bacterial fever with eruption of red spots on the chest and abdomen and severe intestinal irritation; a similar disease of animals. [f. TYPHUS]

typhoon /taɪˈfu:n/ *n.* a violent hurricane in the East Asian seas. [partly f. Chin., = great wind, partly f. Port. f. Arab.]

typhus /ˈtaɪfəs/ *n.* a rickettsial infectious fever with eruption of purple spots, great prostration, and usually delirium. [f. Gk *tuphos* smoke, stupor]

typical /ˈtɪpɪk(ə)l/ *adj.* **1** having the distinctive qualities of a particular type of person or thing; serving as a representative specimen. **2** characteristic. —**typically** *adv.* [f. L (as TYPE)]

typify /ˈtɪpɪfaɪ/ *v.t.* to be a representative

specimen of; to represent by a type. —**typification** /-fɪ'keɪʃ(ə)n/ *n.* [f. L *typus* type]

typist /'taɪpɪst/ *n.* a person who types, especially one employed to do so. [f. TYPE]

typography /taɪ'pɒgrəfɪ/ *n.* **1** printing as an art. **2** the style and appearance of printed matter. —**typographical** /-'græfɪk(ə)l/ *adj.*, **typographically** /-'græfɪkəlɪ/ *adv.* [f. F (as TYPE, -GRAPHY)]

tyrannical /tɪ'rænɪk(ə)l/ *adj.* given to or characteristic of tyranny. —**tyrannically** *adv.* [f. OF f. L f. Gk (as TYRANT)]

tyrannize /'tɪrənaɪz/ *v.t./i.* to exercise tyranny; to rule as or like a tyrant. [f. F (as TYRANT)]

tyrannosaur /tɪ'rænəsɔ:(r)/ *n.* a dinosaur (*Tyrannosaurus rex*) with very short front legs and a large head, that walked on its hind legs, the largest known carnivorous animal. [as TYRANT, after *dinosaur*]

tyrannous /'tɪrənəs/ *adj.* tyrannical. [f. L (as TYRANT)]

tyranny /'tɪrənɪ/ *n.* **1** the oppressive and arbitrary use of authority. **2** rule by a tyrant; a period of this; a State thus ruled. [as foll.]

tyrant /'taɪrənt/ *n.* **1** an oppressive or cruel ruler. **2** a person exercising power arbitrarily or oppressively. **3** (*Gk hist.*) an absolute ruler who seized power without legal right. [f. OF f. L f. Gk *turannos*]

tyre /taɪə(r)/ *n.* a rubber covering, usually inflated, placed round a wheel to form a soft contact with a road (see below). [var. of TIRE[2]]

tyro var. of TIRO.

Uu

U, u /juː/ *n.* (*pl.* **Us, U's**) **1** the twenty-first letter of the alphabet. **2** a U-shaped object or curve.

U *symbol* uranium.

U /juː/ *adj.* (*colloq.*) upper-class; supposedly characteristic of the upper class. [abbr.; coined by A. S. C. Ross (1954)]

UAE *abbr.* United Arab Emirates.

ubiquitous /juːˈbɪkwɪtəs/ *adj.* present everywhere or in several places simultaneously; often encountered. —**ubiquity** *n.* [f. L *ubique* everywhere]

U-boat /ˈjuːbəʊt/ *n.* (*hist.*) a German submarine, especially in the First and Second World War. [f. G (*unterseeboot* under-sea boat)]

udder *n.* the baglike milk-secreting organ of the cow, ewe, female goat, etc., with two or more teats. [OE]

UDI *abbr.* Unilateral Declaration of Independence.

UFO *abbr.*, **ufo** /ˈjuːfəʊ/ *n.* (*pl.* **-os**) an unidentified flying object. [acronym]

ugh /ʌh, ʊh/ *int.* expressing disgust or horror, or the sound of a cough or grunt. [imit.]

Ugli /ˈʌglɪ/ *n.* [P] a mottled green and yellow citrus fruit, a hybrid of the grapefruit and tangerine developed in Jamaica *c.*1930. [f. UGLY]

uglify /ˈʌglɪfaɪ/ *v.t.* to make ugly. [f. UGLY]

ugly /ˈʌglɪ/ *adj.* **1** unpleasing or repulsive to see or hear. **2** unpleasant in any way; hostile and threatening; discreditable. —**ugly customer,** an unpleasantly formidable person. **ugly duckling,** a person who at first seems unpromising but later becomes much admired or very able (like the cygnet in the brood of ducks in Hans Andersen's story). —**ugliness** *n.* [f. ON, = to be dreaded]

UHF *abbr.* ultra-high frequency.

UHT *abbr.* ultra heat treated (of milk, for long keeping).

UK *abbr.* United Kingdom.

ukase /juːˈkeɪz/ *n.* **1** an arbitrary command. **2** (*hist.*) an edict of the Russian government. [f. Russ. *ukaz*]

ukiyo-e /uːkiːˈjəʊjeɪ/ *n.* a school of Japanese art using subjects from everyday life and simple treatment. [Jap., = genre picture]

Ukrainian /juːˈkreɪnɪən/ *adj.* of a district (*the Ukraine*) north of the Black Sea, now the Ukrainian SSR. —**Ukrainian** *n.* a Ukranian person. [f. Russ., = frontier region (*u* at, *krai* edge)]

ukulele /juːkəˈleɪlɪ/ *n.* a small four-stringed (originally Portuguese) guitar. [Hawaiian]

ulcer *n.* **1** an open sore on the external or internal surface of the body or one of its organs. **2** a corroding or corrupting influence. —**ulcerous** *adj.* [f. L *ulcus*]

ulcerate /ˈʌlsəreɪt/ *v.t./i.* to form an ulcer (in or on). —**ulceration** /-ˈreɪʃ(ə)n/ *n.* [f. L *ulcerare* (as prec.)]

ulna /ˈʌlnə/ *n.* (*pl.* **-ae** /-iː/) the thinner and longer bone in the forearm on the side opposite to the thumb; a corresponding bone in an animal's foreleg or bird's wing. —**ulnar** *adj.* [L, rel. to Gk *ōlenē* and ELL]

ulster *n.* a long loose overcoat of rough cloth, often with a belt, of a kind originally sold in Belfast. [f. *Ulster* in Ireland.]

Ulsterman /ˈʌlstəmən/ *n.* (*pl.* **-men**) a native of Ulster. —**Ulsterwoman** *n. fem.* (*pl.* **-women**)

ult. *abbr.* ultimo.

ulterior /ʌlˈtɪərɪə(r)/ *adj.* (esp. of a motive) beyond what is obvious or admitted. [L, = further (as ULTRA-)]

ultimate /ˈʌltɪmət/ *adj.* **1** last, final, beyond which no other exists or is possible. **2** basic, fundamental. —**ultimately** *adv.* [f. L (*ultimus* last)]

ultimatum /ʌltɪˈmeɪtəm/ *n.* (*pl.* **-ums**) a final statement of terms, the rejection of which may lead to war or the end of co-operation etc. [L (as prec.)]

ultimo /ˈʌltɪməʊ/ *adj.* (in commerce) of last month. [L, = in the last (*mense* month)]

ultra- *prefix* **1** extremely, excessively (*ultra-conservative, ultra-modern*). **2** beyond. [f. L *ultra* beyond]

ultracentrifuge /ʌltrəˈsentrɪfjuːdʒ/ *n.* a high-speed centrifuge used to determine the size of small particles and large molecules by their rate of sedimentation.

ultra-high /ˈʌltrəhaɪ/ *adj.* (of frequency) between 300 and 3,000 MHz.

ultramarine /ʌltrəməˈriːn/ *n.* a brilliant blue pigment originally obtained from lapis lazuli;

the colour of this. —*adj.* of this colour. [f. obs. It. & L., = beyond the sea (because imported)]

ultramicroscope /ʌltrəˈmaɪkrəskəʊp/ *n.* an optical microscope used to detect particles smaller than a wavelength of light by illuminating them at an angle, so that the light scattered by the particles can be observed against a dark background.

ultramicroscopic /ʌltrəmaɪkrəˈskɒpɪk/ *adj.* **1** of such minute size as to be invisible under the ordinary microscope. **2** of or involving the use of the ultramicroscope.

ultrasonic /ʌltrəˈsɒnɪk/ *adj.* of or using sound waves with a pitch above the upper limit of human hearing. —**ultrasonics** *n.* the science and application of ultrasonic waves; (as *pl.*) these waves. —**ultrasonically** *adv.*

ultrasound /ˈʌltrəsaʊnd/ *n.* ultrasonic waves (see SOUND).

ultraviolet /ʌltrəˈvaɪələt/ *adj.* (of radiation) just beyond the violet end of the visible spectrum; of or using such radiation.

ululate /ˈju:ljʊleɪt/ *v.i.* to howl, to wail. —**ululation** /-ˈleɪʃ(ə)n/ *n.* [f. L *ululare* (imit.)]

umbel /ˈʌmb(ə)l/ *n.* a flower-cluster in which stalks nearly equal in length spring from a common centre and form a flat or curved surface, as in the carrot. —**umbellate** *adj.* [f. obs. F or L *umbella* sunshade]

umbellifer /ʌmˈbelɪfə(r)/ *n.* a plant of the order Umbelliferae, bearing umbels, to which the carrot, parsnip, celery, etc., belong. —**umbelliferous** /-bəˈlɪfərəs/ *adj.* [as prec. + *-fer* f. L *ferre* bear]

umber *n.* a pigment like ochre but darker and browner; the colour of this. —*adj.* of this colour. [f. F or It., = shadow, or f. L, = of the province Umbria]

umbilical /ʌmˈbɪlɪk(ə)l/ *adj.* of the navel. —**umbilical cord**, the flexible cordlike structure attaching the foetus to the placenta; an essential connecting-line in various technologies. [obs. F, or f. foll.]

umbilicus /ʌmˈbɪlɪkəs/ *n.* the navel; a navel-like formation. [L]

umbra /ˈʌmbrə/ *n.* (*pl.* **-ae** /-i:/ or **-as**) **1** a region of complete shadow where no light reaches a surface etc., especially that cast by the moon or the earth in an eclipse. **2** the dark central part of a sunspot. [L, = shadow]

umbrage /ˈʌmbrɪdʒ/ *n.* a sense of being offended. [f. OF f. L *umbraticus* (as prec.)]

umbrella /ʌmˈbrelə/ *n.* **1** a light collapsible usually circular canopy of cloth mounted on radial ribs attached to a central stick, used for protection against sunshine or (especially) as a portable protection against rain, or as a symbol of rank and authority in some Oriental and African countries. **2** any kind of general protecting force or influence; a co-ordinating or unifying agency. [f. It. *ombrella* dim. of *ombra* shade f. L *umbra*]

umlaut /ˈʊmlaʊt/ *n.* **1** a vowel-change in related words in Germanic languages, e.g. *man/men* in English, *mann/männer* in German. **2** the mark like a diaeresis used to mark this in German etc. [G (*um* about, *laut* sound)]

umpire /ˈʌmpaɪə(r)/ *n.* a person appointed to see that the rules of a game or contest are observed and to settle disputes (e.g. in a game of cricket or baseball), or to give a decision on any disputed question. —*v.t./i.* to act as umpire (in). [later form of *noumpere* f. OF *non per* not equal (*non* NON-, *per* PEER[2])]

umpteen /ʌmpˈti:n, ˈʌm-/ *adj.* (*slang*) many; an indefinite number of. —**umpteenth** *adj.* [joc. formation on -TEEN]

UN *abbr.* United Nations.

'un /ən/ *pron.* (*colloq.*) one (*a good 'un*). [dial. var. of ONE]

un- *prefix* added to (1) adjectives and their derivative nouns and adverbs, in the sense 'not' (*unusable, uneducated, unyielding, unofficial*), or in the sense 'the reverse of' with the implication of praise or blame (*unselfish, unsociable*); (2) verbs, denoting an action contrary to or annulling that of the simple verb (*unlock, untie*); (3) nouns, forming verbs in the senses 'deprive of', 'divest (oneself) of', 'release from' (*unfrock, unleash*), or 'cause to be no longer' (*unman*); (4) nouns, in the senses 'lack of' or 'the reverse of' (*unbelief, unemployment*). [OE]

The number of words that can be formed with this prefix is unlimited and only a selection can be given here.

unable /ʌnˈeɪb(ə)l/ *adj.* not able (to do a specified thing).

unaccompanied /ʌnəˈkʌmpənɪd/ *adj.* **1** not accompanied; alone, without an escort. **2** without musical accompaniment.

unaccountable /ʌnəˈkaʊntəb(ə)l/ *adj.* **1** that cannot be explained or accounted for. **2** not accountable for one's actions etc. —**unaccountably** *adv.*

unaccustomed /ʌnəˈkʌstəmd/ *adj.* not accustomed; not usual.

unadopted /ʌnəˈdɒptɪd/ *adj.* (of a road) not taken over for maintenance by a local authority.

unadulterated /ʌnəˈdʌltəreɪtɪd/ *adj.* pure.

unadvised /ʌnədˈvaɪzd/ *adj.* **1** indiscreet, rash. **2** not advised. —**unadvisedly** /-zɪdlɪ/ *adv.*

unalloyed /ʌnəˈlɔɪd/ *adj.* (of pleasure etc.) pure, sheer.

un-American *adj.* **1** not in accordance with American characteristics. **2** contrary to the ideals and interests of the USA.

unanimous /juːˈnænɪməs/ *adj.* all agreeing in an opinion or decision; (of an opinion or decision etc.) held or given by all. —**unanimity** /juːnəˈnɪmɪtɪ/ *n.*, **unanimously** *adv.* [f. L (*unus* one, *animus* mind)]

unanswerable /ʌnˈɑːnsərəb(ə)l/ *adj.* that cannot be refuted. —**unanswerably** *adv.*

unarmed /ʌnˈɑːmd/ *adj.* not armed, without weapons.

unashamed /ʌnəˈʃeɪmd/ *adj.* feeling no guilt, shameless. —**unashamedly** /-mɪdlɪ/ *adv.*

unasked /ʌnˈɑːskt/ *adj.* not asked (for), not requested or invited.

unassailable /ʌnəˈseɪləb(ə)l/ *adj.* that cannot be attacked or questioned. —**unassailably** *adv.*

unassuming /ʌnəˈsjuːmɪŋ/ *adj.* not arrogant, unpretentious.

unattached /ʌnəˈtætʃt/ *adj.* **1** not engaged or married. **2** not belonging to a particular regiment, church, club, college, etc.

unattended /ʌnəˈtendɪd/ *adj.* **1** not attended (*to*). **2** not accompanied; (of a vehicle) with no person in charge of it.

unavailing /ʌnəˈveɪlɪŋ/ *adj.* ineffectual.

unavoidable /ʌnəˈvɔɪdəb(ə)l/ *adj.* unable to be avoided. —**unavoidably** *adv.*

unaware /ʌnəˈweə(r)/ *adj.* not aware.

unawares /ʌnəˈweəz/ *adv.* unexpectedly, without noticing.

unbacked /ʌnˈbækt/ *adj.* **1** not supported, having no backers (especially in betting). **2** having no back or no backing.

unbalanced /ʌnˈbælənst/ *adj.* **1** not balanced. **2** mentally unsound.

unbar /ʌnˈbɑː(r)/ *v.t.* (**-rr-**) to remove the bar from (a gate etc.); to unlock.

unbearable /ʌnˈbeərəb(ə)l/ *adj.* that cannot be endured. —**unbearably** *adv.*

unbeatable /ʌnˈbiːtəb(ə)l/ *adj.* impossible to defeat or surpass.

unbeaten /ʌnˈbiːt(ə)n/ *adj.* not beaten; (of a record etc.) not surpassed.

unbecoming /ʌnbɪˈkʌmɪŋ/ *adj.* **1** not suitable, not befitting a person's status etc. **2** not suited to the wearer.

unbeknown /ʌnbɪˈnəʊn/ *adj.* (also **unbeknownst**) (*colloq.*) not known. —**unbeknown to,** without the knowledge of. [f. UN- + archaic *beknown* known]

unbelief /ʌnbɪˈliːf/ *n.* incredulity, disbelief especially in divine revelation or in a particular religion. —**unbeliever** *n.*

unbelievable /ʌnbəˈliːvəb(ə)l/ *adj.* not believable. —**unbelievably** *adv.*

unbeliever /ʌnbɪˈliːvə(r)/ *n.* a person who does not believe, especially one not believing in Christianity or Islam.

unbelieving /ʌnbɪˈliːvɪŋ/ *adj.* **1** atheistic; agnostic. **2** unduly incredulous.

unbend /ʌnˈbend/ *v.t./i.* (*past* & *p.p.* **unbent**) **1** to change or become changed from a bent position, to straighten. **2** to relax (the mind etc.) from strain, exertion, or severity; to become affable. **3** (*Naut.*) to unfasten (a cable), to untie (a rope).

unbending *adj.* **1** inflexible; refusing to alter one's demands. **2** austere; not becoming relaxed or affable.

unbidden /ʌnˈbɪd(ə)n/ *adj.* not commanded or invited.

unbind /ʌnˈbaɪnd/ *v.t.* (*past* & *p.p.* **unbound**) to release from bonds or from binding; to unfasten, to untie.

unblock /ʌnˈblɒk/ *v.t.* to remove an obstruction from.

unblushing /ʌnˈblʌʃɪŋ/ *adj.* shameless.

unbolt /ʌnˈbəʊlt/ *v.t.* to release (a door etc.) by drawing back the bolt(s).

unborn /ʌnˈbɔːn/ *adj.* not yet born; future.

unbosom /ʌnˈbʊz(ə)m/ *v.t.* to disclose (secrets etc.). —**unbosom oneself,** to disclose one's thoughts, feelings, secrets, etc.

unbounded /ʌnˈbaʊndɪd/ *adj.* infinite.

unbreakable /ʌnˈbreɪkəb(ə)l/ *adj.* not breakable.

unbridle /ʌnˈbraɪd(ə)l/ *v.t.* to remove the bridle from (a horse) or (*fig.*) restraint from (the tongue etc.).

unbridled /ʌnˈbraɪd(ə)ld/ *adj.* (of insolence, the tongue, etc.) unrestrained.

unbroken /ʌnˈbrəʊkən/ *adj.* **1** not broken. **2** not tamed. **3** not interrupted. **4** not surpassed.

unbuckle /ʌnˈbʌk(ə)l/ *v.t.* to release the buckle(s) of (a strap, shoe, etc.).

unburden /ʌnˈbɜːd(ə)n/ *v.t.* to relieve (oneself or one's conscience etc.) by confession.

unbutton /ʌnˈbʌt(ə)n/ *v.t.* to unfasten the buttons of.

uncalled-for /ʌnˈkɔldfɔː(r)/ *adj.* offered or intruded impertinently or unjustifiably.

uncanny /ʌnˈkænɪ/ *adj.* **1** strange and rather frightening. **2** extraordinary, beyond what is reckoned to be normal. —**uncannily** *adv.*, **uncanniness** *n.*

uncared-for /ʌnˈkeədfɔː(r)/ *adj.* neglected.

unceasing /ʌnˈsiːsɪŋ/ *adj.* not ceasing. —**unceasingly** *adv.*

unceremonious /ʌnserɪˈməʊnɪəs/ *adj.* without proper formality or dignity; abrupt in manner. —**unceremoniously** *adv.*

uncertain /ʌnˈsɜːt(ə)n/ *adj.* **1** not certainly knowing or known. **2** not to be depended on. **3** changeable. —**uncertainly** *adv.*

uncertainty *n.* being uncertain. —**uncertainty principle,** the principle that the momentum and position of a particle cannot both be precisely determined at the same time; any of various similar restrictions on the accuracy of measurement.

unchain /ʌnˈtʃeɪn/ *v.t.* to release from chains.

unchangeable /ʌnˈtʃeɪndʒəb(ə)l/ *adj.* that may not be changed.

uncharitable /ʌnˈtʃærɪtəb(ə)l/ *adj.* censorious, severe in judgement. —**uncharitably** *adv.*

unchristian /ʌnˈkrɪstjən/ *adj.* contrary to Christian principles, uncharitable.

uncial /ˈʌnsɪəl, ˈʌnʃ(ə)l/ *adj.* of or written in the kind of writing with characters partly resembling modern capitals, found in manuscripts of 4th-8th c. —*n.* an uncial letter or manuscript. [f. L (*uncia* inch)]

uncivil /ʌnˈsɪvɪl/ *adj.* ill-mannered, rude. —**uncivilly** *adv.*

unclasp /ʌnˈklɑːsp/ *v.t.* **1** to loosen the clasp(s) of. **2** to release the grip of (the hand(s) etc.).

uncle /ˈʌŋk(ə)l/ *n.* **1** a brother or brother-in-law of one's father or mother. **2** (*colloq.*) an unrelated friend of a parent. **3** (*slang*) a pawn broker. —**Uncle Sam,** a personification of the government or people of the United States of America. **Uncle Tom,** the name of the hero of Harriet Beecher Stowe's novel *Uncle Tom's Cabin* (1851-2), used allusively for a Black man who is submissively loyal or servile to Whites. [f. AF & OF f. L *avunculus*]

unclean /ʌnˈkliːn/ *adj.* **1** not clean; foul. **2** ceremonially impure. **3** unchaste.

unclose /ʌnˈkləʊz/ *v.t./i.* to open.

unclothe /ʌnˈkləʊð/ *v.t.* to remove the clothes from, to uncover.

uncoil /ʌnˈkɔɪl/ *v.t./i.* to draw out or become drawn out after having been coiled, to unwind.

uncommon /ʌnˈkɒmən/ *adj.* not common, unusual, remarkable.

uncommunicative /ʌnkəˈmjuːnɪkətɪv/ *adj.* not inclined to give information or an opinion etc., silent.

uncompromising /ʌnˈkɒmprəmaɪzɪŋ/ *adj.* refusing to compromise, unyielding, inflexible.

unconcern /ʌnkənˈsɜːn/ *n.* **1** freedom from anxiety. **2** indifference, apathy. —**unconcerned** *adj.*, **unconcernedly** /-nɪdlɪ/ *adv.*

unconditional /ʌnkənˈdɪʃən(ə)l/ *adj.* not subject to conditions or limitations, absolute. —**unconditionally** *adv.*

unconditioned *adj.* not subject to or determined by conditions. —**unconditioned reflex,** an instinctive response to a stimulus.

unconformity /ʌnkənˈfɔːmɪtɪ/ *n.* an instance of a break in the chronological sequence of layers of rock.

unconscionable /ʌnˈkɒnʃənəb(ə)l/ *adj.* **1** having no conscience, unscrupulous. **2** contrary to what one's conscience feels is right; unreasonably excessive. —**unconscionably** *adv.* [f. UN- + *conscion* obs. var. of CONSCIENCE]

unconscious /ʌnˈkɒnʃəs/ *adj.* **1** not conscious, not aware. **2** done or spoken etc. without conscious intention. —*n.* the part of the mind not normally accessible to consciousness. —**unconsciously** *adv.*, **unconsciousness** *n.*

unconstitutional /ʌnkɒnstɪˈtjuːʃən(ə)l/ *adj.* (of measures or acts etc.) not in accordance with a country's constitution. —**unconstitutionally** *adv.*

uncooperative /ʌnkəʊˈɒpərətɪv/ *adj.* not co-operative.

uncoordinated /ʌnkəʊˈɔːdɪneɪtɪd/ *adj.* not co-ordinated.

uncork /ʌnˈkɔːk/ *v.t.* **1** to draw the cork from (a bottle). **2** (*colloq.*) to give vent to (feelings).

uncouple /ʌnˈkʌp(ə)l/ *v.t.* to release from couples or couplings.

uncouth /ʌnˈkuːθ/ *adj.* awkward or clumsy in manner, boorish. [OE, = unknown (UN- + *cūth* p.p. of *cunnan* know, CAN[1])]

uncover /ʌnˈkʌvə(r)/ *v.t./i.* **1** to remove the cover or covering from. **2** to reveal, to disclose. **3** to take off one's cap or hat.

uncrowned /ʌnˈkraʊnd/ *adj.* not crowned. —**uncrowned king,** a person having the power but not the title of a king.

unction /ˈʌŋkʃ(ə)n/ *n.* **1** anointing for medical purposes or as a religious rite. **2** a substance used in this. **3** soothing words, thought, or quality. **4** pretended earnestness; excessive politeness. [f. L (*unguere* anoint)]

unctuous /ˈʌŋktjʊəs/ *adj.* **1** having an oily manner; smugly earnest or virtuous. **2** greasy, oily. —**unctuously** *adv.*, **unctuousness** *n.* [as prec.]

uncurl /ʌnˈkɜːl/ *v.t./i.* to straighten out from a curled state or position.

uncut /ʌnˈkʌt/ *adj.* not cut; (of a book) with the leaves not cut open or with untrimmed margins; (of a film) not censored; (of a diamond) not shaped; (of a fabric) with the loops of the pile not cut.

undeceive /ʌndɪˈsiːv/ *v.t.* to disillusion.

undecided /ʌndɪˈsaɪdɪd/ *adj.* **1** not yet settled or certain. **2** not yet having made up one's mind, irresolute. —**undecidedly** *adv.*

undemonstrative /ʌndɪˈmɒnstrətɪv/ *adj.* not given to showing strong feelings, reserved.

undeniable /ʌndɪˈnaɪəb(ə)l/ *adj.* that cannot be denied or disputed. —**undeniably** *adv.*

under *prep.* **1** in or to a position lower than, below; within or on the inside of (a surface etc.); at the foot of (a high wall). **2** less than. **3** inferior to; of lower rank than. **4** in the position or act of supporting or sustaining. **5** governed or commanded by. **6** on condition of; subject to an obligation imposed by. **7** in accordance with; as determined by; designated or indicated by. **8** in the category of. **9** (of a field etc.) planted with (a crop). **10** propelled by. **11** attested by. —*adv.* **1** in or into a lower position or subordinate condition. **2** in or into unconsciousness. **3** below a certain quantity, rank, age, etc. —*adj.* lower, situated underneath. [OE]

under- *prefix* in the senses (1) UNDER; (2) lower, inner; (3) inferior, subordinate; (4) insufficient, insufficiently; incomplete, incompletely. [OE (as prec.)]

underachieve /ʌndərəˈtʃi:v/ *v.i.* to do less well than was expected (esp. scholastically). —**underachiever** *n.*

underarm *adj.* & *adv.* **1** in the armpit. **2** (in cricket etc.) bowling or bowled etc. with the hand brought forward and upwards and not raised above shoulder level; (in tennis etc.) with the racket moved similarly.

underbelly *n.* the under-surface of an animal etc., especially as vulnerable to attack.

underbid /ʌndəˈbɪd/ *v.t.* (**-dd-**; *past* & *p.p.* **underbid**) **1** to make a lower bid than. **2** (in bridge) to bid less on (one's hand, or *absol.*) than its strength warrants. —/ˈʌndəbɪd/ *n.* such a bid.

undercarriage *n.* **1** an aircraft's landing-wheels etc. and their supports. **2** the supporting frame of a vehicle.

undercharge /ʌndəˈtʃɑ:dʒ/ *v.t.* **1** to charge too little for (a thing) or to (a person). **2** to put too little (explosive, electric, etc.) charge into.

underclass *n.* a subordinate social class; the lowest social stratum in a community, consisting of the poor and the unemployed.

undercliff *n.* a terrace or lower cliff formed by a landslip.

underclothes *n.pl.* garments worn under indoor clothing.

underclothing *n.* underclothes collectively.

undercoat *n.* **1** a layer of paint under a finishing coat; the paint used for this. **2** (in animals) a coat of hair under another. —*v.t.* to apply an undercoat to.

undercover /ʌndəˈkʌvə(r)/ *adj.* **1** surreptitious. **2** spying, especially by working among those observed.

undercroft *n.* a crypt. [f. UNDER- + obs. *croft* (f. MDu. f. L, = CRYPT)]

undercurrent *n.* **1** a current that is below the surface or below another current. **2** an underlying trend, influence, or feeling, especially one opposite to the one perceived.

undercut /ʌndəˈkʌt/ *v.t.* (**-tt-**; *past* & *p.p.* **undercut**) **1** to sell or work at a lower price than. **2** to strike (a ball) to make it rise high. **3** to cut away a part below. —/ˈʌndəkʌt/ *n.* an under-side of sirloin.

underdeveloped /ʌndədɪˈveləpt/ *adj.* not fully developed; (of a film) not developed enough to give a satisfactory image; (of a country) not having reached its potential level in economic development.

underdog *n.* a person etc. losing a fight or in a state of inferiority or subjection.

underdone /ʌndəˈdʌn/ *adj.* not thoroughly done; (of meat) not completely cooked throughout.

underemployed /ʌndərɪmˈplɔɪd/ *adj.* not fully employed. —**underemployment** *n.*

underestimate /ʌndəˈrestɪmeɪt/ *v.t.* to form too low an estimate of. —/-mət/ *n.* an estimate that is too low. —**underestimation** /-ˈmeɪʃ(ə)n/ *n.*

underexpose /ʌndərɪkˈspəʊz/ *v.t.* to expose for too short a time. —**underexposure** *n.*

underfed /ʌndəˈfed/ *adj.* insufficiently fed.

underfelt *n.* felt for laying under a carpet.

underfloor *adj.* situated beneath the floor.

underfoot /ʌndəˈfʊt/ *adv.* under one's feet, on the ground.

undergarment *n.* a piece of underclothing.

undergo /ʌndəˈgəʊ/ *v.t.* (*past* **underwent**; *p.p.* **undergone** /-ˈgɒn/) to be subjected to, to experience, to endure.

undergraduate /ʌndəˈgrædʊət/ *n.* a member of a university who has not yet taken a first degree.

underground /ʌndəˈgraʊnd/ *adv.* **1** beneath the surface of the ground. **2** in secret; into secrecy or hiding. —/ˈʌn-/ *adj.* **1** situated underground. **2** secret, hidden; of a secret political organization or one for resisting enemy forces controlling a country. **3** (of the press, cinema, etc.) involved in producing unconventional or experimental material. —/ˈʌn-/ *n.* **1** an underground railway. **2** an underground organization.

undergrowth *n.* a dense growth of shrubs etc., especially under large trees.

underhand *adj.* **1** acting or done in a sly or secret way. **2** (in cricket etc.) underarm. —**underhanded** *adj.*

underlay /ʌndəˈleɪ/ *v.t.* (*past* & *p.p.* **underlaid**) to lay a thing under (another) in order to support or raise it. —/ˈʌn-/ *n.* a layer of material (e.g. felt, rubber) laid under another as a protection or support.

underlie /ʌndəˈlaɪ/ *v.t.* (*past* **underlay**; *p.p.* **underlain**; *partic.* **underlying**) **1** to lie under (a stratum etc.). **2** to be the basis of (a doctrine or conduct etc.). **3** to exist beneath the superficial aspect of.

underline /ʌndəˈlaɪn/ *v.t.* **1** to draw a line under

(a word etc.). **2** to emphasize. —/ˈʌndəlaɪn/ *n.* **1** a line placed under a word. **2** a caption below an illustration.

underling /ˈʌndəlɪŋ/ *n.* (usu. *derog.*) a subordinate. [f. UNDER- + -LING]

undermanned /ʌndəˈmænd/ *adj.* having too few people as crew or staff.

undermentioned /ʌndəˈmenʃənd/ *adj.* mentioned at a later place in a book etc.

undermine /ʌndəˈmaɪn/ *v.t.* **1** to make an excavation under; to wear away the base of. **2** to weaken or wear out (the health etc.) gradually. **3** to injure (a person etc.) by secret or insidious means.

undermost *adj.* lowest, furthest underneath. —*adv.* in or to the undermost position.

underneath /ʌndəˈniːθ/ *prep.* **1** at or to a lower place than. **2** on the inside of. —*adv.* **1** at or to a lower place. **2** inside. —*n.* a lower surface or part. [OE (as UNDER, BENEATH)]

undernourished /ʌndəˈnʌrɪʃt/ *adj.* insufficiently nourished. —**undernourishment** *n.*

underpants *n.pl.* a man's undergarment covering the lower body and part of the legs.

under-part *n.* a lower or subordinate part.

underpass *n.* a road etc. passing under another; a crossing of this kind.

underpay /ʌndəˈpeɪ/ *v.t.* (*past* & *p.p.* **underpaid**) to pay too little to (a person) or in discharge of (a debt).

underpin /ʌndəˈpɪn/ *v.t.* (**-nn-**) **1** to support from below with masonry etc. **2** to strengthen.

underprivileged /ʌndəˈprɪvɪlɪdʒd/ *adj.* less privileged than others, not enjoying a normal standard of living or rights in a community.

underproof *adj.* containing less alcohol than proof spirit does.

underrate /ʌndəˈreɪt/ *v.t.* to have too low an opinion of.

underscore /ʌndəˈskɔ(r)/ *v.t.* to underline. —/ˈʌn-/ *n.* an underline below a word etc.

undersea *adj.* below the sea, below its surface.

underseal *v.t.* to coat the under-part of (a motor vehicle etc.) with a protective sealing layer. —*n.* a substance used for this.

under-secretary *n.* an official who is directly subordinate to one with the title 'secretary', especially a senior civil servant.

undersell /ʌndəˈsel/ *v.t.* (*past* & *p.p.* **undersold**) to sell at a lower price than (another seller).

under-sexed /ʌndəˈsekst/ *adj.* having less than the normal degree of sexual desire.

undershirt *n.* an undergarment worn under a shirt, a vest.

undershoot /ʌndəˈʃuːt/ *v.t.* (*past* & *p.p.* **undershot**) (of an aircraft) to land short of (a runway etc.).

undershot *adj.* **1** (of a water-wheel) turned by water flowing under it. **2** (of the lower jaw) projecting beyond the upper jaw.

under-side *n.* the side or surface underneath.

undersigned *adj.* whose signature(s) is or are appended.

undersized *adj.* of less than the usual size.

underskirt *n.* a skirt worn under another, a petticoat.

underslung *adj.* supported from above.

underspend /ʌndəˈspend/ *v.t./i.* (*past* & *p.p.* **underspent**) to spend less than (a specified amount); to spend too little.

understaffed /ʌndəˈstɑːft/ *adj.* having too few staff.

understand /ʌndəˈstænd/ *v.t./i.* (*past* & *p.p.* **understood**) **1** to perceive the meaning of (words, a language, or a person). **2** to perceive the significance, explanation, or cause of. **3** to be sympathetically aware of the character or nature of, to know how to deal with. **4** to infer, especially from information received; to take as implied or granted; to supply (a word or words) mentally. **5** to have understanding in general or in particular. [OE (as UNDER-, STAND)]

understandable *adj.* that may be understood. —**understandably** *adv.* [f. prec.]

understanding *n.* **1** the power of thought, intelligence. **2** the ability to understand. **3** an agreement; a thing agreed upon. **4** harmony in opinion or feeling. **5** sympathetic awareness or tolerance. —*adj.* having or showing understanding, insight, or good judgement; able to be sympathetic to others' feelings or points of view. [f. UNDERSTAND]

understate /ʌndəˈsteɪt/ *v.t.* to express in greatly or unduly restrained terms, to represent as being less than it really is. —**understatement** *n.*

understeer *v.i.* (of a vehicle) to have a tendency to turn less sharply than was intended. —*n.* this tendency.

understudy *n.* one who studies the role in a play or the duties etc. of another in order to be able to take his or her place at short notice if necessary. —*v.t.* to study (a role etc.) thus; to act as understudy to (a person).

undertake /ʌndəˈteɪk/ *v.t.* (*past* **undertook** /-ˈtʊk/; *p.p.* **undertaken**) **1** to agree or promise to do something; to make oneself responsible for, to engage in. **2** to guarantee, to affirm.

undertaker /ˈʌndəteɪkə(r)/ *n.* one who professionally makes arrangements for funerals.

undertaking /ʌndəˈteɪkɪŋ/ *n.* **1** work etc. undertaken, an enterprise. **2** a promise or guarantee. **3** /ˈʌn-/ the management of funerals.

undertone *n.* **1** a low or subdued tone. **2** a colour that modifies another. **3** an underlying quality or implication; an undercurrent of feeling.

undertow *n.* a current below the surface of the sea, moving in a direction opposite to that of the surface current.

undervalue /ʌndəˈvælju:/ *v.t.* to value insufficiently. —**undervaluation** /-ˈeɪʃ(ə)n/ *n.*

undervest *n.* a vest (undergarment).

underwater /ʌndəˈwɔ:tə(r)/ *adj.* situated, used, or done beneath the surface of water. —*adv.* beneath the surface of water.

underwear *n.* underclothes.

underweight /ʌndəˈweɪt/ *adj.* below the normal, required, or suitable weight. —/ˈʌn-/ *n.* insufficient weight.

underwood *n.* undergrowth.

underworld *n.* **1** (also **Underworld**; in mythology) the abode of the spirits of the dead, under the earth. **2** the section of society that is habitually engaged in crime.

underwrite *v.t.* (*past* **underwrote**; *p.p.* **underwritten**) **1** to sign and accept liability under (an insurance policy, especially on shipping etc.); to accept (a liability) thus. **2** to undertake to finance or support. **3** to agree to take up, in a new company or new issue (a certain number of shares if not applied for by the public). —**underwriter** *n.*

undeserved /ʌndɪˈzɜ:vd/ *adj.* not deserved (as a reward or punishment). —**undeservedly** /-vɪdlɪ/ *adv.*

undesirable /ʌndɪˈzaɪərəb(ə)l/ *adj.* not desirable, objectionable. —*n.* an undesirable person. —**undesirability** /-ˈbɪlɪtɪ/ *n.*, **undesirably** *adv.*

undetermined /ʌndɪˈtɜ:mɪnd/ *adj.* undecided.

undies /ˈʌndɪz/ *n.pl.* (*colloq.*) women's underclothes. [abbr.]

undignified /ʌnˈdɪgnɪfaɪd/ *adj.* not dignified.

undine /ˈʌndi:n/ *n.* a female water-spirit. [invented by Paracelsus f. L *unda* wave]

undo /ʌnˈdu:/ *v.t.* (*past* **undid**; *p.p.* **undone** /-ˈdʌn/) **1** to unfasten; to unfasten the garment(s) of. **2** to annul, to cancel the effect of. **3** to ruin the prospects, reputation, or morals etc. of. [OE (as UN-, DO¹)]

undoing /ʌnˈdu:ɪŋ/ *n.* **1** ruin; a cause of this. **2** a reversal of what has been done. [f. UNDO]

undone /ʌnˈdʌn/ *adj.* **1** not done. **2** not fastened. **3** (*archaic*) brought to ruin. [f. UNDO]

undoubted /ʌnˈdaʊtɪd/ *adj.* not regarded as doubtful, not disputed. —**undoubtedly** *adv.*

undreamed /ʌnˈdri:md/ *adj.* (also **undreamt** /-ˈdremt/) not (even) dreamed; (with *-of*) not imagined, not thought to be possible.

undress /ʌnˈdres/ *v.t./i.* to take off one's clothes; to take off the clothes of (a person). —*n.* ordinary dress or uniform as opposed to full dress or uniform for ceremonial occasions; casual or informal dress. —/ˈʌn-/ *adj.* constituting such dress or uniform.

undue /ʌnˈdju:/ *adj.* excessive, disproportionate. —**unduly** *adv.*

undulate /ˈʌndjʊleɪt/ *v.i.* to have a wavy motion or look. —**undulation** /-ˈleɪʃ(ə)n/ *n.*, **undulatory** *adj.* [f. L (*unda* wave)]

undying /ʌnˈdaɪɪŋ/ *adj.* immortal; everlasting, never-ending.

unearned /ʌnˈɜ:nd/ *adj.* not earned. —**unearned income,** income from interest payments etc. as opposed to salary, wages, or fees.

unearth /ʌnˈɜ:θ/ *v.t.* **1** to uncover or obtain from the ground or by digging. **2** to bring to light, to find by searching.

unearthly /ʌnˈɜ:θlɪ/ *adj.* **1** not earthly. **2** supernatural, mysterious and frightening. **3** (*colloq.*) absurdly early or late, inconvenient. —**unearthliness** *n.*

uneasy /ʌnˈi:zɪ/ *adj.* **1** not comfortable. **2** not confident, worried. **3** worrying. —**uneasily** *adv.*, **uneasiness** *n.*

uneatable /ʌnˈi:təb(ə)l/ *adj.* not fit to be eaten, especially because of its condition.

uneconomic /ʌni:kəˈnɒmɪk/ *adj.* not profitable, not likely to be profitable.

uneducated /ʌnˈedjʊkeɪtɪd/ *adj.* not educated, ignorant.

unemployable /ʌnɪmˈplɔɪəb(ə)l/ *adj.* unfitted by character etc. for paid employment.

unemployed /ʌnɪmˈplɔɪd/ *adj.* **1** temporarily out of work; lacking employment. **2** not in use. —**unemployment** *n.*

unencumbered /ʌnɪnˈkʌmbəd/ *adj.* (of an estate) having no liabilities on it.

unending /ʌnˈendɪŋ/ *adj.* having or apparently having no end.

unequal /ʌnˈi:kw(ə)l/ *adj.* **1** not equal. **2** of varying quality. **3** not with equal advantage to both sides; not well matched. —**unequally** *adv.*

unequalled *adj.* superior to all others.

unequivocal /ʌnɪˈkwɪvək(ə)l/ *adj.* not ambiguous, clear and unmistakable. —**unequivocally** *adv.*

unerring /ʌnˈɜ:rɪŋ/ *adj.* not erring, not failing or missing the mark. —**unerringly** *adv.*

UNESCO /ju:ˈneskəʊ/ *abbr.* (also **Unesco**) United Nations Educational, Scientific, and Cultural Organization.

unethical /ʌnˈeθɪk(ə)l/ *adj.* not ethical; unscrupulous in professional conduct. —**unethically** *adv.*

uneven /ʌnˈi:v(ə)n/ *adj.* **1** not level or smooth. **2** not uniform or equable, varying. **3** (of a contest) unequal. —**unevenly** *adv.*, **unevenness** *n.*

unexampled /ʌnɪgˈzɑːmp(ə)ld/ *adj.* having no precedent or nothing else that can be compared with it.

unexceptionable /ʌnɪkˈsepʃ(ə)nəb(ə)l/ *adj.* with which no fault can be found. —**unexceptionably** *adv.*

unexceptional /ʌnɪkˈsepʃən(ə)l/ *adj.* not exceptional, quite ordinary. —**unexceptionally** *adv.*

unexpected /ʌnɪkˈspektɪd/ *adj.* not expected. —**unexpectedly** *adv.*

unfailing /ʌnˈfeɪlɪŋ/ *adj.* not failing; not running short; constant; reliable.

unfair /ʌnˈfeə(r)/ *adj.* not impartial; not in accordance with justice. —**unfairly** *adv.*, **unfairness** *n.*

unfaithful /ʌnˈfeɪθfʊl/ *adj.* **1** not loyal, not keeping one's promise. **2** adulterous. —**unfaithfully** *adv.*, **unfaithfulness** *n.*

unfamiliar /ʌnfəˈmɪljə(r)/ *adj.* not familiar. —**unfamiliarity** /-lɪˈærətɪ/ *n.*

unfasten /ʌnˈfɑːs(ə)n/ *v.t./i.* to make or become loose; to open the fastening(s) of; to detach.

unfeeling /ʌnˈfiːlɪŋ/ *adj.* **1** lacking the power of sensation or sensitivity. **2** unsympathetic, not caring about the feelings of others. —**unfeelingly** *adv.*, **unfeelingness** *n.*

unfetter /ʌnˈfetə(r)/ *v.t.* to release from fetters.

unfit /ʌnˈfɪt/ *adj.* **1** not fit, unsuitable. **2** not in perfect health or physical condition. —*v.t.* (**-tt-**) to make unsuitable.

unfix /ʌnˈfɪks/ *v.t.* to release or loosen from a fixed state; to detach.

unflappable /ʌnˈflæpəb(ə)l/ *adj.* (*colloq.*) imperturbable. —**unflappability** /-ˈbɪlɪtɪ/ *n.*

unfledged /ʌnˈfledʒd/ *adj.* **1** (of a bird) not fledged. **2** (of a person) inexperienced.

unfold /ʌnˈfəʊld/ *v.t./i.* **1** to open the fold(s) of; to spread or become spread out. **2** to reveal (thoughts etc.). **3** to become visible or known; (of a story etc.) to develop.

unforgettable /ʌnfəˈgetəb(ə)l/ *adj.* that may not be forgotten.

unformed /ʌnˈfɔːmd/ *adj.* not formed; shapeless.

unfortunate /ʌnˈfɔːtjʊnət, -tʃənət/ *adj.* **1** unlucky; unhappy. **2** regrettable. —*n.* an unfortunate person. —**unfortunately** *adv.*

unfounded /ʌnˈfaʊndɪd/ *adj.* with no foundation of fact(s).

unfreeze /ʌnˈfriːz/ *v.t./i.* (*past* **unfroze**; *p.p.* **unfrozen**) **1** to thaw; to cause to thaw. **2** to make (frozen assets) available again.

unfrock /ʌnˈfrɒk/ *v.t.* to deprive (a clergyman) of ecclesiastical status.

unfurl /ʌnˈfɜːl/ *v.t./i.* to unroll; to spread out.

unfurnished /ʌnˈfɜːnɪʃt/ *adj.* **1** without furniture. **2** not supplied *with*.

ungainly /ʌnˈgeɪnlɪ/ *adj.* awkward-looking, clumsy, ungraceful. —**ungainliness** *n.* [f. UN- + obs. *gain* (OE f. ON *gegn* straight)]

unget-at-able /ʌngetˈætəb(ə)l/ *adj.* (*colloq.*) inaccessible.

ungird /ʌnˈgɜːd/ *v.t.* to release the girdle of.

ungodly /ʌnˈgɒdlɪ/ *adj.* **1** not giving reverence to God; not religious; wicked. **2** (*colloq.*) absurdly early or late, inconvenient. —**ungodliness** *n.*

ungovernable /ʌnˈgʌvənəb(ə)l/ *adj.* uncontrollable, violent.

ungracious /ʌnˈgreɪʃəs/ *adj.* not kindly or courteous.

ungrammatical /ʌngrəˈmætɪk(ə)l/ *adj.* contrary to the rules of grammar. —**ungrammatically** *adv.*

ungrateful /ʌnˈgreɪtf(ə)l/ *adj.* feeling no gratitude.

unguarded /ʌnˈgɑːdɪd/ *adj.* **1** not guarded. **2** incautious, thoughtless.

unguent /ˈʌŋgwənt/ *n.* an ointment; a lubricant. [f. L *unguentum* (*unguere* anoint)]

ungulate /ˈʌŋgjʊlət/ *adj.* hoofed. —*n.* a hoofed mammal. [f. L (*ungula* hoof)]

unhallowed /ʌnˈhæləʊd/ *adj.* not consecrated; not sacred, wicked.

unhand /ʌnˈhænd/ *v.t.* (*rhetorical*) to take one's hands off (a person), to let go of.

unhappy /ʌnˈhæpɪ/ *adj.* **1** not happy, sad. **2** unfortunate. **3** unsuitable; unsuccessful. —**unhappily** *adv.*, **unhappiness** *n.*

unharness /ʌnˈhɑːnɪs/ *v.t.* to remove the harness from.

unhealthy /ʌnˈhelθɪ/ *adj.* **1** not having or not showing good health. **2** unwholesome. **3** (of a place etc.) harmful to health; unwholesome; (*slang*) dangerous to life. —**unhealthily** *adv.*, **unhealthiness** *n.*

unheard *adj.* not heard. —**unheard-of** *adj.* unprecedented.

unhinge /ʌnˈhɪndʒ/ *v.t.* **1** to take (a door etc.) off its hinges. **2** (esp. in *p.p.*) to cause to become mentally unbalanced.

unhitch /ʌnˈhɪtʃ/ *v.t.* to release from a hitched state; to unhook, to unfasten.

unholy /ʌnˈhəʊlɪ/ *adj.* **1** impious, wicked. **2** (*colloq.*) very great, outrageous. —**unholiness** *n.*

unhook /ʌnˈhʊk/ *v.t.* **1** to remove from a hook or hooks. **2** to unfasten by releasing a hook or hooks.

unhoped-for /ʌnˈhəʊptfɔː(r)/ *adj.* not hoped for, not expected.

unhorse /ʌnˈhɔːs/ *v.t.* to throw or drag (a rider) from a horse.

unhuman /ʌn'hju:mən/ *adj.* not human; superhuman; inhuman.

uni- /ju:nɪ-/ *in comb.* one, having or consisting of one. [L (*unus* one)]

Uniat /'ju:nɪæt/ *adj.* of the Churches in eastern Europe and the Near East that acknowledge the pope's supremacy and are in communion with Rome but retain their respective languages, rites, and canon law in accordance with the terms of their union. —*n.* a member of such a Church. [f. Russ. *uniyat* f. L *unio* union]

unicameral /ju:nɪ'kæmər(ə)l/ *adj.* with one legislative chamber. [f. UNI- + L *camera* chamber]

UNICEF /'ju:nɪsef/ *abbr.* United Nations (International) Children's (Emergency) Fund.

unicellular /ju:nɪ'seljʊlə(r)/ *adj.* (of an organism) consisting of one cell. [f. UNI- + CELLULAR]

unicorn /'ju:nɪkɔ:n/ *n.* a mythical animal usually regarded as having the body of a horse with a single straight horn projecting from its forehead. [f. OF f. L, transl. Gk *monokerōs* (= single horn)]

unidentified /ʌnaɪ'dentɪfaɪd/ *adj.* not identified.

unification /ju:nɪfɪ'keɪʃ(ə)n/ *n.* unifying, being unified. [f. UNIFY]

uniform /'ju:nɪfɔ:m/ *adj.* **1** not changing in form or character, unvarying. **2** conforming to the same standard or rule. —*n.* distinctive clothing worn by members of the same school or organization. —**uniformly** *adv.* [f. F or L *uniformis* (UNI-, *forma* form)]

uniformed *adj.* wearing a uniform. [f. prec.]

uniformity /ju:nɪ'fɔ:mɪtɪ/ *n.* being uniform, sameness, consistency. [f. UNIFORM]

unify /'ju:nɪfaɪ/ *v.t.* to form into a single unit, to unite. [f. F or L *unificare* (*unus* one, *facere* make)]

unilateral /ju:nɪ'lætər(ə)l/ *adj.* done by or affecting only one side or party. —**Unilateral Declaration of Independence,** the declaration of independence from the United Kingdom made by Rhodesia under Ian Smith in 1965. —**unilaterally** *adv.* [f. UNI- + LATERAL]

unimpeachable /ʌnɪm'pi:tʃəb(ə)l/ *adj.* not open to doubt or question, completely trustworthy. —**unimpeachably** *adv.*

uninformed /ʌnɪn'fɔ:md/ *adj.* not informed; ignorant.

uninhabitable /ʌnɪn'hæbɪtəb(ə)l/ *adj.* not suitable for habitation.

uninhibited /ʌnɪn'hɪbɪtɪd/ *adj.* not inhibited; having no inhibitions.

uninspired /ʌnɪn'spaɪəd/ *adj.* not inspired; (of a speech or performance etc.) commonplace, not outstanding.

unintelligible /ʌnɪn'telɪdʒəb(ə)l/ *adj.* not intelligible, impossible to understand. —**unintelligibly** *adv.*

uninterested /ʌn'ɪntrəstɪd/ *adj.* not interested; showing or feeling no concern.

uninviting /ʌnɪn'vaɪtɪŋ/ *adj.* unattractive, repellent.

union /'ju:njən, 'ju:nɪən/ *n.* **1** uniting, being united. **2** a whole formed by uniting parts; an association formed by the uniting of people or groups. **3** a trade union. **4** a coupling for pipes or rods. **5** (*Math.*) the set containing every element that is a member of at least one of two or more other sets. —**the Union,** the union of the English and Scottish crowns in 1603 or of their parliaments in 1707, or of Great Britain and Ireland in 1801. **union catalogue,** a catalogue showing the combined holdings of several libraries. **Union Jack** *or* **flag,** the national flag or ensign of the United Kingdom (formerly of Great Britain), formed by combining the crosses of the three patron saints. **Union Territory,** any of the six administrative territories within the Republic of India. [f. OF or L *unio* unity (*unus* one)]

unionist /'ju:njənɪst/ *n.* **1** (in specific uses **Unionist**) an advocate of political or organizational union, esp. between Britain and Ireland; (*US*) a supporter or advocate of the Federal Union of the United States of America, especially one who during the Civil War (1861-5) was opposed to secession. **2** a member of a trade union. —**unionism** *n.* [f. UNION]

unionize /'ju:njənaɪz/ *v.t.* to bring under trade-union organization or rules. —**unionization** /-'zeɪʃ(ə)n/ *n.* [f. UNION]

unique /jʊ'ni:k/ *adj.* **1** being the only one of its kind, having no like or equal or parallel. **2** (D) unusual. —**uniquely** *adv.* [F f. L *unicus* (*unus* one)]

unisex /'ju:nɪseks/ *n.* the tendency of the human sexes to become indistinguishable in dress etc. —*adj.* designed to be suitable for both sexes. [f. UNI- + SEX]

unison /'ju:nɪs(ə)n/ *n.* **1** (*Mus.*) coincidence in pitch of sounds or notes; (esp. **in unison**) combination of voices or instruments at the same pitch or in a different octave. **2** agreement. [OF or f. L *unisonus* (UNI-, *sonus* sound)]

unit /'ju:nɪt/ *n.* **1** an individual thing, person, or group regarded for purposes of calculation etc. as single and complete or as part of a complex whole. **2** a quantity chosen as a standard in terms of which other quantities may be expressed, or for which a stated charge is made. **3** the smallest share in a unit trust. **4** a part or group with a specified function within a complex machine or organization. **5** a piece of furniture for fitting with others like it or made of complementary parts. —**unit price,** the price charged for each unit of goods supplied. **unit trust,** an investment company investing contributions from a number of people in varied stocks and paying contributors a dividend (calculated on the average return on the stocks) in proportion to their holdings. [f. L *unus* one, prob. after *digit*]

unitarian /ju:nɪˈteərɪən/ *n.* **1** an advocate of unity or centralization, e.g. in politics. **2** **Unitarian,** a person who believes that God is one person not a Trinity; a member of a religious body maintaining this. —**Unitarianism** *n.* [f. L *unitas* unity]

unitary /ˈju:nɪtərɪ/ *adj.* **1** of a unit or units. **2** marked by unity or uniformity. [f. UNIT or UNITY]

unite /jʊˈnaɪt/ *v.t./i.* **1** to join together, to make or become one. **2** to agree, combine, or co-operate. —**United Kingdom,** Great Britain and Northern Ireland. **United Nations,** an international peace-seeking organization. **United Reformed Church,** the Church formed in 1972 by the union of the English Presbyterian and Congregational Churches. **United States (of America),** a republic in North America. [f. L *unire* (*unus* one)]

unity /ˈju:nɪtɪ/ *n.* **1** the state of being one or a unit. **2** a thing forming a complex whole. **3** (*Math.*) the number 'one'. **4** harmony; agreement in feelings, ideas, or aims etc. [f. OF f. L *unitas* (*unus* one)]

univalent /ju:nɪˈveɪlənt/ *adj.* having a chemical valence of one. [f. UNI- + VALENCE]

univalve /ˈju:nɪvælv/ *adj.* having one valve. —*n.* a univalve mollusc. [f. UNI- + VALVE]

universal /ju:nɪˈvɜ:s(ə)l/ *adj.* of, for, or done by all; applicable to all cases. —*n.* (*Philos.*) a general notion or idea; a thing that by its nature may be predicated of many. —**universal coupling** *or* **joint,** one that can transmit power by a shaft coupled at any selected angle. **universal time,** that used for astronomical reckoning at all places. —**universality** /-ˈsælɪtɪ/ *n.*, **universally** *adv.* [f. OF or L (as UNIVERSE)]

universe /ˈju:nɪvɜ:s/ *n.* (also **Universe**) all existing things including the Earth and its creatures and all the heavenly bodies; all mankind. [f. F f. L *universus* combined into one (UNI-, *vertere* turn)]

university /ju:nɪˈvɜ:sɪtɪ/ *n.* an educational institution that provides instruction and facilities for research in many branches of advanced learning, and confers degrees; its members collectively. [f. OF f. L (as prec.)]

unjust /ʌnˈdʒʌst/ *adj.* not just, not fair. —**unjustly** *adv.*

unkempt /ʌnˈkempt/ *adj.* of untidy or uncared-for appearance. [f. UN- + archaic *kempt* combed]

unkind /ʌnˈkaɪnd/ *adj.* not kind; harsh, cruel. —**unkindly** *adv.*, **unkindness** *n.*

unknot /ʌnˈnɒt/ *v.t.* (**-tt-**) to release the knot(s) of, to untie.

unknown /ʌnˈnəʊn/ *adj.* not known, unfamiliar; not identified. —*n.* **1** an unknown thing or person. **2** an unknown quantity. —**unknown quantity,** a person or thing whose nature or significance etc. cannot be determined. **Unknown Soldier** *or* (in Britain) **Warrior,** an unnamed representative of a country's armed services killed in battle, buried in a tomb serving as a national memorial. **unknown to,** without the knowledge of.

unlace /ʌnˈleɪs/ *v.t.* to undo the lace(s) of; to unfasten or loosen thus.

unladen /ʌnˈleɪd(ə)n/ *adj.* not laden. —**unladen weight,** the weight of a vehicle etc. when not loaded with goods.

unlatch /ʌnˈlætʃ/ *v.t.* to release the latch of; to open thus.

unlearn /ʌnˈlɜ:n/ *v.t.* to discard from one's memory; to rid oneself of (a habit, false information, etc.).

unlearned[1] /ʌnˈlɜ:nɪd/ *adj.* not well educated.

unlearned[2] /ʌnˈlɜ:nd/ *adj.* (also **unlearnt**) (of a lesson etc.) not learnt.

unleash /ʌnˈli:ʃ/ *v.t.* **1** to release from a leash or restraint. **2** to set free to engage in pursuit or attack (*lit.* or *fig.*).

unleavened /ʌnˈlev(ə)nd/ *adj.* not leavened; made without yeast or other raising agent.

unless /ʌnˈles/ *conj.* if not; except when. [f. LESS preceded by *on* or *in*]

unlettered /ʌnˈletəd/ *adj.* illiterate.

unlike /ʌnˈlaɪk/ *adj.* **1** not like, different from. **2** uncharacteristic of. —*prep.* differently from. —**unlike signs,** (*Math.*) plus and minus.

unlikely /ʌnˈlaɪklɪ/ *adj.* **1** not likely to happen or be true; not to be expected (to do a specified thing). **2** not likely to be successful.

unlimited /ʌnˈlɪmɪtɪd/ *adj.* not limited; very great or numerous.

unlined /ʌnˈlaɪnd/ *adj.* **1** not marked with lines. **2** without a lining.

unlisted /ʌnˈlɪstɪd/ *adj.* not in a published list, especially of telephone numbers or Stock Exchange prices.

unload /ʌnˈləʊd/ *v.t.* **1** to remove the load from (a ship etc., or *absol.*); to remove (the load) from a ship etc. **2** to remove the charge from (a firearm etc.). **3** (*colloq.*) to get rid of.

unlock /ʌnˈlɒk/ *v.t.* to release the lock of (a door etc.); to release (as if) by unlocking.

unlooked-for /ʌnˈlʊktfɔ(r)/ *adj.* unexpected.

unloose /ʌnˈlu:s/ *v.t.* (also **unloosen**) to loose.

unlucky /ʌnˈlʌkɪ/ *adj.* **1** not lucky; wretched; having or bringing bad luck. **2** ill-judged. —**unluckily** *adv.*

unmake /ʌnˈmeɪk/ *v.t.* (*past* & *p.p.* **unmade**) **1** to destroy, to annul. **2** (in *p.p.*) not made.

unman /ʌnˈmæn/ *v.t.* (**-nn-**) to weaken the manly qualities (e.g. self-control, courage) of; to cause to weep etc.

unmanageable /ʌnˈmænɪdʒəb(ə)l/ *adj.* not (easily) managed or manipulated or controlled. —**unmanageably** *adv.*

unmanned /ʌnˈmænd/ *adj.* not manned; operated without a crew.

unmannerly /ʌnˈmænəlɪ/ *adj.* without good manners, showing a lack of good manners. —**unmannerliness** *n.*

unmarked /ʌnˈmɑːkt/ *adj.* **1** not marked. **2** not noticed.

unmarried /ʌnˈmærɪd/ *adj.* not married.

unmask /ʌnˈmɑːsk/ *v.t./i.* **1** to remove the mask from; to remove one's mask. **2** to expose the true character of.

unmeaning /ʌnˈmiːnɪŋ/ *adj.* without meaning.

unmeant /ʌnˈment/ *adj.* not intended.

unmentionable /ʌnˈmenʃənəb(ə)l/ *adj.* so bad, embarrassing, or shocking that it cannot (properly) be spoken of.

unmistakable /ʌnmɪˈsteɪkəb(ə)l/ *adj.* that cannot be mistaken for another or doubted, clear and obvious. —**unmistakably** *adv.*

unmitigated /ʌnˈmɪtɪgeɪtɪd/ *adj.* not modified; absolute.

unmoral /ʌnˈmɒr(ə)l/ *adj.* not concerned with morality. —**unmorally** *adv.*

unmoved /ʌnˈmuːvd/ *adj.* not moved; not changed in one's purpose; not affected by emotion.

unmusical /ʌnˈmjuːzɪk(ə)l/ *adj.* **1** not pleasing to the ear. **2** unskilled in or indifferent to music. —**unmusically** *adv.*

unmuzzle /ʌnˈmʌz(ə)l/ *v.t.* to remove the muzzle from.

unnameable /ʌnˈneɪməb(ə)l/ *adj.* too bad etc. to be named.

unnatural /ʌnˈnætʃər(ə)l/ *adj.* **1** not natural, not normal. **2** lacking natural feelings of affection; extremely cruel, wicked, monstrous. **3** artificial; affected. —**unnaturally** *adv.*

unnecessary /ʌnˈnesəsərɪ/ *adj.* **1** not necessary. **2** more than is necessary. —**unnecessarily** *adv.*

unnerve /ʌnˈnɜːv/ *v.t.* to cause to lose courage or resolution.

unnumbered /ʌnˈnʌmbəd/ *adj.* not marked with a number; not counted; countless.

unobtrusive /ʌnəbˈtruːsɪv/ *adj.* not making oneself or itself noticed. —**unobtrusively** *adv.*

unoccupied /ʌnˈɒkjʊpaɪd/ *adj.* not occupied.

unoffending /ʌnəˈfendɪŋ/ *adj.* harmless, innocent.

unofficial /ʌnəˈfɪʃ(ə)l/ *adj.* not officially authorized or confirmed. —**unofficial strike**, a strike not formally approved by the strikers' trade union. —**unofficially** *adv.*

unpack /ʌnˈpæk/ *v.t.* to open and remove the contents of (luggage etc., or *absol.*); to take (a thing) out thus.

unpaged /ʌnˈpeɪdʒd/ *adj.* with the pages not numbered.

unpaid /ʌnˈpeɪd/ *adj.* **1** (of a debt) not yet paid. **2** (of a person) not receiving payment.

unparalleled /ʌnˈpærəleld/ *adj.* not yet parallelled or equalled.

unparliamentary /ʌnpɑːləˈmentərɪ/ *adj.* contrary to parliamentary custom. —**unparliamentary language**, oaths, abuse.

unperson /ˈʌnpɜːsən/ *n.* one whose name or existence is denied or ignored.

unpick /ʌnˈpɪk/ *v.t.* to undo the stitching of.

unpin /ʌnˈpɪn/ *v.t.* (**-nn-**) to unfasten or detach by removing a pin or pins.

unplaced /ʌnˈpleɪst/ *adj.* not placed as one of the first three in a race etc.

unplayable /ʌnˈpleɪəb(ə)l/ *adj.* (of a ball in games) that cannot be played or returned etc.

unpleasant /ʌnˈplezənt/ *adj.* not pleasant. —**unpleasantly** *adv.*, **unpleasantness** *n.*

unplug /ʌnˈplʌg/ *v.t.* (**-gg-**) **1** to disconnect (an electrical device) by removing its plug from the socket. **2** to unstop.

unplumbed /ʌnˈplʌmd/ *adj.* **1** not plumbed. **2** not fully explored or understood.

unpointed /ʌnˈpɔɪntɪd/ *adj.* **1** having no point(s). **2** not punctuated; (of written Hebrew etc.) having no vowel points marked. **3** (of masonry) not pointed.

unpolitical /ʌnpəˈlɪtɪk(ə)l/ *adj.* not concerned with politics.

unpopular /ʌnˈpɒpjʊlə(r)/ *adj.* not popular; disliked by the public or by people in general. —**unpopularity** /-ˈlærɪtɪ/ *n.*, **unpopularly** *adv.*

unpractical /ʌnˈpræktɪk(ə)l/ *adj.* not practical; (of a person) without practical skill.

unpractised /ʌnˈpræktɪst/ *adj.* **1** not experienced or skilled. **2** not put into practice.

unprecedented /ʌnˈpresɪdentɪd/ *adj.* for which there is no precedent; unparalleled; novel.

unpredictable /ʌnprɪˈdɪktəb(ə)l/ *adj.* impossible to predict.

unpremeditated /ʌnprɪˈmedɪteɪtɪd/ *adj.* not deliberately planned.

unprepared /ʌnprɪˈpeəd/ *adj.* not prepared beforehand, not ready or equipped to do something.

unprepossessing /ʌnpriːpəˈzesɪŋ/ *adj.* unattractive, not making a good impression.

unpretending /ʌnprɪˈtendɪŋ/ *adj.* unpretentious.

unpretentious /ʌnprɪˈtenʃəs/ *adj.* not pretentious, not showy or pompous.

unprincipled /ʌnˈprɪnsɪpəld/ *adj.* lacking or not based on good moral principles, unscrupulous.

unprintable /ʌnˈprɪntəb(ə)l/ *adj.* too indecent, libellous, or blasphemous to be printed.

unprofessional /ʌnprəˈfeʃən(ə)l/ *adj.* **1** contrary to professional etiquette. **2** not belonging to a profession. —**unprofessionally** *adv.*

unprofitable /ʌnˈprɒfɪtəb(ə)l/ *adj.* **1** not producing a profit. **2** serving no useful purpose. —**unprofitably** *adv.*

unprompted /ʌnˈprɒmptɪd/ *adj.* spontaneous.

unputdownable /ʌnpʊtˈdaʊnəb(ə)l/ *adj.* (*colloq.*) (of a book) so engrossing that the reader cannot put it down.

unqualified /ʌnˈkwɒlɪfaɪd/ *adj.* **1** not competent; not legally or officially qualified. **2** not restricted or modified, complete.

unquestionable /ʌnˈkwestʃənəb(ə)l/ *adj.* too clear to be questioned or doubted. —**unquestionably** *adv.*

unquestioning /ʌnˈkwestʃənɪŋ/ *adj.* asking no questions; done etc. without asking questions.

unquote /ʌnˈkwəʊt/ *v.imper.* (in dictation etc.) end the quotation, close the quotation-marks.

unravel /ʌnˈræv(ə)l/ *v.t.* (**-ll-**) **1** to disentangle. **2** to undo (knitted fabric etc.). **3** to probe and solve (a mystery etc.). **4** to become unravelled.

unread /ʌnˈred/ *adj.* **1** (of a book etc.) not read. **2** (of a person) not well read.

unreadable /ʌnˈri:dəb(ə)l/ *adj.* not readable; too dull or too difficult to be worth reading.

unready /ʌnˈredɪ/ *adj.* not ready; not prompt in action. —**unreadily** *adv.*, **unreadiness** *n.*

unreal /ʌnˈrɪəl/ *adj.* not real; imaginary, illusory. —**unreality** /-ˈælɪtɪ/ *n.*

unreason /ʌnˈri:z(ə)n/ *n.* lack of reasonable thought or action.

unreasonable /ʌnˈri:z(ə)nəb(ə)l/ *adj.* **1** not reasonable in attitude etc. **2** excessive, going beyond the bounds of what is reasonable or just. —**unreasonably** *adv.*

unreel /ʌnˈri:l/ *v.t./i.* to unwind from a reel.

unrelenting /ʌnrɪˈlentɪŋ/ *adj.* **1** not relenting or yielding; unmerciful. **2** not abating or relaxing.

unrelieved /ʌnrɪˈli:vd/ *adj.* lacking the relief given by contrast or variation.

unremitting /ʌnrɪˈmɪtɪŋ/ *adj.* incessant, never slackening.

unremunerative /ʌnrɪˈmju:nərətɪv/ *adj.* not (sufficiently) profitable.

unrepeatable /ʌnrɪˈpi:təb(ə)l/ *adj.* **1** that cannot be repeated or done etc. again. **2** too indecent etc. to be said again.

unrequited /ʌnrɪˈkwaɪtɪd/ *adj.* (of love etc.) not returned or rewarded.

unreserved /ʌnrɪˈzɜ:vd/ *adj.* **1** not reserved. **2** without reserve or reservation. —**unreservedly** /-vɪdlɪ/ *adv.*

unrest /ʌnˈrest/ *n.* disturbed or agitated condition.

unrighteous /ʌnˈraɪtʃəs/ *adj.* not righteous, wicked.

unrip /ʌnˈrɪp/ *v.t.* (**-pp-**) to open by ripping.

unripe /ʌnˈraɪp/ *adj.* not yet ripe.

unrivalled /ʌnˈraɪvəld/ *adj.* having no equal, peerless.

unroll /ʌnˈrəʊl/ *v.t./i.* to open out from a rolled-up state; to display or be displayed thus.

unruly /ʌnˈru:lɪ/ *adj.* not easily controlled or disciplined, refractory. —**unruliness** *n.* [f. UN- + RULE]

unsaddle /ʌnˈsæd(ə)l/ *v.t.* **1** to remove the saddle from. **2** to throw (a rider) from the saddle.

unsaid /ʌnˈsed/ *adj.* not spoken or expressed.

unsaleable /ʌnˈseɪləb(ə)l/ *adj.* not saleable.

unsalted /ʌnˈsɔltɪd, -ˈsɒltɪd/ *adj.* not seasoned with salt.

unsaturated /ʌnˈsætʃəreɪtɪd/ *adj.* (*Chem.*) able to combine with hydrogen to form a third substance by the joining of molecules.

unsavoury /ʌnˈseɪvərɪ/ *adj.* **1** disagreeable to taste or smell. **2** morally unpleasant or disgusting. —**unsavouriness** *n.*

unsay /ʌnˈseɪ/ *v.t.* (*past & p.p.* **unsaid** /ʌnˈsed/) to retract (a statement).

unscathed /ʌnˈskeɪðd/ *adj.* without suffering injury.

unscientific /ʌnsaɪənˈtɪfɪk/ *adj.* not in accordance with scientific principles. —**unscientifically** *adv.*

unscramble /ʌnˈskræmb(ə)l/ *v.t.* to restore from a scrambled state, to make (a scrambled transmission etc.) intelligible.

unscreened /ʌnˈskri:nd/ *adj.* (of coal) not passed through a sieve.

unscrew /ʌnˈskru:/ *v.t.* to unfasten by removing a screw or screws; to loosen (a screw).

unscripted /ʌnˈskrɪptɪd/ *adj.* (of a speech etc.) delivered without a prepared script.

unscrupulous /ʌnˈskru:pjʊləs/ *adj.* having no moral scruples, not prevented from doing wrong by scruples of conscience. —**unscrupulously** *adv.*, **unscrupulousness** *n.*

unseal /ʌnˈsi:l/ *v.t.* to break the seal of, to open (a sealed letter, receptacle, etc.).

unseasonable /ʌnˈsi:z(ə)nəb(ə)l/ *adj.* not

seasonable; untimely, inopportune. —**unseasonably** *adv.*

unseat /ʌn'si:t/ *v.t.* 1 to dislodge (a rider) from a seat on horseback or a bicycle etc. 2 to remove from a parliamentary seat.

unseeded /ʌn'si:dɪd/ *adj.* (of a tennis-player etc.) not seeded (see SEED *v.* 5).

unseeing /ʌn'si:ɪŋ/ *adj.* unobservant; blind.

unseemly /ʌn'si:mlɪ/ *adj.* not seemly, improper. —**unseemliness** *n.*

unseen /ʌn'si:n/ *adj.* 1 not seen, invisible. 2 (of translation) to be done without preparation. —*n.* an unseen translation.

unselfconscious /ʌnself'kɒnʃəs/ *adj.* not self-conscious.

unselfish /ʌn'selfɪʃ/ *adj.* not selfish, considering the interests of others before one's own. —**unselfishly** *adv.*, **unselfishness** *n.*

unsettle /ʌn'set(ə)l/ *v.t.* to make uneasy, to disturb the settled calm or stability of.

unsex /ʌn'seks/ *v.t.* to deprive of the qualities of her or his sex.

unshackle /ʌn'ʃæk(ə)l/ *v.t.* to release from shackles; to set free.

unshakeable /ʌn'ʃeɪkəb(ə)l/ *adj.* not shakeable, firm.

unsheathe /ʌn'ʃi:ð/ *v.t.* to remove (a knife etc.) from a sheath.

unshockable /ʌn'ʃɒkəb(ə)l/ *adj.* not able to be shocked.

unshrinkable /ʌn'ʃrɪŋkəb(ə)l/ *adj.* (of a fabric etc.) not liable to shrink.

unshrinking /ʌn'ʃrɪŋkɪŋ/ *adj.* unhesitating, fearless.

unsightly /ʌn'saɪtlɪ/ *adj.* unpleasant to look at, ugly. —**unsightliness** *n.*

unskilled /ʌn'skɪld/ *adj.* not having or needing special skill or training.

unsociable /ʌn'səʊʃəb(ə)l/ *adj.* not sociable, withdrawing oneself from the company of others. —**unsociably** *adv.*

unsocial /ʌn'səʊʃ(ə)l/ *adj.* 1 not social. 2 not suitable for or seeking society. 3 outside the normal working day(s). —**unsocially** *adv.*

unsolicited /ʌnsə'lɪsɪtɪd/ *adj.* not asked for; given or done voluntarily.

unsophisticated /ʌnsə'fɪstɪkeɪtɪd/ *adj.* not sophisticated, simple and natural or naïve.

unsound /ʌn'saʊnd/ *adj.* not sound or strong; not free from defects or mistakes; ill-founded. —**of unsound mind,** insane.

unsparing /ʌn'speərɪŋ/ *adj.* 1 giving freely and lavishly. 2 merciless. —**unsparingly** *adv.*

unspeakable /ʌn'spi:kəb(ə)l/ *adj.* that words cannot express; indescribably bad or good. —**unspeakably** *adv.*

unspecified /ʌn'spesɪfaɪd/ *adj.* not specified.

unstable /ʌn'steɪb(ə)l/ *adj.* 1 not stable, changeable. 2 mentally or emotionally unbalanced. —**unstably** *adv.*

unsteady /ʌn'stedɪ/ *adj.* not steady or firm; changeable, fluctuating; not uniform or regular. —**unsteadily** *adv.*, **unsteadiness** *n.*

unstick /ʌn'stɪk/ *v.t.* (*past* & *p.p.* **unstuck**) to separate (a thing stuck to another). —**come unstuck,** (*colloq.*) to fail, to suffer disaster.

unstinted /ʌn'stɪntɪd/ *adj.* given freely and lavishly.

unstitch /ʌn'stɪtʃ/ *v.t.* to undo the stitches of.

unstop /ʌn'stɒp/ *v.t.* (**-pp-**) 1 to free from an obstruction. 2 to remove the stopper from.

unstoppable /ʌn'stɒpəb(ə)l/ *adj.* that cannot be stopped or prevented.

unstressed /ʌn'strest/ *adj.* not pronounced with a stress.

unstring /ʌn'strɪŋ/ *v.t.* (*past* & *p.p.* **unstrung**) 1 to remove or relax the string(s) of (a bow, harp, etc.). 2 to take (beads etc.) off a string. 3 (esp. in *p.p.*) to unnerve.

unstructured /ʌn'strʌktʃəd/ *adj.* not structured, informal.

unstudied /ʌn'stʌdɪd/ *adj.* natural in manner, not affected.

unsubstantial /ʌnsəb'stɑ:nʃ(ə)l/ *adj.* 1 not substantial, flimsy. 2 having little or no factual basis.

unsuitable /ʌn'su:təb(ə)l, -sju:t-/ *adj.* not suitable. —**unsuitably** *adv.*

unsuited /ʌn'sju:tɪd/ *adj.* not fit (for a purpose); not adapted (to a specified thing).

unsullied /ʌn'sʌlɪd/ *adj.* not sullied, pure.

unsung /ʌn'sʌŋ/ *adj.* not celebrated in song.

unsuspecting /ʌnsə'spektɪŋ/ *adj.* feeling no suspicion.

unswerving /ʌn'swɜ:vɪŋ/ *adj.* not turning aside; unchanging.

untangle /ʌn'tæŋg(ə)l/ *v.t.* to free from a tangle, to disentangle.

untapped /ʌn'tæpt/ *adj.* not (yet) tapped or used.

untaught /ʌn'tɔt/ *adj.* 1 not instructed by teaching. 2 not acquired by teaching.

untenable /ʌn'tenəb(ə)l/ *adj.* (of a theory) not tenable, not able to be held, because strong arguments can be produced against it.

untether /ʌn'teðə(r)/ *v.t.* to release from a tether.

unthink /ʌn'θɪŋk/ *v.t.* (*past* & *p.p.* **unthought** /ʌn'θɔt/) to retract in thought.

unthinkable /ʌn'θɪŋkəb(ə)l/ *adj.* 1 that cannot be imagined or grasped by the mind. 2 (*colloq.*) highly unlikely or undesirable.

unthinking /ʌn'θɪŋkɪŋ/ *adj.* thoughtless; unintentional, inadvertent. —**unthinkingly** *adv.*

unthread /ʌnˈθred/ *v.t.* to take the thread out of (a needle).

unthrone /ʌnˈθrəʊn/ *v.t.* to dethrone.

untidy /ʌnˈtaɪdɪ/ *adj.* not tidy. —**untidily** *adv.*, **untidiness** *n.*

untie /ʌnˈtaɪ/ *v.t.* (*partic.* **untying**) **1** to undo (a knot etc.); to undo the cords of (a parcel etc.). **2** to liberate from bonds or an attachment.

until /ʌnˈtɪl/ *prep.* up to (a specified time); as late as; up to the time of. —*conj.* **1** up to the time when. **2** so long that. [f. ON *und* as far as + TILL[1]]

untimely /ʌnˈtaɪmlɪ/ *adj.* **1** happening at an unsuitable time. **2** happening too soon or sooner than is normal. —**untimeliness** *n.*

unto /ˈʌntʊ, ˈʌntə/ *prep.* (*archaic*) = TO (in all uses except as a sign of the infinitive). [formed f. UNTIL, with substitution of *to* for *til*]

untold /ʌnˈtəʊld/ *adj.* **1** not told. **2** not counted, too much or too many to be measured or counted.

untouchable /ʌnˈtʌtʃəb(ə)l/ *adj.* that may not be touched; non-caste. —*n.* a member of a hereditary Hindu group (non-caste), held to defile members of a caste on contact.

untoward /ʌntəˈwɔːd/ *adj.* inconvenient, awkward, unlucky; perverse, refractory. [f. UN- + *toward* docile (as TOWARDS)]

untraceable /ʌnˈtreɪsəb(ə)l/ *adj.* that may not be traced.

untrammelled /ʌnˈtræm(ə)ld/ *adj.* not trammelled, not hampered.

untravelled /ʌnˈtrævəld/ *adj.* **1** that has not travelled. **2** that has not been travelled over or through.

untried /ʌnˈtraɪd/ *adj.* not yet tried or tested; inexperienced.

untroubled /ʌnˈtrʌbəld/ *adj.* not troubled; calm, tranquil.

untrue /ʌnˈtruː/ *adj.* **1** not true; contrary to fact. **2** not faithful or loyal. **3** deviating from an accepted standard. —**untruly** *adv.*

untruth /ʌnˈtruːθ/ *n.* **1** lack of truth, being untrue. **2** an untrue statement, a lie.

untruthful /ʌnˈtruːθf(ə)l/ *adj.* not truthful. —**untruthfully** *adv.*

untuck /ʌnˈtʌk/ *v.t.* to free (bedclothes etc.) from being tucked in or up.

untwine /ʌnˈtwaɪn/ *v.t./i.* to untwist, to unwind.

untwist /ʌnˈtwɪst/ *v.t./i.* to open from a twisted or spiralled state.

unused /ʌnˈjuːzd/ *adj.* **1** not in use; not yet used. **2** /-ˈjuːst/ not accustomed.

unusual /ʌnˈjuːʒʊəl/ *adj.* not usual; remarkable. —**unusually** *adv.*

unutterable /ʌnˈʌtərəb(ə)l/ *adj.* inexpressible, beyond description. —**unutterably** *adv.*

unvarnished /ʌnˈvɑːnɪʃt/ *adj.* **1** not varnished. **2** (of a statement etc.) plain and straightforward.

unveil /ʌnˈveɪl/ *v.t./i.* **1** to remove the veil from; to remove one's veil. **2** to remove concealing drapery from (a statue etc.) as part of a ceremony when the statue etc. is displayed to the public for the first time. **3** to disclose; to make publicly known.

unversed /ʌnˈvɜːst/ *adj.* not experienced or not skilled (*in* a specified thing).

unvoiced /ʌnˈvɔɪst/ *adj.* **1** not spoken. **2** (of a consonant etc.) not voiced.

unwanted /ʌnˈwɒntɪd/ *adj.* not wanted.

unwarrantable /ʌnˈwɒrəntəb(ə)l/ *adj.* unjustifiable. —**unwarrantably** *adv.*

unwarranted /ʌnˈwɒrəntɪd/ *adj.* unauthorized; unjustified.

unwary /ʌnˈweərɪ/ *adj.* **1** not cautious. **2** not aware (of a possible danger etc.). —**unwarily** *adv.*, **unwariness** *n.*

unwearying /ʌnˈwɪərɪɪŋ/ *adj.* not tiring; persistent.

unwell /ʌnˈwel/ *adj.* not in good health; indisposed.

unwholesome /ʌnˈhəʊlsəm/ *adj.* **1** harmful to or not promoting health or moral well-being. **2** unhealthy-looking. —**unwholesomeness** *n.*

unwieldy /ʌnˈwiːldɪ/ *adj.* awkward to move or control because of its size, shape, or weight. —**unwieldily** *adv.*, **unwieldiness** *n.* [UN- + dial. *wieldy* active (f. WIELD)]

unwilling /ʌnˈwɪlɪŋ/ *adj.* not willing; reluctant, hesitating to do something. —**unwillingly** *adv.*

unwind /ʌnˈwaɪnd/ *v.t./i.* (*past & p.p.* **unwound**) **1** to draw out or become drawn out after being wound. **2** (*colloq.*) to relax.

unwinking /ʌnˈwɪŋkɪŋ/ *adj.* **1** not winking; gazing or (of a light) shining steadily. **2** watchful. —**unwinkingly** *adv.*

unwisdom /ʌnˈwɪzdəm/ *n.* lack of wisdom.

unwise /ʌnˈwaɪz/ *adj.* not wise, foolish. —**unwisely** *adv.*

unwished /ʌnˈwɪʃt/ *adj.* not wished (usu. *for*).

unwitting /ʌnˈwɪtɪŋ/ *adj.* **1** unaware of the state of the case. **2** unintentional. —**unwittingly** *adv.* [OE (as UN-, WIT)]

unwonted /ʌnˈwəʊntɪd/ *adj.* not customary or usual. —**unwontedly** *adv.*

unworkable /ʌnˈwɜːkəb(ə)l/ *adj.* not workable.

unworkmanlike /ʌnˈwɜːkmənlaɪk/ *adj.* amateurish.

unworldly /ʌnˈwɜːldlɪ/ *adj.* not worldly; spirituallyminded. —**unworldliness** *n.*

unworn /ʌnˈwɔːn/ *adj.* **1** that has not yet been worn. **2** not impaired by wear.

unworthy /ʌnˈwɜːðɪ/ *adj.* **1** not worthy, lacking worth or excellence. **2** not deserving.

3 unsuitable to the character of a person or thing. —**unworthily** *adv*., **unworthiness** *n*.

unwrap /ʌn'ræp/ *v.t./i*. (**-pp-**) to open or become opened after being wrapped.

unwritten /ʌn'rɪt(ə)n/ *adj*. **1** not written. **2** (of a law etc.) resting on custom or judicial decision, not on statute.

unyielding /ʌn'ji:ldɪŋ/ *adj*. firm, not yielding to pressure or influence.

unyoke /ʌn'jəʊk/ *v.t./i*. **1** to release (as) from a yoke. **2** to cease work.

unzip /ʌn'zɪp/ *v.t./i*. (**-pp-**) to open or become opened by the undoing of a zip-fastener.

up *adv*. **1** at, in, or towards a higher place, level, value, or condition, or a place etc. regarded as higher; to a larger size; northwards, further north; at or towards a central place or capital city; at or to a university; in a stronger or winning position or condition; (of a jockey) mounted, in the saddle. **2** in or to an erect or vertical position. **3** so as to be inflated. **4** to the place or time in question or where the speaker etc. is. **5** into a condition of activity, progress, efficiency, etc.; out of bed. **6** apart, into pieces; (of a road) with the surface broken or removed during repairs. **7** into a compact or accumulated state; securely. **8** so as to be finished. **9** happening, especially of an unusual or undesirable event etc. —*prep*. **1** upwards along, through, or into; from the bottom to the top of; along. **2** at or in a higher part of. —*adj*. **1** directed upwards. **2** (of travel) towards a capital or centre. —*v.t./i*. (**-pp-**) (*colloq*.) **1** to begin abruptly or unexpectedly to say or do something. **2** to raise, to pick up. **3** to increase. —*n*. a spell of good fortune. —**all up with**, hopeless for (a person). **on the up-and-up**, (*colloq*.) steadily improving; honest, honestly. **up against**, close to; in or into contact with; (*colloq*.) confronted with (a difficulty etc.). **up and about** *or* **up and doing**, having risen from bed; active. **up-and-coming** *adj*. (*colloq*., of a person) making good progress and likely to succeed. **up and down**, to and fro (along). **up-and-over** *adj*. (of a door) opened by being raised and pushed back into a horizontal position. **up for**, available for or being considered for (sale, office, etc.). **up in**, (*colloq*.) knowledgeable about. **ups and downs**, rises and falls; alternate good and bad fortune. **up stage**, at or to the back of a theatre stage. **up to**, until; not more than; equal to; incumbent on; capable of; occupied or busy with. **up to date**, see DATE[1]. **up (with)**, may (the stated person or thing) prosper. [OE]

up- *prefix* in the senses of UP, added (1) as an adverb to verbs and verbal derivatives, = 'upwards' (*upcurved, update*); (2) as a preposition to nouns forming adverbs and adjectives (*up-country, uphill*); (3) as an adjective to nouns (*upland, up-stroke*). [OE]

upas /'ju:pəs/ *n*. **1** (also **upas-tree**) a Javanese tree yielding a poisonous sap. **2** (in mythology) a Javanese tree thought to be fatal to whatever came near it. **3** the poisonous sap of the upas and other trees. [Malay *ūpas* poison]

upbeat *n*. an unaccented beat in music, when the conductor's baton moves upwards. —*adj*. (*colloq*.) optimistic, cheerful.

upbraid /ʌp'breɪd/ *v.t*. to reproach. [OE (UP-, BRAID in obs. sense 'brandish')]

upbringing *n*. the bringing up (of a child), education and training during childhood.

up-country *adv*. & *adj*. inland.

update /ʌp'deɪt/ *v.t*. to bring up to date.

up-end /ʌp'end/ *v.t./i*. to set or rise up on end.

upfield *adv*. in or to a position further along the field.

upgrade /ʌp'greɪd/ *v.t*. to raise to a higher grade or rank.

upheaval /ʌp'hi:v(ə)l/ *n*. **1** a sudden heaving upwards. **2** a violent change or disruption. [f. foll.]

upheave /ʌp'hi:v/ *v.t*. to lift forcibly.

uphill /ʌp'hɪl/ *adv*. up a slope. —/'ʌphɪl/ *adj*. **1** sloping upwards; ascending. **2** arduous.

uphold /ʌp'həʊld/ *v.t*. (*past* & *p.p*. **upheld**) **1** to support, to keep from falling. **2** to confirm (a decision etc.).

upholster /ʌp'həʊlstə(r)/ *v.t*. to provide (a chair etc.) with upholstery. —**upholsterer** *n*. [back-formation f. *upholsterer* f. UPHOLD in obs. sense 'keep in repair']

upholstery *n*. **1** textile covering, padding, springs, etc., for furniture. **2** the work of upholstering. [f. prec.]

upkeep *n*. maintenance in good condition; the cost or means of this.

upland /'ʌplənd/ *n*. (usu. in *pl*.) the higher part of a country. —*adj*. of this part.

uplift /ʌp'lɪft/ *v.t*. to raise. —/'ʌp-/ *n*. (*colloq*.) a mentally or morally elevating influence.

upon /ə'pɒn/ *prep*. on (*upon* is sometimes more formal, and is preferred in *once upon a time* and *upon my word*). [f. UP + ON]

upper *adj*. **1** higher in place or position. **2** situated on higher ground or to the north. **3** ranking above others. **4** (of a geological or archaeological period) later (called 'upper' because its rock formations or remains lie above those of the period called 'lower'). —*n*. the upper part of a boot or shoe, above the sole. —**on one's uppers**, (*colloq*.) extremely short of money. **upper case**, see CASE[2]. **Upper Chamber**, = Upper House. **upper circle**, that next above the dress circle in a theatre. **upper crust**, (*colloq*.) the aristocracy. **upper-cut** *n*. a hit upwards with the arm bent; (*v.t.*) to hit thus. **the upper hand,** dominance, control. **Upper House,** the higher (sometimes non-elected) body in a legislature, especially the House of Lords. [compar. of UP]

uppermost *adj.* highest in place or rank; predominant. —*adv.* at or to the highest or most prominent position. [f. prec. + -MOST]

uppish *adj.* self-assertive, arrogant. [f. UP]

uppity /ˈʌpɪtɪ/ *adj.* (*colloq.*) uppish. [fancifully f. UP]

upright *adj.* **1** in a vertical position; having such a posture or attitude. **2** (of a piano) with the strings mounted vertically. **3** strictly honest or honourable. —*n.* **1** a post or rod fixed upright, especially as a support. **2** an upright piano. —**uprightness** *n.*

uprising *n.* an insurrection.

uproar *n.* an outburst of noise and excitement or anger. [f. Du. (*op* up, *roer* confusion)]

uproarious /ʌpˈrɔːrɪəs/ *adj.* very noisy; provoking loud laughter. —**uproariously** *adv.*

uproot /ʌpˈruːt/ *v.t.* **1** to pull (a plant) up from the ground together with its roots. **2** to force to leave a native or accustomed place. **3** to eradicate.

uprush *n.* an upward rush.

upset /ʌpˈset/ *v.t.* (**-tt-**; *past* & *p.p.* **upset**) **1** to overturn; to become overturned. **2** to disturb the feelings, composure, or digestion of. **3** to disrupt. —/ˈʌpset/ *n.* **1** upsetting, being upset. **2** a surprising result in a contest etc.

upshot *n.* an outcome.

upside-down /ʌpsaɪdˈdaʊn/ *adv.* & *adj.* **1** with the upper part where the lower part should be, inverted. **2** in or into great disorder. [orig. *up so down*, perh. = 'up as if down']

upsilon /ʌpˈsaɪlən/ *n.* the twentieth letter of the Greek alphabet, = u. [Gk, = slender U (*psilos* slender), to distinguish it from the diphthong *oi* (*n* and *oi* being pronounced alike in late Gk)]

upstage /ʌpˈsteɪdʒ/ *adj.* & *adv.* **1** nearer the back of a theatre stage. **2** snobbish, snobbishly. —*v.t.* to move upstage from (an actor) and thus make him face away from the audience; to divert attention from (a person) to oneself.

upstairs /ʌpˈsteəz/ *adv.* up the stairs; to or on an upper floor. —*adj.* situated upstairs. —*n.* an upper floor.

upstanding /ʌpˈstændɪŋ/ *adj.* **1** standing up. **2** strong and healthy. **3** honest.

upstart *n.* a person who has risen suddenly to prominence, especially one who behaves arrogantly. —*adj.* that is an upstart; of upstarts.

upstate *adj.* (*US*) of the part of a State remote from large cities, especially the northern part. —*n.* this part.

upstream *adv.* against the flow of a stream etc. —*adj.* moving upstream.

up-stroke *n.* a stroke made or written upwards.

upsurge *n.* an upward surge.

upswept *adj.* (of the hair) combed to the top of the head.

upswing *n.* an upward movement or trend.

upsy-daisy /ˈʌpsɪdeɪzɪ/ *int.* of encouragement to a child who is rising after a fall or who is being lifted. [orig. *up-a-daisy*, f. UP]

uptake *n.* (*colloq.*) understanding (usu. in **quick** or **slow in the uptake**).

upthrust *n.* an upward thrust; an upward displacement of part of the earth's crust.

uptight /ˈʌptaɪt, ʌpˈtaɪt/ *adj.* **1** (*colloq.*) nervously tense, annoyed. **2** (*US colloq.*) rigidly conventional.

uptown *adj.* (*US*) of the residential part of a town or city. —*adv.* (*US*) in or into this part. —*n.* (*US*) this part.

upturn /ˈʌptɜːn/ *n.* **1** an upward trend, an improvement. **2** an upheaval. —/ʌpˈtɜːn/ *v.t.* to turn up or upside-down.

upward /ˈʌpwəd/ *adv.* (also **upwards**) towards what is higher, superior, more important, or earlier. —*adj.* moving or extending upwards. [OE (as UP, -WARD)]

upwind *adj.* & *adv.* against the wind; in the direction from which the wind is blowing.

uranium /jʊəˈreɪnɪəm/ *n.* a heavy grey radioactive metallic element, symbol U, atomic number 92, used as a source of nuclear energy. —**uranic** /jʊəˈrænɪk/ *adj.* [f. *Uranus*, planet; cf. *tellurium*]

urban /ˈɜːbən/ *adj.* of, living in, or situated in a town or city. —**urban guerrilla,** a terrorist operating in an urban area. [f. L (*urbs* city)]

urbane /ɜːˈbeɪn/ *adj.* having manners that are courteous and elegant. —**urbanely** *adv.*, **urbanity** /ɜːˈbænɪtɪ/ *n.* [f. F or L, = prec.]

urbanize /ˈɜːbənaɪz/ *v.t.* to render urban; to remove the rural quality of (a district). —**urbanization** /-ˈzeɪʃ(ə)n/ *n.* [f. F (as URBAN)]

urchin /ˈɜːtʃɪn/ *n.* **1** a mischievous or needy boy. **2** a sea-urchin. [orig. = hedgehog, f. OF *herichon* f. L (*h*)*ericius*]

Urdu /ˈʊədu:, ˈɜː-/ *n.* an Indic language allied to Hindi. [f. Hindustani, = (language of the) camp, rel. to HORDE]

urea /ˈjʊərɪə, -ˈrɪə/ *n.* a soluble colourless crystalline compound contained especially in urine. [f. F *urée* f. Gk *ouron* urine]

ureter /jʊəˈriːtə(r)/ *n.* a duct by which urine passes from the kidney to the bladder or cloaca. [f. F f. Gk (*oureō* urinate)]

urethra /jʊəˈri:θrə/ *n.* the duct by which urine passes from the bladder. [L f. Gk (as prec.)]

urge *v.t.* **1** to drive onward, to encourage to proceed. **2** to try hard or persistently to persuade. **3** to recommend strongly with reasoning or entreaty; to mention earnestly as a reason or justification. —*n.* an urging impulse or tendency; a strong desire. [f. L *urgēre*]

urgent *adj.* **1** requiring immediate action or attention. **2** importunate. —**urgency** *n.*, **urgently** *adv.* [f. F (as prec.)]

uric /ˈjʊərɪk/ *adj.* of urine. —**uric acid,** a constituent of urine. [f. F *urique* (as URINE)]

urinal /jʊəˈraɪn(ə)l, ˈjʊərɪn(ə)l/ *n.* a place or receptacle for urination. [as URINE]

urinary /ˈjʊərɪnərɪ/ *adj.* of or relating to urine. [as URINE]

urinate /ˈjʊərɪneɪt/ *v.i.* to discharge urine. —**urination** /-ˈneɪʃ(ə)n/ *n.* [f. L (as foll.)]

urine /ˈjʊərɪn/ *n.* the pale-yellow fluid secreted by the blood from the kidneys and (in man and the higher animals) stored in the bladder and discharged at intervals. [f. OF f. L *urina*]

urn *n.* **1** a vase with a foot and usually a rounded body, especially for storing the ashes of the dead or as a vessel or measure. **2** a large vessel with a tap, in which tea or coffee etc. is made or kept hot. [f. L *urna*]

urogenital /jʊərəˈdʒenɪt(ə)l/ *adj.* of the urinary and reproductive systems. [as foll. + GENITAL]

urology /jʊəˈrɒlədʒɪ/ *n.* the study of the urinary system. [f Gk *ouron* urine + -LOGY]

ursine /ˈɜ:saɪn/ *adj.* of or like a bear. [f. L (*ursus* bear)]

US *abbr.* United States (of America).

us /əs, *emphat.* ʌs/ *pron.* **1** the object case of WE. **2** (*colloq.*) we. **3** (*colloq.*) me. [OE]

USA *abbr.* United States of America.

usable /ˈju:zəb(ə)l/ *adj.* that may be used.

usage /ˈju:sɪdʒ/ *n.* **1** the manner of using or treating something. **2** a customary practice, especially in the use of a language. [f. OF (as USE²)]

use[1] /ju:z/ *v.t./i.* **1** to cause to act or serve for a purpose; to bring into service. **2** to treat in a specified manner; to behave towards. **3** to exploit selfishly. **4** (in *past*; often /ju:st/) had as one's or its constant or frequent practice or state. —**be used to** /ju:st/, to be familiar with by practice or habit. **use up,** to use the whole of; to find a use for (remaining material or time); to exhaust or tire out. [f. OF, ult. f. L *uti* use]

use[2] /ju:s/ *n.* **1** using, being used. **2** the right or power of using. **3** ability to be used; the purpose for which a thing can be used. **4** custom, usage. —**have no use for,** to be unable to find a use for; to dislike; to be contemptuous of. **in use,** being used. **make use of,** to use; to benefit from; to exploit. **out of use,** not being used. [f. OF f. L *usus* (as prec.)]

used /ju:zd/ *adj.* second-hand.

useful /ˈju:sf(ə)l/ *adj.* **1** able to be used for some practical purpose; producing or able to produce good results. **2** (*colloq.*) creditable, efficient. —**make oneself useful,** to perform useful services. —**usefully** *adv.*, **usefulness** *n.* [f. USE² + -FUL]

useless /ˈju:slɪs/ *adj.* serving no practical purpose; not able to produce good results. —**uselessly** *adv.*, **uselessness** *n.* [f. USE² + -LESS]

user /ˈju:zə(r)/ *n.* one who uses something. —**user-friendly** *adj.* (in computers) easy to use; designed with the needs of users in mind. [f. USE¹]

usher *n.* **1** a person who shows people to their seats in a hall or theatre etc. **2** the door-keeper of a lawcourt etc. **3** an officer walking before a person of rank. —*v.t.* **1** to escort as an usher. **2** to announce or show (in or out etc.; *lit.* or *fig.*). [f. AF f. L *ostiarius* (*ostium* door)]

usherette /ʌʃəˈret/ *n.* a female usher, especially in a cinema. [f. prec. + -ETTE]

usquebaugh /ˈʌskɪbɔ:/ *n.* whisky. [f. Ir. & Sc. Gael. *uisge beatha* water of life]

USSR *abbr.* Union of Soviet Socialist Republics.

usual /ˈju:ʒʊəl/ *adj.* such as occurs or is done or used etc. in many or most instances. —**as usual,** as commonly occurs. —**usually** *adv.* [f. OF or L (as USE²)]

usurer /ˈju:ʒərə(r)/ *n.* one who practises usury. [as USURY]

usurious /jʊˈzʊərɪəs/ *adj.* of, involving, or practising usury. [f. USURY]

usurp /jʊˈzɜ:p/ *v.t.* to seize or assume (a throne or power etc.) wrongfully or by force. —**usurpation** /ju:zəˈpeɪʃ(ə)n/ *n.*, **usurper** *n.* [f. OF f. L *usurpare* seize for use]

usury /ˈju:ʒərɪ/ *n.* the lending of money at interest, especially at an exorbitant or illegal rate; interest at this rate. [f. AF f. L *usura* (as USE¹)]

UT *abbr.* universal time.

UTC *abbr.* co-ordinated universal time.

utensil /ju:ˈtens(ə)l/ *n.* an implement or vessel, especially for domestic use. [f. OF f. L, = usable (as USE¹)]

uterine /ˈju:təraɪn/ *adj.* of the uterus. [f. L (as foll.)]

uterus /ˈju:tərəs/ *n.* (*pl.* **-i** /-aɪ/) the womb. [L]

utilitarian /ju:tɪlɪˈteərɪən/ *adj.* **1** designed to be useful for a purpose rather than decorative or luxurious; severely practical. **2** of utilitarianism. —*n.* an adherent of utilitarianism. [f. UTILITY]

utilitarianism /ju:tɪlɪˈteərɪənɪz(ə)m/ *n.* the theory that the guiding principle of conduct should be to achieve the greatest happiness of the greatest number; the theory that the usefulness (or otherwise) of an action is the criterion of whether it is right (or wrong). [f. prec.]

utility /ju:ˈtɪlɪtɪ/ *n.* **1** usefulness, profitableness. **2** a useful thing; a public service such as the supply of water, gas, or electricity. —*adj.* severely practical and standardized; made or serving for utility. —**utility room,** a room containing large fixed domestic appliances, e.g. a washing-machine. **utility vehicle,** a vehicle serving various functions. [f. OF f. L (*utilis* useful, as USE[1])]

utilize /ˈju:tɪlaɪz/ *v.t.* to make use of, to turn to account. —**utilization** /-ˈzeɪʃ(ə)n/ *n.* [f. F f. It. (as prec.)]

utmost /ˈʌtməʊst/ *adj.* furthest, extreme, greatest. —*n.* the utmost point or degree etc. —**do one's utmost,** to do all that one can. [OE, = OUTMOST]

Utopia /ju:ˈtəʊpɪə/ *n.* an imagined perfect place or state of things. —**Utopian** *adj.* [name of imaginary island, governed on a perfect political and social system, in book of that title by Sir Thomas More (1516)]

utricle /ˈju:trɪk(ə)l/ *n.* a cell or small cavity in an animal or plant. [f. F or L *utriculus* dim. of *uter* leather bag)]

utter[1] *attrib. adj.* complete, absolute. —**utterly** *adv.* [OE, = OUTER]

utter[2] *v.t./i.* **1** to make (a sound or words) with the mouth or voice. **2** to speak. **3** to put (a forged banknote or coin etc.) into circulation. [f. MDu. *ūteren* make known]

utterance /ˈʌtərəns/ *n.* **1** uttering. **2** the power or manner of speaking. **3** a thing spoken. [f. prec.]

uttermost *adj.* utmost. [f. UTTER[1]]

U-turn /ˈju:tɜ:n/ *n.* **1** turning a vehicle in a U-shaped course so as to face the opposite direction. **2** a reversal of policy.

UV *abbr.* ultraviolet.

uvula /ˈju:vjʊlə/ *n.* (*pl.* **-ae** /-i:/) the fleshy part of the soft palate hanging from the back of the roof of the mouth above the throat. —**uvular** *adj.* [L, dim. of *uva* grape]

uxorious /ʌkˈsɔ:rɪəs/ *adj.* greatly or obsessively fond of one's wife. [f. L (*uxor* wife)]

Vv

V, v /viː/ *n.* (*pl.* **Vs, V's**) **1** the twenty-second letter of the alphabet. **2** a V-shaped thing. **3** (as a Roman numeral) 5.

V *symbol* vanadium.

V *abbr.* volt(s).

v. *abbr.* **1** verse. **2** versus. **3** very. **4** *vide.*

vac *n.* (*colloq.*) **1** a vacation. **2** a vacuum cleaner. [abbr.]

vacancy /ˈveɪkənsɪ/ *n.* **1** being vacant, emptiness. **2** an unoccupied position of employment or place of accommodation. [f. foll. or L *vacantia*]

vacant /ˈveɪkənt/ *adj.* **1** empty, not filled or occupied. **2** not mentally active, having a blank expression. —**vacant possession,** (of a house etc.) the state of being empty of occupants and available for the purchaser to occupy immediately. —**vacantly** *adv.* [f. OF or L (as foll.)]

vacate /vəˈkeɪt/ *v.t.* to cease to occupy (a place or position). [f. L *vacare* be empty]

vacation /vəˈkeɪʃ(ə)n/ *n.* **1** any of the intervals between terms in universities and lawcourts. **2** (*US*) a holiday. **3** vacating. —*v.i.* (*US*) to take a holiday. [f. OF or L (as prec.)]

vaccinate /ˈvæksɪneɪt/ *v.t.* to inoculate with a vaccine. —**vaccination** /-ˈneɪʃ(ə)n/ *n.*, **vaccinator** *n.* [f. foll.]

vaccine /ˈvæksiːn, -sɪn/ *n.* a preparation of cowpox virus introduced into the bloodstream to procure immunity against smallpox; any preparation of an organism or substance causing a disease, specially treated or synthesized and injected or administered orally against an infection. [f. L (*vacca* cow)]

vacillate /ˈvæsɪleɪt/ *v.i.* to fluctuate in opinion or resolution. —**vacillation** /-ˈleɪʃ(ə)n/ *n.*, **vacillator** *n.* [f. L *vacillare* sway]

vacuole /ˈvækjʊəʊl/ *n.* a tiny cavity in an organ or cell, containing air or fluid etc. [F, dim. of L *vacuus* empty]

vacuous /ˈvækjʊəs/ *adj.* **1** expressionless; unintelligent. **2** empty. —**vacuity** /vəˈkjuːɪtɪ/ *n.*, **vacuously** *adv.*, **vacuousness** *n.* [f. L *vacuus* empty]

vacuum /ˈvækjʊəm/ *n.* (*pl.* **vacua** or **vacuums**) **1** space entirely devoid of matter; a space or vessel from which the air has been completely or partly removed by a pump etc. **2** absence of normal or previous contents. **3** (*pl.* **-s**) (*colloq.*) a vacuum cleaner. —*v.t./i.* (*colloq.*) to use a vacuum cleaner (on). —**vacuum brake,** a brake in which pressure is produced by exhaustion of air. **vacuum cleaner,** an electric appliance for taking up dust, dirt, etc. by suction. **vacuum flask,** a vessel with a double wall enclosing a vacuum so that liquid in the inner receptacle retains its temperature. **vacuum-packed** *adj.* sealed after partial removal of the air. **vacuum tube,** a tube with a near-vacuum for the free passage of electric current. [neut. of L *vacuus* empty]

vade-mecum /vɑːdɪˈmeɪkəm, veɪdɪˈmiːkəm/ *n.* a handbook or other small useful work of reference. [F f. L, = go with me]

vagabond /ˈvægəbɒnd/ *n.* a wanderer, especially an idle or dishonest one. —*adj.* having no fixed habitation, wandering. [f. OF or L *vagabundus* (*vagari* wander)]

vagary /ˈveɪgərɪ/ *n.* a capricious act, idea, or fluctuation. [f. L *vagari* wander]

vagina /vəˈdʒaɪnə/ *n.* (*pl.* **-ae** /-iː/ or **-as**) the passage leading from the vulva to the womb in a female mammal. —**vaginal** *adj.* [L, = sheath]

vagrant /ˈveɪgrənt/ *n.* a person without a settled home or regular work. —*adj.* wandering, roving. —**vagrancy** *n.* [f. AF *vag(a)raunt* (cf. L *vagari* wander)]

vague /veɪg/ *adj.* **1** of uncertain or ill-defined meaning or character. **2** (of a person or mind) imprecise, inexact in thought, expression, or understanding —**vaguely** *adv.*, **vagueness** *n.* [F or f. L *vagus* wandering]

vain *adj.* **1** conceited, especially about one's appearance. **2** having no value or significance, unsubstantial. **3** useless, futile, followed by no good result. —**in vain,** without result or success. —**vainly** *adv.* [f. OF f. L *vanus* empty]

vainglory /veɪnˈglɔːrɪ/ *n.* extreme vanity, boastfulness. —**vainglorious** *adj.* [after OF *vaine gloire*, L *vana gloria*]

valance /ˈvæləns/ *n.* a short curtain round the frame or canopy of a bedstead or above a window or under a shelf. [perh. f. AF *valer* descend]

vale *n.* (*archaic* exc. in place-names) a valley. [f. OF *val* f. L *vallis*]

valediction /vælɪˈdɪkʃ(ə)n/ *n.* bidding farewell; the words used in this. —**valedictory** *adj.* [f. L *valedicere* bid farewell (*vale* farewell, *dicere* say), after *benediction*]

valence /ˈveɪləns/ *n.* the combining or replacing power of an atom as compared with that of the hydrogen atom. [f. L *valentia* power]

valency /ˈveɪlənsɪ/ *n.* the unit of the combining power of an atom; this power. [as VALENCE]

valentine /ˈvæləntaɪn/ *n.* **1** a card or picture etc. sent (often anonymously) to a person of the opposite sex on St Valentine's day (14 Feb.). **2** a sweetheart chosen on this day. [f. *Valentine*, name of two saints]

valerian /vəˈlɪərɪən/ *n.* **1** any of various herbaceous plants of the widely-distributed genus *Valeriana*, many of which have been used medicinally as stimulants or antispasmodics. **2** the dried roots of such a plant used in medicine or scents etc. [f. OF f. L, app. f. *Valerianus* of Valerius]

valet /ˈvælɪt, -leɪ/ *n.* a man's personal attendant who takes care of clothes etc. —*v.t./i.* to act as valet (to). [F, = VARLET]

valetudinarian /vælɪtju:dɪˈneərɪən/ *n.* a person who pays excessive attention to preserving his health. —*adj.* that is a valetudinarian. —**valetudinarianism** *n.* [f. L (*valetudo* health)]

valiant /ˈvæljənt/ *adj.* (of a person or conduct) brave, courageous. —**valiantly** *adv.* [f. AF f. L *valēre* be strong]

valid /ˈvælɪd/ *adj.* **1** (of a reason, objection, etc.) sound and to the point, logical. **2** legally acceptable or usable; executed with the proper formalities. —**validity** /vəˈlɪdɪtɪ/ *n.*, **validly** *adv.* [f. F or L *validus* strong]

validate /ˈvælɪdeɪt/ *v.t.* to make valid, to ratify. —**validation** /-ˈdeɪʃ(ə)n/ *n.* [f. L (as prec.)]

valise /vəˈli:z/ *n.* a kitbag; (*US*) a small suitcase. [F f. It. *valigia*; orig. unkn.]

valley /ˈvælɪ/ *n.* **1** a long low area between hills. **2** a region drained by a river. **3** the internal angle formed by intersecting planes of a roof. [f. AF f. L. *vallis* (as VALE)]

valour /ˈvælə(r)/ *n.* courage, especially in battle. —**valorous** *adj.* [f. OF f. L *valor* (*valēre* be strong)]

valuable /ˈvæljʊəb(ə)l/ *adj.* of great value, price, or worth. —*n.* (usu. in *pl.*) a valuable thing. —**valuably** *adv.* [f. VALUE]

valuation /væljʊˈeɪʃ(ə)n/ *n.* estimation of a thing's value (especially by a professional valuer) or of a person's merit; the value so estimated. [f. foll.]

value /ˈvælju:/ *n.* **1** the amount of money, goods, or services etc. considered to be equivalent to a thing or for which it can be exchanged. **2** desirability, usefulness, importance. **3** the ability of a thing to serve a purpose or cause an effect. **4** (in *pl.*) one's principles or standards; one's judgement of what is valuable or important in life. **5** the amount or quantity denoted by a figure etc.; the duration of a musical sound indicated by a note; the relative importance of each playing-card, chess piece, etc., in a game; (in painting) the relative lightness and darkness of tones. —*v.t.* **1** to estimate the value of; to appraise professionally. **2** to have a high or specified opinion of; to attach importance to. —**value added tax**, a tax on the amount by which the value of an article has been increased at each stage of its production. **value judgement**, a subjective estimate of quality etc. [f. OF, p.p. of *valoir* be worth f. L *valēre* be strong]

valueless *adj.* having no value. [f. VALUE + -LESS]

valuer *n.* one who estimates or assesses values, especially as a professional. [f. VALUE]

valve *n.* **1** a device for controlling the passage of a fluid through a pipe etc., especially an automatic device allowing movement in one direction only. **2** a membranous structure in the heart or in a blood-vessel allowing blood to flow in one direction only. **3** a thermionic valve (see THERMIONIC). **4** a device to vary the length of tube in a trumpet etc. **5** each of the two shells of an oyster or mussel etc. [f. L. *valva* leaf of folding-door]

valvular /ˈvælvjʊlə(r)/ *adj.* **1** of or like a valve. **2** forming or having a valve or valves. [f. dim. of L *valva* (see prec.)]

vamoose /vəˈmu:s/ *v.i.* (*US slang*) to depart hurriedly. [f. Sp. *vamos* let us go]

vamp[1] *n.* the upper front part of a boot or shoe. —*v.t./i.* **1** to repair, to furbish. **2** to make by patching or from odds and ends. **3** to improvise (a musical accompaniment). [f. OF *avantpié* (*avant* before, *pied* foot)]

vamp[2] *n.* (*colloq.*) a seductive woman who uses her attractiveness to exploit men; an unscrupulous flirt. —*v.t./i.* (*colloq.*) to exploit or flirt with (a man) unscrupulously; to act as a vamp. [abbr. of foll.]

vampire /ˈvæmpaɪə(r)/ *n.* **1** a ghost or reanimated corpse supposed to leave a grave at night and suck the blood of living persons. **2** a person who preys ruthlessly on others. —**vampire bat**, a tropical bat, especially of South America, actually or supposedly biting animals and persons and lapping their blood. [F or G f. Magyar perh. f. Turk. *uber* witch]

van[1] *n.* **1** a covered vehicle for transporting goods or horses etc. or prisoners. **2** a railway carriage for luggage or for the use of the guard. [abbr. of CARAVAN]

van[2] *n.* the vanguard; the forefront. [abbr.]

vanadium /vəˈneɪdɪəm/ *n.* a hard grey metallic element, symbol V, atomic number 23. [f. ON *vanadis* name of the Scandinavian goddess Freya]

Van Allen belt /væn ˈælən/ (also **Van Allen layer**) each of the two regions of intense radiation partly surrounding the earth at heights of several thousand kilometres. [f. J. A. *Van Allen*, Amer. physicist (1914–)]

vandal /ˈvænd(ə)l/ *n.* one who wilfully or ignorantly destroys or damages works of art or other property or the beauties of nature. —**vandalism** *n.* [f. prec.]

vandalize /ˈvændəlaɪz/ *v.t.* to destroy or damage (property etc.) as a vandal. [f. *Vandals*, Germanic tribe that sacked Rome in 5th c.]

Vandyke /vænˈdaɪk/ *adj.* in the style of dress etc. common in portraits by Van Dyck. —**Vandyke beard,** a neat pointed beard. **Vandyke brown,** deep rich brown. [anglicized f. *Van Dyck*, Flemish painter (d. 1641)]

vane *n.* **1** a weather-vane. **2** the blade of a screw propeller, sail of a windmill, or similar device acted on or moved by water or wind. **3** the flat part of a bird's feather formed by barbs. [var. of obs. *fane* f. OE *fana* banner]

vanguard /ˈvængɑːd/ *n.* **1** the foremost part of an army or fleet advancing or ready to do so. **2** the leaders of a movement, opinion, etc. [f. OF *avan(t)garde* (*avant* before, *garde* guard)]

vanilla /vəˈnɪlə/ *n.* **1** a substance obtained from the vanilla-pod or synthetically and used to flavour ices, chocolate, etc. **2** a tropical climbing orchid of the genus *Vanilla* with fragrant flowers; the fruit of this. —**vanilla-pod** *n.* this fruit. [f. Sp. *vainilla* pod, dim. of *vaina* sheath, pod, f. L *vagina* sheath]

vanish /ˈvænɪʃ/ *v.t./i.* **1** to disappear completely; to cease to exist. **2** to cause to disappear. —**vanishing-point** *n.* the point at which receding parallel lines viewed in perspective appear to meet; the stage of complete disappearance. [f. OF *evanir* f. L (as EVANESCE)]

vanity /ˈvænɪtɪ/ *n.* **1** conceit, especially about one's appearance. **2** futility, worthlessness; something vain. —**vanity bag** *or* **case,** a bag or case carried by a woman and containing a small mirror, cosmetics, etc. [f. OF f. L *vanitas* (as VAIN)]

vanquish /ˈvæŋkwɪʃ/ *v.t.* (*literary*) to conquer. [f. OF f. L *vincere*]

vantage /ˈvɑːntɪdʒ/ *n.* advantage, especially as a score in tennis. —**vantage-point** *n.* a place from which one has a good view of something. [f. AF (as ADVANTAGE)]

vapid /ˈvæpɪd/ *adj.* insipid, uninteresting. —**vapidity** /vəˈpɪdɪtɪ/ *n.*, **vapidly** *adv.*, **vapidness** *n.* [f. L. *vapidus*]

vaporize /ˈveɪpəraɪz/ *v.t./i.* to convert or be converted into vapour. —**vaporization** /-ˈzeɪʃ(ə)n/ *n.*, **vaporizer** *n.* [f. foll.]

vapour /ˈveɪpə(r)/ *n.* **1** moisture or other substance diffused or suspended in air. **2** the gaseous form of a normally liquid or solid substance. —**vaporous** *adj.*, **vapoury** *adj.* [f. OF or L *vapor* steam]

variable /ˈveərɪəb(ə)l/ *adj.* **1** varying, changeable. **2** that may be varied. **3** (of a mathematical quantity) indeterminate, that may assume different numerical values. —*n.* a variable thing or quantity. —**variable star,** any star whose brightness changes. —**variability** /-ˈbɪlɪtɪ/ *n.*, **variably** *adv.* [f. OF f. L (as VARY)]

variance /ˈveərɪəns/ *n.* a discrepancy. —**at variance,** disagreeing, conflicting; in a state of discord or enmity. [f. OF f. L (as VARY)]

variant /ˈveərɪənt/ *adj.* differing in form or details from that named or from a standard; differing thus among themselves. —*n.* a variant form, spelling, type, etc. [as VARY]

variation /veərɪˈeɪʃ(ə)n/ *n.* **1** varying; the extent to which a thing varies. **2** a thing that varies from a type. **3** music produced by repeating a theme in a different (usually more elaborate) form. [as VARY]

varicoloured /ˈveərɪkʌləd/ *adj.* **1** variegated in colour. **2** of various or different colours. [f. L *varius* (as VARIOUS) + COLOURED]

varicose /ˈværɪkəʊs/ *adj.* (of a vein etc.) permanently and abnormally dilated. —**varicosity** /-ˈkɒsɪtɪ/ *n.* [f. L (*varix* varicose vein)]

varied /ˈveərɪd/ *adj.* showing variety. [f. VARY]

variegated /ˈveərɪgeɪtɪd/ *adj.* marked with irregular patches of different colours. —**variegation** /-ˈgeɪʃ(ə)n/ *n.* [f. L *variegare* (as VARIOUS)]

variety /vəˈraɪətɪ/ *n.* **1** absence of uniformity; the quality of not being the same or of not being the same at all times. **2** a quantity, collection, or range of different things. **3** a class of things differing from others in the same general group; a specimen or member of such a class; a different form of a thing, quality, etc. **4** an entertainment consisting of a mixed series of short performances of different kinds (e.g. singing, dancing, comedy acts, acrobatics). [f. F or L (as foll.)]

various /ˈveərɪəs/ *adj.* **1** of several kinds, unlike one another. **2** more than one, several; individual and separate. —**variously** *adv.* [f. L *varius* changing, diverse]

varlet /ˈvɑːlɪt/ *n.* (*archaic*) a menial, a rascal. [f. OF, var. of *vaslet* (cf. VALET)]

varnish /ˈvɑːnɪʃ/ *n.* **1** a resinous solution used to give a hard shiny transparent coating; some other preparation for a similar purpose. **2** an external appearance or display without underlying reality. —*v.t.* **1** to apply varnish to. **2** to gloss over (a fact). [f. OF *vernis* f. L or Gk, prob. f. *Berenice* in Cyrenaica]

varsity /ˈvɑːsɪtɪ/ *n.* **1** (*colloq.*, esp. with ref. to sports) university. **2** (*US*) the team representing a school or college etc. in a sport. [abbr.]

varve *n.* a pair of layers of silt deposited in lakes where a glacier melts, one being of fine silt (deposited in winter, when there is little melting) and one of coarser silt (deposited in summer, when the ice melts more freely). [f. Sw. *varv* layer]

vary /ˈveərɪ/ *v.t./i.* **1** to make or become different. **2** to be different or of different kinds. [f. OF or L *variare* (as VARIOUS)]

vas /væs/ *n.* (*pl.* **vasa** /ˈveɪsə/) a duct, a vessel. —**vas deferens** /ˈdefərenz/ (*pl.* **vasa deferentia** /defəˈrentɪə/), the spermatic duct of the testicle. [L, = vessel]

vascular /ˈvæskjʊlə(r)/ *adj.* of or containing vessels for conveying blood, sap, etc. [f. L *vasculum*, dim. of VAS]

vase /vɑːz/ *n.* an open usually tall vessel of glass, pottery, etc., used for holding cut flowers or as an ornament. [F f. L *vas* vessel]

vasectomy /vəˈsektəmɪ/ *n.* surgical removal of a part of each vas deferens, especially to sterilize a patient. [f. VAS + -ECTOMY]

Vaseline /ˈvæsəliːn/ *n.* [P] a type of petroleum jelly used as an ointment etc. [f. G *wasser* water + Gk *elaion* oil]

vaso- /ˈveɪsəʊ/ *comb. form* vessel, blood-vessel. —**vaso-motor** *adj.* causing constriction or dilatation of blood-vessels. [f. L *vas* vessel]

vassal /ˈvæs(ə)l/ *n.* **1** a humble servant or dependant. **2** (*hist.*) a holder of land by feudal tenure. —**vassalage** *n.* [f. OF f. L *vassallus* retainer; of Celtic origin]

vast /vɑːst/ *adj.* immense, very great in area or size. —**vastly** *adv.*, **vastness** *n.* [f. L *vastus*]

VAT /viː eɪ ˈtiː, væt/ *abbr.* value added tax.

vat *n.* a tank or other great vessel, especially for holding liquids in the process of brewing, tanning, dyeing, etc. —**vatful** *n.* [dial. var. of obs. *fat*, OE *fæt*]

vaudeville /ˈvɔːd(ə)vɪl, ˈvəʊ-/ *n.* variety entertainment, popular from about 1880 to 1932. [F, orig. of convivial song, esp. any of those composed by O. Basselin, 15th-c. poet born at *Vau de Vire* in Normandy]

vault[1] /vɔːlt, vɒlt/ *n.* **1** an arched roof. **2** a vault-like covering. **3** an underground room used as a place of storage. **4** a burial chamber. —*v.t.* (esp. in *p.p.*) to make in the form of a vault; to furnish with a vault or vaults. [f. OF, ult. f. L *volvere* roll]

vault[2] /vɔːlt, vɒlt/ *v.t./i.* to leap (over), especially while resting on the hand(s) or with the help of a pole. —*n.* a leap performed thus. —**vaulting-horse** *n.* a padded structure for vaulting over in a gymnasium. [f. OF *vo(u)lter* leap (as prec.)]

vaulting *n.* the arched work in a vaulted roof or ceiling. [f. VAULT[1]]

vaunt *v.t./i.* (*literary*) to boast. —*n.* (*literary*) a boast. [f. AF f. L *vanitare* (*vanus* vain)]

VC *abbr.* Victoria Cross.

VD *abbr.* venereal disease.

VDU *abbr.* visual display unit.

've *v.t./i.* (*colloq.*, usu. after pronouns) = HAVE. [abbr.]

veal *n.* calf's flesh as food. [f. AF f. L *vitellus* dim. of *vitulus* calf]

vector /ˈvektə(r)/ *n.* **1** a quantity having direction as well as magnitude (e.g. velocity = speed in a given direction). **2** a carrier of disease or infection. —**vectorial** /-ˈtɔːrɪəl/ *adj.* [L, = carrier (*vehere* convey)]

Veda /ˈveɪdə, ˈviː-/ *n.* (also **Vedas**) the most ancient and sacred literature of the Hindus. —**Vedic** *adj.* [f. Skr., = (sacred) knowledge]

veer *v.i.* to change direction or course; (of the wind) to change gradually in a clockwise direction. —*n.* a change of direction. [f. F *virer*, perh. ult. f. L *gyrare* gyrate]

veg /vedʒ/ *n.* (*colloq.*) vegetable(s). [abbr.]

vegan /ˈviːgən/ *n.* a strict vegetarian who eats neither meat nor animal products (e.g. eggs). —*adj.* of vegans or their diet. [f. VEGETARIAN]

vegetable /ˈvedʒɪtəb(ə)l/ *n.* **1** a plant of which some part is used (raw or cooked) for food, especially as an accompaniment to meat. **2** a person living a dull monotonous life; one who is physically alive but mentally inert owing to injury, illness, or abnormality. —*adj.* of, from, or relating to plant life. [f. OF or L (as VEGETATE)]

vegetal /ˈvedʒɪt(ə)l/ *adj.* of plants; of the nature of plants. [as VEGETATE]

vegetarian /vedʒɪˈteərɪən/ *n.* a person who eats no meat and whose diet includes vegetables, cereals, seeds, fruit, and nuts, with (or in strict observance without) eggs and dairy products. —**vegetarianism** *n.* [f. VEGETABLE]

vegetate /ˈvedʒɪteɪt/ *v.i.* **1** to lead a dull existence devoid of intellectual or social acitivity; to live in comfortably uneventful retirement or seclusion. **2** to grow as plants do. [f. L *vegetare* to animate (*vegetus* active)]

vegetation /vedʒɪˈteɪʃ(ə)n/ *n.* plants collectively, plant life. [as prec.]

vegetative /ˈvedʒɪtətɪv/ *adj.* **1** concerned with growth and development rather than (sexual) reproduction. **2** of vegetation. [f. OF or L (as VEGETATE)]

vehement /ˈviːəmənt/ *adj.* showing or caused

by strong feeling, ardent. —**vehemence** *n.*, **vehemently** *adv.* [f. F or L *vehemens*]

vehicle /ˈviːɪk(ə)l/ *n.* **1** a conveyance for transporting passengers or goods on land or in space. **2** a medium by which thought, feeling, or action is expressed or displayed. **3** a liquid etc. as a medium for suspending pigments, drugs, etc. —**vehicular** /vɪˈhɪkjʊlə(r)/ [f. F or L *vehiculum* (as VECTOR)]

veil /veɪl/ *n.* **1** a piece of fine net or other fabric worn as part of a head-dress or to protect or conceal the face. **2** a piece of linen etc. as part of a nun's head-dress. **3** a curtain, especially that separating the sanctuary in the Jewish Temple. **4** a disguise, a pretext. —*v.t.* **1** to cover (as) with a veil. **2** to conceal partly. —**beyond the veil,** in the unknown state of life after death. **draw a veil over,** to avoid discussing or calling attention to. **take the veil,** to become a nun. [f. AF f. L *velum*]

vein /veɪn/ *n.* **1** any of the tubes by which blood is conveyed from all parts of the body to the heart; (*pop.*) any blood-vessel. **2** a rib of a leaf or insect's wing. **3** a streak or stripe of a different colour in wood, marble, cheese, etc. **4** a fissure in rock filled with ore. **5** a distinctive character or tendency, a mood. —**veined** *adj.*, **veiny** *adj.* [f. OF f. L *vena*]

Velcro /ˈvelkrəʊ/ *n.* [P] a fastener for clothes etc., consisting of two strips of fabric with tiny loops on one and hooks on the other which cling together when pressed one upon the other. [f. F *velours croché* hooked velvet]

veld /velt/ *n.* (also **veldt**) open grassland in southern Africa. [Afrik., = FIELD]

veleta /vəˈliːtə/ *n.* an old-fashioned ballroom dance in triple time. [Sp., = weather-vane (*vela* cloth, veil)]

vellum /ˈveləm/ *n.* **1** fine parchment originally from the skin of the calf; a manuscript on this. **2** smooth writing-paper imitating vellum. [f. OF *velin* (as VEAL)]

velocipede /vɪˈlɒsɪpiːd/ *n.* (*hist.*) a light vehicle propelled by the rider, especially an early form of bicycle or tricycle. [f. F f. L *velox* swift + *pes* foot]

velocity /vɪˈlɒsɪtɪ/ *n.* speed, especially in a given direction (usually of inanimate things). [f. F or L (*velox* swift)]

velour /vəˈlʊə(r)/ *n.* (also **velours**) a plush-like woven fabric or felt. [F, = velvet]

velvet /ˈvelvɪt/ *n.* **1** a closely woven fabric (originally of silk) with a thick short pile on one side. **2** a furry skin on a growing antler. —*adj.* of, like, or as soft as velvet. —**on velvet,** in an advantageous or prosperous position. **velvet glove,** outward gentleness cloaking sternness or inflexibility. —**velvety** *adj.* [f. OF *veluotte*, ult. f. L *villus* down]

velveteen /velvɪˈtiːn/ *n.* cotton velvet. [f. prec.]

Ven. *abbr.* Venerable (as the title of an archdeacon).

vena cava /viːnə ˈkeɪvə/ each of the (usually two) veins carrying deoxygenated blood into the heart. [L, = hollow vein]

venal /ˈviːn(ə)l/ *adj.* (of a person) that may be bribed; (of conduct etc.) characteristic of a venal person. —**venality** /viːˈnælɪtɪ/ *n.*, **venally** *adv.* [f. L *venalis* (*venum* thing for sale)]

vend *v.t.* to offer (small wares) for sale. —**vending-machine** *n.* a slot-machine for the automatic retail of small articles. [f. F or L *vendere* sell (as VENAL)]

vendetta /venˈdetə/ *n.* a blood feud; prolonged bitter hostility. [It. f. L *vindicta* (as VINDICTIVE)]

vendor *n.* **1** (esp. *Law*) one who sells. **2** a vending-machine. [f. AF (as VEND)]

veneer /vɪˈnɪə(r)/ *v.t.* **1** to cover (wood) with a thin layer of a finer wood. **2** (esp. in *p.p.*) to disguise (character etc.) superficially. —*n.* **1** a layer used in veneering. **2** a superficial show of some good quality. [earlier *fineer* f. G *furni(e)ren* f. OF (as FURNISH)]

venerable /ˈvenərəb(ə)l/ *adj.* **1** entitled to veneration on account of character, age, associations, etc. **2** the title of an archdeacon in the Church of England. —**venerability** /-ˈbɪlɪtɪ/ *n.*, **venerably** *adv.* [f. OF or L (as foll.)]

venerate /ˈvenəreɪt/ *v.t.* to regard with deep respect; to honour as hallowed or sacred. —**veneration** /-ˈreɪʃ(ə)n/ *n.*, **venerator** *n.* [f. L *venerari* adore, revere]

venereal /vɪˈnɪərɪəl/ *adj.* of sexual desire or intercourse; relating to venereal disease. —**venereal disease,** a disease contracted chiefly by sexual intercourse with a person already infected. —**venereally** *adv.* [f. L *venereus* (*venus* sexual love)]

Venetian /vɪˈniːʃ(ə)n/ *adj.* of Venice. —*n.* a native or the dialect of Venice. —**venetian blind,** a window-blind of horizontal slats that can be adjusted to let in or exclude light. [f. OF, assim. to L *Venetianus* (*Venetia* Venice)]

vengeance /ˈvendʒəns/ *n.* revenge for hurt or harm to oneself or to a person etc. whose cause one supports. —**with a vengeance,** to an extreme degree, more than was expected. [f. OF (*venger* avenge f. L, as VINDICATE)]

vengeful *adj.* vindictive, seeking vengeance. —**vengefully** *adv.*, **vengefulness** *n.* [f. obs. *venge* avenge (as prec.) + -FUL]

venial /ˈviːnɪəl/ *adj.* (of a sin or fault) pardonable, excusable, not mortal. —**veniality** /viːnɪˈælɪtɪ/ *n.*, **venially** *adv.* [f. OF f. L (*venia* forgiveness)]

venison /ˈvenɪsən/ *n.* deer's flesh as food. [f. OF f. L *venatio* hunting]

Venn diagram a diagram using overlapping and intersecting circles etc. to show the relationships between mathematical sets. [f. J. *Venn*, British logician (d. 1923)]

venom /ˈvenəm/ *n.* **1** poisonous fluid secreted by certain snakes, scorpions, etc., and injected into a victim by a bite or sting. **2** virulence of feeling, language, or conduct. [f. OF f. L *venenum* poison]

venomous /ˈvenəməs/ *adj.* **1** secreting venom. **2** full of venom in feeling etc. —**venomously** *adv.* [as prec.]

venous /ˈviːnəs/ *adj.* of, full of, or contained in veins. [f. L *venosus* (*vena* vein)]

vent[1] *n.* **1** a hole or opening allowing air, gas, or liquid to pass out of or into a confined space. **2** the anus, especially of a lower animal. **3** an outlet; free passage or play. —*v.t.* **1** to make a vent in. **2** to give vent or free expression to. —**vent light,** a small window, hinged at the top edge. [f. F f. L *ventus* wind]

vent[2] *n.* a slit in a garment, especially in the lower edge of the back of a coat. [f. OF *fente* f. L *findere* cleave]

ventilate /ˈventɪleɪt/ *v.t.* **1** to cause air to circulate freely in (a room etc.). **2** to express (a question, grievance, etc.) publicly for consideration and discussion. —**ventilation** /-ˈleɪʃ(ə)n/ *n.* [f. L *ventilare* blow, winnow (*ventus* wind)]

ventilator *n.* **1** an appliance or aperture for ventilating a room etc. **2** equipment for maintaining breathing artificially. [f. prec.]

ventral /ˈventr(ə)l/ *adj.* of or on the abdomen. —**ventrally** *adv.* [f. L *venter* abdomen]

ventricle /ˈventrɪk(ə)l/ *n.* a cavity in the body, the hollow part of an organ, especially each of four in the brain or of two in the heart that pump blood into the arteries by contracting. —**ventricular** /-ˈtrɪkjʊlə(r)/ *adj.* [f. L *ventriculus* dim. of *venter* belly]

ventriloquist /venˈtrɪləkwɪst/ *n.* an entertainer who produces voice-sounds so that they seem to come from a source other than himself. —**ventriloquism** *n.* [f. L *ventriloquus* (*venter* belly, *loqui* speak)]

ventriloquize /venˈtrɪləkwaɪz/ *v.i.* to use ventriloquism. [f. prec.]

venture /ˈventʃə(r)/ an undertaking that involves risk; a commercial speculation. —*v.t./i.* **1** to dare, not to be afraid; to dare to go, do, or utter. **2** to expose to risk, to stake. **3** to take risks. —**at a venture,** at random; without previous consideration. **venture on,** to dare to engage in or make etc. **Venture Scout,** a member of the senior section of the Scout Association. [as ADVENTURE]

venturesome *adj.* **1** willing to take risks, daring. **2** risky. [f. prec. + -SOME]

venturi tube /venˈtjʊərɪ/ a device consisting of a short section of tube which is narrower than the parts at each end, so that gas or liquid under pressure flows through it faster, used to produce an effect of suction or in measuring the rate of flow. [f. G. B. *Venturi*, Italian physicist (d. 1822)]

venue /ˈvenjuː/ *n.* **1** an appointed place of meeting, especially for a sports match. **2** the county etc. within which a jury must be gathered and a cause tried. [F, = coming (*venir* come)]

veracious /vəˈreɪʃəs/ *adj.* **1** truthful. **2** (of a statement etc.) that is or is meant to be true. —**veraciously** *adv.*, **veracity** /vəˈræsɪtɪ/ *n.* [f. L *verax* (*verus* true)]

veranda /vəˈrændə/ *n.* a roofed terrace along the side of a house. [f. Hindi f. Port. *varanda*]

verb *n.* a word used to indicate an action, state, or occurrence (e.g. *bring*, *become*, *happen*). [f. OF or L *verbum*, lit. 'word']

verbal *adj.* **1** of or in words. **2** spoken, not written. **3** of a verb. **4** (of a translation) literal. —*n.* (*colloq.*) a verbal statement, especially one made to the police. —**verbal noun,** a noun (e.g. *singing*, *dancing*, or other nouns ending in *-ing*) derived from a verb and partly sharing its constructions. —**verbally** *adv.* [f. F or L (as prec.)]

verbalism /ˈvɜːbəlɪz(ə)m/ *n.* minute attention to words. [f. prec.]

verbalize /ˈvɜːbəlaɪz/ *v.t./i.* **1** to express in words. **2** to be verbose. —**verbalization** /-ˈzeɪʃ(ə)n/ *n.* [f. VERBAL]

verbatim /vɜːˈbeɪtɪm/ *adv.* & *adj.* in exactly the same words, word for word. [f. L (*verbum* word)]

verbena /vɜːˈbiːnə/ *n.* a herb or small shrub of the genus *Verbena*. —**lemon verbena,** a similar plant (*Lippia citriodora*) with lemon-scented leaves. [L, orig. = sacred bough of olive]

verbiage /ˈvɜːbɪɪdʒ/ *n.* an excessive number of words used to express an idea. [F (obs. *verbeier* chatter f. *verbe* word, as VERB)]

verbose /vɜːˈbəʊs/ *adj.* using or expressed in more words than are needed. —**verbosely** *adv.*, **verbosity** /vɜːˈbɒsɪtɪ/ *n.* [f. L *verbosus* (*verbum* word)]

verdant /ˈvɜːd(ə)nt/ *adj.* (of grass etc.) green, freshcoloured; (of a field etc.) covered with green grass etc. —**verdancy** *n.* [perh. f. OF *verdoier* be green f. L *viridis* green]

verdict /ˈvɜːdɪkt/ *n.* **1** the decision of a jury on an issue of fact in a civil or criminal cause. **2** a decision or opinion given after examining, testing, or experiencing something. [f. AF *verdit* (*veir* true f. L *verus*, *dit* = DICTUM)]

verdigris /ˈvɜːdɪgrɪs, -riːs/ *n.* a green deposit on copper or brass. [f. OF, = green of Greece]

verdure /ˈvɜːdjə(r), -djʊə(r)/ *n.* green vegetation;

the greenness of this. —**verdurous** *adj.* [f. OF (*verd* green f. L *viridis*)]

verge[1] *n.* **1** a brink or border (usu. *fig.*). **2** a grass edging of a road, flower-bed, etc. [f. OF f. L *virga* rod]

verge[2] *v.i.* to incline downwards or in a specified direction. —**verge on,** to border on, to approach closely. [f. L *vergere* incline]

verger *n.* an official in a church who acts as caretaker and attendant; an officer who bears a staff before a bishop or other dignitary. [as VERGE[1]]

verifiable /ˈverɪfaɪəb(ə)l/ *adj.* that may be verified. [f. foll.]

verify /ˈverɪfaɪ/ *v.t.* to establish the truth or correctness of by examination or demonstration; (of an event etc.) to bear out, to fulfil (a prediction or promise). —**verification** /-fɪˈkeɪʃ(ə)n/ *n.*, **verifier** *n.* [f. OF f. L *verificare* (*verus* true, *facere* make)]

verily /ˈverɪlɪ/ *adv.* (*archaic*) really, truly. [f. VERY]

verisimilitude /verɪsɪˈmɪlɪtjuːd/ *n.* the appearance of being true or real. [f. L, = resemblance to the truth (*verus* true, *similis* like)]

veritable /ˈverɪtəb(ə)l/ *adj.* real, rightly so called. —**veritably** *adv.* [OF (as foll.)]

verity /ˈverɪtɪ/ *n.* a true statement; truth. [f. OF f. L *veritas* truth (*verus* true)]

vermicelli /vɜːmɪˈselɪ, -tʃelɪ/ *n.* pasta made in long slender threads. [It., dim. of *verme* f. L *vermis* worm]

vermicide /ˈvɜːmɪsaɪd/ *n.* a drug that kills worms. [f. L *vermis* worm + -CIDE]

vermiform /ˈvɜːmɪfɔːm/ *adj.* worm-shaped. —**vermiform appendix,** a small blind tube extending from the caecum in man and some other mammals. [f. L *vermis* worm + FORM]

vermilion /vəˈmɪljən/ *n.* **1** cinnabar. **2** a brilliant red pigment made by grinding this or artificially. **3** the colour of this. —*adj.* of this colour. [f. OF *vermeillon* (*vermeil* f. L *vermiculus* dim. of *vermis* worm)]

vermin /ˈvɜːmɪn/ *n.* **1** (usu. treated as *pl.*) common mammals and birds injurious to game, crops, etc., e.g. foxes, mice, owls. **2** noxious or parasitic worms or insects. **3** vile persons, those harmful to society. [f. OF, ult. f. L *vermis* worm]

verminous /ˈvɜːmɪnəs/ *adj.* of the nature of vermin; infested with vermin. [f. prec. or L *verminosus*]

vermouth /ˈvɜːməθ/ *n.* a wine flavoured with aromatic herbs. [f. F f. G *wermut* wormwood]

vernacular /vəˈnækjʊlə(r)/ *n.* **1** the language or dialect of the country. **2** the language of a particular class or group. **3** homely speech. —*adj.* (of a language) of one's native country, not of foreign origin or of learned formation. [f. L *vernaculus* domestic, native (*verna* home-born slave)]

vernal /ˈvɜːn(ə)l/ *adj.* of, occurring in, or appropriate to spring. —**vernally** *adv.* [f. L *vernalis* (*vernus* f. *ver* spring)]

vernier /ˈvɜːnɪə(r)/ *n.* a small movable graduated scale for obtaining fractional parts of subdivisions on the fixed scale of a barometer etc. [f. P. *Vernier*, French mathematician (d. 1637)]

veronica /vəˈrɒnɪkə/ *n.* **1** a plant of the genus *Veronica*, speedwell. **2** a vernicle. [L, f. woman's name *Veronica*]

verruca /vəˈruːkə/ *n.* (*pl.* **-cae** /-siː/ or **-cas**) a wart or similar protuberance. [L]

versatile /ˈvɜːsətaɪl/ *adj.* able to do or to be used for many different things. —**versatility** /-ˈtɪlɪtɪ/ *n.* [F, or f. L (*versare* turn)]

verse *n.* **1** a metrical form of composition. **2** a stanza of metrical lines; a metrical line. **3** each of the short numbered divisions of the Bible. [OE & f. OF f. L *versus* turn of plough, furrow, line of writing (*vertere* turn)]

versed /vɜːst/ *adj.* (with *in*) experienced or skilled in, having a knowledge of. [f. F or L *versatus* (*versari* be engaged in)]

versicle /ˈvɜːsɪk(ə)l/ *n.* each of the short sentences in a liturgy said or sung by a priest etc. and alternating with the responses. [f. OF or L *versiculus* dim. of *versus* (see VERSE)]

versify /ˈvɜːsɪfaɪ/ *v.t./i.* to turn into or express in verse; to compose verses. —**versification** /-fɪˈkeɪʃ(ə)n/ *n.* [f. OF f. L *versificare* (as VERSE, *facere* make)]

version /ˈvɜːʃ(ə)n/ *n.* **1** an account of a matter from a particular person's point of view. **2** a book or work etc. in a particular edition or translation. **3** a particular variant. [F or f. L (*vertere* turn)]

verso *n.* (*pl.* **-os**) the left-hand page of an open book, the back of a leaf of a book etc. (cf. RECTO). [f. L *verso* (*folio*) = turned (leaf) (*vertere* turn)]

versus /ˈvɜːsəs/ *prep.* (esp. *Law* and in sport) against. [L, = against]

vert *n.* (in heraldry) green. [f. OF f. L *viridis* green]

vertebra /ˈvɜːtɪbrə/ *n.* (*pl.* **-ae** /-iː/) each segment of the backbone. —**vertebral** *adj.* [L (*vertere* turn)]

vertebrate /ˈvɜːtɪbrət, -reɪt/ *adj.* having a spinal column, and thus belonging to the subphylum Vertebrata of the phylum Chordata, which includes fish, amphibians, reptiles, birds, and mammals. —*n.* a vertebrate animal. [f. L. *vertebratus* jointed (as prec.)]

vertex /ˈvɜːteks/ *n.* (*pl.* **vertices** /-ɪsiːz/ or **vertexes**) **1** the highest point of a hill or structure; the apex. **2** each angular point of a triangle, polygon, etc.; the meeting-point of the lines that form an angle. [L, = whirlpool, crown of head]

vertical /ˈvɜːtɪk(ə)l/ *adj.* **1** at right angles to the plane of the horizon. **2** in the direction from top to bottom of a picture etc. **3** of or at the vertex. —*n.* a vertical line or plane. —**vertical take-off,** the take-off of an aircraft directly upwards. —**vertically** *adv.* [F or f. L (as prec.)]

vertiginous /vɜːˈtɪdʒɪnəs/ *adj.* of or causing vertigo. [f. L (as foll.)]

vertigo /ˈvɜːtɪɡəʊ/ *n.* (*pl.* **-os**) dizziness. [L, = whirling (*vertere* turn)]

vervain /ˈvɜːveɪn/ *n.* a herbaceous plant of the genus *Verbena*, especially *V. officinalis* with small blue, white, or purple flowers. [f. OF f. L, = VERBENA]

verve *n.* enthusiasm, vigour, especially in artistic or literary work. [F, orig. = form of expression, f. L *verba* words]

very /ˈverɪ/ *adv.* **1** in a high degree. **2** (with superlative adjectives or *own*) in the fullest sense. **3** exactly. **4** (*archaic*) genuine, truly so called. —*adj.* **1** itself or himself etc. and no other; actual, truly such. **2** extreme, utter. —**not very,** in a low degree; far from being. **very good** *or* **well,** an expression of approval or consent. **very high frequency,** (in radio) 30-300 megahertz. [f. OF *verai* f. L *verus* truth]

Very light /ˈverɪ, ˈvɪərɪ/ a flare projected from a pistol for signalling or temporarily illuminating part of a battlefield etc. [f. E. W. *Very*, Amer. inventor (d. 1910)]

vesica /ˈvesɪkə, vɪˈsaɪkə/ *n.* a pointed oval used as an aureole in medieval sculpture and painting. [L, = bladder, blister]

vesicle /ˈvesɪk(ə)l/ *n.* a small bladder, blister, or bubble. [f. F or L *vesicula* dim. of *vesica* bladder]

vespers /ˈvespəz/ *n.pl.* the evening service in the Western (Roman Catholic) Church. [f. OF f. L (*vesper* evening, evening star]

vessel /ˈves(ə)l/ *n.* **1** a hollow receptacle, especially for liquid. **2** a hollow structure designed to travel on water and carry people or goods, a ship or boat. **3** a tubelike structure holding or conveying blood or sap etc. in the body of an animal or plant. [f. AF f. L *vascellum* dim. of *vas* vessel]

vest[1] *n.* **1** a knitted or woven undergarment covering the trunk of the body. **2** (*US* & in commerce) a waistcoat. —**vest-pocket** *adj.* of a very small size, as if suitable for carrying in a waistcoat pocket. [f. F f. It. f. L *vestis* garment]

vest[2] *v.t./i.* **1** to confer (on) as a firm or legal right. **2** (of property or a right etc.; with *in*) to come into the possession of. **3** (usu. *archaic*) to clothe. —**vested interest** *or* **right,** one securely held by right or by long association. **a vested interest in,** an expectation of benefiting from. [f. OF f. L *vestire* clothe (as prec.)]

vestibule /ˈvestɪbjuːl/ *n.* **1** an antechamber, entrance hall, or lobby next to the outer door of a building. **2** (*US*) an enclosed entrance to a railway-carriage. [F, or f. L *vestibulum* entrance-court]

vestige /ˈvestɪdʒ/ *n.* **1** a trace, a small remaining part of what once existed. **2** a very small amount. **3** a part or organ (of a plant or animal) that is now degenerate but was well developed in the ancestors. —**vestigial** /-ˈtɪdʒɪəl/ *adj.* [F, f. L *vestigium* footprint]

vestment /ˈvestmənt/ *n.* **1** any of the official garments of the clergy, choristers, etc., worn during divine service, especially the chasuble. **2** a garment, especially an official or State robe. [f. OF f. L *vestimentum* (as VEST[2])]

vestry /ˈvestrɪ/ *n.* **1** a room or building attached to a church, where vestments are kept and where clergy and choir robe themselves. **2** (*hist.*) a meeting of parishioners, usually in the vestry, for parochial business; the body of parishioners meeting thus. [f. OF f. L *vestiarium* (as VEST[1])]

vet *n.* (*colloq.*) a veterinary surgeon. —*v.t.* (**-tt-**) **1** to examine carefully and critically for faults or errors etc. **2** to examine or treat (an animal). [abbr.]

vetch *n.* a plant of the pea family especially of the genus *Vicia*, largely used for fodder. [f. AF f. L *vicia*]

vetchling *n.* a plant of the genus *Lathyrus*, allied to vetch. [f. VETCH + -LING]

veteran /ˈvetərən/ *n.* **1** a person with long experience, especially in the armed forces. **2** (*US*) an ex-serviceman. —**veteran car,** a car made before 1916, especially before 1905. [f. F or L *veteranus* (*vetus* old)]

veterinarian /vetərɪˈneərɪən/ *n.* a veterinary surgeon. [as foll.]

veterinary /ˈvetərɪnərɪ/ *adj.* of or for the diseases of farm and domestic animals or their treatment. —*n.* a veterinary surgeon. —**veterinary surgeon,** one skilled in such treatment. [f. L *veterinarius* (*veterinae* cattle)]

veto /ˈviːtəʊ/ *n.* (*pl.* **-oes**) **1** the constitutional right to reject a legislative enactment; the right of a permanent member of the UN Security Council to reject a resolution. **2** such a rejection; an official message conveying this. **3** a prohibition. —*v.t.* to exercise one's veto against; to forbid authoritatively. [L, = I forbid]

vex *v.t.* **1** to annoy, to irritate. **2** (*archaic*) to grieve, to afflict. —**vexed question,** a problem that is much discussed. [f. OF f. L *vexare* shake, disturb]

vexation /vek'seɪʃ(ə)n/ *n.* **1** vexing, being vexed; a state of irritation or worry. **2** an annoying or distressing thing. [f. OF or L (as prec.)]

vexatious /vek'seɪʃəs/ *adj.* causing vexation, annoying; (*Law*) not having sufficient grounds for action and seeking only to annoy the defendant. —**vexatiously** *adv.*, **vexatiousness** *n.* [as prec.]

VHF *abbr.* very high frequency.

via /'vaɪə/ *prep.* by way of, through. [L, abl. of *via* way]

viable /'vaɪəb(ə)l/ *adj.* capable of living or existing successfully; (of a foetus) sufficiently developed to be able to survive after birth; (of a plan etc.) feasible, especially from an economic standpoint. —**viability** /-'bɪlɪtɪ/ *n.*, **viably** *adv.* [F (*vie* life f. L *vita*)]

viaduct /'vaɪədʌkt/ *n.* a bridgelike structure, especially a series of arches, carrying a railway or road across a valley or dip in the ground. [f. L *via* way, after *aqueduct*]

vial /'vaɪəl/ *n.* a small (usually cylindrical glass) vessel especially for holding liquid medicines. [as PHIAL]

viand /'vaɪənd/ *n.* (*archaic*, usu. in *pl.*) an article of food. [f. OF f. L *vivenda* (gerundive of *vivere* live)]

viaticum /vaɪ'ætɪkəm/ *n.* the Eucharist given to a person dying or in danger of death. [L, = provision for a journey (*via* way)]

vibes /vaɪbz/ *n.pl.* (*colloq.*) **1** a vibraphone. **2** mental or emotional vibrations. [abbr.]

vibrant /'vaɪbrənt/ *adj.* vibrating, resonant; thrilling with energy or activity. [as VIBRATE]

vibraphone /'vaɪbrəfəʊn/ *n.* a percussion instrument of metal bars and tubular resonators surmounted by small circular fans mechanically rotated to give a vibrato effect. [f. VIBRATO + -PHONE]

vibrate /vaɪ'breɪt/ *v.t./i.* **1** to move rapidly and continuously to and fro; to move to and fro like a pendulum, to oscillate. **2** to cause to do this. **3** to resound; to sound with a rapid slight variation of pitch. [f. L *vibrare* shake]

vibration /vaɪ'breɪʃ(ə)n/ *n.* **1** vibrating; a vibrating movement, sensation, or sound. **2** (in *pl.*) mental stimuli thought to be given out by a person or place; the emotional sensations these produce. [as prec.]

vibrato /vɪ'brɑ:təʊ/ *n.* (*pl.* **-os**) the slight wavering of pitch used to enrich and intensify the tone of the voice and of many (esp. stringed) instruments. [It. (as VIBRATE)]

vibrator /vaɪ'breɪtə(r)/ *n.* a thing that vibrates or causes vibration, especially an electric or other instrument used in massage. [f. VIBRATE]

vibratory /'vaɪbrətərɪ/ *adj.* causing vibration. [as prec.]

viburnum /vɪ'bɜ:nəm/ *n.* a shrub of the genus *Viburnum*, usually with white flowers. [L, = wayfaring-tree]

vicar /'vɪkə(r)/ *n.* an incumbent of a Church of England parish where the tithes formerly belonged to a chapter or religious house or to a layman. —**vicar apostolic**, a Roman Catholic missionary or titular bishop. **vicar-general** *n.* an official assisting or representing a bishop, especially in administrative matters. **Vicar of Christ**, the pope. [f. AF f. L *vicarius* substitute]

vicarage /'vɪkərɪdʒ/ *n.* the house provided for a vicar. [f. VICAR]

vicarious /vɪ'keərɪəs/ *adj.* **1** experienced through sharing imaginatively in the feelings or emotions etc. of another person. **2** acting or done for another; deputed, delegated. —**vicariously** *adv.*, **vicariousness** *n.* [f. L (as VICAR)]

vice[1] *n.* **1** evil or grossly immoral conduct, depravity. **2** an evil habit; a particular form of depravity. **3** a defect or blemish. —**vice squad**, the police department enforcing the laws against criminal and immoral practices such as prostitution. [f. OF f. L *vitium*]

vice[2] *n.* an instrument with two jaws between which a thing may be gripped so as to leave the hands free to work on it. [orig. = screw, f. OF *vis* f. L *vitis* vine]

vice[3] /'vaɪsɪ/ *prep.* in the place of, in succession to. [L, abl. of (*vix*) *vicis* change]

vice- *prefix* forming nouns in the senses 'acting as a substitute or deputy for' (*vice-president*), 'next in rank to' (*vice-admiral*). [f. VICE[3]]

vice-chancellor /vaɪs'tʃɑ:nsələ(r)/ *n.* a deputy chancellor (especially of a university, discharging most of the chancellor's administrative duties).

vicegerent /vaɪs'dʒerənt/ *adj.* exercising delegated power. —*n.* a vicegerent person, a deputy. [f. L (VICE-, *gerere* carry on)]

viceregal /vaɪs'ri:g(ə)l/ *adj.* of a viceroy. —**viceregally** *adv.* [f. REGAL, after VICEROY]

vicereine /'vaɪsreɪn/ *n.* a viceroy's wife; a woman viceroy. [F (VICE-, *reine* queen)]

viceroy /'vaɪsrɔɪ/ *n.* a ruler on behalf of a sovereign in a colony, province, etc. [F (VICE-, *roy* king)]

viceroyalty /vaɪs'rɔɪəltɪ/ *n.* the office of viceroy. [f. F (as prec.)]

vice versa /'vaɪsɪ 'vɜ:sə/ with the order of the terms changed, the other way round. [L, = the position being reversed]

vicinage /'vɪsɪnɪdʒ/ *n.* **1** the neighbourhood, the surrounding district. **2** the relation of neighbours. [f. OF f. L *vicinus* neighbour]

vicinity /vɪ'sɪnɪtɪ/ *n.* **1** the surrounding district. **2** nearness, closeness. —**in the vicinity (of)**, near. [f. L *vicinitas* (as prec.)]

vicious /ˈvɪʃəs/ *adj.* **1** acting or done with evil intentions. **2** brutal, strongly spiteful; bad-tempered; (of animals) savage and dangerous. **3** violent, severe. **4** (of language or reasoning) faulty, unsound. —**vicious circle,** a state of affairs in which a cause produces an effect which itself produces or intensifies the original cause. **vicious spiral,** a similar interaction causing a continuous increase or decrease (see SPIRAL 2). —**viciously** *adv.*, **viciousness** *n.* [f. OF or L *vitiosus* (as VICE[1])]

vicissitude /vɪˈsɪsɪtju:d/ *n.* a change of circumstances, especially of fortune. [F or f. L *vicissitudo* (*vicissim* by turns)]

victim /ˈvɪktɪm/ *n.* **1** a person who is injured or killed by another or as the result of an event or circumstance. **2** a prey; a person who suffers because of a trick. **3** a living creature sacrificed to a deity or in a religious rite. [f. L *victima*]

victimize *v.t.* to single out (a person) for punishment or unfair treatment; to make (a person etc.) a victim. —**victimization** /-ˈzeɪʃ(ə)n/ *n.* [f. prec.]

victor /ˈvɪktə(r)/ *n.* the winner in a battle or contest. [f. AF or L (*vincere* conquer)]

victoria /vɪkˈtɔ:rɪə/ *n.* **1** a low light four-wheeled horse-drawn carriage with a seat for two and a raised driver's seat and with a collapsible top. **2** (in full **victoria plum**) a large red luscious variety of plum. —**Victoria Cross,** a decoration awarded to members of the Commonwealth armed services for a conspicuous act of bravery. [f. Queen *Victoria* (d. 1901)]

Victorian /vɪkˈtɔ:rɪən/ *adj.* belonging to or characteristic of the reign of Queen Victoria. —*n.* a person of this period. —**Royal Victorian Order,** an order founded by Queen Victoria in 1896 and awarded for personal service to the sovereign. [as prec.]

Victoriana /vɪktɔ:rɪˈɑ:nə/ *n.pl.* objects from Victorian times. [as prec.]

victorious /vɪkˈtɔ:rɪəs/ *adj.* having gained the victory. [as VICTORY]

victory /ˈvɪktərɪ/ *n.* success in a battle, contest, or game etc. achieved by gaining mastery over one's opponent(s) or by achieving the highest score. [f. AF f. L *victoria* (as VICTOR)]

victual /ˈvɪt(ə)l/ *n.* (usu. in *pl.*) food, provisions. —*v.t./i.* (**-ll-**) **1** to supply with victuals. **2** to obtain stores; to eat victuals. [f. OF *vitaille* f. L *victualia* (*victus* food)]

victualler /ˈvɪtlə(r)/ *n.* one who furnishes victuals. —**licensed victualler,** an innkeeper licensed to sell alcoholic liquor etc. [as prec.]

vicuña /vɪˈkju:nə/ *n.* **1** a South American mammal (*Vicugna vicugna*) related to the llama, with fine silky wool. **2** cloth made from its wool; an imitation of this. [Sp. f. Quechua]

vide /ˈvɪdeɪ, ˈvaɪdɪ/ *v.t.* (as an instruction in a reference to a passage in a book etc.) see, consult. [L, imper. of *vidēre* see]

videlicet /vɪˈdelɪset/ *adv.* = VIZ. [L, = it is permitted to see]

video /ˈvɪdɪəʊ/ *adj.* relating to the recording or broadcasting of photographic images. —*n.* (*pl.* **-os**) **1** such a recording or broadcasting. **2** an apparatus for recording or playing videotapes. **3** a videotape. —**video game,** a game played by electronically manipulating images displayed on a television screen. [L, = I see]

videotape *n.* a magnetic tape containing or suitable for records of television pictures and sound. —*v.t.* to make a recording of (broadcast material etc.) with this.

vie /vaɪ/ *v.i.* (*partic.* **vying** /ˈvaɪɪŋ/) to carry on a rivalry, to compete. [prob. as ENVY]

view /vju:/ *n.* **1** what can be seen from a specified point; fine natural scenery. **2** range of vision. **3** visual inspection of something. **4** a mental survey of a subject etc. **5** a manner of considering a subject; a mental attitude; an opinion. —*v.t./i.* **1** to survey with the eyes or mind. **2** to inspect, to look over (a house etc.) with the idea of buying it. **3** to watch television. **4** to regard or consider. —**have in view,** to have as one's object; to bear in mind in forming a judgement etc. **in view of,** having regard to, considering. **on view,** being shown (for observation or inspection). **with a view to,** with the hope or intention of. [f. AF f. *vēoir* see f. L *vidēre*]

viewdata *n.* a news and information service provided by a computer source to which a television screen is connected by a telephone link.

viewer *n.* **1** one who views. **2** a person watching television. **3** a device for looking at photographic transparencies etc. [f. VIEW]

viewfinder *n.* a device on a camera showing the area that will be included in a photograph.

viewpoint *n.* a point of view, a standpoint.

vigil /ˈvɪdʒɪl/ *n.* **1** staying awake during the time usually given to sleep, especially to keep watch or pray. **2** the eve of a religious festival, especially an eve that is a fast. [f. OF f. L *vigilia* (*vigil* wakeful)]

vigilance /ˈvɪdʒɪləns/ *n.* watchfulness, being on the lookout for possible danger etc. —**vigilance committee,** (*US*) a self-appointed body for the maintenance of order etc. —**vigilant** *adj.*, **vigilantly** *adv.* [F or f. L (as prec.)]

vigilante /vɪdʒɪˈlæntɪ/ *n.* a member of a vigilance committee or similar body. [Sp., = vigilant]

vignette /vi:nˈjet/ *n.* **1** an illustration not in a definite border. **2** a photograph etc. with the background gradually shaded off. **3** a short description, a character-sketch. —*v.t.* to shade off in the style of a vignette. [F, dim. of *vigne* vine]

vigorous /ˈvɪgərəs/ *adj.* full of vigour. —**vigorously** *adv.*, **vigorousness** *n.* [as foll.]

vigour /ˈvɪgə(r)/ *n.* **1** active physical or mental strength, energy; flourishing physical condition. **2** forcefulness of language or composition etc. [f. OF f. L *vigor* (*vigēre* be lively)]

Viking /ˈvaɪkɪŋ/ *n.* a member of the Scandinavian traders and pirates who ravaged much of northern Europe between the 8th and 11th centuries. [f. ON perh. f. OE (*wīc* camp)]

vile *adj.* **1** extremely disgusting. **2** despicable on moral grounds. **3** (*colloq.*) abominably bad. —**vilely** *adv.*, **vileness** *n.* [f. OF f. L *vilis* cheap, base]

vilify /ˈvɪlɪfaɪ/ *v.t.* to defame, to speak evil of. —**vilification** /-fɪˈkeɪʃ(ə)n/ *n.* [f. L *vilificare* (as prec.)]

villa /ˈvɪlə/ *n.* **1** a detached or semi-detached house in a residential district. **2** a country residence, especially in Italy or southern France. **3** a house for holiday-makers at the seaside etc. [It. & L]

village /ˈvɪlɪdʒ/ *n.* a group of houses etc. in a country district, smaller than a town and usually having a church. [f. OF f. L *villa*]

villager /ˈvɪlɪdʒə(r)/ *n.* an inhabitant of a village. [f. prec.]

villain /ˈvɪlən/ *n.* **1** a person who is guilty of or capable of great wickedness; a wrongdoer, a criminal. **2** a character in a story or play whose evil actions or motives are important in the plot. **3** (*colloq.*) a rascal. —**villainy** *n.* [f. OF f. L *villa*; cf. VILLEIN]

villainous /ˈvɪlənəs/ *adj.* **1** worthy of a villain; wicked. **2** (*colloq.*) abominably bad. —**villainously** *adv.* [f. prec.]

villein /ˈvɪlɪn/ *n.* (*hist.*) a feudal tenant entirely subject to a lord or attached to a manor. —**villeinage** *n.* [var. of VILLAIN]

vim *n.* (*colloq.*) vigour. [perh. L, accusative of *vis* energy]

vina /ˈviːnə/ *n.* an Indian four-stringed musical instrument with a fretted finger-board and a half-gourd at each end. [f. Skr. & Hindi]

vinaigrette /vɪnɪˈgret/ *n.* **1** vinaigrette sauce. **2** a small bottle for smelling-salts. —**vinaigrette sauce,** a salad dressing of oil and vinegar. [F, dim. of *vinaigre* vinegar]

vindicate /ˈvɪndɪkeɪt/ *v.t.* **1** to clear of blame or suspicion. **2** to establish the existence, merits, or justice of (one's courage, conduct, assertion, etc.). —**vindication** /-ˈkeɪʃ(ə)n/ *n.*, **vindicator** *n.*, **vindicatory** *adj.* [f. L *vindicare* (*vindex* claimant, avenger)]

vindictive /vɪnˈdɪktɪv/ *adj.* tending to seek revenge. —**vindictively** *adv.*, **vindictiveness** *n.* [f. L *vindicta* vengeance (as prec.)]

vine *n.* **1** a climbing or trailing plant of the genus *Vitis* (especially *V. vinifera*) with a woody stem, bearing grapes. **2** a slender trailing or climbing stem. [f. OF f. L *vinea* vineyard (*vinum* wine)]

vinegar /ˈvɪnɪgə(r)/ *n.* **1** a sour liquid made from wine, cider, etc., by fermentation and used as a condiment or for pickling. **2** sour behaviour or character. —**vinegary** *adj.* [f. OF *vyn egre* f. L *vinum* wine, *acer* sour]

vinery /ˈvaɪnərɪ/ *n.* a greenhouse for grape-vines. [f. VINE]

vineyard /ˈvɪnjɑːd/ *n.* a plantation of grape-vines, especially for wine-making.

vingt-et-un /vætеɪˈœ̃/ *n.* pontoon (PONTOON[1]). [F, = twenty-one]

vinous /ˈvaɪnəs/ *adj.* **1** of, like, or due to wine. **2** addicted to wine. [f. L *vinosus* (*vinum* wine)]

vintage /ˈvɪntɪdʒ/ *n.* **1** the gathering of grapes for wine-making; the season of this. **2** the season's produce of grapes; wine made from this. **3** wine of high quality (from a single year) kept separate from others. **4** the year or period when a thing was made or existed; a thing made etc. in a particular year etc. —*adj.* of high quality, especially of a past season. —**vintage car,** a car made between 1917 and 1930. [f. OF f. L *vindemia* (*vinum* wine, *demere* remove)]

vintner /ˈvɪntnə(r)/ *n.* a wine-merchant. [f. AF *vineter* f. L *vinetarius* (*vinetum* vineyard)]

vinyl /ˈvaɪnɪl/ *n.* one of a group of plastics, made by polymerization, especially polyvinyl chloride. [f. L *vinum* wine]

viol /ˈvaɪəl/ *n.* a bowed string instrument of the Renaissance and baroque periods, with six strings. [f. OF f. Prov., prob. ult. f. L *vitulari* be joyful; cf. FIDDLE]

viola[1] /vɪˈəʊlə/ *n.* **1** a bowed stringed instrument of the violin family, larger and deeper-pitched than the violin itself, and sometimes known as the 'alto' or 'tenor violin' because of this. **2** a viol. —**viola da gamba,** a viol held between a seated player's legs, especially corresponding to the modern cello. **viola d'amore** /dæˈmɔreɪ/, a sweet-toned tenor viol. [It. & Sp., prob. f. Prov. (see prec.)]

viola[2] /ˈvaɪələ/ *n.* any plant of the group including the violet and pansy, especially a cultivated hybrid. [L, = violet]

violable /ˈvaɪələb(ə)l/ *adj.* that may be violated. [f. foll.]

violate /ˈvaɪəleɪt/ *v.t.* **1** to break or act contrary to (an oath, treaty, conscience, etc.). **2** to treat (a sacred place) with irreverence or disrespect. **3** to disturb (a person's privacy etc.). **4** to rape. —**violation** /-ˈleɪʃ(ə)n/ *n.*, **violator** *n.* [f. L *violare* treat violently]

violence /ˈvaɪələns/ *n.* being violent; violent acts, conduct, or treatment; the unlawful use of force. —**do violence to,** to act contrary to, to be a breach of. [f. OF f. L *violentia* (as foll.)]

violent /ˈvaɪələnt/ *adj.* **1** involving great force, strength, or intensity. **2** (of a death) caused by physical force or by poison, not natural. —**violently** *adv.* [f. OF f. L *violentus*]

violet /ˈvaɪələt/ *n.* **1** a plant of the genus *Viola* with usually purple, blue, or white flowers. **2** the colour seen at the end of the spectrum opposite red, blue with a slight admixture of red. **3** a pigment, clothes or material of this colour. —*adj.* of this colour. [f. OF, dim. of *viole* = VIOLA[2]]

violin /vaɪəˈlɪn/ *n.* **1** a musical instrument of treble pitch with four strings played with a bow. **2** a player of this. —**violinist** *n.* [f. It. *violino* dim. of VIOLA[1]]

violist[1] /ˈvaɪəlɪst/ *n.* a viol-player. [f. VIOL]

violist[2] /vɪˈəʊlɪst/ *n.* a viola-player. [f. VIOLA[1]]

violoncello /vaɪələnˈtʃeləʊ, viːə-/ *n.* (*pl.* **-os**) a cello. [It., dim. of foll.]

violone /vɪəˈləʊnɪ/ *n.* a double-bass viol. [It. (as VIOLA[1])]

VIP *abbr.* very important person.

viper /ˈvaɪpə(r)/ *n.* **1** a small venomous snake of the family Viperidae, especially the common viper or adder. **2** a malignant or treacherous person. [f. F or L *vipera* (*vivus* alive, *parere* bring forth)]

virago /vɪˈrɑːgəʊ/ *n.* (*pl.* **-os**) a fierce or abusive woman. [L, = female warrior (*vir* man)]

viral /ˈvaɪər(ə)l/ *adj.* of or caused by a virus. [f. VIRUS]

virgin /ˈvɜːdʒɪn/ *n.* **1** a person (especially a woman) who has never had sexual intercourse. **2** a picture or statue of the Virgin Mary. **3 the Virgin,** the constellation or sign of the zodiac Virgo. —*adj.* **1** virginal. **2** spotless, undefiled. **3** untouched, in its original state; not yet used. —**the (Blessed) Virgin (Mary),** the mother of Christ. **Virgin birth,** the doctrine that Christ had no human father but was conceived by the Virgin Mary by the power of the Holy Spirit. **Virgin Queen,** Elizabeth I of England. —**virginity** /vəˈdʒɪnɪtɪ/ *n.* [f. AF & OF f. L *virgo*]

virginal *adj.* that is or befits a virgin. —*n.* (usu. in *pl.*) a legless spinet in a box. [f. OF or L (as prec.)]

Virgo /ˈvɜːgəʊ/ a constellation and the sixth sign of the zodiac, the Virgin, which the sun enters about 23 Aug. —**Virgoan** *adj.* & *n.* [OE f. L, = virgin]

virile /ˈvɪraɪl/ *adj.* **1** having masculine vigour or strength. **2** of or having procreative power. **3** of a man as distinct from a woman or child. —**virility** /vɪˈrɪlɪtɪ/ *n.* [f. F or L *virilis* (*vir* man)]

virology /vaɪəˈrɒlədʒɪ/ *n.* the study of viruses. —**virological** /-rəˈlɒdʒɪk(ə)l/ *adj.*, **virologist** *n.* [f. VIRUS + -LOGY]

virtual /ˈvɜːtjʊəl/ *adj.* that is such in effect though not in name or according to strict definition. —**virtually** *adv.* [f. L (as VIRTUE)]

virtue /ˈvɜːtjuː/ *n.* **1** moral excellence, goodness; a particular form of this. **2** chastity, especially in a woman. **3** a good quality, an advantage. —**by** *or* **in virtue of,** by reason of; because of. [f. OF f. L *virtus* (*vir* man)]

virtuoso /vɜːtjʊˈəʊsəʊ/ *n.* (*pl.* **-si** /-siː/) a person skilled in the technique of a fine art, especially music. —**virtuosity** /-ˈɒsɪtɪ/ *n.* [It., = skilful, f. L (as foll.)]

virtuous /ˈvɜːtjʊəs/ *adj.* having or showing moral virtue, chaste. —**virtuously** *adv.*, **virtuousness** *n.* [f. OF f. L *virtuosus* (as VIRTUE)]

virulent /ˈvɪrʊlənt/ *adj.* **1** (of poison or disease) extremely strong, violent. **2** strongly and bitterly hostile. —**virulence** *n.*, **virulently** *adv.* [f. L *virulentus* (as foll.)]

virus /ˈvaɪərəs/ *n.* **1** any of a group of minute infective and disease-producing agents. **2** a hidden destructive code in a computer. [L, = poison]

visa /ˈviːzə/ *n.* an endorsement on a passport etc. especially as permitting the holder to enter or leave a country. —**visaed** *adj.* [F f. L, p.p. of *vidēre* see]

visage /ˈvɪzɪdʒ/ *n.* (*literary*) a person's face, a countenance. [f. OF f. L *visus* sight]

vis-à-vis /viːzɑːˈviː/ *prep.* **1** in relation to. **2** so as to face, opposite to. —*adv.* facing one another. —*n.* a person or thing facing another. [F, = face to face (as prec.)]

viscera /ˈvɪsərə/ *n.pl.* the internal organs of the body. —**visceral** *adj.* [L, pl. of *viscus*]

viscid /ˈvɪsɪd/ *adj.* (of liquid) thick and gluey. —**viscidity** /-ˈsɪdɪtɪ/ *n.* [f. L *viscidus* (*viscum* birdlime)]

viscose /ˈvɪskəʊz/ *n.* cellulose in a highly viscous state (for making into rayon etc.); fabric made from this. [f. L (as VISCOUS)]

viscosity /vɪsˈkɒsɪtɪ/ *n.* the quality or degree of being viscous. [f. OF or L (as VISCOUS)]

viscount /ˈvaɪkaʊnt/ *n.* **1** a British nobleman ranking between earl and baron. **2** the courtesy title of an earl's eldest son. —**viscountcy** *n.* [f. AF f. L (as VICE-, COUNT[2])]

viscountess /ˈvaɪkaʊntɪs/ *n.* a viscount's wife or widow; a woman holding the rank of viscount in her own right.

viscous /ˈvɪskəs/ *adj.* thick and gluey; semifluid; not flowing freely. [f. AF or L *viscosus* (as VISCID)]

visibility /vɪzɪˈbɪlɪtɪ/ *n.* **1** being visible. **2** the range or possibility of vision as determined by conditions of light and atmosphere. [f. F or L (as foll.)]

visible /ˈvɪzɪb(ə)l/ *adj.* **1** that can be seen or noticed. **2** (of exports etc.) consisting of actual goods. —**visibly** *adv.* [f. OF or L *visibilis* (*vidēre* see)]

vision /ˈvɪʒ(ə)n/ *n.* **1** the faculty of seeing, sight. **2** a thing seen in the imagination or in a dream etc. **3** imaginative insight into a subject or problem etc.; foresight and wisdom in planning. **4** a person etc. of unusual beauty. **5** what is seen on a television screen. [f. OF f. L (as VISIBLE)]

visionary /ˈvɪʒənərɪ/ *adj.* **1** given to seeing visions or to indulging in fanciful theories. **2** existing only in vision or in imagination; not practicable. —*n.* a visionary person. [f. prec.]

visit /ˈvɪzɪt/ *v.t./i.* **1** to go or come to see (a person or place etc., or *absol.*) socially or on business etc. **2** to reside temporarily with (a person) or at (a place). **3** to be a visitor. **4** (of a disease or calamity etc.) to come upon, to attack. **5** to inflict punishment for (a sin) upon a person. —*n.* an act of visiting; temporary residence with a person or at a place. [f. OF or L *visitare* go to see, frequent. of *visare* view f. *vidēre* see]

visitant /ˈvɪzɪt(ə)nt/ *n.* **1** a visitor, especially a supposedly supernatural one. **2** a migratory bird that is a visitor to an area. [F, or f. L *visitare* (see prec.)]

visitation /vɪzɪˈteɪʃ(ə)n/ *n.* **1** an official visit of inspection. **2** trouble or disaster regarded as divine punishment. **3 the Visitation,** the visit of the Virgin Mary to her kinswoman Elizabeth; the festival on 2 July commemorating this. [as VISIT]

visitor /ˈvɪzɪtə(r)/ *n.* **1** one who visits a person or place. **2** a migratory bird that lives in an area temporarily or at a certain season. **3** (in a college etc.) an official with the right or duty of occasionally inspecting and reporting. —**visitors' book,** a book in which visitors to a hotel or church etc. record their visit by writing their names and addresses and sometimes remarks. [f. AF & OF (as VISIT)]

visor /ˈvaɪzə(r)/ *n.* **1** a movable part of a helmet covering the face. **2** a shield at the top of a vehicle windscreen to protect the eyes from bright sunshine. **3** the projecting front part of a cap. [f. AF *viser* (as VISAGE)]

vista /ˈvɪstə/ *n.* **1** a long narrow view as between rows of trees. **2** a mental view of a long succession of events. [It., = view]

visual /ˈvɪzjʊəl, ˈvɪʒj-/ *adj.* of or used in seeing; received through sight. —**visual aid,** a film etc. as an aid to learning. **visual display unit,** a device containing a screen, used for output or input in a computer. —**visually** *adv.* [f. L *visualis* (*visus* sight)]

visualize /ˈvɪzjʊəlaɪz, ˈvɪʒ-/ *v.t.* **1** to form a mental picture of. **2** to make visible to the eye. —**visualization** /-ˈzeɪʃ(ə)n/ *n.* [f. prec.]

vital /ˈvaɪt(ə)l/ *adj.* **1** of, concerned with, or essential to organic life. **2** essential to the existence of a thing or to the matter in hand. **3** full of vitality. **4** affecting life; fatal to life or to success etc. —*n.* (in *pl.*) the vital organs of the body (e.g. heart, lungs, brain). —**vital statistics,** statistics relating to population figures or births and deaths; (*colloq.*) the measurements of a person's bust, waist, and hips. [f. OF f. L *vitalis* (*vita* life)]

vitalism /ˈvaɪtəlɪz(ə)m/ *n.* the doctrine that life originates in a vital principle distinct from physical forces. —**vitalist** *n.*, **vitalistic** /-ˈlɪstɪk/ *adj.* [f. F or prec.]

vitality /vaɪˈtælɪtɪ/ *n.* liveliness, vigour, persistent energy; the ability to sustain life. [f. L (as VITAL)]

vitalize /ˈvaɪtəlaɪz/ *v.t.* to endow with life; to infuse with vitality. —**vitalization** /-ˈzeɪʃ(ə)n/ *n.* [f. VITAL]

vitally /ˈvaɪtəlɪ/ *adv.* essentially, indispensably. [f. VITAL]

vitamin /ˈvɪtəmɪn, ˈvaɪ-/ *n.* any of a number of unrelated organic compounds essential for normal growth and nutrition. [f. G f. L *vita* life + AMINE, because orig. thought to contain an amino acid]

vitaminize /ˈvɪtəmɪnaɪz, ˈvaɪ-/ *v.t.* to add vitamins to (food). [f. prec.]

vitiate /ˈvɪʃɪeɪt/ *v.t.* **1** to impair the quality or efficiency of, to debase. **2** to make invalid or ineffectual. —**vitiation** /-ˈeɪʃ(ə)n/ *n.* [f. L *vitiare* (as VICE¹)]

viticulture /ˈvɪtɪkʌltʃə(r), ˈvaɪt-/ *n.* grape-growing. [f. L *vitis* vine + CULTURE]

vitreous /ˈvɪtrɪəs/ *adj.* of or like glass. —**vitreous humour,** see HUMOUR. [f. L *vitreus* (*vitrum* glass)]

vitrify /ˈvɪtrɪfaɪ/ *v.t./i.* to change into glass or a glassy substance, especially by heat. —**vitrifaction** /-ˈfækʃ(ə)n/ *n.*, **vitrification** /-fɪˈkeɪʃ(ə)n/ *n.* [f. F (as prec.)]

vitriol /ˈvɪtrɪəl/ *n.* **1** sulphuric acid or a sulphate. **2** caustic or hostile speech or criticism. —**vitriolic** /-ˈɒlɪk/ *adj.* [f. OF or L *vitriolum* (as VITREOUS)]

vituperate /vɪˈtju:pəreɪt, vaɪ-/ *v.t./i.* to revile, to abuse; to use abusive language. —**vituperation** /-ˈreɪʃ(ə)n/ *n.*, **vituperative** /-ətɪv/ *adj.*, **vituperator** *n.* [f. L *vituperare* (*vitium* VICE¹)]

viva /ˈvaɪvə/ *n.* & *v.t.* (*past* & *p.p.* **vivaed**) (*colloq.*) = VIVA VOCE. [abbr.]

viva /ˈvi:və/ *int.* long live. —*n.* a cry of this as a salute etc. [It., pres. subj. of *vivere* live]

vivacious /vɪˈveɪʃəs/ *adj.* lively, high-spirited. —**vivaciously** *adv.*, **vivacity** /vɪˈvæsɪtɪ/ *n.* [f. L *vivax* (*vivere* live)]

vivarium /vaɪˈveərɪəm/ *n.* (*pl.* **-ia**) a place artificially prepared for keeping animals in (nearly) their natural state. [L (*vivere* live)]

viva voce /vaɪvə ˈvəʊtʃɪ/ *adj.* oral. —*adv.* orally. —*n.* an oral examination. —**viva-voce** *v.t.* to examine viva voce. [L, = with the living voice]

vivid /ˈvɪvɪd/ *adj.* **1** (of light or colour) bright and strong, intense. **2** (of a description etc.) producing strong and clear mental pictures; (of a mental impression) clearly produced; (of the imagination) creating ideas etc. in an active and lively way. —**vividly** *adv.*, **vividness** *n.* [f. L *vividus* (*vivere* live)]

vivify /ˈvɪvɪfaɪ/ *v.t.* to give life to (esp. *fig.*), to enliven, to animate. [f. F f. L *vivificare* (*vivus* alive, *facere* make)]

viviparous /vɪˈvɪpərəs, vaɪ-/ *adj.* bringing forth young that are in a developed state when they leave the mother's body, not hatching by means of an egg (cf. *oviparous*). [f. L (*vivus* alive, *parere* bear)]

vivisect /ˈvɪvɪsekt/ *v.t.* to perform vivisection on. [f. foll.]

vivisection /vɪvɪˈsekʃ(ə)n/ *n.* performance of surgical or other experiments on living animals for scientific research. —**vivisectionist** *n.*, **vivisector** /ˈvɪvɪsektə(r)/ *n.* [f. L *vivus* alive, after *dissection*]

vixen /ˈvɪks(ə)n/ *n.* **1** a female fox. **2** a spiteful woman. [f. earlier *fixen*, fem. of FOX]

viz. /vɪz, or by substitution ˈneɪmlɪ/ *adv.* namely, that is to say, in other words. [abbr. of VIDELICET]

vizier /vɪˈzɪə(r), ˈvɪz-/ *n.* an official of high rank in some Muslim countries. [ult. f. Arab. *wazīr* caliph's chief counsellor]

V neck a V-shaped neckline on a pullover or other garment.

vocable /ˈvəʊkəb(ə)l/ *n.* a word, especially with reference to its form not its meaning. [F or f. L *vocabulum* (*vocare* call)]

vocabulary /vəˈkæbjʊlərɪ/ *n.* **1** the words used in a language, book, or branch of science, or by an author. **2** a list of these arranged alphabetically with definitions or translations. **3** the range of words known to an individual person. **4** a set of artistic or stylistic forms or techniques. [f. L *vocabularius* (as prec.)]

vocal /ˈvəʊk(ə)l/ *adj.* **1** of, for, or uttered by the voice. **2** expressing one's feelings freely in speech. —*n.* (in *sing.* or *pl.*) the sung part or a sung piece of music. —**vocal cords,** the folds of the lining membrane of the larynx at the opening of the glottis, with edges that vibrate in the air-stream to produce the voice. —**vocally** *adv.* [f. L *vocalis* (as VOICE)]

vocalic /vəˈkælɪk/ *adj.* of or consisting of a vowel or vowels. [f. VOCAL]

vocalist /ˈvəʊkəlɪst/ *n.* a singer. [f. VOCAL]

vocalize /ˈvəʊkəlaɪz/ *v.t.* to form (a sound) or utter (a word) with the voice. —**vocalization** /-ˈzeɪʃ(ə)n/ *n.* [f. VOCAL]

vocation /vəˈkeɪʃ(ə)n/ *n.* **1** a divine call to or a sense of one's fitness for a certain career or occupation. **2** a person's trade or profession. —**vocational** *adj.* [f. OF or L (*vocare* call)]

vocative /ˈvɒkətɪv/ *n.* the case of a noun used in addressing or invoking a person or thing. —*adj.* of or in the vocative. [f. OF or L (*vocare* call)]

vociferate /vəˈsɪfəreɪt/ *v.t./i.* to utter noisily; to shout. —**vociferation** /-ˈreɪʃ(ə)n/ *n.*, **vociferator** *n.* [f. L *vociferari* (*vox* voice, *ferre* bear)]

vociferous /vəˈsɪfərəs/ *adj.* making a great outcry; expressing one's views loudly and insistently in speech. —**vociferously** *adv.*, **vociferousness** *n.* [as prec.]

vodka /ˈvɒdkə/ *n.* an alcoholic spirit distilled especially in Russia from rye etc. [Russ., dim. of *voda* water]

vogue /vəʊg/ *n.* prevailing fashion; popular favour or acceptance. —**in vogue,** in fashion; generally current. **vogue-word** *n.* a word currently fashionable. [F f. It. *voga* rowing, fashion]

voice *n.* **1** sound formed in the larynx and uttered by the mouth, especially human utterance in speaking or singing etc.; ability to produce this. **2** use of the voice; an utterance in spoken or (*fig.*) written form; an opinion so expressed; the right to express an opinion; the agency by which an opinion is expressed. **3** (*Gram.*) a set of verbal forms showing whether a verb is active or passive. —*v.t.* **1** to give utterance to; to express in words. **2** to utter with vibration of the vocal cords (e.g. *b*, *d*). —**in good voice,** in proper vocal condition for singing or speaking. **voice-over** *n.* narration in a film etc. not accompanied by a picture of the speaker. **with one voice,** unanimously. [f. AF *voiz* f. L *vox*]

voiceless *adj.* **1** dumb, speechless, mute. **2** (of a sound) uttered without vibration of the vocal cords (e.g. *f*, *p*). [f. VOICE + -LESS]

void *adj.* **1** empty, vacant. **2** (of a contract etc.) invalid, not legally binding. —*n.* empty space, a vacuum. —*v.t.* **1** to render void. **2** to excrete. —**void of,** lacking; free from. [f. OF, ult. f. L (as VACATE)]

voile /vɔɪl, vwɑːl/ *n.* a thin semi-transparent dress-material. [F, = veil]

vol. *abbr.* volume.

volatile /ˈvɒlətaɪl/ *adj.* **1** evaporating rapidly. **2** changing quickly or easily from one mood or interest to another; transient; lively; apt to break out into violence. —**volatility** /-ˈtɪlɪtɪ/ *n.* [f. OF or L *volatilis* (*volare* fly)]

volatilize /vəˈlætɪlaɪz/ *v.t./i.* to turn into vapour. —**volatilization** /-ˈzeɪʃ(ə)n/ *n.* [f. prec.]

vol-au-vent /ˈvɒləʊvɑ̃/ *n.* a (usually small) round case of puff pastry filled with a savoury mixture. [F, lit. 'flight in the wind']

volcanic /vɒlˈkænɪk/ *adj.* of, like, or produced by a volcano. —**volcanically** *adv.* [f. F (as foll.)]

volcano /vɒlˈkeɪnəʊ/ *n.* (*pl.* **-oes**) **1** an opening in the earth's crust through which lava, steam, etc., are or have been expelled; a mountain or hill formed round such an opening. **2** a state of things likely to cause a violent outburst. [It. f. L *Volcanus* Vulcan, Roman god of fire]

vole *n.* a small herbivorous rodent of the family Cricetidae. [orig. *vole-mouse*, f. Norw. *voll* field]

volition /vəˈlɪʃ(ə)n/ *n.* the act or faculty of willing. —**volitional** *adj.*, **volitionally** *adv.* [F or f. L (*volo* I wish)]

volley /ˈvɒlɪ/ *n.* **1** a simultaneous discharge of a number of weapons; the bullets etc. thus discharged. **2** a noisy emission of questions or curses etc. in quick succession. **3** return of a ball in tennis, football, etc., before it touches the ground; a full toss. —*v.t.* **1** to discharge or fly in a volley. **2** to return (a ball) by a volley. —**volley-ball** *n.* a game for two teams of 6 persons, volleying a large ball by hand over a net. [f. F *volée* f. L *volare* fly]

volt /vəʊlt/ *n.* a unit of electromotive force, the difference of potential that would carry one ampere of current against one ohm resistance. [f. A. *Volta*, Italian physicist (d. 1824)]

voltage /ˈvəʊltɪdʒ/ *n.* electromotive force expressed in volts. [f. VOLT]

volte-face /vɒltˈfɑːs/ *n.* a complete reversal of position in an argument or opinion. [F f. It. *voltafaccia* (*voltare* to turn f. L *volvere* roll)]

voltmeter /ˈvəʊltmiːtə(r)/ *n.* an instrument measuring electric potential in volts. [f. VOLT + -METER]

voluble /ˈvɒljʊb(ə)l/ *adj.* with a vehement or incessant flow of words. —**volubility** /-ˈbɪlɪtɪ/ *n.*, **volubly** *adv.* [F or f. L *volubilis* (*volvere* roll)]

volume /ˈvɒljuːm/ *n.* **1** a book, especially one of a set. **2** the amount of space (often expressed in cubic units) that a three-dimensional object occupies or contains or that a gas or liquid occupies. **3** the amount of a thing, a quantity. **4** the strength or power of a sound. [f. OF f. L *volumen* (as prec., ancient books being in roll form)]

volumetric /vɒljʊˈmetrɪk/ *adj.* of measurement by volume. —**volumetrically** *adv.* [f. prec. + METRIC]

voluminous /vəˈljuːmɪnəs, vəˈluː-/ *adj.* **1** having great volume, bulky; of (drapery etc.) loose and ample. **2** (of writings) great in quantity; (of a writer) producing many works, copious. —**voluminously** *adv.*, **voluminousness** *n.* [f. L (as VOLUME)]

voluntary /ˈvɒləntərɪ/ *adj.* **1** acting, done, or given etc. of one's own free will, not under compulsion. **2** working or done without payment. **3** (of an institution) maintained by voluntary contributions or voluntary workers; (of a school) originally built by such an institution but maintained by a Local Education Authority. **4** (of a movement, muscle, or limb) controlled by the will. —*n.* an organ solo played before, during, or after a church service. —**voluntarily** *adv.*, **voluntariness** *n.* [f. OF or L *voluntarius* (*voluntas* will)]

volunteer /vɒlənˈtɪə(r)/ *n.* a person who voluntarily undertakes a task or enters military etc. service. —*v.t./i.* **1** to undertake or offer voluntarily. **2** to be a volunteer. [f. F *volontaire* (as prec.)]

voluptuary /vəˈlʌptjʊərɪ/ *n.* a person given up to luxury and sensual pleasure. [f. L (as foll.)]

voluptuous /vəˈlʌptjʊəs/ *adj.* of, tending to, occupied with, or derived from sensuous or sensual pleasure; (of a woman) having a full and attractive figure. —**voluptuously** *adv.*, **voluptuousness** *n.* [f. OF or L (*voluptas* pleasure)]

volute /vəˈljuːt/ *n.* a spiral scroll in stonework forming the chief ornament of Ionic capitals and used also in Corinthian and composite capitals. [F, or f. L *voluta* (*volvere* roll)]

vomit /ˈvɒmɪt/ *v.t./i.* **1** to eject (matter) from the stomach through the mouth; to be sick. **2** (of a volcano, chimney, etc.) to eject violently, to belch forth. —*n.* matter vomited from the stomach. [f. OF or L *vomitus*, *vomitare*]

voodoo /ˈvuːduː/ *n.* **1** use of or belief in a form of religious witchcraft practised among Blacks in Haiti and elsewhere in the Caribbean area. **2** a person skilled in this. **3** a voodoo spell. —*v.t.* to affect by voodoo, to bewitch. —**voodooism** *n.*, **voodooist** *n.* [f. Dahomey *vodu*]

voracious /vəˈreɪʃəs/ *adj.* **1** greedy in eating, ravenous. **2** very eager in some activity. —**voraciously** *adv.*, **voracity** /vəˈræsɪtɪ/ *n.* [f. L *vorax* (*vorare* devour)]

vortex /ˈvɔːteks/ *n.* (*pl.* **vortexes** or **vortices** /-ɪsiːz/) **1** a whirlpool, a whirlwind, a whirling motion or mass. **2** a thing viewed as swallowing those who approach it. —**vortical** /-ɪk(ə)l/ *adj.*, **vortically** /-ɪkəlɪ/ *adv.* [L *vortex* -*icis* eddy, var. of VERTEX]

votary /ˈvəʊtərɪ/ *n.* a person vowed or devoted

to the service of a god, cult, or pursuit. —**votaress** *n.fem.* [f. L (as foll.)]

vote *n.* **1** a formal expression of choice of opinion in the election of a candidate, passing of a law, etc., signified by a ballot or show of hands etc. **2** the right to vote, especially in a State election. **3** an opinion expressed by a majority of votes; the collective votes given by or for a particular group. —*v.t./i.* **1** to give one's vote. **2** to enact or resolve by a majority of votes; to grant (a sum of money etc.) by a vote. **3** (*colloq.*) to pronounce by general consent; to announce one's proposal (that). —**vote down,** to defeat (a proposal etc.) by votes. **vote in,** to elect by votes. —**voter** *n.* [f. L *votum* (*vovēre* vow)]

votive /ˈvəʊtɪv/ *adj.* given or consecrated in fulfilment of a vow. [f. L *votivus* (as VOTE)]

vouch *v.i.* (with *for*) to guarantee the certainty, accuracy, or reliability of. [f. OF *vo(u)cher* summon, ult. f. L *vocare* call]

voucher *n.* **1** a document (issued in token of payment made or promised) exchangeable for certain goods or services. **2** a document establishing that money has been paid or goods etc. delivered. [AF or f. prec.]

vouchsafe /vaʊtʃˈseɪf/ *v.t.* to condescend to grant or do a thing. [f. VOUCH in sense 'warrant' + SAFE]

voussoir /ˈvu:swɑ:(r)/ *n.* each of the wedge-shaped or tapered stones forming an arch. [f. OF, ult. f. L *volvere* roll]

vow *n.* a solemn promise especially in the form of an oath to a deity or saint. —*v.t.* **1** to promise solemnly. **2** (*archaic*) to declare solemnly. [f. AF *vou* f. L (as VOTE)]

vowel /ˈvaʊəl/ *n.* a speech-sound made with vibration of the vocal cords but without audible friction (cf. CONSONANT); a letter or letters representing this, as *a, e, i, o, u, aw, ah*. [f. OF f. L *vocalis* (*littera*) vocal (letter)]

vox populi /vɒks ˈpɒpjʊli:, -laɪ/ public opinion, the general verdict, popular belief. [L, = the people's voice]

voyage /ˈvɔɪɪdʒ/ *n.* an expedition to a distance, especially by water or in space. —*v.i.* to make a voyage. —**voyager** *n.* [f. AF f. L *viaticum* (*via* road)]

voyeur /vwɑ:ˈjɜ:(r)/ *n.* one who obtains sexual gratification from looking at others' sexual actions or organs. —**voyeurism** *n.* [F (*voir* see)]

vs. *abbr.* versus.

V sign a gesture made with the raised hand with the first and second fingers forming a V, expressing victory or approval, or vulgar derision.

VTO *abbr.* vertical take-off.

VTOL *abbr.* vertical take-off and landing.

vulcanite /ˈvʌlkənaɪt/ *n.* hard black vulcanized rubber. [as foll.]

vulcanize /ˈvʌlkənaɪz/ *v.t.* to make (rubber etc.) stronger and more elastic by treating with sulphur at a high temperature. —**vulcanization** /-ˈzeɪʃ(ə)n/ *n.* [f. *Vulcan*, Roman god of fire]

vulcanology /vʌlkəˈnɒlədʒɪ/ *n.* the study of volcanoes. [as prec. + -LOGY]

vulgar /ˈvʌlgə(r)/ *adj.* **1** characteristic of the common people; lacking in refinement or good taste, coarse. **2** commonly used. —**vulgar fraction,** a fraction expressed by a numerator and a denominator, not decimally. **vulgar tongue,** *the* national or vernacular language. —**vulgarity** /-ˈgærɪtɪ/ *n.*, **vulgarly** *adv.* [f. L *vulgaris* (*vulgus* common people)]

vulgarian /vʌlˈgeərɪən/ *n.* a vulgar person, especially a rich one. [f. prec.]

vulgarism *n.* a word or expression in coarse or uneducated use; an instance of coarse or uneducated behaviour. [f. VULGAR]

vulgarize /ˈvʌlgəraɪz/ *v.t.* **1** to make vulgar. **2** to spoil by making too common or frequented or too well known. —**vulgarization** /-ˈzeɪʃ(ə)n/ *n.* [as prec.]

Vulgate /ˈvʌlgət/ *n.* the Latin version of the Bible prepared mainly by Jerome in the late 4th c., translated directly from the Hebrew text of the Old Testament. [f. L (*editio*) *vulgata* (*vulgare* make public)]

vulnerable /ˈvʌlnərəb(ə)l/ *adj.* **1** that may be hurt, wounded, or injured. **2** unprotected, exposed to danger, attack, or criticism etc. **3** having won a game towards a rubber at contract bridge and therefore liable to higher penalties. —**vulnerability** /-ˈbɪlɪtɪ/ *n.*, **vulnerably** *adv.* [f. L *vulnerabilis* (*vulnus* wound)]

vulpine /ˈvʌlpaɪn/ *adj.* of or like a fox; crafty, cunning. [f. L *vulpinus* (*vulpes* fox)]

vulture /ˈvʌltʃə(r)/ *n.* **1** a large bird of prey of the order Raptores, feeding chiefly on carrion and reputed to gather with others in anticipation of a death. **2** a rapacious person seeking to profit from the misfortunes of others. [f. AF f. L]

vulva /ˈvʌlvə/ *n.* the external parts of the female genitals. [L, = womb]

vv. *abbr.* **1** verses. **2** volumes.

vying *partic.* of VIE.

Ww

W, w /ˈdʌb(ə)lju:/ *n.* (*pl.* **Ws, W's**) the twenty-third letter of the alphabet.

W *abbr.* **1** watt(s). **2** west(ern).

W *symbol* tungsten. [f. *wolframium*, Latinized name]

W. *abbr.* **1** wicket(s). **2** wide(s). **3** with.

WA *abbr.* Western Australia.

wacky *adj.* (*slang*) crazy. —*n.* (*slang*) a crazy person. [orig. dial., = left-handed]

wad /wɒd/ *n.* **1** a lump or bundle of soft material to keep things apart or in place or to block a hole. **2** a collection of banknotes or documents placed together. **3** (*slang*) a bun; a sandwich. —*v.t.* (**-dd-**) to fix or stuff with a wad; to stuff, line, or protect with wadding. [perh. rel. to Du. *watten*, F *ouate* padding]

wadding /ˈwɒdɪŋ/ *n.* soft fibrous material used for padding, packing, or lining things. [f. WAD]

waddle /ˈwɒd(ə)l/ *v.i.* to walk with short steps and a swaying motion. —*n.* a waddling walk. [perh. frequent. of WADE]

wade *v.t./i.* **1** to walk through water or some impeding medium; to cross (a stream) thus. **2** to progress slowly or with difficulty. —*n.* a spell of wading. —**wade in,** (*colloq.*) to make a vigorous intervention or attack. **wade into,** (*colloq.*) to attack (a person or task) vigorously. **wade through,** to read through (a book etc.) in spite of its difficulty, dullness, or length. **wading-bird** *n.* a long-legged water-bird that wades in shallow water. [OE]

wader *n.* **1** a wading-bird. **2** (in *pl.*) high waterproof fishing-boots. [f. WADE]

wadi /ˈwɒdɪ/ *n.* a rocky watercourse in North Africa and neighbouring countries that is dry except in the rainy season. [f. Arab.]

wafer /ˈweɪfə(r)/ *n.* **1** a kind of thin light crisp sweet biscuit. **2** a thin disc of unleavened bread used in the Eucharist. **3** a disc of red paper stuck on law papers instead of a seal. —*v.t.* to fasten or seal with a wafer. —**wafer-thin** *adj.* very thin. [f. AF *wafre* f. MLG *wāfel* WAFFLE²]

waffle¹ /ˈwɒf(ə)l/ *n.* aimless verbose talk or writing. —*v.i.* to indulge in waffle. [orig. dial., f. *waff* yelp (imit.)]

waffle² /ˈwɒf(ə)l/ *n.* a small crisp batter cake. —**waffle-iron** *n.* a utensil, usually of two hinged shallow metal pans, for baking waffles. [f. Du. *wafel* f. MLG; cf. WAFER]

waft /wɒft/ *v.t.* to convey smoothly (as) through air or along water. —*n.* a wafted odour. [orig. = convoy (ship), f. obs. *wafter* armed convoy-ship f. Du. or LG *wachter* (*wachten* guard)]

wag *v.t./i.* (**-gg-**) to shake or move briskly to and fro. —*n.* **1** a single wagging movement. **2** a person who is given to joking or playing practical jokes. —**tongues wag,** there is talk. [f. root of OE *wagian* sway]

wage *n.* (in *sing.* or *pl.*) a regular payment to an employee in return for his work or services. —*v.t.* to carry on (a war etc.). —**wage-earner** *n.* one who works for a wage. **wage freeze,** a ban on wage-increases. [f. AF; cf. GAGE¹, WED]

wager /ˈweɪdʒə(r)/ *n.* a bet. —*v.t./i.* to bet. [f. AF (as prec.)]

waggish *adj.* playful, facetious. —**waggishly** *adv.*, **waggishness** *n.* [f. WAG]

waggle *v.t./i.* (*colloq.*) to wag. —*n.* (*colloq.*) a waggling movement. —**waggle dance,** a movement performed by honey-bees at their hive or nest, believed to indicate to other bees the site of a source of food. —**waggly** *adj.* [f. WAG]

wagon /ˈwægən/ *n.* (also **waggon**) **1** a four-wheeled vehicle for heavy loads drawn by horses or oxen. **2** an open railway truck. **3** a trolley for carrying food etc. —**hitch one's wagon to a star,** to utilize powers higher than one's own. **on the (water-)wagon,** (*slang*) abstaining from alcohol. [f. Du. *wag(h)en*, rel. to WAIN]

wagoner *n.* (also **waggoner**) the driver of a wagon. [f. prec.]

wagonette /wægəˈnet/ *n.* (also **waggonette**) a four-wheeled open horse-drawn carriage with facing side-seats. [f. WAGON + -ETTE]

wagtail *n.* a kind of small bird of the genus *Motacilla* with a long tail that is in frequent motion when the bird is standing.

waif *n.* **1** a homeless and helpless person, especially an abandoned child. **2** an ownerless object or animal. —**waifs and strays,** homeless or neglected children; odds and ends. [f. AF, prob. of Scand. orig.]

wail *n.* a long sad inarticulate cry of pain or grief; a sound resembling this. —*v.i.* **1** to utter a wail; to make such a sound. **2** to lament or complain persistently. [f. ON (rel. to WOE)]

wain *n.* (*archaic*) a wagon. [OE]

wainscot /ˈweɪnskət/ *n.* the boarding or wooden panelling on the lower part of a room-wall. [f. MLG *wagenschot* (app. as WAGON)]

wainscoting *n.* wainscot; material for this. [f. prec.]

waist *n.* **1** the part of the human body below the ribs and above the hips; the narrowness marking this; its circumference. **2** a similar narrow part in the middle of a long object (e.g. a violin) or of a wasp etc. **3** the part of a garment corresponding to the waist. **4** (*US*) a blouse; a bodice. —**waist-deep** *or* **-high** *adjs.* & *advs.* immersed up to the waist; so high as to reach the waist. [orig. *wast*, perh. f. root of WAX²]

waistband *n.* a strip of cloth forming the waist of a garment.

waistcoat *n.* a close-fitting waist-length garment without sleeves or a collar, worn (especially by men) over a shirt and under a jacket.

waistline *n.* the outline or size of the body at the waist.

wait *v.t./i.* **1** to defer an action or departure until an expected event occurs; to do this for (a specified time). **2** to await (an opportunity, one's turn, etc.). **3** to defer (a meal) until a person's arrival. **4** to park a vehicle for a short time at the side of the road etc. **5** to act as a waiter or attendant. —*n.* **1** an act or period of waiting. **2** waiting for an enemy. **3** (in *pl.*) street singers of Christmas carols. —**lie in wait,** to be hidden and ready. **wait and see,** to await the progress of events. **waiting-game** *n.* postponing an action for greater effect. **waiting-list** *n.* a list of applicants etc. for a thing not immediately available. **waiting-room** *n.* a room where people can wait, e.g. at a railway station or surgery. **wait on** *or* **upon,** to await the convenience of; to be an attendant or respectful visitor to. **wait up (for),** not to go to bed (until the arrival or happening of). **you wait!** an expression of threat or warning. [f. OF (rel. to WAKE¹)]

waiter *n.* a man who takes orders and brings food etc. at hotel or restaurant tables. —**waitress** *n.fem.* [f. WAIT]

waive *v.t.* to refrain from insisting on or using (a right or claim etc.). [f AF *weyver*, OF *gaiver* allow to become a waif, abandon]

waiver *n.* the waiving of a legal right; a document recording this. [f. prec.]

wake¹ *v.t./i.* (*past* **woke** or **waked**; *p.p.* **waked** or **woken**) **1** (often with *up*) to cease or cause to cease to sleep; to make or become alert or attentive. **2** (archaic exc. in **waking**) to be awake. **3** to disturb with noise. **4** to evoke (an echo). —*n.* **1** (in Ireland) a watch by a corpse before burial; the attendant lamentations and merry-making. **2** (usu. in *pl.*) an annual holiday in (industrial) northern England. [OE (rel. to WATCH)]

wake² *n.* **1** the track left on the water's surface by a moving ship etc. **2** turbulent air left by a moving aircraft. —**in the wake of,** following; as a result of; in imitation of. [prob. f. MLG f. ON, = hole or opening in ice]

wakeful /ˈweɪkfʊl/ *adj.* **1** unable to sleep; (of a night etc.) with little sleep. **2** vigilant. —**wakefully** *adv.* [f. WAKE¹ + -FUL]

waken /ˈweɪkən/ *v.t./i.* to wake (*lit.* or *fig.*). [f. ON (as WAKE¹)]

wale *n.* **1** a weal (WEAL¹). **2** a ridge on corduroy etc. **3** (*Naut.*) a broad thick timber along a ship's side. [OE, = stripe, ridge]

walk /wɔːk/ *v.t./i.* **1** to move by lifting and setting down each foot in turn so that one foot is always on the ground at any time. **2** to travel or go on foot; to take exercise thus. **3** to traverse (a distance) in walking. **4** to tread the floor or surface of. **5** to cause to walk with one, to accompany in walking; to ride or lead (a horse) or lead (a dog) at a walking pace. —*n.* **1** the act or style of walking; a walking pace. **2** a journey on foot, especially for pleasure or exercise. **3** a route or track for walking. —**walk (all) over,** (*colloq.*) to defeat easily; to take advantage of. **walk away from,** to outdistance easily. **walk away** *or* **off with,** (*colloq.*) to steal; to win easily. **walk into,** (*colloq.*) to encounter through unwariness. **walk of life,** one's occupation. **walk on air,** to feel elated. **walk-on part,** a part involving an appearance on stage but no speaking. **walk out,** to depart suddenly or angrily. **walk-out** *n.* a sudden angry departure, especially as a protest or strike. **walk out on,** to desert, to leave in the lurch. **walk-over** *n.* an easy victory. **walk the streets,** to be a prostitute. [OE, = roll, toss]

walkabout *n.* **1** an informal stroll among a crowd by a visiting royal person etc. **2** a period of wandering by an Australian Aboriginal.

walker /ˈwɔːkə(r)/ *n.* **1** one who walks. **2** a framework for a person unable to walk without support. [f. WALK]

walkie-talkie /ˈwɔːkɪˈtɔːkɪ/ *n.* a small portable radio transmitting and receiving set. [f. WALK + TALK]

walking-stick *n.* a stick held or used as a support when walking.

walkway *n.* a passage for walking along,

especially one connecting sections of a building; a wide path in a garden etc.

wall /wɔːl/ *n.* **1** a continuous upright structure of stone or brick etc. enclosing, protecting, or separating a building, room, field, or town etc. **2** a thing like a wall in appearance or effect; the steep side of a mountain; the outermost part of a hollow structure; the outermost layer of an animal or plant organ or cell. —*v.t.* to surround, enclose, or block with a wall. —**go to the wall,** to suffer defeat, failure, or ruin. **up the wall,** (*colloq.*) crazy, furious. **wall-board** *n.* board made from wood-pulp etc. and used to cover walls. **wall game,** a ball-game played at Eton beside a wall. **walls have ears,** beware of eaves-droppers. **wall-to-wall** *adj.* covering the whole floor of a room. **with one's back to the wall,** at bay. —**wall-less** *adj.* [OE]

wallaby /ˈwɒləbɪ/ *n.* **1** a kind of small kangaroo. **2 Wallabies,** an Australian international Rugby Union team, so called from the animal found extensively in Australia. [f. Aboriginal *wolabā*]

wallah /ˈwɒlə/ *n.* (*slang*) a person employed or concerned in a specific occupation or task. [f. Hindi]

wallet /ˈwɒlɪt/ *n.* a small flat folding case for holding banknotes or small documents etc. [earlier *walet*; orig. unkn.]

wall-eye /ˈwɔːlaɪ/ *n.* an eye with the iris whitish or streaked, or with an outward squint. —**wall-eyed** *adj.* [f. ON; cf. Icel. *vagl* film over eye]

wallflower *n.* **1** a plant of the genus *Cheiranthus*, especially *C. cheiri*, with fragrant flowers. **2** (*colloq.*) a woman sitting out dances for lack of partners.

Walloon /wɒˈluːn/ *n.* **1** a member of a people living in southern Belgium and neighbouring parts of France. **2** their language. —*adj.* of the Walloons or their language. [f. F f. L (rel. to Welsh)]

wallop /ˈwɒləp/ *v.t.* (*slang*) **1** to thrash, to beat. **2** (in *partic.*) big. —*n.* (*slang*) **1** a heavy resounding blow. **2** beer or other drink. [earlier sense 'gallop', 'boil', f. OF *waloper* (as gallop)]

wallow /ˈwɒləʊ/ *v.i.* **1** to roll about in mud, sand, water, etc. **2** to take unrestrained pleasure in a specified thing. —*n.* **1** the act of wallowing. **2** a place where animals go to wallow. [OE]

wallpaper *n.* paper for pasting on the interior walls of rooms, often decoratively printed.

walnut /ˈwɔːlnʌt/ *n.* **1** a nut containing an edible kernel with a wrinkled surface. **2** the tree (*Juglans regia*) bearing this; its timber used in making furniture. [OE, = foreign nut]

walrus /ˈwɔːlrəs/ *n.* a large amphibious mammal (*Odobenus rosmarus*) of Arctic seas, with two long tusks. —**walrus moustache,** a long thick drooping moustache. [prob. f. Du.]

waltz /wɔːls, wɒls/ *n.* a ballroom dance for couples, with a graceful flowing melody in triple time; the music for this. —*v.t./i.* **1** to dance a waltz. **2** to move (a person) in or as in a waltz. **3** to dance round in joy etc.; to move easily or casually. [f. G *walzer* (*walzen* revolve)]

wampum /ˈwɒmpəm/ *n.* strings of shell-beads formerly used by North American Indians for money or ornament. [f. Algonquin]

wan /wɒn/ *adj.* pallid, especially from illness or exhaustion. —**wanly** *adv.*, **wanness** *n.* [OE, = dark]

wand /wɒnd/ *n.* a slender rod for carrying in the hand, especially one associated with the working of magic; a music conductor's baton; a slender rod or staff carried as a sign of office etc. [f. ON]

wander /ˈwɒndə(r)/ *v.i.* **1** to go from place to place without a settled route or aim; to go aimlessly *in*, *off*, etc. **2** to diverge from the right way (*lit.* or *fig.*). **3** to digress from a subject; to be inattentive or incoherent through illness or weakness. —**wanderer** *n.* [OE (as wend)]

wanderlust *n.* an eager desire or fondness for travelling or wandering. [G]

wane *v.i.* **1** (of the moon) to show a gradually decreasing area of brightness after being full. **2** to decrease in vigour, strength, or importance. —*n.* **1** the process of waning. **2** a defect in a plank etc. when the corners are not square. —**on the wane,** declining. [OE *wanian* lessen]

wangle *v.t.* (*slang*) to obtain or arrange by using trickery, improper influence, or persuasion etc. —*n.* (*slang*) an act of wangling. [19th-c. printers' slang; orig. unkn.]

wank *v.i.* (*vulgar*) to masturbate. —*n.* (*vulgar*) an act of masturbation. —**wanker** *n.* [orig. unkn.]

want /wɒnt/ *v.t./i.* **1** to desire, to wish for. **2** to require or need; should, ought. **3** to lack, to be insufficiently supplied with; to fall short of. **4** to be without the necessaries of life. —*n.* **1** a desire for something, a requirement. **2** lack or need of something, deficiency. **3** lack of the necessaries of life. —**in want of,** needing. **wanted (by the police),** sought by the police as a suspected criminal. [f. ON (*vanr* lacking), OE *wana* (as wane)]

wanting *adj.* lacking; deficient; not equal to requirements. [f. want]

wanton /ˈwɒnt(ə)n/ *adj.* **1** licentious, unchaste. **2** (of cruelty, damage, etc.) purposeless, unprovoked. **3** capricious, playful; unrestrained, luxuriant. —*n.* a licentious person. —*v.i.* to behave capriciously or playfully. —**wantonly** *adv.*, **wantonness** *n.* [orig. *wantowen* = undisciplined (as UN-, *tēon* team)]

wapiti /ˈwɒpɪtɪ/ *n.* a North American elk (*Cervus canadensis*) resembling the red deer but larger. [f. Cree, = white deer]

war /wɔ:(r)/ *n.* **1** strife (especially between countries) involving military, naval, or air attacks; the period of this. **2** open hostility between persons. **3** strong efforts to combat crime, disease, poverty, etc. —*v.i.* (**-rr-**) (*archaic*) to make war. —**at war,** engaged in a war. **go to war,** to begin hostile operations. **have been in the wars,** (*colloq.*) to show signs of injury. **war-cry** *n.* a phrase or name shouted in battle; the slogan of a political or other party. **war-dance** *n.* a dance performed by certain primitive peoples before war or after victory. **war-game** *n.* a game simulating warfare, using models or blocks moved about on a map etc.; a set of military exercises designed to examine or test a military strategy. **war-horse** *n.* a trooper's horse; a veteran soldier. **war-lord** *n.* (in China, esp. in 1916–28) a military commander with a regional power base, acting independently of the central government. **war memorial,** a monument to those killed in a war. **war of nerves,** an attempt to wear down an opponent by gradual destruction of his morale. **war-paint** *n.* paint put on the body (especially by North American Indians) before battle. **war-path** *n.* a march of North American Indians to make war; *on the war-path,* engaged in conflict, taking a hostile attitude. [f. AF, OF *guerre* (cf. OHG *werra* confusion, strife)]

War. *abbr.* Warwickshire.

warble /ˈwɔ:b(ə)l/ *v.t./i.* to sing, especially with a gentle trilling note as certain birds do. —*n.* a warbling sound. [f. OF *werbler* f. Frankish, = whirl, trill]

warble-fly *n.* a kind of fly whose larvae burrow under the skin of cattle etc. and produce tumours. [orig. unkn.]

warbler *n.* any of several small birds of the family Sylviidae or (*US*) Parulidae (not necessarily one noted for its song). [f. WARBLE]

ward /wɔ:d/ *n.* **1** a separate room or division in a hospital or (hist.) workhouse. **2** an administrative division, especially for elections. **3** a minor etc. under the care of a guardian or court. **4** (in *pl.*) the notches and projections in a key and lock designed to prevent opening by a key other than the right one. **5** (*archaic*) guarding, defending, guardianship; the bailey of a castle. —*v.t.* **1** (usu. with *off*) to parry (a blow), to avert (a danger etc.). **2** (*archaic*) to guard, to defend. [OE, = guard]

-ward /-wɔ:d/ *suffix* (also **-wards**) added to nouns of place or destination and to adverbs of direction and forming adverbs (usu. in *-wards*) meaning 'towards the place etc.' (*backwards, homewards*), adjectives (usu. in *-ward*) meaning 'turned or tending towards' (*downward, onward*), and less commonly nouns meaning 'the region towards or about' (*look to the eastward*). [OE]

warden /ˈwɔ:d(ə)n/ *n.* **1** the president or governor of an institution (e.g. a hospital or college). **2** an official with supervisory duties. **3** a churchwarden. [f. AF & OF, = guardian]

warder /ˈwɔ:də(r)/ *n.* an official in charge of prisoners in a prison. —**wardress** *n.fem.* [f. AF (as GUARD)]

wardrobe /ˈwɔ:drəʊb/ *n.* **1** a place where clothes are kept, especially a large cupboard usually with pegs or rails etc. from which they hang. **2** a person's or persons' stock of clothes. —**wardrobe master** *or* **mistress,** one who has charge of an actor's or a company's costumes. [f. OF (as GUARD, ROBE)]

wardroom /ˈwɔ:dru:m/ *n.* a room for commissioned officers in a warship.

-wards see -WARD.

wardship *n.* tutelage, a guardian's care. [f. WARD + -SHIP]

ware *n.* **1** manufactured articles (especially pottery) of the kind specified. **2** (in *pl.*) what one has for sale. [OE, perh. orig. = 'object of care']

warehouse /ˈweəhaʊs/ *n.* a building in which goods are stored or shown for sale. —/also -haʊz/ *v.t.* to place or keep in warehouses.

warfare *n.* making war, fighting; a particular form of this.

warhead *n.* the explosive head of a missile, torpedo, or similar weapon.

warlike *adj.* **1** fond of or skilful in war, aggressive. **2** of or for war.

warlock /ˈwɔ:lɒk/ *n.* (*archaic*) a sorcerer. [OE, = traitor]

warm /wɔ:m/ *adj.* **1** moderately hot, not cold or cool. **2** (of clothes etc.) keeping the body warm; (of exertion) making one warm. **3** enthusiastic, hearty; (of a reception) vigorous by being either heartily friendly or strongly hostile. **4** kindly and affectionate. **5** (of colours) suggesting warmth, especially by containing reddish shades. **6** (of the scent in hunting) still fairly fresh and strong; (of the seeker in a children's game etc.) close to the object sought or guessed at. —*v.t./i.* to make or become warm or warmer. —*n.* **1** the act of warming. **2** warmth of atmosphere. —**keep a position warm,** to occupy it temporarily so that it can be available (for a specified person) at a later date. **warm-blooded** *adj.* having blood that remains warm (36–42° C) permanently; passionate. **warm-hearted** *adj.* having a kindly and affectionate disposition. **warming-pan** *n.* a covered metal pan with a long handle, formerly filled with live coals and used for warming beds. **warm to,** to become cordial or well-disposed to (a person) or more animated about (a task). **warm up,** to make or become warm; to reach or cause to reach the temperature of efficient working; to prepare for a performance by exercise or practice; to reheat (food). **warm-up** *n.* the process of warming up. —**warmly** *adv.*, **warmness** *n.* [OE]

warmonger /ˈwɔːmʌŋgə(r)/ *n.* one who seeks to cause war.

warmth /wɔːmθ/ *n.* warmness, being warm. [f. WARM]

warn /wɔːn/ *v.t.* to inform (a person) about a present or future danger or about something to be reckoned with; to advise about action in such circumstances. —**warn off,** to tell (a person) to keep away (from); to prohibit from taking part in race-meetings (at). [OE]

warning /ˈwɔːnɪŋ/ *n.* what is said or done or occurs to warn a person. [f. WARN]

warp /wɔːp/ *v.t./i.* **1** to make or become crooked or twisted especially by uneven shrinkage or expansion. **2** to distort or pervert (a person's judgement or principles); to suffer such distortion. **3** to haul (a ship) along by means of a rope fixed to an external point; to progress thus. —*n.* **1** a warped condition. **2** threads stretched lengthwise in a loom, to be crossed by the weft. **3** a mental perversion or bias. **4** a rope used in warping a ship. [OE, = throw]

warrant /ˈwɒrənt/ *n.* **1** a thing that authorizes an action; a written authorization to receive or supply money, goods, or services, or to carry out an arrest or search. **2** a certificate of the service rank held by a warrant-officer. —*v.t.* **1** to serve as a warrant for, to justify. **2** to guarantee, to answer for the genuineness etc. of. —**I('ll) warrant (you),** I am certain, I assure you. **warrant-officer** *n.* an officer ranking between commissioned officers and NCOs. [f. OF *warant* f. Frankish (*giwerēn* be surety for)]

warranty *n.* **1** authority or justification for doing something. **2** a seller's undertaking that a thing sold is his and fit for use etc., often accepting responsibility for repairs needed over a specified period. [f. AF *warantie* (as prec.)]

warren /ˈwɒrən/ *n.* **1** a piece of ground abounding in rabbit burrows. **2** a densely populated or labyrinthine building or district. [f. AF *warenne*, OF *garenne*, game-park]

warring /ˈwɔːrɪŋ/ *adj.* engaged in a war; rival, antagonistic. [f. WAR]

warrior /ˈwɒrɪə(r)/ *n.* a person who fights in battle; a distinguished or veteran soldier; a member of any of the armed services. [f. OF (*guerreier* make war)]

warship *n.* a ship for use in war.

wart /wɔːt/ *n.* **1** a small hard roundish growth on the skin, caused by a virus. **2** a protuberance on the skin of an animal or on the surface of a plant. **3** (*colloq.*) an objectionable person. —**wart-hog** *n.* an African wild pig of the genus *Phacochoerus*, with warty lumps on the face and large curved tusks. **warts and all,** (*colloq.*) with no attempt to conceal blemishes or inadequacies. —**warty** *adj.* [OE]

wartime *n.* a period when war is being waged.

wary /ˈweərɪ/ *adj.* cautious, in the habit of looking out for possible danger or difficulty. —**warily** *adv.*, **wariness** *n.* [f. *ware* cognizant (as AWARE)]

was see BE.

wash /wɒʃ/ *v.t./i.* **1** to cleanse with water or other liquid. **2** to remove (a stain) by washing; (of a stain) to be removed thus. **3** to wash oneself; to wash clothes etc. **4** to be washable; (of reasoning) to be valid. **5** to moisten; (of a river etc.) to flow past or against. **6** (of a moving liquid) to carry in a specified direction; to go splashing or flowing. **7** to sift (ore) by the action of water. **8** to coat with a wash of paint or wall-colouring etc. —*n.* **1** washing, being washed; the process of laundering; clothes etc. that are being washed or to be washed or have just been washed. **2** the motion of disturbed water or air behind a moving ship or aircraft etc. **3** liquid food or swill for pigs etc. **4** a thin coating of colour painted over a surface; a cleansing or healing liquid for external use. —**come out in the wash,** (of mistakes etc.) to be eliminated during the process of work etc. **wash-basin** *n.* a basin (usually fixed to a wall) for washing one's hands etc. in. **wash dirty linen in public,** to discuss private quarrels or difficulties publicly. **wash down,** to clean by washing; to accompany or follow (food) with a drink. **washed out,** faded by washing; faded-looking; pallid; enfeebled. **washed up,** (*slang*) defeated, having failed. **wash one's hands (of),** to renounce responsibility (for). **wash-leather** *n.* chamois or similar leather for washing windows etc.; a piece of this. **wash out,** to clean the inside of by washing; (*colloq.*) to cancel. **wash-out** *n.* a breach in a railway or road caused by a flood; (*slang*) a complete failure. **wash up,** to wash (dishes etc., or *absol.*) after use; (of the sea) to cast up on the shore. [OE]

washable *adj.* that may be washed without being damaged. [f. WASH]

washer /ˈwɒʃə(r)/ *n.* **1** a flat ring of leather,

rubber, or metal etc. to tighten a joint and prevent leakage. **2** a washing-machine. [f. WASH]

washerwoman *n.* (*pl.* **-women**) a woman whose occupation is washing clothes etc.

washing /ˈwɒʃɪŋ/ *n.* clothes etc. that are being washed or to be washed or have just been washed. —**washing-machine** *n.* a machine for washing clothes. **washing-powder** *n.* a powder of soap or detergent for washing clothes etc. **washing-soda** *n.* sodium carbonate, used (dissolved in water) for washing and cleaning things. **washing-up** *n.* the process of washing dishes etc. after use; the dishes etc. for washing. [f. WASH]

washy /ˈwɒʃɪ/ *adj.* **1** (of liquids) thin, watery. **2** (of colours) washed-out. **3** lacking vigour. —**washily** *adv.*, **washiness** *n.* [f. WASH]

wasn't /ˈwɒz(ə)nt/ (*colloq.*) was not.

WASP /wɒsp/ *abbr.* (*US*, usu. *derog.*) White Anglo-Saxon Protestant, a member of the American white Protestant middle or upper class descended from early European settlers in North America.

wasp /wɒsp/ *n.* a stinging insect of the superfamily Vespoidea, especially the common kind (of the genus *Vespa*) with black and yellow stripes, a slender waist, and buzzing flight. —**wasp-waist** *n.* a very slender waist. [OE]

waspish /ˈwɒspɪʃ/ *adj.* snappish, making sharp comments. —**waspishly** *adv.*, **waspishness** *n.* [f. WASP]

wassail /ˈwɒseɪl/, -s(ə)l/ *n.* (*archaic*) merry-making, festive drinking. —*v.i.* (*archaic*) to make merry. [f. ON *ves heill* 'be in good health', form of salutation (cf. HALE¹)]

wastage /ˈweɪstɪdʒ/ *n.* **1** loss by waste; the amount of this. **2** (in full **natural wastage**) loss of employees through retirement or resignation, not by redundancy. [f. foll.]

waste /weɪst/ *v.t./i.* **1** to use to no purpose, for an inadequate result, or extravagantly; to fail to use (an opportunity). **2** to give (advice etc.) without effect on a person. **3** to run to waste. **4** to wear away gradually; to make or become gradually weaker. **5** to lay waste; to treat as waste. —*adj.* **1** superfluous, no longer serving a purpose; not wanted. **2** (of land) not used, not cultivated or built on. —*n.* **1** an act of wasting. **2** waste material. **3** a waste region. **4** diminution by use or wear. **5** a waste-pipe. —**go** *or* **run to waste**, to be wasted. **waste paper**, spoiled or valueless paper. **waste-paper basket**, a receptacle for waste paper. **waste-pipe** *n.* a pipe to carry off waste liquid, especially from washing etc. **waste product**, a useless by-product of an organism or manufacture. [f. OF *waster* f. L *vastare* (as VAST)]

wasteful *adj.* using more than is needed, causing or showing waste. —**wastefully** *adv.*, **wastefulness** *n.* [f. prec. + -FUL]

wasteland *n.* an unproductive or useless area of land.

waster *n.* **1** a wasteful person. **2** (*slang*) a wastrel. [f. WASTE]

wastrel /ˈweɪstr(ə)l/ *n.* a good-for-nothing person. [f. WASTE]

watch /wɒtʃ/ *n.* **1** a small portable device indicating the time, usually worn on the wrist or carried in the pocket. **2** the act of watching, especially to see that all is well; constant observation or attention. **3** (*Naut.*) a spell of duty (usually four hours) on board ship; the part of a crew taking this. **4** (*hist.*) a watchman or watchmen. —*v.t./i.* **1** to look at, to keep one's eyes fixed on; to keep under observation. **2** to be on the alert; to take heed. **3** to be careful about; to safeguard, to exercise protective care. **4** to look out for (an opportunity). **5** (*archaic*) to remain awake for devotions etc. —**on the watch**, alert for an occurrence. **watch-dog** *n.* a dog kept to guard property etc.; a person etc. acting as guardian of others' rights etc. **watches of the night**, a time when one lies awake. **watching brief**, the brief of a barrister who follows a case for a client not directly concerned. **watch it**, (*colloq.*) be careful. **watch-night service**, a religious service on the last day of the year. **watch out**, to be on one's guard. **watch over**, to look after, to protect. **watch-tower** *n.* a tower from which observation can be kept. —**watcher** *n.* [OE (as WAKE¹)]

watchful *adj.* watching or observing closely; on the watch. —**watchfully** *adv.*, **watchfulness** *n.* [f. prec. + -FUL]

watchmaker *n.* a person who makes and repairs watches and clocks.

watchman *n.* (*pl.* **-men**) a man employed to look after an empty building etc. at night.

watchword *n.* a phrase summarizing a principle of a party etc.

water /ˈwɔːtə(r)/ *n.* **1** a colourless odourless tasteless liquid that is a compound of hydrogen and oxygen, convertible into steam by heat and into ice by cold; liquid consisting chiefly of this (in seas and rivers, rain, tears, sweat, saliva, urine), (*usu. in pl.*) amniotic fluid, etc.); a body of this as a sea, lake, or river; water as supplied for domestic use; (in *pl.*) part of a sea or river, the mineral water at a spa etc. **2** the state of the tide. **3** a solution of specified substance in water. **4** the transparency and brilliance of a diamond or other gem. —*attrib.* **1** found in or near water. **2** of, for, or worked by water. **3** involving, using, or yielding water. —*v.t./i.* **1** to give drinking-water to (an animal); to supply (a plant etc.) with water. **2** to take in a supply of water. **3** to dilute with water. **4** to secrete saliva or tears. **5** (in *p.p.*, of silk etc.) having irregular wavy markings. —**by water,** using a ship etc. for travel or transport. **like water,** lavishly, recklessly. **make one's mouth water,** to cause a flow of saliva; to create an appetite or desire. **make** *or* **pass water,** to urinate. **mouth-watering** *adj*. appetizing. **under water,** in or covered by water. **water-bed** *n*. a mattress of rubber or plastic etc. filled with water. **water-bird** *n*. a bird that swims on or wades in water. **water-biscuit** *n*. a thin crisp unsweetened biscuit made from flour and water. **water-buffalo** *n*. the common domestic Indian buffalo. **water bus,** a boat carrying passengers on a regular route on a lake or river. **water-cannon** *n*. a device giving a powerful water-jet to disperse a crowd etc. **Water-carrier** *n*. the constellation and sign of the zodiac Aquarius. **water-clock** *n*. a device for measuring time by the flow of water. **water-closet** *n*. a lavatory with a pan that is flushed by water. **water-colour** *n*. a pigment diluted with water and not oil; a picture painted or the art of painting with this. **water-cooled** *adj*. cooled by the circulation of water. **water down,** to dilute; to make less forceful or horrifying. **water-glass** *n*. a solution of sodium or potassium silicate, especially for preserving eggs. **water-hammer** *n*. a knocking noise in a pipe when a tap is turned off. **water-hole** *n*. a shallow depression in which water collects. **water-ice** *n*. an edible concoction of frozen flavoured water. **watering-can** *n*. a portable container with a long tubular spout, holding water for watering plants. **watering-place** *n*. a pool where animals drink; a spa or seaside resort. **water-jump** *n*. a place where a horse in a steeplechase etc. must jump over water. **water-level** *n*. the surface of water in a reservoir etc.; the height of this; the water-table; a level using water to determine the horizontal. **water-lily** *n*. an aquatic plant of the family Nymphaeaceae with floating leaves and flowers. **water-line** *n*. the line along which the surface of the water touches a ship's side. **water-main** *n*. a main pipe in a water-supply system. **water-meadow** *n*. a meadow periodically flooded by a stream. **water-melon** *n*. a large melon (*Citrullus vulgaris*) with a smooth green skin, red pulp, and watery juice. **water-mill** *n*. a mill worked by a water-wheel. **water-pistol** *n*. a toy pistol shooting a jet of water. **water polo,** a game played by swimmers with a ball like a football. **water-power** *n*. mechanical force from the weight or motion of water. **water-rat** *n*. a water-vole. **water-rate** *n*. a charge for the use of a public water-supply. **water-ski** *n*. a ski on which a person towed by a motor boat can skim the water-surface. **water-softener** *n*. an apparatus for softening hard water. **water-table** *n*. the plane below which the ground is saturated with water. **water-tower** *n*. a tower with an elevated tank to give pressure for distributing water. **water under the bridge,** the irrevocable past. **water-vole** *n*. an aquatic rat-like vole (*Arvicola amphibius*). **water-wheel** *n*. a wheel driven by water to work machinery, or used to raise water. **water-wings** *n.pl.* inflated supports worn on the shoulders by a person learning to swim. [OE]

watercourse *n*. a brook or stream; the bed of this.

watercress *n*. a cress of the genus *Rorippa* growing in springs etc., with pungent leaves used in salads.

waterfall *n*. a stream falling over a precipice or down a steep height.

waterfowl *n*. (usu. as *pl.*) water birds, especially game-birds that can swim.

waterfront *n*. the part of a town that borders on a river or lake or on the sea.

waterlogged *adj*. saturated with water; (of a boat etc.) barely able to float from being saturated or filled with water. [f. WATER + LOG[1]; connection with *log* obscure]

waterman *n*. (*pl.* **-men**) **1** a boatman plying for hire. **2** an oarsman as regards skill in keeping the boat balanced.

watermark *n*. a manufacturer's design in some kinds of paper, visible when the paper is held against light. —*v.t.* to mark with this.

waterproof *adj*. impervious to water. —*n*. a waterproof coat, cape or covering. —*v.t.* to make waterproof.

watershed *n*. **1** a line of high land where streams on one side flow into one river or sea and streams on the other side flow into another. **2** a turning-point in the course of events.

waterside *n*. the margin of a river, lake, or sea.

waterspout *n*. a funnel-shaped column of water and spray between sea and cloud, formed when a whirlwind draws up a gyrating mass of water.

watertight *adj*. **1** closely fastened or fitted so as to prevent the passage of water. **2** (of an argument etc.) unassailable; (of an agreement) with inescapable provisions.

waterway *n*. a route for travel by water; a navigable channel.

waterworks *n*. **1** an establishment for the management of a water-supply. **2** (*slang*) the shedding of tears. **3** (*slang*) the urinary system.

watery *adj*. **1** of or like water. **2** containing too much water; thin in consistency. **3** full of water or moisture. **4** (of a colour) pale; (of the sun, moon, or sky) looking as if rain will come. —**watery grave,** death by drowning. —**wateriness** *n.* [f. OE]

watt /wɒt/ *n.* a unit of power, the rate of working of one joule per second, corresponding to an electric circuit where the electromotive force is one volt and the current one ampere. —**watt-hour** *n.* the energy of one watt applied for one hour. [f. James *Watt*, Scottish engineer (d. 1819)]

wattage /ˈwɒtɪdʒ/ *n.* an amount of electrical power expressed in watts. [f. WATT]

wattle[1] /ˈwɒt(ə)l/ *n.* **1** an Australian acacia with pliant boughs and golden flowers, used as the national emblem. **2** interlaced rods and twigs for fences etc. —**wattle and daub,** this plastered with mud or clay to make huts etc. [OE; orig. unkn.]

wattle[2] /ˈwɒt(ə)l/ *n.* a red fleshy fold of skin on the head or throat of certain birds (e.g. the turkey). [orig. unkn.]

wave *v.t./i.* **1** to move (the arm, hand, or something held) to and fro as a signal or in greeting; to signal or express thus. **2** to move loosely to and fro or up and down. **3** to give a wavy form to; to have such a form. —*n.* **1** a ridge of water moving along the surface of the sea etc. or curling into an arched form and breaking on the shore. **2** a thing compared to this, e.g. an advancing group of attackers, a temporary increase of an influence or condition; a spell of hot or cold weather. **3** a wave-like curve or arrangement of curves; waving of the hair. **4** a gesture of waving. **5** a rhythmic disturbance of a fluid or solid substance in which successive portions of it undergo alternate displacement and recovery, so that a state of motion travels through it without any continued advance of the substance itself; an analogous variation of an electromagnetic field in the propagation of light or other radiation; a single curve in this plotted graphically against time. —**wave aside,** to dismiss as intrusive or irrelevant. **wave down,** to wave to (a vehicle or driver) as a signal to stop. **wave mechanics,** a particular mathematical formulation of quantum mechanics in which particles such as electrons are regarded as having some of the properties of waves. [OE]

waveband *n.* a range of wavelengths between specified limits.

wavelength *n.* the distance between the crests of successive waves; a corresponding distance between points in a sound wave or electromagnetic wave; this as a distinctive feature of waves from a particular transmitter or (*fig.*) of a person's way of thinking.

wavelet *n.* a small wave. [WAVE + -LET]

waver /ˈweɪvə(r)/ *v.i.* **1** to be or become unsteady, to begin to give way. **2** to show hesitation or uncertainty. **3** (of light) to flicker. —**waverer** *n.* [f. ON, = flicker; cf. WAVE]

wavy /ˈweɪvɪ/ *adj.* having waves or alternate contrary curves. —**wavily** *adv.*, **waviness** *n.* [f. WAVE]

wax[1] *n.* **1** a sticky plastic yellowish substance secreted by bees as the material of honeycomb; this bleached and purified for candles, modelling, etc., or used in polishes. **2** any similar substance. —*v.t.* to cover or treat with wax. —**be wax in a person's hands,** to be entirely subservient to him. [OE]

wax[2] *v.i.* **1** (of the moon) to show a gradually increasing area of brightness before becoming full. **2** to increase in vigour, strength, or importance. **3** (*archaic*) to pass into a specified state, to become. —**wax and wane,** to undergo alternate increases and decreases. [OE]

wax[3] *n.* (*slang*) a fit of anger. [orig. unkn.]

waxen *adj.* **1** like wax, having a smooth pale translucent surface as of wax. **2** (*archaic*) made of wax. [f. WAX[1]]

waxwing *n.* any of several small birds of the genus *Bombycilla* with red tips like sealing-wax to some wingfeathers.

waxwork *n.* an object modelled in wax; a model of a person with the face etc. made in wax, clothed to look lifelike and to be exhibited; (in *pl.*) an exhibition of such models.

waxy *adj.* **1** resembling wax in consistency or surface. **2** (*slang*) angry; easily enraged. —**waxily** *adv.*, **waxiness** *n.* [f. WAX[1,3]]

way *n.* **1** a line of communication, e.g. a road or track. **2** a course or route for reaching a place; the best route, the one taken or intended. **3** a method or plan for attaining an object; a person's desired or chosen course of action. **4** travelling-distance; the amount of difference between two states or conditions. **5** an unimpeded opportunity to advance; a space free of obstacles so that people etc. can pass; a region over which advance is proceeding, desired, or natural. **6** an advance in some direction, impetus, progress. **7** a specified direction. **8** a manner; habitual manner; the normal course of action or events; a talent or skill. **9** a scope or range; a line of occupation or business. **10** a specified condition or state; a respect. **11** (in *pl.*) a structure of timber etc. down which a new ship is launched. —*adv.* (*colloq.*) far. —**by the way,** by the roadside during a journey; incidentally, as a more or less irrelevant comment. **by way of,** by means of; as a form of or substitute for; as a method of; passing through. **come one's way,** to become available to one. **go out of one's way,** to make a special effort; to act without compulsion. **in a way,** to a limited extent; in some respects. **in no way,** not at all. **in the way,** forming an obstacle or hindrance. **lead** *or* **show the way,** to act as guide or leader. **look the other way,** to ignore deliberately. **make one's way,** to go; to prosper. **make way for,** to allow to pass; to be superseded by. **on one's way,** in the process of travelling or approaching. **on the way,** travelling or approaching; having progressed; (of a baby) conceived but not yet born. **on the way out,** (*colloq.*) going down in status or favour; disappearing. **out of the way,** unusual; not obstructing; remote; disposed of. **under way,** in motion or progress. **way back,** (*colloq.*) long ago. **way-bill** *n.* a list of the passengers or parcels conveyed. **way-leave** *n.* a right of way rented to another. **way of life,** the principles or habits governing one's actions. **way-out** *adj.* (*colloq.*) exaggeratedly unusual in style, exotic; progressive. **ways and means,** methods of achieving something; (in Parliament) a means of providing money. [OE; adv. f. AWAY]

wayfarer /ˈweɪfeərə(r)/ *n.* a traveller, especially on foot. —**wayfaring** *n.*

wayfaring-tree *n.* a shrub (*Viburnum lantana*) that grows commonly along roadsides, with white flowers and with berries that turn red and then black.

waylay /weɪˈleɪ/ *v.t.* (*past* & *p.p.* **waylaid**) to lie in wait for, especially so as to talk to or rob.

-ways *suffix* forming adjectives and adverbs of direction or manner (*sideways*). [f. WAY]

wayside *n.* the side of a road; the land bordering a road.

wayward *adj.* childishly self-willed, capricious. —**waywardness** *n.* [f. obs. *awayward* turned away (AWAY, -WARD)]

Wb *abbr.* weber.

WC *abbr.* **1** water-closet. **2** West Central.

we /wiː, wɪ/ *pron.* (obj. US; poss. OUR, OURS). **1** pl. of I, used by a person referring to himself and another or others, or speaking on behalf of a nation, group, firm, etc. **2** used instead of 'I' by a royal person in formal proclamations and by the writer of a newspaper editorial etc. [OE]

weak *adj.* **1** lacking strength, power, or number; easily broken, bent, or defeated. **2** lacking vigour, not acting strongly. **3** not convincing or forceful. **4** (of a solution or drink) dilute, having a large proportion of water or other solvent. —**weaker sex,** women. **weak-kneed** *adj.* lacking determination, giving way easily when intimidated. **weak-minded** *adj.* mentally deficient; lacking determination. **weak verb,** a verb forming inflexions by a suffix, not by vowel-change only. —**weakly** *adv.* [f. ON *veikr* = OE *wāc* pliant, insignificant]

weaken *v.t./i.* to make or become weaker. [f. WEAK]

weakling *n.* a feeble person or animal. [f. WEAK + -LING]

weakly *adj.* sickly, not robust. —**weakliness** *n.* [f. WEAK]

weakness *n.* **1** being weak. **2** a weak point, a defect or fault. **3** a self-indulgent liking, inability to resist a particular temptation. [f. WEAK]

weal[1] *n.* a ridge raised on the flesh by a stroke of a whip etc. —*v.t.* to mark with a weal. [var. of WALE]

weal[2] *n.* welfare. [OE (as WELL[1])]

weald /wiːld/ *n.* the formerly wooded district including parts of Kent, Surrey, and East Sussex. [OE, = wold]

wealth /welθ/ *n.* **1** riches, possession of these. **2** a great quantity, plenty. [f. WEAL[2] or WELL[1], after *health*]

wealthy /ˈwelθɪ/ *adj.* having wealth, rich. —**wealthily** *adv.*, **wealthiness** *n.* [f. prec.]

wean *v.t.* **1** to accustom (an infant or other young mammal) to take food other than (its mother's) milk. **2** (with *of*) to cause (a person) to give up a habit or interest etc. gradually. [OE, = accustom]

weapon /ˈwepən/ *n.* **1** a thing designed, used, or usable as a means of inflicting bodily harm. **2** a means employed for getting the better of someone in a conflict. [OE]

weaponry /ˈwepənrɪ/ *n.* weapons collectively. [f. prec.]

wear /weə(r)/ *v.t./i.* (*past* **wore**; *p.p.* WORN) **1** to have on one's body, e.g. as clothing, ornaments, or make-up. **2** to have (a specified look) on one's face. **3** (*colloq.*, usu. with neg.) to accept or tolerate. **4** to injure the surface of or become injured by rubbing, stress, or use; to make (a hole etc.) thus. **5** to exhaust or (with *down*) overcome by persistence. **6** to endure continued use or life (well or badly etc.). **7** (of time) to pass gradually. **8** (of a ship) to fly (a specified flag). —*n.* **1** wearing or being worn as clothing etc. **2** (esp. as suffix) clothing, suitable apparel (*sportswear*). **3** (also **wear and tear**) damage resulting from ordinary use. **4** capacity to endure being worn. —**wear one's heart on one's sleeve,** to show one's affections openly. **wear off,** to lose effectiveness or intensity. **wear out,** to use or to be used until no longer usable; to tire or be tired out. **wear thin,** (of patience etc.) to begin to fail. —**wearer** *n.* [OE]

wearable /ˈweərəb(ə)l/ *adj.* that may be worn. [f. WEAR]

wearisome /ˈwɪərɪsəm/ *adj.* tedious, tiring by monotony or length. [f. foll. + -SOME]

weary /ˈwɪərɪ/ *adj.* **1** very tired, especially from exertion or endurance. **2** (with *of*) tired of (a specified thing). **3** tiring, tedious. —*v.t./i.* to make or become weary. —**wearily** *adv.*, **weariness** *n.* [OE]

weasel /ˈwi:z(ə)l/ *n.* a small fierce carnivorous animal (*Mustela nivalis*) with a slender body and reddish-brown fur, living on small animals, birds' eggs, etc. —**weasel word,** an equivocating or ambiguous word that takes away the force of the expression containing it (said to allude to the weasel's alleged habit of sucking out the contents of an egg and leaving only the shell). [OE]

weather /ˈweðə(r)/ *n.* **1** the state of the atmosphere at a certain place and time, with reference to heat, cloudiness, dryness, sunshine, wind, rain, etc. **2** (*attrib.*) windward. —*v.t./i.* **1** to expose to or affect by atmospheric changes; to be discoloured or worn thus. **2** to come safely through (a storm, *lit.* or *fig.*). **3** to get to windward of (a cape etc.). —**keep a weather eye open,** to be watchful. **make heavy weather of,** to find trying or needlessly difficult. **under the weather,** (*colloq.*) indisposed. **weather-beaten** *adj.* affected by exposure to the weather. **weather-board** *n.* a sloping board at the bottom of a door to keep out rain; (in *pl.*, also **weatherboarding**) a series of boards each overlapping the one below, fixed to the outside walls of light buildings. *weather-vane* *n.* a weathercock. [OE]

weathercock *n.* **1** a revolving pointer, often in the form of a cockerel, mounted in a high place and turning easily in the wind to show from which direction the wind is blowing. **2** an inconstant person.

weatherly *adj.* (*Naut.*) making little leeway, capable of keeping close to the wind. —**weatherliness** *n.* [f. WEATHER]

weatherman *n.* (*pl.* **-men**) a meteorologist, especially one who broadcasts a weather forecast.

weatherproof *adj.* resistant to wind and rain.

weave[1] *v.t./i.* (*past* **wove**; *p.p.* **woven**) **1** to make (fabric etc.) by passing crosswise threads or strips under and over lengthwise ones; to form (thread etc.) into fabric thus. **2** to put (facts etc.) together into a story or connected whole; to make (a story etc.) thus. —*n.* a style or pattern of weaving. [OE]

weave[2] *v.i.* to move repeatedly from side to side; to take an intricate course to avoid obstructions. —**get weaving,** (*slang*) to begin an action, to hurry. [prob. f. ON (as WAVE)]

weaver *n.* **1** one whose occupation is weaving. **2** a tropical bird of the family Ploceidae that builds a nest of elaborately interwoven twigs etc. [f. WEAVE[1]]

web *n.* **1** the network of fine strands made by a spider etc. **2** a network. **3** woven fabric; an amount woven in one piece. **4** a membrane filling the spaces between the toes of swimming birds (e.g. ducks) and animals (e.g. frogs). **5** a large roll of paper for printing. **6** a thin flat connecting part in machinery. —**web-footed** *adj.* having the toes connected by a web. —**webbed** *adj.* [OE (as WEAVE)]

webbing *n.* strong narrow closely-woven fabric used for belts or in upholstery etc. [f. WEB]

weber /ˈveɪbə(r)/ *n.* a unit of magnetic flux, causing an electromotive force of one volt in a circuit of one turn when generated or removed in one second. [f. W. E. *Weber*, German physicist (d. 1891)]

wed *v.t./i.* (**-dd-**; *p.p.* occas. **wed**) **1** to marry. **2** (*fig.*) to unite; **3** (in *p.p.*) of marriage; (with *to*) devoted to and unable to abandon (an occupation or opinion etc.). [OE, = pledge]

Wed. *abbr.* Wednesday.

wedding *n.* a marriage ceremony and festivities. —**wedding breakfast,** a meal after the wedding ceremony and before departure for the honeymoon. **wedding-cake** *n.* a rich iced cake cut and eaten at a wedding. **wedding march,** a march (especially one by Mendelssohn) for a wedding procession. **wedding-ring** *n.* a ring worn by a married person from the time of the wedding ceremony. [OE (as WED)]

wedge *n.* **1** a piece of wood or metal etc. thick at one end and tapered to a thin edge at the other, thrust between things to force them apart or prevent free movement etc. **2** a wedge-shaped thing. —*v.t.* **1** to force apart or fix firmly by using a wedge. **2** to thrust or pack tightly between other things or people or in a limited space; to be made immovable thus. —**thin end of the wedge,** a change or procedure etc. that appears small or insignificant but will open the way to greater changes etc. [OE]

Wedgwood /ˈwedʒwʊd/ *n.* **1** [P] a kind of fine pottery, especially with a white cameo design. **2** its characteristic blue colour. [f. J. *Wedgwood*, English potter (d. 1795)]

wedlock /ˈwedlɒk/ *n.* the married state. —**born in wedlock,** legitimate. **born out of wedlock,** illegitimate. [OE, = marriage vow]

Wednesday /ˈwenzdeɪ, -dɪ/ *n.* the day of the week following Tuesday. —*adv.* (*colloq.*) on Wednesday. [OE, = day of (the god) Odin, transl. of L *Mercurii dies* day of the planet Mercury]

wee *adj.* **1** (esp. *Sc.*) little. **2** (*colloq.*) tiny. [orig. Sc., f. obs. *wei* (small) quantity (as WEIGH)]

weed *n.* **1** a wild plant growing where it is not

wanted. **2** a thin weak-looking person or horse. **3** (*slang*) marijuana. **4** (*archaic*) tobacco. —*v.t./i.* **1** to remove weeds from; to uproot weeds. **2** (with *out*) to remove as inferior or undesirable. —**weed-killer** *n.* a substance used to destroy weeds. [OE; orig. unkn.]

weeds /wi:dz/ *n.pl.* the deep mourning formerly worn by widows. [OE, = garment]

weedy *adj.* **1** full of weeds. **2** growing freely like a weed. **3** thin and weak-looking. [f. WEED]

week *n.* **1** a period of seven successive days, especially one reckoned from midnight at the end of Saturday. **2** the six days between successive Sundays; the five days other than Saturday and Sunday. **3** the period for which one regularly works during a week. —**a week (from) today, Monday,** etc. (*or* **today, Monday,** etc., **week**), seven days after today, Monday, etc. [OE]

weekday *n.* a day other than Sunday.

weekend /wi:kˈend, ˈwi:-/ *n.* Sunday and (part of) Saturday (or a slightly longer period) especially for a holiday or visit.

weekly *adj.* done, produced, occurring, or payable etc. every week. —*adv.* every week. —*n.* a weekly newspaper or periodical. [f. WEEK]

weeny /ˈwi:nɪ/ *adj.* (*colloq.*) tiny. [f. WEE, after *tiny*]

weep *v.t./i.* (*past* & *p.p.* **wept**) **1** to shed tears. **2** to shed or ooze moisture in drops; to send forth in drops. **3** (of a tree, usu. in *partic.*) to have drooping branches. —*n.* a spell of weeping. —**Weeping Cross,** (*hist.*) a wayside cross for penitents to pray at. [OE]

weepy *adj.* (*colloq.*) inclined to weep, tearful. [f. WEEP]

weevil /ˈwi:vɪl/ *n.* a destructive granary-beetle of the family Curculionidae. [f. MLG *wevel* = OE *wifel* beetle]

wee-wee /ˈwi:wi:/ *n.* (*children's colloq.*) urination; urine. —*v.i.* (*children's colloq.*) to urinate. [orig. unkn.]

weft *n.* crosswise threads woven over and under the warp threads to make fabric. [OE (as WEAVE)]

weigh /weɪ/ *v.t./i.* **1** to measure the weight of, especially by means of scales or a similar instrument. **2** to have (a specified weight). **3** to consider carefully the relative importance or value of; to compare (a thing with or against another). **4** to have importance or influence. **5** to be burdensome. —**weigh anchor,** take up the anchor. **weigh down,** to bring or keep down by weight; to depress or make troubled. **weigh in,** to be weighed (of a boxer before a contest, or a jockey after a race). **weigh in with,** (*colloq.*) to advance (an argument etc.) confidently. **weigh out,** to take a specified weight of; (of a jockey) to be weighed before a race. **weigh up,** (*colloq.*) to form an estimate of. **weigh one's words,** to choose those which precisely express one's meaning. [OE; rel. to WAIN, WAY]

weighbridge *n.* a weighing-machine set into a road etc., with a plate on to which vehicles can be driven to be weighed.

weight /weɪt/ *n.* **1** the force with which a body tends to a centre of gravitational attraction, especially the tendency of bodies to fall to earth. **2** relative mass giving such force; (*pop.*) mass. **3** a quantitative expression of a body's mass; a scale for expressing weights. **4** a heavy object, especially one used to bring or keep something down; an object of known weight for use in weighing. **5** a load to be supported; a burden of responsibility or worry. **6** influence, importance. **7** (in athletics) a shot (SHOT[1]). —*v.t.* **1** to attach a weight to; to hold down with a weight or weights. **2** to burden with a load. **3** to bias or arrange the balance of. —**throw one's weight about,** (*colloq.*) to use one's influence aggressively. **weight-lifting** *n.* the athletic sport of lifting heavy objects. **weight training,** a system of physical training using weights in the form of barbells or dumb-bells. [OE (as WEIGH)]

weighting /ˈweɪtɪŋ/ *n.* extra pay given in special cases. [f. prec.]

weightless *adj.* having no weight, or with no weight relative to the surroundings (e.g. in a spacecraft moving under the action of gravity). —**weightlessness** *n.* [f. WEIGHT + -LESS]

weighty /ˈweɪtɪ/ *adj.* **1** having great weight, heavy. **2** burdensome. **3** showing or deserving earnest thought. **4** important, influential. —**weightily** *adv.*, **weightiness** *n.* [f. WEIGHT]

weir /wɪə(r)/ *n.* a small dam built across a river or canal to raise the level of water upstream or regulate its flow. [OE *wer* f. *werian* dam up]

weird /wɪəd/ *adj.* **1** strange and uncanny or bizarre. **2** connected with fate (obs. exc. in **the weird sisters,** the Fates; witches). —**weirdly** *adv.*, **weirdness** *n.* [f. OE *wyrd* destiny]

welcome /ˈwelkəm/ *int.* of greeting expressing pleasure at a person's coming. —*n.* saying 'welcome'; a kind or glad reception. —*v.t.* to receive with signs of pleasure. —*adj.* that one receives with pleasure; (*predic.*) ungrudgingly permitted or given the right (to a thing). [orig. OE *wilcuma* one whose coming is a pleasure (as WELL[1], COME)]

weld *v.t.* **1** to unite or fuse (pieces of metal) by hammering or pressure, usually after softening by heat. **2** to make (an article) thus. **3** to be able to be welded. **4** to unite effectively into a whole. —*n.* a welded joint. —**welder** *n.* [alt. f. WELL[2] in obs. sense 'melt']

welfare /ˈwelfeə(r)/ *n.* **1** good health, happiness, and prosperity. **2** the maintenance of persons in such a condition; money given for this purpose. —**Welfare State,** a country ensuring the welfare of its citizens by social services operated by the government. **welfare work,** organized efforts for the welfare of a class or group. [f. WELL[1] + FARE]

welkin *n.* (*poetic*) the sky. [OE, = cloud]

well[1] *adv.* (*compar.* BETTER; *superl.* BEST) **1** in the right or a satisfactory way. **2** favourably, kindly. **3** thoroughly, carefully. **4** to a considerable extent. **5** with good reason; easily; probably. —*adj.* **1** in good health. **2** (*attrib.*) in a satisfactory state or position. **3** (*attrib.*) advisable. —*int.* expressing surprise or resignation etc., used especially after a pause in speaking. —**let well alone,** to avoid needless change or disturbance. **well-advised** *adj.* prudent. **well and truly,** decisively, completely. **well away,** having made considerable progress. **well-being** *n.* welfare. **well-born** *adj.* born of good family. **well-bred** *adj.* having or showing good breeding or manners. **well-connected** *adj.* related to good families. **well-disposed** *adj.* having kindly or favourable feelings (towards a person or plan etc.). **well done!** a cry of commendation. **well-groomed** *adj.* with carefully tended hair, clothes, etc. **well-heeled** *adj.* (*colloq.*) wealthy. **well-intentioned** *adj.* having or showing good intentions. **well-judged** *adj.* opportunely, skilfully, or discreetly done. **well-known** *adj.* known to many; known thoroughly. **well-mannered** *adj.* having good manners. **well-meaning** *or* **-meant** *adj.* well-intentioned (but ineffective). **well off,** fortunately situated; fairly rich. **well-oiled** *adj.* (*slang*) drunk. **well-preserved** *adj.* in good condition; (of an old person) showing little sign of age. **well-read** *adj.* having read much literature. **well-spoken** *adj.* speaking in a polite and correct way. **well-to-do** *adj.* fairly rich. **well-tested** *adj.* often tested with good results. **well-trodden** *adj.* much frequented. **well-wisher** *n.* a person who wishes one well. **well-worn** *adj.* much worn by use; (of a phrase etc.) hackneyed. [OE]

well[2] *n.* **1** a shaft sunk into the ground to obtain water or oil from below the earth's surface. **2** an enclosed space like a well-shaft, e.g. in the middle of a building for stairs or a lift, or to admit light or air. **3** (*fig.*) a source. **4** (in *pl.*) a spa. **5** an ink-well. **6** (*archaic*) a water-spring —*v.i.* to spring as from a fountain. [OE]

wellies /ˈwelɪz/ *n.pl.* (*colloq.*) wellingtons. [abbr.]

wellington /ˈwelɪŋt(ə)n/ *n.* a boot of rubber or similar waterproof material, usually reaching almost to the knee. [f. Duke of *Wellington* (d. 1852)]

Welsh *adj.* of Wales or its people or language. —*n.* the Celtic language of Wales. —**the Welsh,** the Welsh people. **Welsh rabbit** (*or* by folk etym. **rarebit**), a dish of melted cheese on toast. [OE, ult. f. L *Volcae* name of a Celtic people]

welsh *v.i.* **1** (of one who loses a bet, esp. a bookmaker at a racecourse) to decamp without paying out winnings. **2** (with *on*) to break an agreement with (a person); to fail to honour (an obligation). —**welsher** *n.* [orig. unkn.]

Welshman *n.* (*pl.* **-men**) one who is Welsh by birth or descent. —**Welshwoman** *n.fem.* (*pl.* **-women**).

welt *n.* **1** a leather rim sewn to a shoe-upper for the sole to be attached to. **2** a weal (WEAL[1]). **3** a heavy blow. **4** a ribbed or reinforced border of a garment. —*v.t.* **1** to provide with a welt. **2** to raise weals on, to thrash. [orig. unkn.]

welter[1] *v.i.* **1** (of a ship) to be tossed to and fro on the waves. **2** to roll or lie prostrate, to be soaked (in blood etc.). —*n.* a state of turmoil; a disorderly mixture. [f. MDu. or MLG]

welter[2] *n.* a heavy rider or boxer. [orig. unkn.]

welterweight *n.* the boxing-weight between lightweight and middleweight (see BOXING-WEIGHT).

wen *n.* a benign tumour on the skin, esp. of the scalp. [OE]

wench *n.* (*archaic*) a girl or young woman. [f. OE *wencel* child]

wend *v.t.* **wend one's way,** to go. [OE, = turn]

Wendy house /ˈwendɪ/ a children's small houselike structure for playing in. [character in J. M. Barrie's *Peter Pan* (1904)]

went *past* of GO[1].

wept *past* & *p.p.* of WEEP.

were see BE.

weren't /wɜːnt/ (*colloq.*) = were not.

werewolf /ˈwɪəwʊlf/ *n.* (also **werwolf;** *pl.* **-wolves**) a mythical being who at times changes from a person to a wolf. [OE; first element perh. f. *wer* man = L *vir*]

Wesleyan /ˈwezlɪən/ *adj.* (*hist.*) of the Protestant denomination founded by John Wesley. —*n.* a member of this denomination. [f. J. *Wesley* (d. 1791)]

west *n.* **1** the point of the horizon where the sun sets at the equinoxes, opposite east; the compass point corresponding to this; the direction in which this lies. **2** (usu. **West**) the western part of a country etc.; European civilization; the non-Communist States of Europe and North America. —*adj.* towards, at, or facing the west; (of a wind) blowing from the west. —*adv.* towards, at, or near the west. —**go west,** (*slang*) to be killed or destroyed etc. **West Country,** south-western England. **West End,** the part of London near Piccadilly, containing famous theatres, restaurants, shops, etc. **West Side,** (*US*) the western part of Manhattan. **west-north-west, west-south-west** *adjs.* & *advs.* midway between west and north-west or south-west; (*ns.*) the compass point in this position. [OE]

westering *adj.* (of the sun) nearing the west. [f. WEST]

westerly /ˈwestəlɪ/ *adj.* & *adv.* in a western position or direction (of a wind) blowing from the west (approximately). [as prec.]

western /ˈwestən/ *adj.* of or in the west. —*n.* a film or novel about life in western North America during the wars with the Indians, or involving cowboys etc. —**Western Church,** the Churches of western Christendom as distinct from the Eastern or Orthodox Church. —**westernmost** *adj.* [OE (as WEST)]

westerner *n.* a native or inhabitant of the west. [f. WESTERN]

westernize /ˈwestənaɪz/ *v.t.* to make (an Oriental person etc.) more like the West in ideas and institutions etc. —**westernization** /-ˈzeɪʃ(ə)n/ *n.* [f. WESTERN]

westing *n.* (*Naut.* etc.) **1** a distance travelled or measured westward. **2.** a westerly direction. [f. WEST]

westward /ˈwestwəd/ *adj.* & (also **westwards**) *adv.* towards the west. —*n.* a westward direction or region. [f. WEST + -WARD]

wet *adj.* **1** soaked, covered, or moistened with water or other liquid. **2** (of weather etc.) rainy. **3** (of ink or paint etc.) not yet dried. **4** used with water. **5** (*slang*) lacking good sense or mental vitality, feeble, dull. —*v.t.* (**-tt-**; *past* & *p.p.* **wet** or **wetted**) to make wet. —*n.* **1** liquid that wets something. **2** rainy weather. **3** (*slang*) a dull or feeble person. **4** (*slang*) a drink. —**wet behind the ears,** immature, inexperienced **wet blanket,** a person or thing damping or discouraging enthusiasm, cheerfulness, etc. **wet dream,** an erotic dream with involuntary emission of semen. **wet-nurse** *n.* a woman employed to suckle another's child; (*v.t.*) to suckle thus; to treat as if helpless. **wet suit,** a rubber garment worn by skin-divers etc. to keep warm. —**wetly** *adv.*, **wetness** *n.* [OE, rel. to WATER]

wether /ˈweðə(r)/ *n.* a castrated ram. [OE]

whack *v.t.* (*colloq.*) to strike or beat forcefully. —*n.* **1** (*colloq.*) a sharp or resounding blow. **2** (*slang*) a share. —**have a whack at,** (*slang*) to attempt. [imit.]

whacked *adj.* (*colloq.*) tired out. [f. prec.]

whacking *adj.* (*slang*) very large. —*adv.* (*slang*) very (*great* etc.). [f. WHACK]

whale *n.* a marine mammal of the order Cetacea, especially a large one hunted for oil, whalebone, etc. —*v.i.* to hunt whales. —**a whale of a time,** (*colloq.*) an exceedingly good or fine etc. time. **whale-oil** *n.* oil from the blubber of whales. [OE]

whalebone *n.* an elastic horny substance from the upper jaw of some whales, formerly used as stiffening.

whaler /ˈweɪlə(r)/ *n.* a person or ship engaged in hunting whales. [f. WHALE]

wham *int.* expressing forcible impact. [imit.]

whang *v.t./i.* to strike heavily and loudly. —*n.* a whanging sound or blow. [imit.]

wharf /wɔːf/ *n.* (*pl.* **wharfs**) a platform to which a ship may be moored to load and unload. —*v.t.* to moor (a ship) at or store (goods) on a wharf. [OE]

wharfage *n.* accommodation at a wharf; the fee for this. [f. prec.]

wharfinger /ˈwɔːfɪndʒə(r)/ *n.* the owner or keeper of a wharf. [f. WHARF; cf. *messenger*]

what *interrog. adj.* asking for a choice from an indefinite number (*what books have you read?*) or for a statement of amount, number, or kind (*what stores have we got?*); (*colloq.*) which? (*what book have you chosen?*). —*excl. adj.* how great or remarkable. —*rel. adj.* the or any . . . that. —*interrog. pron.* **1** what thing(s)? **2** (a request for a remark to be repeated) what did you say? —*excl. pron.* what thing(s)!, how much!, etc. —*rel. pron.* that or those which; the thing(s) or anything that. —*adv.* to what extent or degree. —*int.* expressing surprise. —**what about,** what is the news about (a subject); what is your opinion of; how would you deal with; shall we do or have etc. **what d'you call it** *or* **what's his** (*or* **its**) **name?** a substitute for a name that one cannot remember. **what for?** for what reason or purpose? (*give a person what for*, (*slang*) to punish or scold him or her). **what have you,** anything else similar. **what not,** other similar things. **what's what,** what is useful or important etc. **what with,** because of (various specified causes). [OE]

whatever /wɒtˈevə(r)/ *adj.* & *pron.* **1** = WHAT (in relative uses) with emphasis on indefiniteness. **2** though anything. **3** (with neg. or interrog.) at all, of any kind.

whatnot *n.* **1** something trivial or indefinite. **2** a stand with shelves for small objects.

whatsoever /wɒtsəʊˈevə(r)/ *adj.* & *pron.* = WHATEVER.

wheat *n.* a cereal of the genus *Triticum* bearing dense four-sided seed-spikes from which much bread is made; its grain. [OE]

wheatear *n.* a small migratory bird of the genus *Oenanthe*, especially a species with a white belly and rump. [app. f. *wheatears* (as WHITE, ARSE)]

wheaten *adj*. made of wheat. [as WHEAT]

wheatmeal *n*. wholemeal flour made from wheat.

wheedle *v.t*. to coax; to persuade or obtain by coaxing. [perh. f. G *wedeln* fawn, cringe (*wedel* tail)]

wheel *n*. **1** a circular frame or disc arranged to revolve on an axle and used to facilitate the motion of a vehicle or for various mechanical purposes; a wheel-like thing. **2** a machine etc. of which a wheel is an essential part. **3** motion like that of a wheel; movement of a line of men that pivots on one end. —*v.t./i*. **1** to turn or cause to turn like a wheel; to change direction and face another way. **2** to push or pull (a bicycle or cart etc. with wheels, or its contents) along. **3** to move in circles or curves. —**at the wheel,** driving a vehicle or directing a ship's course; in control of affairs. **on (oiled) wheels,** smoothly. **wheel and deal,** (*US*) to engage in political or commercial scheming so as to exert influence. **wheel-spin** *n*. rotation of a vehicle's wheels without traction. **wheels within wheels,** secret or indirect motives and influences interacting with one another. [OE]

wheelbarrow *n*. an open container for moving small loads in gardening, building, etc., with a wheel beneath one end and two handles (by which it is pushed) at the other.

wheelbase *n*. the distance between the axles of a vehicle.

wheelchair *n*. a disabled person's chair on wheels.

wheel-house *n*. a steersman's shelter.

wheelie *n*. the stunt of riding a bicycle or motor cycle for a short distance with the front wheel off the ground.

wheelwright *n*. a maker or repairer of wooden wheels.

wheeze *v.i*. to breathe with an audible hoarse whistling sound. —*n*. **1** a sound of wheezing. **2** (*slang*) a clever scheme. —**wheezy** *adj*. [prob. f. ON = hiss]

whelk *n*. a spiral-shelled marine mollusc of the genus *Bucinum* etc., especially one used as food. [OE; orig. unkn.]

whelm *v.t*. (*poetic*) to engulf, to crush with a weight. [cf. OE *hwylfan*]

whelp *n*. **1** a young dog, a pup. **2** (*archaic*) a cub. —*v.t./i*. to give birth to (a whelp or whelps). [OE]

when *interrog. adv*. at what time?, on what occasion?, how soon? —*rel. adv*. (with ref. to time) at or on which. —*conj*. **1** at the or any time that; as soon as. **2** although; considering that; since. —*pron*. what or which time. —*n*. the time, the occasion (*fix the where and when*). [OE]

whence *interrog. adv*. from what place or source? —*rel. adv*., & *conj*. (with ref. to place) from which; to the place from which. —*pron*. what place?; which place. —*n*. source. [OE, rel. to prec.]

whenever /wenˈevə(r)/ *conj*. & *adv*. at whatever time, on whatever occasion; every time that.

whensoever /wensəʊˈevə(r)/ *conj*. & *adv*. = WHENEVER.

where /weə(r)/ *interrog. adv*. in or to what place or position (*lit*. or *fig*.)?; in what direction?; in what respect? —*rel. adv*., & *conj*. (with ref. to place) in or to which; in the direction, part, or respect, in which; and there. —*pron*. what place? —*n*. the place (see WHEN). [OE]

whereabouts /weərəˈbaʊts/ *adv*. approximately where. —/ˈweər-/ *n*. (as *sing*. or *pl*.) a person's or thing's location roughly defined.

whereas /weərˈæz/ *conj*. **1** in contrast or comparison with the fact that. **2** (esp. in legal preambles) taking into consideration the fact that.

whereby /weəˈbaɪ/ *conj*. by what or which means.

wherefore *adv*. (*archaic*) for what reason?; for which reason. —*n*. a reason (see WHY).

wherein /weərˈɪn/ *conj*. (*formal*) in what or which place or respect.

whereof /weərˈɒv/ *adv*. & *conj*. (*formal*) of what or which.

whereupon /weərəˈpɒn/ *conj*. immediately after which.

wherever /weərˈevə(r)/ (also **wheresoever**) *adv*. in or to whatever place. —*conj*. in every place that.

wherewithal /ˈweəwɪðɔ:l/ *n*. (*colloq*.) the money or things needed for a purpose.

wherry /ˈwerɪ/ *n*. a light rowing-boat usually for carrying passengers; a large light barge. [orig. unkn.]

whet *v.t*. (**-tt-**) **1** to sharpen by rubbing against a stone etc. **2** to stimulate (an appetite or interest). [OE]

whether /ˈweðə(r)/ *conj*. introducing the first or both of alternative possibilities. —**whether or no,** whether it is so or not. [OE]

whetstone *n*. a shaped stone for sharpening tools.

whew /hwju:/ *int*. expressing surprise, consternation, or relief. [imit.]

whey /weɪ/ *n*. the watery liquid left when milk forms curds. [OE]

which *interrog. adj*. asking for a choice from a definite or known number (*which way shall we go?*). —*rel. adj*. (usu. with noun) being the one just referred to, and this or these (*for ten* *years, during which time he spoke to nobody*). —*interrog. pron.* which person(s) or thing(s)? —*rel. pron.* which thing(s), used (esp. of an incidental description rather than a defining one) of the thing, or animal, or (*archaic*) person referred to (*the house, which is empty, has been damaged*; *Our Father, which art in heaven*), or in place of THAT after *in* or *that*. [OE]

whichever /wɪtʃˈevə(r)/ *adj. & pron.* any which, that or those which.

whiff *n.* **1** a puff of air, smoke, or odour; a trace of scandal etc. **2** a small cigar. [imit.]

Whig /wɪg/ *n.* (*hist.*) **1** a 17th-c. Scottish Presbyterian. **2** a member of a former British political group. **3** (*US*) a supporter of the American Revolution. **4** (*US*) a member of a political party of 1834-56, succeeded by the Republicans. —*adj.* of the Whigs. —**Whiggery** *n.* [prob. abbr. of *whiggamer*, Scottish rebel of 1648 (*whig* drive)].

while *n.* a space of time, the time spent in some action. —*conj.* **1** during the time that, for as long as, at the same time as. **2** in spite of the fact that, at the same time. —*v.t.* (with *away*) to pass (time etc.) in a leisurely or interesting manner. —*adv.* (preceded by *time* etc.) during which. —**between whiles,** in the intervals. **for a while,** for some time. **in a while,** soon. **once in a while,** occasionally. **the while,** during some other action. **worth (one's) while,** worth the time or effort spent. [OE]

whiles /waɪlz/ *conj.* (*archaic*) while. [f. prec.]

whilom /ˈwaɪləm/ *adv.* (*archaic*) formerly. —*adj.* (*archaic*) former. [f. WHILE]

whilst /waɪlst/ *adv. & conj.* while. [f. WHILES]

whim *n.* a sudden unreasoning desire or impulse, a caprice. [orig. unkn.]

whimper *v.i.* to make feeble querulous or frightened sounds. —*n.* such a sound. [imit.]

whimsical /ˈwɪmzɪk(ə)l/ *adj.* **1** impulsive and playful. **2** fanciful, quaint. —**whimsicality** /-ˈkælɪtɪ/ *n.*, **whimsically** *adv.* [f. foll.]

whimsy /ˈwɪmzɪ/ *n.* a whim. [rel. to *whim-wham* toy; orig. unkn.]

whin *n.* (in *sing.* or *pl.*) furze. [prob. Scand.]

whinchat *n.* a small brownish songbird (*Saxicola rubetra*).

whine *v.t./i.* **1** to make a long-drawn complaining cry like that of a child or dog. **2** to make a similar shrill sound. **3** to complain in a petty or feeble way; to utter thus. —*n.* a whining cry, sound, or complaint. —**whiner** *n.*, **whiny** *adj.* [OE]

whinge /wɪndʒ/ *v.i.* to whine, to grumble persistently. [OE]

whinny /ˈwɪnɪ/ *n.* a gentle or joyful neigh. —*v.i.* to give a whinny. [imit.]

whip *n.* **1** a cord or strip of leather fastened to a stick that serves as a handle, used for urging animals on or for striking a person or animal in punishment. **2** an official of a political party in Parliament with authority to maintain discipline among members of his party; his written notice requesting attendance at a division etc. (variously underlined according to the degree of urgency: *three-line whip*); party discipline and instructions. **3** a food made with whipped cream etc. **4** a whipper-in. —*v.t./i.* (**-pp-**) **1** to strike or urge on with a whip. **2** to beat (cream or eggs etc.) into a froth. **3** to move suddenly, or unexpectedly, or rapidly. **4** (*slang*) to excel, to defeat. **5** to bind with spirally wound twine. **6** to sew with overcast stitches. —**have the whip hand,** to have the advantage or control. **whip in,** to bring (hounds) together. **whip on,** to urge into action. **whip-round** *n.* (*colloq.*) an appeal for contributions from a group of people. **whip up,** to incite, to stir up. [prob. f. MLG & MDu. *wippen* swing]

whipcord *n.* **1** cord made of tightly twisted strands. **2** a kind of twilled fabric with prominent ridges.

whiplash *n.* the lash of a whip. —**whiplash injury,** injury to the neck caused by a jerk of the head in a collision.

whipper-in *n.* a huntsman's assistant who manages hounds.

whipper-snapper /ˈwɪpəsnæpə(r)/ *n.* a small child; an insignificant but presumptuous person.

whippet /ˈwɪpɪt/ *n.* a cross-bred dog of greyhound type used for racing. [perh. f. obs. *whippet* move briskly, f. *whip it*]

whipping-boy *n.* a scapegoat; (*hist.*) a boy educated with a young prince and punished for the prince's faults.

whipping-top *n.* a top kept spinning by blows of a lash.

whippoorwill /ˈwɪppʊəwɪl/ *n.* the American nightjar (*Caprimulgus vociferus*). [imit. of its cry]

whippy *adj.* flexible, springy. —**whippiness** *n.* [f. WHIP]

whipstock *n.* the handle of a whip.

whirl *v.t./i.* **1** to swing round and round, to revolve rapidly. **2** to send or travel swiftly in a curved course. **3** to convey or go rapidly in a vehicle. **4** (of the brain, senses, etc.) to seem to spin round. —*n.* **1** a whirling movement. **2** a state of intense activity or confusion. [f. ON (*hvirfill* circle) or MLG & MDu. *wervel* spindle]

whirligig /ˈwɜːlɪgɪg/ *n.* **1** a spinning or whirling toy. **2** a merry-go-round. **3** a revolving motion. [f. prec. + obs. *gig* whipping-top]

whirlpool *n.* a circular eddy of water, often drawing floating objects towards its centre.

whirlwind *n.* **1** a whirling mass or column of air. **2** (*attrib.*) very rapid.

whirlybird /ˈwɜːlıbɜːd/ *n.* (*slang*) a helicopter.

whirr *n.* a continuous rapid buzzing or softly clicking sound. —*v.i.* to make this sound. [prob. Scand.]

whisk *v.t./i.* **1** to brush or sweep lightly from a surface. **2** to move with a quick light sweeping movement; to convey or go rapidly. **3** to beat (eggs etc.) into a froth. —*n.* **1** a whisking movement. **2** a utensil for beating eggs etc. **3** a bunch of strips of straw etc. tied to a handle, used for flicking flies away. [prob. Scand.]

whisker *n.* **1** (usu. in *pl.*) the hair growing on a man's face, especially on the cheeks. **2** bristle(s) on the face of a cat etc. **3** (*colloq.*) a very small distance. —**whiskery** *adj.* [f. prec.]

whiskey var. of foll. (esp. *US* and of Irish whisky).

whisky *n.* spirit distilled from malted grain, especially barley; a drink of this. [abbr. of obs. *whiskybae*, var. of USQUEBAUGH]

whisper *v.t./i.* **1** to speak or utter softly, using the breath but not the vocal cords. **2** to converse confidentially or secretly; to spread (a tale) thus. **3** (of leaves or fabric etc.) to rustle. —*n.* **1** a whispering sound or remark; whispering speech. **2** a rumour. —**whispering gallery,** a gallery or dome in which the slightest sound made at a particular point can be heard at another far off. [OE (imit.)]

whist *n.* a card-game of mingled skill and chance, using a pack of 52 cards, usually played between two pairs of players. —**whist drive,** a progressive whist party, usually with prizes. [f. earlier *whisk*, influenced by the cry of *whist!* for silence in the game]

whistle /ˈwɪs(ə)l/ *n.* **1** a clear shrill sound made by forcing the breath through a small hole between nearly closed lips; a similar sound made by a bird, wind, missile, or instrument. **2** an instrument used to produce this sound as a signal etc. —*v.t./i.* to emit a whistle; to summon or signal thus; to produce (a tune) by whistling. —**whistle for,** (*colloq.*) to seek or desire in vain. **whistle-stop** *n.* (*US*) a small unimportant town on a railway; a politician's brief pause for an electioneering speech on a tour. —**whistler** *n.* [OE (imit.)]

Whit *adj.* connected with, belonging to, or following Whit Sunday. —**Whit Sunday,** the seventh Sunday after Easter, commemorating the descent of the Holy Spirit upon the Apostles at Pentecost. [OE, = White (Sunday), prob. f. white robes of newly-baptized; in the Western Church the festival became a date for baptisms]

whit *n.* the least possible amount. [app. alt. f. WIGHT]

white *adj.* **1** reflecting all light, of the colour of fresh snow or common salt; approaching this colour; pale from illness, fear, or other emotion. **2 White,** of the human group characterized by light-coloured skin; of or reserved for such persons. **3** (of magic etc.) of a harmless kind. —*n.* **1** white colour or pigment; white clothes or material. **2** the white part of something (e.g. of the eyeball round the iris); the translucent or white part round the yolk of an egg. **3** a white ball or piece in a game; the player using this. **4 White,** a White person. —**white admiral,** see ADMIRAL. **white ant,** a termite. **white Christmas,** one with snow. **white coffee,** coffee with milk or cream. **white-collar worker,** one not engaged in manual labour. **white elephant,** a useless possession. [from the story that the kings of Siam were accustomed to present an elephant of a rare white albino kind (venerated in some Asian countries) to courtiers who had rendered themselves obnoxious, in order to ruin the recipient by the cost of its maintenance] **white feather,** a symbol of cowardice. **white flag,** a symbol of surrender. **White Friars,** Carmelites (so called from their white cloaks). **white gold,** a pale alloy of gold with nickel etc. **white-headed boy,** a highly favoured person. **white heat,** the temperature at which metal looks white; a state of intense passion or activity. **white hope,** a person expected to achieve much. **white horses,** white-crested sea-waves. **white-hot** *adj.* at white heat. **white lead,** a mixture of lead carbonate and hydrated lead oxide used as a pigment. **white lie,** a harmless or trivial untruth. **white light,** colourless light, e.g. ordinary daylight. **white noise,** noise containing many frequencies with about equal energies. **white-out** *n.* a dense blizzard, especially in polar regions. **White Paper,** a government report giving information on a subject. **white pepper,** pepper made by grinding the ripe or husked berry. **white sale,** a sale of household linen. **white sauce,** a sauce of flour, melted butter, and milk or cream. **white slave,** a woman tricked or forced into prostitution. **white spirit,** light petroleum as a solvent. **white sugar,** purified sugar. **white tie,** a man's white bow-tie worn with full evening dress. **white whale,** a northern whale (*Delphinapterus leucas*), white when adult. —**whitely** *adv.*, **whiteness** *n.*, **whitish** *adj.* [OE]

whitebait *n.* a small silvery-white food-fish, probably the young of herring, sprat, etc.

whiten /ˈwaɪt(ə)n/ *v.t./i.* to make or become white or whiter. [f. WHITE]

whitewash *n.* **1** a solution of lime or whiting

for whitening walls etc. **2** the concealing of mistakes or faults. —*v.t.* **1** to cover with whitewash. **2** to conceal the mistakes or faults of or in.

whitewood *n.* a light-coloured wood, especially one prepared for staining etc.

whither /ˈwɪðə(r)/ *adv.* (*archaic*) to what place or state?; (preceded by *place* etc.) to which. —*conj.* (*archaic*) to the or any place to which; and thither. [OE]

whiting[1] /ˈwaɪtɪŋ/ *n.* a small white-fleshed food-fish (*Merlangus merlangus*). [f. MDu., app. as WHITE]

whiting[2] *n.* (also **whitening**) ground chalk used in whitewashing, plate-cleaning, etc. [f. WHITE]

whitlow /ˈwɪtləʊ/ *n.* a small abscess under or near a nail. [earlier *whitflaw*, app. = WHITE + FLAW[1] in sense 'crack']

Whitsun /ˈwɪts(ə)n/ *n.* (also **Whitsuntide**) the weekend or week including Whit Sunday. [f. *Whitsun Day* = Whit Sunday]

whittle /ˈwɪt(ə)l/ *v.t./i.* **1** to pare (wood) with repeated slicings of a knife; to use a knife thus. **2** reduce by repeated subtractions. [var. of dial. *thwittle*]

whiz *n.* the sound made by a body moving through the air at great speed. —*v.i.* (**-zz-**) to move with or make this sound; to move very quickly. —**whiz-kid** *n.* (*colloq.*) a brilliant or highly successful young person. [imit.]

WHO *abbr.* World Health Organization.

who /hu:/ *pron.* (*obj.* **whom**, *colloq.* **who**; *poss.* **whose** /hu:z/) **1** (*interrog.*) what or which person(s)? **2** (*rel.*) the particular person(s) that; and or but he, they, etc. (*sent it to Jones, who sent it on to Smith*). —**who's who,** who or what each person is; a list with facts about notable persons. [OE]

whoa /wəʊ/ *int.* used to stop a horse etc. [var. of HO]

whodunit /hu:ˈdʌnɪt/ *n.* (*colloq.*) a detective or mystery story or play etc. [= *who done* (illiterate for *did*) *it?*]

whoever /hu:ˈevə(r)/ *pron.* (*obj.* **whomever,** (*colloq.*) **whoever**; poss. **whosever** /hu:z-/ **1** the or any person(s) who. **2** though anyone.

whole /həʊl/ *adj.* **1** with no part removed or left out. **2** not injured or broken. —*n.* **1** the full or complete amount, all the parts or members. **2** a complete system made up of parts. —**on the whole,** taking everything relevant into account; in respect of the whole though some details form exceptions. **whole foods,** foods not processed or refined. **whole-hearted** *adj.* without doubts or reservations; done with all possible effort. **a whole lot,** (*colloq.*) a great amount. **whole number,** a number consisting of one or more units with no fractions. **whole wheat,** wheat not separated into parts by bolting. [OE]

wholemeal *adj.* made from the whole grain of (unbolted) wheat etc.

wholesale *n.* the selling of things in large quantities to be retailed by others. —*adj.* & *adv.* **1** by wholesale. **2** on a large scale. —*v.t.* to sell wholesale. —**wholesaler** *n.* [orig. *by whole sale*]

wholesome /ˈhəʊlsəm/ *adj.* promoting good physical or mental health or moral condition; showing good sense. —**wholesomeness** *n.* [as WHOLE, -SOME]

wholly /ˈhəʊllɪ/ *adv.* entirely, with nothing excepted or removed. [as WHOLE]

whom *pron.* the objective case of WHO.

whoop /hu:p/ *n.* **1** a loud cry (as) of excitement etc. **2** a long rasping indrawn breath in whooping cough. —*v.i.* to utter a whoop. —**whooping cough,** an infectious bacterial disease, especially of children, with a short violent cough followed by a whoop. **whoop it up,** (*colloq.*) to engage in revelry; (*US*) to make a stir. [imit.]

whoopee /wʊˈpi:/ *int.* expressing exuberant joy. —**make whoopee** /ˈwʊpɪ/, (*colloq.*) to rejoice noisily or hilariously. [f. prec.]

whoops /wʊps/ *int.* on making an obvious mistake or losing balance. [var. of OOPS]

whop *v.t.* (**-pp-**) (*slang*) to thrash, to defeat. [var. of (dial.) *wap*; orig. unkn.]

whopper *n.* (*slang*) a big specimen; a great lie. [f. WHOP]

whopping *adj.* (*slang*) very big. [f. WHOP]

whore /hɔ:(r)/ *n.* a prostitute; a sexually immoral woman. —**whore-house** *n.* a brothel. [OE]

whorl /wɜ:l/ *n.* **1** a coiled form; one turn of a spiral. **2** a ring of leaves or petals round a stem or central point. **3** a complete circle formed by ridges in a fingerprint. [app. var. of WHIRL]

whortleberry /ˈwɜ:t(ə)lberɪ/ *n.* a bilberry. [dial. form of *hurtleberry*]

whose /hu:z/ *interrog.* & *rel. pron.* & *adj.* of whom; of which. [OE, genitive case of WHO]

whosoever /hu:səʊˈevə(r)/ *pron.* (*obj.* **whomsoever**; *poss.* **whosesoever** /hu:zsəʊˈevə(r)/) = WHOEVER.

why /waɪ/ *interrog. adv.* for what reason or purpose? —*rel. adv.* preceded by *reason* etc.) for which. —*int.* expressing surprised discovery or recognition, impatience, reflection, objection, etc. —*n.* a reason (*the whys and wherefores*). [OE]

WI *abbr.* **1** West Indies. **2** Women's Institute.

wick *n.* a strip or thread feeding a flame with fuel. [OE]

wicked /ˈwɪkɪd/ *adj.* **1** morally bad, offending against what is right. **2** (*colloq.*) very bad or formidable, severe. **3** malicious, mischievous

—**wickedly** *adv.*, **wickedness** *n.* [f. obs. *wick* in same sense]

wicker *n.* thin canes or osiers woven together as material for making furniture, baskets, etc. [f. Scand.; cf. Sw. *viker* willow rel. to *vika* bend]

wickerwork *n.* wicker; things made of this.

wicket /ˈwɪkɪt/ *n.* **1** a small door or gate especially beside or in a larger one or closing the lower part only of a doorway. **2** (in cricket) the stumps (orig. two, now three) with the bails in position defended by a batsman; the ground between the two wickets; the state of this; a batsman's tenure of the wicket. —**wicket-keeper** *n.* a fieldsman stationed close behind the batsman's wicket. [f. AF *wiket*, OF *guichet*; orig. unkn.]

widdershins var. of WITHERSHINS.

wide *adj.* **1** having the sides far apart, not narrow. **2** extending far; having great range. **3** open to the full extent. **4** far from the target etc., not within a reasonable distance. **5** (appended to a measurement) in width; (as *suffix*) extending to the whole of (*worldwide*). —*adv.* widely, to the full extent; far from the target etc. —*n.* a wide ball. —**give a wide berth to,** see BERTH. **to the wide,** completely. **wide awake,** (*colloq.*) wary, knowing. **wide ball,** (in cricket) one judged by an umpire to be beyond the batsman's reach. **wide-eyed** *adj.* with eyes wide open in amazement or innocent surprise. **wide of the mark,** incorrect; irrelevant. **wide open,** exposed to attack; (of a contest) with no contestant who can be predicted as a certain winner. **the wide world,** the whole world, great as it is. —**widely** *adv.*, **wideness** *n.* [OE]

widen /ˈwaɪd(ə)n/ *v.t./i.* to make or become wider. [f. WIDE]

widespread *adj.* widely distributed.

widgeon /ˈwɪdʒ(ə)n/ *n.* a kind of wild duck, especially *Anas penelope* or (US) *A. americana*. [perh. f. imit. *wi-*, after *pigeon*]

widow /ˈwɪdəʊ/ *n.* a woman who has lost her husband by death and not married again. —*v.t.* to make into a widow or widower; (in *p.p.*) bereft by the death of a husband or wife. —**widowhood** *n.* [OE]

widower *n.* a man who has lost his wife by death and not married again. [f. prec.]

width *n.* **1** distance or measurement from side to side. **2** a strip of material of full width as woven. **3** a large extent. **4** liberality of views etc. —**widthways** *adv.* [f. WIDE]

wield /wi:ld/ *v.t.* **1** to hold and use (a weapon or tool etc.). **2** to have and use (power). [OE]

Wiener schnitzel /ˈvi:nə ˈʃnɪts(ə)l/ a veal cutlet breaded, fried, and garnished. [G, = Viennese cutlet]

wife *n.* (*pl.* **wives**) **1** a married woman, especially in relation to her husband. **2** (*archaic*) a woman. —**wifely** *adv.* [OE]

wig[1] *n.* an artificial head of hair. [abbr. of PERIWIG]

wig[2] *v.t.* (**-gg-**) (*colloq.*) to rebuke lengthily (esp. in *a wigging*). [app. slang use of prec.]

wiggle *v.t./i.* (*colloq.*) to move or cause to move repeatedly from side to side; to wriggle. —*n.* a wiggling movement. [f. MLG & MDu. *wiggelen*; cf. WAG, WAGGLE]

wight /waɪt/ *n.* (*archaic*) a person. [OE, = thing, creature]

wigwam /ˈwɪgwæm/ *n.* a hut or tent made by fastening skins or mats over a framework of poles, as formerly used by American Indians. [Amer. Ind., = their house]

wilco /ˈwɪlkəʊ/ *int.* expressing compliance or agreement. [abbr. of *will comply*]

wild /waɪld/ *adj.* **1** living or growing in its original natural state, not domesticated or tame or cultivated. **2** not civilized, barbarous. **3** unrestrained, disorderly, uncontrolled. **4** tempestuous, stormy. **5** full of strong unrestrained feeling, intensely eager, frantic; (*colloq.*) infuriated. **6** extremely foolish or unreasonable; random, ill-aimed. —*adv.* in a wild manner. —*n.* a wild tract, a desert. —**in the wilds,** (*colloq.*) far from towns etc. **run wild,** to grow or stray unchecked or undisciplined. **sow one's wild oats,** to indulge in youthful follies before maturity. **wild-goose chase,** a foolish or useless search; a hopeless quest. **wild silk,** silk from wild silkworms; an imitation of this. **Wild West,** the western regions of the USA at the time when they were lawless frontier districts. —**wildly** *adv.*, **wildness** *n.* [OE]

wildcat *n.* a hot-tempered or violent person. —*adj.* **1** reckless, financially unsound. **2** (of a strike) sudden and unofficial.

wildebeest /ˈwɪldəbi:st, v-/ *n.* the gnu. [Afrik. (as WILD, BEAST)]

wilderness /ˈwɪldənɪs/ *n.* **1** a desert, an uncultivated region. **2** a confused assemblage. —**voice in the wilderness,** an unheeded advocate of reform (with ref. to Matt. 3:3 etc.). [f. OE (*wil(d)deor* wild deer)]

wildfire *n.* (*hist.*) a combustible liquid used in war. —**spread like wildfire,** to spread with extraordinary speed.

wildfowl *n.* a game-bird or game-birds (e.g. ducks and geese, quail, pheasants).

wildlife *n.* wild animals collectively.

wile *n.* (usu. in *pl.*) a piece of trickery intended to deceive or attract. —*v.t.* to lure. [perh. f. Scand. (ON *vél* craft)]

wilful /ˈwɪlfʊl/ *adj.* **1** intentional, deliberate. **2** selfwilled. —**wilfully** *adv.*, **wilfulness** *n.* [f. WILL[2] + -FUL]

will[1] *v.aux.* (3 *sing. pres.* **will**; 2 *sing.* (*archaic*) **wilt**; *past* WOULD) **1** (strictly only in 2nd and 3rd persons) expressing a future statement or an order (*they will attack at dawn*; *you will do as you are told*). **2** expressing the speaker's intention (*I will support you!*). [OE]

will[2] *n.* **1** the mental faculty by which a person decides or conceives himself as deciding upon and initiating his actions. **2** (also **will-power**) control exercised by one's will. **3** determination, fixed desire or intention. **4** (*archaic*) that which is desired or ordained. **5** a person's disposition in wishing good or bad to others. **6** written directions made by a person for the disposal of his or her property after his or her death. —*v.t.* **1** to exercise one's will-power; to influence or compel thus. **2** to intend unconditionally. **3** to bequeath by a will. —**at will,** however one pleases. [OE]

willies /ˈwɪlɪz/ *n.pl.* (*slang*) nervous discomfort. [orig. unkn.]

willing *adj.* **1** ready to consent or to undertake what is required. **2** given or done etc. by a willing person. —*n.* a cheerful intention (*to show willing*). —**willingly** *adv.*, **willingness** *n.* [f. WILL[2]]

will-o'-the-wisp /wɪləðəˈwɪsp/ *n.* **1** a phosphorescent light seen on marshy ground. **2** an elusive person. **3** a delusive hope or plan. [orig. *Will* (William) *with the wisp* (*wisp* = bundle of (lighted) hay)]

willow /ˈwɪləʊ/ *n.* a waterside tree of the genus *Salix* with pliant branches yielding osiers and timber for cricketbats. —**willow-herb** *n.* a plant of the genus *Epilobium* with leaves like the willow. [OE]

willow-pattern *n.* a conventional 'Chinese' design of blue on white china etc., in which a willow-tree is a prominent feature.

willowy /ˈwɪləʊɪ/ *adj.* **1** full of willow trees. **2** lithe and slender. [f. prec.]

willy-nilly /wɪlɪˈnɪlɪ/ *adv.* whether one likes it or not. [= *will I, nill* (obs. for *will not*) *I*]

wilt *v.t./i.* **1** (of plants) to lose freshness and droop. **2** to cause to do this. **3** (of persons) to become limp from exhaustion. —*n.* a plant-disease that causes wilting. [orig. dial., perh. f. LDu.]

Wilton /ˈwɪlt(ə)n/ *n.* a kind of carpet with loops cut into thick pile, first made at Wilton in Wiltshire.

Wilts. *abbr.* Wiltshire.

wily /ˈwaɪlɪ/ *adj.* full of wiles, crafty, cunning. —**wilily** *adv.*, **wiliness** *n.* [f. WILE]

wimple *n.* a head-dress of linen or silk folded round the head and neck so as to cover all but the front of the face, worn by women in medieval times and retained in the dress of nuns. [OE]

win *v.t./i.* (**-nn-**; *past* & *p.p.* **won** /wʌn/) **1** to obtain or achieve as the result of a battle, contest, bet, or effort; to be the victor. **2** to be victorious in (a battle, game, race, etc.). **3** to make one's way or become (free etc.) by successful effort. —*n.* victory in a game or contest. —**win over,** to gain the favour or support of. **win one's spurs,** (*hist.*) to gain a knighthood; (*fig.*) to prove one's ability, to gain distinction. **win through** *or* **out,** to overcome obstacles. **you can't win,** (*colloq.*) there is no way to succeed. [OE]

wince *n.* a start or involuntary shrinking movement showing pain or distress. —*v.i.* to make such a movement. [cf. OF *guenchir* turn aside]

wincey /ˈwɪnsɪ/ *n.* a lightweight fabric of wool and cotton or linen. [app. f. *woolsey* in LINSEY-WOOLSEY]

winceyette /wɪnsɪˈet/ *n.* a soft napped fabric woven of cotton and wool. [f. prec. + -ETTE]

winch *n.* **1** the crank of a wheel or axle. **2** a windlass. —*v.t.* to lift with a winch. [OE]

wind[1] /wɪnd/ *n.* **1** air in natural motion; a scent carried by this and indicating a presence. **2** an artificially produced air-current especially for sounding a wind instrument. **3** the wind instruments in an orchestra etc. **4** breath as needed in exertion or speech; the power of breathing without difficulty. **5** a point below the centre of the chest where a blow temporarily paralyses the breathing. **6** gas generated in the stomach or bowels. **7** empty talk. —*v.t.* **1** to exhaust the wind of by exertion or a blow. **2** to renew the wind of by a rest. **3** to make breathe quickly and deeply by exercise. **4** to detect the presence of by scent. —**get wind of,** to begin to suspect. **get** *or* **have the wind up,** (*slang*) to feel frightened. **in the wind,** about to happen. **like the wind,** swiftly. **put the wind up,** (*slang*) to frighten. **take the wind out of a person's sails,** to frustrate him by anticipating his action or remark. **wind-break** *n.* a row of trees etc. to break the force of the wind. **wind-cheater** *n.* a jacket designed to give protection against the wind. **wind instrument,** a musical instrument sounded by a current of air, especially that produced by the player's breath. **wind-jammer** *n.* a merchant sailing-ship. **wind-sock** *n.* a canvas cylinder or cone on a mast to show the direction of the wind. **wind-swept** *adj.* exposed to high winds. **wind-tunnel** *n.* a tunnel-like device to produce an air-stream past models of aircraft etc. for the study of wind effects. [OE]

wind[2] /waɪnd/ *v.t./i.* (*past* & *p.p.* **wound**) **1** to go or cause to go in a curving, twisting, or spiral course; to make (one's way) thus. **2** to coil; to wrap closely; to provide with a coiled thread etc.; to surround (as) with a coil. **3** to haul, hoist, or move by turning a handle or windlass etc. **4** to wind up (a clock etc.). —*n.* **1** a bend or turn in a course. **2** a single turn in winding. —**wind down,** to unwind (*lit.* or *fig.*). **winding-sheet** *n.* a sheet in which a corpse is wrapped for burial. **wind off,** to unwind. **wind up,** to set or keep (a clock etc.) going by tightening its spring or adjusting its weights; to bring or come to an end; to settle and finally close the business affairs of (a company); (*colloq.*) to arrive finally. —**winder** *n.* [OE]

windbag *n.* (*colloq.*) a person who talks at length and without value.

windfall n. **1** a fruit blown to the ground by the wind. **2** a piece of unexpected good fortune, especially a sum of money acquired.

windlass /ˈwɪndləs/ *n.* a machine with a horizontal axle for hauling or hoisting things. [f. AF f. ON (*vinda* WIND², *áss* pole)]

windmill *n.* a mill worked by the wind acting on its sails. —**tilt at windmills,** to attack an imaginary enemy (with ref. to Don Quixote, who attacked windmills, thinking that they were giants).

window /ˈwɪndəʊ/ *n.* **1** an opening in a wall etc. usually with glass for the admission of light etc.; the glass itself; the space for display behind the window of a shop. **2** a window-like opening. **3** an interval during which the positions of planets etc. allow a specified journey by a spacecraft. —**window-box** *n.* a trough fixed outside a window for cultivating ornamental plants. **window-dressing** *n.* the art of arranging a display in a shop-window etc.; adroit presentation of facts etc. to give a falsely favourable impression. **window-shopping** *n.* looking at the goods displayed in shop-windows without buying anything. [f. ON (as WIND¹, EYE)]

windpipe *n.* the air-passage from the larynx to the bronchial tubes.

windscreen *n.* a screen of glass at the front of a motor vehicle.

Windsurfer *n.* [P] a board like a surf-board with a sail. —**windsurfer** *n.* one engaged in the sport of riding on such a board. —**windsurfing** *n.*

windward /ˈwɪndwəd/ *adj.* & *adv.* in the direction from which the wind is blowing. —*n.* the windward direction. [f. WIND¹ + -WARD]

windy *adj.* **1** with much wind. **2** exposed to wind. **3** generating or characterized by flatulence. **4** full of useless talk. **5** (*slang*) nervous, frightened. —**windily** *adv.*, **windiness** *n.* [f. WIND¹]

wine *n.* **1** fermented grape-juice as an alcoholic drink; a fermented drink resembling it made from other fruits etc. **2** the dark red colour of red wine. —*v.t./i.* **1** to drink wine. **2** to entertain to wine. —**wine-bibber** *n.* a tippler. **wine-cellar** *n.* a cellar for storing wine; its contents. [OE f. L *vinum*]

wineglass *n.* a glass for wine, usually with a stem and foot.

winepress *n.* a press in which grapes are squeezed in making wine.

wineskin *n.* the whole skin of a goat etc. sewn up and used to hold wine.

wing *n.* **1** each of a pair of projecting parts by which a bird. bat, or insect etc. is able to fly; a corresponding part in a non-flying bird or insect. **2** a winglike part of an aircraft, supporting it in flight. **3** a part resembling a wing in appearance or position; a projecting part of a building, battle array, etc.; (in *pl.*) the sides of a theatre stage out of sight of the audience. **4** (in football etc.) the player at either end of the forward line; the side part of the playing area. **5** a section of a political party or other group, with more extreme views than those of the majority. **6** the mudguard of a motor vehicle, the part of the bodywork immediately above each wheel. **7** an air-force unit of several squadrons or groups. —*v.t./i.* **1** to fly, to travel by means of wings; to make (its way) thus. **2** to equip with wings; to enable to fly; to send in flight. **3** to wound in the wing or arm. —**on the wing,** flying. **spread one's wings,** to develop one's powers fully. **take under one's wing,** to treat as a protégé. **take wing,** to fly away. **wing-case** *n.* the horny cover of an insect's wing. **wing-chair** *n.* one with side pieces at the top of a high back. **wing-collar** *n.* a high stiff collar with turned-down corners. **wing commander,** an RAF officer next below group captain. **wing-nut** *n.* a nut with projections for the finger to turn it on a screw. **wing-span** *or* **-spread** *n.* the measurement right across the wings. [f. ON]

winger *n.* (in football etc.) a wing player.

wink *v.t./i.* **1** to close and open one eye deliberately, especially as a private signal to someone. **2** (of a light) to twinkle. —*n.* **1** an act of winking. **2** a short sleep. —**tip a person the wink,** to give him information privately. **wink at,** to pretend not to notice (something that should be stopped or condemned). [OE; cf. WINCE]

winker *n.* a flashing indicator on a motor vehicle. [f. WINK]

winkle *n.* a small edible sea snail of the genus *Littorina.* —*v.t.* (with *out*) to extract or eject. —**winkle-picker** *n.* (*slang*) a shoe with a long pointed toe. [abbr. of PERIWINKLE]

winner *n.* **1** one who wins. **2** a successful thing. [f. WIN]

winning *adj.* **1** having or bringing victory. **2** attractive. —*n.* (in *pl.*) money won.

—**winning-post** *n.* a post marking the end of a race. [f. WIN]

winnow /ˈwɪnəʊ/ *v.t.* **1** to expose (grain) to a current of air by tossing or fanning it so that the loose dry outer part is blown away; to separate (chaff) thus. **2** to sift or separate (evidence etc.) from worthless or inferior elements. [OE (as WIND¹)]

wino /ˈwaɪnəʊ/ *n.* (*pl.* **-os**) (*slang*) an alcoholic. [f. WINE]

winsome /ˈwɪnsəm/ *adj.* (of a person, looks, or manner) winning, engaging. [OE (*wyn* joy)]

winter *n.* the coldest and last season of the year, from December to February in the northern hemisphere. —*adj.* characteristic of or fit for winter. —*v.i.* to spend the winter. —**winter garden,** a garden or conservatory of plants kept flourishing in winter. **winter sports,** sports performed on snow or ice, e.g. skiing. [OE]

wintergreen *n.* any of various creeping or low shrubby plants with leaves remaining green in winter, especially the North American *Gaultheria procumbens* with drooping white flowers, edible scarlet berries, and aromatic leaves yielding an oil used in medicine and for flavouring.

wintry *adj.* **1** characteristic of winter. **2** (of a smile etc.) lacking warmth or vivacity. —**wintriness** *n.* [f. WINTER]

winy /ˈwaɪnɪ/ *adj.* wine-flavoured. [f. WINE]

wipe *v.t./i.* **1** to clean or dry the surface of by rubbing; to rub (a cloth) over a surface; to put (a liquid etc.) on to a surface by rubbing. **2** to clear or remove by wiping. —*n.* the act of wiping. —**wipe the floor with,** (*slang*) to inflict a humiliating defeat on. **wipe off,** to annul (a debt). **wipe out,** to avenge (an insult etc.); to destroy, to annihilate. [OE]

wiper /ˈwaɪpə(r)/ *n.* a device for keeping a windscreen clear of rain etc. [f. WIPE]

wire *n.* **1** metal drawn out into a slender flexible rod or thread; a piece of this. **2** a length of wire used for fencing or to carry an electric current etc. **3** (*colloq.*) a telegram. —*v.t./i.* **1** to provide, fasten, or strengthen with wire. **2** (*colloq.*) to telegraph. —**get one's wires crossed,** to become confused and misunderstand. **wire-haired** *adj.* (esp. of a dog) with stiff or wiry hair. **wire-tapping** *n.* the tapping of telephone wires. **wire wheel,** a vehicle wheel with wire spokes. **wire wool,** a mass of fine wire for cleaning kitchen utensils etc. **wire-worm** *n.* the destructive larva of a beetle of the family Elateridae. [OE]

wireless *n.* radio, a radio receiving set. [f. WIRE + -LESS]

wiring /ˈwaɪrɪŋ/ *n.* a system of wires providing electrical circuits. [f. WIRE]

wiry /ˈwaɪrɪ/ *adj.* tough and flexible as wire; (of a person) lean and strong. —**wirily** *adv.*, **wiriness** *n.* [f. WIRE]

wisdom /ˈwɪzdəm/ *n.* **1** experience and knowledge together with the power of applying them; sagacity, prudence, common sense. **2** wise sayings. —**wisdom tooth,** the third and hindmost molar tooth on each side of the upper and lower jaws, usually cut (if at all) after the age of 20. [OE (as WISE¹)]

wise¹ /waɪz/ *adj.* **1** having, or showing, or dictated by wisdom; having knowledge; suggestive of wisdom. **2** (*US slang*) alert, crafty. —**none the wiser,** knowing no more than before. **wise man,** a wizard; each of the Magi. —**wisely** *adv.* [OE]

wise² /waɪz/ *n.* (*archaic*) way, manner, degree. —**in no wise,** not at all. [OE]

-wise /-waɪz/ *suffix* forming adjectives and adverbs of manner (*clockwise, crosswise, lengthwise*) or respect (*moneywise*). [as prec.]

wiseacre /ˈwaɪzeɪkə(r)/ *n.* one who affects to be wise. [f. MDu., = soothsayer]

wisecrack *n.* (*colloq.*) a smart pithy remark. —*v.i.* (*colloq.*) to make a wisecrack.

wish *n.* **1** a desire or ambition. **2** an expression of desire about another person's welfare. —*v.t./i.* **1** to have or express as a wish; to formulate a wish. **2** to hope or express hope for (specified fortune) to befall someone; to hope that (a person) will fare (*well* or *ill*). **3** (*colloq.*) to foist (a specified thing etc. on a person). [OE]

wishbone *n.* **1** a forked bone between the neck and breast of a bird (pulled in two between two persons, the one who gets the larger part having the supposed right to magic fulfilment of any wish). **2** a thing shaped like this.

wishful *adj.* desiring. —**wishful thinking,** belief founded on wishes rather than facts. —**wishfully** *adv.* [f. WISH + -FUL]

wishy-washy /ˈwɪʃɪwɒʃɪ/ *adj.* feeble in quality or character. [redupl. of WASHY]

wisp *n.* **1** a small bundle or twist of straw etc.; a small separate quantity of smoke or hair etc. **2** a small thin person. —**wispy** *adj.* [orig. unkn.]

wistaria /wɪˈsteərɪə/ *n.* (also **wisteria**) a climbing shrub of the genus *Wistaria* with blue, purple, or white hanging flowers. [f. C. *Wistar* (or *Wister*), Amer. anatomist (d. 1818)]

wistful *adj.* full of sad or vague longing. —**wistfully** *adv.*, **wistfulness** *n.* [app. assim. of obs. *wistly* adv. (= intently) to *wishful*]

wit *n.* **1** (in *sing.* or *pl.*) intelligence, quick understanding. **2** the ability to combine words or ideas etc. ingeniously so as to produce a kind of clever humour that appeals to the intellect. **3** a person with such ability. —*v.t./i.* (*sing. pres.* **wot**; *past & p.p.* **wist**; *partic.* **witting**) (*archaic*) to know. —**at one's wit's**

(*or* **wits'**) **end,** utterly at a loss or in despair. **have** *or* **keep one's wits about one,** to be alert. **live by one's wits,** to live by ingenious or crafty expedients, without a settled occupation. **out of one's wits,** mad. **to wit,** that is to say, namely. [OE]

witch *n.* **1** a sorceress, a woman supposed to have dealings with the Devil or evil spirits. **2** an ugly old woman. **3** a fascinating woman. —**witch ball,** a coloured glass ball of the kind formerly hung up to keep witches away. **witch-doctor** *n.* a tribal magician of a primitive people. **witches' sabbath,** a supposed midnight orgy of the Devil and witches. **witch-hunt** *n.* a search for and the persecution of supposed witches or persons suspected of unpopular or unorthodox views. [OE]

witch- var. of WYCH-.

witchcraft *n.* the use of magic.

witchery *n.* witchcraft, the power exercised by beauty or eloquence or the like. [f. WITCH]

with /wɪð/ *prep.* expressing (1) instrumentality or means, cause, possession, circumstances, manner, material, agreement and disagreement, (2) company and parting of company, (3) antagonism. —**in** (*or* **out** etc.) **with,** take, send, or put (a person or thing) in (or out etc.). **with it,** (*colloq.*) up to date, conversant with modern ideas etc. [OE]

withal /wɪˈðɔːl/ *adv.* (*archaic*) in addition, moreover. [f. WITH + ALL]

withdraw /wɪðˈdrɔː/ *v.t./i.* (*past* **-drew**; *p.p.* **-drawn**) **1** to pull or take back or away. **2** to remove (deposited money) from a bank etc. **3** to discontinue; to cancel (a promise or statement etc.). **4** to go away from company or from a place etc. **5** (in *p.p.*, of a person) unresponsive, unsociable. —**withdrawal** *n.* [f. *with-* away (as WITH) + DRAW]

withe /wɪθ, wɪð, waɪð/ *n.* a tough flexible shoot used for tying a bundle of wood etc. [OE]

wither /ˈwɪðə(r)/ *v.t./i.* **1** to make or become dry and shrivelled; to lose or cause to lose vigour or freshness. **2** to blight with scorn etc. [app. var. of WEATHER]

withers /ˈwɪðəz/ *n.pl.* the ridge between a horse's shoulderblades. [app. f. obs. *widersome* (*wider-*, *wither* against)]

withershins /ˈwɪðəʃɪnz/ *adv.* (esp. *Sc.*) in a direction contrary to the apparent course of the sun (considered unlucky), anticlockwise. [f. MLG f. MHG (*wider* against, *sin* direction]

withhold /wɪðˈhəuld/ *v.t.* (*past* & *p.p.* **-held**) **1** to hold back, to restrain. **2** to refuse to give or grant or allow. [f. *with-* away (as WITH) + HOLD]

within /wɪˈðɪn/ *adv.* inside; indoors. —*prep.* **1** inside, not out of or beyond. **2** not transgressing or exceeding. **3** not further off than. —**within one's grasp,** close enough to be grasped or obtained. **within reach** (*or* **sight**) **of,** near enough to be reached (or seen). [OE (as WITH, IN)]

without /wɪˈðaut/ *prep.* **1** not having, not feeling or showing; with freedom from. **2** in the absence of. **3** with neglect or avoidance of. **4** (*archaic*) outside. —*adv.* (*archaic*) outside. [OE (as WITH, OUT)]

withstand /wɪðˈstænd/ *v.t.* (*past* & *p.p.* **-stood** /-ˈstud/) to endure successfully, to resist. [OE (as WITH, STAND)]

withy /ˈwɪðɪ/ *n.* = WITHE.

witless *adj.* foolish, crazy. —**witlessly** *adv.*, **witlessness** *n.* [f. WIT + -LESS]

witness /ˈwɪtnɪs/ *n.* **1** a person giving sworn testimony; a person attesting another's signature to a document. **2** a person present, one who sees or hears what happens. **3** testimony, evidence, confirmation. **4** a person or thing whose existence etc. serves as testimony or proof. —*v.t./i.* **1** to be a witness to the authenticity of (a document or signature). **2** to be a spectator of. **3** to serve as evidence or indication of. **4** to be a witness. —**bear witness to** *or* **of,** to attest the truth of. **call to witness,** to appeal to for confirmation etc. **witness-box** *or* (*US*) **-stand** *n.* an enclosure in a lawcourt from which a witness gives evidence. [OE (as WIT)]

witter *v.i.* (*colloq.*) to speak with annoying lengthiness on trivial matters. [prob. imit.]

witticism /ˈwɪtɪsɪz(ə)m/ *n.* a witty remark. [coined by Dryden f. WITTY]

wittingly /ˈwɪtɪŋlɪ/ *adv.* with knowledge of what one is doing. [f. WIT]

witty /ˈwɪtɪ/ *adj.* showing verbal wit. —**wittily** *adv.*, **wittiness** *n.* [OE (as WIT)]

wives *pl.* of WIFE.

wizard /ˈwɪzəd/ *n.* **1** a magician. **2** a person of extraordinary ability. —**wizardry** *n.* [f. WISE[1]]

wizened /ˈwɪzənd/ *adj.* (of a person or face) full of wrinkles. [p.p. of *wizen* shrivel, f. OE]

WNW *abbr.* west-north-west.

woad *n.* a plant (*Isatis tinctoria*) of the mustard family, yielding a blue dye; the dye itself. [OE]

wobble *v.i.* **1** to rock from side to side; to stand or go unsteadily. **2** (of the voice) to quiver. —*n.* a wobbling movement; a quiver. —**wobbly** *adj.* [cf. LG *wabbeln*, ON *vafla* waver]

wodge *n.* (*colloq.*) a chunk, a lump. [alt. f. WEDGE]

woe *n.* **1** sorrow, distress. **2** (in *pl.*) trouble causing this, misfortune. [OE]

woebegone /ˈwəubɪgɒn/ *adj.* dismal-looking. [f. WOE + obs. *bego* surround (BE-, GO)]

woeful *adj.* **1** full of woe, sad. **2** deplorable. —**woefully** *adv.* [f. WOE + -FUL]

wok *n.* a bowl-shaped frying-pan used especially in Chinese cookery. [Chinese]

woke *past* of WAKE¹.

woken *p.p.* of WAKE¹.

wold /wəʊld/ *n.* a high open uncultivated or moorland tract. [OE, = OHG *wald* forest, ON *völlr* field]

wolf /wʊlf/ *n.* (*pl.* **wolves**) **1** a carnivorous doglike mammal of the genus *Canis* (esp. *Canis lupus*), with coarse tawny-grey fur and erect ears, preying on sheep etc. or combining in packs to hunt larger animals. **2** (*slang*) a man who aggressively seeks to attract women for sexual purposes. —*v.t.* to devour greedily. —**cry wolf,** to raise a false alarm (like the shepherd-boy in the fable, so that eventually a genuine alarm is ignored). **keep the wolf from the door,** to avert starvation. **wolf in sheep's clothing,** a hypocrite. **wolf-whistle** *n.* a whistle by a man sexually admiring a woman. [OE]

wolfhound *n.* a dog of a kind used (originally) to hunt wolves.

wolfram /ˈwʊlfrəm/ *n.* tungsten (ore). [G, perh. f. *wolf* wolf + *rahm* cream, or MHG *rām* dirt, soot]

wolverine /ˈwʊlvəriːn/ *n.* an animal (*Gulo gulo*), also known as the glutton, that is the largest of the weasel family, living in the cold pine forests of the northern continents, especially North America. [orig. *wolvering* f. WOLF]

woman /ˈwʊmən/ *n.* (*pl.* **women** /ˈwɪmɪn/) **1** an adult human female. **2** women in general. **3** feminine emotions. **4** (*attrib.*) female. **5** (*colloq.*) a charwoman. —**Women's Lib,** a movement urging the liberation of women from domestic duties and subservient status. **women's rights,** the right of women to have a position of legal and social equality with men. [OE (as WIFE, MAN)]

-woman *suffix* denoting a woman concerned or skilful with (*needlewoman*) or describable as (*Welshwoman*).

womanhood *n.* **1** female maturity. **2** womanly instinct. **3** womankind. [f. WOMAN + -HOOD]

womanish *adj.* like a woman; (usu. *derog.*) effeminate, unmanly. [f. WOMAN]

womanize *v.i.* to philander, to consort illicitly with women. —**womanizer** *n.* [as prec.]

womankind *n.* (also **womenkind**) women in general.

womanly *adj.* having or showing the qualities befitting a woman. —**womanliness** *n.* [f. WOMAN]

womb /wuːm/ *n.* the hollow organ (in women and other female animals) in which children or young are conceived and nourished while developing before birth, the uterus. [OE]

wombat /ˈwɒmbæt/ *n.* a burrowing herbivorous Australian marsupial, especially of the genus *Phascolomis*, resembling a small bear. [Aboriginal]

women *pl.* of WOMAN.

womenfolk *n.* **1** women in general. **2** the women in a family.

won *past* & *p.p.* of WIN.

wonder /ˈwʌndə(r)/ *n.* **1** a feeling of surprise mingled with admiration, curiosity, or bewilderment. **2** something that arouses this, a marvel, a remarkable thing or event. —*v.t./i.* **1** to feel wonder or surprise. **2** to feel curiosity about; to desire to know; to try to form an opinion about. —**for a wonder,** as a welcome exception. **I wonder!** I very much doubt it. **no** *or* **small wonder,** it is not surprising. **work** *or* **do wonders,** to produce remarkably successful results. [OE]

wonderful /ˈwʌndəf(ə)l/ *adj.* remarkable, surprisingly fine or excellent. —**wonderfully** *adv.* [f. prec. + -FUL]

wonderland *n.* a land or place full of marvels or wonderful things.

wonderment *n.* surprise. [f. WONDER]

wondrous /ˈwʌndrəs/ *adj.* (*poetic*) wonderful. —*adv.* (*poetic*) wonderfully. —**wondrously** *adv.* [f. obs. *wonders* (f. WONDER), after *marvellous*]

wonky *adj.* (*slang*) unsteady; unreliable. [fanciful formation]

wont /wəʊnt/ *predic. adj.* (*archaic*) accustomed. —*n.* (*archaic*) what is customary, one's habit. [OE]

won't /wəʊnt/ (*colloq.*) = will not.

wonted /ˈwəʊntɪd/ *attrib. adj.* habitual, usual. [f. WONT]

woo *v.t.* **1** (*archaic*) to court (a woman). **2** to try to achieve or obtain (fame, fortune, etc.). **3** to seek the favour of; to try to coax or persuade. [OE]

wood /wʊd/ *n.* **1** the hard fibrous substance in the trunks and branches of a tree or shrub; timber or fuel of this. **2** (in *sing.* or *pl.*) growing trees densely occupying a tract of land. **3** a wooden cask for wine etc. **4** a wooden-headed golf-club. **5** a bowl (BOWL²). —**cannot see the wood for the trees,** cannot get a clear view of the main issue because of over-attention to details. **out of the wood,** out of danger or difficulty. **wood-louse** *n.* a small land crustacean of the genus *Oniscus* etc. with many legs, found in old wood etc. **wood-pigeon** *n.* the ring-dove. **wood-pulp** *n.* wood fibres prepared for paper-making. **wood-shed** *n.* a shed where wood for fuel is stored. **wood sorrel,** a plant of the genus *Oxalis* with trifoliate leaves and white or pink flowers. [OE]

woodbine *n.* honeysuckle.

woodchuck *n.* a reddish-brown and grey North American marmot (*Marmota monax*). [f. Amer. Ind. name]

woodcock *n.* a game-bird (*Scolopax rusticola*) related to the snipe.

woodcut *n.* a relief cut on wood; a print made from this.

wooded *adj.* having woods or many trees. [f. WOOD]

wooden /ˈwʊd(ə)n/ *adj.* **1** made of wood. **2** stiff and unnatural in manner, showing no expression or animation. —**wooden horse,** (*Gk legend*) that by use of which Troy was taken. **wooden spoon,** a spoon made of wood, used in cookery or given as a prize to the competitor with the lowest score. —**woodenly** *adv.*, **woodenness** *n.* [f. WOOD]

woodland *n.* wooded country, woods.

woodman *n.* (*pl.* **-men**) a forester.

woodpecker *n.* a bird of the family Picidae that clings to tree-trunks and taps them in search of insects.

woodwind *n.* orchestral wind instruments made (originally) of wood.

woodwork *n.* the making of things in wood; things made of wood.

woodruff *n.* a white-flowered plant (*Galium odoratum*) with fragrant leaves.

woodworm *n.* the larva of a beetle (*Anobium punctatum*) that bores into wooden furniture and fittings.

woody /ˈwʊdɪ/ *adj.* **1** like wood; consisting of wood. **2** wooded. —**woodiness** *n.* [f. WOOD]

woof[1] /wʊf/ *n.* the gruff bark of a dog. —*v.i.* to give a woof. [imit.]

woof[2] /wu:f/ *n.* the weft. [OE (as A[3], WEB)]

woofer /ˈwʊfə(r)/ *n.* a loudspeaker for accurately reproducing low-frequency signals. [f. WOOF[1]]

wool /wʊl/ *n.* **1** the fine soft hair that forms the fleece of sheep and goats etc. **2** yarn made from this; fabric made from such yarn. **3** something resembling wool in texture. —**pull the wool over a person's eyes,** to deceive him. **wool-gathering** *n.* being in a dreamy or absent-minded state. [OE]

woollen /ˈwʊlən/ *adj.* made wholly or partly of wool. —*n.* a woollen fabric; (in *pl.*) woollen garments. [OE (as WOOL)]

woolly /ˈwʊlɪ/ *adj.* **1** covered with wool or wool-like hair. **2** like wool; woollen. **3** not thinking clearly; not clearly expressed or thought out, vague. —*n.* (*colloq.*) a knitted woollen garment; a jumper or cardigan etc. —**woolly-bear** *n.* a hairy caterpillar, especially of the tiger-moth. —**woolliness** *n.* [f. WOOL]

Woolsack *n.* the usual seat, without back or arms, of the Lord Chancellor in the House of Lords, made of a large square bag of wool and covered with cloth.

word /wɜ:d/ *n.* **1** any sound or combination of sounds (or its written or printed symbol, usually shown with a space on either side of it but none within it) forming a meaningful element of speech, conveying an idea or alternative ideas, and capable of serving as a member of, the whole of, or a substitute for a sentence; a unit of expression in a computer. **2** speech, especially as distinct from action. **3** one's promise or assurance. **4** (in *sing.* or *pl.*) a thing said, a remark; a conversation. **5** (in *pl.*) the text of a song or of an actor's part. **6** (in *pl.*) angry talk. **7** news; a message. **8** a command; a password; a motto. —*v.t.* to put into words, to select words to express. —**in a** *or* **one word,** briefly. **in other words,** expressing the same thing differently. **in so many words,** explicitly, bluntly. **take a person's word for it,** to believe his statement without investigation etc. **take a person at his word,** to act on the assumption that he meant exactly what he said. **(upon) my word,** an exclamation of surprise or consternation. **word for word,** in exactly the same or (of a translation) corresponding words. **word-game** *n.* a game involving the making, selection, or guessing etc. of words. **the Word (of God),** the Bible or a part of it; the title of the Second Person of the Trinity, = LOGOS. **word of honour,** an assurance given upon one's honour. **word of mouth,** speech (only). **word-perfect** *adj.* knowing one's part etc. by heart. **word processor,** a device for storing text entered from a keyboard, incorporating corrections, and providing a printout. [OE]

wording /ˈwɜ:dɪŋ/ *n.* the form of words used. [f. WORD]

wordless *adj.* without words, not expressed in words. —**wordlessly** *adv.* [f. WORD + -LESS]

wordy /ˈwɜ:dɪ/ *adj.* using many or too many words. —**wordily** *adv.*, **wordiness** *n.* [f. WORD]

wore *past* of WEAR.

work /wɜ:k/ *n.* **1** the application of mental or physical effort in order to do or make something, especially as contrasted with play or recreation; use of energy. **2** (in physics) the exertion of force overcoming resistance or producing molecular change. **3** something to be undertaken; the materials for this. **4** a thing done or produced by work; the result of action; a piece of literary or musical composition. **5** doings or experiences of a specified kind. **6** employment or occupation, what a person does to earn a living. **7** things or parts made of specified material or with specified tools; ornamentation of a specified kind. **8** (in *pl.*) operations in building etc. **9** (in *pl.*) the operative parts of a clock or machine; (*slang*) all that is available. **10** (in *pl.*, often treated as *sing.*) a place where industrial or manufacturing processes are carried out. **11** (usu. in *pl.* or *comb.*) a defensive structure (*earthwork*). —*v.t./i.* **1** to perform work, to be engaged in bodily or mental activity. **2** to make efforts. **3** to be employed, to have a job. **4** to operate or function; to do this effectively. **5** to carry on, to manage, to control. **6** to put or keep in operation so as to obtain material or benefit etc.; to cause to work or function. **7** to bring about, to accomplish. **8** to shape, knead, or hammer etc. into the desired shape or consistency. **9** to do or make by needlework, fretwork, etc. **10** to make (a way) or cause to pass gradually or by effort; to become (loose etc.) through repeated stress, movement, or pressure. **11** to excite artificially. **12** to solve (a sum) by mathematics. **13** to purchase with one's labour instead of with money. **14** to be in motion or agitated; to ferment; to have an influence. —**at work,** in action; engaged in work. **give a person the works,** to give or tell him everything; to treat him harshly. **have one's work cut out,** to be faced with a hard task. **make short work of,** to accomplish or dispose of quickly. **work-basket** *n.* a basket containing sewing materials. **work-force** *n.* the workers engaged or available; the number of these. **work in,** to find a place for in a composition or structure. **work-load** *n.* the amount of work to be done. **work of art,** a fine picture, poem, building, etc. **work off,** to get rid of by work or activity. **work out,** to solve (a sum) or find (an amount) by calculation; to be calculated; to have a result; to provide for all the details of; to attain with difficulty; to exhaust with work. **work-out** *n.* a practice or test, especially in boxing. **work over,** to examine thoroughly; (*colloq.*) to treat with violence. **work-room** *n.* a room in which work is done. **work-shy** *adj.* disinclined to work. **work study,** a system of assessing jobs so as to get the best results for employees and employers. **work to rule,** to follow the rules of one's occupation with excessive strictness so as to reduce efficiency, usually as a protest. **work-to-rule** *n.* this process. **work up,** to bring gradually to an efficient state; to advance gradually (to a climax); to elaborate or excite by degrees; to mingle (ingredients); to learn (a subject) by study. [OE]

workable /ˈwɜːkəb(ə)l/ *adj.* that may be worked, used, or acted upon successfully. [f. WORK]

workaday *adj.* ordinary, everyday, practical.

workaholic /wɜːkəˈhɒlɪk/ *n.* (*colloq.*) a person who is addicted to working. [f. WORK, after *alcoholic*]

workday *n.* a day on which work is regularly done.

worker /ˈwɜːkə(r)/ *n.* **1** a person who works; one who works well or in a specified way. **2** a neuter or undeveloped bee or ant etc. that does the work of the hive or colony but cannot reproduce. **3** a member of the working class. [f. WORK]

workhouse *n.* (*hist.*) a public institution where people unable to support themselves were housed and (if able-bodied) made to work.

working /ˈwɜːkɪŋ/ *adj.* **1** engaged in work, especially in manual or industrial labour; working-class. **2** functioning, able to function. —*n.* **1** the activity of work. **2** functioning. **3** a mine or quarry etc.; a part of this in which work is or has been carried on. —**working capital,** capital actually used in a business. **working class,** the class of people who are employed for wages, especially in manual or industrial work. **working day,** a workday; the part of the day devoted to work. **working knowledge,** knowledge adequate to work with. **working order,** the condition in which a machine works satisfactorily. **working party,** a group of people appointed to advise on some question. [f. WORK]

workman *n.* (*pl.* **-men**) **1** a man employed to do manual labour. **2** a person in respect of his skill in a job.

workmanlike *adj.* showing practised skill.

workmanship *n.* degree of skill in doing a task or of finish in a product made. [f. WORKMAN + -SHIP]

workmate *n.* one engaged in the same work as another.

workpeople *n.pl.* people employed in labour for wages.

workpiece *n.* a thing worked on with a tool or machine.

worksheet *n.* **1** a paper for recording work done or in progress. **2** a paper listing questions or activities for students etc. to work through.

workshop *n.* **1** a room or building in which manual work or manufacture is done. **2** a place for concerted activity; such activity.

world /wɜːld/ *n.* **1** the earth, or a heavenly body like it. **2** the universe, all that exists. **3** the time, state, or scene of human existence. **4** secular interests and affairs. **5** human affairs; the active life. **6** average or respectable people; their customs or opinions. **7** all that concerns or all who belong to a specified class or sphere of activity. **8** a vast amount. **9** (*attrib.*) affecting many nations; of all nations. —**bring** (*or* **come**) **into the world,** to give birth to (or be born). **in the world,** of all or at all. **man** *or* **woman of the world,** a person experienced and practical in human affairs. **out of this world,** (*colloq.*) extremely good etc. **think the world of,** to have a very high regard for. **world-beater** *n.* a person or thing surpassing all others. **world-famous** *adj.* known throughout the world. **world war,** a war involving many important nations (*First World War* 1914-18, *Second World War* 1939-45). **world-wide** *adj.* covering or known in all parts of the world. [OE]

worldly /ˈwɜːldlɪ/ *adj.* **1** of or belonging to life on earth, not spiritual. **2** engrossed in worldly affairs, especially the pursuit of pleasure or material gains. —**worldly-wise** *adj.* prudent in dealing with worldly affairs. —**worldliness** *n.* [OE (as prec.)]

worm /wɜːm/ *n.* **1** any of many types of invertebrate slender burrowing or creeping animal; the wormlike larva of an insect, especially one feeding on fruit or wood etc.; (in *pl.*) internal (intestinal) parasites. **2** an insignificant or contemptible person. **3** the spiral part of a screw. —*v.t./i.* **1** to move with a twisting movement like a worm; to make (one's way) by wriggling or with slow or patient progress. **2** to obtain (a secret) by crafty persistence. **3** to rid of parasitic worms. **4** (*Naut.*) to make (a rope etc.) smooth by winding thread between the strands. —**worm-cast** *n.* a convoluted pile of earth sent up by an earthworm on to the surface of the ground. **worm-eaten** *adj.* full of worm-holes. **worm-hole** *n.* a hole left in fruit or wood etc. by the passage of a worm. **worm's-eye view,** a view from below or from a humble position. [OE]

wormwood /ˈwɜːmwʊd/ *n.* **1** a plant (*Artemisia abrotanum*) with a bitter aromatic taste. **2** bitter mortification; the source of this. [alt. f. obs. *wormod* f. OE (ult. orig. unkn.); cf. VERMOUTH]

wormy /ˈwɜːmɪ/ *adj.* full of worms; worm-eaten. —**worminess** *n.* [f. WORM]

worn *p.p.* of WEAR. —*adj.* **1** damaged by use or wear. **2** looking tired and exhausted. —**worn-out** *adj.* [f. WEAR]

worrisome /ˈwʌrɪsəm/ *adj.* causing worry. [f. foll. + -SOME]

worry /ˈwʌrɪ/ *v.t./i.* **1** to give way to anxiety. **2** to harass, to importune; to be a trouble or anxiety to. **3** (of a dog etc.) to shake or pull about with the teeth. **4** (in *p.p.*) feeling or showing worry, uneasy. —*n.* **1** a state of worrying, mental uneasiness. **2** a thing that causes this. —**worry beads,** a string of beads manipulated by the fingers to occupy or calm oneself. **worry out,** to obtain (a solution to a problem etc.) by persistent effort. —**worrier** *n.* [OE, = strangle]

worse /wɜːs/ *adj.* **1** more bad. **2** (*predic.*) in or into worse health; in a worse condition. —*adv.* more badly or ill. —*n.* a worse thing or things. —**from bad to worse,** into an even worse state. **the worse,** a worse condition. **the worse for wear,** damaged by use; injured or exhausted. **worse luck,** see LUCK. [OE]

worsen /ˈwɜːs(ə)n/ *v.t./i.* to make or become worse. [f. prec.]

worship /ˈwɜːʃɪp/ *n.* **1** homage or service paid to a deity. **2** the acts, rites, or ceremonies of this. **3** adoration of or devotion to a person or thing. —*v.t./i.* **(-pp-) 1** to honour as a deity, to pay worship to. **2** to take part in an act of worship. **3** to idolize, to regard with adoration. —**Your** (*or* **His** etc.) **Worship,** the title of respect used to or of a mayor or certain magistrates. —**worshipper** *n.* [OE (as WORTH, -SHIP)]

worshipful /ˈwɜːʃɪpf(ə)l/ *adj.* (*archaic*, esp. in old titles of companies or officers) honourable, distinguished. —**worshipfully** *adv.* [f. prec. + -FUL]

worst /wɜːst/ *adj.* most bad. —*adv.* most badly. —*n.* the worst part or possibility. —*v.t.* to get the better of, to defeat. —**at its** etc. **worst,** in the worst state. **at (the) worst,** in the worst possible case. **do your worst,** an expression of defiance. **get the worst of it,** to be defeated. **if the worst comes to the worst,** if the worst happens. [OE (as WORSE)]

worsted /ˈwʊstɪd/ *n.* fine smooth yarn spun from long strands of wool which has been combed so that the fibres lie parallel; fabric made from this. [f. *Worste(a)d* in Norfolk]

wort /wɜːt/ *n.* **1** (*archaic* exc. in names) a plant (*liverwort*). **2** an infusion of malt before it is fermented into beer. —**St John's wort,** a plant of the genus *Hypericum*, with yellow flowers. [f. OE, rel. to ROOT]

worth /wɜːθ/ *predic. adj.* (governing a noun like a *prep.*) **1** of a value equivalent to. **2** such as to justify or repay. **3** possessing, having property amounting to. —*n.* **1** what a person or thing is worth; (high) merit; usefulness. **2** the amount that a specified sum will buy. —**for all one is worth,** (*colloq.*) making every effort. **for what it is worth,** with no guarantee of its truth or value. **worth one's salt,** having merit. **worth (one's) while,** see WHILE. [OE]

worthless *adj.* without value or merit. —**worthlessly** *adv.*, **worthlessness** *n.* [f. prec. + -LESS]

worthwhile /wɜːθˈwaɪl/ *adj.* that is worth the time or effort spent.

worthy /ˈwɜːðɪ/ *adj.* **1** having great merit, deserving respect or support. **2** having sufficient worth or merit, deserving (of); adequate or suitable to the dignity etc. (of a specified person or thing). **3** (as *suffix* forming adjectives) deserving of, suitable for (*noteworthy*, *seaworthy*). —*n.* a worthy person; a person of some distinction in his country, time, etc. —**worthily** *adv.*, **worthiness** *n.* [f. WORTH]

wot see WIT.

would /wəd, *emphat.* wʊd/ *v. aux.* (3 *sing.* **would**) past tense of WILL, used especially in reported speech or to express a habitual action or a condition, question, polite request, or probability. —**would-be** *adj.* desiring or aspiring to be. [as WILL]

wouldn't /ˈwʊd(ə)nt/ (*colloq.*) = would not.

wound[1] /wu:nd/ *n.* **1** an injury done to living tissue by a cut or blow etc. **2** an injury to a person's reputation or feelings. —*v.t.* to inflict a wound on. [OE]

wound[2] *past* & *p.p.* of WIND[2].

wove *past* of WEAVE[1].

woven *p.p.* of WEAVE[1].

wow[1] *int.* expressing astonishment or admiration. —*n.* (*slang*) a sensational success. [imit.]

wow[2] *n.* a slow pitch-fluctuation in sound-reproduction, perceptible in long notes. [imit.]

w.p.b. *abbr.* waste-paper basket.

WPC *abbr.* woman police constable.

w.p.m. *abbr.* words per minute.

WRAC *abbr.* Women's Royal Army Corps.

wrack *n.* **1** seaweed cast up or growing on the shore, used for manure. **2** destruction. [f. MDu. or MLG; cf. WRECK, RACK[4]]

WRAF *abbr.* Women's Royal Air Force.

wraith *n.* a ghost; a spectral appearance of a living person supposed to portend his death. [orig. unkn.]

wrangle *n.* a noisy angry argument or quarrel. —*v.i.* to engage in a wrangle. —**wrangler** *n.* [prob. f. LDu.; cf. LG *wrangelen* frequent. of *wrangen* to struggle]

wrap *v.t./i.* (**-pp-**) **1** to enclose in soft or flexible material used as a covering. **2** to arrange (such a covering or a garment etc.) round a person or thing. —*n.* a shawl, coat, or cloak etc. worn for warmth. —**under wraps,** in concealment or secrecy. **wrap over,** (of a garment) to overlap at the edges when worn. **wrapped up in,** with one's attention deeply occupied by; deeply involved in. **wrap up,** to envelop in wrappings; to put on warm clothing; (*slang*) to finish, to cease talking. [orig. unkn.]

wrapper *n.* **1** a cover of paper etc. wrapped round something. **2** a loose enveloping robe or gown. [f. WRAP]

wrapping *n.* (esp. in *pl.*) wraps, wrappers, enveloping garments. —**wrapping paper** strong or decorative paper for wrapping parcels. [f. WRAP]

wrasse /ræs/ *n.* a bright-coloured sea-fish of the family Labridae with thick lips and strong teeth. [f. Cornish *wrach* mutated rel. to Welsh *gwrach* (lit. 'old woman')]

wrath /rɒθ, rɔ:θ/ *n.* extreme anger. [OE (as WROTH)]

wrathful *adj.* extremely angry. —**wrathfully** *adv.* [f. prec. + -FUL]

wreak *v.t.* to give play to (vengeance, anger, etc.) upon an enemy etc.; to inflict (damage etc.). [OE, = drive, avenge]

wreath *n.* (*pl.* /ri:θs, ri:ðz/) **1** flowers or leaves fastened in a ring especially as an ornament for the head or a building or for laying on a grave etc. as a mark of respect. **2** a curl or ring of smoke, cloud, or soft fabric. [OE (as WRITHE)]

wreathe /ri:ð/ *v.t./i.* **1** to encircle as, with, or like a wreath. **2** to wind (one's arms etc.) round a person etc. **3** (of smoke etc.) to move in wreaths. [partly back-formation f. earlier *wrethen* writhe, partly f. prec.]

wreck *n.* **1** destruction or disablement, especially of a ship by storm or accidental damage. **2** a ship that has suffered wreck. **3** a greatly damaged or disabled building, thing, or person; a wretched remnant. —*v.t./i.* **1** to cause the wreck of (a ship, hopes, etc.). **2** to suffer wreck; (in *p.p.*) involved in a wreck. [f. AF *wrec* etc.; cf. WREAK]

wreckage *n.* wrecked material; the remnants of a wreck. [f. prec.]

wrecker *n.* **1** one who wrecks something, one who tries from the shore to bring about a shipwreck in order to plunder or profit by wreckage. **2** a person employed in demolition work. [f. WRECK]

wren *n.* a small short-winged usually brown songbird of the family Troglodytidae, with a short erect tail. [OE]

wrench *n.* **1** a violent twist or oblique pull. **2** an adjustable tool like a spanner for gripping and turning nuts, bolts, etc. **3** a painful parting. —*v.t.* **1** to twist or pull violently round; to damage or pull (away etc.) thus. **2** to distort (facts) to suit a theory etc. [f. OE, = twist]

wrest *v.t.* **1** to wrench away. **2** to obtain by effort or with difficulty. **3** to distort into accordance with one's own views or interests etc. [OE, rel. to WRIST]

wrestle /ˈres(ə)l/ *v.t./i.* **1** to fight (especially as a sport) by grappling with a person and trying to throw him to the ground; to fight with (a person) thus. **2** (with *with*) to struggle to deal with or overcome. —*n.* **1** a wrestling-match. **2** a hard struggle. —**wrestler** *n.* [OE].

wretch *n.* **1** an unfortunate or pitiable person. **2** a despicable person; (in playful use) a rascal. [OE, = OHG *reccho* exile, adventurer]

wretched /ˈretʃɪd/ *adj.* **1** unhappy, miserable. **2** of bad quality or no merit, contemptible. **3** unsatisfactory, displeasing. —**wretchedly** *adv.*, **wretchedness** *n.* [f. prec.]

wriggle *v.t./i.* to move with short twisting movements; to make (one's way) thus. —*n.* a wriggling movement. —**wriggle out of,** to avoid on some pretext. —**wriggly** *adj.* [f. MLG]

wright /raɪt/ *n.* (*archaic* exc. in *comb.*) a maker or builder (*playwright, wheelwright*). [OE (as WORK)]

wring *v.t.* (*past* & *p.p.* **wrung**) **1** to twist and squeeze in order to remove liquid; to remove (liquid) thus. **2** to squeeze firmly or forcibly; to clasp (one's hands) together emotionally. **3** to extract or obtain (a promise etc.) with effort or difficulty. —*n.* a wringing movement; a squeeze or twist. —**wringing wet,** so wet that water can be wrung out. **wring the neck of,** to kill (a chicken etc.) by twisting its head round. [OE, rel. to WRONG]

wringer *n.* a device with a pair of rollers between which washed clothes etc. are passed so that water is squeezed out. [f. prec.]

wrinkle *n.* **1** a small crease; a small furrow or ridge in the skin such as is produced by age. **2** (*colloq.*) a useful hint about how to do something. —*v.t./i.* to make wrinkles in; to form wrinkles. —**wrinkly** *adj.* [f. OE, = sinuous]

wrist *n.* **1** the joint connecting the hand with the arm. **2** the part of a garment covering this. **3** (also **wrist-work**) working the hand without moving the arm. —**wrist-watch** *n.* a small watch worn on a strap etc. round the wrist. [OE, = ON *rist* instep]

wristlet *n.* a band or bracelet etc. worn round the wrist. [f. prec. + -LESS]

writ[1] *n.* a form of written command to act or not act in some way. [OE (as WRITE)]

writ[2] *archaic p.p.* of WRITE. —**writ large,** in a magnified or emphasized form. [f. foll.]

write /raɪt/ *v.t./i.* (*past* **wrote**; *p.p.* **written**) **1** to mark letters or other symbols or words on a surface, especially with a pen or pencil on paper. **2** to form (such symbols etc. or a message) thus; to fill or complete (a sheet or cheque etc.) with writing. **3** to put (data) into a computer store. **4** to compose for written or printed reproduction or publication; to be engaged in such literary composition. **5** to write and send a letter; (*US* or *colloq.*) to write and send a letter to (a person); to convey (news etc.) by letter. **6** to state in a book etc. —**write down,** to record in writing; to write as if for inferiors, to disparage in writing; to reduce the nominal value of. **write off,** to write and send a letter; to cancel the record of (a bad debt, sum absorbed by depreciation, etc.); to ignore (a person) as now of no account. **write-off** *n.* a thing written off; a vehicle too badly damaged to be worth repairing. **write out,** to write in full or in a finished form. **write up,** to write a full account of; to praise in writing. **write-up** *n.* a written or published account, a review. [OE, = scratch, score, write; orig. of symbols inscribed with sharp tools on stone or wood]

writer *n.* one who writes or has written something; one who writes books, an author. —**writer's cramp,** a muscular spasm caused by excessive writing. [f. prec.]

writhe /raɪð/ *v.i.* **1** to twist or roll oneself about (as) in acute pain; to suffer. **2** to suffer because of great shame or embarrassment. [OE]

writing /ˈraɪtɪŋ/ *n.* **1** the process of marking letters or other symbols or words on a surface. **2** written symbols or words; a written document; (in *pl.*) an author's works; **the Writings,** the Jewish name for the parts of the Old Testament other than the Law and the Prophets. —**in writing,** in written form. **writing on the wall,** an ominous event or sign that something is doomed (with allusion to the Biblical story of the writing that appeared on the wall at Belshazzar's feast (Dan. 5: 5, 25–8), foretelling his doom). **writing-paper** *n.* paper for writing (especially letters) on. [f. WRITE]

written *p.p.* of WRITE.

WRNS *abbr.* Women's Royal Naval Service.

wrong *adj.* **1** (of conduct etc.) morally bad, contrary to justice, equity, or duty. **2** incorrect, not true; less or least desirable; (of a side of a fabric) not meant for show or use. **3** not in a normal condition, not functioning normally. —*adv.* in a wrong manner or direction; with an incorrect result. —*n.* what is morally wrong; a wrong or unjust action or treatment. —*v.t.* **1** to do wrong to, to treat unjustly. **2** to attribute bad motives to (a person) mistakenly. —**get (hold of) the wrong end of the stick,** to misunderstand completely. **get a person wrong,** to misunderstand him or her. **go wrong,** to take the wrong path; to stop functioning properly; to cease virtuous behaviour. **in the wrong,** not having justice or truth on one's side. **on the wrong side of,** out of favour with or not liked by (a person); somewhat more than (a stated age). **wrong-foot** *v.t.* to catch (a person) unprepared. **wrong-headed** *adj.* perverse and obstinate. **wrong 'un,** (*colloq.*) a person of bad character. —**wrongly** *adv.*, **wrongness** *n.* [OE]

wrongdoer *n.* a person guilty of a breach of law or morality. —**wrongdoing** *n.*

wrongful *adj.* contrary to what is fair, just, or legal. —**wrongfully** *adv.* [f. WRONG + -FUL]

wrote *past* of WRITE.

wroth /rəʊθ, rɒθ/ *predic. adj.* (*literary*) angry. [OE]

wrought /rɔːt/ *archaic past & p.p.* of WORK. —*adj.* (of metals) beaten out or shaped by hammering. —**wrought iron,** see IRON. [as WORK]

wrung *past & p.p.* of WRING.

WRVS *abbr.* Women's Royal Voluntary Service.

wry /raɪ/ *adj.* (*compar.* **wryer**; *superl.* **wryest**) **1** distorted, turned to one side. **2** (of a face, smile, etc.) contorted in disgust, disappointment, or mockery. **3** (of humour) dry and mocking. —**wryly** *adv.*, **wryness** *n.* [f. *wry* v. f. OE, = tend, incline (later = deviate, contort)]

wryneck *n.* a small bird of the genus *Jynx*, able to turn its head over its shoulder.

WSW *abbr.* west-south-west.

wt. *abbr.* weight.

wych- *prefix* in names of trees with pliant branches (*wych-alder*, *-elm*). —**wych-hazel** *n.* an American shrub of the genus *Hamamelis* whose bark yields an astringent lotion; this lotion. [OE, = bending (rel. to WEAK)]

wyvern /ˈwaɪvən/ *n.* (in heraldry) a winged two-legged dragon with a barbed tail. [f. OF f. L *vipera* viper]

X, x /eks/ *n.* (*pl.* **Xs, X's**) **1** the twenty-fourth letter of the alphabet. **2** (as a Roman numeral) 10. **3** (in algebra) **x,** the first unknown quantity. **4** a cross-shaped symbol, especially used to indicate a position or incorrectness or to symbolize a kiss or vote, or as the signature of a person who cannot write.

Xe *symbol* xenon.

xenon /ˈzenɒn/ *n.* a colourless odourless element of the noble gas group, symbol Xe, atomic number 54. [Gk, neut. of *xenos* strange]

xenophobia /zenəˈfəʊbɪə/ *n.* strong dislike or distrust of foreigners. —**xenophobic** *adj.* [f. Gk *xenos* foreigner + -PHOBIA]

xerography /zɪəˈrɒgrəfɪ, zeˈr-/ *n.* a dry copying process in which powder adheres to areas remaining electrically charged after exposure of the surface to light from the image of the document to be copied. [f. Gk *xēros* dry + -GRAPHY]

Xerox /ˈzɪərɒks, ˈzer-/ *n.* [P] a certain process of xerography; a copy made by this. —**xerox** *v.t.* to reproduce by a process of this kind. [f. prec.]

xi /ksaɪ, gzaɪ, zaɪ/ *n.* the fourteenth letter of the Greek alphabet, = x. [Gk]

Xmas /ˈkrɪsməs/ *n.* = CHRISTMAS. [abbr., with X for initial chi of Gk *Khristos* Christ]

X-ray /ˈeksreɪ/ *n.* **1** (in *pl.*) electromagnetic radiation of short wavelength, able to pass through opaque bodies. **2** a photograph made by X-rays, especially one showing the position of bones etc. by their greater absorption of the rays. —*v.t.* to photograph, examine, or treat with X-rays. [transl. of G *X-strahlen*, so called from their unknown nature]

xylem /ˈzaɪləm/ *n.* woody tissue (opp. PHLOEM) in the stem of a plant, that carries water and dissolved minerals upwards from the ground. [f. Gk *xulon* wood]

xylophone /ˈzaɪləfəʊn/ *n.* a musical instrument of graduated wooden bars with tubular resonators suspended vertically beneath them, struck with small wooden etc. hammers. —**xylophonist** /-ˈlɒfənɪst/ *n.* [f. Gk *xulon* wood + -PHONE]

Yy

Y, y /waɪ/ *n.* (*pl.* **Ys, Y's**) **1** the twenty-fifth letter of the alphabet. **2** (in algebra) **y**, the second unknown quantity. **3** a Y-shaped thing.

Y *symbol* yttrium.

yacht /jɒt/ *n.* **1** a light sailing-vessel kept, and usually specially built and rigged, for racing; a similar vessel for use on sand or ice. **2** a vessel propelled by sails, steam, electricity, or motive power other than oars, and used for private pleasure excursions, cruising, travel, etc. [f. Du. *jachte* = *jaghtship* fast pirate-ship (*jagen* to hunt)]

yachting /ˈjɒtɪŋ/ *n.* racing or cruising in a yacht. [f. prec.]

yachtsman *n.* (*pl.* **-men**) a person who goes yachting.

yah *int.* expressing derision or defiance. [imit.]

yahoo /jəˈhuː/ *n.* a bestial person. [name of race of brutes in Swift's *Gulliver's Travels*]

yak *n.* a long-haired Tibetan ox (*Bos grunniens*), wild or domesticated. [f. Tibetan *gyag*]

Yale *n.* [P] (in full **Yale lock**) a type of lock for doors etc., with a revolving barrel. [f. L. *Yale*, Amer. inventor (d. 1868)]

yam *n.* **1** a tropical or subtropical climbing plant of the genus *Dioscorea*; its edible starchy tuber. **2** the sweet potato. [f. Port. or Sp. *iñame* (orig. unkn.)]

yammer *n.* (*colloq.* or *dial.*) a lament, a wail, a grumble; voluble talk. —*v.i.* (*colloq.* or *dial.*) to utter a yammer. [OE (*geōmor* sorrowful)]

yang *n.* (in Chinese philosophy) the active principle of the universe, characterized as heaven, male, light, and penetrating (complemented by YIN). [Chinese]

Yank *n.* (*colloq.*) a Yankee. [abbr.]

yank *v.t.* (*colloq.*) to pull with a jerk. —*n.* (*colloq.*) such a pull. [orig. unkn.]

Yankee /ˈjæŋkɪ/ *n.* **1** (*colloq.*) an American. **2** (*US*) an inhabitant of New England; an inhabitant of the northern States, a Federal soldier in the Civil War. **3** a type of bet on four or more horses to win (or be placed) in different races. [perh. f. Du. *Janke* dim. of *Jan* John used derisively; or perh. f. *Jengees*, Amer. Ind. pronunc. of *English*]

yap *v.i.* (**-pp-**) **1** to bark shrilly or fussily. **2** (*colloq.*) to chatter. —*n.* a sound of yapping. [imit.]

yapp *n.* a bookbinding with a projecting limp leather cover. [name of London bookseller *c.*1860, for whom it was first made]

yarborough /ˈjɑːbərə/ *n.* a whist or bridge hand with no card above a 9. [f. Earl of *Yarborough* (d. 1897), said to have betted against its occurrence]

yard[1] *n.* **1** a unit of linear measure, = 3 ft. or 36 inches (0.9144 metre); this length of material; a square or cubic yard. **2** a spar slung across a mast for a sail to hang from. —**yard-arm** *n.* a ship's yard; either end of this. [OE, = OS *gerdia* twig]

yard[2] *n.* **1** a piece of enclosed ground, especially one attached to a building or used for a particular purpose. **2** (*US*) the garden of a house. [OE (as GARTH, GARDEN)]

yardage *n.* the number of yards of material etc. [f. YARD[1]]

yardstick *n.* **1** a rod a yard long, usually divided into inches etc. **2** a standard of comparison.

yarmulka /ˈjɑːmʌlkə/ *n.* a skull-cap worn by Jewish men. [Yiddish]

yarn *n.* **1** spun thread, esp. of the kinds prepared for knitting or weaving etc. **2** (*colloq.*) a tale, esp. one that is exaggerated or invented. —*v.i.* (*colloq.*) to tell yarns. [OE]

yarrow /ˈjærəʊ/ *n.* a perennial herb of the genus *Achillea*, especially milfoil (*A. millefolium*). [OE]

yashmak /ˈjæʃmæk/ *n.* a veil concealing the face except the eyes, worn in public by Muslim women in certain countries. [f. Arab.]

yaw *v.i.* **1** (of a ship or aircraft etc.) to fail to hold a straight course, to go unsteadily, esp. turning from side to side. **2** a yawing course or movement. [orig. unkn.]

yawl *n.* **1** a two-masted fore-and-aft sailing-boat with the mizen-mast stepped far aft. **2** a kind of small fishing-boat. [f. MLG or Du. *jol* (orig. unkn.); cf. *jolly-boat*]

yawn *v.i.* **1** to open the mouth wide and inhale, especially in sleepiness or boredom. **2** to have a wide opening, to form a chasm. —*n.* the act of yawning. [OE]

yaws /jɔːz/ *n.pl.* (usu. treated as *sing.*) a contagious tropical skin-disease with raspberry-like swellings. [orig. unkn.]

Yb *symbol* ytterbium.

yd(s). *abbr.* yard(s).

ye[1] /jɪ, jiː/ *pron.* (*archaic*) *pl.* of THOU.

ye[2] /jiː, or as THE/ *adj.* (*pseudo-archaic*) = THE (*ye olde tea-shoppe*). [f. old use of obs. y-shaped letter for *th*]

yea /jeɪ/ *adv.* (*archaic*) yes. —*n.* the word 'yea'. —**yeas and nays,** affirmative and negative votes. [OE]

yeah /jeə/ *adv.* (*colloq.*) yes. [casual pronunc. of YES]

year /jɪə(r), jɜː(r)/ *n.* **1** the time occupied by the earth in one revolution round the sun, approximately 365¼ days. **2** the period from 1 Jan. to 31 Dec. inclusive. **3** a period of the same length as this starting at any point. **4** (in *pl.*) age, time of life. **5** (usu. in *pl.*) a very long time. **6** a group of students entering a college etc. in the same academic year. —**year-book** *n.* an annual publication containing current information about a specified subject. [OE]

yearling /ˈyɜːlɪŋ/ *n.* an animal between one and two years old. [f. YEAR]

yearly /ˈyɜːlɪ/ *adj.* **1** done, produced, or occurring etc. every year. **2** of, for, or lasting a year. —*adv.* once every year. [OE (as YEAR)]

yearn /jɜːn/ *v.i.* to be filled with great longing. [OE]

yeast *n.* a greyish-yellow fungous substance that causes alcohol and carbon dioxide to be produced when it is developing, used to cause fermentation in making beer and wines and as a raising agent in baking. —**yeast cake,** one in which the raising agent used is yeast. [OE]

yeasty *adj.* frothy like yeast when it is developing. —**yeastiness** *n.* [f. prec.]

yell *n.* a loud sharp cry of pain, anger, fright, encouragement, delight, etc.; a shout. —*v.t./i.* to make or utter with a yell. [OE]

yellow /ˈjeləʊ/ *adj.* **1** of the colour of buttercups and ripe lemons, or a colour approaching this. **2** having a yellow skin or complexion. **3** (*colloq.*) cowardly. —*n.* **1** yellow colour or pigment. **2** yellow clothes or material. —*v.t./i.* to turn yellow. —**yellow card,** such a card shown by the referee at a football match to a player whom he is cautioning. **yellow fever,** a tropical disease with fever and jaundice. **yellow flag,** that displayed by a ship in quarantine. **yellow pages,** a section of a telephone directory, printed on yellow paper, listing business subscribers according to the goods or services they offer. —**yellowish** *adj.*, **yellowness** *n.* [OE (rel. to GOLD)]

yellowhammer *n.* a bunting (*Emberiza citrinella*), the male of which has a yellow head, neck, and breast.

yelp *n.* a sharp shrill cry or bark. —*v.i.* to utter a yelp. [OE, = boast (imit.)]

yen[1] *n.* (*pl.* same) the Japanese monetary unit. [Jap. f. Chin. *yuan* round, dollar]

yen[2] *n.* a longing or yearning. —*v.i.* (**-nn-**) to feel a longing. [Chin. dial.]

yeoman /ˈjəʊmən/ *n.* (*pl.* **-men**) **1** a man holding and cultivating a small landed estate. **2** a member of a yeomanry force. —**Yeoman of the Guard,** a member of the British sovereign's bodyguard, first established by Henry VII, commonly known as beefeaters. **yeoman('s) service,** efficient or useful help in need. —**yeomanly** *adj.* [prob. f. YOUNG + MAN]

yeomanry /ˈjəʊmənrɪ/ *n.* **1** a body of yeomen. **2** (*hist.*) a volunteer cavalry force raised from the yeoman class. [f. prec.]

yes *adv.* **1** serving to indicate that the answer to the question is affirmative, the statement etc. made is correct, the request or command will be complied with, or the person summoned or addressed is present. **2** (*interrog.*) indeed?; is that so?; what do you want? —*n.* the word or answer 'yes'. —**yes-man** *n.* (*colloq.*) a weakly acquiescent person. [OE, prob. = yea let it be]

yester- *in comb.* (*literary*) of yesterday, that is last past (*yester-eve*, *yestermorn*). —**yester-year** *n.* last year; the recent past. [OE]

yesterday /ˈjestədeɪ, -dɪ/ *adv.* on the day before today; in the recent past. —*n.* the day before today; the recent past. [OE (as prec. + DAY)]

yet *adv.* **1** up to this or that time and continuing, still. **2** (with neg. or interrog.) by this or that time, so far. **3** besides, in addition. **4** before the matter is done with, eventually. **5** (with compar.) even. **6** nevertheless. —*conj.* nevertheless, but in spite of that. [OE]

yeti /ˈjetɪ/ *n.* the Abominable Snowman (see ABOMINABLE). [Tibetan]

yett *n.* (*Sc.*) a type of gate or portcullis with interlocking bands. [= GATE]

yew *n.* a dark-leaved evergreen coniferous tree (*Taxus baccata*) with needle-like leaves and red berries; its wood, used formerly as material for bows and still in cabinet-making. [OE]

Yiddish /ˈjɪdɪʃ/ *n.* a language used by Jews of or from central Europe. of this language. [f. G *jüdisch* Jewish]

yield *v.t./i.* **1** to give or return as fruit or as gain or result. **2** to surrender; to do what is requested or ordered. **3** to be inferior, to confess inferiority. **4** (of traffic) to give the right of way to other traffic. **5** to be able to be forced out of the natural or usual shape, e.g.

under pressure. —*n.* the amount yielded or produced. [OE, = pay]

yin *n.* (in Chinese philosophy) the passive principle of the universe, characterized as earth, female, dark, and absorbing (complemented by YANG). [Chinese]

yippee /'jɪpɪ/ *int.* expressing delight or excitement. [cf. HIP[3]]

YMCA *abbr.* Young Men's Christian Association.

yob *n.* (also **yobbo** /'jɒbəʊ/) (*pl.* **-os**) (*slang*) a lout, a hooligan. [back slang for BOY]

yodel /'jəʊd(ə)l/ *v.t./i.* (**-ll-**) to sing, or utter a musical call, with the voice alternating continually between falsetto and its normal pitch, in the manner of Swiss and Tyrolean mountain-dwellers. —*n.* a yodelling cry. —**yodeller** *n.* [f. G *jodeln*]

yoga /'jəʊgə/ *n.* a Hindu system of philosophic meditation and asceticism designed to effect reunion with the universal spirit; the system of physical exercises and breathing-control used in this. [Hind. f. Skr., = union]

yoghurt /'jɒgət/ *n.* a semi-solid sourish food prepared from milk fermented by added bacteria. [f. Turk.]

yogi/ 'jəʊgɪ/ *n.* a devotee of yoga. [Hind. (as YOGA)]

yoicks *int.* used by a fox-hunter to urge on hounds. [orig. unkn.]

yoke *n.* **1** a wooden cross-piece fastened over the necks of two oxen etc. and attached to a plough or wagon to be drawn. **2** a pair of oxen etc. **3** an object like a yoke in form or function; a piece of wood shaped to fit a person's shoulders and to hold a pail or other load slung from each end; the top section of a dress or skirt etc. from which the rest hangs. **4** oppression, burdensome restraint. **5** a bond of union, especially of marriage. —*v.t./i.* **1** to put a yoke upon; to harness by means of a yoke. **2** to unite, to link. [OE]

yokel /'jəʊk(ə)l/ *n.* a rustic, a country bumpkin. [perh. f. dial. *yokel* green woodpecker]

yolk /jəʊk/ *n.* the yellow internal part of an egg. [OE (as YELLOW)]

Yom Kippur /jɒm kɪ'pʊə(r)/ the Day of Atonement (see ATONE). [Heb.]

yomp *v.i.* to march with heavy equipment over difficult terrain. [orig. unkn.]

yon *adj.* & *adv.* (*archaic* or *dial.*) yonder. —*n.* (*archaic* or *dial.*) yonder person or thing. [OE]

yonder *adv.* over there. —*adj.* situated or able to be seen over there. [cf. OS *gendra*]

yore *n.* **of yore,** formerly, in or of old days. [OE]

yorker *n.* (in cricket) a ball that pitches immediately under the bat. [prob. as foll., with ref. to practice of Yorkshire cricketers]

Yorkist /'jɔ:kɪst/ *adj.* of the family descended from the 1st Duke of York or of the White Rose party supporting it in the Wars of the Roses (cf. LANCASTRIAN). —*n.* a member or adherent of the Yorkist family. [f. YORK]

Yorkshire pudding /'jɔ:kʃə(r)/ baked batter eaten with roast beef. [*Yorkshire*, former county of England]

Yorkshire terrier /'jɔ:kʃə(r)/ a small shaggy blue and tan toy kind of terrier. [as prec.]

Yoruba /'jɒrəbə/ *n.* (*pl.* same or **-s**) **1** a member of a Black people on the coast of West Africa, especially in Nigeria. **2** their language. [native name]

you /ju:, jʊ/ *pron.* of the second person singular and plural (*obj.* **you**; *poss.* YOUR, YOURS) **1** the person(s) or thing(s) addressed; (as *voc.* with a noun in an exclamatory statement: *you fools!*). **2** (in general statements) one, a person, anyone, everyone. —**you and yours,** you together with your family, property, etc. [OE, orig. acc. & dat. of YE[1]]

young /jʌŋ/ *adj.* **1** having lived or existed for only a short time, not yet old; (of the night or a year etc.) still near its beginning. **2** immature; having little experience. **3** representing young people; characteristic of youth. **4** distinguishing the son from the father or (in *compar.*) one person from another of the same name. —*n. collect.* offspring, especially of animals before or soon after birth. —**the young,** young people. **Young Pretender,** see PRETENDER. [OE]

youngster *n.* a child, a young person. [f. prec.]

your /jɔ:(r), jʊə(r)/ *poss. adj.* of or belonging to you. [OE, orig. gen. of YE[1]]

yours /jɔ:z, jʊəz/ *poss. pron.* of or belonging to you; the thing or things belonging to you. — —**yours ever, faithfully, sincerely, truly,** etc., formulas preceding the signature of a letter. [f. YOUR]

yourself /jɔ:'self, jʊə'self/ *pron.* (*pl.* **yourselves**) the emphatic and reflexive form of YOU.

youth /ju:θ/ *n.* (*pl.* /ju:ðz/) **1** being young; the period between childhood and adult age; the vigour, enthusiasm, inexperience, or other characteristic of this period. **2** a young man. **3** (as *pl.*) young people collectively. —**youth club,** a place where leisure activities are provided for young people. **youth hostel,** a place where (young) holiday-makers can stay cheaply for the night. **youth hosteller,** a user of a youth hostel. [OE (as YOUNG)]

youthful *adj.* young or (still) having the characteristics of youth. —**youthfully** *adv.*, **youthfulness** *n.* [f. prec. + -FUL]

yowl *n.* a loud wailing cry, a howl. —*v.i.* to utter a yowl. [imit.]

Yo-Yo /'jəʊjəʊ/ *n.* (*pl.* **Yo-Yos**) [P] a toy consisting of a pair of discs with a deep groove between them in which a string is attached and wound, and which can be made to fall and rise on the string when this is jerked by a finger. [orig. unkn.]

yr. *abbr.* **1** year(s). **2** younger. **3** your.

yrs. *abbr.* **1** years. **2** yours.

ytterbium /ɪ'tɜːbɪəm/ *n.* a soft metallic element of the lanthanide series, symbol Yb, atomic number 70. [f. *Ytterby* village in Sweden]

yttrium /'ɪtrɪəm/ *n.* a metallic element, symbol Y, atomic number 39, included among the rare-earth metals. The metal itself is used in certain alloys. [as prec.]

yucca /'jʌkə/ *n.* a tall American plant of the genus *Yucca*, with white bell-like flowers and spiky leaves. [Carib]

yule *n.* (in full **yule-tide**) (*archaic*) the Christmas festival. **—yule-log** *n.* a large log traditionally burnt in the hearth on Christmas Eve. [OE]

yummy *adj.* (*colloq.*) tasty, delicious. [f. foll.]

yum-yum /jʌm'jʌm/ *int.* expressing pleasure from eating or the prospect of eating. [natural excl.]

yuppie *n.* (*colloq.*) young urban professional person. [abbr.]

YWCA *abbr.* Young Women's Christian Association.

Zz

Z, z /zed/ *n.* (*pl.* **Zs, Z's**) **1** the twenty-sixth letter of the alphabet. **2** (in algebra) **z,** the third unknown quantity.

zabaglione /zɑ:bɑ:ˈljəʊneɪ/ *n.* an Italian sweet of whipped and heated egg yolks, sugar, and Marsala or other wine. [It.]

zany /ˈzeɪnɪ/ *adj.* crazily funny or ridiculous. —*n.* **1** a comical or eccentric person. **2** (*hist.*) an attendant clown awkwardly mimicking the chief clown in shows. [f. F or It. *zan(n)i*, Venetian form of *Giovanni* John]

zap *v.t.* (**-pp-**) (*slang*) to hit, to attack, to kill. [imit.]

zeal *n.* enthusiasm, hearty and persistent effort. [f. L f. Gk *zēlos*]

zealot /ˈzelət/ *n.* **1** a zealous person; an uncompromising or extreme partisan, a fanatic. **2 Zealot,** a member of a Jewish sect aiming at world Jewish theocracy and resisting the Romans until AD 70. —**zealotry** *n.* [as prec.]

zealous /ˈzeləs/ *adj.* full of zeal. —**zealously** *adv.* [f. ZEAL]

zebra /ˈzebrə, ˈzi:brə/ *n.* **1** an African quadruped of the genus *Equus*, related to the ass and the horse, with a body entirely covered by black and white (or dark-brown and cream) stripes. **2** (*attrib.*) with alternate dark and pale stripes. —**zebra crossing,** a striped street-crossing where pedestrians have precedence over vehicles. [It. or Port. f. Congolese]

zebu /ˈzi:bu:/ *n.* a humped ox (*Bos indicus*) of India, East Asia, and Africa. [f. F *zébu*; orig. unkn.]

zed *n.* the letter Z. [f. F f. L f. Gk, = ZETA]

zee *n.* (*US*) the letter Z. [var. of ZED]

Zen *n.* a sect of Japanese Buddhism that teaches the attainment of enlightenment through meditation and intuition rather than through study of the scriptures. [Jap., = meditation]

zenana /zɪˈnɑ:nə/ *n.* the part of the house for the seclusion of women of high-caste families in India and Iran. [f. Hind. f. Pers. (*zan* woman)]

Zend /zend/ *n.* an interpretation of the Avesta, each Zend being part of the **Zend-Avesta**, Zoroastrian scriptures consisting of Avesta (= text) and Zend (= commentary). [f. Pers. *zand* interpretation]

zenith /ˈzenɪθ, ˈzi:-/ *n.* **1** the point of the heavens directly above the observer. **2** the highest point (of power or prosperity etc.). [f. OF or L ult. f. Arab., = path (over the head)]

zephyr /ˈzefə(r)/ *n.* a soft mild gentle wind or breeze. [f. F or L f. Gk *zephuros* (god of the) west wind]

zero /ˈzɪərəʊ/ *n.* (*pl.* **-os**) **1** nought; the figure 0. **2** the point on the graduated scale of a thermometer etc. from which a positive or negative quantity is reckoned. **3** (in full **zero-hour**) the hour at which a planned military or other operation is timed to begin; the crucial or decisive moment. —**zero in on,** to take aim at; to focus attention on. **zero-rated** *adj.* on which no value added tax is charged. [f. F or It. ult. f. Arab. (as CIPHER)]

zest *n.* **1** piquancy, stimulating flavour or quality. **2** keen enjoyment or interest. **3** the coloured part of orange or lemon peel as flavouring. —**zestful** *adj.*, **zestfully** *adv.* [f. F *zeste* orange or lemon peel; orig. unkn.]

zeta /ˈzi:tə/ *n.* the sixth letter of the Greek alphabet, = z. [f. Gk]

zeugma /ˈzju:gmə/ *n.* a figure of speech using a verb or adjective with two nouns, to one of which it is strictly applicable while the word appropriate to the other is not used (e.g. *with weeping eyes and* [sc. *grieving*] *hearts*); (*loosely*) syllepsis. [L f. Gk (*zeugnumi* to yoke, *zugon* yoke)]

ziggurat /ˈzɪgəræt/ *n.* a pyramidal stepped tower in ancient Mesopotamia, built in several stages which diminish in size towards the summit on which there may have been a shrine. [f. Assyrian, = pinnacle]

zigzag /ˈzɪgzæg/ *adj.* with abrupt alternate right and left turns. —*n.* a zigzag line; a thing forming this or having sharp turns. —*adv.* with a zigzag course. —*v.i.* (**-gg-**) to move in a zigzag course. [F f. G *zickzack* (symbolic formation)]

zillion /ˈzɪljən/ *n.* (*US*) an indefinite large number. [f. *z* (perh. = unknown quantity) + MILLION]

zinc *n.* a white metallic element, symbol Zn,

atomic number 30. —*v.t.* to coat or treat with zinc. [f. G *zink*, orig. unkn.]

zing *n.* (*colloq.*) vigour, energy. —*v.i.* (*colloq.*) to move swiftly or shrilly. [imit.]

zinnia /ˈzɪnɪə/ *n.* a garden plant of the genus *Zinnia* with brightly-coloured flowers. [f. J. G. *Zinn*, German botanist (d. 1759)]

Zion /ˈzaɪən/ **1** ancient Jerusalem; its holy hill; the heavenly city or kingdom of heaven. **2** the Jewish religion. **3** the Christian Church. **4** a non-conformist chapel. [OE f. L f. Heb.]

Zionism /ˈzaɪənɪz(ə)m/ *n.* a political movement that sought and has achieved the re-establishment of a Jewish nation in Palestine. —**Zionist** *n.* [f. ZION]

zip *n.* **1** a short sharp sound like that of a bullet going through the air. **2** energy, vigour. **3** a zip-fastener. —*v.t./i.* (**-pp-**) **1** to move with a zip or at high speed. **2** to fasten with a zip-fastener. —**zip-fastener** *n.* a fastening device of two flexible strips with interlocking projections closed or opened by a sliding clip pulled along them. [imit.]

Zip code (*US*) a system of postal codes. [f. *z*one *i*mprovement *p*lan]

zipper *n.* a zip-fastener. [f. ZIP]

zircon /ˈzɜːkən/ *n.* zirconium silicate of which some translucent varieties are used as gems. [f. G *zirkon*]

zirconium /zɜːˈkəʊnɪəm/ *n.* a grey metallic element, symbol Zr, atomic number 40. [f. prec.]

zither /ˈzɪðə(r)/ *n.* **1** a plucked stringed folk instrument of Austria and Bavaria, in its present most common form comprising a shallow wooden sound-box over which are stretched five melody strings and two sets of accompaniment strings tuned to form chords. [G, ult. f. Gk *kithara* kind of harp (cf. GUITAR)]

zloty /ˈzlɒtɪ/ *n.* the monetary unit of Poland. [Polish lit. 'golden']

Zn *symbol* zinc.

zodiac /ˈzəʊdɪæk/ *n.* **1** a band of the heavens close to the sun's apparent annual path through the celestial sphere, as viewed from Earth, and including about 8° on each side of the ecliptic, divided into twelve equal parts (the **signs of the zodiac**), each named after a prominent constellation situated in it. **2** a diagram of these signs. —**zodiacal** /ˈzəˈdaɪək(ə)l/ *adj.* [f. OF f. L f. Gk (*zōidion* animal-figure)]

zombie /ˈzɒmbɪ/ *n.* **1** (in voodoo) a corpse said to be revived by witchcraft. **2** (*colloq.*) a dull or apathetic person. [West African]

zone *n.* **1** an area having particular features, properties, purpose, or use. **2** any well-defined region of more or less beltlike form. **3** the area between two concentric circles. **4** an encircling band of colour etc. **5** (*archaic*) a girdle or belt. —*v.t.* **1** to encircle as or with a zone. **2** to arrange or distribute by zones; to assign to a particular area. —**zonal** *adj.* [F or f. L f. Gk *zōnē* girdle]

zoo *n.* a zoological garden. [abbr.]

zoological /zəʊəˈlɒdʒɪk(ə)l, zuːə-/ *adj.* of zoology. —**zoological garden(s)**, a public garden or park with a collection of animals for exhibition and study. —**zoologically** *adv.* [f. foll.]

zoology /zəʊˈɒlədʒɪ, zuː-/ *n.* the study of animal structure, physiology, classification, habits, behaviour, and distribution. —**zoologist** *n.* [f. Gk *zōion* animal + -LOGY]

zoom *v.i.* **1** to move quickly, especially with a buzzing sound. **2** to rise quickly or steeply. **3** (in photography) to alter the size of the image continuously from long shot to close-up. —*n.* an aeroplane's steep climb. —**zoom lens**, a lens allowing a camera to zoom by varying the focus. [imit.]

zoomorphic /zəʊəˈmɔfɪk/ *adj.* **1** imitating or representing animal forms; having the form of an animal. **2** attributing the form or nature of an animal to a deity etc. —**zoomorphism** *n.* [f. Gk *zōion* animal + *morphē* form]

zoophyte /ˈzəʊəfaɪt/ *n.* a plantlike animal, especially a coral, jellyfish, or sponge. [f. Gk (*zōion* animal, *phuton* plant)]

Zoroastrianism /zɒrəʊˈæstrɪənɪz(ə)m/ *n.* a monotheistic religion of ancient Iran founded by Zoroaster (or Zarathustra) in the 6th c. BC. —**Zoroastrian** *adj.* & *n.* [f. *Zoroaster*, Persian prophet]

Zr *symbol* zirconium.

zucchini /zuːˈkiːnɪ/ *n.* (*pl.* same or **-is**) a courgette. [It., pl. of *zucchino* dim. of *zucca* gourd]

Zulu /ˈzuːluː/ *n.* **1** a member of a South African Bantu people inhabiting the north-eastern part of Natal. **2** their Bantu language. —*adj.* of the Zulus or their language. [native name]

zygote /ˈzaɪgəʊt/ *n.* a cell formed by the union of two gametes. [f. Gk *zugōtos* yoked (as ZEUGMA)]

Appendices

APPENDIX I

Countries of the World

Country	*Capital*	*Currency unit*
Afghanistan	Kabul	afghani = 100 puls
Albania	Tiranë	lek = 100 qindarka
Algeria	Algiers	dinar = 100 centimes
		franc = 100 centimes
Andorra	Andorra la Vella	peseta = 100 céntimos
Angola	Luanda	kwanza = 100 lweis
Antigua and Barbuda	St John's	dollar = 100 cents
Argentina	Buenos Aires	austral
Australia	Canberra	dollar = 100 cents
Austria	Vienna	schilling = 100 groschen
Bahamas	Nassau	dollar = 100 cents
Bahrain	Manama	dinar = 1,000 fils
Bangladesh	Dhaka	taka = 100 poisha
Barbados	Bridgetown	dollar = 100 cents
Belgium	Brussels	franc = 100 centimes
Belize	Belmopan	dollar = 100 cents
Benin	Porto Novo	franc
Bhutan	Thimphu	ngultrum = 100 paisa
Bolivia	La Paz	peso = 100 centavos
Botswana	Gaborone	pula = 100 thebe
Brazil	Brasilia	cruzado = 1,000 cruzeiros
Brunei	Bandar Seri Begawan	dollar = 100 sen
Bulgaria	Sofia	lev = 100 stotinki
Burkina	Ouagadougou	franc
Burma see Myanmar		
Burundi	Bujumbura	franc
Cambodia	Phnom Penh	riel = 100 sen
Cameroon	Yaoundé	franc
Canada	Ottawa	dollar = 100 cents
Cape Verde Islands	Praia	escudo = 100 centavos
Central African Republic	Bangui	franc
Chad	N'Djamena	franc
Chile	Santiago	peso = 100 centavos
China	Peking	yuan = 10 jiao or 100 fen
Colombia	Bogotá	peso = 100 centavos
Comoros	Moroni	franc
Congo	Brazzaville	franc
Costa Rica	San José	colón = 100 céntimos
Cuba	Havana	peso = 100 centavos
Cyprus	Nicosia	pound = 1,000 cents
Czechoslovakia	Prague	koruna = 100 haléru
Denmark	Copenhagen	krone = 100 öre

Country	*Capital*	*Currency unit*
Djibouti	Djibouti	franc
Dominica	Roseau	dollar = 100 cents
Dominican Republic	Santo Domingo	peso = 100 centavos
Ecuador	Quito	sucre = 100 centavos
Egypt	Cairo	pound = 100 piastres or 1,000 millièmes
El Salvador	San Salvador	colón = 100 centavos
Equatorial Guinea	Malabo	franc
Ethiopia	Addis Ababa	birr = 100 cents
Fiji	Suva	dollar = 100 cents
Finland	Helsinki	markka = 100 penniä
France	Paris	franc = 100 centimes
Gabon	Libreville	franc
Gambia, the	Banjul	dalasi = 100 bututs
German Democratic Republic (East Germany)	East Berlin	Deutschmark = 100 pfennig
Germany, Federal Republic of (West Germany)	Bonn	Deutschmark = 100 pfennig
Ghana	Accra	cedi = 100 pesewa
Greece	Athens	drachma = 100 lepta
Grenada	St George's	dollar = 100 cents
Guatemala	Guatemala	quetzal = 100 centavos
Guinea	Conakry	franc
Guinea-Bissau	Bissau	peso = 100 centavos
Guyana	Georgetown	dollar = 100 cents
Haiti	Port-au-Prince	gourde = 100 centimes
Honduras	Tegucigalpa	lempira = 100 centavos
Hungary	Budapest	forint = 100 fillér
Iceland	Reykjavik	króna = 100 aurer
India	New Delhi	rupee = 100 paise
Indonesia	Jakarta	rupiah = 100 sen
Iran	Teheran	rial = 100 dinars
Iraq	Baghdad	dinar = 1,000 fils
Ireland, Republic of	Dublin	pound (punt) = 100 pence
Israel	Jerusalem	new shekel
Italy	Rome	lira
Ivory Coast	Abidjan	franc
Jamaica	Kingston	dollar = 100 cents
Japan	Tokyo	yen
Jordan	Amman	dinar = 1,000 fils
Kampuchea = Cambodia		
Kenya	Nairobi	shilling = 100 cents
Kiribati	Tarawa	dollar = 100 cents
Korea, North	Pyongyang	won = 100 chon
Korea, South	Seoul	won = 100 jeon
Kuwait	Kuwait	dinar = 1,000 fils
Laos	Vientiane	kip = 100 ats
Lebanon	Beirut	pound = 100 piastres
Lesotho	Maseru	maluti

Country	*Capital*	*Currency unit*
Liberia	Monrovia	dollar = 100 cents
Libya	Tripoli	dinar = 1,000 dirhams
Liechtenstein	Vaduz	franc = 100 centimes
Luxemburg	Luxemburg	franc = 100 centimes
Madagascar	Antananarivo	franc malgache
Malawi	Lilongwe	kwacha = 100 tambala
Malaysia	Kuala Lumpur	dollar (ringgit) = 100 cents
Maldives	Malé	rufiyaa = 100 laris
Mali	Bamako	franc
Malta	Valletta	lira = 100 cents
Mauritania	Nouakchott	ouguiya = 5 khoums
Mauritius	Port Louis	rupee = 100 cents
Mexico	Mexico City	peso = 100 centavos
Monaco	Monaco	franc = 100 centimes
Mongolia	Ulan Bator	tugrik = 100 mongo
Morocco	Rabat (summer capital, Tangier)	dirham = 100 centimes
Mozambique	Maputo	metical = 100 centavos
Myanmar (until 1989 called *Burma*)	Yangon (formerly *Rangoon*)	kyat = 100 pyas
Namibia	Windhoek	rand = 100 cents
Nauru	Yaren	dollar = 100 cents
Nepal	Kathmandu	rupee = 100 paisa
Netherlands	Amsterdam (seat of government, The Hague)	guilder = 100 cents
New Zealand	Wellington	dollar = 100 cents
Nicaragua	Managua	córdoba = 100 centavos
Niger	Niamey	franc
Nigeria	Lagos	naira = 100 kobo
Norway	Oslo	krone = 100 öre
Oman	Muscat	rial = 1,000 baiza
Pakistan	Islamabad	rupee = 100 paisa
Panama	Panama	balboa = 100 cents
Papua New Guinea	Port Moresby	kina = 100 toea
Paraguay	Asunción	guarani = 100 céntimos
Peru	Lima	inti = 1,000 soles
Philippines	Manila	peso = 100 centavos
Poland	Warsaw	zloty = 100 groszy
Portugal	Lisbon	escudo = 100 centavos
Qatar	Doha	riyal = 100 dirhams
Romania	Bucharest	leu = 100 bani
Rwanda	Kigali	franc
St Kitts and Nevis	Basseterre	dollar = 100 cents
St Lucia	Castries	dollar = 100 cents
St Vincent	Kingstown	dollar = 100 cents
San Marino	San Marino	lira
São Tomé and Principe	São Tomé	dobra = 100 centimos
Saudi Arabia	Riyadh	riyal = 20 qursh or 100 halalas

Country	*Capital*	*Currency unit*
Senegal	Dakar	franc
Seychelles	Victoria	rupee = 100 cents
Sierra Leone	Freetown	leone = 100 cents
Singapore	Singapore	dollar = 100 cents
Solomon Islands	Honiara	dollar = 100 cents
Somalia	Mogadishu	shilling = 100 cents
South Africa	Pretoria (administrative); seat of Legislature, Cape Town	rand = 100 cents
Spain	Madrid	peseta = 100 céntimos
Sri Lanka	Colombo	rupee = 100 cents
Sudan	Khartoum	pound = 100 piastres or 1,000 millièmes
Suriname	Paramaribo	guilder = 100 cents
Swaziland	Mbabane	lilangeni = 100 cents
Sweden	Stockholm	krona = 100 öre
Switzerland	Berne	franc = 100 centimes
Syria	Damascus	pound = 100 piastres
Tanzania	Dodoma	shilling = 100 cents
Thailand	Bangkok	baht = 100 stangs
Togo	Lomé	franc
Tonga	Nuku'alofa	pa'anga = 100 seniti
Trinidad and Tobago	Port of Spain	dollar = 100 cents
Tunisia	Tunis	dinar = 1,000 millimes
Turkey	Ankara	lira = 100 kurus
Tuvalu	Funafuti	dollar = 100 cents
Uganda	Kampala	shilling = 100 cents
Union of Soviet Socialist Republics	Moscow	rouble = 100 copecks
United Arab Emirates	Abu Dhabi	dirham = 100 fils
United Kingdom	London	pound = 100 pence
England	London	
Northern Ireland	Belfast	
Scotland	Edinburgh	
Wales	Cardiff	
United States of America	Washington	dollar = 100 cents
Uruguay	Montevideo	peso = 100 centésimos
Vanuatu	Vila	vatu
Vatican City	—	lira
Venezuela	Caracas	bolivar
Vietnam	Hanoi	dong = 10 hào or 100 xu
Western Samoa	Apia	tala = 100 sene
Yemen Arab Republic	Sana'a	riyal = 100 fils
Yemen, People's Democratic Republic of	Aden	dinar = 1,000 fils
Yugoslavia	Belgrade	dinar = 100 paras
Zaïre	Kinshasa	zaire = 100 makuta or 10,000 senghi
Zambia	Lusaka	kwacha = 100 ngwee
Zimbabwe	Harare	dollar = 100 cents

APPENDIX II

Counties of the United Kingdom

(with abbreviations in general use)

England

Avon
Bedfordshire (Beds.)
Berkshire (Berks.)
Buckinghamshire (Bucks.)
Cambridgeshire (Cambs.)
Cheshire (Ches.)
Cleveland
Cornwall (Corn.)
Cumbria
Derbyshire (Derby.)
Devon
Dorset
Durham (Dur.)
East Sussex
Essex
Gloucestershire (Glos.)
Greater London
Greater Manchester
Hampshire (Hants)
Hereford & Worcester
Hertfordshire (Herts.)
Humberside
Isle of Wight (IOW)
Kent
Lancashire (Lancs.)
Leicestershire (Leics.)
Lincolnshire (Lincs.)
Merseyside
Norfolk
Northamptonshire (Northants)
Northumberland (Northumb.)
North Yorkshire
Nottinghamshire (Notts.)
Oxfordshire (Oxon.)
Shropshire
Somerset (Som.)
South Yorkshire
Staffordshire (Staffs.)
Suffolk
Surrey
Tyne and Wear
Warwickshire (War.)
West Midlands
West Sussex
West Yorkshire
Wiltshire (Wilts.)

Northern Ireland

Antrim
Armagh
Down
Fermanagh (Ferm.)
Londonderry
Tyrone

(For administrative purposes smaller unit areas are used.)

Scotland

Regions

Borders
Central
Dumfries & Galloway
Fife
Grampian
Highland
Lothian
Strathclyde
Tayside

Islands Areas

Orkney
Shetland
Western Isles

Wales

Clwyd
Dyfed
Gwent
Gwynedd
Mid Glamorgan
Powys
South Glamorgan
West Glamorgan

APPENDIX III

States of the United States of America

(with official and postal abbreviations)

State	*Capital*	*Popular name*
Alabama (Ala., AL)	Montgomery	Yellowhammer State, Heart of Dixie, Cotton State
Alaska (Alas., AK)	Juneau	Great Land
Arizona (Ariz., AZ)	Phoenix	Grand Canyon State
Arkansas (Ark., AR)	Little Rock	Land of Opportunity
California (Calif., CA)	Sacramento	Golden State
Colorado (Col., CO)	Denver	Centennial State
Connecticut (Conn., CT)	Hartford	Constitution State, Nutmeg State
Delaware (Del., DE)	Dover	First State, Diamond State
Florida (Fla., FL)	Tallahassee	Sunshine State
Georgia (Ga., GA)	Atlanta	Empire State of the South, Peach State
Hawaii (HI)	Honolulu	The Aloha State
Idaho (ID)	Boise	Gem State
Illinois (Ill., IL)	Springfield	The Inland Empire
Indiana (Ind., IN)	Indianapolis	Hoosier State
Iowa (Ia., IA)	Des Moines	Hawkeye State
Kansas (Kan., KS)	Topeka	Sunflower State
Kentucky (Ky., KY)	Frankfort	Bluegrass State
Louisiana (La., LA)	Baton Rouge	Pelican State
Maine (Me., ME)	Augusta	Pine Tree State
Maryland (Md., MD)	Annapolis	Old Line State, Free State
Massachusetts (Mass., MA)	Boston	Bay State, Old Colony
Michigan (Mich., MI)	Lansing	Great Lake State, Wolverine State
Minnesota (Minn., MN)	St Paul	North Star State, Gopher State
Mississippi (Miss., MS)	Jackson	Magnolia State
Missouri (Mo , MO)	Jefferson City	Show Me State
Montana (Mont., MT)	Helena	Treasure State
Nebraska (Nebr., NB)	Lincoln	Cornhusker State
Nevada (Nev., NV)	Carson City	Sagebrush State, Battleborn State, Silver State
New Hampshire (NH)	Concord	Granite State
New Jersey (NJ)	Trenton	Garden State
New Mexico (N. Mex., NM)	Santa Fe	Land of Enchantment
New York (NY)	Albany	Empire State
North Carolina (NC)	Raleigh	Tar Heel State, Old North State
North Dakota (N. Dak., ND)	Bismarck	Peace Garden State
Ohio (OH)	Columbus	Buckeye State
Oklahoma (Okla., OK)	Oklahoma City	Sooner State

State	*Capital*	*Popular name*
Oregon (Oreg., OR)	**Salem**	**Beaver State**
Pennsylvania (Pa., PA)	**Harrisburg**	**Keystone State**
Rhode Island (RI)	**Providence**	**Little Rhody, Ocean State**
South Carolina (SC)	**Columbia**	**Palmetto State**
South Dakota (S. Dak., SD)	**Pierre**	**Coyote State, Sunshine State**
Tennessee (Tenn., TN)	**Nashville**	**Volunteer State**
Texas (Tex., TX)	**Austin**	**Lone Star State**
Utah (UT)	**Salt Lake City**	**Beehive State**
Vermont (Vt., VT)	**Montpelier**	**Green Mountain State**
Virginia (Va., VA)	**Richmond**	**Old Dominion**
Washington (Wash., WA)	**Olympia**	**Evergreen State**
West Virginia (W. Va., WV)	**Charleston**	**Mountain State**
Wisconsin (Wis., WI)	**Madison**	**Badger State**
Wyoming (Wyo., WY)	**Cheyenne**	**Equality State**

APPENDIX IV

Rulers of England and of the United Kingdom

Saxon Line

Edwy	955–959
Edgar	959–975
Edward the Martyr	975–978
Ethelred the Unready	978–1016
Edmund Ironside	1016

Danish Line

Canute (Cnut)	1017–1035
Harold I	1035–1040
Hardicanute (Harthacnut)	1040–1042

Saxon Line

Edward the Confessor	1042–1066
Harold II (Godwinson)	1066

House of Normandy

William I (the Conqueror)	1066–1087
William II	1087–1100
Henry I	1100–1135
Stephen	1135–1154

House of Plantagenet

Henry II	1154–1189
Richard I	1189–1199
John	1199–1216
Henry III	1216–1272
Edward I	1272–1307
Edward II	1307–1327
Edward III	1327–1377
Richard II	1377–1399

House of Lancaster

Henry IV	1399–1413
Henry V	1413–1422
Henry VI	1422–1461

House of York

Edward IV	1461–1483
Edward V	1483
Richard III	1483–1485

House of Tudor

Henry VII	1485–1509
Henry VIII	1509–1547
Edward VI	1547–1553
Mary I	1553–1558
Elizabeth I	1558–1603

House of Stuart

James I of England and VI of Scotland	1603–1625
Charles I	1625–1649

Commonwealth (declared 1649)

Oliver Cromwell, Lord Protector	1653–1658
Richard Cromwell	1658–1659

House of Stuart

Charles II	1660–1685
James II	1685–1688
William III and Mary II (Mary d. 1694)	1689–1702
Anne	1702–1714

House of Hanover

George I	1714–1727
George II	1727–1760
George III	1760–1820
George IV	1820–1830
William IV	1830–1837
Victoria	1837–1901

House of Saxe-Coburg-Gotha

Edward VII	1901–1910

House of Windsor

George V	1910–1936
Edward VIII	1936
George VI	1936–1952
Elizabeth II	1952–

APPENDIX V

Prime Ministers of Great Britain and of the United Kingdom

Sir Robert Walpole	Whig	[1721]–1742
Earl of Wilmington	„	1742–1743
Henry Pelham	„	1743–1754
Duke of Newcastle	„	1754–1756
Duke of Devonshire	„	1756–1757
Duke of Newcastle	„	1757–1762
Earl of Bute	Tory	1762–1763
George Grenville	Whig	1763–1765
Marquis of Rockingham	„	1765–1766
Earl of Chatham	„	1766–1768
Duke of Grafton	„	1768–1770
Lord North	Tory	1770–1782
Marquis of Rockingham	Whig	1782
Earl of Shelburne	„	1782–1783
Duke of Portland	coalition	1783
William Pitt	Tory	1783–1801
Henry Addington	„	1801–1804
William Pitt	„	1804–1806
Lord William Grenville	Whig	1806–1807
Duke of Portland	Tory	1807–1809
Spencer Perceval	„	1809–1812
Earl of Liverpool	„	1812–1827
George Canning	„	1827
Viscount Goderich	„	1827–1828
Duke of Wellington	„	1828–1830
Earl Grey	Whig	1830–1834
Viscount Melbourne	„	1834
Duke of Wellington	Tory	1834
Sir Robert Peel	Conservative	1834–1835
Viscount Melbourne	Whig	1835–1841
Sir Robert Peel	Conservative	1841–1846
Lord John Russell	Whig	1846–1852
Earl of Derby	Conservative	1852
Earl of Aberdeen	coalition	1852–1855
Viscount Palmerston	Liberal	1855–1858
Earl of Derby	Conservative	1858–1859
Viscount Palmerston	Liberal	1859–1865
Earl Russell	„	1865–1866
Earl of Derby	Conservative	1866–1868
Benjamin Disraeli	„	1868
William Ewart Gladstone	Liberal	1868–1874
Benjamin Disraeli	Conservative	1874–1880

William Ewart Gladstone	Liberal	1880–1885
Marquis of Salisbury	Conservative	1885–1886
William Ewart Gladstone	Liberal	1886
Marquis of Salisbury	Conservative	1886–1892
William Ewart Gladstone	Liberal	1892–1894
Earl of Rosebery	„	1894–1895
Marquis of Salisbury	Conservative	1895–1902
Arthur James Balfour	„	1902–1905
Sir Henry Campbell-Bannerman	Liberal	1905–1908
Herbert Henry Asquith	„	1908–1916
David Lloyd George	coalition	1916–1922
Andrew Bonar Law	Conservative	1922–1923
Stanley Baldwin	„	1923–1924
James Ramsay MacDonald	Labour	1924
Stanley Baldwin	Conservative	1924–1929
James Ramsay MacDonald	coalition	1929–1935
Stanley Baldwin	„	1935–1937
Neville Chamberlain	„	1937–1940
Winston Spencer Churchill	„	1940–1945
Clement Richard Attlee	Labour	1945–1951
Sir Winston Spencer Churchill	Conservative	1951–1955
Sir Anthony Eden	„	1955–1957
Harold Macmillan	„	1957–1963
Sir Alexander Douglas-Home	„	1963–1964
Harold Wilson	Labour	1964–1970
Edward Heath	Conservative	1970–1974
Harold Wilson	Labour	1974–1976
James Callaghan	„	1976–1979
Margaret Thatcher	Conservative	1979–

APPENDIX VI

Presidents of the United States of America

1. George Washington	Federalist	1789–1797
2. John Adams	„	1797–1801
3. Thomas Jefferson	Democratic-Republican	1801–1809
4. James Madison	„	1809–1817
5. James Monroe	„	1817–1825
6. John Quincy Adams	Independent	1825–1829
7. Andrew Jackson	Democrat	1829–1837
8. Martin Van Buren	„	1837–1841
9. William H. Harrison	Whig	1841
10. John Tyler	Whig, then Democrat	1841–1845
11. James K. Polk	Democrat	1845–1849
12. Zachary Taylor	Whig	1849–1850
13. Millard Fillmore	„	1850–1853
14. Franklin Pierce	Democrat	1853–1857
15. James Buchanan	„	1857–1861
16. Abraham Lincoln	Republican	1861–1865
17. Andrew Johnson	Democrat	1865–1869
18. Ulysses S. Grant	Republican	1869–1877
19. Rutherford B. Hayes	„	1877–1881
20. James A. Garfield	„	1881
21. Chester A. Arthur	„	1881–1885
22. Grover Cleveland	Democrat	1885–1889
23. Benjamin Harrison	Republican	1889–1893
24. Grover Cleveland	Democrat	1893–1897
25. William McKinley	Republican	1897–1901
26. Theodore Roosevelt	„	1901–1909
27. William H. Taft	„	1909–1913
28. Woodrow Wilson	Democrat	1913–1921
29. Warren G. Harding	Republican	1921–1923
30. Calvin Coolidge	„	1923–1929
31. Herbert Hoover	„	1929–1933
32. Franklin D. Roosevelt	Democrat	1933–1945
33. Harry S Truman	„	1945–1953
34. Dwight D. Eisenhower	Republican	1953–1961
35. John F. Kennedy	Democrat	1961–1963
36. Lyndon B. Johnson	„	1963–1969
37. Richard M. Nixon	Republican	1969–1974
38. Gerald R. Ford	„	1974–1977
39. James Earl Carter	Democrat	1977–1981
40. Ronald W. Reagan	Republican	1981–1989
41. George H. W. Bush	„	1989–

APPENDIX VII

Books of the Bible

Old Testament

Genesis (Gen.)
Exodus (Exod.)
Leviticus (Lev.)
Numbers (Num.)
Deuteronomy (Deut.)
Joshua (Josh.)
Judges (Judg.)
Ruth
First Book of Samuel (1 Sam.)
Second Book of Samuel (2 Sam.)
First Book of Kings (1 Kgs.)
Second Book of Kings (2 Kgs.)
First Book of Chronicles (1 Chr.)
Second Book of Chronicles (2 Chr.)
Ezra
Nehemiah (Neh.)
Esther
Job
Psalms (Ps.)
Proverbs (Prov.)
Ecclesiastes (Eccles.)
Song of Songs, Song of Solomon, Canticles (S. of S., Cant.)
Isaiah (Isa.)
Jeremiah (Jer.)
Lamentations (Lam.)
Ezekiel (Ezek.)
Daniel (Dan.)
Hosea (Hos.)
Joel
Amos
Obadiah (Obad.)
Jonah
Micah (Mic.)
Nahum (Nah.)
Habakkuk (Hab.)
Zephaniah (Zeph.)
Haggai (Hag.)
Zechariah (Zech.)
Malachi (Mal.)

Apocrypha

First Book of Esdras (1 Esd.)
Second Book of Esdras (2 Esd.)
Tobit
Judith
Rest of Esther (Rest of Esth.)
Wisdom of Solomon (Wisd.)
Ecclesiasticus, Wisdom of Jesus the Son of Sirach (Ecclus., Sir.)
Baruch
Song of the Three Children (S. of III Ch.)
Susanna (Sus.)
Bel and the Dragon (Bel & Dr.)
Prayer of Manasses (Pr. of Man.)
First Book of Maccabees (1 Macc.)
Second Book of Maccabees (2 Macc.)

New Testament

Gospel according to St Matthew (Matt.)
Gospel according to St Mark (Mark)
Gospel according to St Luke (Luke)
Gospel according to St John (John)
Acts of the Apostles (Acts)
Epistle to the Romans (Rom.)
First Epistle to the Corinthians (1 Cor.)
Second Epistle to the Corinthians (2 Cor.)
Epistle to the Galatians (Gal.)
Epistle to the Ephesians (Eph.)
Epistle to the Philippians (Phil.)
Epistle to the Colossians (Col.)
First Epistle to the Thessalonians (1 Thess.)
Second Epistle to the Thessalonians (2 Thess.)
First Epistle to Timothy (1 Tim.)

Second Epistle to Timothy (2 Tim.)
Epistle to Titus (Tit.)
Epistle to Philemon (Philem.)
Epistle to the Hebrews (Heb.)
Epistle of James (Jas.)
First Epistle of Peter (1 Pet.)
Second Epistle of Peter (2 Pet.)
First Epistle of John (1 John)
Second Epistle of John (2 John)
Third Epistle of John (3 John)
Epistle of Jude (Jude)
Revelation, Apocalypse (Rev., Apoc.)

APPENDIX VIII

Days of the Week

The days of the week were named more than a thousand years ago, in Anglo-Saxon times, and the English names are based on those given by the ancient Romans. They are named after the planets, taking the order of these from ancient astronomy.

Sunday from Old English *sunnandaeg* = day of the sun; the Latin name was *solis dies.*

Monday from Old English *monandaeg* = day of the moon; the Latin name was *lunae dies*. Compare French *lundi.*

Tuesday from Old English *Tiwesdaeg* = day of Tiw, the Norse god of war, whose name was substituted for that of Mars, the Roman god of war; the Latin name was *Martis dies* = day of Mars. Compare French *Mardi.*

Wednesday from Old English *Wodnesdaeg* = day of Odin or Woden, the chief Norse god, whose name was substituted for that of Mercury, the Roman messenger-god; the Latin name was *Mercurii dies.* Compare French *Mercredi.*

Thursday from Old English *thuresdaeg* = day of thunder, named after Thor, the Norse god of thunder, whose name was substituted for that of Jove or Jupiter, the Roman god who controlled thunder and lightning; the Latin name was *Jovis dies* = day of Jupiter. Compare French *Jeudi.*

Friday from Old English *Frigedaeg* = day of Frigg, wife of the god Odin (see *Wednesday*); the Latin name was *Veneris dies* = day of Venus. Compare French *Vendredi.*

Saturday from Old English *Saeternesdaeg* = day of Saturn, a Roman god; the Latin name was *Saturni dies*. Compare French *Samedi.*

Months of the Year

The names of the months go back to ancient Roman times, and some are named after Roman gods and goddesses.

January is named after Janus, god of gates and beginnings, who faced two ways (past and future), whose festival was held on 9 January.

February is named after *februa*, an ancient Roman feast of purification held in this month.

March is named after Mars, god of war, several of whose festivals were held in this month. It was originally the first month of the year and the months September–December were counted from here.

April	is from its Latin name *Aprilis*. The Romans considered this month to be sacred to Venus, goddess of love, and its name may be taken from that of her Greek equivalent Aphrodite.
May	is named after the goddess Maia, who was worshipped in this month.
June	is named after Juno, queen of the gods.
July	is named after Julius Caesar, who was born in this month.
August	is named after Augustus Caesar, the first Roman emperor, who was given the name Augustus (Latin, = majestic) in 27 BC.
September	is from Latin *septem* = seven, because it was the seventh month in the ancient Roman calendar (see the note on *March*).
October	is from Latin *octo* = eight (eighth month).
November	is from Latin *novem* = nine (ninth month).
December	is from Latin *decem* = ten (tenth month).

Signs of the zodiac

The strip of sky called the *zodiac* is divided into twelve equal sections, each named after a group of stars (its *sign*) that was formerly situated in it. When seen from the Earth, the sun appears to move through each section in turn during one year. The dates given below are the approximate times when it enters and leaves each sign.

In ancient times, people believed that stars and planets influenced the entire world and all that happened in it, including crops, medicine, and people's lives. The key to a person's whole life was thought to lie in the way the planets were arranged (called a *horoscope*) at his or her birth. Many newspapers and magazines print forecasts of what is about to happen to those born under each sign, but only a few people treat them seriously.

The names of the signs are derived from the Latin word with the same meaning.

Aries	the Ram	21 March–20 April
Taurus	the Bull	21 April–20 May
Gemini	the Twins	21 May–20 June
Cancer	the Crab	21 June–21 July
Leo	the Lion	22 July–22 August
Virgo	the Virgin	23 August–21 September
Libra	the Scales	22 September–22 October
Scorpio	the Scorpion	23 October–21 November
Sagittarius	the Archer	22 November–21 December
Capricorn	the Goat	22 December–20 January
Aquarius	the Water-carrier	21 January–19 February
Pisces	the Fishes	20 February–20 March

APPENDIX IX

Wedding Anniversaries

The principal anniversaries are the twenty-fifth, fiftieth, and sixtieth. Since few couples can hope to reach their seventy-fifth anniversary the diamond wedding (like Queen Victoria's Diamond Jubilee) is celebrated after sixty years. The popular idea is that the names attached to the anniversaries indicate the material appropriate to a gift for the occasion. There is considerable variation in the lesser anniversaries among those listed below.

1st	cotton or paper wedding
2nd	paper or cotton wedding
3rd	leather wedding
4th	fruit or flower wedding
5th	wooden wedding
6th	iron or sugar wedding
7th	woollen wedding
8th	bronze wedding
9th	copper or pottery wedding
10th	tin wedding
11th	steel wedding
12th	silk and fine linen wedding
13th	lace wedding
14th	ivory wedding
15th	crystal wedding
20th	china wedding
25th	silver wedding
30th	pearl or ivory wedding
35th	coral wedding
40th	ruby wedding
45th	sapphire wedding
50th	golden wedding
55th	emerald wedding
60th	diamond wedding
75th	diamond wedding

APPENDIX X

Some Terms for Groups of Animals, Birds, etc.

Terms marked † belong to 15th-c. lists of 'proper terms', notably that in the *Book of St Albans* attributed to Dame Juliana Barnes (1486). Many of these are fanciful or humorous terms which probably never had any real currency, but have been taken up by Joseph Strutt in *Sports and Pastimes of England* (1801) and by other antiquarian writers.

a †shrewdness of apes
a herd or †pace of asses
a †cete of badgers
a †sloth or †sleuth of bears
a hive of bees; a swarm, drift, or bike of bees
a flock, flight, (*dial.*) parcel, pod (= small flock), †fleet, or †dissimulation of (small) birds; a volary of birds in an aviary
a sounder of wild boar
a †blush of boys
a herd or gang of buffalo
a †clowder or †glaring of cats; a †dowt (= ?do-out) or †destruction of wild cats
a herd, drove, (*dial.*) drift, or (*US* & *Austral.*) mob of cattle
a brood, (*dial.*) cletch or clutch, or †peep of chickens
a †chattering or †clattering of choughs
a †drunkship of cobblers
a †rag or †rake of colts
a †hastiness of cooks
a †covert of coots
a herd of cranes
a litter of cubs
a herd of curlew
a †cowardice of curs
a herd or mob of deer
a pack or kennel of dogs
a trip of dotterel
a flight, †dole, or †piteousness of doves
a raft, bunch, or †paddling of ducks on water; a team of wild ducks in flight
a fling of dunlins
a herd of elephants
a herd or (*US*) gang of elk
a †business of ferrets
a charm or †chirm of finches
a shoal of fish; a run of fish in motion
a cloud of flies
a †stalk of foresters
a †skulk of foxes
a gaggle or (in the air) a skein, team, or wedge of geese
a herd of giraffes
a flock, herd, or (*dial.*) trip of goats
a pack or covey of grouse
a †husk or †down of hares
a cast of hawks let fly
an †observance of hermits
a †siege of herons
a stud or †haras of (breeding) horses; (*dial.*) a team of horses
a kennel, pack, cry, or †mute of hounds
a flight or swarm of insects
a mob or troop of kangaroos
a kindle of kittens
a bevy of ladies
a †desert of lapwing
an †exaltation or bevy of larks
a †leap of leopards
a pride of lions
a †tiding of magpies
a †sord or †sute (= suit) of mallard
a †richesse of martens
a †faith of merchants
a †labour of moles
a troop of monkeys
a †barren of mules
a †watch of nightingales
a †superfluity of nuns
a covey of partridges
a †muster of peacocks
a †malapertness (= impertinence) of pedlars
a rookery of penguins

a head or (*dial.*) nye of pheasants
a kit of pigeons flying together
a herd of pigs
a stand, wing, or †congregation of plovers
a rush or flight of pochards
a herd, pod, or school of porpoises
a †pity of prisoners
a covey of ptarmigan
a litter of pups
a bevy or drift of quail
a string of racehorses
an †unkindness of ravens
a bevy of roes
a parliament or †building of rooks
a hill of ruffs
a herd or rookery of seals; a pod (= small herd) of seals
a flock, herd, (*dial.*) drift or trip, or (*Austral.*) mob of sheep
a †dopping of sheldrake
a wisp or †walk of snipe
a †host of sparrows
a †murmuration of starlings
a flight of swallows
a game or herd of swans; a wedge of swans in the air
a herd of swine; a †sounder of tame swine, a †drift of wild swine
a †glozing (= fawning) of taverners
a †spring of teal
a bunch or knob of waterfowl
a school, herd, or gam of whales; a pod (= small school) of whales; a grind of bottle-nosed whales
a company or trip of widgeon
a bunch, trip, or plump of wildfowl; a knob (less than 30) of wildfowl
a pack or †rout of wolves
a gaggle of women (*derisive*)
a †fall of woodcock
a herd of wrens

APPENDIX XI

Some Foreign Words and Phrases used in English

(Many words that are in frequent use, and are not now thought of as being 'foreign', are in the text of the dictionary.)

---

ab initio /æb ɪ'nɪʃɪəʊ/ from the beginning. [Latin]

ad hoc /æd hɒk/ for this purpose, special(ly). [Latin]

ad infinitum /æd ɪnfɪ'naɪtəm/ without limit, for ever. [Latin, = to an unlimited extent]

ad nauseam /æd 'nɔ:zɪæm/ to an excessive or sickening degree. [Latin, = to sickness]

affaire de cœur /æ'feər də 'kɜ:(r)/ love-affair. [French, = affair of the heart]

agent provocateur /æʒɑ̃ prəvɒkə'tɜ:(r)/ a person employed to detect suspected offenders by tempting them to overt action. [French, = provocative agent]

aide de camp /eɪd də 'kɑ̃/ an officer assisting a senior officer. [French, = camp assistant]

aide-memoire /'eɪdmemwɑ:(r)/ *n.* an aid to the memory. [French]

à la carte /ɑ: lɑ: 'kɑ:t/ ordered as separate items from a menu. (Cf. *table d'hôte.*) [French, = according to the menu]

alfresco /æl'freskəʊ/ *adj.* & *adv.* in the open air. [from Italian *al fresco* = in the fresh air]

alter ego /æltər 'i:gəʊ/ an intimate friend; another aspect of oneself. [Latin, = other self]

amende honorable /æmɑ̃d ɒnɔ:'rɑ:bl/ a public or open apology and reparation. [French, = honourable reparation]

amour propre /æmʊə 'prɒpr/ self-esteem, vanity. [French, = self-love]

ancien régime /ɑ̃nsjɑ̃ reɪ'ʒi:m/ a regime that has been superseded; (orig.) the system of government in France before the Revolution. [French, = old regime]

Anno Domini /'ænəʊ 'dɒmɪnaɪ/ in the year of the Christian era; (*colloq.*) advancing age. [Latin, = in the year of the Lord]

à outrance /æ u:'trɑ̃s/ to the death; to the bitter end. [French, = to the utmost]

argumentum ad hominem /ɑ:gu:'mentəm æd 'hɒmɪnem/ reasoning that appeals to a particular person's feelings, not to his or her intellect. [Latin, = argument to the person]

a posteriori /eɪ pɒsterɪ'ɔ:raɪ/ reasoning from effects back to their causes. (Cf. *a priori.*) [Latin, = from what comes after]

après-ski /æpreɪ'ski:/ *adj.* done or worn after skiing. [French]

a priori /eɪ praɪ'ɔ:raɪ/ reasoning from causes to effects; assumed without investigation; (of knowledge) existing in the mind independently of sensory experience. [Latin, = from what is before]

aqua fortis /ækwə 'fɔ:tɪs/ nitric acid. [Latin, = strong water]

aqua vitae /ækwə 'vaɪti:, 'vi:taɪ/ alcoholic spirits, especially of the first distillation. [Latin, = water of life (orig. an alchemists' term)]

arrière-pensée /ærɪeər'pɑ̃seɪ/ *n.* an ulterior motive; a mental reservation. [French, = behind thought]

au courant /əʊ 'ku:rɑ̃/ acquainted with what is going on. [French, = in the (regular) course]

au fait /əʊ 'feɪ/ well acquainted with a subject. [French]

au fond /əʊ fɔ̃/ at bottom, basically. [French]

au grand sérieux /əʊ grɑ̃ serɪ'ɜ:/ quite seriously. [French]

au gratin /əʊ 'grætæ̃/ cooked with a crust of breadcrumbs and grated cheese. [French (*gratter* = to grate)]

au naturel /əʊ nætu:'rel/ uncooked, or cooked in the most natural or simplest way. [French, = in the natural state]

au revoir /əʊ rə'vwɑ:r/ goodbye for the moment. [French, = to see again]

avant-garde /ævɑ̃'gɑ:d/ *n.* a leading group of innovators, especially in art and literature. —*adj.* (of ideas) new, progressive. [French, = vanguard]

bête noire /beɪt 'nwɑ:(r)/ a person's chief dislike. [French, = black beast]

bona-fide /bəʊnə'faɪdɪ/ *adj.* genuine, sincere. [Latin, = in good faith]

bona fides /bəʊnə 'faɪdi:z/ honest intention, sincerity. [Latin, = good faith]

bonhomie /'bɒnəmi:/ *n.* friendly geniality. [French, from *bonhomme* = good-natured man]

bon mot /bɔ̃ 'məʊ/ a witty saying. [French, = good word]

bon vivant /bɔ̃ vi:'vɑ̃/ a gourmand. [French, = one who lives well (*vivre*=to live)]

bon voyage /bɔ̃ vwɑ:'jɑ:ʒ/ an expression of good wishes to someone beginning a journey. [French, = pleasant journey]

carte blanche /kɑ:t 'blɑ̃ʃ/ full discretionary power given to a person. [French, = blank paper]

c'est la vie /se læ 'vi:/ life is like that. [French, = that's life]

chargé d'affaires /ʃɑ:ʒeɪ dæ'feə(r)/ an ambassador's deputy; an envoy to a minor country. [French, = entrusted with affairs]

chef-d'œuvre /ʃeɪ'dɜ:vr/ *n.* a masterpiece. [French, = chief work]

chez /ʃeɪ/ *prep.* at the home of. [French]

ci-devant /si:də'vɑ̃/ *adj.* & *adv.* former; formerly. [French, = before this time]

circa /'sɜ:kə/ *prep.* about (a specified date or number). [Latin]

compos mentis /'kɒmpəs 'mentɪs/ in one's right mind; sane. (The opposite is *non compos mentis.*) [Latin, = having control of the mind]

contretemps /'kɔ̃trətɑ̃/ *n.* an unfortunate occurrence; an unexpected mishap. [French]

cordon bleu /kɔ:dɔ̃ 'blɜ:/ of the highest class in cookery; a cook of this class. [French, = blue ribbon]

corps de ballet /kɔ: də 'bæleɪ/ a company of ballet-dancers. [French]

corps diplomatique /kɔ: dɪpləmæ'ti:k/ the diplomatic corps. [French]

coup de grâce /ku: də 'grɑ:s/ a finishing stroke. [French, = mercy-blow]

coup d'état /ku: deɪ'tɑ:/ the sudden overthrow of a government, especially by force. [French, = blow of State]

crème de la crème /krem də læ 'krem/ the very best of something. [French, = cream of the cream]

curriculum vitae /kə'rɪkjʊləm 'vi:taɪ/ an account of one's previous career. [Latin, = course of life]

de facto /di: 'fæktəʊ, deɪ/ in fact, existing in fact (whether by right or not. [Latin, = from what has been done]

de haut en bas /də əʊt ɑ̃ 'bɑ:/ in a condescending or superior manner. [French, = from above to below]

déjà vu /deɪʒɑ: 'vu:/ the illusory feeling of having already experienced a present situation; something tediously familiar. [French, = already seen]

démodé /deɪ'məʊdeɪ/ *adj.* out of fashion. [French]

de mortuis nil nisi bonum /deɪ 'mɔ:tu:i:s nɪl nɪzɪ 'bəʊnəm/ say nothing but good about the dead. [Latin]

de novo /di: 'nəʊvəʊ, deɪ/ afresh, starting again. [Latin, = from new]

de rigueur /də rɪ'gɜ:(r)/ required by custom or etiquette. [French, = of strictness]

de trop /də 'trəʊ/ not wanted, in the way. [French, = excessive]

deus ex machina /'deɪəs eks 'mækɪnə/ an unexpected power or event saving a seemingly impossible situation. [Latin, = god from the machinery (with reference to the machinery by which, in ancient Greek theatre, gods were shown in the air)]

distingué /dɪ'stæŋgeɪ/ *adj.* having a distinguished air or manners. [French]

distrait /dɪ'streɪ/ *adj.* (fem. **distraite**) inattentive, distraught. [French]

doppelgänger /'dɒp(ə)lgeŋə(r)/ *n.* the wraith of a living person. [German, = double-goer]

double entendre /du:bl ãtãdr/ a phrase affording two meanings, one usually indecent. [obsolete French, = double understanding]

douceur /du:'sɜ:(r)/ *n.* a gratuity; a bribe. [French, from Latin *dulcor* = sweetness]

dramatis personae /'dræmətɪs pɜ:'səʊnaɪ/ the characters in a play; a list of these. [Latin, = persons of the drama]

embarras de richesse /ãbɑ:rɑ: də ri:'ʃes/ more wealth than one knows how to deal with. [French, = embarrassment of riches]

embonpoint /ãbɔ̃'pwæ̃/ *n.* plumpness of body. [from French *en bon point* = in good condition]

éminence grise /emınãs 'gri:z/ one who exercises power or influence without holding office. [French, = grey cardinal (originally applied to Cardinal Richlieu's secretary)]

empressment /ã'presmã/ *n.* a display of cordiality or eagerness. [French]

en bloc /ã 'blɒk/ in a block, all at the same time. [French]

en brosse /ã 'brɒs/ (of hair) cut short and bristly. [French, = in a brush]

en clair /ã 'kleə(r)/ in ordinary language, not in code or cipher. [French, = in clear]

en famille /ã fæ'mi:ə/ at home; in or with one's family. [French, = in family]

enfant terrible /ãfã te'ri:bl/ a person who causes embarrassment by indiscreet behaviour; an unruly child. [French, = terrible child]

en masse /ã mæs/ all together. [French, = in a mass]

en passant /ã 'pæsã/ by the way. [French, = in passing]

en route /ã 'ru:t/ on the way. [French]

en suite /ã 'swi:t/ forming a single unit. [French, = in sequence]

entente /ã'tãt/ *n.* a friendly understanding or association, especially between States. [French, = understanding]

entre nous /ãtrə 'nu:/ between you and me, in private. [French, = between ourselves]

esprit de corps /'espri: də 'kɔ:/ devotion and loyalty to a body by its members. [French, = spirit of the body]

eureka /jʊə'ri:kə/ *int.* I have found it. [Greek]

ex cathedra /eks kə'θi:drə/ with full authority (especially of a papal pronouncement). [Latin, = from the chair]

exceptis excipiendis /ek'septi:s eksɪpɪ'endi:s/ with the appropriate exceptions. [Latin, = with things excluded that should be excluded]

exempli gratia /eg'zemplɪ 'greɪʃə/ for the sake of an example. [Latin]

exeunt /'eksɪʊnt/ *v.i.* (as a stage direction) they leave the stage. [Latin, = they go out]

ex gratia /eks 'greɪʃə/ done or given as a concession, not from (legal) obligation. [Latin, = from kindness]

ex hypothesi /eks haɪ'pɒθəsaɪ/ according to the hypothesis proposed. [Latin]

exit /eksɪt/ *v.i.* (as a stage direction) he or she leaves the stage. [Latin, = he or she goes out]

ex officio /eks ə'fɪʃɪəʊ/ by virtue of one's office. [Latin]

ex post facto /eks pəʊst 'fæktəʊ/ retrospective, retrospectively. [Latin, = from what is done afterwards]

ex silentio /eks sɪ'lenʃɪəʊ/ by absence of contrary evidence. [Latin, = from silence]

ex voto /eks 'vəʊtəʊ/ in pursuance of a vow. [Latin, = out of a vow]

facile princeps /'fæsɪlɪ 'prɪnseps/ easily first; an acknowledged leader. [Latin]

fait accompli /feɪt ə'kɒmpli:/ a thing that has been done and is past arguing against. [French]

faute de mieux /fəʊt də 'mjɜ:/ for lack of any better alternative. [French]

faux pas /fəʊ 'pɑ:/ a tactless mistake, a blunder. [French, = false step]

femme fatale /fæm fæ'tɑ:l/ a dangerously attractive woman. [French]

fête champêtre /feɪt ʃɑ̃'peɪtr/ an outdoor entertainment, a rural festival. [French]

fils /fi:s/ (added to a name to distinguish a person from a father who has the same name) son. (Cf. *père*) [French]

fin de siécle /fæ̃ də sɪ'eɪkl/ characteristic of the end of the 19th century. [French, = end of century]

folie à deux /'fɒli: ɑ: 'dɜ:/ delusion shared by two emotionally associated persons. [French, = folly of two]

folie de grandeur /'fɒlɪ də grɑ̃'dɜ:(r)/ delusions of grandeur. [French, = folly of grandeur]

force majeure /fɔ:s mæ'ʒɜ:(r)/ irresistible force; unforeseen circumstances excusing a person from the fulfilment of a contract. [French, = superior strength]

frisson /'fri:sɔ̃/ *n.* an emotional thrill. [French, = shiver]

gemütlichkeit /gə'mu:tlɪkkeɪt/ *n.* cheerfulness, cosiness; geniality. [German]

Götterdammerung /gɜ:tə'demərʊŋ/ *n.* the twilight of the gods, the complete downfall of a regime etc. [German]

grande dame /grɑ̃d dɑ:m/ a dignified lady of high rank, or one whose manner corresponds to this. [French, = great lady]

grande passion /grɑ̃d 'pæsjɔ̃/ an overwhelming love affair. [French]

grande tenue /grɑ̃d tə'nu:/ full dress. [French]

grand mal /grɑ̃ mæl/ epilepsy with loss of consciousness. [French, = great sickness]

grand seigneur /grɑ̃ semjɜ:(r)/ a dignified man of high rank, or one whose manner corresponds to this. [French, = great lord]

habeas corpus /'heɪbɪəs 'kɔ:pəs/ a writ requiring a person under arrest to be brought before a judge or into court, especially to investigate the lawfulness of the restraint. [Latin, = you must have the body]

hapax legomenon /'hæpæks lɪ'gɒmɪnɒn/ a word of which only one instance is recorded. [Greek, = thing said once]

hara-kiri /hærə'kɪrɪ/ *n.* ritual suicide involving disembowelment with the sword, formerly practised by samurai to avoid dishonour. [from Japanese *hara* = belly, *kiri* = cutting]

hoi polloi /hɔɪ pə'lɔɪ/ the masses, the common people. [Greek, = the many]

Homo sapiens /'həʊməʊ 'sæpɪenz/ modern mankind regarded as a species. [Latin, = wise man]

honoris causa /ɒ'nɔ:rɪs 'kaʊzə/ as a mark of esteem. [Latin, = for the sake of honour]

hors concours /ɔ:r kɔ̃'kʊə(r)/ not competing for a prize. [French, = outside the contest]

hors de combat /ɔ:r də 'kɔ̃bɑ:/ out of the fight; disabled by an injury etc. [French]

hors d'œuvre /ɔ:r 'dɜ:vr/ an appetizer served at the beginning of a meal. [French, = outside the work]

ignotum per ignotius /ɪg'nəʊtəm pɜ: ɪg'nəʊtɪəs/ an explanation that is more obscure than the thing it is meant to explain. [Latin, = the unknown by the still less known]

imperium /ɪm'perɪəm/ *n.* absolute power. [Latin, = command, dominion]

in absentia /ɪn æb'sentɪə/ in (his or her or their) absence. [Latin]

in camera /ɪn ˈkæmərə/ in a judge's private room; privately, not in public. [Latin, = in the vault]

in extenso /ɪn eksˈtensəʊ/ at full length. [Latin]

in extremis /ɪn eksˈtri:mɪs/ at the point of death; in great difficulties. [Latin, = in the greatest danger]

in flagrante delicto /ɪn flæˈgræntɪ deˈlɪktəʊ/ in the very act of committing an offence. [Latin, = in blazing crime]

infra /ˈɪnfrə/ *adv.* below or further on in a book etc. [Latin, = below]

infra dig /ˈɪnfrə ˈdɪg/ beneath one's dignity. [abbreviation of Latin *infra dignitatem*]

in loco parentis /ɪn lɒkəʊ pəˈrentɪs/ in the position of a parent, with a parent's responsibility. [Latin]

in medias res /ɪn medɪɑ:s ˈrez/ into the midst of things; into the middle of a narrative etc. [Latin]

in memoriam /ɪn mɪˈmɔ:rɪæm/ in memory of. [Latin]

in re /ɪn ri:/ in the matter of. [Latin]

in situ /ɪn ˈsɪtju:/ in its original place. [Latin]

in statu pupillari /ɪn ˈstætu: pu:pɪˈlɑ:rɪ/ under guardianship; in junior status at a university, not having a master's degree. [Latin]

in statu quo /ɪn ˈstætu: ˈkwəʊ/ in the same state as formerly. [Latin]

inter alia /ɪntər ˈeɪlɪə/ among other things. [Latin]

in utero /ɪn ˈju:tərəʊ/ in the womb; before birth. [Latin]

in vitro /ɪn ˈvɪtrəʊ/ in a test-tube or other laboratory environment. [Latin, = in glass]

in vivo /ɪn ˈvi:vəʊ/ in the living body. [Latin]

ipse dixit /ˈɪpsɪ ˈdɪksɪt/ a dogmatic statement resting solely on the speaker's authority. [Latin, = he himself said it]

ipsissima verba /ɪpˈsɪsɪmə ˈvɜ:bə/ the precise words. [Latin]

ipso facto /ˈɪpsəʊ ˈfæktəʊ/ by that very fact. [Latin]

j'adoube /ʒɑ:ˈdu:b/ (in chess) a statement indicating that one does not intend to move the man one is about to touch. [French, = I adjust]

je ne sais quoi /ʒə nə seɪ ˈkwɑ:/ an indefinable something. [French, = I do not know what]

jeu d'esprit /ʒɜ: desˈpri:/ a witty or humorous trifle; a witticism. [French, = sport of wit]

jeunesse dorée /ˈʒɜ:nes ˈdɔ:reɪ/ gilded youth, wealthy fashionable young people. [French]

joie de vivre /ʒwɑ: də ˈvi:vr/ a feeling of exuberant enjoyment of life; high spirits. [French, = joy of living]

laissez-aller /leɪseɪˈæleɪ/ *n.* unconstrained freedom; lack of constraint. [French, = allow to go]

laissez-faire /leɪseɪˈfeə(r)/ *n.* a policy of non-interference. [French, = allow to act]

laissez-passer /leɪseɪˈpɑ:seɪ/ *n.* a document allowing the holder to pass. [French, = allow to pass]

langue de chat /lɑ̃ŋ də ˈʃɑ:/ a very thin finger-shaped piece of chocolate or crisp biscuit. [French, = cat's tongue]

lebensraum /ˈleɪbənzraʊm/ *n.* territory which the Germans (in the 1930s) believed was needed for their natural development as a nation. [German, = living-space]

lèse-majesté /leɪzˈmæʒestɪ/ *n.* treason; an insult to a sovereign or ruler; presumptuous conduct. [French, = injury to the sovereign]

lusus naturae /ˈlu:zəs næˈtʊəraɪ/ a sport or freak of nature, a strikingly abnormal natural production. [Latin]

magnum opus /mægnəm ˈəʊpəs/ a great work of literature etc.; an author's greatest work. [Latin, = great work]

maître d'hôtel /meɪtr dəʊˈtel/ a major-domo; a head waiter. [French, = master of house]

mal de mer /mæl də ˈmer/ seasickness. [French, = sickness of sea]

mariage de convenance /'mærɪɑ:ʒ də 'kɔ̃vənɑ̃s/ marriage of convenience. [French]

matériel /mətɪərɪ'el/ *n.* stock-in-trade; available means; materials and equipment (opp. *personnel*) for use in warfare. [French, = material, stores]

mauvais quart d'heur /məʊveɪ kær 'dɜ:r/ a short but unpleasant experience, interview, etc. [French, = bad quarter of an hour]

mésalliance /meɪ'zælɪɑ̃s/ *n.* marriage with a social inferior. [French, = misalliance]

mirabile dictu /mɪ'rɑ:bɪleɪ 'dɪktu:/ wonderful to relate. [Latin]

mise en scène /mi:z ɑ̃ 'seɪn/ the scenery and properties of an acted play; the surroundings of an event. [French, = put on the stage]

modus operandi /'məʊdəs ɒpə'rændɪ/ the way a person goes about a task; the way a thing operates. [Latin, = mode of working]

modus vivendi /'məʊdəs vɪ'vendɪ/ a way of living or coping. [Latin, = mode of living]

mot juste /məʊ 'ʒu:st/ the expression that conveys a desired shade of meaning more precisely than any other. [French, = correct word]

multum in parvo /'mʊltəm ɪn 'pɑ:vəʊ/ much in a small compass. [Latin, = much in little]

mutatis mutandis /mu:'tɑ:ti:s mu:'tændi:s/ with due alteration of details (in comparing cases). [Latin, = with things changed that need to be changed]

nem. con. /nem 'kɒn/ *abbr.* nemine contradicente = with no one dissenting. [Latin]

noblesse oblige /nəʊ'bles ɒ'bli:ʒ/ privilege entails responsibility. [French, = nobility has obligations]

nolens volens /'nəʊlenz 'vəʊlenz/ willy-nilly, perforce. [Latin, = being unwilling, being willing]

noli me tangere /'nəʊlɪ meɪ 'tæŋgerɪ/ touch me not, a warning against meddling or approach. [Latin; cf. John 20:17]

nom de guerre /nɒm də 'ger/ an assumed name under which a person fights, plays, writes, etc. [French, = war-name]

nom de plume /nɒm də 'plu:m/ a writer's assumed name. [sham French, = pen-name]

non compos mentis see *compos mentis.*

non est /nɒn 'est/ non-existent; absent. [Latin]

non sequitur /nɒn 'sekwɪtə(r)/ a conclusion that does not logically follow from the premises. [Latin, = it does not follow]

nota bene /'nəʊtə 'beneɪ/ take notice, observe what follows. [Latin, = note well]

nouveau riche /nu:vəʊ 'ri:ʃ/ one who has acquired wealth only recently, especially one who displays this ostentatiously. [French, = new rich]

nouvelle cuisine /nu:vel kwɪ'zi:n/ a style of cooking that avoids traditional rich sauces and emphasizes fresh ingredients and attractive presentation. [French, = new cookery]

obiter dictum /'ɒbɪtə(r) 'dɪktəm/ a judge's expression of opinion that does not have binding authority; an incidental remark. [Latin, = thing said by the way]

objet d'art /ɒbʒeɪ 'dɑ:(r)/ a small decorative object. [French, = object of art]

obscurum per obscurius /ɒb'skʊərəm pər ɒb'skʊrɪəs/ an explanation that is more obscure than the thing it is meant to explain. [Latin, = the obscure by the still more obscure]

on dit /ɔ̃ 'di:/ a piece of gossip or hearsay. [French, = they say]

pace /'peɪsɪ, 'pɑ:tʃeɪ/ *prep.* (in announcing a contrary opinion) with all due deference to (the person named). [Latin, = with peace]

par excellence /pɑ:r ekse'lɑ̃s/ above all others that may be so called. [French, = by virtue of special excellence]

passé /'pæseɪ/ *adj.* behind the times; past the prime. [French, = past]

passim /'pæsɪm/ *adv.* throughout or at many points in a book or article etc. [Latin]

per annum /pɜːr 'ænəm/ for each year. [Latin]

per capita /pɜː 'kæpɪtə/ for each person. [Latin, = by heads]

per pro. /pɜː 'prəʊ/ *abbr.* per procurationem, by proxy. [Latin]

per se /pɜː 'seɪ/ by or in itself, intrinsically. [Latin]

persona grata /pɜː'səʊnə 'grɑːtə/ a person acceptable to certain others, especially a diplomat acceptable to a foreign government. (The opposite is *persona non grata*.) [Latin, = pleasing person]

petit bourgeois /pəti: 'bʊəʒwɑː/ a member of the lower middle classes. [French]

petit four /pəti: 'fʊə(r)/ a very small fancy cake. [French, = little oven]

petit mal /pəti: 'mæl/ a mild form of epilepsy without loss of consciousness. [French, = small sickness]

petit point /pəti: 'pwæ̃/ embroidery on canvas using small stitches. [French]

pièce de résistance /pɪəs də re'zɪstɑ̃s/ the most important or remarkable item; the main dish at a meal. [French]

pied-à-terre /pjeɪdɑː'te(r)/ *n.* a place kept available as temporary quarters when needed. [French, = foot to earth]

pietà /pɪeɪ'tɑː/ *n.* a picture or sculpture of the Virgin Mary holding the dead body of Christ on her lap. [Italian, from Latin *pius* = dutiful]

pis aller /piːz æ'leɪ/ a course of action etc. followed because nothing better is available. [French, *pis* = worse, *aller* = to go]

plein air /plen 'eə(r)/ (in painting) representing effects of atmosphere and light that are not observable in a studio. [French, = open air]

post hoc /pəʊst 'hɒk/ the (false) reasoning that because something happened after something else it was caused by the earlier event. [Latin, short for *post hoc ergo propter hoc* = after this therefore because of this]

prima donna /'priːmə 'dɒnə/ the chief female singer in an opera. [Italian, = first lady]

prima facie /'praɪmə 'feɪʃiː/ at first sight; (of evidence) based on the first impression. [Latin, = on first appearance]

primus inter pares /'priːməs ɪntə 'pɑːrez/ first among equals; the senior member of a group whose members are notionally of equal status. [Latin]

pro bono publico /prəʊ 'bəʊnəʊ 'pʊblɪkəʊ/ for the public good. [Latin]

pro rata /prəʊ 'rɑːtə/ proportional; in proportion. [Latin, = according to the rate]

pro tempore /prəʊ 'tempərɪ/ (abbr. *pro tem*) for the time being. [Latin, = for the time]

proxime accessit /'prɒksɪmɪ æk'sesɪt/ (he or she is) the runner-up, the person finishing next to the prizewinner in an examination etc. [Latin, = came very near]

quand même /kɑ̃ 'mem/ despite any consequences, even so. [French, = all the same]

quid pro quo /kwɪd prəʊ 'kwəʊ/ a thing given as compensation. [Latin, = something for something]

qui vive /ki: 'viːv/ on the qui vive, on the alert. [French, = (long) live who? (at sentry's challenge), i.e. whom do you support?]

quod erat demonstrandum /kwɒd er'æt demən'strændəm/ which was the thing to be proved. [Latin]

raison d'être /reɪzɔ̃ 'detr/ the purpose or reason that accounts for or justifies or originally caused a thing's existence. [French, = reason for being]

reductio ad absurdum /rɪ'dʌktɪəʊ æd əb'sɜːdəm/ proof that something is false by showing its absurd logical consequence. [Latin, = reduction to the absurd]

requiescat in pace /rekwɪ'eskæt ɪn 'pɑːtʃeɪ/ may he or she rest in peace. [Latin]

rigor mortis /'raɪgə(r) 'mɔːtɪs/ stiffening of the body after death. [Latin, = stiffness of death]

sang-froid /sɑ̃'frwɑː/ *n.* calmness in danger or difficulty. [French, = cold blood]

sans peur et sans reproche /sɑ̃ pɜːr eɪ sɑ̃ rə'prɒʃ/ chivalrous in character. [French, = without fear and without reproach]

sauve qui peut /səʊv ki: 'pɜ:/ precipitate flight. [French, = save (himself) who can]

savoir faire /sævwɑ: 'feə(r)/ knowledge of how to behave in any situation that may arise; tact. [French, = know how to do]

schadenfreude /'ʃɑ:dənfrɔɪdə/ *n.* malicious enjoyment of others' misfortunes. [German (*schaden* = harm, *freude* = joy)]

sic /sɪk/ *adv.* thus used or spelt etc. (used in brackets to confirm or call attention to the form of quoted words). [Latin, = thus]

simpliciter /sɪm'plɪsɪtə(r)/ *adv.* universally, without limitation. [Latin, = simply]

soi-disant /swɑ:'di:zɑ̃/ *adj.* self-styled, pretended. [French (*soi* = oneself, *disant* = saying)]

sotto voce /'sɒtəʊ 'vəʊtʃɪ/ in an undertone. [Italian, = under the voice]

status quo /'steɪtəs 'kwəʊ/ the state of affairs as it is or as it was before a recent change. [Latin *status* = standing, *quo* = in which (*ante* = before)]

sub finem /sʌb 'fi:nem/ towards the end. [Latin]

sub judice -sʌb 'dʒu:dɪsɪ/ under judicial consideration, not yet decided. [Latin, = under a judge]

sub rosa /sʌb 'rəʊzə/ in confidence, secretly. [Latin, = under the rose, as emblem of secrecy]

succès de scandale /sʊkseɪ də skɑ̃'dɑ:l/ an eager reception given to a work because of its scandalous nature or associations. [French, = success of scandal]

succès d'estime /sʊkseɪ des'ti:m/ a cordial reception given to a performance or work because of respect for its performer or author rather than appreciation of its merits. [French, = success of respect]

succès fou /sʊkseɪ 'fu:/ a success marked by wild enthusiasm. [French, = wild or unbelievable success]

suggestio falsi /sə'dʒestɪəʊ 'fælsaɪ/ misrepresentation that does not involve a direct lie but goes beyond concealment of the truth. (Cf. *suppressio veri.*) [Latin, = supplying a falsehood]

sui generis /su:aɪ 'dʒenərɪs/ of its own kind, peculiar, unique. [Latin]

summum bonum /sʊməm 'bəʊnəm/ the chief good. [Latin]

suppressio veri /sə'presɪəv 'veəraɪ/ concealment of the truth; misrepresentation by concealment of facts that ought to be made known. (Cf. *suggestio falsi.*) [Latin]

tableau vivant /tæbləʊ 'vi:vɑ̃/ a silent and motionless group of persons etc. representing a scene. [French, = living picture]

table d'hôte /tɑ:bl 'dəʊt/ a meal at a fixed price in a hotel etc., with less choice of dishes than à la carte. [French, = host's table]

terra firma /terə 'fɜ:mə/ dry land, firm ground. [Latin]

terra incognita /terə ɪn'kɒgnɪtə/ an unknown or unexplored region. [Latin]

tête-à-tête /teɪtɑ:'teɪt/ *n.* a private conversation or interview, usually between two persons. [French, = head-to-head]

tour de force /tʊə də 'fɔ:s/ a great feat of strength or skill. [French]

tout ensemble /tu:t ɑ̃'sɑ̃bl/ a thing viewed as a whole. [French, = all the group]

tu quoque /tu: 'kwɒkweɪ/ the retort 'and so are you' or 'and so did you'. [Latin, = you too]

urbi et orbi /ɜ:bɪ et 'ɔ:bɪ/ to the city (i.e. Rome) and for the world (the Pope's solemn blessing given from a balcony of St Peter's church, Rome). [Latin]

verboten /vɜ:'bəʊt(ə)n/ *adj.* forbidden. [German]

vers libre /veər 'li:br/ verse composition using variable rhythm or mixing different metres or disregarding prosodic conventions. [French, = free verse]

vice /'vaɪsɪ/ *prep.* in the place of, in succession to. [Latin, = by change]

vide /'vi:deɪ, 'vaɪdɪ/ *v.t.* see, consult. [Latin]

vieux jeu /vjɜ: 'ʒɜ:/ old-fashioned, hackneyed. [French, = old game]

vin ordinaire /væ̃ ɔ:dɪ'neə(r)/ cheap wine. [French]

vis-à-vis /viːzɑːˈviː/ *prep.* in relation to; facing, opposite to. [French, = face to face]

vivat /ˈvaɪvæt/ *v.i.* long live (the king or queen etc.). [Latin]

viva voce /ˈvaɪvə ˈvəʊtʃɪ/ a spoken examination. [Latin, = with the living voice]

volte-face /vɒltˈfɑːs/ *n.* a complete reversal of position in an argument or opinion. [French, = turn of face]

vox populi /vɒks ˈpɒpjʊlɪ, -laɪ/ public opinion, the general verdict, popular belief. [Latin, = the people's voice]

Weltschmerz /ˈveltʃmeərts/ *n.* an apathetic or vaguely yearning outlook on life. [German (*welt* = world, *schmerz* = pain)]

APPENDIX XII

The Chemical Elements

Element	*Symbol*	*Atomic number*	*Element*	*Symbol*	*Atomic number*
actinium	Ac	89	iridium	Ir	77
aluminium	Al	13	iron	Fe	26
americium	Am	95	krypton	Kr	36
antimony	Sb	51	lanthanum	La	57
argon	Ar	18	lawrencium	Lr	103
arsenic	As	33	lead	Pb	82
astatine	At	85	lithium	Li	3
barium	Ba	56	lutetium	Lu	71
berkelium	Bk	97	magnesium	Mg	12
beryllium	Be	4	manganese	Mn	25
bismuth	Bi	83	mendelevium	Md	101
boron	B	5	mercury	Hg	80
bromine	Br	35	molybdenum	Mo	42
cadmium	Cd	48	neodymium	Nd	60
caesium	Cs	55	neon	Ne	10
calcium	Ca	20	neptunium	Np	93
californium	Cf	98	nickel	Ni	28
carbon	C	6	niobium	Nb	41
cerium	Ce	58	nitrogen	N	7
chlorine	Cl	17	nobelium	No	102
chromium	Cr	24	osmium	Os	76
cobalt	Co	27	oxygen	O	8
copper	Cu	29	palladium	Pd	46
curium	Cm	96	phosphorus	P	15
dysprosium	Dy	66	platinum	Pt	78
einsteinium	Es	99	plutonium	Pu	94
erbium	Er	68	polonium	Po	84
europium	Eu	63	potassium	K	19
fermium	Fm	100	praseodymium	Pr	59
fluorine	F	9	promethium	Pm	61
francium	Fr	87	protactinium	Pa	91
gadolinium	Gd	64	radium	Ra	88
gallium	Ga	31	radon	Rn	86
germanium	Ge	32	rhenium	Re	75
gold	Au	79	rhodium	Rh	45
hafnium	Hf	72	rubidium	Rb	37
hahnium	Ha	105	ruthenium	Ru	44
helium	He	2	rutherfordium	Rf	104
holmium	Ho	67	samarium	Sm	62
hydrogen	H	1	scandium	Sc	21
indium	In	49	selenium	Se	34
iodine	I	53	silicon	Si	14

Element	*Symbol*	*Atomic number*
silver	Ag	47
sodium	Na	11
strontium	Sr	38
sulphur	S	16
tantalum	Ta	73
technetium	Tc	43
tellurium	Te	52
terbium	Tb	65
thallium	Tl	81
thorium	Th	90
thulium	Tm	69
tin	Sn	50
titanium	Ti	22
tungsten	W	74
uranium	U	92
vanadium	V	23
xenon	Xe	54
ytterbium	Yb	70
yttrium	Y	39
zinc	Zn	30
zirconium	Zr	40

APPENDIX XIII

Weights and Measures

Note. The conversion factors are not exact unless so marked. They are given only to the accuracy likely to be needed in everyday calculations.

1. British and American, with metric equivalents

Linear Measure

1 inch	=25.4 millimetres exactly
1 foot = 12 inches	=0.3048 metre exactly
1 yard = 3 feet	=0.9144 metre exactly
1 (statute) mile = 1,760 yards	= 1.609 kilometres

Square Measure

1 square inch	=6.45 sq. centimetres
1 square foot = 144 sq. in.	=9.29 sq. decimetres
1 square yard = 9 sq. ft.	=0.836 sq. metre
1 acre = 4,840 sq. yd.	=0.405 hectare
1 square mile = 640 acres	=259 hectares

Cubic Measure

1 cubic inch	=16.4 cu. centimetres
1 cubic foot = 1,728 cu. in.	=0.0283 cu. metre
1 cubic yard = 27 cu. ft.	=0.765 cu. metre

Capacity Measure

British

1 pint = 20 fluid oz. = 34.68 cu. in.	=0.568 litre
1 quart = 2 pints	= 1.136 litres
1 gallon = 4 quarts	=4.546 litres
1 peck = 2 gallons	=9.092 litres
1 bushel = 4 pecks	=36.4 litres
1 quarter = 8 bushels	=2.91 hectolitres

American dry

1 pint = 33.60 cu. in.	=0.550 litre
1 quart = 2 pints	= 1.101 litres
1 peck = 8 quarts	=8.81 litres
1 bushel = 4 pecks	=35.3 litres

American liquid

1 pint = 16 fluid oz. = 28.88 cu. in.	=0.473 litre
1 quart = 2 pints	=0.946 litre
1 gallon = 4 quarts	=3.785 litres

Avoirdupois Weight

1 grain	=0.065 gram
1 dram	=1.772 grams
1 ounce = 16 drams	=28.35 grams
1 pound = 16 ounces = 7,000 grains	=0.4536 kilogram (0.45359237 exactly)
1 stone = 14 pounds	=6.35 kilograms
1 quarter = 2 stones	=12.70 kilograms
1 hundredweight = 4 quarters	=50.80 kilograms
1 (long) ton = 20 hundredweight	=1.016 tonnes
1 short ton = 2,000 pounds	=0.907 tonne

2. Metric, with British equivalents

Linear Measure

1 millimetre	=0.039 inch
1 centimetre = 10 mm	=0.394 inch
1 decimetre = 10 cm	=3.94 inches
1 metre = 10 dm	=1.094 yards
1 decametre = 10 m	=10.94 yards
1 hectometre = 100 m	=109.4 yards
1 kilometre = 1,000 m	=0.6214 mile

Square Measure

1 square centimetre	=0.155 sq. inch
1 square metre = 10,000 sq. cm	=1.196 sq. yards
1 are = 100 sq. metres	=119.6 sq. yards
1 hectare = 100 ares	=2.471 acres
1 square kilometre = 100 hectares	=0.386 sq. mile

Cubic Measure

1 cubic centimetre	= 0.061 cu. inch
1 cubic metre = 1,000,000 cu. cm	= 1.308 cu. yards

Capacity Measure

1 millilitre	= 0.002 pint (British)
1 centilitre = 10 ml	= 0.018 pint
1 decilitre = 10 cl	= 0.176 pint
1 litre = 10 dl	= 1.76 pints
1 decalitre = 10 l	= 2.20 gallons
1 hectolitre = 100 l	= 2.75 bushels
1 kilolitre = 1,000 l	= 3.44 quarters

Weight

1 milligram	= 0.015 grain
1 centigram = 10 mg	= 0.154 grain
1 decigram = 10 cg	= 1.543 grains
1 gram = 10 dg	= 15.43 grains
1 decagram = 10 g	= 5.64 drams
1 hectogram = 100 g	= 3.527 ounces
1 kilogram = 1,000 g	= 2.205 pounds
1 tonne (metric ton) = 1,000 kg	= 0.984 (long) ton

3. Power notation

This expresses concisely any power of ten (any number that is composed of factors 10), and is sometimes used in the dictionary. 10^2 or ten squared = $10 \times 10 = 100$; 10^3 or ten cubed = $10 \times 10 \times 10 = 1{,}000$. Similarly, $10^4 = 10{,}000$ and $10^{10} = 1$ followed by ten noughts = 10,000,000,000. Proceeding in the opposite direction, dividing by ten and subtracting one from the index, we have $10^2 = 100$, $10^1 = 10$, $10^0 = 1$, $10^{-1} = \frac{1}{10}$, $10^{-2} = \frac{1}{100}$, and so on; $10^{-10} = 1/10^{10} = 1/10{,}000{,}000{,}000$.

4. Temperature

Fahrenheit: Water boils (under standard conditions) at 212° and freezes at 32°.

Celsius or Centigrade: Water boils at 100° and freezes at 0°.

Kelvin: Water boils at 373.15 K and freezes at 273.15 K.

Celsius	*Fahrenheit*
−17.8°	0°
−10°	14°
0°	32°
10°	50°
20°	68°
30°	86°
40°	104°
50°	122°
60°	140°
70°	158°
80°	176°
90°	194°
100°	212°

To convert Celsius into Fahrenheit: multiply by 9, divide by 5, and add 32.

To convert Fahrenheit into Celsius: subtract 32, multiply by 5, and divide by 9.

5. Metric prefixes

	Abbreviation or Symbol	*Factor*
deca-	da	10
hecto-	h	10^2
kilo-	k	10^3
mega-	M	10^6
giga-	G	10^9
tera-	T	10^{12}
peta-	P	10^{15}
exa-	E	10^{18}
deci-	d	10^{-1}
centi-	c	10^{-2}
milli-	m	10^{-3}
micro-	μ	10^{-6}
nano-	n	10^{-9}
pico-	p	10^{-12}
femto-	f	10^{-15}
atto-	a	10^{-18}

Pronunciations and derivations of these are given at their alphabetical places in the dictionary. They may be applied to any units of the metric system: hectogram (abbr. hg) = 100 grams; kilowatt (abbr. kW) = 1,000 watts; megahertz (MHz) = 1 million hertz; centimetre (cm) = $\frac{1}{100}$ metre; microvolt (μV) = one millionth of a volt; picofarad (pF) = 10^{-12} farad, and are sometimes applied to other units (megabit, microinch).

6. Chemical notation

The symbol for a molecule (such as H_2O, CH_4, H_2SO_4) shows the symbols for the elements contained in it (C = carbon, H = hydrogen, etc.), followed by a subscript numeral denoting the number of atoms of each element in the molecule where this number is more than one. For example, the water molecule (H_2O) contains two atoms of hydrogen and one of oxygen.

7. SI units

Base Units

Physical quantity	*Name*	*Abbreviation or Symbol*
length	metre	m
mass	kilogram	kg
time	second	s
electric current	ampere	A
temperature	kelvin	K
amount of substance	mole	mol
luminous intensity	candela	cd

Supplementary Units

Physical quantity	*Name*	*Abbreviation or Symbol*
plane angle	radian	rad
solid angle	steradian	sr

Derived Units with Special Names

Physical quantity	*Name*	*Abbreviation or Symbol*
frequency	hertz	Hz
energy	joule	J
force	newton	N
power	watt	W
pressure	pascal	Pa
electric charge	coulomb	C
electromotive force	volt	V
electric resistance	ohm	Ω
electric conductance	siemens	S
electric capacitance	farad	F
magnetic flux	weber	Wb
inductance	henry	H
magnetic flux density	tesla	T
luminous flux	lumen	lm
illumination	lux	lx

8. Binary system

Only two units (0 and 1) are used, and the position of each unit indicates a power of two.

One to ten written in binary form:

	eights (2^3)	*fours* (2^2)	*twos* (2^1)	*one*
1				1
2			1	0
3			1	1
4		1	0	0
5		1	0	1
6		1	1	0
7		1	1	1
8	1	0	0	0
9	1	0	0	1
10	1	0	1	0

i.e. ten is written as 1010 (2^3+0+2^1+0); one hundred is written as 1100100 ($2^6+2^5+0+0+2^2+0+0$).

APPENDIX XIV

Roman Numerals

I	=	1	XX	=	20
II	=	2	XXX	=	30
III	=	3	XL	=	40
IV	=	4	L	=	50
V	=	5	LX	=	60
VI	=	6	LXX	=	70
VII	=	7	LXXX	=	80
VIII	=	8	XC	=	90
IX	=	9	C	=	100
X	=	10	CC	=	200
XI	=	11	CCC	=	300
XII	=	12	CD	=	400
XIII	=	13	D	=	500
XIV	=	14	DC	=	600
XV	=	15	DCC	=	700
XVI	=	16	DCCC	=	800
XVII	=	17	CM	=	900
XVIII	=	18	M	=	1000
XIX	=	19	MM	=	2000

MCMXC = 1990

APPENDIX XV

Some Points of English Usage

What follows is intended as guidance on a number of uses that, although widely found, are the subject of adverse comment by informed users. They should be avoided, especially in formal speech or writing. For further information see *The Oxford Miniguide to English Usage* by E. S. C. Weiner (1983).

1. Pronunciation

The following words are often mispronounced:

capitalist	/'kæpɪtəlɪst/	not /kə'pɪt-/
comparable	/'kɒmpərəb(ə)l/	not /kəm'pær-/
contribute	/kən'trɪbju:t/	not /'kɒn-/
controversy	/'kɒntrəvɜ:sɪ/	is preferable to /kən'trɒv-/
deity	/'di:ɪtɪ/	not /'deɪ-/
dispute	/dɪ'spju:t/	not /'dɪs-/
distribute	/dɪ'strɪbju:t/	not /'dɪs-/
exquisite	/'ekskwɪzɪt/	not /ɪks'kwɪz-/
formidable	/'fɔ:mɪdəb(ə)l/	not /fə'mɪd-/
harass(ment)	/'hærəs/	not /hə'ræs/
irreparable	/ɪ'repərəb(ə)l/	not /ɪrɪ'pær-/
irrevocable	/ɪ'revəkəb(ə)l/	not /ɪrɪ'vəʊk-/
kilometre	/'kɪləmi:tə(r)/	is preferable to /kɪ'lɒm-/
lamentable	/'læmɪntəb(ə)l/	not /lə'ment-/
length	/leŋθ/	not /lenθ/
preferable	/'prefərəb(ə)l/	not /prɪ'fɜ:rəb(ə)l/
primarily	/'praɪmərɪlɪ/	not /praɪ'meər-/
reputable	/'repjʊtəb(ə)l/	not /rɪ'pju:t-/
secretary	/'sekrətrɪ/	not /'sekɪteərɪ/
strength	/streŋθ/	not /strenθ/
surveillance	/sɜ:'veɪləns/	not /sə'veɪjəns/
temporarily	/'tempərərɪlɪ/	not /tempə're-/
trait	/treɪ/	not /treɪt/
vulnerable	/'vʌlnərəb(ə)l/	not /'vʌn-/

2. Spellings

Avoid these common misspellings:

alright the correct form is **all right**
barbeque the correct form is **barbecue**
onto the correct form is **on to**
'til the correct form is **till** (it is not a contraction of **until**)

3. Meanings

The following words are often misused:

alibi is not a synonym for 'excuse'
anticipate is not a synonym for 'expect'
dilemma is not a synonym for 'problem'
disinterested does not mean 'uninterested'
enormity does not mean 'largeness' or 'magnitude'
fulsome is not a synonym for 'full' or 'copious'
parameter does not mean 'limit'
protagonist does not mean 'advocate' or 'champion'
refute is not a synonym for 'repudiate' or 'deny'
transpire does not mean 'happen'

Do not confuse:

alternate	*and*	alternative
comprise	*and*	compose
deprecate	*and*	depreciate
derisive	*and*	derisory
flaunt	*and*	flount
infer	*and*	imply
militate	*and*	mitigate
seasonable	*and*	seasonal

4. Plurals

bacteria is the plural of **bacterium**
criteria is the plural of **criterion**
data is the plural of **datum** (see below)
graffiti is the plural of **graffito**
media is the plural of **medium**
referendums is the recommended plural of **referendum**, not *referenda*
strata is the plural of **stratum**

None of these plurals should be used with a singular verb or with *that* or *this*. Correct use is *these bacteria* (the singular is *this bacterium*). The word *data* is now often used (like 'information') with a singular verb in the context of computers, e.g. *the data is entered here*; in other contexts it should be used (like 'facts') with a plural verb, e.g. *these data are correct*.

5. Grammar

The following points often cause confusion:

less means 'a smaller amount or quantity of' and is used with nouns such as *money* or *porridge*, whereas
fewer means 'a smaller number of' and is used with plural nouns such as *people* or *buttons*.

shall and **will** should be used in the following way:

(i) To express the simple future, use
I/we **shall**
you **will**
he/she/it/they **will**
as in 'I shall be at home tomorrow'; 'he will arrive later'

(ii) To express determination or a promise, use
I/we **will**
you **shall**
he/she/it/they **shall**
as in 'I *will* be heard'; 'you *shall* go to the ball'

These are the rules for strictly correct usage, but nowadays many people use *will* for the simple future after *I* and *we*, and it is not usually regarded as wrong.

should and **would** should be used in the following way:
I/we **should** like to come
I/we **should** say so
you/he/she/they **would** like to come
you/he/she/they **would** say so
it **would** be correct

In polite statements (such as *I should like to come*), although *should* is strictly correct many people nowadays use *would* after *I* and *we* as well as after other pronouns, and this is not regarded as wrong.

When the meaning is *ought to*, **should** is used in all cases:
I/you/he/she/we/you/they **should** be able to find it
it **should** be quite easy

APPENDIX XVI

Punctuation

Apostrophe

1. Used to indicate the possessive case:

singular	*a boy's book; a day's work; the boss's chair*
plural with *s*	*a girls' school; two weeks' holiday; the bosses' chairs*
plural without *s*	*children's books; women's liberation*
names: singular	*Bill's book; Thomas's coat*
	Barnabas' (or *Barnabas's*) *book; Nicholas'* (or *Nicholas's*) *coat*

names ending in *-es* pronounced /-ɪz/ are treated like plurals: *Bridges' poems; Moses' mother*

before the word *sake*: *for God's sake; for goodness' sake; for Charles's sake*

business names often omit the apostrophe: *Debenhams; Barclays Bank*

2. Used to mark an omission of one or more letters:

e'er (=ever); *he's* (=he is or he has); *we'll* (=we shall or we will); '88 (=1988)

- Incorrect uses: (i) the apostrophe must not be used with a plural where there is no possessive sense, as in *tea's are served here*; (ii) there is no such word as *her's, our's, their's, your's*
- Confusions: *it's*=it is or it has (not 'belonging to it'); correct uses are *it's here* (=it is here); *it's gone* (=it has gone); but *the dog wagged its tail* (no apostrophe)
  who's=who is or who has; correct uses are *who's there?*; *who's taken my pen?*; but *whose book is this?* (*whose*=belonging to whom)

Colon

1. Used to introduce an example or a list:

Please send the following items: passport, two photographs, the correct fee.

2. Used to introduce an interpretation or description of what precedes it:

There is one thing we need: money.

I have news for you: we have won!

3. Used to introduce speech in a play or in a newspaper report where quotation marks are omitted:
   Defence lawyer: Objection!
   Judge: Objection overruled.

Comma

The comma marks a slight break between words or phrases etc. Among its specific uses are the following:

1. to separate items in a list:
   red, white, and blue
   bread, butter, jam, and cake
2. to separate main clauses:
   Cars will park here, coaches will turn left.
3. after (or before and after) a vocative or a clause etc. with no finite verb:
   Reader, I married him.
   Well, Mr Jones, we meet again.
   Having had lunch, we went back to work.
4. to separate phrases etc. in order to clarify meaning:
   In the valley below, the villages looked very small.
   In 1988, 1918 seems a long time ago.
5. following words that introduce direct speech, or after direct speech where there is no question mark or exclamation mark:
   They answered, 'Here we are'.
   'Here we are,' they answered.
6. after *Dear Sir*, *Dear John*, etc. in letters, and after *Yours faithfully*, *Yours sincerely*, etc.; after a vocative such as *My Lord*.
7. to separate a parenthetical word, phrase, or clause:
   I am sure, however, that it will not happen.
   Autumn, the season of mists, is here again.

- No comma is needed between month and year in dates (e.g. *in December 1988*) or between number and road in addresses (e.g. *17 Belsyre Court*).

Dash

1. Used to mark the beginning and end of an interruption in the structure of a sentence:
   My son—where has he gone?—would like to meet you.

2. In print, a line slightly longer than a hyphen is used to join pairs or groups of words where it is often equivalent to *to* or *versus*:
   the 1914–18 war; the London–Horsham–Brighton route; the Marxist–Trotskyite split

(See also **hyphen**.)

Exclamation mark

Used after an exclamatory word, phrase, or sentence, or an interjection:
Well! If it isn't John!
Order! Order!

Full stop

1. Used at the end of all sentences that are not questions or exclamations.
2. Used after abbreviations:
   H. G. Wells; B.Litt.; Sun. (=Sunday); *Jan.* (=January); p. 7 (=page 7); *e.g.; etc.; a.m.; p.m.*

- A full stop should not be used with the numerical abbreviations *1st, 2nd, 3rd,* etc., nor with acronyms such as *Aslef, Naafi,* nor with words that are colloquial abbreviations (e.g. *Co-op, demo, recap, vac*).
- Full stops are not essential in abbreviations consisting entirely of capitals (e.g. *BBC, NNE, AD, BC, PLC*), nor with *C* (=Celsius), *F* (=Fahrenheit), chemical symbols, and measures of length, weight, time, etc. (except for *in.* =inch), nor for *Dr, Revd, Mr, Mrs, Ms, Mme, Mlle, St, Hants, Northants, p* (=penny or pence).

Hyphen

1. Used to join two or more words so as to form a single expression:
   father-in-law; happy-go-lucky; non-stick; self-control
2. Used to join words in an attributive compound:
   a well-known man (but 'the man is well known')
   an out-of-date list (but 'the list is out of date')
3. Used to join a prefix etc. to a proper name:
   anti-Darwinian; half-Italian; non-German

4. Used to prevent misconceptions, by linking words:
   a poor-rate collection; a poor rate-collection
   or by separating a prefix:
   re-cover/recover; re-present/represent; re-sign/resign
5. Used to separate two similar consonant or vowel sounds, as a help to understanding and pronunciation:
   pre-empt; pre-exist; Ross-shire
6. Used to represent a common second element in the items of a list:
   two-, three-, or fourfold
7. Used at the end of a line of print to show that a word not usually hyphenated has had to be divided.

Question mark

1. Used after every question that expects a separate answer:
   Why is he here? Who invited him?
2. Placed before a word or date etc. whose accuracy is doubted:
   T. Tallis ?1505–85

- It is not used in indirect questions, e.g. *We asked why he was there and who had invited him.*

Quotation marks

Used round a direct quotation:

'That is nonsense,' he said.

The commas stand outside the quotation marks when *he said* interrupts the quotation:

'That', he said, 'is nonsense.'

Semicolon

Used to separate those parts of a sentence between which there is a more distinct break than would be called for by a comma but which are too closely connected to be made into separate sentences:

To err is human; to forgive, divine.

16 19 24 11 33 44 39

11 16 19 24 33 44 39

2 13 20 36 34 40 34